MW00616061

HENRETTA'S

AMERICA'S HISTORY

TENTH EDITION

FOR THE AP® COURSE

Rebecca Edwards
Vassar College

Eric Hinderaker
University of Utah

Robert O. Self
Brown University

James A. Henretta
University of Maryland

TEACHER'S EDITION

Dave Neumann
California State Polytechnic University, Pomona

Nicki Griffin
South Central High School, North Carolina

Kyle VanderWall
Grandville High School, Michigan

bedford, freeman & worth
high school publishers
Boston | New York

Sr. Vice President, Humanities and Social Sciences and High School: *Charles Linsemeier*
Senior Executive Program Manager for History: *William J. Lombardo*
Senior Program Director, HS: *Ann Heath*
Executive Program Manager, HS Humanities: *Nathan Odell*
Senior Marketing Manager, HS: *Janie Pierce-Bracher*
Director of Content Development: *Jane Knetzger*
Senior Development Editor: *Heidi L. Hood*
Assistant Editor: *Carly Lewis*
Associate Editor, HS: *Kelly Noll*
Director of Media Editorial: *Adam Whitehurst*
Media Editor: *Mollie Chandler*
Senior Media Editor, HS: *Kim Morté*
Marketing Manager: *Melissa Rodriguez*
Marketing Coordinator, HS: *Tiffani Tang*
Senior Director, Content Management Enhancement: *Tracey Kuehn*
Senior Managing Editor: *Michael Granger*
Senior Content Project Manager: *Kendra LeFleur*
Senior Workflow Project Manager: *Lisa McDowell*
Production Supervisor: *Robin Besofsky*
Director of Design, Content Management: *Diana Blume*
Interior Design: *Maureen McCutcheon*
Cover Design: *William Boardman*
Text Permissions Editor: *Michael McCarty*
Text Permissions Researcher: *Elaine Kosta, Lumina Datamatics*
Director of Rights and Permissions: *Hilary Newman*
Senior Photo Permissions Editor: *Sheena Goldstein*
Photo Researcher: *Naomi Kornhauser*
Director of Digital Production: *Keri deManigold*
Copy Editor: *Dana Richards*
Indexer: *Sonya Dintaman*
Composition: *Lumina Datamatics, Inc.*
Cover Image: *Lily Furedi, Subway, 1934, oil on canvas, Smithsonian American Art Museum, Washington, DC/ART Resource, NY*
Printing and Binding: *Transcontinental Printing*

Copyright © 2021, 2018, 2014, 2011 by Bedford, Freeman & Worth High School Publishers. All rights reserved. No part of this book may be reproduced, stored in a retrieval system, or transmitted in any form or any means, electronic, mechanical, photocopying, recording, or otherwise, except as may be permitted by law or expressly permitted in writing by the Publisher.

Library of Congress Control Number: 2021932784
ISBN: 978-1-319-33520-5

Printed in Canada.
1 2 3 4 5 6 25 24 23 22 21

Acknowledgments
Acknowledgments and copyrights appear on the same page as the text and art selections they cover; these acknowledgments and copyrights constitute an extension of the copyright page.

AP® is a trademark registered by the College Board, which is not affiliated with, and does not endorse, this product.

For information, write: BFW Publishers, One New York Plaza, Suite 4500, New York, NY 10004
hsmarketing@bfwpub.com

About the Contributors

Dave Neumann (*California State Polytechnic University, Pomona*)
Dave Neumann (PhD, University of Southern California) is Assistant Professor of History Education at California State Polytechnic University in Pomona. As Director of the History Project at CSU Long Beach, he oversaw professional development on various topics for K–12 teachers. A lecturer in the History Department at CSU Long Beach for eight years, he taught American and world history, and capstone courses in elementary and secondary education programs. He began his career as a high school history teacher, working in Southern California urban schools for over a decade. He has presented at many history and education conferences, including the American Historical Association, the Organization of American Historians, the World History Association, the National Council for the Social Studies, and the National Council for History Education.

Sarah Neumann

Nicki Griffin (*Georgia Virtual School; Onslow County Schools, North Carolina*)
Nicki Griffin, National Board Certified Teacher, teaches AP® U.S. History and AP® European History with the Georgia Virtual School and teaches social studies with Onslow County Schools in North Carolina. Ms. Griffin has served as Facilitating Teacher for AP® U.S. History in the Pitt County School system. She has also served as Course Lead and teacher for AP® European History for the North Carolina Virtual Public School. She has served as an AP® Reader for six years and is a College Board Consultant. Over the past decade, she has provided training for hundreds of teachers in AP® U.S. and European History.

Robyn Barnes

Kyle VanderWall (*Grandville High School, Michigan*)
Kyle VanderWall has taught history for eighteen years at Grandville High School in Grandville, MI. For sixteen of those years, he has taught AP® U.S. History. Over that span, the program has grown significantly. The AP® U.S. History course at Grandville is designed for sophomores and has no prerequisites for admission. During the last ten years, Kyle has led numerous workshops around the country to help improve historical pedagogy. His instructional design and work focuses on increasing students' self-efficacy of historical inquiry. For the past ten years, he has participated in the AP® Reading as both a Reader and Table Leader scoring the Long-Essay and Document-Based Questions.

Kyle VanderWall

Brief Contents

Introduction to the AP® U.S. History Course

Welcome to *America's History* and the AP® United States History course. The survey design of this course seeks to mirror two semesters of content through both historical events and disciplinary practices. *America's History* is organized around the basic framework of the AP® structure and provides support for teachers and students for both instructional and assessment practices.

AP® U.S. History is sometimes described as more of an experience than a course. Whether this is your first year teaching AP® U.S. History or you are a returning veteran, the course will reward and challenge you. *America's History* is a book designed to augment and support your instruction this year.

History is a subject and discipline. Inasmuch as you are teaching United States history, you are concurrently facilitating students' ability to learn how to learn. The disciplinary aspects of the course require students who are intellectually curious and possess a desire to become critical readers and writers. Since the original iterative of the redesigned AP® history courses, first launched in the fall of 2014, the goal has been to privilege disciplinary historical skills. One of the central goals of AP® United States History is to identify what students need to know and be able to do with the historical events and skills learned throughout the year. The content of U.S. history is still important; however, without disciplinary skills, students will unfortunately see history as an exercise in rote memorization. Moreover, incorporating the reading and writing skills concomitant to the AP® course design is a more interesting experience.

Prepare to Teach AP® United States History

If you have not done so already, be sure to visit the College Board's AP® Central U.S. History course website. AP® Central houses germane resources such as information on the AP® United States History Course and Exam Description, AP® Classroom, and the course audit procedures. Additionally, you will find information related to professional development through one- or two-day workshops as well as week-long summer institutes called AP® Summer Institutes (APSI).

It is also essential to familiarize yourself with the ancillary resources from *America's History*. This book, along with the ancillary resources, provides you with a generous amount of help in the way of resources, assessment items, suggested responses, notes, and materials for scope and sequence. You will likely answer many questions you have by perusing the book and resources.

About the AP® United States History Exam

The exam currently consists of two main sections:

Section 1 (95 minutes, 60 percent of the total exam score)

- 55 multiple-choice questions (55 minutes; 40 percent of the total exam score)
- 3 short-answer questions chosen from four options (40 minutes total; 20 percent of the total exam score)

Section 2 (100 minutes, 40 percent of the total exam score)

- 1 document-based question (DBQ) (60 minutes; 25 percent of the total exam score)
- 1 long-essay question chosen from three options on the same theme (40 minutes; 15 percent of the total exam score)

The **multiple-choice questions** are designed to assess a student's ability to employ reasoning skills using historical evidence, so all multiple-choice questions are stimulus-based and organized in groups of three to four questions per stimulus. Some questions do not ask directly about the stimulus, but use the historical context of the stimulus as a springboard. Some questions will be attached to two documents with differing points of view, e.g. two historians with different interpretations on a historical development or process.

The **short-answer questions** ask students to apply specific historical thinking skills to historical source material and historical problems. They do not require a thesis statement. Short-answer questions 1 and 2 are required. SAQ 1 includes a secondary source attached and covers a development or process from between 1754 and 1980. SAQ 2 has a primary source attached and also covers a development or process from between 1754 and 1980.

Students may pick between SAQ 3 and 4. Neither has a stimulus attached. SAQ 3 will come from 1491 to 1877 and SAQ 4 from 1865 to 2001.

The **document-based question** requires analysis of seven primary sources, and will come from historical developments or processes between 1754 to 1980.

For **long-essay questions**, students will be given the option to select from three with prompts using the same reasoning process (e.g. continuity and change), but with different time periods and topics. They will write a thesis-based essay using relevant historical evidence to support their thesis. The first LEQ choice will come from 1491 to 1800, the second from 1800 to 1898, and the third from 1890 to 2001.

There are nine units in the curriculum framework. Exam coverage varies. For example, Units 1 (1491–1607) and 9 (1980—Present) each constitute 4–6% of the exam. Unit 2 (1607–1754), 6–8%. Units 3–8 are 10–17% of the exam each. You must pace your course and content accordingly.

More information on the exam, including rubrics and a complete sample exam can be found in the AP® United States History Course and Exam Description.

Professional Development and Online Support

Learning and teaching are recursive actions; therefore, consider the value in attending professional development specific to Advanced Placement®. Taking advantage of these resources will help prepare you for success in the classroom.

- College Board–approved AP® Summer Institutes (APSI). These institutes are either four or five days long and are intended to be an in-depth look at the purpose and structure of the course. You will network with other teachers and learn from an endorsed AP® Workshop Consultant. There are also one-day and online workshops available for teachers, too. New teachers are highly encouraged to attend a workshop before they teach the course. It is also best practice for veterans to return every few years to stay current with the exam and instructional practices. Search AP® Central to find more information on APSI opportunities.
- There are several ways to connect with support online. Each of these are located on AP® Central.
  - AP® United States History Teacher Community Forum
  - AP® Mentoring
  - AP® Daily
  - AP® Classroom

Pace Your Course

The AP® Course and Exam Description, which includes the Course Framework, is an effort to be transparent about what students need to know and be able to do at the conclusion of the course. This document is essential for pacing your course. Additionally, *America's History* provides information that will help you envision how you will organize the course. Every history teacher must make a distinction between what information is nice to know and what is essential to know and understand. This involves choice on the part of instructors. Bear in mind, academic freedom does not equate to the role of an independent contractor in this case. Instead, we commit to the disciplinary skills and essential historical content of the AP® US History Course. Equitable classrooms facilitate courses that allow students to learn all the requisite information and disciplinary practices.

The commitment to teaching the core structure of the course does not mean you will have a rigid structure. Instead, it means when you make choices, select items immediately relevant to the course. Making decisions in this vein means you will be curating a course that enlivens students' understandings of the past. The reading, writing, and thinking skills attendant to the AP® U.S. History courses are challenging. This is part of what makes this course so much fun to teach. Moreover, this Teacher's Edition will help you prepare your students for success in the course and on exams.

Whether you adopt pre-established pacing guides or construct your own, be sure to choose some postholes that will act as non-negotiables for you and your students. School schedules, which vary widely from state-to-state, are an important factor when you determine these postholes. However, there are a few common to most teachers. For example, many teachers will finish Period 5 before January and will wrap up Period 7 before the middle of March. The benefit of using postholes is you will maintain flexibility with students while also recognizing the need to finish the curriculum.

You Are a Writing Instructor

The most successful courses recognize scope and sequence is not just about historical events, developments, and processes. Rather, it is about the combination of historical writing, primary and secondary source analysis, and discrete historical events that make for a dynamic experience.

It is highly recommended that you create a schedule that details the various writing skills of the course. For example, students will need to demonstrate proficiency with two-to-three-sentence responses to Short Answer questions, where theses are not required. Instead, students will explain historical evidence that addresses a broad concept in U.S. History. Students will also be required to write historically sound thesis statements, establish historical context, and develop historical arguments. Moreover, students will need to analyze and incorporate primary sources in their writing in addition to demonstrating complexity. Start by examining the writing rubrics for the Long-Essay, Document-Based, and Short-Answer Questions. After you are familiar with the requisite skills, determine which areas will be sources of strength and areas of concern for your students. This will help you prioritize your in-class time. Regardless, develop a plan, be confident, and help students understand the nuance of historical writing.

Assess Throughout the Year

It is important for you to assess your students' progress regularly. Frequent, daily, and informal formative assessments are crucial for success. The style and purpose of the assessment will vary, but the frequency and consistency should remain the same. The goal is to alert students to their place within both the current unit of study as well as the overall skills of the course. *America's History* has strong in-text assessment questions that prepare students for the quizzes and tests you will administer. The in-text questions are excellent fodder for discussion about how questions are structured, possible answers, and queries students might possess. Moreover, the ancillary resources for *America's History* have questions that can make up larger unit assessments. Think of formative assessments as *for* learning and summative assessments *of* learning. While routine is good, it is also important to avoid rote processes. I find establishing a menu of options prevents rote assessment practices.

- Reading Quizzes: Minimally, one or two per chapter means regular practice for students on reading comprehension.
- Short-Answer Questions: These can be administered in parts or whole to assess students' understanding of a particular topic or process. Similar to quizzes, these questions take less than fifteen minutes and can serve as excellent check-ins with students.
- Document Analysis: Primary source analysis can elucidate broad or discrete historical developments. Done well, they serve as excellent contextual sources.
- Secondary Sources: Abbreviated secondary source excerpts, which are included in *America's History*, can help generate helpful discussion at the beginning of a class period.

Consider the potential rhythms of a week in class. Using one of these for each class period means, in the course of a week, students are beginning class with a 5-15 minute exercise that informally assesses their understanding, briefly captures the content of class, and prepares them for the remainder of class.

Writing is recursive. Students need time, practice, and patience when they work through the writing portions of this course. This also means you will need to establish a routine that allows you to provide timely feedback. I make a pledge to my students the first week of class about when they will receive their written responses back from me. This practice is part of a culture of commitment. We are truly all in this journey together, and when I work hard for my students, they typically reciprocate that practice. It is an expectation we have of and for one another. Choose a timeframe realistic to your teaching situation and stick to it throughout the year.

Think about when and how you will assess Multiple-Choice, Short-Answer, Long-Essay, and Document-Based Questions. For instance, a DBQ takes a full 60 minutes, whereas a Long Essay takes no more than 40 minutes. This is an important consideration when creating unit tests. Also, refer back to the section on pacing the course to consider what this might look like for your students. Some may choose to concentrate on SAQs and LEQs early in the year and wait until students have gleaned the requisite skills for DBQs. Regardless, the earlier you can establish a schedule for these items, the better you will feel as you work your way through the course.

Help Students Establish Habits of Mind with the Textbook

Students need to embrace the idea of this course as a two-way street with you, their instructor. Students need to actively read the text, consistently engage with the text, and regularly ask questions about what they read. You can and should play an active role in this process. Many students will benefit from direct instruction in the practice of note-taking strategies. Think about carving time into your schedule to model different methods of note-taking. Moreover, creating daily reading schedules can help truncate students' focus for the reading. For the two-way street to operate well, you need to model the practice and reinforce the benefits of good notes.

Historical Context

Aside from the contextualization point on the LEQ and DBQ rubric, this disciplinary skill represents one of the more important aspects of studying history. Encourage students to make connections both within and across chapters. One of the new features for *America's History* is a section called "Making Connections Across Chapters." This section is really about understanding how context can change the purpose of and answers for historical queries. Moreover, you can help students understand historical context through writing instruction, examining secondary sources, and evaluating the claims in primary sources helps students understand the importance of historical context. Historical inquiry is really about evaluating how historical context shapes events. Providing students with consistent practice makes them critical consumers of information and helps prepare them for success on the AP® Exam.

Course and Exam Success

Course culture is not to be underestimated as a critical component for success. While results on the AP® Exam are important, those data points illustrate part, not all, of students' experiences with the course. The book and materials will support that endeavor, but you need to think about ways to create a culture that promotes the course and goals therein. Historical literacy is something open to every student. In many ways, this course can be an epistemological journey for students. You are likely not teaching a class full of future history majors. Therefore, what are your goals? How can this course help further intellectually curious citizens who are capable of and possess a desire to understand a variety of perspectives on various issues? Who will matriculate in your course? Look around your school and think about how your course can mirror the student population, if it does not already. Removing barriers to populations historically underrepresented can help create better learning environment and reinforce a commitment to all students. These questions are important considerations for your course's culture.

The broad goal of historical inquiry is to inculcate habits of mind for critical reading and writing. While varying secondary sources are a part of the exam, they also provide students with an example of how professionals view similar evidence, but arrive at different conclusions. In this way, yes, you are preparing students for the exam, but you are also encouraging them to understand the validity of different perspectives. Historians build interpretations based on evidence. Teaching students the art of accounting for evidence, in support of and contrary to their arguments, will serve them well in whatever field of study they enter. Disciplinary skills facilitate this action. History is not rote memorization of dates and events to be forgotten by students. Instead, history affords us the opportunity to help students see a broader, complex world. We limit ourselves when we only see history as the objective.

Reviewing for the AP® Exam

Similar to the goal of establishing non-negotiable post-holes to ensure finishing the course curriculum, consider creating time for review at the end of the year. Most teachers will spend two or three weeks reviewing for the course. When you create your pacing model, be sure to consider this factor. Work backwards from the AP® Exam date and stick to the plan. Review will look different for everyone because of the variance in school calendars. Therefore, consider some broad review principles, relevant for every teacher.

Test Prep

Test prep should include all question types:

- Multiple-Choice Practice Questions
- Short-Answer Questions
- Document-Based Questions
- Long-Essay Questions

Students should write the entire Free Response Section (3 SAQs, 1 LEQ, 1 DBQ) in one sitting before the May test. Some teachers schedule after-school writing sessions, while others schedule a practice test on a Saturday in April. Regardless, the first time a student writes the entire exam should not be on test day. Simulate the timing by giving students this opportunity so they can adjust before the actual test.

Similar to the writing section of the test, you should consider how you provide students with full-length practice exams. *America's History* comes with full-length practice tests, and AP® Classroom and the AP® Course Audit page provide full-length, secured tests. Create a schedule that gives students multiple opportunities to practice this section of the test.

Course Concepts

The AP® Course Framework is a document to use throughout the year and especially during review. The learning objectives, historical developments, and topics delineated throughout the Course Framework represent precisely what a student needs to know and be able to do on the AP® Exam. The requisite content and historical thinking and reasoning skills are addressed as you work your way through this document.

Distilling information to the essentials is vital for a strong review, and the Course Framework distills the information for you. Remind students the items found in that document are the essentials. Shear away from the peripheral information covered in the course and concentrate on the non-negotiables.

Establishing a review schedule will help keep you and your students on pace. As a personal anecdote, since 2005, I have used the same routine. During class, I administer three full-length multiple-choice tests and the remaining days I review content. In the evenings, for 90 to 120 minutes (four evenings during the first week of review and three evenings during the second week), I review the writing portion of the exam. At least once before the test, students have the opportunity to write a full-length free response section. This schedule has worked for my students and it is a source of course culture, too. Again, we are all in this endeavor together.

Regardless of what you choose for a review schedule, select something that fits your personality and embrace the challenge with your students.

A Final Note

Remember why you went into this profession. You entered this career to make a difference with students and share your love of history. Be patient. The course may take you a few years to develop some level of comfort with the class and exam. Each year, select a few items you will concentrate on and work to make those foundational pieces of your course. Remember, historical inquiry promotes learning in novel manners for students and the disciplinary skills are a significant part of what make the course so valuable. Share your love of history, have fun, and the rest will fall in place. The co-authors of this book hope the notes herein help you in this endeavor.

Kyle VanderWall
AP® United States History Teacher
Grandville High School
Grandville, Michigan

How to Use This Teacher's Edition

Prepare with Ease

This Teacher's Edition was developed to be your ultimate teaching tool. Every tip, activity, and reference was written with one thing in mind: to provide support and guidance to help you teach a successful AP® U.S. History course. By using this Teacher's Edition and accompanying Teacher's Resource Materials, you will have at your fingertips everything you need to be effective and efficient in your AP® U.S. History instruction.

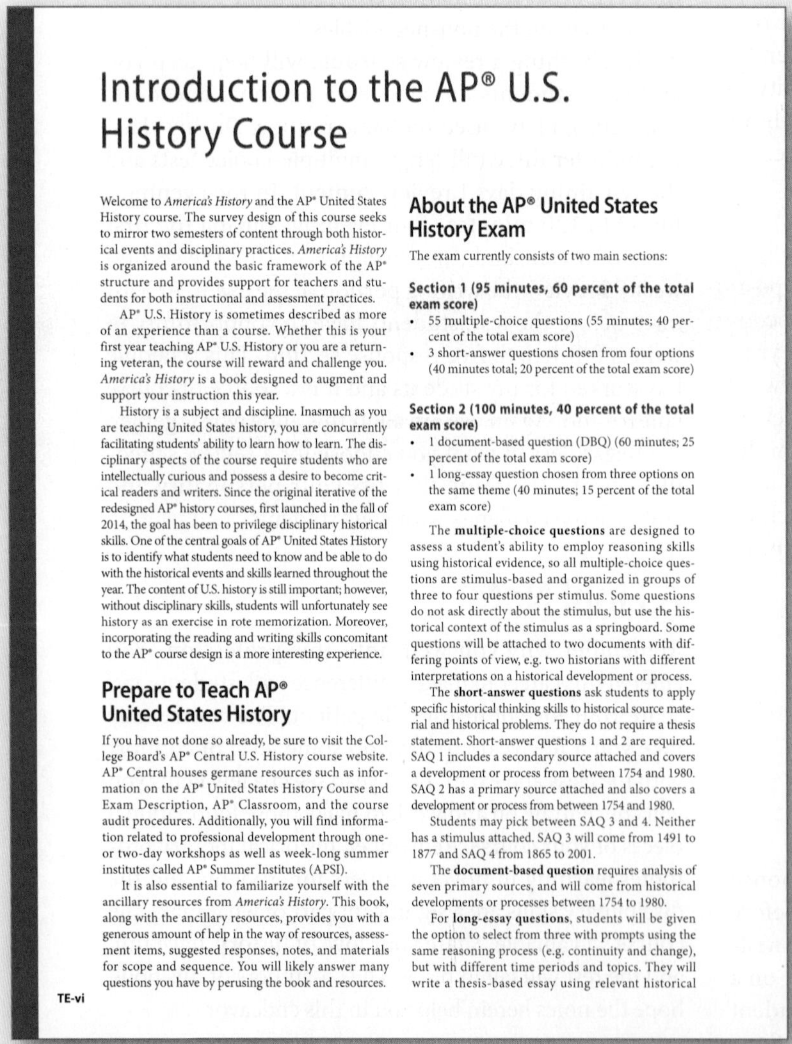

Introduction to the AP® U.S. History Course

Welcome to *America's History* and the AP® United States History course. The survey design of this course seeks to mirror two semesters of content through both historical events and disciplinary practices. *America's History* is organized around the basic framework of the AP® structure and provides support for teachers and students for both instructional and assessment practices.

AP® U.S. History is sometimes described as more of an experience than a course. Whether this is your first year teaching AP® U.S. History or you are a returning veteran, the course will reward and challenge you. *America's History* is a book designed to augment and support your instruction this year.

History is a subject and discipline. Inasmuch as you are teaching United States history, you are concurrently facilitating students' ability to learn how to learn. The disciplinary aspects of the course require students who are intellectually curious and possess a desire to become critical readers and writers. Since the original iterative of the redesigned AP® history courses, first launched in the fall of 2014, the goal has been to privilege disciplinary historical skills. One of the central goals of AP® United States History is to identify what students need to know and be able to do with the historical events and skills learned throughout the year. The content of U.S. history is still important; however, without disciplinary skills, students will unfortunately see history as an exercise in rote memorization. Moreover, incorporating the reading and writing skills concomitant to the AP® course design is a more interesting experience.

Prepare to Teach AP® United States History

If you have not done so already, be sure to visit the College Board's AP® Central U.S. History course website. AP® Central houses germane resources such as information on the AP® United States History Course and Exam Description, AP® Classroom, and the course audit procedures. Additionally, you will find information related to professional development through one- or two-day workshops as well as week-long summer institutes called AP® Summer Institutes (APSI).

It is also essential to familiarize yourself with the ancillary resources from *America's History*. This book, along with the ancillary resources, provides you with a generous amount of help in the way of resources, assessment items, suggested responses, notes, and materials for scope and sequence. You will likely answer many questions you have by perusing the book and resources.

About the AP® United States History Exam

The exam currently consists of two main sections:

Section 1 (95 minutes, 60 percent of the total exam score)

- 55 multiple-choice questions (55 minutes; 40 percent of the total exam score)
- 3 short-answer questions chosen from four options (40 minutes total; 20 percent of the total exam score)

Section 2 (100 minutes, 40 percent of the total exam score)

- 1 document-based question (DBQ) (60 minutes; 25 percent of the total exam score)
- 1 long-essay question chosen from three options on the same theme (40 minutes; 15 percent of the total exam score)

The **multiple-choice questions** are designed to assess a student's ability to employ reasoning skills using historical evidence, so all multiple-choice questions are stimulus-based and organized in groups of three to four questions per stimulus. Some questions do not ask directly about the stimulus, but use the historical context of the stimulus as a springboard. Some questions will be attached to two documents with differing points of view, e.g. two historians with different interpretations on a historical development or process.

The **short-answer questions** ask students to apply specific historical thinking skills to historical source material and historical problems. They do not require a thesis statement. Short-answer questions 1 and 2 are required. SAQ 1 includes a secondary source attached and covers a development or process from between 1754 and 1980. SAQ 2 has a primary source attached and also covers a development or process from between 1754 and 1980.

Students may pick between SAQ 3 and 4. Neither has a stimulus attached. SAQ 3 will come from 1491 to 1877 and SAQ 4 from 1865 to 2001.

The **document-based question** requires analysis of seven primary sources, and will come from historical developments or processes between 1754 to 1980.

For **long-essay questions**, students will be given the option to select from three with prompts using the same reasoning process (e.g. continuity and change), but with different time periods and topics. They will write a thesis-based essay using relevant historical

TE-vi

INTRODUCTION TO THE AP® U.S. HISTORY COURSE

Before you begin working with this text, review the **Introduction to the AP® U.S. History Course**, which offers valuable tips for course preparation, suggestions on course planning and pacing, class projects, and exam review information to help you prepare your students for the rigors of reading and writing in this college-level course.

2 CHAPTER

American Experiments

1521–1700

Chapter 2 — AP® Assessment Weight and Pacing Guide

The assessment weight on the AP® U.S. History Exam for Chapters 1–2 is 4–6 percent. This chapter falls at the end of Unit 1 of the AP® U.S. History Curriculum, covering Period 1: 1491–1607 and the beginning of Unit 2 of the AP® U.S. History Curriculum, covering Period 2: 1607–1754.

This pacing guide is based on a schedule with 120 sessions of 50 minutes each before the AP® U.S. History Exam. If you have a different number of sessions before the exam, you can modify the pacing to meet your needs. If you have additional time, consider incorporating quizzes, released AP® U.S. History questions, practice exams, writing practice, and other instructional activities.

	Traditional Schedule	Block Schedule
Chapter 2	4 days	2–3 days

Daily Pacing Guide

	Focus Content	Essential Question
Day 1	Spain's Tribute Colonies	How did Spanish colonization affect people in the Americas and in Europe?
Day 2	Plantation Colonies	How did the labor demands of plantation colonies transform the process of colonization?
Day 3	Neo-European Colonies	What conditions were necessary to establish successful neo-European colonies?
Day 4	War and Rebellion in North America	What did these three rebellions — Metacom's War, the Pueblo Revolt, and Bacon's Rebellion — have in common?

AP® Alignment

Section Heading	AP® Topic	AP® Theme
Spain's Tribute Colonies	1.5, 2.2	SOC, MIG
Plantation Colonies	2.3, 2.4, 2.5, 2.6	GEO, WXT, WOR
Neo-European Colonies	2.2, 2.3	MIG, GEO
War and Rebellion in North America	2.5, 2.7	WOR, ARC

* Should changes be made to the Course Framework in the future, an updated alignment will be placed on our AP® updates page at go.bfwpub.com/ap-course-updates.

40-a

BLUE PAGES

As you prepare your lessons, look to each chapter's **BLUE PAGES** for help with relevant resources, AP® Pacing Guides, and Bell Ringers activities. Need to move quickly through a chapter? The Essential Activity is the least you should do to cover chapter content.

Chapter 2 — Overview

This chapter begins with a look at the Columbian Exchange and growing challenges to Spanish power in the New World (Unit 1 in the AP® U.S. History Curriculum). As settlement of the New World grows, the chapter turns its attention to the important development of plantation colonies in South America and the Caribbean islands. Competition between European nations leads to a push to establish settlements in New France, New Netherland, and New England, with each nation attempting to incorporate Native American groups into alliances and military exchanges. The chapter closes with a focus on instability and conflicts in the colonies between Europeans and Native Americans and between the British colonists and their colonial governments and British policy (Unit 2 in the AP® U.S. History Curriculum).

Chapter 2 — Resources

The following resources can be found in the Teacher's Resource Materials (TRM) that accompany the book. You can access the TRM via the book's digital platform, by clicking the TRM links found here in your Teacher's Edition e-book or by contacting your representative to access the resources online. Visit **bfwpub.com/henretta10e** to learn more.

- TRM Chapter 2 Lecture Presentation Slides
- TRM Chapter 2 Outline with AP® Focus
- TRM Chapter 2 Lecture Strategies
- TRM Chapter 2 Suggested Responses
- TRM Handout 2.1 — Comparison: Early Settlements
- TRM Handout 2.2 — Thematic Analysis: Introduction of Tobacco in the Chesapeake Colonies
- TRM Handout 2.3 — Comparison: European Settlements in North America
- TRM Handout 2.4 — Causation: Religious Tolerance in British North America
- TRM Handout 2.5 — Contextualization: Bacon's Rebellion

Chapter 2 — Essential Activity

Ask students to provide six specific events that connect Columbus's landing in the Caribbean (1492) to the founding of Jamestown (1607) based on one AP® Theme. Students should explain the connection between the events they choose using AP® Historical Thinking Skills and Reasoning Processes (contextualization; comparison; causation; and continuity and change). Students should also provide evidence for each event that helps to support the connections between events. Finally, require students to provide contextualization for the events by looking at the broad processes and developments that influenced the events from 1491 to 1607.

40-b

Teach with Confidence

Whether you are new to AP® U.S. History or a venerable pro, you'll find useful tips in the chapter wraparound material. Plan your lessons faster with our point-of-use teaching tips, activities, AP® course connections, and more.

Immigrants flooded into Philadelphia, which grew from 2,000 people in 1700 to 25,000 by 1760. Many families came in search of land; for them, Philadelphia was only a temporary way station. Other migrants came as laborers, including a large number of indentured servants. Some were young, unskilled men, but the colony's explosive growth also created a strong demand for all kinds of skilled laborers, especially in the construction trades.

Pennsylvania and New Jersey grew prosperous but contentious. New Jersey was plagued by contested land titles, and ordinary settlers rioted against the proprietors in the 1740s and the 1760s. By the 1760s, eastern Pennsylvania landowners with large farms were using slaves and poor Scots-Irish migrants to grow wheat. Other ambitious men were buying up land and dividing it into small tenancies, which they lent out on profitable leases. Still others sold manufactured goods, including farm equipment, or ran mills. These large-scale farmers, rural landlords, speculators, storekeepers, and gristmill operators formed a distinct class of agricultural capitalists. They built large stone houses for their families, furnishing them with four-poster beds and expensive mahogany tables, on which they laid elegant linen and imported Dutch dinnerware.

Ethnic Diversity and Material Culture As non-English migrants arrived in greater numbers in British North America, they brought craft traditions with them that transformed the colonies' material culture. This eighteenth-century chest, made of yellow pine and tulip poplar and intricately hand-painted, was built by a German craftsman in Berks County, Pennsylvania. The central panel features two unicorns, while the two side panels portray men on horseback. Floral patterns surround the panels and decorate the drawers. These motifs are commonly found on marriage chests from the region.

The Metropolitan Museum of Art, Rogers Fund, 1923.

By contrast, one-half of the Middle colonies' white men owned no land and little personal property. Some were the sons of smallholding farmers and would eventually inherit some land. But many were Scots-Irish or German "inmates" — single men or families, explained a tax assessor, "such as live in small cottages and have no taxable property, except a cow." In the predominantly German township of Lancaster, Pennsylvania, a merchant noted an "abundance of Poor people" who "maintain their Families with great difficulty by day Labour." Although these workers hoped eventually to become landowners, rising land prices prevented many from realizing their dreams.

AP® SKILLS & PROCESSES

CAUSATION

How did rapid immigration and economic growth trigger conflict in the Middle colonies?

Cultural Diversity

The Middle Atlantic colonies were not a melting pot. Most European migrants held tightly to their traditions, creating a patchwork of ethnically and religiously diverse communities (Figure 4.2). In 1748, a Swedish traveler counted no fewer than twelve religious denominations in Philadelphia, including Anglicans, Baptists, Quakers, Swedish and German Lutherans, Mennonites, Scots-Irish Presbyterians, and Roman Catholics.

Migrants preserved their cultural identity by marrying within their ethnic groups. A major exception was the Huguenots, Calvinists who had been expelled from Catholic France in the 1680s and resettled in Holland, England, and the British colonies. Huguenots in American port cities such as Boston, New York, and Charleston quickly lost their French identities by intermarrying with other Protestants.

AP® EXAM TIP

Evaluate the relationship between diversity and tolerance in the Middle colonies and compare to other colonial regions.

AP® THEME

ARC: American and Regional Culture

Students are responsible for understanding how a nascent colonial culture expanded culturally and intellectually because of demographic shifts. Help students understand the larger historical processes by explaining the following concepts: cultural pluralism, intellectual exchanges, and demographic shifts. After explaining these ideas, have students examine the picture of the eighteenth-century chest in groups. Ask them to think of how the picture represents either cultural pluralism, intellectual exchanges, and/or demographic shifts.

CHECK FOR UNDERSTANDING

Ask students: **How did economic growth, opportunity, and conflict characterize the Middle colonies?** *The rising prices of grain lured migrants while raising the hope for many that they could improve their lives and own their own property. The simultaneous rise of land prices frustrated these hopes, leading to strong tensions. Some attempted to acquire land by settling on Native American territory, fueling conflict with them.*

AP® SKILLS & PROCESSES

CAUSATION

Use the **CAUSATION** question to explore how demographic and economic trends affected social stability in the Middle colonies. Students may need some guidance to grasp the idea that

AP® NOTES

Look for the gray, blue, and red bands for specific connections to the AP® Course.

GRAY BANDS offer support for teaching AP® Themes.

BLUE BANDS provide tips for teaching AP® Skills & Processes.

RED BANDS suggest activities for extending the AP® Exam Tips in the Student Edition.

authority in families and society but did not overturn it. Rejecting the pleas of evangelical women, Baptist men kept church authority in the hands of "free born male members," and Anglican slaveholders retained control of the political system. Still, the Baptist insurgency infused the lives of poor tenant families with spiritual meaning and empowered yeomen to defend their economic interests. Moreover, as Baptist ministers spread Christianity among slaves, they undermined a key justification for slavery while giving some blacks a new religious identity. Within a generation, African Americans would develop distinctive versions of Protestant Christianity.

THE MIDCENTURY CHALLENGE: WAR, TRADE, AND SOCIAL CONFLICT, 1750–1763

How did midcentury developments reflect Britain's deepening connections to North America?

Between 1750 and 1763, three significant events transformed colonial life. First, Britain went to war against the French in America, sparking a worldwide conflict: the Great War for Empire. Second, a surge in trade boosted colonial consumption but caused Americans to become deeply indebted to British creditors. Third, westward migration sparked warfare with Indian peoples, violent disputes between settlers and land speculators, and backcountry rebellions against eastern-controlled governments.

AP® EXAM TIP

Compare the impact of colonial rivalries in the Ohio Valley on American Indian populations to earlier imperial rivalries involving Native groups.

The French and Indian War

In 1754, overlapping French and British claims in North America came to a head (Map 4.2). The French maintained their vast claims through a network of forts and trading posts that sustained alliances with neighboring Indians. The soft underbelly of this sprawling empire was the Ohio Valley, where French claims were tenuous. Native peoples were driven out of the valley by Iroquois attacks in the seventeenth century, but after 1720 displaced Indian populations — especially Delawares and Shawnees from Pennsylvania — resettled there in large numbers. In the 1740s, British traders from Pennsylvania began traveling down the Ohio River. They traded with Delawares and Shawnees in the upper valley and began to draw French-allied Indians into their orbit and away from French posts. Then, in 1749, the Ohio Company of Virginia, a partnership of prominent colonial planters and London merchants, received a 200,000-acre grant from the crown to establish a new settlement on the upper Ohio, threatening French claims to the region.

Conflict in the Ohio Valley By midcentury, Britain relied on the Iroquois Confederacy as its partner in Indian relations throughout the Northeast. By extending the Covenant Chain, the Iroquois had become a kind of Indian empire in their own right, claiming to speak for other groups throughout the region based on their seventeenth-century conquests. The Delawares, Shawnees, and other groups who repopulated the Ohio Valley did so in part to escape the Iroquois yoke. To maintain influence on the Ohio, the Iroquois sent two "half-kings," Tanaghrisson (an adopted Seneca) and Scarouady (an Oneida), to the Native settlement of Logstown, a trading town on the upper Ohio, where Britain recognized them as leaders.

French authorities, alarmed by British inroads, built a string of forts from Lake Erie to the headwaters of the Ohio, culminating with Fort Duquesne on the site of present-day Pittsburgh. To reassert British claims, Governor Dinwiddie dispatched an expedition led by Colonel George Washington, a twenty-two-year-old Virginian whose half-brothers were Ohio Company stockholders. Washington discovered that most of the Ohio Indians had decided to side with the French; only the Iroquois half-kings and a few of their followers supported his efforts. After Washington's party fired on a French

CHECK FOR UNDERSTANDING

Ask students: **How did the accelerating pace of travel and communication affect colonial society and culture?** *Greater infrastructure (e.g. port facilities and roads) as well as the rise of print culture in the colonies led to religious upheavals in the British North American colonies. This period was known as the Great Awakening.*

AP® APPLY THE TIP

Ask students to create a Venn diagram comparing the conflict over the Ohio Valley in the mid-eighteenth century to imperial conflicts involving Native populations in the seventeenth century (e.g., Beaver Wars, Chickasaw Wars, etc.). Ask students to focus on the causes of the conflicts, the role of European powers in the conflicts, and the impact on Native populations in their comparison.

TEACHING STRATEGY

To supplement your discussion of "The Midcentury Challenge" section, use the Educator's Guide that accompanies the PBS film *The War That Made America*. The guide contains standards-based lessons and activities, discussion questions, small and large group role-plays, mock trials, and collaborative research suggestions. Access this film by searching "PBS The War That Made America Education Outreach."

TEACHING STRATEGIES AND CHECK FOR UNDERSTANDING ANNOTATIONS

For support in teaching the course, look for the purple and green bands. PURPLE BANDS offer teaching strategies, including discussion and activity ideas as well as online, video, and literary suggestions to supplement your class discussion. GREEN BANDS provide questions to ensure your students understand the material before moving on to a new topic.

TEACHING STRATEGY

The chapter introduction lays out the major question facing the nation in its first years after drafting the Constitution. The United States had avoided the pitfalls of other republican-inspired rebellions, but it faced the task of putting a viable independent republic into place. While American leaders agreed on the desirability of republican government, they differed on the details of the kind of republic they should form, asking the question: Should the American republic be a representative institution led by able elites or a genuinely democratic polity in which ordinary citizens participated? For a complete suggested response to the **AP® LEARNING FOCUS** question, see p. 242.

7
CHAPTER

Hammering Out a Federal Republic
1787–1820

AP® LEARNING FOCUS

Why did the United States survive the challenges of its first three decades to become a viable, growing independent republic?

Like an earthquake, the American Revolution shook the European monarchical order, and its aftershocks reverberated for decades. By "creating a new republic based on the rights of the individual, the North Americans introduced a new force into the world," the eminent German historian Leopold von Ranke warned the king of Bavaria in 1854, a force that might cost the monarch his throne. Before 1776, "a king who ruled by the grace of God had been the center around which everything turned. Now the idea emerged that power should come from below [from the people]."

Other republican-inspired upheavals — England's Puritan Revolution of the 1640s and the French Revolution of 1789 — ended in political chaos and military rule. Similar fates befell many Latin American republics that won independence from Spain in the early nineteenth century. But the American states escaped both anarchy and dictatorship. Having been raised in a Radical Whig political culture that viewed standing armies and powerful generals as instruments of tyranny, General George Washington left public life in 1783 to manage his plantation, astonishing European observers but bolstering the authority of elected Patriot leaders. "'Tis a Conduct so novel," American painter John Trumbull reported from London, that it is "inconceivable to People [here]."

The great task of fashioning representative republican governments absorbed the energy and intellect of an entire generation and was rife with conflict. Seeking to perpetuate the elite-led polity of the colonial era, Federalists celebrated "natural aristocrats" such as Washington and condemned the radical republicanism of the French Revolution. In response, Jefferson and his Republican followers claimed the Fourth of July as their holiday and "we the people" as their political language. "There was a grand democrat procession in Town on the 4th of July," came a report from Baltimore: "All the farmers, tanners, black-smiths, shoemakers, etc. were there . . . and afterwards they went to a grand feast."

Many people of high status worried that the new state governments were too attentive to the demands of such ordinary workers and their families. When considering a bill, Connecticut conservative Ezra Stiles grumbled, every elected official "instantly thinks how it will affect his constituents" rather than how it would enhance the general welfare. What Stiles criticized as irresponsible, however, most Americans welcomed. The concerns of ordinary citizens were now paramount, and traditional elites trembled.

210

210 CHAPTER 7

TEACHER'S RESOURCE MATERIALS

The TRM icon indicates extension materials — such as handouts, maps, and suggested responses — that are available in the Teacher's Resource Materials.

CHAPTER 7 Hammering Out a Federal Republic, 1787–1820 213

Devising the New Government Once the military savior of his country, Washington now became its political father. At age fifty-seven, the first president possessed great personal dignity and a cautious personality. To maintain continuity, he adopted many of the administrative practices of the Confederation and asked Congress to reestablish the existing executive departments: Foreign Affairs (State), Finance (Treasury), and War. To head the Department of State, Washington chose Thomas Jefferson, a fellow Virginian and an experienced diplomat. For secretary of the treasury, he turned to Alexander Hamilton, a lawyer and his former military aide. The president designated Jefferson, Hamilton, and Secretary of War Henry Knox as his cabinet, or advisory body.

AP® SKILLS & PROCESSES

DEVELOPMENTS AND PROCESSES
How did the debate over the balance between liberty and order influence the formation of political parties?

TRM Find complete suggested responses in the Teacher's Resource Materials.

The Constitution mandated a supreme court, but the Philadelphia convention gave Congress the task of creating a national court system. The Federalists wanted strong national institutions, and the **Judiciary Act of 1789** reflected their vision. The act established a three-tiered system: it created federal district courts in each state and three circuit courts above them to which the decisions of the district courts could be appealed. The Supreme Court would then serve as the appellate court of last resort in the federal system. The Judiciary Act also specified that cases arising in state courts that involved federal laws could be appealed to the Supreme Court. This provision ensured that federal judges would determine the meaning of the Constitution.

Judiciary Act of 1789
Act that established federal district courts in each state and three circuit courts to hear appeals from the districts, with the Supreme Court serving as the highest appellate court in the federal system.

The Bill of Rights The Federalists kept their promise to consider amendments to the Constitution. James Madison, now a member of the House of Representatives, submitted nineteen amendments to the First Congress; by 1791, ten had been approved by Congress and ratified by the states. These ten amendments, known as the **Bill of Rights**, safeguard fundamental personal rights, including freedom of speech and religion, and mandate legal procedures, such as trial by jury. By protecting individual citizens, the amendments eased Antifederalists' fears of an oppressive national government and secured the legitimacy of the Constitution. They also addressed the issue of federalism: the proper balance between the authority of the national and state governments. But that question was repeatedly contested until the Civil War and remains important today.

Bill of Rights
The first ten amendments to the Constitution, officially ratified by 1791. The amendments safeguarded fundamental personal rights, including freedom of speech and religion, and mandated legal procedures, such as trial by jury.

CHECK FOR UNDERSTANDING

Ask students: **What were the main features of the Federalists' implementation of the Constitution?** *Washington appointed the first cabinet, whose positions were carried over from the Confederation government; Congress established a strong federal judiciary, including the Supreme Court; and Federalists upheld their promise to Antifederalists to create a Bill of Rights.*

Hamilton's Financial Program

George Washington's most important decision was choosing Alexander Hamilton as secretary of the treasury. An ambitious self-made man of great intelligence, Hamilton was a prominent lawyer in New York City who had married into the influential Schuyler family, which owned land in the Hudson River Valley. At the Philadelphia convention, he condemned the "democratic spirit" and called for an authoritarian government and a president with near-monarchical powers.

AP® EXAM TIP
Consider the ways that Hamilton's Financial Plan helped spur the growth of the first political party system in the U.S.

AP® APPLY THE TIP

To help students understand the connections between Hamilton's financial plan and the development of the first political parties, ask students to complete **Handout 7.1 — Causation: Impact of Hamilton's Financial Plan (TRM)**. To extend the discussion, ask students to predict the reaction of the first two parties to the following issues: war between Great Britain and France; limitations of freedom of speech; and federal support for building roads and railroads.

TRM Find **Handout 7.1 — Causation: Impact of Hamilton's Financial Plan** in the Teacher's Resource Materials.

As treasury secretary, Hamilton devised bold policies to enhance national authority and to assist financiers and merchants. He outlined his plans in three pathbreaking reports to Congress: on public credit (January 1790), on a national bank (December 1790), and on manufactures (December 1791). These reports outlined a coherent program of national mercantilism — government-assisted economic development. Hamilton's system immediately sparked disagreement and eventually drove a wedge between him and fellow Federalists Jefferson and James Madison.

Public Credit: Redemption and Assumption The financial and social implications of Hamilton's "**Report on the Public Credit**" made it instantly controversial. Hamilton asked Congress to redeem at face value the $55 million in Confederation securities held by foreign and domestic investors (Figure 7.1). His reasons were simple: as an underdeveloped nation, the United States needed good credit to secure loans from Dutch and British financiers. However, Hamilton's redemption plan would

Report on the Public Credit
Alexander Hamilton's 1790 report recommending that the federal government should assume all state debts and fund the national debt — that is, offer interest on it rather than repaying it — at full value. Hamilton's goal was to make the new country creditworthy, not debt-free.

AP® SKILLS & PROCESSES

DEVELOPMENTS AND PROCESSES

Hamilton's financial program is a complex design and many students spend too much time focusing on a microanalysis of the program, as opposed to remembering the macro view of his proposals. Provide students with two historical ideas such as commercialism and nationalism. Remind students in this context, nationalism is connected to Hamilton's desire to have the United States compete on a global stage. As students study the concepts of Hamilton's financial program, have them connect the details to either nationalism or commercialism. In this way, students will remember to think through a macroanalysis of Hamilton's proposals.

HAMMERING OUT A FEDERAL REPUBLIC, 1787–1820 213

Assess for Readiness

Ensure that your students are ready for the exam with tools built specifically for the updated AP® course.

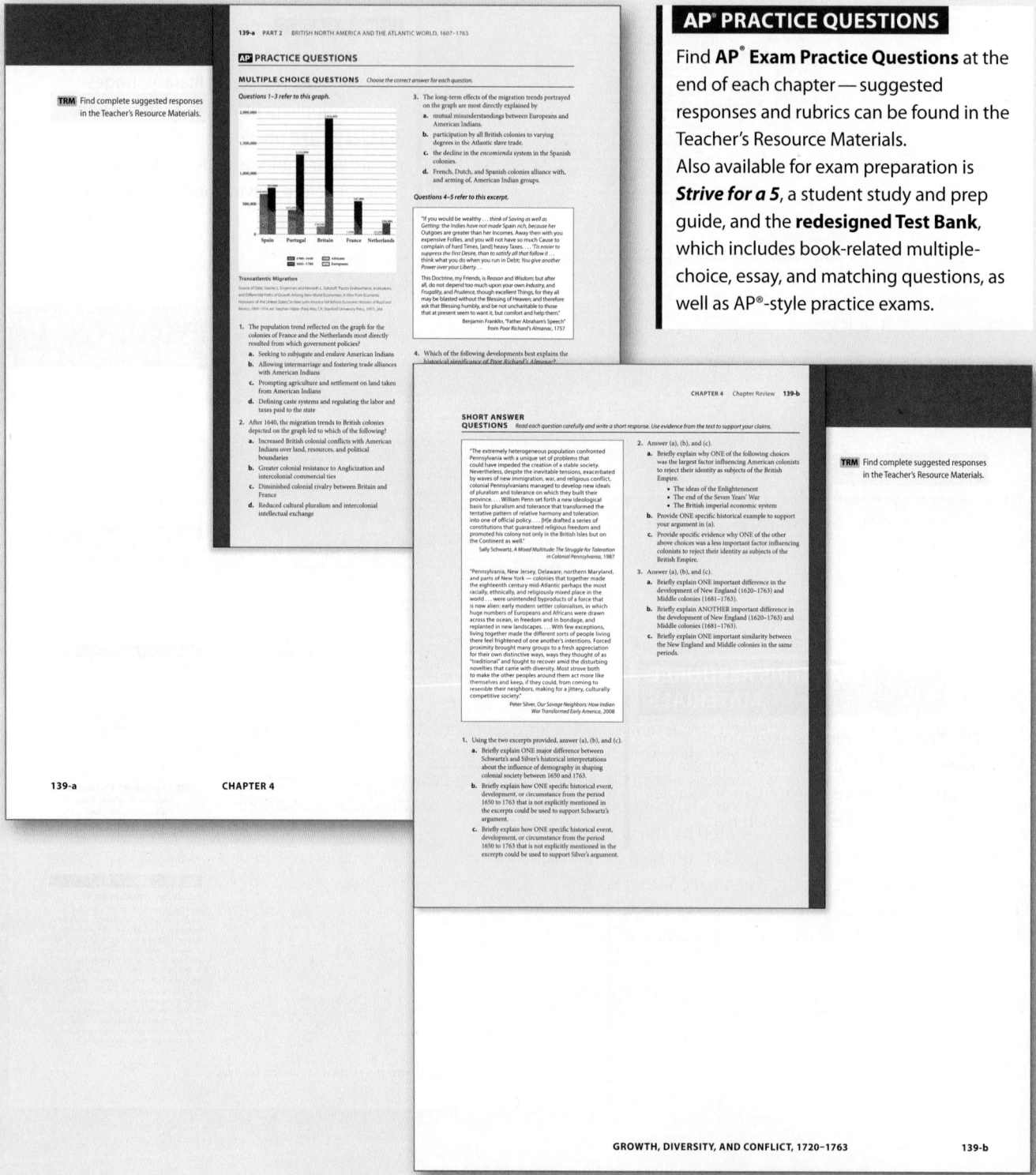

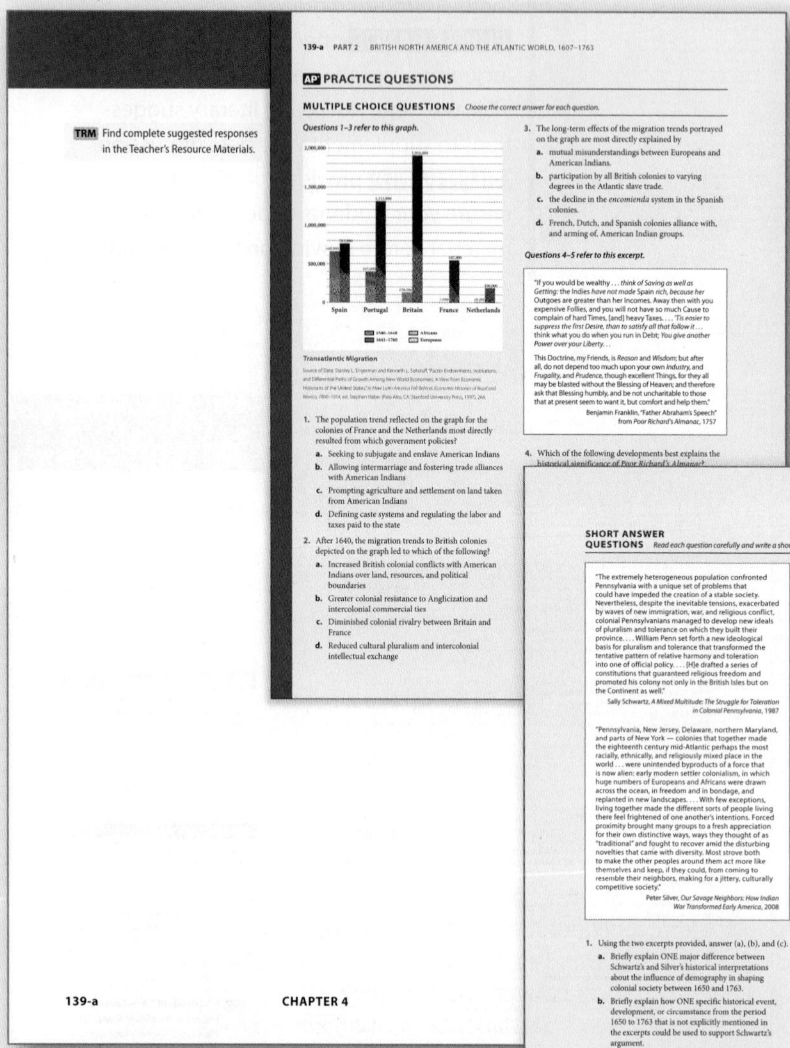

TRM Find complete suggested responses in the Teacher's Resource Materials.

139-a PART 2 BRITISH NORTH AMERICA AND THE ATLANTIC WORLD, 1607–1763

AP PRACTICE QUESTIONS

MULTIPLE CHOICE QUESTIONS *Choose the correct answer for each question.*

Questions 1–3 refer to this graph.

Transatlantic Migration

Source of Data: Stanley L. Engerman and Kenneth L. Sokoloff, "Factor Endowments, Institutions, and Differential Paths of Growth Among New World Economies: A View from Economic Historians of the United States," in *How Latin America Fell Behind: Economic Histories of Brazil and Mexico, 1800–1914*, ed. Stephen Haber (Palo Alto, CA: Stanford University Press, 1997), 264.

1. The population trend reflected on the graph for the colonies of France and the Netherlands most directly resulted from which government policies?
   a. Seeking to subjugate and enslave American Indians
   b. Allowing intermarriage and fostering trade alliances with American Indians
   c. Prompting agriculture and settlement on land taken from American Indians
   d. Defining caste systems and regulating the labor and taxes paid to the state
2. After 1640, the migration trends to British colonies depicted on the graph led to which of the following?
   a. Increased British colonial conflicts with American Indians over land, resources, and political boundaries
   b. Greater colonial resistance to Anglicization and intercolonial commercial ties
   c. Diminished colonial rivalry between Britain and France
   d. Reduced cultural pluralism and intercolonial intellectual exchange
3. The long-term effects of the migration trends portrayed on the graph are most directly explained by
   a. mutual misunderstandings between Europeans and American Indians.
   b. participation by all British colonies to varying degrees in the Atlantic slave trade.
   c. the decline in the *encomienda* system in the Spanish colonies.
   d. French, Dutch, and Spanish colonies alliance with, and arming of, American Indian groups.

Questions 4–5 refer to this excerpt.

"If you would be wealthy . . . *think of Saving as well as Getting:* the Indies *have not made* Spain *rich, because her* Outgoes are greater than her Incomes. Away then with you expensive Follies, and you will not have so much Cause to complain of hard Times, [and] heavy Taxes. . . . *'Tis easier to suppress the first Desire, than to satisfy all that follow it . . .* think what you do when you run in Debt; *You give another Power over your Liberty. . .*

This Doctrine, my Friends, is *Reason* and *Wisdom*; but after all, do not depend too much upon your own *Industry*, and *Frugality*, and *Prudence*, though excellent Things, for they all may be blasted without the Blessing of Heaven; and therefore ask that Blessing humbly, and be not uncharitable to those that at present seem to want it, but comfort and help them."

Benjamin Franklin, "Father Abraham's Speech" from *Poor Richard's Almanac*, 1757

4. Which of the following developments best explains the historical significance of *Poor Richard's Almanac*?

139-a CHAPTER 4

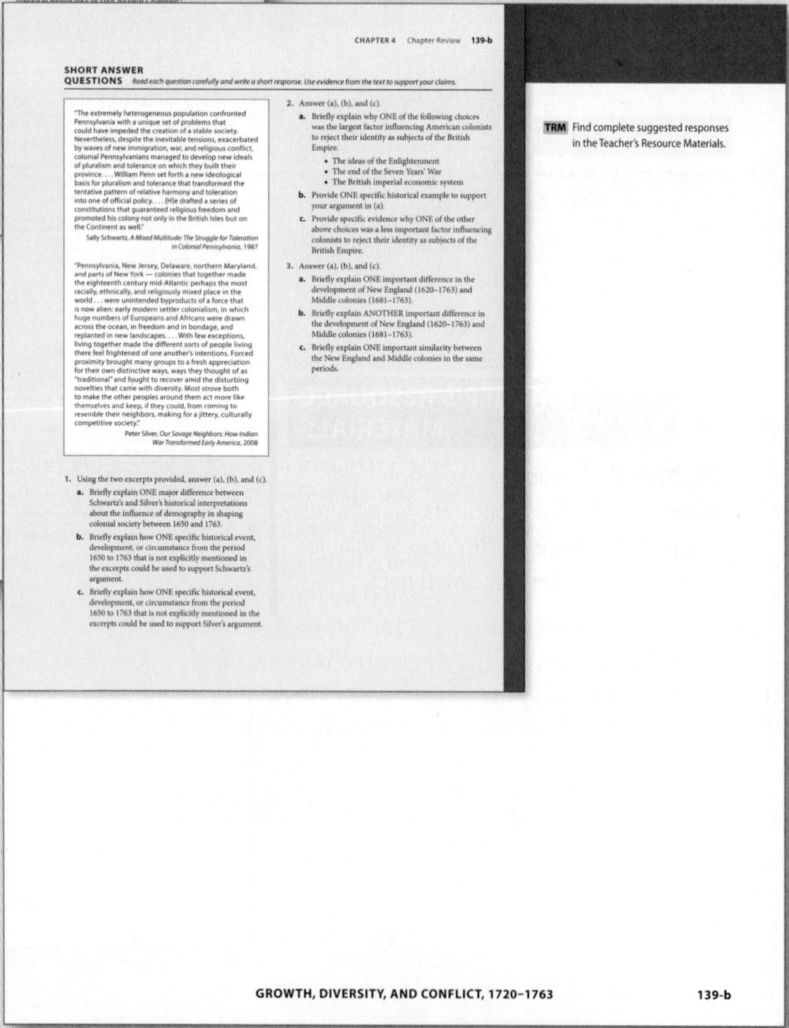

CHAPTER 4 Chapter Review 139-b

SHORT ANSWER QUESTIONS *Read each question carefully and write a short response. Use evidence from the text to support your claims.*

"The extremely heterogeneous population confronted Pennsylvania with a unique set of problems that could have impeded the creation of a stable society. Nevertheless, despite the inevitable tensions, exacerbated by waves of new immigration, war, and religious conflict, colonial Pennsylvanians managed to develop new ideals of pluralism and tolerance on which they built their province. . . . William Penn set forth a new ideological basis for pluralism and tolerance that transformed the tentative pattern of relative harmony and toleration into one of official policy. . . . [H]e drafted a series of constitutions that guaranteed religious freedom and promoted his colony not only in the British Isles but on the Continent as well."

Sally Schwartz, *A Mixed Multitude: The Struggle for Toleration in Colonial Pennsylvania*, 1987

"Pennsylvania, New Jersey, Delaware, northern Maryland, and parts of New York — colonies that together made the eighteenth century mid-Atlantic perhaps the most racially, ethnically, and religiously mixed place in the world . . . were unintended byproducts of a force that is now alien: early modern settler colonialism, in which huge numbers of Europeans and Africans were drawn across the ocean, in freedom and in bondage, and replanted in new landscapes. . . . With few exceptions, living together made the different sorts of people living there feel frightened of one another's intentions. Forced proximity brought many groups to a fresh appreciation for their own distinctive ways, ways they thought of as "traditional" and fought to recover amid the disturbing novelties that came with diversity. Most strove both to make the other peoples around them act more like themselves and keep, if they could, from coming to resemble their neighbors, making for a jittery, culturally competitive society."

Peter Silver, *Our Savage Neighbors: How Indian War Transformed Early America*, 2008

1. Using the two excerpts provided, answer (a), (b), and (c).
   a. Briefly explain ONE major difference between Schwartz's and Silver's historical interpretations about the influence of demography in shaping colonial society between 1650 and 1763.
   b. Briefly explain how ONE specific historical event, development, or circumstance from the period 1650 to 1763 that is not explicitly mentioned in the excerpts could be used to support Schwartz's argument.
   c. Briefly explain how ONE specific historical event, development, or circumstance from the period 1650 to 1763 that is not explicitly mentioned in the excerpts could be used to support Silver's argument.
2. Answer (a), (b), and (c).
   a. Briefly explain why ONE of the following choices was the largest factor influencing American colonists to reject their identity as subjects of the British Empire.
      - The ideas of the Enlightenment
      - The end of the Seven Years' War
      - The British imperial economic system
   b. Provide ONE specific historical example to support your argument in (a).
   c. Provide specific evidence why ONE of the other above choices was a less important factor influencing colonists to reject their identity as subjects of the British Empire.
3. Answer (a), (b), and (c).
   a. Briefly explain ONE important difference in the development of New England (1620–1763) and Middle colonies (1681–1763).
   b. Briefly explain ANOTHER important difference in the development of New England (1620–1763) and Middle colonies (1681–1763).
   c. Briefly explain ONE important similarity between the New England and Middle colonies in the same periods.

TRM Find complete suggested responses in the Teacher's Resource Materials.

GROWTH, DIVERSITY, AND CONFLICT, 1720–1763 139-b

AP® PRACTICE QUESTIONS

Find **AP® Exam Practice Questions** at the end of each chapter — suggested responses and rubrics can be found in the Teacher's Resource Materials.
Also available for exam preparation is ***Strive for a 5***, a student study and prep guide, and the **redesigned Test Bank**, which includes book-related multiple-choice, essay, and matching questions, as well as AP®-style practice exams.

About the cover image

Subway, c. 1934

The Subway (1934) depicts a common scene of life in New York City during the Great Depression of the 1930s. Artist Lily Furedi captures a wide diversity of social class, race, and economic status that made up the American demographic landscape at the time. Furedi presents bow-tie wearing upper class riders sitting beside blue collar workers, highlighting the range of work and labor done at the time, and reflecting a sense of community created by the challenges of the Great Depression. The juxtaposition of individuals from various racial and ethnic backgrounds challenges many commonly held beliefs around the United States at the time, which supported segregation in public transportation, and also illustrates changes in the role of women as the three women in the foreground are clearly engaging in society independently. *Subway*, Lily Furedi, Public Works of Art Project, New York, c. 1934

50°N
120°W
110°W
100°W
CANADA
Columbia River
Seattle
Olympia
WASHINGTON
Mt. Rainier
(14,411 ft.; 4,392 m)
Mt. St. Helens
(8,366 ft.; 2,550 m)
Portland
Columbia River
Salem
Eugene
CASCADE MTS.
OREGON
COAST RANGES
Missouri River
Helena
MONTANA
Yellowstone River
Billings
NORTH DAKOTA
Bismarck
BADLANDS
SOUTH DAKOTA
Pierre
Boise
IDAHO
Snake River
ROCKY MOUNTAINS
WYOMING
BLACK HILLS
GREAT PLAINS
40°N
Sacramento River
SIERRA NEVADA
Carson City
Great Salt Lake
Salt Lake City
GREAT DIVIDE BASIN
Cheyenne
NEBRASKA
Platte River
San Francisco
Sacramento
Oakland
San Jose
GREAT BASIN
NEVADA
UTAH
COLORADO
Denver
Mt. Elbert
(14,433 ft.; 4,399 m)
Colorado Springs
Pikes Peak
(14,110 ft.; 4,301 m)
KANSAS
Wichita
San Joaquin River
Fresno
Mt. Whitney
(14,494 ft.; 4,418 m)
Las Vegas
Colorado River
Arkansas River
CALIFORNIA
MOJAVE DESERT
OKLAHOMA
Santa Fe
Los Angeles
Albuquerque
ARIZONA
Oklahoma City
NEW MEXICO
Red River
PACIFIC OCEAN
San Diego
Phoenix
Lubbock
Pecos River
LLANO ESTACADO
Tucson
Fort Worth
TEXAS
El Paso
Colorado River
30°N
EDWARDS PLATEAU
Austin
Rio Grande
San Antonio
MEXICO
170°W
130°W
ARCTIC OCEAN
RUSSIA
70°N
BROOKS RANGE
ALASKA
Arctic Circle
Mt. McKinley
(20,320 ft.; 6,194 m)
Yukon River
ALASKA RANGE
CANADA
Anchorage
60°N
Bering Sea
Gulf of Alaska
Juneau
ALEUTIAN ISLANDS
0 250 500 miles
0 250 500 kilometers
160°W
150°W
140°W
Kauai
Niihau
22°N
HAWAII
Oahu
Honolulu
Molokai
PACIFIC OCEAN
Lanai
Maui
Kahoolawe
20°N
Hawaii
0 50 100 miles
0 50 100 kilometers
160°W
158°W
156°W

CANADA
90°W
80°W
70°W
N
S
E
W
0
150
300 miles
0
150
300 kilometers
Lake Superior
Lake Michigan
Lake Huron
Lake Ontario
Lake Erie
St. Lawrence River
Hudson River
Missouri River
Mississippi River
Ohio River
Cumberland River
Tennessee River
Alabama River
Potomac River
Chesapeake Bay
MINNESOTA
WISCONSIN
MICHIGAN
IOWA
MISSOURI
ILLINOIS
INDIANA
OHIO
KENTUCKY
TENNESSEE
ARKANSAS
LOUISIANA
MISSISSIPPI
ALABAMA
GEORGIA
FLORIDA
SOUTH CAROLINA
NORTH CAROLINA
VIRGINIA
W. VA.
PENNSYLVANIA
NEW YORK
VERMONT
MAINE
NEW HAMPSHIRE
MASS.
R.I.
CONNECTICUT
NEW JERSEY
DELAWARE
MARYLAND
WASHINGTON, D.C.
CENTRAL LOWLAND
APPALACHIAN MTS.
TIDEWATER
St. Paul
Minneapolis
Milwaukee
Madison
Lansing
Detroit
Chicago
Des Moines
Omaha
Topeka
Kansas City
St. Louis
Jefferson City
Springfield
Indianapolis
Cincinnati
Columbus
Cleveland
Wheeling
Pittsburgh
Harrisburg
Buffalo
Albany
Burlington
Montpelier
Mt. Washington (6,288 ft.; 1,917 m)
Concord
Manchester
Augusta
Portland
Boston
Providence
Hartford
New York
Trenton
Philadelphia
Dover
Baltimore
Annapolis
Richmond
Norfolk
Charleston
Frankfort
Louisville
Knoxville
Mt. Mitchell (6,684 ft.; 2,037 m)
Nashville
Raleigh
Charlotte
Columbia
Charleston
Atlanta
Memphis
Birmingham
Montgomery
Little Rock
Tulsa
Dallas
Jackson
Baton Rouge
New Orleans
Houston
Tallahassee
Jacksonville
Orlando
Miami
Lake Okeechobee
Gulf of Mexico
ATLANTIC OCEAN
BAHAMAS
CUBA
THE UNITED STATES
Elevation
Feet
Meters
Over 13,001
Over 3,001
6,561–13,000
2,001–3,000
3,281–6,560
1,001–2,000
1,641–3,280
501–1,000
661–1,640
201–500
0–660
0–200
Below sea level
Below sea level
67°W
65°W
18°N
ATLANTIC OCEAN
San Juan
PUERTO RICO
VIRGIN ISLANDS
Caribbean Sea
0
50
100 miles
0
50
100 kilometers

HENRETTA'S

AMERICA'S HISTORY

TENTH EDITION

FOR THE AP® COURSE

Rebecca Edwards
Vassar College

Eric Hinderaker
University of Utah

Robert O. Self
Brown University

James A. Henretta
University of Maryland

bedford, freeman & worth
high school publishers
Boston | New York

Sr. Vice President, Humanities and Social Sciences and High School: *Charles Linsemeier*
Executive Program Director, HS: *Ann Heath*
Executive Program Manager, HS Humanities: *Nathan Odell*
Executive Marketing Manager, HS: *Janie Pierce-Bracher*
Senior Executive Program Manager for History: *William J. Lombardo*
Director of Content Development: *Jane Knetzger*
Senior Development Editor: *Heidi L. Hood*
Assistant Editor: *Carly Lewis*
Assistant Editor, HS: *Carla Duval*
Director of Media Editorial: *Adam Whitehurst*
Media Editor: *Mollie Chandler*
Senior Media Editor, HS: *Kim Morté*
Marketing Manager: *Melissa Rodriguez*
Marketing Coordinator, HS: *Tiffani Tang*
Senior Director, Content Management Enhancement: *Tracey Kuehn*
Senior Managing Editor: *Michael Granger*
Senior Content Project Manager: *Kendra LeFleur*
Senior Workflow Project Manager: *Lisa McDowell*
Production Supervisor: *Robin Besofsky*
Director of Design, Content Management: *Diana Blume*
Interior Design: *Maureen McCutcheon*
Cover Design: *William Boardman*
Text Permissions Editor: *Michael McCarty*
Text Permissions Researcher: *Elaine Kosta, Lumina Datamatics*
Director of Rights and Permissions: *Hilary Newman*
Senior Photo Permissions Editor: *Sheena Goldstein*
Photo Researcher: *Naomi Kornhauser*
Director of Digital Production: *Keri deManigold*
Copy Editor: *Dana Richards*
Indexer: *Sonya Dintaman*
Composition: *Lumina Datamatics, Inc.*
Cover Image: *Lily Furedi,* Subway, *1934, oil on canvas, Smithsonian American Art Museum, Washington, DC/ART Resource, NY*
Printing and Binding: *Transcontinental Printing*

Copyright © 2021, 2018, 2014, 2011 by Bedford, Freeman & Worth High School Publishers All rights reserved. No part of this book may be reproduced, stored in a retrieval system, or transmitted in any form or any means, electronic, mechanical, photocopying, recording, or otherwise, except as may be permitted by law or expressly permitted in writing by the Publisher.

Library of Congress Control Number: 2020945298
ISBN: 978-1-319-28115-1

Printed in Canada.
1 2 3 4 5 6 25 24 23 22 21

Acknowledgments

Acknowledgments and copyrights appear on the same page as the text and art selections they cover; these acknowledgments and copyrights constitute an extension of the copyright page.

AP® is a trademark registered by the College Board, which is not affiliated with, and does not endorse, this product.

For information, write: BFW Publishers, One New York Plaza, Suite 4500, New York, NY 10004 hsmarketing@bfwpub.com

Preface
Why This Book This Way

How do we teach our students to think like historians? As scholars and teachers who go into the classroom every day, the authors of *America's History* know these challenges well and have written the tenth edition to help teachers meet them. Combining breadth with balance, *America's History* has long been recognized for its big-picture, analytic focus and its commitment to an integrated narrative—one that does not privilege either "top down" institutions *or* "bottom up" social changes and Americans' rich diversity of experiences, but instead reveals their interdependency. In each chapter we also situate U.S. history in global context, showing students how events and trends elsewhere shaped the colonies and the American nation.

For the tenth edition, we intensified our focus on helping students understand **not just what happened, but *why***. *Why*, for example, did the outcome of the Seven Years' War result in an imperial crisis that ultimately led to the separation of thirteen North American colonies from Great Britain? *Why* did the United States double its territory between 1800 and 1848? *Why* did the rise of large corporations transform workers' experiences and trigger conflict? *Why* did the United States fight a Cold War with the Soviet Union and ascend to global leadership? You'll find these questions and many more, embedded at the start of chapters and presented in the thematic Part Openers. As they read the narrative, students can use these guiding questions to trace themes, explore causes and consequences, and understand change over time.

One of the most exciting developments in this edition is the attention we have devoted to capitalism and economic history. For example, we now highlight more clearly the role of indentured servitude in early colonization. Having introduced the idea of the cotton complex in the ninth edition, we have now strengthened our emphasis on the importance of western lands and trade protectionism in the early development of the U.S. economy. We give more emphasis to ideas about capitalism, especially Social Darwinism, and to the emergence of a self-conscious "middle class" and urban "working class." We have also expanded our coverage of the emergence of a mass consumer economy in the twentieth century, detailing that economy's rise in the 1920s and its consolidation in the 1950s. And finally, we have provided more emphasis on the economics of globalization in the last two chapters. As authors, together we strive to ensure that the most recent scholarship, and the liveliest historical narratives, infuse every page of the text.

In students' Wikipedia-driven world, facts and data are everywhere. What they crave is analysis—frameworks to help them organize and prioritize information. As it has since its inception, *America's History* provides students with a comprehensive explanation and interpretation of events, a road map for understanding the world in which we live. The core of a textbook is its narrative. We have endeavored to keep ours clear, accessible, and lively. In it, we focus not only on the marvelous diversity of peoples who came to call themselves Americans but also on the political, legal, and military institutions that have forged a common national identity. As we write this preface, a novel coronavirus is spreading worldwide, reinforcing our keen awareness of the fragility of our institutions and the shrinking distance between Americans and others around the globe. To help students understand the challenges we face today, we call attention to connections with the histories of our neighbors in North and South America as well as Europe, Africa, and Asia, in all eras of our past.

A Nine-Part Framework Highlights Key Developments

One of the great strengths of *America's History* is its part structure, which helps students identify key forces and major developments that shaped each era. A four-page part opener introduces each of the nine parts, starting with an overview followed by three broad thematic questions with accompanying analysis and striking images. In the tenth edition these are followed by a new, streamlined **thematic visual timeline** that orients students to the most important developments and themes of the period and helps them see the big picture and relationships among events. The part openers conclude with new questions, **"AP® Making Connections Across Chapters,"** that ask students to consider large-scale developments, assess periodization and change over time, and make connections among chapters—questions that serve both as preparation for reading the part and as assignments for post-reading reflection.

Part 1, "Transformations of North America, 1491–1700," highlights the diversity and complexity of Native Americans prior to European contact, examines the transformative impact of European intrusions and the Columbian Exchange, and emphasizes the experimental quality of colonial ventures. **Part 2, "British North America and the Atlantic World, 1607–1763,"** explains the diversification of British North America and the rise of the British Atlantic world and emphasizes the importance of contact between colonists and Native Americans and imperial rivalries among European powers. **Part 3, "Revolution and Republican Culture, 1754–1800,"** traces the rise of colonial protest against British imperial reform, outlines the ways that the American Revolution challenged the social order, and explores the processes of conquest, competition, and consolidation that followed it.

Part 4, "Overlapping Revolutions, 1800–1848," traces the transformation of the economy, society, and culture of the new nation; the creation of a democratic polity; and growing sectional divisions. **Part 5, "Consolidating a Continental Union, 1844–1877,"** covers the conflicts generated by America's empire building in the West, including sectional political struggles that led to the Civil War and national consolidation of power during and after Reconstruction. **Part 6, "Industrializing America: Upheavals and Experiments, 1877–1917,"** examines the transformations brought about by the rise of corporations and a powerhouse industrial economy; immigration and a diverse, urbanizing society; and movements for progressive reform.

Part 7, "Global Ambitions and Domestic Turmoil, 1890–1945," explores America's rise to world power, the cultural transformations and political conflicts of the 1920s, the Great Depression, and the creation of the New Deal welfare state. **Part 8, "The Modern State and the Age of Liberalism, 1945–1980,"** addresses the postwar period, including America's new global leadership role during the Cold War; the expansion of federal responsibility during a new "age of liberalism"; and the growth of mass consumption and the middle class. Finally, **Part 9, "Globalization and the End of the American Century, 1980 to the Present,"** discusses the conservative political ascendancy of the 1980s; the end of the Cold War and rising conflict in the Middle East; and globalization and increasing economic and social inequality.

Helping Students Work with Primary and Secondary Sources, Maps, and Visuals

America's History emphasizes the importance of both primary and secondary sources, not only as a means to enliven and extend the narrative but to help students sharpen their skills in interpreting historical evidence. In addition to weaving lively quotations throughout the narrative, we offer students substantial excerpts from historical documents—letters, diaries, autobiographies, public testimony, and more—plus numerous figures that give students practice working with data. These documents allow students to experience the past through the words and perspectives of those who lived it and to gain skill in interpreting historical evidence. Five types of special features appear that provide either primary or secondary sources for comparison and interpretation.

To help students understand that history is an ongoing process of interpretation, we include excerpts from diverse scholarly views in a secondary-source feature called **AP® Comparing Interpretations,** which brings historical argumentation directly into the book. Students read accessible passages—many expanded in this edition for more fruitful comparisons—from two scholars who offer different interpretations of the same event or period. By examining the passages side by side and responding to the questions we pose, students learn how historians interpret evidence, weigh facts, and arrive at their conclusions. This feature, appearing in sixteen of the book's thirty chapters, highlights how history is a way of thinking and analyzing, rather than an inert set of facts. This edition includes the new feature "How Rational Were the Great Railroad Empires?" as well as other favorites such as "Did British Administrators Try to Protect or Exploit Native Americans?" "Did the Market Revolution Expand Opportunities for Women?" "Were the 'Gilded Age' and 'Progressive Era' Separate Periods?" and "Was Martin Luther King Jr. a Radical or a Reformer?"

AP® Firsthand Accounts, a two-page feature in each chapter, helps students learn to think critically by comparing primary source texts written or spoken from two or more perspectives. New topics include "The First National Debate over Slavery," "Sex Workers, Libertines, and Reformers," "Three Reform Platforms—Populist, Progressive, and Socialist," and "African American Leaders React to the Great Migration."

The **AP® America in the World** feature, which appears in fourteen chapters, uses primary sources and data to situate U.S. history in a global context while giving students practice in comparison and data analysis. These features address topics as diverse as transatlantic migration from 1500 to 1760, the fight for women's rights in France and the United States, post-emancipation labor laws in Haiti and the United States, the loss of human life in World War I, economic nationalism in the United States and Mexico, and the worldwide economic malaise of the 1970s.

Finally, we are proud to retain and refresh our signature **AP® Thinking Like a Historian** feature, which appears in every chapter to aid students with their historical thinking skills. Each of these features includes five to eight brief primary sources organized around a central theme. Students are asked to analyze the documents and complete an "AP® DBQ Practice" assignment that asks them to synthesize and use the evidence to create an argument. The themes are engaging and important topics, such as "Women's Labor," "Becoming Literate: Public Education and Democracy," "Making Modern Presidents," and "Debating Vietnam." The tenth edition brings in fresh topics for exploration, including "Claiming the Oregon Country," "The Power and the Appeal of the Ward Boss," and "The Automobile Transforms America."

As in past editions, an outstanding visual program engages students' attention and gives them practice in working with visual sources. We have added in each chapter one new guided **Visual Activity**. Captions provide necessary context; "Reading the Image" questions prompt students to study the image closely, while "Making Connections" questions link it to wider issues in the narrative. The tenth edition features an abundance of additional opportunities for considering visual evidence, with more than four hundred paintings, cartoons, illustrations, photographs, and charts, most in full color and more than a quarter new to this edition. Informative captions set the illustrations in context and provide students with background for making their own analysis of the images in the book.

Keenly aware that students lack geographic literacy as well as map interpretation skills, we have added in each chapter a **new Mapping the Past activity** that pairs a map with two levels of questions. "Reading the Map" requires students to examine the map carefully and "Making Connections" asks them to interpret its implications in the context of the chapter. To further aid students with their understanding of the geography of American history, we have included more than 120 full-color **maps** that show major developments in the narrative, each with a caption to help students interpret what they see.

Because we understand how important primary sources are to the study of history, we are also pleased to offer for packaging the companion reader, *Sources for America's History*, featuring a wealth of additional documents. For more information, see Versions and Supplements, which follows this preface.

Taken together, these documents, figures, maps, and illustrations provide teachers with a multitude of prepared, carefully curated teaching materials, so that *America's History* offers not only a compelling narrative, but also—right in the textbook—the rich documentary materials that teachers need to bring the past alive and introduce students to historical analysis.

Helping Students Understand the Narrative

Study aids in the tenth edition have been strengthened to support students' understanding of the material and development of historical thinking skills. **AP® Learning Focus** questions at the start of every chapter, guide student reading and focus their attention on identifying not just what happened, but why. **New part and chapter visual timelines** help students see how events relate to one another. In each chapter, a variety of learning tools support this big idea focus. As they read, students will gain proficiency with the AP® Reasoning Processes and Historical Thinking Skills via **AP® Skills and Processes** margin questions that ask students to answer "Causation," "Contextualization," and "Continuity and Change" questions, among other skills. Additionally, students will gain key insights into the AP® Exam with the **AP® Exam Tip** margin notes that point out important topics and ideas to focus on while reading the chapter. Where students are likely to stumble over a key concept, we boldface it in the text where it is first mentioned and now provide a **new marginal glossary** that defines each term.

The Chapter Review section provides a set of **AP® Content Review questions** that restate the individual section preview questions and **AP® Making Connections** questions that ask students to consider broader historical issues, developments, and continuities and changes over time. **AP® Terms to Know** provides a list of **Key Concepts and Events** and **Key People** students should review and remember. Lastly, a **Key Turning Points** question reminds students of important developments and asks them to consider periodization.

AP® Practice Questions at the end of each chapter and part allow students to practice answering Multiple Choice Questions, Short Answer Questions, Document-Based Questions, and Long Essay Questions like those they will see on the AP® U.S. History Exam. Additionally, students will have the opportunity to take a full-length practice exam in the **AP® U.S. History Practice Exam** that sits at the back of the book. In addition, whenever a teacher assigns the book's **digital platform** (which is available bundled with the print book or on its own), students get full access to **LearningCurve**, an online adaptive learning tool that promotes mastery of the book's content and diagnoses students' trouble spots. With this adaptive quizzing, students accumulate points toward a target score as they go, giving the interaction a game-like feel. Feedback for incorrect responses explains why the answer is mistaken and directs students back to the text to review before they attempt to answer the question again. The end result is a better understanding of the key elements of the text. Teachers who actively assign LearningCurve report that their students enjoy using it and come to class more prepared for discussion. In addition, LearningCurve's reporting feature allows teachers to quickly diagnose which concepts their students are struggling with, so they can adjust lectures and activities accordingly.

Helping Teachers Teach with Digital Resources

As noted, *America's History* is offered in Macmillan's premier digital platform, which includes an intuitive, interactive e-book and course space with a comprehensive set of options for engaging and assessing students. Available packaged with the print text or at a low price when used alone, the digital platform grants students and teachers access to a wealth of online tools and resources built specifically for our text to enhance reading comprehension and promote in-depth study. The course space and interactive e-book are ready to use as is, or they can be edited and customized with the teacher's own materials and assigned right away.

Developed with extensive feedback from history teachers and students, the digital platform for *America's*

History includes the complete narrative of the print book, the companion reader, *Sources for America's History*, and **LearningCurve**, an adaptive learning tool that is designed to get students to read before they come to class. With **new source-based questions in the test bank and in LearningCurve,** teachers now have more ways to test students on their understanding of sources and narrative in the book.

The digital platform also includes **Guided Reading Exercises** that prompt students to be active readers of the chapter narrative and auto-graded **primary source quizzes** to test comprehension of written and visual sources. These features, plus **additional primary source documents, video sources and tools for making video assignments, map activities, flash cards,** and **customizable test banks,** make this the premium platform for teachers who want a multifaceted teaching tool for enlivening their courses and assessing their students.

These new learning platforms have not changed the central mission of the book but seek to enhance it by reaching students wherever they are in their learning and give teachers new ways to invigorate their courses. To learn more about the benefits of the digital platform, see the "Versions and Supplements" section on page xi.

New Updates to the Narrative

In the new edition, we continue to offer teachers a bold account of U.S. history that reflects the latest, most exciting scholarship in the field. As noted earlier, we have highlighted the history of capitalism throughout. We have updated and augmented a number of other areas in the narrative as well. The tenth edition also gives revised or expanded coverage of:

- Colonial resistance to British reforms after the Seven Years' War (chapter 5)
- The relationship between the French Revolution and American politics (chapter 7)
- Organization and labor activism among women working in the Waltham-Lowell mills (chapter 8)
- Americans' religious experiences in the Second Great Awakening (chapter 10)
- Free African American communities in the antebellum era (chapter 10)
- Slave resistance, including the 1811 German Coast uprising in Louisiana (chapter 11)
- Eugenic ideas and their real-world consequences (chapter 17)
- The aftermath of World War I and the devastating worldwide consequences of the Treaty of Versailles (chapter 20)
- The rise and flourishing of youth culture in the twentieth century (chapter 25)
- Key developments (such as growth of the black middle class and the advent of television) that made the Civil Rights Movement possible (chapter 26)
- The role of religion in social and political life after the 1970s (chapter 28)
- Environmental and economic crises in the early twenty-first century (chapter 30)
- The presidency of Donald Trump (chapter 30)

Acknowledgments

We are grateful to the following scholars and teachers who reported on their experiences with the ninth edition or reviewed features of the new edition. Their comments often challenged us to rethink or justify our interpretations and always provided a check on accuracy down to the smallest detail.

Harry Asana Akoh, *Atlanta Metropolitan State College*
Karen Auman, *Brigham Young University*
James Paul Beil, *Luna Community College*
Colt Chaney, *Murray State College*
Eric D. Duchess, *Finger Lakes Community College*
Linda Graham, *Wharton County Junior College*
George Jarrett, *Cerritos College*
Jeffrey Kleiman, *University of Wisconsin – Stevens Point*
Lynne Nelson Manion, *Eastern Maine Community College*
John G. McCurdy, *Eastern Michigan University*
James Miller, *Carleton University*
David Raley, *El Paso Community College*
Nancy J. Rosenbloom, *Canisius College*
Scott Seagle, *University of Tennessee at Chattanooga*
Scott M. Williams, *Weatherford College*

As the authors of *America's History*, we know better than anyone else how much this book is the work of other hands and minds. We are greatly indebted to the team at Bedford/St. Martin's (Macmillan Learning): Michael Rosenberg, William J. Lombardo, and Heidi Hood, who guided us through the revision process and suggested many improvements. Kerri Cardone did a masterful job seeing the book through the production process. Melissa Rodriguez in the marketing department understood how to communicate our vision to teachers; they and the members of college and high school sales forces did wonderful work in helping this edition reach the classroom. We also thank the rest of our editorial and production team for their dedicated efforts: Media Editor Mollie Chandler; Assistant Editor Carly Lewis; copyeditor Dana Richards; proofreaders Joe Ford and Jananee Sekar; indexer Sonya Dintaman; art researcher Naomi Kornhauser; and text permissions researcher Eve Lehmann. Many thanks to all of you for your contributions to this new edition of *America's History*.

Rebecca Edwards
Eric Hinderaker
Robert O. Self

Versions and Supplements

Adopters of *America's History* and their students have access to abundant print and digital resources and tools, the acclaimed *Bedford Series in History and Culture* volumes, and much more. The digital course space for *America's History* provides access to the narrative as well as a wealth of primary sources and other features, along with assignment and assessment opportunities at the ready. See below for more information, visit the book's catalog site at **bfwpub.com/henretta10e**, or contact your local BFW High School Publishers representative.

Digital Options

Access the Interactive E-book with Sources on the Book's Digital Platform

Available for purchase on its own or for packaging with new books, the digital platform for *America's History for the AP® Course* is a breakthrough solution for history courses. Intuitive and easy to use for students and teachers alike, it is ready to use as is and can be edited, customized with your own material, and assigned quickly. LaunchPad for *Henretta's America's History* for the AP® Course includes the entire program all in one place, including the full interactive e-book and the companion reader *Sources for America's History*, a downloadable e-book for reading offline, plus LearningCurve adaptive quizzing, guided reading activities designed to help students read actively for key concepts, autograded quizzes for each primary source, and chapter summative quizzes. Through a wealth of formative and summative assessments, including the adaptive learning program of LearningCurve (see the full description ahead), students gain confidence and mastery of course content. These features, plus additional primary source documents, video sources and tools for making video assignments, map activities, flashcards, and customizable test banks integrated in into each chapter for teacher use, make the book's digital platform an invaluable asset for any teacher.

For more information, or to arrange a demo or class test, contact us at **hsmarketing@bfwpub.com**.

LearningCurve

Assign LearningCurve So Your Students Come to Class Prepared

Students using the book's digital platform receive access to LearningCurve for *America's History*. Assigning LearningCurve in place of reading quizzes is easy for teachers, and the reporting features help them track overall class trends and spot topics that are giving students trouble so they can adjust their lectures and class activities. This online learning tool is popular with students because it was designed to help them rehearse content at their own pace in a nonthreatening, game-like environment. The feedback for wrong answers provides instructional coaching and sends students back to the book for review. Students answer as many questions as necessary to reach a target score, with repeated chances to revisit material they haven't mastered. When LearningCurve is assigned, students come to class better prepared.

Teacher's Edition for Henretta's America's History

The Teacher's Edition provides a wealth of guidance and support for AP® teachers. Developed for the updated AP® U.S. History course, annotations include teaching tips, AP® Reasoning Processes and Historical Thinking Skills practice, pacing guides, exam alerts, and more. The Teacher's Edition helps teachers at all levels build the most successful AP® U.S. History course they can. Kyle VanderWall, a dedicated and experienced high school teacher who has served as an AP® Reader for ten years, built off the work of previous edition authors Nicki Griffin and Dave Neumann, as well as his own invaluable classroom experience, to create resources that every teacher will find useful in preparing their students for the AP® U.S. History Exam.

Strive for a 5: Preparing for the AP® U.S. History Examination

Revised for the updated AP® U.S. History course, this print guide provides students with narrative and thematic overviews of each historical period, chapter reviews organized around AP® key concepts, and AP®-style practice exams, including source-based multiple-choice and document-based questions as well as short- and long-answer essay questions. The guide is authored by Warren Hierl of the Career Center, Winston-Salem, NC (retired) and Louisa Moffitt of Marist School, Atlanta, GA, both experienced AP® teachers, exam readers, and workshop leaders.

Take Advantage of Teacher Resources

Bedford/St. Martin's has developed a rich array of teaching resources for this book and for this course. They range from lecture and presentation materials and assessment tools to course management options. Most can be found in the digital platform or can be downloaded or ordered at **bfwpub.com/henretta10e**.

Guide to Changing Editions. Designed to facilitate a teacher's transition from the previous edition of *America's History* to this new edition, this guide presents an overview of major changes as well as of changes in each chapter.

Computerized Test Bank. The test bank includes both **content quizzes** for each chapter and **AP®-Style Practice Exams**. The test bank is available on the book's digital platform, and via third-party software that quickly create paper, Internet, and LAN-based tests. Not only can you create and format a test in minutes, but the platform is fully customizable, allowing you to enter your own questions, edit existing questions, set time limits, incorporate multimedia, and scramble answers and change the order of questions to prevent plagiarism. Detailed results reports feed into a gradebook.

Teacher's Resource Materials. The Teacher's Resource Materials, easily downloadable from our digital platform, contains resources to help teachers structure and navigate the course, such as lecture presentation slides, handouts, and suggested responses. Because every instructor teaches history differently, these resources are designed to be used in a variety of ways, giving teachers many options for designing and redesigning a course to focus on specific topics or areas of interest.

More Package Options for More Choice and Value

For information on packages, visit **bfwpub.com/henretta10e**, or contact your local BFW High School Publishers representative.

***Sources for America's History*, Tenth Edition.** This primary source collection provides a revised selection of sources to accompany *America's History*, Tenth Edition. *Sources for America's History* offers a broad selection of approximately 225 primary source documents as well as pedagogy to help students understand the sources. Five to six documents per chapter, ranging from speeches by celebrated historical figures to personal letters and diary entries by ordinary people, foster historical thinking skills while emphasizing the first-person experience and putting a human face on America's diverse history. The tenth edition features over thirty new image sources including colonial tobacco advertisements, political cartoons, and photographs of women's rights marches. Added immigration-related tweets from President Trump bring the collection up to the present moment. To support the structure of the parent text, unique part document sets at the end of each part present sources that illustrate the major themes of each section. Brief introductions place each document in historical context, and questions for analysis help students practice historical thinking skills and link individual sources to larger themes. This companion reader is an exceptional value for students and offers plenty of assignment options for teachers. Available packaged with the print text and included in the e-book with auto-graded quizzes for each source. Also available on its own as a downloadable e-book.

Bedford Document Collections. These affordable, brief document projects provide 5 to 7 primary sources, an introduction, historical background, and other pedagogical features. Each curated project—designed for use in a single class period and written by a historian about a favorite topic—poses a historical question and guides students through analysis of the sources. More than 35 document collections in U.S. history cover the breadth of the survey course on engaging topics such as "Witch Accusations in Seventeenth-Century New England"; "The California Gold Rush: A Trans-Pacific Phenomenon"; "Bleeding Kansas: A Small Civil War"; "Sand Creek: Battle or Massacre?"; "The Legend of John Henry Folklore and the Lives of African Americans in the Postwar South"; "The Chinese Exclusion Act of 1882"; and "The Texas Rangers: Vanguard of Anglo Settlements in the Lone Star State"; "The Decision to Intern the Japanese Americans during World War II"; "War Stories: Black Soldiers and the Long Civil Rights Movement"; and "The Cuban Missile Crisis: And International History," and "Black Power." These primary source projects are available in a low-cost, easy-to-use digital format or can be combined with other course materials in Bedford Select to create an affordable, personalized print product.

The Bedford Series in History and Culture. More than 100 titles in this highly praised series combine first-rate scholarship, historical narrative, and important primary documents for undergraduate courses. Each book is brief, inexpensive, and focused on a specific topic or period. Recently published titles include *The Chinese Exclusion Act and Angel Island: A Brief History with Documents* by Judy Yung; *American Working Women in World War II: A Brief History with Documents* by Lynn Dumenil; *Brown v. Board of Education: A Brief History with Documents,* Second Edition, by Waldo E. Martin Jr.; and *Defending Slavery: Proslavery Thought in the Old South* by Paul Finkelman. For a complete list of titles, visit **bfwpub.com/henretta10e**. Package discounts are available.

Trade Books. History titles published by sister companies Hill and Wang; Farrar, Straus and Giroux; Henry Holt and Company; St. Martin's Press; Picador; and Palgrave Macmillan are available at a 50% discount when packaged with Bedford/St. Martin's textbooks. For more information, visit **macmillanlearning.com/tradeup**.

A Pocket Guide to Writing in History. Updated to reflect changes made in the 2017 *Chicago Manual of Style* revision, this portable and affordable reference tool by Mary Lynn Rampolla provides reading, writing, and research advice useful to students in all history courses. Concise yet comprehensive advice on approaching typical history assignments, developing critical reading skills, writing effective history papers, conducting research, using and documenting sources, and avoiding plagiarism—enhanced with practical tips and examples throughout—has made this slim reference a bestseller. Deep discounts are available when bundled with a survey textbook.

About the Authors

Karl Rabe.

Rebecca Edwards is Eloise Ellery Professor of History at Vassar College, where she teaches courses on nineteenth-century politics, the Civil War, the frontier West, and women, gender, and sexuality. She is the author of, among other publications, *Angels in the Machinery: Gender in American Party Politics from the Civil War to the Progressive Era*; *New Spirits: Americans in the "Gilded Age," 1865–1905*; and the essay "Women's and Gender History" in *The New American History*. She is currently working on a book about the role of childbearing in the expansion of America's nineteenth-century empire.

Jeff Hanson, University of Utah.

Eric Hinderaker is Distinguished Professor of History at the University of Utah. His research explores early modern imperialism, relations between Europeans and Native Americans, military-civilian relations in the Atlantic world, and comparative colonization. His most recent book, *Boston's Massacre*, was awarded the Cox Book Prize from the Society of the Cincinnati and was a finalist for the George Washington Prize. His other publications include *Elusive Empires: Constructing Colonialism in the Ohio Valley, 1673–1800*; *The Two Hendricks: Unraveling a Mohawk Mystery*, which won the Herbert H. Lehman Prize for Distinguished Scholarship in New York History from the New York Academy of History; and, with Peter C. Mancall, *At the Edge of Empire: The Backcountry in British North America*.

Peter Goldberg.

Robert O. Self is Mary Ann Lippitt Professor of American History at Brown University. His research focuses on urban history, American politics, and the post-1945 United States. He is the author of *American Babylon: Race and the Struggle for Postwar Oakland*, which won four professional prizes, including the James A. Rawley Prize from the Organization of American Historians, and *All in the Family: The Realignment of American Democracy Since the 1960s*. He is currently at work on a book about the centrality of houses, cars, and children to family consumption in the twentieth-century United States.

National Humanities Center.

James A. Henretta is Professor Emeritus of American History at the University of Maryland, College Park, where he taught Early American History and Legal History. His publications include *"Salutary Neglect": Colonial Administration under the Duke of Newcastle*; *Evolution and Revolution: American Society, 1600–1820*; and *The Origins of American Capitalism*. His most recent publication is a long article, "Magistrates, Lawyers, Legislators: The Three Legal Systems of Early America," in *The Cambridge History of American Law*.

About the AP® Contributors

Jeff Hanson, University of Utah.

Nicki Griffin National Board Certified Teacher, teaches AP® U.S. History, AP® European History, and AP® Art History at South Central High School in Winterville, North Carolina, where she serves as Facilitating Teacher for AP® U.S. History in the Pitt County School system. She also serves as Course Lead and teacher for AP® European History for the North Carolina Virtual Public School. She has served as an AP® Reader for seven years and is a College Board Consultant. Over the past decade, she has provided training for hundreds of teachers in AP® U.S. and European History.

Naomi Stanaland.

Marika Manos is the History/Social Science/Civics Coordinator at the Orange County Department of Education and has been an educator for over 19 years. In her previous work, she was a History/Social Science methods instructor at California State University, Long Beach, the K–12 History/Social Science Curriculum Leader for Long Beach Unified School District, and a classroom teacher for 12 years. She has a doctorate in Education from the University of Southern California with an emphasis in curriculum. Her current research interests include Culturally Sustaining Pedagogies, Historical Thinking Practices, and Inquiry-Based Learning.

Kyle VanderWall.

Kyle VanderWall has taught history for eighteen years at Grandville High School in Grandville, MI. For sixteen of those years, he has taught AP® U.S. History. Over that span, the program has grown significantly. The AP® U.S. History course at Grandville is designed for sophomores and has no prerequisites for admission. During the last ten years, Kyle has led numerous workshops around the country to help improve historical pedagogy. His instructional design and work focuses on increasing students' self-efficacy of historical inquiry. For the past ten years, he has participated in the AP® Reading as both a Reader and Table Leader scoring the Long-Essay and Document-Based Questions.

Brief Contents

Contents

Why did contact among Native Americans, Europeans, and Africans cause such momentous changes?

Private Collection/Bridgeman Images

Why did the American colonies develop the social, political, and economic institutions they did, and why were some colonial experiments more successful than others?

Private Collection/Peter Newark American Pictures/Bridgeman Images

PART 2 British North America and the Atlantic World, 1607–1763 *74*

CHAPTER 3
The British Atlantic World, 1607–1750 *78*

The Granger Collection, New York

Why and how did the South Atlantic System reshape the economy, society, and culture of British North America?

CHAPTER 4
Growth, Diversity, and Conflict, 1720–1763 *110*

George Whitefield Preaching/Collet, John (c. 1725–1780)/ Private Collection/Bridgeman Images

Why did transatlantic travel and communication reshape Britain's American colonies so dramatically?

PART 3 Revolution and Republican Culture, 1754–1800 *140*

CHAPTER 5
The Problem of Empire, 1754–1776 *144*

Historic New England, Boston, Massachusetts, USA/Bridgeman Images

Why did the imperial crisis lead to war between Britain and the United States?

CHAPTER 6
Making War and Republican Governments, 1776–1789 *176*

Anne S. K. Brown Military Collection, Brown University Library

Why did the American independence movement succeed, and what changes did it initiate in American society and government?

PART 4 Overlapping Revolutions, 1800–1848 *244*

CHAPTER 10
Religion, Reform, and Culture,
1820–1848 *314*

Library of Congress, LC-USZC4-772

Why did new intellectual, religious, and social movements emerge in the early nineteenth century, and how did they change American society?

CHAPTER 11
Imperial Ambitions,
1820–1848 *346*

Library of Congress

Why did the ideology of Manifest Destiny unite ordinary Americans and shape U.S. policies?

PART 5 Consolidating a Continental Union, 1844–1877 *376*

CHAPTER 12
Sectional Conflict and Crisis, 1844–1861 *380*

Artokoloro Quint Lox Limited/Alamy Stock Photo

Why did the new Republican Party arise, and what events led to Democratic division and southern secession?

CHAPTER 13
Bloody Ground: The Civil War, 1861–1865 *414*

The Granger Collection, New York

Why and how did the Union win the Civil War?

CHAPTER 14
Reconstruction, 1865–1877 *450*

Library of Congress, LC-USZC4-973

Why did freedpeople, Republican policymakers, and ex-Confederates all end up dissatisfied with Reconstruction — or with its aftermath? To what degree did each group succeed in fulfilling its goals?

CHAPTER 15
Conquering a Continent, 1860–1890 *480*

Library of Congress, 3g04085

Why and how did the United States build a continental empire, and how did this affect people living in the West?

PART 6 Industrializing America: Upheavals and Experiments,

CHAPTER 16
Industrial America: Corporations and Conflicts, 1877–1911 *514*

Library of Congress, LC-DIG-ggbain-03008

Why did large corporations arise and thrive in late nineteenth-century America, and how did they reshape trade, work, and politics?

CHAPTER 17
Making Modern American Culture, 1880–1917 *544*

The Granger Collection

Why and how did Americans' identities, beliefs, and culture change in the early industrial era?

CHAPTER 18
"Civilization's Inferno": The Rise and Reform of Industrial Cities, 1880–1917 *576*

Why and how did the rise of big cities shape American society and politics?

Collection of Mr. and Mrs. Paul Mellon, National Gallery of Art. Courtesy National Gallery of Art, Washington

CHAPTER 19
Whose Government? Politics, Populists, and Progressives, 1880–1917 *604*

Why and how did Progressive Era reformers seek to address the problems of industrial America, and to what extent did they succeed?

Library of Congress, 1s09215

PART 7 Global Ambitions and Domestic Turmoil, 1890–1945 *636*

CHAPTER 22

Managing the Great Depression, Forging the New Deal, 1929–1938 *702*

Keystone-France/Gamma-Keystone via Getty Images

Why did the New Deal change the role of government in American life, and what were the economic and social consequences?

CHAPTER 23

The World at War, 1937–1945 *734*

Afro American Newspapers/Gado/Getty Images

Why and how did World War II transform the United States domestically and internationally?

PART 8 The Modern State and the Age of Liberalism, 1945–1980 *768*

CHAPTER 24
The Cold War Dawns, 1945–1963 *772*

swin ink 2/Corbis via Getty Images

Why did the international rivalry of the Cold War create a climate of fear at home, and how did it affect politics and society in the United States?

CHAPTER 25
Triumph of the Middle Class, 1945–1963 *804*

Justin Locke/National Geographic Creative

Why did consumer culture become such a fixture of American life in the postwar decades, and how did it affect politics and society?

CHAPTER 26

The Civil Rights Movement, 1941–1973 *834*

AP Photo

Why did the civil rights movement change over time, and how did competing ideas and strategies evolve within the movement itself?

CHAPTER 27

Liberal Crisis and Conservative Rebirth, 1961–1972 *870*

Private Collection/Peter Newark American Pictures/Bridgeman Images

Why did debates over liberal values in the 1960s lead to social conflict and divide the country?

PART 8 (continued)

CHAPTER 28
The Search for Order in an Era of Limits, 1973–1980 *904*

Owen Franken/Getty Images

Why did the social changes of the 1960s — such as civil rights, shifting gender roles, and challenges to the family — create both new opportunities and political clashes in the 1970s?

PART 9 Globalization and the

CHAPTER 29
Conservative America in the Ascent, 1980–1991 *938*

Ronald Reagan Presidential Library

Why was the New Right able to ascend to national political power in the 1980s and reshape both government and society?

End of the American Century, 1980 to the Present *934*

CHAPTER 30
National and Global Dilemmas, 1989 to the Present *968*

Raphael GAILLARDE/Gamma-Rapho via Getty Images

Why did the shape of American politics, economics, and society shift in response to post–Cold War globalization?

AP® United States History Practice Exam

DOCUMENTS

Maps, Figures, and Tables

How to Get the Most from This Program

START SMART!

Notice that this book is organized into nine parts. **These parts align with the nine time periods established by the College Board for the AP® U.S. History course.** Each part and chapter of this text is structured around a common set of features designed to convey the rich story of humankind while helping you develop the skills required to realize success on the AP® U.S. History Exam.

America's History	AP® U.S. History Time Periods	% Tested
Part 1	1491–1607	5%
Part 2	1607–1754	10%
Part 3	1754–1800	12%
Part 4	1800–1848	10%
Part 5	1844–1877	13%
Part 6	1865–1898	13%
Part 7	1890–1945	17%
Part 8	1945–1980	15%
Part 9	1980–Present	5%

FOCUS YOUR LEARNING

The AP® symbol is your cue that the content or skill practice is specifically designed to help students succeed in the AP® U.S. History course and on the AP® Exam. Look for these special features throughout the book for focused study and targeted practice.

AP® CONCEPT CONNECTIONS

AP® THEMATIC UNDERSTANDING

AP® LEARNING FOCUS

AP® SKILLS & PROCESSES

AP® EXAM TIP

AP® PRACTICE QUESTIONS

AP® PRACTICE ESSAY QUESTIONS

Put Concepts in Context

AP® CONCEPT CONNECTIONS

Why Did the Colonists Revolt?

To administer the vast new American territory it gained in 1763, Britain had to reform its empire. Until that time, its colonies had been left largely free to manage their own affairs. Now, Parliament hoped to pay the costs of empire by taxing the colonies, while at the same time extending control over its new lands in the continental interior. Colonial radicals resisted these reforms. Calling themselves Patriots, they insisted on preserving local control over taxes. As Britain pressured local communities, colonists created intercolonial institutions and developed a broad critique of British rule that combined older, republican political principles with radical ideas of natural rights and the equality of all men. Their protests grew more strident, eventually resulting in open warfare with Great Britain and a declaration of independence.

The Granger Collection, New York.

Why Did Americans Create Republican Governments?

At the same time they fought a war against Great Britain, Patriot leaders in the newly independent states had to create new governments. They drafted constitutions for their states while maintaining a loose confederacy to bind them together. In 1787, reformers put forward a new plan of government, in the form of a constitution that would bind the states into a single nation. At both the state and the national level, leaders sought to create republics: systems of government grounded in the sovereignty of the people.

The new American republic emerged fitfully. Experiments in government took shape across an entire generation, and it took still longer to decide how much power the federal republic should wield over the states. Political culture was unformed and slow to develop. Political parties, for example, were an unexpected development. At first they were widely regarded as illegitimate, but by 1800 they had become essential to managing political conflict, heightening some forms of competition while blunting others. In the last half of the eighteenth century, American political culture was transformed as newly created governments gained the allegiance of their citizens.

The Granger Collection, New York.

AP® Concept Connections appear in every Part Opener and connect striking images to the important AP® U.S. history concepts that students will explore in each part of the textbook.

AP® THEMATIC UNDERSTANDING

Revolution and Republican Culture, 1754–1800

1760 | 1780 | 1800 | 1820

AMERICA IN THE WORLD

- **1763** France and Spain cede all their territories east of the Mississippi to Great Britain in the first Treaty of Paris
- **1775–1783** American Revolutionary War
- **1778–1779** U.S. alliances with France and Spain virtually ensure a Patriot victory
- **1793–1798** The French Revolution divides Americans
- **1812** The War of 1812
- **1823** The Monroe Doctrine asserts American leadership in the Western Hemisphere

POLITICS AND POWER

- **1765** Stamp Act Congress petitions the king
- **1774** First Continental Congress debates responses to the Coercive Acts
- **1775–1781** Second Continental Congress organizes for war
- **1776** Declaration of Independence
- **1787** U.S. Constitution drafted
- **1790** Indians form Western Confederacy
- **1796–1815** First national parties: Federalists and Republicans

ECONOMY

- **1765–1774** Patriots mount three boycotts of British goods
- **1790–1792** Conflict over Alexander Hamilton's economic policies
- **1791** Bank of the United States founded
- **1794** Whiskey producers rebel against taxes
- **1794** Invention of cotton gin stimulates boom in cotton production
- **1807** Jefferson enacts embargo against U.S. shipping to foreign ports to pressure Britain and France to recognize U.S. neutrality

SOCIETY AND CULTURE

- **1765–1780** The idea of natural rights challenges the institution of chattel slavery
- **1779** Judith Sargent Murray publishes "On the Equality of the Sexes"
- **1791** Bill of Rights ratified; guarantees freedom of assembly, worship, speech, press
- **1793–1803** Thousands of refugees from the Haitian Revolution arrive in American ports
- **1798** Sedition Act limits freedom of the press

GEOGRAPHY AND THE ENVIRONMENT

- **1763–1775** The trans-Appalachian west attracts the interest of settlers and investors
- **1770–1781** Ohio Indians resist Anglo-American expansion
- **1784–1789** Western land ordinances and sham Indian treaties open the Ohio country to settlement
- **1803** The Louisiana Purchase nearly doubles the size of the United States
- **1804–1806** Lewis and Clark explore the far west

AP® THEMATIC UNDERSTANDING

AP® Thematic Understanding timelines orient students to major developments and AP® themes of the period.

Read with a Purpose

AP LEARNING FOCUS

AP® Learning Focus questions guide student reading and highlight key historical themes in the chapter by focusing students on not just what happened, but why.

7
CHAPTER

Hammering Out a Federal Republic

1787–1820

AP LEARNING FOCUS

Why did the United States survive the challenges of its first three decades to become a viable, growing independent republic?

Like an earthquake, the American Revolution shook the European monarchical order, and its aftershocks reverberated for decades. By "creating a new republic based on the rights of the individual, the North Americans introduced a new force into the world," the eminent German historian Leopold von Ranke warned the king of Bavaria in 1854, a force that might cost the monarch his throne. Before 1776, "a king who ruled by the grace of God had been the center around which everything turned. Now the idea emerged that power should come from below [from the people]."

Other republican-inspired upheavals — England's Puritan Revolution of the 1640s and the French Revolution of 1789 — ended in political chaos and military rule. Similar fates befell many Latin American republics that won independence from Spain in the early nineteenth century. But the American states escaped both anarchy and dictatorship. Having been raised in a Radical Whig political culture that viewed standing armies and powerful generals as instruments of tyranny, General George Washington left public life in 1783 to manage his plantation, astonishing European observers but bolstering the authority of elected Patriot leaders. "'Tis a Conduct so novel," American painter John Trumbull reported from London, that it is "inconceivable to People [here]."

The great task of fashioning representative republican governments absorbed the energy and intellect of an entire generation and was rife with conflict. Seeking to perpetuate the elite-led polity of the colonial era, Federalists celebrated

AP EXAM TIP

AP® Exam Tip margin notes (and related **AP® Apply the Tip** margin notes in the Teacher's Edition) highlight important concepts and questions that students should focus on to prepare for the AP® Exam as they read through the textbook.

AP SKILLS & PROCESSES

AP® Skills & Processes margin notes identify key historical disciplinary practices and reasoning skills that students will need to perform well on the AP® Exam.

The French Revolution Divides Americans

Proclamation of Neutrality
A proclamation issued by President George Washington in 1793, allowing U.S. citizens to trade with all belligerents in the war between France and Great Britain.

AP EXAM TIP
The impact of conflicts in Europe on the economy, politics, and foreign policy of the U.S. is important to know on the AP® Exam.

American merchants profited even more handsomely from the war between France and Great Britain. In 1793, President Washington issued a **Proclamation of Neutrality**, allowing U.S. citizens to trade with all belligerents. As neutral carriers, American merchant ships claimed a right to pass through Britain's naval blockade of French ports, and American firms quickly took over the lucrative sugar trade between France and its West Indian islands. Commercial earnings rose spectacularly, averaging $20 million annually in the 1790s — twice the value of cotton and tobacco exports. As the American merchant fleet increased from 355,000 tons in 1790 to 1.1 million tons in 1808, northern shipbuilders and merchants provided work for thousands of shipwrights, sailmakers, dockhands, and seamen. Carpenters, masons, and cabinetmakers in Boston, New York, and Philadelphia easily found work building warehouses and fashionable "Federal-style" town houses for newly affluent merchants.

French Revolution
A revolution in France (1789–1799) that was initially welcomed by most Americans because it began by abolishing feudalism and establishing a constitutional monarchy, but eventually came to seem too radical to many.

AP SKILLS & PROCESSES
CONTEXTUALIZATION
How did the French Revolution challenge the United States in domestic and foreign policy?

Ideological Politics As Americans profited from Europe's struggles, they argued passionately over its ideologies. Most Americans had welcomed the **French Revolution** (1789–1799) because it began by abolishing feudalism and establishing a constitutional monarchy. The creation of the First French Republic (1792–1804) was more controversial. Many Americans embraced the democratic ideology of the radical Jacobins, forming political clubs and beginning to address one another as "citizen" to declare their shared values. However, Americans with strong religious beliefs condemned the new French government for closing Christian churches and promoting a rational religion based on "natural morality." And for many, the Reign of Terror (1793–1794) offered proof that the revolution had gone too far. Fearing social revolution at home, wealthy Americans condemned revolutionary leader Robespierre and his followers for executing King Louis XVI and three thousand aristocrats.

Whiskey Rebellion
A 1794 uprising by farmers in western Pennsylvania in response to enforcement of an unpopular excise tax on whiskey.

Their fears were well founded, because Hamilton's economic policies quickly sparked a domestic insurgency. In 1794, western Pennsylvania farmers mounted the so-called **Whiskey Rebellion** to protest Hamilton's excise tax on spirits (see "Thinking Like a Historian," p. 219). This tax had cut demand for the corn whiskey the farmers distilled and bartered for eastern manufactures. Like the Sons of Liberty in 1765 and the Shaysites in 1786, the Whiskey Rebels assailed the tax collectors who sent the farmers' hard-earned money to a distant government. Protesters waved banners proclaiming the French revolutionary slogan "Liberty, Equality, Fraternity!" To deter popular rebellion and uphold national authority, President Washington raised a militia force of 12,000 troops and dispersed the Whiskey Rebels.

Build AP® Skills

AP® AMERICA IN THE WORLD

The Haitian Revolution and the Problem of Race

The slave uprising on the French island of Saint-Domingue triggered international war, created a refugee crisis, and ended with the creation of a new republic. The American Revolution did all these things as well, yet the United States did not support either the rebellion or the republic of Haiti. Some 25,000 refugees from Saint-Domingue arrived in American ports between 1791 and 1810, about two-thirds of them black. Though all were fleeing the insurrection, many Americans feared that the new arrivals might carry the contagion of slave rebellion. Yet the refugees were also objects of charitable relief, and many were welcomed in their adoptive communities.

SAVANNAH CITY COUNCIL'S RESOLUTION IN RESPONSE TO THE HAITIAN UPRISING, 1795

Whereas, from the mischiefs which the people of St. Domingo, and other French islands, have experienced, from the insurrection of their Negroes and People of Colour, the precautions taken by the people of South Carolina . . . to prevent the importation or landing of any such Negroes or Mulattoes amongst them, and the information the Citizens now assembled have received, that a vessel is now lying at Cockspur, recently from Kingston, [Jamaica], with near one hundred Negroes on board, whose landing may be dangerous to the inhabitants of this state, with the daily expectation of many more; therefore, to prevent the evils that may arise from suffering people of this description, under any pretense whatever, from being introduced amongst us, the Citizens pledge them-

everything. Some French patriots here, and a number of Americans, have already made up a small sum of their relief; no doubt the generosity of the Philadelphians and of the inhabitants of every city on the continent will prompt them to follow the example. Among these unfortunate people are a number of French patriotic Captains who have been obliged to fly and abandon their vessels and property; numbers of old men and heads of families, once wealthy, but now reduced to misery and want. Some among them may have by their guilt drawn the misfortunes they feel on their own heads, but they are all unfortunate, and pity is the only sentiment that their heart breaking situation can inspire.". . .

Source: "Extract of a Letter from a Gentleman in Baltimore to His Friend in This City, Containing Some Important Details Relative to the Unfortunate Affair at Cape-François, July 9," *Pennsylvania Gazette*, July 17, 1793, 1.

EXCERPTS FROM THE CONSTITUTION OF 1801

AP® AMERICA IN THE WORLD

The **AP® America in the World** feature uses primary sources and data to situate U.S. history in a global context, giving students practice in comparison and data analysis, which are key to success on the AP® Exam.

AP® FIRSTHAND ACCOUNTS

Factional Politics and the War of 1812

In the quarter-century following the ratification of the U.S. Constitution, American leaders had to deal with the wars of the French Revolution and Napoleon. These European conflicts posed two dangers to the United States. First, the naval blockades imposed by the British and the French hurt American commerce and prompted calls for a military response. Second, European ideological and political struggles intensified party conflicts in the United States. On three occasions, the American republic faced danger from the combination of an external military threat and internal political turmoil. In 1798, the Federalist administration of John Adams almost went to war with France to help American merchants and to undermine the Republican Party. In 1807, Thomas Jefferson's embargo on American commerce shocked Federalists and sharply increased political tensions. And, as the following selections show, the political divisions during the War of 1812 threatened the very existence of the American republic.

GEORGE WASHINGTON
Farewell Address, 1796

Washington's support for Alexander Hamilton's economic policies promoted political factionalism. Ignoring his own role in creating that political divide, Washington condemned factionalism and, as his presidency proceeded, tried to stand above party conflicts. In his farewell address, Washington warned Americans to stand

those of the popular form, it is seen in its greatest rankness, and is truly their worst enemy.

The alternate dominion of one faction over another, sharpened by the spirit of revenge . . . , is itself a frightful despotism; but this leads at length to a more formal and permanent despotism. ”

AP® FIRSTHAND ACCOUNTS

AP® Firsthand Accounts, a two-page feature in each chapter, helps students learn to think critically and develop key AP® comparison skills by juxtaposing primary source texts written or spoken from two or more perspectives.

AP® COMPARING INTERPRETATIONS

Did British Administrators Try to Protect or Exploit Native Americans?

In the summer of 1763, Indian warriors throughout the Great Lakes and the Ohio Valley attacked the outposts that France had just ceded to Great Britain at the end of the Great War for Empire in an event known as Pontiac's War. They captured nine forts and besieged two others — Detroit and Fort Pitt — throughout the summer. In the fall, King George III issued the Royal Proclamation of 1763, which prohibited settlement west of the Allegheny Ridge. Nevertheless, Anglo-American colonists continued to push into the Ohio Valley (see Map 5.5, p. 170). Not surprisingly, the Indian peoples living in the Ohio Valley continued to be alarmed at the influx. In an effort to manage the empire and reduce the potential for conflict, British officials had to maintain or initiate alliances with the Indian nations while also preventing conflict between Indians and Anglo-American colonists. In the following excerpts, historians Eric Hinderaker (one of the authors of this textbook) and Gregory Evans Dowd highlight one aspect of this conflict: British imperial policy toward the Indian nations.

ERIC HINDERAKER

Source: Eric Hinderaker, *Elusive Empires: Constructing Colonialism in the Ohio Valley, 1673–1800* (Cambridge: Cambridge University Press, 1997), 134–135, 170–171, 175.

Britain's victory [in the Great War for Empire] placed enormous new administrative demands on the empire; to succeed in managing affairs in the Ohio Valley, its agents needed far-

Though Fort Pitt was imposed on the Indians of the upper Ohio Valley against their will, it served as an important center of diplomatic accommodation and, at least in theory, as an important restraint on the activities of western squatters. . . . In response to requests from Indian leaders, the fort commander, Charles Edmonstone, repeatedly warned settlers off of Indian lands; in the summer of 1767 a detachment of soldiers from the fort chased away hundreds

AP® COMPARING INTERPRETATIONS

The **AP® Comparing Interpretations** feature brings historical argumentation directly into each chapter, helping students understand how to work with secondary sources.

AP® THINKING LIKE A HISTORIAN

The Social Life of Alcohol

Alcohol was ubiquitous in post-Revolutionary America. Expensive wines and distilled spirits traveled through the channels of Atlantic trade; molasses was imported from the West Indies and distilled into rum in American port towns; and cider, beer, and whiskey were produced on a small scale everywhere in the countryside. Taverns were centers of social and political activity. Alcohol both mirrored and reinforced the economic and geographical divisions in American life.

1. **James Newport's ad in the *Pennsylvania Gazette*, 1790.** *This advertisement illustrates the connections between the trade in alcohol and the Atlantic world. While cheap whiskey, cider, and beer were made in American homes, fine wines and spirits were articles of international trade.*

   JAMES NEWPORT, At his *Wine, Spirit and Cordial Stores*, in Second street, at the upper corner of Carter's alley, has, by Wholesale and Retail, MADEIRA, Sherry, Lisbon, Teneriffe, Malaga, Fayal, and Port Wines, Jamaica spirits, Antigua rum, Philadelphia ditto, Holland gin, Philadelphia ditto, very excellent, in cases, Coniac [*sic*] brandy, American ditto, good flavor, choice shrub. CORDIALS, &c. Anniseed water, clove water, all-fours, Cinnamon water, prime wine and rum colouring, wine bitters, Spirits of wine. Retail Stores and Tavern-keepers

2. **Benjamin Chew on providing alcohol to his slaves, 1794.** *The instructions of a prominent Philadelphia lawyer and landowner to his overseer about giving rum to his slaves during the harvest.*

   I have written . . . to let you have [illegible] Rum & other necessaries for the Harvest. But as these articles are so [illegible] dear I must recommend it to you to be as sparing of them as possible. . . . I must rely on you good man [to conduct] the Business. . . . I would have you let the People have a little Rum — let them be cautious in using too much Spirits during Harvest — it will be well to mix some molasses with water to drink — it is very wholesome & much recommended. . . . I need not caution you that a great deal depends upon your own proper attention to yourself and that you are careful of good Conduct

AP® THINKING LIKE A HISTORIAN

An **AP® Thinking like a Historian** feature in every chapter includes five to eight brief primary sources organized around a central theme that helps students learn to work with evidence and to build the critical habits of mind key to success for the DBQ on the AP® Exam.

Chapter Review Material

CHAPTER 2 REVIEW

AP® CONTENT REVIEW

Answer these questions to demonstrate your understanding of the chapter's main ideas.

1. How did Spanish colonization affect people in the Americas and in Europe?
2. How did the labor demands of plantation colonies transform the process of colonization?
3. What conditions were necessary to establish successful neo-European colonies?
4. What did these three rebellions — Metacom's War, the Pueblo Revolt, and Bacon's Rebellion — have in common?

AP® TERMS TO KNOW

Identify and explain the significance of each term below.

Key Concepts and Events

chattel slavery (p. 40)
neo-Europes (p. 40)
encomienda (p. 43)
casta system (p. 43)
Columbian Exchange (p. 43)
mercantilism (p. 46)
joint-stock corporation (p. 48)
House of Burgesses (p. 49)
royal colony (p. 49)
freeholds (p. 53)
headright system (p. 53)
indentured servitude (p. 55)
Pilgrims (p. 62)
Puritans (p. 62)
toleration (p. 63)
covenant of works (p. 63)
covenant of grace (p. 63)
town meeting (p. 67)
Metacom's War (p. 69)
Pueblo Revolt (p. 70)
Bacon's Rebellion (p. 72)

Key People

Philip II (p. 45)
Opechancanough (p. 49)
Lord Baltimore (p. 49)
John Winthrop (p. 62)
Roger Williams (p. 63)
Anne Hutchinson (p. 63)
Metacom (p. 69)

AP® MAKING CONNECTIONS

Recognize the larger developments and continuities within and across chapters by answering these questions.

1. In Chapter 1, we saw that there were many parallels between Native American, European, and African societies on the eve of contact. Yet Europeans ended up dominating both Native American and African populations in colonial American settings. Based on evidence from in Chapter 2, what factors help to explain that dominance?
2. This chapter has emphasized the experimental and unstable nature of colonization. Each type of colony—tribute, plantation, and neo-European —faced its own distinct challenges. Identify one important source of instability that affected the early development of each type of colony.

KEY TURNING POINTS

Refer to the timeline at the start of the chapter for help in answering the following questions.

The Chesapeake tobacco boom (1620–1660), Opechancanough's uprising (1622), and the takeover of Virginia by the crown (1624): How were these events related to each other? What was their cumulative result? Make a historically defensible claim and support your argument with evidence from the text.

73

CHAPTER REVIEW

The Chapter Review section provides a set of **AP® Content Review** questions that restate the individual section review questions. **AP® Terms to Know** provides a list of Key Concepts and Events as well as Key People students should know. **AP® Making Connections** questions ask students to consider broader historical issues, developments, and continuities and changes over time. Lastly, a **Key Turning Points** question reminds students of important events.

Practice for the AP® Exam

AP® PRACTICE QUESTIONS

MULTIPLE CHOICE QUESTIONS *Choose the correct answer for each question.*

Questions 1–3 refer to this excerpt.

> "The powers not delegated to the United States by the Constitution, nor prohibited by it to the States, are reserved to the States respectively, or to the people."
>
> United States Constitution, Amendment 10

1. The ideology of which of the following groups showed the greatest similarity to the position endorsed by the Tenth Amendment?
   - **a.** Abolitionists
   - **b.** Antifederalists
   - **c.** American Indians
   - **d.** Federalists

2. The creation of the Tenth Amendment was most immediately motivated by the desire to
   - **a.** ensure ratification of the Constitution.
   - **b.**
   - **c.**
   - **d.**

3. T
   w
   - **a.**
   - **b.**
   - **c.**
   - **d.**

3 PART — AP® PRACTICE ESSAY QUESTIONS

DOCUMENT-BASED QUESTION *Suggested reading period: 15 minutes. Suggested writing time: 45 minutes*

DIRECTIONS: Question 1 is based on the accompanying documents. The documents have been edited for the purpose of this exercise.

1. Evaluate the extent to which revolutionary ideals changed American society in the period 1776 to 1800.

DOCUMENT 1

> Source: The Declaration of Independence, 1776.
>
> "When in the Course of human events, it becomes necessary for one people to dissolve the political bands which have connected them with another, and to assume among the powers of the earth, the separate and equal station to which the Laws of Nature and of Nature's God entitle them, a decent respect to the opinions of mankind requires that they should declare the causes which impel them to the separation.
>
> We hold these truths to be self-evident, that all men are created equal, that they are endowed by their Creator with certain unalienable Rights, that among these are Life, Liberty and the pursuit of Happiness. — That to secure these rights, Governments are instituted among Men, deriving their just powers from the consent of the governed, —That whenever any Form of Government becomes destructive of these ends, it is the Right of the People to alter or to abolish it, and to institute new Government, laying its foundation on such principles and organizing its powers in such form, as to them shall seem most likely to effect their Safety and Happiness."

AP® PRACTICE QUESTIONS

AP® Practice Questions follow every chapter, including multiple-choice and short answer questions after every chapter, and long essay and document-based questions after every part, to build deep familiarity with the tasks and format of AP® Exam items.

AP® UNITED STATES HISTORY PRACTICE EXAM

EXAM OVERVIEW

Section	Question Type	Number of Questions	Timing	% of Total Exam Score
Section I	Part A: Multiple Choice Questions	55 questions	55 minutes	40%
	Part B: Short Answer Questions	3 questions	40 minutes	20%
Section II	Part A: Document-Based Question	1 question	60 minutes	25%
	Part B: Long Essay Question	1 question	40 minutes	15%

SECTION I
PART A: MULTIPLE CHOICE QUESTIONS
55 minutes

DIRECTIONS: Choose the correct answer for each question.

Questions 1–3 refer to the excerpt provided.

> "The extremely heterogeneous population confronted Pennsylvania with a unique set of problems that could have impeded the creation of a stable society. Nevertheless, despite the inevitable tensions, exacerbated by waves of new immigration, wars, and religious conflict, colonial Pennsylvanians managed to develop new ideals of pluralism and tolerance on which they built their province. . . . William Penn . . . set forth a new, ideological basis for pluralism and tolerance that transformed the tentative pattern of relative harmony and toleration into one of official policy.
>
> . . . [H]e drafted a series of constitutions that guaranteed religious freedom and promoted his colony not only in the British Isles but on the Continent as well."
>
> Sally Schwartz, *"A Mixed Multitude": The Struggle for Toleration in Colonial Pennsylvania*, 1987

1. Which of the following later developments can best be used to support Schwartz's argument regarding the colonial culture in Pennsylvania?
   - **a.** A strong abolitionist movement developed in Pennsylvania in the eighteenth and nineteenth centuries.
   - **b.** Relations with American Indians deteriorated over time as colonists demanded more land.
   - **c.** Pennsylvania's nineteenth-century leaders rejected the development of a strong national government.
   - **d.** The overt resistance of African Americans revolting against slavery.

AP® UNITED STATES HISTORY PRACTICE EXAM

Students can test themselves before taking the AP® Exam by using the full-length **AP® United States History Practice Exam** at the end of the book.

HENRETTA'S

AMERICA'S HISTORY

TENTH EDITION

FOR THE AP® COURSE

PART 1

CHAPTER 1
Colliding Worlds, 1491–1600

CHAPTER 2
American Experiments, 1521–1700

Transformations of North America

1491–1700

Each of the nine parts in *America's History* covers a particular period of time. The choice of beginning and ending dates is called *periodization*: the process of deciding how to break down history into pieces with coherent themes. Throughout this book, each choice of periodization represents a form of historical argument, and we'll explain each periodization choice as we go.

Part 1 of *America's History* is about collisions and experiments. Our choice to begin in 1491 is symbolic: it represents the moment before Columbus's first voyage in 1492 bridged the Atlantic Ocean. At this time, North America, Europe, and Africa were home to complex societies with distinctive cultures. But their histories were about to collide, bringing vast changes to all three continents. Sustained contact among Native Americans, Europeans, and Africans was one of the most momentous developments in world history.

No one knew what European colonies in the Americas would be like. Only by experimenting did new societies gradually emerge. These experiments were neither easy nor peaceful. Warfare, mass enslavement, death, and destruction lay at the heart of colonial enterprise. Native Americans, Europeans, and Africans often clashed violently as they struggled to control their fates.

But colonies also created opportunities for new societies to flourish. Across two centuries, five European nations undertook colonial experiments in dozens of places. Some failed miserably; some prospered beyond anyone's imagining. We bring Part 1 to a close in 1700, when the first fruits of these experiments were clear, though colonial societies remained insecure and unstable. Would other concluding dates be possible for this part — for example, 1607? Yes, but to our minds, it's best to consider the early decades of British and French colonization — 1607 to 1700 — in tandem with a deep exploration of precontact Native American and African societies. Here, in brief, are three key interpretive questions to keep in mind as you read Chapters 1 and 2. ▶

2

AP® CONCEPT CONNECTIONS

How did the diversity of Native American societies shape colonization?

National Museum of the American Indian, Smithsonian Institution 9/7990.

Native American societies ranged from vast, complex imperial states to small, kin-based bands of hunters and gatherers: a spectrum much too broad for the familiar term *tribe* to cover. Native Americans' economic and social systems were adapted to the ecosystems they inhabited. Many were productive farmers, and some hunted bison and deer, while others were expert salmon fishermen who plied coastal waters in large oceangoing boats. Native American religions and cultures also differed, though many had broad characteristics in common.

These variations in Native American societies shaped colonial enterprise. Europeans conquered and co-opted the Native American empires in Mexico and the Andes with relative ease, but smaller societies were harder to exploit. Mobile hunter-gatherers were especially formidable opponents of colonial expansion.

Why did colonization of the Americas transform life on earth?

Sarin Images/Granger, NYC.

European colonization triggered a series of sweeping changes that historians have labeled the Columbian Exchange. Plants, animals, and germs crossed the Atlantic. European grains and weeds were carried westward, while American foods like potatoes and maize (corn) transformed diets in Europe and Asia. Native Americans had domesticated very few animals; the Columbian Exchange introduced many new creatures to the Americas. Germs also made the voyage, especially deadly pathogens like smallpox, influenza, and bubonic plague, which took an enormous toll. Having lost on average 90 percent of their populations from disease over the first century of contact, Native American societies were forced to cope with European and African newcomers in a weakened and vulnerable state.

Inanimate materials crossed oceans as well: enough gold and silver traveled from the Americas to Europe and Asia to transform the world's economies, intensifying competition and empire building in Europe.

Why did colonization disrupt traditional ideas and practices in American, European, and African worlds so profoundly?

Private Collection/© Look and Learn/Peter Jackson Collection/Bridgeman Images.

The collisions of American, European, and African worlds challenged the beliefs and practices of all three groups. Colonization was, above all, a long and tortured process of experimentation that brought Europeans, Native Americans, and Africans into contact in a variety of ways. Over time, Europeans carved out three distinct types of colonies in the Americas. Where Native American societies were organized into densely settled empires, Europeans conquered the ruling class and established tribute-based empires of their own. In tropical and subtropical settings, colonizers created plantation societies that demanded large, imported labor forces—a need that was met through the African slave trade. And in temperate regions, colonists came in large numbers hoping to create societies similar to the ones they knew in Europe.

Everywhere, core beliefs were shaken by contact with radically unfamiliar peoples and circumstances. Native American population loss challenged the most basic aspects of their societies and belief systems. The enslavement of Africans meant that their ability to sustain social and cultural systems was dramatically circumscribed. Europeans, too, struggled to maintain familiar social and cultural norms, even though they dominated the new colonies they had created. Traditional elites were hard-pressed to sustain their authority, while religious traditions and scientific knowledge were strained by new circumstances and new discoveries. These transformations are the subject of Part 1.

Organized around a single theme, the Part 1 Document Set in *Sources for America's History* can be used to teach the AP® theme Work, Exchange, and Technology (WXT), how patterns of exchange developed as a result of European contact with Native Americans and Africans.

AP® THEMATIC UNDERSTANDING

Transformations of North America 1491–1700

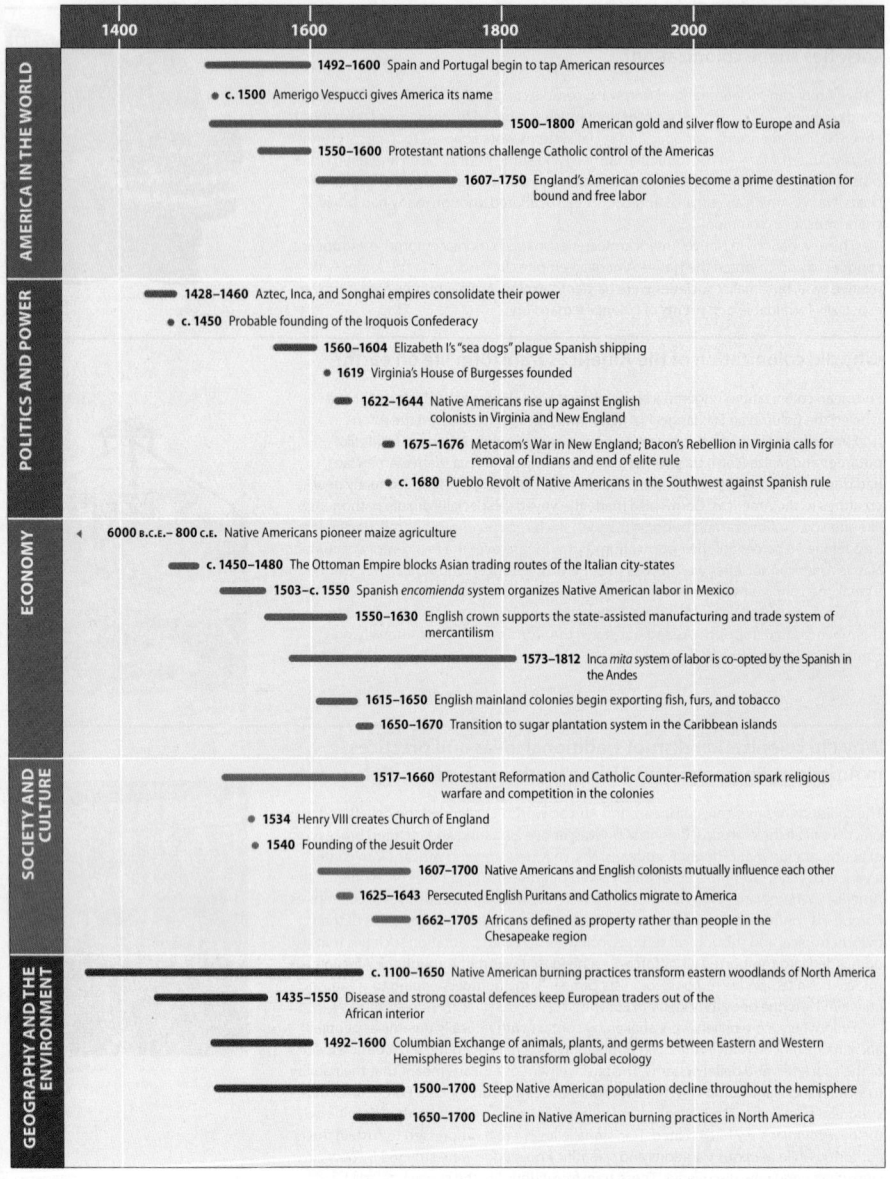

1400 | 1600 | 1800 | 2000

AMERICA IN THE WORLD

- **1492–1600** Spain and Portugal begin to tap American resources
- **c. 1500** Amerigo Vespucci gives America its name
- **1500–1800** American gold and silver flow to Europe and Asia
- **1550–1600** Protestant nations challenge Catholic control of the Americas
- **1607–1750** England's American colonies become a prime destination for bound and free labor

POLITICS AND POWER

- **1428–1460** Aztec, Inca, and Songhai empires consolidate their power
- **c. 1450** Probable founding of the Iroquois Confederacy
- **1560–1604** Elizabeth I's "sea dogs" plague Spanish shipping
- **1619** Virginia's House of Burgesses founded
- **1622–1644** Native Americans rise up against English colonists in Virginia and New England
- **1675–1676** Metacom's War in New England; Bacon's Rebellion in Virginia calls for removal of Indians and end of elite rule
- **c. 1680** Pueblo Revolt of Native Americans in the Southwest against Spanish rule

ECONOMY

- **6000 B.C.E.– 800 C.E.** Native Americans pioneer maize agriculture
- **c. 1450–1480** The Ottoman Empire blocks Asian trading routes of the Italian city-states
- **1503–c. 1550** Spanish *encomienda* system organizes Native American labor in Mexico
- **1550–1630** English crown supports the state-assisted manufacturing and trade system of mercantilism
- **1573–1812** Inca *mita* system of labor is co-opted by the Spanish in the Andes
- **1615–1650** English mainland colonies begin exporting fish, furs, and tobacco
- **1650–1670** Transition to sugar plantation system in the Caribbean islands

SOCIETY AND CULTURE

- **1517–1660** Protestant Reformation and Catholic Counter-Reformation spark religious warfare and competition in the colonies
- **1534** Henry VIII creates Church of England
- **1540** Founding of the Jesuit Order
- **1607–1700** Native Americans and English colonists mutually influence each other
- **1625–1643** Persecuted English Puritans and Catholics migrate to America
- **1662–1705** Africans defined as property rather than people in the Chesapeake region

GEOGRAPHY AND THE ENVIRONMENT

- **c. 1100–1650** Native American burning practices transform eastern woodlands of North America
- **1435–1550** Disease and strong coastal defences keep European traders out of the African interior
- **1492–1600** Columbian Exchange of animals, plants, and germs between Eastern and Western Hemispheres begins to transform global ecology
- **1500–1700** Steep Native American population decline throughout the hemisphere
- **1650–1700** Decline in Native American burning practices in North America

AP® Making Connections Across Chapters

Read these questions and think about them as you read the chapters in this part. Then when you have completed reading this part, return to these questions and answer them.

1 How did the structure of Native American societies help to determine the types of colonies that developed alongside them? How did Spain's encounter with the Aztec and Inca empires make its colonial system fundamentally different from that of the English?

Private Collection/Archives Charmet/ Bridgeman Images

2 Why did European kingdoms involve themselves with overseas colonization in the Americas? What did they hope to gain?

Neue Galerie, Kessel, Germany© Museumslandschaft Hessen Kassel/ Bridgeman Images

3 How did England's mainland colonies interact with their Native American neighbors? How successful or effective were those interactions? What were their results?

Culture Club/Getty Images

4 To what extent were European migrants to the Americas able to sustain traditional societies and economies, and how did they change as a result of colonization?

Worcester Art Museum, Massachusetts, USA/Bridgeman Images

5 What developments led to instability, war, and rebellion in North America in the late seventeenth century?

Jim Feliciano/Shutterstock.com

TRM Find complete suggested responses in the Teacher's Resource Materials.

1 CHAPTER

Colliding Worlds

1491–1600

Chapter 1 — AP® Assessment Weight and Pacing Guide

The assessment weight on the AP® U.S. History Exam for Chapters 1–2 is 4–6 percent. This chapter falls in Unit 1 of the AP® U.S. History Curriculum, covering Period 1: 1491–1607.

This pacing guide is based on a schedule with 120 sessions of 50 minutes each before the AP® U.S. History Exam. If you have a different number of sessions before the exam, you can modify the pacing to meet your needs. If you have additional time, consider incorporating quizzes, released AP® U.S. History questions, practice exams, writing practice, and other instructional activities.

	Traditional Schedule	Block Schedule
Chapter 1	4 days	2–3 days

Daily Pacing Guide

	Content Focus	Essential Question
Day 1	The Native American Experience	What factors best explain the variations among Native American societies and cultures?
Day 2	Western Europe: The Edge of the Old World	How had recent developments changed Western Europe by 1491?
Day 3	West and Central Africa: Origins of the Atlantic Slave Trade	How was sub-Saharan Africa affected by the arrival of European traders?
Day 4	Exploration and Conquest	What motivated Portuguese and Spanish expansion into the Atlantic, and what were its unintended consequences?

AP® Alignment

Section Heading	AP® Topic	AP® Theme
The Native American Experience	1.2	GEO
Western Europe: The Edge of the Old World	1.3, 1.4	WOR, GEO
West and Central Africa: Origins of the Atlantic Slave Trade	1.5	SOC
Exploration and Conquest	1.4, 1.5, 1.6	GEO, SOC, WOR

*Should changes be made to the Course Framework in the future, an updated alignment will be placed on our AP® updates page at go.bfwpub.com/ap-course-updates.

Chapter 1 — Overview

Chapter 1 covers the period from 1491 to around 1600. Beginning the chapter at 1491 is significant because it implies the importance of understanding Native American groups before the arrival of Columbus and the dramatic changes that followed. This chapter focuses on the political, economic, and religious characteristics of Native American groups. In addition, this chapter provides an overview of European and African society, politics, and economy before the Age of Exploration to provide students with context for the dramatic changes that occurred after 1492. After providing an overview of the New World, Europe, and Africa before Columbus, the chapter concludes with a look at the initial contact and conflict between Native groups and European explorers and conquerors.

Chapter 1 — Resources

The following resources can be found in the Teacher's Resource Materials (TRM) that accompany the book. You can access the TRM via the book's digital platform, by clicking the TRM links found here in your Teacher's Edition e-book, or by contacting your representative to access the resources online. Visit **bfwpub.com/henretta10e** to learn more.

TRM Chapter 1 Lecture Presentation Slides

TRM Chapter 1 Outline with AP® Focus

TRM Chapter 1 Lecture Strategies

TRM Chapter 1 Suggested Responses

TRM Handout 1.1 — Comparison: Native Societies before Columbus

TRM Handout 1.2 — Causation: Creating the Atlantic World

TRM Handout 1.3 — Thematic Analysis: African Slave Trade

Chapter 1 — Essential Activity

Divide students into small, collaborative groups to conduct research and develop an oral presentation on an assigned topic using the PechaKucha format. In a PechaKucha presentation, students will develop a slide show with 20 slides that are pre-set to run for 20 seconds each. In addition to the time limits, the content of the slide is limited to one image or one word/phrase. Provide each student with one of the following Native groups to research: Anasazi/Pueblo, Mississippians, Iroquois, Algonquin, Great Basin, Olmec, Aztec, Maya, and Inca. Based on their research, each group should develop four questions based on one AP® Theme and answer their questions using the AP® Historical Thinking Skills and Reasoning Processes. Students should design their presentation to present the questions and answers regarding their assigned Native American group.

Chapter 1 — Bell Ringers

The following activities take no more than 5–15 minutes of your class period and offer an effective and engaging way to begin your lessons and for students to apply AP® Skills & Processes:

- Provide students with a short excerpt from Charles Mann's introduction to his book *1491: New Revelations of the Americas before Columbus* (Alfred A. Knopf, 2005). Ask students to write down the historical argument being made by the historian. You can use this Bell Ringer to introduce the idea of thesis writing and/or to introduce the lesson on pre-Columbian Native American societies. *Answers will vary.*
- Project two images of Columbus in the New World — one positive (Columbus as hero) and one negative (Columbus as villain). Ask students to work with a partner or small group to create a narration of the event from the point of view of the artist who created the image. Use this activity to begin a lesson on the age of exploration or to introduce analyzing historical evidence considering point of view. *Answers will vary.*

NOTES

TEACHING STRATEGY

Lead students in a discussion on how contact between Native Americans, Europeans, and Africans — and the change that resulted from this contact — contributed to the major development of the era, noting that at the moment of contact, these three "worlds" shared rough equality, but they would soon be transforming each other's societies. For a complete suggested response to the **AP® LEARNING FOCUS** question, see p. 38.

1 CHAPTER

Colliding Worlds
1491–1600

AP® LEARNING FOCUS

Why did contact among Native Americans, Europeans, and Africans cause such momentous changes?

In April 1493, a Genoese sailor of humble origins appeared at the court of Queen Isabella of Castile and King Ferdinand of Aragon along with six Caribbean natives, numerous colorful parrots, and "samples of finest gold, and many other things never before seen or heard tell of in Spain." The sailor was Christopher Columbus, just returned from his first voyage into the Atlantic. He and his party entered Barcelona's fortress in a solemn procession. The monarchs stood to greet Columbus; he knelt to kiss their hands. They talked for an hour and then adjourned to the royal chapel for a ceremony of thanksgiving. Columbus, now bearing the official title *Admiral of the Ocean Sea*, remained at court for more than a month. The highlight of his stay was the baptism of the six natives, whom Columbus called Indians because he mistakenly believed he had sailed westward all the way to Asia.

In the spring of 1540, the Spanish explorer Hernando de Soto met the Lady of Cofachiqui, ruler of a large Native American province in present-day South Carolina. Though an epidemic had carried away many of her people, the lady of the province offered the Spanish expedition as much corn, and as many pearls, as it could carry. As she spoke to de Soto, she unwound "a great rope of pearls as large as hazelnuts" and handed them to the Spaniard; in return he gave her a gold ring set with a ruby. De Soto and his men then visited the temples of Cofachiqui, which were guarded by carved statues and held storehouses of weapons and chest upon chest of pearls. After loading their horses with corn and pearls, they continued on their way.

A Portuguese traveler named Duarte Lopez visited the African kingdom of Kongo in 1578. "The men and women are black," he reported, "some approaching olive colour, with black curly hair, and others with red. The men are of middle height, and, excepting the black skin, are like the Portuguese." The royal city of Kongo sat on a high plain that was "entirely cultivated," with a population of more than 100,000. The city included a separate commercial district, a mile around, where Portuguese traders acquired ivory, wax, honey, palm oil, and slaves from the Kongolese.

Three glimpses of three lost worlds. Soon these peoples would be transforming one another's societies, often through conflict and exploitation. But at the moment they first met, Europeans, Native Americans, and Africans stood on roughly equal terms. Even a hundred years after Columbus's discovery of the Americas, no one could have foreseen the shape that their interactions would take in the generations to come. To begin, we need to understand the three worlds as distinct places, each home to unique societies and cultures.

6

Village of Secoton, 1585 English colonist John White painted this view of an Algonquian village on the outer banks of present-day North Carolina. Its cluster of houses surrounded by fields of crops closely resembled European farming communities of the same era. White captured everyday details of the town's social life, including food preparation and a ceremony or celebration in progress (lower right). Private Collection/Bridgeman Images.

AP® THEME

GEO: Geography and the Environment

Discuss how the illustration of the Village of Secoton reveals geographic and environmental features that shaped the development of Eastern Woodland Indian communities, such as the Algonquins. The ability to grow corn (maize), a technological skill that diffused from Mexico, allowed for a semisedentary lifestyle and, as the caption notes, the construction of villages that Europeans found to look a lot like their own.

AP® SKILLS & PROCESSES

CONTINUITY AND CHANGE

Use the **TIMELINE** table in each chapter to help students begin thinking about the ways historical events and processes can be organized into discrete historical periods. Provide tips to help students interpret this table. For example, precise years like 1491 are usually an indication of a very specific, significant event, whereas round years, such as 1600, are often rough markers of a less decisive transition. Encourage students to consider the title of the chapter as they attempt to answer the question of what "worlds" are "colliding," helping students to recognize that Africa was part of this interaction, not just Europe and the Americas.

TEACHING STRATEGY

Divide students into small groups and assign each group one pre-Columbian society: Inca, Aztec, Maya, Pueblo (Anasazi), Mississippian, Algonquin, Iroquois, etc. Have students research and develop a brief presentation based on the AP® History Reasoning Skills (contextualization, comparison, causation, and continuity and change over time). Groups should write four questions based on each skill and provide the answers based on their research. This exercise will give students practice in learning to apply these skills to content. Provide students with guidance as they formulate questions and do research to answer the questions. Provide students with **Handout 1.1 — Comparison: Native Societies before Columbus (TRM)** to complete as each group presents.

TRM Find **Handout 1.1 — Comparison: Native Societies before Columbus** in the Teacher's Resource Materials.

TIMELINE

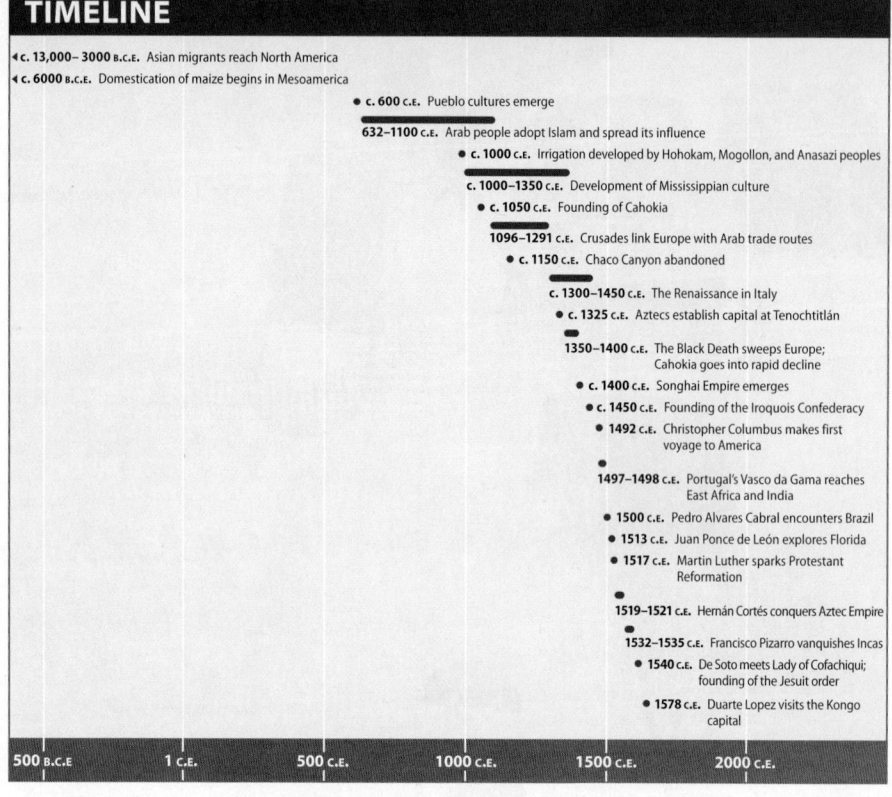

- **c. 13,000–3000 B.C.E.** Asian migrants reach North America
- **c. 6000 B.C.E.** Domestication of maize begins in Mesoamerica
- **c. 600 C.E.** Pueblo cultures emerge
- **632–1100 C.E.** Arab people adopt Islam and spread its influence
- **c. 1000 C.E.** Irrigation developed by Hohokam, Mogollon, and Anasazi peoples
- **c. 1000–1350 C.E.** Development of Mississippian culture
- **c. 1050 C.E.** Founding of Cahokia
- **1096–1291 C.E.** Crusades link Europe with Arab trade routes
- **c. 1150 C.E.** Chaco Canyon abandoned
- **c. 1300–1450 C.E.** The Renaissance in Italy
- **c. 1325 C.E.** Aztecs establish capital at Tenochtitlán
- **1350–1400 C.E.** The Black Death sweeps Europe; Cahokia goes into rapid decline
- **c. 1400 C.E.** Songhai Empire emerges
- **c. 1450 C.E.** Founding of the Iroquois Confederacy
- **1492 C.E.** Christopher Columbus makes first voyage to America
- **1497–1498 C.E.** Portugal's Vasco da Gama reaches East Africa and India
- **1500 C.E.** Pedro Alvares Cabral encounters Brazil
- **1513 C.E.** Juan Ponce de León explores Florida
- **1517 C.E.** Martin Luther sparks Protestant Reformation
- **1519–1521 C.E.** Hernán Cortés conquers Aztec Empire
- **1532–1535 C.E.** Francisco Pizarro vanquishes Incas
- **1540 C.E.** De Soto meets Lady of Cofachiqui; founding of the Jesuit order
- **1578 C.E.** Duarte Lopez visits the Kongo capital

500 B.C.E | 1 C.E. | 500 C.E. | 1000 C.E. | 1500 C.E. | 2000 C.E.

THE NATIVE AMERICAN EXPERIENCE

> **What factors best explain the variations among Native American societies and cultures?**

hunters and gatherers
Societies whose members gather food by hunting, fishing, and collecting wild plants rather than relying on agriculture or animal husbandry. Because hunter-gatherers are mobile, moving seasonally through their territory to exploit resources, they have neither fixed townsites nor weighty material goods.

semisedentary societies
Societies whose members combine slash-and-burn agriculture with hunting and fishing. Semisedentary societies often occupy large village sites near their fields in the summer, then disperse during the winter months into smaller hunting, fishing, and gathering camps, regathering again in spring to plant their crops.

When Europeans arrived, perhaps 60 million people occupied the Americas, 7 million of whom lived north of Mexico. In Mesoamerica (present-day Mexico and Guatemala) and the Andes, empires that rivaled the greatest civilizations in world history ruled over millions of people. At the other end of the political spectrum, **hunters and gatherers** were organized into kin-based bands. Between these extremes, **semisedentary societies** planted and tended crops in the spring and summer, fished and hunted, made war, and conducted trade. Though we often see this spectrum as a hierarchy in which the empires are most impressive and important while hunter-gatherers deserve scarcely a mention, this bias toward civilizations that left behind monumental architecture and spawned powerful ruling classes is misplaced. To be fully understood, the Americas must be treated in all their complexity, with an appreciation for their diverse societies and cultures.

The First Americans

Archaeologists believe that migrants from Asia crossed a 100-mile-wide land bridge connecting Siberia and Alaska during the last Ice Age sometime between 13,000 and

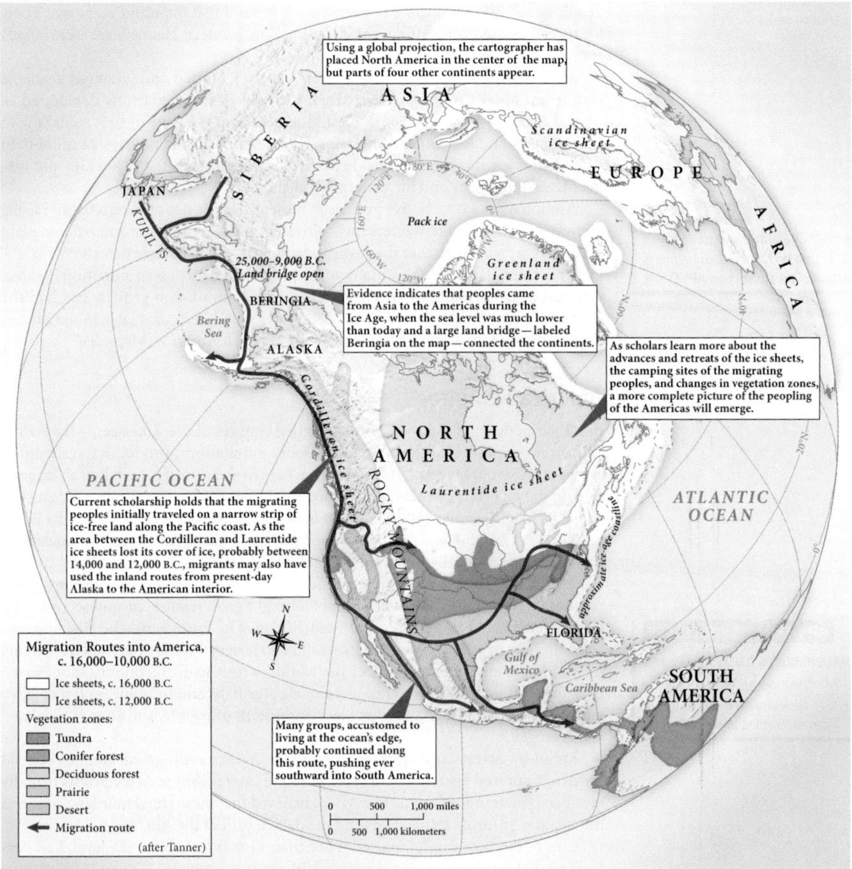
Using a global projection, the cartographer has placed North America in the center of the map, but parts of four other continents appear.
ASIA
SIBERIA
Scandinavian ice sheet
EUROPE
AFRICA
JAPAN
KURIL IS.
Pack ice
Greenland ice sheet
25,000–9,000 B.C. Land bridge open
BERINGIA
Evidence indicates that peoples came from Asia to the Americas during the Ice Age, when the sea level was much lower than today and a large land bridge — labeled Beringia on the map — connected the continents.
Bering Sea
ALASKA
As scholars learn more about the advances and retreats of the ice sheets, the camping sites of the migrating peoples, and changes in vegetation zones, a more complete picture of the peopling of the Americas will emerge.
Cordilleran ice sheet
NORTH AMERICA
Laurentide ice sheet
PACIFIC OCEAN
ATLANTIC OCEAN
approximate ice-age coastline
ROCKY MOUNTAINS
Current scholarship holds that the migrating peoples initially traveled on a narrow strip of ice-free land along the Pacific coast. As the area between the Cordilleran and Laurentide ice sheets lost its cover of ice, probably between 14,000 and 12,000 B.C., migrants may also have used the inland routes from present-day Alaska to the American interior.
FLORIDA
Gulf of Mexico
Caribbean Sea
SOUTH AMERICA
Migration Routes into America, c. 16,000–10,000 B.C.
Ice sheets, c. 16,000 B.C.
Ice sheets, c. 12,000 B.C.
Vegetation zones:
Tundra
Conifer forest
Deciduous forest
Prairie
Desert
Migration route
(after Tanner)
Many groups, accustomed to living at the ocean's edge, probably continued along this route, pushing ever southward into South America.
0 500 1,000 miles
0 500 1,000 kilometers

MAP 1.1 The Ice Age and the Settling of the Americas
Some sixteen thousand years ago, a sheet of ice covered much of Europe and North America. As the ice lowered the level of the world's oceans, a broad bridge of land was created between Siberia and Alaska. Using that land bridge, hunting peoples from Asia migrated to North America as they pursued woolly mammoths and other large game animals and sought ice-free habitats. By 10,000 B.C.E., the descendants of these migrant peoples had moved south to present-day Florida and central Mexico. In time, they would settle as far south as the tip of South America and as far east as the Atlantic coast of North America.

3000 B.C.E. and thus became the first Americans. The first wave of this migratory stream from Asia lasted from about fifteen thousand to eleven thousand years ago. Then the glaciers melted, and the rising ocean submerged the land bridge beneath the Bering Strait (Map 1.1). Around eight thousand years ago, a second movement of peoples, traveling by water across the same narrow strait, brought the ancestors of the Navajos and the Apaches to North America. The forebears of the Aleut and Inuit

AP® THEME

GEO: Geography and the Environment

MAP 1.1 provides a view of probable migration routes Asian peoples took in their movement into the Americas. This map and corresponding details about the Ice Age reveal how scholars have reconstructed the ways that geographic and environmental factors shaped migration and settlement. Show students the map and lead them in a discussion on how the lack of contact with the Eurasian landmass affected the Western Hemisphere.

CHECK FOR UNDERSTANDING

Ask students: **Where did the first Americans come from and when did they begin to arrive in North America? When did they first domesticate crops?** *The first migrants to the Americas likely came across a land bridge that connected Asia and North America. They arrived sometime between 13,000 B.C.E. and 3,000 B.C.E. and gradually moved throughout the continent. Most moved south, where crops were domesticated in Mexico and Peru around 6,000 B.C.E.*

AP® APPLY THE TIP

Ask students: **How would developing an economic system based on maize cultivation allow for the growth of a civilization?** *Maize cultivation allows for a large amount of food to be produced by a distinct group within a civilization. This specialization allows for others to focus on other tasks including warfare, tool production, religious leadership, etc. In addition, producing a surplus of maize would give a civilization a commodity that can be used in trade, which would also lead to the spread of maize cultivation. Moreover, at the time of the conquest of the Aztecs, Tenochtitlán had a population of 250,000 while London at the same time was 50,000 and Paris was 200,000.*

AP® SKILLS & PROCESSES

DEVELOPMENTS AND PROCESSES

Use the **DEVELOPMENTS AND PROCESSES** question to help students identify some long-term causes for the development of empires in Mesoamerica and the Andes. Students may need some assistance in understanding that factors spanning hundreds or even thousands of years, including the development of agriculture, might be necessary prerequisites for empires. Extend this prompt by asking students to compare and contrast the factors that allowed the empires in Mexico and the Andes to flourish.

TRM Find complete suggested responses in the Teacher's Resource Materials.

CHECK FOR UNDERSTANDING

Use the "American Empires" section to introduce students to using social, political, and economic categories as analytical tools. Ask students: **What characteristics made Aztec and Inca civilizations empires?** *Each had dense populations, agricultural surpluses, and strong bureaucracies. Their governments built and maintained roads and controlled trade. Each had subject peoples who paid them tribute.*

peoples, the "Eskimos," came in a third wave around five thousand years ago. Then, for three hundred generations, the peoples of the Western Hemisphere were largely cut off from the rest of the world.

Migrants moved across the continents as they hunted and gathered available resources. Most flowed southward, and the densest populations developed in central Mexico — home to some 20 million people at the time of first contact with Europeans — and the Andes Mountains, with a population of perhaps 12 million. In North America, a secondary trickle pushed to the east, across the Rockies and into the Mississippi Valley and the eastern woodlands.

AP® EXAM TIP

Knowledge of the impact of maize cultivation on Native populations is essential for success on AP® Exam.

Around 6000 B.C.E., Native peoples in present-day Mexico and Peru began raising domesticated crops. Mesoamericans cultivated maize (corn) into a nutritious plant with a higher yield per acre than wheat, barley, or rye, the staple cereals of Europe. In Peru, they also bred the potato, a root crop of unsurpassed nutritional value. The resulting agricultural surpluses encouraged population growth and laid the foundation for wealthy, urban societies in Mexico and Peru, and later in the Mississippi Valley and the southeastern woodlands of North America (Map 1.2).

American Empires

In Mesoamerica and the Andes, the two great empires of the Americas — the Aztecs and Incas — dominated the landscape. Dense populations, productive agriculture, and aggressive bureaucratic states were the keys to their power. Each had an impressive capital city. Tenochtitlán, established in 1325 at the center of the Aztec Empire, had at its height around 1500 a population of about 250,000, at a time when the European cities of London and Seville each had perhaps 50,000. The Aztec state controlled the fertile valleys in the highlands of Mexico, and Aztec merchants forged trading routes that crisscrossed the empire. Trade, along with tribute demanded from subject peoples (comparable to taxes in Europe), brought gold, textiles, turquoise, obsidian, tropical bird feathers, and cacao to Tenochtitlán. The Europeans who first encountered this city in 1519 marveled at its wealth and beauty. "Some of the soldiers among us who had been in many parts of the world," wrote Spanish conquistador Bernal Díaz del Castillo, "in Constantinople, and all over Italy, and in Rome, said that [they had never seen] so large a market place and so full of people, and so well regulated and arranged."

AP® SKILLS & PROCESSES

DEVELOPMENTS AND PROCESSES

What factors allowed for the development of empires in central Mexico and the Andes?

Ruled by priests and warrior-nobles, the Aztecs subjugated most of central Mexico. Captured enemies were brought to the capital, where Aztec priests brutally sacrificed thousands of them. The Aztecs believed that these ritual murders sustained the cosmos, ensuring fertile fields and the daily return of the sun.

Cuzco, the Inca capital located more than 11,000 feet above sea level, had perhaps 60,000 residents. A dense network of roads, storehouses, and administrative centers stitched together this improbable high-altitude empire, which ran down the 2,000-mile-long spine of the Andes Mountains. A king claiming divine status ruled the empire through a bureaucracy of nobles. As with the Aztecs, the empire consisted of subordinate kingdoms that had been conquered by the Incas, and tribute flowed from local centers of power to the imperial core.

Chiefdoms and Confederacies

Nothing on the scale of the Aztec and Inca empires ever developed north of Mexico, but maize agriculture spread from Mesoamerica across much of North America, laying a foundation for new ways of life there as well.

AP® EXAM TIP

The impact of geography on the diversity of North American cultures is important to know for the AP® Exam.

The Mississippi Valley The spread of maize to the Mississippi River Valley and the Southeast around C.E. 800 led to the development of a large-scale northern Native American culture. The older Adena and Hopewell cultures had already introduced

TEACHING STRATEGY

To enhance students' understanding of the scale and grandeur of the Aztec civilization, use Hernán Cortés's description of Tenochtitlán. Cortés's text includes a description of the city's layout, practices in agriculture, trade, architecture, and religion as well as the lifestyle of Moctezuma and the nobility. Available through the Internet Modern History Sourcebook, you can access this document by searching "Sourcebook Hernán Cortés." (Note: Including the accent marks in your search is not necessary.) Given the length of the document, you can select portions to read aloud or divide the class into small groups to read different selections.

TEACHING STRATEGY

Use The Great Inka Road: Engineering an Empire, an interactive Web site created by the National Museum of the American Indian, to help students grasp the scale and sophistication of the Inca Empire. The site provides information on environment, geography, art, architecture, governance, and religion using maps, photographs, and short videos. Search "NMAI Inka Road" to access this site.

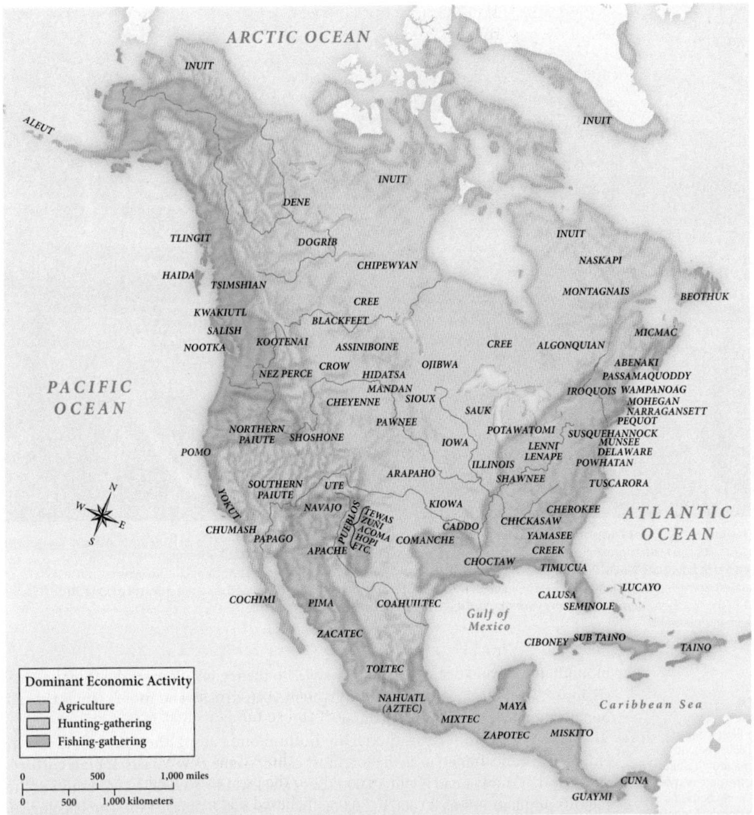

MAPPING THE PAST

MAP 1.2 Native American Peoples, 1492

Having learned to live in many environments, Native Americans populated the entire Western Hemisphere. They created cultures that ranged from centralized empires (the Incas and Aztecs) to societies that combined farming with hunting, fishing, and gathering (the Iroquois and Algonquians) to nomadic tribes of hunter-gatherers (the Micmacs and Shoshones). The great diversity of Native American peoples — in language, tribal identity, and ways of life — and the long-standing rivalries among neighboring peoples usually prevented them from uniting to resist the European invaders.

ANALYZING THE MAP: Look carefully at the broad divisions of this map represented by its three colors. Which type of economic activity occupied most of North America? Where was agriculture most important?

MAKING CONNECTIONS: This map contains the names of dozens of Native American groups, but they are only a small fraction of the hundreds who actually populated the continent in 1492. Why is it important to recognize that a map like this offers only an approximation of the information it claims to present? Can you identify any Native American groups that are named in the chapter narrative but do not appear on the map? Why do you think there are more groups' names on some parts of this map than others?

AP® THEME

MIG: Migration and Settlement

Use **MAP 1.2** to help students analyze the causes of migration and settlement in the Americas in 1492. In combination with climate and elevation maps, help students identify the connection between geographic features and the dominant economic patterns of Native Americans who settled in different regions.

TRM Find complete suggested responses in the Teacher's Resource Materials.

AP® THEME

MIG: Migration and Settlement

Use the image of the Great Serpent Mound to lead a discussion on the patterns of settlement in different regions of North America. Emphasize to students how a task of this size suggests an agrarian society with a predictable food surplus and a social hierarchy to command labor.

The Great Serpent Mound Scholars long believed that this mound was the work of the Adena peoples (500 B.C.E.–200 C.E.) because of its proximity to an Adena burial site in present-day southern Ohio. Recent research places the mound at a much later date (950–1200 C.E.) and, because of the serpent imagery, ties it to the Fort Ancient culture, which is closely related to the Mississippian complex. The head of the serpent is aligned with the sunset of the summer solstice (June 20 or 21 in the Northern Hemisphere), an event of great religious significance to a sun-worshipping culture. Richard A. Cooke/Corbis Documentary/Getty Images.

TEACHING STRATEGY

Show *City of the Sun*, a 14-minute film that explores the Cahokia site and the people who built it, to supplement your discussion of Native American life in the Mississippi Valley. Search "Cahokia Mounds Educate" and click "Videos" to access the film.

Mississippian culture
A Native American culture complex that flourished in the Mississippi River basin and the Southeast from around 850 to around 1700 C.E.. Characterized by maize agriculture, moundbuilding, and distinctive pottery styles, Mississippian communities were complex chiefdoms usually located along the floodplains of rivers. The largest of these communities was Cahokia, in modern-day Illinois.

eastern woodlands
A culture area of Native Americans that extended from the Atlantic Ocean westward to the Great Plains, and from the Great Lakes to the Gulf of Mexico. The eastern woodlands could be subdivided into the southeastern and northeastern woodlands. Eastern woodlands peoples were generally semisedentary, with agriculture based on maize, beans, and squash. Most, but not all, were chiefdoms.

Algonquian cultures/languages
A Native American language family whose speakers were widespread in the eastern woodlands, Great Lakes, and subarctic regions of eastern North America. The Algonquian language family should not be confused with the Algonquins, who were a single nation inhabiting the St. Lawrence Valley at the time of first contact.

moundbuilding and distinctive pottery styles to the region. Now residents of the Mississippi River Valley experienced the greater urban density and more complex social organization that agriculture encouraged.

The city of Cahokia, in the fertile bottomlands along the Mississippi River, emerged around 1000 C.E. as the foremost center of the new **Mississippian culture**. At its peak, Cahokia had about 10,000 residents; including satellite communities, the region's population was 20,000 to 30,000. In an area of 6 square miles, archaeologists have found 120 mounds of varying size, shape, and function. Some contain extensive burials; others, known as platform mounds, were used as bases for ceremonial buildings or rulers' homes. Cahokia had a powerful ruling class and a priesthood that worshipped the sun. After peaking in size around 1350, it declined rapidly. Why did Cahokia, once an impressive city, decline and disappear? Scholars speculate that its fall was caused by a period of ruinous warfare, made worse by environmental changes that made the site less habitable. It had been abandoned by the time Europeans arrived in the area.

Mississippian culture endured, however, and was still in evidence throughout much of the Southeast at the time of first contact with Europeans. The Lady of Cofachiqui encountered by Hernando de Soto in 1540 ruled over a Mississippian community, and others dotted the landscape between the Carolinas and the lower Mississippi River. In Florida, sixteenth-century Spanish explorers encountered the Apalachee Indians, who occupied a network of towns built around mounds and fields of maize.

Eastern Woodlands In the **eastern woodlands**, the Mississippian-influenced peoples of the Southeast interacted with other groups, many of whom adopted maize agriculture but did not otherwise display Mississippian characteristics. **Algonquian**

The Kincaid Site Located on the north bank of the Ohio River 140 miles from Cahokia, the Kincaid site was a Mississippian town from 1050 to 1450 C.E.. It contains at least nineteen mounds topped by large buildings thought to have been temples or council houses. Now a state historic site in Illinois, it has been studied by anthropologists and archaeologists since the 1930s. Artist Herb Roe depicts the town as it may have looked at its peak. Illustration by Herb Roe, ©2004.

and **Iroquoian** speakers shared related languages and lifeways but were divided into dozens of distinct societies. Most occupied villages built around fields of maize, beans, and squash during the summer months; at other times of the year, they dispersed in smaller groups to hunt, fish, and gather. Throughout the eastern woodlands, as in most of North America, women tended crops, gathered plants, and oversaw affairs within the community, while men were responsible for activities beyond it, especially hunting, fishing, and warfare.

In this densely forested region, Indians regularly set fires — in New England, twice a year, in spring and fall — to clear away underbrush, open fields, and make it easier to hunt big game. The catastrophic population decline accompanying European colonization quickly put an end to seasonal burning, but in the years before Europeans arrived in North America, bison roamed east as far as modern-day New York and Georgia. Early European colonists remarked upon landscapes that "resemble[d] a stately Parke," where men could ride among widely spaced trees on horseback and even a "large army" could pass unimpeded (see "America in the World," p. 14).

Algonquian and Iroquoian peoples had no single style of political organization. Many were chiefdoms, with one individual claiming authority. Some were paramount chiefdoms, in which numerous communities with their own local chiefs banded together under a single, more powerful ruler. For example, the Powhatan Chiefdom,

Iroquoian cultures/languages
A Native American language family whose speakers were concentrated in the eastern woodlands. The Iroquoian language family should not be confused with the nations of the Iroquois Confederacy, which inhabited the territory of modern-day upstate New York at the time of first contact.

AP® THEME

MIG: Migration and Settlement

The image of the Kincaid site reflects a complex society with large-scale settlement and well laid out buildings and fortifications. Emphasize to students how the artist's reconstruction illustrates the ways that scholars extrapolate from archaeological remains and other evidence to envision what these centuries-old sites might have looked like.

AP® SKILLS & PROCESSES

ANALYZING HISTORICAL EVIDENCE

The **AP® AMERICA IN THE WORLD** feature helps students situate the practice of Indian alteration of their landscape within the global contexts of European practice and the earth's temperature. Use the **QUESTIONS FOR ANALYSIS** prompts to help students analyze point of view, including the limitations of a primary source. Help students appreciate that Morton, as an outsider reporting on a foreign custom, might not fully understand Native Americans' purposes and practices. To extend the discussion, ask students to make connections between the claim that the decline in burning provoked an Ice Age with contemporary concerns about global warming.

TRM Find complete suggested responses in the Teacher's Resource Materials.

AP® AMERICA IN THE WORLD

Altered Landscapes

In the eastern woodlands, Native Americans set fires once or twice a year to clear underbrush and open up landscapes that would otherwise have been densely wooded. The burnings made it easier to plant corn, beans, and squash and drew big game animals into the clearings, where hunters could fell them. As European colonization displaced Indian populations, this practice ended. Some scholars have even suggested that the decline in burning caused a drop of carbon in the atmosphere large enough to account for the Little Ice Age, an episode of global cooling that lasted from about 1550 to 1850, though careful analysis suggests this claim is overstated.

THOMAS MORTON, OF THE CUSTOME IN BURNING THE COUNTRY, AND THE REASON THEREOF (1637)

The Savages are accustomed to set fire of the Country in all places where they come, and to burne it twize a yeare, viz: at the Spring, and the fall of the leafe. The reason that mooves them to doe so, is because it would other wise be so overgrowne with underweedes that it would be all a coppice wood, and the people would not be able in any wise to passe through the Country out of a beaten path.

The meanes that they do it with, is with certaine minerall stones, that they carry about them in baggs made for that purpose of the skinnes of little beastes, which they convert into good lether, carrying in the same a peece of touch wood, very excellent for that purpose, of their owne making. These minerall stones they have from the Piquenteenes, (which is to the Southward of all the plantations in New England,) by trade and trafficke with those people.

The burning of the grasse destroyes the underwoods, and so scorcheth the elder trees that it shrinkes them, and hinders their grouth very much: so that hee that will looke to finde large trees and good tymber, must not depend upon the help of a woodden prospect to finde them on the upland-ground; but must seeke for them, (as I and others have done,) in the lower grounds, where the grounds are wett, when the Country is fired, by reason of the snow water that remaines there for a time, untill the Sunne by continuance of that hath exhaled the vapoures of the earth, and dried up those places where the fire, (by reason of the moisture,) can have no power to doe them any hurt: and if he would endevoure to finde out any goodly Cedars, hee must not seeke for them on the higher grounds, but make his inquest for them in the vallies, for the Savages, by this custome of theirs, have spoiled all the rest: for this custome hath bin continued from the beginninge.

And least their firing of the Country in this manner should be an occasion of damnifying us, and indaingering our habitations, wee our selves have used carefully about the same times to observe the winds, and fire the grounds about our owne habitations; to prevent the Dammage that might happen by any neglect thereof, if the fire should come neere those howses in our absence.

For, when the fire is once kindled, it dilates and spreads it selfe as well against, as with the winde; burning continually night and day, untill a shower of raine falls to quench it.

And this custome of firing the Country is the meanes to make it passable; and by that meanes the trees growe here and there as in our parks: and makes the Country very beautifull and commodious.

SOURCE: Thomas Morton, *The New English Canaan* (1637; Boston: John Wilson and Son, 1883), 172–173.

QUESTIONS FOR ANALYSIS

1. What benefits and dangers does Morton attribute to the practice of Indian burning? How did he and his fellow colonists respond to the practice? Identify the author's point of view.
2. Since Europeans did not practice widespread burning in the Indian manner, they achieved deforestation only slowly, through many years of backbreaking labor. Use historical reasoning to compare European and Native American approaches to landscape management, how would you assess the benefits and challenges of each approach?

which dominated the Chesapeake Bay region, was made up of more than thirty subordinate chiefdoms, and some 20,000 people, when Englishmen established the colony of Virginia. Powhatan himself, according to the English colonist John Smith, was attended by "a guard of 40 or 50 of the tallest men his Country affords."

Elsewhere, especially in the Mid-Atlantic region, the power of chiefs was strictly local. Along the Delaware and Hudson rivers, Lenni Lenape (or Delaware) and Munsee Indians lived in small, independent communities without overarching political organizations. Early European maps of this region show a landscape dotted with a bewildering profusion of Indian names. Colonization would soon drive many of these communities into oblivion and force survivors to coalesce into larger groups.

Some Native American groups were not chiefdoms at all but instead granted political authority to councils of sachems, or leaders. This was the case with the **Iroquois Confederacy**. Sometime shortly before the arrival of Europeans, probably around 1500, five nations occupying the region between the Hudson River and Lake Erie — the Mohawks, Oneidas, Onondagas, Cayugas, and Senecas — banded together to form the Iroquois, or, as they called themselves, the Haudenosaunee (People of the Longhouse).

These nations had been fighting among themselves for years. Then, according to legend, a Mohawk man named Hiawatha lost his family in one of these wars. Stricken by grief, he met a spirit who taught him a series of condolence rituals. He returned to his people preaching a new gospel of peace and power, and the condolence rituals he taught became the foundation for the Iroquois League. Once bound by these rituals, the Five Nations began acting together as a political confederacy. They made peace among themselves and became one of the most powerful Native American groups in the Northeast.

The Iroquois did not recognize chiefs; instead, councils of sachems made decisions. These were matriarchal societies, with power inherited through female lines of authority. Women were influential in local councils, though men served as sachems, made war, and conducted diplomacy.

Along the southern coast of the region that would soon be called New England, a dense network of powerful chiefdoms — including the Narragansetts, Wampanoags, Mohegans, Pequots, and others — competed for resources and dominance. When the Dutch and English arrived, they were able to exploit these rivalries and pit Indian groups against one another. Farther north, in northern New England and much of present-day Canada, the short growing season and thin, rocky soil were inhospitable to maize agriculture. Here the Native peoples were hunters and gatherers and therefore had smaller and more mobile communities.

Iroquois Confederacy
A league of five Native American nations — the Mohawks, Oneidas, Onondagas, Cayugas, and Senecas — probably formed around 1450 C.E.. A sixth nation, the Tuscaroras, joined the confederacy around 1720. Condolence ceremonies introduced by a Mohawk named Hiawatha formed the basis for the league. Positioned between New France and New Netherland (later New York), the Iroquois played a central role in the era of European colonization.

AP® SKILLS & PROCESSES
COMPARISON
Explain differences in the ways various Native populations interacted with the natural environment in North America.

The Great Lakes To the west, Algonquian-speaking peoples dominated the **Great Lakes**. The tribal groups recognized by Europeans in this region included the Ottawas, Ojibwas, and Potawatomis. Collectively, these groups thought of themselves as a single people: the Anishinaabeg. Clan identities — beaver, otter, sturgeon, deer, and others — crosscut tribal affiliations and were in some ways more fundamental. The result was a social landscape that could be bewildering to outsiders. Here lived, one French official remarked, "an infinity of undiscovered nations."

The extensive network of lakes and rivers, and the use of birchbark canoes, made Great Lakes peoples especially mobile. "They seem to have as many abodes as the year has seasons," wrote one observer. They traveled long distances to hunt and fish, to trade, or to join in important ceremonies or military alliances. Groups negotiated access to resources and travel routes. Instead of an area with clearly delineated tribal territories, it is best to imagine the Great Lakes as a porous region, where "political power and social identity took on multiple forms," as one scholar has written.

Great Lakes
Five enormous, interconnected freshwater lakes — Ontario, Erie, Huron, Michigan, and Superior — that dominate eastern North America. In the era before long-distance overland travel, they comprised the center of the continent's transportation system.

The Great Plains and Rockies Farther west lies the vast, arid steppe region known as the **Great Plains**, which was dominated by small, dispersed groups of hunter-gatherers. The world of these Plains Indians was transformed by a European import — the horse — long before Europeans themselves arrived on the plains. Horses were introduced in the Spanish colony of New Mexico in the late sixteenth century and gradually dispersed across the plains. Bison hunters who had previously relied on stealth became much more successful on horseback.

Indians on horseback were also more formidable opponents in war than their counterparts on foot, and some Plains peoples leveraged their control of horses to gain power over their neighbors. The Comanches were a small Shoshonean band on the northern plains that migrated south in pursuit of horses. They became expert raiders,

Great Plains
A broad plateau region that stretches from central Texas in the south to the Canadian plains in the north, bordered on the east by the eastern woodlands and on the west by the Rocky Mountains. Averaging around 20 inches of rainfall a year, the Great Plains are primarily grasslands that support grazing but not crop agriculture.

TEACHING STRATEGY

Culture Quest, an interactive Web site from the National Museum of the American Indian, is a great tool that allows students to engage further with Native American culture and artifacts from each major region in North and South America. Assign this site for independent student work or use for classroom discussion. Search "NMAI Culture Quest" to access this site.

AP® SKILLS & PROCESSES

COMPARISON

Provide students with a physical map of North America and ask them to label important geographic features including (but not limited to) the Mississippi River, Great Lakes, Rocky Mountains, Great Basin, Eastern Woodlands, Appalachian Mountains, and Central Lowlands. Ask students to discuss with a partner the advantages and/or disadvantages that each region would present to people living there in 1491. Have students label the Native American groups who populated North America and identify the ways they took advantage of the region they occupied and/or dealt with the challenges presented by geography and environment. After students have labeled and discussed maps, ask students to address the following questions (*answers will vary*):

- **How did differences in geography and environment influence the development of technology and innovation?**
- **How did interactions between native groups influence migrations?**
- **How did geography and environment influence beliefs, ideas, and culture?**

Encourage students to see connections to the modern world by leading a class discussion on the ways these same questions would be answered in the U.S. today.

TRM Find complete suggested responses in the Teacher's Resource Materials.

TEACHING STRATEGY

This note pairs well with the questions about the regions where American Indians lived and how geography influenced the settlements they created. Think about providing students with the following systems: agricultural, hunter-gatherer, and settled communities. The goal is for students to recognize these systems as not fixed, but rather fluid processes where indigenous populations continually adapted to their environment. Ask students to match geographic areas for agricultural, hunter-gatherer, and settled communities.

capturing people and horses alike and trading them for weapons, food, clothing, and other necessities. Eventually they controlled a vast territory. Their skill in making war on horseback transformed the Comanches from a small group to one of the region's most formidable peoples.

Similarly, horses allowed the Sioux, a confederation of seven distinct peoples who originated in present-day Minnesota, to move west and dominate a vast territory ranging from the Mississippi River to the Black Hills. The Crow Indians moved from the Missouri River to the eastern slope of the **Rocky Mountains**, where they became nomadic bison hunters. Beginning in the mid-eighteenth century, they became horse breeders and traders as well.

Rocky Mountains
A high mountain range that spans some 3,000 miles, the Rocky Mountains are bordered by the Great Plains on the east and the Great Basin on the west. Native peoples fished; gathered roots and berries; and hunted elk, deer, and bighorn sheep there. Silver mining boomed in the Rockies in the nineteenth century.

In some places, farming communities were embedded within the much wider territories of hunter-gatherers. The Hidatsa and Mandan Indians, for example, maintained settled agricultural villages along the Missouri River, while the more mobile Sioux dominated the region around them. Similarly, the Caddos, who lived on the edge of the southern plains, inhabited farming communities that were like islands in a sea of more mobile peoples.

Great Basin
An arid basin-and-range region bounded by the Rocky Mountains on the east and the Sierra Mountains on the west. All of its water drains or evaporates within the basin. A resource-scarce environment, the Great Basin was thinly populated by Native American hunter-gatherers who ranged long distances to support themselves.

Three broad swaths of Numic-speaking peoples occupied the **Great Basin** that separated the Rockies from the Sierra Mountains: Bannocks and Northern Paiutes in the north, Shoshones in the central basin, and Utes and Southern Paiutes in the south. Resources were varied and spread thin on the land. Kin-based bands traveled great distances to hunt bison along the Yellowstone River (where they shared territory with the Crows) and bighorn sheep in high altitudes, to fish for salmon, and to gather pine nuts when they were in season. Throughout the Great Basin, some groups adopted horses and became relatively powerful, while others remained foot-borne and impoverished in comparison with their more mobile neighbors.

The Arid Southwest In the part of North America that appears to be most hostile to agriculture — the canyon-laced country of the arid Southwest — surprisingly large farming settlements developed. Anasazi peoples were growing maize by the first century earlier than anywhere else north of Mexico, and Pueblo cultures emerged around 600 C.E.. By 1000 C.E., the Hohokams, Mogollons, and Anasazis (all Pueblo peoples) had developed irrigation systems to manage scarce water, enabling them to build sizable villages and towns of adobe and rock that were often molded to sheer canyon walls. Chaco Canyon, in modern New Mexico, supported a dozen large Anasazi towns, while beyond the canyon a network of roads tied these settlements together with hundreds of small Anasazi villages.

Extended droughts and soil exhaustion caused the abandonment of Chaco Canyon and other large settlements in the Southwest after 1150, but smaller communities still dotted the landscape when the first Europeans arrived. It was the Spanish who called these groups Pueblos: *pueblo* means "town" in Spanish, and the name refers to their distinctive building style. When Europeans arrived, Pueblo peoples, including the Acomas, Zuñis, Tewas, and Hopis, were found throughout much of modern New Mexico, Arizona, and western Texas.

Anasazi Ladle Crafted between 1300 and 1600 C.E. and found in a site in central Arizona, this Anasazi dipper was coiled and molded by hand and painted with a geometric motif. Anasazi pottery is abundant in archaeological sites, thanks in part to the Southwest's dry climate. Clay vessels and ladles helped Anasazi peoples handle water — one of their most precious resources — with care. National Museum of the American Indian, Smithsonian Institution 21/5025.

The Pacific Coast Hunter-gatherers inhabited the Pacific coast. Before the Spanish arrived, California was home to more than 300,000 people, subdivided into dozens of small, localized groups and speaking at least a hundred distinct languages. This diversity of languages and cultures discouraged intermarriage and kept these societies independent. Despite their differences, many groups did

TEACHING STRATEGY

Use the image of the Anasazi artifact to lead a discussion on tool-making and artistry in Southwestern Indian communities, as well as how preserved materials help archaeologists reconstruct past societies. Supplement this discussion with high-quality images of other artifacts from the region. The National Museum of the American Indian's *Infinity of Nations* Web site provides a brief overview of the region's culture and links to high-resolution images and details about roughly twenty objects' construction and use. Search "Infinity of Nations Southwest" to access this resource.

CHECK FOR UNDERSTANDING

Ask students: **What types of political organization characterized each of the following regions?**

- **The Mississippi Valley?** *The Mississippi Valley saw chiefdoms with extensive settlements, most prominently Cahokia, but this culture peaked around 1000 A.D. and declined centuries before Europeans arrived.*
- **Eastern Woodlands?** *The Eastern Woodlands region consisted largely of Algonquian and Iroquoian peoples, who adopted seasonal agriculture and a semisedentary lifestyle. Their political organizations primarily consisted of chiefdoms, some of which included larger confederacies while others had purely local authority.*
- **Great Lakes?** *Great Lakes peoples were also Algonquian-speaking and thought of themselves as one people, the Anishinaabeg, though they were split into different clans.*
- **Great Plains and Rockies?** *The peoples of the Great Plains and Rockies largely consisted of small groups of hunter-gatherers.*
- **Southwest?** *Using irrigation, Southwest Indian groups were able to adopt maize agriculture and establish towns and road networks, although drought and soil exhaustion led to the decline of these cultures.*
- **Pacific Coast?** *The Pacific Coast largely consisted of hundreds of small, localized groups speaking different languages engaged in hunter-gatherer economies.*

share common characteristics, including clearly defined social hierarchies separating elites from commoners. They gathered acorns and other nuts and seeds, caught fish and shellfish, and hunted game.

The Pacific Northwest also supported a dense population that was divided into many distinct groups who controlled small territories — both on land and on the sea — and spoke different languages. Their stratified societies were ruled by wealthy families. To maintain control of their territories, the more powerful nations, including the Chinooks, Coast Salishes, Haidas, and Tlingits, nurtured strong warrior traditions. They developed sophisticated fishing technologies and crafted oceangoing dugout canoes, made from enormous cedar trees, that ranged up to 60 feet in length. Their distinctive material culture included large longhouses that were home to dozens of people and totem poles representing clan lineages or local legends.

Chilkat Tlingit Bowl This bowl in the form of a brown bear, which dates to the mid-nineteenth century, is made of alder wood and inlaid with snail shells. The brown bear is a Tlingit clan totem. Animal-form bowls like this one, which express an affinity with nonhuman creatures, are a common feature of Tlingit culture. National Museum of the American Indian, Smithsonian Institution 9/7990.

Patterns of Trade

Expansive trade networks tied together regions and carried valuable goods hundreds and even thousands of miles. Trade goods included food and raw materials, tools, ritual artifacts, and decorative goods. Trade enriched diets, enhanced economies, and allowed the powerful to set themselves apart with luxury items.

In areas where Indians specialized in a particular economic activity, regional trade networks allowed them to share resources. Thus nomadic hunters of the southern plains, including the Navajos and Apaches, conducted annual trade fairs with Pueblo farmers, exchanging hides and meat for maize, pottery, and cotton blankets. Similar patterns of exchange occurred throughout the Great Plains, wherever hunters and farmers coexisted. In some parts of North America, a regional trade in war captives who were offered as slaves helped to sustain friendly relations among neighboring groups. One such network developed in the Upper Mississippi River basin, where Plains Indian captives were traded, or given as diplomatic gifts, to Ottawas and other Great Lakes and eastern woodlands peoples.

Rare and valuable objects traveled longer distances. Great Lakes copper, Rocky Mountain mica, jasper from Pennsylvania, obsidian from New Mexico and Wyoming, and pipestone from the Midwest have all been found in archaeological sites hundreds of miles from their points of origin. Seashells — often shaped and polished into beads and other artifacts — were highly prized and widely distributed. Grizzly bear claws and eagle feathers were valuable, high-status objects. After European contact, Indian hunters often traveled long distances to trade for cloth, iron tools, and weapons.

Powerful leaders controlled much of a community's wealth and redistributed it to prove their generosity and strengthen their authority. In small, kin-based bands, the strongest hunters possessed the most food, and sharing it was essential. In chiefdoms, rulers filled the same role, often collecting the wealth of a community and then redistributing it to their followers. Powhatan, the powerful Chesapeake Bay chief, reportedly collected nine-tenths of the produce of the communities he oversaw — "skins, beads, copper, pearls, deer, turkeys, wild beasts, and corn" — and then gave much of it back to his subordinates. His generosity was considered a mark of good leadership. In the Pacific Northwest, the Chinook word *potlatch* refers to periodic festivals in which wealthy residents gave away belongings to friends, family, and followers.

AP® SKILLS & PROCESSES

CAUSATION

How did landscape, climate, and resources influence the development of Native American societies?

TEACHING STRATEGY

Use the image of a Tlingit artifact to deepen students' understanding of culture and beliefs in the Pacific Northwest. Supplement this discussion with high-quality images of other artifacts from this region on the National Museum of the American Indian's Infinity of Nations Web site. Search "Infinity of Nations Northwest" to access this resource.

AP® SKILLS & PROCESSES

CAUSATION

Use the **CAUSATION** question to help students identify the long-term effects of environmental factors on social development. Ask students to consider how climate and natural resources helped shape the size and nature of social groups. It might be helpful for them to chart each region, its dominant environmental factors, and the resulting social organization. To extend this prompt, ask students to make a generalization about the influence of environmental factors on social patterns.

TRM Find complete suggested responses in the Teacher's Resource Materials.

CHECK FOR UNDERSTANDING

Ask students: **What major patterns of trade characterized precontact North America?**
A variety of specialized goods were traded, and valuable objects — like minerals and precious metals — often traveled great distances. Trade served political and diplomatic purposes, as leaders distributed wealth to strengthen their authority.

AP® SKILLS & PROCESSES

CAUSATION

Use the **CAUSATION** question to help students understand diverse perspectives. Students may need guidance in understanding animism and its implications for everyday patterns of behavior given most students tend to be much less familiar with Native American views of spirituality. To extend this prompt, ask students to compare animist views with monotheistic views.

TRM Find complete suggested responses in the Teacher's Resource Materials.

Sacred Power

Most Native North Americans were animists who believed that the natural world was suffused with spiritual power. They interpreted dreams and visions to understand the world, and their rituals appeased guardian spirits to ensure successful hunts and other forms of good fortune. Although their views were subject to countless local variations, certain patterns were widespread.

Women and men interacted differently with these spiritual forces. In farming communities, women grew crops and maintained hearth, home, and village. Native American ideas about female power linked their bodies' generative functions with the earth's fertility, and rituals like the Green Corn Ceremony — a summer ritual of purification and renewal — helped to sustain the life-giving properties of the world around them.

AP® SKILLS & PROCESSES

CAUSATION

How did Native Americans' conceptions of the spiritual world influence their daily lives?

For men, spiritual power was invoked in hunting and war. To ensure success in hunting, men took care not to offend the spirits of the animals they killed. They performed rituals before, during, and after a hunt to acknowledge the power of those guardian spirits, and they believed that, when an animal had been killed properly, its spirit would rise from the earth unharmed. Success in hunting and prowess in war were both interpreted as signs of sacred protection and power.

Ideas about war varied widely. War could be fought for geopolitical reasons — to gain ground against an enemy — but for many groups, warfare was a crucial rite of passage for young men, and raids were conducted to allow warriors to prove themselves in battle. Motives for war could be highly personal; war was often more like a blood feud between families than a contest between nations. If a community lost warriors in battle, it might retaliate by capturing or killing a like number of warriors in response — a so-called mourning war. Some captives were adopted into new communities, while others were enslaved or tortured.

WESTERN EUROPE: THE EDGE OF THE OLD WORLD

How had recent developments changed Western Europe by 1491?

AP® EXAM TIP

Consider the ways that European societies were similar to and different from Native societies in the Americas.

In 1491, Western Europe lay at the far edge of the Eurasian and African continents. It had neither the powerful centralized empires nor the hunter-gatherer bands and semisedentary societies of the Americas. Western Europe was, instead, a patchwork of roughly equivalent kingdoms, duchies, and republics vying with one another and struggling to reach out effectively to the rest of the world. No one would have predicted that Europeans would soon become overlords of the Western Hemisphere. A thousand years after the fall of the Roman Empire, Europe's populations still relied on subsistence agriculture and were never far from the specter of famine. Moreover, around 1350, a deadly plague was introduced from Central Asia — the Black Death — that killed one-third of Europe's people. The lives of ordinary people were afflicted by poverty, disease, and uncertainty, and the future looked as difficult and dark as the past.

Hierarchy and Authority

In traditional hierarchical societies — American or European — authority came from above. In Europe, kings and princes owned vast tracts of land, forcibly conscripted men for military service, and lived off the peasantry's labor. Yet monarchs were far from supreme: local nobles also owned large estates and controlled hundreds of peasant families. Collectively, these nobles challenged royal authority with both their military power and their legislative institutions, such as the French *parlements* and the English House of Lords.

Just as kings and nobles ruled society, men governed families. These were patriarchies, in which property and social identity descended in male family lines. Rich or poor, the man was the head of the house, his power justified by the teachings of the Christian Church. As one English clergyman put it, "The woman is a weak creature not embued with like strength and constancy of mind"; law and custom "subjected her to the power of man." Once married, an Englishwoman assumed her husband's surname, submitted to his orders, and surrendered the right to her property.

Men also controlled the lives of their children, who usually worked for their father into their middle or late twenties. Then landowning peasants would give land to their sons and dowries (property or money given by a bride's family to her husband) to their daughters and choose marriage partners of appropriate wealth and status. In many regions, fathers bestowed all their land on their eldest son — a practice known as primogeniture — forcing many younger children to join the ranks of the roaming poor. Few men and even fewer women had much personal freedom.

Powerful institutions — nobility, church, and village — enforced hierarchy and offered ordinary people a measure of security in a violent and unpredictable world. Carried by migrants to America, these security-conscious institutions would shape the character of family and society well into the eighteenth century.

Peasant Society

Most Europeans were **peasants**, farmworkers who lived in small villages surrounded by fields farmed cooperatively by different families. On manorial lands, farming rights were given in exchange for labor on the lord's estate, an arrangement that turned peasants into serfs. Gradually, obligatory manorial services gave way to paying rent or, as in France, landownership. Once freed from the obligation to labor for their farming rights, European farmers began to produce surpluses and created local market economies.

peasants
The traditional term for farmworkers in Europe. Some peasants owned land, whereas others leased or rented small plots from landlords.

As with Native Americans, the rhythm of life followed the seasons. In March, villagers began the exhausting work of plowing and then planting wheat, rye, and oats. During the spring, the men sheared wool, which the women washed and spun into yarn. In June, peasants cut hay and stored it as winter fodder for their livestock. During the summer, life was more relaxed, and families repaired their houses and barns. Fall brought the harvest, followed by solemn feasts of thanksgiving and riotous bouts of merrymaking. As winter approached, peasants slaughtered excess livestock and salted or smoked the meat. During the cold months, they threshed grain and wove textiles, visited friends and relatives, and celebrated the winter solstice or the birth of Christ. Just before the cycle began again in the spring, they held carnivals, celebrating the end of the long winter with drink and dance.

For most peasants, survival meant constant labor, and poverty corroded family relationships. Malnourished mothers fed their babies sparingly, calling them "greedy and gluttonous," and many newborn girls were "helped to die" so that their brothers would have enough to eat. Half of all peasant children died before the age of twenty-one, victims of malnourishment and disease. Many peasants drew on strong religious beliefs, "counting blessings" and accepting their harsh existence. Others hoped for a better life. It was the peasants of Spain, Germany, and Britain who would supply the majority of white migrants to the Western Hemisphere.

AP® SKILLS & PROCESSES
COMPARISON
In what ways were the lives of Europeans similar to and different from those of Native Americans?

Expanding Trade Networks

In the millennium before contact with the Americas, Western Europe was the barbarian fringe of the civilized world. In the Mediterranean basin, Arab scholars synthesized and expanded on the intellectual achievements of Greek, Roman, Persian, and Asian cultures to develop sophisticated systems of mathematical, medical, and

CHECK FOR UNDERSTANDING

Ask students: **What structures of hierarchy and authority characterized early modern Europe?** *Kings, princes, and other nobility ruled European society, often competing with each other for power. Men ruled their wives and children. Church teaching reinforced this political and family hierarchy.*

TEACHING STRATEGY

Introduce students to the concept of using a pyramid to model division and power in human societies. Have students work in pairs, and ask one student to complete the social pyramid for European society and the other to complete the pyramid for Native societies. Students can use the text, information from pre-Columbian notes, and online sources as needed for this activity. After the partners complete their assigned pyramids, ask them to share them and discuss the similarities and differences in European and Native societies and the reasons why these similarities and differences might exist. Next, ask them to consider the ways that Europeans and Native people would react to each other based on their similarities and differences. When students have finished discussing the comparisons, ask them to individually answer the following questions: Did European and Native societies share more similarities or differences? Did this make a difference in the interactions between them in the early period of colonization?

CHECK FOR UNDERSTANDING

Ask students: **What was peasant society in Europe like?** *Generally, life was very difficult. Though there was some seasonal variation, labor was typically year-round and taxing. With part of rent going to landlords, poverty, malnourishment, sickness, and high mortality were common.*

AP® SKILLS & PROCESSES

COMPARISON

Use the **COMPARISON** question to help students make broad comparisons across different geographical locations. Scaffold this question by identifying the points of comparison outlined in the text: social hierarchies, economic production, cultural traditions, and gender patterns. To extend this prompt, ask students how patterns in both of these premodern cultures differ from these patterns in modern societies.

TRM Find complete suggested responses in the Teacher's Resource Materials.

European Peasant Life This painting by Pieter Bruegel the Elder shows a summer farm scene in which a community of laborers is harvesting a hay crop. Two men are cutting plants with hand scythes in the foreground and two women are bundling them into sheaves in the background, while the rest of the group takes a lunch break in the shade. Though the landscape is beautiful and idyllic, peasant labor was a slow, backbreaking affair that required many pairs of hands working together. The Metropolitan Museum of Art, Rogers Fund, 1919.

scientific knowledge, while Arab merchants controlled trade in the Mediterranean, Africa, and the Near East. This control gave them access to spices from India and silks, magnetic compasses, water-powered mills, and mechanical clocks from China.

AP® EXAM TIP

Take good notes on the changing structure of the European economy from the fourteenth to sixteenth centuries and how that in turn impacted European society.

In the twelfth century, merchants from the Italian city-states of Genoa, Florence, Pisa, and especially Venice began to push their way into the Arab-dominated trade routes of the Mediterranean. Trading in Alexandria, Beirut, and other eastern Mediterranean ports, they carried the luxuries of Asia into European markets. At its peak, Venice had a merchant fleet of more than three thousand ships. This enormously profitable commerce created wealthy merchants, bankers, and textile manufacturers who expanded trade, lent vast sums of money, and spurred technological innovation in silk and wool production.

republic
A state without a monarch or prince that is governed by representatives of the people.

Italian moneyed elites ruled their city-states as **republics**, states that had no prince or king but instead were governed by merchant coalitions. They celebrated civic humanism, an ideology that praised public virtue and service to the state; over time, this tradition profoundly influenced European and American conceptions of government. They sponsored great artists — Michelangelo, Leonardo da Vinci, and others — who produced an unprecedented flowering of genius. Historians have labeled the arts and learning associated with this cultural transformation from 1300 to 1450 the Renaissance.

AP® SKILLS & PROCESSES

CONTEXTUALIZATION

Using the Bruegel painting as the backdrop for discussion, ask students to define feudalism. The transition from feudalism to capitalism is a significant historical change during this period. For both the Long-Essay and the Document-Based Question on the AP® Exam, students will need to describe broader contextual processes. To begin this conversation, consider providing students with characteristics of what it looks like to describe a broader historical process. Start with a broad process such as the transition from feudalism to capitalism. After students are familiar with this concept, ask them to brainstorm two pieces of historical evidence that could substantiate their statement about the economic changes attendant to the movement toward capitalism. Factors such as the Columbian Exchange, merchant capitalism, and colonization are among the many possible answers. The goal is to have students start conceptualizing what it means to establish historical context.

AP® APPLY THE TIP

With students, discuss the Renaissance and economic revolution as factors that contributed to colonization. Emphasize the role of the failure of Europeans in the Crusades as a driving force in "discovery" and colonization of the New World. Ask students the following questions:

- **Even though they failed, how did the Crusades impact Europe's economy?** *The Crusades introduced new luxury goods in Europe including, but not limited to, silk, porcelain, spices, sugar, gold/silver goods, paints, and dyes. In addition, innovations such as checks as a form of currency and banking systems were introduced from the Arab world. These practices allowed for the rise of bankers in Italian city-states who then funded the growth of nation-states and exploration to the New World.*
- **How did the influence of ideas from the Byzantine world influence the worldview of Italians and then Europeans in general?** *The conquest of Byzantine areas by Muslim forces led to migration of scholars, scientists, writers, mathematicians, etc., to Italy. This influx of scholarly work and ideas reintroduced ideas from the Greek world and ideas related to the Age of Exploration, such as the size of the Earth and understanding of geography. In addition, Europeans are introduced to innovations including the caravel and astrolabe, which supports navigation.*
- **How did the rise of merchants influence the "discovery" and colonization of the New World?** *The rise of a powerful merchant class supported the power of kings as they formed powerful nation-states in France, England, and eventually Spain. Merchants undermined the traditional power of the nobility. Kings encouraged merchants and trade by granting royal charters to guilds, safeguarding trade in their realms, and using tax money to support bureaucracies to support trade.*

Procession in St. Mark's Square in Venice, 1496 Venice was one of the world's great trading centers in the fifteenth century. Its merchant houses connected Europe to Asia and the Middle East, while its complex republican government aroused both admiration and mistrust. Here, Venetian painter Gentile Bellini (c. 1429–1507) depicts a diplomatic procession celebrating the League of Venice, a union of European states opposed to French expansion into Italy. Galleria dell 'Accademia, Venice, Italy/Giraudon/The Bridgeman Art Library.

The economic revolution that began in Italy spread slowly to northern and western Europe. England's principal export was woolen cloth, which was prized in the colder parts of the continent but had less appeal in southern Europe and beyond. Northern Europe had its own trade system, controlled by an alliance of merchant communities called the Hanseatic League. Centered on the Baltic and North seas, it dealt in timber, furs, wheat and rye, honey, wax, and amber.

As trade picked up in Europe, merchants and artisans came to dominate its growing cities and towns. While the Italian city-states ruled themselves without a powerful monarch, in much of Europe the power of merchants stood in tension with that of kings and nobles. In general, the rise of commerce favored the power of kings at the expense of the landed nobility. Why did the growth of a merchant class buttress royal power? The kings of Western Europe established royal law courts that gradually eclipsed the manorial courts controlled by nobles; they also built bureaucracies that helped them centralize power while they forged alliances with merchants and urban artisans. Monarchs allowed merchants to trade throughout their realms; granted privileges to guilds, or artisan organizations that regulated trades; and safeguarded commercial transactions, thereby encouraging domestic manufacturing and foreign trade. In return, they extracted taxes from towns and loans from merchants to support their armies and officials.

AP® SKILLS & PROCESSES

CONTINUITY AND CHANGE

How did the growth of commerce shift the structure of power in Western European societies?

Myths, Religions, and Holy Warriors

The oldest European religious beliefs drew on a form of animism similar to that of Native Americans, which held that the natural world — the sun, wind, stones, animals — was animated by spiritual forces. As in North America, such beliefs led ancient European peoples to develop localized cults of knowledge and spiritual practice. Wise men and women created rituals to protect their communities, ensure abundant harvests, heal illnesses, and bring misfortunes to their enemies.

The pagan traditions of Greece and Rome overlaid animism with elaborate myths about gods interacting directly with the affairs of human beings. As the Roman

AP® THEME

WXT: Work, Exchange, and Technology

Ask students: **How does the image of the procession in St. Mark's Square in Venice show patterns of exchange intersected with governmental actions and religious traditions?** *The image reveals the role of religion in European culture, as the procession takes place in the plaza in front of the opulent St. Mark's Basilica — a cathedral gilded with wealth accumulated through Venetian commerce. The diplomatic gathering in the church plaza of an economic powerhouse suggests how political, economic, and religious concerns often overlapped.*

TRM Find complete suggested responses in the Teacher's Resource Materials.

CHECK FOR UNDERSTANDING

Ask students: **How did European trade networks expand from the medieval period, through the Renaissance, and into the early modern era?** *Italian city-states began to break into the Arab-dominated world of trade in the thirteenth century. Their profits led to the development of banking, which in turn generated more capital for expanded commercial ventures. The practices Italians introduced spread northward through Europe, and trade grew there as well. The expansion of trade led to the elevation of merchants and artisans as the leading town authorities. The growth of trade also favored monarchs, who could tax trade, at the expense of nobles, whose wealth came from land rents.*

Empire expanded, it built temples to its gods wherever it planted new settlements. Thus peoples throughout Europe, North Africa, and the Near East were exposed to the Roman pantheon. Soon the teachings of Christianity began to flow in these same channels.

Christianity
A religion that holds the belief that Jesus Christ was himself divine. For centuries, the Roman Catholic Church was the great unifying institution in Western Europe, and it was from Europe that Christianity spread to the Americas.

The Rise of Christianity **Christianity**, which grew out of Jewish monotheism (the belief in one god), held that Jesus Christ was himself divine. As an institution, Christianity benefitted enormously from the conversion of the Roman emperor Constantine in 312 C.E.. Prior to that time, Christians were an underground sect at odds with the Roman Empire. After Constantine's conversion, Christianity became Rome's official religion, temples were abandoned or remade into churches, and noblemen who hoped to retain their influence converted to the new state religion.

For centuries, the Roman Catholic Church was the great unifying institution in Western Europe. The pope in Rome headed a vast hierarchy of cardinals, bishops, and priests. Catholic theologians preserved Latin, the language of classical scholarship, and imbued kingship with divine power. Christian dogma provided a common understanding of God and human history, and the authority of the Church buttressed state institutions. Every village had a church, and holy shrines served as points of contact with the sacred world. Often those shrines had their origins in older, animist practices, now largely forgotten and replaced with Christian ritual.

Christian doctrine penetrated deeply into the everyday lives of peasants. While animist traditions held that spiritual forces were alive in the natural world, Christian priests taught that the natural world was flawed and fallen. Spiritual power came from outside nature, from a supernatural God who had sent his divine son, Jesus Christ, into the world to save humanity from its sins. The Christian Church devised a religious calendar that transformed animist festivals into holy days. The winter solstice, which had for millennia marked the return of the sun, became the feast of Christmas.

The Church also taught that Satan, a wicked supernatural being, was constantly challenging God by tempting people to sin. People who spread heresies — doctrines that were inconsistent with the teachings of the Church — were seen as the tools of Satan, and suppressing false doctrines became an obligation of Christian rulers.

TEACHING STRATEGY

Ask students to create a mind map with "Exploration" in the center and branches reading "political causes," "economic causes," and "religious causes." Working with the textbook and primary sources, have students provide supporting details for each cause of exploration. Primary sources could include an excerpt from Bartolomé de las Casas, a map of major religions in the New World, an excerpt from "City upon a Hill," a map of trade routes before 1492, or an excerpt from Richard Hakluyt on reasons for English settlement of the New World. Once students have added significant supporting details, have them use dotted lines to connect supporting details to one another. Students should write an explanation for the connection on the dotted lines. After students have completed this activity, have them present their findings and explanations in groups to facilitate a class discussion of the changing political, economic, and religious causes of exploration.

Islam
A religion that considers Muhammad to be God's last prophet. Following the death of Muhammad in 632 C.E., the newly converted Arab peoples of North Africa used force and fervor to spread the Muslim faith into sub-Saharan Africa, India, Indonesia, Spain, and the Balkan regions of Europe.

Crusades
A series of wars undertaken by Christian armies between 1096 and 1291 C.E. to reverse the Muslim advance in Europe and win back the holy lands where Christ had lived.

The Crusades In their work suppressing false doctrines, Christian rulers were also obliged to combat **Islam**, the religion whose followers considered Muhammad to be God's last prophet. Islam's reach expanded until it threatened European Christendom. Following the death of Muhammad in 632 C.E., the newly converted Arab peoples of North Africa used force and fervor to spread the Muslim faith into sub-Saharan Africa, India, and Indonesia, as well as deep into Spain and the Balkan regions of Europe. Between 1096 and 1291 C.E., Christian armies undertook a series of **Crusades** to reverse the Muslim advance in Europe and win back the holy lands where Christ had lived. Under the banner of the pope and led by Europe's Christian monarchs, crusading armies aroused great waves of popular piety as they marched off to combat. New orders of knights, like the Knights Templar and the Teutonic Knights, were created to support them.

The crusaders had some military successes, but their most profound impact was on European society. Religious warfare intensified Europe's Christian identity and prompted the persecution of Jews and their expulsion from many European countries. The Crusades also introduced Western European merchants to the trade routes that stretched from Constantinople to China along the Silk Road and from the Mediterranean Sea through the Persian Gulf to the Indian Ocean. And crusaders encountered sugar for the first time. Returning soldiers brought it back from the Middle East, and as Europeans began to conquer territory in the eastern Mediterranean, they experimented with raising it themselves. These early experiments with sugar would have a profound impact on European enterprise in the Americas — and European

European Crusaders Conquer Constantinople This miniature from a fifteenth-century chronicle, created by David Aubert for Philip, the duke of Burgundy, depicts the capture of Constantinople in 1204, the culminating act of the Fourth Crusade. Because Constantinople was the capital of the Byzantine Empire and headquarters of the Orthodox Christian Church, the Crusaders' decision to besiege, capture, and loot the city was controversial. It dramatically weakened the Byzantine Empire and ultimately left it vulnerable to conquest by the Ottoman Turks. Leemage/Corbis via Getty Images.

involvement with the African slave trade — in the centuries to come. Although Western Europe in 1491 remained relatively isolated from the centers of civilization in Eurasia and Africa, the Crusades and the rise of Italian merchant houses had introduced it to a wider world.

The Reformation In 1517, Martin Luther, a German monk and professor at the university in Wittenberg, took up the cause of reform in the Catholic Church. Luther's *Ninety-five Theses* condemned the Church for many corrupt practices. More radically, Luther downplayed the role of priests as mediators between God and believers and said that Christians must look to the Bible, not to the Church, as the ultimate authority in matters of faith. So that every literate German could read the Bible, previously available only in Latin, Luther translated it into German.

Meanwhile, in Geneva, Switzerland, French theologian John Calvin established a rigorous Christian community. Even more than Luther, Calvin stressed human weakness and God's omnipotence. His *Institutes of the Christian Religion* (1536) depicted God as an absolute ruler. Calvin preached the doctrine of predestination, the idea that God chooses certain people for salvation before they are born and condemns the rest to eternal damnation. Calvin's Geneva was ruled by ministers who prohibited frivolity and luxury. "We know," wrote Calvin, "that man is of so perverse and crooked a nature, that everyone would scratch out his neighbor's eyes if there were no bridle to hold them in." Calvin's authoritarian doctrine won converts all over Europe, including the Puritans in Scotland and England.

AP® SKILLS & PROCESSES

CONTINUITY AND CHANGE

How did the evolution of Christianity bring changes to Europe?

AP® EXAM TIP

It's important to recognize the relationship of religious changes in Europe to the exploration and conquest of the New World.

AP® SKILLS & PROCESSES

ANALYZING HISTORICAL EVIDENCE

Too often, students repeat specific information from historical sources instead of drawing conclusions about the purposes of the document. Students should be taught to capture broad claims, especially in non-text documents. Using the painting of the conquering of Constantinople, have students identify one way in which the painting depicts the long-term historical processes of the Crusades.

AP® SKILLS & PROCESSES

CONTINUITY AND CHANGE

Use the **CONTINUITY AND CHANGE** question to help students understand the growth and eventual division of Christianity in relation to changes in political organization. Scaffold this question by asking students to identify the major developments in European Christianity in the "The Rise of Christianity," "The Crusades," and "The Reformation" sections of the text. Then ask them what political developments took place in each period. Finally, ask students to connect the religious changes to the political changes.

TRM Find complete suggested responses in the Teacher's Resource Materials.

AP® APPLY THE TIP

"Lesson 2: The Counter Reformation and the Religious Struggle in Europe" on The World History for Us All's Web site offers an overview of the difference between Protestants and Catholics, a summary of the religious wars in France and Spain, and a student chart that can be purposed for an in-class activity. Access the lesson by searching "World History for Us All Counter Reformation."

CHECK FOR UNDERSTANDING

Ask students: **How had recent developments changed Western Europe by 1491?** *The major transformation that catalyzed change in Europe before 1491 was the inauguration of large-scale trading networks begun by the Italian city-states of Genoa, Florence, Pisa, and Venice. Beginning in the twelfth century, merchants from these areas began penetrating the Arab-dominated Mediterranean, in turn selling their goods to continental Europeans. The wealth created allowed merchant families to patronize the arts and to seek new answers to existing questions, leading to the cultural transformation known as the Renaissance (ca. 1300 to 1450), the ideas from which were propagated along the new trade routes into the rest of Europe.*

Protestant Reformation
The reform movement that began in 1517 with Martin Luther's critiques of the Roman Catholic Church and that precipitated an enduring schism that divided Protestants from Catholics.

Counter-Reformation
A reaction in the Catholic Church triggered by the Reformation that sought change from within and created new monastic and missionary orders, including the Jesuits (founded in 1540), who saw themselves as soldiers of Christ.

Luther's criticisms triggered a war between the Holy Roman Empire and the northern principalities in Germany, and soon the controversy between the Roman Catholic Church and radical reformers like Luther and Calvin spread throughout much of Western Europe. The **Protestant Reformation**, as this movement came to be called, triggered a **Counter-Reformation** in the Catholic Church that sought change from within and created new monastic and missionary orders, including the Jesuits (founded in 1540), who saw themselves as soldiers of Christ. The competition between these divergent Christian traditions did much to shape European colonization of the Americas. Roman Catholic powers — Spain, Portugal, and France — sought to win souls in the Americas for the Church, while Protestant nations — England and the Netherlands — viewed the Catholic Church as corrupt and exploitative and hoped instead to create godly communities attuned to the true gospel of Christianity.

WEST AND CENTRAL AFRICA: ORIGINS OF THE ATLANTIC SLAVE TRADE

How was sub-Saharan Africa affected by the arrival of European traders?

Homo sapiens originated in Africa. Numerous civilizations had already risen and fallen there, and contacts with the Near East and the Mediterranean were millennia old, when Western Europeans began sailing down Africa's Atlantic coast. Home to perhaps 100 million in 1400, Africa was divided by the vast expanse of the Sahara Desert. North Africa bordered on the Mediterranean, and its peoples fell under the domination of Christian Byzantium until the seventh century, when Muslim conquests brought the region under Islamic influence. In its coastal seaports, the merchandise of Asia, the Near East, Africa, and Europe converged. South of the Sahara, by contrast, the societies of West and Central Africa bordering on the Atlantic were relatively isolated. After 1400, that would quickly change.

Empires, Kingdoms, and Ministates

West Africa — the part of the continent that bulges into the Atlantic — can be visualized as a broad horizontal swath divided into three climatic zones. The Sahel is the mostly flat, semiarid zone immediately south of the Sahara. Below it lies the savanna, a grassland region dotted with trees and shrubs. South of the savanna, in a band 200 to 300 miles wide along the West African coast, lies a tropical rain forest. A series of four major watersheds — the Senegal, Gambia, Volta, and Niger — dominate West Africa (Map 1.3).

Sudanic civilization took root at the eastern end of West Africa beginning around 9000 B.C.E. and traveled westward. Sudanic peoples domesticated cattle (8500–7500 B.C.E.) and cultivated sorghum and millet (7500–7000 B.C.E.). Over several thousand years, these peoples developed a distinctive style of pottery, began to grow and weave cotton (6500–3500 B.C.E.), and invented techniques for working copper and iron (2500–1000 B.C.E.). Sudanic civilization had its own tradition of monotheism distinct from that of Christians, Muslims, and Jews. Most Sudanic peoples in West Africa lived in stratified states ruled by kings and princes who were regarded as divine.

From these cultural origins, three great empires arose in succession in the northern savanna. The first, the Ghana Empire, appeared sometime around 800 C.E.. Ghana capitalized on the recently domesticated camel to pioneer trade routes across the Sahara to North Africa, where Ghana traders carried the wealth of West Africa. The Ghana Empire gave way to the Mali Empire in the thirteenth century, which was

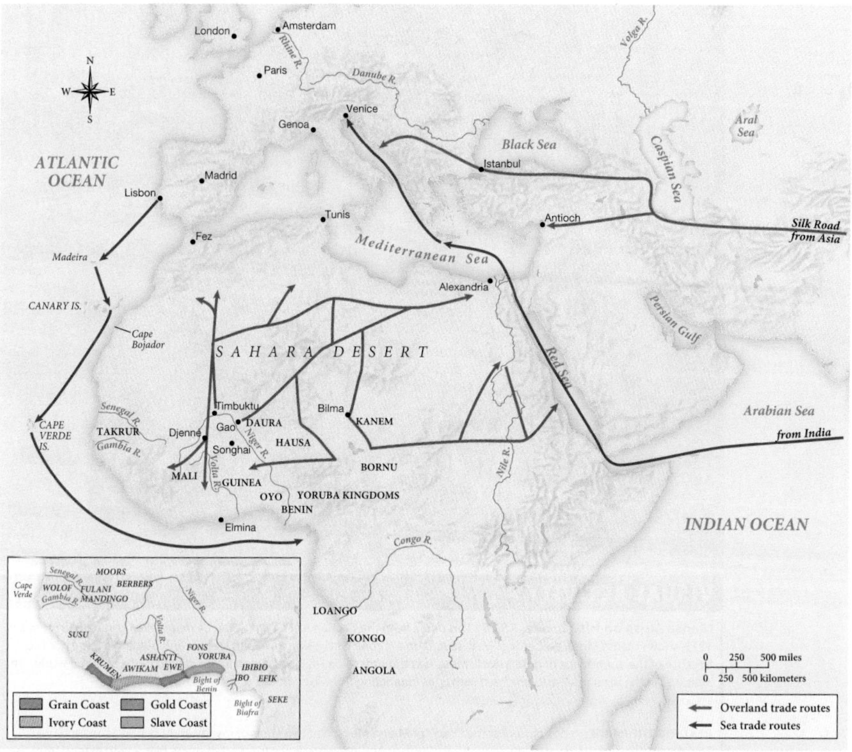

MAP 1.3 West Africa and the Mediterranean in the Fifteenth Century
Trade routes across the Sahara had long connected West Africa with the Mediterranean region. Gold, ivory, and slaves moved north and east; fine textiles, spices, and the Muslim faith traveled south. Beginning in the 1430s, the Portuguese opened up maritime trade with the coastal regions of West Africa, which were home to many peoples and dozens of large and small states. Over the next century, the movement of gold and slaves into the Atlantic would surpass that across the Sahara.

eclipsed in turn by the Songhai Empire in the fifteenth century. All three empires were composed of smaller vassal kingdoms, not unlike the Aztec and Inca empires, and relied on military might to control their valuable trade routes.

Gold, abundant in West Africa, was the cornerstone of power and an indispensable medium of international trade. By 1450, West African traders had carried so much of it across the Sahara that it constituted one-half to two-thirds of all the gold in circulation in Europe, North Africa, and Asia. Mansa Musa, the tenth emperor of Mali, was a devout Muslim famed for his construction projects and his support of mosques and schools. In 1326, he went on a pilgrimage to Mecca with a vast retinue that crossed the Sahara and passed through Egypt. They spent so much gold along the way that the region's money supply was devalued for more than a decade after their visit.

TEACHING STRATEGY

Show **MAP 1.3** to students and ask the following questions:

- **Which African groups likely grew in power as a result of European maritime trade? Why?** *The Krumen, Awikam, Ewe, and Yoruba grew in power because they controlled access to the coast.*
- **What is the advantage of maritime trade compared with land trade?** *Though sea routes covered more distance, ships' larger capacity and use of wind power allowed them to carry much larger loads at lower costs than goods traveling slowly across the desert.*
- **What geographic locations were strategic for Europeans to control to ensure the continuation of their maritime routes?** *Portugal used the coastal islands to move up and down the coast of West Africa and resupply their ships. Venetian sailors relied on access through the Red Sea, including the isthmus near the source of the Nile.*

TEACHING STRATEGY

Leo Africanus's "Description of Timbuktu" from his 1526 work, *The Description of Africa*, provides a glimpse into the infrastructure, court, economy, and culture of the Songhai kingdom. Use this text to help deepen students' understanding of the sophistication and complexity of sub-Saharan Africa in the early modern period. Available through the *Internet History Sourcebook*, you can access the document by searching "Internet History Sourcebook Leo Africanus."

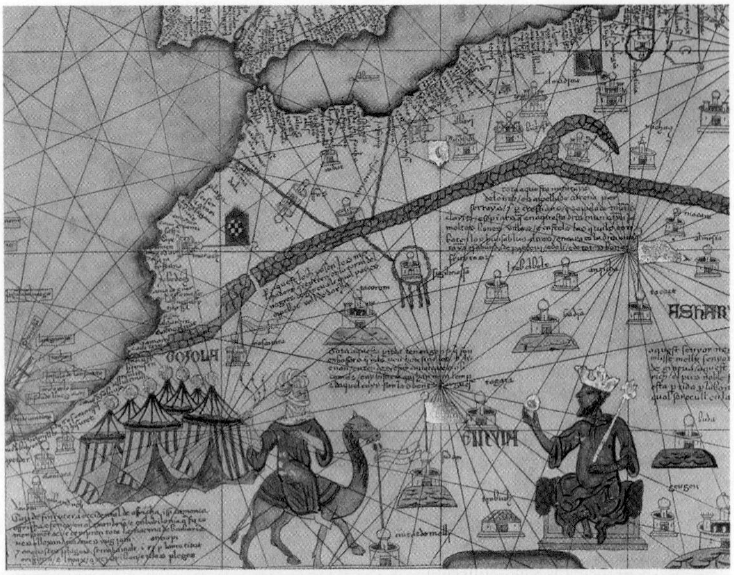

VISUAL ACTIVITY

Mansa Musa on His Throne, 1375 This detail from the Catalan Atlas, completed by mapmaker Abraham Cresques in 1375, shows Mansa Musa, emperor of Mali, seated on a throne with gold crown and scepter and holding a large gold coin. Because of the abundance of gold in Mali, Musa was thought to be the richest man in Africa (and perhaps in the world). The atlas was in the form of a Portolan chart, with lines emanating from fixed points to assist in navigation.

Bibliothèque Nationale, Paris, France/Bridgeman Images.

READING THE IMAGE: Look closely at the image of Mansa Musa. What symbols of royalty identify him as an emperor? This detail is part of a large atlas made for Prince John of Aragon, who requested a set of maps that would extend from the Straits of Gibraltar all the way across Asia. Cresques's atlas reflects centuries of European contact with Asia. What value do you think this atlas would have had to a monarch of Western Europe?

MAKING CONNECTIONS: The gold of Mali was a critically important medium of exchange throughout the Mediterranean basin. When Musa made his pilgrimage to Mecca (along with tens of thousands of followers), he distributed so much of it that the region's economy was dramatically affected. How do you think the massive influx of gold and silver from the Americas might have compared to the effect of Mansa Musa's fourteenth-century pilgrimage?

TRM Find complete suggested responses in the Teacher's Resource Materials.

AP® SKILLS & PROCESSES

COMPARISON

How do the states of the savanna compare to those of the Americas and Europe?

To the south of these empires, the lower savanna and tropical rain forest of West Africa were home to a complex mosaic of kingdoms that traded among themselves and with the empires to the north. In such a densely populated, resource-rich region, they also fought frequently in a competition for local power. A few of these coastal kingdoms were quite large in size, but most were small enough that they have been termed ministates by historians. Comparable to the city-states of Italy, they were often about the size of a modern-day county in the United States. The tropical ecosystem prevented them from raising livestock, since the tsetse fly (which carries a parasite deadly to livestock) was endemic to the region, as was malaria. In place of the grain crops of the savanna, these peoples pioneered the cultivation of yams; they also gathered resources from the rivers and seacoast.

AP® SKILLS & PROCESSES

COMPARISON

Use the **COMPARISON** question to help students compare three different geographical locations. Scaffold the question by identifying the points of comparison in the text: cultural traditions, economic patterns, and political power structures. Extend this prompt by asking students to make inferences about how savanna cultures might have changed as a result of extensive contact with Europe.

TRM Find complete suggested responses in the Teacher's Resource Materials.

CHECK FOR UNDERSTANDING

Ask students: **What features characterized the three empires of West Africa? What kinds of political organization characterized West Africa's other two regions: the lower savanna and tropical rain forest?** *Ghana, Mali, and Songhai established large Muslim empires with vassal states, using their military strength to control and tax trade routes. Most lower savanna and tropical rain forest kingdoms were mini-states with local power.*

Trans-Saharan and Coastal Trade

For centuries, the primary avenue of trade for West Africans passed through the Ghana, Mali, and Songhai empires, whose power was based on the monopoly they enjoyed over the trans-Saharan trade. Their caravans carried West African goods — including gold, copper, salt, and slaves — from the south to the north across the Sahara, then returned with textiles and other products. For the smaller states clustered along the West African coast, merchandise originating in the world beyond the Sahara was scarce and expensive, while markets for their own products were limited.

Beginning in the mid-fifteenth century, a new coastal trade with Europeans offered many West African peoples a welcome alternative. As European sailors made their way along the coast of West and then Central Africa, they encountered a bewilderingly complicated political landscape. Around the mouths of the Senegal and Gambia rivers, numerous Mande-speaking states controlled access to the trade routes into the interior. Proceeding farther along the coast, they encountered the Akan states, a region of several dozen independent but culturally linked peoples. The Akan states had goldfields of their own, and this region soon became known to Europeans as the Gold Coast. East of the Akan states lay the Bight of Benin, which became an early center of the slave trade and thus came to be called the Slave Coast. Bending south, fifteenth-century sailors encountered the Kingdom of Kongo in Central Africa, the largest state on the Atlantic seaboard, with a coastline that ran for some 250 miles. It was here in 1578 that Duarte Lopez visited the capital city of more than 100,000 residents. Wherever they went ashore along this route, European traders had to negotiate contacts on local terms (see "Thinking Like a Historian," p. 28).

Terracotta Figure from Mali Dating to the thirteenth or fourteenth century, this terracotta figure came from an archaeological site near Djenné. The rider wears a large, ornate necklace, while the horse has a decorative covering on its head. The Mali Empire relied on a large cavalry to expand and defend its borders, and the horse was an important symbol of Mali's wealth and power. Werner Forman/Art Resource, NY.

The Spirit World

Some West Africans who lived immediately south of the Sahara — the Fulanis in Senegal, the Mande-speakers in Mali, and the Hausas in northern Nigeria — learned about Islam from Arab merchants and Muslim leaders called imams. Converts to Islam knew the Koran and worshipped only a single God. Some of their cities, like Timbuktu, the legendary commercial center on the Niger River, became centers of Islamic learning and instruction. But most West Africans acknowledged multiple gods, as well as spirits that lived in the earth, animals, and plants.

Like animists in the Americas and Europe, African communities had wise men and women adept at manipulating these forces for good or ill. The Sudanic tradition of divine kingship persisted, and many people believed that their kings could contact the spirit world. West Africans treated their ancestors with great respect, believing that the dead resided in a nearby spiritual realm and interceded in their lives. Most West African peoples had secret societies, such as the Poro for men and the Sande for women, that united people from different lineages and clans. These societies conducted rituals that celebrated male virility and female fertility. "Without children you are naked," said a Yoruba proverb. Happy was the man with a big household, many wives, many children, and many relatives — and, in a not very different vein, many slaves.

AP® SKILLS & PROCESSES

MAKING CONNECTIONS

Why were West African leaders eager to engage in trade with Europeans?

TEACHING STRATEGY

Use the photo of the terracotta figure from Mali to help students understand Mali culture. Ask students: **What purpose might this terracotta sculpture of a warrior have served?** *It might have honored soldiers and glorified their role in Mali's society.*

CHECK FOR UNDERSTANDING

Ask students to compare trans-Saharan trade patterns with the coastal trade that developed in the mid-fifteenth century. *Major African exports remained the same: gold and slaves. European coastal trade benefitted the small coastal states that had largely been cut out of the trans-Sahara trade.*

AP® SKILLS & PROCESSES

MAKING CONNECTIONS

Use the **MAKING CONNECTIONS** question to help students understand how the broader regional context can be used to situate historical developments. Students may need guidance in answering this question, since it is not explicitly addressed in the text. You can extend this question prompt by asking students to explore the possible consequences to African traders of the discovery of gold and silver in the Americas.

TRM Find complete suggested responses in the Teacher's Resource Materials.

AP® SKILLS & PROCESSES

ANALYZING HISTORICAL EVIDENCE

Direct students to read the sources and answer the questions in the **AP® THINKING LIKE A HISTORIAN** feature to investigate the relevance of medium in analyzing different types of sources. Since many of the Native American and African societies discussed in this chapter did not have writing systems, this feature provides an opportunity to discuss the tools scholars have for understanding these people groups. Encourage students to think carefully about comparisons and connections between these very different sources.

AP® THINKING LIKE A HISTORIAN

Colliding Cultures

Carefully consider each of the following objects or texts. What meanings might you—thinking like a historian—impart to them?

1. **Mississippian warrior gorget (neck guard), 1250–1350 C.E.** *This large mollusk-shell medallion is inscribed with the figure of a warrior with a severed head in his right hand and a war club in his left. His face is inscribed with the likeness of a hawk, symbol of his speed, power, and precision.*

SOURCE: National Museum of the American Indian, Smithsonian Institution 15/853.

2. **Portuguese officer's account of de Soto's expedition, 1557.** *This excerpt describes Indian resistance in the face of de Soto's campaign of conquest against Indians in the southeastern United States.*

[Spanish soldiers] went over a swampy land where the horsemen could not go. A half league from camp they came upon some Indian huts near the river; [but] the people who were inside them plunged into the river. They captured four Indian women, and twenty Indians came at us and attacked us so stoutly that we had to retreat to the camp, because of their being (as they are) so skillful with their weapons. Those people are so warlike and so quick that they make no account of foot soldiers; for if these go for them, they flee, and when their adversaries turn their backs they are immediately on them. The farthest they flee is the distance of an arrow shot. They are never quiet but always running and crossing from one side to another so that the crossbows or the arquebuses can not be aimed at them; and before a crossbowman can fire a shot, an Indian can shoot three or four arrows, and very seldom does he miss what he shoots at. If the arrow does not find armor, it penetrates as deeply as a crossbow. The bows are very long and the arrows are made of certain reeds like canes, very heavy and so tough that a sharpened cane passes through a shield. Some are pointed with a fish bone, as sharp as an awl, and others with a certain stone like a diamond point.

3. **Duarte Lopez, *A Report on the Kingdom of Kongo*, 1591.** *A Portuguese explorer's account of his travels in southern Africa in the sixteenth century.*

[T]he Kingdom of Sofala lies between the two rivers, Magnice and Cuama, on the sea-coast. It is small in size, and has but few villages and towns.... It is peopled by Mohammedans, and the king himself belongs to the same sect. He pays allegiance to the crown of Portugal, in order not to be subject to the government of Monomotapa [Mutapa]. On this account the Portuguese have a fortress at the mouth of the River Cuama, trading with those countries in gold, amber, and ivory, all found on that coast, as well as in slaves, and giving in exchange silk stuffs and taffetas.... It is said, that from these regions the gold was brought by sea which served for Solomon's Temple at Jerusalem, a fact by no means improbable, for in these countries of Monomotapa are found several ancient buildings of stone, brick, and wood, and of such wonderful workmanship, and architecture, as is nowhere seen in the surrounding provinces.

The Kingdom of Monomotapa is extensive, and has a large population of Pagan heathens, who are black, of middle stature, swift of foot, and in battle fight with great bravery, their weapons being bows and arrows, and light darts. There are numerous kings tributary to Monomotapa, who constantly rebel and wage war against it. The Emperor maintains large armies, which in the provinces are divided into legions, after the manner of the Romans, for, being a great ruler, he must be at constant warfare in order to maintain his dominion. Amongst his warriors, those most renowned for bravery, are the female legions, greatly valued by the Emperor, being the sinews of his military strength.

28

4. **Benin figurine of a Portuguese soldier from the seventeenth century.** *This brass figure would have been kept on an altar or on the roof of the royal palace of Benin.*

Source: © The Trustees of the British Museum/Art Resource, NY.

5. **Sixteenth-century Portuguese coin made from African gold.** *Before the discovery of the Americas, half of the Old World's gold came from sub-Saharan Africa.*

Source: © The Trustees of the British Museum/Art Resource, NY.

6. **Sixteenth- or seventeenth-century Spanish silver real.** *Spain minted enormous quantities of American silver; much of it was shipped to Manila, where it was exchanged for Asian luxury goods.*

Source: ©The Trustees of the British Museum/Art Resource, NY.

Sources: (2) John E. Worth, "Account of the Northern Conquest and Discovery of Hernando de Soto by Rodrigo Rangel," trans. John E. Worth, in Lawrence A. Clayton et al., eds., *The De Soto Chronicles: The Expedition of Hernando de Soto to North America in 1539–1543* (University of Alabama Press, 1993), 59; (3) Filippo Pigafetta, *A Report of the Kingdom of Congo*, trans. Margarite Hutchinson (London: John Murray, 1881), 117–119.

ANALYZING THE EVIDENCE

1. What can you infer about cultural values among Mississippian peoples from source 1? About the cultural values of the Spanish and Portuguese from sources 5 and 6? What arguments may not be BEST supported by these sources?
2. How does de Soto describe the Native peoples he encounters in Florida (source 2)? How does that compare to the traits of the African kingdoms that Lopez comments upon in source 3? Use historical reasoning to explain why the king of Sofala might prefer a Portuguese alliance to subjection to Monomotapa.
3. What does source 4 suggest about Benin relations with the Portuguese?

AP® DBQ PRACTICE

Using these sources, along with what you have learned in this chapter, write a short essay that considers the connection between the impulses of warfare and commerce, which appear again and again in contact settings.

29

TRM Find complete suggested responses in the Teacher's Resource Materials.

AP® SKILLS & PROCESSES

ARGUMENTATION

The **AP® DBQ PRACTICE** prompt may be challenging for some students, so it might be useful to focus the question only on the misunderstandings and potential sources of conflict that the documents suggest.

EXPLORATION AND CONQUEST

What motivated Portuguese and Spanish expansion into the Atlantic, and what were its unintended consequences?

Beginning around 1400, the Portuguese monarchy propelled Europe into overseas expansion. Portugal soon took a leading role in the African slave trade, while the newly unified kingdom of Spain undertook Europe's first conquests in the Americas. These two ventures, though not initially linked, eventually became cornerstones in the creation of the "Atlantic World," which connected Europe, Africa, and the Americas.

Portuguese Expansion

AP® EXAM TIP

Take good notes on the impact of technology on European's ability to navigate the Atlantic Ocean and reach the Americas.

As a young soldier fighting in the Crusades, Prince Henry of Portugal (1394–1460) learned about the trans-Saharan trade in gold and slaves. Seeking a maritime route to the source of this trade in West Africa, Henry founded a center for oceanic navigation. Henry's mariners, challenged to find a way through the treacherous waters off the northwest African coast, designed a better-handling vessel, the caravel, which was rigged with a lateen (triangular) sail that enabled the ship to tack into the wind. This innovation allowed them to sail far into the Atlantic, where they discovered and colonized the Madeira and Azore islands. From there, they sailed in 1435 to sub-Saharan Sierra Leone, where they exchanged salt, wine, and fish for African ivory and gold.

Henry's efforts were soon joined to those of Italian merchants, who were blocked from eastern Mediterranean trade routes to Asia by the Ottoman Empire in the second half of the fifteenth century (c. 1450–1480). Cut off from Asia, Genoese traders sought an Atlantic route to the lucrative markets of the Indian Ocean. They began to work with Portuguese and Castilian mariners and monarchs to finance trading voyages, and the African coast and its offshore islands opened to their efforts. European voyagers discovered the Canaries, the Cape Verde Islands, and São Tomé; all of them became laboratories for the expansion of Mediterranean agriculture.

On these Atlantic islands, planters transformed local ecosystems to experiment with a variety of familiar cash crops: wheat, wine grapes, and woad, a blue dye plant; livestock and honeybees; and, where the climate permitted, sugar. By 1500, Madeira was producing 2,500 metric tons a year, and Madeira sugar was available — in small, expensive quantities — in London, Paris, Rome, and Constantinople. Most of the islands were unpopulated. The Canaries were the exception; it took Castilian adventurers decades to conquer the Guanches who lived there. Once defeated, they were enslaved to labor in the Canaries or on Madeira, where they carved irrigation canals into the island's steep rock cliffs.

Europeans made no such inroads on the continent of Africa itself. The coastal kingdoms were well defended, and yellow fever, malaria, and dysentery quickly struck down Europeans who spent any time in the interior of West Africa. Instead they maintained small, fortified trading posts on offshore islands or along the coast, usually as guests of the local king.

Portuguese sailors continued to look for an Atlantic route to Asia. In 1488, Bartolomeu Dias rounded the Cape of Good Hope, the southern tip of Africa. Vasco da Gama reached East Africa in 1497 and India in the following year; his ships were mistaken for those of Chinese traders, the last pale-skinned men to arrive by sea. Although da Gama's inferior goods — tin basins, coarse cloth, honey, and coral beads — were snubbed by the Arab and Indian merchants along India's Malabar Coast, he managed to acquire a highly profitable cargo of cinnamon and pepper. Da Gama returned to India in 1502 with twenty-one fighting vessels, which outmaneuvered and outgunned the Arab fleets. Soon the Portuguese government set up fortified trading posts for its merchants at key points around the Indian Ocean, in Indonesia, and along the coast of China (Map 1.4). In a transition that sparked the momentous

AP® APPLY THE TIP

Ask students to sketch out Europe, Africa, North, Central, and South America, and the major islands in the Caribbean Sea on a large sheet of paper. Assign different color markers to represent Portugal's and Spain's claims in the Americas and Africa in the fifteenth and sixteenth centuries. Then have students indicate the commodities that each nation traded and the origin of the commodities, and use arrows to represent the routes of trade. Students can then layer their map with areas claimed by England and France in the seventeenth century with different colors and add the commodities controlled by England and France along with arrows that indicate patterns of trade. Finally, ask students to use a symbol (e.g., star) to indicate areas where conflicts occurred between European nations in the sixteenth and seventeenth centuries. When students have completed maps, ask them to complete **Handout 1.2 — Causation: Creating the Atlantic World (TRM)**.

TRM Find **Handout 1.2 — Causation: Creating the Atlantic World** in the Teacher's Resource Materials.

TEACHING STRATEGY

"Lesson 1: What Was Needed to Link Continents?" on *The World History for Us All*'s Web site provides a brief reading with illustrations that explain the innovations in ship design that allowed European vessels to sail from Europe to the Indian Ocean and across the Atlantic Ocean. Access the lesson by searching "World History for Us All Great Global Convergence."

AP® THEME

WXT: Work, Exchange, and Technology

Discuss the ways that technological innovations in ship construction facilitated the growth of European trade and exploration.

CHECK FOR UNDERSTANDING

Ask students: **Where and why did Portuguese expansion take place beginning in the early fifteenth century?** *Prince Henry sponsored a center to develop maritime technologies to take advantage of the African trade, hoping to bypass trans-Saharan middlemen and trade directly with coastal Africans. From there, Portugal established colonies on islands off the coast of Africa and looked to reach Asia by sea.*

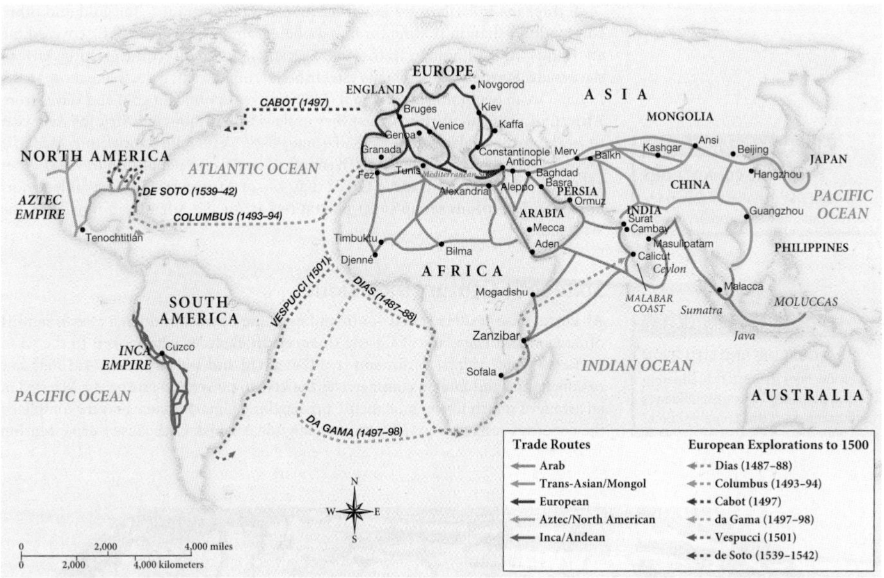

MAP 1.4 The Eurasian Trade System and European Maritime Ventures, c. 1500
For centuries, the Mediterranean Sea was the meeting point for the commerce of Europe, North Africa, and Asia—via the Silk Road from China and the Spice Route from India. Beginning in the 1490s, Portuguese, Spanish, and Dutch rulers and merchants subsidized Christian maritime explorers who discovered new trade routes around Africa and new sources of wealth in the Americas. These initiatives undermined the commercial primacy of the Arab Muslim–dominated Mediterranean.

growth of European wealth and power, the Portuguese and then the Dutch replaced the Arabs as the leaders in Asian commerce.

The African Slave Trade

Portuguese traders also ousted Arab merchants as the leading suppliers of African slaves. Coerced labor—through slavery, serfdom, or indentured servitude—was the norm in most premodern societies, and in Africa slavery was widespread. Some Africans were held in bondage as security for debts; others were sold into servitude by their kin in exchange for food in times of famine; many others were war captives. Slaves were a key commodity, sold as agricultural laborers, concubines, or military recruits. Sometimes their descendants were freed, but others endured hereditary bondage. Sonni Ali (r. 1464–1492), the ruler of the powerful Songhai Empire, personally owned twelve "tribes" of hereditary agricultural slaves, many of them seized in raids against neighboring peoples.

Slaves were also central to the trans-Saharan trade. When the renowned Tunisian adventurer Ibn Battuta crossed the Sahara from the Kingdom of Mali around 1350, he traveled with a caravan of six hundred female slaves, destined for domestic service or concubinage in North Africa, Egypt, and the Ottoman Empire. Between 700 and 1900 C.E., it is estimated that as many as nine million Africans were sold in the trans-Saharan slave trade.

AP® SKILLS & PROCESSES

DEVELOPMENTS AND PROCESSES

How did Europe's desire for an ocean route to Asia shape its contacts with Africa?

AP® EXAM TIP

Understanding the origins of the slave trade system in the "Atlantic World" is critical to success on the AP® Exam.

AP® THEME

WXT: Work, Exchange, and Technology

Use **MAP 1.4** to discuss the global patterns of trade that developed as a result of European exploration of the African coast and the attempt to reach China by sailing west.

AP® SKILLS & PROCESSES

DEVELOPMENTS AND PROCESSES

Use the **DEVELOPMENTS AND PROCESSES** question to help students recognize the causes behind Europe's relationship with Africa. Help students recognize that this process should be understood through identifying long-term factors given the pattern that unfolded over more than a half-century. Students who have some knowledge of later European imperialism in the African interior might consider what factors changed between the fifteenth and eighteenth centuries, since in the earlier period, Europeans were confined to the coast.

TRM Find complete suggested responses in the Teacher's Resource Materials.

AP® APPLY THE TIP

To help students understand the origin of the slave system, ask them to create a flow chart as they read "The African Slave Trade" section to illustrate how the slave trade within Africa evolved into the African slave trade in the Atlantic world (Africa, Europe, and the Americas). After students have completed the flow chart, ask them to read the primary source "Slave Trade: The African Connection," available online at *Eyewitness to History*. In their reading, students should identify the methods used to acquire slaves for the slave trade and the point of view of the historical source. Then ask students to complete **Handout 1.3—Thematic Analysis: African Slave Trade (TRM)**.

TRM Find **Handout 1.3—Thematic Analysis: African Slave Trade** in the Teacher's Resource Materials.

CHECK FOR UNDERSTANDING

Ask students: **How did the African slave trade with Europe begin?** *Slavery was widespread in Africa and in the trans-Sahara trade. Europeans gradually came to see slaves as a valuable export for plantation labor, first on Atlantic islands and later in Brazil and the West Indies.*

AP® SKILLS & PROCESSES

MAKING CONNECTIONS

Use the **MAKING CONNECTIONS** question to help students understand the development of the transatlantic slave trade. By framing the issue as a pattern of continuity and change, this question reminds students that the enslavement of Africans was a continuity. Assist students in identifying the major features of African slavery and transatlantic slavery as well as the similarities and differences between the two.

TRM Find complete suggested responses in the Teacher's Resource Materials.

AP® THEME

WOR: America in the World

Lead a class discussion on the ways a combination of competition between European rivals and the desire to spread Christianity influenced the movement of the Spanish and Portuguese into the Americas.

Europeans initially were much more interested in trading for gold and other commodities than in trading for human beings, but gradually they discovered the enormous value of human trafficking. To exploit and redirect the existing African slave trade, Portuguese merchants established fortified trading posts like those in the Indian Ocean beginning at Elmina in 1482, where they bought gold and slaves from African princes and warlords. First they enslaved a few thousand Africans each year to work on sugar plantations on São Tomé, Cape Verde, the Azores, and Madeira; they also sold slaves in Lisbon, which soon had an African population of 9,000. After 1550, the Atlantic slave trade, a forced diaspora of African peoples, expanded enormously as Europeans set up sugar plantations across the Atlantic, in Brazil and the West Indies.

AP® SKILLS & PROCESSES
MAKING CONNECTIONS
How was the African slave trade adapted to European needs?

Sixteenth-Century Incursions

As Portuguese traders sailed south and east, the Spanish monarchs Ferdinand II of Aragon and Isabella I of Castile financed an explorer who looked to the west. As Renaissance rulers, Ferdinand (r. 1474–1516) and Isabella (r. 1474–1504) saw national unity and foreign commerce as the keys to power and prosperity. Married in an arranged match to combine their Christian kingdoms, the young rulers completed the centuries-long *reconquista*, the campaign by Spanish Catholics to drive Muslim

AP® SKILLS & PROCESSES
SOURCING AND SITUATION
How does the historical situation and purpose of the artist influence understanding of this primary source?

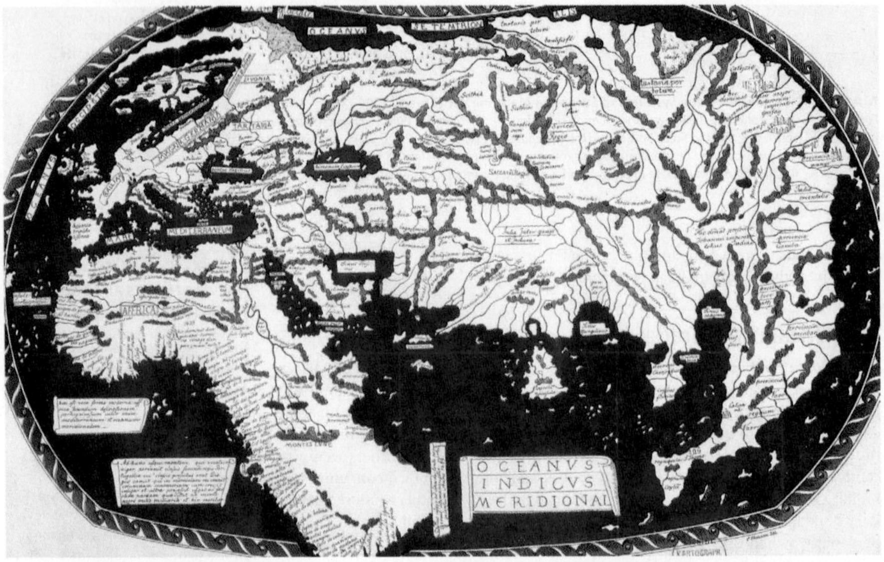

The Map Behind Columbus's Voyage In 1489, Henricus Martellus, a German cartographer living in Florence, produced this huge (4 feet by 6 feet) view of the known world, probably working from a map devised by Christopher Columbus's brother, Bartholomew. The map uses the spatial projection of the ancient Greek philosopher Claudius Ptolemy (90–168 C.E.) and incorporates information from Marco Polo's explorations in Asia and Bartolomeu Dias's recent voyage around the tip of Africa. Most important, it greatly exaggerates the width of Eurasia, thereby suggesting that Asia lies only 5,000 miles west of Europe (rather than the actual distance of 15,000 miles). Using Martellus's map, Columbus persuaded the Spanish monarchs to support his westward voyage. bpk Bildagentur/Staatsbibliothek zu Berlin, Stiftung Preussischer Kulturbesitz/Ruth Schacht/Art Resource, NY.

Arabs from the European mainland, by capturing Granada, the last Islamic territory in Western Europe, in 1492. Using Catholicism to build a sense of "Spanishness," they launched the brutal Inquisition against suspected Christian heretics and expelled or forcibly converted thousands of Jews and Muslims.

Columbus and the Caribbean Simultaneously, Ferdinand and Isabella sought trade and empire by subsidizing the voyages of Christopher Columbus, an ambitious and daring mariner from Genoa. Columbus believed that the Atlantic Ocean, long feared by Arab merchants as a 10,000-mile-wide "green sea of darkness," was a much narrower channel of water separating Europe from Asia. After six years of lobbying, Columbus persuaded Genoese investors and Ferdinand and Isabella to accept his dubious theories and finance a western voyage to Asia.

Columbus set sail in three small ships in August 1492. Six weeks later, after a perilous voyage of 3,000 miles, he disembarked on an island in the present-day Bahamas. Believing that he had reached Asia — "the Indies," in fifteenth-century parlance — Columbus called the native inhabitants Indians and the islands the West Indies. He was surprised by the crude living conditions but expected the Native peoples "easily [to] be made Christians." He claimed the islands for Spain and then explored the neighboring Caribbean islands, demanding tribute from the local Taino, Arawak, and Carib peoples. Columbus left forty men on the island of Hispaniola (present-day Haiti and the Dominican Republic) and returned triumphantly to Spain (Map 1.5).

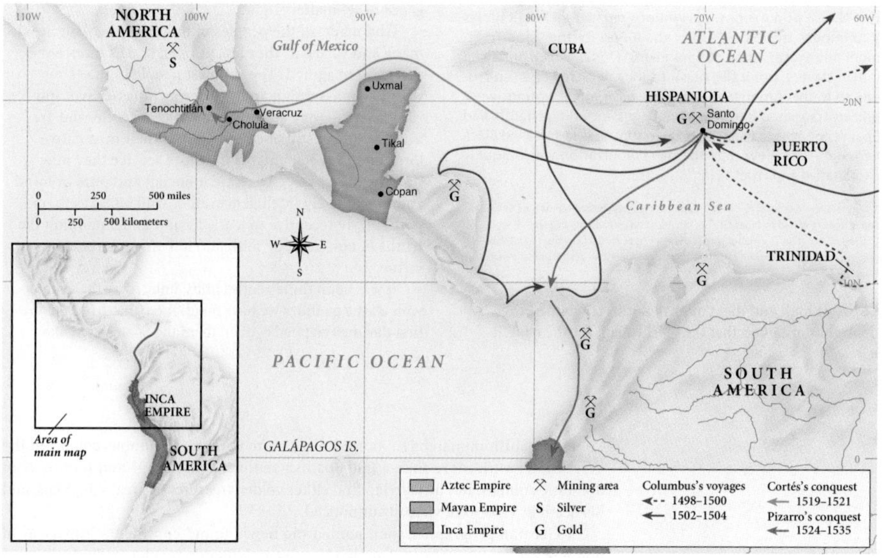

MAP 1.5 The Spanish Conquest of America's Great Empires
The Spanish first invaded the islands of the Caribbean, largely wiping out the Native peoples. Rumors of a gold-rich civilization led to Cortés's invasion of the Aztec Empire in 1519. By 1535, other Spanish conquistadors had conquered the Mayan temple cities and the Inca Empire in Peru, completing one of the great conquests in world history.

AP® THEME

MIG: Migration and Settlement

Use **MAP 1.5** to explore the routes and patterns of Spanish conquest of North and South America. As indicated on the map, note the precious metals located in or near areas of conquest.

AP® THEME

SOC: Social Structures

One of the more crucial aspects of Spanish colonization was the focus on extracting mineral resources from the Americas. Provide students with three terms such as exploration, mineral wealth, and enslavement. In this activity, students need to write one to three sentences that use at least two of the terms to explain how Spanish colonization affected social structures. In this way, you are providing students with the correct historical information so they can work on the explanations.

AP® SKILLS & PROCESSES

ANALYZING HISTORICAL EVIDENCE

The **AP® FIRSTHAND ACCOUNTS** feature provides a clear, useful introduction to students on how to read primary sources critically. In addition to the analysis questions offered in the introduction, students could consider the point of view of de las Casas. Extend this prompt by having students consider how his purpose in creating this text differed from the use the English later made of it.

AP® FIRSTHAND ACCOUNTS

A Spanish Priest Criticizes His Fellow Colonists

Primary sources are documents, images, or artifacts that were created during the time you are studying. To analyze a primary source, you need to ask some basic questions about the source:

- Who is the author, and what circumstances led to the document's creation?
- Who was the author's intended audience?
- What was the author's goal in creating the document?
- What ideas, arguments, and images does the author use to make his or her point? How effective are they?
- What outside information can you bring to bear on this document? How does the primary source enhance your understanding of the textbook, and how does the textbook enhance your understanding of the source?
- What does this source tell you about the society in which it was produced?

These are general questions that you should have in mind whenever you read a primary source. Try to answer them for yourself as you read the following document. Then, once you have read it, answer the Questions for Analysis that follow.

BARTOLOMÉ DE LAS CASAS

A Short Account of the Destruction of the Indies

Bartolomé de las Casas first emigrated from Spain to the island of Hispaniola as a colonist and slave owner. After determining that Spain's treatment of Native Americans was cruel and unjust, Las Casas became a Dominican friar, or preacher, and argued that the Spanish king should intervene to protect Native populations. His writings persuaded King Charles V to impose the "New Laws of the Indies for the Good Treatment and Preservation of the Indians" (1542), which outlawed Indian slavery. Ironically, because they depicted Spanish cruelty to Native Americans so vividly, Las Casas's writings were quickly translated into other languages, including English, and Spain's enemies used these texts to support the so-called Black Legend — the view that Spanish colonization was uniquely exploitative and cruel.

SOURCE: *A Short Account of the Destruction of the Indies* by Bartolomé De Las Casas, edited and translated by Nigel Griffin, introduction by Anthony Pagden (Penguin Classics, 2008). The Translation and Notes copyright © Nigel Griffin, 1992. Introduction copyright © Anthony Pagden, 1992. Reproduced by permission of Penguin Books Ltd.

" Most high and most mighty Lord: As Divine Providence has ordained that the world shall, for the benefit and proper government of the human race, be divided into kingdoms and peoples and that these shall be ruled by kings, who are . . . the noblest and most virtuous of beings, there is no doubt . . . that these kings entertain nothing save that which is morally unimpeachable. It follows that if the commonwealth suffers from some . . . evil, the reason can only be that the ruler is unaware of it; once the matter is brought to his notice, he will work with the utmost diligence to set matters right. . . .

God made all the peoples of this area [the Americas], many and varied as they are, as open and as innocent as can be imagined. The simplest people in the world — unassuming, long-suffering, unassertive, and submissive — they are without malice or guile, and are utterly faithful and obedient both to their own native lords and to the Spaniards in whose service they now find themselves. . . . They are innocent and pure in mind and have a lively intelligence, all of which makes them particularly receptive to learning and understanding the truths of our Catholic faith and to being instructed in virtue. . . .

It was upon these gentle lambs, imbued by the Creator with all the qualities we have mentioned, that from the very first day they clapped eyes on them the Spanish fell like

The Spanish monarchs supported three more voyages. Columbus colonized the West Indies with more than 1,000 Spanish settlers — all men — and hundreds of domestic animals. But he failed to find either golden treasures or great kingdoms, and his death in 1506 went virtually unnoticed.

A German geographer soon named the newly found continents "America" in honor of a different explorer. Amerigo Vespucci, a Florentine explorer who had visited the coast of present-day South America around 1500, denied that the region was part of Asia. He called it a *nuevo mundo*, a "new world." The Spanish crown called the two continents *Las Indias* ("the Indies") and wanted to make them a new Spanish world.

34

ravening wolves upon the fold, or like tigers and savage lions who have not eaten meat for days. The pattern established at the outset has remained unchanged to this day, and the Spaniards still do nothing save tear the natives to shreds, murder them and inflict upon them untold misery, suffering and distress, tormenting, harrying and persecuting them mercilessly. . . .

When the Spanish first journeyed there, the indigenous population of the island of Hispaniola stood at some three million; today only two hundred survive. The island of Cuba . . . is now to all intents and purposes uninhabited; and two other large, beautiful and fertile islands, Puerto Rico and Jamaica, have been similarly devastated. Not a living soul remains today on any of the islands of the Bahamas. . . . On the mainland, we know for sure that our fellow-countrymen have, through their cruelty and wickedness, depopulated and laid waste an area which once boasted more than ten kingdoms, each of them larger in area than the whole of the Iberian Peninsula. . . .
At a conservative estimate, the despotic and diabolical behaviour of the Christians has, over the last forty years, led to the unjust and totally unwarranted deaths of more than twelve million souls, women and children among them, and there are grounds for believing my own estimate of more than fifteen million to be nearer the mark.

There are two main ways in which those who have travelled to this part of the world pretending to be Christians have uprooted these pitiful peoples and wiped them from the face of the earth. First, they have waged war on them: unjust, cruel, bloody and tyrannical war. Second, they have murdered anyone and everyone who has shown the slightest sign of resistance, or even of wishing to escape the torment to which they have subjected him. This latter policy has been instrumental in suppressing the native leaders, and, indeed, given that the Spaniards normally spare only women and children, it has led to the annihilation of all adult males, whom they habitually subject to the harshest and most iniquitous and brutal slavery that man has ever devised for his fellow-men, treating them, in fact, worse than animals. . . .

The reason the Christians have murdered on such a vast scale and killed anyone and everyone in their way is purely and simply greed. They have set out to line their pockets with gold and to amass private fortunes as quickly as possible so that they can then assume a status quite at odds with that into which they were born. Their insatiable greed and overweening ambition know no bounds. ”

JUAN GINÉS DE SEPULVEDA

Democrates Alter

Theologian Juan Ginés de Sepulveda responded to Las Casas, arguing that it was appropriate to subjugate and enslave Native Americans.

SOURCE: Juan Ginés de Sepulveda, "Democrates Alter, Or, on the Just Causes for War Against the Indians" (1547), in *Boletín de la Real Academia de la Historia*, vol. 21 (Oct. 1892). Originally translated for *Introduction to Contemporary Civilization in the West* (NY: Columbia University Press, 1946, 1954, 1961), online at http://www.columbia.edu/acis/ets/CCREAD/sepulved.htm.

“ Whether the war by means of which the rulers of Spain and our countrymen have brought and are attempting to bring under their domination the barbarian inhabitants, commonly known as Indians . . . is just or unjust . . . is . . . a most important question. . . . Those who surpass the rest in prudence and talent, although not in physical strength, are by nature the masters. Those, on the other hand, who are retarded or slow to understand, although they may have the physical strength necessary for the fulfillment of all their necessary obligations, are by nature slaves. . . . [T]he Spanish have a perfect right to rule these barbarians of the New World and the adjacent islands, who in prudence, skill, virtues, and humanity are as inferior to the Spanish as children to adults, or women to men, for there exists between the two as great a difference as between savage and cruel races and the most merciful, between the most intemperate and the moderate and temperate and, I might even say, between apes and men. ”

QUESTIONS FOR ANALYSIS

1. Who is Las Casas's intended audience? What does the opening passage tell you about his view of royal authority?
2. What moral qualities does Las Casas attribute to Native Americans and to the Spanish colonists? What evidence does he use to make his point?
3. How does Sepulveda justify Spain's war against Native Americans? What evidence does he use to make his point?

TRM Find complete suggested responses in the Teacher's Resource Materials.

The Spanish Invasion After brutally subduing the Arawaks and Tainos on Hispaniola, the Spanish probed the mainland for gold and slaves. In 1513, Juan Ponce de León explored the coast of Florida and gave that peninsula its name. In the same year, Vasco Núñez de Balboa crossed the Isthmus of Darien (Panama) and led the first party of Europeans who saw the Pacific Ocean. Rumors of rich Indian kingdoms encouraged other Spaniards, including hardened veterans of the *reconquista*, to invade the mainland. The Spanish monarchs offered successful conquistadors noble titles, vast estates, and Indian laborers (see "Firsthand Accounts," p. 34).

AP® EXAM TIP

The patterns established by the early conflicts between the Spanish and Native populations are critical understandings for evaluating colonial systems.

With these inducements before him, in 1519 Hernán Cortés (1485–1547) led an army of 600 men to the Yucatán Peninsula. Gathering allies among Native peoples who chafed under Aztec rule, he marched on Tenochtitlán and challenged its ruler, Moctezuma. Awed by the Spanish invaders, Moctezuma received Cortés with great ceremony. But Cortés soon took the emperor captive, and after a long siege he and his men captured the city. The conquerors cut off the city's supply of food and water, causing great suffering for the residents of Tenochtitlán. By 1521, Cortés and his men had toppled the Aztec Empire.

The Spanish had a silent ally: disease. Having been separated from Eurasia for thousands of years, the inhabitants of the Americas had no immunities to common

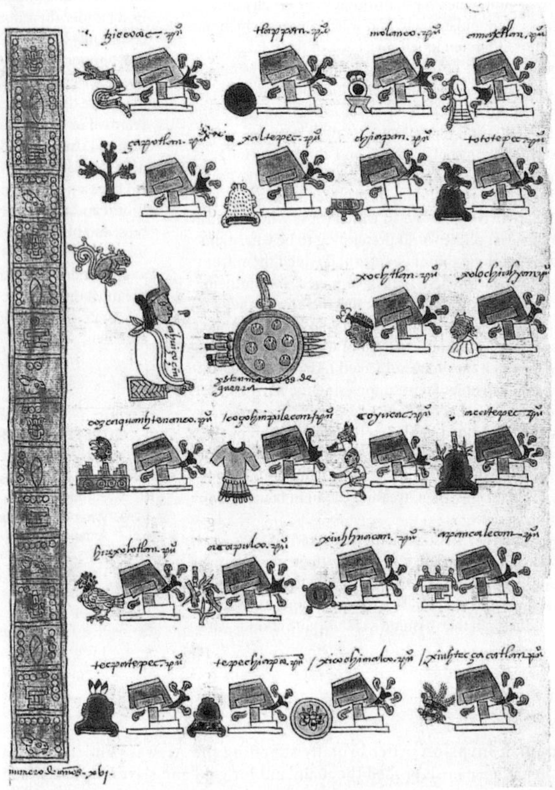

The Codex Mendoza Millions of people spoke Nahuatl, the language of the Aztec Empire. It was also a written language: a pictographic system allowed scribes to record histories, tribute lists, and other official texts. Spanish colonizers systematically destroyed Aztec records but later encouraged Native scribes to re-create them. The Codex Mendoza, which dates to the 1540s, gives a history of the Aztec Empire. This page depicts the conquests of Ahuitzotl, the figure in a white cloak and turquoise crown. The toppling temples surrounding him symbolize the city-states he conquered. The History Collection/Alamy Stock Photo.

European diseases. After the Spaniards arrived, a massive smallpox epidemic ravaged Tenochtitlán, "striking everywhere in the city," according to an Aztec source, and killing Moctezuma's brother and thousands more. "They could not move, they could not stir.... Covered, mantled with pustules, very many people died of them." Subsequent outbreaks of smallpox, influenza, and measles killed hundreds of thousands of Indians and sapped the survivors' morale. Exploiting this advantage, Cortés quickly extended Spanish rule over the Aztec Empire. His lieutenants then moved against the Mayan city-states of the Yucatán Peninsula, eventually conquering them as well.

In 1524, Francisco Pizarro set out to accomplish the same feat in Peru. By the time he and his small force of 168 men and 67 horses finally reached their destination in 1532, half of the Inca population had already died from European diseases. Weakened militarily and divided between rival claimants to the throne, the Inca nobility was easy prey. Pizarro killed Atahualpa, the last Inca emperor, and seized his enormous wealth. Although Inca resistance continued for a generation, the conquest was complete by 1535, and Spain was now the master of the wealthiest and most populous regions of the Western Hemisphere.

The Spanish invasion changed life forever in the Americas. Why was the impact of the invasion so devastating? Disease and warfare wiped out virtually all of the Indians of Hispaniola — at least 300,000 people. In Peru, the population of 9 million in 1530 plummeted to fewer than 500,000 a century later. Mesoamerica suffered the greatest losses: in one of the great demographic disasters in world history, its population of 20 million Native Americans in 1500 had dwindled to just 3 million in 1650.

AP® SKILLS & PROCESSES

CAUSATION

How did Spanish colonization affect Native American societies?

Cabral and Brazil At the same time, Portuguese efforts to sail around the southern tip of Africa led to a surprising find. As Vasco da Gama and his contemporaries experimented with winds and currents, their voyages carried them ever farther away from the African coast and into the Atlantic. On one such voyage in 1500, the Portuguese commander Pedro Alvares Cabral and his fleet were surprised to see land loom in the west. Cabral named his discovery Ihla da Vera Cruz — the Island of the True Cross — and continued on his way toward India. Others soon followed and changed the region's name to Brazil after the indigenous tree that yielded a valuable red dye; for several decades, Portuguese sailors traded with the Tupi Indians for brazilwood. Then in the 1530s, to secure Portugal's claim, King Dom João III sent settlers, who began the long, painstaking process of carving out sugar plantations in the coastal lowlands.

AP® EXAM TIP

Take good notes on the Portuguese plantation system since it will be important to compare it to the Spanish *encomienda* system that will be introduced in Chapter 2.

For several decades, Native Americans supplied most of the labor for these operations, but African slaves gradually replaced them. Brazil would soon become the world's leading producer of sugar; it would also devour African lives. By introducing the **plantation system** to the Americas — a form of estate agriculture using slave labor that was pioneered by Italian merchants and crusading knights in the twelfth century and transplanted to the islands off the coast of Africa in the fifteenth century — the Portuguese set in motion one of the most significant developments of the early modern era.

plantation system
A system of production characterized by unfree labor producing cash crops for distant markets. The plantation complex developed in sugar-producing areas of the Mediterranean world and was transferred to the Americas, where it took hold in tropical and subtropical areas, including Brazil, the West Indies, and southeastern North America. In addition to sugar, the plantation complex was adapted to produce tobacco, rice, indigo, and cotton.

By the end of the sixteenth century, the European colonization of the Americas had barely begun. Yet several of its most important elements were already taking shape. Spanish efforts demonstrated that densely populated empires were especially vulnerable to conquest and were also especially valuable sources of wealth. The Portuguese had discovered the viability of sugar plantations in the tropical regions of the Americas and pioneered the transatlantic slave trade as a way of manning them. And contacts with Native peoples revealed their devastating vulnerabilities to Eurasian diseases — one part of the larger phenomenon of the Columbian Exchange (discussed in Chapter 2).

AP® THEME

MIG: Migration and Settlement

Lead students in a discussion on the effect of European immigration on Native populations with the outbreak of deadly epidemics.

AP® SKILLS & PROCESSES

CAUSATION

To help students understand the brutality with which the Spanish conquered Native populations, provide them with brief excerpts from primary sources, including Columbus's journals, that illustrate Spanish attitudes toward the Natives, excerpts from Francisco Pizarro's letter on the conquest of Incas, and a page from the Codex Mendoza. In pairs, ask students to read and analyze the sources and look for evidence to address the following prompt: How did early conflicts between the Spanish and Native populations establish a pattern of interaction that dominated their relationship? Once students have found evidence to use, lead a whole group discussion in addressing this question.

TRM Find complete suggested responses in the Teacher's Resource Materials.

AP® APPLY THE TIP

Ask students to use a variety of sources to create a Venn diagram comparing the Portuguese plantation system to the Spanish *encomienda* system. Ask students to consider the ways that geographic and environmental factors influenced these systems as well as the impact of both systems on migrations to and within the Americas. Finally, ask students to consider the ways that each system influenced the development of labor systems in the Americas. To supplement this activity, consider incorporating primary sources such as "The Sugar Trade in the West Indies and Brazil between 1492 and 1700" by Mark Johnson and "The First Plantation Colony: Early Latin America" by Peter Stearns, 1999, both available online.

AP® THEME

SOC: Social Structures

In groups, assign each student one of the following: Enslaved Africans, Spanish, and American Indians. Each student is responsible for defining how the group he or she were assigned helped define the Spanish caste system. Better responses will move beyond simple definitions to explanations about the role race, religion, and/or gender played in this system.

AP® THEME

WXT: Work, Exchange, and Technology

Discuss how the combination of plantation crops and a declining Native population created a labor shortage that helped spawn the transatlantic slave trade.

✓ LearningCurve

Remind students to go online to complete the LearningCurve quiz for this chapter.

CHECK FOR UNDERSTANDING

Use the **AP® LEARNING FOCUS** question from the beginning of the chapter to assess students' understanding of the chapter as a whole: **How did the political, economic, and religious systems of Native Americans, Europeans, and Africans compare, and how did things change as a result of contacts among them?** *Points of comparison between the three cultures prior to contact include: the primary importance of religion and agriculture; the existence of smaller as well as more complex societies; and a larger range of economic conditions, from great wealth to dire poverty. After contact, the three continents traded natural resources, disease, and slaves. Native Americans suffered from European conquest and the widespread dispersion of European diseases. Africa lost many souls to the Atlantic slave trade, which fueled warfare along the western coast of the continent. In general, Europe gained from the increased trade networks.*

TRM Find complete suggested responses in the Teacher's Resource Materials.

AP® SKILLS & PROCESSES

COMPARISON

AP® CONTENT REVIEW QUESTION 1 encourages students to compare Native Americans in different geographic regions, explaining differences between them.

AP® SKILLS & PROCESSES

CONTINUITY AND CHANGE

AP® CONTENT REVIEW QUESTION 2 provides an opportunity for students to describe changes in Europe on the eve of contact with the Americas.

AP® SKILLS & PROCESSES

CAUSATION

AP® CONTENT REVIEW QUESTION 3 invites students to consider the effects of the historical development of European traders arriving by sea.

AP® SKILLS & PROCESSES

CAUSATION

AP® CONTENT REVIEW QUESTION 4 addresses both the causes and effects of Iberian expansion, but the focus on unintended consequences provides an opportunity to explore contingency with students.

SUMMARY

AP® SKILLS & PROCESSES

CAUSATION

How did the search for wealth, competition between nations, and changes in Christianity influence conquest of the New World?

Native American, European, and African societies developed independently over thousands of years before they experienced direct contacts with one another. In the Americas, residents of Mesoamerica and the Andes were fully sedentary (with individual ownership of land and intensive agriculture), but elsewhere societies were semisedentary (with central fields and villages that were occupied seasonally) or nonsedentary (hunter-gatherers). West and Central Africa also had a mix of sedentary, semisedentary, and nonsedentary settlements. Western Europe, by contrast, was predominantly sedentary. All three continents had a complex patchwork of political organizations, from empires, to kingdoms and chiefdoms, to principalities, duchies, and ministates; everywhere, rulership was imbued with notions of spiritual power. Ruling classes relied on warfare, trade, and tribute (or taxes) to dominate those around them and accumulate precious goods that helped to set them apart from ordinary laborers, but they also bore responsibility for the well-being of their subjects and offered them various forms of protection.

As sailors pushed into the Atlantic, they set in motion a chain of events whose consequences they could scarcely imagine. From a coastal trade with Africa that was secondary to their efforts to reach the Indian Ocean, from the miscalculations of Columbus and the happy accident of Cabral, developed a pattern of transatlantic exploration, conquest, and exploitation that no one could have foretold or planned. In the tropical zones of the Caribbean and coastal Brazil, invading Europeans enslaved Native Americans and quickly drove them into extinction or exile. The demands of plantation agriculture soon led Europeans to import slaves from Africa, initiating a transatlantic trade that would destroy African lives on both sides of the ocean. And two of the greatest empires in the world — the Aztec and Incan empires — collapsed in response to unseen biological forces that acted in concert with small invading armies.

CHAPTER 1 REVIEW

AP® CONTENT REVIEW *Answer these questions to demonstrate your understanding of the chapter's main ideas.*

1. What factors best explain the variations among Native American societies and cultures?
2. How had recent developments changed Western Europe by 1491?
3. How was sub-Saharan Africa affected by the arrival of European traders?
4. What motivated Portuguese and Spanish expansion into the Atlantic, and what were its unintended consequences?

AP® TERMS TO KNOW *Identify and explain the significance of each term below.*

Key Concepts and Events

hunters and gatherers (p. 8)
semisedentary societies (p. 8)
Mississippian culture (p. 12)
eastern woodlands (p. 12)
Algonquian cultures/languages (p. 12)
Iroquoian cultures/languages (p. 13)
Iroquois Confederacy (p. 15)
Great Lakes (p. 15)
Great Plains (p. 15)
Rocky Mountains (p. 16)
Great Basin (p. 16)
peasants (p. 19)
republic (p. 20)
Christianity (p. 22)
Islam (p. 22)
Crusades (p. 22)
Protestant Reformation (p. 24)
Counter-Reformation (p. 24)
plantation system (p. 37)

Key People

Hiawatha (p. 15)
Martin Luther (p. 23)
Christopher Columbus (p. 33)
Hernán Cortés (p. 36)
Moctezuma (p. 36)
Pedro Alvares Cabral (p. 37)

TRM Find definitions for these terms in the **Glossary/Glosario** in the Teacher's Resource Materials.

AP® MAKING CONNECTIONS

Recognize the larger developments and continuities within and across chapters by answering these questions.

1. The century following the first contacts among Europe, sub-Saharan Africa, and the Americas brought some of the most momentous changes in world history: a dramatic reconfiguration of human populations across the globe, new patterns of trade and warfare, and immense challenges to peoples' worldviews. Thinking about our contemporary world, what monumental changes currently affect our lives? How would you compare them with the events described in this chapter?
2. How is Christianity different from animism? How might faith in such a religious system shape the values and priorities of believers? Use evidence from at least two geographic regions to support your claim.

KEY TURNING POINTS

Refer to the timeline at the start of the chapter for help in answering the following questions.

The domestication of maize (6000 B.C.E.–800 C.E.), the founding of Tenochtitlán (1325), and the conquest of the Aztec Empire (1519–1521): How did the domestication of maize make the city of Tenochtitlán possible? What characteristics of the Aztec Empire and its capital city made it vulnerable to conquest?

AP® PRACTICE QUESTIONS

MULTIPLE CHOICE QUESTIONS

Choose the correct answer for each question.

Questions 1–3 refer to this image.

***The New World as Paradise*, engraving by Theodore de Bry, 1588.**

Library of Congress.

1. Which of the following BEST describes the point of view of this image:
   - **a.** Europeans believed that American Indians lived in complex urban societies.
   - **b.** Many European thought American Indian populations were able to modify and adapt to their geography.
   - **c.** Indigenous peoples had diverse cultural beliefs and practices.
   - **d.** The New World provided an opportunity for Europeans to Christianize native societies.
2. The image would be most useful as a source of information about which of the following?
   - **a.** The role of the African slave trade in the development of plantation-based agriculture
   - **b.** Improvements in maritime technologies that fueled the Columbian Exchange
   - **c.** Development of European attitudes regarding the culture of Native Americans
   - **d.** Exchanges of goods between Europe and the Americas that stimulated the growth of European capitalism

AP® SKILLS & PROCESSES

COMPARISON

MAKING CONNECTIONS 1 invites students to consider how momentous changes 500 years ago might compare with the present.

AP® SKILLS & PROCESSES

ARGUMENTATION

MAKING CONNECTIONS 2 asks students to evaluate a particular type of evidence, a piece of visual propaganda, and explain its relevance to a larger claim about religious views.

AP® SKILLS & PROCESSES

CONTINUITY AND CHANGE

The **KEY TURNING POINTS** question encourages students to consider the domestication of maize as one turning point in Aztec development and its conquest as a final turning point.

TRM Find complete suggested responses in the Teacher's Resource Materials.

3. The engraving was most likely intended to
   - **a.** convince American Indians to defend their political sovereignty.
   - **b.** justify the poor treatment of American Indians by Europeans.
   - **c.** stimulate European interest in the settlement and development of the New World.
   - **d.** illustrate American Indian religious traditions to Europeans.

Questions 4–6 refer to this excerpt.

> "Widely dispersed over the great land mass of the Americas, [American Indians] numbered 15 or 20 million people by the time Columbus came, perhaps 5 million in North America. Responding to the different environments of soil and climate, they developed hundreds of different tribal cultures, perhaps two thousand different languages. They perfected the art of agriculture, and figured out how to grow maize (corn), which cannot grow by itself and must be planted, cultivated, fertilized, harvested, husked, shelled. They ingeniously developed a variety of other vegetables and fruits, as well as peanuts and chocolate and tobacco and rubber."
>
> Howard Zinn, *A People's History of the United States: 1492–Present*, 1980

4. The passage describes which of the following historical developments in the period 1491 to 1607?
   - **a.** Prior to the arrival of Europeans, American Indians had developed advanced systems of cultivation.
   - **b.** Spanish exploration of the Americas stemmed from a search for new sources of economic competition.
   - **c.** The Spanish developed a refined caste system that defined the status of Europeans, Africans, and American Indians.
   - **d.** American Indians in present-day California supported themselves by hunting and gathering.

5. Which of the below arguments BEST characterizes Zinn's perspective on the contributions of Native Americans in this passage:
   - **a.** Native Americans had diverse cultures and languages.
   - **b.** American Indians had complex patterns of trade and commerce.
   - **c.** Indigenous populations were well-equipped to deal with changes in the environment.
   - **d.** Native American systems of agriculture were well-developed and innovative.

6. Which of the following pieces of evidence would best support Zinn's description of economic changes of this era?
   - **a.** Written accounts of early transatlantic voyages to the Americas
   - **b.** Archeological evidence of permanent, indigenous villages in the American Northeast
   - **c.** European testimony of mutual misunderstandings between Europeans and American Indians
   - **d.** European debates by religious and political leaders about the treatment of American Indians

Questions 7–8 refer to this excerpt.

> "The reason the Christians have murdered on such a vast scale and killed anyone and everyone in their way is purely and simply greed. They have set out to line their pockets with gold and to amass private fortunes as quickly as possible so that they can then assume a status quite at odds with that into which they were born. Their insatiable greed and overweening ambition know no bounds."
>
> Bartolomé de las Casas, *A Short Account of the Destruction of the Indies*, 1552.

7. The excerpt from de las Casas can be used most directly to prove which of the following arguments about the period 1491 to 1607?
   - **a.** Many Europeans adopted aspects of American Indian culture and tradition.
   - **b.** European settlers often misunderstood American Indian cultures and traditions.
   - **c.** American Indians often sought diplomatic solutions to conflict.
   - **d.** Europeans disagreed about how American Indians should be treated.

8. Which of the following contributed most directly to the developments described by de las Casas?
   - **a.** Advances in European maritime technologies
   - **b.** European encroachment on American Indians' land
   - **c.** Widespread epidemics
   - **d.** The importation of enslaved labor

SHORT ANSWER QUESTIONS

Read each question carefully and write a short response. Use evidence from the text to support your claims.

> "The first residents of the Americas were by modern estimates divided into at least two thousand cultures and more societies, practiced a multiplicity of customs and lifestyles, held an enormous variety of values and beliefs, spoke numerous languages mutually unintelligible to the many speakers, and did not conceive of themselves as a single people — if they knew about each other at all."
>
> Robert F. Berkhofer Jr., *The White Man's Indian*, 1978
>
> "Given the archaeological record, North American 'prehistory' can hardly be characterized as a multiplicity of discrete micro histories. Fundamental to the social and economic patterns . . . were exchanges that linked peoples across geographic, cultural, and linguistic boundaries. The effects of these links are apparent in the spread of raw materials and finished goods, of beliefs and ceremonies, and of techniques for food production and for manufacturing. . . . Exchange constitutes an important key to conceptualizing American history before Columbus."
>
> Neal Salisbury, *The Indians' Old World*, 1966

1. Using the two excerpts provided, answer (a), (b), and (c).
   - **a.** Briefly explain ONE major difference between Berkhofer's and Salisbury's historical interpretations of the lives of American Indians in the period 1491 to 1607.
   - **b.** Briefly explain how ONE specific historical event or development in the period 1491 to 1607 that is not explicitly mentioned in the excerpts could be used to support Berkhofer's interpretation.
   - **c.** Briefly explain how ONE specific historical event or development in the period 1491 to 1607 that is not explicitly mentioned in the excerpts could be used to support Salisbury's interpretation.

2. Answer (a), (b), and (c).
   - **a.** Briefly explain ONE important way in which the Columbian Exchange transformed interactions between American Indian societies prior to 1607.
   - **b.** Briefly explain ONE important way in which the Columbian Exchange transformed European societies prior to 1607.
   - **c.** Briefly explain ANOTHER important way in which the Columbian Exchange transformed European societies prior to 1607.

3. Answer (a), (b), and (c).
   - **a.** Briefly explain ONE important technological change that led to the growth of Spanish colonies in the Americas prior to 1607.
   - **b.** Briefly explain ONE important economic change that led to the development of colonies in the Americas prior to 1607.
   - **c.** Briefly explain ONE way in which Spanish colonization changed the environment of the Americas.

TRM Find complete suggested responses in the Teacher's Resource Materials.

AP® SKILLS & PROCESSES

ANALYZING HISTORICAL EVIDENCE

Especially early in the year, students may struggle with academic or historical vocabulary used by historians. Therefore, think about providing students with the definitions of the following words or phrases for the excerpt by Salisbury: "multiplicity of discrete microhistories," "linguistic boundaries," and "conceptualizing American history." Once students are familiar with the language, they are better able to make meaningful connections.

2 CHAPTER American Experiments

1521–1700

Chapter 2 — AP® Assessment Weight and Pacing Guide

The assessment weight on the AP® U.S. History Exam for Chapters 1–2 is 4–6 percent. This chapter falls at the end of Unit 1 of the AP® U.S. History Curriculum, covering Period 1: 1491–1607 and the beginning of Unit 2 of the AP® U.S. History Curriculum, covering Period 2: 1607–1754.

This pacing guide is based on a schedule with 120 sessions of 50 minutes each before the AP® U.S. History Exam. If you have a different number of sessions before the exam, you can modify the pacing to meet your needs. If you have additional time, consider incorporating quizzes, released AP® U.S. History questions, practice exams, writing practice, and other instructional activities.

	Traditional Schedule	Block Schedule
Chapter 2	4 days	2–3 days

Daily Pacing Guide

	Focus Content	Essential Question
Day 1	Spain's Tribute Colonies	How did Spanish colonization affect people in the Americas and in Europe?
Day 2	Plantation Colonies	How did the labor demands of plantation colonies transform the process of colonization?
Day 3	Neo-European Colonies	What conditions were necessary to establish successful neo-European colonies?
Day 4	War and Rebellion in North America	What did these three rebellions — Metacom's War, the Pueblo Revolt, and Bacon's Rebellion — have in common?

AP® Alignment

Section Heading	AP® Topic	AP® Theme
Spain's Tribute Colonies	1.5, 2.2	SOC, MIG
Plantation Colonies	2.3, 2.4, 2.5, 2.6	GEO, WXT, WOR
Neo-European Colonies	2.2, 2.3	MIG, GEO
War and Rebellion in North America	2.5, 2.7	WOR, ARC

*Should changes be made to the Course Framework in the future, an updated alignment will be placed on our AP® updates page at go.bfwpub.com/ap-course-updates.

Chapter 2 — Overview

This chapter begins with a look at the Columbian Exchange and growing challenges to Spanish power in the New World (Unit 1 in the AP® U.S. History Curriculum). As settlement of the New World grows, the chapter turns its attention to the important development of plantation colonies in South America and the Caribbean islands. Competition between European nations leads to a push to establish settlements in New France, New Netherland, and New England, with each nation attempting to incorporate Native American groups into alliances and military exchanges. The chapter closes with a focus on instability and conflicts in the colonies between Europeans and Native Americans and between the British colonists and their colonial governments and British policy (Unit 2 in the AP® U.S. History Curriculum).

Chapter 2 — Resources

The following resources can be found in the Teacher's Resource Materials (TRM) that accompany the book. You can access the TRM via the book's digital platform, by clicking the TRM links found here in your Teacher's Edition e-book or by contacting your representative to access the resources online. Visit **bfwpub.com/henretta10e** to learn more.

TRM Chapter 2 Lecture Presentation Slides

TRM Chapter 2 Outline with AP® Focus

TRM Chapter 2 Lecture Strategies

TRM Chapter 2 Suggested Responses

TRM Handout 2.1 — Comparison: Early Settlements

TRM Handout 2.2 — Thematic Analysis: Introduction of Tobacco in the Chesapeake Colonies

TRM Handout 2.3 — Comparison: European Settlements in North America

TRM Handout 2.4 — Causation: Religious Tolerance in British North America

TRM Handout 2.5 — Contextualization: Bacon's Rebellion

Chapter 2 — Essential Activity

Ask students to provide six specific events that connect Columbus's landing in the Caribbean (1492) to the founding of Jamestown (1607) based on one AP® Theme. Students should explain the connection between the events they choose using AP® Historical Thinking Skills and Reasoning Processes (contextualization; comparison; causation; and continuity and change). Students should also provide evidence for each event that helps to support the connections between events. Finally, require students to provide contextualization for the events by looking at the broad processes and developments that influenced the events from 1491 to 1607.

Chapter 2 — Bell Ringers

The following activities take no more than 5–15 minutes of your class period and offer an effective and engaging way to begin your lessons and for students to apply AP® Skills & Processes:

- Project an image that illustrates the *casta* system in Spanish colonies. Ask students to explain how this image reflected attitudes toward race in the Spanish colonies. *Answers will vary, but should include the following: an established hierarchy based on paternity and race created a system that allowed for marriage of European and non-Europeans, allowed for non-Europeans to be mobile in social system, blurred lines between European and non-European, and reflected ideas of racial superiority of Europeans.*
- Provide students with a copy of the Virginia Charter and the Mayflower Compact without any identifying source information. Let students know the names of the two documents they are reading, and then ask them to read and analyze the sources and guess which source is which. Use this activity to introduce a comparison of Jamestown and Plymouth (Massachusetts Bay Colony).
- Ask students: What should America's role be in the world? Allow students to discuss and write their ideas on the board. Use this discussion as an introduction to a document analysis activity based on John Winthrop's "City upon a Hill" sermon. *Answers will vary.*

NOTES

TEACHING STRATEGY

Use the chapter opener material to help students identify the three major developments of the era: European transplantation of familiar patterns to the Americas, the creation of new patterns (largely through plantations), and the responses of Native Americans to the European presence. For a complete suggested response to the **AP® LEARNING FOCUS** question, see p. 72.

2 CHAPTER

American Experiments 1521–1700

AP® LEARNING FOCUS

Why did the American colonies develop the social, political, and economic institutions they did, and why were some colonial experiments more successful than others?

Beginning in the 1660s, legislators in Virginia and Maryland hammered out the legal definition of **chattel slavery**: the ownership of human beings as property. The institution of slavery — which would profoundly affect African Americans and shape much of American history — had been obsolete in England for centuries, and articulating its logic required lawmakers to reverse some of the most basic presumptions of English law. For example, in 1662 a Virginia statute declared, "all children borne in this country shalbe held bond or free only according to the condition of the mother." This idea — that a child's legal status derived from the mother, rather than the father — ran contrary to the patriarchal foundations of English law. The men who sat in Virginia's House of Burgesses would not propose such a thing lightly. Why would they decide that the principle of patriarchal descent, which was so fundamental to their own worlds, was inappropriate for their slaves?

The question needed to be addressed, according to the statute's preamble, since "doubts have arisen whether children got by an Englishman upon a negro woman should be slave or free." One such case involved Elizabeth Key, a woman whose father was a free Englishman and mother was an African slave. She petitioned for her freedom in 1656, based on her father's status. Her lawyer was an Englishman named William Greensted. He not only took Key's case, but he also fathered two of her children and, eventually, married her. Key won her case and her freedom from bondage. Elizabeth Key escaped her mother's fate — a life in slavery — because her father and her husband were both free Englishmen. The 1662 statute aimed to close Key's avenue to freedom.

The process by which the institution of chattel slavery was molded to the needs of colonial planters is just one example of the way Europeans adapted the principles they brought with them to the unfamiliar demands of their new surroundings. In the showdown between people like Elizabeth Key and William Greensted, on the one hand, and the members of Virginia's House of Burgesses on the other, we see how people in disorienting circumstances — some in positions of power, others in various states of subjection to their social and political superiors — scrambled to make sense of their world and bend its rules to their advantage. Through countless contests of power and authority like this one, the outlines of a new world gradually began to emerge from the collision of cultures.

By 1700, three distinct types of colonies had developed in the Americas. The tribute colonies created in Mexico and Peru relied initially on the wealth and labor of indigenous peoples. Plantation colonies produced sugar and other tropical and subtropical crops with bound labor. Finally, **neo-Europes** sought to replicate, or at least approximate, economies and social structures that colonists knew at home.

chattel slavery
A system of bondage in which a slave has the legal status of property and so can be bought and sold like property.

neo-Europes
Term for colonies in which colonists sought to replicate, or at least approximate, economies and social structures they knew at home.

Power and Race in the Chesapeake In this 1670 painting by Gerard Soest, proprietor Lord Baltimore holds a map of Maryland, the colony he owned and that would soon belong to his grandson Cecil Calvert, shown in the painting as already grasping his magnificent inheritance. The presence of a young African servant foretells the importance of slave labor in the post-1700 economy of the Chesapeake colonies. Private Collection/Peter Newark American Pictures/Bridgeman Images.

TEACHING STRATEGY

Students may not know that the formal painting depicting power and race in the Chesapeake was likely commissioned by a patron, probably Lord Baltimore himself, and would have been very expensive. Guide students' analysis with the following questions:

- **What do you see in the painting, besides the three figures identified in the caption?** *Lord Baltimore stands authoritatively and stares confidently at the viewer, as does the toddler, Cecil Calvert. The African servant bows his head in a gesture of humility and subservience. The luxurious quality of the fabrics is evident from the sheen on Lord Baltimore and Cecil Calvert's clothing, which is probably silk, as well as the soft fabric covering the table, likely velvet. The intricate patterns in the clothing required expensive, time-consuming weaving.*
- **Why do you think this painting was made?** *The painting was likely commissioned by Baltimore to celebrate his power and authority.*
- **What does it reveal about plantation colonies like Maryland?** *As the caption suggests, it reveals the importance of race and race-based slavery. It also suggests the vast disparities in wealth that separated elites from the rest of the colonists and the importance of inherited wealth in maintaining power.*

AP® SKILLS & PROCESSES

CONTINUITY AND CHANGE

Use the **TIMELINE** table to explore how 1521 to 1692 could constitute a definitive historical period. Remind students that very precise years like 1521 and 1692 are often indications of a very specific significant event. Referring students to the chapter title will help them think further about the reasoning for this periodization. Remind them that "American" has a broader geographic meaning than they typically think of when they hear the term. Discuss the connotations of "experiments" as something new and untried in contrast to something settled or fixed. As students skim the events, they can look for who was in the Americas, where they settled, and what the outcomes of their settlement seemed to be.

AP® THEME

WOR: America in the World; WXT: Work, Exchange, and Technology

Ask students: **How did the cultural interaction between Spain and the Aztec and Inca empires they conquered influence political, economic, and social developments in those regions?** *The Spanish imposed new forms of government, including municipal councils, legal code, and the Catholic Church. The Spanish also imposed economic systems, including the* encomienda *and* mita *systems, using Native American labor to support plantation agriculture and extract precious metals and other resources. Note: the Inca* mita *system was coopted and expanded by the Spanish so this was not an entirely new economic pattern.*

TEACHING STRATEGY

Episode 2 of *Guns, Germs, and Steel*, a PBS film based on Jared Diamond's book of the same name, provides useful materials for illustrating the initial confrontation between Pizarro and Inca leader Atahualpa. The site also provides a lesson plan titled "Steel: The Great Conqueror," which looks at the difference in technology between the two empires. While Diamond's overall thesis has been controversial among historians, this segment avoids contested issues. Search "PBS Episode 2 Guns, Germs, and Steel" to access the film.

TIMELINE

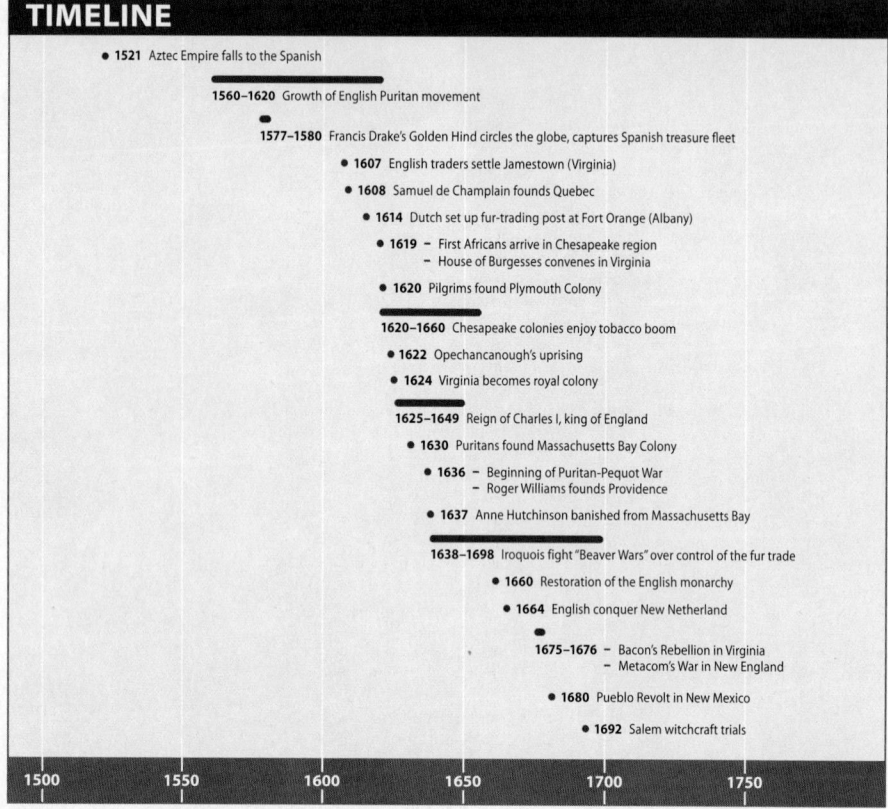

- **1521** Aztec Empire falls to the Spanish
- **1560–1620** Growth of English Puritan movement
- **1577–1580** Francis Drake's Golden Hind circles the globe, captures Spanish treasure fleet
- **1607** English traders settle Jamestown (Virginia)
- **1608** Samuel de Champlain founds Quebec
- **1614** Dutch set up fur-trading post at Fort Orange (Albany)
- **1619** – First Africans arrive in Chesapeake region
  – House of Burgesses convenes in Virginia
- **1620** Pilgrims found Plymouth Colony
- **1620–1660** Chesapeake colonies enjoy tobacco boom
- **1622** Opechancanough's uprising
- **1624** Virginia becomes royal colony
- **1625–1649** Reign of Charles I, king of England
- **1630** Puritans found Massachusetts Bay Colony
- **1636** – Beginning of Puritan-Pequot War
  – Roger Williams founds Providence
- **1637** Anne Hutchinson banished from Massachusetts Bay
- **1638–1698** Iroquois fight "Beaver Wars" over control of the fur trade
- **1660** Restoration of the English monarchy
- **1664** English conquer New Netherland
- **1675–1676** – Bacon's Rebellion in Virginia
  – Metacom's War in New England
- **1680** Pueblo Revolt in New Mexico
- **1692** Salem witchcraft trials

1500 | 1550 | 1600 | 1650 | 1700 | 1750

SPAIN'S TRIBUTE COLONIES

How did Spanish colonization affect people in the Americas and in Europe?

European interest in the Americas took shape under the influence of Spain's conquest of the Aztec and Inca empires. There, Spanish colonizers capitalized on preexisting tribute systems and labor regimes to tap the enormous wealth of Mesoamerica and the Andes. Once native rulers were overthrown, the Spanish monarchs transferred their institutions — municipal councils, the legal code, the Catholic Church — to America; the empire was centrally controlled to protect the crown's immensely valuable holdings. The Spanish conquest also set in motion a global ecological transformation through a vast intercontinental movement of plants, animals, and diseases that historians call the Columbian Exchange. And the conquest triggered hostile responses from Spain's European rivals, especially the Protestant Dutch and English.

A New American World

After Cortés toppled Moctezuma and Pizarro defeated Atahualpa (see Chapter 1), leading conquistadors received ***encomiendas*** from the crown, which allowed them to claim tribute in labor and goods from Indian communities. Later these grants were repartitioned, but the pattern was set early: prominent men controlled vast resources and monopolized Indian labor. The value of these grants was dramatically enhanced by the discovery of gold and, especially, silver deposits in both Mexico and the Andes. In the decades after the conquest, mines were developed in Zacatecas, in Guanajuato, and — most famously — at Potosí, high in the Andes. There, Spanish officials co-opted the *mita* system, which had made laborers available to the Inca Empire, to force Indian workers into the mines. At its peak, Potosí alone produced 200 tons of silver per year, accounting for half the world's supply.

encomienda
A grant of Indian labor in Spanish America given in the sixteenth century by the Spanish kings to prominent men. *Encomenderos* extracted tribute from these Indians in exchange for granting them protection and Christian instruction.

The two great indigenous empires of the Americas thus became the core of an astonishingly wealthy European empire. Vast amounts of silver poured across the Pacific Ocean to China, where it was minted into money; in exchange, Spain received valuable Chinese silks, spices, and ceramics. In Europe, the gold that had formerly honored Aztec and Inca gods now flowed into the countinghouses of Spain and gilded the Catholic churches of Europe. The Spanish crown benefitted enormously from all this wealth — at least initially. In the long run, it triggered ruinous inflation. As a French traveler noted in 1603, "Everything is dear [expensive] in Spain, except silver."

A new society took shape on the conquered lands. Between 1500 and 1650, at least 350,000 Spaniards migrated, most to Mesoamerica and the Andes. About two-thirds were males drawn from a cross section of Spanish society, many of them skilled tradesmen; the other one-third were female. Also arriving were 250,000 to 300,000 enslaved Africans. Racial mixture was widespread, and such groups as mestizos (Spaniard-Indian) and mulattos (Spaniard-African) grew rapidly. Zambo (Indian-African) populations developed gradually as well. Over time, a system of increasingly complex racial categories developed — the **casta system** — buttressed by a legal code that differentiated among the principal groups.

AP® EXAM TIP
The relationship between the encomienda system and the casta system is important to know for the AP® Exam.

casta system
A hierarchical system of racial classification developed by colonial elites in Latin America to make sense of the complex patterns of racial mixing that developed there.

Indians were always in the majority in Mexico and Peru, but profound changes came as their numbers declined and peoples of Spanish and mixed-race descent grew in number. Spaniards initially congregated in cities, but gradually they moved into the countryside, creating large estates (known as haciendas) and regional networks of market exchange. Most Indians remained in their Native communities, under the authority of Native rulers and speaking Native languages. However, Spanish priests suppressed religious ceremonies and texts and converted Natives to Christianity *en masse*. Catholicism was transformed in the process: Catholic parishes took their form from Indian communities; indigenous ideas and expectations reshaped Church practices; and new forms of Native American Christianity emerged in both regions.

The Columbian Exchange

The Spanish invasion permanently altered the natural as well as the human environment. Smallpox, influenza, measles, yellow fever, and other silent killers carried from Europe and Africa ravaged Indian communities, whose inhabitants had never encountered these diseases before and thus had no immunities to them. In the densely populated core areas, populations declined by 90 percent or more in the first century of contact with Europeans. On islands and in the tropical lowlands, the toll was even heavier; Native populations were often wiped out altogether. Syphilis was the only significant illness that traveled in the opposite direction: Columbus's sailors carried a virulent strain of the sexually transmitted disease back to Europe with them.

AP® EXAM TIP
Differentiate the impact of the Columbian Exchange on European and on Native populations.

The movement of diseases and peoples across the Atlantic was part of a larger pattern of biological transformation that historians call the **Columbian Exchange**

Columbian Exchange
The massive global exchange of living things, including people, animals, plants, and diseases, between the Eastern and Western Hemispheres that began after the voyages of Columbus.

AP® APPLY THE TIP

Ask students to analyze an image of the *casta* system painted in the eighteenth century — *Las castas.* Anonymous, 18th century, Museo Nacional del Virreinato, Mexico — to create a social pyramid for the Spanish colonies. Students may be unfamiliar with the names or terms on the image so be prepared to talk about terms such as "mestizo" and "mulatto." Guide students' analysis through the following questions:

- **What factor determines who occupies the highest social classes in Spanish colonies?** *The casta system is a patriarchal system with the father's nationality having the largest impact on class; there are also distinctions between interracial children who are ethnically Native and ethnically African with those of African descent occupying the lower of the classes in comparison with Native or European.*
- **Why was the development of a complicated social class system necessary in the Spanish colonies?** *The Spanish accepted that interracial relationships were inevitable in this system of colonization and therefore developed a social system that acknowledged the children produced from these relationships. While the Spanish developed a system legitimizing interracial marriage, the system still discriminated based on race.*
- **In what ways does the *casta* system illustrate continuity with the social class system of Europe in the sixteenth through eighteenth centuries? In what way does the casta system show a major change from the dominant social system in Europe in this period?** *Social systems in Europe in this era drew sharp distinctions in class and privilege based on patriarchy. However, relationships between ethnic groups or races were not accepted in European society in this era. The casta system, therefore, would only develop in the New World.*

CHECK FOR UNDERSTANDING

Ask students: **What features characterized Spanish America?** *Spain expropriated the vast silver and gold reserves of Mexico and Peru, which made it fabulously wealthy. The imports of African slaves along with relationships between Spanish and Indians led to a complex racial mixture.*

AP® THEME

SOC: Social Structures

The encomienda system is a central aspect of Spain's efforts to use the New World for mineral wealth. Students are required to know this as both an economic and social system. Consider the following activity to build out this concept: In groups of two, students select either economic or social and individually define encomienda within the boundaries of their category. Each pair then shares responses. Students then use their definitions to answer the following prompt: Identify and explain how the encomienda system altered the lives of American Indians in the New World.

AP® THEME

GEO: Geography and the Environment; WOR: America in the World

Use **MAP 2.1** to discuss how the Columbian Exchange had significant consequences for both Europe and the Americas. Remind students that this phenomenon was a function of geographic and environmental features stemming from the Americas' isolation from Eurasia. In Europe, new crops stimulated population growth, while new sources of wealth aided the European transition from feudalism to capitalism. In the Americas, new crops and animals changed the economy, while deadly epidemics decimated Native populations.

AP® SKILLS & PROCESSES

DEVELOPMENTS AND PROCESSES

Use the **DEVELOPMENTS AND PROCESSES** question to help students think about the global context in which colonization occurred. Remind students how the geographical isolation of the Americas from the Eurasian landmass prevented Native Americans from benefiting from the spread of crops and livestock, but also prevented their exposure to diseases that would have allowed them to develop forms of immunity. As a result, the Columbian Exchange spurred population collapse in the Americas, in contrast to a population explosion in Eurasia due to the spread of new food crops.

TRM Find complete suggested responses in the Teacher's Resource Materials.

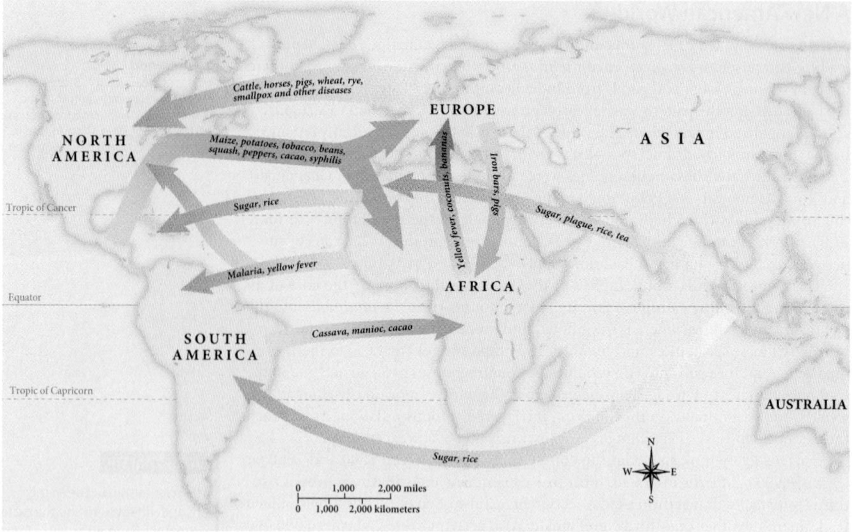

MAP 2.1 The Columbian Exchange
As European traders and adventurers traversed the world between 1430 and 1600, they began what historians call the Columbian Exchange, a vast intercontinental movement of plants, animals, and diseases that changed the course of historical development. The nutritious, high-yielding American crops of corn and potatoes enriched the diets of Europeans, Africans, and Asians. However, the Eurasian and African diseases of smallpox, diphtheria, malaria, and yellow fever nearly wiped out the native inhabitants of the Western Hemisphere and virtually ensured that they would lose control of their lands.

AP® SKILLS & PROCESSES
DEVELOPMENTS AND PROCESSES
How did the ecological context of colonization shape interactions between Europeans and Native Americans?

(Map 2.1). Foods of the Western Hemisphere — especially maize (corn), potatoes, manioc, sweet potatoes, and tomatoes — significantly increased agricultural yields and population growth in other continents. Maize and potatoes, for example, reached China around 1700; in the following century, the Chinese population tripled from 100 million to 300 million. At the same time, many animals, plants, and germs were carried to the Americas. European livestock transformed American landscapes. Though Native Americans domesticated very few animals — dogs and llamas were the principal exceptions — Europeans brought an enormous Old World bestiary to the Americas, including cattle, pigs, horses, oxen, chickens, and honeybees. Eurasian grain crops — wheat, barley, rye, and rice — made the transatlantic voyage along with inadvertent imports like dandelions and other weeds.

AP® EXAM TIP
Take good notes on how religion drove imperial competition between European nations.

The Protestant Challenge to Spain

Beyond the core regions of its empire, Spain claimed vast American dominions but struggled to hold them. Controlling the Caribbean basin, which was essential for Spain's transatlantic shipping routes, was especially difficult, since the net of tiny islands spanning the eastern Caribbean — the Lesser Antilles — provided many safe harbors for pirates and privateers. Fortified outposts in Havana (Cuba) and St. Augustine (Florida) provided some protection, but they were never sufficient to keep enemies at bay.

And Spain had powerful enemies, their animosity sharpened by the Protestant Reformation and the resulting split in European Christendom (see Chapter 1). In the wake of Martin Luther's attack on the Catholic Church, the Protestant critique of Catholicism broadened and deepened. Gold and silver from Mexico and Peru

AP® APPLY THE TIP

Have students work in small groups to construct a timeline of events illustrating the impact of religion on imperial competition between Spain, France, England, and the Dutch Republic. For each event on the timeline, ask students to provide a brief description of the event, its relationship to religion, and then a direct effect on colonization of the Americas. After students complete timelines, ask each group to rank the events on the timeline from most to least religiously motivated. Discuss the impact of religion as a driving force and as a justification for imperial policies. Extend the discussion by asking students to compare the impact of religion on imperial competition and colonization by different European nations. Ask students to consider the impact of religion in competition between nations in the world today.

The Columbian Exchange in Action This image, which combines Nahuatl alphabetic writing with elaborate pictographs, depicts a sixteenth-century scene in which Maxixcatzin, the *cacique* (or head man) of Tlaxcala, presents gifts to Hernán Cortés. They include flowers, birds, and — at the upper right — large baskets of maize (corn), an American food crop previously unfamiliar to Europeans. Private Collection/Archives Charmet/Bridgeman Images.

made Spain the wealthiest nation in Europe, and King Philip II (r. 1556–1598) — an ardent Catholic — its most powerful ruler. Philip was determined to root out challenges to the Catholic Church wherever they appeared. One such place was in the Spanish Netherlands, a collection of Dutch- and Flemish-speaking provinces that had grown wealthy from textile manufacturing and trade with Portuguese outposts in Africa and Asia. To protect their Calvinist faith and political liberties, they revolted against Spanish rule in 1566. After fifteen years of war, the seven northern provinces declared their independence, becoming the Dutch Republic (or Holland) in 1581.

The English king Henry VIII (r. 1509–1547) initially opposed Protestantism. However, when the pope refused to annul his marriage to the Spanish princess Catherine of Aragon in 1534, Henry broke with Rome, confiscated church properties, and placed himself at the head of the new Church of England, which promptly granted an annulment. Although Henry's new church maintained most Catholic doctrines and practices, Protestant teachings continued to spread. Faced with popular pressure for reform, Henry's daughter and successor, Queen Elizabeth I (r. 1558–1603), approved a Protestant confession of faith. But she also retained the Catholic ritual of Holy Communion and left the Church in the hands of Anglican bishops and archbishops. Elizabeth's compromises angered radical Protestants, but the independent Anglican Church was an affront to Spain's Philip II, Europe's foremost defender of the Catholic Church.

Elizabeth supported a generation of English seafarers who took increasingly aggressive actions against Spanish control of American wealth. The most famous of these Elizabethan "sea dogs" was Francis Drake, a rough-hewn, devoutly Protestant farmer's son from Devon who took to the sea and became a scourge to Philip's American interests. In 1577, he ventured into the Pacific to disrupt Spanish shipping to Manila. Drake's fleet lost three ships and a hundred men, but the survivors captured two Spanish treasure ships and completed the first English circumnavigation of the globe. When Drake's flagship, the *Golden Hind,* returned to England in 1580, it brought enough silver, gold, silk, and spices to bring his investors a 4,700 percent return on their investment.

AP® SKILLS & PROCESSES

CONTEXTUALIZATION

How did the new resources from the Columbian Exchange facilitate the shift from feudalism to capitalism?

AP® THEME

AMERICAN AND REGIONAL CULTURE

As the sixteenth century ended, more European nations looked to the New World for the opportunity to colonize. In particular, the English sought to extend their economic and political influence to the New World. Have students compare the American regions in which the Spanish and English colonized, or sought to colonize. Specifically, ask students to compare the goals of colonization and how the regions that were colonized aligned with Europeans' goals.

TRM Find complete suggested responses in the Teacher's Resource Materials.

Queen Elizabeth Receiving Dutch Ambassadors This sixteenth-century Dutch painting by an anonymous artist depicts a pair of Dutch ambassadors being received by England's Queen Elizabeth I. The seventeen provinces that constituted the Dutch Republic were in rebellion against Spanish rule in the later decades of the sixteenth century and hoped for Elizabeth's support. In 1585 Elizabeth signed the Treaty of Nonsuch, pledging her support for the Dutch cause. An undeclared war with Spain ensued, punctuated by the defeat of the Spanish Armada in 1588. Neue Galerie, Kessel, Germany © Museumslandschaft Hessen Kassel/Bridgeman Images.

At the same time, Elizabeth imposed English rule over Gaelic-speaking Catholic Ireland. Calling the Irish "wild savages" who were "more barbarous and more brutish in their customs . . . than in any other part of the world," English soldiers brutally massacred thousands, prefiguring the treatment of Indians in North America.

To meet Elizabeth's challenges, Philip sent a Spanish Armada — 130 ships and 30,000 men — against England in 1588. Philip intended to restore the Roman Church in England and then wipe out Calvinism in Holland. But he failed utterly: a fierce storm and English ships destroyed the Spanish fleet. Philip continued to spend his American gold and silver on religious wars, an ill-advised policy that diverted workers and resources from Spain's fledgling industries. The gold was like a "shewer of Raine," complained one critic, that left "no benefite behind." Oppressed by high taxes on agriculture and fearful of military service, more than 200,000 residents of Castile, once the most prosperous region of Spain, migrated to America. By the time of Philip's death in 1598, Spain was in serious economic decline.

By contrast, England's population soared from 3 million in 1500 to 5 million in 1630. English merchants had long supplied European weavers with high-quality wool; around 1500, they created their own textile industry. Merchants bought wool from the owners of great estates and sent it to landless peasants in small cottages to spin and weave into cloth. The government aided textile entrepreneurs by setting low wage rates and helped merchants by giving them monopolies in foreign markets.

mercantilism
A system of political economy based on government regulation. Beginning in 1650, Britain enacted Navigation Acts that controlled colonial commerce and manufacturing for the enrichment of Britain.

This system of state-assisted manufacturing and trade became known as **mercantilism**. By encouraging textile production, Elizabeth reduced imports and increased exports. The resulting favorable balance of trade caused gold and silver to flow into England and stimulated further economic expansion. Increased trade with Turkey and India also boosted import duties, which swelled the royal treasury and the monarch's power. By 1600, Elizabeth's mercantile policies had laid the foundations for overseas colonization. Now the English had the merchant fleet and wealth needed to challenge Spain's control of the Western Hemisphere.

AP® SKILLS & PROCESSES
CAUSATION
Why did Spain's economy deteriorate and England's economy improve in the sixteenth century?

PLANTATION COLONIES

How did the labor demands of plantation colonies transform the process of colonization?

As Spain hammered out its American empire and struggled against its Protestant rivals, Portugal, England, France, and the Netherlands created successful plantation settlements in Brazil, Jamestown, Maryland, and the Caribbean islands (Map 2.2). Worldwide demand for sugar and tobacco fueled the growth of these new colonies, and the resulting influx of colonists diminished Spain's dominance in the New World. At the same time, they imposed dramatic new pressures on Native populations, who scrambled to survive and carve out pathways to the future.

TEACHING STRATEGY

This painting of Queen Elizabeth receiving Dutch ambassadors reveals her significant role in European affairs, which set the stage for England's exploration of North America. The British Library provides a high-quality reproduction and transcript of the text of her famous address to English troops before the invasion that was expected with the arrival of the Spanish Armada. The site also provides a two-minute clip from a librarian explaining the context and significance of the document. Search "British Library Spanish Armada Speech" to access this resource.

AP® SKILLS & PROCESSES

CAUSATION

Use the **CAUSATION** question to invite students to trace two different patterns of change, the economy of Spain and that of England, and to compare their different trajectories. Assist students by identifying the religious, economic, political, and demographic factors involved in England's rise relative to Spain. Extend this prompt by asking students to examine how different choices by the Spanish government might have stopped or at least limited its decline.

TRM Find complete suggested responses in the Teacher's Resource Materials.

AP® SKILLS & PROCESSES

CONTEXTUALIZATION

In the previous chapter, students worked on recognizing the characteristics of contextualization. Mercantilism presents an opportunity to develop this important historical thinking skill. Review with students that contextualization represents a broader understanding of historical developments. Students studying the processes of colonization can use mercantilism to explain the broader economic considerations made by European powers. Consider providing two pieces of historical evidence such as textiles and merchant capitalism. Next, have students write a two-or three-sentence explanation connecting mercantilism, textiles, and merchant capitalism to the process of colonization. In doing this, students are moving from a conceptual understanding of contextualization to one grounded in their ability to describe the historical context of colonization.

CHECK FOR UNDERSTANDING

Ask students: **How did Spanish colonization affect people in the Americas and in Europe?** *In the Americas, Spanish colonization brought social and economic dislocations. Socially, as almost 350,000 Spanish migrants arrived in the Americas, new social leveling based on race, known as the* casta *system, emerged. Native Americans were converted to Catholicism en masse. Eonomically, the Americans were re-oriented to serve Spanish and European needs and its transoceanic trading partners. In Europe, the Spanish Crown as well as Spain's merchants became fantastically wealthy. Money flowed into Spain then into Europe, especially the Catholic Church.*

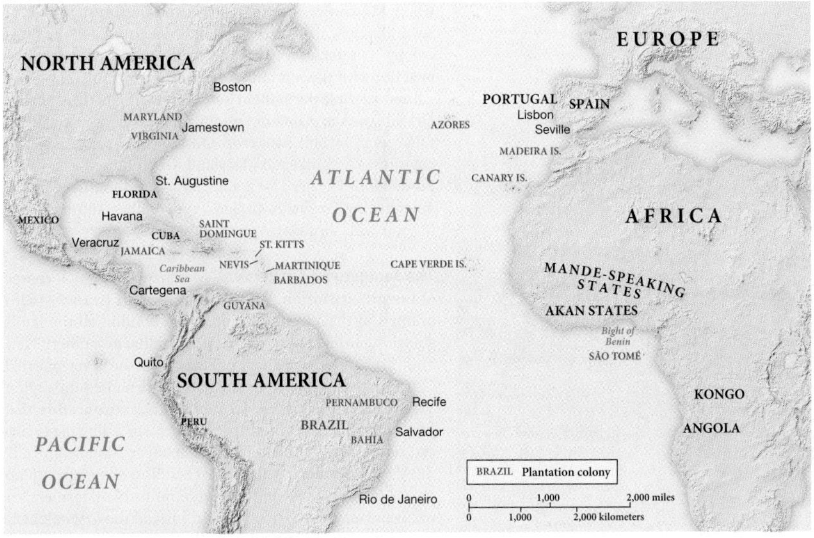

MAP 2.2 The Plantation Colonies
The plantation zone in the Americas extended from the tropical coast of Brazil northwestward through the West Indies and into the tropical and subtropical lowlands of southeastern North America. Sugar was the most important plantation crop in the Americas, but where the soil or climate could not support it planters experimented with a wide variety of other possibilities, including tobacco, indigo, cotton, cacao, and rice.

Brazil's Sugar Plantations

Portuguese colonists transformed the tropical lowlands of coastal Brazil into a sugar plantation zone like the ones they had recently created on Madeira, the Azores, the Cape Verdes, and São Tomé. The work proceeded slowly, but by 1590 more than a thousand sugar mills had been established in Pernambuco and Bahia. Each large plantation had its own milling operation: because sugarcane is extremely heavy and rots quickly, it must be processed on-site. Thus sugar plantations combined back-breaking agricultural labor with milling, extracting, and refining processes that made them look like Industrial Revolution–era factories.

Initially, Portuguese planters hoped that Brazil's indigenous peoples would supply the labor required to operate their sugar plantations. But, beginning with a smallpox epidemic in 1559, unfamiliar diseases ravaged the coastal Indian population. As a result, planters turned to African slaves in ever-growing numbers; by 1620, the switch was complete. While Spanish colonies in Mexico and Peru took shape with astonishing speed following conquest, Brazil's development required both trial and error and prolonged hard work.

England's Chesapeake Colonies

England was slow to pursue colonization in the Americas. There were fumbling attempts in the 1580s in Newfoundland and Maine, privately organized and poorly funded. Sir Walter Raleigh's three expeditions to North Carolina ended in disaster

AP® THEME

GEO: Geography and the Environment

Use **MAP 2.2** to help students recognize the geography of plantation colonies. Ask students: **What generalization can you make about the location of plantation colonies? Why did they share these features?** *The plantation colonies were all in tropical and subtropical climates and all located on islands or near the coast. The latitude reflected the location where valuable plantation crops could be grown, while the proximity to the coast indicated the need to easily ship these cash crops to market.*

CHECK FOR UNDERSTANDING

Ask students: **What were Brazil's sugar plantations like?** *The sugar plantations were large-scale operations requiring a factory-like process based on division of labor and requiring many workers. Since disease devastated Native populations, the Portuguese turned to African slaves for labor.*

Carolina Indians Fishing, 1585 Though maize was a mainstay of the Indian diet, Native peoples along the Atlantic coast also harvested protein-rich fish, crabs, and oysters. In this watercolor by the English adventurer John White, Indians gather fish (in their "cannow," or dugout canoe) in the shallow waters of the Albemarle Sound, off present-day North Carolina. On the left, note the weir used both to catch fish and to store them live for later consumption. © The Trustees of the British Museum/Art Resource, NY.

when 117 settlers on Roanoke Island, left unsupplied for several years, vanished. The fate of Roanoke — the "lost colony" — remains a compelling puzzle for modern historians. But with the founding of Jamestown in 1607, England gained its first permanent settlement in North America. Drawing on the plantation colony model, early settlers hit on tobacco as a viable cash crop. On the Chesapeake Bay, two colonies — Virginia and Maryland — committed to tobacco production. The need for arable land caused conflict with the neighboring Powhatan Indians, eventually resulting in all-out war with Virginia.

The Jamestown Settlement Merchants then took charge of English expansion. In 1606, King James I (r. 1603–1625) granted to the Virginia Company of London all the lands stretching from present-day North Carolina to southern New York. To honor the memory of Elizabeth I, the never-married "Virgin Queen," the company's directors named the region Virginia (Map 2.3). This was a **joint-stock corporation** that pooled the resources of many investors, spreading the financial risk widely. Influenced by the Spanish example, in 1607 the Virginia Company dispatched an all-male group with no ability to support itself: there were no women, farmers, or ministers among the first arrivals. Instead the first colonists hoped to demand tribute from the region's Indian population while it searched out valuable commodities like pearls and gold. All they wanted, one of them said, was to "dig gold, refine gold, load gold."

But there was no gold, and the men fared poorly in their new environment. Arriving in Virginia after an exhausting four-month voyage, they settled on a swampy peninsula, which they named Jamestown to honor the king. There the adventurers lacked access to fresh water, failed to plant crops, and quickly died off; only 38 of the 120 men were alive nine months later. Death rates remained high: by 1611, the Virginia Company had dispatched 1,200 colonists to Jamestown, but fewer than half remained alive. "Our men were destroyed with cruell diseases, as Swellings, Fluxes, Burning Fevers, and by warres," reported one of the settlement's leaders, "but for the most part they died of meere famine."

joint-stock corporation
A financial organization devised by English merchants around 1550 that facilitated the colonization of North America. In these companies, a number of investors pooled their capital and received shares of stock in the enterprise in proportion to their share of the total investment.

Their plan to dominate the local Indian population ran up against the presence of Powhatan, the powerful paramount chief who oversaw some thirty subordinate chiefdoms between the James and Potomac rivers. He was willing to treat the English traders as potential allies who could provide valuable goods, but — just as the Englishmen expected tribute from the Indians — Powhatan expected tribute from the English. He provided the hungry English adventurers with corn; in return, he demanded "hatchets . . . bells, beads, and copper" as well as "two great guns" and expected Jamestown to become a dependent community within his chiefdom. Subsequently, Powhatan arranged a marriage between his daughter Pocahontas and John Rolfe, an English colonist (see "Thinking Like a Historian," p. 50). But these tactics failed. The inability to decide who would pay tribute to whom led to more than a decade of uneasy relations, followed by a long era of ruinous warfare.

The war was precipitated by the discovery of a cash crop that — like sugar in Brazil — offered colonists a way to turn a profit but required steady expansion onto Indian lands. Tobacco was a plant native to the Americas, long used by Indians as a

AP® EXAM TIP

Compare the demographics of the Jamestown settlement to Spanish, Dutch, and French settlements.

AP® EXAM TIP

Understanding the impact of the introduction of tobacco on the development of the Chesapeake colonies is important to know on the AP® Exam.

TEACHING STRATEGY

John White provided some of the earliest visual testimony of the Native Americans of the eastern coast of North America, providing an ethnographic representation of Native American life. Ask students: **What does White show in this image? What does his attitude seem to be toward the Carolina Indians he depicts? What conclusion can you draw from this image about English attitudes toward Native Americans?** *White depicts a variety of forms of fishing. The Native Americans are not portrayed in a judgmental or condescending way, and White seems to acknowledge the effectiveness of their ingenuity, as the canoe and weir are both full of large fish, suggesting that the English sometimes showed openness and respect for Native peoples.*

AP® APPLY THE TIP

Ask students to use their notes or text to complete **Handout 2.1 — Comparison: Early Settlements (TRM)** in order to distinguish characteristics of the English settlement at Jamestown from settlements established by the Spanish, Dutch, and French. Then ask students to consider whether the English settlement at Jamestown was more similar or different in comparison to other European settlements. Extend this activity by having students make a generalization across all the European styles of settlement.

TRM Find **Handout 2.1 — Comparison: Early Settlements** in the Teacher's Resource Materials.

AP® THEME

WOR: America in the World

Use the description of conflict and cooperation between Jamestown settlers and Powhatan Indians to explore the misunderstandings that often resulted when two empires with different cultures came into contact. Jamestown's encroachment on Powhatan lands prompted a forceful response, as the Native Americans sought to defend their political sovereignty and economic prosperity. The resulting violence, in which one-third of the Virginia settlers died, led to the revoking of Virginia's charter.

medicine and a stimulant. John Rolfe found a West Indian strain that could flourish in Virginia soil and produced a small crop — "pleasant, sweet, and strong" — that fetched a high price in England and spurred the migration of thousands of new settlers. The English soon came to crave the nicotine that tobacco contained. James I initially condemned the plant as a "vile Weed" whose "black stinking fumes" were "baleful to the nose, harmful to the brain, and dangerous to the lungs." But the king's attitude changed as taxes on imported tobacco bolstered the royal treasury. Powhatan, however, now accused the English of coming "not to trade but to invade my people and possess my country."

To encourage immigration, the Virginia Company allowed individual settlers to own land, granting 100 acres to every freeman and more to those who imported servants. The company also created a system of representative government: the **House of Burgesses**, first convened in 1619, could make laws and levy taxes, although the governor and the company council in England could veto its acts. By 1622, landownership, self-government, and a judicial system based on "the lawes of the realme of England" had attracted some 4,500 new recruits. To encourage the transition to a settler colony, the Virginia Company recruited dozens of "Maides young and uncorrupt to make wifes to the Inhabitants."

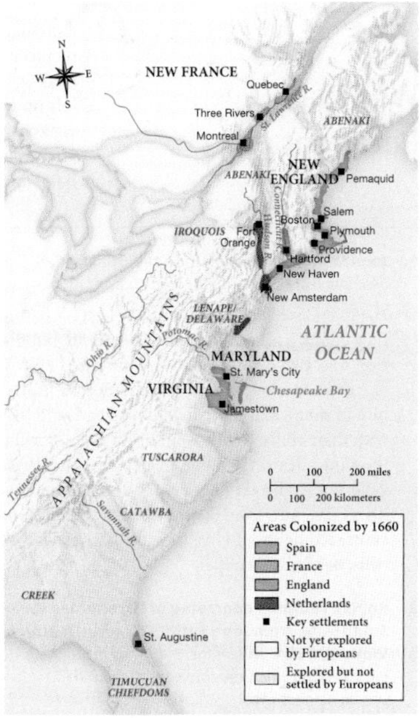

MAP 2.3 Eastern North America, 1650
By 1650, four European nations had permanent settlements along the eastern coast of North America, but only England had substantial numbers of settlers, some 25,000 in New England and another 15,000 in the Chesapeake region. French, Dutch, Swedish, and English colonists were also trading European manufactures to Native Americans in exchange for animal furs and skins, with far-reaching implications for Indian societies.

The Indian War of 1622 The influx of migrants sparked war with the neighboring Indians. The struggle began with an assault led by Opechancanough, Powhatan's younger brother and successor. In 1607, Opechancanough had attacked some of the first English invaders; subsequently, he "stood aloof" from the English settlers and "would not be drawn to any Treaty." In particular, he resisted English proposals to place Indian children in schools to be "brought upp in Christianytie." Upon becoming the paramount chief in 1621, Opechancanough told the leader of the neighboring Potomack Indians: "Before the end of two moons, there should not be an Englishman in all their Countries."

Opechancanough almost succeeded. In 1622, he coordinated a surprise attack by twelve Indian chiefdoms that killed 347 English settlers, nearly one-third of the population. The English fought back by seizing the fields and food of those they now called "naked, tanned, deformed Savages" and declared "a perpetual war without peace or truce" that lasted for a decade. They sold captured warriors into slavery, "destroy[ing] them who sought to destroy us" and taking control of "their cultivated places."

Shocked by the Indian uprising, James I revoked the Virginia Company's charter and, in 1624, made Virginia a **royal colony**. Now the king and his ministers appointed the governor and a small advisory council, retaining the locally elected House of Burgesses but stipulating that the king's Privy Council (a committee of political advisors) must ratify all legislation. The king also decreed the legal establishment of the Church of England in the colony, which meant that residents had to pay taxes to support its clergy. These institutions — an appointed governor, an elected assembly, a formal legal system, and an established Anglican Church — became the model for royal colonies throughout English America.

House of Burgesses
Organ of government in colonial Virginia made up of an assembly of representatives elected by the colony's inhabitants.

royal colony
In the English system, a royal colony was chartered by the crown. The colony's governor was appointed by the crown and served according to the instructions of the Board of Trade.

AP® SKILLS & PROCESSES

CAUSATION
How did the proximity of the Powhatan Chiefdom affect development in early Virginia?

Lord Baltimore Settles Catholics in Maryland A second tobacco-growing colony developed in neighboring Maryland. King Charles I (r. 1625–1649), James's successor, was secretly sympathetic toward Catholicism, and in 1632 he granted lands bordering the vast Chesapeake Bay to Catholic aristocrat Cecilius Calvert, Lord Baltimore. Thus

AP® THEME

WOR: America in the World

Use **MAP 2.3** to help students understand the geographical dimensions of European empires in North America. Ask students the following questions:

- **What settlement pattern can you identify from this map based on geography?** *The location and extent of settlement clearly indicates the importance of waterways and harbors, specifically the St. Lawrence River, Massachusetts Bay, Connecticut River, Hudson River, New York Harbor, and the Chesapeake Bay.*
- **How does the location of the colonies of different empires help explain conflicts between them?** *The location of Dutch settlements immediately adjacent to New England colonies and between New England and Virginia helps explain the English impetus for taking over New Amsterdam.*
- **How does the position of Indian groups relative to European empires explain the policies they adopted toward Europeans?** *The location of Abenaki and Iroquois Indians between the French, English, and Dutch settlements illustrates their ability to serve as mediators between different European empires.*

AP® THEME

NAT: American and National Identity

Discuss with students the ways that the House of Burgesses set a precedent for American ideas of freedom through representative political institutions. Encourage them to identify the ways in which this early form of representative government was limited in how much authority it had and in who was allowed to participate.

AP® SKILLS & PROCESSES

CAUSATION

Use the **CAUSATION** question to discuss the effects of the Virginia Company settlers choosing to locate their colony in the midst of Powhatan's chiefdom. Students might be able to answer this question better by considering a counterfactual question: How might the early years of the colony have been different if settlers had located their colony further from Powhatan's center of power? Point out that there were both positive and negative consequences for the English in their relationship with Powhatan. Extend this prompt by having students weigh the benefits and costs of this relationship to both the English and the Powhatan Indians.

TRM Find complete suggested responses in the Teacher's Resource Materials.

Who Was Pocahontas?

Matoaka — nicknamed Pocahontas — was born around 1596 in the region the English would soon name Virginia. A daughter of Chief Powhatan, her interactions with colonists were important at the time and have been mythologized ever since. Pocahontas left no writings, so what we know of her comes from others. From these accounts, we know that she acted as a mediator with the Jamestown settlers; she was the first Native American to marry an Englishman; and she traveled to England with her husband and son. Pocahontas fell ill and died in Gravesend, England, in June 1617.

1. **John Smith, *Generall Historie of Virginia*, 1624.** *Smith's description of being a captive of Powhatan in 1607.*

Having feasted [Smith] after their best barbarous manner they could, a long consultation was held, but the conclusion was, two great stones were brought before Powhatan: then as many as could layd hands on him, dragged him to them, and thereon laid his head, and being ready with their clubs, to beate out his braines, Pocahontas the Kings dearest daughter, when no entreaty could prevaile, got his head in her armes, and laid her owne upon his to save him from death: whereat the Emperour was contented he should live to make him hatchets, and her bells, beads, and copper.

2. **Robert Vaughn's engraving of Pocahontas saving Smith's life, from John Smith's *Generall Historie of Virginia*, 1624.** *This image, published in Smith's history of early Virginia, imagines the scene that Smith described in the preceding passage.*

Source: The New York Public Library/Art Resource, NY

3. **John Smith, *Generall Historie of Virginia*, 1624.** *Pocahontas visited Jamestown regularly in the years following Smith's capture. Smith returned to England in 1609; four years later Captain Samuel Argall kidnapped Pocahontas and held her captive in Jamestown.*

[S]he too James towne [was brought.] A messenger forthwith was sent to her father, that his daughter Pocahontas he loved so dearely, he must ransome with our men, swords, peeces, tooles, &c. he treacherously had stolen. . . . [H]e . . . sent us word, that when we would deliver his daughter, he would make us satisfaction for all injuries done to us, and give us five hundred bushels of Corne, and for ever be friends with us. . . . [W]e could not believe the rest of our armes were either lost or stolen from him, and therefore till he sent them, we would keep his daughter. . . . [W]e heard no more from him a long time after. . . . .

[Long before this, Master John Rolfe, an honest Gentleman of good behavior had been in love with Pocahontas, and she with him. . . . T]his marriage came soone to the knowledge of Powhatan, a thing acceptable to him, as appeared by his sudden consent, for within ten daies he sent Opachisco, an old Uncle of hers, and two of his sons, to see the manner of the marriage, and to do in that behalf what they were requested . . . which was accordingly done about the first of April: And ever since we have had friendly trade and commerce.

4. **John Rolfe, Letter to Sir Thomas Dale, 1614.** *Pocahontas and John Rolfe married in April 1614. In June, Rolfe defended his motives in this letter to Virginia's deputy-governor.*

I freely subject my selfe to your grave and mature judgment, deliberation, approbation and determination. . . . [I am not led by] the unbridled desire of carnal affection: but for the good of this plantation, for the honour of our countrie, for the glory of God, for my owne salvation, and for the converting to the true knowledge of God and Jesus Christ, an unbeleeving creature, namely Pocahontas. To whom my hartie and best

50

AP® SKILLS & PROCESSES

ANALYZING HISTORICAL EVIDENCE

The **AP® THINKING LIKE A HISTORIAN** feature explores the fragmentary, sometimes contradictory nature of evidence about Pocahontas. This topic and these sources provide an example of the limitations of a primary source and the need to consider an author's point of view. Corroborating evidence from different documents is an important part of this exercise as well.

thoughts are, and have [for] a long time bin so intangled, and inthralled in so intricate a labyrinth, that I was even awearied to unwinde my selfe thereout. . . . [I have often thought]: surely these are wicked instigations, hatched by him who seeketh and delighteth in man's destruction[.]

I say the holy spirit of God has often demanded of me, why I was created . . . but to labour in the Lord's vineyard. . . . Likewise adding hereunto her great appearance of love to me, her desire to be taught and instructed in the knowledge of God, her capableness of understanding, her aptness and willingness to receive any good impression, and also the spirituall, besides her owne incitements stirring me up hereunto. . . .

Now if the vulgar sort, who square all men's actions by the base rule of their owne filthiness, shall tax or taunt me in this my godly labour: let them know, it is not any hungry appetite, to gorge my selfe with incontinency; sure (if I would, and were so sensually inclined) I might satisfy such desire, though not without a seared conscience.

5. **Portrait of Pocahontas by Simon Van De Pass, 1616.** *In 1616, the Virginia Company of London sent Pocahontas, John Rolfe, and their son Thomas to England, where she met King James and sat for this portrait, the only surviving image of Pocahontas.*

MATOAKA ALS REBECCA FILIA POTENTISS: PRINC: POWHATANI IMP: VIRGINIÆ.
Matoaks als Rebecka daughter to the mighty Prince Powhatan Emperour of Attanoughkomouck als virginia converted and baptized in the Christian faith, and wife to the wor.ll Mr. Joh Rolff.
Compton Holland excud.

Source: Library of Congress, 3a10723.

6. **John Smith, *Generall Historie of Virginia*, 1624.** *In 1624, John Smith recalled a meeting he had with Pocahontas during her 1616 tour of England.*

[H]earing shee was at Branford with divers of my friends, I went to see her: After a modest salutation, without any word, she turned about, obscured her face, as not seeming well contented; and in that humour her husband, with divers others, we all left her two or three houres. . . . But not long after, she began to talke, and remembred mee well what courtesies she had done: saying, ["]You did promise Powhatan what was yours should bee his, and he the like to you; you called him father being in his land a stranger, and by the same reason so must I doe you:["] which though I would have excused, I durst not allow of that title, because she was a Kings daughter; with a well set countenance she said, ["]Were you not afraid to come into my fathers Countrie, and caused feare in him and all his people (but mee) and feare you here I should call you father; I tell you then I will, and you shall call mee childe, and so I will bee for ever and ever your Countrieman. They did tell us [always] you were dead, and I knew no other till I came to [Plymouth]; yet Powhatan did command Uttamatomakkin to seeke you, and know the truth, because your Countriemen will lie much.["]

Sources: (1, 3, 6) John Smith, *Generall Historie of Virginia* (Glasgow: James MacLehose and Sons, 1907), 101, 218, 220, 238–239; (4) J. Franklin Jameson, *Narratives of Early Virginia* (New York: Charles Scribner's Sons, 1907), 237–244.

ANALYZING THE EVIDENCE

1. Most historians now believe that the event described and shown in sources 1 and 2 was a Powhatan ritual to make Smith an ally and that his life was not actually in danger. Cite the evidence from source 1 and 2 demonstrating the validity of this interpretation.
2. How does Vaughn (source 2) depict power relations and social hierarchy among the Powhatans? Where does Pocahontas fit within this hierarchy? What messages about Pocahontas do you think Van De Pass (source 5) intended to convey? What is similar about the images' portrayal of Pocahontas?
3. How does Rolfe explain his interest in Pocahontas (source 4)? Explain the point of Rolfe and the historical significance of this source.
4. Assess the reliability of sources 1, 3, and 6 and consider Smith's motive in including them in his Historie. Source 6 purports to record an actual conversation between Pocahontas and Smith. What is the tone of this encounter? Why does the author include Pocahontas's remarks?

AP® DBQ PRACTICE

Imagine the various encounters Pocahontas experienced with the Jamestown Englishmen from her point of view. Reflect on who Pocahontas was as described in these documents—savior and friend, captive, baptized wife, Virginia Company prize, and betrayed ally—and in a brief essay, use Pocahontas's experience to explore the uncertain nature of English-Powhatan relations in the first decade of contact.

TRM Find complete suggested responses in the Teacher's Resource Materials.

AP® SKILLS & PROCESSES

ARGUMENTATION

The **AP® DBQ PRACTICE** prompt asks a sophisticated question some students may need support in understanding and answering. Given the partial, conflicting nature of the evidence regarding English-Powhatan relations, use this prompt as an exercise to teach students how to use diverse historical evidence in a cohesive way to illustrate contradiction and corroboration.

AP® SKILLS & PROCESSES

SOURCING AND SITUATION

This wood engraving, made in 1672, more than fifty years after the successful cultivation of tobacco in the New World, provides an example of a connected Atlantic world. To help students develop an awareness of what it means to understand the historical situation of a document, start by asking about the different types of cash crops from colonies in the New World by the 1670s. Answers will vary, but students are likely to mention tobacco, rice, and sugar. Have students write a draft answer consisting of one or two sentences to the following prompt: In what ways did the mercantilist system of Great Britain further the interdependence of the Atlantic world from 1607–1700?

TRM Find complete suggested responses in the Teacher's Resource Materials.

CHECK FOR UNDERSTANDING

Ask students: **How did Virginia and Maryland compare as tobacco colonies?** *Virginia's location in the midst of Powhatan's confederacy led to severe conflict very quickly, which Maryland largely avoided. Maryland instituted religious toleration to protect its Catholic elites from a growing Protestant majority. However, through their adoption of tobacco, their economies and social structures became very similar.*

TRM Find complete suggested responses in the Teacher's Resource Materials.

VISUAL ACTIVITY

Anti-Smoking Pamphlet, 1672 Coffee and tobacco were often consumed together in coffeehouses, which were still a novelty in 1672. This woodcut comes from a publication that warned against the dangerous pleasures of tobacco (which came from the colonies) and coffee (a Turkish import). The pamphlet warned readers that coffee and tobacco were harmful to their health. But this image goes farther in offering a moral critique of the coffeehouse, where it was said that foreign influences poisoned English culture. Here, a Turkish man in a turban smokes and drinks alongside two English patrons, while an African slave serves coffee. Private Collection/Bridgeman Images.

READING THE IMAGE: Analyze the coat of arms in the center of the image at the top. What is the significance of the black face and the two tobacco pipes? How is the engraver criticizing the coffeehouse as an institution?

MAKING CONNECTIONS: How does this image connect the health dangers of tobacco and coffee with the cultural threat of foreign influences in English life?

Maryland became a refuge for Catholics, who were subject to persecution in England. In 1634, twenty gentlemen, mostly Catholics, and two hundred artisans and laborers, mostly Protestants, established St. Mary's City at the mouth of the Potomac River.

Maryland grew quickly because Baltimore imported many artisans and offered ample lands to wealthy migrants. But political conflict threatened the colony's stability. Disputing Baltimore's powers, settlers elected a representative assembly and insisted on the right to initiate legislation, which Baltimore grudgingly granted. Anti-Catholic agitation by Protestants also threatened his religious goals. To protect his coreligionists, Lord Baltimore persuaded the assembly to enact the Toleration Act (1649), which granted all Christians the right to follow their beliefs and hold church services. In Maryland, as in Virginia, tobacco quickly became the main crop, and that similarity, rather than any religious difference, ultimately made the two colonies very much alike in their economic and social systems.

The Laboratory of the Caribbean

AP® SKILLS & PROCESSES

MAKING CONNECTIONS

How did the development of slavery in Barbados influence the slave system in British North America?

Virginia's experiment with a cash crop that created a land-intensive plantation society ran parallel to developments in the Caribbean, where English, French, and Dutch sailors began looking for a permanent toehold. In 1624, a small English party under the command of Sir Thomas Warner established a settlement on St. Christopher (St. Kitts). A year later, Warner allowed a French group to settle the other end of the island so they could better defend their position from the Spanish. Within a few years, the English and French colonists on St. Kitts had driven the native Caribs from the island, weathered a Spanish attack, and created a common set of bylaws for mutual occupation of the island.

After St. Kitts, a dozen or so colonies were founded in the Lesser Antilles, including the French islands of Martinique, Guadeloupe, and St. Bart's; the English outposts of Nevis, Antigua, Montserrat, Anguilla, Tortola, and Barbados; and the Dutch colony of St. Eustatius. In 1655, an English fleet captured the Spanish island of Jamaica — one of the large islands of the Greater Antilles — and opened it to settlement as well. A few of these islands were unpopulated before Europeans settled there; elsewhere, native populations were displaced, and often wiped out, within a decade or so. Only on the largest islands did native populations hold out longer.

Why were these island colonies attractive? Because colonists could experiment with a wide variety of cash crops, including tobacco, indigo, cotton, cacao, and ginger. Beginning in the 1640s — and drawing on the example of Brazil — planters on many of the islands shifted to sugar cultivation. Where conditions were right, as they were in Barbados, Jamaica, Nevis, and Martinique, these colonies were soon producing substantial crops of sugar and, as a consequence, claimed some of the world's most valuable real estate. Daily life in plantation colonies was often miserable, but investors grew rich on the backs of their laborers.

A Sugar Mill in the French West Indies, 1655 Making sugar required both hard labor and considerable expertise. Field slaves labored strenuously in the hot tropical sun to cut the sugarcane and carry or cart it to an oxen- or wind-powered mill, where it was pressed to yield the juice. Then skilled slave artisans took over. They carefully heated the juice and, at the proper moment, added ingredients that granulated the sugar and separated it from the molasses, which was later distilled into rum. Sarin Images/Granger, NYC.

Plantation Life

In North America and the Caribbean, plantations were initially small **freeholds**, farms of 30 to 50 acres owned and farmed by families or male partners. But the logic of plantation agriculture soon encouraged consolidation: large planters engrossed as much land as they could and experimented with new forms of labor discipline that maximized their control over production. In Virginia, the **headright system** guaranteed 50 acres of land to anyone who paid the passage of a new immigrant to the colony; thus, by buying additional indentured servants and slaves, the colony's largest planters also amassed ever-greater claims to land.

European demand for tobacco set off a forty-year economic boom in the Chesapeake. "All our riches for the present do consist in tobacco," a planter remarked in 1630. Exports rose from 3 million pounds in 1640 to 10 million pounds in 1660. After 1650, wealthy migrants from gentry or noble families established large estates along the coastal rivers, then acquired English indentured servants and enslaved Africans to work their lands. At about the same time, the switch to sugar production in Barbados caused the price of land there to quadruple, driving small landowners out.

For rich and poor alike, life in the plantation colonies of North America and the Caribbean was harsh. The scarcity of towns deprived settlers of community (Map 2.4). Families were equally scarce because there were few women, and marriages often ended with the early death of a spouse. Pregnant women were especially vulnerable to malaria, spread by mosquitoes that flourished in tropical and subtropical climates (see "Comparing Interpretations," p. 54). Many mothers died after bearing a first or second child, so orphaned children (along with unmarried young men) formed a large segment of the society. Sixty percent of the children born in Middlesex County, Virginia, before 1680 lost one or both parents before they were thirteen. Death was pervasive. Although 15,000 English migrants arrived in Virginia between

freeholds
Land owned in its entirety, without feudal dues or landlord obligations. Freeholders had the legal right to improve, transfer, or sell their landed property.

headright system
A system of land distribution, pioneered in Virginia and used in several other colonies, that granted land — usually 50 acres — to anyone who paid the passage of a new arrival. By this means, large planters amassed huge landholdings as they imported large numbers of servants and slaves.

AP® SKILLS & PROCESSES

COMPARISON

How were the motivations and characteristics of the social classes in the plantation colonies distinguished?

TEACHING STRATEGY

Use the image of the sugar mill in the French West Indies to help students understand the labor-intensive nature of sugar production. Ask students: **How does this image convey the notion that sugar production looked like "Industrial Revolution–era factories," as the text describes? What were the implications of this type of enterprise for planters and for workers?** *Sugar production required complex, specialized equipment and relied on division of labor, with different workers concentrating on individual tasks. The equipment costs and the scale of labor indicate that planters needed wealth or investors to begin such an operation. Work was difficult and dangerous, especially in tropical conditions.*

CHECK FOR UNDERSTANDING

Ask students: **What were the English Caribbean colonies like?** *Most experimented with different cash crops. Those that could successfully grow sugar did so, making landowners there very wealthy through the exploitation of labor.*

AP® THEME

GEO: Geography and the Environment; WXT: Work, Exchange, and Technology

Ask students to explore the relationship between climate and economy and to compare the nature of plantation economies and the labor systems they created. *Sugar crops require year-round warm weather and cannot be cultivated as far north as Virginia, otherwise Virginia planters might have shifted to this crop, just as planters in the Caribbean shifted from tobacco to sugar because it was more lucrative. But the regions did have some similarities, with both economies coming to be characterized by race-based slavery.*

TRM Find complete suggested responses in the Teacher's Resource Materials.

TEACHING STRATEGY

Prompt students to complete **Handout 2.2 — Thematic Analysis: Introduction of Tobacco in the Chesapeake Colonies (TRM)**. Then ask them to add at least two specific pieces of evidence related to the impact of the introduction of tobacco in the Chesapeake, such as a key term, event, or person's name, etc. Once students have completed their Thematic Analysis, recreate the diagram on the board (or project the handout) and ask students to volunteer to add specific points with each theme to guide them in a discussion of the impact of tobacco on the Chesapeake colonies.

Alternatively, use **Handout 2.2** to facilitate collaborative discussion by dividing students into groups and assigning each group one theme. Ask each group to focus exclusively on the theme they have been assigned in order to identify specific effects of tobacco on the Chesapeake. After each group has completed their assigned theme, share the ideas on the board to generate a whole class discussion.

TRM Find **Handout 2.2 — Thematic Analysis: Introduction of Tobacco in the Chesapeake Colonies** in the Teacher's Resource Materials.

AP® SKILLS & PROCESSES

ANALYZING HISTORICAL EVIDENCE

The **AP® COMPARING INTERPRETATIONS** feature provides students with an opportunity to analyze two diverse historical interpretations by scholars focusing on a similar subject — climate's effect on colonization in different parts of North America. To analyze and compare these arguments, students should recognize that the authors are not in direct disagreement with each other because they focus on different eras, different regions with diverse climates, and different people groups. The point of comparison is the pattern of new climate situations and the way people groups responded to them.

AP® COMPARING INTERPRETATIONS

What Role Did Climate and Ecology Play in American Colonization?

Colonization brought Europeans into contact with extreme environments in the Americas, ranging from the very cold arctic to the very hot tropics. In all but the most obvious cases, however, we usually tell the stories of colonization without reference to climate and ecology; we focus on what people intended to do, without fully considering the ways in which nature defeated or altered their purposes. Recently, historians have paid more sustained attention to these forces. Colonization took place in the era of the Little Ice Age, when many parts of the globe were experiencing the coldest temperatures and most erratic weather in hundreds, if not thousands, of years. Because they assumed that climate followed latitude, colonial promoters expected much of North America to be warmer than it was; the extreme cold of the Little Ice Age only magnified their miscalculation. In the Caribbean, Europeans had no real understanding of the tropical diseases that largely determined who would live and who would die. The roles of climate and ecology — the power of nonhuman forces in human history — are coming into focus through the work of scholars like Sam White and John McNeill, whose books are briefly excerpted here.

SAM WHITE

A Cold Welcome

Source: Sam White, *A Cold Welcome: The Little Ice Age and Europe's Encounter with North America* (Cambridge, MA: Harvard University Press, 2017), 9–11, 19, 21–23.

As historian Karen Kupperman has put it, Europeans crossing the Atlantic faced a "puzzle of the American climate." It was not simply that the climate of the New World was different from that of Europe, or that European settlers had first to come to grips with a novel environment. It was that the climate of North America defied European preconceptions handed down across the centuries from classical Greece and Rome.

In the work of the geographer Ptolemy (ca. 90-168 CE), still influential in early modern Europe, climate *was* latitude. The words were more or less synonymous. . . . In the Ptolemaic vision, as it was simplified and popularized in Renaissance geography, the world was divided by parallel concentric bands: from a "frozen zone" at the poles to a dry, burning "torrid zone" in the tropics, with "temperate zones" in between. It was a view of climates taken from ancient Greek and Roman experiences of northern Europe, the Sahara, and the Mediterranean, but one that proved entirely misleading when extended across the Atlantic. . . .

Even the briefest glance at a map of the Atlantic reveals the dangers of this approach. Today it is common to forget just how far north most of Europe lies compared to the populous parts of America and Canada. Britain is well above the continental United States. Even Paris lies north of Quebec City. The Mediterranean, from southern France to northern Tunisia, lines up with the coast from Maine to North Carolina. Nevertheless, given prevailing ideas about latitude and climate, it was only natural for educated Europeans to assume that today's eastern United States would grow the crops of Italy or Israel and that Canada might have the mild winters of France. . . .

When severe weather was encountered during brief expeditions, the promoters of colonization could always find ways to write it off as an aberration, insisting that the true climates of North America were similar to those along the same latitudes across the Atlantic. The argument may have been especially persuasive during the Little Ice Age, an era of climate instability and change.

For many readers, the expression "Little Ice Age" suggests an age of perpetual cold and human misery, stretching imprecisely from the late Middle Ages to the dawn of the industrial age. . . . [B]reakthroughs in climate reconstruction make it clear that the Little Ice Age was in reality more than one phenomenon, with more than one cause. Over several millennia, slight changes in the earth's orbit around the sun very slowly reduced the intensity of solar radiation reaching the Northern Hemisphere, leading to the very slow cooling of summer temperatures. . . . Medium- and short-term events changed climate more dramatically on the scale of decades or years. . . .

Such phenomena happened more or less independently of one another. . . . For some decades, even generations,

1622 and 1640, the population rose only from 2,000 to 8,000. It was even harsher in the islands, where yellow fever epidemics killed indiscriminately. On Barbados, burials outnumbered baptisms in the second half of the seventeenth century by 4 to 1.

Indentured Servitude Still, the prospect of owning land continued to lure settlers. By 1700, more than 100,000 English migrants had come to Virginia and Maryland and more than 200,000 had migrated to the islands of the West Indies, principally to Barbados; the vast majority to both destinations traveled as indentured servants. They took a huge risk in emigrating, but a growing population and shrinking temperatures in Europe and North America were not much different than in the early twentieth century. At other times, when these oscillations and forcings aligned, the impact was considerable.

Moreover, the climate data are not the whole story. What we call the Little Ice Age was as much a human event as an atmospheric one. . . . It mattered how people experienced and perceived the climate, and how it influenced their history. . . . The Little Ice Age played a major role in Europe's encounter with North America not because the climate was unrelentingly cold but because it was variable and unpredictable, and Europe's colonial enterprises were often at their most vulnerable when the climate was most extreme. . . .

Most contemporaries did not notice climatic change per se. They felt the greater frequency and intensity of weather extremes and disasters. . . . Many people during the Little Ice Age perceived the disruption of the seasons as divine warnings or punishments.

JOHN R. McNEILL

Mosquito Empires

SOURCE: John R. McNeill, *Mosquito Empires: Ecology and War in the Greater Caribbean, 1620–1914* (New York: Cambridge University Press, 2010), 1–3.

In 1727, the British Vice-Admiral Francis Hosier sailed with a naval squadron to the shores of what is now Colombia and Panama. His superiors had instructed him to blockade this coast in hopes of preventing a Spanish treasure fleet laden with South American silver from reaching Spain. Yellow fever broke out on Hosier's ships while they were cruising off Portobelo, killing almost the entire crew. Hosier soon scraped together another crew from Jamaica and returned to his duty, whereupon yellow fever killed the second crew along with the Vice-Admiral. Some 4,000 sailors died without a shot fired. Fourteen years later, Admiral Edward Vernon brought an amphibious strike force of about 29,000 men to the Colombia coast to besiege the Spanish stronghold of Cartagena. Within a few months 22,000 were dead, almost all from diseases, mainly yellow fever but probably malaria as well. The population of the Spanish colonies remained unaffected, and Spain's grip on its American empire remained firm.

The enormous mortality of these expeditions and many more like them was remarkably one-sided. Yellow fever and malaria attacked some people much more often than others, which had political consequences. Although always evolving, the ecological conditions that prevailed in the Greater Caribbean after the 1640s reliably included these twin killers. Strictly speaking, they did not determine the outcomes of struggles for power, but they governed the probabilities of success and failure in military expeditions and settlement schemes. . . .

. . . [Q]uests for wealth and power changed ecologies in the Greater Caribbean, and . . . ecological changes in turn shaped the fortunes of empire, war, and revolution in the years between 1620 and 1914. By "Greater Caribbean" I mean the Atlantic coastal regions of South, Central, and North America, as well as the Caribbean islands themselves, that in the course of the seventeenth and eighteenth centuries became plantation zones: from Surinam to the Chesapeake. [This] perspective . . . takes into account nature — viruses, plasmodia, mosquitoes, monkeys, swamps — as well as humankind in making political history. . . .

The geopolitical struggles of the Greater Caribbean were fought out mainly in landscapes undergoing rapid environmental change, replete with deforestation, soil erosion, and the installation of plantation agro-ecosystems based on crops such as sugar and rice. The unstable evolving ecologies of the Greater Caribbean provided ideal incubators for the species of mosquitoes that carry two of humankind's most lethal diseases, yellow fever and malaria. . . . Ecological change resulting from the establishment of a plantation economy improved breeding and feeding conditions for both mosquito species, helping them become key actors in the geopolitical struggles of the early modern Atlantic world. . . .

AP® SHORT ANSWER PRACTICE

1. White and McNeill both suggest that natural forces played an independent role in shaping historical events. What forces, specifically, does each historian refer to? Identify and describe the claim of each source.
2. White refers to climate in his excerpt, while McNeill refers to ecology. How were these two aspects of the natural world different from each other? Support your reasoning with evidence from each source.
3. Chapter 2 describes colonization as a series of experiments. What role did the natural world play in determining the limits and outcomes of colonial experimentation? Make a historically defensible claim.

economic opportunity in England drove many people, especially unskilled laborers, to take this desperate step. Shipping registers from the English port of Bristol reveal the backgrounds of 5,000 servants embarking for the Chesapeake. Three-quarters were young men. They came to Bristol searching for work; once there, merchants persuaded them to sign contracts to labor in America. **Indentured servitude** contracts bound the men — and the quarter who were women — to work for a master for four or five years, after which they would be free to marry and work for themselves.

For merchants, servants were valuable cargo: their contracts fetched high prices from Chesapeake and West Indian planters. For the plantation owners, indentured

indentured servitude
System in which workers contracted for service for a specified period. In exchange for agreeing to work for four or five years (or more) without wages in the colonies, indentured workers received passage across the Atlantic, room and board, and status as a free person at the end of the contract period.

TRM Find complete suggested responses in the Teacher's Resource Materials.

AP® SKILLS & PROCESSES

DEVELOPMENTS AND PROCESSES

Especially early in the year, students need ways to formulate understandings of discrete historical information that will be harnessed to advance interpretations to free response questions. Enslavement is a topic central to the development of the British Empire, and, by extension, the broader Atlantic world. Consider having students differentiate among the following types of forced labor: chattel slavery, indentured servitude, and the enslavement of American Indians. Even though this is strictly focused on understanding historical developments, reinforce to students that it is a necessary component of successful interpretations.

AP® THEME

GEO: Geography and the Environment; MIG: Migration and Settlement

Use **MAP 2.4** to help students understand the English settlement pattern in Virginia, which was a function of the geography of the Chesapeake Bay itself with its many rivers and inlets, as well as of the economy it adopted, where large plantations made for dispersed settlements and access to waterfront property facilitated shipping tobacco to market.

TEACHING STRATEGY

"The Terrible Transformation" Web site page, available as part of PBS's series *Africans in America*, explains indentured servitude in theory and practice, the reasons for the shift from servitude to slavery, and the social fluidity that existed for blacks before this transition. The teacher's companion site provides a series of activities, lesson ideas, and other resources, including an extensive list of related primary sources. Access this resource by searching "PBS Terrible Transformation."

AP® SKILLS & PROCESSES

COMPARISON

Use the **COMPARISON** question to help students analyze how slavery and indentured servitude were similar and different. Help students see the similarities and differences more clearly by having them create a table describing the situation and characteristics of four different groups: indentured servants and slaves in the Chesapeake as well as in the Caribbean. Once students learn about indentured servitude, they tend to minimize its differences with slavery, so it is important to emphasize the distinctions in status and condition.

TRM Find complete suggested responses in the Teacher's Resource Materials.

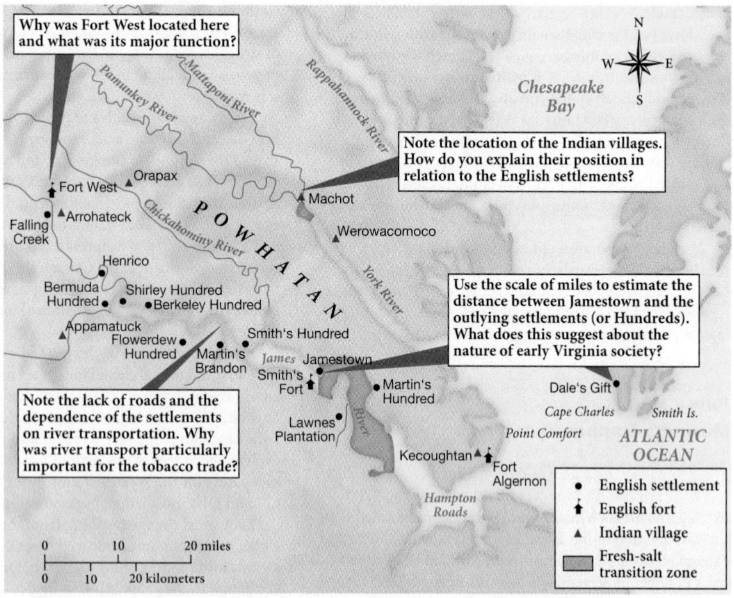

MAP 2.4 River Plantations in Virginia, c. 1640
The first migrants settled in widely dispersed plantations along the James River, a settlement pattern promoted by the tobacco economy. From their riverfront plantations wealthy planter-merchants could easily load heavy hogsheads of tobacco onto oceangoing ships and offload supplies that they then sold to smallholding planters. Consequently, few substantial towns or trading centers developed in the Chesapeake region.

servants were a bargain if they survived the voyage and their first year in a harsh new disease environment, a process called "seasoning." During the Chesapeake's tobacco boom, a male servant could produce five times his purchase price in a single year. To maximize their gains, many masters ruthlessly exploited servants, forcing them to work long hours, beating them without cause, and withholding permission to marry. If servants ran away or became pregnant, masters went to court to increase the term of their service. Female servants were especially vulnerable to abuse. A Virginia law of 1692 stated that "dissolute masters have gotten their maids with child; and yet claim the benefit of their service." In such cases, the law stipulated that the churchwardens of the parish would step in to manage the woman's remaining term of service. Planters got rid of uncooperative servants by selling their contracts. In Virginia, an Englishman remarked in disgust that "servants were sold up and down like horses."

AP® SKILLS & PROCESSES
COMPARISON
How were the experiences of indentured servants and slaves in the Chesapeake and the Caribbean similar? How were they different?

Few indentured servants escaped poverty. In the Chesapeake, half the men died before completing the term of their contract, and another quarter remained landless. Only one-quarter achieved their quest for property and respectability. Female servants generally fared better. Because men had grown "very sensible of the Misfortune of Wanting Wives," many propertied planters married female servants. Thus a few — very fortunate — men and women escaped early death or a life of landless poverty.

African Laborers The rigors of indentured servitude paled before the brutality that accompanied the large-scale shift to African slave labor. In Barbados and the other English islands, deadly working conditions devoured laborers, and the supply of indentured servants quickly became inadequate to planters' needs. By 1690, blacks

AP® THEME

SOC: Social Structures

The explanation of the shift to slavery provides an opportunity to talk about race as a social construct that developed particular associations and legal restrictions. Students may tend to assume that racism preceded enslavement, but the dominant pattern seems to have developed in the opposite direction: the demand for slaves created a need for a reliable, identifiable, easily controlled workforce, which made a racialized system attractive.

outnumbered whites on Barbados nearly 3 to 1, and white slave owners were developing a code of force and terror to keep sugar flowing and maintain control of the black majority that surrounded them. The first comprehensive slave legislation for the island, adopted in 1661, was called an "Act for the better ordering and governing of Negroes."

In the Chesapeake, the shift to slave labor was more gradual. In 1619, John Rolfe noted that "a Dutch man of warre . . . sold us twenty Negars" — slaves originally shipped by the Portuguese from the port of Luanda in Angola. For a generation, the number of Africans remained small. About 400 Africans lived in the Chesapeake colonies in 1649, just 2 percent of the population. By 1670, that figure had reached 5 percent. Most Africans served their English masters for life. However, since English common law did not acknowledge chattel slavery, it was possible for some Africans to escape bondage. Some were freed as a result of Christian baptism; some purchased their freedom from their owners; some — like Elizabeth Key, whose story was related at the beginning of the chapter — won their freedom in the courts. Once free, some ambitious Africans became landowners and purchased slaves or the labor contracts of English servants for themselves.

AP® EXAM TIP

Understanding the origins of the slave trade system in the "Atlantic World" is critical to success on the AP® Exam.

Social mobility for Africans ended in the 1660s with the collapse of the tobacco boom and the increasing political power of the gentry. Tobacco had once sold for 30 pence a pound; now it fetched less than one-tenth of that. The "low price of Tobacco requires it should bee made as cheap as possible," declared Virginia planter-politician Nicholas Spencer, and "blacks can make it cheaper than whites." As they imported more African workers, the English-born political elite grew more race-conscious. Increasingly, Spencer and other leading legislators distinguished English from African residents by color (white-black) rather than by religion (Christian-pagan). By 1671, the Virginia House of Burgesses had forbidden Africans to own guns or join the militia. It also barred them — "tho baptized and enjoying their own Freedom" — from owning English servants. Being black was increasingly a mark of inferior legal status, and slavery was fast becoming a permanent and hereditary condition. As an English clergyman observed, "These two words, Negro and Slave had by custom grown Homogeneous and convertible."

NEO-EUROPEAN COLONIES

What conditions were necessary to establish successful neo-European colonies?

While Mesoamerica and the Andes emerged at the heart of a tribute-based empire in Latin America, and tropical and subtropical environments were transformed into plantation societies, a series of colonies that more closely replicated European patterns of economic and social organization developed in the temperate zone along North America's Atlantic coast. Dutch, French, and English sailors probed the continent's northern coastline, initially searching for a Northwest Passage through the continent to Asia. Gradually, they developed an interest in the region on its own terms. They traded for furs with coastal Native American populations, fished for cod on the Grand Banks off the coast of Newfoundland, and established freehold family farms and larger manors where they reproduced European patterns of agricultural life. Many migrants also came with aspirations to create godly communities, places of refuge where they could put religious ideals into practice. New France, New Netherland, and New England were the three pillars of neo-European colonization in the early seventeenth century.

AP® EXAM TIP

Take good notes that compare the settlements in New France, New Netherland, and New England.

New France

In the 1530s, Jacques Cartier ventured up the St. Lawrence River and claimed it for France. Cartier's claim to the St. Lawrence languished for three-quarters of a century, but in 1608 Samuel de Champlain returned and founded the fur-trading post of

AP® APPLY THE TIP

Provide students with **Handout 2.3 — Comparison: European Settlements in North America (TRM)** and ask them to consider key characteristics of the settlers in each region and the role of the "mother country" in each settlement. Once students have completed the chart, they should discuss which European nation best illustrates the system of mercantilism in these settlements.

TRM Find **Handout 2.3 — Comparison: European Settlements in North America** in the Teacher's Resource Materials.

TEACHING STRATEGY

The *New France, New Horizons* online exhibition offers dozens of high-quality primary sources and the context related to the exploration and settlement of New France, and relations between colonists and Native peoples. Search "New France, New Horizons" to access the exhibition.

The Fur Trade Luxuriant pelts like ermine and silver fox were always desirable, but the humble beaver dominated the early trade between Europeans and Indians in the Northeast. It had thick, coarse hair, but beneath that outer layer was soft "underfur." Those fine hairs were covered in microscopic barbs that allowed them to mat into a dense mass. European hatmakers pressed this fur into felt so strong and pliable that even broad-brimmed hats would hold their shape. As such hats became fashionable in Europe and the colonies, beavers were hunted to near-extinction in North America. Library and Archives Canada/NLC-3269.

Quebec. Trade with the Cree-speaking Montagnais; Algonquian-speaking Micmacs, Ottawas, and Ojibwas; and Iroquois-speaking Hurons gave the French access to furs — mink, otter, and beaver — that were in great demand in Europe. To secure plush beaver pelts from the Hurons, who controlled trade north of the Great Lakes, Champlain provided them with manufactured goods. Selling pelts, an Indian told a French priest, "makes kettles, hatchets, swords, knives, bread." It also made guns, which Champlain sold to the Hurons.

The Hurons also became the first focus of French Catholic missionary activity. Hundreds of priests, most of them Jesuits, fanned out to live in Indian communities. They mastered Indian languages and came to understand, and sometimes respect, Indian values. Many Native peoples initially welcomed the French "Black Robes" as spiritually powerful beings, but when prayers to the Christian god did not protect them from disease, the Indians grew skeptical. A Peoria chief charged that a priest's "fables are good only in his own country; we have our own [beliefs], which do not make us die as his do." When a drought struck, Indians blamed the missionaries. "If you cannot make rain, they speak of nothing less than making away with you," lamented one Jesuit.

Although New France became an expansive center of fur trading and missionary work, it languished as a farming settlement. In 1662, King Louis XIV (r. 1643–1714) turned New France into a royal colony and subsidized the migration of indentured servants. French servants labored under contract for three years, received a salary, and could eventually lease a farm — far more generous terms than those for indentured servants in the English colonies.

Nonetheless, few people moved to New France, a cold and forbidding country "at the end of the world," as one migrant put it. And some state policies discouraged migration. Louis XIV drafted tens of thousands of men into military service and barred Huguenots (French Calvinist Protestants) from migrating to New France, fearing they might win converts and take control of the colony. Moreover, the French legal system gave peasants strong rights to their village lands, whereas migrants to New France faced an oppressive, aristocracy- and church-dominated feudal system. In the village of Saint Ours in Quebec, for example, peasants paid 45 percent of their wheat crop to nobles and the Catholic Church. By 1698, only 15,200 Europeans lived in New France, compared to 100,000 in England's North American colonies.

Despite this small population, France eventually claimed a vast inland arc, from the St. Lawrence Valley through the Great Lakes and down the course of the Ohio and Mississippi rivers. Explorers and fur traders drove this expansion. In 1673, Jacques Marquette reached the Mississippi River in present-day Wisconsin; then, in 1681, Robert de La Salle traveled down the majestic river to the Gulf of Mexico. To honor Louis XIV, La Salle named the region Louisiana. By 1718, French merchants had founded the port of New Orleans at the mouth of the Mississippi. Eventually a network of about two dozen forts grew up around the Great Lakes and along the Mississippi. Soldiers and missionaries used them as bases of operations, while Indians, traders, and their métis (mixed-race) offspring created trading communities alongside them.

AP® SKILLS & PROCESSES

DEVELOPMENTS AND PROCESSES

Even though the focus of this chapter includes the processes by which Europeans established colonies in the New World, American Indians were not passive historical actors in this development. Instead, American Indians such as the Iroquois and Huron, in addition to many more, negotiated, accommodated, and resisted both European and other indigenous nations. Students can select one American Indian group and explain how they successfully negotiated or resisted European encroachment.

CHECK FOR UNDERSTANDING

Ask students: **What features characterized New France?** *Established by fur traders and Catholic missionaries, New France was slow to grow into a settler colony, as the cold climate discouraged migrants. The massive land it claimed was thinly populated by French colonists.*

New Netherland

By 1600, Amsterdam had become the financial and commercial hub of northern Europe, and Dutch financiers dominated the European banking, insurance, and textile industries. Dutch merchants owned more ships and employed more sailors than did the combined fleets of England, France, and Spain. Indeed, the Dutch managed much of the world's commerce. During their struggle for independence from Spain and Portugal (ruled by Spanish monarchs, 1580–1640), the Dutch seized Portuguese forts in Africa and Indonesia and sugar plantations in Brazil. These conquests gave the Dutch control of the Atlantic trade in slaves and sugar and the Indian Ocean commerce in East Indian spices and Chinese silks and ceramics (Map 2.5).

In 1609, Dutch merchants sent the English mariner Henry Hudson to locate a navigable route to the riches of the East Indies. What he found as he probed the rivers of northeast America was a fur bonanza. Following Hudson's exploration of the river

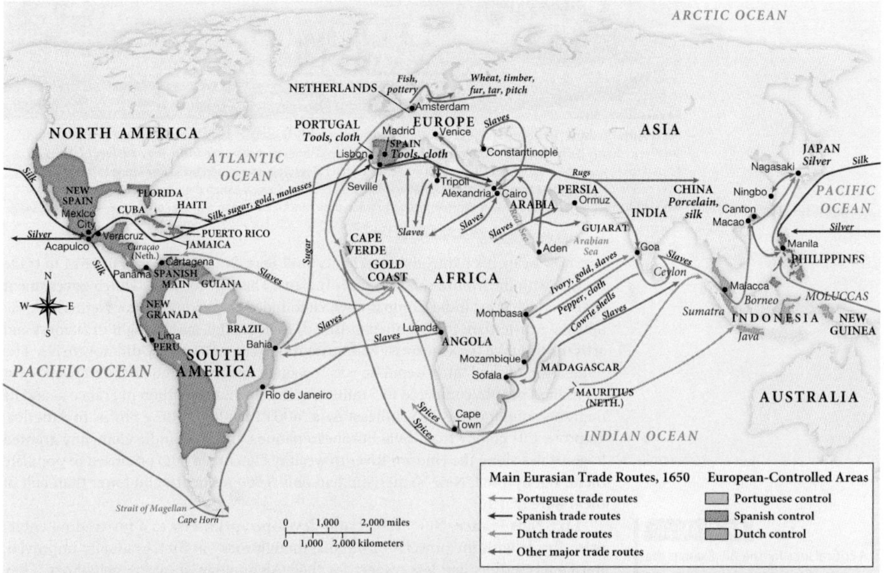

MAPPING THE PAST

MAP 2.5 The Eurasian Trade System and European Spheres of Influence, 1650

Between 1550 and 1650, Spanish, Portuguese, and Dutch merchants took control of the maritime trade routes between Europe and India, Indonesia, and China. They also created two new trading connections. The South Atlantic System carried slaves, sugar, and manufactured goods between Europe, Africa, and the valuable plantation settlements in Brazil and the Caribbean islands. And a transpacific trade carried Spanish American silver to China in exchange for silks, ceramics, and other manufactures. (To trace long-term changes in trade and empires, see Map 1.4 on p. 31 and Map 5.1 on p. 147.)

ANALYZING THE MAP: What were the primary commodities traded by the Portuguese, Spanish, and Dutch traders? How did trade with the Americas connect to trade with Asia?

MAKING CONNECTIONS: Compare this map to Map 2.3 (p. 49). Why are the French, English, and Dutch colonies depicted in Map 2.3 absent from this map of the Eurasian trade system?

AP® THEME

WXT: Work, Exchange, and Technology

Use **MAP 2.5** to illustrate the complex trade network driven by acquiring, producing, and exporting commodities, in which North and South America were included. Discuss with students how this map makes clear that the Atlantic economy was part of a larger global economy.

TRM Find complete suggested responses in the Teacher's Resource Materials.

TEACHING STRATEGY

This image of New Amsterdam provides an opportunity to discuss the potential unreliability of primary sources. Ask students: **How is the image "fictionalized"? Why might the artist have wanted to "reassure the viewer that all was well in the American colony"?** *It depicts a large, thriving village with strong defenses. It portrays friendly relations with Native Americans, despite the vicious warfare between the Dutch and local Algonquins. The artist may have wanted to reassure investors or prospective investors that New Amsterdam was a worthwhile venture, where opportunities for wealth outweighed possible dangers.*

AP® THEME

WOR: America in the World

Point out to students that Native Americans were not simply victims of French, Dutch, and English colonies, but fostered alliances with them, often against other Indian peoples.

CHECK FOR UNDERSTANDING

Ask students: **How did New Netherland compare with New France?** *Like New France, New Netherland was founded largely as a fur-trading colony and it was slow to grow as a settler colony. Unlike New France, however, its commercial founders had little interest in evangelizing Indians. New France's lifespan was much more limited, as it was taken over by the English less than a half-century after it was founded.*

New Amsterdam This early image of New Amsterdam shows a fictionalized scene. Although New Netherland was small and poorly defended, with nothing more than wooden palisades to protect the town, the engraver of this print hoped to reassure the viewer that all was well in the American colony. It is dominated by a large stone fort that appears to conform to the highest standards of European military engineering. Several Dutch merchant vessels ride at anchor, while Indians approach the shore in canoes hoping to trade their furs for European manufactures. Culture Club/Getty Images.

that now bears his name, the merchants built Fort Orange (Albany) in 1614 to trade for furs with the Munsee and Iroquois Indians. Then, in 1621, the Dutch government chartered the West India Company, which founded the colony of New Netherland, set up New Amsterdam (on Manhattan Island) as its capital, and brought in farmers and artisans to make the enterprise self-sustaining. The new colony did not thrive. The population of the Dutch Republic was too small to support much emigration — just 1.5 million people, compared to 5 million in Britain and 20 million in France — and its migrants sought riches in Southeast Asia rather than fur-trading profits in America. To protect its colony from rival European nations, the West India Company granted huge estates along the Hudson River to wealthy Dutchmen who promised to populate them. But by 1664, New Netherland had only 5,000 residents, and fewer than half of them were Dutch.

AP® EXAM TIP

A critical idea for the AP® Exam is the role of European rivals in altering conflicts between Native American groups in North America.

Like New France, New Netherland developed primarily as a fur-trading enterprise. Trade with the powerful Iroquois, though rocky at first, gradually improved. But Dutch settlers had less respect for their Algonquian-speaking neighbors. They seized prime farming land and disrupted Native American trade. In response, in 1643 the Algonquians launched attacks that nearly destroyed the colony. "Almost every place is abandoned," a settler lamented, "whilst the Indians daily threaten to overwhelm us." To defeat the Algonquians, the Dutch waged vicious warfare — maiming, burning, and killing hundreds of men, women, and children — and formed an alliance with the Mohawks, who were no less brutal. The grim progression of Euro-Indian relations — an uneasy welcome, followed by rising tensions and war — afflicted even the Dutch, who had only limited designs on Indians' lands, sent no missionaries to convert them, and were looking primarily for trading partners.

After the crippling Indian war, the West India Company ignored New Netherland and expanded its profitable trade in African slaves and Brazilian sugar. In New Amsterdam, Governor Peter Stuyvesant ruled in an authoritarian fashion, rejecting demands for a representative system of government and alienating the colony's diverse Dutch, English, and Swedish residents. Consequently, the residents of New Netherland offered little resistance when England invaded the colony in 1664. New Netherland became New York and fell under English control.

AP® SKILLS & PROCESSES

MAKING CONNECTIONS

Why did New France and New Netherland struggle to attract colonists?

The Rise of the Iroquois

Like other Native groups decimated by European diseases and warfare, the Five Nations of the Iroquois suffered as a result of colonization, but they were able to capitalize on their strategic location in central New York to dominate the region between the French and Dutch colonies. Obtaining guns and goods from Dutch merchants at Fort Orange, Iroquois warriors inflicted terror on their neighbors. Partly in response to a virulent smallpox epidemic in 1633, which cut their number by one-third, and subsequent waves of epidemic disease, the Five Nations waged a series of devastating wars against other Iroquoian-speaking neighbors, including the Hurons (1649), Neutrals (1651), Eries (1657), and Susquehannocks (1660). Warriors razed villages and killed many residents, but they also took many captives back to their own communities, where they were adopted to help restore the Five Nations' declining numbers. The conquered Hurons ceased to exist as a distinct people; survivors trekked westward with displaced Algonquian peoples and formed a new nation, the Wyandots. Iroquois warriors pressed still farther — eastward into New England, south to the Carolinas, north to Quebec, and west via the Great Lakes to the Mississippi —dominating Indian groups along the way. Collectively known as the Beaver Wars, these Iroquois campaigns dramatically altered the map of northeastern North America.

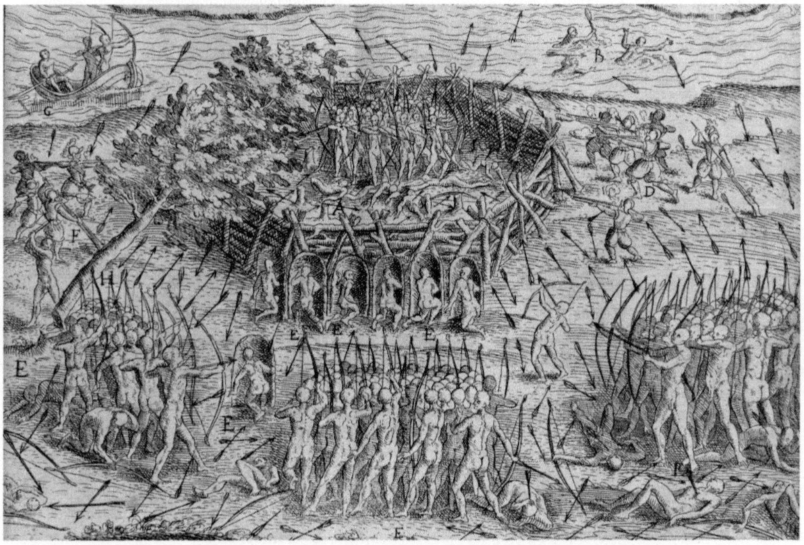

Attack on a Mohawk Fort, 1610 The Iroquois were at odds with New France and its Algonquian-speaking allies from the earliest years of French colonization. In this image, Samuel de Champlain and five French soldiers (on the upper right) assist a party of Montagnais, Algonquin, and Huron warriors in an attack on a Mohawk fort. Iroquois towns were so well fortified that Europeans commonly referred to them as "castles," but in this case Champlain and his allies overran the fort, killing nearly a hundred Mohawk warriors and taking more than a dozen captives. Encounters like this one laid the foundation for the prolonged warfare of the later seventeenth century. Beinecke Rare Book and Manuscript Library, Yale University.

AP® SKILLS & PROCESSES

MAKING CONNECTIONS

Use the **MAKING CONNECTIONS** question to challenge students' ability to make inferences about causation. Explain to students that this is a somewhat unusual causation question that essentially asks them to identify the factors that explain why something *failed* to happen. Besides comparing New France and New Netherland, this question makes an implicit comparison with the colonies that *did* succeed in attracting settlers. Extend this prompt by asking students to directly compare the factors that drew settlers to the English colonies and how those factors differed in the French and Dutch colonies.

TRM Find complete suggested responses in the Teacher's Resource Materials.

TEACHING STRATEGY

Divide students into small groups and assign each group to investigate either the Beaver Wars or the Chickasaw War, and create an illustration (in the tradition of Theodore de Bry) that shows the impact of European rivalries on conflicts between Native American groups. This illustration should emphasize the role of Europeans in changing the conflicts in North America. Give students a time limit for their research and illustration. When time is up, ask all groups to post their illustrations on the board (or somewhere everyone can easily see them). Ask students to analyze the visual representations and draw conclusions about the impact of Europeans on Native American conflicts. As a summary activity, ask students to choose an illustration they did not draw and write a causation argument.

Many Iroquois raids came at the expense of French-allied Algonquian Indians, and in the 1660s New France committed to all-out war against the Iroquois. In 1667, the Mohawks were the last of the Five Nations to admit defeat. As part of the peace settlement, the Five Nations accepted Jesuit missionaries into their communities. A minority of Iroquois — perhaps 20 percent of the population — converted to Catholicism and moved to the St. Lawrence Valley, where they settled in mission communities near Montreal (where their descendants still live today).

The Iroquois who remained in New York did not collapse, however. Forging a new alliance with the Englishmen who had taken over New Netherland, they would continue to be a dominant force in the politics of the Northeast for generations to come.

AP® THEME

SOC: Social Structures

Point out to students that the conversion of a significant minority of the Iroquois to Catholicism, through the tenacious efforts of Jesuit missionaries, represented a significant shift in their identity as a people.

CHECK FOR UNDERSTANDING

Ask students: **What were the causes and effects of the rise of the Iroquois?** *The Iroquois took advantage of their location between French and Dutch settlements to acquire goods and weapons that allowed them to expand their territory dramatically, defeating a number of other tribes along the way. New France eventually launched a war against them, which significantly reduced their power; in response, they began to ally with the English.*

New England

AP® EXAM TIP

Understanding conflicts between the interests of European governments and the colonists they sent to the New World is a key idea for the AP® Exam.

In 1620, 102 English Protestants landed at a place they called Plymouth, near Cape Cod. A decade later, a much larger group began to arrive just north of Plymouth, in the newly chartered Massachusetts Bay Colony. By 1640, the region had attracted more than 20,000 migrants. Unlike the early arrivals in Virginia and Barbados, these were not parties of young male adventurers seeking their fortunes or bound to labor for someone else. They came in family groups to create communities like the ones they left behind, except that they intended to establish them according to Protestant principles, as John Calvin had done in Geneva. Their numbers were small compared to the Caribbean and the Chesapeake, but their balanced sex ratio and organized approach to community formation allowed them to multiply quickly. By distributing land broadly, they built a society of independent farm families. And by establishing a "holy commonwealth," they gave a moral dimension to American history that survives today.

Pilgrims
One of the first Protestant groups to come to America, seeking a separation from the Church of England. They founded Plymouth, the first permanent community in New England, in 1620.

The Pilgrims The **Pilgrims** were religious separatists — committed Protestants who had left the Church of England. When King James I threatened to drive them "out of the land, or else do worse," some chose to live among Dutch Calvinists in Holland. Subsequently, 35 of these exiles resolved to maintain their English identity by moving to America. Led by William Bradford and joined by 67 migrants from England, the Pilgrims sailed to America in 1620 aboard the *Mayflower.* Because they lacked a royal charter, they combined themselves "together into a civill body politick," as their leader explained. This Mayflower Compact used the Pilgrims' self-governing religious congregation as the model for their political structure.

Only half of the first migrant group survived until spring, but thereafter Plymouth thrived; the cold climate inhibited the spread of mosquito-borne disease, and the Pilgrims' religious discipline encouraged a strong work ethic. Moreover, a smallpox epidemic in 1618 had devastated the local Wampanoags, minimizing the danger they posed. By 1640, there were 3,000 settlers in Plymouth. To ensure political stability, they established representative self-government, broad political rights, property ownership, and religious freedom of conscience.

AP® APPLY THE TIP

Ask students to read and analyze the Mayflower Compact of 1620 and the First Charter of Virginia, April 10, 1606, to examine the conflicts between settlers and the government of England. Then lead a discussion of the main ideas in each document. Ask students to source these documents by identifying the historical context, intended audience, purpose, and point of view of each document. (If you have already introduced the AP® DBQ Rubric, remind students of what sourcing a document entails. If not, this activity can be used to introduce sourcing.) To extend this discussion, ask students to compare the documents, focusing on the ideas expressed in each, the expectations of the settlers, and the differences and similarities of the English settlements in Jamestown and Plymouth.

Meanwhile, England plunged deeper into religious turmoil. When King Charles I repudiated certain Protestant doctrines, English Puritans, now powerful in Parliament, accused the king of "popery" — of holding Catholic beliefs. In 1629, Charles dissolved Parliament. When his archbishop, William Laud, began to purge Protestant ministers, thousands of **Puritans** — Protestants who (unlike the Pilgrims) did not separate from the Church of England but hoped to purify it of its ceremony and hierarchy — fled to America.

Puritans
Dissenters from the Church of England who wanted a genuine Reformation rather than the partial Reformation sought by Henry VIII. The Puritans' religious principles emphasized the importance of an individual's relationship with God developed through Bible study, prayer, and introspection.

John Winthrop and Massachusetts Bay The Puritan exodus began in 1630 with the departure of 900 migrants led by John Winthrop, a well-educated country squire who became the first governor of the Massachusetts Bay Colony. Calling England morally corrupt and "overburdened with people," Winthrop sought land for his children and a place in Christian history for his people. "We must consider that we shall be as a City upon a Hill," Winthrop told the migrants. "The eyes of all people are upon us." Like the

AP® THEME

MIG: Migration and Settlement

Remind students that the demographic pattern of migrants to New England was very different from that of New France or New Netherland. This was in part a function of the motivations of the migrants, which included the desire for prosperity, social mobility, and religious freedom.

Pilgrims, the Puritans envisioned a reformed Christian society with "authority in magistrates, liberty in people, purity in the church," as minister John Cotton put it. By their example, they hoped to inspire religious reform throughout Christendom.

Winthrop and his associates governed the Massachusetts Bay Colony from the town of Boston. Like the Virginia Company, the Massachusetts Bay Company was a joint-stock corporation. But the colonists transformed the company into a representative political system with a governor, council, and assembly. To ensure rule by the godly, the Puritans limited the right to vote and hold office to men who were church members. Rejecting the Plymouth Colony's policy of religious tolerance, the Massachusetts Bay Colony established Puritanism as the state-supported religion, barred other faiths from conducting services, and used the Bible as a legal guide. "Where there is no Law," they said, magistrates should rule "as near the law of God as they can." Over the next decade, about 10,000 Puritans migrated to the colony, along with 10,000 others fleeing hard times in England.

Seeing bishops as "traitours unto God," the New England Puritans placed power in the congregation of members — hence the name *Congregationalist* for their churches. Inspired by John Calvin, many Puritans embraced predestination, the idea that God saved only a few chosen people. Church members often lived in great anxiety, worried that God had not placed them among the "elect." Some hoped for a conversion experience, the intense sensation of receiving God's grace and being "born again." Other Puritans relied on "preparation," the confidence in salvation that came from spiritual guidance by their ministers. Still others believed that they were God's chosen people, the new Israelites, and would be saved if they obeyed his laws.

Roger Williams and Rhode Island To maintain God's favor, the Massachusetts Bay magistrates purged their society of religious dissidents. One target was Roger Williams, the Puritan minister in Salem, a coastal town north of Boston. Williams opposed the decision to establish an official religion and praised the Pilgrims' separation of church and state. He advocated **toleration**, arguing that political magistrates had authority over only the "bodies, goods, and outward estates of men," not their spiritual lives. Williams also questioned the Puritans' seizure of Indian lands. The magistrates banished him from the colony in 1636.

Williams and his followers settled 50 miles south of Boston, founding the town of Providence on land purchased from the Narragansett Indians. Other religious dissidents settled nearby at Portsmouth and Newport. In 1644, these settlers obtained a corporate charter from Parliament for a new colony — Rhode Island — with full authority to rule themselves. In Rhode Island, as in Plymouth, there was no legally established church, and individuals could worship God as they pleased.

Anne Hutchinson The Massachusetts Bay magistrates saw a second threat to their authority in Anne Hutchinson. The wife of a merchant and mother of seven, Hutchinson held weekly prayer meetings for women and accused various Boston clergymen of placing undue emphasis on good behavior. Like Martin Luther, Hutchinson denied that salvation could be earned through good deeds. There was no "**covenant of works**" that would save the well-behaved, only a "**covenant of grace**" through which God saved those he predestined for salvation. Hutchinson likewise declared that God "revealed" divine truth directly to individual believers, a controversial doctrine that the Puritan magistrates denounced as heretical.

The magistrates also resented Hutchinson because of her sex. Like other Christians, Puritans believed that both men and women could be saved. But gender equality stopped there. Women were inferior to men in earthly affairs, said leading Puritan divines, who told married women: "Thy desires shall bee subject to thy husband, and he shall rule over thee." Puritan women could not be ministers or lay preachers, nor could they vote in church affairs. In 1637, the magistrates accused Hutchinson of teaching that inward grace freed an individual from the rules of the Church and

AP® EXAM TIP

The impacts of the sentiments expressed in "A City upon a Hill" on American identity is important to know for the AP® Exam.

AP® SKILLS & PROCESSES

ARGUMENTATION

What made New England different from New France and New Netherland?

toleration
The allowance of different religious practices. Lord Baltimore persuaded the Maryland assembly to enact the Toleration Act (1649), which granted all Christians the right to follow their beliefs and hold church services. The crown imposed toleration on Massachusetts Bay in its new royal charter of 1691.

AP® SKILLS & PROCESSES

SOURCING AND SITUATION

How did reactions to Roger Williams and Anne Hutchinson illustrate importance of point of view?

covenant of works
The Christian idea that God's elect must do good works in their earthly lives to earn their salvation.

covenant of grace
The Christian idea that God's elect are granted salvation as a pure gift of grace. This doctrine holds that nothing people do can erase their sins or earn them a place in heaven.

AP® APPLY THE TIP

Provide students with an excerpt from "A Model of Christian Charity" by John Winthrop. Ask students: To what extent did John Winthrop's reference to "a city upon a hill" contribute to the idea of American exceptionalism? Have students read and analyze the document in pairs. Show them excerpts from modern speeches that use the words from Winthrop (John F. Kennedy's "City upon a Hill" speech; Reagan's Farewell Speech, or others). Lead a class discussion that focuses on the impact of religion on ideas of American exceptionalism. As a follow-up assignment, ask students to complete **Handout 2.4 — Causation: Religious Tolerance in British North America.**

TRM Find **Handout 2.4 — Causation: Religious Tolerance in British North America** in the Teacher's Resource Materials.

AP® SKILLS & PROCESSES

ARGUMENTATION

Use the **ARGUMENTATION** question to help students identify differences in colonies established by various European powers. Because much more detail is provided about New England, not all parts of the text can be compared directly. Factors that could be compared include population patterns, economy, and relations with Native Americans. Extend this prompt by asking students to make an inference about how New Netherland changed after the English takeover in 1664.

TRM Find complete suggested responses in the Teacher's Resource Materials.

AP® APPLY THE TIP

Ask students to create a Venn diagram to compare Metacom's War (King Philip's War) and the Pequot War. Direct students to include information about the causes of the conflict, the nature of the fighting, and the impact of the conflicts on both the Native populations and the settlers. You can illustrate the brutality of these conflicts for students through short videos available on YouTube, including "Massacre at Mystic (May 26, 1637)." Lead students in a discussion of the ways in which these early conflicts were similar to relations in Spanish areas of South America and different from relations between the French and Native population in Canada.

found her guilty of holding heretical views. Banished, she followed Roger Williams into exile in Rhode Island.

Other Puritan groups moved out from Massachusetts Bay in the 1630s and settled on or near the Connecticut River. For several decades, the colonies of Connecticut, New Haven, and Saybrook were independent of one another; in 1660, they secured a charter from King Charles II (r. 1660–1685) for the self-governing colony of Connecticut. Like Massachusetts Bay, Connecticut had a legally established church and an elected governor and assembly; however, it granted voting rights to most property-owning men, not just to church members as in the original Puritan colony.

AP® EXAM TIP

Take notes on the causes and effects of conflicts between British settlers and American Indians.

Puritan-Pequot War Many rival Indian groups lived in New England before Europeans arrived; by the 1630s, these groups were bordered by the Dutch colony of New Netherland to their west and the various English settlements to the east — Plymouth, Massachusetts Bay, Rhode Island, Connecticut, New Haven, and Saybrook. The region's Indian leaders created various alliances for the purposes of trade and defense: Wampanoags with Plymouth, Mohegans with Massachusetts and Connecticut, Pequots with New Netherland, and Narragansetts with Rhode Island.

Because of their alliance with the Dutch, the Pequots became a thorn in the side of English traders. A series of violent encounters began in July 1636 and escalated until May 1637, when a combined force of Massachusetts and Connecticut militiamen, accompanied by Narragansett and Mohegan warriors, attacked a Pequot village and massacred some 500 men, women, and children. In the months that followed, the New Englanders drove the surviving Pequots into oblivion and divided their lands.

Believing they were God's chosen people, Puritans considered their presence to be divinely ordained. Initially, they pondered the morality of acquiring Native American lands. "By what right or warrant can we enter into the land of the Savages?" they asked themselves. Responding to such concerns, John Winthrop detected God's hand in a recent smallpox epidemic: "If God were not pleased with our inheriting these parts," he asked, "why doth he still make roome for us by diminishing them as we increase?" Experiences like the Pequot War confirmed New Englanders' confidence in their enterprise. "God laughed at the Enemies of his People," one soldier boasted after the 1637 massacre, "filling the Place with Dead Bodies."

Like Catholic missionaries, Puritans believed that their church should embrace all peoples. However, their strong emphasis on predestination — the idea that God saved only a few chosen people — made it hard for them to accept that Indians could be counted among the elect. "Probably the devil" delivered these "miserable savages" to America, Cotton Mather suggested, "in hopes that the gospel of the Lord Jesus Christ would never come here." A few Puritan ministers committed themselves to the effort to convert Indians. On Martha's Vineyard, Jonathan Mayhew helped to create an Indian-led community of Wampanoag Christians. John Eliot translated the Bible into Algonquian and created fourteen Indian praying towns. By 1670, more than 1,000 Indians lived in these settlements, but relatively few Native Americans were ever permitted to become full members of Puritan congregations.

The Puritan Revolution in England Meanwhile, a religious civil war engulfed England. Archbishop Laud had imposed the Church of England prayer book on Presbyterian Scotland in 1637; five years later, a rebel Scottish army invaded England. Thousands of English Puritans (and hundreds of American Puritans) joined the Scots, demanding religious reform and parliamentary power. After years of civil war, parliamentary forces led by Oliver Cromwell emerged victorious. In 1649, Parliament beheaded King Charles I, proclaimed a republican Commonwealth, and banished bishops and elaborate rituals from the Church of England.

The Puritan triumph in England was short-lived. Popular support for the Commonwealth ebbed after Cromwell took dictatorial control in 1653. Following his death in 1658, moderate Protestants and a resurgent aristocracy restored the

The Execution of Charles I, 1649 Charles I led the royalist army in the English Civil War until he was captured by Oliver Cromwell's rebelling New Model Army. Tried by members of the so-called Rump Parliament for treason, Charles was found guilty after three days of deliberation. On a platform erected in the street outside Whitehall, the royal palace in London, the king was beheaded on January 30, 1649. In this image, Charles — dressed in black, with head bowed — approaches the executioner and the chopping block as members of Parliament and throngs of Londoners look on. Private Collection/© Look and Learn/Peter Jackson Collection/Bridgeman Images.

monarchy and the hierarchy of bishops. With Charles II (r. 1660–1685) on the throne, England's experiment in radical Protestant government came to an end.

For the Puritans in America, the restoration of the monarchy began a new phase of their "errand into the wilderness." They had come to New England expecting to return to Europe in triumph. When the failure of the English Revolution dashed that sacred mission, ministers exhorted congregations to create a godly republican society in America. The Puritan colonies now stood as outposts of Calvinism and the Atlantic republican tradition.

Puritanism and Witchcraft Like Native Americans, Puritans believed that the physical world was full of supernatural forces. Devout Christians saw signs of God's (or Satan's) power in blazing stars, birth defects, and other unusual events. Noting after a storm that the houses of many ministers "had been smitten with Lightning," Cotton Mather, a prominent Puritan theologian, wondered "what the meaning of God should be in it."

Puritans were hostile toward people who they believed tried to manipulate these forces, and many were willing to condemn neighbors as Satan's "wizards" or "witches." People in the town of Andover "were much addicted to sorcery," claimed one observer, and "there were forty men in it that could raise the Devil as well as any astrologer." Between 1647 and 1662, civil authorities in New England hanged 14 people for witchcraft, most of them older women accused of being "double-tongued" or of having "an unruly spirit" (see "Firsthand Accounts," p. 66).

The most dramatic episode of witch-hunting occurred in Salem in 1692. Several girls who had experienced strange seizures accused neighbors of bewitching them. When judges at the accused witches' trials allowed the use of "spectral" evidence — visions of evil beings and marks seen only by the girls — the accusations spun out of control. Eventually, Massachusetts Bay authorities tried 175 people for witchcraft and executed 19 of them. Why did Salem become the focus for this mass hysteria? The causes were complex and are still debated. Some historians point

AP® EXAM TIP

Note the differences in the ways that historians interpret evidence related to the Salem Witch Trials.

AP® APPLY THE TIP

Ask students to work with a partner to analyze at least two historians' interpretations of the Salem witchcraft trials. (One good source is an excerpt from "The Easiest Room in Hell" in *The Devil in Massachusetts* by Marion Starkey.) Help students to understand that historians use a variety of evidence to formulate historical arguments, therefore all historical arguments can be analyzed for supporting evidence. Ask students to explain the historical arguments in their excerpts to each other by citing evidence given in the excerpt and evidence not in the source that could be used to support each historical argument. Ask students to discuss how the historians came to different interpretations of the same events. Use the following questions to guide students' analysis (*answers will vary*):

- **What evidence was most important to each historian?**
- **Did either historian omit evidence in his or her argument?**
- **What bias, if any, influenced the historian in making his or her argument?**
- **Which historical argument do you find most convincing? Why?**

AP® SKILLS & PROCESSES

ANALYZING HISTORICAL EVIDENCE

The primary sources in the **AP® FIRSTHAND ACCOUNTS** feature address a controversial issue in colonial history, one in which the presuppositions of the historical actors often differ from those of modern scholars. Analysis of these sources provides an opportunity for students to explore the importance of perspective and the need to read between the lines — asking questions of a source that may differ from the author's original reason for creating it.

AP® FIRSTHAND ACCOUNTS

Susanna Martin, Accused Witch

Before reading the following document, review questions one uses to interrogate a source (p. 34). Consider the nature of the document and the motives of its creators as you read.

COTTON MATHER

Tryal of Susanna Martin in Salem, June 29, 1692

Susanna Martin was tried for witchcraft in Salem, Massachusetts, in the summer of 1692, during the height of the crisis there. Cotton Mather, a prominent Boston minister, published summaries of the testimony against her in the following year in *The Wonders of the Invisible World*, a book that sought to defend the colony's effort to root out the witches who he believed were doing the devil's work. "The New-Englanders are a people of God settled in those, which were once the Devil's Territories," he wrote. "The devil is now making one Attempt more upon us." Mather compiled the following testimony, but he is quoting witnesses who also must be treated, in a sense, as authors: witnesses with their own ideas and purposes, which may have been similar to Mather's but were not identical. In the bizarre stories they tell, we get a glimpse of how early New Englanders believed that the devil used people like Susanna Martin to act in the world.

SOURCE: "Tryal of Susanna Martin in Salem, June 29, 1692," in Cotton Mather, *The Wonders of the Invisible World* (London: J. R. Smith, 1862), 138–148.

❝ Susanna Martin, pleading *Not Guilty* to the Indictment of *Witchcraft*, brought in against her, there were produced the Evidences of many Persons very sensibly and grievously Bewitched; who all complained of the Prisoner at the Bar, as the Person whom they believed the cause of their Miseries. . . .

IV. *John Atkinson* testifi'd, That he exchanged a Cow with a Son of *Susanna Martin's*, whereat she muttered, and was unwilling he should have it. Going to receive this Cow, tho he Hamstring'd her, and Halter'd her, she, of a Tame Creature, grew so mad, that they could scarce get her along. She broke all the Ropes that were fastned unto her, and though she were ty'd fast unto a Tree, yet she made her escape, and gave them such further trouble, as they could ascribe to no cause but Witchcraft.

V. *Bernard Peache* testifi'd, That being in Bed, on the Lord's-day Night, he heard a scrabbling at the Window, whereat he then saw *Susanna Martin* come in, and jump down upon the Floor. She took hold of this Deponent's Feet, and drawing his Body up into an Heap, she lay upon him near Two Hours; in all which time he could neither speak nor stir. At length, when he could begin to move, he laid hold on her Hand, and pulling it up to his Mouth, he bit three of her Fingers, as he judged, unto the Bone. Whereupon she went from the Chamber, down the Stairs, out at the Door. This Deponent thereupon called unto the People of the House, to advise them of what passed; and he himself did follow her. The People saw her not; but there being a Bucket at the Left-hand of the Door, there was a drop of Blood found upon it; and several more drops of Blood upon the Snow newly fallen abroad: There was likewise the print of her 2 Feet just without the Threshold; but no more sign of any Footing further off. . . .

VI. *Robert Downer* testified, That this Prisoner being some Years ago prosecuted at Court for a Witch, he then said unto her, *He believed she was a Witch*. Whereat

to group rivalries: many accusers were the daughters or servants of poor farmers, whereas many of the alleged witches were wealthier church members or their friends. Because 18 of those put to death were women, other historians see the episode as part of a broader Puritan effort to subordinate women. Still others focus on political instability in Massachusetts Bay in the early 1690s and on fears raised by recent Indian attacks in nearby Maine, which had killed the parents of some of the young accusers. It is likely that all of these causes played some role in the executions.

Whatever the cause, the Salem episode marked a major turning point. Shaken by the number of deaths, government officials now discouraged legal prosecutions for witchcraft. Moreover, many influential people embraced the outlook of the European Enlightenment, a major intellectual movement that began around 1675 and promoted a rational, scientific view of the world. Increasingly, educated men and women explained strange happenings and sudden deaths by reference to "natural causes," not witchcraft. Unlike Cotton Mather (1663–1728), who believed that lightning was a supernatural sign, Benjamin Franklin (1706–1790) and other well-read men of his generation would investigate it as a natural phenomenon.

she being dissatisfied, said, *That some She-Devil would shortly fetch him away*! Which words were heard by others, as well as himself. The Night following, as he lay in his Bed, there came in at the Window, the likeness of a *Cat*, which flew upon him, took fast hold of his Throat, lay on him a considerable while, and almost killed him. At length he remembered what *Susanna Martin* had threatned the Day before; and with much striving he cried out, *Avoid, thou She-Devil! In the Name of God the Father, the Son, and the Holy Ghost, Avoid!* Whereupon it left him, leap'd on the Floor, and flew out at the Window. . . .

VIII. *William Brown* testifi'd, That Heaven having blessed him with a most Pious and Prudent Wife, this Wife of his, one day met with *Susanna Martin*; but when she approach'd just unto her, *Martin* vanished out of sight, and left her extreamly affrighted. After which time, the said *Martin* often appear'd unto her, giving her no little trouble; and when she did come, she was visited with Birds, that sorely peck'd and prick'd her; and sometimes, a Bunch, like a Pullet's Egg, would rise in her Throat, ready to choak her, till she cry'd out, *Witch, you shan't choak me!* While this good Woman was in this extremity, the Church appointed a Day of Prayer, on her behalf; whereupon her Trouble ceas'd; she saw not *Martin* as formerly; and the Church, instead of their Fast, gave Thanks for her Deliverance. But a considerable while after, she being Summoned to give in some Evidence at the Court, against this *Martin*, quickly thereupon, this Martin came behind her, while she was milking her Cow, and said unto her, *For thy defaming her at Court, I'll make thee the miserablest Creature in the World.* Soon after which, she fell into a strange kind of distemper, and became horribly frantick, and uncapable of any reasonable Action; the Physicians declaring, that her Distemper was preternatural, and that some Devil had certainly bewitched her; and in that condition she now remained.

IX. *Sarah Atkinson* testify'd, That *Susanna Martin* came from *Amesbury* to their House at *Newbury*, in an extraordinary Season, when it was not fit for any to Travel. She came (as she said, unto *Atkinson*), all that long way on Foot. She brag'd and shew'd how dry she was; nor could it be perceived that so much as the Soles of her Shoes were wet. *Atkinson* was amazed at it; and professed, that she should her self have been wet up to the knees, if she had then came so far; but *Martin* reply'd, *She scorn'd to be Drabbled!* It was noted, that this Testimony upon her Trial, cast her in a very singular Confusion. . . .

Note, this Woman was one of the most imprudent, scurrilous, wicked Creatures in the World; and she did now throughout her whole Tryal, discover [reveal] her self to be such an one. Yet when she was asked, what she had to say for her self? Her chief Plea was, *That she had lead a most virtuous and holy Life.* ❞

QUESTIONS FOR ANALYSIS

1. Who is Mather's intended audience? What is the purpose of sharing this information?
2. How might the motives of the witnesses in Susanna Martin's trial have differed from Mather's? Describe the purposes and perspectives of both witnesses and Mather.
3. What kinds of actions alienated Martin from her neighbors? What occurrences do her neighbors blame her for, and why? Use evidence from the source to describe your reasoning.
4. Consider the discussion of New England culture on pages 62–69. How would you put this testimony in context? What aspects of New England society and culture predisposed people to view some of their neighbors as witches?

TRM Find complete suggested responses in the Teacher's Resource Materials.

A Yeoman Society, 1630–1700 In building their communities, New England Puritans consciously rejected the feudal practices of English society. Many Puritans came from middling families in East Anglia, a region of pasture lands and few manors, and had no desire to live as tenants of wealthy aristocrats or submit to oppressive taxation by a distant government. They had "escaped out of the pollutions of the world," the settlers of Watertown in Massachusetts Bay declared, and vowed to live "close togither" in self-governing communities. Accordingly, the General Courts of Massachusetts Bay and Connecticut bestowed land on groups of settlers, who then distributed it among the male heads of families.

Widespread ownership of land did not mean equality of wealth or status. "God had Ordained different degrees and orders of men," proclaimed Boston merchant John Saffin, "some to be Masters and Commanders, others to be Subjects, and to be commanded." Town proprietors normally awarded the largest plots to men of high social status who often became selectmen and justices of the peace. However, all families received some land, and most adult men had a vote in the **town meeting**, the main institution of local government (Map 2.6).

AP® SKILLS & PROCESSES

MAKING CONNECTIONS

How did differences in geography and environment impact the development of social systems in colonial regions?

TRM Find complete suggested responses in Teacher's Resource Materials.

town meeting
A system of local government in New England in which all male heads of households met regularly to elect selectmen; levy local taxes; and regulate markets, roads, and schools.

AP® THEME

NAT: American and National Identity

Point out to students that, like the House of Burgesses, the New England town meeting was a precursor to later forms of self-governing American political institutions based on participation by free citizens. More than in Virginia, town meetings were atypically democratic for the time.

AP® THEME

MIG: Migration and Settlement

Analysis of **MAP 2.6** will help students understand the unique settlement patterns of New England, with dozens of small towns based on an economy driven by small-scale, private agriculture. Students can compare this map with **MAP 2.4** of Virginia to draw a clear contrast between the patterns of the two regions, based on environment, economy, and the values of the settlers.

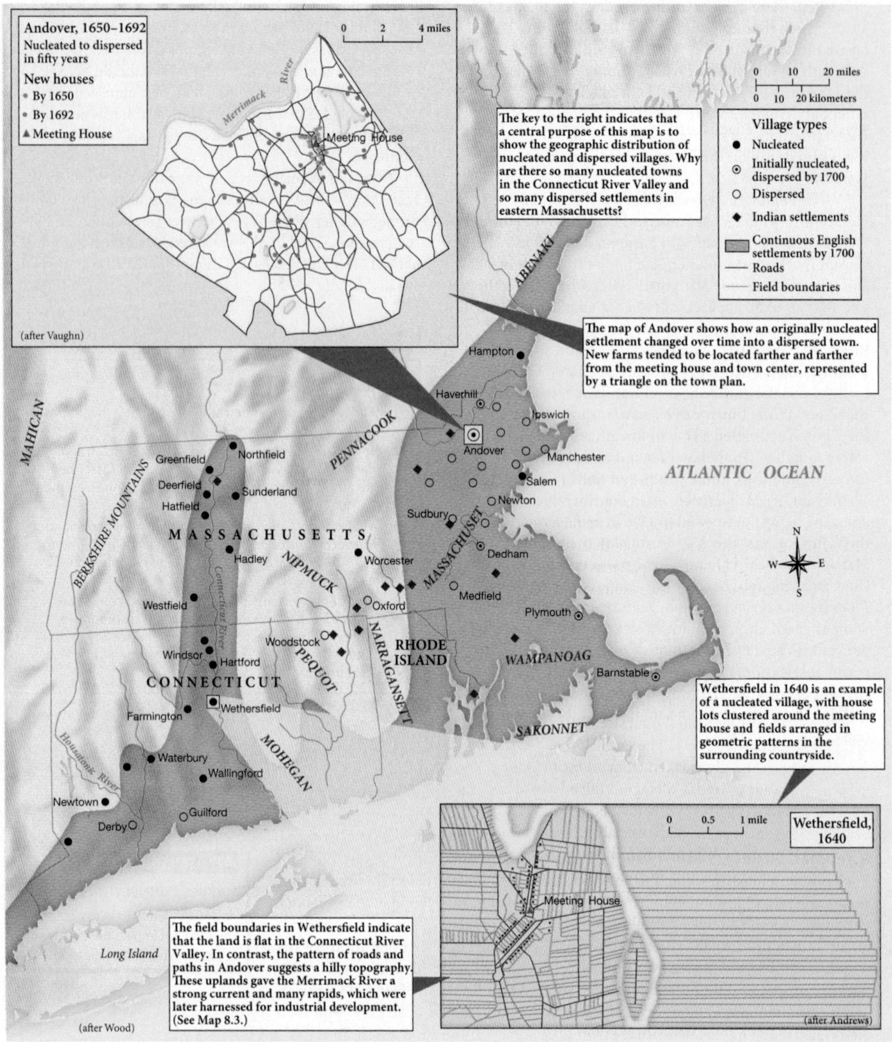

MAP 2.6 Settlement Patterns in New England Towns, 1630–1700

Throughout New England, colonists pressed onto desirable Indian lands. Initially, most Puritan towns were compact, or nucleated: families lived close to one another in village centers and traveled daily to work in the surrounding fields. This 1640 map of Wethersfield, Connecticut, a town situated on the broad plains of the Connecticut River Valley, shows this pattern clearly. The first settlers in Andover, Massachusetts, also chose to live in the village center. However, the rugged topography of eastern Massachusetts encouraged the townspeople to disperse. By 1692 (as the varied location of new houses shows), many Andover residents were living on farms distant from the village center.

In this society of independent households and self-governing communities, ordinary farmers had much more political power than Chesapeake yeomen and European peasants did. Although Nathaniel Fish was one of the poorest men in the town of Barnstable — he owned just a two-room cottage, 8 acres of land, an ox, and a cow — he was a voting member of the town meeting. Each year, Fish and other Barnstable farmers levied taxes; enacted ordinances governing fencing, roadbuilding, and the use of common fields; and chose the selectmen who managed town affairs. The farmers also selected the town's representatives to the General Court (the colony's legislature), which gradually displaced the governor as the center of political authority. For Fish and thousands of other ordinary settlers, New England had proved to be a new world of opportunity.

Mrs. Elizabeth Freake and Baby Mary This portrait, completed around 1674 by an unknown artist, depicts the wife and youngest daughter of a wealthy Bostonian. Their clothes and surroundings illustrate the growing prosperity of well-to-do households. Mother and child both wear fine linen edged with fine lace. Elizabeth Freake's sleeve is decorated with colorful red and black ribbons and she wears a beaded bracelet on her wrist. They are seated on a chair colorfully upholstered in a style intended to imitate a Turkish carpet. Worcester Art Museum, Massachusetts, USA/Bridgeman Images.

WAR AND REBELLION IN NORTH AMERICA

What did these three rebellions — Metacom's War, the Pueblo Revolt, and Bacon's Rebellion — have in common?

Everywhere in Europe's American colonies, conflicts arose over the control of resources, the legitimacy of colonial leaders' claims to power, and attempts to define social and cultural norms. Periodically, these conflicts flared spectacularly into episodes of violence. In New England and the Southwest, Native Americans rose up to challenge the legitimacy of the colonial order. In Virginia, colonists clashed with Native Americans and the colonial government in pursuit of opportunity and status. Each episode has its own story — its own unique logic and narrative — but taken together, they also illustrate the way that, in their formative stages, colonial societies pressured people to accept new patterns of authority and new claims to power. When these claims were contested, the results could quickly turn deadly.

AP® SKILLS & PROCESSES

DEVELOPMENTS AND PROCESSES

What made New England's yeoman society relatively democratic?

Metacom's War, 1675–1676

In New England, Wampanoags and other Indian groups had maintained alliances with neighboring colonies for years. But these relations were unstable, and the potential for violence was never far from the surface. By the 1670s, Europeans in New England outnumbered Indians by 3 to 1. The English population had multiplied to 55,000, while Native peoples had diminished from an estimated 120,000 in 1570 to barely 16,000. To the Wampanoag leader Metacom (also known as King Philip), the prospects for coexistence looked dim. When his people copied English ways by raising hogs and selling pork in Boston, Puritan officials accused them of selling at "an under rate" and restricted their trade. When Indians killed wandering hogs that devastated their cornfields, authorities prosecuted them for violating English property rights.

AP® EXAM TIP

Compare attempts by native populations to maintain autonomy in the face of European encroachment in British North America.

Metacom concluded that the English colonists had to be expelled. In 1675, the Wampanoag leader forged a military alliance with the Narragansetts and Nipmucks and attacked white settlements throughout New England. Almost every day, settler William Harris fearfully reported, he heard new reports of the Indians' "burneing houses, takeing cattell, killing men & women & Children: & carrying others captive." Bitter fighting continued into 1676, ending only when the Indian warriors ran short of gunpowder and the Massachusetts Bay government hired Mohegan and Mohawk warriors, who killed Metacom.

Metacom's War of 1675–1676 (which English settlers called King Philip's War) was a deadly affair. Indians destroyed one-fifth of the English towns in Massachusetts and Rhode Island and killed 1,000 settlers, nearly 5 percent of the adult population; for a time the Puritan experiment hung in the balance. But the Natives' losses — from famine and disease, death in battle, and sale into slavery — were much larger: about 4,500 Indians died, one-quarter of an already diminished population. Many of the surviving Wampanoag, Narragansett, and Nipmuck peoples moved west, intermarrying

Metacom's War
Also known as King Philip's War, it pitted a coalition of Native Americans led by the Wampanoag leader Metacom against the New England colonies in 1675–1676. A thousand colonists were killed and twelve colonial towns destroyed, but the colonies prevailed. Metacom and his allies lost some 4,500 people.

CHECK FOR UNDERSTANDING

Ask students: **What conditions were necessary to establish successful neo-European colonies?** *As opposed to Spain's tribute colonies or plantation colonies, neo-European colonies had a number of traits that distinguished them, making them successful. First was yeoman-based small-scale agriculture, which allowed for settlement but not an export-oriented incentive that would have led to consolidation of farms. Second was a purpose other than export-oriented agriculture. Religion (e.g., Puritanism in New England) provided the greatest prominent examples of a rationale. Finally, the arrival of women from Europe, continuing and replicating the family and social structure of European societies, was important. Many tribute and plantation colonies did not seek to replicate European social structures below the elite level and thus relied on Native American women or an influx of African labor to perpetuate the economically centered colonies.*

TRM Find complete suggested responses in the Teacher's Resource Materials.

AP® APPLY THE TIP

Ask students to create a timeline that illustrates attempts by various Native American groups to maintain autonomy in the face of encroachment by settlers in British North America. Under each event on the timeline, ask students to identify the main cause of the conflict and the outcome of the conflict as well as note which colonial region is involved in the conflict. After students complete the timeline, discuss what these attempts to maintain autonomy have in common and the similarities and differences across the different regions.

AP® THEME

WOR: America in the World

Help students recognize that Metacom's War (King Philip's War) and the Pueblo Revolt both represented resistance to the colonizing efforts of the English and Spanish.

TEACHING STRATEGY

"King Philip's War," a lesson from the Stanford History Education Group's Reading Like a Historian Web site, provides students the opportunity to evaluate different primary sources representing divergent points of view on the causes of Metacom's War. Access this lesson by searching "Stanford King Philip's War."

AP® APPLY THE TIP

Ask students to compare the causes and outcome of the Pueblo Revolt to the attempts by Native populations in the east to maintain autonomy. Discuss the tactics used by the Pueblo that led to their initial success against the Spanish. Guide this discussion through the following questions:

- **What conditions led to the Pueblo Revolt? Are these conditions examples of continuity or change over time in Spanish settlements?** *Attempts by the Spanish to impose imperial policies converting natives to Christianity and using forced labor led to the Pueblo Revolt. These conditions are an example of continuity given the same policies were implemented in Central and South America under the encomienda system.*
- **How did the Pueblo organize a successful revolt against the Spanish?** *Native leader Pope organized a military offensive by unifying many Pueblo groups in the surrounding region.*
- **Was the Pueblo Revolt a "success"?** *Militarily, the Spanish defeated the rebellion. However, the revolt did lead to changes in Spanish policies that lessened forced labor and led to better treatment of the Pueblos. Ultimately, disease ravaged these communities as it had other Native groups.*

CHECK FOR UNDERSTANDING

Ask students: **What prompted Native American resistance, as expressed in Metacom's War and the Pueblo Revolt?** *European claims to power and territory threatened Native Americans' economy and way of life, leading to violent resistance by Native groups.*

with Algonquian tribes allied to the French. Over the next century, these displaced Indian peoples would take their revenge, joining with French Catholics to attack their Puritan enemies. Metacom's War did not eliminate the presence of Native Americans in southern New England, but it effectively destroyed their existence as independent peoples.

AP® EXAM TIP

Evaluate the impact of the Pueblo Revolt on Spanish policy in the North American Southwest.

The Pueblo Revolt

From the time of their first arrival in Pueblo country in 1540, Spanish soldiers and Franciscan missionaries in the colony of New Mexico had attempted to dominate its Indian communities. They demanded tribute, labor, and forced conversions to Catholicism, and they ferociously suppressed resistance. A small minority ruling over a population of some 17,000 people, the Spanish were mistrusted and often hated. A drought beginning in 1660 compounded the Pueblos' misery; one priest wrote, "a great many Indians perished of hunger, lying dead along the roads, in the ravines, and in their huts." In this period of suffering, many Pueblos turned away from Christianity and back to their own holy men and traditional ceremonies. Seeking to suppress these practices, in 1675 Spanish officials hanged three Pueblo priests and whipped dozens of others as punishment for sorcery.

Pueblo Revolt Also known as Popé's Rebellion, the revolt in 1680 was an uprising of forty-six Native American pueblos against Spanish rule. Spaniards were driven out of New Mexico. When they returned in the 1690s, they granted more autonomy to the pueblos they claimed to rule.

One of the convicted sorcerers was a religious leader from San Juan Pueblo named Popé. Five years later in 1680, he organized a complex military offensive against the Spanish that came to be known as the **Pueblo Revolt** (also called Popé's Rebellion). Drawing on warriors from two dozen pueblos spread across several hundred miles and speaking six languages, Popé orchestrated an uprising that liberated the pueblos and culminated in the capture of Santa Fe; 400 Spaniards were killed; the remaining 2,100 fled south. New Mexico was in Pueblo hands. Under the leadership of Diego de Vargas, the Spanish returned and recaptured Santa Fe in 1693; three years later, they had reclaimed most of the pueblos of New Mexico. But Spanish policy was redirected by the revolt. Officials reduced their labor demands on Pueblo communities, and across the Southwest—from Baja California to Tejas y Coahuila—Spain relied on Indian missions to create a defensive perimeter against their Ute, Apache, and Navajo neighbors.

The Taos Pueblo After he was released from Spanish custody, Popé made Taos Pueblo his base of operations while he organized the Pueblos' revolt against Spanish rule. Between 1675 and 1680, he traveled to more than forty pueblos to recruit participants in the uprising. This photo shows the oldest portion of modern-day Taos, which is believed to appear much as it did in the era of Spanish occupation. Constructed entirely of adobe, Taos was founded more than a thousand years ago and is considered the oldest continuously occupied settlement in North America. Jim Feliciano/Shutterstock.com.

In the century that followed, Jesuit and Franciscan missionaries built a dense network of missions extending north from Mexico along the coast of Baja and Alta (or lower and upper) California. From San José del Cabo in the south to San Francisco in the north, these institutions sought to pacify Native peoples and transform their ways of life. Massive waves of smallpox, typhus, and other diseases drove surviving Indians to the missions; their desperation often accomplished what the faithful labors of missionaries could not. Throughout coastal California, remnant Indian populations gravitated toward mission communities and the sustenance and protection they could offer.

Bacon's Rebellion

At about the same time that New England fought its war with Metacom and the Pueblos took up arms with Popé, Virginia was wracked by a rebellion that nearly toppled its government. It, too, grew out of a conflict with neighboring Indians, but this one inspired a popular uprising against the colony's royal governor. Like Metacom's War, it highlighted the way that a land-intensive settler colony created friction with Native American populations; in addition, it dramatized the way that ordinary colonists could challenge the authority of a new planter elite to rule over them.

By the 1670s, economic and political power in Virginia was in the hands of a small circle of men who amassed land, slaves, and political offices. Through headrights and royal grants, they controlled nearly half of all the settled land in Virginia. What they could not plant themselves, they leased to tenants. Freed indentured servants found it ever harder to get land of their own; many were forced to lease lands, or even sign new indentures, to make ends meet. To make matters worse, the price of tobacco fell until planters received only a penny a pound for their crops in the 1670s.

At the top of Virginia's narrow social pyramid was William Berkeley, governor between 1642 and 1652 and again after 1660. To consolidate power, Berkeley bestowed large land grants on members of his council. The councilors exempted these lands from taxation and appointed friends as justices of the peace and county judges. To win support in the House of Burgesses, Berkeley bought off legislators with land grants and lucrative appointments as sheriffs and tax collectors. But social unrest erupted when the Burgesses took the vote away from landless freemen, who by now constituted half the adult white men. Although property-holding yeomen retained their voting rights, they were angered by falling tobacco prices, political corruption, and "grievous taxations" that threatened the "utter ruin of us the poor commonalty." Berkeley and his allies were living on borrowed time.

Frontier War An Indian conflict ignited the flame of social rebellion. In 1607, when the English intruded, 30,000 Native Americans resided in Virginia; by 1675, the Native population had dwindled to only 3,500. By then, Europeans numbered some 38,000 and Africans another 2,500. Most Indians lived on treaty-guaranteed territory along the frontier, where poor freeholders and landless former servants now wanted to settle, demanding that the Natives be expelled or exterminated. Their demands were ignored by wealthy planters, who wanted a ready supply of tenants and laborers, and by Governor Berkeley and the planter-merchants, who traded with the Occaneechee Indians for beaver pelts and deerskins.

Fighting broke out late in 1675, when a vigilante band of Virginia militiamen murdered thirty Indians. Defying Berkeley's orders, a larger force then surrounded a fortified Susquehannock village and killed five leaders who came out to negotiate. The Susquehannocks retaliated by attacking outlying plantations and killing three hundred whites. In response, Berkeley proposed a defensive strategy: a series of frontier forts to deter Indian intrusions. The settlers dismissed this scheme as a militarily useless plot by planter-merchants to impose high taxes and take "all our tobacco into their own hands."

Challenging the Government Enter Nathaniel Bacon, a young, well-connected migrant from England who emerged as the leader of the rebels. Bacon held a position on the governor's council, but he was shut out of Berkeley's inner circle and differed with Berkeley on Indian policy. When the governor refused to grant him a military commission, Bacon mobilized his neighbors and attacked any Indians he could find. Condemning the frontiersmen as "rebels and mutineers," Berkeley expelled

AP® SKILLS & PROCESSES

ARGUMENTATION

Compare the pressures that Native American groups faced from colonists in New England and New Mexico. What was similar, and in what ways did their circumstances differ?

AP® SKILLS & PROCESSES

DEVELOPMENTS AND PROCESSES

Why did Bacon's Rebellion lead to greater dependence on the African slave trade?

AP® SKILLS & PROCESSES

ARGUMENTATION

Use the **ARGUMENTATION** question to help students compare similarities and differences in Native Americans' experiences with two different European groups. Students could brainstorm major differences between Spanish and English culture and society, as well as differences in their patterns of colonization. Then they could make a Venn diagram indicating how Native Americans' experiences compared in the two regions. Extend this prompt by asking students which similarities or differences were more significant and to explain their reasoning.

TRM Find complete suggested responses in the Teacher's Resource Materials.

AP® SKILLS & PROCESSES

DEVELOPMENTS AND PROCESSES

To further students' understanding of how Bacon's Rebellion is connected to the creation of new social groups in colonial America, consider having students create a visual representation of the social hierarchy in Virginia because of the conflict. Their visuals must include the following groups: yeoman farmers, enslaved Africans, white property owners, and landed-gentry.

TRM Find complete suggested responses in the Teacher's Resource Materials.

AP® SKILLS & PROCESSES

CONTEXTUALIZATION

Use the **CONTEXTUALIZATION** question to help students situate Bacon's Rebellion in the broader regional context in which it occurred and draw conclusions about the rebellion's significance. Use **Handout 2. Contextualization: Bacon's Rebellion** to help students situate Bacon's Rebellion in the historical period. Students could brainstorm the grievances that led to Bacon's Rebellion and the consequences of its collapse. They could connect each factor they identify to a larger pattern in Virginia. Students could also consider whether Bacon's Rebellion was a turning point in the development of colonial Virginia.

TRM Find **Handout 2.5 Contextualization: Bacon's Rebellion** in the Teacher's Resource Materials.

TRM Find complete suggested responses in the Teacher's Resource Materials.

CHECK FOR UNDERSTANDING

Use the **AP® LEARNING FOCUS** questions from the beginning of the chapter to assess students' understanding of the chapter as a whole: **In what ways did European migrants transfer familiar patterns and institutions to their colonies in the Americas, and in what ways did they create new American worlds? How did Native Americans adapt to the growing presence of Europeans among them?** *In the Americas, Spanish colonization brought social and economic dislocations. Socially, as almost 350,000 Spanish migrants arrived in the Americas, new social leveling based on race, known as the casta system, emerged. Native Americans were converted to Catholicism en masse. Economically, the Americans were re-oriented to serve Spanish and European needs and its transoceanic trading partners. In Europe, the Spanish Crown as well as Spain's merchants became fantastically wealthy. Money flowed into Spain, then into Europe, especially the Catholic Church.*

LearningCurve

Remind students to go online to complete the LearningCurve quiz for this chapter.

AP® SKILLS & PROCESSES

CONTEXTUALIZATION

In what ways was Bacon's Rebellion symptomatic of social tensions in the colony of Virginia?

Bacon's Rebellion
The rebellion in 1675-1676 in Virginia that began when vigilante colonists started a war with neighboring Indians. When Governor William Berkeley refused to support them, the rebels — led by Nathaniel Bacon — formed an army that marched on the capital. The rebellion was finally crushed but prompted reforms in Virginia's government.

Bacon from the council and had him arrested. But Bacon's army forced the governor to release their leader and hold legislative elections. The newly elected House of Burgesses enacted far-reaching reforms that curbed the powers of the governor and council and restored voting rights to landless freemen.

These much-needed reforms came too late. Poor farmers and servants resented years of exploitation by wealthy, well-connected planters. As one yeoman rebel complained, "A poor man who has only his labour to maintain himself and his family pays as much [in taxes] as a man who has 20,000 acres." Backed by 400 armed men, Bacon issued a "Manifesto and Declaration of the People" that demanded the removal of Indians and an end to the rule of wealthy "parasites." "All the power and sway is got into the hands of the rich," Bacon proclaimed as his army burned Jamestown to the ground and plundered the plantations of Berkeley's allies. When Bacon died suddenly of dysentery in October 1676, the governor took revenge, dispersing the rebel army, seizing the estates of well-to-do rebels, and hanging twenty-three men.

In the wake of **Bacon's Rebellion**, Virginia's leaders worked harder to appease their humble neighbors. But the rebellion also coincided with the time when Virginia planters were switching from indentured servants, who became free after four years, to slaves, who labored for life. In the years to come, wealthy planters would make common cause with poorer whites, while slaves became the colony's most exploited workers. That fateful change eased tensions within the free population but committed subsequent generations of Americans to a labor system based on racial exploitation. Bacon's Rebellion, like Metacom's War, reminds us that these colonies were unfinished worlds, still searching for viable foundations.

SUMMARY

During the sixteenth and seventeenth centuries, three types of colonies took shape in the Americas. In Mesoamerica and the Andes, Spanish colonists made indigenous empires their own, capitalizing on preexisting labor systems and using tribute and the discovery of precious metals to generate enormous wealth, which Philip II used to defend the interests of the Catholic Church in Europe. In tropical and subtropical regions, colonizers transferred the plantation complex — a centuries-old form of production and labor discipline — to places suited to growing exotic crops like sugar, tobacco, and indigo. The rigors of plantation agriculture demanded a large supply of labor, which was first filled in English colonies by indentured servants and later supplemented and eclipsed by African slaves. The third type of colony, neo-European settlement, developed in North America's temperate zone, where European migrants adapted familiar systems of social and economic organization in new settings.

Everywhere in the Americas, colonization was, first and foremost, a process of experimentation. As resources from the Americas flowed to Europe, monarchies were strengthened and the competition among them — sharpened by the schism between Protestants and Catholics — gained new force and energy. Establishing colonies demanded political, social, and cultural innovations that threw Europeans, Native Americans, and Africans together in bewildering circumstances, triggered massive ecological change through the Columbian Exchange, and demanded radical adjustments. In the Chesapeake and New England — the two earliest regions of English settlement on mainland North America — the adjustment to new circumstances sparked conflict with neighboring Indians and waves of instability within the colonies. These external and internal crises were products of the struggle to adapt to the rigors of colonization.

CHAPTER 2 REVIEW

AP® CONTENT REVIEW

Answer these questions to demonstrate your understanding of the chapter's main ideas.

1. How did Spanish colonization affect people in the Americas and in Europe?
2. How did the labor demands of plantation colonies transform the process of colonization?
3. What conditions were necessary to establish successful neo-European colonies?
4. What did these three rebellions — Metacom's War, the Pueblo Revolt, and Bacon's Rebellion — have in common?

AP® TERMS TO KNOW

Identify and explain the significance of each term below.

Key Concepts and Events

chattel slavery (p. 40)
neo-Europes (p. 40)
encomienda (p. 43)
casta system (p. 43)
Columbian Exchange (p. 43)
mercantilism (p. 46)
joint-stock corporation (p. 48)
House of Burgesses (p. 49)
royal colony (p. 49)
freeholds (p. 53)
headright system (p. 53)
indentured servitude (p. 55)
Pilgrims (p. 62)
Puritans (p. 62)
toleration (p. 63)
covenant of works (p. 63)
covenant of grace (p. 63)
town meeting (p. 67)
Metacom's War (p. 69)
Pueblo Revolt (p. 70)
Bacon's Rebellion (p. 72)

Key People

Philip II (p. 45)
Opechancanough (p. 49)
Lord Baltimore (p. 49)
John Winthrop (p. 62)
Roger Williams (p. 63)
Anne Hutchinson (p. 63)
Metacom (p. 69)

AP® MAKING CONNECTIONS

Recognize the larger developments and continuities within and across chapters by answering these questions.

1. In Chapter 1, we saw that there were many parallels between Native American, European, and African societies on the eve of contact. Yet Europeans ended up dominating both Native American and African populations in colonial American settings. Based on evidence from in Chapter 2, what factors help to explain that dominance?
2. This chapter has emphasized the experimental and unstable nature of colonization. Each type of colony—tribute, plantation, and neo-European —faced its own distinct challenges. Identify one important source of instability that affected the early development of each type of colony.

KEY TURNING POINTS

Refer to the timeline at the start of the chapter for help in answering the following questions.

The Chesapeake tobacco boom (1620–1660), Opechancanough's uprising (1622), and the takeover of Virginia by the crown (1624): How were these events related to each other? What was their cumulative result? Make a historically defensible claim and support your argument with evidence from the text.

TRM Find complete suggested responses in the Teacher's Resource Materials.

AP® SKILLS & PROCESSES

CAUSATION

AP® CONTENT REVIEW QUESTION 1 asks students to explain the effects of Spain's colonizing efforts and the effects on people in two different regions, in the areas they colonized and in Europe. Note: This is the same question as on p. 42.

AP® SKILLS & PROCESSES

CAUSATION

AP® CONTENT REVIEW QUESTION 2 encourages students to describe the effects of labor needs on the larger pattern of colonization — the development of governance, the economy, and settlement patterns. Note: This is the same question as on p. 46.

AP® SKILLS & PROCESSES

CAUSATION

AP® CONTENT REVIEW QUESTION 3 asks students to identify long-term causes of a generalized pattern of colonization. Note: This is the same question as on p. 57.

AP® SKILLS & PROCESSES

COMPARISON

AP® CONTENT REVIEW QUESTION 4 asks students to identify the similarities in three rebellions that occurred within a few short years of each other. Note: This is the same question as on p. 69.

TRM Find definitions for these terms in the **Glossary/Glosario** in the Teacher's Resource Materials.

AP® SKILLS & PROCESSES

COMPARISON

AP® MAKING CONNECTIONS 1 invites students to make connections between related patterns in three different regions.

AP® SKILLS & PROCESSES

CONTINUITY AND CHANGE

KEY TURNING POINTS invites students to draw connections between three events that happened in close proximity and explain their effect on developments in colonial Virginia.

TRM Find complete suggested responses in the Teacher's Resource Materials.

AP® PRACTICE QUESTIONS

MULTIPLE CHOICE QUESTIONS *Choose the correct answer for each question.*

Questions 1–2 refer to this excerpt.

> "I must now speak of the skilled workmen whom Montezuma employed in all the crafts they practiced, beginning with the jewelers and workers in silver and gold . . . which excited the admiration of our great silversmiths at home. . . . There were other skilled craftsmen who worked with precious stones . . . and very fine painters and carvers.
>
> But why waste so many words on the goods in their great market? If I describe everything in detail I shall never be done. . . . Having examined and considered all that we had seen, we turned back to the great market and the swarm of buying and selling. The mere murmur of their voices talking was loud enough to be heard more than three miles away. Some of our soldiers who had been in many parts of the world, in Constantinople, in Rome, and all over Italy, said that they had never seen a market so well laid out, so orderly, and so full of people."
>
> Bernal Díaz del Castillo, *The Conquest of New Spain,* 1632

1. Which of the following best describes the historical situation of the author?
   - **a.** A debate among European religious and political leaders about how non-Europeans should be treated
   - **b.** The Columbian Exchange facilitating the European shift from feudalism to capitalism
   - **c.** The mutual misunderstandings between Europeans and Native Americans as each group sought to make sense of the other
   - **d.** The development of a caste system by the Spanish that defined the status of the diverse population in their empire

2. The events described in the passage most directly foreshadowed which of the following developments?
   - **a.** Spanish attempts to convert Native populations to Christianity
   - **b.** Native peoples seeking to maintain their economic prosperity through diplomatic negotiations and military resistance
   - **c.** The Europeans' and American Indians' adoptions of useful aspects of each other's culture
   - **d.** Spanish efforts to extract wealth from the New World

Questions 3–5 refer to this excerpt.

> "We cannot in our hearts find one single spot of Rebellion of Treason or that we have in any manner aimed at subverting the settled Government. . . . We appeal to the Country itself . . . of what nature their Oppressions have been . . . let us trace the men in Authority and Favor [here] . . . let us observe the sudden rise of their Estates composed with the Quality in which they first entered this country . . . let us [also] consider whether any Public work for our safety and defense or for the Advancement of and propagation of [our] trade . . . is here . . . in [any] way adequate to our vast charge. . . .
>
> Another main article of our guilt is our open and manifest aversion of all . . . Indians, this we are informed is a Rebellion . . . we do declare and can prove that they have been for these Many years enemies to the King and Country . . . but yet have by persons in authority [here] been defended and protected even against His Majesties loyal Subjects. . . .
>
> . . . may all the world know that we do unanimously desire to represent our sad and heavy grievances to his most sacred Majesty . . . where we do well know that our Causes will be impartially heard and Equal justice administered to all men."
>
> Nathaniel Bacon, *Declaration,* 1676

3. The excerpt is best understood in the context of
   - **a.** the gradual Anglicization of the British colonies over time.
   - **b.** the first Great Awakening and the spread of Enlightenment ideas.
   - **c.** the diverging goals and interests of European leaders and colonists.
   - **d.** the development of plantation economies in the British West Indies.

4. Which of the following was most likely to have supported the perspective expressed in Bacon's *Declaration*?
   - **a.** Male indentured servants
   - **b.** Plantation-owning colonial politicians
   - **c.** Colonial representative assemblies
   - **d.** Fur trading American Indians

5. Which of the following was an important consequence of the historical processes discussed in the excerpt?
   - **a.** A decrease in British conflicts with American Indians over land, resources, and political boundaries
   - **b.** An increasing attempt of the British government to incorporate North American colonies into a coherent imperial structure in pursuit of mercantilist aims
   - **c.** Expanded use of enslaved labor in the plantation systems of the Chesapeake
   - **d.** The development of autonomous political communities influenced by the spread of Protestant evangelism

SHORT ANSWER QUESTIONS

Read each question carefully and write a short response. Use evidence from the text to support your claims.

"Throughout the early period of colonization, there was continuing tension between hope that the environment might meet English expectations and requirements and accommodation by the English settlers to the environment actually encountered. The steady accumulation and assimilation of facts about the climate of eastern North America threatened the classical concept of climates — the belief that climate is constant in any latitude around the world. Yet colonists and promoters struggled to adapt the old concept to fit new evidence. . . . Newfoundland came to be rejected for colonization, although its importance as a fishing ground continued. New England was finally perceived as a rough country where settlement was possible. . . . In the early seventeenth-century southern mainland colonies, settlers continued to base their expectations on latitude and to hope they could eventually produce commodities comparable to those England imported from southern Europe."

Karen Kupperman, "The Puzzle of the American Climate in the Early Colonial Period," *American Historical Review* 87 (1982): 1288–1289.

"Summer and winter, rain and snow, ceased to come predictably in the Southwest somewhat earlier than elsewhere in the northern hemisphere. . . . [D]ense populations had been living at the edge of the land's agricultural carrying capacity. . . . Perhaps the extraordinary religious fervor, political capital and material resources devoted to agricultural ceremonies . . . shows a cultural recognition of just how unstable the balance was. In the arid Southwest, the balance had always been particularly delicate, and collapse appears to have come suddenly — not with the onset of global cooling in the 1300s, but after a fifty-year-long local drought struck the Chaco Canyon area after 1130. . . . All of the major Puebloan and Hohokam urban centers were gradually abandoned in favor of new pueblos . . . the former, stratified system of smaller supporting villages apparently disappeared in favor of a more egalitarian settlement pattern."

Daniel K. Richter, *Before the Revolution: America's Ancient Pasts*, 2010

1. Using the two excerpts provided, answer (a), (b), and (c).
   - **a.** Briefly explain how ONE specific historical event or development supports one of the following as the most significant factor contributing to increased British colonization of North America prior to 1700.
     - The desire for religious freedom
     - Social mobility
     - An Atlantic economy of extensive trade networks
   - **b.** Briefly explain how ONE specific historical event, development, or circumstance from the period before 1700 that is not explicitly mentioned in the excerpts could be used to support Kupperman's argument.
   - **c.** Briefly explain how ONE specific historical event, development, or circumstance from the period before 1700 that is not explicitly mentioned in the excerpts could be used to support Richter's argument.
2. Answer (a), (b), and (c).
   - **a.** Briefly explain ONE important difference in the development of British and French colonies in North America between 1500 and 1700.
   - **b.** Briefly explain ANOTHER important difference in the development of British and French colonies in North America between 1500 and 1700.
   - **c.** Briefly explain ONE important similarity in the development of British and French colonies in North America between 1500 and 1700.
3. Answer (a), (b), and (c).
   - **a.** Briefly explain how ONE specific historical event or development supports one of the following as the most significant factor contributing to increased British colonization of North America prior to 1700.
     - Desires of colonists for religious freedom
     - Royal economic and legal policies
     - Extensive transatlantic trade networks
   - **b.** Briefly explain how ANOTHER specific historical event or development supports your choice in (a).
   - **c.** Briefly explain why ONE of the other developments had a less significant effect as your choice in part (1).

TRM Find complete suggested responses in the Teacher's Resource Materials.

TRM Find complete suggested responses in the Teacher's Resource Materials.

PART 1 AP® PRACTICE ESSAY QUESTIONS

DOCUMENT-BASED QUESTION *Suggested reading period: 15 minutes. Suggested writing time: 45 minutes*

DIRECTIONS: Question 1 is based on the accompanying documents. The documents have been edited for the purpose of this exercise.

1. Evaluate the extent to which transatlantic interactions changed Atlantic world societies from 1491–1607.

DOCUMENT 1

Source: Portuguese chronicler Duarte Lopez, *A Report on the Kingdom of Kongo*, 1491.

"The King of Portugal, Don Giovanni the Second, being desirous to discover the East Indies, sent forth diverse ships by the coast of Africa to search out this Navigation . . . and running all along that coast did light upon the River Zaire . . . [T] o entertain this traffic with Congo . . . finding the trade there to be so free and profitable, and the people so friendly, left certain Portuguese behind them, to learn the language and to [trade] with them, among whom one was a Mass-Priest. These Portuguese were very well entertained and esteemed by the Prince [of Congo], and reverenced as though they had become earthly Gods, and [had] descended down from heaven into those Countries. But the Portuguese told them that they were men as they themselves were, and professors of Christianity. And when they perceived in how great estimation the people held them, the foresaid Priest and others began to reason with the Prince, touching the Christian religion, and to show unto them the errors of the Pagan superstition, and by little and little teach them the faith which we profess . . . [and] that which the Portuguese spoke unto them, greatly pleased the Prince, and so he became converted. . . .

And now the Portuguese ships departed from Congo, and returned to Portugal; and by them did the King of Congo write to the King of Portugal . . . with earnest request, that he would send some Priests, with all other orders and ceremonies to make him a Christian . . . and so the King [of Portugal] took order for sundry religious persons, to be sent to him accordingly, with all ornaments for the Church and other services, as Crosses and Images, so that he was fully furnished with all things that were necessary and needful for such an action. . . ."

DOCUMENT 2

Source: *Aztec Account of the Siege of Tenochtitlan*, 1520.

"While the Spaniards were in Tlaxcala, a great plague broke out here in Tenochtitlan. It . . . lasted for seventy days, striking everywhere in the city and killing a vast number of our people. Sores erupted on our faces, our breasts, our bellies; we were covered with agonizing sores from head to foot.

The illness was so dreadful that no one could walk or move. The sick were so utterly helpless that they could only lie on their beds like corpses, unable to move their limbs or even their heads. They could not lie face down or roll from one side to the other. If they did move their bodies, they screamed with pain.

A great many died from this plague, and many others died of hunger. They could not get up to search for food, and everyone else was too sick to care for them, so they starved to death in their beds.

Some people came down with a milder form of the disease; they suffered less than the others and made a good recovery. But they could not escape entirely. Their looks were ravaged, for wherever a sore broke out, it gouged an ugly pockmark in the skin. And a few of the survivors were left completely blind."

DOCUMENT 3

Source: Letter from King Nzinga Mbemba of the Congo to King Joao III of Portugal, 1526.

"Sir, your highness should know how our Kingdom is being lost in so many ways. . . . We cannot reckon how great the damage is, since [your Portuguese] merchants are taking every day our natives, sons of the land and sons of our noblemen and vassals and our relatives. . . . So great, Sir, is the corruption and licentiousness that our country is being completely depopulated, and your highness should not agree with this or accept in your service. . . . That is why we beg of Your Highness to help and assist us in this matter, commanding your factors [representatives] that they should not send here either merchants or wares, because it is our will that in these Kingdoms there should not be any trade of slaves nor outlet for them. . . .

Moreover, Sir, in our Kingdoms there is another great inconvenience which is of little service to God, and this is that many of our people [are] keenly desirous . . . of the wares and things of your Kingdoms, which are brought here by your people. In order to satisfy their voracious appetite . . . very often it happens that they kidnap even noblemen and the sons of noblemen, and our relatives, and take them to be sold to the white men or are in our Kingdoms. . . ."

DOCUMENT 4

Source: Spanish priest and historian Bartolomé de las Casas, *History of the Indies*, 1528.

"In that year of 1500 . . . the King determined to send a new governor to Hispaniola, which at that time was the only seat of government in the Indies. . . .

At first the Indians were forced to stay six months away at work; later the time was extended to eight months and this was called a shift, at the end of which they brought all the gold for minting . . . during the minting period, the Indians were allowed to go home, a few days' journey on foot. One can imagine their state when they arrived after eight months, and those who found their wives must have cried, lamenting their condition together. How could they even rest, since they had to provide for the needs of their family when their land had gone to weeds? Of those who had worked in the mines, a bare 10 percent had survived to start the journey home. . . .

The [Commander] arranged to have wages paid as follows, which I swear is the truth: in exchange for his life of services, an Indian received . . . 225 maravedis, paid to them once a year. . . . This sum bought a comb, a small mirror, and a string of green or blue glass beads . . . although in truth, they offered their labor up for nothing, caring only to fill their stomachs to appease their raging hunger and find ways to escape their desperate lives. . . .

I believe the above clearly demonstrates that the Indians were totally deprived of their freedom and put in the harshest, fiercest, most horrible servitude and captivity which no one who has not seen it can understand. Even beasts enjoy more freedom when they are allowed to graze in the fields."

DOCUMENT 5

Source: Michel de Montaigne, French philosopher, reflecting upon the meaning of Barbarism in his essay *Des Cannibales*, 1580.

"I had with me for a long time a man who had lived ten or twelve years in that other [New] world which had been discovered in our century. . . .

. . . I think there is nothing barbarous and savage in that [American Indian] nation, from what I have been told, except each man calls barbarous whatever is not his own practice; for indeed it seems we have no other test of truth and reason than the example and pattern of opinions and customs of the country we live in. There is always the perfect religion, the perfect government, the perfect and accomplished manners in all things. . . .

These [American Indian] nations, then, seem barbarous in this sense, that they have been fashioned very little by the human mind, and are still close to their original naturalness. The laws of nature still rule them, very little corrupted by ours; and they are in such a state of purity that I am sometimes vexed that they were unknown earlier, in the days when there were men able to judge them better than we. . . . This is a nation, I should say to Plato, in which there is no sort of traffic [business], no knowledge of letters, no science or numbers . . . no custom of servitude, no riches or poverty, no care for any but common kinship, no clothes, no agriculture, no metal, no use of wine or wheat. . . .

. . . I am heartily sorry that, judging their faults rightly, we should be so blind to our own. I think there is more barbarity . . . in tearing by tortures and the rack a body still full of feeling, in roasting a man bit by bit, in having him bitten and mangled by dogs and swine (as we have not only read but seen within fresh memory . . . and what is worse, on the pretext of piety and religion). . . ."

DOCUMENT 6

Source: Englishman Richard Hakluyt, *Discourse Concerning the Western Planting*, 1584.

"It is well worth the observation to see and consider what the like voyages of discovery and planting in the East and West Indies have wrought in the kingdoms of Portugal and Spain, both which realms, being of themselves poor and barren and hardly able to sustain their inhabitants, by their discoveries have found such occasion of employment, that these many years we have not heard scarcely of any pirate of those two nations; whereas we and the French are most infamous for our outrageous, common, and daily piracies. . . .

. . . [W]e are grown more populous than ever heretofore; so that now there are of every art and science so many . . . having no way to be set on work, [who] be either mutinous and seek alteration in the state, or at the very least burdensome to the commonwealth . . . whereby all the prisons of the land . . . are stuffed full of them. . . .

Whereas if this voyage were put into execution, these petty thieves might be condemned for certain years to the western parts . . . in sawing and felling of timber for masts of ships . . . in burning of the firs and pine trees to make pitch, tar, rosin and soap ashes . . . in planting of sugar cane . . . in gathering of cotton whereof there is plenty, in tilling of the soil for grain . . . trees for oranges, lemons, almonds, figs , and other fruits, all which are found to grow there already . . . in fishing, salting and drying of . . . cod, salmon, and herring; in making of honey, wax, and turpentine. . . ."

DOCUMENT 7

Source: Number of Cities in Europe (10,000 inhabitants or more), Selected Regions, 1400–1600.

	England (Wales)	Netherlands	France	Northern Italy	Spain	Portugal
1400	4	0	24	21	12	2
1500	5	14	31	31	28	3
1600	7	21	42	37	43	5

LONG ESSAY QUESTIONS *Suggested writing time: 40 minutes*

DIRECTIONS: Please choose one of the following three questions to answer. Make a historically defensible claim and support your reasoning with specific and relevant evidence.

2. Evaluate the extent to which the British and Spanish shared similar views about the role of religion in colonization.
3. Evaluate the extent to which American Indians and Europeans differed in political systems from 1491–1607.
4. Evaluate the extent to which American Indians and Europeans held divergent economic views in the period prior to 1607.

2 PART

CHAPTER 3
The British Atlantic World, 1607–1750

CHAPTER 4
Growth, Diversity, and Conflict, 1720–1763

British North America and the Atlantic World
1607–1763

Between 1607 and 1763, English North America took root and flourished. From its unpromising beginnings in Jamestown, where colonists struggled simply to survive, England's colonies grew quickly in number and then, after 1680, became dramatically more populous and diverse. To begin Part 2, we reach back to 1607, the date when Jamestown was founded and permanent English colonization began. We end Part 2 a century and a half later, in 1763, with Britain's victory in the Great War for Empire. The choice to include the Great War in Part 2 — thus ending in 1763 rather than 1754 — allows us to understand how imperial rivalry and warfare underlay the colonial North American experience in the eighteenth century. By 1763, Britain became the dominant power in eastern North America, and its colonies contained nearly two million subjects.

The rise of British North America occurred amid great changes. Instead of a barrier to contact, the Atlantic Ocean became a watery highway carrying people, merchandise, and ideas. Britain's growing strength in manufacturing and commerce dramatically affected colonists, as both producers and consumers. Trade caused more intensive interactions with Europe that knit together the increasingly diverse societies of British North America. After 1689, Europe plunged into a century of warfare that spilled over into North America. British, French, and Spanish colonies all turned to Indian allies for help, fundamentally changing the character of cross-cultural relations. The Great War for Empire transformed the map of North America, making Great Britain ascendant in eastern North America, while also creating new challenges for everyone living there.

We give particular attention in Part 2 to three central questions that help define this period. Keep them in mind as you read Chapters 3 and 4. ▶

AP® CONCEPT CONNECTIONS

Why did British North America become so diverse?

Europe's American colonies gradually diverged from each other in character. The core of Spanish America developed into complex multiracial societies; Portuguese Brazil was dominated by plantations and mining; the Dutch kept only a few tropical plantation colonies; the French also had valuable plantation colonies but struggled to populate their vast North American holdings. Britain's mainland colonies, by contrast, gradually stabilized and then grew and diversified rapidly. Britain came to dominate the Atlantic slave trade and brought more than two million slaves across the Atlantic. Most went to Jamaica and Barbados, but half a million found their way to the mainland.

Many non-English Europeans also came to British North America, including more than 200,000 Germans and Scots-Irish. Most immigrated to Pennsylvania, which soon had the most ethnically diverse population of Europeans on the continent. These groups struggled to maintain their identities in a rapidly changing landscape.

National Maritime Museum, London/The Image Works.

How was colonial culture shaped by ties to Great Britain?

These population movements were part of the larger growth of the British Atlantic world. Britain's transatlantic shipping networks laid the foundation for rising economic productivity and dramatic cultural transformations. The cultural impact of this change grew out of two further developments: the print revolution, which brought many ideas into circulation, and the consumer revolution, which flooded the Atlantic world with a variety of newly available merchandise. Previously, observers believed that colonies were useful primarily for the goods they produced. But as they grew and prospered, colonies also became important markets for British exports. Colonists were consumers as well as producers, and they constituted Britain's fastest-growing market.

Four new cultural developments emerged in the British Atlantic world. A transatlantic community interested in science and rationalism shared Enlightenment ideas; Pietists promoted the revival and expansion of Christianity; well-to-do colonists gained access to genteel values and the finery needed to put them into action; and colonial consumers went further into debt than they ever had before.

The Granger Collection, New York.

Why did imperial warfare transform relations with Native Americans?

After 1689, Britain, France, and their European allies went to war against each other repeatedly. As these conflicts came to the North American theater, they decisively influenced Indian relations. Colonization and the Columbian Exchange had devastated Native American populations. The rise of imperial warfare encouraged the process of tribalization, whereby Indians regrouped and, where it was necessary, modified their political structures — called tribes by Europeans — to deal with their colonial neighbors and strike alliances in times of war. Native Americans benefitted from these alliances by gaining resources and strengthening their hands against traditional enemies. Europeans, in turn, used Indian allies as proxy warriors in their conflicts over North American territory.

This pattern culminated in the Great War for Empire, which began in North America and reshaped its map. The Treaty of Paris of 1763 gave Britain control of the entire continent east of the Mississippi. Events would soon show what a mixed blessing that outcome was, for Native Americans, colonists, and British administrators alike.

Courtesy of the John Carter Brown Library at Brown University.

Organized around a single theme, the Part 2 Document Set in *Sources for America's History* can be used to teach AP® Theme MIG: Migration and Settlement, how and why people migrated to and within the Americas in the period after contact.

AP® THEMATIC UNDERSTANDING

British North America and the Atlantic World 1607–1763

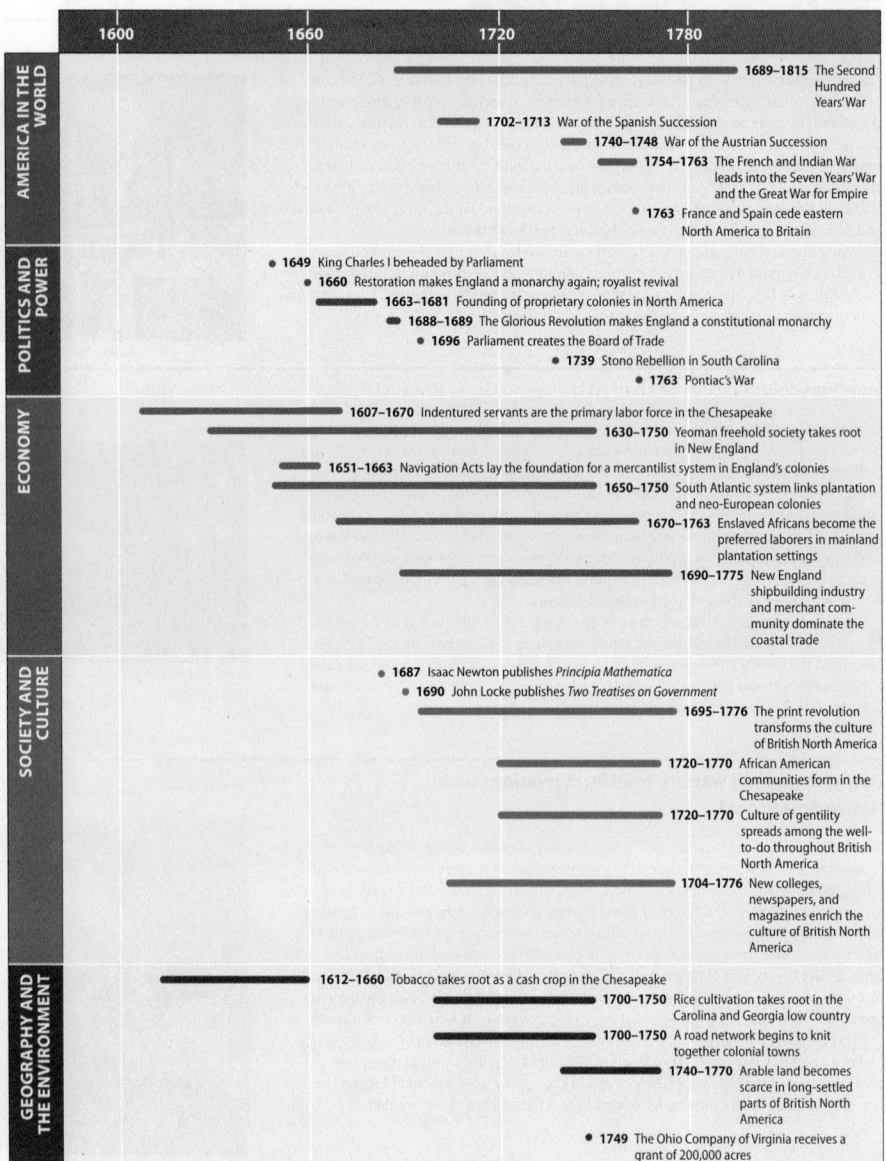

Timeline: 1600 · 1660 · 1720 · 1780

AMERICA IN THE WORLD

- **1689–1815** The Second Hundred Years' War
- **1702–1713** War of the Spanish Succession
- **1740–1748** War of the Austrian Succession
- **1754–1763** The French and Indian War leads into the Seven Years' War and the Great War for Empire
- **1763** France and Spain cede eastern North America to Britain

POLITICS AND POWER

- **1649** King Charles I beheaded by Parliament
- **1660** Restoration makes England a monarchy again; royalist revival
- **1663–1681** Founding of proprietary colonies in North America
- **1688–1689** The Glorious Revolution makes England a constitutional monarchy
- **1696** Parliament creates the Board of Trade
- **1739** Stono Rebellion in South Carolina
- **1763** Pontiac's War

ECONOMY

- **1607–1670** Indentured servants are the primary labor force in the Chesapeake
- **1630–1750** Yeoman freehold society takes root in New England
- **1651–1663** Navigation Acts lay the foundation for a mercantilist system in England's colonies
- **1650–1750** South Atlantic system links plantation and neo-European colonies
- **1670–1763** Enslaved Africans become the preferred laborers in mainland plantation settings
- **1690–1775** New England shipbuilding industry and merchant community dominate the coastal trade

SOCIETY AND CULTURE

- **1687** Isaac Newton publishes *Principia Mathematica*
- **1690** John Locke publishes *Two Treatises on Government*
- **1695–1776** The print revolution transforms the culture of British North America
- **1720–1770** African American communities form in the Chesapeake
- **1720–1770** Culture of gentility spreads among the well-to-do throughout British North America
- **1704–1776** New colleges, newspapers, and magazines enrich the culture of British North America

GEOGRAPHY AND THE ENVIRONMENT

- **1612–1660** Tobacco takes root as a cash crop in the Chesapeake
- **1700–1750** Rice cultivation takes root in the Carolina and Georgia low country
- **1700–1750** A road network begins to knit together colonial towns
- **1740–1770** Arable land becomes scarce in long-settled parts of British North America
- **1749** The Ohio Company of Virginia receives a grant of 200,000 acres

AP® Making Connections Across Chapters

Read these questions and think about them as you read the chapters in this part. Then when you have completed reading this part, return to these questions and answer them.

1 How did warfare between Great Britain and its European rivals affect relations with Native Americans?

Anne S. K. Brown Military Collection, Brown University Library.

2 What were Great Britain's priorities in governing its American colonies? How did colonial governments develop in response?

DEA PICTURE LIBRARY/Getty Images.

3 What was the South Atlantic System, and how did it shape economic development in Great Britain's colonies?

Library of Congress.

4 How and why did the societies and cultures of British North America grow more diverse and complex during the first two-thirds of the eighteenth century?

Private Collection/Bridgeman Images.

5 How did the challenges that developed in the colonies in the mid-eighteenth century place new pressures on the colonies and strain relations with Great Britain?

Museum of Fine Arts, Boston, Massachusetts, USA/Bridgeman Images.

TRM Find complete suggested responses in the Teacher's Resource Materials.

3 CHAPTER The British Atlantic World

1607–1750

Chapter 3 — AP® Assessment Weight and Pacing Guide

The assessment weight on the AP® U.S. History Exam for Chapters 3–4 is 6–8 percent. This chapter falls in Unit 2 of the AP® U.S. History Curriculum, covering Period 2: 1607–1754.

This pacing guide is based on a schedule with 120 sessions of 50 minutes each before the AP® U.S. History Exam. If you have a different number of sessions before the exam, you can modify the pacing to meet your needs. If you have additional time, consider incorporating quizzes, released AP® U.S. History questions, practice exams, writing practice, and other instructional activities.

	Traditional Schedule	Block Schedule
Chapter 3	5 days	2–3 days

Daily Pacing Guide

	Content Focus	Essential Question
Day 1	Colonies to Empire, 1607–1713	Why did changes in England between 1660 and 1690 reshape its American Empire?
Day 2	Imperial Wars and Native Peoples	What was tribalization, and how did it help Native Americans cope with their European neighbors?
Day 3	The Imperial Slave Economy	How did their ties to Great Britain and Africa change the lives of American planters?
Day 4	The Northern Maritime Economy	What economic activities drove the northern maritime economy?
Day 5	The New Politics of Empire, 1713–1750	How could Great Britain maintain its mercantilist policies and permit the "salutary neglect" of its colonies at the same time?

AP® Alignment

Section Heading	AP® Topic	AP® Theme
Colonies to Empire, 1607–1713	2.2, 2.3	MIG, GEO
Imperial Wars and Native Peoples	2.4, 2.5	WXT, WOR
The Imperial Slave Economy	2.4, 2.6	WXT, SOC
The Northern Maritime Economy	2.4, 2.7	WXT, ARC
The New Politics of Empire, 1713–1750	2.4, 2.7	WXT, NAT

*Should changes be made to the Course Framework in the future, an updated alignment will be placed on our AP® updates page at go.bfwpub.com/ap-course-updates.

Chapter 3 — Overview

Chapter 3 begins by focusing on the reasons for resistance to British policies in the British North American colonies. This chapter begins to describe the unique development of individual colonies and the characteristics of colonial regions. While this chapter focuses on the development within the colonies, attention is also given to the impact of the exchange of ideas in the Atlantic world, including the beginning of the Enlightenment. It is important that students understand the development of the slave trade and the system of slavery in the British North American colonies. As the development of the colonies proceeds, the chapter engages students in an analysis of colonial economic development and its relationship to social hierarchy. Finally, the chapter examines the differences in the colonial elite and popular action, both of which often operate in opposition to the policy of mercantilism.

Chapter 3 — Resources

The following resources can be found in the Teacher's Resource Materials (TRM) that accompany the book. You can access the TRM via the book's digital platform, by clicking the TRM links found here in your Teacher's Edition e-book or by contacting your representative to access the resources online. Visit **bfwpub.com/henretta10e** to learn more.

TRM Chapter 3 Lecture Presentation Slides

TRM Chapter 3 Outline with AP® Focus

TRM Chapter 3 Lecture Strategies

TRM Chapter 3 Suggested Responses

TRM Handout 3.1 — Thematic Analysis: Sugar

TRM Handout 3.2 — Causation: Salutary Neglect

Chapter 3 — Essential Activity

Show students images of the Chesapeake and Massachusetts Bay Colony, and prompt them to discuss the ideas or perceptions the images emphasize about these two early regions. Then ask students to create a Venn diagram by identifying specific differences and similarities between the settlements. Provide students with the following categories to consider: population/demographics, government, moral order, credit base/economy, and defense. Then ask students to write a thesis statement in response to the following prompt: Compare the development of the Chesapeake and the Massachusetts Bay Colony as unique regions within British North America.

Chapter 3 — Bell Ringers

The following activities take no more than 5–15 minutes of your class period and offer an effective and engaging way to begin your lessons and for students to apply AP® Skills & Processes:

- To help students understand reactions to attempts to change salutary neglect by the British, pretend to announce that a policy or rule that is not strongly enforced (maybe dress code, no cell phone policy, etc.) will now be strictly enforced and put a list of penalties on the board for violations. Students will likely be "outraged" by this change in policy. Give students a few minutes to express their "grievances" at this change in policy. Then, relate their reactions to the reactions of colonists at the Navigation Acts. This is a great way to introduce a lesson on increasing tensions between colonists and the British government.
- Divide the class into three large groups, designating each group to represent students, teachers, and administrators, respectively. Give each group 3 minutes to come up with a list of goals the group they are representing has at school each day. After 3 minutes, ask groups to share lists with each other and discuss as time permits. Use this to introduce students to thinking about the goals of the three groups in the colonies: colonists, colonial governments, and the British government. Ask students to consider how the goals of these groups might show similar differences and discuss reasons for those differences.

NOTES

3
CHAPTER

The British Atlantic World
1607–1750

TEACHING STRATEGY

Assist students in understanding how the South Atlantic System created interconnections that shaped the development of the British colonies. The term "Atlantic world" emphasizes the notion that the ocean acted as a sphere of interaction, largely through trade, that linked not only Britain and its colonies but also connected colonies to each other. Beyond trade, the growing Atlantic world included the English government's efforts to extend greater control over the colonies in the late seventeenth and early eighteenth centuries as the colonists became increasingly aware of being British subjects, even as they paradoxically experienced a measure of autonomy. For an overview of the Atlantic world, approaches to teaching it, and suggestions for additional reading, see the College Board's *Teaching About the Atlantic World in the AP® U.S. History Classroom.* Access this resource by searching "AP® Central Teaching Atlantic World." For a complete model answer to the **AP® LEARNING FOCUS** question, see p. 108.

AP® LEARNING FOCUS

Why and how did the South Atlantic System reshape the economy, society, and culture of British North America?

For two weeks in June 1744, the town of Lancaster, Pennsylvania, hosted more than 250 Iroquois men, women, and children for a diplomatic conference with representatives from Pennsylvania, Maryland, and Virginia. Crowds of curious observers thronged Lancaster's streets and courthouse. The conference grew out of a diplomatic system between the colonies and the Iroquois designed to air grievances and resolve conflict: the Covenant Chain. Participants welcomed each other, exchanged speeches, and negotiated agreements in public ceremonies whose minutes became part of the official record of the colonies.

At Lancaster, the colonies had much to ask of their Iroquois allies. For one thing, they wanted them to confirm a land agreement. The Iroquois often began such conferences by resisting land deals; as the Cayuga orator Gachradodon said, "You know very well, when the White people came first here they were poor; but now they have got our Lands, and are by them become rich, and we are now poor; what little we have had for the Land goes soon away, but the Land lasts forever." In the end, however, they had little choice but to accept merchandise in exchange for land, since colonial officials were unwilling to take no for an answer. The colonists also announced that Britain was once again going to war with France, and they requested military support from their Iroquois allies. Canassatego — a tall, commanding Onondaga orator, about sixty years old, renowned for his eloquence — replied, "We shall never forget that you and we have but one Heart, one Head, one Eye, one Ear, and one Hand. We shall have all your Country under our Eye, and take all the Care we can to prevent any Enemy from coming into it."

The Lancaster conference, and dozens of others like it, demonstrate that the British colonies, like those of France and Spain, relied ever more heavily on alliances with Native Americans as they sought to extend their power in North America. Indian nations remade themselves in these same years, creating political structures — called "tribes" by Europeans — that allowed them to regroup in the face of population decline and function more effectively alongside neighboring colonies. The colonies, meanwhile, were drawn together into an integrated economic sphere — the South Atlantic System — that brought prosperity to British North America, while they achieved a measure of political autonomy that became essential to their understanding of what it meant to be British subjects.

English Tobacco Label, c. 1700 This label, which was used to advertise Virginia tobacco to London consumers, illustrates the growth of plantation economies in North America. Three well-to-do planters, bewigged and dressed in fashionable, colorful coats, take their ease with pipes of tobacco and glasses of liquor while slaves labor for them in the fields. The product's name — London's Virginia — highlights the relationship between production on colonial plantations and consumption in the English metropolis. The Granger Collection, New York.

AP® THEME

WXT: Work, Exchange, and Technology

Use this advertisement to discuss how the British Atlantic world was shaped by the production and trade of cash crops. Guide students' analysis with the following questions:

- **What does this image indicate about Europeans' perceptions of how tobacco was grown?** *The image reflects perceptions of the exotic American location where tobacco was grown by slaves laboring under a hot sun.*
- **What does this advertisement suggest about tobacco and its uses?** *The image is a reminder that tobacco — like other cash crops — was a luxury consumer item. Elites used it, but it was also an "aspirational" product, as middle-rank people seeing an ad like this might consider tobacco use to emulate the lifestyle of elites.*

AP® SKILLS & PROCESSES

CONTINUITY AND CHANGE

Use the **TIMELINE** table to explore how 1642 to 1751 might constitute a definable historical era associated with the notion of a "British Atlantic World." Extend this discussion by asking students to identify specific events from the timeline that especially highlight the notion of a British Atlantic system.

TIMELINE

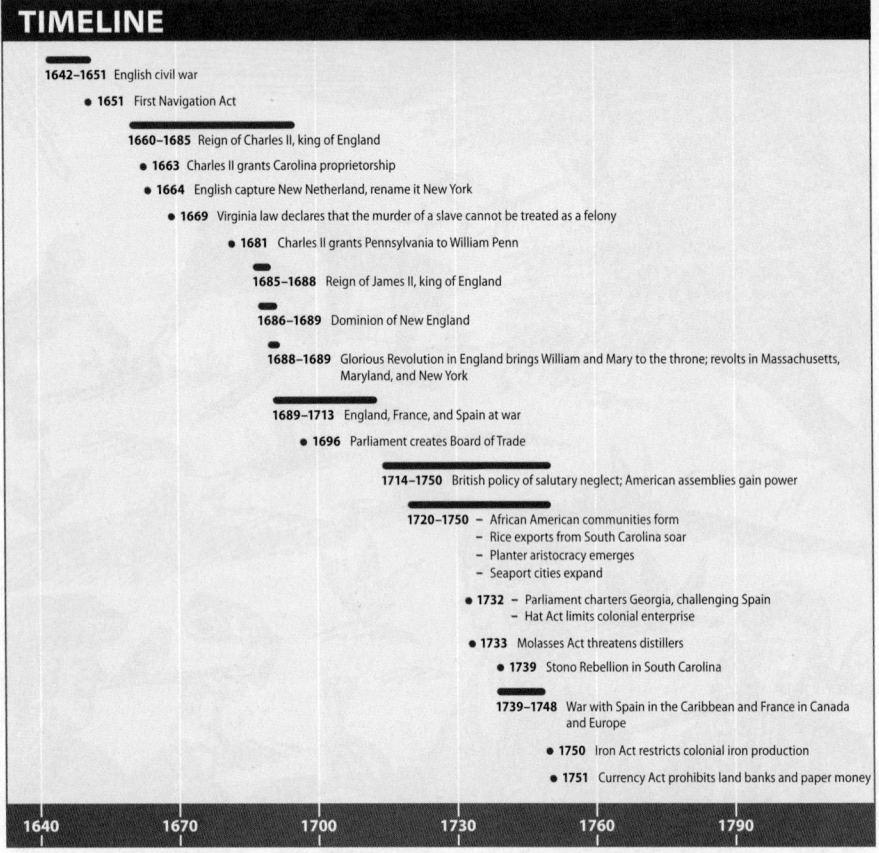

- **1642–1651** English civil war
- **1651** First Navigation Act
- **1660–1685** Reign of Charles II, king of England
- **1663** Charles II grants Carolina proprietorship
- **1664** English capture New Netherland, rename it New York
- **1669** Virginia law declares that the murder of a slave cannot be treated as a felony
- **1681** Charles II grants Pennsylvania to William Penn
- **1685–1688** Reign of James II, king of England
- **1686–1689** Dominion of New England
- **1688–1689** Glorious Revolution in England brings William and Mary to the throne; revolts in Massachusetts, Maryland, and New York
- **1689–1713** England, France, and Spain at war
- **1696** Parliament creates Board of Trade
- **1714–1750** British policy of salutary neglect; American assemblies gain power
- **1720–1750**
  - African American communities form
  - Rice exports from South Carolina soar
  - Planter aristocracy emerges
  - Seaport cities expand
- **1732**
  - Parliament charters Georgia, challenging Spain
  - Hat Act limits colonial enterprise
- **1733** Molasses Act threatens distillers
- **1739** Stono Rebellion in South Carolina
- **1739–1748** War with Spain in the Caribbean and France in Canada and Europe
- **1750** Iron Act restricts colonial iron production
- **1751** Currency Act prohibits land banks and paper money

1640 1670 1700 1730 1760 1790

COLONIES TO EMPIRE, 1607–1713

Why did changes in England between 1660 and 1690 reshape its American Empire?

AP® EXAM TIP

Explaining the difficulty experienced in British North America is critical for success on the AP® Exam.

Before 1660, England governed its New England and Chesapeake colonies haphazardly. Taking advantage of that laxness and the English civil war, local "big men" (Puritan magistrates and tobacco planters) ran their societies as they wished. Following the restoration of the monarchy in 1660, royal bureaucrats tried to impose order on the unruly settlements and, enlisting the aid of Indian allies, warred with rival European powers.

Self-Governing Colonies and New Elites, 1607–1660

In the years after its first American colonies were founded, England experienced a wrenching series of political crises. Disagreements between King Charles I and Parliament grew steadily worse until they culminated in the English civil war, which lasted from 1642 to 1651. A parliamentary army led by Oliver Cromwell fought against royalist forces for control of the country. Charles I was captured by Cromwell's army, tried for treason, and beheaded in 1649. Charles II, his son and successor, carried on the war for two more years but was defeated in 1651 and fled to France. England was no longer a monarchy. It was ruled by Parliament as a commonwealth, then fell under the personal rule of Oliver Cromwell, who was known as the Lord Protector. Cromwell's death in 1658 triggered a political crisis that led Parliament to invite Charles II to restore the monarchy and take up the throne.

During the long period of instability and crisis in England, its American colonies largely managed their own affairs. Neither crown nor Parliament devised a consistent system of imperial administration; in these years, England had colonies but no empire. Moreover, these were difficult years for all the colonies, when important decisions about the nature of the economy, the government, and the social system had to be worked out through trial and error. In this era of intense experimentation and struggle, emerging colonial elites often had to arrive at their own solutions to pressing problems. Leading men in Virginia, Maryland, the New England colonies, and the islands of the West Indies claimed authority and hammered out political systems that allowed the colonies to be largely self-governing. Even in colonies with crown-appointed governors, such as Sir William Berkeley in Virginia, it soon became apparent that those appointees had to make alliances with local leaders in order to be effective.

Charles II Ascends the Throne When Parliament invited Charles Stuart to take up the throne, it brought a return to traditional forms and symbols of royal authority. This coronation portrait by John Michael Wright features all the trappings of monarchy, including robes trimmed with ermine, a crown, a scepter, and an orb. Those objects had been destroyed after Parliament beheaded Charles's father, and so they had to be remade for the coronation. DEA PICTURE LIBRARY/Getty Images.

The restoration of the crown in 1660 marked a decisive end to this period of near-independence in the colonies. Charles II (r. 1660–1685) and his brother and successor, James II (r. 1685–1688), were deeply interested in England's overseas possessions and dramatically reshaped colonial enterprise. From England's early, prolonged, halting efforts to sponsor overseas activity, an empire finally began to take shape.

AP® SKILLS & PROCESSES

CAUSATION

How did the turmoil of the English Civil War affect England's colonial enterprises?

The Restoration Colonies and Imperial Expansion

Charles II expanded English power in Asia and America. In 1662, he married the Portuguese princess Catherine of Braganza, whose dowry included the islands of Bombay (present-day Mumbai, India). Then, in 1663, Charles initiated new outposts in America by authorizing eight loyal noblemen to settle Carolina, an area that had long been claimed by Spain and was populated by thousands of Indians. The following year, he awarded the just-conquered Dutch colony of New Netherland to his brother James, the Duke of York, who renamed the colony New York and then re-granted a portion of it, called New Jersey, to another group of proprietors. Finally, in 1681, Charles granted a vast tract to — Pennsylvania, or "Penn's Woods." In a great land grab, England had ousted the Dutch from North America (see "New Netherland" in Chapter 2), intruded into Spain's northern empire, and claimed all the land in between.

AP® SKILLS & PROCESSES

CONTEXTUALIZATION

How did the establishment of the Restoration colonies compare to earlier colonies established in British North America?

The Carolinas In 1660, English settlement was concentrated in New England and the Chesapeake. Five corporate colonies coexisted in New England: Massachusetts Bay, Plymouth, Connecticut, New Haven, and Rhode Island. (Connecticut absorbed

CHECK FOR UNDERSTANDING

Ask students: **How did the colonies become functionally self-governing in the first half of the seventeenth century?** *The civil war caused turmoil in England, culminating in the execution of Charles I. This left the colonies to largely govern themselves. When the monarchy was restored in 1660, this autonomy ended.*

AP® SKILLS & PROCESSES

CAUSATION

Use the **CAUSATION** question to help students consider the effects of the English civil war on the colonies. Remind them that despite the tendency to view the colonies as independent, they were in fact part of the English empire and deeply affected by events that happened there. Extend this prompt by asking students to make an inference about how Charles II and James II "dramatically reshaped colonial enterprise," since they "were deeply interested in England's overseas possessions."

TRM Find complete suggested responses in the Teacher's Resource Materials.

TEACHING STRATEGY

Present students with the following quote from Edmund Burke's *An Account of the European Settlements in America* (1757): "The settlement of our colonies was never pursued upon any regular plan; but they were formed, grew, and flourished, as accidents, the nature of the climate, or the dispositions of private men happened to operate" (Burke, 408). Ask students to classify colonies according to Burke's classifications: accidents, climate, or private men. Lead students in a discussion on the importance of salutary neglect in the development of the British North American colonies as it relates to this quote. Since there was "no regular plan," British colonists developed independent ideas about self-government and colonial administration. Then discuss the English civil war, Commonwealth period, and restoration as influences on the development of British colonies in North America.

AP® APPLY THE TIP

Ask pairs of students to work collaboratively to provide supporting details of the key characteristics identified for each British colony in **TABLE 3.1**. Alternatively, complete this activity using a jigsaw format by dividing the colonies among different groups of students and then rearranging groups to allow each student to act as an "expert" on a specific colony. Ask groups to determine which characteristics are most important for distinguishing colonies and colonial regions from each other. In addition to organizing by colonial region, ask students to determine other ways to organize the colonies into meaningful groups based on specific similarities and differences.

TEACHING STRATEGY

Use **TABLE 3.1** as a template for charting the earlier English colonies in North America in Virginia, Massachusetts, and Maryland by having students identify patterns in colony type, religion, and economic activity across time and regions for all of the English colonies.

proprietorship
A colony created through a grant of land from the English monarch to an individual or group who then set up a form of government largely independent from royal control.

New Haven in 1662, while Massachusetts Bay became a royal colony and absorbed Plymouth in 1692.) In the Chesapeake, Virginia was controlled by the crown while Maryland was in the hands of a Lord Proprietor. Like Lord Baltimore's Maryland, the new settlements in Carolina, New York, New Jersey, and Pennsylvania — the Restoration Colonies, as historians call them — were **proprietorships**. The Carolina and Jersey grantees, the Duke of York, and William Penn owned all the land in their new colonies and could rule them as they wished, provided that their laws conformed broadly to those of England (Table 3.1). Indeed, in New York, James II refused to allow an elective assembly and ruled by decree. The Carolina proprietors envisioned a traditional European society; they hoped to implement a manorial system, with a mass of serfs governed by a handful of powerful nobles.

The manorial system proved a fantasy. The first North Carolina settlers were a mixture of poor families and runaway servants from Virginia and English Quakers, an equality-minded Protestant sect (also known as the Society of Friends). Quakers "think there is no difference between a Gentleman and a labourer," complained an Anglican clergyman. Refusing to work on large manors, the settlers raised corn, hogs, and tobacco on modest family farms. Inspired by Bacon's Rebellion, they rebelled in 1677 against taxes on tobacco and again in 1708 against taxes to support the Anglican Church. Through their stubborn independence, residents forced the proprietors to abandon their dreams of a manorial society.

In South Carolina, the colonists also went their own way. The leading white settlers there were migrants from overcrowded Barbados. Hoping to re-create that island's hierarchical slave society, they used enslaved workers — both Africans and Native Americans — to raise cattle and food crops for export to the West Indies. Carolina merchants opened a lucrative trade in deerskins and Indian slaves with neighboring peoples. Then, around 1700, South Carolina planters hit upon rice cultivation. The swampy estuaries of the coastal low country could be modified with sluices, floodgates, and check dams to create ideal rice-growing conditions, and slaves could do the backbreaking work. By 1708, white South Carolinians relied upon a few thousand slaves to work their coastal plantations; thereafter, the African population exploded. Blacks outnumbered whites by 1710 and constituted two-thirds of the population by 1740.

AP® EXAM TIP
Expand upon the chart below as you read to compare the development of Massachusetts Bay, Virginia, South Carolina, and Pennsylvania.

TABLE 3.1

English Colonies Established in North America, 1660–1750

Colony	Date	Original Colony Type	Religion	Status in 1775	Chief Export/ Economic Activity
Carolina	1663	Proprietary	Church of England		
North	1691	Proprietary	Church of England	Royal	Farming, naval stores
South	1691	Proprietary	Church of England	Royal	Rice, indigo
New Jersey	1664	Proprietary	Church of England	Royal	Wheat
New York	1664	Proprietary	Church of England	Royal	Wheat
Pennsylvania	1681	Proprietary	Quaker	Proprietary	Wheat
Georgia	1732	Trustees	Church of England	Royal	Rice
New Hampshire (separated from Massachusetts)	1741	Royal	Congregationalist	Royal	Mixed farming, lumber, naval stores
Nova Scotia	1749	Royal	Church of England	Royal	Fishing, mixed farming, naval stores

TEACHING STRATEGY

Because the English focused primarily on a proprietary model of colonization in North America, each region developed unique economies due to the pressure to produce a profit. Profitability lead to viability and this circumstance was a sharp contrast from the Spanish attempts to colonize. Have students work on connecting this concept through the idea of agriculture-based economies. Have students select two proprietary colonies whose inhabitants focused on agriculture, and provide a brief two- or three-sentence explanation connecting proprietary, agriculture, and labor.

William Penn and Pennsylvania In contrast to the Carolinas, which languished for decades with proprietors and colonists at odds, William Penn's colony was marked by unity of purpose: all who came hoped to create a prosperous neo-European settlement similar to the societies they knew at home. Penn, though born to wealth — he owned substantial estates in Ireland and England and lived lavishly — joined the **Quakers**, who condemned extravagance. Penn designed his colony as a refuge for his fellow Quakers, who were persecuted in England because they refused to serve in the military or pay taxes to support the Church of England. Penn himself had spent more than two years in jail in England for preaching his beliefs.

Like the Puritans, the Quakers sought to restore Christianity to its early simple spirituality. But they rejected the Puritans' pessimistic Calvinist doctrines, which restricted salvation to a small elect. The Quakers followed the teachings of two English visionaries, George Fox and Margaret Fell, who argued that God had imbued all men — and women — with an "inner light" of grace or understanding. Reflecting the sect's emphasis on gender equality, 350 Quaker women would serve as ministers in the colonies.

Mindful of the catastrophic history of Indian relations in the Chesapeake and New England, Penn exhorted colonists to "sit downe Lovingly" alongside the Native American inhabitants of the Delaware and Susquehanna valleys. He wrote a letter to the leaders of the Iroquois Confederacy alerting them to his intention to settle a colony, and in 1682 he arranged a public treaty with the Delaware Indians to purchase the lands that Philadelphia and the surrounding settlements would soon occupy.

Penn's Frame of Government (1681) applied the Quakers' radical beliefs to politics. It ensured religious freedom by prohibiting a legally established church, and it promoted political equality by allowing all property-owning men to vote and hold office. Cheered by these provisions, thousands of English Quakers flocked to Pennsylvania. To attract European Protestants, Penn published pamphlets in Germany promising cheap land and religious toleration. In 1683, migrants from Saxony founded Germantown (just outside Philadelphia), and thousands of other Germans soon followed. Ethnic diversity, pacifism, and freedom of conscience made Pennsylvania the most open and democratic of the Restoration Colonies.

From Mercantilism to Imperial Dominion

As Charles II distributed American land, his advisors devised policies to keep colonial trade in English hands. Since the 1560s, the English crown had pursued mercantilist policies, using government subsidies and charters to stimulate English manufacturing and foreign trade. Now it extended these mercantilist strategies to the American settlements through the **Navigation Acts**.

Quakers
Epithet for members of the Society of Friends. Their belief that God spoke directly to each individual through an "inner light" and that neither the Bible nor ministers were essential to discovering God's Word put them in conflict with both the Church of England and orthodox Puritans.

Navigation Acts
English laws passed, beginning in the 1650s and 1660s, requiring that certain English colonial goods be shipped through English ports on English ships manned primarily by English sailors in order to benefit English merchants, shippers, and seamen.

PENNS TREATY with the INDIANS. made 1681 with out an Oath and never broken. The foundation of Religious and Civil LIBERTY, in the U.S. of AMERICA.

VISUAL ACTIVITY

Edward Hicks, *Penn's Treaty*, c. 1830–1835 Edward Hicks was a Pennsylvania-born painter and preacher whose art expressed a religiously infused understanding of early Pennsylvania history. In more than a hundred paintings, Hicks depicted the colony as a "peaceable kingdom," in which lions lay down with lambs and colonists met peacefully with Native Americans. This painting, which features Hicks's characteristic folk art style, depicts William Penn's first meeting with the Lenni-Lenape peoples in 1683. A Quaker pacifist, Penn refused to seize Indian lands by force and instead negotiated their purchase. This spirit of peaceful cooperation eroded in the later colonial era, but Hicks chose to portray Penn's meeting with the Indians as the foundation of religious and civil liberty in America. Private Collection/Bridgeman Images.

READING THE IMAGE: Look carefully at this painting. Who are the principal figures, and what have they brought to this meeting? What is the large sheet of paper that Penn is pointing to?

MAKING CONNECTIONS: This painting is not a contemporary document; it was made in the 1830s, 150 years after the event it is supposed to depict. Why do you think Edward Hicks thought this moment was especially significant? Why would he call it "the foundation of Religious and Civil Liberty, in the U.S. of America"?

TEACHING STRATEGY

Use the lesson plan "William Penn's Peaceable Kingdom" from the National Endowment for the Humanities' EDSITEment! Web site to supplement your discussion on William Penn. The lesson plan provides excerpts of Penn's *Frame for Government* mentioned in the text and guided reading questions that give a brief introduction to his vision for his colony. Access this resource by searching "EDSITEment William Penn."

AP® THEME

WOR: America in the World

Use Hicks's painting to discuss the cultural cooperation that characterized early Pennsylvania's relationship with Native Americans. Ask students: **How does this image indicate Pennsylvania's self-understanding in terms of its relationship with Native Americans?** *In contrast to the pattern established by most other English colonies, whose relationships with Native Americans were often characterized by violence, this image reflects a conscious self-identity of Pennsylvania as uniquely respectful toward Indians. As the caption indicates, that relationship broke down long before Hicks painted this, so he is commemorating that earlier period.*

CHECK FOR UNDERSTANDING

Ask students: **What were the Restoration Colonies and how did they represent imperial expansion?** *Charles II, king during the "Restoration" of the monarchy, allowed proprietors, mostly nobility, to found their own colonies. This included Carolina, New York (captured from the Dutch), and Pennsylvania. These new ventures represented a significant geographical expansion of British North America.*

TRM Find complete suggested responses in the Teacher's Resource Materials.

AP® APPLY THE TIP

Ask students to create a flow chart that illustrates both British colonial policies and the reactions of colonists to these policies from 1650 to 1688. In addition, the flow chart should illustrate the consequences of different reactions to British policy in the colonies. Students should note when multiple effects can be seen from one policy or action in their chart. Then lead students in a discussion exploring the reasons why the colonists reacted so strongly to the imposition of mercantilism when it was the dominant economic philosophy of all European nations in this era.

AP® EXAM TIP

Take notes on the ways that colonists responded to British attempts to impose mercantilist economic policies on the colonies.

The Navigation Acts Dutch and French shippers were often buying sugar and other colonial products from English colonies and carrying them directly into foreign markets. To counter this practice, the Navigation Act of 1651 required that goods be carried on ships owned by English or colonial merchants. New parliamentary acts in 1660 and 1663 strengthened the ban on foreign traders: colonists could export sugar and tobacco only to England and import European goods only through England; moreover, three-quarters of the crew on English vessels had to be English. To pay the customs officials who enforced these laws, the Revenue Act of 1673 imposed a "plantation duty" on American exports of sugar and tobacco.

The English government backed these policies with military force. In three wars between 1652 and 1674, the English navy drove the Dutch from New Netherland and contested Holland's control of the Atlantic slave trade by attacking Dutch forts and ships along the West African coast. Meanwhile, English merchants expanded their fleets, which increased in capacity from 150,000 tons in 1640 to 340,000 tons in 1690. This growth occurred on both sides of the Atlantic; by 1702, only London and Bristol had more ships registered in port than did the town of Boston.

Though colonial ports benefitted from the growth of English shipping, many colonists violated the Navigation Acts. Planters continued to trade with Dutch shippers, and New England merchants imported sugar and molasses from the French West Indies. The Massachusetts Bay assembly boldly declared: "The laws of England are bounded within the seas [surrounding it] and do not reach America." Outraged by this insolence, customs official Edward Randolph called for troops to "reduce Massachusetts to obedience." Instead, the Lords of Trade — the administrative body charged with colonial affairs — chose a less violent, but no less confrontational, strategy. In 1679, it denied the claim of Massachusetts Bay to New Hampshire and eventually established a separate royal colony there. Then, in 1684, the Lords of Trade persuaded an English court to annul the Massachusetts Bay charter by charging the Puritan government with violating the Navigation Acts and virtually outlawing the Church of England.

Dominion of New England
A royal province created by King James II in 1686 that would have absorbed Connecticut, Rhode Island, Massachusetts Bay, Plymouth, New York, and New Jersey into a single colony and eliminated their chartered rights. James's plan was canceled by the Glorious Revolution, which removed him from the throne.

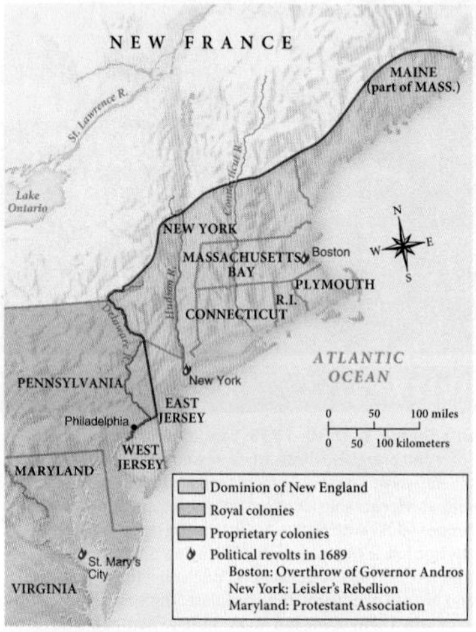

MAP 3.1 The Dominion of New England, 1686–1689
In the Dominion, James II created a vast royal colony that stretched nearly 500 miles along the Atlantic coast. During the Glorious Revolution in England, politicians and ministers in Boston and New York City led revolts that ousted Dominion officials and repudiated their authority. King William and Queen Mary replaced the Dominion with governments that balanced the power held by imperial authorities and local political institutions.

The Dominion of New England The Puritans' troubles had only begun, thanks to the accession of King James II (r. 1685–1688), an aggressive and inflexible ruler. During the reign of Oliver Cromwell, James had grown up in exile in France, and he admired its authoritarian king, Louis XIV. James wanted stricter control over the colonies and targeted New England for his reforms. In 1686, the Lords of Trade revoked the charters of Connecticut and Rhode Island and merged them with Massachusetts Bay and Plymouth to form a new royal province, the **Dominion of New England**. James II appointed Sir Edmund Andros, a hard-edged former military officer, as governor of the Dominion. Two years later, James II added New York and New Jersey to the Dominion, creating a vast colony that stretched from Maine to Pennsylvania (Map 3.1).

The Dominion extended to America the authoritarian model of colonial rule that the English government had imposed on Catholic Ireland. James II ordered Governor Andros to abolish the existing legislative assemblies. In Massachusetts, Andros banned town meetings, angering villagers who prized local self-rule. Andros also advocated public worship in the Church of England, offending Puritan Congregationalists. Even worse, from the colonists' perspective, the governor invalidated all land titles granted under the original Massachusetts Bay charter. Andros offered to provide new deeds, but only if the colonists would pay an annual fee. James's plan for the

AP® THEME

WOR: America in the World

Use **MAP 3.1** to illustrate the conflict between the colonies and Britain that erupted during the Glorious Revolution. Ask students: **What does this map reveal about imperial government during the Dominion and colonial responses to it?** *The map shows the vast swath of territory contained by the Dominion, including the tremendous length of coastline. The Dominion encompassed diverse colonial backgrounds — Puritan-dominated New England, a former Dutch colony, and Quaker East Jersey and West Jersey. Apart from resentment over the loss of town meetings, New Englanders had a very different culture from the others. Violent rebellion broke out in port towns across the northern British colonies.*

CHECK FOR UNDERSTANDING

Ask students: **How did mercantilism and imperial "dominion" affect the colonies?** *The Navigation Acts, first instituted during the reign of Oliver Cromwell, extended British authority over the colonies by requiring that most trade take place directly with and through England, and enforcing these policies militarily. The Dominion of New England also dramatically expanded government power, ending self-governing through town hall meetings.*

AP® SKILLS & PROCESSES

DEVELOPMENTS AND PROCESSES

Mercantilism is an essential and required historical concept to understand. Not only is it crucial for students to understand a basic definition, but students need to develop their comprehension to the extent they can make connections across Period 2 and Period 3 of the AP® Course Framework. Mercantilism has been the central focus of multiple AP® free response questions. Therefore, have students work on defining mercantilism using the two or three following terms: *colonization, natural resources, Atlantic world, Navigation Laws, economic self-sufficiency.* Connecting these terms enables students to see the breadth of importance relevant to mercantilism.

Dominion of New England made it clear that he intended to rule his overseas possessions as an absolute monarch, rejecting the institutions and rights that colonists had come to expect.

The Glorious Revolution in England and America

Fortunately for the colonists, James II angered English political leaders as much as Andros alienated colonists. The king revoked the charters of English towns, rejected the advice of Parliament, and aroused popular opposition by openly practicing Roman Catholicism. Then, in 1688, James's Spanish Catholic wife gave birth to a son. Faced with a Catholic heir to the English throne, Protestant bishops and parliamentary leaders in the Whig Party invited William of Orange, a staunchly Protestant Dutch prince who was married to James's Protestant daughter, Mary Stuart, to come to England at the head of an invading army. With their support, William led a quick and nearly bloodless coup, and King James II was overthrown in an event dubbed the **Glorious Revolution** by its supporters. Whig politicians forced King William and Queen Mary to accept the Declaration of Rights, creating a **constitutional monarchy** that enhanced the powers of the House of Commons at the expense of the crown. The Whigs wanted political power, especially the power to levy taxes, to reside in the hands of the gentry, merchants, and other substantial property owners.

To justify their coup, the members of Parliament relied on political philosopher John Locke. In his *Two Treatises on Government* (1690), Locke rejected the divine-right monarchy celebrated by James II, arguing that the legitimacy of government rests on the consent of the governed and that individuals have inalienable natural rights to life, liberty, and property. Locke's celebration of individual rights and representative government had a lasting influence in America, where many political leaders wanted to expand the powers of the colonial assemblies.

The Glorious Revolution sparked rebellions by Protestant colonists in Massachusetts, Maryland, and New York. When news of the coup reached Boston in April 1689, Puritan leaders and 2,000 militiamen seized Governor Andros and shipped him back to England. Heeding American complaints of authoritarian rule, the new monarchs broke up the Dominion of New England. However, they refused to restore the old Puritan-dominated government of Massachusetts Bay, instead creating in 1692 a new royal colony (which absorbed Plymouth and Maine). The new charter empowered the king to appoint the governor and customs officials, gave the vote to all male property owners (not just Puritan church members), and eliminated Puritan restrictions on the Church of England.

In Maryland, the uprising had economic as well as religious causes. Since 1660, falling tobacco prices had hurt poorer farmers, who were overwhelmingly Protestant, while taxes and fees paid to mostly Catholic proprietary officials continued to rise. When Parliament ousted James II, a Protestant association mustered 700 men and forcibly removed the Catholic governor. The Lords of Trade supported this Protestant initiative: they suspended Lord Baltimore's proprietorship, imposed royal government, and made the Church of England the legal religion in the colony. This arrangement lasted until 1715, when Benedict Calvert, the fourth Lord Baltimore, converted to the Anglican faith and the king restored the proprietorship to the Calvert family.

In New York, a Dutchman named Jacob Leisler led the rebellion against the Dominion of New England. Initially he enjoyed broad support, but he soon alienated many English-speaking New Yorkers and well-to-do Dutch residents. Leisler's heavy-handed tactics made him vulnerable; when William and Mary appointed Henry Sloughter as governor in 1691, Leisler was indicted for treason, hanged, and decapitated.

AP® SKILLS & PROCESSES

CAUSATION

How did the ambitions of Charles II and James II remake English North America?

Glorious Revolution
A quick and nearly bloodless coup in 1688 in which members of Parliament invited William of Orange to overthrow James II. Whig politicians forced the new King William and Queen Mary to accept the Declaration of Rights, creating a constitutional monarchy that enhanced the powers of the House of Commons at the expense of the crown.

constitutional monarchy
A monarchy limited in its rule by a constitution — in England's case, the Declaration of Rights (1689), which formally limited the power of its king.

AP® EXAM TIP

Comparing the ideas of John Locke to existing ideas of self-government in the colonies is a good way to contextualize the Enlightenment.

AP® SKILLS & PROCESSES

CAUSATION

The **CAUSATION** question situates developments within North America in the broader context of royal restoration-era policies. To appreciate the significance of the imperial policies of the restoration, students may need to be reminded of the small-scale nature of the previous colonies in Virginia, Massachusetts, and Maryland, which had begun with little support from the Crown.

TRM Find complete suggested responses in the Teacher's Resource Materials.

AP® APPLY THE TIP

Help students to place the Glorious Revolution (1688) and the start of the Enlightenment (1690) into context by explaining John Locke's role as political theorist justifying the Glorious Revolution in what would become the first treatise of the Enlightenment. Remind students that in context, the theories of John Locke regarding natural rights, sovereignty of citizens, and social contract theory were describing the existing government of England after the Glorious Revolution. Provide students with one or more excerpts from Locke's *Second Treatise on Civil Government*. Ask them to read and analyze the excerpts and make a historical argument regarding the extent to which Locke's ideas described the conditions, governments, and social systems that were in place in the colonies by 1690. Ask students to consider why Locke's ideas would have such a profound effect on the development of political ideas in the British North American colonies.

AP® SKILLS & PROCESSES

CAUSATION

The **CAUSATION** question asks students to explore both the short- and long-term consequences of the Glorious Revolution. Assist students in finding these consequences and identifying the language that helps them distinguish between the short-term effect of greater self-government and the long-term effect of Locke's notions of individual rights and representative government, which had a "lasting influence" in America.

TRM Find complete suggested responses in the Teacher's Resource Materials.

CHECK FOR UNDERSTANDING

Ask students to do the following: **Identify three new developments between 1660 and 1690 that helped shape England's American Empire.** *New proprietary colonies expanded British North America, the Navigation Acts tied the colonies more closely to England, and the Glorious Revolution reinforced the notion of self-governance in the colonies.*

AP® APPLY THE TIP

Have students work in pairs to create a T-chart labeled "Conflict" and "Cooperation." Ask them to use their textbook to classify the ways that European imperial rivalries impacted American Indian groups. Students should indicate the ways that both cooperation and conflicts between American Indian groups illustrated attempts to maintain autonomy in the face of the growing presence of settlers in North America in their chart. Then lead a discussion considering the impact of technology, disease, and European ideas on conflict and cooperation in British North America.

AP® SKILLS & PROCESSES

CAUSATION
How did the Glorious Revolution affect relations between England and its colonies?

The Glorious Revolution of 1688–1689 began a new era in the politics of both England and its American colonies. In England, William and Mary ruled as constitutional monarchs; overseas, they promoted an empire based on commerce. They accepted the overthrow of James's disastrous Dominion of New England and allowed Massachusetts (under its new charter) and New York to resume self-government. In 1696, Parliament created a new body, the Board of Trade, to oversee colonial affairs. While the Board of Trade continued to pursue the mercantilist policies that made the colonies economically beneficial, it permitted local elites to maintain a strong hand in colonial affairs. As England plunged into a new era of European warfare, its leaders had little choice but to allow its colonies substantial autonomy.

IMPERIAL WARS AND NATIVE PEOPLES

What was tribalization, and how did it help Native Americans cope with their European neighbors?

The price that England paid for bringing William of Orange to the throne was a new commitment to warfare on the continent. England wanted William because of his unambiguous Protestant commitments; William wanted England because of the resources it could bring to bear in European wars. Beginning with the War of the League of Augsburg in 1689, England embarked on an era sometimes called the **Second Hundred Years' War**, which lasted until the defeat of Napoleon at Waterloo in 1815. In that time, England (which became Great Britain in 1707, when the Act of Union joined the English and Scottish Parliaments) fought in seven major wars; the longest era of peace lasted only twenty-six years.

Second Hundred Years' War An era of warfare between England and France beginning in 1689 and lasting until 1815. In that time, England fought in seven major wars; the longest era of peace lasted only twenty-six years.

Imperial wars transformed North America. Prior to 1689, American affairs were distant from those of Europe, but the recurrent wars of the eighteenth century spilled over repeatedly into the colonies. Governments were forced to arm themselves and create new alliances with neighboring Native Americans, who tried to turn the fighting to their own advantage. Although war brought money to the American colonies in the form of war contracts, it also placed new demands on colonial governments to support the increasingly militant British Empire. To win wars in Western Europe, the Caribbean, and far-flung oceans, British leaders created a powerful central state that spent three-quarters of its revenue on military and naval expenses.

AP® EXAM TIP
The impact of European imperial rivalries on American Indian populations illustrated conflict and cooperation in North America.

Tribalization

For Native Americans, the rise of war intersected with a process scholars have called **tribalization**: the adaptation of stateless peoples to the demands imposed on them by neighboring states. In North America, tribalization occurred in catastrophic circumstances. Eurasian diseases rapidly killed off broad swaths of Native communities, disproportionately victimizing the old and the very young. In oral cultures, old people were irreplaceable repositories of knowledge, while the young were literally the future. With populations in free fall, many polities disappeared altogether. By the eighteenth century, the groups that survived had all been transformed. Some new tribes, like the Catawbas, had not existed before and were pieced together from remnants of formerly large groups. Other nations, like the Iroquois, declined in numbers but sustained themselves by adopting many war captives. In the Carolina borderlands, a large number of Muskogean-speaking communities came together as a nation known to the British as the "Creek" Indians, so named because some of them lived on Ochese Creek. Similarly, the Cherokees, the Delawares, and other groups that were culturally linked but politically fragmented became coherent "tribes" to deal more effectively with their European neighbors.

tribalization The adaptation of stateless peoples to the demands imposed on them by neighboring states.

The rise of imperial warfare exposed Native American communities to danger, but it also gave them newfound leverage. The Iroquois were radically endangered by imperial conflict. A promised English alliance failed them, and in 1693 a combined force of French soldiers, militiamen, and their Indian allies burned all three Mohawk villages to the ground. Thereafter, the Iroquois devised a strategy for playing French and English interests against each other. In 1701, they made alliances with both empires, declaring their intention to remain neutral in future conflicts between them. This did not mean that the Iroquois stayed on the sideline. Iroquois warriors often participated in raids during wartime, and Iroquois spokesmen met regularly with representatives of New York and New France to affirm their alliances and receive diplomatic gifts that included guns, powder, lead, clothing, and rum (from the British) or brandy (from the French). Their neutrality, paradoxically, made them more sought after as allies. For example, their alliance with New York, known as the **Covenant Chain**, soon became a model for relations between the British Empire and other Native American peoples.

Imperial warfare also reshaped Indian relations in the Southeast. During the War of the Spanish Succession (1702–1713), which pitted Britain against France and Spain, English settlers in the Carolinas armed the Creeks, whose 15,000 members farmed the fertile lands along the present-day border of Georgia and Alabama. A joint English-Creek expedition attacked Spanish Florida, burning the town of St. Augustine but failing to capture the fort. To protect Havana in nearby Cuba, the Spanish reinforced St. Augustine and unsuccessfully attacked Charleston, South Carolina.

The "Four Indian Kings" in London, 1710 After a failed invasion of Canada in 1709, a colonial delegation went to London to ask the queen to try again. They brought four Indians with them — three Mohawks and a Mahican — and presented them in London as the "Four Indian Kings" of the Iroquois. The four kings met Queen Anne, dined with nobility, attended the theater, and toured the sites. They sat for several portraits, which were engraved for prints like this one. The queen agreed to make another try for Canada, but the 1711 invasion failed again. Collection of the New-York Historical Society, USA/Bridgeman Images.

AP® THEME

WOR: America in the World

Use the image of the "Four Indian Kings" to discuss the nature of alliances the British Empire and Native American groups formed together against the French Empire. For some students, the notion of Native Americans as allies of the British may be surprising. Ask students: **What does this image suggest about the relationship between the British Empire and Iroquois in the early eighteenth century? Why do you think so?** *The British accorded some respect to their allies. This is indicated by their willingness to bring them to England, host them, and have their portraits created. In other words, the British treated them as another empire.*

Indian Goals

The Creeks had their own agenda: to become the dominant tribe in the region, they needed to vanquish their longtime enemies, the pro-French Choctaws to the west and the Spanish-allied Apalachees to the south. Beginning in 1704, a force of Creek and Yamasee warriors destroyed the remaining Franciscan missions in northern Florida, attacked the Spanish settlement at Pensacola, and captured a thousand Apalachees, whom they sold to South Carolinian slave traders for sale in the West Indies. Simultaneously, a Carolina-supported Creek expedition attacked the Iroquois-speaking Tuscarora people of North Carolina, killing hundreds, executing 160 male captives, and sending 400 women and children into slavery. The surviving Tuscaroras moved north to join the Iroquois in New York (who now became the Six Nations of the Iroquois). The Carolinians, having used the Creeks to kill Spaniards, now died at the hands of their former allies: when English traders demanded payment for trade debts in 1715, the Creeks and Yamasees revolted, killing 400 colonists before being overwhelmed by the Carolinians and their new Indian allies, the Cherokees.

Covenant Chain
The alliance of the Iroquois, first with the colony of New York, then with the British Empire and its other colonies. The Covenant Chain became a model for relations between the British Empire and other Native American peoples.

AP® SKILLS & PROCESSES

ARGUMENTATION

How did competition over resources encourage change and conflict in relations between native populations and Europeans?

TRM Find complete suggested responses in the Teacher's Resource Materials.

AP® SKILLS & PROCESSES

ANALYZING HISTORICAL EVIDENCE

The **AP® FIRSTHAND ACCOUNTS** feature introduces the practice of "reading against the grain," a key analytical skill historians routinely employ to derive evidence from documents by reading them in ways their authors did not intend. Tease out this metaphor for students by talking about how woodworkers typically sand and paint with the grain, so going "against the grain" implies resisting the natural pattern. In the case of primary sources, this means identifying the author's original purpose, noting the author's likely biases and distortions in the evidence that might result from this bias through a careful reading. As the text notes, this is a particularly important strategy when dealing with sources about Native Americans since they did not have written languages and their own words are rarely available to corroborate the claims made in European sources.

AP® FIRSTHAND ACCOUNTS

Native Americans and European Empires

Analyzing primary sources in which Europeans recorded Native American speech or actions can be especially challenging. In many cases, historians believe that recorded accounts of Native American speeches from the colonial era are essentially accurate. But often scholars consider it necessary to read *against the grain* of such sources — the document should be read closely and skeptically. Were the Native Americans speaking for themselves, or were others speaking for them? Who recorded their speech, and did they have any reason to alter the words they heard? What silences or contradictions can you see? These are good questions to apply to any primary source, but it's especially important when reading accounts of early Native Americans, who did not have written languages of their own to counterbalance the texts that were produced and archived by colonial powers. Try reading the two documents below "against the grain," and then answer the Questions for Analysis.

A BRITISH ACCOUNT OF INDIAN "KINGS" FROM THE SIX NATIONS VISITING LONDON, 1710

In 1710, four "Indian kings" traveled to London to strengthen the imperial alliance between Great Britain and the Iroquois. A London periodical printed the following account of their visit, including the speech they made to Queen Anne.

Source: [Abel Boyer], *The History of the Reign of Queen Anne. Digested into Annals. Year the Ninth* (London, 1711), 189–192.

“On the 19th of *April*, . . . Four *Kings*, or *Chiefs* of the Six Nations in the *West-Indies*, which lye between *New-England*, and *New-France*, or *Canada*: Who lately came over with the *West-India* Fleet, and were Cloath'd and Entertain'd at the Queen's Expence, had a Publick Audience of Her Majesty at the Palace of St. *James's*. . . . They made a Speech by their Interpreter, which Major *Pidgeon*, who was one of the Officers that came with them, read in *English* to Her Majesty, being as follows:

Great Queen!

We have undertaken a long and tedious Voyage, which none of our Predecessors could ever be prevail'd upon to undertake. The Motive that induc'd us was that we might see our *Great Queen*, and relate to Her those Things we thought absolutely necessary, for the Good of Her, and us, Her Allies, on the other side of the Great Water.

We doubt not but our *Great Queen* has been acquainted with our long and tedious War, in Conjunction with Her Children, (meaning Subjects) against Her Enemies the French; and that we have been as a strong Wall for their Security, even to the Loss of our best Men. The Truth of which . . . Colonel *Schuyler*, and . . . Colonel *Nicholson*, can testify, they having all our Proposals in Writing.

We were mightily rejoiced when we heard . . . that our Great Queen had resolved to send an Army to reduce *Canada*; . . . and in Token of our Friendship, we hung up the *Kettle*, and took up the *Hatchet*; and with one Consent, joined . . . Colonel *Schuyler*, and . . . Colonel *Nicholson*, in making Preparations . . . by building Forts, Store-Houses, Canows [canoes], and Battows [flat-bottomed boats]; whilst . . . Colonel *Vetch*, at the same time raised an Army at *Boston*, of which we were informed by our Ambassadors, who we sent thither for that Purpose. We waited long in Expectation of the Fleet from *England*, to join . . . Colonel *Vetch*, to go against *Quebec* by Sea, whilst [Nicholson, Schuyler], and we, went to *Port-Royal* by Land; but at last we were told, that our *Great Queen*, by some important Affair, was prevented in Her Design for that Season. This made us extream sorrowful, lest the *French*, who hitherto had dreaded us, should now think us unable to make War against them. The Reduction of *Canada* is of such Weight, that after the effecting

Native Americans also joined in the warfare between French Catholics in Canada and English Protestants in New England. With French aid, Catholic Mohawk and Abenaki warriors attacked their Puritan neighbors. They destroyed English settlements in Maine and, in 1704, attacked the western Massachusetts town of Deerfield, where they killed 48 residents and carried 112 into captivity. In response, New England militia attacked French settlements and, in 1710, joined with British naval forces to seize Port Royal in French Acadia (Nova Scotia). However, a major British–New England expedition against the French stronghold at Quebec, inspired in part by the visit of four Indian "kings" to London, failed miserably (see "Firsthand Accounts," above).

thereof, we should have *Free Hunting*, and a great Trade with our *Great Queen's* Children; and as a Token of the Sincerity of the Six Nations, we do here, in the Name of all, present Our *Great Queen* with the *Belts* of *Wampum*.

Since we have been in Alliance with our *Great Queen's* Children, we have had some Knowledge of the *Saviour* of the World; and have often been importuned by the *French*, both by the insinuations of their Priests, and by Presents, to come over to their Interest, but have always esteem'd them *Men of Falshood*: But if our *Great Queen* will be pleas'd to send over some Persons to instruct us, they shall find a most hearty Welcome. . . .

On *Friday*, the 21st of *April*, the Four *Indian* Princes went to see Dr. *Flamstead's* House, and Mathematical Instruments in *Greenwich* Park; after which they were nobly treated by some of the Lords Commissioners of the Admiralty, in One of Her Majesty's Yachts. They staid about a Fortnight longer in *London*, where they were entertain'd by several Persons of Distinction, particularly by the Duke of *Ormond*, who regaled them likewise with a Review of the Four Troops of Life-Guards; And having seen all the Curiosities in and about this Metropolis, they went down to Portsmouth, through *Hampton-Court*, and *Windsor*, and embark'd on Board the *Dragon*, . . . and on the 15th of *July* arrived at *Boston* in *New England*. ❞

FRENCH ACCOUNT OF A MEETING WITH ALLIED NATIVE AMERICAN LEADERS, 1730

In 1725, French officials in Louisiana organized a similar trip to Paris for five Native leaders representing the Missouris, Osages, Otos, and the Illinois confederacy. Jesuit missionaries had been active among the Illinois Indians for decades and had made many converts. Among them was Chikagou, a Michigamea headman (the Michigameas were one member nation of the Illinois confederacy) who was a staunch ally of the French. After a group of Natchez warriors attacked a French outpost in 1729, Chikagou and Mamantouensa, a headman of the Kaskaskias (another Illinois nation), appeared before the governor of Louisiana to offer their support in a counterattack. This account was recorded by a Jesuit missionary in attendance and included in a letter to his superior in Paris.

Source: Father le Petit to Father d'Avaugour, July 12, 1730, in *Jesuit Relations and Allied Documents*, ed. Reuben G. Thwaites, 73 vols. (Cleveland, 1896–1901), 68: 201–203.

❝ [The Illinois spokesman assured the governor,] 'We always place ourselves . . . before the enemies of the French; it is necessary to pass over our bodies to go to them, and to strike us to the heart before a single blow can reach them.' Their conduct is in accordance with this declaration, and has not in the least contradicted their words. . . . Chikagou, whom you saw in Paris, was at the head of the *Mitchigamias*, and *Mamantouensa* at the head of the *Kaskaskias*.

Chikagou spoke first. He spread out in the hall a carpet of deerskin, bordered with porcupine quills, on which he placed two calumets, with different savage ornaments, accompanying them with a present according to the usual custom. 'There,' said he, in showing these two calumets, 'are two messages which we bring you, the one of Religion, and the other of peace or war, as you shall determine. We have listened with respect to the Governors, because they bring us the word of the King our Father, and much more to the black Robes [Jesuit missionaries], because they bring us the word of God himself, who is the King of Kings. We have come from a great distance to weep with you for the death of the French, and to offer our Warriors to strike those hostile Nations whom you may wish to designate. You have but to speak. When I went over to France, the King promised me his protection for the Prayer, and recommended me never to abandon it. I will always remember it. Grant then your protection to us and to our black Robes.' He then gave utterance to the edifying sentiments with which he was impressed with regard to the Faith, as the Interpreter Baillarjon enabled us to half understand them in his miserable French. ❞

QUESTIONS FOR ANALYSIS

1. What language was the speech of the "four kings" delivered in? What requests did the "four kings" make of Queen Anne? Use evidence from the source to support your answer.
2. How large a role do you think the four men played in shaping its content? Use evidence from the source to support your answer.
3. What language was Chikagou's speech delivered in? What points did he seek to make? Use evidence from the source to support your answer.
4. Compare the accounts. Which of these texts do you consider most reliable? Support your argument using specific and relevant evidence.

TRM Find complete suggested responses in the Teacher's Resource Materials.

Stalemated militarily in America, Britain won major territorial and commercial concessions through its victories in Europe. In the Treaty of Utrecht (1713), Britain obtained Newfoundland, Acadia, and the Hudson Bay region of northern Canada from France, as well as access through Albany to the western Indian trade. From Spain, Britain acquired the strategic fortress of Gibraltar at the entrance to the Mediterranean and a thirty-year contract to supply slaves to Spanish America. These gains advanced Britain's quest for commercial supremacy and brought peace to eastern North America for a generation (Map 3.2).

AP® SKILLS & PROCESSES

MAKING CONNECTIONS

What did Native Americans have to gain by participating in imperial wars?

AP® SKILLS & PROCESSES

MAKING CONNECTIONS

The **MAKING CONNECTIONS** question asks students to consider Native Americans' motives. Remind students how Native Americans lacked written language, so we often have to infer their motives or learn about them through the mediation of European reports of their words.

TRM Find complete suggested responses in the Teacher's Resource Materials.

TEACHING STRATEGY

Use **MAP 3.2** to help students draw conclusions about the geographic reach of British North America, the form of government in each region, the racial makeup of each region, and the export volume of each region. Point out the tremendous value of West Indies exports, as well as the vast disproportion of blacks to whites in the colonies.

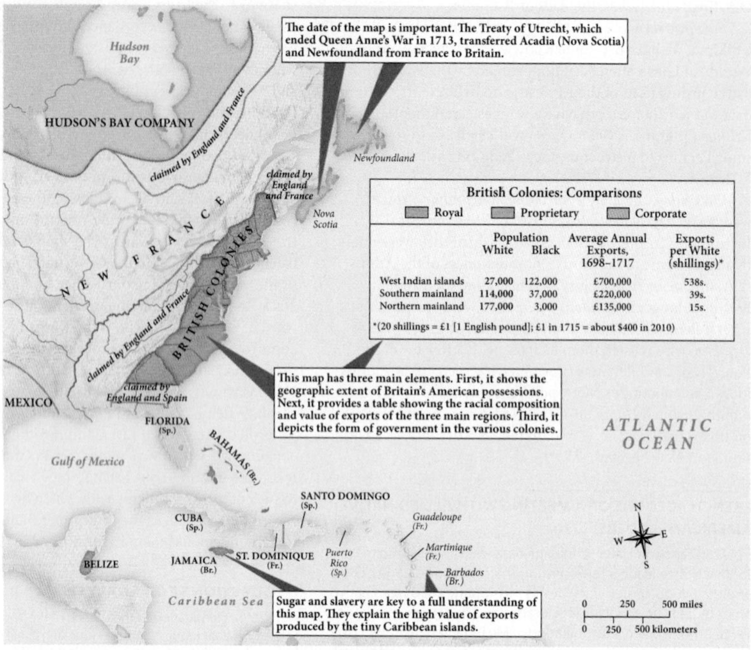
The date of the map is important. The Treaty of Utrecht, which ended Queen Anne's War in 1713, transferred Acadia (Nova Scotia) and Newfoundland from France to Britain.
Hudson Bay
HUDSON'S BAY COMPANY
claimed by England and France
Newfoundland
claimed by England and France
Nova Scotia
NEW FRANCE
BRITISH COLONIES
claimed by England and France
claimed by England and Spain
MEXICO
FLORIDA (Sp.)
Gulf of Mexico
BAHAMAS (Br.)
This map has three main elements. First, it shows the geographic extent of Britain's American possessions. Next, it provides a table showing the racial composition and value of exports of the three main regions. Third, it depicts the form of government in the various colonies.
ATLANTIC OCEAN
SANTO DOMINGO (Sp.)
CUBA (Sp.)
Guadeloupe (Fr.)
Martinique (Fr.)
BELIZE
JAMAICA (Br.)
ST. DOMINIQUE (Fr.)
Puerto Rico (Sp.)
Barbados (Br.)
Caribbean Sea
Sugar and slavery are key to a full understanding of this map. They explain the high value of exports produced by the tiny Caribbean islands.
N
W
E
S
0 250 500 miles
0 250 500 kilometers
British Colonies: Comparisons
Royal
Proprietary
Corporate

	Population White	Population Black	Average Annual Exports, 1698–1717	Exports per White (shillings)*
West Indian islands	27,000	122,000	£700,000	538s.
Southern mainland	114,000	37,000	£220,000	39s.
Northern mainland	177,000	3,000	£135,000	15s.

*(20 shillings = £1 [1 English pound]; £1 in 1715 = about $400 in 2010)

MAP 3.2 Britain's American Empire, 1713
Many of Britain's possessions in the West Indies were tiny islands, mere dots on the Caribbean Sea. However, in 1713, these small pieces of land were by far the most valuable parts of the empire. Their sugar crops brought wealth to English merchants, commerce to the northern colonies, and a brutal life and early death to the hundreds of thousands of African slaves working on the plantations.

THE IMPERIAL SLAVE ECONOMY

How did their ties to Great Britain and Africa change the lives of American planters?

Britain's focus on America reflected the growth of a new agricultural and commercial order — the **South Atlantic System** — that produced sugar, tobacco, rice, and other tropical and subtropical products for an international market. Its plantation societies were ruled by European planter-merchants and worked by hundreds of thousands of enslaved Africans (Figure 3.1).

South Atlantic System
A new agricultural and commercial order that produced sugar, tobacco, rice, and other tropical and subtropical products for an international market. Its plantation societies were ruled by European planter-merchants and worked by hundreds of thousands of enslaved Africans.

AP® EXAM TIP
Understanding the causes for the development and expansion of the African Slave Trade is important to know for the AP® Exam.

The South Atlantic System

The South Atlantic System had its center in Brazil and the West Indies, and sugar was its primary product. Before 1500, there were few sweet foods in Europe — mostly honey and fruits — so when European planters developed vast sugarcane plantations in America, they found a ready market for their crop. (The craving for the potent new sweet food was so intense that, by 1900, sugar accounted for an astonishing 20 percent of the calories consumed by the world's people.)

AP® APPLY THE TIP

Provide students with **Handout 3.1 — Thematic Analysis: Sugar (TRM)** that focuses on the impact of sugar on the development of the African slave trade. (Note: You could also put African slave trade in the center of this thematic analysis, but it is important to focus students on the importance of sugar and the comparison of slavery in different regions of the New World.) Then ask students to provide at least two pieces of specific evidence to illustrate the growth of the South Atlantic economy and African slave trade that can be tied back to the importance of sugar as a commodity in international trade.

TRM Find **Handout 3.1 — Thematic Analysis: Sugar** in the Teacher's Resource Materials.

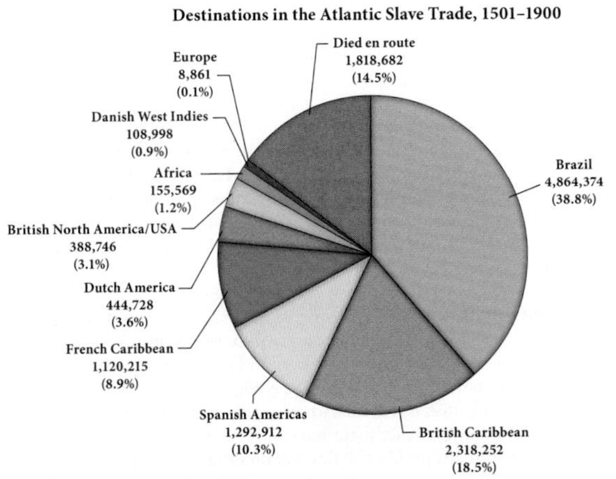

FIGURE 3.1 The Transit of Africans to the Americas
About 12.5 million enslaved Africans were forced into Atlantic slavery. Of those, about 1.8 million—almost 15 percent—died en route, while 10.7 million reached American destinations. The vast majority of the survivors went to Brazil or the West Indies, where they worked primarily on sugar plantations. About 388,000 arrived directly from Africa in the present-day United States, and tens of thousands more were traded to the North American mainland from the West Indies. Data from the Trans-Atlantic Slave Trade Database, at https://www.slavevoyages.org/, accessed July 15, 2019.

European merchants, investors, and planters reaped the profits of the South Atlantic System. Following mercantilist principles, they provided the plantations with tools and equipment to grow and process the sugarcane and ships to carry it to Europe. But it was the Atlantic slave trade that made the system run. Between 1520 and 1650, Portuguese traders carried about 820,000 Africans across the Atlantic—about 4,000 enslaved people a year before 1600 and 10,000 annually thereafter. Over the next half century, the Dutch dominated the Atlantic slave trade; then, between 1700 and 1800, the British transported about 2.5 million of the total of 6.1 million Africans carried to the Americas.

England and the West Indies England was a latecomer to the plantation economy, but from the beginning the prospect of a lucrative cash crop drew large numbers of migrants. On St. Kitts, Nevis, Montserrat, and Barbados, most early settlers were small-scale English farmers (and their indentured servants) who exported tobacco and livestock hides; on this basis, they created small but viable colonies. In 1650, there were more English residents in the West Indies (some 44,000) than in the Chesapeake (20,000) and New England (23,000) colonies combined.

After 1650, sugar transformed Barbados and the other islands into slave-based plantation societies, a change facilitated by English capital combined with the knowledge and experience of Dutch merchants. By 1680, an elite group of 175 planters, described by one antislavery writer of the time as "inhumane and barbarous," dominated Barbados's economy; they owned more than half of the island, thousands of indentured servants, and half of its more than 50,000 slaves. In 1692, exploited Irish servants and island-born African slaves staged a major uprising, which was brutally suppressed. The "leading principle" in a slave society, declared one West Indian planter, was to instill "fear" among workers and a commitment to "absolute coercive" force among masters. As social inequality and racial conflict increased, hundreds of

AP® EXAM TIP

Take good notes on the distinctions between the slave systems that developed in different British colonies.

AP® THEME

WXT: Work, Exchange, and Technology

FIGURE 3.1 provides useful information about the proportion of slaves that ended up in various locations throughout the Atlantic world. Guide students' analysis with the following questions:

- **What does the size of each wedge indicate?** *The size of each wedge represents the proportion of slaves out of the roughly 12 million who left Africa that went to each location.*
- **What major conclusions can you draw about the slave trade from this graphic representation?** *From this image, it is clear that more went to Brazil than to any other location, but that the West Indies comes in a very close second. While students rarely think of slaves going to Europe, a very small number did. The grey wedge indicates the percentage of those who died on board ship—approximately 1.8 million.*

TEACHING STRATEGY

Use prize-winning historian Philip Morgan's essay "Origins of American History" to provide an overview of the developments of slavery in an Atlantic context. Assign this as outside reading for advanced students or use as reference material for a lecture. Access this resource by searching "AP Central Origins of American History."

AP® THEME

SOC: Social Structures

The South Atlantic System and the Middle Passage are inextricably connected, as the economic well-being of British colonies in the Caribbean were heavily dependent upon laborers from Africa. Use video clip "Slave ship in 3D video" from slavevoyages.org and challenge students to brainstorm how enslaved persons could create new identities out of the horrors of commodification and the Middle Passage.

English farmers fled to South Carolina and the large island of Jamaica. But the days of Caribbean smallholders were numbered. English sugar merchants soon invested heavily in Jamaica; by 1750, it had seven hundred large sugar plantations, worked by more than 105,000 slaves, and had become the wealthiest British colony.

Sugar was a rich man's crop because it could be produced most efficiently on large plantations. Scores of enslaved laborers planted and cut the sugarcane, which was then processed by expensive equipment — crushing mills, boiling houses, distilling apparatus — into raw sugar, molasses, and rum. The affluent planter-merchants who controlled the sugar industry drew annual profits of more than 10 percent on their investment. As Scottish economist Adam Smith noted in his famous treatise *The Wealth of Nations* (1776), sugar was the most profitable crop grown in America or Europe.

The Impact on Britain The South Atlantic System generated enormous wealth and helped Europeans achieve world economic leadership. Most British West Indian plantations belonged to absentee owners who lived in England, where they spent their profits and formed a powerful sugar lobby. The Navigation Acts kept the British sugar trade in the hands of British merchants, who exported sugar to foreign markets, and by 1750 reshipments of American sugar and tobacco to Europe accounted for half of British exports. Enormous profits also flowed into Britain from the slave trade. The value of the guns, iron, rum, and cloth that were used to buy slaves was only about one-tenth (in the 1680s) to one-third (by the 1780s) of the value of the crops those enslaved workers produced in America, allowing English traders to sell slaves in the West Indies for three to five times what they paid for them in Africa.

These massive profits drove the slave trade. At its height in the 1790s, Britain annually exported three hundred thousand guns to Africa, and a British ship carrying 300 to 350 slaves left an African port every other day. This commerce stimulated the entire British economy. English, Scottish, and American shipyards built hundreds of vessels, and many thousands of people worked in trade-related industries: building port facilities and warehouses, refining sugar and tobacco, distilling rum from molasses, and manufacturing textiles and iron products for the growing markets in Africa and America. More than one thousand British merchant ships were plying the Atlantic by 1750, providing a supply of experienced sailors and laying the foundation for the supremacy of the Royal Navy.

AP® SKILLS & PROCESSES

CAUSATION

How did the South Atlantic System affect the British economy?

Africa, Africans, and the Slave Trade

As the South Atlantic System enhanced European prosperity, it imposed enormous costs on West and Central Africa. Between 1550 and 1870, the Atlantic slave trade uprooted 11 million Africans, draining lands south of the Sahara of people and wealth and changing African society (Map 3.3). By directing commerce away from the savannas and the Islamic world on the other side of the Sahara, the Atlantic slave trade changed the economic and religious dynamics of the African interior. It also fostered militaristic, centralized states in the coastal areas.

Africans and the Slave Trade Warfare and slaving had been part of African life for centuries, but the South Atlantic System made slaving a favorite tactic of ambitious kings and plundering warlords. "Whenever the King of Barsally wants Goods or Brandy," an observer noted, "the King goes and ransacks some of his enemies' towns, seizing the people and selling them." Supplying slaves became a way of life in the West African state of Dahomey, where the royal house monopolized the sale of slaves and used European guns to create a military despotism. Dahomey's army, which included a contingent of 5,000 women, raided the interior for captives; between 1680 and 1730, Dahomey annually exported 20,000 slaves from the ports of Allada and Whydah. The Asante kings likewise used slaving to conquer states along the Gold Coast as well as

CHECK FOR UNDERSTANDING

Ask students: **What was the South Atlantic System?** *The South Atlantic System was a trade network that linked merchants, investors, and planters across the Atlantic in Portuguese, Dutch, and British empires, as well as West African kingdoms. The network centered on sugar production and exportation, and on the African slave labor that made it possible.*

AP® SKILLS & PROCESSES

CAUSATION

Use the **CAUSATION** question to have students explore the long-term effects of the formation of the South Atlantic System on the British economy. Point out to students that since the question is about the effects on the economy, they should be looking for changes in trade and investment patterns, and on the profits that resulted from the shipment and trade of sugar and slaves. Because the British resided on both sides of the Atlantic, students' answers should address effects in England and the colonies.

TRM Find complete suggested responses in the Teacher's Resource Materials.

TEACHING STRATEGY

The Web site Voyages: The Trans-Atlantic Slave Trade Database provides an outstanding collection of resources for teaching every dimension of the slave trade, including essays, several detailed maps, and estimates of the volume of the slave trade by region and by year from 1500 to 1875. Interactive features allow students to use the database of all known slave voyages to conduct specialized searches using two dozen different variables. Access this site by searching "Slave Voyages."

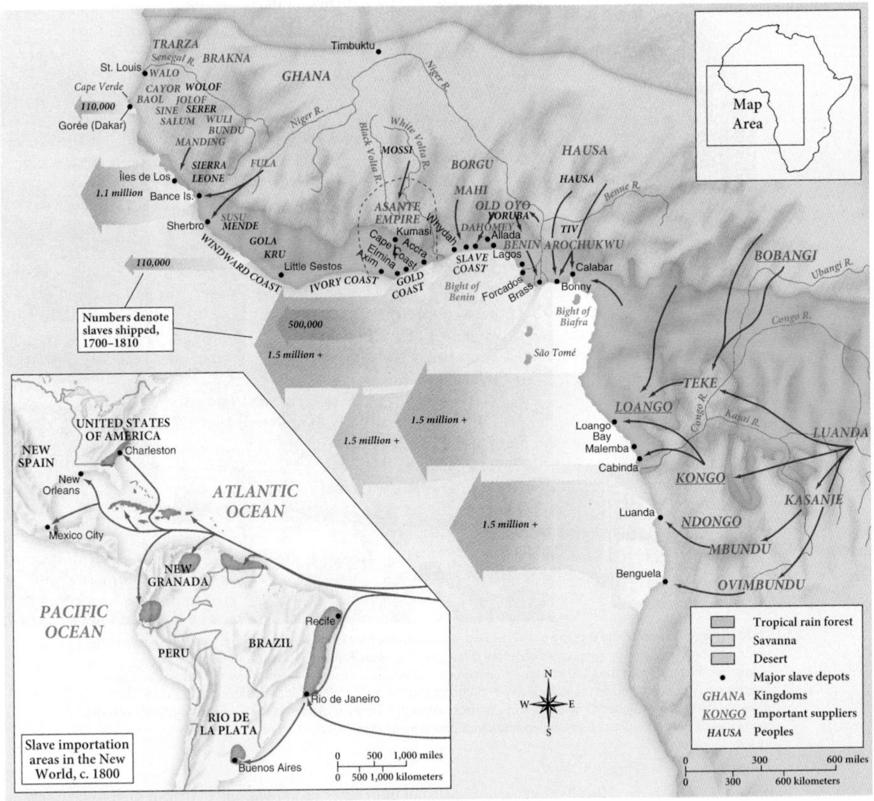

MAP 3.3 Africa and the Atlantic Slave Trade, 1700–1810

The tropical rain forest of West Africa was home to scores of peoples and dozens of kingdoms. With the rise of the slave trade, some of these kingdoms became aggressive slavers. Dahomey's army, for example, seized tens of thousands of captives in wars with neighboring peoples and sold them to European traders. About 14 percent of the captives died during the grueling Middle Passage, the transatlantic voyage between Africa and the Americas. Most of the survivors labored on sugar plantations in Brazil and the British and French West Indies.

Muslim kingdoms in the savanna. By the 1720s, they had created a prosperous empire of 3 to 5 million people. Yet participation in the transatlantic slave trade remained a choice for Africans, not a necessity. The powerful kingdom of Benin, famous for its cast bronzes and carved ivory, prohibited for decades the export of all slaves, male and female.

The trade in humans produced untold misery. Hundreds of thousands of young Africans died, and millions more endured a brutal life in the Americas. In Africa itself, class divisions hardened as people of noble birth enslaved and sold those of lesser status. Gender relations shifted as well. Two-thirds of the slaves sent across the Atlantic were men, partly because European planters paid more for men and "stout men boys" and partly because Africans were more likely to sell enslaved women

AP® THEME

MIG: Migration and Settlement; WXT: Work, Exchange, and Technology

Use **MAP 3.3** to discuss slave importation to the New World. Guide students' analysis with the following questions:

- **What period of time does this map cover? And why?** *The map highlights English involvement in the transatlantic slave trade. It starts at the time that slave trade volume began to increase dramatically, which was also the time of greatest British involvement in the trade. The map extends through British abolition of the slave trade.*
- **Roughly how many Africans does the map account for in raw numbers in proportion to the total transatlantic slave trade of 12 million? If about one and a half million were transported before this period, what does that tell you about the history of the trade after British abolition?** *Just under 8 million, so roughly two thirds of the total transatlantic slave trade volume. Another 3 million slaves were transported in the half-century after British abolition of the slave trade, so they were unable to enforce the end of the trade.*
- **What broad pattern about the identity of African slaves does this map reveal?** *Slaves were drawn from a wide range of sub-Saharan Africa, often from deep in the interior. The map hints at how ethnically and geographically diverse the slave population on any particular plantation might have been.*

TEACHING STRATEGY

These illustrations of the Middle Passage indicate both the conditions as well as humanitarian efforts to end the practice by publicizing its nature. Guide students' analysis through the following questions:

- **What do these two images reveal about the Middle Passage?** *The images reveal the ways that slaves suffered miserable conditions in tight quarters as they were transported as chattel, sometimes with other cargo.*
- **Who made these illustrations? Why?** *The illustration on the left is an effort from abolitionists to publicize the horrors of the Middle Passage. The illustration on the right was painted by the ship's officer and minimizes the horrific conditions of the Middle Passage given it doesn't depict the chains slaves were transported in.*

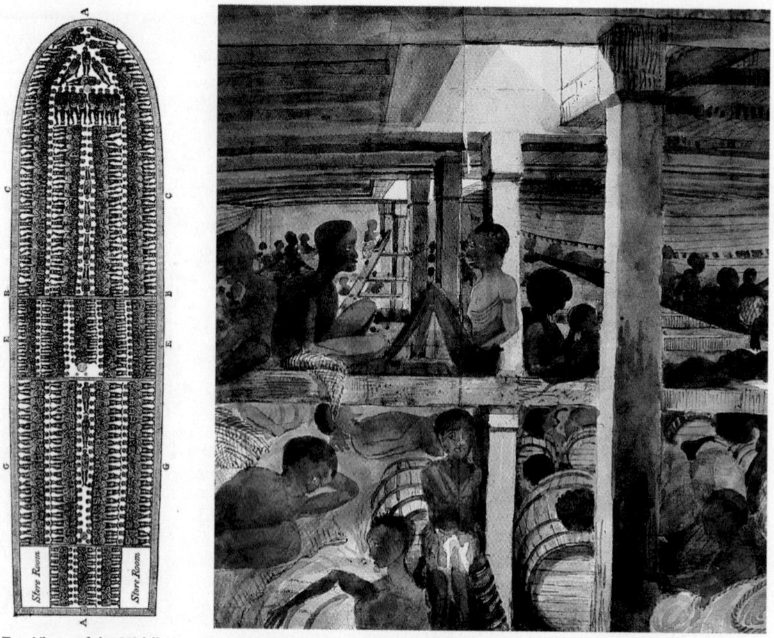

Two Views of the Middle Passage An 1846 watercolor (on the right) shows the cargo hold of a slave ship en route to Brazil, which imported large numbers of African slaves until the 1860s. Painted by a ship's officer, the work minimizes the brutality of the Middle Passage — none of the slaves are in chains — and captures the Africans' humanity and dignity. The illustration on the left, which was printed by England's Abolitionist Society, shows the plan of a Liverpool slave ship designed to hold 482 Africans, packed in with no more respect than that given to hogsheads of sugar and tobacco. Records indicate that the ship actually carried as many as 609 Africans at once. Left: Private Collection © Michael Graham-Stewart/Bridgeman Images. Right: © National Maritime Museum, London/The Image Works.

locally. The resulting sexual imbalance prompted more African men to take several wives. Finally, the expansion of the Atlantic slave trade increased the extent of slavery in Africa. Sultan Mawlay Ismail of Morocco (r. 1672–1727) owned 150,000 black slaves, obtained by trade in Timbuktu and in wars he waged in Senegal. In Africa, as in the Americas, slavery eroded the dignity of human life.

Middle Passage
The brutal sea voyage that carried about 12.5 million Africans toward enslavement in the Americas, of whom about 1.8 million died en route.

The Middle Passage and Beyond Africans sold into the South Atlantic System suffered the bleakest fate. Torn from their villages, they were marched in chains to coastal ports, their first passage in slavery. Then they endured the perilous **Middle Passage** to the New World in hideously overcrowded ships. The captives had little to eat or drink, and some died from dehydration. The feces, urine, and vomit below decks prompted outbreaks of dysentery, which took more lives. "I was so overcome by the heat, stench, and foul air that I nearly fainted," reported a European doctor. Some slaves jumped overboard to drown rather than endure more suffering. Others staged violent shipboard revolts. Slave uprisings occurred on two thousand voyages, roughly one of every ten Atlantic passages. Nearly 100,000 enslaved Africans died in these insurrections, and more than 1.8 million others — almost 15 percent of those who were transported — died of disease or illness on the month-long journey (see "America in the World," p. 95).

Olaudah Equiano: The Brutal "Middle Passage"

Olaudah Equiano claimed to have been born in Igboland (present-day southern Nigeria). But Vincent Carretta of the University of Maryland has discovered strong evidence that Equiano was born in South Carolina. He suggests that Equiano drew on conversations with African-born slaves to create a fictitious account of his kidnapping at the age of eleven and a traumatic passage across the Atlantic. After being purchased by an English sea captain, Equiano bought his freedom in 1766. In London, he became an antislavery activist, and in 1789 he published the memoir from which the following selections are drawn. His autobiographical narrative is the fullest and best-known account of the experience of slavery in British North America.

My father, besides many slaves, had a numerous family. . . . I was trained up from my earliest years in the art of war, . . . and my mother adorned me with emblems after the manner of our greatest warriors. One day, when all our people were gone out to their works as usual and only I and my dear sister were left to mind the house, two men and a woman got over our walls, and in a moment seized us both. . . .

I was . . . sold and carried through a number of places till . . . at the end of six or seven months after I had been kidnapped I arrived at the sea coast.

The first object which saluted my eyes when I arrived on the coast was the sea, and a slave ship, which was then riding at anchor, and waiting for its cargo. These filled me with astonishment, which was soon converted into terror when I was carried on board. . . . I now saw myself deprived of all chance of returning to my native country. . . . I was soon put down under the decks, and there I received such a salutation in my nostrils as I had never experienced in my life; so that with the loathsomeness of the stench and crying together, I became so sick and low that I was not able to eat, nor had I the least desire to taste anything. I now wished for the last friend, death, to relieve me; but soon, to my grief, two of the white men offered me eatables, and on my refusing to eat, one of them held me fast by the hands and . . . tied my feet while the other flogged me severely. I had never experienced anything of this kind before, and . . . could I have got over the nettings, I would have jumped over the side. . . . One day, when we had a smooth sea and moderate wind, two of my wearied countrymen who were chained together . . . , preferring death to such a life of misery, somehow made it through the nettings and jumped into the sea. . . .

At last we came in sight of the island of Barbados; the white people got some old slaves from the land to pacify us. They told us we were not to be eaten but to work, and were soon to go on land where we should see many of our country people. This report eased us much; and sure enough soon after we were landed there came to us Africans of all languages. On a signal given, . . . the buyers rush at once into the yard where the slaves are confined, and make choice of that parcel they like best. The noise and clamour with which this is attended, and the eagerness visible in the countenances of the buyers, serve not a little to increase the apprehensions of the terrified Africans. . . . In this manner, without scruple, are relations and friends separated, most of them never to see each other again. . . . O, ye nominal Christians! might not an African ask you, learned you this from your God, who says unto you, Do unto all men as you would men should do unto you? Is it not enough that we are torn from our country and friends to toil for your luxury and lust of gain? Must every tender feeling be likewise sacrificed to your avarice? . . . Why are parents to lose their children, brothers their sisters, or husbands their wives? Surely this is a new refinement in cruelty, which, while it has no advantage to atone for it, thus aggravates distress, and adds fresh horrors even to the wretchedness of slavery.

SOURCE: *The Interesting Narrative of the Life of Olaudah Equiano, or Gustavus Vassa, the African, Written by Himself* (London, 1789), 15, 22–23, 28–29.

QUESTIONS FOR ANALYSIS

1. What evidence from Equiano's account might explain the average slave mortality rate of about 14 percent during the Atlantic crossing?
2. Assuming that Carretta is correct, and Equiano was not born in Africa, why do you think he composed this fictitious narrative of his childhood instead of describing his own childhood in slavery? In your answer describe Equiano's historical situation and/or purpose for writing the account.

For those who survived the Atlantic crossing, things only got worse as they passed into endless slavery. Life on the sugar plantations of northwestern Brazil and the West Indies was one of relentless exploitation. Slaves worked ten hours a day under the hot tropical sun; slept in flimsy huts; and lived on a starchy diet of corn, yams, and dried fish. They were subjected to pitiless discipline: "The fear of punishment is the

AP® SKILLS & PROCESSES

ANALYZING HISTORICAL EVIDENCE

The **AP® AMERICA IN THE WORLD** feature places the experience of American slaves in the broader Atlantic context of the slave trade. The **QUESTIONS FOR ANALYSIS** prompts provide opportunities for students to practice two different historical skills using evidence. The first question asks students to corroborate a narrative account with evidence resulting from historical research, a statistic about slave mortality. The second question invites students to consider the usefulness of a source that may not provide completely truthful information.

TRM Find complete suggested responses in the Teacher's Resource Materials.

CHECK FOR UNDERSTANDING

Ask students: **What were Africans' roles in the slave trade?** *African leaders in some kingdoms and chiefdoms actively participated in the selling of Africans from other polities in the interior. Those sold into slavery suffered miserably from the Middle Passage and endured oppressive conditions after they arrived in the Americas.*

TRM Find complete suggested responses in the Teacher's Resource Materials.

TEACHING STRATEGY

Create a chart on the board to illustrate the differences in slave systems in different areas of the British colonies. Ask students to look at types of jobs or tasks assigned to slaves, laws directed at slaves, and treatment of slaves in each area. Compare these conditions to the descriptions of slave systems in Barbados, Brazil, and other areas in the Americas.

principle [we use] . . . to keep them in awe and order," one planter declared. When punishments came, they were brutal. Flogging was commonplace; some planters rubbed salt, lemon juice, or urine into the resulting wounds.

Planters often took advantage of their power by raping enslaved women. Sexual exploitation was a largely unacknowledged but ubiquitous feature of master-slave relations, something that many slave masters considered to be an unquestioned privilege of their position. "It was almost a constant practice with our clerks, and other whites," Olaudah Equiano wrote, "to commit violent depredations on the chastity of the female slaves." Thomas Thistlewood was a Jamaica slave owner who kept an unusually detailed journal in which he noted every act of sexual exploitation he committed. In thirty-seven years in the colony, Thistlewood recorded 3,852 sex acts with 138 enslaved women.

AP® SKILLS & PROCESSES

CONTEXTUALIZATION

How did the high price of sugar shape the experience of enslaved African laborers?

With sugar prices high and the cost of slaves low, many planters worked their slaves to death and then bought more. Between 1708 and 1735, British planters on Barbados imported about 85,000 Africans; however, in that same time the island's black population increased by only 4,000 (from 42,000 to 46,000). The constant influx of new slaves kept the population thoroughly African in its languages, religions, and culture. "Here," wrote a Jamaican observer, "each different nation of Africa meet and dance after the manner of their own country . . . [and] retain most of their native customs."

Slavery in the Chesapeake and South Carolina

West Indian–style slavery came to Virginia and Maryland following Bacon's Rebellion. Taking advantage of the expansion of the British slave trade (following the end of the Royal African Company's monopoly in 1698), elite planter-politicians led a "tobacco revolution" and bought more Africans, putting these slaves to work on ever-larger plantations. By 1720, Africans made up 20 percent of the Chesapeake population; by 1740, nearly 40 percent. Slavery had become a core institution, no longer just one of several forms of unfree labor. Moreover, slavery was now defined in racial terms. Virginia legislators prohibited sexual intercourse between English and Africans and defined virtually all resident Africans as slaves: "All servants imported or brought into this country by sea or land who were not Christians in their native country shall be accounted and be slaves."

On the mainland as in the islands, slavery was a system of brutal exploitation. Violence was common, and the threat of violence always hung over master-slave relationships. In 1669, Virginia's House of Burgesses decreed that a master who killed a slave in the process of "correcting" him could not be charged with a felony, since it would be irrational to destroy his own property. From that point forward, even the most extreme punishments were permitted by law. Slaves could not carry weapons or gather in large numbers. Slaveholders were especially concerned to discourage slaves from running away. Punishments for runaways commonly included not only brutal whipping but also branding or scarring to make recalcitrant slaves easier to identify. Virginia laws spelled out the procedures for capturing and returning runaway slaves in detail. If a runaway slave was killed in the process of recapturing him, the county would reimburse the slave's owner for his full value. In some cases, slave owners could put runaway slaves up for trial; if they were found guilty and executed, the owner would be compensated for his loss (see "Thinking Like a Historian," p. 98).

Despite the inherent brutality of the institution, slaves in Virginia and Maryland worked under better conditions than those in the West Indies. Many lived relatively long lives. Unlike sugar and rice, which were "killer crops" that demanded strenuous labor in a tropical climate, tobacco cultivation required steadier and less demanding labor in a more temperate environment. Workers planted young tobacco seedlings in spring, hoed and weeded the crop in summer, and in fall picked and hung the leaves to cure over the winter. Nor did diseases spread as easily in the Chesapeake, because plantation quarters were less crowded and more dispersed than those in the West Indies. Finally, because tobacco profits were lower than those from sugar, planters treated their slaves less harshly than West Indian planters did.

Many tobacco planters increased their workforce by buying female slaves and encouraging them to have children. In 1720, women made up more than one-third of the Africans in Maryland, and the black population had begun to increase naturally. "Be kind and indulgent to the breeding wenches," one slave owner told his overseer, "[and do not] force them when with child upon any service or hardship that will be injurious to them." By midcentury, more than three-quarters of the enslaved workers in the Chesapeake were American-born.

Slaves in South Carolina labored under much more oppressive conditions. The colony grew slowly until 1700, when planters began to plant and export rice to southern Europe, where it was in great demand. Between 1720 and 1750, rice production increased fivefold. To expand production, planters imported thousands of Africans, some of them from rice-growing societies. By 1710, Africans formed a majority of the total population, eventually rising to 80 percent in rice-growing areas.

Most rice plantations lay in inland swamps, and the work was dangerous and exhausting. Enslaved workers planted, weeded, and harvested the rice in ankle-deep mud. Pools of stagnant water bred mosquitoes, which transmitted diseases that claimed hundreds of African lives. Others, forced to move tons of dirt to build irrigation works, died from exhaustion. "The labour required [for growing rice] is only fit for slaves," a Scottish traveler remarked, "and I think the hardest work I have seen them engaged in." In South Carolina, as in the West Indies and Brazil, there were many slave deaths and few births, and the arrival of new slaves continually "re-Africanized" the black population.

An African American Community Emerges

Slaves came from many peoples in West Africa and the Central African regions of Kongo and Angola. White planters welcomed ethnic diversity to deter slave revolts. "The safety of the Plantations," declared a widely read English pamphlet, "depends upon having Negroes from all parts of Guiny, who do not understand each other's languages and Customs and cannot agree to Rebel." By accident or design, most plantations drew laborers of many languages, including Kwa, Mande, and Kikongo. Among Africans imported after 1730 into the upper James River region of Virginia, 41 percent came from ethnic groups in present-day Nigeria, and another 25 percent from West-Central Africa. The rest hailed from the Windward and Gold coasts, Senegambia, and Sierra Leone. In South Carolina, plantation owners preferred laborers from the Gold Coast and Gambia, who had a reputation as hardworking farmers. But as African sources of slaves shifted southward after 1730, more than 30 percent of the colony's workers later came from Kongo and Angola.

Initially, the slaves did not think of themselves as Africans or blacks but as members of a specific family, clan, or people — Wolof, Hausa, Ibo, Yoruba, Teke, Ngola — and they sought out those who shared their language and customs. In the upper James River region, Ibo men and women arrived in equal numbers, married each other, and maintained their Ibo culture. In most places, though, this was impossible. Slaves from varying backgrounds were thrown together and only gradually discovered common ground.

Building Community Through painful trial and error, enslaved people eventually discovered what limited freedoms their owners would allow them. Those who were not too rebellious or too recalcitrant were able to carve out precarious family lives — though they were always in danger of being disrupted by sale or life-threatening punishment — and build the rudiments of a slave community.

One key to the development of families and communities was a more or less balanced sex ratio that encouraged marriage and family formation. In South Carolina, the high death rate among slaves undermined ties of family and kinship; but in the Chesapeake, after 1725 some enslaved workers, especially on larger plantations, were able to

CHECK FOR UNDERSTANDING

Ask students to compare and contrast slavery in the Chesapeake with slavery in South Carolina. *Over time, the percentage of the enslaved population in Virginia and Maryland increased, as slaves became the dominant form of labor on ever-larger plantations. As slave populations grew, the use of violence increased to control them. Despite the ways the Chesapeake colonies became more like the West Indies, the tobacco regime remained much less harsh than South Carolina's rice production system.*

AP® THEME

SOC: Social Structures

Use the text's discussion of community and resistance in the "An African American Community Emerges" section to help students understand the variety of ways Africans resisted the dehumanization of slavery and attempted to retain their family and culture.

AP® SKILLS & PROCESSES

ANALYZING HISTORICAL EVIDENCE

The set of sources in the **AP® THINKING LIKE A HISTORIAN** feature helps students analyze primary sources to make a clear comparison between two related but distinct forms of unfree labor: indentured servitude and slavery. As students read these documents, encourage them to take the specific details from individual cases and make generalizations about the features of indentured servitude and slavery.

AP® THINKING LIKE A HISTORIAN

Servitude and Slavery

Britain's American colonies relied heavily on bound labor. Two forms predominated: indentured servitude and African slavery. The idea of being bound to a master is alien to most of us today; the following texts allow us to glimpse some aspects of the experience. In what ways were these two institutions similar, and how did they differ?

1. **Slave advertisement from Charleston, South Carolina, July 24, 1769.** *By the 1760s, Charleston was the leading slave trading port in British North America.*

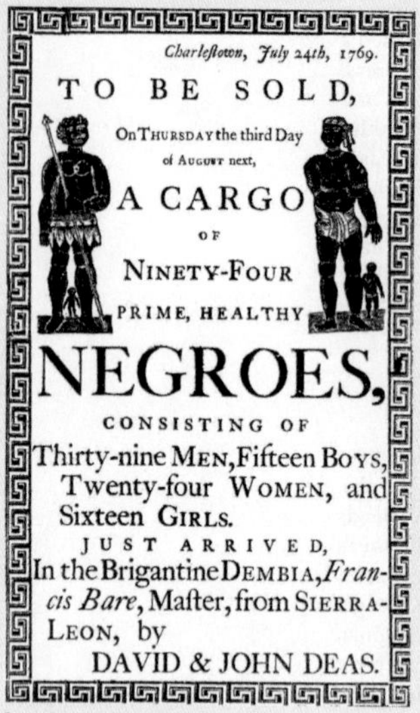

Charleſtown, July 24th, 1769.

TO BE SOLD,

On THURSDAY the third Day of AUGUST next,

A CARGO OF NINETY-FOUR PRIME, HEALTHY

NEGROES,

CONSISTING OF

Thirty-nine MEN, Fifteen BOYS, Twenty-four WOMEN, and Sixteen GIRLS.

JUST ARRIVED,

In the Brigantine DEMBIA, *Francis Bare*, Maſter, from SIERRA-LEON, by

DAVID & JOHN DEAS.

SOURCE: American Antiquarian Society, Worcester, Massachusetts, USA/Bridgeman Images.

2. **Indentured servant advertisement from the *Pennsylvania Gazette*, 1770.** *This advertisement offers to sell the remainder of a servant girl's indenture.*

TO BE SOLD, A HEALTHY servant GIRL'S Time, about 17 Years old, who has between 3 and 4 years to serve. She is sold for no other Reason, only there being more Servants than are needful in the family where she is.

N. B. She has had the Small pox, can wash, and do all Sorts of Housework. Enquire of the Printers.

3. **Poem by James Revel, c. 1680.** *James Revel was an Englishman convicted of theft and transported to Virginia, where he served fourteen years as an indentured servant. Upon returning he published* A Poor Unhappy Transported Felon's Sorrowful Account of His Fourteen Years' Transportation at Virginia, in America *(1680).*

At last to my new master's house I came,
At the town of Wicocc[o]moco call'd by name,
Where my Europian clothes were took from me,
Which never after I again could see.
A canvas shirt and trowsers then they gave,
With a hop-sack frock in which I was to slave:
No shoes nor stockings had I for to wear,
Nor hat, nor cap, both head and feet were bare.
Thus dress'd into the Field I nex[t] must go,
Amongst tobacco plants all day to hoe,
At day break in the morn our work began,
And so held to the setting of the Sun.
My fellow slaves were just five Transports more,
With eighteen Negroes, which is twenty four . . .
We and the Negroes both alike did fare,
Of work and food we had an equal share.

4. **Mechanisms used to control slaves, from Thomas Branagan, *The Penitential Tyrant; or, slave trader reformed*, 1807.** *The shackles and spurs (lower left) were intended to prevent escape; the faceguard with spiked collar (top and lower right) kept its wearer from either eating or lying down.*

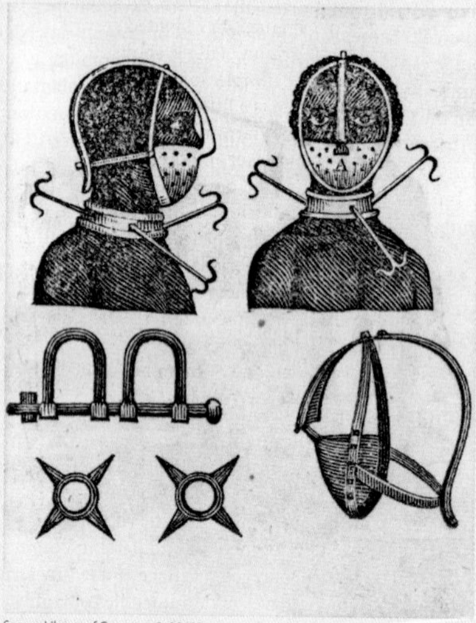

SOURCE: Library of Congress, 3a32403.

98

5. **Court deposition of Joseph Mulders, July 31, 1649.** *In a court case in Lower Norfolk County, Virginia indentured servant Joseph Mulders testified that his mistress, Deborah Fernehaugh, brutally beat her maidservant, Charity Dallen.*

[Mulders testified] That Deborah Fernehaugh, the Mistress of this deponent, did beate her mayd Sarvant in the quartering house before the dresser more Liken a dogge then a Christian, and that at a Certaine time, I felt her head, which was beaten as soft as a sponge, in one place, and that as there shee was a weeding, shee complained and sayd, her backe bone as shee thought was broken with beating, and that I did see the mayds arme naked which was full of blacke and blew bruises and pinches, and her necke Likewise and that after wards, I tould my Mistress of it and said, that two or three blowes, could not make her in such a Case, and after this my speeches shee Chidge [i.e., chided] the said mayd, for shewing her body to the men, and very often afterwards she [the maid] would have shoen mee, how shee had been beaten, but I refused to have seene it, saying it concernes me not, I will doe my worke and if my Mistress abuse you; you may complaine, and about 8 dayes since, being about the time shee last went to Complaine, I knew of her goeing, but would not tell my mistress of it, although shee asked mee, and sayd I could not chuse but know of it.

6. **Runaway slave advertisement, Chestertown, Maryland, March 12, 1755.** *Absconding from their masters was a common method of resistance for both slaves and servants, and masters frequently posted runaway advertisements in local newspapers.*

Chestertown, Maryland, March 12, 1755. TEN PISTOLES Reward. RAN away last night, from James Ringgold, of Eastern Neck, in Kent county, in the province of Maryland, the two following servant men; one named James Francis, an indented servant for five years, a middle siz'd young fellow, about 26 years of age, of a smooth fair complexion, his hair cut off, is an Englishman, and speaks a little in the west country dialect; was brought up to farming and husbandry: Had on, a country kersey jacket and breeches, blue fearnought jacket, and an old dark colour'd coat. The other a lusty young Mulatto fellow, named Toby, a slave about the same age, he is a well set, clean limb'd, stout fellow neither a very bright or very dark Mulatto, has large nostrils, is a likely fellow, and when he talks drawls his words out in a very slow manner, is no other way remarkable; he had on the same sort of clothes with the other servant, and one of them has a check or striped green and red everlasting jacket on or with them; and perhaps the Mulatto may set up for a cooper or carpenter, having work at both those business, and also understands plantation affairs. Whoever takes up and secures the above persons, and gives notice, so as their master gets them again, shall have Four Pistoles reward for the white servant, and Six Pistoles for the Mulatto. . . . That this slave should runaway, and attempt getting his liberty, is very alarming, as he has always been too kindly used, if any thing by his master, and one in whom his master has put great confidence, and depended on him to overlook the rest of his slaves, and he had no kind of provocation to go off. It seems to be the interest at least of every gentleman that has slaves, to be active in the beginning of these attempts . . . THOMAS RINGGOLD.

SOURCE: (2) *Pennsylvania Gazette*, May 3, 1770; (3) John Melville Jennings, ed., *The Virginia Magazine of History and Biography* 56 (April 1948), 187–194; (5) *Second to None: A Documentary History of American Women*, Vol. 1 (University of Nebraska Press, 1993), 67–68; (6) *Pennsylvania Gazette*, March 12, 1755.

ANALYZING THE EVIDENCE

1. What information do the traders in sources 1 and 2 want to convey to prospective buyers, and why? What similarities and differences do you see in the way sellers might choose to market servants and slaves? Use historical reasoning to compare the accounts.
2. What aspects of servitude did James Revel object to (source 3)? How did he compare the experiences of servants and slaves? Use evidence to support your answer.
3. Source 4 appeared in an abolitionist work published in New York in 1807. How does the historical context influence your interpretation of the images?
4. How does Mulders grapple with his position as a fellow servant as he testifies against his mistress (source 5)? Based on Mulders's testimony, the court removed Dallen from Fernehaugh's household. How might the position of Mulders or Dallen as an indentured servant inform the conclusion of the case?
5. In source 6, what characteristics of each man does the ad emphasize? What does Ringgold's plea to other slaveholders tell us about slaveholding culture? Describe specific examples from the text.

AP® DBQ PRACTICE

Using these sources, along with what you learned in class and in Chapter 3, write a short essay that compares servitude and slavery. In what ways did African slavery in the British colonies grow out of servitude and bear close similarities to it, and in what ways were slaves set apart and treated fundamentally differently than their servant counterparts? Write a claim and support it with evidence from the sources and textbook.

TRM Find complete suggested responses in the Teacher's Resource Materials.

AP® SKILLS & PROCESSES

ARGUMENTATION

The **AP® DBQ PRACTICE** prompt asks students to respond to a comparison question using evidence from the documents, from the text, and from lecture and other materials. In comparing the two systems, this prompt also suggests that students make causal links between them, explaining how slavery grew out of servitude.

AP® SKILLS & PROCESSES

COMPARISON

Use the **COMPARISON** question to have students compare two different plantation-based slave systems on mainland British colonies at the same time. Students should identify not only the nature of the respective labor regime, but also the effect of these regimes on family formation and cultural patterns. Extend this prompt by having students weigh whether the institutions were more alike or more different.

TRM Find complete suggested responses in the Teacher's Resource Materials.

TEACHING STRATEGY

The argument that West Africans introduced a rice cultivation "knowledge system" to North American plantations was first made by geographer Judith A. Carney. Historian Drew Gilpin Faust reviewed Carney's book titled *Black Rice: The African Origins of Rice Cultivation in the Americas*, laying out the book's argument and its significance. This review also provides a link to the first part of Carney's first chapter, which introduces key evidence from Portuguese sailors who first visited the Senegal and Gambia rivers in the mid-fifteenth century. Access the review by searching "NY Times Seeds of History."

create strong nuclear families and extended kin relations. On one of Charles Carroll's estates in Maryland, 98 of the 128 slaves were members of two extended families. These African American kin groups passed on family names, traditions, and knowledge to the next generation, and thus a distinct culture gradually developed. As one observer suggested, blacks had created a separate world, "a Nation within a Nation."

As enslaved laborers forged a new identity, they carried on certain African practices but let others go. Many Africans arrived in America with ritual scars that white planters called "country markings"; these signs of ethnic identity fell into disuse on culturally diverse plantations. (Ironically, on some plantations these African markings were replaced by brands or scars that identified them with their owners.) But other tangible markers of African heritage persisted, including hairstyles, motifs used in wood carvings and pottery, the large wooden mortars and pestles used to hull rice, and the design of houses, in which rooms were arranged from front to back in a distinctive "I" pattern, not side by side as was common in English dwellings. Musical instruments — especially drums, gourd rattles, and a stringed instrument called a "molo," forerunner of the banjo — helped Africans preserve cultural traditions and, eventually, shape American musical styles.

AP® SKILLS & PROCESSES

COMPARISON

How did the experiences of slaves in the Chesapeake differ from their experiences in South Carolina?

African values also persisted. Some slaves passed down Muslim beliefs, and many more told their children of the spiritual powers of conjurers, called *obeah* or *ifa*, who knew the ways of the African gods. Enslaved Yorubas consulted Orunmila, the god of fate, and other Africans (a Jamaican planter noted) relied on *obeah* "to revenge injuries and insults, discover and punish thieves and adulterers; [and] to predict the future."

AP® EXAM TIP

Compare the ways that enslaved Africans overtly and covertly resisted slavery's dehumanizing effects.

Resistance and Accommodation Slaves' freedom of action was always dramatically circumscribed. It became illegal to teach slaves to read and write, and most enslaved people owned no property of their own. Because the institution of slavery rested on fear, planters had to learn a ferocious form of cruelty. Slaves might be whipped, restrained,

Hulling Rice in West Africa and Georgia Cultural practices often extend over time and space. The eighteenth-century engraving on the left shows West African women using huge wooden mortars and pestles to strip the tough outer hull from rice kernels. In the photo on the right, taken a century and a half later, African American women in Georgia use similar tools to prepare rice for their families. Left: Library of Congress. Right: Georgetown County Library, Georgetown, South Carolina.

or maimed for any infraction, large or small. Olaudah Equiano observed a female cook in a Virginia household who "was cruelly loaded with various kinds of iron machines; she had one particularly on her head, which locked her mouth so fast that she could scarcely speak; and could not eat nor drink." Thomas Jefferson, who witnessed such punishments on his father's Virginia plantation, noted that each generation of whites was "nursed, educated, and daily exercised in tyranny," and he concluded that the relationship "between master and slave is a perpetual exercise of the most unremitting despotism on the one part, and degrading submission on the other." A fellow Virginian, planter George Mason, agreed: "Every Master is born a petty tyrant."

The extent of white violence often depended on the size and density of the slave population. As Virginia planter William Byrd II complained of his slaves in 1736, "Numbers make them insolent." In the northern colonies, where slaves were few, white violence was sporadic. But plantation owners and overseers in the sugar- and rice-growing areas, where Africans outnumbered Europeans 8 or more to 1, routinely whipped assertive slaves. They also prohibited their workers from leaving the plantation without special passes and called on their poor white neighbors to patrol the countryside at night.

Despite the constant threat of violence, some slaves ran away, a very small number of them successfully. In some parts of the Americas — for example, in Jamaica — runaway slaves were able to form large, independent Maroon communities. But on the mainland, planters had the resources necessary to reclaim runaways, and such communities were unusual and precarious. More often, slaves who spoke English and possessed artisanal skills fled to colonial towns, where they tried to pass as free; occasionally they succeeded. Slaves who did not run away were engaged in a constant tug-of-war with their owners over the terms of their enslavement. Some blacks bartered extra work for better food and clothes; others seized a small privilege and dared the master to revoke it. In this way, Sundays gradually became a day of rest — asserted as a right, rather than granted as a privilege. When bargaining failed, enslaved workers silently protested by working slowly or stealing.

Slave owners' greatest fear was that their regime of terror would fail and slaves would rise up to murder them in their beds. Occasionally that fear was realized. In the 1760s, in Amherst County, Virginia, a slave killed four whites; in Elizabeth City County, eight slaves strangled their master in bed. But the circumstances of slavery made any larger-scale uprising all but impossible. To rebel against their masters, slaves would have to be able to communicate secretly but effectively across long distances; choose leaders they could trust; formulate and disseminate strategy; accumulate large numbers of weapons; and ensure that no one betrayed their plans. This was all but impossible: in plantation slavery, the preponderance of force was on the side of the slave owners, and blacks who chose to rise up did so at their peril.

AP® SKILLS & PROCESSES

MAKING CONNECTIONS

How much autonomy could slaves attain, and what did slave owners do to control them?

The Stono Rebellion The largest slave uprising in the mainland colonies, South Carolina's **Stono Rebellion** of 1739, illustrates the impossibility of success. The Catholic governor of Spanish Florida instigated the revolt by promising freedom to fugitive slaves. By February 1739, at least 69 slaves had escaped to St. Augustine, and rumors circulated "that a Conspiracy was formed by Negroes in Carolina to rise and make their way out of the province." When war between England and Spain broke out in September, 75 Africans rose in revolt and killed a number of whites near the Stono River. According to one account, some of the rebels were Portuguese-speaking Catholics from the Kingdom of Kongo who hoped to escape to Florida. Displaying their skills as soldiers — decades of brutal slave raiding in Kongo had militarized the society there — the rebels marched toward Florida "with Colours displayed and two Drums beating."

Stono Rebellion
Slave uprising in 1739 along the Stono River in South Carolina in which a group of slaves armed themselves, plundered six plantations, and killed more than twenty colonists. Colonists quickly suppressed the rebellion.

Though their numbers and organization were impressive, the Stono rebels were soon met by a well-armed, mounted force of South Carolina militia. In the ensuing battle, 44 slaves were killed and the rebellion was suppressed, preventing any general uprising. In response, frightened South Carolinians cut slave imports and tightened plantation discipline.

TEACHING STRATEGY

Use excerpts from William Byrd's diary to give students insight into the life of a male member of the southern gentry. In the midst of describing his daily reading and other leisure activities, Byrd casually mentions the routine whipping of various slaves for a range of offenses. These excerpts show not only his patriarchal authority but the racial violence he oversaw in the midst of his genteel plantation life. Access Byrd's diary by searching "PBS Africans in America William Byrd's Diary."

CHECK FOR UNDERSTANDING

Ask students: **In the face of almost certain punishment, why was resistance to slavery critically important?** Give students several minutes to think and compose their responses without talking or sharing ideas with classmates. Then in small groups or with a partner, have students share their responses and combine their answers into an effective thesis statement. Next, ask the small groups or partners to find evidence of both overt and covert resistance that supports their thesis statement. As a whole class, discuss the goals of overt or covert resistance to slavery and which method of resistance was more effective.

AP® SKILLS & PROCESSES

MAKING CONNECTIONS

Use the **MAKING CONNECTIONS** question to help students link changes in slave autonomy to the larger economic and social system in which their lives were embedded. Students should recognize that autonomy was by definition circumscribed, given that slaves were rarely freed. Students may be drawn to the few examples of large-scale rebellions, but daily resistance was also important. On that small, day-to-day scale, autonomy probably increased over time in general, as slaves often won accommodations from their masters.

TRM Find complete suggested responses in the Teacher's Resource Materials.

AP® THEME

SOC: Social Structures

In this section, students examine the role of environment and the ability of enslaved persons to resist enslavement. Ask students to compare the dynamics of resisting enslavement in urban vs. rural areas. Students should focus their responses on how the environments shaped the contours of some of the experiences of enslaved persons.

CHECK FOR UNDERSTANDING

Ask students: **How would you characterize the African American community that emerged in the early 1700s?** *African Americans married and established both nuclear and extended families, especially on larger plantations. They adopted some European practices while maintaining African beliefs, particularly religious beliefs. They resisted oppression in small ways when they could, seen through running away or outright rebellion when they thought they stood a chance of success.*

AP® EXAM TIP

It's important to make connections between the economy that developed in various colonies and the social hierarchy that came to dominate British North America.

The Rise of the Southern Gentry

As the southern colonies became full-fledged slave societies, life changed for whites as well as for blacks. Consider the career of William Byrd II (1674–1744). Byrd's father, a successful planter-merchant in Virginia, hoped to marry his children into the English gentry. To smooth his son's entry into landed society, Byrd sent him to England for his education. But his status-conscious classmates shunned young Byrd, calling him a "colonial," a first bitter taste of the gradations of rank in English society.

Other English rejections followed. Lacking aristocratic connections, Byrd was denied a post with the Board of Trade, passed over three times for the royal governorship of Virginia, and rejected as a suitor by a rich Englishwoman. In 1726, at age fifty-two, Byrd finally gave up and moved back to Virginia, where he sometimes felt he was "being buried alive." Accepting his lesser destiny as a member of the colony's elite, Byrd built an elegant brick mansion on the family's estate at Westover, sat in "the best pew in the church," and won an appointment to the governor's council.

William Byrd II's experience mirrored that of many planter-merchants, trapped in Virginia and South Carolina by their inferior colonial status. They used their wealth to rule over white yeomen families and tenant farmers and relied on violence to exploit enslaved blacks. Planters used Africans to grow food, as well as tobacco; to build houses, wagons, and tobacco casks; and to make shoes and clothes. By making their plantations self-sufficient, the Chesapeake elite survived the depressed tobacco market between 1670 and 1720.

AP® SKILLS & PROCESSES

CONTEXTUALIZATION

How did the planter elite maintain alliances with their smallholder neighbors?

White Identity and Equality To prevent uprisings like Bacon's Rebellion, the Chesapeake gentry found ways to assist middling and poor whites. They gradually lowered taxes; in Virginia, for example, the annual head tax (on each adult man) fell from 45 pounds of tobacco in 1675 to just 5 pounds in 1750. Many smallholders responded to their improved circumstances by becoming slaveholders themselves. By 1770, 60 percent of English families in the Chesapeake owned at least one slave. On the political front, planters now allowed poor yeomen and some tenants to vote. The strategy of the leading families — the Carters, Lees, Randolphs, and Robinsons — was to bribe these voters with rum, money, and the promise of minor offices in county governments. In return, they expected the yeomen and tenants to elect them to office and defer to their rule. This horse-trading solidified the authority of the planter elite, which used its control of the House of Burgesses to limit the power of the royal governor. Hundreds of yeomen farmers benefitted as well, tasting political power and claiming substantial fees and salaries as deputy sheriffs, road surveyors, estate appraisers, and grand jurymen.

An Overseer Doing His Duty By the mid-eighteenth century, the race-based system of chattel slavery was well-established in the Chesapeake and the low country of South Carolina and Georgia. Enslaved Africans did the most demanding labor in these colonies, while middling and poorer whites cooperated with wealthy planters in maintaining a system of labor discipline. Here, Benjamin Henry Latrobe has sketched a white overseer — presumably an employee of the wealthy landowner — watching two enslaved women work the ground with hoes. The Picture Art Collection/Alamy Stock Photo.

Even as wealthy Chesapeake gentlemen formed political ties with smallholders, they took measures to set themselves apart culturally. As late as the 1720s, leading planters were boisterous, aggressive men who lived much like the common folk — hunting, drinking, gambling on horse races, and demonstrating their manly prowess by forcing themselves on female servants and slaves. As time passed, however, planters like William Byrd II began to

AP® SKILLS & PROCESSES

CONTEXTUALIZATION

The **CONTEXTUALIZATION** question asks students to identify the activities planters engaged in that caused smallholders to be loyal to them. Extend this prompt by asking how elites would have communicated their desire for relationships with these smallholders in more subtle ways than the "bribery" the text describes.

TRM Find complete suggested responses in the Teacher's Resource Materials.

AP® SKILLS & PROCESSES

CLAIMS AND EVIDENCE IN SOURCES

When students are presented with non-text-based documents such as this painting, it can be challenging to identify what historical evidence to use in a description of the document. Encourage students to think about "reading" the painting with the big picture in mind. For instance, while this painting clearly illustrates enslavement, the artist carefully selected enslaved women. Ask students to draw a connection between enslavement and gender in the eighteenth century Chesapeake region.

model themselves on the English aristocracy, remaining sexual predators but learning from advice books how to act like gentlemen in other regards: "I must not sit in others' places; Nor sneeze, nor cough in people's faces. Nor with my fingers pick my nose, Nor wipe my hands upon my clothes." Cultivating **gentility** — a lifestyle that stressed refinement and self-control — they replaced their modest wooden houses with mansions of brick and mortar. Planters educated their sons in London as lawyers and gentlemen. But unlike Byrd's father, they expected them to return to America, marry local heiresses, and assume their fathers' roles: managing plantations, socializing with fellow gentry, and running the political system.

gentility
A refined style of living and elaborate manners that came to be highly prized among well-to-do English families after 1600 and strongly influenced leading colonists after 1700.

Wealthy Chesapeake and South Carolina women likewise emulated the English elite. They read English newspapers and fashionable magazines, wore the finest English clothes, and dined in the English fashion, including an elaborate afternoon tea. To enhance their daughters' gentility (and improve their marriage prospects), parents hired English tutors and dancing masters. Once married, planter women deferred to their husbands, reared pious children, and maintained complex social networks, in time creating a new ideal: the southern gentlewoman. Using the profits generated by enslaved Africans in the South Atlantic System of commerce, wealthy planters formed an increasingly well-educated, refined, and stable ruling class.

CHECK FOR UNDERSTANDING

Ask students: **How did their ties to Great Britain and Africa change the lives of American planters?** *Rejected by English society as "colonials," many planters attempted to carve out elite status in the colonies, albeit one that largely mimicked the social and cultural norms of Britain, calling it "gentility," i.e. a lifestyle that stressed refinement and self-control.*

THE NORTHERN MARITIME ECONOMY

What economic activities drove the northern maritime economy?

The South Atlantic System had a broad geographical reach. As early as the 1640s, New England farmers supplied the sugar islands with most of the necessities of life, including bread, lumber, fish, and meat. As a West Indian explained, planters "had rather buy foode at very deare rates than produce it by labour, soe infinite is the profitt of sugar works." By 1700, the economies of the West Indies and New England were closely interwoven. Soon farmers and merchants in New York, New Jersey, and Pennsylvania were also shipping wheat, corn, and bread to the Caribbean. By the 1750s, about two-thirds of New England's exports and half of those from the Middle Atlantic colonies went to the British and French sugar islands.

The sugar economy linked Britain's entire Atlantic empire. In return for the sugar they sent to England, West Indian planters received credit, in the form of bills of exchange, from London merchants. The planters used these bills to buy slaves from Africa and to pay North American farmers and merchants for their provisions and shipping services. The mainland colonists then exchanged the bills for British manufactures, primarily textiles and iron goods.

The Urban Economy

The West Indian trade created the first American merchant fortunes and the first urban industries. Merchants in Boston, Newport, Providence, Philadelphia, and New York invested their profits in new ships; some set up manufacturing enterprises, including twenty-six refineries that processed raw sugar into finished loaves. Mainland distilleries turned West Indian molasses into rum, producing more than 2.5 million gallons in Massachusetts alone by the 1770s. Merchants in Salem, Marblehead, and smaller New England ports built a major fishing industry by selling salted mackerel and cod to the sugar islands and to southern Europe. Baltimore merchants transformed their town into a major port by developing a bustling export business in wheat, while traders in Charleston shipped deerskins, indigo, and rice to European markets (Map 3.4).

As transatlantic commerce expanded — from five hundred voyages a year in the 1680s to fifteen hundred annually in the 1730s — American port cities grew in size and complexity. By 1750, the populations of Newport and Charleston were nearly

AP® THEME

WXT: Work, Exchange, and Technology

MAP 3.4 shows the complex trade of the British Atlantic world in 1750, at the end of the period this chapter covers. This map provides annotations to guide students in proper interpretation of the data that can be derived from the map. Spend some time helping students develop their ability to interpret this important map.

TRM Find complete suggested responses in the Teacher's Resource Materials.

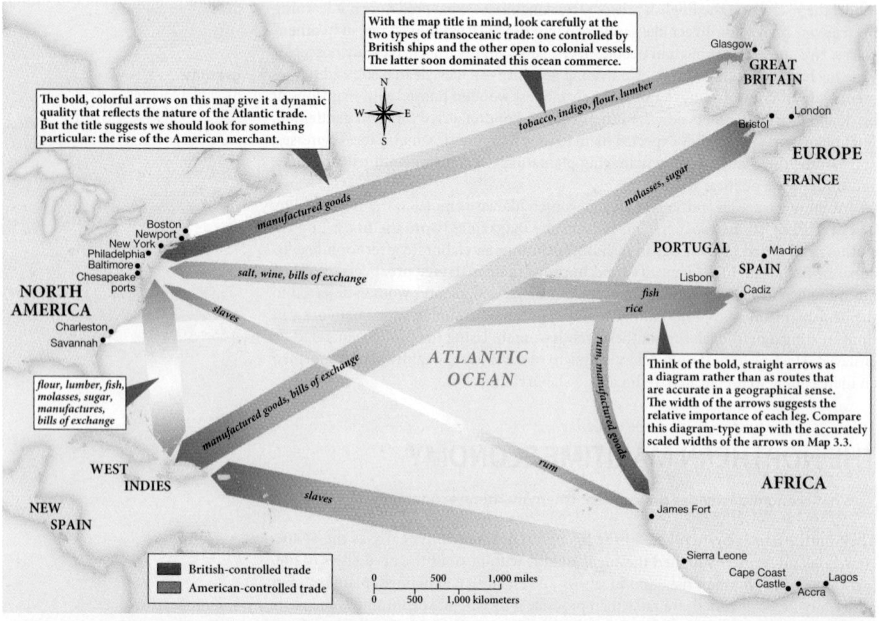

With the map title in mind, look carefully at the two types of transoceanic trade: one controlled by British ships and the other open to colonial vessels. The latter soon dominated this ocean commerce.
The bold, colorful arrows on this map give it a dynamic quality that reflects the nature of the Atlantic trade. But the title suggests we should look for something particular: the rise of the American merchant.
N
W
E
S
Glasgow
GREAT BRITAIN
Bristol
London
EUROPE
FRANCE
PORTUGAL
Madrid
SPAIN
Lisbon
Cadiz
tobacco, indigo, flour, lumber
molasses, sugar
manufactured goods
Boston
Newport
New York
Philadelphia
Baltimore
Chesapeake ports
NORTH AMERICA
Charleston
Savannah
salt, wine, bills of exchange
slaves
fish
rice
ATLANTIC OCEAN
manufactured goods, bills of exchange
rum, manufactured goods
rum
Think of the bold, straight arrows as a diagram rather than as routes that are accurate in a geographical sense. The width of the arrows suggests the relative importance of each leg. Compare this diagram-type map with the accurately scaled widths of the arrows on Map 3.3.
flour, lumber, fish, molasses, sugar, manufactures, bills of exchange
WEST INDIES
NEW SPAIN
slaves
AFRICA
James Fort
Sierra Leone
Cape Coast Castle
Accra
Lagos
British-controlled trade
American-controlled trade
0 500 1,000 miles
0 500 1,000 kilometers

MAPPING THE PAST

MAP 3.4 The Growing Power of American Merchants, 1750

Throughout the colonial era, British merchant houses dominated the transatlantic trade in manufactures, sugar, tobacco, and slaves. However, by 1750, American-born merchants in Boston, New York, and Philadelphia had seized control of the commerce between the mainland and the West Indies. In addition, Newport traders played a small role in the slave trade from Africa, and Boston and Charleston merchants grew rich carrying fish and rice to southern Europe.

ANALYZING THE MAP: This map represents the flow of trade goods in the British Atlantic. Colonial merchants were involved in commerce throughout the Atlantic by 1750, but the trade with one region was especially important. Based on the width of the arrow, which trading destination was most valuable to North American merchants?

MAKING CONNECTIONS: Consider this map in relation to "The Northern Maritime Economy." How was the growing power of American merchants reflected in changes that were taking place in North American seaports?

10,000; Boston had 15,000 residents; and New York had almost 18,000. The largest port was Philadelphia, whose population by 1776 had reached 30,000, the size of a large European provincial city. Smaller coastal towns emerged as centers of the lumber and shipbuilding industries. Seventy sawmills lined the Piscataqua River in New Hampshire, providing low-cost wood for homes, warehouses, and especially shipbuilding. Hundreds of shipwrights turned out oceangoing vessels, while other artisans made ropes, sails, and metal fittings to outfit them. By the 1770s, colonial-built ships made up one-third of the British merchant fleet.

The South Atlantic System extended far into the interior. A fleet of small vessels sailed back and forth on the Hudson and Delaware rivers, delivering cargoes of European manufactures and picking up barrels of flour and wheat to carry to New York and Philadelphia for export to the West Indies and Europe. By the 1750s, hundreds of professional teamsters in Maryland were transporting 370,000 bushels of

The Rising Ports of British North America As the South Atlantic System matured, colonial port towns grew rapidly to become bustling centers of intercoastal and transatlantic commerce. In this 1738 painting by Scottish-born artist John Smibert, three figures look across the harbor at the town of Boston. Church steeples dot the background, but the scene is dominated by symbols of commerce. Oceangoing vessels come into port or ride at anchor while the shoreline is studded with merchants' wharves. In the left center of the painting we can see Long Wharf, built by the town in the 1710s to accommodate even the largest ships. The Granger Collection, New York.

wheat and corn and 16,000 barrels of flour to urban markets each year — more than 10,000 wagon trips. To service this traffic, entrepreneurs and artisans set up taverns, horse stables, and barrel-making shops in towns along the wagon roads. Lancaster (the town that hosted the Iroquois conference described in the chapter opening), in a prosperous wheat-growing area of Pennsylvania, boasted more than 200 German and English artisans and a dozen merchants.

AP® SKILLS & PROCESSES

MAKING CONNECTIONS

How did the rise of the South Atlantic System impact economic development in the northern colonies?

Urban Society

Wealthy merchants dominated the social life of seaport cities. In 1750, about forty merchants controlled more than 50 percent of Philadelphia's trade. Like the Chesapeake gentry, urban merchants imitated the British upper classes, importing architectural design books from England and building Georgian-style mansions to display their wealth. Their wives strove to create a genteel culture by buying fine furniture and entertaining guests at elegant dinners.

Artisan and shopkeeper families, the middle ranks of seaport society, made up nearly half the population. Innkeepers, butchers, seamstresses, shoemakers, weavers, bakers, carpenters, masons, and dozens of other skilled workers toiled to gain an income sufficient to maintain their families in modest comfort. Wives and husbands often worked as a team and taught the "mysteries of the craft" to their children. Some artisans aspired to wealth and status, an entrepreneurial ethic that prompted them to hire apprentices and expand production. However, most artisans were not well-to-do. During his working life, a tailor was lucky to accumulate £30 worth of property, far less than the £2,000 owned at death by an ordinary merchant or the £300 listed in the probate inventory of a successful blacksmith.

Laboring men and women formed the lowest ranks of urban society. Merchants needed hundreds of dockworkers to unload manufactured goods and molasses from inbound ships and reload them with barrels of wheat, fish, and rice. For these demanding jobs, merchants used enslaved blacks and indentured servants, who together made up 30 percent of the workforce in Philadelphia and New York City until the 1750s; otherwise, they hired unskilled wageworkers. Poor white and black women eked out a living by washing clothes, spinning wool, or working as servants or prostitutes. To make ends meet, laboring families sent their children out to work.

Periods of stagnant commerce threatened the financial security of merchants and artisans alike. For laborers, seamen, and seamstresses — whose household budgets left no margin for sickness or unemployment — depressed trade meant hunger, dependence

AP® SKILLS & PROCESSES

CAUSATION

How did the development of an urban economy and society influence the development of the Northern area of British North America?

AP® THEME

ARC: American and Regional Culture

Use the painting by John Smibert as the backdrop for a bell-ringer activity that focuses on the theme of American and Regional Culture. After debriefing the description of the painting, ask students to define each of the following terms: South Atlantic System, Atlantic world, colonial interdependence, and merchant capitalism. After defining each term, students select two terms to explain how port cities contributed to regional economic trends.

CHECK FOR UNDERSTANDING

Ask students: **How did their ties to Great Britain and Africa change the lives of American planters?** *Rejected by English society as "colonials," many planters attempted to carve out elite status in the colonies, albeit one that largely mimicked the social and cultural norms of Britain, calling it "gentility," i.e. a lifestyle that stressed refinement and self-control.*

TRM Find complete suggested responses in the Teacher's Resource Materials.

TEACHING STRATEGY

Ask students to create a general social class pyramid diagram that can be applied to all the British North American colonies despite the differences that existed by region and colony. Ask students to include a label for each social class and a list of distinguishing characteristics of each social class. Have students draw arrows between social classes to indicate where and how social mobility (up or down in class) was possible. On these arrows, ask students to note the ways in which individuals would move across the indicated social classes. On the outside of the social class pyramid diagram, ask students to indicate what events, conditions, or actions could influence the social class system.

TEACHING STRATEGY

Supplement the discussion of the transatlantic economy with historian Carole Shammas's article entitled "America, the Atlantic, and Global Consumer Demand, 1500–1800," which provides an excellent overview of the entire scope of the transatlantic economy — not just British participation — in a long-term perspective from 1500 through 1800. Access this resource by searching "AP® Central Carole Shammas."

CHECK FOR UNDERSTANDING

Ask students: **What economic activities drove the northern maritime economy?** *The northern maritime economy was driven by producing ships, rum (from West Indies sugar), fish, wheat, deerskins, indigo, and rice as well as delivering these products to Britain.*

AP® APPLY THE TIP

Ask students to complete **Handout 3.2 — Thematic Analysis: Salutary Neglect (TRM)** in small groups. Students may also complete this activity in a jigsaw format with different groups assigned to investigate salutary neglect as it related to one AP® Theme. Reorganize the groups so that each objective is represented by one student who explains that objective to the large group. After students have shared their thematic analysis in small groups, lead a class discussion addressing the ways salutary neglect supported the development of self-government in the colonies.

TRM Find **Handout 3.2 — Causation: Salutary Neglect** in the Teacher's Resource Materials.

AP® SKILLS & PROCESSES

DEVELOPMENTS AND PROCESSES

Use the **DEVELOPMENTS AND PROCESSES** question to help students identify the causes of political autonomy. Students may need assistance identifying links between the Glorious Revolution's effects in Europe and the colonies. Assemblies were in effect local versions of Parliament, while governors' roles resembled the king. So assemblies' limitations on governors' power paralleled Parliament's limiting of royal power.

TRM Find complete suggested responses in the Teacher's Resource Materials.

on public charity, and (for the most desperate) petty thievery or prostitution. The sugar- and slave-based South Atlantic System, and cycles of imperial warfare, brought economic uncertainty as well as opportunity to the people of the northern colonies.

THE NEW POLITICS OF EMPIRE, 1713–1750

How could Great Britain maintain its mercantilist policies and permit the "salutary neglect" of its colonies at the same time?

The South Atlantic System also changed the politics of empire. British ministers, pleased with the wealth produced by the trade in slaves, sugar, rice, and tobacco, ruled the colonies with a gentle hand. The colonists took advantage of that leniency to strengthen their political institutions and eventually to challenge the rules of the mercantilist system.

The Rise of Colonial Assemblies

AP® EXAM TIP

Take good notes as you read through this section on the reasons colonists opposed British policies under the mercantilist system.

After the Glorious Revolution, representative assemblies in America copied the English Whigs and limited the powers of crown officials. In Massachusetts during the 1720s, the assembly repeatedly ignored the king's instructions to provide the royal governor with a permanent salary, and legislatures in North Carolina, New Jersey, and Pennsylvania did the same. Using such tactics, the legislatures gradually took control of taxation and appointments, angering imperial bureaucrats and absentee proprietors. "The people in power in America," complained William Penn during a struggle with the Pennsylvania assembly, "think nothing taller than themselves but the Trees."

Leading the increasingly powerful assemblies were members of the colonial elite. Although most property-owning white men had the right to vote, only men of wealth and status stood for election. In New Jersey in 1750, 90 percent of assemblymen came from influential political families. In Virginia, seven members of the wealthy Lee family sat in the House of Burgesses and, along with other powerful families, dominated its major committees. In New England, affluent descendants of the original Puritans formed a core of political leaders. "Go into every village in New England," John Adams wrote in 1765, "and you will find that the office of justice of the peace, and even the place of representative, have generally descended from generation to generation, in three or four families at most."

However, neither elitist assemblies nor wealthy property owners could impose unpopular edicts on the people. Purposeful crowd actions were a fact of colonial life. An uprising of ordinary citizens overthrew the Dominion of New England in 1689. In New York, mobs closed houses of prostitution; in Salem, Massachusetts, they ran people with infectious diseases out of town; and in New Jersey in the 1730s and 1740s, mobs of farmers battled with proprietors who were forcing tenants off disputed lands. When officials in Boston restricted the sale of farm produce to a single public market, a crowd destroyed the building, and its members defied the authorities to arrest them. "If you touch One you shall touch All," an anonymous letter warned the sheriff, "and we will show you a Hundred Men where you can show one." These expressions of popular discontent, combined with the growing authority of the assemblies, created a political system that was broadly responsive to popular pressure and increasingly resistant to British control.

AP® SKILLS & PROCESSES

DEVELOPMENTS AND PROCESSES

What explains the increasing political autonomy of the colonies in the eighteenth century?

Salutary Neglect

salutary neglect
A term used to describe British colonial policy during the reigns of George I and George II. By relaxing their supervision of internal colonial affairs, royal bureaucrats inadvertently assisted the rise of self-government in North America.

British colonial policy during the reigns of George I (r. 1714–1727) and George II (r. 1727–1760) allowed for this rise of American self-government as royal bureaucrats, pleased by growing trade and import duties, relaxed their supervision of internal colonial affairs. In 1775, British political philosopher Edmund Burke would praise this strategy as **salutary neglect**.

AP® THEME

PCE: Politics and Power

Point out to students how salutary neglect was a political institution that developed gradually and inadvertently, reflecting the erratic enforcement of imperial policies as the British government attempted to create a coherent empire.

Salutary neglect was a by-product of the political system developed by Sir Robert Walpole, the Whig leader in the House of Commons from 1720 to 1742. Walpole relied on **patronage** — the practice of giving offices and salaries to political allies — to create a strong Court Party. Under his leadership, Britain's government achieved a new measure of financial and political stability. But critics — the so-called Country Party — charged that Walpole's policies of high taxes and a bloated royal bureaucracy threatened British liberties.

These arguments were echoed in North America, where colonial legislators complained that royal governors abused their patronage powers. To preserve American liberty, the colonists strengthened the powers of the representative assemblies, unintentionally laying the foundation for the American independence movement.

patronage
The power of elected officials to grant government jobs and favors to their supporters; also the jobs and favors themselves.

Protecting the Mercantile System

In 1732, Walpole provided parliamentary funding for the new colony of Georgia. While Georgia's reform-minded trustees envisioned the colony as a refuge for Britain's poor, Walpole had little interest in social reform. He supported the new colony because it would serve as a military buffer to protect the valuable rice-growing colony of South Carolina from Spanish Florida. But the new colony had the opposite effect. Britain's expansion into Georgia outraged Spanish officials, who were already angry about the rising tide of smuggled British manufactures in New Spain. To counter Britain's commercial imperialism, Spanish naval forces stepped up their seizure of illegal traders, in the process cutting off the ear of an English sea captain, Robert Jenkins.

AP® SKILLS & PROCESSES

ARGUMENTATION

In what ways did British decisions to protect mercantilist policies lead to conflict between British government and colonial leaders and governments?

Yielding to parliamentary pressure, Walpole declared war on Spain in 1739. The so-called War of Jenkins's Ear (1739–1741) was a fiasco for Britain. In 1740, British regulars failed to capture St. Augustine because South Carolina whites, still shaken by the Stono Rebellion, refused to commit militia units to the expedition. A year later, a British assault on the prosperous seaport of Cartagena (in present-day Colombia) also failed; 20,000 British sailors and soldiers and 2,500 colonial troops died in the attack, mostly from tropical diseases.

The War of Jenkins's Ear quickly became part of a general European conflict, the War of the Austrian Succession (1740–1748). Massive French armies battled British-subsidized German forces in Europe, and French naval forces roamed the West Indies, vainly trying to conquer a British sugar island. In 1745, three thousand New England militiamen and a British naval squadron captured Louisbourg, the French fort guarding the entrance to the St. Lawrence River. To the dismay of New England Puritans, who feared invasion from Catholic Quebec, the Treaty of Aix-la-Chapelle (1748) returned Louisbourg to France. The treaty made it clear to colonial leaders that England would act in its own interests, not theirs.

The Siege and Capture of Louisbourg, 1745 In 1760, as British and colonial troops moved toward victory in the French and Indian War (1754–1763), the London artist J. Stevens sought to bolster imperial pride by celebrating an earlier Anglo-American triumph. In 1745, a British naval squadron led a flotilla of colonial ships and thousands of New England militiamen in an attack on the French fort at Louisbourg, on Cape Breton Island, near the mouth of the St. Lawrence River. After a siege of forty days, the Anglo-American force captured the fort, long considered impregnable. The victory was bittersweet because the Treaty of Aix-la-Chapelle (1748) returned the island to France. Anne S. K. Brown Military Collection, Brown University Library.

Mercantilism and the American Colonies

Though Parliament prohibited Americans from manufacturing textiles (Woolen Act, 1699), hats

CHECK FOR UNDERSTANDING

Ask students: **What was salutary neglect?** *Salutary neglect was the British policy in the first half of the eighteenth century of purposely allowing the colonies greater latitude in self-government and trade.*

TRM Find complete suggested responses in the Teacher's Resource Materials.

AP® THEME

ARC: American and Regional Culture

Although the mercantilist system was an imperial economic design, the colonists enjoyed a relative amount of autonomy known as salutary neglect. During the years of salutary neglect, the colonists continued to expand their economy largely because Great Britain remained a commercial empire in North America. Remind students that Anglicization in the colonies was in many ways buttressed by the policy of salutary neglect.

(Hat Act, 1732), and iron products such as plows, axes, and skillets (Iron Act, 1750), and also curbed the colonies' ability to print their own paper money (Currency Act, 1751), it could not prevent the colonies from maturing economically. American merchants soon controlled over 75 percent of the transatlantic trade in manufactures and 95 percent of the commerce between the mainland and the British West Indies (see Map 3.4).

Moreover, by the 1720s, the British sugar islands could not absorb all the flour, fish, and meat produced by mainland settlers. So, ignoring Britain's intense rivalry with France, colonial merchants sold their produce to the French sugar islands. When American rum distillers began to buy cheap molasses from the French islands, the West Indian sugar lobby in London persuaded Parliament to pass the Molasses Act of 1733. The act placed a high tariff on French molasses, so high that it would no longer be profitable for American merchants to import it. Colonists protested that the Molasses Act would cripple the distilling industry; cut farm exports; and, by slashing colonial income, reduce the mainland's purchases of British goods. When Parliament ignored these arguments, American merchants smuggled in French molasses by bribing customs officials.

These conflicts angered a new generation of English political leaders. In 1749, Charles Townshend of the Board of Trade charged that the American assemblies had assumed many of the "ancient and established prerogatives wisely preserved in the Crown," and he vowed to replace salutary neglect with more rigorous imperial control.

The wheel of empire had come full circle. In the 1650s, England had set out to create a centrally managed Atlantic empire and, over the course of a century, achieved the military and economic aspects of that goal. Mercantilist legislation, maritime warfare, commercial expansion, and the forced labor of a million African slaves brought prosperity to Britain. However, internal unrest (the Glorious Revolution) and a policy of salutary neglect had weakened Britain's political authority over its American colonies. Recognizing the threat self-government posed to the empire, British officials in the late 1740s vowed to reassert their power in America — an initiative with disastrous results.

SUMMARY

In this chapter, we examined processes of change in politics and society. The political story began in the 1660s as Britain imposed controls on its American possessions. Parliament passed the Acts of Trade and Navigation to keep colonial products and trade in English hands. Then King James II abolished representative institutions in the northern colonies and created the authoritarian Dominion of New England. Following the Glorious Revolution, the Navigation Acts remained in place and tied the American economy to that of Britain. But the uprisings of 1688–1689 overturned James II's policy of strict imperial control, restored colonial self-government, and ushered in an era of salutary political neglect. It also initiated a long era of imperial warfare, in which Native American peoples allied themselves to the colonies and often served as proxy warriors against French- and Spanish-allied peoples, pursuing their own goals in the process.

The social story centers on the development of the South Atlantic System of production and trade, which involved an enormous expansion in African slave raiding; the Atlantic slave trade; and the cultivation of sugar, rice, and tobacco in America. This complex system created an exploited African American labor force in the southern mainland and West Indian colonies, while it allowed European American farmers, merchants, and artisans on the North American mainland to prosper. How would the two stories play out? In 1750, slavery and the South Atlantic System seemed firmly entrenched, but the days of salutary neglect appeared numbered.

CHECK FOR UNDERSTANDING

Ask students: **How did Parliament attempt to protect its mercantile system?** *It launched a disastrous war against Spain in an effort to protect shipping as Spain increased its seizing of ships engaged in illegal trade.*

CHECK FOR UNDERSTANDING

Use the **AP® LEARNING FOCUS** question from the beginning of the chapter to assess students' understanding of the chapter as a whole: **What was the South Atlantic System, and how did it shape economic development of Great Britain's colonies?** *The South Atlantic System brought Europeans, Native Americans, and Africans together through the exploitation of land in South America and labor from Africans. This benefitted the mercantilist economic system of Great Britain, but it wrought human tragedy and political disruption and brought economic decline to West Africa and parts of East Africa. Because of climate and location, some colonies, such as Brazil, the Carolinas, Barbados, and Jamaica, were more suitable to plantation agriculture, and as a result they grew rapidly into slave-based agricultural plantation colonies. Beyond initial settlements, the plantation economy of the Carolinas had a distinct and direct connection to Barbados. Moreover, even though the New England economy of Massachusetts focused on lumber, shipping, and the fishing industry, they too were connected to the South Atlantic System due to the trade in fish and molasses. The interconnectedness of the South Atlantic System was inextricably connected to the financial health and growth of Great Britain's colonies in the New World.*

LearningCurve

Remind students to go online to complete the LearningCurve quiz for this chapter.

CHAPTER 3 REVIEW

AP® CONTENT REVIEW *Answer these questions to demonstrate your understanding of the chapter's main ideas.*

1. Why did changes in England between 1660 and 1690 reshape its American Empire?
2. What was tribalization, and how did it help Native Americans cope with their European neighbors?
3. How did their ties to Great Britain and Africa change the lives of American planters?
4. What economic activities drove the New England maritime economy?
5. How could Great Britain maintain its mercantilist policies and permit the "salutary neglect" of its colonies at the same time?

AP® TERMS TO KNOW *Identify and explain the significance of each term below.*

Key Concepts and Events

proprietorship (p. 82)
Quakers (p. 83)
Navigation Acts (p. 83)
Dominion of New England (p. 84)
Glorious Revolution (p. 85)
constitutional monarchy (p. 85)
Second Hundred Years' War (p. 86)
tribalization (p. 86)
Covenant Chain (p. 87)
South Atlantic System (p. 90)
Middle Passage (p. 94)
Stono Rebellion (p. 101)
gentility (p. 103)
salutary neglect (p. 106)
patronage (p. 107)

Key People

William Penn (p. 81)
Edmund Andros (p. 84)
William of Orange (p. 85)
John Locke (p. 85)
Jacob Leisler (p. 85)
William Byrd II (p. 101)
Robert Walpole (p. 107)

AP® MAKING CONNECTIONS *Recognize the larger developments and continuities within and across chapters by answering these questions.*

1. In Chapter 2, we traced the emergence of three distinct colonial types in the Americas during the sixteenth and seventeenth centuries: tribute, plantation, and neo-European colonies. In Chapter 3, we have seen how Britain's plantation and neo-European colonies became more closely interconnected after 1700. What developments caused them to become more closely tied to each other? How did they benefit from these ties? Can you see any disadvantages to the colonies in a more fully integrated Atlantic system? Use evidence to support a historically defensible claim.
2. Part 1 emphasized the unstable and unpromising origins of England's American colonies. In Chapter 3, we examined key developments that contributed to the growth and stability of the colonies. What were the most important changes contributing to the rise of the British Atlantic world, and how did they change the character of the colonies? Support your argument using specific and relevant evidence.

KEY TURNING POINTS *Refer to the timeline at the start of the chapter for help in answering the following questions.*

The Glorious Revolution (1688–1689), salutary neglect and the rise of the assemblies (1714–1750), and the Hat, Molasses, Iron, and Currency Acts (1732–1751): How do these developments reflect Britain's new attitude toward its colonies? In what matters did Parliament seek to control the colonies, and in what did it grant them autonomy? Use historical reasoning to describe patterns of continuity and change over time.

109

TRM Find complete suggested responses in the Teacher's Resource Materials.

AP® SKILLS & PROCESSES

CAUSATION

AP® CONTENT REVIEW QUESTION 1 asks students to explain the effects of changes in England on the character of British America. Note: This is the same question as the prompt on p. 80.

AP® SKILLS & PROCESSES

CAUSATION

AP® CONTENT REVIEW QUESTION 2 asks students to explain the effects of tribalization on Native Americans' diplomacy. Note: This is the same question as the prompt on p. 86.

AP® SKILLS & PROCESSES

CAUSATION

AP® CONTENT REVIEW QUESTION 3 asks students to explain the effects of connections to both Britain and Africa on planters. Note: This is the same question as the prompt on p. 90.

AP® SKILLS & PROCESSES

CAUSATION

AP® CONTENT REVIEW QUESTION 4 asks students to identify particular economic activities that caused the growth of the maritime economy. Note: This is the same question as the prompt on p. 103.

AP® SKILLS & PROCESSES

CAUSATION

AP® CONTENT REVIEW QUESTION 5 asks students to explain the causes of British leaders adopting similarly contradictory policies. Note: This is the same question as the prompt on p. 106.

TRM Find definitions for these terms in the **Glossary/Glosario** in the Teacher's Resource Materials.

AP® SKILLS & PROCESSES

CONTINUITY AND CHANGE

AP® MAKING CONNECTIONS 1 invites students to make connections between three different settlement patterns that developed in an earlier period and trace their changes through the period addressed in this chapter.

AP® SKILLS & PROCESSES

CONTINUITY AND CHANGE

Use the **KEY TURNING POINTS** question to prompt students to draw connections between three events that explain how they reveal developments in Britain's relationship with its colonies.

AP® SKILLS & PROCESSES

ARGUMENTATION

AP® MAKING CONNECTIONS 2 encourages students to examine changes contributing to the rise of the British Atlantic world. The questions also ask students to examine how the character of the colonies changed. The British Atlantic world experienced the continuity of the reliance on the mercantile system of government, whereby Great Britain relied on colonies to produce a profit, most often through a focus on agricultural goods. As a result, the use of enslaved labor increased over time, which changed the character of several colonies from "societies with slaves" to "slave societies." Moreover, because Great Britain loosely enforced mercantilism through a series of navigation laws, colonists were allowed some relative autonomy and diversified their economies.

TRM Find complete suggested responses in the Teacher's Resource Materials.

AP PRACTICE QUESTIONS

MULTIPLE CHOICE QUESTIONS *Choose the correct answer for each question.*

Questions 1–4 refer to this excerpt.

> "I know what is said by the several admirers of monarchy, aristocracy, and democracy, which are the rule of one, a few, and many, and are the three common ideas of government, when men discourse on the subject. But I choose to solve the controversy with this small distinction, and it belongs to all three: Any government is free to the people under it (whatever be the frame) where the laws rule, and the people are a party to those laws, and more than this is tyranny, oligarchy, or confusion."
>
> William Penn, "Frame of Government of Pennsylvania," 1682

1. The ideas expressed by William Penn in the excerpt most directly reflect the influence of
   - **a.** transatlantic print culture.
   - **b.** the First Great Awakening.
   - **c.** European Enlightenment ideas.
   - **d.** British mercantilist policies.
2. The ideas expressed in the excerpt contributed most to which of the following developments in colonial Pennsylvania?
   - **a.** The abolition of slavery
   - **b.** The influx of large numbers of European immigrants in the early 1700s
   - **c.** British government efforts to exert more direct control over the colony
   - **d.** Widespread violence between Pennsylvania colonists and American Indians
3. What characteristic of Pennsylvania is best suited to the type of government described by Penn?
   - **a.** Plantation economies based on exporting staple crops such as tobacco and rice
   - **b.** Relatively homogeneous population of self-sufficient family farmers
   - **c.** High degree of cultural and ethnic diversity
   - **d.** Lack of organized religion and low levels of church attendance
4. Which of the following approaches toward governing most aligns to Penn's argument?
   - **a.** The local governments created in the Spanish and French colonies
   - **b.** The establishment of colonial legislatures such as the Virginia House of Burgesses
   - **c.** The constitutional monarchy created in England after the Glorious Revolution
   - **d.** The use of town hall meetings in colonial New England

Questions 5–6 refer to this excerpt.

> "When I came [in 1714] there was not so much as one proper carpenter, nor mason, nor tailor, nor butcher in the town, nor . . . a market worth naming. . . . But now we abound in artificers [skilled craftsmen], and some of the best, and our markets large, even to a full supply. And, what above all I would remark, there was not so much as one foreign trading vessel belonging to the town, nor for several years after I came into it. . . .
>
> [N]ow we have between thirty and forty ships . . . engaged in foreign trade. From so small a beginning the town has risen into its present flourishing circumstances. . . ."
>
> *The Autobiography of the Reverend John Barnard*, 1766

5. The excerpt could best be used as historical evidence to support an argument that British colonization of North America grew most significantly due to the influence of which of the following?
   - **a.** The imperial enforcement of mercantilist policies
   - **b.** An intensification of the Atlantic system of trade
   - **c.** An Anglicization of the British colonies
   - **d.** The borrowing of improved naval technology
6. Which of the following most directly resulted from the pattern of change described in the excerpt?
   - **a.** The British colonies attracted larger numbers of settlers than the French, Spanish, or Dutch colonies in North America.
   - **b.** The British government attempted to incorporate the colonies into a coherent, hierarchical imperial structure.
   - **c.** British colonial plantations grew increasingly reliant on the transatlantic trade in enslaved labor.
   - **d.** The relative prosperity of the British colonies stimulated peaceful trade relations with American Indians.

SHORT ANSWER QUESTIONS *Read each question carefully and write a short response. Use evidence from the text to support your claims.*

"That Europeans used only non-Europeans as slaves . . . for primarily economic reasons has wide support [among scholars]. . . . [E]lites would surely use the cheapest option possible within the limits of mercantilist policies. . . . Yet such motives operated under the aegis of fundamental non-economic values. . . . One central issue here is perception of race, ethnicity, or, less controversially, who is to be considered an outsider and is therefore enslavable and who is an insider and thus unenslavable. . . . [F]rom the strictly economic standpoint there were strong arguments in support of using European rather than African slave labor. The crux of the matter was shipping costs. . . . [But] the barrier to European slaves in the Americas lay not only beyond shipping and enslavement costs but also beyond any strictly economic sphere. . . ."

David Eltis, *The Rise of African Slavery in the Americas*, 2000

"The decision for slavery was implicit in the competitive commercial structure of planters and merchants. . . . Once planters and merchants competed to bring plantation produce to the market by the swiftest means possible, with a free hand to import slaves and exploit them, the transition to the slave-worked plantations was inevitable. The Atlantic slave trade option was supported by governments, deferring to the wishes of the main actors in the matter. For the planter who was seriously interested in maximizing output, and in the fortune this promised to make him, the decision to buy African slaves became a natural one."

Robin Blackburn, *The Making of New World Slavery: From the Baroque to the Modern, 1492–1800*, 2010

1. Using the two excerpts provided, answer (a), (b), and (c).
   - **a.** Briefly explain ONE major difference between Eltis's and Blackburn's historical interpretations of the origins of slavery in the Americas.
   - **b.** Briefly explain how ONE specific historical event or development from the period 1607 to 1754 that is not mentioned directly in the excerpts could be used to support Eltis's interpretation.
   - **c.** Briefly explain how ONE specific historical event or development from the period 1607 to 1754 that is not explicitly mentioned in the excerpts could be used to support Blackburn's interpretation.

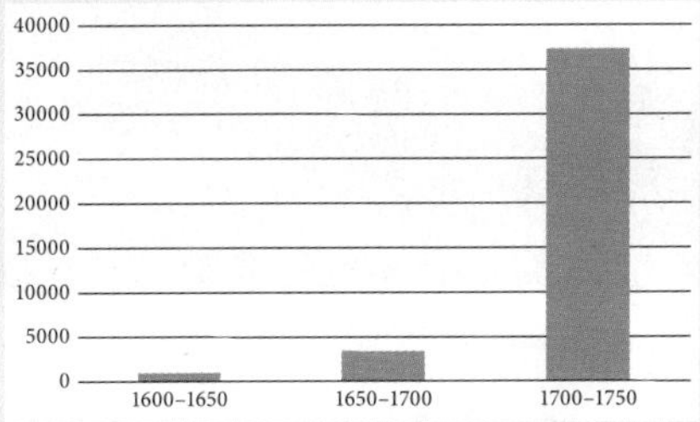

Slaves Imported to the British North American Colonies

Source of data: www.slavevoyages.org/assessment/estimates

2. Using the graph provided, answer (a), (b), and (c).
   - **a.** Briefly explain ONE specific historical factor that accounts for the change illustrated in the graph.
   - **b.** Briefly explain ONE specific historical event or development resulting from the change illustrated in the graph.
   - **c.** Briefly explain ONE specific historical response of enslaved African laborers to the conditions they experienced in the colonies prior to 1750.
3. Answer (a), (b), and (c).
   - **a.** Briefly explain ONE specific historical similarity between the New England colonies and the Middle colonies in the period from 1660 to 1750.
   - **b.** Briefly explain ONE specific historical difference between the New England colonies and the Middle colonies in the period from 1660 to 1750.
   - **c.** Briefly explain ONE specific historical cause that accounts for the difference you indicated in (b).

TRM Find complete suggested responses in the Teacher's Resource Materials.

4 CHAPTER Growth, Diversity, and Conflict

1720–1763

Chapter 4 — AP® Assessment Weight and Pacing Guide

The assessment weight on the AP® U.S. History Exam for Chapters 3–4 is 6–8 percent. This chapter falls at the end of Unit 2 of the AP® U.S. History Curriculum, covering Period 2: 1607–1754, and the beginning of Unit 3 of the AP® U.S. History Curriculum, covering Period 3: 1754–1800.

This pacing guide is based on a schedule with 120 sessions of 50 minutes each before the AP® U.S. History Exam. If you have a different number of sessions before the exam, you can modify the pacing to meet your needs. If you have additional time, consider incorporating quizzes, released AP® U.S. History questions, practice exams, writing practice, and other instructional activities.

	Traditional Schedule	Block Schedule
Chapter 4	5 days	3 days

Daily Pacing Guide

	Content Focus	Essential Question
Day 1	New England's Freehold Society	What goals and values shaped New England society in the eighteenth century?
Day 2	Diversity in the Middle Colonies	How were the goals of immigrants to the Middle colonies similar to those of New England colonists, and how did they differ?
Day 3	Cultural Transformations	How did the accelerating pace of travel and communication affect colonial society and culture?
Days 4 and 5	The Midcentury Challenge: War, Trade, and Social Conflict, 1750–1763	How did midcentury developments reflect Britain's deepening connections to North America?

AP® Alignment

Section Heading	AP® Topic	AP® Theme
New England's Freehold Society	2.3	GEO
Diversity in the Middle Colonies	2.3, 2.7, 3.12	GEO, ARC, MIG
Cultural Transformation	2.7	ARC
The Midcentury Challenge: War, Trade, and Social Conflict, 1750–1763	3.2	WOR

*Should changes be made to the Course Framework in the future, an updated alignment will be placed on our AP® updates page at go.bfwpub.com/ap-course-updates.

Chapter 4 — Overview

Chapter 4 focuses on the development of the New England colonies, including the unique demographics of family life and the role of religion in creating both unity and diversity. The chapter focuses on the unique characteristics of the Middle colonies, especially the characteristics that encouraged tolerance and the impact of increasing diversity on the region. While the development of unique regions is one focus, the chapter also places emphasis on the impact of two major movements on the colonies as a whole: the Enlightenment and the Great Awakening. The chapter concludes with a discussion of the French and Indian War.

Chapter 4 — Resources

The following resources can be found in the Teacher's Resource Materials (TRM) that accompany the book. You can access the TRM via the book's digital platform, by clicking the TRM links found here in your Teacher's Edition e-book, or by contacting your representative to access the resources online. Visit **bfwpub.com/henretta10e** to learn more.

TRM Chapter 4 Lecture Presentation Slides

TRM Chapter 4 Outline with AP® Focus

TRM Chapter 4 Lecture Strategies

TRM Chapter 4 Suggested Responses

TRM Handout 4.1 — Thematic Analysis: Diversity in the Middle Colonies

TRM Handout 4.2 — Comparison: Ideas in the Atlantic World

TRM Handout 4.3 — Causation: Impact of the Proclamation of 1763

Chapter 4 — Essential Activity

Help students develop the skill of contextualization by placing key events and processes in Chapter 4 within the context of events occurring in Europe. Using the text and outside resources, ask students to create a chart of events in Europe that had an impact on the development of the British North American colonies. For each event, students should provide a statement of contextualization. A helpful interactive timeline that allows students to compare events in Europe and the New World is available through the Annenberg Learner Web site. To access this resource, search "Annenberg interactive timeline colonial settlement."

Chapter 4 — Bell Ringers

The following activities take no more than 5–15 minutes of your class period and offer an effective and engaging way to begin your lessons and for students to apply AP® Skills & Processes:

- Provide students with a copy or project the image of the "Join or Die" cartoon without revealing the source date, and ask students to explain the historical context of the cartoon. The typical misconception is that this cartoon was created to promote unity in the American Revolution. Use this activity to clarify the creation of this cartoon in response to the French and Indian War and the Albany Congress, and introduce the lesson on the French and Indian War.
- Ask students: Does the U.S. believe in separation of church and state? Require students to provide evidence to support their answer. Use this discussion to have students think about the role of religion in the founding and development of the colonies. This activity is also effective for introducing a lesson on the Great Awakening or differences in colonial regions. *Answers will vary, but should include the following examples of church and state: references to the First Amendment; debates over limiting immigration based on religion or nationality; use of public funds to support private, church-based schools; pledge of allegiance in schools, etc.*

NOTES

TEACHING STRATEGY

As students read the chapter introduction, they can try to identify the specific forms of "growth, diversity, and conflict" that the chapter addresses by looking at the chapter headings and subheadings. Point out how the **AP® LEARNING FOCUS** question reveals a paradox: Britain continued to influence the colonies even while their distinctive American identity continued to grow simultaneously. For a complete suggested response to the **AP® LEARNING FOCUS** question, see p. 138.

4

CHAPTER

Growth, Diversity, and Conflict

1720–1763

AP® LEARNING FOCUS

Why did transatlantic travel and communication reshape Britain's American colonies so dramatically?

In 1736, Alexander MacAllister left the Highlands of Scotland for the backcountry of North Carolina, where his wife and three sisters soon joined him. MacAllister prospered as a landowner and mill proprietor and had only praise for his new home. Carolina was "the best poor man's country," he wrote to his brother Hector, urging him to "advise all poor people . . . to take courage and come." In North Carolina, there were no landlords to keep "the face of the poor . . . to the grinding stone," and so many Highlanders were arriving that "it will soon be a new Scotland." Here, on the far margins of the British Empire, people could "breathe the air of liberty, and not want the necessarys of life." Some 300,000 European migrants — primarily Highland Scots, Scots-Irish, and Germans — heeded MacAllister's advice and helped swell the population of Britain's North American settlements from 400,000 in 1720 to almost 2 million by 1765.

MacAllister's "air of liberty" did not last forever, as the rapid increase in white settlers and the arrival of nearly 300,000 enslaved Africans transformed life throughout mainland British North America. Long-settled towns in New England became overcrowded. In the Middle Atlantic colonies, diverse ethnic and religious communities sometimes became antagonistic with each other; in 1748, there were more than a hundred German Lutheran and Reformed congregations in Quaker-led Pennsylvania. By then, the MacAllisters and thousands of other Celtic and German migrants had altered the social landscape and introduced religious conflict into the southern backcountry.

Everywhere, two European cultural movements, the Enlightenment and Pietism, changed the tone of intellectual and spiritual life. Advocates of "rational thought" viewed human beings as agents of moral self-determination and urged Americans to fashion a better social order. Religious Pietists outnumbered them and had more influence. Convinced of the weakness of human nature, evangelical ministers told their followers to seek regeneration through divine grace. Amidst this intellectual and religious ferment, migrants and the landless children of long-settled families moved inland and sparked wars with the Native peoples and with France and Spain. A generation of dynamic growth produced a decade of deadly warfare that would set the stage for a new era in American history.

John Collet, *George Whitefield Preaching* No painting could capture English minister George Whitefield's charismatic appeal, although this image conveys his open demeanor and religious intensity. When Whitefield spoke to a crowd near Philadelphia, an observer noted that his words were "sharper than a two-edged sword. . . . Some of the people were pale as death; others were wringing their hands . . . and most lifting their eyes to heaven and crying to God for mercy." An astute businessman as well as a charismatic preacher, Whitefield tirelessly promoted the sale of his sermons and books. *George Whitefield Preaching*/Collet, John (c. 1725–1780)/Private Collection/Bridgeman Images.

TEACHING STRATEGY

Use the following questions to guide students' analysis of the painting *George Whitefield Preaching*. How does Collet portray Whitefield's audience? Consider the postures and facial expressions of individual members of the crowd and imagine what might have been running through their minds as they listened. What do the various elements of this painting (the crowd, tankard of ale, sleeping dog, setting) suggest about the Great Awakening's appeal? About Collet's attitude toward evangelical preaching?

TEACHING STRATEGY

Use Collet's painting as an opportunity to discuss religious trends of the time. Supplement your discussion with the Library of Congress's *Religion in the Eighteenth Century* exhibit, which provides an overview of religious trends in the colonies during the eighteenth century. Short essays and over thirty primary sources introduce the architecture of churches, deism, the Great Awakening, and the emergence of evangelicalism. Search for "Library of Congress Religion eighteenth century" to access the Web site.

AP® SKILLS & PROCESSES

CONTINUITY AND CHANGE

Use the **TIMELINE** table to explore how 1687 to 1771 could constitute a definable historical era. Have students identify at least one specific example each of growth, diversity, and conflict in the chronology. Extend this discussion by asking students why the events at the beginning (1687) and end (1771) of the chronology are included despite the fact that they fall outside the larger chapter time boundaries.

TEACHING STRATEGY

Use the lesson plan "Gender and Opportunity" on the Elizabeth Murray Project Web site to explore the roles of seventeenth- and eighteenth-century women in colonial New England. The lesson offers a nuanced understanding of women's roles by focusing on several primary and secondary source excerpts that not only look at women's most common roles as housewives on farms but also public and commercial ventures like shop-keeping. To access the site, search "Elizabeth Murray Project Gender Opportunity."

AP® APPLY THE TIP

Ask students to use the sources in the **AP® THINKING LIKE A HISTORIAN** feature on pp. 114–115 to analyze the role of women in the development of a thriving mixed economy in New England. In small groups, students should identify how the roles of women were critical in shaping the economy of New England. Students should also note the limitations placed on women in the colonial society compared to men, examining how women responded and the justifications provided for limiting the rights and participation of women in civil society. Lead a class discussion and call upon each group to report their findings and discuss.

TIMELINE

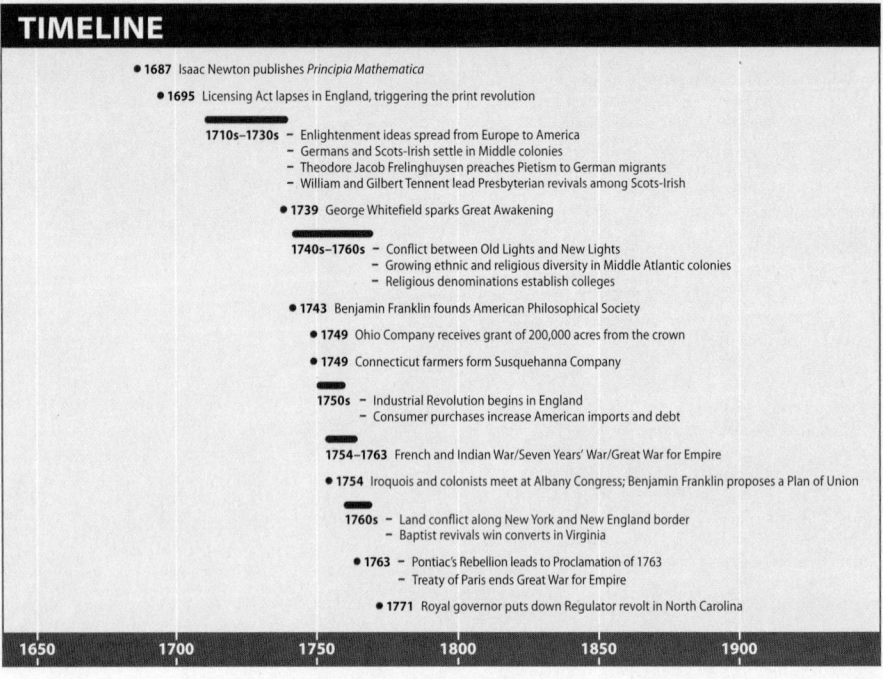

- **1687** Isaac Newton publishes *Principia Mathematica*
- **1695** Licensing Act lapses in England, triggering the print revolution
- **1710s–1730s**
  - Enlightenment ideas spread from Europe to America
  - Germans and Scots-Irish settle in Middle colonies
  - Theodore Jacob Frelinghuysen preaches Pietism to German migrants
  - William and Gilbert Tennent lead Presbyterian revivals among Scots-Irish
- **1739** George Whitefield sparks Great Awakening
- **1740s–1760s**
  - Conflict between Old Lights and New Lights
  - Growing ethnic and religious diversity in Middle Atlantic colonies
  - Religious denominations establish colleges
- **1743** Benjamin Franklin founds American Philosophical Society
- **1749** Ohio Company receives grant of 200,000 acres from the crown
- **1749** Connecticut farmers form Susquehanna Company
- **1750s**
  - Industrial Revolution begins in England
  - Consumer purchases increase American imports and debt
- **1754–1763** French and Indian War/Seven Years' War/Great War for Empire
- **1754** Iroquois and colonists meet at Albany Congress; Benjamin Franklin proposes a Plan of Union
- **1760s**
  - Land conflict along New York and New England border
  - Baptist revivals win converts in Virginia
- **1763**
  - Pontiac's Rebellion leads to Proclamation of 1763
  - Treaty of Paris ends Great War for Empire
- **1771** Royal governor puts down Regulator revolt in North Carolina

1650 1700 1750 1800 1850 1900

NEW ENGLAND'S FREEHOLD SOCIETY

What goals and values shaped New England society in the eighteenth century?

In the 1630s, the Puritans had fled England, where a small elite of nobles and gentry owned 75 percent of the arable land, while tenants and propertyless workers farmed it. In New England, the Puritans created a yeoman society of relatively equal freeholders — landowning farm families who weren't beholden to landlords. But by 1750, the migrants' numerous descendants had parceled out the best farmland, threatening the future of their freehold society.

Farm Families: Women in the Household Economy

AP® EXAM TIP

Take good notes throughout this chapter on the role of women in New England families as they developed a thriving mixed economy based on farming and commerce.

The Puritans' vision of social equality did not extend to women, and their ideology placed the husband firmly at the head of the household. In *The Well-Ordered Family* (1712), the Reverend Benjamin Wadsworth of Boston advised women, "Since he is thy Husband, God has made him the head and set him above thee." It was a wife's duty "to love and reverence" her husband.

Women learned this subordinate role throughout their lives. Small girls watched their mothers defer to their fathers, and as young women, they were told to be "silent in company." They saw the courts prosecute more women than men for the crime of fornication (sex outside of marriage), and they found that their marriage portions would be inferior to those of their brothers. Thus Ebenezer Chittendon of Guilford, Connecticut, left his land to his sons, decreeing that "Each Daughter [shall] have half so much as Each Son, one half in money and the other half in Cattle."

Throughout the colonies, women assumed the role of dutiful helpmeets (helpmates) to their husbands. In addition to tending gardens, farmwives spun thread and yarn from flax and wool and then wove it into cloth for shirts and gowns. They knitted sweaters and stockings, made candles and soap, churned milk into butter, fermented malt for beer, preserved meats, and mastered dozens of other household tasks. "Notable women"—those who excelled at domestic arts—won praise and high status (see "Thinking Like a Historian," p. 114).

Bearing and rearing children were equally important tasks. Most women in New England married in their early twenties and by their early forties had given birth to six or seven children, delivered with the help of a female neighbor or a midwife. One Massachusetts mother confessed that she had little time for religious activities because "the care of my Babes takes up so large a portion of my time and attention." Yet most Puritan congregations were filled with women: "In a Church of between *Three* and *Four* Hundred *Communicants*," the eminent minister Cotton Mather noted, "there are but few more than *One* Hundred *Men*; all the Rest are Women."

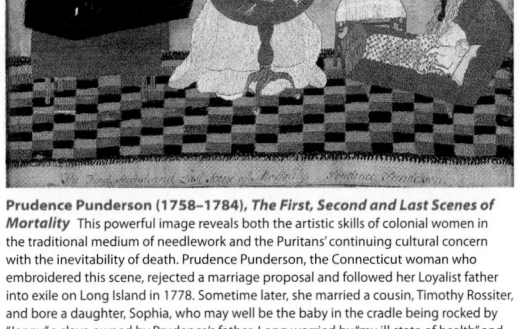

Prudence Punderson (1758–1784), *The First, Second and Last Scenes of Mortality* This powerful image reveals both the artistic skills of colonial women in the traditional medium of needlework and the Puritans' continuing cultural concern with the inevitability of death. Prudence Punderson, the Connecticut woman who embroidered this scene, rejected a marriage proposal and followed her Loyalist father into exile on Long Island in 1778. Sometime later, she married a cousin, Timothy Rossiter, and bore a daughter, Sophia, who may well be the baby in the cradle being rocked by "Jenny," a slave owned by Prudence's father. Long worried by "my ill state of health" and perhaps now anticipating her own death, Prudence has inscribed her initials on the coffin—and, in creating this embroidery, transformed her personal experience into a broader meditation on the progression from birth, to motherhood, to death. Embroidery, 1776–1783, Gift of Newton C. Brainard, accession no. 1962.28.4, the Connecticut Historical Society.

Women's lives remained tightly bound by a web of legal and cultural restrictions. Ministers praised women for their piety but excluded them from an equal role in the church. When Hannah Heaton, a Connecticut farmwife, grew dissatisfied with her Congregational minister, thinking him unconverted and a "blind guide," she sought out equality-minded Quaker and evangelist Baptist churches that welcomed questioning women such as herself and treated "saved" women equally with men. However, by the 1760s, many evangelical congregations had reinstituted men's dominance over women. "The government of Church and State must be . . . family government" controlled by its "king," declared the Danbury (Connecticut) Baptist Association.

AP® SKILLS & PROCESSES

MAKING CONNECTIONS

What ideas, institutions, and responsibilities shaped New England farm women's lives?

Farm Property: Inheritance

By contrast, European men who migrated to the colonies escaped many traditional constraints, including the curse of landlessness. "The hope of having land of their own & becoming independent of Landlords is what chiefly induces people into America," an official noted in the 1730s. Owning property gave formerly dependent peasants a new social identity.

Unlike the adventurers seeking riches in other parts of the Americas, most New England migrants wanted farms that would provide a living for themselves and ample land for their children. In this way, they hoped to secure a **competency** for their families: the ability to keep their households solvent and independent and to pass that ability on to the next generation. A father's duty was to provide inheritances for his children so that one day they could "be for themselves." Men who failed to do so lost status in the community. Some fathers willed the family farm to a single son and provided other children with money, an apprenticeship, or uncleared frontier tracts. Other yeomen moved their families to the frontier, where life was hard but land was cheap and abundant enough to provide for all sons.

competency
The ability to keep households solvent and independent and to pass that ability on to the next generation.

TEACHING STRATEGY

As the caption suggests, this image of Prudence Punderson provides an opportunity to discuss the common lifecycle of colonial women. It also illustrates a uniquely Puritan focus on the ever-present reality of death. In this way, Puritans would always be ready to throw themselves on God's mercy when their death actually approached. Guide students' analysis with the following question: **What effect might having her casket prepared in advance have had on Prudence's outlook as a Puritan?** *It would have reminded her that she was mortal and that her hope of heaven depended on God's grace.*

CHECK FOR UNDERSTANDING

Ask students: **What role did women play in the household economy?** *Women tended gardens; spun, wove, and knitted clothing; prepared food; and cared for children.*

AP® SKILLS & PROCESSES

MAKING CONNECTIONS

The **MAKING CONNECTIONS** question provides an opportunity for students to consider the ways gender roles uniquely shaped women's experiences. Students may need help in understanding the time-consuming, difficult nature of daily farm chores in a premodern world; refer students to the **AP® THINKING LIKE A HISTORIAN** feature (pp. 114–115), which gives a glimpse of this work routine. Students might also consider whether women in early industrial societies had greater or less latitude as their roles changed in a society shaped by a new economy.

TRM Find complete suggested responses in the Teacher's Resource Materials.

AP® SKILLS & PROCESSES

ANALYZING HISTORICAL EVIDENCE

The variety of sources in the **AP® THINKING LIKE A HISTORIAN** feature provides students with an opportunity to differentiate between expectations and reality, especially on an important issue like gender roles. Linking the format of a particular primary source to its reliability and limitations can be a useful exercise. Help students recognize that advice manuals only reveal what a particular authority figure — in this case, typically a male authority — thought cultural norms ought to be. The very fact that an advice manual was deemed necessary at all suggests that these norms were neither automatic nor understood by all. Letters and diary entries, by contrast, tend to provide more accurate insight regarding women's actual lives.

Women's Labor

As these documents show, women bore the responsibility for a wide variety of work, from keeping up households to supporting themselves independently.

1. **Thomas Tusser, *Five Hundred Pointes of Good Husbandrie*, 1557.** *Advice manuals like Tusser's circulated for generations and offered guidance on household management. In this couplet, Tusser stresses the virtues of a wife's economy and hard work.*

Wife, make thine own candle,
Spare penny to handle.
Provide for thy tallow ere frost cometh in,
And make thine own candle ere winter begin.

2. **Eliza Lucas, letters, 1740–1742.** *George Lucas owned three South Carolina plantations, but, as lieutenant governor of Antigua, he was frequently absent. When his daughter was sixteen, he gave her responsibility for managing them. She introduced indigo cultivation in South Carolina, and it soon became the colony's second-leading cash crop. These letters were written when she was between the ages of eighteen and twenty.*

May 2, 1740

"I have the business of 3 plantations to transact, which requires much writing and more business and fatigue of other sorts than you can imagine. But least you should imagine it too burthensom to a girl at my early time of life, give me leave to answer you: I assure you I think myself happy that I can be useful to so good a father, and by rising very early I find I can go through much business."

July 1740

"Wrote my Father a very long letter on his plantation affairs and on . . . the pains I had taken to bring the Indigo, Ginger, Cotton and Lucerne and Casada to perfection, and had greater hopes from the Indigo . . . than any of the rest of the things I tried."

February 6, 1741

". . . I have a Sister to instruct and a parcel of little Negroes whom I have undertaken to teach to read."

April 23, 1741

"Wrote to my Father informing him of the loss of a Negro man — also the boat being overset in Santilina [Saint Helena] Sound and 20 barrels of Rice lost."

[1742]

"Wont you laugh at me if I tell you I am so busey in providing for Posterity I hardly allow my self time to Eat or sleep. . . . I am making a large plantation of Oaks which I look upon as my own property, whether my father gives me the land or not; and therefore I design many years hence when oaks are more valueable than they are now — which you know they will be when we come to build fleets."

[c. June 1742]

"I am engaged with the rudiments of the law to which I am yet but a stranger. . . . If You will not laugh too immoderately at me I'll Trust you with a secrett. I have made two wills already."

3. **Mary Vial Holyoke, diary excerpts, 1761.** *Mary Vial Holyoke, wife of a prominent physician in Salem, Massachusetts, kept a diary that offers a glimpse of the range of household tasks women faced.*

[1761]

Jan. 16: Began upon the firkin of butter of 40 lb. . . .
22: Bo't hog, weighed 182 pounds, at 2/5. Salted hog with half Lisbon & half saltertudas [Tortugas] salt. . . .
Mar. 4: Ironing. . . .
7: Scower'd pewter. . . .
17: Made the Dr. six Cravats marked H. . . .
Apr. 17: Made soap. . . .
23: Dressed a Calves Head turtle fashion. . . .
May 20: Began to whitewash. . . .
28: Ironed. . . .
30: Scower'd pewter. . . .
July 7: Scowered rooms. . . .

4. **Colonial house interiors in Germantown, Pennsylvania, and Augusta, Maine.** *These images show the dining room of Benjamin Chew, a wealthy Philadelphia lawyer (below), and the kitchen of the Howards, an extended family of soldiers and merchants on the Maine frontier (opposite).*

SOURCE: © Ron Blunt.

114

Source: Old Fort Western, Augusta, Maine.

5. **Business advertisement in the *Pennsylvania Gazette*, 1758.** *Not all women's work was done in the home. Hannah Breintnall, a Philadelphia widow, ran a tavern before opening a shop specializing in eyeglasses.*

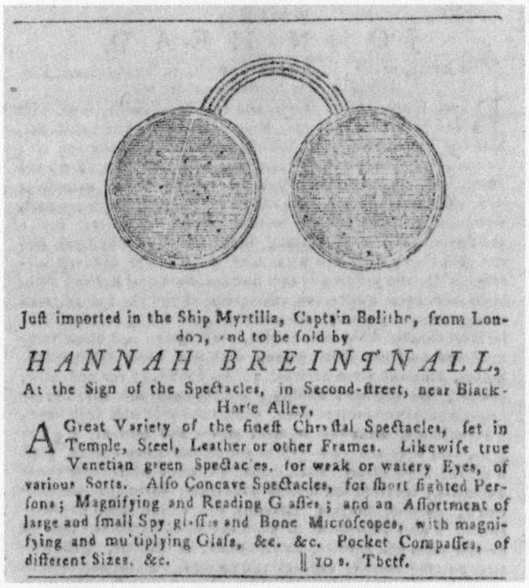
Juſt imported in the Ship Myrtilla, Captain Bolithr, from London, and to be ſold by
HANNAH BREINTNALL,
At the Sign of the Spectacles, in Second-ſtreet, near Black-Horſe Alley,
A Great Variety of the fineſt Chryſtal Spectacles, ſet in Temple, Steel, Leather or other Frames. Likewiſe true Venetian green Spectacles, for weak or watery Eyes, of various Sorts. Alſo Concave Spectacles, for ſhort ſighted Perſons; Magnifying and Reading Glaſſes; and an Aſſortment of large and ſmall Spy-glaſſes and Bone Microſcopes, with magnifying and multiplying Glaſs, &c. &c. Pocket Compaſſes, of different Sizes. &c.
10 s. Tbetf.

Source: The Library Company of Philadelphia, www.librarycompany.org.

6. ***Hilliad Magna: Being the Life and Adventures of Moll Placket-Hole*, 1765.** *Moll Placket-Hole was a satirical, seven-page pamphlet that purported to describe the life of a Philadelphia prostitute. Moll was an eighteenth-century term for a loose woman or prostitute, while placket-hole referred to a slit that might be found in a woman's skirt.*

MOLL PLACKET-HOLE was born in a *Bawdy House* in a *Lane* in the City of *Brotherly Love*. . . . [A]t the Age of twelve (Shocking to consider!) . . . [her] Mother *sold* her Virginity — *sold* it for the Trifling Consideration of *Ten Pounds*. Her Purchaser was soon cloyed and abandoned her. Virtue lost and good Reputation (if ever she had it) gone, she commenced open Prostitute and dealt out her Favours to the highest Bidder. . . . [S]he understood the Trade and set up a *Bawdy-House*. . . . It was necessary, however, that a Man should live with her, that they might appear to the Publick, as *honest* Housekeepers. . . . The Trade became at last so publick, that it gave Offence to her sober Neighbours. . . . [T]he Town tired out with her Insolence, and her Escape from Justice in a regular Manner, set a Mob (many of whom had been her Beneficiaries) upon her. They pulled down her House, and destroyed her Furniture &c. She stormed and raged and swore if her Customers would not build her a better House, she would expose them. . . . They opened a Subscription, and a hundred Pounds were subscribed in one Day.

Sources: (1) Alice Morse Earle, *Home Life in the Colonial Days* (New York: The Macmillan Company, 1898), 35; (2) From *The Letterbook of Eliza Lucas Pinckney, 1739–1762*, edited by Elise Pinckney, University of North Carolina Press, 1972. Based on original documents from the South Carolina Historical Society. Courtesy of the South Carolina Historical Society; (3) George Francis Dow, ed., *The Holyoke Diaries, 1709–1856* (Salem, MA: The Essex Institute, 1911), 49–51; (6) *Hilliad Magna: Being the Life and Adventures of Moll Placket-Hole* ([Philadelphia]: Printed [by Anthony Armbruster], 1765).

ANALYZING THE EVIDENCE

1. Compare the advice manual (source 1) with Eliza Lucas's letters and Mary Vial Holyoke's diary. What themes do the sources share? How do the experiences of women in sources two and three deviate from the expectations of the advice book authors?
2. Eliza Lucas supervised slave labor, and Mary Vial Holyoke very likely employed servants. How does this historical situation affect the way you interpret sources 2 and 3? Make a historically defensible claim.
3. Compare the two house interiors (source 4). What work would women have done in these spaces? The Chews were a slaveholding family, and the Howards probably employed servants. How might relationships and work completed be affected by access to manual labor?
4. Hannah Breintnall was a well-to-do widow, while Moll Placket-Hole was a fictional stereotype. What does Breintnall's experience tell us about the prospects of a single woman? How does Moll Placket-Hole shed light on popular attitudes toward single women? Compare how social status affects how each woman fared during colonial times.

AP® DBQ PRACTICE

With all these sources in mind, write a short essay that considers the role of hierarchy and social power in women's work. How did economic and social status affect the work that was expected of women? Use historical reasoning to compare how the women here navigate the challenges and opportunities they faced. And how does the satire of Moll Placket-Hole illuminate popular attitudes toward women's work and its place in colonial society? Use evidence from source 6 and the textbook to describe colonial attitudes toward women's work.

TRM Find complete suggested responses in the Teacher's Resource Materials.

AP® SKILLS & PROCESSES

ARGUMENTATION

The **AP® DBQ PRACTICE** prompt requires students to integrate evidence of the constraints on women's behavior with evidence of ways they sought opportunity despite those constraints.

Parents who could not give their offspring land placed these children as indentured servants in more prosperous households. When the indentures ended at age eighteen or twenty-one, propertyless sons faced a decades-long climb up the agricultural ladder, from laborer to tenant and finally to freeholder.

Sons and daughters in well-to-do farm families were luckier: they received a marriage portion when they were in their early twenties. That portion — land, livestock, or farm equipment — repaid them for their past labor and allowed parents to choose their marriage partners. Parents' security during old age depended on a wise choice of son- or daughter-in-law. Although the young people could refuse an unacceptable match, they did not have the luxury of falling in love with and marrying whomever they pleased.

coverture
A principle in English law that placed wives under the protection and authority of their husbands, so that they did not have independent legal standing.

Marriage under eighteenth-century English common law was not a contract between equals. Under the legal principle of **coverture**, which placed married women under the protection and authority of their husbands, a bride relinquished to her husband the legal ownership of all her property. After his death, she received a dower right, the right to use (though not sell) one-third of the family's property. On the widow's death or remarriage, her portion was divided among the children. Thus the widow's property rights were subordinate to those of the family line, which stretched across the generations.

Freehold Society in Crisis

AP® EXAM TIP
Compare the impact of demographic change in the colonial regions.

Because of rapid natural increase, New England's population doubled each generation, from 100,000 in 1700, to nearly 200,000 in 1725, to almost 400,000 in 1750. After being divided and then subdivided, farms became so small — 50 acres or less — that parents could provide only one child with an adequate inheritance. In the 1740s, the Reverend Samuel Chandler of Andover, Massachusetts, was "much distressed for land for his children," seven of them young boys. A decade later, in nearby Concord, about 60 percent of the farmers owned less land than their fathers had.

Because parents had less to give their sons and daughters, they had less control over their children's lives. As the traditional system of arranged marriages broke down, young people were more likely to engage in premarital sex. Why? One reason is that they could use the urgency of pregnancy to win permission to marry. Throughout New England, premarital conceptions rose dramatically, from about 10 percent of firstborn children in the 1710s to more than 30 percent in the 1740s. Given another chance, young people "would do the same again," an Anglican minister observed, "because otherwise they could not obtain their parents' consent to marry."

Even as New England families changed, they maintained the freeholder ideal: the ability to remain independent and to ensure independence for their children. Some parents chose to have smaller families and used birth control to do so: abstention, coitus interruptus, or primitive condoms. Other families petitioned the provincial government for frontier land grants and hacked new farms out of the forests of central Massachusetts, western Connecticut, and eventually New Hampshire and Vermont. Still others improved their farms' productivity by replacing the traditional English crops of wheat and barley with high-yielding potatoes and maize (Indian corn). Corn was an especially wise choice: good for human consumption, as well as for feeding cattle and pigs, which provided milk and meat. Gradually, New England changed from a grain to a livestock economy, becoming a major exporter of salted meat to the plantations of the West Indies.

household mode of production
The system of exchanging goods and labor that helped eighteenth-century New England freeholders survive on ever-shrinking farms as available land became more scarce.

As the population swelled, New England farmers developed the full potential of what one historian has called the "**household mode of production**," in which families swapped labor and goods. Women and children worked in groups to spin yarn, sew quilts, and shuck corn. Men loaned neighbors tools, draft animals, and grazing land. Farmers plowed fields owned by artisans and shopkeepers, who repaid them with shoes, furniture, or store credit. Partly because currency was in short supply, no cash changed hands. Instead, farmers, artisans, and shopkeepers recorded debits and credits and "balanced" the books every few years. This system helped New Englanders to maximize agricultural output and preserve the freehold ideal.

AP® SKILLS & PROCESSES
CONTINUITY AND CHANGE
What factors threatened the freeholder ideal in midcentury New England, and what strategies did farming families use to preserve this ideal?

CHECK FOR UNDERSTANDING

Ask students: **What was the relationship between inheritance and property in New England?** *Parents sought to provide an adequate means for all of their children to live on independent farms, through inheritances of land or money, and through arranged marriages.*

AP® APPLY THE TIP

Ask students to create a Venn diagram comparing the impact of demographic change on the southern colonies following Bacon's Rebellion (1676) to the New England colonies in the eighteenth century. In their comparison, ask students to define the demographic changes, explain the causes of these demographic changes, and explain ways people adapted to the changes.

TEACHING STRATEGY

Benjamin Franklin's 1751 essay "Observations Concerning the Increase of Mankind" is an astute analysis of the reasons for population growth in the colonies and the likely consequences of this growth. It is also an outstanding example of an Enlightenment-era intellectual applying his understanding to practical problems. Access this document by searching "Franklin Increase of Mankind."

AP® SKILLS & PROCESSES

CONTINUITY AND CHANGE

The **CONTINUITY AND CHANGE** question asks students to identify changes in farm families' behavior that were caused by threats to their status. Students may not understand that the dilemma created by rapid population growth was in some ways unique to New England, where the custom of inheritance prevailed. In other colonies, like Virginia, where primogeniture was the norm, a profit-based economy provided an opportunity to buy more land as well as a greater range of real property to pass on to descendants. Some students might be surprised by the seemingly modern notion of forcing parents' hands regarding their marriage choice. Extend this prompt by asking students to make inferences about other social consequences of rapid population growth, apart from its effects on families and their economic position.

TRM Find complete suggested responses in the Teacher's Resource Materials.

CHECK FOR UNDERSTANDING

Ask students: **What goals and values shaped New England society in the eighteenth century?** *Eighteenth-century New England society was structured around the freehold — outright ownership of farmland — with the ability to pass that land to one's descendants. Gender roles were strictly defined. Women were supposed to be subordinate to men and to serve as dutiful helpmates. A man's job was to tend the farm successfully so he could pass it on to his sons.*

DIVERSITY IN THE MIDDLE COLONIES

How were the goals of immigrants to the Middle colonies similar to those of New England colonists, and how did they differ?

The Middle colonies — New York, New Jersey, and Pennsylvania — became home to peoples of differing origins, languages, and religions. Scots-Irish Presbyterians, English and Welsh Quakers, German Lutherans and Moravians, Dutch Reformed Protestants, and others all sought to preserve their cultural and religious identities as they pursued economic opportunity. At the same time, rapid population growth throughout the region strained public institutions, pressured Indian lands, and created a dynamic but unstable society.

AP® EXAM TIP

Understanding the causes of diversity in the Middle colonies and its impact on the region's development is important to know on the AP® Exam.

Economic Growth, Opportunity, and Conflict

Previously home to New Netherland and New Sweden, the Mid-Atlantic region was already ethnically diverse before England gained control of it. The founding of Pennsylvania and New Jersey amplified this pattern. Fertile land seemed abundant, and grain exports to Europe and the West Indies financed the colonies' rapid settlement (see "America in the World," p. 118). Between 1720 and 1770, a growing demand for wheat, corn, and flour doubled their prices and brought people and prosperity to the region. Yet that very growth led to conflict, both within the Middle colonies and in their relations with Native American neighbors.

Tenancy in New York In New York's fertile Hudson River Valley, wealthy Dutch and English families presided over the huge manors created by the Dutch West India Company and English governors and relied on **tenancy** to work their land. Like Chesapeake planters, the New York landlords aspired to live in the manner of the European gentry but found that few migrants wanted to labor as peasants. To attract tenants, the manorial lords granted long leases, with the right to sell improvements such as houses and barns to the next tenant. They nevertheless struggled to populate their estates.

Most tenant families hoped that with hard work and ample sales they could eventually buy their own farmsteads. But preindustrial technology limited output. A worker with a hand sickle could reap only half an acre of wheat, rye, or oats a day. The cradle scythe, a tool introduced during the 1750s, doubled or tripled the amount of grain one worker could cut. Even so, a family with two adult workers could reap only about 12 acres of grain, or roughly 150 to 180 bushels of wheat. After saving enough grain for food and seed, the surplus might be worth £15 — enough to buy salt and sugar, tools, and cloth, but little else. The road to landownership was not an easy one.

tenancy
The rental of property. To attract tenants in New York's Hudson River Valley, Dutch and English manorial lords granted long tenancy leases, with the right to sell improvements — houses and barns, for example — to the next tenant.

Conflict in the Quaker Colonies In Quaker-dominated Pennsylvania and New Jersey, wealth was initially distributed more evenly than in New York, but the proprietors of each colony, like the manor lords of New York, had enormous land claims. The first migrants lived simply in small, one- or two-room houses with a sleeping loft, a few benches or stools, and some wooden platters and cups. Economic growth brought greater prosperity, along with conflicts between ordinary settlers and the proprietors who tried to control their access to land, resources, and political power.

William Penn's early appeals to British Quakers and European Protestants led to a boom in immigrants. When these first arrivals reported that Pennsylvania and New Jersey were "the best poor man's country in the world," thousands more followed. Soon the proprietors of both colonies were overwhelmed by the demand for land. By the 1720s, many new migrants were forced to become **squatters**, establishing themselves illegally on land that had not yet been surveyed in the hope that they would have the first right to purchase it when it became available for sale.

squatter
Someone who settles on land he or she does not own or rent. Many eighteenth-century migrants settled on land before it was surveyed and entered for sale, requesting the first right to purchase the land when sales began.

TEACHING STRATEGY

Ask students to work in small groups to complete **Handout 4.1 — Thematic Analysis: Diversity in the Middle Colonies (TRM)** to analyze the causes and effects of diversity by utilizing AP® Themes. You may also have students complete this activity in a jigsaw format with different groups assigned to investigate Middle colonies diversity as it related to one AP® Theme. Reorganize the groups so that each theme is represented by one student who explains his or her theme to the new group. After students have discussed their thematic analysis in small groups, lead a class discussion about what led to the development of diversity and the limits of tolerance in the Middle colonies.

TRM Find complete suggested responses and **Handout 4.1 — Thematic Analysis: Diversity in the Middle Colonies** in the Teacher's Resource Materials.

AP® SKILLS & PROCESSES

ANALYZING HISTORICAL EVIDENCE

FIGURE 4.1 situates migration to the British colonies in the larger transatlantic context of the European empires. Though consisting of only ten columns, this chart provides a significant amount of information that students may need help unpacking. First, it allows for comparison in volume between five different empires. Second, it gives information about the type of immigrant — African and European. Third, it provides for analysis of changes in the scale and makeup of migrants over time. The dramatic explosion in the population of the British colonies reveals a majority of these migrants were enslaved Africans, but the number of European migrants still significantly exceeds that of any other empire. Extend this discussion by asking students to identify the most significant trend in the figure.

TRM Find complete suggested responses in the Teacher's Resource Materials.

AP® AMERICA IN THE WORLD

Transatlantic Migration, 1500–1760

The following graph compares the number of European and African migrants who arrived in the American colonies of Spain, Portugal, Britain, France, and the Netherlands. It also charts change over time: while immigrants in the sixteenth and early seventeenth centuries went predominantly to the colonies of Spain and Portugal, Britain's colonies became the principal destination for both Europeans and Africans between 1640 and 1760.

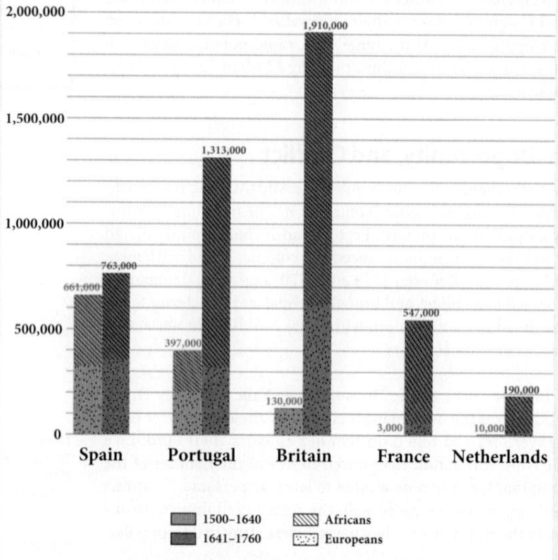

FIGURE 4.1 Transatlantic Migration

Source of data: Stanley L. Engerman and Kenneth L. Sokoloff, "Factor Endowments, Institutions, and Differential Paths of Growth Among New World Economies: A View from Economic Historians of the United States," in *How Latin America Fell Behind: Economic Histories of Brazil and Mexico*, 1800–1914, ed. Stephen Haber (Palo Alto, CA: Stanford University Press, 1997), 264.

QUESTIONS FOR ANALYSIS

1. What relationship do you see between the number of European emigrants and the importation of African slaves? Which nation's colonies had the highest percentage of Africans relative to Europeans? Which had the lowest? Which time periods had the highest and lowest percentages of Africans?
2. Compare France and the Netherlands to Spain, Portugal, and Britain. Why do you suppose that the ratio of Africans to Europeans is so much higher in French and Dutch colonies than in the other nations? Choose examples from the chapter to support your claim. Which type of colony — tribute, plantation, or neo-European — was likely to have been most important to the French and Dutch?

Frustration over the lack of land led the Penn family to perpetrate one of the most infamous land frauds of the eighteenth century, the so-called Walking Purchase of 1737, in which they ruthlessly exploited an Indian deed to claim more than a million acres of prime farmland north of Philadelphia. This purchase, while opening new lands to settlement, poisoned Indian relations in the colony. Delaware and Shawnee migration to western Pennsylvania and the Ohio Valley, which was already under way, accelerated rapidly in response.

Immigrants flooded into Philadelphia, which grew from 2,000 people in 1700 to 25,000 by 1760. Many families came in search of land; for them, Philadelphia was only a temporary way station. Other migrants came as laborers, including a large number of indentured servants. Some were young, unskilled men, but the colony's explosive growth also created a strong demand for all kinds of skilled laborers, especially in the construction trades.

Ethnic Diversity and Material Culture As non-English migrants arrived in greater numbers in British North America, they brought craft traditions with them that transformed the colonies' material culture. This eighteenth-century chest, made of yellow pine and tulip poplar and intricately hand-painted, was built by a German craftsman in Berks County, Pennsylvania. The central panel features two unicorns, while the two side panels portray men on horseback. Floral patterns surround the panels and decorate the drawers. These motifs are commonly found on marriage chests from the region.
The Metropolitan Museum of Art, Rogers Fund, 1923.

Pennsylvania and New Jersey grew prosperous but contentious. New Jersey was plagued by contested land titles, and ordinary settlers rioted against the proprietors in the 1740s and the 1760s. By the 1760s, eastern Pennsylvania landowners with large farms were using slaves and poor Scots-Irish migrants to grow wheat. Other ambitious men were buying up land and dividing it into small tenancies, which they lent out on profitable leases. Still others sold manufactured goods, including farm equipment, or ran mills. These large-scale farmers, rural landlords, speculators, storekeepers, and gristmill operators formed a distinct class of agricultural capitalists. They built large stone houses for their families, furnishing them with four-poster beds and expensive mahogany tables, on which they laid elegant linen and imported Dutch dinnerware.

By contrast, one-half of the Middle colonies' white men owned no land and little personal property. Some were the sons of smallholding farmers and would eventually inherit some land. But many were Scots-Irish or German "inmates" — single men or families, explained a tax assessor, "such as live in small cottages and have no taxable property, except a cow." In the predominantly German township of Lancaster, Pennsylvania, a merchant noted an "abundance of Poor people" who "maintain their Families with great difficulty by day Labour." Although these workers hoped eventually to become landowners, rising land prices prevented many from realizing their dreams.

AP® SKILLS & PROCESSES

CAUSATION

How did rapid immigration and economic growth trigger conflict in the Middle colonies?

Cultural Diversity

The Middle Atlantic colonies were not a melting pot. Most European migrants held tightly to their traditions, creating a patchwork of ethnically and religiously diverse communities (Figure 4.2). In 1748, a Swedish traveler counted no fewer than twelve religious denominations in Philadelphia, including Anglicans, Baptists, Quakers, Swedish and German Lutherans, Mennonites, Scots-Irish Presbyterians, and Roman Catholics.

Migrants preserved their cultural identity by marrying within their ethnic groups. A major exception was the Huguenots, Calvinists who had been expelled from Catholic France in the 1680s and resettled in Holland, England, and the British colonies. Huguenots in American port cities such as Boston, New York, and Charleston quickly lost their French identities by intermarrying with other Protestants.

AP® EXAM TIP

Evaluate the relationship between diversity and tolerance in the Middle colonies and compare to other colonial regions.

AP® THEME

ARC: American and Regional Culture

Students are responsible for understanding how a nascent colonial culture expanded culturally and intellectually because of demographic shifts. Help students understand the larger historical processes by explaining the following concepts: cultural pluralism, intellectual exchanges, and demographic shifts. After explaining these ideas, have students examine the picture of the eighteenth-century chest in groups. Ask them to think of how the picture represents either cultural pluralism, intellectual exchanges, and/or demographic shifts.

CHECK FOR UNDERSTANDING

Ask students: **How did economic growth, opportunity, and conflict characterize the Middle colonies?** *The rising prices of grain lured migrants while raising the hope for many that they could improve their lives and own their own property. The simultaneous rise of land prices frustrated these hopes, leading to strong tensions. Some attempted to acquire land by settling on Native American territory, fueling conflict with them.*

AP® SKILLS & PROCESSES

CAUSATION

Use the **CAUSATION** question to explore how demographic and economic trends affected social stability in the Middle colonies. Students may need some guidance to grasp the idea that change — even positive change, like economic prosperity — can be disruptive to a society if it happens too rapidly.

TRM Find complete suggested responses in the Teacher's Resource Materials.

AP® THEME

MIG: Migration and Settlement

Use **FIGURE 4.2** to explore the effects of European migration on the diversity of the colonial population. Guide students' analysis of this chart with the following questions:

- **What trend in the volume of immigrants does this chart indicate over the course of the eighteenth century?** *The volume of immigrants increased steadily, until about mid-century, when it leveled off.*
- **Which two groups migrated in the largest numbers?** *Germans and Northern Irish (Scots-Irish) made up just over half of the migrants.*
- **What conclusion does this chart suggest about the European makeup of the colonies?** *Though the vast majority of the migrants were British, less than 15 percent were English. The colonies were very ethnically diverse overall — though this diversity varied according to region, and this chart only includes Europeans, not Africans.*

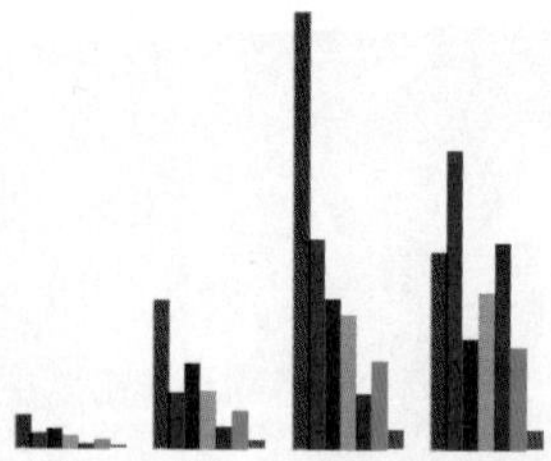

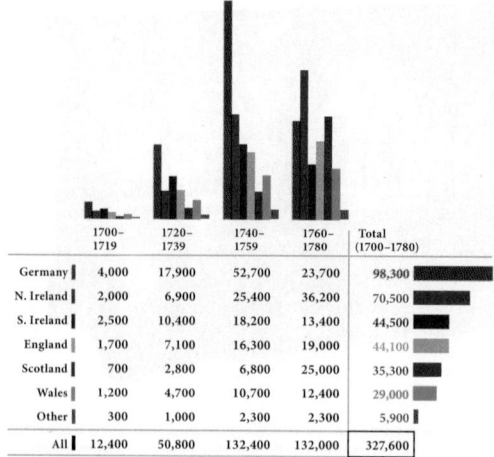

	1700–1719	1720–1739	1740–1759	1760–1780	Total (1700–1780)
Germany	4,000	17,900	52,700	23,700	98,300
N. Ireland	2,000	6,900	25,400	36,200	70,500
S. Ireland	2,500	10,400	18,200	13,400	44,500
England	1,700	7,100	16,300	19,000	44,100
Scotland	700	2,800	6,800	25,000	35,300
Wales	1,200	4,700	10,700	12,400	29,000
Other	300	1,000	2,300	2,300	5,900
All	12,400	50,800	132,400	132,000	327,600

FIGURE 4.2 Estimated European Migration to the British Mainland Colonies, 1700–1780

After 1720, European migration to British North America increased dramatically, peaking between 1740 and 1780, when more than 264,000 settlers arrived in the mainland colonies. Emigration from Germany peaked in the 1740s, but the number of migrants from Ireland, Scotland, England, and Wales continued to increase during the 1760s and early 1770s. Most migrants, including those from Ireland, were Protestants.

More typical were the Welsh Quakers in Chester County, Pennsylvania: 70 percent of the children of the original Welsh migrants married other Welsh Quakers, as did 60 percent of the third generation.

In Pennsylvania and western New Jersey, Quakers shaped the culture because of their numbers, wealth, and social cohesion. Most Quakers came from English counties with few landlords and brought with them traditions of local village governance, popular participation in politics, and social equality. But after 1720, the growth of German and Scots-Irish populations challenged their dominance.

The German Influx The Quaker vision of a "peaceable kingdom" attracted 100,000 German migrants who had fled their homelands because of military conscription, religious persecution, and high taxes. First to arrive, in 1683, were the Mennonites, religious dissenters drawn by the promise of freedom of worship. In the 1720s, a larger wave of German migrants arrived from the overcrowded villages of southwestern Germany and Switzerland. "Wages were far better" in Pennsylvania, Heinrich Schneebeli reported to his friends in Zurich, and "one also enjoyed there a free unhindered exercise of religion." A third wave of Germans and Swiss — nearly 40,000 strong — landed in Philadelphia between 1749 and 1756. To help pay the costs of the expensive trip from the Rhine Valley, German immigrants pioneered the **redemptioner** system, a flexible form of indentured servitude that allowed families to negotiate their own terms upon arrival. Families often indentured one or more children while their parents set up a household of their own.

redemptioner
A type of indentured servant in the Middle colonies in the eighteenth century who did not sign a contract before leaving Europe but instead negotiated employment after arriving in America.

Germans soon dominated many districts in eastern Pennsylvania, and thousands more moved down the fertile Shenandoah Valley into the western backcountry of Maryland, Virginia, and the Carolinas (Map 4.1). Many migrants preserved their cultural identity by settling in German-speaking Lutheran and Reformed communities that endured well beyond 1800. A minister in North Carolina admonished young people "not to contract any marriages with the English or Irish," arguing that "we owe it to our native country to do our part that German blood and the German language be preserved in America."

These settlers were willing colonial subjects of Britain's German-born and German-speaking Protestant monarchs, George I (r. 1714–1727) and George II (r. 1727–1760). They generally avoided politics except to protect their cultural practices; for example, they insisted that married women have the legal right to hold property and write wills, as they did in Germany.

Scots-Irish Settlers Migrants from Ireland, who numbered about 115,000, were the most numerous of the incoming Europeans. Some were Irish and Catholic, but most were Scots and Presbyterian, the descendants of the Calvinist Protestants sent to Ireland during the seventeenth century to solidify English rule there. Once in Ireland, the Scots faced hostility from both Irish Catholics and English officials and landlords. The Irish Test Act of 1704 restricted voting and office holding to members of the Church of England. English mercantilist regulations placed heavy import duties on

CHECK FOR UNDERSTANDING

Ask students: **What kinds of cultural diversity characterized the Middle colonies?** *Though Germans and Scots-Irish were the most prominent non-English groups, the Middle colonies also contained large numbers of Dutch and Swedes. With this ethnic and linguistic diversity came a wide range of religious traditions.*

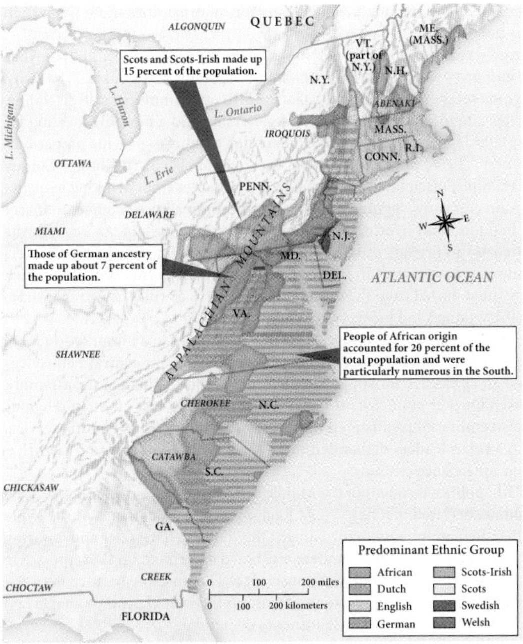

MAPPING THE PAST

MAP 4.1 Ethnic and Racial Diversity in the British Colonies, 1775

In 1700, most colonists in British North America were of English origin; by 1775, settlers of English descent constituted only about 50 percent of the total population. African Americans now accounted for one-third of the residents of the South, while tens of thousands of German and Scots-Irish migrants added ethnic and religious diversity in the Middle colonies, the southern backcountry, and northern New England (see Figure 4.2).

ANALYZING THE MAP: Based on a careful examination of this map, why is it appropriate to say that British North America was not a melting pot, but a patchwork of ethnic, religious, and racial groups?

MAKING CONNECTIONS: Consider this map in relation to Map 4.4 and the accompanying discussion of western rebels and regulators. Based on a comparison of the two maps, why do you think Scots-Irish colonists were disproportionately involved in the frontier conflicts depicted on the map and in the text?

linens made by Scots-Irish weavers, and farmers paid heavy taxes. This persecution made America seem desirable. "Read this letter, Rev. Baptist Boyd," a migrant to New York wrote back to his minister, "and tell all the poor folk of ye place that God has opened a door for their deliverance . . . all that a man works for is his own; there are no revenue hounds to take it from us here."

Lured by such reports, thousands of Scots-Irish families sailed for the colonies. By 1720, most migrated to Philadelphia, attracted by the religious tolerance there. Seeking cheap land, they moved to central Pennsylvania and to the fertile Shenandoah Valley to the south. Governor William Gooch of Virginia welcomed the Scots-Irish presence to secure "the Country against the Indians." An Anglican planter, however, thought them as dangerous as "the Goths and Vandals of old" had been to the Roman Empire. Like the Germans, the Scots-Irish retained their culture, living in ethnic communities and holding firm to the Presbyterian Church.

AP® SKILLS & PROCESSES

CONTEXTUALIZATION

What attracted German and Scots-Irish migrants to Pennsylvania in such large numbers?

Religion and Politics

In Western Europe, the leaders of church and state condemned religious diversity. "To tolerate all [religions] without controul is the way to have none at all," declared an Anglican clergyman. Orthodox church officials carried such sentiments to Pennsylvania. "The preachers do not have the power to punish anyone, or to force anyone to go to church," complained Gottlieb Mittelberger, an influential German minister. As a result, "Sunday is very badly kept. Many people plough, reap, thresh, hew or split

AP® SKILLS & PROCESSES

DEVELOPMENTS AND PROCESSES

How did the religious changes in the colonies contribute to the development of pluralism in American identity?

AP® THEME

SOC: Social Structure; MIG: Migration and Settlement

Use **MAP 4.1** in conjunction with **FIGURE 4.1** (p. 118) to show where different ethnic groups settled, including Africans as well as Europeans. Guide students' analysis through the following questions:

- **In which region did English settlers predominate?** *New England.*
- **How would you characterize the region from the Chesapeake south to Florida?** *It is mixed English and African, reflecting the heavy reliance on slaves.*
- **In what regions of British North America did Germans and Scots-Irish predominate?** *On the frontier margins of British North America, in the Appalachians and the edges of New England.*
- **What does the map suggest about religious diversity? Why?** *Because ethnicity and religion were strongly related, the ethnic diversity also shows where particular religious groups predominated. Mixed colors on the map suggest places where religious syncretism was most likely — for example, with English and African religions influencing each other.*

TRM Find complete suggested responses in the Teacher's Resource Materials.

AP® SKILLS & PROCESSES

CONTEXTUALIZATION

The **CONTEXTUALIZATION** question is in effect two separate questions: What caused a large migration of Germans to Pennsylvania? And what caused a large migration of Scots-Irish to Pennsylvania? Students might think about these two migrations in terms of push-pull factors, where the push factors were somewhat distinctive, while the pull factor — ethnic and religious tolerance — was essentially the same. Extend this prompt by having students identify how Germans and Scots-Irish might have learned about Pennsylvania and what the demographic patterns of those who migrated might have looked like.

TRM Find complete suggested responses in the Teacher's Resource Materials.

CHECK FOR UNDERSTANDING

Ask students: **How were the goals of immigrants to the Middle colonies similar to those of New England colonists, and how did they differ?** *The goals of immigrants of the Middle colonies, at least the Quakers and the Moravians, were similar to their New England neighbors in as much as religion primarily catalyzed their emigration. At the same time, other immigrants in the Middle colonies, especially the Scots-Irish, were fleeing political and economic persecution, unlike their New England neighbors.*

AP® SKILLS & PROCESSES

COMPARISON

The **COMPARISON** question asks students to compare the perspectives of different groups in the same region. Scaffold this question by asking the following: How did their cultural values and religious beliefs cause division? How did other values create a countervailing tendency toward unity? Extend this prompt by asking students to make an argument regarding why the "broad agreement on the importance of economic opportunity and liberty of conscience" was insufficient to quell tensions between different groups.

TRM Find complete suggested responses in the Teacher's Resource Materials.

AP® THEME

ARC: American and Regional Culture

This short but important discussion about the emergence of a transatlantic print culture explains one important way that ideas about Protestant evangelicalism and the Enlightenment made their way to the colonies. This point is again raised on p. 128 regarding evangelical religious texts.

wood and the like." He concluded: "Liberty in Pennsylvania does more harm than good to many people, both in soul and body."

Mittelberger was mistaken. Although ministers in Pennsylvania could not invoke government authority to uphold religious values, the result was not social anarchy. Instead, religious sects enforced moral behavior through communal self-discipline. Quaker families attended a weekly meeting for worship and a monthly meeting for business; every three months, a committee reminded parents to provide proper religious instruction. The committee also supervised adult behavior; a Chester County meeting, for example, disciplined a member "to reclaim him from drinking to excess and keeping vain company." Significantly, Quaker meetings allowed couples to marry only if they had land and livestock sufficient to support a family. As a result, the children of well-to-do Friends usually married within the sect, while poor Quakers remained unmarried, wed later in life, or married without permission — in which case they were often ousted from the meeting. These marriage rules helped the Quakers build a self-contained and prosperous community.

In the 1740s, the flood of new migrants reduced Quakers to a minority — a mere 30 percent of Pennsylvanians. Moreover, Scots-Irish settlers in central Pennsylvania demanded an aggressive Indian policy, challenging the pacifism of the assembly. To retain power, Quaker politicians sought an alliance with those German religious groups that also embraced pacifism and voluntary (not compulsory) militia service. In response, German leaders demanded more seats in the assembly and laws that respected their inheritance customs.

AP® SKILLS & PROCESSES

COMPARISON

What issues divided the various ethnic and religious groups of the Middle colonies? What core values did they agree upon?

By the 1750s, politics throughout the Middle colonies roiled with conflict. In New York, a Dutchman declared that he "Valued English Law no more than a Turd," while in Pennsylvania, Benjamin Franklin disparaged the "boorish" character and "swarthy complexion" of German migrants. Yet there was broad agreement on the importance of economic opportunity and liberty of conscience. The unstable balance between shared values and mutual mistrust prefigured tensions that would pervade an increasingly diverse American society in the centuries to come.

CULTURAL TRANSFORMATIONS

How did the accelerating pace of travel and communication affect colonial society and culture?

After 1720, transatlantic shipping grew more frequent and Britain and its colonies more closely connected, while a burgeoning print culture flooded the colonies with information and ideas. Two great European cultural movements — the **Enlightenment**, which emphasized the power of human reason to understand and shape the world; and **Pietism**, an evangelical Christian movement that stressed the individual's personal relationship with God — reached America as a result. At the same time, an abundance of imported goods began to reshape material culture, bringing new comforts into the lives of the middling sort while allowing prosperous merchants and landowners to set themselves apart from their neighbors in new ways.

Enlightenment
An eighteenth-century philosophical movement that emphasized the use of reason to reevaluate previously accepted doctrines and traditions and the power of reason to understand and shape the world.

Pietism
A Christian revival movement characterized by Bible study, the conversion experience, and the individual's personal relationship with God that became widely influential in Britain and its colonies in the eighteenth century.

Transportation and the Print Revolution

In the eighteenth century, improved transportation networks opened Britain's colonies in new ways, and British shipping came to dominate the North Atlantic. In 1700, Britain had 40,000 sailors; by 1750, the number had grown to 60,000, while many more hailed from the colonies. An enormous number of vessels plied Atlantic waters: in the late 1730s, more than 550 ships arrived in Boston annually. About a tenth came directly from Britain or Ireland; the rest came mostly from other British colonies, either on the mainland or in the West Indies.

AP® SKILLS & PROCESSES

DEVELOPMENTS AND PROCESSES

As students examine the demographic shifts and concomitant cultural transformations, encourage work on the skill of understanding historical developments. This activity can be a bell-ringer for class. Organize students into four groups; two groups will be assigned Enlightenment and two groups will be assigned Great Awakening. Have each group develop an interpretation arguing why their historical development was the most significant cultural transformation in mid-eighteenth-century colonial society. After groups finish, have the Enlightenment groups exchange answers and select the best answer. Students in the Great Awakening groups do the same. Students then present the best argument for each development to the class.

A road network slowly took shape as well, though roadbuilding was expensive and difficult. In 1704, Sarah Kemble Knight traveled from Boston to New York on horseback. The road was "smooth and even" in some places, treacherous in others; it took eight days of hard riding to cover 200 miles. Forty years later, a physician from Annapolis, Maryland, traveled along much better roads to Portsmouth, New Hampshire, and back — more than 1,600 miles in all. He spent four months on the road, stopping frequently to meet the locals and satisfy his curiosity. By the mid-eighteenth century, the "Great Wagon Road" carried migrating families down the Shenandoah Valley as far as the Carolina backcountry.

All of these water and land routes carried people, produce, and finished merchandise. They also carried information, as letters, newspapers, pamphlets, and crates of books began to circulate widely. The trip across the Atlantic took seven to eight weeks on average, so the news arriving in colonial ports was not fresh by our standard, but compared to earlier years, the colonies were awash in information.

Until 1695, the British government had the power to censor all printed materials. In that year, Parliament let the Licensing Act lapse, and the floodgates opened. Dozens of new printshops opened in London and Britain's provincial cities. They printed newspapers and pamphlets; poetry, ballads, and sermons; and handbills, tradesman's cards, and advertisements. Larger booksellers also printed scientific treatises, histories, travelers' accounts, and novels. The result was a print revolution. In Britain and throughout Europe, print was essential to the transmission of new ideas, and both the Enlightenment and Pietism took shape in part through its growing influence.

All this material crossed the Atlantic and filled the shops of colonial booksellers. The colonies also began printing their own newspapers. In 1704, the *Boston Newsletter* was founded; by 1720, Boston had five printing presses and three newspapers; and by 1776, the thirteen colonies that united in declaring independence had thirty-seven newspapers among them. This world of print was essential to their ability to share grievances and join in common cause.

AP® EXAM TIP

The flow of ideas through print culture common in the "Atlantic World," and its impact on development of the colonies, is important to know on AP® Exam.

The Enlightenment in America

To explain the workings of the natural world, some colonists relied on folk wisdom. Swedish migrants in Pennsylvania attributed magical powers to the great white mullein, a common wildflower, and treated fevers by tying the plant's leaves around their feet and arms. Traditionally, Christians believed that the earth stood at the center of the universe, and God (and Satan) intervened directly and continuously in human affairs. The scientific revolution of the sixteenth and seventeenth centuries challenged these ideas, and educated people — most of them Christians — began to modify their views accordingly.

AP® EXAM TIP

Compare the impact of Enlightenment rationalism and Pietism (Evangelical Protestantism) on colonial development.

The European Enlightenment In 1543, the Polish astronomer Copernicus published his observation that the earth traveled around the sun, not vice versa. Copernicus's discovery suggested that humans occupied a more modest place in the universe than Christian theology assumed. In the next century, Isaac Newton, in his *Principia Mathematica* (1687), used the sciences of mathematics and physics to explain the movement of the planets around the sun (and invented calculus in the process). Though Newton was profoundly religious, his work challenged the traditional Christian understanding of the cosmos.

In the century between the *Principia Mathematica* and the French Revolution of 1789, the philosophers of the European Enlightenment used empirical research and scientific reasoning to study all aspects of life, including social institutions and human behavior. Enlightenment thinkers advanced four fundamental principles: the lawlike order of the natural world, the power of human reason, the "natural rights" of individuals (including the right to self-government), and the progressive improvement of society.

AP® APPLY THE TIP

Divide students into groups and give each group a large sheet of paper. Ask groups to sketch the Atlantic world (North America, South America, Europe, and Africa). Have students use information from the textbook (pp. 118–125) to create a map that illustrates the exchange of ideas and goods that shows the print revolution, growth of transportation, and exchange of ideas between the colonies and Europe. Provide students with colored pencils or markers so they can create a key that shows understanding of the exchange of Enlightenment ideas versus the exchange of religious ideas. Ask students to create a key to illustrate items, topics, and commodities being exchanged (books, pamphlets, luxury products, religious movements, etc.). After completing their maps, ask students to complete **Handout 4.2 — Comparison: Ideas in the Atlantic World (TRM)**.

TRM Find **Handout 4.2 — Comparison: Ideas in the Atlantic World** in the Teacher's Resource Materials.

CHECK FOR UNDERSTANDING

Ask students: **What were the transportation and print revolutions?** *The expiration of the Licensing Act led to a flood of publications across the Atlantic. The building of ports and roads facilitated the spread of these texts and the ideas they contained.*

TEACHING STRATEGY

Illustrate the tensions between Enlightenment rationalism and Christian theistic understandings through a series of letters to the editor about smallpox, which show the ways these views were invoked on both sides of the debate. Access these letters by searching "National Humanities Center Smallpox."

English philosopher John Locke was a major contributor to the Enlightenment. In his *Essay Concerning Human Understanding* (1690), Locke stressed the impact of environment and experience on human behavior and beliefs, arguing that the character of individuals and societies was not fixed but could be changed through education, rational thought, and purposeful action. Locke's *Two Treatises of Government* (1690) advanced the revolutionary theory that political authority was not given by God to monarchs, as James II had insisted. Instead, it derived from social compacts that people made to preserve their **natural rights** to life, liberty, and property. In Locke's view, the people should have the power to change government policies — or even their form of government.

natural rights
The rights to life, liberty, and property. John Locke argued that political authority was not given by God to monarchs but instead derived from social compacts that people made to preserve their natural rights.

Some clergymen responded to these developments by devising a rational form of Christianity. Rejecting supernatural interventions and a vengeful Calvinist God, Congregational minister Andrew Eliot maintained that "there is nothing in Christianity that is contrary to reason." The Reverend John Wise of Ipswich, Massachusetts, used Locke's philosophy to defend giving power to ordinary church members. Just as the social compact formed the basis of political society, Wise argued, so the religious covenant among the lay members of a congregation made them — not the bishops of the Church of England or even ministers like himself — the proper interpreters of religious truth. The Enlightenment influenced Puritan minister Cotton Mather as well. When a measles epidemic ravaged Boston in the 1710s, Mather thought that only God could end it; but when smallpox struck a decade later, he used his newly acquired knowledge of inoculation — gained in part from a slave, who told him of the practice's success in Africa — to advocate this scientific preventive for the disease.

deism
The Enlightenment-influenced belief that God created the universe and then left it to run according to natural laws. Deists relied on reason rather than scripture to interpret God's will.

Franklin's Contributions Benjamin Franklin was the exemplar of the American Enlightenment. Born in Boston in 1706 to devout Calvinists, he grew to manhood during the print revolution. Apprenticed to his brother, a Boston printer, Franklin educated himself through voracious reading. At seventeen, he abandoned his brother and fled to Philadelphia, where he became a prominent printer, and in 1729 he founded the *Pennsylvania Gazette*, which became one of the colonies' most influential newspapers. Franklin also formed a "club of mutual improvement" that met weekly to discuss "Morals, Politics, or Natural Philosophy." These discussions, as well as Enlightenment literature, shaped his thinking. As Franklin explained in his *Autobiography* (1771), "From the different books I read, I began to doubt of Revelation [God-revealed truth]."

Benjamin Franklin's Rise This portrait of Benjamin Franklin, attributed to Robert Feke and executed around 1746, portrays Franklin as a successful businessman. His ruffled collar and cuffs, his fashionably curly wig, and his sober but expensive suit reveal his social ambitions. In later portraits, after he gained fame as an Enlightenment sage, he dispensed with the wig and chose more unaffected poses; but in 1746, he was still establishing his credentials as a young Philadelphia gentleman on the rise. Fogg Art Museum, Harvard Art Museums, USA/Bridgeman Images.

Like a small number of urban artisans, wealthy Virginia planters, and affluent seaport merchants, Franklin became a deist. **Deism** was a way of thinking, not an established religion. "My own mind is my own church," said deist Thomas Paine. "I am of a sect by myself," added Thomas Jefferson. Influenced by Enlightenment science, deists such as Jefferson believed that a Supreme Being (or Grand Architect) created the world and then allowed it to operate by natural laws but did not intervene in people's lives. Rejecting the divinity of Christ and the authority of the Bible, deists relied on "natural reason," their innate moral sense, to define right and wrong. Thus Franklin, a onetime slave owner, came to question the morality of slavery, repudiating it once he recognized the parallels between racial bondage and the colonies' political bondage to Britain.

Franklin popularized the practical outlook of the Enlightenment in *Poor Richard's Almanack* (1732–1757), an annual publication that was read by thousands. He also founded the American Philosophical Society (1743–present) to promote

TEACHING STRATEGY

Supplement your discussion of the Enlightenment with Benjamin Franklin's description of George Whitefield's ministry, which provides a classic intersection between the greatest evangelist of the colonial era and the most prominent Enlightenment thinker. In his assessment of Whitefield, Franklin perceptively describes the evangelist's strategies and his appeal to audiences. In the process, he demonstrates his own analytical intellect at work — as well as his self-deprecating wit. Access this text by searching "Franklin on Reverend George Whitefield."

"useful knowledge." Adopting this goal in his own life, Franklin invented bifocal lenses for eyeglasses, the Franklin stove, and the lightning rod. His book on electricity, published in England in 1751, won praise as the greatest contribution to science since Newton's discoveries. Inspired by Franklin, ambitious printers in America's seaport cities published newspapers and gentlemen's magazines, the first significant nonreligious periodicals to appear in the colonies. The European Enlightenment, then, added a secular dimension to colonial cultural life, foreshadowing the great contributions to republican political theory by American intellectuals of the Revolutionary era: John Adams, James Madison, and Thomas Jefferson.

Enlightenment Philanthropy: Pennsylvania Hospital, Philadelphia Using public funds and private donations, Philadelphia reformers built this imposing structure in 1753. The new hospital embodied two principles of the Enlightenment: that purposeful actions could improve society, and that the products of these actions should express reason and order, exhibited here in the building's symmetrical facade. Etchings like this one from the 1760s (*A Perspective View of the Pennsylvania Hospital*, by John Streeper and Henry Dawkins) circulated widely and bolstered Philadelphia's reputation as the center of the American Enlightenment. The New York Public Library/Art Resource, NY.

American Pietism and the Great Awakening

As some colonists turned to deism, thousands of others embraced Pietism, a Christian movement originating in Germany around 1700 and emphasizing pious behavior (hence the name). In its emotional worship services and individual striving for a mystical union with God, Pietism appealed to believers' hearts rather than their minds (see "Firsthand Accounts," p. 126). In the 1720s, German migrants carried Pietism to America, sparking a religious **revival** (or renewal of religious enthusiasm) in Pennsylvania and New Jersey, where Dutch minister Theodore Jacob Frelinghuysen preached passionate sermons to German settlers and encouraged church members to spread the message of spiritual urgency. A decade later, William Tennent and his son Gilbert copied Frelinghuysen's approach and led revivals among Scots-Irish Presbyterians throughout the Middle Atlantic region, in the process stirring controversy with more conservative preachers.

Simultaneously, an American-born Pietist movement appeared in New England. Revivals of Christian zeal were built into the logic of Puritanism. In the 1730s, Jonathan Edwards, a minister in Northampton, Massachusetts, encouraged a revival there that spread to towns throughout the Connecticut River Valley. Edwards guided and observed the process and then published an account entitled *A Faithful Narrative of the Surprising Work of God*, printed first in London (1737), then in Boston (1738), and then in German and Dutch translations. Its publication history highlights the transatlantic network of correspondents that gave Pietism much of its vitality.

English minister George Whitefield transformed the local revivals of Edwards and the Tennents into a Great Awakening. After Whitefield had his personal awakening upon reading the German Pietists, he became a follower of John Wesley, the founder of English Methodism. In 1739, Whitefield carried Wesley's fervent message to America, where he attracted huge crowds from Georgia to Massachusetts.

Why was Whitefield so effective? It began with his appearance. "He looked almost angelical; a young, slim, slender youth . . . cloathed with authority from the Great God," wrote a Connecticut farmer. Like most evangelical preachers, Whitefield did not read his sermons but spoke from memory. Because he was a traveling preacher, he could deliver the same sermons over and over again, gradually perfecting his

AP® SKILLS & PROCESSES

CONTEXTUALIZATION

What conditions and ideas lay behind the emergence of the Enlightenment in America?

revival
A renewal of religious enthusiasm in a Christian congregation. In the eighteenth century, revivals were often inspired by evangelical preachers who urged their listeners to experience a rebirth.

AP® EXAM TIP

Analyze the impact of the Great Awakening on increasing pluralism in the British colonies.

AP® THEME

WOR: America in the World; SOC: Social Structures

Show students the image of the Pennsylvania Hospital and ask them to identify how it illustrates the following core tenets of the Enlightenment: (1) the lawlike order of the natural world, (2) the power of human reason, (3) the "natural rights" of individuals (including the right to self-government), and (4) the progressive improvement of society. *The symmetry of the building reflects the order of the natural world; the hospital reflects the notion that humans can identify a problem and solve it rationally; while the philanthropic concern for all people does not reveal a "natural right" to health, it does suggest related ideas about the value of the individual; the notion of reform reflects an optimistic notion about the possibility of progress.*

CHECK FOR UNDERSTANDING

Ask students: **What characterized the Enlightenment in America?** *It was often characterized by Deism, rather than atheism, and a practical effort to improve living conditions.*

AP® SKILLS & PROCESSES

CONTEXTUALIZATION

The **CONTEXTUALIZATION** question invites students to situate Enlightenment in its broader context. Students might use the text's four fundamental principles of the Enlightenment to identify contextual features that aided the emergence of those ideas in America. In particular, they might explore the question of how significant Franklin's role was, as the text devotes significant attention to his efforts. Students might also consider the broader Atlantic context of the Enlightenment and identify the mechanisms by which European ideas were introduced to American society.

TRM Find complete suggested responses in the Teacher's Resource Materials.

TEACHING STRATEGY

The National Humanities Center's Divining Religion: Religion in American History Web site page provides excellent resources for teaching about colonial religion. The site contains separate materials for Deism, the Great Awakening, the Anglican Church in colonial America, and religion and women. For each topic, the site provides a detailed background essay, suggestions for teaching and discussion, and a brief historiographical overview on debates regarding this topic. Access this site by searching "NHC Divining America."

AP® SKILLS & PROCESSES

ANALYZING HISTORICAL EVIDENCE

The **AP® FIRSTHAND ACCOUNTS** feature invites students to compare diverse perspectives from primary sources to draw conclusions about two distinct religious trends. All the authors, regardless of their views, were aware of both Enlightenment ideas and the Great Awakening, but their awareness did not automatically lead to predictable responses. Use this exercise to counter the tendency many students have to simplify historical trends. This can happen when they assume a mechanical understanding: the emergence of new ideas automatically forces people to change their views. It can also happen when students create sharp dichotomies — people were either for a particular development or against it. These documents reveal a more nuanced understanding of the complex ways people reacted. Extend this activity by having students explain why Enlightenment ideas have had such a lasting hold on American culture.

AP® FIRSTHAND ACCOUNTS

Evangelical Religion and Enlightenment Rationalism

Analyzing primary sources often involves comparing and contrasting documents that represent multiple points of view. In such cases, we ask the same analytical questions of each document, but we also think about the sources in relation to each other. How does one person's perspective on an important issue shed light on other points of view? In the documents that follow, four individuals offer statements that describe formative experiences and link them to core beliefs. As you read, consider the ways in which each person's experience shapes his or her views.

Two great historical movements, Enlightenment thought and Christian Pietism, swept across British North America in the eighteenth century and offered radically different — indeed, almost completely contradictory — worldviews. Pietism sparked religious revivals based on passion and emotion, while Enlightenment rationalism encouraged personal restraint and intellectual logic. Both movements shaped American cultural development: Pietism transformed American religious life, and Enlightenment thinking influenced the principles of the American government.

SARAH LIPPET

Death as a Passage to Life

Sarah Lippet was a longtime member of the Baptist church of Middletown in eastern New Jersey. She died in October 1767 at the age of sixty-one; fellow parishioners reported her sentiments as she lay, for four days, on her deathbed.

SOURCE: "The Triumphant Christian," in *Historical and Genealogical Miscellany*, ed. John E. Stillwell (New York, 1964), 3: 465–466.

" All my lifetime I have been in fears and doubts, but now am delivered. He hath delivered them who through fear of death were all their lifetime subject to bondage. For the love I have for Christ I am willing to part with all my friends to be with Him, for I love Him above all; yet it is nothing in me, for I know if I had my desert I should be in Hell. I believe in Christ, and I know that I put my whole trust in Him, and he that believeth in Him shall not be ashamed nor be confounded. . . .

Why do you mourn when I rejoice? You should not; it is no more for me to die and leave my friends for the great love I have for Christ than for me to go to sleep. I have no fears of death in my mind. Christ has the keys of death and hell, and blessed are the dead that die in the Lord. I can't bear to see a tear shed. You should not mourn. "

NATHAN COLE

The Struggle for Salvation

Connecticut farmer Nathan Cole found God after listening to a sermon by George Whitefield, the great English evangelist. But Cole's spiritual quest was not easy. He struggled for two years before coming to believe that he was saved.

SOURCE: "The Spiritual Travels of Nathan Cole, 1741" in *The Great Awakening: Documents on the Revival of Religion, 1740–1745*, ed. Richard L. Bushman (New York: Atheneum, 1970), 68–70.

" [After hearing Whitefield] I began to think I was not Elected, and that God made some for heaven and me for hell. And I thought God was not Just in so doing. . . . My heart then rose against God exceedingly, for his making me for hell; Now this distress lasted Almost two years — Poor Me — Miserable me. . . . I was loaded with the guilt of Sin. . . .

Hell fire was most always in my mind; and I have hundreds of times put my fingers into my pipe when I have been smoaking to feel how fire felt: And to see how my Body could bear to lye in Hell fire for ever and ever. . . . And while these thoughts were in my mind God appeared unto me and made me Skringe: before whose face the heavens and the earth fled away; and I was Shrinked into nothing; I knew not whether I was in the body or out, I seemed to hang in open Air before God, and he seemed to Speak to me in an angry and Sovereign way[:] What? Won't you trust your Soul with God?; My heart answered O yes, yes, yes. . . .

When God disappeared or in some measure withdrew, every thing was in its place again and I was on my Bed. . . . I was set free, my distress was gone, and I was filled with a pineing desire to see Christs own words in the bible; . . . I got the bible up under my Chin and hugged it; it was sweet and lovely; the word was nigh [near] me in my hand, then I began to pray and to praise God. "

BENJAMIN FRANKLIN

The Importance of a Virtuous Life

Franklin stood at the center of the American Enlightenment. In his *Autobiography*, he outlined his religious views and his human-centered moral principles.

SOURCE: Louis P. Masur, ed., *The Autobiography of Benjamin Franklin, with Related Documents*, 3rd ed. (Boston: Bedford/St. Martin's, 2016), 66–67, 86, 101.

126

“My Parent's had early given me religious Impressions, and brought me through my Childhood piously in the Dissenting Way. But I was scarce 15 when, after doubting by turns of several Points as I found them disputed in the different Books I read, I began to doubt of Revelation itself. Some Books against Deism fell into my Hands. . . . It happened that they wrought an Effect on me quite contrary to what was intended by them: For the Arguments of the Deists [that were quoted in those books] appeared to me much Stronger than the Refutations. In short I soon became a thorough Deist. . . .

I grew convinc'd that Truth, Sincerity & Integrity in Dealings between Man & Man, were of the utmost Importance to the Felicity of Life, and I form'd written Resolutions, (which still remain in my Journal Book) to practice them ever while I lived. . . .

I never was without some religious Principles; I never doubted, for instance, the Existance of the Deity, that he made the World, & govern'd it by his Providence; that the most acceptable Service of God was the doing Good to Man; that our Souls are immortal; and that all Crime will be punished & Virtue rewarded either here or hereafter; these I esteem'd the Essentials of every Religion.

About the Year 1734. There arrived among us from Ireland, a young Presbyterian Preacher named Hemphill, who delivered with a good Voice, & apparently extempore, most excellent Discourses, which drew together considerable Numbers of different Persuasions, who join'd in admiring them. Among the rest I became one of his constant Hearers, his Sermons pleasing me as they had little of the dogmatical kind, but inculcated strongly the Practice of Virtue, or what in the religious Stile are called Good Works. Those however, of our Congregation, who considered themselves as orthodox Presbyterians, disapprov'd his Doctrine, and were join'd by most of the old Clergy, who arraign'd him of Heterodoxy before the Synod, in order to have him silenc'd. I became his zealous Partisan. . . . ”

JOHN WISE

The Primacy of Human Reason and Natural Laws

Reverend John Wise (1652–1725) served for many years as a pastor in Ipswich, Massachusetts. A graduate of Harvard College, Wise used the Enlightenment doctrines of John Locke and Samuel von Pufendorf to justify the democratic structure of New England Congregational churches.

SOURCE: John Wise, *A Vindication of the Government of New England Churches* (Boston: J. Allen, for N. Boone, 1717), 32–40.

“I Shall disclose several Principles of Natural Knowledge; plainly discovering the Law of Nature; or the true sentiments of Natural Reason, with Respect to Mans Being and Government. . . . I shall consider Man in a state of Natural Being, as a Free-Born Subject under the Crown of Heaven, and owing Homage to none but God himself. It is certain Civil Government in General, is a very Admirable Result of Providence, and an Incomparable Benefit to Mankind, yet must needs be acknowledged to be the Effect of Humane Free-Compacts and not of Divine Institution; it is the Produce of Mans Reason, of Humane and Rational Combinations, and not from any direct Orders of Infinite Wisdom. . . .

The Prime Immunity in Mans State, is that he is most properly the Subject of the Law of Nature. He is the Favourite Animal on Earth; in that this Part of Gods Image, viz. Reason is Congenate with his Nature, wherein by a Law Immutable, Instampt upon his Frame, God has provided a Rule for Men in all their Actions; obliging each one to the performance of that which is Right, not only as to Justice, but likewise as to all other Moral Vertues, which is nothing but the Dictate of Right Reason founded in the Soul of Man. . . .

The Second Great Immunity of Man is an Original Liberty Instampt upon his Rational Nature. He that intrudes upon this Liberty, Violates the Law of Nature. . . .

The Third Capital Immunity belonging to Mans Nature, is an equality amongst Men; Which is not to be denyed by the Law of Nature, till Man has Resigned himself with all his Rights for the sake of a Civil State; and then his Personal Liberty and Equality is to be cherished, and preserved to the highest degree. ”

QUESTIONS FOR ANALYSIS

1. All of these writers declare a belief in God. How do their perspectives differ?
2. These writers were variously influenced by the Great Awakening, the Enlightenment, and rational Christianity. How are these movements reflected in the preceding passages? Describe how the relevant historical context likely influenced each author.
3. What roles do fear and anxiety play in the experiences of Sarah Lippet and Nathan Cole? To what extent does fear influence Franklin and Wise? Explain why this is historically significant.
4. Benjamin Franklin and John Wise stress the importance of reason and virtue as guides to human conduct. How would Nathan Cole and Sarah Lippet react to that emphasis?

TRM Find complete suggested responses in the Teacher's Resource Materials.

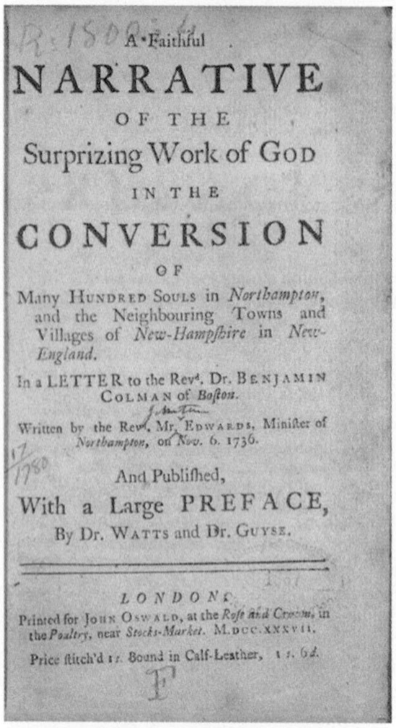
A Faithful
NARRATIVE
OF THE
Surprizing Work of GOD
IN THE
CONVERSION
OF
Many HUNDRED SOULS in *Northampton*, and the Neighbouring Towns and Villages of *New-Hampſhire* in *New-England*.
In a LETTER to the Revd. Dr. BENJAMIN COLMAN of *Boſton*.
Written by the Revd. Mr. EDWARDS, Miniſter of *Northampton*, on *Nov.* 6. 1736.
And Publiſhed,
With a Large PREFACE,
By Dr. WATTS and Dr. GUYSE.
LONDON:
Printed for JOHN OSWALD, at the *Roſe and Crown*, in the *Poultry*, near *Stocks-Market*. M.DCC.XXXVII.
Price ſtitch'd 1*s*. Bound in Calf-Leather, 1*s*. 6*d*.

The Print Revolution and the Great Awakening A local revival in Northampton, Massachusetts, gained transatlantic importance through the power of print. Jonathan Edwards's *A Faithful Narrative of the Surprising Works of God* began as a letter to a fellow clergyman describing events in his congregation. Two English evangelicals, Isaac Watts and John Guyse, learned of the letter and encouraged Edwards to expand it into a book. Edwards sent them an enlarged version; Watts and Guyse gave it a title and shepherded it into print in London in 1737, complete with extensive editorial commentary. A year later the first American edition was published in Boston. It became an important evangelical text in England, Scotland, and North America, and Dutch and German translations also made the book available to Pietists on the continent. Rare Book and Special Collections Division, Library of Congress.

performance. More like an actor than a theologian, he gestured eloquently, raised his voice for dramatic effect, and at times assumed a female persona — as a woman in labor struggling to deliver the word of God. When the young preacher told his spellbound listeners that they had sinned and must seek salvation, some suddenly felt a "new light" within them. As "the power of god come down," Hannah Heaton recalled, "my knees smote together . . . [and] it seemed to me I was a sinking down into hell . . . but then I resigned my distress and was perfectly easy quiet and calm . . . [and] it seemed as if I had a new soul & body both." Strengthened and self-confident, these converts, the so-called New Lights, were eager to spread Whitefield's message.

The rise of print intersected with this enthusiasm. "Religion is become the Subject of most Conversations," the *Pennsylvania Gazette* reported. "No books are in Request but those of Piety and Devotion." Whitefield and his circle did their best to answer the demand for devotional reading. As he traveled, Whitefield regularly sent excerpts of his journal to be printed in newspapers. Franklin printed Whitefield's sermons and journals by subscription and found them to be among his best-selling titles. Printed accounts of Whitefield's travels, conversion narratives, sermons, and other devotional literature helped to confirm Pietists in their faith and strengthen the communication networks that sustained them.

Religious Upheaval in the North

Like all cultural explosions, the Great Awakening was controversial. Conservative ministers — passionless **Old Lights**, according to the evangelists — condemned the "cryings out, faintings and convulsions" in revivalist meetings and the New Lights' claims of "working Miracles or speaking with Tongues." Boston minister Charles Chauncy attacked the Pietist **New Lights** for allowing women to speak in public: it was "a plain breach of that commandment of the lord, where it is said, Let your women keep silence in the churches." In Connecticut, Old Lights persuaded the legislature to prohibit evangelists from speaking to a congregation without the minister's permission. But the New Lights refused to be silenced. Dozens of farmers, women, and artisans roamed the countryside, condemning the Old Lights as "unconverted" and willingly accepting imprisonment: "I shall bring glory to God in my bonds," a dissident preacher wrote from jail.

The Great Awakening undermined legally established churches and their tax-supported ministers. In New England, New Lights left the Congregational Church and founded 125 "separatist" churches that supported their ministers through voluntary contributions (Figure 4.3). Other religious dissidents joined Baptist congregations, which also condemned government support of churches: "God never allowed any civil state upon earth to impose religious taxes," declared Baptist preacher Isaac Backus. In New York and New Jersey, the Dutch Reformed Church split in two as New Lights refused to accept doctrines imposed by conservative church authorities in Holland.

The Great Awakening also appealed to Christians whose established churches could not serve their needs. By 1740, Pennsylvania's German Reformed and Lutheran congregations suffered from a severe lack of university-trained pastors. In the colony's Dutch Reformed, Dutch and Swedish Lutheran, and even its Anglican congregations, half the pulpits were empty. In this circumstance, itinerant preachers who stressed the power of "heart religion" and downplayed the importance of formal ministerial training found a ready audience.

Old Lights
Conservative ministers opposed to the passion displayed by evangelical New Light preachers; they preferred to emphasize the importance of cultivating a virtuous Christian life.

New Lights
Evangelical preachers who decried a Christian faith that was merely intellectual; they emphasized instead the importance of a spiritual rebirth.

TEACHING STRATEGY

This image provides students with an opportunity to discuss the role of print in spreading religious and other ideas in the colonies. Ask students: **How did the print revolution affect ministers like Whitefield?** *As an Englishman, Whitefield was virtually unknown in the colonies until he began publishing his works there.*

CHECK FOR UNDERSTANDING

Ask students: **What were American Pietism and the Great Awakening?** *They were revivalist Protestant movements that emphasized the experience of God through devotional practices and emotion, rather than intellect.*

TEACHING STRATEGY

Give students an excerpt from Benjamin Franklin's discussion of the Great Awakening from his 1771 autobiography (an excerpt is available on the Digital History Web site). Ask students to read and analyze this primary source, underlining key words or phrases that address the impact of the Great Awakening on developing pluralism in the colonies. Then ask students to extend their analysis of the document by looking at the historical context, intended audience, purpose, and author's point of view. Ask students to then use the text to outline the denominations established as a result of the Great Awakening. For each denomination identified, ask students to identify at least one defining characteristic that allowed colonists to distinguish the religious sects from one another.

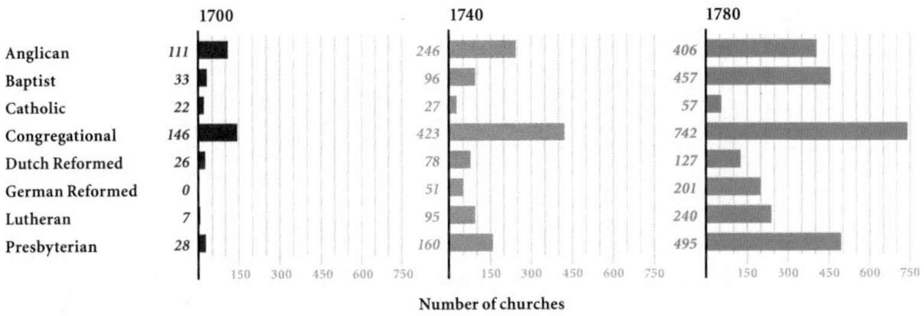

FIGURE 4.3 Church Growth by Denomination, 1700–1780
In 1700, and again in 1740, the Congregational and Anglican churches had the most members. By 1780, however, largely because of their enthusiastic evangelical message, Presbyterian and Baptist congregations outnumbered those of the Anglicans. The growth of immigrant denominations, such as the German Reformed and Lutheran, was equally impressive.

Why was the Great Awakening a threat to traditional Christian ministers? Because it challenged the authority of all ministers whose status rested on respect for their education and knowledge of the Bible. In an influential pamphlet, *The Dangers of an Unconverted Ministry* (1740), Gilbert Tennent asserted that ministers' authority should come not from theological knowledge but from the conversion experience. Reaffirming Martin Luther's belief in the priesthood of all Christians, Tennent suggested that anyone who had felt God's redeeming grace could speak with ministerial authority. Sarah Harrah Osborn, a New Light "exhorter" in Rhode Island, refused "to shut up my mouth . . . and creep into obscurity" when silenced by her minister.

As religious enthusiasm spread, churches founded new colleges to educate their young men and to train ministers. New Light Presbyterians established the College of New Jersey (Princeton) in 1746, and New York Anglicans founded King's College (Columbia) in 1754. Baptists set up the College of Rhode Island (Brown) in 1764; two years later, the Dutch Reformed Church subsidized Queen's College (Rutgers) in New Jersey. However, the main intellectual legacy of the Great Awakening was not education for the privileged few but a new sense of authority among the many. A European visitor to Philadelphia remarked in surprise, "The poorest day-laborer . . . holds it his right to advance his opinion, in religious as well as political matters, with as much freedom as the gentleman."

AP® SKILLS & PROCESSES

COMPARISON

What did the Enlightenment and Pietism have in common, and how did they differ?

Social and Religious Conflict in the South

In the southern colonies, where the Church of England was legally established, religious enthusiasm triggered social conflict. Anglican ministers generally ignored the spiritual needs of African Americans and landless whites, who numbered 40 percent and 20 percent of the population, respectively. Middling white freeholders (35 percent of the residents) formed the core of most Church of England congregations. But prominent planters (just 5 percent) held the real power, using their control of parish finances to discipline ministers. One clergyman complained that dismissal awaited any minister who "had the courage to preach against any Vices taken into favor by the leading Men of his Parish."

The Presbyterian Revival Democratic religious movements challenged the dominance of both the Anglican Church and the planter elite. In 1743, bricklayer Samuel Morris, inspired by reading George Whitefield's sermons, led a group of Virginia Anglicans out of their congregation. Seeking a deeper religious experience, Morris

AP® THEME

ARC: American and Regional Culture

Use **FIGURE 4.3** to illustrate the growing religious diversity across the British colonies. Guide students' analysis through the following questions:

- **How did the number of Anglican and Congregational churches, the two largest denominations in 1700, change over time?** *Both denominations grew substantially in total numbers. Congregationalism remained the largest denomination in 1780.*
- **Which denomination was the smallest in 1780? Why is this significant?** *Roman Catholicism remained the smallest. Despite growing diversity in the colonies, they remained overwhelmingly Protestant.*
- **What are the limitations of this data?** *The graphs look at the colonies as a whole, so regional differences are not taken into consideration. The graphs measure number of churches, not numbers of members, so these numbers may not accurately capture the members of each denomination.*

AP® SKILLS & PROCESSES

COMPARISON

The **COMPARISON** question asks students to compare two different intellectual trends, one philosophical and the other religious. Students will more easily identify differences and will need assistance recognizing commonalities. As students learned in the **AP® FIRSTHAND ACCOUNTS** feature, these views were not simple dichotomies. Students may need to broaden their framework for similarities to answer this question, and to consider effects of these trends, not simply the trends themselves.

TRM Find complete suggested responses in the Teacher's Resource Materials.

CHECK FOR UNDERSTANDING

Ask students: **What kinds of religious upheavals did the Great Awakening cause in the North?** *The Great Awakening led to splits within existing churches, the undermining of tax support for established churches, devaluing of educated ministry, and the formation of new colleges to train ministers.*

TRM Find complete suggested responses in the Teacher's Resource Materials.

AP® SKILLS & PROCESSES

ARGUMENTATION

How did the religious developments in British North America encourage greater autonomy among colonists?

invited New Light Presbyterian Samuel Davies to lead their prayer meetings. Davies's sermons, filled with erotic devotional imagery and urging Christians to feel "ardent Passion," sparked Presbyterian revivals across the Tidewater region that threatened the social authority of the Virginia gentry. Traditionally, planters and their well-dressed families arrived at Anglican services in fancy carriages drawn by well-bred horses and flaunted their power by sitting in the front pews. Such ritual displays of power were meaningless if freeholders attended other churches. At the same time, members of dissenting congregations complained about paying taxes to support the Anglican Church.

To halt the spread of New Light ideas, Virginia governor William Gooch denounced them as "false teachings," and Anglican justices of the peace closed Presbyterian churches. This harassment kept most white yeomen and poor tenant families in the Church of England.

The Baptist Insurgency During the 1760s, the vigorous preaching and democratic message of New Light Baptist ministers converted thousands of white farm families in Virginia and North Carolina. The Baptists were radical Protestants whose central ritual was adult (rather than infant) baptism. Once men and women had experienced the infusion of grace — had been "born again" — they were baptized in an emotional public ceremony, often involving complete immersion in water.

AP® SKILLS & PROCESSES

SOURCING AND SITUATION

Sometimes students overthink historical sources, particularly documents from the seventeenth and eighteenth century. Therefore, think about having students work on developing an awareness of Sourcing and Situation. Students will answer two main prompts: 1) What eighteenth-century religious movement is connected to this document? 2) Briefly describe one way in which this document is evidence of the historical development you described.

TRM Find complete suggested responses in the Teacher's Resource Materials.

AP® SKILLS & PROCESSES

SOURCING AND SITUATION

What was the artist's purpose in creating the woodcut below? Who was the artist's intended audience?

AP® SKILLS & PROCESSES

DEVELOPMENTS AND PROCESSES

How did the rise of new religious movements threaten the authority of Virginia planters and Anglican ministers?

Slaves were welcome at Baptist revivals. During the 1740s, George Whitefield had urged Carolina planters to bring their slaves into the Christian fold, but white opposition and the Africans' commitment to their ancestral religions kept the number of converts low. However, in the 1760s, native-born African Americans in Virginia welcomed the Baptists' message that all people were equal in God's eyes. Sensing a threat to the system of racial slavery, the House of Burgesses imposed heavy fines on Baptists who preached to slaves without their owners' permission.

Baptists threatened gentry authority because they repudiated social distinctions and urged followers to call one another "brother" and "sister." They also condemned the planters' decadent lifestyle. As planter Landon Carter complained, the Baptists were "destroying pleasure in the Country; for they encourage ardent Prayer . . . & an intire Banishment of *Gaming, Dancing*, & Sabbath-Day Diversions." The gentry responded with violence. In Caroline County, an Anglican posse attacked Brother John Waller at a prayer meeting. Waller "was violently jerked off the stage; they caught him by the back part of his neck, beat his head against the ground, and a gentleman gave him twenty lashes with his horsewhip."

Baptism in the Schuylkill River The Baptist movement, which made adult baptism central to its religious practice, gained enormous influence during the Great Awakening. Baptists challenged the social order in New England, where Isaac Backus and other leaders vigorously opposed the power of established Congregationalist churches. They presented an even greater threat to established authority in Virginia, where they ministered to enslaved African Americans and challenged the status of the gentry. This woodcut, from an eighteenth-century history of the Baptist movement, shows a congregation gathered on the banks of the Schuylkill River in Pennsylvania to witness the baptism of a new convert. Fotosearch/Getty Images.

Despite these attacks, Baptist congregations multiplied. By 1775, about 15 percent of Virginia's whites and hundreds of enslaved blacks had joined Baptist churches. To signify their state of grace, some Baptist men "cut off their hair, like Cromwell's round-headed chaplains." Others forged a new evangelical masculinity, "crying, weeping, lifting up the eyes, groaning" when touched by the Holy Spirit.

The Baptist revival in the Chesapeake challenged customary

AP® SKILLS & PROCESSES

DEVELOPMENTS AND PROCESSES

Historical developments such as the Great Awakening are useful events to teach students about the historical reasoning skill of Developments and Processes. Beyond just "knowing history," this skill is about being able to both identify and describe historical events. Therefore, ask students to describe the following two prompts: 1) What was the Great Awakening ? 2) Identify two regions of the British North American colonies and describe how colonists' religious experience in the Great Awakening varied by region. In this way, you are requiring students to know the basic information while also encouraging them to describe an outcome of an event.

authority in families and society but did not overturn it. Rejecting the pleas of evangelical women, Baptist men kept church authority in the hands of "free born male members," and Anglican slaveholders retained control of the political system. Still, the Baptist insurgency infused the lives of poor tenant families with spiritual meaning and empowered yeomen to defend their economic interests. Moreover, as Baptist ministers spread Christianity among slaves, they undermined a key justification for slavery while giving some blacks a new religious identity. Within a generation, African Americans would develop distinctive versions of Protestant Christianity.

THE MIDCENTURY CHALLENGE: WAR, TRADE, AND SOCIAL CONFLICT, 1750–1763

How did midcentury developments reflect Britain's deepening connections to North America?

Between 1750 and 1763, three significant events transformed colonial life. First, Britain went to war against the French in America, sparking a worldwide conflict: the Great War for Empire. Second, a surge in trade boosted colonial consumption but caused Americans to become deeply indebted to British creditors. Third, westward migration sparked warfare with Indian peoples, violent disputes between settlers and land speculators, and backcountry rebellions against eastern-controlled governments.

AP® EXAM TIP

Compare the impact of colonial rivalries in the Ohio Valley on American Indian populations to earlier imperial rivalries involving Native groups.

The French and Indian War

In 1754, overlapping French and British claims in North America came to a head (Map 4.2). The French maintained their vast claims through a network of forts and trading posts that sustained alliances with neighboring Indians. The soft underbelly of this sprawling empire was the Ohio Valley, where French claims were tenuous. Native peoples were driven out of the valley by Iroquois attacks in the seventeenth century, but after 1720 displaced Indian populations — especially Delawares and Shawnees from Pennsylvania — resettled there in large numbers. In the 1740s, British traders from Pennsylvania began traveling down the Ohio River. They traded with Delawares and Shawnees in the upper valley and began to draw French-allied Indians into their orbit and away from French posts. Then, in 1749, the Ohio Company of Virginia, a partnership of prominent colonial planters and London merchants, received a 200,000-acre grant from the crown to establish a new settlement on the upper Ohio, threatening French claims to the region.

Conflict in the Ohio Valley By midcentury, Britain relied on the Iroquois Confederacy as its partner in Indian relations throughout the Northeast. By extending the Covenant Chain, the Iroquois had become a kind of Indian empire in their own right, claiming to speak for other groups throughout the region based on their seventeenth-century conquests. The Delawares, Shawnees, and other groups who repopulated the Ohio Valley did so in part to escape the Iroquois yoke. To maintain influence on the Ohio, the Iroquois sent two "half-kings," Tanaghrisson (an adopted Seneca) and Scarouady (an Oneida), to the Native settlement of Logstown, a trading town on the upper Ohio, where Britain recognized them as leaders.

French authorities, alarmed by British inroads, built a string of forts from Lake Erie to the headwaters of the Ohio, culminating with Fort Duquesne on the site of present-day Pittsburgh. To reassert British claims, Governor Dinwiddie dispatched an expedition led by Colonel George Washington, a twenty-two-year-old Virginian whose half-brothers were Ohio Company stockholders. Washington discovered that most of the Ohio Indians had decided to side with the French; only the Iroquois half-kings and a few of their followers supported his efforts. After Washington's party fired on a French

CHECK FOR UNDERSTANDING

Ask students: **How did the accelerating pace of travel and communication affect colonial society and culture?** *Greater infrastructure (e.g. port facilities and roads) as well as the rise of print culture in the colonies led to religious upheavals in the British North American colonies. This period was known as the Great Awakening.*

AP® APPLY THE TIP

Ask students to create a Venn diagram comparing the conflict over the Ohio Valley in the mid-eighteenth century to imperial conflicts involving Native populations in the seventeenth century (e.g., Beaver Wars, Chickasaw Wars, etc.). Ask students to focus on the causes of the conflicts, the role of European powers in the conflicts, and the impact on Native populations in their comparison.

TEACHING STRATEGY

To supplement your discussion of "The Midcentury Challenge" section, use the Educator's Guide that accompanies the PBS film *The War That Made America*. The guide contains standards-based lessons and activities, discussion questions, small and large group role-plays, mock trials, and collaborative research suggestions. Access this film by searching "PBS The War That Made America Education Outreach."

AP® SKILLS & PROCESSES

DEVELOPMENTS AND PROCESSES

Students need to understand even though there were a series of imperial wars and Great Britain and France would battle for European supremacy in North America, indigenous groups had agency throughout this process. Ask students to identify one American Indian nation from **MAP 4.2** and describe how they were able to negotiate or resist European encroachment from 1754–1763. The historical takeaway for students is that even though American Indians were threatened by European wars, they nevertheless were central historical actors who also shaped the contours of imperial wars.

AP® THEME

WOR: America in the World

MAP 4.2 illustrates the imperial conflict that spawned the French and Indian War and "The Great War for Empire." Students should note the massive territories disputed between the British and the French, as well as the much smaller — but still substantial — disputed claims between the English and Spanish.

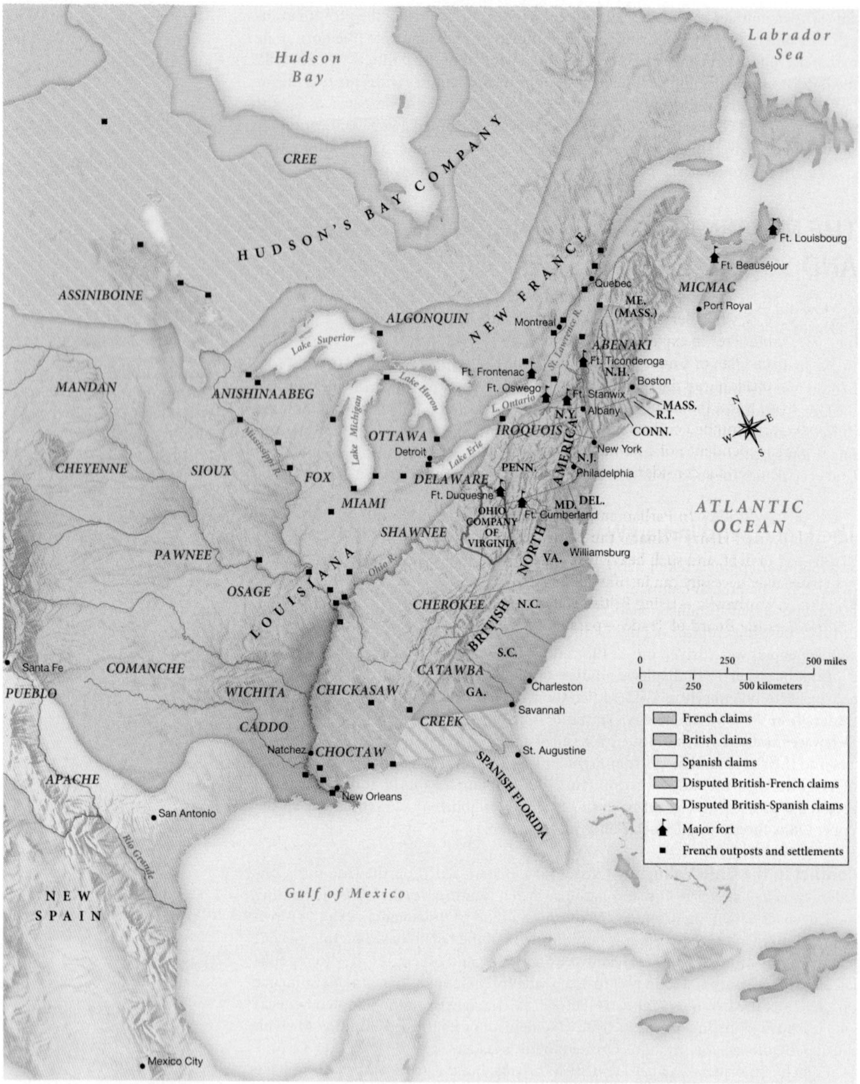

MAP 4.2 European Spheres of Influence in North America, 1754
In the mid-eighteenth century, France, Spain, and the British-owned Hudson's Bay Company laid claim to the vast areas of North America still inhabited primarily by Indian peoples. British settlers had already occupied much of the land east of the Appalachian Mountains. To safeguard their lands west of the mountains, Native Americans played off one European power against another. As a British official remarked: "To preserve the Ballance between us and the French is the great ruling Principle of Modern Indian Politics." When Britain expelled France from North America in 1763, Indians had to face encroaching Anglo-American settlers on their own.

detachment, Tanaghrisson rushed in and killed a French officer to ensure war — a prospect that would force British arms to support Iroquois interests in the valley.

Washington's party was soon defeated by a larger French force. The result was an international incident that prompted Virginian and British expansionists to demand war. But war in North America was a worrisome prospect: the colonies were notoriously incapable of cooperating in their own defense, and the Covenant Chain was badly in need of repair.

The Albany Congress Why was the Covenant Chain in need of repair? Iroquois leaders believed that the British were neglecting them while settlers from New York pressed onto their lands. Moreover, they worried that the British were losing ground to the French in the Ohio Valley. To mend relations with the Iroquois, the British Board of Trade called a meeting at Albany in June 1754. There, a prominent Mohawk leader named Hendrick Peters Theyanoguin challenged Britain to defend its interests more vigorously, while Benjamin Franklin proposed a "Plan of Union" among the colonies to counter French expansion.

The Albany Plan of Union proposed that "one general government . . . be formed in America, including all the said colonies." It would have created a continental assembly to manage trade, Indian policy, and the colonies' defense. Though it was attractive to a few reform-minded colonists and administrators, the plan would have compromised the independence of colonial assemblies and the authority of Parliament. It never received serious consideration, but that did not stop the push toward war.

The War Hawks Win In Parliament, the fight for the Ohio prompted a debate over war with France. Henry Pelham, the British prime minister, urged calm: "There is such a load of debt, and such heavy taxes already laid upon the people, that nothing but an absolute necessity can justifie our engaging in a new War." But two expansionist-minded war hawks — rising British statesman William Pitt and Lord Halifax, the new head of the Board of Trade — persuaded Pelham to launch an American war.

VISUAL ACTIVITY

Hendrick Peters Theyanoguin, Chief of the Mohawks Great Britain's alliance with the Iroquois Confederacy — the Covenant Chain — was central to its Indian policy in the mid-eighteenth century, and the Mohawk warrior and sachem Hendrick Peters Theyanoguin emerged as its most powerful spokesman. His speech at the Albany Congress of 1754, in which he urged Great Britain toward war, was reported in newspapers in Britain and the colonies and made him a transatlantic celebrity. This print was advertised for sale in London bookstalls just as his death at the Battle of Lake George (1755) was being reported in newspapers there. Hendrick wears a rich silk waistcoat, an overcoat trimmed with gold lace, a ruffled shirt, and a tricorn hat — gifts from his British allies — while he holds a wampum belt in one hand and a tomahawk in the other. Courtesy of the John Carter Brown Library at Brown University.

READING THE IMAGE: What historical situation is illustrated with the expensive suit of clothes? Who is the intended audience: colonists and British officials, or his fellow Mohawk Indians? Why?

MAKING CONNECTIONS: This image, based on a portrait that was painted in North America, was printed and colored in London, then advertised for sale both in London and in the colonies. How does the passage of this image back and forth across the Atlantic make connections to the print revolution?

AP® THEME

WOR: America in the World

This print of Theyanoguin provides insight into the ways Native Americans selectively embraced European traditions. Guide students' analysis through the following questions:

- **What elements of Theyanoguin's clothing are European?** *The hat and coat.*
- **Which elements are Native American?** *The tomahawk and wampum belt.*
- **What conclusion can you draw about his identity from this image?** *Native Americans selectively incorporated elements of European culture while retaining their own distinctive sense of identity.*

TRM Find complete suggested responses in the Teacher's Resource Materials.

In June 1755, British and New England troops captured Fort Beauséjour in the disputed territory of Nova Scotia (which the French called Acadia). Soldiers from Puritan Massachusetts then forced nearly 10,000 French settlers from their lands, arguing they were "rebels" without property rights, and deported them to France, the West Indies, and Louisiana (where "Acadians" became "Cajuns"). English and Scottish Protestants took over the farms the French Catholics left behind.

This Anglo-American triumph was quickly offset by a stunning defeat. In July 1755, General Edward Braddock advanced on Fort Duquesne with a force of 1,500 British regulars and Virginia militiamen. Braddock and his fellow officers believed that they could easily triumph in the American backcountry, but instead they were routed by a French and Indian force. Braddock was killed, and more than half his troops were dead or wounded. "We have been beaten, most shamefully beaten, by a handfull of Men," George Washington complained bitterly as he led the survivors back to Virginia.

CHECK FOR UNDERSTANDING

Ask students: **How did the French and Indian War begin?** *The war started as a contest over overlapping French and British claims west of the Appalachians in the Ohio Valley. The outbreak of fighting at Fort Duquesne quickly became a larger war between the two empires.*

TRM Find complete suggested responses in the Teacher's Resource Materials.

The Great War for Empire

By 1756, the American conflict had spread to Europe, where it was known as the Seven Years' War, and pitted Britain and Prussia against France, Spain, and Austria. When Britain mounted major offensives in India, West Africa, and the West Indies as well as in North America, the conflict became the Great War for Empire.

William Pitt emerged as the architect of the British war effort. Pitt was a committed expansionist with a touch of arrogance. "I know that I can save this country and that I alone can," he boasted. A master strategist, he planned to cripple France by seizing its colonies. In North America, he enjoyed a decisive demographic advantage, since George II's 2 million subjects outnumbered the French 14 to 1. To mobilize the colonists, Pitt paid half the cost of their troops and supplied them with arms and equipment, at a cost of £1 million a year. He also committed a fleet of British ships and 30,000 British soldiers to the conflict in America.

AP® SKILLS & PROCESSES

CONTEXTUALIZATION

How did the beginning of the French and Indian War illustrate broader context of colonial conflicts and developments?

Beginning in 1758, the powerful Anglo-American forces moved from one triumph to the next, in part because they brought Indian allies back into the fold. They forced the French to abandon Fort Duquesne (renamed Fort Pitt) in western Pennsylvania and then captured Fort Louisbourg, the stronghold at the mouth of the St. Lawrence that had previously been captured in 1745, only to be returned at the close of the previous war. In 1759, an armada led by British general James Wolfe sailed down the St. Lawrence and took Quebec, the heart of France's American Empire. The Royal Navy prevented French reinforcements from crossing the Atlantic, allowing British forces to complete the conquest of Canada in 1760 by capturing Montreal (Map 4.3).

AP® THEME

WOR: America in the World;
SOC: Social Structures

Negotiation and accommodation were two hallmarks of British policy toward both American colonists and American Indians in the years before the Seven Years' War. Each side fought in the war, but ultimately had varying motivations for their participation. Ask students to identify and describe one reason American Indians (have them narrow their focus to no more than two indigenous nations), American colonists, and the British fought in the Seven Years' War.

Elsewhere in this global war for empire, the British likewise had great success. From Spain, the British won Cuba and the Philippine Islands. Fulfilling Pitt's dream, the East India Company ousted French traders from India, and British forces seized French Senegal in West Africa. They also captured the rich sugar islands of Martinique and Guadeloupe in the French West Indies, but at the insistence of the West Indian sugar lobby (which wanted to protect its monopoly), the ministry returned the islands to France in the Treaty of Paris of 1763. Despite that controversial decision, the treaty confirmed Britain's triumph. It granted Britain sovereignty over half of North America, including French Canada, all French territory east of the Mississippi River, Spanish Florida, and the recent conquests in Africa and India. Britain had forged a commercial and colonial empire that was nearly worldwide.

AP® EXAM TIP

Identifying the reasons that limitations set by the Proclamation of 1763 angered colonists is critical on the AP® Exam.

Though Britain had won cautious support from some Native American groups in the late stages of the war, its territorial acquisitions in North America alarmed many Native peoples from New York to the Mississippi, who preferred the presence of a few French traders to an influx of thousands of Anglo-American settlers. To encourage the French to return, the Ottawa chief Pontiac declared, "I am French, and I want to die French." Neolin, a Delaware prophet, went further, calling for the expulsion of all white-skinned invaders: "If you suffer the English among you, you are dead men. Sickness, smallpox,

CHECK FOR UNDERSTANDING

Ask students: **In what ways did the Seven Years' War become "the Great War for Empire"?** *It was a large-scale, expensive war fought in Europe, India, Africa, and the Caribbean, as well as in North America — where it involved several Native American groups as well. The British won not only French North America, but territories in the other theaters of war as well.*

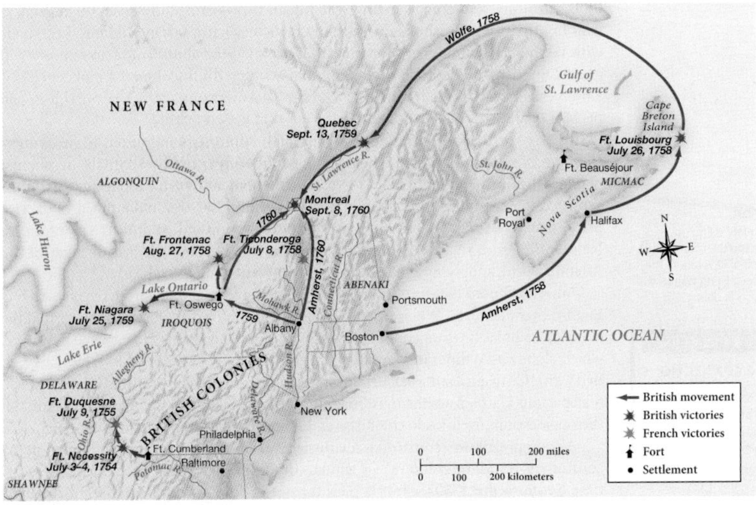

MAP 4.3 The Anglo-American Conquest of New France
After full-scale war with France began in 1756, it took almost three years for the British ministry to equip colonial forces and dispatch a sizable army to far-off America. In 1758, British and colonial troops attacked the heartland of New France, capturing Quebec in 1759 and Montreal in 1760. This conquest both united and divided the allies. Colonists celebrated the great victory: "The Illuminations and Fireworks exceeded any that had been exhibited before," reported the *South Carolina Gazette*. However, British officers had little respect for colonial soldiers. Said one, "[They are] the dirtiest, most contemptible, cowardly dogs you can conceive."

and their poison [rum] will destroy you entirely." In 1763, inspired by Neolin's nativist vision, Pontiac led a major uprising at Detroit. Following his example, Indians throughout the Great Lakes and Ohio Valley seized nearly every British military garrison west of Fort Niagara, besieged Fort Pitt, and killed or captured more than 2,000 settlers.

British military expeditions defeated the Delawares near Fort Pitt and broke the siege of Detroit, but it took the army nearly two years to reclaim all the posts it had lost. In the peace settlement, Pontiac and his allies accepted the British as their new political "fathers." The British ministry, having learned how expensive it was to control the trans-Appalachian west, issued the Royal Proclamation of 1763, which confirmed Indian control of the region and declared it off-limits to colonial settlement. It was an edict that many colonists would ignore.

AP® SKILLS & PROCESSES

CAUSATION

How did the Seven Years' War reshape Britain's empire in North America and affect Native peoples?

British Industrial Growth and the Consumer Revolution

Britain owed its military and diplomatic success to its unprecedented economic resources. Since 1700, when it had wrested control of many oceanic trade routes from the Dutch, Britain had become the dominant commercial power in the Atlantic and Indian oceans. By 1750, it was also becoming the first country to use new manufacturing technology and work discipline to expand output. This combination of commerce and industry would soon make Britain the most powerful nation in the world.

Mechanical power was key to Britain's Industrial Revolution. British artisans designed and built water mills and steam engines that efficiently powered a wide array of machines: lathes for shaping wood, jennies and looms for spinning and weaving textiles, and hammers for forging iron. Compared with traditional manufacturing methods, the new power-driven machinery produced woolen and linen textiles, iron

AP® THEME

WOR: America in the World

MAP 4.3 reveals the key locations where the clash between the British and French empires led to ultimate British victory. Guide students' analysis through the following questions:

- **What were the sites of major British victories?** *Ft. Louisbourg, Quebec, Montreal, Fr. Fontenac, and Ft. Niagara.*
- **What routes did British forces take?** *They entered the St. Lawrence after defeating Louisbourg, came up the Hudson to Montreal, and went overland to Lake Ontario.*
- **Strategically, what made the locations of British victories important sites?** *They were located at strategic points that were important for defense. Louisbourg controlled access to the Gulf of St. Lawrence and from there into the St. Lawrence River. The other sites are major French settlements or chokepoints along the St. Lawrence River.*

AP® SKILLS & PROCESSES

CAUSATION

The **CAUSATION** question identifies two distinct but related effects of the Seven Years' War: effects on the structure of the British Empire, and effects on Native American peoples. For analytical purposes, it is probably useful to separate these two consequences, but students should be asked to connect the two as well.

TRM Find complete suggested responses in the Teacher's Resource Materials.

AP® SKILLS & PROCESSES

MAKING CONNECTIONS

The **MAKING CONNECTIONS** question identifies two distinct effects of growing British prosperity: improvement and endangerment. Students should probably spend more time considering the second effect because it is paradoxical and unexpected. This provides an opportunity to explore the nature of historical contingency — that not all consequences are anticipated. Indeed, sometimes the opposite of what anyone wants or expects to happen is what transpires nonetheless. Students who may already know that the American Revolution began shortly after this period may infer how the consequences of colonial debt helped to pave the way for the American independence movement.

TRM Find complete suggested responses in the Teacher's Resource Materials.

CHECK FOR UNDERSTANDING

Ask students: **What was the relationship between British industrial growth and the consumer revolution?** *Innovations in British manufacturing made many consumer goods cheaper, and the vibrant transatlantic trade soon made those goods available in the colonies, which in turn led to a trade deficit and personal debt.*

TEACHING STRATEGY

The Elizabeth Murray Project Web site provides two related lessons on the consumer revolution, "The Consumer Revolution: American Identity" and "The Consumer Revolution: America and Britain." The lessons provide a detailed background essay for teachers with references to scholarly sources and a separate essay for students. The lesson provides several primary and secondary source excerpts, including data on per capita income in the colonies that flesh out the nature of the consumer revolution in the colonial period. Search for "Elizabeth Murray Project High School."

tools, furniture, and chinaware in greater quantities — and at lower cost. The owners running the new workshops drove their employees hard, forcing them to keep pace with the machines and work long hours. To market the abundant factory-produced goods, English and Scottish merchants extended credit to colonial shopkeepers for a full year instead of the traditional six months. Americans soon were purchasing 30 percent of all British exports.

To pay for British manufactures, mainland colonists increased their exports of tobacco, rice, indigo, and wheat. Using credit advanced by Scottish merchants, planters in Virginia bought land, slaves, and equipment to grow tobacco, which they exported to expanding markets in France and central Europe. In South Carolina, rice planters used British government subsidies to develop indigo and rice plantations. New York, Pennsylvania, Maryland, and Virginia became the breadbasket of the Atlantic world, supplying Europe's exploding population with wheat.

consumer revolution
An increase in consumption of English manufactures in Britain and the colonies that was fueled by the Industrial Revolution. The consumer revolution raised living standards but landed many colonists in debt.

AP® SKILLS & PROCESSES
MAKING CONNECTIONS
How did the prosperity of the British Empire improve and endanger the lives and interests of colonists?

Americans used their profits and the generous credit extended from overseas to buy English manufactures. When he was practicing law in Boston, John Adams visited the home of Nicholas Boylston, one of the city's wealthiest merchants, "to view the Furniture, which alone cost a thousand Pounds sterling," he wrote. "[T]he Marble Tables, the rich Beds with Crimson Damask Curtains and Counterpins, the Beautiful Chimny Clock, the Spacious Garden, are the most magnificent of any Thing I have ever seen." Through their possessions, well-to-do colonists set themselves apart from their poorer neighbors.

Although Britain's **consumer revolution** raised living standards, it landed many consumers — and the colonies as a whole — in debt (Figure 4.4). Even during the wartime boom of the 1750s, exports paid for only 80 percent of British imports. Britain financed the remaining 20 percent — the Americans' trade deficit — through the extension of credit and Pitt's military expenditures. When the military subsidies ended in 1763, the colonies fell into an economic recession. Merchants looked anxiously at their overstocked warehouses and feared bankruptcy. "I think we have a gloomy prospect before us," a Philadelphia trader noted in 1765. The increase in transatlantic trade had made Americans more dependent on overseas credit and markets.

Nicholas Boylston, c. 1769
Merchants in the coastal and transatlantic trades gained enormous wealth in the mid-eighteenth century and displayed it in new ways. Among the most flamboyant was Nicholas Boylston. Of Boylston's home John Adams wrote, "A Seat it is for a noble Man, a Prince." In this portrait, painted by John Singleton Copley in 1769, Boylston flaunts his exotic possessions. In place of the wig he would have worn outside his home, Boylston wears a red velvet turban to keep his shaved head warm. His morning gown of heavy silk damask covers a rich waistcoat, casually unbuttoned in the middle to reveal his elegant ruffled shirt. Boylston rests his left elbow on two thick account books, an unmistakable reminder of the source of his wealth. Museum of Fine Arts, Boston, Massachusetts, USA/Bridgeman Images.

The Struggle for Land in the East

In good times and bad, the population continued to grow, intensifying the demand for arable land. Consider the experience of Kent, Connecticut. Like earlier generations, Kent's residents had moved inland to establish new farms, but Kent stood at the colony's western boundary. To provide for the next generation, many Kent families joined the Susquehanna Company (1749), which speculated in lands in the Wyoming Valley in present-day northeastern Pennsylvania. As settlers took up farmsteads there, the company urged the Connecticut legislature to claim the region on the basis of Connecticut's "sea-to-sea" royal charter of 1662. However, Charles II had also granted the Wyoming Valley to William Penn, and the Penn family had sold farms there to Pennsylvania residents. By the late 1750s, settlers from Connecticut and Pennsylvania were at war, burning down their rivals' houses and barns. Delawares with their own claim to the valley were caught in the crossfire. In April 1763, the Delaware headman Teedyuscung was burned to death in his cabin; in retaliation, Teedyuscung's son Captain Bull led a war party that destroyed a community of Connecticut settlers.

Simultaneously, three distinct but related land disputes broke out in the Hudson River Valley (Map 4.4). Dutch tenant farmers, Wappinger Indians, and migrants from Massachusetts asserted ownership rights to lands long claimed by manorial families such as the Van Rensselaers and the Livingstons. When the manor lords turned to the legal system to uphold their claims, Dutch and English farmers in Westchester, Dutchess, and Albany counties rioted to close the courts. In response, New York's royal governor ordered British troops to assist local sheriffs and manorial bailiffs: they suppressed the tenant uprisings, intimidated the Wappingers, and evicted the Massachusetts squatters.

TEACHING STRATEGY

Ask students to complete each row in **Handout 4.3 — Causation: Impact of the Proclamation of 1763 (TRM)** by filling in the boxes to show causes and effects of the Proclamation of 1763. Students should focus on identifying the motivations behind the decision to issue the proclamation and how that action revealed distinct differences in the interests of the colonists versus those of the British imperial government.

TRM Find **Handout 4.3 — Causation: Impact of the Proclamation of 1763** in the Teacher's Resource Materials.

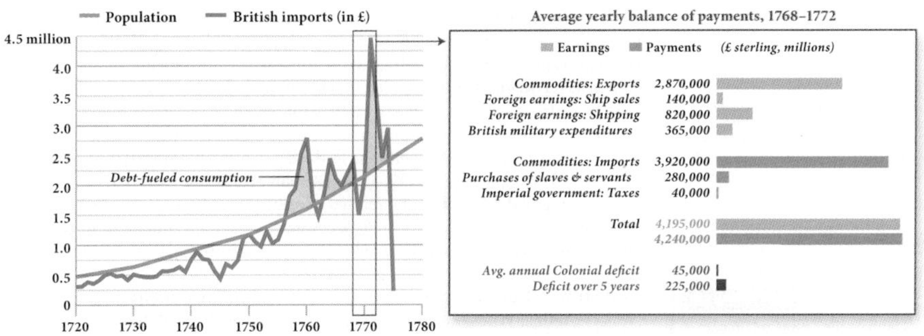

FIGURE 4.4 Mainland Population and British Imports

Around 1750, British imports were growing at a faster rate than the American population, indicating that the colonists were consuming more per capita. But Americans went into debt to pay for these goods, running an annual trade deficit with their British suppliers that by 1772 had created a cumulative debt of £2 million.

Other land disputes erupted in New Jersey and the southern colonies, where landlords and English aristocrats had successfully revived legal claims based on long-dormant seventeenth-century charters. One court decision allowed Lord Granville, the heir of an original Carolina proprietor, to collect an annual tax on land in North Carolina; another decision awarded ownership of the entire northern neck of Virginia (along the Potomac River) to Lord Fairfax.

The revival of these proprietary claims by manorial lords and English nobles testified to the rising value of land along the Atlantic coastal plain. It also underscored the increasing similarities between rural societies in Europe and America. To avoid the status of European peasants, native-born yeomen and tenant families joined the stream of European migrants searching for cheap land near the Appalachian Mountains.

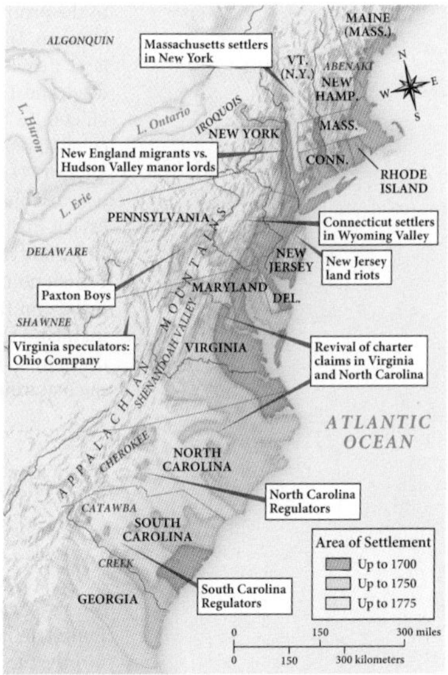

MAP 4.4 Westward Expansion and Land Conflicts, 1750–1775

Between 1750 and 1775, the mainland colonial population more than doubled—from 1.2 million to 2.5 million—triggering westward migrations and legal battles over land, which had become increasingly valuable. Violence broke out in eastern areas, where tenant farmers and smallholders contested landlords' property claims based on ancient titles; and in the backcountry, where migrating settlers fought with Indians, rival claimants, and the officials of eastern-dominated governments.

Western Rebels and Regulators

As would-be landowners moved west, they sparked conflicts over Indian policy, political representation, and debts. During the war with France, Delaware and Shawnee warriors had exacted revenge for Thomas Penn's land swindle of 1737 by destroying frontier farms in Pennsylvania and killing hundreds of residents. Scots-Irish settlers demanded the expulsion of all Indians, but Quaker leaders refused. So in 1763, a group of Scots-Irish frontiersmen called the Paxton Boys massacred twenty Conestoga Indians, an assimilated community that had lived alongside their colonist neighbors peacefully for many years. When Governor John Penn tried to bring the murderers to justice, 250 armed Scots-Irishmen advanced on Philadelphia. Benjamin Franklin intercepted the angry mob at Lancaster and arranged a truce, averting a battle with the militia. Prosecution of the Paxton Boys failed for lack of witnesses, and the episode gave their defenders the opportunity to excoriate Pennsylvania's government for protecting Indians while it neglected the interests of backcountry colonists.

AP® THEME

WXT: Work, Exchange, and Technology

FIGURE 4.4 illustrates an important point hinted at in the text: colonial debt derived largely from the purchase of English manufactured goods, largely consumer goods, like the kinds of items Boylston displays in his portrait, and those used to furnish his house, as described in the text. Ask students: **What does the bar graph reveal about the source of the colonists' debt?** *Commodities imports far outweigh any other colonial expense and are substantially larger than British commodity imports.*

CHECK FOR UNDERSTANDING

Ask students: **Why was there a struggle for land in the East?** *Population growth made arable land increasingly valuable, especially land near the Atlantic coast or fronting major rivers. Migrants and tenant farmers lost their claims to land long claimed by aristocrats.*

AP® THEME

MIG: Migration and Settlement

MAP 4.4 provides a geographical representation of tensions over westward expansion within particular colonies, between colonies, and between colonists and Native Americans. It is important to note for students that some of these tensions preceded the more overt defiance of the British government that came later with the Proclamation of 1763, mentioned briefly on p. 131 and discussed in more depth in Chapter 5. In part, the Proclamation responded to a problem that was already underway before the Seven Years' War.

Regulators
Landowning protestors who organized in North and South Carolina in the 1760s and 1770s to demand that the eastern-controlled government provide western districts with more courts, fairer taxation, and greater representation in the assembly.

The South Carolina Regulators Violence also broke out in the backcountry of South Carolina, where land-hungry colonists clashed repeatedly with Cherokees during the war with France. After the fighting ended in 1763, a group of landowning vigilantes known as the **Regulators** demanded that the eastern-controlled government provide western districts with more courts, fairer taxation, and greater representation in the assembly. "We are *Free-Men* — British Subjects — Not Born *Slaves*," declared a Regulator manifesto. Fearing slave revolts, the lowland rice planters who ran the South Carolina assembly compromised. In 1767, the assembly created western courts and reduced the fees for legal documents; but it refused to reapportion the legislature or lower western taxes. Like the Paxton Boys in Pennsylvania, the South Carolina Regulators won attention to backcountry needs but failed to wrest power from the eastern elite.

AP® EXAM TIP
Compare the causes and impact of the Regulator Movement of the 1760's to Bacon's Rebellion in the 1670's.

Civil Strife in North Carolina In 1766, a more radical Regulator movement arose in North Carolina. When the economic recession of the early 1760s brought a sharp fall in tobacco prices, many farmers could not pay their debts. When creditors sued these farmers for payment, judges directed sheriffs to seize the debtors' property. Many backcountry farmers lost their property or ended up in jail for resisting court orders.

To save their farms, North Carolina's debtors defied the government's authority. Disciplined mobs intimidated judges, closed courts, and freed their comrades from jail. The Regulators proposed a series of reforms, including greater representation in the assembly and a fairer revenue system that would tax each person "in proportion to the profits arising from his estate." All to no avail. In May 1771, Royal Governor William Tryon mobilized British troops and the eastern militia, which defeated a large Regulator force at the Alamance River. When the fighting ended, thirty men lay dead, and Tryon executed seven insurgent leaders. Not since Bacon's Rebellion in Virginia in 1675 and the colonial uprisings during the Glorious Revolution of 1688 had a colonial rebellion been suppressed so violently.

In 1771, as in 1675 and 1688, colonial conflicts became linked with imperial politics. In Connecticut, the Reverend Ezra Stiles defended the North Carolina Regulators. "What shall an injured & oppressed people do," he asked, "[when faced with] Oppression and tyranny?" Stiles's remarks reflected growing resistance to recently imposed British policies of taxation and control. The American colonies still depended primarily on Britain for their trade and military defense. However, by the 1760s, the mainland settlements had evolved into complex societies with the potential to exist independently. British policies would play a crucial role in determining the direction the maturing colonies would take.

SUMMARY

In this chapter, we observed dramatic changes in British North America between 1720 and 1763. An astonishing surge in population — from 400,000 to almost 2 million — was the combined result of natural increase, European migration, and the African slave trade. The print revolution and the rise of the British Atlantic world brought important new influences: the European Enlightenment and European Pietism transformed the world of ideas, while a flood of British consumer goods and the genteel aspirations of wealthy colonists reshaped the colonies' material culture.

Colonists confronted three major regional challenges. In New England, crowded towns and ever-smaller farms threatened the yeoman ideal of independent farming, prompting families to limit births, move to the frontier, or participate in an "exchange" economy. In the Middle Atlantic colonies, Dutch, English, German, and Scots-Irish residents maintained their religious and cultural identities while they competed for access to land and political power. Across the backcountry, new interest in western lands triggered conflicts with Indian peoples, civil unrest among whites, and, ultimately, the Great War for Empire. In the aftermath of the fighting, Britain stood triumphant in Europe and America.

AP® APPLY THE TIP

Ask students to create a Venn diagram comparing the Regulator movement and Bacon's Rebellion. Ask students to consider the participants, causes, conflict, and outcome as they complete the Venn diagram. Lead a class discussion that focuses on similarities and differences between these events. Ask students to consider how both represent conflicts with British imperial policies and conflicts between colonial elites and popular movements.

CHECK FOR UNDERSTANDING

Ask students: **How did midcentury developments reflect Britain's deepening connections to North America?** *Britain's deepening connections to North America occurred in three manners. First, the French and Indian War brought British military to the colonies for the first time on a large scale. Second, trade and European industrialization brought greater colonial consumption and attendant debt. Third, westward migration forced London to develop a significant western policy for the first time.*

CHECK FOR UNDERSTANDING

Use the **AP® LEARNING FOCUS** question from the beginning of the chapter to check students' understanding of the chapter as a whole: **Why did transatlantic travel and communication reshape Britain's American colonies so dramatically?** *The uniformity of British economic policies, such as salutary neglect, and the spread of the ideas of the Enlightenment and the Great Awakening increasingly brought the regions politically and culturally closer despite marked ethnic differences in population. The Enlightenment and the Great Awakening motivated Americans to use experience and knowledge to formulate their own beliefs. Americans began to challenge the omnipotence of monarchy over representative government.*

LearningCurve

Remind students to go online to complete the LearningCurve quiz for this chapter.

CHAPTER 4 REVIEW

AP® CONTENT REVIEW *Answer these questions to demonstrate your understanding of the chapter's main ideas.*

1. What goals and values shaped much of New England society in the eighteenth century?
2. How were the goals of many immigrants to the Middle colonies similar to those of New England colonists, and how did they differ?
3. How did the accelerating pace of travel and communication affect colonial society and culture?
4. How did midcentury developments reflect Britain's deepening connections to North America?

AP® TERMS TO KNOW *Identify and explain the significance of each term below.*

Key Concepts and Events

competency (p. 113)
coverture (p. 116)
household mode of production (p. 116)
tenancy (p. 117)
squatters (p. 117)
redemptioner (p. 120)
Enlightenment (p. 122)
Pietism (p. 122)
natural rights (p. 124)
deism (p. 124)
revival (p. 125)
Old Lights (p. 128)
New Lights (p. 128)
consumer revolution (p. 136)
Regulators (p. 138)

Key People

Benjamin Franklin (p. 122)
Isaac Newton (p. 123)
John Locke (p. 124)
Jonathan Edwards (p. 125)
George Whitefield (p. 125)
Tanaghrisson (p. 131)
William Pitt (p. 133)
Pontiac (p. 134)

AP® MAKING CONNECTIONS *Recognize the larger developments and continuities within and across chapters by answering these questions.*

1. In Chapter 3 we saw the rise of the South Atlantic System, an engine of economic growth that tied Britain's colonies more closely together and generated prosperity throughout the British Atlantic world. What are the consequences of that integration and prosperity? Identify specific examples from the chapter. For example, how was the Great War for Empire grounded in earlier economic developments? And how did the postwar debt crisis grow out of the South Atlantic System?
2. This chapter highlights population growth and ethnic diversification in British North America. Considering what you know about the unpromising origins of English colonization from Chapters 2 and 3, why did Britain's colonies attract so many European migrants in the first half of the eighteenth century? How did their arrival transform the societies and cultures of mainland British North America by the 1760s? Describe the changes over time.

KEY TURNING POINTS *Refer to the timeline at the start of the chapter for help in answering the following questions.*

The Ohio Company grant (1748), the formation of the Susquehanna Company (1749), land conflict along the New York and New England border (1760s), and the defeat of the North Carolina Regulators (1771): How do these events reveal tensions over the question of who would control the development of frontier lands in Britain's mainland North American colonies? What were the effects of these conflicts on Native American populations? Use evidence from the text to support your claim.

139

TRM Find complete suggested responses in the Teacher's Resource Materials.

AP® SKILLS & PROCESSES

CAUSATION

AP® CONTENT REVIEW 1 asks students to identify the long-term effects of New England values on the shape of their society.

AP® SKILLS & PROCESSES

COMPARISON

AP® CONTENT REVIEW 2 asks students to recognize similarities and differences in the motives of migrants to the two regions.

AP® SKILLS & PROCESSES

CAUSATION

AP® CONTENT REVIEW 3 invites students to consider the effects of changes in travel and communication on colonial society and culture.

AP® SKILLS & PROCESSES

CONTEXTUALIZATION

AP® CONTENT REVIEW 4 encourages students to situate the relationship between Britain and its colonies in the broader context of mid-eighteenth century developments.

TRM Find definitions for these terms in the **Glossary/Glosario** in the Teacher's Resource Materials.

AP® SKILLS & PROCESSES

CONTINUITY AND CHANGE

AP® MAKING CONNECTIONS 1 invites students to draw connections between the South Atlantic System described in the previous chapter and developments that followed in the early eighteenth century — economic trends, the Seven Years' War, and the debt that followed it.

AP® SKILLS & PROCESSES

ARGUMENTATION

AP® MAKING CONNECTIONS 2 encourages students to closely analyze the image of Whitefield to consider the larger context in which he preached and how that reveals the appeal of his message.

AP® SKILLS & PROCESSES

CONTINUITY AND CHANGE

The **KEY TURNING POINTS** question prompt invites students to draw connections between four events that happened over more than two decades and explain their relationship to British-American relations and the situation of Native American communities.

TRM Find complete suggested responses in the Teacher's Resource Materials.

AP® PRACTICE QUESTIONS

MULTIPLE CHOICE QUESTIONS *Choose the correct answer for each question.*

Questions 1–3 refer to this graph.

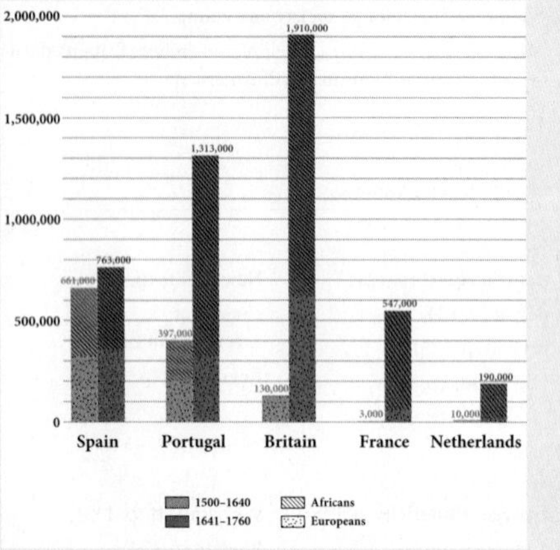

Transatlantic Migration

Source of Data: Stanley L. Engerman and Kenneth L. Sokoloff, "Factor Endowments, Institutions, and Differential Paths of Growth Among New World Economies: A View from Economic Historians of the United States," in *How Latin America Fell Behind: Economic Histories of Brazil and Mexico, 1800–1914*, ed. Stephen Haber (Palo Alto, CA: Stanford University Press, 1997), 264.

1. The population trend reflected on the graph for the colonies of France and the Netherlands most directly resulted from which government policies?
   a. Seeking to subjugate and enslave American Indians
   b. Allowing intermarriage and fostering trade alliances with American Indians
   c. Prompting agriculture and settlement on land taken from American Indians
   d. Defining caste systems and regulating the labor and taxes paid to the state

2. After 1640, the migration trends to British colonies depicted on the graph led to which of the following?
   a. Increased British colonial conflicts with American Indians over land, resources, and political boundaries
   b. Greater colonial resistance to Anglicization and intercolonial commercial ties
   c. Diminished colonial rivalry between Britain and France
   d. Reduced cultural pluralism and intercolonial intellectual exchange

3. The long-term effects of the migration trends portrayed on the graph are most directly explained by
   a. mutual misunderstandings between Europeans and American Indians.
   b. participation by all British colonies to varying degrees in the Atlantic slave trade.
   c. the decline in the *encomienda* system in the Spanish colonies.
   d. French, Dutch, and Spanish colonies alliance with, and arming of, American Indian groups.

Questions 4–5 refer to this excerpt.

"If you would be wealthy . . . *think of Saving as well as Getting:* the Indies *have not made* Spain *rich, because her* Outgoes are greater than her Incomes. Away then with you expensive Follies, and you will not have so much Cause to complain of hard Times, [and] heavy Taxes. . . . *'Tis easier to suppress the first Desire, than to satisfy all that follow it . . .* think what you do when you run in Debt; *You give another Power over your Liberty. . .*

This Doctrine, my Friends, is *Reason* and *Wisdom*; but after all, do not depend too much upon your own *Industry*, and *Frugality*, and *Prudence*, though excellent Things, for they all may be blasted without the Blessing of Heaven; and therefore ask that Blessing humbly, and be not uncharitable to those that at present seem to want it, but comfort and help them."

Benjamin Franklin, "Father Abraham's Speech" from *Poor Richard's Almanac*, 1757

4. Which of the following developments best explains the historical significance of *Poor Richard's Almanac*?
   a. The rise of Protestant evangelism in the mid-eighteenth century
   b. The cultural exchanges generated by transatlantic print culture
   c. The experiences and experiments in colonial self-government
   d. Romantic beliefs in human perfectibility spreading in reaction to the Enlightenment

5. All of the following persons or groups would have been likely to agree with the point of view of the excerpt EXCEPT
   a. a Baptist minister.
   b. members of the colonial commercial elite.
   c. an Enlightenment scholar.
   d. an indentured servant.

SHORT ANSWER QUESTIONS

Read each question carefully and write a short response. Use evidence from the text to support your claims.

"The extremely heterogeneous population confronted Pennsylvania with a unique set of problems that could have impeded the creation of a stable society. Nevertheless, despite the inevitable tensions, exacerbated by waves of new immigration, war, and religious conflict, colonial Pennsylvanians managed to develop new ideals of pluralism and tolerance on which they built their province. . . . William Penn set forth a new ideological basis for pluralism and tolerance that transformed the tentative pattern of relative harmony and toleration into one of official policy. . . . [H]e drafted a series of constitutions that guaranteed religious freedom and promoted his colony not only in the British Isles but on the Continent as well."

Sally Schwartz, *A Mixed Multitude: The Struggle for Toleration in Colonial Pennsylvania*, 1987

"Pennsylvania, New Jersey, Delaware, northern Maryland, and parts of New York — colonies that together made the eighteenth century mid-Atlantic perhaps the most racially, ethnically, and religiously mixed place in the world . . . were unintended byproducts of a force that is now alien: early modern settler colonialism, in which huge numbers of Europeans and Africans were drawn across the ocean, in freedom and in bondage, and replanted in new landscapes. . . . With few exceptions, living together made the different sorts of people living there feel frightened of one another's intentions. Forced proximity brought many groups to a fresh appreciation for their own distinctive ways, ways they thought of as "traditional" and fought to recover amid the disturbing novelties that came with diversity. Most strove both to make the other peoples around them act more like themselves and keep, if they could, from coming to resemble their neighbors, making for a jittery, culturally competitive society."

Peter Silver, *Our Savage Neighbors: How Indian War Transformed Early America*, 2008

1. Using the two excerpts provided, answer (a), (b), and (c).
   - **a.** Briefly explain ONE major difference between Schwartz's and Silver's historical interpretations about the influence of demography in shaping colonial society between 1650 and 1763.
   - **b.** Briefly explain how ONE specific historical event, development, or circumstance from the period 1650 to 1763 that is not explicitly mentioned in the excerpts could be used to support Schwartz's argument.
   - **c.** Briefly explain how ONE specific historical event, development, or circumstance from the period 1650 to 1763 that is not explicitly mentioned in the excerpts could be used to support Silver's argument.

2. Answer (a), (b), and (c).
   - **a.** Briefly explain why ONE of the following choices was the largest factor influencing American colonists to reject their identity as subjects of the British Empire.
     - The ideas of the Enlightenment
     - The end of the Seven Years' War
     - The British imperial economic system
   - **b.** Provide ONE specific historical example to support your argument in (a).
   - **c.** Provide specific evidence why ONE of the other above choices was a less important factor influencing colonists to reject their identity as subjects of the British Empire.

3. Answer (a), (b), and (c).
   - **a.** Briefly explain ONE important difference in the development of New England (1620–1763) and Middle colonies (1681–1763).
   - **b.** Briefly explain ANOTHER important difference in the development of New England (1620–1763) and Middle colonies (1681–1763).
   - **c.** Briefly explain ONE important similarity between the New England and Middle colonies in the same periods.

TRM Find complete suggested responses in the Teacher's Resource Materials.

TRM Find complete suggested responses in the Teacher's Resource Materials.

PART 2 AP® PRACTICE ESSAY QUESTIONS

DOCUMENT-BASED QUESTION *Suggested reading period: 15 minutes. Suggested writing time: 45 minutes*

DIRECTIONS: Question 1 is based on the accompanying documents. The documents have been edited for the purpose of this exercise.

1. Evaluate the extent of change in the labor systems of the British North American colonies between 1600 and 1750.

DOCUMENT 1

Source: The General Court of Massachusetts, *An Act of Assessment on Spinning*, 1655.

"This Court . . . Does therefore Order . . . That all hands not necessarily employed on other occasions, as Women, Girls and Boys, shall and hereby are enjoined to Spin according to their skill and ability; and that the Select men in every Town do consider the condition and capacity of every family, and accordingly do assess them at one or more Spinners; And because Several Families are necessarily employed the greatest part of their time in other business, yet if opportunities were attended, some time might be spared, at least be some of them for this work. . . ."

DOCUMENT 2

Source: Gabriel Thomas, *An Historical Description [of Pennsylvania]*, 1698.

"I must say, even the present encouragements are very great and inviting for poor people (both men and women) of all kinds, can here get three times the wages for their Labor they can in England or Wales.

I shall instance in a few. . . . The first was a blacksmith (my next neighbor) who himself and one Negro man he had, got fifty shillings in one day, by working up a hundred pound weight of iron. . . . And for carpenters, both house and ship, bricklayers, masons, either of these tradesmen will get between five and six shillings every day constantly. As to journeymen shoemakers, they have two shillings per pair both for men and women's shoes; and journeymen tailors have 12 shillings per week. . . .

The maidservant's wages is commonly between six and ten pounds per annum, with very good accommodation. And for the women who get their livelihood by their own industry, their Labor is very dear. . . .

[T]he chief reason why wages of servants of all sorts is much higher here than there, arises from the great fertility and produce of the place; if these large stipends were refused them, they would quickly set up for themselves. . . .

First, their land costs them little or nothing in comparison [to] the farmers in England. . . . In the second place, they have constantly good price for their corn, by reason of the great and quick vent [trade] into Barbados and other Islands; through which means silver is become more plentiful than here in England. . . . Thirdly they pay no tithes and their Taxes are inconsiderable. . . ."

DOCUMENT 3

Source: Estimated Number of White and Black Headrights to Virginia.

Years	White Headrights	Black Headrights
1650–1659	18,836	317
1660–1669	18,369	609
1670–1679	13,867	411
1680–1689	10,401	619
1690–1699	9,379	1,847

DOCUMENT 4

Source: Robert Beverley, *The History and Present State of Virginia*, 1705.

"Slaves are the Negroes . . . following the condition of the Mother, . . . They are called Slaves, in respect of the time of their Servitude, because it is for Life.

Servants, are those which serve for only a few years, according to the time of the Indenture, or the Custom of the Country. . . .

The Male-Servants, and Slaves of both Sexes, are employed together in Tilling and Manuring the Ground, in Sowing and Planting Tobacco, Corn, etc. Some Distinction indeed is made between them in the Clothes, and Food; but the Work of both, is no other than what the Overseers, the Freemen, and the Planters themselves do.

Sufficient Distinction is also made between the Female-Servants and Slaves; for a White Woman is rarely or never put to work in the Ground [fields], if she be good for anything else. . . .

The work of their Servants and Slaves, is no other than what every common Freeman does. Neither is any freeman required to do more in a day than his Overseer. And I can assure you with a great deal of Truth, that generally their Slaves are not worked near so hard, nor so many Hours in a day, as the Husbandmen [Farmers], and Day-Laborers in *England*. An Overseer is a Man, that having served his time, has acquired the Skill and Character of an experienced Planter, and is therefore entrusted with the Direction of the Servants and Slaves."

DOCUMENT 5

Source: *An Indentured Contract of Apprenticeship between William Matthews and Thomas Windover*, 1718.

"I, William Mathews . . . of the city of New York . . . does voluntarily and of his own free will . . . put himself as an apprentice cordwainer [shoemaker] to Thomas Windover. . . .

[William Mathews] will live and . . . serve from August 15, 1718, until the full term of seven years be completed and ended. . . . [He] shall faithfully serve his master, shall faithfully keep his secrets, and gladly obey his lawful commands everywhere. . . . He shall not waste his said master's goods nor lend them unlawfully to any. He shall not . . . contract matrimony within the [seven years].

At cards, dice, or any other unlawful game, he shall not play. . . with his own goods or the goods of others. Without a license from his master he shall neither buy nor sell during the said term. He shall not absent himself day or night from his master's service without his leave, not haunt alehouses, but in all things he shall behave himself as a faithful apprentice toward his master. . . .

The master . . . shall, by the best means or methods, teach or cause the apprentice to be taught the art or mystery of a cordwainer. He shall find and provide unto the said apprentice sufficient meat, drink, apparel, lodging, and washing fit for an apprentice. During the said term, every night in winter he shall give the apprentice one quarter of schooling. At the expiration of the said term he shall provide him with a sufficient new suit of apparel, four shirts, and two necklets."

DOCUMENT 6

Source: South Carolina Assembly, *An Act for the Better Ordering and Governing of Negroes and Other Slaves in This Province*, 1740.

"I. *And be it enacted* . . . That all Negroes and Indians . . . mullatoes or mestizos who now are, or shall hereafter be, in this Province, and all their issue and offspring, born or to be born, shall be, and they are hereby declared to be, and remain forever hereafter, absolute slaves. . . .

II. . . . *Be it further enacted* . . . That no person whatsoever shall permit or suffer any slave under his or their care or management . . . to go out of the plantation . . . without a letter. . . .

XXX. *And be it further enacted* . . . That no slave who shall dwell, reside, inhabit, or be usually employed in Charlestown, shall presume to buy, sell, deal, traffic, barter, exchange or use commerce for any goods, wares, provisions, grain, victuals [foodstuffs], or commodities, of any sort or kind whatsoever. . . .

XLIII. . . . *Be it therefore enacted* . . . That no men slaves exceeding seven in number, shall herein be permitted to travel together in any high road in this Province, without some white person with them; and it shall and may be lawful for any [white] person or persons . . . to apprehend all and every such slaves, and shall and may whip them, not exceeding twenty lashes on the bare back.

LVI. And whereas, several Negroes did lately rise in rebellion, and did commit many barbarous murders at Stono and in other parts adjacent thereto; and whereas, in suppressing the said rebels, several of them were killed and others taken alive and executed. . . . Be it enacted . . . That all and every act . . . committed, and executed, in and about suppressing and putting all . . . the said . . . Negroes to death, is and are hereby declared lawful, to all intents and purposes whatsoever. . . ."

DOCUMENT 7

Source: Benjamin Franklin, observations on the population of Pennsylvania in his essay "Observations Concerning the Increasing of Mankind, Peopling of Countries, &c," 1751.

"Land being thus plenty in America, and so cheap as that a laboring Man, that understands Husbandry [agriculture], can in a short Time save Money enough to purchase a Piece of new Land sufficient for a Plantation, whereon he may subsist a family; such are not afraid to marry. . . .

Labor will never be cheap here, where no man continues long a laborer for others, but gets a plantation of his own; no man continues long a journeyman to a trade, but goes among those new settlers, and sets up for himself, etc. Hence labor is no cheaper now in Pennsylvania than it was thirty years ago, though so many thousand laboring people have been imported. . . .

The labor of slaves can never be so cheap here as the labor of workingmen is in Britain. . . . Why then will Americans purchase slaves? Because slaves may be kept as long as a man pleases, or has occasion for their labor; while hired men are continually leaving their masters (often in the midst of business) and setting up for themselves."

LONG ESSAY QUESTIONS *Suggested writing time: 40 minutes*

DIRECTIONS: Please choose one of the following three questions to answer. Make a historically defensible claim and support your reasoning with specific and relevant evidence.

2. Evaluate the extent to which Great Britain's mercantilist policies affected the economic development of the British North American colonies from 1620–1754.
3. Evaluate the extent to which the chattel slave system affected social developments in the British North American Colonies from 1619–1754.
4. Evaluate the extent to which European imperial rivalries affected relations with American Indians from 1607–1754.

3

PART

Revolution and Republican Culture

1754–1800

Although Part 3 is dominated by the causes and consequences of the War of Independence, it opens in 1754 to capture the changes wrought by the Great War for Empire, which were revolutionary in themselves — Britain had triumphed in the war, only to see its American empire unravel and descend into rebellion. Against all odds, thirteen colonies first united to win their independence, and then formed a federal republic that could claim a place among the nations of the world. "The American war is over," Philadelphia Patriot Benjamin Rush declared in 1787, "but this is far from being the case with the American Revolution. On the contrary, nothing but the first act of the great drama is closed. It remains yet to establish and perfect our new forms of government."

The republican revolution extended far beyond politics. It challenged many of the values and institutions that had prevailed for centuries in Europe and the Atlantic world. After 1776, Americans reconsidered basic assumptions that structured their societies, cultures, families, and communities. Moreover, the new nation had to establish its economic independence and viability as it sought to secure western lands for American citizens and protect American manufacturing from foreign competition. These effects of the Revolution were only beginning to take shape by 1800, but we end Part 3 there, when the essential characteristics of the United States were becoming clear. (Chapter 7 carries the political story forward to 1820 in order to trace key themes to their conclusion, but Part 4 takes 1800 as its start date.) This periodization — 1754 to 1800 — captures a critical phase in American history: the transition from imperial rivalry and wars among European powers and Native societies to the founding of a new nation-state and its political institutions. Here are three key questions to keep in mind as you read the chapters in this part: ▶

AP® CONCEPT CONNECTIONS

Why Did the Colonists Revolt?

To administer the vast new American territory it gained in 1763, Britain had to reform its empire. Until that time, its colonies had been left largely free to manage their own affairs. Now, Parliament hoped to pay the costs of empire by taxing the colonies, while at the same time extending control over its new lands in the continental interior. Colonial radicals resisted these reforms. Calling themselves Patriots, they insisted on preserving local control over taxes. As Britain pressured local communities, colonists created intercolonial institutions and developed a broad critique of British rule that combined older, republican political principles with radical ideas of natural rights and the equality of all men. Their protests grew more strident, eventually resulting in open warfare with Great Britain and a declaration of independence.

The Granger Collection, New York.

Why Did Americans Create Republican Governments?

At the same time they fought a war against Great Britain, Patriot leaders in the newly independent states had to create new governments. They drafted constitutions for their states while maintaining a loose confederacy to bind them together. In 1787, reformers put forward a new plan of government, in the form of a constitution that would bind the states into a single nation. At both the state and the national level, leaders sought to create republics: systems of government grounded in the sovereignty of the people.

The new American republic emerged fitfully. Experiments in government took shape across an entire generation, and it took still longer to decide how much power the federal republic should wield over the states. Political culture was unformed and slow to develop. Political parties, for example, were an unexpected development. At first they were widely regarded as illegitimate, but by 1800 they had become essential to managing political conflict, heightening some forms of competition while blunting others. In the last half of the eighteenth century, American political culture was transformed as newly created governments gained the allegiance of their citizens.

The Granger Collection, New York.

How Did the United States Secure and Expand Its Borders?

One uncontested value of the Revolutionary era was a commitment to economic opportunity. To achieve this, people migrated in large numbers, creating new pressures on the United States to meet the needs of its citizens. The federal government acted against westerners who tried to rebel or secede, fought Indian wars to claim new territory, and turned back challenges from Britain and France to maintain its control over western lands. By 1820, the United States had dramatically expanded its boundaries and extended control far beyond the original seaboard states.

Even as the borders of the United States expanded, its diversity inhibited the effort to define an American culture and identity. Native Americans still lived in their own clans and nations; black Americans were developing a distinct African American culture; and white Americans were enmeshed in vigorous regional ethnic communities. But by 1800, to be an American meant, for many members of the dominant white population, to be a republican, a Protestant, and an enterprising individual.

Smithsonian American Art Museum, Washington, D.C. / Art Resource, NY.

Organized around a single theme, the Part 3 Document Set in ***Sources for America's History*** can be used to teach the AP® Theme American and National Identity (NAT), which explores the competing conceptions of national identity that emerged in the colonial period.

AP® THEMATIC UNDERSTANDING

Revolution and Republican Culture, 1754–1800

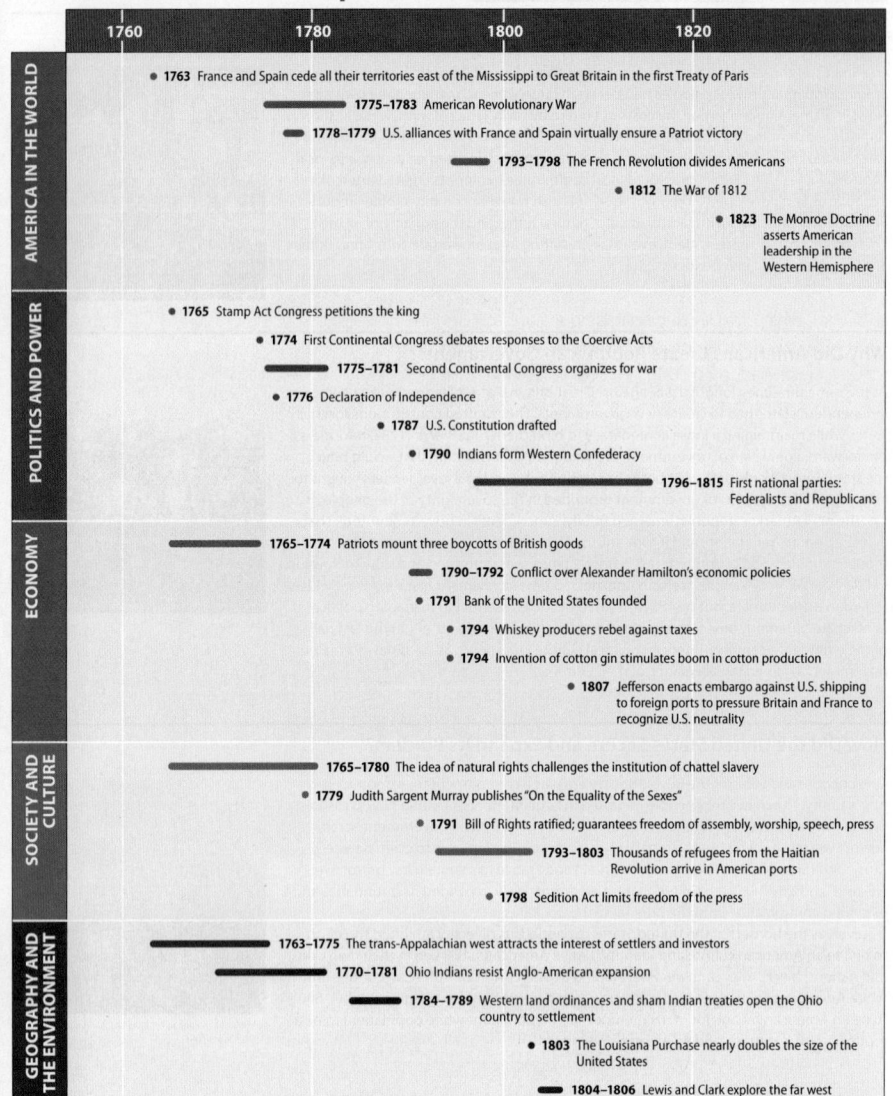

1760 | 1780 | 1800 | 1820

AMERICA IN THE WORLD

- **1763** France and Spain cede all their territories east of the Mississippi to Great Britain in the first Treaty of Paris
- **1775–1783** American Revolutionary War
- **1778–1779** U.S. alliances with France and Spain virtually ensure a Patriot victory
- **1793–1798** The French Revolution divides Americans
- **1812** The War of 1812
- **1823** The Monroe Doctrine asserts American leadership in the Western Hemisphere

POLITICS AND POWER

- **1765** Stamp Act Congress petitions the king
- **1774** First Continental Congress debates responses to the Coercive Acts
- **1775–1781** Second Continental Congress organizes for war
- **1776** Declaration of Independence
- **1787** U.S. Constitution drafted
- **1790** Indians form Western Confederacy
- **1796–1815** First national parties: Federalists and Republicans

ECONOMY

- **1765–1774** Patriots mount three boycotts of British goods
- **1790–1792** Conflict over Alexander Hamilton's economic policies
- **1791** Bank of the United States founded
- **1794** Whiskey producers rebel against taxes
- **1794** Invention of cotton gin stimulates boom in cotton production
- **1807** Jefferson enacts embargo against U.S. shipping to foreign ports to pressure Britain and France to recognize U.S. neutrality

SOCIETY AND CULTURE

- **1765–1780** The idea of natural rights challenges the institution of chattel slavery
- **1779** Judith Sargent Murray publishes "On the Equality of the Sexes"
- **1791** Bill of Rights ratified; guarantees freedom of assembly, worship, speech, press
- **1793–1803** Thousands of refugees from the Haitian Revolution arrive in American ports
- **1798** Sedition Act limits freedom of the press

GEOGRAPHY AND THE ENVIRONMENT

- **1763–1775** The trans-Appalachian west attracts the interest of settlers and investors
- **1770–1781** Ohio Indians resist Anglo-American expansion
- **1784–1789** Western land ordinances and sham Indian treaties open the Ohio country to settlement
- **1803** The Louisiana Purchase nearly doubles the size of the United States
- **1804–1806** Lewis and Clark explore the far west

AP® Making Connections Across Chapters

Read these questions and think about them as you read the chapters in Part 3. Then when you have completed the chapters, return to these questions and answer them.

1 Why did the outcome of the Seven Years' War result in an imperial crisis that ultimately led to the separation of thirteen North American colonies from Great Britain?

Library of Congress, LC-DIG-ppmsca-17521.

2 What ideas lay behind the independence movement, and how did they influence the systems of government that were adopted during and after the Revolutionary War?

Everett Collection.

3 Why were the American Patriots able to defeat Great Britain and win their independence?

Architect of the Capitol.

4 How did relations between the United States and European nations develop during the first three decades after the Treaty of Paris?

The Granger Collection, New York.

5 How did the American Revolution affect the fortunes of Native Americans and enslaved people? What impact did it have on the place of women in American society?

Chicago History Museum/Getty Images.

TRM Find complete suggested responses in the Teacher's Resource Materials.

5 CHAPTER The Problem of Empire

1754–1776

Chapter 5 — AP® Assessment Weight and Pacing Guide

The assessment weight on the AP® U.S. History Exam for Chapters 5–7 is 10–17 percent. This chapter falls in Unit 3 of the AP® U.S. History Curriculum, covering Period 3: 1754–1800.

This pacing guide is based on a schedule with 120 sessions of 50 minutes each before the AP® U.S. History Exam. If you have a different number of sessions before the exam, you can modify the pacing to meet your needs. If you have additional time, consider incorporating quizzes, released AP® U.S. History questions, practice exams, writing practice, and other instructional activities.

	Traditional Schedule	Block Schedule
Chapter 5	5 days	2–3 days

Daily Pacing Guide

	Content Focus	Essential Question
Day 1	An Empire Transformed	What changes in Britain's imperial policy were triggered by its victory in the Great War for Empire?
Day 2	The Dynamics of Rebellion, 1765–1770	What was the relationship between formal protests against Parliament and popular resistance in the years between 1765 and 1770?
Day 3	The Road to Independence, 1771–1776	What actions did the Continental Association take to support the efforts of the Continental Congress?
Days 4 and 5	Violence East and West	How did the colonies' long controversy with Parliament influence the ideals that shaped the independence movement?

AP® Alignment

Section Heading	AP® Topic	AP® Theme
An Empire Transformed	3.2, 3.3	WOR
The Dynamics of Rebellion, 1765–1770	3.2, 3.3, 3.4, 3.5	WOR, NAT
The Road to Independence, 1771–1776	3.3	WOR
Violence East and West	3.4, 3.5	NAT, WOR

*Should changes be made to the Course Framework in the future, an updated alignment will be placed on our AP® updates page at go.bfwpub.com/ap-course-updates.

Chapter 5 — Overview

Chapter 5 engages students in the study of the period from the start of the French and Indian War to the Declaration of Independence. The first part of the chapter focuses on the changes in British policy toward the colonies as a result of the French and Indian War and the reactions of colonial leaders and popular action in response. The chapter also asks students to consider the problem of reconciling the existence of slavery and the ideals expressed in response to British policy regarding natural rights and liberty. Finally, the chapter engages students in the events that led to the American Revolution and unified the colonists behind the writing of the Declaration of Independence.

Chapter 5 — Resources

The following resources can be found in the Teacher's Resource Materials (TRM) that accompany the book. You can access the TRM via the book's digital platform, by clicking the TRM links found here in your Teacher's Edition e-book, or by contacting your representative to access the resources online. Visit **bfwpub.com/henretta10e** to learn more.

TRM Chapter 5 Lecture Presentation Slides

TRM Chapter 5 Outline with AP® Focus

TRM Chapter 5 Lecture Strategies

TRM Chapter 5 Suggested Responses

TRM Handout 5.1 — Causation: Road to the American Revolution

TRM Handout 5.2 — Comparison: Colonial Congress

TRM Handout 5.3 — Comparison: *Common Sense* and the Declaration of Independence

Chapter 5 — Essential Activity

Understanding the role of the French and Indian War in the events leading to the conflict between the British government and the British colonists is critical for students. To help students make the connections visually, organize them into collaborative groups and give each group a piece of poster paper on which they should write "French and Indian War" in the center of the paper. Off this title, ask students to create a web with four parts: British, French, colonists, and Natives. Ask students to use the textbook and other resources to identify actions and policies of each group during and immediately after the war. Once students have added details for each part of the web, ask them to identify and explain connections between the supporting details by using colors or dotted lines. Consider using a color code that identifies connections that supported the relationship between the British and the colonies versus events that strained the relationship between the British and the colonies.

Chapter 5 — Bell Ringers

The following activities take no more than 5–15 minutes of your class period and offer an effective and engaging way to begin your lessons and for students to apply AP® Skills & Processes:

- Project an image of North America in 1754 that focuses student attention on the Ohio Valley and shows areas controlled by the British, French, and Native groups. Ask students to point out reasons for conflict over this region. *Answers will vary, but should include the following reasons for conflict: access to trade on the Great Lakes, control of border regions, access to the St. Lawrence River, competition for trade with Native groups, conflicts between Native groups, and dangers to people on the British "frontier."*
- Provide students with Paul Revere's engraving of the Boston Massacre (on p. 162 of the text). Ask students to explain the historical context, intended audience, purpose, and point of view (HIPP) for this image. Then have students compare the image to the events that occurred in the Boston Massacre. *Answers will vary.*
- Project an image of the Revolutionary-era flag stating "Resistance to Tyrants Is Obedience to God." Ask students to contextualize the image by identifying the historical processes and developments in colonial history that explain the significance of this image. Ask students to also contextualize beyond the American Revolution for the ways the sentiment expressed would impact the development of American government. *Answers will vary.*

NOTES

5

CHAPTER

The Problem of Empire

1754–1776

TEACHING STRATEGY

Use "The Reluctant Revolutionaries," a lesson plan available on the PBS Liberty! The American Revolution Web site, to help students understand Americans' reluctant shift from loyal subjects to rebels. The lesson directs teachers to show clips from a documentary, followed by a few discussion questions. Access this lesson plan by searching "PBS Liberty Reluctant Revolutionaries." You can also use the first three questions from the lesson to complement your discussion of the "An Empire Transformed" section beginning on p. 146. For a complete suggested response to the **AP® LEARNING FOCUS** question, see p. 174.

AP® LEARNING FOCUS

Why did the imperial crisis lead to war between Britain and the United States?

In June 1775, the city of New York faced a perplexing dilemma. Word arrived that George Washington, who had just been named commander in chief of the newly formed Continental army, was coming to town. But on the same day, William Tryon, the colony's crown-appointed governor, was scheduled to return from Britain. Local leaders orchestrated a delicate dance. Though the Provincial Congress was operating illegally in the eyes of the crown, it did not wish to offend Governor Tryon. It instructed the city's newly raised volunteer battalion to divide in two. One company awaited Washington's arrival, while another prepared to greet the governor. The "residue of the Battalion" was to be "ready to receive either the General or Governour *Tryon*, which ever shall first arrive." Washington arrived first. He was met by nine companies of the volunteer battalion and a throng of well-wishers, who escorted him to his rooms in a local tavern. Many of this same crowd then crossed town to join the large group assembled to greet the governor, whose ship was just landing. The crowd met him with "universal shouts of applause" and accompanied him home.

This awkward moment in the history of one American city reflects a larger crisis of loyalty that plagued colonists throughout British North America in the years between 1763 and 1776. The outcome of the Great War for Empire left Great Britain the undisputed master of eastern North America. But that success pointed the way to catastrophe. Convinced of the need to reform the empire and tighten its administration, British policymakers imposed a series of new administrative measures on the colonies. Accustomed as they were to governing their own affairs, colonists could not accept these changes. Yet the bonds of loyalty were strong, and the unraveling of British authority was tortuous and complex. Only gradually — as militancy slowly mounted on both sides — were the ties of empire broken and independence declared.

Troops Arrive in Boston, 1768 During the Stamp Act riots, Boston earned a reputation among British administrators as a "mobbish town." Fearing a resurgence of mob activity, Massachusetts Governor Francis Bernard asked for troops to be stationed in town. General Thomas Gage concurred, and in fall 1768 four battalions and an artillery company — more than 2,000 troops in all — took up residence; two of the battalions remained in Boston for more than seventeen months. Their stay ended abruptly after a detachment of soldiers fired into a crowd on March 5, 1770, in an event Patriots called a "bloody massacre." Soon after, Paul Revere engraved and printed this image of the troops arriving in Boston to emphasize that their purpose had been aggressive from the start. With warships positioned broadside, cannons pointing at the town, and transport boats filled with redcoats, the print vividly portrayed the hostile intent of the town's occupation. Historic New England, Boston, Massachusetts, USA/Bridgeman Images.

TEACHING STRATEGY

One of the most significant outcomes of the Seven Years' War was the transformation of Great Britain from a commercial to a territorial empire, which is implicitly referenced in this picture. Have students identify the characteristics of both a commercial and a territorial empire. After students successfully identify each, ask them to describe one way in which this transition affected the relationship between Great Britain and the North American colonists.

AP® SKILLS & PROCESSES

CONTINUITY AND CHANGE

Use the **TIMELINE** to explore how 1763 to 1776 could constitute a definable historical era during which "the problem of empire" set Americans on the path to independence. Even though 1754 is not included in the **TIMELINE**, encourage students to ask what happened in 1754 and in 1776, and why these two events might be considered turning points. Extend this exercise by asking students to consider alternatives to these starting and ending dates.

AP® THEME

WOR: America in the World

Discuss with students the text's explanation of how competition between two empires, Britain and France, influenced political developments in North America.

AP® APPLY THE TIP

Using close reading of the text, ask students to create a flow chart that traces the changes in British policy toward the colonists starting with Britain's victory in the French and Indian War in 1763 to the Battle of Lexington and Concord in 1775. Make sure students show reactions and decisions made by colonists in response. Then ask students to think about ways in which colonial reactions show both attempts to reconcile with Britain and attempts to challenge British authority.

TIMELINE

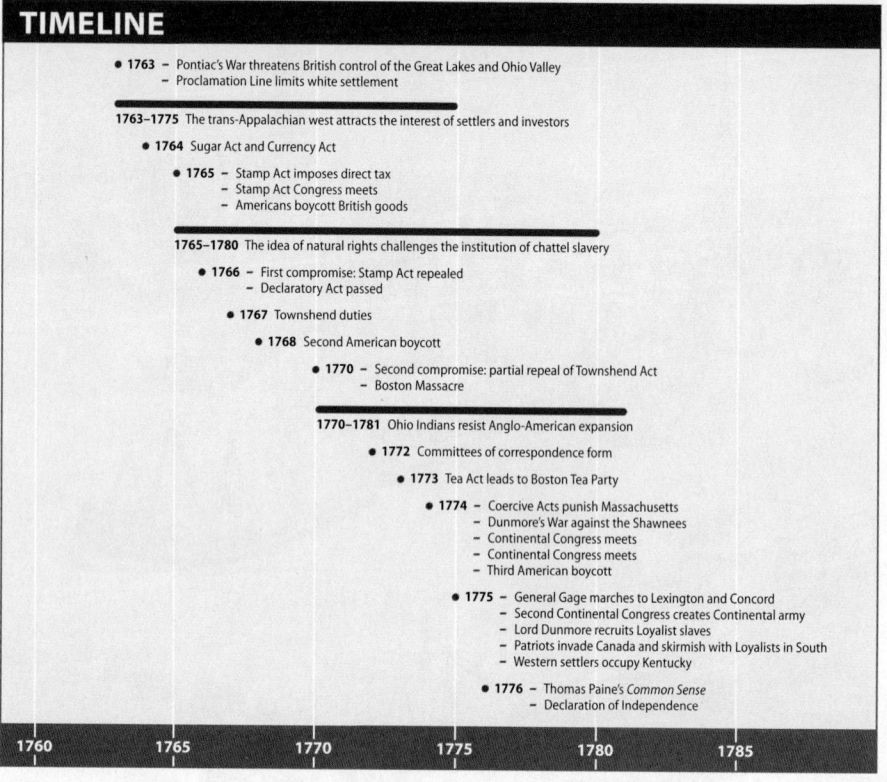

- **1763** – Pontiac's War threatens British control of the Great Lakes and Ohio Valley
  – Proclamation Line limits white settlement
- **1763–1775** The trans-Appalachian west attracts the interest of settlers and investors
- **1764** Sugar Act and Currency Act
- **1765** – Stamp Act imposes direct tax
  – Stamp Act Congress meets
  – Americans boycott British goods
- **1765–1780** The idea of natural rights challenges the institution of chattel slavery
- **1766** – First compromise: Stamp Act repealed
  – Declaratory Act passed
- **1767** Townshend duties
- **1768** Second American boycott
- **1770** – Second compromise: partial repeal of Townshend Act
  – Boston Massacre
- **1770–1781** Ohio Indians resist Anglo-American expansion
- **1772** Committees of correspondence form
- **1773** Tea Act leads to Boston Tea Party
- **1774** – Coercive Acts punish Massachusetts
  – Dunmore's War against the Shawnees
  – Continental Congress meets
  – Continental Congress meets
  – Third American boycott
- **1775** – General Gage marches to Lexington and Concord
  – Second Continental Congress creates Continental army
  – Lord Dunmore recruits Loyalist slaves
  – Patriots invade Canada and skirmish with Loyalists in South
  – Western settlers occupy Kentucky
- **1776** – Thomas Paine's *Common Sense*
  – Declaration of Independence

1760 | 1765 | 1770 | 1775 | 1780 | 1785

AN EMPIRE TRANSFORMED

What changes in Britain's imperial policy were triggered by its victory in the Great War for Empire?

The war that began as the French and Indian War in 1754 and culminated in the Great War for Empire of 1756–1763 transformed the British Empire in North America. The British ministry could no longer let the colonies manage their own affairs while it minimally oversaw Atlantic trade. Its interests and responsibilities now extended far into the continental interior — a much more costly and complicated proposition than it had ever faced before. And neither its American colonies nor their Native American neighbors were inclined to cooperate in the transformation.

British administrators worried about their American colonists, who, according to former Georgia governor Henry Ellis, felt themselves "entitled to a greater measure of Liberty than is enjoyed by the people of England." Ireland had been closely ruled for decades, and recently the East India Company set up dominion over millions of non-British peoples (Map 5.1). Britain's American possessions were likewise filled with aliens and "undesirables": "French, Dutch, Germans innumerable, Indians, Africans, and a multitude of felons from this country," as one member of Parliament put it. Consequently, declared Lord Halifax, "The people of England" considered Americans "as foreigners."

AP® EXAM TIP

Identifying the reasons for changes in British policies toward colonies after the French and Indian War is critical for the AP® Exam.

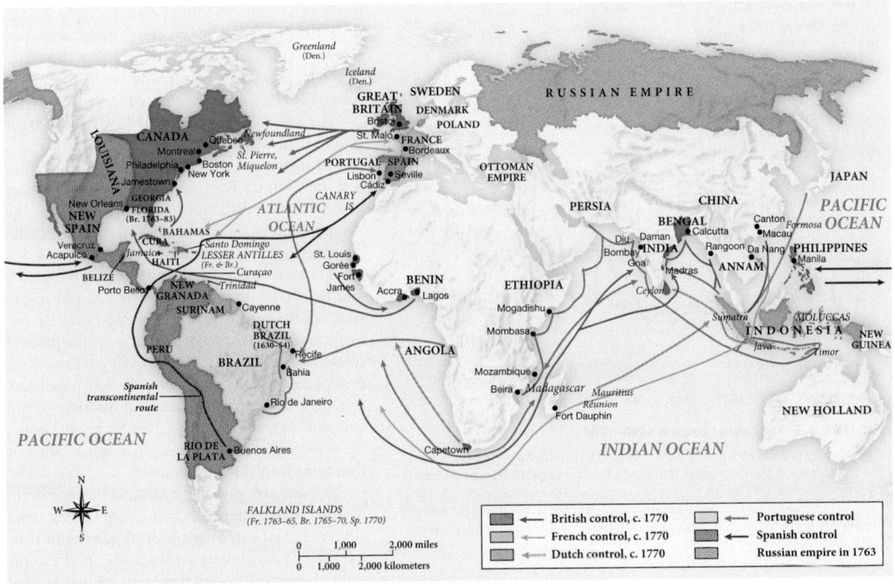

MAP 5.1 Eurasian Trade and European Colonies, c. 1770
By 1770, the Western European nations that had long dominated maritime trade had created vast colonial empires and spheres of influence. Spain controlled the western halves of North and South America, Portugal owned Brazil, and Holland ruled Indonesia. Britain, a newer imperial power, boasted settler societies in North America, rich sugar islands in the West Indies, slave ports in West Africa, and a growing presence on the Indian subcontinent. France had lost its possessions on mainland North America but retained lucrative sugar islands in the Caribbean.

Contesting that status, wealthy Philadelphia lawyer John Dickinson argued that his fellow colonists were "not [East Indian] Sea Poys, nor Marattas, but *British subjects* who are born to liberty, who know its worth, and who prize it high." Thus was the stage set for a struggle between the conceptions of identity — and empire — held by British ministers, on the one hand, and many American colonists on the other.

AP® SKILLS & PROCESSES

CAUSATION

What was the impact of the Great War for Empire on British policymakers and the colonies?

The Costs of Empire

The Great War for Empire imposed enormous costs on Great Britain. The national debt soared from £75 million to £133 million and was, an observer noted, "becoming the alarming object of every British subject." By war's end, interest on the debt alone consumed 60 percent of the nation's budget, and the ministry had to raise taxes. During the eighteenth century, taxes were shifting from land — owned by the gentry and aristocracy — to everyday items that were consumed by middling and poor Britons, and successive ministries became ever more ingenious in devising new ways to raise money. Excise (or sales) taxes were levied on salt and beer, bricks and candles, paper (in the form of a stamp tax), and many other ordinary goods. In the 1760s, the per capita tax burden was 20 percent of income.

To collect the taxes, the government doubled the size of the tax bureaucracy (Figure 5.1). Customs agents patrolled the coasts of southern Britain, seizing tons of contraband French wines, Dutch tea, and Flemish textiles. Convicted smugglers faced

AP® EXAM TIP

Be sure to highlight in your notes the ways that British laws were designed to enhance British power in North America after the French and Indian War.

AP® THEME

WOR: America in the World

Use **MAP 5.1** to illustrate how the competition between Britain and France in North America was part of a larger global contest for colonial empires and spheres of influence.

AP® SKILLS & PROCESSES

CAUSATION

Pose the **CAUSATION** question to help students address the short-term effects of the Great War for Empire on British policymakers and colonies. Scaffold this question by asking students to draw a cause-effect chart with separate effects for policymakers and colonies. You can additionally ask students to infer possible long-term effects of the war and think about why short- and long-term effects might have differed.

TRM Find complete suggested responses in the Teacher's Resource Materials.

AP® APPLY THE TIP

As Great Britain transitioned to a territorial empire, they needed to account for the tremendous increase in debt, as a result of winning the Seven Years' War. Even though colonists interpreted these new taxes as an affront to colonial freedoms, challenge students to think broadly about the reasons for new imperial economic policies. As a result, students will move beyond simplistic generalizations about taxation and move toward understanding how Great Britain's policies were designed to enhance their control in North America, which as students should recall came at the expense of both British citizens and American colonists.

In the **TEACHING STRATEGY** note on p. 82, students were asked to analyze a quote by Edmund Burke. Remind students of Burke's statement and review how it is essentially describing the result of the policy of salutary neglect, which was not so much an imperial policy as the result of not imposing a policy on the colonies. Ask students to use this quote to illustrate the colonists' reactions to British laws that illustrated an end to salutary neglect, including the reasons for colonial discontent with the Currency Act, the Sugar Act, and the Stamp Act.

TEACHING STRATEGY

FIGURE 5.1 offers students practice in reading data for patterns and drawing inferences from those trends. Guide students' analysis with the following questions:

- **How does this graph provide evidence that the British Empire was in debt?** *Civil spending remains essentially flat and consistently falls well below military spending.*
- **What evidence does it provide that military spending — particularly wars — caused this debt?** *Military spending frequently rises above net tax income, with wars creating massive spikes where spending dramatically outpaces revenue.*

CHECK FOR UNDERSTANDING

Ask students: **How did Britain's empire become costly?** *Supplying, provisioning, and paying troops to fight for seven years, thousands of miles from home, was extremely expensive, as was stationing troops afterward to protect the colonies.*

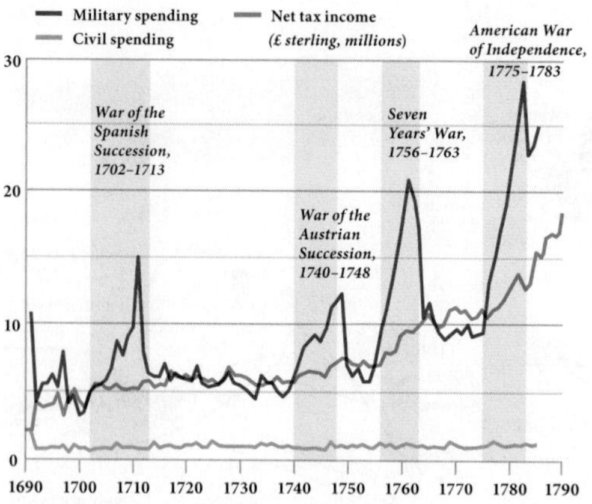

FIGURE 5.1 The Cost of Empire, 1690–1790

It cost money to build and maintain an empire. As Britain built a great navy, subsidized the armies of European allies, and fought four wars against France and Spain between 1702 and 1783, military expenditures soared. Tax revenues did not keep pace, so the government created a large national debt by issuing bonds for millions of pounds. This policy created a class of wealthy financiers, led to political protests, and eventually prompted attempts to tax the American colonists.

heavy penalties, including death or forced "transportation" to America as indentured servants. (Despite colonial protests, nearly fifty thousand English criminals had already been shipped to America to be sold as indentured servants.)

The price of empire abroad was thus larger government and higher taxes at home. Members of two British opposition parties, the Radical Whigs and the Country Party, complained that the huge war debt placed the nation at the mercy of the "monied interests," the banks and financiers who reaped millions of pounds in interest from government bonds. To reverse the growth of government and the threat to personal liberty and property rights, British reformers demanded that Parliament represent a broader spectrum of the property-owning classes. The Radical Whig John Wilkes condemned rotten boroughs — sparsely populated, aristocratic-controlled electoral districts — and demanded greater representation for rapidly growing commercial and manufacturing cities. The war thus transformed British politics.

The war also revealed how little power Britain wielded in its American colonies. In theory, royal governors had extensive political powers; in reality, they shared power with the colonial assemblies, which outraged British officials. Moreover, colonial merchants had evaded trade duties for decades by bribing customs officials. To end that practice, Parliament passed the Revenue Act of 1762, which required absentee customs officers to take up their posts in the colonies, rather than hiring underpaid assistants to do their work. The ministry also instructed the Royal Navy to seize American vessels carrying food crops from the mainland colonies to the French West Indies. It was absurd, declared a British politician, that French armies attempting "to Destroy one English province . . . are actually supported by Bread raised in another."

Britain's military victory brought another fundamental shift in policy: a new peacetime deployment of 15 royal battalions — some 7,500 troops — in North America. In part the move was strategic. The troops would maintain Britain's hold on its vast new North American territory: they would prevent colonists from settling in the trans-Appalachian west in defiance of the Proclamation of 1763 (see "The Great War for Empire" in Chapter 4), while managing relations with Native Americans and 60,000 French residents of Canada, Britain's newly conquered colony (Map 5.2).

In part, too, the decision to deploy peacetime troops had financial implications. The cost of supporting these troops was estimated at £225,000 per year, and Parliament expected that the colonies would bear the cost of the troops stationed in America. The king's ministers agreed that Parliament could no longer let them off the hook for the costs of empire. The greatest gains from the war had come in North America, where the specter of French encirclement had finally been lifted, and the greatest new postwar expenses were being incurred in North America as well.

George Grenville and the Reform Impulse

The challenge of raising revenue from the colonies fell first to George Grenville. Widely regarded as "one of the ablest men in Great Britain," Grenville understood the need for far-reaching imperial reform. He first passed the Currency Act of 1764, which banned the American colonies from using paper money as legal tender.

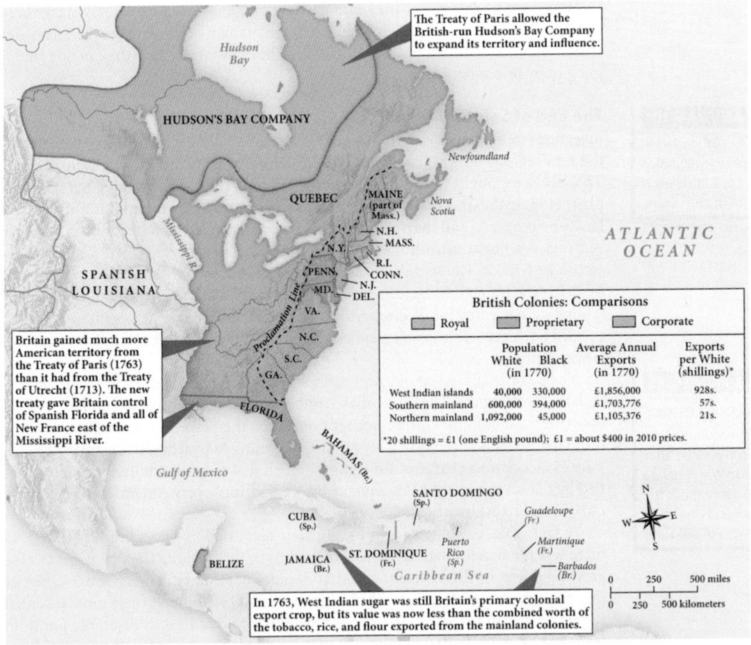

MAP 5.2 Britain's American Empire in 1763
The Treaty of Paris gave Britain control of the eastern half of North America and returned a few captured sugar islands in the West Indies to France. To protect the empire's new mainland territories, British ministers dispatched troops to Florida and Quebec. They also sent troops to uphold the terms of the Proclamation of 1763, which prohibited Anglo-American settlement west of the Appalachian Mountains.

AP® THEME

WOR: America in the World

Use **MAP 5.2** to help students see the major expansion of British territorial holdings that resulted from defeat of the French.

Colonial shopkeepers, planters, and farmers had used local currency, which was worth less than British pounds sterling, to pay their debts to British merchants. The Currency Act ensured that merchants would no longer be paid in money printed in the colonies, boosting their profits and British wealth.

The Sugar Act Grenville also won parliamentary approval of the **Sugar Act of 1764** to replace the widely ignored Molasses Act of 1733 (see "Mercantilism and the American Colonies" in Chapter 3). The earlier act had set a tax rate of 6 pence per gallon on French molasses, in effect outlawing the trade, since such a high tax made it unprofitable — which was Parliament's intention, since trade with the French sugar colonies violated the spirit of the Navigation Acts and enriched Britain's perennial European enemy. But French molasses was cheap and abundant, so colonial merchants bought it anyway and, instead of paying the tax, bribed customs officials at the going rate of 1.5 pence per gallon to look the other way. The 1764 act was intended to make the trade in foreign molasses legal for the first time and collect a duty of 3 pence per gallon, which merchants could pay and still turn a profit.

Sugar Act of 1764
British law that lowered the duty on French molasses and raised penalties for smuggling. New England merchants opposed both the tax and the provision that they would be tried in a vice-admiralty court.

This carefully crafted policy received little support in America. New England merchants, among them John Hancock of Boston, had made their fortunes smuggling French molasses. In 1754, Boston merchants paid customs duties on a mere 400

AP® APPLY THE TIP

Divide students into 5–6 groups and assign each a significant colonial leader, including Benjamin Franklin, James Otis, John Hancock, Patrick Henry, Samuel Adams, Paul Revere, and others as needed. Ask each team to briefly research the actions of their assigned colonial leader and make a case for that individual to be awarded the title "Leader of the People" for their contributions leading to the American Revolution. Ask groups to provide specific supporting details and at least one primary source reference for the importance of their assigned leader in energizing ideas of independence and resistance to British law. Next, have each group present their case to the class and conduct a class vote on the colonial leader who deserves the title "Leader of the People."

TRM Find complete suggested responses in the Teacher's Resource Materials.

CHECK FOR UNDERSTANDING

Ask students: **How did Grenville attempt to raise revenue? What was the result?** *The Currency Act enforced payment in pounds sterling, not paper currency, and the Sugar Act attempted to end sugar smuggling by reducing the tax rate on sugar imports. Colonists protested the laws as unjust and continued their smuggling operations.*

AP® SKILLS & PROCESSES

CONTEXTUALIZATION

Ask the **CONTEXTUALIZATION** question to assess students' ability to compare diverse perspectives on the same historical event. Scaffold this question by pointing out that Franklin proposed this idea, which was seen as radical by many on both sides of the Atlantic. Ask students to identify the different reasons that leaders in Parliament and in the colonies came to the same conclusion.

TRM Find complete suggested responses in the Teacher's Resource Materials.

hogsheads of molasses, yet they imported 40,000 hogsheads for use by sixty-three Massachusetts rum distilleries. Publicly, the merchants claimed that the Sugar Act would ruin the distilling industry; privately, they vowed to evade the duty by smuggling or by bribing officials.

AP® EXAM TIP

The role of colonial leaders in energizing ideas of independence and resistance to British law is important to know for the AP® Exam.

The End of Salutary Neglect More important, colonists raised constitutional objections to the Sugar Act. In Massachusetts, the leader of the assembly argued that the new legislation was "contrary to a fundamental Principall of our Constitution: That all Taxes ought to originate with the people." In Rhode Island, Governor Stephen Hopkins warned: "They who are taxed at pleasure by others cannot possibly have any property, and they who have no property, can have no freedom." The Sugar Act raised other constitutional issues as well. Merchants prosecuted under the act would be tried in vice-admiralty courts, tribunals governing the high seas and run by British-appointed judges. Previously, merchants accused of Navigation Acts violations were tried by local common-law courts, where friendly juries often acquitted them. The Sugar Act instead extended the jurisdiction of the vice-admiralty courts to all customs offenses.

AP® SKILLS & PROCESSES

MAKING CONNECTIONS

How did the reactions of the colonists to British policies after the French and Indian War illustrate relationships to ideas about the rights of British subjects, rights of individuals, and traditions of self-rule?

The Sugar Act revived old American fears that colonists would not be treated as equals of the English. The influential Virginia planter Richard Bland emphasized that the American colonists "were not sent out to be the Slaves but to be the Equals of those that remained behind." John Adams, the young Massachusetts lawyer defending John Hancock on a charge of smuggling, argued that the vice-admiralty courts specified by the act diminished this equality by "degrad[ing] every American . . . below the rank of an Englishman."

In fact, accused smugglers in Britain were also tried in vice-admiralty courts, so there was no discrimination against Americans in that regard. The real issue was the growing power of the British state. After decades of salutary neglect, Americans saw that the new imperial regime would deprive them "of some of their most essential Rights as British subjects," as a committee of the Massachusetts assembly put it. In response, Royal Governor Francis Bernard replied: "The rule that a British subject shall not be bound by laws or liable to taxes, but what he has consented to by his representatives must be confined to the inhabitants of Great Britain only." To Bernard, Grenville, and other imperial reformers, Americans were second-class subjects of the king, with rights limited by the Navigation Acts, parliamentary laws, and British interests.

An Open Challenge: The Stamp Act

Stamp Act of 1765
British law imposing a tax on all paper used in the colonies. Widespread resistance to the Stamp Act prevented it from taking effect and led to its repeal in 1766.

Another new tax, the **Stamp Act of 1765**, sparked the first great imperial crisis. Grenville hoped the Stamp Act would raise £60,000 per year. The act would require a tax stamp on all printed items, from college diplomas, court documents, land titles, and contracts to newspapers, almanacs, and playing cards. It was ingeniously designed. Like its counterpart in England, it bore more heavily on the rich, since it charged only a penny a sheet for newspapers and other common items but up to £10 for a lawyer's license. It also required no new bureaucracy; stamped paper would be delivered to colonial ports and sold to printers in lieu of unstamped stock.

AP® SKILLS & PROCESSES

CONTEXTUALIZATION

Why did most British and colonial leaders reject the idea that the colonies should be represented in Parliament?

Benjamin Franklin, agent of the Pennsylvania assembly, proposed a different solution: American representation in Parliament. "If you chuse to tax us," he wrote, "give us Members in your Legislature, and let us be one People." With the exception of William Pitt, British politicians rejected Franklin's idea as too radical. They argued that the colonists already had virtual representation in Parliament because some of its members were transatlantic merchants and West Indian sugar planters. Colonial leaders were equally skeptical of Franklin's plan. Americans were "situate at a great Distance from their Mother Country," the Connecticut assembly declared, and therefore "cannot participate in the general Legislature of the Nation."

AP® SKILLS & PROCESSES

MAKING CONNECTIONS

To help students make connections, consider having students match broader historical processes with the specific historical ideas of self-rule, rights of British subjects, and rights of individuals. For example, if you provide students with developments and ideas such as Enlightenment, Salutary Neglect, and political autonomy, students can make connections between a broad historical development such as the Enlightenment and the concept of self-rule. By providing students with possible answers, students can focus on making connections.

The House of Commons ignored American opposition and passed the act by an overwhelming majority of 205 to 49. At the request of General Thomas Gage, the British military commander in America, Parliament also passed the **Quartering Act of 1765**, which ensured that British troops could not be boarded in private homes but required colonial governments to provide barracks and food for them. New York's colonial assembly regarded this requirement as another form of taxation and refused to pay the cost of housing and feeding its soldiers. Finally, Parliament approved Grenville's proposal that violations of the Stamp Act be tried in vice-admiralty courts.

Protesting the Stamp Act in Portsmouth, New Hampshire Throughout the colonies, disciplined mobs protesting the Stamp Act forced stamp distributors to resign their offices. In this engraving, protesters in the small city of Portsmouth, New Hampshire, stone an effigy of the distributor as other members of the mob carry off a coffin representing the death of American "Liberty." Illustration from "Interesting Events in the History of the U.S." by J. W. Barber, 1829/Picture Research Consultants & Archives.

Using the doctrine of parliamentary supremacy, Grenville had begun to fashion a centralized imperial system in America much like that already in place in Ireland: British officials would govern the colonies with little regard for the local assemblies. Consequently, the prime minister's plan provoked a constitutional confrontation on the specific issues of taxation, jury trials, and military quartering as well as on the general question of representative self-government.

Quartering Act of 1765
A British law passed by Parliament at the request of General Thomas Gage, the British military commander in America, that required colonial governments to provide barracks and food for British troops.

THE DYNAMICS OF REBELLION, 1765–1770

What was the relationship between formal protests against Parliament and popular resistance in the years between 1765 and 1770?

In the name of reform, Grenville had thrown down the gauntlet to the Americans. The colonists had often resisted unpopular laws and aggressive governors, but they had faced an all-out attack on their institutions only once before — in 1686, when James II had unilaterally imposed the Dominion of New England. Now the danger was even greater because both the king and Parliament backed reform. But the Patriots, as the defenders of American rights came to be called, met the challenge posed by Grenville and his successor, Charles Townshend. They organized protests — formal and informal, violent as well as peaceful — and fashioned a compelling ideology of resistance.

AP® EXAM TIP
Evaluate the role of popular movements that incorporated activism by laborers, artisans, and women in energizing the push for independence.

Formal Protests and the Politics of the Crowd

Virginia's House of Burgesses was the first formal body to complain. In May 1765, hotheaded young Patrick Henry denounced Grenville's legislation and attacked King George III (r. 1760–1820) for supporting it. He compared the king to Charles I, whose tyranny had led to his overthrow and execution in the 1640s. These remarks, which bordered on treason, frightened the Burgesses; nonetheless, they condemned the Stamp Act's "manifest Tendency to Destroy American freedom." In Massachusetts, James Otis, another republican-minded firebrand, persuaded the House of Representatives to call a meeting of all the mainland colonies "to implore Relief" from the act.

AP® THEME

PCE: Politics and Power

Ask students: **How does the image of the Stamp Act protest illustrate the way political activism by popular movements energized American resistance to British policies?** *The image illustrates an example of mob action of large numbers, which threatened violence. During this time, popular opposition often took violent forms, which proved an effective form of protest to nullify the Stamp Act through the intimidation of royal officials.*

AP® SKILLS & PROCESSES

DEVELOPMENTS AND PROCESSES

Students are required to distinguish between both real and perceived constraints as Great Britain imposed its imperial authority. Have students define what would encompass a real and perceived threat. After they have defined each, have students identify an example of a real threat and perceived threat in the American colonies from 1754–1766.

AP® APPLY THE TIP

Provide students with primary source images of the Boston Massacre, Edenton Tea Party, and Sons of Liberty attacks on Andrew Oliver and Thomas Hutchinson. With each image, provide students with a brief historical sketch of the events surrounding the image. Ask students to analyze the images as historical sources, noting the point of view of the artists, their intended audience, and the purpose behind creating the image. Use the images to engage students in a discussion of the role of laborers and artisans (the "middling" and poor class) as well as women in energizing the push for independence. Next, ask students to write a response to each image from an opposing point of view.

TEACHING STRATEGY

For a loyalist perspective on Britain's imperial policy, assign Peter Oliver's "Origin and Progress of the American Rebellion" in Chapter 5 of the companion reader, *Sources for America's History*.

Stamp Act Congress
A congress of delegates from nine assemblies that met in New York City in October 1765 to protest the loss of American "rights and liberties." The congress challenged Parliament by declaring that only the colonists' elected representatives could tax them.

The Stamp Act Congress Nine assemblies sent delegates to the **Stamp Act Congress**, which met in New York City in October 1765. The congress protested the loss of American "rights and liberties," especially the right to trial by jury. It also challenged the constitutionality of both the Stamp and Sugar Acts by declaring that only the colonists' elected representatives could tax them. Still, moderate-minded delegates wanted compromise, not confrontation. They assured Parliament that Americans "glory in being subjects of the best of Kings" and humbly petitioned for repeal of the Stamp Act. Other influential Americans favored active (but peaceful) resistance, organizing a boycott of British goods.

Sons of Liberty
Colonists — primarily middling merchants and artisans — who banded together to protest the Stamp Act and other imperial reforms of the 1760s. The group originated in Boston in 1765 but soon spread to all the colonies.

Crowd Actions Popular opposition also took a violent form, however. When the Stamp Act went into effect on November 1, 1765, disciplined mobs demanded the resignation of stamp-tax collectors. In Boston, a group calling itself the **Sons of Liberty** burned an effigy of collector Andrew Oliver and then destroyed Oliver's new brick warehouse. Two weeks later, Bostonians attacked the house of Lieutenant Governor Thomas Hutchinson, Oliver's brother-in-law and a prominent defender of imperial authority, breaking his furniture, looting his wine cellar, and setting fire to his library. Soon, groups calling themselves Sons of Liberty were organizing crowd activities in cities and towns throughout the colonies.

Wealthy merchants and Patriot lawyers, such as John Hancock and John Adams, encouraged the mobs, which were usually led by middling artisans and minor merchants. In New York City, nearly three thousand shopkeepers, artisans, laborers, and seamen marched through the streets breaking windows and crying "Liberty!" Resistance to the Stamp Act spread far beyond the port cities. In nearly every colony, angry crowds — the "rabble," their detractors called them — intimidated royal officials. Near Wethersfield, Connecticut, five hundred farmers seized tax collector Jared Ingersoll and forced him to resign his office in "the Cause of the People."

AP® SKILLS & PROCESSES

COMPARISON

Why did the Stamp Act arouse so much more resistance than the Sugar Act?

The Motives of the Crowd Such crowd actions were common in both Britain and America, and protesters had many motives. Roused by the Great Awakening, evangelical Protestants resented arrogant British military officers and corrupt royal bureaucrats. In New England, where rioters invoked the antimonarchy sentiments of their great-grandparents, an anonymous letter sent to a Boston newspaper promising to save "all the Freeborn Sons of America" was signed "Oliver Cromwell," the English republican revolutionary of the 1650s. In New York City, Sons of Liberty leaders Isaac Sears and Alexander McDougall were minor merchants and Radical Whigs who feared that imperial reform would undermine political liberty. The mobs also included apprentices, day laborers, and unemployed sailors: young men with their own notions of liberty who — especially if they had been drinking — were quick to resort to violence.

Nearly everywhere popular resistance nullified the Stamp Act. Fearing an assault on Fort George, New York, lieutenant governor Cadwallader Colden called on General Gage to use his small military force to protect the stamps. Gage refused. "Fire from the Fort might disperse the Mob, but it would not quell them," he told Colden, and the result would be "an Insurrection, the Commencement of Civil War." The tax was collected in Barbados and Jamaica, but frightened collectors resigned their offices in all thirteen colonies that would eventually join in the Declaration of Independence. This popular insurrection gave a democratic cast to the emerging Patriot movement. "Nothing is wanting but your own Resolution," declared a New York rioter, "for great is the Authority and Power of the People."

The Ideological Roots of Resistance

Some Americans couched their resistance in constitutional terms. Many were lawyers or well-educated merchants and planters. Composing pamphlets of remarkable

AP® SKILLS & PROCESSES

COMPARISON

The **COMPARISON** question allows students to compare the different effects of two events that happened in close proximity to each other. Help students to recognize that this question begins from the assumption that these two laws were similar — both were taxes on imports, passed a year apart — but that they caused significantly different reactions. Why did the Sugar Act provoke relatively little response, while the Stamp Act generated major protests? Extend this prompt by having students examine the motives of each law, not just the stated purpose of each.

TRM Find complete suggested responses in the Teacher's Resource Materials.

AP® THEME

PCE: Politics and Power

Discuss with students how the text reveals the ways that American resistance was energized by colonial leaders, as well as by the political activism of laborers and artisans.

CHECK FOR UNDERSTANDING

Ask students to compare and contrast formal protests and crowd actions in response to the Stamp Act. *Both expressed dissatisfaction with this law, but formal protests relied on rational argument by a few education leaders through legal channels, while mob action relied on larger numbers and the threat of violence — though Patriot leaders also backed this approach.*

political sophistication, they gave the resistance movement its rationale, its political agenda, and its leaders.

Patriot writers drew on three intellectual traditions. The first was **English common law**, the centuries-old body of legal rules and procedures that protected the lives and property of the monarch's subjects. In the famous *Writs of Assistance* case of 1761, Boston lawyer James Otis invoked English legal precedents to challenge open-ended search warrants. In demanding a jury trial for John Hancock in the late 1760s, John Adams appealed to the Magna Carta (1215), the ancient document that, said Adams, "has for many Centuries been esteemed by Englishmen, as one of the . . . firmest Bulwarks of their Liberties." Other lawyers protested that new strictures violated specific "liberties and privileges" granted in colonial charters or embodied in Britain's "ancient constitution."

English common law
The centuries-old body of legal rules and procedures that protected the lives and property of the British monarch's subjects.

AP® EXAM TIP
Explain the context in which common law, Enlightenment thought, and Whig ideals influenced calls for independence.

Enlightenment rationalism provided Patriots with a second important intellectual resource. Virginia planter Thomas Jefferson and other Patriots drew on the writings of John Locke, who had argued that all individuals possessed certain **natural rights** — life, liberty, and property — that governments must protect (see "The Enlightenment in America" in Chapter 4). Locke contended further that governments originated in social compacts among ordinary people, not in the divine right of kings, and that when they failed to protect these rights, the people had a right to rebel against them. Patriots were also influenced by the French philosopher Montesquieu, who had maintained that a "separation of powers" among government departments prevented arbitrary rule. In Britain, they feared, this separation had broken down, allowing corrupt government officials to gain too much influence in Parliament.

natural rights
The rights to life, liberty, and property. According to John Locke, governments derived from social compacts that people made to preserve their natural rights.

The republican and Whig strands of the English political tradition provided a third ideological source for American Patriots. Puritan New England had long venerated the Commonwealth era (1649–1660), when England had been a republic. After the Glorious Revolution of 1688–1689, many colonists praised the English Whigs for creating a constitutional monarchy that prevented the king from imposing taxes and other measures. John Dickinson's *Letters from a Farmer in Pennsylvania* (1768) urged colonists to "remember your ancestors and your posterity" and oppose parliamentary taxes. The letters circulated widely and served as an early call to resistance. If Parliament could tax the colonies without their consent, he wrote, "our boasted liberty is but A sound and nothing else."

Such arguments, widely publicized in newspapers and pamphlets, gave intellectual substance to the Patriot movement and turned a series of impromptu riots, tax protests, and boycotts of British manufactures into a formidable political force.

Phillis Wheatley Born in West Africa and enslaved as a child, Phillis Wheatley was purchased by Boston merchant and tailor John Wheatley when she was eight. Tutored by Wheatley's children, Phillis learned to read English, Greek, and Latin by the age of twelve. This engraving, which pictures her at a writing desk, was the frontispiece for her *Poems on Various Subjects, Religious and Moral* (1773), which was praised by George Washington and gained attention in both Britain and the colonies. Freed upon the death of her master, Wheatley married John Peters, a free black man. He was later imprisoned for debt, forcing Wheatley to take employment as a maid. She died in 1784 at age thirty-one; none of her three children survived infancy. Library of Congress, 3b04682.

Another Kind of Freedom

"We are taxed without our own consent," Dickinson wrote in one of his *Letters*. "We are therefore — SLAVES." As Patriot writers argued that taxation without representation made colonists the slaves of Parliament, many, including Benjamin Franklin in Philadelphia and James Otis in Massachusetts, also began to condemn the institution of chattel slavery itself as a violation of slaves' natural rights. African Americans made the connection as well. In Massachusetts, enslaved laborers submitted at least four petitions to the legislature asking that slavery be abolished. As one petition noted, slaves "have in common with other men,

AP® APPLY THE TIP

Ask students to consider what turns a rebellion into a revolution and allow them to discuss possible answers. Help students understand that rebellions not only include political actions like protests and riots but occur in the ideas that justify these actions. Then ask students to write the word "Revolution" in the center of a sheet of paper with three corresponding topics reading "English Common Law," "Enlightenment Thought," and "Whig Ideals." Have students closely read the "The Ideological Roots of Resistance" section and identify the ways in which each of these three topics helped to create the American Revolution. Then ask students to connect at least one "rebellious" action by the colonists to the ideology of "revolution" as illustrated by these three sources of ideology.

AP® THEME

NAT: American and National Identity

Point out to students that though Phillis Wheatley became famous among colonial leaders in 1773 for writing about freedom, she gained her own freedom only in 1778 after the death of her master.

AP® THEME

NAT: American and National Identity

While students are reading "The Ideological Roots of Resistance" section, help them understand how ideas about freedom and individualism, including Enlightenment ideas, helped to develop a sense of American identity.

CHECK FOR UNDERSTANDING

Ask students to identify different intellectual traditions that inspired American rebellion.

Intellectual traditions included the English common law's protection of rights and property, Enlightenment notions of natural rights, and Whig and republican ideas of limited government.

TEACHING STRATEGY

Complement the text's discussion of the "Another Kind of Freedom" section with "Episode 2: Revolution" (31:00-38:00) of the *Africans in America* video series on PBS. This video series provides a perspective on the experience of black Americans beginning in the early seventeenth century. This episode explores blacks' response to Stamp Act protests, including consequences of the Patriots' use of the language of slavery. After viewing the segment, ask students to discuss what the effects of the Stamp Act were for African Americans and why. Access the video by searching "PBS Africans in America Revolution."

TEACHING STRATEGY

Use John Dickinson's *Letters from a Farmer in Pennsylvania* to illustrate Patriot ideas, and have students analyze his argument about taxation and representation. Access this document by searching "Dickinson Letters from a Farmer in Pennsylvania."

AP® APPLY THE TIP

In Letter VII of his *Letters from a Farmer in Pennsylvania* (1768), Patriot leader John Dickinson wrote, "We are taxed without our own consent. We are therefore – SLAVES" (Dickinson, 78). Use this statement and other arguments by Patriot leaders against the British government to have students write a petition to a colonial government to end slavery. Students should outline the ways in which the system of slavery in the colonies contradicted the revolutionary ideals of the Patriot cause. Then ask volunteers to read their petition aloud while you record their list of arguments. Help students connect the arguments against slavery to the ideals expressed by the Enlightenment, Great Awakening, Radical Whigs, etc. Once several students have read, ask the class to consider why the arguments to end slavery at the time of the American Revolution failed as well as the long-term impact of the decision to ignore the issue of slavery in the Revolutionary Era.

AP® SKILLS & PROCESSES

COMPARISON

Use the **COMPARISON** question to invite students to compare diverse reactions to the same historical development, namely challenges to the institution of slavery. Begin by reminding students that all colonies had slavery, so regional differences in reaction were more complicated than a slave-free dichotomy. Hints about course themes, such as economic self-interest versus intellectual ideas, might help students make the contrast. Extend this prompt by asking students to consider whether economics, not just ideas, influenced northern reactions just as it did southern reactions.

TRM Find complete suggested responses in the Teacher's Resource Materials.

AP® EXAM TIP

Illustrating the contradictions between the ideals of the American Revolution and the system of slavery in the colonies is critical to success on AP® Exam.

AP® SKILLS & PROCESSES

COMPARISON

Why were southerners more threatened by challenges to the institution of slavery than northerners?

a natural right to be free, and without molestation, to enjoy such property, as they may acquire by their industry."

In the southern colonies, where enslaved people constituted half or more of the population and the economy depended on their servitude, the quest for freedom alarmed slaveholders. In November 1773, a group of Virginia slaves hoped to win their freedom by supporting British troops that, they heard, would soon arrive in the colony. Their plan was uncovered, and, as James Madison wrote, "proper precautions" were taken "to prevent the Infection" from spreading. He fully understood how important it was to defend the colonists' liberties without allowing the idea of natural rights to undermine the institution of slavery. "It is prudent," he wrote, "such things should be concealed as well as suppressed." Throughout the Revolution, the quest for African American rights and liberties would play out alongside that of the colonies, but unlike national independence, the liberation of African Americans would not be fulfilled for many generations.

Parliament and Patriots Square Off Again

When news of the Stamp Act riots and the boycott reached Britain, Parliament was already in turmoil. Disputes over domestic policy had led George III to dismiss Grenville as prime minister. However, Grenville's allies demanded that imperial reform continue, if necessary at gunpoint.

Yet a majority in Parliament was persuaded that the Stamp Act was cutting deeply into British exports and thus doing more harm than good. "The Avenues of Trade are all shut up," a Bristol merchant told Parliament: "We have no Remittances and are at our Witts End for want of Money to fulfill our Engagements with our Tradesmen." Grenville's successor, the Earl of Rockingham, forged a compromise. He repealed the Stamp Act and reduced the duty on molasses imposed by the Sugar Act to a penny a gallon. Then he pacified imperial reformers and hard-liners with the **Declaratory Act of 1766**, which explicitly reaffirmed Parliament's "full power and authority to make laws and statutes . . . to bind the colonies and people of America . . . in all cases whatsoever." By swiftly ending the Stamp Act crisis, Rockingham hoped it would be forgotten just as quickly.

Declaratory Act of 1766
Law asserting Parliament's unassailable right to legislate for its British colonies "in all cases whatsoever."

Townshend Act of 1767
British law that established new duties on tea, glass, lead, paper, and painters' colors imported into the colonies. The Townshend duties led to boycotts and heightened tensions between Britain and the American colonies.

Celebrating Repeal This British cartoon mocking supporters of the Stamp Act—"The Repeal, or the Funeral Procession of Miss Americ-Stamp"—was probably commissioned by merchants trading with America. Preceded by two flag bearers, George Grenville, the author of the legislation, carries a miniature coffin (representing the act) to a tomb, as a dog urinates on the leader of the procession. Two bales on the wharf, labeled "Stamps from America" and "Black cloth return'd from America," testify to the failure of the act. The Granger Collection, New York.

Charles Townshend Steps In Often the course of history is changed by a small event — an illness, a personal grudge, a chance remark. That was the case in 1767, when George III named William Pitt to head a new government. Pitt, chronically ill and often absent from parliamentary debates, left chancellor of the exchequer Charles Townshend in command. Pitt was sympathetic toward America; Townshend was not. He had strongly supported the Stamp Act, and in 1767 he promised to find a new source of revenue in America.

The new tax legislation, the **Townshend Act of 1767**, had both fiscal and political goals. It imposed duties on colonial imports of tea, glass, lead paper, and painters' colors that were expected to raise about £40,000 a year. Though Townshend did allocate some of this revenue for American military expenses, he

TEACHING STRATEGY

Studying the image of the British cartoon can help students deepen their understanding of point of view, as a cartoonist in Britain (rather than America) mocks parliamentary policy. Guide students' analysis with the following questions:

- **Who is depicted in this British cartoon?** *George Grenville and supporters of the Stamp Act.*
- **The caption indicates that the cartoonist is mocking Stamp Act supporters. What in the image provides evidence for this assumption?** *The image uses exaggeration to mock the figures. This includes the extreme emotion of some, including the man wiping tears from his eyes; the oversized Anglican priests; and the absurdity of holding a funeral procession for a law, complete with a miniature coffin. The dog urinating on the procession's leader is also an obvious clue.*
- **How does knowing that a cartoonist in Britain made this image help you understand points of view in this conflict?** *It suggests that not everyone in Britain supported government policies, just as not all Americans supported Patriot actions. In this case, those who benefitted from commerce with the colonies had a direct interest in seeing the law repealed.*

earmarked most of it to pay the salaries of royal governors, judges, and other imperial officials, who had always previously been paid by colonial assemblies. Now, he hoped, royal appointees would be financially independent of the colonies and could therefore enforce parliamentary laws and carry out the king's instructions without regard for local opinion. Townshend next devised the Revenue Act of 1767, which created a board of customs commissioners in Boston and vice-admiralty courts in Halifax, Boston, Philadelphia, and Charleston. By using parliamentary taxes to finance imperial administration, Townshend intended to undermine American political institutions.

The Townshend duties revived the constitutional debate over taxation. During the hearings to repeal the Stamp Act, Benjamin Franklin and others claimed that Americans only objected to internal taxes like the Stamp Act. They had always been willing to pay external taxes — that is, duties on trade such as those long mandated by the Navigation Acts. In fact, most colonists opposed all parliamentary taxation and would not have recognized a distinction between external and internal taxes. Townshend himself thought this distinction was "perfect nonsense," but he took Franklin at his word and laid duties only on trade.

A Second Boycott and the Daughters of Liberty Most colonial leaders rejected the legitimacy of Townshend's measures. In February 1768, the Massachusetts assembly condemned the Townshend Act, and Boston and New York merchants began a new boycott of British goods. Throughout Puritan New England, ministers and public officials discouraged the purchase of "foreign superfluities" and promoted the domestic manufacture of cloth and other necessities.

American women, ordinarily excluded from public affairs, became crucial to the **nonimportation movement**. They reduced their households' consumption of imported goods and produced large quantities of homespun cloth to help fill the gap left by boycotted textiles. Pious farmwives spun yarn at their ministers' homes. In Berwick, Maine, "true Daughters of Liberty" celebrated American products by "drinking rye coffee and dining on bear venison." Other women's groups supported the boycott with charitable work, spinning flax and wool for the needy. Just as Patriot men followed tradition by joining crowd actions, so women's protests reflected their customary concern for the well-being of the community (Figure 5.2).

nonimportation movement
The effort to protest parliamentary legislation by boycotting British goods. This occurred in 1766, in response to the Stamp Act; in 1768, after the Townshend duties; and in 1774, after the Coercive Acts.

AP® SKILLS & PROCESSES

DEVELOPMENTS AND PROCESSES

How did the nonimportation movement bring women into the political sphere?

Newspapers celebrated these exploits of the Daughters of Liberty. One Massachusetts town proudly claimed an annual output of 30,000 yards of cloth; East Hartford, Connecticut, reported 17,000 yards. This surge in domestic production did not offset the loss of British imports, which had averaged about 10 million yards of cloth annually, but it brought thousands of women into the public arena.

The boycott mobilized many American men as well. In the seaport cities, the Sons of Liberty published the names of merchants who imported British goods and harassed their employees and customers. By March 1769, the nonimportation movement had spread to Philadelphia; two months later, the members of the Virginia House of Burgesses vowed not to buy dutied articles, luxury goods, or imported slaves. Reflecting colonial self-confidence, Benjamin Franklin called for a return to the pre-1763 mercantilist system: "Repeal the laws, renounce the right, recall the troops, refund the money, and return to the old method of requisition."

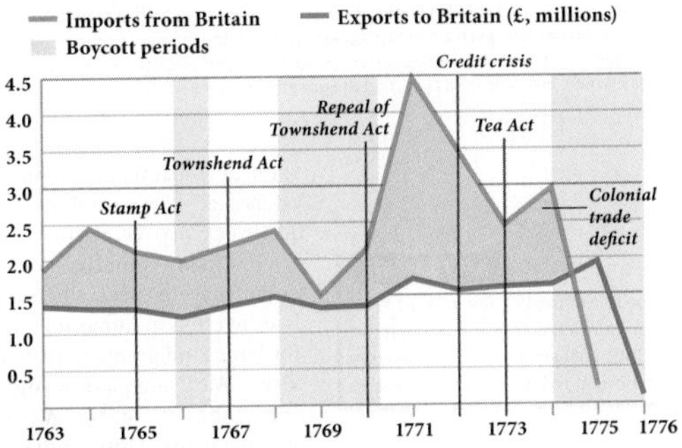

FIGURE 5.2 Trade as a Political Weapon, 1763–1776
Political upheaval did not affect the mainland colonies' exports to Britain, which rose slightly over the period, but imports fluctuated greatly. The American boycott of 1765–1766 prompted a dip in imports, but the second boycott of 1768–1770 led to a sharp drop in imports of British textiles, metal goods, and ceramics. Imports of manufactures soared after the repeal of the Townshend duties, only to plummet when the First Continental Congress proclaimed a third boycott in 1774.

AP® THEME

PCE: Politics and Power

The Daughters of Liberty offer a good example of political activism by women that strengthened American protests.

AP® SKILLS & PROCESSES

DEVELOPMENTS AND PROCESSES

Use the **DEVELOPMENTS AND PROCESSES** question to ask students to explain how ushering women into the political sphere was one short-term effect of nonimportation agreements. Remind students that women were not typically part of the public political sphere: What was it about their relationship to consumer goods that made boycotts a legitimate form of protest for them? Extend this prompt by having students consider the extent of women's public role by discussing the limitations to boycott as a means of political participation.

TRM Find complete suggested responses in the Teacher's Resource Materials.

TEACHING STRATEGY

The lesson plan "Shopkeepers in Revolutionary Boston" available through The Elizabeth Murray Project Web site uses the life of one female shopkeeper to explore how some shopkeepers debated whether to participate in boycotts. In addition to adding complexity to students' understanding of popular protest, the lesson explores the role of women in boycotts. Apart from teaching the entire lesson, teachers may find a variety of primary and secondary sources in the lesson to be useful. Access this lesson plan by searching "Elizabeth Murray Project Shopkeepers in Revolutionary Boston."

TEACHING STRATEGY

FIGURE 5.2 offers students practice in reading data for patterns and drawing inferences from those trends. Guide students' analysis with the following questions:

- **Before 1775, how would you characterize American exports to Britain? How and why did patterns change after 1775?** *From 1763 to 1775, American exports to Britain remained relatively flat. After 1775, as conflict with Britain intensified, trade in both directions suffered.*
- **In what year did the colonies suffer the worst trade deficit — the gap in value between exports and imports? What factor was primarily responsible for this deficit? How do you know?** *1771. While exports remain relatively flat (as discussed in the previous question), imports shot up dramatically, as indicated by the steep import curve.*
- **The caption indicates that the third boycott was the most effective. How does the graph confirm this conclusion?** *The first boycott period shows a modest increase in British imports, the second shows a steep decline, but the third shows an even steeper and longer decline.*

TEACHING STRATEGY

Use the image of the Edenton Ladies' Tea Party to further analyze women's roles in Patriot resistance to British policy, revealing the ways some critics perceived women's behavior as violating gender norms. Guide students' analysis with the following questions:

- **The caption indicates that the cartoonist is mocking women's participation in boycott activities. What in the image provides evidence for this assumption?** *One man and woman are kissing, suggesting that the presence of women leads to inappropriate public behavior. The woman with the gavel is depicted as unattractive and, as the caption says, "mannish." Finally, the child under the table is being neglected, licked by a urinating dog with no mother to provide protection.*
- **What does this image reveal about contemporary views of women's roles?** *The image suggests that some thought that gender norms providing a distinction between public and private spheres should be maintained. When women entered the public sphere, they disrupted orderly proceedings, while necessarily abandoning their maternal responsibilities.*

CHECK FOR UNDERSTANDING

Ask students: **What did the Townshend Act do? How did Patriots respond and what was the result?** *It imposed new taxes on colonial imports of items like paper, paint, glass, and tea. The result was a new wave of constitutional debate and boycotts.*

AP® APPLY THE TIP

Review the restrictions placed on the colonists by the Proclamation of 1763 and the reactions of the colonists. Then ask students to analyze documents in the **AP® THINKING LIKE A HISTORIAN** feature (pp. 158–159). Have students explain how reactions to the Proclamation Line by colonists antagonized both Native Americans on the frontier and British leaders in England.

AP® THEME

MIG: Migration and Settlement

Point out to students that settlement in the West was a form of migration. It affected American life by creating conflict with Britain, as imperial officials attempted to prevent settlement out West to maintain order.

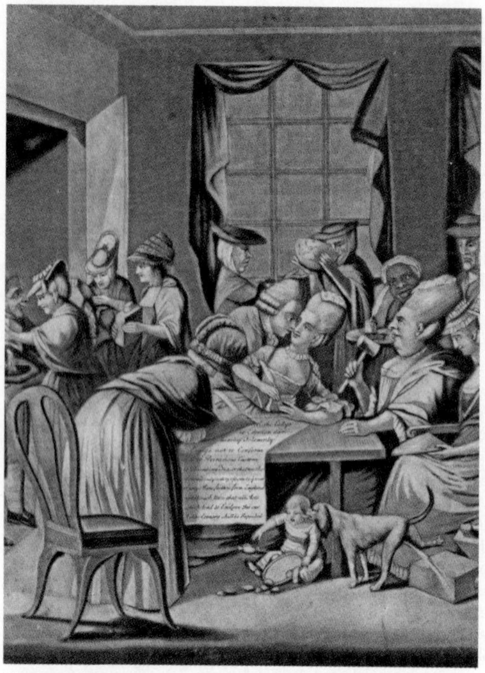

Edenton Ladies' Tea Party In October 1774, a group of fifty-one women from Edenton, North Carolina, led by Penelope Barker, created a local association to support a boycott of British goods. Patriots in the colonies praised the Edenton Tea Party, which was one of the first formal female political associations in North America, but it was ridiculed in Britain, where this cartoon appeared in March 1775. The women are given a mannish appearance, and the themes of promiscuity and neglect to their female duties are suggested by the presence of a slave and an amorous man, the neglected child, and the urinating dog. Library of Congress, 19468.

Despite the enthusiasm of Patriots, nonimportation—accompanied by pressure on merchants and consumers who resisted it—exposed and heightened social conflict. Not only royal officials but also merchants, farmers, and ordinary folk were subject to new forms of surveillance and coercion imposed by Patriot leaders—a pattern that would only become more pronounced as the imperial crisis unfolded.

Troops to Boston American resistance only increased British determination. When the Massachusetts assembly's letter opposing the Townshend duties reached London, Lord Hillsborough, the secretary of state for American affairs, branded it "unjustifiable opposition to the constitutional authority of Parliament." To strengthen the "Hand of Government" in Massachusetts, Hillsborough dispatched General Thomas Gage and 2,000 British troops to Boston (Map 5.3). Once in Massachusetts, Gage accused its leaders of "Treasonable and desperate Resolves" and advised the ministry to "Quash this Spirit at a Blow." In 1765, American resistance to the Stamp Act had sparked a parliamentary debate; in 1768, it provoked a plan for military coercion.

The Problem of the West

At the same time that successive ministries addressed the problem of raising a colonial revenue, they quarreled over how to manage the vast new inland territory—about half a billion acres—acquired in the Treaty of Paris in 1763 (see "The Great War for Empire" in Chapter 4). The Proclamation Line had drawn a boundary between the colonies and Indian country. The line was originally intended as a temporary barrier. It prohibited settlement in Indian country "for the present, and until our further Pleasure be known." The Proclamation also created three new mainland colonies—Quebec, East Florida, and West Florida—and thus opened new opportunities at the northern and southern extremities of British North America (Map 5.4), p. 164.

AP® EXAM TIP

The role of the Proclamation of 1763 in growing animosity between the British government and colonists is important to know on the AP® Exam.

But many colonists looked west rather than north or south. Four groups in the colonies were especially interested in westward expansion. First, gentlemen who had invested in numerous land speculation companies were petitioning the crown for large land grants in the Ohio country. Second, officers who served in the Seven Years' War were paid in land warrants—up to 5,000 acres for field officers—and some, led by George Washington, were exploring possible sites beyond the Appalachians. Third, Indian traders who had received large grants from the Ohio Indians hoped to sell land titles. And fourth, thousands of squatters were following the roads cut to the Ohio by the Braddock and Forbes campaigns during the Seven Years' War to take up lands in the hope that they could later receive a title to them. "The roads are . . . alive with Men, Women, Children, and Cattle from Jersey, Pennsylvania, and Maryland," wrote one astonished observer (see "Thinking Like a Historian," p. 158).

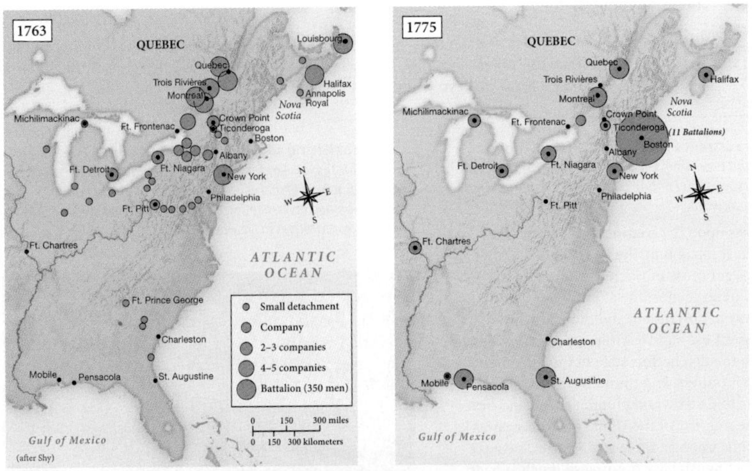

MAPPING THE PAST

MAP 5.3 British Troop Deployments, 1763 and 1775

As the imperial crisis deepened, British military priorities changed. In 1763, most British battalions were stationed in formerly French and Spanish territories, where soldiers could maintain alliances with Native peoples, support trade, and deter revolts. After the Stamp Act riots of 1765, the British placed large garrisons in New York and Philadelphia. By 1775, eleven battalions of British regulars occupied Boston, the center of the Patriot movement.

ANALYZING THE MAP: Consider the way troops were distributed in 1763. What was the strategic significance of the places supported by troops? What functions might they have served in the places they were deployed?

MAKING CONNECTIONS: Based on your reading of the chapter, what had changed by 1775? How do the changes illustrated in the maps show connections to changing British policies regarding the colonies?

All of this activity antagonized the Ohio Indians. In 1770, Shawnees invited hundreds of Indian leaders to gather at the town of Chillicothe on the Scioto River. There they formed the Scioto Confederacy, which pledged to oppose any further expansion into the Ohio country. Some British officers and administrators tried to protect Indian interests, while others encouraged their exploitation, leading to interpretive disagreements among historians about whether the British Empire slowed or accelerated the mistreatment of Indians in the trans-Appalachian west (see "Comparing Interpretations," p. 160).

Meanwhile, in London, the idea that the Proclamation Line was only temporary gave way to the view that it should be permanent. Hillsborough, who became colonial secretary in 1768, adamantly opposed westward expansion, believing it would antagonize the Indians without benefitting the empire. Moreover, he owned vast Irish estates, and he was alarmed by the number of tenants who were leaving Ireland for America. To preserve Britain's laboring class, as well as control costs, Hillsborough wanted to make the Proclamation Line permanent.

For colonists who were already moving west to settle in large numbers, this shift in policy caused confusion and frustration. Eventually, like the Patriots along the seaboard, they would take matters into their own hands.

AP® SKILLS & PROCESSES

MAKING CONNECTIONS

What groups were most interested in western lands, and why did Hillsborough oppose them?

TEACHING STRATEGY

MAP 5.3 allows students to analyze the relationship between geography and military conflict, as well as change over time. Guide students' analysis with the following questions:

- **What areas did the British Empire most need to defend at the end of the Seven Years' War?** *The British needed to defend the borders between the two former empires. These were formed largely by natural boundaries, the St. Lawrence River, the Great Lakes, and the Ohio River. Though militarily defeated, French Canadians and their former Indian allies might rise in revolt, causing tremendous turmoil even though they were not sufficiently powerful to achieve independence.*
- **Apart from Boston, where did British troops relocate to in 1775? Why?** *Many shifted to Florida and the Gulf of Mexico, to protect British loyalists who had moved there after the Seven Years' War.*
- **What areas retained a sizable British presence from 1763 to 1775? Why?** *Locations like Ft. Detroit, Ft. Niagara, Montreal, and Quebec remained centers of British troop presence. As strategic chokepoints, these fortified, easily defended places remained crucial to British defense, whether the perceived enemy was thought to be American Indian, French, or Patriot.*

TRM Find complete suggested responses in the Teacher's Resource Materials.

AP® SKILLS & PROCESSES

MAKING CONNECTIONS

Use the **MAKING CONNECTIONS** question to encourage students to evaluate the relative significance of the potential availability of western lands for different groups of people. Support students by encouraging them to identify four types of colonists interested in the West by social class and specific economic interest. Extend this prompt by asking students to weigh the relative consequences of the Proclamation of 1763 for these four groups.

TRM Find complete suggested responses in the Teacher's Resource Materials.

CHECK FOR UNDERSTANDING

Ask students: **How did the British government and the colonies' view of westward settlement differ?** *The government primarily saw it as a problem to manage, while colonists thought of it as an opportunity to advance their fortunes.*

ANALYZING HISTORICAL EVIDENCE

Direct students to read the sources and answer the questions in the **AP® THINKING LIKE A HISTORIAN** feature to investigate the relevance of point of view, purpose, and context, as well as evaluate the usefulness of these sources in understanding differences in American and British perspectives. Encourage them to pay careful attention to the identity of each author and to the date of each document relative to the larger context. Extend this exercise by having students consider this debate from the perspective of American Indians, whose point of view is only represented directly in one document.

AP® THINKING LIKE A HISTORIAN

Beyond the Proclamation Line

Though the Royal Proclamation of 1763 called the territory between the Appalachian Mountains and the Mississippi River "Indian country," the reality was more complex than this phrase indicates. The following documents illustrate some of the patterns that shaped life beyond the Proclamation Line between 1763 and 1776.

1. **Colonel John Bradstreet's Thoughts on Indian Affairs, 1764.** *Colonel John Bradstreet led a force of British redcoats to Fort Niagara in response to Pontiac's Rebellion. He drafted these remarks shortly afterward.*

   Of all the Savages upon the continent, the most knowing, the most intriguing, the less useful, and the greatest Villains, are those most conversant with the Europeans, and deserve most the attention of Govern[men]t by way of correction, and these are the Six Nations, Shawanese and Delawares; they are well acquainted with the defenceless state of the Inhabitants, who live on the Frontiers, and think they will ever have it in their power to distress and plunder them, and never cease raising the jealousy of the Upper Nations against us, by propagating amongst them such stories, as make them believe the English have nothing so much at heart as the extirpation of all Savages. The apparent design of the Six Nations, is to keep us at war with all Savages, but themselves, that they may be employed as mediators between us and them.

2. **William Johnson to the British Lords of Trade, 1763.** *William Johnson, a New Yorker with extensive experience in Indian relations, was the crown's superintendent for Indian affairs in the northern colonies.*

   [T]he Colonies, had all along neglected to cultivate a proper understanding with the Indians, and from a mistaken notion, have greatly dispised them, without considering, that it is in their power at pleasure to lay waste and destroy the Frontiers. . . . Without any exageration, I look upon the Northern Indians to be the most formidable of any uncivilized body of people in the World. Hunting and War are their sole occupations, and the one qualifies them for the other, they have few wants, and those are easily supplied, their properties of little value, consequently, expeditions against them however successful, cannot distress them, and they have courage sufficient for their manner of fighting, the nature and situation of their Countrys, require not more.

3. **"Indians Giving a Talk to Colonel Bouquet," 1766.** *Based on a painting by Benjamin West, this engraving from a book about Bouquet's campaign to the Ohio following Pontiac's Rebellion depicts a meeting with Delaware, Seneca, and Shawnee representatives in October 1764.*

SOURCE: The Granger Collection, New York.

4. **David Jones's journal, 1773.** *David Jones was a Baptist minister who traveled down the Ohio River in 1772 and 1773. His journal offers a compelling glimpse of life in the valley's trading communities.*

   FRIDAY [January] 22, in company with Mr. Irwine, set out for Chillicaathee. . . . Here Mr. Irwine kept

158

an assortment of goods, and for that purpose rented an house from an Indian whose name is *Waappee Monneeto*, often called the White Devil. . . . Went to see Mr. Moses Henry a gunsmith and trader from Lancaster. This gentleman has lived for some years in this town, and is lawfully married to a white woman, who was captivated so young that she speaks the language as well as any Indian. . . . Mr. Henry lives in a comfortable manner, having plenty of good beef, pork, milk, &c. . . . Chillicaathee is the chief town of the Shawanee Indians — it is situated north of a large plain adjacent to a branch of Paint Creek. This plain is their corn-field, which supplies great part of their town. Their houses are made of logs. . . .

WEDNESDAY [February] 10. . . . This is a small town consisting of Delawares and Shawanees. The chief is a Shawanee woman, who is esteemed very rich — she entertains travelers — there were four of us in company, and for our use, her negro quarter was evacuated this night, which had a fire in the middle without any chimney. This woman has a large stock, and supplied us with milk. Here we also got corn for our horses at a very expensive price. . . .

FRIDAY [February] 12 . . . We passed [the Delaware chief] Captain White Eye's Town. . . . He told me that he intended to be religious, and have his children educated. He saw that their way of living would not answer much longer — game grew scarce — they could not much longer pretend to live by hunting, but must farm, &c. — But said, he could not attend to matters of religion now, for he intended to make a great *hunt* down Ohio, and take the skins himself to Philadelphia.

5. **Killbuck to the governors of Pennsylvania, Maryland, and Virginia, December 1771.** *John Killbuck Jr., or Gelelemend, a Delaware headman, aired grievances on behalf of Ohio Delaware, Munsie, and Mahican Indians.*

Great numbers more of your people have come over the Great Mountains and settled throughout this country, and we are sorry to tell you, that several quarrels have happened between your people and ours, in which people have been killed on both sides, and that we now see the nations round us and your people ready to embroil in a quarrel, which gives our nations great concerns, as we, on our parts, want to live in friendship with you. As you have always told us, you have laws to govern your people by, — but we do not see that you have; therefore, brethren, unless you can fall upon some method of governing your people who live between the Great Mountains and the Ohio River and who are now very numerous, it will be out of the Indians' power to govern their young men, for we assure you the black clouds begin to gather fast in this country. . . . We find your people are very fond of our rich land. We see them quarrelling every day about land and burning one another's houses, so that we do not know how soon they may come over the river Ohio and drive us from our villages, nor do we see you, brothers, take any care to stop them.

6. **Aeneas MacKay to Pennsylvania governor John Penn, April 4, 1774.** *MacKay, a magistrate of Pennsylvania's Westmoreland County, reported on Virginia's effort to create a competing jurisdiction in the vicinity of Pittsburgh. Dr. John Connolly, appointed by Governor Dunmore as commander of the militia in Pittsburgh, was at the center of the controversy.*

Since the return of the Celebrated Doctor Connelly from Virginia last to this place, which he did on the 28th of March, our village is become the scene of anarchy and Confusion. . . .

The Doctor now is in actual possession of the Fort, with a Body Guard of Militia about him, Invested, as we are told, with both Civil & military power, to put the Virginia Law in Force in these parts, and a considerable Number of the Inhabitants of these back Parts of this Country, Ready to join him on any emergency, every artifice are used to seduce the people, some by being promoted to Civil or military employments, and others with the promises of grants of Lands, on easy Terms, & the giddy headed mobs are so Infatuated as to suffer themselves to be carried away by these Insinuating Delusions. . . .

The Indians are greatly alarmed at seeing parties of armed men patrolling through our streets Daily, not knowing but there is hostility intended against them and their country.

Sources: (1, 2) E. B. O'Callaghan and Berthold Fernow, eds., *Documents Relative to the Colonial History of the State of New York*, 15 vols. (Albany, 1856–1887), 7: 690–694, 574; (4) David Jones, *A Journal of Two Visits Made to Some Nations of Indians on the West Side of the River Ohio, in the Years 1772 and 1773* (Burlington, 1774 [rep. NY, 1971]); (5) K. G. Davies, ed., *Documents of the American Revolution, 1770–1783*, 19 vols. (Shannon and Dublin, 1972–1981), 3: 254–255; (6) Samuel Hazard, ed., *Pennsylvania Archives*, series 1, 12 vols. (Philadelphia: Joseph Severns & Co., 1856), 4: 484–486.

ANALYZING THE EVIDENCE

1. John Bradstreet, a career British army officer, based his observations (source 1) on his wartime experiences in the West. William Johnson (source 2) had lived in close proximity to Iroquois Indians for many years. Use historical reasoning to compare their views: what do they agree upon, and where do they differ? Use evidence to explain your comparisons.
2. Charles Grignion's engraving (source 3) appeared in print a short time after Pontiac's Rebellion. How does it portray the Ohio Indians? Identify the perspectives and historical situation of sources 1, 2, 3, and 5. Use historical reasoning to describe the differences and similarities among the sources.
3. What is the historical context of the author of source 4? What details of trading communities does he share? In what ways is that related to his perspective? Use evidence from the text in your answer.
4. Sources 5 and 6 describe the state of affairs on the upper Ohio shortly before the outbreak of Dunmore's War. What concerns does Killbuck express? Why was Virginia's willingness to organize a militia so important to the residents of the region? In your answer, explain the power relations between differing groups.

AP® DBQ PRACTICE

Using these documents and what you have learned in Chapter 5, write a short essay that surveys British and Anglo-American attitudes toward the Ohio Indians and use examples from the textbook and these sources to explain how attitudes and the reality of life in the Ohio country contradict.

TRM Find complete suggested responses in the Teacher's Resource Materials.

AP® SKILLS & PROCESSES

ARGUMENTATION

The **AP® DBQ PRACTICE** prompt challenges students to develop an argument using diverse evidence to illustrate contradictions between settlers' attitudes and the reality of life in the Ohio region. Scaffold this question by telling students to start with a chart where they identify for each document the evidence it provides for "attitudes" and the evidence it provides for "reality of life." Extend this prompt by having students explore the reasons for such contradictions between perception and reality in this historical situation.

AP® SKILLS & PROCESSES

ANALYZING HISTORICAL EVIDENCE

The **AP® COMPARING INTERPRETATIONS** feature helps students analyze two historians' arguments and their effectiveness, and to analyze the diversity in interpretation the two arguments provide. Scaffold this discussion by asking students to paraphrase the text of each historian verbally and in writing, to verify that they understand the argument each is making.

AP® THEME

MIG: Migration and Settlement

Use the **AP® COMPARING INTERPRETATIONS** feature to provide an in-depth investigation of the ways colonial migration to the West created tension with Britain and with Native Americans.

AP® SKILLS & PROCESSES

ANALYZING HISTORICAL EVIDENCE

Sometimes students need help identifying a claim made by a historian. Therefore, provide students with a scaffolded approach so they can better interpret the excerpt. For instance, highlight the question in the heading, "Did British Administrators Try to Protect or Exploit Native Americans?" You can also have students use the title of the book referenced, *Elusive Empires: Constructing Colonialism in the Ohio Valley, 1673–1800*, to help students brainstorm the topic. From this simple approach students focus on locating arguments about protection vs. exploitation, empires, colonialism, and the Ohio Valley.

TRM Find complete suggested responses in the Teacher's Resource Materials.

AP® COMPARING INTERPRETATIONS

Did British Administrators Try to Protect or Exploit Native Americans?

In the summer of 1763, Indian warriors throughout the Great Lakes and the Ohio Valley attacked the outposts that France had just ceded to Great Britain at the end of the Great War for Empire in an event known as Pontiac's War. They captured nine forts and besieged two others — Detroit and Fort Pitt — throughout the summer. In the fall, King George III issued the Royal Proclamation of 1763, which prohibited settlement west of the Allegheny Ridge. Nevertheless, Anglo-American colonists continued to push into the Ohio Valley (see Map 5.5, p. 170). Not surprisingly, the Indian peoples living in the Ohio Valley continued to be alarmed at the influx. In an effort to manage the empire and reduce the potential for conflict, British officials had to maintain or initiate alliances with the Indian nations while also preventing conflict between Indians and Anglo-American colonists. In the following excerpts, historians Eric Hinderaker (one of the authors of this textbook) and Gregory Evans Dowd highlight one aspect of this conflict: British imperial policy toward the Indian nations.

ERIC HINDERAKER

SOURCE: Eric Hinderaker, *Elusive Empires: Constructing Colonialism in the Ohio Valley, 1673–1800* (Cambridge: Cambridge University Press, 1997), 134–135, 170–171, 175.

Britain's victory [in the Great War for Empire] placed enormous new administrative demands on the empire; to succeed in managing affairs in the Ohio Valley, its agents needed far-sighted policies and cooperative, influential Indian leaders. But the complex demands of western development defeated administrators' efforts to devise a workable imperial strategy, and powerful, accommodating Indian leaders were hard to come by. . . . Under these circumstances, the terrible energies of colonial adventurers and Indian warriors overwhelmed attempts to impose structure on imperial expansion, and in place of mediation the aggressive initiatives of ambitious individuals increasingly shaped intercultural relations in the Ohio Valley. . . .

Though Fort Pitt was imposed on the Indians of the upper Ohio Valley against their will, it served as an important center of diplomatic accommodation and, at least in theory, as an important restraint on the activities of western squatters. . . . In response to requests from Indian leaders, the fort commander, Charles Edmonstone, repeatedly warned settlers off of Indian lands; in the summer of 1767 a detachment of soldiers from the fort chased away hundreds of squatters and destroyed "as Many Hutts as they could find." . . .

Pressed by crises in the colonies' port towns and the need for imperial economy, the king's advisors were more interested in saving money than solving the problems of the west. To this end, troops dismantled, razed, and abandoned Fort Pitt [in 1772]. . . . [T]he withdrawal of British power made the Ohio Valley a kind of Hobbesian world, where only sheer force could effectively determine the outcome of events. . . .

AP® SKILLS & PROCESSES

CLAIMS AND EVIDENCE IN SOURCES

What is the historical argument being made in the excerpt above? What evidence does the author give to support the historical argument?

Parliament Wavers

In Britain, the colonies' nonimportation agreement was taking its toll. In 1768, the colonies had cut imports of British manufactures in half; by 1769, the mainland colonies had a trade surplus with Britain of £816,000. Hard-hit by these developments, British merchants and manufacturers petitioned Parliament to repeal the Townshend duties. Early in 1770, Lord North became prime minister. A witty man and a skillful politician, North designed a new compromise. Arguing that it was foolish to tax British exports to America (thereby raising their price and decreasing consumption), he persuaded Parliament to repeal most of the Townshend duties. However, North retained the tax on tea as a symbol of Parliament's supremacy.

The Boston Massacre Even as Parliament was debating North's repeal, events in Boston guaranteed that reconciliation between Patriots and Parliament would be hard to achieve. Between 1,200 and 2,000 troops had been stationed in Boston for a year and a half. Soldiers were also stationed in New York, Philadelphia, several towns in New Jersey, and various frontier outposts in these years, with a minimum of conflict or violence. But in Boston — a small port town on a tiny peninsula — the troops numbered 10 percent of the local population, and their presence wore on the locals.

Officers of empire and Indian leaders had consistently sought, through long years of association, to create patterns of leadership and diplomacy that would mute conflict and encourage accommodation. . . . The collapse of British authority in the Ohio Valley dealt the final blow to the already badly weakened principles of accommodation and mediation.

GREGORY EVANS DOWD

SOURCE: Gregory Evans Dowd, *War Under Heaven: Pontiac, the Indian Nations, & the British Empire* (Baltimore: The Johns Hopkins University Press, 2002), 174–175, 211–212.

To the degree that the issue has been examined, backcountry settlers wishing only to drive Indians out appear to have squared off against imperial administrators willing to incorporate them (in relationships of power that would be reciprocal, if asymmetrical) into the empire; such distinctions between farmers and officials grow largely out of the administrative record, which masks both a vast imperial failure of imagination and a much darker reality. Though there were debates and even violent confrontations over Indian policy, settlers and authorities shared in the conviction of British superiority and in the expectation that Indians would, before long, surrender their homelands to British subjects who were racially white. . . .

The issue was not, as it is too often portrayed, a matter of contention between officers supporting a benevolent rule of law that might protect Indians and unruly backcountry Indian killers bent on doing what killers do best. Official policy, highly confused though it was, tended to place Indians far beyond the rule of law, and it intended, even in the long run, to keep them there by pushing them away from any civil jurisdiction in the colonies. . . .

During [Pontiac's W]ar . . . officers urged, ordered, and approved the indiscriminate slaughter of Indians. . . . [T]he top echelons of the army, whose own arrogant disregard for Indian honor, custom, and right had brought on the war in the first place, not only contemplated but also committed and sanctioned atrocities of the first order. Officers and superintendents ordered that no quarter be given to captured Indians, and the army obeyed. Fort Pitt deliberately infected negotiators with smallpox in a manner approved by two commanders in chief, [General Jeffery] Amherst and [General Thomas] Gage. The smallpox-infected blankets were handed out by William Trent, himself a gentleman. . . .

[A]s the British and the British colonists contemplated and fought over the status of Indians within their emerging empire, they came up with nothing satisfactory for the Indians involved. Almost all people, Indian, colonist, or imperial officer, could agree that Indians were not British subjects in the fully charged meaning of the word. Almost all contemplated, with sentiments that ranged from desire to fury, the continued westward expansion of the British Empire, at Indian expense. The idea of the Indians as inhabiting a kind of protectorate within the realm was, even in the minds of its proponents and progenitors, at best a temporary solution implying a current Indian dependence and a foreseeable Indian reduction that no Indian nation could gladly abide.

AP® SHORT ANSWER PRACTICE

1. Identify the major difference between these two historians' arguments concerning British policy toward Native Americans.
2. How does each historian assess the effectiveness of British imperial officials in managing relations with Native Americans? Explain what evidence each author uses to bolster their respective claim.
3. How does the textbook's discussion of Anglo-American settlers in the Ohio Valley support or challenge each of the historians' arguments regarding British policy? Corroborate the sources and the textbook's interpretations of Ohio Valley politics.

On the night of March 5, 1770, a group of nine British redcoats fired into a crowd and killed five townspeople. A subsequent trial exonerated the soldiers, but Boston's Radical Whigs, convinced of a ministerial conspiracy against liberty, labeled the incident a "massacre" and used it to rally sentiment against imperial power. One of the victims was an African American sailor and laborer named Crispus Attucks. In the nineteenth century, he was rediscovered by abolitionists and identified as the first black martyr of American liberty, though little is known of his life or his political commitments.

Sovereignty Debated When news of North's compromise arrived in the colonies in the wake of the Boston Massacre, the reaction was mixed. Most of Britain's colonists remained loyal to the empire, but five years of conflict had taken their toll. In 1765, American leaders had accepted Parliament's authority; the Stamp Act Resolves had opposed only certain "unconstitutional" legislation. By 1770, the most outspoken Patriots — Benjamin Franklin in Pennsylvania, Patrick Henry in Virginia, and Samuel Adams in Massachusetts — repudiated parliamentary supremacy and claimed equality for the American assemblies within the empire. Franklin suggested that the colonies were now "distinct and separate states" with "the same Head, or Sovereign, the King."

TEACHING STRATEGY

Ask students the following additional questions regarding the **AP® COMPARING INTERPRETATIONS** feature:

- **How does information about the books' full titles help you understand the authors' arguments better?** *"Constructing colonialism" hints that Hinderaker's focus rests on imperial policy, while his long periodization might provide a perspective that includes trade and cooperation, which often characterized European-Indian interactions, not just conflict. "War under heaven" seems to focus on conflict and violence, and the mention of heaven suggests that perhaps this conflict was religiously motivated.*
- **What's at stake in these different interpretations?** *The debates hinge on the nature of the relationship between British and Native Americans. Was it characterized by mutual respect and exchange, only occasionally marred by war? Or was it inherently conflicted and violent? This sets the stage for considering the degree to which American policy toward American Indians was a continuation of British policies.*

TRM Find complete suggested responses in the Teacher's Resource Materials.

AP® SKILLS & PROCESSES

ANALYZING HISTORICAL EVIDENCE

Encourage a close analysis of Revere's famous engraving to provide practice in using relevant historical evidence. Direct students to identify audience and purpose, and then consider the usefulness and limitations of this type of propaganda as historical evidence. Extend this exercise by asking students to make inferences about the potential impact of Revere's text on its audience.

TRM Find complete suggested responses in the Teacher's Resource Materials.

VISUAL ACTIVITY

Patriot Propaganda Silversmith Paul Revere issued this engraving of the confrontation between British redcoats and snowball-throwing Bostonians in the days after it occurred. To whip up opposition to the military occupation of their town, Revere and other Patriots labeled the incident "The Boston Massacre." The shooting confirmed their Radical Whig belief that "standing armies" were instruments of tyranny. Anne S. K. Brown Military Collection, Brown University Library.

READING THE IMAGE: This image was not an accurate portrayal of the shootings; it was instead an instrument of political propaganda. What features of the image are most important to its political purpose? Consider his depiction of both the soldiers and the townspeople. Look, too, at the buildings surrounding the crowd, especially the Custom House on the right. Identify the ways in which Revere invokes the idea of tyranny in this image.

MAKING CONNECTIONS: Who was the intended audience of this print? What historical events led to the event portrayed? One of the lawyers who defended the soldiers in their trial worried that Revere's image would prejudice a local jury against them. Do you think this is likely? Why or why not?

AP® SKILLS & PROCESSES

SOURCING AND SITUATION

What was Benjamin Franklin's position on colonial representation in 1765, and why had his view changed by 1770?

Franklin's suggestion outraged Thomas Hutchinson, the American-born royal governor of Massachusetts. Hutchinson emphatically rejected the idea of "two independent legislatures in one and the same state." He told the Massachusetts assembly, "I know of no line that can be drawn between the supreme authority of Parliament and the total independence of the colonies."

There the matter rested. The British had twice imposed revenue acts on the colonies, and American Patriots had twice forced a retreat. If Parliament insisted on a policy of constitutional absolutism by imposing taxes a third time, some Americans were prepared to pursue violent resistance. Nor did they flinch when reminded that George

AP® SKILLS & PROCESSES

SOURCING AND SITUATION

Use the **SOURCING AND SITUATION** question to help students identify the change in perspective of one individual. Students needing help identifying why Franklin's views on parliamentary representation changed should read carefully the text's discussion of his views in 1770, as that is where reasons for the change will be explained. Extend this prompt by asking students to explain the significance in the change in Franklin's views.

TRM Find complete suggested responses in the Teacher's Resource Materials.

CHECK FOR UNDERSTANDING

Ask students: **What was the relationship between formal protests against Parliament and popular resistance in the years between 1765 and 1770?** *While both formal protests, e.g., the Stamp Act Congress of 1765, and popular protests both sought to counter the new taxes Parliament passed after the Great War for Empire, the methods, composition, and tactics differed. Methodologically, the formal protest asserted loyalty to the Crown and the natural rights of Englishmen while popular resistance was often anti-monarchical. Compositionally, formal protests largely came from the elites while popular protests were just that, from the masses. Finally, tactically they differed; formal protests were often non-violent while popular protests were violent.*

III condemned their agitation. As the Massachusetts House replied to Hutchinson, "There is more reason to dread the consequences of absolute uncontrolled supreme power, whether of a nation or a monarch, than those of total independence." Fearful of civil war, Lord North's ministry hesitated to force the issue.

THE ROAD TO INDEPENDENCE, 1771–1776

What actions did the Continental Association take to support the efforts of the Continental Congress?

Repeal of the Townshend duties in 1770 restored harmony to the British Empire, but strong feelings and mutual distrust lay just below the surface. In 1773, those emotions erupted, destroying any hope of compromise. Within two years, the Americans and the British clashed in armed conflict. Despite widespread resistance among loyal colonists, Patriot legislators created provisional governments and military forces, the two essentials for independence.

AP® EXAM TIP

To practice identifying examples of cause and effect relationships, trace events from 1771 to 1776 that weakened ties between Britain and its colonies as you read through this section.

A Compromise Repudiated

Once aroused, political passions are not easily quieted. In Boston, Samuel Adams and other radical Patriots continued to warn Americans of imperial domination and, late in 1772, persuaded the town meeting to set up a committee of correspondence "to state the Rights of the Colonists of this Province." Soon, eighty Massachusetts towns had similar committees. When British officials threatened to seize the Americans responsible for the burning of the customs vessel *Gaspée* and prosecute them in Britain, the Virginia House of Burgesses and several other assemblies set up their own **committees of correspondence**. These standing committees allowed Patriots to communicate with leaders in other colonies when new threats to liberty occurred. By 1774, among the colonies that would later declare independence, only Pennsylvania was without one.

committees of correspondence
A communications network established among colonial assemblies between 1772 and 1773 to provide for rapid dissemination of news about important political developments.

The East India Company and the Tea Act Committees of correspondence sprang into action when Parliament passed the **Tea Act of May 1773**. The act provided financial relief for the East India Company, a royally chartered private corporation that served as the instrument of British imperialism. The company was deeply in debt; it also had a huge surplus of tea as a result of high import duties, which led Britons and colonists alike to drink smuggled Dutch tea instead. The Tea Act gave the company a government loan and, to boost its revenue, canceled the import duties on tea the company exported to Ireland and the American colonies. Now even with the Townshend duty of 3 pence a pound on tea, high-quality East India Company tea would cost less than the Dutch tea smuggled into the colonies by American merchants.

Tea Act of May 1773
British act that lowered the existing tax on tea and granted exemptions to the East India Company to make their tea cheaper in the colonies and entice boycotting Americans to buy it.

Radical Patriots accused the British ministry of bribing Americans with the cheaper East India Company tea so they would give up their principled opposition to the tea tax. As an anonymous woman wrote to the *Massachusetts Spy*, "The use of [British] tea is considered not as a private but as a public evil . . . a handle to introduce a variety of . . . oppressions amongst us." Merchants joined the protest because the East India Company planned to distribute its tea directly to shopkeepers, excluding American wholesalers from the trade's profits. "The fear of an Introduction of a Monopoly in this Country," British general Frederick Haldimand reported from New York, "has induced the mercantile part of the Inhabitants to be very industrious in opposing this Step and added Strength to a Spirit of Independence already too prevalent."

AP® SKILLS & PROCESSES

MAKING CONNECTIONS

Why did colonists react so strongly against the Tea Act, which actually lowered the price of tea?

The Tea Party and the Coercive Acts The Sons of Liberty prevented East India Company ships from delivering their cargoes in New York, Philadelphia, and Charleston. In Massachusetts, Royal Governor Hutchinson was determined to land the tea

AP® APPLY THE TIP

Ask students to consider the cause and effect relationships of each event listed on **Handout 5.1 — Causation: Road to the American Revolution (TRM)**. To help students think about point of view, have one partner take the point of view of the British in explaining the causation relationships and the other partner take the point of view of the Patriots. Ask both students to provide specific evidence to support their interpretation of events. Then ask partners to explain their interpretation of events to each other, emphasizing the role of point of view in their causation relationships. Lead a class discussion to address the following questions:

- **Why was British interpretation of events so different from Patriot interpretation?** *The use of propaganda on both sides of the Atlantic influenced the interpretation of the events. British mercantilist policies were seen as part of legitimate imperial policy by British, while the same policies were interpreted as violations of rights and liberty by colonists.*
- **Did the goals of the British government change from 1763 to 1771? What about from 1771 to 1775? If so, why did the goals change?** *From 1763 to 1771, the goals of the British were largely to enforce tax (economic) policies on the colonies by forcing colonists to pay taxes and end smuggling. From 1771 to 1775, the goals of the British were largely focused on imposing imperial control over the colonies to suppress colonial rebellion. These goals changed as the colonists" protests and actions against British policy became more active and violent.*
- **How did colonial reaction to British laws change between 1763 to 1771? From 1771 and 1775?** *In the period from 1763 to 1771, colonial reactions were largely economic protests in the form of boycotts that were sometimes supported by political actions such as the Stamp Act Congress. After 1771, the protests and demands of the colonists were dominated by political arguments that questioned the authority and legitimate right of the British to govern the colonies.*

TRM Find **Handout 5.1 — Causation: Road to the American Revolution** in the Teacher's Resource Materials.

AP® THEME

SOC: Social Structures

Encourage students to think about the breadth of colonial resistance and how this was an essential reason why political protest was successful. For instance, provide students with three categories: rural yeoman farmers, urban merchants, wealthy aristocracy. Have students provide one historical example of colonial protest for each category.

AP® SKILLS & PROCESSES

MAKING CONNECTIONS

Use the **MAKING CONNECTIONS** question to help students probe reasons for colonists' perspective. Students needing support in answering this question might consider the paradox implied in this question: The colonists' reaction seems counterintuitive, so why did they react this way?

TRM Find complete suggested responses in the Teacher's Resource Materials.

and collect the tax. To foil the governor's plan, artisans and laborers disguised as Indians boarded three ships — the *Dartmouth*, the *Eleanor*, and the *Beaver* — on December 16, 1773, broke open 342 chests of tea (valued at about £10,000, or about $1.5 million today), and threw them into the harbor. "This destruction of the Tea . . . must have so important Consequences," John Adams wrote in his diary, "that I cannot but consider it as an Epoch in History."

The king was outraged. "Concessions have made matters worse," George III declared. "The time has come for compulsion." Early in 1774, Parliament passed four **Coercive Acts** to force Massachusetts to pay for the tea and to submit to imperial authority. The Boston Port Bill closed Boston Harbor to shipping; the Massachusetts Government Act annulled the colony's charter and prohibited most town meetings; a new Quartering Act mandated new barracks for British troops; and the Justice Act allowed trials for capital crimes to be transferred to other colonies or to Britain.

Coercive Acts
Four British acts of 1774 meant to punish Massachusetts for the destruction of three shiploads of tea. Known in America as the Intolerable Acts, they led to open rebellion in the northern colonies.

Continental Congress
September 1774 gathering of delegates in Philadelphia to discuss the crisis caused by the Coercive Acts. The Congress issued a declaration of rights and agreed to a boycott of trade with Britain.

Patriot leaders throughout the colonies branded the measures "Intolerable" and rallied support for Massachusetts. In Georgia, a Patriot warned the "Freemen of the Province" that "every privilege you at present claim as a birthright, may be wrested from you by the same authority that blockades the town of Boston." "The cause of Boston," George Washington declared in Virginia, "now is and ever will be considered as the cause of America." The committees of correspondence had created a firm sense of Patriot unity.

In 1774, Parliament also passed the Quebec Act, which allowed the practice of Roman Catholicism in Quebec. This concession to Quebec's predominantly Catholic population reignited religious passions in New England, where Protestants associated Catholicism with arbitrary royal government. Because the act extended Quebec's boundaries into the Ohio River Valley, it also angered influential land speculators in Virginia and Pennsylvania and ordinary settlers by the thousands (see Map 5.4). Although the ministry did not intend the Quebec Act as a coercive measure, many colonists saw it as further proof of Parliament's intention to control American affairs.

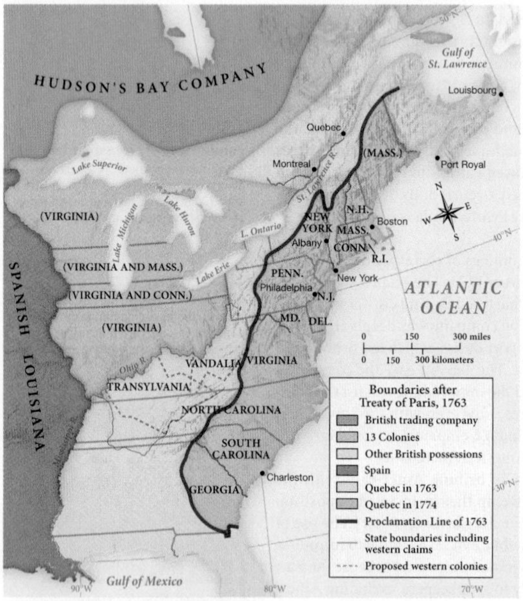

MAP 5.4 British Western Policy, 1763–1774
The Proclamation of 1763 prohibited white settlement west of the Appalachian Mountains. Nonetheless, Anglo-American settlers and land speculators proposed the new colonies of Vandalia and Transylvania to the west of Virginia and North Carolina. The Quebec Act of 1774 designated most western lands as Indian reserves and vastly enlarged the boundaries of Quebec, dashing speculators' hopes and eliminating the old sea-to-sea land claims of many seaboard colonies. The act especially angered New England Protestants, who condemned it for allowing French residents to practice Catholicism, and colonial political leaders, who protested its failure to provide Quebec with a representative assembly.

The Continental Congress Responds

In response to the Coercive Acts, Patriot leaders convened a new continent-wide body, the **Continental Congress**. Twelve mainland colonies sent representatives. Four recently acquired colonies — Florida, Quebec, Nova Scotia, and Newfoundland — refused to send delegates, as did Georgia, where the royal governor controlled the legislature. The assemblies of Barbados, Jamaica, and the other sugar islands, although wary of British domination, were even more fearful of revolts by their predominantly African populations and therefore declined to attend.

The delegates who met in Philadelphia in September 1774 had different agendas. Southern representatives, fearing a British plot "to

AP® THEME

MIG: Migration and Settlement

Use **MAP 5.4** to illustrate the conflict over western migration by revealing the amount of territory in dispute: the difference between the Proclamation Line and the proposed western colonies boundaries reveals what was at stake.

TEACHING STRATEGY

MAP 5.4 provides a lot of data that might prove so complicated that some students choose to ignore it. Guide students' analysis with the following questions:

- **Based on the map, which colonies would have been most disappointed by the Quebec Act of 1774? Why?** *Virginia, Massachusetts, and Connecticut. All three claimed vast territories in the area that was set aside for French Catholics in the Quebec Act.*
- **How might colonial claims to lands in Canada have led to intercolonial conflict if Britain had not passed the Quebec Act? What might have made governing these lands difficult for the colonies?** *Colonies had overlapping claims to Western territories, which would likely have led to conflict if Britain had not provided the land to French Canadians. The western lands were often several hundred miles from their colonial centers and, in the case of Virginia, not even contiguous with the colony's existing territory. Since all communication had to be hand-carried, western settlers would learn about policies very slowly and would be hard to govern if they refused to comply with directives.*
- **Why did American colonists see the Proclamation Line of 1763 as an affront to their individual freedom?** *Even though Great Britain designed the proclamation as a way to accommodate American Indian resistance and the cost of a territorial empire after the Seven Years' War, colonists interpreted this action as an attempt by Great Britain to control their access to new lands.*

overturn the constitution and introduce a system of arbitrary government," advocated a new economic boycott. Independence-minded representatives from New England demanded political union and defensive military preparations. Many delegates from the Middle Atlantic colonies favored compromise.

Led by Joseph Galloway of Pennsylvania, these men of "loyal principles" proposed a new political system similar to Benjamin Franklin's proposal at the Albany Congress of 1754: each colony would retain its assembly to legislate on local matters, and a new continent-wide body would handle general American affairs. The king would appoint a president-general to preside over a legislative council selected by the colonial assemblies. Galloway's plan failed by a single vote; a bare majority thought it was too conciliatory (see "Firsthand Accounts," p. 166).

Instead, the delegates demanded the repeal of the Coercive Acts and stipulated that British control be limited to matters of trade. They also approved a program of economic retaliation: Americans would stop importing British goods in December 1774. If Parliament did not repeal the Coercive Acts by September 1775, the Congress vowed to cut off virtually all colonial exports to Britain, Ireland, and the British West Indies. Ten years of constitutional conflict had culminated in a threat of all-out commercial warfare.

A few British leaders still hoped for compromise. In January 1775, William Pitt, now sitting in the House of Lords as the Earl of Chatham, asked Parliament to renounce its power to tax the colonies and to recognize the Continental Congress as a lawful body. In return, he suggested, the Congress should acknowledge parliamentary supremacy and provide a permanent source of revenue to help defray the national debt.

The British ministry rejected Pitt's plan. Why did Lord North choose not to accept this compromise solution? Twice Parliament had backed down in the face of colonial resistance; a third retreat was impossible. Branding the Continental Congress an illegal assembly, the ministry rejected Lord Dartmouth's proposal to send commissioners to negotiate a settlement. Instead, Lord North set stringent terms:

America Ravaged This political cartoon, published in London in 1774, presents a deeply critical view of Parliament's Coercive Acts. Entitled "The able doctor, or, America swallowing the bitter draught," it depicts Lord North forcibly administering medicine (from a teapot) to a female figure representing America. In his pocket is the Boston Port Bill, which closed the port to all traffic until the town paid for the tea it had destroyed. Two key allies assist North in his efforts: Lord Mansfield holds her arms, while Lord Sandwich peers up her skirt. Britannia, a female figure representing Great Britain, stands nearby, covering her eyes in shame. To the left, a Frenchman and a Spaniard — Britain's traditional enemies — look on with interest. In the background, ships surround and cannonade Boston. Every detail of this image is critical of the Coercive Acts. From The New York Public Library, https://digitalcollections.nypl.org/items/510d47da-e46f-a3d9-e040-e00a18064a99.

AP® EXAM TIP

Compare the Continental Congress to earlier attempts to unify colonies in the Albany Congress and Stamp Act Congress.

AP® APPLY THE TIP

Ask students to complete **Handout 5.2 — Comparison: Colonial Congress (TRM)** to compare and contrast the Albany Congress, Stamp Act Congress, and Continental Congress. Students should find details to illustrate the similarities and differences between each of these attempts to unify the colonies. Ask students to include at least three points to illustrate differences and at least one point to emphasize similarities. Next, ask students to draw a conclusion by writing a thesis statement that addresses the following prompt: Compare the actions and outcomes of attempts by the colonists to unify in the period 1754–1775. Ask students to volunteer their thesis statements and record the first shared thesis on the board. Then ask other students to add to, modify, or change parts of the thesis to clarify and strengthen the historical argument. Once a thesis statement is established, list evidence that could be used to support the thesis statement as a class.

TRM Find **Handout 5.2 — Comparison: Colonial Congress** in the Teacher's Resource Materials.

TEACHING STRATEGY

Colonial reaction to British imperial policies affected British merchants throughout this period. Have students identify one historical reason why this cartoon, published in London, would be critical of British imperial policies, specifically the Coercive Acts of 1774.

AP® SKILLS & PROCESSES

ANALYZING HISTORICAL EVIDENCE

Help students recognize that the **AP® FIRST-HAND ACCOUNTS** feature asks them to demonstrate their understanding of the significance of primary sources related to the Stamp Act. Support students' analysis by asking them to identify the central question this set of sources is designed to answer, drawing their attention to the title of this section and the questions posed in the first paragraph about taxation, representation, and sovereignty. As they read each document, they should consider specifically how the document provides evidence for the central question. Extend this prompt by having students make inferences about Parliament's likely response to Ingersoll.

AP® FIRSTHAND ACCOUNTS

The Debate over Representation and Sovereignty

These two documents offer formal statements of political principles. To analyze them effectively, think carefully about the ways in which the abstract ideas they express might shape the lives of ordinary people. Why did Parliament believe the taxing power was essential to its authority? Why would colonists disagree? And why would people like Joseph Galloway want to find a way to reconcile their differences? Consider what motivated the authors of these documents as you read them; then turn to the Questions for Analysis that follow.

Speaking before the House of Commons, Benjamin Franklin declared that before 1763 Americans had paid little attention to the question of Parliament's "right to lay taxes and duties" in the colonies. The reason was simple, Franklin said: "A right to lay internal taxes was never supposed to be in Parliament, as we are not represented there." Franklin recognized that representation was central to the imperial debate. As the following selections show, the failure to solve the problem of representation, and the closely related issue of parliamentary sovereignty, led to the American rebellion.

JARED INGERSOLL

Report on the Debates in Parliament, 1765

Connecticut lawyer Jared Ingersoll (1722–1781) served as his colony's agent, or lobbyist, in Britain. In this 1765 letter to the governor of Connecticut, Ingersoll summarizes the debate then under way in Parliament over the Stamp Act. When the act passed, he returned home to become the stamp distributor in Connecticut. A mob forced him to resign that post. Ingersoll later served as a vice-admiralty judge in Philadelphia and, during the Revolution, remained loyal to Britain.

SOURCE: New Haven Colony Historical Society, *Papers* (1918), 9: 306–315.

❝ The principal Attention has been to the Stamp bill that has been preparing to Lay before Parliament for taxing America. The Point of the Authority of Parliament to impose such Tax I found on my Arrival here was so fully and Universally yielded [accepted], that there was not the least hopes of making any impressions that way. . . .

I beg leave to give you a Summary of the Arguments which are made use of in favour of such Authority. The House of Commons, say they, is a branch of the supreme legislature of the Nation, and which in its Nature is supposed to represent, or rather to stand in the place of, the Commons, that is, of the great body of the people. . . .

That this house of Commons, therefore, is now . . . a part of the Supreme unlimited power of the Nation, as in every State there must be some unlimited Power and Authority. . . .

They say a Power to tax is a necessary part of every Supreme Legislative Authority, and that if they have not that Power over America, they have none, and then America is at once a Kingdom of itself.

On the other hand those who oppose the bill say, it is true the Parliament have a supreme unlimited Authority over every Part and Branch of the Kings dominions and as well over Ireland as any other place.

Yet [they say] we believe a British parliament will never think it prudent to tax Ireland [or America]. Tis true they say, that the Commons of England and of the British Empire are all represented in and by the house of Commons, but this representation is confessedly on all hands by Construction and Virtual [because most British subjects] . . . have no hand in choosing the representatives. . . .

[They say further] that the Effects of this implied Representation here and in America must be infinitely different in the Article of Taxation. . . . By any Mistake an act of Parliament is made that prove injurious and hard the Member of Parliament here [in Britain] sees with his own Eyes and is moreover very accessible to the people. . . . [Also,] the taxes are laid equally by one Rule and fall as well on the Member himself as on the people. But as to America, from the great distance in point of Situation [they are not represented in the same way]. . . .

[Finally, the opponents of the Act say] we already by the Regulations upon their trade draw from the Americans all that they can spare. . . . This Step [of taxation] should not take place until or unless the Americans are allowed to send Members to Parliament.

Thus I have given you, I think, the Substance of the Arguments on both sides of that great and important

AP® SKILLS & PROCESSES

ARGUMENTATION

Why did Parliament prefer North's solution to the Boston Tea Party to William Pitt's?

Americans must pay for their own defense and administration and acknowledge Parliament's authority to tax them. To put teeth in these demands, North imposed a naval blockade on American trade with foreign nations and ordered General Gage to suppress dissent in Massachusetts. "Now the case seemed desperate," the prime minister told Thomas Hutchinson, whom the Patriots had forced into exile in London. "Parliament would not — could not — concede." North predicted that the crisis "must come to violence."

166

AP® SKILLS & PROCESSES

ARGUMENTATION

Use the **ARGUMENTATION** question to direct students to compare two different proposed solutions to the Boston Tea Party. Ask students how the two solutions differed in character. Then ask why Parliament favored the solution it did. Extend this prompt by having students consider the significance of Pitt's alternate proposal, which suggests that some in Parliament remained sympathetic to the colonists.

TRM Find complete suggested responses in the Teacher's Resource Materials.

CHECK FOR UNDERSTANDING

Ask students to describe the Continental Congress's demands and Parliament's response.

The Continental Congress demanded retraction of the Coercive Acts; Parliament imposed a naval blockade and sent troops to quell Massachusetts dissent.

Question of the right and also of the Expediency of taxing America by Authority of Parliament. . . . [But] upon a Division of the house upon the Question, there was about 250 to about 50 in favour of the Bill. ❞

JOSEPH GALLOWAY

Plan of Union, 1775

Speaker of the Pennsylvania assembly Joseph Galloway was a delegate to the First Continental Congress, where he proposed a plan that addressed the issue of representation. The colonies would remain British but operate under a continental government with the power to veto parliamentary laws that affected America. Radical Patriots in the Congress, who favored independence, prevented a vote on Galloway's plan and suppressed mention of it in the records. Galloway remained loyal to the crown, fought on the British side in the War for Independence, and moved to England in 1778.

SOURCE: Joseph Galloway, *Historical and Political Reflections on the Rise and Progress of the American Rebellion* (London, 1780), 70.

❝ If we sincerely mean to accommodate the difference between the two countries, . . . we must take into consideration a number of facts which led the Parliament to pass the acts complained of. . . . [You will recall] the dangerous situation of the Colonies from the intrigues of France, and the incursions of the Canadians and their Indian allies, at the commencement of the last war. . . . Great-Britain sent over her fleets and armies for their protection. . . .

In this state of the Colonies, it was not unreasonable to expect that Parliament would have levied a tax on them proportionate to their wealth, . . . Parliament was naturally led to exercise the power which had been, by its predecessors, so often exercised over the Colonies, and to pass the Stamp Act. Against this act, the Colonies petitioned Parliament, and denied its authority . . . [declaring] that the Colonies could not be represented in that body. This justly alarmed the British Senate. It was thought and called by the ablest men [in] Britain, a clear and explicit declaration of the American Independence, and compelled the Parliament to pass the Declaratory Act, in order to save its ancient and incontrovertible right of supremacy over all the parts of the empire. . . .

Having thus briefly stated the arguments in favour of parliamentary authority, . . . I am free to confess that the exercise of that authority is not perfectly constitutional in respect to the Colonies. We know that the whole landed interest of Britain is represented in that body, while neither the land nor the people of America hold the least participation in the legislative authority of the State. . . . Representation, or a participation in the supreme councils of the State, is the great principle upon which the freedom of the British Government is established and secured.

I wish to see . . . the right to participate in the supreme councils of the State extended, in some form . . . to America . . . [and therefore] have prepared the draught of a plan for uniting America more intimately, in constitutional policy, with Great-Britain. . . . I am certain when dispassionately considered, it will be found to be the most perfect union in power and liberty with the Parent State, next to a representation in Parliament, and I trust it will be approved of by both countries.

The Plan

That the several [colonial] assemblies shall [form an American union and] choose members for the grand council. . . .

That the Grand Council . . . shall hold and exercise all the like rights, liberties and privileges, as are held and exercised by and in the House of Commons of Great-Britain. . . .

That the President-General shall hold his office during the pleasure of the King, and his assent shall be requisite to all acts of the Grand Council, and it shall be his office and duty to cause them to be carried into execution. . . .

That the President-General, by and with the advice and consent of the Grand-Council, hold and exercise all the legislative rights, powers, and authorities, necessary for regulating and administering all the general police and affairs of the colonies. . . .

That the said President-General and the Grand Council, be an inferior and distinct branch of the British legislature, united and incorporated with it, . . . and that the assent of both [Parliament and the Grand Council] shall be requisite to the validity of all such general acts or statutes [that affect the colonies]. ❞

QUESTIONS FOR ANALYSIS

1. According to Ingersoll, what were the main arguments of those in Parliament who opposed the Stamp Act? Did those opposing the Stamp Act agree with the act's supporters that Parliament had the right to tax the colonies?
2. How did Galloway's plan solve the problem of colonial representation in Parliament? How would the British ministers who advocated parliamentary supremacy have reacted to the plan? Use evidence form the sources or the textbook to support your claim.
3. The framers of the U.S. Constitution addressed the problem of dividing authority between state governments and the national government by allowing the states to retain legal authority over most matters and delegating limited powers to the national government. Could such a solution have been implemented in the British Empire? Make an argument and support your argument with relevant evidence.

The Rising of the Countryside

The fate of the urban-led Patriot movement would depend on the colonies' large rural population. Most farmers had little interest in imperial affairs. Their lives were deeply rooted in the soil, and their prime allegiance was to family and community. But imperial policies had increasingly intruded into the lives of farm families by sending their sons to war and raising their taxes. In 1754, farmers on Long Island, New York, had

TRM Find complete suggested responses in the Teacher's Resource Materials.

AP® SKILLS & PROCESSES

ARGUMENTATION

The third **QUESTIONS FOR ANALYSIS** prompt asks students to make connections between two issues: framing the Constitution and the challenges of governing the British Empire. Students will need to make a specific claim in response to this counterfactual question. Support students by asking them to cite a specific line from one or both documents and then explaining clearly how this evidence allows them to make an inference that supports their claim. Extend this prompt by asking students to offer examples of ways that dividing authority between state and national governments has continued to challenge the United States.

paid an average tax of 10 shillings; by 1756, thanks to the Great War for Empire, their taxes had jumped to 30 shillings.

Continental Association
An association established in 1774 by the First Continental Congress to enforce a boycott of British goods.

The Continental Association The boycotts of 1765 and 1768 raised the political consciousness of rural Americans. When the First Continental Congress established the **Continental Association** in 1774 to enforce a third boycott of British goods, it quickly set up a rural network of committees to do its work. In Concord, Massachusetts, 80 percent of the male heads of families and a number of single women signed a "Solemn League and Covenant" supporting nonimportation. In other farm towns, men blacked their faces, disguised themselves in blankets "like Indians," and threatened violence against shopkeepers who traded "in rum, molasses, & Sugar, &c." in violation of the boycott.

Patriots likewise warned that British measures threatened the yeoman tradition of landownership. In Petersham, Massachusetts, the town meeting worried that new British taxes would drain "this People of the Fruits of their Toil." Arable land was now scarce and expensive in older communities, and in new settlements merchants were seizing farmsteads for delinquent debts. By the 1770s, many northern yeomen felt personally threatened by British policies, which, a Patriot pamphlet warned, were "paving the way for reducing the country to lordships" (Table 5.1).

Southern Planters Fear Dependency Despite their higher standard of living, southern slave owners had similar fears. Many Chesapeake planters were deeply in debt to British merchants. Accustomed to being absolute masters on their slave-labor plantations and seeing themselves as guardians of English liberties, planters resented their financial dependence on British creditors and dreaded the prospect of political subservience to British officials.

That danger now seemed real. If Parliament used the Coercive Acts to subdue Massachusetts, then it might turn next to Virginia, dissolving its representative assembly and assisting British merchants to seize debt-burdened properties. Consequently, the Virginia gentry supported demands by indebted yeomen farmers to close the law courts so that they could bargain with merchants over debts without the threat of

TABLE 5.1

Patriot Resistance, 1762–1776

Date	British Action	Patriot Response
1762	Revenue Act	Merchants complain privately
1763	Proclamation Line	Land speculators voice discontent
1764	Sugar Act	Merchants and Massachusetts legislature protest
1765	Stamp Act	Sons of Liberty riot; Stamp Act Congress; first boycott of British goods
1765	Quartering Act	New York assembly refuses to fund until 1767
1767–1768	Townshend Act; military occupation of Boston	Second boycott of British goods; harassment of pro-British merchants
1772	Royal commission to investigate *Gaspée* affair	Committees of correspondence form
1773	Tea Act	Widespread resistance; Boston Tea Party
1774	Coercive Acts; Quebec Act	First Continental Congress; third boycott of British goods
1775	British raids near Boston; king's Proclamation for Suppressing Rebellion and Sedition	Armed resistance; Second Continental Congress; invasion of Canada; cutoff of colonial exports
1776	Military attacks led by royal governors in South	Paine's *Common Sense*; Declaration of Independence

CHECK FOR UNDERSTANDING

Ask students: **How and why did Patriots attempt to win farmers to their cause?** *Though many farmers felt disengaged from the controversy with Parliament, they constituted the vast majority of the colonial population, so no rebellion could succeed without their support.*

TEACHING STRATEGY

Timelines provide an opportunity for students to consider the ways historians determine eras, especially how they identify turning points. Teachers might point out that a timeline like **TABLE 5.1** provides a stripped-down version of events that is less complex than the textbook narrative, making a sequence of events easier to trace. Guide students' analysis with the following questions:

- **According to TABLE 5.1, when did broad resistance to British policies begin?** *The Stamp Act shows the first broad resistance; before that, complaints are limited to specific groups.*
- **When did opposition become effective?** *The Tea Act indicates the first "widespread resistance," while the Coercive Acts led to the calling of the First Continental Congress. Either of these might be considered effective opposition.*
- **At what point, if any, did war become inevitable? Why?** *In 1775, the colonists first engaged in armed resistance, including the invasion of Canada. For many, this was a point of no return, although perhaps reconciliation might still have been possible after that. It wasn't until after Paine's* Common Sense *the following year that war was actually declared.*

legal action. "The spark of liberty is not yet extinct among our people," declared one planter, "and if properly fanned by the Gentlemen of influence will, I make no doubt, burst out again into a flame."

Loyalists and Neutrals

Yet in many places, the Patriot movement was a hard sell. In Virginia, Patriot leaders were nearly all wealthy planters, and many of their poorer neighbors regarded the movement with suspicion. In regions where great landowners became Patriots — the Hudson River Valley of New York, for example — many tenant farmers supported the king because they hated their landlords. Similar social conflicts prompted some Regulators in the North Carolina backcountry and many farmers in eastern Maryland to oppose the Patriots there.

There were many reasons to resist the Patriot movement. Skeptics believed that Patriot leaders were subverting British rule only to advance their own selfish interests. Peter Oliver wrote of Samuel Adams, for example, "He was so thorough a Machiavilian, that he divested himself of every worthy Principle, & would stick at no Crime to accomplish his Ends." Some "Gentlemen of influence" worried that resistance to Britain would undermine all political institutions and "introduce Anarchy and disorder and render life and property here precarious." Their fears increased when the Sons of Liberty used intimidation and violence to uphold the boycotts. One well-to-do New Yorker complained, "No man can be in a more abject state of bondage than he whose Reputation, Property and Life are exposed to the discretionary violence . . . of the community." As the crisis deepened, such men became Loyalists — so called because they remained loyal to the British crown.

Many other colonists simply hoped to stay out of the fray. Some did so on principle: in New Jersey and Pennsylvania, thousands of pacifist Quakers and Germans resisted conscription and violence out of religious conviction. Others were ambivalent or confused about the political crisis unfolding around them. The delegate elected to New York's Provincial Congress from Queen's County, on Long Island, chose not to attend since "the people [he represented] seemed to be much inclined to remain peaceable and quiet." More than three-fourths of Queen's County voters, in fact, opposed sending any delegate at all. Many loyal or neutral colonists hoped, above all, to preserve their families' property and independence, whatever the outcome of the imperial crisis.

Historians estimate that some 15 to 20 percent of the white population — perhaps as many as 400,000 colonists — were loyal to the crown. Some managed to avoid persecution, but many were pressured by their neighbors to join the boycotts and subjected to violence and humiliation if they refused. As Patriots took over the reins of local government throughout the colonies, Loyalists were driven out of their homes or forced into silence. At this crucial juncture, Patriots commanded the allegiance, or at least the acquiescence, of the majority of white Americans.

VIOLENCE EAST AND WEST

How did the colonies' long controversy with Parliament influence the ideals that shaped the independence movement?

By 1774, British authority was wavering. At the headwaters of the Ohio, the abandonment of Fort Pitt left a power vacuum that was filled by opportunistic men, led by a royally appointed governor acting in defiance of his commission. In Massachusetts, the attempt to isolate and punish Boston and the surrounding countryside backfired as Patriots resisted military coercion. Violence resulted in both places, and with it the collapse of imperial control.

TEACHING STRATEGY

Use "Revolutionary America: Choosing Sides," a lesson plan from The Elizabeth Murray Project Web site, to help students better understand the dilemmas colonists experienced in deciding which side to support in the conflict. This lesson plan reveals the tense personal relationships that sometimes resulted. Apart from teaching the entire lesson, teachers may find a variety of primary and secondary sources in the lesson to be useful. Access this lesson plan by searching "Elizabeth Murray Project Choosing Sides lesson."

CHECK FOR UNDERSTANDING

Ask students: **What actions did the Continental Association take to support the efforts of the Continental Congress?** *The Continental Association of 1774 enforced the Continental Congress's third boycott of British goods by creating and maintaining a network of rural committees to ensure enforcement.*

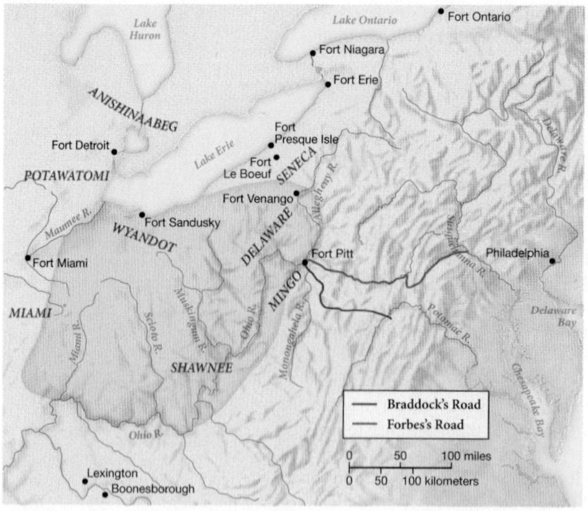

MAP 5.5 The Ohio Country, 1774–1775
The erosion of British imperial authority caused chaos in the Ohio country. Pennsylvania and Virginia each claimed Pittsburgh and the surrounding countryside, while the Indian communities on the upper Ohio increasingly feared colonist aggression. Their fears were realized in the summer of 1774, when Lord Dunmore led a force of Virginia militia into the valley. After defeating a Shawnee force in the Battle of Point Pleasant, many Virginians began surveying and staking claims to land in the Kentucky bluegrass. In the summer of 1775, perhaps a dozen new towns were settled there, in violation of the Royal Proclamation of 1763 and the Quebec Act of 1774.

Lord Dunmore's War

In the years since the end of Pontiac's Rebellion, at least 10,000 people had traveled along Braddock's and Forbes's Roads to the headwaters of the Ohio River, where Fort Pitt had replaced Fort Duquesne during the Great War for Empire, and staked claims to land around Pittsburgh (Map 5.5). They relied for protection on Fort Pitt, which remained one of Britain's most important frontier outposts. But the revenue crisis forced General Gage to cut expenses, and in October 1772, the army pulled down the fort's log walls and left the site to the local population. Settler relations with the neighboring Ohio Indians were tenuous and ill-defined, and the fort's abandonment left them exposed and vulnerable.

In the ensuing power vacuum, Pennsylvania and Virginia both claimed the region. Pennsylvania had the better claim on paper. It had organized county governments, established courts, and collected taxes there. But — in keeping with its pacifist Quaker roots — it did not organize a militia. In this omission, Virginia's royal governor, the Earl of Dunmore, recognized an opportunity. Appointed to his post in 1771, Dunmore was an irascible and unscrupulous man who clashed repeatedly with the House of Burgesses. But when it suited him, he was just as willing to defy the crown. In 1773, he traveled to Pittsburgh, where, he later wrote, "the people flocked about me and beseeched me . . . to appoint magistrates and officers of militia." He organized a local militia; soon, men armed by Virginia were drilling near the ruins of Fort Pitt.

Dunmore's War
A 1774 war led by Virginia's governor, the Earl of Dunmore, against the Ohio Shawnees, who claimed Kentucky as a hunting ground. The Shawnees were defeated and Virginians claimed Kentucky as their own.

AP® SKILLS & PROCESSES
CONTEXTUALIZATION
What led to Dunmore's War, and why did western settlers support it?

In the summer of 1774, Dunmore took the next step. In defiance of both his royal instructions and the House of Burgesses, he called out Virginia's militia and led a force of 2,400 men against the Ohio Shawnees, who had a long-standing claim to Kentucky as a hunting ground. They fought a single battle, at Point Pleasant; the Shawnees were defeated, and Dunmore and his militia forces claimed Kentucky as their own. A participant justified his actions shortly afterward: "When without a king," he wrote, "[one] doeth according to the freedom of his own will." Years of neglect left many colonists in the backcountry feeling abandoned by the crown. **Dunmore's War** was their declaration of independence.

Armed Resistance in Massachusetts

Meanwhile, as the Continental Congress gathered in Philadelphia in September 1774, Massachusetts was also defying British authority. In August, a Middlesex County Congress had urged Patriots to close the existing royal courts and to transfer their political allegiance to the popularly elected House of Representatives. Subsequently, armed crowds harassed Loyalists and ensured Patriot rule in most of New England.

In response, General Thomas Gage, now the military governor of Massachusetts, ordered British troops in Boston in September 1774 to seize Patriot armories in nearby Charlestown and Cambridge. An army of 20,000 militiamen quickly mobilized to safeguard other Massachusetts military depots. The Concord town meeting

TEACHING STRATEGY

Guide students' analysis of **MAP 5.5** with the following questions:

- **From a geographic standpoint, why might both Pennsylvania and Virginia have wanted to claim Pittsburgh?** *It was located at a strategic point, right at a bend on the Ohio River. This location provided access to travel throughout the region by water, as well as control of anyone else who attempted to travel the river. Both colonies had already invested time and effort building roads to the town to facilitate communication and trade.*
- **Of the various American Indian communities in the Ohio Valley, why did the Virginians come into conflict with the Shawnee?** *Located on the eastern end of the Ohio Valley, the Shawnee were the closest community to the encroachment of Virginia settlers, which spawned conflict.*

AP® SKILLS & PROCESSES

CONTEXTUALIZATION

Though teachers could use the **CONTEXTUALIZATION** question to address causation, this prompt also provides an opportunity for students to situate Dunmore's War in a broader regional context by considering why colonists in a particular place supported the war more than other colonists. Help students to recognize that there are two separate causal questions: Why did the war start? Why did Westerners support it? Extend this prompt by asking students to make an inference about what colonists outside the West thought about the war and why.

TRM Find complete suggested responses in the Teacher's Resource Materials.

CHECK FOR UNDERSTANDING

Ask students: **What was Dunmore's War and what was its outcome?** *It was a fight Virginia governor Lord Dunmore launched against the Shawnee with the support of the Virginia militia. Defeat of the Shawnee opened Kentucky for colonial settlement.*

raised a defensive force, the famous **Minutemen**, to "Stand at a minutes warning in Case of alarm." Increasingly, Gage's authority was limited to Boston, where it rested on the bayonets of his 3,500 troops. Meanwhile, the Patriot-controlled Massachusetts assembly met in nearby Salem in open defiance of Parliament, collecting taxes, bolstering the militia, and assuming the responsibilities of government.

In London, the colonial secretary, Lord Dartmouth, proclaimed Massachusetts to be in "open rebellion" and ordered Gage to march against the "rude rabble." On the night of April 18, 1775, Gage dispatched 700 soldiers to capture colonial leaders and supplies at Concord. However, Paul Revere and a series of other riders warned Patriots in many towns, and at dawn, militiamen confronted the British regulars first at Lexington and then at Concord. Those first skirmishes took a handful of lives, but as the British retreated to Boston, militia from neighboring towns repeatedly ambushed them. By the end of the day, 73 British soldiers were dead, 174 wounded, and 26 missing. British fire had killed 49 Massachusetts militiamen and wounded 39. Twelve years of economic and constitutional conflict had ended in violence.

Minutemen
Colonial militiamen ready to mobilize on short notice during the imperial crisis of the 1770s. These volunteers formed the core of the citizens' army that met British troops at Lexington and Concord in April 1775.

CHECK FOR UNDERSTANDING

Ask students: **How did the confrontation between Minutemen and British troops lead to bloodshed?** *Britain instructed General Gage to forcibly put down colonial rebellion in Massachusetts, while Minutemen were willing to confront British troops with armed force.*

The Second Continental Congress Organizes for War

A month later, in May 1775, Patriot leaders gathered in Philadelphia for the **Second Continental Congress**. As the Congress opened, 3,000 British troops attacked American fortifications on Breed's Hill and Bunker Hill overlooking Boston. After three assaults and 1,000 casualties, they finally dislodged the Patriot militia. Inspired by his countrymen's valor, John Adams exhorted the Congress to rise to the "defense of American liberty" by creating a continental army. He nominated George Washington to lead it. After bitter debate, the Congress approved the proposals, but, Adams lamented, only "by bare majorities."

Second Continental Congress
Legislative body that governed the United States from May 1775 through the war's duration. It established an army, created its own money, and declared independence.

The Contest for Bunker Hill With Boston occupied by British troops in the spring of 1775, Bunker Hill dominated the nearby Charlestown peninsula and therefore had great strategic value. On the night of June 16, 1,200 colonial militiamen moved into position on the adjacent Breed's Hill. On the following day, British troops conducted a series of attacks on the Patriot position, while Charlestown was cannonaded and set on fire. This image shows Patriot fortifications at the top of the hill as British troops mass along the shore. The British won the battle, but at a terrible cost. Assessing the results, General Henry Clinton concluded, "A few more such victories would have shortly put an end to British dominion in America." Yale University Art Gallery.

TEACHING STRATEGY

Use the image depicting the contest for Bunker Hill to emphasize how important port cities were to the war strategy of Great Britain and use this as an opportunity to address how the Americans needed naval assistance to combat the British fleet.

AP® SKILLS & PROCESSES

CAUSATION

Use the **CAUSATION** question to help students explain the effects of Boston violence on Congress's deliberations. Provide support for students by reminding them of the Boston violence that preceded the convention, the battles of Lexington and Concord. Ask students how the fighting on Breed's Hill compared in scale and outcome. In answering this question, students might weigh Parliament's response to the Boston violence, not just the delegates' reaction to the violence itself.

TRM Find complete suggested responses in the Teacher's Resource Materials.

Congress Versus King George Despite the bloodshed in Massachusetts, a majority in the Congress still hoped for reconciliation. Led by John Dickinson of Pennsylvania, these moderates won approval of a petition expressing loyalty to George III and asking for repeal of oppressive parliamentary legislation. But Samuel Adams, Patrick Henry, and other zealous Patriots drummed up support for a Declaration of the Causes and Necessities of Taking Up Arms. Americans dreaded the "calamities of civil war," the declaration asserted, but were "resolved to die Freemen rather than to live [as] slaves." George III failed to exploit the divisions among the Patriots; instead, in August 1775, he issued a Proclamation for Suppressing Rebellion and Sedition.

AP® SKILLS & PROCESSES

CAUSATION

How did the violence around Boston in the spring of 1775 affect proceedings in the Second Continental Congress?

Before the king's proclamation reached America, the radicals in the Congress had won support for an invasion of Canada to prevent a British attack from the north. Patriot forces easily defeated the British at Montreal; but in December 1775, they failed to capture Quebec City and withdrew. Meanwhile, American merchants waged the financial warfare promised at the First Continental Congress by cutting off exports to Britain and its West Indian sugar islands. Parliament retaliated with the Prohibitory Act, which outlawed all trade with the rebellious colonies.

Fighting in the South Skirmishes between Patriot and Loyalist forces now broke out in the southern colonies. In Virginia, Patriots ousted Governor Dunmore and forced him to take refuge on a British warship in Chesapeake Bay. Branding the rebels "traitors," the governor organized two military forces: one white, the Queen's Own Loyal Virginians; and one black, the Ethiopian Regiment, which enlisted 1,000 slaves who had fled their Patriot owners. In November 1775, Dunmore issued a controversial proclamation promising freedom to black slaves and white indentured servants who joined the Loyalist cause. White planters denounced this "Diabolical scheme," claiming it "point[ed] a dagger to their Throats." A new rising of the black and white underclasses, as in Bacon's Rebellion in the 1670s, seemed a possibility. In Fincastle County in southwestern Virginia, Loyalist planter John Hiell urged workers to support the king, promising "a Servant man" that soon "he and all the negroes would get their freedom." Frightened by Dunmore's aggressive tactics, Patriot yeomen and tenants called for a final break with Britain.

In North Carolina, too, military clashes prompted demands for independence. Early in 1776, Josiah Martin, the colony's royal governor, raised a Loyalist force of 1,500 Scottish Highlanders in the backcountry. In response, Patriots mobilized the low country militia and, in February, defeated Martin's army at the Battle of Moore's Creek Bridge, capturing more than 800 Highlanders. Following this victory, radical Patriots in the North Carolina assembly told its representatives to the Continental Congress to join with "other Colonies in declaring Independence, and forming foreign alliances." In May, the Virginia gentry followed suit: led by James Madison, Edmund Pendleton, and Patrick Henry, the Patriots met in convention and resolved unanimously to support independence.

Occupying Kentucky Beginning in the spring of 1775, in the wake of Dunmore's War, independent parties of adventurers began to occupy the newly won lands of Kentucky. Daniel Boone led one group to the banks of the Kentucky River, where they established the town of Boonesborough; nearby was Lexington, named in honor of the Massachusetts town that had resisted British troops a few months earlier. The Shawnees and other Ohio Indians opposed the settlers, and colonists built their tiny towns in the form of stations to protect themselves — groups of cabins connected by palisades to form small forts.

These western settlers had complex political loyalties. Many had marched under Dunmore and hoped to receive recognition for their claims from the crown. But as the rebellion unfolded, most recognized that the Patriots' emphasis on liberty and equality squared with their view of the world. They soon petitioned Virginia's rebel government, asking it to create a new county that would include the Kentucky settlements. They had

CHECK FOR UNDERSTANDING

Ask students: **How did the Second Continental Congress prepare for war?** *It created a Continental Army.*

"Fought and bled" for the land in Dunmore's War and now wanted to fight against the crown and its Indian allies in the Ohio country. Virginia agreed: in 1776, it organized six new frontier counties and sent arms and ammunition to Kentucky. In July, the Continental Congress followed suit, dispatching troops and arms to the Ohio River as well.

Thomas Paine's *Common Sense*

As military conflicts escalated, Americans were divided in their opinions of King George III. Many blamed him for supporting oppressive legislation and ordering armed retaliation, but other influential colonists held out the hope that he might mediate their conflict with Parliament. John Dickinson, whose *Letters* did so much to arouse Patriot resistance in 1768, nevertheless believed that war with Great Britain would be folly. In July 1775, he persuaded Congress to send George III the Olive Branch Petition, which pleaded with the king to negotiate. John Adams, a staunch supporter of independence, was infuriated by Dickinson's waffling. But Dickinson had many supporters, both inside and outside of Congress. For example, many of Philadelphia's Quaker and Anglican merchants were neutrals or Loyalists. In response to their passivity, Patriot artisans in the city organized a Mechanics' Association to protect America's "just Rights and Privileges."

AP® EXAM TIP

Outline the ideals expressed in Thomas Paine's *Common Sense* and the Declaration of Independence.

With popular sentiment in flux, a single brief pamphlet helped tip the balance. In January 1776, Thomas Paine published *Common Sense*, a rousing call for independence and a republican form of government. Paine had served as a minor customs official in England until he was fired for joining a protest against low wages. In 1774, Paine migrated to Philadelphia, where he met Benjamin Rush and other Patriots who shared his republican sentiments.

In *Common Sense*, Paine assaulted the traditional monarchical order in stirring language. "Monarchy and hereditary succession have laid the world in blood and ashes," Paine proclaimed, leveling a personal attack at George III, "the hard hearted sullen Pharaoh of England." Mixing insults with biblical quotations, Paine blasted the British system of "mixed government" that balanced power among the three estates of king, lords, and commoners. Paine granted that the system "was noble for the dark and slavish times" of the past, but now it yielded only "monarchical tyranny in the person of the king" and "aristocratical tyranny in the persons of the peers."

Paine argued for American independence by turning the traditional metaphor of patriarchal authority on its head: "Is it the interest of a man to be a boy all his life?" he asked. Within six months, *Common Sense* had gone through twenty-five editions and reached hundreds of thousands of people. "There is great talk of independence," a worried New York Loyalist noted, "the unthinking multitude are mad for it. . . . A pamphlet called Common Sense has carried off . . . thousands." Paine urged Americans to create independent republican states: "A government of our own is our natural right, 'tis time to part."

Independence Declared

Inspired by Paine's arguments and beset by armed Loyalists, Patriot conventions urged a break from Britain. In June 1776, Richard Henry Lee presented Virginia's resolution to the Continental Congress: "That these United Colonies are, and of right ought to be, free and independent states." Faced with certain defeat, staunch Loyalists and anti-independence moderates withdrew from the Congress, leaving committed Patriots to take the fateful step. On July 4, 1776, the Congress approved the **Declaration of Independence** (see the Declaration of Independence at the end of the book in Documents, p. D-1).

The Declaration's main author, Thomas Jefferson of Virginia, had mobilized resistance to the Coercive Acts with the pamphlet *A Summary View of the Rights of British America* (1774). Now, in the Declaration, he justified independence and

Declaration of Independence
A document containing philosophical principles and a list of grievances that declared separation from Britain. Adopted by the Second Continental Congress on July 4, 1776, it ended a period of intense debate with moderates still hoping to reconcile with Britain.

AP® APPLY THE TIP

Provide students with excerpts from Thomas Paine's *Common Sense* and the Declaration of Independence. Ask students to complete **Handout 5.3 — Comparison: *Common Sense* and the Declaration of Independence (TRM)** in order to record the ideas expressed in each document. After students complete the T-chart, have them work in small groups to connect the ideas expressed by Thomas Paine in *Common Sense* to the philosophy expressed by Thomas Jefferson in the Declaration of Independence, focusing on their arguments for independence from Great Britain and the style, tone, influence, and intended audience of each document.

TRM Find **Handout 5.3 — Comparison: *Common Sense* and the Declaration of Independence** in the Teacher's Resource Materials.

AP® THEME

NAT: American and National Identity

Help students understand how Paine's *Common Sense* shaped an American identity based on ideas of freedom, as it argued for the superiority of republican forms of government. His argument helped to unite the colonists to defend their political rights.

CHECK FOR UNDERSTANDING

Ask students: **What did Paine argue and why was it so effective?** *He called for independence and republicanism; its use of insults, biblical quotes, and metaphors made arguments for independence accessible to a wide range of Americans.*

AP® THEME

NAT: American and National Identity

Discuss with students how the Declaration of Independence became the nation's founding document, creating a sense of unity as it shaped an American identity based on ideas of freedom and the superiority of republican forms of government.

TEACHING STRATEGY

This image depicting the destruction of a statue of King George III was printed in Paris and the title is written in both French and German. Teachers could point out that the American rebellion did not remain an intra-empire affair with Britain, but quickly became international news.

Destruction of the King's Statue On July 9, 1776—just days after the Continental Congress approved the Declaration of Independence—a New York crowd removed symbols of the monarchy from buildings throughout the city and smashed or burned them. The crowd then proceeded to Bowling Green on the southern end of Manhattan and pulled down a statue of King George III on horseback. Constructed of gilded lead, the two-ton statue was beheaded. The horse and its headless rider were melted down to make bullets. Patriots intended to place the king's head on a spike, but British soldiers recovered it and shipped it to England. In this engraving, printed in Paris, the work is being done by slaves, suggesting how Europeans imagined life in the American colonies. Library of Congress, LC-DIG-ppmsca-17521.

republicanism to Americans and the world by vilifying George III: "He has plundered our seas, ravaged our coasts, burned our towns, and destroyed the lives of our people." Such a prince was a "tyrant," Jefferson concluded, and "is unfit to be the ruler of a free people."

Employing the ideas of the European Enlightenment, Jefferson proclaimed a series of "self-evident" truths: "that all men are created equal"; that they possess the "unalienable rights" of "Life, Liberty, and the pursuit of Happiness"; that government derives its "just powers from the consent of the governed" and can rightly be overthrown if it "becomes destructive of these ends." By linking these doctrines of individual liberty, popular sovereignty (the principle that ultimate power lies in the hands of the electorate), and republican government with American independence, Jefferson established them as the defining political values of the new nation.

For Jefferson, as for Paine, the pen proved mightier than the sword. The Declaration won wide support in France and Germany; at home, it sparked celebrations in rural hamlets and seaport cities, as crowds burned effigies and toppled statues of the king. On July 8, 1776, in Easton, Pennsylvania, a "great number of spectators" heard a reading of the Declaration, "gave their hearty assent with three loud huzzahs, and cried out, 'May God long preserve and unite the Free and Independent States of America.'"

SUMMARY

Chapter 5 has focused on a short span of time—little more than a decade—and outlined the plot of a political drama. Act I of that drama resulted from the Great War for Empire, which prompted British political leaders to implement a program of imperial reform and taxation. Act II is full of dramatic action, as colonial mobs riot, colonists chafe against restrictions on western lands, Patriot pamphleteers articulate ideologies of resistance, and British ministers search for compromise between claims of parliamentary sovereignty and assertions of colonial autonomy. Act III takes the form of tragedy: the once-proud British Empire dissolves into civil war, an imminent nightmare of death and destruction.

Why did this happen? More than two centuries later, the answers still are not clear. Certainly, the lack of astute leadership in Britain was a major factor. But British leaders faced circumstances that limited their actions: a huge national debt, an enormous new territory to administer in North America, and deep commitments to both a powerful fiscal-military state and the absolute supremacy of Parliament. Moreover, in America, decades of salutary neglect strengthened Patriots' demands for a return to political autonomy and economic opportunity. Artisans, farmers, and aspiring western settlers all feared an oppressive new era in imperial relations. The trajectories of their conflicting intentions and ideas placed Britain and its American possessions on course for a disastrous and fatal collision.

CHECK FOR UNDERSTANDING

Use the **AP® LEARNING FOCUS** question from the beginning of the chapter to check students' understanding of the chapter as a whole: **Why did the imperial crisis lead to war between Britain and the United States?** *Independence was not inevitable in the eighteenth century. If parliamentary leaders in the mid-1760s had granted colonial requests for a direct system of representation, more local control over the function of government bodies, and less internal taxation, the colonists might have remained British subjects and agreed to increase their economic share of paying for the costs of empire. Great Britain's movement from a commercial to a territorial empire necessitated new imperial policies to control the territory gained from France. Moreover, the war created new policies with American Indians, which exacerbated political tensions between the American colonists and American Indians. In the end, American colonists, as a result of an extended period of relative autonomy before the Seven Years' War, had become too accustomed to their own sense of self-rule, representation, and opportunity.*

LearningCurve

Remind students to go online to complete the LearningCurve quiz for this chapter.

CHAPTER 5 REVIEW

AP® CONTENT REVIEW *Answer these questions to demonstrate your understanding of the chapter's main ideas.*

1. What changes in Britain's imperial policy were triggered by its victory in the Great War for Empire?
2. What was the development of formal protests against Parliament and popular resistance in the years between 1765 and 1770?
3. What actions did the Continental Association take to support the efforts of the Continental Congress?
4. How did the colonies' long controversy with Parliament influence the ideals that shaped the independence movement?

AP® TERMS TO KNOW *Identify and explain the significance of each term below.*

Key Concepts and Events

Sugar Act of 1764 (p. 149)
Stamp Act of 1765 (p. 150)
Quartering Act of 1765 (p. 151)
Stamp Act Congress (p. 152)
Sons of Liberty (p. 152)
English common law (p. 153)
natural rights (p. 153)
Declaratory Act of 1766 (p. 154)
Townshend Act of 1767 (p. 154)
nonimportation movement (p. 155)
committees of correspondence (p. 163)
Tea Act of May 1773 (p. 163)
Coercive Acts (p. 164)
Continental Congress (p. 164)
Continental Association (p. 168)
Dunmore's War (p. 170)
Minutemen (p. 171)
Second Continental Congress (p. 171)
Declaration of Independence (p. 173)

Key People

John Dickinson (p. 147)
George Grenville (p. 148)
Charles Townshend (p. 151)
Lord North (p. 160)
Samuel Adams (p. 161)
Lord Dunmore (p. 170)
Thomas Paine (p. 173)
Thomas Jefferson (p. 153)

AP® MAKING CONNECTIONS *Recognize the larger developments and continuities within and across chapters by answering these questions.*

1. Chapter 4 presented a turbulent era, marked by social and cultural conflict and imperial warfare, during which the regions of British North America were disparate and without unity. Yet by 1776—only thirteen years after the Treaty of Paris ending the Great War for Empire—thirteen of Britain's mainland colonies were prepared to unite in a Declaration of Independence. What happened in that intervening time to strengthen and deepen colonists' sense of common cause? As they drew together to resist imperial authority, what political and cultural resources did they have in common? common? Using specific and relevant examples, explain the short- and long-term causes, as well as the relevant context shaping actions toward independence.
2. Consider what you have learned about British North America and the British Atlantic World in Chapters 3, 4, and 5. The British Empire oversaw dramatic growth and prosperity in its mainland colonies after 1700, but its control of North America unraveled after its decisive triumph in the Great War for Empire. What were the greatest strengths of the British Empire in these years? What were its fatal weaknesses? Describe the patterns of changes in the British Empire using evidence from the text.

KEY TURNING POINTS *Refer to the timeline at the start of the chapter for help in answering the following questions.*

What did Parliament hope to achieve with the Coercive Acts? How did the decision to convene a continent-wide congress demonstrate the failure of Parliament's efforts?

175

TRM Find complete suggested responses in the Teacher's Resource Materials.

AP® SKILLS & PROCESSES

CAUSATION

Use **AP® CONTENT REVIEW 1** to help students identify the effects of the Seven Years' War on British policy. Note: This is the same question as the section-opening question on p. 146.

AP® SKILLS & PROCESSES

COMPARISON

AP® CONTENT REVIEW 2 asks students to compare similarities and differences in two forms of protest against British policies.

AP® SKILLS & PROCESSES

CAUSATION

AP® CONTENT REVIEW 3 prompts students to evaluate the significance of the Continental Association's aid to the Continental Congress. Note: This is the same question as the section-opening question on p. 163.

AP® SKILLS & PROCESSES

CAUSATION

AP® CONTENT REVIEW 4 assists students in explaining the effects of conflict with Parliament on the ideology of independence. This is the same question as the section-opening question on p. 169.

TRM Find definitions for these terms in the **Glossary/Glosario** in the Teacher's Resource Materials.

AP® THEME

NAT: American and National Identity

Use **AP® MAKING CONNECTIONS 1** to consolidate students' understanding of the way that a sense of American identity was forged in the period from 1754 to 1776.

AP® SKILLS & PROCESSES

CONTINUITY AND CHANGE

AP® MAKING CONNECTIONS 2 asks students to consider continuity and change in the power of the British Empire. The strength of the British imperial system in the period before the Seven Years' War was the emphasis it placed on commercial success and the attendant mercantile economic system. Due to this emphasis, Great Britain was able to not overextend its military and instead focused on allowing some relative autonomy—both commercial and political—in the colonies, which also increased a belief in Anglicization among colonists. The weaknesses of a territorial empire were exposed in the period immediately following the Seven Years' War. The victory in the imperial contest for control of North America caused changes in policies toward American colonists and American Indians. Britain's new territorial empire increased political control, taxation, and military control in the colonies. These changes altered not only the relationship between the British and the American colonists; it altered the meaning of self-rule and independence.

AP® SKILLS & PROCESSES

CONTINUITY AND CHANGE

The **KEY TURNING POINTS** question encourages students to consider the Coercive Acts as a possible turning point in the relationship between Britain and the colonies.

TRM Find complete suggested responses in the Teacher's Resource Materials.

AP® PRACTICE QUESTIONS

MULTIPLE CHOICE QUESTIONS *Choose the correct answer for each question.*

Questions 1–3 refer to this graph.

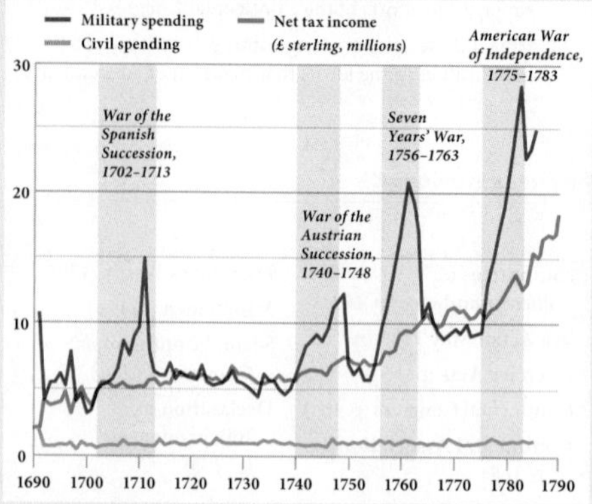

The Cost of Empire, 1690–1790

1. Which of the following most directly contributed to the trends seen in the graph between 1740 and 1765?
   - **a.** Inability of the British navy to secure trade on the high seas
   - **b.** Failure of the British government to recognize colonial dissatisfaction with imperial policy
   - **c.** Decreased British imperial interest in governing its North American colonies
   - **d.** Intensifying rivalries in North America between European powers seeking to expand

2. The graph would be most useful as a source of information about which of the following?
   - **a.** European and American Indian alliances during the Seven Years' War
   - **b.** British attempts to consolidate control over its American colonies
   - **c.** American colonists' increasing demands for self-rule
   - **d.** British efforts to collect taxes without direct colonial consent

3. Which of the following additional evidence would best support economic changes summarized in this graph?
   - **a.** Ship logs recording the goods carried between the colonies and the Caribbean
   - **b.** Political pamphlets calling for increased resistance to British imperial policies
   - **c.** Parliamentary records detailing the cost of stationing troops in the colonies
   - **d.** The diary of an American merchant describing the collection of customs duties

Questions 4–6 refer to this engraving.

Protesting the Stamp Act in Portsmouth, New Hampshire

Illustration from "Interesting Events in the History of the U.S." by J. W. Barber, 1829/Picture Research Consultants & Archives.

4. The activities of the colonists in the 1760s depicted in the engraving could best be used as evidence to support which of the following arguments?
   - **a.** Colonial elites feared the dangers of self-rule and popular sovereignty.
   - **b.** Commoners sought to preserve policies favoring Protestantism in the colonies.
   - **c.** Colonists of all classes protested Britain's pro-expansion policies.
   - **d.** British efforts to raise revenue from the colonies sparked major resistance.

5. Political protests of the 1760s, such as the one depicted in the engraving, flourished for all of the following reasons EXCEPT
   - **a.** parliament's adoption of a policy of salutary neglect after the Seven Years' War.
   - **b.** colonial leaders such as Benjamin Franklin organized resistance to British imperial policy.
   - **c.** the spread of a transatlantic print literature across the colonies.
   - **d.** British efforts to restrict colonists' westward expansion into unsecured areas.

6. In response to events in the 1760s, American colonists most commonly
   a. embraced ideas of hereditary privilege.
   b. argued for natural rights and republicanism.
   c. demanded abolition of slavery.
   d. departed from ideas popularized by the Enlightenment.

Questions 7–8 refer to this excerpt.

> "This widespread ownership of property is perhaps the most important single fact about the Americans of the Revolutionary period. It meant that they were not divided so widely between rich and poor as the people of the Old World. Most of the men and women who settled the colonies had come with expectations of a better life for themselves and their children, and most had achieved it . . . [T]here was as yet no professed belief in social equality . . . in every colony there were aristocrats . . . , [but] there were no peasants for them to lord it over — except always the slaves."
>
> Edmund Morgan, *The Birth of the Republic: 1763–1789*, 1992

7. Which of the following social organizations most likely resulted in the period from 1754 to 1776 from the trend described in the excerpt?
   a. The colonies began to unite after perceived constraints on their political and economic activities.
   b. Colonists provided financial and material support for the Revolution despite economic hardships.
   c. The American Revolution was energized by laborers and women, as well as elites and intellectuals.
   d. The Patriots succeeded in overthrowing Britain because of their overwhelming financial advantages.

8. The passage would be most useful as a source of information about which of the following?
   a. The importance of egalitarianism as an American ideal
   b. Radical agitators and extralegal violence
   c. Changing notions of family and gender roles
   d. Growing sectionalism and regional specialization

SHORT ANSWER QUESTIONS

Read each question carefully and write a short response. Use evidence from the text to support your claims.

> "Officers of empire and Indian leaders had consistently sought, through long years of association, to create patterns of leadership and diplomacy that would mute conflict and encourage accommodation. . . . The collapse of British authority in the Ohio Valley dealt the final blow to the already badly weakened principles of accommodation and mediation."
>
> Eric Hinderaker, *Elusive Empires: Constructing Colonialism in the Ohio Valley, 1673–1800*, 1997
>
> "Official policy, highly confused though it was, tended to place Indians far beyond the rule of law, and it intended, even in the long run, to keep them there by pushing them away from any civil jurisdiction in the colonies. . . . During the war . . . officers urged, ordered, and approved the indiscriminate slaughter of Indians."
>
> Gregory Evans Dowd, *War Under Heaven: Pontiac, the Indian Nations, & the British Empire*, 2002

1. Using the two excerpts provided, answer (a), (b), and (c).
   a. Briefly explain ONE major difference between Hinderaker's and Dowd's historical interpretations of British policies toward Native American Indians.
   b. Briefly explain how ONE specific historical event or development during the period 1754 to 1776 that is not explicitly mentioned in the excerpts could be used to support Hinderaker's argument.
   c. Briefly explain how ONE specific historical event or development during the period 1754 to 1776 that is not explicitly mentioned in the excerpts could be used to support Dowd's argument.

2. Answer (a), (b), and (c).
   a. Briefly explain ONE specific historical cause of British participation in the Seven Years' War (1754–1763).
   b. Briefly explain ONE specific historical event or development that resulted from British participation in the Seven Years' War (1754–1763).
   c. Briefly explain how ONE specific British imperial policy resulting from the Seven Years' War (1754–1763) changed relations between Britain and its North American colonies.

3. Answer (a), (b), and (c).
   a. Briefly explain ONE specific historical factor that changed American philosophical ideas about government in the period from 1763–1776.
   b. Briefly explain ANOTHER specific historical factor that changed American philosophical ideas about government in the period from 1763–1776.
   c. Briefly explain ONE way in which the changes you explained in part (a) or (b) were challenged in the period from 1763 to 1776.

TRM Find complete suggested responses in the Teacher's Resource Materials.

6 CHAPTER Making War and Republican Governments 1776–1789

Chapter 6 — AP® Assessment Weight and Pacing Guide

The assessment weight on the AP® U.S. History Exam for Chapters 5–7 is 10–17 percent. This chapter falls in Unit 3 of the AP® U.S. History Curriculum, covering Period 3: 1754–1800.

This pacing guide is based on a schedule with 120 sessions of 50 minutes each before the AP® U.S. History Exam. If you have a different number of sessions before the exam, you can modify the pacing to meet your needs. If you have additional time, consider incorporating quizzes, released AP® U.S. History questions, practice exams, writing practice, and other instructional activities.

	Traditional Schedule	Block Schedule
Chapter 6	5 days	2–3 days

Daily Pacing Guide

	Content Focus	Essential Question
Day 1	The Trials of War, 1776–1778	What challenges did Patriot forces confront in the first two years of the war, and what were their key achievements?
Day 2	The Path to Victory, 1778–1783	Why did the Patriots win the American Revolution?
Days 3 and 4	Creating Republican Institutions, 1776–1787	What were the most important challenges facing governments in the 1780s?
Day 5	The Constitution of 1787	What were the most important compromises struck in the Philadelphia convention of 1787?

AP® Alignment

Section Heading	AP® Topic	AP® Themes
The Trials of War, 1776–1778	3.5	WOR
The Path to Victory, 1778–1783	3.5, 3.7	WOR, PCE
Creating Republican Institutions, 1776–1787	3.6, 3.7	SOC, PCE
The Constitution of 1787	3.8, 3.9	PCE

*Should changes be made to the Course Framework in the future, an updated alignment will be placed on our AP® updates page at go.bfwpub.com/ap-course-updates.

Chapter 6 — Overview

Chapter 6 begins by looking at the factors that led to the victory of the Patriots over the British in the American Revolution by examining battles, leaders, and the importance of alliances. Even before the final victory in the American Revolution, colonial leaders began to focus on establishing a new government based on the principles of republicanism. The chapter chronicles the challenges of establishing a new government, including the successes and failures of the Articles of Confederation. Finally, the writing of the U.S. Constitution is discussed and the debate that ensued between Federalists and Antifederalists ultimately resulting in ratification.

Chapter 6 — Resources

The following resources can be found in the Teacher's Resource Materials (TRM) that accompany the book. You can access the TRM via the book's digital platform, by clicking the TRM links found here in your Teacher's Edition e-book, or by contacting your representative to access the resources online. Visit **bfwpub.com/henretta10e** to learn more.

TRM Chapter 6 Lecture Presentation Slides

TRM Chapter 6 Outline with AP® Focus

TRM Chapter 6 Lecture Strategies

TRM Chapter 6 Suggested Responses

TRM Handout 6.1 — Continuity and Change over Time: American Revolution

TRM Handout 6.2 — Causation: Articles of Confederation

TRM Handout 6.3 — Contextualization: Ratification Debate

Chapter 6 — Essential Activity

Engage students in an activity in which they will visually represent the events, choices, and challenges that led to the American Revolution as a road map complete with road signs (warnings, directions, etc.), billboards (sponsored by different groups), exits (choices and their results), road hazards, etc. Provide students with large sheets of bulletin board paper on which to create the road map. Instruct students to begin their road map on one corner with the Proclamation of 1763 and Treaty of Paris in 1783. Display the road maps in the classroom and have students view and make comments with sticky notes on the effectiveness of their classmates' maps and suggestions for improvement.

Chapter 6 — Bell Ringers

The following activities take no more than 5–15 minutes of your class period and offer an effective and engaging way to begin your lessons and for students to apply AP® Skills & Processes:

- Ask students: Did the states or federal government come first? This should be a fairly simple question for students to answer. Extend the question by asking: Why is it important that states came before the federal government? *Answers will vary but should include the following: It is important because the state constitutions influenced the establishment of federal government. Also, differences between states led to conflicts when trying to create federal government.*
- Project an image of the sculpture "George Washington" by Jean-Antoine Houdon. Ask students to analyze the image by identifying the elements in the sculpture and what they represent. Then ask them to explain the way the sculpture was used to represent the leadership of Washington in early U.S. history. *Answers will vary, but should identify the following elements: the fasces represents the unity of the 13 colonies; the plow shows Washington as a farmer or common man; his civilian clothes show him giving up military power; his belly reveals he is no longer a young man; the keys reference Cincinnatus; the sword shows he willingly gave up military power for service.*
- Write the following names on the board: Montesquieu, Voltaire, Locke, and Rousseau. Ask students to brainstorm the connection of each of the Enlightenment thinkers to the establishment of the new republic. Ask students to provide specific evidence that shows the influence of each thinker.

NOTES

TEACHING STRATEGY

Use the chapter opener material to help students identify the main themes of the period between the Declaration of Independence in 1776 and the start of a new government under the Constitution in 1789. When colonies rejected the Crown's authority, they needed to form their own governments. Having criticized monarchical tyranny using republican arguments, it was no surprise that they founded republican governments of their own. Students tend to assume that the creation of a national government was the first order of business but, as the chapter makes clear, creating individual state governments came first in time and in importance. American society experienced historical continuities and changes as they designed new governments. Students should be attentive to both developments as they read this chapter. For a complete suggested response to the **AP® LEARNING FOCUS** question, see p. 208.

6

CHAPTER

Making War and Republican Governments

1776–1789

AP® LEARNING FOCUS

Why did the American independence movement succeed, and what changes did it initiate in American society and government?

When Patriots in Frederick County, Maryland, demanded his allegiance to their cause in 1776, Robert Gassaway would have none of it. "It was better for the poor people to lay down their arms and pay the duties and taxes laid upon them by King and Parliament than to be brought into slavery and commanded and ordered about [by you]," he told them. The story was much the same in Farmington, Connecticut, where Patriot officials imprisoned Nathaniel Jones and seventeen other men for "remaining neutral." In Pennsylvania, Quakers accused of Loyalism were rounded up, jailed, and charged with treason, and some were hanged for aiding the British cause. Everywhere, the outbreak of fighting in 1776 forced families to choose the Loyalist or the Patriot side.

The Patriots' control of most local governments gave them an edge in this battle. Patriot leaders organized militia units and recruited volunteers for the Continental army, a ragtag force that surprisingly held its own on the battlefield. "I admire the American troops tremendously!" exclaimed a French officer. "It is incredible that soldiers composed of every age, even children of fifteen, of whites and blacks, almost naked, unpaid, and rather poorly fed, can march so well and withstand fire so steadfastly."

Military service created political commitment, and vice versa. Many Patriot leaders encouraged Americans not only to support the war but also to take an active role in government. As more people did so, their political identities changed. Previously, Americans had lived within a social world dominated by the links of family, kinship, and locality. Now, the abstract bonds of citizenship connected them directly to more distant institutions of government. "From subjects to citizens the difference is immense," remarked South Carolina Patriot David Ramsay. By repudiating monarchical rule and raising a democratic army, the Patriots launched the age of republican revolutions.

Soon republicanism would throw France into turmoil and inspire revolutionaries in Spain's American colonies. The independence of the Anglo- American colonies, remarked the Venezuelan political leader Francisco de Miranda, who had been in New York and Philadelphia at the end of the American Revolution, "was bound to be . . . the infallible preliminary to our own [independence movement]." The Patriot uprising of 1776 set in motion a process that gradually replaced an Atlantic colonial system that spanned the Americas with an American system of new nations.

General Washington, 1781 By war's end, George Washington was a hero on both sides of the Atlantic. This engraving, printed in Paris in 1781, shows him with various British bills and declarations in tatters at his feet while he holds copies of the Declaration of Independence and the Treaty of Alliance with France. In the background of this vaguely Orientalized scene, a black slave — presumably William Lee, Washington's valet and constant companion during the Revolution — saddles his horse. Anne S. K. Brown Military Collection, Brown University Library.

TEACHING STRATEGY

The portrait of George Washington illustrates many significant themes of the Revolution and its consequences. Guide students' analysis with the following questions:

- **How is Washington characterized?** *He is depicted as a noble, confident military leader. He is well-dressed, carries a sword, and wears a uniform coat with epaulets. His warhorse is being readied in the background.*
- **How do the documents included in the image hint at the reasons for rebellion and hopes for success?** *Washington is trampling documents that represent Britain's broken promises of reconciliation with its colonies. He holds the Declaration of Independence, which catalogs American grievances. Beneath it is the Franco-American Treaty of Alliance, which promises the hope of success for the rebellion.*
- **What details in the picture suggest contradictions in the colonies' fight for independence and republicanism?** *The slave presented in the literal and metaphorical background of the painting illustrates the ways that freedom for slaves was largely ignored by those complaining of being enslaved by Britain. Washington's depiction as an American nobleman suggests tensions between the potentially egalitarian values of republicanism and a long American tradition of deference to colonial elites.*

AP® SKILLS & PROCESSES

CONTINUITY AND CHANGE

Use the **TIMELINE** to explore how 1776 to 1788 could constitute a definable historical era. Ask students why the Declaration of Independence in 1776 is one of the few generally uncontested turning points in American history. Inform students that historians identify different ending dates for this era depending on what they focus on, such as the drafting of the Constitution (1787), its ratification (1788), or the start of the new government under the Constitution (1789). Students might consider the significance of the textbook's choice of the last of these three dates. Extend this exercise by asking students to explain why the Constitution, rather than the ratification of the Articles of Confederation, is typically considered the end of this era.

TEACHING STRATEGY

Ask students: **In what ways did Joseph Brant adopt a hybrid identity?** *He converted to Christianity, helped translate the Bible into Mohawk (which relied on French missionaries' work creating an alphabet for the oral Mohawk language), wore some Western clothing, and had a European-style portrait commissioned for himself by one of Britain's most famous artists.*

TIMELINE

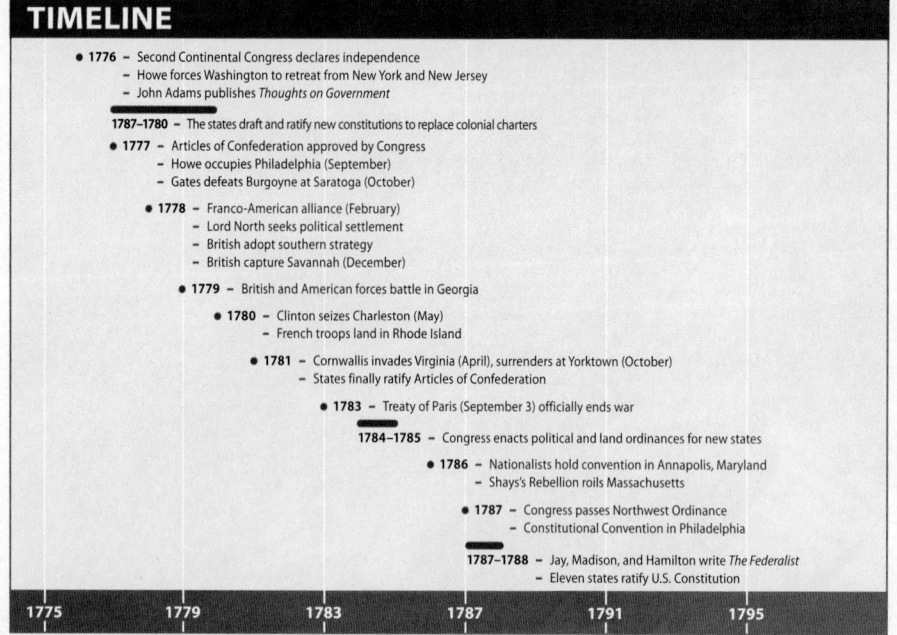

- **1776** – Second Continental Congress declares independence
  - Howe forces Washington to retreat from New York and New Jersey
  - John Adams publishes *Thoughts on Government*
- **1787–1780** – The states draft and ratify new constitutions to replace colonial charters
- **1777** – Articles of Confederation approved by Congress
  - Howe occupies Philadelphia (September)
  - Gates defeats Burgoyne at Saratoga (October)
- **1778** – Franco-American alliance (February)
  - Lord North seeks political settlement
  - British adopt southern strategy
  - British capture Savannah (December)
- **1779** – British and American forces battle in Georgia
- **1780** – Clinton seizes Charleston (May)
  - French troops land in Rhode Island
- **1781** – Cornwallis invades Virginia (April), surrenders at Yorktown (October)
  - States finally ratify Articles of Confederation
- **1783** – Treaty of Paris (September 3) officially ends war
- **1784–1785** – Congress enacts political and land ordinances for new states
- **1786** – Nationalists hold convention in Annapolis, Maryland
  - Shays's Rebellion roils Massachusetts
- **1787** – Congress passes Northwest Ordinance
  - Constitutional Convention in Philadelphia
- **1787–1788** – Jay, Madison, and Hamilton write *The Federalist*
  - Eleven states ratify U.S. Constitution

1775 1779 1783 1787 1791 1795

Joseph Brant Mohawk chief Thayendanegea, known to whites as Joseph Brant, was a devout member of the Church of England and helped to translate the Bible into the Mohawk language. Brant persuaded four of the six Iroquois nations to support Britain in the war. He received a captain's commission in the British army and led Iroquois warriors and Tory rangers in devastating attacks on American settlements in the Wyoming Valley of Pennsylvania and Cherry Valley in New York. After the war, he was instrumental in resettling Mohawks and other British-allied Indians on the Grand River in Ontario, Canada. Brant was depicted many times by painters and sculptors. In this 1786 portrait, painted during one of his trips to England, Gilbert Stuart depicts his hybrid identity and captures a haunting sense of melancholy. Corbis Historical/Getty Images.

THE TRIALS OF WAR, 1776–1778

What challenges did Patriot forces confront in the first two years of the war, and what were their key achievements?

The Declaration of Independence appeared just as the British launched a full-scale military assault. For two years, British troops manhandled the Continental army. A few inspiring American victories kept the rebellion alive, but during the winters of 1776 and 1777, the Patriot cause hung in the balance.

War in the North

Once the British resorted to military force, few Europeans gave the rebels a chance. The population of Great Britain was 11 million; the colonies, 2.5 million, 20 percent of whom were enslaved Africans. Moreover, the British government had access to the immense wealth generated by the South Atlantic System and the emerging Industrial Revolution. Britain also had the most powerful navy in the world, a standing army of 48,000 Britons plus thousands of German (Hessian) soldiers, and the support of thousands of American Loyalists and powerful Indian coalitions. In the Carolinas, the Cherokees resisted colonists' demands for their lands by allying with the British, as did four of the six Iroquois nations of New York (Map 6.1). In the Ohio country, Shawnees and their allies, armed by the British, attacked the new Kentucky settlements.

By contrast, the Americans were economically and militarily weak. They lacked a strong central government and a reliable source of tax revenue. Their new Continental army, commanded by General George Washington, consisted of 18,000 poorly trained and inexperienced recruits.

AP® SKILLS & PROCESSES

DEVELOPMENTS AND PROCESSES

Remind students of the relationship between the imperial powers of France and Great Britain and the alliances they developed with American Indian groups in the years preceding and during the Seven Years' War. Ask students to identify one historical change in the alliances of American Indians with Europeans after the Seven Years' War and how that affected the Americans during the Revolutionary War.

To demonstrate Britain's military superiority, Prime Minister Lord North ordered General William Howe to capture New York City. His strategy was to seize control of the Hudson River and thereby isolate the radical Patriots in New England from the colonies to the south. As the Second Continental Congress declared independence in Philadelphia in July 1776, Howe landed 32,000 troops — British regulars and German mercenaries — outside New York City. In August 1776, Howe defeated the Americans in the **Battle of Long Island** and forced their retreat to Manhattan Island. There, Howe outflanked Washington's troops and nearly trapped them. Outgunned and outmaneuvered, the Continental army again retreated, eventually crossing the Hudson River to New Jersey. By December, the British army had pushed the rebels across New Jersey and over the Delaware River into Pennsylvania.

From the Patriots' perspective, winter came just in time. Following eighteenth-century custom, the British halted their military campaign for the cold months, allowing the Americans to catch them off guard. On Christmas night 1776, Washington crossed the Delaware River and staged a successful surprise attack on Trenton, New Jersey, where he forced the surrender of 1,000 German soldiers. In early January 1777, the Continental army won a small victory at nearby Princeton (Map 6.2). But these minor triumphs could not mask British military superiority. "These are the times," wrote Thomas Paine, "that try men's souls."

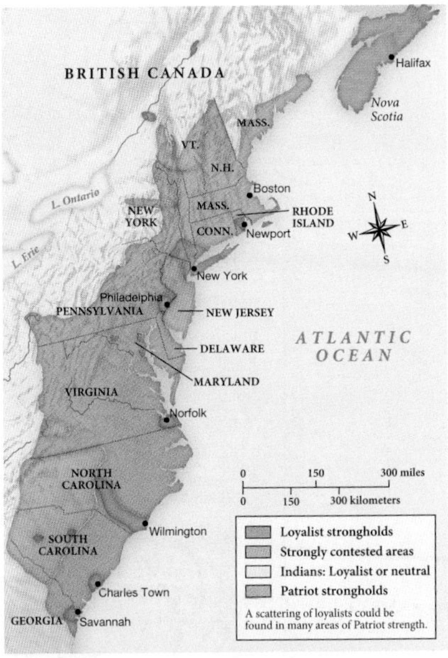

MAP 6.1 Patriot and Loyalist Strongholds
Patriots were in the majority in most of the thirteen mainland colonies and used their control of local governments to funnel men, money, and supplies to the rebel cause. Although Loyalists could be found in every colony, their strongholds were limited to Nova Scotia, eastern New York, New Jersey, and certain areas in the South. However, most Native American peoples favored the British cause and bolstered the power of Loyalist militias in central New York (see Map 6.3) and in the Carolina backcountry.

Armies and Strategies

Thanks in part to General Howe, the rebellion survived. Howe had opposed the Coercive Acts of 1774 and still hoped for a political compromise. So he did not try to destroy the American army but instead tried to show its weakness and persuade the Continental Congress to give up the struggle. Howe's restrained tactics cost Britain the opportunity to nip the rebellion in the bud. For his part, Washington acted cautiously to avoid a major defeat: "On our Side the War should be defensive," he told Congress. His strategy was to draw the British away from the seacoast, extend their lines of supply, and sap their morale.

Congress had promised Washington a regular force of 75,000 men, but the Continental army never reached even a third of that number. Why were American men reluctant to join the army? Yeomen, refusing to be "Haras'd with callouts" that took them away from their families and farms, would serve only in local militias. When the Virginia gentry imposed a military draft and three years of service on propertyless men — the "Lazy fellows who lurk about and are pests to Society" — they resisted so fiercely that the legislature had to pay them substantial bounties and agree to shorter terms of service. The Continental soldiers recruited in Maryland by General William Smallwood were poor American youths and older foreign-born men, often British ex-convicts and former indentured servants. Most enlisted for the $20 cash bonus (about $2,000 today) and the promise of 100 acres of land.

Molding such recruits into an effective fighting force was nearly impossible. Inexperienced soldiers panicked in the face of British attacks; thousands deserted, unwilling to submit to the discipline of military life. The soldiers who stayed resented the contempt their officers had for the "camp followers," the women who made do with

Battle of Long Island (1776)
First major engagement of the new Continental army against 32,000 British troops; Washington's army was defeated and forced to retreat to Manhattan Island.

AP® SKILLS & PROCESSES

DEVELOPMENTS AND PROCESSES

Why was control of New York City Britain's first military objective in the emerging war?

AP® EXAM TIP

Identify the ways that men and women mobilized resources in support of the Patriot movement in the American Revolution.

TEACHING STRATEGY

PBS provides several lesson plans to accompany segments of the documentary *Liberty! The American Revolution*. "Lesson 3: The Continental Army & Washington" offers a firsthand understanding of the conditions faced by Washington's Continental Army and explores how Washington was able to hold his troops together. Lesson materials include discussion points for teachers, a viewing guide and a separate answer key, links to other resources, and extension ideas. Access this lesson plan by searching "PBS Continental Army Washington."

CHECK FOR UNDERSTANDING

Ask students: **What characterized war in the north between 1776 and 1778?** *The larger and better-supplied British took Long Island and then Manhattan, forcing several Patriot retreats. Washington won minor victories at Trenton and Princeton.*

AP® SKILLS & PROCESSES

DEVELOPMENTS AND PROCESSES

The **DEVELOPMENT AND PROCESSES** question asks students to consider the perspective of British military planners, which implies a contrast with Washington and Patriot military tactics. Students can be asked to explain why the British identified particular locations as strategic. Extend this prompt by asking students to explore why Washington's goal was essentially one of attrition — avoid defeat while attempting to wear the British out.

TRM Find complete suggested responses in the Teacher's Resource Materials.

AP® APPLY THE TIP

Remind students that fighting wars requires much more than just guns and ammunition. Ask students, individually or in small groups, to make a list of resources needed to support a war effort and have them consider the ways in which the Continental Army could acquire the goods needed to fight the British in the American Revolution. Provide students with excerpts from primary sources that shed light on the issue of providing needed supplies to the Patriot cause (many can be found online at the Library of Congress's teacher's resources Web site, including "Washington to Pennsylvania Governor Joseph Reed, May 28, 1780" and "Recruiting African Americans into the Continental Army"). Ask students to analyze the documents for the historical evidence they provide related to the issues of supporting the Patriot movement. Have students engage in an extended analysis as required on the AP® DBQ Rubric by asking them to consider the historical context of each source, the intended audience, purpose, and point of view of the author.

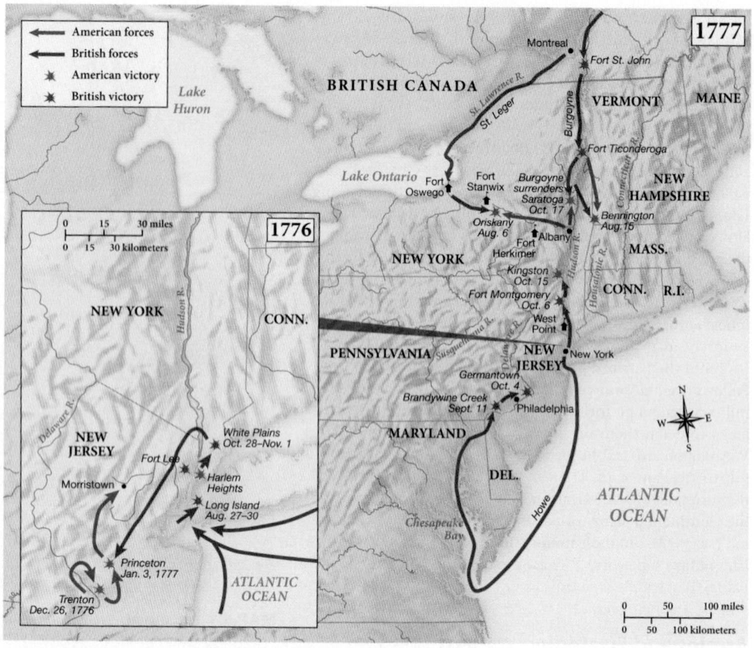

MAP 6.2 The War in the North, 1776–1777
In 1776, the British army drove Washington's forces across New Jersey into Pennsylvania. The Americans counterattacked successfully at Trenton and Princeton and then set up winter headquarters in Morristown. In 1777, British forces stayed on the offensive. General Howe attacked the Patriot capital, Philadelphia, from the south and captured it in early October. Meanwhile, General Burgoyne and Colonel St. Leger launched simultaneous invasions from Canada. With the help of thousands of New England militiamen, American troops commanded by General Horatio Gates defeated Burgoyne in August at Bennington, Vermont, and in October at Saratoga, New York, the military turning point in the war.

the meager supplies provided to feed and care for the troops. General Philip Schuyler of New York complained that his troops were "destitute of provisions, without camp equipage, with little ammunition, and not a single piece of cannon."

The Continental army was not only poorly supplied but was also held in suspicion by Radical Whig Patriots, who believed that a standing army was a threat to liberty. Even in wartime, they preferred militias to a professional fighting force and often resisted Washington's pleas for stronger support. Given these handicaps, Washington and his army were fortunate to have survived.

AP® SKILLS & PROCESSES

DEVELOPMENTS AND PROCESSES

What factors made it difficult for the Continental Congress to create an effective army?

Victory at Saratoga

After Howe failed to achieve an overwhelming victory, Lord North and his colonial secretary, Lord George Germain, launched another major military campaign in 1777. Isolating New England remained the primary goal. To achieve it, Germain planned a three-pronged attack converging on Albany, New York. General John Burgoyne would lead a large contingent of regulars south from Quebec, Colonel Barry St. Leger and a

AP® SKILLS & PROCESSES

DEVELOPMENTS AND PROCESSES

Use the **DEVELOPMENTS AND PROCESSES** question to help students evaluate the relative significance of factors that caused the American army's weakness. Some students may have learned a patriotic account of the Revolution that makes the problems of the Continental Army surprising. Extend this prompt by asking students to consider how the rebellion might have turned out differently if General Howe had fought more aggressively. Though the book suggests that this course of action could have nipped the Revolution in the bud, it's also possible that it would have stiffened colonial resistance and/or won over some moderates.

TRM Find complete suggested responses in the Teacher's Resource Materials.

CHECK FOR UNDERSTANDING

Ask students: **What was the Continental army like and what was its strategy?** *Consisting of less than 25,000 poorly trained and poorly supplied troops, the best the Continental army could hope for was to avoid a major defeat.*

force of Iroquois would attack from the west, and General Howe would lead troops north from New York City.

Howe instead decided to attack Philadelphia, the home of the Continental Congress, hoping to end the rebellion with a single decisive blow. Howe's troops easily outflanked the American positions along Brandywine Creek in Delaware and, in late September, marched triumphantly into Philadelphia. However, the capture of the rebels' capital did not end the uprising; the Continental Congress, determined to continue the struggle, fled to the countryside.

Victory at Saratoga The surrender of General John Burgoyne to American forces at Saratoga, New York, in October 1777 was the most important Patriot victory in the early years of the war. General Horatio Gates, wearing the blue and buff officers' uniform of the Continental army, stands at the center of this painting by John Trumbull, which hangs in the U.S. Capitol. Burgoyne, in the scarlet uniform of the British army, forlornly offers Gates his sword as Gates invites him into his tent. The Patriots' victory at Saratoga, which unfolded over several weeks in a complex set of military maneuvers, proved to their allies and enemies alike that they could defeat a British army in the field. Architect of the Capitol

In the north, Burgoyne's troops had at first advanced quickly, overwhelming the American defenses at Fort Ticonderoga in early July and driving south toward the Hudson River. Then they stalled. Burgoyne — nicknamed "Gentleman Johnny" — was used to high living and had fought in Europe in a leisurely fashion; underestimating the extent of popular support for the rebels, he stopped early each day to pitch comfortable tents and eat elaborate dinners with his officers. The American troops led by General Horatio Gates also slowed Burgoyne's progress by felling huge trees in his path and raiding British supply lines to Canada.

At summer's end, Burgoyne's army of 6,000 British and German troops and 600 Loyalists and Indians was stuck near Saratoga, New York. Desperate for food and horses, in August the British raided nearby Bennington, Vermont, but were beaten back by 2,000 American militiamen. Patriot forces in the Mohawk Valley also threw St. Leger and the Iroquois into retreat. Making matters worse, the British commander in New York City recalled 4,000 troops he had sent toward Albany and ordered them to Philadelphia to bolster Howe's force. While Burgoyne waited in vain for help, thousands of Patriot militiamen from Massachusetts, New Hampshire, and New York joined Gates. The Patriots "swarmed around the army like birds of prey," reported an English sergeant, and in October 1777, they forced Burgoyne to surrender.

The victory at the **Battle of Saratoga** was the turning point of the war. The Patriots captured more than 5,000 British troops and ensured the diplomatic success of American representatives in Paris, who won a military alliance with France.

AP® EXAM TIP

Explaining the importance of European allies in the Patriot victory over the superior British Army is essential for success on the AP® Exam.

AP® SKILLS & PROCESSES

CAUSATION

What were the most important results of the Patriot victory at Saratoga?

Battle of Saratoga (1777)
A multistage battle in New York ending with the surrender of British general John Burgoyne. The victory ensured the diplomatic success of American representatives in Paris, who won a military alliance with France.

The Perils of War

The Patriots' triumph at Saratoga was tempered by wartime difficulties. A British naval blockade cut off supplies of European manufactures and disrupted the New England fishing industry; meanwhile, the British occupation of Boston, New York, and Philadelphia reduced trade. As Patriots, along with unemployed artisans and laborers, moved to the countryside, New York City's population declined from 21,000 to 10,000. The British blockade cut tobacco exports in the Chesapeake, so planters grew grain to sell to the contending armies. All across the land, farmers and artisans adapted to a war economy.

With goods now scarce, governments requisitioned military supplies directly from the people. In 1776, Connecticut officials asked the citizens of Hartford to provide 1,000 coats and 1,600 shirts, and soldiers echoed their pleas. After losing

AP® APPLY THE TIP

To contextualize the alliance between the French and the Patriot cause that was established by the Treaty of Alliance of 1778, divide students into two groups, one group representing France and one group representing the Patriots. Ask the groups to brainstorm their goals and objectives in the conflict between the colonies and Great Britain. Remind students that every treaty involves the goals and objectives of all parties involved. Provide a few minutes to brainstorm and then have the two groups negotiate terms of the Treaty of Alliance of 1778. To guide students' "negotiations," prompt both sides to consider the following hypothetical questions (*answers will vary*):

- **What would the Patriots be willing to offer to the French in exchange for support?**
- **What would the French be willing to offer to the Patriots? What would the French want in exchange?**
- **What problems might a treaty between France and an independent Patriot nation cause after the American Revolution ends?**
- **How would a treaty between France and the Patriots increase connections in the Atlantic world? How would this benefit or harm a new American nation?**

AP® SKILLS & PROCESSES

CAUSATION

Use the **CAUSATION** question to help students practice evaluating the significance of multiple effects. While many students can identify multiple effects, they may have trouble weighing them. Provide support by asking students to identify the most important effect of Saratoga and justify their answer with evidence from the text. Extend this prompt by having students explore the significance of Parliament's response to the defeat at Saratoga, since the Patriots ignored Parliament's offer. Can anything of historical value be learned from this path that was not taken?

TRM Find complete suggested responses in the Teacher's Resource Materials.

TEACHING STRATEGY

This painting depicting the victory of Saratoga provides an opportunity to explore the ways artistic depictions may serve nationalistic purposes. Ask students: **How does this painting, which celebrates the American victory at Saratoga, celebrate American nationalism?** *Gates is positioned at the very center of the painting. He and other American troops have a confident bearing. An American cannon, pointed toward the defeated British, is prominently depicted in the right-hand corner. The American flag waves proudly at the top of the picture. Very few British appear and those that do are depicted clearly in a posture of defeat.*

CHECK FOR UNDERSTANDING

Ask students: **How did the Patriots achieve victory at Saratoga?** *Burgoyne's leisurely pace and underestimation of Patriot sympathy led his army to be stalled at Saratoga en route to Albany. While he waited for reinforcements, Patriot forces swarmed him and forced his surrender.*

AP® THEME

PCE: Politics and Power

The drawing of two American militiamen illustrates the economic shortages caused by the British military occupation and the ways Patriot women mobilized to provide material support. Ask students: **What does this drawing reveal about the Patriot cause?** *It shows the resourcefulness of Patriot soldiers, as well as the support of Patriot women who made clothing out of whatever materials were available.*

CHECK FOR UNDERSTANDING

Ask students: **What wartime perils did Americans face?** *Lack of work and/or income for products or services, requisitioning of supplies by the military, scarcity of goods, violence to civilians, and divided communities.*

American Militiamen Beset by continuing shortages of cloth, the Patriot army dressed in a variety of uniforms and fabrics. This German engraving, taken from a drawing by a Hessian officer, shows two American militiamen (one of them barefoot) wearing hunting shirts and trousers made of ticking, the strong linen fabric often used to cover mattresses and pillows. Anne S. K. Brown Military Collection, Brown University Library.

all his shirts "except the one on my back" in the Battle of Long Island, Captain Edward Rogers told his wife that "the making of Cloath . . . must go on." Patriot women responded; in Elizabeth, New Jersey, they promised "upwards of 100,000 yards of linnen and woolen cloth." Other women assumed the burdens of farmwork while their men were away at war and acquired a taste for decision making. "We have sow'd our oats as you desired," Sarah Cobb Paine wrote to her absent husband. "Had I been master I should have planted it to Corn." Their self-esteem boosted by wartime activities, some women expected greater legal rights in the new republican society.

Still, goods remained scarce and pricey. Hard-pressed consumers assailed shopkeepers as "enemies, extortioners, and monopolizers" and called for government regulation. But when the New England states imposed price ceilings in 1777, many farmers and artisans refused to sell their goods. Ultimately, a government official admitted, consumers had to pay the higher market prices "or submit to starving."

The fighting endangered tens of thousands of civilians. A British officer, Lord Rawdon, favored giving "free liberty to the soldiers to ravage [the country] at will, that these infatuated creatures may feel what a calamity war is." As British and American armies marched back and forth across New Jersey, they forced Patriot and Loyalist families to flee their homes to escape arrest — or worse. Soldiers and partisans looted farms, and disorderly troops harassed and raped women and girls. "An army, even a friendly one, are a dreadful scourge to any people," wrote one Connecticut soldier. "You cannot imagine what devastation and distress mark their steps."

The war divided many communities. Patriots formed committees of safety to collect taxes and seized the property of those who refused to pay. "Every Body submitted to our Sovereign Lord the Mob," lamented a Loyalist preacher. In parts of Maryland, the number of "nonassociators" — those who refused to join either side — was so large that they successfully defied Patriot mobs. "Stand off you dammed rebel sons of bitches," shouted Robert Davis of Anne Arundel County, "I will shoot you if you come any nearer."

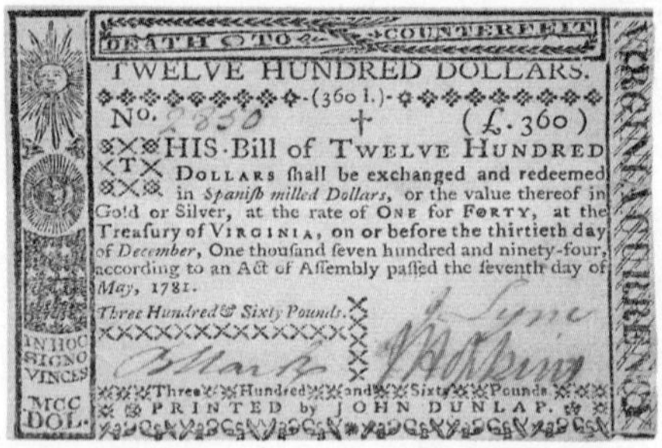

Paper Currency Testifying to their independent status, the new state governments printed their own currencies. Rejecting the English system of pounds and shillings, Virginia used the Spanish gold dollar as its basic unit of currency, although the equivalent in English pounds is also shown. Initially, $1,200 was equal to £360 — a ratio of 3.3 to 1. By 1781, Virginia had printed so much paper money to pay its soldiers and wartime expenses that the value of its currency had depreciated. It now took $40 in Virginia currency to buy the same amount of goods as £1 sterling. Courtesy of the American Numismatic Society.

Financial Crisis

Such defiance exposed the weakness of Patriot governments. Most states were afraid to raise taxes, so officials issued bonds to secure gold or silver from wealthy individuals. When those funds ran out, individual states financed the war by issuing so much paper money — some $260 million all told — that it lost worth, and most people refused to accept it at face value. In North Carolina, even tax collectors eventually rejected the state's currency.

The finances of the Continental Congress collapsed, too, despite the efforts of Philadelphia merchant Robert Morris, the government's chief treasury official. Why was the financial position of the United States so precarious? Because the Congress lacked the authority to impose taxes, Morris relied on funds requisitioned from the states, but the states paid late or not at all. So Morris secured loans from France and Holland and sold Continental loan certificates to some thirteen thousand firms and individuals. All the while, the Congress was issuing paper money — some $200 million between 1776 and 1779 — which, like state currencies, quickly fell in value. In 1778, a family needed $7 in Continental bills to buy goods worth $1 in gold or silver. As the exchange rate deteriorated — to 42 to 1 in 1779, 100 to 1 in 1780, and 146 to 1 in 1781 — it sparked social upheaval. In Boston, a mob of women accosted merchant Thomas Boylston, "seazd him by his Neck," and forced him to sell his wares at traditional prices. In rural Ulster County, New York, women told the committee of safety to lower food prices or "their husbands and sons shall fight no more." As morale crumbled, Patriot leaders feared the rebellion would collapse.

Valley Forge

Fears reached their peak during the winter of 1777. While Howe's army lived comfortably in Philadelphia, Washington's army retreated 20 miles to **Valley Forge**, where 12,000 soldiers and hundreds of camp followers suffered horribly. "The army . . . now begins to grow sickly," a surgeon confided to his diary. "Poor food — hard lodging — cold weather — fatigue — nasty clothes — nasty cookery. . . . Why are we sent here to starve and freeze?" Nearby farmers refused to help. Some were pacifists, Quakers and German sectarians unwilling to support either side. Others looked out for their own families, selling grain for gold from British quartermasters but refusing depreciated Continental currency. "Such a dearth of public spirit, and want of public virtue," lamented Washington. By spring, more than 200 officers had resigned, 1,000 hungry soldiers had deserted, and another 3,000 had died from malnutrition and disease. That winter at Valley Forge took as many American lives as had two years of fighting.

Valley Forge
A military camp in which George Washington's army of 12,000 soldiers and hundreds of camp followers suffered horribly in the winter of 1777–1778.

In this dark hour, Baron von Steuben raised the readiness of the American army. A former Prussian military officer, von Steuben was one of a handful of republican-minded foreign aristocrats who joined the American cause. Appointed as inspector general of the Continental army, he instituted a strict drill system and encouraged officers to become more professional. Thanks to von Steuben, the smaller army that emerged from Valley Forge in the spring of 1778 was a much tougher and better-disciplined force.

THE PATH TO VICTORY, 1778–1783

Why did the Patriots win the American Revolution?

Wars are often won by astute diplomacy, and so it was with the War of Independence. The Patriots' prospects improved dramatically in 1778, when the Continental Congress concluded a military alliance with France, the most powerful nation in Europe. The alliance gave the Americans desperately needed money, supplies, and, eventually, troops. And it confronted Britain with an international war that challenged its domination of the Atlantic and Indian oceans.

AP® EXAM TIP
Evaluate the degree to which allies, George Washington's leadership, and popular support led to Patriot victory in the American Revolution.

The French Alliance

France and America were unlikely partners. France was Catholic and a monarchy; the United States was Protestant and a federation of republics. From 1689 to 1763, the two peoples had been enemies: New Englanders had brutally uprooted the French population from Acadia (Nova Scotia) in 1755, and the French and their Indian allies had raided British settlements. But the Comte de Vergennes, the French foreign minister, was determined to avenge the loss of Canada during the Great War for Empire

CHECK FOR UNDERSTANDING

Ask students: **What financial crisis did the war cause?** *Both states and the Continental Congress struggled to raise the funds they needed to fight the war, so they resorted to printing paper money — which became severely inflated — and European loans.*

CHECK FOR UNDERSTANDING

Ask students: **What challenges did Patriot forces confront in the first two years of the war, and what were their key achievements?** *The challenges the Patriot forces confronted in the first two years included a weak central government with no reliable method for raising funds, few Native American allies, as well as poorly trained and inexperienced soldiers, especially in comparison to the British forces. As a result, they lost many key battles and some major port cities, including New York and Philadelphia. Despite these handicaps, the Patriot forces maintained themselves on the battlefield and won a few key victories, including at Trenton (1776) and especially Saratoga (1777).*

AP® APPLY THE TIP

Victory of the Patriot cause in the American Revolution can be attributed to many factors, including allies, especially France; George Washington's leadership; and popular support for the war effort. Organize students into small groups and ask them to determine which factor was most important for the Patriot victory. Students should engage in academic debate using specific supporting details to argue for each of the factors listed. The group should record arguments in favor of each factor as the most important in the Patriot victory. After allowing time for debate, ask each group to write a thesis statement that addresses the prompt: Which factor was most important in the Patriot victory in the American Revolution? Have groups share their thesis statements and explain how the evidence they discussed in small group supports their thesis. Engage the class in a discussion of the use of evidence to support a historical argument.

AP® SKILLS & PROCESSES

DEVELOPMENTS AND PROCESSES

French assistance during the war is required information for students. Have students quickly identify one military reason the alliance with France was crucial to the American victory.

CHECK FOR UNDERSTANDING

Ask students: **Why did the French ally with the Patriots? What were the consequences?** *The Patriots exploited the British-French rivalry and French hopes of winning territory in the Caribbean. The alliance renewed Patriot hopes while demoralizing many British.*

and persuaded King Louis XVI to provide the rebellious colonies with a secret loan and much-needed gunpowder. When news of the rebel victory at Saratoga reached Paris in December 1777, Vergennes sought a formal alliance.

Benjamin Franklin and other American diplomats craftily exploited France's rivalry with Britain to win an explicit commitment to American independence. The Treaty of Alliance of February 1778 specified that once France entered the war, neither partner would sign a separate peace without the "liberty, sovereignty, and independence" of the United States. In return, the Continental Congress agreed to recognize any French conquests in the West Indies. "France and America," warned Britain's Lord Stormont, were "indissolubly leagued for our destruction."

The alliance gave new life to the Patriots' cause. "There has been a great change in this state since the news from France," a Patriot soldier reported from Pennsylvania. Farmers — "mercenary wretches," he called them — were "as eager for Continental Money now as they were a few weeks ago for British gold." Its confidence bolstered, the Continental Congress addressed the demands of the officer corps. Most officers were gentlemen who equipped themselves and raised volunteers; in return, they insisted on lifetime military pensions at half pay. John Adams condemned the officers for "scrambling for rank and pay like apes for nuts," but General Washington urged the Congress to grant the pensions: "The salvation of the cause depends upon it." The Congress reluctantly granted the officers half pay, but only for seven years.

Meanwhile, the war had become unpopular in Britain. At first, George III was determined to crush the rebellion. If America won independence, he warned Lord North, "the West Indies must follow them. Ireland would soon follow the same plan and be a separate state, then this island would be reduced to itself, and soon would be a poor island indeed." Stunned by the defeat at Saratoga, however, the king changed his mind. To thwart an American alliance with France, he authorized North to seek a negotiated settlement. In February 1778, North persuaded Parliament to repeal the Tea and Prohibitory Acts and, amazingly, to renounce its power to tax the colonies. But the Patriots, now allied with France and committed to independence, rejected North's overture.

War in the South

The French alliance did not bring a rapid end to the war. When France entered the conflict in June 1778, it hoped to seize all of Britain's sugar islands. Spain, which joined the war against Britain in 1779, aimed to regain Florida and the fortress of Gibraltar at the entrance to the Mediterranean Sea.

Britain's Southern Strategy For its part, the British government revised its military strategy to defend the West Indies and capture the rich tobacco- and rice-growing colonies: Virginia, the Carolinas, and Georgia. Once conquered, the ministry planned to use the Scottish Highlanders in the Carolinas and other Loyalists to hold them. It had already mobilized the Cherokees and Delawares against the land-hungry Americans and knew that the Patriots' fears of slave uprisings weakened them militarily (Map 6.3). As South Carolina Patriots admitted to the Continental Congress, they could raise only a few recruits "by reason of the great proportion of citizens necessary to remain at home to prevent insurrection among the Negroes."

The large number of slaves in the South made the Revolution a "triangular war," in which enslaved African Americans constituted a strategic problem for Patriots and a tempting, if dangerous, opportunity for the British. Britain actively recruited slaves to its cause. The effort began with Dunmore's controversial proclamation in November 1775 recruiting slaves to his Ethiopian Regiment. In 1779, the **Philipsburg Proclamation** declared that any slave who deserted a rebel master would receive protection, freedom, and land from Great Britain. Together, these proclamations

Philipsburg Proclamation
A 1779 proclamation that declared that any slave who deserted a rebel master would receive protection, freedom, and land from Great Britain.

led some 30,000 African Americans to take refuge behind British lines. George Washington initially barred blacks from the Continental army, but he relented in 1777. By war's end, African Americans could enlist in every state but South Carolina and Georgia, and some 5,000 — slave and free — fought for the Patriot cause (see "Thinking Like a Historian," p. 186).

It fell to Sir Henry Clinton — acutely aware of the role enslaved people might play — to implement Britain's southern strategy. From the British army's main base in New York City, Clinton launched a seaborne attack on Savannah, Georgia. Troops commanded by Colonel Archibald Campbell captured the town in December 1778. Mobilizing hundreds of blacks to transport supplies, Campbell moved inland and captured Augusta early in 1779. By year's end, Clinton's forces and local Loyalists controlled coastal Georgia and had 10,000 troops poised for an assault on South Carolina.

In 1780, British forces marched from victory to victory (Map 6.4). In May, Clinton forced the surrender of Charleston, South Carolina, and its garrison of 5,000 troops. Then Lord Charles Cornwallis assumed control of the British forces and, at Camden, defeated an American force commanded by General Horatio Gates, the hero of Saratoga. Only 1,200 Patriot militiamen joined Gates at Camden, a fifth of the number at Saratoga. Cornwallis took control of South Carolina, and hundreds of African Americans fled to freedom behind British lines. The southern strategy was working.

Then the tide of battle turned. Thanks to another republican-minded European aristocrat, the Marquis de Lafayette, France finally dispatched troops to the American mainland. A longtime supporter of the American cause, Lafayette persuaded King Louis XVI to send General Comte de Rochambeau and 5,500 men to Newport, Rhode Island, in 1780. There, they threatened the British forces holding New York City.

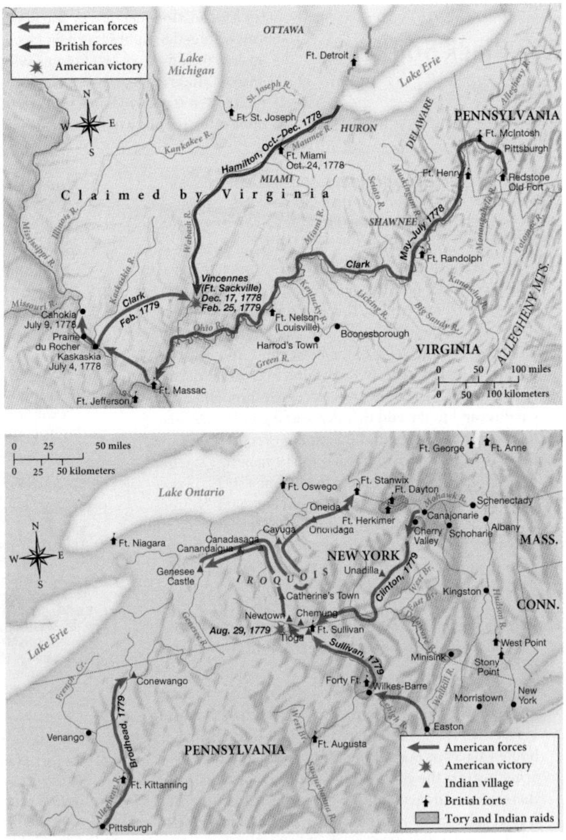

MAP 6.3 Native Americans and the War in the West, 1778–1779
Many Indian peoples remained neutral, but others, fearing land-hungry Patriot farmers, used British-supplied guns to raid American settlements. To thwart attacks by militant Shawnees, Cherokees, and Delawares, a Patriot militia led by George Rogers Clark captured the British fort and supply depot at Vincennes on the Wabash River in February 1779. To the north, Patriot generals John Sullivan and James Clinton defeated pro- British Indian forces near Tioga (on the New York–Pennsylvania border) in August 1779 and then systematically destroyed villages and crops throughout the lands of the Iroquois.

Guerrilla Warfare in the Carolinas Meanwhile, Washington dispatched General Nathanael Greene to recapture the Carolinas, where he found "a country that has been ravaged and plundered by both friends and enemies." Greene put local militiamen,

AP® SKILLS & PROCESSES

ANALYZING HISTORICAL EVIDENCE

The **AP® THINKING LIKE A HISTORIAN** feature helps students explore the challenges of understanding the point of view of marginalized and oppressed people. The question posed focuses on the decisions slaves faced and the ways they attempted to evaluate their options. The collection of documents suggests the challenges of recovering their voices, as most of the documents are about slaves, rather than by them. Extend this prompt by asking students to think about the limitations in a source such as Jehu Grant's and brainstorm other possible sources of evidence for slave behavior during the war. The **AP® DBQ PRACTICE** prompt challenges students to think of the Revolution from a perspective that differs from convention, as they consider slaves' struggle for independence as a separate subject of analysis.

TEACHING STRATEGY

Lesson plans associated with PBS's *Africans in America* series provide several resources to explore the Revolution's consequences for enslaved Americans. "Freedom Fire" is based on a 27-minute segment of the documentary that looks at runaways and those who served in the military on both sides during the war. The lesson plan includes questions for viewing and discussion as well as several primary sources, including the text of Lord Dunmore's proclamation and a half-dozen other primary sources that link slavery and rebellion. Access this resource by searching "PBS Africans in America Freedom Fire."

AP® THINKING LIKE A HISTORIAN

The Black Soldier's Dilemma

For African American slaves, the Revolution offered no clear path to freedom. Some slaves agreed to fight for Britain because of its promise to liberate slaves who fought against their masters. While some were freed, many others died fighting, were forced into servitude in the army, or even sold into slavery in the West Indies. Patriots at first refused the service of black soldiers, then enlisted them in small numbers, but always upheld the property rights of masters.

1. **Dunmore's Proclamation, 1775.** *Virginia's governor Dunmore issued this proclamation in response to the emerging rebellion and formed his recruits into the so-called Ethiopian Regiment.*

   To defeat such unreasonable Purposes . . . that the Peace, and good Order of this Colony may be again restored . . . I have thought fit to issue this my Proclamation, hereby declaring, that until the aforesaid good Purposes can be obtained, I do in Virtue of the Power and Authority to me given, by His majesty, determine to execute Martial Law, and cause the same to be executed throughout this Colony: and to the end that Peace and good Order may the sooner be [effected], I do require every Person capable of bearing Arms, to [resort] to His majesty's standard, or be looked upon as Traitors to His [majesty] . . . I do hereby further declare all indentured Servants, Negroes, or others, (appertaining to Rebels,) free that are able and willing to bear Arms, they joining His majesty's Troops as soon as may be, for the more speedily reducing this Colony to a proper Sense of their Duty.

2. **Virginia's response to Dunmore's Proclamation, 1775.** *A month later, Virginia's General Assembly issued the following response.*

   WHEREAS lord Dunmore, by his proclamation, dated on board the ship William, off Norfolk, the 7th day of November 1775, hath offered freedom to such able-bodied slaves as are willing to join him, and take up arms, against the good people of this colony, giving thereby encouragement to a general insurrection . . . it is enacted, that all negro or other slaves, conspiring to rebel or make insurrection, shall suffer death. . . . We think it proper to declare, that all slaves who have been, or shall be seduced, by his lordship's proclamation, or other arts, to desert their masters' service, and take up arms against the inhabitants of this colony, shall be liable to such punishment as shall hereafter be directed by the General Convention. . . . [A]ll such, who have taken this unlawful and wicked step, may return in safety to their duty, and escape the punishment due their crimes. . . . And we do farther earnestly recommend it to all humane and benevolent persons in this colony to explain and make known this our offer of mercy to those unfortunate people.

3. **Runaway advertisement, 1775.** *Titus—or, as he was later known, Captain Tye of the Ethiopian Regiment—abandoned his Delaware master in response to Dunmore's Proclamation.*

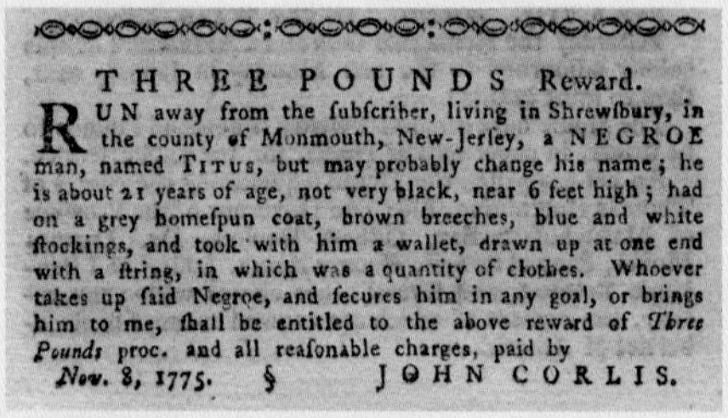

THREE POUNDS Reward.

RUN away from the subscriber, living in Shrewsbury, in the county of Monmouth, New-Jersey, a NEGROE man, named TITUS, but may probably change his name; he is about 21 years of age, not very black, near 6 feet high; had on a grey homespun coat, brown breeches, blue and white stockings, and took with him a wallet, drawn up at one end with a string, in which was a quantity of clothes. Whoever takes up said Negroe, and secures him in any goal, or brings him to me, shall be entitled to the above reward of *Three Pounds* proc. and all reasonable charges, paid by

Nov. 8, 1775. § JOHN CORLIS.

SOURCE: American Antiquarian Society, Worcester, Massachusetts, USA/Bridgeman Images.

4. **Report of Bernardo de Gálvez, 1780.** *Fighting against the British in support of the Patriots, Louisiana governor Bernardo de Gálvez raised a mixed regiment, almost half of whom were slaves and free people of color from New Orleans. He praised their efforts in this report of his campaign.*

   No less deserving of eulogy are the companies of Negroes and free Mulattoes who were continually occupied in the outposts, in false attacks, and discoveries, exchanging

who had been "without discipline and addicted to plundering," under strong leaders and unleashed them on less mobile British forces. In October 1780, Patriot militia defeated a regiment of Loyalists at King's Mountain, South Carolina, taking about one thousand prisoners. American guerrillas commanded by the "Swamp Fox," General Francis Marion, also won a series of small but fierce battles. Then, in January 1781, General Daniel Morgan led an American force to a bloody victory at Cowpens, South Carolina. In March, Greene's soldiers fought Cornwallis's seasoned army to a draw at North Carolina's Guilford Court House. Weakened by this war of attrition, the British

186

shots with the enemy . . . conduct[ing] themselves with as much valor and generosity as the whites.

5. **Boston King gains his freedom, 1783.** *In 1780, Boston King, like many other southern slaves, escaped to the British army. Here he describes his experiences at war's end.*

About this time, peace was restored between America and Great Britain which diffused universal joy among all parties except us, who had escaped slavery and taken refuge in the English army; for a report prevailed at New-York that all the slaves, in number two thousand, were to be delivered up to their masters, altho' some of them had been three or four years among the English. This dreadful rumour filled us with inexpressible anguish and terror, especially when we saw our old masters coming from Virginia, North-Carolina and other parts and seizing upon slaves in the streets of New-York, or even dragging them out of their beds. Many of the slaves had very cruel masters, so that the thought of returning home with them embittered life to us. For some days we lost our appetite for food, and sleep departed from our eyes. The English had compassion upon us in the day of our distress, and issued out a Proclamation importing "That all slaves should be free who had taken refuge in the British lines and claimed the sanction and privileges of the Proclamations respecting the security and protection of Negroes." In consequence of this, each of us received a certificate from the commanding officer at New-York, which dispelled our fears and filled us with joy and gratitude.

6. **Jehu Grant is re-enslaved, 1778.** *Jehu Grant of Narragansett, Rhode Island, was owned by a Loyalist. In August 1777 he escaped and joined the Patriot side; ten months later, his master tracked him down and reclaimed him. In 1837 Grant applied for a pension from the U.S. government and supplied the following narrative of his experience. His application was denied.*

[I] enlisted as a soldier but was put to the service of a teamster in the summer and a waiter in the winter . . . I was then grown to manhood, in the full vigor and strength of life, and heard much about the cruel and arbitrary things done by the British. Their ships lay within a few miles of my master's house, which stood near the shore, and I was confident that my master traded with them, and I suffered much from fear that I should be sent aboard a ship of war. This I disliked. But when I saw liberty poles and the people all engaged for the support of freedom, I could not but like and be pleased with such thing (God forgive me if I sinned in so feeling). And living on the borders of Rhode Island, where whole companies of colored people enlisted, it added to my fears and dread of being sold to the British. These considerations induced me to enlist into the American army, where I served faithful about ten months, when my master found and took me home. Had I been taught to read or understand the precepts of the Gospel, "Servants obey your master," I might have done otherwise, notwithstanding the songs of liberty that saluted my ear, thrilled through my heart.

Sources: (1) Lord Dunmore's Proclamation, Learn NC, North Carolina Digital History "Revolutionary North Carolina," www.learn nc.org; (2) J. N. Brenaman, *A History of Virginia Conventions* (Richmond: J. L. Hill Printing Company, 1902), 30; (4) Thomas Truxtun Moebs, *Black Soldiers-Black Sailors-Black Ink: Research Guide on African-Americans in U. S. Military History, 1526–1900* (Chesapeake Bay, Paris: Moebs Publishing Company, 1994), 1125; (5) Boston King, *Book of Negroes* (New York, 1783), in Simon Schama, *Rough Crossings: Britain, the Slaves and the American Revolution* (New York: HarperCollins, 2006), 107, 150; (6) Jehu Grant, To Hon. J. L. Edwards, Commissioner of Pension, 1836, in *The Revolution Remembered: Eyewitness Accounts of the War for Independence*, ed. John C. Dann (Chicago: University of Chicago Press, 1980), 27–28.

ANALYZING THE EVIDENCE

1. Why was Dunmore willing to offer freedom to slaves (source 1) when they were a recognized form of property under the British Empire? Describe the historical context of the Empire's decision with evidence from the textbook. What assumptions about the loyalties of slaves underlie the response of the Virginia assembly (source 2)? What is the purpose and historical situation of the author of source 2?
2. Why might Louisiana governor Bernardo de Gálvez (source 4) have made a point of praising the contributions of black soldiers to the Patriot cause? How does the author's historical situation influence his perspective (source 4)?
3. Compare the runaway ad for Titus (source 3) and the narratives of Boston King and Jehu Grant (sources 5 and 6). What goals did British officers hope to achieve in their relations with slaves? What Patriot values trumped slaves' individual liberties during and after the war? Use ideas from the textbook and the sources to support your answer.

AP® DBQ PRACTICE

Considering these sources along with the chapter contents and what you've learned in class, write a short essay that explains how the presence of slaves created a "triangular war" in the South. Use historical reasoning to explain how the choices that individual slaves had to make during the Revolution, and regional differences in the institution of slavery informed this so-called "triangular war."

TRM Find complete suggested responses in the Teacher's Resource Materials.

general decided to concede the Carolinas to Greene and seek a decisive victory in Virginia. There, many Patriot militiamen had refused to take up arms, claiming that "the Rich wanted the Poor to fight for them."

Exploiting these social divisions, Cornwallis moved easily through the Tidewater region of Virginia in the early summer of 1781. Reinforcements sent from New York and commanded by General Benedict Arnold, the infamous Patriot traitor, bolstered his ranks. As Arnold and Cornwallis sparred with an American force led by Lafayette near the York Peninsula, Washington was informed that France had finally sent

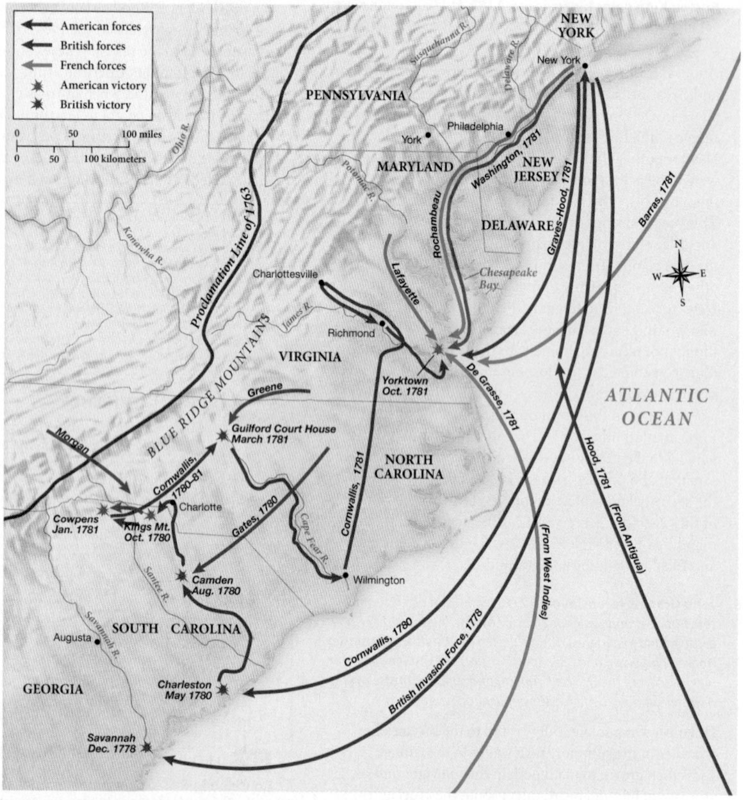

MAP 6.4 The War in the South, 1778–1781
Britain's southern military strategy started well. British forces captured Savannah in December 1778, took control of Georgia during 1779, and vanquished Charleston in May 1780. Over the next eighteen months, brutal warfare between the British troops and Loyalist units and the Continental army and militia raged in the interior of the Carolinas and ended in a stalemate. Hoping to break the deadlock, British general Charles Cornwallis carried the battle into Virginia in 1781. A Franco-American army led by Washington and Lafayette, with the help of the French fleet under Admiral de Grasse, surrounded Cornwallis's forces on the Yorktown Peninsula and forced their surrender.

Battle of Yorktown (1781)
A battle in which French and American troops and a French fleet trapped the British army under the command of General Charles Cornwallis at Yorktown, Virginia. The Franco-American victory broke the resolve of the British government and led to peace negotiations.

AP® SKILLS & PROCESSES
CAUSATION
What were the keys to the Patriot victory in the South?

its powerful West Indian fleet to North America, and he devised an audacious plan. Feigning an assault on New York City, he secretly marched General Rochambeau's army from Rhode Island to Virginia. Simultaneously, the French fleet took control of Chesapeake Bay. By the time the British discovered Washington's scheme, Cornwallis was surrounded, his 9,500-man army outnumbered 2 to 1 on land and cut off from reinforcement or retreat by sea. In a hopeless position, at the conclusion of the **Battle of Yorktown** Cornwallis surrendered in October 1781.

The Franco-American victory broke the resolve of the British government. "Oh God! It is all over!" Lord North exclaimed. Isolated diplomatically in Europe, stymied militarily in America, and lacking public support at home, the British ministry gave up active prosecution of the war on the American mainland.

TEACHING STRATEGY

"Lesson 4: Factors That Handicapped the British" accompanying the PBS documentary *Liberty! The American Revolution* explores how the strongest military force in the world was defeated by comparatively weak, nonprofessional American soldiers. Lesson materials include discussion points for teachers, a ready-to-use viewing guide, links to other resources, and extension ideas. Access this lesson plan by searching "Liberty Factors That Handicapped the British."

AP® SKILLS & PROCESSES

CAUSATION

Use the **CAUSATION** question to help students identify multiple causes of the Patriots' southern victory and evaluate its relative significance. To scaffold this question, students can identify each factor, explain why that factor was important, and then rank the factors in terms of significance. Extend this prompt by having students identify one or more of these factors as indispensable for Patriot victory—without which the war in the South might have been lost. Students should explain the reasoning for their answer.

TRM Find complete suggested responses in the Teacher's Resource Materials.

CHECK FOR UNDERSTANDING

Ask students: **What was the nature of the war in the South?** *The British relied on Native American alliances and the fear of slave uprisings to defeat the South, capturing Savannah, Augusta, Charleston, and Camden. Patriot guerrilla warriors had some success, but the tide only turned with Washington's secret plan to march troops to Virginia, which—with French naval support—led to the defeat of Cornwallis at Yorktown.*

The Patriot Advantage

How could mighty Britain, victorious in the Great War for Empire, lose to a motley rebel army? The British ministry pointed to a series of blunders by the military leadership. Why had Howe not ruthlessly pursued Washington's army in 1776? Why had Howe and Burgoyne failed to coordinate their attacks in 1777? Why had Cornwallis marched deep into the Patriot-dominated state of Virginia in 1781?

Historians acknowledge British mistakes, but they also attribute the rebels' victory to French aid and the inspired leadership of George Washington. Astutely deferring to elected officials, Washington won the support of the Continental Congress and the state governments. Confident of his military abilities, he pursued a defensive strategy that minimized casualties and maintained the morale of his officers and soldiers through five difficult years of war. Moreover, the Patriots' control of local governments gave Washington a greater margin for error than the British generals had. Local militiamen provided the edge in the 1777 victory at Saratoga and forced Cornwallis from the Carolinas in 1781.

In the end, it was the American people who decided the outcome, especially the one-third of white colonists who were zealous Patriots. Tens of thousands of these farmers and artisans accepted Continental bills in payment for supplies, and thousands of soldiers took them as pay, even as the currency literally depreciated in their pockets. Rampant inflation meant that every paper dollar held for a week lost value, imposing a hidden "**currency tax**" on those who accepted the paper currency. Each individual tax was small — a few pennies on each dollar. But as millions of dollars changed hands multiple times, the currency taxes paid by ordinary citizens financed the American military victory.

VISUAL ACTIVITY

Francis Marion Crossing the Pedee River Francis Marion was a master of the ferocious guerrilla fighting that characterized the war in South Carolina. Though Patriot general Horatio Gates had little confidence in him, Marion led an irregular militia brigade in several successful attacks. After chasing Marion into a swamp, British general Banastre Tarleton declared, "As for this damned old fox, the Devil himself could not catch him." Soon Patriots began calling Marion the Swamp Fox. In 1851, William T. Ranney painted Marion (on horseback, second from left, with his blue coat covered by a mantle) and his men crossing the Pedee River in flatboats. Ranney included an unidentified (and possibly fictionalized) black oarsman. William T. Ranney, *Marion Crossing the Pedee*, 1850, oil on canvas. Amon Carter Museum, Fort Worth, Texas, 1983.126.

READING THE IMAGE: This painting presents a complex and jumbled scene. The flatboat is overcrowded with people, horses, and dogs. Many of the men on the boat have their backs turned to the viewer, and it is difficult to identify Marion with certainty. Why do you think the artist chose to represent Marion and his army in this way?

MAKING CONNECTIONS: Considering what you learned about Marion and the significance of guerrilla fighting in the Carolinas in this chapter, what features of this painting best illustrate their character as a military unit? How does it capture the spirit of the American Revolution in the Carolinas?

currency tax
A hidden tax on farmers and artisans who accepted Continental bills in payment for supplies and on the thousands of soldiers who took them as pay. Rampant inflation caused Continental currency to lose much of its value during the war, implicitly taxing those who accepted it as payment.

Diplomatic Triumph

After Yorktown, diplomats took two years to conclude a peace treaty. Talks began in Paris in April 1782, but the French and Spanish, still hoping to seize a West Indian island or Gibraltar, stalled for time. Their tactics infuriated American diplomats Benjamin Franklin, John Adams, and John Jay. So the Americans negotiated secretly with the British, prepared if necessary to ignore the Treaty of Alliance and sign a separate peace. British ministers were equally eager: Parliament wanted peace, and they feared the loss of a rich sugar island.

AP® SKILLS & PROCESSES

DEVELOPMENTS AND PROCESSES

What turning points in the war were most important to the Patriot victory?

TEACHING STRATEGY

Created more than a half-century after the events it depicts, this painting provides an opportunity to discuss popular remembrances of the past and the tendency to romanticize particular events. Guide students' analysis with the following questions:

- **Why might you be cautious in using this text as a source of historical evidence?** *It was painted decades after the event it depicts. The romantic landscape hints that the event itself might be romanticized.*
- **In what ways does this illustration romanticize Marion and his guerrilla warriors?** *Marion is dramatically highlighted as a hero, remaining on horseback as he crosses the river. His clothing reveals both a uniform and a more rakish cap, suggesting his identity as part of the Patriot army as well as his renegade status. The painter has chosen a wide color palette to emphasize the ragtag nature of the group. Including a black figure who may not have been a part of the group may suggest romanticizing relations between blacks and whites.*
- **In what way can a painting like this be useful for historical inquiry?** *Paintings like this tell us how Marion was viewed in the 1850s and how the Revolution was remembered at the time.*

CHECK FOR UNDERSTANDING

Ask students: **What was the Patriots' advantage?** *Apart from the French alliance and Washington's strategic leadership, local support from local governments supplied militia and farmers and artisans provided financial support.*

TRM Find complete suggested responses in the Teacher's Resource Materials.

AP® THEME

NAT: American and National Identity; PCE: Politics and Power

The "Diplomatic Triumph" section explains how the Patriots succeeded despite Loyalist opposition and Britain's overwhelming advantages, identifying Washington's leadership, the support of colonial militias, and Patriot commitment and sacrifice. The French alliance, mentioned elsewhere, played a significant role as well.

The U.S. Delegation at the Treaty of Paris The United States were represented at the Paris treaty negotiations by (from left) Henry Laurens, John Adams, Benjamin Franklin, John Jay, and William Temple Franklin. This image is based on an unfinished sketch by Benjamin West, an accomplished painter who was born in Pennsylvania but had moved to London in 1763 to pursue his craft. He hoped to complete a large-scale painting that depicted the Paris negotiators; in his original plan, the British delegation would have occupied the right side of his canvas. The British commissioners refused to sit for the painting, however, so West had to abandon his plan and the painting was never completed. National Park Service.

Treaty of Paris of 1783
The treaty that ended the Revolutionary War. By its terms, Great Britain formally recognized American independence and relinquished its claims to lands south of the Great Lakes and east of the Mississippi River.

Consequently, the American diplomats secured extremely favorable terms. In the **Treaty of Paris of 1783**, signed in September, Great Britain formally recognized American independence and relinquished its claims to lands south of the Great Lakes and east of the Mississippi River. The British negotiators did not insist on a separate territory for their Indian allies. "In endeavouring to assist you," a Wea Indian complained to a British general, "it seems we have wrought our own ruin." The Cherokees were forced to relinquish claims to 5 million acres — three-quarters of their territory — in treaties with Georgia, the Carolinas, and Virginia, while New York and the Continental Congress pressed the Iroquois and Ohio Indians to cede much of their land as well. British officials, like those of other early modern empires, found it easy to abandon allies they had never really understood.

The Paris treaty also granted Americans fishing rights off Newfoundland and Nova Scotia, prohibited the British from "carrying away any negroes or other property," and guaranteed freedom of navigation on the Mississippi to American citizens "forever." In return, the American government allowed British merchants to pursue legal claims for prewar debts and encouraged the state legislatures to return confiscated property to Loyalists and grant them citizenship.

In the Treaty of Versailles, signed simultaneously, Britain made peace with France and Spain. Neither American ally gained very much. Spain reclaimed Florida from Britain, but not the strategic fortress at Gibraltar. France received the Caribbean island of Tobago, small consolation for a war that had sharply raised taxes and quadrupled France's national debt. Just six years later, cries for tax relief and political liberty would spark the French Revolution. Only Americans profited handsomely; the treaties gave them independence and access to the trans-Appalachian west.

AP® SKILLS & PROCESSES

MAKING CONNECTIONS

The contestations over space in the Great Lakes region was a long-term historical process. Have students identify how the region surrounding the Great Lakes — including the Great Lakes, west to the Mississippi and east to the Ohio River Valley — exchanged hands from 1754–1783. Amidst the exchanges, American Indians continued to assert their agency and presence in the region. Have students identify and explain one way in which American Indians, despite the agreements among Europeans and Americans, retained some level of sovereignty.

CHECK FOR UNDERSTANDING

Ask students: **What were the keys to Patriot victory in the American revolution?** *Answers will vary, but students should highlight the expense of the war for Great Britain, the naval assistance of the French, the political leadership of the colonies, the leadership of George Washington, and the fact that American colonists could fight a defensive war aimed at prolonging the conflict.*

CREATING REPUBLICAN INSTITUTIONS, 1776–1787

What were the most important challenges facing governments in the 1780s?

When the Patriots declared independence, they confronted the issue of political authority. "Which of us shall be the rulers?" asked a Philadelphia newspaper. The question was multifaceted. Would power reside in the national government or the states? Who would control the new republican institutions: traditional elites or average citizens? Would women have greater political and legal rights? What would be the status of enslaved people in the new republic?

The State Constitutions: How Much Democracy?

In May 1776, the Second Continental Congress urged Americans to reject royal authority and establish republican governments. Most states quickly complied. "Constitutions employ every pen," an observer noted. Within six months, Virginia, Maryland, North Carolina, New Jersey, Delaware, and Pennsylvania had all ratified new constitutions, and Connecticut and Rhode Island had revised their colonial charters to delete references to the king.

Republicanism meant more than ousting the king. The Declaration of Independence stated the principle of popular sovereignty: governments derive "their just powers from the consent of the governed." In the heat of revolution, many Patriots gave this clause a further democratic twist. In North Carolina, the backcountry farmers of Mecklenburg County told their delegates to the state's constitutional convention to "oppose everything that leans to aristocracy or power in the hands of the rich." In Virginia, voters elected a new assembly in 1776 that, an eyewitness remarked, "was composed of men not quite so well dressed, nor so politely educated, nor so highly born" as colonial- era legislatures (Figure 6.1).

AP® EXAM TIP

Recognizing the impact of state constitutions on the development of the Constitution of the United States is essential for success on the AP® Exam.

Pennsylvania constitution of 1776
It granted all taxpaying men the right to vote and hold office and created a unicameral (one-house) legislature with complete power; there was no governor to exercise a veto. It also mandated a system of elementary education and protected citizens from imprisonment for debt.

Pennsylvania's Controversial Constitution

This democratic impulse flowered in Pennsylvania, thanks to a coalition of Scots-Irish farmers, Philadelphia artisans, and Enlightenment- influenced intellectuals. In 1776, these insurgents ousted every officeholder of the Penn family's proprietary government, abolished property ownership as a qualification for voting, and granted all taxpaying men the right to vote and hold office. The **Pennsylvania constitution of 1776** also created a unicameral (one-house) legislature with complete power; there was no governor to exercise a veto. Other provisions mandated a system of elementary education and protected citizens from imprisonment for debt.

Pennsylvania's democratic constitution alarmed many leading Patriots. Why would Revolutionary leaders oppose the idealism that shaped this new system of government? From Boston, John Adams denounced the unicameral legislature as "so democratical that it must produce confusion and every evil work." Along with other conservative Patriots, Adams wanted to restrict office holding to "men of learning, leisure and easy circumstances" and warned of oppression under majority rule: "If you give [ordinary citizens] the command or

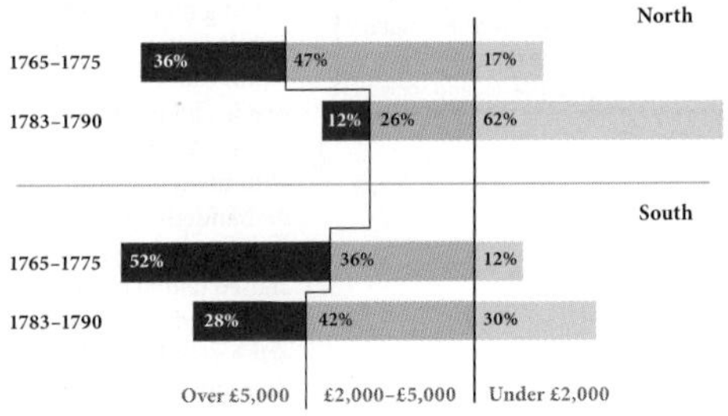

FIGURE 6.1 Middling Men Enter the Halls of Government, 1765–1790
Before the Revolution, wealthy men (with assets of £2,000 or more, as measured by tax lists and probate records) dominated most colonial assemblies. The power of money was especially apparent in the southern colonies, where representatives worth at least £5,000 formed a majority of the legislators. However, in the new American republic, the proportion of middling legislators (yeomen farmers and others worth less than £2,000) increased dramatically, especially in the northern states. Adapted from Jackson T. Main, "Government by the People: The American Revolution and the Democratization of the Legislatures," *William and Mary Quarterly*, series 3, 23 (1966). Used by permission of *William and Mary Quarterly*.

AP® APPLY THE TIP

Begin by reviewing who attended the Constitutional Convention — 55 delegates representing 12 states — and the goals of the meeting, which was at first to revise but ultimately to replace the Articles of Confederation with a stronger central government. Ask students to consider the "baggage" that the 55 delegates brought with them to this meeting discussing a new form of government, specifically what/who each delegate was representing and the models on which the delegates had to base their ideas about an effective government.

After clarifying the objectives of the Constitutional Convention, assign small groups of students to briefly investigate state constitutions from Pennsylvania, New York, North Carolina, Virginia, Massachusetts, and Connecticut. After a brief period of research, ask students to identify characteristics of the state constitutions that likely influenced the delegates in writing the U.S. Constitution. Together as a class, discuss what the state constitutions have in common and how their origin in the colonial period influenced the ideals of the U.S. Constitution.

AP® THEME

NAT: American and National Identity; PCE: Politics and Power

The "Creating Republican Institutions" section explores basic patterns of state government in the post–Revolutionary era. There is a brief but important discussion about Pennsylvania's radical experiment in democracy, inspired in part by Enlightenment ideals. This provides a dramatic example of the tendency of state governments to place power in the hands of legislatures at the expense of governors. Later text in this section highlights the tendency to maintain property qualifications for voting and citizenship that predated the Revolution.

AP® THEME

NAT: American and National Identity; PCE: Politics and Power

Use **FIGURE 6.1** to illustrate the movement toward political democracy that emerged in state governments after the Revolution. Guide students' analysis with the following questions:

- **What does this chart measure?** *Changes in the relative wealth of those elected to state legislatures in the North and South.*
- **What percent of northern legislators came from the highest rank before the Revolution? The lowest? How dramatically did those percentages change after the war?** *36%; 17%. The top rank was reduced by two thirds, while the bottom rank grew more than 3½ times larger.*
- **What percent of southern legislators came from the highest rank before the Revolution? The lowest? How do changes here compare with those in the North?** *52%; 12%. The top rank was cut almost in half, while the bottom rank more than doubled.*
- **What generalization can you make about changes in the status of those elected to legislatures caused by the Revolution?** *Though changes in the North were far more dramatic, in both regions there was a decisive shift toward the lower classes.*

AP® SKILLS & PROCESSES

MAKING CONNECTIONS

What aspects of the Pennsylvania constitution were most objectionable to John Adams, and what did he advocate instead?

mixed government
A political theory that called for three branches of government, each representing one function: executive, legislative, and judicial. This system of dispersed authority was devised to maintain a balance of power in government.

preponderance in the . . . legislature, they will vote all property out of the hands of you aristocrats."

Tempering Democracy To counter the appeal of the Pennsylvania constitution, Adams published *Thoughts on Government* (1776). In that treatise, he adapted the British Whig theory of **mixed government** (a sharing of power among the monarch, the House of Lords, and the Commons) to a republican society. To disperse authority and preserve liberty, he insisted on separate institutions: legislatures would make laws, the executive would administer them, and the judiciary would enforce them. Adams also demanded a bicameral (two-house) legislature with an upper house of substantial property owners to offset the popular majorities in the lower one. As further curbs on democracy, he proposed an elected governor with veto power and an appointed — not elected — judiciary.

Conservative Patriots endorsed Adams's governmental system. In New York's constitution of 1777, property qualifications for voting excluded 20 percent of white men from assembly elections and 60 percent from casting ballots for the governor and the upper house. In South Carolina, elite planters used property rules to disqualify about 90 percent of white men from office holding. The 1778 constitution required candidates for governor to have a debt-free estate of £10,000 (about $700,000 today), senators to be worth £2,000, and assemblymen to own property valued at £1,000. Even in traditionally democratic Massachusetts, the 1780 constitution, authored primarily by Adams, raised property qualifications for voting and office holding and skewed the lower house toward eastern, mercantile interests.

AP® EXAM TIP

Debating the degree to which the American Revolution brought political, economic, and social change is a key idea for the AP® Exam.

The political legacy of the Revolution was complex. Only in Pennsylvania and Vermont were radical Patriots able to create truly democratic institutions. Yet in all the new states, representative legislatures had acquired more power, and average citizens now had greater power at the polls and greater influence in the halls of government.

Women Seek a Public Voice

AP® SKILLS & PROCESSES

ARGUMENTATION

How did women's participation in the American Revolution impact the roles of women in American politics and society?

The extraordinary excitement of the Revolutionary era tested the dictum that only men could engage in politics. Men controlled all public institutions — legislatures, juries, government offices — but upper-class women engaged in political debate and, defying men's scorn, filled their letters, diaries, and conversations with opinions on public issues. "The men say we have no business [with politics]," Eliza Wilkinson of South Carolina complained in 1783. "They won't even allow us liberty of thought, and that is all I want."

As Wilkinson's remark suggests, most women did not insist on civic equality with men; many sought only an end to restrictive customs and laws. Abigail Adams demanded equal legal rights for married women, who under common law could not own property, enter into contracts, or initiate lawsuits. The war bonds she purchased had to be held in a trust run by a male relative. "Men would be tyrants" if they continued to hold such power over women, Adams declared to her husband, John, criticizing him and other Patriots for "emancipating all nations" from monarchical despotism while "retaining absolute power over Wives."

Most politicians ignored women's requests, and most men insisted on traditional sexual and political prerogatives. Long-married husbands remained patriarchs who dominated their households, and even young men who embraced the republican ideal of "companionate marriage" did not support legal equality for their wives and daughters. Except in New Jersey, which until 1807 allowed unmarried and widowed female property holders to vote, women remained disenfranchised. In the new American republic, only white men enjoyed full citizenship.

Nevertheless, the republican belief in an educated citizenry created opportunities for some women. In her 1779 essay "On the Equality of the Sexes," Judith Sargent Murray argued that men and women had equal capacities for memory and that

AP® SKILLS & PROCESSES

MAKING CONNECTIONS

The **MAKING CONNECTIONS** question highlights the diversity of views among Patriots about the best kind of government to form as independent people. Students may need help considering why different groups favored unicameral and bicameral options and what they thought was at stake. Extend this prompt by asking students to consider how Adams's background and values might have shaped his views of Pennsylvania's constitution.

TRM Find complete suggested responses in the Teacher's Resource Materials.

AP® APPLY THE TIP

Help students evaluate the American Revolution as a turning point in history by considering the degree to which change occurred before and after the Revolution by asking students to complete **Handout 6.1 — Continuity and Change: American Revolution (TRM)**. With partners, have students list the characteristics of the U.S. (British colonies) before and after the American Revolution. After students have had the opportunity to discuss these issues related to the American Revolution, ask each group to develop a thesis statement that addresses how "revolutionary" the American Revolution was.

TRM Find **Handout 6.1 — Continuity and Change: American Revolution** in the Teacher's Resource Materials.

CHECK FOR UNDERSTANDING

Ask students: **Why did leaders drafting state constitutions debate how much democracy they wanted?** *While Patriots were uniformly opposed to monarchy, there were many versions of republicanism, which agreed primarily on some idea of representative government. But while radicals wanted genuine democracy, many wealthier Patriots feared governments led by the masses and favored a more moderate form of representation.*

TEACHING STRATEGY

Supplement your discussion of the Argumentation question with the writing of Judith Sargent Murray. The National Women's History Museum provides a detailed biography of Judith Sargent Murray, including links to her text "On the Equality of the Sexes" and other resources. Access these resources by searching "NWHM Judith Sargent Murray."

AP® THEME

SOC: Social Structures

Causation historians have varied interpretations about the role of women during the revolution. To provide one interpretation of how womens' lives were affected by the revolution, have students go to ap.gilderlehrman.org and read the essay in period 3 by Marylynn Salmon titled "The Legal Status of Women, 1776–1830" women had superior imaginations. She conceded that most women were inferior to men in judgment and reasoning, but only from lack of training: "We can only reason from what we know," she argued, and most women had been denied "the opportunity of acquiring knowledge." That situation changed in the 1790s, when the attorney general of Massachusetts declared that girls had an equal right to schooling under the state constitution. By 1850, the literacy rates of women and men in the northeastern states were equal, and educated women again challenged their subordinate legal and political status.

The War's Losers: Loyalists, Native Americans, and Slaves

The success of republican institutions was assisted by the departure of as many as 100,000 Loyalists, many of whom suffered severe financial losses. Some Patriots demanded Revolutionary justice: the seizure of all Loyalist property and its distribution to needy Americans. But most officials were unwilling to go so far. When state governments did seize Loyalist property, they often auctioned it to the highest bidders; only rarely did small-scale farmers benefit. In the cities, Patriot merchants replaced Loyalists at the top of the economic ladder, supplanting a traditional economic elite — who often invested profits from trade in real estate — with republican entrepreneurs who tended to promote new trading ventures and domestic manufacturing. This shift facilitated America's economic development in the years to come.

Though the Revolution did not result in widespread property redistribution, it did encourage yeomen, middling planters, and small-time entrepreneurs to believe that their new republican governments would protect their property and ensure widespread access to land. In western counties, former Regulators demanded that the new governments be more responsive to their needs; beyond the Appalachians, thousands of squatters who had occupied lands in Kentucky and Tennessee expected their claims to be recognized and lands to be made available on easy terms. If the United States were to secure the loyalty of westerners, it would have to meet their needs more effectively than the British Empire had.

This meant, among other things, extinguishing Native American claims to land as quickly as possible. At war's end, George Washington commented on the "rage for speculating" in Ohio Valley lands. "Men in these times, talk with as much facility of fifty, a hundred, and even 500,000 Acres as a Gentleman formerly would do of 1000 acres." "If we make a right use of our natural advantages," a Fourth of July orator observed, "we soon must be a truly great and happy people." Native American land claims stood as a conspicuous barrier to the "natural advantages" he imagined.

For southern slaveholders, the Revolution was fought to protect property rights, and any sentiment favoring slave emancipation met with violent objections. When Virginia Methodists called for general emancipation in 1785, slaveholders used Revolutionary principles to defend their right to human property. They "risked [their] Lives and Fortunes, and waded through Seas of Blood" to secure "the Possession of [their] Rights of Liberty and Property," only to hear of "a very subtle and daring Attempt" to "dispossess us of a very important Part of our Property." Emancipation would bring "Want, Poverty, Distress, and Ruin to the Free Citizen." The liberties coveted by ordinary white Americans bore hard on the interests of Native Americans and enslaved laborers.

The Articles of Confederation

As Patriots embraced independence in 1776, they envisioned a central government with limited powers. Carter Braxton of Virginia thought the Continental Congress should "regulate the affairs of trade, war, peace, alliances, &c." but "should by no

Judith Sargent Murray Judith Sargent Murray was perhaps the most accomplished female essayist of the Revolutionary era. Publishing under various pen names, she advocated for economic independence and better educational opportunities for women. Two years before Mary Wollstonecraft's *A Vindication of the Rights of Woman* (1792), she published "On the Equality of the Sexes" in the *Massachusetts Magazine*. Her letter books, which run to twenty volumes, were discovered only in 1984; the Judith Sargent Murray Society (http://www.jsmsociety.com/Home.html) is now transcribing and indexing them for publication. This striking portrait by John Singleton Copley hints at her intelligence and sardonic wit. John Singleton Copley, *Portrait of Mrs. John Stephens (Judith Sargent, later Mrs. John Murray)*. Daniel J. Terra Art Acquisition Endowment Fund, 2000.6. Terra Foundation for American Art, Chicago/Art Resource, NY.

AP® SKILLS & PROCESSES

CONTINUITY AND CHANGE

What impact did republican ideals have on gender roles and expectations during the Revolutionary era?

AP® SKILLS & PROCESSES

CONTEXTUALIZATION

How did the Revolutionary commitment to liberty and the protection of property affect enslaved African Americans and western Indians?

AP® THEME

NAT: American and National Identity; PCE: Politics and Power

Judith Sargent Murray appealed for an expanded role for women to teach republican values in postrevolutionary America. Her arguments helped pave the way for "republican motherhood," which is discussed on p. 287 of Chapter 9.

CHECK FOR UNDERSTANDING

Ask students: **How did women seek a public voice during the Revolution?** *Abigail Adams lobbied her husband unsuccessfully for married women's legal equality, while Judith Sargent Murray argued that equal access to education would allow women to strengthen republican ideals.*

AP® SKILLS & PROCESSES

CONTINUITY AND CHANGE

Scaffold the **CONTINUITY AND CHANGE** question by reviewing colonial gender roles, particularly as they developed in the eighteenth century, and then identify regional differences between New England shaped by Puritanism, Middle colonies like Pennsylvania shaped by egalitarian Quakerism, and the largely Anglican southern colonies. In particular, students should reflect on the position of women with respect to the law, government, and the public sphere in general. Then they should define specific features of republicanism and explain why republicanism might be thought to have a bearing on the status of women.

TRM Find complete suggested responses in the Teacher's Resource Materials.

CHECK FOR UNDERSTANDING

Ask students: **What consequences did the war's losers face?** *Some Loyalists lost their property and positions of leadership, Native Americans lost land to western settlers, while slaves in the South experienced a harsher regime as planters reinforced their right to property.*

AP® APPLY THE TIP

Have students work in pairs and ask them to consider the cause and effect relationships of each event listed on **Handout 6.2 — Causation: Articles of Confederation (TRM).** Students should focus on the ways that the Articles of Confederation caused conflict in the new republic as well as influenced a pattern of western settlement in the U.S.

TRM Find **Handout 6.2 — Causation: Articles of Confederation** in the Teacher's Resource Materials.

Articles of Confederation
The written document defining the structure of the government from 1781 to 1788, under which the Union was a confederation of equal states, with no executive and limited powers, existing mainly to foster a common defense.

AP® EXAM TIP

It's important to be able to explain the ways that the Articles of Confederation led to the writing of the Constitution while also encouraging migration to the West.

means have authority to interfere with the internal police [governance] or domestic concerns of any Colony."

That idea informed the **Articles of Confederation**, which were approved by the Continental Congress in November 1777. The Articles provided for a loose union in which "each state retains its sovereignty, freedom, and independence." As an association of equals, each state had one vote regardless of its size, population, or wealth. Important laws needed the approval of nine of the thirteen states, and changes in the Articles required unanimous consent. Though the Confederation had significant powers on paper — it could declare war, make treaties with foreign nations, adjudicate disputes between the states, borrow and print money, and requisition funds from the states "for the common defense or general welfare" — it had major weaknesses as well. It had neither a chief executive nor a judiciary. Though it could make treaties, it could not enforce their provisions, since the states remained sovereign. Most important, it lacked the power to tax either the states or the people.

Although the Congress exercised authority from 1776 — raising the Continental army, negotiating the treaty with France, and financing the war — the Articles won formal ratification only in 1781. The delay stemmed from conflicts over western lands. The royal charters of Virginia, Massachusetts, Connecticut, and other states set boundaries stretching to the Pacific Ocean. States without western lands — Maryland and Pennsylvania — refused to accept the Articles until the land-rich states relinquished these claims to the Confederation. Threatened by Cornwallis's army in 1781, Virginia gave up its claims, and Maryland, the last holdout, finally ratified the Articles (Map 6.5).

Continuing Fiscal Crisis By 1780, the central government was nearly bankrupt, and General Washington called urgently for a national tax system; without one, he warned, "our cause is lost." Led by Robert Morris, who became superintendent of finance in 1781, nationalist-minded Patriots tried to expand the Confederation's authority. They persuaded Congress to charter the Bank of North America, a private institution in Philadelphia, arguing that its notes would stabilize the inflated Continental currency. Morris also created a central bureaucracy to manage the Confederation's finances and urged Congress to enact a 5 percent import tax. Rhode Island and New York rejected the tax proposal. His state had opposed British import duties, New York's representative declared, and it would not accept them from Congress. To raise revenue, Congress looked to the sale of western lands. In 1783, it asserted that the recently signed Treaty of Paris had extinguished the Indians' rights to those lands and made them the property of the United States.

The Northwest Ordinance By 1784, more than 30,000 settlers had already moved to Kentucky and Tennessee, despite the uncertainties of frontier warfare, and after the war their numbers grew rapidly. In that year, the residents of what is now eastern Tennessee organized a new state, called it Franklin, and sought admission to the Confederation. To preserve its authority over the West, Congress refused to recognize Franklin. Subsequently, Congress created the Southwest and Mississippi Territories (the future states of Tennessee, Alabama, and Mississippi) from lands ceded by North Carolina and Georgia. Because these cessions carried the stipulation that "no regulation . . . shall tend to emancipate slaves," these states and all those south of the Ohio River allowed human bondage.

However, the Confederation Congress banned slavery north of the Ohio River. Between 1784 and 1787, it issued three important ordinances organizing the "Old Northwest." The Ordinance of 1784, written by Thomas Jefferson, established the principle that territories could become states as their populations grew. The Land Ordinance of 1785 mandated a rectangular-grid system of surveying and specified a minimum price of $1 an acre. It also required that half of the townships be sold in single blocks

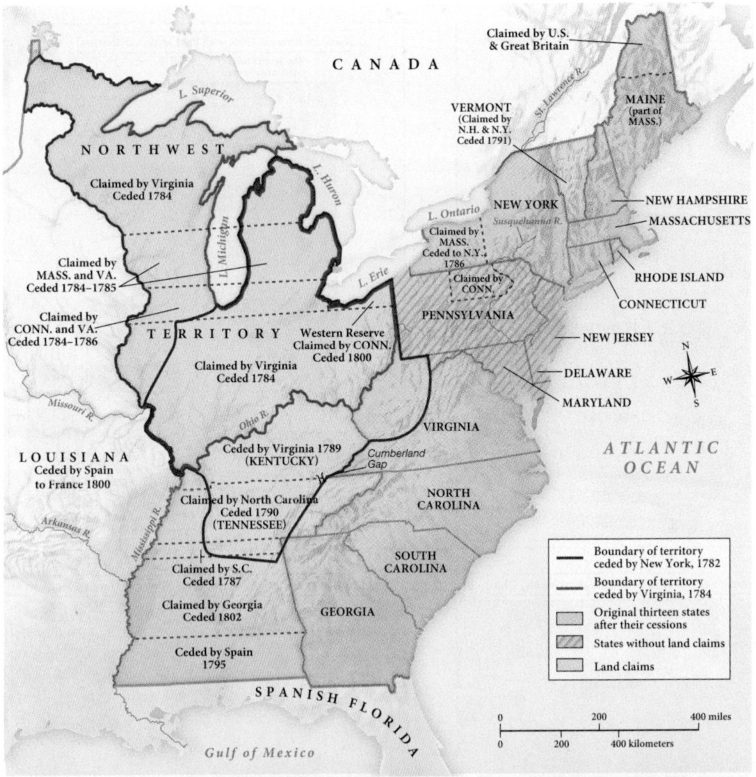

MAPPING THE PAST

MAP 6.5 The Confederation and Western Land Claims, 1781–1802

The Congress formed by the Articles of Confederation had to resolve conflicting state claims to western lands. For example, the territories claimed by New York and Virginia on the basis of their royal charters overlapped extensively. Beginning in 1781, the Confederation Congress and, after 1789, the U.S. Congress persuaded all of the states to cede their western claims, creating a "national domain" open to all citizens. In the Northwest Ordinance (1787), the Congress divided the domain north of the Ohio River into territories and set up democratic procedures by which they could eventually join the Union as states. South of the Ohio River, the Congress allowed the existing southern states to play a substantial role in settling the ceded lands.

ANALYZING THE MAP: After agreeing to cede western lands during the war, states formally completed their cessions between 1784 and 1802. Which states gave up the largest claims to western lands, and which gave up the least?

MAKING CONNECTIONS: Based on your reading of the narrative, what explains the decision of states with extensive claims to give up their western lands? Why was this issue central to the survival of the Confederation and, subsequently, the United States?

AP® THEME

PCE: Politics and Power

Even though students often remember the Articles government as a failure, **MAP 6.5** provides an opportunity to discuss some of the ways the Articles of Confederation succeeded in unifying the independent states and creating a national government with limited power. Guide students' analysis with the following questions:

- **Which states had competing claims to territory?** *All states except Pennsylvania, New Jersey, Delaware, and Maryland.*
- **Roughly how large was the volume of land in the West compared with the existing states?** *Roughly the same size.*
- **If these claims had not been ceded to the Continental Congress, what would have been the likely result?** *States would have continued to argue over them, squatters from each state might have settled there, and conflict might have led to outright war.*
- **Why was it so important to the survival of the Confederation that individual states give up their claims to these western lands?** *Land disputes were a serious obstacle to unity, as well as to the uninhibited settlement of the West, which eventually strengthened the U.S. economically.*

TRM Find complete suggested responses in the Teacher's Resource Materials.

AP® THEME

MIG: Migration and Settlement; PCE: Politics and Power

Use **MAP 6.6** to discuss a major success of the Articles of Confederation. Guide students' analysis with the following questions:

- **How did the Northwest Ordinance help settlement of the West?** *It provided for division of the Northwest Territory into six separate states and determined their boundaries.*
- **How did the Land Ordinance aid in settlement of the West?** *It created a linear division of land based on survey, breaking the land into continuously smaller chunks: townships, sections, and parts of sections.*
- **In what way might the Land Ordinance survey pattern reflect Enlightenment principles?** *The linear grid pattern reflects an imposition of rational order on natural variation. This might be more disruptive than divisions (like Baltimore County) that follow the natural contours of the land.*

AP® THEME

MIG: Migration and Settlement

The text highlights how ordinances governing the Northwest created a means for admitting new states, promoted public education, protected private property, and banned slavery.

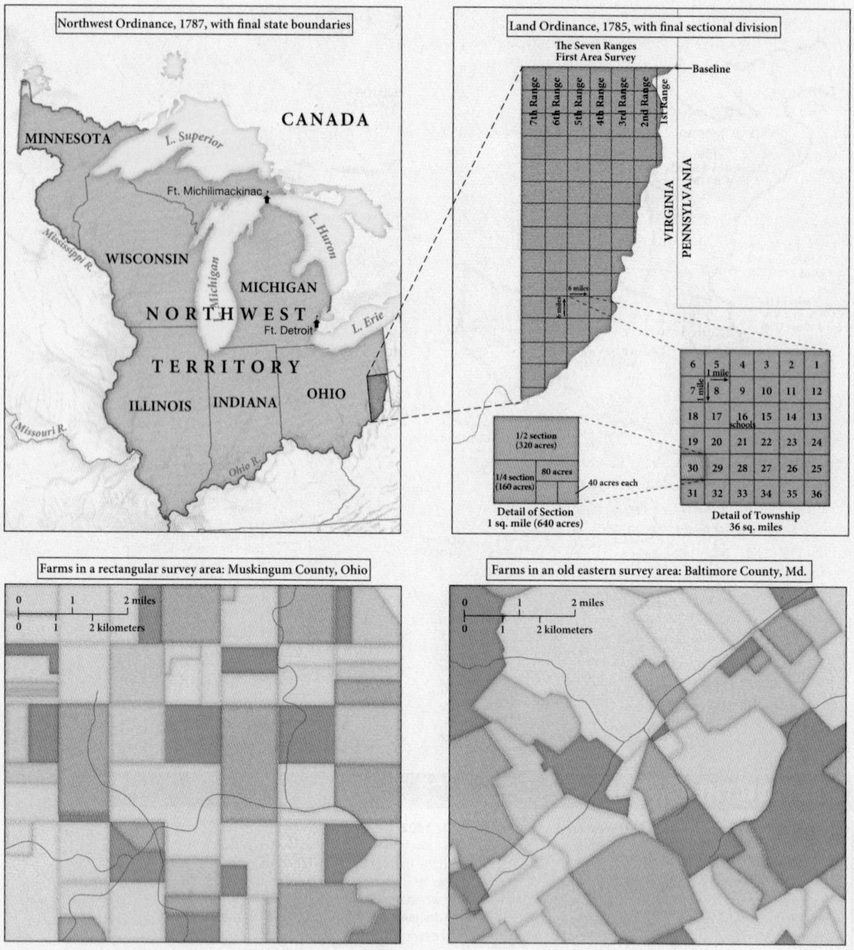

MAP 6.6 Land Division in the Northwest Territory

Throughout the Northwest Territory, government surveyors imposed a rectangular grid on the landscape, regardless of the local topography, so that farmers bought neatly defined tracts of land. The right-angled property lines in Muskingum County, Ohio (lower left), contrasted sharply with those in Baltimore County, Maryland (lower right), where—as in most of the eastern and southern states—boundaries followed the contours of the land.

Northwest Ordinance of 1787
A land act that provided for orderly settlement and established a process by which settled territories would become the states of Ohio, Indiana, Illinois, Michigan, and Wisconsin. It also banned slavery in the Northwest Territory.

of 23,040 acres each, which only large-scale speculators could afford, and the rest in parcels of 640 acres each, which restricted their sale to well-to-do farmers (Map 6.6).

Finally, the **Northwest Ordinance of 1787** created the territories that would eventually become the states of Ohio, Indiana, Illinois, Michigan, and Wisconsin. The ordinance prohibited slavery and earmarked funds from land sales for the support of schools. It also specified that Congress would appoint a governor and judges to administer each new territory until the population reached 5,000 free adult men, at which point the citizens could elect a territorial legislature. When the population reached 60,000, the legislature could devise a republican constitution and apply to join the Confederation.

The land ordinances of the 1780s were a great and enduring achievement of the Confederation Congress. They provided for orderly settlement and the admission of new states on the basis of equality; there would be no politically dependent "colonies" in the West. But they also extended the geographical division between slave and free areas that would haunt the nation in the coming decades. And they implicitly invalidated Native American claims to an enormous swath of territory—a corollary that would soon lead the newly independent nation, once again, into war.

AP® SKILLS & PROCESSES

COMPARISON

In what ways did the Confederation function effectively, and what were its greatest failings?

Shays's Rebellion

Though many national leaders were optimistic about the long-term prospects of the United States, postwar economic conditions were grim. The Revolution had crippled American shipping and cut exports of tobacco, rice, and wheat. The British Navigation Acts, which had nurtured colonial commerce, now barred Americans from legal trade with the British West Indies. Moreover, low-priced British manufactures (and some from India as well) were flooding American markets, driving urban artisans and wartime textile firms out of business.

AP® EXAM TIP

Evaluate the arguments that led to the call for revising the Articles of Confederation.

The fiscal condition of the state governments was dire, primarily because of war debts. Well-to-do merchants and landowners (including Abigail Adams) had invested in state bonds during the war; others had speculated in debt certificates, buying them on the cheap from hard-pressed farmers and soldiers. Now creditors and speculators demanded that the state governments redeem the bonds and certificates quickly and at full value, a policy that would require tax increases and a decrease in the amount of paper currency. Most legislatures—now including substantial numbers of middling farmers and artisans—refused. Instead they authorized new issues of paper currency and allowed debtors to pay private creditors in installments. Although wealthy men deplored these measures as "intoxicating Draughts of Liberty" that destroyed "the just rights of creditors," such political intervention prevented social upheaval.

In Massachusetts, however, the new constitution placed power in the hands of a mercantile elite that owned the bulk of the state's war bonds. Ignoring the interests of ordinary citizens, the legislature increased taxes fivefold to pay off wartime debts—and it stipulated that they be paid in hard currency. Moreover, it specified that 90 percent of the revenue would come from property and poll taxes, while only 10 percent was borne by a tax on imports that merchants would have to pay. Even for substantial farmers, this was a crushing burden. When cash-strapped farmers could not pay both their taxes and their debts, creditors threatened lawsuits. Debtor Ephraim Wetmore heard a rumor that merchant Stephan Salisbury "would have my Body Dead or Alive in case I did not pay." To protect their livelihoods, farmers called extralegal conventions to protest high taxes and property seizures. Then mobs of angry farmers, including men of high status, closed the courts by force. "[I] had no Intensions to Destroy the Publick Government," declared Captain Adam Wheeler, a former town selectman; his goal was simply to prevent "Valuable and Industrious members of Society [being] dragged from their families to prison" because of their debts. These crowd actions grew into a full-scale revolt led by Captain Daniel Shays, a Continental army veteran.

As a revolt against taxes imposed by an unresponsive government, **Shays's Rebellion** resembled American resistance to the British Stamp Act. Consciously linking themselves to the Patriot movement, Shays's men placed pine twigs in their hats just as Continental troops had done. "The people have turned against their teachers the doctrines which were inculcated to effect the late revolution," complained Fisher Ames, a conservative Massachusetts lawmaker. Some of the radical Patriots of 1776

Shays's Rebellion
A 1786–1787 uprising led by dissident farmers in western Massachusetts, many of them Revolutionary War veterans, protesting the taxation policies of the eastern elites who controlled the state's government.

AP® SKILLS & PROCESSES

COMPARISON

The **COMPARISON** question is really an evaluation, rather than a comparison, but it essentially asks students to weigh the strengths of the Confederation relative to its weaknesses. Since students already know that the Articles were replaced by the Constitution, they may need to be pressed to identify the strengths of the document and the government it created. Students might be asked to explain how this was precisely the kind of government many rebels wanted, rather than an oversight.

TRM Find complete suggested responses in the Teacher's Resource Materials.

CHECK FOR UNDERSTANDING

Ask students: **How did the Articles of Confederation government lead the new nation?** *A loose association only ratified late in the war after several states gave up claims to western lands, it successfully passed two ordinances that guided orderly settlement of the West. Hampered in its ability to tax, it continued to face financial difficulties.*

AP® APPLY THE TIP

Provide students with several primary source excerpts that support and oppose the calling of the Constitutional Convention. (Suggested sources include Patrick Henry's address to the Virginia Convention in 1788, Alexander Hamilton, and James Madison.) Ask students to outline the arguments of those who supported creating a stronger central government and those who opposed these changes.

AP® SKILLS & PROCESSES

MAKING CONNECTIONS

The **MAKING CONNECTIONS** question asks students to consider Shays's Rebellion in the larger context of the Revolution. While the question focuses on the "inspiration" of the Revolution, students should consider the context of the Revolution both in terms of the ideals it reflected and the problems it created. Ask students to evaluate the persuasiveness of the Shaysite claims — was this opportunism or did their complaints fit within debates raised by the Revolution?

TRM Find complete suggested responses in the Teacher's Resource Materials.

CHECK FOR UNDERSTANDING

Ask students**: What were the most important challenges facing governments in the 1780s?** *The most important challenges facing the 1780s governments were two-fold. First was the nature of political power; mainly how to balance both elite and popular rights as well as the states and national government. Second was the disposition of the new lands acquired in the West, which was largely accomplished by the 1787 Northwest Ordinance.*

TEACHING STRATEGY

Constitutional Conversations, a video series sponsored by the James Madison Foundation, offers several dozen short discussions by leading scholars about the principles, framing, ratification, and implementation of constitutional government in the United States. Access this series by searching "James Madison Foundation Constitutional Conversations."

likewise condemned the Shaysites: "[Men who] would lessen the Weight of Government lawfully exercised must be Enemies to our happy Revolution and Common Liberty," charged Samuel Adams. To put down the rebellion, the Massachusetts legislature passed the Riot Act, and wealthy bondholders equipped a formidable fighting force, which Governor James Bowdoin used to disperse Shays's ragtag army during the winter of 1786–1787.

Although Shays's Rebellion failed, it showed that many middling Patriot families felt that American oppressors had replaced British tyrants. Massachusetts voters turned Governor Bowdoin out of office, and debt-ridden farmers in New York, northern Pennsylvania, Connecticut, and New Hampshire closed courthouses and forced their governments to provide economic relief. British officials in Canada predicted the imminent demise of the United States, while American leaders urged purposeful action to save their republican experiment. Events in Massachusetts, declared nationalist Henry Knox, formed "the strongest arguments possible" for the creation of "a strong general government."

AP® SKILLS & PROCESSES
MAKING CONNECTIONS
How did the Shaysites draw on the Revolution for inspiration?

THE CONSTITUTION OF 1787

What were the most important compromises struck in the Philadelphia convention of 1787?

These issues ultimately led to the drafting of a national constitution. From its creation, the U.S. Constitution was a controversial document, both acclaimed for solving the nation's woes and condemned for perverting its republican principles. Critics charged that republican institutions worked only in small political units — the states. Advocates replied that the Constitution extended republicanism by adding another level of government elected by the people. In the new two-level political federation created by the Constitution, the national government would exercise limited, delegated powers, and the existing state governments would retain authority over all other matters.

The Rise of a Nationalist Faction

Money questions — debts, taxes, and tariffs — dominated the postwar political agenda. Americans who had served the Confederation as military officers, officials, and diplomats viewed these issues from a national perspective and advocated a stronger central government. George Washington, Robert Morris, Benjamin Franklin, John Jay, and John Adams wanted Congress to control foreign and interstate trade and tariff policy. However, lawmakers in Massachusetts, New York, and Pennsylvania — states with strong commercial traditions — insisted on controlling their own tariffs, both to protect their artisans from low-cost imports and to assist their merchants. Most southern states opposed tariffs because planters wanted to import British textiles and ironware at the lowest possible prices.

Nonetheless, some southern leaders became nationalists because their state legislatures had cut taxes and refused to redeem state war bonds. Such policies, lamented wealthy bondholder Charles Lee of Virginia, led taxpayers to believe they would "never be compelled to pay" the public debt. Creditors also condemned state laws that "stayed" (delayed) the payment of mortgages and other private debts. "While men are madly accumulating enormous debts, their legislators are making provisions for their nonpayment," complained a South Carolina merchant. To undercut the democratic majorities in the state legislatures, creditors joined the movement for a stronger central government.

Delegates from five states met in Annapolis, Maryland, in September 1786 to consider solutions to the Confederation's economic problems. They recommended that another convention, with representatives from all the states, meet in Philadelphia in 1787. Spurred on by Shays's Rebellion, nationalists in Congress secured a resolution calling for such a convention to revise the Articles of Confederation. Only an "efficient plan from the Convention," a fellow nationalist wrote to James Madison, "can prevent anarchy first & civil convulsions afterwards."

The Philadelphia Convention

In May 1787, fifty-five delegates arrived in Philadelphia. They came from every state except Rhode Island, where the legislature opposed increasing central authority. Most were strong nationalists; forty-two had served in the Confederation Congress. They were also educated and propertied: merchants, slaveholding planters, and "monied men." There were no artisans, backcountry settlers, or tenants, and only a single yeoman farmer.

Some influential Patriots missed the convention. John Adams and Thomas Jefferson were serving as American ministers to Britain and France, respectively. The Massachusetts General Court rejected Samuel Adams as a delegate because he opposed a stronger national government, and his fellow firebrand from Virginia, Patrick Henry, refused to attend because he "smelt a rat." Just as politically engaged citizens disagreed in 1787 whether a new form of government was needed, historians have argued ever since about whether the Constitution was necessary (see "Comparing Interpretations," p. 200).

The absence of experienced leaders and contrary-minded delegates allowed capable younger nationalists to set the agenda. Declaring that the convention would "decide for ever the fate of Republican Government," James Madison insisted on increased national authority. Alexander Hamilton of New York likewise demanded a strong central government to protect the republic from "the imprudence of democracy."

James Madison, Statesman Throughout his long public life, Madison kept the details of his private life to himself. His biography, he believed, should be a record of his public accomplishments, not his private affairs. Future generations celebrated him not as a great man (like Hamilton or Jefferson) or as a great president (like Washington), but as an original and incisive political thinker. The chief architect of the U.S. Constitution and the Bill of Rights, Madison was the preeminent republican political theorist of his generation. Mead Art Museum, Amherst College, MA, USA/Bequest of Herbert L. Pratt (Class of 1895)/ Bridgeman Images.

The Virginia and New Jersey Plans The delegates elected George Washington as their presiding officer and voted to meet behind closed doors. Then — momentously — they decided not to revise the Articles of Confederation but rather to consider the so-called **Virginia Plan**, a scheme for a powerful national government devised by James Madison. Just thirty-six years old, Madison was determined to fashion national political institutions run by men of high character. A graduate of Princeton, he had read classical and modern political theory and served in both the Confederation Congress and the Virginia assembly. Once an optimistic Patriot, Madison had grown discouraged because of the "narrow ambition" and outlook of state legislators.

Virginia Plan
A plan drafted by James Madison that was presented at the Philadelphia Constitutional Convention. It designed a powerful three-branch government, with representation in both houses of the congress tied to population; this plan would have eclipsed the voice of small states in the national government.

Madison's Virginia Plan differed from the Articles of Confederation in three crucial respects. First, the plan rejected state sovereignty in favor of the "supremacy of national authority," including the power to overturn state laws. Second, it called for the national government to be established by the people (not the states) and for national laws to operate directly on citizens of the various states. Third, the plan proposed a three-tier election system in which ordinary voters would elect only the lower house of the national legislature. This lower house would then select the upper house, and both houses would appoint the executive and judiciary.

AP® EXAM TIP

Take good notes on the ways that negotiation and compromise led to the establishment of federalism and a system of checks and balances in U.S. government.

From a political perspective, Madison's plan had two fatal flaws. First, most state politicians and citizens resolutely opposed allowing the national government to veto state laws. Second, the plan based representation in the lower house on population; this provision, a Delaware delegate warned, would allow the populous

CHECK FOR UNDERSTANDING

Ask students: **What prompted the rise of a nationalist faction?** *Financial problems created by conflicting tax and tariff policies of different states led some to desire a national government to bring order and stability.*

AP® THEME

PCE: Politics and Power; NAT: American and National Identity

Discuss with students how Madison was the most influential figure during the Philadelphia Convention as delegates created a limited government with centralized power and a separation of powers after much negotiation and compromise.

AP® APPLY THE TIP

Help students to understand that one of the most basic debates at the Constitutional Convention was over the balance of power between the federal government and the states. Have students practice contextualization by asking them to consider the traditions, precedents, and experiences that led many Americans to see state governments as the most natural source of power in the new republic. Help students to connect the power of the states to the idea of colonial charters, regional differences, early forms of self-government in the colonies, role of colonies in organizing militias, etc. Ask students to consider the reasons that colonial leaders like Patrick Henry would be suspicious of the creation of a stronger central (federal) government. Guide students in a point-by-point comparison of Madison's Virginia Plan and Paterson's New Jersey Plan. Ask the students to give special consideration to Madison's point of view and purpose in proposing the strong central government. Ask students to work with partners to research the Great (Connecticut) Compromise and explain how it balanced the interests of those who wanted a stronger central government and those who supported leaving power in the hands of the states.

AP® SKILLS & PROCESSES

ANALYZING HISTORICAL EVIDENCE

In the **AP® COMPARING INTERPRETATIONS** feature, highlight the summaries provided in the introduction and present students with a question to further their understanding of the differences in interpretation. You can ask students to identify where Maier emphasizes the goal of addressing the weaknesses of the Articles of Confederation and where Holton highlights the fear some of the aristocracy held over the democratic features of the state governments.

AP® COMPARING INTERPRETATIONS

What Did the Framers Intend When They Drafted the Constitution?

Historians have long debated the motives of the fifty-five men who hammered out the details of the new Constitution of the United States in Philadelphia in the summer of 1787. One interpretation has held that the Articles of Confederation were insufficient because they did not grant the Continental Congress certain powers that were essential to its ability to function, especially the power to levy taxes, conduct diplomacy, and regulate foreign and interstate trade. In the first excerpt that follows, Pauline Maier emphasizes the weakness of Congress and the consequent danger, feared by George Washington and others, that the American experiment in democratic government might fail altogether. It was the Framers' primary intention, she implies, to remedy the defects of the Articles.

Another long-standing interpretive tradition stresses a very different set of motives for the new Constitution. Woody Holton argues that James Madison and the rest of the Framers were more concerned about the democratic excesses of state governments than they were the weakness of the Articles of Confederation. In particular, they feared that the property rights of more well-to-do citizens were threatened by the inflationary and debtor-friendly policies of many of the states. In response, they hoped to devise a national government that would take control of the money supply, guarantee the obligation of contracts, and insulate government from too much popular input or interference.

PAULINE MAIER

SOURCE: Pauline Maier, *Ratification: The People Debate the Constitution* (New York: Simon and Schuster, 2010), 11–15, 17–18.

Under the Articles of Confederation, Congress had no power to levy taxes. The struggle with Britain began when colonists denied Parliament the right to tax them on the principle of "no taxation without representation." With independence, it seemed safest to keep the right to tax in the state legislatures, where the people were directly represented. The Continental Congress could legally print money, and it did so to finance the opening years of the war, but its currency depreciated to the point of uselessness. Congress could also borrow money, which it did. And in the 1780s it began to make arrangements for surveying and selling government lands in the west, but it would take time before those sales produced a substantial revenue stream.

In the meantime, Congress depended on annual payments — requisitions — from the states to make interest and principal payments on the war debt and to cover current expenses. But none of the states paid all of their requisitions, and Georgia paid nothing. . . .

In 1783 [George] Washington had called on the country to pay the debts Congress had incurred during the Revolutionary War as a matter of justice and honesty. To default on the foreign debt would also undermine the country's capacity to borrow abroad in the event of another military crisis. "We have it in our power to be one of the most respectable Nations upon Earth," he wrote in October 1785, when the problems of national finance were already abundantly clear. Nobody could deny that "our resources are ample, & encreasing," but by denying Congress a share of that wealth "we give the vital stab to public credit, and must sink into contempt in the eyes of Europe." . . .

Congress could not enforce the powers it clearly had under the Articles of Confederation. . . . Meanwhile the Confederation Congress remained in a state of paralysis. Under the Articles of Confederation, Congress could not engage in war, enter into treaties or alliances, coin money and regulate its value, determine the expenses necessary for the country's welfare, appropriate money, or essentially do anything of significance without the consent of nine state delegations. . . .

By 1786 Washington's dream of a "respectable nation" — that is, a nation that could be "considered on a respectable footing by the powers of Europe" — seemed increasingly remote. The very future of the republic — a government without hereditary rulers, in which all power came from the people — seemed in doubt. . . .

[In] Massachusetts, where the event remembered as Shays's Rebellion was underway, "everything" was "in a state of confusion." Was America following the pattern of previous republics, which ended after a plague of anarchy led law-abiding people to invest power in some strong leader who could restore order? . . .

A crippled national government; state authority trampled into the dust; a people incapable of self-government;

a revolutionary cause on the brink of failure: The situation amounted to a crisis of unprecedented importance in the young republic. . . .

Now, in late 1786 and early 1787, some of Washington's correspondents mused on what changes in national government would resolve the country's problems and shared their ideas with him. To a man they proposed giving the national government a more complex structure, with separate legislative, executive, and judiciary department. They also proposed a more centralized national government, one to which the states would be clearly subordinate.

WOODY HOLTON

SOURCE: Woody Holton, *Unruly Americans and the Origins of the Constitution* (New York: Hill and Wang, 2007), 3–5, 7–10.

Today politicians as well as judges profess an almost religious reverence for the Framers' original intent. And yet what do we really know about the motives that set fifty-five of the nation's most prominent citizens — men like George Washington, Ben Franklin, and Alexander Hamilton — on the road to Philadelphia? . . .

High school textbooks and popular histories of the Revolutionary War locate the origins of the Constitution in the nasty conflicts that kept threatening to tear the convention apart — and in the brilliant compromises that, again and again, brought the delegates back together. . . .

The textbooks and the popular histories give surprisingly short shrift to the Framers' motivations. What almost all of them do say is that harsh experience had exposed the previous government, under the Articles of Confederation (1781–89), as too weak. What makes this emphasis strange is that the Framers' own statements reveal another, more pressing motive. Early in the Constitutional Convention, James Madison urged his colleagues to tackle "the evils . . . which prevail within the States individually as well as those which affect them collectively." The "mutability" and "injustice" of "the laws of the States" had, Madison declared shortly after leaving Philadelphia, "contributed more to that uneasiness which produced the Convention, and prepared the public mind for a general reform, than those which accrued to our national character and interest from the inadequacy of the Confederation." . . .

What these men were saying was that the American Revolution had gone too far. Their great hope was that the federal convention would find a way to put the democratic genie back in the bottle. Alexander Hamilton, the most ostentatiously conservative of the convention delegates, affirmed that many Americans — not just himself — were growing "tired of an excess of democracy." Others identify the problem as "a headstrong democracy," a "prevailing rage of excessive democracy," a "republican frenzy," "democratical tyranny," and "democratic licentiousness." . . .

What really alarmed Madison was the specific legislation the [state] assemblies had adopted. More than anything else, it was the desire to overturn these state laws that set him on the road to Philadelphia. . . . Most glaringly, [state] representatives had shown excessive indulgence to debtors and taxpayers. They had refused to force farmers to pay what they owed. . . .

The Framers believed the only way to prevent state assemblymen from giving the taxpayer a free ride was to get them out of the business of collecting — or not collecting — "Continental" taxes. Article I, Section 8 [of the Constitution] gave the national government what it had never had before, its own power to tax. Article I, Section 10 imposed a similar crackdown on private debtors. It prohibited the states from rescuing farmers by issuing paper money or by "impairing the obligation of contracts" using any of the other devices they had discovered during the 1780s.

As a result of the protection that Section 10 afforded creditors, more [Federalists] proclaimed that clause "the best in the Constitution" than any other in the document. . . . [But t]he danger would have remained that the new national government would itself go easy on debtors and taxpayers. . . . It was largely in order to eliminate these possibilities that the Framers made the Constitution considerably less responsive to the popular will than any of the states. Only one element of the new government, the House of Representatives, would be elected directly by the people, and its initiatives could be derailed by the senators (who would not be chosen directly by the voters until 1913), the president, or the Supreme Court. . . .

A month before writing *Federalist* Number 10, Madison privately summarized it, employing an expression he did not dare use in that public essay: "Divide et impera, the reprobated axiom of tyranny, is under certain qualifications, the only policy, by which a republic can be administered on just principles." "Divide et impera" is Latin for "divide and conquer."

AP® SHORT ANSWER PRACTICE

1. Identify the arguments of each historian and explain two differences between their interpretations of the concerns and motives of the Framers.
2. Using the two historians' explanations of the Framers' goals, explain why some Americans were especially likely to support the new Constitution, while others were more likely to oppose it. Use examples from the source to justify your answer.
3. Corroborate the chapter's interpretation of "The Articles of Confederation" and "The Constitution of 1787" with these sources. Choose which historian's interpretation of the Constitutional Convention most parallels the textbook's interpretation. Make a historically defensible claim.

TRM Find complete suggested responses in the Teacher's Resource Materials.

states to "crush the small ones whenever they stand in the way of their ambitious or interested views."

New Jersey Plan
Alternative to the Virginia Plan drafted by delegates from small states, retaining the Confederation's single-house congress with one vote per state. It shared with the Virginia Plan enhanced congressional powers to raise revenue, control commerce, and make binding requisitions on the states.

So delegates from Delaware and other small states rallied behind a plan devised by William Paterson of New Jersey. The **New Jersey Plan** gave the Confederation the power to raise revenue, control commerce, and make binding requisitions on the states. But it preserved the states' control of their own laws and guaranteed their equality: as in the Confederation Congress, each state would have one vote in a unicameral legislature. Delegates from the more populous states vigorously opposed this provision. After a month-long debate on the two plans, a bare majority of the states agreed to use Madison's Virginia Plan as the basis of discussion.

This decision raised the odds that the convention would create a more powerful national government. Outraged by this prospect, two New York delegates, Robert Yates and John Lansing, accused their colleagues of exceeding their mandate to revise the Articles and left the convention. The remaining delegates met six days a week during the summer of 1787, debating both high principles and practical details. Experienced politicians, they looked for a plan that would be acceptable to most citizens and existing political interests. Pierce Butler of South Carolina invoked a classical Greek precedent: "We must follow the example of Solon, who gave the Athenians not the best government he could devise but the best they would receive."

Philadelphia Delegates Debate the Constitution, 1787 The fifty-five men who debated plans for a new Constitution in Philadelphia in the summer of 1787 kept their deliberations secret. But Americans have been fascinated by the proceedings ever since, and many artists have imagined the scene. In this early engraving, which appeared in Charles Augustus Goodrich, *A History of the United States of America* (1823), convention president George Washington stands on a raised dais and towers over the other delegates, in keeping with his popularity and stature. When Washington agreed to attend, it was a foregone conclusion that his fellow delegates would elect him president of the proceedings, and he was selected unanimously for that role. Though he offered little input in the debates, his presence reassured many Americans that the convention would not betray the ideals of the Revolution. Everett Collection.

The Great Compromise As the convention grappled with the central problem of the representation of large and small states, the Connecticut delegates suggested a possible solution. They proposed that the national legislature's upper chamber (the Senate) have two members from each state, while seats in the lower chamber (the House of Representatives) be apportioned by population (determined every ten years by a national census). After bitter debate, delegates from the populous states reluctantly accepted this "Great Compromise."

Other state-related issues were quickly settled by restricting (or leaving ambiguous) the extent of central authority. Some delegates opposed a national system of courts, predicting that "the states will revolt at such encroachments" on their judicial authority. This danger led the convention to vest the judicial power "in one supreme Court" and allow the new national legislature to decide whether to establish lower courts within the states. The convention also refused to set a property requirement for voting in

AP® THEME

NAT: American and National Identity

"The Great Compromise" section explains the way the Philadelphia delegates struck a compromise over the representation of slave states and the federal government's role in regulating slavery and the slave trade. For a more in-depth investigation of this subject, see the **AP® FIRSTHAND ACCOUNTS** feature on pp. 204–205.

TEACHING STRATEGY

Using the engraving of the Philadelphia Convention, have students examine how Goodrich chose to capture the scene at Independence Hall. To give students a comparison, have them visit Independence Hall online by using the National Park Service's site devoted to providing pictures and descriptions of the scene in Philadelphia (https://www.nps.gov/inde/learn/historyculture/places-independencehall.html). Students can compare the engraving with the historical accounts of what took place to better understand the events at the convention.

national elections. "Eight or nine states have extended the right of suffrage beyond the freeholders," George Mason of Virginia pointed out. "What will people there say if they should be disfranchised?" Finally, the convention specified that state legislatures would elect members of the upper house, or Senate, and the states would select the electors who would choose the president. By allowing states to have important roles in the new constitutional system, the delegates hoped that their citizens would accept limits on state sovereignty.

Negotiations over Slavery The shadow of slavery hovered over many debates, and Gouverneur Morris of New York brought it into view. To safeguard property rights, Morris wanted life terms for senators, a property qualification for voting in national elections, and a strong president with veto power. Nonetheless, he rejected the legitimacy of two traditional types of property: the feudal dues claimed by aristocratic landowners and the ownership of slaves. An advocate of free markets and personal liberty, Morris condemned slavery as "a nefarious institution."

Many slave-owning delegates from the Chesapeake region, including Madison and George Mason, recognized that slavery contradicted republican principles and hoped for its eventual demise. They supported an end to American participation in the Atlantic slave trade, a proposal the South Carolina and Georgia delegates angrily rejected. Unless the importation of African slaves continued, these rice planters and merchants declared, their states "shall not be parties to the Union." At their insistence, the convention denied Congress the power to regulate immigration — and so the slave trade — until 1808 (see "Firsthand Accounts," p. 204).

The delegates devised other slavery- related compromises. To mollify southern planters, they wrote a "fugitive clause" that allowed masters to reclaim enslaved blacks (or white indentured servants) who fled to other states. But in acknowledgment of the antislavery sentiments of Morris and other northerners, the delegates excluded the words *slavery* and *slave* from the Constitution; it spoke only of citizens and "all other Persons." Because slaves lacked the vote, antislavery delegates wanted their census numbers excluded when apportioning seats in Congress. Southerners — ironically, given that they considered slaves property — demanded that slaves be counted in the census the same as full citizens, to increase the South's representation. Ultimately, the delegates agreed that each slave would count as three-fifths of a free person for purposes of representation and taxation, a compromise that helped southern planters dominate the national government until 1860.

AP® EXAM TIP

Being able to explain the way that slavery was included in the U.S. Constitution is critical to success on the AP® Exam.

National Authority Having addressed the concerns of small states and slave states, the convention created a powerful national government. The Constitution declared that congressional legislation was the "supreme" law of the land. It gave the new government the power to tax, raise an army and a navy, and regulate foreign and interstate commerce, with the authority to make all laws "necessary and proper" to implement those and other provisions. To assist creditors and establish the new government's fiscal integrity, the Constitution required the United States to honor the existing national debt and prohibited the states from issuing paper money or enacting "any Law impairing the Obligation of Contracts."

The proposed constitution was not a "perfect production," Benjamin Franklin admitted, as he urged the delegates to sign it in September 1787. But the great statesman confessed his astonishment at finding "this system approaching so near to perfection." His colleagues apparently agreed; all but three signed the document.

AP® SKILLS & PROCESSES

DEVELOPMENTS AND PROCESSES

How did the Constitution, in its final form, differ from the plan originally proposed by James Madison?

The People Debate Ratification

The procedure for ratifying the new constitution was as controversial as its contents. Knowing that Rhode Island (and perhaps other states) would reject it, the delegates did not submit the Constitution to the state legislatures for their unanimous

AP® APPLY THE TIP

The delegates at the Constitutional Convention debated the issue of slavery and ultimately included it in the U.S. Constitution. However, the delegates were careful not to use the word "slave" or "slavery" in the actual document. Ask students to discuss the reason for choosing to exclude the word "slave" or "slavery" even when everyone knew the references to slavery existed. Ask students to point out the specific ways that slavery was included in the Constitution by identifying specific clauses and phrases. After students identify evidence of slavery in the Constitution, lead a class discussion examining why slavery was included in the Constitution through issues of the slave trade, the "fugitive clause," and representation.

CHECK FOR UNDERSTANDING

Ask students: **What were the major debates at the Philadelphia Convention? What was the outcome?** *Fifty-five delegates debated representation, the slave trade, and judicial authority to create a constitution that provided a true national government with centralized power.*

AP® SKILLS & PROCESSES

DEVELOPMENTS AND PROCESSES

The **DEVELOPMENTS AND PROCESSES** question asks students to distinguish between Madison's original governmental frame and the version finally adopted in the Constitution. Because Madison is regularly discussed as the Father of the Constitution or its chief architect, students may have a difficult time recognizing that the Constitution diverged from his vision. Extend this prompt by having students explain how the country might have been different if Madison had gotten his way.

TRM Find complete suggested responses in the Teacher's Resource Materials.

AP® SKILLS & PROCESSES

ANALYZING HISTORICAL EVIDENCE

The **AP® FIRSTHAND ACCOUNTS** feature invites students to compare diverse perspectives to draw conclusions about the fate of slavery in light of the Revolution. As the introduction indicates, the debate over slavery at the Philadelphia Convention reveals how slavery was a source of controversy from the nation's birth. Help students to recognize that Martin is not advocating the abolition of slavery but only of the slave trade. This less invasive measure might have been thought more appropriate to the federal government given the status of slavery was generally considered a state matter. Extend this prompt by asking students to consider why Martin and other Chesapeake slave owners argued for abolition of the slave trade. In answering this question, students should recognize that many plantations in this region were shifting away from tobacco to food crops, which marked a shift from year-round labor to more seasonal labor.

AP® THEME

PCE: Politics and Power; NAT: American and National Identity

The **AP® FIRSTHAND ACCOUNTS** feature explores in detail the way that the American Revolution increased awareness of social inequities, prompting some to advocate abolition and/or an end to the slave trade.

AP® FIRSTHAND ACCOUNTS

The First National Debate over Slavery

How did republican ideology affect American politics and society? In some contexts, Revolutionary idealism led Americans to challenge long-standing principles and institutions. Elsewhere, however, existing practices were too valuable or important to be altered or discarded. The institution of slavery offers an especially complex case study in the interplay between Revolutionary ideals and economic and social realities. During the Revolution, the Pennsylvania assembly adopted a gradual emancipation law; a few years later, the Massachusetts courts found slavery to be unconstitutional. But in 1787, slavery was legal in the rest of the Union and was the bedrock of social order and agricultural production in the southern states. A look at the debates on the issue of the African slave trade at the Philadelphia convention and in a state ratifying convention shows that slavery was an extremely divisive issue at the birth of the nation — a dark cloud threatening the bright future of the young republic.

THE CONSTITUTIONAL CONVENTION, 1787

Slavery was not a major topic of discussion at the Philadelphia convention, but it surfaced a number of times, notably in the important debate over representation (which produced the three-fifths clause). A discussion of the Atlantic slave trade began when Luther Martin, a delegate from Maryland, proposed a clause allowing Congress to impose a tax on or prohibit the importation of slaves.

SOURCE: Max Farrand, ed., *The Records of the Federal Convention of 1787* (New Haven: Yale University Press, 1911), 2: 364–365, 369–372.

" Mr. Martin proposed to vary article 7, sect. 4 so as to allow a prohibition or tax on the importation of slaves. . . . [He believed] it was inconsistent with the principles of the Revolution, and dishonorable to the American character, to have such a feature [promoting the slave trade] in the Constitution.

Mr. [John] Rutledge [of South Carolina declared that] religion and humanity had nothing to do with this question. Interest alone is the governing principle with nations. The true question at present is whether the Southern states shall or shall not be parties to the Union. . . . Mr. [Oliver] Ellsworth [of Connecticut] was for leaving the clause as it stands. Let every state import what it pleases. The morality or wisdom of slavery are considerations belonging to the states themselves. . . . The old Confederation had not meddled with this point, and he did not see any greater necessity for bringing it within the policy of the new one.

Mr. [Charles C.] Pinckney [said] South Carolina can never receive the plan [for a new constitution] if it prohibits the slave trade. In every proposed extension of the powers of Congress, that state has expressly and watchfully excepted that of meddling with the importation of Negroes. . . .

Mr. [Roger] Sherman [of Connecticut] was for leaving the clause as it stands. He disapproved of the slave trade; yet, as the states were now possessed of the right to import slaves, . . . and as it was expedient to have as few objections as possible to the proposed scheme of government, he thought it best to leave the matter as we find it.

Col. [George] Mason [of Virginia stated that] this infernal trade originated in the avarice of British merchants. The British government constantly checked the attempts of Virginia to put a stop to it. The present question concerns not the importing states alone, but the whole Union. . . . Maryland and Virginia, he said, had already prohibited the importation of slaves expressly. North Carolina had done the same in substance. All this would be in vain if South Carolina and Georgia be at liberty to import. The Western people are already calling out for slaves for their new lands, and will fill that country with slaves, if they can be got through South Carolina and Georgia. Slavery discourages arts and manufactures. The poor despise labor when performed by slaves. They prevent the immigration of whites, who really enrich and strengthen a country. . . .

Every master of slaves is born a petty tyrant. They bring the judgment of Heaven on a country. As nations cannot be rewarded or punished in the next world, they must be in

consent, as required by the Articles of Confederation. Instead, they arbitrarily — and cleverly — declared that it would take effect when ratified by conventions in nine of the thirteen states. Moreover, they insisted that the conventions could only approve or disapprove the plan; they could not suggest alterations. As George Mason put it, the conventions would "take this or take nothing."

As the constitutional debate began in the fall of 1787, the nationalists seized the initiative with two bold moves. First, they called themselves **Federalists**, suggesting that they supported a federal union — a loose, decentralized system — and obscuring their commitment to a strong national government. Second, they launched a

Federalists
Supporters of the Constitution of 1787, which created a strong central government; their opponents, the Antifederalists, feared that a strong central government would corrupt the nation's newly won liberty.

this. By an inevitable chain of causes and effects, Providence punishes national sins by national calamities. . . . He held it essential, in every point of view, that the general government should have power to prevent the increase of slavery.

Mr. Ellsworth, as he had never owned a slave, could not judge of the effects of slavery on character. He said, however, that if it was to be considered in a moral light, we ought to go further, and free those already in the country. . . . Let us not intermeddle. As population increases, poor laborers will be so plenty as to render slaves useless. Slavery, in time, will not be a speck in our country. . . .

Gen. [Charles C.] Pinckney [argued that] South Carolina and Georgia cannot do without slaves. As to Virginia, she will gain by stopping the importations. Her slaves will rise in value, and she has more than she wants. It would be unequal to require South Carolina and Georgia to confederate on such unequal terms. . . . He contended that the importation of slaves would be for the interest of the whole Union. The more slaves, the more produce to employ the carrying trade; the more consumption also; and the more of this, the more revenue for the common treasury. . . . [He] should consider a rejection of the [present] clause as an exclusion of South Carolina from the Union. ❞

THE MASSACHUSETTS RATIFYING CONVENTION, JANUARY 1788

In Philadelphia, the delegates agreed on a compromise: they gave Congress the power to tax or prohibit slave imports, as Luther Martin had proposed, but withheld that power for twenty years. In the Massachusetts convention, the delegates split on this issue and on many others. They ratified the Constitution by a narrow margin, 187 to 168.

SOURCE: Jonathan Elliot, ed., *The Debates . . . on the Adoption of the Federal Constitution* (Philadelphia: J. B. Lippincott, 1836), 1: 103–105, 107, 112, 117.

❝ Mr. Neal (from Kittery) [an Antifederalist] went over the ground of objection to . . . the idea that slave trade was allowed to be continued for 20 years. His profession, he said, obliged him to bear witness against any thing that should favor the making merchandize of the bodies of men, and unless his objection was removed, he could not put his hand to the constitution. Other gentlemen said, in addition to this idea, that there was not even a proposition that the negroes ever shall be free: and Gen. Thompson exclaimed—'Mr. President, shall it be said, that after we have established our own independence and freedom, we make slaves of others? Oh! Washington . . . he has immortalized himself! but he holds those in slavery who have a good right to be free as he is. . . .'

On the other side, gentlemen said, that the step taken in this article, towards the abolition of slavery, was one of the beauties of the constitution. They observed, that in the confederation there was no provision whatever for its ever being abolished; but this constitution provides, that Congress may after twenty years, totally annihilate the slave trade. . . .

Mr. Heath (Federalist): . . . I apprehend that it is not in our power to do anything for or against those who are in slavery in the southern states. No gentleman within these walls detests every idea of slavery more than I do: it is generally detested by the people of this commonwealth, and I ardently hope that the time will soon come, when our brethren in the southern states will view it as we do, and put a stop to it; but to this we have no right to compel them.

Two questions naturally arise: if we ratify the Constitution, shall we do anything by our act to hold the blacks in slavery or shall we become the partakers of other men's sins? I think neither of them: each state is sovereign and independent to a certain degree, and they have a right, and will regulate their own internal affairs, as to themselves appears proper. . . . We are not in this case partakers of other men's sins. . . .

The federal convention went as far as they could; the migration or immigration &c. is confined to the states, now existing only, new states cannot claim it. Congress, by their ordinance for erecting new states, some time since, declared that there shall be no slavery in them. But whether those in slavery in the southern states, will be emancipated after the year 1808, I do not pretend to determine: I rather doubt it. ❞

QUESTIONS FOR ANALYSIS

1. At the Constitutional Convention in Philadelphia, what were the main arguments for and against federal restrictions on the Atlantic slave trade? How do you explain the position taken by the Connecticut delegates in Philadelphia and Mr. Heath in the Massachusetts debate? Identify the evidence used to support each claim.
2. What argument does George Mason, a Virginia slave owner, make in favor of prohibiting the Atlantic slave trade? Describe his claim.
3. What evidence of regional tensions appears in the documents? Explain your reasoning with examples from men from different states—Mason from Virginia, Ellsworth from Connecticut, and Heath from Massachusetts—offered predictions about the future of slavery.

TRM Find complete suggested responses in the Teacher's Resource Materials.

coordinated campaign in pamphlets and newspapers to explain and justify the Philadelphia constitution.

The Antifederalists The opponents of the Constitution, called by default the **Antifederalists**, had diverse backgrounds and motives. Some, like Governor George Clinton of New York, feared that state governments would lose power. Rural democrats protested that the proposed document, unlike most state constitutions, lacked a declaration of individual rights; they also feared that the central government would be run by wealthy men. "Lawyers and men of learning and monied men expect to be

Antifederalists
Opponents of ratification of the Constitution. Antifederalists feared that a powerful and distant central government would be out of touch with the needs of citizens. They also complained that it failed to guarantee individual liberties in a bill of rights.

TEACHING STRATEGY

"Lesson 6: Creating a New Nation" from PBS's *Liberty! The American Revolution* examines postwar tensions between Federalists and Antifederalists and ways their debate shaped the Constitution and the U.S. government. Lesson materials include discussion points for teachers, a viewing guide and a separate answer key, links to other resources, and extension ideas. Access this lesson plan by searching "PBS Liberty Creating a New Nation."

managers of this Constitution," worried a Massachusetts farmer. "[T]hey will swallow up all of us little folks . . . just as the whale swallowed up Jonah." Giving political substance to these fears, Melancton Smith of New York argued that the large electoral districts prescribed by the Constitution would restrict office holding to wealthy men, whereas the smaller districts used in state elections usually produced legislatures "composed principally of respectable yeomanry." John Quincy Adams agreed: if only "*eight* men" would represent Massachusetts, "they will infallibly be chosen from the aristocratic part of the community."

Smith summed up the views of Americans who held traditional republican values. To keep government "close to the people," they wanted the states to remain small sovereign republics tied together only for trade and defense — not the "United States" but the "States United." Citing the French political philosopher Montesquieu, Antifederalists argued that republican institutions were best suited to small polities. "No extensive empire can be governed on republican principles," declared James Winthrop of Massachusetts. Patrick Henry worried that the Constitution would re-create British rule: high taxes, an oppressive bureaucracy, a standing army, and a "great and mighty President . . . supported in extravagant munificence." As another Antifederalist put it, "I had rather be a free citizen of the small republic of Massachusetts than an oppressed subject of the great American Empire." Many Americans found themselves somewhere in the middle, supporting a stronger central government in principle but worried about countless details that made the Constitution appear flawed.

Federalists Respond In New York, where ratification was hotly contested, James Madison, John Jay, and Alexander Hamilton defended the proposed constitution in a series of eighty-five essays written in 1787 and 1788, collectively titled *The Federalist*. This work influenced political leaders throughout the country and subsequently won acclaim as an important treatise of practical republicanism. Its authors denied that a centralized government would lead to domestic tyranny. Drawing on Montesquieu's theories and John Adams's *Thoughts on Government*, Madison, Jay, and Hamilton pointed out that authority would be divided among the president, a bicameral legislature, and a judiciary. Each branch of government would "check and balance" the others and so preserve liberty.

Federalist No. 10
An essay by James Madison in *The Federalist* (1787–1788) that challenged the view that republican governments only worked in small polities; it argued that a geographically expansive national government would better protect republican liberty.

In "**Federalist No. 10**," Madison challenged the view that republican governments only worked in small polities, arguing that a large state would better protect republican liberty. It was "sown in the nature of man," Madison wrote, for individuals to seek power and form factions. Indeed, "a landed interest, a manufacturing interest, a mercantile interest, a moneyed interest, with many lesser interests, grow up of necessity in civilized nations." A free society should welcome all factions but keep any one of them from becoming dominant — something best achieved in a large republic. "Extend the sphere and you take in a greater variety of parties and interests," Madison concluded, inhibiting the formation of a majority eager "to invade the rights of other citizens."

AP® EXAM TIP

It's important to recognize the Ratification Debate as a continuing example of negotiation and compromise on the establishment of U.S. government.

The Constitution Ratified The delegates debating these issues in the state ratification conventions included untutored farmers and middling artisans as well as educated gentlemen. Generally, backcountry delegates were especially skeptical, while those from coastal areas were more likely to support the new constitution. In Pennsylvania, a coalition of Philadelphia merchants and artisans and commercial farmers ensured its ratification. Other early Federalist successes came in four less populous states — Delaware, New Jersey, Georgia, and Connecticut — where delegates hoped that a strong national government would offset the power of large neighboring states (Map 6.7).

The Constitution's first real test came in January 1788 in Massachusetts, a hotbed of Antifederalist sentiment. Influential Patriots, including Samuel Adams and Governor John Hancock, opposed the new constitution, as did many followers of Daniel Shays. But Boston artisans, who wanted tariff protection from British imports, supported ratification. To win over other delegates, Federalist leaders suggested nine

AP® APPLY THE TIP

Ask small groups of students to work collaboratively to complete **Handout 6.3 — Contextualization: Ratification Debate (TRM)** to outline the main arguments of the Federalists and Antifederalists, using pp. 203–206 in the text as well as primary source excerpts from the Federalists and Antifederalists. Once students have completed the handout, ask them to discuss the ways that the arguments on each side of the debate could be supported using Enlightenment ideals. Then, ask students to analyze the map on p. 207 and make an argument that explains the regional differences in support of ratification of the Constitution.

TRM Find **Handout 6.3 — Contextualization: Ratification Debate** in the Teacher's Resource Materials.

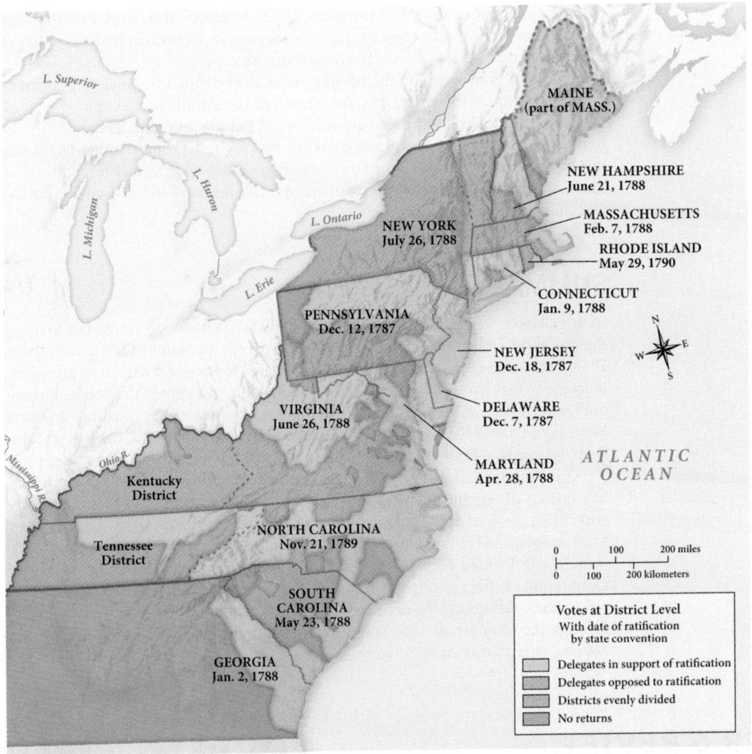

MAP 6.7 Ratifying the Constitution of 1787
In 1907, geographer Owen Libby mapped the votes of members of the state conventions that ratified the Constitution. His map showed that most delegates from seaboard or commercial farming districts (which sent many delegates to the conventions) supported the Constitution, while those from sparsely represented, subsistence-oriented backcountry areas opposed it. Subsequent research has confirmed Libby's socioeconomic interpretation of the voting patterns in North and South Carolina and in Massachusetts. However, other states' delegates were influenced by different factors. For example, in Georgia, delegates from all regions voted for ratification.

amendments that the Massachusetts delegation would submit to the new Congress for consideration once the Constitution was ratified. By a close vote of 187 to 168, the Federalists carried the day.

Spring brought Federalist victories in Maryland, South Carolina, and New Hampshire, reaching the nine- state quota required for ratification. But it took the powerful arguments advanced in *The Federalist* and more talk of amendments to secure the Constitution's adoption in the essential states of Virginia and New York. The votes were again close: 89 to 79 in Virginia and 30 to 27 in New York.

Testifying to their respect for popular sovereignty and majority rule, most Americans accepted the verdict of the ratifying conventions. "A decided majority" of the New Hampshire assembly had opposed the "new system," reported Joshua Atherton, but now they said, "It is adopted, let us try it." In Virginia, Patrick Henry vowed to "submit as a quiet citizen" and fight for amendments "in a constitutional way."

AP® THEME

NAT: American and National Identity; PCE: Politics and Power

MAP 6.7 shows the divisions between Antifederalists and Federalists over ratification. Because students know that the Constitution was ultimately ratified — and because ratification is often celebrated — they may tend to see this outcome as a foregone conclusion. Ask students: **What can you conclude about ratification of the Constitution from this map?** *The nation was deeply — and fairly evenly — divided. Many individual states were divided internally. In general, coastal residents supported ratification and westerners opposed it. Ratification stretched from early December 1787 (Delaware) through late May 1790 (Rhode Island), nearly two and a half years.*

CHECK FOR UNDERSTANDING

Ask students: **What were the most important compromises struck in the Philadelphia convention of 1787?** *The major compromises in 1787 consisted of those dealing with the nature of each state's congressional representation as well as the status of slavery. On the first matter, the Great Compromise was adopted—creating a bicameral legislature with one chamber based on a state's population and another with two senators from each state. On the second matter, the 3/5th compromise was developed, wherein slavery was legalized but slaves were counted for the census (and thus congressional reputation) as 3/5th of a person. The slave trade could also not be regulated until 1808 at the earliest.*

CHECK FOR UNDERSTANDING

Use the **AP® LEARNING FOCUS** question from the beginning of the chapter to check students' understanding of the chapter as a whole: **Why did the American independence movement succeed, and what changes did it initiate in American society and government?** *The war prompted many changes, including the cultural fragmentation of the British world. Federalism and republicanism replaced monarchy and deference as fundamental principles of the Revolution. The colonial relationship with Britain was destroyed. The Atlantic slave trade was condemned and outlawed by 1808. Non-elite men achieved a greater role in determining the government system that ruled over them. But even as these changes took place, much remained the same. Women remained second-class citizens, slavery remained a legal institution for African American people, Native Americans continued to be viewed as outsiders who had a minimal role to play in the independence movement, and elite white men continued to control national affairs.*

✓ LearningCurve

Remind students to go online to complete the LearningCurve quiz for this chapter.

TRM Find complete suggested responses in the Teacher's Resource Materials.

AP® SKILLS & PROCESSES

CAUSATION

AP® CONTENT REVIEW 1 asks students to identify the challenges faced by Americans in the first two years of the war. Ask students how Americans overcame having a nascent central government and lack of naval force at the beginning of the war.

And during the first session of Congress, James Madison set to work drafting a set of amendments to satisfy some of the most pressing concerns that had arisen in the ratification process (see "The Bill of Rights" in Chapter 7).

Unlike in France, where the Revolution of 1789 divided the society into irreconcilable factions for generations, the American Constitutional Revolution of 1787 created a national republic that enjoyed broad popular support. Federalists celebrated their triumph by organizing great processions in the seaport cities. By marching in an orderly fashion—in conscious contrast to the riotous Revolutionary mobs—Federalist-minded citizens affirmed their allegiance to a self-governing but elite-ruled republican nation.

SUMMARY

In this chapter, we examined the unfolding of two related sets of events. The first was the war between Britain and its rebellious colonies that began in 1776 and ended in 1783. The two great battles of Saratoga (1777) and Yorktown (1781) determined the outcome of that conflict. Surprisingly, given the military might of the British Empire, both were American victories. These triumphs testify to the determination of George Washington, the resilience of the Continental army, and support for the Patriot cause from hundreds of local militias and tens of thousands of taxpaying citizens.

This popular support reflected the Patriots' second success: building effective institutions of republican government. These elected institutions of local and state governance evolved out of colonial-era town meetings and representative assemblies. They were defined in the state constitutions written between 1776 and 1781, and their principles informed the first national constitution, the Articles of Confederation. Despite the challenges posed by conflicts over suffrage, women's rights, and fiscal policy, these self-governing political institutions carried the new republic successfully through the war-torn era and laid the foundation for the Constitution of 1787, the national charter that endures today.

CHAPTER 6 REVIEW

AP® CONTENT REVIEW

Answer these questions to demonstrate your understanding of the chapter's main ideas.

1. What challenges did Patriot forces confront in the first two years of the war, and what were their key achievements?
2. Why did the Patriots win the American Revolution?
3. What were the most important challenges facing governments in the 1780s?
4. What were the most important compromises struck in the Philadelphia convention of 1787?

AP® TERMS TO KNOW

Identify and explain the significance of each term below.

Key Concepts and Events

Battle of Long Island (1776) (p. 179)
Battle of Saratoga (1777) (p. 181)
Valley Forge (p. 183)
Philipsburg Proclamation (p. 184)
Battle of Yorktown (1781) (p. 188)
currency tax (p. 189)
Treaty of Paris of 1783 (p. 190)
Pennsylvania constitution of 1776 (p. 191)
mixed government (p. 192)
Articles of Confederation (p. 194)
Northwest Ordinance of 1787 (p. 196)
Shays's Rebellion (p. 197)
Virginia Plan (p. 199)
New Jersey Plan (p. 202)
Federalists (p. 204)
Antifederalists (p. 205)
Federalist No. 10 (p. 206)

AP® SKILLS & PROCESSES

CAUSATION

AP® CONTENT REVIEW 2 asks students to identify both the short- and long-term causes of American victory. Note: This is the same question as the section-opening prompt on p. 178.

AP® SKILLS & PROCESSES

DEVELOPMENTS AND PROCESSES

AP® CONTENT REVIEW 3 focuses on the "Critical Period" of 1781–1787, the period in which the Americans were governed under the Articles of Confederation.

AP® SKILLS & PROCESSES

DEVELOPMENTS AND PROCESSES

AP® CONTENT REVIEW 4 asks students to identify the major compromises of the Constitutional Convention such as the Great Compromise.

TRM Find definitions for these terms in the **Glossary/Glosario** in the Teacher's Resource Materials.

Key People

General George Washington (p. 178)
General William Howe (p. 179)
Robert Morris (p. 182)
General Horatio Gates (p. 185)
Baron von Steuben (p. 183)
Judith Sargent Murray (p. 192)
James Madison (p. 199)

AP MAKING CONNECTIONS

Recognize the larger developments and continuities within and across chapters by answering these questions.

1. In Chapter 5, we saw the way that protests against imperial policy grew until colonists chose to declare their independence rather than submit to Parliament's authority. By 1787, the problems created by the Revolutionary War forced leaders of the newly independent states to consider plans for their own powerful central government. What problems led nationalists to believe such a step was necessary? How did Antifederalists draw on Revolutionary ideas to make their case against the Constitution? What claims did nationalists make in response to dampen Antifederalist fears? Use historical reasoning to discuss arguments of both factions.

2. Chapters 4 and 5 traced the rise of slavery and the growing importance of western lands in British North America. What role did these two forms of property—human property in enslaved laborers, and lands controlled by Native Americans beyond the Proclamation Line but desired by speculators and yeoman farmers—play in the progress and outcomes of the American Revolution? How did the Revolution's emphasis on liberty, equality, and republican government help to justify the persistence of slavery in the tobacco- and rice-growing colonies and the displacement of Native Americans in the trans-Appalachian west? Describe relevant and specific examples to support the perspectives identified.

KEY TURNING POINTS

Refer to the timeline at the start of the chapter for help in answering the following questions.

Gates defeats Burgoyne at Saratoga (1777), the Franco- American alliance (1778), and Cornwallis surrenders at Yorktown (1781): How were these three events linked? How important was the French alliance to the Patriot victory?

AP PRACTICE QUESTIONS

MULTIPLE CHOICE QUESTIONS

Choose the correct answer for each question.

Questions 1–3 refer to this excerpt.

> "These are the times that try men's souls. The summer soldier and the sunshine patriot will, in this crisis, shrink from the service of their country; but he that stands it now, deserves the love and thanks of man and woman. Tyranny, like hell, is not easily conquered; yet we have this consolation with us, that the harder the conflict, the more glorious the triumph. What we obtain too cheap, we esteem too lightly: it is dearness only that gives every thing its value. Heaven knows how to put a proper price upon its goods; and it would be strange indeed if so celestial an article as freedom should not be highly rated. Britain, with an army to enforce her tyranny, has declared that she has a right (not only to tax) but to 'bind us in all cases whatsoever,' and if being bound in that manner, is not slavery, then is there not such a thing as slavery upon earth. Even the expression is impious; for so unlimited a power can belong only to God."
>
> Thomas Paine, "The American Crisis," December 19, 1776

1. Which of the following best explains the challenge faced by Patriots as described in the excerpt?
   a. Debates between the states over the fate of slavery
   b. Early military struggles against the British army
   c. Criticisms levied in Parliament by those opposed to the colonial war
   d. The Enlightenment ideal of freedom as the highest of all virtues

2. The sentiments expressed in the excerpt are most similar to sentiments expressed by which of the following groups?
   a. Women advocating a greater role in American society
   b. Frontier settlers in favor of seizing American Indian lands

AP® SKILLS & PROCESSES

CONTINUITY AND CHANGE

AP® MAKING CONNECTIONS 1 invites students to draw a connection between Patriot protests against central power, as described in a previous chapter, and the decision by some Patriots to form just such a government. This question further asks students to explain how both Federalists and Antifederalists relied on revolutionary ideas to justify their positions.

AP® SKILLS & PROCESSES

CAUSATION

AP® MAKING CONNECTIONS 2 asks students to identify how the ideals of the revolution affected enslavement and American Indians, and how these ideals were challenged by the continuation of enslavement and the persistent attacks on American Indian territory.

AP® SKILLS & PROCESSES

CONTINUITY AND CHANGE

The **KEY TURNING POINTS** question prompt invites students to draw connections between three major events that happened during the war and use them to determine the significance of the French alliance in leading to the turning point of American victory.

TRM Find complete suggested responses in the Teacher's Resource Materials.

c. Protestant evangelists during the First Great Awakening

d. Antifederalists opposed to ratification of the Constitution

3. As evidenced by the sentiments in this excerpt, which of the following most significantly contributed to the defeat of the British in the Revolutionary War?

a. The American public's willingness to endure economic shortages and inflation

b. The technological and military superiority of the Continental Army

c. The lack of dissent against the war effort in the American colonies

d. The ingenuity of American mechanics in bolstering industrial output

Questions 4–6 refer to this map.

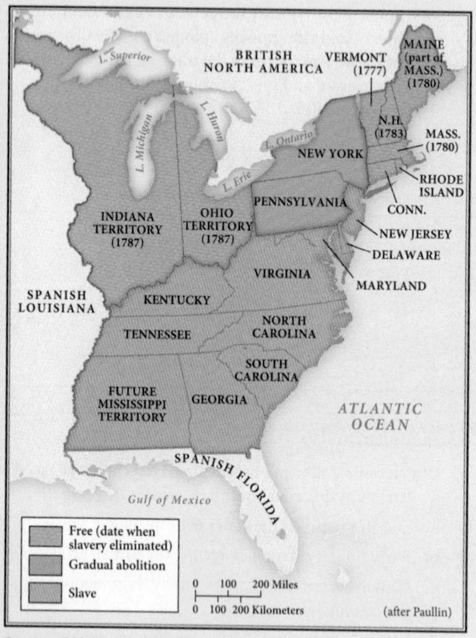

Status of Slavery in the United States Following the American Revolution Macmillan Learning.

4. The map could be best used to support a characterization of the dominant national attitude regarding slavery in the United States in the 1780s as

a. abolitionist seeking emancipation.

b. free-soil opposing the westward expansion of slavery.

c. sectional resulting from early federal and state government policies.

d. perfectionist avoiding compromise in favor of principle.

5. Using the dates in the map, which of the following most directly contributed to the status of the Indiana and Ohio Territories as shown in the map?

a. Federal treaty obligations with American Indian tribes

b. Compromises at the Constitutional Convention

c. The end of the Seven Years' War

d. Passage of the Northwest Ordinance

6. In the years immediately following the Revolutionary War, the regional differences depicted in the map posed the greatest threat to

a. maintaining existing systems of labor.

b. creating a sense of national identity and unity.

c. promoting peaceful relations with neighboring countries.

d. solving the nation's financial crisis.

SHORT ANSWER QUESTIONS

Read each question carefully and write a short response. Use evidence from the text to support your claims.

TRM Find complete suggested responses in the Teacher's Resource Materials.

"[T]he often violent expression of such discontents in politics should not blind us to the fact that the period was one of extraordinary economic growth. Merchants owned more ships at the end of the 1780s than they had at the beginning of the Revolution . . . [and] the export of agricultural produce was double. . . . American cities grew rapidly. . . . There can be no question but that freedom from the British Empire resulted in a surge of activity in all phases of American life. . . . [T]here is no evidence of stagnation and decay in the 1780s. Instead the story is one of a newly free people who seized upon every means to improve and enrich themselves in a nation which they believed had a golden destiny."

Merrill Jensen, *The New Nation: A History of the United States During the Confederation, 1781–1789*, 1950

"Viewing the state as analogous to the human body, Americans saw their country stricken by a serious sickness. The 1780s seemed to mark the point in the life of the young nation where a decisive change had to occur, leading either to recovery or death. . . . The signs of disease spread everywhere. Merchants and farmers were seeking their own selfish ends; hucksters were engrossing products to raise prices. Even government officials . . . were using their public positions to fill their own pockets. The fluctuation in the value of money . . . was putting a premium on selfishness. . . . Instead of bringing about the moral reformation they had anticipated from victory, the Revolution had only aggravated America's corruption and sin."

Gordon S. Wood, *The Creation of the American Republic, 1776–1787*, 1969

1. Using the two excerpts provided, answer (a), (b), and (c).
   a. Briefly explain ONE major difference between Jensen's and Wood's historical interpretations of American politics during the 1780s.
   b. Briefly explain how ONE specific historical event or development from the 1780s that is not explicitly mentioned in the excerpts could be used to support Jensen's interpretation.
   c. Briefly explain how ONE specific historical event or development from the 1780s that is not explicitly mentioned in the excerpts could be used to support Wood's interpretation.

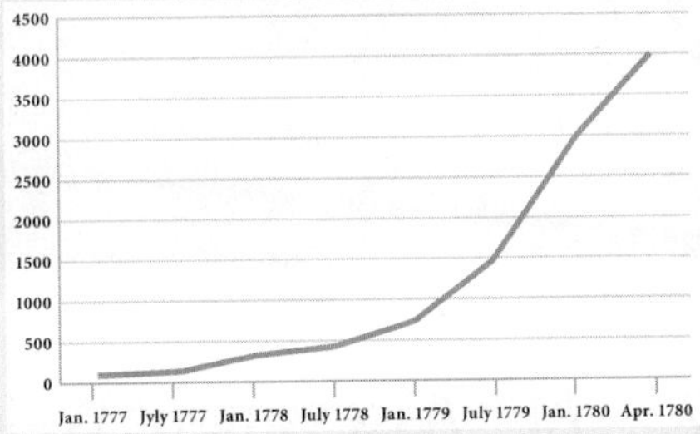

Graph of Massachusetts Paper Dollars Needed to Equal $100 of Gold

2. Using the graph provided, answer (a), (b), and (c).
   a. Briefly explain ONE specific historical factor that caused the change illustrated in the graph.
   b. Briefly explain ONE significant historical event or development resulting from the change illustrated in the graph.
   c. Briefly explain ANOTHER significant historical event or development resulting from the change illustrated in the graph.

3. Answer (a), (b), and (c).
   a. Briefly explain ONE specific historical similarity between the Articles of Confederation and the Constitution.
   b. Briefly explain ONE specific historical difference between the Articles of Confederation and the Constitution.
   c. Briefly explain ONE specific historical event, development, or circumstance that led to the difference you indicated in (b).

7 CHAPTER

Hammering Out a Federal Republic

1787–1820

Chapter 7 — AP® Assessment Weight and Pacing Guide

The assessment weight on the AP® U.S. History Exam for Chapters 5–7 is 10–17 percent. This chapter falls at the end of Unit 3 of the AP® U.S. History Curriculum, covering Period 3: 1754–1800, and the beginning of Unit 4, covering Period 4: 1800–1848. Periods 3 and 4 both account for 10–17 percent of the AP® U.S. History Exam.

This pacing guide is based on a schedule with 120 sessions of 50 minutes each before the AP® U.S. History Exam. If you have a different number of sessions before the exam, you can modify the pacing to meet your needs. If you have additional time, consider incorporating quizzes, released AP® U.S. History questions, practice exams, writing practice, and other instructional activities.

	Traditional Schedule	Block Schedule
Chapter 7	5 days	2–3 days

Daily Pacing Guide

	Content Focus	Essential Question
Days 1 and 2	The Political Crisis of the 1790s	What were the most important differences between Federalists and Republicans in the 1790s?
Days 3 and 4	A Republican Empire Is Born	How were the principles of the Jeffersonian Republicans reflected in this era of dramatic growth and development?
Day 5	The War of 1812 and the Transformation of Politics	What elements of Federalist political philosophy survived the end of the First Party System?

AP® Alignment

Section Heading	AP® Topic	AP® Theme
The Political Crisis of the 1790s	3.6, 3.10, 4.2	WOR, PCE
A Republican Empire Is Born	3.12, 4.2, 4.4, 4.8	MIG, WOR, PCE
The War of 1812 and the Transformation of Politics	4.2, 4.3, 4.4	PCE, WOR

*Should changes be made to the Course Framework in the future, an updated alignment will be placed on our AP® updates page at go.bfwpub.com/ap-course-updates.

Chapter 7 — Overview

Chapter 7 begins by focusing on the challenges and crises faced by the new government of the U.S. as leaders implemented the U.S. Constitution. The chapter emphasizes the different visions and actions of Alexander Hamilton and Thomas Jefferson, whose ideas led to the emergence of the first political party system in the U.S. The chapter then turns attention to the beginnings of imperial development of the U.S. by looking at conflicts and treaties with Native Americans that were designed to give the U.S. more land while at the same time seeing the expansion of U.S. territory through the Louisiana Purchase during Jefferson's administration. Finally, the chapter looks at the causes and effects of the War of 1812 on America's relationship with Europe as well as on the political party system and the decline of the Federalist Party.

Chapter 7 — Resources

The following resources can be found in the Teacher's Resource Materials (TRM) that accompany the book. You can access the TRM via the book's digital platform, by clicking the TRM links found here in your Teacher's Edition e-book, or by contacting your representative to access the resources online. Visit **bfwpub.com/henretta10e** to learn more.

TRM Chapter 7 Lecture Presentation Slides

TRM Chapter 7 Outline with AP® Focus

TRM Chapter 7 Lecture Strategies

TRM Chapter 7 Suggested Responses

TRM Handout 7.1 — Causation: Impact of Hamilton's Financial Plan

TRM Handout 7.2 — Comparison: First Party System

TRM Handout 7.3 — Contextualization: Louisiana Purchase

Chapter 7 — Essential Activity

Provide students with excerpts from Washington's Farewell Address. Ask students to read and analyze the arguments made by Washington regarding domestic and foreign policy. Ask students to extend their analysis by explaining the significance of the historical context, intended audience, purpose, and Washington's point of view. Lead a class discussion that clarifies questions regarding the analysis and extended analysis of this document. Next, ask students to think about current political policy, which includes allowing the other political party to give a response to a presidential address. Ask students to work in pairs to produce a "Democratic-Republican Response" to Washington's Farewell Address from the point of view of Thomas Jefferson. In this response, students should provide an assessment of Washington's administration and respond to his advice on domestic and foreign policy. Ask students to deliver their responses as time allows. Lead a discussion on the differences in the interpretation of events and policies by the first political parties.

Chapter 7 — Bell Ringers

The following activities take no more than 5–15 minutes of your class period and offer an effective and engaging way to begin your lessons and for students to apply AP® Skills & Processes:

- Ask students to create an "agenda" for George Washington's first day as president that lists (in order of priority) the problems and issues that he needs to address as the President of the newly formed United States. Lead a discussion of the problems and their level of priority. Use this as an introduction to a class discussion on Washington's administration.
- Provide students with a list of quotes from both Thomas Jefferson and Alexander Hamilton (without the author's names provided). Allow students to work in teams or individually to see who can correctly identify the author of each quote first. To get credit, students must provide an explanation that relates the quote to the ideas of each leader.

NOTES

TEACHING STRATEGY

The chapter introduction lays out the major question facing the nation in its first years after drafting the Constitution. The United States had avoided the pitfalls of other republican-inspired rebellions, but it faced the task of putting a viable independent republic into place. While American leaders agreed on the desirability of republican government, they differed on the details of the kind of republic they should form, asking the question: Should the American republic be a representative institution led by able elites or a genuinely democratic polity in which ordinary citizens participated? For a complete suggested response to the **AP® LEARNING FOCUS** question, see p. 242.

7

CHAPTER

Hammering Out a Federal Republic

1787–1820

AP® LEARNING FOCUS

Why did the United States survive the challenges of its first three decades to become a viable, growing independent republic?

Like an earthquake, the American Revolution shook the European monarchical order, and its aftershocks reverberated for decades. By "creating a new republic based on the rights of the individual, the North Americans introduced a new force into the world," the eminent German historian Leopold von Ranke warned the king of Bavaria in 1854, a force that might cost the monarch his throne. Before 1776, "a king who ruled by the grace of God had been the center around which everything turned. Now the idea emerged that power should come from below [from the people]."

Other republican-inspired upheavals — England's Puritan Revolution of the 1640s and the French Revolution of 1789 — ended in political chaos and military rule. Similar fates befell many Latin American republics that won independence from Spain in the early nineteenth century. But the American states escaped both anarchy and dictatorship. Having been raised in a Radical Whig political culture that viewed standing armies and powerful generals as instruments of tyranny, General George Washington left public life in 1783 to manage his plantation, astonishing European observers but bolstering the authority of elected Patriot leaders. "'Tis a Conduct so novel," American painter John Trumbull reported from London, that it is "inconceivable to People [here]."

The great task of fashioning representative republican governments absorbed the energy and intellect of an entire generation and was rife with conflict. Seeking to perpetuate the elite-led polity of the colonial era, Federalists celebrated "natural aristocrats" such as Washington and condemned the radical republicanism of the French Revolution. In response, Jefferson and his Republican followers claimed the Fourth of July as their holiday and "we the people" as their political language. "There was a grand democrat procession in Town on the 4th of July," came a report from Baltimore: "All the farmers, tanners, black-smiths, shoemakers, etc. were there . . . and afterwards they went to a grand feast."

Many people of high status worried that the new state governments were too attentive to the demands of such ordinary workers and their families. When considering a bill, Connecticut conservative Ezra Stiles grumbled, every elected official "instantly thinks how it will affect his constituents" rather than how it would enhance the general welfare. What Stiles criticized as irresponsible, however, most Americans welcomed. The concerns of ordinary citizens were now paramount, and traditional elites trembled.

Election Day in Philadelphia, 1815 Though election days were an old tradition in England and its American colonies, the democratic character of the new republic made them a special object of fascination. This painting by German immigrant John Lewis Krimmel captures the boisterous spirit of election day proceedings outside of the Philadelphia State House, where voters passed their ballots through the building's window to cast their votes. Krimmel depicts a mixed crowd, with gentlemen gathered on the building's steps while women, children, dogs, and intoxicated tradesmen crossed paths on Chestnut Street. A man on the balcony gazes down on the scene while the American flag waves above his head. Here was American democracy in all its chaotic glory. Winterthur Museum, purchased with funds provided by Henry Francis du Pont.

TEACHING STRATEGY

Show students the engraving to illustrate the nation's uncertainty about the appropriate emblem for the new nation and its conflicted sense of identity in its early years. Ask students: **What processes facilitated the democratization of politics in the early nineteenth century?** *Though the first generation of American political leaders consistently expressed worries about the long-term viability of democratic nations, the system they designed allowed political processes to experience increased political participation over time. The framers were adamant about producing a republican form of government, which meant the eligible body politic elected people to make decisions for them. However, factors such as the evolution of political parties and suffrage requirement changes at the state level meant that a national transformation would happen. Indeed, by the early nineteenth century, American politics was experiencing increased democratization, as expressed in this painting.*

AP® SKILLS & PROCESSES

CONTINUITY AND CHANGE

Use the **TIMELINE** table to explore how 1784 to 1819 could constitute a distinct era running from the drafting of the Constitution through the end of the War of 1812. As students skim the events on the timeline, you might prompt them to make a generalization about the types of events that helped early leaders to "hammer out" a federal republic. This can include the establishment of a Bill of Rights (which students know from the previous chapter was key to securing Antifederalist support for the Constitution), dealing with issues of credit and debt, major federal court decisions, treaties with Native Americans and European powers, as well as military struggles — several battles and at least one war. Extend this exercise by asking students to create a label for this era and justify its appropriateness.

TIMELINE

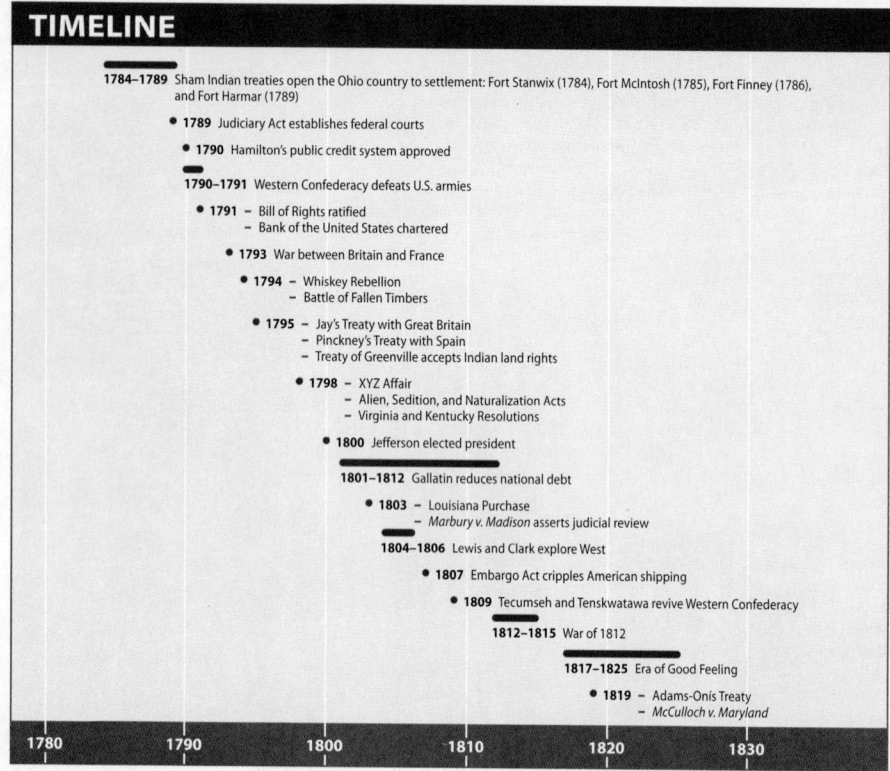

- **1784–1789** Sham Indian treaties open the Ohio country to settlement: Fort Stanwix (1784), Fort McIntosh (1785), Fort Finney (1786), and Fort Harmar (1789)
- **1789** Judiciary Act establishes federal courts
- **1790** Hamilton's public credit system approved
- **1790–1791** Western Confederacy defeats U.S. armies
- **1791** – Bill of Rights ratified
  – Bank of the United States chartered
- **1793** War between Britain and France
- **1794** – Whiskey Rebellion
  – Battle of Fallen Timbers
- **1795** – Jay's Treaty with Great Britain
  – Pinckney's Treaty with Spain
  – Treaty of Greenville accepts Indian land rights
- **1798** – XYZ Affair
  – Alien, Sedition, and Naturalization Acts
  – Virginia and Kentucky Resolutions
- **1800** Jefferson elected president
- **1801–1812** Gallatin reduces national debt
- **1803** – Louisiana Purchase
  – *Marbury v. Madison* asserts judicial review
- **1804–1806** Lewis and Clark explore West
- **1807** Embargo Act cripples American shipping
- **1809** Tecumseh and Tenskwatawa revive Western Confederacy
- **1812–1815** War of 1812
- **1817–1825** Era of Good Feeling
- **1819** – Adams-Onís Treaty
  – *McCulloch v. Maryland*

1780 | 1790 | 1800 | 1810 | 1820 | 1830

THE POLITICAL CRISIS OF THE 1790S

What were the most important differences between Federalists and Republicans in the 1790s?

AP® EXAM TIP

Identifying the ways that Washington and Adams put the Constitution into practice is essential to success on the AP® Exam.

The final decade of the eighteenth century brought fresh challenges for American politics. The Federalists split into two factions over financial policy and the French Revolution, and their leaders, Alexander Hamilton and Thomas Jefferson, offered contrasting visions of the future. Would the United States remain an agricultural nation governed by local officials, as Jefferson hoped? Or would Hamilton's vision of a strong national government and an economy based on manufacturing become reality?

The Federalists Implement the Constitution

The Constitution expanded the dimensions of political life by allowing voters to choose national leaders as well as local and state officials. The Federalists swept the election of 1788, winning forty-four seats in the House of Representatives; only eight Antifederalists won election. As expected, members of the electoral college chose George Washington as president. John Adams received the second-highest number of electoral votes and became vice president.

212

AP® APPLY THE TIP

Ask students to work with a partner to generate a list of public concerns present when George Washington was inaugurated as President of the U.S. Students might include fear that government was too powerful, fear that the new government was not powerful enough to keep order in a large nation, fear that other nations would take advantage of the new nation, and concern over the debt the new nation faced. Once students have a list of concerns, ask them to identify problems or issues that caused these (or other) concerns to grow in the early Federal period. Then have students identify the ways that the administrations of George Washington and John Adams attempted to address these concerns.

TEACHING STRATEGY

The Web site for Mt. Vernon, George Washington's home, provides many teaching resources about his role in the young U.S. The site includes a digital encyclopedia with many entries on topics from Washington's presidency and the early republic. There are links to dozens of paintings, drawings, and artifacts related to Washington, as well as a number of primary source-based lesson plans and teaching resources. Lessons include an examination of his foreign policy, using political cartoons to understand his presidency, an examination of his views on slavery, and a study of his "apotheosis." Access these resources by searching "Mount Vernon Education."

Devising the New Government Once the military savior of his country, Washington now became its political father. At age fifty-seven, the first president possessed great personal dignity and a cautious personality. To maintain continuity, he adopted many of the administrative practices of the Confederation and asked Congress to reestablish the existing executive departments: Foreign Affairs (State), Finance (Treasury), and War. To head the Department of State, Washington chose Thomas Jefferson, a fellow Virginian and an experienced diplomat. For secretary of the treasury, he turned to Alexander Hamilton, a lawyer and his former military aide. The president designated Jefferson, Hamilton, and Secretary of War Henry Knox as his cabinet, or advisory body.

The Constitution mandated a supreme court, but the Philadelphia convention gave Congress the task of creating a national court system. The Federalists wanted strong national institutions, and the **Judiciary Act of 1789** reflected their vision. The act established a three-tiered system: it created federal district courts in each state and three circuit courts above them to which the decisions of the district courts could be appealed. The Supreme Court would then serve as the appellate court of last resort in the federal system. The Judiciary Act also specified that cases arising in state courts that involved federal laws could be appealed to the Supreme Court. This provision ensured that federal judges would determine the meaning of the Constitution.

The Bill of Rights The Federalists kept their promise to consider amendments to the Constitution. James Madison, now a member of the House of Representatives, submitted nineteen amendments to the First Congress; by 1791, ten had been approved by Congress and ratified by the states. These ten amendments, known as the **Bill of Rights**, safeguard fundamental personal rights, including freedom of speech and religion, and mandate legal procedures, such as trial by jury. By protecting individual citizens, the amendments eased Antifederalists' fears of an oppressive national government and secured the legitimacy of the Constitution. They also addressed the issue of federalism: the proper balance between the authority of the national and state governments. But that question was repeatedly contested until the Civil War and remains important today.

Hamilton's Financial Program

George Washington's most important decision was choosing Alexander Hamilton as secretary of the treasury. An ambitious self-made man of great intelligence, Hamilton was a prominent lawyer in New York City who had married into the influential Schuyler family, which owned land in the Hudson River Valley. At the Philadelphia convention, he condemned the "democratic spirit" and called for an authoritarian government and a president with near-monarchical powers.

As treasury secretary, Hamilton devised bold policies to enhance national authority and to assist financiers and merchants. He outlined his plans in three pathbreaking reports to Congress: on public credit (January 1790), on a national bank (December 1790), and on manufactures (December 1791). These reports outlined a coherent program of national mercantilism — government-assisted economic development. Hamilton's system immediately sparked disagreement and eventually drove a wedge between him and fellow Federalists Jefferson and James Madison.

Public Credit: Redemption and Assumption The financial and social implications of Hamilton's "**Report on the Public Credit**" made it instantly controversial. Hamilton asked Congress to redeem at face value the $55 million in Confederation securities held by foreign and domestic investors (Figure 7.1). His reasons were simple: as an underdeveloped nation, the United States needed good credit to secure loans from Dutch and British financiers. However, Hamilton's redemption plan would

AP® SKILLS & PROCESSES

DEVELOPMENTS AND PROCESSES

How did the debate over the balance between liberty and order influence the formation of political parties?

Judiciary Act of 1789
Act that established federal district courts in each state and three circuit courts to hear appeals from the districts, with the Supreme Court serving as the highest appellate court in the federal system.

Bill of Rights
The first ten amendments to the Constitution, officially ratified by 1791. The amendments safeguarded fundamental personal rights, including freedom of speech and religion, and mandated legal procedures, such as trial by jury.

AP® EXAM TIP

Consider the ways that Hamilton's Financial Plan helped spur the growth of the first political party system in the U.S.

Report on the Public Credit
Alexander Hamilton's 1790 report recommending that the federal government should assume all state debts and fund the national debt — that is, offer interest on it rather than repaying it — at full value. Hamilton's goal was to make the new country creditworthy, not debt-free.

TRM Find complete suggested responses in the Teacher's Resource Materials.

CHECK FOR UNDERSTANDING

Ask students: **What were the main features of the Federalists' implementation of the Constitution?** *Washington appointed the first cabinet, whose positions were carried over from the Confederation government; Congress established a strong federal judiciary, including the Supreme Court; and Federalists upheld their promise to Antifederalists to create a Bill of Rights.*

AP® APPLY THE TIP

To help students understand the connections between Hamilton's financial plan and the development of the first political parties, ask students to complete **Handout 7.1 — Causation: Impact of Hamilton's Financial Plan (TRM).** To extend the discussion, ask students to predict the reaction of the first two parties to the following issues: war between Great Britain and France; limitations of freedom of speech; and federal support for building roads and railroads.

TRM Find **Handout 7.1 — Causation: Impact of Hamilton's Financial Plan** in the Teacher's Resource Materials.

AP® SKILLS & PROCESSES

DEVELOPMENTS AND PROCESSES

Hamilton's financial program is a complex design and many students spend too much time focusing on a microanalysis of the program, as opposed to remembering the macro view of his proposals. Provide students with two historical ideas such as commercialism and nationalism. Remind students in this context, nationalism is connected to Hamilton's desire to have the United States compete on a global stage. As students study the concepts of Hamilton's financial program, have them connect the details to either nationalism or commercialism. In this way, students will remember to think through a macroanalysis of Hamilton's proposals.

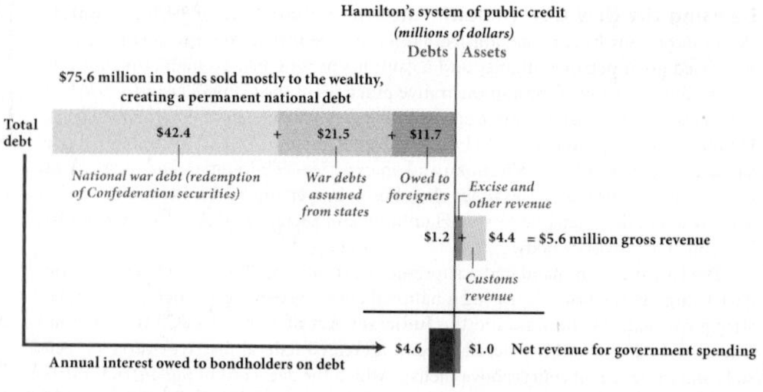

FIGURE 7.1 Hamilton's Fiscal Structure, 1792
As treasury secretary, Alexander Hamilton established a national debt by issuing government bonds and using the proceeds to redeem Confederation securities and assume the war debts of the states. To pay the annual interest due on the bonds, he used the revenue from excise taxes and customs duties. Hamilton deliberately did not attempt to redeem the bonds because he wanted to tie the interests of the wealthy Americans who owned them to the new national government.

AP® SKILLS & PROCESSES

MAKING CONNECTIONS

Why did Hamilton believe a national debt would strengthen the United States and help to ensure its survival?

give enormous profits to speculators, who had bought up depreciated securities. For example, the Massachusetts firm of Burrell & Burrell had paid $600 for Confederation notes with a face value of $2,500; it stood to reap a profit of $1,900. Such windfall gains offended a majority of Americans, who condemned the speculative practices of capitalist financiers. Equally controversial was Hamilton's proposal to pay the Burrells and other note holders with new interest-bearing securities, thereby creating a permanent national debt and tying the interests of wealthy creditors to the survival of the new nation.

Patrick Henry condemned this plan "to erect, and concentrate, and perpetuate a large monied interest" and warned that it would prove "fatal to the existence of American liberty." James Madison demanded that Congress recompense those who originally owned Confederation securities: the thousands of shopkeepers, farmers, and soldiers who had bought or accepted them during the dark days of the war. However, it would have been difficult to trace the original owners; moreover, nearly half the members of the House of Representatives owned Confederation securities and would profit personally from Hamilton's plan. Melding practicality with self-interest, the House rejected Madison's suggestion.

Hamilton then proposed that the national government further enhance public credit by assuming the war debts of the states. This assumption plan, costing $22 million, also favored well-to-do creditors such as Abigail Adams, who had bought depreciated Massachusetts government bonds with a face value of $2,400 for only a few hundred dollars and would reap a windfall profit. Still, Adams was a long-term investor, not a speculator like Assistant Secretary of the Treasury William Duer. Knowing Hamilton's intentions in advance, Duer and his associates secretly bought up $4.6 million of the war bonds of southern states at bargain rates. Congressional critics condemned Duer's speculation. They also pointed out that some states had already paid off their war debts; in response, Hamilton promised to reimburse those states. To win the votes of congressmen from Virginia and Maryland, the treasury chief arranged another deal: he agreed that the permanent national capital would be built along the Potomac River, where suspicious southerners could easily watch its operations. Such astute bargaining gave Hamilton the votes he needed to enact his redemption and assumption plans.

AP® THEME

NAT: American and National Identity; PCE: Politics and Power

Use **FIGURE 7.1** to discuss how Hamilton's economic policies played a significant role in launching debates in the following decade regarding the appropriate relationship between the national government and the economy. Guide students' analysis with the following questions:

- **How much total debt did the U.S. government owe? What was the largest source of debt?** *$75.6 million. National war debt owed to individuals who redeemed Confederation bonds.*
- **What was the annual revenue? Where did this revenue come from?** *$5.6 million. From excise taxes on whiskey distillers and others, and customs duties on imports.*
- **Roughly what percent of annual revenue went to paying off the debt?** *Over 80 percent ($4.6 million/$5.6 million).*
- **Based on revenue available for government spending, what can you conclude about the size of the federal government?** *Relying on a budget of $1 million, less than 20 percent of annual revenue suggests that the government was fairly small by today's standards, even under a conservative like Washington.*
- **The U.S. government is much bigger now than in Washington's time. What major source of revenue does the government have now that Hamilton did not use?** *Income tax and payroll tax constitute about 80 percent of revenue today, while the remainder is collected fairly evenly between corporate income taxes and excise taxes.*

AP® SKILLS & PROCESSES

MAKING CONNECTIONS

The **MAKING CONNECTIONS** question asks students to consider Hamilton's perspective on the crucial historical question of the appropriate federal response to the national debt. Students need to understand how his outlook compared to that of his critics. Scaffold this prompt with the following questions: Why did he think this funding strategy was essential while others were sure it would be disastrous? What was at stake — why was the method of retiring the debt such an important topic for the early nation? Extend this prompt by asking students to determine whether Hamilton was correct in this economic assessment according to the text.

TRM Find complete suggested responses in the Teacher's Resource Materials.

Creating a National Bank In December 1790, Hamilton asked Congress to charter the **Bank of the United States**, which would be jointly owned by private stockholders and the national government. Hamilton argued that the bank would provide stability to the American economy, which was chronically short of capital, by making loans to merchants, handling government funds, and issuing bills of credit — much as the Bank of England had done in Great Britain. These potential benefits persuaded Congress to grant Hamilton's bank a twenty-year charter and to send the legislation to the president for his approval.

Bank of the United States
A bank chartered in 1790 and jointly owned by private stockholders and the national government. Alexander Hamilton argued that the bank would provide stability to the American economy, which was chronically short of capital, by making loans to merchants, handling government funds, and issuing bills of credit.

At this critical juncture, Secretary of State Thomas Jefferson joined with James Madison to oppose Hamilton's financial initiatives. Jefferson charged that Hamilton's national bank was unconstitutional. "The incorporation of a Bank," Jefferson told President Washington, was not a power expressly "delegated to the United States by the Constitution." Jefferson's argument rested on a *strict* interpretation of the Constitution. Hamilton preferred a *loose* interpretation; he told Washington that Article 1, Section 8, empowered Congress to make "all Laws which shall be necessary and proper" to carry out the provisions of the Constitution. Agreeing with Hamilton, the president signed the legislation.

Raising Revenue Through Tariffs Hamilton now sought revenue to pay the annual interest on the national debt. At his insistence, Congress imposed excise taxes, including a duty on whiskey distilled in the United States. These taxes would yield $1 million a year. To raise another $4 million to $5 million, the treasury secretary proposed higher tariffs on foreign imports. Although Hamilton's "**Report on Manufactures**" (1791) urged the expansion of American manufacturing, he did not support high protective tariffs that would exclude foreign products. Rather, he advocated moderate revenue tariffs that would pay the interest on the debt and other government expenses.

Report on Manufactures
A proposal by treasury secretary Alexander Hamilton in 1791 calling for the federal government to urge the expansion of American manufacturing while imposing tariffs on foreign imports.

Hamilton's scheme worked brilliantly. As American trade increased, customs revenue rose steadily and paid down the national debt. Controversies notwithstanding, the treasury secretary had devised a strikingly modern and successful fiscal system; as entrepreneur Samuel Blodget Jr. declared in 1801, "the country prospered beyond all former example."

Jefferson's Agrarian Vision

Hamilton paid a high political price for his success. As Washington began his second four-year term in 1793, Hamilton's financial measures had split the Federalists into bitterly opposed factions. Most northern Federalists supported the treasury secretary, while most southern Federalists joined a group headed by Madison and Jefferson. By 1794, the two factions had acquired names. Hamiltonians remained Federalists; the allies of Madison and Jefferson called themselves Democratic Republicans or simply Republicans.

Thomas Jefferson spoke for southern planters and western farmers. Well-read in architecture, natural history, agricultural science, and political theory, Jefferson embraced the optimism of the Enlightenment. He believed in the "improvability of the human race" and deplored the corruption and social divisions that threatened its progress. Having seen the poverty of laborers in British factories, Jefferson doubted that wageworkers had the economic and political independence needed to sustain a republican polity.

Two Men, Two Visions of America Thomas Jefferson (left) and Alexander Hamilton confront each other in these portraits, as they did in the political battles of the 1790s. Jefferson was pro-French, Hamilton pro-British. Jefferson favored farmers and artisans; Hamilton supported merchants and financiers. Jefferson believed in democracy and rule by legislative majorities; Hamilton argued for strong executives and judges. Still, in the contested presidential election of 1800, Hamilton (who detested candidate Aaron Burr) threw his support to Jefferson and secured the presidency for his longtime political foe. Left: White House Collection/White House Historical Association. Right: Yale University Art Gallery.

CHECK FOR UNDERSTANDING

Ask students: **What were the key elements of Hamilton's financial program? Why were they controversial?** *He proposed redeeming inflated Confederation currency at face value, which outraged critics who saw the policy as a windfall for speculators. He proposed assuming the states' war debts, though critics complained that some states had already paid off their debts. He also proposed creation of a national bank, which some worried would create an undesirable alliance between investors and government officials. Finally, he proposed creation of a tariff and an excise tax to fund the federal debt.*

AP® THEME

PCE: Politics and Power

Use the portraits of Hamilton and Jefferson to discuss the two basic divisions in American political culture in the 1790s. In broad terms, they disagreed on the extent of national government power and on economic policy. In particular, they disagreed about the Bank of the U.S., foreign policy, and whether government policies should prioritize order or liberty, which eventually led to the formation of political parties in the Adams administration.

AP® SKILLS & PROCESSES

COMPARISON

Students are required to understand how competing political parties debated policies over the power of the federal government. Ask students to identify and describe three ways in which the Jeffersonian Democratic-Republicans represented a break from the Federalist vision for the United States.

TRM Find complete suggested responses in the Teacher's Resource Materials.

CHECK FOR UNDERSTANDING

Ask students: **What was Jefferson's agrarian vision?** *He wanted the U.S. to become a democratic nation of small independent farmers.*

AP® APPLY THE TIP

Provide students with an outline map of the U.S. in 1789. Ask students to label the following features: Atlantic Ocean, United States, British Territory, Spanish Territory, Mississippi River, New Orleans, Great Lakes, and the Ohio Valley. Ask students to carefully read pp. 216–223 in order to mark areas on the map where the U.S. came into conflict with Great Britain, France, and Spain. Students should then add notes about the ways in which these conflicts were solved by the Proclamation of Neutrality, Jay's Treaty, Pinckney's Treaty, and the Treaty of Greenville. Then as a class discuss what these conflicts reveal about the important foreign policy goals in the U.S. during the early Federal period. Also, examine how the foreign policy agreements exacerbated political party conflicts.

TRM Find complete suggested responses in the Teacher's Resource Materials.

AP® SKILLS & PROCESSES

COMPARISON

How did Jefferson's idea of an agrarian republic differ from the economic vision put forward by Alexander Hamilton?

Jefferson therefore set his democratic vision of America in a society of independent yeomen farm families. "Those who labor in the earth are the chosen people of God," he wrote. The grain and meat from their homesteads would feed European nations, which "would manufacture and send us in exchange our clothes and other comforts." Jefferson's notion of an international division of labor resembled that proposed by Scottish economist Adam Smith in *The Wealth of Nations* (1776).

Turmoil in Europe brought Jefferson's vision closer to reality. The French Revolution began in 1789; four years later, the First French Republic (1792–1804) went to war against a British-led coalition of monarchies. As fighting disrupted European farming, wheat prices leaped from 5 to 8 shillings a bushel and remained high for twenty years, bringing substantial profits to Chesapeake and Middle Atlantic farmers. "Our farmers have never experienced such prosperity," remarked one observer. Simultaneously, a boom in the export of raw cotton, fueled by the invention of the cotton gin and the mechanization of cloth production in Britain, boosted the economies of Georgia and South Carolina. As Jefferson had hoped, European markets brought prosperity to American agriculture.

The French Revolution Divides Americans

Proclamation of Neutrality
A proclamation issued by President George Washington in 1793, allowing U.S. citizens to trade with all belligerents in the war between France and Great Britain.

American merchants profited even more handsomely from the war between France and Great Britain. In 1793, President Washington issued a **Proclamation of Neutrality**, allowing U.S. citizens to trade with all belligerents. As neutral carriers, American merchant ships claimed a right to pass through Britain's naval blockade of French ports, and American firms quickly took over the lucrative sugar trade between France and its West Indian islands. Commercial earnings rose spectacularly, averaging $20 million annually in the 1790s — twice the value of cotton and tobacco exports. As the American merchant fleet increased from 355,000 tons in 1790 to 1.1 million tons in 1808, northern shipbuilders and merchants provided work for thousands of shipwrights, sailmakers, dockhands, and seamen. Carpenters, masons, and cabinetmakers in Boston, New York, and Philadelphia easily found work building warehouses and fashionable "Federal-style" town houses for newly affluent merchants.

AP® EXAM TIP

The impact of conflicts in Europe on the economy, politics, and foreign policy of the U.S. is important to know on the AP® Exam.

French Revolution
A revolution in France (1789–1799) that was initially welcomed by most Americans because it began by abolishing feudalism and establishing a constitutional monarchy, but eventually came to seem too radical to many.

Ideological Politics As Americans profited from Europe's struggles, they argued passionately over its ideologies. Most Americans had welcomed the **French Revolution** (1789–1799) because it began by abolishing feudalism and establishing a constitutional monarchy. The creation of the First French Republic (1792–1804) was more controversial. Many Americans embraced the democratic ideology of the radical Jacobins, forming political clubs and beginning to address one another as "citizen" to declare their shared values. However, Americans with strong religious beliefs condemned the new French government for closing Christian churches and promoting a rational religion based on "natural morality." And for many, the Reign of Terror (1793–1794) offered proof that the revolution had gone too far. Fearing social revolution at home, wealthy Americans condemned revolutionary leader Robespierre and his followers for executing King Louis XVI and three thousand aristocrats.

AP® SKILLS & PROCESSES

CONTEXTUALIZATION

How did the French Revolution challenge the United States in domestic and foreign policy?

Whiskey Rebellion
A 1794 uprising by farmers in western Pennsylvania in response to enforcement of an unpopular excise tax on whiskey.

Their fears were well founded, because Hamilton's economic policies quickly sparked a domestic insurgency. In 1794, western Pennsylvania farmers mounted the so-called **Whiskey Rebellion** to protest Hamilton's excise tax on spirits (see "Thinking Like a Historian," p. 219). This tax had cut demand for the corn whiskey the farmers distilled and bartered for eastern manufactures. Like the Sons of Liberty in 1765 and the Shaysites in 1786, the Whiskey Rebels assailed the tax collectors who sent the farmers' hard-earned money to a distant government. Protesters waved banners proclaiming the French revolutionary slogan "Liberty, Equality, Fraternity!" To deter popular rebellion and uphold national authority, President Washington raised a militia force of 12,000 troops and dispersed the Whiskey Rebels.

CHECK FOR UNDERSTANDING

Ask students: **How did the French Revolution divide Americans?** *Many Americans initially favored the Revolution's overthrow of feudalism and establishment of a constitutional monarchy, but others were bothered by the rejection of traditional Christianity. Jay's Treaty, negotiated in the midst of British-French conflict, seemed too pro-British to some Americans. Americans were also torn about how to respond to the Haitian Revolution.*

VISUAL ACTIVITY

The Whiskey Rebellion, 1794 This painting shows George Washington reviewing the militia forces raised by New Jersey, Pennsylvania, Maryland, and Virginia to march against the Whiskey Rebels in western Pennsylvania. Washington, astride a white horse, dominates the scene; subordinate army officers, including Daniel Morgan and "Light-Horse" Harry Lee, accompany him as he greets an officer of one of the militia units. It expresses a Federalist vision of hierarchy (in the form of officers on horseback) and order (represented by the ranks of troops). The reality was messier: militias were called up from four states, but when volunteers were too few the states resorted to a draft, which prompted protests and riots. In the end, the militia force of more than 12,000 men was larger than the Continental army itself had been through much of the Revolution. Upon its approach, the rebellion evaporated. Twenty-four men were indicted for treason; two were sentenced to hang, but Washington pardoned them to encourage peaceful reconciliation. The Granger Collection, New York.

READING THE IMAGE: This painting, attributed to James Peale, shows both the strength and the diversity of America's militia forces, but it masks the difficulties involved in raising men to march against their fellow American citizens. What conclusion can be drawn on the point of view of the artist? What was the artist's purpose in portraying Washington and the militia in this way? How might this image have been influenced by other developments in Washington's administration?

MAKING CONNECTIONS: At the same time that Washington was raising a militia force to suppress the rebels in western Pennsylvania, U.S. Army troops under the command of General Anthony Wayne were marching against the Western Confederacy of Indians in the Ohio country (see "Sham Treaties and Indian Lands"). Why would the Washington administration use federal troops to displace Native Americans from their Ohio lands, but rely on state militias to suppress the rebellion in western Pennsylvania?

Jay's Treaty Britain's maritime strategy intensified political divisions in America. Beginning in late 1793, the British navy seized 250 American ships carrying French sugar and other goods. Hoping to protect merchant property through diplomacy, Washington dispatched John Jay to Britain. But Jay returned with a controversial treaty that ignored the American claim that "free ships make free goods" and accepted Britain's right to stop neutral ships. The treaty also required the U.S. government to make "full and complete compensation" to British merchants for pre–Revolutionary War debts owed by American citizens. In return, the agreement allowed Americans to submit claims for illegal seizures and required the British to remove their troops and Indian agents from the Northwest Territory. Despite Republican charges that **Jay's Treaty** was too conciliatory, the Senate ratified it in 1795, but only by the two-thirds majority required by the Constitution. As long as the Federalists were in power, the United States would have a pro-British foreign policy.

Jay's Treaty
A 1795 treaty between the United States and Britain, negotiated by John Jay. The treaty accepted Britain's right to stop neutral ships and required the U.S. government to provide restitution for the pre–Revolutionary War debts of British merchants. In return, it allowed Americans to submit claims for illegal seizures and required the British to remove their troops and Indian agents from the Northwest Territory.

TEACHING STRATEGY

The painting of the Whiskey Rebellion provides an opportunity to explore the ways art expresses cultural values, including political values. Ask students: **How does this painting illustrate a Federalist view of the nation?** *Washington, the nation's first and unanimously elected president, is positioned at the very center of the painting. As commander in chief, he authoritatively guides the army on horseback as he points commandingly. Washington's head is higher than anyone else in the painting. Washington and the other officers wearing matching uniforms, while the troops are also in matching uniforms according to their unit and lined up in a way that illustrates order and discipline. The painting symbolizes strong, authoritative leadership by an elite, the importance of order for a peaceful society, and the willingness to use military force to achieve it.*

TRM Find complete suggested responses in the Teacher's Resource Materials.

AP® THINKING LIKE A HISTORIAN

The Social Life of Alcohol

Alcohol was ubiquitous in post-Revolutionary America. Expensive wines and distilled spirits traveled through the channels of Atlantic trade; molasses was imported from the West Indies and distilled into rum in American port towns; and cider, beer, and whiskey were produced on a small scale everywhere in the countryside. Taverns were centers of social and political activity. Alcohol both mirrored and reinforced the economic and geographical divisions in American life.

1. James Newport's ad in the *Pennsylvania Gazette*, 1790. *This advertisement illustrates the connections between the trade in alcohol and the Atlantic world. While cheap whiskey, cider, and beer were made in American homes, fine wines and spirits were articles of international trade.*

JAMES NEWPORT, At his *Wine, Spirit and Cordial Stores*, in Second street, at the upper corner of Carter's alley, has, by Wholesale and Retail, MADEIRA, Sherry, Lisbon, Teneriffe, Malaga, Fayal, and Port Wines, Jamaica spirits, Antigua rum, Philadelphia ditto, Holland gin, Philadelphia ditto, very excellent, in cases, Coniac [*sic*] brandy, American ditto, good flavor, choice shrub. CORDIALS, &c. Anniseed water, clove water, all-fours, Cinnamon water, prime wine and rum colouring, wine bitters. Spirits of wine. Retail Stores and Tavern-keepers will in particular, find their interest in buying here, the articles being all the best in their kind, and selling at the most reduced prices. Philadelphia, April 30, 1790.

2. Benjamin Chew on providing alcohol to his slaves, 1794. *The instructions of a prominent Philadelphia lawyer and landowner to his overseer about giving rum to his slaves during the harvest.*

I have written . . . to let you have [illegible] Rum & other necessaries for the Harvest. But as these articles are so [illegible] dear I must recommend it to you to be as sparing of them as possible. . . . I must rely on you good man [to conduct] the Business. . . . I would have you let the People have a little Rum — let them be cautious in using too much Spirits during Harvest — it will be well to mix some molasses with water to drink — it is very wholesome & much recommended. . . . I need not caution you that a great deal depends upon your own proper attention to yourself and that you are careful of good Conduct during Harvest.

3. Anonymous, *The Toast*, c. 1810–1815. *In this painting, a group of well-to-do gentlemen are drinking wine out of fine crystal stemware, and several are smoking clay pipes. Someone has just proposed a toast.*

Source: John P. Nugent Collection, Newburgh, Indiana.

218

AP® SKILLS & PROCESSES

ANALYZING HISTORICAL SOURCES

The **AP® THINKING LIKE A HISTORIAN** feature helps students understand the role of alcohol in the early republic and, therefore, why Hamilton's excise tax on whiskey made sense — and why it generated such anger. As the introduction explains, alcohol was ubiquitous in the early republic. Far from functioning as a simple form of entertainment, alcohol served a number of political, economic, and social roles. If students understand these more abstract functions, they will have an easier time working with the **AP® DBQ PRACTICE** prompt that emphasizes alcohol's ability to both unify and divide people.

4. **John Lewis Krimmel, *Village Tavern*, 1814.** *This painting of a postman arriving at a Pennsylvania tavern with letters and newspapers reminds us that taverns were not merely places to drink.*

SOURCE: John Lewis Krimmel (American, 1786–1821) ***Village Tavern***, 1813–1814, oil on canvas, 16 7/8 x 22 1/2 inches, Toledo Museum of Art (Toledo, Ohio). Purchased with funds from the Florence Scott Libbey Bequest in Memory of her Father, Maurice A. Scott, 1954.13. Photo Credit: Richard Goodbody, New York.

5. **Public notice from the *Pennsylvania Gazette*, 1794.** *Here, a tavern serves as the gathering place for citizens interested in nominating candidates for election to office.*

THE INHABITANTS of the County of Chester, are hereby requested to meet at the Centre house, kept by Abraham Marshall, in West Bradford, on FRIDAY the 10th Day of October next, at 10 o'clock, A. M. in order to form a TICKET for the ensuing Election.

6. **Tom the Tinker demands compliance, July 23, 1794.** *During the Whiskey Rebellion, "Tom the Tinker" pinned this notice to a tree near John Reed's distillery. Reed had it published in a Pittsburgh newspaper.*

In taking a survey of the troops under my direction in the late expedition against that insolent exciseman, John Neville, I find there were a great number of delinquents, even among those who carry on distilling. It will, therefore, be observed that I, Tom the Tinker, will not suffer any certain class or set of men to be excluded [from] the service of this my district, when notified to attend on any expedition carried on in order to obstruct the execution of the excise law, and obtain a repeal thereof.

And I do declare on my solemn word, that if such delinquents do not come forth on the next alarm, with equipments, and give their assistance in opposing the execution and obtaining a repeal of the excise law, he or they will be deemed as enemies and stand opposed to virtuous principles of republican liberty, and shall receive punishment according to the nature of the offense.

And whereas, a certain John Reed, now resident in Washington, and being at his place near Pittsburgh, called Reedsburgh, and having a set of stills employed at said Reedsburgh, entered on the excise docket, contrary to the will and good pleasure of his fellow citizens, and came not forth to assist in the suppression of the execution of said law, by aiding and assisting in the late expedition, have, by delinquency, manifested his approbation to the execution of the aforesaid law, is hereby charged forthwith to cause the contents of this paper, without adding or diminishing, to be published in the Pittsburgh Gazette, the ensuing week, under the no less penalty than the consumption of his distillery.

Given under my hand, this 19th day of July, one thousand seven hundred and ninety-four.

SOURCES: (1) James Newport, *Pennsylvania Gazette*, May 5, 1790; (2) Chew Family Papers, Box 773, ff. 25, 10, Historical Society of Pennsylvania; (5) *Pennsylvania Gazette*, October 1, 1794; (6) *Pennsylvania Archives*, 2nd ser., 4:61–62 (Harrisburg: E. K. Meyers, State Printer, 1890).

ANALYZING THE EVIDENCE

1. Who is the intended audience for an advertisement like James Newport's (source 1)? How many Atlantic ports of call are represented in the products he advertises? Use your answer as reasoning for the audience chosen.
2. The two paintings (sources 3 and 4), set in the interiors of a private home and a tavern, depict mostly men. What have they gathered for in each case? *Village Tavern* is set during the War of 1812. How does that fact influence your interpretation of the scene? What do you think the woman and child are doing in the tavern? Use additional examples from the textbook to support your argument.
3. *Village Tavern* (source 4) and the ad calling for a political gathering (source 5) both suggest the way that politics and drinking often mixed. How might the fact that taverns were gathering places for political discussion and decision making have influenced outcomes? Consider demographic position in your answer.
4. What concerns does Benjamin Chew express in his correspondence with his overseer (source 2)? Given those worries, why do you think he provides rum to his slaves at all? Support your reasoning with at least one example from the textbook.
5. Tom the Tinker expressed the collective will of whiskey distillers in western Pennsylvania during the Whiskey Rebellion (source 6). Why would it have been important to enforce unanimous action during the uprising? Make a historically defensible claim.

AP® DBQ PRACTICE

Using the sources here and what you learned in this chapter about the trade and consumption of alcohol, social stratification in the early republic, and differences between urban and rural communities, write a short essay about the ways in which taverns and alcohol helped unite people in some ways while differentiating or dividing them in others. Describe how tavern culture influences social organization.

TRM Find complete suggested responses in the Teacher's Resource Materials.

Toussaint L'Ouverture, Haitian Revolutionary and Statesman The American Revolution of 1776 constituted a victory for republicanism; the Haitian revolt of the 1790s represented a triumph of liberty over slavery and a demand for racial equality. After leading the black army that ousted French planters and British invaders from Haiti, Toussaint formed a constitutional government in 1801. A year later, when French troops invaded the island, he negotiated a treaty that halted Haitian resistance in exchange for a pledge that the French would not reinstate slavery. Subsequently, the French seized Toussaint and imprisoned him in France, where he died in 1803. This image, engraved in France in 1802, places Toussaint on horseback to emphasize his military prowess. Photo12/UIG/Getty Images.

The Haitian Revolution The French Revolution inspired a revolution closer to home that would also impact the United States. The wealthy French plantation colony of Saint-Domingue in the West Indies was deeply divided: a small class of elite planters stood atop the population of 40,000 free whites and dominated the island's half million slaves. In between, some 28,000 *gens de couleur* — free men of color — were excluded from most professions, forbidden from taking the names of their white relatives, and prevented from dressing like whites. The French Revolution intensified conflict between planters and free blacks, giving way to a massive slave uprising in 1791 that aimed to abolish slavery. The uprising touched off years of civil war, along with Spanish and British invasions. In 1798, black Haitians led by Toussaint L'Ouverture — himself a former slave-owning planter — seized control of the country. After five more years of fighting, in 1803, Saint-Domingue became the independent nation of Haiti: the first black republic in the Atlantic world.

The **Haitian Revolution** profoundly impacted the United States. In 1793, thousands of refugees — planters, slaves, and free blacks alike — fled the island and traveled to Charleston, Norfolk, Baltimore, Philadelphia, and New York, while newspapers detailed the horrors of the unfolding war. Many slaveholders panicked, fearful that the "contagion" of black liberation would undermine their own slave regimes. U.S. policy toward the rebellion presented a knotty problem. Why was it so difficult for U.S. political leaders to decide how to regard Saint-Domingue? Because the war stirred conflicting values. The first instinct of the Washington administration was to supply aid to the island's white population. Adams — strongly antislavery and no friend of France — changed course, aiding the rebels and strengthening commercial ties. Jefferson, though sympathetic to moral arguments against slavery, was himself a southern slaveholder; he was, moreover, an ardent supporter of France. When he became president, he cut off aid to the rebels, imposed a trade embargo, and refused to recognize an independent Haiti. For many Americans, an independent nation of liberated citizen-slaves was a horrifying paradox, a perversion of the republican ideal (see "America in the World," p. 221).

Haitian Revolution
An uprising against French colonial rule in Saint-Domingue (1791–1804) involving *gens de coleur* and liberated slaves from the island and armies from three European countries. In 1803, Saint-Domingue became the independent black republic of Haiti, in which former slaves were citizens.

The Rise of Political Parties

The appearance of Federalists and Republicans marked a new stage in American politics — what historians call the First Party System. Colonial legislatures had factions based on family, ethnicity, or region, but they did not have organized political parties. Nor did the new state and national constitutions make any provision for political societies. Indeed, most Americans believed that parties were dangerous because they looked out for themselves rather than serving the public interest.

But a shared understanding of the public interest collapsed in the face of sharp conflicts over Hamilton's fiscal policies. Most merchants and creditors supported the Federalist Party, as did wheat-exporting slaveholders in the Tidewater districts of the Chesapeake. The emerging Republican coalition included southern tobacco and rice planters, debt-conscious western farmers, Germans and Scots-Irish in the southern backcountry, and subsistence farmers in the Northeast.

AP® SKILLS & PROCESSES

CAUSATION

How did events abroad during the 1790s sharpen political divisions in the United States?

Party identity crystallized in 1796. To prepare for the presidential election, Federalist and Republican leaders called caucuses in Congress and conventions in the states. They also mobilized popular support by organizing public festivals and processions: the Federalists held banquets in February to celebrate Washington's birthday, and the Republicans marched through the streets on July 4 to honor the Declaration of Independence.

In the election, voters gave Federalists a majority in Congress and made John Adams president. Jefferson, narrowly defeated, became vice president. Adams continued Hamilton's pro-British foreign policy and strongly criticized French seizures of American merchant ships. When American diplomats insisted that France respect U.S. neutrality, the French foreign minister Talleyrand instructed his agents to

AP® THEME

NAT: American and National Identity

The American Revolution and ideals in the Declaration of Independence helped to inspire the Haitian Revolution. Americans' negative reactions to this unintended consequence of their own rebellion are explored in the **AP® AMERICA IN THE WORLD** feature on p. 221. Ask students: **How did the American Revolution inspire the Haitian revolt, led by Toussaint L'Ouverture?** *The colonies declared independence, embraced republicanism and constitutional government, and used the language of slavery, freedom, and equality to justify their cause.*

AP® SKILLS & PROCESSES

CAUSATION

The **CAUSATION** question asks students to identify the way global events contributed to domestic political disagreements. To scaffold this question, students can create a cause-effect chart indicating specific foreign events and their consequences for domestic politics. Extend this prompt by asking students to explain why foreign events played such a crucial role in the young nation.

TRM Find complete suggested responses in the Teacher's Resource Materials.

TEACHING STRATEGY

Use "The First American Party System: Events, Issues, and Positions," a three-lesson sequence from the National Endowment for the Humanities' EDSITEment! Web site to explore the emergence of the Federalist-Republican dispute in the 1790s, providing a detailed timeline, links to primary sources, and an activity that requires students to sort the issues that divided the factions into "party platforms" in an era before such statements were produced. Access this lesson plan by searching "EDSITEment First American Party System."

AP® AMERICA IN THE WORLD

The Haitian Revolution and the Problem of Race

The slave uprising on the French island of Saint-Domingue triggered international war, created a refugee crisis, and ended with the creation of a new republic. The American Revolution did all these things as well, yet the United States did not support either the rebellion or the republic of Haiti. Some 25,000 refugees from Saint-Domingue arrived in American ports between 1791 and 1810, about two-thirds of them black. Though all were fleeing the insurrection, many Americans feared that the new arrivals might carry the contagion of slave rebellion. Yet the refugees were also objects of charitable relief, and many were welcomed in their adoptive communities.

SAVANNAH CITY COUNCIL'S RESOLUTION IN RESPONSE TO THE HAITIAN UPRISING, 1795

Whereas, from the mischiefs which the people of St. Domingo, and other French islands, have experienced, from the insurrection of their Negroes and People of Colour, the precautions taken by the people of South Carolina . . . to prevent the importation or landing of any such Negroes or Mulattoes amongst them, and the information the Citizens now assembled have received, that a vessel is now lying at Cockspur, recently from Kingston, [Jamaica], with near one hundred Negroes on board, whose landing may be dangerous to the inhabitants of this state, with the daily expectation of many more; therefore, to prevent the evils that may arise from suffering people of this description, under any pretense whatever, from being introduced amongst us, the Citizens pledge themselves unanimously to support the City Council in any salutary measures they may adopt[.]...

Resolved, That any vessel that has arrived, or may arrive, in this port, with seasoned Negroes, or People of Colour, from any of the West India, Windward, Leeward, or Bahama Islands, East or West Florida, or any other port whatever, . . . shall not be permitted to come over the Bar, nor anchor within the anchorage ground of this port. . . .

SOURCE: Schomburg Center for Research in Black Culture, Manuscripts, Archives and Rare Books Division, Image ID 1243998, digitalgallery.nypl.org.

***PENNSYLVANIA GAZETTE,* RELIEF EFFORTS IN BALTIMORE, JULY 1793**

Extract of a letter from a gentleman in Baltimore to his friend in this city, containing some important details relative to the unfortunate affair at Cape-Francois. . . .

"One hundred and twenty vessels have entered the Chesapeake bay, with upwards of 1,200 passengers, men, women and children, on board, many of whom have escaped by swimming from fire and sword, naked and in want of everything. Some French patriots here, and a number of Americans, have already made up a small sum of their relief; no doubt the generosity of the Philadelphians and of the inhabitants of every city on the continent will prompt them to follow the example. Among these unfortunate people are a number of French patriotic Captains who have been obliged to fly and abandon their vessels and property; numbers of old men and heads of families, once wealthy, but now reduced to misery and want. Some among them may have by their guilt drawn the misfortunes they feel on their own heads, but they are all unfortunate, and pity is the only sentiment that their heart breaking situation can inspire.". . .

SOURCE: "Extract of a Letter from a Gentleman in Baltimore to His Friend in This City, Containing Some Important Details Relative to the Unfortunate Affair at Cape-Francois, July 9," *Pennsylvania Gazette*, July 17, 1793, 1.

EXCERPTS FROM THE CONSTITUTION OF 1801 ESTABLISHED BY THE CENTRAL ASSEMBLY OF SAINT-DOMINGUE

Article 1. – Saint-Domingue in its entire expanse, and Samana, La Tortue, La Gonave, Les Cayemites, L'Ile-a-Vache, La Saone and other adjacent islands form the territory of a single colony, which is part of the French Empire, but ruled under particular laws. . . .

Article 3. – There cannot exist slaves on this territory, servitude is therein forever abolished. All men are born, live and die free and French.

Article 4. – All men, regardless of color, are eligible to all employment.

Article 5. – There shall exist no distinction other than those based on virtue and talent, and other superiority afforded by law in the exercise of a public function.

The law is the same for all whether in punishment or in protection.

SOURCE: *Haitian Constitution of 1801* (English), The Louverture Project, thelouvertureproject.org.

QUESTIONS FOR ANALYSIS

1. How does the first document express the fears of American slaveholders? Why do you suppose the Savannah City Council perceived Haitian refugees to be a danger? And why do you think their resolution prohibited the importation of enslaved people from other islands, including Jamaica? Describe the historical context of Savannah City as part of your reasoning.
2. Why did the residents of Baltimore described in the second document respond so differently from the refugees who arrived there in 1793. Use historical reasoning to compare the historical context of Savannah City to Baltimore.
3. How does the excerpt from the 1801 Constitution echo themes of the American Revolution? What differences do you see?
4. Comparing the second document to the first, how would you say that the two revolutions impacted views of race in Georgia and in Haiti?

AP® SKILLS & PROCESSES

ANALYZING HISTORICAL EVIDENCE

In terms of format, the primary sources in the **AP® AMERICA IN THE WORLD** feature are similar as legal documents, but they tend in opposite directions. Students might consider why, in effect, race trumped republican government in Americans' attitudes toward Haiti.

AP® SKILLS & PROCESSES

CONTEXTUALIZATION

The **AP® AMERICA IN THE WORLD** feature places American events in a global context. In this case, students explore the reverberations of the American Revolution outside of the nation's borders. The Patriots' revolt helped inspire the Haitian Revolution. This, in turn, forced the U.S. to respond to a neighbor republic composed largely of former slaves.

TRM Find complete suggested responses in the Teacher's Resource Materials.

demand a loan and a bribe from the United States to stop the seizures. American diplomats refused to pay, Talleyrand ignored their pleas, and Adams charged that Talleyrand's agents, whom he dubbed X, Y, and Z, had insulted America's honor. In response to the **XYZ Affair**, Congress cut off trade with France in 1798 and authorized American privateering (licensing private ships to seize French vessels). This undeclared maritime war curtailed American trade with the French West Indies and resulted in the capture of nearly two hundred French and American merchant vessels.

XYZ Affair
A 1797 incident in which American negotiators in France were rebuffed for refusing to pay a substantial bribe. The incident led the United States into an undeclared war that curtailed American trade with the French West Indies.

The Naturalization, Alien, and Sedition Acts of 1798 As Federalists became more hostile to the French Republic, they also took a harder line against their Republican critics. When Republican-minded immigrants from Ireland vehemently attacked Adams's policies, a Federalist pamphleteer responded in kind: "Were I president, I would hang them for otherwise they would murder me." To silence the critics, the Federalists enacted three coercive laws — the **Naturalization, Alien, and Sedition Acts** — limiting individual rights and threatening the fledgling party system. The Naturalization Act lengthened the residency requirement for American citizenship from five to fourteen years, the Alien Act authorized the deportation of foreigners, and the Sedition Act prohibited the publication of insults or malicious attacks on the president or members of Congress. "He that is not for us is against us," thundered the Federalist *Gazette of the United States*. Using the Sedition Act, Federalist prosecutors arrested more than twenty Republican newspaper editors and politicians, accused them of sedition, and convicted and jailed a number of them.

Naturalization, Alien, and Sedition Acts
Three laws passed in 1798 that limited individual rights and threatened the fledgling party system. The Naturalization Act lengthened the residency requirement for citizenship, the Alien Act authorized the deportation of foreigners, and the Sedition Act prohibited the publication of insults or malicious attacks on the president or members of Congress.

This repression sparked a constitutional crisis. Republicans charged that the Sedition Act violated the First Amendment's prohibition against "abridging the freedom of speech, or of the press." However, they did not appeal to the Supreme Court because the Court's power to review congressional legislation was uncertain and because most of the justices were Federalists. Instead, Madison and Jefferson looked to the state legislatures. At their urging, the Kentucky and Virginia legislatures issued resolutions in 1798 declaring the Alien and Sedition Acts to be "unauthoritative, void, and of no force." The **Virginia and Kentucky Resolutions** set forth a states' rights interpretation of the Constitution, asserting that the states had a "right to judge" the legitimacy of national laws; the Kentucky resolution, authored by Jefferson, even argued that states could nullify unconstitutional federal laws if necessary.

Virginia and Kentucky Resolutions
Resolutions by the Virginia and Kentucky state legislatures in 1798 condemning the Alien and Sedition Acts. The resolutions tested the idea that state legislatures could judge the legitimacy of federal laws.

The conflict over the Sedition Act set the stage for the presidential election of 1800. Jefferson, once opposed on principle to political parties, now asserted that they could "watch and relate to the people" the activities of an oppressive government. Meanwhile, John Adams reevaluated his foreign policy. Rejecting Hamilton's advice to declare war against France (and benefit from the resulting upsurge in patriotism), Adams put country ahead of party and used diplomacy to end the maritime conflict.

The "Revolution of 1800" The campaign of 1800 was a bitter, no-holds-barred contest. The Federalists launched personal attacks on Jefferson, branding him an irresponsible pro-French radical and, because he opposed state support of religion in Virginia, "the arch-apostle of irreligion and free thought." Both parties changed state election laws to favor their candidates, and rumors circulated of a Federalist plot to stage a military coup.

The election did not end these worries. Thanks to a surprising Republican victory in New York, low Federalist turnout in Virginia and Pennsylvania, and the three-fifths rule (which boosted electoral votes in the southern states), Jefferson won a narrow 73-to-65 victory over Adams in the electoral college. However, the Republican electors also gave 73 votes to Aaron Burr of New York, who was Jefferson's vice-presidential running mate (Map 7.1). The Constitution specified that in the case of a tie vote, the House of Representatives would choose between the candidates. For thirty-five rounds of balloting, Federalists in the House blocked Jefferson's election, prompting rumors that Virginia would raise a military force to put him into office.

AP® EXAM TIP
Recognizing the outcome of the Election of 1800 as an effect of the political party actions is essential for success on the AP® Exam.

AP® APPLY THE TIP

Organize students into small groups and provide each group with **Handout 7.2 — Comparison: First Party System (TRM)**. After the groups have completed the handout, lead a discussion to contextualize the events listed on the handout.

TRM Find **Handout 7.2 — Comparison: First Party System** in the Teacher's Resource Materials.

AP® THEME

ARC: American and Regional Culture

Jefferson's election offers an opportunity for students to evaluate how regional interests affect politics. Ask students to identify and explain at least two pieces of historical evidence that explain why Jefferson and the Democratic-Republican vision for the United States was appealing to southerners. Be sure to encourage students to include the regional aspect of his appeal as a political candidate.

Ironically, arch-Federalist Alexander Hamilton ushered in a more democratic era by supporting Jefferson. Calling Burr an "embryo Caesar" and the "most unfit man in the United States for the office of president," Hamilton persuaded key Federalists to allow Jefferson's election. The Federalists' concern for political stability also played a role. As Senator James Bayard of Delaware explained, "It was admitted on all hands that we must risk the Constitution and a Civil War or take Mr. Jefferson."

Jefferson called the election the "Revolution of 1800," and so it was. The bloodless transfer of power showed that popularly elected governments could be changed in an orderly way, even in times of bitter partisan conflict. In his inaugural address in 1801, Jefferson praised this achievement, declaring, "We are all Republicans, we are all Federalists."

A REPUBLICAN EMPIRE IS BORN

How were the principles of the Jeffersonian Republicans reflected in this era of dramatic growth and development?

In the Treaty of Paris of 1783, Great Britain gave up its claims to the trans-Appalachian region and, said one British diplomat, left the Indian nations "to the care of their [American] neighbours." *Care* was hardly the right word: many white Americans wanted to destroy Native communities. "Cut up every Indian Cornfield and burn every Indian town," proclaimed Congressman William Henry Drayton of South Carolina, so that their "nation be extirpated and the lands become the property of the public." Other leaders, including Henry Knox, Washington's first secretary of war, favored assimilating Native peoples into Euro-American society. Knox proposed the division of tribal lands among individual Indian families, who would become citizens of the various states. Indians resisted both forms of domination and fought to retain control of their lands and cultures. In the ensuing struggle, the United States emerged as an expansive power, determined to control the future of the continent.

Sham Treaties and Indian Lands

As in the past, conflicts between Natives and Europeans centered on land rights. Invoking the Paris treaty and regarding Britain's Indian allies as conquered peoples, the U.S. government asserted both sovereignty over and ownership of the trans-Appalachian west. Indian nations rejected both claims, pointing out they had not been conquered and had not signed the Paris treaty. "Our lands are our life and our breath," declared Creek chief Hallowing King; "if we part with them, we part with our blood." Brushing aside such objections and threatening military action, U.S. commissioners forced the pro-British Iroquois peoples — Mohawks, Onondagas, Cayugas, and Senecas — to cede huge tracts in New York and Pennsylvania in the Treaty of Fort Stanwix (1784). New York land speculators used liquor and bribes to take a million more acres, confining the once powerful Iroquois to reservations — essentially colonies of subordinate peoples.

American negotiators used similar tactics to grab Ohio Valley lands. At the Treaties of Fort McIntosh (1785) and Fort Finney (1786), they pushed the Chippewas,

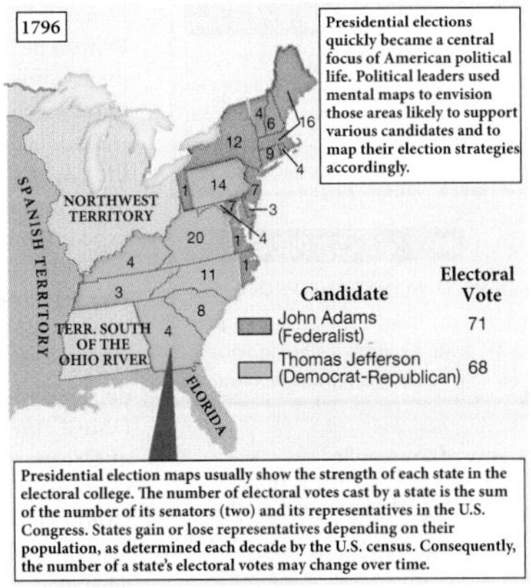

1796
Presidential elections quickly became a central focus of American political life. Political leaders used mental maps to envision those areas likely to support various candidates and to map their election strategies accordingly.
SPANISH TERRITORY
NORTHWEST TERRITORY
TERR. SOUTH OF THE OHIO RIVER
FLORIDA
Candidate
Electoral Vote
John Adams (Federalist) 71
Thomas Jefferson (Democrat-Republican) 68
Presidential election maps usually show the strength of each state in the electoral college. The number of electoral votes cast by a state is the sum of the number of its senators (two) and its representatives in the U.S. Congress. States gain or lose representatives depending on their population, as determined each decade by the U.S. census. Consequently, the number of a state's electoral votes may change over time.

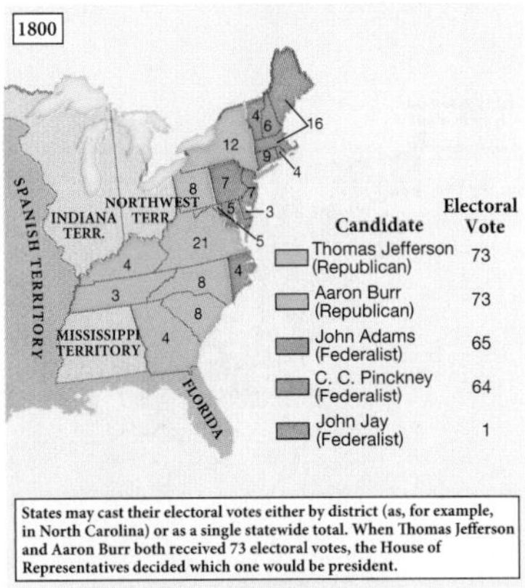

MAP 7.1 The Presidential Elections of 1796 and 1800
Both elections pitted Federalist John Adams of Massachusetts against Republican Thomas Jefferson of Virginia, and both saw voters split along regional lines. Adams carried every New England state and, reflecting Federalist strength in maritime and commercial areas, the eastern districts of the Middle Atlantic states; Jefferson won most of the agricultural-based states of the South and West (Kentucky and Tennessee). New York was the pivotal swing state. It gave its 12 electoral votes to Adams in 1796 and, thanks to the presence of Aaron Burr on the Republican ticket, bestowed them on Jefferson in 1800.

AP® SKILLS & PROCESSES

CONTEXTUALIZATION

Why did Jefferson consider his election in 1800 to be revolutionary?

AP® THEME

PCE: Politics and Power

The election maps of 1796 and 1800 depicted in **MAP 7.1** reveal the nature of political divisions after Washington's administration. Guide students' analysis with the following questions:

- **What voting patterns are evident from the maps?** *Federalist support was strongest in the north and along the coast, while Republican support was greatest in the south and west.*
- **How large were the margins of victory between parties?** *Very narrow — Adams had a 3-vote margin in 1796, while Jefferson and Burr beat Adams by an 8-vote margin (though based on the procedures at the time, the tie between Jefferson and Burr led to a vote by the House).*
- **What conclusion can you draw about political divisions based on these maps and the election outcomes? Why should caution be exercised in drawing conclusions about the general populace?** *The electorate was relatively evenly divided. The vote was made by a handful of relatively elite electors rather than a broadly based popular vote; this outcome does not necessarily reflect the views of many landless Americans who couldn't vote.*

AP® SKILLS & PROCESSES

CONTEXTUALIZATION

In calling his election a "revolution," Jefferson implicitly invoked the American Revolution and, perhaps, the French Revolution as well. To answer the **CONTEXTUALIZATION** question, students might consider the ways in which Jefferson's election fit extended values of the Revolution or overturned the tyranny of an "aristocratic" Federalist Party. To extend this prompt ask students to evaluate the textbook's claim that the election was indeed revolutionary because its "bloodless transfer of power showed that popularly elected governments could be changed in an orderly way."

TRM Find complete suggested responses in the Teacher's Resource Materials.

AP® APPLY THE TIP

Ask students to choose one conflict between Native populations and the U.S. government during the Federal period. Students should define the conflict and the outcome of the conflict for both the Native population and the U.S. Have students work in pairs to brainstorm the ways that this conflict illustrates both continuity and change in relations between Europeans (Americas) and the Native populations. Students should then make a historical argument illustrating both continuity and change.

AP® SKILLS & PROCESSES

DEVELOPMENTS AND PROCESSES

Use the **DEVELOPMENTS AND PROCESSES** question to have students consider actions toward Native Americans in the context of ongoing tensions with Britain. Some students may need guidance connecting this context to the government's perceived urgency to respond forcefully to Native Americans. Extend this prompt by asking students to consider alternatives to the nation's course of actions toward Native Americans by examining what other policies the U.S. could have pursued and the outcomes that might have followed.

TRM Find complete suggested responses in the Teacher's Resource Materials.

AP® EXAM TIP

As you read through this section, compare the relationship between the new U.S. government and natives to earlier periods of interaction between Europeans and Natives.

AP® SKILLS & PROCESSES

DEVELOPMENTS AND PROCESSES

Why did the United States go to war against western Indians so quickly after the Revolution?

Treaty of Greenville
A 1795 treaty between the United States and various Indian tribes in Ohio. American negotiators acknowledged Indian ownership of the land, and, in return for various payments, the Western Confederacy ceded most of Ohio to the United States.

Delawares, Ottawas, Wyandots, and Shawnees to cede most of the future state of Ohio. The tribes quickly repudiated the agreements, justifiably claiming they were made under duress. Recognizing the failure of these agreements, American negotiators arranged for a comprehensive agreement at Fort Harmar (1789), but many Indian leaders refused to attend and it, too, was repudiated. To defend their lands, these tribes joined with the Miami and Potawatomi Indians to form the Western Confederacy. Led by Miami chief Little Turtle, confederacy warriors crushed American expeditionary forces sent by President Washington in 1790 and 1791.

The Treaty of Greenville Fearing an alliance between the Western Confederacy and the British in Canada, Washington doubled the size of the U.S. Army and ordered General "Mad Anthony" Wayne to lead a new expedition. In August 1794, Wayne defeated the confederacy in the Battle of Fallen Timbers (near present-day Toledo, Ohio). However, continuing Indian resistance forced a compromise. In the **Treaty of Greenville** (1795), American negotiators acknowledged Indian ownership of the land, and, in return for various payments, the Western Confederacy ceded most of Ohio (Map 7.2). The Indian peoples also agreed to accept American sovereignty, placing themselves "under the protection of the United States, and no other Power whatever." These American advances caused Britain to agree, in Jay's Treaty (1795), to reduce its trade and military aid to Indians in the trans-Appalachian region.

The Greenville treaty sparked a wave of white migration. Kentucky already had a population of 73,000 in 1790, and in 1792 it was admitted to the Union as the fifteenth state (Vermont entered a year earlier). Tennessee, Kentucky's neighbor to the south, was admitted in 1796. By 1800, more than 375,000 people had moved into the Ohio and Tennessee valleys; in 1805, the new state of Ohio alone had more than 100,000 residents. Thousands more farm families moved into the future states of Indiana and Illinois, sparking new conflicts with Native peoples over land and hunting rights. Between 1790 and 1810, farm families settled as much land as they had during the entire colonial period. The United States "is a country in flux," a visiting French aristocrat observed in 1799, and "that which is true today as regards its population, its establishments, its prices, its commerce will not be true six months from now."

MAP 7.2 Indian Cessions and State Formation, 1776–1840
By virtue of the Treaty of Paris (1783) with Britain, the United States claimed sovereignty over the entire trans-Appalachian west. The Western Confederacy contested this claim, but the U.S. government upheld it with military force. By 1840, armed diplomacy had forced most Native American peoples to move west of the Mississippi River. White settlers occupied their lands, formed territorial governments, and eventually entered the Union as members of separate — and equal — states. By 1860, the trans-Appalachian region constituted an important economic and political force in American national life.

Assimilation Rejected To dampen further conflicts, the U.S. government encouraged Native Americans to assimilate into white society. The goal, as one Kentucky Protestant minister put it, was to make the Indian "a farmer, a citizen of the United States, and a Christian." Most Indians rejected wholesale assimilation; even those who joined Christian churches retained many ancestral values and religious beliefs. Why was assimilation so unappealing to most Native Americans? To think of themselves as individuals or members of a nuclear family, as white Americans were

AP® THEME

MIG: Migration and Settlement; WOR: America in the World

MAP 7.2 illustrates the ways that continued westward migration created tensions between the federal government and American Indian tribes over land seizure and treaty terms. Guide students' analysis with the following questions:

- **From the map, which region functioned as an American foothold, where the earliest westward migration after the Revolution forced Indian cessions of land?** *Indians had already given up most of Kentucky to the Ohio River by 1784.*
- **Which areas represent strong pockets of Indian resistance despite being surrounded by American settlers?** *Indians in Georgia, Alabama, and Florida held out until after 1820, despite the fact that they were surrounded by American settlers.*
- **When and where did tensions lead to battles between Indians and the federal government, which acted to protect white settlers? Do they fit any pattern?** *Harmar's Defeat (1790), St. Clair's Defeat (1791), Fallen Timbers (1794), Tippecanoe (1811), and Horseshoe Bend (1814). Many of these battles took place in the 1790s, most were in the Ohio and Great Lakes country, and most were in areas where Indians had not ceded territory to the U.S. government.*

demanding, meant repudiating the clan, the very essence of Indian life. To preserve "the old Indian way," many Native communities expelled white missionaries and forced Christianized Indians to participate in tribal rites. As a Munsee prophet declared, "There are two ways to God, one for the whites and one for the Indians."

A few Indian leaders sought a middle path in which new beliefs overlapped with old practices. Among the Senecas, the prophet Handsome Lake encouraged traditional animistic rituals that gave thanks to the sun, the earth, water, plants, and animals. But he included Christian elements in his teachings — the concepts of heaven and hell and an emphasis on personal morality — to deter his followers from alcohol, gambling, and witchcraft. Handsome Lake's teachings divided the Senecas into hostile factions. Led by Chief Red Jacket, traditionalists condemned European culture as evil and demanded a complete return to ancestral ways.

The Treaty of Greenville, 1795 Coming at the conclusion of several years of punishing warfare, this treaty was the first meaningful diplomatic agreement between the United States and the Native peoples of the trans-Appalachian west. The Western Confederacy ceded most of Ohio to the United States in exchange for a recognition of Indian ownership of lands beyond the cession, a large gift of merchandise, and the promise of an annual payment of federal funds. The United States also received permission to establish army posts at strategic locations in Indian country. This painting, attributed to an officer on General Anthony Wayne's staff, shows Wayne and William Henry Harrison at the head of the American delegation, while Little Turtle speaks for the Western Confederacy. Captain William Wells, kneeling nearby, acted as translator and scribe for the proceedings. Chicago History Museum/Getty Images.

Most Indians also rejected the efforts of American missionaries to turn warriors into farmers and women into domestic helpmates. Among eastern woodland peoples, women grew corn, beans, and squash — the mainstays of the Indians' diet — and land cultivation rights passed through the female line. Consequently, women exercised considerable political influence, which they were eager to retain. Nor were Indian men interested in becoming farmers. When war raiding and hunting were no longer possible, many turned to grazing cattle and sheep.

Migration and the Changing Farm Economy

Native American resistance slowed the advance of white settlers but did not stop it. Nothing "short of a Chinese Wall, or a line of Troops," Washington declared, "will restrain . . . the Incroachment of Settlers, upon the Indian Territory." During the 1790s, two great streams of migrants moved out of the southern states, while a third flowed from New England.

AP® EXAM TIP

Compare the frontier culture of the Federal Period in the U.S. to the frontier culture of the Colonial Era in North America.

Southern Migrants One stream, composed primarily of white tenant farmers and struggling non-slaveowning families, flocked through the Cumberland Gap into Kentucky and Tennessee. "Boundless settlements open a door for our citizens to run off and leave us," a worried Maryland landlord lamented, "depreciating all our landed property and disabling us from paying taxes." In fact, many migrants were fleeing from this planter-controlled society. They wanted more freedom and hoped to prosper by growing cotton and hemp, which were in great demand.

Many settlers in Kentucky and Tennessee lacked ready cash to buy land. Like the North Carolina Regulators in the 1770s, poorer migrants claimed a customary right to occupy "back waste vacant Lands" sufficient "to provide a subsistence to themselves and their

AP® SKILLS & PROCESSES

MAKING CONNECTIONS

Use the image depicting the Treaty of Greenville to brainstorm a possible answer to the following prompt: From 1763–1795, evaluate the extent to which American Indians were successful in negotiating and resisting encroachment by Americans. Students should build out separate answers for both negotiating and resisting with specific evidence for each category.

CHECK FOR UNDERSTANDING

Ask students: **How and why did the U.S. create "sham treaties" with Native Americans?** *The federal government used alcohol and bribery to pressure Native Americans to cede territory so more Americans could move west to farm.*

AP® APPLY THE TIP

To better draw conclusions about the continuity and change associated with the "frontier" in American development, have students create a Venn diagram labeled "Frontier: Colonial Period" on one side and "Frontier: Federal Period" on the other side. Ask students to identify ways in which the role of the frontier illustrates continuity across time periods in the center of the Venn diagram and examples of change between the periods on the outside of the Venn diagram.

AP® THEME

SOC: Social Structures

The "Migration and Changing Farm Economy" section describes the very different forms of westward migration that took place in this period, helping to explain how frontier cultures continued to grow, which fueled social, political, and ethnic tensions.

AP® THEME

SOC: Social Structures

In many ways, migration patterns can be used to better understand social structures in the United States. Have students focus on developing contextualization by using the theme of social structures. As mentioned earlier, contextualization can be accomplished by developing a broader historical process such as migration while including accompanying details. Have students use migration and use supporting evidence of white and American Indian migration patterns to explain social structures. Using the following question will help guide students in their response: To what extent do migration patterns in the early nineteenth century explain social structures on the western edge of the United States?

TRM Find complete suggested responses in the Teacher's Resource Materials.

AP® SKILLS & PROCESSES

MAKING CONNECTIONS

How did the migration of Americans in the Federal Period help to establish new forms of national culture and form new ideas about national identity?

Posterity." Virginia legislators, who administered the Kentucky Territory, had a more elitist vision. Although they allowed poor settlers to buy up to 1,400 acres of land at reduced prices, they sold or granted huge tracts of 100,000 acres to twenty-one groups of speculators and leading men. In 1792, this landed elite owned one-fourth of the state, while half the white men owned no land and lived as quasi-legal squatters or tenant farmers.

Widespread landlessness — and in some cases, opposition to slavery — prompted a new migration across the Ohio River into the future states of Ohio, Indiana, and Illinois. In a free community, thought Peter Cartwright, a Methodist lay preacher from southwestern Kentucky who moved to Illinois, "I would be entirely clear of the evil of slavery . . . [and] could raise my children to work where work was not thought a degradation." Yet land distribution in Ohio was almost exactly as unequal as in Kentucky: in 1810, a quarter of its real estate was owned by 1 percent of the population, while more than half of its white men were landless.

Meanwhile, a second stream of southern planters and slaves from the Carolinas moved along the coastal plain toward the Gulf of Mexico. Some set up new estates in the interior of Georgia and South Carolina, while others moved into the future states of Alabama, Mississippi, and Louisiana. "The Alabama Feaver rages here with great violence," a North Carolina planter remarked, "and has carried off vast numbers of our Citizens."

Cotton was the key to this migratory surge. Around 1750, the demand for raw wool and cotton increased dramatically as water-powered spinning jennies, weaving mules, and other technological innovations of the Industrial Revolution boosted textile production in England. South Carolina and Georgia planters began growing cotton, and American inventors, including Connecticut-born Eli Whitney, built machines (called gins) that efficiently extracted seeds from its strands. To grow more cotton, white planters imported about 115,000 Africans between 1776 and 1808, when Congress cut off the Atlantic slave trade. The cotton boom financed the rapid settlement of Mississippi and Alabama — in a single year, a government land office in Huntsville, Alabama, sold $7 million of uncleared land — and the two states entered the Union in 1817 and 1819, respectively.

Exodus from New England As southerners moved across the Appalachians and along the Gulf Coast, a third stream of migrants flowed out of the overcrowded communities of New England. Previous generations of Massachusetts and Connecticut farm families had moved north and east, settling New Hampshire, Vermont, and Maine. Now New England farmers moved west. Seeking land for their children, thousands of farmers migrated to New York with their families. "The town of Herkimer," noted one traveler, "is entirely populated by families come from Connecticut." By 1820, almost 800,000 New Englanders lived in a string of settlements stretching from Albany to Buffalo, and many others had traveled on to Ohio and Indiana. Soon, much of the Northwest Territory consisted of New England communities that had moved inland.

In New York, as in Kentucky and Ohio, well-connected speculators snapped up much of the best land, leasing farms to tenants for a fee. Imbued with the "homestead" ethic, many New England families preferred to buy farms. They signed contracts with the Holland Land Company, a Dutch-owned syndicate of speculators that allowed settlers to pay for their farms as they worked them, or moved west again in an elusive search for land on easy terms.

Innovation on Eastern Farms The new farm economy in New York, Ohio, and Kentucky forced major changes in eastern agriculture. Unable to compete with lower-priced western grains, farmers in New England switched to potatoes, which were high yielding and nutritious. To make up for the labor of sons and daughters who had moved inland, Middle Atlantic farmers bought more efficient farm equipment. They replaced metal-tipped wooden plows with cast-iron models that dug deeper and required a single yoke of oxen instead of two. Such changes in crop mix and technology kept production high.

Cutting Hay on a New Hampshire Farm This painting, attributed to Francis Alexander, illustrates the growing productivity of many New England farmsteads. In this idyllic scene, a group of men loads hay onto an overflowing cart on the Leete family farm in West Claremont, New Hampshire, nestled in the foothills between the White and Green mountain ranges. Though this was marginal agricultural land, the Leete farm appears snug and prosperous. A large house is dwarfed by a series of outbuildings for livestock and storage. The barn nearest the house is filled with fodder to feed livestock during the winter months. The Metropolitan Museum of Art, Gift of Edgar William and Bernice Chrysler Garbisch, 1972.

Easterners also adopted the progressive farming methods touted by British agricultural reformers and shifted land and resources to livestock production. "Improvers" in Pennsylvania doubled their average yield per acre by rotating their crops. Many farmers raised sheep and sold the wool to textile manufacturers. Others adopted a year-round planting cycle, sowing corn in the spring for animal fodder and then planting winter wheat in September for market sale. Women and girls took advantage of new urban markets by milking the family cows and making butter and cheese to sell in the growing towns and cities.

Whether hacking fields out of western forests or carting manure to replenish eastern soils, farmers now worked harder and longer, but their increased productivity brought them a better standard of living. European demand for American produce was high in these years, and westward migration — the settlement and exploitation of Indian lands — boosted the farming economy throughout the country.

AP® SKILLS & PROCESSES

CAUSATION

Why were westward migration and agricultural improvement so widespread in the late eighteenth and early nineteenth centuries?

The Jefferson Presidency

From 1801 to 1825, three Republicans from Virginia — Thomas Jefferson, James Madison, and James Monroe — each served two terms as president. Supported by farmers in the South and West and strong Republican majorities in Congress, this "Virginia Dynasty" completed what Jefferson had called the Revolution of 1800. It reversed many Federalist policies and actively supported westward expansion.

When Jefferson took office in 1801, he inherited an old international conflict. Beginning in the 1780s, the Barbary States of North Africa had raided merchant ships in the Mediterranean, and like many European nations, the United States had paid an annual bribe — massive in relation to the size of the federal budget — to protect its vessels. Initially Jefferson refused to pay this "tribute" and ordered the U.S. Navy to attack the pirates' home ports. After four years of intermittent fighting, in which the United States bombarded Tripoli and captured the city of Derna, the Jefferson administration cut its costs. It signed a peace treaty that included a ransom for returned

AP® SKILLS & PROCESSES

MAKING CONNECTIONS

Using the painting of a New Hampshire Farm, have students identify and describe at least one connection between fledgling industry in the east and established farming in the hinterland areas of the northeast. Students' main goal is to establish a historical connection that can be used as evidence of an economy experiencing both continuity and change.

CHECK FOR UNDERSTANDING

Ask students: **Why did southerners and New Englanders migrate west in the 1790s? How did their new farms force agricultural innovations in the east?** *All sought economic opportunity through landownership in the west, though some were poor and landless, while others were already wealthy planters. Western farmers grew grain crops on a large scale, lowering prices beyond eastern farmers' ability to compete. So they switched crops, used more efficient farm equipment, and adopted techniques like crop rotation and fertilization.*

AP® SKILLS & PROCESSES

CAUSATION

The **CAUSATION** question implicitly asks students to identify the shared causes of two distinct, but related, phenomena during the same time period. Students may need some assistance recognizing the relationship between the two. Since the vast majority of westward migrants engaged in farming — typically commercial farming — they were part of the same effort to improve quality of life through economic opportunities provided by commercial farming.

TRM Find complete suggested responses in the Teacher's Resource Materials.

TEACHING STRATEGY

This lithograph, painted the same year the U.S. went to war with Mexico, reflects a nationalistic assessment of American power, as it commemorates a relatively minor conflict two generations after the events took place. The **AP® MAKING CONNECTIONS 2** on p. 243 provides questions to guide students' analysis. Below are additional questions to use:

- **What does this image depict?** *The American attack on the North African port of Tripoli using great American force.*
- **Why might it have been made 40 years after the attack?** *It seems to reflect American pride through a desire to commemorate the nation's first overseas military conflict.*
- **How does it compare with the image of Washington on p. 217?** *They both celebrate American force and strength. The Tripoli image depicts battle from a distance, with no individuals visible, while the Whiskey Rebellion image places Washington and his officers in the center. While the Tripoli attack was a fight against a foreign threat, Washington threatened to crush domestic rebels. Though Jefferson reduced the size of the military, his military engagement is still being remembered 40 years later.*

AP® APPLY THE TIP

Divide students into small groups and assign each group to analyze excerpts from one of the following court cases: *Marbury v. Madison*, *Gibbons v. Ogden*, *McCulloch v. Maryland*, *Dartmouth College v. Woodward*, and *Fletcher v. Peck*. Students should identify the constitutional issue in their assigned case, the decision of the Supreme Court, and the impact of the decision on the power of federal government and state governments. As a class, create a chart on the board that brings together all the court cases, and prompt students to make broader conclusions about the Federalist Party. Discuss how the decisions of these cases illustrated the philosophy of the Federalist Party and the impact of the Marshall Court on state and federal government.

America in the Middle East, 1804 To protect American merchants from capture and captivity in the Barbary States, President Thomas Jefferson sent in the U.S. Navy. This 1846 lithograph, created by the famous firm of Currier & Ives, depicts one of the three attacks on the North African port of Tripoli by Commodore Edward Preble in August 1804. As the USS *Constitution* and other large warships lob shells into the city, small American gunboats defend the fleet from Tripolitan gunboats. "Our loss in Killed & Wounded has been considerable," Preble reported, and "the Enemy must have suffered very much . . . among their Shipping and on shore." The Granger Collection, New York.

prisoners, and Algerian ships were soon taking American sailors hostage again. Finally, in 1815, President Madison sent a fleet of ten warships to the Barbary Coast under the command of Commodore Stephen Decatur, which forced leaders in Algiers, Tunis, and Tripoli to sign a treaty respecting American sovereignty.

At home, Jefferson inherited a national judiciary filled with Federalist appointees, including the formidable John Marshall of Virginia, the new chief justice of the Supreme Court. To add more Federalist judges, the outgoing Federalist Congress had passed the Judiciary Act of 1801. The act created sixteen new judgeships and various other positions, which President Adams filled at the last moment with "midnight appointees." The Federalists "have retired into the judiciary as a stronghold," Jefferson complained, "and from that battery all the works of Republicanism are to be beaten down and destroyed."

AP® EXAM TIP

The continuity of Federalist power through the courts is important to know on the AP® Exam.

***Marbury v. Madison* (1803)**
A Supreme Court case that established the principle of judicial review in finding that parts of the Judiciary Act of 1789 were in conflict with the Constitution. For the first time, the Supreme Court assumed legal authority to overrule acts of other branches of the government.

Jefferson's fears were soon realized. When Republican legislatures in Kentucky and Virginia repudiated the Alien and Sedition Acts as unconstitutional, John Marshall, chief justice of the Supreme Court, declared that only the Supreme Court held the power of constitutional review. The Court claimed this authority for itself when James Madison, the new secretary of state, refused to deliver the commission of William Marbury, one of Adams's midnight appointees. In ***Marbury v. Madison* (1803)**, Marshall asserted that Marbury had the right to the appointment under the Judiciary Act of 1789, but the clause of the act that gave him the right to bring his claim to the Supreme Court conflicted with Article III, Section 2, of the Constitution. By finding that a clause of the Judiciary Act of 1789 was unconstitutional, Marshall established the Court's authority to review congressional legislation and interpret the Constitution. "It is emphatically the province and duty of the judicial department to say what the law is," the chief justice declared, directly challenging the Republican view that the state legislatures had that power.

Ignoring this setback, Jefferson and the Republicans reversed other Federalist policies. When the Alien and Sedition Acts expired in 1801, Congress branded them unconstitutional and refused to extend them. It also amended the Naturalization Act, restoring the original waiting period of five years for resident aliens to become citizens. Charging the Federalists with grossly expanding the national government's size and power, Jefferson had the Republican Congress shrink it. He abolished all internal taxes, including the excise tax that had sparked the Whiskey Rebellion of 1794. To quiet Republican fears of a military coup, Jefferson reduced the size of the permanent army. He also secured repeal of the Judiciary Act of 1801, ousting forty of Adams's midnight appointees. Still, Jefferson retained competent Federalist officeholders, removing only 69 of 433 properly appointed Federalists during his eight years as president.

Jefferson likewise governed tactfully in fiscal affairs. He tolerated the economically important Bank of the United States, which he had once condemned as unconstitutional. But he chose as his secretary of the treasury Albert Gallatin, a fiscal conservative who believed that the national debt was "an evil of the first magnitude." By limiting expenditures and using customs revenue to redeem government bonds,

Gallatin reduced the debt from $83 million in 1801 to $45 million in 1812. With Jefferson and Gallatin at the helm, the nation's fiscal affairs were no longer run in the interests of northeastern creditors and merchants.

Jefferson and the West

Jefferson had long championed settlement of the West. He celebrated the yeoman farmer in *Notes on the State of Virginia* (1785); wrote one of the Confederation's western land ordinances; and supported Pinckney's Treaty (1795), the agreement between the United States and Spain that reopened the Mississippi River to American trade and allowed settlers to export crops via the Spanish-held port of New Orleans.

As president, Jefferson pursued policies that made it easier for farm families to acquire land. In 1796, a Federalist-dominated Congress had set the price of land in the national domain at $2 per acre; by the 1830s, Jefferson-inspired Republican Congresses had enacted more than three hundred laws that cut the cost to $1.25, eased credit terms, and allowed illegal squatters to buy their farms. Eventually, in the Homestead Act of 1862, Congress gave farmsteads to settlers for free.

The Louisiana Purchase International events challenged Jefferson's vision of westward expansion. In 1799, Napoleon Bonaparte seized power in France and sought to reestablish France's American Empire. In 1801, he coerced Spain into signing a secret treaty that returned Louisiana to France and restricted American access to New Orleans, violating Pinckney's Treaty. Napoleon also launched an invasion to restore French rule in Saint-Domingue. It was once the richest sugar colony in the Americas, but its civil war had ruined the economy and cost France a fortune. Napoleon wanted to crush the rebellion and restore its planter class.

Napoleon's actions in Haiti and Louisiana prompted Jefferson to question his pro-French foreign policy. "The day that France takes possession of New Orleans, we must marry ourselves to the British fleet and nation," the president warned, dispatching James Monroe to Britain to negotiate an alliance. To keep the Mississippi River open to western farmers, Jefferson told Robert Livingston, the American minister in Paris, to negotiate the purchase of New Orleans.

Jefferson's diplomacy yielded a magnificent prize: the entire territory of Louisiana. By 1802, the French invasion of Saint-Domingue was faltering in the face of disease and determined black resistance, a new war threatened in Europe, and Napoleon feared an American invasion of Louisiana. Acting with characteristic decisiveness, the French ruler offered to sell the entire territory of Louisiana for $15 million (about $500 million today). "We have lived long," Livingston remarked to Monroe as they concluded the **Louisiana Purchase** in 1803, "but this is the noblest work of our lives."

The Louisiana Purchase forced Jefferson to reconsider his strict interpretation of the Constitution. He had long believed that the national government possessed only the powers expressly delegated to it in the Constitution, but there was no provision for adding new territory. So Jefferson pragmatically accepted a loose interpretation of the Constitution and used its treaty-making powers to complete the deal with France. The new western lands, Jefferson wrote, would be "a means of tempting all our Indians on the East side of the Mississippi to remove to the West."

Secessionist Schemes The acquisition of Louisiana brought new political problems. Some New England Federalists, fearing that western expansion would hurt their region and party, talked openly of leaving the Union and forming a confederacy of northeastern states. The secessionists won the support of Aaron Burr, the ambitious vice president. After Alexander Hamilton accused Burr of planning to destroy the Union, the two fought an illegal pistol duel that led to Hamilton's death.

AP® EXAM TIP

A key idea to trace starting with the Louisiana Purchase is the conflict between national and sectional interests as a result of western expansion.

Louisiana Purchase
The 1803 purchase of French territory west of the Mississippi River that stretched from the Gulf of Mexico to Canada and nearly doubled the size of the United States. The purchase required President Thomas Jefferson to exercise powers not explicitly granted to him by the Constitution.

CHECK FOR UNDERSTANDING

Ask students: **What were the most significant features of the Jefferson presidency?** *He defeated the Barbary pirates and reversed Federalist policies like the Alien and Sedition Acts and amended the Naturalization Act, abolished internal taxes, and reduced the size of the military. He also left some Federalist policies in place — he left the Bank of the United States alone and allowed many Federalists to stay in office.*

AP® APPLY THE TIP

Help students to understand that western expansion was a source of political conflict in the U.S. beginning in the colonial period. Lead students in a discussion of conflicts that were related to western expansion, including Bacon's Rebellion, Proclamation of 1763, Northwest Ordinance, Treaty of Greenville, and the Whiskey Rebellion. Ask students to place each of these events in context to explain why western expansion created conflict between various factions by completing **Handout 7.3 — Contextualization: Louisiana Purchase (TRM)**.

TRM Find **Handout 7.3 — Contextualization: Louisiana Purchase (TRM)** in the Teacher's Resource Materials.

TEACHING STRATEGY

Ask students: **How was Jefferson's agrarian vision reflected in his policies affecting western lands?** In answering this question, students are linking an ideology, or "vision," to its implementation in practice. This question also provides an opportunity to consider contingency, specifically to what extent was Jefferson's implementation of his vision a matter of happenstance and luck rather than careful planning. Extend this prompt by having students consider why this part of Jefferson's ideological system remained unchanged, even while he showed more pragmatism later in his exercise of national power.

A Mandan Village This Mandan settlement in North Dakota, painted by George Catlin around 1837, resembled those in which the Lewis and Clark expedition spent the winter of 1804–1805. Note the palisade of logs that surrounds the village, as protection from the Sioux and other marauding Plains peoples, and the solidly built mud lodges that provided warm shelter from the bitter cold of winter on the northern Great Plains. Smithsonian American Art Museum, Washington, DC/Art Resource, NY.

This tragedy propelled Burr into another secessionist scheme, this time in the Southwest. When his term as vice president ended in 1805, Burr moved west to avoid prosecution. There, he conspired with General James Wilkinson, the military governor of the Louisiana Territory, either to seize territory in New Spain or to establish Louisiana as a separate nation. But Wilkinson, himself a Spanish spy and incipient traitor, betrayed Burr and arrested him. In a highly politicized trial presided over by Chief Justice John Marshall, the jury acquitted Burr of treason.

The Louisiana Purchase had increased party conflict and generated secessionist schemes in both New England and the Southwest. Such sectional differences would continue, challenging Madison's argument in "Federalist No. 10" that a large and diverse republic was more stable than a small one.

Lewis and Clark Meet the Mandans and Sioux A scientist as well as a statesman, Jefferson wanted information about Louisiana: its physical features, plant and animal life, and Native peoples. He was also worried about intruders: the British-run Hudson's Bay Company and Northwest Company were actively trading for furs on the upper Missouri River. So in 1804, Jefferson sent his personal secretary, Meriwether Lewis, to explore the region with William Clark, an army officer. From St. Louis, Lewis, Clark, and their party of American soldiers and frontiersmen traveled up the Missouri for 1,000 miles to the fortified, earth-lodge towns of the Mandan and Hidatsa peoples (near present-day Bismarck, North Dakota), where they spent the winter.

The Mandans lived primarily by horticulture, growing corn, beans, and squash. They had acquired horses by supplying food to nomadic Plains Indians and secured guns, iron goods, and textiles by selling buffalo hides and dried meat to European traders. However, the Mandans (and neighboring Arikaras) had been hit hard by the smallpox epidemics that swept across the Great Plains in 1779–1781 and 1801–1802. Now they were threatened by Sioux peoples: Tetons, Yanktonais, and Oglalas. Originally, the Sioux had lived in the prairie and lake region of northern Minnesota. As their numbers rose and fish and game grew scarce, the Sioux moved westward, acquired horses, and hunted buffalo, living as nomads in portable skin tepees. The Sioux became ferocious fighters who tried to reduce the Mandans and other farming tribes to subject peoples. According to Lewis and Clark, they were the "pirates of the Missouri." Soon the Sioux would dominate the buffalo trade throughout the upper Missouri region.

In the spring of 1805, Lewis and Clark began an epic 1,300-mile trek into unknown country. Their party now included Toussaint Charbonneau, a French Canadian fur trader, and his Shoshone wife, Sacagawea, who served as a guide and translator. After following the Missouri River to its source on the Idaho-Montana border, they crossed the Rocky Mountains, and — venturing far beyond the Louisiana Purchase — traveled down the Columbia River to the Pacific Ocean. Nearly everywhere, Indian peoples

TEACHING STRATEGY

The PBS documentary *Lewis and Clark: The Journey of the Corps of Discovery* provides many resources to accompany the film. Lesson plans address the historical context of the expedition, analysis of William Clark's maps, close reading of Lewis's journals, and investigation of Lewis and Clark's interactions with Dakota and Lakota Indians. The Web site also includes extensive information about the Native Americans of the region, an interactive trail map, and clips from historians reflecting on the expedition. Access the documentary by searching "PBS Lewis and Clark."

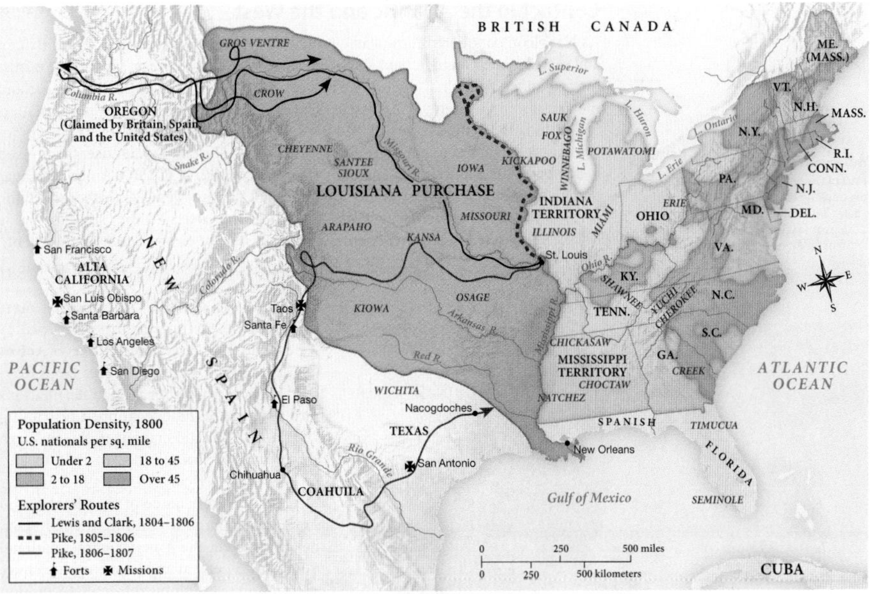

MAP 7.3 U.S. Population Density in 1803 and the Louisiana Purchase
When the United States purchased Louisiana from France in 1803, much of the land to its east — the vast territory between the Appalachian Mountains and the Mississippi River — remained in Indian hands. The equally vast lands beyond the Mississippi were virtually unknown to Anglo-Americans, even after the epic explorations of Meriwether Lewis and William Clark and of Captain Zebulon Pike Jr., who led an exploratory expedition to the south of Lewis and Clark's route beginning in the summer of 1806. (Pike's party lost its way and unintentionally ventured far into New Spain.) Still, President Jefferson predicted quite accurately that the huge Mississippi River Valley "from its fertility . . . will ere long yield half of our whole produce, and contain half of our whole population."

asked for guns so they could defend themselves from other armed tribes. In 1806, Lewis and Clark capped off their pathbreaking expedition by providing Jefferson with the first maps of the immense wilderness and a detailed account of its natural resources and inhabitants (Map 7.3). Their report prompted some Americans to envision a nation that would span the continent.

THE WAR OF 1812 AND THE TRANSFORMATION OF POLITICS

What elements of Federalist political philosophy survived the end of the First Party System?

The Napoleonic Wars that ravaged Europe after 1802 brought new attacks on American merchant ships. American leaders struggled desperately to protect the nation's commerce while avoiding war. When this effort finally failed, it sparked dramatic political changes that destroyed the Federalist Party and split the Republicans into National and Jeffersonian factions.

AP® EXAM TIP

Trace the events that resulted in the War of 1812 against Great Britain despite America's proclaimed neutrality in European affairs.

TEACHING STRATEGY

Use **MAP 7.3** to help students examine American expansionist foreign policy geographically. Guide students' analysis with the following questions:

- **Which part of the U.S. was the most densely settled? Why?** *From Massachusetts to Delaware. Shipping and manufacturing created urban centers, especially around ports.*
- **West of the Appalachians, which region was most densely settled? Why?** *Kentucky and other pockets along the Ohio River. Settlers like Daniel Boone were drawn to fertile land there even before the American Revolution, so because it was one of the earliest Western locations to be settled it also became the most densely populated.*
- **What route did Lewis and Clark follow from St. Louis?** *They followed the Missouri River most of the way and then went west to the Pacific coast.*
- **How many major Indian groups lived in the area encompassed by the Louisiana Purchase? Which Indian groups did Lewis and Clark encounter?** *Nearly a dozen. Missouri, Sioux, Crow, and Gros Ventre.*
- **What does Lewis and Clark's destination tell you about its purpose and about American ambitions?** *The only reason to go to the Pacific coast was to see if there was a viable route across the continent. This suggests that the U.S. had plans to take over Oregon, which at the time was disputed with Britain. The U.S. had a continental vision, which included subsuming all of the Indian peoples there under American leadership.*

CHECK FOR UNDERSTANDING

Ask students: **How were the principles of the Jeffersonian Republicans reflected in this era of dramatic growth and development?** *Jeffersonian Republicans, upon gaining power in 1801, put into practice policies that reflected their small-government agrarian roots. Though Jefferson tolerated the First Bank of the United States, he limited federal expenditures, especially in the military, and used Hamilton's tariff revenues to pay off, rather than increase, debt. He also abolished internal taxes, so detested by his supporters. Jefferson and his fellow Virginians also expanded the land available for agrarian settlement with the 1803 Louisiana Purchase.*

AP® APPLY THE TIP

Lead a class discussion on the War of 1812 and the historical concept of a "turning point" event. Ask students to identify and explain events that created conflicts between the U.S. and Great Britain in the years 1800–1812. As students name and explain events, list them on the board in a timeline format. Help students identify the major issues, including impressments, British attacks on U.S. shipping, the Battle of Tippecanoe, and the Louisiana Purchase. Once the class has identified events from 1800–1812, ask students to choose one event and make a historical argument that it was the turning point leading to war between the U.S. and Great Britain. Remind students that they must explain what was different before and after the events that led to the War of 1812. After giving students some time to formulate their argument, lead a class discussion in which different students share their turning point event and defend their choice with evidence. Encourage other students to challenge the turning point and counter with arguments in favor of a different event.

Conflict in the Atlantic and the West

As Napoleon conquered European countries, he cut off their commerce with Britain and seized American merchant ships that stopped in British ports. The British ministry responded with a naval blockade and seized American vessels carrying sugar and molasses from the French West Indies. The British navy also searched American merchant ships for British deserters and used these raids to replenish its crews, a practice known as impressment. Between 1802 and 1811, British naval officers impressed nearly eight thousand sailors, including many U.S. citizens. In 1807, American anger boiled over when a British warship attacked the U.S. Navy vessel *Chesapeake*, killing three, wounding eighteen, and seizing four alleged deserters. "Never since the battle of Lexington have I seen this country in such a state of exasperation as at present," Jefferson declared.

Embargo Act of 1807
An act of Congress that prohibited U.S. ships from traveling to foreign ports in an attempt to deter Britain and France from halting U.S. ships at sea. The embargo caused grave hardships for Americans engaged in overseas commerce.

The Embargo of 1807 To protect American interests, Jefferson pursued a policy of peaceful coercion. The **Embargo Act of 1807** prohibited American ships from leaving their home ports for foreign destinations until Britain and France stopped restricting U.S. trade. A drastic maneuver, the embargo overestimated the reliance of Britain and France on American shipping and underestimated the resistance of merchants, who feared the embargo would ruin them. In fact, the embargo cut the American gross national product by 5 percent and weakened the entire economy. Exports plunged from $108 million in 1806 to $22 million in 1808, hurting farmers as well as merchants. "All was noise and bustle" in New York City before the embargo, one visitor remarked; afterward, everything was closed up as if "a malignant fever was raging in the place."

Despite popular discontent over the embargo, voters elected Republican James Madison — Jefferson's heir and closest political ally — to the presidency in 1808. A powerful advocate for the Constitution, the architect of the Bill of Rights, and a prominent congressman and party leader, Madison had served the nation well. But the conflict he inherited with Britain and France appeared unresolvable. Just before he took office, Congress replaced the Embargo Act with the less restrictive Non-Intercourse Act of 1807, which restored some overseas trade while attempting to pressure Britain and France more directly. This act failed as well, both in its effort to ensure U.S. neutrality and in its attempt to restore and protect American commerce.

Western War Republican congressmen from the West had additional grievances

Tenskwatawa, "The Prophet," 1830 Tenskwatawa added a spiritual dimension to Native American resistance by urging a holy war against the invading whites and calling for a return to sacred ancestral ways. His dress reflects his teachings: note the animal-skin shirt and the heavily ornamented ears. However, some of Tenskwatawa's religious rituals reflected the influence of French Jesuits; he urged his followers to finger a sacred string of beads (such as those in his left hand) that were similar to the Catholic rosary, thereby "shaking hands with the Prophet." Whatever its origins, Tenskwatawa's message transcended the cultural differences among Indian peoples and helped his brother Tecumseh create a formidable political and military alliance. Smithsonian American Art Museum, Washington, DC/Art Resource, NY.

AP® THEME

WOR: America in the World

Tenskwatawa's spiritual vision helped provide unity among a variety of Indian groups to form an alliance against the migration of white settlers in an attempt to maintain control of their tribal lands and natural resources.

with Great Britain. They pointed to its trade with Indians in the Ohio River Valley in violation of the Treaty of Paris and Jay's Treaty. Bolstered by British guns and supplies, the Shawnee war chief Tecumseh revived the Western Confederacy in 1809. His brother, the prophet Tenskwatawa, provided the confederacy with a powerful nativist ideology. He urged Indian peoples to shun Americans, "the children of the Evil Spirit . . . who have taken away your lands"; renounce alcohol; and return to traditional ways. The Shawnee leaders found their greatest support among Kickapoo, Potawatomi, Winnebago, Ottawa, and Chippewa warriors: Indians of the western Great Lakes who had so far been largely shielded from the direct effects of U.S. westward expansion. They flocked to Tenskwatawa's holy village, Prophetstown, in the Indiana Territory.

As Tecumseh mobilized the western Indian peoples for war, William Henry Harrison, the governor of the Indiana Territory, decided on a preemptive strike. In November 1811, when Tecumseh went south to seek support from the Chickasaws, Choctaws, and Creeks, Harrison took advantage of his absence and attacked Prophetstown. The governor's 1,000 troops and militiamen traded heavy casualties with the confederacy's warriors at the **Battle of Tippecanoe** and then destroyed the holy village.

Battle of Tippecanoe
An attack on Shawnee Indians and their allies at Prophetstown on the Tippecanoe River in 1811 by American forces headed by William Henry Harrison, Indiana's territorial governor. The governor's troops traded heavy casualties with the confederacy's warriors and then destroyed the holy village.

The War of 1812

With Britain assisting Indians in the western territories and seizing American ships in the Atlantic, Henry Clay of Kentucky, the new Speaker of the House of Representatives, and John C. Calhoun, a rising young congressman from South Carolina, pushed Madison toward war. Like other Republican "war hawks" from the West and South, they wanted to seize territory in British Canada and Spanish Florida. With national elections approaching, Madison issued an ultimatum to Britain. When Britain failed to respond quickly, the president asked Congress for a declaration of war. In June 1812, a sharply divided Senate voted 19 to 13 for war, and the House of Representatives concurred, 79 to 49.

The causes of the War of 1812 have been much debated. Officially, the United States went to war because Britain had violated its commercial rights as a neutral nation. But the Federalists in Congress who represented the New England and Middle Atlantic merchants voted against the war; and in the election of 1812, those regions cast their 89 electoral votes for the Federalist presidential candidate, De Witt Clinton of New York. Madison amassed most of his 128 electoral votes in the South and West, where voters and congressmen strongly supported the war. Many historians therefore argue that the conflict was actually "a western war with eastern labels" (see "Firsthand Accounts," p. 234).

AP® SKILLS & PROCESSES

ARGUMENTATION

What do you think is the most persuasive explanation for the United States's declaration of war on Great Britain in 1812?

The War of 1812 was a near disaster for the United States. An invasion of British Canada in 1812 quickly ended in a retreat to Detroit. Nonetheless, the United States stayed on the offensive in the West. In 1813, American raiders burned the Canadian capital of York (present-day Toronto), Commodore Oliver Hazard Perry defeated a small British flotilla on Lake Erie, and General William Henry Harrison overcame a British and Indian force at the Battle of the Thames, taking the life of Tecumseh, now a British general.

In the East, political divisions prevented a wider war. New England Federalists opposed the war and prohibited their states' militias from attacking Canada. Boston merchants and banks refused to lend money to the federal government, making the war difficult to finance. In Congress, Daniel Webster, a dynamic young politician from New Hampshire, led Federalists opposed to higher tariffs and national conscription of state militiamen.

Gradually, the tide of battle turned in Britain's favor. When the war began, American privateers had captured scores of British merchant vessels, but by 1813 British

TEACHING STRATEGY

The PBS documentary *The War of 1812* provides a variety of lessons to accompany the film that give multiple perspectives on the war. Lessons explore the causes of the war, the role of race in the war, and the Treaty of Ghent. Access these resources at "PBS War of 1812 Classroom."

CHECK FOR UNDERSTANDING

Ask students: **How did the U.S. face conflict in the Atlantic and the West in the Jeffersonian era?** *The U.S. was caught in the Napoleonic wars between Britain and France. Though attempting to be neutral, U.S. ships were routinely stopped and searched by the British navy. Supplied by the British, Tecumseh and Tenskwatawa threatened to attack the U.S., but William Harrison preemptively attacked them in the Battle of Tippecanoe.*

AP® SKILLS & PROCESSES

ARGUMENTATION

In answering the **ARGUMENTATION** question, students have an opportunity to weigh causes, determining which were primary and which were secondary. Students could begin by listing the factors. Then they could rank them in order of importance. Finally, they could explain why the factor they listed first was the most important. Extend this prompt by having students identify the factors that argued against war and what kept those factors from having more influence than they did.

TRM Find complete suggested responses in the Teacher's Resource Materials.

AP® SKILLS & PROCESSES

ANALYZING HISTORICAL EVIDENCE

The **AP® FIRSTHAND ACCOUNTS** feature gives students a chance to weigh the perspectives of various political leaders as they consider the relationship between foreign crises and domestic stability. Students might consider how realistic Washington's idea of neutrality might have been over the long term. Given all the dire warnings about the dangers of war, students might consider whether the outcome of the War of 1812 bore out these concerns.

AP® THEME

NAT: American and National Identity

The **AP® FIRSTHAND ACCOUNTS** feature explores how Washington's Farewell Address encouraged national unity by cautioning against political factions.

AP® FIRSTHAND ACCOUNTS

Factional Politics and the War of 1812

In the quarter-century following the ratification of the U.S. Constitution, American leaders had to deal with the wars of the French Revolution and Napoleon. These European conflicts posed two dangers to the United States. First, the naval blockades imposed by the British and the French hurt American commerce and prompted calls for a military response. Second, European ideological and political struggles intensified party conflicts in the United States. On three occasions, the American republic faced danger from the combination of an external military threat and internal political turmoil. In 1798, the Federalist administration of John Adams almost went to war with France to help American merchants and to undermine the Republican Party. In 1807, Thomas Jefferson's embargo on American commerce shocked Federalists and sharply increased political tensions. And, as the following selections show, the political divisions during the War of 1812 threatened the very existence of the American republic.

GEORGE WASHINGTON

Farewell Address, 1796

Washington's support for Alexander Hamilton's economic policies promoted political factionalism. Ignoring his own role in creating that political divide, Washington condemned factionalism and, as his presidency proceeded, tried to stand above party conflicts. In his farewell address, Washington warned Americans to stand united and avoid the "Spirit of Party."

Source: James D. Richardson, ed., *A Compilation of the Messages and Papers of the Presidents, 1789–1896* (Washington, D.C.: U.S. Government Printing Office, 1896), 1: 213–215.

“ A solicitude for your welfare [prompts me] . . . to offer . . . the disinterested warnings of a parting friend, who can possibly have no personal motive to bias his counsels. . . .

The Unity of Government which constitutes you one people . . . is a main Pillar in the Edifice of your real independence . . . your tranquility at home; your peace abroad. . . . But it is easy to foresee, that, from different causes, and from different quarters, much pains will be taken, many artifices employed, to weaken in your minds the conviction of this truth. . . .

I have already intimated to you the danger of parties in the State, with particular reference to founding them on geographical discriminations. Let me now take a more comprehensive view, and warn you, in the most solemn manner, against the baneful effects of the Spirit of Party, generally.

This spirit, unfortunately, is inseparable from our nature, having its root in the strongest passions of the human mind. It exists under different shapes, in all governments, more or less stifled, controlled or repressed; but in those of the popular form, it is seen in its greatest rankness, and is truly their worst enemy.

The alternate dominion of one faction over another, sharpened by the spirit of revenge . . . , is itself a frightful despotism; but this leads at length to a more formal and permanent despotism. ”

JOSIAH QUINCY ET AL.

Federalists Protest "Mr. Madison's War"

The United States — and its two political parties — divided sharply over the War of 1812. As Congress debated the issue of going to war against Great Britain, Josiah Quincy and other antiwar Federalist congressmen published a manifesto that questioned the justifications for the war offered by President Madison and the military strategy proposed by Republican war hawks.

Source: *Annals of Congress*, 12th Cong., 1st sess., vol. 2, cols. 2219–2221.

“ How will war upon the land [an invasion of British Canada] protect commerce upon the ocean? What balm has Canada for wounded honor? How are our mariners benefited by a war which exposes those who are free, without promising release to those who are impressed?

But it is said that war is demanded by honor. Is national honor a principle which thirsts after vengeance, and is appeased only by blood? . . . If honor demands a war with England, what opiate lulls that honor to sleep over the wrongs done us by France? On land, robberies, seizures, imprisonments, by French authority; at sea, pillage, sinkings, burnings, under French orders. These are notorious. Are they unfelt because they are French? . . .

warships were disrupting American commerce and threatening seaports along the Atlantic coast. In 1814, a British fleet sailed up the Chesapeake Bay, and troops stormed ashore to attack Washington City. Retaliating for the destruction of York, the invaders burned the U.S. Capitol and government buildings. After two years of fighting, the United States was stalemated along the Canadian frontier and on the

There is . . . a headlong rushing into difficulties, with little calculation about the means, and little concern about the consequences. With a navy comparatively [small], we are about to enter into the lists against the greatest marine [power] on the globe. With a commerce unprotected and spread over every ocean, we propose to make a profit by privateering, and for this endanger the wealth of which we are honest proprietors. An invasion is threatened of the [British colonies in Canada, but Britain] . . . without putting a new ship into commission, or taking another soldier into pay, can spread alarm or desolation along the extensive range of our seaboard. . . .

What are the United States to gain by this war? Will the gratification of some privateersmen compensate the nation for that sweep of our legitimate commerce by the extended marine of our enemy which this desperate act invites? Will Canada compensate the Middle states for [the loss of] New York; or the Western states for [the loss of] New Orleans?

Let us not be deceived. A war of invasion may invite a retort of invasion. When we visit the peaceable, and as to us innocent, colonies of Great Britain with the horrors of war, can we be assured that our own coast will not be visited with like horrors? ❞

HEZEKIAH NILES

A Republican Defends the War

In 1814, what the Federalists feared had come to pass: British ships blockaded American ports, and British troops invaded American territory. In January 1815, Republican editor Hezekiah Niles used the pages of his influential Baltimore newspaper, *Niles' Weekly Register*, to explain current Republican policies and blame the Federalists for American reverses.

❝ It is universally known that the causes for which we declared war are no obstruction to peace. The practice of blockade and impressment having ceased by the general pacification of Europe, our government is content to leave the principle as it was. . . .

We have no further business in hostility, than such as is purely defensive; while that of Great Britain is to humble or subdue us. The war, on our part, has become a contest for life, liberty and property — on the part of our enemy, of revenge or ambition. . . .

What then are we to do? Are we to encourage him by divisions among ourselves — to hold out the hope of a separation of the states and a civil war — to refuse to bring forth the resources of the country against him? . . . I did think that in a defensive war — a struggle for all that is valuable — that all parties would have united. But it is not so — every measure calculated to replenish the treasury or raise men is opposed [by Federalists] as though it were determined to strike the 'star spangled banner' and exalt the bloody cross. Look at the votes and proceedings of congress — and mark the late spirit [to secede from the Union] . . . that existed in Massachusetts, and see with what unity of action everything has been done [by New England Federalists] to harass and embarrass the government. Our loans have failed; and our soldiers have wanted their pay, because those [New England merchants] who had the greater part of the monied capital covenanted with each other to refuse its aid to the country. They had a right, legally, to do this; and perhaps, also, by all the artifices of trade or power that money gave them, to oppress others not of their 'stamp' and depress the national credit — but history will shock posterity by detailing the length to which they went to bankrupt the republic. . . .

To conclude — why does the war continue? It is not the fault of the government — we demand no extravagant thing. I answer the question, and say — *it lasts because Great Britain depends on the exertions of her 'party' in this country to destroy our resources, and compel 'unconditional submission.'*

Thus the war began, and is continued, by our divisions. ❞

SOURCE: *Niles' Weekly Register*, January 28, 1815.

QUESTIONS FOR ANALYSIS

1. According to Washington, what is the ultimate cause of political factionalism? Why does Washington believe that factionalism is most dangerous in "popular" — that is, republican — governments?
2. Compare and contrast the Quincy and Niles documents. What specific dangers did Josiah Quincy and the Federalists foresee with regard to Republican war policies? According to Hezekiah Niles, what were the war goals of the Republican administration? Corroborate the sources to compare their perspectives on the parties.
3. Read the section on the War of 1812 on pages 233–235, and then discuss the accuracy of the Federalists' predictions. What historical situation influences Federalist arguments?
4. How had Republican war goals changed since the start of the war? Niles charged the Federalists and their supporters with impeding the American war effort. What were his specific charges? Did they have any merit? How might the Federalists have defended their stance with respect to the war? Identify relevant examples from the textbook and sources.

TRM Find complete suggested responses in the Teacher's Resource Materials.

defensive in the Atlantic, and its new capital city lay in ruins. The only U.S. victories came in the Southwest. There, the rugged slave-owning planter General Andrew Jackson and a force of Tennessee militiamen defeated British- and Spanish-supported Creek Indians in the Battle of Horseshoe Bend (1814) and forced the Creeks to cede 23 million acres of land (Map 7.4).

AP® THEME

WOR: America in the World

The War of 1812 was the culmination of tensions created by the war between France and Britain that resulted from the French Revolution. Ask students: **Based on MAP 7.4, what were the main features of the War of 1812?** *With no large-scale military campaigns, most fighting took place on the border between the U.S. and Canada. The British invasion of the Chesapeake led to the burning of Washington, D.C. but a failed attack on Baltimore.*

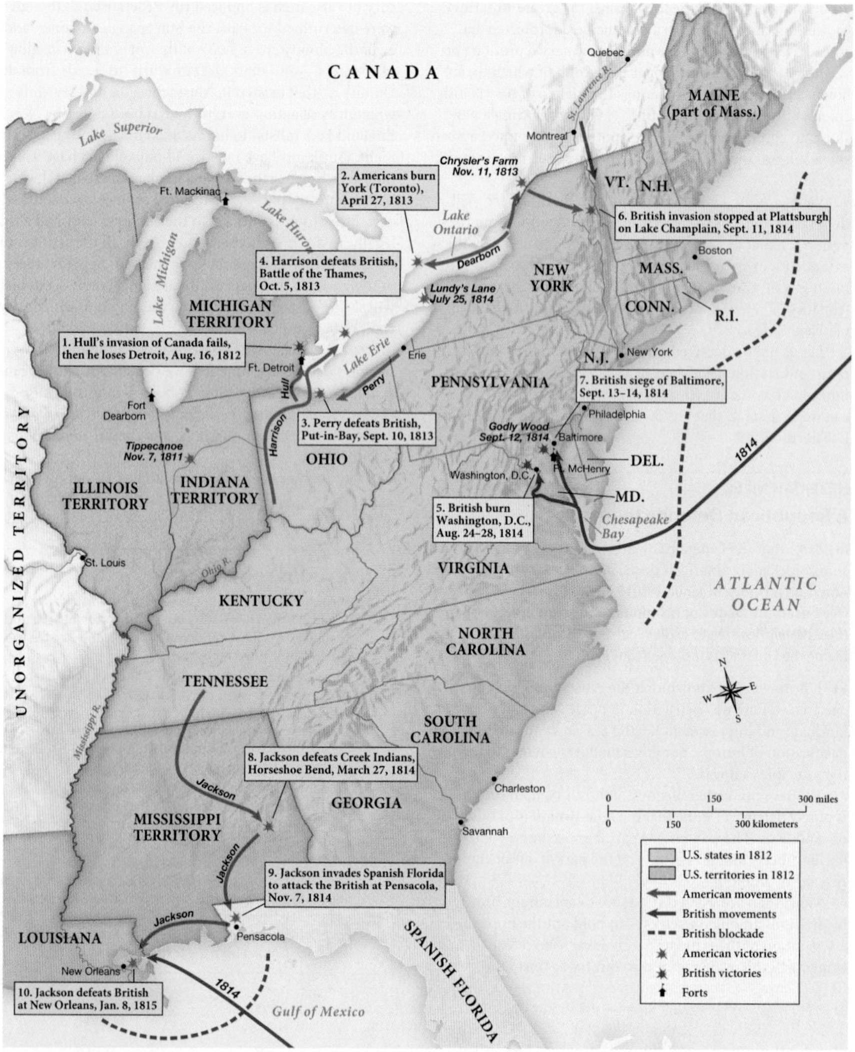

MAP 7.4 The War of 1812

Unlike the War of Independence, the War of 1812 had few large-scale military campaigns. In 1812 and 1813, most of the fighting took place along the Canadian border, as small American military forces attacked British targets with mixed success (nos. 1–4). The British took the offensive in 1814, launching a successful raid on Washington, but their attack on Baltimore failed, and they suffered heavy losses when they invaded the United States along Lake Champlain (nos. 5–7). Near the Gulf of Mexico, American forces moved from one success to another: General Andrew Jackson defeated the pro-British Creek Indians at the Battle of Horseshoe Bend, won a victory in Pensacola, and, in the single major battle of the war, routed an invading British army at New Orleans (nos. 8–10).

Washington, D.C., Burns, 1814 This chaotic image depicts the events of August 24, 1814, when British forces under the command of Major-General Robert Ross captured Washington, D.C. Ross and his men, with three cannons captured from American forces, command the heights above the city (right). The American flotilla (foreground) is defeated and the dockyard and arsenal are in flames. In the background, more of the city is burning, including a bridge over the Potomac River, the War Office, the Treasury, the Senate building, and the White House (center, far background). Ross's army then proceeded to Baltimore, where American forces at Fort McHenry held out against the British. A lawyer named Francis Scott Key, observing the fort's bombardment, dashed off a poem entitled "Defense of Fort McHenry." Later set to music, it came to be known as "The Star-Spangled Banner." Library of Congress, LC-DIG-ppmsca-31113.

Federalists Oppose the War American military setbacks increased opposition to the war in New England. In 1814, Massachusetts Federalists called for a convention "to lay the foundation for a radical reform in the National Compact." When New England Federalists met in Hartford, Connecticut, some delegates proposed secession, but most wanted to revise the Constitution. To end Virginia's domination of the presidency, the Hartford Convention proposed a constitutional amendment limiting the office to a single four-year term and rotating it among citizens from different states. The convention also suggested amendments restricting commercial embargoes to sixty days and requiring a two-thirds majority in Congress to declare war, prohibit trade, or admit a new state to the Union.

As a minority party, the Federalists could prevail only if the war continued to go badly — a very real prospect. The war had cost $88 million, raising the national debt to $127 million. And now, as Albert Gallatin warned Henry Clay in May 1814, Britain's triumph over Napoleon in Europe meant that a "well organized and large army is [now ready] . . . to act immediately against us." When an attack from Canada came in the late summer of 1814, only an American naval victory on Lake Champlain stopped the British from marching down the Hudson River Valley. A few months later, thousands of seasoned British troops landed outside New Orleans, threatening American

AP® EXAM TIP

Evaluate the role of the War of 1812 in defining and ultimately undermining the first two-party system.

AP® APPLY THE TIP

Provide students with excerpts from the Hartford Convention that illustrate the arguments of Federalists in New England during the War of 1812. As a comparison to the arguments for state autonomy, give students excerpts from the Virginia and Kentucky Resolutions arguing in favor of nullification. Ask students to compare the motives and philosophy of these documents.

CHECK FOR UNDERSTANDING

Ask students: **What were the major consequences of the War of 1812?** *The Treaty of Ghent restored the prewar borders of the U.S., prompted a faction of Republicans to support Federalist-like policies of a new Bank of the United States and internal improvements, while Federalist opposition to the war led to its demise as a party.*

TEACHING STRATEGY

"John Marshall, *Marbury v. Madison*, and Judicial Review," a lesson on the NEH's ESDITEment! Web site, provides an in-depth analysis of the development of judicial review and its significance through a close reading of Article III of the Constitution, selections from *Marbury*, and Federalist #78, which provides Hamilton's views on judicial review. Access this site by searching "EDSITEment John Marshall Marbury Madison."

***John Marshall*, by Chester Harding, c. 1830** Even at the age of seventy-five, John Marshall (1755–1835) had a commanding personal presence. After he became chief justice of the U.S. Supreme Court in 1801, Marshall elevated the Court from a minor department of the national government to a major institution in American legal and political life. His decisions on judicial review, contract rights, the regulation of commerce, and national banking permanently shaped the character of American constitutional law. © Boston Athenaeum, USA/Bridgeman Images.

Treaty of Ghent
The treaty signed on Christmas Eve 1814 that ended the War of 1812. It retained the prewar borders of the United States.

control of the Mississippi River. With the nation politically divided and under attack from north and south, Gallatin feared that "the war might prove vitally fatal to the United States."

Peace Overtures and a Final Victory Fortunately for the young American republic, by 1815 Britain wanted peace. The twenty-year war with France had sapped its wealth and energy, so it began negotiations with the United States in Ghent, Belgium. At first, the American commissioners — John Quincy Adams, Gallatin, and Clay — demanded territory in Canada and Florida, while British diplomats sought an Indian buffer state between the United States and Canada. Both sides quickly realized that these objectives were not worth the cost of prolonged warfare. The **Treaty of Ghent**, signed on Christmas Eve 1814, retained the prewar borders of the United States.

That result hardly justified three years of war, but before news of the treaty reached the United States, a final military victory lifted Americans' morale. On January 8, 1815, General Jackson's troops crushed the British forces attacking New Orleans. Fighting from carefully constructed breastworks, the Americans rained "grapeshot and cannister bombs" on the massed British formations. The British lost 700 men, and 2,000 more were wounded or taken prisoner; just 13 Americans died, and only 58 suffered wounds. A newspaper headline proclaimed: "Almost Incredible Victory!! Glorious News." The victory made Jackson a national hero, redeemed the nation's battered pride, and undercut the Hartford Convention's demands for constitutional revision.

The Federalist Legacy

The War of 1812 ushered in a new phase of the Republican political revolution. Before the conflict, Federalists had strongly supported Alexander Hamilton's program of national mercantilism — a funded debt, a central bank, and tariffs — while Jeffersonian Republicans had opposed it. After the war, the Republicans split into two camps. Led by Henry Clay, National Republicans pursued Federalist-like policies. In 1816, Clay pushed legislation through Congress creating the Second Bank of the United States and persuaded President Madison to sign it. In 1817, Clay won passage of the Bonus Bill, which created a national fund for roads and other internal improvements. Madison vetoed it. Reaffirming traditional Jeffersonian Republican principles, he argued that the national government lacked the constitutional authority to fund internal improvements.

Meanwhile, the Federalist Party crumbled. As one supporter explained, the National Republicans in the eastern states had "destroyed the Federalist party by the adoption of its principles" while the favorable farm policies of Jeffersonians maintained the Republican Party's dominance in the South and West. "No Federal character can run with success," Gouverneur Morris of New York lamented, and the election of 1818 proved him right: Republicans outnumbered Federalists 37 to 7 in the Senate and 156 to 27 in the House. Westward expansion and the success of Jefferson's Revolution of 1800 had shattered the First Party System.

Marshall's Federalist Law However, Federalist policies lived on thanks to John Marshall's long tenure on the Supreme Court. Appointed chief justice by President John Adams in January 1801, Marshall had a personality and intellect that allowed him to dominate the Court until 1822 and strongly influence its decisions until his death in 1835.

Three principles informed Marshall's jurisprudence: judicial authority, the supremacy of national laws, and traditional property rights (Table 7.1). Marshall claimed the right of judicial review for the Supreme Court in *Marbury v. Madison*

TABLE 7.1

Major Decisions of the Marshall Court

	Date	Case	Significance of Decision
Judicial Authority	1803	*Marbury v. Madison*	Asserts principle of judicial review
Property Rights	1810	*Fletcher v. Peck*	Protects property rights through broad reading of Constitution's contract clause
	1819	*Dartmouth College v. Woodward*	Safeguards property rights, especially of chartered corporations
Supremacy of National Law	1819	*McCulloch v. Maryland*	Interprets Constitution to give broad powers to national government
	1824	*Gibbons v. Ogden*	Gives national government jurisdiction over interstate commerce

(1803), and the Court frequently used that power to overturn state laws that, in its judgment, violated the Constitution.

Asserting National Supremacy The important case of ***McCulloch v. Maryland* (1819)** involved one such law. When Congress created the Second Bank of the United States in 1816, it allowed the bank to set up state branches that competed with state-chartered banks. In response, the Maryland legislature imposed a tax on notes issued by the Baltimore branch of the Second Bank. The Second Bank refused to pay, claiming that the tax infringed on national powers and was therefore unconstitutional. The state's lawyers then invoked Jefferson's argument: that Congress lacked the constitutional authority to charter a national bank. Even if a national bank was legitimate, the lawyers argued, Maryland could tax its activities within the state.

***McCulloch v. Maryland* (1819)** A Supreme Court case that denied the right of states to tax the Second Bank of the United States, thereby asserting the dominance of national over state statutes.

Marshall and the nationalist-minded Republicans on the Court firmly rejected both arguments. The Second Bank was constitutional, said the chief justice, because it was "necessary and proper," given the national government's control over currency and credit, and Maryland did not have the power to tax it.

The Marshall Court again asserted the dominance of national over state statutes in *Gibbons v. Ogden* (1824). The decision struck down a New York law granting a monopoly to Aaron Ogden for steamboat passenger service across the Hudson River to New Jersey. Asserting that the Constitution gave the federal government authority over interstate commerce, the chief justice sided with Thomas Gibbons, who held a federal license to run steamboats between the two states.

AP® SKILLS & PROCESSES

DEVELOPMENTS AND PROCESSES

How did the Supreme Court influence the debate over the powers of the federal government in the Federal Period?

Upholding Vested Property Rights Finally, Marshall used the Constitution to uphold Federalist notions of property rights. During the 1790s, Jefferson Republicans had celebrated "the will of the people," prompting Federalists to worry that popular sovereignty would result in a "tyranny of the majority." If state legislatures enacted statutes infringing on the property rights of wealthy citizens, Federalist judges vowed to void them.

Like other Federalist judges, Marshall was determined to protect individual property rights, and he invoked the contract clause of the Constitution to do it. The contract clause (in Article I, Section 10) prohibits the states from passing any law "impairing the obligation of contracts." Economic conservatives at the Philadelphia convention had inserted the clause to prevent "stay" laws, which kept creditors from seizing the lands and goods of delinquent debtors (see "Comparing Interpretations," in Chapter 6). In *Fletcher v. Peck* (1810), Marshall greatly expanded its scope. The Georgia legislature had granted a huge tract of land to the Yazoo Land Company.

AP® THEME

NAT: American and National Identity

Use **TABLE 7.1** to review the highlights of John Marshall's leadership of the Supreme Court, which established the primacy of the judiciary in determining the Constitution's meaning and asserted the precedence of federal laws over state laws. Guide students' analysis with the following questions:

- **What is the span of these decisions?** *More than 20 years.*
- **Why is *Marbury v. Madison* the necessary prelude to the other decisions?** *Without asserting the right of judicial review, the Court could not have made its later rulings, which all hinged on the legitimacy of that principle.*
- **What principles did the Marshall Court uphold?** *Protection of private property rights and the power of the national government.*

TRM Find complete suggested responses in the Teacher's Resource Materials.

TRM Find complete suggested responses in the Teacher's Resource Materials.

When a new legislature cancelled the grant, alleging fraud and bribery, speculators who had purchased Yazoo lands appealed to the Supreme Court to uphold their titles. Marshall did so by ruling that the legislative grant was a contract that could not be revoked. His decision was controversial and far-reaching. It limited state power; bolstered vested property rights; and, by protecting out-of-state investors, promoted the development of economic interests on a national scale.

The Court extended its defense of vested property rights in *Dartmouth College v. Woodward* (1819). Dartmouth College was a private institution created by a royal charter issued by King George III. In 1816, New Hampshire's Republican legislature enacted a statute converting the school into a public university. The Dartmouth trustees opposed the legislation and hired Daniel Webster to plead their case. A renowned constitutional lawyer and a leading Federalist, Webster cited the Court's decision in *Fletcher v. Peck* and argued that the royal charter was an unalterable contract. The Marshall Court agreed and upheld Dartmouth's claims.

AP® SKILLS & PROCESSES

CLAIMS AND EVIDENCE IN SOURCES

Why do historians think the decisions of the Marshall Court constitute a Federalist legacy?

AP® SKILLS & PROCESSES

DEVELOPMENTS AND PROCESSES

How did the foreign policy initiatives of John Quincy Adams expand control over North America and support an independent global presence for the United States?

The Diplomacy of John Quincy Adams Even as John Marshall incorporated important Federalist principles into the American legal system, voting citizens and political leaders embraced the outlook of the Republican Party. The political career of John Quincy Adams was a case in point. Although he was the son of Federalist president John Adams, John Quincy Adams had joined the Republican Party before the War of 1812. He came to national attention for his role in negotiating the Treaty of Ghent, which ended the war.

Adams then served brilliantly as secretary of state for two terms under James Monroe (1817–1825). Ignoring Republican antagonism toward Great Britain, in 1817, Adams negotiated the Rush-Bagot Treaty, which limited American and British naval forces on the Great Lakes. In 1818, he concluded another agreement with Britain setting the forty-ninth parallel as the border between Canada and the lands of the Louisiana Purchase. Then, in the **Adams-Onís Treaty** of 1819, Adams persuaded Spain to cede the Florida territory to the United States (Map 7.5). In return, the American government accepted Spain's claim to Texas and agreed to a compromise on the western boundary for the state of Louisiana, which had entered the Union in 1812.

Adams-Onís Treaty
An 1819 treaty in which John Quincy Adams persuaded Spain to cede the Florida territory to the United States. In return, the American government accepted Spain's claim to Texas and agreed to a compromise on the western boundary for the state of Louisiana.

Finally, Adams persuaded President Monroe to declare American national policy with respect to the Western Hemisphere. At Adams's behest, Monroe warned Spain and other European powers to keep their hands off the newly independent republics in Latin America. The American continents were not "subject for further colonization," the president declared in 1823—a policy that thirty years later became known as the **Monroe Doctrine**. In return, Monroe pledged that the United States would not "interfere in the internal concerns" of European nations. Thanks to John Quincy Adams, the United States had successfully asserted its diplomatic leadership in the Western Hemisphere and won international acceptance of its northern and western boundaries.

Monroe Doctrine
The 1823 declaration by President James Monroe that the Western Hemisphere was closed to any further colonization or interference by European powers. In exchange, Monroe pledged that the United States would not become involved in European struggles.

The appearance of political consensus after two decades of bitter party conflict prompted observers to dub James Monroe's presidency (1817–1825) the "Era of Good Feeling." This harmony was real but transitory. The Republican Party was now split between the National faction, led by Clay and Adams, and the Jeffersonian faction, soon to be led by Martin Van Buren and Andrew Jackson. The two groups differed sharply over federal support for roads and canals and many other issues. As the aging Jefferson himself complained, "You see so many of these new [National] republicans maintaining in Congress the rankest doctrines of the old federalists." This division in the Republican Party would soon produce the Second Party System, in which national-minded Whigs and state-focused Democrats would confront each other. By the early 1820s, one cycle of American politics and economic debate had ended, and another was about to begin.

CHECK FOR UNDERSTANDING

Ask students: **What elements of Federalist political philosophy survived the end of the First Party System?** *Even though the War of 1812 effectively killed the Federalists as a political force, especially after the failed 1814 Hartford Convention, the conflict convinced many Republicans of the wisdom of many Federalist policies, which survived after the end of the First Party System. These surviving policies included a strong central bank (the Second Bank of the United States was chartered in 1817), federal supremacy (as evidenced in the 1819 decision in* McCulloch v. Maryland *and* Gibbons v. Ogden *in 1824), and an emphasis on state-run internal improvements such as roads and canals.*

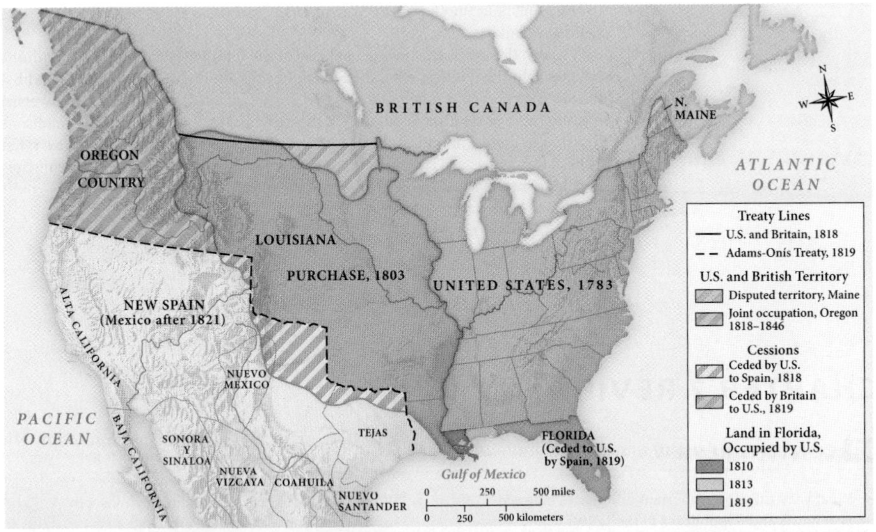

MAPPING THE PAST

MAP 7.5 Defining the National Boundaries, 1800–1820
After the War of 1812, American diplomats negotiated treaties with Great Britain and Spain that defined the boundaries of the Louisiana Purchase, with British Canada to the north and New Spain (which in 1821 became the independent nation of Mexico) to the south and west. These treaties eliminated the threat of border wars with neighboring states for a generation, giving the United States a much-needed period of peace and security.

ANALYZING THE MAP: Look carefully at this map, which illustrates the territorial claims of the United States, Great Britain, and Spain in North America. How does this map illustrate efforts of the United States to claim territory throughout North America? How did this expansion influence relations with Native American nations?

MAKING CONNECTIONS: This map puts the diplomatic achievements of John Quincy Adams in clear perspective. How can the achievements of Adams's administration be related to diplomatic efforts of earlier American presidents?

SUMMARY

In this chapter, we traced four interrelated themes: public policy, westward expansion, party politics, and the persistence of Federalist values in the actions of the Marshall Court. We began by examining the contrasting public policies advocated by Alexander Hamilton and Thomas Jefferson. A Federalist, Hamilton supported a strong national government and created a fiscal infrastructure (the national debt, tariffs, and a national bank) to spur trade and manufacturing. By contrast, Jefferson wanted to preserve the authority of state governments, and he envisioned an America enriched by farming rather than industry.

Jefferson and the Republicans promoted a westward movement that transformed the agricultural economy and sparked new wars with Indian peoples. Expansion westward also shaped American diplomatic and military policy, leading

AP® THEME

WOR: America in the World

Ask students: **How does MAP 7.5 indicate the successes of the U.S. government in diplomatic initiatives dealing with the continued British and Spanish presence in North America? What tensions remained in 1820?** *The Louisiana Purchase created a buffer of new American territory between the U.S. and Spain. Spain ceded Florida to the U.S. Treaties in 1818 and 1819 clarified borders between the U.S. and Spain and British Canada. Territory in northern Maine and in the Oregon country remained disputed.*

TRM Find complete suggested responses in the Teacher's Resource Materials.

to the Louisiana Purchase, the War of 1812, and the treaties negotiated by John Quincy Adams.

Finally, there was the unexpected rise of the First Party System. As Hamilton's policies split the political elite, the French Revolution divided Americans into hostile ideological groups. The result was two decades of bitter conflict and controversial measures: the Federalists' Sedition Act, the Republicans' Embargo Act, and Madison's decision to go to war with Britain. Although the Federalist Party faded away, it left as its enduring legacy Hamilton's financial innovations and John Marshall's constitutional jurisprudence.

CHECK FOR UNDERSTANDING

Use the **AP® LEARNING FOCUS** question from the beginning of the chapter to check on students' understanding of the chapter as a whole: **Why did the United States survive the challenges of its first three decades to become a viable, growing independent republic?** *More than anything else, compromise was required to make the early nation viable — compromise between state and national governance; between wealthy, middle-class, and poor interests; and between urban and agricultural workers. The debate over the Constitution provided balance between the federal and state powers and guaranteed a bill of rights to the new American citizens.*

✓ LearningCurve

Remind students to go online to complete the LearningCurve quiz for this chapter.

TRM Find complete suggested responses in the Teacher's Resource Materials.

CHAPTER 7 REVIEW

AP CONTENT REVIEW

Answer these questions to demonstrate your understanding of the chapter's main ideas.

1. What were the most important differences between Federalists and Republicans in the 1790s?
2. How were the principles of the Jeffersonian Republicans reflected in this era of dramatic growth and development?
3. What elements of Federalist political philosophy survived the end of the First Party System?

AP SKILLS & PROCESSES

COMPARISON

AP® CONTENT REVIEW 1 asks students to compare the values and policies of the two opposing members of the First Party System.

AP SKILLS & PROCESSES

CONTEXTUALIZATION

AP® CONTENT REVIEW 2 encourages students to place the Republican Party in the larger economic context in which it emerged and explain its principles in light of that context. Note: This is the same question as the **CHECK FOR UNDERSTANDING** prompt on p. 231.

AP SKILLS & PROCESSES

CONTINUITY AND CHANGE

AP® CONTENT REVIEW 3 invites students to consider continuity in the political ideology of Federalism — even after the party itself had disappeared. Note: This is the same question as the **CHECK FOR UNDERSTANDING** prompt on p. 240.

AP TERMS TO KNOW

Identify and explain the significance of each term below.

Key Concepts and Events

Judiciary Act of 1789 (p. 213)
Bill of Rights (p. 213)
Report on the Public Credit (p. 213)
Bank of the United States (p. 215)
Report on Manufactures (p. 215)
Proclamation of Neutrality (p. 216)
French Revolution (p. 216)
Whiskey Rebellion (p. 216)
Jay's Treaty (p. 217)
Haitian Revolution (p. 220)
XYZ Affair (p. 222)
Naturalization, Alien, and Sedition Acts (p. 222)
Virginia and Kentucky Resolutions (p. 222)
Treaty of Greenville (p. 224)
***Marbury v. Madison* (1803)** (p. 228)
Louisiana Purchase (p. 229)
Embargo Act of 1807 (p. 232)
Battle of Tippecanoe (p. 233)
Treaty of Ghent (p. 238)
***McCulloch v. Maryland* (1819)** (p. 239)
Adams-Onís Treaty (p. 240)
Monroe Doctrine (p. 240)

Key People

John Adams (p. 212)
Alexander Hamilton (p. 212)
Thomas Jefferson (p. 213)
Little Turtle (p. 224)
John Marshall (p. 228)
Tecumseh (p. 233)
Henry Clay (p. 233)
John Quincy Adams (p. 238)

TRM Find definitions for these terms in the **Glossary/Glosario** in the Teacher's Resource Materials.

AP® MAKING CONNECTIONS

Recognize the larger developments and continuities within and across chapters by answering these questions.

1. In Chapter 6, thirteen former British colonies cooperated in war and established new republican institutions of self-government. After 1789, unforeseen divisions developed in American politics. Why did Hamiltonians and Jeffersonians disagree so sharply on key questions of national policy? Which of the factions in the First Party System — Federalists or Republicans — best embodied the principles of the Revolution? How did westward expansion and international relations force the United States to modify its Revolutionary republican ideals? Make an argument about changes to and continuity of American Revolutionary ideals and support it with specific evidence.

2. In Chapters 3, 4, and 5, we traced the growing competition among Britain, France, and Spain for claims to North American territory. What allowed the United States — newly formed and relatively weak — to enter into this competition and succeed in claiming so much of the continent's territory? What military and diplomatic initiatives secured American boundaries, and why did the nations of Europe choose to concede so many of their claims to the new nation? Be sure to include the global context in your answer.

KEY TURNING POINTS

Refer to the timeline at the start of the chapter for help in answering the following questions.

The sham Indian treaties (1784–1789), Kentucky and Tennessee join the Union (1792, 1796), and Jefferson is elected president (1800): How were developments in the West tied into national politics in the 1790s? Why did the Federalists steadily lose ground to the Republicans?

AP® PRACTICE QUESTIONS

MULTIPLE CHOICE QUESTIONS

Choose the correct answer for each question.

Questions 1–3 refer to this excerpt.

> "The powers not delegated to the United States by the Constitution, nor prohibited by it to the States, are reserved to the States respectively, or to the people."
>
> United States Constitution, Amendment 10

1. The ideology of which of the following groups showed the greatest similarity to the position endorsed by the Tenth Amendment?
   - **a.** Abolitionists
   - **b.** Antifederalists
   - **c.** American Indians
   - **d.** Federalists

2. The creation of the Tenth Amendment was most immediately motivated by the desire to
   - **a.** ensure ratification of the Constitution.
   - **b.** secure individual rights of free speech against government abuse.
   - **c.** bolster the powers of the federal government.
   - **d.** restrict the powers of state government.

3. The passage could best be used as evidence to support which of the following claims?
   - **a.** The Constitution grants the federal government supremacy over the states.
   - **b.** Americans disagreed about how much power should be granted to the federal government.
   - **c.** Many states maintained property qualifications for voting and citizenship after the American Revolution.
   - **d.** The Articles of Confederation created a central government with limited power.

AP® SKILLS & PROCESSES

CONTINUITY AND CHANGE

AP® MAKING CONNECTIONS 1 asks students to consider patterns of continuity and change over time as they consider a shift from "cooperation" to "division."

AP® SKILLS & PROCESSES

ANALYZING HISTORICAL EVIDENCE

Have students use the painting on p. 228 to answer **AP® MAKING CONNECTIONS 2**. Ask students to derive historical relevant information from the primary source — distinguishing what actually happened from what is depicted — and to use that information to explain how the source provides information about the broader historical setting of the early nineteenth century.

AP® SKILLS & PROCESSES

CONTINUITY AND CHANGE

The **KEY TURNING POINTS** question invites students to draw connections between three major events that happened during the war and relate them to the emergence of the First Party System, and its quick decline with the demise of the Federalist Party.

TRM Find complete suggested responses in the Teacher's Resource Materials.

Questions 4–6 refer to this excerpt.

> "*Be it enacted by the Senate and House of Representatives of the United States of America in Congress assembled*, That whenever there shall be a declared war between the United States and any foreign nation or government, or any invasion or predatory incursion shall be perpetrated, attempted, or threatened against the territory of the United States, by any foreign nation or government, and the President of the United States shall make public proclamation of the event, all natives, citizens, denizens, or subjects of the hostile nation or government, being males of the age of fourteen years and upwards, who shall be within the United States, and not actually naturalized, shall be liable to be apprehended, restrained, secured and removed, as alien enemies."
>
> Alien Act, 1798

4. Which of the following most actively resisted the policies of the Alien Act of 1798?

a. Democratic Republicans
b. Antifederalists
c. Merchants
d. Federalists

5. Which of the following contributed most directly to the conflicts addressed in the passage?

a. Political tensions between Federalists and Democratic-Republicans
b. Westward expansion and the development of frontier culture
c. State alliances with American Indian tribes on the eastern seaboard
d. War with Great Britain

6. The passage of the legislation in the excerpt above most directly resulted in which of the following?

a. Supreme Court decisions that enhanced the power of the federal government at the expense of the states
b. A long-term decline in foreign immigration to the United States
c. Control of the federal government shifting to the Democratic Republican Party
d. Expansion of slavery in the United States

Questions 7–8 refer to this map.

Indian Cessions and State Formation, 1776–1840

7. Which of the following contributed LEAST to the events and developments depicted on the map?

a. Diminishing fertility of plantation lands
b. Government policies coercing American Indian treaties
c. Extension of slavery into the Northwest Territories
d. Population growth along the Atlantic coast

8. The most important political motivation leading to expansionist policies of the federal government resulted from

a. desires to minimize conflicts within the American two-party system over the Bill of Rights.
b. international rivalries with the British and Spanish for control of North America.
c. popular expectations that politicians follow the advice of George Washington's Farewell Address.
d. the declining numbers of Americans laboring in agriculture as a result of the market revolution.

SHORT ANSWER QUESTIONS

Read each question carefully and write a short response. Use evidence from the text to support your claims.

"Hamilton's assigned duty, upon becoming minister of the nation's finances, would be to devise a way of managing the Revolutionary War debts so as to place public credit upon firm foundations. . . . Hamilton set for himself 'the task of making the citizens in every regard more well-behaved, healthier, wiser, richer, and more secure.' Specifically, he proposed to use his administration of the public finances as an instrument for forging the American people into a prosperous, happy, and respected nation."

Forrest McDonald, *Alexander Hamilton: A Biography*, 1979

"His [Alexander Hamilton's] plans . . . were not only a catalyst for sectional confrontation. They seemed an excellent confirmation of persistent Antifederalist suspicions of an engulfing federal power. . . . Coming in conjunction with the high style of the new government, the antipopulistic pronouncements of some of its supporters, and measures such as an excise tax and a professional army, the Hamiltonian program might as well have been designed to awaken specific expectations about the course and nature of governmental decay that were never very far beneath the surface of revolutionary minds."

Lance Banning, *The Jeffersonian Persuasion: Evolution of a Party Ideology*, 1978

1. Using the two excerpts provided, answer (a), (b), and (c).
   - **a.** Briefly explain ONE major difference between McDonald's and Banning's historical interpretations about Alexander Hamilton.
   - **b.** Briefly explain how ONE specific historical event or development from the period 1787 to 1820 that is not explicitly mentioned in the excerpts could be used to support McDonald's interpretation.
   - **c.** Briefly explain how ONE historical event or development from the period 1787 to 1820 that is not explicitly mentioned in the excerpts could be used to support Banning's interpretation.

2. Answer (a), (b), and (c).
   - **a.** Briefly explain ONE specific historical argument used to oppose ratifying the Constitution in the 1780s.
   - **b.** Briefly explain ONE specific historical argument used to support ratifying the Constitution in the 1780s.
   - **c.** Briefly explain how ONE specific historical event or development represents an accomplishment of the national government under the Constitution between 1787 and 1820.

3. Answer (a), (b), and (c).
   - **a.** Briefly explain ONE specific way in which the development of the two-party political system transformed the government of the United States between 1787 and 1820.
   - **b.** Briefly explain ONE important way in which the development of the two party system between 1787 and 1820 transformed the relationship between the United States and European nations.
   - **c.** Briefly explain ONE specific historical transformation in the United States society resulting from the development of the two-party political system between 1787 and 1820.

TRM Find complete suggested responses in the Teacher's Resource Materials.

TRM Find complete suggested responses in the Teacher's Resource Materials.

3 PART — AP® PRACTICE ESSAY QUESTIONS

DOCUMENT-BASED QUESTION *Suggested reading period: 15 minutes. Suggested writing time: 45 minutes*

DIRECTIONS: Question 1 is based on the accompanying documents. The documents have been edited for the purpose of this exercise.

1. Evaluate the extent to which revolutionary ideals changed American society in the period 1776 to 1800.

DOCUMENT 1

Source: The Declaration of Independence, 1776.

"When in the Course of human events, it becomes necessary for one people to dissolve the political bands which have connected them with another, and to assume among the powers of the earth, the separate and equal station to which the Laws of Nature and of Nature's God entitle them, a decent respect to the opinions of mankind requires that they should declare the causes which impel them to the separation.

We hold these truths to be self-evident, that all men are created equal, that they are endowed by their Creator with certain unalienable Rights, that among these are Life, Liberty and the pursuit of Happiness. — That to secure these rights, Governments are instituted among Men, deriving their just powers from the consent of the governed, —That whenever any Form of Government becomes destructive of these ends, it is the Right of the People to alter or to abolish it, and to institute new Government, laying its foundation on such principles and organizing its powers in such form, as to them shall seem most likely to effect their Safety and Happiness."

DOCUMENT 2

Source: The New Jersey State Constitution, 1776.

"That all inhabitants of this Colony, of full age, who are worth fifty pounds proclamation money, clear estate in the same, and have resided within the county in which they claim a vote for twelve months immediately preceding the election, shall be entitled to vote for Representatives in Council and Assembly; and also for all other public offices, that shall be elected by the people of the county at large."

DOCUMENT 3

Source: Letter from Henry Knox to George Washington, 1786.

"This dreadful situation has alarmed every man of principle and property in New England. . . . Our government must be braced, changed, or altered to secure our lives and property. We imagined that the mildness of our government and the virtue of the people were so correspondent, that we were not as other nations requiring brutal force to support the laws — But we find that we are men, actual men, possessing all the turbulent passions belonging to that animal and that we must have a government proper and adequate for him — The people of Massachusetts for instance, are far advanced in this doctrine, and the men of reflection, and principle, are determined to endeavor to establish a government which shall have the power to protect them in their lawful pursuits, and which will be efficient in all cases of internal commotions or foreign invasions. . . ."

243-c

DOCUMENT 4

Source: The Northwest Ordinance, 1787.

"Art. 3. Religion, morality, and knowledge, being necessary to good government and the happiness of mankind, schools and the means of education shall forever be encouraged. . . .

Art. 6. There shall be neither slavery nor involuntary servitude in the said territory, otherwise than in the punishment of crimes whereof the party shall have been duly convicted: *Provided, always,* That any person escaping into the same, from whom labor or service is lawfully claimed in any one of the original States, such fugitive may be lawfully reclaimed and conveyed to the person claiming his or her labor or service as aforesaid."

DOCUMENT 5

Source: The Fugitive Slave Law of 1793.

"For the better security of the peace and friendship now entered into by the contracting parties, against all infractions of the same, by the citizens of either party, to the prejudice of the other, neither party shall proceed to the infliction of punishments on the citizens of the other, otherwise than by securing the offender, or offenders, by imprisonment, or any other competent means, till a fair and impartial trial can be had by judges or juries of both parties, as near as can be, to the laws, customs, and usage's of the contracting parties, and natural justice. . . . And it is further agreed between the parties aforesaid, that neither shall entertain, or give countenance to, the enemies of the other, or protect, in their respective states, criminal fugitives, servants, or slaves, but the same to apprehend and secure, and deliver to the state or states, to which such enemies, criminals, servants, or slaves, respectively below."

DOCUMENT 6

Source: "Keep Within Compass," circa 1795.

Text at top reads: "How blest the Maid whose bosom no headstrong passion knows, Her days in Joy she Passes, her nights in soft repose."

Text at bottom reads: "Virtuous Woman is a Crown to her Husband."

"Keep Within Compass," engraving, c. 1795. Courtesy of Winterthur Museum, Garden & Library, Gift of Henry Francis du Pont, 1954.0093.001 A.

DOCUMENT 7

Source: Years States Eliminated Established Churches

Connecticut	1818
Delaware	never had established church
Georgia	1789
Maryland	1776
Massachusetts	1780
New Hampshire	1790
New Jersey	1776
New York	1777
North Carolina	1776
Pennsylvania	never had established church
Rhode Island	never had established church
South Carolina	1790
Virginia	1786

LONG ESSAY QUESTIONS *Suggested writing time: 40 minutes*

DIRECTIONS: Please choose one of the following three questions to answer. Make a historically defensible claim and support your reasoning with specific and relevant evidence.

2. Evaluate the extent to which the Seven Years' War fostered changes in the relationship between Great Britain and the North American colonies in the period from 1754–1783.
3. Evaluate the extent to which migration patterns fostered changes in American society in the period from 1776–1820.
4. Evaluate the extent to which the American Revolution fostered changes in the lives of women and African Americans in the period from 1775–1800.

4

PART

Overlapping Revolutions
1800–1848

Four transformations reshaped the United States in the early nineteenth century. One was economic: the rise of manufacturing and the growth of commercial agriculture — including the spectacular expansion of cotton — brought unprecedented economic growth. Another was political, as democratic participation expanded and mass-based parties arose. A third transformation was the emergence of new forms of evangelical Christianity, which inspired reform movements and utopian experiments that remade American culture and society. Finally, the United States aggressively expanded its geographical boundaries. Part 4 of *America's History* explains how these momentous changes happened and how closely they were intertwined.

We begin Part 4 in 1800 because at that time, important structural changes were beginning to reshape American life. They included new banking, credit, and transportation systems; invention of the cotton gin and the transformation of American slavery; innovations in government and politics; and new religious and cultural expressions. The Louisiana Purchase of 1803 also powerfully expanded the geographic scope of the United States and, in turn, widened American aspirations for expansion to the Pacific. We have chosen 1848 as a useful end point for this period because in that year the U.S.-Mexico War concluded, fulfilling many of those ambitions for continental conquest and expanded political and economic power.

Historians often call these decades the antebellum (prewar) era because, looking back, we know that soon afterward, in 1861, the Civil War began. But Americans at the time, of course, did not know a civil war was coming between North and South. On the contrary, many developments between 1800 and 1848 worked to unify northern and southern interests. Policymakers and entrepreneurs built canals and banks, expanded the reach of plantation slavery, opened textile factories in the North to process slave-grown cotton from the South, and sold northern products back to southern planters. By the 1830s this system created vast prosperity — and new inequalities. Radical abolitionists criticized the new economy for enabling "Lords of the Loom" and "Lords of the Lash" to build one vast cycle of exploitative enterprise. ▶

AP® CONCEPT CONNECTIONS

Why did economic innovations and territorial expansion trigger such dramatic growth?

Bettmann/Getty Images.

The economic revolution of the early 1800s rested on advances in technology, from the cotton gin to the steam-powered loom. It also relied on displacing native peoples through relentless acquisition of frontier lands. On the lands taken, Midwestern farmers specialized in growing products that could be shipped to an increasingly industrial Northeast.

In the South, the rise of the "cotton complex" vastly expanded slavery. It also sharpened class divisions among business and professional elites, planters, middle-class merchants, artisans, wageworkers, and the urban poor. At first, Americans hoped manufacturing would increase prosperity for all, but by the end of the period some desperate immigrants from Ireland, and others who could only access low-skill jobs, lived in shocking poverty. Like other transformations, the commercial revolution had unintended consequences.

Why did mass-based political parties and reform movements arise in this era?

Private Collection/Bridgeman Images.

Americans celebrated the expansion of political rights and the rise of mass parties, starting with Democrats under the charismatic leadership of Andrew Jackson. Jacksonian Democrats cut government aid to financiers, merchants, and corporations. Beginning in the 1830s, Democrats faced challenges from the Whigs, who devised a competing program stressing state-sponsored economic development, moral reform, and individual opportunity. The parties wrestled over such issues as Jackson's Indian Removal Act of 1830 and high protective tariffs on manufactured goods, the latter of which many farmers and planters opposed.

New democratic forms flourished in culture as well as politics. The expanding urban middle class created a distinct religious culture and an ideal of domesticity for women, as well as an array of reform movements, from temperance to abolitionism. Wage earners in the growing cities, including poor immigrants from Germany and Ireland, built their own vibrant popular culture. New England intellectuals launched the distinctly American movement of transcendentalism, while utopians founded cooperative experiments and religious communities such as those of the Shakers and Mormons.

Why did the United States double its territory between 1800 and 1848?

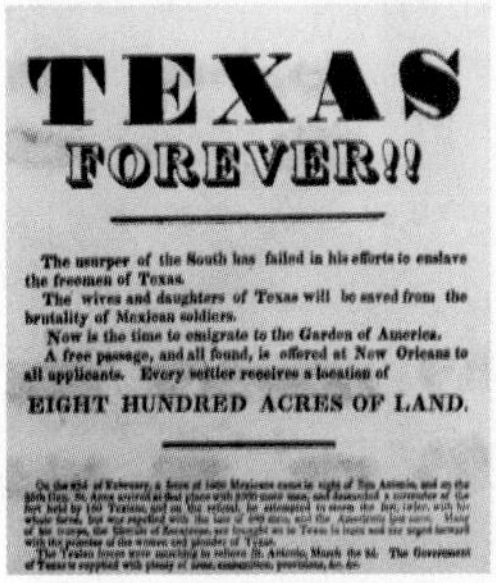

The Granger Collection, New York.

Territorial expansion was vast and violent. In the decades after the Louisiana Purchase, the United States continued to seize ancestral lands from Native peoples and forcibly push them westward. Moving into Texas at the invitation of Mexican authorities, who were struggling to populate Mexico's northern areas, southern cotton planters brought slavery and a desire for autonomy that soon triggered the Texas revolution for separation from Mexico. Other Americans, especially on the midwestern frontier, pushed for annexation of Oregon. In the decisive election of 1844, Democrat James K. Polk won election on promises to claim all of Oregon from the United States's chief rival — Britain — and to annex Texas even if that precipitated war with Mexico. Though the former conflict was arbitrated, the latter triggered a war in which the United States seized not only Texas but also California and the Southwest.

245

Organized around a single theme, the Part 4 Document Set in *Sources for America's History* can be used to teach the AP® Theme Geography and the Environment (GEO), which explores the role of environmental factors in shaping regional economic and political identities in the nineteenth century.

AP® THEMATIC UNDERSTANDING

Overlapping Revolutions, 1800–1848

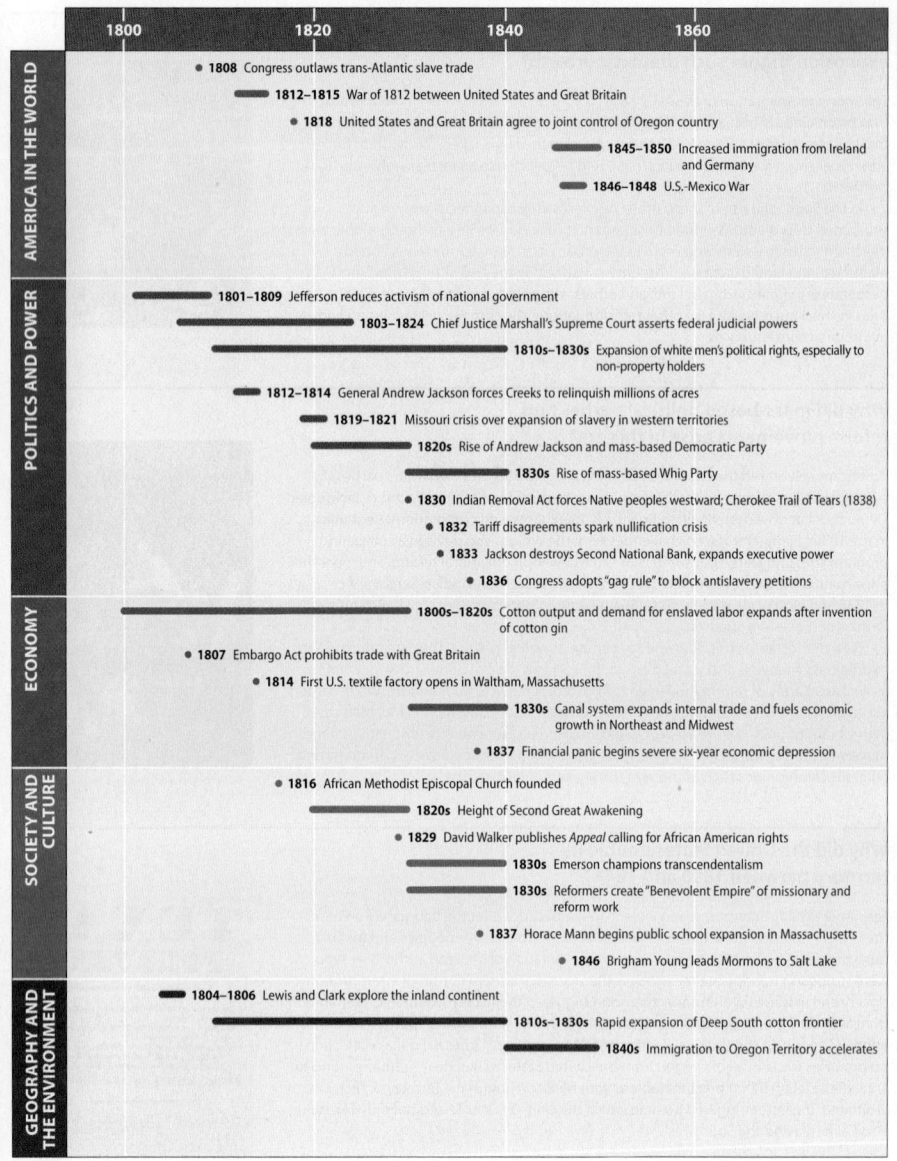

1800 | 1820 | 1840 | 1860

AMERICA IN THE WORLD

- **1808** Congress outlaws trans-Atlantic slave trade
- **1812–1815** War of 1812 between United States and Great Britain
- **1818** United States and Great Britain agree to joint control of Oregon country
- **1845–1850** Increased immigration from Ireland and Germany
- **1846–1848** U.S.-Mexico War

POLITICS AND POWER

- **1801–1809** Jefferson reduces activism of national government
- **1803–1824** Chief Justice Marshall's Supreme Court asserts federal judicial powers
- **1810s–1830s** Expansion of white men's political rights, especially to non-property holders
- **1812–1814** General Andrew Jackson forces Creeks to relinquish millions of acres
- **1819–1821** Missouri crisis over expansion of slavery in western territories
- **1820s** Rise of Andrew Jackson and mass-based Democratic Party
- **1830s** Rise of mass-based Whig Party
- **1830** Indian Removal Act forces Native peoples westward; Cherokee Trail of Tears (1838)
- **1832** Tariff disagreements spark nullification crisis
- **1833** Jackson destroys Second National Bank, expands executive power
- **1836** Congress adopts "gag rule" to block antislavery petitions

ECONOMY

- **1800s–1820s** Cotton output and demand for enslaved labor expands after invention of cotton gin
- **1807** Embargo Act prohibits trade with Great Britain
- **1814** First U.S. textile factory opens in Waltham, Massachusetts
- **1830s** Canal system expands internal trade and fuels economic growth in Northeast and Midwest
- **1837** Financial panic begins severe six-year economic depression

SOCIETY AND CULTURE

- **1816** African Methodist Episcopal Church founded
- **1820s** Height of Second Great Awakening
- **1829** David Walker publishes *Appeal* calling for African American rights
- **1830s** Emerson champions transcendentalism
- **1830s** Reformers create "Benevolent Empire" of missionary and reform work
- **1837** Horace Mann begins public school expansion in Massachusetts
- **1846** Brigham Young leads Mormons to Salt Lake

GEOGRAPHY AND THE ENVIRONMENT

- **1804–1806** Lewis and Clark explore the inland continent
- **1810s–1830s** Rapid expansion of Deep South cotton frontier
- **1840s** Immigration to Oregon Territory accelerates

AP Making Connections Across Chapters

Read these questions and think about them as you read the chapters in this part. Then when you have completed reading this part, return to these questions and answer them.

1 Many historians have celebrated the early nineteenth century as a period of new opportunities — economic, political, and social — for people outside the elite. To what extent was that true? Who benefitted from new opportunities, who did not, and why?

Cincinnati Art Museum, Ohio, USA/Gift of the Proctor & Gamble Company/ Bridgeman Images.

2 How and why did the United States expand geographically in these decades? What new territories and states joined the Union? In what ways did this influence political decisions in Washington, D.C.?

Library of Congress, LC-DIG ppmsca-09855.

3 How did Americans' ideals of family life change in this era, especially for wives and mothers but also for husbands and fathers, children, and young women before marriage? How did those ideals differ by region and by social and economic class, and what was their impact on politics and society?

The Granger Collection, New York.

4 Amid the dramatic economic changes of this era, what new religious and cultural movements arose? Which ones arose in tandem with economic change, and which arose in opposition to emerging forms of capitalism and labor organization?

The Metropolitan Museum of Art, Gilman Collection, Purchase, Mr. and Mrs. Henry R. Kravis Gift, 2005.

5 Andrew Jackson was such an influential president, and embodied so many key themes of his generation, that historians often call this period the "Jacksonian Era." Some use that name even though they take a negative view of Jackson's practices and policies. Do you agree that this should be called the "Jacksonian Era"? Why or why not? If not, what other name might you propose, to better capture the spirit of the age?

William L. Clements Library, University of Michigan.

TRM Find complete suggested responses in the Teacher's Resource Materials.

8 CHAPTER

Economic Transformations

1800–1848

Chapter 8 — AP® Assessment Weight and Pacing Guide

The assessment weight on the AP® U.S. History Exam for Chapters 8–11 is 10–17 percent. This chapter is part of Unit 4 of the AP® U.S. History Curriculum, covering Period 4: 1800–1848.

This pacing guide is based on a schedule with 120 sessions of 50 minutes each before the AP® U.S. History Exam. If you have a different number of sessions before the exam, you can modify the pacing to meet your needs. If you have additional time, consider incorporating quizzes, released AP® U.S. History questions, practice exams, writing practice, and other instructional activities.

	Traditional Schedule	Block Schedule
Chapter 8	3 days	1–2 days

Daily Pacing Guide

	Content Focus	Essential Question
Day 1	Foundations of a New Economic Order	What was the relationship between government support and private enterprise in economic development?
Day 2	The Cotton Complex: Northern Industry and Southern Agriculture and New Social Classes and Cultures	How were industrial development in the North and the expansion of cotton agriculture in the South connected? How was the structure of American society different in 1848 than it had been in 1800?
Day 3	Technological Innovation and Labor	How did technological innovation improve the lives of ordinary people, and what challenges did it present to them?

AP® Alignment

Section Heading	AP® Topic	AP® Theme
Foundations of a New Economic Order	4.2, 4.5, 4.6	PCE, WXT, SOC
The Cotton Complex: Northern Industry and Southern Agriculture	4.6, 4.12, 4.13	SOC, GEO
New Social Classes and Cultures	4.12, 4.13	SOC, GEO
Technological Innovation and Labor	4.5, 4.6, 4.9	WXT, SOC, ARC

*Should changes be made to the Course Framework in the future, an updated alignment will be placed on our AP® updates page at go.bfwpub.com/ap-course-updates.

Chapter 8 — Overview

Chapter 8 covers the economic development of the U.S. in the early nineteenth century and its impact on U.S. society. The chapter begins with a focus on the Market Revolution and its impact on credit, banking, and transportation that connected previously divergent regions of the U.S. The chapter examines the development of the Industrial Revolution and its connection to the growth of the dependence of the South on cotton production and slavery. In addition, this chapter focuses on technological innovations that spurred economic growth and the impact of all of these changes on the social class system in the U.S.

Chapter 8 — Resources

The following resources can be found in the Teacher's Resource Materials (TRM) that accompany the book. You can access the TRM via the book's digital platform, by clicking the TRM links found here in your Teacher's Edition e-book, or by contacting your representative to access the resources online. Visit **bfwpub.com/henretta10e** to learn more.

TRM Chapter 8 Lecture Presentation Slides

TRM Chapter 8 Outline with AP® Focus

TRM Chapter 8 Lecture Strategies

TRM Chapter 8 Suggested Responses

TRM Handout 8.1 — Causation: Innovations in the Early Nineteenth Century

TRM Handout 8.2 — Thematic Analysis: Cotton Kingdom

TRM Handout 8.3 — Causation: Early Nineteenth-Century Urbanization

Chapter 8 — Essential Activity

Provide students with a blank outline map of the U.S. in 1800 (with states). Ask students to label the Mississippi River, Rocky Mountains, Great Lakes, and Appalachian Mountains. Next, discuss with students the regions that existed in the early nineteenth century: North, South, and West. Discuss the changes that occurred in transitioning from colonial regions (New England, Middle, Southern). Discussion might possibly include the importance of slavery in defining regions and the importance of the westward movement of settlers. Guide students in labeling the North, South, and West on the map by showing the dividing line between North and South at Maryland and the dividing line for West at the Appalachian Mountains. Ask students to label the main economic activity of each region on their maps. *North — textiles/manufactured goods, South — cotton, West — food.* On the board, list the three major components of the American System: national bank, protective tariffs, and internal improvements. Ask students to illustrate with arrows on their maps the ways that these components would unify the nation into one market despite the regional differences. Lead a class discussion on the ways in which the economic policies of the American System supported the Market Revolution.

Chapter 8 — Bell Ringers

The following activities take no more than 5–15 minutes of your class period and offer an effective and engaging way to begin your lessons and for students to apply AP® Skills & Processes:

- Ask students: What is a market? *Possible answers could include "a place to buy and sell," "a place goods are exchanged," etc.* Then ask students to explain what the market is today for any good or service. What are the limits on markets today? Then have students explain the limits of markets in the early nineteenth century. Discuss the growth in markets by projecting maps that show markets in the early nineteenth century and how they expanded by 1848.
- Project an image of cotton and the cotton gin. Ask students to explain the function of the cotton gin and why it was necessary. *Cotton seeds are difficult to remove and took a great deal of labor — mostly slave labor — to remove. The cotton gin was a simple invention that removed seeds from cotton by forcing the cotton through prongs that resembles a comb. This sped up the cleaning of cotton, allowed for the greater production of cotton, and conversely caused a greater demand for slaves to plant, tend, and harvest cotton.*
- Project a blank social pyramid diagram. Ask students to label the pyramid with social classes in the U.S. today. As students discuss and debate current social classes, ask them to provide defining characteristics of each class. Use this activity to introduce discussion of social classes in the early nineteenth century.

NOTES

TEACHING STRATEGY

Help students understand the main themes of the chapter, namely the dramatic changes in the economy over a very short period of time that affected most Americans. Though "Market Revolution" is a somewhat contested term among historians, it captures the essence of the historical developments this chapter addresses. The term is first introduced on p. 256; however, the Chapter Summary (p. 280) conveys the scale of the changes implied by this revolution. It might make sense for students to read that section now to identify the most significant factors that constituted the Market Revolution and its major social consequences. For a complete model answer of the **AP® LEARNING FOCUS** question, see p. 280.

8 CHAPTER

Economic Transformations 1800–1848

AP® LEARNING FOCUS

Why and how did the economic transformations of the first half of the nineteenth century reshape northern and southern society and culture?

In 1804, life turned grim for eleven-year-old Chauncey Jerome. His father died suddenly, and Jerome became an indentured servant on a Connecticut farm. Quickly learning that few farmers "would treat a poor boy like a human being," Jerome bought out his indenture by making dials for clocks and then found a job with clockmaker Eli Terry. A manufacturing wizard, Terry used water power to drive precision saws and woodworking lathes. Soon his shop, and dozens of outworkers, were turning out thousands of tall clocks with wooden works. Then, in 1816, Terry patented an enormously popular desk clock with brass parts, an innovation that turned Waterbury, Connecticut, into the clockmaking center of the United States.

In 1822, Chauncey Jerome set up his own clock factory. By organizing work more efficiently and using new machines that stamped out interchangeable metal parts, he drove down the price of a simple clock from $20 to $5 and then to less than $2. By the 1840s, Jerome was selling his clocks in England, the hub of the Industrial Revolution; a decade later, his workers were turning out 400,000 clocks a year. By 1860, the United States was not only the world's leading exporter of cotton and wheat but also the third-ranked manufacturing nation behind Britain and France.

"Business is the very soul of an American: the fountain of all human felicity," author Francis Grund observed shortly after arriving from Europe. Stimulated by America's entrepreneurial culture, thousands of artisan-inventors like Chauncey Jerome propelled the country into the Industrial Revolution, a new system of production based on water and steam power and machine technology. To bring their products to market, they relied on important innovations in travel and communication. By 1848, northern entrepreneurs — and their southern counterparts who invested in cotton planting — had created a new economic order.

Not all Americans embraced the new business-dominated society, and many failed to share in the new prosperity. The increase in manufacturing, commerce, and finance created class divisions that challenged the founders' vision of an agricultural republic with few distinctions of wealth. As the philosopher Ralph Waldo Emerson warned in 1839: "The invasion of Nature by Trade with its Money, its Credit, its Steam, [and] its Railroad threatens to . . . establish a new, universal Monarchy."

248

South Street, New York City, 1827 The revolution in economic productivity that came to the United States in the first several decades of the nineteenth century is captured in the bustle of commercial activity on South Street along the New York City wharf. Laborers guide horse-drawn sledges, hoist heavy loads, or stop to chat while merchants oversee their efforts. The human figures in this 1827 watercolor, painted by British immigrant William James Bennett, are dwarfed by the forest of masts rising from the ships in the harbor, testimony to the commercial power and vitality of America's greatest port city. The Metropolitan Museum of Art, The Edward W. C. Arnold Collection of New York Prints, Maps, and Pictures, Bequest of Edward W. C. Arnold, 1954.

TEACHING STRATEGY

This painting presents an opportunity for students to examine the Market Revolution. Even though this painting is at the beginning of the chapter, think about carving time out of your schedule at the end of the chapter to examine how this painting, explicitly and implicitly, illustrates many concepts related to the Market Revolution. You could ask students to connect any one of the following issues to the painting: regionalism, merchants, international trade, interregional trade, technological advancements, and urbanization. The goal is for students to connect what they have learned in a more abstract manner.

AP® SKILLS & PROCESSES

CONTINUITY AND CHANGE

Use the **TIMELINE** to explore how 1790 to 1842 is a distinct era based on the major economic developments and their social consequences during this time. Some students may think of the development of a capitalist economy as largely a matter of private businesses. As they skim the events on the timeline, they could note evidence that actions by the federal government shaped the economy in this era: abolition of the slave trade, protective tariffs, and Supreme Court decisions protecting trade. Extend this discussion by asking students to explain what "transformations" characterized the era based on the timeline.

TIMELINE

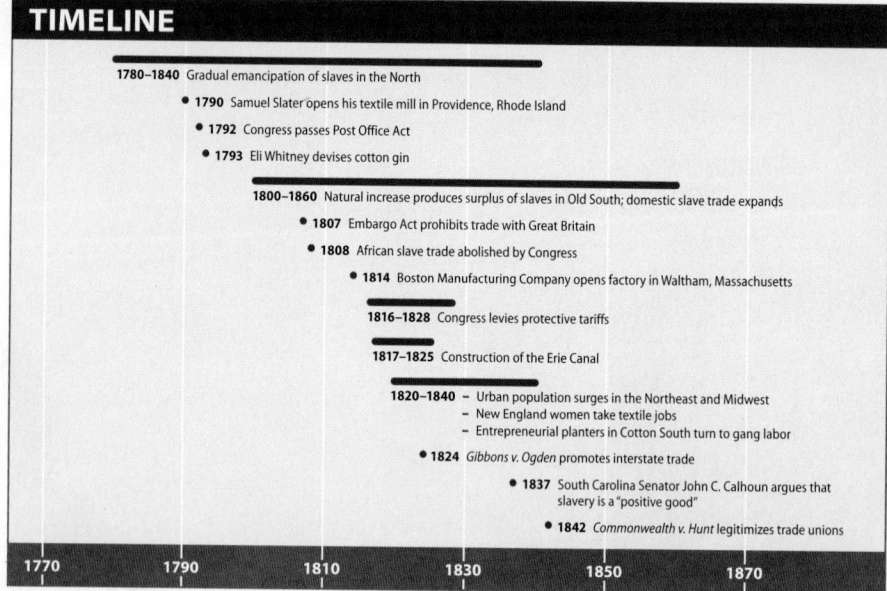

- **1780–1840** Gradual emancipation of slaves in the North
- **1790** Samuel Slater opens his textile mill in Providence, Rhode Island
- **1792** Congress passes Post Office Act
- **1793** Eli Whitney devises cotton gin
- **1800–1860** Natural increase produces surplus of slaves in Old South; domestic slave trade expands
- **1807** Embargo Act prohibits trade with Great Britain
- **1808** African slave trade abolished by Congress
- **1814** Boston Manufacturing Company opens factory in Waltham, Massachusetts
- **1816–1828** Congress levies protective tariffs
- **1817–1825** Construction of the Erie Canal
- **1820–1840**
  - Urban population surges in the Northeast and Midwest
  - New England women take textile jobs
  - Entrepreneurial planters in Cotton South turn to gang labor
- **1824** *Gibbons v. Ogden* promotes interstate trade
- **1837** South Carolina Senator John C. Calhoun argues that slavery is a "positive good"
- **1842** *Commonwealth v. Hunt* legitimizes trade unions

1770 1790 1810 1830 1850 1870

FOUNDATIONS OF A NEW ECONOMIC ORDER

What was the relationship between government support and private enterprise in economic development?

AP® EXAM TIP

As you read through this section, take notes on the degree to which the elite, middle class, and laboring poor benefited from economic change in the early nineteenth century.

neomercantilism
A system of government-assisted economic development embraced by state legislatures in the first half of the nineteenth century, especially in the Northeast. This system of activist government encouraged entrepreneurs to enhance the public welfare through private economic initiatives.

The emerging economic order was based on core principles grounded in the ideals of republicanism, a political philosophy that valued representative government and sought to implement "commonwealth" principles, in which government assisted private businesses in advancing economic development. Private property, market exchange, and individual opportunity were widely shared values, and throughout the nation, activist state governments pursued **neomercantilist** policies to help achieve them. New systems of banking and credit, often supported by state charters, increased the money supply and made capital more widely available to American entrepreneurs. State legislatures also issued charters to turnpike and canal companies, whose new roads and waterways reduced the cost of transportation and stimulated economic activity. As a result, beginning around 1800 the average per capita income of Americans increased by more than 1 percent a year — more than 30 percent in a single generation.

Credit and Banking

America was "a Nation of Merchants," a British visitor reported from Philadelphia in 1798, "keen in the pursuit of wealth in all the various modes of acquiring it." Acquire it they did, making spectacular profits as the wars of the French Revolution and Napoleon (1793–1815) crippled European firms. Merchants John Jacob Astor and Robert Oliver became the nation's first millionaires. After working for an Irish-owned linen firm in Baltimore, Oliver struck out on his own, achieving affluence by trading West Indian sugar and coffee. Astor, who migrated from Germany to New York in

The China Trade Following the Revolution, New England merchants traded actively with the major Asian manufacturing centers of China and India. In Canton (modern Guangzhou), merchants exchanged bundles of American furs for cargoes of Chinese teas, silks, and porcelain plates, cups, and serving dishes. In this image of a Canton tea warehouse, painted in a Chinese studio, laborers haul, sort, and pack tea for shipping while, in the foreground, an American merchant negotiates his purchase. akg-images/Pictures From History.

1784, began by selling dry-goods and became wealthy carrying furs from the Pacific Northwest to China and investing in New York City real estate (see "Thinking Like a Historian," p. 252).

To finance their ventures, Oliver, Astor, and other merchants needed capital, from either their own savings or loans. Before the American Revolution, colonial merchants often relied on credit from British suppliers. In 1781, the Confederation Congress chartered the Bank of North America in Philadelphia, and traders in Boston and New York soon founded similar institutions to raise and loan money. "Our monied capital has so much increased from the Introduction of Banks, & the Circulation of the Funds," Philadelphia merchant William Bingham boasted in 1791, "that the Necessity of Soliciting Credits from England will no longer exist."

That same year, Federalists in Congress chartered the Bank of the United States (see "Creating a National Bank" in Chapter 7). By 1805, the bank had branches in eight seaport cities, profits that averaged a handsome 8 percent annually, and clients with easy access to capital. As trader Jesse Atwater noted, "the foundations of our [merchant] houses are laid in bank paper."

But Jeffersonians attacked the bank as an unconstitutional expansion of federal power "supported by public creditors, speculators, and other insidious men." When the bank's charter expired in 1811, the Jeffersonian Republican–dominated Congress refused to renew it. Merchants, artisans, and farmers quickly persuaded state legislatures to charter banks — in Pennsylvania, no fewer than forty-one. By 1816, when Congress (now run by National Republicans) chartered a new national bank (the Second Bank of the United States), there were 246 state-chartered banks with tens of thousands of stockholders and $68 million in banknotes in circulation. These state banks were often shady operations that issued notes without adequate specie reserves, made loans to insiders, and lent generously to farmers buying overpriced land.

AP® EXAM TIP

It's important to recall the federal and state laws that supported the growth of markets, the transportation network, and tariffs.

TEACHING STRATEGY

Soon after the Revolution, the United States was, in many ways, seeking to further its economic strength by engaging in international trade. Inasmuch as this was the result of creating a nation independent of Great Britain, it also aligned with Hamilton's goal of having the United States be a global economic leader, and trading with Asian countries furthered that desire. The Gilder Lehrman Institute provides a helpful historical essay on America's early China trade. Access this essay by searching "Gilder Lehrman Institute America and China Trade."

AP® APPLY THE TIP

To help students understand the importance of both state and federal support of economic growth in the early nineteenth century, prompt students to identify specific ways that the federal and state governments supported the building of transportation networks and the banking system. Students should identify the charter of the Second Bank of the U.S., charters to state banks, the postal system, and charters for turnpikes and canals, such as the Erie Canal, etc. Then have students think about the way in which these federal and state initiatives worked together to generate economic growth and ask them to explain the role of a protective tariff in this system. Students should identify that the tariffs insured domestic manufacturers that they would have a domestic market by limiting foreign competition.

AP® SKILLS & PROCESSES

ANALYZING HISTORICAL EVIDENCE

The **AP® THINKING LIKE A HISTORIAN** feature helps students understand the tension between perception and reality. The introduction of a vibrant capitalist economy in the Market Revolution introduced millions of Americans to the notion that anyone could get ahead through honest hard work. Jacob Astor provides a case study to consider how accurate that popular perception was in the early nineteenth century.

AP® THINKING LIKE A HISTORIAN

The Entrepreneur and the Community

Americans of the early republic believed that with hard work and virtue, even the lowliest of white men might rise to economic and political respectability, if not prominence. In the Revolutionary generation, Benjamin Franklin, born into a large and impoverished Boston family, had become a successful businessman and an international celebrity. Franklin's success reflected the optimism that laboring men felt when contemplating the new nation's seemingly boundless opportunity.

1. **Banner of the Society of Pewterers of the City of New York, carried in the Federal Procession, July 23, 1788, celebrating the ratification of the U.S. Constitution.** *The ribbon at top right reads "The Federal Plan Most Solid & Secure/Americans Their Freedom Will Endure/All Art Shall Flourish in Columbia's Land/And All her Sons Join as One Social Band."*

SOURCE: © Collection of the New-York Historical Society, USA/Bridgeman Images.

2. **John Jacob Astor quoted in Elbert Hubbard, *Little Journeys to the Homes of Great Business Men*, 1909.** *John Jacob Astor's (1763–1848) story is a parable of American entrepreneurial triumph. Arriving in America in 1783 from Germany, Astor worked in the fur industry treating pelts and, with capital borrowed from his brother, started up a musical instrument shop and fur business in 1786. Over the next three decades, Astor's American Fur Company prospered by trading furs in China, making Astor America's first millionaire. Apparently influenced by Benjamin Franklin's aphorism "Early to bed and early to rise, makes a man healthy wealthy and wise," Astor wrote:*

The man who makes it the habit of his life to go to bed at nine o'clock, usually gets rich and is always reliable. Of course, going to bed does not make him rich — I merely mean that such a man will in all probability be up early in the morning and do a big day's work . . . good habits in America make any man rich.

3. **Anonymous, "A Working Man's Recollections of America," *Knight's Penny Magazine*, 1846.** *A cabinetmaker penned this account after returning to England following an unsuccessful stint seeking success in New York.*

I was a cabinet-maker by trade, and one of the many who, between the years 1825–35, expatriated themselves in countless thousands, drawn by the promise of fair wages for faithful work, and driven by the scanty remuneration offered to unceasing toil at home. . . . On landing in New York I made up my mind to lose none of the advantages it uttered by want of diligence on my part. During the first two years I took but one holiday. . . . In summer we began work at six; at eight took half an hour for breakfast, and then worked till twelve, when one an hour for dinner; after which we kept on till six, seven, or eight. . . . A relative who arrived from England held out to me bright prospects of advantages to be realized by the employment of a little capital, combined with a

Panic of 1819
First major economic crisis of the United States. Farmers and planters faced an abrupt 30 percent drop in world agricultural prices, and as farmers' income declined, they could not pay debts owed to stores and banks, many of which went bankrupt.

AP® SKILLS & PROCESSES
CAUSATION
What effects did banks have on American economic development?

Bad banking policies helped bring on the **Panic of 1819** (just as they caused the financial crisis of 2008), but broader forces were equally important. As the Napoleonic Wars ended in 1815, American imports of English woolen and cotton goods spiked and demand for U.S.-produced cloth plummeted. Then, in 1818, farmers and planters faced an abrupt 30 percent drop in world agricultural prices. As farmers' income declined, they could not pay debts owed to stores and banks, many of which went bankrupt. "A deep shadow has passed over our land," lamented one New Yorker, as land prices dropped by 50 percent. The panic gave Americans their first taste of a business cycle, the periodic boom and bust inherent to a modern market economy.

AP® SKILLS & PROCESSES

CAUSATION

There are many possible answers to the question regarding the effects banks have on economic development. Therefore, give students a parameter for their answers such as 1794–1819.

TRM Find complete suggested responses in the Teacher's Resource Materials.

CHECK FOR UNDERSTANDING

Ask students: **What role did credit and banking play in the early 1800s?** *Merchants relied on state banks and the Bank of the United States for capital to expand their businesses. Without such credit, the growth of businesses would not have been possible in this era. Bad banking policies, however, helped lead to the Panic of 1819.*

removal to some inland town. I sold off nearly the whole of our moveables . . . [and committed all my savings to this enterprise. However,] our scheme . . . completely failed, and I had no resources but my industry and chest of tools to meet the impending difficulties.

4. **Diary entry by Philip Hone, March 29, 1848.** *Philip Hone (1780–1851), a conservative Whig, was a successful merchant and entrepreneur and mayor of New York City from 1826 to 1827. Hone's marvelous diary (1828–1851) records the changing character of New York City, as well as his contempt for Jacksonian Democracy and its Irish immigrant supporters.*

   John Jacob Astor died this morning, at nine o'clock, in the eighty-fifth year of his age . . . and left reluctantly his unbounded wealth. His property is estimated at $20,000,000, some judicious persons say $30,000,000; but, at any rate, he was the richest man in the United States in productive and valuable property; and this immense, gigantic fortune was the fruit of his own labor, unerring sagacity, and far-seeing penetration. He came to this country at twenty years of age; penniless, friendless, without inheritance, without education . . . but with a determination to be rich, and ability to carry it into effect. His capital consisted of a few trifling musical instruments, which he got from his brother, George Astor, in London, a dealer in music. . . . The fur trade was the philosopher's stone of this modern Croesus; beaver-skins and musk-rats furnished the oil for the supply of Aladdin's lamp. His traffic was the shipment of furs to China, where they brought immense prices, for he monopolized the business; and the return cargoes of teas, silks, and rich productions of China brought further large profits. . . . My brother and I found in Mr. Astor a valuable customer. . . . All he touched turned to gold.

5. **Editorial in the *New York Herald*, April 5, 1848.** *John Jacob Astor's will included a bequest of $400,000 for the establishment of what became the New York Public Library. This editorial questioned whether this relatively meager bequest adequately repaid residents.*

   If we had been an associate of John Jacob Astor the first idea that we should have put into his head would have been that one-half of his immense property—ten million at least—belonged to the people of the city of New York. During the last fifty years of the life of John Jacob Astor, his property has been augmented and increased in the value by the aggregate intelligence, industry, enterprise and commerce of New York, fully to the amount of one-half its value. The farms and lots of ground which he bought forty, twenty and ten and five years ago, have all increased in value entirely by the industry of the citizens of New York . . . half of his immense estate, in its actual value, has accrued to him by the industry of the community.

SOURCES: (2) Elbert Hubbard, *Little Journeys to the Homes of Great Business Men* (New York: Wm. H. Wise & Co., 1916), 201; (3) *Knight's Penny Magazine*, Vol. 1 (London: Charles Knight & Co., 1846), 97, 107, 108; (4) Philip Hone, *The Diary of Philip Hone, 1828–1851*, Vol. 2 (New York: Dodd, Mead and Company, 1889), 347–348; (5) Gustavus Myers, *History of the Great American Fortunes*, Vol. 1 (Chicago: Charles H. Kerr & Company, 1910), 199–200.

ANALYZING THE EVIDENCE

1. What does the Pewterers' Banner (source 1) suggest about personal and by extension national identity in the post-Revolutionary era? Use evidence from the image to describe the values portrayed.
2. According to John Jacob Astor (source 2) and the cabinetmaker (source 3), what traits are important in work? Corroborate the source messages.
3. Sources 2, 4, and 5 all deal with John Jacob Astor. What do these sources suggest about the road to wealth in America, and in what ways can do they account for the development of national identity?
4. Compare and contrast Hone's view of Astor (source 4) with that of the *Herald*'s editorial (source 5). Use historical reasoning to compare the sources.

AP® DBQ PRACTICE

As these sources indicate, Americans had a divided view of the place of wealth in their society. For many, the opportunity to reap the benefits of hard work was essential to American liberty, and the wealth of John Jacob Astor was his just reward. Others, in keeping with older, republican values, believed that Astor's great wealth came at the expense of others, and that the fortunes of the individual and the community should rise together. Considering these sources and what you have learned in Chapter 8, write an essay that explores this tension in American economic ideals.

Transportation and the Market Revolution

Economic expansion also depended on improvements in transportation, where governments once again played a crucial role. As with bank charters, legislative charters for turnpikes and canal companies reflected the ideology of mercantilism—government-assisted economic development. Just as Parliament had used the Navigation Acts to spur British prosperity, so American legislatures enacted laws "of great public utility" to increase the "common wealth." Following Jefferson's embargo of 1807, which cut off goods and credit from Europe, the New England states awarded charters to two hundred iron-mining, textile-manufacturing, and banking

AP® EXAM TIP

Differentiating the impact of the Market Revolution on the North, West, and South is essential for success on the AP® Exam.

253

AP® THEME

SOC: Social Structures

The **AP® THINKING LIKE A HISTORIAN** feature explores the way that the Market Revolution led to increased social mobility with the emergence of a large middle class and a small, wealthy business elite.

TRM Find complete suggested responses in the Teacher's Resource Materials.

AP® APPLY THE TIP

Ask students to work with a partner to answer the following questions:

- **Based on the maps and images, which region or regions of the U.S. benefitted the most from the American System?** *The North and West benefitted the most because the majority of roads, railroads, and canals were constructed to connect those regions and the trading and manufacturing centers were within these regions. Fewer railroads, roads, and canals were built in the South because of its more extensive, natural system of rivers and streams, which allowed for transportation within the region and to coastal ports as well as a system of plantations that did not encourage the development of manufacturing centers.*
- **Why were state governments in the North more willing to sponsor canal and railroad building than states in the South?** *State governments in the North saw the investments as directly related to their interest in developing a more industrial economy and supporting the growth of textiles and manufacturing.*
- **How did the protective tariffs impact the economy of the North? The economy of the South?** *The economy of the North benefitted from protective tariffs that allowed them to compete with British manufactured goods; the economy of the South was negatively impacted as the tariffs led to higher consumer prices and Southern planters faced paying tariffs to ship cotton to the British or other European states.*
- **In what way did the economic changes generate a new conflict between state and federal power?** *Southern leaders argued that the construction of internal improvements should be a state power while Northern leaders tended to support the use of federal power and tax dollars to support internal improvements.*

Finally, ask students to write a thesis statement and outline that compares the goals and the effects of the American System and Hamilton's financial plan.

Commonwealth System
The republican system of political economy implemented by state governments in the early nineteenth century that funneled aid to private businesses whose projects would improve the general welfare.

companies, while Pennsylvania granted more than eleven hundred. By 1820, state governments had created a republican political economy: a **Commonwealth System** that funneled state aid to private businesses whose projects would improve the general welfare.

Transportation projects were among the greatest beneficiaries of the Commonwealth System. Between 1793 and 1812, for example, the Massachusetts legislature granted charters to more than one hundred private turnpike corporations. These charters gave the companies special legal status and often included monopoly rights to a transportation route. Pennsylvania issued fifty-five charters, including one to the Lancaster Turnpike Company, which built a 65-mile graded and graveled toll road to Philadelphia. The road quickly boosted the regional economy. A farm woman noted, "The turnpike is finished and we can now go to town at all times and in all weather." New turnpikes soon connected dozens of inland market centers to seaport cities. Westward migration beyond the seaboard states created a rapidly growing demand for new transportation routes.

The vital precondition for westward migration was the dispossession of Native American peoples. In the War of 1812, the United States defeated the confederation of Great Lakes and Ohio Indians led by Tecumseh and Tenskwatawa and claimed their lands, along with 23 million acres ceded by the Creeks after the Battle of Horseshoe Bend. Subsequent treaties with the Creeks, Cherokees, Chickasaws, and Choctaws in the South and with the Miamis, Ottawas, Sauks, Fox, and other nations in the North brought millions more acres into the public domain. (See Map 7.2, p. 224.)

For farmers, artisans, and merchants to capitalize on these new lands, however, they needed access to transportation routes. Farmers in Kentucky, Tennessee, southern Ohio, Indiana, and Illinois settled near the Ohio River and its many tributaries, so they could easily get goods to market. Similarly, speculators hoping to capitalize on the expansion of commerce bought up property in the cities along the banks of major rivers: Cincinnati, Louisville, Chattanooga, and St. Louis. Farmers and merchants built barges to carry cotton, grain, and meat downstream to New Orleans, which by 1815 was exporting about $5 million in agricultural products yearly.

But natural waterways were not enough, by themselves, to connect East and West. To link westward migrants to the seaboard states, Congress approved funds for a National Road constructed of compacted gravel. The project began in 1811 at Cumberland in western Maryland, at the head of navigation of the Potomac River; reached Wheeling, Virginia (now West Virginia), on the Ohio River in 1818; and ended in Vandalia, Illinois, in 1839. As migrants traveled west on the National Road and other interregional highways, they passed livestock herds heading in the opposite direction, destined for eastern markets.

Shrinking Space: Canals Even on well-built gravel roads, overland travel was slow and expensive. As U.S. territory expanded and artisans, farmers, and manufacturers produced an ever-expanding array of goods, legislators and businessmen created faster and cheaper ways to get those products to consumers. To carry people, crops, and manufactures to and from the great Mississippi River basin, public money and private businesses developed a water-borne transportation system of unprecedented size, complexity, and cost. State governments and private entrepreneurs dredged shallow rivers and constructed canals to bypass waterfalls and rapids. Around 1820, they began constructing a massive system of canals and roads linking states along the Atlantic coast with new states in the trans-Appalachian west.

This transportation system set in motion a mass migration of people to the Greater Mississippi River basin. This huge area, drained by six river systems (the Missouri, Arkansas, Red, Ohio, Tennessee, and Mississippi), contains the largest and most productive contiguous acreage of arable land in the world. By 1860, nearly one-third of the nation's citizens lived in eight of its states — the "Midwest," consisting of the five states carved out of the Northwest Territory (Ohio, Indiana, Illinois, Michigan,

AP® THEME

WXT: Work, Exchange, and Technology
Students should be aware that social structures of American citizens changed over time in concert with new realities for American Indians. Have students explain how social structures of Americans changed as a result of expansion while American Indians also changed as a result of expansion. In their response, students should delineate who was migrating westward and how that may relate to social structures.

TEACHING STRATEGY

The National Park Service's Web site on the Chesapeake & Ohio Canal includes links to a wealth of historical materials under its "Learn About the Park" tab that you can use to help students understand the mechanics of a canal and its use. In addition to images and photos, there are a number of detailed historical studies of various canal structures, including towpaths, locks, and bridges. The site also provides links to other primary sources and short videos with historical reenactments and CGI illustrations that explain the mechanics of canals, locks, and the use of mules. Access the site by searching "NPS Chesapeake Ohio Canal."

View of the Erie Canal This pastoral view of the Erie Canal near Lockport, New York, painted by artist John William Hill, hints at this waterway's profound impact on American life. Without the canal, the town in the background would not exist and farmers such as the man in the foreground would not have a regional market for their cattle and grain. The success of the Erie Canal had led to the construction of a vast system of canals by 1860. This infrastructure was as important to the nation as the railroad network of the late nineteenth century and the interstate highway and airport transportation systems of the late twentieth century. Bettmann/Getty Images.

and Wisconsin) along with Missouri, Iowa, and Minnesota. There they created a rich agricultural economy and an industrializing society.

The key event was the New York legislature's 1817 financing of the **Erie Canal**, a 364-mile waterway connecting the Hudson River and Lake Erie. Previously, the longest canal in the United States was just 28 miles long — reflecting the huge capital cost of canals and the lack of American engineering expertise. New York's ambitious project had three things working in its favor: the vigorous support of New York City's merchants, who wanted access to western markets; the backing of New York's governor, De Witt Clinton, who proposed to finance the waterway from tax revenues, tolls, and bond sales to foreign investors; and the relatively gentle terrain west of Albany. Even so, the task was enormous. Workers — many of them Irish immigrants — dug out millions of cubic yards of soil, quarried thousands of tons of rock for the huge locks that raised and lowered the boats, and constructed vast reservoirs to ensure a steady supply of water.

Erie Canal
A 364-mile waterway connecting the Hudson River and Lake Erie. The Erie Canal brought prosperity to the entire Great Lakes region, and its benefits prompted civic and business leaders in Philadelphia and Baltimore to propose canals to link their cities to the Midwest.

The first great engineering project in American history, the Erie Canal altered the ecology of an entire region. As farming communities and market towns sprang up along the waterway, settlers cut down millions of trees to provide wood for houses and barns and to open the land for growing crops and grazing animals. Cows and sheep foraged in pastures that had recently been forests occupied by deer and bears, and spring rains caused massive erosion of the denuded landscape.

AP® EXAM TIP
Recognizing the role of innovations on increased efficiency is important to know on the AP® Exam.

Whatever its environmental consequences, the Erie Canal was an instant economic success. The first 75-mile section opened in 1819 and quickly yielded enough revenue to repay its construction cost. When workers finished the canal in 1825, a 40-foot-wide ribbon of water stretched from Buffalo, on the eastern shore of Lake Erie, to Albany, where it joined the Hudson River for the 150-mile trip to New York City. The canal's water "must be the most fertilizing of all fluids," suggested novelist

AP® THEME

WXT: Work, Exchange, and Technology

This illustration of the Erie Canal conveys the way that labor changed in the Market Revolution, as increasing numbers of Americans shifted from reliance on subsistence agriculture to supporting themselves by producing goods for distant markets. Students may not know that a "pastoral" scene usually depicts rural life as pure and simple, in contrast to urban life. Ask students: **What elements of the image depict the presence of the market and make the pastoralism seem ironic or misleading?** *The waterway that dominates the picture was an artificial "road" created by a huge labor force paid for by the state of New York. The town, as the caption notes, only exists because of the canal. The products on the boat are doubtless going to market, as are the other animals that appear in the picture.*

TEACHING STRATEGY

Episode 1 of PBS's *New York: A Documentary Film* includes a short segment on the political, engineering, and labor efforts involved in surveying the route, hiring labor, clearing the land, and digging the Erie Canal. Access the film by searching "PBS New York: A Documentary Film."

AP® APPLY THE TIP

Ask students to work in pairs and consider the cause and effect relationships of each event listed on **Handout 8.1 — Causation: Innovations in the Early Nineteenth Century (TRM).** Ask students to focus on the ways that the innovations caused change in American society and led to conflict between regions. Then lead a class discussion addressing the ways innovations brought more attention to regional divides in the U.S. and how the changes associated with the Industrial Revolution and the cotton complex had a dramatic impact on women and workers.

TRM Find **Handout 8.1 — Causation: Innovations in the Early Nineteenth Century** in the Teacher's Resource Materials.

Nathaniel Hawthorne, "for it causes towns with their masses of brick and stone, their churches and theaters, their business and hubbub, their luxury and refinement, their gay dames and polished citizens, to spring up."

The Erie Canal brought prosperity to the farmers of central and western New York and the entire Great Lakes region. Why did the canal have such an immense impact? It allowed northeastern manufacturers to ship clothing, boots, and agricultural equipment to farm families; in return, farmers sent grain, cattle, hogs, and raw materials (leather, wool, and hemp, for example) to eastern cities and foreign markets. Two horses pulling a wagon overland could tow 4 tons of freight; now, those same two horses working the towpaths of the Erie Canal could pull 100-ton freight barges at a steady 30 miles a day, cutting transportation costs and accelerating the flow of goods. In 1818, the mills in Rochester, New York, processed 26,000 barrels of flour for export. Ten years later their output soared to 200,000 barrels, and by 1840 it was at 500,000 barrels.

The spectacular benefits of the Erie Canal prompted a national canal boom. Civic and business leaders in Philadelphia and Baltimore proposed waterways to link their cities to the Midwest. Copying New York's fiscal innovations, they persuaded their state legislatures to invest directly in canal companies or to force state-chartered banks to do so, and to offer guarantees that encouraged British and Dutch investors. Soon, artificial waterways connected Philadelphia and Baltimore, via the Pennsylvania Canal and the Chesapeake and Ohio Canal, to the Great Lakes region. The Michigan and Illinois Canal (finished in 1848), which linked Chicago to the Mississippi River, completed an inland all-water route from New York City to New Orleans, the two most important port cities in North America (Map 8.1). Historians have labeled the economic boom resulting from these new banking and transportation systems the **Market Revolution**. Americans had greater access to capital, more financial liquidity, and more opportunities to buy and sell products over long distances, than they had ever had before.

Market Revolution
The dramatic increase between 1820 and 1850 in the exchange of goods and services in market transactions. The Market Revolution reflected the increased output of farms and factories, the entrepreneurial activities of traders and merchants, and the creation of a transportation network of roads, canals, and railroads.

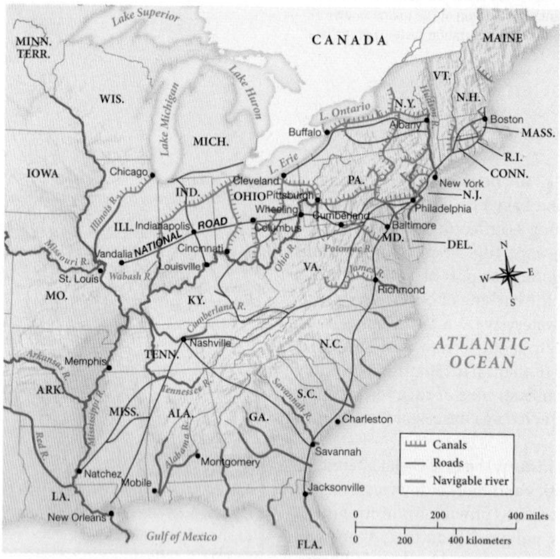

MAP 8.1 The Transportation Revolution: Roads and Canals, 1820–1850
By 1850, the United States had an efficient system of water-borne transportation with three distinct parts. Short canals and navigable rivers carried cotton, tobacco, and other products from the countryside of the southern seaboard states into the Atlantic commercial system. A second system, centered on the Erie, Chesapeake and Ohio, and Pennsylvania Mainline canals, linked northeastern seaports to the vast trans-Appalachian region. Finally, a set of regional canals in the Midwest connected most of the Great Lakes region to the Ohio and Mississippi rivers and the port of New Orleans.

Shrinking Space: Steamboats The steamboat, another product of the industrial age, added crucial flexibility to the Mississippi basin's river-based transportation system. In 1807, engineer-inventor Robert Fulton piloted the first American steamboat, the *Clermont*, up the Hudson River. To navigate shallow western rivers, engineers broadened steamboats' hulls to reduce their draft and enlarge their cargo capacity. These vessels halved the cost of upstream river transport and dramatically increased the flow of goods, people, and news. In 1830, a traveler or a letter from New York could reach Buffalo or Pittsburgh by water in less than a week and Detroit, Chicago, or St. Louis in two weeks. In 1800, the same journeys had taken twice as long.

Aspiring slaveholders from the Upper South — Kentucky, Tennessee, and Virginia — settled in Missouri (admitted to the Union in 1821) and pushed on to Arkansas (admitted in 1836). Simultaneously, nonslaveholding

AP® THEME

PCE: Politics and Power; WXT: Work, Exchange, and Technology

Use **MAP 8.1** to illustrate the ways that a transportation infrastructure developed in a very short time with strong financial support from individual states. While the map conveys a tremendous amount of information about the extent of the transportation network, it also has significant limitations. Guide students' analysis with the following questions:

- **How much time did it take this infrastructure to be built?** *Roughly thirty years, from 1820 to 1850.*
- **Roughly how many miles does the transportation network extend North to South? East to West?** *At least one thousand miles in both directions, if navigable rivers are included.*
- **What patterns do you notice?** *Canals are chiefly in the North. Navigable rivers basically consist of the Mississippi and its tributaries (especially the Missouri and Ohio) and coastal rivers in the South.*
- **Where does the network seem densest? Least dense?** *The Northeast and Northwest are both dense, and the South is much less connected to the rest of the country.*
- **What important points about the development of infrastructure does the map fail to convey?** *The labor and financing it took to build, the conquest of Native American lands involved, the physical barriers that builders encountered, and the development of steamboats that made two-way traffic on the Mississippi possible.*

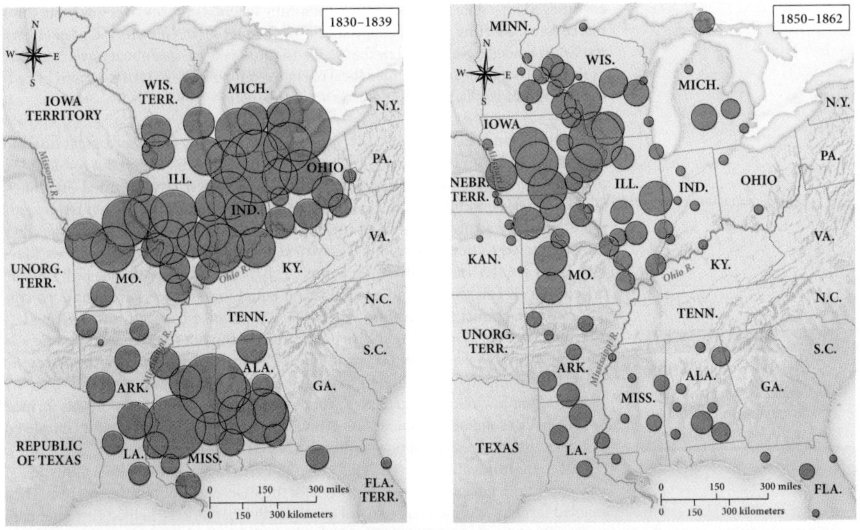

MAPPING THE PAST

MAP 8.2 Western Land Sales, 1830–1839 and 1850–1862
The federal government set up local offices to sell land in the national domain to settlers. During the 1830s, the offices sold huge amounts of land in the corn and wheat belt of the Midwest (Ohio, Indiana, Illinois, and Michigan) and the cotton belt to the south (especially Alabama and Mississippi). As settlers moved westward in the 1850s, most sales were in the Upper Mississippi River Valley (particularly Iowa and Wisconsin). Each circle indicates the relative amount of land sold at a local office.

ANALYZING THE MAP: How do sales in the North compare to sales in the South for 1830–1839? How do they compare for 1850–1862? How can the changes illustrated in these maps be related to innovations such as the cotton gin? How can the changes be related to U.S. policies towards Native American nations?

MAKING CONNECTIONS: Compare the pattern of land sales represented in these maps with the network of roads, canals, and rivers illustrated in Map 8.1. What is the relationship between land sales and transportation routes?

families from those same states joined migrants from New England and New York in farming the fertile lands near the Great Lakes. Once Indiana and Illinois were settled, American-born farmers poured into Michigan (1837), Iowa (1846), and Wisconsin (1848) — where they resided among tens of thousands of hardworking immigrants from Germany. To meet the demand for cheap farmsteads, Congress in 1820 reduced the price of federal land from $2.00 an acre to $1.25. For $100, a farmer could buy 80 acres, the minimum required under federal law. By the 1840s, this generous policy had enticed about 5 million people to states and territories west of the Appalachians (Map 8.2).

While state legislatures subsidized canals, the national government created a vast postal system, the first network for the exchange of information. Thanks to the Post Office Act of 1792, there were more than eight thousand post offices by 1830, and the postal service had more employees than all the rest of the government's civilian employees combined. They safely delivered thousands of letters and banknotes worth millions of dollars, along with newspapers that carried information from the Atlantic seaboard to the Mississippi basin. The U.S. Supreme Court, headed by John Marshall, likewise

AP® THEME

MIG: Migration and Settlement; PCE: Politics and Power

MAP 8.2 provides a quick snapshot of patterns of settlement in the period before the Civil War. Students might need to be reminded that these land sales reflect the process for the orderly purchase and settlement of Western lands established by the Land Ordinance of 1785. Ask students: **What settlement patterns do you notice in the maps?** *Based on the size and number of circles, the greater volume of land sales took place in the 1830s. In the later period, there is a shift farther west and north, as much (though not all) of the earlier land had already been acquired.*

TRM Find complete suggested responses in the Teacher's Resource Materials.

AP® THEME

NAT: American and National Identity

The text offers a brief discussion of a very important point about the Supreme Court's role in encouraging the Market Revolution, in part through decisions that established the principle that federal laws took precedence over state laws.

AP® SKILLS & PROCESSES

CAUSATION

The **CAUSATION** question asks students to identify particular innovations that transformed the economy. For each innovation students identify, they should clearly explain its significance and how it advanced the Market Revolution. Extend this prompt by having students sort these developments into those that were primary to the economy's growth and those that played a more secondary role.

TRM Find complete suggested responses in the Teacher's Resource Materials.

TEACHING STRATEGY

Divide students into three groups representing the North, South, and West. Ask each group to determine if they support or oppose continuing the American System based on their region. Each group should consider the goals and impact of the American System on each region and on the nation as a whole. Once groups have determined their position on the American System, ask them to list three important supporting details for their position. Each group should appoint one person as their spokesperson. Engage students in a debate in response to the following statement: The American System disproportionately benefitted the North. Allow each spokesperson to present their group's argument. Then allow students in the groups to present questions to the spokespersons. After a period of debate, ask students to write their own response to the debate resolution based on their interpretation of the evidence presented.

AP® THEME

WXT: Work, Exchange, and Technology

The discussion of "the cotton complex" introduces a key concept: cotton production and northern manufacturing, banking, and shipping were deeply intertwined and together created a national and international market.

encouraged interstate trade by firmly establishing federal authority over interstate commerce (see "Asserting National Supremacy" in Chapter 7). In *Gibbons v. Ogden* (1824), the Court voided a New York law that created a monopoly on steamboat travel into New York City. That decision prevented local or state monopolies — or tariffs — from impeding the flow of goods, people, and news across the nation.

Shrinking Space: The Telegraph An efficient postal service was a great boon to merchants and manufacturers doing business across long distances. But for decades, inventors who were familiar with the properties of electricity dreamed of a much faster form of communication: electrical telegraphy. Across Europe, scientists experimented with various methods of using electrical impulses to send messages, but they struggled to devise a practical way to represent the alphabet. In 1837, a Massachusetts painter-turned-inventor, Samuel F. B. Morse, devised a telegraph capable of sending signals through miles of wire. Of equal importance, Morse and his collaborator, machinist and inventor Alfred Vail, invented a code for transmitting letters and numbers along a single wire by means of a contact key. A telegraph line was strung between Washington, D.C., and Baltimore in 1844; a year later, the Magnetic Telegraph Company was founded to create the first network of telegraph lines. By 1848, telegraph wires connected New York and Chicago. Western Union was formed in 1856 to consolidate the operations of smaller companies, and in 1861 it completed a transcontinental telegraph line connecting New York with San Francisco.

AP® SKILLS & PROCESSES
CAUSATION
How did advances in technology and engineering contribute to the Market Revolution?

All these innovations — roads and turnpikes, canals and steamboats, the postal service and the telegraph — helped to shrink the vast spaces of North America. They enabled farmers and merchants to sell goods in distant markets, helped entrepreneurs to coordinate business activity, aided immigrants as they relocated, and created a network of information that shaped politics and culture on a national scale. Together, they constituted the foundation of a new social order.

THE COTTON COMPLEX: NORTHERN INDUSTRY AND SOUTHERN AGRICULTURE

How were industrial development in the North and the expansion of cotton agriculture in the South connected?

In 1800, the economy of the United States remained overwhelmingly agricultural, and manufacturing was still in its infancy. Nevertheless, in the first half of the nineteenth century, the **Industrial Revolution** came to the United States. Between 1790 and 1860, merchants and manufacturers reorganized work routines, built factories, and exploited a wide range of natural resources. At the center of this transformation was the **cotton complex**: the relationship between northern industry and southern agriculture that drove a major economic transformation. In the Northeast, merchants and manufacturers invested in new textile mills that relied on the labor of young women drawn from nearby farms. Because they produced high-quality textiles quickly and cheaply, these northeastern mills, and many more like them in Great Britain, created vast demand for cotton, which transformed the southern economy as well. As northern merchants and manufacturers reorganized work routines and increased output, goods that were once luxury items became part of everyday life. Southern planters poured capital into land and slaves, revolutionizing agricultural production and sentencing additional generations of African American slaves to the miseries of plantation life.

Industrial Revolution
A burst of major inventions and economic expansion based on water and steam power, reorganized work routines, and the use of machine technology that transformed certain industries, such as cotton textiles and iron, between 1790 and 1860.

cotton complex
The economic system that developed in the first half of the nineteenth century binding together southern cotton production with northern clothmaking, shipping, and capital.

The American Industrial Revolution

The Industrial Revolution had its roots in Great Britain, where textile manufacturing had undergone major changes in the last half of the eighteenth century. Clothmaking was an ancient enterprise common to Asia, Africa, Europe, and the Americas, but until this time it was driven by small-scale production. For millennia, spinning and weaving—whether wool, cotton, linen, or silk—were crafts that were plied in the home, using technology that had been very slow to change. Strands of fiber were spun into thread and yarn by hand or using foot-driven spinning wheels, while yarn was woven into cloth on foot-powered looms.

A series of technical innovations in Britain in the eighteenth century made cloth-making increasingly efficient. The flying shuttle, invented in 1733, made it possible to weave cloth much more rapidly than yarn could be spun. Then, beginning in the 1760s, a series of devices for spinning fibers into yarn were invented: first a spinning jenny, then a water frame, and then a mule. Because the water frame and the mule were machines that relied on water or steam power, spinning moved out of households and into factories built alongside rivers that could drive the apparatus. Water-powered spinning mills could now produce abundant yarn, and cloth production soared. In India, it took 50,000 hours of labor to spin 100 pounds of raw cotton. In Britain in 1790, workers using a spinning mule could do the same work in 1,000 hours; by 1825, it took only 135 hours. This was a revolution in productivity.

To protect its textile industry from American competition, Great Britain prohibited the export of textile machinery and the emigration of the skilled craftsmen who could replicate the mills. But the promise of higher wages brought thousands of these skilled **mechanics** to the United States illegally.

mechanics
A term used in the nineteenth century to refer to skilled craftsmen and inventors who built and improved machinery and machine tools for industry.

Samuel Slater, the most important émigré mechanic, came to America in 1789 after working for Richard Arkwright, who had invented the most advanced British machinery for spinning cotton. A year later, Slater reproduced Arkwright's innovations in merchant Moses Brown's cotton mill in Providence, Rhode Island—the first in North America. The fast-flowing rivers that cascaded down from the Appalachian foothills to the coastal plain provided a cheap source of energy. From Massachusetts to Delaware, these waterways were soon lined with industrial villages and textile mills as large as 150 feet long, 40 feet wide, and four stories high (Map 8.3). The Industrial Revolution had arrived on American shores.

American and British Advantages British textile manufacturers nevertheless easily undersold their American competitors, for two reasons. First, they enjoyed the benefit of efficient shipping networks, which brought raw cotton to Britain at bargain prices, and low interest rates, which enabled mill owners to borrow money cheaply to support and expand their operations. Second, Britain had cheap labor: it had a larger population—about 12.6 million in 1810 compared to 7.3 million Americans—and thousands of landless laborers prepared to accept low-paying factory jobs, while in the United States labor was scarce and well paid.

To offset these advantages, American entrepreneurs relied on help from the federal government: in 1816, 1824, and 1828, Congress passed tariff bills that placed high taxes on imported cotton and woolen cloth. However, in the 1830s, Congress reduced tariffs because southern planters, western farmers, and urban consumers demanded inexpensive imports.

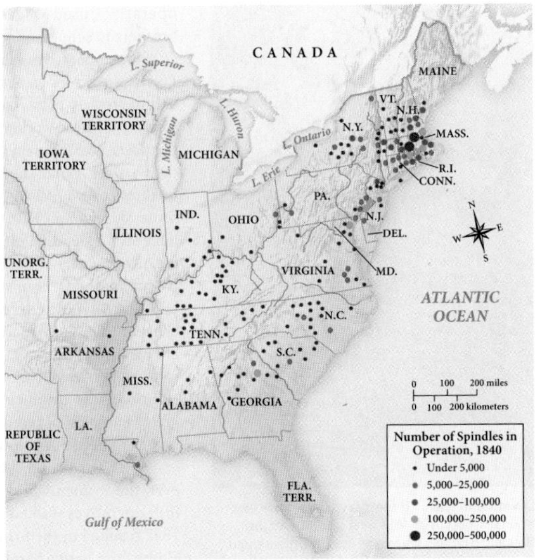

MAP 8.3 New England's Dominance in Cotton Spinning, 1840
Although the South grew the nation's cotton, it did not process it. Prior to the Civil War, entrepreneurs in Massachusetts and Rhode Island built most of the factories that spun and wove raw cotton into cloth. Their factories made use of the abundant water power available in New England and the region's surplus labor force. Initially, factory managers hired young farmwomen to work the machines; later, they relied on immigrants from Ireland and the French-speaking Canadian province of Quebec.

AP® THEME

WXT: Work, Exchange, and Technology

MAP 8.3 illustrates the significance of one particular new technology, spinning machines. While the map confirms the dominance of New England, it also reveals that some spinning took place throughout much of the country. Guide students' analysis with the following questions:

- **According to the caption, what region dominated in cotton spinning and why?** *New England, because of its abundant, fast-flowing rivers and surplus labor source.*
- **What can you conclude about the number of spindles in operation by 1840?** *Based on the number of the two largest circles, there were at least 1 million spindles in operation.*
- **How widespread was cotton spinning in the U.S.?** *More than twenty states from Maine to Georgia and from Massachusetts to Arkansas spun some cotton.*
- **Outside of New England, what region had the next largest production?** *Middle Atlantic states like Pennsylvania and Maryland.*

AP® THEME

SOC: Social Structures

In this section, the text provides a brief discussion of the role of tariffs in protecting infant American industries from British competition.

Migration patterns have produced economic opportunity for both the people migrating to the United States and industry within. Have students develop at least one reason why social structures for immigrant populations would change due to industrialization in the United States.

AP® APPLY THE TIP

Provide students with excerpts from the Lucy Larcom document (available in *Sources for America's History*) and other primary source documents from women who worked in the Waltham-Lowell System. After the students read the excerpts, ask them to write a paragraph explaining how the changes associated with the Industrial Revolution and the Waltham-Lowell System show continuity as well as change in the view of women in American society.

AP® SKILLS & PROCESSES

COMPARISON

The **COMPARISON** question would best be answered by creating a chart listing the specific advantages of each nation. Extend this prompt by having students explain why, despite Jefferson's claim that the U.S. was "nearly on a footing" with England by 1825, the British economy continued to outpace the American economy.

TRM Find complete suggested responses in the Teacher's Resource Materials.

TEACHING STRATEGY

The Lowell National Historical Park Web site provides a number of resources to explore the nature of early textile production in New England. Resources include information about the history of Lowell, the nature and mechanics of water power and textile machines, the nature of women's work, and the immigrant Irish community that developed. Some of these materials are downloadable PDFs that could be assigned as a group project or for additional reading. Access this resource by searching "Lowell National Historical Park."

CHECK FOR UNDERSTANDING

Ask students: **What elements made the American industrial revolution successful?** *British immigrants replicated English mills, fast-flowing rivers powered machines, federal tariffs protected Americans from British competition, cheap labor (in the form of single farm women) made American mills more competitive, and American innovators made their machines more efficient than British ones. Together, these factors helped Americans compete against Britain, which had a tremendous head start.*

AP® EXAM TIP

Explaining the impact of the Industrial Revolution on gender roles and family life is essential on the AP® Exam.

AP® SKILLS & PROCESSES

COMPARISON

What were the advantages and strategies of British and American textile manufacturers?

Waltham-Lowell System
A labor system employing young farm women in New England factories that originated in 1822 and declined after 1860, when immigrant labor became predominant. The women lived in company boardinghouses with strict rules and curfews and were often required to attend church.

Better Machines, Cheaper Workers American producers used two other strategies to compete with their British rivals. First, they improved on British technology. In 1811, Francis Cabot Lowell, a wealthy Boston merchant, toured British textile mills, secretly making detailed drawings of their power machinery. Paul Moody, an experienced American mechanic, then copied the machines and improved their design. In 1814, Lowell joined with merchants Nathan Appleton and Patrick Tracy Jackson to form the Boston Manufacturing Company. Having raised the staggering sum of $400,000, they built a textile plant in Waltham, Massachusetts — the first American factory to perform all clothmaking operations under one roof. Thanks to Moody's improvements, Waltham's power looms operated at higher speeds than British looms and needed fewer workers.

The second strategy was to tap a cheaper source of labor. In the 1820s, the Boston Manufacturing Company recruited thousands of young women from farm families, providing them with rooms in boardinghouses and with evening lectures and other cultural activities. To reassure parents about their daughters' moral welfare, the mill owners enforced strict curfews, prohibited alcoholic beverages, and required regular church attendance. At Lowell (1822), Chicopee (1823), and other sites in Massachusetts and New Hampshire, the company built new factories that used this labor system, known as the **Waltham-Lowell System**.

By the early 1830s, more than 40,000 New England women were working in textile mills. As an observer noted, the wages were "more than could be obtained by the hitherto ordinary occupation of housework," the living conditions were better than those in crowded farmhouses, and the women had greater independence. Lucy Larcom became a Lowell textile operative at age eleven to avoid being "a trouble or burden or expense" to her widowed mother. Other women operatives used wages to pay off their father's farm mortgages, send brothers to school, or accumulate a marriage dowry for themselves.

Lowell Mill Girls These two young women who labored in the Lowell Mills wear smocks over their clothing to protect it from the dust, lint, grease, and moving machinery that surrounded them during their workday. Looking past the photographer, they strike a pose that conveys their solidarity and fierce independence. The image is a tintype, an early form of photography that became popular in the 1850s and 1860s; this picture is thought to date to c. 1870. Lowell Historical Society.

Some operatives just had a good time. Susan Brown, who worked as a Lowell weaver for eight months, spent half her earnings on food and lodging and the rest on plays, concerts, lectures, and a two-day excursion to Boston. Like most textile workers, Brown soon tired of the rigors of factory work and the never-ceasing clatter of the machinery, which ran twelve hours a day, six days a week. After she quit, she lived at home for a time and then moved to another mill. Whatever the hardships, waged work gave young women a sense of freedom. "Don't I feel independent!" a woman mill worker wrote to her sister. "The thought that I am living on no one is a happy one indeed to me." The owners of the Boston Manufacturing Company were even happier. By combining tariff protection with improved technology and cheap female labor, they could undersell their British rivals. Their textiles were also cheaper than those made in New York and Pennsylvania, where farmworkers were paid more than in New England and textile wages consequently were higher. Manufacturers in those states earned profits by using advanced technology to produce higher-quality cloth. Even Thomas Jefferson, the great champion of yeoman farming, was impressed. "Our manufacturers are now very nearly on a footing with those of England," he boasted in 1825.

When the Boston Manufacturing Company reduced their wages, however, the women workers struck back. In 1834, and again in 1836, female mill operatives walked off the job to protest wage cuts. Another strike in 1842 resulted in the firing of seventy workers. Under the leadership of New Hampshire native Sarah George Bagley, in 1844, a group of workers organized the Lowell Female Labor Reform Association to agitate for ten-hour workdays and to publicize their poor working conditions. Although the strikes and the Reform Association petitions were unsuccessful, they provided a valuable education for a generation of female mill workers. Owners soon looked elsewhere for cheap labor. Beginning about 1860, Irish and

Canadian immigrants entered the mills in large numbers and soon replaced farm women in the New England factories.

Origins of the Cotton South

As its industrial capacity grew in the eighteenth century, Great Britain began to import cotton in larger quantities. But the world supply was relatively small because cotton production was immensely labor-intensive. A revolution in cotton cloth production would require a revolution in cotton agriculture, based on new forms of cheap labor. The black belt of the American Southeast — an arc of fertile soil stretching from western South Carolina through central Georgia, Alabama, Mississippi, and east Texas — provided a landscape that was ideal for cotton cultivation, and the slave plantation complex offered a system of labor discipline that could bring cotton to world markets on an entirely new scale.

AP® EXAM TIP

Understand the debate that developed over the benefits of the American System to the regions of the U.S.

gradual emancipation
The practice of ending slavery in the distant future while recognizing white property rights to the slaves they owned. Gradual emancipation statutes only applied to enslaved laborers born after the passage of the statute, and only after they had first labored for their owners for a term of years.

The Decline of Slavery, 1776–1800 The possibility that cotton production would lead to a boom in African slavery would have come as a surprise to the generation that lived through the American Revolution, because in that era slavery was in a steep decline. Whites and blacks alike perceived a contradiction between the colonies' pursuit of liberty and the institution of slavery. "I wish most sincerely there was not a Slave in the province," Abigail Adams confessed to her husband, John. "It always appeared a most iniquitous Scheme to me — to fight ourselves for what we are daily robbing and plundering from those who have as good a right to freedom as we do."

The North Ends Slavery — Slowly Beginning in the 1750s, Quaker evangelist John Woolman urged Friends to free their slaves, and many did so. In 1780, antislavery activists in Pennsylvania passed the first **gradual emancipation** law in the United States. Though it freed no one, the law set an important precedent. In subsequent years, legislators in Connecticut (1784), Rhode Island (1784), New York (1799), and New Jersey (1804) adopted gradual emancipation statutes as well (Map 8.4). These laws recognized white property rights by requiring slaves to buy their freedom by years — even decades — of additional labor. For example, the New York Emancipation Act of 1799 allowed slavery to continue until 1828 and freed slave children only at the age of twenty-five. Consequently, as late as 1810, almost 30,000 blacks in the northern states — nearly one-fourth of the African Americans living there — were still enslaved.

Freed blacks faced severe prejudice from whites who feared job competition and racial melding. When Massachusetts judges abolished slavery through case law in 1784, the legislature

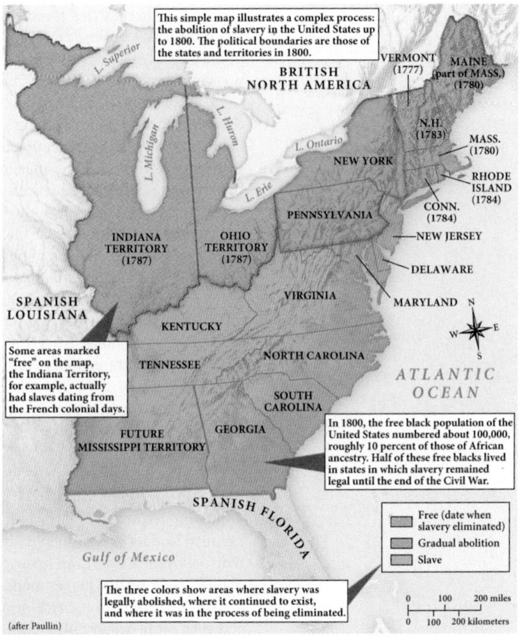

MAP 8.4 The Status of Slavery, 1800
In 1775, racial slavery was legal in all of the British colonies in North America. By the time the confederated states achieved their independence in 1783, the New England region was mostly free of slavery. By 1800, all of the states north of Maryland had provided for the gradual abolition of slavery except New Jersey, whose legislature finally acted in 1804, but the process of gradual emancipation dragged on until the 1830s. Some slave owners in the Chesapeake region manumitted a number of their slaves, leaving only the whites of the Lower South firmly committed to racial bondage.

AP® SKILLS & PROCESSES

DEVELOPMENTS AND PROCESSES

The American System was a contentious issue due to the fact that different regions of the United States would not benefit as much from such an economic vision. Have students identify at least one region that would have benefitted from the American System and one region that would not benefit as much from the American System.

AP® THEME

GEO: Geography and the Environment; WXT: Work, Exchange, and Technology

MAP 8.4 provides guidance for student interpretation as they investigate geographical patterns of slavery across the U.S. They should note that the map date is the beginning of the period covered in the chapter, before slavery began to grow dramatically. One result is that New Jersey is the only state north of the Mason-Dixon line, the later barrier demarcating free and slave states, that still had slaves. The state passed a gradual emancipation law in 1804. Ask students: **How does this map illustrate the relationship between slavery and state and federal governments?** *Because the Constitution left slavery up to the states, the nation became a crazy quilt of slave state, free state, and states on their way to being free. The Northwest Ordinance, passed before the Constitutional Convention, outlawed slavery in that territory, so even though portions are due west of slave states like Virginia and Kentucky, Ohio and Indiana still became free states.*

AP® APPLY THE TIP

Ask students to carefully read pp. 261–263 in order to create a timeline that illustrates laws and policies related to slavery in the North. Students should note changes in arguments as well as laws in the period from 1776–1800. After students have added events and laws to their timeline for the North, ask them to use a different color pen or marker to add important developments in the South for the same time period. When students have completed their timeline, ask them to answer the following questions:

- **Was there a common philosophical belief about slavery at the time of the American Revolution?** *Yes, most leaders in 1776 understood and believed slavery to be in opposition to republican ideals. Even slave owners like Jefferson viewed it as a "necessary evil."*
- **How did gradual emancipation laws show continuity of belief in property rights in the North and the South?** *Gradual emancipation laws were seen as a way to limit and eventually end slavery without threatening long-held beliefs in the protection of private property.*
- **How did arguments in both the North and South change over time?** *In the early Federal Period, most leaders in both the North and the South recognized that slavery violated the principles of republican government and ideals of liberty expressed in the Declaration of Independence. However, as the South became more economically dependent on slavery, arguments began to develop justifying slavery as a moral and political good. Over time, a vocal minority developed in opposition to slavery and gained momentum in the North as slavery began to grow in the South with the invention of the cotton gin and expansion of slavery to the West.*

AP® EXAM TIP

Trace the changes in laws and policies regarding African slaves in the North from the American Revolution (Chapter 5) to the invention of the cotton gin.

reenacted an old statute that prohibited whites from marrying blacks, mulattos, or Indians. For African Americans in the North, freedom meant second-class citizenship; nevertheless, the institution of slavery was being ushered slowly out of existence.

Manumission in the Chesapeake The coming of war encouraged many southern slaves to expect that the Revolution would bring their freedom. A black preacher in Georgia told his fellow slaves that King George III "was about to alter the World, and set the Negroes free." Similar rumors, prompted in part by Royal Governor Lord Dunmore's proclamation of 1775 and the Philipsburg Proclamation of 1779, led thousands of African Americans to flee behind British lines. Two neighbors of Virginia Patriot Richard Henry Lee lost "every slave they had in the world," as did many other planters. In 1781, when the British army evacuated Charleston, more than 6,000 former slaves went with them; another 4,000 left from Savannah. All told, about 30,000 blacks fled their owners.

Yet thousands of African Americans supported the Patriot cause as well. In Maryland, some slaves took up arms for the rebels in return for the promise of freedom. Enslaved Virginians struck informal bargains with their Patriot owners, trading loyalty in wartime for the hope of liberty. Following the Virginia legislature's passage of a **manumission** act in 1782, allowing owners to free their slaves, 10,000 enslaved people won their freedom.

manumission
The legal act of relinquishing property rights in slaves. Worried that a large free black population would threaten the institution of slavery, the Virginia assembly repealed Virginia's 1782 manumission law in 1792.

The southern states faced the most glaring contradiction between liberty and property rights because enslaved blacks represented a huge financial investment. But in the Chesapeake, slavery was in decline for three reasons. First, the tobacco economy was chronically depressed, and many tobacco planters were shifting to wheat and livestock production, a less labor-intensive form of farming that gave them an oversupply of slaves. Second, many leading planters were committed to the principle of human liberty and saw, in the institution of slavery, the same contradiction that their northern counterparts did. Third, evangelical Christianity encouraged some planters to regard their slaves as spiritual equals. In 1784, a conference of Virginia Methodists declared that slavery was "contrary to the Golden Law of God on which hang all the Law and the Prophets." Under these influences, many Chesapeake slave owners manumitted their slaves or allowed them to buy their freedom by working as artisans or laborers. In 1785, a Powhatan planter named Joseph Mayo manumitted all of his slaves, 150 to 170 in number; in the 1790s, Robert "Councillor" Carter manumitted more than 500 slaves and provided them with land. John Randolph of Roanoke manumitted hundreds of slaves in his will, and also left money to buy them land. Widespread manumission gradually brought freedom to one-third of the African Americans in Maryland.

Slavery Resurgent But slavery still had powerful advocates. In Virginia, slave owners pushed back against the wave of manumissions. Fearing the possibility of total emancipation, hundreds of slave owners petitioned the Virginia legislature to repeal the manumission act and thereby protect "the most valuable and indispensible Article of our Property, our Slaves." In 1792, legislators forbade further manumissions. Following the lead of Thomas Jefferson, who owned more than a hundred slaves, political leaders now argued that slavery was a "necessary evil" required to maintain white supremacy and the luxurious planter lifestyle. In North Carolina, legislators condemned private Quaker manumissions as "highly criminal and reprehensible."

Farther south, in the rice-growing states of South Carolina and Georgia, slavery was even more deeply entrenched. Yet, rice plantations were confined to the seaboard; at the time of the Revolution, there was no cash crop that could support plantation agriculture farther inland. Cotton was about to change that. In 1786, responding to rising prices resulting from Great Britain's mechanized processing, Georgia planters on the Sea Islands harvested their first crop of long-staple cotton. Its silky fibers produced a high grade of cotton, but — like rice and indigo — Sea Island cotton would not grow in the uplands. Hardier varieties of short-staple cotton could thrive in rich inland soils, but their bolls, with tightly packed fibers, were prohibitively difficult to process by hand. American inventors immediately put their minds to the problem.

CHECK FOR UNDERSTANDING

Ask students: **What were the origins of the Cotton South?** *After the Revolution, slavery began to die out in the North and declined in the Chesapeake as well. This decline was offset by the migration of planters to the Southwest's Black Belt, where cotton growing was ideal, as well as by slavery's entrenched status in the rice-growing states of South Carolina and Georgia.*

In 1793, Massachusetts native Eli Whitney devised a machine, called a cotton engine (or cotton "gin" for short), that could quickly separate the seeds of a short-staple cotton boll from their delicate fibers, an innovation that increased the speed of cotton processing fiftyfold. The cotton rush was on.

AP® SKILLS & PROCESSES

CONTEXTUALIZATION

Why was slavery in retreat in the Revolutionary era, and what caused its resurgence?

The Cotton Boom and Slavery

In the early nineteenth century, slave plantations pushed into the interior of North America in two directions at once: westward, from the coastal states of South Carolina and Georgia; and northward from New Orleans up the Mississippi (Map 8.5). In the lower Mississippi Valley, sugar was a viable crop; thus, a combination of sugar and cotton drove the development of formerly French Louisiana (admitted as a state in 1812) and Mississippi (admitted in 1817). After crossing the Appalachians, westward-moving cotton planters settled in southern Tennessee (admitted 1796) and Alabama (1819), then pushed into Missouri (1821), Arkansas (1836), and Texas (1845). These migratory streams converged in the rich alluvial soils of the black belt, which stretched from western South Carolina all the way to east Texas. Between 1800 and 1848, the new cotton-growing lands of the American South became some of the most valuable real estate in the world.

The cotton boom immediately tripled the value of good southern farmland. As the federal government forcibly removed Creeks, Choctaws, and Chickasaws from their land, officials made it available to southern planters as quickly as possible. Capital investments from overseas helped to speed the process, as wealthy British investors like banker and cotton merchant Thomas Baring loaned money to bring the lands under cultivation. Cotton was wildly profitable; in 1807, a Mississippi cotton

AP® EXAM TIP

Identifying the causes and effects of Southern dependency on cotton to the development of a regional Southern identity is important to know on the AP® Exam.

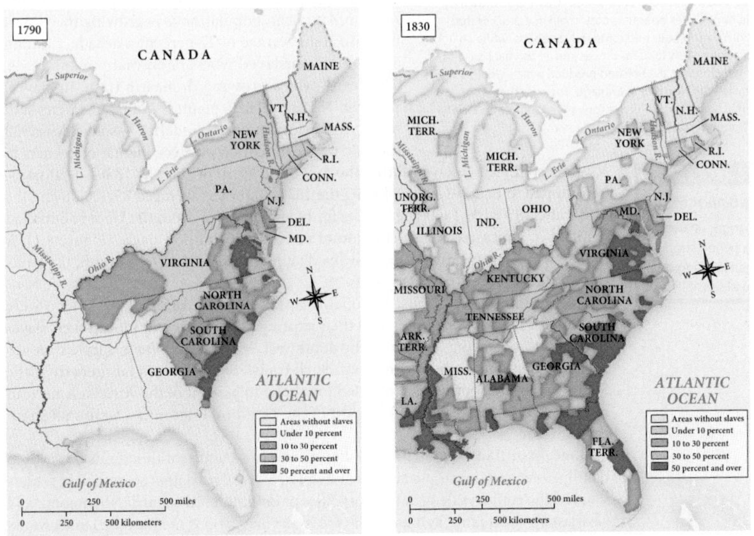

MAP 8.5 Distribution of the Slave Population in 1790 and 1830
The cotton boom shifted the African American population to the South and West. In 1790, most slaves lived and worked on Chesapeake tobacco and Carolina rice and indigo plantations. By 1830, those areas were still heavily populated by black families, but hundreds of thousands of slaves also labored on the cotton and sugar lands of the lower Mississippi Valley and on cotton plantations in Georgia, northern Florida, and Alabama. In the decades to come, the cotton frontier would push across Mississippi and Louisiana and into Texas.

AP® SKILLS & PROCESSES

CONTEXTUALIZATION

The **CONTEXTUALIZATION** question asks students to identify the historical contexts that explain the decline and resurgence of slavery. Students may need guidance to recognize that this question is asking about slavery in aggregate national terms. In the Deep South, slavery was never "in decline," for example. Students could classify the reasons for decline and resurgence by category — cultural/ideological v. economic — and identify the type of evidence that could confirm which type of factor was more significant. Extend this prompt by asking students to explain why the growth of slavery so dramatically outpaced its decline.

TRM Find complete suggested responses in the Teacher's Resource Materials.

AP® THEME

GEO: Geography and the Environment; WXT: Work, Exchange, and Technology

MAP 8.5 provides an excellent opportunity for students to explore continuity and change over time by looking at the geography of slavery. Guide students' analysis with the following questions:

- **How many northern states still had some slaves in 1830?** *Every northern state and territory except Vermont, New Hampshire, Maine, and Massachusetts.*
- **How many states had dense slave populations (represented in red) in 1790? In 1830? Where were the new states with dense slave populations located?** *Five. Nine. In the deep South — Florida, Alabama, Mississippi, and Louisiana.*
- **What can you conclude about continuity and change regarding slavery in the early 1800s?** *Slavery died slowly in the North and expanded dramatically in scale and distribution in the South.*

For a deeper explanation of this topic, use several animated maps of slavery's expansion available through the Smithsonian. The accompanying article provides a commentary on things for students to notice as they view the maps. Access this Web site by searching "Smithsonian maps slavery expansion."

AP® SKILLS & PROCESSES

DEVELOPMENTS AND PROCESSES

Using the image of the first cotton gin, have students answer the following question: In what ways did the interdependence of northern industry and southern agricultural staples change the lives of enslaved persons?

TRM Find complete suggested responses in the Teacher's Resource Materials.

The First Cotton Gin The economic lives of northerners and southerners alike were transformed by technological innovation and new forms of labor discipline in the years between 1800 and 1848. In this image drawn by William L. Sheppard, two male slaves operate a cotton gin in a process that crushed the hard, stubborn cotton bolls and removed the seeds, while an enslaved woman brings a heavy new load for processing. In the background, a planter and a buyer closely inspect the finished product, which would soon be shipped to a textile mill in the North or in England. This was the cotton complex, a set of economic activities that drove forward economic change in both the northern and southern states. Bettmann/Getty Images.

plantation returned 22.5 percent a year on its investment. As cotton cultivation expanded, it became the cornerstone of the nation's economy: between 1815 and 1860, it accounted for more than half of all U.S. exports. By 1840, the South produced and exported 1.5 million bales of raw cotton a year, over two-thirds of the world's supply. The cotton-producing capacity of the South dwarfed the industrial capacity of the Northeast. In the first half of the nineteenth century, more than 85 percent of the U.S. cotton crop was sold in Liverpool to be processed in Great Britain, while only a small fraction could be absorbed by American mills. "Cotton is King," boasted the *Southern Cultivator*.

To plant this vast new inland frontier, white planters first imported enslaved laborers from Africa. Between 1776 and 1808, when Congress outlawed the Atlantic slave trade, planters purchased about 115,000 Africans. "The Planter will . . . Sacrifice every thing to attain Negroes," declared one slave trader. But demand far exceeded the supply. Planters also imported new African workers illegally, through the Spanish colony of Florida until 1819 and then through the Mexican province of Texas. Yet these Africans — about 50,000 between 1810 and 1865 — did not satisfy the demand either.

The Upper South Exports Slaves Planters seeking labor also looked to the Chesapeake region, where the African American population was growing by natural increase at an average of 27 percent a decade, creating a surplus of enslaved workers on many plantations. The result was a growing domestic trade in slaves. Between 1818 and 1829, planters in just one Maryland tobacco-growing county — Frederick — sold at least 952 slaves to traders or cotton planters. Plantation owners in Virginia sold 75,000 slaves during the 1810s and again during the 1820s. That number jumped to nearly 120,000 during the 1830s and then averaged 85,000 during the 1840s and 1850s. By 1860, the "mania for buying negroes" from the Upper South had resulted in a massive transplantation of more than 1 million slaves (Figure 8.1). A majority of African Americans now lived and worked in the Deep South, the lands that stretched from Georgia to Texas.

AP® SKILLS & PROCESSES

DEVELOPMENTS AND PROCESSES

How did the changes related to slavery in this period support the emergence of regional cultural sensibilities?

At the same time, thousands of Chesapeake and Carolina planters who were looking for new opportunities sold their existing plantations and moved their slaves to the cotton-growing frontier of the Southwest. Many other planters gave slaves to sons and daughters who moved west. Such transfers of enslaved laborers from the Southeast to the Southwest accounted for about 40 percent of the African American migrants. The rest — about 60 percent of the 1 million migrants — were sold south through traders.

One set of trading routes ran to the Atlantic coast and sent thousands of slaves to rapidly developing sugar plantations in Louisiana. As sugar output soared, slave traders scoured the countryside near the port cities of Baltimore, Alexandria, Richmond, and Charleston — searching, as one of them put it, for "likely young men such as I think would suit the New Orleans market." Because this **coastal trade** in laborers was highly visible, it elicited widespread condemnation by northern abolitionists. Sugar was a "killer" crop, and Louisiana (like the eighteenth-century West Indies) soon had a well-deserved reputation among African Americans "as a place of slaughter." Maryland farmer John Anthony

coastal trade
The domestic slave trade with routes along the Atlantic coast that sent thousands of slaves to sugar plantations in Louisiana and cotton plantations in the Mississippi Valley.

Munnikhuysen refused to allow his daughter Priscilla to marry a Louisiana sugar planter, declaring: "Mit has never been used to see negroes flayed alive and it would kill her."

The **inland system** that fed enslaved workers to the Cotton South was less visible than the coastal trade but more extensive. Professional slave traders went from one rural village to another buying "young and likely Negroes." The traders marched their purchases in coffles — columns of slaves bound to one another — to Alabama, Mississippi, and Missouri in the 1830s and to Arkansas and Texas in the 1850s.

Chesapeake and Carolina planters provided the human cargo. Some planters sold slaves when they ran into debt. "Trouble gathers thicker and thicker around me," Thomas B. Chaplin of South Carolina lamented in his diary. "I will be compelled to send about ten prime Negroes to Town on next Monday, to be sold." Many more planters doubled as slave traders, earning substantial profits by traveling south to sell some of their slaves and those of their neighbors. Colonel E. S. Irvine, a member of the South Carolina legislature and "a highly respected gentleman" in white circles, traveled frequently "to sell a drove of Negroes." Prices marched in step with those for cotton; during a boom year in the 1850s, a planter noted that a slave "will fetch $1000, cash, quick."

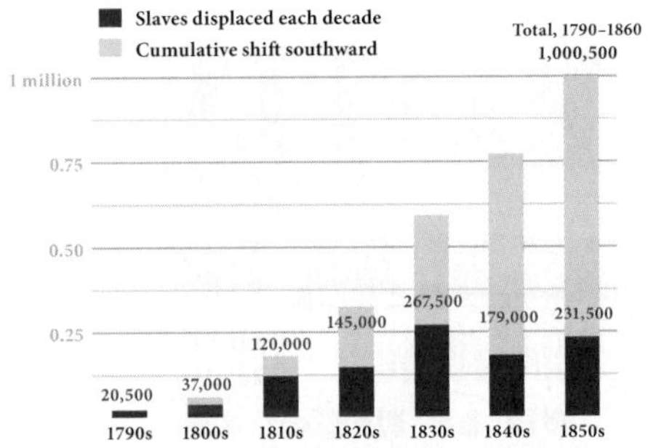

FIGURE 8.1 Forced Slave Migration to the Lower South, 1790–1860
The cotton boom set in motion a vast redistribution of the African American population. Between 1790 and 1860, white planters moved or sold more than a million enslaved people from the Upper to the Lower South, a process that broke up families and long-established black communities. Data from Robert William Fogel, et al., 1974 and Tadman, 1996.

inland system
The slave trade system in the interior of the country that fed slaves to the Cotton South.

The domestic slave trade was crucial to the prosperity of the fast-developing Cotton South. Equally important, it sustained the wealth of slave owners in the East. By selling surplus black workers, planters in the Chesapeake and Carolinas added about 20 percent to their income. As a Maryland newspaper remarked in 1858, "[The trade serves as] an almost universal resource to raise money. A prime able-bodied slave is worth three times as much to the cotton or sugar planter as to the Maryland agriculturalist."

The Impact on Blacks For African American families, the domestic slave trade was a personal disaster that underlined their status — and vulnerability — as chattel slaves. In law, they were the movable personal property of the whites who owned them. As Lewis Clark, a fugitive from slavery, noted: "Many a time i've had 'em say to me, 'You're my property.'" "The being of slavery, its soul and its body, lives and moves in the chattel principle, the property principle, the bill of sale principle," declared former slave James W. C. Pennington. As a South Carolina master put it, "[The slave's earnings] belong to me because I bought him."

Slave property underpinned the entire southern economic system. Whig politician Henry Clay noted that the "immense amount of capital which is invested in slave property . . . is owned by widows and orphans, by the aged and infirm, as well as the sound and vigorous. It is the subject of mortgages, deeds of trust, and family settlements."

The Inland Slave Trade Mounted whites escort a convoy of slaves from Virginia to Tennessee in Lewis Miller's *Slave Trader, Sold to Tennessee* (1853). For white planters, the interstate trade in slaves was lucrative; it pumped money into the declining Chesapeake economy and provided young workers for the expanding plantations of the cotton belt. For blacks, it was a traumatic journey, a new Middle Passage that broke up their families and communities. "Arise! Arise! and weep no more, dry up your tears, we shall part no more," the slaves sing sorrowfully as they journey to new lives in Tennessee. The Colonial Williamsburg Foundation. Gift of Dr. Richard M. Kain in memory of George Hay Kain.

TEACHING STRATEGY

Together the features on this page attempt to capture the nature of the internal slave trade. Use **FIGURE 8.1** to convey the scale of this forced migration, while the image depicts the way a convoy of slaves was forced to march hundreds of miles from their home and remaining family in the Chesapeake into the Deep South.

TEACHING STRATEGY

Though students have already learned that slaves were legally defined as property, the stark language of this ad might provide an opportunity for a brief discussion about the consequences for slaves and masters of a system that treated human beings as chattel.

AP® THEME

SOC: Social Structures

The Web site that accompanies PBS's *Slavery and the Making of America* provides resources to help students understand the nature of slave families and the role of gender in shaping slaves' experiences. Access this resource by searching "PBS Slavery and the Making of America gender."

The Chattel Principle This public notice for a New Orleans raffle in which the prizes are a horse and buggy and a female slave named Sarah dramatically illustrates the "chattel principle" governing the institution of slavery, which made enslaved laborers the property of their owners. Joseph Jennings, the store owner conducting the raffle, has valued Sarah at $900. The Granger Collection, New York.

As a slave owner, Clay also knew that property rights were key to slave discipline. "I govern them . . . without the whip," another master explained, "by stating . . . that I should sell them if they do not conduct themselves as I wish." The threat was effective. "The Negroes here dread nothing on earth so much as this," a Maryland observer noted. "They regard the south with perfect horror, and to be sent there is considered as the worst punishment." Thousands of slaves suffered that fate, which destroyed about one in every four slave marriages. "Why does the slave ever love?" asked black abolitionist Harriet Jacobs in her autobiography, *Incidents in the Life of a Slave Girl*, when her partner "may at any moment be wrenched away by the hand of violence?" After being sold, one Georgia slave lamented, "My Dear wife for you and my Children my pen cannot Express the griffe I feel to be parted from you all."

The interstate slave trade often focused on young adults. In northern Maryland, planters sold away boys and girls at an average age of seventeen years. "Dey sole my sister Kate," Anna Harris remembered decades later, "and I ain't seed or heard of her since." The trade also separated almost a third of all slave children under the age of fourteen from one or both of their parents. Sarah Grant remembered, "Mamma used to cry when she had to go back to work because she was always scared some of us kids would be sold while she was away."

Despite the constant threat of being sold, 75 percent of slave marriages remained unbroken, and the majority of children lived with one or both parents until puberty. Consequently, the sense of family among African Americans remained strong. Sold from Virginia to Texas in 1843, Hawkins Wilson carried with him a mental picture of his family. Twenty-five years later and now a freedman, Wilson set out to find his "dearest relatives" in Virginia. "My sister belonged to Peter Coleman in Caroline County and her name was Jane. . . . She had three children, Robert, Charles and Julia, when I left — Sister Martha belonged to Dr. Jefferson. . . . Sister Matilda belonged to Mrs. Botts."

During the decades between sale and freedom, Hawkins Wilson and thousands of other African Americans constructed new lives for themselves in the Mississippi Valley. Undoubtedly, many did so with a sense of foreboding, knowing from personal experience that their owners could disrupt their lives at any moment. Like Charles Ball, some "longed to die, and escape from the bonds of my tormentors." The darkness of slavery shadowed even moments of joy. Knowing that sales often ended slave marriages, a white minister blessed one couple "for so long as God keeps them together."

"positive good"
In 1837, South Carolina Senator John C. Calhoun argued on the floor of the Senate that slavery was not a necessary evil, but a positive good, "indispensable to the peace and happiness" of blacks and whites alike.

The Ideology and Reality of "Benevolence" The planter aristocracy flourished around the periphery of the South's booming Cotton Belt — in Virginia, South Carolina, and Louisiana — and took the lead in defending slavery. Within a generation after the Revolution, southern apologists rejected the view that slavery was, at best, a "necessary evil." In 1837, South Carolina Senator John C. Calhoun argued that the institution was a **"positive good"** because it subsidized an elegant lifestyle for a white elite and provided tutelage for genetically inferior Africans. "As a race, the African is inferior to the white man," declared Alexander Stephens, the future vice president of the Confederacy. "Subordination to the white man is his normal condition." Apologists depicted planters and their wives as aristocratic models of "disinterested benevolence," who provided food and housing for their workers and cared for them in old age. One wealthy Georgian declared, "Plantation government should be eminently patriarchal. . . . The pater-familias, or head of the family, should, in one sense, be the father of the whole concern, negroes and all."

Those planters who embraced Christian stewardship tried to shape the religious lives of the people they enslaved. They built churches on their plantations, welcomed evangelical preachers, and required their slaves to attend services. A few encouraged African Americans with spiritual "gifts" to serve as exhorters and deacons. Most of these planters acted from sincere Christian belief, but they also hoped to counter abolitionist criticism and to use religious teachings to control their workers.

Indeed, slavery's defenders increasingly used religious justifications for human bondage. Protestant ministers in the South pointed out that the Hebrews, God's chosen people, had owned slaves and that Jesus Christ had never condemned slavery. As James Henry Hammond told a British abolitionist in 1845: "What God ordains and Christ sanctifies should surely command the respect and toleration of man." In making their case, slavery's advocates rarely acknowledged its day-to-day brutality and exploitation. "I was at the plantation last Saturday and the crop was in fine order," a son wrote to his absentee father, "but the negroes are most brutally scarred & several have run off."

Despite the violence inherent in the chattel principle, many white planters considered themselves benevolent masters, committed to the welfare of "my family, black and white." Historians have labeled this idea **paternalism**. Some masters gave substance to the paternalist ideal by giving kind treatment to "loyal and worthy" slaves — black overseers, the mammy who raised their children, and trusted house servants. By preserving the families of these slaves, many planters could believe that they "sold south" only "coarse" troublemakers who had "little sense of family." Other owners were more honest about the human cost of their pursuit of wealth. "Tomorrow the negroes are to get off [to Kentucky]," a slave-owning woman in Virginia wrote to a friend, "and I expect there will be great crying and moaning, with children Leaving there mothers, mothers there children, and women there husbands."

Whether or not they acknowledged the slaves' pain, few southern whites questioned the morality of the slave trade. Responding to abolitionists' criticism, the city council of Charleston, South Carolina, declared that "the removal of slaves from place to place, and their transfer from master to master, by gift, purchase, or otherwise" was completely consistent "with moral principle and with the highest order of civilization" (see "Firsthand Accounts," p. 270).

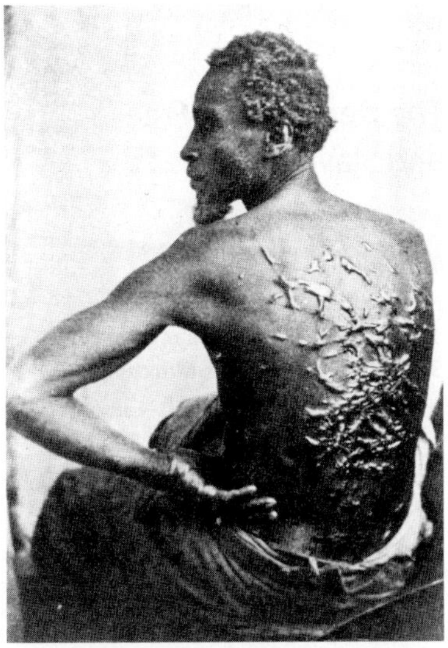

The Inherent Brutality of Slavery Like all systems of forced labor, American racial slavery relied ultimately on physical coercion. Slave owners and overseers routinely whipped slaves who worked slowly or defied their orders. On occasion, they applied the whip with such ferocity that the slave was permanently injured or killed. This photograph of a Mississippi slave named Gordon, taken after he fled to the Union army in Louisiana in 1863 and published in *Harper's Weekly*, stands as graphic testimony to the inherent brutality of the system. Smith Collection/Gado/Getty Images.

paternalism
The ideology held by slave owners who considered themselves committed to the welfare of their slaves.

AP® SKILLS & PROCESSES
CAUSATION
How did the internal slave trade affect planter-slave relations and black families?

AP® EXAM TIP
Define the changes that occurred in arguments justifying slavery as the South developed a regional identity known as the "Cotton Kingdom."

TECHNOLOGICAL INNOVATION AND LABOR

How did technological innovation improve the lives of ordinary people, and what challenges did it present to them?

The technical advances that spurred the rise of cotton mills in the North were part of a larger pattern of economic innovation and change. Americans became inventive, seeking countless ways to improve and simplify production. Machines were at the center of many of these improvements, and American mechanics led the world in creating devices that worked faster and better than before. But workers did not always benefit. Skilled laborers formed unions to strengthen their bargaining position with employers. Lower-skilled workers in factory jobs, who often performed repetitive labor under close supervision, tried to organize as well, but they often faced legal obstacles. In the first half of the nineteenth century, many Americans struggled to understand their place in an increasingly complex social order. Urban growth was one sign of change, as wage-workers swelled the size of older cities and prompted the creation of many new ones.

TEACHING STRATEGY

This image of a slave's scarred back graphically depicts the brutality of the enslaved experience. The National Humanities Center's *Making of African American Identity* Web site provides a variety of primary sources, including photographs, transcripts of WPA interviews, and nineteenth-century slave narratives, letters, and other documents that address daily life, sale, the plantation experience, slave drivers, the nature of slave labor, the master-slave relationship, and forms of resistance. Each set of primary sources begins with a short essay that provides historical context and teaching suggestions, as well as discussion questions for use with students. Access this resource by searching "NHC Making of African American Identity Vol 1."

TEACHING STRATEGY

To see a longer excerpt of the city council of Charleston, South Carolina, document, along with other primary sources from this period, see *Sources for America's History*.

CHECK FOR UNDERSTANDING

Ask students: **How were industrial development in the North and the expansion of cotton agriculture in the South connected?** *While many in the North denigrated slavery, the industrialization of the North provided both the technology and the industrial capacity to help entrench the cotton economy in the South. After all, it was a Massachusetts inventor, Eli Whitney, who developed the cotton gin in 1793. Moreover, textile mills in the North spun Southern cotton into clothing for export. Despite an increasing number of textile mills, however, the South still exported most of its cotton to European mills, so successful was the cotton economy.*

AP® SKILLS & PROCESSES

CAUSATION

The **CAUSATION** question requires students to identify two distinct effects of the internal slave trade. The text is explicit about the effects on families. However, determining the relationship between the slave trade and planter-slave relations requires some inference. Students could consider the relationship between the two consequences.

TRM Find complete suggested responses in the Teacher's Resource Materials.

AP® APPLY THE TIP

Provide students with excerpts from a variety of sources on slavery. (Suggested sources include excerpts from Thomas Jefferson, Abigail Adams, John Calhoun, John Quincy Adams, George Fitzhugh, etc.) Students should read and analyze the sources to identify the arguments regarding slavery. Ask students to group the documents into those making political, economic, or social arguments regarding slavery. Once students have read the documents, have them work in small groups to discuss their organization of the sources and identify the historical context, including intended audience, purpose, and point of view. Finally, ask each student to write a thesis statement that compares the arguments regarding slavery in the Revolutionary era (1770–1790) to arguments regarding slavery in the mid-nineteenth century (1830–1860). Extend this activity by asking students to complete **Handout 8.2 — Thematic Analysis: Cotton Kingdom (TRM).**

TRM Find **Handout 8.2 — Thematic Analysis: Cotton Kingdom** in the Teacher's Resource Materials.

AP® FIRSTHAND ACCOUNTS

AP® SKILLS & PROCESSES

ANALYZING HISTORICAL EVIDENCE

The **AP® FIRSTHAND ACCOUNTS** feature encourages students to consider competing regional economic systems in the early nineteenth century. Though students tend to distinguish between the urban northern economy and rural southern economy, they should be reminded that these regional economies were inextricably linked to each other in the Market Revolution. Also, they may need to understand that the emergence of "free labor" (discussed on pp. 270–271) was often exploitative and repudiated the paternalism often found in the apprenticeship system — just as southern planters were beginning to articulate their own paternalistic views.

The Debate over Free and Slave Labor

As the abolitionist assault on slavery mounted, its rhetoric shaped the debate over the emergent system of wage labor in the northern states. By the 1850s, New York senator William Seward starkly contrasted the political systems of the South and the North in terms of their labor systems: "the one resting on the basis of servile or slave labor, the other on voluntary labor of freemen." Seward strongly favored the "free-labor system," crediting to it "the strength, wealth, greatness, intelligence, and freedom, which the whole American people now enjoy." As the following documents show, some Americans agreed with Seward, while others, such as *New York Tribune* editor Horace Greeley and South Carolina senator James Henry Hammond (who is quoted often in this chapter), contested his premises and conclusions.

SOUTH CAROLINA SENATOR JAMES HENRY HAMMOND

Speech to the Senate, March 4, 1858

In response to New York senator Seward, Senator Hammond urged admission of Kansas under the proslavery Lecompton Constitution and, by way of argument, celebrated the success of the South's cotton economy and its political and social institutions.

Source: *The Congressional Globe* (Washington, DC, March 6, 1858), 962.

“ In all social systems there must be a class to do the menial duties, to perform the drudgery of life. . . . Such a class you must have, or you would not have that other class which leads progress, civilization, and refinement. It constitutes the very mud-sill of society and of political government. . . . Fortunately for the South, she found a race adapted to that purpose to her hand. A race inferior to her own, but eminently qualified in temper, in vigor, in docility, in capacity to stand the climate, to answer all her purposes. We use them for our purpose, and call them slaves. . . .

The Senator from New York said yesterday that the whole world had abolished slavery. Aye, the name, but not the thing; . . . for the man who lives by daily labor, and scarcely lives at that, and who has to put out his labor in the market, and take the best he can get for it; in short, your whole hireling class of manual laborers and 'operatives,' as you call them, are essentially slaves. The difference between us is, that our slaves are hired for life and well compensated; there is no starvation, no begging, no want of employment among our people, and not too much employment either. Yours are hired by the day, not cared for, and scantily compensated, which may be proved in the most painful manner, at any hour in any street in any of your large towns. ”

NEW YORK PROTESTANT EPISCOPAL CHURCH MISSION SOCIETY

Sixth Annual Report, 1837

This excerpt demonstrates the society's belief that a class-bound social order could be avoided by encouraging "a spirit of independence and self-estimation" among the poor.

Source: New York Protestant Episcopal Church Mission Society, Sixth Annual Report (New York, 1837), 15–16.

“ In the older countries of Europe, there is a CLASS OF POOR: families born to poverty, living in poverty, dying in poverty. With us there are none such. In our bounteous land individuals alone are poor; but they form no poor class, because with them poverty is but a transient evil . . . save [except] paupers and vagabonds . . . all else form one common class of citizens; some more, others less advanced in the career of honorable independence. ”

HORACE GREELEY

Public Letter Declining an Invitation to Attend an Antislavery Convention in Cincinnati, Ohio, June 3, 1845

This letter from the editor of the *New York Tribune* explains his broad definition of slavery.

Source: Horace Greeley, *Hints Toward Reform in Lectures, Addresses, and Other Writings* (New York: Harper & Brothers, 1850), 352–355.

AP® EXAM TIP

Recognizing the impact of individual entrepreneurs and the inventions they created is essential for success on the AP® Exam.

The Spread of Innovation

By the 1820s, American-born artisans had replaced British immigrants at the cutting edge of technological innovation. In the Philadelphia region, the remarkable Sellars family produced the most important inventors. Samuel Sellars Jr. invented a machine for twisting worsted woolen yarn to give it an especially smooth surface. His son John improved the efficiency of the waterwheels powering the family's sawmills and built a machine to weave wire sieves. John's sons and grandsons ran machine shops that turned out riveted leather fire hoses, papermaking equipment, and eventually locomotives. In 1824, the Sellars and other mechanics founded the Franklin Institute in

“ Dear Sir: — I received, weeks since, your letter inviting me to be present at a general convention of opponents of Human Slavery. . . . What is Slavery? You will probably answer; 'The legal subjection of one human being to the will and power of another.' But this definition appears to me inaccurate. . . .

I understand by Slavery, that condition in which one human being exists mainly as a convenience for other human beings. . . . In short, . . . where the relation [is one] of authority, social ascendency and power over subsistence on the one hand, and of necessity, servility, and degradation on the other — there, in my view, is Slavery. . . . If I am less troubled concerning the Slavery prevalent in Charleston or New-Orleans, it is because I see so much Slavery in New-York. . . .

Wherever Opportunity to Labor is obtained with difficulty, and is so deficient that the Employing class may virtually prescribe their own terms and pay the Laborer only such share as they choose of the produce, there is a strong tendency to Slavery. ”

EDITORIAL IN THE *STAUNTON SPECTATOR*, 1859

Entitled "Freedom and Slavery," this editorial argues that "the black man's lot as a slave, is vastly preferable to that of his free brethren at the North."

SOURCE: *Staunton Spectator*, December 6, 1859, p. 2, c. 1.

“ The intelligent, christian slave-holder at the South is the best friend of the negro. He does not regard his bonds-men as mere chattel property, but as human beings to whom he owes duties. While the Northern Pharisee will not permit a negro to ride on the city railroads, Southern gentlemen and ladies are seen every day, side by side, in cars and coaches, with their faithful servants. Here the honest black man is not only protected by the laws and public sentiment, but he is respected by the community as truly as if his skin were white. Here there are ties of genuine friendship and affection between whites and blacks, leading to an interchange of all the comities of life. The slave nurses his master in sickness, and sheds tears of genuine sorrow at his grave. ”

JAMES HENRY HAMMOND

Private Letter to His Son Harry Hammond, 1856

This letter regards the future of Hammond's slave mistress, Sally Johnson, her son Henderson, and her daughter Louisa, who was the common mistress of father and son, and Louisa's children whom they sired.

SOURCE: James Hammond to Harry Hammond, February 19, 1856, in JHH Papers, SCL, quoted in Drew Gilpin Faust, *James Henry Hammond and the Old South: A Design for Mastery* (Baton Rouge: Louisiana State University Press, 1982), 87.

“ In the last will I made I left to you . . . Sally Johnson the mother of Louisa & all the children of both. Sally says Henderson is my child. It is possible, but I do not believe it Yet act on her's rather than my opinion. Louisa's first child may be mine. I think not. Her second I believe is mine. Take care of her & her children who are both of your blood if not of mine. . . . The services of the rest will compensate for indulgence to these. I cannot free these people & send them North. It would be cruelty to them. Nor would I like that any but my own blood should own as slaves my own blood or Louisa. I leave them to your charge, believing that you will best appreciate & most independently carry out my wishes in regard to them. Do not let Louisa or any of my children or possible children be the Slaves of Strangers. Slavery in the family will be their happiest earthly condition. ”

QUESTIONS FOR ANALYSIS

1. Which of these documents argue for slave owners as benevolent paternalists and the institution of slavery as a "positive good"? Identify the perspectives represented in these sources.
2. Given the discussion of "class" and "honorable independence" in the Mission Society statement (source 2), how would an Episcopalian reply to Hammond's critique of the northern labor system? Use evidence from at least one source to develop your response.
3. How can we understand Hammond's treatment of Sally Johnson and her daughter, as well as his refusal to free his and his son's children, in the context of his 1858 speech and the *Staunton Spectator*'s editorial?
4. Using the principles asserted in his letter, how would Horace Greeley (source 3) analyze the southern labor system, as described by Hammond and the *Staunton Spectator*? Why does Greeley suggest that the northern system has only "a strong tendency to Slavery"? Explain Greeley's historical situation and purpose.
5. Consider the sources above in the light of this Abraham Lincoln comment: "although volume upon volume is written to prove slavery a very good thing, we never hear of the man who wishes to take the good of it, by being a slave himself." What historical context influences many proponents of slavery?

TRM Find complete suggested responses in the Teacher's Resource Materials.

Philadelphia. Named after Benjamin Franklin, whom the mechanics admired for his work ethic and scientific accomplishments, the institute published a journal; provided high-school-level instruction in chemistry, mathematics, and mechanical design; and organized exhibits of new products. Craftsmen in Ohio and other states established similar institutes to disseminate technical knowledge and encourage innovation. Between 1820 and 1860, the number of patents issued by the U.S. Patent Office rose from two hundred to four thousand a year.

American craftsmen pioneered the development of **machine tools** — machines that made parts for other machines. Eli Whitney was a key innovator. At the age of fourteen, Whitney began fashioning nails and knife blades; later, he made women's

machine tools
Machines that made standardized metal parts for other machines, like textile looms and sewing machines. The development of machine tools by American inventors in the early nineteenth century accelerated industrialization.

CHECK FOR UNDERSTANDING

Ask students: **How did innovation spread in this era?** *Mass production techniques led to improvements in textile manufacturing, but also spread to other industries that affected farms and factories throughout the U.S.*

AP® SKILLS & PROCESSES

DEVELOPMENTS AND PROCESSES

While American factories in the 1840s and '50s represented a continuity with mechanized labor that had existed for decades, the **DEVELOPMENTS AND PROCESSES** question prompt asks students to identify changes in the products being produced.

TRM Find complete suggested responses in the Teacher's Resource Materials.

AP® THEME

WXT: Work, Exchange, and Technology

This illustration provides a reminder that just as technological innovations shaped the economy of New England (textile production) and the South (the cotton gin), the West was also impacted by machines that increased the speed and efficiency of production, assisting efforts to farm commercially and thus participate in the Market Revolution.

hatpins. Aspiring to wealth and status, Whitney won admission to Yale College and subsequently worked as a tutor on a Georgia cotton plantation. He capitalized on his expertise in making hatpins to design his cotton gin. Although Whitney patented the machine, other manufacturers improved on his design and captured the market.

Still seeking his fortune, Whitney decided in 1798 to manufacture military weapons. He eventually designed and built machine tools that could rapidly produce interchangeable musket parts, bringing him the wealth and fame he had long craved. After Whitney's death in 1825, his partner John H. Hall built an array of metalworking machine tools, such as turret lathes, milling machines, and precision grinders.

Technological innovation now swept through American manufacturing. Mechanics in the textile industry invented lathes, planers, and boring machines that turned out standardized parts for new spinning jennies and weaving looms. Despite being mass-produced, these jennies and looms were precisely made and operated at higher speeds than British equipment. Richard Garsed nearly doubled the speed of the power looms in his father's Delaware factory and patented a cam-and-harness device that allowed damask and other elaborately designed fabrics to be machine-woven. Meanwhile, the mechanics employed by Samuel W. Collins built a machine for pressing and hammering hot metal into dies (cutting forms). Using this machine, a worker could make three hundred ax heads a day — compared to twelve using traditional methods. In Richmond, Virginia, Welsh- and American-born mechanics at the Tredegar Iron Works produced low-cost parts for complicated manufacturing equipment. As a group of British observers noted admiringly, many American products were made "with machinery applied to almost every process . . . all reduced to an almost perfect system of manufacture."

AP® SKILLS & PROCESSES
DEVELOPMENTS AND PROCESSES
What new types of products came out of American factories by the 1840s and 1850s?

As mass production spread, the American Industrial Revolution came of age. Reasonably priced products such as Remington rifles, Singer sewing machines, and Yale locks became household names in the United States and abroad. After winning praise at the Crystal Palace Exhibition in London in 1851 — the first major international display of industrial goods — Remington, Singer, and other American firms became multinational businesses, building factories in Great Britain and selling goods throughout Europe. By 1877, the Singer Manufacturing Company controlled 75 percent of the world market for sewing machines.

artisan republicanism
An ideology of production that celebrated small-scale producers and emphasized liberty and equality. It flourished after the American Revolution and gradually declined as a result of industrialization.

McCormick's Reaper The economic revolution was the result, in part, of increased output created by power-driven machinery used in factories. However, machines also dramatically increased farm productivity. The mechanical reaper invented by Cyrus McCormick, first patented in 1834, revolutionized the harvesting process. Using McCormick's reaper and a horse, a farmer and his son could cut as much grain in a day as seven men with scythes. They could now plant more acres and not worry about the wheat sprouting (and becoming worthless) before it could be harvested. Threshing machines similarly allowed farmers to use animal power to process the grain. Eventually, a single horse-drawn machine — the combine harvester, or combine — could execute both operations. Oxford Science Archive/Print Collector/Getty Images.

Wageworkers and the Labor Movement

As the Industrial Revolution gathered momentum, it changed the nature of workers' lives. Following the American Revolution, many craft workers espoused **artisan republicanism**, an ideology of production based on liberty and equality. They saw themselves as small-scale producers, equal to one another and free to work for themselves. The poet Walt Whitman summed up their outlook: "Men must be masters, under themselves."

Free Workers Form Unions However, as the outwork and factory systems spread, more and more workers became wage earners who labored under the control of an employer. Unlike young women, who embraced factory work because it freed them from parental control and domestic service, men bridled at their status as supervised wageworkers. To assert their independence, male wageworkers rejected the traditional terms of *master* and *servant* and used the Dutch word *boss* to refer to their employer. Likewise, lowly apprentices refused to allow masters to control their private (nonwork) lives and joined their mates in building an independent, often rowdy, working-class culture. Still, as hired hands, they received meager wages and had little job security. The artisan-republican ideal of "self-ownership" confronted the harsh reality of waged work in an industrializing capitalist society. Labor had become a commodity, to be bought and sold.

Some wage earners worked in carpentry, stonecutting, masonry, and cabinetmaking — traditional crafts that required specialized skills. Their strong sense of identity, or trade consciousness, enabled these workers to form **unions** and bargain with their master-artisan employers over wages, hours, benefits, and control of the workplace. They resented low wages and long hours, which restricted their family life and educational opportunities. In Boston, six hundred carpenters went on strike in 1825. That protest failed, but in 1840, craft workers in St. Louis secured a ten-hour day, and President Van Buren issued an executive order setting a similar workday for federal workers.

Artisans in other occupations were less successful in preserving their pay and working conditions. As aggressive entrepreneurs and machine technology took command, shoemakers, hatters, printers, furniture makers, and weavers faced low-paid factory work. In response, some artisans in these trades moved to small towns, while in New York City, 800 highly skilled cabinetmakers made fashionable furniture. In status and income, these cabinetmakers outranked a group of 3,200 semitrained wageworkers who made cheaper tables and chairs in factories. Thus, the new industrial system split the traditional artisan class into self-employed craftsmen and wage-earning workers.

Woodworker, c. 1850 Skilled craftsmen took great pride in their furniture, which was often intricately designed and beautifully executed. To underline the dignity of his occupation, this woodworker poses in formal dress and proudly displays the tools of his craft. A belief in the value of their labor was an important ingredient of the artisan-republican ideology held by many workers. Library of Congress.

When wage earners banded together to form unions, they faced a legal hurdle: English and American common law branded such groups as illegal "combinations." Why were unions often considered to be illegal? As a Philadelphia judge put it, unions interfered with a "master's" authority over his "servant" — echoing the logic of an earlier, pre-democratic age. Other lawsuits accused unions of "conspiring" to raise wages and thereby injure employers. "It is important to the best interests of society that the price of labor be left to regulate itself," the New York Supreme Court declared in 1835. But employers were not bound by the same rule against conspiring among themselves: clothing manufacturers in New York City collectively agreed to set wage rates and to dismiss members of the Society of Journeymen Tailors.

unions
Organizations of workers that began during the Industrial Revolution to bargain with employers over wages, hours, benefits, and control of the workplace.

Labor Ideology Despite such obstacles, during the 1830s journeymen shoemakers founded mutual benefit societies in Lynn, Massachusetts, and other shoemaking centers. As the workers explained, "The capitalist has no other interest in us, than to get as much labor out of us as possible." To exert more pressure on their employers, in 1834 local unions from Boston to Philadelphia formed the National Trades Union, the first regional union of different trades.

AP® EXAM TIP
It's important to explain the changes in the identity of the "worker" that were the result of the Market Revolution in the early 19th century.

Workers found considerable popular support for their cause. When a New York City court upheld a conspiracy verdict against their union, tailors warned that the "Freemen of the North are now on a level with the slaves of the South," and organized a mass meeting of 27,000 people to denounce the decision. In 1836, local juries hearing conspiracy cases acquitted shoemakers in Hudson, New York; carpet makers in Thompsonville, Connecticut; and plasterers in Philadelphia. Then, in *Commonwealth v. Hunt* (1842), Chief Justice Lemuel Shaw of the Massachusetts Supreme Judicial Court upheld the right of workers to form unions and call strikes to enforce closed-shop agreements that limited employment to union members. But many judges continued to resist unions by forbidding strikes.

Union leaders expanded artisan republicanism to include wageworkers. Arguing that wage earners were becoming "slaves to a monied aristocracy," they condemned

TEACHING STRATEGY

This image provides an opportunity to discuss some of the challenges laborers faced in shifting from high-skilled labor to less complex tasks. Ask students: **What does this image reveal about how workers might have felt in shifting to lower-skill work?** *Given how much pride they seemed to take in the skill of their craft, they likely felt disappointed and frustrated doing less-skilled work.*

AP® APPLY THE TIP

To help students understand the changes that occurred in the identity of the "worker" in the nineteenth century, ask them to examine how workers viewed themselves before and after the Market Revolution. Provide students with a blank sheet of paper that they can fold in half, marking two sides: "before" and "after." Ask them to label the "before" side "Artisan Republicanism" (the dominant idea before the Market Revolution) and the "after" side "Wageworkers." Students should then provide an illustration that reflects the ways that workers' identity changed over time. Encourage students to use symbols and simple images to convey the changes. Each side of the illustration should have a caption that explains the evolution.

AP® SKILLS & PROCESSES

ANALYZING HISTORICAL EVIDENCE

Though the **AP® COMPARING INTERPRETATIONS** feature focuses specifically on opportunities for women, this question is part of a broader argument about whether we should think about the emergence of capitalism — then or now — as a generally beneficial dynamic and/or one that distributed benefits widely, or as a primarily exploitative force that needs to be managed. Because the Market Revolution was the beginning of the nation's large-scale introduction to capitalism, much historical debate about capitalism has centered here. As women's history began to develop in the late 1970s in the wake of the feminist movement, scholars began to ask about how the economy affected women.

AP® COMPARING INTERPRETATIONS

Did the Market Revolution Expand Opportunities for Women?

The Market Revolution of the early nineteenth century produced important changes in patterns of work. Two opportunities that the revolution opened for women are highlighted by Paul E. Johnson and Mary H. Blewett. Johnson describes the emergence of the factory system in Lowell, Massachusetts, pioneered by the Boston Manufacturing Company, which employed young, unmarried women in the production of textiles. Mostly from rural New England towns, the "Lowell girls" worked in the factories and lived together in the company's boardinghouses until they married and left the wage economy. The New England farmwomen whom Blewett describes also participated in the market economy but indirectly and from home. Often wives and mothers, these women squeezed piecework between their domestic chores to supplement the family income. In this case, they stitched the leather uppers of a shoe and then shipped them to a "shoe boss" whose shop finished the shoe's manufacture by stitching the upper to its leather sole.

PAUL E. JOHNSON

SOURCE: Paul E. Johnson, *The Early American Republic, 1789–1829* (New York: Oxford University Press, 2007), 78–79.

[Francis Cabot] Lowell joined with wealthy friends to form the Boston Manufacturing Company — soon known as the Boston Associates. In 1813 they built their first mill in Waltham, Massachusetts, and then expanded into Lowell, Lawrence, and other new towns near Boston in the 1820s. . . . [T]he operatives who tended their machines were young, single women recruited from the farms of northern New England — farms that were switching to livestock raising and thus had little need for the labor of daughters. The company provided carefully supervised boarding houses for them and enforced rules of conduct both on and off the job. The young women worked steadily, never drank, seldom stayed out late, and attended church faithfully. They dressed neatly — often stylishly — and read newspapers and attended lectures. They impressed visitors, particularly those who had seen factory workers in other places, as a dignified and self-respecting workforce.

The brick mills and prim boarding houses set within landscaped towns and occupied by sober, well-behaved farm girls signified the Boston Associates' desire to build a profitable textile industry without creating a permanent working class. The women would work for a few years in a carefully controlled environment, send their wages back to their family, and return home to live as country housewives. These young farm women did in fact form an efficient, decorous workforce. But the decorum was imposed less by the owners than by the women themselves. To protect their own reputations, they punished misbehavior and shunned fellow workers whose behavior was questionable. Nor did they send their wages home or, as was popularly believed, use them to pay for their brothers' college education. Some saved their money to use as dowries that their fathers could not afford. More, however, spent their wages on themselves — particularly on clothes and books.

The owners of the factories expected that the young women's sojourn would reinforce their own parternalistic position and that of the girls' fathers. Instead, it produced a self-respecting sisterhood of independent, wage-earning women. Twice in the 1830s the women of Lowell went out on strike, proclaiming that they were not wage slaves but "the daughters of freemen." After finishing their stint in the

labor theory of value
The belief that human labor produces economic value. Adherents argued that the price of a product should be determined not by the market but by the amount of work required to make it, and that most of the price should be paid to the person who produced it.

the new factory system in which "capital and labor stand opposed." To create a just society in which workers could "live as comfortably as others," they advanced a **labor theory of value**. Under this theory, the price of goods should reflect the labor required to make them, and the income from their sale should go primarily to the producers, not to factory owners, middlemen, or storekeepers. "The poor who perform the work, ought to receive at least half of that sum which is charged" to the consumer, declared minister Ezra Stiles Ely. Union activists agreed, organizing nearly fifty strikes for higher wages in 1836. Appealing to the spirit of the American Revolution, which had destroyed the aristocracy of birth, they called for a new revolution to demolish the aristocracy of capital.

Women textile operatives were equally active. Competition in the woolen and cotton textile industries was fierce because mechanization caused output to grow faster than consumer demand. As textile prices fell, manufacturers' revenues declined. To maintain profits, employers reduced workers' wages and imposed tougher work rules. In 1828 and again in 1834, women mill workers in Dover, New Hampshire, went

CHECK FOR UNDERSTANDING

Ask students: **How did wage work and the labor movement emerge?** *The new outwork and factory system led to the decline of apprenticeship and the rise of wage work. As pay and work conditions declined for wage workers, they began to form unions to resist their slide in status.*

mills, many Lowell women entered public life as reformers. Most of them married and became housewives but not on the same terms their mothers had known. One in three married Lowell men and became city dwellers. Those who returned home to rural neighborhoods remained unmarried longer than their sisters who had stayed at home and then married men about their own age who worked at something other than farming. Thus the Boston Associates kept their promise to produce cotton cloth profitably without creating a permanent working class. But they did not succeed in shuttling young women between rural and urban paternalism and back again. Wage labor, the ultimate degradation for agrarian-republican men, opened a road to independence for thousands of young women.

MARY H. BLEWETT

SOURCE: From Mary H. Blewett, "Work, Gender and the Artisan Tradition in New England Shoemaking, 1780–1860," *Journal of Social History* 17 (1983), 222–239 by George Mason University. Reproduced with permission of George Mason University in the format Book via Copyright Clearance Center.

For women workers, the pre-industrial period was a time of submersion in the family and in the family wage economy. The sexual division of labor placed them outside the vitality of life, politics and work which centered in the artisan shop. . . . The introduction of the sexual division of labor into an artisan craft represented a major change in the mode of production. Work was redefined and relocated, new words were coined and new procedures devised for supervision. The work assigned to women took on social meanings appropriate to their gender. Female family members adapted their traditional needle skills to hand sew the leather uppers of shoes in their kitchens without disrupting their domestic duties or their child care tasks. . . .

By 1833 there were about 1,500 women in Lynn [Massachusetts] who earned wages as shoebinders. . . . Sharing the bonds of womanhood both in work and in their domestic sphere, shoebinders in 1834 tried to organize themselves in terms of a female community of workers. . . . [B]ut . . . the conditions under which many shoebinders labored — isolated from each other, employed by the shoe boss outside a group labor system and combining wage work with domestic responsibilities — discouraged collective activity. The tensions between their relationship to the artisan system and its equal rights ideology and their subordinate role as females in the family were exposed by their arguments for a just wage for women. Neither the social relations of the artisan family nor the realities of working as a woman for a shoe boss encouraged . . . [her] . . . to identify with her working sister in the Lowell mills or conceive of herself as a worker capable of supporting herself who could unite with her peers to protest mistreatment. . . .

[T]ension between women workers and the family values of artisan culture remained constant and unresolved as work reorganized during the shift toward industrialization from 1780 to 1860. Contradictions between perceptions of the proper gender role for women in the family and their consciousness as workers in production prolonged these tensions for women workers into the early factory system. . . . This struggle, most visible during moments of labor protest, had been initiated by the recruitment of women into production in the artisan system and maintained by the differences in the location of work and the exposure of the individual worker to the increasing control of the work process by the employer.

AP® SHORT ANSWER PRACTICE

1. Identify two factors that explain the different conclusions drawn by Johnson and Blewett regarding women's opportunities in the market economy.
2. To what extent did the women these two historians describe see their work as a means to claim political, social, or economic rights? Support your argument with specific examples.
3. Comparing these excerpts with Chapter 8's discussion of the development of the market economy, identify two ways women's work experiences differed from men's.

TRM Find complete suggested responses in the Teacher's Resource Materials.

on strike and won some relief. In Lowell, two thousand women operatives backed a strike by withdrawing their savings from an employer-owned bank. "One of the leaders mounted a pump," the *Boston Transcript* reported, "and made a flaming . . . speech on the rights of women and the iniquities of the 'monied aristocracy.'" Increasingly, young New England women refused to enter the mills, and impoverished Irish (and later French Canadian) immigrants took their places (see "Comparing Interpretations," p. 272).

AP® SKILLS & PROCESSES

MAKING CONNECTIONS

How did the capitalist-run industrial economy conflict with artisan republicanism, and how did workers respond?

The Growth of Cities and Towns

The expansion of industry and trade dramatically increased America's urban population. In 1820, there were 58 towns with more than 2,500 inhabitants; by 1840, there were 126 such towns, located mostly in the Northeast and Midwest. During those two decades, the total number of city dwellers grew more than fourfold, from 443,000 to 1,844,000 (Map 8.6).

AP® EXAM TIP

Be able to summarize the causes and effects of the process of urbanization beginning in the early nineteenth century.

AP® SKILLS & PROCESSES

MAKING CONNECTIONS

In order for students to engage in a discussion of the differences between artisan republican and capitalist-run industry, have students define the broader contexts of each idea. For instance, when you ask students about artisan republican, ask them to identify what artisan means. When you ask them about capitalist-run industry, require students to define that term in the context of the Market Revolution. In this way, you are rooting students in a specific time and place, which will help them develop better responses.

TRM Find complete suggested responses in the Teacher's Resource Materials.

AP® APPLY THE TIP

Have students work in pairs to consider the cause and effect relationships of each event listed on **Handout 8.3 — Causation: Early Nineteenth-Century Urbanization (TRM)**. Students should focus on the types of cities that developed and their connection to expanded markets and transportation networks. Lead a class discussion on how urbanization caused greater regional division in the U.S. and how it impacted workers.

TRM Find **Handout 8.3 — Causation: Early Nineteenth-Century Urbanization** in the Teacher's Resource Materials.

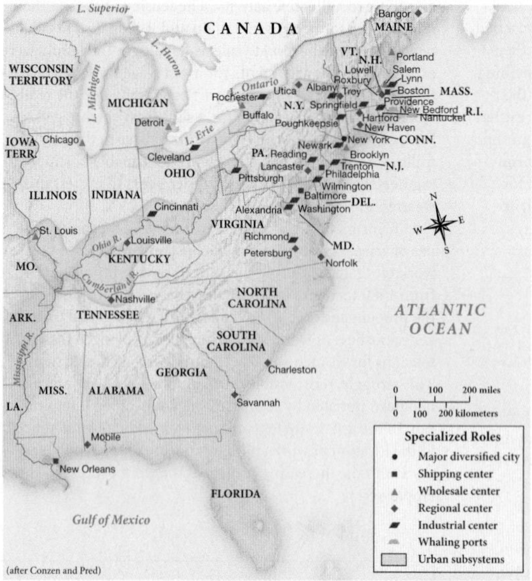

MAP 8.6 The Nation's Major Cities, 1840

By 1840, the United States boasted three major conglomerations of cities. The long-settled ports on the Atlantic — from Boston to Baltimore — served as centers for import merchants, banks, insurance companies, and manufacturers of ready-made clothing, and their financial reach extended far into the interior — nationwide in the case of New York City. A second group of cities stretched along the Great Lakes and included the commercial hubs of Buffalo, Detroit, and Chicago, as well as the manufacturing center of Cleveland. A third urban system extended along the Ohio River, comprising the industrial cities of Pittsburgh and Cincinnati and the wholesale centers of Louisville and St. Louis.

AP® THEME

MIG: Migration and Settlement

Use **MAP 8.6** to encourage students to move beyond familiar depictions of individual cities to consider larger interconnected regions. Discuss how this map helps students to conceptualize patterns of migration and urbanization in the era of the Market Revolution.

The fastest growth occurred in the new industrial towns that sprouted along the "fall line," where rivers descended rapidly from the Appalachian Mountains to the coastal plain. In 1822, the Boston Manufacturing Company built a complex of mills in a sleepy Merrimack River village that quickly became the bustling textile factory town of Lowell, Massachusetts. The towns of Hartford, Connecticut; Trenton, New Jersey; and Wilmington, Delaware, also became urban centers as mill owners exploited the water power of their rivers and recruited workers from the countryside.

Western commercial cities such as Pittsburgh, Cincinnati, and New Orleans grew almost as fast. They began as transit centers, where workers transferred goods from farmers' rafts and wagons to flatboats or steamboats. As the midwestern population grew during the 1830s and 1840s, St. Louis, Detroit, and especially Buffalo and Chicago also emerged as dynamic centers of commerce. "There can be no two places in the world," journalist Margaret Fuller wrote from Chicago in 1843, "more completely thoroughfares than this place and Buffalo. . . . The life-blood [of commerce] rushes from east to west, and back again from west to east." Chicago's merchants and bankers developed the marketing, provisioning, and financial services essential to farmers and small-town shopkeepers in its vast hinterland. "There can be no better [market] any where in the Union," declared a farmer in Paw Paw, Illinois.

These midwestern hubs quickly became manufacturing centers. Capitalizing on the cities' links to rivers and canals, entrepreneurs built warehouses, flour mills, packing plants, and machine shops, creating work for hundreds of artisans and factory laborers. In 1846, Cyrus McCormick moved his reaper factory from western Virginia to Chicago to be closer to his midwestern customers.

The old Atlantic seaports — Boston, Philadelphia, Baltimore, Charleston, and especially New York City — remained important for their foreign commerce and, increasingly, as centers of finance and small-scale manufacturing. New York City and nearby Brooklyn grew at a phenomenal rate: between 1820 and 1860, their combined populations increased nearly tenfold to 1 million people, thanks to the arrival of hundreds of thousands of German and Irish immigrants. Drawing on these workers, New York became a center of the ready-made clothing industry, which relied on thousands of low-paid seamstresses. "The wholesale clothing establishments are . . . absorbing the business of the country," a "Country Tailor" complained to the *New York Tribune*, "casting many an honest and hardworking man out of employment [and helping] . . . the large cities to swallow up the small towns."

New York City had the best harbor in the United States and, thanks to the Erie Canal, was the best gateway to the Midwest and the best outlet for western grain. Recognizing the city's advantages, in 1818 four English Quaker merchants founded the Black Ball Line to carry cargo, people, and mail between New York and London,

VISUAL ACTIVITY

***View of Cincinnati*, by John Caspar Wild, c. 1835** Thanks to its location on the Ohio River (a tributary of the Mississippi), Cincinnati quickly became one of the major processing centers for grain and hogs in the trans-Appalachian west. By the 1820s, passenger steamboats and freight barges connected the city with Pittsburgh to the north and the ocean port of New Orleans far to the south. Cincinnati Museum Center/Getty Images.

READING THE IMAGE: What economic activities do you imagine were going on in the many large brick buildings near the waterfront?

MAKING CONNECTIONS: Why did Cincinnati's geographical advantage become less important with the passage of time?

Liverpool, and Le Havre, establishing the first regularly scheduled transatlantic shipping service. By 1840, its port handled almost two-thirds of foreign imports into the United States, almost half of all foreign trade, and much of the immigrant traffic. New York likewise monopolized trade with the newly independent South American nations of Brazil, Peru, and Venezuela, and its merchants took over the trade in cotton by offering finance, insurance, and shipping to southern planters and merchants.

AP® SKILLS & PROCESSES

COMPARISON

What different types of cities emerged between 1820 and the 1840s, and what caused their growth?

NEW SOCIAL CLASSES AND CULTURES

How was the structure of American society different in 1848 than it had been in 1800?

The economic changes of the early nineteenth century improved the lives of many Americans, who now lived in larger houses, cooked on iron stoves, and wore better-made clothes, but they also created a more stratified society. In 1800, white Americans thought of their society in terms of rank: "notable" families had higher status

TEACHING STRATEGY

Have students compare the *View of Cincinnati* by John Caspar Wild with the image of the Erie Canal on p. 255, since both depict commercial waterways — one natural and the other artificial — and the communities that grew up around them.

TRM Find complete suggested responses in the Teacher's Resource Materials.

AP® SKILLS & PROCESSES

COMPARISON

The **COMPARISON** question combines causation — why cities grew — alongside comparison of the different types of cities. This question can be combined into one as students compare the reasons for the growth of different types of cities. Students may need to be cautioned not to exaggerate these changes — Americans remained overwhelmingly rural in this era, as only 11 percent of Americans lived in towns of 2,500 or more in 1840 after the urban boom the text describes. Extend this prompt by having students explore links between the different types of cities, considering how the growth of one influenced the growth of another.

TRM Find complete suggested responses in the Teacher's Resource Materials.

CHECK FOR UNDERSTANDING

Ask students: **How did technological innovation improve the lives of ordinary people, and what challenges did it present to them?** *Technological innovation made the ordinary worker's labor easier, relying less on his or her physical prowess and more on the machine's use of energy. Technology's efficiency also made products cheaper, meaning an ordinary person could afford more of the new goods like sewing machines. On the contrary, it altered his or her relationship to their labor. Under the new factory system, labor became a commodity like any other and the independent merchant or service provider gradually disappeared into the dehumanizing factory and its poor standardized wages.*

than those from the "lower orders." Yet in rural areas, people of different ranks often shared a common culture. Gentlemen farmers talked easily with yeomen about crop yields, while their wives conversed about the art of quilting. In the South, humble tenants and aristocratic slave owners enjoyed the same amusements: gambling, cockfighting, and horse racing. Rich and poor attended the same Quaker meetinghouse or Presbyterian church. "Almost everyone eats, drinks, and dresses in the same way," a European visitor to Hartford, Connecticut, reported in 1798, "and one can see the most obvious inequality only in the dwellings."

The rise of the cotton complex heightened economic inequality. In the South, the cotton boom sharpened distinctions between poorer and wealthier whites and concentrated slaves on larger plantations. In the booming cities, the new economic order spawned distinct social classes: a small but wealthy business elite, a substantial middle class, and a mass of propertyless wage earners. By creating a class-divided society, industrialization posed a momentous challenge to America's republican ideals.

Inequality in the South

gang-labor system
A system of work discipline used on southern cotton plantations in the mid-nineteenth century in which white overseers or black drivers supervised gangs of enslaved laborers to achieve greater productivity.

By the time of the American Revolution, tobacco and rice planting in the South had already created a three-tiered slave society. Large planters who owned dozens, or even hundreds, of slaves dominated the life of the Chesapeake and the Carolina low country, while poorer whites with less land and fewer slaves deferred to their wealthy neighbors' leadership. Enslaved African Americans possessed little or nothing of their own and lived at the mercy of their owners. After 1800, South Carolina rice planters remained at the apex of the seaboard plantation aristocracy. In 1860, the fifteen proprietors of the vast plantations in All Saints Parish in South Carolina owned 4,383 slaves — nearly 300 apiece — who annually grew and processed 14 million pounds of rice. As inexpensive Asian rice entered the world market in the 1820s, the Carolina rice planters sold some slaves and worked the others harder to maintain their lifestyle.

A Slave Family Picking Cotton Picking cotton — thousands of small bolls attached to 3-foot-high woody and often prickly stalks — was a tedious and time-consuming task, taking up to four months on many plantations. However, workers of both sexes and all ages could pick cotton, and masters could measure output by weighing the baskets of each picker or family, chastising those who failed to meet their quotas. What does this early photograph of a family of pickers, taken on a plantation near Savannah, Georgia, and believed to date to the 1860s, suggest about women's and children's lives, family relations, and living conditions? © Collection of the New-York Historical Society, USA/Bridgeman Images.

In tobacco-growing regions, the planter aristocracy followed a different path. Slave ownership had always been more widely diffused: in the 1770s, about 60 percent of white families in the Chesapeake owned at least one slave. As wealthy tobacco planters moved their estates and slaves to the Cotton South, middling whites (who owned between five and twenty slaves) came to dominate the Chesapeake economy. The descendants of the old tobacco aristocracy remained influential, but increasingly as slave-owning grain farmers, lawyers, merchants, industrialists, and politicians. They hired out surplus slaves, sold them south, or allowed them to purchase their freedom.

In the Cotton South, ambitious planters worked their slaves ferociously as they sought to establish themselves. A Mississippi planter put it plainly: "Everything has to give way to large crops of cotton." It was a demanding crop. Frederick Law Olmsted, the future architect of New York's Central Park, noted during his travels that slaves in the Cotton South worked "much harder and more unremittingly" than those in the tobacco regions. To increase output, profit-seeking cotton planters began during the 1820s to use a rigorous **gang-labor system**. Previously, many planters

AP® THEME

SOC: Social Structures

The photo of the slave family and the accompanying caption capture the fact that cotton labor was not just an economic activity but a central part of family life for enslaved people. The question posed in the caption encourages students to think about the experiences of men, women, and children, their relationships, and their daily experiences.

had supervised workers only sporadically, or had assigned them tasks to complete at their own pace. Now masters with twenty or more slaves organized disciplined teams, or "gangs," supervised by black drivers and white overseers. They worked the gangs at a steady pace, clearing and plowing land or hoeing and picking cotton.

The gang-labor system enhanced profits by increasing productivity. Because slaves in gangs finished tasks in thirty-five minutes that took a white farmer an hour to complete, gang labor became ever more prevalent. As the price of raw cotton surged after 1846, the wealth of the planter class skyrocketed. And no wonder: nearly 2 million enslaved African Americans now labored on the plantations of the Cotton South and annually produced 4 million bales of the valuable fiber.

On the eve of the Civil War, southern slave owners accounted for nearly two-thirds of all American men with wealth of $100,000 or more. But wealth was concentrated at the top of society, along with southern capital: only about one-quarter of southern households were slave owning; three-fourths owned no slaves and participated in only limited ways in the economic revolution that cotton brought to the South. Other white southerners — backcountry farmers on marginal lands and cotton-planting tenants in particular — occupied some of the lowest rungs of the nation's social order. The expansion of southern slavery, like the flowering of northern capitalism, increased inequalities of wealth and status.

AP® SKILLS & PROCESSES

MAKING CONNECTIONS

How did the rise of cotton agriculture affect the social structure of the South?

The Northern Business Elite

In the North, the Industrial Revolution altered the older agrarian social order. The urban economy made a few city residents — the merchants, manufacturers, bankers, and landlords who made up the business elite — very rich. In 1800, the richest 10 percent of the nation's families owned about 40 percent of the wealth; by 1860, they held nearly 70 percent. In New York, Chicago, Baltimore, and New Orleans, the superrich — the top 1 percent — owned more than 40 percent of the land, buildings, and other tangible property and an even higher share of intangible property, such as stocks and bonds.

Government tax policies facilitated the accumulation of wealth. There were no federal taxes on individual and corporate income. Rather, the U.S. Treasury raised most of its revenue from tariffs: regressive taxes on textiles and other imported goods purchased mostly by ordinary citizens. State and local governments also favored the wealthy. They taxed real estate (farms, city lots, and buildings) and tangible personal property (furniture, tools, and machinery), but almost never taxed stocks and bonds or the inheritances the rich passed on to their children.

As cities expanded in size and wealth, affluent families set themselves apart. They dressed in well-tailored clothes, rode in fancy carriages, and bought expensively furnished houses tended by butlers, cooks, and other servants. The women no longer socialized with those of lesser wealth, and the men no longer labored side by side with their employees. Instead, they became managers and directors and relied on trusted subordinates to supervise their employees. Merchants, manufacturers, and bankers placed a premium on privacy and lived in separate neighborhoods, often in exclusive central areas or at the city's edge. The geographic isolation of privileged families and the massive flow of immigrants into separate districts divided cities spatially along lines of class, race, and ethnicity.

AP® EXAM TIP

It's important to recognize the impact of the Market Revolution on the distinctions between classes in American society.

AP® SKILLS & PROCESSES

CONTINUITY AND CHANGE

To what degree did elite families change between 1800 and 1848?

The Middle Class

Standing between wealthy owners and propertyless wage earners was a growing **middle class** — the social product of increased commerce. The "middling class," a Boston printer explained, was made up of "the farmers, the mechanics, the manufacturers, the traders, who carry on professionally the ordinary operations of buying, selling, and exchanging merchandize." Professionals with other skills — building contractors, lawyers, surveyors, and so on — were suddenly in great demand and

middle class
An economic group of prosperous farmers, artisans, and traders that emerged in the early nineteenth century. Its rise reflected a dramatic increase in prosperity. This surge in income, along with an abundance of inexpensive mass-produced goods, fostered a distinct middle-class urban culture.

AP® SKILLS & PROCESSES

MAKING CONNECTIONS

The **MAKING CONNECTIONS** question asks students what cotton's role was in shaping the southern social structure. Students need to identify the ways economic changes modified the relationship between whites in the region's class hierarchy. This text calls for close reading and would benefit from drawing a social pyramid, labeling the groups, and annotating the relationship between each level. Extend this prompt by asking students to compare these changes to the social structure in the Chesapeake region and explain reasons for similarities and differences between the two social structures.

TRM Find complete suggested responses in the Teacher's Resource Materials.

AP® APPLY THE TIP

Divide students into small groups and assign each group to focus on the social class system of either the North or the South. Ask students to develop a social class pyramid diagram based on a close reading of pp. 275–280. Divide the pyramid so that the size of the space is relative to the size of the social class and ask students to label each social class. Under the label, students should list the characteristics of the social class, including the relative number of people in the class, typical occupations, common cultural features, etc. After groups have created the pyramid for their social class, ask students to pair up so they can compare the social systems of the North and South. Ask students to write a paragraph on the similarities and differences in the social class systems of North and South.

CHECK FOR UNDERSTANDING

Ask students: **Who made up the northern business elite and how did they live?** *They were merchants, manufacturers, bankers, and landlords who owned a majority of the nation's wealth by the start of the Civil War. They lived in expensively furnished houses, owned fancy carriages, and wore well-tailored clothes.*

AP® SKILLS & PROCESSES

CONTINUITY AND CHANGE

The **CONTINUITY AND CHANGE** question requires students to chart changes over time in the nature of elite families. This could be represented graphically through a T-chart with the first column for elite families in 1800 and the second for elite families in 1848.

TRM Find complete suggested responses in the Teacher's Resource Materials.

Hartford Family Completely at home in their elegant drawing room, this elite family in Hartford, Connecticut, enjoys the fruits of the father's business success. As the father lounges in his silk robe, his eldest son (and presumptive heir) adopts an air of studied nonchalance, and his daughter fingers a piano, signaling her musical accomplishments and the family's gentility. A diminutive African American servant (her size suggesting her status) serves fruit to the lavishly attired woman of the house. The sumptuously appointed drawing room reflects the owners' prosperity and their aesthetic and cultural interests. White House Collection/White House Historical Association.

AP® THEME

SOC: Social Structures

The portrait of the Hartford family, which contrasts dramatically with the photo of a slave family on page 276, illustrates the emergence of a larger middle class as the growth of manufacturing increased prosperity for some. The caption points out the indicators of wealth depicted in the picture, both the quality of the material goods and the leisure time to enjoy them.

AP® APPLY THE TIP

To better understand the distinctions that increasingly differentiated middle class and urban poor women, have students create a Venn diagram. Ask students to note the distinctions in the social classes and the ways in which this especially differentiated women's roles. Although there are many differences, ask students to clarify what women in both classes had in common as well.

AP® EXAM TIP

A helpful exercise in prepping for the AP® Exam is to compare the impact of economic change on women in the middle class and the urban poor class.

well compensated, as were middling business owners and white-collar clerks. In the Northeast, men with these qualifications numbered about 30 percent of the population in the 1840s. But they also could be found in small towns of the agrarian Midwest and South. In 1854, the cotton boomtown of Oglethorpe, Georgia (population 2,500), boasted eighty "business houses" and eight hotels.

The emergence of the middle class reflected a dramatic rise in prosperity. Between 1830 and 1857, the per capita income of Americans increased by about 2.5 percent a year, a remarkable rate that has never since been matched. This surge in income, along with an abundance of inexpensive mass-produced goods, fostered a distinct middle-class urban culture. Middle-class husbands earned enough to save about 15 percent of their income, which they used to buy well-built houses in a "respectable part of town." Middle-class wives became purveyors of genteel culture, buying books, pianos, lithographs, and comfortable furniture for their front parlors. Upper-middle-class families hired Irish or African American domestic servants, while less prosperous folk enjoyed the comforts provided by new industrial goods. For their homes they acquired furnaces (to warm the entire house and heat water for bathing), cooking stoves with ovens, and Singer's treadle-operated sewing machines. Some urban families now kept their perishable food in iceboxes, which ice-company wagons periodically refilled.

If material comfort was one distinguishing mark of the middle class, moral and mental discipline was another. Middle-class writers denounced raucous carnivals and festivals as a "chaos of sin and folly, of misery and fun" and, by the 1830s, had largely suppressed them. Ambitious parents were equally concerned with their children's moral and intellectual development, providing a high school education (in an era when most white children received only five years of schooling) and stressing the importance of discipline and hard work. American Protestants had long believed that diligent work in an earthly "calling" was a duty owed to God. Now the business elite and the middle class gave this idea a secular twist by celebrating work as the key to individual social mobility and national prosperity.

Young, middle-class men saved their money, adopted temperate habits, and aimed to rise in the world. There was an "almost universal ambition to get forward," observed Hezekiah Niles, editor of *Niles' Weekly Register*. Warner Myers, a Philadelphia housepainter, rose from poverty by saving his wages, borrowing from his family and friends, and becoming a builder, eventually constructing and selling sixty houses. Countless children's books, magazine stories, self-help manuals, and novels recounted the tales of similar individuals. The **self-made man** became a central theme of American popular culture. Just as the yeoman ethic had served as a unifying ideal in pre-1800 agrarian America, so the gospel of personal achievement linked the middle and business classes of the new industrializing society.

The Emerging Middle Class This young family from York, Pennsylvania, displays all the hallmarks of a comfortable middle-class existence. The colorful carpet, wallpaper, framed mirrors and painting, and furniture attest to both their aesthetic taste and their economic means. The African American nursemaid tending the youngest child was probably hired labor, though it is possible she was enslaved, since the institution was not completely abolished until 1848. The mother reads a book — symbol of the family's commitment to education and culture — while her children attend at her knees. Her husband appears relaxed and self-satisfied in a fine suit of clothes. The setting is modest compared to the splendor of the Hartford family pictured on the previous page, but this painting, executed by an unknown artist in about 1828, reflects the values and growing wealth of America's new middle class. Saint Louis Art Museum, Missouri, USA/Gift of Edgar William and Bernice Chrysler Garbisch/Bridgeman Images.

self-made man
A nineteenth-century ideal that celebrated men who rose to wealth or social prominence from humble origins through self-discipline, hard work, and temperate habits.

AP® SKILLS & PROCESSES

DEVELOPMENTS AND PROCESSES

What were the moral values and material culture of the urban middle class?

Urban Workers and the Poor

As thoughtful business leaders surveyed their society, they concluded that the yeoman farmer and artisan-republican ideal — a social order of independent producers — was no longer possible. "Entire independence ought not to be wished for," Ithamar A. Beard, the paymaster of the Hamilton Manufacturing Company (in Lowell, Massachusetts), told a mechanics' association in 1827. "In large manufacturing towns, many more must fill subordinate stations and must be under the immediate direction and control of a master or superintendent, than in the farming towns."

Beard had a point. In 1840, all of the nation's slaves, some 2.5 million people, and about half of its adult white workers, another 3 million (of a total population of 17 million), were laboring for others. The bottom 10 percent of white wage earners consisted of casual workers hired on a short-term basis for arduous jobs. Poor women washed clothes; their husbands and sons carried lumber and bricks for construction projects, loaded ships, and dug out dirt and stones to build canals. Even when they could find jobs, they could never save enough "to pay rent, buy fire wood and eatables" when the job market or the harbor froze up. During business depressions, casual laborers suffered and died; in good times, their jobs were temporary and dangerous.

Other laborers had greater security of employment, but few were prospering. In Massachusetts in 1825, an unskilled worker earned about two-thirds as much as a mechanic did; two decades later, it was less than half as much. A journeyman carpenter in Philadelphia reported that he was about "even with the World" after several years of work but that many of his coworkers were in debt. Only the most fortunate working-class families could afford to educate their children, buy apprenticeships for their sons, or accumulate small dowries for their daughters. Most families sent ten-year-old children out to work, and the death of a parent often threw the survivors into dire poverty. As a charity worker noted, "What can a bereaved widow do, with 5 or 6 little children, destitute of every means of support but what her own hands can furnish (which in a general way does not amount to more than 25 cents a day)?"

Impoverished workers congregated in dilapidated housing in bad neighborhoods. Single men and women lived in crowded boardinghouses, while families jammed themselves into tiny apartments in the basements and attics of small houses. As immigrants poured in after 1840, urban populations soared, and developers squeezed more and more dwellings and foul-smelling outhouses onto a single lot. By 1848, America's

CHECK FOR UNDERSTANDING

Ask students: **Who made up the northern middle class and how did they live?** *Farmers, mechanics, manufacturers, traders, and professionals made up the northern middle class. They enjoyed well-built homes, inexpensive art and furniture, and could afford to hire domestic servants.*

TRM Find complete suggested responses in the Teacher's Resource Materials.

CHECK FOR UNDERSTANDING

Ask students: **How was the structure of American society different in 1848 than it had been in 1800?** *The industrialization of the Market Revolution in both North and South drastically stratified American society. While ranks had predated the early 1800s, the Market Revolution made such distinctions more astute. Even as all lives improved, a small but wealthy merchant class and plantation class controlled most wealth. A small but growing middle class did exist, but many found themselves as propertyless wage earners or, in the South, as poor farmers. This analysis, of course, discounts African slaves.*

The Five Points, New York City As New York City grew rapidly larger and became increasingly segregated by class, poorer neighborhoods gained unsavory reputations among the middling and upper classes. This painting by an unknown artist depicts the Five Points, one of the city's most notorious locales, in about 1828. The artist has placed a bemused gentleman in the center of the image, surrounded by a chaotic and riotous street scene. Both people and animals run wild, while groups of African Americans congregate to draw water, talk, sing, and fight. This painting was reproduced as a lithograph in the 1850s, at about the same time the *New York Herald* called the Five Points a "nest of drunkenness, roguery, debauchery, vice, and pestilence." The Metropolitan Museum of Art. Bequest of Mrs. Screven Lorillard (Alice Whitney), from the collection of Mrs. J. Insley Blair, 2016.

AP® SKILLS & PROCESSES

MAKING CONNECTIONS

How did the increasingly urban, capitalist economy of the northeastern states affect the lives of poor workers?

largest cities were growing more divided between the genteel dwellings of the middle and upper classes and the impoverished neighborhoods of the working poor.

SUMMARY

This chapter began by examining the structural changes that transformed the American economy in the first half of the nineteenth century. The Market Revolution enabled long-distance travel, trade, and communication, while a revolution in productivity — the Industrial Revolution in the North and the expansion of cotton production in the South — dramatically increased economic output. Water, steam, and minerals such as coal and iron were essential to this transformation; so, too, were technological innovation and labor discipline. Together they helped the United States to master and exploit its vast new territory.

The chapter went on to explore the consequences of that transformation. In the South, the institution of slavery expanded its geographical reach, with millions of new laborers exploited more intensively than ever before. In the North, where new urban centers developed and older cities grew, workers struggled to control the terms of their employment. The Northeast and the Midwest shared important cultural affinities, while the resurgence of slavery in the South set it apart, but in every region the social order was growing more divided by race and class. As the next chapter suggests, Americans looked to their political system, which was becoming increasingly democratic, to address these social divisions. In fact, the tensions among economic inequality, cultural diversity, and political democracy became a troubling — and enduring — part of American life.

TRM Find complete suggested responses in the Teacher's Resource Materials.

CHECK FOR UNDERSTANDING

Use the **AP® LEARNING FOCUS** question from the beginning of the chapter to check students' understanding of the chapter as a whole: **Why and how did the economic transformations of the first half of the nineteenth century reshape northern and southern society and culture?** *The economic transformations of the so-called Market Revolution drastically altered the northern and southern society and culture. In the North, increasing infrastructure, especially banks, canals, roadways, and the telegraph, allowed for the beginnings of industrialization. Industrialization brought with it a culture of innovation, increased mobility, urbanization, greater class divisions, and the transformation of labor from free workers to unionization, with an emphasis on the labor theory of value. In the South, the economic transformations of this period, with a concurrent emphasis on innovation, further entrenched the plantation system, but now based on cotton instead of tobacco, which revived the slave system and, like in the North, stratified the class system.*

LearningCurve

Remind students to go online to complete the LearningCurve quiz for this chapter.

CHAPTER 8 REVIEW

AP CONTENT REVIEW *Answer these questions to demonstrate your understanding of the chapter's main ideas.*

1. What was the relationship between government support and private enterprise in economic development?
2. How were industrial development in the North and the expansion of cotton agriculture in the South connected?
3. How did technological innovation improve the lives of ordinary people, and what challenges did it present to them?
4. How was the structure of American society different in 1848 than it had been in 1800?

AP TERMS TO KNOW *Identify and explain the significance of each term below.*

Key Concepts and Events

neomercantilism (p. 250)
Panic of 1819 (p. 252)
Commonwealth System (p. 254)
Erie Canal (p. 255)
Market Revolution (p. 256)
Industrial Revolution (p. 258)
cotton complex (p. 258)
mechanics (p. 259)
Waltham-Lowell System (p. 260)
gradual emancipation (p. 261)
manumission (p. 262)
coastal trade (p. 264)
inland system (p. 265)
"positive good" (p. 266)
paternalism (p. 267)
machine tools (p. 269)
artisan republicanism (p. 270)
unions (p. 271)
labor theory of value (p. 272)
gang-labor system (p. 276)
middle class (p. 277)
self-made man (p. 279)

Key People

John Jacob Astor (p. 250)
Samuel F. B. Morse (p. 258)
Samuel Slater (p. 259)
Francis Cabot Lowell (p. 260)
Sellars Family (p. 268)
Eli Whitney (p. 263)
Cyrus McCormick (p. 274)

AP MAKING CONNECTIONS *Recognize the larger developments and continuities within and across chapters by answering these questions.*

1. How did the economic revolution described in this chapter affect the lives of women in various social groups, and how did it make their experiences different from those of their mothers, whose political and social lives were explored in Chapter 6 on the American Revolution, and their grandmothers, whose work lives and cultural experiences were considered in Chapter 4? Describe patterns of change and continuity from generation to generation.
2. In Chapters 3 and 5, we discussed the role of mercantilism in the colonial policies of the seventeenth and eighteenth centuries. We used the same term to describe government policies relating to economic development in the early republic. How were these more recent forms of mercantilism similar to those of the colonial era? In what ways were they different? Explain relevant similarities and differences.

KEY TURNING POINTS *Refer to the timeline at the start of the chapter for help in answering the following question.*

Many of the early chronology entries concern economic matters, while later entries refer to other subjects. Based on your reading of the chapter, when and why does this change in emphasis occur?

281

TRM Find complete suggested responses in the Teacher's Resource Materials.

AP SKILLS & PROCESSES

CAUSATION

AP® CONTENT REVIEW 1 asks students to identify the effects of government policies on economic development. Note: This is the same question as the section-opening prompt on p. 250.

AP SKILLS & PROCESSES

CONTEXTUALIZATION

AP® CONTENT REVIEW 2 encourages students to consider the relationship between economic developments in the North and in the South by viewing them both in the larger context of the Market Revolution. Note: This is the same question as the section-opening prompt on p. 258.

AP SKILLS & PROCESSES

CAUSATION

AP® CONTENT REVIEW 3 requires students to describe the positive and negative effects of technological changes on the lives of non-elites. Note: This is the same question as the section-opening prompt on p. 267.

AP SKILLS & PROCESSES

CONTINUITY AND CHANGE

AP® CONTENT REVIEW 4 asks students to identify ways that American social structure changed over the course of the early nineteenth century. Note: This is the same question as the section-opening prompt on p. 275.

TRM Find definitions for these terms in the **Glossary/Glosario** in the Teacher's Resource Materials.

AP SKILLS & PROCESSES

CONTINUITY AND CHANGE

The **KEY TURNING POINTS** question asks students to identify a turning point within the larger era the chapter considers: Why does the focus shift from economy to urbanization, emergence of the labor movement, emergence of a middle-class culture, and development of a defense of slavery?

AP SKILLS & PROCESSES

ARGUMENTATION

AP® MAKING CONNECTIONS 2 challenges students to explain how disparate economic systems worked in concert. Students need to concentrate on the interdependency between the North and South.

AP SKILLS & PROCESSES

COMPARISON & CONTINUITY

AP® MAKING CONNECTIONS 1 essentially poses a question about changes in women's position from 1750 to 1850 by comparing their role and status at three different points in time.

TRM Find complete suggested responses in the Teacher's Resource Materials.

AP® PRACTICE QUESTIONS

MULTIPLE CHOICE QUESTIONS *Choose the correct answer for each question.*

Questions 1–3 refer to this excerpt.

> "Use of terms like white slavery and slavery of wages in the 1830s and 1840s presents an intriguing variation on the theme of American exceptionalism. . . . [O]ne might regard the antebellum US labor movement as exceptional in being the world leader in militant criticisms of wage work as slavery.
>
> Of course, concern over 'slavery' was very much in the air in Jacksonian America. . . [N]onetheless, the use of the white slave metaphor for wage workers ought not be dismissed as merely another example of the 'paranoid' style of antebellum politics. It might instead be profitable to view the paranoid style itself as a republican tradition much enlivened by the horrific example of chattel slavery and fears engendered by the growing failure of the American republic to produce a society of independent farmers and mechanics among whites."
>
> David Roediger, *The Wages of Whiteness: Race and the Making of the American Working Class*, 2007

1. Which of the following historical developments of the antebellum period had the LEAST to do with the social fears of the antebellum working class?
   - **a.** Debates in the 1800s over the powers of the federal government
   - **b.** Mechanical innovations in production and agriculture
   - **c.** The increasing numbers of Americans that no longer relied upon semisubsistence agriculture
   - **d.** The large numbers of immigrants moving to northern cities

2. Which of the following late nineteenth century developments resulted most directly from the antebellum ideas described in the excerpt?
   - **a.** The organization of workers into local and national unions
   - **b.** The articulation of the belief that the wealthy had a moral obligation to help the less fortunate and improve society
   - **c.** The use of Social Darwinism to justify the success of those at the top of the American social order
   - **d.** The development of political machines in urban areas

3. The changes in labor relations evidenced in the source caused by changing techniques during the Market Revolution first impacted which of the following industries in the United States?
   - **a.** Textiles
   - **b.** Steel
   - **c.** Farm machinery
   - **d.** Meatpacking

Questions 4–5 refer to this map.

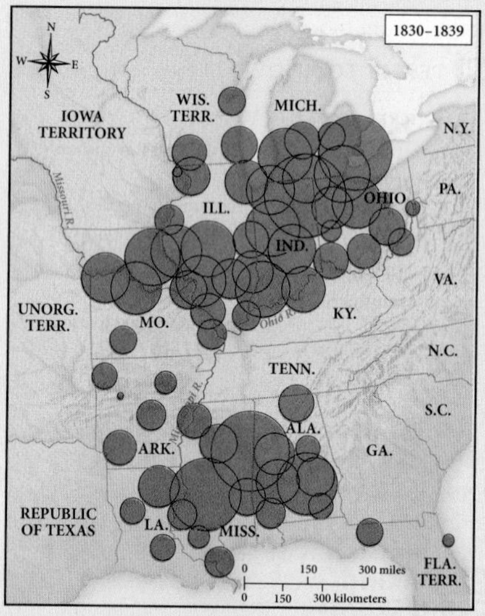

Western Land Sales, 1830–1839

4. Which of the following factors MOST directly contributed to the activity shown on the map?
   - **a.** Overcultivation of land in the Southeast
   - **b.** American Indian resistance to expansion efforts
   - **c.** The increasing antislavery efforts in the North
   - **d.** Congressional attempts at political compromise, such as the Missouri Compromise

5. The map most strongly supports which of the following arguments about the first half of the nineteenth century?
   - **a.** Property qualifications for voting were a major incentive to land settlement north of the Ohio River.
   - **b.** Federal efforts to control and relocate American Indian populations were largely successful.
   - **c.** Plans such as the "American System" were of limited value in developing the nation's economy.
   - **d.** The market revolution meant that slavery had a limited future west of the Mississippi River.

SHORT ANSWER QUESTIONS

Read each question carefully and write a short response. Use evidence from the text to support your claims.

"Sharing the bonds of womanhood both at work and in their domestic sphere, shoebinders in 1834 tried to organize themselves in terms of a female community of workers. . . . [But] . . . the conditions under which many shoebinders labored — isolated from each other, employed by the shoe boss outside a group labor system and combining wage work with domestic responsibilities — discouraged collective activity. The tensions between their relationship to the artisan system and its equal rights ideology and their subordinate roles as females in the family were exposed by their arguments for a just wage for women. Neither the social relations of the artisan family nor the realities of working as a woman for the shoe boss encouraged . . . [her] . . . to identify with her working sister in the Lowell mills or conceive of herself as a worker capable of supporting herself who could unite with her peers to protest mistreatment."

Mary Hewitt, "Wage, Gender and the Artisan Tradition in Shoemaking 1780–1860," 1983

"The brick mills and prim boarding houses . . . occupied by sober, well-behaved farm girls . . . produced a self-respecting sisterhood of independent, wage-earning women. Twice in the 1830s the women of Lowell went out on strike, proclaiming that they were not wage slaves but 'the daughters of freemen.' . . . [M]any [former] Lowell women entered public life as reformers. Most of them married and became housewives but not on the same terms their mothers had known. . . . Thus the [male factory owners] kept their promise to produce cotton cloth profitably without creating a permanent working class. But they did not succeed in shuttling young women between rural and urban paternalism and back again. Wage labor, the ultimate degradation for agrarian-republican men, opened a road to independence for thousands of young women."

Paul Johnson, *The Early American Republic, 1789–1829*, 2007

1. Using the two excerpts provided, answer (a), (b), and (c).
   a. Briefly explain ONE major difference between Johnson's and Hewitt's historical interpretations of how work affected women in the first half of the nineteenth century.
   b. Briefly explain how ONE specific historical event or development between 1800 and 1850 that is not explicitly mentioned in the excerpts could be used to support Johnson's argument.
   c. Briefly explain how ONE specific historical event or development between 1800 and 1850 that is not explicitly mentioned in the excerpts could be used to support Hewitt's argument.

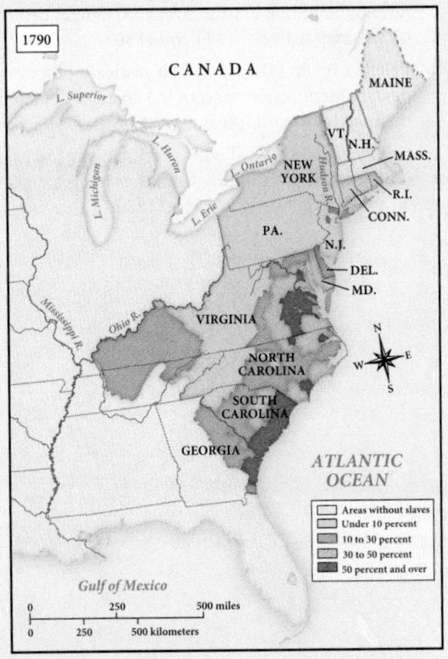

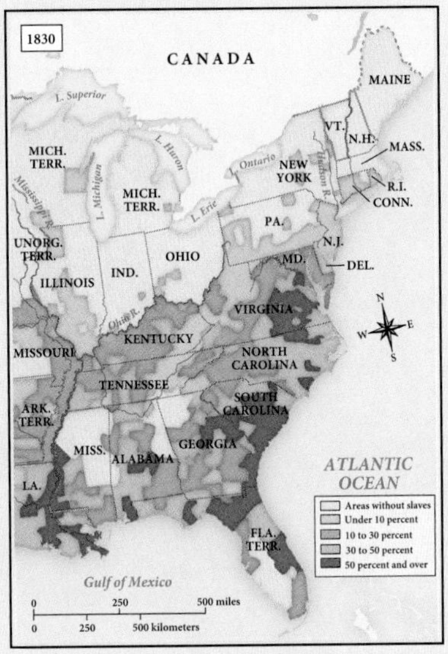

Distribution of the Slave Population in 1790 and 1830

TRM Find complete suggested responses in the Teacher's Resource Materials.

2. Using the two maps provided on the previous page, answer (a), (b), and (c).
   a. Briefly explain ONE specific historical event or development that accounts for the changes depicted on the map between 1790 and 1830.
   b. Briefly explain ONE specific historical event or development resulting from the changes depicted on the map between 1790 and 1830.
   c. Briefly explain ANOTHER specific historical event or development resulting from the changes depicted on the map between 1790 and 1830.

3. Answer (a), (b), and (c).
   a. Briefly explain why ONE of the following developments exerted the greatest influence in promoting the economic development of the United States in the period from 1800 to 1850.
      - Tariff policy
      - Transportation networks
      - Interchangeable parts
   b. Provide ONE specific historical event or development to support your explanation in (a).
   c. Briefly explain why ONE of the other developments exerted less influence in promoting the economic development of the United States than your choice in (a).

9 CHAPTER

A Democratic Revolution

1800–1848

Chapter 9 — AP® Assessment Weight and Pacing Guide

The assessment weight on the AP® U.S. History Exam for Chapters 8–11 is 10–17 percent. This chapter falls in Unit 4 of the AP® U.S. History Curriculum, covering Period 4: 1800–1848.

This pacing guide is based on a schedule with 120 sessions of 50 minutes each before the AP® U.S. History Exam. If you have a different number of sessions before the exam, you can modify the pacing to meet your needs. If you have additional time, consider incorporating quizzes, released AP® U.S. History questions, practice exams, writing practice, and other instructional activities.

	Traditional Schedule	Block Schedule
Chapter 9	3 days	1–2 days

Daily Pacing Guide

	Content Focus	Essential Question
Day 1	The Rise of Popular Politics	How did Jackson and the new Democratic Party overcome sectional differences?
Day 2	Jackson in Power, 1829–1837	What were the constitutional arguments for and against internal improvements, the tariff, and nullification?
Day 3	Class, Culture, and the Second Party System	What principles united the Whig Party and how did they differ from those of the Democratic Party?

AP® Alignment

Section Heading	AP® Topic	AP® Theme
The Rise of Popular Politics	3.6, 4.7, 4.8, 4.11	PCE, SOC, ARC
Jackson in Power, 1829–1837	4.7, 4.8	PCE
Class, Culture, and the Second Party System	4.7	PCE

*Should changes be made to the Course Framework in the future, an updated alignment will be placed on our AP® updates page at go.bfwpub.com/ap-course-updates.

Chapter 9 — Overview

It is important to help students understand that the developments discussed in this chapter happened simultaneously with those in Chapter 8. While the previous chapter focused on economic developments from 1800 to 1848, Chapter 9 focuses on the dramatic political developments within the same time period. The chapter begins with the transition of the American political system from one dominated by notables from the elite class of planters, merchants, and landlords to popular politics dominated by political parties and personalities. While major changes occurred as a result of the expansion of suffrage in this period, women and African Americans remained excluded from direct political participation. In addition, the Missouri Compromise and the election of 1824 quickly undermined the feelings of unity and nationalism that were created by the War of 1812 in the "Era of Good Feelings." The rise of Andrew Jackson to the White House marked the victory of party politics and ushered in a Second Party System in the U.S. Jackson's policies on the national bank, Native American policy, and tariffs caused conflicts that would last throughout the period.

Chapter 9 Resources

The following resources can be found in the Teacher's Resource Materials (TRM) that accompany the book. You can access the TRM via the book's digital platform, by clicking the TRM links found here in your Teacher's Edition e-book, or by contacting your representative to access the resources online. Visit **bfwpub.com/henretta10e** to learn more.

TRM Chapter 9 Lecture Presentation Slides

TRM Chapter 9 Outline with AP® Focus

TRM Chapter 9 Lecture Strategies

TRM Chapter 9 Suggested Responses

TRM Handout 9.1 — Causation: Rise of Popular Politics

TRM Handout 9.2 — Contextualization: Missouri Compromise

TRM Handout 9.3 — Continuity and Change: Second Party System

Chapter 9 — Essential Activity

Provide students with a blank map of the United States at the time of the Missouri Compromise. Ask students to label the major components of the compromise, including Missouri (a slave state), Maine (a free state), and the 36°30′ line. Ask students to label which states (as represented in the Senate) voted in favor of the compromise and which opposed it. (Students should note that all southern Senators except two voted against the Missouri Compromise prohibition of slavery north of 36°30′.) Provide students with several excerpts from letters and other primary sources that illustrate reactions to the Missouri Compromise as it was debated and passed in Congress. These can include Thomas Jefferson to John Holmes, April 22, 1820; Thomas Jefferson to James Monroe, March 3, 1820; James Madison to Robert Walsh, November 27, 1819; John Henry Eaton to Andrew Jackson, March 11, 1820; John C. Calhoun to Andrew Jackson, June 1, 1820, all available at the Library of Congress Web site. Then ask students to analyze the excerpts and identify the key arguments in the Missouri Compromise.

Chapter 9 — Bell Ringers

The following activities take no more than 5 to 15 minutes of your class period and offer an effective and engaging way to begin your lessons and for students to apply AP® Skills & Processes:

- Provide students with an excerpt from Thomas Jefferson's letter to John Holmes on April 22, 1820. Ask students to contextualize the letter by explaining the historical developments and processes that influenced Jefferson's letter. Use this activity as an introduction to a lesson on the Missouri Compromise.
- Provide students with a copy of the political cartoon "King Andrew I" (on p. 297 of the text). Ask them to circle and label each element in the cartoon (e.g., crown, scepter, shield, documents, robes, etc.). Ask students to explain the historical context, intended audience, purpose, and point of view of the artist of the cartoon. Discuss the use of this cartoon as an outline of Whig Party policies. *Answers will vary.*

NOTES

TEACHING STRATEGY

The chapter's title, "A Democratic Revolution," reflects one way of framing the era between roughly 1800 and 1850, while the **AP® LEARNING FOCUS** question adds to this discussion by hinting at the significant role of Andrew Jackson in this era's politics. For a complete suggested response to the **AP® LEARNING FOCUS** question, see p. 312.

9

CHAPTER

A Democratic Revolution

1800–1848

AP® LEARNING FOCUS

Why did Andrew Jackson's election mark a turning point in American politics?

Europeans who visited the United States in the 1830s mostly praised its republican society but not its political parties and politicians. "The gentlemen spit, talk of elections and the price of produce, and spit again," Frances Trollope reported in *Domestic Manners of the Americans* (1832). In her view, American politics was the sport of self-serving party politicians who reeked of "whiskey and onions." Other Europeans lamented the low intellectual level of American political debate. The "clap-trap of praise and pathos" from a Massachusetts politician "deeply disgusted" Harriet Martineau, while the shallow arguments advanced by the inept "farmers, shopkeepers, and country lawyers" who sat in the New York assembly astonished Basil Hall.

The negative verdict was nearly unanimous. "The most able men in the United States are very rarely placed at the head of affairs," French aristocrat Alexis de Tocqueville concluded in *Democracy in America* (1835). The reason, said Tocqueville, lay in the character of democracy itself. Most citizens ignored important policy issues, jealously refused to elect their intellectual superiors, and listened in awe to "the clamor of a mountebank [a charismatic fraud] who knows the secret of stimulating their tastes."

These Europeans were witnessing the American Democratic Revolution. Before 1815, men of ability had sat in the seats of government, and the prevailing ideology had been republicanism, or rule by "men of TALENTS and VIRTUE," as a newspaper put it. Many of those leaders feared popular rule, so they wrote constitutions with Bills of Rights, bicameral legislatures, and independent judiciaries, and they criticized overambitious men who campaigned for public office. But history took a different course. By the 1820s and 1830s, the watchwords were *democracy* and *party politics*, a system run by men who avidly sought office and rallied supporters through newspapers, broadsides, and great public processions. Politics became a sport — a competitive contest for the votes of ordinary men. "That the majority should govern was a fundamental maxim in all free governments," declared Martin Van Buren, the most talented of the new breed of professional politicians. By encouraging ordinary Americans to burn with "election fever" and support party principles, he and other politicians redefined the meaning of democratic government and made it work.

The Politics of Democracy As ordinary American men asserted a claim to a voice in government affairs, politicians catered to their preferences and prejudices. Aspiring candidates took their messages to voters, in rural hamlets as well as large towns. This detail from George Caleb Bingham's *Stump Speaking* (1855) shows a swanky, tail-coated politician on an improvised stage seeking the votes of an audience of well-dressed gentlemen and local farmers — identified by their broad-brimmed hats and casual attire. Private Collection/Bridgeman Images.

TEACHING STRATEGY

This painting by George Caleb Bingham illustrates one of his common themes of popular politics in the "age of democracy." Apart from the class differences between the politician and his audience indicated by the caption, students analyzing this painting might identify the informal outdoor setting and that the audience consists solely of white males paying varying levels of attention to the speaker. Have students compare this painting with other election-themed Bingham prints online such as the *Country Politician, The County Election, Canvassing for a Vote,* and *The Verdict of the People* to identify common themes. Students could discuss how these common elements reveal the nature of political participation in the early nineteenth century. If time permits, show students some of Bingham's paintings of everyday experiences of frontier families, fur traders, and boatmen, and discuss how these two categories of paintings relate to each other.

AP® SKILLS & PROCESSES

CONTINUITY AND CHANGE

Use the **TIMELINE** to explore how 1810 to 1841 could constitute a definable historical era. Ensure that students understand that this chapter covers the same chronological period as the previous chapter, but now from a primarily political perspective. Ask students to identify what elements from the chronology point to "revolutionary" democratic changes as the chapter title indicates. Extend this discussion by asking students to draw connections between developments listed in this timeline and those listed in the previous chapter: How did economic and political developments influence each other?

TIMELINE

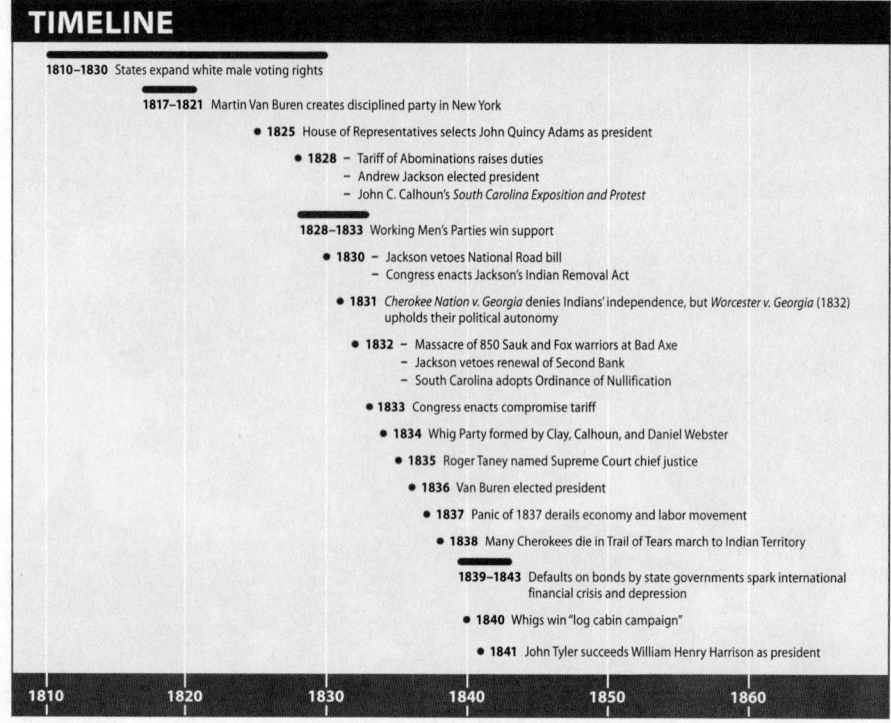

- **1810–1830** States expand white male voting rights
- **1817–1821** Martin Van Buren creates disciplined party in New York
- **1825** House of Representatives selects John Quincy Adams as president
- **1828**
  - Tariff of Abominations raises duties
  - Andrew Jackson elected president
  - John C. Calhoun's *South Carolina Exposition and Protest*
- **1828–1833** Working Men's Parties win support
- **1830**
  - Jackson vetoes National Road bill
  - Congress enacts Jackson's Indian Removal Act
- **1831** *Cherokee Nation v. Georgia* denies Indians' independence, but *Worcester v. Georgia* (1832) upholds their political autonomy
- **1832**
  - Massacre of 850 Sauk and Fox warriors at Bad Axe
  - Jackson vetoes renewal of Second Bank
  - South Carolina adopts Ordinance of Nullification
- **1833** Congress enacts compromise tariff
- **1834** Whig Party formed by Clay, Calhoun, and Daniel Webster
- **1835** Roger Taney named Supreme Court chief justice
- **1836** Van Buren elected president
- **1837** Panic of 1837 derails economy and labor movement
- **1838** Many Cherokees die in Trail of Tears march to Indian Territory
- **1839–1843** Defaults on bonds by state governments spark international financial crisis and depression
- **1840** Whigs win "log cabin campaign"
- **1841** John Tyler succeeds William Henry Harrison as president

1810 1820 1830 1840 1850 1860

THE RISE OF POPULAR POLITICS

How did Jackson and the new Democratic Party overcome sectional differences?

franchise
The right to vote. Between 1820 and 1860, most states revised their constitutions to extend the vote to all adult white males. Black adult men gained the right to vote with the passage of the Fourteenth Amendment. The Nineteenth Amendment granted adult women the right to vote.

Expansion of the **franchise** (the right to vote) dramatically symbolized the Democratic Revolution. By the 1830s, most states allowed nearly all white men to vote. Nowhere else in the world did ordinary farmers and wage earners exercise such political influence; in England, the Reform Bill of 1832 extended the vote to only 600,000 out of 6 million men — a mere 10 percent. Equally important, political parties provided voters with the means to express their preferences. At the same time, state legislatures barred women and free African Americans from exercising the franchise. As political democracy took shape in the United States, participation was restricted to white men.

The Decline of the Notables and the Rise of Parties

notables
Northern landlords, slave-owning planters, and seaport merchants who dominated the political system of the early nineteenth century.

The American Revolution weakened the elite-run society of the colonial era but did not overthrow it. Only two states — Pennsylvania and Vermont — gave the vote to all male taxpayers, and many families of low rank continued to defer to their social "betters." Consequently, wealthy **notables** — northern landlords, slave-owning planters, and seaport merchants — dominated the political system in the new republic. And rightly so, said John Jay, the first chief justice of the Supreme Court: "Those who own the country are the most fit persons to participate in the government of it." Jay and other notables managed local elections by building up an "interest": lending money to small farmers, giving business to storekeepers, and treating their tenants to rum. An outlay of $20 for refreshments, remarked one poll watcher, "may produce about 100 votes." This gentry-dominated system kept men who lacked wealth and powerful family connections from seeking office.

The Rise of Democracy To broaden voting rights, Maryland reformers in the 1810s invoked the equal rights rhetoric of republicanism. They charged that property qualifications for voting were a "tyranny" because they endowed "one class of men with privileges which are denied to another." In response, legislators in Maryland and other seaboard states grudgingly expanded the franchise. The new voters often rejected candidates who wore "top boots, breeches, and shoe buckles," their hair in "powder and queues." Instead, they elected men who dressed simply and endorsed popular rule.

Farmers and laborers in the Midwest and Southwest also challenged the old order. The constitutions of the new states of Indiana (1816), Illinois (1818), and Alabama (1819) prescribed a broad male franchise, and voters usually elected middling men to local and state offices. A well-to-do migrant in Illinois was surprised to learn that the man who plowed his fields "was a colonel of militia, and a member of the legislature." Once in public office, men from modest backgrounds restricted imprisonment for debt, kept taxes low, and allowed farmers to claim squatters' rights to unoccupied land.

By 1830, most state legislatures had given the vote to all white men or to all men who paid taxes or served in the militia. Only two — North Carolina and Rhode Island — still required the possession of freehold property (Map 9.1). Equally

AP® EXAM TIP

Trace the expansion of participatory democracy as a critical element in the development of a national identity in the U.S.

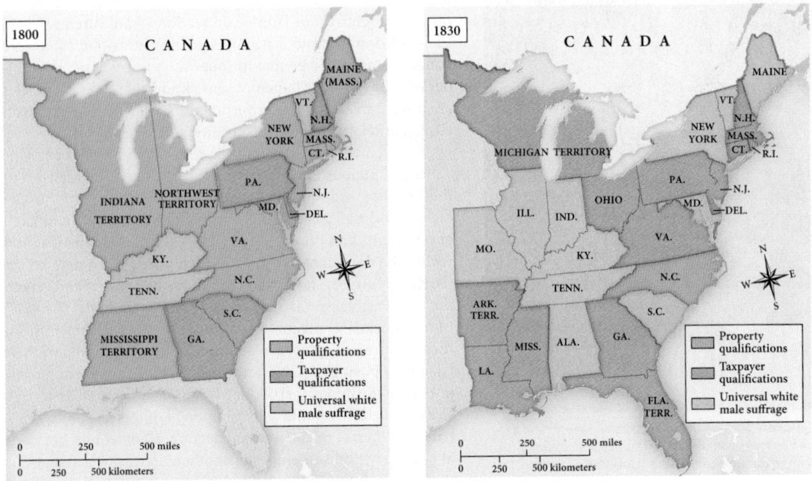

MAP 9.1 The Expansion of Voting Rights for White Men, 1800 and 1830
Between 1800 and 1830, the United States moved steadily toward political equality for white men. Many existing states revised their constitutions and replaced a property qualification for voting with less restrictive criteria, such as paying taxes or serving in the militia. Some new states in the West extended the suffrage to all adult white men. As parties sought votes from a broader electorate, the tone of politics became more open and competitive — swayed by the interests and values of ordinary people.

AP® APPLY THE TIP

To help students better understand the changes that occurred in participatory democracy in the age of Jackson, ask them to complete **Handout 9.1 — Causation: Rise of Popular Politics (TRM)** to identify the cause and effect relationships that led to the rise of popular politics. After students have completed the handout, lead a discussion that addresses the rise of the Democratic Party and the appeal to new voters.

TRM Find **Handout 9.1 — Causation: Rise of Popular Politics** in the Teacher's Resource Materials.

TEACHING STRATEGY

Use **MAP 9.1** for students to identify political changes at a glance through geographical representations. Guide students' analysis with the following questions:

- **In 1800, how many states or territories required property qualifications for voting? In 1830?** *In 1800, eleven; in 1830, two.*
- **Why might the pattern of universal male suffrage have spread most widely in the West?** *In the West, migrants were often ordinary settlers who did not represent the social hierarchy of established states and could shape political requirements in their own interests more easily.*
- **Why might demands for political equality have grown in the early 1800s?** *The American Revolution remained a defining feature of the young nation's culture, as the Fourth of July became a national holiday. The rhetoric of independence and equality continued to be appropriated by ordinary Americans and applied to their own circumstances.*
- **What is the significance of the change this map indicates?** *The scale and nature of political participation changed dramatically, forcing candidates to rethink their means of getting elected and maintaining power.*

significant, between 1818 and 1821, Connecticut, Massachusetts, and New York wrote more democratic constitutions that reapportioned legislative districts on the basis of population and stipulated that judges and justices of the peace would be elected rather than appointed.

Democratic politics was contentious and, because it attracted ambitious men, often corrupt. Powerful entrepreneurs and speculators — both notables and self-made men — demanded government assistance and paid bribes to get it. Speculators won land grants by paying off the members of important committees, and bankers distributed shares of stock to key legislators. When the Seventh Ward Bank of New York City received a legislative charter in 1833, the bank's officials set aside one-third of the 3,700 shares of stock for themselves and their friends and almost two-thirds for state legislators and bureaucrats, leaving just 40 shares for public sale.

AP® EXAM TIP

Recognizing the connection between participatory democracy and the American political parties is essential for success on the AP® Exam.

political machine
A highly organized group of insiders that directs a political party. As the power of notables waned in the 1820s, disciplined political parties usually run by professional politicians appeared in a number of states.

caucus
A meeting held by a political party to choose candidates, make policies, and enforce party discipline.

Parties Take Command The appearance of political parties encouraged vigorous debates over government policy. Revolutionary-era Americans had condemned political "factions" as antirepublican, and the new state and national constitutions made no mention of political parties. However, as the power of notables waned in the 1820s, disciplined political parties appeared in a number of states. Usually they were run by professional politicians, often middle-class lawyers and journalists. One observer called the new parties **political machines** because, like the new power-driven textile looms, they efficiently wove together the interests of diverse social and economic groups.

Martin Van Buren Martin Van Buren's skills as a lawyer and a politician won him many admirers, as did his personal charm, sharp intellect, and imperturbable composure. "Little Van" — a mere 5 feet 6 inches in height — had almost as many detractors. Davy Crockett, Kentucky frontiersman, land speculator, and congressman, labeled him "an artful, cunning, intriguing, selfish lawyer," concerned only with "office and money." In truth, Van Buren was a complex man, a middle-class lawyer with republican values and aristocratic tastes who nonetheless created a democratic political party. © Huntington Library, Art Museum, and Botanical Gardens/Bridgeman Images.

Martin Van Buren of New York was the chief architect of the emerging system of party government. The ambitious son of a Jeffersonian tavern keeper, Van Buren grew up in the landlord-dominated society of the Hudson River Valley. Trained as a lawyer, he sought an alternative to the system of deferring to local notables. He wanted to create a political order based on party identity, not family connections. Van Buren rejected the traditional republican belief that political factions were dangerous and claimed that the opposite was true. In his autobiography he wrote, "All men of sense know that political parties are inseparable from free government," because they restrain an elected official's inherent "disposition to abuse power."

Between 1817 and 1821 in New York, Van Buren turned his "Bucktail" supporters (who wore a deer's tail on their hats) into the first statewide political machine. Taking shape in the "era of good feeling," when the Jeffersonian Republicans dominated government, Van Buren's Bucktails rose as a disciplined faction within the dominant party. Van Buren purchased a newspaper, the *Albany Argus*, and used it to promote his policies and get out the vote. Patronage was an even more important tool. When Van Buren's Bucktails won control of the New York legislature in 1821, they acquired the power to appoint some six thousand of their friends to positions in New York's legal bureaucracy of judges, justices of the peace, sheriffs, deed commissioners, and coroners. Critics called this ruthless distribution of offices a spoils system, but Van Buren argued it was fair, operating "sometimes in favour of one party, and sometimes of another." Party government was thoroughly republican, he added, because it reflected the preferences of a majority of the citizenry. To ensure the passage of the Bucktails' legislative program, Van Buren insisted on disciplined voting as determined by a **caucus**, a meeting of key leaders who made policy decisions on behalf of the group. On one crucial occasion, the "Little Magician" — a nickname reflecting Van

CHECK FOR UNDERSTANDING

Ask students: **How did political participation change in the early nineteenth century?** *The role of notables declined as adult white males gained the right to vote, regardless of property ownership. Corruption was widespread. Political parties with strict discipline emerged in many states, enforcing discipline on their members' voting.*

Buren's short stature and political dexterity—honored seventeen New York legislators for sacrificing "individual preferences for the general good" of the party.

Racial Exclusion and Republican Motherhood

The rise of a more democratic political system did not lead to universal voting rights. Old cultural rules—and new laws—denied the vote to most women and free African American men. When women and free blacks asked for voting rights, legislators wrote explicit race and gender restrictions into the law. In 1802, Ohio disenfranchised African Americans, and the New York constitution of 1821 imposed a property-holding requirement on black voters. A striking case of sexual discrimination occurred in New Jersey, where the state constitution of 1776 had granted the voting franchise to all property holders. As Federalists and Republicans competed for power, they ignored customary gender rules and urged property-owning single women and widows to vote. Sensing a threat to men's monopoly on politics, the New Jersey legislature in 1807 invoked both biology and custom to limit voting to men only: "Women, generally, are neither by nature, nor habit, nor education, nor by their necessary condition in society fitted to perform this duty with credit to themselves or advantage to the public."

Republican Motherhood The controversy over women's political rights mirrored a debate over authority within the household. Traditionally, most American women had spent their active adult years working as farmwives and bearing and nurturing children. However, after 1800, the birthrate in the northern states dropped significantly. In the farming village of Sturbridge in central Massachusetts, women now bore an average of six children; their grandmothers had usually given birth to eight or nine. In the growing seaport cities, native-born white women now bore an average of only four children.

The United States was among the first nations to experience this sharp decline in the birthrate—what historians call the **demographic transition**. There were several causes. Thousands of young men migrated to the trans-Appalachian west, which increased the number of never-married women in the East and delayed marriage for many more. Women who married in their late twenties had fewer children. In addition, white urban middle-class couples deliberately limited the size of their families. Fathers wanted to leave children an adequate inheritance, while mothers, influenced by new ideas of individualism and self-achievement, refused to spend their entire adulthood rearing children. After having four or five children, these couples used birth control or abstained from sexual intercourse.

Even as women bore fewer children, they accepted greater responsibility for the welfare of the family. In his *Thoughts on Female Education* (1787), Philadelphia physician Benjamin Rush argued that young women should ensure their husbands' "perseverance in the paths of rectitude" and called for loyal "republican mothers" who would instruct "their sons in the principles of liberty and government."

Christian ministers readily embraced this idea of **republican motherhood**. "Preserving virtue and instructing the young are not the fancied, but the real 'Rights of Women,' " the Reverend Thomas Bernard told the Female Charitable Society of Salem, Massachusetts. He urged his audience to dismiss public roles for women, such as voting or serving on juries, that English feminist Mary Wollstonecraft had advocated in *A Vindication of the Rights of Woman* (1792). Instead, women should care for their children, a responsibility that gave them "an extensive power over the fortunes of man in every generation." As ordinary white men voted in unprecedented numbers, their wives were expected to exercise influence in their homes, not in public.

Debates over Education Although families provided most moral and intellectual training, republican ideology encouraged publicly supported schooling. Bostonian

AP® SKILLS & PROCESSES

MAKING CONNECTIONS

What was the relationship between the growth of democracy and the emergence of political parties?

AP® EXAM TIP

The changing role of women and the family in the face of major demographic change is important to know on the AP® Exam.

demographic transition
The sharp decline in birthrate in the United States beginning in the 1790s that was caused by changes in cultural behavior, including the use of birth control. The migration of thousands of young men to the trans-Appalachian west was also a factor in this decline.

republican motherhood
The idea that the primary political role of American women was to instill a sense of patriotic duty and republican virtue in their sons and husbands and mold them into exemplary citizens.

AP® SKILLS & PROCESSES

MAKING CONNECTIONS

Use the **MAKING CONNECTIONS** question to have students identify the ways democratic ideas caused the emergence of (particular) political parties. Some students may need to be reminded that the primary focus is on extending political power to individuals irrespective of social class. White men, far from seeing any contradiction in limiting the political rights of blacks or women, typically viewed their own rights as being based on their gender and racial identities.

TRM Find complete suggested responses in the Teacher's Resource Materials.

AP® APPLY THE TIP

Provide students with excerpts from Benjamin Rush's "Thoughts upon Female Education." Divide students into groups and ask them to analyze the source and consider its relationship to citizenship, the rights of women, and the idea of republican motherhood. After they read, have students answer the following questions:

- **Is Rush making an argument for the equality of women or for their subordination to husbands?** *While the ideal of "republican motherhood" led to the expansion of access to education for some women, this is a system of inequality because women are not educated for their own self-fulfillment or success, but to serve as mothers and wives.*
- **In what way does Rush's argument illustrate both change and continuity in the relationship of women to the American republic?** *Rush's argument illustrates change because it advocates for the role of women to be limited despite their active role in the Colonial Period and American Revolution, as seen with Abigail Adams and Phyllis Wheatley. His arguments represent continuity because the economic and political rights of women were limited in most colonies before the American Revolution.*

AP® THEME

SOC: Social Structures

"Republican motherhood," which emerged in response to the American Revolution, is often addressed in discussions of the early republic. While scholars generally agree on what it was—granting women a specific, limited civic role of training their children to be good citizens—they have disagreed on its significance. Republican motherhood represented a paradoxical role, since by definition citizenship has been defined as participation in the public realm, while women exercised this role exclusively in the home. Prompt students to discuss the significance of this development through the following questions: Did it represent a significant step toward political equality for women? Or was its main purpose to pacify the demands of patriotic women for political equality without offering anything of substance? Did it provide an opportunity for women to join the public sphere of politics, or did it solidify the notion of separate spheres further?

***The Wedding*, 1805** Bride and groom stare intently into each other's eyes as they exchange vows, suggesting that their union was a love match, not an arranged marriage based on economic calculation. The plain costumes of the guests and the sparse furnishings of the room suggest that the unknown artist may have provided us with a picture of a rural Quaker wedding. The Granger Collection, New York.

Caleb Bingham, an influential textbook author, called for "an equal distribution of knowledge to make us emphatically a 'republic of letters.'" Farmers, artisans, and laborers wanted elementary schools that would instruct their children in the "three Rs" — reading, 'riting, and 'rithmetic — and make them literate enough to read the Bible. In New England, locally funded public schools offered basic instruction to most boys and some girls. In other regions, there were few publicly supported schools, and only 25 percent of the boys and perhaps 10 percent of the girls attended private institutions or had personal tutors.

Although many state constitutions encouraged support for education, few legislatures acted until the 1820s. Then a new generation of educational reformers established statewide standards. To encourage students, the reformers chose textbooks such as Parson Mason Weems's *The Life of George Washington* (c. 1800), which praised honesty and hard work and condemned gambling, drinking, and laziness. To bolster patriotism and shared cultural ideals, reformers required the study of American history. As a New Hampshire schoolboy, Thomas Low recalled: "We were taught every day and in every way that ours was the freest, the happiest, and soon to be the greatest and most powerful country of the world."

Slavery and National Politics As the northern states ended human bondage, the South's commitment to slavery became a political issue. At the Philadelphia convention in 1787, northern delegates had reluctantly accepted clauses allowing slave imports for twenty years and guaranteeing the return of fugitive slaves. Seeking even more protection for their "peculiar institution," southerners in the new national legislature won approval of James Madison's resolution that "Congress have no authority to interfere in the emancipation of slaves, or in the treatment of them within any of the States."

TEACHING STRATEGY

The caption to this illustration of a wedding suggests that the eye contact between bride and groom reflects a love match. With students, you might discuss whether the slim evidence of that gaze is sufficient to draw the conclusion provided, which can raise questions about visual sources as a type of evidence and how they are to be read properly. Also, students may tend to assume that the choice of marriage partners has been a feature of American life for longer than has been the case. In fact, the early 1800s saw the emergence of the largely middle-class notion of "companionate marriage" that would become more fully formed by the late nineteenth century. Though gender norms prevented any expectation of equality between husband and wife, notions of autonomy and choice, fueled in part by the Revolution, helped to establish the ideal of a freely chosen partnership characterized by mutual respect and compatibility.

AP® THEME

SOC: Social Structures; NAT: American and National Identity; PCE: Politics and Power

The text introduces ways that free blacks engaged in political efforts aimed at changing their status. Though many free blacks eventually rejected colonization, the American Colonization Society discussed on p. 289 represented a form of abolitionism. Later calls by William Lloyd Garrison and others for immediate abolition represented a direct repudiation of the notion of gradual, compensated emancipation — and of colonization.

Nonetheless, slavery remained a contested issue. When Congress outlawed the Atlantic slave trade in 1808, some northern representatives demanded an end to the trade in slaves between states. Southern leaders responded with a forceful defense of their labor system. "A large majority of people in the Southern states do not consider slavery as even an evil," declared one congressman. The South's political clout, which was an ironic consequence of the decision to count enslaved people as three-fifths of a person for the purposes of representation, ensured that the national government would protect slavery.

AP® SKILLS & PROCESSES

ARGUMENTATION

How did the leadership of African Americans establish strategies to protect African American communities and political challenges to the institution of slavery?

African Americans Speak Out Heartened by the end of the Atlantic slave trade, black abolitionists spoke out. In speeches and pamphlets, Henry Sipkins and Henry Johnson pointed out that slavery — "relentless tyranny," they called it — was a central legacy of America's colonial history. For inspiration, they looked to the Haitian Revolution; for collective support, they joined in secret societies, such as Prince Hall's African Lodge of Freemasons in Boston. Initially, black (and white) antislavery advocates hoped that slavery would die out naturally as the tobacco economy declined. The cotton boom ended that hope.

As some Americans campaigned against slavery, a group of prominent citizens, including Speaker of the House Henry Clay, founded the **American Colonization Society** in 1817. Its leaders argued for gradual emancipation plans such as the ones adopted in northern states after the Revolution. Most believed that emancipation should include compensation to masters and that freedpeople, conceived as alien "Africans," should be deported from the United States. According to Henry Clay — a society member, Speaker of the House of Representatives, and a slave owner himself — racial bondage hindered economic progress, but emancipation without removal would cause "a civil war that would end in the extermination or subjugation of the one race or the other." Though the Society was popular with many white Americans who held moderate antislavery views, it had little effect on the institution of slavery or the lives of enslaved people. With help from the U.S. Navy, a Society representative coerced Dey and Bassa leaders on the west coast of Africa to sell the group a strip of land that could serve as a colony for resettled American blacks. But high death rates plagued the colony; between 1820 and 1843, some 4,500 people made the voyage, but only about 1,800 survived. Conflicts between residents and Society leaders also caused the colony to struggle. In 1847, the residents declared themselves the independent nation of Liberia.

American Colonization Society Founded by Henry Clay and other prominent citizens in 1817, the society argued that slaves had to be freed and then resettled, in Africa or elsewhere.

Most free blacks strongly opposed such colonization schemes because they saw themselves as Americans. As the African American minister Richard Allen put it, "This land which we have watered with our tears and our blood is now our mother country." Allen spoke from experience. Born into slavery in Philadelphia in 1760 and sold to a farmer in Delaware, Allen grew up in bondage. In 1777, Freeborn Garretson, an itinerant preacher, converted Allen to Methodism and convinced Allen's owner that on Judgment Day, slaveholders would be "weighted in the balance, and . . . found wanting." Allowed to buy his freedom, Allen became a Methodist minister in Philadelphia. In 1795, Allen formed a separate black congregation, the Bethel Church; in 1816, he became the first bishop of a new denomination: the African Methodist Episcopal Church (see "Free Black Communities, South and North" in Chapter 10). Two years later, 3,000 African Americans met in Allen's church to condemn colonization and to claim American citizenship.

The Reverend Richard Allen Born into slavery on a Delaware plantation, Allen converted to Methodism, taught himself to read and write, and purchased his freedom by the age of twenty. Relocating to Philadelphia, he was ordained as a Methodist minister in 1784, about the time this pastel portrait is thought to have been executed. He went on to serve as the first bishop of the African Methodist Episcopal Church, one of the most influential African American institutions in American history. The Granger Collection, New York.

CHECK FOR UNDERSTANDING

Ask students: **What impact did early-nineteenth-century democratization have on women and African Americans?** *Women were explicitly excluded from political participation, but the ideology of "Republican Motherhood" granted women an indirect civic role of instilling virtue in their children. This ideology paved the way for girls' access to education in the emerging public school system. As northern states abolished slavery, southern states reaffirmed it. African Americans spoke out for abolition and against colonization, while forming their own independent congregations.*

AP® SKILLS & PROCESSES

ARGUMENTATION

Students should recognize the work of African Americans in the fight against enslavement. Absalom Jones and Richard Allen were key figures in Philadelphia at the end of the eighteenth through the beginning of the nineteenth century. In New York City, David Ruggles proved to be a key African American leader. Have students choose one of these leaders and connect one of the following to the respective leader: mutual aid societies, churches, education reform, or vigilance committees. Each of these topics were key ways African Americans used networks within and around northern urban areas, where African Americans experienced success in combating enslavement and discrimination. The use of any one of these leaders will help students understand the agency of African Americans in the battle over enslavement.

TRM Find complete suggested responses in the Teacher's Resource Materials.

TEACHING STRATEGY

Colonization was a complex phenomenon in the early republic, sometimes supported by free blacks as a solution to racism and slavery, and often advocated by sympathetic reform-minded ministers, not just white racists. The PBS companion site for *Africans in America* provides several useful resources for exploring this issue in more depth. The Web site includes a short background essay, several primary sources about the American Colonization Society, and short excerpts from three different historians commenting on various aspects of the Society, including reasons blacks sometimes supported it. Access this resource by searching "Africans in America American Colonization Society."

AP® THEME

ARC: American and Regional Culture

Teachers looking to further their understanding of Richard Allen can use Gary B. Nash's *Forging Freedom: The Formation of Philadelphia's Black Community, 1720–1840* to elucidate details about the role Allen played in Philadelphia. In particular, Chapter 4, "To Arise Out of the Dust," is especially helpful in detailing the pivotal role Allen had in the formation of free institutions for African Americans.

AP® APPLY THE TIP

Provide students with **Handout 9.2 — Contextualization: Missouri Compromise (TRM)**. Once students have completed their contextualization analysis, ask students the following questions:

- **How did the Missouri Compromise show both continuity and change in American government policy toward slavery?** *Continuity is revealed through the power of Congress to limit slavery as in the Northwest Ordinance, an agreement among the founding fathers that slavery was an evil — even if a "necessary evil." Change is revealed through the emphasis on geographical division based on slavery, emphasis on regional interests over national interests, and the debate on morality of slavery.*
- **Based on the voting in the U.S. Senate in 1820, is it accurate to call this agreement the Missouri Compromise, i.e., was this really a compromise?** *Answers will vary.*

TRM Find **Handout 9.2 — Contextualization: Missouri Compromise** in the Teacher's Resource Materials.

AP® THEME

NAT: American and National Identity

The debate over Missouri represents the emergence of an ongoing political division based on region and economy. Partly a debate over the status of slavery, this larger division included debates over the tariff, which tended to benefit northern manufacturers over southern farmers, and funding for internal improvements, which likewise disproportionately benefitted the North. Though political parties were not organized by regional interest (both Democrats and Whigs could be found throughout both regions), regional concerns consistently shaped political debates from this period to the outbreak of the Civil War.

Sounding the principles of democratic republicanism, they vowed to defy racial prejudice and advance in American society using "those opportunities . . . which the Constitution and the laws allow to all."

The Missouri Crisis, 1819–1821

AP® EXAM TIP

The role of the Missouri Compromise in illustrating the divergence of regional identity and interpretations of federal power is important to know on the AP® Exam.

The abject failure of colonization set the stage for a major battle over slavery. In 1818, Congressman Nathaniel Macon of North Carolina warned that radical members of the "bible and peace societies" intended to place "the question of emancipation" on the national political agenda. When Missouri applied for admission to the Union in 1819, Congressman James Tallmadge of New York did just that: he declared that he would support statehood for Missouri only if its constitution banned the entry of new slaves and provided for the emancipation of existing bonds-people. Missouri whites rejected Tallmadge's proposals, and the northern majority in the House of Representatives blocked the territory's admission.

White southerners were horrified. "It is believed by some, & feared by others," Alabama senator John Walker reported from Washington, that Tallmadge's amendment was "merely the entering wedge and that it points already to a total emancipation of the blacks." Underlining their commitment to slavery, southerners used their power in the Senate — where they held half the seats — to withhold statehood from Maine, which was seeking to separate itself from Massachusetts.

Missouri Compromise
A series of agreements devised by Speaker of the House Henry Clay. Maine entered the Union as a free state and Missouri followed as a slave state, preserving a balance in the Senate between North and South. Farther west, it set the northern boundary of slavery at the southern boundary of Missouri.

In the ensuing debate, southerners advanced three constitutional arguments. First, they invoked the principle of "equal rights," arguing that Congress could not impose conditions on Missouri that it had not imposed on other territories. Second, they maintained that the Constitution guaranteed a state's sovereignty with respect to its internal affairs and domestic institutions, such as slavery and marriage. Finally, they insisted that Congress had no authority to infringe on the property rights of individual slaveholders. Southern leaders began to justify slavery on religious grounds. "Christ himself gave a sanction to slavery," declared Senator William Smith of South Carolina.

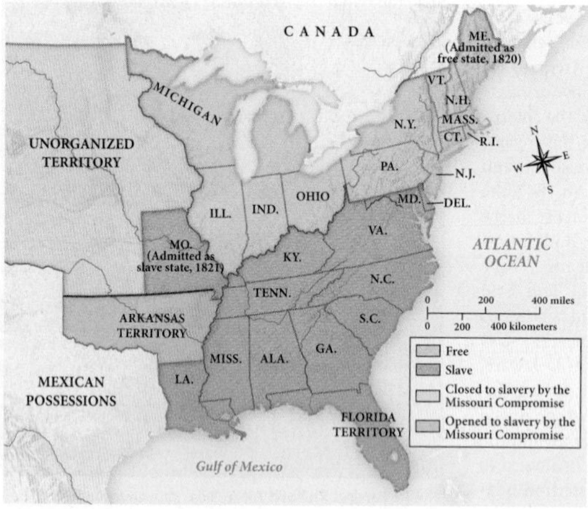

MAP 9.2 The Missouri Compromise, 1820–1821
The Missouri Compromise resolved for a generation the issue of slavery in the lands of the Louisiana Purchase. The agreement prohibited slavery north of the Missouri Compromise line (36°30′ north latitude), with the exception of the state of Missouri. To maintain an equal number of senators from free and slave states in the U.S. Congress, the compromise provided for the nearly simultaneous admission to the Union of Missouri and Maine.

Controversy raged in Congress and the press for two years before Henry Clay devised a series of political agreements known collectively as the **Missouri Compromise**. Faced with unwavering southern opposition to Tallmadge's amendment, a group of northern congressmen deserted the antislavery coalition. They accepted a deal that allowed Maine to enter the Union as a free state in 1820 and Missouri to follow as a slave state in 1821. This bargain preserved a balance in the Senate between North and South and set a precedent for future admissions to the Union. For their part, southern senators accepted the prohibition of slavery in most of the Louisiana Purchase, all the lands north of latitude 36°30′ except for the state of Missouri (Map 9.2).

As they had in the Philadelphia convention of 1787, white politicians preserved the Union by compromising over slavery. However, the delegates in Philadelphia had resolved their differences in two months; it took Congress two years to work out the Missouri Compromise, which even then did not

AP® THEME

POL: Politics and Power

MAP 9.2 reveals the geography of political controversy over the extension of slavery. Guide students' analysis with the following questions:

- **What natural feature formed the boundary between slave and free states in territory east of the Mississippi River?** *The Ohio River.*
- **Why couldn't this boundary serve as a guideline for the extension of slavery farther west?** *The river joins the Mississippi at southern Illinois, so it couldn't serve as a boundary farther west. Simply extending the terminal point of the Ohio River due west would not have provided an easy solution. Because the Ohio River moves southwest as it joins the Mississippi, southern Illinois, a free state, is farther south than Virginia, a slave state.*
- **How could each side draw on precedent to argue for or against the extension of slavery?** *The North could claim that the Louisiana Purchase, like the Northwest Territory, should be closed to slavery. The South could argue that the Constitution had permitted states to decide on the issue of slavery.*

command universal support. "[B]eware," the *Richmond Enquirer* protested sharply as southern representatives agreed to exclude slavery from most of the Louisiana Purchase: "What is a territorial restriction to-day becomes a state restriction tomorrow." The fate of western lands, enslaved blacks, and the Union itself were now intertwined, raising the specter of civil war and the end of the American experiment. As the aging Thomas Jefferson exclaimed during the Missouri crisis, "This momentous question, like a fire-bell in the night, awakened and filled me with terror."

The Election of 1824

These pressing political concerns came to the fore as the structure of national politics fractured, bringing the "era of good feeling" to an abrupt end. The advance of political democracy had led to the demise of the Federalist Party, while the Republican Party splintered into competing factions. Now, as the election of 1824 approached, five Republican candidates campaigned for the presidency. Three were veterans of President James Monroe's cabinet: Secretary of State John Quincy Adams, the son of former president John Adams; Secretary of War John C. Calhoun; and Secretary of the Treasury William H. Crawford. The other candidates were Henry Clay of Kentucky, the hard-drinking, dynamic Speaker of the House of Representatives; and General Andrew Jackson, now a senator from Tennessee. When the Republican caucus in Congress selected Crawford as the party's official nominee, the other candidates took their case to the voters. Thanks to democratic reforms, eighteen of the twenty-four states required popular elections (rather than a vote of the state legislature) to choose their representatives to the electoral college.

Each candidate had strengths. John Quincy Adams enjoyed national recognition for his diplomatic successes as secretary of state, and his family's prestige in Massachusetts ensured him the electoral votes of New England. Henry Clay based his candidacy on the **American System**, his integrated mercantilist program of national economic development. Clay wanted to strengthen the Second Bank of the United States, raise tariffs, and use tariff revenues to finance **internal improvements**, that is, public works such as roads and canals. His nationalistic program won praise in the Northwest, which needed better transportation, but elicited sharp criticism in the South, which relied on rivers to market its cotton and had few manufacturing industries to protect. William Crawford of Georgia, an ideological heir of Thomas Jefferson, denounced Clay's American System as a scheme to "consolidate" political power in Washington. Concluding that he could not defeat Crawford, John C. Calhoun of South Carolina withdrew from the race and endorsed Andrew Jackson.

As the hero of the Battle of New Orleans, Jackson benefitted from the surge of patriotism after the War of 1812. Born in the Carolina backcountry, Jackson settled in Nashville, Tennessee, where he formed ties to influential families through marriage and a career as an attorney and a slave-owning cotton planter. His rise from common origins symbolized the new democratic age, and his reputation as a "plain solid republican" attracted voters in all regions. Still, Jackson's strong showing in the electoral college surprised most political leaders. The Tennessee senator received 99 electoral votes; Adams, 84 votes; Crawford, struck down by a stroke during the campaign, won 41; and Clay finished with 37 (Map 9.3).

Because no candidate received an absolute majority, the Twelfth Amendment to the Constitution (ratified in 1804) set

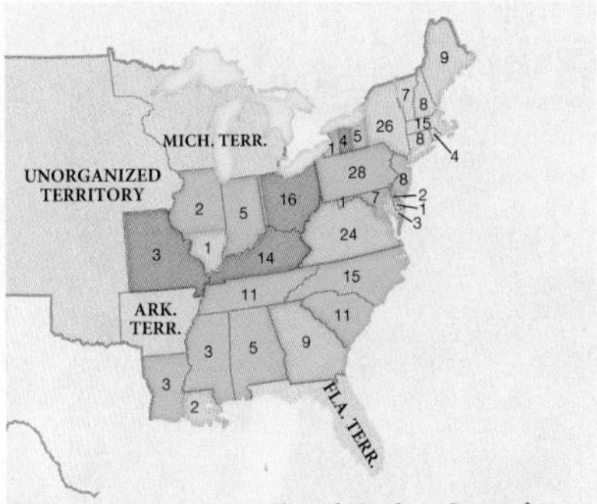

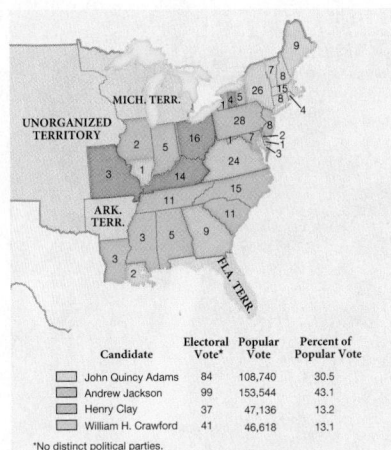

Candidate	Electoral Vote*	Popular Vote	Percent of Popular Vote
John Quincy Adams	84	108,740	30.5
Andrew Jackson	99	153,544	43.1
Henry Clay	37	47,136	13.2
William H. Crawford	41	46,618	13.1

*No distinct political parties.

MAP 9.3 The Presidential Election of 1824
Regional voting was the dominant pattern in 1824. John Quincy Adams captured every electoral vote in New England and most of those in New York; Henry Clay carried Ohio and Kentucky, the most populous trans-Appalachian states, as well as Missouri; and William Crawford took the southern states of Virginia and Georgia. Only Andrew Jackson claimed a national constituency, winning Pennsylvania and New Jersey in the East, Indiana and most of Illinois in the Midwest, and much of the South. Only 356,000 Americans voted, about 27 percent of the eligible electorate.

AP® EXAM TIP

Identifying the ways that the American System both united and divided regions is essential for success on the AP® Exam.

American System
The mercantilist system of national economic development advocated by Henry Clay and adopted by John Quincy Adams, with a national bank to manage the nation's financial system; protective tariffs to provide revenue and encourage industry; and a nationally funded network of roads, canals, and railroads.

internal improvements
Government-funded public works such as roads and canals.

CHECK FOR UNDERSTANDING

Ask students: **What was the Missouri Crisis? How was it resolved?** *A proposal to admit Missouri on the condition that it gradually become a free state caused panic among southerners, who claimed that this violated the sovereign right of states to determine the status of slavery free from intervention by the federal government. The crisis was resolved by admitting Missouri as a slave state, while admitting Maine (then part of Massachusetts) as a free state to maintain a balance between slave and free states in the Senate. Slavery in the remainder of the Louisiana Purchase was banned north of latitude 36°30′.*

AP® APPLY THE TIP

Ask students to use a blank map of the United States to illustrate the three main parts of the American System: the new Bank of the United States, internal improvements, and a protective tariff. On the map of the U.S., help students to label the North, South, West, Appalachian Mountains, and Great Lakes. Then lead students in a discussion of the main economic activities of each region. The North produced cotton textiles and manufactured goods; the South produced cotton; and the West produced food (wheat, grains, livestock). Draw arrows on the map to show how the American System was designed to strengthen the U.S. as a national market. Draw roads to connect northern manufacturing centers, turnpikes/roads to connect North to West through the Appalachian Mountains, canals to connect eastern rivers to the Great Lakes, and railroads to connect regions. Display students' maps that show internal improvement expansion by 1850 and lead a class discussion on the impact of the American System on both nationalism and sectionalism in the early nineteenth century. Be sure to discuss how the National Bank's use of one currency of exchange inspired confidence in trade and how protective tariffs prevented competition from cheaper British products.

CHECK FOR UNDERSTANDING

Ask students: **Why did the election of 1824 become controversial?** *Andrew Jackson received more electoral votes (and more popular votes) than John Quincy Adams, but because neither won a majority, the House of Representatives determined the election. Led by Henry Clay, the House chose Adams, who then made Clay secretary of state (often considered a steppingstone to being nominated for president). Jackson's supporters charged that Adams and Clay had made a "corrupt bargain."*

TRM Find complete suggested responses in the Teacher's Resource Materials.

AP® SKILLS & PROCESSES

DEVELOPMENTS AND PROCESSES

Why did Jacksonians consider the political deal between Adams and Clay "corrupt"?

corrupt bargain
When Speaker of the House Henry Clay used his influence to select John Quincy Adams as president in 1824, and then Adams appointed Clay secretary of state, Andrew Jackson's supporters called it a corrupt bargain.

the rules: the House of Representatives would choose the president from among the three highest vote-getters. This procedure hurt Jackson because many congressmen feared that the rough-hewn "military chieftain" might become a tyrant. Excluded from the race, Henry Clay used his influence as Speaker of the House to thwart Jackson's election. Clay assembled a coalition of representatives from New England and the Ohio River Valley that voted Adams into the presidency in 1825. Adams showed his gratitude by appointing Clay his secretary of state, the traditional stepping-stone to the presidency. Clay's appointment was politically fatal for both men: Jackson's supporters accused Clay and Adams of making a **corrupt bargain**, and they vowed to oppose Adams's policies and to prevent Clay's rise to the presidency.

The Last Notable President: John Quincy Adams

As president, Adams called for bold national action. "The moral purpose of the Creator," he told Congress, was to use the president to "improve the conditions of himself and his fellow men." Adams called for the establishment of a national university in Washington, scientific explorations in the Far West, and a uniform standard of weights and measures. Most important, he endorsed Henry Clay's American System and its three key elements: protective tariffs to stimulate manufacturing, federally subsidized roads and canals to facilitate commerce, and a national bank to control credit and provide a uniform currency.

American Textile Merchant The rising tariffs of the 1810s and 1820s benefitted northern textile merchants at the expense of southern planters and western farmers. The elegant suit of clothes and brightly colored fabrics depicted in this anonymous portrait emphasize the merchant's growing wealth and gentility, a phenomenon that southern planters argued was achieved at their expense. Sepia Times/Getty Images.

The Demise of the American System Manufacturers, entrepreneurs, and farmers in the Northeast and Midwest welcomed Adams's proposals. However, his policies won little support in the South, where planters opposed protective tariffs because these taxes raised the price of manufactures. Southern smallholders also feared powerful banks that could force them into bankruptcy. From his deathbed, Thomas Jefferson condemned Adams for promoting the rule of a monied "aristocracy" over "the plundered ploughman and beggared yeomanry."

Other politicians objected to the American System on constitutional grounds. In 1817, President Madison had vetoed the Bonus Bill, which proposed using the national government's income from the Second Bank of the United States to fund improvement projects in the states. Such projects, Madison argued, were the sole responsibility of the states, a sentiment shared by the Republican followers of Thomas Jefferson. In 1824, Martin Van Buren likewise declared his allegiance to the constitutional "doctrines of the Jefferson School" and his opposition to "consolidated government," a powerful and potentially oppressive national administration. Now a member of the U.S. Senate, Van Buren helped to defeat most of Adams's proposed subsidies for roads and canals.

The Tariff Battle The major battle of the Adams administration came over tariffs. The Tariff of 1816 had placed relatively high duties on imports of cheap English cotton cloth, allowing New England textile producers to control that segment of the market. In 1824, Adams and Clay secured a new tariff that protected New England and Pennsylvania manufacturers from more expensive woolen and cotton textiles and also English iron goods. Without these tariffs, British imports would have dominated the market and slowed American industrial development.

AP® SKILLS & PROCESSES

DEVELOPMENTS AND PROCESSES

Students need to be aware of the intermediate and short-term controversies protective tariffs had on national politics. For many southerners, this was a point of contention as they felt tariffs assisted manufacturing interests at the expense of farmers. Ask students to make a historical connection between the tariffs of 1816, 1824, and 1828 to sectional partisanship. Remind students the key is to make a connection between tariffs and partisan politics and not to give an overly detailed explanation of the tariffs.

Recognizing the appeal of tariffs, Van Buren and his Jacksonian allies hopped on the bandwagon. By increasing duties on wool, hemp, and other imported raw materials, they hoped to win the support of farmers in New York, Ohio, and Kentucky for Jackson's presidential candidacy in 1828. The tariff had become a political weapon. "I fear this tariff thing," remarked Thomas Cooper, the president of the College of South Carolina and an advocate of free trade. "By some strange mechanical contrivance [it has become] . . . a machine for manufacturing Presidents, instead of broadcloths, and bed blankets." Disregarding southern protests, northern Jacksonians joined with supporters of Adams and Clay to enact the Tariff of 1828, which raised duties significantly on raw materials, textiles, and iron goods.

Why did southerners resent tariffs so deeply? The new tariff, simply put, cost them about $100 million a year. Planters had to buy either higher-cost American textiles and iron goods, thus enriching northeastern businesses and workers, or highly taxed British imports, thus paying the expenses of the national government. The new tariff was "little less than legalized pillage," an Alabama legislator declared, calling it a **Tariff of Abominations**. Ignoring the Jacksonians' support for the Tariff of 1828, most southerners heaped blame on President Adams.

Tariff of Abominations
A tariff enacted in 1828 that raised duties significantly on raw materials, textiles, and iron goods. It enraged the South, which had no industries that needed protection and resented the higher cost of imported goods.

Southern governments also criticized Adams's Indian policy. A deeply moral man, the president supported the treaty-guaranteed land rights of Native Americans against expansion-minded whites. In 1825, U.S. commissioners had secured a treaty from one faction of Creeks ceding its lands in Georgia to the United States for eventual sale to the state's citizens. When the Creek National Council claimed the treaty was fraudulent, Adams called for new negotiations. In response, Georgia governor George M. Troup attacked the president as a "public enemy . . . the unblushing ally of the savages." Mobilizing Georgia's congressional delegation, Troup persuaded Congress to extinguish the Creeks' land titles, forcing most Creeks to leave the state.

Elsewhere, Adams's primary weakness was his out-of-date political style. He was aloof, inflexible, and paternalistic. When Congress rejected his economic policies, Adams accused its members of following the whims of public opinion and told them not to be enfeebled "by the will of our constituents." Rather than "run" for reelection in 1828, Adams "stood" for it, telling friends, "If my country wants my services, she must ask for them."

AP® SKILLS & PROCESSES

ARGUMENTATION

What were the successes and failures of John Adams's presidency, and what accounted for those outcomes?

TRM Find complete suggested responses in the Teacher's Resource Materials.

"The Democracy" and the Election of 1828

Martin Van Buren and the politicians handling Andrew Jackson's campaign for the presidency had no reservations about running for office. To put Jackson in the White House, Van Buren revived the political coalition created by Thomas Jefferson, championing policies that appealed to both southern planters and northern farmers and artisans, the "plain Republicans of the North." John C. Calhoun, Jackson's running mate, brought his South Carolina allies into Van Buren's party, and Jackson's close friends in Tennessee rallied voters throughout the Old Southwest. The Little Magician hoped that a national party would reconcile the diverse "interests" that, as James Madison suggested in Federalist No. 10, inevitably existed in a large republic. Equally important, added Jackson's ally Duff Green, it would put the "anti-slave party in the North . . . to sleep for twenty years to come."

AP® EXAM TIP

Compare the rise of the Democratic Party in the 1820s to the first two political parties in the Federal Period (Chapter 7).

AP® APPLY THE TIP

Have students work in pairs to review the platforms of the first political parties and complete **Handout 9.3 — Continuity and Change Over Time: Second Party System (TRM)**. Then ask students to respond to the following prompt using pp. 293–303 for reference: With which of the original political parties from the Federal period was the Democratic Party that developed in the age of Jackson most closely aligned? After students have read and analyzed the text, lead a class discussion on different responses to this prompt.

TRM Find **Handout 9.3 — Continuity and Change Over Time: Second Party System** in the Teacher's Resource Materials.

Van Buren and the Jacksonians orchestrated a massive publicity campaign. In New York, fifty newspapers declared their support for Jackson. Elsewhere, Jacksonians used mass meetings, torchlight parades, and barbecues to celebrate the candidate's frontier origin and rise to fame. They praised "Old Hickory" as a "natural" aristocrat, a self-made man.

The Jacksonians called themselves Democrats or "the Democracy" to convey their egalitarian message. As Thomas Morris told the Ohio legislature, the Democratic Party was fighting for equality: the republic had been corrupted by legislative charters

AP® SKILLS & PROCESSES

CONTEXTUALIZATION

Jackson lost the presidential election of 1824 and won in 1828: what changes explain these different outcomes?

AP® SKILLS & PROCESSES

CONTEXTUALIZATION

The **CONTEXTUALIZATION** question requires students to note changes in the electorate, particularly the expansion of the popular vote. Extend this prompt by asking students to identify the continuity between the two elections.

TRM Find complete suggested responses in the Teacher's Resource Materials.

AP® THEME

POL: Politics and Power

FIGURE 9.1 indicates the growth in political participation — not eligibility for participation. Students can explore these charts to consider how and why participation grew. Guide students' analysis with the following questions:

- **Roughly what percentage of eligible voters turned out to vote in 1824? In 1844?** *In 1824, just over 25 percent; in 1844, just over 75 percent.*
- **How much did support for Jackson and his successor, Van Buren, grow between 1828 and 1836?** *Use the Web site 270 to win.com and locate the historical presidential election maps. Compare the 1828 election with the 1836 election to determine whether the data suggests that support for Democrats increased, the percentage of voters participating increased, or the Two-Party System likely increased participation.*
- **Overall, why did participation grow so dramatically in these two decades?** *Eligible voters came to see that national politics — which often intersected with economic issues — had important implications for their own lives.*

CHECK FOR UNDERSTANDING

Ask students: **What were John Quincy Adams's political goals? How was he the "last notable president"?** *He supported Clay's American System of protective tariffs, a federal transportation network, and a national bank. He was the last elite candidate and the last one to follow the older style of campaigning that had become outdated in the era of democratic participation.*

TRM Find complete suggested responses in the Teacher's Resource Materials.

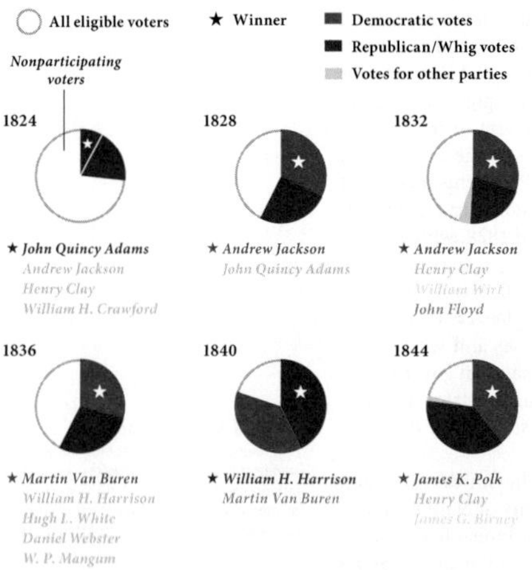

FIGURE 9.1 The Rise of Voter Turnout, 1824–1844
As the shrinking white sections of these pie graphs indicate, the proportion of eligible voters who cast ballots in presidential elections increased dramatically over time. In 1824, 27 percent voted; in 1840 and thereafter, about 80 percent went to the polls. Voter participation soared first in 1828, when Andrew Jackson and John Quincy Adams contested for the White House, and again in 1840, as competition heated up between Democrats and Whigs, who advocated different policies and philosophies of government. Democrats won most of these contests because their policies had greater appeal to ordinary citizens.

that gave "a few individuals rights and privileges not enjoyed by the citizens at large." Morris promised that the Democracy would destroy such "artificial distinction." Jackson himself declared that "equality among the people in the rights conferred by government" was the "great radical principle of freedom."

Jackson's message appealed to many social groups. His hostility to corporations and to Clay's American System won support from northeastern artisans and workers who felt threatened by industrialization. Jackson captured the votes of Pennsylvania ironworkers and New York farmers who had benefitted from the controversial Tariff of Abominations. Yet, by astutely declaring his support for a "judicious" tariff that would balance regional interests, Jackson remained popular in the South. In the Southeast and Midwest, Jackson's well-known hostility toward Native Americans reassured white farmers seeking Indian removal.

The Democrats' celebration of popular rule carried Jackson into office. In 1824, about one-quarter of the electorate had voted; in 1828, more than one-half went to the polls, and 56 percent voted for the Tennessee senator — the first president from a trans-Appalachian state (Figure 9.1 and Map 9.4). Jackson's popularity and sharp temper frightened men of wealth. Senator Daniel Webster of Massachusetts, a former Federalist and now a corporate lawyer, warned his clients that the new president would "bring a breeze with him. Which way it will blow, I cannot tell [but] . . . my fear is stronger than my hope." Supreme Court justice Joseph Story shared Webster's apprehensions. Watching an unruly Inauguration Day crowd climb over the elegant White House furniture to congratulate Jackson, Story lamented that "the reign of King 'Mob' seemed triumphant."

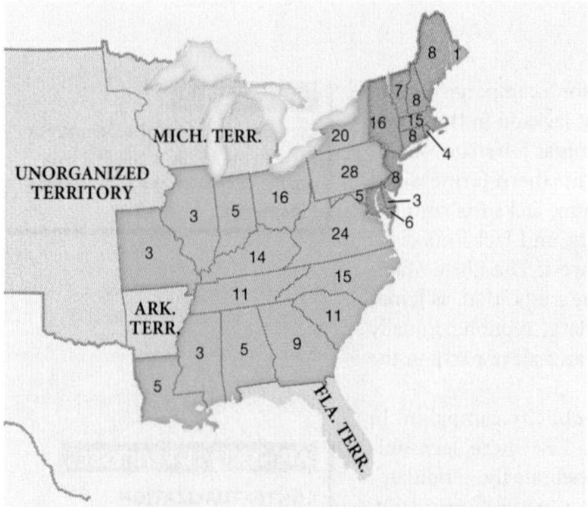

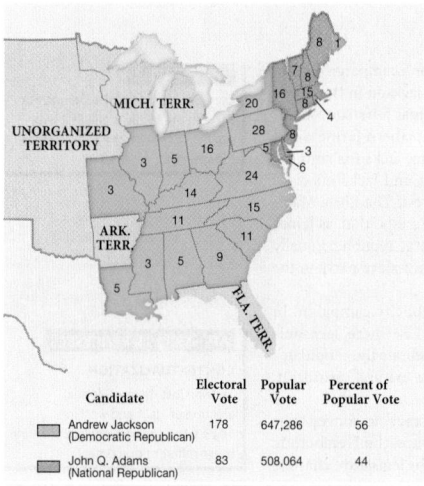

	Candidate	Electoral Vote	Popular Vote	Percent of Popular Vote
	Andrew Jackson (Democratic Republican)	178	647,286	56
	John Q. Adams (National Republican)	83	508,064	44

MAPPING THE PAST

MAP 9.4 The Presidential Election of 1828
As in 1824, John Quincy Adams carried all of New England and some of the Mid-Atlantic states. However, Andrew Jackson swept the rest of the nation and won a resounding victory in the electoral college. Over 1.1 million American men cast ballots in 1828, more than three times the number who voted in 1824.

ANALYZING THE MAP: Compare this map to Map 9.3, which depicts voting patterns in the 1824 election. What had changed in the intervening four years to explain the decline of regional candidates and the consolidation of party politics?

MAKING CONNECTIONS: This map vividly demonstrates the widespread support for Andrew Jackson in the 1828 election. How did the Jackson campaign reflect the nation's transition to a more participatory democracy? How did Jackson appeal show the influence of new political parties? Why was Adams's popularity limited to his home region of the northeast?

AP® THEME

PCE: Politics and Power

MAP 9.4 indicates the regional nature of political divisions in early 1800s, though students should also recognize that parties were national. Guide students' analysis with the following questions:

- **What issues divided the two parties? What differences in values did these issues reflect?** *They disagreed over the American System, including tariffs and funding for infrastructure. Whigs tended to favor manufacturing and economic development, while Democrats were more egalitarian (in terms of social class) and sympathetic to white workers.*
- **How does MAP 9.4 indicate the regional nature of these divisions?** *Jackson won nearly all the southern states and all of the northwestern states.*
- **What cautions need to be kept in mind when considering regionalism and national political parties?** *Electoral victory in a particular state means that a majority in the state supported the party or candidate, not that the candidate was uncontested. Jackson lost Delaware and parts of Maryland, both southern states, as well as New Jersey. Also, both parties were broadly national, and Clay, the leader of the Whigs, was a southerner.*

JACKSON IN POWER, 1829–1837

What were the constitutional arguments for and against internal improvements, the tariff, and nullification?

American-style political democracy — a broad franchise, a disciplined political party, and policies favoring specific interests — ushered Andrew Jackson into office. Jackson used his popular mandate to transform the national government. During his two terms, he enhanced presidential authority, destroyed the mercantilist and nationalist American System, established a new ideology of limited government, and supported Indian removal. An Ohio supporter summed up Jackson's vision: "the Sovereignty of the People, the Rights of the States, and a Light and Simple Government."

Jackson's Agenda: Rotation and Decentralization

To make policy, Jackson relied primarily on his so-called Kitchen Cabinet. Its most influential members were two Kentuckians, Francis Preston Blair, who edited the *Washington Globe*, and Amos Kendall, who wrote Jackson's speeches; Roger B. Taney (pronounced "tawny") of Maryland, who became attorney general, treasury secretary, and then chief justice of the Supreme Court; and Martin Van Buren, whom Jackson named secretary of state.

Following Van Buren's example in New York, Jackson used patronage to create a disciplined national party. He rejected the idea of "property in office" (that a qualified official held a position permanently) and insisted on a rotation of officeholders when a new administration took power. Rotation would not lessen expertise, Jackson insisted, because public duties were "so plain and simple that men of intelligence may readily qualify themselves for their performance." William L. Marcy, a New York Jacksonian, offered a more realistic explanation for rotation: government jobs were like the spoils of war, and "to the victor belong the spoils of the enemy." Jackson used this **spoils system** to reward his allies and win backing for his policies.

spoils system
The widespread award of public jobs to political supporters after an electoral victory. In 1829, Andrew Jackson instituted the system on the national level, arguing that the rotation of officeholders was preferable to a permanent group of bureaucrats.

Jackson's highest priority was to destroy the American System. He believed that government-sponsored plans for national economic development were unconstitutional. Declaring that the "voice of the people" called for "economy in the expenditures of the Government," Jackson vetoed four internal improvement bills in 1830, including an extension of the National Road, arguing that they infringed on "the reserved powers of states." By eliminating expenses, these vetoes also undermined the case for protective tariffs. As Jacksonian senator William Smith of South Carolina pointed out, "Destroy internal improvements and you leave no motive for the tariff."

The Tariff and Nullification

The Tariff of 1828 had helped Jackson win the presidency, but it saddled him with a major political crisis. There was fierce opposition to high tariffs throughout the South and especially in South Carolina. That state was the only one with an African American majority — 56 percent of the population in 1830 — and its slave owners, like the white sugar planters in the West Indies, feared a black rebellion. Even more, they worried about the legal abolition of slavery. The British Parliament had declared that slavery in its West Indian colonies would end in 1833; South Carolina planters, vividly recalling northern efforts to end slavery in Missouri, worried that the U.S. Congress would follow the British lead. So they attacked the tariff, both to lower rates and to discourage the use of federal power to attack slavery.

The crisis began in 1832, when Congress reenacted the Tariff of Abominations. In response, leading South Carolinians called a state convention that boldly

AP® EXAM TIP

Be able to summarize the role of political leaders in defining regional interests in the early nineteenth century.

AP® APPLY THE TIP

Divide the class into groups and assign each group to research one of the following leaders: Andrew Jackson, John C. Calhoun, Henry Clay, Martin Van Buren, Roger B. Taney, Francis Preston Blair, Nicholas Biddle, or John Quincy Adams. Ask students to determine the role of each individual in representing regional interests. Students should present their findings to the class in a brief presentation. In their presentations, students should note whether the leaders determined the interests of their regions or simply represented them. Once all groups have presented, ask the class to group the leaders according to region and define the region's interests. Additionally, discuss how the regional interests in the early nineteenth century grew more defined and the root cause of the differences.

AP® SKILLS & PROCESSES

DEVELOPMENTS AND PROCESSES

One essential task is for students to understand the extent to which Jacksonian Democrats defended the interests of the so-called "common man." The spoils system, bank war, nullification crisis, and Indian Removal are all topics students can use to evaluate this question. This could be a brief bell-ringer exercise to get students thinking about whether or not the Jacksonians represented a significant change in American politics.

TRM Find complete suggested responses in the Teacher's Resource Materials.

AP® SKILLS & PROCESSES

MAKING CONNECTIONS

Divide students into groups and have them select two of the steps from the image. Ask students to connect the words on the step with the idea of nullification. After students make the connection, ask them to provide the artist's point of view about what nullification meant in this period.

CHECK FOR UNDERSTANDING

Ask students: **What was nullification, and how did Jackson respond to it?** *Reacting against the high tariff duties in the 1832 Tariff of Abominations, John C. Calhoun drafted a statement declaring that states could nullify unconstitutional federal laws. Jackson requested a Force Bill to use military power to compel southern states to comply with the law, while working to gradually lower the tariff rate over several years.*

adopted an Ordinance of Nullification declaring the tariffs of 1828 and 1832 to be null and void. The ordinance prohibited the collection of those duties in South Carolina after February 1, 1833, and threatened secession if federal officials tried to collect them.

nullification
The constitutional argument advanced by John C. Calhoun that a state legislature or convention could void a law passed by Congress.

South Carolina's act of **nullification** — the argument that a state has the right to void, within its borders, a law passed by Congress — rested on the constitutional arguments developed in *The South Carolina Exposition and Protest* (1828). Written anonymously by Vice President John C. Calhoun, the *Exposition* contended that protective tariffs and other national legislation that operated unequally on the various states lacked fairness and legitimacy. "Constitutional government and the government of a majority," Calhoun concluded, "are utterly incompatible."

Calhoun's argument echoed the claims made by Jefferson and Madison in the Kentucky and Virginia Resolutions of 1798. Those resolutions asserted that, because state-based conventions had ratified the Constitution, sovereignty lay in the states, not in the people. Beginning from this premise, Calhoun argued that a state convention could declare a congressional law to be void within the state's borders. Replying to this states' rights interpretation of the Constitution, which had little support in the text of the document, Senator Daniel Webster of Massachusetts presented a nationalist interpretation that celebrated popular sovereignty and Congress's responsibility to secure the "general welfare."

AP® SKILLS & PROCESSES
DEVELOPMENTS AND PROCESSES
How did South Carolina justify nullification on constitutional grounds?

Jackson hoped to find a middle path between Webster's strident nationalism and Calhoun's radical doctrine of localist federalism. Jackson declared that South Carolina's Ordinance of Nullification violated the letter of the Constitution and was "destructive of the great object for which it was formed." At his request, Congress in early 1833 passed a military Force Bill, authorizing the president to compel South Carolina's obedience to national laws. At the same time, Jackson addressed the South's objections to high import duties with a new tariff act that, over the course of a decade, reduced rates to the modest levels of 1816. Export-hungry midwestern wheat farmers joined southern planters in advocating low duties to avoid retaliatory tariffs by foreign nations. "Illinois wants a market for her agricultural products," declared Senator Sidney Breese in 1846. "[S]he wants the market of the world."

Second Bank of the United States
National bank with multiple branches chartered in 1816 for twenty years. Intended to help regulate the economy, the bank became a major issue in Andrew Jackson's reelection campaign in 1832.

Nullification Equals Despotism This highly critical cartoon shows John C. Calhoun, author of the *South Carolina Exposition and Protest* (1828), having ascended a stairway that leads from nullification to treason, civil war, deception, and disunion. He reaches toward the crown of despotism as figures representing the United States — one with a banner declaring "E Pluribus Union," the other "Constitution" — lie in the foreground with swords protruding from their lifeless bodies. From The New York Public Library, https://digitalcollections.nypl.org/items/8f4ae1d3-b464-3973-e040-e00a180607fe.

Having won the political battle by securing a tariff reduction, the South Carolina convention did not press its constitutional stance on nullification. Jackson was satisfied. He had assisted the South economically while upholding the constitutional principle of national authority — a principle that Abraham Lincoln would embrace to defend the Union during the secession crisis of 1861.

The Bank War

In the midst of the tariff crisis, Jackson faced a major challenge from politicians who supported the **Second Bank of the United States**. Founded in Philadelphia in 1816 (see "The Federalist Legacy" in Chapter 7) with regional branches in thirteen states, the bank was privately managed and operated under a twenty-year charter from the federal government, which owned 20 percent of its stock. The bank's most important roles were to increase the availability of credit and stabilize the nation's money supply, which consisted primarily of paper money issued by state-chartered banks. The state banks promised to redeem the notes on demand with "hard" money (or "specie") — that is, gold or silver coins minted by the U.S. or foreign governments — but there were few coins in circulation. By collecting those notes and regularly demanding specie, the Second Bank kept the state banks from issuing too much paper money and depreciating its value.

This cautious monetary policy pleased creditors — the bankers and entrepreneurs in Boston, New York, and Philadelphia, whose capital investments were underwriting economic development. However, expansion-minded bankers, including friends of Jackson's in Nashville, demanded an end to central oversight. Moreover, many ordinary Americans worried that the Second Bank would force weak banks to close, leaving them holding worthless paper notes. Many politicians resented the arrogance of the bank's president, Nicholas Biddle. "As to mere power," Biddle boasted, "I have been for years in the daily exercise of more personal authority than any President habitually enjoys."

Jackson's Bank Veto Although the Second Bank had many enemies, a political miscalculation by its friends brought its downfall. In 1832, Henry Clay and Daniel Webster persuaded Biddle to seek an early extension of the bank's charter (which still had four years to run). They had the votes in Congress to enact the required legislation and hoped to lure Jackson into a veto that would split the Democrats just before the 1832 elections.

Jackson turned the tables on Clay and Webster. He vetoed the rechartering bill with a masterful message that blended constitutional arguments with class rhetoric and patriotic fervor. Adopting the position taken by Thomas Jefferson in 1793, Jackson declared that Congress had no constitutional authority to charter a national bank. He condemned the bank as "subversive of the rights of the States," "dangerous to the liberties of the people," and a privileged monopoly that promoted "the advancement of the few at the expense of . . . farmers, mechanics, and laborers." Finally, the president noted that British aristocrats owned much of the bank's stock. Such a powerful institution should be "purely American," Jackson declared with patriotic zeal.

Jackson's attack on the bank carried him to victory in 1832. Old Hickory and Martin Van Buren, his new running mate, overwhelmed Henry Clay, who headed the National Republican ticket, by 219 to 49 electoral votes. Jackson's most fervent supporters were eastern workers and western farmers, who blamed the Second Bank for high prices and stagnant farm income. Other Jackson supporters had prospered during a decade of strong economic growth. Thousands of middle-class Americans — lawyers, clerks, shopkeepers, and artisans — had used the opportunity to rise in the world and cheered Jackson's attack on privileged corporations.

King Andrew the First, 1833
Jackson's decision to veto the rechartering of the Second Bank of the United States helped him win reelection, but for his opponents it confirmed the fear that he was an autocrat. This political cartoon portrays Jackson as a king. He wears a crown and holds a scepter in one hand and his veto power in the other. Underfoot lie a tattered copy of the Constitution, the bank charter, and an internal improvements bill. The cartoon appeared in the fall of 1833, after his treasury secretary, Roger B. Taney, removed federal deposits from the Bank of the United States. Library of Congress, LC-DIG-ppmsca-15771.

The Bank Destroyed Early in 1833, Jackson met their wishes by appointing Roger B. Taney, a strong opponent of corporate privilege, as head of the Treasury Department. Taney promptly transferred the federal government's gold and silver from the Second Bank to various state banks, which critics labeled Jackson's "pet banks." To justify this abrupt (and probably illegal) transfer, Jackson declared that his reelection represented "the decision of the people against the bank" and gave him a mandate to destroy it. This sweeping claim of presidential power was new and radical. Never before had a president claimed that victory at the polls allowed him to pursue a controversial policy or to act independently of Congress (see "Firsthand Accounts," p. 298).

The "bank war" escalated into an all-out political battle. In March 1834, Jackson's opponents in the Senate passed a resolution composed by Henry Clay that censured

TEACHING STRATEGY

Guide students' analysis of the cartoon of King Andrew the First with the following questions:

- **What point of view does the cartoonist support?** *The cartoonist is critical of Andrew Jackson's use of presidential power through the veto.*
- **How do you know?** *He has torn up the Constitution and trampled it underfoot. He is depicted as a king — the epitome of bad government for a nation that celebrated its rebellion against the King of England and its subsequent independence.*
- **How effective are the cartoons in championing that view?** *Like many political cartoons, this one was probably most compelling to those who already shared the artist's views. It would have been an effective critique for many Americans worried about maintaining the Revolution's legacy or suspicious of Jackson. For Jackson's supporters, it would probably have been dismissed as the grumbling of those who stood to lose power by a president who appropriately exercised his authority to protect the people.*

AP® SKILLS & PROCESSES

ANALYZING HISTORICAL EVIDENCE

The **AP® FIRSTHAND ACCOUNTS** feature provides another opportunity to consider point of view in primary sources, since it offers a variety of perspectives on the same individual. Ask students to consider why Jackson, more than some other presidents, drew such strong and varied opinions from his contemporaries.

AP® FIRSTHAND ACCOUNTS

The Character and Goals of Andrew Jackson

From the start of his career, Andrew Jackson was a controversial figure. "Hot-tempered," "Indian-hater," "military despot," said his critics, while his friends praised him as a forthright statesman. His contemporary biographer, the journalist James Parton, found him a man of many faces, an enigma. Others thought they understood his personality and policies: James Hamilton, a loyal Jacksonian congressman, recalled Jackson's volatile temper. Henry Clay, his archrival, warned that Jackson's quest for power threatened American republicanism, while wealthy New York Whig Philip Hone accused him of inciting class warfare. After talking with dozens of Americans, Frenchman Alexis de Tocqueville offered a balanced interpretation of the man and his goals.

JAMES PARTON

Preface to *The Life of Andrew Jackson* (1860)

SOURCE: James Parton, *The Life of Andrew Jackson. In Three Volumes* (New York: Mason Brothers, 1860), vol. 1, vii–viii.

"If any one . . . had asked what I had yet discovered respecting General Jackson, I might have answered thus: 'Andrew Jackson, I am given to understand, was a patriot and a traitor. He was one of the greatest of generals, and wholly ignorant of the art of war. . . . The first of statesmen, he never devised, he never framed a measure. He was the most candid of men, and was capable of the profoundest dissimulation. A most law-defying, law-obeying citizen. A stickler for discipline, he never hesitated to disobey his superior. A democratic autocrat. An urbane savage. An atrocious saint.'"

JAMES HAMILTON JR.

Recalling an Event in 1827, as Jackson Campaigns for the Presidency

SOURCE: Sean Wilentz, ed., *Major Problems in the Early Republic, 1787–1848* (Lexington, MA: D. C. Heath, 1991), 374.

"The steamer Pocahontas was chartered by citizens of New Orleans to convey the General and his party from Nashville to that city. She was fitted out in the most sumptuous manner. The party was General and Mrs. Jackson, . . . Governor Samuel Houston, Wm. B. Lewis, Robert Armstrong, and others. . . . The only freight was the General's cotton-crop. . . .

In the course of the voyage an event occurred, which I repeat, as it is suggestive of [his] character. A steamer of greater speed than ours, going in the same direction, passed us, crossed our bow; then stopped and let us pass her and then passed us again in triumph. This was repeated again and again, until the General, being excited by the offensive course, ordered a rifle to be brought to him; hailed the pilot of the other steamer, and swore that if he did the same thing again he would shoot him."

PHILIP HONE

Ruminating in His Diary on the Jacksonians' Victory in the New York Elections of 1834

SOURCE: Sean Wilentz, ed., *Major Problems in the Early Republic, 1787–1848* (Lexington, MA: D. C. Heath, 1991), 392–393.

"I apprehend that Mr. Van Buren [Jackson's vice president] and his friends have no permanent cause of triumph in their victory. They . . . have mounted a vicious horse, who, taking the bit in his mouth, will run away with [them]. . . . This battle had been fought upon the ground of the poor against the rich, and this unworthy prejudice, this dangerous delusion, has been encouraged by the leaders of

the president and warned of executive tyranny: "We are in the midst of a revolution, hitherto bloodless, but rapidly descending towards a total change of the pure republican character of the Government, and the concentration of all power in the hands of one man." The censure did not deter Jackson. "The Bank is trying to kill me but I will kill it," he vowed to Van Buren. And so he did. When the Second Bank's national charter expired in 1836, Jackson prevented its renewal.

Jackson had destroyed both national banking — the handiwork of Alexander Hamilton — and the American System of protective tariffs and public works created by Henry Clay and John Quincy Adams. The result was a profound check on economic activism and innovative policymaking by the national government. "All is gone," observed a Washington newspaper correspondent. "All is gone, which the General Government was instituted to create and preserve."

AP® SKILLS & PROCESSES

MAKING CONNECTIONS

Why — and how — did Jackson destroy the Second National Bank?

298

AP® SKILLS & PROCESSES

MAKING CONNECTIONS

The **MAKING CONNECTIONS** question asks students to place Jackson's actions in the larger context of his era. Students may need guidance to recognize that his actions were shaped by ideology, political party disputes, and by the interests of his Nashville friends. Also, without state banks, he would have found it difficult to defeat the Bank of the United States. Extend this prompt by asking students to consider how Jackson's context differed from Madison's, who came to embrace the formation of a new national bank.

TRM Find complete suggested responses in the Teacher's Resource Materials.

CHECK FOR UNDERSTANDING

Ask students: **What was the bank war and how did it end?** *Jackson thought the Second Bank of the United States, chartered in 1816, represented an unconstitutional extension of power. When Clay and Webster tried to pass a bill reauthorizing the bank four years early (to help divide Democrats before the 1832 election and ensure Jackson's defeat), Jackson vetoed the bill. This action helped him win reelection. Treating his victory as a mandate, he set about destroying the bank by diverting its deposits to state banks.*

the triumphant party, and fanned into a flame by the polluted breath of the hireling press in their employ. . . .

The cry of 'Down with the aristocracy!' mingled with the shouts of victory. . . . They have succeeded in raising this dangerous spirit [of the mob], and have gladly availed themselves of its support to accomplish a temporary object; but can they allay it at pleasure? . . . Eighteen thousand men in New York have voted for the high-priest of the party whose professed design is to bring down the property, the talents, the industry, the steady habits of that class which constituted the real strength of the Commonwealth, to the common level of the idle, the worthless, and the unenlightened. Look to it, ye men of respectability in the Jackson party, are ye not afraid of the weapons ye have used in this warfare? ❞

HENRY CLAY

Introducing a Senate Resolution Censuring Jackson, December 26, 1833

SOURCE: Calvin Colton, ed., *The Life . . . of Henry Clay*, 6 vols. (New York: A. Barnes, 1857), 576–580.

❝ We are in the midst of a revolution, hitherto bloodless, but rapidly tending toward a total change of the pure republican character of the government, and to the concentration of all power in the hands of one man. The powers of Congress are paralyzed, except when exerted in conformity with his will, by frequent and an extraordinary exercise of the executive veto, not anticipated by the founders of our Constitution, and not practiced by any of the predecessors of the present chief magistrate. . . .

The judiciary has not been exempt from the prevailing rage for innovation. Decisions of the tribunals, deliberately pronounced, have been contemptuously disregarded. . . . Our Indian relations, coeval with the existence of the government, and recognized and established by numerous laws and treaties, have been subverted. . . . The system of protection of improvement lies crushed beneath the veto. The system of protection of American industry [will soon meet a similar fate]. . . . In a term of eight years, a little more than equal to that which was required to establish our liberties [as an independent republic between 1776 and 1783], the government will have been transformed into an elective monarchy — the worst of all forms of government. ❞

ALEXIS DE TOCQUEVILLE

Analysis of Jackson in *Democracy in America* (1835)

SOURCE: Alexis de Tocqueville, *Democracy in America*, abr. by Thomas Bender (New York: Modern Library, 1981), 271–273.

❝ We have been told that General Jackson has won battles; that he is an energetic man, prone by nature and habit to the use of force, covetous of power and a despot by inclination.

All this may be true; but the inferences which have been drawn from these truths are very erroneous. It has been imagined that General Jackson is bent on establishing a dictatorship in America, introducing a military spirit, and giving a degree of influence to the central authority that cannot but be dangerous to provincial [state] liberties. . . .

Far from wishing to extend the Federal power, the President belongs to the party which is desirous of limiting that power to the clear and precise letter of the Constitution and which never puts a construction upon that act favorable to the government of the Union; far from standing forth as the champion of centralization, General Jackson is the agent of the state jealousies; and he was placed in his lofty station by the passions that are most opposed to the central government. ❞

QUESTIONS FOR ANALYSIS

1. Was Jackson a "democratic autocrat," as Parton puts it? Would the authors of the other excerpts agree? Did Jackson instigate class warfare, as Hone suggests? Corroborate evidence from each source to develop a historically defensible claim.
2. In your judgment, which writer, Clay or Tocqueville, offers the more accurate assessment of Jackson and his policies? Evaluate the extent to which each claim is effective.
3. Do you agree with Philip Hone's view that the Jacksonian Democrats mobilized "poor against the rich"? What evidence would support or contradict Hone's assertion? Use relevant examples to make a claim and refute a counterclaim.

TRM Find complete suggested responses in the Teacher's Resource Materials.

Indian Removal

The status of Native American peoples posed an equally complex political problem. By the late 1820s, white voices throughout the South and Midwest demanded the resettlement of Indian peoples west of the Mississippi River. Many whites who were sympathetic to Native Americans also favored resettlement. Removal to the West seemed the only way to protect Indians from alcoholism, financial exploitation, and cultural decline (see "Comparing Interpretations," p. 300).

However, most Indians did not want to leave their ancestral lands. For centuries, Cherokees and Creeks had lived in Georgia, Tennessee, and Alabama; Chickasaws and Choctaws in Mississippi and Alabama; and Seminoles in Florida. During the War of 1812, Andrew Jackson had forced the Creeks to relinquish millions of acres, but Indian nations still controlled vast tracts and wanted to keep them.

AP® EXAM TIP

A helpful exercise to prep for the AP® Exam is to evaluate the ways that Indian Removal illustrates both change and continuity in relations with Native Americans.

AP® APPLY THE TIP

Ask students to closely read an excerpt from Andrew Jackson's message to Congress "On Indian Removal" from 1830 (available on the Our Documents Web site) and explain Jackson's historical argument regarding Indian removal. Students should provide historical evidence to support Jackson's argument. Remind students that a common practice in modern politics is for an opposing party or group to write a response to a president's address to Congress. Ask students to write a response to Jackson's message to Congress from the point of view of the Whig Party.

AP® SKILLS & PROCESSES

ANALYZING HISTORICAL EVIDENCE

Some students may need clarification on the question posed in the **AP® COMPARING INTERPRETATIONS** feature. The focus is not on whether or not Indian Removal was humanitarian, but rather about whether Jackson believed that it was. In answering this question, students will need to be able to avoid present beliefs as most will probably sympathize with the Cherokees' plight and be critical of Jackson's motives, and attempt to evaluate Jackson according to the standards of humanitarianism in his own time. Students should also consider the critiques of removal by both American Indians and whites that might call into question Jackson's claims of humanitarianism.

TEACHING STRATEGY

Extend the **AP® COMPARING INTERPRETATIONS** feature by examining further Remini's claim that Jackson acted in a humanitarian way. The National Humanities Center provides more detailed background information about the effects of the removal by scholar Clara Sue Kidwell, including several illustrations, documents, and maps. Access this site by searching "NHC Effects of Removal on American Indian Tribes."

TRM Find complete suggested responses in the Teacher's Resource Materials.

AP® COMPARING INTERPRETATIONS

Was Indian Removal Humanitarian or Racist?

The Indian Removal Act, passed by Congress in 1830 at Andrew Jackson's request, has polarized historians' assessments of his presidency more than any other issue. Unlike some earlier presidents who encouraged the assimilation of Native groups, Jackson supported a policy of moving Native Americans from their lands in the American Southeast to unoccupied federal lands beyond the Mississippi River. The issue came to a head in the late 1820s, just as Jackson's presidency began, when the Cherokees, living within the borders of Georgia, declared themselves to be a sovereign nation. Neither the state, nor Jackson, nor the Supreme Court agreed with them. The 1830 Indian Removal Act granted Jackson authority to negotiate treaties with Native tribes to achieve his policy of removing them. Some tribes agreed to move. When others, like the Seminoles, Creeks, and Cherokees, resisted, the federal government used a forced removal policy. The result was great suffering as Indians died on the Trail of Tears.

Historians agree on the basic narrative of Jackson's Indian policy, but they debate his motivations. Robert V. Remini and Anthony F. C. Wallace interpret Jackson's policies regarding Native Americans in different ways. Was Jackson motivated by a humanitarian concern for Native Americans, or were his policies reflective of the era's racial discrimination against "savages"?

ROBERT V. REMINI

SOURCE: Robert V. Remini, *Andrew Jackson and the Course of American Freedom, 1822–1832* (New York: Harper & Row, 1981), 2: 221–222, 228.

There is no doubt that Jackson believed absolutely that he was pursuing a "just and humane policy towards the Indians." Given the greed of the white man and the certitude that the two races could not intermingle or live side by side, Jackson contended that only through removal could the Indians escape inevitable annihilation. Once relocated beyond the Mississippi the federal government might then exercise "parental control" over their interests and in that way "perpetuate their race." Most Americans probably agreed with this policy. As "hard and cruel as it was then thought," wrote one contemporary a short time afterward, it "is now universally felt to have been as kind as it was necessary."

To implement this "hard and cruel" yet "kind" and "necessary" action, [William] Carroll and [John] Coffee were instructed by Jackson to learn first who controlled the will of the Creeks and Cherokees. "Go to them," he directed, explain the dangers facing their people, enlarge on their "comparative degradation as a people" and the utter impossibility of their ever attaining high privileges if they stay, and that their own laws were soon to be superseded by the laws of at least four states. Then describe to them, Jackson continued, "the fine and fertile and abundant country" west of the Mississippi where the federal government "could and *would* protect them more fully in the possession of the soil, and their right of self government." There, in succeeding generations, they would grow "to be our equals in privileges, civil and religious"; if they refused to go, however, then "they must necessarily entail destruction upon their race." . . .

AP® SKILLS & PROCESSES

DEVELOPMENTS AND PROCESSES

How did American Indian resistance respond to federal policies in the Era of Jackson?

Cherokee Resistance But on what terms? Some Indians had adopted white ways. An 1825 census revealed that various Cherokees owned 33 gristmills, 13 sawmills, 2,400 spinning wheels, 760 looms, and 2,900 plows. Many of these owners were mixed-race, the offspring of white traders and Indian women. They had grown up in a bicultural world, knew the political and economic ways of whites, and often favored assimilation into white society. Indeed, some of these mixed-race people were indistinguishable from southern planters. At his death in 1809, Georgia Cherokee James Vann owned one hundred black slaves, two trading posts, and a gristmill. Three decades later, forty other mixed-blood Cherokee families each owned ten or more African American workers.

Prominent mixed-race Cherokees believed that integration into American life was the best way to protect their property and the lands of their people. In 1821, Sequoyah, a part-Cherokee silversmith, perfected a system of writing for the Cherokee language; six years later, mixed-race Cherokees devised a new charter of Cherokee government modeled directly on the U.S. Constitution. "You asked us to throw off the hunter and warrior state," Cherokee John Ridge told a Philadelphia audience in 1832. "We did so. You asked us to form a republican government: We did so. . . . You asked us to learn to

But what about protecting the Indians with federal power in the lands they still occupied? "It is too late" for that, Jackson declared. "It is too late to inquire whether it was just in the United States to include them and their territories within the bounds of new States, whose limits they could control. That step can not be retraced. A State can not be dismembered by Congress or restricted in the exercise of her constitutional power." . . .

Given the past atrocities and the present continued greed of white men the only sane policy for a just government, Jackson declared, was to get the Indian to a place of safety, which he fervently believed existed west of the Mississippi River.

ANTHONY F. C. WALLACE

SOURCE: Anthony F. C. Wallace, *The Long Bitter Trail: Andrew Jackson and the Indians* (New York: Hill & Wang, -1993), 5–6, 56.

The hunger for Indian land was most intense in the Southern slave-owning states, and Jackson as a politician generally reflected Southern economic interests. He became the political prime mover of the Indian-removal process. In 1824 he ran unsuccessfully for President on the Democratic ticket. In 1828 he tried again, and won, and one of his first actions as President was to call, in his inaugural address of 1829, for the passage of a Removal Act that would effectively dislodge the Native Americans — and especially the Southern tribes — from their ancestral lands east of the Mississippi River and colonize them in an Indian territory west of the Mississippi. The Act was passed in 1830, and during the remainder of his presidency, and for several years thereafter, the government proceeded to persuade — with force when necessary — the tribes to "voluntarily" surrender their territories and emigrate to allocated tracts, primarily in what is now the state of Oklahoma. . . .

Jackson never proposed exterminating the Indians or at least in public rhetoric, removing by force of arms those who wished to remain. But he was adept at devising conditions that would make those who chose not to remove so miserable that they would emigrate eventually anyway. Like many others, he seems to have regarded as inevitable the ultimate extinction of the Native Americans as a culturally distinct entity. Their doom was not to be regretted, however: the present race of Indians had destroyed the once great civilization of the "mound builders," he argued (along with others of his time, including Joseph Smith and the Mormons), and now their own decline was only one more episode in the history of the human race.

But whatever were Jackson's private reasons for promoting Indian removal — some combination of political ambition, financial greed, and philosophical rationalization — there remained the political forces that he mobilized under the banner of the Democratic Party. The exaltation of the common man (meaning, on the frontier, the settler and speculator hungry for Indian land), the sense of America as the redeemer nation destined for continental expansion, the open acceptance of racism as a justification not only for the enslavement of blacks but also for the exploitation of Native Americans — these were popular, politically powerful themes that would have driven any Democratic President to press for a policy of Indian removal.

AP® SHORT ANSWER PRACTICE

1. Identify one key difference between Remini and Wallace in their interpretation of Jackson's attitude toward Native Americans. Compare the main of ideas of their arguments.
2. To what extent does each of these historians believe Jackson's view of Native Americans was widely shared by white Americans at the time? Justify your claim with specific examples from each source.
3. In considering these two excerpts and Chapter 9's discussion, why do you think Indian removal became a leading issue during Jackson's presidency? Describe the political, social, economic circumstances driving Indian policy.

TRM Find complete suggested responses in the Teacher's Resource Materials.

read: We did so. You asked us to cast away our idols, and worship your God: We did so." Full-blood Cherokees, who made up 90 percent of the population, resisted many of these cultural and political innovations but were equally determined to retain their ancestral lands. "We would not receive money for land in which our fathers and friends are buried," one full-blood chief declared. "We love our land; it is our mother."

What the Cherokees did or wanted carried no weight with the Georgia legislature. In 1802, Georgia had given up its western land claims in return for a federal promise to extinguish Indian landholdings in the state. Now it demanded fulfillment of that pledge. Having spent his military career fighting Indians and seizing their lands, Andrew Jackson gave full support to Georgia. On assuming the presidency, he withdrew the federal troops that had protected Indian enclaves there and in Alabama and Mississippi. The states, he declared, were sovereign within their borders.

The Removal Act and Its Aftermath Jackson then pushed the **Indian Removal Act of 1830** through Congress over the determined opposition of evangelical Protestant men — and women. To block removal, Catharine Beecher and Lydia Sigourney composed a Ladies Circular that urged "benevolent ladies" to use "prayers and exertions

Indian Removal Act of 1830
Act that directed the mandatory relocation of eastern tribes to territory west of the Mississippi. Jackson insisted that his goal was to save the Indians and their culture. Indians resisted the controversial act, but in the end most were forced to comply.

AP® THEME

ARC: American and Regional Culture

Think about engaging students in an activity that requires them to think about the changes in American cultural and political practices over time. Have students go to Period 4 on Gilder-Lehrman's Web site (ap.gilderlehrman.org) and select the essay on Indian Removal by historian Theda Perdue, which will focus students' attention on the generational, cultural, and political changes regarding how Americans viewed American Indians. Couple this reading with an analysis of the map on page 303 to illustrate the national attitude toward American Indians in the early nineteenth century.

VISUAL ACTIVITY

Andrew Jackson as the Great Father, 1835 Jackson championed the Indian Removal Act of 1830, which created the Indian Territory on lands obtained in the Louisiana Purchase and forced dozens of Native American nations throughout the eastern United States to move across the Mississippi. Jackson professed a concern for Native American welfare, prompting this sarcastic portrayal as the "Great Father" tending to the needs of his diminutive Native American "children." Jackson is portrayed unflatteringly, with dark skin that seems to suggest his own racial ambiguity. William L. Clements Library, University of Michigan.

READING THE IMAGE: Look closely at the figures surrounding Jackson. What details can you identify, and how do you interpret them? Above his left shoulder, Columbia (a female personification of the United States) rests her foot on the head of a fallen enemy. What is the point of view of the artist regarding Jackson and the Indian Removal Act? What is the artist's purpose in creating this image?

MAKING CONNECTIONS: Considering what you have read about Jackson's Indian policy, how does the representation of Jackson in this cartoon illustrate continuity and change in relations between the United States and American Indian nations?

to avert the calamity of removal." Women from across the nation flooded Congress with petitions. Nonetheless, Jackson's bill squeaked through the House of Representatives by a vote of 102 to 97.

The Removal Act created the Indian Territory on national lands acquired in the Louisiana Purchase and located in present-day Oklahoma and Kansas. It promised money and reserved land to Native American peoples who would give up their ancestral holdings east of the Mississippi River. Government officials promised the Indians that they could live on their new land, "they and all their children, as long as grass grows and water runs." However, as one Indian leader noted, on the Great Plains "water and timber are scarcely to be seen." When Chief Black Hawk and his Sauk and Fox followers refused to leave rich, well-watered farmland in western Illinois in 1832, Jackson sent troops to expel them by force. Eventually, the U.S. Army pursued Black Hawk into the Wisconsin Territory and, in the brutal eight-hour Bad Axe Massacre, killed 850 of his 1,000 warriors. Over the next five years, American diplomatic pressure and military power forced seventy Indian peoples to sign treaties and move west of the Mississippi (Map 9.5).

In the meantime, the Cherokees had carried the defense of their lands to the Supreme Court, where they claimed the status of a "foreign nation." In *Cherokee Nation v. Georgia* (1831), Chief Justice John Marshall denied that claim and declared that Indian peoples were "domestic dependent nations." However, in *Worcester v. Georgia* (1832), Marshall and the Court sided with the Cherokees against Georgia. Voiding Georgia's extension of state law over the Cherokees, the Court held that Indian nations were "distinct political communities, having territorial boundaries, within which their authority is exclusive [and is] guaranteed by the United States."

But Jacksonians had little sympathy for the position the Marshall Court had taken, and instead of guaranteeing the Cherokees' territory, the U.S. government took it from them. In 1835, American officials and a minority Cherokee faction negotiated the Treaty of New Echota, which specified that Cherokees would resettle in Indian Territory. When only 2,000 of 17,000 Cherokees had moved by the May 1838 deadline,

Blackhawk This portrait of Black Hawk (1767–1838), by George Catlin, shows the Indian leader holding his namesake, a black hawk and its feathers. When Congress approved Andrew Jackson's Indian Removal Act in 1830, Black Hawk mobilized Sauk and Fox warriors to protect their ancestral lands in Illinois. "It was here, that I was born — and here lie the bones of many friends and relatives," the aging chief declared. "I . . . never could consent to leave it." National Portrait Gallery, Smithsonian Institution, USA/Bridgeman Images.

TEACHING STRATEGY

Show students the cartoon of Andrew Jackson, and ask the following questions:

- **What point of view does the cartoonist support?** *The cartoonist depicts Jackson visually in an unflattering way.*
- **How do you know?** *As the caption suggests, it depicts his skin as dark, hinting with veiled racism at his uncertain racial origins. His hair seems exaggerated, and his posture arrogant.*
- **How effective are the cartoons in championing that view?** *Again, this cartoon probably didn't change many people's views, but it did effectively express the outrage of those who criticized Indian Removal as unjust and un-American.*
- **Compare this cartoon with the cartoon on p. 297. What similarities and differences do they have? Which seems more persuasive? Why?** *Both depict Jackson in an unflattering light. Both seem to highlight his authority or use of power — whether by depicting him as a monarch or showing him as an adult tending Native American "children," who are adults themselves. (Note: Students will have varying opinions about the relative persuasiveness of the cartoons, but they should justify whatever answers they provide.)*

TRM Find complete suggested responses in the Teacher's Resource Materials.

TEACHING STRATEGY

The National Park Service, in consultation with Cherokee groups, created a 26-minute film about the Trail of Tears available on YouTube. The film provides a detailed historical narrative with some dramatic reenactments by Cherokees in period dress. The last several minutes of the film discuss the status and condition of Cherokees in the contemporary U.S. Access the film by searching "NPS Trail of Tears National Historic Trail."

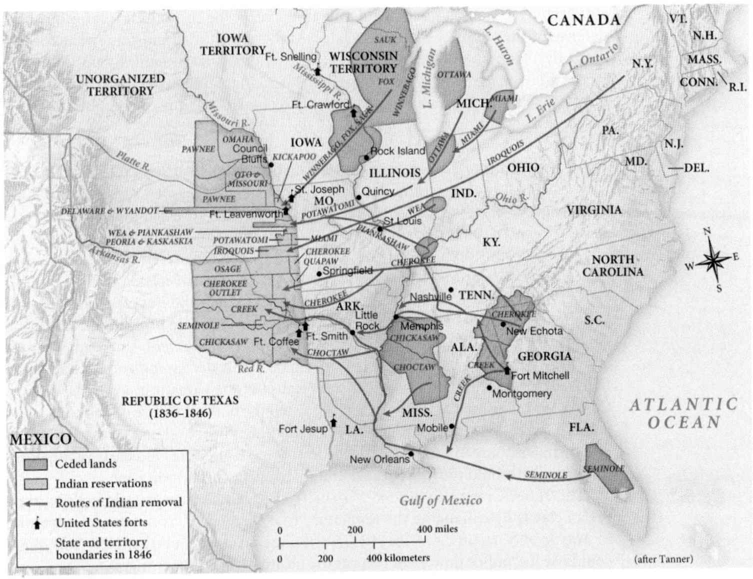

MAP 9.5 The Removal of Native Americans, 1820–1846
As white settlers moved west, the U.S. government forced scores of Native American communities to leave their ancestral lands. Andrew Jackson's Indian Removal Act of 1830 formalized this policy. Subsequently, many Indian peoples signed treaties that exchanged their lands in the East, Midwest, and Southeast for money and designated reservations in an Indian Territory west of the Mississippi River. When the Sauk, Fox, Cherokees, and Seminoles resisted resettlement, the government used the U.S. Army to enforce the removal policy.

President Martin Van Buren (who succeeded Jackson in the election of 1836) ordered General Winfield Scott to enforce the treaty. Scott's army rounded up 14,000 Cherokees (including mixed-race African Cherokees) and marched them 1,200 miles, an arduous journey that became known as the **Trail of Tears**. Along the way, 3,000 Indians died of starvation and exposure. Once in Oklahoma, the Cherokees excluded anyone of "negro or mulatto parentage" from governmental office, thereby affirming that full citizenship in their nation was racially defined. Just as the United States was a "white man's country," so Indian Territory would be a "red man's country."

Trail of Tears
Forced westward journey of Cherokees from their lands in Georgia to present-day Oklahoma in 1838. Nearly a quarter of the Cherokees died en route.

Pressed by their white neighbors, the Creeks, Chickasaws, and Choctaws accepted grants of land west of the Mississippi, leaving the Seminoles in Florida as the only numerically significant Indian people remaining in the Southeast. Government pressure persuaded about half of the Seminoles to migrate to Indian Territory, but families whose ancestors had intermarried with runaway slaves feared the emphasis on "blood purity" there. During the 1840s, they fought a successful guerrilla war against the U.S. Army and retained their lands in central Florida. These Seminoles were the exception: the Jacksonians had forced the removal of most eastern Indian peoples.

AP® SKILLS & PROCESSES
COMPARISON
How did the views of Jackson and John Marshall differ regarding the status and rights of Indian peoples?

Jackson's Impact

Jackson's legacy is complex. He expanded the authority of the nation's chief executive: as Jackson put it, "The President is the direct representative of the American people." Assuming that role during the nullification crisis, he upheld national

TEACHING STRATEGY

Use **MAP 9.5** to enhance students' understanding of Indian removal and its consequences. Guide students' analysis with the following questions:

- **What does the map show about Indian land cessions between 1820 and 1846?** *Indians ceded land throughout the northwest, not just in the south. Some Iroquois from as far north as New York moved to reservations in this period.*
- **Looking at the locations of Indian reservations, what inference can you make about the consequences relocation had for American Indians?** *They were relocated hundreds or more miles from their homelands to areas with a different climate and topography, which would have made familiar ways of life more difficult. Reservations placed previously distant tribes in close proximity, likely leading to some tensions and possibly social and cultural interactions.*

CHECK FOR UNDERSTANDING

Ask students: **What was Jackson's Indian Removal policy? Who opposed it? What was the outcome?** *He wanted to use the U.S. military to forcibly remove Native Americans from southern states to free up land for whites and relocate Native Americans farther West. Many Cherokees, Christian missionaries, and the Supreme Court opposed the policy. Van Buren carried out Jackson's plans in what came to be known as the Trail of Tears.*

AP® SKILLS & PROCESSES

COMPARISON

Students tend to focus simply on the outcome of the rulings, rather than the reasoning — particularly in Marshall's case. Ask them to clearly explain why each ruled the way he did in responding to the **COMPARISON** question. Students could additionally identify the factors in the background of each individual that might have helped to shape their perspective.

TRM Find complete suggested responses in the Teacher's Resource Materials.

authority by threatening the use of military force, laying the foundation for Lincoln's defense of the Union a generation later. At the same time (and somewhat contradictorily), Jackson curbed the reach of the national government. By undermining Henry Clay's American System of national banking, protective tariffs, and internal improvements, Jackson reinvigorated the Jeffersonian tradition of a limited and frugal central government.

The Taney Court Jackson also undermined the constitutional jurisprudence of John Marshall by appointing Roger B. Taney as his successor in 1835. During his long tenure as chief justice (1835–1864), Taney partially reversed the nationalist and vested-property-rights decisions of the Marshall Court and gave constitutional legitimacy to Jackson's policies of states' rights and free enterprise. In the landmark case *Charles River Bridge Co. v. Warren Bridge Co.* (1837), Taney declared that a legislative charter — in this case, to build and operate a toll bridge — did not necessarily bestow a monopoly, and that a legislature could charter a competing bridge to promote the general welfare: "While the rights of private property are sacredly guarded, we must not forget that the community also has rights." This decision directly challenged Marshall's interpretation of the contract clause of the Constitution in *Dartmouth College v. Woodward* (1819), which had stressed the binding nature of public charters and the sanctity of "vested rights." By limiting the property claims of existing canal and turnpike companies, Taney's decision allowed legislatures to charter competing railroads that would provide cheaper and more efficient transportation.

The Taney Court also limited Marshall's nationalistic interpretation of the commerce clause by enhancing the regulatory role of state governments. For example, in *Mayor of New York v. Miln* (1837), the Taney Court ruled that New York State could use its "police power" to inspect the health of arriving immigrants. The Court also restored to the states some of the economic powers they had exercised prior to the Constitution of 1787. In *Briscoe v. Bank of Kentucky* (1837), the justices allowed a bank owned by the state of Kentucky to issue currency, despite the wording of Article 1, Section 10 of the Constitution, which prohibits states from issuing "bills of credit."

States Revise Their Constitutions Inspired by Jackson and Taney, Democrats in the various states mounted their own constitutional revolutions. Between 1830 and 1860, twenty states called conventions that furthered democratic principles by reapportioning state legislatures on the basis of population and giving the vote to all white men. Voters also had more power because the new documents mandated the election, rather than the appointment, of most public officials, including sheriffs, justices of the peace, and judges.

classical liberalism, or laissez-faire The political ideology of individual liberty, private property, a competitive market economy, free trade, and limited government. The ideal is a *laissez faire* or "let alone" policy, in which government does as little as possible to regulate the economy.

The new constitutions also embodied the principles of **classical liberalism, or laissez-faire**, by limiting the government's role in the economy. (Twenty-first-century social-welfare liberalism endorses the opposite principle: that government should intervene in economic and social life.) As president, Jackson had destroyed the American System, and his disciples now attacked the state-based Commonwealth System, which had used chartered corporations and state funds to promote economic development. Most Jackson-era constitutions prohibited states from granting special charters to corporations and extending loans and credit guarantees to private businesses. "If there is any danger to be feared in . . . government," declared a New Jersey Democrat, "it is the danger of associated wealth, with special privileges." The revised constitutions also protected taxpayers by setting strict limits on state debt. Said New York reformer Michael Hoffman, "We will not trust the legislature with the power of creating indefinite mortgages on the people's property."

"The world is governed too much," the Jacksonians proclaimed as they embraced a small-government, laissez-faire outlook and celebrated the power of ordinary people to make decisions in the voting booth and the marketplace.

AP® SKILLS & PROCESSES

DEVELOPMENTS AND PROCESSES

How did the Taney court and the Jacksonian state constitutions alter the American legal and constitutional systems?

AP® SKILLS & PROCESSES

DEVELOPMENTS AND PROCESSES

Scaffold the **DEVELOPMENTS AND PROCESSES** question by asking students to consider how the Taney Court rulings undermined the Marshall Court and how state constitutions undermined the American System. Extend this prompt by having students describe the overall character of the Taney Court.

TRM Find complete suggested responses in the Teacher's Resource Materials.

CLASS, CULTURE, AND THE SECOND PARTY SYSTEM

What principles united the Whig Party and how did they differ from those of the Democratic Party?

The rise of the Democracy and Jackson's tumultuous presidency sparked the creation in the mid-1830s of a second national party: the Whigs. For the next two decades, Whigs and Democrats competed fiercely for votes and appealed to different cultural groups. Many evangelical Protestants became Whigs, while most Catholic immigrants and traditional Protestants joined the Democrats. By debating issues of economic policy, class power, and moral reform, party politicians offered Americans a choice between competing programs and political leaders. The First Party System in United States politics, pitting Federalists against Jeffersonian Republicans, had ended with the collapse of the Federalist Party and the "era of good feeling." The Second Party System, pitting Whigs against Democrats, persisted until the Whig Party fractured in the 1850s.

AP® EXAM TIP

It's important to note that opposition to the leadership of Andrew Jackson led to changes in the political party system and to realignment of a new two party system.

The Whig Worldview

The **Whig Party** arose in 1834, when a group of congressmen contested Andrew Jackson's policies and his high-handed, "kinglike" conduct. They took the name *Whigs* to identify themselves with the pre-Revolutionary American and British parties — also called Whigs — that had opposed the arbitrary actions of British monarchs. The Whigs accused "King Andrew I" of violating the Constitution by creating a spoils system and undermining elected legislators, whom they saw as the true representatives of the sovereign people. One Whig accused Jackson of ruling in a manner "more absolute than that of any absolute monarchy of Europe."

Whig Party
The Whig Party arose in 1834 when a group of congressmen contested Andrew Jackson's policies and conduct. The party identified itself with the pre-Revolutionary American and British parties — also called Whigs — that had opposed the arbitrary actions of British monarchs.

Initially, the Whigs consisted of political factions with distinct points of view. However, guided by Senators Webster of Massachusetts, Clay of Kentucky, and Calhoun of South Carolina, they gradually coalesced into a party with a distinctive stance and coherent ideology. The Whigs celebrated the entrepreneur and the enterprising individual: "This is a country of self-made men," they boasted, pointing to the relative absence of permanent distinctions of class and status among white citizens. Embracing the Industrial Revolution, northern Whigs welcomed the investments of "moneyed capitalists," which provided workers with jobs and "bread, clothing and homes." Whig congressman Edward Everett championed a "holy alliance" among laborers, owners, and governments and called for a return to Henry Clay's American System. Many New England and Pennsylvania textile and iron workers shared Everett's vision because they benefitted directly from protective tariffs.

John C. Calhoun (1782–1850) This daguerreotype, made close to the time of Calhoun's death, suggests his emotional intensity and thwarted ambition. The prime advocate of the doctrines of nullification and states' rights, a founder of the Whig Party, and a steadfast defender of slavery, Calhoun found his lifelong pursuit of the presidency frustrated by Martin Van Buren's political skills and sectional divisions over tariffs and slavery. Image courtesy of the Gibbes Museum of Art/Carolina Art Association.

Calhoun's Dissent Support for the Whigs in the South — less widespread than that in the North — rested on the appeal of specific policies and politicians. Some southern Whigs were wealthy planters who invested in railroads and banks or sold their cotton to New York merchants. But the majority were poorer whites who resented the power and policies of low-country planters, most of whom were Democrats.

Southern Whigs rejected their party's enthusiasm for high tariffs and social mobility, and John C. Calhoun was their spokesman. Extremely conscious of class divisions in society, Calhoun believed that northern Whigs' rhetoric of equal opportunity was contradicted not only by slavery, which he considered a fundamental American institution, but also by the wage-labor system of industrial capitalism. "There is and always has been in an advanced state of wealth and civilization a conflict between labor and capital," Calhoun declared in 1837. He urged slave owners and factory owners to unite against their common foe: the working class of enslaved blacks and propertyless whites.

TEACHING STRATEGY

Teachers and students looking to gain a deeper understanding of the origins and development of the Whig Party should go to Gilder-Lehrman's Web site (ap.gilderlehrman.org) and select Period 4. Look for the video by historian Michael Holt in which he discusses the importance of the Whig Party in the context of the expansion of political participation.

Most northern Whigs denied Calhoun's class-conscious social ideology. "A clear and well-defined line between capital and labor" might fit the slave South or class-ridden Europe, Daniel Webster conceded, but in the North "this distinction grows less and less definite as commerce advances." Ignoring the ever-increasing numbers of propertyless immigrants and native-born wageworkers, Webster focused on the growing size of the middle class, whose members generally favored Whig candidates. In the election of 1834, the Whigs took control of the House of Representatives by appealing to evangelical Protestants and upwardly mobile families — prosperous farmers, small-town merchants, and skilled industrial workers in New England, New York, and the new communities along the Great Lakes.

Anti-Masons Become Whigs Many Whig voters in 1834 had previously supported the Anti-Masons, a powerful but short-lived party that formed in the late 1820s. As its name implies, Anti-Masons opposed the Order of Freemasonry. Freemasonry began in Europe as an organization of men seeking moral improvement by promoting the welfare and unity of humanity. Many Masons espoused republicanism, and the Order spread rapidly in America after the Revolution. Its ideology, mysterious symbols, and semisecret character gave the Order an air of exclusivity that attracted ambitious businessmen and political leaders, including George Washington, Henry Clay, and Andrew Jackson. In New York State alone by the mid-1820s, there were more than 20,000 Masons, organized into 450 local lodges. However, after the kidnapping and murder in 1826 of William Morgan, a New York Mason who had threatened to reveal the Order's secrets, the Freemasons fell into disrepute. Thurlow Weed, a newspaper editor in Rochester, New York, spearheaded an Anti-Masonic Party, which condemned the Order as a secret aristocratic fraternity. The new party quickly ousted Freemasons from local and state offices, and just as quickly ran out of political steam.

Because many Anti-Masons espoused temperance, equality of opportunity, and evangelical morality, they gravitated to the Whig Party. Throughout the Northeast and Midwest, Whig politicians won election by proposing legal curbs on the sale of alcohol and local ordinances that preserved Sunday as a day of worship. The Whigs also secured the votes of farmers, bankers, and shopkeepers, who favored Henry Clay's American System. For these citizens of the growing Midwest, the Whigs' program of government subsidies for roads, canals, and bridges was as important as their moral agenda.

In the election of 1836, the Whig Party faced Martin Van Buren, the architect of the Democratic Party and Jackson's handpicked successor. Like Jackson, Van Buren denounced the American System and warned that its revival would create a "consolidated government." Positioning himself as a defender of individual rights, Van Buren also condemned the efforts of Whigs and moral reformers to enact state laws imposing temperance and national laws abolishing slavery. "The government is best which governs least" became his motto in economic, cultural, and racial matters.

To oppose Van Buren, the Whigs ran four candidates, each with a strong regional reputation. They hoped to win enough electoral votes to throw the contest into the House of Representatives. However, the Whig tally — 73 electoral votes collected by William Henry Harrison of Ohio, 26 by Hugh L. White of Tennessee, 14 by Daniel Webster of Massachusetts, and 11 by W. P. Mangum of Georgia — fell short of Van Buren's 170 votes. Still, the four Whigs won 49 percent of the popular vote, showing that the party's message of economic and moral improvement had broad appeal.

AP® SKILLS & PROCESSES

COMPARISON

How did the ideology of the Whigs differ from that of the Jacksonian Democrats?

Labor Politics and the Depression of 1837–1843

As the Democrats battled Whigs on the national level, they faced challenges from urban artisans and workers. Between 1828 and 1833, artisans and laborers in fifteen states formed Working Men's Parties. "Past experience teaches us that we have nothing to hope from the aristocratic orders of society," declared the New York Working

CHECK FOR UNDERSTANDING

Ask students: **What were key features of the Whig worldview?** *With Webster's support, they formed a coherent program in support of reviving the American System. They tended to support entrepreneurship and personal effort, and to endorse temperance, equality of opportunity, and Protestant morality.*

AP® SKILLS & PROCESSES

COMPARISON

To help students answer the **COMPARISON** question, have them create a chart that lists the Whigs and Jacksonian Democrats at the top and broad issues on the left. Students can fill out the chart by indicating each party's views on the respective issues. Extend this prompt by having students compare the Whig Party to the earlier Federalist Party.

TRM Find complete suggested responses in the Teacher's Resource Materials.

Men's Party. It vowed "to send men of our own description, if we can, to the Legislature at Albany."

The new parties' agenda reflected the values and interests of ordinary urban workers. The Philadelphia Working Men's Party set out to secure "a just balance of power . . . between all the various classes." It called for the abolition of private banks, chartered monopolies, and debtors' prisons, and it demanded universal public education and a fair system of taxation (see "Thinking Like a Historian," p. 308). It won some victories, electing a number of assemblymen and persuading the Pennsylvania legislature in 1834 to authorize tax-supported schools. Elsewhere, Working Men's candidates won office in many cities, but their parties' weakness in statewide contests soon took a toll. By the mid-1830s, most politically active workers had joined the Democratic Party.

The Working Men's Parties left a mixed legacy. They mobilized craft workers and gave political expression to their ideology of artisan republicanism. As labor intellectual Orestes Brownson defined their distinctive vision, "All men will be independent proprietors, working on their own capitals, on their own farms, or in their own shops." However, this emphasis on proprietorship inhibited alliances between the artisan-based Working Men's Parties and the rapidly increasing class of dependent wage earners. As Joseph Weydemeyer, a close friend of Karl Marx, reported from New York in the early 1850s, many American craft workers "are incipient bourgeois, and feel themselves to be such."

The **Panic of 1837** threw the American economy — and the workers' movement — into disarray. The panic began when the Bank of England tried to boost the faltering British economy by sharply curtailing the flow of money and credit to the United States. Since 1822, British manufacturers had extended credit to southern planters to expand cotton production, and British investors had purchased millions

AP® EXAM TIP

It's important to take notes on the impact of the realignment of political groups on the working class and women in the early nineteenth century.

Panic of 1837
Triggered by a sharp reduction in English capital and credit flowing into the United States, the cash shortage caused a panic while the collapse of credit led to a depression — the second major economic crisis of the United States — that lasted from 1837 to 1843.

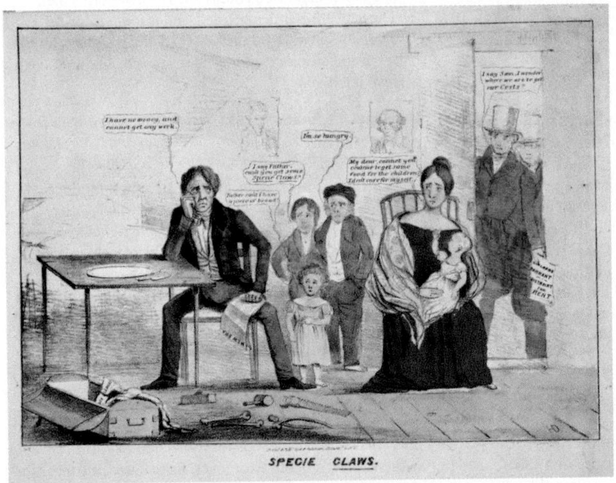

"I Have No Money, and Cannot Get Any Work" The Panic of 1837 struck hard at Americans of all social ranks. This cartoon blames Jackson's Specie Circular for the woes of a forlorn tradesman. Unable to find work, he is surrounded by a hungry wife and children while the landlord's agents appear at the door, intending to collect his overdue rent. Posters of Andrew Jackson and Martin Van Buren on the wall indicate that he is a Democrat who has been betrayed by his own party's restrictive monetary policy. Library of Congress, 3g03240.

AP® THEME

WXT: Work, Exchange, and Technology

In analyzing the weakness of Working Men's parties in this era, the text identifies organizers' unwillingness to work with the growing number of dependent laborers, who were increasing in number as the Market Revolution brought more and more to produce goods for the market and led to a growing population of laboring poor. For a better understanding of the views of the Working Men's parties, have students read the *Working Men's Declaration of Independence*, available online.

AP® SKILLS & PROCESSES

ANALYZING HISTORICAL EVIDENCE

This painting captures the increased politicization of American society in the early-mid nineteenth century. To help students make historical connections, ask them to look at the captions and the pictures hanging on the wall. What connections can be made between the captions and the images on the wall? Students should connect this with partisanship and the Panic of 1837.

AP® SKILLS & PROCESSES

ANALYZING HISTORICAL EVIDENCE

Use the primary sources in the **AP® THINKING LIKE A HISTORIAN** feature to help students consider differing arguments about the role of education in a democratic society.

AP® THINKING LIKE A HISTORIAN

Becoming Literate: Public Education and Democracy

The struggle for a genuinely *democratic* polity—"government of the people, by the people, and for the people," as Lincoln put it—played out at the local and state level in battles over who should participate in the political arena. As legislators argued over extending the franchise, they considered the knowledge that citizens needed to participate responsibly in politics. Although primary education was publicly supported in most New England towns (giving that region nearly universal literacy), it received only spotty funding in the other northern states and almost none in the South (restricting literacy there to one-third of the white population). The following documents address the resulting debate over publicly supported education and citizenship.

1. **Editorial from the *Philadelphia National Gazette*, 1830.** *Pennsylvania was one of the first states to debate legislation regarding universal free public education.*

   The scheme of Universal Equal Education . . . is virtually "Agrarianism" [redistribution of land from rich to poor]. It would be a compulsory application of the means of the richer, for the direct use of the poorer classes. . . . One of the chief excitements to industry . . . is the hope of earning the means of educating their children respectably . . . that incentive would be removed, and the scheme of state and equal education be a premium for comparative idleness, to be taken out of the pockets of the laborious and conscientious.

2. **Thaddeus Stevens, speech before the Pennsylvania General Assembly, February 1835.** *Pennsylvania's Free Public School Act of 1834 was the handiwork of the Working Men's Party of Philadelphia. When over half of Pennsylvania's school districts refused to implement the law, the legislature threatened to repeal it. Thaddeus Stevens, later a leading antislavery advocate, turned back that threat through this speech to the Pennsylvania General Assembly.*

   It would seem to be humiliating to be under the necessity, in the nineteenth century, of entering into a formal argument to prove the utility, and to free governments, the absolute necessity of education. . . . Such necessity would be degrading to a Christian age and a free republic. If an elective republic is to endure for any great length of time, every elector must have sufficient information, not only to accumulate wealth and take care of his pecuniary concerns, but to direct wisely the Legislatures, the Ambassadors, and the Executive of the nation; for some part of all these things, some agency in approving or disapproving of them, falls to every freeman. If, then, the permanency of our government depends upon such knowledge, it is the duty of government to see that the means of information be diffused to every citizen. This is a sufficient answer to those who deem education a private and not a public duty—who argue that they are willing to educate their own children, but not their neighbor's children.

3. **"Letter from a Teacher" in Catharine E. Beecher, *The True Remedy for the Wrongs of Women*, 1851.** *The public school movement created new opportunities not just for children of middle and lower classes but also for the young Protestant women who contributed to the "Benevolent Empire" as professional educators. Beecher's academy in Hartford, Connecticut, sent out dozens of young women to establish schools.*

   I am now located in this place, which is the county-town of a newly organized county [in a midwestern state]. . . . The Sabbath is little regarded, and is more a day for diversion than devotion. . . . My school embraces both sexes and all ages from five to seventeen, and not one can read intelligibly.

4. **"Popular Education," 1833.** *This piece appeared in the* North American Review, *the nation's first literary and cultural journal and the mouthpiece of New England's intellectual elite.*

   [T]he mind of a people, in proportion as it is educated, will not only feel its own value, but will also perceive its rights. We speak now of those palpable rights which are recognised by all free states. . . . [T]he palpable rights of men, those of personal security, of property and of the free and unembarrassed pursuit of individual welfare, it is obviously impossible to conceal from an educated and

of dollars of the canal bonds from the northern states. Suddenly deprived of British funds, American planters, merchants, and canal corporations had to withdraw gold from domestic banks to pay their foreign debts. Moreover, British textile mills drastically reduced their purchases of raw cotton, causing its price to plummet from 20 cents a pound to 10 cents or less.

Falling cotton prices and the drain of specie to Britain set off a financial panic. On May 8, the Dry Dock Bank of New York City ran out of specie, prompting worried depositors to withdraw gold and silver coins from other banks. Within two weeks, reading people. Such a people rises at once above the condition of feudal tenants. . . . It directs its attention to the laws and institutions that govern it. It compels public office to give an account of itself. It strips off the veil of secrecy from the machinery of power. . . . And when all this is spread abroad in newspaper details . . . of a people that can read; when the estimate is freely made, of what the government tax levies upon the daily hoard, and upon apparel, and upon every comfort of life, can it be doubted that such a people will demand and obtain an influence in affairs that so vitally concern it? This would be freedom.

5. Judge Baker, sentencing hearing in the court case against Mrs. Margaret Douglass of Norfolk, Virginia, January 10, 1854. *Southern whites considered the acquisition of literacy by blacks, whether slave or free, as a public danger, especially after the Nat Turner uprising in Southampton County, Virginia, in 1831 (Chapter 10). A Virginia court sent Mrs. Margaret Douglass to jail for a month "as an example to all others" for teaching free black children to read so they might have access to books on religion and morality.*

There are persons, I believe, in our community, opposed to the policy of the law in question. They profess to believe that universal intellectual culture is necessary to religious instruction and education, and that such culture is suitable to a state of slavery. . . .

Such opinions in the present state of our society I regard as manifestly mischievous. It is not true that our slaves cannot be taught religious and moral duty, without being able to read the Bible and use the pen. Intellectual and religious instruction often go hand in hand, but the latter may well be exist without the former; . . . among the whites one-fou[r]th or more are entirely without a knowledge of letters, [nonetheless,] respect for the law, and for moral and religious conduct and behavior, are justly and prope[r]ly appreciated and practiced. . . .

The first legislative provision upon this subject was introduced in the year 1831, immediately succeeding the bloody scenes of the memorable Southampton insurrection; and . . . was re-enacted with additional penalties in the year 1848. . . . After these several and repeated recognitions of the wisdom and propriety of the said act, it may well be said that bold and open opposition to it [must be condemned] . . . as a measure of self-preservation and protection.

6. Working Men's Party poster for immigrant voters, New York, 1830.

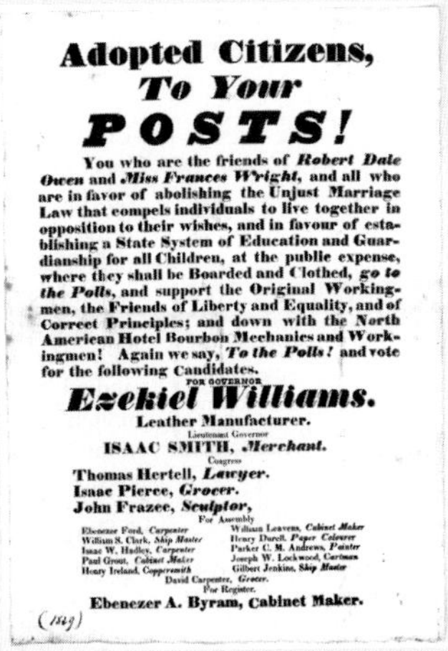
Adopted Citizens,
To Your
POSTS!
You who are the friends of Robert Dale Owen and Miss Frances Wright, and all who are in favor of abolishing the Unjust Marriage Law that compels individuals to live together in opposition to their wishes, and in favour of establishing a State System of Education and Guardianship for all Children, at the public expense, where they shall be Boarded and Clothed, go to the Polls, and support the Original Workingmen, the Friends of Liberty and Equality, and of Correct Principles; and down with the North American Hotel Bourbon Mechanics and Workingmen! Again we say, To the Polls! and vote for the following Candidates.
FOR GOVERNOR
Ezekiel Williams.
Leather Manufacturer.
Lieutenant Governor
ISAAC SMITH, Merchant.
Congress
Thomas Hertell, Lawyer.
Isaac Pierce, Grocer.
John Frazee, Sculptor,
For Assembly
Ebenezer Ford, Carpenter
William S. Clark, Ship Master
Isaac W. Hadley, Carpenter
Paul Grout, Cabinet Maker
Henry Ireland, Coppersmith
William Leavens, Cabinet Maker
Henry Durell, Paper Colourer
Parker C. M. Andrews, Painter
Joseph W. Lockwood, Cartman
Gilbert Jenkins, Ship Master
David Carpenter, Grocer.
For Register.
Ebenezer A. Byram, Cabinet Maker.
(1829)

SOURCE: Joshua R. Greenberg, Advocating the Man/Picture Research Consultants & Archives.

ANALYZING THE EVIDENCE

1. What arguments does the editorial in the *Philadelphia National Gazette* (source 1) advance? How does Stevens (source 2) reframe this argument? Describe the main differences in each argument.
2. What does the letter from a former student of Beecher's (source 3) tell us about educational reform? Compare this development to other social movements, such as Sabbatarianism (p. 319)?
3. How is the argument of the author in source 4 similar to, or different from, that in sources 1 and 2? Compare the main ideas of each source.
4. How does Judge Baker (source 5) justify the denial of education to African Americans? Identify the historical circumstance contributing to the perspective.
5. What do the occupations of the Working Men's Party candidates suggest about its definition of "worker" (source 6)?

AP® DBQ PRACTICE

Using these documents and materials in this chapter, write an essay that identifies arguments for and against public education in America between 1800 and 1854. Explain which arguments were most compelling to which groups of people and regions.

every American bank had stopped trading specie and called in its loans, turning a financial panic into an economic crisis. "This sudden overthrow of the commercial credit" had a "stunning effect," observed Henry Fox, the British minister in Washington. "The conquest of the land by a foreign power could hardly have produced a more general sense of humiliation and grief."

To stimulate the economy, state governments increased their investments in canals and railroads. However, as governments issued (or guaranteed) more bonds to finance these ventures, they were unable to pay the interest charges, sparking a severe financial

TRM Find complete suggested responses in the Teacher's Resource Materials.

AP® SKILLS & PROCESSES

ARGUMENTATION

The link between education and citizenship in the **AP® DBQ PRACTICE** prompt may not be intuitive for some students. Provide guidance as needed.

AP® SKILLS & PROCESSES

CAUSATION

Use the **CAUSATION** question to have students identify the causes of the defeat of the Anti-Masonic and Working Men's political parties. Because most students have never heard of these parties before, they may automatically assume that the parties were never viable, so it may be helpful to tease out reasons some Americans were drawn to such parties at a particular time. Extend this prompt by having students evaluate the relative strengths of each party and determine whether their views inevitably doomed them or if, under different circumstances, one or both of them might have survived into the 1850s.

TRM Find complete suggested responses in the Teacher's Resource Materials.

CHECK FOR UNDERSTANDING

Ask students: **What were the labor politics of the 1820s and 1830s? What caused the depression of 1837? And what were its effects?** *Artisan-based labor groups formed political parties to lobby for the interests of everyday workers. They opposed private banks, government-chartered monopolies, and debtors' prisons. As defenders of private property, they lost out on the opportunity to ally with wage earners.*

TEACHING STRATEGY

Use the image of Harrison's campaign banner to explore the techniques of the 1840 election, typically viewed as the beginning of modern campaigning.

crisis on both sides of the Atlantic in 1839. Nine state governments defaulted on their debts, and hard-pressed European lenders cut the flow of new capital to the United States.

The American economy fell into a deep depression. By 1843, canal construction had dropped by 90 percent, prices and wages had fallen by 50 percent, and unemployment in seaports and industrial centers had reached 20 percent. Bumper crops drove down cotton prices, pushing hundreds of planters and merchants into bankruptcy. Minister Henry Ward Beecher described a land "filled with lamentation . . . its inhabitants wandering like bereaved citizens among the ruins of an earthquake, mourning for children, for houses crushed, and property buried forever."

AP® SKILLS & PROCESSES
CAUSATION
What factors led to the demise of the Anti-Masonic and Working Men's political parties?

By creating a surplus of unemployed workers, the depression finished off the union movement and the Working Men's Parties. In 1837, six thousand masons, carpenters, and other building-trades workers lost their jobs in New York City, destroying their unions' bargaining power. By 1843, most local unions, all the national labor organizations, and all the workers' parties had disappeared.

"Tippecanoe and Tyler Too!"

Specie Circular
An executive order in 1836 that required the Treasury Department to accept only gold and silver in payment for lands in the national domain.

Many Americans blamed the Democrats for the depression of 1837–1843. They criticized Jackson for destroying the Second Bank and directing the Treasury Department in 1836 to issue the **Specie Circular**, an executive order that required the Treasury Department to accept only gold and silver in payment for lands in the national domain. Critics charged — mistakenly — that the Circular drained so much specie from the economy that it sparked the Panic of 1837.

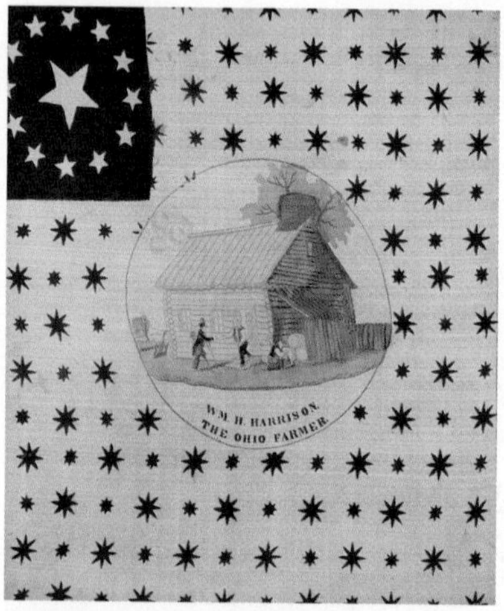

Harrison's Log Cabin and Cider Campaign To boost the chances that William Henry Harrison would be elected president in 1840, Whig political strategists promoted him as the "log cabin and hard cider" candidate, in contrast to the aristocratic Martin Van Buren. On this patriotic cotton banner, Harrison, coming out the door of his cabin in shirtsleeves, greets a veteran who has lost a leg in service to his country. A third man bends down before a keg of hard cider, presumably intending to offer the visitor a drink. Despite Harrison's well-to-do background — the son of a prominent Virginia slaveowner, he had served as territorial governor of Indiana and in both the House and the Senate — the campaign presented him as a simple Ohio farmer. The populist appeal of the Whig campaign was misleading, but it succeeded in elevating Harrison to the White House. © Collection of the New-York Historical Society, USA/Bridgeman Images.

The public turned its anger on Van Buren, who took office just before the panic struck. Ignoring the pleas of influential bankers, the new president refused to revoke the Specie Circular or take actions to stimulate the economy. Holding to his philosophy of limited government, Van Buren advised Congress that "the less government interferes with private pursuits the better for the general prosperity." As the depression deepened in 1839, this laissez-faire outlook commanded less and less political support. Worse, Van Buren's major piece of fiscal legislation, the Independent Treasury Act of 1840, delayed recovery by pulling federal specie out of Jackson's pet banks (where it had backed loans) and placing it in government vaults, where it had little economic impact.

The Log Cabin Campaign The Whigs exploited Van Buren's weakness. In 1840, they organized their first national convention and nominated William Henry Harrison of Ohio for president and John Tyler of Virginia for vice president. A military hero of the Battle of Tippecanoe and the War of 1812, Harrison was well advanced in age (sixty-eight) and had little political experience. However, the Whig leaders in Congress, Henry Clay and Daniel Webster, wanted a president who would rubber-stamp their program for protective tariffs and a national bank. An unpretentious, amiable man, Harrison told voters that Whig policies were "the only means, under Heaven, by which a poor industrious man may become a rich man without bowing to colossal wealth."

The depression stacked the political cards against Van Buren, but the election turned as much on style as on substance. It became the great "log cabin campaign" — the first time two well-organized parties competed for votes through a new style of campaigning. Whig songfests, parades, and mass meetings drew new voters into politics. Whig speakers assailed "Martin Van Ruin" as a manipulative politician with aristocratic tastes — a devotee of fancy wines, elegant clothes, and polite refinement, as indeed he was. Less truthfully, they portrayed Harrison as a self-made man who lived contentedly in a log cabin and quaffed hard cider, a drink of the common people. In fact, Harrison's father was a wealthy Virginia planter who had signed the Declaration of Independence, and Harrison himself lived in a series of elegant mansions.

The Whigs boosted their electoral hopes by welcoming women to campaign festivities — a "first" for American politics. Many Jacksonian Democrats had long embraced an ideology of aggressive manhood, likening politically minded females to "public" women, prostitutes who plied their trade in theaters and other public places. Whigs took a more restrained view of masculinity and recognized that Christian women had already entered American public life through the temperance movement and other benevolent activities. In October 1840, Daniel Webster celebrated moral reform to an audience of twelve hundred women and urged them to back Whig candidates. "This way of making politicians of their women is something new under the sun," exclaimed one Democrat, worried that it would bring more Whig men to the polls. And it did: more than 80 percent of the eligible male voters cast ballots in 1840, up from fewer than 60 percent in 1832 and 1836 (see Figure 9.1). Heeding the Whigs' campaign slogan "Tippecanoe and Tyler Too," they voted Harrison into the White House with 53 percent of the popular vote and gave the party a majority in Congress.

AP® SKILLS & PROCESSES

CONTEXTUALIZATION

How did Whigs and Democrats view women in politics, and why did they hold those views?

TRM Find complete suggested responses in the Teacher's Resource Materials.

Tyler Subverts the Whig Agenda Led by Clay and Webster, the Whigs in Congress prepared to reverse the Jacksonian revolution. Their hopes were short-lived; barely a month after his inauguration in 1841, Harrison died of pneumonia, and the nation got "Tyler Too." But in what capacity: as acting president or as president? The Constitution was vague on the issue. Ignoring his Whig associates in Congress, who wanted a weak chief executive, Tyler took the presidential oath of office and declared his intention to govern as he pleased. As it turned out, that would not be like a Whig.

Tyler had served in the House and the Senate as a Jeffersonian Democrat, firmly committed to slavery and states' rights. He had joined the Whigs only to protest Jackson's stance against nullification. On economic issues, Tyler shared Jackson's hostility to the Second Bank and the American System. He therefore vetoed Whig bills that would have raised tariffs and created a new national bank. Outraged by this betrayal, most of Tyler's cabinet resigned in 1842, and the Whigs expelled Tyler from their party. "His Accidency," as he was called by his critics, was now a president without a party.

The split between Tyler and the Whigs allowed the Democrats to regroup. The party vigorously recruited small farmers in the North, smallholding planters in the South, and former members of the Working Men's Parties in the cities. It also won support among Irish and German Catholic immigrants — whose numbers had increased during the 1830s — by backing their demands for religious and cultural liberty, such as the freedom to drink beer and whiskey. A pattern of ethnocultural politics, as historians refer to the practice of voting along ethnic and religious lines, now became a prominent feature of American life. Thanks to these urban and rural recruits, the Democrats remained the majority party in most parts of the nation. Their program of equal rights, states' rights, and cultural liberty was attractive to more white Americans than the Whig platform of economic nationalism, moral reform, temperance laws, and individual mobility.

CHECK FOR UNDERSTANDING

Ask students: **What principles united the Whig Party, and why did the Tyler presidency fail to fulfill its leaders' wishes?** *The Whigs, initially a sectional disparate group that rose in opposition to Jackson's policies, coalesced under the leadership of Henry Clay, Daniel Webster, and to a lesser extent John C. Calhoun. They celebrated the entrepreneurial spirit of Americans, embraced the so-called "moneyed interests" as job creation engines, and the reinvigoration of Henry Clay's American System, especially its emphasis on internal improvements and high tariffs. Once they won the White House in 1840, however, they were unable to implement their vision since their candidate, William Henry Harrison, died in office within a month. Harrison's vice president, John Tyler, was a compromise candidate, effectively a Democrat in policy, and subverted much of the Whig program.*

SUMMARY

In this chapter, we examined the causes and the consequences of the democratic political revolution. We saw that the expansion of the franchise weakened the political system run by notables of high status and encouraged the transfer of power

CHECK FOR UNDERSTANDING

Use the **AP® LEARNING FOCUS** question prompt from the beginning of the chapter to check students' understanding of the chapter as a whole: **Why did Andrew Jackson's election mark a turning point in American politics?** *The Jackson era gave rise to a new democratic political revolution, with an expansion of the franchise that weakened the political system run by notables of high status. Party politics increased the growth of democracy through an increase in party competition, white male voter interest, and participation in national elections. Modern political parties were now run by professional politicians, mostly of middle-class origins. Jackson dismantled the political foundation of the mercantilist system, the American System of national improvements through state support, and the Commonwealth System of government charters and subsidies to private businesses.*

✓ LearningCurve

Remind students to go online to complete the LearningCurve quiz for this chapter.

TRM Find complete suggested responses in the Teacher's Resource Materials.

AP® SKILLS & PROCESSES

CAUSATION

AP® CONTENT REVIEW 1 encourages students to identify the actions that caused the overcoming of sectional differences. Note: This is the same question as the section-opening question on p. 284.

AP® SKILLS & PROCESSES

CONTEXTUALIZATION

AP® CONTENT REVIEW 2 encourages students to examine how political parties and specific individuals interpreted the constitutionality of internal improvements, tariffs, and nullification. While it is easy to focus on President Jackson, remind students to see a more holistic view of the question. Note: This is the same question as the section-opening question on p. 295.

AP® SKILLS & PROCESSES

COMPARISON

AP® CONTENT REVIEW 3 encourages students to identify what united the Whig Party and how their views differed from the Democrats. It is important to remember the Whigs had their own agenda, aside from simply opposing the Democrats. Note: This is the same question as the section-opening question on p. 305.

to professional politicians — men like Martin Van Buren, who were mostly of middle-class origin.

We also witnessed a revolution in government policy, as Andrew Jackson and his Democratic Party dismantled the mercantilist economic system of government-supported economic development. On the national level, Jackson destroyed Henry Clay's American System; on the state level, Democrats wrote new constitutions that ended the Commonwealth System of government charters and subsidies to private businesses. Jackson's treatment of Native Americans was equally revolutionary; the Removal Act of 1830 forcefully resettled eastern Indian peoples west of the Mississippi River, opening their ancestral lands to white settlement.

Finally, we watched the emergence of the Second Party System. Following the split in the Republican Party during the election of 1824, two new parties — the Democrats and the Whigs — developed on the national level and eventually absorbed the members of the Anti-Masonic and Working Men's Parties. The new party system established universal suffrage for white men and a mode of representative government that was responsive to ordinary citizens. In their scope and significance, these political innovations matched the economic advances of both the Industrial Revolution and the Market Revolution.

CHAPTER 9 REVIEW

AP® CONTENT REVIEW *Answer these questions to demonstrate your understanding of the chapter's main ideas.*

1. How did Jackson and the new Democratic Party overcome sectional differences?
2. What were the constitutional arguments for and against internal improvements, the tariff, and nullification?
3. What principles united the Whig Party and how did they differ from those of the Democratic Party?

AP® TERMS TO KNOW *Identify and explain the significance of each term below.*

Key Concepts and Events

franchise (p. 284)
notables (p. 284)
political machine (p. 286)
caucus (p. 286)
demographic transition (p. 287)
republican motherhood (p. 287)
American Colonization Society (p. 289)
Missouri Compromise (p. 290)
American System (p. 291)
internal improvements (p. 291)
corrupt bargain (p. 292)
Tariff of Abominations (p. 293)
spoils system (p. 295)
nullification (p. 296)
Second Bank of the United States (p. 296)
Indian Removal Act of 1830 (p. 301)
Trail of Tears (p. 303)
classical liberalism, or laissez-faire (p. 304)
Whig Party (p. 305)
Panic of 1837 (p. 307)
Specie Circular (p. 310)

Key People

Martin Van Buren (p. 286)
Mary Wollstonecraft (p. 287)
Richard Allen (p. 289)
Henry Clay (p. 289)
John Quincy Adams (p. 291)
Andrew Jackson (p. 291)
John C. Calhoun (p. 291)
Roger B. Taney (p. 295)
Sequoyah (p. 300)
John Tyler (p. 310)

TRM Find definitions for these terms in the **Glossary/Glosario** in the Teacher's Resource Materials.

AP® MAKING CONNECTIONS

Recognize the larger developments and continuities within and across chapters by answering these questions.

1. This chapter argues that a democratic revolution swept America in the decades after 1820 and uprooted the old system of politics. After reviewing the discussions of politics in Chapters 6 and 7, explain how party systems and political alignments had patterns of continuity and change. Evaluate the extent to which there was a democratic revolution after 1820.
2. Look again at the cartoon depictions of Andrew Jackson, as King Andrew (p. 298) and the Great Father (p. 302). What point of view does each cartoonist support, and how effective are the cartoons in championing that view? Use evidence from the sources and chapter to describe the relative effectiveness of each cartoon.

KEY TURNING POINTS

Refer to the timeline at the start of the chapter for help in answering the following question.

Based on the events in the timeline (and your reading of this chapter), which five-year period brought more significant changes to American political and economic life: 1829–1833, Andrew Jackson's first term as president, or 1837–1842, the years of panic and depression? Explain and defend your choice.

AP® PRACTICE QUESTIONS

MULTIPLE CHOICE QUESTIONS

Choose the correct answer for each question.

Questions 1–4 refer to this excerpt.

"Be it enacted that whenever, by reason of unlawful obstructions, combinations, or assemblages of persons, it shall become impracticable . . . to execute the revenue laws, and collect the duties on imports in the ordinary way, in any collection district, . . . it shall and may be lawful for the President of the United States . . . to employ . . . land or naval forces, or militia of the United States, as may be deemed necessary for the purpose of preventing the removal of such vessel or cargo, and protecting the officers of the customs in retaining the custody thereof. . . .

[T]he President shall be, and hereby is, authorized, promptly to employ such means to suppress the same, and to . . . cause the said laws or process to be duly executed. . . ."

The Force Bill, 1833

1. The context of the passage of the Force Bill reflected ongoing debates in the United States over
   - **a.** the power of the presidency.
   - **b.** federalism and states' rights.
   - **c.** the legal use of military force.
   - **d.** First Amendment rights of assembly and protest.
2. The provisions in the excerpt would have been most widely condemned by
   - **a.** Massachusetts merchants.
   - **b.** Pennsylvania small farmers.
   - **c.** New York textile workers.
   - **d.** South Carolina plantation owners.
3. Which of the following was the most important result of the enactment of the Force Bill?
   - **a.** An increase in federal tariff revenues
   - **b.** An expansion of semisubsistence agriculture
   - **c.** An increase in sectionalism
   - **d.** An expansion of white male suffrage
4. The underlying principles in the excerpt are most consistent with those expressed in
   - **a.** *Common Sense* (1776).
   - **b.** the Northwest Ordinance (1787).
   - **c.** the *Federalist Papers* (1787).
   - **d.** Washington's Farewell Address (1796).

Questions 5–6 refer to this excerpt.

"We believe the present plan of the General Government to effect our removal West of the Mississippi, and thus obtain our lands for the use of the State of Georgia, to be highly oppressive, cruel and unjust. And we sincerely hope there is no consideration which can induce our citizens to forsake the land of our fathers of which they have been in possession from time immemorial, and thus compel us, against our will, to undergo the toils and difficulties of removing with our helpless families hundreds of miles to unhealthy and unproductive country. We hope therefore the committee and Council will take into deep consideration our deplorable situation, and do everything in their power to avert such a state of things. And we trust by a prudent course their transactions with the General Government will enlist in our behalf the sympathies of the good people of the United States."

Cherokee Women's Petition, 1831

AP® SKILLS & PROCESSES

CONTINUITY AND CHANGE

AP® MAKING CONNECTIONS 1 asks students to identify the scale of change in the nature of the political party system to determine whether it is appropriate to characterize this era as revolutionary.

AP® SKILLS & PROCESSES

ANALYZING HISTORICAL EVIDENCE

AP® MAKING CONNECTIONS 2 asks students to analyze two political images, and to identify the ways their creators conveyed their negative point of view about Jackson through illustration rather than words.

AP® SKILLS & PROCESSES

CONTINUITY AND CHANGE

The **KEY TURNING POINTS** question asks students to weigh the relative significance of two different periods. To scaffold this question, have students list the major events that transpired in the years immediately following each of these events, determine which might be attributed directly to either Jackson or the depression, and then evaluate which event was more consequential.

TRM Find complete suggested responses in the Teacher's Resource Materials.

TRM Find complete suggested responses in the Teacher's Resource Materials.

5. All of the following historical developments contributed to the concerns expressed in the petition EXCEPT
   a. the overcultivation of arable land in the Southeast.
   b. federal efforts to relocate Indian settlements.
   c. the expansion of frontier settlements.
   d. attempts by American Indians to retain control of tribal lands and natural resources.

6. Which of the following groups would have been most likely to support the sentiments expressed in the petition?
   a. Southern plantation owners
   b. Frontier settlers
   c. Leaders of rival American Indian nations
   d. States rights advocates

SHORT ANSWER QUESTIONS

Read each question carefully and write a short response. Use evidence from the text to support your claims.

"There is no doubt that Jackson believed absolutely that he was pursuing a 'just and humane policy towards the Indians.' Given the greed of the white man and the certitude that the two races could not intermingle or live side by side, Jackson contended that only through removal could the Indians escape inevitable annihilation. Once relocated beyond the Mississippi the federal government might then exercise 'parental control' over their interests and in that way 'perpetuate their race.' Most Americans probably agreed with this policy. As 'hard and cruel as it was then thought,' wrote one contemporary . . . it 'is now universally felt to have been as kind as it was necessary.' . . . [T]he only sane policy for a just government, Jackson declared, was to get the Indian to a place of safety, which he fervently believed existed west of the Mississippi River."

Robert V. Remini, *Andrew Jackson and the Course of American Freedom*, 1822–1832, 1981

"Jackson never proposed exterminating the Indians or at least in public rhetoric, removing by force of arms those who wished to remain. But he was adept at devising conditions that would make those who chose not to remove . . . miserable. . . . [H]e seems to have regarded as inevitable the ultimate extinction of the Native Americans. . . . [T]heir doom was not to be regretted, however. . . . But whatever were Jackson's private reasons for . . . Indian removal — . . . political ambition, financial greed, and philosophical rationalization — there remained the political forces that he mobilized under the banner of the Democratic Party. The exaltation of the common man . . . the sense of America as . . . destined for continental expansion, the open acceptance of racism — these were popular, politically powerful themes that would have driven any Democratic President to press for a policy of Indian removal."

Anthony F. C. Wallace, *The Long Bitter Trail: Andrew Jackson and the Indians*, 1993

1. Using the two excerpts provided, answer (a), (b), and (c).
   a. Briefly explain ONE major difference between Remini's and Wallace's historical interpretations of President Jackson's attitude toward American Indians.
   b. Briefly explain how ONE specific historical event or development from the period 1820 to 1840 that is not mentioned directly in the excerpts could be used to support Remini's interpretation.
   c. Briefly explain how ONE specific historical event or development from the period 1820 to 1840 that is not explicitly mentioned in the excerpts could be used to support Wallace's interpretation.

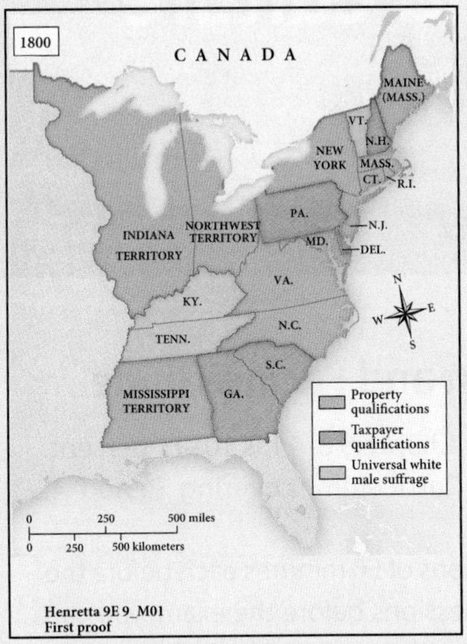

The Expansion of Voting Rights for White Men, 1800

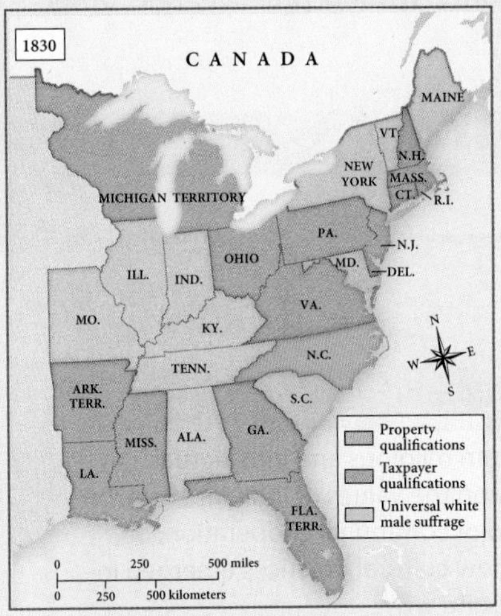

The Expansion of Voting Rights for White Men, 1830

2. Using the two maps provided, answer (a), (b), and (c).
   - **a.** Briefly explain ONE specific historical event or development that caused the change in voting rights for white men illustrated in the maps.
   - **b.** Briefly explain ONE specific historical effect of the change in voting rights for white men illustrated in the maps.
   - **c.** Briefly explain ANOTHER specific historical effect of the change in voting rights for white men illustrated in the maps.
3. Answer (a), (b), and (c).
   - **a.** Briefly explain ONE specific historical similarity between the first two-party system in the United States featuring political rivalry between the Federalist and Democratic Republican Parties prior to the 1820s and the Second American Party System featuring the rival Democratic and Whig Parties in the period after 1828.
   - **b.** Briefly explain ONE specific historical difference between the first two-party system in the United States featuring political rivalry between the Federalist and Democratic-Republican Parties prior to 1820 and the Second American Party System featuring the rival Democratic and Whig Parties in the period after 1828.
   - **c.** Briefly explain ANOTHER specific historical difference between the first two-party system in the United States featuring political rivalry between the Federalist and Democratic-Republican Parties prior to 1820 and the Second American Party System featuring the rival Democratic and Whig Parties in the period after 1828.

10 CHAPTER Religion, Reform, and Culture

1820–1848

Chapter 10 — AP® Assessment Weight and Pacing Guide

The assessment weight on the AP® U.S. History Exam for Chapters 8–11 is 10–17 percent. This chapter falls in Unit 4 of the AP® U.S. History Curriculum, covering Period 4: 1800–1848.

This pacing guide is based on a schedule with 120 sessions of 50 minutes each before the AP® U.S. History Exam. If you have a different number of sessions before the exam, you can modify the pacing to meet your needs. If you have additional time, consider incorporating quizzes, released AP® U.S. History questions, practice exams, writing practice, and other instructional activities.

	Traditional Schedule	Block Schedule
Chapter 10	3 days	1–2 days

Daily Pacing Guide

	Content Focus	Essential Question
Day 1	Spiritual Awakenings and Urban Cultures and Conflicts	How did antebellum religious and intellectual movements draw on the values of individualism, on the one hand, and of communal cooperation, on the other? What new cultural practices emerged in antebellum cities, and why?
Day 2	African Americans and the Struggle for Freedom	What communal and political goals did free blacks pursue in this period, and how did their actions influence debates over slavery and race?
Day 3	The Women's Rights Movement	Why did women gain new rights in the early nineteenth century, and how and why were these rights limited?

AP® Alignment

Section Heading	AP® Topic	AP® Theme
Spiritual Awakenings	4.9, 4.10, 4.11	ARC
Urban Cultures and Conflicts	4.9	ARC
African Americans and the Struggle for Freedom	4.11, 4.12, 4.13	ARC, SOC, GEO
The Women's Rights Movement	4.10, 4.11	ARC

*Should changes be made to the Course Framework in the future, an updated alignment will be placed on our AP® updates page at go.bfwpub.com/ap-course-updates.

Chapter 10 — Overview

Chapter 10 focuses on the changes in American culture that took place as the new nation developed and expanded. Students should understand how the Second Great Awakening initiated a revival of religious fervor, but also instigated an outpouring of reform movements designed to address the evils in American society and culture. In addition, because the Second Great Awakening allowed and even encouraged the activism of women, the women's rights movement grew, which culminated in the Declaration of Sentiments at Seneca Falls. At the same time, the development of an urban culture in the U.S. challenged traditional views and popularized a national press. Finally, African Americans who were still excluded from representation and protection in the new republic responded by developing strong, independent communities in both the North and the South from which the abolitionist movement rose.

Chapter 10 — Resources

The following resources can be found in the Teacher's Resource Materials (TRM) that accompany the book. You can access the TRM via the book's digital platform, by clicking the TRM links found here in your Teacher's Edition e-book, or by contacting your representative to access the resources online. Visit **bfwpub.com/henretta10e** to learn more.

TRM Chapter 10 Lecture Presentation Slides

TRM Chapter 10 Outline with AP® Focus

TRM Chapter 10 Lecture Strategies

TRM Chapter 10 Suggested Responses

TRM Handout 10.1 — Causation: Temperance Movement

TRM Handout 10.2 — Causation: Free Black Communities and the Struggle for Freedom

TRM Handout 10.3 — Contextualization: Seneca Falls Convention of 1848

Chapter 10 — Essential Activity

After students have read and discussed most of Chapter 10, divide the class into small groups and provide each group with excerpts from a variety of sources without any identifying source information. Some suggested excerpts could include: Dorothea Dix's Declaration of Sentiments, Angelina and Sarah Grimké on slavery, an American anti-slavery image, Horace Mann on education, David Walker, Ralph Waldo Emerson, Henry David Thoreau, excerpts from property laws impacting women, William Lloyd Garrison, Margaret Fuller, Joseph Smith, Paul Cuffee, African Methodist Episcopal Church charters, and James Birney. Provide students with a chart on which they can record their analysis of the documents in order to identify the author or organization, keys words or ideas, historical context, intended audience, purpose, and point of view. To encourage active participation, this activity can be turned into a class competition to see which group can identify the most documents correctly.

Chapter 10 — Bell Ringers

The following activities take no more than 5–15 minutes of your class period and offer an effective and engaging way to begin your lessons and for students to apply AP® Skills & Processes:

- Provide students with several images from the Second Great Awakening, and ask them to identify the common characteristics of the images. You can use the image on p. 315 of the text or use other options found online. Then ask students how they think the Second Great Awakening could challenge American society. *Answers will vary, but common characteristics could include the following: outdoor settings, crowds showing emotional response, women in prominent positions, and the inclusion of African Americans.*
- Ask students to make a list of problems that are threatening American society today. Give students a couple of minutes to brainstorm aloud while you list the problems on the board. Ask students to think about organizations or leaders who are trying to address these problems. Discuss the role of private organizations in responding to social evils as a way to introduce a lesson on reform movements of the early nineteenth century. *Answers will vary.*
- Project a set of images that were commonly used as part of the Underground Railroad, including stones (drumming stones to send messages), quilts, lanterns (lighted meant house was safe), door knockers (coded knocks), owls (hoots used to convey messages). Ask students: What do these items have in common? Engage in a discussion of possible ideas. Use this as a way to introduce a lesson on responses to slavery and the rise of abolitionism. *Answers will vary.*

NOTES

TEACHING STRATEGY

As the penultimate paragraph in the introduction indicates, an upsurge of religious activity in the midst of dramatic economic and social changes, new leadership roles for women in those religious organizations, and a flowering of utopian communities that fundamentally reconsidered the nature of human social organization characterized this time period. For a complete suggested response to the **AP® LEARNING FOCUS** question, see p. 344.

10 CHAPTER

Religion, Reform, and Culture 1820–1848

AP® LEARNING FOCUS

Why did new intellectual, religious, and social movements emerge in the early nineteenth century, and how did they change American society?

Amid a wild thunderstorm in the summer of 1830, an African American seamstress in Philadelphia awoke to hear God speaking. "I rose up and walked the floor wringing my hands and crying under great fear," Rebecca Cox Jackson wrote later. She prayed for hours, plunged in "the chamber of death." Suddenly she felt ecstasy: "my spirit was light, my heart filled with love for God and all mankind. . . . I ran downstairs and opened the door to let the lightning in the house, for it was like sheets of glory to my soul." Jackson reported that God had told her sexual relations caused sin: she should leave her husband. Sharing this news with her astonished spouse, Jackson was reportedly so full of spiritual power that she placed her hands on a hot stove over and over and removed them unhurt.

Jackson left home and became a traveling preacher. In upstate New York she discovered the communal movement of Shakers, or United Society of Believers in Christ's Second Appearing, whose popular nickname came from their ecstatic dances in worship. Like Jackson, Shakers practiced sexual abstinence. They also recognized women as religious and community leaders. Inspired by visions of a "mother spirit," Jackson returned to Philadelphia and built her own African American Shaker community, which endured for decades after her death in 1871.

Like Rebecca Cox Jackson, many Americans of the 1830s and 1840s found new callings. Inspired by the era's economic and political transformations, they believed they could perfect their lives and the society around them. Much seemed to need fixing. The rise of saloons, prostitution, and a boisterous working-class street culture in cities, especially in the Northeast, prompted middle-class men and women to work to restore moral and religious order. Other reformers, like Jackson, rejected mainstream religion and advocated such radical ideas as common ownership of property, immediate emancipation of slaves, and sexual equality. These activists challenged legal, economic, and social norms and provoked horrified opposition. As one fearful southerner argued, radicals favored a world with "No-Marriage, No-Religion, No-Private Property, No-Law and No-Government."

Such fears were grounded in the economic, social, and political upheavals Americans were experiencing. Rapid economic growth had weakened traditional institutions, which opened new opportunities but also increased poverty and inequality, forcing individuals to fend for themselves. In 1835, Alexis de Tocqueville coined the word ***individualism*** to describe a new set of ideas that resulted. Native-born white Americans were "no longer attached to each other by any tie of caste, class, association, or family," the French aristocrat lamented. But while Tocqueville mourned the loss of social ties, some Americans embraced those changes, while others built new movements for community, worship, and reform.

individualism
Word coined by Alexis de Tocqueville in 1835 to describe Americans as people no longer bound by social attachments to classes, castes, associations, and families.

Great American Revivals As shown in this painting of an 1819 Methodist camp meeting, the Second Great Awakening attracted large crowds of men, women, and children to revivals in outdoor venues. In the South, many African Americans also attended. In an atmosphere of intense excitement, some people (like the man in the foreground) were helped by friends and family members after being overcome with awareness of their sins and the spiritual power of redemption and grace. The tents in the background show that participants camped for the duration of the meeting as preaching, prayer, and conversions continued for several days. Library of Congress, LC-USZC4-772.

AP® THEME

NAT: American and National Identity

The illustration of a Methodist camp meeting suggests some of the emotional fervor during the Second Great Awakening and provides an opportunity for students to consider links between revival and the era's democratic spirit. Guide students' analysis with the following questions:

- **How would you describe the scene depicted in this image?** *It is a very large gathering, despite the fact that it is taking place in the woods. It is crowded, disorderly, and emotional.*
- **How does this gathering suggest ways that revivalists' focus on redemption and grace had democratic features?** *The gathering brought men and women, blacks and whites, and adults and children together, all of whom could hear and respond to the message.*
- **Evangelical revivalists rejected Calvin's idea of predestination and emphasized free will instead. How might that fit with the democratic spirit of the age?** *Free will fits with the ideas of choice, autonomy, and equality — everyone can determine their own fate.*

AP® SKILLS & PROCESSES

CONTINUITY AND CHANGE

Use the **TIMELINE** table to explore how 1816 to 1855 could constitute a distinct historical era. Ensure that students understand that this chapter covers the same chronological period as the previous two chapters, but now from a primarily cultural perspective. Ask students to consider the relationship between religion and reform in this era based on the events provided in the chronology. Extend this activity by asking students to make inferences about how the cultural developments of this era relate to the political and economic developments discussed in the previous two chapters.

TIMELINE

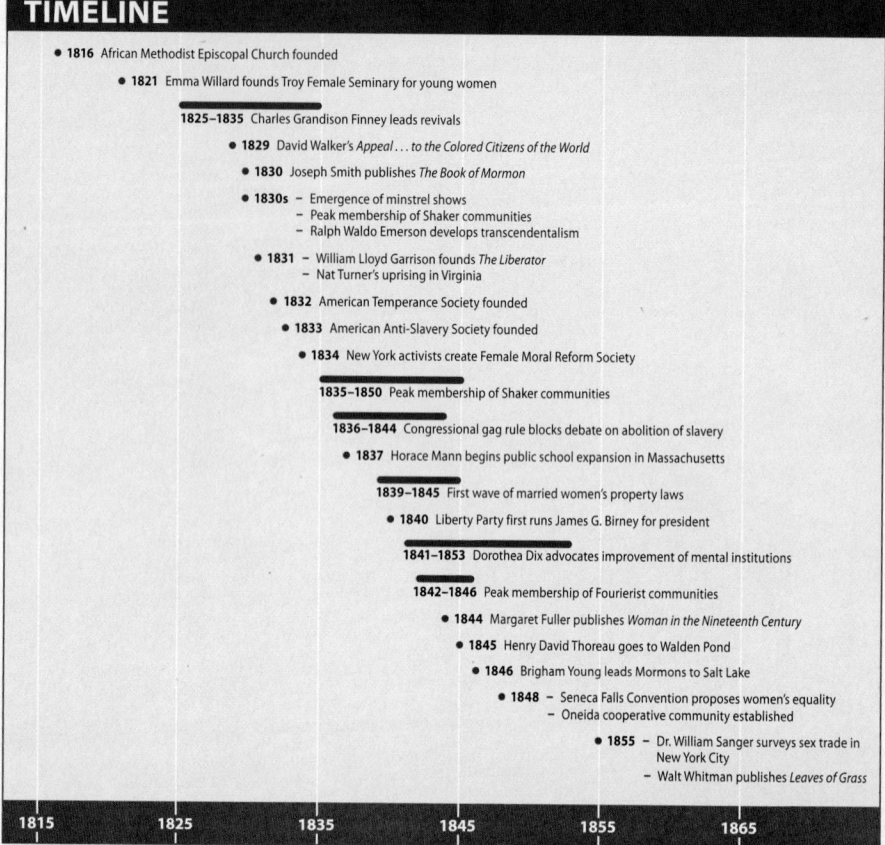

- **1816** African Methodist Episcopal Church founded
- **1821** Emma Willard founds Troy Female Seminary for young women
- **1825–1835** Charles Grandison Finney leads revivals
- **1829** David Walker's *Appeal . . . to the Colored Citizens of the World*
- **1830** Joseph Smith publishes *The Book of Mormon*
- **1830s** – Emergence of minstrel shows
  – Peak membership of Shaker communities
  – Ralph Waldo Emerson develops transcendentalism
- **1831** – William Lloyd Garrison founds *The Liberator*
  – Nat Turner's uprising in Virginia
- **1832** American Temperance Society founded
- **1833** American Anti-Slavery Society founded
- **1834** New York activists create Female Moral Reform Society
- **1835–1850** Peak membership of Shaker communities
- **1836–1844** Congressional gag rule blocks debate on abolition of slavery
- **1837** Horace Mann begins public school expansion in Massachusetts
- **1839–1845** First wave of married women's property laws
- **1840** Liberty Party first runs James G. Birney for president
- **1841–1853** Dorothea Dix advocates improvement of mental institutions
- **1842–1846** Peak membership of Fourierist communities
- **1844** Margaret Fuller publishes *Woman in the Nineteenth Century*
- **1845** Henry David Thoreau goes to Walden Pond
- **1846** Brigham Young leads Mormons to Salt Lake
- **1848** – Seneca Falls Convention proposes women's equality
  – Oneida cooperative community established
- **1855** – Dr. William Sanger surveys sex trade in New York City
  – Walt Whitman publishes *Leaves of Grass*

1815 | 1825 | 1835 | 1845 | 1855 | 1865

SPIRITUAL AWAKENINGS

How did antebellum religious and intellectual movements draw on the values of individualism, on the one hand, and of communal cooperation, on the other?

At the time of the American Revolution, every state except Pennsylvania and Rhode Island had a legally established church that claimed everyone as a member and collected compulsory religious taxes. In the years that followed, the combined pressure of Enlightenment principles and religious dissent eliminated most state support for religion and allowed voluntary church membership. Americans in large numbers joined evangelical Methodist and Baptist churches that preached spiritual equality and developed egalitarian, outwardly emotional worship cultures.

Second Great Awakening
A series of evangelical Protestant revivals extending from the 1790s to the 1830s that prompted thousands of conversions and widespread optimism about Americans' capacity for progress and reform.

From the 1790s through the 1830s, the country experienced powerful waves of religious revival. One of the largest frontier camp meetings, at Cane Ridge in Kentucky in 1801, lasted for nine electrifying days and attracted almost 20,000 people. Similar religious excitement swept all regions of the country. Known to historians as the **Second Great Awakening**, this upheaval lasted several decades and stimulated an array of long-lasting reform movements. By the time the Awakening subsided, New England intellectuals led by Ralph Waldo Emerson

316

were developing a radical individualist theology known as transcendentalism. Other spiritual seekers, like Rebecca Cox Jackson, joined utopian communities to remake the world.

The Second Great Awakening and Reform

Evangelical revivals depended on an intense personal experience of salvation. The first step was to reflect on your sins and reach a state of *conviction* — certainty that God, truly seeing and judging you, found you deserving of punishment and damnation. Penitents at revival meetings, surrounded by others praying for them, sat on the "anxious seat," a prominent bench just below the pulpit, where everyone hoped the pastor's words would provoke *conversion* — a profound experience of the presence of God's love, inspiring sinners to shed their former ways and emerge reborn, spiritually redeemed and psychologically transformed. Conversion was both an individual and a collective act. Christians who had experienced being "born again" worked to help family members and friends achieve the same joy and confidence in salvation.

Unlike the First Great Awakening, which split churches into warring factions, the second fostered cooperation among denominations, because evangelicals labored together, optimistically believing they could "perfect" their society. In a true church, declared Christian reformer Lydia Maria Child, members' "heads and hearts unite in working for the welfare of the human race." Between 1815 and 1826, religious leaders founded five major interdenominational societies: the American Education Society, Bible Society, Sunday School Union, Tract Society, and Home Missionary Society. Based in northeastern cities, these societies dispatched hundreds of missionaries to the West and distributed thousands of Bibles and religious pamphlets.

One of the Awakening's most successful leaders was Presbyterian minister Charles Grandison Finney. Born into a poor farm family in Connecticut, Finney planned to become a lawyer before he underwent an intense religious experience in 1823 and chose the ministry. Beginning in towns along the Erie Canal, the young minister conducted emotional revival meetings. Finney's central message was that "God has made man a moral free agent" who could choose salvation. This doctrine of free will was particularly attractive to members of the new middle class, who emphasized self-examination, self-discipline, and striving for advancement.

Finney's greatest triumph came in 1830 when he moved his revivals to Rochester, New York, a new commercial city on the Erie Canal. Preaching every day for six months and promoting group prayer in family homes, Finney converted influential merchants and manufacturers of Rochester. They promised to attend church, give up intoxicating beverages, and work hard. To encourage their employees to do the same, businessmen founded a Free Presbyterian Church — "free" because members did not have to pay for pew space. Other evangelicals founded churches to serve transient canal laborers, while pious businessmen set up a savings bank to encourage thrift among workers. Finney's wife, Lydia, and other middle-class women set up Sunday schools for poor children and formed a Female Charitable Society to assist the unemployed.

Finney's efforts were not completely successful. Skilled workers in strong craft organizations — boot makers, carpenters, stonemasons — protested that they needed higher wages and better schools more than sermons and prayers. Most poor people ignored Finney's revival, as did Irish Catholic immigrants, many of whom hated Protestants as religious heretics and political oppressors. Nonetheless, revivalists from New England to the Midwest copied Finney's message and techniques. In New York City, wealthy silk merchants Arthur and Lewis Tappan founded the *Journal of Commerce* to promote business enterprise while advocating Finney's evangelical and reform ideas. Revivals swept through Pennsylvania, North Carolina, Tennessee, and Indiana, where a convert reported, "you could not go upon the street and hear any conversation, except upon religion."

AP® EXAM TIP

As you read through this section, compare the Second Great Awakening of the early nineteenth century to the First Great Awakening that occurred in the early eighteenth century (Chapter 4).

AP® SKILLS & PROCESSES

SOURCING AND SITUATION

What was Charles Finney's central message, and how did it change the customs of society?

AP® APPLY THE TIP

To help students compare the First and Second Great Awakenings, provide or project an image of the painting "George Whitefield Preaching in Boston, June 1750" by Thomas Walley, and ask students to compare this to the image captioned "Great American Revivals" on p. 315 of the text. Ask students to describe the similarities and differences that can be seen in the images of these events. Have students then read the "Spiritual Awakenings" section (pp. 316–325) and create a list of key characteristics of the Second Great Awakening. Students should then write a paragraph comparing the effects of the First and Second Great Awakenings on the development of American society. (Remind students that comparison requires a discussion of both similarities and differences.)

TEACHING STRATEGY

The Library of Congress's online exhibit on religion in the early republic provides many high-quality primary sources, including several images that explore evangelical religion, black and white preachers, the role of emotion, and the establishment of benevolent societies. Access the site by searching "Library of Congress Religion and the Early Republic."

TEACHING STRATEGY

The National Humanities Center's Web site provides a helpful introduction to the emergence of African American Christianity. A short scholarly essay introduces the major themes, provides a guide to student discussion, and offers links to two dozen related primary sources. Access this resource by searching "NHC Divining America."

AP® SKILLS & PROCESSES

SOURCING AND SITUATION

Use the **SOURCING AND SITUATION** question to explore the effects of Finney's preaching. It might be helpful to frame this question for students in a broader way: How did the Second Great Awakening affect American society? Extend this prompt by asking students to evaluate whether the text characterizes these changes as generally beneficial, detrimental, or neutral to American society.

TRM Find complete suggested responses in the Teacher's Resource Materials.

AP® SKILLS & PROCESSES

DEVELOPMENTS AND PROCESSES

The bifurcated nature of the Second Great Awakening was part of its success. Indeed, the fact that both wealthy merchants and those who lived in the hinterlands participated in the spiritual awakening speaks to the breadth of the movement. Have students identify one geographical location that represents a wealthier segment of the awakening and one geographical location that represents a middle-to-lower class segment of the movement.

TEACHING STRATEGY

Ask students: **What was the Benevolent Empire, and why did it emerge at this historical moment?** Some students may need clarification that, despite the image created by the label "benevolent empire," reform was not one entity but a combination of overlapping and competing groups. Extend this prompt by having students identify a wider range of causes beyond the influence of evangelicalism, including the social upheaval created by the Market Revolution and the increasing cachet of democratic ideas as contributing factors.

AP® APPLY THE TIP

Have students work in pairs and consider the cause and effect relationship of the events listed on **Handout 10.1—Causation: Temperance Movement (TRM)**. Students should focus on the ways that the temperance movement built on the Second Great Awakening and encouraged more participation by women in the movement. Prompt students to use their findings to explain how the methods of the temperance movement show influences from the Second Great Awakening and why the methods of the temperance movement had less success with the working class.

TRM Find **Handout 10.1—Causation: Temperance Movement** in the Teacher's Resource Materials.

AP® THEME

POL: Politics and Power

The "Benevolent Empire" refers to the overlapping connection of voluntary organizations that attempted to change the behavior of individuals and improve society through various reforms. This section discusses temperance, adultery, prostitution, and crime. The rise of abolition, public education reform, "moral" reform that aimed to end prostitution, and prison reform are discussed later on in the chapter.

Benevolent Empire
A web of reform organizations, heavily Whig in their political orientation, built by evangelical Protestant men and women influenced by the Second Great Awakening.

AP® EXAM TIP

Be able to explain the conditions in the early nineteenth century that influenced the rise of the Temperance Movement for the AP® Exam.

Maine Law
The nation's first state law for the prohibition of liquor manufacture and sales, passed in 1851.

The Second Great Awakening inspired profound social transformations in the North. Members of the rising middle classes wanted to make the world more humane and just; they also wanted safe cities and a disciplined workforce. By the 1820s, led by Congregational and Presbyterian ministers, reformers created a network of organizations that historians call the **Benevolent Empire**. Their goal was to establish "the moral government of God" by reducing consumption of alcohol and other vices they believed caused poverty. Reform-minded individuals had pledged to regulate their own behavior; now they tried to control the lives of working people — by persuasion if possible, by law if necessary.

The Benevolent Empire targeted age-old evils such as drunkenness, adultery, prostitution, and crime, but its methods were new. Instead of relying on sermons, reformers created large-scale organizations such as the Prison Discipline Society and the General Union for Promoting the Observance of the Christian Sabbath. Each organization had a managing staff, a network of hundreds of chapters, thousands of volunteer members, and a newspaper. Often acting in concert, these groups encouraged people to exercise self-control and acquire "regular habits." They persuaded local governments to ban public carnivals of drink and dancing, such as Negro Election Day (festivities in which African Americans symbolically took control of the government), which had been enjoyed by working-class whites as well as blacks. Reformers created homes for abandoned children and asylums for the insane, who previously had often been confined by their families in attics and cellars.

"And I heard a voice from heaven, saying, write henceforth blessed are the dead who die in the Lord."—Rev. xiv.
"Verily I say unto you there is more joy in Heaven over one sinner that repenteth, than over ninety and nine just persons."

"Rescuing" Fallen Women This illustration from the first annual report of the New York Magdalen Society, published in 1831, suggests how reformers saw themselves and the women they sought to help. A minister prays at the deathbed of one former sex worker (perhaps attended by her child, who sits at her feet) while several friends watch and weep. The Society, seeking to convey to the public and potential donors the importance of their work, emphasizes repentance and redemption from sin: "Blessed are those who die in the Lord." The term "Magdalen" referred to the New Testament friend of Christ who was said to have been a prostitute. Library Company of Philadelphia.

Temperance advocates built the most energetic and successful movement. Beer and rum had long been a standard part of American holidays and everyday life, and grogshops dotted almost every block in working-class districts. During the 1820s and 1830s, alcohol consumption reached new heights, even among the elite. Heavy drinking was devastating for wage earners and their families, who could ill afford the costs. Though Methodist craftsmen swore off liquor to protect their skills, health, and finances, other workingmen drank heavily on the job — and not just during the traditional 11 A.M. and 4 P.M. "refreshers."

Evangelical Protestants who took over the American Temperance Society in 1832 set out to curb consumption of alcohol through voluntary abstinence. The society grew quickly to two thousand chapters and more than 200,000 members. Its campaigns succeeded through revivalist methods — group confession, prayer, and using women as spiritual guides. On one day in New York City in 1841, more than 4,000 people took the temperance pledge. Annual consumption of spirits fell dramatically, from an average of 5 gallons per person in 1830 to 2 gallons in 1845.

Despite this trend, temperance advocates were frustrated that thousands of Americans — especially working-class men — refused to join the cause. By the early 1850s they turned toward prohibition — laws to forbid the manufacture and sale of alcohol. In 1851, the Maine legislature outlawed the sale of alcoholic beverages in the state. The Maine Supreme Court upheld the statute, arguing that the legislature had the "right to regulate by law the sale of any article, the use of which would be detrimental of the morals of the people." The success of this **Maine Law** shaped the reformers' goals for decades, all the way up to the adoption of national prohibition in 1919.

Temperance ideas met resistance among workers who enjoyed their "refreshers" and Sunday beer. Even more controversial was Sabbatarianism, a movement to require business closings on the Christian Sabbath. As the economy grew, merchants and storekeepers began conducting business more often on Sundays. Sabbatarians pressured state legislatures to halt such practices and urged Congress to repeal an 1810 law allowing mail to be transported — though not delivered — on Sundays. Members boycotted shipping companies that did business on the Sabbath and campaigned for municipal laws forbidding games and festivals on the Lord's day.

Provoking opposition from workers and freethinkers, these efforts had limited success. Men who labored twelve to fourteen hours a day, six days a week, wanted the freedom to spend their one day of leisure as they wished. Pressured by shipping companies, the Erie Canal provided lockkeepers on Sundays. Using laws to enforce a particular set of religious beliefs, business leaders said, was "contrary to the free spirit of our institutions."

AP® SKILLS & PROCESSES

CAUSATION

What factor(s) contributed to the rise of the Second Great Awakening?

American Renaissance
A literary explosion during the 1840s inspired in part by Emerson's ideas on the liberation of the individual.

romanticism
A European philosophy that rejected the ordered rationality of the eighteenth-century Enlightenment, embracing human passion, spiritual quest, and self-knowledge. Romanticism strongly influenced American transcendentalism.

transcendentalism
A nineteenth-century American intellectual movement that posited the importance of an ideal world of mystical knowledge and harmony beyond the immediate grasp of the senses. Influenced by romanticism, transcendentalists Ralph Waldo Emerson and Henry David Thoreau called for the critical examination of society and emphasized individuality, self-reliance, and nonconformity.

Transcendentalism

Influential New England philosopher Ralph Waldo Emerson ranged far beyond benevolent reform. He celebrated the overthrow of old hierarchies and the spiritual power of individuals, influencing thousands of ordinary Americans and a generation of writers in the **American Renaissance**, a mid-nineteenth-century flourishing of literature and philosophy. Its roots lay with Unitarian ministers from well-to-do New England families who questioned the constraints of their Puritan heritage. For inspiration, they turned to European **romanticism**, a new conception of self and society. Romantic thinkers, such as German philosopher Immanuel Kant and English poet Samuel Taylor Coleridge, rejected the ordered, rational world of the eighteenth-century Enlightenment. They embraced human passion and sought deeper insight into the mysteries of existence. Through spiritual quest and self-knowledge, young Unitarians believed each individual could experience the infinite and eternal.

The Founder of Transcendentalism As this painting of Ralph Waldo Emerson by an unknown artist indicates, the young philosopher was an attractive man, his face brimming with confidence and optimism. With his radiant personality and incisive intellect, Emerson deeply influenced dozens of influential writers, artists, and scholars and enjoyed great success as a lecturer to the emerging middle class. The Metropolitan Museum of Art, Gilman Collection, Purchase, Mr. and Mrs. Henry R. Kravis Gift, 2005.

Emerson's Individualism As a Unitarian, Emerson already stood outside the mainstream of American Protestantism. In 1832, he took a more radical step by resigning his Boston pulpit and rejecting organized religion. He moved to Concord, Massachusetts, and wrote influential essays probing what he called "the infinitude of the private man," the radically free person. In doing so, Emerson launched the intellectual movement of **transcendentalism**. He argued that people needed to shake off inherited customs and institutions and discover their "original relation with Nature," in order to enter a mystical union with the "currents of Universal Being."

Emerson's individualistic ethos spoke to the experiences of many middle-class Americans who had left family farms to make their way in the urban world. His pantheistic, nature-centered view of God encouraged Unitarians in Boston to create Mount Auburn Cemetery, a beautiful landscape with burial markers for the dead of all faiths. Despite his own rejection of organized religion, Emerson's optimism also inspired many Protestant leaders of the Second Great Awakening, such as Finney, who urged believers to reject old doctrines and seek direct experiences of God's power.

Transcendentalists' message of self-realization reached hundreds of thousands of people through Emerson's writings

TRM Find complete suggested responses in the Teacher's Resource Materials.

CHECK FOR UNDERSTANDING

Ask students: **What was the Second Great Awakening?** *It was a widespread religious revival, primarily in the North, among Protestant evangelicals between the 1790s and the 1830s. The label distinguishes this revival from a similar movement, the Great Awakening, in the 1730s and 1740s.*

AP® THEME

NAT: American and National Identity

The text calls attention to the influence of European romanticism on the philosophy and literature produced by the transcendentalists, despite the fact that the movement is often associated with Emerson's call to reject European influence and create a distinctive American style.

AP® THEME

ARC: American and Regional Culture

Even though Transcendentalism was an American intellectual movement, its roots and rhythms were concentrated in northern communities. Have students identify three reasons why the movement was centered in northern communities and were largely absent in southern communities. (Possible answers would include: utopian communities, abolitionism, advocacy of public education, and civil disobedience.)

AP® EXAM TIP

It's important to identify European influences that continued to impact the U.S. even as Americans developed their own unique cultural heritage.

and lectures. He became the most popular speaker in the lyceum movement, which was modeled on the public forum of the ancient Greek philosopher Aristotle and which in 1826 began to arrange speaking tours by poets, preachers, scientists, and reformers. The lyceum became an important cultural institution in the North and Midwest, though not in the South, where the middle class was smaller and popular education had a lower priority. Emerson eventually delivered fifteen hundred lectures in twenty states.

Thoreau, Fuller, and Whitman New England intellectual Henry David Thoreau heeded Emerson's call to seek inspiration from the natural world. In 1845, depressed by his beloved brother's death, Thoreau built a cabin near Walden Pond in Concord, Massachusetts, and lived alone there for two years. In 1854, he published *Walden, or Life in the Woods*, an account of his search for meaning beyond the artificiality of civilized society:

> I went to the woods because I wished to live deliberately, to front only the essential facts of life, and see if I could not learn what it had to teach, and not, when I came to die, discover that I had not lived.

Walden's most famous metaphor provides an enduring justification for independent thinking: "If a man does not keep pace with his companions, perhaps it is because he hears a different drummer." Beginning from this premise, Thoreau urged readers to avoid unthinking conformity and peacefully resist unjust laws. He soon opposed both slavery and the U.S.-Mexico War (Chapter 11).

***Margaret Fuller*, 1848** At the age of thirty-eight, American transcendentalist author Margaret Fuller moved to Italy, where she reported on the Revolution of 1848 for the *New York Tribune*. There she fell in love with Thomas Hicks (1823–1890), a much younger American artist. Hicks rebuffed Fuller's romantic advances but painted this flattering portrait, softening her features and giving her a pensive look. Fuller took as a lover a petty noble and republican revolutionary, Giovanni Angelo, Marchese d'Ossoli, and gave birth to a son in September 1848. Two years later, the entire family died in a shipwreck while in route to the United States. Niday Picture Library/Alamy Stock Photo.

As Thoreau sought self-realization for men, Margaret Fuller explored the possibilities of freedom for women. Born into a wealthy Boston family, Fuller mastered six languages and read broadly. Embracing Emerson's ideas, she started a transcendental discussion group for educated Boston women in 1839. While editing *The Dial*, the leading transcendentalist journal, Fuller also published *Woman in the Nineteenth Century* (1844). In it, Fuller endorsed the transcendental principle that all people could develop a life-affirming mystical relationship with God. Every woman therefore deserved psychological and social independence: the ability "to grow, as an intellect to discern, as a soul to live freely and unimpeded." She also called for equality in education and work. Fuller traveled to Italy to report on the Revolution of 1848, only to drown in a shipwreck on her way home to the United States. Her life and writings inspired a rising generation of women writers and reformers.

Emerson urged American authors to reject European influences and find inspiration in everyday life — "the ballad in the street; . . . the form and gait of the body" — and no one responded to that call more vibrantly than poet Walt Whitman. While working as a printer, teacher, journalist, and publicist for the Democratic Party, Whitman recalled that he had been "simmering, simmering"; Emerson "brought me to a boil." In *Leaves of Grass*, a collection of wild, exuberant poems first published in 1855 and constantly revised and expanded, Whitman recorded in verse his efforts to transcend various "invisible boundaries": between solitude and community, between humans seeking sexual connection, even between the living and the dead. At the center of *Leaves of Grass* is the individual: "I celebrate myself, and sing myself." Through his Emersonian "original relation" with nature, Whitman claimed perfect communion with others: "Every

TEACHING STRATEGY

Provide students with excerpts from Immanuel Kant's "What is Enlightenment?" and Ralph Waldo Emerson's "Self-Reliance," and ask them to analyze both of these sources to answer the question "What is Enlightenment?" from the point of view of Kant and Emerson, respectively. Finally, provide students with an excerpt from Margaret Fuller's "Woman in the Nineteenth Century" and ask them to compare her views to those of Kant and Emerson. Lead the class in a discussion of the ways in which the rise of transcendentalism in the U.S., romanticism in Europe, and the Second Great Awakening challenged traditional roles and values in American cultural heritage and national identity.

AP® SKILLS & PROCESSES

COMPARISON

Romanticism is a concept students are required to know. Therefore, have students define the ideas of Romanticism within the context of the Transcendentalist movement. In this way students might be better equipped to define two otherwise abstract concepts.

atom belonging to me as good belongs to you." Whitman's aims, however, were not only individualistic. He believed America's collective democracy was sacred and needed a distinctive culture to match its political forms. He urged Americans to reject European models in literature and the arts and create new forms to capture the energy and diversity of American life. He rejected aristocratic traditions and celebrated the lives and passions of ordinary people, including workingmen, women, and even slaves.

While Whitman roamed the streets of New York, another poet took the American Renaissance in a very different direction. In Amherst, Massachusetts, the reclusive Emily Dickinson never married. She maintained lively correspondences with many religious and literary figures. When she died at age fifty-six in 1886, her family found a trunk full of neatly bound poems that she had labored over all her life. After her death, Dickinson's unique and powerful voice shaped the future of American literature. Though more conventionally religious than Whitman, and writing often of her loneliness and unrequited love, Dickinson also took Transcendentalist-style inspiration from the natural world, as in her poem "To Make a Prairie":

> To make a prairie it takes a clover.
> One clover, and a bee.
> And revery.
> The revery alone will do,
> If bees are few.

In an isolated but intensely emotional and creative life, Dickinson pursued her own experiment in Transcendentalist observation and self-knowledge.

Limits of Transcendentalism Like many others, transcendentalists worried that the new market society — focused on work, profits, and consumption — was debasing Americans' spiritual lives. "Things are in the saddle," Emerson wrote, "and ride mankind." Seeking to reject profit-seeking and revive intellectual life, transcendentalists created communal experiments. The most important was Brook Farm, just outside Boston, where Emerson, Thoreau, and Fuller were residents or frequent visitors. Members recalled that they "inspired the young with a passion for study, and the middle-aged with deference and admiration." Brook Farm's residents planned to produce their own food and exchange surplus milk, vegetables, and hay for manufactures. However, most members had few farming skills; only cash from affluent residents kept the enterprise afloat for five years. After a devastating fire in 1846, the community disbanded and sold the farm. With this failure, transcendentalists abandoned their quest for new social institutions. They accepted the emerging commercial order but tried to reform it, especially through the education of workers and the movement to abolish slavery.

In the meantime, Emerson's writings influenced two great novelists, Nathaniel Hawthorne and Herman Melville, with more pessimistic worldviews. Both sounded powerful warnings about the dangers of individualism when it became unfettered egoism. The main characters of Hawthorne's novel *The Scarlet Letter* (1850), Hester Prynne and Arthur Dimmesdale, challenge their seventeenth-century New England community by committing adultery and producing a child. Their decision to ignore social restraints results not in liberation but in a profound sense of guilt and condemnation by the community.

Melville explored the limits of individualism in even more extreme and tragic terms and became a critic of transcendentalism. His most powerful work, *Moby-Dick* (1851), tells the story of Captain Ahab's obsessive hunt for a mysterious white whale, which ends in the destruction of Ahab and almost his entire crew. Here, the quest for spiritual meaning in nature — and perhaps also for economic profits — brings death, not transcendence, because Ahab lacks discipline and self-restraint. *Moby-Dick* won

AP® EXAM TIP

It's important to note that liberal ideas about the perfectibility of man and Romanticism influenced the rise of a distinctive American culture.

CHECK FOR UNDERSTANDING

Ask students: **How was transcendentalism a "spiritual awakening"?** *Influenced by German romanticism's embrace of "the mysteries of existence," transcendentalists encouraged a self-realization of mystical union with, as Emerson said, the "currents of Universal Being."*

AP® APPLY THE TIP

Ask students to create a chart that illustrates the impact of liberal ideas and romanticism on American culture. Students' charts should include Walt Whitman, Nathaniel Hawthorne, Herman Melville, Brook Farm, Shakerism, Fourierist socialism, Oneida, and Mormonism. For each of these developments in American culture, students should identify the following: ideas about perfectibility of man, ideas about man's responsibility to society, and influences on/challenges to national identity.

AP® SKILLS & PROCESSES

COMPARISON

The **COMPARISON** question requires students to consider the differences between two contemporary spiritual belief systems. Students should identify the Christian roots of transcendentalism, as well as the influences of European romanticism. They may need help recognizing the features that distinguish Catholic and Protestant Christianity. Then have students consider similarities in these systems of thought — particularly in their shared rejection of Calvinist predestination and the Calvinist assumption of an intrinsically evil human nature — and in their affirmation of feeling as a guide toward spiritual development.

TRM Find complete suggested responses in the Teacher's Resource Materials.

AP® THEME

POL: Politics and Culture

Use **MAP 10.1** to discuss the geographic dispersion of the utopian movements that characterized the era. Guide students' analysis with the following questions:

- **Which type of utopian experiment prompted the greatest number of communities?** *Fourierists were the most numerous utopian community.*
- **What conclusions can you draw about the geographic dispersion of utopian communities?** *Shakers had the greatest strength in New England. Utopian communities clustered around the newly settled growth regions of the Market Revolution.*
- **Why did this era give rise to so many utopian experiments?** *The upheaval of the Market Revolution's capitalist economy, combined with an optimism about human ability to freely join in communities and perfect society, led to a large number of experiments.*

AP® SKILLS & PROCESSES

COMPARISON

What were the main principles of transcendentalism, and how did they differ from the beliefs of most Protestant Christians?

recognition as a landmark in American literature, but it was not a bestseller. Middle-class readers who devoured sentimental fiction refused to follow Melville into the dark, dangerous realm of individualism gone mad. They emphatically preferred the optimistic views of Emerson or Finney.

Utopian Communities and New Religious Movements

utopias
Communities founded by reformers and transcendentalists to help realize their spiritual and moral potential and to escape from the competition of modern industrial society.

Like the founders of Brook Farm, thousands of less affluent Americans rejected America's emerging market society and sought to create ideal communities, or **utopias**, in rural parts of the Northeast and Midwest (Map 10.1). They hoped to build models for different ways of living. Many were farmers and artisans seeking refuge from the economic depression of 1837–1843. Others were religious idealists. By advocating common ownership of property (socialism) and unconventional forms of family life, communalists challenged traditional property rights and gender roles.

AP® EXAM TIP

Analyze the impact of utopian and religious movements that resulted from the Second Great Awakening.

The first successful American communal movement was Shakerism. In 1770, Ann Lee Stanley (Mother Ann Lee), a young cook in Manchester, England, had a vision that she was a second Christ — the female aspect of God, whereas Jesus represented the male aspect. Four years later, Lee led a few disciples to America and established a church near Albany, New York. After her death in 1784, her followers formed disciplined religious communities. Members embraced common ownership of property; accepted strict oversight by church leaders; and pledged to abstain from alcohol, tobacco, politics, and war. Shakers' repudiation of sexual pleasure and marriage followed Mother Ann's teaching that "lustful gratifications of the flesh" were "the foundation of human corruption." Holding that God was "a dual person, male and female," Shakers placed community governance in the hands of both women and men — elderesses and elders.

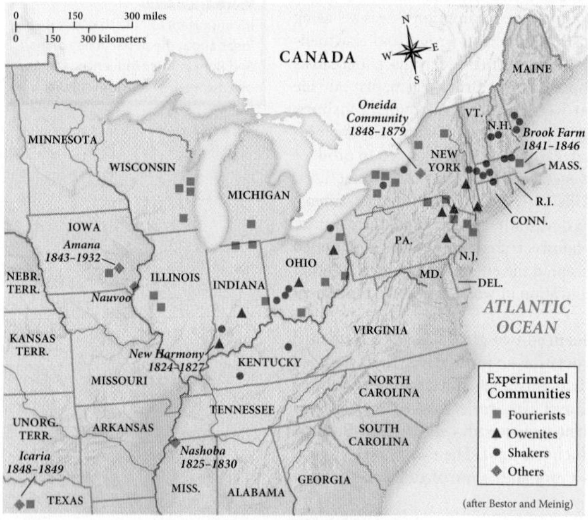

MAP 10.1 Major Communal Experiments Before 1860
Some experimental communities settled along the frontier, but the vast majority chose rural areas in settled regions of the North and Midwest. Because they opposed slavery, communalists usually avoided the South. Most secular experiments failed within a few decades, as conflicts arose within the communities, or as founders lost their reformist enthusiasm or died off; some tightly knit religious communities, such as the Shakers and the Mormons, were longer-lived.

Shakers founded twenty communities, mostly in New England, New York, and Ohio. Their agriculture and crafts, especially furniture making, acquired a reputation for quality that made them self-sustaining and even comfortable. Because Shakers disdained sexual intercourse, they relied on conversions and the adoption of thousands of young orphans to increase their numbers. During the 1830s, 3,000 adults, mostly women, joined the Shakers, attracted by their communalism and sexual equality. However, as the Benevolent Empire expanded the availability of public and private orphanages during the 1840s and 1850s, Shaker communities began to decline and, by 1900, virtually disappeared.

Other Americans championed the ideas of French reformer Charles Fourier, who devised an eight-stage theory of social evolution predicting the imminent decline of individual property rights and capitalism, through the creation of cooperative communities. Fourier's leading

Shakers at Prayer Most Americans viewed the Shakers with a mixture of fascination and suspicion. They feared the sect's radical aspects, such as a commitment to celibacy and communal property, and considered the Shakers' dancing more an invitation to debauchery than a form of prayer. Those apprehensions surface in this engraving, *The Shakers of New Lebanon* (New York), which expresses both the powerful intensity and the collective character of this Shaker spiritual ritual. The work of the journalist-engraver Joseph Becker, the picture appeared in Frank Leslie's *Illustrated Newspaper* in 1873. Bettmann/Getty Images.

disciple in America, Albert Brisbane, argued that Fourier's methods would liberate workers from low wages and servitude to capitalist employers. Fourierists also called for "associated households" in which both sexes shared domestic labor, emancipating women from "slavish domestic duties."

Following the Panic of 1837, Fourierism found a receptive audience among educated farmers and craftsmen who yearned for economic stability and communal solidarity. In the 1840s, Fourierists started nearly a hundred cooperative communities, mostly in western New York and the Midwest. Members owned property in common, including stores, banks, schools, and libraries. Most communities quickly collapsed as members fought over work responsibilities and social policies. Fourierism's rapid decline revealed how economic challenges and internal conflicts made it difficult to maintain a utopian community.

John Humphrey Noyes ascribed the Fourierists' failure to their secular outlook and praised Shakers as the true "pioneers of modern Socialism." Noyes, a well-to-do graduate of Dartmouth, developed his own belief system, centered — like those of many other radical utopians — on reforming family and household relationships. Noyes rejected marriage, but instead of Shaker-style celibacy he proposed a system of "complex marriage," in which all members of a community married one another.

AP® SKILLS & PROCESSES

DEVELOPMENTS AND PROCESSES

Explain the influence of uniquely American elements, European influences, and regional cultural identity in the development of an American culture.

TEACHING STRATEGY

This engraving provides an example of the distinctive Shaker practices that outsiders found disturbing. Students might note that it comes from an 1879 magazine, so it raises a question students could discuss about how useful the engraving is as evidence for Shaker activities during the 1820s and 1830s. Students could discuss whether they find the caption's assessment convincing that the image depicts the Shakers as "menacing." This question addresses the larger issue of whether the Shakers were considered odd but harmless or threatening.

TRM Find complete suggested responses in the Teacher's Resource Materials.

TEACHING STRATEGY

Use the illustration of the burning of the Nauvoo Temple to discuss why Mormonism was the target of such violence, which no other utopian movement experienced on this scale. The National Humanities Center's *Divining America* Web site offers a background essay, "Mormonism and the American Mainstream," that explains Mormon doctrine in greater detail and explores reasons for American hostility to the movement. The site also offers a guide to student discussion and a link to primary sources on Mormonism from the Library of Congress's exhibit on religion in the early republic. Access this essay by searching "Divining America Mormonism American Mainstream."

AP® SKILLS & PROCESSES

MAKING CONNECTIONS

The **MAKING CONNECTIONS** question asks students to identify causes for the growth of several different utopian communities. It might be helpful to create a basic chart that indicates the year, location, and type of community, followed by a brief description of reasons people joined it. It would probably also be helpful for students to include one utopian group from each of several different types. Some students might offer a generalization about why people in the early nineteenth century joined utopian communities at all.

TRM Find complete suggested responses in the Teacher's Resource Materials.

The Burning of Nauvoo Temple After the lynching of founding prophet Joseph Smith in 1844, and facing ongoing hostility and violence, Mormons were forced to flee Nauvoo, Illinois. Most fled to Utah in 1846 under the leadership of Brigham Young. They left behind not only homes and businesses but also the 53,000-square-foot Nauvoo Temple, built over six years at an immense price in building materials and human labor. With no ready non-Mormon buyers, church leaders were forced to sell the Temple for $500, a tiny fraction of the cost. On the night of October 8–9, 1848, as shown in this dramatic lithograph, arsonists burned the temple to the ground. Everett Collection.

He rejected monogamy partly to free women from their status as the property of their husbands.

In 1839, Noyes set up a utopian community near his hometown of Putney, Vermont. Local outrage forced the colony to relocate in 1848 to an isolated site near Oneida, New York. To give women time and energy to participate fully in community affairs, Noyes urged them to avoid multiple pregnancies. He instructed men to help by avoiding orgasm during intercourse. Eventually, he began to encourage sexual relations at a very early age and used his position of power to manipulate the sexual lives of his followers. When dissenters finally reported on such practices to outsiders, Noyes fled to Canada in 1879 to avoid prosecution for adultery. The community abandoned complex marriage but remained a successful cooperative silverware venture until the mid-twentieth century.

The historical significance of the Shaker, Fourierist, and Oneida projects does not lie in the numbers of participants, which were small, or in their fine crafts. Rather, they posed radical questions about traditional sexual norms and marriage, and about the capitalist values and class divisions of the emerging market society. Their utopian communities stood as countercultural blueprints for a more egalitarian social and economic order.

AP® SKILLS & PROCESSES

MAKING CONNECTIONS

Name three communal utopias of the 1830s and 1840s. How did the founders of each group propose to organize society, and why?

The era's most successful religious utopian movement emerged, like several others, from religious ferment among families of Puritan descent who lived along the Erie Canal. The founder of Mormonism, Joseph Smith, was born in Vermont to a poor farming and shop-keeping family who migrated to Palmyra in central New York. In 1820, Smith began to have religious experiences: "A pillar of light above the brightness of the sun at noonday came down from above and rested upon me and I was filled with the spirit of God." Smith believed God had singled him out for special revelations. In 1830, he published *The Book of Mormon*, which he said he translated from ancient hieroglyphics on gold plates shown to him by an angel. *The Book of Mormon* told the story of ancient Jews from the Middle East who had migrated to the Western Hemisphere and were visited by Jesus Christ soon after his Resurrection. Smith's account of New World history integrated it into the Judeo-Christian tradition.

Church of Jesus Christ of Latter-day Saints, or Mormons
Founded by Joseph Smith in 1830. After Smith's death at the hands of an angry mob, in 1846 Brigham Young led many followers of Mormonism to lands in present-day Utah.

Smith organized the **Church of Jesus Christ of Latter-day Saints, or Mormons**. Seeing himself as a prophet in a sinful, excessively individualistic society, he emphasized the family as the heart of religious and social life. Like many Protestants, Smith encouraged practices that led to individual success in the market economy: frugality, hard work, and enterprise. But Smith also stressed communal discipline. His goal was a church-directed society that would restore primitive Christianity and encourage moral perfection.

Constantly harassed by violent threats, Smith struggled to find a secure place to settle. After he identified Jackson County in Missouri as the site of the "City of Zion," and his followers began to move there, they met extreme hostility. Mormons were "enemies of mankind and ought to be destroyed," said one minister. Missouri's governor agreed, issuing an order for Mormons to be "exterminated or driven out." Smith and his growing congregation eventually settled in Nauvoo, Illinois, a town they founded on the Mississippi River. By the early 1840s, Nauvoo had 30,000 residents. Mormons' prosperity and their secret rituals and rigid discipline — including bloc voting in Illinois elections — fueled resentment among their neighbors. Antagonism increased when Smith asked Congress to make Nauvoo a separate federal territory and declared himself a candidate for president of the United States.

Like other religious visionaries of his era, Smith also proposed a radical change in the structure of the family. Secretly, at first, he preached a new revelation justifying polygamy, the practice of a man having multiple wives. Smith pointed to biblical precedent for this practice of patriarchal or **plural marriage**. The revelation caused some of Smith's followers to break with him; when word got out, polygamy enraged church enemies. In 1844, Illinois officials arrested Smith and charged him with treason for allegedly conspiring to create a Mormon colony in Mexican territory. An anti-Mormon mob stormed the jail in Carthage, Illinois, seized Smith and his brother Hyrum, and murdered them.

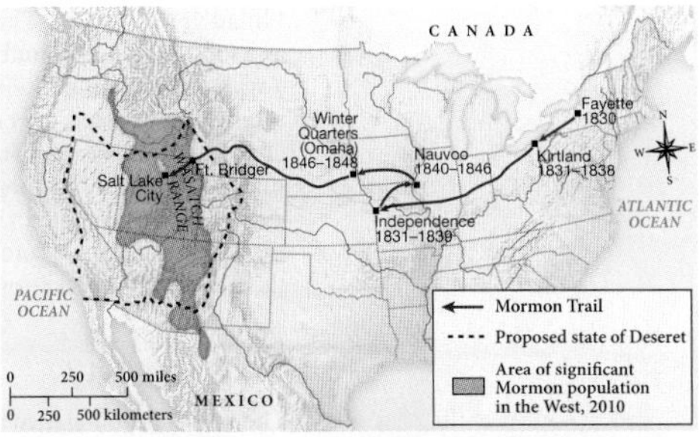

MAPPING THE PAST

MAP 10.2 The Mormon Trek, 1830–1848

Because of their unorthodox religious views and communal solidarity, Mormons faced hostility first in New York and then in Missouri and Illinois. After the murder of church founder Joseph Smith in 1844, Brigham Young led the majority of Latter-day Saints from Illinois westward to Omaha, Nebraska. From Omaha the migrants followed the path of the Oregon Trail to Fort Bridger and then struck off to the southwest to settle in the basin of the Great Salt Lake, along the Wasatch Range in what is now Utah. At the time, this land was part of northern Mexico and was occupied by Utes, Paiutes, and Shoshones. The United States' victory in the U.S.-Mexico War (Chapter 11) turned Deseret into U.S. territory only two years later.

ANALYZING THE MAP: Compare the area of the proposed state of Deseret with the area of the state of Utah (created in 1896) and areas of significant Mormon population in 2010. What do you conclude about the goals of the LDS settlement, its incorporation into the United States, and its long-term legacies?

MAKING CONNECTIONS: Compare this map with Map 10.1 of other communal antebellum experiments. What patterns did those communities and early Mormonism share? In what ways did they differ geographically?

Some Mormons who rejected polygamy remained in the Midwest, led by Smith's son, Joseph Smith III. About 6,500 Mormons, however, fled the United States under the guidance of Brigham Young, Smith's leading disciple. Beginning in 1846, they crossed the Great Plains into Mexican territory and occupied the Great Salt Lake Valley and nearby lands centered on present-day Utah, an area they called "Deseret" (Map 10.2). Using cooperative labor and an irrigation system based on communal water rights, Mormon pioneers quickly built successful agricultural communities. Unlike most other American utopias, Deseret survived and grew. For the rest of the nineteenth century its relationship with — and soon, Utah's role in — the expanding U.S. empire became an issue of bitter national debate.

plural marriage
The practice of men taking multiple wives, which Mormon prophet Joseph Smith argued was biblically sanctioned and divinely ordained as a family system.

AP® SKILLS & PROCESSES
COMPARISON
In what ways was early Mormonism similar to, and different from, other utopian movements of its era?

URBAN CULTURES AND CONFLICTS

What new cultural practices emerged in antebellum cities, and why?

As utopians organized in the countryside, rural migrants and foreign immigrants plunged into the exciting and risky world of the growing cities. In 1800, American cities had been overgrown towns: New York had only 60,000 residents and

TRM Find complete suggested responses in the Teacher's Resource Materials.

AP® SKILLS & PROCESSES

COMPARISON

The **COMPARISON** question requires students to recognize unique features of Mormonism. Some students may struggle to recognize Mormonism as a form of utopianism, given they are likely familiar with it as a well-established religion. A Venn diagram provides a simple framework for identifying similarities and differences to answer this question, though it might be helpful to add categories for comparison, like origins, leadership structure, and major beliefs to assist students in making their comparison. Students could then identify features of Mormonism that help explain its longevity relative to other utopian movements.

TRM Find complete suggested responses in the Teacher's Resource Materials.

CHECK FOR UNDERSTANDING

Ask students: **To what extent did antebellum intellectual and religious movements draw on the values of individualism, on the one hand, and of communal cooperation, on the other?** *All antebellum intellectual and religious movements embraced both individualism and communal cooperation to differing extents. They stressed individual perfection and self-correction based on Charles Finney's ideas about man's moral free-agency. Some ideas, like transcendentalism, felt that such perfection could be accomplished by living the simple life largely in solitude. Most, however, created communities for both societal needs and accountability. These included Fourierists, Shakers, Owenites, and Mormons.*

Philadelphia, 41,000. Then urban growth accelerated as the economy expanded, and jobs lured huge numbers of native and foreign-born newcomers. By 1850, New York's population ballooned to more than half a million, despite the high death rates that persisted for city dwellers, especially infants and children. Five other cities — Baltimore, Boston, Philadelphia, New Orleans, and Cincinnati — had more than 100,000 each. As they grew, cities began to play more central roles in American culture. They generated vibrant, popular new ideas and practices, especially among the working classes, scandalizing more wealthy and pious residents and intensifying their calls for "moral reform."

Sex in the City

Thousands of young men and women flocked to the city searching for adventure and fortune, but many found hardship. Young men labored for meager wages, building tenements, warehouses, and workshops. Others worked as low-paid clerks or operatives in mercantile and manufacturing firms. Young women faced even greater deprivation and danger. Thousands toiled as live-in domestic servants, ordered about by the mistress of the household and often sexually exploited by the master. Others scraped out a bare living as needlewomen in New York City's booming ready-made clothes industry or doing other forms of "piecework." Unwilling to endure domestic service or subsistence wages, many young girls turned to prostitution (see "Firsthand Accounts," p. 328). New York had two hundred brothels in the 1820s and five hundred by the 1850s.

Not all urban sex was commercial. Freed from family oversight, men formed homoerotic relationships; as early as 1800, the homosexual "fop" was an acknowledged character in Philadelphia. Heterosexual young people sometimes moved from partner to partner until they chanced on an ideal mate. City streets were an ideal place for young people to flaunt their fashions and check each other out. Middle-class young men strolled Broadway in flowing capes, boots, and silver-plated walking sticks, eyeing young women in elaborate bonnets and silk dresses. Rivaling the elegance on Broadway were the colorful costumes of the working-class Bowery, the broad avenue that ran along the east side of lower Manhattan. By day, a Bowery Boy or "B'hoy" worked as an apprentice or journeyman. By night, he prowled the streets as a "dandy," hair cropped at the back of the head "as close as scissors could cut," with long front locks "matted by a lavish application of *bear's grease*, the ends tucked under so as to form a roll and brushed until they shone like glass bottles." The B'hoy cut a dashing figure walking with a "Bowery Gal" in a bright dress and shawl. To some shocked observers, such couples represented disorder and disrespect for middle-class values of respectability and piety.

Urban Entertainments

AP® EXAM TIP

The rise of the popular press and entertainment influenced the development of a unique American culture.

When they dressed up for a night on the town, young city dwellers enjoyed many options. In New York, working men could partake of traditional blood sports — rat and terrier fights, boxing matches — at Sportsmen's Hall, or they could seek drink and fun in billiard and bowling saloons. Other workers crowded the pit of the Bowery Theatre to see the "Mad Tragedian," Junius Brutus Booth, perform Shakespeare's *Richard III*. Reform-minded couples enjoyed evenings at the huge Broadway Tabernacle, where they could hear a temperance lecture or see the renowned Hutchinson Family Singers lead a roof-raising rendition of their antislavery anthem "Get Off the Track." Families could visit the museum of oddities (and hoaxes) created by P. T. Barnum, the great cultural entrepreneur and founder of Barnum & Bailey Circus.

CHECK FOR UNDERSTANDING

Ask students: **What was the nature of "sex in the city"?** *The anonymous character of the nation's growing cities, where young people often lived unsupervised, led to freer experimentation with sex outside of marriage, including prostitution and same-sex relationships. The commercial sex trade was fueled by young women who could not find work for appropriate wages in factories or domestic service.*

AP® APPLY THE TIP

As students read the "Urban Entertainments" and "Popular Fiction and the Penny Press" sections, prompt them to begin thinking about the influence of the popular press and entertainment on American culture in the early twentieth century through the following open-ended questions *(answers will vary)*:

- **How do popular media and entertainment influence American culture today?**
- **Do you have to participate in popular media and entertainment to be influenced by it?**
- **How does popular media and entertainment define or alter American national identity?**

Then ask students to create a list of groups who produced popular media and groups who consumed popular media in the early nineteenth century. Prompt students to use the examples from the text to discuss the role the popular press and entertainment played in the Second Great Awakening. Students should address how the ideals and values encouraged in popular media and entertainment clashed with the Second Great Awakening and the ways in which it challenged traditional American culture and facilitated racist and sexist attitudes in the U.S.

AP® THEME

SOC: Social Structures

At the beginning of this section, it may be worthwhile to have students make some concrete connections so as they study the material they can remember the broader historical processes. In this bell-ringer activity, have students connect the growth of urbanization to migration patterns. After students have connected these concepts, ask students to explain how international migrants' social opportunities changed because of migration. The goal is for students to see a broader historical concept before they study the details of some aspects of urbanization.

The most popular theatrical entertainments were **minstrel shows**, which featured white actors in blackface presenting comic routines that combined racist caricature and social criticism. Minstrelsy began around 1830, when a few white actors put on blackface and performed song-and-dance routines (see "Thinking Like a Historian," p. 332). The most famous was John Dartmouth Rice, whose "Jim Crow" blended a shuffle-dance-and-jump with unintelligible lyrics delivered in "Negro dialect." By the 1840s hundreds of minstrel troupes toured the country. Minstrel players used African musical instruments, including banjos and castanets, blending them with other musical traditions and styles. Many minstrel tunes — such as "O Susanna" and "Camptown Races" — remain well-known today.

minstrel shows
Popular theatrical entertainment begun around 1830 in which white actors in blackface presented comic routines that combined racist caricature and social criticism.

At least one traveling group, Gavitt's Original Ethiopian Serenaders, was actually composed of black musicians. But in the vast majority of shows, white performers used rambling lyrics and vicious stereotypes to depict African Americans as lazy, sensual, and irresponsible. Minstrel singers simultaneously criticized white society: their songs ridiculed the alleged drunkenness of Irishmen, parodied the halting English of German immigrants, denounced women's demands for political rights, and mocked the arrogance of upper-class men. Still, minstrelsy declared white supremacy most of all. The racial stereotypes of minstrelsy — which can be traced up through radio, film, television, and beyond — had an immense and enduring impact on American popular culture.

Popular Fiction and the Penny Press

Minstrelsy was not the only new form of popular consumer culture. Fostered by high literacy rates and advances in technology, publishing became one of the American city's most lucrative industries. By 1850, more than six hundred magazines were being published in the United States. Boston and Philadelphia specialized in religious devotionals, sentimental and reform literature, and magazines for the growing middle class. Most Protestant denominations communicated with followers through monthly publications, as did homeopathic doctors, leaders of the Sunday School movement, and temperance advocates. For affluent women, *Godey's Lady's Book* depicted the latest Paris fashions and offered uplifting stories, poems, and advice on wifely and motherly duties. Because they published novels in serial form, magazines became an important springboard for popular fiction. Print culture also provided a forum for newly arrived groups to assert their American identities. Jewish authors included poet Penina Moïse of Charleston, South Carolina, and Reform Rabbi Isaac Mayer Wise, editor of *The Israelite* and author of historical novels such as *The Jewish Heroine* (1855).

Print culture helped Americans navigate the chaotic, unstable world of the market economy. Advice books guided young men on how to dress and comport

A Violent Death Imagined in the Penny Press This cover of an 1843 New York almanac shows the commercial appeal of the sensational case of Mary Rogers, who is depicted here being abducted and thrown over a cliff by two sinister gentlemen. After it was discovered that Rogers, whose body was found floating in the East River, had likely died of a botched abortion, sympathy turned against the former "cigar girl." Even as the narrative of her death changed, her fate continued to suggest the risks of sexual danger and violence that faced young women in the growing cities. © Collection of the New-York Historical Society, USA/Bridgeman Images.

TEACHING STRATEGY

The illustration of the penny press indicates the lurid, sensationalist nature of its stories. As the text indicates, Edgar Allen Poe's writing emerged from this context. Students who have read his work in their English classes may be able to discuss ways that he addresses themes found in the penny press. This topic also seems ripe for comparison with contemporary "fake news," often a combination of fact and fantasy. Students comparing the pulp writing of both eras should think about differences as well as similarities between the two.

AP® FIRSTHAND ACCOUNTS

Sex Workers, Libertines, and Reformers

What caused prostitution? Under what circumstances did women (and some men, though we know little about them) take up sex work? Sources like these, from those who encountered sex workers, offer clues.

FEMALE MORAL REFORM SOCIETY OF THE CITY OF NEW YORK

First Annual Report, 1835

Inspired by the Second Great Awakening and the ideals of domesticity, the Female Moral Reform Society was an organization of middle-class women who worked to suppress sex work. In comparison with their male counterparts who also condemned prostitution these women reformers emphasized holding men accountable for sexual assault and exploitation.

SOURCE: *First Annual Report of the Female Moral Reform Society of the City of New York* (New York: William Newell, 1835), 13–14, 9–10.

WARNING TO THE COUNTRY. The Board have ascertained that there are annually brought into the larger cities from the country, a large number of young women under various pretences, but *really* for the purpose of supplying the market of sin. Some are brought in under the promise of marriage; and here, friendless and destitute, their seducers abandon them to infamy to hide their own guilt. . . .

In one portion of the city to which missionary efforts were principally directed, many of the guilty inhabitants would hide themselves on the approach of the missionaries, and some broke up their houses, and *professed* to give up their business but perhaps left, only to find another place, where they might carry on their wretched calling undisturbed by the messengers of God. . . .

There is quite as little hope in reforming "strange women," as in reforming drunkards. Indeed, they are intimately connected, for a "strange woman" is almost always a drunkard. . . . Many of the poor creatures who are its victims acknowledge that they are going to hell, and weep and tremble when compelled to look at the fact, but like the drunkard, whose mind is under the influence of beastly bodily appetites, they seem not to have the power to break the chains that bind them to their sins. Very few of those that *might* be reclaimed, *can* be induced to enter a Magdalen asylum. . . .

During the last six months, 30 females have been received into the society's house; of these, 3 have gone to [domestic] service, 4 have been sent to the asylum of the N. Y. Female Benevolent society, and one, . . . being in ill health, having partially recovered, is now taking care of herself. The others after staying some a longer and some a shorter time have returned to their sins. No one has been permitted to leave the house without being solemnly warned of the consequences, and told that she was deliberately preferring eternal misery to a life of virtue; and many, as they left would acknowledge that they believed it to be the last opportunity they might have to save their souls, and yet they would deliberately return to their haunts of vice. . . . Some pains have been taken to ascertain their history after they left the society's house, and it has been found that two or three have died sudden and awful deaths. One, within a few days, three times endeavored to drown herself.

The Sunday Flash, October 17, 1841

Published for and by libertines — men who visited brothels and flaunted respectable social norms — these underground newspapers were frequently prosecuted under obscenity statutes; to escape the law they closed down in a "flash" but often popped up under a new title. This article reports on the background of a New York sex worker.

SOURCE: *The Sunday Flash*, October 17, 1841, from *The Flash Press*, ed. Patricia Cline Cohen, Timothy J. Gilfoyle, and Helen Lefkowitz Horowitz (Chicago: University of Chicago Press, 2008), 148–150.

Amanda Green. This celebrated nymph was born in this city, . . . somewhere in the North side of town, her mother was a . . . [dress]maker. . . . Amanda was sent to school and achieved that invaluable accomplishment possessed by so few cyprians [sex workers] in this city, of being able to read. . . . By and by, she grew up, and right pretty did she grow too and many a grocer's clerk and amorous shop boy, would find his mouth water and his heart beat as she went about the neighborhood on errands, and many a liquorish old goat and salacious young one, would wear out his ineffectual leather in

themselves and how to recognize deception and fraud. Other guidebooks counseled women and men on how to choose marriage partners and manage their domestic lives, for example, by limiting family size. Despite repeated indictments for "obscenity," Massachusetts physician Charles Knowlton sold thousands of copies of *The Fruits of Philosophy* (1832), the first published American guide to contraception.

Knowlton's sales were modest in comparison with those of urban newspapers, which gained huge audiences as the cost of printing fell and entrepreneurs developed new

AP® SKILLS & PROCESSES

ANALYZING HISTORICAL EVIDENCE

Use the primary sources in the **AP® FIRSTHAND ACCOUNTS** feature to help students understand the broader implications of prostitution as it relates to American society and urbanization. Have students connect the causes of prostitution to any one of the following categories of analysis: urbanization, poverty, subjugation, or employment. Students should be aware of the immediate causes referenced in the documents as well as the broader societal causes.

AP® THEME

SOC: Social Structures

Two ideas required of students are the differences between public and private spheres. Remind students that common law traditions had long defined differences between men and women. For instance, public sphere work meant the world of economics, politics, and government whereas the private sphere connoted life at home. If students can start this section with these clear societal definitions, they may interact with the information in a way that keeps the history in the context of the nineteenth century.

following her about. . . . But Amanda had not yet felt the throb of passion in a high degree, or if she had, had the discretion to master it . . . and so she battled off the annoyance.

One [winter] evening a dress had been finished for a lady in Hudson Street and Amanda was to take it. . . . On her return home [she] was about to cross Hudson Street when the jingle of a fast approaching sleigh warned her to stand back. The person driving, seeing a pretty female on the road, stopped the sleigh and apologizing for endangering her safety begged her to allow him to drive her home as a recompense. This Amada refused and was about slipping to the other side, when the gentleman sprang out, clasped her in his arms, lifted her in, whistled to his horse and the next moment was flying along like mad; her complaints drowned by the clatter of the bells. . . . The kidnapper appeared anxious to convince Amanda of his kind intentions toward her and to that end clasped her again and again in his arms and pressed upon her unwilling (so says Amanda) lips, a thousand kisses. After the proper quantum of struggling and crying she became subdued and reposed unresistingly in his arms. . . . [At the man's house or "Chateau"], finding herself housed in a strange place, with no prospect of getting home, another fit of crying came on, but this assiduous stranger, whom we shall now call Chambers, silenced and persuaded her to drink a glass of . . . [mulled wine]. . . . A sumptuous supper followed this, and exhilarated by the share of a bottle of champagne, she submitted without further opposition to his advances. . . .

Amanda remained at the Chateau some three months, when she discovered by a letter that Chambers was unfaithful to her. . . . She left his establishment, returned to her mother, told her story and asked forgiveness. . . . For six months did Amanda lead a most exemplary life; but alas, who can control their fate! At the end of that time she fell in with a young German, and soon fell victim to his seductive arts. . . . Amanda and her paramour were . . . turned out of doors. . . . No resource was left her but open prostitution and she accordingly took to that degraded calling, has followed it two years and now remains in it, another unhappy victim sacrificed at the altar of man's brutal passions. [She is] very handsome. She resides at Mrs. Shannon's, No. 74 West Broadway.

DR. WILLIAM SANGER

History of Prostitution, 1858

Sanger, born in Virginia, moved to New York City in the 1840s and became resident physician at Blackwell's Island prison. Asked by city officials to investigate the causes of prostitution, Sanger participated in hundreds of interviews with sex workers entering the jail. Stressing economic motives for sex work, Sanger's book included charts of wages taken from the 1850 census: men in the cotton textile trade, for example, earned an average $16.79 per month, women $9.24. In this passage, Sanger comments on the surge in prostitution during the severe economic downturn of 1853.

Source: William Sanger, *History of Prostitution* (New York: Harper & Bros., 1858), 577–578.

Trade was literally dead; operatives, never too well paid, were threatened with starvation; females, particularly, felt the rigid pressure of the times. In many families the embarrassments of the fathers compelled a reduction of the servants employed, and a large number of domestics were added to the aggregate of that class already out of situations. The occupations of the army of seamstresses, dress-makers, milliners, and tailoresses were suspended. . . . But one resort seemed available; the poor workless, houseless, foodless woman must have recourse to prostitution as a means of preserving life. . . .

That female virtue was yielded in many instances cannot, unfortunately, be doubted, but the sufferers did not become public prostitutes. Poor creatures! They surrendered themselves unwillingly to some temporary acquaintance, probably in gratitude for assistance already rendered, or anticipating aid. . . . It is but charity to conclude that the woman who thus acted, if her subsequent course was not a continuous life of abandonment, was impelled by the stern necessity of the times rather than induced by a laxity of moral feeling.

QUESTIONS FOR ANALYSIS

1. What causes does each account identify for women's entry into sex work? Compare the ideas of each source.
2. Many antebellum Americans believed that when a young unmarried woman lost her virginity she was "ruined": rejected by her family and turned away from respectable occupations and marriage, she would inevitably sell her body. Would the authors of these documents agree? How might each writer have responded to the above prevailing assumptions? Explain your reasoning with evidence from each source.
3. What alternative words or euphemisms do these authors use instead of "prostitute"? What do those tell us about each author's point of view toward prostitution?

TRM Find complete suggested responses in the Teacher's Resource Materials.

models for marketing and delivery. Within two years of its first issue in 1835, the *New York Herald* sold 11,500 copies a day, the largest circulation of any American newspaper. By the 1830s, young boys in New York City hawked daily newspapers on the streets; four major **penny papers** had a combined circulation of fifty thousand, reaching many more readers as copies passed from hand to hand in tenements, workshops, and saloons.

penny papers
Sensational and popular urban newspapers that built large circulations by reporting crime and scandals.

The *Herald*'s editor was colorful and controversial James Gordon Bennett, a brilliant businessman adept at attracting advertisement dollars. Bennett pitched his paper to "the great masses of the community — the merchant, mechanic, working people." Unabashedly racist and strongly proslavery, Bennett won loyalty through his ardent support for building an "Empire in the West." The *Herald* also featured gossip, exposés, and, above all, lurid and sensational accounts of violent crime, often falsified for dramatic effect. Disgusted, Walt Whitman denounced Bennett as a "midnight ghoul, preying on rottenness and repulsive filth." Undeterred, Bennett built the *Herald* into a political force that exerted national influence by the time of the Civil War.

Fascinated by the urban underworld of crime, author Edgar Allan Poe drew on such sensational journalism to develop a new genre of popular fiction. Deserted by his father and orphaned at age three, Poe had a tumultuous relationship with the Virginia family who adopted him. He found a position at *The Southern Literary Messenger* before moving north to edit a series of gentlemen's magazines in Philadelphia and New York, quarreling all the time with owners and coworkers. Disdaining those who wrote for small literary audiences, Poe sought to represent and reach what he called "the popular mind." Despite his tormented career and early death from complications of alcoholism, Poe's dark stories of supernatural terror and secret crime, like "The Murders in the Rue Morgue," helped establish the genres of mystery and detective fiction.

CHECK FOR UNDERSTANDING

Ask students: **What were the themes of the penny press?** *Fueled by growing literacy rates, various forms of cheap literature developed in the early 1800s, some with religious themes and others offering advice. But the most prominent form was the "penny press," which offered gossip, exposés, and sensationalized tales of crime.*

CHECK FOR UNDERSTANDING

Ask students: **What new working-class cultural practices emerged in large antebellum cities, and why?** *New working-class cultural practices before the Civil War included sexual promiscuity, popular fiction, and new urban entertainments, especially theatrical shows like minstrel shows. They emerged primarily because of the increasing urbanization catalyzed by industrialization, which also increased the working man's pay, allowing him to afford such amusements.*

AFRICAN AMERICANS AND THE STRUGGLE FOR FREEDOM

What communal and political goals did free blacks pursue in this period, and how did their actions influence debates over slavery and race?

Between 1820 and 1840, in northern states that abolished slavery, free African American communities found their political voices. Chief among their goals were voting rights for black men, access to the growing network of public schools, and abolition of slavery. By the 1830s, they began to work with white allies, who like other reformers drew on the religious enthusiasm of the Second Great Awakening. After the American Revolution, white antislavery activists had assailed human bondage as contrary to republicanism and liberty, but most had called for gradual emancipation with compensation to slave owners. Three decades later, white and black abolitionists built the nation's first interracial movement for justice, demanding immediate, uncompensated emancipation: an uncompromising stance that met with fierce denunciations and violence.

Free Black Communities, South and North

AP® EXAM TIP

Recognizing the role of free black communities in the anti-slavery movement is important to know for the AP® Exam.

The free black population of the slave states lived primarily in coastal cities — Mobile, Memphis, New Orleans — and in the Upper South. Partly because skilled Europeans avoided the South, free blacks formed the backbone of the urban artisan workforce, laboring as carpenters, blacksmiths, barbers, butchers, and shopkeepers. Whatever their skills, free blacks faced many dangers. White officials often denied jury trials to free blacks accused of crimes; sometimes they forced people charged with vagrancy back into slavery. Some free blacks were simply kidnapped and sold.

Seeking opportunity and protection, some free blacks distanced themselves from plantation slaves and assimilated white culture and values. Indeed, mixed-race individuals sometimes joined the planter class. David Barland, one of twelve children born to a white Mississippi planter and his black slave Elizabeth, himself owned no

AP® APPLY THE TIP

Place students in collaborative groups to create an annotated timeline of African Americans' response to slavery from 1789 to1850. Ask students to read the "African Americans and the Struggle for Freedom" section (pp. 330–339) and choose the ten most important events that illustrate reactions to slavery in the African American community. For each event on the timeline, students should provide a brief explanation and a quick example to portray the importance of the event. As a follow-up, ask students to complete **Handout 10.2 — Causation: Free Black Communities and the Struggle for Freedom (TRM).**

TRM Find **Handout 10.2 — Causation: Free Black Communities and the Struggle for Freedom** in the Teacher's Resource Materials.

African American Worship in the South After the 1831 revolt led by enslaved preacher Nat Turner, few southern African Americans were permitted to worship by themselves without whites' presence and supervision. In this rare sketch of a South Carolina church service, published in London in 1863, the plantation owners preside over the meeting, sharing the religious message while also making sure that the preacher's words don't challenge the hierarchies of slavery. Hulton Archive/Getty Images.

fewer than eighteen slaves. But such men and women were rare. Most free African Americans identified with the great mass of slaves, some of whom were their relatives. Calls by white planters in the 1840s to re-enslave free African Americans reinforced black unity.

The Second Great Awakening profoundly reshaped black spirituality, greatly expanding the number of African Americans who embraced Christianity. Before it began, most blacks, especially in the South, continued practices brought from Africa — in some cases Islam, but more often animism. These religious traditions never fully faded. In 1842, Charles C. Jones, a Presbyterian minister in Georgia, reported disapprovingly that the enslaved men and women on his family's plantation believed in "second-sight, in apparitions, charms, and witchcraft." Fearing for their own souls if they withheld the "means of salvation" from African Americans, Jones and other zealous preachers and planters set out to convert slaves.

Black Protestant leaders, who emerged across the South in this period, also developed traditions of emotional conversion and communal spirituality. They adapted Protestantism to black needs. The optimistic theology of the Second Great Awakening had a special appeal, because African American Protestants tended to ignore the doctrines of original sin and predestination, as well as slaveholders' exhortations to be obedient and submissive. A white minister in Liberty County, Georgia, reported that when he urged slaves to obey their masters, "one half of my audience deliberately rose up and walked off." Indeed, many black converts envisioned God as the Old

AP® EXAM TIP

Compare actions of blacks in the South to those in the North in efforts to resist and end slavery.

AP® THINKING LIKE A HISTORIAN

Dance and Social Identity in Antebellum America

Styles of dance and attitudes toward them tell us a great deal about cultural and social norms. When nineteenth-century Americans had a party, their dances — regardless of the class or ethnic identity of the dancers — focused more on individual couples and allowed more room for improvisation and intimacy than the dance forms of the previous century.

1. **William Sidney Mount, *Rustic Dance After a Sleigh Ride*, 1830.** *In the eighteenth century, wealthy, fashionable Americans danced the French minuet, a ceremonious and graceful dance in which couples executed prescribed steps while barely touching. Ordinary white folks preferred the country dances brought by their ancestors from Europe, which also involved intricate steps, line formations, and limited physical contact. William Sydney Mount (1807–1868) was self-taught, lived in rural Long Island, and depicted scenes of everyday life. This painting, replete with amorous pursuits, depicts a traditional contra dance in which the lead couple advances a few steps and then sashays to the back of the line, as another couple takes its place.*

SOURCE: Museum of Fine Arts, Boston, Massachusetts, USA/Bequest of Martha C. Karolik for the M. and M. Karolik/Collection of American Paintings, 1815-65/Bridgeman Images.

2. **"The Polka Fashions," from *Godey's Lady's Book*, 1845.** *"A magazine of elegant literature," according to its publisher, Louis A. Godey, the* Lady's Book *had a wide circulation and became an arbiter of good taste among the aspiring middle classes. Each issue contained a sheet of music for the latest dance craze. The* Lady's Book *cautiously endorsed the waltz, a sensuous dance that required a close embrace, but enthusiastically welcomed its cousin, the polka, whose lively tempo and rapid spinning had a wholesome and joyful quality. Introduced from Bohemia, the polka dominated the ballrooms of America's upper and middle classes in the 1840s and 1850s.*

SOURCE: Private Collection/Bridgeman Images.

3. **George Templeton Strong, diary entry, December 23, 1845.** *Strong, an elite young New Yorker who had just joined his father's law practice, recorded his first impression of the polka in high society. (Despite his apparent dislike of the new dance, he successfully courted and married three years later, at age 28.)*

Well, last night I spent at Mrs. Mary Jones's great ball. Very splendid affair — "the Ball of the Season." . . . Two houses open, standing supper table, "dazzling array of beauty and fashion." "Polka" for the first time brought under my inspection. It's a kind of insane Tartar jig performed to disagreeable music of an uncivilized character.

Testament warrior who had liberated the Jews and who would liberate them. They saw themselves as Chosen people, marked by suffering but, like the ancient Israelites, destined for redemption.

Almost half of free blacks in the United States in 1840 (some 170,000) lived in the free states of the North. However, few enjoyed unfettered freedom. In rural

4. Description of juba dancing from Charles Dickens, *American Notes for General Circulation*, 1842. *In New York's Five Points slum in 1842, Charles Dickens described a challenge dance featuring William Henry Lane, or Master Juba, a young African American who created juba dancing, a blend of Irish jig and African dance moves.*

The corpulent black fiddler, and his friend who plays the tambourine, stamp upon the boarding of the small raised orchestra in which they sit, and play a lively measure. Five or six couples come upon the floor, marshalled by a lively young negro, who is the wit of the assembly, and the greatest dancer known. . . . Instantly the fiddler grins, and goes at it tooth and nail; there is new energy in the tambourine. . . . Single shuffle, double shuffle, cut and cross-cut; snapping his fingers, rolling his eyes, turning in his knees, presenting the backs of his legs in front, spinning about on his toes and heels like nothing but the man's fingers on the tambourine; dancing with two left legs, two right legs, two wooden legs, two wire legs, two spring legs — all sorts of legs and no legs — . . . having danced his partner off her feet, and himself too, he finishes by leaping gloriously on the bar-counter, and calling for something to drink.

5. Poster advertising Barlow, Wilson, Primrose, and West's "Mammoth Minstrels' Colored Masquerade." *Unlike slavery, minstrelsy survived the Civil War and remained popular until the early twentieth century, when it evolved into vaudeville. Barlow, Wilson, Primrose, and West's Mammoth Minstrels toured the United States, Europe, and Australia between 1877 and 1882, thrilling audiences with the clog dances that had evolved out of juba.*

Source: Private Collection/Photo © Barbara Singer/Bridgeman Images.

Sources: (3) Luther S. Harris, *Around Washington Square: An Illustrated History of Greenwich Village* (Baltimore, 2003), 41; (4) Charles Dickens, *American Notes and Pictures from Italy* (C. Scribner: New York, 1868), 107.

ANALYZING THE EVIDENCE

1. What do sources 1 and 2 suggest about the social interactions among rural folk and genteel urbanites? Compare the sources.
2. What does the polka (sources 3 and 4) reveal about changing cultural practices among the social elite? Describe patterns of change and continuity.
3. Compare the juba and minstrelsy dances (sources 4 and 5) with the polka and contra dance forms (sources 1 and 2). How do each of the images reflect broader social changes? Use examples from each dance type to explain patterns of social change.
4. The waltz, polka, and juba dances were popular during the Second Great Awakening, when (and long after) preachers often complained that "dance is destructive to Christian life." Why might ministers (and priests) take such a view? Support your claim with evidence from the chapter and sources.

AP® DBQ PRACTICE

Using these sources, along with what you have learned in this chapter, write a short essay showing what dance and other entertainments revealed about differing American social groups. Use historical reasoning to make comparisons.

areas, blacks worked as farm laborers or tenant farmers; in towns and cities, they toiled as domestic servants, laundresses, or day laborers. Only a small number owned land. "You do not see one out of a hundred . . . that can make a comfortable living, own a cow, or a horse," a traveler in New Jersey noted. In most states, law or custom prohibited northern blacks from voting or attending public schools. They

TRM Find complete suggested responses in the Teacher's Resource Materials.

AP® SKILLS & PROCESSES

ARGUMENTATION

The **AP® DBQ PRACTICE** prompt requires students to synthesize evidence from a variety of primary sources to understand the role of dance in American culture and how that connected to varying social groups. Students may need assistance in thinking about dance abstractly as a form of social communication and interaction. It might help to begin the discussion by explicitly asking students why they might have attended dances, how the structure of dances might affect the kinds of interactions people had, and how the growth of ideas about individualism and choice played a role in changing dance styles. Students might also consider how different gender roles shaped expected dance behavior. Students should be careful to illustrate trends without generalizing too much. This can be a difficult concept for students, so be sure to emphasize that trends are illustrations of factual evidence whereas a generalization is rooted less in fact and more in assumption.

AP® SKILLS & PROCESSES

COMPARISON

The **COMPARISON** question focuses on differences, but it hinges on a fundamental similarity: the existence of free blacks in both regions. Some students may need to be reminded that a free black population was a relatively new phenomenon in the early 1800s, a consequence of abolition and slave owners freeing their slaves in the wake of the Revolution. Students might also consider why free blacks in the North chose to create independent societies and churches.

TRM Find complete suggested responses in the Teacher's Resource Materials.

Free African Societies
Organizations in northern free black communities that sought to help community members and work against racial discrimination, inequality, and slavery.

African Methodist Episcopal Church
Church founded in 1816 by African Americans who were discriminated against by white Protestants. The church spread across the Northeast and Midwest.

AP® SKILLS & PROCESSES
COMPARISON
How were the lives of free African Americans different in the northern and southern states?

could testify in court against whites only in Massachusetts. The federal government did not allow African Americans to work for the postal service, claim public lands, or hold a passport. Furthermore, the Fugitive Slave Law (1793) allowed owners and hired slave catchers to seize suspected runaways and return them to bondage. As black activist Martin Delaney remarked in 1852: "We are slaves in the midst of freedom."

Confronting these deep prejudices, African American leaders in the North encouraged free blacks to "elevate" themselves through piety, education, temperance, and hard work. By securing respectability, they argued, blacks could become the social equals of whites. Some African Americans achieved great distinction. Mathematician and surveyor Benjamin Banneker published an almanac and helped lay out the new capital in the District of Columbia; Joshua Johnston won praise for his portraiture; and John Russwurm and Samuel D. Cornish of New York published the first African American newspaper, *Freedom's Journal*, in 1827.

Freedom's Journal was a signal of African Americans' determined community building across the North. Throughout the North, largely unknown men and women founded schools, mutual-benefit organizations, and fellowship groups, often called **Free African Societies**. In addition, they founded vibrant religious congregations, independent of white oversight for the first time. Ceasing to tolerate the second-class roles they were assigned in white-dominated churches, they formed their own Baptist and Methodist congregations and a new denomination, the **African Methodist Episcopal Church**. Founded in 1816, this new church spread across the Northeast and Midwest. A few AME leaders even founded congregations in the slave states of Missouri, Kentucky, Louisiana, and South Carolina.

Paul Cuffee The life of merchant Paul Cuffee (1759–1817) illustrates how African Americans who achieved business success could use their newfound prosperity for community building and political activism. Born in Massachusetts, Cuffee was the son of a freed slave and a Wampanoag Indian woman. Like his parents and nine brothers and sisters, he was a devout Quaker. Cuffee became a boatbuilder and trader along the Massachusetts coast. After working on a whaling ship, he captained a blockade-running vessel during the American Revolution and spent several months in a British prison in New York. By the 1810s, Cuffee had built a transatlantic merchant fleet crewed by black and Indian sailors. One of the wealthiest men of color in the United States, Cuffee built an interracial school for his children and those of white, black, and Native American neighbors. He also helped persuade the Massachusetts legislature to grant voting rights to black men. Library of Congress, LC-DIG-ppmsca-07615.

The Rise of Abolitionism

Free blacks' quest for respectability and equity met violent responses from whites. In Boston, Pittsburgh, and other northern cities, angry whites refused to accept African Americans as social equals. Motivated by racial contempt, white mobs terrorized black communities. White workers in northern towns laid waste to taverns and brothels where blacks and whites mixed and vandalized African American churches, temperance halls, and orphanages.

Responding to such attacks, David Walker published a stirring pamphlet, *An Appeal . . . to the Colored Citizens of the World* (1829), protesting black "wretchedness in this Republican Land of Liberty!!!!!" Walker was a free African American from North Carolina who had moved to Boston, where he sold second-hand clothes and copies of *Freedom's Journal*. Self-educated, he denounced northern discrimination as well as southern slavery, declaring that "we must and shall be free, . . . and woe, woe, will be it to you if we have to obtain our freedom by fighting." He called for global solidarity among people of African descent: "Oh! my coloured brethren, all over the world, when shall we arise from this death-like apathy? — And be men!!" Walker's call represented a radical challenge to the beliefs of white citizens, both North and South, including those who led the American Colonization Society (Chapter 9). **David Walker's *Appeal*** quickly went through three printings and, carried by black merchant sailors, reached free blacks in the South.

Nat Turner's Revolt While David Walker called for a violent rebellion, Nat Turner, a slave in Southampton County, Virginia, staged one — a chronological coincidence that had far-reaching consequences. As a child, Turner had taught himself to read and hoped for emancipation, but one master forced him into the fields, while another separated him from his wife. Becoming deeply spiritual, Turner had a religious vision in which "the Spirit" explained that "Christ had laid down the yoke he had borne for the sins of men, and that I should take it on and fight against the Serpent, for the time was fast approaching when the first should be last and the last should be first." In August 1831, Turner and a group of relatives and friends rose in rebellion and killed at least 55 white men, women, and children. Turner, apparently hoping to seize weapons from a nearby armory and take up a defensive position in the Great Dismal Swamp, hoped hundreds of slaves would rally to his cause and may have sought to coordinate with other groups of rebels across southern Virginia and northern North Carolina. His plan failed: the white militia dispersed his poorly armed force and took their revenge, which included the slaughter of many local slaves who had no role in the rebellion. One company of cavalry killed 40 blacks in two days and put fifteen of the severed heads on poles to warn "all those who should undertake a similar plot." Turner died by hanging, still identifying his mission with that of his Savior. "Was not Christ crucified?" he asked.

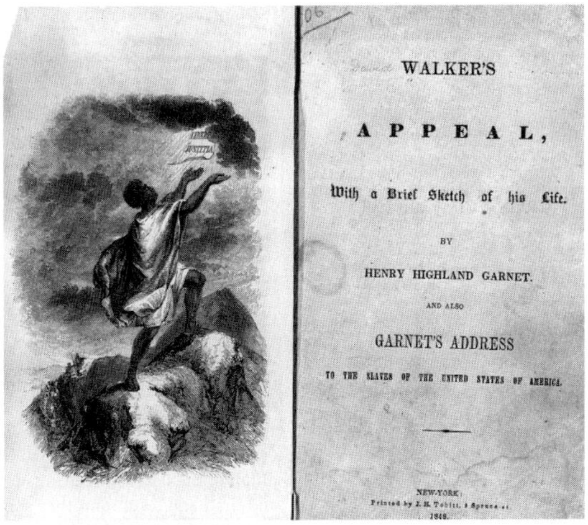

A Call for Revolution David Walker, who ran a used clothing shop in Boston, spent his hard-earned savings to publish *An Appeal . . . to the Colored Citizens of the World* (1829), a learned and passionate attack on racial slavery. Walker depicted Christ as an avenging "God of justice and of armies" and raised the banner of slave rebellion. A year later, a passerby found Walker in the doorway of his shop, dead from unknown causes. Library of Congress 3c05530.

David Walker's *Appeal*
A radical 1829 pamphlet by free African American David Walker in which he protested slavery and racial oppression, called for solidarity among people of African descent, and warned that slaves would revolt if the cause of freedom was not served.

Turner's Rebellion sowed terror among whites across the South. For a brief moment, the American Colonization Society became wildly popular, as Americans debated remedies for the violence inherent in the slave system. Deeply shaken, Virginia's legislature debated a law providing for gradual emancipation and colonization abroad. When the bill failed by a vote of 73 to 58, it closed off the possibility that southern planters would voluntarily end slavery. Instead, because of Turner's revolt, slaveholders clamped down hard, making their political and social order much harsher. Southern states toughened their slave codes, limited black movement, banned independent slave preaching, and prohibited anyone from teaching slaves to read. Any questioning of slavery met denunciation and suppression. Blaming northern "agitation" for Turner's Rebellion, the slave states met Walker's radical *Appeal* with radical measures of their own.

AP® SKILLS & PROCESSES

DEVELOPMENTS AND PROCESSES

How did the emancipation that was gradually accomplished in the North contribute to the growth of abolitionism throughout the nation?

The American Anti-Slavery Society Rejecting Turner's and Walker's strategy of armed rebellion, a small cadre of northern white Protestants launched a moral crusade to abolish the slave regime by pacifist means. If planters did not allow blacks their God-given status as free moral agents, these radicals warned, they faced eternal damnation at the hands of a just God. The most determined white advocate of **abolitionism** was William Lloyd Garrison. A Massachusetts-born printer, Garrison had worked during the 1820s in Baltimore on an antislavery newspaper, the *Genius of Universal Emancipation*. In 1830 he went to jail, convicted of libeling a New England merchant engaged in the domestic slave trade. After his release, Garrison moved to Boston and started his own weekly, *The Liberator* (1831–1865). Inspired by a bold pamphlet written by an English Quaker, Garrison demanded immediate abolition

abolitionism
The social reform movement to end slavery immediately and without compensation that began in the United States in the 1830s.

AP® THEME

POL: Politics and Power

Walker's Appeal is an example of political activism by free blacks in the early nineteenth century. As the illustration and caption indicate, Walker invoked God in his cause. The illustration shows Walker, like a new Moses on the mountaintop, receiving liberty and justice from God. Walker viewed Christ as a liberating warrior. This is a reminder that African Americans often understood Christianity in distinct ways from whites, often viewing God as a liberating and empowering force. You can find a selection from Walker's text on PBS's *Africans in America* Web site, along with many other resources for teaching about the free black community. Access this site by searching "PBS Africans in America Judgment Day."

AP® THEME

POL: Politics and Power

Nat Turner's rebellion and other rebellions by black leaders from this time are discussed on the PBS's *Africans in America* Web site, along with primary sources, historical sketches, and commentary by historians on conspiracy and rebellion. Access this site by searching "PBS Africans in America Brotherly Love."

TRM Find complete suggested responses in the Teacher's Resource Materials.

without compensation to slaveholders. "I will not retreat a single inch," he declared, "AND I WILL BE HEARD."

Garrison accused the American Colonization Society of perpetuating slavery, and he assailed the U.S. Constitution as "a covenant with death and an agreement with Hell" because it implicitly accepted racial bondage. In 1833, Garrison and sixty other religious abolitionists, black and white, established the **American Anti-Slavery Society (AA-SS)**. It won financial support from influential New York merchants and editors Arthur and Lewis Tappan. Women abolitionists established separate groups, including the Philadelphia Female Anti-Slavery Society, founded by Lucretia Mott in 1833.

American Anti-Slavery Society (AA-SS)
The first interracial social justice movement in the United States, which advocated the immediate, unconditional end of slavery on the basis of human rights, without compensation to slave masters.

These multiracial abolitionist groups were small at first, but they launched a three-pronged attack. Using new steam-powered presses to print a million pamphlets, they first carried out a "great postal campaign" in 1835, flooding the nation, including the South, with antislavery literature. More publications followed, including Theodore Weld's *The Bible Against Slavery* (1837). Two years later, Weld teamed up with the Grimké sisters — Angelina, whom he married, and Sarah, who had left their father's plantation in South Carolina, converted to Quakerism, and taken up the abolitionist cause. In *American Slavery as It Is: Testimony of a Thousand Witnesses* (1839), Weld and the Grimkés addressed a simple question: "What is the actual condition of the slaves in the United States?" Using evidence from southern newspapers and firsthand testimony, they showed slavery's inherent violence. Angelina Grimké told of a whipping house used by South Carolina slave owners: "One poor girl, [who was] sent there to be flogged, and who was accordingly stripped naked and whipped, showed me the deep gashes on her back — I might have laid my whole finger in them — large pieces of flesh had actually been cut out by the torturing lash." Filled with such images of suffering, the book sold more than one hundred thousand copies in a single year.

Abolitionists' second tactic was to aid fugitive slaves. They provided lodging and jobs for escaped blacks in free states and helped build the **Underground Railroad**, an informal network of blacks and whites who assisted fugitives. In Baltimore, a free African American sailor loaned his identification papers to future abolitionist Frederick Douglass, who used them to escape to New York. Harriet Tubman and other runaways risked re-enslavement or death by returning repeatedly to the South to help others escape. "I should fight for . . . liberty as long as my strength lasted," Tubman explained, "and when the time come for me to go, the Lord let them take me."

Underground Railroad
An informal network of whites and free blacks in the South that assisted fugitive slaves to reach freedom in the North.

A petition campaign was the final element of abolitionists' program. Between 1835 and 1838, the AA-SS bombarded Congress with nearly 500,000 signatures of citizens demanding abolition of slavery in the District of Columbia, an end to the interstate slave trade, and a ban on admission of new slave states. Along with many free blacks, thousands of deeply religious white farmers and small-town proprietors began to support these efforts. The number of local abolitionist societies grew from two hundred in 1835 to two thousand by 1840, with nearly 200,000 members. The transcendentalist thinker Emerson condemned Americans for supporting slavery, while Thoreau, viewing the U.S.-Mexico War as a naked scheme to extend slavery, refused to pay taxes and submitted to arrest. In 1848, he published "Resistance to Civil Government," a foundational text for later advocates of civil disobedience. African American minister Henry Highland Garnet went further; his *Address to the Slaves of the United States of America* (1841) urged "Resistance! Resistance!"

The Impact of Abolitionism The rhetoric of Walker and the AA-SS, combined with the shock of Turner's Rebellion, alarmed white Americans. Abolitionist agitation, ministers warned, risked "setting friend against friend" and "embittering one portion of the land against the other." Northern merchants and

CHECK FOR UNDERSTANDING

Ask students: **How did the ideology and tactics of the Garrisonian abolitionists differ from those of the American Colonization Society?** *Students need to identify differences in the beliefs and strategies of two groups that sought to end American slavery. Students might begin by considering the members of each group. Students might also explain reasons for the differences between these two groups.*

textile manufacturers supported southern planters who supplied them with cotton, as did hog farmers in Ohio, Indiana, and Illinois and pork packers in Cincinnati and Chicago who profited from lucrative sales in the South. Wealthy men feared that attacks on slave property might become an assault on all property rights. Conservative clergymen condemned the public roles assumed by abolitionist women. Northern white working men, both native-born and immigrant, feared freed blacks would work for lower wages and take their jobs. Finally, whites almost universally opposed the racial mixing and intermarriage that Garrison seemed to support by holding meetings of blacks and whites of both sexes together. Fear of interracial sex, or "amalgamation," was a bedrock argument against abolitionism and black equality. As African Americans began to organize and press for a larger civic role, white supremacist arguments emerged full force.

Racial fears and hatreds led to violent mob actions. In 1829, working-class whites in Cincinnati drove more than a thousand African Americans from the city — enforcing, through vigilantism, an 1807 law that had banned all blacks from Ohio. Four years later, an armed group of 1,500 New Yorkers stormed a church in search of Garrison and Arthur Tappan. Another white mob swept through Philadelphia's African American neighborhoods, clubbing and stoning residents and destroying homes and churches. In 1835, "gentlemen of property and standing" — lawyers, merchants, and

Mob Burning of Pennsylvania Hall After several years of struggling to find places where they could meet, reform-minded Philadelphians formed a joint-stock company and raised $40,000 to build and open Pennsylvania Hall, a place to discuss "the evils of slavery" and other questions of the day. It included a lecture hall, meeting rooms, and a bookstore. While the Hall's dedication ceremonies were taking place in May 1838, broadsides were already circulating through Philadelphia, denouncing abolitionism and women's public speaking, and calling for a violent response to protect "property" and the Constitution. Four days after the Hall opened, during a meeting of the Antislavery Convention of American Women, a mob surrounded the building and began throwing rocks through the windows. Abolitionists, such as African American Maria Chapman of Boston and Angelina Grimké Weld, continued speaking despite the attack; after finishing their meeting, the white and black women linked arms and left the building, enduring insults and blows. The mob then torched the building. For several days afterward men roamed the streets, attacking a black orphanage and church, among other targets. Even in the "City of Brotherly Love," with its many Quakers, abolitionist ideas met with violence. Library Company of Philadelphia, PA, USA/Bridgeman Images.

AP® APPLY THE TIP

To help students understand the evolving debate over slavery in the U.S., ask them to consider the differences between political, economic, and moral arguments regarding slavery. Provide students with a variety of quotes from American leaders from the Constitutional Convention through the Missouri Compromise debate and finally the debate over slavery in the 1840s and 1850s. Ask students to categorize the arguments as political, economic, or moral. Guide students into a discussion of the evolution of debates over slavery from largely political to largely moral by the 1850s. Draw a political spectrum on the board with proslavery on the right, antislavery on the left, and unconcerned in the middle. Ask students to consider how the evolution of the debate on slavery moved Americans from the middle of this spectrum to more radical positions toward the left and right.

TRM Find complete suggested responses in the Teacher's Resource Materials.

AP® EXAM TIP

Take notes comparing the debate over slavery in the 1840s–1850s to the debate that occurred over the Missouri Compromise prior to 1820.

bankers — broke up an abolitionist convention in Utica, New York. Two years later, a mob in Alton, Illinois, shot and killed Elijah P. Lovejoy, editor of the abolitionist *Alton Observer*. By pressing for emancipation and equality, abolitionists had revealed the extent of whites' race hatred.

Southern states, while passing laws for more restrictions on slaves, also banned all abolitionist writings, sermons, and lectures. Georgia's legislature offered a $5,000 reward to anyone who would kidnap Garrison and bring him to the South to be tried (or lynched) for inciting rebellion. In Nashville, vigilantes whipped a northern college student for distributing abolitionist pamphlets; in Charleston, a mob attacked the post office and destroyed sacks of abolitionist mail. After 1835, southern postmasters simply refused to deliver mail suspected to be of abolitionist origin. When abolitionists protested, President Andrew Jackson, a longtime slave owner, asked Congress to restrict use of the mail by antislavery groups. Congress refused, but in practice the federal government allowed southern postmasters to discard or burn any abolitionist mail. In 1836, the House of Representatives adopted the so-called **gag rule**. Under this informal agreement, which remained in force until 1844, the House automatically tabled abolitionist petitions, refusing even to discuss the explosive issue of slavery.

gag rule
A procedure in the House of Representatives from 1836 to 1844 by which antislavery petitions were automatically tabled when they were received so that they could not become the subject of debate.

Assailed from the outside, abolitionists also divided internally over gender issues and political strategy. Many antislavery clergymen opposed public roles for

VISUAL ACTIVITY

Fear of Interracial Sexuality, 1839 This cartoon, drawn by Edward Williams Clay and published in New York, shows how central fears of interracial sexuality were to antebellum racism. Clay made his reputation selling caricatures of African American life in Philadelphia. Library Company of Philadelphia.

READING THE IMAGE: What is happening in the picture? How does the image illustrate the artist's point of view? What is the artist's purpose in creating this image?

MAKING CONNECTIONS: The cartoon includes three mini-portraits of abolitionists, hanging above the sofa: Arthur Tappan of New York, Daniel O'Connell of Ireland, and John Quincy Adams of Massachusetts. Why did the cartoonist include these? What relationship does he imply between their work for emancipation and what is happening in the parlor? Based on your reading of the chapter, who was the intended audience of this image? Why?

women, but Garrison championed women's rights: "Our object is universal emancipation, to redeem women as well as men from a servile to an equal condition." In 1840, this issue split the movement. Women's rights advocates remained in the AA-SS, while opponents founded a new organization, the American and Foreign Anti-Slavery Society.

At the same time, dissenters from Garrison's strategy of "moral suasion" focused their energies on electoral politics. Led by key African Americans who had escaped from slavery, this group broke with Garrison and organized the **Liberty Party**, the first antislavery political party. In 1840, they nominated James G. Birney, a former Alabama slave owner, for president. Birney won few votes, but his campaign began to open the way for further electoral action against slavery. In 1844, Birney's second run for president would have a far-ranging impact (Chapter 11). Political abolitionists would, over the next two decades, transform the political system.

Liberty Party
An antislavery political party that ran its first presidential candidate in 1844, controversially challenging both the Democrats and Whigs.

AP® SKILLS & PROCESSES

CAUSATION

How and why did a radical abolitionist movement emerge in the 1830s and 1840s?

THE WOMEN'S RIGHTS MOVEMENT

Why did women gain new rights in the early nineteenth century, and how and why were these rights limited?

Controversies over abolitionist women's work reflected a broad shift in American culture. The post-Revolutionary ideal of republican motherhood (Chapter 9) recognized a limited civic role for women. By the 1830s and 1840s, religious revivals and rapid expansion of the middle class intensified Americans' emphasis on women's moral authority and capacity to inspire change. The result was **domesticity**, a set of ideals that emerged first among middle-class and elite families in the Northeast. Advocates of domesticity hailed "Woman's Sphere of Influence," celebrating women's special role as mothers and homemakers. Some even praised women's charitable efforts — as long as they didn't go too far. Almost all Americans believed married women should remain under their husbands' authority and that women should stay in the "separate sphere" of the home, away from politics. As one minister put it, women had no place in "the markets of trade, the scenes of politics and popular agitation, the courts of justice and the halls of legislation."

But women's education and reform work raised questions about these long-standing norms of marriage and family authority. At the same time, the obvious plight of working-class women — especially those in the growing cities, struggling to survive by sewing or selling their bodies — made it clear that "domesticity" was a fragile ideal, unavailable to thousands of young white women. So did slavery, with its inherent brutality and sexual exploitation of enslaved women. Were these acts of individual sin, as reformers suggested, or the workings of a patriarchal order? By the 1840s, a small group of northern women began to advocate women's equal rights.

domesticity
A middle-class ideal of "separate spheres" that celebrated women's special mission as homemakers, wives, and mothers who exercised a Christian influence on their families and communities; it excluded women from professional careers, politics, and civic life.

AP® EXAM TIP

Study the ways that expanded opportunities outside the home associated with the Second Great Awakening and Market Revolution altered the role of women in the United States.

Origins of the Women's Rights Movement

Women formed a crucial part of the Second Great Awakening and the Benevolent Empire. After 1800, more than 70 percent of the members of New England Congregational churches were female. This shift prompted Congregational ministers to end traditional gender-segregated prayer meetings, while evangelical Methodist and Baptist preachers actively promoted mixed-sex praying. "Our prayer meetings have been one of the greatest means of the conversion of souls," a minister in central New York reported in the 1820s, "especially those in which brothers and sisters have prayed together."

Far from leading to sexual promiscuity, as critics feared, mixing men and women in religious activities seems to have promoted greater self-discipline. Believing in female

AP® EXAM TIP

A helpful exercise for the AP® Exam is to trace the arguments for greater equality and opportunities for women in the early nineteenth century that ultimately would be expressed in the Seneca Falls Convention (see page 343).

CHECK FOR UNDERSTANDING

Ask students: **How did free African American communities shape American life and culture, and how did black civic leadership transform debates over slavery and race?** *Free African communities, constructed mostly outside the dominant white culture because free blacks were largely rejected by that society, caused tension in both North and South as whites refused to accept blacks as social equals. Even though some whites in the North embraced abolitionism — 10 percent by one estimate — most whites took a hard line against abolitionism as a result of African American civic leadership.*

AP® SKILLS & PROCESSES

CAUSATION

The **CAUSATION** question encourages students to consider opponents to abolition. Students will likely assume that opponents were basically southern slave owners, and should be encouraged to identify northern opponents and the reasons for their opposition. Extend this prompt by asking students to make an inference about how southern opponents might have used the democratic rhetoric of the era to bolster their critiques.

TRM Find complete suggested responses in the Teacher's Resource Materials.

virtue, young women and the men who courted them more often postponed sexual intercourse until after marriage — previously a much rarer form of self-restraint. In many New England towns, more than 30 percent of the women who married between 1750 and 1800 bore a child within eight months of their wedding day; by the 1820s, the rate had dropped to 15 percent.

As women claimed spiritual authority, men tried to curb their power. In both the North and the South, evangelical Baptist churches that had once advocated spiritual equality now prevented women from voting on church matters or offering public accounts of their faith. Testimonies by women, one layman declared, were "directly opposite to the apostolic command in [Corinthians] xiv, 34, 35, 'Let your women learn to keep silence in the churches.'" Despite such warnings, Christian women throughout the United States founded maternal associations to encourage proper child rearing. By the 1820s, popular journals, such as *Mother's Magazine*, gave women a sense of shared identity and purpose. Women undertook missionary fund-raising, Sunday School teaching, and other religious activities. The ideal of domesticity justified such work, since it celebrated women as more pious, caring, patient, and self-sacrificing than men could be. In towns and on prosperous farms in the Northeast and Midwest, women drew on domesticity to claim new roles.

TRM Find complete suggested responses in the Teacher's Resource Materials.

AP® SKILLS & PROCESSES

COMPARISON

In what ways was the idea of domesticity in the nineteenth century similar to and different from the ideal of Republican Motherhood in the eighteenth century?

Domesticity and Education Outside the South — where literacy lagged for white women and was banned altogether for enslaved women — a post-Revolutionary surge in women's education gave the rising generation tools and confidence to pursue reform. Religious activism also advanced female education, as churches sponsored academies for girls from the middling classes. Emma Willard, the first American advocate of higher education for women, opened the Middlebury Female Seminary in Vermont in 1814 and later founded girls' academies in Waterford and, famously, at Troy, New York, in 1821.

The intellectual leader of the new women educators was Catharine Beecher, whose *Treatise on Domestic Economy* (1841) advised women on how to make their homes examples of middle-class efficiency and domesticity. Though Beecher largely upheld woman's "separate sphere," she made an exception for teaching, arguing that "energetic and benevolent women" were better qualified than men to instruct the young.

By the 1820s, women educated in the nation's growing number of female seminaries and academies participated in a remarkable expansion of public education that increased women's opportunities for paid work and civic engagement. From Maine to Wisconsin, women vigorously supported the movement led by reformer Horace Mann to increase elementary schooling and improve the quality of instruction. As secretary of the Massachusetts Board of Education from 1837 to 1848, Mann lengthened the school year, established standards in key subjects, and recruited well-educated women as teachers. By the 1850s, a majority of teachers were women, both because local school boards heeded Catharine Beecher's arguments and because they discovered they could hire women at much lower wages than men. A female teacher earned $12 to $14 a month with room and board — less than a male farm laborer. But among the employments open to women, teaching became a respectable and relatively well-paid option, as well as a route into public life.

AP® THEME

ARC: American and Regional Culture

As the caption to this illustration indicates, education for girls and women was a slow process. Students should be able to connect this development with the emergence of Republican Motherhood, discussed in the previous chapter.

Women's Education Even in education-conscious New England, before 1800 few girls attended free public primary schools for more than a few years. Subsequently, as this detail from *Scenes from a Seminary for Young Ladies* (c. 1810–1820) indicates, some girls stayed in school into their teenage years and studied a wide variety of subjects, including geography. Many graduates of these female academies became teachers, a new field of employment for women. Saint Louis Art Museum, Missouri, USA/Bridgeman Images.

Moral Reform Keenly aware of the dangers around them, women in the growing cities made particularly bold efforts at reform. In 1834, middle-class women in New York City founded the **Female Moral Reform Society** and elected Lydia Finney, wife of revivalist Charles Grandison Finney, as its president. Rejecting the sexual double standard, its members demanded chaste behavior by men. Employing only women as agents, society members provided moral guidance for young female factory operatives, seamstresses, and servants. They visited brothels where they sang hymns, searched for runaway girls, and pointedly recorded the names of clients. By 1840, the society had blossomed into a national association with 555 chapters and 40,000 members throughout the North and Midwest. Many local chapters founded homes of refuge for prostitutes; in New York and Massachusetts they won passage of laws that made seduction a crime.

Female Moral Reform Society
An organization led by middle-class Christian women who viewed prostitutes as victims of male lust and sought to expose their male customers while "rescuing" sex workers and encouraging them to pursue respectable trades.

Dorothea Dix became a model for women who set out to improve public institutions. Dix's paternal grandparents were prominent Bostonians, but her father, a Methodist minister, ended up an impoverished alcoholic. Emotionally abused as a child, Dix grew into a compassionate young woman with a strong sense of moral purpose. She used money from her grandparents to set up charity schools to "rescue some of America's miserable children from vice." By 1832, she had published seven popular books, including *Conversations on Common Things* (1824), an enormously successful treatise on natural science and moral improvement.

In 1841, Dix took up a new cause. Discovering that insane women were jailed alongside male criminals, she persuaded Massachusetts lawmakers to enlarge the state hospital to house indigent mental patients. Exhilarated by that success, Dix began a national movement to establish public asylums for the mentally ill. By 1854, she had traveled more than 30,000 miles and had visited eighteen state penitentiaries, three hundred county jails, and more than five hundred almshouses and hospitals. Dix's reports and agitation prompted many states to improve their prisons and public hospitals. Like women's entry into education, Dix's career showed that ideas about women's "natural" maternalism and self-sacrifice did not necessarily confine them at home.

AP® SKILLS & PROCESSES

DEVELOPMENTS AND PROCESSES

How did the ideal of domesticity limit the lives of middle-class women, and what new opportunities did it offer?

From Antislavery to Women's Rights

Women joined the antislavery movement, in part, because they understood the special horrors of slavery for women. In her autobiography, *Incidents in the Life of a Slave Girl*, former slave Harriet Jacobs described how enslaved women were sexually coerced and raped by masters. "I cannot tell how much I suffered in the presence of these wrongs," she wrote. She reported that sexual assaults incited additional cruelty by slave owners' wives, who were enraged by their husbands' promiscuity. Jacobs and others made pointed appeals to northern women. Angelina Grimké denounced the slave system in which "women are degraded and brutalized, . . . forcibly plundered of their virtue and their offspring." "*They are our sisters*," she wrote, "and to us, as women, they have a right to look for sympathy with their sorrows, and effort and prayer for their rescue."

AP® EXAM TIP

A good exercise to prepare for the AP® Exam is to compare the arguments made for abolitionism and women's rights in the early nineteenth century.

As Garrisonian women attacked slavery, they frequently violated social taboos by speaking publicly. Maria W. Stewart, an African American abolitionist, spoke to mixed crowds in Boston in the early 1830s. Soon other women began delivering lectures condemning slavery. When Congregationalist clergymen in New England assailed Angelina and Sarah Grimké for such activism in a pastoral letter in 1837, Sarah Grimké turned to the Bible for justification: "The Lord Jesus defines the duties of his followers . . . without any reference to sex or condition," she observed. "Men and women were created equal; both are moral and accountable beings."

In a pamphlet debate with Catharine Beecher, Angelina Grimké pushed the argument beyond religion by invoking Enlightenment principles to claim equal civic rights: "It is a woman's right to have a voice in all the laws and regulations by which she is governed, whether in Church or State." By 1840, female abolitionists were asserting that traditional gender roles resulted in the domestic slavery of women. They focused particularly on the law of coverture (Chapter 4), which gave husbands all rights of property and child custody and even declared a wife's body to belong to her husband. Having acquired a public voice and political skills in the crusade for

TEACHING STRATEGY

The PBS companion site for the documentary *Not for Ourselves Alone* provides a wealth of information about famous women reformers through their own writings and speeches, biographical articles, and critical essays by noted scholars. The Web site also provides lesson plans, lists of related sites, and recommended reading. Access this site by searching "PBS Not for Ourselves Alone Seneca Falls Convention."

AP® SKILLS & PROCESSES

DEVELOPMENTS AND PROCESSES

In order to answer the **DEVELOPMENTS AND PROCESSES** question, students need to consider the conditions of women's lives preceding this period. Some students may need support in recognizing that women gained opportunities to participate in reform movements because particular issues were considered extensions of the domestic sphere.

TRM Find complete suggested responses in the Teacher's Resource Materials.

AP® APPLY THE TIP

Ask students to work with a partner to create a Venn diagram comparing the abolitionist movement and the women's rights movement in the early nineteenth century, considering similarities and differences in arguments, methods, goals, actions, and leadership. Then lead a class discussion examining how the two movements supported each other and why conflict developed.

CHECK FOR UNDERSTANDING

Ask students: **What were the origins of the women's rights movement?** *Participation and leadership in churches and benevolent organizations created during the Second Great Awakening gave women new authority. Increased opportunities for education, especially in the North, provided an informed, articulate cadre of women advocating for greater rights.*

AP® SKILLS & PROCESSES

ANALYZING HISTORICAL EVIDENCE

The **AP® AMERICA IN THE WORLD** feature places women's rights in the context of transatlantic dialogue. Just as American women were interested in British abolitionism, so French women were interested in American developments in women's rights. Students could discuss how their understanding of the women's rights movement is affected by knowing that it was part of a transatlantic phenomenon.

TRM Find complete suggested responses in the Teacher's Resource Materials.

AP AMERICA IN THE WORLD

Women's Rights in France and the United States, 1851

Europe was convulsed with political uprisings in 1848; after those protests were suppressed, the hopes of women's rights advocates were crushed. In France, Pauline Roland and Jeanne Deroine had unsuccessfully sought voting rights and an equal civil status for French women. Imprisoned for their activism, they dispatched a letter to the second national Woman's Rights Convention in the United States, which met in Worcester, Massachusetts, in 1851.

When their letter was read to the Convention, Ernestine Potowsky Rose (1810–1892) offered the following response.

PAULINE ROLAND AND JEANNE DEROINE

Letter to the Convention of the Women of America, 1851

SOURCE: *History of Woman Suffrage*, ed. Elizabeth Cady Stanton, Susan B. Anthony, and Matilda Joslyn Gage (New York: Fowler & Wells, 1887), 1: 234–242.

Dear Sisters: Your courageous declaration of Woman's Rights has resounded even to our prison and has filled our souls with inexpressible joy. In France the [conservative] reaction [to the uprising of 1848] has suppressed the cry of liberty of the women of the future. . . . The Assembly kept silence in regard to the right of one half of humanity. . . . No mention was made of the right of woman in a Constitution framed in the name of Liberty, Equality, and Fraternity. . . .

[However,] the right of woman has been recognized by the laborers and they have consecrated that right by the election of those who had claimed it in vain for both sexes. . . . It is by labor; it is by entering resolutely into the ranks of the working people that women will conquer the civil and political equality on which depends the happiness of the world. . . . Sisters of America! your socialist sisters of France are united with you in the vindication of the right of woman to civil and political equality. . . . [Only] by the union of the working classes of both sexes [can we achieve] . . . the civil and political equality of woman.

ERNESTINE ROSE

Speech to the Second Woman's Rights Convention, 1851

SOURCE: *History of Woman Suffrage*, ed. Elizabeth Cady Stanton, Susan B. Anthony, and Matilda Joslyn Gage (New York: Fowler & Wells, 1887), 1: 234–242.

After having heard the letter read from our poor incarcerated sisters of France, well might we exclaim, Alas poor France! Where is thy glory?

. . . But need we wonder that France, governed as she is by Russian and Austrian despotism, does not recognize . . . the Rights of Woman, when even here, in this far-famed land of freedom . . . woman, the mockingly so-called "better half" of man, has yet to plead for her rights. . . . In the laws of the land, she has no rights; in government she has no voice. . . . From the cradle to the grave she is subject to the power and control of man. Father, guardian, or husband, one conveys her like some piece of merchandise over to the other.

. . . Carry out the republican principle of universal suffrage, or strike it from your banners and substitute "Freedom and Power to one half of society, and Submission and Slavery to the other." Give women the elective franchise. Let married women have the same right to property that their husbands have. . . .

There is no reason against woman's elevation, but . . . prejudices. The main cause is a pernicious falsehood propagated against her being, namely that she is inferior by her nature. Inferior in what? What has man ever done that woman, under the same advantages could not do?

QUESTIONS FOR ANALYSIS

1. What strategy to achieve women's rights do Roland and Deroine advocate? What strategy can be detected in Rose's remarks? In what ways are their perspectives similar to or different from one another? Include specific examples from the source.
2. What does this French-American comparison, along with your reading of this chapter, suggest about the values of reformers who were part of the American women's rights movement?

African American freedom, thousands of northern women now advocated greater rights for themselves.

Unlike radical utopians, women's rights advocates of the 1840s did not reject the institution of marriage or conventional divisions of labor within the family. Instead, they tried to strengthen the legal rights of married women by seeking legislation that permitted them to own property (see "America in the World," p. 342). This initiative won crucial support from affluent men, who feared bankruptcy in the volatile market economy and wanted to protect family assets by putting them in their wives' names. Fathers also desired their married daughters to have property rights to shield them (and their paternal inheritances) from financially irresponsible husbands. Such motives prompted legislatures in three states — Mississippi, Maine, and Massachusetts — to enact **married women's property laws** between 1839 and 1845. Then, in 1848, women activists in New York won a comprehensive statute that gave women full legal control over any property they brought to a marriage. This law became the model for similar laws in fourteen other states.

married women's property laws
Laws enacted between 1839 and 1860 in New York and other states that permitted married women to own, inherit, and bequeath property.

In the same year of 1848, Elizabeth Cady Stanton and Lucretia Mott organized a gathering of women's rights activists in the small New York town of Seneca Falls. Seventy women and thirty men attended the **Seneca Falls Convention**, which issued a rousing manifesto extending to women the egalitarian republican ideology of the Declaration of Independence. "All men and women are created equal," the Declaration of Sentiments declared. It denounced coverture and asserted that no man had the right to tell a woman what her "sphere" should be — a decision that belonged to "her conscience and her God." The Declaration called for women's higher education, property rights, access to the professions, the opportunity to divorce, and an end to the sexual double standard. It also claimed women's "right to the elective franchise." The authors acknowledged that their struggle would be difficult, because society worked to "destroy [woman's] confidence in her own powers, to lessen her self-respect." But they called Americans to work for gender equality.

Seneca Falls Convention
The first women's rights convention in the United States. Held in Seneca Falls, New York, in 1848, it resulted in a manifesto extending to women the egalitarian republican ideology of the Declaration of Independence.

AP® EXAM TIP

The role of the Seneca Falls Convention in the expansion of women's rights is important to know on the AP® Exam.

Dress Reform Amelia Jenks Bloomer (1818–1894) wrote for her husband's newspaper in Seneca Falls, New York, until she attended the women's convention there in 1848. Afterward she founded her own biweekly newspaper, *The Lily*, focusing on temperance and women's rights. In 1851, Bloomer enthusiastically promoted — and serendipitously gave her name to — a comfortable form of women's clothing devised by another temperance activist: loose trousers gathered at the ankles topped by a short skirt. Bloomer and her allies argued that their "reform costume" allowed freer movement and more physical activity while also protecting women's health, because long skirts picked up grime from the streets. Fearing women's quest for equal dress and equal rights, humorists ridiculed the proposal. This cartoon warns radical women of the reaction they may encounter on the streets if they wear the "Bloomer costume": children jeer and thumb their noses, while a modest woman turns away. Fototeca Gilardi/Getty Images.

AP® APPLY THE TIP

Provide students with excerpts of the Declaration of Sentiments from the Seneca Falls Convention of 1848. Ask students to analyze the excerpts to identify the goals of the women's rights movement and generate a list of grievances. Once students have completed their primary source analysis, ask students to explain the ways that the authors were attempting to create a continuity argument with the ideals professed in the Declaration of Independence of 1776. Lastly, ask students to complete **Handout 10.3 — Contextualization: Seneca Falls Convention of 1848 (TRM).**

TRM Find **Handout 10.3 — Contextualization: Seneca Falls Convention of 1848** in the Teacher's Resource Materials.

TEACHING STRATEGY

This illustration provides insight into negative popular reactions toward women's rights advocates of the early nineteenth century. Guide students' analysis with the following questions:

- **How are the women depicted in this illustration?** *One woman, noted as a "modest woman" in the caption, is dressed in clothes more traditional to the time period whereas the other woman is wearing a bloomer. This is meant to have students think about the reactions people had toward women, solely based on their clothing.*
- **What does this image suggest about the fears of those who opposed women's rights?** *This image suggests that critics assumed that the subordination of women to men was part of a larger order of gendered behavior, where certain behaviors and modes of fashion were expected. Many of the fears opponents to women's rights possessed were in fact tied to their preconceived notions of femininity and masculinity. Any definitions outside of the cultural norms were often attacked.*

AP® SKILLS & PROCESSES

CONTEXTUALIZATION

Students might think about the **CONTEXTUALIZATION** question in both broad and narrower contexts. Both movements were part of the larger dynamic that stressed equality, individualism, and social perfection. More narrowly, the women's rights movement was a direct outgrowth of participation in abolitionism. Students might also weigh which movement was a more radical application of democratic notions that developed from the American Revolution and its ideology.

TRM Find complete suggested responses in the Teacher's Resource Materials.

CHECK FOR UNDERSTANDING

Ask students: **What new rights did women gain in the early nineteenth century, and which women most benefitted from these changes? What rights remained out of reach?** *Women gained a few legal rights, generally at the state level, in the early nineteenth century. In Mississippi, Maine, Massachusetts, and later New York, married women gained property rights over the property they brought to their marriages. In 1860, New York lawmakers gave women control of their own wages, their own property acquired by their trade, and to assume sole guardianship over their children if widowed. However, these were small steps. Full political equality and the vote, though advocated starting with the 1848 Seneca Falls Convention, proved illusory for a few generations.*

CHECK FOR UNDERSTANDING

Use the **AP® LEARNING FOCUS** question from the beginning of the chapter to check students' understanding of the chapter as a whole: **Why did new intellectual, religious, and social movements emerge in the early nineteenth century, and how did they change American society?** *The Market Revolution had profound changes to American culture. New popular forms of entertainment emerged, financially underwritten by an increasingly literate and wealthier working class. The Second Great Awakening (i.e., the spread of evangelical faiths) led directly to the abolitionist movement, which caused increasing sectional rift and catalyzed the women's movement that sought political representation for women.*

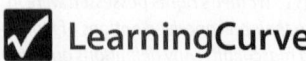

LearningCurve

Remind students to go online to complete the LearningCurve quiz for this chapter.

AP® SKILLS & PROCESSES

CONTEXTUALIZATION

What was the relationship between the abolitionist and women's rights movements?

Most Americans — both male and female — dismissed the Seneca Falls declaration as nonsense. In her diary, one small-town mother lashed out at the female reformer who "talks of her wrongs in harsh tone, who struts and strides, and thinks that she proves herself superior to the rest of her sex." Still, the women's rights movement grew. In 1850, delegates to the first national women's rights convention in Worcester, Massachusetts, called on churches to eliminate theological notions of female inferiority. Addressing state legislatures, they proposed laws to allow married women to institute lawsuits and testify in court. After 1850, the movement held national conventions each year — though few southern-born women attended. Women's rights continued to have a strong abolitionist bent. Passionate speeches by African American women, in particular, reminded convention delegates of the continued plight of women in slavery.

Legislative campaigns for women's rights required talented organizers and speakers. The most prominent was Susan B. Anthony, a Quaker who had acquired political skills in the temperance and antislavery movements. Those experiences, Anthony reflected, taught her "the great evil of woman's utter dependence on man." Joining the women's rights movement, she worked closely with Elizabeth Cady Stanton, an elite New Yorker who wrote some of the movement's most eloquent manifestos. Anthony created an activist network of political "captains," all women, who relentlessly lobbied state legislatures. In 1860, her efforts secured a New York law granting women the right to control their own wages; to own property acquired by "trade, business, labors, or services"; and, if widowed, to assume sole guardianship of their children. Genuine individual equality for women, the dream of transcendentalist Margaret Fuller, had advanced a small step closer to reality. In ways large and small, new thinkers and reform movements had altered the character of American culture.

SUMMARY

Between the 1820s and the 1840s, Americans developed new republican ideas and practices. A sweeping series of Protestant revivals, known to historians as the Second Great Awakening, inspired thousands of Americans to evangelize and reform the world. In doing so, they built movements to shelter orphans, reform prisons, combat prostitution, discourage alcohol consumption, and close businesses on the Christian Sabbath. Many of these efforts were aimed at the urban working classes, whom middle-class reformers viewed as undisciplined and sinful. Urban workers, however, often ignored reformers and built their own vibrant cultures of leisure and entertainment, including such enduring institutions as minstrel shows and the penny press.

African American communities, largely enslaved in the South but emerging from slavery in the North, developed their own vibrant Protestant traditions. Some religious leaders and reformers pushed in radical directions. Critics of the emerging market economy, ranging from pious Shakers to Fourierist socialists, founded utopian communities to experiment with different ways of organizing labor and family life. The most successful of these, Mormons, met such hostility and violence from non-Mormons that they eventually trekked west to resettle in what is now Utah. New England intellectuals, led by Ralph Waldo Emerson, articulated transcendentalism, a romantic movement that emphasized spiritual connections with nature and the individual autonomy of each human soul. Transcendentalist thinkers joined the growing movement for immediate abolition of slavery, which originated in free African American communities in the North and also found support among some white northern evangelicals and Quakers. Some whites responded to abolitionist ideas — and to African American business success and political activism — with threats and riots. But the antislavery movement survived external pressures and internal disagreements. By the 1840s, a small group of northern abolitionist women, inspired by ideals of equality and by the growth of women's education and reform activism, argued for women's rights.

CHAPTER 10 REVIEW

AP® CONTENT REVIEW
Answer these questions to demonstrate your understanding of the chapter's main ideas.

1. How did antebellum religious and intellectual movements draw on the values of individualism, on the one hand, and of communal cooperation, on the other?
2. What new cultural practices emerged in antebellum cities, and why?
3. What communal and political goals did free blacks pursue in this period, and how did their actions influence debates over slavery and race?
4. Why did women gain new rights in the early nineteenth century, and how and why were these rights limited?

AP® TERMS TO KNOW
Identify and explain the significance of each term below.

Key Concepts and Events

individualism (p. 314)
Second Great Awakening (p. 316)
Benevolent Empire (p. 318)
Maine Law (p. 318)
American Renaissance (p. 319)
romanticism (p. 319)
transcendentalism (p. 319)
utopias (p. 322)
Church of Jesus Christ of Latter-day Saints, or Mormons (p. 324)
plural marriage (p. 325)
minstrel shows (p. 327)
penny papers (p. 329)
Free African Societies (p. 334)
African Methodist Episcopal Church (p. 334)
David Walker's *Appeal* (p. 335)
abolitionism (p. 335)
American Anti-Slavery Society (AA-SS) (p. 336)
Underground Railroad (p. 336)
gag rule (p. 338)
Liberty Party (p. 339)
domesticity (p. 339)
Female Moral Reform Society (p. 341)
married women's property laws (p. 343)
Seneca Falls Convention (p. 343)

Key People

Charles Grandison Finney (p. 317)
Ralph Waldo Emerson (p. 319)
Henry David Thoreau (p. 320)
Margaret Fuller (p. 320)
Walt Whitman (p. 320)
Emily Dickinson (p. 321)
Joseph Smith (p. 324)
David Walker (p. 334)
Nat Turner (p. 335)
William Lloyd Garrison (p. 335)
Angelina and Sarah Grimké (p. 341)
Dorothea Dix (p. 341)
Susan B. Anthony (p. 344)
Elizabeth Cady Stanton (p. 343)

AP® MAKING CONNECTIONS
Recognize the larger developments and continuities within and across chapters by answering these questions.

1. How did Americans begin to define themselves, in this period, as members of the middle class or urban working class? How did each group expect men and women to behave, dress, and spend their time? What tensions and conflicts did these differences provoke? Use varied examples to compare social groups.
2. Historians often refer to the decades between 1820 and 1850 as the era of "white men's democracy." What tools and strategies did African Americans use to seek inclusion? How did women, white and black, seek inclusion as well?
3. In what ways did the era of reform (1820–1848) increase the social and cultural freedoms that existed during the Revolutionary era (1770–1820), and for whom? Do you see any ways in which such freedoms diminished? If so, how and for whom? Describe patterns of continuity and change.

KEY TURNING POINTS
Refer to the timeline at the start of the chapter for help in answering the following question.

Transformative social and political movements that arose in the United States between 1820 and 1848 included temperance, antislavery, and women's emancipation. What events in the timeline were landmark moments for each of these reform efforts? To what extent did each succeed or meet resistance to its demands, and why?

345

TRM Find complete suggested responses in the Teacher's Resource Materials.

AP® SKILLS & PROCESSES

COMPARISON

AP® CONTENT REVIEW 1 asks students to compare ways in which religious and intellectual movements were able to draw on both individual and communal aspects of reform. Note: This is a similar question to the **CHECK FOR UNDERSTANDING** prompt on p. 325.

AP® SKILLS & PROCESSES

CAUSATION

AP® CONTENT REVIEW 2 asks students to identify new cultural practices and explain what caused them. Note: This is a similar question to the **CHECK FOR UNDERSTANDING** prompt on p. 330.

AP® SKILLS & PROCESSES

CAUSATION

Use **AP® CONTENT REVIEW 3** to explore the effects of free black communities on American culture and politics. Note: This is a similar question to the **CHECK FOR UNDERSTANDING** prompt on p. 339.

AP® SKILLS & PROCESSES

CONTINUITY AND CHANGE

AP® CONTENT REVIEW 4 asks students to weigh changes in women's status against continuities in their situation. Note: This is a similar question to the **CHECK FOR UNDERSTANDING** prompt on p. 344.

TRM Find definitions for these terms in the **Glossary/Glosario** in the Teacher's Resource Materials.

AP® SKILLS & PROCESSES

COMPARISON

AP® MAKING CONNECTIONS 1 asks students to compare gender norms of middle- and working-class Americans.

AP® SKILLS & PROCESSES

CONTINUITY AND CHANGE

AP® MAKING CONNECTIONS 2 asks a question about the degree to which this particular label accurately characterizes religion in the early 1800s.

AP® SKILLS & PROCESSES

CONTINUITY AND CHANGE

AP® MAKING CONNECTIONS 3 asks students to consider continuity and change in the longer context of the period from 1770 to 1848.

AP® SKILLS & PROCESSES

CONTINUITY AND CHANGE

The **KEY TURNING POINTS** question asks students to identify and explain "landmark" events for each movement.

TRM Find complete suggested responses in the Teacher's Resource Materials.

AP PRACTICE QUESTIONS

MULTIPLE CHOICE QUESTIONS *Choose the correct answer for each question.*

Questions 1–2 refer to this excerpt.

> "What is popularly called Transcendentalism among us, is Idealism; Idealism as it appears in 1842. As thinkers, mankind have ever divided into two sects, Materialists and Idealists; the first class founding on experience, the second on consciousness; the first class beginning to think from the data of the senses, the second class perceive that the senses are not final, and say, the senses give us representations of things, but what are the things themselves, they cannot tell. The materialist insists on facts, on history, on the force of circumstances, and the animal wants of man; the idealist on the power of Thought and of Will, on inspiration, on miracle, on individual culture."
>
> Ralph Waldo Emerson, "The Transcendentalist," 1842

1. Which of the following contributed to the rise of ideas reflected in the passage during this period?
- **a.** European Romanticism
- **b.** The spread of mercantilism
- **c.** The presence of only one major political party
- **d.** Limited immigration

2. The excerpt was written primarily to
- **a.** criticize immigration policies after 1800.
- **b.** respond to the creation of the two-party political system.
- **c.** challenge traditional beliefs about American society.
- **d.** address injustices to American Indians.

Questions 3–5 refer to this excerpt.

> "Above all, [Mormonism] provided desperately desired structure for lives beset by unpredictability, disorder, and change. It gave its adherents enormous social, psychological, and economic support. In social terms, in fact, Mormonism can be seen as perhaps the most successful, dynamic, and enduring version of the communitarianism of the l830s and 1840s. It provided isolated, struggling, often desperate families like the Smiths and Youngs from economically changing or declining countryside and small towns from the Northeast and Midwest with a new kind of economic security and cooperation."
>
> Donald Scott, "Mormonism and the Mainstream," 2004

3. The excerpt describes which of the following developments in the United States at the beginning of the nineteenth century?
- **a.** Efforts to bolster the reemerging market economy
- **b.** Conflicts among Americans over slavery
- **c.** The emergence of a distinctly American style of art
- **d.** The growth of utopian movements

4. Which of the following was the most direct cause leading to the developments described by Scott in the excerpt?
- **a.** The rise of a Second Great Awakening
- **b.** Growing regional separation between North and South
- **c.** Federally funded internal improvements
- **d.** The rise of Jacksonian democracy

5. The developments described by Scott could best be used to argue that during the antebellum period in the United States
- **a.** the expansion of universal white male suffrage limited religious expression.
- **b.** many Americans advanced their ideals by working independently of government institutions.
- **c.** technological advances favored factory production methods.
- **d.** federal and local governments effectively protected religious dissenters from persecution.

Questions 6–7 refer to this lithograph.

The Drunkards Progress. From the First Glass to the Grave

Text within image reads: STEP 1. A glass with a Friend. STEP 2. A glass to keep the cold out. STEP 3. A glass too much. STEP 4. Drunk and riotous. STEP 5. The summit attained / Jolly companions / A confirmed drunkard. STEP 6. Poverty and Disease. STEP 7. Forsaken by Friends. STEP 8. Desperation and crime. STEP 9. Death by suicide. Library of Congress.

6. The most likely purpose of the artist in creating the image was to
   - **a.** promote the efforts of temperance societies to change the behavior of individuals.
   - **b.** advocate for political rights and gender equality throughout the United States.
   - **c.** support the efforts of the nativist American Party to limit Irish immigration.
   - **d.** advance the work of early labor unions seeking wage equality for working women.

7. All of the following are true of the period pictured EXCEPT
   - **a.** women's roles in social movements increased.
   - **b.** Americans engaged in voluntary organizations to reform society.
   - **c.** alcohol was prohibited by the U.S. Constitution.
   - **d.** women sought increased equality and opportunities.

SHORT ANSWER QUESTIONS

Read each question carefully and write a short response. Use evidence from the text to support your claims.

"Evangelicalism was a middle-class solution to problems . . . generated in the early stages of manufacturing. Revivals provided entrepreneurs with a means of imposing new standards of work discipline and personal comportment upon themselves and the men who worked for them, and thus they functioned as powerful social controls. . . . A significant minority of workingmen participated willingly in that process. And that, of course, is the most total and effective social control."

Paul Johnson, *A Shopkeeper's Millennium*, 1978

"[A] growing number of Americans believed that the only way to stabilize the social order was to internalize self-restraint within the depths of individual character through religion and moral reform. But the roots of reform did not lie exclusively in fear and anxiety. Reform also arose out of a millennialist sense of possibilities that was both secular and religious in its origins. . . . [A] new "middle-class" reform gospel . . . sought simultaneously to free individuals from various forms of bondage; to eradicate such 'relics of barbarism' as chattel slavery and corporal punishment; and to create a sober, educated, self-disciplined citizenry."

Steven Mintz, *Moralists and Modernizers: America's Pre-Civil War Reformers*, 1995

1. Using the two excerpts provided, answer (a), (b), and (c).
   - **a.** Briefly explain ONE major difference between Johnson's and Mintz's historical interpretations of reform in the period 1820 to 1848.
   - **b.** Briefly explain how ONE specific historical event or development in the period 1820 to 1848 that is not explicitly mentioned in the excerpts could be used to support Johnson's interpretation.
   - **c.** Briefly explain how ONE specific historical event or development in the period 1820 to 1848 that is not explicitly mentioned in the excerpts could be used to support Mintz's interpretation.

2. Answer (a), (b), and (c).
   - **a.** Briefly explain ONE specific historical change in United States society that resulted from the efforts of female reformers between 1820 and 1848.
   - **b.** Briefly explain ONE specific historical change in United States society that resulted from the efforts of abolitionist reformers between 1820 and 1848.
   - **c.** Briefly explain ONE specific historical change in United States society that resulted from the efforts of artists OR writers between 1820 and 1848.

3. Answer (a), (b), and (c).
   - **a.** Briefly explain ONE historical factor that led African Americans to increased access to freedom in northern communities in the period 1800–1848.
   - **b.** Briefly explain ONE historical factor that led to a continuity in the limitations of access to freedom in northern communities for African Americans in the period 1800–1848.
   - **c.** Briefly explain ONE historical factor that accounts for changes in the abolitionist movement in the period 1800–1848.

TRM Find complete suggested responses in the Teacher's Resource Materials.

11 CHAPTER

Imperial Ambitions

1820–1848

Chapter 11 — AP® Assessment Weight and Pacing Guide

The assessment weight on the AP® U.S. History Exam for Chapters 8–11 is 10–17 percent. This chapter falls in Unit 4 of the AP® U.S. History Curriculum, covering Period 4: 1800–1848.

This pacing guide is based on a schedule with 120 sessions of 50 minutes each before the AP® U.S. History Exam. If you have a different number of sessions before the exam, you can modify the pacing to meet your needs. If you have additional time, consider incorporating quizzes, released AP® U.S. History questions, practice exams, writing practice, and other instructional activities.

	Traditional Schedule	Block Schedule
Chapter 11	5 days	2–3 days

Daily Pacing Guide

	Focus Content	Essential Question
Day 1	The Expanding South	What were the strengths and limitations of the South's economy and social structure?
Day 2	The World of Enslaved African Americans	What resources and strategies gave African American slaves a measure of control over their lives?
Days 3 and 4	Manifest Destiny, North and South *Note: Manifest Destiny is included in Period 5: 1844–1877 of the AP® U.S. History Curriculum Framework	How did the idea of Manifest Destiny help to unite the otherwise divided interests of northerners and southerners?
Day 5	The U.S.-Mexico War, 1846–1848 *Note: The U.S.-Mexico War is included in Period 5: 1844–1877 of the AP® U.S. History Curriculum Framework	What factors sparked the U.S.-Mexico War?

AP® Alignment

Section Heading	AP* Topic	AP* Theme
The Expanding South	4.8, 4.13	PCE, GEO
The World of Enslaved African Americans	4.10, 4.11, 4.12	ARC, SOC
Manifest Destiny, North and South	5.2	GEO
The U.S.-Mexico War, 1846–1848	5.2, 5.3	GEO, WOR

*Should changes be made to the Course Framework in the future, an updated alignment will be placed on our AP® updates page at go.bfwpub.com/ap-course-updates

Chapter 11—Overview

Chapter 11 focuses on the development and divisions that occurred in the United States as it expanded to the West. The chapter opens with a focus on the South as the Cotton Kingdom expands to the West. The accentuation of the social hierarchy in the South between planters, freeholders, and freemen is examined in relationship to the growth of democracy in the U.S. In response to the growth of slavery, African Americans in both the North and South sought ways to preserve their cultural heritage through church and family as well as expand their opportunities and rights in the U.S. The chapter also focuses on the development of Manifest Destiny as both an idea and a policy of the U.S. government. Finally, the chapter examines the U.S.-Mexico War and its impact on expansionist policies of President James K. Polk.

Chapter 11 — Resources

The following resources can be found in the Teacher's Resource Materials (TRM) that accompany the book. You can access the TRM via the book's digital platform, by clicking the TRM links found here in your Teacher's Edition e-book, or by contacting your representative to access the resources online. Visit **bfwpub.com/henretta10e** to learn more.

TRM Chapter 11 Lecture Presentation Slides

TRM Chapter 11 Outline with AP® Focus

TRM Chapter 11 Lecture Strategies

TRM Chapter 11 Suggested Responses

TRM Handout 11.1 — Causation: Southern Identity

TRM Handout 11.2 — Thematic Analysis: Manifest Destiny

TRM Handout 11.3 — Contextualization: The Mexican War

Chapter 11 — Essential Activity

Organize students into collaborative groups and provide each group with a large sheet of paper. Instruct the groups to draw the outline of the United States and then to draw the Mississippi River, Great Lakes, Appalachian Mountains, and Rocky Mountains. Students should add markers and/or features to the map that would be important for understanding America's imperial ambitions in the early nineteenth century. Students can identify issues such as slavery, Cotton Kingdom, invention of cotton gin, Missouri Compromise, settlement of Texas, Louisiana Purchase, Indian Removal Act, and the Erie Canal, among others. As students work, circulate among the groups and encourage students to think of topics from earlier periods that might impact the idea of Manifest Destiny. Once students have generated their list, they should add those items to their maps and tie those items to one of the AP® Themes. (For example, if they include the Missouri Compromise, they would tie it to Politics and Power.) Then direct students to use pp. 359–374 of the text to add additional events and developments to their map to illustrate the impact of Manifest Destiny on expansion and development of the U.S. At the end of this activity, display the maps and use students' findings to lead a class discussion that focuses on the thematic understanding of Manifest Destiny.

Chapter 11 — Bell Ringers

The following activity takes no more than 5–15 minutes of your class period and offers an effective and engaging way to begin your lessons and for students to apply AP® Skills & Processes:

- Provide students with census data regarding slavery in the United States. To access this data, search "U.S. census statistics of slaves." Ask students to analyze the data provided and to use it as evidence to draw conclusions regarding the impact of expansion on slavery in the U.S. in the early nineteenth century. Discuss the conclusions and evidence used by students as well as the use of quantitative data in historical arguments.

NOTES

TEACHING STRATEGY

Help students identify the major theme of the chapter: the notion of American imperialism within the context of other imperial powers — Britain, France, Mexico, and Russia. Students may struggle to accept this idea because the U.S. has traditionally distinguished its actions from those of European empires and/or they may think of empire as taking place overseas rather than with contiguous territory. Remember, students need to move beyond simply listing factors that explain how the ideology of Manifest Destiny shaped policies and united ordinary people. Instead, encourage students to offer an analysis rooted in historical understanding. It might be helpful to introduce the question of the United States as an empire with Niall Ferguson's essay "America as Empire, Now and in the Future." This piece is definitely provocative, as Ferguson celebrates the virtue of American empire, while encouraging Americans to face up to this identity and handle it responsibly. Access Ferguson's essay by searching "The National Interest America as Empire." For a complete suggested response to the **AP® LEARNING FOCUS** question, see p. 374.

11 CHAPTER

Imperial Ambitions 1820–1848

AP® LEARNING FOCUS

Why did the ideology of Manifest Destiny unite ordinary Americans and shape U.S. policies?

Since the nation's founding in 1776, visionaries believed that it would become both a republic and an empire, predicting a glorious expansion across the continent. "It belongs of right to the United States to regulate the future destiny of North America," declared the *New-York Evening Post* in 1803. Politicians soon took up the refrain. "Our natural boundary is the Pacific Ocean," asserted Massachusetts congressman Francis Baylies in 1823. "The swelling tide of our population must and will roll on until that mighty ocean interposes its waters." Missouri senator Thomas Hart Benton concurred. "All obey the same impulse — *that of going to the West*," he wrote, "which, from the beginning of time has been the course of heavenly bodies, of the human race, and of science, civilization, and national power following in their train." Northerners and southerners alike viewed westward expansion as the durable foundation of American identity.

But in the 1820s, the United States was only one of the imperial powers vying for control of western North America. Mexico, which gained its independence from Spain in 1821, claimed a broad swath of the Southwest that stretched from Coahuila y Tejas on the Gulf coast to Alta California on the Pacific, and France, Mexico's principal creditor, had an interest in helping it to defend that claim. North of Alta California, Great Britain and the United States competed for control of a vast region known as the Oregon Country. Still farther north, Russia laid claim to a coastal strip stretching north to the arctic circle and west to the Bering Strait. And throughout these lands, Native American groups controlled access to resources. In particular, U.S. expansion directly threatened the sovereignty and independence of the Plains Indians, many of whom were formidable and well armed. Despite the confidence of politicians, U.S. control of the North American West was far from assured (Map 11.1).

President James Polk, an ardent imperialist, willingly assumed the risks associated with expansion. "I would meet the war which either England or France . . . might wage and fight until the last man," he told Secretary of State James Buchanan in 1846. Polk's aggressive expansionism sparked conflict. A war with Mexico intended to be "brief, cheap, and bloodless" became "long, costly, and sanguinary," complained Senator Benton. Polk oversaw massive territorial acquisitions — New Mexico, California, and the Oregon Country — but, in so doing, set the stage for a bitter debate over slavery.

John Gast, *American Progress* In 1845, journalist John O'Sullivan coined the term *Manifest Destiny* to describe Americans' suddenly urgent longing to extend the boundaries of the republic to the Pacific Ocean. More than a quarter century later, John Gast's *American Progress* (1872) gave visual form to that aspiration in an allegorical painting that was widely distributed through color lithographs. The goddess Liberty floats westward, holding a "School Book" in one hand and telegraph lines trailing from the other as symbols of the advance of Anglo-American civilization across the continent. Library of Congress.

TEACHING STRATEGY

This painting by John Gast is often used as a shorthand for American notions of Manifest Destiny, though students should recognize that it dates to several years after the Civil War. Use the commentary from historian Martha A. Sandweiss of Amherst College on how she uses it in her own history instruction to supplement your discussion. Access this essay by searching "Sandweiss John Gast."

AP® SKILLS & PROCESSES

CONTINUITY AND CHANGE

Use the **TIMELINE** to help students begin thinking about how the period from 1820 to 1848 could constitute a distinct historical period. It is crucial that students understand that this chapter covers exactly the same chronological period as Chapter 10, but now from the standpoint of "foreign policy," exploring the nation's expansion across the continent. Students should identify nations the U.S. had conflicts with during this period and reasons for those conflicts. Students could make inferences about how the expansion in this era related to the political and economic developments discussed in Chapters 8 and 9, as well as to the cultural trends of the previous chapter.

TEACHING STRATEGY

MAP 11.1 illustrates the notion of competing empires introduced in the chapter opener. Students should note the overlapping claims between the U.S. and Britain not just in Oregon, but in the western Great Lakes region and in upper Maine as well. Because this map represents 1821, it does not show the later dispute between the U.S. and Mexico over the Texas territory.

TIMELINE

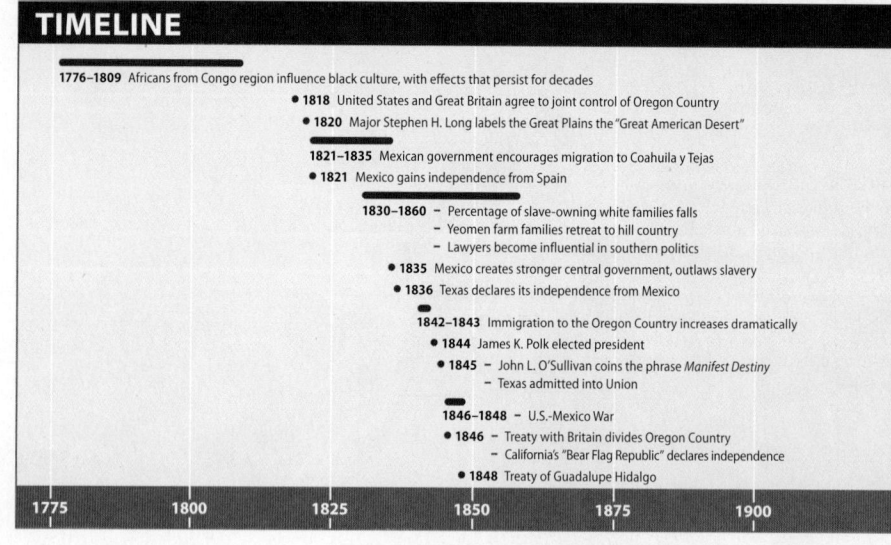

1776–1809 Africans from Congo region influence black culture, with effects that persist for decades

- **1818** United States and Great Britain agree to joint control of Oregon Country
- **1820** Major Stephen H. Long labels the Great Plains the "Great American Desert"

1821–1835 Mexican government encourages migration to Coahuila y Tejas

- **1821** Mexico gains independence from Spain

1830–1860
- Percentage of slave-owning white families falls
- Yeomen farm families retreat to hill country
- Lawyers become influential in southern politics

- **1835** Mexico creates stronger central government, outlaws slavery
- **1836** Texas declares its independence from Mexico

1842–1843 Immigration to the Oregon Country increases dramatically

- **1844** James K. Polk elected president
- **1845** – John L. O'Sullivan coins the phrase *Manifest Destiny*
  – Texas admitted into Union

1846–1848 – U.S.-Mexico War

- **1846** – Treaty with Britain divides Oregon Country
  – California's "Bear Flag Republic" declares independence
- **1848** Treaty of Guadalupe Hidalgo

1775 | 1800 | 1825 | 1850 | 1875 | 1900

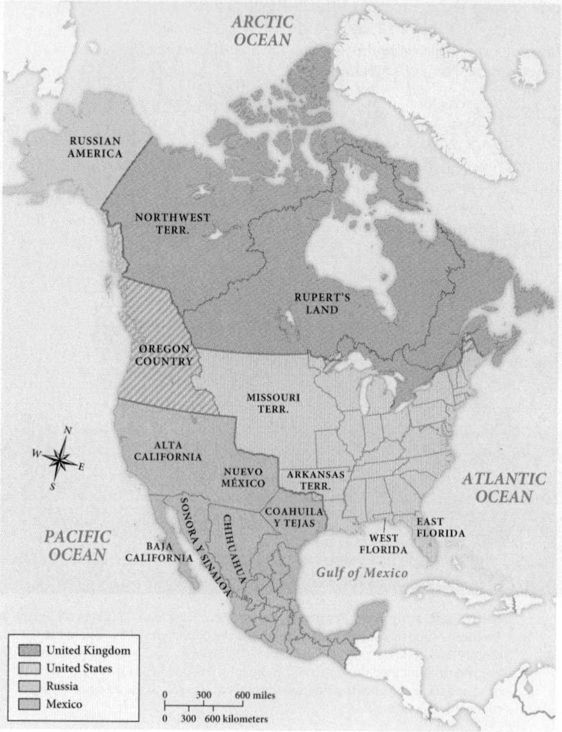

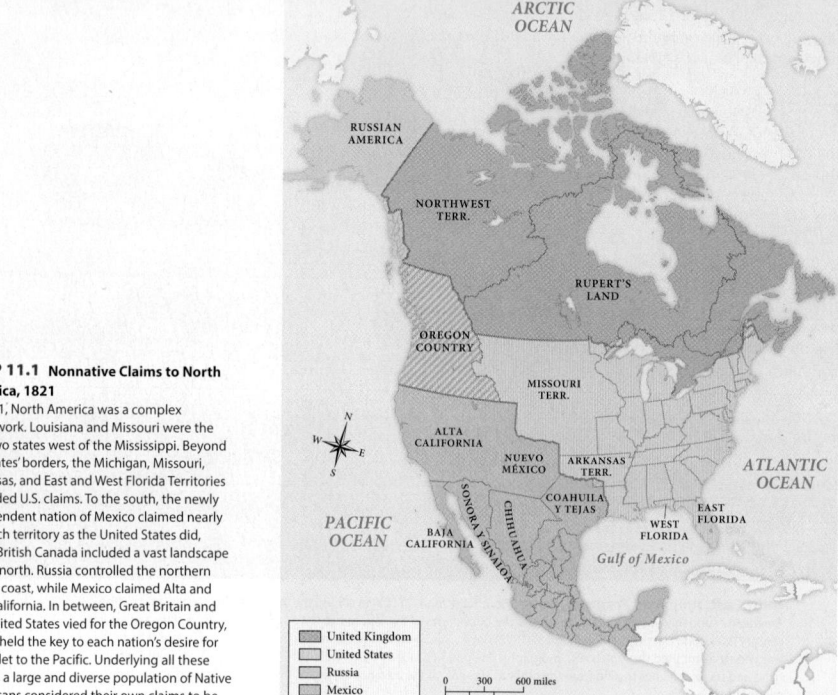

MAP 11.1 Nonnative Claims to North America, 1821
In 1821, North America was a complex patchwork. Louisiana and Missouri were the first two states west of the Mississippi. Beyond the states' borders, the Michigan, Missouri, Arkansas, and East and West Florida Territories extended U.S. claims. To the south, the newly independent nation of Mexico claimed nearly as much territory as the United States did, while British Canada included a vast landscape to the north. Russia controlled the northern Pacific coast, while Mexico claimed Alta and Baja California. In between, Great Britain and the United States vied for the Oregon Country, which held the key to each nation's desire for an outlet to the Pacific. Underlying all these claims, a large and diverse population of Native Americans considered their own claims to be sovereign.

THE EXPANDING SOUTH

What were the strengths and limitations of the South's economy and social structure?

For southerners, imperial ambitions meant territorial expansion and a commitment to the slave plantation system. With slavery's resurgence in the early nineteenth century, the social and political order of the South settled into new patterns. A small minority of planter elites came to dominate southern society, while a larger number of middling planters and aspiring slaveholders supported their ambitions. But the growing number of poor and propertyless whites separated themselves from the plantation economy by moving onto marginal lands. Southern expansionists pushed into east Texas in the 1820s, while the planters of the Cotton South who dominated state legislatures adapted their aristocratic ideals to the demands of a democratic political order.

AP® EXAM TIP

Recognizing the impact of slavery on all classes in the South is important to know on the AP® Exam.

Planters, Small Freeholders, and Poor Freemen

Although the South was a **slave society**—a society in which the institution of slavery affected all aspects of life—most white southerners did not own slaves. The percentage of white families who held blacks in bondage steadily decreased—from 36 percent in 1830, to 31 percent in 1850, to about 25 percent a decade later. However, slave ownership varied by region. In some cotton-rich counties, 40 percent of the white families owned slaves; in the hill country near the Appalachian Mountains, the proportion dropped to 10 percent.

slave society
A society in which the institution of slavery affects all aspects of life.

republican aristocracy
The Old South gentry who envisioned themselves as an American aristocracy and feared federal government interference with their slave property.

Planter Elites A privileged minority of 395,000 southern families owned slaves in 1860, their ranks divided into a strict hierarchy. The top one-fifth of these families owned twenty or more slaves. This elite—just 5 percent of the South's white population—dominated the economy, owning more than 50 percent of the entire slave population of 4 million and growing 50 percent of the South's cotton crop (Map 11.2). The average wealth of these planters was $56,000 (about $1.6 million in purchasing power today); by contrast, a prosperous southern yeoman or northern farmer owned property worth a mere $3,200.

Wealthy southerners cast themselves as a **republican aristocracy**. "The planters here are essentially what the nobility are in other countries," declared James Henry Hammond of South Carolina. "They stand at the head of society & politics . . . [and form] an aristocracy of talents, of virtue, of generosity and courage." Wealthy planters feared federal government interference with their slave property, while on the state level, they worried about populist politicians who would mobilize poorer whites.

Many southern leaders criticized the growth of middle-class democracy in the Northeast and Midwest. "Inequality is the fundamental

James Henry Hammond and Redcliffe, His South Carolina Plantation House
Hammond was an influential defender of slavery who is quoted both in this chapter and in Chapter 8. Born into a middling family, Hammond was a lawyer and newspaper editor before marrying Catherine Fitzsimmons in 1831, through whom he acquired more than 10,000 acres and 147 slaves, as well as the Redcliffe mansion. Hammond argued that slavery was the surest foundation of a republican society. He was elected to the U.S. Congress in 1834 and served as governor of South Carolina from 1842 to 1844. In 1843 his niece accused him of sexual assault, triggering rumors that hurt his political career. But in 1857 he was selected to serve in the U.S. Senate, a seat he resigned in 1860 upon the election of Abraham Lincoln as president. House: Courtesy of South Caroliniana Library, University of South Carolina, Columbia, S.C.; Portrait: Library of Congress, 26689.

AP® APPLY THE TIP

To help students better understand social class and its relationship to slavery in the South, ask them to use a close reading of the text to create a social pyramid of the South in 1850. On their pyramids, ask students to indicate percentage of population and other distinguishing characteristics of each class and to use arrows connecting different classes in the pyramid to show which way the South's classes were most mobile—up or down. Then ask students to answer the following questions:

- **How did the most elite class in the South compare to the upper class in the North?** *The elite class in the South based its power on land ownership rather than capital. Southern elites viewed themselves as an aristocracy while in the North there was less emphasis on a European-style hierarchy.*
- **How did economic power translate to political power in the South? How did political changes challenge this power?** *Land ownership was required to vote or serve in office in most of the South. Therefore, economic power was synonymous with political power; control by the planter class led to passage of laws requiring all white men to serve in militias or patrols. The popularization of universal suffrage challenged this power as it would allow small freeholders and even poor freemen to vote.*
- **How did slave ownership influence relationships in the South?** *Slave ownership distinguished classes and was encouraged by the planter class as a way to ensure protection of the system of slavery. Ownership of five or fewer slaves distinguished the small freeholder from the planter class. The former were encouraged to join the ranks of the planter class to attain political and economic power. Small freeholders and poor freemen were encouraged to see the distinctions between themselves and slaves or free blacks even when their conditions were more similar than to the planter class.*
- **How did the legal system of the South support this social class system?** *Laws were passed to regulate and control the slave population with the required assistance of the poor freeman; laws protected property inheritance and gave absolute power over slaves to slave owners.*

TEACHING STRATEGY

Have students use the picture of Hammond's house as a piece of historical context for the following question: **In what ways did slaveholders seek to create a distinctive regional identity?**

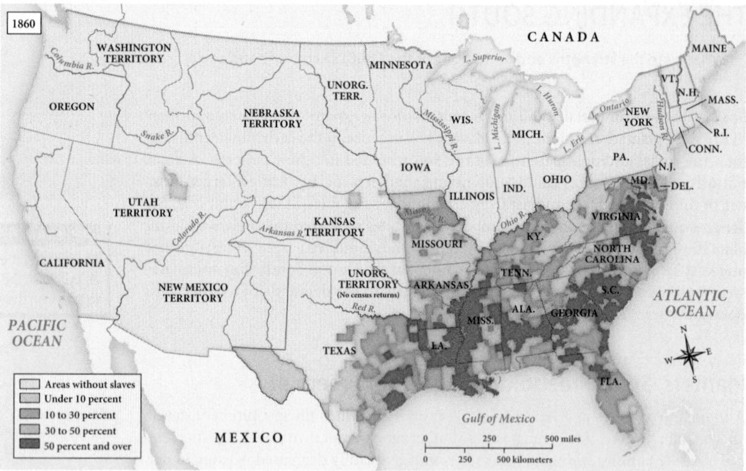

MAP 11.2 Distribution of the Slave Population in 1860
The center of the African American population shifted steadily westward, following the cotton boom. By 1860 the slave plantation system had pushed into east Texas, while the majority of blacks lived and worked along the Mississippi River and in an arc of fertile cotton lands — the "black belt" — sweeping from Mississippi through South Carolina.

AP® EXAM TIP

Identifying the political, economic, and cultural causes for the development of regional identity of the South is essential for success on the AP® Exam.

law of the universe," declared one planter. Others condemned professional politicians as "a set of demagogues" and questioned the legitimacy of universal suffrage. "Times are sadly different now to what they were when I was a boy," lamented David Gavin, a prosperous South Carolinian. Then, the "Sovereign people, alias mob" had little influence; now they vied for power with the elite. "[How can] I rejoice for a freedom," Gavin thundered, "which allows every bankrupt, swindler, thief, and scoundrel, traitor and seller of his vote to be placed on an equality with myself?"

Substantial proprietors, another fifth of the slave-owning population, held title to six to twenty bondsmen and -women. These middling planters owned almost 40 percent of the enslaved laborers and produced more than 30 percent of the cotton. Often they pursued dual careers as skilled artisans or professional men. Thus some of the fifteen slaves owned by Georgian Samuel L. Moore worked in his brick factory, while others labored on his farm. Dr. Thomas Gale used the income from his medical practice to buy a Mississippi plantation that annually produced 150 bales of cotton. In Alabama, lawyer Benjamin Fitzpatrick used his legal fees to buy ten slaves.

Like Fitzpatrick, lawyers acquired wealth by managing the affairs of the slave-owning elite, representing planters and merchants in suits for debt, and helping smallholders and tenants register their deeds and contracts. Standing at the legal crossroads of their small towns, they rose to prominence and regularly won election to public office. Less than 1 percent of the male population, lawyers made up 16 percent of the Alabama legislature in 1828 and an astounding 26 percent in 1849.

Small Freeholders Smallholding slave owners were much less visible than the wealthy grandees and the middling lawyer-planters. These planters held from one to five black laborers in bondage and owned a few hundred acres of land. Some smallholders were well-connected young men who would rise to wealth when their fathers' deaths blessed them with more land and slaves. Others were poor but ambitious men

TEACHING STRATEGY

MAP 11.2 illustrates the growth of slavery in the early nineteenth century. While the "black belt" included regions where more than half of the population was enslaved, so did the older southern states, like the Carolinas. This included the Chesapeake states, Virginia, and Maryland, which, at the turn of the nineteenth century, had been moving toward abolition.

AP® APPLY THE TIP

Ask students to complete the cause and effect relationships in **Handout 11.1 — Causation: Southern Identity (TRM)** to examine the development of Southern identity in the nineteenth century. Then lead a class discussion on the political, economic, and cultural causes that led to the creation of regional identities.

TRM Find **Handout 11.1 — Causation: Southern Identity** in the Teacher's Resource Materials.

AP® THEME

ARC: American and Regional Culture

Have students compare the emerging Free Labor society of the Northern states, which espoused a belief in social mobility, with the southern states using enslavement as the bedrock of their economy. In what ways did Free Labor entice new internal and international migrants? Why would the system of enslavement repel such a migration pattern?

trying to pull themselves up by their bootstraps, often encouraged by elite planters and proslavery advocates. "Ours is a proslavery form of Government, and the proslavery element should be increased," declared a Georgia newspaper. "We would like to see every white man at the South the owner of a family of negroes." Some aspiring planters achieved modest prosperity. A German settler reported from Alabama in 1855 that "nearly all his countrymen" who emigrated with him were slaveholders. "They were poor on their arrival in the country; but no sooner did they realize a little money than they invested it in slaves."

Bolstered by the patriarchal ideology of the planter class, middling farmers ruled with a firm hand. The male head of the household had legal authority over all the dependents — wives, children, and slaves — and, according to one South Carolina judge, the right on his property "to be as churlish as he pleases." Their wives had little power; like women in the North, under the laws of coverture, they lost their legal identity when they married. To express their concerns, many southern women joined churches, where they usually outnumbered men by a margin of two to one. Women especially welcomed the message of spiritual equality preached in evangelical Baptist and Methodist churches, and they hoped that the church community would hold their husbands to the same standards of Christian behavior to which they conformed. However, most churches supported patriarchal rule and told female members to remain in "wifely obedience" to their husbands.

Whatever their authority within the household, most southern freeholders lived and died as hardscrabble farmers. They worked alongside their slaves in the fields, struggled to make ends meet as their families grew, and moved regularly in search of opportunity. In 1847, James Buckner Barry left North Carolina with his new wife and two slaves to settle in Bosque County, Texas. There he worked part-time as an Indian fighter while his slaves toiled on a drought-ridden farm that barely kept the family in food. In South Carolina, W. J. Simpson struggled for years as a smallholding cotton planter and then gave up. He hired out one of his two slaves and went to work as an overseer on his father's farm.

Poor Freemen Less fortunate smallholders fell from the privileged ranks of the slave-owning classes. Selling their land and slaves to pay off debts, they joined the mass of propertyless tenants who farmed the estates of wealthy landlords. In 1860, in Hancock County, Georgia, there were 56 slave-owning planters and 300 propertyless white farm laborers and factory workers; in nearby Hart County, 25 percent of the white farmers were tenants. Across the South, about 40 percent of the white population worked as tenants or farm laborers. As the *Southern Cultivator* observed, they had "no legal right nor interest in the soil [and] no homes of their own."

Propertyless whites suffered the ill consequences of living in a slave society that accorded little respect to hardworking white laborers. Nor could they hope for a better life for their children, because slave owners refused to pay taxes to fund public schools. Moreover, the competitive bidding of wealthy planters drove up the price of slaves, depriving white laborers and tenants of easy access to the labor required to accumulate wealth. Finally, planter-dominated legislatures forced all white men, whether they owned slaves or not, to serve in the patrols and militias that deterred black uprisings. After touring the South, the future architect of New York's Central Park, Frederick Law Olmsted, concluded that the majority of white southerners "are poor. They . . . have little — very little — of

North Carolina Emigrants: *Poor White Folks* Completed in 1845, James Henry Beard's (1811–1893) painting depicts a family moving north to Ohio. Unlike many optimistic scenes of emigration, the picture conveys a sense of resigned despair. The family members, led by a sullen, disheveled father, pause at a water trough while their cow drinks and their dog chews a bone. The mother looks apprehensively toward the future as she cradles a child; two barefoot older children listlessly await their father's command. New York writer Charles Briggs interpreted the painting as an "eloquent sermon on Anti-Slavery . . . , the blight of Slavery has paralyzed the strong arm of the man and destroyed the spirit of the woman." Although primarily a portrait painter, Beard questioned the ethics and optimism of American culture in *Ohio Land Speculator* (1840) and *The Last Victim of the Deluge* (1849), as well as in *Poor White Folks*. Cincinnati Art Museum, Ohio, USA/Gift of the Proctor & Gamble Company/Bridgeman Images.

AP® THEME

ARC: American and Regional Culture

This painting of North Carolina emigrants provides a good opportunity to help students see beyond the stereotypes of the white South as dominated by planters. While planters did dominate the region politically, they made up only a small portion of the population compared to the individuals depicted here. It might be helpful to have students draw a social pyramid of white southerners that indicates the rough size of each group and that clearly delineates the slaveholding classes from the majority that owned no slaves. Students could also discuss why the white majority accepted slavery — directly or tacitly — when it was against their own economic interests. Additionally, to gain a sense of the southern freeholding perspective, students could read "'So Cheapened the White Man's Labor': White Artisans Contest the Labor of Black Workers, 1838," accessed online by searching "History Matters So Cheapened."

AP® SKILLS & PROCESSES

DEVELOPMENTS AND PROCESSES

Ask students to define one commonality among Planter Elite, Small Freeholders, and Poor Freeman. Students need to be able to explain how and why the system of enslavement — which economically benefitted those at the top disproportionately — was defended across classes of white southerners.

CHECK FOR UNDERSTANDING

Ask students: **How were the lives of planters, small freeholders, and poor freemen in the South different?** *Between one-third and one-fifth of planters owned slaves; the planter elite, roughly 5% of the white population, dominated the economy and owned 50% of the slaves while middling planters owned 40% of the slaves. Small freeholders owned the remaining 10% of the region's slaves, each owning between one and five. They typically worked alongside their slaves and just scraped by. The majority of the southern white population consisted of poor people, many without property. Many southern whites relocated to the hill country, beyond the reach of planter control.*

AP® SKILLS & PROCESSES

MAKING CONNECTIONS

Have students use the subheadings in this section, Planter Elite, Small Freeholders, and Poor Freemen, to structure their response. By no means is this list exhaustive, but it does give students a chance to work on making historical connections.

TRM Find complete suggested responses in the Teacher's Resource Materials.

the common comforts and consolations of civilized life. Their destitution is not material only; it is intellectual and it is moral."

Marking this moral destitution, poor whites enjoyed the psychological satisfaction that they ranked above blacks. As Alfred Iverson, a U.S. senator from Georgia, explained: a white man "walks erect in the dignity of his color and race, and feels that he is a superior being, with the more exalted powers and privileges than others." To reinforce that sense of racial superiority, planter James Henry Hammond told his poor white neighbors, "In a slave country every freeman is an aristocrat."

Rejecting that half-truth, many southern whites fled planter-dominated counties in the 1830s and sought farms in the Appalachian hill country and beyond — in western Virginia, Kentucky, Tennessee, the southern regions of Illinois and Indiana, and Missouri. Living as small farmers, they used family labor to grow foodstuffs for sustenance. To obtain cash or store credit to buy agricultural implements, cloth, shoes, salt, and other necessities, farm families sold their surplus crops, raised hogs for market sale, and — when the price of cotton rose sharply — grew a few bales. Their goals were modest: on the family level, they wanted to preserve their holdings and buy enough land to set up their children as small-scale farmers. As citizens, smallholders wanted to control their local government and elect men of their own kind to public office. But most understood that the slave-based cotton economy sentenced family farmers to a subordinate place in the social order. They could hope for a life of independence and dignity only by moving north or farther west, where labor was "free" and hard work was respected.

AP® SKILLS & PROCESSES

MAKING CONNECTIONS

What social groups made up white southern society, and how did they interact?

Great American Desert
A term coined by Major Stephen H. Long in 1820 to describe the grasslands of the southern plains from the ninety-fifth meridian west to the Rocky Mountains, which he believed was "almost wholly unfit for cultivation."

By the 1830s, settlers from the South had carried both small farming and plantation slavery into Arkansas and Missouri. Between those states and the Rocky Mountains stretched great grasslands. An army explorer, Major Stephen H. Long, thought the plains region "almost wholly unfit for cultivation" and in 1820 labeled it the **Great American Desert**. The label stuck. Americans looking for land turned south, to Mexican territory. At the same time, elite planters struggled to control state governments in the Cotton South.

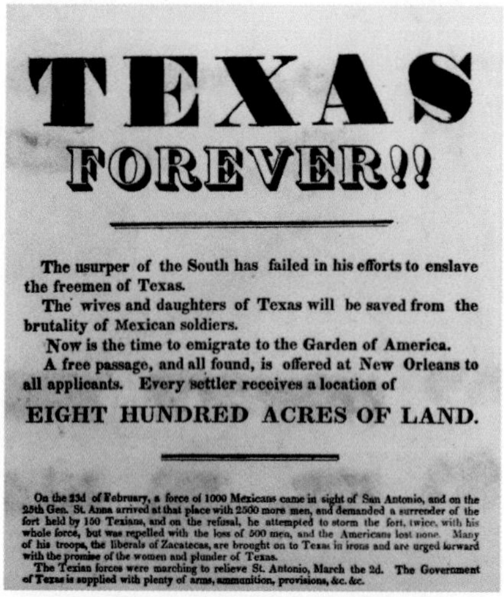

TEXAS FOREVER!!

The usurper of the South has failed in his efforts to enslave the freemen of Texas.

The wives and daughters of Texas will be saved from the brutality of Mexican soldiers.

Now is the time to emigrate to the Garden of America.

A free passage, and all found, is offered at New Orleans to all applicants. Every settler receives a location of

EIGHT HUNDRED ACRES OF LAND.

On the 23d of February, a force of 1000 Mexicans came in sight of San Antonio, and on the 25th Gen. St. Anna arrived at that place with 2500 more men, and demanded a surrender of the fort held by 150 Texians, and on the refusal, he attempted to storm the fort, twice, with his whole force, but was repelled with the loss of 500 men, and the Americans lost none. Many of his troops, the liberals of Zacatecas, are brought on to Texas in irons and are urged forward with the promise of the women and plunder of Texas.

The Texian forces were marching to relieve St. Antonio, March the 2d. The Government of Texas is supplied with plenty of arms, ammunition, provisions, &c. &c.

Texas Forever! After gaining its independence from Mexico in 1836, the independent republic of Texas aggressively recruited additional settlers from the United States. This broadside proclaims that Santa Anna — the "usurper of the South" — failed in his effort to enslave the Texans. "Now is the time," it urges, "to emigrate to the Garden of America." Anyone applying in New Orleans is promised free passage and eight hundred acres of land. The Granger Collection, New York.

The Settlement of Texas

After winning independence from Spain in 1821, the Mexican government pursued an activist settlement policy. To encourage migration to the newly reconfigured state of Coahuila y Tejas, it offered sizable land grants both to its own citizens and to American emigrants. Moses Austin, an American land speculator, settled smallholding farmers on his large grant, and his son, Stephen F. Austin, acquired even more land — some 180,000 acres — which he sold to newcomers. By 1835, about 27,000 white Americans and their 3,000 African American slaves were raising cotton and cattle in the well-watered plains and hills of eastern and central Texas. They far outnumbered the 3,000 Mexican residents, who lived primarily near the southwestern Texas towns of Goliad and San Antonio.

When Mexico in 1835 adopted a new constitution creating a stronger central government and dissolving state legislatures, the Americans split into two groups. The "war party," led by Sam Houston and recent migrants from Georgia, demanded independence for Texas. Members of the "peace party," led by Stephen Austin, negotiated with the central government in Mexico City for greater political autonomy. They believed Texas could flourish within a decentralized Mexican republic, a "federal" constitutional system favored by the Liberal Party in Mexico (and advocated in the United States by Jacksonian Democrats). Austin won significant concessions for the Texans, including an exemption from a law ending slavery, but in 1835 Mexico's president, General Antonio López de Santa Anna, nullified them. Santa Anna wanted to impose national authority throughout Mexico. Fearing central control, the war party provoked a rebellion that most of the American settlers ultimately supported. On March 2, 1836, the American rebels proclaimed the independence of Texas and adopted a constitution legalizing slavery.

To put down the rebellion, President Santa Anna led an army that wiped out the Texan garrison defending the **Alamo** in San Antonio and then captured Goliad, executing about 350 prisoners of war (Map 11.3). Santa Anna thought that he had crushed the rebellion, but New Orleans and New York newspapers romanticized the deaths at the Alamo of folk heroes Davy Crockett and Jim Bowie. Drawing on anti-Catholic sentiment aroused by Irish immigration and the massacre at Goliad, they urged Americans to "Remember the Alamo" and depicted the Mexicans as tyrannical butchers in the service of the pope. American adventurers, lured by offers of land grants, flocked to Texas to join the rebel forces. Commanded by General Sam Houston, the Texans routed Santa Anna's overconfident army in the Battle of San Jacinto in April 1836, winning de facto independence. The Mexican government refused to recognize the Texas Republic but, for the moment, did not seek to conquer it.

The Texans voted for annexation by the United States, but President Martin Van Buren refused to bring the issue before Congress. As a Texas diplomat reported, the cautious Van Buren and other party politicians feared that annexation would spark a war with Mexico and, beyond that, a "desperate death-struggle . . . between the North and the South [over the extension of slavery]; a struggle involving the probability of a dissolution of the Union."

AP® SKILLS & PROCESSES

DEVELOPMENTS AND PROCESSES

What issues divided the Mexican government and the Americans in Texas, and what proposals sought to resolve them?

Alamo
The 1836 defeat by the Mexican army of the Texan garrison defending the Alamo in San Antonio. Newspapers urged Americans to "Remember the Alamo," and American adventurers, lured by offers of land grants, flocked to Texas to join the rebel forces.

The Politics of Democracy

As national leaders refused admission to Texas, elite planters faced political challenges in the Cotton South. Unlike the planter-aristocrats who ruled the colonial world, they lived in a republican society with a democratic ethos. For example, the Alabama Constitution of 1819 granted suffrage to all white men; it also provided for a **secret ballot** (rather than voice voting); apportionment of legislative seats based on population; and the election of county supervisors, sheriffs, and clerks of court. Given these democratic provisions, political factions in Alabama had to compete for votes. When a Whig newspaper sarcastically asked whether the state's policies should "be governed and controlled by the whim and caprice of the majority of the people," Democrats hailed the power of the common folk. They called on "Farmers, Mechanics, laboring men" to repudiate Whig "aristocrats . . . the soft handed and soft headed gentry."

secret ballot
Form of voting that allows the voter to enter a choice privately rather than making a public declaration for a candidate.

Taxation Policy Whatever the electioneering rhetoric, most Whig and Democrat political candidates were men of means. Alabama is a good example of this pattern. In the early 1840s, nearly 90 percent of Alabama's legislators owned slaves, testimony to the political power of the slave-owning minority. Still, relatively few lawmakers — only about 10 percent — were rich planters, a group voters by and large distrusted. "A rich man cannot sympathize with the poor," declared one candidate. Consequently, the majority of state and county officials in the Cotton South came from the ranks of middle-level planters and planter-lawyers. Astute politicians, they refrained from laying "oppressive" taxes on the people, particularly the white majority who owned no slaves. Between 1830 and 1860, the Alabama legislature obtained about 70 percent of the state's revenue from

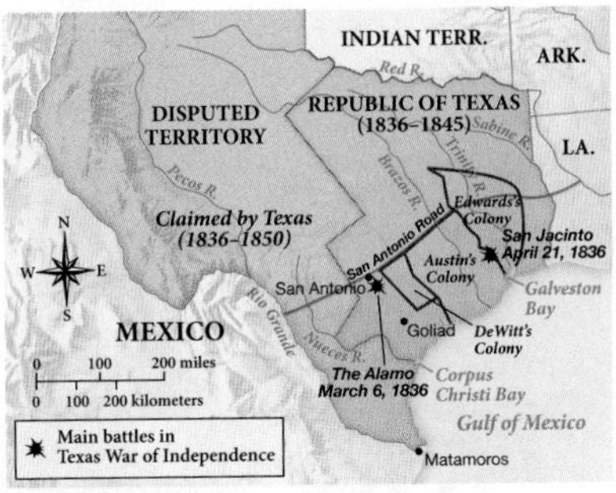

MAP 11.3 American Settlements, Texas War of Independence, and Boundary Disputes
During the 1820s the Mexican government encouraged Americans to settle in the sparsely populated state of Coahuila y Tejas. By 1835 the nearly 30,000 Americans far outnumbered Mexican residents. To put down an American-led revolt, General Santa Anna led 6,000 soldiers into Tejas in 1836. After overwhelming the rebels at the Alamo in March, Santa Anna set out to capture the Texas Provisional Government, which had fled to Galveston. But the Texans' victory at San Jacinto in April ended the war and secured de facto independence for the Republic of Texas (1836–1845). However, the annexation of Texas to the United States sparked a war with Mexico in 1846, and the state's boundaries remained in dispute until the Compromise of 1850.

AP® SKILLS & PROCESSES

DEVELOPMENTS AND PROCESSES

The **DEVELOPMENTS AND PROCESSES** question invites students to compare the Mexican government's perspective on conflicts with Texans and the Texans' own views. Partly because of the well-known story of the Alamo, students may be prone to sympathize with the Texans and could be encouraged to consider specific reasons why the Mexican government felt aggrieved. Extend this prompt by asking students to discuss ways the mythology about Texas has shaped Americans' understanding of events in Texas between the 1820s and 1840s.

TRM Find complete suggested responses in the Teacher's Resource Materials.

CHECK FOR UNDERSTANDING

Ask students: **How did Texas become part of the United States?** *The government of Mexico invited Americans to settle in remote northern regions of the country, under the condition that they accept Mexican laws and Catholicism. After rebelling against Mexico, Texans formed an independent republic for nearly a decade before agreeing to be annexed to the United States.*

AP® SKILLS & PROCESSES

DEVELOPMENTS AND PROCESSES

If Manifest Destiny was an ideology that united many Americans, ask students to determine what foreign policy issues divided Whigs and Democrats from 1840–1850. Many of the differences will be slight and motivated by political exigencies. This is an opportunity to illustrate some nuance to American foreign policy during this period. Remind students that basic, foundational knowledge is needed before they can develop nuance.

taxes on slaves and land. Another 10 to 15 percent came from levies on carriages, gold watches, and other luxury goods and on the capital invested in banks, transportation companies, and manufacturing enterprises.

To win the votes of taxpaying slave owners, Alabama Democrats advocated limited government and low taxes. They attacked their Whig opponents for favoring higher taxes and for providing government subsidies for banks, canals, railroads, and other internal improvements. "Voting against appropriations is the safe and popular side," one Democratic legislator declared, and his colleagues agreed; until the 1850s, they rejected most of the bills that would have granted subsidies to transportation companies or banks.

If tax policy in Alabama had a democratic thrust, elsewhere in the South it did not. In some states, wealthy planters used their political muscle to exempt slave property from taxation. Or they shifted the burden to backcountry freeholders, who owned low-quality pasturelands, by taxing farms according to acreage rather than value. Planter-legislators also spared themselves the cost of building fences around their fields by requiring small farmers to "fence in" their livestock. And, during the 1850s, wealthy legislators throughout the South belatedly pursued state-funded internal improvements, using public funds to subsidize the canals and railroads in which they had invested, while ignoring the protests of yeoman-backed legislators.

The Paradox of Southern Prosperity Even without these internal improvements, the South had a strong economy. Indeed, it ranked fourth in the world in 1860, with a per capita income among whites higher than that of France and Germany. As a contributor to a Georgia newspaper argued in the 1850s, planters and yeomen should not complain about "tariffs, and merchants, and manufacturers" because "the most highly prosperous people now on earth, are to be found in these very [slave] States." Such arguments tell only part of the story. Nearly all African Americans — 40 percent of the population — lived in dire and permanent poverty. And, although the average southern white man was 80 percent richer than the average northerner in 1860, the southerner's *nonslave* wealth was only 60 percent of the northern average. Moreover, the wealth of the industrializing Northeast was increasing at a faster pace than that of the South. Between 1820 and 1860, the trans-Atlantic trade in goods produced by slave labor declined from 12.6 percent of world trade to 5.3 percent.

Influential southerners steadfastly defended their agricultural society, where urbanization and economic diversification developed so slowly in comparison with the north. "We have no cities — we don't want them," boasted U.S. senator Louis Wigfall of Texas in 1861. "We want no manufactures: we desire no trading, no mechanical or manufacturing classes. . . . As long as we have our rice, our sugar, our tobacco, and our cotton, we can command wealth to purchase all we want." So wealthy southerners continued to buy land and slaves, a strategy that neglected investments in the great technological innovations of the nineteenth century — water- and steam-powered factories, machine tools, steel plows, and crushed-gravel roads — that would have raised the South's productivity and wealth.

Rise of the Cotton South By the 1830s, much of the economic energy of the southern states was devoted to cotton agriculture. This painting by William Henry Brown, entitled *Hauling the Whole Week's Picking* (c. 1842), depicts an enslaved worker driving a team of oxen pulling a wagon full of processed cotton. The scene is peaceful, even idyllic, yet the patched clothing and bare feet suggest the poverty of most laboring people in the rural south. The Historic New Orleans Collection/Bridgeman Images.

Urban growth, the key to prosperity in Europe and the North, occurred primarily in the commercial cities around the periphery of the South that specialized in shipping the region's agricultural goods: New Orleans, St. Louis, and

Baltimore. Factories — often staffed by slave labor — appeared primarily in the Chesapeake region, which had a diverse agricultural economy and a surplus of enslaved workers. Within the Cotton South, wealthy planters invested in railroads primarily to grow and sell more cotton; when the Western & Atlantic Railroad reached the Georgia upcountry, the cotton crop there quickly doubled. Cotton and agriculture remained king.

Slavery also deterred Europeans from migrating to the South, because they feared competition from bound labor. Their absence deprived the region of skilled artisans and of hardworking laborers to drain swamps, dig canals, smelt iron, and work on railroads. When entrepreneurs tried to hire slaves for these dangerous tasks, planters replied that "a negro's life is too valuable to be risked." Slave owners also feared that hiring out would make their slaves too independent. As a planter told Frederick Law Olmsted, such workers "had too much liberty . . . and got a habit of roaming about and taking care of themselves."

Thus, despite its increasing size and booming exports, the South remained an economic colony: Great Britain and the North bought its staple crops and provided its manufactures, financial services, and shipping facilities. In 1860, some 84 percent of southerners — more than double the percentage in the northern states — still worked in agriculture, and southern factories turned out only 10 percent of the nation's manufactures. The South's fixation on an "exclusive and exhausting" system of cotton monoculture and slave labor filled South Carolina textile entrepreneur William Gregg with "dark forebodings": "It has produced us such an abundant supply of all the luxuries and elegances of life, with so little exertion on our part, that we have become enervated, unfitted for other and more laborious pursuits."

AP® SKILLS & PROCESSES

CAUSATION

How did the political power of slave owners affect tax policy and economic development in the southern states?

THE WORLD OF ENSLAVED AFRICAN AMERICANS

What resources and strategies gave African American slaves a measure of control over their lives?

By the 1820s, the cultural life of most slaves reflected both the values and customs of their West African ancestors and their long subjection to the laws and culture of the slaveholding South. With the rise of cotton agriculture, the working lives of enslaved African Americans became increasingly regimented and demanding. In response, some slaves tried to escape their owners' plantations or rose up in rebellion, but most remained in their slave communities, negotiating for small accommodations and freedoms that would give them more control over their lives.

AP® EXAM TIP

It's important to know the efforts of free and enslaved blacks to maintain cultural identity as well as thrive in American society.

Forging Families and Communities

In the rural South, African American culture became increasingly homogeneous during the first half of the nineteenth century. Even in South Carolina — a major point of entry for imported slaves — only 20 percent of the black residents in 1820 had been born in Africa. The domestic slave trade mingled blacks from many states, erased regional differences, and prompted the emergence of a core culture in the Lower Mississippi Valley. A prime example was the fate of the **Gullah dialect**, which combined words from English and a variety of African languages in an African grammatical structure. Spoken by blacks in the Carolina low country well into the twentieth century, Gullah did not take root on the cotton plantations of Alabama and Mississippi. There, slaves from Carolina were far outnumbered by migrants from the Chesapeake, who spoke black English. Like Gullah, black English used double negatives and other African grammatical forms, but it consisted primarily of English words rendered with West African pronunciation (for example, with *th* pronounced as *d* — "de preacher").

Gullah dialect
A Creole language that combined English and African words in an African grammatical structure. It remained widespread in the South Carolina and Georgia low country throughout the nineteenth century and is still spoken in a modified form today.

AP® SKILLS & PROCESSES

CAUSATION

The **CAUSATION** question asks students to consider the effects of slave owners' power on the nature of taxation. Some students may be surprised that southerners were subjected to taxes beyond the excise taxes and tariffs described in previous chapters. They should begin by identifying the particular types of taxes levied and then determine the uses of those taxes. Students could also identify the ways that tax policy not only stunted economic development in the South but also exacerbated class hierarchies.

TRM Find complete suggested responses in the Teacher's Resource Materials.

AP® APPLY THE TIP

To help students understand the importance of African American cultural responses to slavery, ask them to brainstorm ways that cultural expression can be seen in their own lives by identifying what is most important for defining their values and beliefs. Students will likely respond with comments about their family, neighborhood, community, religious group, and possibly jobs. Ask students to consider the challenges slaves would face in protecting and defining their cultural values and beliefs in the U.S. in the early nineteenth century. Have students closely read pp. 355–359. Then lead a class discussion that focuses students' attention on the importance of religion and church, communities and families, and "work" in African American culture.

VISUAL ACTIVITY

Black Kitchen Ball In this 1838 painting, *Kitchen Ball at White Sulphur Springs Virginia*, African American slaves dance to the music of a fiddle and a fife (on the right). These men and women were not field hands, but the household slaves of well-to-do plantation families vacationing at a mountain resort. Note the light complexions and Europeanized features of the most prominent figures, the result of either racial mixing or the cultural perspective of the artist. The painter, Christian Mayr, was born in Germany in 1805 and migrated to the United States in 1833. After working for years as a traveling portrait painter, Mayr settled in New York City in 1845 and died there in 1850. DeAgostini/Getty Images.

READING THE IMAGE: Look closely at the figures in this painting. Why do you think the couple in the center of the painting is dressed in white?

MAKING CONNECTIONS: These enslaved workers accompanied their owners on a trip to Sulphur Springs, Virginia, an exclusive resort community. How does the artist's choice of this topic illustrate his point of view regarding slavery? What is the artist's purpose in creating this image? Who was the intended audience for this image? Why?

TRM Find complete suggested responses in the Teacher's Resource Materials.

Nonetheless, African influences remained significant. At least one-third of the slaves who entered the United States between 1776 and 1809 came from the Congo region of West-Central Africa, and they brought their cultures with them. As traveler Isaac Holmes reported in 1821: "In Louisiana, and the state of Mississippi, the slaves . . . dance for several hours during Sunday afternoon. The general movement is in what they call the Congo dance." Similar descriptions of blacks who "danced the Congo and sang a purely African song to the accompaniment of . . . a drum" appeared as late as 1890.

African Americans also continued to respect African incest taboos by shunning marriages between cousins. On the Good Hope Plantation in South Carolina, nearly half of the slave children born between 1800 and 1857 were related by blood to one another; yet when they married, only one of every forty-one unions took place between cousins. White planters were not the source of this taboo: cousin marriages were frequent among the 440 South Carolina men and women who owned at least one hundred slaves in 1860, in part because such unions kept wealth within an extended family.

Unlike white marriages, slave unions were not legally binding. According to a Louisiana judge, "slaves have no legal capacity to assent to any contract . . . because slaves are deprived of all civil rights." Nonetheless, many African Americans took marriage vows before Christian ministers or publicly marked their union in ceremonies that included the West African custom of jumping over a broomstick together. Once married, newly arrived young people in the Cotton South often chose older people in their new communities as fictive "aunts" and "uncles." The slave trade had destroyed their family but not their family values.

The creation of fictive kinship ties was part of a community-building process, a partial substitute for the family ties that sustained whites during periods of crisis. Naming children was another. Recently imported slaves frequently gave their children African names. Males born on Friday, for example, were often called Cuffee — the name of that day in several West African languages. Many American-born parents chose names of British origin, but they usually named sons after fathers, uncles, or grandfathers and daughters after grandmothers. Those transported to the Cotton South often named their children for relatives left behind. Like incest rules and marriage rituals, this intergenerational sharing of names evoked memories of a lost world and bolstered kin ties in the new one.

AP® SKILLS & PROCESSES

CONTEXTUALIZATION

How did African cultural practices affect the lives of enslaved African Americans?

Working Lives

During the Revolutionary era, blacks in the rice-growing lowlands of South Carolina successfully asserted the right to labor by the "task." Under the **task system**, workers had to complete a precisely defined job each day — for example, digging up a quarter-acre of land, hoeing half an acre, or pounding seven mortars of rice. By working hard, many finished their tasks by early afternoon, a Methodist preacher reported, and had "the rest of the day for themselves, which they spend in working their own private fields . . . planting rice, corn, potatoes, tobacco &c. for their own use and profit."

task system A system of labor common in the rice-growing regions of South Carolina in which a slave was assigned a daily task to complete and was allowed to do as he wished upon its completion.

Slaves on sugar and cotton plantations led more regimented lives, thanks to the gang-labor system. As one field hand put it, there was "no time off [between] de change of de seasons. . . . Dey was allus clearin' mo' lan' or sump'. " Many slaves faced bans on growing crops on their own. "It gives an excuse for trading," explained one owner, and that encouraged roaming and independence. Still, many masters hired out surplus workers as teamsters, drovers, steamboat workers, turpentine gatherers, and railroad builders; in 1856, no fewer than 435 hired slaves laid track for the Virginia & Tennessee Railroad. Many owners regretted the result. As an overseer remarked about a slave named John, "He is not as good a hand as he was before he went to Alabamy."

The planters' greatest fear was that enslaved African Americans — a majority of

Antebellum Slave Quarters During the colonial period, owners often housed their slaves by gender in communal barracks. In the nineteenth century, slaves usually lived in family units in separate cabins. The slave huts on this South Carolina plantation were sturdily built but had few windows. Inside, they were sparsely furnished. From The New York Public Library.

CHECK FOR UNDERSTANDING

Ask students: **How did blacks in the rural South forge families and communities?** *They maintained some West African customs, like the taboo against cousin marriage. They formalized marriages by taking vows before ministers or celebrating ceremonies that included broom-jumping. Marriages were tenuous since they were not legally binding. Slaves created fictive kinship groups, calling unrelated people "uncle" and "aunt," to substitute for the destruction of their own blood families.*

TRM Find complete suggested responses in the Teacher's Resource Materials.

TEACHING STRATEGY

Use Johann Blozius's text entitled, "As Much Land as They Can Handle," to explain the task system from the perspective of a contemporary. Access this text by searching "Johann Blozius As Much Land as They Can Handle."

AP® THEME

SOC: Social Structures

As the caption to this photo indicates, housing arrangements in the early nineteenth century shifted toward family units. This change facilitated slaves' efforts to maintain a sense of kinship and reflects the results of their ability to "negotiate rights" with masters over time. This concession should not be exaggerated, however, as family life remained tenuous. Spouses and children could always be sold to distant plantations. The photo also suggests the meagerness of slaves' material circumstances.

AP® APPLY THE TIP

It may help to define the different regions of the South for students. For instance, some scholars use terms such as the Upper South, Lower South, and Border South to distinguish between regions of the South. Maryland, Delaware, Kentucky, and Missouri are often sometimes referred to as the Border South. Virginia, Tennessee, North Carolina, and Arkansas are sometimes referred to as the Upper South. South Carolina, Florida, Georgia, Mississippi, Alabama, Louisiana, and Texas are sometimes referred to as the Lower South.

AP® EXAM TIP

Compare the experiences of enslaved Africans in different regions of the South.

the population in most cotton-growing counties — would rise in rebellion. Legally speaking, owners had virtually unlimited power over their slaves. "The power of the master must be absolute," intoned Justice Thomas Ruffin of the North Carolina Supreme Court in 1829. But absolute power required brutal coercion, and only hardened or sadistic masters had the stomach for such violence. "These poor negroes, receiving none of the fruits of their labor, do not love work," explained one woman who worked her own farm; "if we had slaves, we should have to . . . beat them to make use of them."

Moreover, passive resistance by African Americans seriously limited their owners' power. Slaves slowed the pace of work by feigning illness and losing or breaking tools. One Maryland slave, faced with transport to Mississippi and separation from his wife, flatly refused "to accompany my people, or to be exchanged or sold," his owner reported. Masters ignored such feelings at their peril. A slave (or a relative) might retaliate by setting fire to the master's house and barns, poisoning his food, or destroying his crops. Fear of resistance, as well as critical scrutiny by abolitionists, prompted many masters to reduce their reliance on the lash and use positive incentives such as food and special privileges. Noted Frederick Law Olmsted: "Men of sense have discovered that it was better to offer them rewards than to whip them." Nonetheless, owners could always resort to violence, and countless masters regularly asserted their power by demanding sex from their female slaves. As ex-slave Bethany Veney lamented in her autobiography, from "the unbridled lust of the slave-owner . . . the law holds . . . no protecting arm" over black women.

Contesting the Boundaries of Slavery

German Coast uprising
The largest slave revolt in nineteenth-century North America, it began on January 8, 1811, on Louisiana sugar plantations and involved more than two hundred enslaved workers. About ninety-five slaves were killed in the fighting or executed as a result of their involvement.

Slavery remained an exploitative system grounded in fear and coercion. Over the decades, hundreds of individual slaves responded by attacking their masters and overseers. But only a few blacks — among them Gabriel and Martin Prosser (1800) and Nat Turner (1831) (see Chapter 10, "Nat Turner's Revolt") — plotted mass uprisings. The largest nineteenth-century rebellion, the **German Coast uprising**, illustrates the futility of these efforts. Settled by German immigrants who were recruited to French Louisiana in the 1720s, by the early nineteenth century the German Coast was home to wealthy sugar plantations on the east bank of the Mississippi River about 30 miles upriver from New Orleans. The uprising began on January 8, 1811, and ultimately mobilized at least two hundred enslaved people, who marched toward New Orleans. But they were poorly armed and eventually turned back in hopes of finding refuge. After two days, militia forces had hunted them down and killed more than three dozen of the rebels. The rest were captured. Some were summarily executed, others were tried and then shot or hanged, while the remainder were returned to their owners, who imposed their own punishments. In all, about ninety-five enslaved people lost their lives. The participants were mostly young, unskilled men; more than three-quarters of the enslaved people on the plantations involved chose not to participate. Like most slaves throughout the South, they recognized that revolt would be futile. The tasks of planning, organizing, and assembling weapons for such an action were all but impossible under the constraints of slavery. Whites, by contrast, were readily mobilized, well armed, and determined to maintain their position of racial superiority.

Negro Abraham, Seminole Warrior
Born into slavery in Georgia, Abraham joined the British army in Pensacola during the War of 1812 and was freed for his service. He subsequently fought in the First Seminole War, earning the name Sauanaffe Tustunnagee (Suwanee Warrior). An adopted member of the Seminole nation, he served as an influential advisor and translator in their dealings with U.S. representatives. Everett Collection Historical/Alamy Stock Photo.

Escape was equally problematic. Blacks in the Upper South could flee to the North, but only by leaving their families and kin. Slaves in the Lower South escaped to sparsely settled regions of Florida, where some intermarried with the Seminole Indians. Elsewhere in the South, escaped slaves eked out a meager existence in inhospitable marshy areas or mountain valleys. Consequently, most African Americans remained on plantations; as Frederick Douglass put it, they were "pegged down to one single spot, and must take root there or die."

"Taking root" meant building the best possible lives for themselves. Over time, enslaved African Americans pressed their owners for a greater share of the product of their labor, much like unionized workers in the North were doing. Thus slaves insisted on getting paid for "overwork" and on the right to cultivate a garden and sell its produce. "De menfolks tend to de gardens round dey own house," recalled a Louisiana slave. "Dey raise some cotton and sell it to massa and git li'l money dat way." Enslaved women raised poultry and sold chickens and eggs. An Alabama slave remembered buying "Sunday clothes with dat money, sech as hats and pants and shoes and dresses." By the 1850s, thousands of African Americans were reaping the small rewards of this underground economy, and some accumulated sizable property. Enslaved Georgia carpenter Alexander Steele owned four horses, a mule, a silver watch, two cows, a wagon, and large quantities of fodder, hay, and corn.

Whatever their material circumstances, few slaves accepted the legitimacy of their status. Although he was fed well and never whipped, a former slave told an English traveler, "I was cruelly treated because I was kept in slavery." In an address to a white audience on the Fourth of July, the escaped slave and abolitionist Frederick Douglass asked, "What, to the American slave, is your Fourth of July? I answer: a day that reveals to him, more than all other days in the year, the gross injustice and cruelty to which he is the constant victim."

AP® SKILLS & PROCESSES

MAKING CONNECTIONS

Identify five responses that enslaved people could make to the demands placed upon them. What were the benefits and limitations of each?

MANIFEST DESTINY, NORTH AND SOUTH

How did the idea of Manifest Destiny help to unite the otherwise divided interests of northerners and southerners?

The institution of slavery cast a pall over national politics. The Missouri crisis of 1819–1821 (see Chapter 9, "The Missouri Crisis, 1819-1821") frightened the nation's leaders. For the next two decades, the professional politicians who ran the Second Party System avoided policies, such as the annexation of the slaveholding Republic of Texas, that would prompt regional strife. Then, during the 1840s, many citizens embraced an ideology of expansion and proclaimed a God-given duty to extend American republicanism to the Pacific Ocean. But whose republican institutions: the hierarchical slave system of the South or the more egalitarian, reform-minded, capitalist-managed society of the North and Midwest? Or both? Ultimately, the failure to find a political solution to this question would rip the nation apart.

AP® EXAM TIP

Trace the expansion of slavery that follows the geographic expansion of the U.S. associated with Manifest Destiny.

The Push to the Pacific

As expansionists developed continental ambitions, the term ***Manifest Destiny*** captured those dreams. John L. O'Sullivan, editor of the *Democratic Review*, coined the phrase in 1845: "Our manifest destiny is to overspread the continent allotted by Providence for the free development of our yearly multiplying millions." Underlying the rhetoric of Manifest Destiny was a sense of Anglo-American cultural and racial superiority: the "inferior" peoples who lived in the Far West — Native Americans and Mexicans — would be subjected to American dominion, taught republicanism, and converted to Protestantism.

Manifest Destiny
A term coined by John L. O'Sullivan in 1845 to express the idea that Euro-Americans were fated by God to settle the North American continent from the Atlantic to the Pacific Ocean.

Oregon Long before American politicians became interested in the Far West, however, the region was enmeshed in trade systems that connected Pacific coast settlements with Asia, Europe, and eastern North America (see "Thinking Like a Historian," p. 360). Russian traders made contact with Aleut and Tlingit communities in Alaska in the late eighteenth century and developed a lucrative trade in sea otter pelts, which was controlled after 1799 by the Russian-American Company. British explorer

AP® EXAM TIP

Recognizing the role of Manifest Destiny in the development of American identity and of the United States as a global presence is important to know on the AP® Exam.

AP® THEME

NAT: American and National Identity; WOR: America in the World

This text introduces the important notion of Manifest Destiny, which rested on a belief in the superiority of American institutions. This ideology compelled the U.S. to expand westward to the Pacific. Though attention is typically focused exclusively on the continent of North America, part of the motivation for acquiring California stemmed from the desire for its strategic natural ports that would facilitate expansion of trade with Asia, particularly China. Use the essay "Expansionism and Imperialism" by historian James Hietala to provide further details about Manifest Destiny. Access this essay by searching "PBS Expansionism and Imperialism."

TRM Find complete suggested responses in the Teacher's Resource Materials.

AP® APPLY THE TIP

Provide students with an outline map that indicates territorial expansion of the U.S. through 1853. Ask them to label each territorial area on the map using pp. 352–353 and 359–365 in the text. Students should annotate their maps with details related to the growth and expansion of slavery, note the debates or conflicts that developed related to slavery in each territory, and indicate areas that emancipated slaves over the period of territorial expansion. For example, students could identify the Louisiana Purchase in connection with Jefferson's goal of providing land for expansion of agriculture, including plantation/slave-based agriculture. Use students' maps to lead a class discussion on the relationship between slavery and Western expansion in American history.

AP® APPLY THE TIP

Project the painting *American Progress* by John Gast or direct students to p. 347. Circle or point out specific figures and elements in the painting. Ask students to identify each and to explain why Gast included each element in the painting to help establish historical context. Then ask students to answer the following questions:

- **What is the artist's point of view regarding Manifest Destiny?** *The use of the image of Columbia and the glorification of technology show that the artist supports Manifest Destiny.*
- **How does this painting illustrate changes impacting the U.S. in the early nineteenth century?** *The painting illustrates the spread of canals, railroads, telegraph, farm machinery, steamboats, etc.*
- **What is the artist's purpose in producing this work?** *Answers may vary, but should reference to popularize Manifest Destiny; to justify removal of Native Americans; to encourage people to move west; to glorify technological development of the U.S.*
- **How would this painting look different if it were drawn from a Native American perspective?** *Answers will vary — Columbia (or a different figure) would look menacing or evil; Native Americans would be shown fighting to defend territory; land in the West would be shown in light rather than dark; evils of industrialization such as pollution, crime, overcrowding would be illustrated, etc.*

Follow up this discussion by asking students to complete **Handout 11.2 — Thematic Analysis: Manifest Destiny (TRM)**.

TRM Find **Handout 11.2 — Thematic Analysis: Manifest Destiny** in the Teacher's Resource Materials.

AP® SKILLS & PROCESSES

ANALYZING HISTORICAL EVIDENCE

The primary sources in the **AP® THINKING LIKE A HISTORIAN** provide students with a diverse set of primary sources from which to gather information and analyze a question about larger historical processes. Because this question asks students to think about the perspectives of American Indians, Europeans, and Americans, remind students of the necessity of thinking in advance about these perspectives before they read the sources. Working through the source title can be a good way to promote efficacy among students as they work through each document.

AP® SKILLS & PROCESSES

DEVELOPMENTS AND PROCESSES

Have students use the map on p. 362 to familiarize themselves on the geography of the area in question. Ask students the following warm-up questions: What physical land features would make this a challenging area for settlers? How does this area compare with the land in Texas? The goal is for student to brainstorm about the area before they begin reading the documents.

AP® THINKING LIKE A HISTORIAN

Claiming the Oregon Country

When U.S. interest in the Oregon Country picked up in the 1840s, the dense population of Native Americans in the vicinity of the Puget Sound had been trading and interacting with Europeans for more than half a century. These documents illustrate this history of contact, trade, and occupation.

1. **A sailor on Captain Cook's voyage assesses trade prospects, 1778.** *John Ledyard marveled at the abundance of furbearing mammals at Nootka Sound.*

The light in which this country will appear most to advantage respects the variety of its animals, and the richness of their furr. They have foxes, sables, hares, marmosets, ermines, weazles, bears, wolves, deer, moose, dogs, otters, beavers, and a species of weazle called the glutton; the skin of this animal was sold at Kamchalka, a Russian factory on the Asiatic coast[,] for sixty rubles which is near 12 guineas, and had it been sold in China it would have been worth 30 guineas. We purchased while here about 1500 beaver [sea otter], besides other skins. . . . [S]kins which did not cost the purchaser sixpence sterling sold in China for 100 dollars. Neither did we purchase a quarter part of the beaver and other furrskins we might have done, . . . had we known of meeting the opportunity of disposing of them to such an astonishing profit.

2. **A Russian explorer describes the Tlingit potlatch ceremony, 1834.** *Fyodor Litke, a Russian sailor connected to the Russian-American company, described the role of potlatches, festivals in which wealthy residents gave away belongings, in Tlingit society.*

Koloshi [Tlingit] are the great lovers of feasts. . . . There was no shortage of pretexts for this: new alliances, new acquaintances, peace and war, any notable event, commemoration of relatives and friends—everything is a reason for these [festivals. They] . . . are of two kinds: *domestic*, occurring several times annually between only the closest neighbors, and *public*, in which acquaintances and prominent persons from remote places are invited.

The first are in fall, when food is laid up for winter. The . . . elder of the clan entertains his neighbors for several days, during the course of which they eat and dance without stop, alternating between them; finally, the host endows the guests with animal skins, fine leather, blankets, and the like; and together with the whole company moves to another [elder], then a third, and so on, during which they know how to proportion with great delicacy the number and quality of gifts in order that the preponderance was not too great in any individual's favor.

Public [potlatches] are not given by families, rather by the whole tribe; at them those invited from distant places remain for more than a month. . . . They endow the arriving guests everywhere in proportion to the dignity of each and with the more or less true hope of obtaining from him an equal gift in time.

3. **Interior of a Chinook Indian lodge, 1844.** *This engraving is based on a drawing by Alfred Thomas Agate, a member of the United States Exploring Expedition, 1838–1842.*

Source: Library of Congress.

4. **Hudson's Bay Company official describes Chinook communities on the Columbia River, 1824.** *John McLoughlin penned this description of indigenous life near Fort Vancouver, in what is today southern Washington.*

The population on the banks of the Columbia River is much greater than in any other part of North America that I have visited as from the upper Lake to the Coast it may be said that the shores are actually lined with Indian Lodges; this I account for by the River affording an abundant provision at little trouble for a great part of the year [as] the whole of the Interior population flock to its banks at the Fishing Season. . . . The population is divided into a great variety of tribes or bands speaking different Languages and are generally on Friendly terms with each other as it rarely happens that they have Serious differences or form themselves into War parties.

360

5. **American ethnologist visits Fort Vancouver, 1841.** *This account by Horatio Hale of the pidgin language (or Jargon) spoken at Fort Vancouver highlights the region's far-flung trading ties, which had even brought laborers from the Hawaiian Islands to the Oregon Country.*

The place at which the Jargon is most in use is Fort Vancouver. At this establishment five languages are spoken by about five hundred persons, — namely, the English, the Canadian French, the Tshinuk [Chinook], the Cree or Knisteneau, and the Hawaiian. . . . Cree is the language spoken in the families of many officers and men belonging to the Hudson's Bay Company, who have married half-breed wives at the posts east of the Rocky Mountains. The Hawaiian is in use among about a hundred natives of the Sandwich [Hawaiian] Islands who are employed as labourers about the fort. Besides these five languages there are many others . . . which are daily heard from natives who visit the fort for the purpose of trading. Among all these individuals there are very few who understand more than two languages and many who speak only their own. The general communication is therefore, maintained chiefly by means of the Jargon. . . . There are Canadians and half-breeds married to Chinook women, who can only converse with their wives in this speech, — and it is the fact, strange as it may seem, that many young children are growing up to whom this factitious language is really the mother tongue, and who speak it with more readiness and perfection than any other.

6. **U.S. migrant to the Oregon Country reflects on the region's destiny, 1847.** *J. Henry Brown emigrated as a teenager from Illinois to the Oregon Country. He later wrote an autobiographical account of his experience.*

About the middle [?] of October, 1847, we arrived in Salem, thus finishing our long-journey of over 2000 miles across the American continent. . . .

The Americans came here to make permanent homes, they expected to build a State, by the slow action of numbers, year by year as they should come across the plains. [They expected] to work, make homes by the labor of their hands, live in peace, rear their families in the pursuits of industry and care of stock; — erect school houses, foster education, live under a government not contaminated with slavery and burdened with heavy taxes. . . . They were the Pilgrim fathers of the Pacific coast. . . . They . . . were chosen to fill one of the destinies of nations, to accomplish the grandest achievements of modern emigration of any nation. The advance guard of civilization to the western shore, to wrest a beautiful country from barbarism; the country was ripe, the time had come . . . that it should be occupied by a better people, one who would cultivate the soil and establish intercourse with the Asiatic world. . . . Even the heavy population of natives that settled the Willamette Valley and adjacent districts had mostly disappeared through the instrumentality of "great sick" or some kind of plague.

SOURCES: (1) John Ledyard, "A Journal of Captain Cook's Last Voyage," in *The Last Voyage of Captain Cook: The Collected Writings of John Ledyard* ed. James Zug (Washington, DC: National Geographic Adventure Classics, 2005), 46; (2) F. P. Litke, *Puteshestvie vokrug sveta, sovershennoe . . . na voennom shliupe "Senvanin" v 1826, 1827, 1828 I 1829 godakh* . . . [Voyage around the World, Conducted . . . in the Naval Sloop *Siniavin* in 1826, 1827, 1828, and 1829 . . .] Pt. I. St. Petersburg: Tipografia III Otdeleniia sobstvennoi e.i.v. Kantseliarii [Printing House of the 3rd Division of His Imperial Majesty's Own Chancellory], 1834, 164–165, quoted in Andrei Val'Terovich Grinev, *The Tlingit Indians in Russian America, 1741–1867*, trans. Richard L. Bland and Katerina G. Solovjova (Lincoln: University of Nebraska Press, 2005), 46; (4) John McLoughlin to Edward Ermatinger, February 1, 1836 [from Fort Vancouver], in T. C. Elliott, "Letters of Dr. John McLoughin," *The Quarterly of the Oregon Historical Society* 23 (December 1922), 368; (5) Horatio Hale, *United States Exploring Expedition During the Years 1838, 1839, 1840, 1841, 1842, Under the Command of Charles Wilkes*, Volume 6: Ethnography and Philology (Philadelphia: Lea and Blanchard), 644; (6) J. Henry Brown, *J. Henry Brown* (Oregon, 1938), Library of Congress, U.S. Work Projects Administration, Federal Writers' Project: Folklore Project, Life Histories, 1936–1939.

ANALYZING THE EVIDENCE

1. John Ledyard (source 1) catalogs the abundance of furbearing animals he saw. Use evidence from the source to explain why he considered them to be noteworthy?
2. Consider the descriptions and image of Native American life in the Oregon Country (sources 2, 3, and 4). How would you describe their way of life, based on this evidence?
3. With Horatio Hale's description of the community surrounding Fort Vancouver (source 5) in mind, how did an economy based on cross-cultural trade affect the society and culture of its participants?
4. How did J. Henry Brown (source 6) envision the society of overland emigrants to Oregon, and what was his view of the Native American populations he hoped to displace? Based on the descriptions in the earlier sources, what do you think Brown was correct about, and where was he mistaken? Describe relevant examples form the sources.

AP® DBQ PRACTICE

Using these sources, along with what you have learned in this chapter, write a short essay that compares the values of and assumptions about the societies of Native American, European, and U.S. occupants of the Oregon Territory from 1778 to 1847.

TRM Find complete suggested responses in the Teacher's Resource Materials.

AP® SKILLS & PROCESSES

ARGUMENT DEVELOPMENT

The **AP® DBQ PRACTICE** prompt asks students to compare both the values and assumptions about society among Europeans, Americans, and Native Americans in the Oregon Territory. Students may want to begin by defining the values and assumptions. Have students create a t-chart that breaks down the values and assumptions among Europeans, Americans, and Native Americans. Students will likely need help understanding the periodization of this question, given its breadth. Help students to remember the big picture of the historical question and encourage them to categorize the documents according to the elements of the question before they begin. For instance, Source 4 offers a useful description of what migrants learned about how Natives used the environment to create a stable society.

TEACHING STRATEGY

Guide students' analysis of **MAP 11.4** with the following questions:

- **What features formed the boundaries of the territory disputed between the U.S. and Britain?** *The Pacific Ocean in the west, the Continental Divide of the Rocky Mountains in the east, and Russian claims to Alaska in the north.*
- **Why does the 1846 border not continue westward all the way to the Pacific?** *The British wanted to keep possession of Vancouver Island in its entirety, including Fort Victoria at its southern tip.*
- **How successful was the U.S. in resolving this dispute?** *The U.S. gave up claim to the majority of the land in dispute with Britain. The U.S. did retain a portion of its claim, including a significant natural harbor in Portland without resorting to war.*

AP® THEME

GEO: Geography and the Environment; MIG: Migration and Settlement

Although "the ground along the river was little more than cleared dirt," as the caption indicates, the scale of settlement depicted in this image can be connected to how the environment shaped early settlements. Many features of settled communities are already apparent along the Willamette, including a church and several sites of economic production.

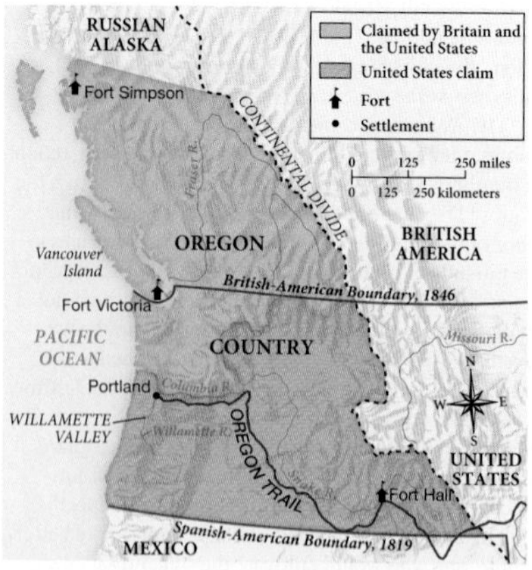

MAP 11.4 Territorial Conflict in Oregon, 1819–1846
As thousands of American settlers poured into the Oregon Country in the early 1840s, British authorities tried to keep them south of the Columbia River. However, the migrants — and fervent expansionists — asserted that Americans could settle anywhere in the territory, raising the prospect of armed conflict. In 1846, British and American diplomats resolved the dispute by dividing most of the region at the forty-ninth parallel while giving both nations access to fine harbors (Vancouver and Seattle) through the Strait of Juan de Fuca.

***Oregon City on the Willamette River*, 1850–1852** Americans quickly populated the Far West and re-created there the small-town life of the eastern states. This painting by John Mix Stanley, completed in 1850–1852, captures Oregon City in an early stage of development, when the ground along the river was little more than cleared dirt. On the south bank are a church, several large merchandise warehouses, and numerous houses. On the riverbank opposite, a few smaller structures have begun to appear. In the foreground are two Native Americans, who had a very different way of life and would be steadily pushed off the lands of their ancestors. Library of Congress.

James Cook mapped the Pacific coast in 1778 and learned of the great demand for sea otter pelts in China, prompting a series of British trading voyages to the Pacific Northwest. Between 1788 and 1814, American traders based in Boston overtook their British rivals and dominated the region's maritime trade. Then, in the nineteenth century, overland traders from the Pacific Fur Company of John Jacob Astor, the North West Company based in Montreal, and the Hudson's Bay Company all pushed westward to establish footholds in the region. Thus, the Native peoples of the Pacific Northwest had had sustained contact with Europeans for two generations before the United States became interested in settlement there.

As a result of their overlapping trading activities, Britain and the United States agreed in 1818 to joint control of the Oregon Country, which allowed settlement by people from both nations. Under its terms, the British-run Hudson's Bay Company developed a lucrative fur business and oversaw Indian relations north of the Columbia River, while Methodist missionaries and a few hundred American farmers settled to the south, in the Willamette Valley (Map 11.4).

In 1842, American interest in Oregon increased dramatically. The U.S. Navy published a glowing report of fine harbors in the Puget Sound, which New England merchants trading with China were already using. Simultaneously, a party of one hundred farmers journeyed along the Oregon Trail, which fur traders and explorers had blazed from Independence, Missouri, across the Great Plains and the Rocky Mountains (Map 11.5). Their letters from Oregon told of a mild climate and rich soil.

"Oregon fever" suddenly raged. A thousand men, women, and children — with a hundred wagons and five thousand oxen and cattle — gathered in Independence in April 1843. As the spring mud dried, they began their six-month trek, hoping to miss the winter snows. Another five thousand settlers, mostly farm families from the southern border states (Missouri, Kentucky, and Tennessee), set out over the next two years. These pioneers overcame floods, dust storms, livestock deaths, and a few armed encounters with Native peoples before reaching Oregon, a journey of 2,000 miles.

By 1860, about 250,000 Americans had braved the **Oregon Trail** or its alternates, including the California, Mormon, and Bozeman trails. Some 65,000 went to Oregon, 185,000 traveled to California, while others stopped in the Utah Territory or somewhere else along the way. More than 34,000 migrants died, mostly from disease and exposure; fewer than five hundred deaths resulted from Indian attacks. The walking migrants wore paths 3 feet deep, and their wagons carved 5-foot ruts across sandstone

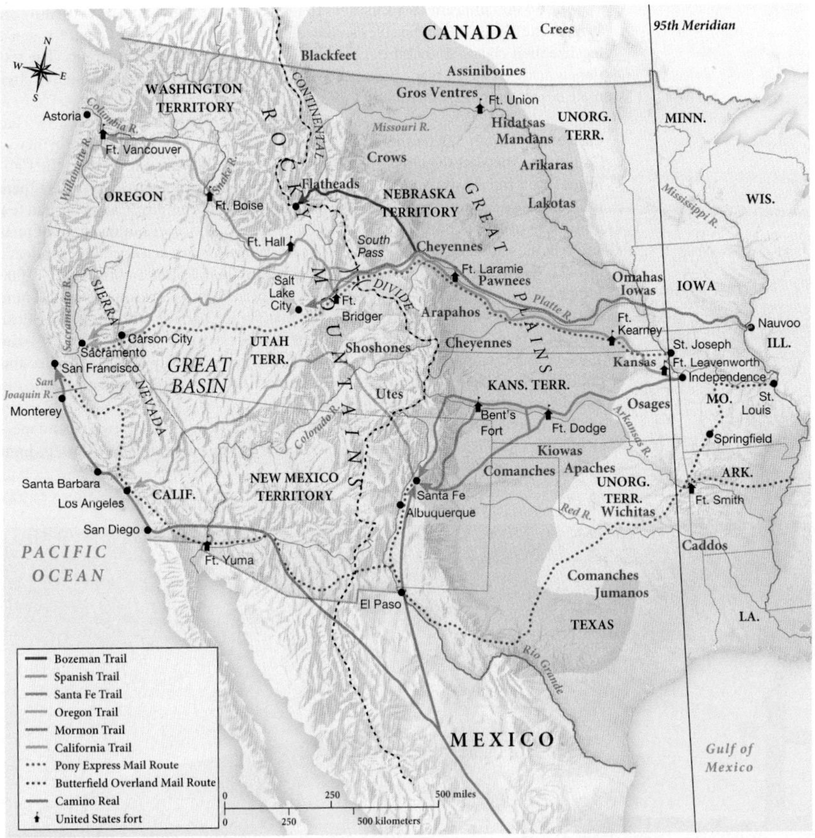

MAP 11.5 The Great Plains: Settler Trails, Indian Raiders, and Traders
By the 1850s, the Mormon, Oregon, and Santa Fe trails ran across "Indian Country," the semiarid, bison-filled Great Plains west of the ninety-fifth meridian, and then through the Rocky Mountains. Tens of thousands of Americans set out on these trails to found new communities in Utah, Oregon, New Mexico, and California. This mass migration exposed sedentary Indian peoples to American diseases, guns, and manufactures. However, raids by Comanches and Sioux affected their lives even more significantly, as did the Euro-American traders who provided a ready market for Indian horses and mules, dried meat, and bison skins.

formations in southern Wyoming—tracks that are visible today. Women found the trail especially difficult; in addition to their usual chores and the new work of driving wagons and animals, they lacked the support of female kin and the security of their domestic space. About 2,500 women endured pregnancy or gave birth during the long journey, and some did not survive. "There was a woman died in this train yesterday," Jane Gould Tortillott noted in her diary. "She left six children, one of them only two days old."

Oregon Trail
An emigrant route that originally led from Independence, Missouri, to the Willamette Valley in Oregon, a distance of some 2,000 miles. Alternate routes included the California Trail, the Mormon Trail, and the Bozeman Trail. Together they conveyed several hundred thousand migrants to the Far West in the 1840s, 1850s, and 1860s.

TEACHING STRATEGY

For vivid accounts of life on the Oregon Trail, students could read excerpts from travelers' diaries available on the Oregon Pioneers Web site. Access the site by searching "Oregon Pioneers diaries."

The 10,000 migrants who made it to Oregon in the 1840s mostly settled in the Willamette Valley. Many families squatted on 640 acres and hoped Congress would legalize their claims so that they could sell surplus acreage to new migrants. The settlers quickly created a race- and gender-defined polity by restricting voting to a "free male descendant of a white man."

California About 3,000 other early migrants ended up in the Mexican province of California. They left the Oregon Trail along the Snake River, trudged down the California Trail, and mostly settled in the interior along the Sacramento River, where there were few Mexicans. A remote outpost of Spain's American empire, California had few nonnative residents until the 1770s, when Spanish authorities built a chain of forts and religious missions along the Pacific coast. When Mexico achieved independence in 1821, its government took over the Franciscan-run missions and freed the 20,000 Indians whom the monks had persuaded or coerced into working on them. Some mission Indians rejoined their tribes, but many intermarried with mestizos (Mexicans of mixed Spanish and Indian ancestry). They worked on huge ranches — the 450 estates created by Mexican officials and bestowed primarily on their families and political allies. The owners of these vast properties (averaging 19,000 acres) mostly raised Spanish cattle, prized for their hides and tallow.

The ranches soon linked California to the American economy. New England merchants dispatched dozens of agents to buy leather for the booming Massachusetts boot

Mission Santa Clara, California, 1849 The Spanish mission system in California dates to the eighteenth century (see "The Pueblo Revolt" in Chapter 2), when Franciscan missionaries founded more than two dozen settlements to "reduce" the Native American population to European-style village life. Mission Santa Clara was founded in 1777 among the Ohlone Indians. Though the mission system imposed coercive discipline on its Indian adherents and remains controversial in the region's history, the structures are among the oldest buildings in California. They were romanticized by early U.S. migrants like Andrew P. Hill, who painted this idyllic scene in 1880 to represent an earlier era. The Granger Collection, New York.

and shoe industry and tallow to make soap and candles. Many agents married the daughters of the elite Mexican ranchers — the **Californios** — and adopted their manners, attitudes, and Catholic religion. A crucial exception was Thomas Oliver Larkin, a successful merchant in the coastal town of Monterey. Although Larkin worked closely with Mexican politicians and landowners, he remained strongly American in outlook.

Like Larkin, the American migrants in the Sacramento River Valley did not assimilate into Mexican society. Some hoped to emulate the Americans in Texas by colonizing the country and then seeking annexation. However, in the early 1840s, these settlers numbered only about 1,000, far outnumbered by the 7,000 Mexicans who lived along the coast.

Californios
The elite Mexican ranchers in the province of California.

AP® SKILLS & PROCESSES
CAUSATION
What developments prompted thousands of Americans to follow the Oregon Trail to the Pacific Coast?

The Plains Indians

As the Pacific-bound wagon trains rumbled across Nebraska along the broad Platte River, the migrants encountered the unique ecology of the Great Plains. A vast sea of wild grasses stretched from Texas to Saskatchewan in Canada, and west from the Missouri River to the Rocky Mountains. Tall grasses flourished in the eastern regions of the future states of Kansas, Nebraska, and the Dakotas, where there was moderate rainfall. To the west, in the semiarid region beyond the ninety-fifth meridian, the migrants found short grasses that sustained a rich wildlife dominated by buffalo and grazing antelopes. Nomadic buffalo-hunting Indian peoples roamed the western plains, while the eastern river valleys were home to semisedentary tribes and, since the 1830s, the Indian peoples whom Andrew Jackson had "removed" to the west. A north-south line of military forts — stretching from Fort Jesup in Louisiana to Fort Snelling, then in the Wisconsin Territory — policed the boundary between white settlements and what Congress in 1834 designated as Permanent Indian Territory.

As they traveled west through Indian Territory, migrants traversed the lands of dozens of Native American nations, from the Fox, Sauk, Shawnee, and Potawatomi nations on the lower Missouri to the Pawnee, Arapaho, Cheyenne, and Sioux Indians of the plains and the Shoshone, Bannock, Paiute, and Ute Indians of the Great Basin. Most of these groups had been in sustained contact with European-descended peoples for generations, and in the early decades conflict with overland migrants was limited and sporadic. That changed in 1854, when a Sioux Indian killed a cow belonging to a migrant on the Oregon Trail. Seeking compensation, a group of soldiers of the 6th Infantry Regiment, led by Lieutenant John Lawrence Grattan, entered the Sioux encampment near Fort Laramie and shot a headman named Conquering Bear. Sioux warriors responded by killing more than two dozen of Grattan's soldiers. The American press labeled this event the "Grattan Massacre." The army retaliated the following summer, initiating an era of warfare between the United States and the Sioux Indians that would continue intermittently for thirty-five years.

AP® SKILLS & PROCESSES
CONTEXTUALIZATION
How were the policies and military actions of the United States in the nineteenth century similar to and different from policies towards Native American nations in the colonial era?

For most Plains peoples, the impact of American expansion was less dramatic but no less devastating. For centuries, the Indians who lived on the eastern edge of the plains, such as the Pawnees and the Mandans on the Upper Missouri River, subsisted primarily on corn and beans, supplemented by buffalo meat. They hunted buffalo on foot, driving them over cliffs or into canyons for the kill. Long before the overland migrations of the nineteenth century, Spanish horses from the colony of New Mexico began to transform life on the plains (see Chapter 1, "The Great Plains and Rockies"). The nomadic Apaches of the southern plains were the first to acquire horses and range widely across the plains. The Comanches, who migrated down the Arkansas River from the Rocky Mountains around 1750, developed both a horse-based culture and imperial ambitions. Skilled buffalo hunters and fierce warriors, the Comanches slowly pushed the Apaches to the southern edge of the plains. They also raided Spanish settlements in New Mexico, incorporating captured women and children into their society.

AP® EXAM TIP
Describe the impact of Manifest Destiny on different American Indian groups.

CHECK FOR UNDERSTANDING

Ask students: **What were the key factors in the American push to the Pacific?** *American ideology of Manifest Destiny was based on an assumption of racial and cultural superiority, while the desire for prosperity played a significant role as well. Competition with Britain — including the fear that the British would beat them to the best land — also contributed.*

AP® SKILLS & PROCESSES

CONTEXTUALIZATION

Help students by narrowing their focus for comparison by providing more specific periodization for the question such as 1607–1750 with that of 1800–1848. In this way, students will have more discrete time periods from which to form their claim.

TRM Find complete suggested responses in the Teacher's Resource Materials.

AP® APPLY THE TIP

Provide students with a map of U.S. territorial expansion by 1853 and ask them to label the territories added to the U.S. at that time. Students should read and analyze textbook pp. 365–367 to help them add labels to the map to indicate the location of American Indian groups, especially on the Great Plains. They should also annotate the way in which these groups utilized the natural environment for subsistence and trade. Once maps are complete, ask students to answer the following questions:

- **How did expansion of the U.S. impact American Indian groups?** *Groups that followed the buffalo on the Great Plains were blocked and attacked. The U.S. government encouraged destruction of buffalo as a way to weaken Native groups as well as the movement of Native Americans onto restricted reservations.*
- **To what degree was the impact of Manifest Destiny on American Indians encouraging continuity in American history? Encouraging change?** *Answers will vary, but should touch upon the continuity in the removal of Native Americans to make way for white expansion, seen with the Pequot War, Anglo-Powhatan War, War of 1812, Indian Removal Act; and the change in the replacement of the removal policy with reservation policy.*
- **How had the lifestyle of American Indian groups on the Great Plains been altered by the introduction of technology and ideas from Europeans in the period of colonization?** *Many Native groups on the Great Plains abandoned farming in favor of hunting and gathering with buffalo as the main staple following the introduction of horses, which made hunting buffalo more feasible.*
- **How did the lifestyle of American Indian groups impact American expansionism in the early nineteenth century?** *The reliance of most Great Plains groups on a hunter-gatherer lifestyle led many Americans to view their land use as "wasteful" and argue for more industrial or agricultural development of the land.*

TEACHING STRATEGY

George Catlin was one of the great chroniclers of Native Americans of the American Midwest. Use the biography of Catlin and the gallery of his paintings available on the Smithsonian Art Museum Web site to help students understand his important role in chronicling the encounter of two different cultures in the frontier region. Access these resources by searching "Smithsonian George Catlin Indian Gallery."

George Catlin, *Comanche Feats of Horsemanship*, 1834 When artist George Catlin accompanied the dragoons of the U.S. Army into Indian Territory in the 1830s, the Comanches were masters of the southern plains. They hunted buffalo, raised horses and mules for sale, and used their skills as horsemen to dominate other Indian peoples and control the passage of Americans along the Santa Fe Trail. Smithsonian American Art Museum, Washington, DC/Art Resource, NY.

After 1800, the Comanches gradually built up a pastoral economy, raising horses and mules and selling them to northern Indian peoples and to Euro-American farmers in Missouri and Arkansas. Many Comanche families owned thirty to thirty-five horses or mules, far more than the five or six required for hunting buffalo and fighting neighboring peoples. The Comanches also exchanged goods with merchants and travelers along the Santa Fe Trail, which cut through their territory as it connected Missouri and New Mexico. By the early 1840s, goods worth nearly $1 million moved along the trail each year.

By the 1830s, the Kiowas, Cheyennes, and Arapahos had also adopted this horse culture and, allied with the Comanches, dominated the plains between the Arkansas and Red rivers. The new culture brought sharper social divisions. Some Kiowa men owned hundreds of horses and had several "chore wives" and captive children who worked for them. Poor men, who owned only a few horses, had difficulty finding marriage partners and often had to work for their wealthy kinsmen.

While European horses made Plains Indians wealthier and more mobile, European diseases and guns thinned their ranks. A devastating smallpox epidemic spread northward from New Spain in 1779–1781 and killed half of the Plains peoples. Twenty years later, another smallpox outbreak left dozens of deserted villages along the Missouri River. Smallpox struck the northern plains again from 1837 to 1840, killing half of the Assiniboines and Blackfeet and nearly a third of the Crows, Pawnees, and Cheyennes. "If I could see this thing, if I knew where it came from, I would go there and fight it," exclaimed a distressed Cheyenne warrior.

European weapons also altered the geography of Native peoples. Around 1750, the Crees and Assiniboines, who lived on the far northern plains, acquired guns by trading wolf pelts and beaver skins to the British-run Hudson's Bay Company. Once armed, they drove the Blackfoot peoples westward into the Rocky Mountains and took control of the Saskatchewan and Upper Missouri river basins. When the Blackfeet obtained guns and horses around 1800, they emerged from the mountains and pushed the Shoshones and Crows to the south. Because horses could not easily find winter forage in the snow-filled plains north of the Platte River, Blackfoot families kept only five to ten horses and remained hunters rather than pastoralists.

The powerful Lakota Sioux, who acquired guns and ammunition from French, Spanish, and American traders along the Missouri River, also remained buffalo hunters. A nomadic war-prone people who lived in small groups, the Lakotas largely avoided major epidemics. They kept some sedentary peoples, such as the Arikaras, in subjection and raided others for their crops and horses. By the 1830s, the Lakotas were the dominant tribe on the central as well as the northern plains. "Those lands once belonged to the Kiowas and the Crows," boasted the Oglala Sioux chief Black Hawk, "but we whipped those nations out of them, and in this we did what the white men do when they want the lands of the Indians."

The Sioux's prosperity also came at the expense of the bison, which provided them with a diet rich in protein and with hides and robes to sell. The number of hides and robes shipped down the Missouri River each year by the American Fur Company and the Missouri Fur Company increased from 3,000 in the 1820s, to 45,000 in the 1830s, and to 90,000 annually after 1840. North of the Missouri, the story was much the same. The 24,000 Indians of that region — Blackfeet, Crees, and Assiniboines — annually killed about 160,000 bison. The women dried the meat to feed their people and to sell to white traders and soldiers. The women also undertook the arduous work of skinning and tanning the hides, which they fashioned into tepees, robes, and sleeping covers. Over time, Indian hunters increased the kill and traded surplus hides and robes — about 40,000 annually by the 1840s — for pots, knives, guns, and other Euro-American manufactures. As among the Kiowas, trade increased social divisions. "It is a fine sight," a traveler noted around 1850, "to see one of those big men among the Blackfeet, who has two or three lodges, five or six wives, twenty or thirty children, fifty to a hundred head of horses; for his trade amounts to upward of $2,000 per year."

Although the Blackfeet, Kiowas, and Lakotas contributed bison hides to the national economy, they did not fully grasp their market value as winter clothes, leather accessories, and industrial drive belts. Consequently, they could not demand the best price. Moreover, the increasing size of the kill diminished the bison herds. Between 1820 and 1870, the northern herd shrank from 5 million to less than 2 million. When the Assiniboines' cultural hero Inkton'mi had taught his people how to kill the bison, he told them that the animals "will live as long as your people. There will be no end of them until the end of time." Meant as a perpetual guarantee, by the 1860s Inkton'mi's words prefigured the end of time — the demise of traditional bison hunting and, perhaps, of the Assiniboines as well.

AP® SKILLS & PROCESSES

CONTINUITY AND CHANGE

Why did some Great Plains peoples flourish between 1750 and 1860 while others did not?

The Fateful Election of 1844

The election of 1844 changed the American government's policy toward the Great Plains, the Far West, and Texas. Since 1836, southern leaders had supported the annexation of Texas, but cautious party politicians, pressured by northerners who opposed the expansion of slavery, had rebuffed them. Now rumors swirled that Great Britain was encouraging Texas to remain independent; wanted California as payment for the Mexican debts owed to British investors; and had designs on Spanish

AP® EXAM TIP

The impact of the election on westward expansion policies of 1844 is important to know on the AP® Exam.

AP® SKILLS & PROCESSES

MAKING CONNECTIONS

Ask students to determine the extent to which Plains Indians successfully resisted European encroachment in the period 1800–1865. Remind students this will likely be a non-linear answer because although groups such as the Lakota Sioux were ultimately forced to reservations by the end of the nineteenth century, prior to that they experienced some level of success at resisting encroachment by the Americans.

CHECK FOR UNDERSTANDING

Ask students: **How did interactions with Europeans affect the lives of Plains Indians?** *European horses made Plains Indians more mobile and helped them hunt buffalo more successfully, which increased their wealth. European guns increased conflict among rival tribes and, along with European diseases, devastated Native populations.*

AP® SKILLS & PROCESSES

CONTINUITY AND CHANGE

The **CONTINUITY AND CHANGE** question requires students to understand the impact horses had on hunting. Horses and the use of guns to hunt extended the range and lethality of Indians' hunting grounds. Indians became increasingly prosperous, but they also became dependent on trade, as buffalo became a kind of cash crop. Their expanded hunting grounds also increased conflict with rival groups, and interaction with whites facilitated the spread of epidemic disease, which often decimated Native populations.

TRM Find complete suggested responses in the Teacher's Resource Materials.

AP® APPLY THE TIP

To help students understand the importance of the election of 1844, begin by writing "Democratic Party" and "Whig Party" on the board. Ask students to review the main platform positions of each party and write down their responses under each heading. Students should also review the leaders of each party and the way in which this two-party system evolved in the 1820s. Once students have an understanding of the parties, ask them to work with a partner to explain the ways in which the election of 1844 challenged each party's leadership and unity. Finally, ask students to form a thesis statement and a contextualization for the following prompt: To what degree was the election of 1844 a turning point in American development in the nineteenth century?

Cuba, which some slave owners wanted to add to the United States. To thwart such imagined schemes, southern expansionists demanded the immediate annexation of Texas.

At this crucial juncture, Oregon fever altered the political landscape in the North. In 1843, Americans in the Ohio River Valley and the Great Lakes states organized "Oregon conventions," and Democratic and Whig politicians alike called for American sovereignty over the entire Oregon Country, from Spanish California to Russian Alaska (which began at 54°40′ north latitude). With northerners demanding Oregon, President John Tyler, a proslavery zealot, called for the annexation of Texas. Disowned by the Whigs because he thwarted Henry Clay's nationalist economic program, Tyler hoped to win reelection in 1844 as a Democrat. To curry favor among northern expansionists, Tyler supported claims to all of Oregon.

In April 1844, Tyler and John C. Calhoun, his proslavery, expansionist-minded secretary of state, sent the Senate a treaty to bring Texas into the Union. However, the two major presidential hopefuls, Democrat Martin Van Buren and Whig Henry Clay, opposed Tyler's initiative. Fearful of raising the issue of slavery, they persuaded the Senate to reject the treaty.

Nonetheless, expansion into Texas and Oregon became the central issue in the election of 1844. Most southern Democrats favored Texas annexation and refused to support Van Buren's candidacy. The party also passed over Tyler, whom they did not trust. Instead, the Democrats selected Governor James K. Polk of Tennessee, a slave owner and an avowed expansionist. Known as "Young Hickory" because he was a protégé of Andrew Jackson, Polk shared his mentor's iron will, boundless ambition, and determination to open up lands for American settlement. Accepting the false claim in the Democratic Party platform that both areas already belonged to the United States, Polk campaigned for the "Re-occupation of Oregon and the Re-annexation of Texas." He insisted that the United States defy British claims and occupy "the whole of the territory of Oregon" to the Alaskan border. **"Fifty-four forty or fight!"** became his jingoistic cry.

"Fifty-four forty or fight!"
Democratic candidate Governor James K. Polk's slogan in the election of 1844 calling for American sovereignty over the entire Oregon Country, which stretched from California to Russian-occupied Alaska and at the time was shared with Great Britain.

The Whigs nominated Henry Clay, who again advocated his American System of high tariffs, internal improvements, and national banking. Clay initially dodged the issue of Texas but, seeking southern votes, ultimately supported annexation. Northern Whigs who opposed the admission of a new slave state refused to vote for Clay and cast their ballots for James G. Birney of the Liberty Party (see Chapter 10, "The Impact of Abolitionism"). Birney garnered less than 3 percent of the national vote but took enough Whig votes in New York to cost Clay that state — and the presidency.

Following Polk's narrow victory, congressional Democrats called for immediate Texas statehood. However, they lacked the two-thirds majority in the Senate needed to ratify a treaty of annexation. So the Democrats admitted Texas using a joint resolution of Congress, which required just a majority vote in each house, and Texas became the twenty-eighth state in December 1845. Polk's strategy of linking Texas and Oregon had put him in the White House and Texas in the Union. Shortly, it would make the expansion of the South — and its system of slavery — the central topic of American politics (see Firsthand Accounts, p. 370).

AP® SKILLS & PROCESSES
CONTEXTUALIZATION
Why did party politicians initially oppose the annexation of Texas, and how did this view change during the election of 1844?

THE U.S.-MEXICO WAR, 1846–1848

What factors sparked the U.S.-Mexico War?

In the Southwest, as in the Oregon Country, dramatic change came quickly in the 1840s. Comanches, Kiowas, Apaches, and Navajos who had traded peacefully with northern Mexicans for decades began, instead, to make war on their ranches and

AP® SKILLS & PROCESSES

CONTEXTUALIZATION

The **CONTEXTUALIZATION** question asks students to compare party politicians' views on a particular topic — annexation of Texas — at two different points in time. Some students may have a teleological view of American westward expansion, including the acquisition of Texas. They need to clearly understand that not all Americans supported expansion and that — as this question implies — Americans' views were not static. This question really hinges on the influence of proslavery southern Democrats, whose views led them to choose Polk over Van Buren (an opponent of Texas annexation); faced with the increasing popularity of this view, Clay was forced by the need to court southern votes to endorse annexation as well. Extend this prompt by having students explore why the views of southern proslavery forces were so influential in the crucial 1844 election, given that they represented a minority of the electorate.

TRM Find complete suggested responses in the Teacher's Resource Materials.

CHECK FOR UNDERSTANDING

Ask students to weigh the following causes of the Mexican-American War: Manifest Destiny ideology, American actions on the frontier, James K. Polk's election, Texas independence, and U.S.-Mexico relations.

AP® THEME

WOR: America in the World

The PBS companion Web site for *The U.S.-Mexican War, 1846–1848* documentary provides a number of teacher resources, including detailed lesson and activity suggestions, an interactive timeline, an extensive video library of clips, and relevant articles, maps, primary sources, and links to further resources. Access this resource by searching "PBS U.S. Mexican War Educators."

towns, ruining the region's economy and devastating many of its settlements. The Mexican government, only two decades old and still preoccupied with challenges in its densely populated center, proved unable to suppress these attacks in the far north. Recognizing an opportunity to gain even more territory, Polk determined to go to war if necessary to acquire all the Mexican lands between Texas and the Pacific Ocean. What he and many Democrats consciously ignored was the domestic crisis that a war of conquest to expand slavery would unleash.

The Mexican North

Since gaining independence in 1821, Mexico had not prospered. Its federal system of government tended to serve the northern frontier states poorly, while two decades of political instability resulted in a stagnant economy and modest tax revenues, which debt payments to European bankers quickly devoured. In the 1830s and 1840s, Comanche warriors conducted dozens of campaigns against the settlements of the Mexican north. Mexico's central government lacked the resources to respond effectively, and the northern territories were devastated (see "America in the World," p. 372). Always sparsely settled — California and New Mexico had a Spanish-speaking population of only 75,000 in 1840 — many northern ranches and communities were abandoned in what one historian has called the "War of a Thousand Deserts." Nevertheless, Mexican officials vowed to preserve their nation's historic boundaries. When its breakaway province of Texas prepared to join the American Union, Mexico suspended diplomatic relations with the United States.

Polk's Expansionist Program

President Polk moved quickly to acquire Mexico's other northern provinces. He hoped to foment a revolution in California that, like the 1836 rebellion in Texas, would lead to annexation. In October 1845, Secretary of State James Buchanan told merchant Thomas Oliver Larkin, now the U.S. consul for the Mexican province, to encourage influential Californios to seek independence and union with the United States. To add military muscle to this scheme, Polk ordered American naval commanders to seize San Francisco Bay and California's coastal towns in case of war with Mexico. The president also instructed the War Department to dispatch Captain John C. Frémont and an "exploring" party of soldiers into Mexican territory. By December 1845, Frémont's force had reached California's Sacramento River Valley.

With these preparations in place, Polk launched a secret diplomatic initiative: he sent Louisiana congressman John Slidell to Mexico, telling him to secure the Rio Grande boundary for Texas and to buy the provinces of California and New Mexico for $30 million. Insulted by U.S. disregard for Mexico's sovereignty, government officials refused to meet with Slidell.

Events now moved quickly toward war. Polk ordered General Zachary Taylor and an American army of 2,000 soldiers to occupy disputed lands between the Nueces River (the historic southern boundary of Spanish Texas) and the Rio Grande, which the Republic of Texas had claimed as its border with Mexico. "We were sent to provoke a fight," recalled Ulysses S. Grant, then a young officer serving with Taylor, "but it was essential that Mexico should commence it." When the armies clashed near the Rio Grande in May 1846, Polk delivered the war message he had drafted long before. Taking liberties with the truth, the president declared that Mexico "has passed the boundary of the United States, has invaded our territory, and shed American blood upon the American soil." Ignoring pleas by some Whigs for a negotiated settlement, an overwhelming majority in Congress voted for war — a decision greeted with great

AP® EXAM TIP

Evaluate the Mexican-American War as a continuation of expansionism that began in the colonial period.

CHECK FOR UNDERSTANDING

Ask students: **What was the "War of a Thousand Deserts"?** *Settlers abandoned ranches and towns in northern Mexico due to Comanche attacks and lack of adequate response from the Mexican government.*

AP® APPLY THE TIP

Ask students to create a political cartoon that illustrates the idea that expansionism through the U.S.-Mexico War was an example of the continuity of expansionism from the earliest colonization by the British in 1607. Emphasize to students that their artistic ability is less important than the argument created by their political cartoon. Refer students back to the "King Andrew the First" cartoon on p. 297 to talk about use of symbols and captions in a cartoon. Once students have created cartoons, have them exchange cartoons with another classmate and discuss similarities and differences in their portrayals. Lastly, ask students to complete **Handout 11.3 — Contextualization: The Mexican War (TRM).**

TRM Find **Handout 11.3 — Contextualization: The Mexican War** in the Teacher's Resource Materials.

AP® SKILLS & PROCESSES

ANALYZING HISTORICAL EVIDENCE

Because the narrative of Manifest Destiny is so well known — and because the U.S. did go to war with Mexico — the views of O'Sullivan and Buchanan in the **AP® FIRSTHAND ACCOUNTS** feature will be much more familiar to students. Students should concentrate on attempting to understand the arguments of Sumner and Whitman, focusing on the particular reasons each opposed the war. Students might additionally be asked why prowar forces overpowered critics of war.

The U.S.-Mexico War: Expansion and Slavery

Conflict with Mexico prompted debates over the Polk administration's aggressive efforts to acquire territory and spread slavery. Here, Polk's critics face off against the expansionists.

JOHN L. O'SULLIVAN, EDITOR

"Manifest Destiny," from United States Magazine and Democratic Review, July 1845

SOURCE: Sean Wilentz, ed., *Major Problems in the Early Republic, 1787–1848* (Lexington, MA: D. C. Heath, 1991), 525–528.

❝ Texas is now ours . . . [Britain and France tried] to intrude themselves [into Texas affairs] . . . for the avowed object of thwarting our policy and hampering our power, limiting our greatness and checking the fulfillment of our manifest destiny to overspread the continent allotted by Providence for the free development of our yearly multiplying millions. . . .

The independence of Texas was complete and absolute. It was an independence, not only in fact, but of right. . . . What then can be more preposterous than all this clamor by Mexico and the Mexican interest, against Annexation, as a violation of any rights of hers . . . ?

Nor is there any just foundation for the charge that Annexation is a great pro-slavery measure — calculated to increase and perpetuate that institution. Slavery had nothing to do with it. . . . That it will tend to facilitate and hasten the disappearance of Slavery from all the northern tier of the present Slave States, cannot surely admit of serious question. The greater value in Texas of the slave labor now employed in those States, must soon produce the effect of draining off that labor southwardly. . . .

California will, probably, next fall away. . . . Already the advance guard of the irresistible army of Anglo-Saxon emigration has begun to pour down upon it, armed with the plough and the rifle, and marking its trail with schools and colleges, courts and representative halls, mills and meeting-houses. A population will soon be in actual occupation of California. . . . And they will have a right to independence — to self-government . . . a better and a truer right than the artificial title of sovereignty in Mexico, a thousand miles distant, inheriting from Spain a title good only against those who have none better. ❞

JAMES BUCHANAN, U.S. SECRETARY OF STATE

Letter to John Slidell, Minister Plenipotentiary to Mexico, November 1845

SOURCE: Victoria Bissell Brown and Timothy J. Shannon, eds., *Going to the Source: The Bedford Reader in American History* (Boston: Bedford/St. Martin's, 2004), 1: 260–262.

❝ In your negotiations with Mexico, the independence of Texas must be considered a settled fact, and is not to be called in question. . . .

It may, however, be contended on the part of Mexico, that the Nueces and not the Rio del Norte [Rio Grande], is the true western boundary of Texas. I need not furnish you arguments to controvert this position. . . . The jurisdiction of Texas has been extended beyond that river [the Nueces] and . . . representatives from the country between it and the Del Norte have participated in the deliberations both of her Congress and her Convention. . . .

The case is different in regard to New Mexico. Santa Fe, its capital, was settled by the Spaniards more than two centuries ago; and that province has been ever since in their possession and that of the Republic of Mexico. The Texans never have conquered or taken possession of it. . . . [However,] a great portion of New Mexico being on this side of the Rio Grande and included within the limits already claimed by Texas, it may hereafter, should it

popular acclaim. To avoid a simultaneous war with Britain, Polk retreated from his demand for "fifty-four forty or fight" and in June 1846 accepted British terms that divided the Oregon Country at the forty-ninth parallel.

American Military Successes

American forces in Texas quickly established their military superiority. Zachary Taylor's army crossed the Rio Grande; occupied the Mexican city of Matamoros;

remain a Mexican province, become a subject of dispute. . . . It would seem to be equally the interest of both Powers, that New Mexico should belong to the United States. . . .

It is to be seriously apprehended that both Great Britain and France have designs upon California. . . . This Government . . . would vigorously interpose to prevent the latter from becoming either a British or a French Colony. . . . The possession of the Bay and harbor of San Francisco, is all important to the United States. . . . Money would be no object. ”

CHARLES SUMNER, CONSCIENCE WHIG AND FUTURE REPUBLICAN SENATOR FROM MASSACHUSETTS

Letter to Robert Winthrop, Whig Congressman from Massachusetts, October 25, 1846

Source: Sean Wilentz, ed., *Major Problems in the Early Republic, 1787–1848* (Lexington, MA: D. C. Heath, 1991), 541.

“ If we regard Texas as a province of Mexico, its boundaries must be sought in the geography of that republic. If we regard it as an independent State, they must be determined by the extent of jurisdiction which the State was able to maintain. Now it seems clear that the river Nueces was always recognized by Mexico as the western boundary; and it is undisputed that the State of Texas, since its Declaration of Independence, never exercised any jurisdiction beyond the Nueces. . . .

In the month of January, 1846, the President of the United States directed the troops under General Taylor, called the Army of Occupation, to take possession of this region [west of the Nueces River]. Here was an act of aggression. As might have been expected, it produced collision. The Mexicans, aroused in self-defence, sought to repel the invaders. . . .

Here the question occurs, What was the duty of Congress in this emergency? Clearly to withhold all sanction to unjust war, — to aggression upon a neighboring Republic. . . . The American forces should have been directed to retreat, not from any human force, but from wrongdoing; and this would have been a true victory.

Alas! This was not the mood of Congress. With wicked speed a bill was introduced, furnishing large and unusual supplies of men and money. . . . This was adopted by a vote of 123 to 67; and the bill then leaped forth, fully armed, as a measure of open and active hostility against Mexico. ”

WALT WHITMAN, POET AND EDITOR OF THE *BROOKLYN EAGLE*

Editorial, September 1, 1847

Source: Sean Wilentz, ed., *Major Problems in the Early Republic, 1787–1848* (Lexington, MA: D. C. Heath, 1991), 543.

“ The question whether or no there shall be slavery in the new territories . . . is a question between the grand body of white workingmen, the millions of mechanics, farmers, and operatives of our country, with their interests on the one side — and the interests of the few thousand rich, 'polished,' and aristocratic owners of slaves at the South, on the other side.

Experience has proved . . . that a stalwart mass of respectable workingmen, cannot exist, much less flourish, in a thorough slave State. Let any one think for a moment what a different appearance New York, Pennsylvania, or Ohio, would present — how much less sturdy independence and family happiness there would be — were slaves the workmen there, instead of each man as a general thing being his own workman. . . .

Slavery is a good thing enough . . . to the rich — the one out of thousands; but it is destructive to the dignity and independence of all who work, and to labor itself. . . . All practice and theory . . . are strongly arrayed in favor of limiting slavery to where it already exists. ”

QUESTIONS FOR ANALYSIS

1. What arguments do Buchanan and Sumner make about the boundaries of Texas, the issue that sparked the fighting? Whose argument is more persuasive and why? Use evidence from the sources and the text to support your reasoning.
2. Do O'Sullivan's and Buchanan's assertions support or undercut the claim that the U.S.-Mexico War was an aggressive act of imperialism? Make a defensible claim.
3. Why does Whitman oppose the expansion of slavery? Given Whitman's views, who might have gotten his vote in the election of 1848? Support your argument with examples from the textbook and source.
4. Two of the sources are newspaper editorials; two are letters written by or addressed to public officials. How does the author's purpose influence its content?

TRM Find complete suggested responses in the Teacher's Resource Materials.

and, after a fierce six-day battle in September 1846, took the interior Mexican town of Monterrey. Two months later, a U.S. naval squadron in the Gulf of Mexico seized Tampico, Mexico's second most important port. By the end of 1846, the United States controlled much of northeastern Mexico (Map 11.6).

Fighting also broke out in California. In June 1846, naval commander John Sloat landed 250 marines in Monterey and declared that California "henceforward will be a portion of the United States." Simultaneously, American settlers in the Sacramento River Valley staged a revolt and, supported by Frémont's force, captured the town

AP® SKILLS & PROCESSES

ANALYZING HISTORICAL EVIDENCE

The **AP® AMERICA IN THE WORLD** feature asks students to use data as evidence from which to make generalizations. Students should identify 1840 as the first year in the "Mexico: Tax Revenues, 1790–1844" table for which data from an independent Mexico is provided; the years before that all represent its time as a Spanish colony. Students should notice that 1816 represents parity in the tax revenues of the two entities. The bottom tables provide the most instructive comparison, as Mexico's deficit increased each year from 1840 on, while the U.S.'s deficit peaked in 1841 and then decreased steadily until it ran a surplus in 1844. Given Mexico's reduced finances as an independent nation, students might also explore whether independence doomed Mexico to defeat at the hands of an increasingly wealthy United States.

TRM Find complete suggested responses in the Teacher's Resource Materials.

AP® AMERICA IN THE WORLD

Financing War

To explain the outcome of war, we usually focus on the combatants' military assets, but a nation's finances also play a crucial role. In the U.S.-Mexico War, the United States benefitted from low federal expenditures and a reliable tax system. Mexico, though it had been one of Spain's most valuable colonies, struggled financially after it gained independence in 1821. Higher expenses and widespread tax evasion caused large deficits, making it difficult to borrow the funds it needed to fight. The United States kept expenses low, nearly eliminated the federal debt, and ran small deficits, which made it easier to finance the war effort. Both nations' finances were dramatically affected by the global economic downturn that began in 1837 (see Chapter 9, "Labor Politics and the Depression of 1837–1843"), but the United States was running a surplus by 1844, while Mexico's revenues still lagged far behind expenses. The following tables illustrate this comparison.

Mexico: Tax Revenues, 1790–1844

1790	$10,466,831
1808	$58,829,740
1816	$47,920,070
1840	$15,452,919
1844	$20,592,058

United States: Tax Revenues, 1790–1844

1792	$3,670,000
1808	$17,061,000
1816	$47,678,000
1840	$19,480,000
1844	$29,321,000

Mexico: Revenues and Expenses, 1840–1844

	Revenues	Expenses	Deficit
1840	$15,452,919	$21,255,097	$5,802,173
1841	$14,724,788	$22,997,219	$8,272,431
1842	$15,968,774	$30,639,711	$14,670,937
1843	$19,602,180	$34,035,277	$14,433,097
1844	$20,592,058	$31,304,102	$10,712,044

United States: Revenues and Expenses, 1840–1844

	Revenues	Expenses	Deficit
1840	$19,480,000	$24,318,000	$4,837,000
1841	$16,860,000	$26,566,000	$9,706,000
1842	$19,976,000	$25,206,000	$5,230,000
1843	$ 8,303,000	$11,858,000	$3,555,000
1844	$29,321,000	$22,338,000	($6,984,000)

SOURCES: Barbara A. Tenenbaum, *The Politics of Penury: Debts and Taxes in Mexico, 1821–1856* (Albuquerque: University of New Mexico Press, 1986); *Historical Statistics of the United States: Millennial Edition Online* (New York: Cambridge University Press).

QUESTIONS FOR ANALYSIS

1. Identify at least one pattern in U.S. taxes, revenues, and expenses, as well as one pattern for Mexico. Note, a pattern has at least three data points in the same direction.
2. Why do you think Mexico's tax collection system might have been more effective when it was a colony of Spain than it was once the nation gained independence? Why did the United States have a different experience? Use evidence from the chapter to support your claim.
3. Compare the nations' revenues, expenses, and deficits in the years 1840–1844. What are the most significant differences in the budgets of U.S. and Mexico?

Bear Flag Republic
A short-lived republic created in California by American emigrants to sponsor a rebellion against Mexican authority in 1846.

of Sonoma, where they hoisted a flag featuring a grizzly bear facing a red star and proclaimed the independence of the "**Bear Flag Republic.**" To cement these victories, Polk ordered army units to capture Santa Fe in New Mexico and then march to southern California. Despite stiff Mexican resistance, American forces secured control of California early in 1847, bringing an end to the short-lived independent republic.

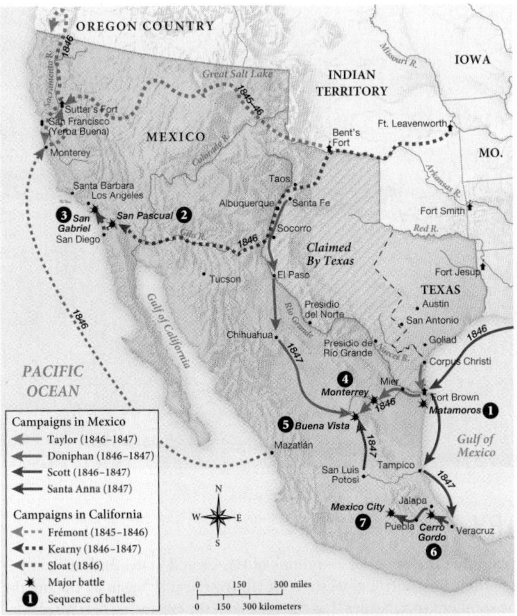

MAPPING THE PAST

MAP 11.6 The U.S.-Mexico War, 1846–1848
After moving west from Fort Leavenworth in present-day Kansas, American forces commanded by Captain John C. Frémont and General Stephen Kearny defeated Mexican armies in California in 1846 and early 1847. Simultaneously, U.S. troops under General Zachary Taylor and Colonel Alfred A. Doniphan won victories over General Santa Anna's forces south of the Rio Grande. In mid-1847, General Winfield Scott mounted a successful seaborne attack on Veracruz and Mexico City, ending the war.

ANALYZING THE MAP: Mexico considered the Nueces River to be the southern boundary of Texas, while Texans insisted that it was the Rio Grande. How did this difference affect the territorial claims of the Republic of Texas?

MAKING CONNECTIONS: President Polk capitalized on the controversy between Texas and Mexico to capture much of northern Mexico for the United States. How was the United States able to conquer so much territory so quickly?

Polk expected these victories to end the war, but he underestimated the Mexicans' national pride and the determination of President Santa Anna. In February 1847 in the Battle of Buena Vista, Santa Anna nearly defeated Taylor's army in northeastern Mexico. With most Mexican troops deployed in the north, Polk approved General Winfield Scott's plan to capture the port of Veracruz and march 260 miles to Mexico City. An American army of 14,000 seized the Mexican capital in September 1847. That American victory cost Santa Anna his presidency, and a new Mexican government made a forced peace with the United States.

AP® SKILLS & PROCESSES

CONTEXTUALIZATION

How was the American acquisition of California similar to, and different from, the American-led creation of the Texas Republic?

TRM Find complete suggested responses in the Teacher's Resource Materials.

AP® SKILLS & PROCESSES

CONTEXTUALIZATION

The **CONTEXTUALIZATION** question asks students to assess similarities and differences in the American acquisition of two territories within a few years of each other. Students could consider motives, methods, and actors — including who took the initiative in each case.

TRM Find complete suggested responses in the Teacher's Resource Materials.

CHECK FOR UNDERSTANDING

Ask students: **What was Polk's expansionist program?** *He instigated war with Mexico to acquire California and the rest of the Mexican northwest. He backed down from his demand for an Oregon boundary at 54°40′ and accepted a compromise with Britain to avoid two simultaneous wars.*

TEACHING STRATEGY

This painting reveals the savage nature of fighting in the Mexican city of Monterrey. Students might be familiar with this type of urban warfare from more contemporary U.S. military conflicts in Afghanistan and Iraq.

CHECK FOR UNDERSTANDING

Use the **AP® LEARNING FOCUS** question from the beginning of the chapter to check students' understanding of the chapter as a whole: **Why did the ideology of Manifest Destiny unite ordinary Americans and shape U.S. policies?** *The ideology of Manifest Destiny, by which the United States expanded westward, achieving a recognized border on the Pacific Ocean by 1848, encouraged policymakers to embrace an expansionist foreign policy with both Britain and Mexico, leading to a boundary treaty with the former and war with the latter. For whites, both North and South, the new Western territories provided lands on which to expand and effectively served as an outlet for population pressures in the East. After this initial rush, however, the new Western lands exacerbated the schism between North and South over the status of slaves in these new lands. For Native Americans and blacks, however, the results were much worse. Native Americans were pushed farther West or increasingly decimated and the new Western lands also led to the expansion of slavery, which led to profound changes in U.S. policies.*

LearningCurve

Remind students to go online to complete the LearningCurve quiz for this chapter.

TRM Find complete suggested responses in the Teacher's Resource Materials.

Street Fighting in the Calle de Iturbide, 1846 Monterrey, which had resisted Spanish troops during Mexico's war for independence (1820–1821), was captured by the Americans only after bloody house-to-house fighting in the U.S.-Mexico War (1846–1848). Protected by thick walls and shuttered windows, Mexican defenders pour a withering fire on the dark-uniformed American troops and buckskin-clad frontier fighters. A large Catholic cathedral looms in the background, its foundations obscured by the smoke from the Mexicans' cannons. West Point Museum, United States Military Academy, West Point, NY.

SUMMARY

This chapter explored the imperial ambitions of the United States and the competition among nations for control of western North America. It began by tracing the contours of the southern social order that emerged with the expansion of slave plantation agriculture. It followed the migration of ambitious slaveholders into the Mexican state of Coahuila y Tejas; considered the challenges that aristocratic planters faced in a democratic political order; and analyzed the patterns of work, family, community life, and culture that structured the African American experience.

The American ideology of Manifest Destiny, which held that God intended that the dominion of the United States should extend across the entire North American continent, informed U.S. efforts to claim the Oregon Country and California and shaped the country's interactions with the independent Plains Indians, many of whom were formidable powers in their own right. Finally, the chapter examined the aftermath of the presidential election of 1844, which brought James K. Polk to power and set the nation's course toward war with Mexico. In Chapter 12, we will consider the effects of that war on American society and politics.

CHAPTER 11 REVIEW

AP® CONTENT REVIEW

Answer these questions to demonstrate your understanding of the chapter's main ideas.

1. What were the strengths and limitations of the South's economy and social structure?
2. What resources and strategies gave African American slaves a measure of control over their lives?
3. How did the idea of Manifest Destiny help to unite the otherwise divided interests of northerners and southerners?
4. What factors caused the U.S.-Mexico War? Differentiate between short-term and long-term causes.

AP® TERMS TO KNOW *Identify and explain the significance of each term below.*

Key Concepts and Events

slave society (p. 349)
republican aristocracy (p. 349)
Great American Desert (p. 352)
Alamo (p. 353)
secret ballot (p. 353)
Gullah dialect (p. 355)
task system (p. 357)
German Coast uprising (p. 358)
Manifest Destiny (p. 359)
Oregon Trail (p. 363)
Californios (p. 365)
"Fifty-four forty or fight!" (p. 368)
Bear Flag Republic (p. 372)

Key People

Sam Houston (p. 352)
Stephen Austin (p. 352)
Antonio López de Santa Anna (p. 353)
James K. Polk (p. 368)
Zachary Taylor (p. 369)
John C. Frémont (p. 369)

TRM Find definitions for these terms in the **Glossary/Glosario** in the Teacher's Resource Materials.

AP® MAKING CONNECTIONS *Recognize the larger developments and continuities within and across chapters by answering these questions.*

1. How were the American territorial acquisitions of the 1840s similar to, and/or different from, those of the Treaty of Paris of 1783 and the Louisiana Purchase (discussed in Chapters 6 and 7)? Explain patterns of continuity and change.
2. How did the experience of enslaved African Americans evolve during the first half of the nineteenth century? How was the institution different than it had been in the eighteenth century (discussed in Chapters 3 and 8)? Use historical reasoning to compare slavery over time.

AP® SKILLS & PROCESSES

COMPARISON

AP® MAKING CONNECTIONS 1 asks students to compare the acquisition of land at three different points in American history.

KEY TURNING POINTS *Refer to the timeline at the start of the chapter for help in answering the following question.*

Focusing on developments in the 1830s and 1840s, what were the similarities and differences between the outcomes of westward expansion in the North and the South?

AP® SKILLS & PROCESSES

COMPARISON

KEY TURNING POINTS encourages students to compare the effects of Manifest Destiny in two regions.

TRM Find complete suggested responses in the Teacher's Resource Materials.

AP® PRACTICE QUESTIONS

MULTIPLE CHOICE QUESTIONS *Choose the correct answer for each question.*

Questions 1–3 refer to the excerpt provided.

> Letter from Frances Kemble of Georgia, the English wife of American plantation owner Pierce Butler, to a friend, 1838–1839:
>
> "Upon my word . . . I used to pity the slaves, and I do pity them with all my soul; but, oh dear! Oh dear! Their case is a bed of roses to that of their owners. . . . I was looking over this morning, with a most indescribable mix of feelings, a pamphlet published in the South upon the subject of the religious instruction of the slaves, and the difficulty of the task undertaken by these reconcilers of God and Mammon [earthly wealth] seems to me nothing short of piteous [pitiful]. 'We must give our involuntary servants (they seldom call them slaves, for it is an ugly word in the American mouth) Christian enlightenment,' they say; and where shall they begin? 'Whatsoever you would that men should do unto you, do you also unto them'? No; but 'Servants, obey your masters;' and there, I think, they naturally come to a full stop. . . . The pamphlet suggested to me the necessity for . . . a slave Bible. If these heaven-blinded Negro enlighteners persist in their pernicious [diabolical] plan of making Christians of their cattle, something of the sort must be done. . . ."
>
> Sean Wilentz, *Major Problems in the Early Republic, 1787–1848*, p. 255

1. The pamphlet described by Kemble best reflects which of the following?
   - **a.** The emergence of a new national culture combining American elements and European influences
   - **b.** The development of a women's rights movement that sought to create greater equality and opportunities
   - **c.** The growth of a distinctive Southern regional identity
   - **d.** Reform efforts aimed at changing Americans' individual behaviors
2. The reformers goals outlined in the pamphlet most directly challenges the belief held by many in the 1830s that
   - **a.** slavery was a positive part of the Southern way of life.
   - **b.** the public and private spheres of daily life should be separate.

TRM Find complete suggested responses in the Teacher's Resource Materials.

c. an emerging wealthy elite resulted in the growth of a laboring poor population.

d. voluntary organizations could successfully change individual behaviors.

3. In the decade following the conflict described by Kemble, which of the following trends was most directly a response to the issues described in the excerpt?

a. The creation of African American communities and strategies to protect their dignity and family structures

b. The rise of democratic and individualistic beliefs and a response to rationalism

c. Regional interests overriding national concerns

d. The overcultivation of arable lands in the Southeast leading to the cultivation of lands further west

Questions 4–6 refer to the excerpt provided.

"The strong desire to establish peace with Mexico on liberal and honorable terms, and the readiness of this government to regulate and adjust our boundary and other causes of difference with that power on such fair and equitable principles as would lead to permanent relations of the most friendly nature, induced me in September last to seek the reopening of diplomatic relations between the two countries. . . . An envoy of the United States repaired to Mexico with full powers to adjust every existing difference. But . . . his mission has been unavailing. The Mexican Government not only refused to receive him or listen to his propositions, but after a long-continued series of menaces have at last invaded our territory and shed the blood of our fellow citizens on our own soil."

President James K. Polk, Message to Congress, 1846

4. The conflict between the United States and Mexico as evidenced by this source was primarily driven by differing

a. forms of government.

b. religious faiths and beliefs.

c. claims to land.

d. economic priorities.

5. Which following ideas contributed most directly to the reasoning behind Polk's message?

a. Transcendentalism

b. Free-Soil ideals

c. Perfectionism

d. Manifest Destiny

6. Which of the following developments likely resulted from the developments described in the excerpt?

a. The arrival of substantial numbers of immigrants to the United States

b. The rise of a strongly anti-Catholic nativist movement

c. Heated controversies over whether to allow slavery in western territories

d. The establishment of the Second Party System in American politics

SHORT ANSWER QUESTIONS

Read each question carefully and write a short response. Use evidence from the text to support your claims.

Distribution of the Slave Population in 1860

1. Using the map provided, answer (a), (b), and (c).

a. Briefly explain ONE specific historical event or development in the nineteenth century that contributed to the emergence of the patterns depicted in the map.

b. Briefly explain ANOTHER specific historical event or development in the nineteenth century that contributed to the patterns depicted in the map.

c. Briefly explain ONE specific historical effect that resulted from the patterns depicted in the map.

2. Answer (a), (b), and (c).

a. Briefly describe ONE historical similarity in the defense of slavery between those who were slaveholders and those who did not profit from the slave system in the period 1800–1860.

b. Briefly describe ONE historical difference in the ways Southerners defended the institution of slavery in the period 1800–1860.

c. Briefly describe ONE historical difference between those who defended slavery in the North and those who defended the institution in the South in the period 1800–1860.

"By 1850 . . . Americans had evidence plain before them that they were a chosen people: from the English they had learned that the Anglo-Saxons had always been peculiarly gifted in the arts of government; from the scientists and ethnologists they were learning that they were of a distinct Caucasian race, innately endowed with abilities that placed them above other races . . . . [M]any Americans found comfort in the strength and status of a distinguished racial heritage. The new racial ideology could be used to force new immigrants to conform to the prevailing political, economic, and social system, and it could also be used to justify the sufferings or deaths of blacks, Indians, or Mexicans. Feelings of guilt could be assuaged by assumptions of historical and scientific inevitability. . . . Agrarian and commercial desires and the search for national and personal wealth and security were at the heart of mid-nineteenth century expansion, but the racial ideology that accompanied and permeated these drives helped determine the nature of America's specific relationships with other peoples encountered in the surge to world power."

Reginald Horsman, *Race and Manifest Destiny: The Origins of American Racial Anglo-Saxonism*, 1981

"[T]he American encounter with potential new territories in the antebellum period was shaped by concerns at home, especially evolving gendered ideals and practices. . . . [A]ggressive expansionism, defined here as support for the use of war to gain new American territory . . . was supported by martial men, and . . . debates over Manifest Destiny also were debates over the meaning of American manhood and womanhood. . . . [T]he restrained men who opposed aggressive expansionism also believed that America's Manifest Destiny was yet to be fulfilled, but they envisioned it unfolding . . . through trade and the spread of American social and religious institutions. . . . But in the 1850s the discourse of aggressive expansionism dominated the discussion of America's proper role in the world . . . and . . . led to an unintended victory for martial manhood. It ended up exacerbating the growing sectional conflict by promoting violence as a solution to discord."

Amy S. Greenberg, *Manifest Manhood and the Antebellum American Empire*, 2005

3. Using the two excerpts provided, answer (a), (b), and (c).

a. Briefly describe ONE major difference between Horsman's and Greenberg's historical interpretations of antebellum expansion.

b. Briefly explain how ONE specific historical event or development during the period 1820 to 1860 that is not explicitly mentioned in the excerpts could be used to support Horsman's interpretation.

c. Briefly explain how ONE specific historical event or development during the period 1820 to 1860 that is not explicitly mentioned in the excerpts could be used to support Greenberg's interpretation.

TRM Find complete suggested responses in the Teacher's Resource Materials.

4 PART

AP® PRACTICE ESSAY QUESTIONS

DOCUMENT-BASED QUESTION

Suggested reading period: 15 minutes. Suggested writing time: 45 minutes.

DIRECTIONS: Question 1 is based on the accompanying documents. The documents have been edited for the purpose of this exercise.

1. Evaluate the extent of change in the practices of political democracy supported by political parties in the period from 1801 to 1840.

DOCUMENT 1

Source: Thomas Jefferson, First Inaugural Address, March 4, 1801.

"[T]hough the will of the majority is in all cases to prevail, that will to be rightful must be reasonable; that the minority possess their equal rights, which equal law must protect, and to violate would be oppression . . . every difference of opinion is not a difference of principle. We have called by different names brethren of the same principle. We are all Republicans, we are all Federalists. . . .

About to enter, fellow-citizens, on the exercise of duties which comprehend everything dear and valuable to you, it is proper you should understand what I deem the essential principles of our Government, and consequently those which ought to shape its Administration. . . . Equal and exact justice to all men, of whatever state or persuasion, religious or political; peace, commerce, and honest friendship with all nations, entangling alliances with none; the support of the State governments in all their rights . . . the preservation of the General Government in its whole constitutional vigor . . . economy in the public expense . . . encouragement of agriculture, and of commerce as its handmaid . . . freedom of religion; freedom of the press, and freedom of person under the protection of the habeas corpus, and trial by juries impartially selected. These principles . . . guided our steps through an age of revolution and reformation. . . . They should be the creed of our political faith[.]"

DOCUMENT 2

Source: Article from The Charleston (South Carolina) newspaper, *L'Oracle Francais-Americain*, July 18, 1807.

"We can make the British People know that all the miseries they may feel in consequence of a suspension of intercourse with us, is to be attributed to the wicked and impolitic conduct of their own ministry.

All of this and much more our government can do by scratch of a pen — by renouncing all intercourse with a government which has shewn to the world that it is totally unworthy of our confidence and connection.

But should any of all those measures fail to restore the British ministry to a sense of justice, and war must be the ultimate resort, we wish them to know that America can be one of her most formidable foes. . . .

We can with ease deprive them of Canada and Nova Scotia and deliver that people from a galling yoke, which they are now willing and only want an opportunity to throw off.

We can expel them from the continent of America."

DOCUMENT 3

Source: John Randolph, a Democratic-Republican congressman from Virginia, in a speech to the House of Representatives on the proposed tariff of 1816.

"[W]e have another proof that the present government have renounced the true republican principles of Jefferson's administration on which they raised themselves to power, and that they have taken up, in their stead, those of John Adams. . . . [T]heir principle now is old Federalism, vamped up into something bearing the superficial appearance of republicanism. . . . I am convinced that it would be impolitic, as well as unjust, to aggravate the burdens of the people for the purpose of favoring the manufacturers; for [in the Constitution] this government created and gave power to Congress to regulate commerce and equalize duties [tariffs] on the whole of the United States. . . . It eventuates in this: whether you, as a planter will consent to be taxed, in order to hire another man to go to work in a shoemaker's shop, or to set up a spinning jenny. For my part I will not agree to it. . . . No, I will buy where I can get manufactures cheapest; I will not agree to lay a duty on the cultivators of the soil to encourage exotic manufactures; because, after all, we should only get much worse things at a much higher price, and we, the cultivators of the country, would in the end pay all."

DOCUMENT 4

Source: Alexis de Tocqueville, *Democracy in America*, 1831.

"In the absence of great parties, the United States abound with lesser controversies; and public opinion is divided into a thousand minute shades of difference upon questions of very little moment. The pains which are taken to create parties are inconceivable, and at the present day it is no easy task. In the United States there is no religious animosity, because all religion is respected, and no sect is predominant; there is no jealousy of rank, because the people is everything, and none can contest its authority; lastly, there is no public indigence to supply the means of agitation, because the physical position of the country opens so wide a field to industry that man is able to accomplish the most surprising undertakings with his own native resources. Nevertheless, ambitious men are interested in the creation of parties, since it is difficult to eject a person from authority upon the mere ground that his place is coveted by others. The skill of the actors in the political world lies therefore in the art of creating parties. A political aspirant in the United States begins by discriminating his own interest, and by calculating upon those interests which may be collected around and amalgamated with it; he then contrives to discover some doctrine or some principle which may suit the purposes of this new association, and which he adopts in order to bring forward his party and to secure his popularity; just as the imprimatur of a King was in former days incorporated with the volume which it authorized, but to which it nowise belonged. When these preliminaries are terminated, the new party is ushered into the political world."

DOCUMENT 5

Source: Senator Henry Clay of Kentucky, Speech in the U.S Senate, July 10, 1832.

"A bill to re-charter the bank [of the United States], has recently passed Congress, after much deliberation. . . . Notwithstanding this state of things, the president has rejected the bill, and transmitted to the Senate an elaborate message, communicating at large his objections. . . .

There are some parts of this message that ought to excite deep alarm; and that especially in which the president announces, that each public officer may interpret the Constitution as he pleases. His language is, 'Each public officer, who takes an oath to support the Constitution, swears that he will support it as he understands it, and not as it is understood by others.'

. . . I conceive . . . that the president has mistaken the purport [meaning] of the oath to support the Constitution of the United States. No one swears to support it as he understands it, but to support it simply as it is in truth. . . . [I]f [every official] . . . is bound to obey the Constitution only *as he understands it;* what would be the consequence? . . . We should have nothing settled, nothing stable, nothing fixed. There would be general disorder and confusion throughout every branch of administration, from the highest to the lowest officers — universal nullification. For what is the doctrine of the president but that of South Carolina applied throughout the Union? The president independent both of Congress and the Supreme Court! only bound to execute the laws of the one and the decisions of the other, as far as they conform to the Constitution of the United States, *as far as he understands it*!

. . . [W]e are about to close one of the longest and most arduous sessions of Congress under the present Constitution; and when we return among our constituents, what account of the operations of their government shall we be bound to communicate? . . . that the president has promulgated a rule of action for those who have taken the oath to support the Constitution of the United States, that must, if there be practical conformity to it, introduce general nullification, and end in the absolute subversion of the government."

DOCUMENT 6

Source: Letter from Fairfax Catlett, member of the Republic of Texas delegation to the United States, to Sam Houston, President of the Republic of Texas, September 5, 1837.

"The proposition for annexation was fairly made. . . . No means were left untried to secure a[n] . . . answer from the Executive. But it was all in vain. As might have been expected from a knowledge of Mr Van Buren's character . . . he has mildly but decisively declined the proposition to treat upon the subject. It is the opinion of most of the members with whom I have conversed, that the question . . . will be forced up [in Congress] by the South some time next winter and will then produce a hurricane in that body more alarming than any which has ever rocked this Union to its centre. The Southern men with but few exceptions appear to regard the annexation of Texas as their last and forlorn hope. Should the measure fail and the Northern Abolitionists gain the ascendancy in Congress . . . it will be a question between the slave holding and non slave holding interests, (and there will be no middle ground upon which the two great parties can meet and compromise their differences). . . . With regard to Mr Van Buren's policy respecting the annexation of Texas I conceive it to be simply as follows[.] He would like to get Texas, but he is afraid of the consequences. . . . For by coming out as an open advocate of the measure, he would lose the North en masse . . . and dash his party into chaos. He would have to change his ground altogether and commence an entirely new system of operations. . . . The question is one of tremendous import, for it involves the destiny of North America for fifty years to come. . . . I doubt not that Mr Van Buren is fully alive to all the momentous bearings of the question upon the future welfare of the Union, and that he dreads the approach of the debate in Congress. . . . Yet it was not the less necessary that the proposition should be made. It has been made, declined, and it now rests with the Congress of the United States to determine whether Texas shall add another star to the cluster of the Union or — commence the conquest of the whole of Mexico. But the negotiation may be regarded as closed for the present."

DOCUMENT 7

Source: The Democratic Party Platform, 1840.

1. Resolved, That the federal government is one of limited powers, derived solely from the constitution, and the grants of power shown therein, ought to be strictly construed by all the departments and agents of the government, and that it is inexpedient and dangerous to exercise doubtful constitutional powers.

2. Resolved, That the constitution does not confer upon the general government the power to commence and carry on, a general system of internal improvements. . . .

4. Resolved, That justice and sound policy forbid the federal government to foster one branch of industry to the detriment of another, or to cherish the interests of one portion to the injury of another portion of our common country — that every citizen and every section of the country, has a right to demand and insist upon an equality of rights and privileges, and to complete and ample protection of person and property from domestic violence, or foreign aggression. . . .

7. Resolved, That congress has no power, under the constitution, to interfere with or control the domestic institutions of the several states, and that such states are the sole and proper judges of everything appertaining to their own affairs, not prohibited by the constitution; that all efforts by abolitionists or others, made to induce congress to interfere with questions of slavery, or to take incipient steps in relation thereto, are calculated to lead to the most alarming and dangerous consequences, and that all such efforts have an inevitable tendency to diminish the happiness of the people, and endanger the stability and permanency of the union, and ought not to be countenanced by any friend to our political institutions.

LONG ESSAY QUESTIONS *Suggested writing time: 40 minutes.*

DIRECTIONS: Please choose one of the following three questions to answer. Make a historically defensible claim and support your reasoning with specific and relevant evidence.

2. Compare the relative significance of the effects the Market Revolution had on regional economies in the period from 1800–1848.
3. Compare the relative significance of the various experiences of both enslaved and free African Americans in the period 1800–1848.
4. Compare the relative significance of the regional interests that contributed to westward expansion in the period from 1800–1848.

5 PART

Consolidating a Continental Union

1844–1877

Should historians of the United States call the mid-nineteenth century the Civil War era? Many do, but in *America's History* we choose a slightly different emphasis. Like other scholars, we argue that the Civil War and emancipation brought extraordinary changes in U.S. politics, law, society, and culture. We devote a chapter to the political crisis of the 1850s; one to the Civil War itself; and one to Reconstruction, the postwar struggle over power and policy in the ex-Confederacy and nationwide. We situate these struggles, however, in the context of U.S. conquest of the West, a process that began before the Civil War and continued during and afterward.

The first Republican president, Abraham Lincoln, engineered the triumph of the Union, but on terms few expected when the Civil War began. Instead of a short, heroic fight between white northerners and southerners, the conflict turned into an agonizing "hard war" that lasted four weary years. Emancipation, which few expected at the start, proved essential to winning the war, as did the participation and sacrifice of African Americans, 180,000 of whom served in the U.S. Army for the first time.

Union victory ended slavery — a momentous achievement. It did not, however, resolve the bitter disagreements that had caused the war in the first place, conflicts that emerged from the United States' expanding claims for territory and continental power. In fact, conflicting points of view multiplied in the decades after Confederate defeat. In one of history's astonishing upsets, the Republican Party — which did not exist until 1854 — not only won the presidency by 1860 but wielded unparalleled power because of the South's secession. During and after the war, Republicans remade the federal government. They increased U.S. control over the trans-Mississippi West, transformed economic and political relationships among the nation's regions, and set the stage for U.S. global influence. As you read about the transformations of the era, here are a few key questions to keep in mind. ▶

AP® CONCEPT CONNECTIONS

Why did the Civil War happen, and why did the Union win?

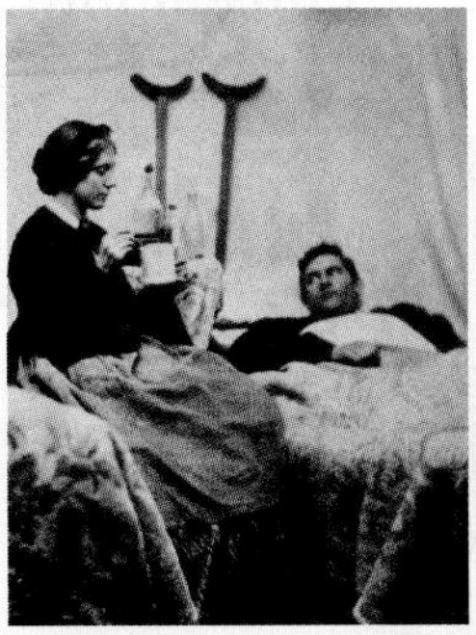

Corbis via Getty Images.

Politicians in the 1840s and 1850s were eager to add new land to the United States, believing that expansion would bring economic growth and military security. Many also hoped geographic expansion would lessen internal conflicts, but instead land acquisitions in the U.S.-Mexico War prompted a decade-long dispute over whether slavery should expand. The Compromise of 1850, a complex legislative agreement designed to solve the impasse, won little support in either North or South, and the Kansas-Nebraska Act of 1854 brought further conflict. Southern Whigs abandoned their party for the Democrats, while northern Whigs became Republicans or anti-immigrant Know-Nothings. By 1860, Democrats also split on sectional lines, enabling the election of Republican president Abraham Lincoln. The United States divided over whether the nation should promote slavery or "free soil" for white farmers with the possibility of eventually ending slavery.

Slaveholders could not tolerate Lincoln's election. In response, eleven southern states seceded and created the Confederate States of America. Elsewhere, citizens rallied to preserve the Union. In the Civil War that followed, the Confederacy began with superior military commanders. The North won, however, because the South did not win quickly: as the conflict became an extended "hard war," the North's superior financial and industrial resources eventually gave it the advantage, as did Lincoln's proclamation of emancipation in 1863. Linking Union victory to the end of slavery undermined European support for the Confederacy and added thousands of African Americans to the northern armies, helping Union forces sweep across the South and end the war.

How did the Civil War and Reconstruction transform American government?

Library of Congress, 3g05606.

The Civil War created a powerful American state, as the Union government mobilized millions of men and billions of dollars. Republicans created an elaborate network of national banks and — for the first time in U.S. history — a significant federal bureaucracy. Congress intervened forcefully to integrate the national economy and promote industrialization. These policies, along with the dynamic postwar economy, committed the United States to a modern capitalist order, one built on massive public investment in public-private partnerships (such as railroad building) that ultimately served corporate ends. The results transformed the nation, extending federal authority to far-flung corners of the continent and setting the United States on a course toward global power.

The federal government asserted its authority in other ways after the war. Three Republican-sponsored constitutional amendments limited the powers of the states and imposed new definitions of citizenship — prohibiting slavery, enfranchising black men, and forbidding state actions that denied people equal protection under the law. These amendments were undercut, however, by ex-Confederates' resistance and violence, indifference among white northerners, and a Supreme Court that refused to authorize the protection of black voting rights. Despite these failures, Reconstruction opened new opportunities for African Americans and created a blueprint for greater future equality.

Why and how did the United States create a continental empire between the 1840s and 1890s?

Allen Memorial Art Museum, Oberlin College, Ohio, USA/Gift of Mrs. Jacob D. Cox/Bridgeman Images.

The United States claimed large swaths of western territory in the 1840s, through victory in the U.S.-Mexico War and the California gold rush that followed. But it was post–Civil War railroad building and economic expansion that truly brought the West into the orbit of federal authority. This expansion intensified conflicts between Native peoples, Mexican Americans, and Anglo newcomers.

The U.S. Army, which occupied parts of the ex-Confederacy as late as 1877, also suppressed Indian resistance and extended national control in the West. By 1890, most Native peoples had been forced onto reservations, while thousands of Mexicans also found themselves dispossessed. The legacies of the Civil War, therefore, were as significant in the West as in the former Confederacy. Western minerals, lumber, cattle, wheat, and oil proved essential to the transformation we will discuss in Part 6: the United States's economic transformation and rise to global economic power.

Organized around a single theme, the Part 5 Document Set in *Sources for America's History* can be used to teach AP® Theme NAT: American and National Identity, which analyzes the debates over the true meaning of the Constitution, the relationship between the federal and state government, and the definition of citizenship.

AP® THEMATIC UNDERSTANDING

Consolidating a Continental Union, 1844–1877

1845 | 1855 | 1865 | 1875

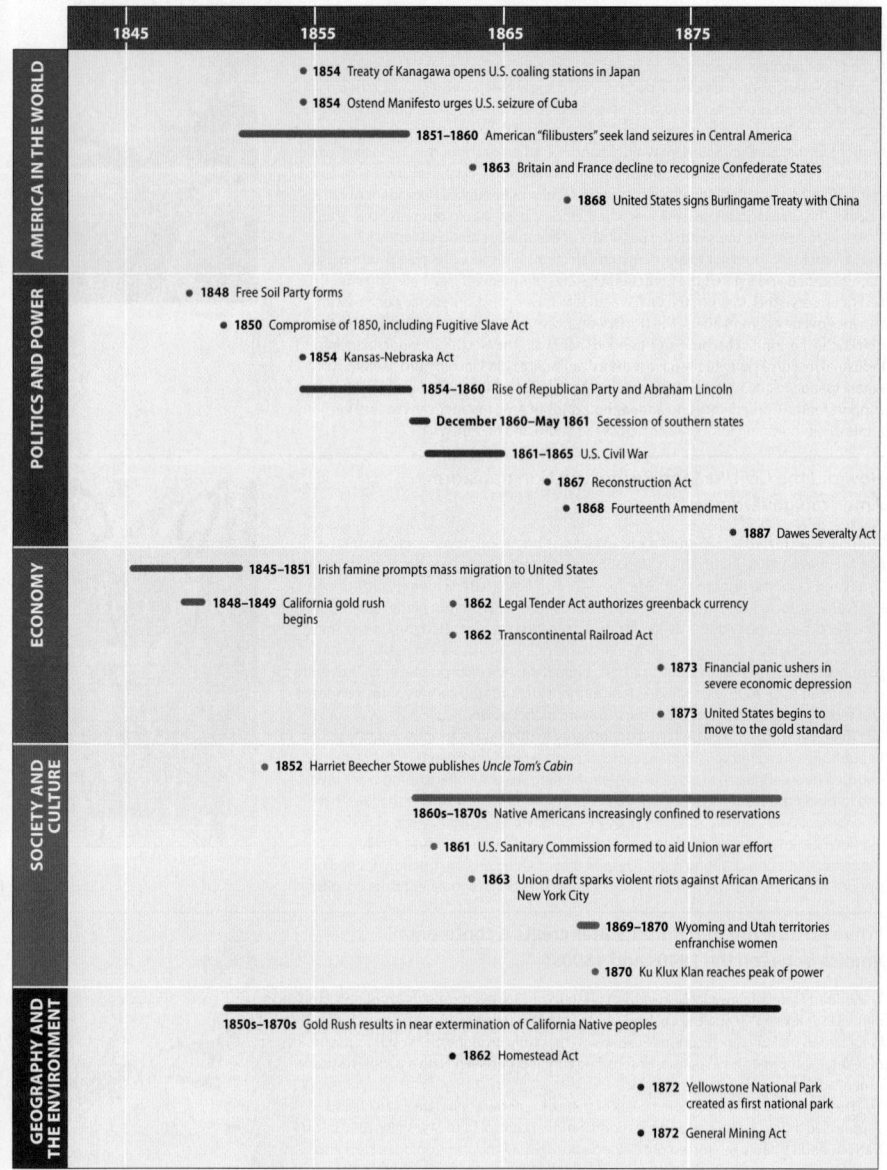

AMERICA IN THE WORLD

- **1854** Treaty of Kanagawa opens U.S. coaling stations in Japan
- **1854** Ostend Manifesto urges U.S. seizure of Cuba
- **1851–1860** American "filibusters" seek land seizures in Central America
- **1863** Britain and France decline to recognize Confederate States
- **1868** United States signs Burlingame Treaty with China

POLITICS AND POWER

- **1848** Free Soil Party forms
- **1850** Compromise of 1850, including Fugitive Slave Act
- **1854** Kansas-Nebraska Act
- **1854–1860** Rise of Republican Party and Abraham Lincoln
- **December 1860–May 1861** Secession of southern states
- **1861–1865** U.S. Civil War
- **1867** Reconstruction Act
- **1868** Fourteenth Amendment
- **1887** Dawes Severalty Act

ECONOMY

- **1845–1851** Irish famine prompts mass migration to United States
- **1848–1849** California gold rush begins
- **1862** Legal Tender Act authorizes greenback currency
- **1862** Transcontinental Railroad Act
- **1873** Financial panic ushers in severe economic depression
- **1873** United States begins to move to the gold standard

SOCIETY AND CULTURE

- **1852** Harriet Beecher Stowe publishes *Uncle Tom's Cabin*
- **1860s–1870s** Native Americans increasingly confined to reservations
- **1861** U.S. Sanitary Commission formed to aid Union war effort
- **1863** Union draft sparks violent riots against African Americans in New York City
- **1869–1870** Wyoming and Utah territories enfranchise women
- **1870** Ku Klux Klan reaches peak of power

GEOGRAPHY AND THE ENVIRONMENT

- **1850s–1870s** Gold Rush results in near extermination of California Native peoples
- **1862** Homestead Act
- **1872** Yellowstone National Park created as first national park
- **1872** General Mining Act

AP® Making Connections Across Chapters

Read these questions and think about them as you read the chapters in this part. When you have completed reading this part, return to these questions and answer them.

1 Between 1844 and 1890, what conflicts and transformations did U.S. expansion bring about in the trans-Mississippi West? How did it shape the nation's geographic scope?

PhotoQuest/Getty Images.

2 In 1850, the United States was—in its constitution, laws, and political and social order—a white man's country. In what ways was that still true in 1877, and in what ways had law, policy, and custom come to acknowledge the United States as a multiracial society?

The Granger Collection, NY.

3 In what ways did the scope and power of the federal government grow in this era, and why? What roles did the Civil War play in this transformation?

Library of Congress, LC-DIG-ppmsca-09398.

4 In addition to the Civil War itself, what other forms of violent conflict arose in this period, and what were their results?

Sarin Images/Granger, NYC.

5 How did events between 1850 and 1877 set the stage for the United States to become a global industrial power? In what ways did political events lead to particular types of economic growth or development, and to what extent did economic shifts drive political changes?

Library of Congress, 3g04588.

TRM Find complete suggested responses in the Teacher's Resource Materials.

12 CHAPTER

Sectional Conflict and Crisis

1844–1861

Chapter 12 — AP® Assessment Weight and Pacing Guide

The assessment weight on the AP® U.S. History Exam for Chapters 12–14 is 10–17 percent. This chapter falls in Unit 5 of the AP® U.S. History Curriculum, covering Period 5: 1844–1877.

This pacing guide is based on a schedule with 120 sessions of 50 minutes each before the AP® U.S. History Exam. If you have a different number of sessions before the exam, you can modify the pacing to meet your needs. If you have additional time, consider incorporating quizzes, released AP® U.S. History questions, practice exams, writing practice, and other instructional activities.

	Traditional Schedule	Block Schedule
Chapter 12	5 days	2–3 days

Daily Pacing Guide

	Content Focus	Essential Question
Day 1	Consequences of the U.S.-Mexico War, 1844–1850	How did U.S. acquisition of lands in the U.S.-Mexico War trigger political conflicts?
Day 2	An Emerging Political Crisis, 1850–1858	Why did Democrats and Whigs fail in their attempts to keep the issue of slavery in the federal territories from creating a sectional rift?
Days 3 and 4	Abraham Lincoln and the Republican Triumph, 1858–1860	Why did the Republican Party win national power in 1860?
Day 5	Secession Winter, 1860–1861	After South Carolina's secession, why were Unionists and Confederates unable to avoid war?

AP® Alignment

Section Heading	AP® Topic	AP® Theme
Consequences of the U.S.-Mexico War, 1844–1850	5.3, 5.4, 5.5	WOR, NAT, ARC
An Emerging Political Crisis, 1850–1858	5.4, 5.5, 5.6	NAT, ARC, SOC, PCE
Abraham Lincoln and the Republican Triumph, 1858–1860	5.6, 5.7	PCE
Secession Winter, 1860–1861	5.8, 5.9	WOR, NAT

*Should changes be made to the Course Framework in the future, an updated alignment will be placed on our AP® updates page at go.bfwpub.com/ap-course-updates.

Chapter 12 — Overview

Chapter 12 opens with an analysis of the results of the U.S.-Mexico War on U.S. politics and the rising debate over both the expansion of slavery and the idea of abolition. The chapter focuses both on the impact of the war on Americans and on Mexican nationals and Native American groups in the West. The Compromise of 1850 altered the debates in the U.S. over slavery and federal supremacy leading to the breakdown of the two-party system. This in turn allowed the Republican Party to rise in power based on a "free soil" platform. Finally, the chapter focuses on the rise of Abraham Lincoln to national prominence largely due to the Lincoln-Douglas debates. The chapter concludes with an analysis of the election of 1860 and the impact of Lincoln's victory on the debate over slavery, "free soil," abolitionism, and states' rights, leading to the secession of eleven southern states.

Chapter 12 — Resources

The following resources can be found in the Teacher's Resource Materials (TRM) that accompany the book. You can access the TRM via the book's digital platform, by clicking the TRM links found here in your Teacher's Edition e-book, or by contacting your representative to access the resources online. Visit **bfwpub.com/henretta10e** to learn more.

TRM Chapter 12 Lecture Presentation Slides

TRM Chapter 12 Outline with AP® Focus

TRM Chapter 12 Lecture Strategies

TRM Chapter 12 Suggested Responses

TRM Handout 12.1 — Causation: Impact of U.S.-Mexico War

TRM Handout 12.2 — Comparison: Courts and Congress on Slavery in the 1850s

TRM Handout 12.3 — Contextualization: Election of 1860

Chapter 12 — Essential Activity

Use a document analysis activity to investigate the ideas of Abraham Lincoln on the issue of slavery with the goal of defining and clarifying Lincoln's political, personal, and moral views. Provide students with excerpts from the following documents (other sources may be used): Personal Letter to Joshua Speed of Kentucky, Chicago, Illinois (July 10, 1858); "House-Divided" Speech in Springfield, Illinois (June 16, 1858); *The Collected Works of Abraham Lincoln*, ed. Roy P. Basler, Vol. II (August 1, 1858); Fourth Debate with Stephen A. Douglas at Charleston, Illinois (September 18, 1858); Sixth Debate with Stephen A. Douglas, Quincy, Illinois (October 13, 1858); Seventh and Last Debate with Stephen A. Douglas, Alton, Illinois (October 15, 1858); Letter to Alexander H. Stephens (December 22, 1860); Letter to William H. Seward (February 1, 1861); Lincoln's First Inaugural Address (March 4, 1861); Letter to Horace Greeley (August 22, 1862); and Speech to One Hundred Fortieth Indiana

Regiment (March 17, 1865). Ask students to work in pairs or in small collaborative groups to provide an extended analysis of each source for the ideas Lincoln expresses regarding slavery, including notes on historical context, intended audience, and purpose. Then ask students to group these ideas into three categories: political, personal, or moral views.

Chapter 12 — Bell Ringers

The following activities take no more than 5–15 minutes of your class period and offer an effective and engaging way to begin your lessons and for students to apply AP® Skills & Processes:

- Have students work in pairs and read the **AP® COMPARING INTERPRETATIONS** feature on pp. 384–385 of the text. One student should read the excerpt by Ramsdell, the other the excerpt by Smith. Then each student should explain the historical argument of each historian to his or her partner. In their discussion, students should explain the difference in the historical interpretations and the reasons/use of evidence that led each historian to his or her conclusion. Ask students to consider evidence that is not provided in the excerpts that could support or challenge each interpretation.
- Project an image of the political cartoon "Forcing Slavery down the Throat of a Free Soiler" or provide students with a copy. To access this cartoon, search "Library of Congress Forcing Slavery." Divide the image into quadrants and ask students to list the elements included in each quadrant. Remind students that every element in a cartoon is likely to have meaning, unlike inadvertent elements that can appear in photographs. Have students explain, with their partner, what each element in the cartoon represents and then come together as a class to discuss.

NOTES

TEACHING STRATEGY

The chapter opener sets the stage for this chapter's exploration of the rapid dissolution of the Union, which took place between the end of the U.S.-Mexico War in 1848 and the election of Abraham Lincoln twelve years later. As the text makes clear, debates about slavery were central to this dissolution. Students should recognize that the issue of slavery had divided the nation since debates at the Philadelphia Convention. It would be useful, therefore, to ask students why events of this period of little more than a decade following the war proved so different from earlier debates. As the **AP® LEARNING FOCUS** question hints, the rise of the Republican Party — facilitated by the demise of the Whig Party — played a significant role. For a complete suggested response to the **AP® LEARNING FOCUS** question, see p. 412.

12 CHAPTER

Sectional Conflict and Crisis 1844–1861

AP® LEARNING FOCUS

Why did the new Republican Party arise, and what events led to Democratic division and southern secession?

The U.S.-Mexico War was immensely popular with millions of Americans. Those who opposed it took big risks, as young Abraham Lincoln discovered to his dismay. In December 1847, as a freshman Whig congressman from Illinois, Lincoln introduced a bill demanding that President Polk identify the exact spot where the war had begun, which Polk claimed had been in U.S. territory. Lincoln, like other critics, believed U.S. troops had been trespassing on Mexican soil. But Lincoln's "spot resolution" went nowhere. Ridiculing the young congressman, a newspaper in his home state nicknamed him "Spotty Lincoln" and a Democrat defeated him in the next election. Lincoln went back to his law practice in Springfield.

Soon afterward, in 1849, tales of California gold generated excitement over the riches waiting in newly taken territories. Thousands of American men rushed west, joining counterparts from Mexico, Chile, Hawaii, Britain, and elsewhere to gather gold from the beds of California's rivers and streams. San Francisco became an overnight boomtown. Alas, few struck it rich, and the chaotic quest for gold led to vigilantism, ugly racial conflicts, and the deliberate near-extermination of California's Native peoples.

Like the lure of California gold, U.S. dreams of territorial expansion gave way to harsher truths in the 1850s. The process of incorporating the **Mexican cession** — lands the United States had acquired in the war — reignited fierce debates over the expansion of slavery. Though only a small minority of white northerners were abolitionists, by the 1850s many feared the "slave power" of southern interests was dominating Washington, D.C. Most northerners wanted western territories reserved as "free soil" for white farmers. Rising politicians — among them Lincoln, who returned to politics to help found the Illinois Republican Party — vowed to block the expansion of slavery, pointing out that the Northwest Ordinance of 1787 barred slavery in the Midwest. Southerners, in turn, insisted that the Constitution protected slaveholders' property rights throughout the nation. As early as 1850, radical proslavery advocates called for secession, while others launched military expeditions into Latin America to add territory to slavery's empire. As conflict accelerated, violence erupted in California, Kansas, Virginia, and even on the Senate floor. The dispute shattered old alliances, ultimately fragmenting both major parties. By 1861 it ignited a political firestorm that engulfed the Union.

Mexican cession
Lands taken by the United States in the U.S.-Mexico War (1846–1848).

Fugitive Slave Law Convention in Cazenovia, New York, 1850 This daguerreotype, a detail from the only known photograph of an abolitionist meeting before the Civil War, shows the movement's diversity and determination. More than 2,000 abolitionists gathered in upstate New York for the convention, including about 50 fugitive slaves. Frederick Douglass, center left, presided. The group denounced the federal Fugitive Slave Act, which Congress was then debating; issued a letter of solidarity with those still enslaved; and raised money to free William Chaplin, a Washington, D.C., man who was imprisoned for helping a slave escape. Though the convention did not stop passage of the Fugitive Slave Act, it showed the growing militancy and political ambition of those who denounced the cruelty of slavery. Artokoloro Quint Lox Limited/Alamy Stock Photo.

TEACHING STRATEGY

Use David Brion Davis's essay "Slavery and Anti-Slavery," available online at the Gilder Lehrman Institute, to supplement your discussion on the abolitionist movement. Davis provides an excellent overview of the abolitionist movement, particularly the roles of blacks within it and its growing intensity in the wake of westward movement in the 1840s. To access the essay, search "Davis Slavery and Anti-Slavery."

TEACHING STRATEGY

Ask students: **What do this photo and caption reveal about the abolitionist movement at the start of the 1850s?** *The movement was diverse and included men and women, blacks and whites — and free people and (runaway) slaves. Though 2,000 people was a tiny number at a time when the national population was 23 million, this represented a critical mass of activists willing to engage in controversial actions. Their actions played a significant role in increasing the tensions that led to the Civil War.*

AP® SKILLS & PROCESSES

CONTINUITY AND CHANGE

Use the **TIMELINE** to help students begin thinking about how the period from 1844 to 1861 could constitute a distinct historical period. Students should note that this chapter moves the timeline forward for the first time in several chapters, as Chapters 8 through 11 all addressed basically the same period. At the same time, however, the chronology of this chapter is not completely new — it overlaps somewhat with that of Chapter 11. Students could explain why Chapter 12 begins with the election of Polk in 1844, rather than picking up in 1848, where Chapter 11 left off with the end of the U.S.-Mexico War. To extend this prompt, students can identify the effects of Lincoln's election at the end of this period.

TIMELINE

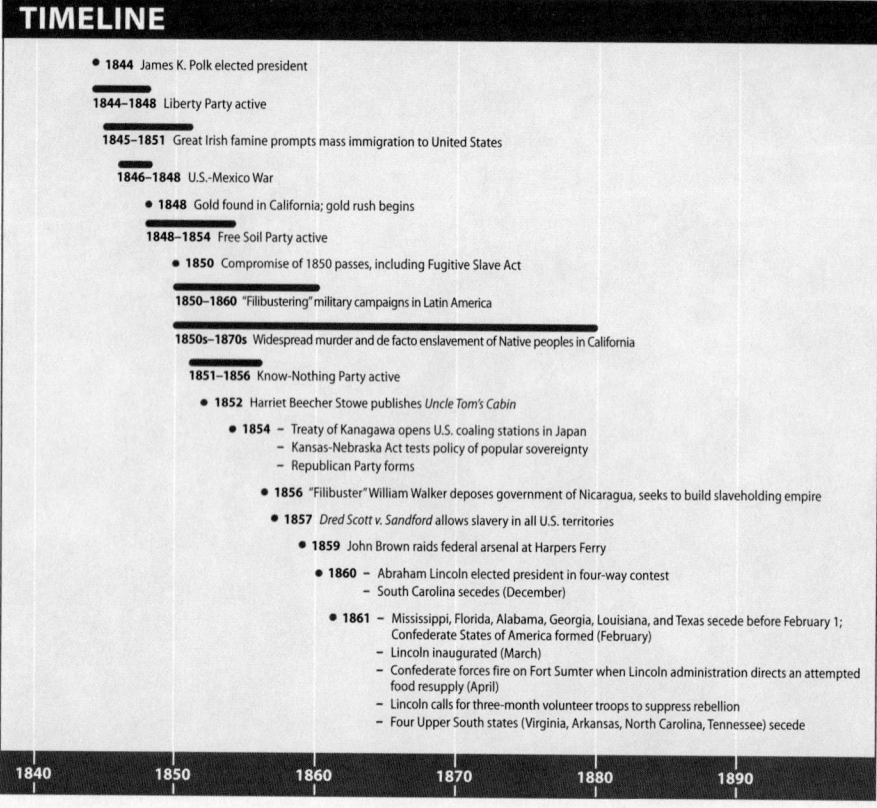

- **1844** James K. Polk elected president
- **1844–1848** Liberty Party active
- **1845–1851** Great Irish famine prompts mass immigration to United States
- **1846–1848** U.S.-Mexico War
- **1848** Gold found in California; gold rush begins
- **1848–1854** Free Soil Party active
- **1850** Compromise of 1850 passes, including Fugitive Slave Act
- **1850–1860** "Filibustering" military campaigns in Latin America
- **1850s–1870s** Widespread murder and de facto enslavement of Native peoples in California
- **1851–1856** Know-Nothing Party active
- **1852** Harriet Beecher Stowe publishes *Uncle Tom's Cabin*
- **1854** – Treaty of Kanagawa opens U.S. coaling stations in Japan
  - Kansas-Nebraska Act tests policy of popular sovereignty
  - Republican Party forms
- **1856** "Filibuster" William Walker deposes government of Nicaragua, seeks to build slaveholding empire
- **1857** *Dred Scott v. Sandford* allows slavery in all U.S. territories
- **1859** John Brown raids federal arsenal at Harpers Ferry
- **1860** – Abraham Lincoln elected president in four-way contest
  - South Carolina secedes (December)
- **1861** – Mississippi, Florida, Alabama, Georgia, Louisiana, and Texas secede before February 1; Confederate States of America formed (February)
  - Lincoln inaugurated (March)
  - Confederate forces fire on Fort Sumter when Lincoln administration directs an attempted food resupply (April)
  - Lincoln calls for three-month volunteer troops to suppress rebellion
  - Four Upper South states (Virginia, Arkansas, North Carolina, Tennessee) secede

1840 | 1850 | 1860 | 1870 | 1880 | 1890

CONSEQUENCES OF THE U.S.-MEXICO WAR, 1844–1850

How did U.S. acquisition of lands in the U.S.-Mexico War trigger political conflicts?

"The United States will conquer Mexico," Ralph Waldo Emerson had predicted as the war began, but "Mexico will poison us." He was right. The U.S.-Mexico War roused bitter sectional conflict even while it was being fought. Afterward, Congress engaged in fierce debates over how to handle the newly seized lands — especially whether to allow slavery there. Political conflict over this issue was so intense that new parties arose to advocate "free soil," following the model of midwestern states, such as Illinois and Indiana, that barred slavery but also barred entry by African Americans. At the same time, the discovery of gold launched thousands of prospectors to California, where in a quest to get rich they fought with one other, excluded immigrants from other countries, and ruthlessly exterminated Native peoples.

382

"Free Soil" in Politics

When voters repudiated Polk's war policy in the election of 1846, Whigs took control of the House. They called for a congressional pledge that the United States would not seek any land from the Mexican republic. Polk's expansionist policies also split the Democrats. As early as 1839, Ohio Democrat Thomas Morris had warned that "the power of slavery is aiming to govern the country." In 1846, David Wilmot, an antislavery Democratic congressman from Pennsylvania, took up that refrain and proposed the **Wilmot Proviso**, a ban on slavery in any territories gained from the war with Mexico. Whigs and antislavery Democrats in the House of Representatives quickly passed the bill, dividing Congress along sectional lines. Fearful that southern voters would heed calls for secession, a few proslavery northern senators joined their southern colleagues to kill the proviso. But the dispute had just begun.

AP® EXAM TIP

Identifying the connection between the Mexican-American War and growing conflict over slavery is essential for the AP® Exam.

Wilmot Proviso
The 1846 proposal by Representative David Wilmot of Pennsylvania to ban slavery in territory acquired from the U.S.-Mexico War.

Slavery in the Mexican Cession At the war's end, President Polk, Secretary of State Buchanan, and Senators Stephen A. Douglas of Illinois and Jefferson Davis of Mississippi called for annexation of a huge swath of Mexican territory south of the Rio Grande. John C. Calhoun and others, however, feared this would require the assimilation of many mixed-race people. They favored only annexation of sparsely settled New Mexico and California. "Ours is a government of the white man," proclaimed Calhoun; it should never welcome "any but the Caucasian race." To unify the Democratic Party, Polk and Buchanan accepted Calhoun's policy. In 1848, Polk signed, and the Senate ratified, the Treaty of Guadalupe Hidalgo, in which the United States agreed to pay Mexico $15 million in return for more than one-third of its territory (Map 12.1).

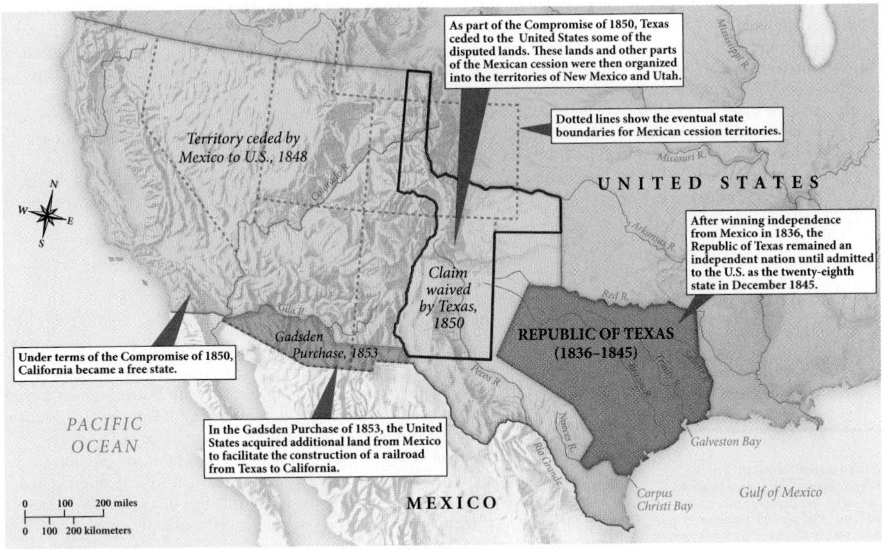

MAP 12.1 The Mexican Cession, 1848
In the Treaty of Guadalupe Hidalgo (1848), Mexico ceded to the United States its vast northern territories — the present-day states of California, Nevada, Utah, Arizona, New Mexico, and half of Colorado. These new territories, President Polk boasted to Congress, "constitute of themselves a country large enough for a great empire, and the acquisition is second in importance only to that of Louisiana in 1803."

AP® APPLY THE TIP

Provide students with an image of a Free Soil Party campaign poster, an advertisement for a meeting of an antislavery society, excerpts from the Wilmot Proviso, Henry David Thoreau's "On Civil Disobedience," and George Fitzhugh's *Sociology of the South*. Ask students to analyze each source to find evidence of growing conflict over slavery in the U.S. Students should also engage in an extended analysis by looking at the historical context related to the U.S.-Mexico War, the purpose of the document, the intended audience, and the point of view of the author of the document. Ask students to use the documents to organize a thesis statement addressing the extent to which the U.S.-Mexico War caused a change in the debate over slavery in the United States.

AP® THEME

NAT: American and National Identity
Use **MAP 12.1** to reveal the ways the Mexican cession led to controversies over whether to allow slavery in the newly acquired territories. Ask students: **Based on the map, why might some southerners have resisted the admission of California as a free state?** *The southern part of the state is due west of the southern states and south of the 36°30′ latitude, so closing the state to slavery set a precedent for not extending the Missouri Compromise line all the way to the West Coast.*

AP® SKILLS & PROCESSES

ANALYZING HISTORICAL EVIDENCE

The **AP® COMPARING INTERPRETATIONS** feature explores the question of slavery's expansion in the West. It implicitly challenges stereotypes about, as Smith says, "the myth that the West was a landscape of liberty." First, students should recognize that Smith is offering a broader assessment of unfree labor in the West — not just African American slavery. Second, students should note the date of Ramsdell's piece. The age of a piece of scholarship should not disqualify its merits from being considered. However, trends in the 1920s demand that any claims involving slavery and race be evaluated critically.

AP® APPLY THE TIP

Provide students with **Handout 12.1 — Causation: Impact of the U.S.-Mexico War (TRM)**. Have students work in pairs to consider the cause and effect relationships of each event listed on the handout. Students should focus on the ways that the American victory in the U.S.-Mexico War impacted American Indians, Mexicans, Chinese immigrants, and others. Then lead a class discussion to address the following questions:

- **How did the discovery of gold in California impact non-American settlers and inhabitants of California?** *Answers will vary but should emphasize the displacement of Native groups and Mexicans from areas sought after for gold mining.*
- **How did the American victory in the war with Mexico compound the problems of minority groups in California?** *American victory resulted in the Mexican cession, which gave the U.S. control over California, and ended protection of the rights of Mexican nationals in the region.*
- **Were events in California part of a larger pattern of U.S. impact on groups in the West? Or something new?** *Answers will vary, but should touch on the following: a larger pattern is evident in American expansion across the continent under the banner of Manifest Destiny, which included adding areas such as Texas and Oregon where Native groups were displaced to allow for American control and settlement. However, the use of military power against another nation to achieve the goal of expansion can be considered new given previously this was largely achieved through negotiation and diplomacy.*

AP® COMPARING INTERPRETATIONS

Did Slavery Have a Future in the West?

During the antebellum period, cotton planters pushed west into the Mississippi Valley in search of the region's rich and fertile soil. This demographic and economic shift west fueled antislavery fears that slavery was poised to spread across the continent. Abraham Lincoln's Republican Party responded to this fear by rejecting popular sovereignty in the territories and decrying the infamous *Dred Scott* decision, calling for slavery's containment in the states where it already existed. To slavery's supporters, the movement west kindled hopes of economic and political survival in the face of mounting abolitionist attacks. Slaveholders also confronted declining soil quality on the lands where they currently farmed, and they feared the consequences of a growing enslaved population, unless planters had a "safety valve" of westward expansion. While slavery's enemies and defenders clashed over the legitimacy of its expansion into the territories, many on both sides accepted the idea that slavery *could* expand even into areas such as the Great Plains, the Southwest, and California. But did slavery have a future in the West? And, if so, what was it? Two scholars, Charles W. Ramsdell and Stacey L. Smith, offer different assessments regarding the limits of slavery's expansion.

CHARLES W. RAMSDELL

SOURCE: Charles W. Ramsdell, "The Natural Limits of Slavery Expansion," *Mississippi Valley Historical Review* 16 (September 1929): 155–157. Reprinted by permission of *The Journal of American History*/The Organization of American Historians, Oxford University Press via Copyright Clearance Center.

The extension of the cotton plantation into the interior of Texas had to wait upon the development of a cheaper and more efficient means of transportation. As all attempts to improve the navigation of the shallow, snag-filled rivers failed, it became more and more evident that the only solution of the problem of the interior planter lay in the building of railroads. Throughout the eighteen-fifties, and indeed for two decades after the [Civil] War, there was a feverish demand for railroads in all parts of the state. The newspapers of the period were full of projects and promises, and scores of railroad companies were organized or promoted. But capital was lacking and the roads were slow in building. Not a single railroad had reached the fertile black-land belt of central Texas by 1860. There can hardly be any question that the cotton plantations with their working forces of slaves would have followed the railroads westward until they reached the black-land prairies of central Texas or the semi-arid plains which cover the western half of the state. But would they have followed on into the prairies and the plains? . . .

The history of the Texas plains region since 1880 affords abundant evidence that it would never have become suitable for plantation slave labor . . . . It took more than twenty years of experimentation and adaptation with wind mills, dry-farming, and new drought-resisting feed crops for the cotton farmer to conquer the plains. There is little reason to believe that the conquest could have been effected earlier; there is even less basis for belief that the region would ever have been filled with plantations and slaves . . . It is likely that the institution of slavery would have declined toward extinction in the Old South before the cotton conquest of the plains could have been

AP® EXAM TIP

Evaluate the impact of American victory in the Mexican War on Mexicans and American Indians in lands ceded to the U.S.

"slave power" conspiracy
The political argument, made by abolitionists, free soilers, and Republicans in the pre–Civil War years, that southern slaveholders were using their unfair representative advantage under the three-fifths compromise of the Constitution, as well as their clout within the Democratic Party, to demand extreme federal proslavery policies (such as annexation of Cuba) that the majority of American voters would not support.

Congress also created the Oregon Territory in 1848 and, two years later, passed the Oregon Donation Land Claim Act, which granted farm-sized plots of land to settlers who took up residence before 1854. Soon, treaties with Native peoples erased Indian titles to much of the new territory. With the claiming of Oregon, New Mexico, and California, American conquest of the Far West rapidly advanced.

Commentators debated whether the arid lands of the Southwest were suitable for slavery or cotton culture. Debates over expansion dominated the election of 1848. The Senate's rejection of the Wilmot Proviso revived charges that southern politicians were leading a **"slave power" conspiracy** to dominate the federal government. They pointed out that the Constitution allowed slaveholding states to count each slave as three-fifths of a person for purposes of electoral representation, though of course slaves did not vote; thus, whites in areas with large numbers of slaves had disproportionate political power. Northerners also argued that Democrats were favoring southern interests in their appointments and policies.

384

TRM Find **Handout 12.1 — Causation: Impact of the U.S.-Mexico War** in the Teacher's Resource Materials.

accomplished, even had there been no Civil War . . . . It would have been almost impossible to establish the plantation system in this semi-arid section where, in the experimental period, complete losses of crops were so frequent. With so much of his capital tied up in unremunerative laborers whom he must feed and clothe, it is hard to see how any planter could have stayed in that country. Moreover, in the later period the use of improved machinery, especially adapted to the plains, would have made slave labor unnecessary and unbearably expensive.

STACEY L. SMITH

SOURCE: Stacey L. Smith, *Freedom's Frontier: California and the Struggle over Unfree Labor, Emancipation, and Reconstruction* (Chapel Hill: University of North Carolina Press, 2013), 2–6.

California's struggle over slavery did not end with its entrance into the Union as a free state as part of the Compromise of 1850. Instead . . . California's free soil was far less solid, its contests over human bondage far more complicated, contentious, and protracted, than historians have usually imagined. Across the antebellum and Civil War decades, Californians saw the rise of a dense tangle of unfree labor systems . . . that undermined and unsettled free-state status. The development of African American slavery, diverse forms of American Indian servitude, sexual trafficking in bound women, and contract labor arrangements involving Latin Americans, Asians, and Pacific Islanders all kept the slavery question alive in California . . . .

The persistence of the slavery question in California . . . challenges us to rethink the broader narrative of nineteenth-century U.S. history. Histories of the sectional crisis invariably focus on politics east of the Mississippi River and treat the Far West as an imagined space, a place onto which northerners and southerners projected their hopes and fears about slavery's future . . . California's story can enhance our understanding of U.S. national history in fundamental ways. A multiracial society with multiple systems of bound and semibound labor, California complicates familiar black-white, slave-free binaries . . . . White Californians were just as likely to express concern about American Indian, Mexican, Chilean, and Chinese "slaves" as they were to discuss the fate of African American bondpeople . . . . Politicians, reformers, and lawyers refashioned the language of antislavery . . . to contest labor systems ranging from peonage to contract labor to prostitution . . . .

[Scholars have] done much to dispel the myth that the West was a landscape of liberty . . . . [They have] demonstrated how the region's vast geography and seemingly limitless opportunities restricted rather than enhanced workers' freedom. Reliant on employers and labor contractors to move them to and across the West's wide-open spaces, immigrant workers often became enmeshed in debt peonage and contract labor . . . . [Historians] have documented the journeys of slaves to the goldfields, California's systems of forced Indian labor, the lives of Chinese women bound in the sex trade, and the debates over imagined Chinese "coolie" slavery on the Pacific coast. In light of this research, the idea that western environments, economies, or social structures were somehow incompatible with bound labor is gradually losing its force.

AP® SHORT ANSWER PRACTICE

1. One of these historians focuses on Texas and the other on California. How does each scholar's geographic focus shape his or her conclusions?
2. To what extent does each historian emphasize geography, environment, and labor systems in assessing slavery's future in the West?
3. Imagine that Smith wrote a review of Ramsdell's article. What strengths and weaknesses might she point out? What factors does she emphasize, in the passage from her book reprinted here, that Ramsdell did not consider in 1929?
4. Why is this debate over the potential for slavery in the West important to historians seeking to understand the sectional crisis described in this chapter?

TRM Find complete suggested responses in the Teacher's Resource Materials.

To protest this perceived bias, thousands of ordinary northerners, such as farmer Abijah Beckwith of Herkimer County, New York, joined the **free soil movement**. Slavery, Beckwith wrote in his diary, was an "aristocratic" institution, a danger to "the great mass of the people [because it] . . . threatens the general and equal distribution of our lands into convenient family farms." Free soil ideas drew on a popular movement for access to public lands that had been growing since the 1820s. Increasingly, frontier congressmen pressured the U.S. government to give land to poor farmers — a demand ultimately fulfilled by the Homestead Act of 1862 (see "Comparing Interpretations," p. 384).

Free soilers quickly organized for the election of 1848. Compared with abolitionists, the new Free Soil Party placed less emphasis on slavery as a sin. Instead, like Beckwith, the new party's leaders depicted slavery as a threat to republicanism and the Jeffersonian ideal of a freeholder society, arguments that won broad support among aspiring white farmers. Hundreds of men and women in the Great Lakes states joined free soil organizations formed by the American and Foreign Anti-Slavery

free soil movement
A political movement that opposed the expansion of slavery. In 1848, the free soilers organized the Free Soil Party, which depicted slavery as a threat to republicanism and to the Jeffersonian ideal of a freeholder society, arguments that won broad support among aspiring white farmers.

AP® THEME

ARC: American and Regional Culture

The U.S. government engaged in conflict with American Indians in regions newly taken from Mexico, altering these groups' economic self-sufficiency and cultures. In some cases, the government supported even uglier behavior by whites toward American Indians. The white campaign against the Yuki will be unfamiliar to most students. In "Patterns of Frontier Genocide 1803–1910," genocide scholar Benjamin Madley reviews the basic narrative of violence in pages 176 to 181 of an article available to the public. To access this article, search "Journal of Genocide Research Patterns of Frontier."

AP® THEME

NAT: American and National Identity

The free soil movement played a significant role in debates during the 1840s and 1850s about the expansion of slavery. Sympathetic to free whites rather than to slaves, the movement's members portrayed the expansion of slavery as incompatible with free labor in a republic.

CHECK FOR UNDERSTANDING

Ask students: **What did the label "Free Soil" mean in national politics during the 1840s?** *Both a movement and a political party, free soil was a popular movement demanding access to public lands. It denounced slavery as a threat to republicanism and Jeffersonian notions of widespread ownership of land.*

AP® SKILLS & PROCESSES

DEVELOPMENTS AND PROCESSES

Immediately attendant to the idea of a "free soil" movement was a belief in free labor. Free Labor was a basic tenet of the Republican Party because they believed that a democratic society, with free labor, offered social mobility and would further economic progress. Ask students to explain how, economically, the northern half of the country embraced a free labor movement.

TRM Find complete suggested responses in the Teacher's Resource Materials.

Society. So did Frederick Douglass, the foremost black abolitionist, who attended the first Free Soil Party convention in the summer of 1848 and endorsed its strategy. Douglass believed Free Soilers could win far more political clout than abolitionists could, ultimately undermining slavery. William Lloyd Garrison and other abolitionists, however, condemned the new party's stress on the rights of freeholders as racist "whitemanism."

AP® EXAM TIP

Outline the ways the debate over slavery after the Mexican-American War illustrates both continuity and change over time.

The Election of 1848 The conflict over slavery took a toll on Polk and the Democratic Party. Scorned by Whigs and Free Soilers and exhausted by his rigorous dawn-to-midnight work regime, Polk declined to run for a second term and died just three months after leaving office. In his place, Democrats nominated Senator Lewis Cass of Michigan, an avid expansionist who had advocated buying Cuba, annexing Mexico's Yucatán Peninsula, and taking all of Oregon. To maintain party unity, Cass promoted a new idea — squatter sovereignty. Under this plan, Congress would allow settlers in each territory to determine its status as free or slave. Cass's doctrine failed to persuade those northern Democrats who opposed any expansion of slavery. They joined the Free Soil Party, as did former Democratic president Martin Van Buren, who became its candidate for president. To attract Whig votes, the new party chose conscience Whig Charles Francis Adams for vice president.

Whigs nominated General Zachary Taylor, a Louisiana slave owner firmly committed to defending slavery in the South but not in the territories, a position that won him support in the North. The general's military exploits in the U.S.-Mexico War had made him a popular hero, known affectionately to his troops as "Old Rough and Ready." In 1848, as in 1840 with the candidacy of William Henry Harrison, the Whigs succeeded by running a military hero. Taylor took 47 percent of the popular vote to Cass's 42 percent. However, Taylor won partly because Van Buren and the Free Soil ticket took away enough Democratic votes in New York to block Cass's victory there. Although their numbers were small, antislavery voters in New York had denied the presidency to Clay in 1844 and to Cass in 1848. Bitter debates over slavery were changing the dynamics of national politics.

AP® SKILLS & PROCESSES

DEVELOPMENTS AND PROCESSES How and why did the idea of "free soil" rise to prominence?

California Gold and Racial Warfare

Even before Taylor took office, events in California shifted the nation's attention westward. In January 1848, workers building a milldam for John A. Sutter in the Sierra Nevada foothills came across flakes of gold. Sutter was a Swiss immigrant who had come to California in 1839, become a Mexican citizen, and accumulated land in the Sacramento Valley. He tried to hide the discovery, but by mid-1848 indigenous Californians, Mexican Californios, and Anglo-Americans from Monterey and San Francisco poured into the foothills, along with scores of Mexicans and Chileans. By January 1849, sixty-one crowded ships had left New York and other northeastern ports to sail around Cape Horn to San Francisco; by May, twelve thousand wagons had crossed the Missouri River bound for the goldfields. Forty-niners from South America, Europe, China, and Australia also converged on California to seek their fortunes.

Forty-Niners The mining prospectors — almost all men — lived in crowded, chaotic towns and camps amid gamblers, saloonkeepers, and prostitutes. They set up "claims clubs" to settle mining disputes and cobbled together informal systems of legal rules. Anglo-American miners ruthlessly expelled Indians, Mexicans, and Chileans from the goldfields or confined them to marginal diggings. When substantial numbers of Chinese miners arrived in 1850, often in the employ of Chinese companies, whites called for laws to expel them from California. Chilean immigrant Vicente Pérez Rosales reported sardonically on affairs in San Francisco: the leading official was "a Yankee, more or less drunk"; in disputes "between a Yankee and someone who speaks Spanish, his job is to declare the Spaniard guilty and make him pay the court costs."

Miners in the Sierras, 1851–1852 The painter of this work, Charles Christian Nahl, emigrated to New York from Germany in 1848 and then rushed west to join the search for gold. He had little success as miners, but Nahl's mother and sister earned money doing laundry for other miners, and Nahl and his brother soon set up a profitable business in San Francisco, painting portraits of successful prospectors. The methods depicted here are typical of early miners, who did the backbreaking labor of sifting through deposits from stream and river beds. Nahl's view, however, is idealized. In reality, wet conditions often caused pneumonia and disease, and most miners lived in makeshift camps, not the neat cabin in the background. If you look closely, you may see that the line of clean laundry hanging outside the cabin happens to be red, white, and blue. Smithsonian American Art Museum, Washington, DC/Art Resource, NY.

AP® SKILLS & PROCESSES

ANALYZING HISTORICAL EVIDENCE

Even though the painting includes an idealized perspective, ask students why someone, who was unable to achieve riches through the Gold Rush, would still portray it in this manner?

A **Foreign Miner's Tax**, implemented in 1850, charged a prohibitive fee that drove out many Latino and Asian miners.

Foreign Miner's Tax
A discriminatory tax, adopted in 1850 in California Territory, that forced Chinese and Latin American immigrant miners to pay high taxes for the right to prospect for gold. The tax effectively drove these miners from the goldfields.

The first miners to exploit a site often met success, scooping up easily reached deposits and leaving small pickings for later arrivals. "High hopes" wrecked, one latecomer saw himself and most other forty-niners as little better than "convicts condemned to exile and hard labor." They faced disease and death as well: "Diarrhea was so general during the fall and winter months" and so often fatal, a Sacramento doctor remarked, that it was called "the disease of California."

By the mid-1850s almost as many people were leaving San Francisco each year as were arriving to seek their fortune. But thousands of disillusioned forty-niners were too ashamed, exhausted, broke, or ambitious to go home. Some became wageworkers for companies engaged in hydraulic or underground mining; others turned to farming. "Instead of going to the mines where fortune hangs upon the merest chance," one frustrated miner advised emigrants, "commence the cultivation of the soil."

Racial Warfare and Land Rights Farming required arable land, and Mexican grantees and Native peoples occupied much of it. American migrants brushed aside both groups, brutally eliminating the Indians and wearing down Mexican claimants with legal tactics and political pressure.

Subjugation of Native peoples came first. When the gold rush began in 1848, California Indians numbered about 150,000; by 1861, there were only 30,000. As elsewhere in the Americas, European diseases took the lives of thousands. Some miners

AP® SKILLS & PROCESSES

DEVELOPMENTS AND PROCESSES

Ask students to identify where American Indians could have found safety within the United States by the end of the 1860s. What areas would have provided the most protection from settlers, migrants, or prospectors?

A California Indian Family, 1868 This engraving, taken from a French traveler's photograph, suggests some of the ways Native people adapted to conquest. Although they wear many items of Anglo-style clothing, the family proudly displays their traditional baskets. During the gold rush, some Native people withdrew into remote parts of the interior to protect their families and communities from murder, sexual violence, and kidnapping. Others sought work in camps or settlements or panned for gold themselves. © Selva/Bridgeman Images.

sexually assaulted Native women and forced them into virtual slavery as domestic workers. White settlers also undertook systematic Indian-killing campaigns, which local leaders did little to stop. "A war of extermination will continue to be waged . . . until the Indian race becomes extinct," predicted Governor Peter Burnett in 1851.

Congress abetted these assaults. At the bidding of white Californians, it repudiated treaties that federal agents had negotiated with 119 tribes, that had allotted California Indians 7 million acres of land. Instead, in 1853, Congress authorized five reservations of only 25,000 acres each and refused to provide Native peoples with military protection. Consequently, some settlers simply murdered Indians to push them off nonreservation lands.

The Yuki people, who lived in the Round Valley in northern California, were one target. As the *Petaluma Journal* reported nonchalantly in April 1857: "Within the past three weeks, from 300 to 400 bucks, squaws and children have been killed by whites." Other white Californians turned to slave trading: "Hundreds of Indians have been stolen and carried into the settlements and sold," the state's Indian Affairs superintendent reported in 1856. Labor-hungry farmers quickly put them to work. Expelled from their lands and widely dispersed, many Indian peoples could no longer sustain distinct communities. Those tribal communities that survived were devastated by population loss. In 1854, at least 5,000 Yuki people lived in the Round Valley; a decade later, only 85 men and 215 women remained.

Mexicans and Californios who held grants to thousands of acres took longer to dislodge. The Treaty of Guadalupe Hidalgo guaranteed that property owned by Mexicans would be "inviolably respected." Though many of the eight hundred grants made by Spanish and Mexican authorities in California were poorly documented or in some cases fraudulent, a Land Claims Commission created by Congress eventually upheld the validity of 75 percent of them. In the meantime, however, hundreds of Anglo-Americans set up farms on the sparsely settled grants. Having come of age in the antimonopoly Jacksonian era, these squatters rejected the legitimacy of Californios' claims to "unimproved" land and successfully pressured local land commissioners and judges to void or reduce the size of many grants. Indeed, Anglos' clamor for land was so intense and their numbers so large that many Californio claimants gave up and sold off their properties at bargain prices.

In northern California, farmers found that they could grow corn and oats to feed work horses, pigs, and chickens; potatoes, beans, and peas for the farm table; and grapes, apples, and peaches. Ranchers gradually replaced Spanish cattle with American breeds that yielded more milk and meat, which found a ready market as newcomers poured in and California's population shot up to 380,000 by 1860 and 560,000 by 1870. Using the latest agricultural machinery and scores of hired workers, California farmers produced huge crops of wheat and barley, which San Francisco merchants exported to Europe at high prices. The gold rush turned into a wheat boom.

AP® SKILLS & PROCESSES

DEVELOPMENTS AND PROCESSES
By 1870, what were the main results in California of the discovery of gold?

1850: Crisis and Compromise

When British miner William Shaw arrived in California in 1849, he brought a Chinese carpenter and a young Malaysian man as his employees. He reported that a posse of armed Anglo-Americans immediately confronted him, demanding to know whether the workers were "in a state of slavery or vassalage to us." Shaw assured them that his men were paid, but he found his group shunned and denied medical care because it included Asians. The Chinese and Malaysian men ended up dying of fever.

As this group's experience suggested — and as the de facto enslavement of Native Californians showed — Americans carried the problem of slavery with them to the Pacific coast. Recognizing these tensions and hoping to avoid an extended debate over slavery, President Taylor advised Californians to skip the territorial phase and immediately apply for statehood. Early in the gold rush, in November 1849, voters ratified a state constitution prohibiting slavery; Taylor urged Congress to admit California as a free state.

AP® EXAM TIP

Trace the controversies that developed over the expansion of slavery in lands acquired in the Mexican Cession.

Constitutional Conflict California's bid for admission produced passionate debate in Congress and four distinct responses. On the verge of death, John C. Calhoun reiterated his deep resentment of the North's "long-continued agitation of the slavery question." He proposed a constitutional amendment to create a dual presidency, permanently dividing executive power between North and South. Calhoun also advanced the radical argument that Congress had no constitutional authority to regulate slavery in the territories. Slaves were property, Calhoun insisted, and the Constitution restricted Congress's power to abrogate or limit property rights. That argument ran counter to a half century of practice: Congress had prohibited slavery in the Northwest Territory in 1787 and had extended that ban to most of the Louisiana Purchase in the Missouri Compromise of 1820. But Calhoun's position — that planters could by right take slave property into new territories — won growing support in the Deep South.

CHECK FOR UNDERSTANDING

Ask students: **How did the California gold rush lead to racial warfare?** *American migrants who flooded into California during the gold rush assaulted Native women and forced them into sexual slavery, while engaging in campaigns of extermination that were abetted by Congress. Anglo settlers also squatted on land that California had legal claim to, but which remained largely "unimproved."*

AP® SKILLS & PROCESSES

DEVELOPMENTS AND PROCESSES

The **DEVELOPMENTS AND PROCESSES** question asks students to identify the effects of the discovery of gold in California. Students may need assistance in distinguishing between immediate effects — like rapid migration and competing claims — to broader effects, like racial violence and the movement toward statehood, which precipitated a major national crisis. Given that Americans had already expressed interest in California before the U.S.-Mexico War, students could also explore the ways the gold rush modified migration patterns that were already underway in the 1840s.

TRM Find complete suggested responses in the Teacher's Resource Materials.

AP® APPLY THE TIP

Provide students with copies of the Compromise of 1850 by Henry Clay. Ask students to work with a partner to analyze each part of the compromise. Students should note which region of the U.S. would support each part of the compromise. Introduce students to the concept of an "omnibus" bill (a bill covering many diverse issues that must be voted on as one piece of legislation). Ask students to consider the advantages of an omnibus bill if the goal is to force competing forces to compromise. *(Henry Clay envisioned the Compromise of 1850 requiring both North and South to compromise, thereby emphasizing the ability of both sides to see national interests. However, when Clay became ill, Stephen Douglas took the Compromise of 1850 as a means to gain favor in both regions in hopes of being elected president.)* Then ask students to debate the decision by Douglas to break the omnibus bill into separate pieces of legislation. Students should look at their notes on which side supported each part of the Compromise of 1850 and explain how the compromise passed in Congress.

Other southerners favored a more moderate proposal to extend the Missouri Compromise line to the Pacific Ocean. This plan won the backing of Pennsylvanian James Buchanan and other influential northern Democrats. It would guarantee slave owners access to some western territory, including a separate state in southern California.

A third alternative was Lewis Cass's earlier proposal of squatter sovereignty — allowing newcomers in a territory to decide the status of slavery. Democratic senator Stephen Douglas of Illinois now championed this approach, renaming it **popular sovereignty** to link it to republican ideology, which placed ultimate power in the hands of voters. Douglas's idea had considerable appeal. Politicians hoped it would relieve Congress from having to make explosive decisions about slavery, and men on the frontier welcomed the power it would give them. However, popular sovereignty was a slippery concept. Could residents accept or ban slavery when a territory was first organized, or must they delay their decision until a territory had enough people to frame a constitution and apply for statehood? Douglas did not say.

popular sovereignty
The principle that ultimate power lies in the hands of the electorate. Also a plan, first promoted by Democratic candidate Senator Lewis Cass as "squatter sovereignty," then revised as "popular sovereignty" by fellow Democratic presidential aspirant Stephen Douglas, under which Congress would allow settlers in each territory to determine its status as free or slave.

Free soilers and opponents of slavery refused to accept any proposal for California or other territories that allowed slavery. Senator Salmon P. Chase of Ohio, elected by a Democratic–Free Soil coalition, and Senator William H. Seward, a New York Whig, urged a fourth plan: federal laws to restrict slavery within its existing boundaries and eventually end it completely. Condemning slavery as "morally unjust, politically unwise, and socially pernicious" and invoking "a higher law than the Constitution," Seward demanded bold action to advance freedom, "the common heritage of mankind."

A Complex Compromise Faced with bitter and potentially disastrous political divisions, senior Whig and Democratic politicians worked desperately to draft bills that could pass Congress. Aided by Millard Fillmore, who became president in 1850 after

Resolving the Crisis of 1850 By 1850, Whig Henry Clay had been in Congress for nearly four decades. Now in partnership with fellow Whig Daniel Webster and Democrat Stephen Douglas, Clay fashioned a complex — and controversial — compromise that preserved the Union. In this engraving, he addresses a crowded Senate chamber, with Webster sitting immediately to his left. Clay addresses his remarks to his prime antagonist, southern advocate John C. Calhoun, the man with the long white hair at the far right of the picture. Library of Congress, LC-DIG-ppmsca-09398.

TEACHING STRATEGY

The Library of Congress offers a lesson plan titled "The Civil War: The Nation Moves Toward War, 1850–61" that explores the path to war in the 1850s. The lesson begins with a clear timeline of events from 1850 to 1861 that led the nation to war, then provides seventeen primary sources from the Library's collection, arranged in chronological order, that illustrate these events. Each source includes a description and a link leading to a high-resolution image of that source on the Library Web site. The lesson also provides questions to guide discussion and includes suggestions for further research from Library materials. Search "LOC Teacher's Guide Nation Moves Toward War."

TEACHING STRATEGY

While highly dramatized, this image of Clay addressing the Senate illustrates the nature of political debate in the antebellum period and particularly the role of long-term leaders Henry Clay, Daniel Webster, and John C. Calhoun. Ask students: **What does the image convey about political debate in the 1840s and 1850s?** *It suggests that senators were deeply engaged in the debates, that a handful of key figures shaped these debates, and that — based on Clay's dramatic posture — oratory played a significant role.*

Zachary Taylor's sudden death, Whig leaders Henry Clay and Daniel Webster and Democrat Stephen A. Douglas managed to win passage of five separate laws known collectively as the **Compromise of 1850**. To mollify southern planters, the compromise included a new Fugitive Slave Act strengthening federal aid to slave catchers. To satisfy various groups of northerners, the legislation admitted California as a free state, resolved a boundary dispute between New Mexico and Texas in favor of New Mexico, and abolished the slave trade (but not slavery) in the District of Columbia. Finally, the compromise organized the rest of the conquered Mexican lands into the territories of New Mexico and Utah and, invoking popular sovereignty, left the issue of slavery in the hands of their residents (Map 12.2).

The Compromise of 1850 preserved national unity by accepting once again the stipulation advanced by the South since 1787: no Union without slavery. Still, southerners feared for the future and threatened secession. While Congress debated the compromise, militant Deep South politicians known as "fire eaters" organized a convention to safeguard "southern rights." Georgia whig Alexander H. Stephens called on delegates to this Nashville Convention to prepare "men and money, arms and munitions, etc. to meet the emergency." Passage of the compromise deflated the secessionist bubble, however: when the convention reconvened for a second meeting, only a small group showed up. Most southerners continued to support the Union, but the convention had spelled out conditions for that support: Congress must protect slavery where it existed and grant statehood to any territory that ratified a proslavery constitution.

Compromise of 1850
Laws passed in 1850 that were meant to resolve the status of slavery in territories acquired in the U.S. Mexico War. Key elements included the admission of California as a free state and a new Fugitive Slave Act.

AP® EXAM TIP

Compare actions taken by courts and Congress to resolve issues related to slavery in the 1850s.

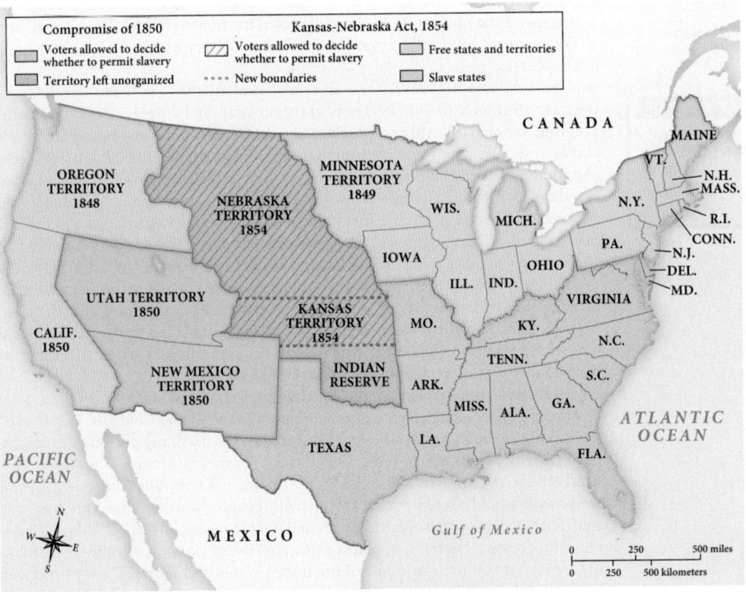

MAP 12.2 The Compromise of 1850 and the Kansas-Nebraska Act of 1854
The contest over the expansion of slavery involved vast territories. The Compromise of 1850 peacefully resolved the status of the Far West: California would be a free state, and settlers in the Utah and New Mexico territories would vote for or against slavery (the doctrine of popular sovereignty). However, the Kansas-Nebraska Act of 1854 (see "The West and the Fate of the Union," p. 399) voided the Missouri Compromise (1820) and instituted popular sovereignty in those territories. That decision sparked a bitter local war and revealed a fatal flaw in the doctrine.

AP® APPLY THE TIP

To help students better understand the role of Congress and the courts in the issues related to slavery, ask them to complete **Handout 12.2 — Comparison: Courts and Congress on Slavery in the 1850s (TRM).** In their analysis, students should review the role of the legislative and judicial branches of government. Then ask students to answer the following questions focused on the Kansas Nebraska Act and Dred Scott decision:

- **How did the Kansas-Nebraska Act alter the agreements made in the Missouri Compromise?** *The Missouri Compromise had prevented the expansion of slavery north of 36°30′ in the territory gained by the Louisiana Purchase; the Kansas-Nebraska Act allowed the expansion of slavery in the same areas through use of popular sovereignty.*
- **How did the decision made in the Dred Scott case support the legislation passed in the Kansas-Nebraska Act?** *Both supported the expansion of slavery and the right of states to protect the institution of slavery.*

TRM Find **Handout 12.2 — Comparison: Courts and Congress on Slavery in the 1850s** in the Teacher's Resource Materials.

CHECK FOR UNDERSTANDING

Ask students: **What political conflicts were triggered by U.S. acquisition of lands in the U.S.-Mexico War?** *The first political conflict had to do with integration of Mexicans and Native Americans into the new American union, as guaranteed by the 1848 Treaty of Guadalupe Hidalgo. The experience of those groups in California, wherein the largest number of those groups lived, is indicative. There, legal codes were altered to favor whites, especially in landholding. Nonetheless, the central political conflict resulting from U.S. acquisition of lands in the U.S.-Mexico War was the status of slavery in these new territories. The passage of five separate laws, known collectively as the Compromise of 1850, was thought to have ameliorated this controversy.*

AP® THEME

PCE: Politics and Power

Use **MAP 12.2** to illustrate the ways national leaders made a variety of attempts to resolve the issue of slavery in the territories, including the Compromise of 1850 and the Kansas-Nebraska Act. Guide students' analysis with the following questions:

- **In the late 1840s, what status was accorded to newly organized federal territories?** *Oregon and Minnesota were admitted as free territories.*
- **How did the Compromise of 1850 attempt to strike a balance on the issue of slavery?** *California was admitted as a free state, but Utah and New Mexico were admitted under the principle of popular sovereignty, where residents would vote to determine the status of slavery.*
- **What resolution did the Kansas-Nebraska Act propose? Based on the location of the boundary the two territories share, what outcome might have been intended?** *The Kansas-Nebraska Act split the remaining unorganized territory into two and allowed residents in each to determine the status of slavery. Given that the northern border of Kansas placed it in line with Missouri, Kentucky, Virginia, and Maryland, it seems that it was hoped that Kansas would vote to become a slave state and Nebraska a free state.*

AN EMERGING POLITICAL CRISIS, 1850–1858

Why did Democrats and Whigs fail in their attempts to keep the issue of slavery in the federal territories from creating a sectional rift?

The Missouri Compromise had endured for a generation, and architects of the Compromise of 1850 hoped their agreement would have an even longer life. Religious leaders, businessmen, and leading judges called on citizens to support the compromise to preserve "government and civil society." Their hopes soon faded. Proslavery southerners openly plotted to extend slavery into the West, the Caribbean, northern Mexico, and Central America. Antislavery northerners, demanding freedom for fugitive slaves and free soil in the West, refused to accept the legitimacy of the compromise. "Free soil" ideas became broadly popular in the North, and the Whig Party disintegrated. At the same time, the arrival of millions of Irish and German immigrants triggered another set of political upheavals. The resulting disputes fragmented both parties and precipitated a crisis.

The Abolitionist Movement Grows

Fugitive Slave Act of 1850
A federal law that set up special federal courts to facilitate capture of anyone accused of being a runaway slave. These courts could consider a slaveowner's sworn affidavit as proof, but defendants could not testify or receive a jury trial. The controversial law led to armed conflict between U.S. marshals and abolitionists.

AP® EXAM TIP
Analyze the reasons that the Fugitive Slave Act can be seen as characterizing the regional divide between North and South in the 1850s.

The **Fugitive Slave Act of 1850** proved the most controversial element of the compromise. To mollify slaveholders, who found it increasingly difficult to capture escaped fugitives in the North, the act set up special federal courts to determine the legal status of alleged runaways. An owner's sworn affidavit was considered proof, while defendants could not receive a jury trial or even the right to testify. U.S. marshals and clerks were paid $10 for each person remanded to slavery and only $5 when they set a captive free.

Under the act's provisions, southern owners located and re-enslaved about 200 fugitives, as well as some free blacks. The plight of runaways and the presence of slave catchers aroused popular hostility in the North and Midwest, broadening support for the abolitionist cause. Ignoring the threat of prison sentences and $1,000 fines, free blacks and white abolitionists protected fugitives. In October 1850, Boston abolitionists helped two slaves escape from Georgia slave catchers. Rioters in Syracuse, New York, broke into a courthouse, freed a fugitive, spirited him to Canada, and then tried to charge the U.S. marshal with kidnapping. Abandoning nonviolence, Frederick Douglass declared that "the only way to make a Fugitive Slave Law a dead letter is to make half a dozen or more dead kidnappers." Precisely such a deadly result occurred in Christiana, Pennsylvania, in September 1851, when twenty African Americans exchanged gunfire with Maryland slave catchers, killing two of them. Federal authorities indicted thirty-six blacks and four whites for treason and other crimes, but a Pennsylvania jury acquitted one defendant, and the government dropped charges against the rest.

Meanwhile, publication of an electrifying novel helped strengthen abolitionist sentiment in the North. Harriet Beecher Stowe's *Uncle Tom's Cabin* (1852) conveyed the moral principles of abolitionism by depicting heartrending personal situations: the barbarity of whippings and sexual abuse; the cruel separation of enslaved husbands and wives, mothers and children; the sin and guilt of white Christian men and women who could not escape the slave system. Touching a nerve, Stowe's book quickly sold 310,000 copies in the United States and double that number in Britain. Promoters soon created theatrical versions of *Uncle Tom's Cabin* — including, improbably, a musical that drew on some of the tropes of minstrel shows. These introduced broad popular audiences to characters such as Uncle Tom, who endures unspeakable cruelties with Christian patience and hope, and Little Eva, an angelic slaveholder's child who, on her deathbed, begs in vain for Tom's freedom. When white southerners indignantly challenged Stowe's portrayal of slavery, she published a *Key to Uncle Tom's Cabin* presenting the evidence she had used, including testimony from those who had escaped slavery.

AP® APPLY THE TIP

Use the video entitled "Sound Smart: The Fugitive Slave Act of 1850," available on History.com, to introduce students to the complexities of the Fugitive Slave Act and the growing regional divisions over slavery. After showing the short video, provide students with excerpts from the Fugitive Slave Act of 1850 and ask them to analyze each part of the law from the point of view of a northern abolitionist and a southern "fire-eater." Then ask students to answer the following questions:

- **How did the Fugitive Slave Act represent continuity in the policy of the federal government on slavery from the Federal Period to the 1850s?** *From the Constitution forward, constitutional provisions and federal law protected the right of slave owners to retrieve runaway slaves.*
- **How did the Fugitive Slave Act illustrate a change in federal government policy in the 1850s?** *The Fugitive Slave Act required federal agents to assist in the return of runaway slaves and gave more power and tools to "slave catchers" in capturing accused runaways.*
- **How did the reliance on the federal Fugitive Slave Act illustrate a contradiction to the states' rights philosophy that was popular in the South?** *Southern politicians typically argued in favor of a state's right to determine its policy on slavery; the federal law limited the ability of northern states to enact laws that protected its citizens from assisting in the return of slaves.*
- **What role did the Fugitive Slave Act play in further involving northerners in the abolitionist movement?** *Prior to passage of the Fugitive Slave Act, most northerners were not overly concerned about the issue of slavery outside of abolitionist groups; after passage of the act, the actions of "slave catchers" and the controversy over personal liberty laws encouraged more northerners to take a position of active support or participation in abolitionist groups.*

AP® THEME

PCE: Politics and Power; SOC: Social Structures

Harriet Beecher Stowe's book *Uncle Tom's Cabin* reveals a dramatic example of ways that popular culture can sometimes dramatically shape national politics. The Harriet Beecher Stowe Center makes the text of *Uncle Tom's Cabin* available online, along with scholarly commentary for each chapter. The Web site also provides more background on Stowe, details about the book's publication, a synopsis of the plot, and information about the book's reception both in the U.S. and overseas. Access these resources by searching "Harriet Beecher Stowe Center Uncle Tom's Cabin."

AP® THEME

SOC: Social Structures

"What to the Slave is the Fourth of July" by Frederick Douglass is an excellent example of how the Fugitive Slave Law of 1850 occasioned changes in the political rhetoric and tenor used by abolitionists. Teachers can curate truncated versions of the speech to help students understand the argument forwarded by Douglass. A copy of the speech is located on the Teaching American History website. (https://teachingamericanhistory.org/)

As Stowe's novel sparked outrage, northern legislators protested that the Fugitive Slave Act violated state sovereignty. Many states passed **personal liberty laws** that guaranteed to all residents, including alleged escapees from slavery, the right to a jury trial. In 1857, the Wisconsin Supreme Court went further, ruling in *Ableman v. Booth* that the Fugitive Slave Act was unconstitutional because it violated the rights of Wisconsin's citizens. Taking a states' rights stance—traditionally a southern position— the Wisconsin court denied the federal judiciary's authority to review its decision. In 1859, Chief Justice Roger B. Taney led a unanimous Supreme Court in affirming the supremacy of federal courts—a position that has withstood the test of time—and upholding the constitutionality of the Fugitive Slave Act.

But popular opposition made the law difficult to enforce. Some African Americans fled temporarily to Canada. Others formed vigilance committees, vowing to defend themselves and their families to the death. Even in far-off San Francisco, networks of abolitionists organized to help local freedom seekers after an 1852 California law declared that southerners who brought slaves to California Territory could take them back in bondage when they departed the state. The resulting Underground Railroad activity showed the complexity of U.S. racial identities: under the law, an African American named Charlotte Gomez was arrested for having rescued an indigenous nine-year-old Yuki girl who had been forced into servitude in a white family. The slavery question now touched every corner of the country.

"Eliza's Flight," 1852 The popularity of Harriet Beecher Stowe's *Uncle Tom's Cabin* prompted the quick marketing of stage productions, board games, music, and even china and wallpaper. This sheet-music cover illustrates the dramatic escape of the enslaved heroine Eliza, who clutches her baby Harry as she jumps from ice floe to ice floe across the Ohio River. Pursuers in the background watch disappointed. The circulation of such images suggests how effectively Stowe appealed to domesticity, urging white readers (and singers) to oppose slavery because it separated loving husbands and wives and parents and children from one another. Eliza's escape and reunion with her husband George provided readers with one of the book's few happy subplots. Courtesy of the Lester S. Levy Collection of Sheet Music, The Sheridan Libraries, The Johns Hopkins University.

Pierce and Expansion

Hoping to unify their party in 1852, Whigs ran yet another war hero, General Winfield Scott, for president. Among Democrats, southerners demanded a candidate who embraced Calhoun's constitutional argument that all territories were open to slavery. However, northern and midwestern Democrats stood behind three leading candidates—Lewis Cass of Michigan, Stephen Douglas of Illinois, and James Buchanan of Pennsylvania—who advocated popular sovereignty. Ultimately, the party settled on Franklin Pierce of New Hampshire, a congenial man sympathetic to the South. The Whigs floundered: as the Free Soil Party ran another spirited campaign, many northerners demanded that Whigs take a stronger stand against slavery expansion, while Democrats strengthened their base in the South by arguing that the Whigs were not doing enough to protect slavery. Pierce swept to victory.

As president, Pierce pursued an expansionist foreign policy. With California and Oregon now firmly in U.S. hands, northern merchants wanted a trans-Pacific commercial empire, and Pierce moved to support them. For centuries, since unpleasant encounters with Portuguese traders in the 1600s, Japan's leaders had adhered to a policy of strict isolation. Americans, who wanted coal stations in Japan, argued that trade would extend what one missionary called "commerce, knowledge, and Christianity, with their multiplied blessings." Whether or not Japan wanted these blessings was irrelevant. In 1854, Commodore Matthew Perry succeeded in getting Japanese officials to sign the **Treaty of Kanagawa**, allowing U.S. ships to refuel at two ports. The Pierce administration rejected Perry's bid to annex more Pacific territories, including Formosa (now Taiwan). But by 1858 the United States and Japan had commenced trade, and a U.S. consul took up residence in Japan's capital, Edo (now known as Tokyo).

Pierce did far more to satisfy southern expansionists. The president and his aggressive secretary of state, William Marcy, first sought to buy extensive Mexican lands south of the Rio Grande. Ultimately, Pierce settled for a smaller slice of territory—the

personal liberty laws
Laws enacted in many northern states that guaranteed to all residents, including alleged fugitives, the right to a jury trial.

Treaty of Kanagawa
An 1854 treaty in which, after a show of military force by U.S. Commodore Matthew Perry, leaders of Japan agreed to permit American ships to refuel at two Japanese ports.

AP® SKILLS & PROCESSES

CAUSATION
How did the Fugitive Slave Act increase sectional conflict?

AP® THEME

PCE: Politics and Power

Though mentioned in the text only briefly, the Underground Railroad represented one important element of abolitionist activism in the 1850s. To supplement students' understanding, use the PBS companion Web site to *Africans in America*, which provides a brief overview of the Underground Railroad as well as a brief biography of Harriet Tubman and two primary sources describing experiences of those who participated in the Underground Railroad. To access this resource, search "Africans in America Underground Railroad."

CHECK FOR UNDERSTANDING

Ask students: **Why did the abolitionist movement grow in the 1850s?** *The Fugitive Slave Law compelled many northerners who were otherwise uninvolved in the issue of slavery to actively participate in recapturing runaways. This heightened the moral dilemma of slavery for many northerners. Harriet Beecher Stowe's* Uncle Tom's Cabin *became an instant classic, and shortly thereafter, a musical play that shaped the views of many northerners.*

AP® SKILLS & PROCESSES

CAUSATION

The **CAUSATION** question asks students to identify the effects of the controversial Fugitive Slave Act. Students could also explore the effects of this law as unintended consequences by examining how and why lawmakers erred so much in their calculations of the law's impact. As part of the Compromise of 1850, the law was designed to quell sectional tension, but it did the opposite.

TRM Find complete suggested responses in the Teacher's Resource Materials.

AP® THEME

WOR: America in the World

These two panels illustrate the robust trade that developed between the U.S. and Japan in the 1850s. Remind students that part of the motivation for Manifest Destiny was to acquire ports in California to facilitate trade with Asia. Ask students: **What do these images reveal about American trade with Japan?** *The images suggest a robust trade, with a steady stream of supplies being loaded onboard. The presence of a Dutch ship suggests that the U.S. was competing with European powers for trade with Japan.*

AP® APPLY THE TIP

To help students contextualize foreign policy in the 1850s, provide each student with a contextualization diagram worksheet. In the center of the diagram, write "American Foreign Policy in the 1850s." Ask students to place major foreign policy events in the circle and explain the importance of each in two to three bullet points (for example, Treaty of Kanagawa, Ostend Manifesto, Gadsden Purchase). In the large box, ask students to explain events in the domestic policy of the U.S. that influenced the foreign policy events. Then ask students to use the contextualization diagram to write a paragraph contextualizing American foreign policy in the 1850s.

An American Merchant Ship in Yokohama Harbor, 1861 After the United States forcibly "opened" Japan to foreign trade in 1854, American and European ships and visitors became a familiar sight in the port of Yokohama. In these 1861 prints — two panels of a five-panel series — artist Hashimoto Sadahide meticulously details activity in Yokohama Harbor. On the left, goods are carried onto an American merchant ship; on the right, two women dressed in Western style watch the arrival of another boat. In the background, a steamship flies the Dutch flag; a rowboat heading to or from another (unseen) ship carries the flag of France. (left) Library of Congress 3g04588; (right) 3g08538.

AP® EXAM TIP

Evaluate foreign policy in the context of the growing debate over slavery in the 1850s.

filibustering
Private paramilitary campaigns, mounted particularly by southern proslavery advocates in the 1850s, to seize additional territory in the Caribbean or Latin America in order to establish control by U.S.-born leaders, with an expectation of eventual annexation by the United States.

Ostend Manifesto
An 1854 manifesto that urged President Franklin Pierce to seize the slave-owning province of Cuba from Spain. Northern Democrats denounced this aggressive initiative, and the plan was scuttled.

Gadsden Purchase of 1853, now part of Arizona and New Mexico — that opened the way for his negotiator, James Gadsden, to build a transcontinental rail line from New Orleans to Los Angeles.

Pierce's most controversial initiatives came in the Caribbean and Central America. Southern expansionists had long urged Cuban slave owners to declare independence from Spain and join the United States. To assist the expansionists and American traders who still supplied enslaved Africans to Cuba, Pierce threatened war with Spain and covertly supported **filibustering** (private military) expeditions. In 1853 John Quitman, a fabulously wealthy cotton planter and former governor of Mississippi, organized a not-so-secret expedition to take Cuba and incorporate it into the United States as proslavery territory. Volunteers and offers of aid poured in from across the South. A Texan hailed Quitman's plan as the "paramount enterprise of the age," while a Mississippian reported that in his area "the desire that Cuba should be acquired as a Southern conquest is almost unanimous."

In 1854, Marcy arranged for American diplomats in Europe to compose the **Ostend Manifesto**, urging Pierce to seize Cuba by force. When the document was exposed, however, Whigs, northern Democrats, and Free Soilers all denounced it, calling it new evidence of southern "slave power" machinations. Pierce saw the political risks of supporting filibusters and withdrew his support for Quitman, who eventually cancelled his plan.

That did not stop William Walker, a Tennessee-born adventurer who had failed as a California forty-niner. Gathering other disappointed gold seekers, Walker first tried to capture Sonora, in northern Mexico. After that failed, he organized three separate expeditions to Central America between 1855 and 1860. In 1856, after being hired as mercenaries to help a faction in a civil war in Nicaragua, Walker and 300 men overthrew the country's government and established their own, with help from

AP® THEME

PCE: Politics and Power

Though the Whig Party does not figure in most Americans' understanding of the early nineteenth century, it nevertheless played a significant role in maintaining national unity in the midst of sectional tensions. The end of the Second Party System is thus a crucial topic. The Whig Party collapsed — and the Democratic Party realigned — when the issues of slavery and anti-immigrant nativism weakened loyalties to the two major parties and fostered the emergence of sectional parties like the Republican Party. Ask students to chart how enslavement, nativism, and sectional issues contributed to the collapse of the Second Party System as they read through this chapter.

New York shipping magnate Cornelius Vanderbilt, who operated a U.S.-Nicaragua steamship line. Walker's new government declared slavery legal in Nicaragua and received immediate recognition from the United States. But Walker could not hold on to power. He fled Nicaragua and then returned to Central America twice more before being captured and executed, apparently by Honduran forces, in 1860. Combined with the expeditions of other filibusters, Walker's exploits confirmed many northerners' belief that the "slave power" would stop at nothing to expand.

AP® SKILLS & PROCESSES

CONTEXTUALIZATION

What actions by Franklin Pierce's administration deepened northerners' fear of the "slave power," and why?

Immigrants and Know-Nothings

While conflict over slavery intensified, another issue vied for center stage in politics. Outside the South, where the slave-labor system discouraged poor immigrants from settling, foreign immigration rose sharply in the 1840s and 1850s. Newcomers arrived almost entirely from northern Europe — England, Ireland, the German states, and Scandinavia — and their circumstances varied widely. German-speaking migrants were a mix of Protestants, Catholics, and Jews, and they included many skilled workers who came in family groups. Often bringing funds they had saved, more than half settled on farms or in small towns. Not so Irish Catholics, who came from an overwhelmingly rural island that was not an independent nation but a colony of Britain. Thus when a catastrophe hit Ireland in the late 1840s, it forced millions to flee or die.

AP® EXAM TIP

Explaining the causes of and reactions to immigration from Germany and Ireland is essential for success on the AP® Exam.

The Irish Famine Ireland's population had grown rapidly during the Napoleonic Wars. Most Irish farmers, working as tenants for English landlords, were required to send their grain crops to England. The poorest third of households ate little but potatoes. Ireland was thus terribly vulnerable to a potato blight in 1845 that destroyed almost the whole crop the following year. Forced to eat their seed potatoes to avoid starvation, and with very little aid offered by the British government, millions of Irish were soon desperate. *An Gorta Mór* — Celtic for "The Great Hunger" — had descended.

The results were horrific. Between 1845 and 1851 over one million people died of malnutrition or diseases that preyed on the hungry, including dysentery and cholera. "Famine and pestilence are sweeping away hundreds," reported a journalist from Bantry on the southwest coast. "The number of deaths is beyond counting." Those who could gathered their meager possessions and took passage. More than 1.5 million — one-sixth of Ireland's people — emigrated, mostly to the United States.

In the 1820s and 1830s, Irish immigrants had largely been poor, unskilled men who came alone and found "heavy, rough work" in northeastern cities and towns, repairing streets or digging canals. The famine refugees came, instead, largely in family groups. Since the famine struck hardest against children and the elderly, the refugees tended to be young, healthy adults — tenant farmers, although not the very poorest. But the Atlantic voyage held new dangers: shipboard conditions in cheap steerage berths were terrible, and typhus and other diseases turned many vessels into "coffin ships." In 1853, when a cholera epidemic raged, 10 percent of Irish immigrants died at sea.

The Irish who came to the United States made up more than a third of all American immigrants in the 1850s. Unable to afford land, they clustered in urban areas. By 1860, a third of Irish-born Americans lived in just ten cities. Finding employment as laborers, factory workers, and domestic servants, the new arrivals faced great hardship. Some, however, through thrift and determination, managed to find their way into the ranks of shopkeepers, policemen, or farmers. Many formed mutual aid groups to support one another. They also found aid through the American Catholic Church, which soon became an Irish-dominated institution.

As early as the 1850s, some Irish began to send positive reports to kin back home (see "Thinking Like a Historian," p. 396). Like many later groups, the Irish developed a pattern of **chain migration**. Once a newcomer settled in, he or she saved carefully and sent for neighbors and family members to join him or her. As a result, steady

chain migration
A pattern by which immigrants find housing and work and learn to navigate a new environment, and then assist other immigrants from their family or home area to settle in the same location.

AP® SKILLS & PROCESSES

CONTEXTUALIZATION

Whenever students are accounting for the historical context of a development or event, they need to consider broader processes. Ask students to think about President Pierce's time in office (1853–1857) and what actions the Slave Power in the South took to deepen sectionalism. Next, ask students to find specific instances of Pierce's administration appealing to southern audiences. Taking a concept such as sectionalism and connecting two pieces of historical evidence can help strengthen students' understanding of this question.

TRM Find complete suggested responses in the Teacher's Resource Materials.

CHECK FOR UNDERSTANDING

Ask students: **What led to the Whig Party's demise?** *The issue of slavery largely destroyed the Whig Party, which had attempted to maintain a middle-of-the-road stance. The Free Soil Party drew abolitionists away from the party, while proslavery southerners gravitated to the Democratic Party.*

AP® APPLY THE TIP

Students can better understand issues related to immigration by a discussion of push and pull factors in any period of history. Ask students to brainstorm a list of factors that might "push" a person or family out of a home country and record these reasons on the board. Then, ask students to brainstorm "pull" factors that might influence a person or family to choose a certain nation to immigrate to. Students should perform a close reading of page 395 to identify specific push and pull factors influencing German and Irish immigration to the U.S. in the nineteenth century. To understand reactions to immigration in this period, students should consider the economic and political changes of the early nineteenth century. Ask students to read the documents in the **AP® THINKING LIKE A HISTORIAN** feature (pp. 396–397). Ask students to work in pairs and answer the **AP® DBQ PRACTICE** and **PUTTING IT ALL TOGETHER** questions on p. 397.

AP® SKILLS & PROCESSES

ANALYZING HISTORICAL EVIDENCE

The **AP® THINKING LIKE A HISTORIAN** feature allows students to understand the consequences of Irish immigration from multiple perspectives. While the views of hostile Americans are included, so are the perspectives of the Irish themselves. For the first document, students may need help in recognizing that Sadlier's presentation of her fellow Irish is shaped by Protestant, middle-class notions of respectability and should be viewed in part as a piece of rhetoric, rather than a simple, straightforward depiction of Irish experiences.

AP® THINKING LIKE A HISTORIAN

The Irish in America

Hardship and hostility accompanied the surge of Irish immigration to the United States, especially when millions began to arrive during the famine. The documents below provide different perspectives on the forms of discrimination and hardship that Irish men and women faced, their reflections on opportunity in America, and the ways they adapted to life in an industrializing economy.

1. **Mary Anne Sadlier, *The Blakes and the Flanagans*, 1855.** *Through her domestic novels, Irish-born author Mary Anne Sadlier defended the respectability of her fellow immigrants. To assert Irish Catholics' readiness to claim equal citizenship, she appealed to the values of American middle-class women: motherhood, piety, hard work, thrift, and selfless community service. This frontispiece from Sadlier's novel* The Blakes and the Flanagans: A Tale, Illustrative of Irish Life in the United States *depicts two Irish-born sisters with pupils from their school.*

Source: Courtesy of the University of Iowa Libraries.

2. **Account by a visiting Scotsman, LaSalle County, Illinois (1840).** *After passing through the town of Utica, Illinois, this traveler commented on a nearby camp along the construction line of the Illinois & Michigan Canal.*

We had scarcely got beyond the edge of town before we came to a colony of Irish laborers employed on the Illinois Canal, and a more repulsive scene we had not for a long time beheld. The number congregated here were about 200, including men, women and children, and these were crowded together in 14 or 15 log huts, temporarily erected for their shelter. I had never been in the south of Ireland and cannot say how far the appearance of this colony differed from that of villages there, but certainly in the north of Ireland, over which I have traveled from Dublin to Londonderry, I never saw anything approaching the scene before us in dirtiness and disorder.

. . . Poverty could be no excuse, as the men were all paid at the rate of a dollar a day for their labor, had houses rent free, and provisions of every kind abundantly cheap. But whiskey and tobacco seemed the chief delights of the men. Of the women and children, no language would give an adequate idea of their filthy condition, in garments and person. It required only a little industry to preserve both in a state of cleanliness, for water was abundant in the river close at hand, and soap abundant and cheaper than in England. It is not to be wondered that Americans conceive a very low estimate of the Irish people generally, when they have such unfavorable specimens of the nation, as these almost constantly before their eyes. Unhappily, of the immigrants who land at New York, the large majority are not merely ignorant and poor . . . but drunken, dirty, indolent, and riotous.

3. **Margaret McCarthy to her family (1850).** *McCarthy, age twenty-three, had emigrated alone from County Cork to New York City the previous year.*

I write these few lines to you hopeing [they] may find you all in as good State of health as I am at present thank God I received your welcome letter To me Dated 22nd. of May . . . My D[ea]r Father I must only say that this is a good place and A good Country for if one place does not Suit A man he can go to Another . . . [But] the Emmigrants has not money enough to Take them to the Interior of the Country which oblidges them to Remain here in New York and the like places for which Reason Causes the less demand for Labour and also the great Reduction in wages for this Reason I would advise no one to Come to America that would not have Some Money after landing here that Enable them to go west in case they would get no work to do here but any man or woman without a family are fools that would not venture and Come to this plentyful Country where no man or woman ever Hungerd or ever will. There are Dangers upon Dangers Attending Comeing here but my Friends . . . Fortune will favour the brave have Courage and prepare yourself. . . . This will be my last remittance until I see you all here. . . . I will have for [Mary] A Silk Dress A Bonnet and Viel . . . Tell my D[ea]r Mother to Bring all her bed Close and also to bring the Kittle and an oven and have handles on them and do not forget the Smoothing Irons. . . .

4. **Advertisement, *Philadelphia Public Record* (1852).**

WANTED — In a private family, a WOMAN, to do general Housework; she must understand plain Cooking, Washing, Ironing, and give the best recent [recom] mendations for honesty, sobriety, cleanliness and smartness. No Irish need apply. Address H.L.D., Ledger Office.

5. **Letter from William Lloyd Garrison to a friend in Dublin, Ireland, July 2, 1852.** *The Boston abolitionist expresses frustration at the failure of Irish immigrants to join his cause, even though an antislavery movement was thriving in Ireland.*

It is now quite apparent that [Irish American voters] will go en masse with Southern men-stealers, and in opposition to the antislavery movement. This will not be done intelligently by them, but will be effectually controlled by a crafty priesthood and unprincipled political demagogues. When we had our great meeting in Faneuil Hall, we took all parties by surprise. Our Irish fellow-citizens, who were then present, acted out their natural love of liberty, to the life; for at that time, they had not been instructed how to act by their leaders, and the Pilot and Diary, and other Irish papers here, had not opened their batteries. Since that time, however, they have kept wholly aloof from us, and it is impracticable to get them to listen. . . .

6. **Advertisements from the *Catholic Herald*, Philadelphia.** *These notices suggest the plight of many families separated by emigration.*

May 20, 1841. Information Wanted — Of John Early of the County Mayo, Ireland. Any person knowing any thing of the said John Early, will oblige his distressed wife by sending information to the office of this paper or to the Clergy of St. John's Church, 13th St., Phila.

July 17, 1844. Information Wanted — of Patrick Lynch, a native of the Parish of Kilberry, County Meath, Ireland. He was in Carthage, N. Y. about a year ago, which place he left for Philadelphia. His wife, Jane Lynch, has arrived in Philadelphia and stops at the house of his nephew, Christopher Nevin, Pearl street above 13th st., where she would be glad to hear from him.

7. ***The Know-Nothing and American Crusader*, 29 July 1854.** *This pamphlet circulated in various eastern cities at the height of anti-immigrant agitation.*

We must not let this fact go-by — the Roman Catholics are bound to serve their Church before their Country. What is the practical and inevitable result of such a system in this country? Why, that every Catholic stands committed as an enemy to the Republic. . . .

Not an office in this whole land should be filled by any but Americans. There is a full supply. They are all capable. They are intelligent, patriotic and all that. Then where is the logic, justice, even decency, of permitting foreigners to hold these places. Many of the best offices [in Washington] . . . are filled by foreigners. And two-thirds of those are IRISH.

8. **Cartoon from *Harper's Weekly*, 1859.** *This caricature illustrates prejudices against the Irish Catholic men who found rapid success in urban politics.*

OUR EDUCATORS.

American School Commissioner: "But, my good Sir, we have always read the Bible in our American Schools." . . Irish School Commissioner: "Worse luck, thin; ye'll rade it no more! Father O'Flaherty says it interfares wid our holy religion, an' by the Vargin it won't and it shan't be read!" SOURCE: The Granger Collection, New York.

SOURCES: (2) John Lamb, "Old Canal Days," *Lockport Free Press*, 15 June 1978; (3) Nancy F. Cott et al., *Root of Bitterness: Documents of the Social History of American Women*, 2nd ed. (Boston: Northeastern University Press, 1992), 152–155; (4) Philadelphia Public Record, Oct. 12, 1852; (5) Quoted in Noel Ignatieff, *How the Irish Became White* (New York: Routledge, 1995), 22; (6 & 7) Historical Society of Pennsylvania.

AP DBQ PRACTICE

1. What hardships did Irish immigrants face after their arrival in the United States, and how did those differ for men and for women?
2. What arguments or assumptions did native-born Americans make in rejecting Irish newcomers? How might immigrants such as Mary Anne Sadlier and Margaret McCarthy have responded to the criticisms of Garrison, the *Know-Nothing and American Crusader*, and *Harper's Weekly*?
3. What explanations do these documents provide as to why immigrant voters might have chosen to vote for political candidates who shared their ethnic backgrounds?

PUTTING IT ALL TOGETHER

Using these documents and what you have learned from Chapter 12, explain how the arrival of large numbers of Irish Americans shaped the U.S. economy and society. What allies and opponents did they find in society and politics, and why?

TRM Find complete suggested responses in the Teacher's Resource Materials.

AP SKILLS & PROCESSES

ARGUMENTATION

The **PUTTING IT ALL TOGETHER** question invites students to consider the social and economic effects of Irish immigration. Some students may need assistance in sorting the cultural critiques of Irish religion and social practices from the economic consequences of their immigration.

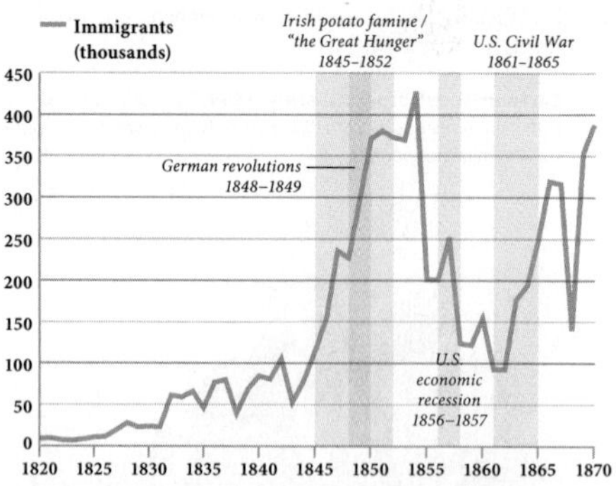

FIGURE 12.1 The Surge in Immigration, 1845–1855
In 1845, failure of the potato crop in Ireland prompted wholesale migration to the United States of peasants from the overcrowded farms of its western counties. Population growth and limited economic prospects likewise spurred the migration of tens of thousands of German peasants, while the failure of the liberal republican political revolution of 1848 prompted hundreds of prominent German politicians and intellectuals to follow them. An American economic recession cut the flow of immigrants, but the booming northern economy during the Civil War again persuaded Europeans to set sail for the United States.

streams of immigrants arrived long after the famine had passed. Between 1860 and 1910, more than 2.6 million Irish would arrive — far more than during the famine itself.

Hostility Toward Immigrants Already by 1850, immigrants were a major presence throughout the Northeast (Figure 12.1). Like other immigrant groups, Irish and Germans boosted the American economy. Factories expanded using low-wage Irish labor. Thousands of elite and middle-class women hired "Bridgets" — Irishwomen — for domestic labor. German-language shop signs filled entire neighborhoods; Irish pubs sprang up all over Boston, while German foods (sausages, hamburgers, sauerkraut) became part of New York culture.

But the scale of immigration prompted a political backlash. Native-born Americans looked with dismay on the crowded tenement districts that sprang up to house low-paid Irish factory workers. They feared the erosion of wages — with some justification, since employers repeatedly used immigrants to break strikes and reduce pay. Advocates of the growing temperance movement condemned Irishmen's tendency to frequent the neighborhood saloon and German families' Sunday afternoons at the *biergarten*. One German observer complained that everywhere three Germans settled together, "one opened a saloon so that the other two might have a place to argue." Some English-speakers also resented the tendency of proud Germans to continue speaking their own language and patronize their own newspapers, businesses, and clubs.

nativism
Opposition to immigration and to full citizenship for recent immigrants or to immigrants of a particular ethnic or national background, as expressed, for example, by anti-Irish discrimination in the 1850s and Asian exclusion laws between the 1880s and 1940s.

AP® SKILLS & PROCESSES
MAKING CONNECTIONS
How did religious intolerance contribute to nativist movements in the nineteenth century?

Perhaps the most significant factor in this era's **nativism** — hostility toward immigrants — was anti-Catholicism. Almost all the newly arrived Irish and perhaps a third of Germans were Catholics. Viewing the pope as authoritarian, some Protestants argued that Catholics could not develop the independent judgment that would make them good citizens and would instead let the pope tell them how to vote. Northerners who mistrusted the "slave power" made such arguments with particular forcefulness. "Slavery and priestcraft," declared one Republican leader in 1854, "have a common purpose: they seek [to add to the United States] Cuba and Hayti and the Mexican States together, because they will be Catholic and Slave. I say they are in alliance by the necessity of their nature — for one denies the right of a man to his body, and the other the right of a man to his soul." Other nativists, believing vows of celibacy were unnatural, provoked hysteria over the alleged secret crimes of Catholic priests and nuns. *The Awful Disclosures of Maria Monk*, a popular exposé originally published in 1836, alleged that sexual debauchery and infanticide went on behind the closed doors of a Montreal convent. Though its claims were debunked, the book circulated for decades, stoking anti-Catholic prejudice.

The actions of some Irish immigrants intensified these fears. In urban areas, groups of Irish men became notorious for organizing mob violence against African Americans, temperance parades, and abolitionist meetings. A much larger number devoted themselves to electoral politics. Most urban Irish forged loyalties with the Democratic Party, which gave them a foothold in the political process. This fueled, in turn, allegations that Irish voters and politicians were corrupt and clannish.

A small number of German immigrants provoked anger in the opposite direction. As radicals who were fleeing oppressive governments after the failed European revolutions of 1848, they brought socialist ideals, and some enrolled in the abolitionist cause. Abraham Lincoln, resuming his political career in the 1850s after his early defeat as

AP® THEME

MIG: Migration and Settlement

FIGURE 12.1 provides graphic evidence for the upsurge in immigrants in a very short period. Students might note that immigration gradually increased in the first decades of the nineteenth century, even accounting for sharp ups and downs. They should also recognize that immigration quadrupled in the late 1840s and only returned to its pre-surge rate in the late 1850s as a result of the Panic of 1857. Students may understand that a dramatic increase in the rate of immigration, rather than immigration per se, often leads to a panicked nativist response.

The PBS documentary *The Irish in America* includes a segment that discusses the immigration caused by the potato famine, patterns of Irish immigration to America — particularly to New York and Boston, but also to the South, and antinativist responses to their arrival. One important point the film makes is that anti-Irish hostility forged an Irish identity among thousands of immigrants whose prior identities had previously been based on the village or community they were from. Access this film online by searching "PBS Irish in America."

AP® SKILLS & PROCESSES

MAKING CONNECTIONS

Have students define both Nativism and the Know-Nothing Party. While nativists were a part of the Know-Nothing Party, nativism is a broader historical process. By starting with a basic definition, students will be equipped to grapple with the historical importance of the Know-Nothing Party in the mid-nineteenth century.

TRM Find complete suggested responses in the Teacher's Resource Materials.

AP® THEME

NAT: American and National Identity

Religious intolerance represents a large umbrella for a very specific historical development. Remind students that although intolerance was directed at many different groups, nativists in particular directed much of their political ire at Catholics. Nativism is a long-term historical process while the development of the Know-Nothing Party is relevant to a very specific period. Students need to be aware of each aspect so they do not conflate topics.

a Whig, discovered that many German Americans in Illinois were eager to prevent slavery's expansion onto "free soil." Lincoln greeted one group in Chicago as "*German Fellow-Citizens*" who were "true to Liberty, not *selfishly*, but upon *principle*." Among whites who supported slavery, though — including many Irish immigrants — the antislavery views of these German immigrants made them politically suspect.

As early as the mid-1830s, nativists called for a halt to immigration and mounted a cultural and political assault on foreign-born residents. Gangs of nativists assaulted Irish youths in the streets. In 1844, a new group calling itself the American Republican Party won the endorsement of local Whigs and swept New York City's elections by stressing temperance, anti-Catholicism, and nativism. Rather than trying to stop immigration, they sought to deny voting and office-holding rights to noncitizens, especially by delaying the waiting period before immigrants could naturalize.

Immigrants and Nativists Clash in New York, 1857 This engraving shows how a backlash against Irish immigration led to gang violence that alarmed Americans. In this street fight, raucous July 4 celebrations escalated into raids and counter-raids between a nativist gang known as the "Bowery Boys" and their Irish immigrant rivals, known popularly as the "Dead Rabbits" (their name for themselves was the "Roach Guards"). Lasting two days, the riot involved hundreds of men and ended with looting and property destruction. Only with help of the New York State militia was order restored.

Sarin Images/Granger, NYC.

By 1850, with immigration swelling, various local nativist societies banded together as the Order of the Star-Spangled Banner. The following year they formed the **American, or Know-Nothing, Party**. When questioned, the party's secrecy-conscious members often replied, "I know nothing" — hence the nickname given by their opponents. The American Party's program was far from secret, however; supporters wanted to mobilize native-born Protestants against the "alien menace" of Irish and German Catholics, discourage further immigration, and institute literacy tests for voting. The new party drew primarily from former Whigs in the South and about equally from Whigs and Democrats in the North. Many northern Know-Nothings had an antislavery or free soil outlook. By the mid-1850s, it was clear that these voters were hostile both to immigrants and to the expansion of slavery. What was unclear, yet, was whether a new national party would take up both of these issues, or which one political leaders would prioritize.

In 1854, voters elected dozens of American Party candidates to the House of Representatives and gave the party control of the state governments of Massachusetts and Pennsylvania. The national emergence of a Protestant-based nativist party to replace the Whigs became a real possibility. At that same moment, Illinois Democrat Stephen Douglas proposed a new application of his idea of popular sovereignty, furthering the Whig Party's collapse and sending the Union spinning toward fragmentation.

American, or Know-Nothing, Party
An anti-immigrant, anti-Catholic political party formed in 1851 that arose in response to mass immigration in the 1840s, especially from Ireland and Germany. In 1854, the party gained control of the state governments of Massachusetts and Pennsylvania.

AP® SKILLS & PROCESSES

CONTEXTUALIZATION
Compare the two major issues Americans debated in the mid-1850s: free soil and slavery, on the one hand, and mass immigration, on the other. What connections do you see between these debates?

The West and the Fate of the Union

Since the Missouri Compromise prohibited new slave states in the Louisiana Purchase north of 36°30′, southern senators had long prevented the creation of new territories there. It remained Permanent Indian Territory. But Douglas wanted to open it up to allow a transcontinental railroad to link Chicago to California. In 1854 he proposed to extinguish Native American rights on the Great Plains and create a large free territory called Nebraska.

Southern politicians opposed Douglas's initiative. They hoped to extend slavery throughout the Louisiana Purchase and have a southern city — New Orleans, Memphis,

AP® THEME

NAT: American and National Identity

The outbreak of violence depicted in the engraving indicates how strong anti-Catholic nativist sentiment was, aimed at limiting new immigrants' political power and cultural influence. Supplement this discussion with the *Smithsonian* article entitled "How the 19th Century Know Nothing Party Reshaped American Politics," which provides an in-depth examination of the Know-Nothing Party and its effects on American political culture. Access this article by searching "Smithsonian Know Nothing Party."

CHECK FOR UNDERSTANDING

Ask students: **What was the platform of the Know-Nothings?** *As large numbers of German and Irish immigrants, the latter overwhelmingly quite poor, flooded into the U.S., a Protestant nativist backlash set in. Opponents of the immigrants and their Catholicism and consumption of alcohol formed the American, or "Know-Nothing," Party. Many Know-Nothings were either antislavery or at least free soil.*

AP® SKILLS & PROCESSES

CONTEXTUALIZATION

The **CONTEXTUALIZATION** note has many essential concepts: Free Soil, Enslavement, and Immigration. As students work through contextualizing these issues, consider providing a broad historical topic such as expansionism. Using a concept such as expansionism helps students organize their ideas around a topic that connects to each term.

TRM Find complete suggested responses in the Teacher's Resource Materials.

or St. Louis — serve as the eastern terminus of a transcontinental railroad. To win their support, Douglas amended his bill so that it explicitly repealed the Missouri Compromise, thus allowing people in new territories to decide for themselves whether to allow slavery and thereby potentially enabling slavery to extend farther west in new areas. He also agreed to the formation of two territories, Nebraska and Kansas, raising the prospect that settlers in the southern one, Kansas, would choose slavery. Knowing the revised bill would "raise a hell of a storm," Douglas insisted to northerners that Kansas, even though it lay next door to the slave state of Missouri, was not suited to plantation agriculture and would become a free state. After weeks of bitter debate, the Senate passed the **Kansas-Nebraska Act** (see Map 12.2). With petitions opposed to the bill flooding the House of Representatives, the measure barely squeaked through.

Kansas-Nebraska Act
A controversial 1854 law that divided Indian Territory into Kansas and Nebraska, repealed the Missouri Compromise, and left the new territories to decide the issue of slavery on the basis of popular sovereignty. Far from clarifying the status of slavery in the territories, the act led to violent conflict in "Bleeding Kansas."

Emergence of the Republican Party The Kansas-Nebraska Act of 1854 jolted the political system. It galvanized thousands of northerners, especially Whigs, to stand up against the "slave power." Cotton textile magnate Amos Lawrence lamented, "We went to bed one night old fashioned, conservative Union Whigs and waked up stark mad abolitionists." In northeastern cities where nativism had been strong, renewed controversy over slavery's expansion in the West deflected attention from immigration. The Kansas-Nebraska Act also crippled the Democratic Party, with northern "anti-Nebraska Democrats" denouncing it as "part of a great scheme for extending and perpetuating supremacy of the slave power." In 1854, these former Democrats joined ex-Whigs and Free Soil supporters to form the Republican Party.

The new party was a coalition of "strange, discordant and even hostile elements," one Republican observed. Many abolitionists refused to join, arguing that the Republicans compromised too much on the need for immediate abolition. However, almost all Republicans disliked and wished to limit slavery, which, they argued, drove down the wages of free workers and degraded the dignity of manual labor. Like Thomas Jefferson, Republicans praised a society based on "the middling classes who own the soil and work it with their own hands." Abraham Lincoln, now a Republican, conveyed the new party's vision of social mobility. "There is no permanent class of hired laborers among us," he declared, ignoring growing economic and social divisions in the industrializing North and Midwest. Lincoln and his fellow Republicans envisioned a society of independent farmers, artisans, and proprietors, and they celebrated middle-class values: domesticity, religious faith, and capitalist enterprise.

Meanwhile, thousands of settlers rushed into the Kansas Territory, putting Douglas's

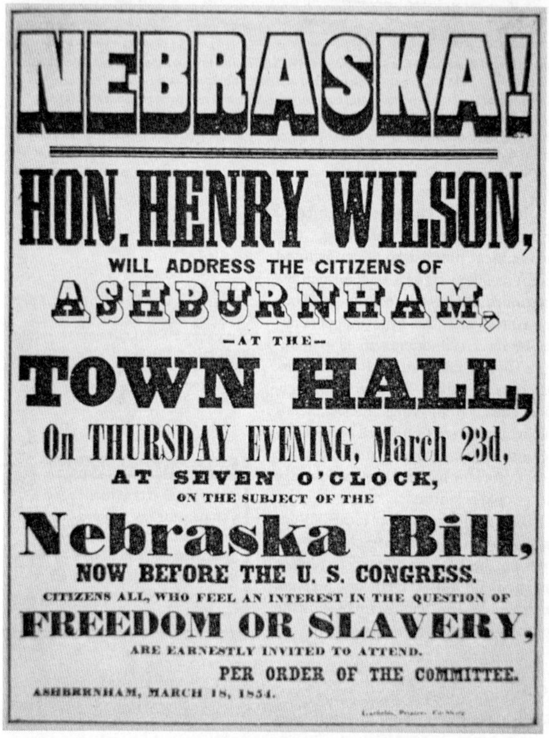

Political Responses to "Nebraska!," 1854 This public notice captures some of the outrage that swept across northern states after passage of the Kansas-Nebraska Act, raising the possibility of slavery in areas where northerners had assumed it was banned. Local "anti-Nebraska" parties created the foundations for a national Republican Party. Henry Wilson, billed to speak at this rally in north-central Massachusetts, was a founder of the Free Soil Party. Kansas-Nebraska launched him onto the national stage: he became a Republican U.S. senator from Massachusetts in 1855, and eventually served as vice president in the administration of Ulysses S. Grant. Private Collection/Peter Newark American Pictures/Bridgeman Images.

TEACHING STRATEGY

In a seven-minute video lecture, historian Eric Foner, whose first book was about the free soil movement, discusses the emergence of the Republican Party, including its roots in the free soil movement, which was less interested in the injustice of slavery than it was in ensuring access to land for free white farmers. Access this video on YouTube by searching "Columbia Learn Free Labor Ideology."

TEACHING STRATEGY

To be anti-slavery did not necessarily mean opposition based on moral queries. Instead, many Americans were anti-slavery for economic or political reasons. Have students differentiate among those who were anti-slavery for moral, economic, and political reasons.

concept of popular sovereignty to the test. On the side of slavery, Missouri senator David R. Atchison encouraged residents of his state to cross temporarily into Kansas to cast illegal votes in crucial elections there. Opposing Atchison was the abolitionist New England Emigrant Aid Society, which dispatched its supporters to Kansas. Adding to the tension, in 1855 the Pierce administration accepted the legitimacy of a proslavery legislature in Lecompton, Kansas, that had been elected with aid from border-crossing Missourians. The majority of Kansas residents favored free soil and refused allegiance to the Lecompton government.

Armed Abolitionists in Kansas, 1859 The confrontation between North and South in Kansas took many forms. In the spring of 1859, Dr. John Doy (seated) slipped across the border into Missouri and tried to lead thirteen escaped slaves to freedom in Kansas, only to be captured and jailed in St. Joseph, Missouri. The serious-looking men standing behind Doy, well armed with guns and Bowie knives, attacked the jail and carried Doy back to Kansas. The photograph celebrated and memorialized their successful exploit. Kansas State Historical Society.

In 1856, both sides turned to violence, prompting Horace Greeley of the *New York Tribune* to label the territory "Bleeding Kansas." A proslavery force, seven hundred strong, looted and burned the antislavery town of Lawrence. The attack enraged John Brown, a fifty-six-year-old abolitionist from New York who commanded a free-state militia. Brown was a complex man with a record of failed businesses, but his intellectual and moral intensity won the trust of influential people. Avenging the sack of Lawrence, Brown and his followers murdered five proslavery settlers at Pottawatomie. Abolitionists must "fight fire with fire" and "strike terror in the hearts of the proslavery people," Brown declared. The attack on Lawrence and the Pottawatomie killings started a guerrilla war in Kansas that took nearly two hundred lives.

In Washington, leaders of the new Republican Party distanced themselves from Brown and radical abolitionists but denounced proslavery maneuvers. In May 1856, in a speech called "The Crime Against Kansas," Massachusetts Republican senator Charles Sumner accused his South Carolina colleague Andrew P. Butler of having taken "the harlot slavery" as his mistress. Butler's cousin Preston Brooks, also a southern congressman, decided to avenge his kinsman, but he disdained to fight a gentleman's duel with any "Black Republican." Instead, he found Sumner working at his desk on the Senate floor and beat him unconscious with a walking cane. Sumner, gravely injured, did not resume his seat for many months. The attack shocked northerners, providing further evidence of the arrogance and outrageousness of proslavery political leaders. Massachusetts voters reelected Sumner even while he remained disabled and could not serve. Brooks, at the same time, resigned his South Carolina seat as a matter of honor but was reelected by a large margin. He received replacement canes and notes of congratulation from allies across the South.

Buchanan's Failed Presidency The violence in Kansas dominated the presidential election of 1856. The new Republican Party stoked anger over Bleeding Kansas. Its platform denounced the Kansas-Nebraska Act and demanded that the federal government prohibit slavery in all the territories. Linking Mormon plural marriage with slavery, it used the language of domesticity and civilization to denounce "those twin relics of barbarism, polygamy and slavery." Republicans also called for federal subsidies to build transcontinental railroads, reviving a Whig economic proposal popular among midwestern Democrats. For president, the Republicans nominated Colonel John C. Frémont, a free soiler who had won fame in the conquest of Mexican California.

The American Party entered the election with equally high hopes, but like the Whigs, it split along sectional lines over slavery. The party's southern faction

AP® EXAM TIP

It's important to identify why the efforts of the courts and Congress failed to address the issue of slavery by the end of the 1850s.

AP® THEME

PCE: Politics and Power

The photograph of armed abolitionists demonstrates the increasingly aggressive dimension of abolitionism in the 1850s. Without reading this caption, students might assume that these men were sheriffs or even outlaws. They are clearly ready to use violence in their confrontation with proslavery forces in Kansas. For good reason, the Kansas Territory was labelled "Bleeding Kansas" in the 1850s.

TEACHING STRATEGY

Though the caning of Charles Sumner by Preston Brooks is only one relatively minor event in a crowded series of incidents that precipitated the Civil War, it provides a useful and engaging case study of sectional tensions. One elected federal official severely beating another constituted an immediate national news story. Not surprisingly, it was reported very differently in the North and the South, and letters to the editor differed dramatically as well. Use these varying responses to offer students a window into the deep sectional differences between the regions in terms of values and beliefs. To access the editorial, search "Secession Era Editorials Project Sumner caning incident."

AP® THEME

PCE: Politics and Power

The Dred Scott case represents another failed effort by national leaders, in this case the Supreme Court, to resolve the issue of slavery in the territories. As part of the Africans in America series on PBS, historian David Blight explains the national significance of the case in a short interview. Search "PBS Africans in America David Blight on Dred Scott Decision" to access this interview. In a four-minute video available through the Gilder Lehrman Institute, historian Matthew Pinsker takes a different approach from Blight. He humanizes this famous historical figure by recounting his story as a family narrative involving his wife, Harriet. Access this video by searching "Gilder Lehrman Dred and Harriet Scott."

AP® APPLY THE TIP

Have students work with a partner to create a Venn diagram comparing the Dred Scott case to the Missouri Compromise. In their Venn diagram, students should include details from close reading of the text, including the following: role of state laws, interpretation of federal power, status of slaves and free African Americans, impact on regions, reactions from state governments, reaction from abolitionists, etc. Then ask students to answer the following questions:

- **What was the main goal of Henry Clay in the Missouri Compromise?** *To unify the regions as an expression of nationalism.*
- **What was the main goal of Roger Taney in the Dred Scott decision?** *To protect the interests of the southern planter class and defend states' rights.*
- **What similarities are evident in both of these events?** *Both emphasized divisions that existed between the North and the South.*
- **What differences are evident between these events?** *The Missouri Compromise created conflict but did not lead to overt division in regions, while the Dred Scott case led to greater conflict over slavery; the motivation behind each differed from the support of nationalism in the Missouri Compromise to the expression of sectionalism in Dred Scott.*
- **Did either event actually achieve its goal?** *Answers will vary: yes, because the Missouri Compromise prevented conflict for a generation; no, because conflict over slavery and its expansion grew after both, etc.*

nominated former Whig president Millard Fillmore, while the northern contingent endorsed Frémont. During the campaign, Republicans won the votes of many northern Know-Nothings by demanding legislation banning foreign immigrants and imposing high tariffs on foreign manufactures. As a Pennsylvania Republican put it, "Let our motto be, protection to everything American, against everything foreign." In New York, Republicans campaigned on a reform platform designed to unite "all of the Anti-Slavery, Anti-Popery, and Anti-Whiskey" voters.

Democrats reaffirmed their support for popular sovereignty and the Kansas-Nebraska Act and nominated James Buchanan of Pennsylvania. A tall, dignified, and experienced politician, Buchanan was staunchly prosouthern. He won the three-way race with 1.8 million popular votes (45.3 percent) and 174 electoral votes. A dramatic restructuring of politics was becoming apparent: with the splintering of the American Party, Republicans replaced the Whigs as the second major party (see Map 12.3, p. 407). However, Frémont had not won a single vote in the South; had he triumphed, one North Carolina newspaper warned, the result would have been "a separation of the states." The fate of the republic hinged on President Buchanan's ability to quiet the passions of the past decade and hold the Democratic Party — the only remaining national party — together. He could not.

Dred Scott: Petitioner for Freedom Events — and his own values and weaknesses — conspired against Buchanan. Early in 1857, the Supreme Court handed down the ***Dred Scott* decision**, which sought to clarify Congress's constitutional authority over slavery. Dred Scott was an enslaved African American who had lived for almost five years with his owner, an army surgeon, in the free state of Illinois and in Wisconsin Territory, both places where the 1820 Missouri Compromise prohibited slavery. Scott argued that residence in a free state and territory had made him free. Buchanan opposed Scott's appeal and, hoping to resolve the slavery controversy, secretly pressured two justices from Pennsylvania to side with their southern colleagues.

***Dred Scott* decision**
The 1857 Supreme Court decision that ruled the Missouri Compromise unconstitutional. The Court ruled against slave Dred Scott, who claimed that travels with his master into free states and territories made him and his family free. The decision also denied the federal government the right to exclude slavery from the territories and declared that African Americans were not citizens.

AP® EXAM TIP
Compare the actions taken in the Dred Scott Case (1857) to those in the Missouri Compromise (1820) to resolve the issue of slavery.

Seven of the nine justices declared that Scott was still a slave, but they disagreed on the legal rationale. Chief Justice Roger B. Taney of Maryland, a slave owner himself, wrote the most influential opinion. He declared that "Negroes," whether enslaved or free, could not be citizens of the United States; notoriously, he added that they had "no rights that a white man was bound to respect." Therefore, no African American could sue in federal court — a controversial argument, given that free blacks were citizens in many northern states. Taney then made two even more radical claims. First, he endorsed John C. Calhoun's argument that the Fifth Amendment, which prohibited "taking" of property without due process, meant that Congress could not prevent southern citizens from moving slave property into the territories. Consequently, the chief justice concluded, the provisions of the Northwest Ordinance and Missouri Compromise that prohibited slavery had *never* been constitutional. Second, Taney declared that Congress could not grant territorial governments the authority to prohibit slavery. Taney thereby endorsed Calhoun's interpretation of popular sovereignty: only when settlers wrote a constitution and requested statehood could they prohibit slavery.

In a single stroke, Taney had declared Republicans' proposals to restrict the expansion of slavery through legislation to be unconstitutional. Republicans could never accept the legitimacy of Taney's constitutional arguments, which indeed had significant flaws. Led by Senator Seward of New York, they accused the chief justice and President Buchanan of a conspiracy to protect slavery by subverting the Constitution.

Buchanan then added fuel to the raging constitutional fire. Ignoring pleas from advisers, who saw that antislavery residents held a clear majority in Kansas, he refused to allow a popular vote on the proslavery Lecompton constitution and in 1858 strongly urged Congress to admit Kansas as a slave state. Angered by Buchanan's machinations, Stephen Douglas, the most influential Democratic senator and architect of the Kansas-Nebraska Act, broke with the president and persuaded Congress to deny Kansas statehood. (Kansas would enter the Union as a free state in 1861, during the Civil War.) Still determined to aid the South, Buchanan resumed negotiations to buy Cuba in December 1858. By pursuing an open proslavery agenda—first in *Dred Scott v. Sandford* and then in Kansas and Cuba—Buchanan widened the split in his party and the nation.

The Mormon War The president's policies in the West provoked further conflict. After the United States acquired Mexico's northern territories in 1848, Salt Lake Mormons had petitioned Congress to create a vast new state, Deseret, stretching from Utah to the Pacific coast. Instead, grudgingly, Congress set up the much smaller Utah Territory in 1850, and President Pierce appointed Mormon leader Brigham Young as governor. Tensions between Mormons and federal authorities simmered in the early 1850s. Pressured by Protestant leaders to end polygamy and angered by Mormons' threat to nullify federal laws, Buchanan dispatched a small army to Utah in 1858. He and other Democrats apparently sought to deflect attention from the slavery question. "I believe," one of the president's advisers wrote him privately, "we can supersede the Negro-Mania with the almost universal excitements of an Anti-Mormon Crusade." Buchanan backed down, however; he decided that forced abolition of polygamy might be a risky precedent for ending slavery, and he offered a pardon to Utah citizens who acknowledged federal authority. The Mormon War ended quietly, turning the nation's attention once again to the question of slavery's expansion.

AP® SKILLS & PROCESSES

CONTEXTUALIZATION

Why did northern Democratic presidents, such as Pierce and Buchanan, adopt prosouthern policies?

ABRAHAM LINCOLN AND THE REPUBLICAN TRIUMPH, 1858–1860

Why did the Republican Party win national power in 1860?

As Democrats divided along sectional lines, Republicans gained support in the North and Midwest, and Abraham Lincoln emerged as one of the party's most eloquent and politically astute candidates. However, few southerners trusted Lincoln, and his presidential candidacy in 1860 revived secessionist agitation.

AP® EXAM TIP

Explaining the end of the Second Party System and the emergence of regional political parties in the 1850s is important to know on the AP® Exam.

Lincoln's Political Career

The middle-class world of storekeepers, lawyers, and entrepreneurs in the small towns of the Ohio River Valley shaped Lincoln's early career. He came from a hardscrabble farm family that was continually on the move—from Kentucky, where Lincoln was born in 1809, to Indiana and then Illinois. In 1831, Lincoln rejected his father's life as a subsistence farmer and became a store clerk in New Salem, Illinois. Socially ambitious, he won entry to the middle class by mastering its culture, joining the New Salem Debating Society, and reading Shakespeare while he studied law. Admitted to the bar in 1837, Lincoln moved to Springfield, the new state capital. There he met Mary Todd, daughter of a Kentucky banker; they married in 1842. Her tastes were aristocratic; his were humble. She was volatile; he was easygoing but suffered bouts of depression that tried her patience and tested his character.

An Ambitious Politician Lincoln became a dexterous party politician, adept in using patronage and getting legislation passed. As a Whig in the Illinois legislature, and an admirer of Henry Clay, he promoted education, banks, canals, and railroads. During his single term in Congress in the U.S.-Mexico War, he voted for military appropriations but also endorsed the Wilmot Proviso's ban on slavery in any acquired territories. Lincoln also introduced legislation that would require the gradual, compensated emancipation of slaves in the District of Columbia. To avoid future racial strife, he favored the colonization of freed blacks in Africa or South America.

AP® SKILLS & PROCESSES

CONTEXTUALIZATION

The **CONTEXTUALIZATION** question invites students to consider the stances of Democratic Party leaders in the context of national politics. Remind students that the Democratic Party was a national coalition that included many northerners who owned no slaves, but the influence of wealthy white southerners required these northern leaders to adopt policies that assuaged their fears that slavery was under siege.

TRM Find complete suggested responses in the Teacher's Resource Materials.

CHECK FOR UNDERSTANDING

Ask students: **Why did Democrats and Whigs fail in their attempts to keep the issue of slavery in the federal territories from creating a sectional rift?** *Because both parties desired to be national institutions rather than sectional parties, both took a vague stance on the issue of slavery, hoping to retain support in both North and South, both to win elections and to avoid a civil war. The Democrats were arguably more electorally successful in this period only because they adopted a policy of nominating a Northerner for president while being largely beholden to Southern interests.*

AP® APPLY THE TIP

Divide the class into small groups and assign each group one of the following political parties of the 1850s: Democrats, Whigs, Free Soil Party, Liberty Party, or American Party. Have the groups research the platforms and candidates of their assigned party, paying special attention to the impact of regional identity in party affiliation, noting when political parties split over the issue of slavery. Ask each group to create a poster that illustrates the most important platform positions of the party as well as a slogan and logo for their assigned political party. Display the posters for the whole class and discuss the breakdown of the Second Party System in the U.S. Prompt students to group the posters according to which group merged into the regional parties of the election of 1860. Then lead a class discussion on the impact of regional political parties in a national presidential election based on winning a majority in the Electoral College.

TEACHING STRATEGY

Abraham Lincoln's views on slavery have been subject to endless examination and debate. He has been variously seen as a saintly egalitarian, well ahead of his time in advocating the full equality of blacks and whites, and a blatant hypocrite for engaging in racial stereotyping and advocating colonization. In the introduction to his Pulitzer Prize–winning book, *The Fiery Trial* (New York: Norton, 2010), historian Eric Foner places Lincoln's views in historical context and dispels notions that he was an abolitionist. Foner's larger point, however, is that Lincoln's views were not static and, as a great leader, he showed the capacity to move toward the abolitionist position.

After his defeat in 1848, Lincoln returned to Illinois and focused on his growing law practice representing railroads and manufacturers. The Kansas-Nebraska Act propelled him back into politics as a Republican. Shocked by the act's repeal of the Missouri Compromise and Senator Douglas's advocacy of popular sovereignty, Lincoln reaffirmed his opposition to slavery in the territories. Although he believed Congress had no power under the Constitution to interfere with slavery in states where it already existed, he likened slavery to a cancer that had to be cut out if the nation's republican ideals and moral principles were to endure.

The Lincoln-Douglas Debates In 1858, Lincoln ran for the U.S. Senate seat held by Stephen Douglas. Lincoln claimed that the proslavery Supreme Court might soon declare that the Constitution "does not permit a state to exclude slavery," just as it had decided in *Dred Scott* that "neither Congress nor the territorial legislature" could ban slavery in a territory. In that event, he warned, "we shall awake to the reality . . . that the Supreme Court has made Illinois a slave state." This prospect informed Lincoln's famous "House Divided" speech. Quoting the biblical adage "A house divided against itself cannot stand," he predicted that American society "cannot endure permanently half slave and half free. . . . It will become all one thing, or all the other."

The Senate race in Illinois attracted national interest because of Douglas's prominence and Lincoln's reputation as a formidable speaker. During a series of seven debates, Douglas declared his support for white supremacy: "This government was made by our

AP® THEME

PCE: Politics and Power

Eric Foner's *Free Soil, Free Labor, Free Men: The Ideology of the Republican Party Before the Civil War* (Oxford University Press, 1970) is still a good starting point for anyone interested in the importance of the Free Labor argument associated with the Republican Party. Teachers looking to further their understanding of this historical development will find it a useful reference.

Wide Awake Club Certificate, 1860 This elaborate print illustrates the themes of the 1860 Republican campaign in a certificate awarded to men who joined marching clubs in support of Lincoln and his running mate Hannibal Hamlin. It calls for "Free Speech, Free Soil, Free Men" and depicts a giant eye keeping watch over the machinations of the "slave power." The figures on the left and right are Wide-Awakes in uniform, ready to march in campaign parades. At the bottom, broken shackles lie in front of the eagle, who spreads his wings over landscapes of rural and urban prosperity. Library of Congress, 06782.

fathers, by white men for the benefit of white men," he said, attacking Lincoln for supporting "negro equality." Lincoln parried Douglas's racist attacks by arguing that free blacks should have equal economic opportunities but not equal political rights. Taking the offensive, he asked how Douglas could accept the *Dred Scott* decision (which protected slave property in the territories) yet advocate popular sovereignty (which allowed settlers to exclude slavery). Douglas responded that a territory's residents could exclude slavery by not adopting laws to protect it. That position pleased neither proslavery nor antislavery advocates. Nonetheless, when Democrats won a narrow majority in the state legislature, they reelected Douglas to the U.S. Senate.

AP® SKILLS & PROCESSES

DEVELOPMENTS AND PROCESSES

Why did Lincoln argue the United States could no longer endure "half slave and half free" when it had already done so for several decades?

The Union Under Siege

The debates with Douglas gave Lincoln a national reputation. In the election of 1858, the Republican Party won control of the U.S. House of Representatives. Shaken by Republicans' advance, southern Democrats divided again. Moderates, who included Senator Jefferson Davis of Mississippi, strongly defended "southern rights" and demanded ironclad political or constitutional protections for slavery. So-called fire-eaters — powerful orators such as Robert Barnwell Rhett of South Carolina and William Lowndes Yancey of Alabama — repudiated the Union and actively promoted secession. President Buchanan's secessionist secretary of war, John B. Floyd, quietly sold ten thousand federal muskets to South Carolina.

Antislavery northerners likewise took a strong stance. Senator William Seward of New York declared that freedom and slavery were locked in "an irrepressible conflict." Ruthless abolitionist John Brown, who had perpetrated the Pottawatomie massacre, showed what that might mean. In October 1859, Brown led eighteen heavily armed black and white men in a raid on the federal arsenal at Harpers Ferry, Virginia. Brown hoped to arm slaves with the arsenal's weapons and mount a major rebellion to end slavery.

The raid was a failure, and Brown was quickly captured. But though he was a poor military strategist, Brown made an excellent martyr. As Virginia rushed to convict and execute him, the wounded Brown came to the courtroom on a stretcher. From the gallows he declared that the New Testament

> teaches me that all things whatsoever I would that men should do to me, I should do even so to them. It teaches me, further, to remember them that are in bonds as bound with them. I endeavored to act up to that instruction. . . . If it is deemed necessary that I should forfeit my life for the furtherance of the ends of justice, and mingle my blood further with the blood of my children and with the blood of millions in this slave country . . . I say, let it be done.

As had happened after the caning of Senator Sumner, onlookers' reactions divided the nation even more than the acts of Brown himself. Southerners were shocked to find that a group of abolitionists — the "Secret Six" — had funded Brown's raid. They were equally outraged that northern church bells tolled on the day of Brown's hanging. "The lesson of the hour is insurrection," thundered abolitionist Wendell Phillips. In Virginia, the *Richmond Enquirer* reported that "the Harpers Ferry invasion has advanced the cause of disunion more than any other event." Republican leaders denounced Brown's plot, but Democrats called it "a natural, logical, inevitable result of the doctrines and teachings of the Republican party." One southern Democratic paper warned that Republicans planned to "put the torch to our dwellings and the knife to our throats."

The Election of 1860

Within months, southern Democrats decided they could no longer count on their northern allies. At the party's convention in April 1860, northern Democrats rejected Jefferson Davis's proposal to protect slavery in the territories. Delegates from eight

AP® EXAM TIP

Evaluate the role of the election of 1860 on the regional divisions leading to the Civil War.

CHECK FOR UNDERSTANDING

Ask students: **How did Lincoln's political career lead him to the White House?** *Largely self-taught, Lincoln learned debate and law, which prepared him for a political career. An extremely ambitious man, he served one term in Congress and then ran for the U.S. Senate. Though Lincoln lost the Senate contest to Douglas, he became a visible figure in the early Republican Party and won candidacy to the presidency in 1860.*

AP® SKILLS & PROCESSES

DEVELOPMENTS AND PROCESSES

Use excerpts from the Second Lincoln-Douglas debates in Freeport, Illinois to help students understand how Lincoln explained the contradiction of Stephen Douglas's support of the Dred Scott decision and the tenets of popular sovereignty. This is often referred to as the Freeport Doctrine. This historical development is essential for students' understanding of how Lincoln lost the Senate race in 1858, yet came out of that contest a national figure.

TRM Find complete suggested responses in the Teacher's Resource Materials.

TEACHING STRATEGY

John Brown's raid on Harpers Ferry provoked dramatically different reactions in the North and the South, which were captured in letters to the editor in both regions. While many northerners joined southerners in expressing outrage, some abolitionists celebrated the attack as the opening battle in a war for freedom. Have students examine these divergent views as one of the final events that paved the way for the Civil War. Access the letters by searching "Secession Era Editorial Project Harpers Ferry."

TEACHING STRATEGY

Use primary sources from the Nineteenth Century Documents Project to have students compare the Democratic and Republican Party platforms for the election of 1860. Access relevant documents by searching "Nineteenth Century Documents Project Election of 1860."

AP® APPLY THE TIP

Provide students with **Handout 12.3 — Contextualization: Election of 1860 (TRM)**. Students should evaluate the outcome of the 1860 election by contextualizing the changes in the U.S. that influenced the election (e.g., Western expansion, Industrial and Market Revolution, immigration, nativism, popular press, etc.) and compare the outcome to the election of 1848 (see maps on p. 407). Finally, ask students to write a paragraph identifying whether the outcome of the election of 1860 was a cause or an effect of regional divisions in the U.S. at the time of the Civil War.

TRM Find **Handout 12.3 — Contextualization: Election of 1860** in the Teacher's Resource Materials.

southern states quit the meeting. At a second Democratic convention, northern and midwestern delegates nominated Stephen Douglas for president. Meeting separately, southern Democrats nominated the sitting vice president, John C. Breckinridge of Kentucky. Democrats — the only remaining party with strong bases in both North and South — had split in half.

With Democrats divided, Republicans sensed victory. They courted white voters with a free soil platform that opposed both slavery and racial equality: "Missouri for white men and white men for Missouri," declared that state's Republican platform. The national Republican convention chose Lincoln as its presidential candidate because he was more moderate on slavery than the best-known Republicans, Senators William Seward of New York and Salmon Chase of Ohio. Lincoln also conveyed a compelling egalitarian image that appealed to smallholding farmers, wage earners, and midwestern voters.

VISUAL ACTIVITY

Lincoln on Home Base Beginning in the 1820s and 1830s, the language and imagery of sports saturated politics, cutting across the lines of class and party. Wielding a long, bat-like rail labeled "Equal Rights and Free Territory," Abraham Lincoln holds a baseball and appears ready to score a victory in the election. His three opponents — from left to right, John Bell (the candidate of a new Constitutional Union Party), Stephen A. Douglas, and John C. Breckinridge — will soon be "out." Indeed, according to the cartoonist, they were about to be "skunk'd." As Douglas laments, their attempt to put a "short stop" to Lincoln's presidential ambitions had failed. Library of Congress, LC-DIG-ppmsca-09311.

READING THE IMAGE: What is written on each player's belt? His bat? What is the point of view of the artist regarding the Election of 1860 and each candidate?

MAKING CONNECTIONS: Part of the mythology of American baseball is that the sport began in Union army camps, amid the struggle of the Civil War. What is the historical situation at the time of this cartoon? How do these events challenge this idea?

AP® THEME

PCE: Politics and Power

This cartoon attests to how Lincoln's victory resulted from divisions among the other three candidates. This split gave Lincoln only a plurality of the popular vote, but a solid majority of the electoral vote. Use this cartoon along with **MAP 12.3** (p. 407) to illustrate the clear regional division of voting patterns, with Lincoln's win being accomplished without any southern electoral votes.

TRM Find complete suggested responses in the Teacher's Resource Materials.

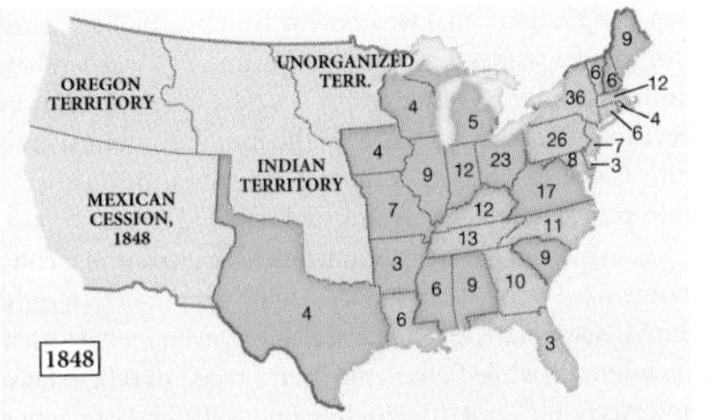

Candidate	Electoral Vote	Popular Vote	Percent of Popular Vote
Zachary Taylor (Whig)	163	1,360,967	47.4
Lewis Cass (Democrat)	127	1,222,342	42.5
Martin Van Buren (Free Soil)	—	291,263	10.1

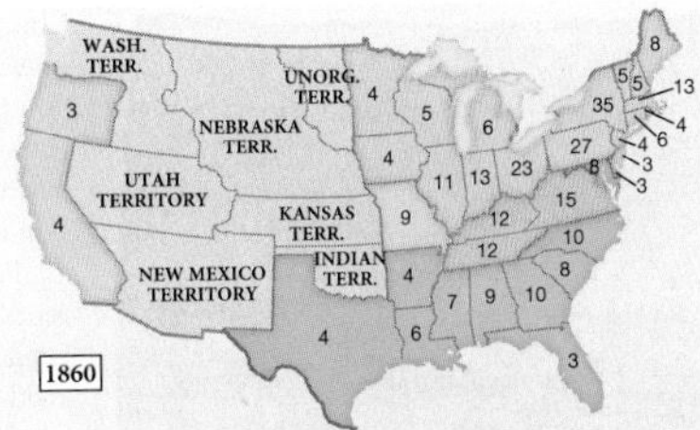

Candidate	Electoral Vote	Popular Vote	Percent of Popular Vote
Abraham Lincoln (Republican)	180	1,865,593	39.8
John C. Breckinridge (Southern Democrat)	72	848,356	18.1
John Bell (Constitutional Union)	39	592,906	12.6
Stephen A. Douglas (Northern Democrat)	12	1,382,713	29.5

MAP 12.3 Political Realignment, 1848 and 1860
In the presidential election of 1848, both the Whig and Democratic candidates won electoral votes throughout the nation. Subsequently, the political conflict over slavery and the Compromise of 1850 destroyed the Whig Party in the South. As the only nationwide party, the Democrats won easily over the Whigs in 1852 and, with the opposition split between the Republican and American parties, triumphed in 1856 as well. However, a new region-based party system appeared by 1860 and persisted for the next seventy years — with Democrats dominant in the South and Republicans usually controlling the Northeast, Midwest, and Far West.

The Republican strategy worked. Although Lincoln was not on the ballot in any Deep South state, and though he received less than 1 percent of the popular vote in the South and only 40 percent of the national vote, he won every northern and western state except New Jersey, giving him 180 (of 303) electoral votes and thus a majority in the electoral college. Breckinridge took 72 electoral votes by sweeping the Deep South and picking up Delaware, Maryland, and North Carolina. Douglas won 30 percent of the popular ballot but only 51 electoral votes. Republicans had united voters in the Northeast and Midwest behind free soil. To his surprise, Lincoln also won California and Oregon by the barest of margins, apparently due in part to public outrage over a duel in which a proslavery California Democrat killed an antislavery rival (Map 12.3).

A revolution was in the making. "Oh My God!!! This morning heard that Lincoln was elected," Keziah Brevard, a widowed South Carolina plantation mistress and owner of two hundred slaves, scribbled in her diary. "Lord save us." Slavery had long been part of the American constitutional order — an order many southerners now believed was under siege. Fearful of a massive slave uprising, Chief Justice Taney recalled "the horrors of St. Domingo [Haiti]." At the very least, warned John Townsend of South Carolina, a Republican administration in Washington would suppress "the inter-State slave trade" and thereby "cripple this vital Southern institution of slavery." To many slaveholders, it seemed time to think carefully about Lincoln's 1858 statement that the Union must "become all one thing, or all the other."

AP® SKILLS & PROCESSES

MAKING CONNECTIONS

What was the relationship between the collapse of the Second Party System and the Republican victory in the election of 1860?

SECESSION WINTER, 1860–1861

After South Carolina's secession, why were Unionists and Confederates unable to avoid war?

Following Lincoln's election, secessionist fervor swept through the Deep South. The Union collapsed first in South Carolina, home of John C. Calhoun and nullification. For Robert Barnwell Rhett and other fire-eaters who had demanded secession since the

AP® EXAM TIP

Trace the debates and actions that resulted in the secession of southern states before the inauguration of Abraham Lincoln.

CHECK FOR UNDERSTANDING

Ask students: **What factors led to the rise of the Republican Party and Lincoln's election in 1860?** *The disgust with the Kansas-Nebraska Act of 1854 fractured the Democratic Party into geographic sections and coalesced antislavery Democrats, Whigs, and Free Soilers under the banner of a new political party, the Republicans. Unlike their Whig predecessors, the Republican Party took a firm stance on slavery and was avowedly against it, at least in the territories. Although the Republican Party ran a candidate for president in 1856, it barely lost. Lincoln's election in 1860 as the Republican candidate owed as much to the splintering of the Democratic Party, with its usual electoral votes divided among three candidates, as any other factor, giving Lincoln a victory.*

AP® SKILLS & PROCESSES

MAKING CONNECTIONS

The **MAKING CONNECTIONS** question addresses the major realignment created by the demise of the Second Party System and the emergence of the Republican Party and the Third Party System. Use **MAP 12.3** to illustrate the differences between the two systems. In 1848, the Whig Zachary Taylor won both northern and Deep South states, while Democrat Lewis Cass won states in the South, far North, and West. By contrast, the 1860 election reveals strictly regional electoral victories.

TRM Find complete suggested responses in the Teacher's Resource Materials.

AP® APPLY THE TIP

Students should work with a partner or in small groups to create a timeline from November 1860 to March 1861 (begin with the election of 1860 and end with the inauguration of Abraham Lincoln). Ask students to place events below the timeline that pushed the South toward secession and the Civil War and place events above the timeline that represented attempts at compromise. Have students read and analyze an excerpt from Lincoln's First Inaugural Address and have students discuss with their partners or groups whether the speech belongs below or above the line. Ask students to provide a justification for their choice. Then lead a class discussion on the speech and its influence on secession.

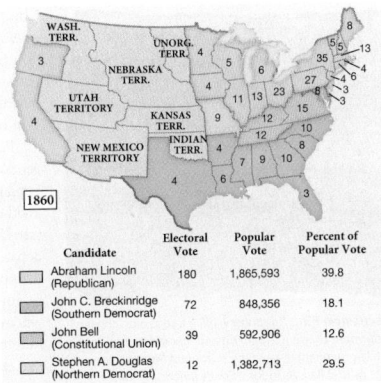

TEACHING STRATEGY

Use primary sources from the Nineteenth Century Documents Project to have students analyze and compare the various arguments provided for secession in the proclamations of several southern states. Access relevant documents by searching "Nineteenth Century Documents Project Secession."

AP® APPLY THE TIP

Have students work in groups of three to complete the **AP® FIRSTHAND ACCOUNTS** document activity and questions on pp. 410–411. Ask each student in the group to be responsible for reading one of the documents for the group. Prompt students to write down the argument being made in each document and provide an extended analysis by focusing on the point of view and purpose of each author.

Alabama Secession Flag In January 1861, a secession convention in Alabama voted to leave the Union and marked its decision by designating this pennant — sewn by a group of Montgomery women — as its official flag. As in John Gast's *American Progress* (p. 347), the Goddess of Liberty forms the central image. Here she holds a sword and a flag with a single star, symbolizing Alabama's new status as an independent republic. Alabama Department of Archives and History.

Compromise of 1850, their goal was now within reach. "Our enemies are about to take possession of the Government," warned one South Carolinian. Frightened by that prospect, a state convention voted on December 20, 1860, to dissolve "the union now subsisting between South Carolina and other States." This unanimous decision resulted in part from the state's unusual political rules.

Fire-eaters elsewhere in the Deep South quickly called similar conventions and organized mobs to attack local Union supporters. In early January, white Mississippians enacted a secession ordinance. Florida and Louisiana followed, while fierce controversy raged in other states (see "Firsthand Accounts," p. 410). Holding out to the end of a bitter debate, over a third of delegates to Alabama's secession convention voted to oppose leaving the Union. In early February, Texans ousted Unionist governor Sam Houston, ignoring his warning that "the North . . . will overwhelm the South." Georgia's prosecession governor waited a month before announcing that a secession referendum had won by 57 percent; returns were never released, and historians now suspect the vote was much closer and a majority may even have opposed secession.

Nevertheless, when the smoke cleared, the Deep South states had all seceded. In February, jubilant secessionists met in Montgomery, Alabama, to proclaim a new nation, the Confederate States of America. Adopting a provisional constitution, the delegates named Mississippian Jefferson Davis, a former U.S. senator and secretary of war, as the Confederacy's president and Georgia congressman Alexander Stephens as vice president.

Secessionist fervor was less intense in four states of the Upper South (Virginia, North Carolina, Tennessee, and Arkansas), where there were fewer slaves. White opinion was especially divided in the four border slave states (Maryland, Delaware, Kentucky, and Missouri), where upcountry, nonslaveholding farmers held substantial political power. Residents of these states also keenly understood that any resulting civil war would likely be fought on their farms and lands and through the streets of their towns and cities. The legislatures of Virginia and Tennessee refused to join the secessionist movement and urged a compromise.

AP® EXAM TIP

The different arguments for war in the North and South at the start of the Civil War is important to know for the AP® Exam.

Meanwhile, President Buchanan's administration floundered. Buchanan declared secession illegal but, in line with his states' rights outlook, claimed that the federal government lacked authority to restore the Union by force. Buchanan's timidity prompted South Carolina's new government to demand the surrender of Fort Sumter (a federal garrison in Charleston Harbor) and cut off its supplies. The president again backed down, refusing to use the navy to supply the fort.

Instead, the outgoing president urged Congress to find a compromise. As legislators scrambled to respond, the plan that emerged with the most support came from Senator John J. Crittenden of Kentucky. His proposal had two parts. The first, which Congress approved, called for a constitutional amendment to protect slavery from federal interference in any state where it already existed. Crittenden's second provision called for the westward extension of the Missouri Compromise line (36°30′ north latitude) to the California border. The provision would have banned slavery north of the line and allowed it to the south, including any territories "hereafter acquired," raising the prospect of expansion into Cuba or Central America.

Congressional Republicans rejected Crittenden's second proposal on strict instructions from president-elect Lincoln. With good reason, Lincoln feared it would unleash new imperialist adventures. "On the territorial question, I am inflexible," he wrote; restoring the Missouri Compromise line would simply invite southerners to keep "filibustering to expand slavery." In 1787, 1821, and 1850, the North and South had resolved their differences over slavery. In 1861, there would be no compromise.

In his March 1861 inaugural address, Lincoln carefully outlined his positions. He promised to safeguard slavery where it existed but vowed to prevent its expansion. He also declared that the Union was "perpetual"; consequently, the secession of the Confederate states was illegal. Lincoln asserted his intention to "hold, occupy, and possess" federal property in the seceded states and "to collect duties and imposts" there. If military force was necessary to preserve the Union, Lincoln—like Democrat Andrew Jackson during the nullification crisis—would use it. The choice was the Deep South's: return to the Union or face war.

Their decision came quickly (Map 12.4). When Lincoln dispatched an unarmed ship to resupply Fort Sumter, Jefferson Davis and his associates in the Provisional Government of the Confederate States decided to seize the fort. Their forces opened fire on April 12, with ardent fire-eater Edmund Ruffin supposedly firing the first cannon. Two days later, the Union defenders capitulated. On April 15, Lincoln called 75,000 state militiamen into federal service for ninety days to put down an insurrection "too powerful to be suppressed by the ordinary course of judicial proceedings."

Northerners responded to Lincoln's call to arms with wild enthusiasm. In western Pennsylvania, a group of lumbermen organized themselves into a regiment, built rafts, and floated down to Harrisburg before the state governor had even requested volunteers. Asked to provide thirteen regiments, Ohio's Republican governor William Dennison sent twenty. Most northern Democrats lent their support. Despite his past differences with Lincoln, Stephen Douglas toured the North urging citizens to support the government. "Every man must be for the United States or against it," he declared. "There can be no neutrals in this war, only patriots—or traitors."

Voters in the Middle and Border South now faced a new situation: war was imminent. Those eight states accounted for two-thirds of whites in the slaveholding states,

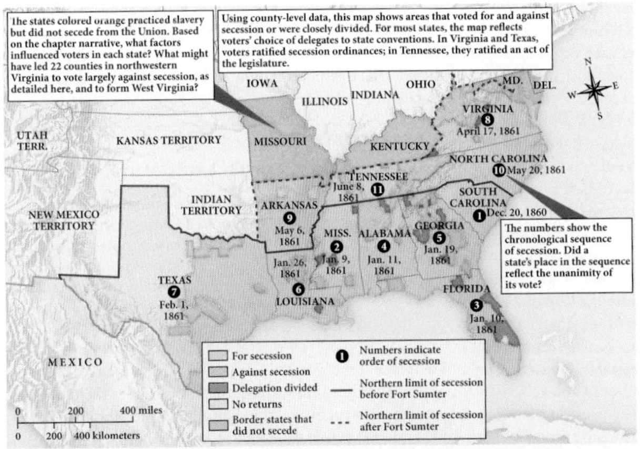

MAPPING THE PAST

MAP 12.4 The Process of Secession, 1860–1861

The states of the Lower South, with the highest concentration of slaves, led the secessionist movement. After the attack on Fort Sumter in April 1861, the states of the Upper South joined the new Confederacy.

ANALYZING THE MAP: Note the order in which eleven states seceded. Which ones helped create the initial Confederate government, in February? Which ones left the Union after that time? In which areas of the South were voters divided or against secession?

MAKING CONNECTIONS: Using this map and the chapter narrative, why did the process of secession extend so long? Why did Missouri, Kentucky, Maryland, and Delaware not secede, and why did Virginia divide? What does this tell us about the strengths and weaknesses of the Confederacy at its founding?

TEACHING STRATEGY

MAP 12.4 provides detailed information about the nature and sequence of secession, including its geographical dimensions. Students should note that most southern states had counties that were either opposed to secession or divided on the issue. Opposition to secession was strongest in the backcountry populated by poor whites who typically owned no slaves. Significant opposition to secession counters the popular misconception that white southerners universally rushed to endorse leaving the Union. Students should also recognize that the Deep South states seceded first. They were not only the most committed to slave labor but also the most geographically buffered from a potential military invasion by the U.S. government. The second wave of secession followed the attack on Fort Sumter. The border states remained in the Union, often in strong part because of their proximity to free states and federal troops.

TRM Find complete suggested responses in the Teacher's Resource Materials.

AP® SKILLS & PROCESSES

ANALYZING HISTORICAL EVIDENCE

The **AP® FIRSTHAND ACCOUNTS** feature provides students with an opportunity to see how many southern politicians were conflicted regarding the issue of secession. To extend this activity, students could look for evidence that the authors reference the revolutionary heritage or the principles of the Constitution.

AP® FIRSTHAND ACCOUNTS

To Secede or Not to Secede?

Across the South, between November 1860 and April 1861, legislators and citizens debated secession. They weighed economic interests and property rights, cultural ties, political loyalties, patriotism, and of course touching on all of these, the question of slavery. In these excerpts three political leaders — a Virginian, Georgian, and Mississippian — explained their positions and tried to influence voters or legislators to heed their warnings.

ALEXANDER STUART

Letter to the *Staunton* (VA) *Spectator*, 1860

Stuart, a Whig from strongly Unionist Augusta County in Virginia's Shenandoah Valley, won election as a delegate to the state's secession convention. In an open letter to constituents, published in the *Staunton Spectator*, Stuart argued that Virginia should stay in the Union.

SOURCE: *Staunton Spectator*, January 22, 1861, from "Valley of the Shadow," University of Virginia, http://valley.lib.virginia.edu/.

" Secession . . . is a doctrine of New England origin. It had its birth among the Federalists of that section of the Union, during the war of 1812, and was nurtured in the celebrated Hartford Convention. . . . In my judgment, it is at war with the whole theory of our institutions. . . .

There is no natural antagonism between the Northern and Southern States. On the contrary, each is necessary to the other. They are the complements of each other, and together constitute the most perfect social, industrial and political systems, that the world has ever seen. . . . The South produces what the North wants, but cannot produce; and the North furnishes what the South needs, but cannot supply for itself. . . . The present condition of antagonism and alienation is unnatural. It is not the legitimate result of any conflict of the social and industrial systems of the two sections, but is the work of those 'DESIGNING MEN,' both North and South, against whom Washington so impressively warned us in his farewell address.

It is true that the Northern States, under the lead of such men, have been guilty of gross outrages on the rights of the South, [but] . . . I believe that all our rights can be secured, and all our wrongs most effectually redressed in the Union, and under the Constitution. . . . I have not been able to perceive how we could add to the security of our slave property by surrendering the guarantees of the Constitution, and substantially bringing down the Canada frontier to the borders of Virginia. It would lead to emancipation and probably to emancipation in blood. Nor can I see how we would secure our rights in the [federal] territories by abandoning them. I am equally at a loss to understand how we will establish any of our demands against the Northern States on a firmer basis, by severing our connection with them, and thereby from us, the million and a half of friends we had in those States at the last election. . . .

Should war follow the dissolution, the consequences must be of the most frightful character. Brother would be arrayed against brother, and the whole land would be drenched with blood. The border country would be ravaged and laid waste with fire and sword. . . . Real estate would be depreciated more than 50 per cent; business in all its departments would be paralyzed; credit destroyed; personal property of all kinds impressed for public use; our slaves incited to insurrection; and ruin and desolation would overwhelm the whole country.

. . . The people should weigh these matters well before they decide to embark on the unknown and tempestuous sea of convulsion and revolution. . . . "

ALEXANDER STEPHENS

Address to the Georgia Legislature, 1860

The Georgia legislature undertook a vigorous debate over secession in December 1860. The Unionist address given by prominent Whig congressman Alexander Stephens was noted throughout the South. When Georgia seceded, Stephens nonetheless went with his state and became vice president of the Confederacy.

SOURCE: William W. Freehling and Craig M. Simpson, eds., *Secession Debated: Georgia's Showdown in 1860* (New York: Oxford University Press, 1992), 51–80.

" It is said that Mr. Lincoln's policy and principles are against the Constitution, and that, if he carries them out, it will be destructive of our rights. Let us not anticipate a threatened evil. If he violates the Constitution, then will come our time to act. Do not let *us* break it, because,

three-fourths of their industrial production, and well over half of their food. They were home to many of the nation's most talented military leaders, including Colonel Robert E. Lee of Virginia, a career officer whom veteran General Winfield Scott recommended to Lincoln to lead the new Union army. Those states were also geographically strategic. Kentucky, with its 500-mile border on the Ohio River, was essential to the movement of troops and supplies. Maryland was vital to the Union's security because it bordered the nation's capital on three sides.

The weight of its history as a slave-owning society decided the outcome in Virginia. On April 17, 1861, a convention approved secession by a vote of 88 to 55, forsooth, *he* may. . . . Mr. Lincoln . . . is bound by the constitutional checks which are thrown around him, which at this time render him powerless to do any great mischief. This shows the wisdom of our system. The President of the United States is no emperor, no dictator,—he is clothed with no absolute power. He can do nothing unless he is backed by power in Congress. . . . The gains in the Democratic party in Pennsylvania, Ohio, New Jersey, New York, Indiana, and other states . . . have been enough to make a majority of nearly thirty in the next House [of Representatives] against Mr. Lincoln. . . . In the Senate he will also be powerless. There will be a majority of four against him. . . .

When I look around and see our prosperity in everything,—agriculture, commerce, art, science, and every department of progress, physical, moral, and mental,—certainly, in the face of such an exhibition, if we can, without the loss of power, or any essential right or interest, remain in the Union, it is our duty to ourselves and to posterity to do so. Let us not unwisely yield to this temptation. . . .

If the policy of Mr. Lincoln and his Republican associates shall be carried out, or attempted to be carried out, no man in Georgia will be more willing or ready than myself to defend our rights, interest, and honor at every hazard and to the last extremity. What is this policy? It is, in the first place, to exclude us, by an act of Congress, from the Territories, with our slave property. . . .

It is the duty of the States to deliver fugitive slaves, as well as it is the duty of the General Government to see that it is done. The Northern States, on entering into the Federal compact, pledged themselves to surrender such fugitives. . . . They have violated their plighted faith. What ought we to do in view of this? . . . We are . . . bound, before proceeding to violent measure, to set forth our grievances, . . . to give them an opportunity to redress the wrong. Has our State yet done this? I think not. . . . ”

WILLIAM HARRIS

Address to the Georgia Legislature, 1860

After seceding, several Deep South states appointed "secession commissioners," whose job was to travel to other slaveholding states to encourage them to join the new Confederacy. In the midst of Georgia's debate, William Harris, one of Mississippi's commissioners, made this impassioned plea to the Georgia legislature.

SOURCE: William L. Harris, commissioner from Mississippi, address to the Georgia legislature, December 17, 1860, in Charles B. Dew, *Apostles of Disunion: Southern Secession Commissioners and the Causes of the Civil War* (Charlottesville: University of Virginia Press, 2001), 83–89.

“ Our fathers made this a government for the white man, rejecting the negro, as an ignorant, inferior, barbarian race, incapable of self-government, and not, therefore, entitled to be associated with the white man upon terms of civil, political, or social equality. This new administration comes into power, under the solemn pledge to overturn and strike down this great feature of our Union . . . and to substitute in its stead their new theory of the universal equality of the black and white races.

Our fathers secured to us, by our Constitutional Union, now being overturned by this Black Republican rule, protection to life, liberty, and property, *all over the Union*. . . . Our Constitution, in unmistakable language, guarantees the return of our fugitive slaves. Congress has recognized her duty in this respect, by enacting proper laws for the enforcement of this right. And yet these laws have been continually nullified. . . .

Mississippi is firmly convinced that there is but one alternative: This *new union* with Lincoln Black Republicans and free negroes, without slavery; or slavery under our old constitutional bond of union, without Lincoln Black Republicans, or free negroes either, to molest us. . . . [For] the latter, then *secession* is inevitable.

. . . Sink or swim, live or die, survive or perish, the part of Mississippi is chosen. She will never submit to the principles and policy of this Black Republican Administration. She had rather see the last of her race, men, women and children, immolated in one common funeral pyre, than see them subjected to the degradation of civil, political and social equality with the negro race. ”

QUESTIONS FOR ANALYSIS

1. All of the authors quoted here were well-to-do southern men who owned slaves. Based on their arguments, what appeared to motivate some of them to advocate secession while others did not?
2. Who was the intended audience for each of these documents? How might that have affected each document's argument, language, and tone?
3. Stuart and Stevens both suggest that, through further negotiations with the Lincoln administration and Congress, a compromise might be reached that would avoid armed conflict. What specific guarantees from Lincoln and Congress does each demand? Based on your reading of this chapter, what might have been the outcome of such negotiations?

TRM Find complete suggested responses in the Teacher's Resource Materials.

with dissenters concentrated in the state's northwestern counties, dominated by poorer, nonslaveholding farmers. Elsewhere, Virginia whites embraced the Confederate cause. "The North was the aggressor," declared Richmond lawyer William Poague as he enlisted. "The South resisted her invaders." Refusing General Scott's offer of the Union command, Robert E. Lee resigned from the U.S. Army. "Save in defense of my native state," Lee told Scott, "I never desire again to draw my sword." Arkansas, Tennessee, and North Carolina quickly joined Virginia in the Confederacy.

Whatever their prior views, the citizens of eleven southern states now committed to separate nationhood on a basis the Deep South had already determined. Two weeks after Lincoln's inauguration, the Confederacy's new vice president, Alexander Stephens of Georgia, outlined its goals in his famous "cornerstone" speech. Jefferson and other founders, he wrote, had considered slavery an evil — an institution they inherited and practiced reluctantly, believing it "wrong in principle, socially, morally, and politically." The new Confederacy, Stephens declared, "is founded upon exactly the opposite idea; its foundations are laid, its corner-stone rests, upon the great truth that the negro is not equal to the white man; that subordination to the superior race is his natural and normal condition. This, our new government, is the first, in the history of the world, based upon this great physical, philosophical, and moral truth."

For millions of loyal Unionists outside the South, secession and the Confederate attack on Fort Sumter automatically meant war. Yet on both sides, few Americans understood what the next four years would bring. At first many thought the South would back down and return to the Union if Republicans stood firm. Republican congressman Thaddeus Stevens scoffed, "They have tried it fifty times, and fifty times they have found weak and recreant tremblers in the north." If war came, northerners were confident of their superior numbers and power. For their part, southerners argued that cotton was "King" and would give them extraordinary economic and political leverage, including likely aid from Britain and France. Many southerners also claimed that "the Yankees are cowards and will not fight," as one put it. A South Carolina congressman promised to drink all the blood that would be shed as a result of secession.

Others expected something different. When Fort Sumter fell, a former army officer named William Tecumseh Sherman was serving as superintendent of a military school in Louisiana. Upon hearing that Lincoln had called up 75,000 troops for three months, Sherman was sure it would not be enough: "You might as well attempt to put out the flames of a burning house with a squirt-gun." He left Louisiana and rejoined the U.S. Army. As volunteers began to mobilize, an enslaved woman in Mississippi named Dora Franks overheard a conversation between her master and his wife: "He feared all the slaves 'ud be took away. She say if dat was true she feel lak jumpin' in de well." Franks added, "I hate to hear her say dat, but from dat minute I started prayin' for freedom."

AP® SKILLS & PROCESSES

CAUSATION

When South Carolina seceded in December 1860, Virginia, North Carolina, Arkansas, and Tennessee declined to do so. What happened over the months that followed, that caused legislators and voters in all four states to change their minds?

SUMMARY

The end of the U.S.-Mexico War set off bitter political conflicts over whether Congress should allow slavery in lands taken from Mexico — a move opposed by many northerners, both Democrats and Whigs. Southern Democrats claimed the constitutional right to carry slaves into all U.S. territories. Congress hoped to placate all sides with the Compromise of 1850, including a new Fugitive Slave Act, but controversy only grew. Discovery of gold, meanwhile, led to rapid settlement of California; though few got rich, gold seekers pushed out Mexican landholders and waged a war of extermination against Native peoples.

Free soilers increasingly called for western lands to be reserved for free white families. As antislavery activists protested the injustice of the Fugitive Slave Act, and with evidence emerging that southerners were working to annex slave Cuba, abolitionists began to warn that southern Democrats' "slave power" conspiracy controlled federal policy. In response, some radical southerners began to advocate secession.

Northern Democratic efforts to implement popular sovereignty in the territories, through the Kansas-Nebraska Act, proved disastrous: increasing violence in Kansas led coalitions of former Democrats, Whigs, and Free Soilers in the North to form the Republican Party. Amid massive immigration from Ireland, it appeared for a while that nativism might eclipse slavery as a national issue. But by 1856, the Republican Party emerged as the main challenger to Democrats in the North. In 1860, the Democratic Party fragmented on sectional lines, leading to a four-way race in which Republican Abraham Lincoln emerged victorious. South Carolina seceded almost immediately, arguing that southern slavery could no longer be protected in the Union. Majorities in the Deep South voted to follow suit. After Confederate forces fired on federal Fort Sumter, Lincoln called up troops to suppress rebellion. Four more states in the Upper South then seceded, leading by April 1861 to civil war.

CHECK FOR UNDERSTANDING

Ask students: **After South Carolina's secession, why were Unionists and Confederates unable to avoid war?** *After Lincoln's election and South Carolina's secession, both in late 1860, neither side seriously entertained compromise over the slavery issue, which had occurred in various forms in 1787, 1821, and 1850. Thus, when the Crittenden Compromise was proposed in 1861, which effectively restored the 1821 Missouri Compromise, it was rejected by Lincoln to invite a final solution to the slavery question, no matter how bloody (and many in 1861 thought it would not be that bloody).*

AP® SKILLS & PROCESSES

CAUSATION

Provide a timeline for students from December, 1860 to April, 1861. Ask students to account for specific responses by these states to federal and southern actions between the dates in question. Making a timeline in this instance can help students focus on discrete causation, as opposed to a broader understanding of causation.

TRM Find complete suggested responses in the Teacher's Resource Materials.

CHECK FOR UNDERSTANDING

Use the **AP® LEARNING FOCUS** question from the beginning of the chapter to check students' understanding of the chapter as a whole: **Why did the new Republican Party arise, and what events led to Democratic division and southern secession?** *The belief in a Free Soil platform, the tacit support among nativists, and the support to stop the expansion of enslavement in the territories west of the Mississippi River, especially those acquired from Mexico in 1848, led to the rise of the Republican Party. The Democratic division occurred in the context of disagreements over popular sovereignty, disagreement over the meaning of the Dred Scott decision, regional differences, and the political intransigence of some members in the Lower South all contributed to the split in the Democratic Party. Southern secession was a complicated mixture of the aforementioned elements, ultimately coming to a head in the winter of 1860–1861.*

LearningCurve

Remind students to go online to complete the LearningCurve quiz for this chapter.

CHAPTER 12 REVIEW

AP® CONTENT REVIEW *Answer these questions to demonstrate your understanding of the chapter's main ideas.*

1. How did U.S. acquisition of lands in the U.S.-Mexico War trigger political conflicts?
2. Why did Democrats and Whigs fail in their attempts to keep the issue of slavery in the federal territories from creating a sectional rift?
3. Why did the Republican Party win national power in 1860?
4. After South Carolina's secession, why were Unionists and Confederates unable to avoid war?

AP® TERMS TO KNOW *Identify and explain the significance of each term below.*

Key Concepts and Events

Mexican cession (p. 380)
Wilmot Proviso (p. 383)
"slave power" conspiracy (p. 384)
free soil movement (p. 385)
Foreign Miner's Tax (p. 387)
popular sovereignty (p. 390)
Compromise of 1850 (p. 391)
Fugitive Slave Act of 1850 (p. 392)
personal liberty laws (p. 393)
Treaty of Kanagawa (p. 393)
filibustering (p. 394)
Ostend Manifesto (p. 394)
chain migration (p. 395)
nativism (p. 398)
American, or Know-Nothing, Party (p. 399)
Kansas-Nebraska Act (p. 400)
***Dred Scott* decision** (p. 402)

Key People

Lewis Cass (p. 386)
Stephen Douglas (p. 390)
Harriet Beecher Stowe (p. 392)
Justice Roger B. Taney (p. 393)
William Walker (p. 394)
John Brown (p. 401)
Abraham Lincoln (p. 403)

AP® MAKING CONNECTIONS *Recognize the larger developments and continuities within and across chapters by answering these questions.*

1. Compare the political realignment of the 1850s with the decline of the Federalists and the first emergence of mass political parties in the 1820s (Chapter 9). Why did well-established parties fragment and disappear, and how did new ones capture the support of millions of voters?
2. The United States had been a nation of immigrants since its founding — and long before. In comparison with earlier periods you have studied, what new factors caused a strong nativist movement to emerge suddenly in the 1850s?

KEY TURNING POINTS *Refer to the timeline at the start of the chapter for help in answering the following questions.*

1. At the beginning of the 1850s, despite sectional tensions, almost no one in the United States expected a civil war between the North and South to result. What events in the 1850s made southern secession and civil war more likely? Which may have constituted a "tipping point" after which secession and war were difficult, if not impossible, to avoid?
2. Some historians view the Civil War as a crisis brewed in Washington, D.C., by politicians who made provocative or dangerous decisions. Others argue that the war's causes emerged from broader conflicts in American economy, society, and culture. In the chapter timeline, what evidence do you see for each of these views?

413

TRM Find complete suggested responses in the Teacher's Resource Materials.

AP® SKILLS & PROCESSES

CAUSATION

AP® CONTENT REVIEW 1 asks students to identify the political effects of the Mexican cession.

AP® SKILLS & PROCESSES

CAUSATION

AP® CONTENT REVIEW 3 asks students to explain the causes of the rise of the Republican Party and its ultimate rise to power in 1860.

TRM Find definitions for these terms in the **Glossary/Glosario** in the Teacher's Resource Materials.

AP® SKILLS & PROCESSES

COMPARISON

AP® MAKING CONNECTIONS 1 asks students to compare the political circumstances that led to the emergence of political parties in the 1820s.

AP® SKILLS & PROCESSES

CONTINUITY AND CHANGE

AP® MAKING CONNECTIONS 2 asks students to explain a new reaction to a seemingly common phenomenon. The graph on p. 398 and accompanying commentary provide suggestions to help students understand what was new about the scale of immigration in this era and how that may explain the nativist reaction.

AP® SKILLS & PROCESSES

CONTINUITY AND CHANGE

KEY TURNING POINTS 1 asks students to identify the point at which the tensions between North and South became an "irrepressible conflict," in the words of Senator William Seward, who became secretary of state under Lincoln.

AP® SKILLS & PROCESSES

CAUSATION

KEY TURNING POINTS 2 asks students to weigh competing arguments about what factors contributed most significantly to the outbreak of the Civil War.

TRM Find complete suggested responses in the Teacher's Resource Materials.

AP® PRACTICE QUESTIONS

MULTIPLE CHOICE QUESTIONS *Choose the correct answer for each question.*

Questions 1–2 refer to this 1850 advertisement.

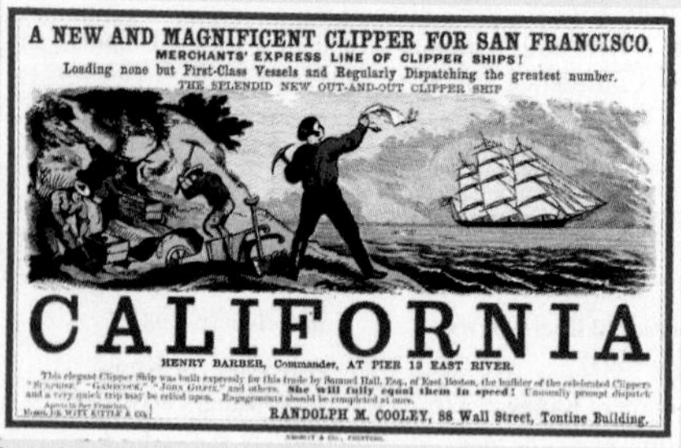

A NEW AND MAGNIFICENT CLIPPER FOR SAN FRANCISCO.
MERCHANTS' EXPRESS LINE OF CLIPPER SHIPS!
Loading none but First-Class Vessels and Regularly Dispatching the greatest number.
THE SPLENDID NEW OUT-AND-OUT CLIPPER SHIP
CALIFORNIA
HENRY BARBER, Commander, AT PIER 13 EAST RIVER.
She will fully equal them in speed!
RANDOLPH M. COOLEY, 88 Wall Street, Tontine Building.

Pictorial Press Ltd/Alamy.

1. The reason for westward expansion summarized by this advertisement can be described best as
   - **a.** free soil.
   - **b.** new markets.
   - **c.** states' rights.
   - **d.** resources.

2. By the early 1850s, all of the following had resulted from migration to California EXCEPT
   - **a.** increased international immigration to the United States.
   - **b.** growing debate over the extension of slavery in the territories.
   - **c.** expanded interest in trade and relations with Asia.
   - **d.** substantial growth in manufacturing in the West.

Questions 3–6 refer to the excerpt provided.

> "[I]t is the opinion of the court that the act of Congress which prohibited a citizen from holding and owning property of this kind in the territory of the United States north of the line therein mentioned is . . . void, and that neither Dred Scott himself nor any of his family were made free by being carried into this territory, even if they had been carried there by the owner with the intention of becoming a permanent resident."
>
> *Dred Scott v. Sandford*, March 1857

3. Based upon this excerpt from the *Dred Scott v. Sandford* decision, which of the following best determines the ruling's significance?
   - **a.** A definition of a territory as free
   - **b.** A definition of a slave
   - **c.** A definition of a citizen
   - **d.** A definition of property

4. The reasoning in the case is most similar to which prior Supreme Court precedent?
   - **a.** The power to determine the meaning of the Constitution established in *Marbury v. Madison* (1803)
   - **b.** The supremacy of federal legislation over state legislation established in *McCullough v. Maryland* (1819)
   - **c.** The sanctity of contracts established in *Dartmouth College v. Woodward* (1819)
   - **d.** The authority of federal government to regulate interstate commerce established in *Gibbons v. Ogden* (1824)

5. The Supreme Court ruling in *Dred Scott v. Sandford* most thoroughly contradicted the provisions of the
   - **a.** Missouri Compromise (1820).
   - **b.** Compromise of 1850.
   - **c.** Fugitive Slave Act (1850).
   - **d.** Kansas-Nebraska Act (1854).

6. The Supreme Court's decision led to
   - **a.** accelerating westward migration.
   - **b.** increasing conflict with American Indian nations.
   - **c.** deepening divisions between the North and South.
   - **d.** strengthening the Second Party System.

SHORT ANSWER QUESTIONS

Read each question carefully and write a short response. Use evidence from the text to support your claims.

"It took more than twenty years of experimentation and adaptation with wind mills, dry-farming, and new drought-resisting feed crops for the cotton farmer to conquer the plains. There is little reason to believe that the conquest could have been effected earlier [than the 1880s]; there is even less basis for belief that the region would ever have been filled with plantations and slaves. . . . [I]t is likely that the institution of slavery would have declined toward extinction in the Old South before the cotton conquest of the plains could have been accomplished, even had there been no Civil War."

Charles W. Ramsdell, "The Natural Limits of Slavery Expansion," *Mississippi Valley Historical Review*, 16 (September 1929): 157

"[Scholars have] done much to dispel the myth that the West was a landscape of liberty. . . . [They have] demonstrated how the region's vast geography and seemingly limitless opportunities restricted rather than enhanced workers' freedom. Reliant on employers and labor contractors to move them to and across the West's wide-open spaces, immigrant workers often became enmeshed in debt peonage and contract labor. . . . [Historians] have documented the journeys of slaves to the goldfields, California's systems of forced Indian labor, the lives of Chinese women bound in the sex trade, and the debates over imagined Chinese 'coolie' slavery on the Pacific coast. . . . [T]he idea that western environments, economies, or social structures were somehow incompatible with bound labor is gradually losing its force."

Stacey L. Smith, *Freedom's Frontier: California and the Struggle over Unfree Labor, Emancipation, and Reconstruction*, 2013

1. Using the two excerpts provided, answer (a), (b), and (c).
   - **a.** Briefly explain ONE major difference between Ramsdell's and Smith's historical interpretations of the nineteenth century in the West.
   - **b.** Briefly explain how ONE specific historical event or development from the period 1844 to 1861 that is not explicitly mentioned in the excerpts could be used to support Ramsdell's interpretation.
   - **c.** Briefly explain how ONE specific historical event or development from the period 1844 to 1861 that is not explicitly mentioned in the excerpts could be used to support Smith's interpretation.

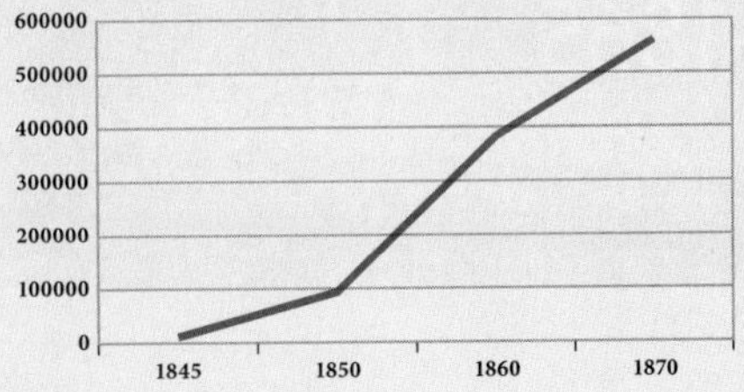

Population in California (Nonnative Americans)

2. Using the graph provided, answer (a), (b), and (c).
   - **a.** Briefly explain ONE specific historical event or development that caused the change illustrated in the graph.
   - **b.** Briefly explain ONE specific historical effect on national politics of the change illustrated in the graph.
   - **c.** Briefly explain ONE specific historical effect on regional attitudes as a result of the change illustrated in the graph.
3. Answer (a), (b), and (c).
   - **a.** Briefly explain ONE specific historical similarity between the free soil and abolitionist movements from the period 1844 to 1860.
   - **b.** Briefly explain ONE specific historical difference between the free soil and abolitionist movements from the period 1844 to 1860.
   - **c.** Briefly explain ONE specific historical effect of EITHER the free soil OR abolitionist movement from the period 1844 to 1860.

TRM Find complete suggested responses in the Teacher's Resource Materials.

13 CHAPTER

Bloody Ground: The Civil War

1861–1865

Chapter 13 — AP® Assessment Weight and Pacing Guide

The assessment weight on the AP® U.S. History Exam for Chapters 12–14 is 10–17 percent. This chapter is part of Unit 5 of the AP® U.S. History curriculum, covering Period 5: 1844–1877.

This pacing guide is based on a schedule with 120 sessions of 50 minutes each before the AP® U.S. History Exam. If you have a different number of sessions before the exam, you can modify the pacing to meet your needs. If you have additional time, consider incorporating quizzes, released AP® U.S. History questions, practice exams, writing practice, and other instructional activities.

	Traditional Schedule	Block Schedule
Chapter 13	4 days	2 days

Daily Pacing Guide

	Content Focus	Essential Question
Day 1	War Begins, 1861–1862	What early political and military strategies did Confederate and Union leaders adopt, and which were most successful?
Days 2 and 3	Toward "Hard War," 1863	Why and how did transformations in the war effort, during 1863, begin to give the Union the upper hand?
Day 4	The Road to Union Victory, 1864–1865	Why and how did the objectives of Lincoln and the Union change by the end of the Civil War?

AP® Alignment

Section Heading	AP® Topic	AP® Theme
War Begins, 1861–1862	5.8, 5.9	WOR, NAT
Toward "Hard War," 1863	5.8, 5.9	WOR, NAT
The Road to Union Victory, 1864–1865	5.8, 5.9	WOR, NAT

*Should changes be made to the Course Framework in the future, an updated alignment will be placed on our AP® updates page at go.bfwpub.com/ap-course-updates.

Chapter 13 — Overview

Chapter 13 focuses on the years of the American Civil War from 1861–1865. The chapter provides analysis of major military engagements, which represented turning points in the war, and explores their impact on the war effort. Another important focus of this chapter is the impact of the Civil War on American politics and society. Students should also understand how the Emancipation Proclamation represented a turning point. The chapter explores how this document dramatically altered the war and had significant political and social consequences. Finally, the chapter analyzes the developments that led to the collapse of the Confederacy and the surrender of the South that led the way for the end of slavery.

Chapter 13 — Resources

The following resources can be found in the Teacher's Resource Materials (TRM) that accompany the book. You can access the TRM via the book's digital platform, by clicking the TRM links found here in your Teacher's Edition e-book, or by contacting your representative to access the resources online. Visit **bfwpub.com/henretta10e** to learn more.

TRM Chapter 13 Lecture Presentation Slides

TRM Chapter 13 Outline with AP® Focus

TRM Chapter 13 Lecture Strategies

TRM Chapter 13 Suggested Responses

TRM Handout 13.1 — Continuity and Change: Federal Power During the Civil War

TRM Handout 13.2 — Causation: Impact of African Americans on the Civil War

TRM Handout 13.3 — Causation: Impact of Women on the Civil War

TRM Handout 13.4 — Contextualization: The Gettysburg Address

Chapter 13 — Essential Activity

Divide students into collaborative groups to create a presentation that explores this question: How did the election of 1864 illustrate divisions within the Union? Students should address the following in their presentations: the political parties in the election and the platforms they represented; the divisions that occurred within political parties and their relationships to divisions in the Union; and the outcome of the election of 1864.

Students should additionally use political cartoons to illustrate the divisions in the Union associated with the election of 1864. When student presentations are complete, ask each group to present their analysis of one of the above requirements. After each presentation, lead a discussion that allows different groups to share different interpretations of evidence. When all the requirements have been presented, ask students to individually write a thesis statement in response to the original question.

Chapter 13 — Bell Ringers

The following activities take no more than 5–15 minutes of your class period and offer an effective and engaging way to begin your lessons and for students to apply AP® Skills and Processes:

- Show students Article I, Section 9 of the U.S. Constitution, which details the writs of habeas corpus. Ask students to discuss the authority granted to or denied to the president by this section of the Constitution; students should also define the use of the term "rebellion" in the section and its application to the Civil War. Then present students with the following scenarios and ask if Lincoln should suspend writs of habeas corpus: (1) citizens in Maryland attack Union troops marching toward Virginia to engage the Confederate army; (2) legislators in the state of Delaware support seceding from the Union; (3) business owners in Kentucky continue trading with southerners after April 1861.
- Divide students into groups and provide each group with a different photograph by Mathew Brady depicting the aftermath of battles in the Civil War. Ask each group to write a caption for the image they were provided. Then project or display each image to discuss the captions and the impact of the war on civilians' understanding of the conflict.

NOTES

TEACHING STRATEGY

The last paragraph of the introduction captures several key features about the Civil War that students should understand. Students should note that the Civil War mobilized populations in the North and South, whether they served as soldiers or not. The war also led to the deaths of probably 750,000 and annihilated the South's economy. Lastly, the war ended slavery — a national debate since the Philadelphia Convention. In reading about the Civil War, it is easy for students to get lost in the details of generals, strategies, and battles — whether they want to or not. Famed Civil War historian James McPherson's "A Defining Time in Our Nation's History" provides a bird's-eye view of the struggle in a helpful and succinct 800-word essay available online. To access this essay, search "Civil War Trust McPherson Overview of Civil War." For a complete model answer to the **AP® LEARNING FOCUS** question, see p. 448.

13

CHAPTER

Bloody Ground: The Civil War

1861–1865

AP® LEARNING FOCUS

Why and how did the Union win the Civil War?

In February 1865, as U.S. troops under General William Tecumseh Sherman completed their destructive march through Georgia and crossed into South Carolina, their pace quickened. They were approaching the state capital, Columbia, where four years earlier South Carolina legislators had passed the ordinance of secession. "Hail Columbia, happy land," some of the soldiers sang, "If we don't burn you, I'll be damned." As the Union army approached, white residents of Columbia fled. Terrified of slaves rebelling, others set up a new whipping post in town, where one enslaved man received a hundred lashes for communicating with federal prisoners held nearby. Local officials dithered: one wanted to defend Columbia house by house, but at the last moment Confederate commanders abandoned the city. Even before Sherman arrived, looting began. Things got worse when arriving Union soldiers discovered 120 barrels of whiskey. One regiment entered the capitol building, voted to revoke secession, and plundered trophies from the senate chamber. More sober soldiers were greeted with glares and curses from whites and shouts of "God bless you" from African Americans. One woman, freed from slavery, gave birth three days later to a son she named Liberty Sherman.

The Union army destroyed all targets of military importance in the city — warehouses, rail stations, machinery. Stacks of cotton bales left on the streets by Confederates caught fire, and a stiff breeze carried the flames from house to house. One southern lady managed to locate Lt. Col. Jeremiah Jenkins, the Union provost marshal, as he hurried around trying to stamp out fires. She begged him to protect her home but Jenkins replied, "The women of the South kept the war alive — and it is only by making them suffer that we can subdue the men."

The burning of Columbia showed how the Civil War unfolded in ways no one expected at the start. In 1861, both Unionists and Confederates believed they were launching a quick and limited conflict they would quickly win. Both proved wrong — it was long and agonizing. As each side hung on fiercely, determined to win, the scale of conflict escalated on battlefields and home fronts. The result, in President Lincoln's words, was "fundamental and astounding": unprecedented political and civilian mobilization, hundreds of thousands dead, the Confederacy's crushing defeat, and the end of slavery.

414

Ruins of Richmond A street scene in Richmond, Virginia, capital of the Confederacy, in 1865. The women's black dresses indicate that they have recently lost husbands, sons, or other close relatives. On the left, the camera's long exposure caught the ghostly image of a man walking by — possibly a veteran in Confederate gray. The Granger Collection, New York.

TEACHING STRATEGY

Southern civilians suffered loss of property and consequent hardship because of their participation in the war effort. The Civil War has sometimes been called the first "total war" because of the mass mobilization of civilians and targeting of the South's war-making ability, not just the defeat of its soldiers on the battlefield. Recently, scholars have become more skeptical of this idea. Attacks on civilians paled in comparison to later wars, like World War II and the Vietnam War, when the development of air power led to large-scale and often intentional bombing of civilians. While calling the Civil War a "total war" may no longer be compelling, it is still helpful to place the war in the context of the industrial era, in which targeting factories and rail lines made strategic sense, and began the logic of blurring distinctions between combatant and civilian. Civil War scholar Aaron Sheehan-Dean provides a brief overview of this issue and of the ways mid-nineteenth-century Americans contemplated moral issues related to war. To access this overview, search "Teaching History American Civil War: Total or Just?"

AP® SKILLS & PROCESSES

CONTINUITY AND CHANGE

Use the **TIMELINE** table to help students begin thinking about how the period from 1861 to 1865 could constitute a distinct historical period. Rather than having a discussion about periodization, it could be more meaningful for students to have a discussion about why the Civil War merits its own chapter. This raises a larger question about the significance of the Civil War in the broad sweep of American history. Students could also consider which year seems to have been the turning point that shifted events toward the Confederacy's defeat.

TEACHING STRATEGY

It may be helpful to begin the study of the war with a discussion of differences between the North and South at the war's outbreak, as those differences played a significant role in the eventual outcome. The lesson plan "On the Eve of War: North vs. South," available on the EDSITEment! Web site, offers useful primary sources on the subject. To access the site, search "NEH Eve of War North vs. South."

TIMELINE

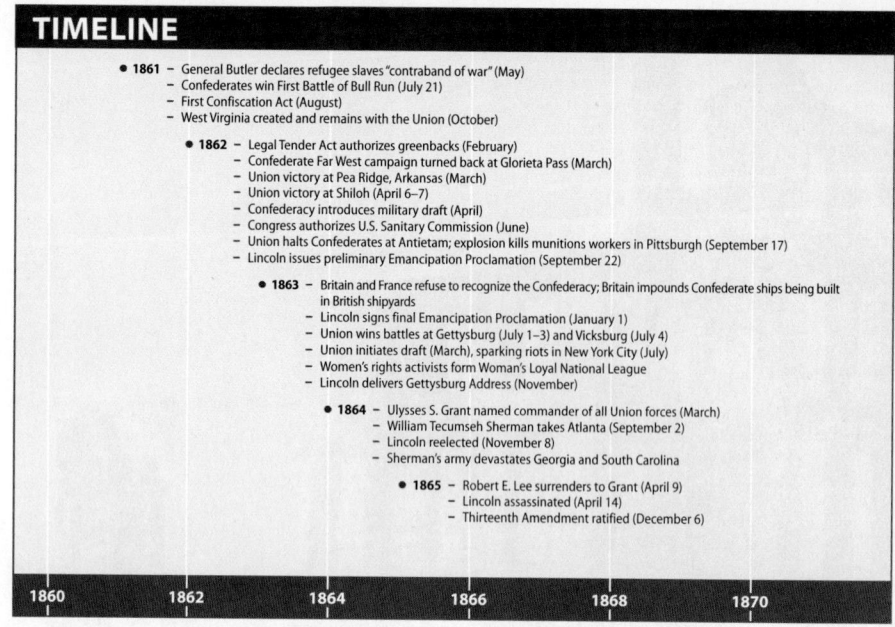

- **1861**
  - General Butler declares refugee slaves "contraband of war" (May)
  - Confederates win First Battle of Bull Run (July 21)
  - First Confiscation Act (August)
  - West Virginia created and remains with the Union (October)
- **1862**
  - Legal Tender Act authorizes greenbacks (February)
  - Confederate Far West campaign turned back at Glorieta Pass (March)
  - Union victory at Pea Ridge, Arkansas (March)
  - Union victory at Shiloh (April 6–7)
  - Confederacy introduces military draft (April)
  - Congress authorizes U.S. Sanitary Commission (June)
  - Union halts Confederates at Antietam; explosion kills munitions workers in Pittsburgh (September 17)
  - Lincoln issues preliminary Emancipation Proclamation (September 22)
- **1863**
  - Britain and France refuse to recognize the Confederacy; Britain impounds Confederate ships being built in British shipyards
  - Lincoln signs final Emancipation Proclamation (January 1)
  - Union wins battles at Gettysburg (July 1–3) and Vicksburg (July 4)
  - Union initiates draft (March), sparking riots in New York City (July)
  - Women's rights activists form Woman's Loyal National League
  - Lincoln delivers Gettysburg Address (November)
- **1864**
  - Ulysses S. Grant named commander of all Union forces (March)
  - William Tecumseh Sherman takes Atlanta (September 2)
  - Lincoln reelected (November 8)
  - Sherman's army devastates Georgia and South Carolina
- **1865**
  - Robert E. Lee surrenders to Grant (April 9)
  - Lincoln assassinated (April 14)
  - Thirteenth Amendment ratified (December 6)

1860 | 1862 | 1864 | 1866 | 1868 | 1870

WAR BEGINS, 1861–1862

What early political and military strategies did Confederate and Union leaders adopt, and which were most successful?

With hindsight we know that the Civil War lasted four years, the Union won, and the war abolished slavery. But if any of these outcomes had been apparent in 1861, the South would not likely have seceded. Southern leaders banked on cotton's centrality to the national and world economy in achieving Confederate independence. They viewed slavery as an asset to the war effort and argued that southern soldiers would be braver and more effective than northern immigrants and urban workers, whom one disdainfully referred to as "mongrel hordes of Yankees." Events on the battlefield, however, proved neither quick nor decisive. By fall 1862, both Union and Confederacy were forced to adopt new military and political strategies.

Early Expectations

In 1861, patriotic fervor filled both Union and Confederate armies with eager young volunteers. One Union recruit wrote that "if a fellow wants to go with a girl now he had better enlist. The girls sing 'I am bound to be a Soldier's Wife or Die an Old Maid.'" Even men of sober minds joined up. "I don't think a young man ever went over all the considerations more carefully than I did," reflected William Saxton of Cincinnatus, New York. "It might mean sickness, wounds, loss of limb, and even life itself. . . . But my country was in danger." The southern call for volunteers was even more successful, thanks to the region's strong military tradition and culture of

AP® EXAM TIP

Take good notes on the early advantages of the South in the Civil War and their impact on the war from April 1861 to July 1863.

AP® APPLY THE TIP

Ask students to list the advantages of the South compared to the North in the Civil War when reading this section. Students should identify defensive war, the use of slaves to produce food and cotton, cotton exports, support from Britain and France, and the Trent Affair. Then have students consider the possible issues with each of these early advantages through the following questions:

- **How does fighting a defensive war possibly become a disadvantage if the war drags on for years and years?** *Destruction of crops, cities, infrastructure will be worse in a defensive war because most of the fighting will occur in the defending region; may become more difficult to move supplies and communicate in the region.*
- **What advantage did the North have that could possibly counter the advantage of slaves to produce goods for export?** *The North had a navy that could be used to blockade the southern ports and prevent export/import of goods.*
- **What kinds of advantages are not included in this list of the South's early advantages? Add these to the matrix under Advantages.** *The North had a more stable political system given it was unified and had an established currency; larger population from which to draw soldiers and supplies; 90% of railroad lines; production of more food in North – others that students generate may be included.*

masculine honor. Confederate soldiers emphasized their duty to protect hearth and home as well as the threat to slavery. If it had not been for "Psalm singing 'brethren' and 'sistern' . . . preaching abolitionism from every northern pulpit," one Alabama infantryman wrote to his wife, "I would never have been soldiering."

Speaking as provisional president of the Confederacy in April 1861, Jefferson Davis identified the Confederate cause with that of Patriots in 1776: like their grandfathers, white southerners were fighting for the "sacred right of self-government." That right included slaveholding. Secessionists did not believe Lincoln when he promised not to interfere "directly or indirectly . . . with the institution of slavery in the States where it exists." Soon, one southern senator warned, "cohorts of Federal office-holders, Abolitionists, may be sent into [our] midst" to encourage slave revolts of the kind John Brown had attempted. Slave rebellion raised the prospect of racial mixture, or amalgamation — by which white southerners meant sexual relations between white *women* and black *men*, given that white masters fathered untold thousands of children by enslaved black women, without legal consequences. "Better, far better! [to] endure all horrors of civil war," insisted a Confederate recruit, "than to see the dusky sons of Ham leading the fair daughters of the South to the altar." To preserve black subordination and white supremacy, radical southerners chose the dangerous enterprise of secession.

Officers of the 57th Georgia Infantry, CSA, and Their Cook
These Confederate officers posed for their portrait while serving with the Army of Tennessee in 1863. First Lieutenant Archibald McKinley and Captain John Richard Bonner smoke pipes and display their swords; Second Lieutenant William S. Stetson holds up his cup. An enslaved man is serving Stetson from a flask. Thousands of African American slaves went with Confederate troops to dig trenches, cook, and otherwise help with the hard work of war. Many were eager to go — in some cases because service at the front provided opportunities for escape to Union lines. GCSU Library Special Collections.

Lincoln responded in a speech to Congress on July 4, 1861, portraying secession as an attack on representative government, America's great contribution to world history. The issue, Lincoln declared, was "whether a constitutional republic" had the will and means to "maintain its territorial integrity against a domestic foe." Living in a world still ruled by monarchies, northern leaders believed that the collapse of the American Union would destroy the possibility of republican government.

AP® SKILLS & PROCESSES

CAUSATION

What motivated volunteers to enlist in the Union and Confederate armies?

Campaigns East and West

Confederates had the advantage of defense: they only needed to preserve their new national boundaries to achieve independence. Moreover, with 9 million people, the Confederacy could mobilize enormous armies. Enslaved blacks, one-third of the population, produced food for the army and raw cotton for export. Southerners counted on sales of **King Cotton** — the leading American export and an essential global commodity — to purchase clothes, boots, blankets, and weapons from abroad. Confederate leaders believed Britain and France, with their large textile industries, were too dependent on cotton not to recognize and assist the Confederacy. Their hopes were boosted in November 1861 when a hot-headed U.S. naval captain intercepted a British steamer, the *Trent*, to seize and detain two Confederate diplomats in route from Cuba to London. The incident nearly precipitated war between the United States and Britain, until the Lincoln administration wisely released the prisoners and the crisis subsided.

King Cotton
The Confederates' belief during the Civil War that their cotton was so important to the British and French economies that those governments would recognize the South as an independent nation and supply it with loans and arms.

In contrast to the Confederacy's defensive stance, the Union had the more difficult job of bringing rebellious states back into the Union. U.S. commander General Winfield Scott proposed a strategy of peaceful persuasion through economic sanctions, combined with a naval blockade of southern ports. Lincoln agreed to the

TEACHING STRATEGY

To shed light onto the ways men viewed war, honor, and death at the outset of war, consider having students read the letter Rhode Island Major Sullivan Ballou wrote, but never sent, to his wife, Sarah, just days before his death in the first Battle of Bull Run. The letter will likely engage many students because of its poignancy. Access this letter by searching "NPS Manassas National Battlefield Park My Very Dear Life."

CHECK FOR UNDERSTANDING

Ask students: **What early expectations about the war did those in the Union and Confederacy have?** *Both sides were eager for war, expecting quick victories. Patriotic young men voluntarily enlisted in large numbers to fight.*

AP® SKILLS & PROCESSES

CAUSATION

Have students identify causes of the Civil War and then trace which causes motivated soldiers in the Union and Confederacy. Did the causes align with the motivation for fighting? Or did only some causes align with soldiers' motivation? This will help students think through the broader, national causes as well as individual reactions to the war.

TRM Find complete suggested responses in the Teacher's Resource Materials.

blockade, which was organized with impressive efficiency through the navy's purchase and charter of merchant vessels. By the start of 1862, more than 260 ships were on blockade duty and another 100 under construction. But Lincoln, determined to crush the rebellion, deemed Scott's blockade too slow and limited. He insisted also on an aggressive military campaign to restore the Union.

Failed Attempts to Take Richmond and Washington Lincoln hoped a quick strike against the Confederate capital of Richmond, Virginia would end the rebellion. Many northerners were equally optimistic. "What a picnic," remarked one New York volunteer, "to go down South for three months and clean up the whole business." In July 1861, Lincoln ordered General Irvin McDowell's army of 30,000 men to attack General P. G. T. Beauregard's force of 20,000 troops at Bull Run (Manassas), a Virginia rail junction 30 miles southwest of Washington. McDowell launched a strong assault near Bull Run, but panic swept his troops when the Confederate soldiers counterattacked, shouting the hair-raising "rebel yell." McDowell's troops — and many civilians who had come to observe the battle — retreated in disarray. Suddenly, Washington, D.C., seemed threatened. For the first of several times during the war, federal officials and residents prepared to flee.

Confederates' victory at Bull Run showed the rebellion's strength. In response, Lincoln replaced McDowell with General George McClellan and enlisted a million men to serve for three years in the new Army of the Potomac. A cautious military engineer, McClellan spent the winter of 1861–1862 training recruits and launched his first major offensive in March 1862. With great logistical skill, the Union general ferried 100,000 troops down the Potomac River to the Chesapeake Bay and landed them on the peninsula between the York and James Rivers (Map 13.1). Ignoring Lincoln's advice to "strike a blow" quickly, however, McClellan advanced slowly toward Richmond, allowing Confederates to mount a counterstrike. General Thomas J. "Stonewall" Jackson marched a Confederate force rapidly northward through the Shenandoah Valley in western Virginia and threatened Washington. When Lincoln recalled 30,000 troops from McClellan's army to protect the Union capital, Jackson returned quickly to Richmond to bolster General Robert E. Lee's army. In late June, Lee launched a ferocious six-day attack that cost 20,000 casualties to the Union's 10,000. When McClellan failed to exploit the Confederates' losses, Lincoln ordered a withdrawal. Richmond remained secure.

AP® EXAM TIP

Evaluate the goals and impact of expansion of executive power during the Civil War.

Border Wars In addition to taking the Confederate capital, Lincoln's second major goal was to hold on to strategic border states where slavery was legal but relatively few whites were slave masters. To secure the railroad connecting Washington to the Ohio River Valley, Lincoln ordered General McClellan to take control of northwestern Virginia. In October 1861, Unionist-leaning voters in that area chose overwhelmingly to create a breakaway territory, West Virginia. Unwilling to "cut our own throats merely to sustain . . . a most unwarrantable rebellion," as one put it, West Virginians formed their own state in 1863. Unionists also maintained political control of Delaware.

In Maryland, where slavery remained entrenched, a pro-Confederate mob attacked Massachusetts troops traveling through Baltimore in late April 1861, causing some of the war's first combat deaths: three soldiers and nine civilians. When Maryland secessionists destroyed railroad bridges and telegraph lines, Lincoln ordered Union troops to occupy the state and arrest Confederate sympathizers, including legislators, releasing them only in November 1861, after Unionists had secured control of Maryland's government. Lincoln's actions provoked bitter debate over this suspension of **habeas corpus** — a legal instrument that protects citizens from arbitrary arrest. The president's opponents pointed to Article I, Section 9 of the U.S. Constitution, which states that "the privilege of the Writ of Habeas Corpus shall not be suspended"; Lincoln argued that the same clause continues, "unless when in Cases of Rebellion or Invasion

habeas corpus
A legal writ forcing government authorities to justify their arrest and detention of an individual. During the Civil War, Lincoln suspended habeas corpus to stop protests against the draft and other anti-Union activities.

TEACHING STRATEGY

As the previous chapter indicated, tensions between northerners and southerners flared from the moment the Kansas-Nebraska Act was passed in 1854. Violence there continued for more than a decade, right to the end of the Civil War. The Kansas City Public Library created an outstanding Web site on the topic, which won four historical awards. Access the site, which provides maps, a timeline, scholarly essays, an interactive feature that allows students to place historical artifacts in their historical context, lesson plans, and links to related primary sources by searching "Kansas City Public Library Civil War on the Western Border."

TEACHING STRATEGY

The University of Chicago Press provides an interview with Daniel Farber, author of a book about Lincoln's relationship to the Constitution. The interview addresses a number of issues regarding Lincoln's constitutional philosophy, including questions of whether Lincoln violated the Constitution by suspending habeas corpus. To access the interview, search "Interview with Daniel Farber."

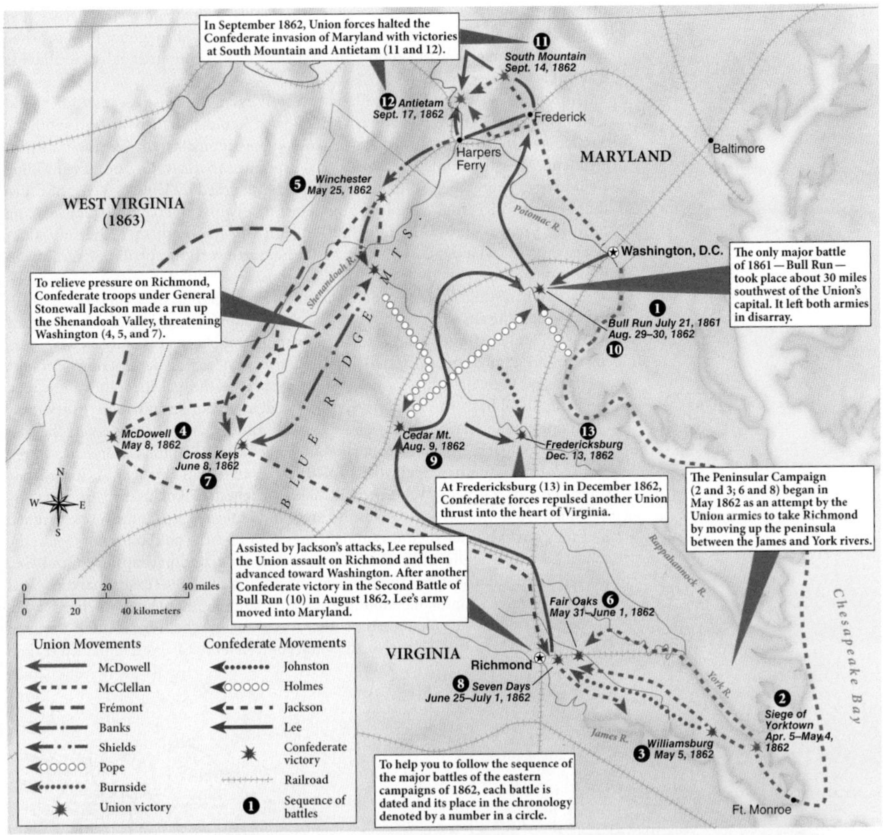
In September 1862, Union forces halted the Confederate invasion of Maryland with victories at South Mountain and Antietam (11 and 12).
South Mountain Sept. 14, 1862
Antietam Sept. 17, 1862
Frederick
Harpers Ferry
MARYLAND
Baltimore
Winchester May 25, 1862
WEST VIRGINIA (1863)
Potomac R.
Washington, D.C.
The only major battle of 1861—Bull Run—took place about 30 miles southwest of the Union's capital. It left both armies in disarray.
To relieve pressure on Richmond, Confederate troops under General Stonewall Jackson made a run up the Shenandoah Valley, threatening Washington (4, 5, and 7).
Shenandoah R.
BLUE RIDGE MTS.
Bull Run July 21, 1861 Aug. 29–30, 1862
McDowell May 8, 1862
Cross Keys June 8, 1862
Cedar Mt. Aug. 9, 1862
Fredericksburg Dec. 13, 1862
At Fredericksburg (13) in December 1862, Confederate forces repulsed another Union thrust into the heart of Virginia.
The Peninsular Campaign (2 and 3; 6 and 8) began in May 1862 as an attempt by the Union armies to take Richmond by moving up the peninsula between the James and York rivers.
Assisted by Jackson's attacks, Lee repulsed the Union assault on Richmond and then advanced toward Washington. After another Confederate victory in the Second Battle of Bull Run (10) in August 1862, Lee's army moved into Maryland.
Rappahannock R.
0 20 40 miles
0 20 40 kilometers
Fair Oaks May 31–June 1, 1862
Chesapeake Bay
VIRGINIA
Richmond
Seven Days June 25–July 1, 1862
York R.
Siege of Yorktown Apr. 5–May 4, 1862
James R.
Williamsburg May 5, 1862
Ft. Monroe
Union Movements
McDowell
McClellan
Frémont
Banks
Shields
Pope
Burnside
Union victory
Confederate Movements
Johnston
Holmes
Jackson
Lee
Confederate victory
Railroad
Sequence of battles
To help you to follow the sequence of the major battles of the eastern campaigns of 1862, each battle is dated and its place in the chronology denoted by a number in a circle.

MAPPING THE PAST

MAP 13.1 The Eastern Campaigns of 1862

Many of the great battles of the Civil War took place in the 125 miles separating the Union capital, Washington, D.C., and the Confederate capital, Richmond, Virginia. During 1862, Confederate generals Thomas Jonathan "Stonewall" Jackson and Robert E. Lee won battles that defended the Confederate capital (3, 6, 8, and 13) and launched offensive strikes against Union forces guarding Washington (1, 4, 5, 7, 9, and 10). They also suffered a defeat—at Antietam (12), in Maryland—that was almost fatal to the Confederate cause. As was often the case in the Civil War, the victors in these battles were either too bloodied or too timid to exploit their advantage.

ANALYZING THE MAP: How many months of military campaigning does this map depict, from the first event (#1) to the last (#13)? In what season did battles *not* take place, and why might this have been the case?

MAKING CONNECTIONS: Note which battles were Confederate victories, and which the Union won. Why did Lincoln choose to announce the Emancipation Proclamation after Antietam, rather than Second Bull Run or Fredericksburg? Compare the number of Union victories here and in Maps 13.3 and 13.4, to trace the course of the war.

AP® THEME

WOR: America in the World

Use **MAP 13.1** to help students recognize that the Confederacy showed military initiative early in the war, even though the Union ultimately succeeded for a variety of reasons, including improvements in leadership and strategy as well as key victories. To supplement this discussion, consider using high-quality maps related to military strategy, available on the companion site to Ken Burns's well-known documentary *The Civil War*. To access these maps, search "PBS The Civil War Maps." Additionally, The Civil War Trust provides a year-by-year overview of the military progress of the Civil War with narration and high-quality animated maps of battles, interspersed with historical photographs and dramatization of events and battles. Access this resource by searching "Civil War Trust Maps."

TRM Find complete suggested responses in the Teacher's Resource Materials.

TEACHING STRATEGY

The border states are central to Lincoln's strategy and handling of the war. Using a blank map of the United States ask students to locate and color the border states during the Civil War. Students should then research how many enslaved persons were in each of the border states. Have students come up with one geographical and one political reason why each border state was essential to Union success. Beginning this way will allow students to understand Lincoln's policies regarding enslavement throughout the war. Teachers looking to further understanding of Lincoln's border state strategy can consult Eric Foner's *The Fiery Trial: Abraham Lincoln and American Slavery*, Chapter 6, "I Must Have Kentucky": The Border Strategy (W.W. Norton, 2010).

AP® SKILLS & PROCESSES

DEVELOPMENTS AND PROCESSES

Have students compare Lincoln's border state strategy with the map of the election of 1860 on p. 407. Lincoln carried no border state in 1860. Remind students about the political nature of the Civil War and ask them to rationalize Lincoln's border state strategy relative to enslavement. In what ways were his policies consistent with his prior positions on enslavement?

the public Safety may require it." To ardent Unionists, a rebellion was clearly under way. Lincoln continued to use habeas corpus suspensions throughout the war when he deemed them essential; Republicans and Democrats continued to disagree bitterly over his actions.

In Kentucky, where political loyalties split evenly between secessionists and Unionists, Lincoln moved cautiously. He allowed Kentucky's thriving trade with the Confederacy to continue until August 1861, when Unionists took over the state government. After the Confederacy unwisely responded to the trade cutoff by invading Kentucky in September, Illinois volunteers commanded by Ulysses S. Grant drove them out, and Kentucky public opinion swung against the Confederacy. Mixing military force with political persuasion, Lincoln had kept three border states (Delaware, Maryland, and Kentucky) and the northwestern portion of Virginia in the Union.

How far west did "border regions" extend? As the territorial conflicts of the 1850s had revealed, the answer was not clear. Lincoln's election roused deep suspicion among many westerners, from Utah Mormons — whom Republicans had alienated by seeking to abolish polygamy — to gold-rush Californians, nearly 40 percent of whom were southern-born. In Oregon, a former U.S. senator praised the "gallant South" and vowed that "the Republican Party will have war enough at home." In Indian Territory (now Oklahoma), many slave-owning Choctaws, Chickasaws, and Cherokees cast their lot with the Confederacy, hoping to secure more autonomy than the Union had allowed them. Thus, the war bitterly divided Native peoples in Indian Territory. A Confederate Cherokee, General Stand Watie, became the war's highest-ranking Native American.

Meanwhile, Texas coveted New Mexico, and enterprising Confederates argued that they could bolster their economy if they captured the gold mines of Colorado, seized Nevada's fabulously rich Comstock silver lode, and perhaps even took San Francisco. In autumn 1861, therefore, an expedition of 3,500 Texans marched west and succeeded in capturing Albuquerque and Santa Fe. But the following March, as the Confederates headed north, Union forces turned them back at the Battle of Glorieta Pass (Map 13.2). Henceforth Union control of the Far West remained secure.

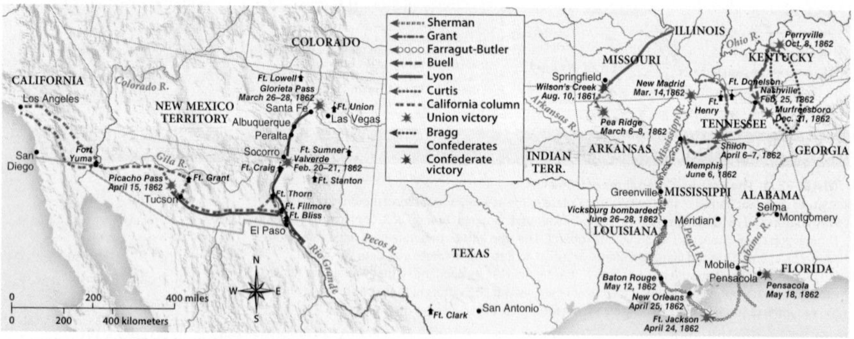

MAP 13.2 The Western Campaigns, 1861–1862
As the Civil War intensified in 1862, Union and Confederate military and naval forces sought control of the great valleys of the Ohio, Tennessee, and Mississippi rivers, as well as the trans-Mississippi west. In fall 1861, a Confederate force marched west from Texas, hoping to seize the rich mining areas of Nevada and Colorado, but they were turned back in March 1862 at the Battle of Glorieta Pass. From February through April 1862, Union armies moved south through western Tennessee. By the end of June, Union naval forces controlled the Mississippi River north of Memphis and from the Gulf of Mexico to Vicksburg. These military and naval victories gave the Union control of crucial transportation routes, kept Missouri in the Union, and carried the war to the borders of the states of the Lower South.

Among the victorious troops were Colorado volunteers whose massacre of friendly Cheyennes at Sand Creek, soon after, embroiled the West in a new round of Indian wars (see Chapter 15).

The Struggle to Control the Mississippi Union commanders in Tennessee also won key victories, dividing the Confederacy and reducing the mobility of its armies. Because Kentucky did not join the rebellion, the Union already dominated the Ohio River Valley. In February 1862, General Grant used an innovative technology, riverboats clad with iron plates, to capture Fort Donelson on the Cumberland River and Fort Henry on the Tennessee River.

Union Gunboats on the Mississippi Steam-powered ironclad gunboats played a key role in the Union war effort, as in the scene depicted here, of the bombardment and capture of Island Number 10, near the far northwest corner of Tennessee, in April 1862. By July 1863, the Union controlled the entire Mississippi River, dividing the Confederacy in two. The Confederate government also built gunboats and eventually deployed a tiny submarine, pointing toward ominous new developments in the technology of destruction. This Currier & Ives lithograph enabled supporters of the Union effort to follow the war's progress. Everett Collection/Alamy.

When Grant moved south to seize critical railroad lines, Confederate troops led by Albert Sidney Johnston and P. G. T. Beauregard caught his army by surprise near a small log church at Shiloh, Tennessee. Grant relentlessly committed troops and forced a Confederate withdrawal.

When it ended on April 7, the Battle of Shiloh left 20,000 men dead or wounded — a shocking total, larger than most of the war's prior battles combined. A Tennessee private wrote of hearing the cries of "the wounded begging piteously for help," while Grant surveyed a large field "so covered with dead that it would have been possible to walk over the clearing in any direction, stepping on dead bodies, without a foot touching the ground." Ambrose Bierce, an Indiana sergeant, was haunted afterward by the hideous sight of charred bodies of Illinois men, too wounded to flee the battlefield, who had burned to death when the woodland caught fire. Some lay in "postures of agony that told of the tormenting flame." Those who survived Shiloh had few illusions about the war's supposed romance and glory.

Farther north and west, the Union barely maintained control of the crucial border slave state of Missouri. At the war's start Lincoln had mobilized the state's German American militia, most of whom strongly opposed slavery. In July 1861, they defeated a force of Confederate sympathizers commanded by the state's governor. In March 1862, at the battle of Pea Ridge, Arkansas, a small Union army defeated a Confederate force that had hoped to capture St. Louis and attack Grant from behind. The Union victory at Pea Ridge kept Missouri in the Union column, though it did not end violent local conflicts that continued through the war.

Meanwhile, Union naval forces commanded by David G. Farragut struck the Confederacy from the Gulf of Mexico. They captured New Orleans, the Deep South's financial center and largest city. The Union army also took control of fifteen hundred plantations and 50,000 enslaved people in the surrounding region, striking a strong blow against slavery. Workers on some plantations looted their owners' mansions; in order to harvest cotton and sugar, planters were forced to pay wages. "[Slavery there] is forever destroyed and worthless," declared a northern reporter. The taking of New Orleans, combined with other Union victories, had significantly undermined Confederate strength in the Mississippi River Valley.

AP® SKILLS & PROCESSES

DEVELOPMENTS AND PROCESSES

What actions did Union and Confederate leaders take in the early part of the war, and what strategic goals did those actions reveal?

Antietam and Its Consequences

In the east, hoping for victories that would humiliate Lincoln's government, Lee went on the offensive. Joining with Jackson in northern Virginia, he routed Union troops in August 1862, in the Second Battle of Bull Run, and then struck north through western

TEACHING STRATEGY

The Civil War Trust provides an essay that places Civil War naval technology in the larger context of industrialization, including the development of steam power and the use of steel. In addition to describing the role of ironclads, the essay explores ramming ships, torpedoes, and submarines, concluding these developments ushered in a new era in naval warfare. Access this essay by searching "Civil War Trust Naval Technology."

CHECK FOR UNDERSTANDING

Ask students: **What campaigns took place in the East and West in 1861 and 1862?** *The Battle of Bull Run was the only battle of 1861 and resulted in Union troops fleeing the battlefield. In 1862, each side attempted to capture their enemy's capital, but each attack was repulsed. In the West, brutal guerrilla campaigns raged. Indians in Oklahoma largely sided with the Confederacy, hoping to improve their circumstances compared with how they had been treated by the U.S. government. In the Gulf of Mexico, the Union destroyed the Confederate navy and captured New Orleans.*

AP® SKILLS & PROCESSES

DEVELOPMENTS AND PROCESSES

Help students narrow a focus by asking them to create categories for representatives in government and members of each military. Public policy and war strategy and action sometimes aligned, while still in other moments came into conflict. If students think through who was making decisions and under what circumstances, it should be easier for them to comprehend what strategic goals those actions revealed.

TRM Find complete suggested responses in the Teacher's Resource Materials.

TEACHING STRATEGY

The Civil War was the first major American military conflict that was photographed on a large scale. These images were significant in shaping the public's perceptions of the war. The Smithsonian provides a five-minute film that describes Mathew Brady's development as a photographer and his transformation into the Civil War's most famous war photographer. Access the film by searching "Smithsonian Mathew Brady's Vision."

Additionally, the *New York Times* offers a written piece providing more detail about Brady's Civil War career. The piece places Brady in the larger context of the developing relationship between war and images, including moving images. Access this essay by searching "NYT The All Seeing Eye."

TRM Find complete suggested responses in the Teacher's Resource Materials.

VISUAL ACTIVITY

Antietam These Confederate soldiers, from General William Starke's Louisiana infantry, died on September 17, 1862, while attacking Union troops along the Hagerstown Pike. This and many other photographs by Alexander Gardner were exhibited in New York by Matthew Brady. Northern commentators were shocked by their immediacy, which brought home the violence of war to civilians far from the battlefield. Frustrated by Brady's failure to recognize the photographers who worked for him, Gardner soon broke with his employer and began to work on his own, becoming one of the war's leading photographers. Library of Congress, LC-DIG-ds-05188.

READING THE IMAGE: Taken by a Union photographer, this image was displayed in the North. How might have civilians reacted if the men depicted were Union soldiers, rather than Confederates? What was the photographer's purpose in creating this image?

MAKING CONNECTIONS: At the time of the Civil War, photographers could only take still images; if a person or horse moved, the result was a blur (as in the picture of Grant and his staff at Spotsylvania Courthouse that appears later in this chapter). To what extent did the limitations on photography impact the artist's purpose?

Maryland. There, he nearly met disaster. When the Confederate commander divided his force, sending Jackson to capture Harpers Ferry in West Virginia, a copy of Lee's orders fell into McClellan's hands. But the Union general again failed to exploit his advantage, delaying an attack against Lee's depleted army and thereby allowing it to secure a strong defensive position west of Antietam Creek, near Sharpsburg, Maryland, before the two armies clashed. Outnumbered 87,000 to 50,000, Lee desperately fought off McClellan's attacks until Jackson's troops arrived and saved the Confederates from a major defeat. Appalled by the Union casualties, McClellan allowed Lee to retreat to Virginia.

The fighting at Antietam was savage. A Wisconsin officer described his men "loading and firing with demoniacal fury." A sunken road — nicknamed Bloody Lane — became filled with Confederate bodies two and three deep, and the advancing Union troops knelt on this "ghastly flooring" to shoot at retreating Confederates. The day of the battle, September 17, 1862, remains the bloodiest single day in U.S. military history. Together, the Confederate and Union dead numbered 4,800 and the wounded 18,500, of whom 3,000 soon died. (By comparison, American troops suffered 6,000 casualties on D-Day, which began the invasion of Nazi-occupied France in World War II.)

In public, Lincoln claimed Antietam as a Union victory; privately, he criticized McClellan for not pursuing Lee to seek a full Confederate surrender. A masterful organizer of men and supplies, McClellan refused to risk his troops, fearing heavy casualties would undermine public support for the war. Lincoln worried more about the danger of a lengthy war. He dismissed McClellan and began a long search for an aggressive commanding general. At the same time, he began building a political and legal framework for ending slavery.

Calls for Emancipation From the war's beginning, northern abolitionists called for slavery's end. Because slave-grown crops sustained the Confederacy, activists justified black emancipation on military grounds. As Frederick Douglass put it, "Arrest that hoe in the hands of the Negro, and you smite the rebellion in the very seat of its life."

In the South, enslaved African Americans exploited wartime chaos to seize freedom for themselves. When three enslaved men liberated themselves and reached the camp of Union general Benjamin Butler in Virginia in May 1861, he labeled them "contraband of war" (enemy property that can be legitimately seized, according to international law) and refused to return them. Butler's term, which turned the logic of "human property" against slaveholders, captured the imagination of northerners. Soon thousands of so-called **contrabands** were camping with Union armies. Near Fredericksburg, Virginia, an average of 200 black refugees appeared every day, "with their packs on their backs and handkerchiefs tied over their heads — men, women, little children, and babies." The influx created a humanitarian crisis. Abolitionist Harriet Jacobs reported that hundreds of former slaves were "packed together in the most miserable quarters," where many died from smallpox and dysentery. To provide legal status to the refugees — some 400,000 by war's end — in August 1861, Congress passed the Confiscation Act, which authorized the seizure of all property, including slave property, used to support the rebellion.

AP® EXAM TIP

Identifying the transition in war aims from maintaining the Union to emancipation of slaves is important to know for the AP® Exam.

contrabands
Slaves who fled plantations and sought protection behind Union lines during the Civil War.

African American Refugees in Virginia This photograph illustrates some of the ways that "contrabands"— formerly enslaved men and women who escaped behind Union lines — survived. The two women posing with their washtubs were undoubtedly paid to do laundry for Union officers or soldiers. The man with the ax is ready to chop wood; the men lying in front might work as messengers or aides. The location was symbolic: a house used by General Lafayette during the Revolutionary War. Library of Congress, 05120.

AP® APPLY THE TIP

Provide students with excerpts from Abraham Lincoln's First Inaugural Address and the text of the Emancipation Proclamation. First, ask students to consider the timing of each document and lead a discussion regarding the contextualization of each document. *(The First Inaugural Address was delivered when the seven states had passed articles of secession. The Upper South had not seceded; there were questions about relations with Europe as well as much opposition to the idea of war in the North. The Emancipation Proclamation was written after victory at Antietam increased pressure from abolitionists in the North like Horace Greeley. Britain and France refused to recognize the South due to slavery. The document also reflects Lincoln's personal views of slavery.)*

Then ask students to read each document and note the goals and arguments made by Lincoln in each. Ask students to create a Venn diagram for the two documents and ask students to note the goals and arguments on the exterior sections of the Venn diagram. Ask students to analyze the information and identify goals and arguments that illustrate similarities between the documents. *(Goals included maintaining the Union, avoiding upsetting loyal areas of the South, relying on executive power, etc.)* Ask students to explain how historical processes, events, and developments other than these documents influenced the goals and arguments (contextualization).

TEACHING STRATEGY

Teachers interested in helping students contextualize President Lincoln's call for emancipation would do well to look up the two confiscation acts passed by Congress in advance of Lincoln's proclamation. First and Second Confiscation Acts can help students understand the change over time relative to emancipation during the Civil War.

Radical Republicans
The members of the Republican Party who were bitterly opposed to slavery and to southern slave owners since the mid-1850s. With the Confiscation Act in 1861, Radical Republicans began to use wartime legislation to destroy slavery.

With the Confiscation Act, **Radical Republicans** — members of the party who had bitterly opposed the "slave power" since the mid-1850s — began to use wartime legislation to destroy slavery. Their leaders were Treasury Secretary Salmon Chase, Senator Charles Sumner of Massachusetts, and Representative Thaddeus Stevens of Pennsylvania. A longtime member of Congress, Stevens was skilled at fashioning legislation that could win majority support. In April 1862, Radicals persuaded Congress to end slavery in the District of Columbia by providing compensation for owners; in June, Congress outlawed slavery in the federal territories (finally enacting the Wilmot Proviso of 1846); in July, it passed a second Confiscation Act, which declared that all enslaved people who managed to reach Union lines or were captured by the Union army became "forever free." Emancipation had become an instrument of war.

AP® SKILLS & PROCESSES

DEVELOPMENTS AND PROCESSES

How did Lincoln's decision to issue the Emancipation Proclamation reframe the purpose of the war and impact diplomacy with European nations?

The Emancipation Proclamation Initially, Lincoln rejected emancipation as a war aim. In August 1861, when Union general John C. Frémont (formerly the Republican presidential candidate in 1856) issued a field order freeing enslaved people held by Missouri Confederates, Lincoln promptly revoked it. But he faced rising Radical Republican pressure and, from his field commanders, reports of overwhelming throngs of African American refugees, most of whom risked their lives to reach Union lines and expressed strong support for the Union. Secretly, the president drafted a general proclamation of emancipation in July 1862. He began to test the waters in his public statements. "If I could save the Union without freeing any slave, I would do it," he wrote to Horace Greeley of the *New York Tribune*, "and if I could save it by freeing all the slaves, I would do it." With this statement Lincoln reassured white Americans, fearful of Radical goals, that his paramount goal was to save the Union — while also getting readers used to the idea that emancipation might be the best way to accomplish that aim.

Secretary of State William Seward, fearful that the Union would look desperate if it threatened emancipation after a string of military losses, advised Lincoln to wait for a Union victory. Lincoln took his advice. Considering the Battle of Antietam "an indication of the Divine Will," Lincoln issued a preliminary proclamation of emancipation on September 22, 1862, basing its legal authority on his duty as commander in chief to suppress rebellion. The proclamation warned that the president would abolish slavery in all states that remained out of the Union on January 1, 1863. Rebel states could preserve slavery by renouncing secession. None chose to do so.

Emancipation Proclamation
President Abraham Lincoln's proclamation issued on January 1, 1863, that legally abolished slavery in all states that remained out of the Union. While the Emancipation Proclamation did not immediately free a single slave, it signaled an end to the institution of slavery.

The proclamation was politically astute. With it, Lincoln conciliated slave owners in the Union-controlled border states, such as Maryland and Missouri, by leaving slavery intact there. He also permitted slavery to continue in areas occupied by Union armies, including western and central Tennessee, western Virginia, and southern Louisiana. Consequently, the **Emancipation Proclamation** did not immediately free a single slave. Yet, as abolitionist Wendell Phillips argued, Lincoln's proclamation had moved slavery to "the edge of Niagara," ready to sweep it over the brink. Advancing Union troops became agents of slavery's destruction. "I became free in 1863, in the summer, when the yankees come by and said I could go work for myself," recalled Jackson Daniel of Maysville, Alabama. On South Carolina's Sea Islands, which were under Union control and largely abandoned by Confederate land owners, an idealistic group of northern abolitionists arrived to bring aid to freedpeople, open schools, and recruit the First South Carolina U.S. Regiment (Colored). As Lincoln now saw it, "the old South is to be destroyed and replaced by new propositions and ideas."

Hailed by reformers in Europe, emancipation helped persuade Britain and France to refrain from recognizing the Confederacy, in a war now being fought between slavery and freedom. Though Britain never recognized the Confederacy as an independent nation, it treated the rebel government as a belligerent power, with the right under international law to borrow money and purchase weapons. King Cotton, however, lost its royal touch: British manufacturers had stockpiled cotton and began to develop new sources of the commodity in Egypt and India. Cotton from the southern United States would never again dominate global markets.

AP® SKILLS & PROCESSES

DEVELOPMENTS AND PROCESSES

The Emancipation Proclamation fundamentally redefined the war and virtually guaranteed there would be no interference from either Great Britain or France with the war. To comprehend how much Lincoln's strategy evolved have students compare the following Lincoln documents: First Inaugural (March, 1861), the Greeley Letter (August, 1862), the Conkling Letter (August, 1863). This spans the time before and immediately following the Emancipation Proclamation. Simple searches online will yield each of these speeches.

TRM Find complete suggested responses in the Teacher's Resource Materials.

AP® THEME

SOC: Social Structures

Students can consult the "Greeley Letter" from August of 1862 in its entirety to see how Lincoln's position on enslavement was both changing and staying the same in the early years of the war. Knowing the timing of Lincoln's announcement is crucial to read the document in historical context, but this brief, well-known document can offer students a glimpse into Lincoln's position on enslavement and the broader societal challenges in the early years of the war.

AP® THEME

NAT: American and National Identity

The Emancipation Proclamation, while not immediately freeing a single slave, as the text notes, had several important consequences. The proclamation reframed the purpose of the war, shifting the focus from an effort to preserve the Union to a fight against slavery. This new moral purpose prevented the Confederacy from gaining full diplomatic support from Britain or France. It also accelerated the pace of African Americans running away from southern plantations and enlisting in the Union army, which helped to undermine the Confederacy.

Confederate president Jefferson Davis denounced the Emancipation Proclamation as the "most execrable measure recorded in the history of guilty man." Even in the Union, the measure was immensely controversial. Democrats used the 1862 midterm elections to attack emancipation as unconstitutional, warn of slave uprisings, and predict that freed blacks would move north and take white men's jobs. Every freed slave, suggested one nativist New Yorker, should "shoulder an Irishman and leave the Continent." Such sentiments propelled Democrat Horatio Seymour into the governor's office in New York; if abolition was a war goal, Seymour argued, the South should not be conquered. Democrats also swept to victory in Pennsylvania, Ohio, and Illinois and gained 34 seats in Congress. However, Republicans still held a 25-seat majority in the House and gained 5 seats in the Senate. Lincoln refused to retreat. Calling emancipation an "act of justice," he signed the final proclamation on New Year's Day 1863. "If my name ever goes into history," he said, "it was for this act."

The proclamation meant little, however, without victory on the battlefield to enforce it. Lincoln's first choice to replace General McClellan, Ambrose E. Burnside, proved to be more daring but woefully incompetent. In December, after heavy losses in futile attacks against well-entrenched Confederate forces at Fredericksburg, Virginia, Burnside resigned his command, and Lincoln replaced him with Joseph "Fighting Joe" Hooker, who would soon prove unsuccessful. As 1862 ended, Confederates were optimistic: the outcome at Fredericksburg demonstrated that the Union still lacked effective generals, and the South had won a stalemate in the East.

AP® SKILLS & PROCESSES

MAKING CONNECTIONS

Explain the roles played by at least five individuals and groups in bringing about the Emancipation Proclamation.

TOWARD "HARD WAR," 1863

Why and how did transformations in the war effort, during 1863, begin to give the Union the upper hand?

The military carnage in 1862 made clear that the war would be long and costly. Grant later remarked that, after Shiloh, he "gave up all idea of saving the Union except by complete conquest." Lincoln committed the Union to mobilizing all its resources — economic, political, and cultural. Aided by the Republican Party and a talented cabinet, Lincoln gradually organized an effective central government that adopted bold policies to pursue victory. In the Confederacy, despite the doctrine of states' rights, Jefferson Davis also exerted centralized authority to harness resources for the fight. Both North and South implemented military drafts — a dramatic change from the all-volunteer forces of 1861. The Union availed itself, also, of a fresh and determined body of volunteers: African American soldiers. What emerged from these developments, and out of the logic of the struggle itself, was a far more ruthless and systemic war. Suddenly the North's greater population, railroads, and industrial infrastructure gave it decisive advantages.

Politics North and South

With double the population of the Confederacy, the Union was far better equipped than the Confederacy to sustain a prolonged, large-scale conflict. Its economy also lent itself better to wartime needs — largely because of recent innovations. As late as 1852, canals had carried twice as much tonnage as the nation's newly emerging railroads. But by 1860, after capitalists in Boston, New York, and London secured state charters and invested heavily, railroads had become the major carriers of wheat and freight from the Midwest to northeastern Atlantic ports, returning with machine tools, hardware, and furniture manufactured in the Northeast. In Confederate states, much less of this infrastructure existed.

Northern entrepreneurs were also modernizing agricultural technology. After 1847, John Deere operated a steel plow factory in Moline, Illinois. Far better than

AP® SKILLS & PROCESSES

MAKING CONNECTIONS

The **MAKING CONNECTIONS** question asks students to identify people who helped to cause the Emancipation Proclamation to be passed. Students need to identify both individuals and larger groups who were involved. To extend this prompt, students could weigh the individuals and groups, rank the two or three they believe were most crucial to the Proclamation's passage, and explain why.

TRM Find complete suggested responses in the Teacher's Resource Materials.

CHECK FOR UNDERSTANDING

Ask students: **What early political and military strategies did Confederate and Union leaders adopt, and which were most successful?** *Confederate political and military strategy was fairly simple early in the war: maintain its borders, fight a defensive war, and obtain European support by manipulating cotton exports ("King Cotton diplomacy"). Union military strategy focused on a plan developed by Winfield Scott, by which the Union military would strangle the Confederacy through a blockade, control the Mississippi River, and capture the Confederate capital at Richmond. Meanwhile, the Union sought to maintain political calm at home by suspending habeas corpus and assuring the public, at least before late 1862, that the war was aimed at restoring the union. Early in the war, at least before 1863, the Confederacy was most successful. The Confederacy's borders were largely intact, and while European support was not yet assured, the Union blockade was ineffectual, Union attacks on Richmond were repeatedly repulsed, and the Mississippi River was not yet controlled by Union forces.*

AP® THEME

WOR: America in the World

The volume of raw materials and the technical competence necessary to build the trestle bridge at Whiteside — constructed quickly in the midst of the war — attests to the Union's industrial capacity. While both the Union and the Confederacy mobilized their economies and societies to wage war, each region had different economies and resource bases, and different social structures. Also, while both faced considerable opposition on the home front, opposition stemmed from different sources. To help students understand these differences, have them create a chart comparing the nature of economic resources, forms of social mobilization, and forms of opposition.

AP® APPLY THE TIP

Ask students to work with a partner or in small groups to complete **Handout 13.1—Continuity and Change: Federal Power During the Civil War (TRM)** to analyze the growth of federal power during the Civil War. Direct students to provide specific factual information to explain the growth of federal power in each of the areas on the handout. Once students have completed this information, ask them to discuss how each area of growth of federal power shows continuity and change over time and record their ideas on the handout. Lead a class discussion on the impact of the Civil War on the power of federal government and the ways this growth reflected continuity and change over time.

TRM Find **Handout 13.1—Continuity and Change: Federal Power During the Civil War** in the Teacher's Resource Materials.

Trestle Bridge at Whiteside This 1864 image from *Photographic Views of Sherman's Campaign* shows a celebrated 780-foot railroad trestle bridge, built by Union engineers (and carefully guarded) after the original bridge was destroyed by Confederate forces seeking to stop a Union advance. Engineering feats such as this one, including pontoon bridges and other innovations, played a central role in supplying troops and enabling them to conquer territory. Confederates, for example, were incredulous when General William T. Sherman launched his march across South Carolina's low country swamps. "When I learned that Sherman's army was marching through the Salk swamps," wrote General Joseph Johnston, "making its own [plank] roads at the rate of a dozen miles a day, I made up my mind that there had been no such army in existence since the days of Julius Caesar." Digital image courtesy of the Getty's Open Content Program.

older cast-iron plows manufactured in New York, Deere plows enabled farmers to cut through deep, tough roots of prairie grasses and open new regions for farming. Other midwestern companies, such as McCormick and Hussey, mass-produced self-raking reapers that harvested 12 acres of grain a day, rather than the 2 acres an adult worker could cut by hand. Such innovations proved to be substantial advantages when the Civil War became long and resource-intensive. Prices rose in the Union, but its food supply did not diminish. Without "reapers, mowers, separators, sowers, drills &c," wrote the *Cincinnati Gazette*, "the wheat, oats, and hay of Ohio, in 1862, could not have been got in safely." "We have seen," one journalist reported in the 1863 harvest season, "a stout matron whose sons are in the army, . . . cut seven acres with ease in a day, riding leisurely upon her cutter."

Republican Economic and Fiscal Policies To mobilize northern resources, the Republican-dominated Congress enacted a program of government-assisted economic development. It imposed high tariffs, averaging nearly 40 percent, on various foreign goods, thereby encouraging domestic industries. To boost agricultural output, it offered free land to farmers through the Homestead Act of 1862. Republicans also created an integrated network of national banks and a transcontinental railroad (see Chapter 15). This economic program won the allegiance of farmers, workers, and entrepreneurs while bolstering the Union's ability to fight a long war.

AP® EXAM TIP

Recognizing the role of a powerful federal government in generating resources for victory in war is a key pattern to know for the AP® Exam.

New industries sprang up to provide the Union's 1.5 million soldiers with guns, clothes, and food. Over the course of the war, soldiers consumed more than half a billion pounds of pork and other packed meats. To meet this demand, Chicago railroads built new lines to carry thousands of hogs and cattle to the city's stockyards and slaughterhouses. By 1862, Chicago had passed Cincinnati as the meatpacking capital of the nation, bringing prosperity to thousands of midwestern farmers and great wealth to Philip D. Armour and other meatpacking entrepreneurs.

Bankers and financiers likewise found themselves pulled into the war effort. Annual U.S. government spending shot up from $63 million in 1860 to more than $865 million in 1864. To raise that enormous sum, Republicans created a modern system of public finance that increased revenue in three ways. First, the government raised money directly by increasing tariffs, placing high duties on alcohol and tobacco, and imposing taxes on business corporations, large inheritances, and the incomes of wealthy citizens. These levies paid about 20 percent of the war's cost. Interest-paying bonds issued by the U.S. Treasury financed another 65 percent. The National Banking Acts of 1863 and 1864 forced most banks to buy those bonds, and Philadelphia banker and Treasury Department agent Jay Cooke used newspaper ads and 2,500 subagents to persuade a million northern families to buy them. For the first time in U.S. history, buying war bonds became a popular patriotic act.

greenbacks
Paper money issued by the U.S. Treasury during the Civil War to finance the war effort.

The Union paid the remaining 15 percent by printing paper money. The Legal Tender Act of 1862 authorized $150 million in paper currency — soon known as **greenbacks** — and required the public to accept them as legal tender. Like the Continental currency of the Revolutionary era, greenbacks could not be exchanged for specie; however, the Treasury issued a limited amount of paper money, so the bills lost only a small part of their face value.

By 1863, then, the Lincoln administration had created an efficient government war machine. Henry Adams, grandson of John Quincy Adams and a future novelist and historian, noted the change from his diplomatic post in London: "Little by little, one began to feel that, behind the chaos in Washington power was taking shape; that it was massed and guided as it had not been before." The short-term results contributed substantially to Union victory. In the longer term, immense concentrations of capital in many industries — meatpacking, steel, coal, railroads, textiles, shoes — gave a few men "command of millions of money," setting up new political conflicts in the postwar era.

AP® SKILLS & PROCESSES

CONTINUITY AND CHANGE

How did the wartime policies of the Republican-controlled Congress redefine the character of the federal government?

AP® EXAM TIP

Be able to explain the impact of a politically weak confederacy in undermining the South's ability to sustain their war effort in the Civil War.

Confederate Policies and Conflicts Economic demands on the South were equally great, but, true to its states' rights philosophy, the Confederacy initially left most matters to state governments. However, as the scale and length of the conflict became clear, Jefferson Davis's administration took extraordinary measures. It built and operated government-owned shipyards, armories, foundries, and textile mills; commandeered food and scarce raw materials such as coal, iron, copper, and lead; set prices; requisitioned enslaved men to work on fortifications; and directly controlled foreign trade.

The Confederate Congress, dominated by wealthy slaveholders, opposed many of Davis's initiatives, particularly taxes. It refused to levy taxes on cotton exports and slaves, the most valuable property held by planters. Consequently, the Confederacy paid less than 10 percent of its expenditures through taxation. The government covered another 30 percent by borrowing, but as Union forces secured control of more and more southern territory, rich planters and foreign bankers grew reluctant to provide loans, fearing they would never be repaid. Consequently, the Confederacy paid 60 percent of its war costs by printing paper money. This flood of currency created spectacular inflation: by 1865, prices had risen to ninety-two times their 1861 level.

Conflicts over government impressment, or borrowing, of slave labor also revealed weaknesses in the Confederacy. Many planters were reluctant to lend their slaves to work on military fortifications, rightly fearing that if these enslaved men found themselves near the battlefront, they would try to flee to Union lines. As a result, wealthy southerners used their political pull to keep their human property in private use. "The planter," wrote the *Mobile Register* angrily in 1863, "is more ready to contribute his sons than his slaves to the war."

Poor whites had no such luxury. The Confederate **one-tenth tax**, adopted in April 1863, required all farmers to turn over a tenth of their crops and livestock to the government for military use. Applied to poor families with husbands and fathers in the army, the policy pushed thousands of civilians to the brink of starvation. In letters and petitions to state officials, women pleaded desperately for help, designating themselves proudly as "S.W.," Soldiers' Wives. "The rich is all at home making great fortunes," wrote an outraged group of Georgia women, "and don't care what becomes of the poor class of people [as long as] they can save there neggroes."

one-tenth tax
A tax adopted by the Confederacy in 1863 that required all farmers to turn over a tenth of their crops and livestock to the government for military use. The tax demonstrated the southern government's strong use of centralized power; it caused great hardship for poor families.

As food prices soared, riots erupted in more than a dozen southern cities and towns. In Richmond, several hundred women broke into bakeries, crying, "our children are starving." In Randolph County, Alabama, women confiscated grain from a government warehouse "to prevent starvation of themselves and their families." As inflation spiraled upward, many southerners refused to accept paper money. When South Carolina storekeeper Jim Harris refused the depreciated currency presented by Confederate troops, the soldiers raided his storehouse and, he claimed, "robbed it of about five thousand dollars' worth of goods." Army supply officers likewise seized goods from merchants and offered payment in worthless IOUs. Facing a public that feared strong government and high taxation, the Confederacy could sustain the war effort only by seizing its citizens' property — including some of its enslaved workforce.

AP® SKILLS & PROCESSES

CONTINUITY AND CHANGE

Use the **CONTINUITY AND CHANGE** question to help students recognize ways that the federal government's role expanded as a result of the war. To fully appreciate the scale of these changes, students may need help recognizing how limited the federal government's reach had been up to this point. Extend this prompt by asking students to explain how or why this changing role was significant.

TRM Find complete suggested responses in the Teacher's Resource Materials.

AP® APPLY THE TIP

To help students understand the impact of a politically weak Confederacy on the South in the Civil War, ask students to review the "Confederate Policies and Conflicts" section (p. 427). Then ask students to complete the **AP® COMPARING INTERPRETATIONS** feature (pp. 430–431). Once students have read the historians' excerpts and answered the questions, ask them to compare answers with a partner. Lead a class discussion of their understanding of the historians' interpretations.

AP® SKILLS & PROCESSES

COMPARISON

The **COMPARISON** question asks students to compare the effects of government policies on civilians in each region. Some may need assistance organizing these comparisons and might find it helpful to create a chart that identifies taxation, military service, and inflation. Students could also explain the degree to which these differing policies were a result of ideological views versus different material circumstances.

TRM Find complete suggested responses in the Teacher's Resource Materials.

TEACHING STRATEGY

As the caption indicates, this print by the famous Currier & Ives represents northern perceptions of southern conscription. Ask students: **What critiques does the image imply about Confederate conscription?** *The image suggests that the southern cause was so unpopular that people had to be compelled to fight. Because the print calls them "volunteers," it mocks the notion that in a republic — and for a just cause — Americans would willingly fight.*

AP® SKILLS & PROCESSES

COMPARISON

How did Union and Confederate civilians' experiences of their wartime governments differ?

Still, after two years of war, the Confederate position was far from weak. The purchase of Enfield rifles from Britain and the capture of 100,000 Union guns at Harpers Ferry near the start of the war helped the Confederacy provide every infantryman with a modern rifle-musket by 1863. Virginia, North Carolina, and Tennessee deployed their substantial industrial capacity. Richmond, with its Tredegar Iron Works, served as an important manufacturing center. Even though civilian life had become difficult, the Confederate military was hardly ready to surrender.

Conscription With battles proving more and more deadly and no end in sight, the supply of military volunteers soon dried up. Still, both the Union and the Confederacy needed more men. The South acted first. In April 1862, following the bloodshed at Shiloh, the Confederate Congress imposed the first legally binding **draft (conscription)** in American history. New laws required existing soldiers to serve for the duration of the war and mandated three years of military service from all men between ages eighteen and thirty-five. In September 1862, after heavy casualties at Antietam, the age limit jumped to forty-five.

draft (conscription)
The system for selecting individuals for conscription, or compulsory military service, first implemented during the Civil War.

The Confederate draft had two loopholes, both controversial. First, wealthier draftees could hire substitutes. By the time the Confederate Congress closed this loophole in 1864, the price of a substitute had soared to $300 in gold, three times the annual wage of a skilled worker. Second, the Confederacy exempted one white man — the planter, a son, or an overseer — in each household that owned more than twenty slaves, allowing some whites on large plantations to avoid military service. This **twenty-Negro rule** was considered essential to maintain order at home — an example of how reliance on forced labor proved to be a liability for the South. Less-affluent whites were furious. One Mississippi legislator warned Jefferson Davis that the twenty-Negro rule "has aroused a spirit of rebellion in some places." Laborers and poor farmers angrily complained that both these measures made the war a "poor man's fight" (see "Comparing Interpretations," p. 430).

twenty-Negro rule
A law adopted by the Confederate Congress that exempted one man from military conscription for every twenty slaves owned by a family. The law showed how dependence on coerced slave labor could be a military disadvantage, and it exacerbated class resentments among nonslaveholding whites who were required to serve in the army.

Some southerners refused to serve. Because the Confederate constitution vested sovereignty in states, the central government in Richmond could not compel military service. Independent-minded governors such as Joseph Brown of Georgia and Zebulon Vance of North Carolina simply ignored President Davis's first draft call in early 1862. Elsewhere, state judges issued writs of habeas corpus and ordered the Confederate army to release reluctant draftees. The Confederate Congress, however, overrode judges' authority to free conscripted men, keeping substantial armies in the field well into 1864. Confederate militia also scoured areas that harbored large groups of deserters, like Jones County and surrounding areas of southeast Mississippi, using bloodhounds to track resisters and conscripting those they could catch — or in some cases, hanging them as an example. In such places, especially the Appalachian upcountry, the Confederacy descended into its own internal civil war.

Military Conscription This Currier & Ives print was likely published soon after the Confederacy instituted a military draft in April 1862. It depicts a "Union man," two wealthy planters, and a barefoot backwoodsman. The Union did not have long to satirize the Confederates' reliance on conscripted troops: within a few months, Lincoln and the Republican Congress instituted a comprehensive military draft for the Union. Library of Congress, 3a12086.

The Union's draft, or Enrollment Act, introduced in March 1863, provoked equally dramatic opposition. Some recent German and Irish immigrants refused to serve; it was not their war, they said. Northern Democrats used the furor to bolster support for their party, which increasingly criticized Lincoln's policies. They accused Lincoln of wielding illegitimate federal power to draft poor whites and liberate enslaved blacks, who would then move north and take white working-class jobs. In July 1863, as conscription went into effect, immigrant and working-class hostility toward the draft and toward blacks sparked virulent **draft riots** in New York City. For five days, working-class men ran rampant, burned draft offices, sacked the homes of influential Republicans, and attacked the police. The rioters lynched and mutilated a dozen African Americans, drove hundreds of black families from their homes, and burned down the Colored Orphan Asylum. To suppress the mobs, Lincoln rushed in Union troops who had just fought at Gettysburg; they killed more than a hundred rioters. In the Union as well as the Confederacy, the war was eroding peace at home.

In contested areas, the Union government treated draft resisters and enemy sympathizers ruthlessly. Union commanders in Missouri and other border states levied special taxes on southern supporters. Lincoln went further, suspending habeas corpus and, over the course of the war, temporarily imprisoning about 15,000 southern sympathizers without trial. He also gave military courts jurisdiction over civilians who discouraged enlistments or resisted the draft, preventing acquittals by sympathetic local juries. However, most Union states used incentives to lure recruits. To meet local quotas set by the Militia Act of 1862, towns, counties, and states offered cash bounties of as much as $600 (about $11,000 today) and signed up nearly a million men.

draft riots
Violent protests against military conscription that occurred in the North, most dramatically in New York City led by working-class men who could not buy exemption from the draft.

AP® SKILLS & PROCESSES

MAKING CONNECTIONS

What made military conscription so controversial in both the Confederacy and the Union?

The Impact of Emancipation

Facing controversy and violent resistance to the draft, the Lincoln administration pursued a novel strategy: enlisting African American soldiers. As early as 1861, free African Americans and fugitives from slavery had volunteered, hoping to end slavery and secure citizenship rights. Abolitionists urged them to press for the right to enlist. "Let the black man get upon his person the brass letter, U.S.," Frederick Douglass predicted, "let him get an eagle on his button, and a musket on his shoulder and bullets in his pocket, there is no power on earth that can deny that he has earned the right to citizenship." Yet many northern whites refused to serve with blacks. One New York soldier told his local newspaper that although he hated slavery, he was "not willing to be put on a level with the negro and fight with them." Union generals also opposed military service by African Americans, doubting they would make good soldiers. Nonetheless, as the war unfolded, free and contraband blacks formed volunteer regiments in New England, South Carolina, Louisiana, and Kansas.

The Emancipation Proclamation changed military policy and popular sentiment. It invited former slaves to serve in the Union army. Northern whites, having suffered thousands of casualties, now accepted that African Americans could share in the fighting and dying. A heroic and costly attack by black troops of the 54th Massachusetts Infantry on Fort Wagner, South Carolina, in 1863 convinced Union officers that African American soldiers could fight bravely. Commentators observed that black soldiers from the seceded states had a triple impact: in addition to strengthening the Union army, their liberation demoralized white southerners and robbed the Confederacy of much-needed labor.

Military service did not end racial discrimination. Black Union soldiers initially earned less than white soldiers ($10 a month versus $13). They served in segregated regiments under white commissioned officers and they died, mostly from disease, at higher rates than white soldiers. Nonetheless, over 180,000 African Americans volunteered by 1865, fighting for emancipation and often their own freedom. "Hello, Massa," said one black Union soldier to his former master, who had been taken prisoner, "bottom rail on top dis time." Raiding a South Carolina town for supplies, a Union colonel

AP® EXAM TIP

The role of African American troops in the Union victory in the Civil War is important to know for the AP® Exam.

African American Soldiers Strengthen the Union Army Determined to end racial slavery, tens of thousands of African Americans volunteered for service in the Union army in 1864 and 1865, boosting the northern war effort at a critical moment. This unknown soldier posed for his studio portrait at Benton Barracks, Saint Louis, Missouri, proudly displaying his weapons while backed by the American flag. Library of Congress, LC-DIG-ppmsca-36456.

CHECK FOR UNDERSTANDING

Ask students: **What was the nature of wartime politics in the North and South?** *The Republican-controlled government instituted high tariffs to raise revenue and encourage domestic manufacture, passed the Homestead Act to promote agricultural production, and increased support for national banks to finance infrastructure and support other costs associated with prosecuting the war.*

In the Confederacy, opposition to centralized government made raising taxes extremely difficult. Dominated by slaveholders, the Confederate government refused to tax cotton or slaves. So the Confederacy was forced to borrow heavily and print paper currency, which became wildly inflated. Slave owners resisted conscription of their slaves for forced labor, while poor whites owed a tenth of their produce as taxation in kind.

Both sides ultimately resorted to conscription, which was unpopular in both regions. Wealthy planters gained exemptions, while recent northern immigrants resisted — sometimes violently — due to the fear that freed blacks would become their economic competitors.

AP® SKILLS & PROCESSES

MAKING CONNECTIONS

The **MAKING CONNECTIONS** question invites students to compare military conscription in the North and the South. Though both resorted to conscription, and the policies were controversial in both regions, they were not controversial for the same reasons. Students should identify the questions of equity that conscription policies raised in both regions.

TRM Find complete suggested responses in the Teacher's Resource Materials.

AP® THEME

WOR: America in the World

Ultimately, roughly 180,000 African Americans served on the Union side in some capacity. This strengthened the North's military capacity, while depriving the South of its labor. At the same time, black leaders like Frederick Douglass argued that those who took the risks associated with citizenship deserved the rights of citizens. Blacks and other ethnic minorities would continue to make this argument in later American wars. The National Archives provides a strong background essay entitled "Black Soldiers in the Civil War," with embedded links to high-quality primary sources detailing various issues associated with black service in the war. Search "National Archives Black Soldiers."

AP® APPLY THE TIP

Provide students with **Handout 13.2 — Causation: Impact of African Americans on the Civil War (TRM)**. Then show students the video "The Civil War in Four Minutes: Black Soldiers" (available on YouTube). Ask students to discuss the similarities and differences in the experience of white soldiers and African American soldiers in the Civil War.

TRM Find **Handout 13.2 — Causation: Impact of African Americans on the Civil War** in the Teacher's Resource Materials.

AP® SKILLS & PROCESSES

ANALYZING HISTORICAL EVIDENCE

Students might need some guidance in identifying the ironies in Gallagher's argument in the **AP® COMPARING INTERPRETATIONS** feature. The changes that southern whites accepted as "necessary to establish nationhood" all contradicted the very reasons they went to war to begin with, including personal freedom, states' rights, and the protection of slavery.

AP® THEME

WOR: America in the World

One of the most compelling stories of African American soldiers is the story of the 54th Regiment from Massachusetts. The Massachusetts Historical Society provides an overview essay describing their story, photographs and brief descriptions of 18 members of the regiment, details about the recruitment of black soldiers (with two broadsides), a description of the attack on Fort Wagner, and sources for further reading. Access this resource by searching "Massachusetts Historical Society 54th Regiment."

AP® COMPARING INTERPRETATIONS

How Divided Was the Confederate Public?

Did the Union army win the Civil War, or did the Confederate army lose it? Was the war won or lost on the battlefield, or because of decisions made by Union and Confederate political leaders, or for other reasons? To explain the outcome, historians have looked at a wide variety of factors, seizing upon one or another as the decisive tipping point. Many have argued that the North's material resources of capital, industry, and population gave it the edge. Others have wondered how the South lasted so long and have pointed to its superior military commanders and its "home field" advantages as well as ideological commitments. Many southerners, for example, believed they were fighting to save their homes and way of life from northern abolitionist aggression.

Historians Gary W. Gallagher and Drew Gilpin Faust focus on the southern civilian population. Did Confederate citizens imagine themselves to be a separate nation? Was their nationalism strong enough to sustain a terrible and costly war?

GARY W. GALLAGHER

Source: Gary W. Gallagher, *The Confederate War* (Cambridge: Harvard University Press, 1997), 63, 71.

Strong feelings of national identity helped spawn the impressive will Confederates exhibited during their war for independence. With the goal of mounting the broad military effort necessary to establish nationhood, soldiers and civilians of the Confederacy tolerated severe intrusions on personal freedom, accepted the erosion of states' rights as the central government sought to equip and feed its armies, and, toward the end, debated openly the possibility of arming and freeing slaves to win the war. Their letters and diaries referred to "my country," "our nation," . . . and otherwise reflected national identification and purpose. . . . Robert E. Lee and his soldiers functioned as the principal focus of Confederate nationalism for much of the war. . . . Testimony from April and May 1865 leaves no doubt that when Lee surrendered his army, many Confederates deeply mourned the death of their four-year-old republic.

Scholarly literature often has slighted the extent to which white southerners identified with one another as Confederates and looked forward to living in a country untrammeled by political interference from the North. . . . The currently dominant thinking about Confederate nationalism assumes a high point early in the war (if ever), followed by a steady dissipation beginning in the months following [the First Battle of Bull Run] and continuing to Appomattox. Too often historians identify an absence of nationalism as both cause and symptom of Confederate failure. . . . Many works that posit an absence of Confederate nationalism overlook or minimize two salient points. First, Confederates by the thousands from all classes exhibited a strong identification with their country and ended the war still firmly committed to the idea of an independent southern nation. Second, although these people finally accepted defeat because Union armies had overrun much of their territory and compelled major southern military forces to surrender, that acceptance should not be confused with an absence of a Confederate identity. . . .

As always, the paucity of testimony from poorer Confederates frustrates efforts to speak confidently about them — although the steadfast military service of scores of thousands of men from those groups certainly implies impressive ties to their country. Members of the slaveholding class left a far richer literary legacy, which, together with testimony from nonslaveholders and the actions of men and

took pleasure in introducing a plantation mistress to Corporal Robert Sutton of his regiment. When the woman recognized the corporal, her former slave, she "drew herself up" and said haughtily, "'*we* called him Bob!'" The worst fears of secessionists had come true. Through the disciplined agency of the Union army, African Americans had risen in a successful rebellion against slavery.

Lincoln, among others, believed the Union could not have won the war without black troops. At the same time, southern responses to the new soldiers transformed the conflict into something more desperate and brutal. Furious Confederate officials vowed to treat black Union prisoners as runaway slaves and execute their officers for inciting slave rebellion. Colonel Thomas Wentworth Higginson, an abolitionist who went south to lead the First South Carolina Regiment (Colored), wrote that his men "fought with ropes round their necks." Confederate threats gave them "grim satisfaction . . . [and] a peculiar sense of self-respect. . . . The First South Carolina must fight it out or be re-enslaved."

Faced with southern intransigence, General Grant suggested that the Union retaliate by shooting Confederate prisoners, man for man. Lincoln declined to women from all ranks of society . . . suggests widespread and tenacious devotion to the Confederate nation.

DREW GILPIN FAUST

SOURCE: From Drew Gilpin Faust, "Altars of Sacrifice: Confederate Women and the Narratives of War," *The Journal of American History* by Mississippi Valley Historical Association; Organization of American Historians. Reproduced with permission of Organization of American Historians in the format Book via Copyright Clearance Center.

Southerners had defined the purpose of secession as the guarantee of personal independence and republican liberty to the citizens and households of the South. Yet the women of the Confederacy found themselves by the late years of the war presiding over the disintegration of those households and the destruction of that vaunted independence. Most white Southern women had long accepted female subordination as natural and just, but growing hardships and women's changed perception of their situation transformed subordination, understood as a justifiable structural reality, into oppression, defined as a relationship of illegitimate power. . . .

The urgency of [civilian] needs yielded a sense of grievance that by 1863 became sufficiently compelling and widespread to erupt into bread riots in communities across the South. . . . Crowds of women banded together to seize bread and other provisions they believed their due. Their actions so controverted prevailing ideology about women that Confederate officials in Richmond requested the press not to report the disturbance at all, thus silencing this expression of female dissent. . . . A Savannah police court charged with disciplining that city's offenders . . . demonstrated the incompatibility of such female behavior with the accepted fiction about Southern women's wartime lives. "When women become rioters," the judge declared baldly, "they cease to be women." Yet in resorting to violence, these women were in a sense insisting on telling — and acting — their own war story. . . . Upper-class women did not usually take to the streets, but they too expressed their objections to the prescriptions of wartime ideology. And, like their lower-class counterparts, they focused much of their protest on issues of consumption and deprivation. . . . Instead of resorting to riots, numbers of more respectable Richmond ladies subverted ideals of wartime sacrifice and female virtue by turning to shoplifting, which a Richmond paper reported to be "epidemic" in the city, especially among women of the better sort. Women, one observer noted in 1865, seemed to be "seeking nothing but their own pleasure while others are baring their bosoms to the storms of war."

The traditional narrative of war had come to seem meaningless to many women; the Confederacy offered them no acceptable terms in which to cast their experience. . . . By the late years of the conflict, sacrifice no longer sufficed as a purpose. By early 1865, countless women of all classes had in effect deserted the ranks. . . . Refusing to accept the economic deprivation further military struggle would have required, resisting additional military service by their husbands and sons . . . Southern women undermined both objective and ideological foundations for the Confederate effort; they directly subverted the South's military and economic effectiveness as well as civilian morale. . . . It may well have been because of its women that the South lost the Civil War.

AP SHORT ANSWER PRACTICE

1. How does each historian discuss wartime unity among Confederates? Compare the claims of the historians.
2. What types of evidence does each author refer to in support of his argument? What limitations do Gallagher and Faust acknowledge in that evidence?
3. How does each author interpret the actions of white southerners who left no written record? How does social organization inform the claim of each historian?
4. From this chapter's discussion of the Confederacy, identify two factors that support or challenge Gallagher and Faust's arguments, respectively, concerning the strength or weakness of Confederate nationalism.
5. What seems to be at stake in this scholarly debate? What are the implications, today, of arguing that Confederate citizens remained loyal to a strongly imagined nation, or that particular groups of civilians challenged the South's political and social order?

TRM Find complete suggested responses in the Teacher's Resource Materials.

carry out this policy, but race warfare nonetheless erupted on the battlefield. At Fort Pillow in Tennessee, in April 1864, Confederate cavalry under Nathan Bedford Forrest (future founder of the Ku Klux Klan) gunned down African American troops as they tried to surrender. After a subsequent battle in Mississippi, one Union lieutenant wrote, "We did not take many prisoners. The Negroes remembered 'Fort Pillow.'"

Confederates' refusal to exchange African American prisoners precipitated a new Union policy: suspending prisoner exchanges, which had taken place regularly since the war's start. As a result, by late 1863 both sides accumulated large numbers of prisoners of war, who suffered horrific conditions in crowded prison camps. Neither side had prepared to manage large prison camps, and both held prisoners in overcrowded, miserable conditions that fostered disease and death. Particularly notorious was the Confederacy's prison at Andersonville, Georgia, where over 13,000 of 45,000 Union prisoners died of disease or malnutrition. Amid public outrage, both Lee and Grant tried to reopen prisoner exchanges, but they could not agree on the treatment of black

CHECK FOR UNDERSTANDING

Ask students: **What was the impact of emancipation?** *The Emancipation Proclamation, while not immediately freeing any slaves, had enormous consequences. It changed the purpose of the war from saving the Union to ending slavery, making it a moral cause. Admired in Europe, this action prevented Britain and France from forming an alliance with the Confederacy. It also encouraged runaways and led to the inclusion of blacks in the Union army.*

AP® APPLY THE TIP

Ask students to review the information in the text on the role of women in the Civil War (pp. 432–433). On the board, draw a timeline that spans the breadth of U.S. history from the Revolutionary War to modern times. On the timeline, ask students to identify major wars in American history. Divide the students into groups and ask each group to investigate the impact of the role of women on society, political opportunities, and economic opportunities. (It is a good idea to time this activity since these topics are broad.) After the assigned time, ask students to share information regarding war and the role of women to put on the timeline. Ask students to draw conclusions regarding the degree to which wars contributed to change and continuity in the role of women in American history. Follow up with **Handout 13.3 — Causation: Impact of Women on the Civil War (TRM).**

TRM Find **Handout 13.3 — Causation: Impact of Women on the Civil War** in the Teacher's Resource Materials.

TEACHING STRATEGY

The human toll of the Civil War is captured well in Drew Gilpin Faust's *This Republic of Suffering: Death and the American Civil War*, 2008, First Vintage Civil War Library. The book details the "work of death" and how death changed America during and after the Civil War. Chapter 5 in particular details how civilians on each side volunteered, worked, and mourned during the year — especially affecting the role of women during the Civil War.

Union troops. Lee argued that "negroes belonging to our citizens" could not be "considered subjects of exchange." Grant responded that his government had a duty "to secure to all persons received into her armies the rights due to soldiers." The effort to renew exchanges failed.

Lieber Code
Union guidelines for the laws of war, issued in April 1863. The code ruled that soldiers and prisoners must be treated equally without respect to color or race; justified a range of military actions if they were based on "necessity" that would "hasten surrender"; and outlawed use of torture. The code provided a foundation for later international agreements on the laws of war.

Grant was guided in these discussions by the Union's **Lieber Code**, an innovative statement of the laws of war drafted by German immigrant law professor Francis Lieber, who had sons serving in both the Union and Confederate armies. Issued in April 1863, the code declared that the "law of nations and of nature" had never recognized slavery and knew "no distinction of color." Anyone who escaped a slaveholding locality was therefore free, and African American soldiers must be treated exactly as whites were. Arguing that the most humane war was one that ended quickly, Lieber defined "military necessity" liberally, permitting many military actions, from shooting spies to starving civilians, if they would "hasten surrender." At the same time, Lieber's code spelled out protections for prisoners of war, outlawed use of torture for any reason, and forbade "the infliction of suffering for the sake of suffering or for revenge." Widely admired in Europe, the code provided a foundation for later international agreements on the laws of war, including the Geneva Conventions.

Citizens and the Work of War

AP® EXAM TIP
Recognizing the impact of war on the role of women in American history is a key pattern to apply to the Civil War.

Lieber was among tens of thousands of civilians who contributed in distinctive ways to the Union war effort, from buying bonds to sewing banners. Unlike the rural Confederacy, northern states had a substantial urban population and stronger infrastructure of schools, press, and reform groups that provided a base for innovative forms of civilian mobilization. On both sides, the conflict was a "people's war" marked by intensive citizen participation.

U.S. Sanitary Commission
An organization that supported the Union war effort through professional and volunteer medical aid.

Medicine and Nursing In 1861, prominent New Yorkers established the **U.S. Sanitary Commission** to provide Union troops with clothing, food, and medical services. By June, Congress officially recognized and funded it. Although paid agents and spokesmen were male, more than 200,000 women supported the commission as volunteers, working through seven thousand local auxiliaries. "I almost weep," reported one agent, "when these plain rural people come to send their simple offerings to absent sons and brothers." The commission also recruited battlefield nurses and doctors for the Union army.

Nursing the Troops At a Union hospital in Nashville, Tennessee, nurse Ann Bell tends to two wounded soldiers. Women on both sides of the conflict volunteered as nurses — a grueling job that included dispensing medication, cleaning wounds, changing bandages, reading to soldiers, and helping them write letters home. The nursing profession was not yet professionalized; some civilians viewed it as "disrespectable" for women, and male doctors often treated nurses with contempt. Women like Bell, however, risked their lives to help the troops, facing exposure to diseases such as typhoid and pneumonia. Corbis via Getty Images.

Despite these efforts, dysentery, typhoid, and malaria spread through the camps, as did mumps and measles. Diseases and infections killed about 250,000 Union soldiers, nearly twice the 135,000 who died in combat. Rural soldiers, who as children had been less exposed to germs than city boys, suffered the worst. Deaths would have been far higher if the Sanitary Commission had not, for example, persuaded key military leaders that their troops should dig latrines for proper waste disposal. The internationally acclaimed U.S. ambulance corps, authorized by Congress in 1864, developed triage protocols for casualties and efficient procedures to evacuate wounded soldiers from the battlefield. As a result of such efforts, one historian estimates that 25 percent of wounded Union soldiers died in 1861 but only 10 percent by 1864 (see "Thinking Like a Historian," p. 434).

Confederate troops were less fortunate because the Confederate army's health system was poorly organized. Scurvy was a special problem for southern soldiers;

lacking vitamin C in their diets, they suffered muscle ailments and had low resistance to camp diseases. Confederate women created dozens of local or state-level relief societies, and thousands volunteered as nurses. "The war is certainly ours as well as that of the men," wrote Kate Cumming, a Scottish-born immigrant to Alabama who served for four years at Confederate hospitals in Georgia. In her diary Cumming recorded the horrors of hospital service, with wounded soldiers groaning in agony among piles of amputated limbs. "I daily witness the same sad scenes — men dying all around me. I do not know who they are, nor have I time to learn."

Emma Edmonds, *Nurse and Spy in the Union Army* Civilians in both the Union and Confederacy had an insatiable appetite for heroic and romantic war stories — an enthusiasm that outlasted the far less romantic experiences of men on the actual battlefield. Sarah Emma Edmonds, a Canadian-born nurse, wrote a sensational postwar autobiography in which she celebrated (and exaggerated) her exploits as a spy. Here she is depicted in disguise as a Union soldier, riding swiftly away from the enemy firing at her from the woods. In other scenes, she infiltrated a Confederate force and defended herself with a pistol. The war helped create a national market for inexpensive, action-packed "dime novels" and adventure stories. The Granger Collection, New York.

Women in the War Effort Far more than Cumming and her fellow Confederate nurses, northern women had a strong base of antebellum public and reform activism on which to build. Freedmen's aid societies, which sent supplies and teachers to black refugees in the South, attracted the energies of religious congregations and of African American abolitionists such as Harriet Tubman and Sojourner Truth. In 1863, women's rights advocates founded the **Woman's Loyal National League**, hoping energetic service for the Union would bring recognition and voting rights.

Woman's Loyal National League An organization of Unionist women that worked to support the war effort, hoping the Union would recognize women's patriotism with voting rights after the war.

The war also drew women into the wage-earning workforce as clerks and factory operatives. Thousands of educated Union women became government clerks in offices such as the Treasury Department — the first women hired to work for the U.S. government. White southern women staffed the efficient Confederate postal service. In both North and South, millions of women took over farm tasks, filled jobs in hospitals and schools, and worked in factories.

Working-class women did some of the war's most grueling, dangerous work in munitions factories, where gunpowder caused over thirty explosions during the war. One of the most horrific occurred in Pittsburgh, Pennsylvania, on September 17, 1862, the same day as the battle of Antietam. With the Allegheny Arsenal's employees — largely female, Irish immigrants — under pressure to increase production of rifle cartridges, a spark triggered a series of explosions that destroyed the building and left seventy-eight dead. The arsenal grounds became an outdoor morgue. One Pittsburgh paper described the "agonizing screams of relatives and friends upon discovering the remains of some loved one whose humble earnings contributed to their comfort." Most were burned beyond recognition.

A few daring women worked as spies and scouts, and at least five hundred disguised themselves as men in order to serve in the Union or Confederate armies. Those who made it through the trauma of battle without being discovered were often accepted afterward by male soldiers who kept their secret. More frequently, women who adhered to the rules of domesticity contributed as writers, penning patriotic songs, poems, editorials, and fiction. Eventually, even the most reluctant Unionist and Confederate men were forced to recognize women's value to the cause. As Union nurse Clara Barton, who later founded the American Red Cross, recalled, "At the war's end, woman was at least fifty years in advance of the normal position which continued peace would have assigned her."

Guerrilla War in the Border States In contested regions like Tennessee, North Carolina, and Missouri, few boundaries existed between home and battlefield. Civilians found themselves trapped between ruthless bands of guerrilla soldiers,

TEACHING STRATEGY

Since a textbook chapter on the Civil War inevitably skews toward coverage of the male experience, it is helpful to find ways to reintroduce women into the narrative. A facsimile edition of Edmonds's *Nurse and Spy in the Union Army*, including a dozen illustrations, is available at Internet Archive. To access this text, search "Internet Archive Nurse and Spy in the Union Army."

TEACHING STRATEGY

Hundreds of women on both sides risked their lives for their respective causes as spies. For information about women spies during the Civil War, see the Smithsonian's "Women Spies of the Civil War" Web site page, which profiles six women spies. To access this site, search "Smithsonian Women Spies of the Civil War."

For a broader perspective on the role of intelligence gathering in both the Union and the Confederacy, see the 50-page booklet compiled by the Central Intelligence Agency. To access this document, search "CIA Intelligence in the Civil War."

AP® SKILLS & PROCESSES

ANALYZING HISTORICAL EVIDENCE

The **AP® THINKING LIKE A HISTORIAN** feature invites students to examine evidence about the scale of death during the Civil War, which largely resulted from infection and disease, rather than being killed in battle. Primary sources provide insights into the nature of injuries and suffering, as well as the state of medicine at the time. In 2012, a scholar recalculated Civil War casualty figures and raised the projection of those who died from the widely accepted figure of 620,000 to about 750,000, or roughly 2.4% of the nation's 1860 population. To get a sense of the scale, students could calculate what 2.4% of the nation's current population would be; more than 7.5 million is a truly staggering number that should give students pause. The *New York Times* provides a helpful overview of this recalculation and its significance. Access this article at "NYT Civil War Toll Up by 20 Percent."

AP® THINKING LIKE A HISTORIAN

Military Deaths — and Lives Saved — During the Civil War

The Civil War, like all wars before and since, encouraged innovation in both the destruction and the saving of human life. More than 620,000 soldiers — 360,000 on the Union side and 260,000 Confederates — died during the war, about 20 percent of those who served. However, thanks to advances in camp hygiene and battlefield treatment, the Union death rate was about 54–58 per 1,000 soldiers per year, less than half the level for British and French troops during the Crimean War of 1854–1855.

1. **Report by surgeon Charles S. Tipler, medical director of the Army of the Potomac, January 4, 1862.** *Most Civil War deaths came from disease. The major killers were bacterial intestinal diseases — typhoid fever, diarrhea, and dysentery — which spread because of unsanitary conditions in the camps.*

The aggregate strength of the forces from which I have received reports is 142,577. Of these, 47,836 have been under treatment in the field and general hospitals, 35,915 of whom have been returned to duty, and 281 have died; 9,281 remained under treatment at the end of the month; . . .

The diseases from which our men have suffered most have been continued remittent and typhoid fevers, measles, diarrhea, dysentery, and the various forms of catarrh [heavy discharge of mucus from the nose]. Of all the scourges incident to armies in the field I suppose that chronic diarrheas and dysenteries have always been the most prevalent and the most fatal. I am happy to say that in this army they are almost unknown. We have but 280 cases of chronic diarrhea and 69 of chronic dysentery reported in the month of November.

2. **Minié ball wounds: femur shot by Springfield 1862 rifle and Private George W. Lemon, 1867.** *Ninety percent of battle casualties were the victims of a new technology: musket-rifles that fired lethal soft-lead bullets called minié balls (after their inventor, Claude-Étienne Minié). The rifle-musket revolutionized military strategy by enormously strengthening defensive forces. Infantrymen could now kill reliably at 300 yards — triple the previous range of muskets. Initially, the new technology baffled commanders, who continued to use the tactics perfected during the heyday of the musket and bayonet charge, sending waves of infantrymen against enemy positions.*

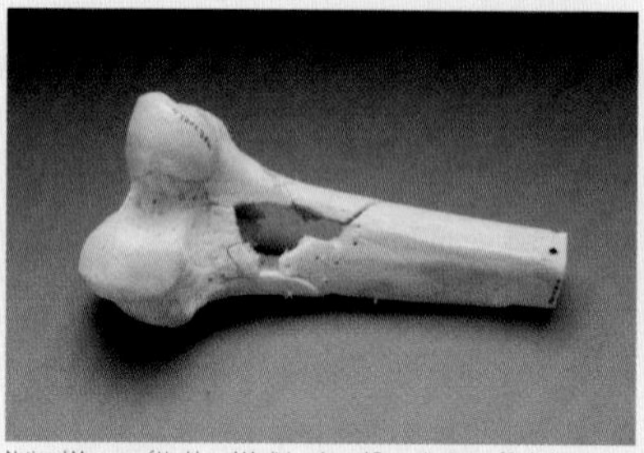

National Museum of Health and Medicine, Armed Forces Institute of Pathology, Washington, D.C.

3. **Private Ludwig Kohn, his wound and its treatment.** *Overwhelmed by the scale of battlefield casualties and the small number of doctors qualified to treat them, surgeons struggled to share effective methods. Photography proved convenient for this purpose. Dr. Reed Bontecou, a Union army surgeon, took this photograph of Private Ludwig Kohn, 214th Pennsylvania Volunteers, treating him for a bullet wound in the right side of the chest, received at Gettysburg on July 1, 1863. "Exit below scapula" Bontecou explained in his notes accompanying the photo, on which he sketched the minié ball's path. Bontecou took dozens of such photographs, hoping to improve medical treatment for future soldiers and civilians. He did not record the opinions of his subjects — some of whom were photographed with horrific wounds, open amputations, and exposed genitals. Private Kohn, unlike most photograph subjects, jauntily wore his Union soldier's cap, suggesting his pride in fighting for the Union cause. Bontecou recorded that Kohn recovered fully.*

U.S. National Library of Medicine.

434

4. **Kate Cumming, April 23, 1862, journal entry on treating a Confederate victim after the Battle of Shiloh.** *Union surgeons performed 29,980 battlefield amputations during the Civil War. Confederate records are less complete, but surgeons apparently undertook about twenty-eight thousand amputations. They quickly removed limbs too shattered to mend, which increased the chances of survival. According to one witness, "surgeons and their assistants, stripped to the waist and bespattered with blood, stood around, some holding the poor fellows while others, armed with long, bloody knives and saws, cut and sawed away with frightful rapidity, throwing the mangled limbs on a pile nearby as soon as removed." This journal entry from a young Confederate nurse in Corinth, Mississippi, describes the plight of one such victim after the Battle of Shiloh.*

A young man whom I have been attending is going to have his arm cut off. Poor fellow! I am doing all I can to cheer him. He says that he knows that he will die, as all who have had limbs amputated in this hospital have died. . . . He lived only a few hours after his amputation.

5. **William Williams Keen, MD, "Surgical Reminiscences of the Civil War," 1905.** *Although 73 percent of the Union amputees survived the war, infected wounds — deadly gangrene — took the lives of most soldiers who suffered certain gunshot injuries in this pre-antibiotic, pre-antiseptic era. Keen, who later became the first brain surgeon in the United States, served as a surgeon in the Union army.*

Not more than one incontestable example of recovery from a gunshot wound of the stomach and not a single incontestable case of wound of the small intestines are recorded during the entire war among the almost 250,000 wounded. . . .

Of 852 amputations of the shoulder-joint, 236 died, a mortality of 28.5 per cent. Of 66 cases of amputation of the hip-joint, 55, or 83.3 per cent died. Of 155 cases of trephining [cutting a hole in the skull to relieve pressure], 60 recovered and 95 died, a mortality of over 61 per cent. Of 374 ligations of the femoral artery, 93 recovered and 281 died, a mortality of over 75 per cent.

These figures afford a striking evidence of the dreadful mortality of military surgery in the days before antisepsis and first-aid packages. Happily such death-rates can never again be seen, at least in civilized warfare.

6. **U.S. Surgeon Jonathan Letterman, Report on Medical Care After Antietam, 1863.** *Letterman introduced several effective innovations, including an ambulance corps and a triage system in which soldiers received immediate first aid and then, as needed, were moved to stabilization centers and long-term care. Here Letterman describes medical efforts after the battle of Antietam on September 17, 1862. Later surgeons hailed him as "The Father of Battlefield Medicine."*

The troops on our left were those among whom no ambulance system existed, but here, owing to the exertions of the medical officers, the wounded were removed by the evening of the day following the battle. . . . Two large camps of hospital tents were formed on the outskirts of [Frederick, Maryland], capable of containing one thousand beds each. . . . All the available buildings in this city (six in number) were taken at once for hospitals [and] fitted up with great rapidity, particularly so when it is considered that the enemy was in possession of the city the day before; . . . the buildings [were] selected and prepared, beds, bedding, dressings, stores, food, cooking arrangements made, surgeons, stewards, cooks, and nurses detailed. . . . [By] the 30th of September these hospitals contained 2,321 patients.

SOURCES: (1) The War of the Rebellion: *A Compilation of the Official Records of the Union and Confederate Armies* (Washington, DC: Government Printing Office, 1889), Series 1, Vol. 5 (Part V), 111–112; (4) Kate Cumming, *A Journal of Hospital Life in the Confederate Army of Tennessee* (Louisville, KY: John P. Morton & Company, 1866), 19; (5) William Williams Keen, "Surgical Reminiscences of the Civil War," in Addresses and Other Papers (Philadelphia: W. B. Saunders, 1905), 433–434; (6) US War Department, The War of the Rebellion (Washington DC: US Government Printing Office, 1880–1901), Vol. 19, 106–117, courtesy Antietam on the Web, antietam.aotw.org/exhibit.php?exhibit_id=73.

ANALYZING THE EVIDENCE

1. Based on Tipler's report (source 1), what is the state of the Union Army? Based on evidence in this source, were the troops ready for battle?
2. Consider sources 2–5. What did battlefield doctors do to save the lives of wounded soldiers? Why did the surgeon use these methods?
3. What do sources 4–6 suggest about the successes and limitations of battlefield medicine during the Civil War?
4. Consider the Civil War in the context of the Industrial Revolution. What was the impact of factory production and technological advances on the number of weapons and their killing power? How are new methods of battlefield triage pioneered by Union doctor Letterman part of industrial revolution?

AP® DBQ PRACTICE

As a "total war" the Civil War involved the citizenry as well as the military, marshaling all of the two societies' resources and ingenuity. Using your understanding of these documents and the textbook, write a response that discusses the relationship between technological advances and the relative effectiveness of medicine.

TRM Find complete suggested responses in the Teacher's Resource Materials.

AP® SKILLS & PROCESSES

ARGUMENTATION

In making an argument about "total war" in response to the **AP® DBQ PRACTICE** question, students may want to refer back to the **AP® COMPARING INTERPRETATIONS** feature (pp. 430–431), which highlights questions about the home front.

CHECK FOR UNDERSTANDING

Ask students: **How did citizens participate in the work of war?** *Many citizens, often women, served as nurses, government clerks, and factory workers. Some served as spies.*

AP® SKILLS & PROCESSES

MAKING CONNECTIONS

The **MAKING CONNECTIONS** question encourages students to place each side's mobilization in the larger political, economic, cultural, and geographical contexts in which each was imbedded, and then to evaluate the effectiveness of each side's strategies. Students could also identify ways that the calculations of each side were based on faulty assumptions or wishful thinking.

TRM Find complete suggested responses in the Teacher's Resource Materials.

AP® APPLY THE TIP

Explain to students that the Gettysburg Address is one of the shortest documents they will study in American History. Therefore, each word is important to understand. Provide students with a copy of the Gettysburg Address. Ask students to read the document and explain the meaning of each sentence. Then, ask students to complete **Handout 13.4 — Contextualization: The Gettysburg Address (TRM)**. Lead a discussion on the impact of this document as an expression of democratic ideals.

TRM Find **Handout 13.4 — Contextualization: The Gettysburg Address** in the Teacher's Resource Materials.

such as William Quantrill's notorious Confederate raiders. Operating often as near-bandits, such "irregulars" on both sides raided, plundered, tortured civilians for information, and carried out revenge killings. In 1863, after a Union commander detained a group of wives and sisters of Quantrill's men, five of the women were killed in a federal building collapse. In retaliation, Quantrill and his men burned the "Free State" town of Lawrence, Kansas, and summarily executed 183 men and boys. The Union responded by evacuating 10,000 people from four Missouri counties that bordered Kansas — while Quantrill continued to wreak destruction in other parts of the state. Like the treatment of black troops, the cruelty of guerrilla warfare shattered any remaining illusions that the war was a heroic adventure.

As battlefield casualties mounted to shocking levels, civilians in both North and South became more and more familiar with the rituals of mourning. The rising tide of death created new industries: embalmers, for example, devised a zinc chloride fluid to preserve soldiers' bodies, allowing them to be shipped home for burial, an innovation that served as the basis for the modern funeral industry. Military cemeteries with hundreds of crosses in neat rows replaced the landscaped "rural cemeteries" that had been in vogue in American cities before the Civil War. Even the poorest bereaved wife, mother, or sister often dyed a dress black so she could mark the loss of a husband, son, or brother. Middle-class women, with greater financial resources, might purchase black-bordered stationery, onyx jewelry, or other tokens of grief. The destructive war, in concert with America's emerging consumer culture and ethic of domesticity, produced a new "cult of mourning" among the middle and upper classes.

AP® SKILLS & PROCESSES

MAKING CONNECTIONS

How did the Union and Confederacy mobilize their populations, and how effective were these methods in influencing the course of the war?

Vicksburg and Gettysburg

AP® EXAM TIP

It's important to recognize the role of Gettysburg and Vicksburg as political and military turning points in the war.

Despite the war's mounting toll, Confederate hopes ran high in the spring of 1863. Union Democrats had made significant gains in the election of 1862, and popular support was growing in the North for a negotiated peace. Two brilliant Confederate victories in Virginia by General Robert E. Lee, at Fredericksburg (December 1862) and Chancellorsville (May 1863), further eroded northern support for the war. At this critical juncture, General Ulysses Grant mounted a major offensive to split the Confederacy in two. Grant drove south along the west bank of the Mississippi in Arkansas and then crossed the river near Vicksburg, Mississippi. There, he defeated two Confederate armies and laid siege to the city. After repelling Union assaults for six weeks, the exhausted and starving Vicksburg garrison surrendered on July 4, 1863.

Five days later, Union forces took Port Hudson, Louisiana, near Baton Rouge, and seized control of the entire Mississippi River. Grant had cut off Louisiana, Arkansas, and Texas from the rest of the Confederacy and prompted thousands of enslaved men and women to desert their plantations. Confederate troops responded by targeting refugees for re-enslavement and massacre. "The battlefield was sickening," a Confederate officer reported from Arkansas, "no orders, threats or commands could restrain the men from vengeance on the negroes, and they were piled in great heaps about the wagons, in the tangled brushwood, and upon the muddy and trampled road." Partly due to the undercounting of civilian casualties on occasions such as this, historians have revised upward their reckoning of the war's total deaths: not 620,000, as was previously thought, but over 750,000.

As Grant advanced toward Vicksburg in May, Confederate leaders argued over the best strategic response. President Davis and other politicians wanted to send an army to Tennessee to relieve Union pressure along the Mississippi River. General Lee, buoyed by his recent victories, favored a new invasion of the North. That strategy, Lee suggested, would either draw Grant's forces to the east or give the Confederacy a major victory that would destroy the North's will to fight.

Lee won out. In June 1863, he maneuvered his army north through Maryland into Pennsylvania. The Army of the Potomac moved along with him, positioning itself between Lee and Washington, D.C. On July 1, the two great armies met by accident at Gettysburg, Pennsylvania, in what became a pivotal confrontation (Map 13.3). On the

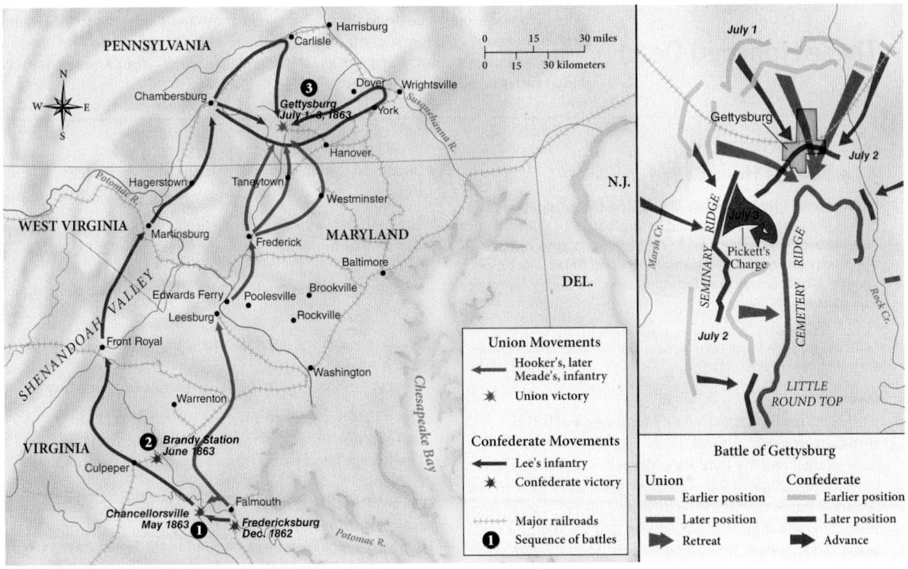

MAP 13.3 Lee Invades the North, 1863
After Lee's victories at Chancellorsville (1) in May and Brandy Station (2) in June, the Confederate forces moved northward, constantly shadowed by the Union army. On July 1, the two armies met accidentally near Gettysburg, Pennsylvania. In the ensuing battle (3), the Union army, commanded by General George Meade, emerged victorious, primarily because it was much larger than the Confederate force and held well-fortified positions along Cemetery Ridge, which gave its units a major tactical advantage.

first day of battle, Lee drove the Union's advance guard to the south of town. There, Union commander George G. Meade placed his troops in well-defended hilltop positions and called for reinforcements. By the morning of July 2, Meade had 90,000 troops to Lee's 75,000. Lee knew he was outnumbered but was determined not to give up; he ordered assaults on Meade's flanks, which failed.

On July 3, Lee decided on a dangerous frontal assault against the center of the Union line. After the heaviest artillery barrage of the war, Lee sent General George E. Pickett and his 14,000 men to take Cemetery Ridge. As Pickett's men charged across a mile of open terrain they faced deadly fire from artillery and massed riflemen. Thousands suffered death, wounds, or capture. As the three-day battle ended, the Confederates counted 28,000 casualties — one-third of Lee's Army of Northern Virginia — while 23,000 of Meade's soldiers lay killed or wounded.

Shocked by the bloodletting, Meade allowed the Confederate units to escape. Lincoln was furious at Meade's caution, perceiving correctly that "the war will be prolonged indefinitely. Still, Gettysburg was a tremendous Union victory and, together with the simultaneous triumph at Vicksburg, marked a military and political turning point. In his **Gettysburg Address**, dedicating a national cemetery at the battlefield, Lincoln dared to hope that the Union might win. Such a victory, he argued, would extend the promise of the Declaration of Independence that "all men are created equal." Without mentioning slavery by name, Lincoln suggested that Americans could draw "from these honored dead" the determination not only to preserve the Union, but also to bring about "a new birth of freedom" in the United States (see "Firsthand Accounts," p. 438).

AP® SKILLS & PROCESSES

CONTEXTUALIZATION

How did Lincoln use the Gettysburg Address to connect the struggle of the Civil War to American identity and democratic ideals?

Gettysburg Address
Abraham Lincoln's November 1863 speech dedicating a national cemetery at the Gettysburg battlefield. Lincoln declared the nation's founding ideal to be that "all men are created equal," and he urged listeners to dedicate themselves out of the carnage of war to a "new birth of freedom" for the United States.

AP® SKILLS & PROCESSES

CONTEXTUALIZATION

Have students consider the month in which Lincoln delivered this address. In November of 1863 almost five months had elapsed since the battle in July. Next, have students do a close read of the document and use the following phrases from the speech to answer the question. Ask students to connect identity and democratic ideals to these parts of the speech.

"to be dedicated here to the unfinished work"
"for us to be here dedicated to the great task remaining before us"
"that this nation, under God, shall have a new birth of freedom"

TRM Find complete suggested responses in the Teacher's Resource Materials.

AP® THEME

NAT: American and National Identity

Lincoln used the Gettysburg Address to portray the struggle against slavery as the fulfillment of America's founding democratic ideals. This required a dramatic reinterpretation of a Declaration of Independence written by a slave owner and a Constitution that implicitly protected slavery at several points. Students may need assistance recognizing that even in the North, this reinterpretation was not greeted with open arms.

The National Park Service provides a brief selection of responses from the press and from civilians to give students a sense of the range of reactions. To access this site, search "NPS Gettysburg National Military Park."

AP® SKILLS & PROCESSES

ANALYZING HISTORICAL EVIDENCE

The **AP® FIRSTHAND ACCOUNTS** feature invites students to consider the varying ways that Americans made sense of death on a vast scale. For some, existing notions of heroic sacrifice, often infused with Christian notions of a good death, sufficed. For others, the carnage forever destroyed traditional understandings of death and dying.

TEACHING STRATEGY

The letter from J.R. Montgomery is the primary source used to contextualize the PBS Documentary "Death and the Civil War." The first 15 minutes can be a powerful introduction for teachers who use these sources in class. Historians Drew Gilpin Faust, David W. Blight, and Vincent Brown are all featured in this powerful documentary.

AP® FIRSTHAND ACCOUNTS

These Honored Dead

The Civil War brought death to the young and healthy, and mourning to those who loved them, on an unprecedented scale. In the following documents — a letter, a poem, a work of fiction, and a famous presidential address — four Americans reckoned with the meaning of soldiers' sacrifice.

JAMES R. MONTGOMERY

A Last Letter Home, 1864

Private James R. Montgomery of Camden, Mississippi, age twenty-five, was mortally wounded at the battle of Spotsylvania Courthouse. This letter, covered with bloodstains, remains in the collections of the Museum of the Confederacy, Richmond, Virginia. Montgomery died four days later. His family was never able to locate his grave.

Source: James Robert Montgomery letter, written May 10, 1864, at Spotsylvania Court House, Civil War Voices, Soldier Studies, http://www.soldierstudies.org/index.php?action=view_letter&Letter=1503.

“Dear Father,

This is my last letter to you. I went into battle this evening as courier for Genl. Heth. I have been struck by a piece of shell and my right shoulder is horribly mangled & I know death is inevitable. I am very weak but I write to you because I know you would be delighted to read a word from your dying son. I know death is near, that I will die far from home and friends of my early youth but I have friends here too who are kind to me. My friend Fairfax will write you at my request and give you the particulars of my death. My grave will be marked so that you may visit it if you desire to do so, but it is optionary with you whether you let my remains rest here or in Miss. I would like to rest in the grave yard with my dear mother and brothers but it's a matter of minor importance. Let us all try to reunite in heaven. I pray my God to forgive my sins and I feel that his promises are true that he will forgive me and save me. Give my love to all my friends. My strength fails me. My horse and my equipments will be left for you. Again, a long farewell to you. May we meet in heaven. Your dying son, J. R. Montgomery”

WALT WHITMAN

Excerpt from "Come Up from the Fields Father," 1865

In this poem, Walt Whitman imagines an Ohio family receiving news of their son.

Source: Walt Whitman, excerpt from "Come Up from the Fields Father," *Civil War Poetry and Prose* (New York: Dover, 1995), 12–14.

Come up from the fields father, here's a letter from our Pete,
And come to the front door mother, here's a letter from thy dear son.

Lo, 'tis autumn, . . . Where apples ripe in the orchards hang and grapes on the trellis'd vines,
(Smell you the smell of the grapes on the vines?
Smell you the buckwheat where the bees were lately buzzing?). . . .

Down in the fields all prospers well,
But now from the fields come father, come at the daughter's call,
And come to the entry mother, to the front door come right away.

Fast as she can she hurries, something ominous, her steps trembling,
She does not tarry to smooth her hair nor adjust her cap.

Open the envelope quickly,
O this is not our son's writing, yet his name is sign'd,
O a strange hand writes for our dear son, O stricken mother's soul!
All swims before her eyes, flashes with black, she catches the main words only,
Sentences broken, gunshot wound in the breast, cavalry skirmish, taken to hospital,
At present low, but will soon be better.
. . . Grieve not so, dear mother, (the just-grown daughter speaks through her sobs,
The little sisters huddle around speechless and dismay'd,)
See, dearest mother, the letter says Pete will soon be better.
Alas poor boy, he will never be better, (nor may-be needs to be better, that brave and simple soul,)
While they stand at home at the door he is dead already,
The only son is dead. . . .

LOUISA MAY ALCOTT

"A Night," from *Hospital Sketches*, 1863

Louisa May Alcott, future author of *Little Women*, launched her career with her immensely popular *Hospital Sketches*, a fictionalized account of her own experiences. Alcott contracted typhoid fever while nursing in a Union hospital and suffered the effects for the rest of her life. In this passage, Nurse Tribulation Periwinkle describes the death of a wounded Virginia blacksmith who fought for the Union.

Source: Louisa May Alcott, *Hospital Sketches* (Boston: James Redpath, 1863), 55–66, University of Pennsylvania Digital Library of Women Writers, http://digital.library.upenn.edu/women/alcott/sketches/sketches.html.

“I had been summoned to many death beds in my life, but to none that made my heart ache as it did then. . . . As I went in, John stretched out both hands:

'I knew you'd come! I guess I'm moving on, ma'am.'

He was; and so rapidly that, even while he spoke, over his face I saw the grey veil falling that no human hand can lift. I sat down by him, wiped the drops from his forehead, stirred the air about him with the slow wave of a fan, and waited to help him die. He stood in sore need of help — and I could do so little; for, as the doctor had foretold, the strong body rebelled against death, and fought every inch of the way. . . . For hours he suffered dumbly, without a moment's respite, or a moment's murmuring; his limbs grew cold, his face damp, his lips white, and, again and again, he tore the covering off his breast, as if the lightest weight added to his agony; yet through it all, his eyes never lost their perfect serenity, and the man's soul seemed to sit therein, undaunted by the ills that vexed his flesh.

One by one, the men woke, and round the room appeared a circle of pale faces and watchful eyes, full of awe and pity; for, though a stranger, John was beloved by all. Each man there had wondered at his patience, respected his piety, admired his fortitude, and now lamented his hard death. . . .

For a little while, there was no sound in the room but the drip of water, from a stump or two, and John's distressful gasps, as he slowly breathed his life away. I thought him nearly gone, and had just laid down the fan, believing its help to be no longer needed, when suddenly he rose up in his bed, and cried out with a bitter cry that broke the silence, sharply startling everyone with its agonized appeal:

'For God's sake, give me air!'

It was the only cry pain or death had wrung from him. . . . Dan flung up the window. The first red streak of dawn was warming the grey east, a herald of the coming sun; John saw it, and with the love of light which lingers in us to the end, seemed to read in it a sign of hope of help, for, over his whole face there broke that mysterious expression, brighter than any smile, which often comes to eyes that look their last. He laid himself gently down; and, stretching out his strong right arm, as if to grasp and bring the blessed air to his lips in a fuller flow, lapsed into a merciful unconsciousness, which assured us that for him suffering was forever past. He died then; for, though the heavy breaths still tore their way up for a little longer, they were but the waves of an ebbing tide that beat unfelt against the wreck, which an immortal voyager had deserted with a smile. He never spoke again.

. . . The lovely expression which so often beautifies dead faces, soon replaced the marks of pain, and I longed for those who loved him best to see him when half an hour's acquaintance with Death had made them friends. . . . I kissed this good son for [his mother's] sake, and laid [an unopened letter from his mother, which had just arrived] in his hand, . . . making myself happy with the thought that, even in his solitary place in the 'Government Lot,' he would not be without some token of the love which makes life beautiful and outlives death. ❞

ABRAHAM LINCOLN

Gettysburg Address, 1863

Abraham Lincoln gave this speech four and a half months after the Battle of Gettysburg, at dedication ceremonies for the national cemetery for U.S. soldiers killed in the battle.

SOURCE: Abraham Lincoln, "Gettysburg Address" (Hay Copy), Gettysburg, Pennsylvania, November 19, 1863, Gettysburg Foundation, http://www.gettysburgfoundation.org/41.

❝ Four score and seven years ago our fathers brought forth, upon this continent, a new nation, conceived in Liberty, and dedicated to the proposition that all men are created equal.

Now we are engaged in a great civil war, testing whether that nation, or any nation so conceived, and so dedicated, can long endure. We are met here on a great battlefield of that war. We have come to dedicate a portion of it, as a final resting place for those who here gave their lives that that nation might live. It is altogether fitting and proper that we should do this.

But, in a larger sense, we can not dedicate — we can not consecrate — we can not hallow — this ground. The brave men, living and dead, who struggled here, have consecrated it far above our poor power to add or detract. The world will little note, nor long remember, what we say here, but can never forget what they did here.

It is for us, the living, rather, to be dedicated here to the unfinished work which they who fought here have, thus far, so nobly carried on. It is rather for us to be here dedicated to the great task remaining before us — that from these honored dead we take increased devotion to that cause for which they gave the last full measure of devotion — that we here highly resolve that these dead shall not have died in vain; that this nation, under God, shall have a new birth of freedom; and that this government of the people, by the people, for the people, shall not perish from the earth. ❞

QUESTIONS FOR ANALYSIS

1. What do these documents tell us about the ways in which religious faith helped Americans cope with wartime death and loss?
2. Historians have argued that nineteenth-century Americans shared an ideal of "a good death": one in which the dying person demonstrated strong character, maintained hope of salvation through his final sufferings, and spoke meaningful last words to the loved ones gathered around. How do these authors, interpreting violent deaths that took place far from home, seek to preserve elements of a "good death"? Integrate examples from at least one source.
3. Which of these authors describe a larger political purpose in soldiers' deaths, and what meanings do they suggest for those sacrifices?

TEACHING STRATEGY

In November of 1863, dead Union and Confederate soldiers were still not all buried. Lincoln was speaking to a town and nation still in mourning. Yet, some of the most analyzed sections of the speech are about what work remained. Have students do a close reading of the document by analyzing what the following excerpts might mean: "unfinished work," "great task remaining before us," "we take increased devotion," and "new birth of freedom." Examining these statements in the final paragraph can help students contextualize the meaning of the document.

TRM Find complete suggested responses in the Teacher's Resource Materials.

AP® SKILLS & PROCESSES

CAUSATION

Use the **CAUSATION** question to address the notion of contingency, the recognition that historical circumstances change and that leaders, including military leaders, modify their strategies according to those changes. Students should recognize that shifting strategies went beyond the battlefield to include, for example, Lincoln's Gettysburg Address and the British decision to impound ironclad warships bound for the Confederacy.

TRM Find complete suggested responses in the Teacher's Resource Materials.

CHECK FOR UNDERSTANDING

Ask students: **Why and how did transformations in the war effort, during 1863, begin to give the Union the upper hand?** *The year 1863 was a turning point in the Civil War. At home, the Union had by this time reorganized its government and its populace to support the war machine while the Confederacy, albeit hampered by states' rights philosophy, was doing the same. Both sides implemented a draft, to the consternation of poor citizens on both sides. Militarily, however, was the area in which 1863 brought the most divergent results. With new African American soldiers, raised after the Emancipation Proclamation took effect on January 1, Union forces won two major victories in July 1863, at Vicksburg and at Gettysburg, and changed the course of the war as they allowed the Union forces to focus on one goal: taking Richmond.*

TEACHING STRATEGY

As discussed with the Mathew Brady image on p. 422, photographs played a significant role in the public's perception of the war. An image like the one shown here on p. 440 created a sense of drama and immediacy, as Americans had never seen a military leader in the midst of planning his strategy.

AP® THEME

WOR: America in the World

The appointment of Grant and Sherman to leadership of the Union military marked a shift in strategy that ultimately led to Union victory, as well as the destruction of the South's infrastructure.

As southern citizens grew increasingly critical of their government, Confederate elections of 1863 went sharply against politicians who supported Jefferson Davis. Meanwhile, northern citizens rallied to the Union, and Republicans swept state elections in Pennsylvania, Ohio, and New York, suggesting citizens' renewed commitment to the war effort. In Europe, the Union victories at Gettysburg and Vicksburg boosted the leverage of U.S. diplomats. Since 1862, a British-built ironclad cruiser, the CSS *Alabama*, had sunk or captured more than a hundred Union merchant ships, and the Confederacy was about to accept delivery of two more ironclads. With a Union victory increasingly likely, the British government decided to impound the warships. British workers and reformers had long condemned slavery and praised emancipation. Moreover, because of poor grain harvests, Britain depended on imports of wheat and flour from the American Midwest. King Cotton diplomacy had failed and King Wheat now stood triumphant. "Rest not your hopes in foreign nations," President Jefferson Davis advised his people. "This war is ours; we must fight it ourselves."

AP® SKILLS & PROCESSES

CAUSATION

How did the battles at Vicksburg and Gettysburg alter Unionists' and Confederates' goals?

THE ROAD TO UNION VICTORY, 1864–1865

Why and how did the objectives of Lincoln and the Union change by the end of the Civil War?

Union victories in 1863 made it less and less likely that the South would win independence through a decisive military triumph. Confederate leaders, however, still hoped for a battlefield stalemate and a negotiated peace — which was a real possibility if Lincoln lost the election of 1864. To remain as president, Lincoln needed to show the northern public he was winning the war — the goal he had pursued for three years with single-minded purpose. Another change of military leaders at last provided the key. When Lincoln's new generals succeeded, the war's impact devastated the South.

Grant Planning a Strategic Maneuver On May 21, 1864, the day this photograph was taken, Grant pulled his forces from Spotsylvania Court House, where a bitter two-week battle (May 8–21) resulted in 18,000 Union and 10,000 Confederate casualties. He moved his army to the southeast, seeking to outflank Lee's forces. Photographer Timothy H. O'Sullivan caught up to the Union army's high command at Massaponax Church, Virginia, and captured this image of Grant (to the left) leaning over a pew and reading a map held by General George H. Meade. As Grant plots the army's movement, his officers smoke their pipes and read reports of the war in newspapers that had just arrived from New York City. Intercepting Grant's forces, Lee took up fortified positions first at the North Anna River and then at Cold Harbor, where the Confederates scored their last major victory of the war (May 31–June 3). Library of Congress, LC-DIG-cwpb-01191.

Grant and Sherman Take Command

Lincoln finally found a ruthless commanding general in March 1864, when he placed Ulysses S. Grant in charge of all Union armies. From then on, the president determined overall strategy and Grant implemented it. Lincoln wanted a simultaneous advance against the major Confederate armies, a strategy Grant had long favored, in order to achieve a decisive victory before the election of 1864.

Grant knew how to fight a war that relied on industrial technology and targeted the enemy's infrastructure. At Vicksburg in July 1863, he had besieged the whole city and forced its surrender. Then, in November, he had used railroads to rescue an endangered Union army near Chattanooga, Tennessee. Grant believed the cautious tactics of previous Union commanders had prolonged the war. He was willing to accept heavy casualties, a stance that earned him a reputation as a butcher. But he followed the tenets of Lieber's code: whatever "military necessity" he might need to invoke, Grant would end the war as swiftly as possible.

In May 1864, Grant ordered two major offensives. Personally taking charge of the 115,000-man Army of the Potomac, he set out to destroy Lee's force of 75,000 troops in Virginia. Grant instructed General William Tecumseh Sherman, who shared his harsh outlook, to invade Georgia and take Atlanta. "All that has gone before is mere skirmish," Sherman wrote as he prepared for battle. "The war now begins." As a young military officer stationed in the South, Sherman had sympathized with the planter class and felt that slavery upheld social stability. However, secession meant "anarchy," he told his southern friends in early 1861: "If war comes . . . I must fight your people whom I best love." Sherman, more than anyone else, developed the philosophy and tactics of **hard war**. When Confederate guerrillas fired on a boat carrying Unionist civilians near Randolph, Tennessee, Sherman had sent a regiment to destroy the town, asserting, "We are justified in treating all inhabitants as combatants." Sherman argued that northerners had had "no hand" in making the war; southern men had caused it by voting for secession. He vowed to "make them so sick of war that generations would pass away before they would again appeal to it."

hard war
The philosophy and tactics used by Union general William Tecumseh Sherman, by which he treated civilians as combatants.

Grant advanced toward Richmond, hoping to force Lee to fight in open fields, where the Union's superior manpower and artillery would prevail. Remembering his tactical errors at Gettysburg, Lee remained in strong defensive positions and attacked only when he held an advantage. The Confederate general seized such opportunities twice in May 1864, winning costly victories at the battles of the Wilderness and Spotsylvania Court House. At Spotsylvania, troops fought at point-blank range; an Iowa recruit recalled "lines of blue and grey [firing] into each other's faces; for an hour and a half." Despite heavy losses in these battles and then at Cold Harbor, Grant drove on (Map 13.4). His attacks severely eroded Lee's forces, which suffered 31,000 casualties, though Union losses were even higher: 55,000 killed or wounded.

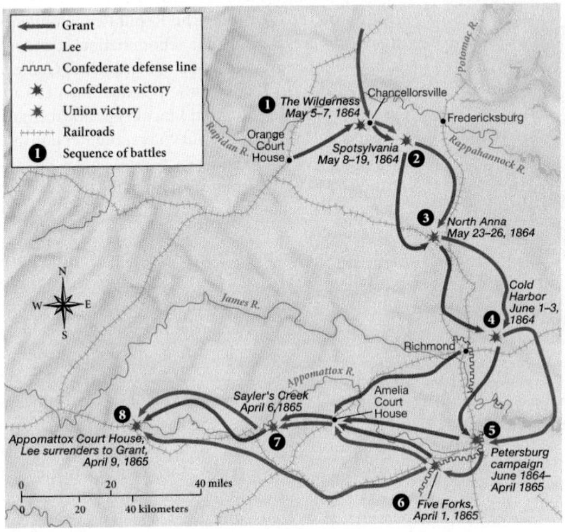

MAP 13.4 The Closing Virginia Campaign, 1864–1865
Beginning in May 1864, General Ulysses S. Grant launched an all-out campaign against Richmond, trying to lure General Robert E. Lee into open battle. Lee avoided a major test of strength. Instead, he retreated to defensive positions and inflicted heavy casualties on Union attackers at the Wilderness, Spotsylvania Court House, North Anna, and Cold Harbor (1–4). From June 1864 to April 1865, the two armies faced each other across defensive fortifications outside Richmond and Petersburg (5). Grant finally broke this ten-month siege by a flanking maneuver at Five Forks (6). Lee's surrender followed shortly.

TEACHING STRATEGY

Students should define "hard war" by using a specific historical example. Give students the option of Vicksburg, Atlanta, or Grant's Virginia Campaign from May of 1864 to April of 1865. Using specific examples will help students understand the importance of hard war during the Civil War.

CHECK FOR UNDERSTANDING

Ask students: **How did the war change when Grant and Sherman took command?** *The war became more brutal and led to more hardships for civilians. It also demoralized the Confederacy and helped to speed Union victory.*

AP® SKILLS & PROCESSES

CAUSATION

Use the **CAUSATION** question to have students evaluate the consequences of Grant's appointment to lead the Union army. It raises the question of the significance of the role of individuals in effecting dramatic change. Students might also explore the question of whether one individual can really make a substantial impact on the outcome of major events, providing evidence for their conclusion.

TRM Find complete suggested responses in the Teacher's Resource Materials.

TEACHING STRATEGY

W. Todd Groce, president of the Georgia Historical Society, reevaluates Sherman's march in an effort to untangle fact from stereotype. In the process, he raises the question of "total war" introduced at the beginning of the chapter. Groce argues emphatically that Sherman did not practice total war. His "hard war," which systematically destroyed foodstuffs, factories, and government property, conscientiously avoided harming civilians. The effect of his march on civilians was, as much as anything, a forerunner of psychological warfare — the fear of his troops destroyed the civilian will to fight and prompted women to urge their loved ones to desert. To access this article, search "NYT Rethinking Sherman's March."

The fighting took a heavy psychological toll. "Many a man has gone crazy since this campaign began from the terrible pressure on mind and body," observed a Union captain. In June 1864, Grant laid siege to Petersburg, an important railroad center near Richmond. As the standoff continued for nine and a half months, Union and Confederate soldiers built complex networks of trenches, tunnels, and artillery emplacements stretching 40 miles along the eastern edge of Richmond and Petersburg, foreshadowing the devastating trench warfare that would emerge in France during World War I. Invoking the intense imagery of the Bible, an officer described the continuous artillery barrages and sniping as "living night and day within the 'valley of the shadow of death.'" The stress was especially great for outnumbered Confederates, who spent months in the muddy, hellish trenches without rotation to the rear.

As time passed, Lincoln and Grant felt pressures of their own. The enormous casualties and military stalemate threatened Lincoln with defeat in the November election. Republicans' outlook worsened in July, when a body of almost 3,000 Confederate cavalrymen raided and burned the town of Chambersburg, in southern Pennsylvania, and threatened Washington. To punish farmers in the Shenandoah Valley who had aided Confederate raiders, Grant ordered General Philip H. Sheridan to turn the region into "a barren waste." Sheridan's troops conducted a scorched-earth campaign, destroying grain, barns, and gristmills and any other resource useful to the Confederates. The war had become hard indeed.

AP® SKILLS & PROCESSES

CAUSATION

How did Grant's appointment as general in chief affect the course of the war?

The Election of 1864 and Sherman's March

William Tecumseh Sherman A man of nervous energy, Sherman smoked cigars and talked continuously. When seated, he crossed and uncrossed his legs incessantly, and a journalist described his fingers as constantly "twitching his red whiskers — his coat buttons — playing a tattoo on the table — or running through his hair." On the battlefield Sherman was a decisive general who commanded the loyalty of his troops. A photographer captured this image of Sherman in 1865, following his devastating march through Georgia and the Carolinas. National Archives, photo no. 525970.

As the siege at Petersburg dragged on, General William Tecumseh Sherman's 90,000 Union men moved methodically toward Atlanta, a railway hub at the heart of the Confederacy. General Joseph E. Johnson's Confederate army of 60,000 stood in Sherman's way and, in June 1864, inflicted heavy casualties on his forces near Kennesaw Mountain, Georgia. By late July, the Union army was poised on the northern outskirts of Atlanta, but the next month brought little gain. Like Grant, Sherman seemed bogged down in a hopeless campaign.

Both Unionists and Confederates pinned their hopes on the election of 1864. In June, the Republican convention rebuffed attempts to prevent Lincoln's renomination. It endorsed the president's war strategy, demanded unconditional Confederate surrender, and called for a constitutional amendment to abolish slavery. Delegates likewise embraced Lincoln's political strategy. To attract border-state and Democratic voters, the Republicans took a new name, the National Union Party, and chose Andrew Johnson, a Tennessee slave owner and Unionist Democrat, as Lincoln's running mate — a choice that proved fateful after Lincoln's assassination (see Chapter 14).

The Democratic Party met in August and nominated George McClellan for president. Lincoln had twice removed McClellan from military commands: first for an excess of caution and then for his opposition to emancipation. Like McClellan, Democratic delegates rejected emancipation and condemned Lincoln's repression of domestic dissent, particularly his suspension of habeas corpus and use of military courts to prosecute civilians. However, they split into two camps over war policy. War Democrats vowed to continue fighting until the rebellion ended, while Peace Democrats called for a "cessation of hostilities" and a constitutional convention to negotiate a peace settlement. Although personally a War Democrat, McClellan promised if elected to recommend to Congress an immediate armistice and a peace convention. Hearing this news, Confederate vice president Alexander Stephens celebrated "the first ray of real light I have seen since the war began." He predicted that if Atlanta and Richmond held out, Lincoln would be defeated and McClellan would eventually accept an independent Confederacy.

AP® EXAM TIP

Analyze the election of 1864 as a reflection of opposition to the war effort in the North and the importance of key victories against the South.

The Fall of Atlanta and Lincoln's Victory Stephens's hopes collapsed on September 2, 1864, as Atlanta fell to Sherman's army. In a stunning move, the Union general pulled his troops from the trenches, swept around the city, and destroyed its rail links to the south. Fearing that Sherman would encircle his army, Confederate general John B. Hood abandoned the city. "Atlanta is ours, and fairly won," Sherman telegraphed Lincoln, sparking hundred-gun salutes and wild Republican celebrations across the North. "We are gaining strength," Lincoln warned Confederate leaders, "and may, if need be, maintain the contest indefinitely."

A deep pessimism settled over the Confederacy. Mary Chesnut, a South Carolina plantation mistress and general's wife, wrote in her diary, "I felt as if all were dead within me, forever," and foresaw the end of the Confederacy: "We are going to be wiped off the earth." Recognizing the dramatically changed military situation, McClellan repudiated the Democratic peace platform. Democrats' fall campaign focused heavily instead on the alleged dangers of emancipation. Cartoonists caricatured Lincoln as an ape; parade floats featured white men in blackface makeup dancing with white women. An anonymous Democratic pamphlet warned of the dangers of race mixing, coining the term **miscegenation** to denounce interracial marriage

miscegenation
A derogatory word for interracial sexual relationships coined by Democrats in the 1864 election, as they claimed that emancipation would allow African American men to gain sexual access to white women and produce mixed-race children.

Southern Refugees A traveling artist made this sketch south of Atlanta, Georgia, where southern civilians were fleeing ahead of Sherman's advance. It appeared in *Harper's Weekly* on October 15, 1864—one of a cascade of images that reassured northerners of the effectiveness of Sherman's strategy. Some of the families depicted were well-to-do enough to own slaves, including the women and children at front left. The Union wagons in the background had most likely been captured and repurposed by Confederates. Three Lions/Getty Images.

AP® APPLY THE TIP

Divide students into collaborative groups and ask each group to create a slide presentation that addresses the following steps to explore the causes behind the outcome of the election of 1864:

- Define the political parties in the election and the platforms they represented.
- Explain the divisions that occurred within political parties and their relationship to divisions in the Union.
- Explore political cartoons to illustrate the divisions in the Union associated with the election of 1864.
- Explain the outcome of the election of 1864.

TEACHING STRATEGY

Mary Chesnut, wife of South Carolina Senator James Chesnut Jr., kept a diary that provides the perspective of an elite, southern white woman from the moment she received news of Lincoln's election through the defeat of the Confederacy. Among other features, the diary provides a glimpse of the hardships civilians in the Confederacy faced, especially after Sherman's advance. To access this diary, search "Documenting the American South Mary Chesnut."

TEACHING STRATEGY

Think about assigning students one of the following roles: Enslaved person, southern citizen, Confederate soldier. Ask students to define one way in which the artist's rendering portrays how the war affected these groups. Remind students to use the artist's rendition and not their own perspective based on what they know and understand. The goal is to have students work on evaluating historical evidence.

and claim that Republican policies would lead to that result. Fear of interracial sexuality, always near the core of American racism, became a central feature of the 1864 campaign.

The National Union Party (the once and future Republicans) went on the offensive, ridiculing McClellan's inconsistency and attacking Peace Democrats as traitors. Boosted by Sherman's victories in Georgia, Lincoln won a clear-cut victory in November. He won 55 percent of the popular vote and 212 of 233 electoral votes. Republicans and National Unionists captured 145 of the 185 seats in the House of Representatives and increased their Senate majority to 42 of 52 seats. Republicans owed their victory in part to the votes of Union troops.

Legal emancipation was already underway at the edges of the South. In 1864, after years of intense pressure, Maryland and Missouri amended their constitutions to end slavery, and the three Confederate states occupied by the Union army — Tennessee, Arkansas, and Louisiana — followed suit. Still, abolitionists worried that the Emancipation Proclamation, based legally on the president's wartime powers, would lose its force at the end of the war. After three attempts, urged on by Lincoln and the National Equal Rights League, Congress finally approved the Thirteenth Amendment in January 1865 (Table 13.1). Once ratified by two-thirds of the states, in December 1865, the amendment officially ended slavery in the United States — except within the prison system, where "involuntary labor" could continue for those convicted of crimes.

TABLE 13.1

The Challenge of Passing the Thirteenth Amendment

This table shows the results of votes in the House of Representatives on amending the Constitution to abolish slavery throughout the United States. The measure needed a 2/3 vote to pass. In 1864, well after Lincoln issued the Emancipation Proclamation as a war measure, Confederate hopes were fading and 180,000 African American troops had fought for the Union. Why did a constitutional amendment abolishing slavery prove, nevertheless, so difficult to pass in Congress? What military and political events happened between June 1864 and January 1865 that made passage possible at last?

	Republican	Democrat	Union	Uncond. Union	Total
Feb. 15, 1864 (trial vote)					
Yea	66	1	1	10	78
Nay	2	52	7	1	62
Absent	17	20	2	3	42
Abstain	1	0	0	0	1
June 15, 1864 (on Senate bill)					
Yea	78	4	0	11	93
Nay	1	58	6	0	65
Absent	6	10	4	3	23
Abstain	1	0	0	0	1
Jan. 31, 1865 (on Senate bill)					
Yea	86	15	4	14	119
Nay	0	50	6	0	56
Absent	0	8	0	0	8
Abstain	0	0	0	0	0

Information from: Michael Vorenberg, *Final Freedom: The Civil War, the Abolition of Slavery, and the Thirteenth Amendment* (New York: Cambridge University Press, 2001), 252.

AP® SKILLS & PROCESSES

ANALYZING HISTORICAL EVIDENCE

TABLE 13.1 allows students to analyze statistical patterns related to the abolition of slavery. Students should be reminded that these votes did not include elected representatives from any Confederate states. The table provides great insight into the stubborn persistence of proslavery sentiment. With only Union states participating, more than fifty officials voted against abolishing slavery as late as January 1865.

Sherman Crosses Georgia Thanks to Sherman, the Confederacy was also reaching its end. After capturing Atlanta, Sherman advocated a bold strategy. Instead of pursuing a retreating Confederate army northward into Tennessee, he proposed to move south, live off the land, and "cut a swath through to the sea." To persuade Lincoln and Grant to approve his unconventional plan, Sherman argued that his march would be "a demonstration to the world, foreign and domestic, that we have a power [Jefferson] Davis cannot resist." The general lived up to his pledge (Map 13.5). "We are not only fighting hostile armies," Sherman wrote, "but a hostile people, and must make old and young, rich and poor, feel the hard hand of war." His soldiers left Atlanta in flames, and during their 300-mile March to the Sea consumed or demolished everything in their path. Though Sherman's army focused on damaging property, not murdering civilians, the havoc so demoralized Confederate soldiers that many deserted their units and returned home. When Sherman reached Savannah in mid-December, the city's 10,000 defenders left without a fight.

Georgia's African Americans treated Sherman as a savior. "They flock to me, old and young," he wrote. "They pray and shout and mix up my name with Moses." To provide for the hundreds of African American families now following his army, Sherman issued **Special Field Order No. 15**, which set aside 400,000 acres of prime rice-growing land for the exclusive use of freedpeople. By June 1865, about 40,000

Special Field Order No. 15
An order by General William T. Sherman, later reversed by policymakers, that granted confiscated land to formerly enslaved families in Georgia and South Carolina so they could farm independently.

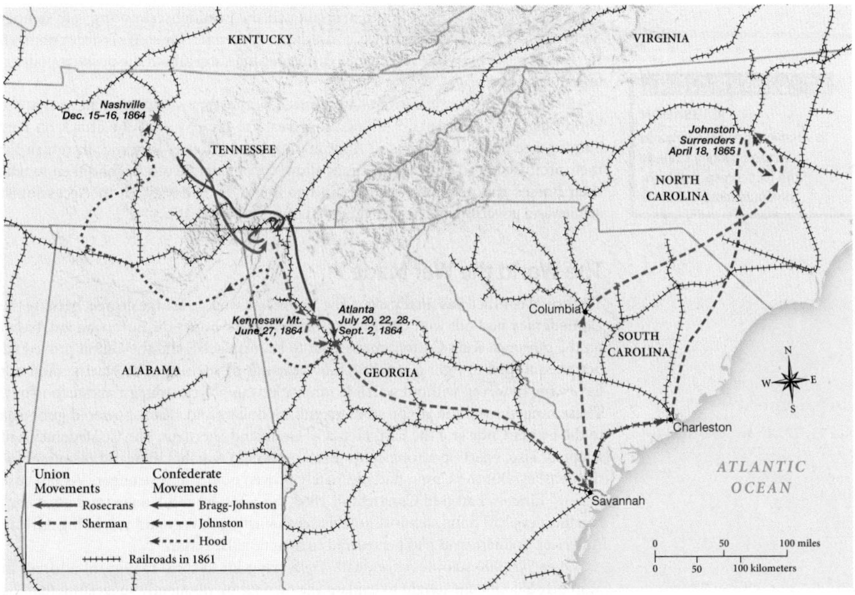

MAP 13.5 Sherman's March Through the Confederacy, 1864–1865
The Union victory in November 1863 at Chattanooga, Tennessee, was almost as critical as the victories in July at Gettysburg and Vicksburg, because it opened up a route of attack into the heart of the Confederacy. In mid-1864, General William Tecumseh Sherman advanced on the railway hub of Atlanta. After taking the city in September 1864, Sherman relied on other Union armies to stem an invasion of Tennessee by Confederate General John Bell Hood, while Sherman began a devastating march across Georgia. By December, Sherman's army reached Savannah, and from there they cut a swath through the Carolinas. Note how Sherman's march followed key rail lines: his troops ripped up, heated, and twisted sections of track to disrupt Confederate transport and communications.

African Americans were cultivating "Sherman lands." Many expected the lands to be theirs forever, a form of payment for generations of unpaid labor. By March, after his devastating march through South Carolina, Sherman was ready to link up with Grant and crush Lee's army.

The Confederacy Collapses

AP® EXAM TIP

Evaluate the importance of attrition and total war on the defeat of the South.

Grant's war of attrition in Virginia exposed a weakness in the Confederacy: rising resentment among poor whites. Angered by slave owners' exemptions from military service and fearing that the Confederacy was doomed, ordinary southern farmers now repudiated the draft. "All they want is to git you . . . to fight for their infurnal negroes," grumbled an Alabama hill farmer. More and more soldiers fled their units. By 1865, at least 100,000 men had deserted from southern armies, prompting reluctant Confederate leaders to approve the enlistment of black soldiers and promise them freedom. It was a hollow offer: tens of thousands had already proved to be excellent soldiers for the Union.

The symbolic end of the war took place in Virginia. In April 1865, Grant finally gained control of the crucial railroad junction at Petersburg and forced Lee to abandon Richmond. As Lincoln made a surprise visit to the ruins of the Confederate capital, greeted by joyful freedmen and women, Grant cut off Lee's escape route to North Carolina. It was one of Lincoln's last acts: on April 14, a pro-Confederate actor named John Wilkes Booth assassinated the president, shouting "Sic semper tyrannis" — Virginia's state motto, *thus always to tyrants*. Lincoln's murder plunged the Union into mourning and opened disturbing questions about the postwar political order (see Chapter 14).

AP® SKILLS & PROCESSES

CAUSATION

To what extent were Grant and Sherman's military strategy and tactics responsible for the Confederacy's defeat?

Just before his death Lincoln had received, with weary satisfaction, news that the Union had won. On April 9, almost four years to the day after the attack on Fort Sumter, Lee had surrendered at Appomattox Court House, Virginia. In return for their promise not to fight again, Grant allowed Confederate officers and men to take their horses and personal weapons and go home. By late May, all the secessionist armies and governments had surrendered or melted away.

The World the War Made

The brutal conflict was finally over. The Union had won, to a large degree, because the Confederacy had not won quickly. Southern leaders' hopes for European aid, based on the power of King Cotton, turned out to be misplaced, and the Union proved far better equipped to fight a grueling four-year war of attrition. The North could not have won, however, without wartime innovations in policy, strategy, and technology. These ranged from the adoption of greenback dollars and steam-powered gunboats to the Lieber Code and the hard tactics of Grant and Sherman. The Confederacy had adapted, also, exerting strong centralized powers to marshal men and resources for the conflict. But the Union had ultimately proven bolder and stronger. "As our case is new," Lincoln had told Congress in 1863, "so we must think anew, and act anew." Northerners had done so, most notably by abolishing slavery and recruiting African American soldiers, and had persevered to maintain the Union.

Over 700,000 people were dead. Delivering his second inaugural address in March 1865, Lincoln sought to explain the carnage by eloquently suggesting that the war's purpose had not been to preserve the Union but to end slavery. That purpose, however long ignored or disavowed by Union leaders, had been a divine plan. "If we shall suppose," Lincoln said,

> that American slavery is one of those offenses which, in the providence of God, must needs come, but which, having continued through His appointed time, He now wills to remove, and that He gives to both North and South this

CHECK FOR UNDERSTANDING

Ask students: **What were the effects of Sherman's march?** *In his march to Savannah, Sherman decimated the countryside and infrastructure, demoralizing civilians and soldiers alike. His success helped earn Lincoln reelection, and his continuity of leadership ensured a Union victory.*

TEACHING STRATEGY

Ford's Theatre, the location where Booth assassinated Lincoln and now a national historic site, provides an engaging online activity that allows students to conduct a crime scene investigation into the questions prompted by his murder. To access the site, search "Ford's Theatre Lincoln's Assassination."

AP® SKILLS & PROCESSES

CAUSATION

The use of "Total War" was a large concept of Grant and Sherman's strategy. Have students define and explain the use of total war in the context of the American Civil War. Next, have students identify battles that changed the tide of the war from 1863–1865. How many of these battles was total war used and what was the result?

TRM Find complete suggested responses in the Teacher's Resource Materials.

CHECK FOR UNDERSTANDING

Ask students: **How did the Confederacy collapse?** *Grant waged a war of attrition against Virginia and finally forced Lee to abandon Richmond, the Confederacy capital.*

AP® THEME

WOR: America in the World

Students should read "The Confederacy Collapses" and "The World the War Made" sections (pp. 446–447) carefully as they provide effective summaries of the reasons the early initiative of the Confederacy proved inadequate to ensure success, as well as reasons the Union did ultimately succeed.

terrible war as the woe due to those by whom the offense came, shall we discern therein any departure from those divine attributes which the believers in a living God always ascribe to Him? Fondly do we hope, fervently do we pray, that this mighty scourge of war may speedily pass away. Yet, if God wills that it continue until all the wealth piled by the bondsman's two hundred and fifty years of unrequited toil shall be sunk, and until every drop of blood drawn with the lash shall be paid by another drawn with the sword, as was said three thousand years ago, so still it must be said, "the judgments of the Lord are true and righteous altogether."

For the first time, Lincoln had named the sin of slavery as the central cause of the war — and proposed, remarkably, that both Union and Confederacy shared guilt for that sin. Abolitionist Frederick Douglass, who heard the address, told Lincoln afterward that it was a "sacred effort." Yet at the same time, Lincoln's second inaugural depicted the catastrophe of war as visited only on *whites* — as if enslaved African Americans had been passive victims and bystanders, rather than participants in the war who, as "contrabands," workers, scouts, and soldiers, had played decisive roles in Union victory. Even Lincoln's most powerful antislavery speech, then, revealed unresolved political problems that would unfold after the war. As southern states returned to the Union, what kind of nation would emerge? Former Confederates wanted a *reunion* of the white North and South, a nation adhering as nearly as possible to prewar principles. African Americans and Radical Republicans wanted *revolution* — a complete economic, social, and political transformation of the South. Neither would get their wish.

As for the future of the United States, an optimistic New York census-taker suggested that the conflict had had an "equalizing effect." In some ways he was right. Slavery was dead: in a transformation of shattering significance, no American could ever again legally claim to own another human being. The same official also reflected that, in the North, "military men from the so called 'lower classes' now lead society, having been elevated by real merit and valor." However perceptive these remarks, they overlooked the simultaneous wartime emergence of a new financial and corporate aristocracy that soon presided over what Mark Twain labeled the Gilded Age. As early as 1863, a journalist warned that when the war was over, "there will be the same wealth in the country, but it will be in fewer hands; we shall have . . . more merchant princes and princely bankers."

Astonishing its European rivals, the United States emerged from the Civil War relatively unscathed. High tariffs put in place by Republicans, for example, paid off the nation's war debt with remarkable speed. And however devastated the South's economy might be, the United States had started on the path to global economic power. In the postwar period, Republicans would wrestle with the limits of that power at home and on the world stage.

SUMMARY

As the Civil War began, both the Union and the Confederacy hoped for a quick, decisive victory, but none was forthcoming. Union commander George B. McClellan proved unable to crush his daring southern equivalent, Robert E. Lee, but as attempts to invade the West and North failed, Confederates proved unable to move the theater of war outside their own territory. From the beginning, also, thousands of African Americans fled to Union lines, undermining Confederates' war effort. Congress soon authorized use of these "contrabands" as scouts, spies, and paid workers.

By 1862 and 1863, new strategies were needed. First the Confederacy and then the Union instituted military conscription. This unprecedented move, along with

TEACHING STRATEGY

Prominent Civil War historian James McPherson argues that the Civil War resolved two problems left unresolved by the American Revolution and the Constitution. His full article, including a more detailed assessment of the war's consequences, is available on the National Archives Web site. To access his article, search "McPherson Out of War, a New Nation."

CHECK FOR UNDERSTANDING

Ask students: **Why and how did the objectives of Lincoln and the Union change by the end of the Civil War?** *At the start of the war, Lincoln made it clear that war was being prosecuted to preserve the Union. As the conflict dragged on, Lincoln reoriented his war aims and the war became about ending slavery, which was accomplished with the passage of the Thirteenth Amendment in early 1865.*

CHECK FOR UNDERSTANDING

Use the **AP® LEARNING FOCUS** question from the beginning of the chapter to check students' understanding of the chapter as a whole: **Why and how did the Union win the Civil War?** *The Union won the Civil War by eventually employing its advantages in men, material, transport, and industry over the Confederacy. It also used diplomatic weapons like the Emancipation Proclamation to prevent European interference.*

LearningCurve

Remind students to go online to complete the LearningCurve quiz for this chapter.

TRM Find complete suggested responses in the Teacher's Resource Materials.

AP® SKILLS & PROCESSES

CONTINUITY AND CHANGE

AP® CONTENT REVIEW 2 asks students to identify changes in the nature of the Civil War. Note: This is the same question as the **CHECK FOR UNDERSTANDING** prompt on p. 440.

AP® SKILLS & PROCESSES

CONTINUITY AND CHANGE

AP® CONTENT REVIEW 3 asks students to identify changes in Lincoln's thinking about the war's purposes. Note: This is the same question as the **CHECK FOR UNDERSTANDING** prompt on p. 447.

TRM Find definitions for these terms in the **Glossary/Glosario** in the Teacher's Resource Materials.

new taxes and inflation, caused considerable civilian unrest, especially in the South, as Union forces made inroads into occupying Confederate land and resources. Even more important was the Emancipation Proclamation, which Lincoln issued after the Union victory at Antietam and put into effect on January 1, 1863. African American troops soon enlisted for the Union, hardening Confederate attitudes but playing a crucial role in Union victory. Two decisive battles in the summer of 1863, Gettysburg and Vicksburg, began to turn the tide toward Union victory. Lincoln then chose an effective commander, Ulysses Grant, to lead U.S. forces, but it took almost two years of grueling, brutal campaigns to defeat the South.

In the fall of 1864, exhausted and shocked by the war's magnitude, Confederates pinned their last hopes on Lincoln's defeat in his campaign for reelection, anticipating that his Democratic opponent would sue for peace and reinstate slavery. But General William T. Sherman's brilliant campaigns helped bolster Union morale and ensure Lincoln's reelection. In the war's final months, as the Confederacy began to collapse, Congress passed the Thirteenth Amendment abolishing slavery.

CHAPTER 13 REVIEW

AP CONTENT REVIEW *Answer these questions to demonstrate your understanding of the chapter's main ideas.*

1. What early political and military strategies did Confederate and Union leaders adopt, and which were most successful?
2. Why and how did transformations in the war effort, during 1863, begin to give the Union the upper hand?
3. Why and how did the objectives of Lincoln and the Union change by the end of the Civil War?

AP TERMS TO KNOW *Identify and explain the significance of each term below.*

Key Concepts and Events

King Cotton (p. 417)
habeas corpus (p. 418)
contrabands (p. 423)
Radical Republicans (p. 424)
Emancipation Proclamation (p. 424)
greenbacks (p. 426)
one-tenth tax (p. 427)
draft (conscription) (p. 428)
twenty-Negro rule (p. 428)
draft riots (p. 429)
Lieber Code (p. 432)
U.S. Sanitary Commission (p. 432)
Woman's Loyal National League (p. 433)
Gettysburg Address (p. 437)
hard war (p. 441)
miscegenation (p. 443)
Special Field Order No. 15 (p. 445)

Key People

Abraham Lincoln (p. 417)
Jefferson Davis (p. 417)
George McClellan (p. 418)
Robert E. Lee (p. 436)
Ulysses S. Grant (p. 420)
William Tecumseh Sherman (p. 441)

AP® MAKING CONNECTIONS

Recognize the larger developments and continuities within and across chapters by answering these questions.

1. Both the American Revolution and the Civil War pitted Americans against each other and were fought on U.S. soil. In the former, however, the far more economically and militarily powerful British Empire lost to the rebellious colonists, while in the latter, it was the seceders who lost. What factors explain these different outcomes? Who made up the armies in each conflict, and what roles did civilians play? Compare the war efforts in each context.

2. The images of southern refugees (p. 443) and Grant planning a strategic maneuver (p. 440) remind us of a world in which people, goods, and soldiers moved either on foot or on horses and mules. How did this limited mobility affect civilians — slave and free — and military forces during the Civil War? How did the emergence of steam-powered naval vessels, railroads, and other new technologies begin to change the nature of war?

KEY TURNING POINTS

Refer to the timeline at the start of the chapter for help in answering the following question.

The Emancipation Proclamation (1863), Union victories at Gettysburg and Vicksburg (1863), and Sherman's taking of Atlanta (1864): historians have seen all of these events as important turning points. Assume that *one* of these events did not happen. What difference would it have made in the military and political struggle between the Union and the Confederacy?

AP® PRACTICE QUESTIONS

MULTIPLE CHOICE QUESTIONS

Choose the correct answer for each question.

Questions 1–3 refer to this excerpt.

> "There is every reason to believe, from present appearances . . . that we shall be short of supplies for one army and people next year. . . . It behooves us therefore to observe the greatest frugality and economy in the use of what we have. It matters not that we have a plethora of money, or that there is an abundance elsewhere to supply our lack, when we are excluded from the markets of the world, and are compelled to rely upon what we have within ourselves. Money cannot produce one grain of corn, or increase by one pound, our quantity of meat. . . . Thousands of our gallant soldiers who were nursed in the lap of plenty, and brought up in the midst of affluence, have known what it is to go for days together without a meal. . . . The season, the condition of the country, the wants of those to whom we have referred, and the prospect before us, all call upon us, trumpet-tongued, to forego every species of luxury during the existence of this war."
>
> Virginia newspaper article from *The Staunton Spectator*, November 4, 1862

1. This passage best serves as evidence of which of the following?
   - **a.** The mobilization of economy and society to wage the Civil War
   - **b.** The failure of the Confederacy from gaining full diplomatic support from European powers
   - **c.** The portrayal of the Civil War as a struggle to fulfill America's democratic ideals
   - **d.** The failure of numerous attempts at compromise to reduce conflict

2. The issues brought up in this passage were primarily a result of which of the following?
   - **a.** The southern economy's dependence on imports
   - **b.** Improvements in Union leadership and strategy
   - **c.** African Americans fleeing southern plantations
   - **d.** Differing forms of government between the North and the South

3. This passage was most likely written in response to the
   - **a.** considerable home front opposition faced by the Confederacy to waging the war.
   - **b.** the initiative and daring shown by the North early in the war.
   - **c.** the wartime destruction of the South's infrastructure.
   - **d.** the greater resources possessed by the North.

AP® SKILLS & PROCESSES

COMPARISON

AP® MAKING CONNECTIONS 1 invites students to compare two rebellions that shared similar features but had different outcomes.

AP® SKILLS & PROCESSES

ARGUMENTATION

AP® MAKING CONNECTIONS 2 asks students to consider the role of transportation technology on the outcome of the war.

AP® SKILLS & PROCESSES

CAUSATION

KEY TURNING POINTS poses a counterfactual question to help students determine which factor was most crucial in the Union's victory.

TRM Find complete suggested responses in the Teacher's Resource Materials.

Questions 4–6 refer to this excerpt.

"...As to the policy I 'seem to be pursuing,' as you say, I have not meant to leave any one in doubt.

I would save the Union. I would save it the shortest way under the Constitution. The sooner the National authority can be restored, the nearer the Union will be 'the Union as it was.' If there be those who would not save the Union unless they could at the same time *save* Slavery, I do not agree with them. If there be those who would not save the Union unless they could *destroy* Slavery, I do not agree with them. My paramount object in this struggle is to save the Union, and is not either to save or destroy Slavery. If I could save the Union without freeing *any* slave, I would do it; and if I could save it by freeing *all* the slaves, I would do it; and if I could save it by freeing some and leave others alone, I would also do that. . . . I have here stated my purpose according to my view of *official* duty; and I intend no modification of my oft-expressed *personal* wish that all men, every-where, could be free."

Letter from Abraham Lincoln to Horace Greeley, August 22, 1862

4. Which of the following developments most directly supports Lincoln's approach in this passage?

a. The enlistment of African Americans in the Union army

b. The issuing of the Emancipation Proclamation

c. The highly visible campaign of African American and white abolitionists against slavery

d. The continued dominance of southern planters in the region after the war

5. Based upon the excerpt, Lincoln would most likely support

a. the reinstatement of the Kansas-Nebraska Act.

b. the Dred Scott decision.

c. the settlement of ex-slaves on former plantation lands.

d. the Thirteenth Amendment.

6. Lincoln's position as referenced in the excerpt is most similar to which of the following?

a. Thomas Jefferson's position on the Louisiana Purchase

b. Ronald Reagan's strong response to countering communism at the beginning of the Cold War

c. George Washington's position on the French Revolution during his presidency

d. James Buchanan's position on the secession of South Carolina

TRM Find complete suggested responses in the Teacher's Resource Materials.

SHORT ANSWER QUESTIONS

Read each question carefully and write a short response. Use evidence from the text to support your claims.

"Strong feelings of national identity helped spawn the impressive will Confederates exhibited during their war for independence. With the goal of mounting the broad military effort necessary to establish nationhood, soldiers and civilians of the Confederacy tolerated severe intrusions on personal freedom, accepted the erosion of states' rights as the central government sought to equip and feed its armies, and, toward the end, debated openly the possibility of arming and freeing slaves to win the war."

Gary W. Gallagher, *The Confederate War*, 1997

"Countless women of all classes had in effect deserted the ranks. . . . Refusing to accept the economic deprivation further military struggle would have required, resisting additional military service by their husbands and sons . . . Southern women undermined both objective and ideological foundations for the Confederate effort; they directly subverted the South's military and economic effectiveness as well as civilian morale. . . . It may well have been because of women that the South lost the Civil War."

Drew Gilpin Faust, "Altars of Sacrifice: Confederate Women and the Narratives of War," *Journal of American History*, 76 (March 1990): 1228

1. Using the two excerpts provided, answer (a), (b), and (c).
   - **a.** Briefly explain ONE major difference between Gallagher's and Faust's historical interpretations about the Confederacy during the Civil War.
   - **b.** Briefly explain how ONE specific event, development, or circumstance not directly mentioned in the excerpts could be used to support Gallagher's argument.
   - **c.** Briefly explain how ONE specific event, development, or circumstance not directly mentioned in the excerpts could be used to support Faust's argument.
2. Answer (a), (b), and (c).
   - **a.** Briefly explain why one of the following developments was the most significant factor contributing to the Union winning the Civil War.
     - Leadership and strategy
     - The emancipation of slaves
     - The greater economic resources of the Union
   - **b.** Provide ONE specific historical example to support your argument in (a).
   - **c.** Provide specific evidence why ONE of the other options is less convincing as a significant factor leading to the Union victory.
3. Answer (a), (b), and (c).
   - **a.** Briefly explain ONE important similarity between the challenges faced by the Confederate and Union governments during the Civil War.
   - **b.** Briefly explain ONE important difference between the challenges faced by the Confederate and Union governments during the Civil War.
   - **c.** Briefly explain ONE important difference in the governmental leadership between the Union and Confederacy during the Civil War.

14 CHAPTER

Reconstruction

1865–1877

Chapter 14 — AP® Assessment Weight and Pacing Guide

The assessment weight on the AP® U.S. History Exam for Chapters 12–14 is 10–17 percent. This chapter is part of Unit 5 of the AP® U.S. History Curriculum, covering Period 5: 1844–1877.

This pacing guide is based on a schedule with 120 sessions of 50 minutes each before the AP® U.S. History Exam. If you have a different number of sessions before the exam, you can modify the pacing to meet your needs. If you have additional time, consider incorporating quizzes, released AP® U.S. History questions, practice exams, writing practice, and other instructional activities.

	Traditional Schedule	Block Schedule
Chapter 14	6 days	3 days

Daily Pacing Guide

	Content Focus	Essential Question
Days 1 and 2	The Struggle for National Reconstruction	What factors explain how Reconstruction policies unfolded between 1865 and 1870, and what was the impact on different groups of Americans?
Days 3 and 4	The Meaning of Freedom	What goals were southern freedmen and freedwomen able to achieve in the post–Civil War years, and why? What goals were they not able to achieve, and why not?
Days 5 and 6	The Undoing of Reconstruction	Why and how did federal Reconstruction policies falter in the South?

AP® Alignment

Section Heading	AP® Topic	AP® Theme
The Struggle for National Reconstruction	5.10	PCE
The Meaning of Freedom	5.10, 5.11	PCE, NAT
The Undoing of Reconstruction	5.11	NAT

*Should changes be made to the Course Framework in the future, an updated alignment will be placed on our AP® updates page at go.bfwpub.com/ap-course-updates.

Chapter 14 — Overview

Chapter 14 begins by comparing Abraham Lincoln's goals and plans for Reconstruction (until his assassination) with the goals and methods of Andrew Johnson. This section of the chapter also investigates the conflicts that arose between the power of Congress and the president to control and administer Reconstruction plans. The impeachment of Andrew Johnson placed Radical Republicans in a position of power in Congress, which allowed them to implement more dramatic changes in the South after the abolition of slavery and implementation of the Fourteenth and Fifteenth Amendments. As a result of these changes, Republicans made significant reforms in education, economic development, and civil rights. Finally, the chapter concludes by examining the ways in which the accomplishments of the Reconstruction era in allowing African Americans to participate in American society and politics were undone, and the lasting legacy of the failures of Reconstruction.

Chapter 14 — Resources

The following resources can be found in the Teacher's Resource Materials (TRM) that accompany the book. You can access the TRM via the book's digital platform, by clicking the TRM links found here in your Teacher's Edition e-book, or by contacting your representative to access the resources online. Visit **bfwpub.com/henretta10e** to learn more.

TRM Chapter 14 Lecture Presentation Slides

TRM Chapter 14 Outline with AP® Focus

TRM Chapter 14 Lecture Strategies

TRM Chapter 14 Suggested Responses

TRM Handout 14.1 — Comparison: Presidential and Congressional Reconstruction

TRM Handout 14.2 — Contextualization: Understanding Thaddeus Stevens

TRM Handout 14.3 — Causation: Sharecropping

TRM Handout 14.4 — Analyzing Historical Evidence: Reconstruction

Chapter 14 — Essential Activity

In this activity, students will create a "road map" that represents the divergent ideas as separate roads in order to illustrate the choices and decisions that led to the failure of Reconstruction and the Compromise of 1877. Students should begin at "1865" and draw three roads that represent Presidential Reconstruction, Radical (Congressional) Reconstruction, and Southern Democrats' Ideas for Reconstruction. Students should use content from Chapter 14 to create a road map that shows the developments along each road from 1865 to 1877. Remind students that road maps have exits, warning signs, information signs, road hazards (such as construction, broken pavement), and roadblocks.

Chapter 14 — Bell Ringers

The following activities take no more than 5–15 minutes of your class period and offer an effective and engaging way to begin your lessons and for students to apply AP® Skills & Processes:

- Ask students: Was the South still part of the U.S. after the Civil War or was it conquered territory? Allow students to discuss this question with a partner and record their answers. Then ask students to answer the same question from the point of view of Abraham Lincoln and jot down their responses. Then answer from the point of view of Thaddeus Stevens. Finally, answer from the point of view of Jefferson Davis. As a class, discuss the answers from various points of view and how they relate to different interpretations of the Constitution.
- Provide students with a copy of the political cartoon "Worse Than Slavery" by Thomas Nast and ask them to divide the cartoon into quadrants to help identify the different elements. Students should explain what each element represents about Reconstruction. Lead a class discussion to discuss Nast's purpose, intended audience, point of view, and historical context of the cartoon.

NOTES

TEACHING STRATEGY

Use the chapter opener material to introduce the central tension that drove the complex process of Reconstruction. On the one hand, through the Fourteenth and Fifteenth Amendments, African Americans were granted full equality and voting rights. This was a major shift away from state-governed voting and citizenship laws. Now the federal government insisted that all states accept that all persons born in the U.S. were citizens, guaranteed due process and equality under the law, and that all men, regardless of race or previous status as slaves, were assured of the right to vote.

On the other hand, white southerners were deeply embittered by their defeat and the imposition of a social revolution in race and were willing to resist, sometimes violently, as in the Memphis incident described in the introduction. White northerners did not wish to remain in a permanently hostile relationship with white southerners.

The federal government sought to address both concerns, protecting newly enfranchised blacks while attempting to soothe the anger of southern whites. But both could not be easily accomplished, and the deterioration of the economy in the 1870s, among other factors, would prompt the federal government to abandon its efforts to achieve full equality for blacks.

TEACHING STRATEGY

The University of Maryland's Freedmen and Southern Society Project Web site provides an outstanding collection of resources for helping students explore the complexities of Reconstruction. The site includes the complete text of more than one hundred letters, state and municipal resolutions, and military orders relating to slavery and emancipation, from 1861 through 1867. The site also provides a month-by-month chronology of emancipation from 1860 through 1865, with hyperlinks to relevant historical documents, as well as a bibliography of relevant scholarship, including four articles for teachers. To access the site, search "Freedmen and Southern Society Project."

14 CHAPTER

Reconstruction

1865–1877

AP® LEARNING FOCUS

Why did freedpeople, Republican policymakers, and ex-Confederates all end up dissatisfied with Reconstruction — or with its aftermath? To what degree did each group succeed in fulfilling its goals?

On the last day of April 1866, black soldiers in Memphis, Tennessee turned in their weapons as they mustered out of the Union army. The next day, whites who resented the soldiers' presence provoked a clash. At a street celebration where African Americans shouted "Hurrah for Abe Lincoln," a white policeman responded, "Your old father, Abe Lincoln, is dead and damned." The scuffle that followed precipitated three days of white violence and rape that left forty-eight African Americans dead and dozens more wounded. Mobs burned black homes and churches and destroyed all twelve of the city's black schools.

Unionists were appalled. They had won the Civil War, but where was the peace? Ex-Confederates murdered freedmen and flagrantly resisted federal authority. After the Memphis attacks, Republicans in Congress proposed a new measure to protect African Americans by defining and enforcing U.S. citizenship rights. Eventually this bill became the most significant law to emerge from Reconstruction, the Fourteenth Amendment to the Constitution.

Andrew Johnson, however — the Unionist Democrat who became president after Abraham Lincoln's assassination — refused to sign the bill. In May 1865, while Congress was adjourned, Johnson had implemented his own Reconstruction plan. It extended amnesty to all southerners who took a loyalty oath, except for a few high-ranking Confederates. It also allowed states to reenter the Union as soon as they revoked secession, abolished slavery, and relieved their new state governments of financial burdens by repudiating Confederate debts. A year later, at the time of the Memphis carnage, all the ex-Confederate states had met Johnson's terms. The president rejected any further intervention in southern states' affairs.

Johnson's vetoes, combined with ongoing violence in the South, angered Unionist voters. In the political struggle that ensued, congressional Republicans seized the initiative from the president and enacted a sweeping program that became known as Radical Reconstruction. One of its key achievements, the Fifteenth Amendment, would have been unthinkable a few years earlier: voting rights for African American men.

Black southerners, though, had additional, urgent needs. "We have toiled nearly all our lives as slaves [and] have made these lands what they are," a group of South Carolina petitioners declared. They pleaded for "some provision by which we as Freedmen can obtain a Homestead." Though northern Republicans and freedpeople agreed that black southerners must have physical safety and the right to vote, formerly enslaved men and women also wanted economic independence. Northerners sought, instead, to revive cash-crop plantations with wage labor. Reconstruction's eventual failure stemmed from the conflicting goals of lawmakers, freedpeople, and relentlessly hostile ex-Confederates.

Celebrating the Fifteenth Amendment, 1870 This lithograph depicts a celebration in Baltimore on May 15, 1870. With perhaps 200,000 people attending, the grand parade and orations marked passage of the Fifteenth Amendment, which enfranchised men irrespective of "race, color, or previous condition of servitude." The heroes depicted at the top are Martin Delany, the first black man to become an officer in the U.S. Army; abolitionist Frederick Douglass, born in slavery on Maryland's Eastern Shore; and Mississippi senator Hiram Rhodes Revels. The images at the bottom carried the following captions: "Liberty Protects the Marriage Altar," "The Ballot Box is open to us," and "Our Representative Sits in the National Legislature." Such lithographs, widely printed and sold, capture the pride, hope, and optimism of Reconstruction — but the optimism was not to last. Library of Congress, LC-USZC4-973.

AP® THEME

NAT: American and National Identity; PCE: Politics and Power

Ask students: **What does the image convey about the hopes and expectations of African Americans at the time of the Fifteenth Amendment's ratification?** *Delany, Douglass, and Revels are depicted with dignity and authority, surrounded by the American flag, suggesting that they are genuine American leaders worthy of respect from all, black or white. The celebration depicts African Americans with horses, a band, a carriage, and marchers wearing formal dress, indicating pride and a measure of prosperity. A number of whites are in attendance, some merely looking on while a few join in the festive atmosphere. The caption indicates some of the reasons for celebration: marriages that could no longer be forcibly separated by masters, access to the vote, and the election of blacks to Congress to represent their people.*

AP® SKILLS & PROCESSES

CONTINUITY AND CHANGE

Use the **TIMELINE** to help students begin thinking about how the period from 1864 to 1877 could constitute a distinct historical period. Students should note that the timeline and text include a few events that overlap with content from Chapter 13, but that the chapter essentially begins where the previous ended — with the end of the Civil War and the death of Lincoln. Students will also see that the chapter's periodization ends very specifically with 1877 and will need to figure out why "Reconstruction officially ends" that year. Students could review the events from the timeline and identify the major characteristics of Reconstruction. To extend this discussion, students might look for events on the timeline that help explain why Reconstruction came to an end.

AP® APPLY THE TIP

Divide the class into three groups and assign each group to research the Reconstruction plans of one of the following: Abraham Lincoln, Andrew Johnson, and Radical Republicans in Congress. Ask students to record their findings in their notebooks. Next, organize the class into collaborative groups of three students so that each group has one student serving as an "expert" to one of the plans for Reconstruction. Provide students with **Handout 14.1 — Comparison: Presidential and Congressional Reconstruction (TRM)**. Students should discuss their research and complete the chart for each of the Reconstruction plans. After students have completed the handout, lead a class discussion on the possible consequences of each plan for Reconstruction.

TRM Find **Handout 14.1 — Comparison: Presidential and Congressional Reconstruction** in the Teacher's Resource Materials.

TIMELINE

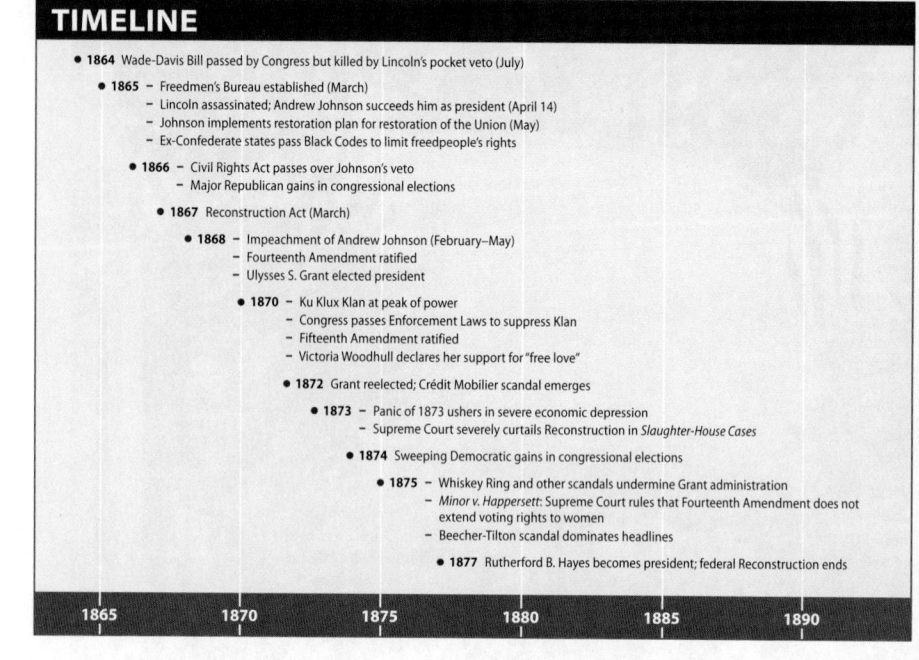

- **1864** Wade-Davis Bill passed by Congress but killed by Lincoln's pocket veto (July)
- **1865** – Freedmen's Bureau established (March)
  – Lincoln assassinated; Andrew Johnson succeeds him as president (April 14)
  – Johnson implements restoration plan for restoration of the Union (May)
  – Ex-Confederate states pass Black Codes to limit freedpeople's rights
- **1866** – Civil Rights Act passes over Johnson's veto
  – Major Republican gains in congressional elections
- **1867** Reconstruction Act (March)
- **1868** – Impeachment of Andrew Johnson (February–May)
  – Fourteenth Amendment ratified
  – Ulysses S. Grant elected president
- **1870** – Ku Klux Klan at peak of power
  – Congress passes Enforcement Laws to suppress Klan
  – Fifteenth Amendment ratified
  – Victoria Woodhull declares her support for "free love"
- **1872** Grant reelected; Crédit Mobilier scandal emerges
- **1873** – Panic of 1873 ushers in severe economic depression
  – Supreme Court severely curtails Reconstruction in *Slaughter-House Cases*
- **1874** Sweeping Democratic gains in congressional elections
- **1875** – Whiskey Ring and other scandals undermine Grant administration
  – *Minor v. Happersett*: Supreme Court rules that Fourteenth Amendment does not extend voting rights to women
  – Beecher-Tilton scandal dominates headlines
- **1877** Rutherford B. Hayes becomes president; federal Reconstruction ends

1865 1870 1875 1880 1885 1890

THE STRUGGLE FOR NATIONAL RECONSTRUCTION

AP® EXAM TIP

Being able to analyze the battle between executive and legislative authority during Reconstruction is critical for success on the AP® Exam.

What factors explain how Reconstruction policies unfolded between 1865 and 1870, and what was the impact on different groups of Americans?

Congress clashed with President Johnson, in part, because the framers of the Constitution did not anticipate a civil war or provide for its aftermath. If Confederate states had legally left the Union when they seceded, then their reentry required action by Congress. If not — if even during secession they had retained U.S. statehood — then restoring them might be an administrative matter, best left to the president. Lack of clarity on this fundamental question made for explosive politics.

Ten Percent Plan
A plan proposed by President Abraham Lincoln during the Civil War, but never implemented, that would have granted amnesty to most ex-Confederates and allowed each rebellious state to return to the Union as soon as 10 percent of its voters had taken a loyalty oath and the state had approved the Thirteenth Amendment.

Wade-Davis Bill
A bill proposed by Congress in July 1864 that required an oath of allegiance by a majority of each state's adult white men, new governments formed only by those who had never taken up arms against the Union, and permanent disenfranchisement of Confederate leaders. The plan was passed but pocket vetoed by President Abraham Lincoln.

Presidential Approaches: From Lincoln to Johnson

As wartime president, Lincoln had offered a plan similar to Johnson's. It granted amnesty to most ex-Confederates and allowed each rebellious state to return to the Union as soon as 10 percent of its voters had taken a loyalty oath and the state had approved the Thirteenth Amendment, abolishing slavery. But even amid defeat, Confederate states rejected this **Ten Percent Plan** — an ominous sign for the future. In July 1864, Congress proposed a tougher substitute, the **Wade-Davis Bill**, that required an oath of allegiance by a majority of each state's adult white men, the creation of new governments formed only by those who had never taken up arms against the Union, and permanent disenfranchisement of Confederate leaders. Lincoln defeated the

452

TEACHING STRATEGY

The PBS companion site to *Slavery and the Making of America* provides the full text of Mississippi's 1865 Black Codes. The text is rather lengthy, so you could split students into groups to analyze and report on specific provisions that limited the freedom and equality of African Americans. To access this site, search "PBS 1865 Black Codes of Mississippi."

TEACHING STRATEGY

The Library of Congress's companion site to the *Reconstruction and Its Aftermath* exhibit provides an essay narrating major developments in the postwar experiences of African Americans with links to nearly two dozen related high-resolution images from the Library's collections. To access the site, search "Library of Congress Reconstruction and Its Aftermath."

Wade-Davis Bill with a pocket veto, leaving it unsigned when Congress adjourned. At the same time, he opened talks with key congressmen, aiming for a compromise.

On April 14, 1865, while watching a play at Ford's Theatre, Lincoln was assassinated by John Wilkes Booth. We will never know what would have happened had he lived. His death precipitated grief and political turmoil. As a special train bore the president's flag-draped coffin home to Illinois, thousands of Americans lined the railroad tracks in mourning. Furious and grief-stricken, many Unionists blamed all Confederates for the acts of southern sympathizer John Wilkes Booth and his accomplices in the murder. At the same time, Lincoln's death left the presidency in the hands of Andrew Johnson, a man utterly lacking in Lincoln's moral sense and political judgment.

Johnson was a self-styled "common man" from the hills of eastern Tennessee. Trained as a tailor, he built his political career on the support of farmers and laborers. Loyal to the Union, Johnson had refused to leave the U.S. Senate when Tennessee seceded. After federal forces captured Nashville in 1862, Lincoln appointed Johnson as Tennessee's military governor. In the election of 1864, placing this border-state War Democrat on the ticket with Lincoln had seemed a smart move, designed to promote unity. But after Lincoln's death, Johnson's disagreements with Republicans, combined with his belligerent and contradictory actions, wreaked political havoc.

Black Codes
Laws passed by southern states after the Civil War that denied ex-slaves the civil rights enjoyed by whites, punished vague crimes such as "vagrancy" or failing to have a labor contract, and tried to force African Americans back to plantation labor systems that closely mirrored those in slavery times.

AP® SKILLS & PROCESSES

COMPARISON

How did Lincoln and Johnson approach Reconstruction differently?

The new president and Congress confronted a set of problems that would have challenged even Lincoln. During the war, Unionists had insisted that rebel leaders were a small minority and most white southerners wanted to rejoin the Union. With even greater optimism, Republicans hoped the defeated South would accept postwar reforms. Ex-Confederates, however, resisted that plan through both violence and political action. New southern state legislatures, created under Johnson's limited Reconstruction plan, moved to restore slavery in all but name. In 1865, they enacted **Black Codes**, designed to force former slaves back to plantation labor. Like similar laws passed in other places after slavery ended, the codes reflected plantation owners' economic interests (see "America in the World," p. 454). They imposed severe penalties on blacks who did not hold full-year labor contracts and also set up procedures for taking black children from their parents and apprenticing them to former slave masters.

Faced with these developments, Johnson gave all the wrong signals. He had long talked tough against southern planters, but in practice he allied himself with ex-Confederate leaders, forgiving them when they appealed for pardons. White southern leaders were delighted. "By this wise and noble statesmanship," wrote a Confederate legislator, "you have become the benefactor of the Southern people." Northerners and freedmen were disgusted. The president had left Reconstruction "to the tender mercies of the rebels," wrote one Republican. An angry Union veteran in Missouri called Johnson "a traitor to the loyal people of the Union." Emboldened by Johnson's indulgence, ex-Confederates began to filter back into the halls of power. When Georgians elected Alexander Stephens, former vice president of the Confederacy, to represent them in Congress, many outraged Republicans saw this as the last straw.

Violence in New Orleans, Louisiana, 1866 Violence against freedmen revealed the lengths that some whites would go to maintain the South's prewar social and political order. In New Orleans, white and African American delegates gathered at the Mechanics Institute on July 30, 1866, to develop a new state constitution. John T. Monroe, a former New Orleans mayor and vocal white supremacist, led a mob of white men—including city police and ex-Confederate soldiers—to attack the convention. Shooting into the windows and then rushing into the building to beat and kill delegates, the mob massacred the largely unarmed delegates. In this image, delegates are shot as they try to flee at the back of the building. By the end of the day, 238 people were killed, including 40 delegates to the convention and at least 200 black Union veterans. The massacre provoked outrage in the North and contributed to the election of a more strongly Republican Congress, in November, which imposed military Reconstruction on the South. The New York Public Library/Art Resource, NY.

Congress Versus the President

Under the Constitution, Congress is "the judge of the Elections, Returns and Qualifications of its own Members" (Article 1, Section 5). Using this power, Republican majorities in both houses refused to admit southern delegations when Congress convened in December 1865, effectively blocking Johnson's program. Hoping to mollify Congress, some southern states dropped the most objectionable provisions from

AP® SKILLS & PROCESSES

COMPARISON

Students should start with a basic overview (such as what follows) and then buttress their broad assertion with specific historical evidence (in bullet points below — some of which detail Congressional plans). *For Lincoln, he never accepted that Southern states had left the Union; instead, he insisted that people in Southern states left the Union and therefore policies should be lenient, through the executive branch, with the idea of restoring the Union. Lincoln did imagine advancing the rights of former enslaved persons much more than President Johnson. Johnson's lenient policies and his efforts to frame Reconstruction debates around the notion of a "Constitution as it is, Union as it was" policy meant, in effect, he argued the only conditions needed for readmission were to accept the Thirteenth Amendment, swear allegiance to the United States, and have high-ranking Confederate officials appeal for pardon. President Johnson's policies enraged Radical Republicans to the extent that leaders in Congress worked around the president and enacted a much more advanced civil rights platform for Reconstruction:*

- *10% Plan*
- *13th Amendment*
- *14th Amendment*
- *Civil Rights Act of 1866*
- *Johnson's "Swing Around the Circle"*

TRM Find complete suggested responses in the Teacher's Resource Materials.

AP® THEME

NAT: American and National Identity; PCE: Politics and Power

Ask students: **What does this image reveal about the relationship between black postwar aspirations and whites' anger?** *The hopes of many blacks were precisely what angered and frightened southern whites. Many southern whites were adamantly opposed to blacks' participation in postwar governance. Many were armed and willing to use their weapons to massacre black elected officials.*

AP® SKILLS & PROCESSES

ANALYZING HISTORICAL EVIDENCE

For many students, the default model of plantation agriculture is the American South. Comparing similar emancipation patterns in the **AP® AMERICA IN THE WORLD** feature can help them recognize the distinctive features of American patterns. Haiti was a neighbor to the U.S., a former European colony, and had a society and economy based on African slave labor.

Labor Laws After Emancipation: Haiti and the United States

Many government officials agreed with former masters on the need to control rural workers. Often planters themselves or allied with the planter class, they believed that economic strength and public revenue depended on plantation export crops and that workers would not produce those without legal coercion.

This was true in the British Caribbean and also Haiti, which eventually, after a successful slave revolt ending in 1803, became an independent republic led by former slaves and, in particular, by propertied free men of color. In the passage below, a British observer describes a rural labor code adopted by Haiti's government in 1826. Despite the law, Haiti's large plantations did not revive; the island's economy, even more than that of the U.S. South, came to be dominated by small-scale, impoverished farmers.

The Code of Laws before us is one that could only have been framed by a legislature composed of proprietors of land, having at their command a considerable military power, of which they themselves were the leaders; for a population whom it was necessary to compel to labour....

The choice of a master, altho' expressly reserved to the labourer, is greatly modified by the clauses which restrain the labourer from quitting the section of country to which he belongs; and from the absence of any clause compelling proprietors to engage him; so that the cultivator must consent to bind himself to whomsoever may be willing to engage him, or remain in prison, to be employed among convicts....

The Code begins (Article 1) by declaring Agriculture to be the foundation of national prosperity; and then decrees (Article 3), That all persons, excepting soldiers, and civil servants of the State, professional persons, artizans, and domestic servants, shall cultivate the soil. The next clause (Article 4), forbids the inhabitants of the country quitting it to dwell in towns or villages; and every kind of wholesale or retail trade is forbidden (Article 7) to be exercised by persons dwelling in the country.

Further articles stipulate that any person dwelling in the country, not being the owner or occupier of land, and not having bound himself in the manner directed, ... shall be considered a vagabond, be arrested, and taken before a Justice, who, after reading the Law to him, shall commit him to jail, until he consent to bind himself according to law.

... Those who are hired from a job-master [labor agent], ... are entitled to receive half the produce, after deducting the expences of cultivation; [those who are bound to the proprietor directly], one-fourth of the gross produce of their labour.... Out of their miserable pittance, these Haitian labourers are to provide themselves and their children with almost every thing, and to lay by a provision for old age....

These, with the regulations already detailed, clearly shew what is intended to be the condition of the labouring population of Haiti. I must not call it slavery; the word is objectionable; but few of the ingredients of slavery seem to be wanting.

QUESTIONS FOR ANALYSIS

1. Compare this Haitian law with the Black Codes briefly adopted by ex-Confederate states, and with the sharecropping system that evolved in the United States during Reconstruction (p. 453). What did these labor systems — or proposed systems — have in common? How did they differ? Support your reasoning with evidence from the source and the chapter.
2. Why would the Haitian government, led by men of color, enact such laws? What social conditions other than race might have shaped their views, and why?

TRM Find complete suggested responses in the Teacher's Resource Materials.

TEACHING STRATEGY

For a follow-up video on the Civil Rights Bill of 1866, have students watch a short video by historian Eric Foner on Gilder-Lehrman's AP Web site (ap.gilderlehrman.org). The Civil Rights Bill of 1866 provides a good historical context for students as they study the early events in Reconstruction.

Freedmen's Bureau
Government organization created in March 1865 to aid displaced blacks and other war refugees. Active until the early 1870s, it was the first federal agency in history that provided direct payments to assist those in poverty and to foster social welfare.

Civil Rights Act of 1866
Legislation passed by Congress that nullified the Black Codes and affirmed that African Americans should have equal benefit of the law.

their Black Codes. But at the same time, racial violence against African Americans erupted in various parts of the South.

Congressional Republicans concluded that the federal government had to intervene. Back in March 1865, Congress had established the **Freedmen's Bureau** to aid displaced blacks and other war refugees. In early 1866, Congress voted to extend the bureau, gave it direct funding for the first time, and authorized its agents to investigate southern abuses. Even more extraordinary was the **Civil Rights Act of 1866**, which declared formerly enslaved people to be citizens and granted them equal protection and rights of contract, with full access to the courts.

These bills provoked bitter conflict with Johnson, who vetoed them both. Johnson's racism, hitherto publicly muted, now blazed forth: "This is a country for white men, and by God, as long as I am president, it shall be a government for white men." Galvanized, Republicans in Congress gathered two-thirds majorities and overrode both vetoes, passing the Civil Rights Act in April 1866 and the Freedmen's Bureau law four months later. Their resolve was reinforced by continued upheaval in the South. In addition to the violence in Memphis, twenty-four black political leaders and their allies in Arkansas were murdered and their homes burned.

Anxious to protect freedpeople and reassert Republican power in the South, in June 1866 Congress took further measures to sustain civil rights. In what became the **Fourteenth Amendment** (ratified in July 1868), it declared that "all persons born or naturalized in the United States" were citizens. No state could abridge "the privileges or immunities of citizens of the United States"; deprive "any person of life, liberty, or property, without due process of law"; or deny anyone "equal protection." In a stunning assertion of federal power, the Fourteenth Amendment declared that when people's essential rights were at stake, national citizenship henceforth took priority over citizenship in a state.

Johnson opposed ratification, but public opinion had swung against him. In the 1866 congressional elections, voters gave Republicans a 3-to-1 majority in Congress. Power shifted to the so-called **Radical Republicans**, who sought sweeping transformations in the defeated South. The Radicals' leader in the Senate was Charles Sumner of Massachusetts, the fiery abolitionist who in 1856 had been nearly beaten to death by South Carolina congressman Preston Brooks. Radicals in the House followed Thaddeus Stevens of Pennsylvania, a passionate advocate of freedmen's political and economic rights. With such men at the fore, and with congressional Republicans now numerous and united enough to override Johnson's vetoes on many questions, Congress proceeded to remake Reconstruction.

Radical Reconstruction

The **Reconstruction Act of 1867**, enacted in March, divided the conquered South into five military districts, each under the command of a U.S. general (Map 14.1). To reenter the Union, former Confederate states had to grant the vote to freedmen and deny it to leading ex-Confederates. The military commander of each district was required to register all eligible adult males, black as well as white; supervise state constitutional conventions; and ensure that new constitutions guaranteed black suffrage. Congress would readmit a state to the Union once these conditions were met and the new state legislature ratified the Fourteenth Amendment. Johnson vetoed the Reconstruction Act, but Congress overrode his veto (Table 14.1).

The Impeachment of Andrew Johnson In August 1867, Johnson fought back by "suspending" Secretary of War Edwin M. Stanton, a Radical, and replacing him with Union general Ulysses S. Grant, believing Grant

Fourteenth Amendment
Constitutional amendment ratified in 1868 that made all native-born or naturalized persons U.S. citizens and prohibited states from abridging the rights of national citizens, thus giving primacy to national rather than state citizenship.

Radical Republicans
The members of the Republican Party who were bitterly opposed to slavery and to southern slave owners since the mid-1850s. With the Confiscation Act in 1861, Radical Republicans began to use wartime legislation to destroy slavery.

AP® SKILLS & PROCESSES

DEVELOPMENTS AND PROCESSES
Under what circumstances did the Fourteenth Amendment win passage, and what problems did its authors seek to address?

Reconstruction Act of 1867
An act that divided the conquered South into five military districts, each under the command of a U.S. general. To reenter the Union, former Confederate states had to grant the vote to freedmen and deny it to leading ex-Confederates.

VISUAL ACTIVITY

"We Accept the Situation" This 1867 *Harper's Weekly* cartoon refers to the Military Reconstruction Act of 1867, which instructed ex-Confederate states to hold constitutional conventions and stipulated that the resulting constitutions must provide voting rights for black men. The cartoonist was Thomas Nast (1840–1902), one of the most influential artists of his era. Nast first drew "Santa Claus" in his modern form, and it was he who began depicting the Democratic Party as a rebellious donkey and Republicans as an elephant — suggesting (since elephants are supposed to have good memories) their long remembrance of the Civil War and emancipation. Library of Congress, 3c31562.

READING THE IMAGE: This cartoon hints at white northerners' views of both ex-Confederates and emancipated slaves. What is the point of view of the artist regarding both groups? What historical events might be related to this cartoon?

MAKING CONNECTIONS: What is the artist's purpose in creating this cartoon? Who is the intended audience? Why?

CHECK FOR UNDERSTANDING

Ask students: **Why did Congress and President Johnson clash over Reconstruction, and what was the outcome?** *Johnson was a racist opposed to equality for African Americans, but congressional Republicans were committed to supporting the Freedmen's Bureau and the Civil Rights Act, while opposing southern Black Codes. The congressional elections of 1866 gave Republicans overwhelming majorities, which allowed them to override Johnson's vetoes.*

AP® SKILLS & PROCESSES

DEVELOPMENTS AND PROCESSES

For students to successfully answer the **DEVELOPMENTS AND PROCESSES** question, it is crucial for them to recognize that, given continued resistance to ending slavery even among many northern members of Congress, achievement of the Fourteenth Amendment was only possible under particular historical circumstances. Some students may also need to be reminded how the amendment process works.

TRM Find complete suggested responses in the Teacher's Resource Materials.

AP® THEME

NAT: American and National Identity; PCE: Politics and Power

Ask students: **What does this image suggest about some white northerners' understanding of the postwar situation in the South?** *The title "We Accept the Situation" is ironic because the body language and scowl of the ex-Confederate suggests anger and resentment. He seems to still be wearing his uniform, suggesting that the war is not yet over for him and, perhaps, that he might still be willing to fight. In contrast, the freedman could not be happier to vote, despite his humble circumstances.*

To extend your discussion of Thomas Nast's cartoons, access nine more high-resolution images of the Reconstruction at the PBS's companion site to *Reconstruction: The Second Civil War.* To access the site, search "PBS Reconstruction Thomas Nast."

TRM Find complete suggested responses in the Teacher's Resource Materials.

AP® THEME

NAT: American and National Identity; PCE: Politics and Power

Guide students' analysis of **MAP 14.1** with the following questions:

- **What range of time was the duration of military occupation after the readmission of each state?** *Republicans began oversight of Virginia in 1870 and lost control the same year; Florida, Louisiana, Mississippi, and South Carolina were all governed from 1868 to 1877.*
- **Why are military districts remarkable in the context of the American political tradition?** *Military rule is the antithesis of free republican institutions and suggests the seriousness of white defiance and the commitment of Radical Republicans to dramatic social change.*

AP® APPLY THE TIP

Show students the excerpt from the movie *Lincoln* that depicts Lincoln in conversation with Thaddeus Stevens in the kitchen to highlight the division between the president and Radical Republicans on the issue of equal rights for African Americans. (Search "The Compass" on YouTube or show the clip from the DVD.) Have students identify the ideas on which Lincoln and Stevens agree and disagree. Then ask students to complete **Handout 14.2 — Contextualization: Understanding Thaddeus Stevens (TRM)** with a partner. Lead a class discussion on the successes of Radical Republicans and the reasons for their eventual failure to maintain their achievements.

TRM Find **Handout 14.2 — Contextualization: Understanding Thaddeus Stevens** in the Teacher's Resource Materials.

TEACHING STRATEGY

Part of the story of Reconstruction is the process by which Congress empowered itself to enforce the Reconstruction Amendments — 13, 14, and 15 — with appropriate legislation. Have students use Section 2 (13) Section 5 (14) and Section 2 (15) to examine the extent to which Congress enforced the provisions of the amendment.

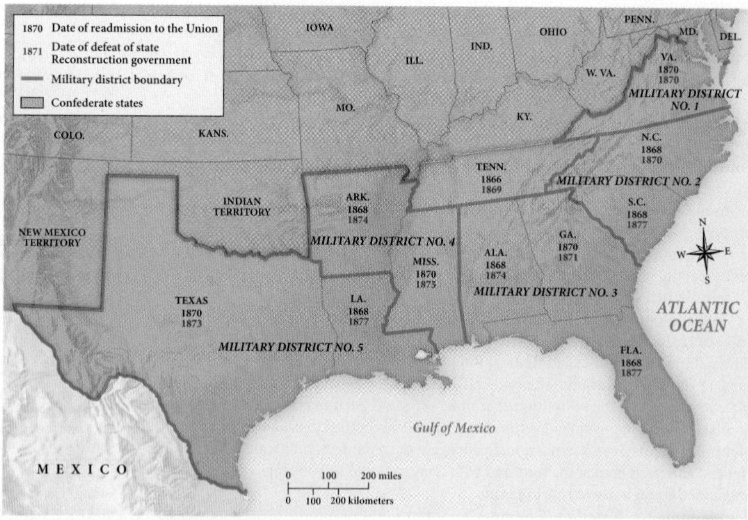

MAP 14.1 Reconstruction

The federal government organized the Confederate states into five military districts during congressional Reconstruction. For the states shown in this map, the first date indicates when that state was readmitted to the Union; the second date shows when Republicans lost control of the state government. All the ex-Confederate states rejoined the Union between 1868 and 1870, but the periods of Radical government varied widely. Republicans lasted only a few months in Virginia; they held on until the end of Reconstruction in Louisiana, Florida, and South Carolina.

AP® EXAM TIP

Recognizing the short-term successes of Radical Republicans in opening opportunities for African Americans is critical on the AP® Exam.

would be a good soldier and follow orders. Johnson, however, had misjudged Grant, who publicly objected to the president's machinations. When the Senate overruled Stanton's suspension, Grant — now an open enemy of Johnson — resigned so Stanton could resume his place as secretary of war. On February 21, 1868, Johnson formally dismissed Stanton. The feisty secretary of war responded by barricading himself in his office, precipitating a crisis.

Three days later, for the first time in U.S. history, legislators in the House of Representatives introduced articles of impeachment against the president, employing their constitutional power to charge high federal officials with "Treason, Bribery, or other high Crimes and Misdemeanors." The House serves, in effect, as the prosecutor in such cases, and the Senate serves as the court. The Republican majority brought eleven counts of misconduct against Johnson, most relating to infringement of the powers of Congress. In May, after an eleven-week trial in the Senate, thirty-five senators voted for conviction — one vote short of the two-thirds majority required. Twelve Democrats and seven Republicans voted for acquittal. The dissenting Republicans felt that removing a president for defying Congress was too damaging to the constitutional system of checks and balances. But despite the president's acquittal, Congress had shown its power. For the brief months remaining in his term, the discredited Johnson was largely irrelevant.

Election of 1868 and the Fifteenth Amendment The impeachment controversy made Grant, already the Union's greatest war hero, a Republican idol as well. He easily won the party's presidential nomination in 1868. Although he supported congressional

TABLE 14.1

Primary Reconstruction Laws and Constitutional Amendments

Law (Date of Congressional Passage)	Key Provisions
Thirteenth Amendment (December 1865*)	Prohibited slavery
Civil Rights Act of 1866 (April 1866)	Defined citizenship rights of freedmen
	Authorized federal authorities to bring suit against those who violated those rights
Fourteenth Amendment (June 1866†)	Established national citizenship for persons born or naturalized in the United States
	Prohibited the states from depriving citizens of their civil rights or equal protection under the law
	Reduced state representation in House of Representatives by the percentage of adult male citizens denied the vote
Reconstruction Act of 1867 (March 1867)	Divided the South into five military districts, each under the command of a Union general
	Established requirements for readmission of ex-Confederate states to the Union
Tenure of Office Act (March 1867)	Required Senate consent for removal of any federal official whose appointment had required Senate confirmation
Fifteenth Amendment (February 1869‡)	Forbade states to deny citizens the right to vote on the grounds of race, color, or "previous condition of servitude"
Ku Klux Klan Act (April 1871)	Authorized the president to use federal prosecutions and military force to suppress conspiracies to deprive citizens of the right to vote and enjoy the equal protection of the law

* Ratified by three-fourths of all states in December 1865.
† Ratified by three-fourths of all states in July 1868.
‡ Ratified by three-fourths of all states in March 1870.

Reconstruction, Grant also urged sectional reconciliation. His Democratic opponent, former New York governor Horatio Seymour, almost declined the nomination because he understood that Democrats could not yet overcome the stain of disloyalty. Grant won by an overwhelming margin, receiving 214 out of 294 electoral votes. Republicans retained two-thirds majorities in both houses of Congress.

In February 1869, following this smashing victory, Republicans produced the era's last constitutional amendment, the Fifteenth, protecting male citizens' right to vote irrespective of race, color, or "previous condition of servitude." Despite Radical Republicans' protests, the amendment left room for a poll tax (paid for the privilege of voting) and literacy requirements. Both were concessions to northern and western states that sought such provisions to keep immigrants and the "unworthy" poor from the polls. Congress required the four ex-Confederate states that remained under federal control to ratify the measure as a condition for readmission to the Union. A year later, the **Fifteenth Amendment** became law.

Passage of the Fifteenth Amendment, despite its limitations, was an astonishing feat. Elsewhere in the Western Hemisphere, lawmakers had left emancipated slaves in a condition of semi-citizenship, with no voting rights. But, like almost all Americans, congressional Republicans had extraordinary faith in the power of the vote. Many African Americans agreed. "The colored people of these Southern states have cast their lot with the Government," declared a delegate to Arkansas's constitutional convention, "and with the great Republican Party.... The ballot is our only means of protection." In the election of 1870, hundreds of thousands of African American men voted across the South, in an atmosphere of collective pride and celebration.

AP® EXAM TIP

The relationship between the Thirteenth, Fourteenth, and Fifteenth Amendments as expansion of the rights of African Americans is important to know on the AP® Exam.

Fifteenth Amendment
Constitutional amendment ratified in 1870 that forbade states to deny citizens the right to vote on grounds of race, color, or "previous condition of servitude."

AP® SKILLS & PROCESSES

DEVELOPMENTS AND PROCESSES

How and why did federal Reconstruction policies evolve between 1865 and 1870?

AP® SKILLS & PROCESSES

ANALYZING HISTORICAL EVIDENCE

TABLE 14.1 offers a compendium of remarkable achievements by Congress in the Reconstruction era. All of the items on the list represent significant extensions of federal power. Ask students to identify specifically how the acts on the list increased federal authority at the expense of the states.

AP® APPLY THE TIP

Provide each student with a copy of a political cartoon related to the Thirteenth, Fourteenth, or Fifteenth Amendments. Suggested cartoons include: "The First Vote" by Thomas Nast, "Worse Than Slavery" by Thomas Nast, "XVth Amendment," "This is a White Man's Government," and others available from the *Harper's Weekly* Web site. Be sure to provide a variety of cartoons from multiple perspectives. Then ask students to analyze the political cartoon to illustrate the artist's point of view, the historical context of the cartoon, the intended audience of the cartoon, and the purpose of the cartoon (this is good practice for students in the skill of sourcing documents). Next, group students so that they can share their analysis of the cartoon with classmates who looked at a different cartoon. Ask groups to discuss each cartoon individually and then to look at the cartoons as a group.

AP® SKILLS & PROCESSES

DEVELOPMENTS AND PROCESSES

The **DEVELOPMENTS AND PROCESSES** question asks students to identify two different issues: how Reconstruction policies changed over time and why these policies changed. The second question is crucial, as Radical Reconstruction policies were so dramatic and unprecedented. Extend this prompt by asking students to identify the features that remained consistent throughout the Reconstruction policies.

TRM Find complete suggested responses in the Teacher's Resource Materials.

CHECK FOR UNDERSTANDING

Ask students: **What was Radical Reconstruction?** *Radical Reconstruction represented an effort to provide full equality for black Americans, including voting rights, in southern states. To achieve this goal, Congress split the former Confederacy into five military districts and ruled through the armed forces to impose its will.*

AP® THEME

SOC: Social Structures

In poking fun at women's efforts to vote, this image also played on racist stereotypes of the era. The Irishman and free black man mock the would-be suffragist, who, like the Chinese man, is locked out of a room that — the cartoonist seems to suggest — ought to be accessible to her before being opened to these men. Many white suffrage advocates had been born in the U.S. and watched recent immigrants and former slaves obtain the vote before themselves, which was improper in their view.

PBS's companion site to *Not for Ourselves Alone: The Story of Elizabeth Cady Stanton and Susan B. Anthony* provides a variety of sources for students to learn more about the life and work of these famous reformers through their own writings and speeches, a biographical article, and critical essays by noted scholars. The site also provides lesson plans and lists of related sites, recommended reading, and links to related organizations that provide information about women's history. To access the site, search "PBS Not for Ourselves Alone."

"Out in the Cold" Though many women, including African American activists in the South, went to the polls in the early 1870s to test whether the new Fourteenth Amendment had given them the vote, federal courts subsequently rejected women's voting rights. Only Wyoming and Utah territories fully enfranchised women. At the same time, revised naturalization laws allowed immigrant men of African descent — though not of Asian descent — to become citizens. With its crude Irish, African, and Chinese racial caricatures, this 1884 cartoon from the humor magazine *The Judge* echoes the arguments of some white suffragists: though men of races stereotyped as inferior had been enfranchised, white women were not. The woman knocking on the door is also a caricature, with her harsh appearance and masculine hat. Library of Congress, LC-USZC4-4119.

Women's Rights Denied

Passage of the Fifteenth Amendment was a bittersweet victory for national women's rights leaders, who had campaigned for the ballot since the Seneca Falls Convention of 1848. They hoped to secure voting rights for women and African American men at the same time. As Elizabeth Cady Stanton put it, women could "avail ourselves of the strong arm and the blue uniform of the black soldier to walk in by his side." The protected categories for voting in the Fifteenth Amendment could have read "race, color, *sex*, or previous condition of servitude." But that word proved impossible to obtain.

Why did women not get voting rights during Reconstruction? For Republican policymakers in Washington, enfranchising black men had clear benefits. It punished ex-Confederates and ensured Republican support in the South. But women's party loyalties were more divided, and a substantial majority of northern voters — all men, of course — opposed women's enfranchisement. Even Radicals feared that this "side issue" would overburden their program. Influential abolitionists such as Wendell Philips refused to campaign for women's suffrage, fearing it would detract from the focus on black men's voting rights. Philips criticized women's leaders for being "selfish." "Do you believe," Stanton hotly replied, "the African race is entirely composed of males?"

By May 1869, the former allies were at an impasse. At a convention of the Equal Rights Association, abolitionist and women's rights advocate Frederick Douglass pleaded for white women to consider the situation in the South and allow black men's suffrage to take priority. "When women, because they are women, are hunted down, . . . dragged from their homes and hung upon lamp posts," Douglass said, "then they will have an urgency to obtain the ballot equal to our own." Some women's suffrage leaders joined Douglass in backing the Fifteenth Amendment without the word *sex*. But many, especially white women, rejected Douglass's plea. One African American woman remarked that these women "all go for sex, letting race occupy a minor position." Embittered, Elizabeth Cady Stanton lashed out against the enfranchisement of uneducated freedmen and immigrants, while educated white women were barred from the polls. Douglass's resolution in support of the Fifteenth Amendment failed, and the convention broke up.

American Woman Suffrage Association
A women's suffrage organization led by Lucy Stone, Henry Blackwell, and others who remained loyal to the Republican Party, despite its failure to include women's voting rights in the Reconstruction amendments. Stressing the urgency of voting rights for African American men, AWSA leaders held out hope that once Reconstruction had been settled, it would be women's turn.

National Woman Suffrage Association (NWSA)
A suffrage group headed by Elizabeth Cady Stanton and Susan B. Anthony that stressed the need for women to lead organizations on their own behalf. The NWSA focused exclusively on women's rights — sometimes denigrating men of color in the process — and took up the battle for a federal women's suffrage amendment.

A rift thus opened in the women's movement. The majority, led by Lucy Stone, reconciled themselves to disappointment. Organized into the **American Woman Suffrage Association**, they remained loyal to the Republican Party in hopes that once Reconstruction had been settled, it would be women's turn. A group led by Elizabeth Cady Stanton and Susan B. Anthony struck out in a new direction. They saw correctly that, once the Reconstruction amendments had passed, women's suffrage was unlikely in the near future. Stanton declared that woman "must not put her trust in man." The new organization she headed, the **National Woman Suffrage Association (NWSA)**, focused exclusively on women's rights and took up the battle for a federal suffrage amendment.

In 1873, NWSA members decided to test the new constitutional amendments that had passed. Suffragists all over the United States, including some African American women in the South, tried to register and vote. Most were turned away. In an ensuing lawsuit, suffrage advocate Virginia Minor of Missouri argued that the registrar who denied her a ballot had violated her rights under the Fourteenth Amendment. In ***Minor v. Happersett*** (1875), the Supreme Court dashed such hopes. It ruled that suffrage rights were not inherent in citizenship; women were citizens, but state legislatures could deny women the vote if they wished.

Women's rights advocates began to focus narrowly on suffrage as their movement suffered backlash from controversies over sexual freedom. After Victoria Woodhull, a flamboyant young woman from Ohio, became the nation's first female stockbroker on Wall Street, she won notoriety by denouncing marriage as a form of tyranny. She urged that women be "trained like men," for independent thought and economic self-sufficiency. Particularly sensational was Woodhull's insistence, in a speech in New York in 1871, that "I am a free lover. I have an inalienable, constitutional, and natural right to love whom I may, to love as long or as short a period as I can; to change that love every day if I please."

Victoria Woodhull Free-love advocate Victoria Woodhull became a controversial figure in the 1870s as she campaigned for universal voting rights, denounced marriage laws for enslaving women, and urged women to work for economic independence. Here, Woodhull and her sister Tennessee Claflin attempt to vote in New York in 1875—seeking, like other women's rights advocates, to trigger legal challenges over their right to do so. Like others, Woodhull and Claflin were turned away from the polls. In 1872 Woodhull had run as the first woman candidate for president on the Equal Rights ticket. Kean Collection/Hulton Archive/Getty Images.

Woodhull helped trigger the Beecher-Tilton scandal, a sensational trial that dominated headlines in the mid-1870s. She accused Brooklyn Congregationalist minister Henry Ward Beecher, a staunch Republican and abolitionist from a famous reform family, of secretly being a free lover himself. For making this allegation of adultery, Woodhull was tried on obscenity charges and briefly jailed. Beecher was then sued by the husband of the congregant with whom he had allegedly had an affair. The results of the trial were inconclusive, but the relentless publicity, including the publication of intimate letters, damaged the reputation of everyone involved. Many Americans concluded that Radical Republicans wanted to go too far, and that, in private, former abolitionists like Beecher and his congregants were behaving immorally. Social conservatives, including ex-Confederates in the South, gleefully watched leading abolitionists get their come-uppance. Women's rights advocates, who had welcomed Victoria Woodhull as an ally, soon distanced themselves from her free love proclamations. Leaders such as Susan B. Anthony decided that the only way to win the vote was to practice and advocate strict sexual respectability.

Despite these defeats and embarrassments, Radical Reconstruction had created the conditions for a nationwide women's rights movement. Some argued for suffrage as part of a broader expansion of democracy. Others, on the contrary, saw white women's votes as a possible counterweight to the votes of African American or Chinese men (while opponents pointed out that black and immigrant women would likely be enfranchised, too). When Wyoming Territory gave women full voting rights in 1869, its governor received telegrams of congratulation from around the world. Afterward, contrary to dire predictions, female voters in Wyoming did not appear to neglect their homes, abandon their children, or otherwise "unsex" themselves. Enfranchisement for Utah women followed in 1870, and referenda for women's suffrage appeared regularly on state ballots in the decades that followed. Women's voting rights had become a serious issue for national debate.

Minor v. Happersett
A Supreme Court decision in 1875 that ruled that suffrage rights were not inherent in citizenship and had not been granted by the Fourteenth Amendment, as some women's rights advocates argued. Women were citizens, the Court ruled, but state legislatures could deny women the vote if they wished.

AP® EXAM TIP

Evaluate the impact of the Fourteenth and Fifteenth Amendments on the women's rights movement in the late nineteenth century.

AP® SKILLS & PROCESSES

MAKING CONNECTIONS

Abolitionists and women's suffrage advocates were generally close allies before 1865. What divisions emerged during Reconstruction and why?

TEACHING STRATEGY

The *Smithsonian* magazine provides an article detailing Woodhull's 1872 campaign for president. The article includes a Thomas Nast depiction of Woodhull as the devil, embedded links to documents by Woodhull, and additional contextual information about women's political aspirations in the postwar era. To access the article, search "Smithsonian Victoria Woodhull."

AP® APPLY THE TIP

Women's rights reformers had long sought to advance the goals of abolitionists and many other social and political reformers throughout the early-to-mid-nineteenth century. Though women generally supported the abolitionist movement, the movement itself split in 1840 over the issue of women's rights. That historical continuity—of African American rights and women's rights creating fissures in reform movements—was also seen with the passage of the Fourteenth and Fifteenth Amendments. Women's reformers were especially bothered by the universal aspect of the Fourteenth and Fifteenth Amendments because they felt many women were more than qualified to participate and were again being denied political equality. The Fourteenth and Fifteenth Amendments complicated reform movements and left many women disappointed by the decision of reformers in Congress to focus solely on race.

AP® SKILLS & PROCESSES

MAKING CONNECTIONS

The **MAKING CONNECTIONS** question asks students to explain change over time: two groups of people who had been closely aligned diverged over time. To extend this prompt, ask students to explain why race ultimately trumped sex in the extension of civil rights in the Reconstruction era. Students could consider why the outcome wasn't reversed, why both groups couldn't achieve victory simultaneously, and the conclusions they can draw about the rate or nature of political or social change at the time.

TRM Find complete suggested responses in the Teacher's Resource Materials.

CHECK FOR UNDERSTANDING

Ask students: **What factors explain how reconstruction policies unfolded between 1865 and 1870, and what was the impact on different groups of Americans?** *The central determinant on Reconstruction policy was the power of the president relative to that of Congress. Under President Andrew Johnson, Reconstruction was fairly lenient and former Confederates were able to effectively recreate the antebellum South, albeit without slavery. Once the midterm elections of 1866 gave Republicans 3-to-1 control of Congress, they were able to assume control of Reconstruction, as Radicals were able to override Johnson's vetoes. Radical Reconstruction was much harsher on former Confederates and, at least legally, was more beneficial to freedpeople.*

TEACHING STRATEGY

Radical Republicans defined the defeated South in varying terms. Lincoln said they were "out of their normal relation," Thaddeus Stevens said they were "conquered provinces," and Charles Sumner claimed the states in rebellion had committed "state suicide." Ask students to define the relationship between the definitions of the South and the goals Republicans had for Reconstruction.

AP® APPLY THE TIP

Provide students with a copy of the 1994 response to the editor of the *New York Times* by historian Eric Foner entitled "'40 Acres' Promise to Blacks Was Broken" (available online). Ask students to identify Foner's historical argument and the evidence he uses to make the argument. Next, provide students with excerpts from Thaddeus Stevens on land redistribution and the Special Field Order 15 by William T. Sherman. Ask students to read and analyze the arguments and goals for land redistribution to African Americans in the South. Then ask students to answer the following questions:

- **What role did landownership play in ideas about citizenship and rights throughout American history?** *Throughout American development, ownership of land had a direct connection to the idea of being a citizen; before popularization of universal suffrage in the early nineteenth century, landownership was required for suffrage; land was equated with power and authority and the ability to protect one's rights as a citizen; "American Dream."*
- **How were the goals and arguments of Sherman and Stevens similar? How were they different?** *Both argue for land redistribution and punishment of southern planters; they differ on the philosophy — Stevens emphasizes rights of African Americans and egalitarian land redistribution; Sherman emphasizes practical management of freed slaves who were following his army at great cost and ensuring power of federal government over the planter class in the South.*
- **What impact did the policies of Johnson have on political power in the South?** *Johnson's policies returned land to previous plantation owners, stripping any possibility of land redistribution to former slaves.*

THE MEANING OF FREEDOM

What goals were southern freedmen and freedwomen able to achieve in the post–Civil War years, and why? What goals were they not able to achieve, and why not?

While political leaders wrangled in Washington, emancipated slaves acted on their own ideas about freedom. Emancipation meant many things: the end of punishment by the lash; the ability to move around and make choices of work and residence; reunion of families; and opportunities to build schools and churches and to publish and read newspapers. Foremost among freedpeople's demands were voting rights and economic autonomy. Former Confederates opposed these goals. Most southern whites believed the proper place for blacks was as "servants and inferiors," as a Virginia planter testified to Congress. Mississippi's governor, elected under President Johnson's plan, vowed that "ours is and it shall ever be, a government of white men." Meanwhile, as Reconstruction unfolded, it became clear that on economic questions, southern blacks and northern Republican policymakers did not see eye to eye.

The Quest for Land

After resettlement became the responsibility of the Freedmen's Bureau, thousands of rural blacks hoped for land distributions. But Johnson's amnesty plan, which allowed pardoned Confederates to recover property seized during the war, blasted such hopes. In October 1865, for example, Johnson ordered General Oliver O. Howard, head of the Freedmen's Bureau, to restore plantations on South Carolina's Sea Islands — so-called Sherman lands, which the Union Army had allotted to freedpeople — to prior white property holders. Dispossessed blacks protested. "Why do you take away our lands?," one group demanded. "You take them from us who have always been true, always true to the Government! You give them to our all-time enemies! That is not right!" Led by black Union veterans they resisted efforts to evict them, fighting pitched battles with former slaveholders and bands of ex-Confederate soldiers. But white landowners, sometimes aided by federal troops, generally prevailed.

AP® EXAM TIP

Evaluate the importance of land ownership as a key to African American self-sufficiency and the continued political power of southern plantation owners.

Freed Slaves and Northerners: Conflicting Goals As the Sea Islands struggle revealed, freedmen in the South and Republicans in Washington seriously differed on questions of land and labor. The economic revolution of the antebellum period had transformed New England and the Mid-Atlantic states. Believing similar development could revolutionize the South, most congressional leaders sought to restore cotton as the country's leading export, and they envisioned former slaves as wageworkers on cash-crop plantations, not independent farmers. Only a handful of Republican leaders, like Thaddeus Stevens, argued that freed slaves had earned a right to land grants, through what Lincoln had referred to as "four hundred years of unrequited toil." Stevens proposed that southern plantations be treated as "forfeited estates of the enemy" and broken up into small farms for those who had survived slavery. "Nothing will make men so industrious and moral," Stevens declared, "as to let them feel that they are above want and are the owners of the soil which they till."

Today, most historians of Reconstruction agree with Stevens: policymakers did not do enough to ensure freedpeople's economic security. Without land, former slaves were left poor and vulnerable. At the time, though, Stevens had few allies. A deep veneration for private property lay at the heart of his vision, but others interpreted the same principle differently: they defined ownership by legal title, not by labor invested. Though often accused of harshness toward the defeated Confederacy, most Republicans — even Radicals — could not imagine "giving" land to former slaves. The same congressmen, of course, had no difficulty granting homesteads on frontier lands that the nation had taken from Indians. But they were deeply reluctant to confiscate white-owned plantations.

Some southern Republican state governments did try, without much success, to use tax policy to break up large landholdings and get them into the hands of poorer whites and blacks. In 1869, South Carolina established a land commission to buy property and resell it on easy terms to the landless; about 14,000 black families acquired farms through the program. But such initiatives were the exception, not the rule. Over time, some rural blacks did succeed in becoming small-scale landowners, especially in Upper South states such as Virginia, North Carolina, and Tennessee. But it was an uphill fight, and policymakers provided little aid.

Wage Labor and Sharecropping Without land, most freedpeople had few options but to work for former slave owners. Landowners wanted to retain the old gang-labor system, with wages replacing the food, clothing, and shelter that slaves had once received. Southern planters — who had recently scorned the North for the cruelties of the wage labor system — now embraced wage work with apparent satisfaction. Maliciously comparing black workers to free-roaming pigs, landowners told them to "root, hog, or die." Former slaves found themselves with rock-bottom wages; it was a shock to find that emancipation and "free labor" did not prevent a hardworking family from nearly starving.

African American workers used a variety of tactics to fight back. As early as 1865, alarmed whites across the South reported that their formerly enslaved neighbors were holding mass meetings to agree on "plans and terms for labor." Such meetings continued through the Reconstruction years. Facing limited prospects at home, some workers left the fields and traveled long distances to seek better-paying jobs on the railroads or in turpentine and lumber camps. Others — from rice cultivators to laundry workers — organized strikes.

At the same time, struggles raged between employers and freedpeople over women's work. In slavery, African American women's bodies had been the sexual property of white men. Protecting black women from such abuse, as much as possible, was a crucial priority for freedpeople. When planters demanded that black women go back into the fields, African Americans resisted resolutely. "I seen on some plantations," one freedman recounted, "where the white men would . . . tell colored men that their wives and children could not live on their places unless they work in the fields. The colored men [answered that] whenever they wanted their wives to work they would tell them themselves." Resisting age-old assumptions about husbands' legal and economic power over their wives, which some African American men now adopted, some black women asserted their independence and headed their own households, though this was often a matter of necessity rather than choice. For many freedpeople, the opportunity for a stable family life was one of the greatest achievements of emancipation. Many enthusiastically accepted the northern ideal of domesticity. Missionaries, teachers, and editors of black newspapers urged men to work diligently and support their families, and they told women (though many worked for wages) to devote themselves to motherhood and the home.

Even in rural areas, former slaves refused to work under conditions that recalled slavery. There would be no gang work, they vowed: no overseers, no whippings, no regulation of their private lives. Across the South, planters who needed labor were forced to yield to what one planter termed the "prejudices of the freedmen, who desire to be masters of their own time." In a few areas, waged work became the norm — for example, on the giant sugar plantations of Louisiana financed by northern capital. But cotton planters lacked money to pay wages, and sometimes, in lieu of a wage, they offered a share of the crop. Freedmen, in turn, paid their rent in shares of the harvest.

Thus the Reconstruction years gave rise to a distinctive system of cotton agriculture known as sharecropping, in which freedmen worked as renters, exchanging their labor for the use of land, house, implements, and sometimes seed and fertilizer. Sharecroppers typically turned over half of their crops to the landlord

AP® EXAM TIP

The impact of the sharecropping system on both African Americans and poor whites in the South is important to know for the AP® Exam.

AP® APPLY THE TIP

Direct students to use the text on pp. 461–463 to complete **Handout 14.3 — Causation: Sharecropping (TRM)**. After completing the handout, lead a class discussion on the impact of sharecropping on the South for African Americans and poor whites. Elaborate by comparing the sharecropping system to the system of tenant farming, which allowed for farmers to rent land rather than engage in the crop-lien system. Ask students to consider the long-term impact on the South as a region and compare this period of development in the South to the rapid industrialization the Civil War brought to the North (Chapter 13).

TRM Find **Handout 14.3 — Causation: Sharecropping** in the Teacher's Resource Materials.

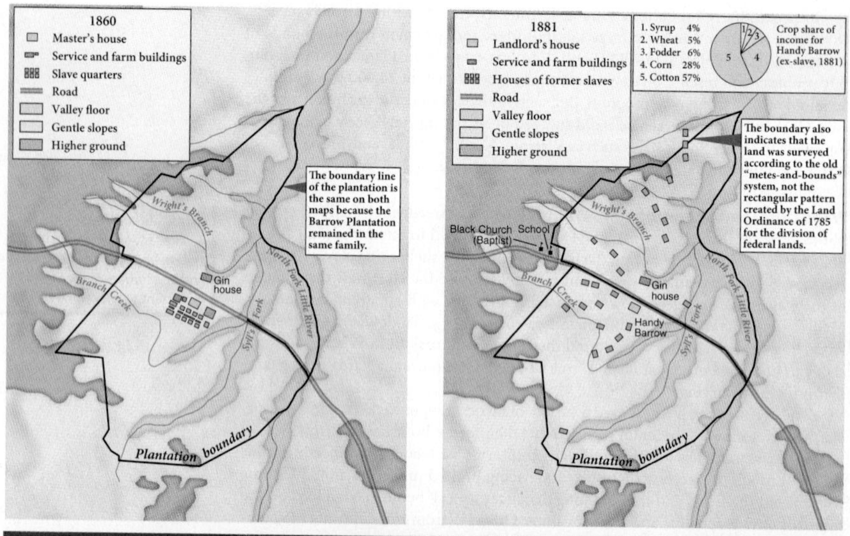

MAPPING THE PAST

MAP 14.2 The Barrow Plantation, 1860 and 1881
This map is a modern redrawing of one that first appeared in the popular magazine *Scribner's Monthly* in April 1881, accompanying an article about the Barrow plantation. The surname *Barrow* was common among the sharecropping families, which means almost certainly that they had been slaves who, years after emancipation, continued to call the plantation home.

ANALYZING THE MAP: Compare the buildings in which members of this community lived and worked in 1860 with those in 1881. What new structures had arisen? What does their existence and location suggest?

MAKING CONNECTIONS: Compare the residential patterns of 1860 with those of sharecroppers in 1881. Based on your reading of this chapter, why do you think these patterns changed the way they did?

AP® THEME

WXT: Work, Exchange, and Technology

MAP 14.2 indicates both the continuities and the changes in labor systems under a plantation with slave labor and in a sharecropping arrangement. Guide students' analysis of this map with the following questions:

- **How does the Barrow Plantation remain the same between 1860 and 1881?** *The boundaries of the plantation remain the same, shaped by natural features like higher ground and creeks, and determined by legal title. The plantation house remains at the center of the plantation, and the gin house is still nearby. There is still only a single road running through the plantation.*
- **How does the plantation change?** *The former slave cabins are more dispersed and, perhaps, somewhat larger. A few are placed outside the bounds of the plantation. A black church and a black school have been added to the 1881 map. Though no indication of crops is provided for 1860, the diversity of crops in 1881 — with cotton making up just over half of the product — seems likely greater than in the earlier period.*
- **What is the significance of those continuities and changes?** *The changes suggest freedpeople's greater autonomy; they no longer live under the direct supervision of the planter, and some technically live outside the plantation. The church and school suggest the importance of community and aspirations for education. The Barrow property remains a plantation and their family home continues to dominate the landscape.*

TRM Find complete suggested responses in the Teacher's Resource Materials.

(Map 14.2). In a credit-starved agricultural region that grew crops for the world economy, sharecropping was an effective strategy, enabling laborers and landowners to share risks and returns. But it was a very unequal relationship. Starting out penniless, sharecroppers had no way to make it through the first growing season without borrowing for food and supplies. They thus started out in debt and often stayed there.

Country storekeepers, bankrolled by northern suppliers, often served as middlemen who furnished sharecroppers with provisions and took as collateral a lien on the crop, effectively assuming ownership of croppers' shares and leaving them only what remained after debts had been paid. **Crop-lien laws** enforced lenders' ownership rights to the crop share. Once indebted at a store, sharecroppers became easy targets for exorbitant prices, unfair interest rates, and crooked bookkeeping. As cotton prices declined in the 1870s, more and more sharecroppers fell into permanent debt. If the merchant was also the landowner or conspired with the landowner, debt became a pretext for forced labor, or peonage.

crop-lien laws
Nineteenth-century laws that enforced lenders' rights to a portion of harvested crops as repayment for debts. Once they owed money to a country store, sharecroppers were trapped in debt and became targets for unfair pricing.

Sharecropping arose in part because it was a good fit for cotton agriculture. Cotton, unlike sugarcane, could be raised efficiently by small farmers (provided they had the lash of indebtedness always on their backs). We can see this in the experience of other regions that became major producers in response to the global cotton shortage set off by the Civil War. In India, Egypt, Brazil, and West Africa, variants of the sharecropping system emerged. Everywhere international merchants and bankers, who put up capital, insisted on passage of crop-lien laws. Indian and Egyptian villagers ended up, like their American counterparts, permanently under the thumb of furnishing merchants.

By 1890, three out of every four black farmers in the South were tenants or sharecroppers; among white farmers, the ratio was one in three. For freedmen, sharecropping was not the worst choice, in a world where former masters threatened to impose labor conditions that were close to slavery. But the costs were devastating. With farms leased on a year-to-year basis, neither tenant nor owner had much incentive to improve the property. The crop-lien system rested on expensive interest payments — money that might otherwise have gone into agricultural improvements or to meet human needs. And sharecropping committed the South inflexibly to cotton, a crop that generated the cash required by landlords and furnishing merchants. The result was a stagnant farm economy that blighted the South's future. As Republican governments tried to remake the region, they confronted not only wartime destruction but also the failure of their hopes that ending slavery would create a modern, prosperous South, built in the image of the industrializing North. Instead, the South's rural economy remained mired in widespread poverty and based on an uneasy compromise between landowners and laborers.

Picking Cotton in Mississippi After emancipation most African Americans in the South, lacking land or capital, continued to work in agriculture. Through sharecropping and other arrangements, they sought as much autonomy and control over their work as they could obtain. Many families made it a priority for women to work in the home and children to attend school. At harvest time, however, everyone was needed in the fields. The Granger Collection, New York.

AP® SKILLS & PROCESSES

CAUSATION

Why did sharecropping emerge, and how did it affect freedpeople and the southern economy?

Republican Governments in the South

Between 1868 and 1871, all the former Confederate states met congressional stipulations and rejoined the Union. Protected by federal troops, Republican administrations in these states retained power for periods ranging from a few months in Virginia to nine years in South Carolina, Louisiana, and Florida. Southern Reconstruction state governments remain some of the most misunderstood institutions in all U.S. history. Ex-Confederates never accepted their legitimacy. Many other whites agreed, focusing particularly on the role of African Americans who began to serve in public office. "It is strange, abnormal, and unfit," declared one British visitor to Louisiana, "that a *negro* Legislature should deal . . . with the gravest commercial and financial interests." During much of the twentieth century, historians echoed such critics, condemning Reconstruction leaders as ignorant and corrupt. These historians shared the racial prejudices of the British observer: black men were simply unfit to govern.

In fact, Reconstruction governments were ambitious. They were hated in part because they undertook impressive reforms in public education, social services, commerce, and transportation. Like their northern allies, southern Republicans admired the economic and social transformations that had occurred in the North before the Civil War and worked energetically to import them. During Reconstruction, opportunities for free public education expanded greatly, across racial lines, for southern children. Some southern cities developed streetcar systems, installed streetlights for safety, and offered free smallpox vaccines.

AP® EXAM TIP

As you read through this section, trace the political opportunities and successes of African Americans during Radical Reconstruction.

CHECK FOR UNDERSTANDING

Ask students: **What was the outcome of freedpeople's quest for land?** *Congressional leaders generally refused to accept the notion that freedpeople had earned the right to land through what Lincoln called their "unrequited toil." As a result, other than a few wartime experiments, plantation land was not confiscated and distributed to former slaves. Without land, they could not earn an independent living and were mostly forced into sharecropping.*

AP® SKILLS & PROCESSES

CAUSATION

Start students off by having them explain the definition of structural racism. Students should work through a definition of sharecropping that explains how it is an example of structural racism. Through this process, students should include an explanation that accounts for the emergence of sharecropping.

TRM Find complete suggested responses in the Teacher's Resource Materials.

AP® APPLY THE TIP

To engage students in a discussion of changing interpretations of Reconstruction, provide each student with **Handout 14.4 — Analyzing Historical Evidence: Reconstruction (TRM)** and ask them to identify the historical argument of each historian, providing evidence that supports or challenges their interpretations of the Reconstruction era. Next, lead a discussion on the use of contextualization to provide possible explanations for the differences in interpretation of the successes and failures of Reconstruction. To supplement this discussion, consider using Eric Foner's essay "Why Reconstruction Matters," which is a wonderful resource for introducing or concluding lessons or units of study on the Civil War and Reconstruction. To access this essay, search "NYT Foner Why Reconstruction Matters."

TRM Find **Handout 14.4 — Analyzing Historical Evidence: Reconstruction** in the Teacher's Resource Materials.

Hiram R. Revels In 1870, Hiram Rhodes Revels (1827–1901) was elected to the U.S. Senate from Mississippi to fill Jefferson Davis's former seat. Revels was a free black from North Carolina who had moved to the North and attended Knox College in Illinois. During the Civil War he had recruited African Americans for the Union army and, as an ordained Methodist minister, served as chaplain of a black regiment in Mississippi, where he settled after the war.
The Granger Collection, New York.

Changes in family law were particularly notable. The link between slavery and patriarchy was strong: on the eve of the Civil War, South Carolina was the only state in the Union where divorce was completely unavailable. During Reconstruction, changes in southern state laws made it easier for both white and African American women to obtain a divorce based on a husband's abandonment or physical or sexual abuse. Some formerly enslaved women sued white men who had fathered their children during slavery, and courts ordered the men to pay child support. Reconstruction governments also recognized the integrity of African American families, protecting children from being forcibly apprenticed to white employers.

Southern Republicans included former Whigs, a few former Democrats, black and white newcomers from the North, and southern African Americans. From the start, its leaders faced the dilemma of racial prejudice. In the upcountry, white Unionists were eager to join the party but sometimes reluctant to work with black allies. In most areas, however, the Republicans also depended on strong support for African Americans, who constituted a majority of registered voters in Alabama, Florida, South Carolina, and Mississippi.

For a brief moment in the late 1860s, black and white Republicans joined forces through the Union League, a secret fraternal order. Formed in border states and northern cities during the Civil War, the league became a powerful political association that spread through the former Confederacy. Functioning as a grassroots wing of Radical Republicanism, Union League members pressured Congress to uphold justice for freedpeople. After blacks won voting rights, the league organized meetings at churches and schoolhouses to instruct freedmen on political issues and voting procedures. League clubs held parades and military drills, giving a public face to the new political order. At the same time, black women and northern allies worked together in the Freedmen's Aid movement, funding schools and sending teachers and much-needed supplies to help formerly enslaved families build economic security.

The federal Freedmen's Bureau also supported grassroots Reconstruction efforts. Though some bureau officials sympathized with planters, most were dedicated, idealistic men who tried valiantly to reconcile opposing interests. Bureau men kept a sharp eye out for unfair labor contracts and often forced landowners to bargain with workers and tenants. They advised freedmen on economic matters; provided direct payments to desperate families, especially women and children; and helped establish schools. In cooperation with northern aid societies, the bureau played a key role in founding African American colleges and universities such as Fisk, Tougaloo, and the Hampton Institute. These institutions, in turn, focused on training teachers. By 1869, more than three thousand teachers were instructing freedpeople in the South, and more than half were themselves African Americans.

Ex-Confederates viewed the Union League, Freedman's Aid movement, Freedmen's Bureau, and Republican Party as illegitimate forces in southern affairs, and they resented the political education of freedpeople. They referred to southern whites who supported Reconstruction as scalawags — an ancient Scots-Irish term for worthless animals — and denounced northern whites as carpetbaggers, self-seeking interlopers who carried all their property in cheap suitcases called carpetbags. Such labels glossed over the actual diversity of white Republicans. Many new arrivals from the North, while motivated by personal profit, also brought capital and skills.

TEACHING STRATEGY

Help familiarize students with the concept of the disparate groups of citizens who were committed to expanding opportunities — political, social, economic, and educational — for African Americans in the South after the Civil War. Students can make a mind map, where they create an illustration, to represent their understanding of the various groups supporting African Americans. Remind students the basic commonality is they were Republican. After that, students should think through carpetbaggers, scalawags, Union League, and Freedmen's Bureau. Detailing each group enables students to see the broad spectrum of support in the South for African Americans by Republicans in the years after the Civil War.

TEACHING STRATEGY

Primary source accounts of African Americans expressing their political and social agency after the Civil War are great pieces of historical evidence for students to examine. Have students go to and read the Jourdan Anderson letter from 1865. Ask students to read the letter, highlighting the sections where Anderson illustrates his sense of agency. Copies of the letter are available in the public domain.

Interspersed with ambitious schemers were reformers hoping to advance freedmen's rights. So-called scalawags were even more varied. Some southern Republicans were former slave owners, including those like sugarcane planters who benefited from Republican tariffs. Others were ex-Whigs or even ex-Democrats who hoped to attract northern capital. But most hailed from the backcountry and wanted to rid the South of its slaveholding aristocracy, believing slavery had victimized whites as well as blacks.

Southern Democrats' contempt for black politicians, whom they regarded as ignorant field hands, was just as misguided as their stereotypes about white Republicans. Many African American leaders in the South came from the ranks of antebellum free blacks. Others were skilled men like Robert Smalls of South Carolina, who in slavery had worked for wages that he turned over to his master. Smalls, a steamer pilot in Charleston harbor, had become a war hero when he escaped with his family and other slaves and brought his ship to the Union navy. Buying property in Beaufort after the war, Smalls became a state legislator and later a congressman. Blanche K. Bruce, another formerly enslaved political leader, had been tutored on a Virginia plantation by his white father; during the war, he escaped and established a school for freedmen in Missouri. In 1869, he moved to Mississippi and became, five years later, Mississippi's second black U.S. senator. Political leaders such as Smalls and Bruce were joined by northern blacks — including ministers, teachers, and Union veterans — who moved south to support Reconstruction.

During Radical Reconstruction, such men fanned out into plantation districts and recruited freedmen to participate in politics. Literacy helped Thomas Allen, a Baptist minister and shoemaker, win election to the Georgia legislature. "The colored people came to me," Allen recalled, "and I gave them the best instructions I could. I took the *New York Tribune* and other papers, and in that way I found out a great deal, and I told them whatever I thought was right." Though never proportionate to their numbers in the population, blacks became officeholders across the South. In South Carolina, African Americans constituted a majority in the lower house of the legislature in 1868. Over the course of Reconstruction, twenty African Americans served in state administrations as governor, lieutenant governor, secretary of state, or lesser offices. More than six hundred became state legislators, and sixteen were congressmen.

Both white and black Republicans had big plans. Their southern Reconstruction governments eliminated property qualifications for the vote and abolished Black Codes. Their new state constitutions expanded the rights of married women in the ways that northern states had done before the Civil War, enabling them to own property and wages — "a wonderful reform," one white woman in Georgia wrote, for "the cause of Women's Rights." Like their counterparts in the North, southern Republicans also believed in using government to foster economic growth. Seeking to diversify the economy beyond cotton agriculture, they poured money into railroads and other projects.

In myriad ways, Republicans brought southern state and city governments up to date. They outlawed corporal punishments such as whipping and branding. They established hospitals and asylums for orphans and the disabled. South Carolina offered free public health services, while Alabama provided free legal representation for defendants who could not pay. Some municipal governments paved streets and installed streetlights. Petersburg, Virginia, established a board of health that offered free medical care during the smallpox epidemic of 1873. Nashville, Tennessee, created soup kitchens for the poor.

Most impressive of all were achievements in public education, where the South had lagged woefully. Republicans viewed education as the foundation of a true democratic order. By 1875, over half of black children were attending school in Mississippi, Florida, and South Carolina. African Americans of all ages rushed to the newly

TEACHING STRATEGY

Despite the rhetoric of southern politicians about the abilities of Radical Republicans and African Americans, political progress occurred in the southern region under the direction of Republicans and African Americans. Have students explain at least three specific ways progress was made by the efforts of these two groups.

AP® SKILLS & PROCESSES

CONTEXTUALIZATION

This is a good point in the chapter to work on the skill of Contextualization. Start by giving students a broad historical process such as regionalism, which helps explain the regional character of Reconstruction and helps students focus on one particular part of the country to explain broader processes. Students need to marshal at least two specific pieces of historical evidence to explain how regionalism helps explain the broader context of Reconstruction. If students are struggling to develop specific evidence, think about providing a brief list such as: 14th Amendment, Radical Republicans, Freedmen's Bureau, Union League, Civil Rights Act of 1866, carpetbaggers, and freedmen.

established schools, even when they had to pay tuition. They understood why slaveholders had criminalized slave literacy: the practice of freedom rested on the ability to read newspapers, labor contracts, history books, and the Bible. A school official in Virginia reported that freedpeople were "*crazy* to learn." One Louisiana man explained why he was sending his children to school, even though he needed their help in the field. It was "better than leaving them a fortune; because if you left them even five hundred dollars, some man having more education than they had would come along and cheat them out of it all." Thousands of white children, particularly girls and the sons of poor farmers and laborers, also benefitted from new public education systems. Young white women's graduation from high school, an unheard-of occurrence before the Civil War, became a celebrated event in southern cities and towns.

Southern Reconstruction governments also had their flaws — weaknessess that became more apparent as the 1870s unfolded. In the race for economic development, for example, state officials allowed private companies to hire out prisoners to labor in mines and other industries, in a notorious system known as **convict leasing**. Corruption was rife and conditions horrific. In 1866, Alabama's governor leased 200 state convicts to a railroad construction company for the grand total of $5. While they labored to build state-subsidized lines such as the Alabama and Chattanooga, prisoners were housed at night in open, rolling cages. Physical abuse was common, sexual violence against women rampant, and medical care nonexistent. At the start of 1869, Alabama counted 263 prisoners available for leasing;

convict leasing
Notorious system, begun during Reconstruction, whereby southern state officials allowed private companies to hire out prisoners to labor under brutal conditions in mines and other industries.

Miners in Coal Creek, Tennessee Like many other southerners, Welsh coal miners in Tennessee took advantage of new economic opportunities in the industrializing postwar South. They began coal mining in Anderson County in 1867 but soon found themselves challenged by the expansion of convict leasing, whereby state prisoners were hired out cheaply to private companies that used them to build railroads and work in quarries and mines under brutal conditions. In Tennessee, the convict leasing system eventually crowded out free miners and led to the so-called Coal Creek War of 1893, in which Welsh American miners protested against competition and intervened to set convict miners free. After subduing the revolt, Tennessee decided to abolish convict labor. Courtesy of Tennessee State Library and Archives.

CHECK FOR UNDERSTANDING

Ask students: **What features characterized Republican governments in the South?** *They had ambitious plans to reform southern city and state laws to outlaw harsh punishment, establish a social support network, increase health, and establish schools. For a short period of time, there was collaboration between black and white Republicans, especially through the Union League, which led to some blacks being elected to office. White racism quickly undermined this cooperation, while examples of Republican corruption reduced their credibility.*

TEACHING STRATEGY

Use the photo on p. 466 as the backdrop for a bell-ringer activity. Students should use the photo and the information they have read to answer the following question: To what extent was the South able to emerge as the "New South" in the decades following the Civil War?

by the end of the year, a staggering 92 of them had died. While convict leasing expanded greatly in later decades, it began during Reconstruction, supported by both Republicans and Democrats.

Building Black Communities

African Americans had built networks of religious worship and mutual aid during slavery, but these operated largely in secret. After emancipation, southern blacks engaged in open community building. In doing so, they cooperated with northern missionaries and teachers, both black and white, who came to help in the great work of freedom. "Ignorant though they may be, on account of long years of oppression, they exhibit a desire to hear and to learn, that I never imagined," reported African American minister Reverend James Lynch, who traveled from Maryland to the Deep South. "Every word you say while preaching, they drink down and respond to, with an earnestness that sets your heart all on fire."

Independent churches quickly became central community institutions, as blacks across the South left white-dominated congregations, where they had sat in segregated balconies, and built churches of their own. These churches joined their counterparts in the North to become denominations of national scope, including most prominently the National Baptist Convention and African Methodist Episcopal Church. Black churches served not only as sites of worship but also as schools, social centers, and meeting halls. Ministers were often political spokesmen as well. As Charles H. Pearce, a black Methodist pastor in Florida, declared, "A man in this State cannot do his whole duty as a minister except he looks out for the political interests of his people." Religious leaders articulated the special destiny of freedpeople as the new "Children of Israel."

The flowering of black churches, schools, newspapers, and civic groups was one of the most enduring initiatives of the Reconstruction era. Dedicated teachers and charity leaders embarked on a project of "race uplift" that never ceased thereafter, while black entrepreneurs were proud to build businesses that served their communities.

AP® SKILLS & PROCESSES

MAKING CONNECTIONS

What policies did southern Reconstruction legislators pursue, and what needs of the postwar South did they seek to serve?

AP® EXAM TIP

The importance of black churches to African American communities before and after the Civil War is a key pattern to understand for the AP® Exam.

Freedmen's School, Petersburg, Virginia, 1870s A Union veteran, returning to Virginia in the 1870s to photograph battlefields, captured this image of an African American teacher and her students at a freedmen's school. Note the difficult conditions in which they study: many are barefoot, and there are gaps in the walls and floor of the school building. Nonetheless, the students have a few books. Despite poverty and relentless hostility from many whites, freedpeople across the South were determined to get a basic education for themselves and their children. William L. Clements Library, University of Michigan.

AP® SKILLS & PROCESSES

MAKING CONNECTIONS

The **MAKING CONNECTIONS** question asks students to consider Reconstruction-era legislation in the context of postwar conditions. It might be helpful for students to categorize these conditions in terms of political, economic, and social factors. They may also need help to recognize the level of resistance Reconstruction legislators faced in implementing progressive policies. To extend this prompt, students could explain why corruption emerged under these circumstances, and what impact it had on legislators' overall Reconstruction goals.

TRM Find complete suggested responses in the Teacher's Resource Materials.

TEACHING STRATEGY

Reconstruction was a combination of small successes and major disappointments for African Americans. This photo illustrates one of the bright spots of Reconstruction: education. Since literacy had been forbidden to slaves, freedpeople eagerly sought to educate their children, even at the cost of losing their valuable labor when their economic status was so tenuous. Assign Brundage's essay "Reconstruction and the Formerly Enslaved" to highlight major questions that Reconstruction raised, followed by an extensive guide to student discussion, and a summary of major historiographical debates about Reconstruction. To access this essay, search "Brundage Reconstruction and the Formerly Enslaved."

Fisk Jubilee Singers, 1873 Fisk University in Nashville, Tennessee, was established in 1865 to provide higher education for African Americans from across the South. When funds ran short in 1871, enterprising students formed the Jubilee Singers choral group (bottom) and toured to raise money for the school. They performed African American spirituals and folk songs, such as "Swing Low, Sweet Chariot," arranged in ways that appealed to white audiences, making this music nationally popular for the first time. In 1872, the group performed for President Grant at the White House. Money raised by this acclaimed group saved Fisk from bankruptcy and built the university's imposing Jubilee Hall (top). Private Collection/© Look and Learn/Illustrated Papers Collection/Bridgeman Images.

The issue of desegregation — sharing public facilities with whites — was trickier. Though some black leaders pressed for desegregation, they were keenly aware of the backlash it was likely to provoke. Others made it clear that they preferred their children to attend all-black schools, especially if they encountered hostile or condescending white teachers and classmates. Many had pragmatic concerns. Asked whether she wanted her boys to attend an integrated school, one woman in New Orleans said no: "I don't want my children to be pounded by . . . white boys. I don't send them to school to fight, I send them to learn." Separate black schools also offered much-needed jobs for African American teachers and principals.

At the national level, congressmen wrestled with these issues as they debated an ambitious civil rights bill championed by Radical Republican senator Charles Sumner. Sumner first introduced his bill in 1870, seeking to enforce, among other things, equal access to schools, public transportation, hotels, and churches. Due to a series of defeats and delays, the bill remained on Capitol Hill for five years. Opponents charged that shared public spaces would lead to race mixing and intermarriage. Some sympathetic Republicans feared a backlash, while others questioned whether, because of the First Amendment, the federal government had the right to regulate churches. On his deathbed in 1874, Sumner exhorted a visitor to remember the civil rights bill: "Don't let it fail." In the end, the Senate removed Sumner's provision for integrated churches, and the House removed the clause requiring integrated schools. But to honor the great Massachusetts abolitionist, Congress passed the **Civil Rights Act of 1875**. The law required "full and equal" access to jury service and to transportation and public accommodations, irrespective of race. It was the last such act for almost a hundred years — until the Civil Rights Act of 1964.

Civil Rights Act of 1875
A law that required "full and equal" access to jury service and to transportation and public accommodations, irrespective of race.

THE UNDOING OF RECONSTRUCTION

Why and how did federal Reconstruction policies falter in the South?

The year of Sumner's death, 1874, marked the waning of Radical Reconstruction. Through both government action and grassroots efforts, it had accomplished more than anyone dreamed a few years earlier. But a chasm had opened between the goals of freedmen, who wanted autonomy, and policymakers, whose first priorities were to reincorporate ex-Confederates into the nation and build a powerful national economy. Meanwhile, the North was flooded with one-sided, racist reports such as James M. Pike's influential book *The Prostrate State* (1873), which claimed South Carolina was in the grip of "black barbarism." Events of the 1870s deepened the northern public's disillusionment. Scandals rocked the Grant administration, and an economic depression curbed both private investment and public spending.

AP® SKILLS & PROCESSES

MAKING CONNECTIONS

Compare the results of African Americans' community building with their struggles to obtain better working conditions. What links do you see between these efforts?

TEACHING STRATEGY

The persistence of racism meant that freedpeople continued to face barriers to achieving an education, especially at the college level. While a few institutions provided education for blacks before the Civil War, the number of black colleges grew during Reconstruction. To explore historically black colleges and universities further, assign students to read "The History of HBCUs in America," an essay from American RadioWorks. The first section provides helpful information about the context and development of the first black colleges in the Reconstruction era. To access the essay, search "American RadioWorks HBCU history."

CHECK FOR UNDERSTANDING

Ask students: **What goals were southern freedmen and freedwomen able to achieve in the post– Civil War years, and why? What goals were they not able to achieve, and why not?** *In the years immediately after the Civil War, when support for Radical Reconstruction was at its height, southern freedwomen and freedmen were able to achieve much advancement largely as a result of the military support of U.S. forces, which inhibited retribution from disgruntled Southern whites. The most prominent of these achievements were in education, politics, infrastructure, civil rights, and the building of distinct black communities. One goal that was unobtainable during this period was economic self-sufficiency, as the ravaged Southern economy did not have enough space for wage earners outside sharecropping and tenant farming, which in many ways replicated the antebellum system without the legality of chattel slavery.*

AP® SKILLS & PROCESSES

MAKING CONNECTIONS

The **MAKING CONNECTIONS** question invites students to compare two different elements of blacks' attempts to improve their circumstances — creating community and improving working conditions. Students could additionally explain reasons for blacks' greater relative success in establishing thriving independent communities than in bettering their labor conditions.

TRM Find complete suggested responses in the Teacher's Resource Materials.

At the same time, northern resolve was worn down by continued ex-Confederate resistance and violence. Only full-scale military intervention could reverse the situation in the South, and by the mid-1870s the North had no willpower to renew the occupation.

The Republicans Unravel

Republicans had banked on economic growth to underpin their ambitious program, but their hopes were dashed in 1873 by the sudden onset of a severe worldwide depression. After both Germany and the United States ceased coining silver as money, the global economy slowed. In September 1873, leading financier Jay Cooke tried to sell millions of dollars of bonds issued by the Northern Pacific Railroad but could not find buyers. Both Cooke's firm and the railroad went bankrupt. Since Cooke's supervision of Union finances during the Civil War had made him a national hero, his downfall was a shock. As dozens of railroads and businesses failed over the next year, officials in the Grant administration rejected pleas to increase the money supply and provide relief from debt and unemployment. Amid the depression, Republicans' allegiance to bankers and big business began to show.

AP® EXAM TIP

Evaluate the impact of waning Northern resolve to implement change in the South on the gradual loss of rights for African Americans.

The impact of the depression varied in different parts of the United States, but everywhere conditions were grim. Farmers suffered a terrible plight as crop prices plunged, while industrial workers faced layoffs and sharp wage reductions. Within a year, 50 percent of American iron manufacturing stopped. By 1877, half the nation's railroad companies had filed for bankruptcy. Workers facing unemployment and severe wage cuts participated in mass protests, including a railroad strike that spread nationwide. Rail construction halted. With hundreds of thousands thrown out of work, people took to the road. Wandering "tramps," who camped by railroad tracks and knocked on doors to beg for work and food, terrified prosperous Americans, who feared the breakdown of social and economic order.

In addition to discrediting Republicans, the depression directly undercut their policies, most dramatically in the South. The ex-Confederacy was still recovering from the ravages of war, and its new economic and social order remained fragile. The bold policies of southern Republicans — for education, public health, and grants to railroad builders — cost a great deal of money. Federal support, through programs like the Freedmen's Bureau, had begun to fade even before 1873. Republicans had anticipated major infusions of northern and foreign investment capital; for the most part, these failed to materialize. Investors who had sunk money into Confederate bonds, only to have those repudiated, were especially wary of supporting southern enterprise. The South's economy grew more slowly than Republicans had hoped, and after 1873, it screeched to a halt. State debts mounted rapidly, and as crushing interest on bonds fell due, public credit collapsed.

Great Railroad Strike Amid a desperate economic depression that started in 1873, a strike against the hated Pennsylvania Railroad led to an attack on the Union Depot in Pittsburgh, Pennsylvania. Here, the aftermath of violence shows, in the foreground, the wreck of the railroad superintendent's luxury palace car. Such bitter conflicts, along with the distress and dislocation caused by the depression, distracted northerners' attention from the South and caused well-to-do northerners to take a strong antilabor stance, reducing their sympathy for the struggles of African American workers in the South.
Carnegie Museum of Art/Historic Pittsburgh.

TEACHING STRATEGY

Use the photo on p. 469 for a bell-ringer activity. Ask students the following question: To what extent did the political fatigue of northerners over Reconstruction policies worsen because economic turmoil in the northern states in 1877?

Not only had Republican officials failed to anticipate a severe depression; during the era of generous spending, considerable funds had also been wasted or had ended up in the pockets of corrupt officials. Two swindlers in North Carolina, one of them a former Union general, were found to have distributed more than $200,000 in bribes and loans to legislators to gain millions in state funds for rail construction. Instead of building railroads, they used the money to travel to Europe and speculate in stocks and bonds. Not only Republicans were on the take. "You are mistaken," wrote one southern Democrat to a northern friend, "if you suppose that all the evils . . . result from the carpetbaggers and negroes. The Democrats are leagued with them when anything is proposed that promises to pay." In South Carolina, when African American congressman Robert Smalls was convicted of taking a bribe, the Democratic governor pardoned him in exchange for an agreement that federal officials would drop an investigation of Democratic election fraud.

One of the depression's most tragic results was the collapse of the Freedman's Savings and Trust Company. This private bank, founded in 1865, had worked closely with the Freedmen's Bureau and Union army across the South. Former slaves associated it with the party of Lincoln, and thousands responded to northerners' call for thrift and savings by bringing their small deposits to the nearest branch. African American farmers, entrepreneurs, churches, and charitable groups opened accounts at the bank. But in the early 1870s, the bank's directors sank their money into risky loans and speculative investments. In June 1874, the bank failed.

Some Republicans believed that, because the bank had been so closely associated with the U.S. Army and federal agencies, Congress had a duty to step in. Even one southern Democrat argued that the government was "morally bound to see to it that not a dollar is lost." But in the end, Congress refused to compensate the 61,000 depositors. About half recovered small amounts — averaging $18.51 — but the others received nothing. The party of Reconstruction was losing its moral gloss.

classical liberalism
The political ideology of individual liberty, private property, a competitive market economy, free trade, and limited government. The ideal is a *laissez faire* or "let alone" policy in which government does the least possible, particularly in reference to economic policies such as tariffs and incentives for industrial development. Attacking corruption and defending private property, late-nineteenth-century liberals generally called for elite governance and questioned the advisability of full democratic participation.

As a result of the depression and rising criticism of Radicals' ambitious goals, a revolt emerged in the Republican Party. It was led by influential intellectuals, journalists, and businessmen who believed in **classical liberalism**: free trade, small government, low property taxes, and limitation of voting rights to men of education and property. Liberals responded to the massive increase in federal power, during the Civil War and Reconstruction, by urging a policy of *laissez faire*, in which government "let alone" business and the economy. In the postwar decades, laissez faire advocates never succeeded in ending federal policies such as the protective tariff and national banking system (see "The Emergence of the Labor Movement" in Chapter 16), but their arguments helped roll back Reconstruction. Unable to block Grant's renomination for the presidency in 1872, the dissidents broke away and formed a new party under the name Liberal Republican. Their candidate was Horace Greeley, longtime publisher of the *New York Tribune* and veteran reformer and abolitionist. The Democrats, still in disarray, also nominated Greeley, notwithstanding his editorial diatribes against them. A poor campaigner, Greeley was assailed so severely that he said, "I hardly knew whether I was running for the Presidency or the penitentiary."

Grant won reelection overwhelmingly, capturing 56 percent of the popular vote and every electoral vote. Yet Liberal Republicans had shifted the terms of debate. The agenda they advanced — smaller government, restricted voting rights, and reconciliation with ex-Confederates — resonated with Democrats, who had long advocated limited government and were working to reclaim their status as a legitimate national party. Liberalism thus crossed party lines, uniting disillusioned conservative Republicans with Democrats who denounced government activism. E. L. Godkin of *The Nation* and other classical liberal editors played key roles in turning northern public opinion against Reconstruction. With unabashed elitism, Godkin and others claimed that freedmen (and women also) were unfit to vote. They denounced universal suffrage, which "can only mean in plain English the government of ignorance and vice."

The second Grant administration gave liberals plenty of ammunition. The most notorious scandal involved **Crédit Mobilier**, a sham corporation set up by shareholders in the Union Pacific Railroad to secure government grants at an enormous profit. Organizers of the scheme protected it from investigation by providing gifts of Crédit Mobilier stock to powerful members of Congress. The *New York Sun* broke news of the scandal in September 1872, amid Grant's reelection campaign; it tainted both Vice President Schuyler Colfax (who was not running for reelection) and Grant's new running mate, Henry Wilson. After the election, Congress censured two leading Republican congressmen who had profited from the scheme. In 1875, another scandal emerged involving the so-called Whiskey Ring, a network of liquor distillers and treasury agents who defrauded the government of millions of dollars of excise taxes on whiskey. The ringleader was Grant's private secretary, Orville Babcock. Others went to prison, but Grant stood by Babcock, possibly perjuring himself to save his secretary from jail. The stench of scandal permeated the White House.

"Grantism" During his second term of office, President Grant was lampooned for the problems of his scandal-ridden administration. Here, the humor magazine *Puck* shows Grant barely defying gravity to keep himself and his corrupt subordinates aloft and out of jail. He hangs from a "third term" bar because many predicted that the Republican party would nominate him yet again in 1876. Due in large part to the administration's scandals, this did not happen, but the Union war hero nonetheless remained personally popular. Library of Congress, 3g05606.

Counterrevolution in the South

While northerners became preoccupied with scandals and the hardships of the economic depression, ex-Confederates seized power in the South. Most believed (as northern liberals had also begun to argue) that southern Reconstruction governments were illegitimate "regimes." Led by the planters, ex-Confederates staged a massive insurgency to take back the South. When they could win at the ballot box, southern Democrats took that route. They got ex-Confederate voting rights restored and campaigned against "negro rule." But when force was necessary, southern Democrats used it. Present-day Americans, witnessing political violence in other countries, seldom remember that our own history includes the overthrow of elected governments by paramilitary groups. But this is exactly how Reconstruction ended in many parts of the South. Ex-Confederates terrorized Republicans, especially in districts with large proportions of black voters. Black political leaders were shot, hanged, beaten to death, and in one case even beheaded (see "Firsthand Accounts," p. 472). Many Republicans, both black and white, went into hiding or fled for their lives. Southern Democrats called this violent process "Redemption" — a heroic name that still lingers today, even though this seizure of power was murderous and undemocratic.

No one looms larger in this bloody story than Nathan Bedford Forrest, a decorated Confederate general. Born in poverty in 1821, Forrest had risen to become a big-time slave trader and Mississippi planter. A fiery secessionist, Forrest had formed a Tennessee Confederate cavalry regiment, fought bravely at the battle of Shiloh, and won fame as a daring raider. On April 12, 1864, at Fort Pillow, Tennessee, his troops perpetrated one of the war's worst atrocities, the massacre of black Union soldiers who were trying to surrender.

After the Civil War, Forrest's determination to uphold white supremacy altered the course of Reconstruction. William G. Brownlow, elected as Tennessee's Republican governor in 1865, was a tough man, a former prisoner of the Confederates who was not shy about calling his enemies to account. Ex-Confederates struck back with a campaign of terror, targeting especially Brownlow's black supporters. Amid the mayhem, ex-Confederates formed the first **Ku Klux Klan** group in late 1865 or early 1866. As it

Crédit Mobilier
A sham corporation set up by shareholders in the Union Pacific Railroad to secure government grants at an enormous profit. Organizers of the scheme protected it from investigation by providing gifts of its stock to powerful members of Congress.

AP® EXAM TIP

Identifying the role of organized violence and terrorist organizations in the loss of constitutional rights of African Americans is important to know for the AP® Exam.

Ku Klux Klan
Secret society that first undertook violence against African Americans in the South after the Civil War but was reborn in 1915 to fight the perceived threats posed by African Americans, immigrants, radicals, feminists, Catholics, and Jews.

CHECK FOR UNDERSTANDING

Ask students: **Why did the Republicans unravel in the 1870s?** *The Panic of 1873 destroyed the economic growth Republicans had counted on to support their programs. The depression, combined with resistance in some quarters to an activist federal government, led to the formation of a liberal Republican faction whose separation weakened the Republican Party. Disgust over corruption in the Grant administration also undermined Republican authority.*

AP® APPLY THE TIP

Begin this activity by asking students to write down the definition of "terrorism." Give students a moment to think about and articulate their definition of "terrorism" on paper without discussing with each other. Then engage the class in a discussion on their definitions to come to a consensus definition on the term. Show students an excerpt from the introduction of the documentary "Aftershock: Beyond the Civil War" (Part 1 is a 10-minute segment available on YouTube.com). After viewing the segment, ask students if the conditions in the South during Reconstruction warrant the use of the term "terrorism" and what this implies about political power in the South.

AP® SKILLS & PROCESSES

ANALYZING HISTORICAL EVIDENCE

The **AP® FIRSTHAND ACCOUNTS** feature provides firsthand testimony of the terror the Ku Klux Klan brought on its victims. Students can use this source to understand the nature of life for freedpeople, the techniques of Klan members, and the role of the federal government in attempting to stop the Klan's violence.

AP® THEME

ARC: American and Regional Culture

Consider using this question to have a class discussion prior to reading the primary document excerpts detailing the activities of the Ku Klux Klan. Ask students: **To what extent did the southern region became an increasingly hostile and distinctive culture in the aftermath of the Civil War?** *Remind students to focus on the developments attendant to culture. The southern region was and continued to be distinctive in the ferocity with which it racialized politics, economic opportunities, and social norms. The end of the war did not witness any easing of these policies. Instead, the southern region amplified its already racially bifurcated system by enacting new laws that sought to further define and separate the two races.*

AP® FIRSTHAND ACCOUNTS

The Impact of Terror

In 1871, thousands of southerners testified before a congressional committee investigating white vigilantism and Ku Klux Klan night-riding in former Confederate states. Their testimony provides a window into the local operations of violence and intimidation. Here, William Coleman, formerly of Winston County, Mississippi, testified to the impact of Klan violence on himself, his family, and his neighbors.

WILLIAM COLEMAN

Testimony on Klan Violence

SOURCE: *Testimony Taken by the Joint Select Committee to Inquire into the Condition of Affairs in the Late Insurrectionary States, Mississippi* (Washington, DC: Government Printing Office, 1872), 1: 482–488.

Macon, Mississippi, November 6, 1871.
William Coleman (colored) sworn and examined.

Q. Where do you live?
A. I live in Macon.
Q. How long have you lived here?
A. I came here about the last of April.
Q. Where did you come from?
A. I came from Winston County.
Q. —What occasioned your coming here?
A. I got run by the Ku-Klux.
Q. Give the particulars to the committee.
A. Give the particulars?
Q. Tell how it occurred. . . .
A. Well, I don't know anything that I had said or done that injured any one, further than being a radical, . . . I had done bought my land and paid for it, and I had . . . —eighteen head of hogs to kill this fall. I had twelve head of sheep, and one good milk-cow, and a yearling, and the cow had a right young calf again, and I had my mule and my filly, and all of it was paid for but my mule. . . . The mule cost me $65, and I had him hired out to pay for him. . . .
Q. Did any of the Ku-Klux come to your house?
A. They did.
Q. In the night-time?
A. They came about a half hour or more before day, as nigh as I can recollect. . . . When they busted the door open, coming in shooting, I was frightened, and I can only tell you as nigh as my recollection will afford. . . . I jumped up and said, "Hallo." Then one at the door said, "Raise a light in there." "What for; who is you?" I said. . . . He says, "God damn you, we didn't come to tell you who we are." I was peeping through the little crack in the door. . . . I saw men out there standing with horns and faces [masks] on all of them, and they all had great, long white cow-tails way down the breast. . . . They told me they rode from Shiloh in two hours, and came to kill me. . . . They shot right smart in that house before they got in, but how many times I don't know, they shot so fast outside; but when they come in, they didn't have but three loads to shoot. . . . I dashed about among them, but they knocked me down several times. Every time I would get up, they would knock me down again. I saw they were going to kill me. . . . I grabbed my ax-handle, and commenced fighting, and then they just took and cut me with knives. They surrounded me in the floor and took my shirt off. They got me out on the floor; some had me by the legs and some by the arms and the neck and anywhere, just like dogs string out a coon, and they took me out to the big road before my gate and whipped me until I couldn't move or holler or do nothing, but just lay there. . . . They left me there for dead, and what it was done for was because I was a radical, and I didn't deny my profession anywhere and I never will. I never will vote that conservative ticket if I die.
Q. Did they tell you they whipped you because you were a radical?
A. They told me, "God damn you, when you meet a white man in the road lift your hat; I'll learn you, God damn you, that you are a nigger, and not to be going about like you thought yourself a white man. . . ." [I believe it was] because I had my filly; I had bought her to ride, not to stay in the stable, but

proliferated across the state, the Klan turned to Forrest, who had been trying unsuccessfully to rebuild his prewar fortune. Late in 1866, at a secret meeting in Nashville, Forrest donned the robes of Grand Wizard. His activities are mostly cloaked in mystery, but there is no mistake about his goals: the Klan would strike blows against the despised Republican government of Tennessee.

In many towns, the Klan became virtually identical to the Democratic Party. Klan members — including Forrest — dominated Tennessee's delegation to the Democratic national convention of 1868. At home, the Klan unleashed a murderous campaign of terror, and though Governor Brownlow responded resolutely, in the end Republicans cracked. The Klan and similar groups — organized under such names as the White to ride when I got ready, like you would do with your property. When I bought her I bought her for $75; she was not nigh grown; a little thing, with flaxen mane and tail, and light cream-color....

Q. Were you working on your own land?
A. Yes sir; that I bought and paid for; $473 for it.
Q. How many men were concerned in beating you?
A. Eight men.
Q. Were they all disguised?
A. Yes sir; every one of them....
Q. Did you know any one that night?
A. Of course I did. I ought to know them, my neighbors; and I knocked off the faces [masks] and horns fighting ... [and saw one without his mask]; of course I knowed him. I would know him again except it was his ashes....
Q. They said they came from Shiloh? ... Did they say they were the spirits of the confederate dead?
A. They didn't tell me nothing about spirits....
Q. When was Nathan Cannon whipped?
A. He was whipped last year.... I went one night to stay with him to go to church [but came late and saw night-riders] stripping him and beating him and knocking him about with pistols.... They whipped him about an hour before he started to holler, and when he started to holler "murder, murder"—every word was murder—I just jumped on my filly and started for home.... I wouldn't tell my wife about it, for fear she would get so uneasy and be tore up in mind, and I didn't tell it, but somebody told it....
Q. Was he badly whipped?
A. He never worked none, to my recollection, in five weeks....
Q. Have you known any teachers of colored schools to be interfered with?
A. Peter Cooper was run from there a short time after I was. He is down here making shoes.
Q. Was he a teacher of a colored school?
A. Yes, sir; they burned up his books and took several dollars of money from him. I know they got $23 from him that night....
Q. Do you know of any colored churches or schools being burned down?
A. There was only one school-house that I ever knew burned down. They teached in it about a week.
Q. Was it a school for colored children?
A. Yes, sir....
Q. Did you ever hear of any colored people sleeping out of their houses in that county?
A. I have heard it and done it myself.
Q. Why?
A. Because I was afraid to stay in my own house.... I have left my house and told my wife to stay in there, for they don't hurt women unless some of the women is sassy to some of their wives, or speak like a white woman, and they call that sass; then they go and whip them nearly to death; but I knew my wife wouldn't say nothing....
Q. Do you think that colored people feel afraid of personal harm and violence in that country?
A. Yes, sir, they do ... and you would, too, if you were most devoured with devils like that.... Here is a knot on my head they did to me that night, [indicating,] and here is one in the edge of my ear, the whole width of the stick, and a long hole over here, in the back of my head. When they took me out of the house I was as bloody as a hog that had been knocked down and stuck in a hog-pen and wallered in his own blood.... They meant to beat me to death....
Q. Are you afraid to go back there?
A. ... My life is better to me than anything there. I would not go back there if there was gold there higher than one of these pines.

QUESTIONS FOR ANALYSIS

1. In this testimony, what achievements does Coleman describe in his life and work in the six years since emancipation? What does Coleman's account tell us about African Americans' priorities and strategies when freedom came?
2. What does Coleman's testimony reveal about the tactics and motivations of night-riders?
3. How does Coleman describe the impact of the riders' violence on his life and those of his neighbors and community?
4. How do you think Winston County was different after the vigilantes had done their work?

TRM Find complete suggested responses in the Teacher's Resource Materials.

League and Knights of the White Camelia—arose in other states. Vigilantes burned freedmen's schools, beat teachers, attacked Republican gatherings, and murdered political opponents. By 1870, Democrats had seized power in Georgia and North Carolina and were making headway across the South. Once they took power, they slashed property taxes and passed other laws favorable to landowners. They terminated Reconstruction programs and cut funding for schools, especially those for black students.

In responding to the Klan between 1869 and 1871, the federal government showed it could still exert power effectively in the South. Determined to end Klan violence, Congress held extensive hearings and in 1870 passed laws designed to protect

Ku Klux Klan Mask White supremacists of the 1870s organized under many names and wore many costumes, not simply (or often) the white cone-shaped hats that were made famous later, in the 1920s, when the Klan underwent a nationwide resurgence. Few masks from the 1870s have survived. The horns and fangs on this one, from North Carolina, suggest how Klan members sought to strike terror in their victims, while also hiding their own identities. SOURCE: North Carolina Museum of History.

freedmen's rights under the Fourteenth and Fifteenth Amendments. These so-called **Enforcement Laws** authorized federal prosecutions, military intervention, and martial law to suppress terrorist activity. Grant's administration made full use of these new powers. In South Carolina, where the Klan was deeply entrenched, U.S. troops occupied nine counties, made hundreds of arrests, and drove as many as 2,000 Klansmen from the state.

This assault on the Klan, while raising the spirits of southern Republicans, revealed how dependent they were on Washington. "No such law could be enforced by state authority," one Mississippi Republican observed, "the local power being too weak." But northern Republicans were growing disillusioned with Reconstruction, while in the South, prosecuting Klansmen was an uphill battle against all-white juries and unsympathetic federal judges. After 1872, prosecutions dropped off. Meanwhile, Democrats seized the Texas government in 1873 and Alabama and Arkansas the following year.

Reconstruction Rolled Back

As divided Republicans debated how to respond, voters in the congressional election of 1874 handed them one of the most stunning defeats of the nineteenth century. Responding especially to the severe depression that gripped the nation, they removed almost half of the party's 199 representatives in the House. Democrats, who had held 88 seats, now commanded an overwhelming majority of 182. "The election is not merely a victory but a revolution," exulted a Democratic newspaper in New York.

Enforcement Laws
Acts passed in Congress in 1870 and signed by President U. S. Grant that were designed to protect freedmen's rights under the Fourteenth and Fifteenth Amendments. Authorizing federal prosecutions, military intervention, and martial law to suppress terrorist activity, the Enforcement Laws largely succeeded in shutting down Klan activities.

AP® SKILLS & PROCESSES

CONTEXTUALIZATION

How did ex-Confederates, freedpeople, Radical Republicans, and classical liberals view the end of Reconstruction?

AP® EXAM TIP

Evaluate the role of the Supreme Court in undermining the rights of African Americans in the Reconstruction Era.

Slaughter-House Cases
A group of decisions begun in 1873 in which the Court began to undercut the power of the Fourteenth Amendment to protect African American rights.

After 1874, with Democrats in control of the House, Republicans trying to shore up their southern wing found they had limited options. Bowing to election results, the Grant administration began to reject southern Republicans' appeals for aid. Events in Mississippi showed the outcome. As state elections neared there in 1875, paramilitary groups such as the Red Shirts operated openly. Mississippi's Republican governor, Adelbert Ames, a Union veteran from Maine, appealed for U.S. troops, but Grant refused. "The whole public are tired out with these annual autumnal outbreaks in the South," complained a Grant official, who told southern Republicans that they were responsible for their own fate. Facing a rising tide of brutal murders, Governor Ames — realizing that only further bloodshed could result — urged his allies to give up the fight. Brandishing guns and stuffing ballot boxes, Democratic "Redeemers" swept the 1875 elections and took control of Mississippi. By 1876, Reconstruction was largely over. Republican governments, backed by token U.S. military units, remained in only three southern states: Louisiana, South Carolina, and Florida. Elsewhere, former Confederates and their allies took power.

Though ex-Confederates seized power in southern states, new landmark constitutional amendments and federal laws remained in force. If the Supreme Court had left these intact, subsequent generations of civil rights advocates could have used the federal courts to combat racial discrimination and violence. Instead, the Court closed off this avenue for the pursuit of justice, just as it dashed the hopes of women's rights advocates.

Beginning in 1873, in a group of decisions known collectively as the ***Slaughter-House Cases***, the Court began to undercut the power of the Fourteenth Amendment. In *Slaughter-House* (1873) and a related ruling, *U.S. v. Cruikshank* (1876), the justices argued that the Fourteenth Amendment offered only a few, rather trivial federal protections to citizens (such as access to navigable waterways). In *Cruikshank* — a case that emerged from the gruesome killing of African American farmers by ex-Confederates in Colfax, Louisiana, followed by a Democratic political coup — the Court ruled that voting rights remained a state matter unless the state itself violated those rights. If former slaves' rights were violated by individuals or private groups (including the Klan), that

CHECK FOR UNDERSTANDING

Ask students: **What was the counterrevolution in the South?** *This was an aggressive effort by southern whites to overthrow the changes brought by Reconstruction. Democrats gradually regained office at various levels of government, while the Ku Klux Klan terrorized freedmen and white Republicans.*

AP® SKILLS & PROCESSES

CONTEXTUALIZATION

The **CONTEXTUALIZATION** question asks students to compare differing reactions to the same event. It might help students to make a simple chart with a row for each of the four groups, and two columns — one for their reactions and another for reasons for those reactions. To extend the prompt, students could identify the group that gained the most from the end of Reconstruction, and the group that lost the most, and then explain their answers.

TRM Find complete suggested responses in the Teacher's Resource Materials.

AP® THEME

NAT: American and National Identity; PCE: Politics and Power

Use a lesson plan from PBS's companion site to *The Supreme Court* to introduce the Fourteenth Amendment and its significance, as well as the role of the Civil Rights Cases of 1883, which undermined the applicability of the amendment in protecting blacks' rights. The lesson plan provides short clips from the film, highlighting both the amendment and the 1883 cases. To access the lesson plan, search "PBS Supreme Court Fourteenth Amendment."

AP® THEME

NAT: American and National Identity; PCE: Politics and Power

The PBS companion site to *The Rise and Fall of Jim Crow* provides an extensive set of resources that encourage students to explore the "redemption" of southern governments by white Democrats and the rise of segregation. Resources include an interactive timeline, interactive maps, primary sources, and interactive activities. To access the site, search "PBS Rise and Fall of Jim Crow."

AP® APPLY THE TIP

Divide the class into three groups and assign each group one of the following Supreme Court cases to research: *Slaughterhouse Cases* (1873), *Cruikshank vs. U.S.* (1876), and *Civil Rights Cases* (1883). Students should explain the background, constitutional issue(s), and decision in each of these cases. Once students have had the opportunity to complete their research, reorganize the class into groups of three with one student representing each case. Have the small groups create a three-part Venn diagram to compare the cases showing both similarities and differences. Ask student groups to write a thesis statement in response to the following prompt: The Supreme Court decisions of the late nineteenth century were transformative events in American history. After groups have formulated their thesis statements, ask one group to share and lead a class discussion. Ask other groups to contribute, modify, or qualify the thesis statement. Continue this whole class activity until the group reaches a consensus on an effective thesis statement. Ask small groups to then briefly outline the supporting evidence they would use to write an essay based on the agreed upon thesis statement.

lay beyond federal jurisdiction. The Fourteenth Amendment did not protect citizens from armed vigilantes, even when those vigilantes seized political power. The Court thus gutted the Fourteenth Amendment. In the ***Civil Rights Cases*** (1883), the justices also struck down the Civil Rights Act of 1875, paving the way for later decisions that sanctioned segregation. The impact of this sweeping repudiation of Reconstruction amendments to protect civil rights endured well into the twentieth century.

Civil Rights Cases
A series of 1883 Supreme Court decisions that struck down the Civil Rights Act of 1875, rolling back key Reconstruction laws and paving the way for later decisions that sanctioned segregation.

The Political Crisis of 1877

After the grim election results of 1874, Republicans faced a major battle in the presidential election of 1876. Abandoning Grant, they nominated Rutherford B. Hayes, a former Union general who was untainted by corruption and hailed from the key swing state of Ohio. Hayes's Democratic opponent was New York governor Samuel J. Tilden, a Wall Street lawyer with a reform reputation. Tilden favored home rule for the South, but so, more discreetly, did Hayes. With enforcement on the wane and the nation in the midst of a severe economic depression, Reconstruction did not figure prominently in the campaign, and little was said about the states still led by Reconstruction governments: Florida, South Carolina, and Louisiana.

Once returns started coming in on election night, however, those states loomed large. Tilden led in the popular vote and seemed headed for victory until campaign leaders at Republican headquarters realized that the electoral vote stood at 184 to 165, with the 20 votes from Florida, South Carolina, and Louisiana still uncertain. If Hayes took those votes, he would win by a margin of 1. Citing ample evidence of Democratic fraud and intimidation, Republican officials certified all three states for Hayes. "Redeemer" Democrats who had taken over the states' governments submitted their own electoral votes for Tilden. When Congress met in early 1877, it confronted two sets of electoral votes from those states.

The Constitution does not provide for such a contingency. All it says is that the president of the Senate (in 1877, a Republican) opens the electoral certificates before the House (Democratic) and the Senate (Republican) and "the Votes shall then be counted" (Article 2, Section 1). Suspense gripped the country. There was talk of inside deals or a new election — even a violent coup. Finally, Congress appointed an electoral commission to settle the question. The commission included seven Republicans, seven Democrats, and, as the deciding member, David Davis, a Supreme Court justice not known to have fixed party loyalties. Davis, however, disqualified himself by accepting an Illinois Senate seat. He was replaced by Republican justice Joseph P. Bradley, and by a vote of 8 to 7, on party lines, the commission awarded the election to Hayes.

In the House of Representatives, outraged Democrats vowed to stall the final count of electoral votes so as to prevent Hayes's inauguration on March 4. But in the end, they went along, partly because Tilden himself urged that they do so. Hayes had publicly indicated his desire to offer substantial patronage to the South, including federal funds for education and internal improvements. He promised "a complete change of men and policy," naively hoping he could count on support from old-line southern Whigs and protect black voting rights. Hayes was inaugurated on schedule. He expressed hope in his inaugural address that the federal government could serve "the interests of both races carefully and equally." But, setting aside the U.S. troops who were serving on border duty in Texas, only 3,000 Union soldiers remained in the South. As soon as the new president ordered them back to their barracks, the last Republican administrations in the South collapsed. Reconstruction had ended.

AP® EXAM TIP
Recognizing the role of political compromise in stripping away African Americans' rights in the South is critical for success on the AP® Exam.

AP® SKILLS & PROCESSES
ARGUMENTATION
To what extent did the resolution of the 1877 presidential crisis bring an end to Reconstruction, and to what extent was Reconstruction already over before election day, 1876?

Lasting Legacies

In the short run, the political events of 1877 made little difference to most southerners, black or white. Most of the work of "Redemption" had already been done. What mattered was the long, slow decline of Radical Republican power and the

AP® EXAM TIP
Defining the ways that the Fourteenth and Fifteenth Amendments established a basis for full equality of all citizens is important to know for the AP® Exam.

CHECK FOR UNDERSTANDING

Ask students: **How was Reconstruction rolled back?** *White Democrats won control of the House after the elections of 1874, while the Supreme Court interpreted the Fourteenth Amendment in a way that undermined its ability to support black rights in the South; the Compromise of 1877 removed the last vestige of federal military presence in the South.*

AP® THEME

ARC: American and Regional Culture

After students have studied the political compromise of 1877 that followed the contested presidential election, ask students to consider how the historical context of reconciliation reflected the regional interests of both northerners and southerners. Students' main task is to define reconciliation while accounting for specific historical factors that explain their assertion. Encourage students to use reconciliation as a vehicle with which to illustrate regional interests.

AP® SKILLS & PROCESSES

ARGUMENTATION

Consider splitting this question in two parts. Ask students to answer the following question: To what extent did political fatigue over Reconstruction in the North exist by the 1876 election and how did the Panic of 1873 add or detract from this fatigue? Next, ask students to use their first answer to help contextualize the response to the question of the political compromise of 1877.

TRM Find complete suggested responses in the Teacher's Resource Materials.

AP® APPLY THE TIP

Show students the TED Ed video "The Fight for Voting Rights" (available online at TED.com and YouTube.com). As the video plays, create a timeline on the board of the key moments highlighted in the fight for voting rights. After the video, focus students' attention on the Fifteenth Amendment and discuss its impact on voters and participatory democracy in the U.S. Next, using the same timeline, ask students to brainstorm the events they would include if they were to create a similar video on civil rights in the U.S. based on the Fourteenth Amendment. Ask students to consider events they would include both before and after passage of the Fourteenth Amendment to show the development of civil rights in the U.S. over time.

AP® SKILLS & PROCESSES

ANALYZING HISTORICAL EVIDENCE

The **AP® THINKING LIKE A HISTORIAN** feature addresses the thorny issue of how Americans have chosen to remember and commemorate the Civil War. Historian David Blight, in his book *Race and Reunion: The Civil War in American Memory* (Cambridge: Belknap/Harvard University Press, 2001), conducted research on how this process developed during the half-century that followed the end of the Civil War. He argues that Americans were torn between two competing imperatives: the need for justice, which implied the extension of equality and economic opportunity to former slaves, and the need for reconciliation, which suggested a need to forgive wrongs on both sides, but particularly Confederate support for slavery. Reconciliation ultimately defeated justice, in Blight's view, and black Americans suffered the price. Consider assigning an excerpt (pp. 1–5) from Blight's book to supplement students' document analysis.

The South's "Lost Cause"

After Reconstruction ended, many white southerners celebrated the Confederacy as a heroic "Lost Cause." Through organizations such as the Sons of Confederate Veterans and United Daughters of the Confederacy, they profoundly influenced the nation's memories of slavery, the Civil War, and Reconstruction.

1. **Commemorative postcard of living Confederate flag, Robert E. Lee Monument, Richmond, Virginia, 1907.** *An estimated 150,000 people gathered in 1890 to dedicate this statue — ten times more than had attended earlier memorial events.*

Library of Virginia

2. **From the United Daughters of the Confederacy Constitution, 1894.** *The United Daughters of the Confederacy (UDC), founded in 1894, grew in three years to 136 chapters and by the late 1910s counted a membership of 100,000.*

The objects of this association are historical, educational, memorial, benevolent, and social: To fulfill the duties of sacred charity to the survivors of the war and those dependent on them; to collect and preserve material for a truthful history of the war; to protect historic places of the Confederacy; to record the part taken by the Southern women . . . in patient endurance of hardship and patriotic devotion during the struggle; to perpetuate the memory of our Confederate heroes and the glorious cause for which they fought; to cherish the ties of friendship among members of this Association; to endeavor to have used in all Southern schools only such histories as are just and true.

3. **McNeel Marble Co. advertisement in *Confederate Veteran* magazine, 1905.** *Companies that manufactured monuments reached out to memorial groups to sell their wares.*

To the Daughters of the Confederacy: In regard to that Confederate monument which your Chapter has been talking about and planning for since you first got organized. Why not buy it NOW and have it erected before all the old veterans have answered the final roll call? Why wait and worry about raising funds? Our terms to U.D.C. Chapters are so liberal and our plans for raising funds are so effective as to obviate the necessity of either waiting or worrying. During the last three or four years we have sold Confederate monuments to thirty-seven of your sister Chapters. . . . Our designs, our prices, our work, our business methods have pleased them, and we can please you. What your sister Chapters have done, you can do. . . . WRITE TO-DAY.

4. **Confederate veteran's letter, *Confederate Veteran* magazine, 1910.** *An anonymous Georgian who had served in Lee's army sent the following letter to the veterans' magazine after attending a reunion in Memphis.*

Reunion gatherings are supposed to be for the benefit of the old veterans; but will you show us where the privates, the men who stood the hardships and did the fighting, have any consideration when they get to the city that is expected to entertain them? . . . [In Memphis, I] stopped at the school building, where there were at least twenty-five or thirty old veterans lying on the ground, and had been there all night. All this while the officers were being

corresponding rise of Democrats in the South and nationally. It was obvious that so-called Redeemers in the South had assumed power through violence. But many Americans, including prominent classical liberals who shaped public opinion, believed the Democrats had overthrown corrupt, illegitimate governments and thus the end justified the means. After Democrats' sweeping victories in the 1874 election, those who deplored the results had little political traction. The only remaining question was how far Reconstruction would be rolled back.

The South never went back to the antebellum status quo. Sharecropping, for all its flaws and injustices, was not slavery. Freedmen and freedwomen managed to resist gang labor and work on their own terms. They also established their right to marry, read and write, worship as they pleased, and travel in search of a better life — rights that were not easily revoked. Across the South, black farmers overcame great odds to banqueted, wined, dined, and quartered in the very best hotels; but the private must shift for himself, stand around on the street, or sit on the curbstone. He must march if he is able, but the officers ride in fine carriages. Pay more attention to the men of the ranks—men who did service! I always go prepared to pay my way; but I do not like to be ignored.

5. **Matthew Page Andrews, *The Women of the South in War Times*, 1923.** *Matthew Page Andrews's* The Women of the South in War Times, *approved by the UDC, was a popular textbook for decades in schools throughout the South.*

The Southern people of the "old regime" have been pictured as engaged primarily in a protracted struggle for the maintenance of negro slavery. . . . Fighting on behalf of slavery was as far from the minds of these Americans as going to war in order to free the slaves was from the purpose of Abraham Lincoln, whose sole object, frequently expressed by him, was to "preserve the Union." . . .

That, in the midst of war, there were almost no instances of arson, murder, or outrage committed by the negroes of the South is an everlasting tribute to the splendid character of the dominant race and their moral uplift of a weaker one . . . . When these negroes were landed on American shores, almost all were savages taken from the lowest forms of jungle life. It was largely the women of the South who trained these heathen people, molded their characters, and, in the second and third generations, lifted them up a thousand years in the scale of civilization.

6. **Susie King Taylor, *Reminiscences of My Life in Camp with the 33d United States Colored Troops, Late 1st S.C. Volunteers*, 1902.** *Susie King Taylor, born in slavery in Georgia in 1848, fled with her uncle during the Civil War and served as a nurse in the Union army.*

I read an article, which said the ex-Confederate Daughters had sent a petition to the managers of the local theatres in Tennessee to prohibit the performance of "Uncle Tom's Cabin," claiming it was exaggerated (that is, the treatment of the slaves), and would have a very bad effect on the children who might see the drama. I paused and thought back a few years of the heart-rending scenes I have witnessed. . . . I remember, as if it were yesterday, seeing droves of negroes going to be sold, and I often went to look at them, and I could hear the auctioneer very plainly from my house, auctioning these poor people off.

Do these Confederate Daughters ever send petitions to prohibit the atrocious lynchings and wholesale murdering and torture of the negro? Do you ever hear of them fearing this would have a bad effect on the children? Which of these two, the drama or the present state of affairs, makes a degrading impression upon the minds of our young generation? In my opinion it is not "Uncle Tom's Cabin." . . . It does not seem as if our land is yet civilized.

SOURCES: (2) *Minutes of the Seventh Annual Meeting of the United Daughters of the Confederacy* (Nashville, TN: Press of Foster & Webb, Printers, 1901), 235; (3) *Confederate Veteran*, 1905; (4) *Confederate Veteran*, Vol. XVIII (Nashville, TN: S. A. Cunningham, 1910); (5) Matthew Page Andrews, ed., *The Women of the South in War Times* (Baltimore: The Norman, Remington Co., 1923), 3–4, 9–10; (6) Susie King Taylor, *Reminiscences of My Life in Camp* (Boston: Published by the author, 1902), 65–66.

ANALYZING THE EVIDENCE

1. What do sources 2 and 3 tell us about the work of local UDC chapters? What does the advertisement suggest about the economy of the postwar South?
2. What can you infer from these sources about the social conditions in the South after the Civil War? Why might women have played a particularly important role in memorial associations?
3. Compare and contrast sources 4 and 6. Who did "Lost Cause" associations serve, and how is this connected to issues of class and race?
4. How does source 5 depict slaves? Slaveholders? Is this an accurate account of the history of the South, and how does this compare to source 4? What do these different interpretations suggest about the legacy of "Redemption"?

AP® DBQ PRACTICE

"Lost Cause" advocates often stated that their work was not political. To what extent was this true, based on the evidence here? What do these documents suggest about the influence of the Lost Cause, and also the limitations and challenges it faced? What do they tell us about the legacies of Reconstruction more broadly? Use evidence from the sources and chapter to support your reasoning.

TRM Find complete suggested responses in the Teacher's Resource Materials.

buy and work their own land. African American businessmen built thriving enterprises. Black churches and community groups sustained networks of mutual aid. Parents sacrificed to send their children to school, and a few proudly watched their sons and daughters graduate from college.

Reconstruction had also shaken, if not fully overturned, the legal and political framework that had made the United States a white man's country. This was a stunning achievement, and though hostile courts and political opponents undercut it, no one ever repealed the Thirteenth, Fourteenth, or Fifteenth Amendments. They remained in the Constitution, as a foundation on which the twentieth-century civil rights movement would return and build (Chapter 26).

Still, in the final reckoning, Reconstruction failed. The majority of freedpeople remained in poverty, and by the late 1870s their political rights were also eroding.

477

Vocal advocates of smaller government argued that Reconstruction had been a mistake; pressured by economic hardship, northern voters abandoned their southern Unionist allies. One of the enduring legacies of this process was the way later Americans remembered Reconstruction itself. After "Redemption," generations of schoolchildren were taught that ignorant, lazy blacks and corrupt whites had imposed illegitimate Reconstruction "regimes" on the South. White southerners won national support for their celebration of a heroic Confederacy and "Redemption" after an era of Reconstruction misrule (see "Thinking Like a Historian," p. 476).

One of the first historians to challenge these views was the great African American intellectual W. E. B. Du Bois. In *Black Reconstruction in America* (1935), Du Bois meticulously documented the history of African American struggle, white vigilante violence, and national policy failure. If northerners had sustained Reconstruction with determination, he wrote, "we should be living today in a different world." His words still ring true, but in 1935 historians ignored him. Not a single scholarly journal reviewed Du Bois's important book. Ex-Confederates had lost the war but won control over the nation's memory of Reconstruction.

Meanwhile, though their programs failed in the South, Republicans carried their nation-building project into the West, where their policies helped consolidate a continental empire. There, the federal power that had secured emancipation created another set of injustices — as well as the conditions for the United States to become an industrial power and a major leader on the world stage.

SUMMARY

Postwar Republicans faced two tasks: restoring rebellious states to the Union and defining the role of emancipated slaves. After Lincoln's assassination, his successor, Andrew Johnson, hostile to Congress, unilaterally offered the South easy terms for reentering the Union. Exploiting this opportunity, southerners adopted oppressive Black Codes and put ex-Confederates back in power. Congress impeached Johnson and, though failing to convict him, seized the initiative and placed the South under military rule. In this second, or radical, phase of Reconstruction, Republican state governments tried to transform the South's economic and social institutions. Congress passed innovative civil rights acts and funded new agencies like the Freedmen's Bureau. The Fourteenth Amendment defined U.S. citizenship and asserted that states could no longer supersede it, and the Fifteenth Amendment gave voting rights to formerly enslaved men. Debate over this amendment precipitated a split among women's rights advocates, since women did not win inclusion.

Freedmen found that their goals conflicted with those of Republican leaders, who counted on cotton to fuel economic growth. Like southern landowners, national lawmakers envisioned former slaves as wageworkers, while freedmen wanted their own land. Sharecropping, which satisfied no one completely, emerged as a compromise suited to the needs of the cotton market and an impoverished, credit-starved region.

Nothing could reconcile ex-Confederates to Republican government, and they staged a violent counterrevolution in the name of white supremacy and "Redemption." Meanwhile, struck by a massive economic depression, northern voters handed Republicans a crushing defeat in the election of 1874. By 1876, Reconstruction was dead. Rutherford B. Hayes's narrow victory in the presidential election of that year resulted in withdrawal of the last Union troops from the South. A series of Supreme Court decisions also undermined the Fourteenth Amendment and civil rights laws, setting up legal parameters through which, over the long term, disenfranchisement and segregation would flourish.

CHECK FOR UNDERSTANDING

Ask students: **Why and how did federal reconstruction policies falter in the south?** *Reconstruction policies faltered under the Grant administration (1869–1877) for a number of reasons. In the North, people became distracted by scandals like Crédit Mobilier (1872) and started demanding smaller government after the Panic of 1873. In the South, resistance activities by whites, e.g., those of the Ku Klux Klan, wore down support for freedmen. By 1876, only three states — South Carolina, Louisiana, and Florida — still had Reconstruction governments. When electoral votes in the 1876 election in those states were disputed, the Compromise of 1877 required the removal of federal troops for those states, ending Reconstruction after twelve years and restoring white rule.*

CHECK FOR UNDERSTANDING

Use the **AP® LEARNING FOCUS** question from the beginning of the chapter to check on students' understanding of the chapter as a whole: **Why did freedpeople, Republican policymakers, and ex-Confederates all end up dissatisfied with Reconstruction — or with its aftermath? To what degree did each group succeed in fulfilling its goals?** *Freedpeople experienced both the rise of promises attendant to freedom such as educational opportunity, political freedom, and social mobility in concert with the tragedy of retrogression through the political terror of the Ku Klux Klan, the decline in support among northerners, and the compromises among Republicans and Democrats for political reconciliation. Republican lawmakers changed over time from being committed to a political revolution in the defeated South to a political fatigue over Reconstruction as they sought reconciliation with southern Democrats. Ex-Confederates, while not able to control the beginning stages of Reconstruction, were able to control the latter stages through the so-called Redeemers. This process was supported by political terror that enabled southerners to enact an economic and political system segregated by race. In many respects, the Redeemers ushered in an era where enslavement existed in all aspects but name.*

✓ LearningCurve

Remind students to go online to complete the LearningCurve quiz for this chapter.

CHAPTER 14 REVIEW

AP CONTENT REVIEW

Answer these questions to demonstrate your understanding of the chapter's main ideas.

1. What factors explain how Reconstruction policies unfolded between 1865 and 1870, and what was the impact on different groups of Americans?
2. What goals were southern freedmen and freedwomen able to achieve in the post–Civil War years, and why? What goals were they not able to achieve, and why not?
3. Why and how did federal Reconstruction policies falter in the South?

AP TERMS TO KNOW

Identify and explain the significance of each term below.

Key Concepts and Events

Ten Percent Plan (p. 452)
Wade-Davis Bill (p. 452)
Black Codes (p. 453)
Freedmen's Bureau (p. 454)
Civil Rights Act of 1866 (p. 454)
Fourteenth Amendment (p. 455)
Radical Republicans (p. 455)
Reconstruction Act of 1867 (p. 455)
Fifteenth Amendment (p. 457)
American Woman Suffrage Association (p. 458)
National Woman Suffrage Association (NWSA) (p. 458)
Minor v. Happersett (p. 459)
crop-lien laws (p. 462)
convict leasing (p. 466)
Civil Rights Act of 1875 (p. 468)
classical liberalism (p. 470)
Crédit Mobilier (p. 471)
Ku Klux Klan (p. 471)
Enforcement Laws (p. 474)
Slaughter-House Cases (p. 474)
Civil Rights Cases (p. 475)

Key People

Andrew Johnson (p. 453)
Charles Sumner (p. 455)
Thaddeus Stevens (p. 455)
Ulysses S. Grant (p. 455)
Victoria Woodhull (p. 459)
Robert Smalls (p. 465)
Blanche K. Bruce (p. 465)
Nathan Bedford Forrest (p. 471)

AP MAKING CONNECTIONS

Recognize the larger developments and continuities within and across chapters by answering these questions.

1. Ex-Confederates were not the first Americans to engage in violent protest against what they saw as tyrannical government power. Imagine, for example, a conversation between a participant in Shays's Rebellion (Chapter 6) and a southern Democrat who participated in the overthrow of a Republican government in his state. How would each describe his grievances? Whom would he name as enemies? Compare and contrast the tactics of these and other violent protests against government power in the United States. To what extent did these groups succeed?
2. Return to the image at the start of this chapter (p. 451), which shows a celebration in Baltimore after ratification of the Fifteenth Amendment. Note the various activities depicted as representations of the impact of emancipation and voting rights for black men. How might an African American family at the time have understood the image? What about a southern white family opposed to the Fifteenth Amendment? Describe and contrast their perspectives.

KEY TURNING POINTS

Refer to the timeline at the start of the chapter for help in answering the question below.

Identify two crucial turning points in the course of Reconstruction. What caused those shifts in direction, and what were the results?

TRM Find complete suggested responses in the Teacher's Resource Materials.

AP® SKILLS & PROCESSES

CAUSATION

AP® CONTENT REVIEW 1 asks students to identify both the causes of particular Reconstruction policies and their effects on different groups.

AP® SKILLS & PROCESSES

CAUSATION

AP® CONTENT REVIEW 2 invites students to explain the causes of success and defeat for particular black goals during Reconstruction.

AP® SKILLS & PROCESSES

CAUSATION

AP® CONTENT REVIEW 3 asks students to provide causes of Reconstruction's failure.

TRM Find definitions for these terms in the **Glossary/Glosario** in the Teacher's Resource Materials.

AP® SKILLS & PROCESSES

COMPARISON

AP® MAKING CONNECTIONS 1 asks students to draw comparisons between rebellious groups after two different major wars, the American Revolution and the Civil War. To scaffold this question, students could chart the grievances, enemies, tactics, and outcomes of each group.

AP® SKILLS & PROCESSES

CONTINUITY AND CHANGE

KEY TURNING POINTS asks students to find two different turning points within the larger period of Reconstruction and explain the cause and effects of those shifts. Students should also explain the significance of these shifts.

TRM Find complete suggested responses in the Teacher's Resource Materials.

AP® PRACTICE QUESTIONS

MULTIPLE CHOICE QUESTIONS *Choose the correct answer for each question.*

Questions 1–3 refer to this excerpt.

"*Sec. 2*. . . All freedmen, free negroes and mulattoes in this State, over the age of eighteen years . . . with no lawful employment or business, or found unlawfully assembling themselves together, either in the day or night . . . shall be deemed vagrants . . . and shall be imprisoned at the discretion of the court. . . ."

Sec. 2. . . it shall not be lawful for any freedman, free negro or mulatto to intermarry with any white person . . . and any person who shall so intermarry, shall be deemed guilty of a felony, and upon conviction thereof shall be confined in the State penitentiary for life. . . .

Sec. 1. . . no freedman, free negro or mulatto, not in the military service of the United States government . . . shall keep or carry firearms of any kind, or any ammunition. . . .

Sec. 5. . . If any freedman, free negro or mulatto, convicted of any of the misdemeanors provided against in this act, shall fail or refuse . . . to pay the fine and costs imposed, such person shall be hired out by the sheriff or other offices . . . to any white person who will pay said fine and all costs, and take said convict. . . ."

The Mississippi Black Code, 1865

1. What is one of the main purposes of the Mississippi Black Codes in the excerpt?
   - **a.** Enforce labor laws
   - **b.** Disenfranchise former slaves
   - **c.** Confiscate property from Mississippi blacks
   - **d.** Establish a social order of segregation
2. The Black Codes emerged most directly from the context of which of the following?
   - **a.** Southern resistance to Reconstruction
   - **b.** A "New South" economy based on sharecropping
   - **c.** The rise of democratic beliefs that influenced moral and social reforms
   - **d.** The spread of the ideology of Social Darwinism
3. Which of the following groups of the period would have most directly opposed the creation of the Black Codes?
   - **a.** Radical Republicans
   - **b.** Labor activists
   - **c.** The U.S. Supreme Court
   - **d.** The Populist Party

Questions 4–6 refer to the image provided.

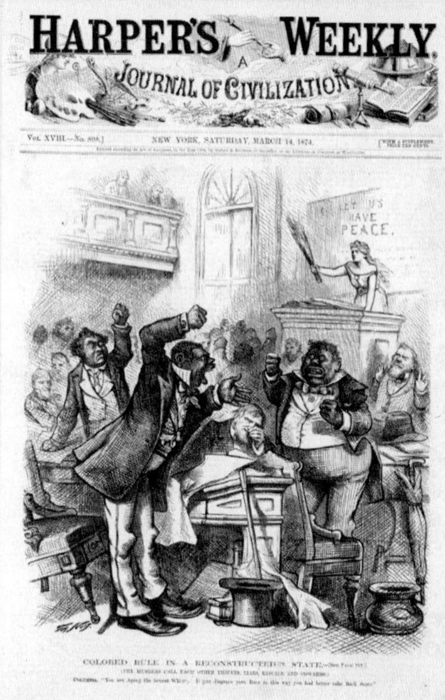

Library of Congress.

4. The image is a response to which of the following developments in the United States?
   - **a.** Republican efforts to reorder race relations in the defeated South
   - **b.** The South's restriction of political opportunities and other leadership roles for former slaves
   - **c.** The abolitionist movement's willingness to use violence to achieve its goals
   - **d.** The support for racial segregation in the *Plessy v. Ferguson* decision

5. An individual who agreed with the artist's perspective as portrayed in the cartoon would express the greatest support for
   - **a.** placing limits on African American rights.
   - **b.** maintaining full legal equality for African Americans.
   - **c.** utilizing systems of patronage at all levels of government.
   - **d.** a moral obligation of wealthy people to help the less fortunate in society.

6. The image best reflects a growing trend in the North supporting policies in the South of political
   - **a.** isolationism.
   - **b.** imperialism.
   - **c.** interventionism.
   - **d.** reconciliation.

SHORT ANSWER QUESTIONS

Read each question carefully and write a short response. Use evidence from the text to support your claims.

1. Answer (a), (b), and (c).
   - **a.** Briefly describe ONE specific historical change in the political behavior of women from after the Civil War to 1898.
   - **b.** Briefly explain ONE specific historical factor that led to the change you identified in (a).
   - **c.** Briefly explain ONE specific historical result of the change you described in (a) on American politics.

2. Answer (a), (b), and (c).
   - **a.** Briefly describe ONE specific historical difference in the economic lives of African Americans from the period before the Civil War to the period after.
   - **b.** Briefly explain ONE specific historical similarity in the economic lives of African Americans from the period before the Civil War to the period after.
   - **c.** Briefly explain ONE specific historical factor that caused the similarity you explained in (b).

> "African-American women decided to quit work over such grievances as low wages, long hours, and unpleasant tasks. . . . [I]t was an effective strategy to deprive employers of complete power over their labor. . . . Occasional refusals to sell their labor or self-imposed limits enabled working class women to conduct their own family and community affairs in ways that mitigated the demands of white supremacy and the market economy."
>
> Tera W. Hunter, *To Joy My Freedom; Black Women's Lives and Labors After the Civil War*, 1997
>
> "[B]lack working women . . . lacked the control over their own productive energies and material resources. . . . Though perhaps "freed" or "liberated" from narrow sex-role conventions, they remained tied to overwhelming wage-earning and child-rearing responsibilities. . . . [W]hen measured against traditional standards of power — usually defined in terms of wealth; personal autonomy; and control over workers, votes, or inheritances — black wives and mothers had little leverage with which to manipulate the behavior of their kinfolk.
>
> Jacqueline Jones, *Labor of Love, Labor of Sorrow; Black Women, Work, and the Family, from Slavery to the Present*, 1986

3. Using the two excerpts provided, answer (a), (b), and (c).
   - **a.** Briefly explain ONE major difference between Hunter's and Jones's historical interpretations of the lives of African American women in the second half of the nineteenth century.
   - **b.** Briefly explain how ONE historical event or development not directly mentioned in the excerpts could be used to support Hunter's argument.
   - **c.** Briefly mention how ONE specific historical event or development not directly mentioned in the excerpts could be used to support Jones's argument.

TRM Find complete suggested responses in the Teacher's Resource Materials.

15 CHAPTER

Conquering a Continent

1860–1890

Chapter 15 — AP® Assessment Weight and Pacing Guide

The assessment weight on the AP® U.S. History Exam for Chapters 15–19 is 10–17 percent. This chapter falls in Unit 6 of the AP® U.S. History Curriculum, covering Period 6: 1865–1898.

This pacing guide is based on a schedule with 120 sessions of 50 minutes each before the AP® U.S. History Exam. If you have a different number of sessions before the exam, you can modify the pacing to meet your needs. If you have additional time, consider incorporating quizzes, released AP® U.S. History questions, practice exams, writing practice, and other instructional activities.

	Traditional Schedule	Block Schedule
Chapter 15	3 days	1–2 days

Daily Pacing Guide

	Content Focus	Essential Question
Day 1	The Republican Economic Program	How did Republicans' economic policies contribute to the rise of America's industrial economy?
Day 2	Incorporating the West	Why and how did federal policies reshape the trans-Mississippi west after the Civil War?
Day 3	A Harvest of Blood: Native Peoples Dispossessed	In the late nineteenth century, how did the United States dispossess Native peoples and attempt to assimilate them, and how did those peoples respond?

AP® Alignment

Section Heading	AP® Topic	AP® Theme
The Republican Economic Program	6.2, 6.3, 6.6, 6.12	MIG, WXT, PCE
Incorporating the West	6.2, 6.3	MIG
A Harvest of Blood: Native Peoples Dispossessed	6.3	MIG

*Should changes be made to the Course Framework in the future, an updated alignment will be placed on our AP® updates page at go.bfwpub.com/ap-course-updates.

Chapter 15 — Overview

With the victory of the Union in the Civil War, a new vision of the U.S. as an economic power and an international power took hold of the nation. The Republican vision of a federally supported, national economy began to come to fruition with federal support for railroad development and the incorporation of the West into the nation's economy and culture. This change in vision altered the view of the natural world as a source of resources and led to controversy over the proper use of the natural environment. Finally, this chapter analyzes the impact of this new national vision on the Native American groups who occupied the West as they attempted to maintain autonomy and resist forced migration to reservations.

Chapter 15 — Resources

The following resources can be found in the Teacher's Resource Materials (TRM) that accompany the book. You can access the TRM via the book's digital platform, by clicking the TRM links found here in your Teacher's Edition e-book, or by contacting your representative to access the resources online. Visit **bfwpub.com/henretta10e** to learn more.

TRM Chapter 15 Lecture Presentation Slides

TRM Chapter 15 Outline with AP® Focus

TRM Chapter 15 Lecture Strategies

TRM Chapter 15 Suggested Responses

TRM Handout 15.1 — Causation: Federal Power and Economic Growth

TRM Handout 15.2 — Comparison: Ranchers and Miners in the West

TRM Handout 15.3 — Thematic Analysis: Homestead Act

Chapter 15 — Essential Activity

For this jigsaw activity, divide students into four collaborative groups. Each group will be responsible for researching one of the following federal actions: Morrill Act, Homestead Act, Dawes Severalty Act, and General Mining Act of 1872. The groups should clearly identify the purposes and provisions of their assigned law and engage in a thematic analysis that looks at the impact of the laws in connection to the AP® Themes.

Once student groups have completed their investigation, reorganize students in a jigsaw fashion so that all the above legislation is represented in each group. In the new groups, ask students to share their research and compare and contrast its purposes, provisions, and impact of implementation.

Chapter 15 — Bell Ringers

The following activities take no more than 5–15 minutes of your class period and offer an effective and engaging way to begin your lessons and for students to apply AP® Skills & Processes:

- Ask students to list the platform positions of the Republican Party in the 1850s, excluding limitation on the expansion of slavery. (*Answers will vary but should include the open sale of public lands in the West, support for industrial growth, higher tariffs, and stronger role of federal government in the economy.*) Then ask students how the Civil War impacted the Republicans' ability to pass legislation from their platform. (*Answers will vary, but students should note that Republicans gained power since Democrats were not represented in Congress because their states seceded, Radicals prevented former Confederates from taking seats in Congress, and the Fifteenth Amendment gave power to the party.*)

- Provide students with a list of states in the order that they granted suffrage rights to women. Students should discuss the reasons for the differences among the states, hypothesizing why western states granted suffrage to women earlier than eastern states.
- Show students Aaron Huey's TED talk entitled "America's Native Prisoners of War," available online. After viewing the video, ask students to identify examples of continuity and change that are evident in the video. Then have students debate the idea proposed in the video that territory in the West should be turned over to Native American tribes. Use this video as an introduction to the discussion of U.S. policy in the West in the late nineteenth century.

NOTES

TEACHING STRATEGY

The chapter introduction conveys the enthusiasm many Americans felt about the completion of the transcontinental railroad because it "meant jobs and money." The economic significance of the railroad and other forms of enterprise in the West — like mining, ranching, and homesteading — is one key theme of the chapter. A related theme is introduced in the penultimate paragraph: the role of the federal government in bringing the railroad and other western projects to fruition, which often resulted in fighting American Indians until they succumbed to demands and settled on reservations. For a complete suggested response to the **AP® LEARNING FOCUS** question, see p. 508.

TEACHING STRATEGY

This chapter provides several important connections to late-nineteenth-century western expansion. In exploring the conquest of the continent, this chapter looks back to Manifest Destiny, where the process began in the 1840s. In linking continental conquest to the growth of trade with Asia, this chapter also looks forward to the War of 1898 — as Richardson indicates — and to the U.S.'s acquisition of the Philippines as a colony. Perhaps the strongest connection is the role of an activist federal government introduced in Reconstruction.

15 CHAPTER

Conquering a Continent

1860–1890

AP® LEARNING FOCUS

Why and how did the United States build a continental empire, and how did this affect people living in the West?

On May 10, 1869, Americans poured into the streets for a giant party. In big cities, the racket was incredible. Cannons boomed and train whistles shrilled. New York fired a hundred-gun salute at City Hall. Congregations sang anthems, while the less pious gathered in saloons to celebrate with whiskey. Philadelphia's joyful throngs reminded an observer of the day, four years earlier, when news had arrived of Lee's surrender. The festivities were prompted by a long-awaited telegraph message: executives of the Union Pacific and Central Pacific railroads had driven a golden spike at Promontory Point, Utah, linking up their lines. Unbroken track now stretched from the Atlantic to the Pacific. A journey across North America could be made in less than a week.

The first **transcontinental railroad** meant jobs and money. San Francisco residents got right to business: after firing a salute, they loaded Japanese tea on a train bound for St. Louis, marking California's first overland delivery to the East. In coming decades, trade and tourism fueled tremendous growth west of the Mississippi. San Francisco, which in 1860 had handled $7.4 million in imports, increased that figure to $49 million over thirty years. The new railroad would, as one speaker predicted in 1869, "populate our vast territory" and make America "the highway of nations."

The railroad was also a political triumph. Victorious in the Civil War, Republicans saw themselves as heirs to the American System envisioned by antebellum Whigs. They believed government intervention in the economy was the key to nation building. But unlike Whigs, whose plans had met stiff Democratic opposition, Republicans enjoyed a decade of unparalleled federal power. They used it vigorously: U.S. government spending per person, after skyrocketing in the Civil War, remained well above antebellum levels. Republicans believed that national economic integration was the best guarantor of lasting peace. As a New York minister declared, the federally supported transcontinental railroad would "preserve the Union."

The minister was wrong on one point. He claimed the transcontinental railroad was a peaceful achievement, in contrast to military battles that had brought "devastation, misery, and woe." In fact, creating a continental empire along with the railroad caused plenty of woe and devastation, to people and also to the environment. Regions west of the Mississippi could only be incorporated if the United States subdued Native peoples and established favorable conditions for international investors — often at great domestic cost. And while conquering the West helped make the United States into an industrial power, it also deepened America's rivalry with European empires and created new patterns of exploitation.

transcontinental railroad The railway line completed on May 10, 1869, that connected the Central Pacific and Union Pacific lines, enabling goods to move by railway from the eastern United States all the way to California.

The Great West In the wake of the Civil War, Americans looked westward. Republicans implemented an array of policies to foster economic development in the "Great West." Ranchers, farmers, and lumbermen cast hungry eyes on the remaining lands held by Native Americans. Steamboats and railroads, both visible in the background of this image, became celebrated as symbols of the expanding reach of U.S. economic might. This 1881 promotional poster illustrates the bountiful natural resources to be found out west, as well as the land available for ranching, farming, and commerce. The men in the lower left corner are surveying land for sale. Library of Congress, 3g04085.

TEACHING STRATEGY

Ask students: **How does this image illustrate Americans' views of the "Great West" as both a wilderness and a place where civilization could flourish?** *The great bluffs, waterfall, and pine trees in the distance suggest a vast wilderness. The economic activity in the foreground — including farm fields, orchards, and livestock — indicates the potential for taming this wilderness. The house and fenced yard seem to belong to a northeastern city, suggesting that Americans could have the best of both worlds. Trains and steamboats provide the link between wilderness and civilization. The whole picture is framed by a cornucopia of produce, highlighting expectations of fruitfulness.*

AP® SKILLS & PROCESSES

CONTINUITY AND CHANGE

Use the **TIMELINE** table to help students begin thinking about how the period from 1859 to 1890 could constitute a distinct historical period related to the expansion of the West. Since 1860 was the year Lincoln, the first Republican president, was elected, students should be aware of the role of Lincoln and his party's pro-development policies in the expansion of the West. To extend this discussion, have students identify events in the timeline that reflect federal government actions and characterize the nature of those actions.

TIMELINE

- **1859** Comstock silver lode discovered in Nevada
- **1862** – Homestead Act
  – Dakota Sioux uprising in Minnesota
  – Morrill Act funds public state universities
- **1864** – Sand Creek massacre of Cheyennes in Colorado (November 29)
  – Yosemite Valley reserved as public park
- **1865** Long Drive of Texas longhorns begins
- **1866** Fetterman massacre
- **1868** Burlingame Treaty with China
- **1869** – Transcontinental railroad completed (May 10)
  – Wyoming grants women suffrage
- **1870** Utah grants women suffrage
- **Early 1870s** Decimation of bison on the Great Plains
- **1872** – General Mining Act
  – Yellowstone National Park created
- **1873** United States begins to move to gold standard
- **1876** Battle of Little Big Horn (June 26–27)
- **1877** – Nez Perce forcibly removed from ancestral homelands in Northwest
  – *Munn v. Illinois* Supreme Court decision
- **1879** – Exoduster migration of black communities from Mississippi and Louisiana to Kansas
  – John Wesley Powell presents *Report on the Lands of the Arid Region of the United States*
- **1880s** Rise of the Ghost Dance movement
- **1885** Sitting Bull tours with Buffalo Bill's Wild West
- **1886** – Dry cycle begins on the plains
  – Chiricahua Apache leader Geronimo surrenders (September)
- **1887** Dawes Severalty Act
- **1890** Massacre of Sioux Ghost Dancers at Wounded Knee, South Dakota (December 29)

1860 | 1870 | 1880 | 1890 | 1900 | 1910

THE REPUBLICAN ECONOMIC PROGRAM

How did Republicans' economic policies contribute to the rise of America's industrial economy?

AP® EXAM TIP

Analyze the ways that the federal government used its power to support the growth of a national economy after the Civil War.

Reshaping the former Confederacy was only part of Republicans' plan for a reconstructed nation. They remembered the era after Andrew Jackson's destruction of the Second National Bank as one of economic chaos, when the United States had become vulnerable to international creditors and market fluctuations. Land speculation on the frontier had provoked extreme cycles of boom and bust. Failure to fund a transcontinental railroad had left different regions of the country disconnected. This, Republicans believed, had helped trigger the Civil War, and they were determined to set a new direction.

Even while the war raged, Congress launched the transcontinental rail project and a new national banking system, as well as raised **protective tariffs** on a range of manufactured goods, from textiles to steel, and on some agricultural products, like wool and sugar. At federal customhouses in each port, foreign manufacturers who brought

protective tariff
A tax or duty on foreign producers of goods imported into the United States; tariffs gave U.S. manufacturers a competitive advantage in America's gigantic domestic market.

482

AP® APPLY THE TIP

Begin this activity by looking at **MAP 15.1** on p. 485, which depicts railroad growth in the U.S. in the late nineteenth century. Ask students to contextualize this map by explaining the historical processes, developments, and/or events that influenced this trend of railroad growth. Guide students to an understanding of the critical role of the federal government in the trend shown on the map. Ask students to consider other ways that the federal government encouraged the growth of a national economy after the Civil War by completing **Handout 15.1 — Causation: Federal Power and Economic Growth (TRM)**. Then lead a class discussion on the impact of federal power on rapid industrialization.

TRM Find **Handout 15.1 — Causation: Federal Power and Economic Growth** in the Teacher's Resource Materials.

merchandise into the United States had to pay import fees. These tariff revenues gave U.S. manufacturers, who did not pay the fees, a competitive advantage in America's vast domestic market.

The economic depression that began in 1873 set limits on Republicans' economic ambitions, just as it hindered their Reconstruction plans in the South. But their policies continued to shape the economy. Though some historians have argued that the late nineteenth century was an era of *laissez faire* or unrestrained capitalism, in which government sat passively by, the industrial United States was actually the product of a massive public-private partnership in which government played critical roles.

The New Union and the World

The United States emerged from the Civil War with new leverage in its negotiation with European countries, especially Great Britain, whose navy dominated the seas. Britain, which had allowed Confederate raiding ships such as CSS *Alabama* to be built in its shipyards, submitted afterward to arbitration and paid the United States $15.5 million in damages. Flush with victory, many Americans expected more British and Spanish territories to drop into the Union's lap as repayment, after international arbitration, for permitting shipbuilding and other support for the Confederacy. Senator Charles Sumner proposed, in fact, that Britain settle the *Alabama* claims by handing over Canada.

Such dreams were a logical extension of pre–Civil War conquests, especially in the U.S.-Mexico War. With the coasts now linked by rail, merchants and manufacturers looked across the Pacific, hungry for trade with Asia.

Union victory also increased U.S. economic influence in Latin America. While the United States was preoccupied with its internal war, France had deposed Mexico's government and installed an emperor. On May 5, 1867, Mexico overthrew the French invaders and executed Emperor Maximilian. But while Mexico regained independence, it lay open to the economic designs of its increasingly powerful northern neighbor.

A new model emerged for asserting U.S. power in Latin America and Asia: not by direct conquest, but through trade. The architect of this vision was William Seward, secretary of state from 1861 to 1869 under presidents Abraham Lincoln and Andrew Johnson. A New Yorker of grand ambition and ego, Seward believed, like many contemporaries, that Asia would become "the chief theatre of [world] events" and that commerce there was key to America's prosperity. He urged the Senate to purchase sites in both the Pacific and the Caribbean for naval bases and refueling stations. When Japan changed policy and tried to close its ports to foreigners, Seward dispatched U.S. naval vessels to join those of Britain, France, and the Netherlands in reopening trade by force. At the same time, Seward urged annexation of Hawaii. He also correctly predicted that the United States would one day claim the Philippines and build a Panama canal.

Seward's short-term achievements were modest. Exhausted by civil war, Americans had little enthusiasm for further military exploits. Seward achieved only two significant victories. In 1868, he secured congressional approval for the **Burlingame Treaty** with China, which guaranteed the rights of U.S. missionaries in China and set official terms for the emigration of Chinese laborers, some of whom were already clearing farmland and building railroads in the West. That same year, Seward negotiated the purchase of Alaska from Russia. After the Senate approved the deal, Seward waxed poetic:

> Our nation with united interests blest
> Not now content to poise, shall sway the rest;
> Abroad our empire shall no limits know,
> But like the sea in endless circles flow.

AP® SKILLS & PROCESSES

CONTINUITY AND CHANGE
In what ways did Republicans use federal power on the world stage, and in what ways did they continue policies from the pre–Civil War era?

Burlingame Treaty
An 1868 treaty that guaranteed the rights of U.S. missionaries in China and set official terms for the emigration of Chinese laborers to work in the United States.

AP® SKILLS & PROCESSES

CONTINUITY AND CHANGE

The **CONTINUITY AND CHANGE** question really asks students to identify what was new in the nation's economic and foreign policies, compared with what was a continuation of earlier policies. Students may hear echoes of Whig policies — particularly the American System — in Republican advocacy for a high tariff and investments in infrastructure. While long-distance railroads required aid on a scale the federal government had never previously supplied, the larger pattern of support for transportation was not new. Students may need to be reminded that the Republican Party grew in large part out of the Whig Party, and that Republican leaders like Seward and Lincoln had previously been Whigs. Students could also explain the links between an expanding economy and a more assertive foreign policy stance.

TRM Find complete suggested responses in the Teacher's Resource Materials.

AP® THEME

WXT: World, Exchange, and Technology

As the text makes clear, businessmen and foreign policymakers in this era increasingly looked outside the U.S. in an effort to increase influence and control over markets in the Pacific Rim and Asia.

CHECK FOR UNDERSTANDING

Ask students: **What effects did Union victory have on the U.S.'s relationship with the world?** *The strength displayed in the Union victory encouraged a bolder foreign policy with efforts to press concessions from Britain for its support of the Confederacy, to indirectly dominate Latin America through trade, and to expand trade with Asia through treaties, military pressure, and the construction of naval fueling stations.*

Many Americans scoffed at the purchase of Alaska, a frigid arctic tract that skeptics nicknamed "Seward's Icebox." But the secretary of state mapped out a path his Republican successors would follow thirty years later in an aggressive bid for global power.

AP® APPLY THE TIP

Connecting government assistance to the railroads is an essential understanding for students. The following can be used as a bell-ringer activity: Which of the following best explains why the federal government provided support for the railroad companies in the late nineteenth century? Transportation of goods, creation of new commercial centers, or migration of people. The goal is for students to work on buttressing interpretations with historical evidence.

Integrating the National Economy

AP® EXAM TIP

Identifying the development of railroads as a partnership between the federal government and private enterprise is critical for success on the AP® Exam.

Closer to home, Republicans focused on transportation infrastructure. Railroad development in the United States began well before the Civil War, with the first locomotives arriving from Britain in the early 1830s. It is hard to overstate their economic impact (see "Comparing Interpretations," p. 486). Unlike canals or roads, railroads offered the promise of year-round, all-weather service. Locomotives could run in the dark and never needed to rest, except to take on coal and water. Steam engines crossed high mountains and rocky gorges where pack animals could find no fodder and canals could never reach. West of the Mississippi, railroads opened vast regions for farming, trade, and tourism. A transcontinental railroad executive was only half-joking when he said, "The West is purely a railroad enterprise."

Governments could choose to build and operate railroads themselves or promote construction by private companies. Unlike most European countries, the United States chose the private approach. The federal government, however, provided essential loans, subsidies, and grants of public land. States and localities also lured railroads with offers of financial aid, mainly by buying railroad bonds. Without this aid, rail networks would have grown much more slowly and would probably have concentrated in urban regions. With it, railroads enjoyed an enormous — and reckless — boom. By 1900, virtually no corner of the country lacked rail service (Map 15.1). At the same time, U.S. railroads built across the border into Mexico, with the goal of bringing up minerals, hemp, and other raw materials to feed the demands of American manufacturing.

Building the Central Pacific Railroad In 1865, Chinese workers had labored to build the 1,100-foot-long, 90-foot-high trestle over the divide between the American and Bear rivers at Secret Town in the Sierra Nevada Mountains. In 1877, the Chinese workers shown in this photograph by Carleton Watkins were again at work on the site, burying the trestle to avoid replacement of the aging timbers, which had become a fire hazard. PhotoQuest/Getty Images.

Railroad companies transformed American capitalism. They adopted a legal form of organization, the corporation, that enabled them to raise private capital in prodigious amounts. In earlier decades, state legislatures had chartered corporations for specific public purposes, binding these creations to government goals and oversight. But over the course of the nineteenth century, legislatures gradually began to allow any business to become a corporation by simply applying for a state charter. Among the first corporations to become large interstate enterprises, private railroads were much freer than earlier companies to do as they pleased. After the Civil War, they received lavish public aid with few strings attached. Their position was like that of American banks in late 2008 after the big federal bailout: even critics acknowledged that public aid to these giant companies was good for the economy, but they observed that it also lent government support to fabulous accumulations of private wealth.

Tariffs and Economic Growth Along with the transformative power of railroads, Republicans' protective tariffs helped build other U.S. industries, including textiles and steel in the Northeast and Midwest and, through tariffs on imported sugar and wool, sugar beet farming and sheep ranching in the West. Tariffs also funded government itself. In an era when the United States did not levy income taxes, tariffs provided the bulk of treasury revenue. The Civil War had left the Union with a staggering debt of \$2.8 billion. Tariff income erased that debt and by the 1880s generated huge budget *surpluses* — a circumstance hard to imagine today.

As Reconstruction faltered, tariffs came under political fire. Democrats argued that tariffs taxed American consumers by

AP® SKILLS & PROCESSES

ANALYZING HISTORICAL EVIDENCE

The development of the transcontinental railroad provides students with the opportunity to explore broader historical processes during the late nineteenth century. When students write contextualization for the Long Essay and Document Based Question, they need to define broader historical processes. Sometimes students struggle with how to organize this concept in writing. Think about having students engage in the following activity. Give students the following broad historical processes attendant to the railroad: expansionism, migration, transportation, or immigration. Students should select the one concept they know the most about. Next, have students connect at least two historical events or developments to their selection of expansionism, migration, transportation, or immigration. Connecting two historical events or developments helps students flesh out the details needed to write contextualization effectively. After students have brainstormed their answers, the next task is to write three sentences that connect the historical developments. The goal is for students to see the development of the railroad in a broader context. Example answer: Migration, Chinese and Irish railroad workers, and Homestead Act.

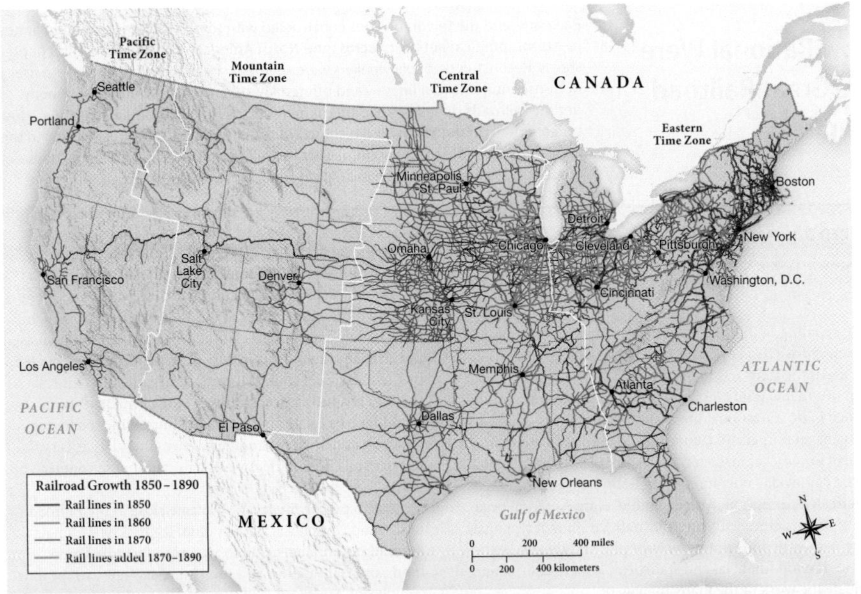

MAPPING THE PAST

MAP 15.1 Expansion of the Railroad System, 1850–1890
In 1850, the United States had 9,000 miles of rail track; by 1890, it had 167,000 miles, including transcontinental lines terminating in San Francisco, Los Angeles, and Seattle. The tremendous burst of construction during the last twenty years of that period essentially completed the nation's rail network, although there would be additional expansion for the next two decades. Time zones—an innovation introduced not by government entities, but by railroad corporations in 1883—are marked by the white lines.

ANALYZING THE MAP: What regions of the United States did the rail network serve in 1850 and in 1890? What does this suggest about the impact of the Civil War (1860s) and Reconstruction (1870s) on American economic development?

MAKING CONNECTIONS: Based on your reading of the narrative, what explains the expansion of railroads across the continent, and what was the impact of that expansion?

denying them access to low-cost imported goods and forcing them to pay subsidies to U.S. manufacturers. Republicans claimed, conversely, that tariffs benefitted workers because they blocked low-wage foreign competition and safeguarded America from the kind of industrial poverty that had arisen in Europe. According to this argument, tariffs helped American men earn enough to support their families; wives could devote themselves to homemaking, and children could go to school instead of the factory. For protectionist Republicans, high tariffs were akin to the abolition of slavery: they protected and uplifted the most vulnerable workers.

In these fierce debates, both sides were partly right. Protective tariffs did play a powerful role in economic growth. They helped transform the United States into a global industrial power. Eventually, though, even protectionist Republicans had to admit that Democrats had a point: tariffs had not prevented industrial poverty in the United States. Corporations accumulated massive benefits from tariffs but failed to pass them along to workers, who often toiled long hours for low wages. Furthermore, tariffs helped foster trusts, corporations that dominated whole sectors of the economy

AP® THEME

PCE: Politics and Power

Use **MAP 15.1** to illustrate the way government subsidies for transportation helped open new markets in the U.S. Guide students' analysis by asking the following questions:

- **How would you describe the distribution of railroads in 1850?** *They were overwhelmingly concentrated in New England and, to a lesser extent, the remainder of the Northeast.*
- **What characterized railroad growth between 1850 and 1870?** *The number of railroads expanded dramatically, creating dense webs from the Atlantic to the Great Plains. Though the far West had fewer, every state was served by at least one railroad.*
- **What economic purposes did railroads serve?** *They allowed farmers, ranchers, and miners to get their products to market, while bringing investors, sightseers, and sometimes settlers west. Railroad construction itself was a central economic activity of the era.*

TRM Find complete suggested responses in the Teacher's Resource Materials.

TEACHING STRATEGY

To make sure students understand the basics of economic growth in concert with the railroad systems, ask them to choose one of the following cities and provide historical evidence as to how that city benefitted from the railroad. Remind students to be as specific as they can be about the industry distinctive to the city of their choice: Pittsburgh, Chicago, or Omaha.

AP® SKILLS & PROCESSES

ANALYZING HISTORICAL EVIDENCE

The **AP® COMPARING INTERPRETATIONS** feature invites students to examine how historians interpret the business practices of the railroad companies of the late nineteenth century. Start by asking students to define the question on p. 486: "How Rational Were the Great Railroad Empires?" Students should focus on the word rational to determine how the historians might focus their interpretations. Next, have students focus on determining a big picture argument presented by each historian. After students have successfully defined each interpretation, invite students to highlight at least two excerpts that support their answer.

AP® COMPARING INTERPRETATIONS

How Rational Were the Great Railroad Empires?

Railroads, and the telegraph lines constructed with them, enabled the United States to extend political authority across the North American continent. As this chapter shows, Reconstruction policymakers were keenly aware of those benefits — especially of transcontinental rail lines — and offered lavish land grants and other benefits to get the railroads built and keep them operating. Alfred D. Chandler, a business historian writing in the 1970s, and Richard White, a historian of the West writing in the 2010s, agree on the profound impact of the railroads. They offer strikingly different accounts, however, of how the railroads developed and were operated.

ALFRED D. CHANDLER

SOURCE: Alfred D. Chandler Jr., *The Visible Hand: The Managerial Revolution in American Business* (Cambridge, MA: Belknap Press of Harvard University Press, 1977), 107, 120–121, 205.

By the coming of the Civil War the modern American business enterprise had appeared among American railroads. The needs of safety and then efficiency had led to the creation of a managerial hierarchy, whose duties were carefully defined in organizational manuals and charts. Middle and top managers supervised, coordinated, and evaluated the work of lower level managers who were directly responsible for the day-to-day operations. . . . [Railroads] were the first American business enterprise to build a large internal organizational structure with carefully defined lines of responsibility, authority, and communication; . . . and they were the first to develop financial and statistical flows to control and evaluate the work of the many managers.

In all this they were the first because they had to be. No other business enterprise up to that time had had to govern a large number of men and offices scattered over wide geographical areas. . . . Nevertheless, the innovations made by the early large intersectional [rail]roads in organization, accounting, and control went beyond mere necessity. . . . Innovations of the 1850s and 1860s, which became standard practice in the 1870s and 1880s, increased the efficiency and productivity of transportation provided by the individual routes. Improved organization and statistical accounting procedures . . . [also] made possible the fuller exploitation of a steadily improving technology which included larger and heavier engines, larger cars, heavier rails, more effective signals, automatic couplers, air brakes, and the like.

. . . No public enterprise . . . came close to the railroad in size and complexity of operation. In the 1890s a single railroad system managed more men and handled more funds and transactions and used more capital than the most complex of American governmental or military organizations. . . . In the United States, the railroad, not government or the military, provided training in modern large-scale administration.

Protective Tariffs Generate a Surplus To encourage industrial expansion in the U. S., Republicans raised import tariffs on overseas goods ranging from textiles to sugar. Importers paid the tax at U.S. Customs Houses in major port cities. This income paid off the nation's Civil War debt within two decades and by the late 1880s generated a large annual surplus. In this 1887 cartoon, the humor magazine Puck illustrates the surplus as a political problem for Congress, depicting the Democrats claiming the extra money promoted corruption. Republicans directed much of the surplus to expanded pensions for Union veterans, a fleet of modern battleships, and other programs. Library of Congress, 3b52971.

and wielded near-monopoly power (see "Innovators in Enterprise" in Chapter 16). The rise of large private corporations and trusts generated enduring political problems.

The Role of Courts While fostering growth, most historians agree, Republicans did not give government enough regulatory power over the new corporations. State legislatures did pass hundreds of regulatory laws after the Civil War, but interstate companies challenged them in federal courts. In ***Munn v. Illinois*** (1877), the Supreme Court affirmed that states could regulate key businesses, such as railroads and grain elevators, that were "clothed in the public interest." However, the justices feared that too many state and local regulations would impede business and fragment the national marketplace. Starting in the 1870s, they interpreted the due process clause of the new Fourteenth Amendment — which

RICHARD WHITE

SOURCE: Richard White, *Railroaded: The Transcontinentals and the Making of Modern America* (New York: W. W. Norton, 2011), xxix–xxxii.

[Railroad] corporations were not the harbingers of order, rationality, and effective large-scale organization. In both Robert Wiebe's *The Search for Order* and Alfred Chandler's *The Visible Hand*, perhaps the two most brilliant and persistently influential books in shaping our ideas of the late nineteenth century, corporations became the architects of what the political scientist James Scott would later call high modernism. Scott identified high modernism as primarily a state project and made its hallmarks radical simplification and legibility. By legibility, he meant the ability of distant bureaucrats and managers to view, measure, and ostensibly control distant places. . . .

Wiebe and Chandler similarly identified the corporation with managerial capitalism and managerial capitalism with . . . order, simplification, and legibility. . . . In both Wiebe's and Chandler's view the corporation emerged as the realm of salaried managers, experts who displaced financiers, entrepreneurs, families, and even stockholders in the control of business enterprises. They were, for better or worse, a force for order.

. . . On the level of aspiration — what the managers of corporations . . . aspired to create — I have little quarrel with Wiebe and Chandler. The achievement is something else again. Managers blamed their failures on accidents and contingent events, but they also used them to cover their mistakes. . . .

Chandler relied on the records of boards of directors and the kinds of materials found in annual stockholders' reports, but mine is not a view from the boardroom. . . . I don't trust annual reports. I try to descend into the bowels of the organization. Move to the presidents' offices or, better yet, to middle management and the workers on and around the trains, and the actual practices of corporations become far more ambiguous and complicated. The corporation was often at war with itself.

. . . . The organizations I describe here not only failed to institute the order they desired; they also just plain failed and repeatedly needed rescuing by the state and the courts. . . .

I wish, if only for simplicity, that I could say, for better or worse, that the [railroad] tycoons dreamed modernity, built empires, and gave us the world we know. They were, however, not that smart. Many were clever enough at soliciting money and not repaying debts. The shrewdest of them were masters at controlling and manipulating information. We have their equivalents today. They were more likely to feel abused and threatened than imperious. . . . These were men whose failures often mattered as much as their successes. . . . They laid hands on a technology they did not fully understand, initiated sweeping changes, and saw these changes often take on purposes they did not intend. . . . They at least gesture toward one of the mysteries of modernity. How, when powerful people can on close examination seem so ignorant and inept; how, when so much work is done stupidly, shoddily, haphazardly, and selfishly; how, then, does the modern world function at all?

AP® SHORT ANSWER PRACTICE

1. In what ways did railroads innovate, according to Chandler? What impacts of those innovations does he identify?
2. How does White describe Chandler's contribution as a historian, and how does he differentiate his own conclusions from Chandler's and from Wiebe's? Compare the perspectives identified.
3. According to White, what types of primary sources did he use in researching his book on the transcontinental railroads, and how did those differ from sources used by earlier historians such as Chandler? Why might these different types of evidence guide historians toward different conclusions?

TRM Find complete suggested responses in the Teacher's Resource Materials.

dictated that no state could "deprive any person of life, liberty, or property, without due process of law" — as shielding corporations from regulation. Ironically, the Court refused to use the same amendment to protect the rights of African Americans.

In the Southwest as well, federal courts promoted economic development at the expense of racial justice. Though the United States had taken control of New Mexico and Arizona after the U.S.-Mexico War, most of the land was inhabited by Native peoples (as discussed later in this chapter); other lands had long been claimed by Mexican farmers and ranchers. Many lived as *peónes*, under long-standing agreements with landowners who held large tracts originally granted by the Spanish crown. The post–Civil War years brought railroads and an influx of land-hungry Anglos. New Mexico's governor reported indignantly that Mexican shepherds were often "asked" to leave their ranges "by a cowboy or cattle herder with a brace of pistols at his belt and a Winchester in his hands."

Existing land claims were so complex that Congress eventually set up a special court to rule on titles. Between 1891 and 1904, the court invalidated most traditional claims, including those of many New Mexico *ejidos* — villages owned collectively by their communities. Mexican Americans lost about 64 percent of the contested lands. In addition, much land was sold or appropriated through legal machinations like those of a notorious cabal of politicians and lawyers known as the Santa Fe Ring. The result was displacement of thousands of Mexican American villagers and farmers. Some found work as railroad builders or mine workers; others, moving into the sparse high country of the Sierras and Rockies where cattle could not survive, developed sheep raising into a major enterprise.

Munn v. Illinois
An 1877 Supreme Court case that affirmed that states could regulate key businesses, such as railroads and grain elevators, if those businesses were "clothed in the public interest."

AP® SKILLS & PROCESSES

MAKING CONNECTIONS

How did the federal government encourage industrial development and respond to problems industrialization created?

AP® SKILLS & PROCESSES

MAKING CONNECTIONS

Making connections requires students to connect one historical topic to another. Therefore, start by having students explain how the government encouraged industrial development. After students define two or three answers have them explain how industrial development created problems in American society. Finally, have students define ways in which the government responded to those problems students identified in step two.

TRM Find complete suggested responses in the Teacher's Resource Materials.

CHECK FOR UNDERSTANDING

Ask students: **What federal policies contributed to the rise of America's industrial economy, and what were their results?** *During and after the Civil War, Republicans took advantage of their political control of the national government and, building on their Whig heritage, created an economy around infrastructure, high tariffs, and a stable monetary supply. Republicans, for example, subsidized railroads by offering land grants and loans, most notably for the First Transcontinental Railroad, completed in 1869, which tied the nation together and moved people and goods more efficiently. They raised tariffs and built customs houses in each port to collect them, which both brought in revenue and protected U.S. manufacturers from foreign competition, allowing for growth. Finally, they put the United States on the gold standard, which though it inhibited the money supply, also encouraged foreign investments. Overall, these policies encouraged business and raised the standard of living, though not equally for all people.*

AP® SKILLS & PROCESSES

CAUSATION

The Republican economic policies ought to be the easy part of this question as students simply need to account for them from their reading of the textbook. However, students should pay particular attention to which groups were affected. Students may need help in developing names of groups for categories of analysis. Groups such as farmers, industrial workers, business tycoons, small business owners, and financiers might help students make better connections.

TRM Find complete suggested responses in the Teacher's Resource Materials.

AP® THEME

WXT: Work, Exchange, and Technology

The significance of the section title "Incorporating the West" may be lost on students. It is a play on words, referring both to the way the West was *integrated* with the rest of the nation and to the role of *corporations* in that growth. Students will likely miss the second connection, which describes the ways businesses made use of technological innovations, access to natural resources, and redesigned management structures to increase the production of goods.

AP® EXAM TIP

Compare the impact of the gold standard on the growth of industries and on farmers and workers.

gold standard
The practice of backing a country's currency with its reserves of gold. In 1873 the United States, following Great Britain and other European nations, began converting to the gold standard.

Silver and Gold In an era of nation building, U.S. and European governments sought new ways to make their economies orderly and stable. Industrializing nations, for example, tried to develop an international system of standard measurements and even a unified currency. Though these proposals failed as each nation succumbed to self-interest, governments did increasingly agree that, for "scientific" reasons, money should be based on gold, which was thought to have an intrinsic worth above other metals. Great Britain had long held to the **gold standard**, meaning that paper notes from the Bank of England could be backed by gold held in the bank's vaults. During the 1870s and 1880s, the United States, Germany, France, and other countries also converted to gold.

Beforehand, these nations had been on a bimetallic standard: they issued both gold and silver coins, with respective weights fixed at a relative value. The United States switched to the gold standard in part because treasury officials and financiers were watching developments out west. Geologists accurately predicted the discovery of immense silver deposits, such as Nevada's Comstock Lode, without comparable new gold strikes. A massive influx of silver would clearly upset the long-standing ratio. Thus, with a law that became infamous as the "Crime of 1873" because of its negative impact on workers and the economy, Congress chose gold. It directed the U.S. Treasury to cease minting silver dollars and, over a six-year period, retire Civil War–era greenbacks (paper dollars) and replace them with notes from an expanded system of national banks. After this process was complete in 1879, the treasury exchanged these notes for gold on request. (Advocates of bimetallism did achieve one small victory: the Bland-Allison Act of 1878 required the U.S. Mint to coin a modest amount of silver.)

By adopting the gold standard, Republican policymakers sharply limited the nation's money supply, to the level of available gold. The amount of money circulating in the United States had been $30.35 per person in 1865; by 1880, it fell to only $19.36 per person. Today, few economists would sanction such a plan, especially for an economy growing at breakneck speed. They would recommend, instead, increasing money supplies to keep pace with development. But at the time, policymakers remembered rampant antebellum speculation and the hardships of inflation during the Civil War. The United States, as a developing country, also needed to attract investment capital from Britain, Belgium, and other European nations that were on the gold standard. Making it easy to exchange U.S. bonds and currency for gold encouraged European investors to send their money to the United States.

AP® SKILLS & PROCESSES
CAUSATION
How did Republicans' economic policies in this era affect different groups of Americans?

Republican policies fostered exuberant growth and a breathtakingly rapid integration of the economy. Railroads and telegraphs tied the nation together. U.S. manufacturers amassed staggering amounts of capital and built corporations of national and even global scope. With its immense, integrated marketplace of workers, consumers, raw materials, and finished products, the United States was poised to become a mighty industrial power. For policymakers, the hardships of low industrial wages and frontier upheaval and displacement were worth the benefits of rapid growth.

INCORPORATING THE WEST

Why and how did federal policies reshape the trans-Mississippi west after the Civil War?

Republicans wanted farms as well as factories. As early as 1860, popular lyrics hailed the advent of "Uncle Sam's Farm":

> A welcome, warm and hearty, do we give the sons of toil,
> To come west and settle and labor on Free Soil;
> We've room enough and land enough, they needn't feel alarmed —
> Oh! Come to the land of Freedom and vote yourself a farm.

Homestead Act
The 1862 act that gave 160 acres of free western land to any applicant who occupied and improved the property. This policy led to the rapid development of the American West after the Civil War; facing arid conditions in the West, however, many homesteaders found themselves unable to live on their land.

The **Homestead Act** (1862) gave 160 acres of federal land to any applicant who occupied and improved the property. Republicans hoped the bill would help build up the interior West, which was inhabited by Indian peoples but remained "empty" on U.S. government survey maps.

Implementing this plan required innovative policies. The same year it passed the Homestead Act, Congress also created the federal Department of Agriculture and, through the Morrill Act, set aside 140 million federal acres that states could sell to raise money for public universities. The goal of these **land-grant colleges** was to broaden educational opportunities and foster technical and scientific expertise. After the Civil War, Congress also funded a series of geological surveys, dispatching U.S. Army officers, scientists, and photographers to chart unknown western terrain and catalog natural resources.

To a large extent, these policies succeeded in incorporating lands west of the Mississippi. The United States began to exploit its western empire for minerals, lumber, and other raw materials. But for ordinary Americans who went west, dreams often outran reality. Well-financed corporations, not individual prospectors, reaped most of the profits from western mines, while the Great Plains environment proved resistant to ranching and farming.

AP® EXAM TIP

Compare the impact of the Homestead Act and the Morrill Act on the development of the West in the late nineteenth century.

land-grant colleges
Authorized by the Morrill Act of 1862, land-grant colleges were public universities founded to broaden educational opportunities and foster technical and scientific expertise.

Comstock Lode
A vein of silver ore discovered in Nevada in 1859, leading to one of the West's most important mining booms. The lode was so rich that a Confederate expedition tried unsuccessfully to capture it during the Civil War; its output significantly altered the ratio of silver in circulation, leading to changes in monetary policy.

Mining Empires

In the late 1850s, as easy pickings in the California gold rush diminished, prospectors scattered in hopes of finding riches elsewhere. They found gold at many sites, including Nevada, the Colorado Rockies, and South Dakota's Black Hills (Map 15.2). As news of each strike spread, remote areas turned overnight into mob scenes of prospectors, traders, prostitutes, and saloon keepers. White prospectors made their own local laws, often using them — as had happened in California in the 1850s — as instruments to exclude Mexicans, Chinese, and blacks.

The silver from Nevada's **Comstock Lode**, discovered in 1859, built the boomtown of Virginia City, which soon acquired fancy hotels, a Shakespearean theater, and even its own stock exchange. In 1870, a hundred saloons operated in Virginia City, brothels lined D Street, and men outnumbered women 2 to 1. In the 1880s, however, as the Comstock ore gave out, Virginia City suffered the fate of many mining camps: it became a ghost town. What remained was a ravaged landscape with mountains of debris, poisoned water sources, and surrounding lands stripped of timber.

In hopes of encouraging development of western resources, Congress passed the General Mining Act of 1872, which allowed those who discovered minerals on federally owned land to work the claim and keep all the proceeds. (The law — including the $5-per-acre fee for filing a claim — remains in force today.) Americans idealized the notion of the lone, hardy mining prospector with his pan and his mule, but tapping deep veins of underground ore required big money. Consortiums of powerful investors, bringing engineers and advanced equipment, generally extracted the most wealth. This was the case for the New York trading firm Phelps Dodge, which invested in massive copper mines and smelting operations on both sides of the U.S.-Mexico border. The mines created jobs in new towns like Bisbee and Morenci, Arizona — but with dangerous conditions and low pay, especially for those who received the segregated "Mexican wage." Anglos, testified one Mexican mine worker, "occupied decorous residences . . . and had large amounts of money," while "the Mexican population and its economic condition offered a pathetic contrast." He protested this affront to "the most elemental principles of justice."

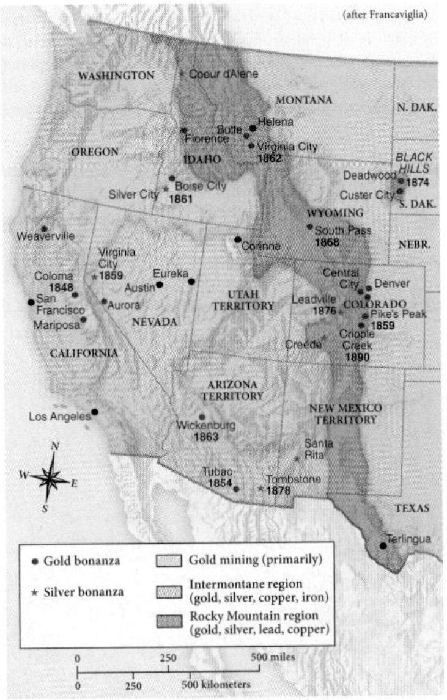

MAP 15.2 Mining Frontiers, 1848–1890
The Far West was America's gold country because of its geological history. Veins of gold and silver form when molten material from the earth's core is forced up into fissures caused by the tectonic movements that create mountain ranges, such as the ones that dominate the far western landscape. It was these veins, the product of mountain-forming activity many thousands of years earlier, that prospectors began to discover after 1848 and furiously exploit. Although widely dispersed across the Far West, the lodes that they found followed the mountain ranges bisecting the region and bypassing the great plateaus not shaped by the ancient tectonic activity.

AP® THEME

GEO: Geography and the Environment

Use **MAP 15.2** to prompt students to examine the ways that geography — in this case, geology — shaped the mining patterns that fueled the nation's economic growth.

CHECK FOR UNDERSTANDING

Ask students: **How did mining create empires?** *Mining operations often involved groups of investors, trained engineers, use of expensive equipment, and low-skill dependent wage labor. The consequent exploitation of the environment is also similar to imperial patterns, where colonial powers give little heed to the destruction of the environment in a search for maximum profits.*

AP® THEME

WXT: Work, Exchange, and Technology

Hydraulic mining is one example of a technological innovation that required significant capital investment. The Oakland Museum of California provides a short but vivid description of the process of hydraulic mining and its varied environmental effects. To access this site, search "Oakland Museum hydraulic mining."

AP® APPLY THE TIP

Working with partners, direct students to provide details from the text (pp. 489–490) to complete **Handout 15.2 — Comparison: Ranchers and Miners in the West (TRM)** to compare the experience of ranching and mining in the West.

TRM Find **Handout 15.2 — Comparison: Ranchers and Miners in the West** in the Teacher's Resource Materials.

Hydraulic Mining This image from 1866 in French Corral, California, northeast of Sacramento in the Sierra Nevada mountains, shows the destructive power of hydraulic mining. Miners used powerful hoses to wash away dirt and look for gold. The process clogged streams and rivers with dirt and reshaped the landscape — as did dam building, tree cutting, and related activities in the pursuit of gold. Library of Congress, 3a12334.

The rise of western mining created an insatiable market for timber and produce from the Pacific Northwest. Seattle and Portland grew rapidly as supply centers, especially during the great gold rushes of California (after 1848) and the Klondike in Canada's Yukon Territory (after 1897). Residents of Tacoma, Washington, claimed theirs was the "City of Destiny" when it became the Pacific terminus for the Northern Pacific, the nation's third transcontinental railroad, in 1887. But rival businessmen in Seattle succeeded in promoting their city as the gateway to Alaska and the Klondike. Seattle, a town with 1,000 residents in 1870, grew over the next forty years to a population of a quarter million.

From Bison to Cattle on the Plains

While boomtowns arose across the West, hunters began transforming the plains. During the Civil War years, great herds of bison (commonly called "buffalo") still roamed this region. But overhunting and the introduction of European animal afflictions, like the bacterial disease brucellosis, were already decimating the herds. In the 1870s and early 1880s, hide hunters finished them off so thoroughly that at one point fewer than two hundred bison remained in U.S. territory, though just a decade earlier they had numbered in the millions (fifteen million being observers' and historians' best guess). Hunters hidden downwind, under the right conditions, could kill four dozen bison at a time without moving from the spot. Using this method one man killed 5,700 bison in two months. These hunters took the tough hides, selling the leather for belts on industrial machines, but left the meat to rot, an act of vast wastefulness that shocked Native peoples.

AP® EXAM TIP

Compare the experiences of settlers in the West who engaged in ranching and in mining in the late nineteenth century.

Bison Skulls on the Plain, 1892 After hunters slaughtered millions of bison and left the carcasses to rot, pioneers gathered the skulls and sold them for processing. The destruction of the great bison herds, then, occurred as part of the broad process of industrialization: buffalo leather was converted into belts that operated industrial machinery, while the skulls were ground up for fertilizer or other uses, such as charcoal for sugar manufacture. The Granger Collection, New York.

Efforts to protect the bison failed, largely due to political and military calculations in Washington. Although Congress passed an 1874 law to criminalize the hunting of female bison by anyone except Indians, President Ulysses S. Grant pocket vetoed the bill. Railroad and telegraph companies found bison to be a nuisance: large herds obstructed train travel, and when bison rubbed against telegraph poles and knocked them over, wire service ended. In addition, U.S. treaties specified that certain Native nations, including the Comanches, Kiowas, Cheyennes, and Arapahos, could continue to live and hunt on the plains as long as there were enough bison on the range "to justify the chase." Killing the bison meant robbing Native peoples of their sustenance, making it far easier to force them onto reservations. One army officer quietly advised a visitor in the West, "kill every buffalo you can. Every buffalo dead is an Indian gone."

Removal of the bison opened opportunities for cattle ranchers. South Texas provided an early model for their ambitious plans. By the end of the Civil War, about five million head of longhorn cattle grazed on Anglo ranches there. In 1865, the Missouri Pacific Railroad reached Sedalia, Missouri, far enough west to be accessible as Texas reentered the Union. A longhorn worth $3 in Texas might command $40 at Sedalia. With this incentive, ranchers inaugurated the Long Drive, hiring cowboys to herd cattle hundreds of miles north to the new rail lines, which soon extended into Kansas. Traveling in spring, when cattle could nibble on fresh grass as they walked, ranchers sold their longhorns at rail hubs such as Abilene and Dodge City, Kansas, while trail-weary cowboys crowded into saloons. These cowtowns captured the nation's imagination as symbols of the Wild West, but the reality was much less exciting. Cowboys, many of them African Americans and Latinos, were really farmhands on horseback who worked long, harsh hours for low pay.

North of Texas, public grazing lands drew investors and adventurers eager for a taste of the West. By the early 1880s, as many as 7.5 million cattle were overgrazing the plains' native grasses. A cycle of good weather postponed disaster, which arrived in 1886: record blizzards and bitter cold. An awful scene of rotting carcasses greeted cowboys as they rode onto the range that spring. Further hit by a severe drought the following summer, the cattle boom collapsed.

Thanks to new strategies, however, cattle ranching survived and became part of the integrated national economy. As railroads reached Texas and ranchers there abandoned the Long Drive, the invention of barbed wire — which enabled ranchers and farmers to fence large areas cheaply and easily on the plains, where wood was scarce and expensive — made it easier for northern cattlemen to fence small areas and feed animals on hay. Stockyards appeared beside the rapidly extending railroad tracks, and trains took these gathered cattle to giant slaughterhouses in cities like Chicago, which turned them into cheap beef for customers back east.

Mythic Outlaws and Cowboys As early as the 1860s, popular dime novels such as this one celebrated the alleged ruggedness, individual freedoms, and gun-slinging capabilities of western cowboys. (Note that this 1888 story, like most dime novels, was published in New York City.) Generations of young Americans grew up on stories of frontier valor and "Cowboys versus Indians." In fact, cowboys were wageworkers on horseback. An ethnically diverse group, including many blacks and Hispanics, they earned perhaps $25 a month, plus meals and a bed in the bunkhouse, in return for long hours of grueling, lonesome work. Denver Public Library, Western History Collection / Bridgeman Images.

Homesteaders

Republicans envisioned the Great Plains dotted with small farms, but farmers had to be persuaded that crops would grow there. Powerful interests worked hard to overcome the popular antebellum idea that the grassland was the Great American Desert. Railroads, eager to sell land the government had granted them, advertised aggressively. Land speculators, transatlantic steamship lines, and western states and territories joined the campaign.

Newcomers found the soil beneath the native prairie grasses deep and fertile. Steel plows enabled them to break through the tough roots, while barbed wire provided cheap, effective fencing. European immigrants brought strains of hard-kernel wheat that tolerated the extreme temperatures of the plains. As if to confirm promoters' optimism, a wet cycle occurred between 1878 and 1886, increasing rainfall in the arid regions east of the Rockies. Americans decided that "rain follows the plow": settlement and farming of the plains was increasing rainfall. Some attributed the rain to soil cultivation and tree planting, while others credited God. One Harvard professor proposed that steel railroad tracks attracted moisture. Such optimists would soon learn their mistake.

The motivation for most settlers, American or immigrant, was to better themselves economically. Union veterans, who received favorable terms in staking homestead claims, played a major role in settling Kansas and other plains states. When

AP® EXAM TIP

Evaluate the opportunities and challenges that homesteading presented to various groups in the late nineteenth century.

TEACHING STRATEGY

Students could explore why the image of cowboys — and the West more generally — continues to have such resonance in American popular culture. "Making Myths: The West in Public and Private Writings," a lesson from PBS's companion site to *The West*, provides an opportunity for students to engage in such an exploration. In this lesson, students read selections from the works of a number of authors, place them on a timeline of writers about the West, and select elements in their works that demonstrate a distinctly Western voice. Students determine how these works came to typify a western mythic image and contrast these versions of the West with the diaries and letters of the pioneers who documented their own travails. Finally, each student can select a work from contemporary Western literature to read and analyze in depth. In their final assignment, they will compare the perspective of the author of their work with the writers read in the first part of the lesson. To access this lesson, search "PBS The West Making Myths."

CHECK FOR UNDERSTANDING

Ask students: **What were the experiences of cattlemen on the Plains?** *The decimation of buffalo herds paved the way for grazing cattle on the Plains. Cowboys, many of whom were African American and Latino, were essentially farmhands on horseback working long hours for relatively low pay. Mature cattle were herded to rail lines to be slaughtered for food in cities. Periods of overgrazing and harsh winters led to occasional disasters but fencing and the use of hay eventually stabilized the process of cattle herding.*

AP® APPLY THE TIP

Help students understand the impact of the Homestead Act of 1862 and the opportunities and challenges of homesteading using **Handout 15.3 — Thematic Analysis: Homestead Act (TRM)**. Students should add at least two specific pieces of evidence related to the Homestead Act and homesteading for each theme as well as try to include a key term, event, person's name, etc., in each point they add to the handout. Remind students that specific supporting details are usually things that have to be capitalized, such as names, place, events. Once students have completed the thematic analysis, recreate the diagram on the board (or project the worksheet) and ask students to volunteer to add specific points with each theme. Guide students in a discussion of the Homestead Act and the opportunities and challenges of homesteading.

TRM Find **Handout 15.3 — Thematic Analysis: Homestead Act** in Teacher's Resource Materials.

severe depression hit northern Europe in the 1870s, Norwegians and Swedes joined German emigrants in large numbers. At the peak of "American fever" in 1882, more than 105,000 Scandinavians left for the United States. Swedish and Norwegian became the primary languages in parts of Minnesota and the Dakotas.

For some African Americans, the plains represented a promised land of freedom. In 1879, a group of black communities left Mississippi and Louisiana in a quest to escape poverty and white violence. Some 6,000 blacks departed together, most carrying little but the clothes on their backs and faith in God. They called themselves **Exodusters**, participants in a great exodus to Kansas. The 1880 census reported 40,000 blacks there, by far the largest African American concentration in the West aside from Texas, where the expanding cotton frontier attracted hundreds of thousands of black migrants.

Exodusters
African Americans who walked or rode out of the Deep South following the Civil War, many settling on farms in Kansas in hopes of finding peace and prosperity.

For newcomers, taming the plains differed from pioneering in antebellum Iowa or Oregon. Dealers sold big new machines — on credit — to help with plowing and harvesting. Western wheat traveled by rail to giant grain elevators and traded immediately on world markets. Hoping frontier land values would appreciate rapidly, many farmers planned to profit from selling acres as much as (or more than) from their crops. In boom times, many rushed into debt to acquire more land and better equipment. All these enthusiasms — for cash crops, land speculation, borrowed money, and new technology — bore witness to the conviction that farming was, as one agricultural journal remarked, a business "like all other business."

Women in the West Early miners, lumbermen, and cowboys were overwhelmingly male, but homesteading was a family affair. The success of a farm depended on the work of wives and children who tended the garden and animals, preserved food, and helped out at harvest time. Some women struck out on their own: a study of North Dakota found between 5 and 20 percent of homestead claims filed by single women, often working land adjacent to that of sisters, brothers, and parents. Family members thus supported one another in the difficult work of farming, while easing the loneliness many newcomers felt. Looking back with pride on her homesteading days, one Dakota woman said simply, "It was a place to stay and it was mine."

While promoting farms in the West, Republicans clashed with the distinctive religious group that had already settled Utah: Mormons, or members of the Church of Jesus Christ of Latter-day Saints (LDS). After suffering persecution in Missouri and Illinois, Mormons had moved west to Utah in the 1840s. Most Americans at the time were deeply hostile to Mormonism, especially the LDS practice of plural marriage — sanctioned by church founder Joseph Smith — through which some Mormon men married more than one wife.

Mormons had their own complex view of women's role, illustrated by the career of Mormon leader Emmeline Wells. Born in New Hampshire, Wells converted to Mormonism at age thirteen along with her mother and joined the exodus to Utah in 1848. After her first husband abandoned her when he left the church, Wells became the seventh wife of a church elder. In 1870, due in part to organized pressure from Wells and other Mormon women, the Utah legislature granted full voting rights to women, becoming the second U.S. territory to do so (after Wyoming, in 1869). The measure increased LDS control, since most Utah women were Mormons, while non-Mormons in mining camps were predominantly male. Suffrage also recognized the central role of women in Mormon life.

Amid the constitutional debates of Reconstruction, polygamy and women's voting rights became intertwined issues (see "Firsthand Accounts," p. 494). Encouraged by other plural wives, Wells began in 1877 to write for a Salt Lake City newspaper, the *Woman's Exponent*. She served as editor for forty years. When Wells entered a local election, Utah's legislature initially blocked her candidacy based on her sex. But when Utah won statehood in 1896, Wells had the pleasure of watching several women win seats in the new legislature, including Dr. Martha Hughes Cannon, a physician and Mormon plural wife who became the first American woman to serve in a state senate.

Like their counterparts in other western states, Utah's white women experienced a combination of severe frontier hardships and striking new opportunities.

Environmental Challenges Homesteaders faced a host of challenges, particularly the natural environment of the Great Plains. Clouds of grasshoppers could descend and destroy a crop in a day; a prairie fire or hailstorm could do the job in an hour. In spring, homesteaders faced sudden, terrifying tornados, while their winter experiences in the 1870s added the word *blizzard* to America's vocabulary. On the plains, also, water and lumber were hard to find. Newly arrived families often cut dugouts into hillsides and then, after a season or two, erected houses made of turf cut from the ground.

Over the long term, homesteaders discovered that the western grasslands did not receive enough rain to grow wheat and other grains. As the cycle of rainfall shifted from wet to dry, farmers as well as ranchers suffered. "A wind hot as an oven's fury . . . raged like a pestilence," reported one Nebraskan, leaving "farmers helpless, with no weapon against this terrible and inscrutable wrath of nature." By the late 1880s, some recently settled lands emptied as homesteaders fled in defeat — 50,000 from the Dakotas alone. It became obvious that farming in the arid West required methods other than those used east of the Mississippi.

Clearly, 160-acre homesteads were the wrong size for the West: farmers needed either small irrigated plots or immense tracts for dry farming, which involved deep planting to bring subsoil moisture to the roots and quick harrowing after rainfalls to slow evaporation. Dry farming developed most fully on huge corporate farms in the Red River Valley of North Dakota. But even family farms, the norm elsewhere, could not survive on less than 300 acres of grain. Crop prices were too low, and the climate too unpredictable, to allow farmers to get by on less.

In this struggle, homesteaders regarded themselves as nature's conquerors, striving, as one pioneer remarked, "to get the land subdued and the wilde nature out of it."

A Family in Their Nebraska Sod House Many immigrants to the Great Plains, arriving with few resources, started in sod houses like this one. Wood had to be brought from afar by railroad and was expensive. The wagon and horses are not on the roof, as it appears, but on the grass behind it; the father of the family almost certainly drove them into the picture to have a record of these prized possessions, which were (along with his plow) essential tools for a better future. Many farm families went "bust," but Solomon Butcher, who took this photograph, returned years later to photograph others living in new frame homes, and using their original sod houses for storage. Solomon D. Butcher/PhotoQuest/Getty Images.

AP® THEME

MIG: Migration and Settlement

This photograph suggests the difficult, austere life of many homesteaders. While the Homestead Act promised free land in fulfillment of the American vision of independent republican farmers, making a go of it was very challenging. "Homesteaders," a lesson created through the Library of Congress's Teaching with Primary Sources Program, explores life on the Nebraska prairie based on images and texts from the 1860s. To access this lesson, search "Teaching with Primary Sources Homesteaders."

AP® SKILLS & PROCESSES

ANALYZING HISTORICAL EVIDENCE

The **AP® FIRSTHAND ACCOUNTS** feature explores the intersection of women's rights and religious history in considering women's suffrage in the context of Mormonism. This exercise provides an opportunity to confront presentism. Many students will find the notion that Mormon culture was "progressive" in giving women the right to vote early counterintuitive, since Mormons also sanctioned plural marriage for men (but not for women), which seemed to indicate the unequal status between men and women in their worldview. The challenge is for students to understand why what may seem contradictory to themselves did not seem so to Mormons at the time. In exploring these documents, students should keep in mind that other western states also gave women the right to vote. Indeed, Wyoming granted the franchise to women the year before Utah.

AP® FIRSTHAND ACCOUNTS

Women's Rights in the West

In 1870, Utah's territorial legislature granted voting rights to women. The decision was a shock to advocates of women's suffrage in the East: they expected their first big victories would come in New England. Furthermore, Utah was overwhelmingly peopled by Mormons — members of the Church of Jesus Christ of Latter-day Saints (LDS). Critics saw Mormonism as a harshly patriarchal religion. They especially loathed the Mormon practice of "plural marriage," in which some Mormon men took more than one wife. Most easterners thought this practice was barbaric and demeaning to women. Over the next two decades, Republicans pressured Mormons to abolish plural marriage. They also disenfranchised Mormon women and required men to take an antipolygamy oath; Congress refused to admit Utah as a state. Only after 1890, when the LDS church officially abolished plural marriage, was Utah statehood possible. In 1896, when Utah became a state, women's voting rights were finally reinstated.

FANNY STENHOUSE

Exposé of Polygamy: A Lady's Life Among the Mormons, 1872

An Englishwoman who converted to the faith and moved to Utah, Stenhouse became disillusioned and published her book to criticize the practice of Mormon polygamy.

SOURCE: *Exposé of Polygamy: A Lady's Life Among the Mormons*, ed. Linda Wilcox DeSimone (Logan: Utah State University Press, 2008), 72–73, 155.

"How little do the Mormon men of Utah know what it is, in the truest sense, to have a wife, though they have so many 'wives,' after their own fashion. Almost imperceptibly to the husband, and even the wife herself, a barrier rises between them the very day that he marries another woman. It matters not how much she believes in the doctrine of plural marriages, or how willing she may be to submit to it; the fact remains the same. The estrangement begins by her trying to hide from him all secret sorrow; for she feels that what has been can not be undone now, and she says, 'I cannot change it; neither would I if I could, because it is the will of God, and I must bear it; besides, what good will it do to worry my husband with all my feelings?'

. . . A man may have a dozen wives; but from the whole of them combined he will not receive as much real love and devotion as he might from one alone, if he had made her feel that she had his undivided affection and confidence. How terribly these men deceive themselves! When peace, or rather quiet, reigns in their homes, they think that the spirit of God is there. But it is not so! It is a calm, not like the gentle silence of sleep, but as the horrible stillness of death — the death of the heart's best affections, and all that is worth calling love. All true love has fled, and indifference has taken its place. The very children feel it. What do they — what can they care about their fathers? They seldom see them.

Whatever, in the providence of God, may be the action of Congress toward Utah, if the word of a feeble woman can be listened to, let me respectfully ask the Honorable Senators and Representatives of the United States that, in the abolition of Polygamy, if such should be the decree of the nation, let no compromise be made where subtlety can bind the woman now living in Polygamy to remain in that condition."

ELIZA SNOW, HARRIET COOK YOUNG, PHOEBE WOODRUFF

A Defense of Plural Marriage, 1870

The vast majority of Mormon women defended their faith and the practice of plural marriage. The statements by Eliza Snow, Harriet Cook Young, and Phoebe Woodruff, below, were made at a public protest meeting in Salt Lake City in 1870. LDS women pointed proudly to their new suffrage rights as proof of their religion's just treatment of women. Why did Mormons, who dominated the Utah legislature, give women full voting rights? In part, they sought to protect their church by increasing Mormon voting power: most of the non-Mormons were single men who worked on ranches

Much about its "wilde nature" was hidden to the newcomers. They did not know that destroying biodiversity, which was what farming the plains really amounted to, opened pathways for exotic, destructive pests and weeds, and that removing native grasses left the soil vulnerable to erosion. By the turn of the twentieth century, about half the nation's cattle and sheep, one-third of its cereal crops, and nearly three-fifths of its wheat came from the Great Plains. But in the drier parts of the region, it was not a sustainable achievement. This renowned breadbasket was later revealed to be, in the words of one historian, "the largest, longest-run agricultural and environmental miscalculation in American history."

John Wesley Powell, a one-armed Union veteran, predicted trouble from an early date. Powell, employed by the new U.S. Geological Survey, led a famous expedition in or in mining camps. But the LDS Church also celebrated women's central role in the family and community. Some women achieved prominence as midwives, teachers, and professionals.

SOURCE: Edward W. Tullidge, *Women of Mormondom* (New York: Tullidge & Crandall, 1877), 390–391, 396, 400.

❝ *Eliza Snow:* Our enemies pretend that, in Utah, woman is held in a state of vassalage — that she does not act from choice, but by coercion — that we would even prefer life elsewhere, were it possible for us to make our escape. What nonsense! We all know that if we wished we could leave at any time — either go singly, or to rise en masse, and there is no power here that could, or would wish to, prevent us. I will now ask this assemblage of intelligent ladies, do you know of anyplace on the face of the earth, where woman has more liberty, and where she enjoys such high and glorious privileges as she does here, as a latter-day saint? No! The very idea of woman here in a state of slavery is a burlesque on good common sense.

Harriet Cook Young: Wherever monogamy reigns, adultery, prostitution and foeticide, directly or indirectly, are its concomitants. . . . The women of Utah comprehend this; and they see, in the principle of plurality of wives, the only safeguard against adultery, prostitution, and the reckless waste of pre-natal life, practiced throughout the land.

Phoebe Woodruff: God has revealed unto us the law of the patriarchal order of marriage, and commanded us to obey it. We are sealed to our husbands for time and eternity, that we may dwell with them and our children in the world to come; which guarantees unto us the greatest blessing for which we are created. If the rulers of the nation will so far depart from the spirit and letter of our glorious constitution as to deprive our prophets, apostles and elders of citizenship, and imprison them for obeying this law, let them grant this, our last request, to make their prisons large enough to hold their wives, for where they go we will go also. ❞

SUSAN B. ANTHONY

Letter to *The Revolution*, July 5, 1871

National women's suffrage leaders responded awkwardly to the Utah suffrage victory. Being associated with Mormons, they understood, damaged their fragile new movement in the eyes of most Americans. But they tried tentatively to forge alliances with Mormon women they viewed as progressive, as well as dissidents in the church. Suffrage leader Susan B. Anthony traveled to Salt Lake City in 1871 to try to forge alliances with Mormon women, especially dissidents such as Fanny Stenhouse. Anthony expressed strong disapproval of polygamy, but she also tried to change the debate to focus on the vulnerability of all married women to exploitation by their husbands. Her report from Utah, published in her journal *The Revolution*, follows.

SOURCE: *The Revolution*, July 20, 1871.

❝ Woman's work in monogamy and polygamy is essentially one and the same — that of planting her feet on the solid ground of self-support; . . . there is and can be no salvation for womanhood but in the possession of power over her own subsistence.

The saddest feature here is that there really is nothing by which these women can earn an independent livelihood for themselves and children. No manufacturing establishments; no free schools to teach. Women here, as everywhere, must be able to live honestly and honorably without men, before it can be possible to save the masses of them from entering into polygamy or prostitution, legal or illegal. Whichever way I turn, whatever phase of social life presents itself, the same conclusion comes — independent bread alone can redeem woman from her sure subjection to man. . . .

Here is missionary ground. Not for 'thus saith the Lord,' divine rights, canting priests, or echoing priestesses of any sect whatsoever; but for great, god-like, humanitarian men and women, who 'feel for them in bonds as bound with them,' . . . a simple, loving, sisterly clasp of hands with these struggling women, and an earnest work with them. Not to modify nor ameliorate, but to ABOLISH the whole system of woman's subjection to man in both polygamy and monogamy. ❞

QUESTIONS FOR ANALYSIS

1. What arguments did the Mormon women make in defense of plural marriage? On what grounds did Stenhouse argue for its abolition? Compare these perspectives.
2. Susan B. Anthony's letter was published in Boston. How might Mormon women have reacted to it? How might non-Mormon women have reacted to the statements by Snow, Young, and Woodruff? Explain the historical situation of Anthony that might lead her to this perspective.
3. Compare the experiences of plural marriage described by Stenhouse, on the one hand, and Snow, Young, and Woodruff, on the other. How do you account for these very different perspectives? How does the purpose of the sources inform their points of view?

TRM Find complete suggested responses in the Teacher's Resource Materials.

the West in which his team navigated the rapids of the Colorado River through the Grand Canyon in wooden boats. In his *Report on the Lands of the Arid Region of the United States* (1879), Powell told Congress bluntly that 160-acre homesteads would not work in dry regions. Impressed with the success of Mormons' irrigation projects in Utah, Powell urged the United States to follow their model. He proposed that the government develop western water resources, building dams and canals and organizing landowners into local districts to operate them. Doubting that rugged individualism would succeed in the West, Powell proposed massive cooperation under government control.

After heated debate, Congress rejected Powell's plan. Critics accused him of playing into the hands of large ranching corporations; boosters were not yet willing to give up the dream of small homesteads. But Powell turned out to be right. Though

AP® SKILLS & PROCESSES

COMPARISON

The **COMPARISON** question asks students to compare three different economic activities and their consequences. It might be helpful for students to create a simple chart with one row for each activity and columns for the development of that activity, where it was concentrated, what role the government played in its growth, and the nature of its environmental impact. To extend this prompt, students could indicate why some forms of economic activity were so much more destructive than others. Alternatively, students could explore the role that beliefs about nature played in the environmental consequences of the West.

TRM Find complete suggested responses in the Teacher's Resource Materials.

CHECK FOR UNDERSTANDING

Ask students: **What were the experiences of homesteaders in the West?** *War veterans, immigrants, and African American "Exodusters" all moved west hoping to improve their economic circumstances. Farming in the West required new plowing and harvesting machines, and access to rail to sell crops. Homesteading required the labor of families — women and children — not single men, as with mining and cattle ranching. Homesteaders faced a host of environmental challenges, including pests, blizzards, and water shortages. The standard lot size of 160 acres was insufficient to produce enough income for a family in many arid portions of the West.*

TEACHING STRATEGY

In a short *National Geographic* article, Nina Strochlic argues that Moran transformed American views of Yellowstone from a harsh, wild place to a sublime landscape. This article helps students see how understandings of the landscape are not simply seen but interpreted through a particular lens or set of cultural values. To access this article, search "National Geographic Thomas Moran Yellowstone Paintings."

AP® SKILLS & PROCESSES

COMPARISON

Compare the development of mining, ranching, and farming in the West. How did their environmental consequences differ?

environmental historians do not always agree with Powell's proposed solutions, they point to his *Report on Arid Lands* as a cogent critique of what went wrong on the Great Plains. Later, federal funding paid for dams and canals that supported intensive agriculture in many parts of the West. But that only happened after severe cycles of drought, suffering, and loss.

The First National Park

Powell was not the only one rethinking land use. The West's incorporation into the national marketplace occurred with such speed that some Americans began to fear rampant overdevelopment. Perhaps the federal government should not sell off all its public land, but instead hold and manage some of it. Amid the heady initiatives of Reconstruction, Congress began to preserve sites of unusual natural splendor. As early as 1864, Congress gave 10 square miles of the Yosemite Valley to California for "public use, resort, and recreation." (In 1890, Yosemite reverted to federal control.) In 1872, Congress set aside 2 million acres of Wyoming's Yellowstone Valley as the world's first national park: preserved as a public holding, it would serve as "a public park or pleasuring ground for the benefit and enjoyment of the people."

Yellowstone National Park Established in 1872 by Congress, Yellowstone was the first national park in the United States.

Railroad tourism, which developed side by side with other western industries, was an important motive for the creation of **Yellowstone National Park**. The Northern Pacific Railroad lobbied Congress vigorously to get the park established. Soon, luxury Pullman cars ushered visitors to Yellowstone's hotel, operated by the railroad itself. But creation of the park was fraught with complications. Since no one knew exactly what a "national park" was or how to operate it, the U.S. Army was dispatched to take charge; only in the early 1900s, after Congress established more parks in the West, did consistent management policies emerge. In the meantime, soldiers spent much of their time arresting Native peoples who sought to hunt on Yellowstone lands.

The creation of Yellowstone was an important step toward an ethic of respect for land and wildlife. So was the 1871 creation of a U.S. Fisheries Commission, which

Thomas Moran, *Grand Canyon of the Yellowstone*, 1872 In 1871, English-born artist Thomas Moran joined Ferdinand Hayden's expedition to the Yellowstone Valley on behalf of the U.S. Geological Survey, an important new federal agency dedicated to mapping and exploring the West, as well as undertaking scientific investigations of flora, fauna, and potential mineral and timber resources. Moran's painting, along with photographs by William Henry Jackson and other eyewitness testimony to Yellowstone's uniqueness and beauty, helped introduce the American public to their first new national park. The painting remains property of the federal government, who commissioned Hayden's expedition, and hangs in the Smithsonian American Art Museum. Artepics / Alamy Stock Photo.

made recommendations to stem the decline in wild fish; by the 1930s, it merged with other federal wildlife bureaus to become the **U.S. Fish and Wildlife Service**. At the same time, eviction of Indians showed that the act of defining small preserves as "uninhabited wilderness" was part of conquest itself. In 1877, for example, the federal government forcibly removed the Nez Perce tribe from their ancestral land in what is now Idaho, Washington, and Oregon. Under the leadership of young Chief Joseph, the Nez Perce tried to flee to Canada. After a journey of 1,100 miles, they were forced to surrender just short of the border. During their trek, five bands crossed Yellowstone; as a Nez Perce named Yellow Wolf recalled, they "knew that country well." For thirteen days, Nez Perce men raided the valley for supplies, waylaying several groups of tourists. The conflict made national headlines. Easterners, proud of their new "pleasuring ground," were startled to find that it remained a site of Native resistance. Americans were not settling an empty West. They were *un*settling it by taking it from Native peoples who already lived there.

U.S. Fish and Wildlife Service
A federal bureau established in 1871 that made recommendations to stem the decline in wild fish. Its creation was an important step toward wildlife conservation and management.

AP® SKILLS & PROCESSES

CAUSATION

What factors led to the creation of the first national park?

A HARVEST OF BLOOD: NATIVE PEOPLES DISPOSSESSED

In the late nineteenth century, how did the United States dispossess Native peoples and attempt to assimilate them, and how did those peoples respond?

Before the Civil War, when most Americans believed the prairie could not be farmed, Congress reserved the Great Plains for Indian peoples. But in the era of steel plows and railroads, policymakers suddenly had the power and desire to incorporate the whole region. During and after the Civil War, the U.S. Army fought against the loosely federated Sioux — the major power on the northern grasslands — as well as other peoples who had agreed to live on reservations but found conditions so desperate that they fled (Map 15.3). These "reservation wars," caused largely by local violence and confused federal policies, were messy and bitter. Pointing to failed military campaigns, army atrocities, and egregious corruption in the Indian Bureau, reformers called for new policies that would destroy Native peoples' traditional lifeways and "civilize" them — or, as one educator put it, "kill the Indian and save the man."

AP® EXAM TIP

As you read through this section, trace violent conflicts in the West that resulted from the U.S. government violating treaties with Native groups and responding to Native resistance with force.

The Civil War and Indians on the Plains

In August 1862, the attention of most Unionists and Confederates was riveted on General George McClellan's failing campaign in Virginia. But in Minnesota, the Dakota Sioux were increasingly frustrated. Four years earlier, when Minnesota secured statehood, they had agreed to settle on a strip of land reserved by the government, in exchange for receiving regular payments and supplies. But Indian agents, contractors, and even Minnesota's territorial governor pocketed most of the funds. When the Dakotas protested that their children were starving, state officials dismissed their appeals. Corruption was so egregious that one leading Minnesotan, Episcopal bishop Henry Whipple, wrote an urgent appeal to President James Buchanan. "A nation which sows robbery," he warned, "will reap a harvest of blood."

Whipple's prediction proved correct. During the summer of 1862, a decade of anger boiled over. In a surprise attack, Dakota fighters fanned out through the Minnesota countryside, killing immigrants and burning farms. They planned to sweep eastward to St. Paul but were stopped at Fort Ridgely. In the end, more than four hundred whites lay dead, including women and children from farms and small towns. Thousands fled; panicked officials telegraphed for aid, spreading hysteria from Wisconsin to Colorado.

AP® SKILLS & PROCESSES

CAUSATION

In answering this **CAUSATION** question about the factors that led to the creation of the first national park, students will likely gravitate toward the actual legislation and those who lobbied for it. They should be encouraged to consider broader factors, including views toward Native Americans and the willingness to dispossess them, the remarkable natural features of the parks themselves, the cultural currents of romanticism that stimulated a celebration of unspoiled sublime landscapes, and the emergence of notions of tourism and recreation. Students could additionally compare the dynamics that led to the establishment of national parks with the desire to exploit natural resources, discussed in the previous section.

TRM Find complete suggested responses in the Teacher's Resource Materials.

CHECK FOR UNDERSTANDING

Ask students: **What factors led to transformation of the trans-Mississippi west after the Civil War?** Students' answers will likely vary, but topics for interpretations could include transportation developments such as the railroad, industrialization and concomitant economic ventures out west, government subsidies, collective dispositions toward American Indians, immigration patterns, and natural resources. This question is a good example of why students should write about what they know. Part of the challenge for students in answering broad questions is possessing the requisite confidence in their inclinations. Encourage students to accept the fact there are many interpretations to this one question.

AP® APPLY THE TIP

To illustrate the impact of U.S. government policies on Native groups, show students the TED talk by Aaron Huey entitled "America's Native Prisoners of War." You can provide students with a transcript of the video as they watch to underline important policies of the U.S. government that impacted this particular group of Native Americans. After the video, lead a class discussion to elaborate on any questions the video brought up or to clarify understanding of government policies referred to in the video. Ask students to articulate the historical argument of Aaron Huey. Then, ask them to extend their analysis by explaining how point of view and historical context influenced this historical argument. Finally, ask students to work in collaborative groups to articulate a thesis statement and outline in response to the following prompt: Compare the policies of the federal government toward Native groups in the West in the late nineteenth century to policies toward Native groups in the period 1789–1840s.

AP® THEME

WXT: Work, Exchange, and Technology

Ask students: **What does MAP 15.3 indicate about the cession of Indian lands between 1850 and 1890?** *During this forty-year period, Native Americans lost the overwhelming majority of their former lands. They were confined to a few dozen reservations scattered across the West, the largest in Nebraska, the so-called Indian Territory, and Arizona–New Mexico.*

AP® SKILLS & PROCESSES

DEVELOPMENTS AND PROCESSES

The nineteenth century witnessed a number of different policies toward American Indians, each of which sought to control land and culture. Have students define each of the following terms: acculturation, removal, reservation. Have students write a two-to-three-sentence answer explaining the historical continuities and changes to the policies of the United States toward American Indians.

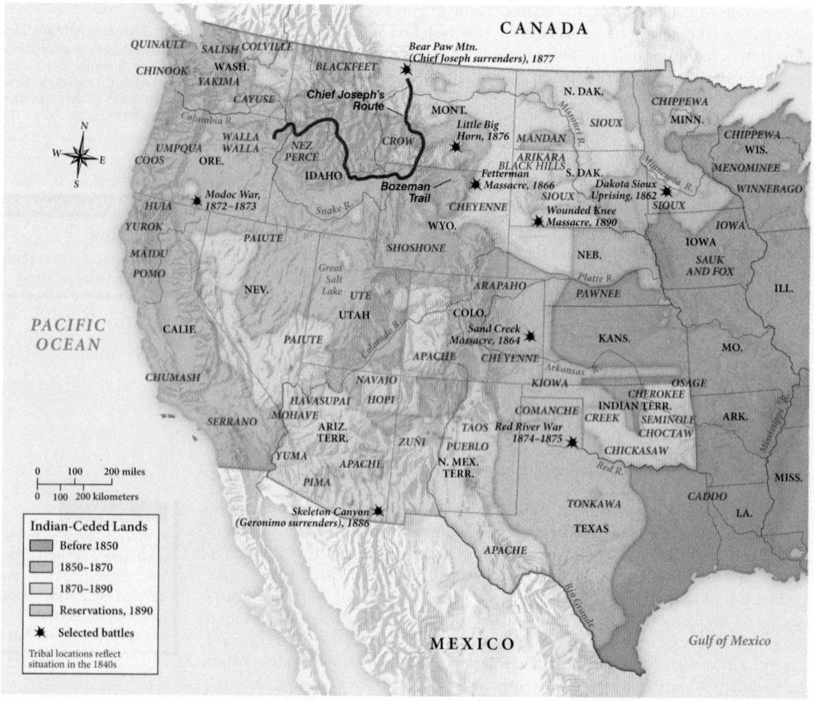

MAP 15.3 Indian Country in the West, to 1890

As settlement pushed onto the Great Plains after the Civil War, Native peoples put up bitter resistance but ultimately to no avail. Over a period of decades, they ceded most of their lands to the federal government, and by 1890 they were confined to scattered reservations.

Minnesotans' ferocious response to the uprising set the stage for further conflict. A hastily appointed military court, bent on revenge, sentenced 307 Dakotas to death, making it clear that rebellious Indians would be treated as criminals rather than military combatants. President Abraham Lincoln reviewed the trial records and commuted most of the sentences but authorized the deaths of 38 Dakota men. They were hanged just after Christmas 1862 in the largest mass execution in U.S. history. Two months later, Congress canceled all treaties with the Dakotas, revoked their annuities, and expelled them from Minnesota. The scattered bands fled west to join nonreservation allies.

As the uprising showed, the Civil War created two dangerous conditions in the West, compounding the problems already caused by corruption. With the Union army fighting the Confederacy, western whites felt vulnerable to Indian attacks. They also discovered they could fight Indians with minimal federal oversight. In the wake of the Dakota uprising, worried Coloradans favored a military campaign against the Cheyennes — allies of the Sioux — even though the Cheyennes had shown little evidence of hostility. Colorado militia leader John M. Chivington, an aspiring politician, determined to quell public anxiety and make his career.

Enclosed Dakota Camp at Fort Snelling, Minnesota, 1862 During the trial of Dakota warriors involved in the 1862 rebellion, and through the harsh Minnesota winter that followed, more than a thousand Dakota people were imprisoned in an enormous enclosure on Pike Island, near St. Paul. A measles epidemic broke out in the crowded camp and dozens died, especially children. Though U.S. soldiers were often unfriendly toward their captives, local sentiment was even more hostile; troops regularly marched through the camp, in part to protect the Dakotas from vigilante violence. In 1863 all members of the tribe were forcibly removed from the state. In November 1862, photographer Benjamin Franklin Upton captured this image of Dakota tents in the Pike Island enclosure. The Granger Collection, New York.

In May 1864, Cheyenne chief Black Kettle, fearing his band would be attacked, consulted with U.S. agents who instructed him to settle his people along Sand Creek in eastern Colorado until a treaty could be signed. On November 29, 1864, Chivington's Colorado militia, on its own initiative, attacked the camp while most of the men were out hunting, slaughtering more than a hundred women and children. "I killed all I could," one officer testified later. "I think and earnestly believe the Indian to be an obstacle to civilization and should be exterminated." Captain Silas Soule, who served under Chivington but refused to give his men the order to fire, dissented. "It was hard to see little children on their knees," he wrote later, "having their brains beat out by men professing to be civilized." Chivington's men rode back for a celebration in Denver, where they hung Cheyenne scalps and women's genitals from the rafters of the Apollo Theater.

The northern plains exploded in conflict. Infuriated by the **Sand Creek massacre**, Cheyennes carried war pipes to the Arapahos and Sioux, who attacked and burned white settlements along the South Platte River. Ordered to subdue these peoples, the U.S. Army failed miserably: officers could not even locate the enemy, who traveled rapidly in small bands and knew the country well. A further shock occurred in December 1866 when 1,500 Sioux warriors executed a perfect ambush, luring Captain William Fetterman and 80 soldiers from a Wyoming fort and wiping them out. With the **Fetterman massacre**, the Sioux succeeded in closing the Bozeman Trail, a private road under army protection that had served as the main route into Montana.

General William Tecumseh Sherman, now commanding the army in the West, swore to defeat defiant Indians. But the Union hero met his match on the plains. Another year of fighting proved expensive and inconclusive. In 1868, the Sioux, led by the Oglala band under Chief Red Cloud, told a peace commission they would not sign any treaty unless the United States pledged to abandon all its forts along the Bozeman Trail. The commission agreed. Red Cloud had won.

Sand Creek massacre
The November 29, 1864, massacre of more than a hundred peaceful Cheyennes, largely women and children, by John M. Chivington's Colorado militia.

Fetterman massacre
A massacre in December 1866 in which 1,500 Sioux warriors lured Captain William Fetterman and 80 soldiers from a Wyoming fort and attacked them. With the Fetterman massacre the Sioux succeeded in closing the Bozeman Trail, the main route into Montana.

AP® THEME

WXT: Work, Exchange, and Technology

The Sand Creek massacre provides an excellent opportunity for students to explore a controversial event and the conflicting ways it can be remembered and commemorated. A variety of resources are available to aid in students' investigation of this topic.

The National Park Service, which designated the location a National Historic Site, provides background information about the massacre and the later efforts to memorialize the event. To access the site, search "NPS Sand Creek Massacre stories."

The PBS film *The West* devotes a segment to the massacre and its aftermath. The companion site provides several primary sources, including editorials from the *Rocky Mountain News*, congressional testimony by eyewitness John Smith, and John Chivington's deposition. To access these resources, search "PBS Sand Creek."

Finally, *Smithsonian* offers a detailed account of the effort to create a national historic site, which could help students understand the labor, expense, and political controversy involved in memorializing past events. To access this site, search "Smithsonian Sand Creek Massacre."

AP® THEME

NAT: American and National Identity

The caption poses an important question about American Indian identity. Use this photograph to discuss with students the ways this identity changed over the course of the late nineteenth century and often embraced elements of white culture and Christianity.

TRM Find complete suggested responses in the Teacher's Resource Materials.

AP® SKILLS & PROCESSES

CAUSATION

In responding to the **CAUSATION** question regarding the causes of violence, students should identify the motives and actions of both whites and Indians, and the larger structural factors (such as the Civil War) that played a role. Students could additionally evaluate the degree to which violence on both sides was planned rather than spontaneous.

TRM Find complete suggested responses in the Teacher's Resource Materials.

CHECK FOR UNDERSTANDING

Ask students: **How did the Civil War impact Indians on the Plains?** *Whites felt vulnerable with federal troops fighting the Confederacy and no longer available to protect them. At the same time, the lack of federal oversight created by the war meant that whites could carry out campaigns against Native Americans with impunity. The Sand Creek massacre and other atrocities soured the American public on the Indian wars.*

VISUAL ACTIVITY

Red Cloud's Bedroom, 1891 Taken on the Pine Ridge Reservation in South Dakota by photographer C. G. Morledge, this photograph shows the bedroom of Red Cloud, a distinguished Oglala Lakota leader. Red Cloud had won a war against the U.S. Army just after the Civil War. He negotiated so tenaciously and shrewdly with what he saw as meddlesome Indian agents, that his people nicknamed Pine Ridge "The Place Where Everything Is Disputed." Denver Public Library, Western History Collection/Bridgeman Images.

READING THE IMAGE: Some of the contents of Red Cloud's bedroom may surprise you. What was the photographer's purpose in capturing and publishing this image? Who do you think was the audience for this photograph? why?

MAKING CONNECTIONS: What aspects of this room suggest Red Cloud's status as a leader of his people? How might a white missionary or Indian agent have responded to the room?

AP® SKILLS & PROCESSES

CAUSATION

What factors led to warfare between whites and Native peoples on the plains?

In the wake of these events, public opinion in the East turned sharply against the Indian wars, which seemed at best ineffective, at worst brutal. Congress held hearings on the slaughter at Sand Creek. Though Chivington, now a civilian, was never prosecuted, the massacre became an infamous example of western vigilantism. By the time Ulysses Grant entered the White House in 1869, the authors of Reconstruction in the South also began to seek solutions to what they called the "Indian problem."

Grant's Peace Policy

Grant inherited an Indian policy in disarray. Federal incompetence was highlighted by yet another mass killing of friendly Indians in January 1870, this time on the Marias River in Montana, by an army detachment that shot and burned to death 173 Piegans (Blackfeet). Having run out of other options, Grant introduced a peace policy, based on recommendations from Christian advisors. He offered selected appointments to the reformers — including many former abolitionists — who had created such groups as the Indian Rights Association and the Women's National Indian Association.

Rejecting the virulent anti-Indian stance of many westerners, reformers argued that Native peoples had the innate capacity to become equal with whites. They believed, however, that Indians could achieve this only if they embraced Christianity and white ways. Reformers thus aimed to destroy indigenous languages, cultures, and religions and force Indians to assimilate. Despite humane intentions, their condescension and racism was obvious. They ignored dissenters like Dr. Thomas Bland of the National Indian Defense Association, who suggested that instead of an "Indian problem" there might be a "white problem" — refusal to permit Indians to follow their own lifeways. To most nineteenth-century Americans, such a notion was uncivilized and unthinkable. Increasingly dismissive of blacks' capacity for citizenship and hostile toward "heathen" Chinese immigrants, white Americans were even less willing to understand and respect Indian cultures. They believed that in the modern world, Native peoples were fated for extinction (see "Thinking Like a Historian," p. 502).

Indian Boarding Schools Assimilationists focused their greatest energy on educating the next generation. Realizing that acculturation — adoption of white ways — was difficult when children lived at home, agents and missionaries created off-reservation schools. Native families were exhorted, bullied, and bribed into sending their children to these schools, where, in addition to school lessons, boys learned farming skills and girls practiced housekeeping. "English only" was the rule; students were punished if they spoke their own languages. Mourning Dove, a Salish girl from what is now Washington State, remembered that her school "ran strictly. We never talked during meals without permission, given only on Sunday or special holidays. Otherwise there was silence — a terrible silent silence. I was used to the freedom of the forest, and it was hard to learn this strict discipline. I was punished many times before I learned." The Lakota boy Plenty Kill, who at boarding school received the new name Luther, remembered his loneliness and fear upon arrival. "The big boys would sing brave songs," he remembered, "and that would start the girls to crying. . . . The girls' quarters were about a hundred and fifty yards from ours, so we could hear them." After having his hair cut short, Plenty Kill felt a profound change in his identity. "None of us slept well that night," he recalled. "I felt that I was no more Indian, but would be an imitation of a white man."

Even in the first flush of reform zeal, Grant's policies faced major hurdles. Most Indians had been pushed off traditional lands and assigned to barren ground that would have defeated the most enterprising farmer. Poverty and dislocation left Indians especially vulnerable to the ravages of infectious diseases like measles and scarlet fever. At the same time, Quaker, Presbyterian, and Methodist reformers fought battles

AP® EXAM TIP

Recognizing the impact of Americanization on Native American populations is important to know on the AP® Exam.

The Impact of Boarding School Tom Torlino, a twenty-two-year-old Navajo man from Arizona, came to the Carlisle Indian School in Pennsylvania in 1882 and stayed for four years. The school took many "before and after" photographs like this one, circulating them to supporters and the general public to demonstrate the school's success in its "civilizing mission." Cutting students' hair and insisting on European-style dress were part of an aggressive program to prevent students from speaking their native languages and forcing them to adopt Christianity. Torlino returned to New Mexico after his graduation in 1886; a school newspaper reported him "doing well." Beinecke Rare Book and Manuscript Library, Yale University.

AP® APPLY THE TIP

Provide students with primary source images that illustrate the impact of Americanization on Native American populations. Ask students to consider the impact of Americanization on the identity of Native American groups. Lead a class discussion on the impact of Americanization and the motivations behind this policy. You can extend this discussion by asking students to consider the ways in which Americanization is still evident in American government policies or society.

AP® SKILLS & PROCESSES

ANALYZING HISTORICAL EVIDENCE

The **AP® THINKING LIKE A HISTORIAN** feature provides students with the opportunity to explore not the actual cultures of nineteenth-century Native Americans, but white *representations* of those cultures. It is crucial that students understand that distinction, so that they recognize that these documents may have little that is accurate to say about American Indians. Scholars like Philip Deloria in his book *Playing Indian* suggest that whites' portrayals of Indians tell us as much about white people as they do about Indians — whites projected onto Native Americans both characteristics they admired and wanted to imitate, and their judgments of Indians as the savage "other."

Representing Indians

The following documents, designed for white audiences, all depict American Indians in the West.

1. **Buffalo Bill Cody's Wild West advertisement, 1899.**
Cody never called the Wild West a "show," placing tremendous emphasis on its allegedly authentic reenactments of events.

Source: Library of Congress, LC-DIG-ppmsca-13514.

2. **Lewis Henry Morgan, *Ancient Society*, 1877.** *Morgan, a leading American anthropologist, studied the Iroquois and other Native peoples. In 1877 he published an influential theory of human development, ranking various peoples in their "progress" from the "lowest stage of savagery" through the pinnacle of "civilization" — northern Europeans.*

Some tribes and families have been left in geographical isolation to work out the problems of progress. . . . [Others] have been adulterated through external influence. Thus, while Africa was and is an ethnical chaos of savagery and barbarism, Australia and Polynesia were in savagery, pure and simple. . . . The Indian family of America, unlike any other existing family, exemplified the condition of mankind in three successive ethnical periods. . . . The far northern Indians and some of the coast tribes of North and South America were in the Upper Status of savagery; the partially Village Indians east of the Mississippi were in the Lower Status of barbarism, and the Village Indians of North and South America were in the Middle Status. . . .

Status of Civilization (from Morgan, *Ancient Society*, 1877)	
I. Lower Status of Savagery	From the Infancy of the Human Race to the commencement of the next Period.
II. Middle Status of Savagery	From the acquisition of a fish subsistence and a knowledge of the use of fire . . .
III. Upper Status of Savagery	From the Invention of the Bow and Arrow . . .
IV. Lower Status of Barbarism	From the Invention of the Art of Pottery . . .
V. Middle Status of Barbarism	From the Domestication of animals on the Eastern hemisphere, and in the Western from the cultivation of maize and plants by Irrigation . . .
VI. Upper Status of Barbarism	From the Invention of the process of Smelting Iron Ore, with the use of iron tools . . .
VII. Civilization	From the Invention of writing, to the present time.

Commencing, then, with the Australians and Polynesians, following with the American Indian tribes, and concluding with the Roman and Grecian, who afford the highest exemplifications respectively of the six great stages of human progress, the sum of their united experiences may be supposed fairly to represent that of the human family. . . . We are dealing substantially, with the ancient history and condition of our own remote ancestors.

3. **Touring Indian Country, 1888 and 1894.** *Hoping to lure eastern tourists, the Northern Pacific Railroad published an annual journal,* Wonderland, *describing the natural splendors and economic progress of the West, as seen from its rail lines.*

We are now in the far-famed Yellowstone Valley. . . . There are but few Indians now to be seen along the line of the railroad, and those are engaged in agricultural and industrial pursuits. The extinction of the buffalo has rendered the Indian much more amenable to the civilizing influences brought to bear upon him than he formerly was, and very fair crops of grain are being raised at some of the agencies. At the Devil's Lake agency, for example, 60,000 bushels of wheat have been raised by the [Sioux and Chippewa] Indians in a single season. . . .

[The Crows'] great reservation is probably the garden spot of Montana, and the throwing open of a large portion of it to [white] settlement, which cannot long be delayed, will assuredly give an immense impetus to the agricultural interests of the Territory. . . .

The Flatheads have probably 10,000 or more horses and 5,000 or 6,000 cattle. . . . As ranchers and farmers the Flatheads are a success. It would be a matter of surprise to some people who think that the only good Indian is a dead Indian, to see the way some of the women handle sewing machines.

4. **Gertrude Käsebier, photograph of Joe Black Fox, 1898.** *One of the first women to become a professional photographer, Käsebier here depicts Joe Black Fox relaxing with a cigarette. Black Fox, an Oglala Sioux, toured with Buffalo Bill's Wild West in 1900.*

Source: Library of Congress, 12100.

Sources: (2) Lewis H. Morgan, *Ancient Society* (New York: Henry Holt and Company, 1878), 12–13, 16–18; (3) John Hyde, *Wonderland* (St. Paul, 1888), 21, and (1894), 27.

AP® DBQ PRACTICE

1. Compare the depiction of the Plains Indians and Buffalo Bill Cody in source 1. How does source 4 differ from source 1? How might these depictions have shaped their audiences' understanding of the West?
2. What bases did Morgan use for his rankings in source 2? How did he define the relationship between American Indians and whites (whom he refers to, in this passage, as "we")? Why did he suggest that Indians offered a unique opportunity for study?
3. A wealthy, well-educated tourist preparing to travel west in 1900 might encounter which of these documents in advance? How might they shape expectations and experiences?
4. These documents had different creators: an artist, a scholar, and two sets of entrepreneurs. How does audience and purpose inform their messages?

PUTTING IT ALL TOGETHER

Using these sources and your knowledge of the period, discuss the myths and realities of Native American life in the late nineteenth century using examples from the above sources and your textbook. Consider how these stereotypes are pervasive today.

TRM Find complete suggested responses in the Teacher's Resource Materials.

AP® SKILLS & PROCESSES

ARGUMENTATION

The **PUTTING IT ALL TOGETHER** prompt asks students to build on the distinction between whites' perceptions of Native American life and the realities. More sophisticated responses will clearly explain the reasons for the gap between these two.

AP® APPLY THE TIP

Ask students to complete the **AP® THINKING LIKE A HISTORIAN** document analysis activity on pp. 502–503. This activity can be assigned for homework the day before or as an in-class group assignment. Once students have completed this activity, ask them if Native Americans had any control over the images presented to the American public in this activity. Then divide students into groups and ask them to research and report back on the ways that Native groups preserved their culture and tribal identities in the late nineteenth century. Note: resources from the Native American History museum in Washington, DC, can be a good place to start this research activity. For large classes, you may want to assign each group a particular tribe to focus on so that you have a variety of ideas for class discussion at the end of the research period.

AP® SKILLS & PROCESSES

CONTEXTUALIZATION

The **CONTEXTUALIZATION** question assumes a contrast between reformers' intentions and the consequences. Students could indicate what factors explain why intention and reality often diverged so dramatically.

TRM Find complete suggested responses in the Teacher's Resource Materials.

CHECK FOR UNDERSTANDING

Ask students: **What was Grant's peace policy?** *Grant supported the views of reformers who sought to assimilate Native Americans by sending children to boarding schools, ending independent tribal governance and treaty making, and dividing tribal lands into family holdings under the Dawes Severalty Act.*

AP® EXAM TIP

Be able to explain the strategies employed by Native Americans to preserve their cultural and tribal identities despite federal government policies.

among themselves and with Catholic missionaries over who had authority. Many traders and agents also continued to steal money and supplies from people they were supposed to protect. In the late 1870s, Rutherford B. Hayes's administration undertook housecleaning at the Bureau of Indian Affairs, but corruption lingered.

From the Indians' point of view, reformers often became just another interest group in a crowded field of whites sending hopelessly mixed messages. The attitudes of individual army representatives, agents, and missionaries ranged from courageous and sympathetic to utterly ruthless. Many times, after chiefs thought they had reached a face-to-face agreement, they found it drastically altered by Washington bureaucrats. Nez Perce leader Joseph observed that "white people have too many chiefs. They do not understand each other. . . . I cannot understand why so many chiefs are allowed to talk so many different ways, and promise so many different things." A Kiowa chief agreed: "We make but few contracts, and them we remember well. The whites make so many they are liable to forget them. The white chief seems not to be able to govern his braves."

Native peoples were nonetheless forced to accommodate, as independent tribal governance and treaty making came to an end. Back in the 1830s, the U.S. Supreme Court had declared Indians no longer sovereign but rather "domestic dependent nations." On a practical basis, however, both the U.S. Senate and agents in the field continued to negotiate treaties as late as 1869. Two years later, the House of Representatives, jealous of Senate privileges, passed a bill to abolish all treaty making with Indians. The Senate agreed, provided that existing treaties remained in force. It was one more step in a long, torturous erosion of Native rights. Eventually, the U.S. Supreme Court ruled in ***Lone Wolf v. Hitchcock*** (1903) that Congress could make whatever Indian policies it chose, ignoring all existing treaties. That same year, in *Ex Parte Crow Dog*, the Court ruled that no Indian was a citizen unless Congress designated him so. Indians were henceforth wards of the government. These rulings remained in force until the New Deal of the 1930s.

Lone Wolf v. Hitchcock
A 1903 Supreme Court ruling that Congress could make whatever Indian policies it chose, ignoring all existing treaties.

Breaking Up Tribal Lands Reformers' most sweeping effort to assimilate Indians was the **Dawes Severalty Act** (1887), the dream of Senator Henry L. Dawes of Massachusetts, a leader in the Indian Rights Association. Dawes saw the reservation system as an ugly relic of the past. Through severalty — division of tribal lands — he hoped to force Indians onto individual landholdings, partitioning reservations into homesteads, just like those of white farmers. Supporters of the plan believed that landownership would encourage Indians to assimilate. It would lead, as Dawes wrote, to "a personal sense of independence." Individual property, echoed another reformer, would make the Indian man "intelligently selfish, . . . with a *pocket that aches to be filled with dollars!*"

Dawes Severalty Act
The 1887 law that gave Native Americans severalty (individual ownership of land) by dividing reservations into homesteads. The law was a disaster for Native peoples, resulting over several decades in the loss of 66 percent of lands held by Indians at the time of the law's passage.

The Dawes Act was a disaster. It played into the hands of whites who coveted Indian land that could be declared "excess" after allotments. The Bureau of Indian Affairs (BIA) implemented the law carelessly, to the outrage of Dawes. In Indian Territory, a commission seized more than 15 million "surplus" acres from Native tribes by 1894, opening the way for whites to create the state of Oklahoma out of the last federal territory set aside for Native peoples. In addition to catastrophic losses of collectively held property, Native peoples lost 66 percent of their individually allotted lands between the 1880s and the 1930s, through fraud, BIA mismanagement, and pressure to sell to whites.

AP® SKILLS & PROCESSES

CONTEXTUALIZATION

How did post–Civil War reformers believe they were improving U.S. Indian policies, and in what ways did that prove to be true and untrue?

The End of Armed Resistance

As the nation consolidated control of the West in the 1870s, Americans hoped that Grant's peace policy was solving the "Indian problem." In the Southwest, such formidable peoples as the Kiowas and Comanches had been forced onto reservations. The Diné or Navajo nation, exiled under horrific conditions during the Civil War but permitted to reoccupy their traditional land, gave up further military resistance. An outbreak among California's Modoc people in 1873 — again, humiliating to the army — was at last subdued. Only Sitting Bull, a leader of the powerful Lakota Sioux on the northern plains, openly refused to go to a reservation. When pressured by U.S. troops, he repeatedly crossed into Canada, where he told reporters that "the life of white men is slavery. . . . I have seen nothing that a white man has, houses or railways or clothing or food, that is as good as the right to move in open country and live in our own fashion."

In 1874, the Lakotas faced direct provocation. Lieutenant Colonel George Armstrong Custer, a brash self-promoter who had graduated last in his class at West Point, led an expedition into South Dakota's Black Hills and loudly proclaimed the discovery of gold. Amid the severe depression of the 1870s, prospectors rushed in. The United States, wavering on its 1868 treaty, pressured Sioux leaders to sell the Black Hills. The chiefs said no. Ignoring this answer, the government demanded in 1876 that all Sioux gather at the federal agencies. The policy backfired: not only did Sitting Bull refuse to report, but other Sioux, Cheyennes, and Arapahos slipped away from reservations to join him. Knowing they might face military attack, they agreed to live together for the summer in one great village numbering over seven thousand people. By June, they were camped on the Little Big Horn River in what is now southeastern Montana. Some of the young men wanted to organize raiding parties, but elders counseled against it. "We [are] within our treaty rights as hunters," they argued. "We must keep ourselves so."

Howling Wolf, Fight Near Ft. Wallace This sketch in colored pencil, crayon, and watercolor by Howling Wolf, a Southern Cheyenne man, illustrates one of the last military engagements in western Kansas in which Southern Cheyenne defeated white invaders. The events likely occurred in 1872. Howling Wolf created this self-portrait (note the wolf above the rider's head) while imprisoned at Fort Marion in St. Augustine, Florida, in the later 1870s. Using paper from ledger books, Howling Wolf and other artists depicted scenes from their lives in "ledger art" that tourists purchased from Native men for very small payments. Howling Wolf, released from prison in 1878, briefly adopted white dress and customs but then chose traditional Cheyenne ways and became a strong advocate for his people. He lived until 1927, when at about age seventy-eight, he died in a car accident while traveling back to Oklahoma from performing in a Wild West show in Texas. Allen Memorial Art Museum, Oberlin College, Ohio, USA; Gift of Mrs. Jacob D. Cox/Bridgeman Images.

The U.S. Army dispatched a thousand cavalry and infantrymen to drive the Indians back to the reservation. Despite warnings from experienced scouts — including Crow Indian allies — most officers thought the job would be easy. Their greatest fear was that the Indians would manage to slip away. But amid the nation's centennial celebration on the Fourth of July 1876, Americans received alarming news. On June 26 and 27, Lieutenant Colonel Custer, leading the 7th Cavalry as part of a three-pronged effort to surround Sitting Bull's camp, had led 210 men in an ill-considered assault. The Sioux and their allies had killed the attackers to the last man. "The Indians," one Oglala woman remembered, "acted just like they were driving buffalo to a good place where they could be easily slaughtered."

As retold by the press in sensational (and often fictionalized) accounts, the story of Custer's "last stand" quickly served to justify American conquest of Indian "savages." Long after Americans forgot the massacres of Cheyenne women and children at Sand Creek and of Piegan people on the Marias River, prints of the **Battle of Little Big Horn** hung in barrooms across the country. William F. "Buffalo Bill" Cody, in his traveling Wild West performances, enacted a revenge killing of a Cheyenne man named Yellow Hand in a tableau Cody called "first scalp for Custer." Notwithstanding that the tableau featured a white man scalping a Cheyenne, Cody depicted it as a triumph for civilization.

Battle of Little Big Horn
The 1876 battle begun when American cavalry under George Armstrong Custer attacked an encampment of Sioux, Arapaho, and Cheyenne Indians who were resisting removal to a reservation. Custer's force was annihilated, but with whites calling for U.S. soldiers to retaliate, the Native American military victory was short-lived.

Little Big Horn proved to be the last military victory of Plains Indians against the U.S. Army. Pursued relentlessly after Custer's death and finding fewer and fewer

TEACHING STRATEGY

The Library of Congress's lesson plan "Assimilation Through Education" uses a variety of primary source documents to present viewpoints on the education and assimilation of Indian peoples in the 1870s and 1880s. Students can learn the perspective of government officials by reading their annual reports and analyzing the Indian schools' population statistics, observe photographs of Indian students, and hear a musical Indian performance. The lesson also allows students to explore the mixed messages in these materials: the desire to eliminate Indian culture and a public fascination with a romanticized version of this culture. To access the site, search "Library of Congress Assimilation Through Education."

CHECK FOR UNDERSTANDING

Ask students: **What led to the end of American Indians' armed resistance?** *The defeat of Custer at the Battle of Little Big Horn was the last great Native American victory on the Plains. Pursued by the U.S. Army and with dwindling buffalo herds, American Indians began to accommodate themselves to life on reservations.*

AP® SKILLS & PROCESSES

ARGUMENTATION

The **ARGUMENTATION** question asks students to identify the results of Grant's policies, particularly the reasons that the goals diverged from the results. Extend this prompt by asking students to evaluate which individuals and groups were most responsible for the implementation of inappropriate policies and explain why they think so.

TRM Find complete suggested responses in the Teacher's Resource Materials.

CHECK FOR UNDERSTANDING

Ask students: **What strategies of survival did Native Americans adopt?** *They selectively adopted white beliefs and practices. Some embraced American education, changed their names, and engaged in professional work. The Ghost Dance represented the hope of returning to life before surrender to whites — the bison would return and the whites would be driven out — and tribes' willingness to join pan-Indian groups.*

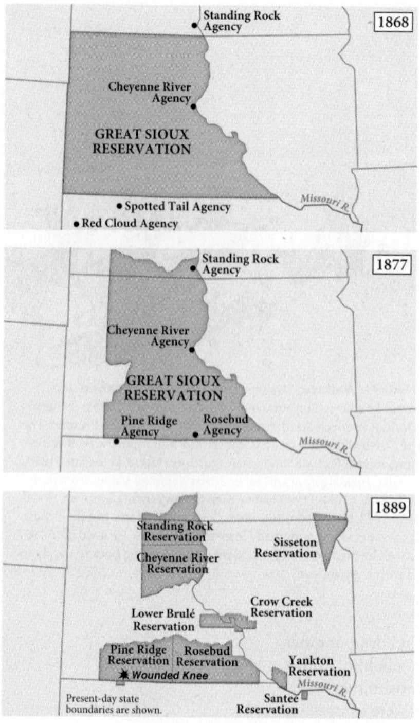

MAP 15.4 The Sioux Reservations in South Dakota, 1868–1889

In 1868, when they bent to the demand that they move onto the reservation, the Sioux thought they had gained secure rights to a substantial part of their ancestral hunting grounds. But harsh conditions on reservations led to continuing military conflicts. Land-hungry whites exerted continuous local pressure, and officials in Washington repeatedly changed the terms of Sioux landholdings — always eroding Native claims.

bison to sustain them, Sioux parents watched their children starve through a bitter winter. Slowly, families trickled into the agencies and accommodated themselves to reservation life (Map 15.4). The next year, the Nez Perce, fleeing for the Canadian border, also surrendered. The final holdouts fought in the Southwest with Chiricahua Apache leader Geronimo. Like many others, Geronimo had accepted reservation life but found conditions unendurable. Describing the desolate land the tribe had been allotted, one Apache said it had "nothing but cactus, rattlesnakes, heat, rocks, and insects. . . . Many, many of our people died of starvation." When Geronimo took up arms in protest, the army recruited other Apaches to track him and his band into the hills; in September 1886, he surrendered for the last time. The Chiricahua Apaches never returned to their homeland. The United States had completed its military conquest of the West.

Strategies of Survival

Though the warpath closed, many Native peoples continued secretly to practice traditional customs. Away from the disapproving eyes of agents and teachers, they passed on their languages, histories, and traditional arts and medicine to younger generations. Frustrated missionaries often concluded that little could be accomplished because bonds of kinship and custom were so strong. Parents hated to relinquish their children to off-reservation boarding schools. Thus more and more Indian schools ended up on or near reservations; white teachers had to accept their pupils' continued participation in the rhythms of Indian community life.

Selectively, most indigenous peoples adopted some white ways. Many parents urged their sons and daughters to study hard, learn English, and develop skills to help them succeed in the new world they confronted. Even Sitting Bull announced in 1885 that he wanted his children "to be educated like the white children are." Some Indian students grew up to be lawyers, doctors, and advocates for their people, including writers and artists who interpreted Native experiences for national audiences. One of the most famous was a Santee Sioux boy named Ohiyesa, who pursued an education at Dartmouth and became Dr. Charles Eastman. Posted to the Pine Ridge Reservation in South Dakota, Eastman practiced medicine side by side with traditional healers, whom he respected, and wrote popular books under his Sioux name. He remembered that when he left for boarding school, his father had said, "We have now entered upon this life, and there is no going back. . . . Remember, my boy, it is the same as if I sent you on your first war-path. I shall expect you to conquer."

Nothing exemplified this syncretism, or cultural blending, better than the **Ghost Dance movement** of the late 1880s and early 1890s, inspired by American Indian peoples' hope that they could, through sacred dances, resurrect the bison and call a great storm to drive whites back across the Atlantic. The Ghost Dance drew on Christian elements as well as Native ones. As the movement spread from reservation to reservation — Paiutes, Arapahos, Sioux — indigenous peoples developed new forms of pan-Indian identity and cooperation.

White responses to the Ghost Dance showed continued misunderstanding and lethal reactions to Native self-assertion. In 1890, a group of Lakota Sioux Ghost

AP® SKILLS & PROCESSES

ARGUMENTATION

How did Grant's peace policy fail to consider the needs of Native Americans in the West, and what were its results?

Ghost Dance movement
Religion of the late 1880s and early 1890s that combined elements of Christianity and traditional Native American religion. It fostered Plains Indians' hope that they could, through sacred dances, resurrect the great bison herds and call up a storm to drive whites back across the Atlantic.

Dancers were pursued by the U.S. Army, who feared that further spread of the religion would provoke war. On December 29, at **Wounded Knee**, the 7th Cavalry caught up with fleeing Lakotas and killed at least 150 — perhaps as many as 300. Like other massacres, this one could have been avoided. The deaths at Wounded Knee stand as an indictment of decades of relentless U.S. expansion, white ignorance and greed, chaotic and conflicting policies, and bloody mistakes.

Wounded Knee
The 1890 massacre of Sioux Indians by American cavalry at Wounded Knee Creek, South Dakota. Sent to suppress the Ghost Dance, soldiers caught up with fleeing Lakotas and killed as many as 300.

Western Myths and Realities

The post–Civil War frontier produced mythic figures who have played starring roles in America's national folklore ever since: "savage" Indians, brave pioneers, rugged cowboys, and gun-slinging sheriffs. Far from being invented by Hollywood in the twentieth century, these oversimplified characters emerged in the very same era when the nation incorporated the West. Pioneers helped develop the mythic ideal. As one Montana woman claimed, they had come west "at peril of their lives" and faced down "scalp dances" and other terrors; in the end, they "conquered the wilderness and transformed it into a land of peace and plenty." Some retired cowboys, capitalizing on the popularity of dime novel Westerns, spiced up their memoirs for sale. Eastern readers were eager for stories like *The Life and Adventures of Nat Love* (1907), written by a Texas cowhand who had been born in slavery in Tennessee and who, as a rodeo star in the 1870s, had won the nickname "Deadwood Dick."

No myth-maker proved more influential than Buffalo Bill Cody. Unlike those who saw the West as free or empty, Bill understood that the United States had taken those lands by conquest. Ironically, his famous Wild West, which he insisted was not a "show" but an authentic representation of frontier experience, provided one of the few employment options for Plains Indians in the 1880s and 1890s. To escape harsh reservation conditions, Sioux and Cheyenne men signed on with Bill and demonstrated their riding skills for cheering audiences across the United States and Europe, chasing buffalo and attacking U.S. soldiers and pioneer wagons in the arena. Buffalo Bill proved to be a good employer to Native men, including Lakota Sioux leader Sitting Bull, who toured with Bill's Wild West in 1885. Black Elk, another Lakota Sioux man who joined Cody's operation, recalled that Bill was generous and "had a strong heart." But Black Elk had a mixed reaction to the Wild West. "I liked the part of the show we made," he told an interviewer, "but not the part the *Wasichus* [white people] made." As he observed, the Wild West of the 1880s was at its heart a celebration of U.S. military conquest.

At this same moment of transition in the 1890s, a young historian named Frederick Jackson Turner reviewed recent census data and proclaimed the end of the frontier. Up until 1890, he wrote, a clear, westward-moving line had existed between "civilization and savagery." The frontier experience, Turner argued, shaped Americans' national character. It left them a heritage of "coarseness and strength, combined with acuteness and inquisitiveness," as well as "restless, nervous energy." But he warned that the frontier had closed and Americans would need to find new ways to build their nation and imagine its future.

Today, historians reject Turner's depiction of Indian "savagery" — and his contradictory idea that white pioneers in the West claimed empty "free land." Many scholars have noted that frontier conquest was both violent and incomplete. The Dust Bowl of the 1930s, as well as more recent cycles of drought, have repeated late-nineteenth-century patterns of hardship and depopulation on the plains. During the 1950s and 1960s, also, uranium mining rushes in the West mimicked earlier patterns of boom and bust, leaving ghost towns in their wake. Turner himself acknowledged that the frontier had both good and evil elements. He noted that in the West, "frontier liberty was sometimes confused with absence of all effective government." But in 1893, when Turner first published "The Significance of the Frontier in American History," eager listeners heard only the positives. They saw pioneering in the West as evidence of

TEACHING STRATEGY

Wounded Knee symbolically represents a turning point: it is the culmination of American violence toward Native Americans, the end of Native American armed resistance, and the consequent acceptance of the reservation system. The Digital Public Library of America provides a teaching guide called "Exploring the Wounded Knee Massacre" that includes a background essay, a set of primary sources, a half-dozen discussion questions, and several suggestions for classroom activities. To access this site, search "Digital Public Library Exploring the Wounded Knee Massacre."

American exceptionalism: of the nation's unique history and destiny. They claimed that "peaceful" American expansion was the opposite of the conquests undertaken by European empires, ignoring the many military and economic similarities between U.S. and European actions. Although politically the American West became a set of states rather than a colony, historians today emphasize the legacy of conquest that is central to its (and America's) history.

Less than two months after the massacre at Wounded Knee, General William T. Sherman died in New York. As the nation marked his passing with pomp and oratory, commentators noted that his career reflected a great era of conquest and consolidation of national power. Known primarily for his role in defeating the Confederacy, Sherman had undertaken his first military exploits against Seminoles in Florida in the early 1840s. Later, during the U.S.-Mexico War, he had gone west with the U.S. Army to help claim California. After the Civil War, the general went west again, supervising the forced removal of Sioux and Cheyennes to reservations.

When Sherman graduated from West Point in 1840, the United States had numbered twenty-six states, none of them west of Missouri. At his death in 1891, the nation boasted forty-four states, stretching to the Pacific coast. The nation now rivaled Britain and Germany as an industrial giant, and its dynamic economy was drawing immigrants from around the world. Over the span of Sherman's career, the United States had become a major player on the world stage. It had done so through the kind of fierce military conquest that Sherman made famous in both the South and West, as well as through bold expansions of federal authority to foster economic expansion. From the wars and policies of Sherman's lifetime, the children and grandchildren of Civil War heroes inherited a vast empire. In the coming decades, it would be up to them to decide how to use the nation's new power.

SUMMARY

Between 1861 and 1877, the United States completed its conquest of the continent. After the Civil War, expansion of railroads fostered integration of the national economy. Republican policymakers promoted this integration through protective tariffs, while federal court rulings facilitated economic growth and strengthened corporations. To attract foreign investment, Congress placed the nation on the gold standard. Federal officials also pursued a vigorous foreign policy, acquiring Alaska and asserting U.S. power indirectly through control of international trade in Latin America and Asia.

An important result of economic integration was incorporation of the West. Mining became a key force for expansion there, at great environmental cost. Cattlemen built an industry linked to the integrated economy, in the process nearly driving native bison to extinction. Homesteaders confronted harsh environmental conditions as they converted the grasslands for agriculture. Republicans championed homesteader families as representatives of domesticity, an ideal opposed to Mormon plural marriage in Utah. Homesteading accelerated the rapid, often violent, transformation of western environments. Perceiving this transformation, federal officials began setting aside natural preserves such as Yellowstone, often clashing with Native Americans who wished to hunt there.

Conflicts led to the dispossession of Native American lands. During the Civil War, whites clashed with the Sioux and their allies. Grant's peace policy sought to end this conflict by forcing Native Americans to acculturate to European-style practices. Indian armed resistance continued through the 1880s, ending with Geronimo's surrender in September 1886. Thereafter, Native Americans survived by secretly continuing their traditions and selectively adopting white ways. Due in part to the determined military conquest of this period, the United States claimed a major role on the world stage. Frontier myths shaped Americans' view of themselves as rugged individualists with a unique national destiny.

CHECK FOR UNDERSTANDING

Ask students: **In the late nineteenth century, what strategies did Native peoples in the West pursue in response to dispossession of their lands and efforts to assimilate them?** to check their understanding of the "A Harvest of Blood: Native Peoples Dispossessed" section. *Native Americans first attempted armed resistance to white encroachments in the late nineteenth century. With the fleeting exception of the success at Little Big Horn (1876), these efforts failed. As a result, many Native Americans attempted to maintain their culture within whites' policies, which entailed selectively accepting some white customs. For instance, they insisted that white schools for indigenous students be placed near reservations and thus Native American parents could still influence their children. They also resurrected sacred dances, such as the Ghost Dances, with tragic results at Wounded Knee (1890).*

CHECK FOR UNDERSTANDING

Use the **AP® LEARNING FOCUS** question from the beginning of the chapter to check students' understanding of the chapter as a whole: **Why and how did the United States build a continental empire, and how did this affect people living in the West?** *U.S. policymakers sought to strengthen the national economy by creating a massive public-private partnership to build railroads, create a national banking system, support domestic manufacturers with a protective tariff, encourage settlement with the Homestead Act, and create markets abroad. The federal government supported the growing industries of the West including mining, ranching, and farming. The result was more than a bifurcated sense of economic agency. Indeed, while industry, mining, ranching, and farming were strengthened through government assistance, those same policies devastated Native people who were violently pushed off their land. Beyond the economic effects, the choice of the federal government to remove Natives from their land enabled further subjugation of Natives, as well as other groups seen by the government as "other."*

LearningCurve

Remind students to go online to complete the LearningCurve quiz for this chapter.

CHAPTER 15 REVIEW

AP® CONTENT REVIEW

Answer these questions to demonstrate your understanding of the chapter's main ideas.

1. How did Republicans' economic policies contribute to the rise of America's industrial economy?
2. Why and how did federal policies reshape the trans-Mississippi west after the Civil War?
3. In the late nineteenth century, how did the United States dispossess Native peoples and attempt to assimilate them, and how did those peoples respond?

AP® TERMS TO KNOW

Identify and explain the significance of each term below.

Key Concepts and Events

transcontinental railroad (p. 480)
protective tariff (p. 482)
Burlingame Treaty (p. 483)
Munn v. Illinois (p. 487)
gold standard (p. 488)
Homestead Act (p. 488)
land-grant colleges (p. 489)
Comstock Lode (p. 489)
Exodusters (p. 492)
Yellowstone National Park (p. 496)
U.S. Fish and Wildlife Service (p. 497)
Sand Creek massacre (p. 499)
Fetterman massacre (p. 499)
Lone Wolf v. Hitchcock (p. 504)
Dawes Severalty Act (p. 504)
Battle of Little Big Horn (p. 505)
Ghost Dance movement (p. 506)
Wounded Knee (p. 507)

Key People

William Seward (p. 483)
John Wesley Powell (p. 494)
Sitting Bull (p. 505)
George Armstrong Custer (p. 505)
William F. "Buffalo Bill" Cody (p. 505)
Geronimo (p. 506)
Ohiyesa (Dr. Charles Eastman) (p. 506)
Frederick Jackson Turner (p. 507)

AP® MAKING CONNECTIONS

Recognize the larger developments and continuities within and across chapters by answering these questions.

1. During the Reconstruction years, Republican policymakers made sweeping policy decisions — especially having to do with land rights, voting rights, and education — that shaped the future of African Americans in the South and American Indians in the West. In an essay, compare U.S. policies toward the two groups. What assumptions and goals underlay each effort to incorporate racial minorities into the United States? To what extent did each effort succeed or fail, and why? How did the actions of powerful whites in each region shape the results?
2. Consider the image at the start of this chapter, "The Great West" (p. 481), which depicts how many Americans of the era thought the West *ought* to look when settlement was complete. Identify at least two other images in Chapter 15 that show what the natural and built environments of the West *really* looked like. What do you conclude from this comparison about the impact or the limits of U.S. policies in the West?

KEY TURNING POINTS

Refer to the timeline at the start of the chapter for help in answering the following question.

The military, political, and economic events of the Civil War years (1861–1865) are often treated as largely occurring in the Northeast and South — at places such as Shiloh, Gettysburg, and Washington, D.C. What impact did these developments have on the West, and what were their legacies?

TRM Find complete suggested responses in the Teacher's Resource Materials.

AP® SKILLS & PROCESSES

CAUSATION

AP® CONTENT REVIEW 1 asks students to assess how Republicans' economic policies both during and after the Civil War affected the new industrial economy.

AP® SKILLS & PROCESSES

CAUSATION

AP® CONTENT REVIEW 2 asks students to evaluate how the federal government's policies changed the land, opportunities, and people west of the Mississippi River after the Civil War.

TRM Find definitions for these terms in the **Glossary/Glosario** in the Teacher's Resource Materials.

AP® SKILLS & PROCESSES

COMPARISON

AP® MAKING CONNECTIONS 1 invites students to compare American policies toward two nonwhite groups who had not previously been assimilated into the nation as full citizens.

AP® SKILLS & PROCESSES

COMPARISON

AP® MAKING CONNECTIONS 2 asks students to compare perceptions of the American West with realities and to draw a larger conclusion about the effects of policies in the West.

AP® SKILLS & PROCESSES

CONTINUITY AND CHANGE

KEY TURNING POINTS asks students to consider the Civil War as a regional turning point, rather than simply a national one.

TRM Find complete suggested responses in the Teacher's Resource Materials.

AP® PRACTICE QUESTIONS

MULTIPLE CHOICE QUESTIONS *Choose the correct answer for each question.*

Questions 1–3 refer to this excerpt.

"[T]he President of the United States . . . is authorized . . . to allot the lands . . . in severalty [individually] to any Indian located thereon in quantities as follows:

> To each head of a family, one-quarter of a section;
> To each single person over eighteen years of age, one-eighth of a section;
> To each orphan child under eighteen years of age, one-eighth of a section; and
> To each other single person under eighteen years now living . . . one-sixteenth of a section. . . .

[E]very member [Indian] to whom allotments have been made shall have the benefit of and be subject to the laws, both civil and criminal, of the State or Territory in which they may reside. . . ."

Dawes Severalty Act, 1887

Questions 4–6 refer to the map provided.

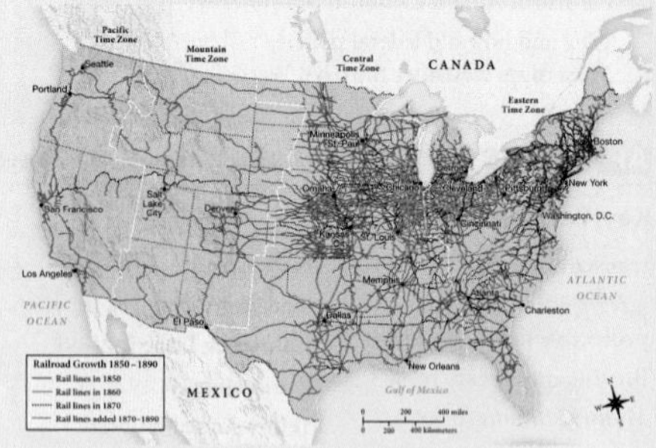

Expansion of the Railroad System, 1850–1890

1. The policy goals endorsed by the Dawes Severalty Act would have been most strongly supported by advocates of
- **a.** assimilation.
- **b.** containment.
- **c.** nativism.
- **d.** Social Darwinism.

2. The policy toward American Indians expressed in the Dawes Severalty Act resulted from all of the following conditions EXCEPT
- **a.** the near extinction of free-roaming bison on the Great Plains.
- **b.** the conflicts over landownership between white settlers and American Indians.
- **c.** the attempts by miners to extract mineral wealth from traditional American Indian lands.
- **d.** the forced relocation of American Indian tribes to lands west of the Mississippi River.

3. In addition to the Dawes Severalty Act, the growth of which of the following historical developments most strongly undermined American Indians' ownership of land during the period between 1850 and 1890?
- **a.** Telegraphs
- **b.** Sharecropping
- **c.** Railroads
- **d.** Newspapers

4. Which of the following most directly contributed to the overall trend depicted in the map?
- **a.** Technological innovations
- **b.** The rise of organized labor
- **c.** Improved standards of living
- **d.** Increased trade with Latin America

5. The federal government most directly contributed to the trend depicted in the map by
- **a.** actively regulating the railroad industry.
- **b.** subsidizing railroad construction through land grants.
- **c.** passing federal income taxes to fund new railroads.
- **d.** taking direct ownership of the major railroad lines.

6. The trend depicted in the map led to all of the following EXCEPT
- **a.** large numbers of migrants moving to the West.
- **b.** the rise of cattle ranching in Texas.
- **c.** an overall increase in consumer prices.
- **d.** the growth of cooperative organizations for farmers.

SHORT ANSWER QUESTIONS

Read each question carefully and write a short response. Use evidence from the text to support your claims.

"The treaty system ended in 1871, when Congress decided that no more treaties would be made with Indian tribes . . . but the paternalism of the federal government toward the Indians continued . . . [under the] Board of Indian Commissioners . . . [which included] a remarkable collection of high-minded Christian philanthropists, suffused with a spirit of benevolence, who epitomized the evangelical religious atmosphere of the nineteenth century. For better or for worse, the American Indians fell into the hands of this group and their successors."

Francis Paul Prucha, *The Indian in American Society: From the Revolutionary War to the Present*, 1985

"[O]fficials often proclaimed that they were ushering in a new age of dealing fairly and kindly with . . . indigenous inhabitants. Yet these new policies actually entailed one of the most draconian measures possible: the removal of indigenous children from their kin . . . to be raised in distant institutions. . . . [I]nstead of watching from the sidelines as male government officials designed and carried out policies of indigenous child removal, many white women reformers campaigned for a greater role in setting public policy for indigenous peoples and became deeply implicated in this phase of settler colonialism."

Margaret D. Jacobs, *White Mother to a Dark Race: Settler Colonialism, Maternalism, and the Removal of Indigenous Children in the American West and Australia, 1880–1940*, 2009

1. Using the two excerpts provided, answer (a), (b), and (c).
   - **a.** Briefly explain ONE major difference between Prucha's and Jacobs's historical interpretations of the federal government's policies toward American Indians.
   - **b.** Briefly explain how ONE specific historical event or development from the period 1865 to 1898 that is not explicitly mentioned in the excerpts could be used to support Prucha's interpretation.
   - **c.** Briefly explain how ONE specific historical event or development from the period 1865 to 1898 that is not explicitly mentioned in the excerpts could be used to support Jacobs's interpretation.

2. Using the map of railroad expansion provided in the multiple choice section, answer (a), (b), and (c).
   - **a.** Briefly explain ONE specific historical event or development that accounts for the pattern of railroad construction illustrated in the map.
   - **b.** Briefly explain ONE specific historical change in the U.S. economy that resulted from the change illustrated in the period from 1850 to 1900.
   - **c.** Briefly explain ONE specific historical environmental result of the change illustrated in the period from 1850 to 1900.

3. Answer (a), (b), and (c).
   - **a.** Briefly explain ONE specific historical similarity in the interactions between the U.S. government and American Indians in the era immediately before the end of the Civil War (1840–1865) and the era immediately after the Civil War (1865–1890).
   - **b.** Briefly explain ONE specific historical difference in the interactions between the U.S. government and American Indians in the era immediately before the end of the Civil War (1840–1865) and the era immediately after the Civil War (1865–1890).
   - **c.** Briefly explain ONE specific historical example of American Indian resistance to U.S. government policies or actions in the era immediately before the end of the Civil War (1840–1865) OR the era immediately after the Civil War (1865–1890).

TRM Find complete suggested responses in the Teacher's Resource Materials.

TRM Find complete suggested responses in the Teacher's Resource Materials.

5 PART AP® PRACTICE ESSAY QUESTIONS

DOCUMENT-BASED QUESTION *Suggested reading period: 15 minutes. Suggested writing time: 45 minutes.*

DIRECTIONS: Question 1 is based on the accompanying documents. The documents have been edited for the purpose of this exercise.

1. Evaluate the extent to which governmental policies during the Civil War altered the lives of Americans in the North and South in the period from 1861–1870.

DOCUMENT 1

Source: Letter from Thomas Drayton, a South Carolina plantation owner, to his brother, a Union naval officer, April 17, 1861.

"Dear Percy,

I have received yours of the 9th last, and as Mr. Lincoln has threatened to stop the mails from us to you after they pass the Confederate Boundary, it is probable this may be a long time in getting to you. . . .

You say I don't yet understand the position you have taken. I do fully — but certainly differ from you when you say that to side with us — would be 'battling for slavery against freedom.' . . .

We are fighting for home & liberty. Can the North say as much? — Good night. And don't say again, that in siding for us — you would be defending slavery and fighting for what is abhorrent to your feelings & convictions. On the contrary, in fighting on our side, you will be battling for law & order & against abstract fanatical ideas which will certainly bring about vastly greater evils upon our race, than could possibly result from the perpetuation of slavery among us. . . .

P.S. Don't imagine that I have meant anything personal in what I have written. . . . I could not help, while alone at this midnight hour, but write in sadness & anguish of heart at the perils which may so soon encompass the orphan children I may so shortly leave behind me. I have meant no unkindness to you. I could not wound one whom I love so well. Goodnight, and pray to God for our country!"

DOCUMENT 2

Source: Letter from Major-General Benjamin Butler to Secretary of War Simon Cameron, July 30, 1861.

"But by the evacuation of Hampton, rendered necessary by the withdrawal of [Union] troops . . . I have therefore now within the Peninsula, this side of Hampton Creek, 900 negroes, 300 of whom are able-bodied men, 30 of whom are men substantially past hard labor, 175 women, 225 children under the age of 10 years, and 170 between 10 and 18 years, and many more coming in. The questions which this state of facts present are very embarrassing.

First — What shall be done with them? and, Second, What is their state and condition? . . . Is it forbidden to the troops to aid or harbor within their lines the negro children who are found therein, or is the soldier, when his march has destroyed their means of subsistence, to allow them to starve because he has driven off the rebel master? Now, shall the commander of regiment or battalion sit in judgment upon the question, whether any given black man has fled from his master, or his master fled from him? Indeed, how are the free born to be distinguished? . . .

In a loyal State I would put down a servile insurrection. In a state of rebellion I would confiscate that which was used to oppose my arms, and take all that property, which constituted the wealth of that State, and furnished the means by which the war is prosecuted, beside being the cause of the war; and if, in so doing, it should be objected that human beings were brought to the free enjoyment of life, liberty and the pursuit of happiness, such objections might not require much consideration."

DOCUMENT 3

Source: Winslow Homer, "Our Women in the War," *Harper's Weekly*, September 6, 1862.

Davis Museum at Wellesley College/Art Resource, NY.

DOCUMENT 4

Source: Enrollment Act, March 3, 1863.

Be it enacted . . . that all able-bodied male citizens of the United States, and persons of foreign birth who shall have declared on oath their intention to become citizens under and in pursuance of the laws thereof, between the ages of twenty and forty-five years, except as hereinafter excepted, are hereby declared to constitute the national forces, and shall be liable to perform military duty in the service of the United States when called out by the President for that purpose. . . .

And, it be further enacted, That any person drafted and notified to appear as aforesaid, may, on or before the day filed for his appearance, furnish an acceptable substitute to take his place in the draft; or he may pay to such person as the Secretary of War may authorize to receive it, such sum, not exceeding three hundred dollars, as the Secretary may determine, for the procuration of each substitute . . . and thereupon such person so furnishing the substitute, or paying the money, shall be discharged from further liability under that draft. . . .

DOCUMENT 5

Source: Letter from Hannah Johnson to President Abraham Lincoln, July 31, 1863.

"My son went in the 54th regiment. I am a colored woman and my son was strong and able as any to fight for his country and the colored people have as much to fight for as any. My father was a Slave and escaped from Louisiana before I was born more than forty years ago. . . . I never went to school, but I know just as well as any what is right between man and man. Now I know it is right that a colored man should go and fight for his country, and so ought to a white man. I know that a colored man ought to run no greater risks than a white, his pay is no greater, his obligation to fight is the same. So why should not our enemies be compelled to treat him the same, Made to do it. . . .

You must put the rebels to work in State prisons to making shoes and things, if they sell our colored soldiers, till they let them all go. And give their wounded the same treatment. It would seem cruel, but there [is] no other way, and a just man must do hard things sometimes, that show him[self] to be a great man. . . .

Will you see that the colored men fighting now, are fairly treated. You ought to do this, and do it at once, Not let the thing run along; meet it quickly and manfully, and stop this, mean cowardly cruelty. We poor oppressed ones, appeal to you, and ask fair play.

DOCUMENT 6

Source: Prices and Real Wages During the Civil War.

Year	Union Prices	Union Real Wages	Confederate Prices	Confederate Real Wages
1860	100	100	100	100
1861	101	100	121	86
1862	113	93	388	35
1863	139	84	1,452	19
1864	176	77	3,992	11

DOCUMENT 7

Source: Black Codes of St. Landry's Parish, Louisiana, 1865.

SECTION 2. . . . That every negro who shall be found absent from the residence of his employer after 10 o'clock at night, without a written permit from his employer, shall pay a fine of five dollars, or in default thereof, shall be compelled to work five days on the public road, or suffer corporeal punishments. . . .

SECTION 4. Be it further ordained, That every negro is required to be in the regular service of some white person, or former owner. . . .

SECTION 6. Be it further ordained, That no negro shall be permitted to preach, exhort, or otherwise declaim to congregations of colored people, without a special permission in writing from the president of the police jury. . . .

SECTION 7. Be it further ordained, That no negro who is not in the military service shall be allowed to carry fire-arms, or any kind of weapons, within the parish, without the special written permission of his employers, approved and endorsed by the nearest or most convenient chief of patrol.

LONG ESSAY QUESTIONS *Suggested writing time: 40 minutes.*

DIRECTIONS: Please choose one of the following three questions to answer. Make a historically defensible claim and support your reasoning with specific and relevant evidence.

2. Evaluate the extent to which western settlement of the United States in the period 1840–1865 affected the economy differently from western settlement of the United States in the period 1865–1900.
3. Evaluate the extent to which Reconstruction fostered changes for African Americans in the South from 1865 to 1877.
4. Evaluate the extent to which the Civil War and Reconstruction expanded the power of the federal government in the period from 1860 to 1890.

PART 6

Industrializing America: Upheavals and Experiments

1877–1917

Touring the United States around 1900, a Hungarian Catholic abbot named Count Péter Vay visited the steel mills of Pittsburgh. "Fourteen-thousand tall chimneys . . . discharge their burning sparks and smoke incessantly," he reported. He was moved by the plight of fellow Hungarians, laboring "wherever the heat is most insupportable, the flames most scorching." One worker had just been killed in a foundry accident. Vay, attending the funeral, worried that immigration was "of no use except to help fill the moneybags of the insatiable millionaires."

Vay witnessed America's emergence as an industrial power, the subject of Part 6 of *America's History*. We begin Part 6 in 1877 because the transformations wrought by capitalism drove the nation's most urgent controversies after the end of the Civil War and Reconstruction. Key working-class reform and protest movements developed new strategies and arguments in the four decades that followed the end of Reconstruction. The Democratic Party, traditionally hostile to strong central government but pressured in new directions by grassroots groups like the People's Party of the 1890s, began to advocate for new measures to address poverty and rein in growing corporate power. By 1910, thousands of middle-class and elite Americans had adopted their own reform visions. As ex-president Theodore Roosevelt declared, American citizens needed to "control the mighty commercial forces which they have called into being."

Part 6 ends in 1917 because U.S. participation in World War I was a key turning point that helped bring about some measures that progressives had sought for decades, such as national women's suffrage, prohibition, and government ownership of railroads. As we shall see in Part 7, the aftermath of World War I also revealed the limits of those reforms. ▶

AP® CONCEPT CONNECTIONS

Why and how did the rise of large corporations transform workers' experiences and provoke intense economic and political conflict?

Library of Congress, LC-DIG-nclc-01151.

Giant corporations developed global networks of production, marketing, and finance by innovating technically and developing ruthless tactics to control labor and markets. Corporations' complex structures opened new careers for managers, salesmen, and "pink-collar" (women) workers. Much labor became unskilled, however, as artisans and craftsmen were marginalized. Laborers, including millions of newly arrived immigrants, endured low pay, health hazards, and frequent unemployment. In addition to creating labor unions to protest such conditions, workers forged political alliances with farmers, who also found themselves economically vulnerable. Along with an eight-hour day and union recognition, workers agitated for, and won, Chinese exclusion. By the 1910s, even well-to-do Americans were forced to acknowledge the "labor question" that industrialization had raised.

Why and how did industrialization transform Americans' social, intellectual, religious, and family life?

Pictorial Press Ltd / Alamy Stock Photo.

The nineteenth-century values of thrift, piety, and domesticity faced challenges in the era of industrialization. Women took prominent roles in public life, while intellectual leaders called for affluent men to build toughness through football and boxing. Charles Darwin's theory of evolution prompted some thinkers to justify economic inequality as a law of nature, whereas others protested that "survival of the fittest" was not a just social goal. Writers and artists experimented with realism and abstraction. People of religious faith developed new forms of religious expression and evangelicalism.

The nation's fast-growing cities proved challenging to govern, as they welcomed newcomers from the American countryside and around the globe. Reformers denounced immigrant-supported political machines and "bosses" who controlled them. But cities offered enticing consumer pleasures, from professional baseball stadiums to the first movie theaters. Life in the big city offered both opportunities and risks for women, who became increasingly visible in workplaces, reform movements, and public spaces. This new female independence contributed to growing support for women's voting rights.

Why did progressive reform movements arise between the 1880s and 1910s, and to what extent did they succeed?

SOUTHERN HORRORS.

LYNCH LAW

IN ALL

ITS PHASES

MISS IDA B. WELLS.

Price, · · · Fifteen Cents.

THE NEW YORK AGE PRINT.

1892.

Schomburg Center, NYPL/Art Resource, NY.

As industrialization progressed, more and more Americans decided that, as the 1892 platform of the People's Party declared, "the power of government — in other words, of the people — should be expanded, . . . to the end that oppression, injustice, and poverty shall eventually cease in the land." Progressive reformers — a diverse group who were not at all united — sought to enhance democracy, improve social welfare, and protect the environment. They argued especially that Americans needed stronger government to rein in the new power of giant corporations. African Americans, who found their political position deteriorating with segregation and disfranchisement, launched new efforts for racial justice. Though President Theodore Roosevelt — a Republican — championed landmark legislation (1901–1909), other parties took on much of the work of national-level reform. During the presidency of Woodrow Wilson (1913–1921), Democrats enacted an impressive slate of laws, including new recognition of labor rights. Meanwhile, the Populist, Socialist, and Progressive parties proposed more radical responses to poverty and concentrated wealth. Although none of these parties won national power, their ideas helped influence the shape of the emerging modern state.

511

Organized around a single theme, the Part 6 Document Set in *Sources for America's History* can be used to teach AP® Theme ARC: American and Regional Culture, which deals with the ways in which cultural values and the arts changed in response to the Civil War and industrialization, and how in the nineteenth and twentieth centuries new philosophical, moral, and scientific ideas were used to defend or challenge the existing economic and social order.

AP® THEMATIC UNDERSTANDING

Industrializing America: Upheavals and Experiments, 1877–1917

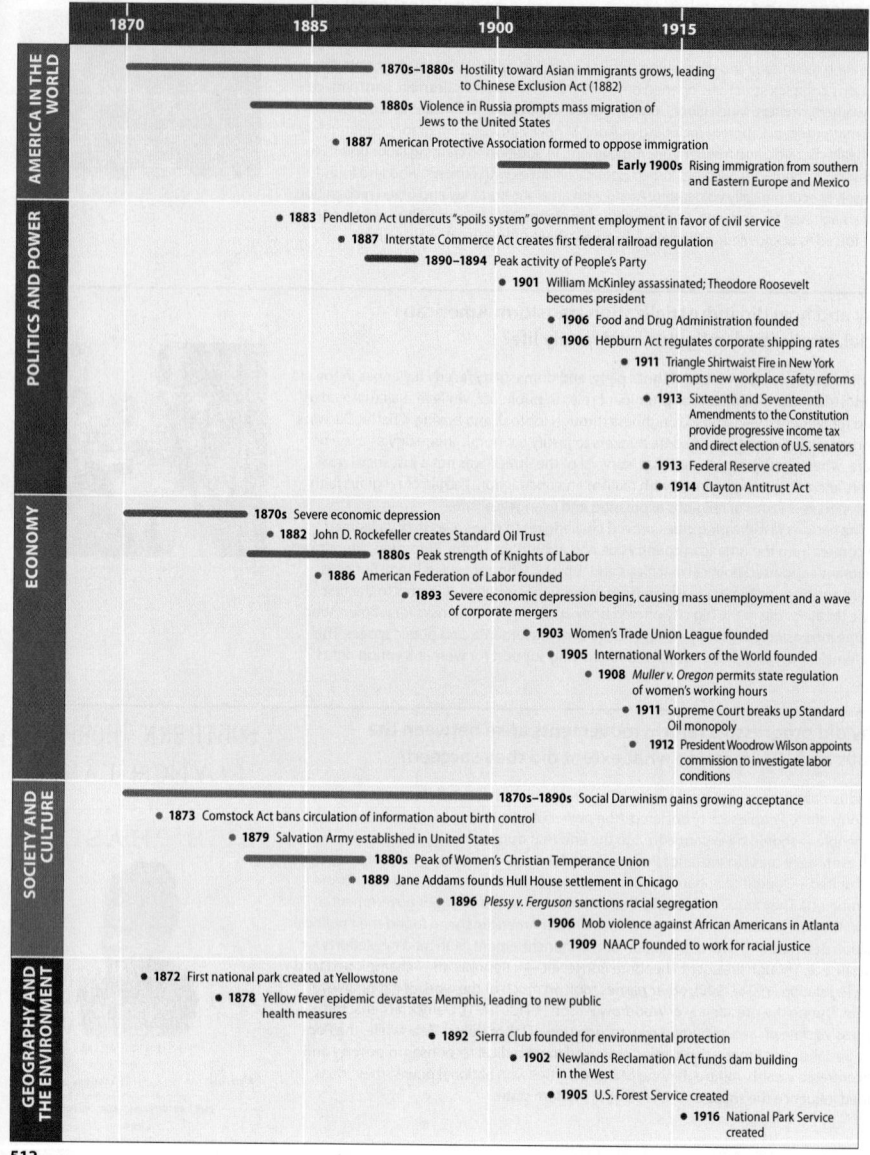

Timeline: 1870 · 1885 · 1900 · 1915

AMERICA IN THE WORLD

- **1870s–1880s** Hostility toward Asian immigrants grows, leading to Chinese Exclusion Act (1882)
- **1880s** Violence in Russia prompts mass migration of Jews to the United States
- **1887** American Protective Association formed to oppose immigration
- **Early 1900s** Rising immigration from southern and Eastern Europe and Mexico

POLITICS AND POWER

- **1883** Pendleton Act undercuts "spoils system" government employment in favor of civil service
- **1887** Interstate Commerce Act creates first federal railroad regulation
- **1890–1894** Peak activity of People's Party
- **1901** William McKinley assassinated; Theodore Roosevelt becomes president
- **1906** Food and Drug Administration founded
- **1906** Hepburn Act regulates corporate shipping rates
- **1911** Triangle Shirtwaist Fire in New York prompts new workplace safety reforms
- **1913** Sixteenth and Seventeenth Amendments to the Constitution provide progressive income tax and direct election of U.S. senators
- **1913** Federal Reserve created
- **1914** Clayton Antitrust Act

ECONOMY

- **1870s** Severe economic depression
- **1882** John D. Rockefeller creates Standard Oil Trust
- **1880s** Peak strength of Knights of Labor
- **1886** American Federation of Labor founded
- **1893** Severe economic depression begins, causing mass unemployment and a wave of corporate mergers
- **1903** Women's Trade Union League founded
- **1905** International Workers of the World founded
- **1908** *Muller v. Oregon* permits state regulation of women's working hours
- **1911** Supreme Court breaks up Standard Oil monopoly
- **1912** President Woodrow Wilson appoints commission to investigate labor conditions

SOCIETY AND CULTURE

- **1870s–1890s** Social Darwinism gains growing acceptance
- **1873** Comstock Act bans circulation of information about birth control
- **1879** Salvation Army established in United States
- **1880s** Peak of Women's Christian Temperance Union
- **1889** Jane Addams founds Hull House settlement in Chicago
- **1896** *Plessy v. Ferguson* sanctions racial segregation
- **1906** Mob violence against African Americans in Atlanta
- **1909** NAACP founded to work for racial justice

GEOGRAPHY AND THE ENVIRONMENT

- **1872** First national park created at Yellowstone
- **1878** Yellow fever epidemic devastates Memphis, leading to new public health measures
- **1892** Sierra Club founded for environmental protection
- **1902** Newlands Reclamation Act funds dam building in the West
- **1905** U.S. Forest Service created
- **1916** National Park Service created

AP Making Connections Across Chapters

Read these questions and think about them as you read the chapters in this part. Then when you have completed reading this part, return to these questions and answer them.

1 Historians often refer to the late nineteenth and early twentieth century as the era of *industrialization*. In what ways does that word accurately describe the transformations that capitalism wrought during this period? What changes took place that might not be captured by the term *industrialization*, or might require us to expand our understanding of what it was?

Library of Congress, 1s13665.

2 Americans endured two severe economic depressions in the late nineteenth century, one starting in 1873 and one in 1893. How did workers, voters, and reformers respond to each of these depressions differently? What does that suggest about how American politics changed over time?

Library of Congress, 3a24380.

3 Farmers, wageworkers, African Americans, women, and different groups of immigrants experienced the "Progressive Era" differently. Which groups might have argued that the early twentieth century was, indeed, "progressive," and which might not?

Keystone-France/Gamma-Keystone via Getty Images.

4 After the Civil War, the United States sought to fully incorporate the former Confederacy and the trans-Mississippi west into its economy and politics—a process explored in Part 6. What immigration patterns, economic developments, and protest movements arose in the South and West during the industrial era? How did they impact national policy and politics?

Picture Research Consultants & Archives.

5 How did industrialization reshape men's and women's roles in the workplace, politics, and the family, among groups of Americans who began to identify themselves as "middle class" and "working class"?

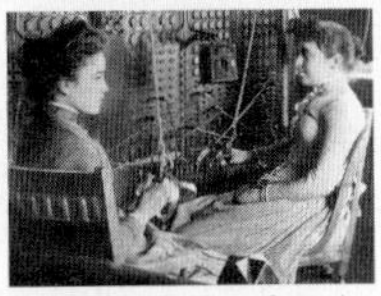

Courtesy of the Ohio History Connection, AL00129.

TRM Find complete suggested responses in the Teacher's Resource Materials.

16 CHAPTER Industrial America: Corporations and Conflicts 1877–1911

Chapter 16 — AP® Assessment Weight and Pacing Guide

This chapter falls at the end of Unit 6 of the AP® U.S. History Curriculum, covering Period 6: 1865–1898, and the beginning of Unit 7, covering Period 7: 1890–1945. Periods 6 and 7 are both weighted 10–17 percent of the AP® Exam.

This pacing guide is based on a schedule with 120 sessions of 50 minutes each before the AP® U.S. History Exam. If you have a different number of sessions before the exam, you can modify the pacing to meet your needs. If you have additional time, consider incorporating quizzes, released AP® U.S. History questions, practice exams, writing practice, and other instructional activities.

	Traditional Schedule	Block Schedule
Chapter 16	3 days	1–2 days

Daily Pacing Guide

	Content Focus	Essential Question
Day 1	The Rise of Big Business	How did corporations come to dominate the American economic landscape in this period, and what impact did industrialization have on employees, consumers, and the environment?
Day 2	Immigrants, East and West	Why did so many immigrants come to the United States in this era, and how did their experiences differ?
Day 3	Labor Gets Organized	How did working people organize to protect their interests in this period, and why and how did their strategies change between 1877 and 1900?

AP® Alignment

Section Heading	AP® Topic	AP® Theme
The Rise of Big Business	6.5, 6.6, 6.7, 6.12	WXT, PCE
Immigrants, East and West	6.7, 6.8, 6.9	WXT, MIG
Labor Gets Organized	6.7, 6.12	WXT, PCE

*Should changes be made to the Course Framework in the future, an updated alignment will be placed on our AP® updates page at go.bfwpub.com/ap-course-updates.

Chapter 16 — Overview

Chapter 16 focuses on the dramatic changes to the American economy, society, and government that arose from the consolidation of wealth and power in large corporations in the late nineteenth and early twentieth century. The chapter analyzes the push and pull factors that encouraged immigration to the U.S. as well as the nativist reactions within the U.S., which were expressed by the exclusion of certain Asian groups. Finally, this chapter focuses on the reaction of labor to the consolidation of wealth and power in large corporations and the laissez-faire policies that supported that growth.

Chapter 16 — Resources

The following resources can be found in the Teacher's Resource Materials (TRM) that accompany the book. You can access the TRM via the book's digital platform, by clicking the TRM links found here in your Teacher's Edition e-book, or by contacting your representative to access the resources online. Visit **bfwpub.com/henretta10e** to learn more.

TRM Chapter 16 Lecture Presentation Slides

TRM Chapter 16 Outline with AP® Focus

TRM Chapter 16 Lecture Strategies

TRM Chapter 16 Suggested Responses

TRM Handout 16.1 — Causation: Trusts and the Consolidation of Wealth

TRM Handout 16.2 — Thematic Analysis: National Consumer Culture

TRM Handout 16.3 — Comparison: Impact of Scientific Management

TRM Handout 16.4 — Comparison: European and Asian Immigrants

TRM Handout 16.5 — Causation: Impact of Farmers' Organizations

Chapter 16 — Essential Activity

Divide the class into collaborative groups and assign each group one of the following labor/farmer organizations: National Grange, Greenback-Labor Party, Knights of Labor, Farmers' Alliance, and American Federation of Labor. Ask each group to summarize their research into a clearly articulated platform of goals and methods, and create a poster that features a unique slogan and logo as well as the ideas supported by the organization. After students have prepared their platform and poster, engage students in a debate articulating the ideas of their group. Allow students to question other groups to clarify similarities and differences in the ideas supported by each group. Finally, lead a class discussion on the reasons these groups did not effectively unify in the late nineteenth century despite the common interests often expressed between workers and farmers.

Chapter 16 — Bell Ringers

The following activities take no more than 5–15 minutes of your class period and offer an effective and engaging way to begin your lessons and for students to apply AP® Skills & Processes:

- Working with partners, direct students to complete **Handout 16.4 — Comparison: European and Asian Immigrants (TRM)** to discuss similarities and differences in immigrant communities in the U.S. in the late nineteenth to early twentieth centuries. Then ask students to write a thesis statement that addresses to what degree immigration in the late nineteenth century represents a dramatic change from earlier periods of immigration.
- Provide groups of students with images of workers in the late nineteenth to early twentieth centuries, including children, women, factory workers, sharecroppers, etc. Ask students to brainstorm a list of problems facing the workers in each image. Then, building upon their lists, students should create a list of issues facing the working class during this period. (Note: You can use this activity as an introduction to the Chapter 16 Essential Activity.)

NOTES

TEACHING STRATEGY

The dramatic account of the Homestead Strike serves as an appropriate opener for the chapter, which covers the conflicts in the industrial era. This incident illustrates the intensity of conflict between workers and managers, which occasionally led to bloodshed but more often led to poverty for workers. Teachers who want to explore the Homestead episode in more depth could use the Digital Public Library's primary source set, which includes more than a dozen photographs and documents, a teacher's guide with discussion questions and suggestions for classroom activities, and links to related resources. To access this site, search "Digital Public Library Homestead Strike." For a complete model answer to the **AP® LEARNING FOCUS** question, see p. 542.

16 CHAPTER

Industrial America: Corporations and Conflicts 1877–1911

AP® LEARNING FOCUS

Why did large corporations arise and thrive in late nineteenth-century America, and how did they reshape trade, work, and politics?

For millions of his contemporaries, Andrew Carnegie exemplified American success. Arriving from Scotland as a poor twelve-year-old in 1848, Carnegie found work as an errand boy for the Pennsylvania Railroad and rapidly scaled the managerial ladder. In 1865, he struck out on his own as an iron manufacturer, selling to friends in the railroad business. Encouraged to enter the steel industry by passage of the Republican tariff, he soon built a massive steel mill outside Pittsburgh where a state-of-the-art Bessemer converter made steel refining dramatically more efficient. With Carnegie leading the way, steel became a major U.S. industry, reaching annual production of 10 million metric tons by 1900 — almost as much as the *combined* output of the world's other top producers, Germany (6.6 million tons) and Britain (4.8 million).

At first, skilled workers at Carnegie's mill in Homestead, Pennsylvania, earned good wages. They had a strong union, and Carnegie affirmed workers' right to organize. But Carnegie — confident that new machinery enabled him to replace many skilled laborers — eventually decided that collective bargaining was too expensive. In the summer of 1892, he withdrew to his estate in Scotland, leaving his partner Henry Clay Frick in command. A former coal magnate and veteran foe of labor, Frick was well qualified to do the dirty work. He announced that after July 1, members of the Amalgamated Association of Iron and Steel Workers would be locked out of the Homestead mill. If they wanted to return to work, they would have to abandon the union and sign new individual contracts. Frick fortified the mill and prepared to hire replacement workers. The battle was on.

At dawn on July 6, barges chugging up the Monongahela River brought dozens of private armed guards from the Pinkerton Detective Agency, hired by Carnegie to defend the plant. Locked-out workers opened fire, starting a gunfight that left seven workers and three Pinkertons dead. Frick appealed to Pennsylvania's governor, who sent the state militia to arrest labor leaders on charges of riot and murder. Most of the locked-out workers lost their jobs. The union was dead.

As the Homestead lockout showed, industrialization was a controversial and often bloody process. During the half century after the Civil War, more and more Americans worked not as independent farmers or artisans but as employees of large corporations. Conditions of work changed for people of all economic classes. Drawn by the dynamic economy, immigrants arrived from around the globe. These transformations provoked working people, including farmers as well as industrial workers, to organize and defend their interests in politics and in the streets.

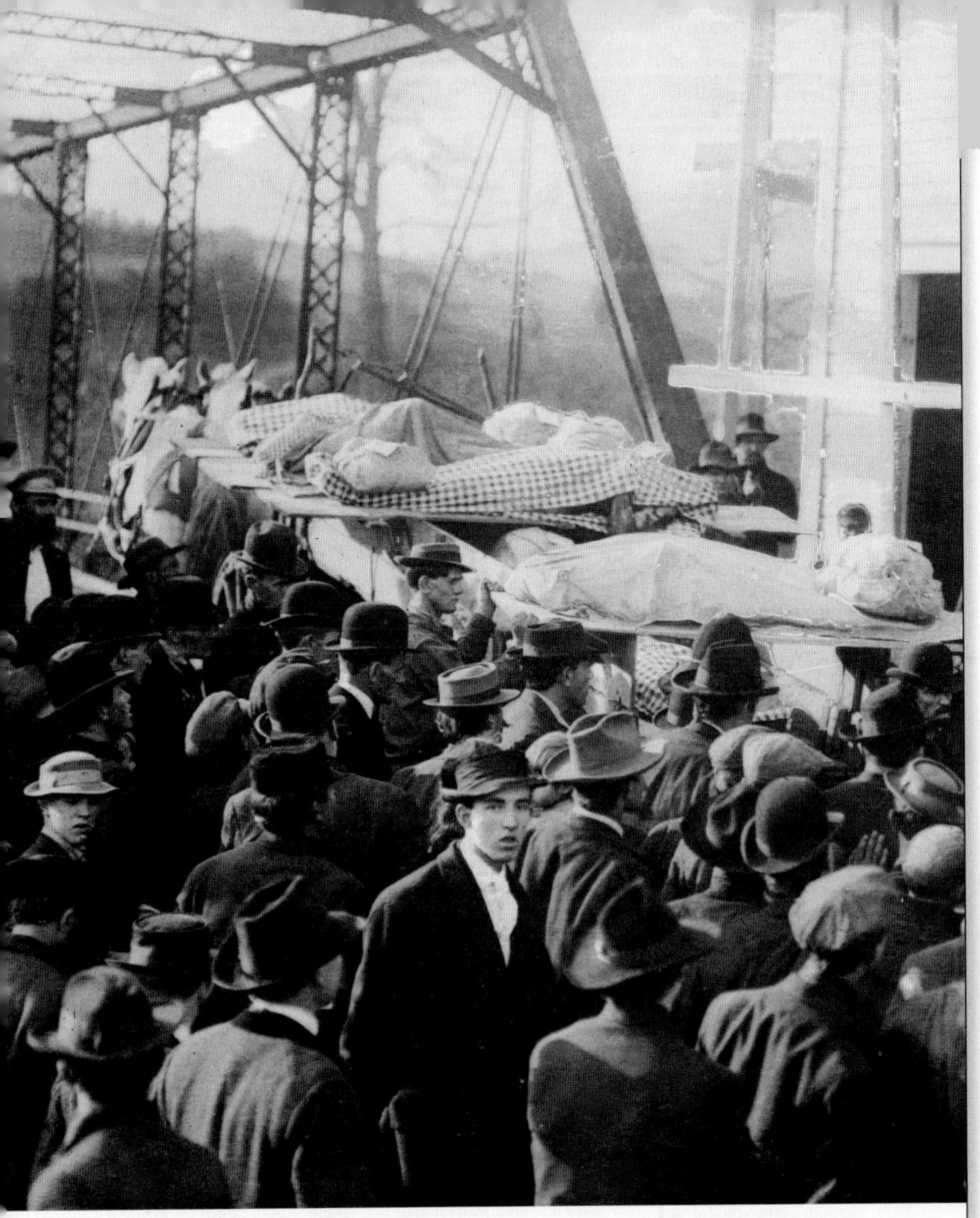

Marianna Mine Disaster The bituminous mines of Marianna, Pennsylvania, and many other rich sites provided the coal that fueled American industrial growth. On November 28, 1908, an explosion in the mine killed 158 workers. Many were American-born; some were Irish, Welsh, Italian, and Polish immigrants. Here, a horse-drawn wagon carries bodies recovered from the mine. Such catastrophes laid bare the human cost of industrialization. Marianna was one among many: in the same decade, disasters at Scofield, Utah; Jacobs Creek, Pennsylvania; Monongah, West Virginia; and Cherry, Illinois, each killed more than 200 men. Library of Congress, LC-DIG-ggbain-03008.

TEACHING STRATEGY

This photo of the Marianna mine disaster provides a snapshot of the difficult, dangerous conditions coal miners routinely faced. The *American Experience* film *Mine Wars*, available online from PBS, explores these conditions in detail. The companion site to the film offers an image gallery with detailed captions for each photo, oral histories from miners and their offspring, and scholarly articles on women, racial and ethnic minorities, industrial democracy, and violence and political expression. To access this site, search "American Experience Mine Wars."

AP® SKILLS & PROCESSES

CONTINUITY AND CHANGE

Use the **TIMELINE** table to help students begin thinking about how the period from 1863 to 1908 could constitute a distinct historical period related to the growth of industry. Students should note that both the starting and ending dates are specific years, and therefore indicate particular events. Students should recognize that this starting point does not suggest that industrial America began precisely at that point, but that the developments associated with industrialization — and particularly the conflicts it brought — came to the forefront as Civil War tensions began to recede. Since no event in the chronology took place in 1911, two events need to be supplied to students from the Part 6 opener: the fire at the Triangle Shirtwaist Company in New York, which highlighted the exploitative conditions workers often faced, and the Supreme Court's ruling against Standard Oil, which forced it to divide to lessen its monopoly power. Students could additionally make inferences about the ways Civil War issues continued to shape the economy in the late nineteenth century.

AP® APPLY THE TIP

Direct students to use The Rise of Big Business section of the text to complete **Handout 16.1 — Causation: Trusts and the Consolidation of Wealth (TRM)**. After completing the handout, lead a class discussion on the impact of trusts and consolidation of wealth on the U.S. economy as well as its probable effects on politics and society. Extend the discussion by asking students to consider the power that corporations have in American politics, economy, and society today. Ask students to compare the development of monopolies in the late nineteenth century with industries that dominate economic development today, including electronics, automobiles, and entertainment.

TRM Find **Handout 16.1 — Causation: Trusts and the Consolidation of Wealth** in the Teacher's Resource Materials.

TIMELINE

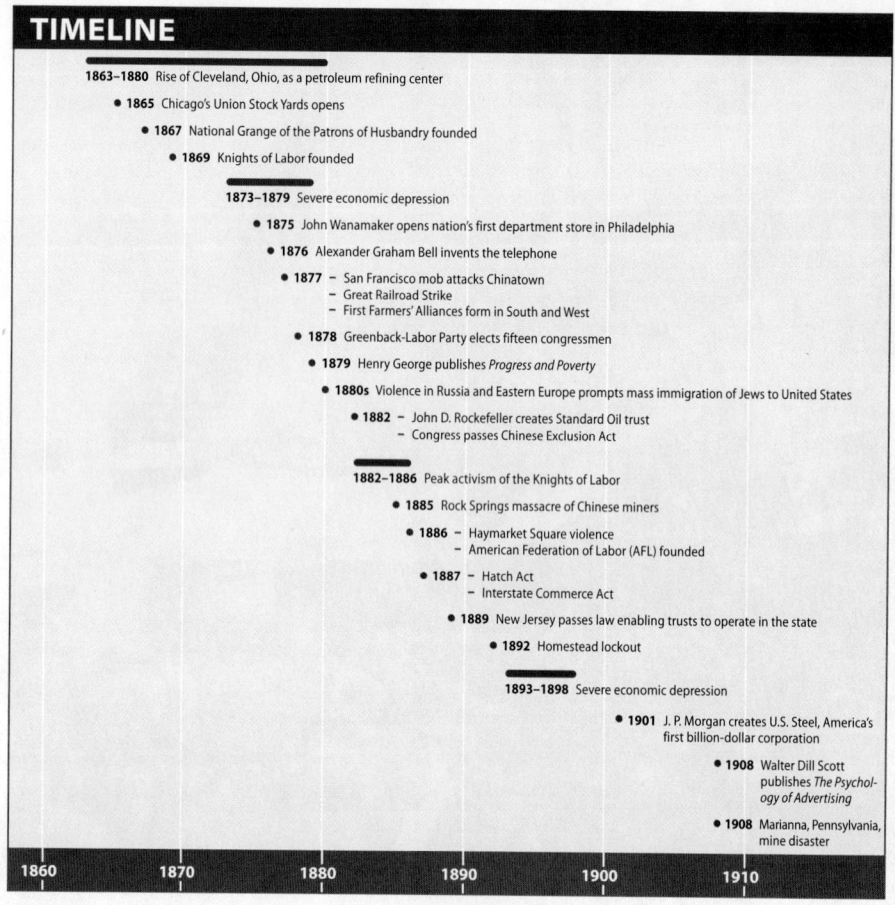

- **1863–1880** Rise of Cleveland, Ohio, as a petroleum refining center
- **1865** Chicago's Union Stock Yards opens
- **1867** National Grange of the Patrons of Husbandry founded
- **1869** Knights of Labor founded
- **1873–1879** Severe economic depression
- **1875** John Wanamaker opens nation's first department store in Philadelphia
- **1876** Alexander Graham Bell invents the telephone
- **1877**
  - San Francisco mob attacks Chinatown
  - Great Railroad Strike
  - First Farmers' Alliances form in South and West
- **1878** Greenback-Labor Party elects fifteen congressmen
- **1879** Henry George publishes *Progress and Poverty*
- **1880s** Violence in Russia and Eastern Europe prompts mass immigration of Jews to United States
- **1882**
  - John D. Rockefeller creates Standard Oil trust
  - Congress passes Chinese Exclusion Act
- **1882–1886** Peak activism of the Knights of Labor
- **1885** Rock Springs massacre of Chinese miners
- **1886**
  - Haymarket Square violence
  - American Federation of Labor (AFL) founded
- **1887**
  - Hatch Act
  - Interstate Commerce Act
- **1889** New Jersey passes law enabling trusts to operate in the state
- **1892** Homestead lockout
- **1893–1898** Severe economic depression
- **1901** J. P. Morgan creates U.S. Steel, America's first billion-dollar corporation
- **1908** Walter Dill Scott publishes *The Psychology of Advertising*
- **1908** Marianna, Pennsylvania, mine disaster

1860 1870 1880 1890 1900 1910

THE RISE OF BIG BUSINESS

How did corporations come to dominate the American economic landscape in this period, and what impact did industrialization have on employees, consumers, and the environment?

AP® EXAM TIP

The consolidation of corporations into trusts and the effects of the resulting concentration of wealth is important to know on the AP® Exam.

In the late 1800s, industrialization in Europe and the United States revolutionized the world economy. It brought large-scale commercial agriculture to many parts of the globe and prompted millions of migrants — both skilled workers and displaced peasants — to cross continents and oceans in search of jobs. Industrialization also created a production glut. The immense scale of agriculture and manufacturing caused a long era of deflation, when prices dropped worldwide (Figure 16.1).

Falling prices normally signal low demand for goods and services, and thus stagnation. In England, a mature industrial power, the late nineteenth century did bring economic decline. But in the United States, production expanded. Between 1877 and 1900, Americans' average real per capita income increased from $388 to $573. In this sense, Andrew Carnegie was right when he argued that, even though industrialization increased the gap between rich and poor, everyone's standard of living rose: as he wrote, "the poor enjoy what the rich could not before afford. What were the luxuries have become the necessaries of life."

Technological and business efficiencies allowed American firms to grow, invest in new equipment, and earn profits even as prices for their products fell. Growth depended, in turn, on America's large and growing population, expansion into the West, and an integrated national marketplace. In many fields, large corporations became the dominant form of business.

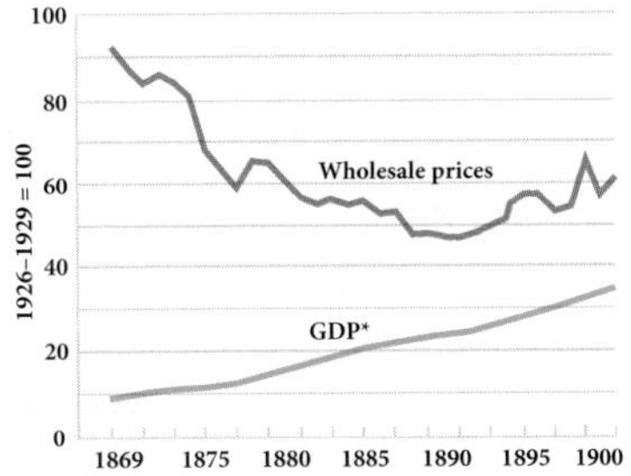

FIGURE 16.1 Business Activity and Wholesale Prices, 1869–1900

This graph shows the key feature of the performance of the late-nineteenth-century economy: while output was booming, wholesale prices were, on the whole, falling. Thus, while workers often struggled with falling wages — especially during decades of severe economic crisis — consumer products also became cheaper to buy.

Innovators in Enterprise

As rail lines stretched westward between the 1850s and 1880s, operators faced a crisis. As one Erie Railroad executive noted, a superintendent on a 50-mile line could personally attend to every detail. But supervising a 500-mile line was impossible; trains ran late, communications failed, and trains crashed. Managers gradually invented systems to solve these problems. They distinguished top executives from those responsible for day-to-day operations. They departmentalized operations by function — purchasing, machinery, freight traffic, passenger traffic — and established clear lines of communication. They perfected cost accounting, which allowed an industrialist like Carnegie to track expenses and revenues carefully and thus follow his Scottish mother's advice: "Take care of the pennies, and the pounds will take care of themselves." This **management revolution** created the internal structure adopted by many large, complex corporations.

management revolution
An internal management structure adopted by large corporations that departmentalized operations and distinguished top executives from those responsible for day-to-day operations.

During these same years, the United States became an industrial power by tapping North America's vast natural resources, particularly in the West. Industries that had once depended on water power began to use prodigious amounts of coal. Steam engines replaced human and animal labor, and kerosene replaced whale oil and wood. By 1900, America's factories and urban homes were converting to electric power. With new management structures and dependency on fossil fuels (oil, coal, natural gas), corporations transformed both the economy and the country's natural and built environments. Fossil fuels were like a giant cup of coffee for the economy — the price of which, in terms of environmental destruction and climate change, Americans did not begin to recognize for more than a century.

Production and Sales After Chicago's Union Stock Yards opened in 1865, middlemen shipped cows by rail from the Great Plains to Chicago and from there to eastern cities, where slaughter took place in local butchertowns. But Gustavus Swift, a shrewd Chicago cattle dealer, saw that local slaughterhouses lacked the scale to utilize waste by-products and cut labor costs. To improve productivity, Swift invented the assembly line, where each wageworker repeated the same slaughtering task over and over.

Swift also pioneered **vertical integration**, a model in which a company controlled all aspects of production from raw materials to finished goods. Once his engineers designed a cooling system, Swift invested in a fleet of refrigerator cars to keep beef fresh as he shipped it eastward, priced below what local butchers could afford. In cities that received his chilled meat, Swift built branch houses and fleets of delivery wagons. He also constructed factories to make fertilizer and chemicals from the by-products

AP® EXAM TIP

Understanding the changes in economic structures and marketing that led to dramatic increase in production of goods is critical for the AP® Exam.

vertical integration
A business model, pioneered by late nineteenth-century entrepreneurs such as Gustavus Swift and Andrew Carnegie, in which a corporation controlled all aspects of production from raw materials to packaged products.

AP® THEME

WXT: Work, Exchange, and Technology

FIGURE 16.1 explores an important economic phenomenon from the industrial era that students often find confusing. Even though workers' wages often fell over time, their relative standard of living did not necessarily decline, as wholesale prices generally fell as well, making products cheaper. Guide students' analysis with the following questions:

- **What does the chart reveal about GDP, the total value of goods and services, in this period?** *GDP steadily rose throughout the period.*
- **What does the chart reveal about wholesale prices?** *Though more uneven than GDP, prices also generally fell throughout most of this period.*
- **What are the limitations of aggregate data like GDP and wholesale prices?** *While useful for understanding broad trends, this data cannot tell more things, like which sectors of the economy were growing, and which items were getting cheaper or by how much.*

TEACHING STRATEGY

The *American Experience* film *Andrew Carnegie: The Richest Man in the World* provides an introduction to both the entrepreneur — with his dramatic tale of immigration and rags-to-riches rise — and to the industrial era as a whole. The companion site to the film offers a timeline, images, and other resources for teachers. To access this site, search "American Experience Andrew Carnegie."

AP® APPLY THE TIP

Provide students with **Handout 16.2 — Thematic Analysis: National Consumer Culture (TRM)**. Students should add at least two specific pieces of evidence, including a key term, person's name, event, etc., related to the development of a national consumer culture in the late nineteenth century for each theme listed in the handout. Once students have completed the handout, re-create the diagram on the board and ask students to volunteer to add specific points with each theme to guide students in a discussion of the rise of a national consumer culture. Extend this activity by asking students to use the information from this thematic analysis to generate a thesis statement and outline based on two themes of history to determine the degree to which the development of a national consumer culture in the U.S. caused changes in the U.S. in the late nineteenth century.

TRM Find **Handout 16.2 — Thematic Analysis: National Consumer Culture** in the Teacher's Resource Materials.

TEACHING STRATEGY

Students are required to know and understand how to explain the concepts of new management structures that were developed by industry during the industrial era. Assign the following terms to groups of students: horizontal integration, vertical integration, trusts, and holding companies. Each group is responsible for one of these terms. After the group has defined their term, they are to meet with each of the other groups and hear the definition of the other terms. Once all terms have been explained and heard, students report back to their original groups and debrief the importance of each historical development. The takeaway is for students to develop a broader understanding of "Industrial Capitalism" and by using these terms, students will be able to use specific evidence.

TEACHING STRATEGY

In order to develop a better understanding of horizontal and vertical integration, have students use an industry of their choice to explain the business practice. For example, one student could select a shoe company — have that student explain vertical integration using shoe companies as their product. Another student could select a coffee company. Have them explain horizontal integration to explain the concept. Using areas of interest can help make these economic terms easier to understand.

predatory pricing
A tactic developed by large corporations in the late nineteenth century, in which a corporation drops prices below cost, in a limited area, to drive small competitors out of business and take control of a local market.

horizontal integration
A business concept invented in the late nineteenth century in which a powerful business forces rivals to merge their companies into a single conglomerate. John D. Rockefeller of Standard Oil pioneered this model.

trust
A small group of associates who hold stock from multiple firms and manage them as a single entity. Trusts quickly evolved into other centralized business forms, but critics continued to refer to giant firms with monopoly power as "trusts."

of slaughter, and he developed marketing strategies for those products as well. Other Chicago packers followed Swift's lead. By 1900, five firms, all vertically integrated, produced nearly 90 percent of the meat shipped in interstate commerce.

Big packers invented new sales tactics. For example, Swift & Company periodically slashed prices in certain markets to below production costs, driving independent distributors to the wall. With profits from its sales elsewhere, a large firm like Swift could survive temporary losses in one locality until competitors went under. Afterward, Swift could raise prices again. This technique, known as **predatory pricing**, helped give a few firms unprecedented market control.

Standard Oil and the Rise of the Trusts No one used ruthless business tactics more skillfully than the king of petroleum, John D. Rockefeller. After inventors in the 1850s figured out how to extract kerosene — a clean-burning fuel for domestic heating and lighting — from crude oil, enormous oil deposits were discovered at Titusville, Pennsylvania. Just then, the Civil War severely disrupted whaling, forcing whale-oil customers to look for alternative lighting sources. Overnight, a forest of oil wells sprang up around Titusville. Connected to these Pennsylvania oil fields by rail in 1863, Cleveland, Ohio, became a refining center. John D. Rockefeller was then an up-and-coming Cleveland grain dealer. (He, like Carnegie and most other budding tycoons, hired a substitute to fight for him in the Civil War.) Rockefeller had strong nerves, a sharp eye for able partners, and a genius for finance. He went into the kerosene business and borrowed heavily to expand. Within a few years, his firm — Standard Oil of Ohio — was Cleveland's leading refiner.

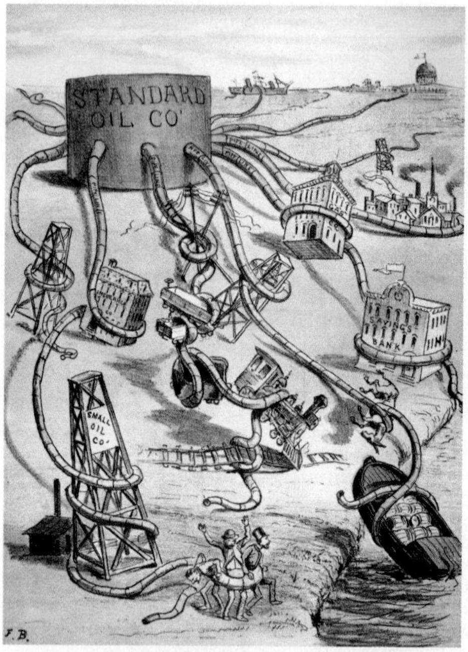

The Reach of Standard Oil Trust. This 1884 cartoon, "The Monster Monopoly," depicts John D. Rockefeller's Standard Oil Company as a giant octopus scooping up oil wells, railroads, ships, telegraph lines, banks, merchant houses — and on the distant horizon, reaching a tentacle toward the U.S. Capitol. The captured men at the bottom of the picture suggest the plight of small businessmen whose enterprises were destroyed by Rockefeller's predatory pricing and other ruthless competitive tactics. Debate over the power of large corporations — referred to in this era as "trusts and monopolies" — became a feature of political debate from the 1880s onward. The Granger Collection, New York.

Like Carnegie and Swift, Rockefeller succeeded through vertical integration: to control production and sales all the way from the oil well to the kerosene lamp, he took a big stake in the oil fields, added pipelines, and developed a vast distribution network. Rockefeller allied with railroad executives, who, like him, hated the oil market's boom-and-bust cycles. What they wanted was predictable, high-volume traffic, and they offered Rockefeller secret rebates that gave him a leg up on competitors.

Rockefeller also pioneered a strategy called **horizontal integration**. After driving competitors to the brink of failure through predatory pricing, he invited them to merge their local companies into his conglomerate. Most agreed, often because they had no choice. Through such mergers, Standard Oil wrested control of 95 percent of the nation's oil refining capacity by the 1880s. In 1882, Rockefeller's lawyers created a new legal form, the **trust**. It organized a small group of associates — the board of trustees — to hold stock from a group of combined firms, managing them as a single entity. Rockefeller soon invested in Mexican oil fields and competed in world markets against Russian and Middle Eastern producers.

Other companies followed Rockefeller's lead, creating trusts to produce such products as linseed oil, sugar, and salt. Many expanded sales and production overseas. As early as 1868, Singer Manufacturing

The Singer Sewing Machine The sewing machine was an American invention that swiftly found markets abroad. The Singer Manufacturing Company, the dominant firm by the time the Civil War began, exported sewing machines to markets as far-flung as Ireland, Russia, China, and India. The company also moved some manufacturing operations abroad, producing 200,000 machines annually at a Scottish plant that employed 6,000 workers. Singer's advertising rightly boasted of the international appeal of a product that the company dubbed "The Universal Sewing Machine." Popperfoto/Getty Images.

Company established a factory in Scotland to produce sewing machines. By World War I, such brands as Ford and General Electric had become familiar around the world. Carnegie, Swift, Rockefeller, Singer, and other corporate empire builders depended on the new fossil fuel infrastructure of railroads and steamships, as well as the rapid long-distance communications made possible by the telegraph.

Distressed by the development of near monopolies, critics began to denounce "the trusts," a term that in popular usage referred to any large corporation that seemed to wield excessive power. Some states outlawed trusts as a legal form. But in an effort to attract corporate headquarters to its state, New Jersey broke ranks in 1889, passing a law that permitted the creation of holding companies and other combinations. Delaware soon followed, providing another legal haven for consolidated corporations. A wave of mergers further concentrated corporate power during the depression of the 1890s, as weaker firms succumbed to powerful rivals. By 1900, America's largest one hundred companies controlled a third of the nation's productive capacity. Purchasing several steel companies in 1901, including Carnegie Steel, the financier J. P. Morgan created U.S. Steel, the nation's first billion-dollar corporation.

AP® SKILLS & PROCESSES

CONTEXTUALIZATION

Why did large corporations arise in the late nineteenth century, and how did leading industrialists consolidate their power?

Assessing the Industrialists The work of men like Swift, Rockefeller, and Carnegie was controversial in their lifetimes and has been ever since. Carnegie, in an essay that became famous as "**The Gospel of Wealth**," argued that corporate titans attained their wealth through talent, proving they deserved their success. He also declared, however, that wealth was a "public trust" and that every successful entrepreneur, after providing for his family, had a patriotic obligation to give away his millions to benefit education and other worthy causes. Carnegie advocated a near 100 percent inheritance tax on privately held wealth: inheriting large sums, he believed, discouraged young people's initiative, just as "handouts" of food or shelter to the poor discouraged them from working. Carnegie rejected both, viewing Social Darwinism or "survival of the fittest" as essential to the success of the new industrial order (see "Darwinism and Its Critics" in Chapter 17).

Gospel of Wealth
Andrew Carnegie's argument that corporate leaders' success showed their "fitness" to lead society and that poverty demonstrated, on the contrary, lack of "fitness" to compete in the new economy. Carnegie advocated, however, that wealthy men should use their fortunes for the public good.

AP® THEME

WXT: Work, Exchange, and Technology

One of the lesser-known aspects of early industrial capitalism is how early industry sought opportunities in foreign markets. Have students use the picture of the advertisement for Singer Sewing Machines to answer the following question: What factors influenced the ability of industrial capitalists to seek out investment opportunities outside of the U.S. borders?

AP® SKILLS & PROCESSES

CONTEXTUALIZATION

The **CONTEXTUALIZATION** question addresses one of the most momentous topics in American history and is worth extended exploration. Many students will gravitate toward examples of exceptional individuals, but encourage students to consider larger structural factors. These factors could include a large country with many natural resources, a sizable population that could serve as both workers and consumers, laws that allowed large-scale immigration, a culture of innovation, a legal system that included tariffs, recognition of corporations' rights, and protection of inventions.

TRM Find complete suggested responses in the Teacher's Resource Materials.

AP® THEME

SOC: Social Structures

Carnegie's "The Gospel of Wealth" helped to establish the idea that wealthy business leaders had a moral obligation to help the less fortunate and improve society through philanthropic contributions that enhanced educational opportunities and urban environments.

AP® EXAM TIP

Evaluate the ways in which economic change improved the standard of living while at the same time increased the gap between the rich and poor.

Historians' opinions of the first industrial titans have tended to be harsh in eras of economic crisis, when the shortcomings of corporate America appear in stark relief. During the Great Depression of the 1930s, a historian coined the term *robber barons*, which is still used today. In periods of prosperity, both scholars and the public have tended to view early industrialists more favorably, calling them *industrial statesmen*. Some scholars have argued that industrialists benefitted the economy by replacing the chaos of market competition with a "visible hand" of planning and management. But one recent study of railroads asserts that the main skills of early tycoons lay in cultivating political friends, defaulting on loans, and lying to the public. Whether we consider the industrialists heroes, villains, or something in between, it is clear that the corporate economy was not the creation of just a few individuals, however famous or influential. It was a systemic transformation of the economy.

A National Consumer Culture As they integrated vertically and horizontally, corporations innovated in other ways. Companies such as Bell Telephone and Westinghouse set up research laboratories. Steelmakers invested in chemistry and materials science to make their products cheaper, better, and stronger. Mass markets brought an appealing array of new goods to consumers who could afford them. Railroads whisked Florida oranges and other fresh produce to the shelves of grocery stores. Retailers such as F. W. Woolworth and the Great Atlantic and Pacific Tea Company (A&P) opened chains of stores that soon stretched nationwide. Corporate power depended not only on production but also on marketing and mass consumption.

The department store was pioneered in 1875 by John Wanamaker in Philadelphia. These megastores displaced small retail shops, tempting customers with large show windows and Christmas displays. Like industrialists, department store magnates developed economies of scale that enabled them to slash prices. They also promised new forms of consumer bliss. An 1898 newspaper advertisement for Macy's Department Store urged shoppers to come right in and "read our books, cook in our saucepans, dine off our china, wear our silks, get under our blankets, smoke our cigars, drink our wines — Shop at Macy's — and Life will Cost You Less and Yield You More Than You Dreamed Possible."

While department stores became urban fixtures, Montgomery Ward and Sears built mail-order empires. Rural families from Vermont to California pored over the companies' annual catalogs, making wish lists of tools, clothes, furniture, and toys. Mail-order companies used money-back guarantees to coax wary customers to buy products they could not see or touch. "Don't be afraid to make a mistake," the Sears catalog counseled. "Tell us what you want, in your own way." By 1900, America counted more than twelve hundred mail-order companies.

The active shaping of consumer demand became, in itself, a new enterprise. Outdoors, advertisements appeared everywhere: in New York's Madison Square, the Heinz Company installed a 45-foot pickle made of green electric lights. Tourists had difficulty admiring Niagara Falls because billboards obscured the view. By 1900, companies were spending more than $90 million a year ($2.3 billion today) on print advertising, as the press itself became a mass-market industry. Rather than charging subscribers the cost of production, magazines began to cover their costs by selling ads. Cheap subscriptions built a mass readership, which in turn attracted more advertisers. In 1903, the *Ladies' Home Journal* became the first magazine with a million subscribers.

The Corporate Workplace

Before the Civil War, most American boys had hoped to become farmers, small-business owners, or independent artisans. Afterward, more and more Americans — both male and female — began working for someone else. Because

CHECK FOR UNDERSTANDING

Ask students: **Who were the major leaders in enterprise, and what were their significant innovations?** *Rail executives created a management structure to run organizations; Swift and Carnegie pioneered vertical integration, where Carnegie's company controlled all aspects of production from raw materials to finished goods; Rockefeller also engaged in vertical integration while innovating with horizontal integration, driving competitors to failure through predatory pricing and then inviting them into a merger.*

they wore white shirts with starched collars, those who held professional positions in corporations became known as white-collar workers, a term differentiating them from blue-collar employees, who labored with their hands. For a range of employees — managers and laborers, clerks and salespeople — the rise of corporate work had wide-ranging consequences.

Managers and Salesmen As the managerial revolution unfolded, the headquarters of major corporations began to house departments handling specific activities such as purchasing and accounting. These departments were supervised by middle managers, something not seen before in American industry. Middle managers took on entirely new tasks, directing the flow of goods, labor, and information throughout the enterprise. They were key innovators, counterparts to the engineers in research laboratories who, in the same decades, worked to reduce costs and improve efficiency.

Corporations also needed a new kind of sales force. In post–Civil War America, the traveling salesman became a familiar sight on city streets and in remote country stores. Riding rail networks from town to town, these salesmen introduced merchants to new products, offered incentives, and suggested sales displays. They built nationwide distribution networks for such popular consumer products as cigarettes and Coca-Cola. By the late 1880s, the leading manufacturer of cash registers produced a sales script for its employees' conversations with local merchants. "Take for granted that he will buy," the script directed. "Say to him, 'Now, Mr. Blank, what color shall I make it?'. . . Handing him your pen say, 'Just sign here where I have made the cross.'"

With such companies in the vanguard, sales became systematized. Managers set individual quotas and awarded prizes to top salesmen, while those who sold too little were singled out for remedial training or dismissal. Executives embraced the ideas of business psychologist Walter Dill Scott, who published *The Psychology of Advertising* in 1908. Scott's principles — which included selling to customers based on their presumed "instinct of escape" and "instinct of combat" — were soon taught at Harvard Business School. Leading thinkers promised that a "scientific attitude" would "attract attention" and "create desire." Corporate growth depended on pressuring people to buy, not just because they needed an item but because advertisers linked it to the customer's identity, fears, and dreams.

AP® EXAM TIP

Explain the impact of economic change in the late nineteenth century on the roles of women in the United States.

Women in the Corporate Office Beneath the ranks of managers emerged a new class of female office workers. Before the Civil War, most clerks at small firms had been young men who expected to rise through the ranks. In a large corporation, secretarial work became a dead-end job, and employers began assigning it to women. By the turn of the twentieth century, 77 percent of all stenographers and typists were female; by 1920, women held half of all low-level office jobs.

For white working-class women, clerking and office work represented new opportunities. In an era before most families had access to day care, mothers most often earned money at home, where they could tend children while also taking in laundry, caring for boarders, or doing piecework (sewing or other assembly projects, paid on a per-item basis). Unmarried daughters could enter domestic service or factory work, but clerking and secretarial work were cleaner and better paid.

New technologies provided additional opportunities for women. The rise of the telephone, introduced by inventor

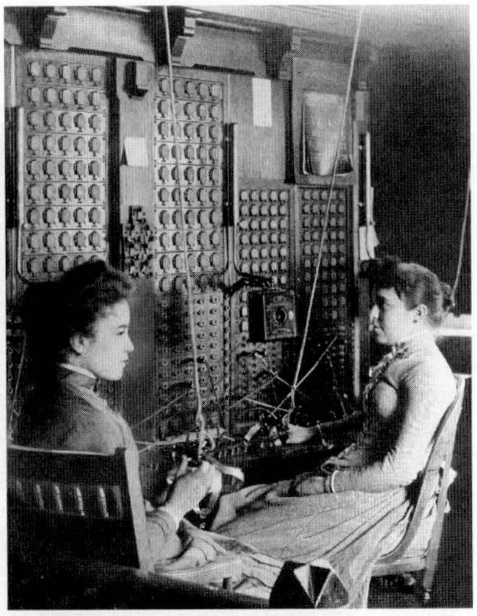

Telephone Operators, 1888 Like other women office workers, these switchboard operators enjoyed relatively high pay and comfortable working conditions — especially in the early years of the telephone industry, before operators' work routines speeded up. These young women worked for the Central Union Telephone Company in Canton, Ohio. Courtesy of the Ohio History Connection, AL00129.

AP® THEME

WXT: Work, Exchange, and Technology

Harvard's Baker Library provides two different online exhibitions that explore the nature of late-nineteenth-century advertising. The online exhibition *The Art of American Advertising, 1865–1910* features extensive detail about trade catalogs, trade cards, novelties, brand management, and other topics alongside numerous high-quality advertisements and other illustrations embedded throughout. To access this site, search "Baker Library American Advertising 1865–1910." The Baker Library also provides the *Marketing in the Modern Era* exhibition, which explores leisure activities and consumer and household goods, and provides dozens of additional advertisements from the late nineteenth century. To access this site, search "Baker Library Marketing in the Modern Era."

AP® APPLY THE TIP

Lead students in a discussion of the historical trends in economic development impacting women up to the late nineteenth century. To begin, draw a timeline that covers the nineteenth century. You might consider including the Lowell system, the Second Great Awakening, and the Civil War era, as well as the development of clerical work. For each of these eras, ask students to identify the changes that were occurring in the U.S. and the specific impact on women. After adding sufficient details to the timeline, ask students to consider the degree to which the roles of women in the workplace in the late nineteenth century represented continuity as well as change over time.

TEACHING STRATEGY

Ask students: **How did female office work in the late nineteenth century compare with work in textile mills?** *While the circumstances were similar in offering some autonomy to women and providing supplemental family income, the comparatively safer and less strenuous work in the late nineteenth century was much more appealing to most women.*

AP® SKILLS & PROCESSES

MAKING CONNECTIONS

Use the **MAKING CONNECTIONS** question to evaluate the effects of industrialization on various classes of corporate employees. Students, who are typically surrounded by these types of jobs today in a service-based economy, may not recognize what a novel development it was to have a (large) class of workers who were neither owner-managers nor physical laborers. Without the emergence of this category, most "middle workers" would have ended up doing physical labor or domestic work. To extend this prompt, students could also identify implications of the quality of life that flowed from this type of job.

TRM Find complete suggested responses in the Teacher's Resource Materials.

CHECK FOR UNDERSTANDING

Ask students: **What were the characteristics of the corporate workplace?** *Large corporations required a new layer of supervision between the owners and the actual workers. Managers directed the flow of goods, labor, and information without participating in the physical labor. Salesmen persuaded customers to buy their products, in part through the use of psychological techniques.*

TEACHING STRATEGY

Examination of the painting *The Ironworkers' Noontime* offers an opportunity to explore connections between labor and gender. Students may need some guidance in shifting their understanding of manliness as a universal quality to an ideological construct that changes over time. The appeal of manliness in the late nineteenth century stemmed from the nature of industrial labor due to the physically demanding nature of work, which encouraged demonstrations of strength like those depicted in this painting. At the same time, the constraints of factory labor and the need to obey a manager — increasingly someone who did not himself perform difficult labor — also challenged conventional understandings of manliness based on autonomy.

AP® SKILLS & PROCESSES

MAKING CONNECTIONS

What opportunities did the rise of corporations offer to different types of "middle workers" — those who were neither top executives nor blue-collar laborers?

Alexander Graham Bell in 1876, was a notable example. Originally intended for business use on local exchanges, telephones were eagerly adopted by residential customers. Thousands of young women found work as telephone operators. By 1900 more than 4 million women worked for wages. About a third worked in domestic service; another third in industry; the rest in office work, teaching, nursing, or sales. As new occupations arose, the percentage of wage-earning women in domestic service dropped dramatically, a trend that continued in the twentieth century.

On the Shop Floor

Despite the managerial revolution at the top, skilled workers — almost all of them men — retained considerable autonomy in many industries. A coal miner, for example, was not an hourly wageworker but essentially an independent contractor, paid by the amount of coal he produced. He provided his own tools, worked at his own pace, and knocked off early when he chose. The same was true for puddlers and rollers in ironworks; molders in stove making; and machinists, glass blowers, and skilled workers in many other industries. Such workers abided by the stint, a self-imposed limit on how much they would produce each day. This informal system of restricting output infuriated efficiency-minded engineers, but to the workers it signified personal dignity, manly pride, and brotherhood with fellow employees. One shop in Lowell, Massachusetts, posted regulations requiring all employees to be at their posts by the time of the opening bell and to remain, with the shop door locked, until the closing bell. A machinist promptly packed his tools, declaring that he had not "been brought up under such a system of slavery."

Skilled craftsmen and foremen often doled out unskilled tasks to workers they chose themselves, paying the helpers from their own pockets. This subcontracting system arose, in part, to enable manufacturers to distance themselves from the consequences of shady labor practices. In Pittsburgh steel mills, foremen were known as "pushers," notorious for driving their gangs mercilessly. On the other hand, industrial

***The Ironworkers' Noontime*, 1880** The ideal qualities of the nineteenth-century craft worker — dignity, brotherhood, manliness — shine through in this painting by Thomas P. Anschutz. *The Ironworkers' Noontime* became a popular painting after it was reproduced as an engraving in *Harper's Weekly* in 1884. Artepics/Alamy Stock Photo.

labor operated on a human scale, through personal relationships that could be close and enduring. Skilled and unskilled workers often went on strike together, and labor gangs sometimes walked out on behalf of a popular foreman.

As industrialization advanced, however, workers lost much of the independence characteristic of craft work. The most important cause of this was the **deskilling** of labor. In the early nineteenth century, shoemaking and other craft work had become divided into discrete parts: rather than a master craftsman creating a whole pair of shoes, unskilled workers assembled soles, tongues, and other parts. These practices expanded under the new system of mechanized manufacturing that men like meat-packer Gustavus Swift pioneered and automobile maker Henry Ford soon called mass production. Everything from typewriters to automobiles came to be assembled from standardized parts, using machines that operated with less and less human oversight. A machinist protested in 1883 that the sewing machine industry was so "subdivided" that "one man may make just a particular part of a machine and may not know anything whatever about another part of the same machine." Such a worker, noted an observer, "cannot be master of a craft, but only master of a fragment." Employers, who originally favored automatic machinery because it increased output, quickly found that it also helped them control workers and cut labor costs. They could pay unskilled workers less and replace them easily.

deskilling
A system in which unskilled workers complete discrete, small-scale tasks to build a standardized item, rather than crafting an entire product. This process accelerated in the late nineteenth century as mechanized manufacturing expanded. With deskilling, employers found they could pay workers less and replace them more easily.

By the early twentieth century, managers sought to further reduce costs through a program of industrial efficiency called **scientific management**. Its inventor, a metal-cutting expert named Frederick W. Taylor, recommended that employers eliminate all brain work from manual labor, hiring experts to develop rules for the shop floor. Workers must be required to "do what they are told promptly and without asking questions or making suggestions." In its most extreme form, scientific management called for engineers to time each task with a stopwatch; companies would pay workers more if they met the stopwatch standard. Taylor assumed that workers would respond automatically to the lure of higher earnings. But scientific management was not, in practice, a great success. It proved expensive, and workers stubbornly resisted it. Corporate managers, however, adopted bits and pieces of Taylor's system, and they enthusiastically agreed that decisions should lie with "management alone." Over time, in comparison with businesses in other countries, American corporations created a particularly wide gap between managers and the blue-collar workers they oversaw. Blue-collar workers had little freedom to negotiate, and their working conditions deteriorated markedly as deskilling and mass production took hold.

scientific management
A system of organizing work, developed by Frederick W. Taylor in the late nineteenth century, designed to coax maximum output from the individual worker, increase efficiency, and reduce production costs.

AP® EXAM TIP

Compare the impact of scientific management on the profits of industrialists and the workplace environment of the working class.

At the same time, industrialization brought cheaper products that enabled Americans to enjoy new consumer products — if they could avoid starvation. From executives down to unskilled workers, the hierarchy of corporate employment contributed to sharper distinctions among three economic classes: the wealthy elite; an emerging, self-defined "middle class"; and a struggling class of workers, who bore the brunt of the economy's new risks and included many Americans living in dire poverty. As it wrought these changes, industrialization prompted intense debates over inequality (see "Thinking Like a Historian," p. 524).

Health Hazards and Pollution Industrialized labor took a severe toll on workers' bodies. In 1884, a study of the Illinois Central Railroad showed that, over the previous decade, one in twenty of its workers had been killed or permanently disabled by an accident on the job. For brakemen — one of the most dangerous jobs — the rate was one in seven. Due to lack of regulatory laws and inspections, mining was 50 percent more dangerous in the United States than in Germany; between 1876 and 1925, an average of more than two thousand U.S. coal miners died each year from cave-ins and explosions. Silver, gold, and copper mines were also not immune from such tragedies, but mining companies resisted demands for safety regulation.

Extractive industries and factories also damaged nearby environments and the people who lived in them. Poor city residents suffered from polluted air

AP® APPLY THE TIP

Direct students to use the On The Shop Floor section of the text to complete **Handout 16.3 — Comparison: Impact of Scientific Management (TRM)**. When the handout is complete, ask students to work in small groups to evaluate the effect of economic changes on the U.S. in the late nineteenth century from a specific assigned perspective: manager, congressman, factory worker, farmer, female clerical worker, sharecropper, or industrialist. Use students' findings to lead a class discussion on the impact of economic change on American society.

TRM Find **Handout 16.3 — Comparison: Impact of Scientific Management** in the Teacher's Resource Materials.

AP SKILLS & PROCESSES

ANALYZING HISTORICAL EVIDENCE

The **AP® THINKING LIKE A HISTORIAN** feature allows students to explore a very specific issue — food — as a marker of class and overall well-being. Students should note that these primary sources span a forty-year period and encompass different kinds of sources, each with its own limitations. Perspective has been mentioned in many chapters, but the issue emerges in a slightly different way in this feature. The authors are all journalists and reformers, members of the middle class who likely did not suffer from inadequate access to food. While they may have been sympathetic to the people they were studying, it's also likely that they did not fully understand the circumstances they observed.

Poverty and Food

Amid rising industrial poverty, food emerged as a reference point. How much was too little, or too much? If some Americans were going hungry, how should others respond? The documents below show some contributions to these debates.

1. **Lewis W. Hine, "Mealtime, New York Tenement," 1910.** *Hine was an influential photographer and reformer. He took a famous series of photographs at Ellis Island, remarking that he hoped Americans would view new immigrants in the same way they thought of the Pilgrims. What does the photographer emphasize in the living conditions of this Italian immigrant family and their relationships with one another? Why do you think Hine photographed them at the table?*

SOURCE: Pictorial Press Ltd./Alamy Stock Photo.

2. **Louisa May Alcott, *Little Women*, 1869.** *Alcott's novel, popular for decades, exemplified the ideal of Christian charity. At the start of this scene, Mrs. March returns from a Christmas morning expedition.*

Merry Christmas, little daughters! . . . I want to say one word before we sit down [to breakfast]. Not far away from here lies a poor woman with a little newborn baby. Six children are huddled into one bed to keep from freezing, for they have no fire. There is nothing to eat. . . . My girls, will you give them your breakfasts as a Christmas present?

. . . For a minute no one spoke, only a minute, for Jo exclaimed impetuously, I'm so glad you came before we began!

May I go and help . . . ? asked Beth eagerly.

I shall take the cream and the muffins, added Amy. . . . Meg was already covering the buckwheats and piling the bread into one big plate.

I thought you'd do it, said Mrs. March, smiling.

. . . A poor, bare, miserable room it was, with broken windows, no fire, ragged bedclothes, a sick mother, wailing baby, and a group of pale, hungry children. . . . Mrs. March gave the mother tea and gruel [while] the girls meantime spread the table [and] set the children round the fire. . . .

That was a very happy breakfast, though they didn't get any of it. And when they went away, leaving comfort behind, I think there were not in all the city four merrier people than the hungry little girls who gave away their breakfasts and contented themselves with bread and milk on Christmas morning.

3. **Mary Hinman Abel, *Promoting Nutrition*, 1890.** *This excerpt is from a cookbook that won a prize from the American Public Health Association. The author had studied community cooking projects in Europe and worked to meet the needs of Boston's poor. How does she propose to feed people on 13 cents a day — her most basic menu? What assumptions does she make about her audience? In what ways was her cookbook, itself, a product of industrialization?*

For family of six, average price 78 cents per day, or 13 cents per person.

. . . I am going to consider myself as talking to the mother of a family who has six mouths to feed, and no more money than this to do it with. Perhaps this woman has never kept accurate accounts. . . . I have in mind the wife [who has] time to attend to the housework and children. If a woman helps earn, as in a factory, doing most of her housework after she comes home at night, she must certainly have more money than in the first case in order to accomplish the same result.

. . . The Proteid column is the one that you must look to most carefully because it is furnished at the most expense, and it is very important that it should not fall below the figures I have given [or] your family would be undernourished.

and the dumping of noxious by-products into the water supply. Mines like those in Leadville, Colorado, contaminated the land and water with mercury and lead. Alabama convicts, forced to work in coal mines, faced not only brutal working conditions but also fatal illnesses caused by the mines' contamination of local water. At the time, people were well aware of many of these dangers, but workers had an even more

[Sample spring menu]
Breakfast. Milk Toast. Coffee.
Dinner. Stuffed Beef's Heart. Potatoes stewed with Milk. Dried Apple Pie. Bread and Cheese. Corn Coffee.
Supper. Noodle Soup (from Saturday). Boiled Herring. Bread. Tea.

Proteids. (oz.)	21.20
Fats. (oz.)	14.39
Carbohydrates. (oz.)	77.08
Cost in Cents.	76

4. **Werner Sombart, *Why Is There No Socialism in the United States?*, 1906.** *Sombart, a German sociologist, compared living conditions in Germany and the United States in order to answer this question. What conclusion did he reach?*

The American worker eats almost three times as much meat, three times as much flour and four times as much sugar as his German counterpart. . . . The American worker is much closer to the better sections of the German middle class than to the German wage-labouring class. He does not merely eat, but dines. . . .

It is no wonder if, in such a situation, any dissatisfaction with the "existing social order" finds difficulty in establishing itself in the mind of the worker. . . . All Socialist utopias come to nothing on roast beef and apple pie.

5. **Helen Campbell, *Prisoners of Poverty*, 1887.** *A journalist, Campbell investigated the conditions of low-paid seamstresses in New York City who did piecework in their apartments. Like Abel (source 3), she tried to teach what she called "survival economics." Here, a woman responds to Campbell's suggestion that she cook beans for better nutrition.*

"Beans!" said one indignant soul. "What time have I to think of beans, or what money to buy coal to cook 'em? What you'd want if you sat over a machine fourteen hours a day would be tea like lye to put a back-bone in you. That's why we have tea always in the pot, and it don't make much odds what's with it. A slice of bread is about all. . . . We'd our tea an' bread an' a good bit of fried beef or pork, maybe, when my husband was alive an' at work. . . . It's the tea that keeps you up."

6. **Julian Street, Show and Extravagance, 1910.** *Street, a journalist, was invited to an elite home in Buffalo, New York, for a dinner that included cocktails, fine wines, caviar, a roast, Turkish coffee, and cigars.*

Before we left New York there was newspaper talk about some rich women who had organized a movement of protest against the ever-increasing American tendency toward show and extravagance. . . . Our hostess [in Buffalo] was the first to mention it, but several other ladies added details. . . .

"We don't intend to go to any foolish extremes," said one. . . . "We are only going to scale things down and eliminate waste. There is a lot of useless show in this country which only makes it hard for people who can't afford things. And even for those who can, it is wrong. . . . Take this little dinner we had tonight. . . . In future we are all going to give plain little dinners like this."

"*Plain*?" I gasped. . . . "But I didn't think it had begun yet! I thought this dinner was a kind of farewell feast — that it was — "

Our hostess looked grieved. The other ladies of the league gazed at me reproachfully. . . . "Didn't you notice?" asked my hostess. . . .

"Notice *what*?"

"That we didn't have champagne!"

SOURCE: (2) Louisa May Alcott, *Little Women*, Part 2, Chapter 2 at xroads.virginia.edu/~HYPER/ALCOTT/ch2.html; (3) Mary Hinman Abel, *Practical, Sanitary, and Economic Cooking Adapted to Persons of Moderate and Small Means* (American Public Health Association, 1890), 143–154; (4) Werner Sombart, *Why Is There No Socialism in the United States?*, trans. Patricia M. Hocking and C. T. Husbands (White Plains, NY: International Arts and Sciences Press, 1976), 97, 105–106; (5) Helen Campbell, *Prisoners of Poverty* (Cambridge, MA: University Press, 1887), 123–124; (6) Julian Street, *Abroad at Home* (New York: The Century Co., 1915), 37–39.

ANALYZING THE EVIDENCE

1. These documents were created by journalists and reformers. What audiences did they seek to reach? Why do you think they all focused on food? Explain the author's situation and purpose of each source in your answer.
2. Compare the perspectives of each source. What are the differences in Sombart's and Campbell's findings? How might Hine, Abel, and Campbell respond to Alcott's vision of charitable Christian acts?
3. What do these documents tell us about how poverty affected women? About strategies that women developed as they began to lead movements for economic and industrial reform? Choose at least two sources to discuss where women understood themselves and others in the social order.

AP® DBQ PRACTICE

Using the documents above and your knowledge from this chapter, write a short essay explaining some challenges and opportunities faced by different Americans in the industrializing era — including those of the wealthy elite, emerging middle class, skilled blue-collar men, and very poorest unskilled laborers. How did labor leaders and reformers seek to persuade prosperous Americans to concern themselves with workers' problems? To what dominant values did they appeal? Relate your discussion to American identity.

urgent priority: work. Pittsburgh's belching smokestacks meant coughing and lung damage, but they also meant running mills and paying jobs.

Unskilled Labor and Discrimination As managers deskilled production, the ranks of factory workers came to include more and more women and children, who were

TRM Find complete suggested responses in the Teacher's Resource Materials.

AP® SKILLS & PROCESSES

ARGUMENTATION

The **AP® DBQ PRACTICE** prompt tackles a much broader topic than the primary sources themselves, so students will need to draw extensively on textbook evidence to complete the essay. Scaffold this prompt by asking students to create a chart with rows for each of the four social groups and one column for challenges and another for opportunities. Students have a tendency to concentrate on the most exploitative conditions for poor workers and might be encouraged to look for evidence that circumstances in the U.S., however meager, may have represented an improvement over immigrants' previous conditions.

AP® EXAM TIP

Explain the continued dominance of the sharecropping system in the South despite popularization of the "New South."

almost always unskilled and low paid. Men often resented women's presence in factories, and male labor unions often worked to exclude women — especially wives, who they argued should remain in the home. Women vigorously defended their right to work. On hearing accusations that married women worked only to buy frivolous luxuries, one female worker in a Massachusetts shoe factory wrote a heated response to the local newspaper: "When the husband and father cannot provide for his wife and children, it is perfectly natural that the wife and mother should desire to work. . . . Don't blame married women if the land of the free has become a land of slavery and oppression."

In 1900, one of every five children under the age of sixteen worked outside the home. Child labor was most widespread in the ex-Confederacy. Here, a low-wage industrial sector emerged after Reconstruction, leading commentators to hail the region as a more economically diversified **New South** (Map 16.1). Textile mills sprouted in the Carolinas and Georgia, recruiting workers from surrounding farms; whole families often worked in the mills. Many children also toiled in Pennsylvania coal fields, where death and injury rates were high. State law permitted children as young as twelve to labor with a family member, but turn-of-the-century investigators estimated that about 10,000 additional boys, at even younger ages, were illegally employed in the mines.

New South
A term describing economic diversification and growth of industry in the post–Civil War South. Because of the region's poverty, much work was extractive (such as coal and timber production), and some (like textiles) was low-wage and involved child labor.

Also at the bottom of the pay scale were most African Americans. Corporations and industrial manufacturers widely discriminated against them on the basis of race, and such prejudice was hardly limited to the South. After the Civil War, African American women who moved to northern cities were largely barred from office work

AP® THEME

NAT: American and National Identity; ARC: American and Regional Culture

The "New South" is a required topic for the AP® U.S. history course. Though the "New South" as imagined by reformers such as Henry Grady ultimately failed, the South after the Civil War did in fact become more industrialized. Yet, the South continued to embrace an agrarian economy buttressed by a racially segregated social system. Have students account for the structural reasons for this historical development. Put another way, be sure students explain governmental (structural) decisions that led the South away from a more comprehensive industrialization.

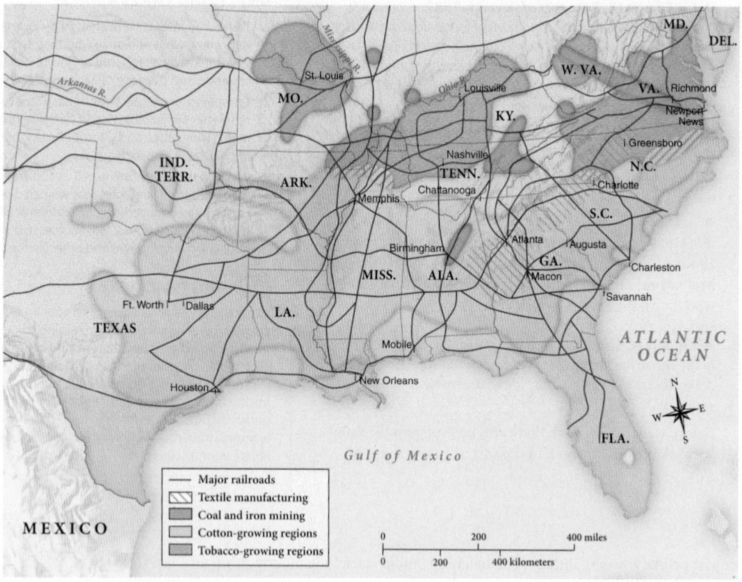

MAP 16.1 The New South, 1900
The economy of the Old South focused on raising staple crops, especially cotton and tobacco. In the New South, staple agriculture continued to dominate, but industrial regions also evolved, producing textiles, coal, and iron. By 1900, the South's industrial pattern was well defined, though the region still served — like the West — as a major producer of raw materials for the industrial region that stretched from New England to Chicago.

Child Labor For many working-class families, children's wages—even though they were low—made up an essential part of the household income. These boys worked the night shift in a glass factory in Indiana. Lewis Hine, an investigative photographer for the National Child Labor Committee, took their picture at midnight, as part of a campaign to educate more prosperous Americans about the widespread employment of child labor and the harsh conditions in which many children worked. Library of Congress, LC-DIG-nclc-01151.

and other new employment options; instead, they remained heavily concentrated in domestic service, with more than half employed as cooks or servants. African American men confronted similar exclusion. America's booming vertically integrated corporations turned black men away from all but the most menial jobs. In 1890, almost a third of black men worked in personal service. Employers in the North and West recruited, instead, a different kind of low-wage labor: newly arrived immigrants.

AP® SKILLS & PROCESSES

CONTINUITY AND CHANGE

How did conditions change for industrial workers in the late nineteenth century, and why?

IMMIGRANTS, EAST AND WEST

Why did so many immigrants come to the United States in this era, and how did their experiences differ?

Across the globe, industrialization set people in motion with the lure of jobs. Between the Civil War and World War I, over 25 million immigrants entered the United States. The American working class became truly global, including not only people of African and Western European descent but also southern and Eastern Europeans, Mexicans, and Asians. In 1900, census-takers found that more than 75 percent of San Francisco and New York City residents had at least one parent who was foreign-born.

In the new industrial order, immigrants made an ideal labor supply. They took the worst jobs at low pay, and during economic downturns tens of thousands returned to their home countries, reducing the shock of unemployment in the United States. But many native-born Americans viewed immigrants with hostility, through the lens of racial, ethnic, and religious prejudices. They also feared that immigrants would take more coveted jobs and erode white men's wages. Political pressure led to policies barring most Asian immigrants from entering the United States, building a new, race-based framework for federal immigration restriction.

AP® EXAM TIP

Evaluate the push and pull factors that accounted for the dramatic increase in immigration to the United States between the Civil War and World War I.

AP® THEME

WXT: Work, Exchange, and Technology

As the caption to the photograph indicates, many parents sent their children to work in order to provide additional income that might allow the family to make ends meet. While their motives may have been understandable, there is no question that children often worked in dangerous and unhealthy conditions. This was a source of concern for reformers, who chronicled child labor in various ways. "The Problem of the Children," a chapter from Jacob Riis's book *How the Other Half Lives*, offers a compelling narrative of the nature of children's work. To access this chapter, search "Bartelby Problem of the Children."

The online exhibition *Child Labor and Child Labor Reform in American History*, available through Ohio State University's eHistory Web site, provides another set of contemporary sources exposing the nature of child labor. To access this site, search "Ohio State University child labor."

CHECK FOR UNDERSTANDING

Ask students: **What new business practices arose in the late nineteenth-century United States, and what impact did they have on employees, consumers, and the environment?** *In the late nineteenth century, industrial corporations embraced new means of management and production, including scientific management and horizontal and/or vertical integration, to great success for stockholders and owners. For employees, results were mixed. New managers and salesmen prospered and women were offered new opportunities as clerks but those on the shop floor suffered from deskilling and lower wages. For consumers, this era brought standardized goods at more affordable prices along with targeted marketing, in what came to be known as the national consumer culture. The environment suffered greatly as corporations did not realize or did not care about the effect of their practices on the Earth and their workers' health.*

AP® APPLY THE TIP

Place students in collaborative groups and ask each group to complete the **AP® AMERICA IN THE WORLD** feature on p. 529. After students have completed this activity, assign each group of students to research one immigrant group from the activity: British, German, Italian, or Swedish. Ask students to use their research to confirm their responses to the activity questions regarding which nations immigrants chose and the conditions they faced after emigrating.

AP® SKILLS & PROCESSES

CONTINUITY AND CHANGE

The **CONTINUITY AND CHANGE** question asks students to identify what factors changed in industrial work and why those changes took place. To answer this question fully, students may need to review Chapter 8 on the Market Revolution, where the nature of labor in the early- to mid-1800s was described. Students should be aware of improvements in conditions, not just their deterioration. Students could also compare late-nineteenth-century deskilling with contemporary discussions about automation and its consequences.

TRM Find complete suggested responses in the Teacher's Resource Materials.

Newcomers from Europe

Mass migration from Western Europe had started in the 1840s, when more than one million Irish fled a terrible famine. In the following decades, as Europe's population grew rapidly and agriculture became commercialized, peasant economies suffered, first in Germany and Scandinavia, then across Austria-Hungary, Russia, Italy, and the Balkans. This upheaval displaced millions of rural people. Some went to Europe's mines and factories; others headed for South America and the United States (Map 16.2; see "America in the World," p. 529).

"America was known to foreigners," remembered one Jewish woman from Lithuania, "as the land where you'd get rich." But the reality was much harsher. Even in the age of steam, a transatlantic voyage was grueling. For ten to twenty days, passengers in steerage class crowded below decks, eating terrible food and struggling with

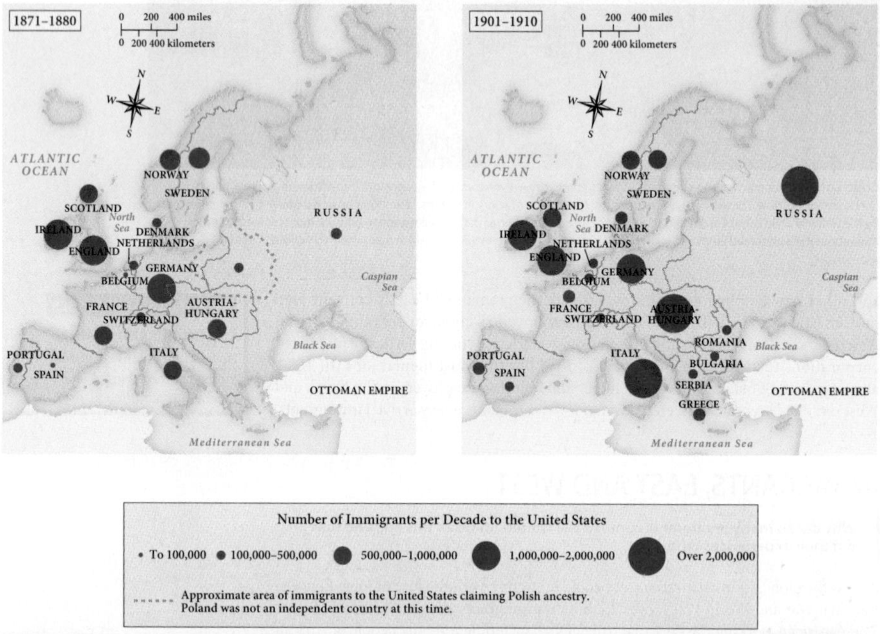

MAPPING THE PAST

MAP 16.2 Sources of European Immigration to the United States, 1871–1910
Around 1900, Americans began to speak of the "new" immigration. They meant the large numbers of immigrants arriving from southern and Eastern Europe — Poles, Slovaks and other Slavic peoples, Yiddish-speaking Jews, Greeks, and Italians — who overwhelmed the still substantial number of immigrants from the British Isles and northern Europe.

ANALYZING THE MAP: Using these two maps, compare immigration in the 1870s and the first decade of the 1900s. From what locations did immigration increase and decrease? What streams of immigration remained largely unchanged over this period?

MAKING CONNECTIONS: Based on your reading of the chapter narrative, what do the geographical limits of this map (excluding the Middle East, Africa, Asia, and Latin America) suggest about U.S. immigration policy and patterns?

AP® SKILLS & PROCESSES

ANALYZING HISTORICAL EVIDENCE

Remind students to look for historical trends when presented with documents that highlight quantitative data. Too often, students recite specific parts of the document or data points and lose sight of the broader historical trends. Guide students through a discussion of what it means to find trends in a document vs. specific data points and why historians find the former more useful.

TRM Find complete suggested responses in the Teacher's Resource Materials.

AP® AMERICA IN THE WORLD

Emigrants and Destinations, 1881–1915

The United States received more new residents than any other nation during the era of industrialization, but it was not the only place where emigrants (those departing) became immigrants (those arriving). With the advent of steamships it became relatively safe, cheap, and easy — compared to earlier eras, at least — for an impoverished, desperate person to relocate to any part of the globe, *if* he or she had access to a port city and a steamship ticket.

A number of factors affected emigrants' decisions as to where they would seek their fortunes. Foremost among them was their home country's political or imperial relationship with other countries or conquered territories. Language also could be a consideration; it was a major advantage to have family members already living in one's destination country, or at least to know that communities from home had settled there.

Equally important was where emigrants could *not* go. Many migrants faced political barriers, such as the Exclusion Act, which barred Asians from emigrating to the United States. The cost of a steamship ticket was a major obstacle, but one that American labor recruiters overcame by offering loans to emigrants — at steep interest rates — to be paid back out of their future earnings. Such recruitment was selective, however. After the Civil War, although the United States opened immigration of "persons of African descent," labor recruiters focused primarily on Europe.

The following graph shows six major destinations for emigrants from four European countries.

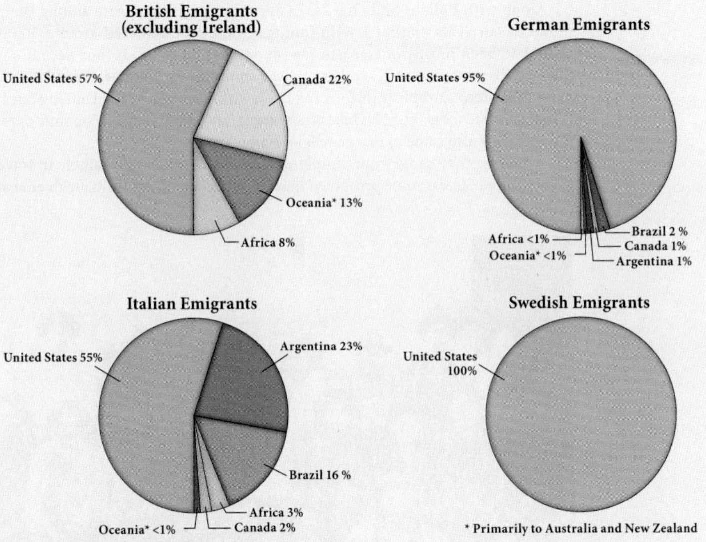

FIGURE 16.2 Major Destinations for Emigrants, 1881–1915

QUESTIONS FOR ANALYSIS

1. Summarize immigration as pictured in each pie chart. What might account for the different emigration patterns shown here?
2. What choices and limitations might each group of emigrants have faced in choosing the country to which they emigrated? What groups are pictured here? Use evidence from the chapter in your answer.
3. Do these figures suggest anything about the conditions various groups may have encountered in different countries, upon arrival? Use evidence from the chapter in your answer.

AP® SKILLS & PROCESSES

ANALYZING HISTORICAL EVIDENCE

Use **FIGURE 16.2** to provide a correction to students' tendency toward American exceptionalism, by reminding them that not all European immigrants went to the U.S. Some students may need to be reminded that pie charts do not indicate absolute size, but only proportional distribution. In other words, the number of Swedish immigrants was not equal to the number of Italian immigrants. Many students will not be surprised that British immigrants went to other Dominion territories, including Canada and Australia, and to British colonies in Africa. Students should note that all Swedes and virtually all Germans *did* go to the U.S. — and the majority of the other groups migrated there as well. It might be useful to rehearse the common push-pull factors that shape immigration. To extend this discussion, students could also offer inferences about why there were so few exceptions to German and Swedish migration patterns.

TRM Find complete suggested responses in the Teacher's Resource Materials.

TEACHING STRATEGY

The Statue of Liberty-Ellis Island Foundation provides an interactive Web site that allows visitors to view a history of Ellis Island and its varied uses and a timeline of American immigration history. By registering for a free account, visitors may also use a searchable database of immigrants processed through Ellis Island and access 2,000 oral histories, many of them in the form of audio recordings. To access the site, search "Statue of Liberty-Ellis Island Foundation."

TEACHING STRATEGY

The Tenement Museum in New York City provides a lesson plan that allows students to explore the experiences of immigrants who lived on the Lower East Side in the late nineteenth century. Through examination of census data, students learn about the birthplaces, dates of immigration, occupations, and other information about family members who resided at one particular location. This provides an opportunity to analyze a particular type of evidence while also humanizing the experiences of European immigrants. To access this lesson plan, search "Tenement Museum primary sources lesson plan."

seasickness. An investigator who traveled with immigrants from Naples asked, "How can a steerage passenger remember that he is a human being when he must first pick the worms from his food?" After 1892, European immigrants were routed through the enormous receiving station at New York's Ellis Island.

Some immigrants brought skills. Many Welshmen, for example, arrived in the United States as experienced tin-plate makers; Germans came as machinists and carpenters, Scandinavians as sailors. But industrialization required, most of all, increasing quantities of unskilled labor. As poor farmers from Italy, Greece, and Eastern Europe arrived in the United States, heavy, low-paid labor became their domain.

In an era of cheap railroad and steamship travel, many immigrants expected to work and save for a few years and then head home. More than 800,000 French Canadians moved to New England in search of textile jobs, often with hopes of scraping together enough savings to return to Quebec and buy a farm. Thousands of men came alone, especially from Ireland, Italy, and Greece. More often than women from other countries, who generally came as part of family groups, many single Irishwomen also immigrated. But some would-be sojourners ended up staying a lifetime, while immigrants who had expected to settle permanently found themselves forced to leave by an accident or sudden economic depression. One historian has estimated that a third of immigrants to the United States in this era returned to their home countries.

Along with Italians and Greeks, Eastern European Jews were among the most numerous arrivals. Earlier Jewish immigrants, who numbered around 50,000 in 1880, had been mostly of German Jewish descent. In the next four decades, more than 3 million poverty-stricken Jews arrived from Russia, Ukraine, Poland, and other parts of Eastern Europe, transforming the Jewish presence in the United States (see "Firsthand Accounts," p. 532). Like other immigrants, they sought economic opportunity, but they also came to escape religious repression.

Wherever they came from, immigrants took a considerable gamble in traveling to the United States. Some prospered quickly, especially if they came with education,

German Beer, Mexican Workers, c. 1900 Immigrants from Germany owned and managed most of the breweries in the United States. But workers at the Maier and Zoblein Brewery in Los Angeles came from many nations, including Mexico. At that time, about 4,000 Mexicans lived in Los Angeles County (about 4 percent of the population); by 1930, 150,000 Mexican-born immigrants lived in Los Angeles, making up about 7 percent of the city's rapidly growing population. Los Angeles Public Library.

money, or well-placed business contacts. Others, by toiling many years in harsh conditions, succeeded in securing a better life for their children or grandchildren. Still others met with catastrophe or early death. One Polish man who came with his parents in 1908 summed up his life over the next thirty years as "a mere struggle for bread." He added: "Sometimes I think life isn't worth a damn for a man like me. . . . Look at my wife and kids — undernourished, seldom have a square meal." But an Orthodox Russian Jewish woman told an interviewer that she "thanked God for America," where she had married, raised three children, and made a good life. She "liked everything about this country, especially its leniency toward the Jews."

Asian Americans and Exclusion

Compared with Europeans, newcomers from Asia faced far harsher treatment. The first Chinese immigrants had arrived in the late 1840s during the California gold rush. After the Civil War, the Burlingame Treaty between the United States and China opened the way for increasing numbers to emigrate. Fleeing poverty and upheaval in southern China, they, like European immigrants, filled low-wage jobs in the American economy. Chinese newcomers confronted threats and violence. "We kept indoors

AP® EXAM TIP

Compare the experiences of Asian and European immigrants in the U.S. in the late nineteenth and early twentieth centuries.

Chinese Workers in a Salmon Cannery, c. 1900 Shut out of many fields of employment by racial discrimination, many Chinese immigrants founded their own restaurants, laundries, and other small businesses. Others, like these cannery workers in Astoria, Oregon, took on some of the most grueling and lowest-paid work in the American economy. Job segregation reinforced, in turn, racial prejudice. Visiting British author Rudyard Kipling, touring canneries along the Columbia River, described Chinese workers in the plants as "blood-besmeared yellow devils." These workers, refuting Kipling's slur, appear clean and respectable. Notice the man in an apron, on the left, who wears his traditional queue, or braided pigtail, tucked into his straw hat. Keystone-France/Gamma-Keystone via Getty Images.

AP® APPLY THE TIP

Direct students to use the section Immigrants, East and West to complete **Handout 16.4 — Comparison: European and Asian Immigrants (TRM)**. When the handout is complete, ask students to work in small groups to develop a thesis statement and outline to compare the responses of the U.S. to immigrants from Europe and Asia in the late nineteenth century.

TRM Find **Handout 16.4 — Comparison: European and Asian Immigrants** in the Teacher's Resource Materials.

TEACHING STRATEGY

The New York Historical Society created classroom materials to accompany its online exhibition *Chinese American Exclusion/Inclusion*. Materials include background information on the relationship between the U.S. and China from the end of the American Revolution through the turn of the twentieth century, an examination of the Chinese experience in the U.S. during the nineteenth century, and the legal "machinery of exclusion" that was not lifted until the middle of World War II. The materials include links to dozens of resources with accompanying reading and discussion questions. To access this site, search "New York Historical Society Chinese American Exclusion/Inclusion."

AP® SKILLS & PROCESSES

ANALYZING HISTORICAL EVIDENCE

The **AP® FIRSTHAND ACCOUNTS** feature gives students a chance to explore the nature of immigrant diasporas through the experiences of turn-of-the-century Jewish settlers. Through the various primary sources, students can see how Jews formed an interlocking network of communities across the nation. They can also see that immigrants' adjustment to their new lives often varied dramatically by region.

AP® FIRSTHAND ACCOUNTS

Jewish Immigrants in the Industrial Economy

Following anti-Semitic violence in Russia during the 1880s, thousands of Jews fled to the United States. Almost a quarter million came between 1881 and 1890, the majority settling in New York City. These poverty-stricken newcomers posed problems for New York's assimilated Jews, most of whom were German- or American-born. Community support networks were quickly overwhelmed; New York's United Hebrew Charities almost went bankrupt. Jewish leaders watched with dismay the expansion of tenement wards. They worried that the presence of so many Eastern European "beggars," as one Reform rabbi put it, would heighten American anti-Semitism.

In 1901, New York's Jewish leaders founded an Industrial Removal Office (IRO) to help disperse Jewish newcomers. By 1922 the office sent over 79,000 Eastern European Jews to locations across the country. IRO correspondence provides a window on how newcomers sought to negotiate places in America's industrial economy. Note that most of the letters are translated from Yiddish. As one immigrant noted, inability to speak English could limit employment opportunities and cause "great distress."

ALEX GRUBMAN

Letter from Portland, Oregon, 1905

“ I write you how fortunate I am in being placed in one of the largest dry goods houses in Oregon by Hon. Sig Sichel. . . . He went personally with me until he procured the present position for me as inside salesman and to start at $60 a month. . . . [Many people here] wish me to thank the I.R.O. for helping them to success. . . . Mr. Lvov or Lvovsky, a tinsmith sent out direct 2 years ago has a stove and hardware store. M. Kaplan a tailor is earning $20–25.00 a week. Mr. Nathan Siegel who arrived only a few days ago is already employed as a clerk earning $10.00 for a start. ”

BARNET MARLIN

Letter from Atlanta, Georgia, 1906

“ Dr. Wildauer secured a place for me to work, at wooden trunks. . . . I could not earn more than 60 cents a day and was working harder than a horse. . . . Atlanta does not pay to work, especially for a foreigner. . . . Several weeks passed by and at the end I was in debt. . . .

During that time I became acquainted with a Jewish policeman and he was the only one who took pity on me. . . . I told my friend the policeman that I had $15.00 (sent to me by my brother) and he advised me to go out peddling. He took me to a store and told the storekeeper to furnish me for over $30.00 worth of goods. He also acted as my reference and prepared me with everything. I went out peddling and gradually I earned enough money to pay all my debts; and so I kept on peddling. I earned enough money and bought a horse and wagon. I now convey goods from the city to the country and sell them there. I thank you very much for sending me to Atlanta. ”

RAPHAEL GERSHONI

Letter from Atlanta, Georgia, 1905

“ Why do you sent people to Atlanta? You give them eight days worth of food and then you let them starve in the street among Negroes. . . . I was given a job to work in a restaurant kitchen, to wait on Negroes, and to clean the Negroes' closets, for three dollars a week. . . . I was then given ten dollars for goods so that I might go around and peddle in Atlanta. But out of this ten dollars, I have to pay four dollars for lodging and three dollars a month for a place just to lay my head. . . . It is hopeless to work in Atlanta. The highest wage is 75 cents a day. And for what kind of work? . . . The competition is difficult here. Why should anyone hire a white greenhorn when they can get a black Negro, who is strong as iron. . . . Everyone says that the only choice here is to go out into the countryside and peddle. But one needs 40–50 dollars worth of goods. How do I get the money? . . . I would like to ask you to help me out. Help me crawl out of black Atlanta and go to Chicago. There I have friends and can make out better. ”

after dark for fear of being shot in the back," remembered one Chinese immigrant to California. During the depression of the 1870s, a rising tide of racism was especially extreme in the Pacific coast states, where the majority of Chinese immigrants lived. "The Chinese must go!" railed Dennis Kearney, leader of the California Workingmen's Party, who referred to Asians as "almond-eyed lepers." Incited by Kearney in July 1877, a mob burned San Francisco's Chinatown and beat up residents. In the 1885 Rock Springs massacre in Wyoming, white miners burned the local Chinatown and murdered at least 28 Chinese men. Despite such atrocities, some Chinese managed to build profitable businesses and farms. Many did so by filling the only niches native-born Americans left open to them: running restaurants and laundries.

CHARLES ZWIRN

Letter from La Crosse, Wisconsin, 1913

❝ [Mr. Goldfish] took me into his house and gave me a very nice welcome. He then led me to the synagogue and introduced me to all the members. Mr. Goldfish is a Jew with a real Jewish heart. He is religiously inclined and the biggest businessman in the city. If any controversy arises, it is always settled by Mr. Goldfish. . . . [He] took me to a shop and they paid me $6 more than I earned in New York. When I wanted to thank him, he said that the only thing he expects of me is that I conduct myself properly and go on the right path so I can eventually succeed. This, he said, was the best reward I can give him. I did as he told me and saved a few hundred dollars. . . .

Another man sent here had been in the country two months. . . . He was sent to Mr. Goldfish, who found him a job sorting corks for $2 a day. . . . He then left. By the way, . . . would you be so kind as to send to me a boy to drive a milk wagon on Mr. Jacob's farm and an older man to work at junk? They must be honest and respectable people. ❞

MARY RUBIN

Letter from New Orleans, Louisiana, 1905

❝ You have sent us out here to starve for hunger and live in the streets. . . . We have arrived in New Orleans about 12 o'clock in the night, and there was nobody to await us there, and we had to go around alnight and look for the address which you had given. . . . They put the nine of us all in one room, with out a bed or a pillow to sleep on. . . . Then they took Mr. Rubin and his wife up to the cigar factory and gave them both a job. Mrs. Rubin is getting about four ($4) a week and Mr. Rubin five ($5). Now we will ask you if a family man can make a living with that. And Mr. Rosenthal they told if he wants work he will have to look for it himself. . . . When he found work, they told him to bring his tools and come to work. He went to the office and asked for the tools; they told him that he can't have them.

. . . [The local Committee] sent mama to be a cook for $4 a month, which she had never done before, and if she wanted to be a cook in N.Y. she could have gotten 3 times that much or more, but it did not suit us to let our mother be a cook, and now we should have to do. ❞

NATHAN TOPLITZKY

Letter from Detroit, Michigan, 1908

❝ I, Nathan Toplitzky, sent to the above city 5 months ago, wish to inform you that a great misfortune has happened to me. Your committee has placed me to work in a machine factory where I have earned $.75 a day, and being unskilled I have had 4 of my fingers torn from my right hand. I now remain a cripple throughout my life. For six weeks my sufferings were indescribable.

When the condition of my health improved a little, I called on the Committee and they advised me to go back to the old employer. I went back to him and he placed me to work at the same machine where the accident occurred. Having lost my fingers I was unable to operate the machine. . . . Kindly write to your Committee to find a position for me. ❞

S. KLEIN

Letter from Cleveland, Ohio, 1905

❝ In the past week something terrible has happened here. Two men sent here by the Removal Office committed suicide out of despair. One took poison and the other hanged himself. . . . That shows the deplorable condition of those who are sent here by the Removal Office. The Cleveland Removal Office is managed by an inexperienced young man who maintains his position merely through favoritism. . . . It was told to me that the one who hanged himself came to this agent and implored him with tears in his eyes to provide some kind of employment. ❞

SOURCE: Letters from the Records of the Industrial Removal Office; 1-91; AJHS, NY, NY and Boston, MA as follows: Alex Grubman, Box 116, Folder 14; Barnet Marlin, Box 95, Folder 4; Raphael Gershoni, Box 95, Folder 4; Charles Zwirn, Box 120, Folder 9; Mary Rubin, Box 99, Folder 17; Nathan Toplitzky, Box 101, Folder 7; S. Klein, Box 114, Folder 5. Reprinted by permission of the American Jewish Historical Society.

QUESTIONS FOR ANALYSIS

1. Based on the accounts above, what factors contributed to a Jewish immigrant's economic success or failure in a new location? Describe the context of historical actors described in each source.
2. In at least ten places, the immigrants above report on wages — daily, weekly, or monthly. For comparison, make a rough conversion of all of these to weekly wages and list them. What do you conclude about compensation for professional, skilled, and unskilled work?
3. Using information from this chapter, as well as the preceding documents, explain why Jewish immigrants sent to the South might have faced more difficulties, on average, than those sent to other parts of the country.

TRM Find complete suggested responses in the Teacher's Resource Materials.

As Pacific Coast Democrats whipped up anti-immigrant fervor, Republicans in the West warned their party's leaders that they had to act. Facing intense political pressure, Congress first passed the 1875 Page Act, which barred the importation of women for prostitution; in practice, the law was largely used to exclude Chinese women, including married women and prospective brides seeking to join husbands in the United States. The far more sweeping **Chinese Exclusion Act** passed in 1882. It specifically barred Chinese laborers from entering the United States. Each decade thereafter, Congress renewed the law and tightened its provisions; it was not repealed until 1943, when U.S. and Chinese soldiers were fighting together against Japan in World War II.

Chinese Exclusion Act
The 1882 race-based law that barred Chinese laborers from entering the United States. Later applied to other Asian immigrants as well, it was not repealed until 1943.

AP® SKILLS & PROCESSES

COMPARISON

The **COMPARISON** question asks students to compare immigrant groups from two different perspectives. First, what were the different expectations immigrants had and what accounted for those differences? Second, what explains why some immigrants succeeded in their new lives while others continued to struggle? It may help some students to point out that many immigrants did not plan to stay in the U.S. Students might differentiate immigrants based on region of origin, sex, level of skill, and level of education.

TRM Find complete suggested responses in the Teacher's Resource Materials.

CHECK FOR UNDERSTANDING

Ask students: **Why did so many immigrants come to the United States, and how did their experiences differ?** *The late nineteenth century witnessed massive immigration from southern and eastern Europe and, before the 1882 Chinese Exclusion Act, China. The push factors that encouraged these immigrants' departures included economic depression caused by commercialized agriculture, religious repression, and, especially in the case of the Chinese, political turmoil in their homelands. The pull factor was primarily the availability of labor, especially in low-skilled factory jobs. For European immigrants, their experiences differed based on their skills, with skilled laborers able to prosper and unskilled laborers barely able to survive, though some escaped poverty after years of hard work. The Chinese, however, were met with significant racism and were forced to work in the poorest of jobs until they were finally excluded in 1882.*

TEACHING STRATEGY

The New York State Library provides a detailed lesson that explores the Great Railroad Strike. The lesson provides a lengthy background essay, more than a dozen primary sources in PDF form, and detailed suggestions for activities. To access this site, search "New York State Library Railroad Strike teacher's guide."

Asian immigrants made vigorous use of the courts to try to protect their rights. In a series of cases brought by Chinese and later Japanese immigrants, the U.S. Supreme Court ruled that all persons born in the United States had citizenship rights that could not be revoked, even if their parents had been born abroad. Nonetheless, well into the twentieth century, Chinese immigrants (as opposed to native-born Chinese Americans) could not apply for citizenship. Meanwhile, Japanese and a few Korean immigrants also began to arrive; by 1909, there were 40,000 Japanese immigrants working in agriculture, 10,000 on railroads, and 4,000 in canneries. In 1906, the U.S. attorney general ruled that Japanese and Koreans, like Chinese immigrants, were barred from citizenship.

The Chinese Exclusion Act created the legal foundations on which far-reaching exclusionary policies would be built in the 1920s and after (see "Culture Wars" in Chapter 21). To enforce the law, Congress and the courts gave broad new powers to immigration officials, transforming the Chinese into America's first "illegal immigrants." Drawn, like others, by the promise of jobs in America's expanding economy, Chinese men stowed away on ships or walked across the borders. Disguising themselves as Mexicans — who at that time could freely enter the United States — some perished in the desert as they tried to reach Arizona or California.

Some would-be immigrants, known as paper sons, relied on Chinese residents in the United States, who generated documents falsely claiming the newcomers as American-born children. Paper sons memorized pages of information about their supposed relatives and hometowns. The San Francisco earthquake of 1906 helped their cause by destroying all the port's records. "That was a big chance for a lot of Chinese," remembered one immigrant. "They forged themselves certificates saying they could go back to China and bring back four or five sons, just like that!" Such persistence ensured that, despite the harsh policies of Chinese exclusion, the flow of Asian immigrants never fully ceased.

AP® SKILLS & PROCESSES

COMPARISON

What factors accounted for the different expectations and experiences of immigrants in this era?

LABOR GETS ORGANIZED

How did working people organize to protect their interests in this period, and why and how did their strategies change between 1877 and 1900?

In the American political system, labor has typically been weak. Industrial workers cluster in cities, near factories and jobs; compared with small towns and rural areas, urban areas have been underrepresented in bodies such as the U.S. Senate and the presidential electoral college, where representation is based on, or weighted by, state. This problem became acute in the era of industrialization, and it has lingered. Even today, the twenty-two U.S. senators elected from Alaska, Idaho, Iowa, Maine, Mississippi, Montana, New Mexico, North Dakota, Vermont, West Virginia, and Wyoming represent a smaller number of people, *combined*, than the two U.S. senators who represent heavily urban California.

Faced with this obstacle, labor advocates could adopt one of two strategies. First, they could try to build political alliances with sympathetic rural voters who shared their problems. Second, they could reject politics and create narrowly focused trade unions to negotiate directly with employers. In general, labor advocates emphasized the first strategy between the 1870s and the early 1890s, and the latter in the early twentieth century, as industrialization brought large-scale conflict between labor and capital.

The Emergence of a Labor Movement

Great Railroad Strike of 1877
A nationwide strike of thousands of railroad workers and labor allies, who protested the growing power of railroad corporations and the steep wage cuts imposed by railroad managers amid a severe economic depression that had begun in 1873.

The problem of industrial labor entered Americans' consciousness dramatically with the **Great Railroad Strike of 1877**. Protesting steep wage cuts amid the depression that had begun in 1873, thousands of railroad workers walked off the job. Broader issues were at stake. "The officers of the road," reported strike leader Barney Donahue in upstate New York, "were bound to break the spirit of the men, and any or all organizations they belonged to." He believed railroad companies wanted to block workers from "all fellowship for mutual aid." The strike brought rail travel and commerce to a halt. Thousands of people poured into the streets of Buffalo, Pittsburgh, and Chicago to protest the economic injustice wrought by railroads — as well as fires caused by stray sparks from locomotives and injuries and deaths on train tracks in urban neighborhoods. When Pennsylvania's governor sent state militia to break the strike, Pittsburgh crowds reacted by burning railroad property and overturning locomotives. Similar clashes between police and protesters occurred in other cities across the country, from Galveston, Texas, to San Francisco.

The 1877 strike left more than 50 people dead and caused $40 million worth of damage, primarily to railroad property. "It seemed as if the whole social and political structure was on the very brink of ruin," wrote one journalist. For their role in the strike, many railroad workers were fired and blacklisted: railroad companies circulated their names on a "do not hire" list to prevent them from getting any work in the industry. In the aftermath of the strike, the U.S. government created the National Guard, intended not to protect Americans against foreign invasion but to enforce order at home.

Watching the upheaval caused by industrialization, some radical thinkers pointed out its injurious impact on workers. Among the most influential was Henry George, whose book *Progress and Poverty* (1879) was a best-seller for decades after publication. George warned that Americans were too optimistic about the impact of railroads and manufacturing, which they hoped would — after an initial period of turmoil — bring prosperity to all. George believed the emerging industrial order brought permanent poverty. Industrialization, he wrote, was driving a wedge through society, lifting the fortunes of professionals and the middle class but pushing the working classes down by forcing them into deskilled, dangerous, and low-wage labor. George's proposed solution, a federal "single tax" on landholdings, did not win widespread support, but his insightful diagnosis of the problem helped encourage radical movements for economic reform.

Many rural people believed they faced problems similar to those of industrial workers. In the new economy, they found themselves at the mercy of large corporations, from equipment dealers who sold them harvesters and plows to railroads and grain elevators that shipped and stored their products. Though farmers appeared to have more independence than corporate employees, many felt trapped in a web of middlemen who chipped away at their profits while international forces robbed them of decision-making power.

Farmers denounced not only corporations but also the previous two decades of government efforts to foster economic development — policies that now seemed wrongheaded. Farmers' advocates argued that high tariffs forced rural families to pay too much for basic necessities while failing to protect America's great export crops, cotton and wheat. At the same time, they charged, Republican financial policies benefitted banks, not borrowers. Farmers blamed railroad companies for taking government grants and subsidies to build their lines but then charging unequal rates that privileged big manufacturers. From the farmers' point of view, public money had been used to build giant railroad companies that turned around and exploited ordinary people.

The most prominent rural protest group of the early postwar decades was the National Grange of the Patrons of Husbandry, founded in 1867. Like industrial workers, Grange farmers sought to counter the rising power of corporate middlemen through cooperation and mutual aid. Local Grange halls brought farm families together for recreation and conversation. The Grange set up its own banks, insurance companies, and grain elevators, and, in Iowa, even a farm implement factory. Many Grange members also advocated political action, building independent local parties that ran on anticorporate platforms.

TEACHING STRATEGY

Students should be aware of how farmers initially reacted to the developments attendant to industrial capitalism. Ask students to define how farmers responded to the following issues: 1. Their own sense of isolation. 2. Industrial capitalists. 3. Government policies toward corporations. In this way, you are having students brainstorm some of the major concepts that will be built out in subsequent parts of the book.

VISUAL ACTIVITY

Farmers' Political Message In this 1875 lithograph, the farmer looms large in comparison with other representative men of the new economy. Note how each man is dressed and how the caption describes his work. Depicted clockwise from the top left are a lawyer, the U.S. president, a military officer, a minister, a ship captain, a merchant, a doctor or pharmacist, a broker ("I fleece you all"), a stock trader ("I bull and bear for all"), and a railroad owner. Library of Congress, LC-DIG-pga-00025.

READING THE IMAGE: What does this image convey about the pride of farmers and others who worked with their hands? About ideals of work and (white) masculinity?

MAKING CONNECTIONS: How do the images in this message illustrate continuity and change in the experiences of farmers throughout the 19th century? What argument does this image convey regarding the role importance of agrarian values in American History?

TRM Find complete suggested responses in the Teacher's Resource Materials.

Greenback-Labor Party
A political movement of the 1870s and 1880s that called on the government to protect worker rights, regulate corporations, continue Reconstruction policies in the South, and increase the money supply in order to assist borrowers.

producerism
An argument, made by late nineteenth-century farmers' and workers' movements, that real economic wealth is created by workers engaged in physical labor, and that merchants, bankers, and other middlemen unfairly gain wealth from such "producers."

During the 1870s depression, Grangers, labor advocates, and local workingmen's parties forged a national political movement, the **Greenback-Labor Party**. Southern Greenbackers, both white and black, protested the collapse of Reconstruction and urged that every man's vote be protected. Across the country, Greenbackers advocated laws to regulate corporations and enforce an eight-hour workday to reduce long, grueling work hours. They called for the federal government to print more greenback dollars and increase the amount of money in circulation; this, they argued, would stimulate the economy, create jobs, and help borrowers by allowing them to pay off debts in dollars that, over time, slowly decreased in value. Greenbackers, like many industrial labor leaders, subscribed to the ideal of **producerism**: they dismissed middlemen, bankers, lawyers, and investors as idlers who lived off the sweat of people who worked with their hands. As a Pittsburgh worker put it in an 1878 poem, it was not the money-handlers or executives at the top but the "noble sons of Labor . . . who with bone, and brain, and fiber make the nation's wealth."

The Greenback movement radicalized thousands of farmers, miners, and industrial workers. In Alabama's coal-mining regions, black and white miners cooperated in the party. Texas boasted seventy African American Greenback clubs. In 1878, Greenback-Labor candidates won more than a million votes, and the party elected fifteen congressmen nationwide. In the Midwest, Greenback pressure helped trigger a wave of economic regulatory actions known as **Granger laws**. By the early 1880s, twenty-nine states had created railroad commissions to supervise railroad rates and policies; others appointed commissions to regulate insurance and utility companies. Such early regulatory efforts were not always effective, but they were crucial starting points for reform. Although short-lived, the Greenback movement created the foundation for more sustained efforts to regulate big business.

Granger laws
Economic regulatory laws that aimed to limit the power of railroads and other corporations, and that midwestern states passed in the late 1870s in response to pressure from farmers and the Greenback-Labor Party.

AP® SKILLS & PROCESSES

COMPARISON

How did the methods used by railroad workers to protest their working conditions compare with the tactics employed by the Greenbackers, who also sought reform?

The Knights of Labor

The most important workers' movement of the late nineteenth century, the **Knights of Labor**, was founded in 1869 as a secret society of garment makers in Philadelphia. In 1878, as the Greenback movement reached its height, some Knights served as delegates to Greenback-Labor conventions. Like Grangers, Knights believed that ordinary people needed control over the enterprises in which they worked. They proposed to set up shops owned by employees, transforming America into what they called a cooperative commonwealth. In keeping with this broad-based vision, the order practiced open membership, irrespective of race, gender, or field of employment — though, like other labor groups, the Knights excluded Chinese immigrants.

Knights of Labor
The first mass labor organization of nationwide scope, which sought to bridge differences of occupation, race, and gender to unite all workers. The Knights peaked in strength in the mid-1880s.

The Knights had a strong political bent. They believed that only electoral action could bring about many of their goals, such as government regulation of corporations and laws requiring employers to negotiate during strikes. Their 1878 platform denounced the "aggressiveness of great capitalists and corporations." "If we desire to enjoy the full blessings of life," the Knights warned, "a check [must] be placed upon unjust accumulation, and the power for evil of aggregated wealth." Among their demands were workplace safety laws, prohibition of child labor, a federal tax on the nation's highest incomes, public ownership of telegraphs and railroads, and government recognition of workers' right to organize. The Knights also advocated personal responsibility and self-discipline. Their leader, Terence Powderly, warned that the abuse of liquor robbed as many workers of their wages as did ruthless employers.

Growing rapidly in the 1880s, the Knights built a sprawling and decentralized movement. It included not only skilled craftsmen such as carpenters, ironworkers, and beer brewers but also textile workers in Rhode Island, domestic workers in Georgia, and tenant farmers in Arkansas. Knights organized workingmen's parties to advocate a host of reforms, ranging from an eight-hour workday to cheaper streetcar fares and better garbage collection in urban areas. One of their key innovations was hiring a full-time women's organizer, Leonora Barry. An Irish American widow who was forced into factory work after her husband's death, Barry became a labor advocate out of horror at the conditions she experienced on the job. To the discomfort of some male Knights, she investigated and exposed not only women's low wages and dangerous working conditions but also widespread evidence of sexual harassment on the job.

The Knights' growth in the 1880s showed the grassroots basis of labor activism. Powderly tried to avoid strikes, which he saw as costly and risky. But the organization's greatest growth resulted from spontaneous, grassroots strikes. In 1885, thousands of workers on the Southwest Railroad walked off the job to protest wage cuts; afterward, they telegraphed the Knights and asked to be admitted as members. The strike enhanced the Knights' reputation among workers and built membership to 750,000.

CHECK FOR UNDERSTANDING

Ask students: **Why did a new labor movement emerge in this era?** *Large corporations attempted to maximize profits by investing in machinery to deskill the workforce and reduce wages. A capitalist economy was subject to dramatic swings in fortune, and during recessions many corporations cut wages severely. As workers came to realize that their conditions were likely to be permanent, many began to band together to lobby for better conditions. They made common cause with farmers, who felt trapped by corporations who sold them equipment and shipped their goods.*

AP® SKILLS & PROCESSES

COMPARISON

The **COMPARISON** question asks students to compare the responses of two reform groups to problems caused by the rise of large corporations. Students may need some help to see why large corporations represented such a formidable challenge. To extend this prompt, ask students to explain the reasons for the differences in these strategies and assess the relative effectiveness of differing strategies.

TRM Find complete suggested responses in the Teacher's Resource Materials.

TEACHING STRATEGY

The Chicago Historical Society's "The Dramas of Haymarket" Web page is a detailed study of the Haymarket affair, organized as a drama in Five Acts. Each "act" provides a background essay, along with numerous primary sources and photos related to the events of the violence that led to the demise of the Knights of Labor. To access this site, search "Chicago Historical Society Dramas of Haymarket."

By the following year, local assemblies had sprung up in every state and almost every county in the United States.

Just as the Knights reached this pinnacle of influence, an episode of violence caused their movement to falter. In 1886, a protest at the McCormick reaper works in Chicago led to a clash with police that left four strikers dead. (Three unions, including a Knights of Labor assembly, had struck, but the Knights had reached an agreement and returned to work. Only the machinists' union remained on strike when the incident occurred.) Chicago was a hotbed of anarchism, the revolutionary advocacy of a stateless society. Local anarchists, many of them German immigrants, called a protest meeting the next day, May 4, 1886, at **Haymarket Square**. When police tried to disperse the crowd, someone threw a bomb that killed several policemen. Officers responded with gunfire. In the trial that followed, eight anarchists were found guilty of murder and criminal conspiracy. All were convicted, despite lack of definitive evidence that one of them threw the bomb (the bomber's identity remains unknown). Four of the eight were executed by hanging, one committed suicide in prison, and the others received long sentences.

Haymarket Square
The May 4, 1886, conflict in Chicago in which both workers and policemen were killed or wounded during a labor demonstration called by local anarchists. The incident created a backlash against all labor organizations, including the Knights of Labor.

Violence in Haymarket Square, Chicago In the pages of *Harper's Weekly*, May 15, 1886, thousands of Americans saw this dramatic depiction of a bomb exploding in Haymarket Square, while British socialist Samuel Fielden addressed the crowd from the back of a wagon. Workers were denouncing police killings of striking workers the previous day and demanding that the federal and state governments enforce laws for an eight-hour day. As more than a hundred armed policemen descended on the square, a dynamite bomb exploded. It was never determined who planted the bomb, which killed at least one Chicago police officer; in the panic that followed, police fired on each other and the crowd. A total of seven policemen and four workers died. Chicago police detectives fed the resulting public alarm by claiming falsely that they had uncovered a vast network of anarchists plotting to bring down the government. The resulting fears discredited the labor movement and led to the hanging or imprisonment of eight Chicago anarchists. Chicago History Museum/Getty Images.

Seizing on resulting antiunion hysteria, which was heightened by Chicago policemen's claims of a vast anarchist conspiracy, employers took the offensive. They broke strikes with mass arrests, tied up the Knights in expensive court proceedings, and forced workers to sign contracts pledging not to join labor organizations. The Knights of Labor never recovered from the damage, which impacted the whole American labor movement. In the view of the press and many prosperous Americans, labor unions were tainted by their alleged links with anarchism. Struggles between industrialists and workers had created bitter divides.

AP® SKILLS & PROCESSES

CAUSATION

What factors contributed to the rapid rise of the Knights of Labor? To its decline?

Farmers and Workers: The Cooperative Alliance

In the aftermath of Haymarket, the Knights' cooperative vision did not entirely fade. A new rural movement, the **Farmers' Alliance**, arose to take up many issues that Grangers and Greenbackers had earlier sought to address. Founded in Texas during the depression of the 1870s, the Farmers' Alliance spread across the plains states and the South, becoming by the late 1880s the largest farmer-based movement in U.S. history. A separate Colored Farmers' Alliance arose to represent rural African Americans. The harsh conditions farmers were enduring — including drought in the West and plunging global prices for corn, cotton, and wheat — intensified the movement's appeal. Traveling Alliance lecturers exhorted farmers to "stand as a great conservative body against . . . the growing corruption of wealth and power." They focused particular anger on the railroads, which arranged special deals for their largest customers and generally charged higher rates for small shipments.

Farmers' Alliance
A rural movement founded in Texas during the depression of the 1870s that spread across the plains and the South. Advocating cooperative stores to circumvent middlemen, the Alliance also called for greater government aid to farmers and stricter regulation of railroads.

Alliance leaders pinned their initial hopes on cooperative stores and exchanges that would circumvent middlemen, including railroads. Cooperatives gathered farmers' orders and bought in bulk at wholesale prices, passing the savings along. Alliance cooperatives achieved notable victories in the late 1880s. The Dakota Alliance, for example, offered members cheap hail insurance and low prices on machinery and farm supplies. The Texas Alliance established a huge cooperative enterprise to market cotton and provide farmers with cheap loans. When cotton prices fell further in 1891, however, the Texas exchange failed. Other cooperatives also suffered from chronic underfunding and lack of credit, and they faced hostility from merchants and lenders they tried to circumvent.

AP® EXAM TIP

Compare the experiences of farmers and workers that led them to organize to confront business and government leaders in the late nineteenth century.

The Texas Farmers' Alliance thus proposed a federal price-support system for farm products, modeled on the national banks. Under this subtreasury plan, the federal government would hold crops in public warehouses and issue loans on their value until they could be profitably sold. When Democrats — still wary of big-government schemes — declared the idea too radical, Alliances in Texas, Kansas, South Dakota, and elsewhere decided to create a new political party, the Populists (see Chapter 19). In this venture, the Alliance cooperated with the weakened Knights of Labor, seeking to use rural voters' substantial clout on behalf of urban workers who shared their vision.

By this time, farmer-labor coalitions were making a considerable impact on state-level politics. But state laws and commissions were proving ineffective against corporations of national and even global scope. It was difficult for Wisconsin, for instance, to enforce new laws against a railroad company whose lines might stretch from Chicago to Seattle and whose corporate headquarters might be in Minnesota. Militant farmers and labor advocates demanded federal action.

In 1887, responding to this pressure, Congress and President Grover Cleveland passed two landmark laws. The Hatch Act provided federal funding for agricultural research and education, meeting farmers' demands for government aid to agriculture. The Interstate Commerce Act counteracted a Supreme Court decision of the previous year, *Wabash v. Illinois* (1886), that had struck down states' authority to regulate railroads. The act created the **Interstate Commerce Commission (ICC)**, charged with

Interstate Commerce Commission (ICC)
Formed in 1887 to oversee the railroad industry and prevent unfair rates, the ICC was an important early effort by Congress to regulate corporate practices.

CHECK FOR UNDERSTANDING

Ask students: **Who were the Knights of Labor and what did they advocate?** *A secret society that developed into an important union in the late nineteenth century, the Knights of Labor had a strong political bent and believed that only legislation could improve their situation through the regulation of corporations. They advocated safety laws, prohibition of child labor, a tax on high incomes, and public ownership of infrastructure. The Knights included all workers regardless of race, gender, or skill — but they excluded Chinese immigrants.*

AP® SKILLS & PROCESSES

CAUSATION

The **CAUSATION** question asks students to explain the rise and fall of the Knights of Labor; the focus is on the pace of change — the organization rose quickly and collapsed equally quickly. Students could additionally compare the Knights of Labor with the views and strategies of the antebellum labor movements described in Chapter 8, particularly their emphasis on the labor theory of value.

TRM Find complete suggested responses in the Teacher's Resource Materials.

AP® APPLY THE TIP

Both farmers and workers were dramatically impacted by the economic changes that occurred in the late nineteenth century. To help students understand the similarities between the issues facing both groups, draw a T-chart on the board labeled "workers" on one side and "farmers" on the other side. Ask students to use Chapter 16 to identify the impact of economic changes on each group in relationship to the following: loss of autonomy, power of corporations, impact of immigration, wages/debt, role of government, actions taken (other areas of comparison may be added as students discuss issues facing both groups). Ask students to create a "platform" based on the T-chart with at least five points that would bring together farmers and workers as a political force in the late nineteenth century. Lead a class discussion on the ways in which the interests of workers and farmers were similar as well as the issues that would limit their ability to unify in the late nineteenth century.

AP® THEME

WXT: Work, Exchange, and Technology

While the Knights of Labor generally avoided strikes in favor of political action, strikes — and acts of violence, as depicted in this photo — increasingly characterized the relationship between management and labor in the late nineteenth century. The online exhibition *Labor-Management Conflict in American History*, available through Ohio State University's eHistory Web site, provides a number of resources on this subject. To access this site, search "Ohio State University labor-management conflict."

Industrial Violence: A Dynamited Mine, 1894 Strikes in the western mining regions pitted ruthless owners, bent on control of their property and workforce, against fiercely independent miners who knew how to use dynamite. Some of the bloodiest conflicts occurred in Colorado mining towns, where the Western Federation of Miners (WFM) had strong support and a series of Republican governors sent state militia to back the mine owners. Violence broke out repeatedly between the early 1890s and the 1910s. At Victor, Colorado, in May 1894, as dozens of armed sheriffs' deputies closed in on angry WFM members occupying the Strong Mine in protest, the miners blew up the mine's shaft house and boiler. Showered with debris, the deputies boarded the next train out of town. Because Colorado then had a Populist governor, Davis Waite, who sympathized with the miners and ordered the deputies to disband, this strike was one of the few in which owners and miners reached a peaceful settlement — a temporary victory for the union. Denver Public Library, Western History Collection/Bridgeman Images.

investigating interstate shipping, forcing railroads to make their rates public, and suing in court when necessary to make companies reduce "unjust or unreasonable" rates.

AP® EXAM TIP

Evaluate the impact of farmers' organizations on state and federal laws to regulate big business.

Though creation of the ICC was a direct response to farmer-labor demands, its final form represented a compromise. Radical leaders wanted Congress to establish a direct set of rules under which railroads must operate. If a railroad did not comply, any citizen could take the company to court; if the new rules triggered bankruptcy, the railroad could convert to public ownership. But getting such a plan through Congress proved impossible. Business-friendly lawmakers called instead for an expert commission to oversee the railroad industry. In a pattern repeated frequently over the next few decades, the commission model proved more acceptable to the majority of congressmen than grassroots legal action with pressure toward public ownership. As had happened with the construction of transcontinental railroads — not publicly owned, as in Europe — policymakers' decision to support for-profit enterprise profoundly shaped the nation's political economy.

AP® SKILLS & PROCESSES

DEVELOPMENTS AND PROCESSES

Why did farmers and industrial workers cooperate, and what political objectives did they achieve?

The ICC faced formidable challenges. Though the new law prohibited railroads from reaching secret rate-setting agreements, evidence was difficult to gather and secret "pooling" continued. A hostile Supreme Court also undermined the commission's powers. In a series of sixteen decisions over two decades after the ICC was created, the Court sided with railroads fifteen times. The justices delivered a particularly hard blow in 1897 when they ruled that the ICC had no power to interfere with shipping rates. Nonetheless, the ICC's existence was a major achievement. In the early twentieth century, Congress would strengthen the commission's powers, and the ICC would become one of the most powerful federal agencies charged with overseeing private business.

AP® APPLY THE TIP

Direct students to use the section "Farmers and Workers: The Cooperative Alliance" to complete **Handout 16.5 — Causation: Impact of Farmers' Organizations (TRM)**. After completing the handout, lead a class discussion on the impact of farmers' organizations on laws and policies passed in the late nineteenth century. Ask students to identify the limitations in the accomplishments of the farmers' organizations in this period.

TRM Find **Handout 16.5 — Causation: Impact of Farmers' Organizations** in the Teacher's Resource Materials.

AP® SKILLS & PROCESSES

DEVELOPMENTS AND PROCESSES

The **DEVELOPMENTS AND PROCESSES** question asks students to identify the historical context that explains why groups that are often thought to have little in common — farmers and urban industrial workers — found common ground in the late 1800s. To extend this prompt, ask students to explain why this partnership proved to be short-lived.

TRM Find complete suggested responses in the Teacher's Resource Materials.

CHECK FOR UNDERSTANDING

Ask students: **How did farmers and workers form a cooperative alliance?** *Farmers' Alliances organized to create cooperative stores and exchanges, and proposed a federal price-support system. Making alliances with urban workers, they put pressure on the federal government. Congress and the president responded by passing the Hatch Act for agricultural research and education and the Interstate Commerce Act to regulate rail rate practices.*

Another Path: The American Federation of Labor

While the Knights of Labor exerted pressure through electoral politics, other workers pursued a different strategy. In the 1870s, printers, ironworkers, bricklayers, and other skilled workers organized nationwide trade unions. These "brotherhoods" focused on the everyday needs of workers in skilled occupations. Trade unions sought a closed shop — with all jobs reserved for union members — that kept out lower-wage workers. Union rules spelled out terms of work and emphasized mutual aid. Because railroading was a high-risk occupation, for example, brotherhoods of engineers, brakemen, and firemen pooled contributions into funds that provided accident and death benefits. Above all, trade unionism asserted craft workers' rights as active decision-makers in the workplace, not just cogs in a management-run machine.

AP® EXAM TIP

Compare the leadership, goals, membership, and methods of the Knights of Labor and the American Federation of Labor.

In the early 1880s, many trade unionists joined the Knights of Labor coalition. But the aftermath of the Haymarket violence persuaded them to leave and create the separate **American Federation of Labor (AFL)**. The man who led them was Samuel Gompers, a Dutch-Jewish cigar maker whose family had immigrated to New York in 1863. Gompers headed the AFL for nearly forty years. He believed the Knights relied too much on electoral politics, where victories were likely to be limited, and he did not share their sweeping critique of capitalism. The AFL, made up of relatively skilled and well-paid workers, was less interested in challenging the corporate order than in winning a larger share of its rewards. The AFL called for the "closed shop" — all employees had to be union members — to keep out low-wage competition and strengthen skilled workers' bargaining power with employers.

American Federation of Labor (AFL) Organization of skilled workers created by Samuel Gompers in 1886 that called for direct negotiation with employers in order to achieve better pay and benefits. The AFL became the largest and most enduring workers' organization of the industrial era.

Having gone to work at age ten, Gompers always contended that what he missed at school he more than made up for in the shop, where cigar makers paid one of their members to read to them while they worked. As a young worker-intellectual, Gompers gravitated to New York's radical circles, where he participated in lively debates over which strategies workingmen should pursue. Partly out of these debates, and partly from his own experience in the Cigar Makers Union, Gompers hammered out a doctrine that he called pure-and-simple unionism. *Pure* referred to membership: strictly limited to workers, organized by craft and occupation, with no reliance on outside advisors or allies. *Simple* referred to goals: only those that immediately benefitted workers — better wages, hours, and working conditions. Pure-and-simple unionists distrusted politics. Their aim was direct collective bargaining with employers.

On one level, pure-and-simple unionism worked. The AFL was small at first, but by 1904 its membership rose to more than two million. In the early twentieth century, it became the nation's leading voice for workers, lasting far longer than movements like the Knights of Labor. The AFL's strategy was well suited to an era when Congress and the courts were hostile to labor. By the 1910s, the political climate would become more responsive; at that later moment, Gompers would soften his antipolitical stance and join the battle for new labor laws and political allies who would enact them.

What Gompers gave up most crucially, in the meantime, was the inclusiveness and dream of a cooperative society that the Knights of Labor and Farmers' Alliance had advanced. By comparison with the Knights, the AFL was far less welcoming to women and blacks; it included mostly skilled craftsmen. There was little room in the AFL for department-store clerks and other service workers, much less the sharecroppers and domestic servants whom the Knights had organized. Despite the AFL's success among skilled craftsmen, the narrowness of its base was a problem that would come back to haunt the labor movement later on. Gompers, however, saw that corporate

Samuel Gompers, c. 1890s Samuel Gompers (1850–1924) was one of the founders of the American Federation of Labor, and its president for nearly forty years. A company detective took this photograph when the labor leader was visiting striking miners in West Virginia, an area where mine operators resisted unions with special fierceness. Labor in America Collection, University of Maryland Libraries.

AP® APPLY THE TIP

Ask students to create a Venn diagram in their notebooks to compare the Knights of Labor and the American Federation of Labor. Students should perform a close reading of the text in order to include specific details in their Venn diagrams that address the similarities and differences in the leadership, goals, membership, and methods of each labor organization. Then ask students to work in collaborative groups to address the following prompt: Why was the American of Federation of Labor more successful over time than the Knights of Labor? After students discuss this prompt, ask them to answer the following questions:

- **What are the most important differences between these two organizations?** *Knights of Labor welcomed both skilled and unskilled workers while the AFL was an organization of skilled workers. Workers joined the Knights individually while the AFL was a "union of unions." The AFL supported the use of strikes while the Knights did not.*
- **What are the most important similarities between these two organizations?** *Both organizations supported the goals of the 8-hour workday, workmen's compensation, minimum wages, and child labor laws.*
- **Why did the Haymarket affair dramatically impact the Knights of Labor?** *The local, state, and federal governments emphasized the role of radical anarchists in the event and tied the event to the Knights of Labor, discrediting the organization.*
- **What role did the actions of governments (local, state, and/or federal) play on these organizations?** *Government agencies supported business and industry — local police broke up rallies, state governors used the National Guard, the federal government sent in troops to break strikes.*

titans and their political allies held tremendous power, and he advocated what he saw as the most practical defensive plan. In the meantime, the upheaval wrought by industrialization spread far beyond the workplace, transforming every aspect of American life.

SUMMARY

The end of the Civil War ushered in the era of American big business. Exploiting the continent's vast resources, vertically integrated corporations emerged as the dominant business form, and giant companies built near monopolies in some sectors of the economy. Corporations devised new modes of production, distribution, and marketing, extending their reach through the department store, the mail-order catalog, and the new advertising industry. These developments laid the groundwork for mass consumer culture. They also offered emerging jobs in management, sales, and office work.

Rapid industrialization drew immigrants from around the world. Until the 1920s, most European and Latin American immigrants were welcome to enter the United States, though they often endured harsh conditions after they arrived. Asian immigrants, by contrast, faced severe discrimination. The Chinese Exclusion Act blocked all Chinese laborers from coming to the United States; it was later extended to other Asians, and it built the legal framework for broader forms of exclusion.

Nationwide movements for workers' rights arose in response to industrialization. During the 1870s and 1880s, coalitions of workers and farmers, notably the Knights of Labor and the Farmers' Alliance, sought political solutions to what they saw as large corporations' exploitation of working people. Pressure from such movements led to the first major attempts to regulate corporations, such as the federal Interstate Commerce Act. Radical protest movements were weakened, however, after public condemnation of anarchist violence in 1886 at Chicago's Haymarket Square. Meanwhile, trade unions such as the American Federation of Labor organized skilled workers and negotiated directly with employers, becoming the most popular form of labor organization in the early twentieth century.

CHAPTER 16 REVIEW

AP® CONTENT REVIEW *Answer these questions to demonstrate your understanding of the chapter's main ideas.*

1. How did corporations come to dominate the American economic landscape in this period, and what impact did industrialization have on employees, consumers, and the environment?
2. Why did so many immigrants come to the United States in this era, and how did their experiences differ?
3. How did working people organize to protect their interests in this period, and why and how did their strategies change between 1877 and 1900?

CHECK FOR UNDERSTANDING

Use the **AP® LEARNING FOCUS** question from the beginning of the chapter to check students' understanding of the chapter as a whole: **Why did large corporations arise and thrive in late nineteenth-century America, and how did they reshape trade, work, and politics?** *The post-Civil War environment accelerated historical processes attendant to industrialization, which began before the war. Industrialization changed the American landscape through the expansion of urban areas, an upsurge in immigration, the concentration of wealth, and the deterioration of working conditions in urban environments. Industrialization created opportunities for men of means as well as jobs for an ever-growing laboring class. It also increased the exploitative processes of business, including corporations, monopolies, and unjust working conditions for men, women, and children. The exploitation and unsafe conditions in American factories facilitated a nascent labor movement. By the close of the nineteenth century, cities were larger and more diverse, classes were more distinct, labor unions were active, and wealth was more concentrated.*

✓ LearningCurve

Remind students to go online to complete the LearningCurve quiz for this chapter.

TRM Find complete suggested responses in the Teacher's Resource Materials.

AP® SKILLS & PROCESSES

CAUSATION

AP® CONTENT REVIEW 1 asks students to describe the effects of new business practices on different groups of people and on the environment. Note: This is the same question as the **CHECK FOR UNDERSTANDING** prompt on p. 527.

AP® SKILLS & PROCESSES

CAUSATION

AP® CONTENT REVIEW 2 asks students to indicate the causes of immigration during the late nineteenth century. The question is implicitly comparative as well, asking how immigrants' experiences differed. Note: This is the same question as the **CHECK FOR UNDERSTANDING** prompt on p. 534.

AP® SKILLS & PROCESSES

CONTINUITY AND CHANGE

AP® CONTENT REVIEW 3 encourages students to identify changes in the labor movement from the end of Reconstruction to the turn of the century.

AP® TERMS TO KNOW *Identify and explain the significance of each term below.*

Key Concepts and Events

management revolution (p. 517)
vertical integration (p. 517)
predatory pricing (p. 518)
horizontal integration (p. 518)
trust (p. 518)
Gospel of Wealth (p. 519)
deskilling (p. 523)
scientific management (p. 523)
New South (p. 526)
Chinese Exclusion Act (p. 533)
Great Railroad Strike of 1877 (p. 534)
Greenback-Labor Party (p. 536)
producerism (p. 536)
Granger laws (p. 537)
Knights of Labor (p. 537)
Haymarket Square (p. 538)
Farmers' Alliance (p. 539)
Interstate Commerce Commission (ICC) (p. 539)
American Federation of Labor (AFL) (p. 541)

Key People

Andrew Carnegie (p. 514)
Gustavus Swift (p. 517)
John D. Rockefeller (p. 518)
Henry George (p. 535)
Terence Powderly (p. 537)
Leonora Barry (p. 537)
Samuel Gompers (p. 541)

AP® MAKING CONNECTIONS *Recognize the larger developments and continuities within and across chapters by answering these questions.*

1. Compare the two phases of industrialization experienced in the nineteenth-century United States: one before the Civil War (see "The American Industrial Revolution" in Chapter 8) and one afterward (discussed in this chapter). What factors drove each period of economic expansion? What kinds of new industries arose, and in which regions and locations? In what ways were workers' experiences similar in the two periods, and how did they differ? What political challenges arose with each wave of industrialization?
2. Before the Civil War, Americans' geographic heritage was primarily from Western Europe and Africa, with a continued presence of American Indians. In the late nineteenth century, millions of working-class immigrants arrived from southern and Eastern Europe and Asia; the United States also integrated former Mexican regions in the Southwest, and more Latin American immigrants began arriving to work in the growing U.S. economy. Thus by 1900, the American working class became truly global in origin. What factors—economic and political—contributed to this shift? How did globalization of the workforce impact the social order in the U.S.? How did native-born Americans respond, politically, to different groups of newcomers?

KEY TURNING POINTS *Refer to the timeline at the start of the chapter for help in answering the following questions.*

In the era of industrialization, what events prompted the rise of labor unions and other reform groups that called for stronger government responses to corporate power? Before 1900, what key events or turning points marked reformers' successes and failures? Explain your reasoning with evidence from the text.

AP® PRACTICE QUESTIONS

MULTIPLE CHOICE QUESTIONS *Choose the correct answer for each question.*

Questions 1–3 refer to this excerpt.

"The recent alarming development and aggression of aggregated wealth, which, unless checked, will inevitably lead to the pauperization and hopeless degradation of the toiling masses, render it imperative, if we desire to enjoy the blessings of the government bequeathed to us by the founders of the republic, that a check should be placed upon its power and unjust accumulation, and a system adopted which will secure to the laborer the fruits of his toil; and as this much desired object can only be accomplished by the thorough unification of labor . . . we have formed the Industrial Brotherhood, with a view of securing the organization and direction, by co-operative effort of power of the industrial classes . . . calling upon all who believe in securing 'the greatest good for the greatest number,' to aid and assist us. . . ."

Terence Powderly, *Thirty Years of Labor*, 1889

TRM Find definitions for these terms in the **Glossary/Glosario** in the Teacher's Resource Materials.

AP® SKILLS & PROCESSES

COMPARISON

AP® MAKING CONNECTIONS 1 invites students to compare two different phases of industrialization. The questions that follow provide a basis for students' comparisons. Students should be sure to include the Civil War itself in their evaluation of the second phase of industrialization.

AP® SKILLS & PROCESSES

CAUSATION

AP® MAKING CONNECTIONS 2 asks students to contemplate intermediate and short-term historical processes that caused the demographics of the United States to change. Additionally, the question also promotes a student awareness of the rationale for migrating and the varied reactions of Americans to the changing demographics of the early twentieth century.

AP® SKILLS & PROCESSES

CAUSATION

KEY TURNING POINTS asks students to identify factors that led to the rise of resistance to corporate power. Since reformers experienced relatively little success, students should explain why reform generally failed in this period.

TRM Find complete suggested responses in the Teacher's Resource Materials.

1. The ideas of Powderly as expressed in the passage had the most in common with the ideas of which of the following?
   a. The Populist Party
   b. Advocates for a "New South"
   c. The Whig Party
   d. The Gospel of Wealth
2. Which of the following developments represents continuity with the concerns expressed in the passage?
   a. Supreme Court decisions regarding slavery in the 1850s
   b. Jeffersonian criticism of industrialization in the early 1800s
   c. Reform efforts of the Second Great Awakening from 1820s–1840s
   d. Criticisms of the War of 1812 by Federalists
3. The ideas expressed in the excerpt were most directly a response to the
   a. decreasing prices of many goods as the real wages of workers increased.
   b. increasing ethnic diversity of an expanding workforce.
   c. greater concentration of wealth through consolidation of corporations into trusts.
   d. growing power of political machines in urban areas.

Questions 4–6 refer to this excerpt.

"It is commonly admitted that while a man or woman who does some small thing in the manufacture of an article . . . may become marvelously expert, the operator runs the risk of becoming more or less of a machine . . . the minute division of labor that makes such wonders possible brutalizes the laborer, and . . . if the girl made the whole article instead of doing one operation out of fifty, she would gain in intelligence if not in expertness. From an economic, or rather an industrial[,] point of view, however, manufacturing has to be carried on at present with the greatest subdivision possible. Fierce competition and a small margin of profit demand it."

Philip Hubert, *The Business of a Factory*, 1897

4. The developments described in this passage most likely originate with which of the following groups?
   a. Newly Arrived Immigrant Groups
   b. Proponents of Cottage Industries
   c. Captains of Industry
   d. Knights of Labor and National Labor Union
5. The process described in this passage most directly led to controversies in the late nineteenth century over
   a. the wages and working conditions of workers.
   b. government intervention during economic downturns.
   c. the political implementation of the Social Gospel.
   d. urban neighborhoods segregated by ethnicity and class.
6. Which of the following would be most supportive of the ideas expressed in the passage?
   a. Populists
   b. The Gospel of Wealth
   c. Members of the American Protective Association
   d. The Knights of Labor

SHORT ANSWER QUESTIONS

Read each question carefully and write a short response. Use evidence from the text to support your claims.

"The visible hand of management replaced the invisible hand of market forces. . . . [S]afe, regular, reliable movement of goods and passengers, as well as the continuing maintenance and repair of locomotives, rolling stock, and track, roadbed, stations, roundhouses, and other equipment, required . . . special skills and training which could only be commanded by a full-time salaried manager. . . . This career orientation and the specialized nature of tasks gave the railroad managers an increasingly professional outlook on their work."

Alfred D. Chandler Jr., *The Visible Hand: The Managerial Revolution in American Business*, 1977

"[Railroads] were not the harbingers of order, rationality, and effective large-scale organization. . . . Managers blamed their failures on accidents and contingent events, but they also used them to cover their mistakes and claim quite fortuitous results as the fruits of their planning. . . . [The railroad corporations] not only failed to institute the order they desired; they also just plain failed and repeatedly needed rescuing by the state and the courts. . . . The transcontinental railroads are sometimes fetishized as the ultimate manifestation of modern rationality, but, when seen from within, these astonishingly mismanaged railroads are the anteroom to mystery."

Richard White, *Railroaded: The Transcontinentals and the Making of Modern America*, 2011

1. Using the two excerpts provided, answer (a), (b), and (c).
   a. Briefly explain ONE major difference between Chandler's and White's historical interpretations of corporate American railroads in the second half of the nineteenth century.
   b. Briefly explain how ONE specific historical event or development not directly mentioned in the excerpts could be used to support Chandler's argument.
   c. Briefly explain how ONE specific historical event or development not directly mentioned in the excerpts could be used to support White's argument.
2. Answer (a), (b), and (c).
   a. Briefly explain ONE specific historical effect of technological innovations on business practices between 1865 and 1900.
   b. Briefly explain ONE specific historical effect industrialization had on western expansion between 1865 and 1900.
   c. Briefly explain ONE specific historical effect of immigration on the United States economy between 1865 and 1900.
3. Answer (a), (b), and (c).
   a. Briefly explain which ONE of the following developments was the most significant factor contributing to political divisions in the United States between 1865 and 1900.
      - Regional interests
      - Industrial capitalism
      - Urban political machines
   b. Briefly explain ONE specific historical event or development that supports your argument in (a).
   c. Briefly explain a specific historical reason that ONE of the other options represents a less significant factor contributing to political divisions in the United States between 1865 and 1900.

TRM Find complete suggested responses in the Teacher's Resource Materials.

17 CHAPTER
Making Modern American Culture
1880–1917

Chapter 17 — AP® Assessment Weight and Pacing Guide

The assessment weight on the AP® U.S. History Exam for Chapters 15–19 is 10–17 percent. Chapter 17 Section 1 falls in Unit 6 of the AP® U.S. History Curriculum, covering Period 6: 1865–1898. Chapter 17 Sections 2 and 3 fall in Unit 7 of the AP® U.S. History Curriculum, covering Period 7: 1890–1945. These sections may be taught together or divided into separate units of study according to College Board periodization.

This pacing guide is based on a schedule with 120 sessions of 50 minutes each before the AP® U.S. History Exam. If you have a different number of sessions before the exam, you can modify the pacing to meet your needs. If you have additional time, consider incorporating quizzes, released AP® U.S. History questions, practice exams, writing practice, and other instructional activities.

	Traditional Schedule	Block Schedule
Chapter 17 Section 1	1 day	1 day
Chapter 17 Sections 2–3	2 days	1 day

Daily Pacing Guide

	Content Focus	Essential Question
Day 1	Science and Faith (Period 6)	How did Charles Darwin's theory of evolution impact American culture and intellectual life, and how did nonscientists make use of such ideas?
Day 2	Commerce and Culture (Period 7)	How did industrialization change the way Americans spent their leisure time, and how did this reflect evolving social identities and divisions?
Day 3	Women, Men, and the Solitude of Self (Period 7)	Why and how did women's public activism arise in the late nineteenth century and how did this impact American politics and society?

AP® Alignment

Section Heading	AP® Topic	AP® Theme
Science and Faith	6.8, 6.9, 6.11	MIG, SOC
Commerce and Culture	6.4, 6.10	NAT, SOC
Women, Men, and the Solitude of Self	6.4, 6.11, 6.13	NAT, SOC, PCE

*Should changes be made to the Course Framework in the future, an updated alignment will be placed on our AP® updates page at go.bfwpub.com/ap-course-updates.

Chapter 17 — Overview

Chapter 17 focuses on the impact of industrialization and urbanization on the beliefs, ideas, and culture of the U.S. The chapter begins by analyzing the impact of scientific ideas, especially the ideas of Charles Darwin, on Americans' beliefs about religion, society, and the economy. These changes in American culture are followed by an examination of the rising class-consciousness that accompanied industrialization and its impact on diverging consumer and leisure activities. Finally, this chapter examines the dramatic changes that industrialization brought for women in the workplace and at home, leading to more demands for political rights for women, including suffrage rights. In this period, the importance of education also dramatically altered life for Americans and led to demands for greater access to schools as well as economic and political activity.

Chapter 17 — Resources

The following resources can be found in the Teacher's Resource Materials (TRM) that accompany the book. You can access the TRM via the book's digital platform, by clicking the TRM links found here in your Teacher's Edition e-book, or by contacting your representative to access the resources online. Visit **bfwpub.com/henretta10e** to learn more.

TRM Chapter 17 Lecture Presentation Slides

TRM Chapter 17 Outline with AP® Focus

TRM Chapter 17 Lecture Strategies

TRM Chapter 17 Suggested Responses

TRM Handout 17.1 — Comparison: Responses to Immigration

TRM Handout 17.2 — Thematic Analysis: Realism and Modernism

TRM Handout 17.3 — Causation: Rise of Feminism

Chapter 17 — Essential Activity

For this activity, provide students with a handful of small slips of paper in two different colors on which they can write a single word or short phrase. Then have students closely listen to the ideas of Washington and Du Bois expressed in excerpts from their most famous works — Washington's "Atlanta Compromise" speech and "Of Booker T. Washington and others" from Du Bois's book *The Souls of Black Folk*. Read each excerpt aloud once while students listen only. Then instruct students to use the small slips of paper in one color to record what they believe are important words and phrases from the excerpt as you reread.

Organize the students into collaborative groups and inform them that they should pool all their words and phrases and use them to create a poem that uses only their slips of paper to effectively express the differences and similarities in the ideas of these two leaders. You can provide students with a large sheet of paper and tape to secure their poems once they are ready to share.

Chapter 17 — Bell Ringers

The following activities take no more than 5–15 minutes of your class period and offer an effective and engaging way to begin your lessons and for students to apply AP® Skills & Processes:

- Provide students with a copy of a cartoon or an illustration in support of eugenics in the 1920s to 1930s. Ask students to analyze the image and discuss the impact new scientific theories, such as Darwin's natural selection, had on political and economic life in the U.S. and the world. Then prompt students to make comparisons to current political debates on issues such as climate change.
- Choose a current environmental issue and ask students to debate the government's policy on that issue. (Examples include offshore oil drilling, pipeline construction, or removing restrictions on hunting certain species.) Ask students to differentiate between established scientific facts related to the issue and the political rhetoric surrounding the issue. Then have students compare various points of view on the issue.

NOTES

TEACHING STRATEGY

Use the chapter opener material to help students explore how the many aspects of the industrial era challenged Americans' traditional beliefs. Some of the biggest challenges were in the area of religious belief, a major theme of this chapter. People responded to these challenges in a variety of ways, from adapting beliefs to the realities of new scientific and intellectual trends, to firmly resisting new views. Consumer goods — aided by developments in advertising — often took on a religious aura. Advertisers seeking to elevate the desirability of their products often subtly evoked familiar sacred imagery to convey the transcendent possibilities of consumption. Together, the changes brought by industrialization, as the chapter title indicates, made American culture "modern." While scholars often disagree about the precise definition of modernity, a number of elements are often included and might be worth explicitly sharing with students: industrial capitalism, rapid transportation and communication, demographic mobility, global trade, growth of science and technology, expansion of education (particularly higher education), bureaucratic rationalism, and an egalitarian ethos. For a complete suggested response to the **AP® LEARNING FOCUS** question, see p. 574.

17

CHAPTER

Making Modern American Culture

1880–1917

AP® LEARNING FOCUS

Why and how did Americans' identities, beliefs, and culture change in the early industrial era?

Between 1888 and 1900, American archaeologists conducted their first explorations in what is now Iraq, at the site of the ancient city of Nippur. Leaders of the expedition included Protestant ministers and the editor of the national *Sunday-School Times*. Their goal was to practice biblical archaeology: to confirm the truth of Old Testament accounts of Babylon. As one participant wrote, they sought to blend a "spirit of Christian enlightenment" with modern "scientific inquiry." The expeditions unearthed thousands of cuneiform tablets, which Jewish and Christian linguists and anthropologists used to reveal much about ancient Assyrian society. Some investigators found that these discoveries strengthened their faith in biblical truth. Others were not so sure.

As shown by the Babylonian expeditions, a passion for scientific inquiry swept the late-nineteenth-century United States, often inspired by religious teachings but ultimately calling into question many tenets of faith. Between the 1870s and the 1910s, a stunning series of scientific discoveries — from dinosaur fossils to telescopic observations of nebulae — challenged long-held beliefs. Biological theories of evolution prompted fierce debate; so did technological innovations such as medical vaccines and electric chairs. While science gained persuasive power, religion hardly faded. In fact, religious diversity grew, as immigrants brought new faiths to the United States and Protestants responded with innovations of their own.

At the same time, industrialization reshaped class identities and generated an alluring consumer culture. Lavish urban department stores catered to middle-class customers, while working-class men and women enjoyed vaudeville shows. Americans of all backgrounds and classes mingled at baseball games and summer amusement parks. An older ethos of duty, self-restraint, and moral uplift gave way to expectations of leisure and fun. As African Americans and women claimed a right to education and public space — the opportunity to shop, dine, and travel freely — they built powerful reform movements. At the same time, the pressures of the industrial workplace led to aggressive calls for masculine fitness, exemplified by the rise of sports. Here, too, scientific research sparked debates over the body, gender, and race. Americans found themselves living in a modern world — one in which their grandparents' beliefs and practices might no longer apply.

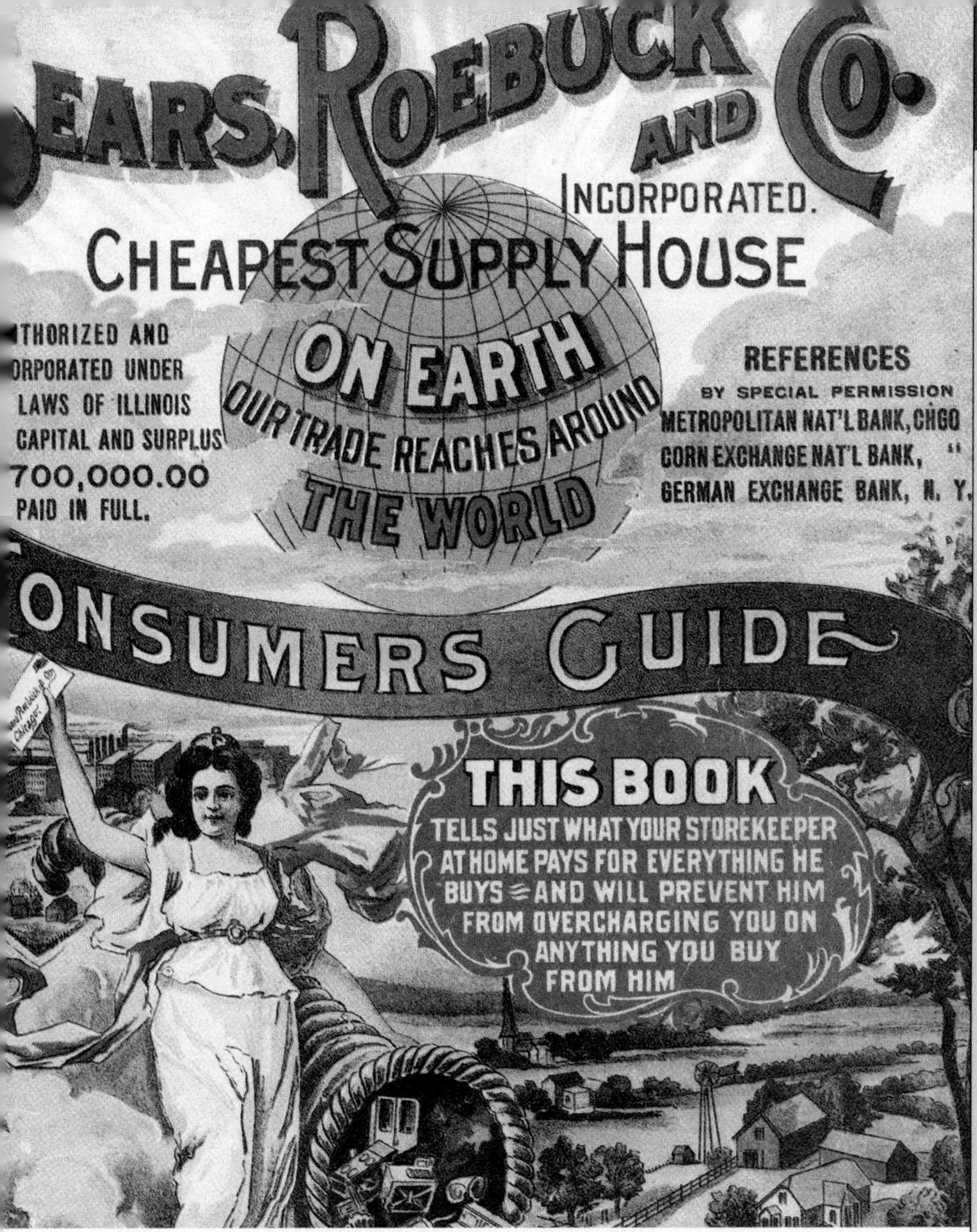

Cornucopia for Consumers, 1896 This Sears, Roebuck catalog provided rural and small-town Americans with access to a dazzling array of products—and provided a direct challenge to the "local storekeeper" by promising to share wholesale prices directly with customers, to "prevent him from overcharging you on anything you buy from him." With its gigantic scale of operation, Sears could price its products lower and undercut small-scale businesses. Rural families learned to pore over the catalog's pages, identifying furniture, clothes, tools, farm equipment, and dolls and toys they'd like to buy. The Granger Collection.

TEACHING STRATEGY

The modernity of growing cities led to the creation of new products and innovative ways of purchasing goods. However, part of the allure of this era for consumers was the novelty of bringing products to those living in rural areas. Though department stores such as Sears, Roebuck and Co. may conjure images of a burgeoning middle class in urban areas, remind students of the broad reach of new consumer goods. Ask students to identify one significant social change for Americans in rural areas occasioned by stores such as Sears, Roebuck and Co.

AP® SKILLS & PROCESSES

CONTINUITY AND CHANGE

Use the **TIMELINE** to help students begin thinking about how the period from the 1870s to 1917 could constitute a distinct historical period. Students will note that the starting date is rounded, and therefore an approximate one. The end date of the chapter, on the other hand, is very precise, indicating a specific event: American entry into World War I. Though the timeline ends with the creation of the National Park Service in 1916, remind students that in 1917 the United States entered World War I. Have students skim through the chronology and identify three to five major patterns that seem to have been most characteristic of American culture in this period. Students could also explain why American entry into World War I provides the end date to this era.

AP® APPLY THE TIP

Use the **AP® FIRSTHAND ACCOUNTS** feature (pp. 548–549) to engage students in a discussion of the impact of Charles Darwin's ideas on society and its implications for the business world. In pairs or small groups, have students answer the questions on p. 549 based on their understanding of the arguments of each author. Then ask students to briefly research the background of each individual, including their areas of expertise, experiences in leadership, and involvement in American politics. After a brief research period, lead a class discussion on the extended analysis of these documents, explaining the importance of the author's point of view, intended audience, purpose, and historical context for each specific document. Finally, ask students to contextualize these documents by identifying historical developments, processes, and/or events that may have influenced each author.

TIMELINE

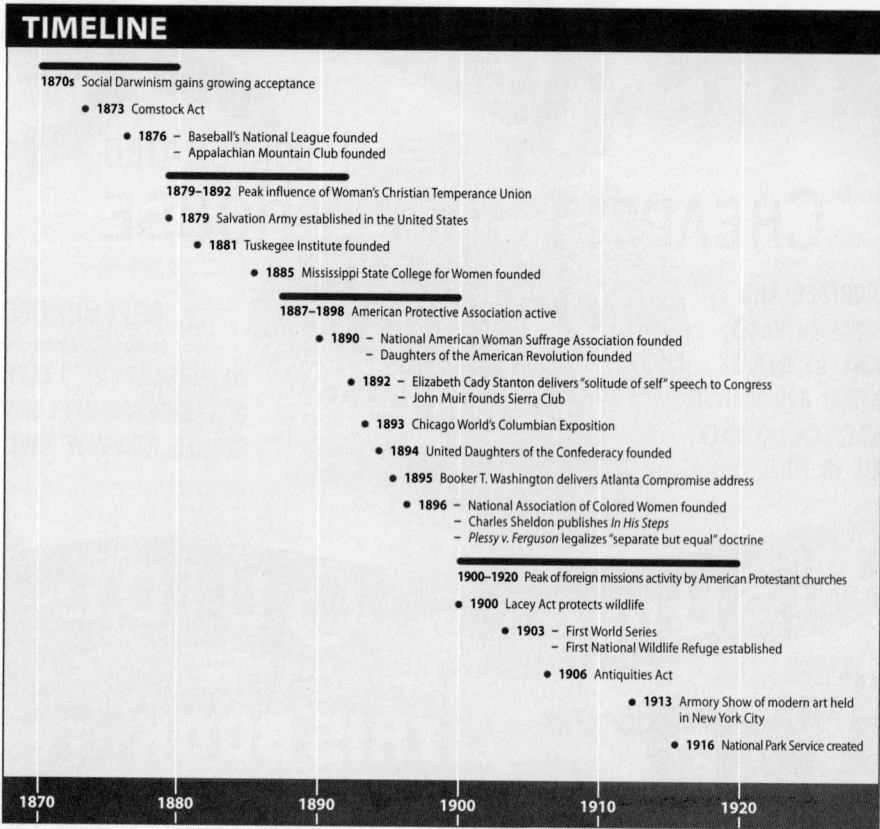

1870s Social Darwinism gains growing acceptance

- **1873** Comstock Act
- **1876** – Baseball's National League founded
  – Appalachian Mountain Club founded

1879–1892 Peak influence of Woman's Christian Temperance Union

- **1879** Salvation Army established in the United States
- **1881** Tuskegee Institute founded
- **1885** Mississippi State College for Women founded

1887–1898 American Protective Association active

- **1890** – National American Woman Suffrage Association founded
  – Daughters of the American Revolution founded
- **1892** – Elizabeth Cady Stanton delivers "solitude of self" speech to Congress
  – John Muir founds Sierra Club
- **1893** Chicago World's Columbian Exposition
- **1894** United Daughters of the Confederacy founded
- **1895** Booker T. Washington delivers Atlanta Compromise address
- **1896** – National Association of Colored Women founded
  – Charles Sheldon publishes *In His Steps*
  – *Plessy v. Ferguson* legalizes "separate but equal" doctrine

1900–1920 Peak of foreign missions activity by American Protestant churches

- **1900** Lacey Act protects wildlife
- **1903** – First World Series
  – First National Wildlife Refuge established
- **1906** Antiquities Act
- **1913** Armory Show of modern art held in New York City
- **1916** National Park Service created

1870 1880 1890 1900 1910 1920

SCIENCE AND FAITH

How did Charles Darwin's theory of evolution impact American culture and intellectual life, and how did nonscientists make use of such ideas?

AP® EXAM TIP

The impact of Darwin's ideas on the thinking about society and the business world is important to know on the AP® Exam

In the early nineteenth century, most Americans believed the world was about six thousand years old. No one knew what lay beyond the solar system. By the 1910s, paleontologists had classified Jurassic dinosaurs, astronomers had identified distant galaxies, and physicists were beginning to measure the speed of light. Many scientists and ordinary Americans accepted Charles Darwin's theory of evolution, though exactly how "natural selection" worked — and its implications for religious belief — remained contested.

Scientific discoveries received widespread publicity through a series of great world's fairs, most famously Chicago's 1893 World's Columbian Exposition, held (a year late) to mark the four-hundredth anniversary of Columbus's first voyage to America. At the fairgrounds, visitors strolled through enormous buildings that displayed the latest inventions in industry, machinery, and transportation. They marveled over steam engines, weather-forecasting equipment, and moving sidewalks. At dusk they gathered to watch the exposition buildings illuminated with strings of electric lights. One observer called the exposition "a vast and wonderful university of the arts and sciences."

It is hardly surprising, amid these achievements, that "fact worship" became a central feature of American intellectual life. Researchers in many fields argued that one could rely only on hard facts to understand the "laws of life." In their enthusiasm, some economists and sociologists rejected all social reform as sentimental. Fiction writers and artists kept a more humane emphasis, but they made use of similar methods — close observation and attention to real-life experience — to create works of realism. Meanwhile, other Americans struggled to reconcile scientific discoveries with religious faith.

Darwinism and Its Critics

Evolution — the idea that species are not fixed, but ever changing — was not a simple idea on which all scientists agreed. In his immensely influential 1859 book, *On the Origin of Species*, British naturalist Charles Darwin argued that all creatures struggle to survive. He argued that when individual members of a species are born with random genetic mutations that better suit them for their environment — for example, camouflage coloring for a moth — these characteristics, since they are genetically transmissible, become dominant in future generations. Many scientists rejected this theory of natural selection. They followed a line of thinking laid out by French biologist Jean Baptiste Lamarck, who argued, unlike Darwin, that individual animals or plants could acquire transmittable traits within a single lifetime. A rhinoceros that fought fiercely, in Lamarck's view, could build up a stronger horn; its offspring would then be born with that trait.

Darwin himself disapproved of the word *evolution* (which does not appear in his book) because it implied upward progress. In his view, natural selection could not be assigned a human moral value: environments and species changed through random mutation.

Evolution and Capitalism Others were less scrupulous about drawing sweeping conclusions from Darwin's work. In the 1870s, British philosopher Herbert Spencer spun out an elaborate theory of how human society advanced through ruthless competitive struggle, resulting in "survival of the fittest." Spencer applied this particularly to capitalism and industry.

The doctrine of **Social Darwinism**, as Spencer's idea became (confusingly) known, found its American champion in William Graham Sumner, a sociology professor at Yale. Competition, said Sumner, was a law of nature, like gravity. Who were the fittest? "Millionaires," Sumner declared. Their success showed they were "naturally selected." Sumner's views bolstered the pride and self-justification of industrial titans such as Andrew Carnegie, who loved Spencer's works and invited him to tour Pittsburgh. (Spencer was not impressed.) "The concentration of capital is necessary for meeting the demands of our day," was the message Carnegie took from Spencer. Similarly, John D. Rockefeller of Standard Oil declared that "the growth of a large business is merely a survival of the fittest. This is not an evil tendency of business. It is merely the working out of a law of nature and a law of God."

Social Darwinism
An idea, actually formulated not by Charles Darwin but by British philosopher and sociologist Herbert Spencer, that human society advanced through ruthless competition and the "survival of the fittest."

Even in the heyday of Social Darwinism, such views were controversial. Many thinkers objected to the application of biological findings to the realm of economics and society. Sociologist Lester Frank Ward argued that humanity "progresses through the *protection* of the weak," not through ruthless competition. "Man," he wrote, "through his intelligence, has labored successfully to resist the law of nature." Ward suggested, tongue in cheek, that if Americans subscribed to a doctrine of "survival of the fittest," they should abolish police and fire departments, irrigation works, and flood control. Social Darwinism, such critics argued, was simply an excuse for the worst excesses of industrialization. By the early twentieth century, intellectuals turned against Sumner and his allies (see "Firsthand Accounts," p. 548).

AP® THEME

SOC: Social Structures

Students should recognize the importance of social commentators' advocacy of "Social Darwinism" as a justification for the appropriateness and inevitability of the position of those at the top of the socioeconomic structure. See the **AP® FIRSTHAND ACCOUNTS** feature (pp. 548–549) for the views of William Graham Sumner, Social Darwinism's preeminent spokesman.

AP® SKILLS & PROCESSES

ANALYZING HISTORICAL EVIDENCE

William Graham Sumner was an Episcopal priest before becoming a sociologist, which suggests one of the many ways that a proper understanding of the era requires attention to religious views. To supplement students' reading in the **AP® FIRSTHAND ACCOUNTS** feature, provide students with a different excerpt of his essay "What Social Classes Owe to Each Other" that captures his defense of the good character of wealthy people. To access this excerpt, search "History Matters Sumner social classes."

AP® SKILLS & PROCESSES

ANALYZING HISTORICAL EVIDENCE

W. E. B. Du Bois was a brilliant scholar and commentator on American life around the turn of the century, particularly on the black experience. His book *Souls of Black Folk* remains a thoughtful and engaging reflection on the "twoness" that American blacks experienced, Reconstruction, and critiques of Booker T. Washington's approach to American racism. An online edition of the book is available through Project Gutenberg, and students could be assigned particular chapters, or sections within chapters. To access the text, search "Gutenberg Souls of Black Folk." Penguin provides an online teacher's guide for the text, with selected quotes for discussion and different sets of reading questions. To access the guide, search "Teacher's Guide Souls of Black Folk."

AP® FIRSTHAND ACCOUNTS

William Graham Sumner and W. E. B. Du Bois on Heredity and Success

In an age of industrialization and bitter class conflict, the idea that human society advanced through "survival of the fittest," referred to by historians as "Social Darwinism," generated fierce debate. Was growing wealth inequality a sign of progress or a menace to democracy? How much did genetics shape individuals' character and achievement? What role did environmental factors play, and what policies should government pursue (or not) when confronting widespread poverty? Leading thinkers offered contrasting answers.

WILLIAM GRAHAM SUMNER

What Social Classes Owe to Each Other, 1883

William Graham Sumner, a professor of sociology at Yale, was a leading U.S. proponent of individualism and Social Darwinism. His book *What Social Classes Owe to Each Other* argued that wealth and poverty resulted from inherent talent, or lack thereof.

SOURCE: William Graham Sumner, *What Social Classes Owe to Each Other* (New York: Harper & Brothers, 1883), 43–57.

❝ There is an old ecclesiastical prejudice in favor of the poor and against the rich.... We all agree that he is a good member of society who works his way up from poverty to wealth, but as soon as he has worked his way up we begin to regard him with suspicion.... Think of the piles of rubbish that one has read about corners, and watering stocks, and selling futures! Undoubtedly there are, in connection with each of these things, cases of fraud, swindling, and other financial crimes; that is to say, the greed and selfishness of men are perpetual.... The criminal law needs to be improved to meet new forms of crime, but to denounce financial devices which are useful and legitimate because use is made of them for fraud, is ridiculous and unworthy of the age in which we live.

... Let any one try to get a railroad built, or to start a factory and win reputation for its products, ... and he will find what obstacles must be overcome, what risks must be taken, what perseverance and courage are required, what foresight and sagacity are necessary.... Persons who possess the necessary qualifications obtain great rewards. They ought to do so. It is foolish to rail at them.... Men who can do what they are told are not hard to find; but men who can think and plan and tell the routine men what to do are very rare. They are paid in proportion to the supply and demand of them.... Labor organizations are formed, not to employ combined effort for a common object, but to indulge in declamation and denunciation, and especially to furnish an easy living to some officers who do not want to work.

The aggregation of large fortunes is not at all a thing to be regretted. On the contrary, it is a necessary condition of many forms of social advance. If we should set a limit to the accumulation of wealth, we should say to our most valuable producers, 'We do not want you to do us the services which you best understand how to perform, beyond a certain point.' It would be like killing off our generals in war. A great deal is said ... about 'ethical views of wealth,' and we are told that some day men will be found of such public spirit that, after they have accumulated a few millions, they will be willing to go on and labor simply for the pleasure of paying the wages of their fellow-citizens. Possibly this is true. It is a prophecy.... There are no such men now.... ❞

W. E. B. DU BOIS

"Heredity and the Public Schools," 1904

W. E. B. Du Bois, an African American sociologist who trained at Harvard and then in Germany, emerged as a leading critic of Social Darwinism. Du Bois also challenged the civic leadership

eugenics
An emerging "science" of human breeding in the late nineteenth century that argued that mentally deficient people should be prevented from reproducing.

Eugenics Meanwhile, though, some of the most dubious applications of evolutionary ideas were codified into new reproductive laws based on **eugenics**, a so-called science of human breeding. Eugenicists argued that so-called mentally deficient people should be prevented from reproducing. They proposed to sterilize those deemed "unfit," especially residents of state asylums for the insane or mentally disabled. In early-twentieth-century America, almost half the states enacted eugenics laws. By the time eugenics subsided in the 1930s, tens of thousands of people had been sterilized, with California and Virginia taking the lead. Women in Puerto Rico and other U.S. imperial possessions also suffered from eugenic policies.

Advocates of eugenics had a broad impact. Because they associated mental unfitness with "lower races"—including people of African, Asian, and Native American descent—their arguments lent support to Jim Crow segregation laws and racial discrimination. In a wave of legislation beginning in the 1870s and peaking in the 1910s,

548

CHECK FOR UNDERSTANDING

Ask students: **What was Darwinism and what did critics say about it?** *Darwin articulated the biological theory of evolutionary change through random genetic ideas, suggesting that species that were best adapted to their environments survived and passed on their genes. Some scientists argued that plants or animals could acquire transmittable traits in a single generation. The notion of "survival of the fittest" was applied to capitalist society in the ideology of Social Darwinism and in the advocacy of eugenics.*

of educator Booker T. Washington and helped found the Niagara movement and the NAACP (Chapter 19). In this excerpt, from a speech given to African American school principals in Washington, D.C., in 1904, Du Bois emphasizes the role of environmental factors in shaping children and society.

SOURCE: W. E. B. Du Bois, "Heredity and the Public Schools," in *Du Bois on Education*, ed. Eugene F. Provenzo Jr. (Walnut Creek, CA: Altamira Press, 2002), 114–121.

❝ The recognition of the wonderful part which heredity and variation play in animal life literally changed the world's language ... and especially did the phrase: '*the survival of the fittest*.' Undoubtedly this phrase led to a hardening of human hearts.... Physical heredity is by no means the only heredity in the world nor is it in all probability the more important heredity. The human child receives its body and the physical bases of life from its parents, but it receives its thoughts, the larger part of its habits, its tricks of doing, of religion; its whole conception of what it is and what the whole world about it is from the society in which it is placed; and this heredity which is not physical at all has been aptly called social heredity.... Nine tenths of what a man is, depends on social rather than on physical heredity.... It is not until the present decade perhaps that [this] idea has received that scientific formulation that enables us to comprehend it broadly, and when people do comprehend it, it is going to revolutionize modern thought and modern conceptions of education....

How does all this apply to the American Negro? In many ways.... As to sheer physical heredity, ... it is an unproved and to all appearance an unprovable thesis that the physical development of men shows any color line.... Nevertheless it is true that if here in the city of Washington we gather haphazard a hundred white children and a hundred black children of the same age, the white would be further advanced, somewhat brighter in intellect and quicker in adaptability. This is not simply true in Washington, in Atlanta, in Chicago, but practically throughout the United States. People who discover this fact usually greet it either with a gasp of astonishment or a word of apology, and many a thoughtless person has without argument or inquiry taken this as self-evident proof of race inferiority....

What does this prove? Let us look at the facts narrowly. Here are two boys being trained for life; six hours a day they are in school; three hours they are in the street; fifteen hours they are at home. The schools they are in are similar — the teachers are of the same sort; but one walks and plays in alleys, with sordid companions, amid poverty and perhaps crime; the other lives on clean streets, with pavements; ... the home of one is dark, cheerless and empty; the home of the other is large, cheerful, filled with books and pictures, music and instruction; the parents of the one are ignorant, driven by the shadow of poverty, harassed by doubt and dream, worn with querulousness, fretting and scolding; the other has hands to lead him, hearts to soothe him, heads to guide him and correct him. Would you expect these two boys after ten years of this training to be equal in endowment and accomplishment? ...

We are so fond of explaining differences of men by the enigmatical word 'heredity' that we forget how far those differences depend upon homely, every day life, and we are so eager to seize any excuse for shirking our great responsibility toward the weak and lowly and unfortunate that we hasten on the slightest pretext to attribute to the act of God or to unknown forces of nature obviously and perfectly intelligible results of the deeds of men.... We must seek not simply to improve the schools but just as strenuously to improve the social surroundings, the social opportunities, and the social heritage. ❞

QUESTIONS FOR ANALYSIS

1. How do Sumner and Du Bois each explain inequalities of wealth and accomplishment? Compare the authors' claims and evidence.
2. What is the historical situation of both authors? How might their positions and purposes influence their arguments?

TRM Find complete suggested responses in the Teacher's Resource Materials.

most states in the South and West passed laws prohibiting interracial marriage, claiming that only separation of the races could foster human advancement. By warning that immigrants from Eastern and Southern Europe would dilute white Americans' racial purity, eugenicists also helped win passage of immigration restriction in the 1920s.

AP® SKILLS & PROCESSES

CONTEXTUALIZATION

How did the ideas of scientists and social scientists reflect events they saw happening around them?

Religion: Diversity and Innovation

By the turn of the twentieth century, emerging scientific and cultural paradigms posed a significant challenge to religious faith. Some Americans argued that science and modernity would sweep away religion altogether. Contrary to such predictions, American religious practice remained vibrant. Protestants developed creative new responses to the challenges of industrialization, while millions of newcomers built institutions for worship and religious education.

AP® SKILLS & PROCESSES

CONTEXTUALIZATION

The **CONTEXTUALIZATION** question asks students to place scholarly and intellectual developments in the context of late nineteenth-century American culture. Students often tend to think of science (natural or social) as a strictly objective pursuit of truth, so they may require some persuading to think of science as developing in the midst of — and in part in response to — a particular cultural milieu. Students might also offer inferences about what larger cultural factors might have led once-popular views, such as eugenics, to eventually fall out of favor.

TRM Find complete suggested responses in the Teacher's Resource Materials.

TEACHING STRATEGY

Religious historian Grant Wacker provides a helpful overview of Protestant liberalism that is both brief and clear. He indicates contexts that explain liberalism's emergence, delineates differing forms of liberalism, and offers a brief summary of historians' debates about liberalism. To access the article, search "Wacker Religious Liberalism."

TEACHING STRATEGY

Eugenics had a powerful and politically connected following in the early twentieth century. This pseudo-science further divided the United States along racial, ethnic, and social strata. Ask students to identify two broad historical factors that contributed to an atmosphere that was receptive to ideas such as eugenics.

TEACHING STRATEGY

Julie Byrne's essay "Roman Catholics and Immigration in Nineteenth-Century America" gives a helpful overview of Catholics' experiences in late nineteenth-century America. She places these experiences in the context of Protestant anti-Catholic sentiment, institutional Catholic support for immigrants, and class differences between Catholics and Protestants. Byrne additionally offers very detailed and thoughtful suggestions of topics for class discussions, and an overview of major themes addressed by scholars of American Catholic history. To access this essay, search "Byrne Roman Catholics and Immigration."

TEACHING STRATEGY

Jonathan Sarna and Jonathan Golden's essay titled "The American Jewish Experience Through the Nineteenth Century: Immigration and Acculturation" offers a synopsis of the Jewish experience in America, beginning with the colonial period and continuing through the end of the nineteenth century. Sarna and Golden additionally provide a substantial guide to student discussion, an overview of historiographical debates about the Jewish American experience, and links to online sources, including the online version of the Library of Congress's exhibition "From Haven to Home: 350 Years of Jewish Life in America." To access this essay, search "Sarna and Golden American Jewish Experience."

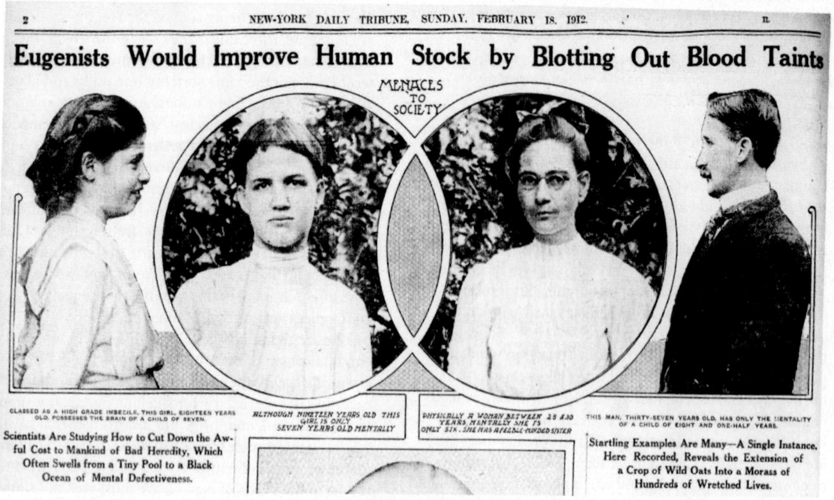
2 NEW-YORK DAILY TRIBUNE, SUNDAY, FEBRUARY 18, 1912. 11

Eugenists Would Improve Human Stock by Blotting Out Blood Taints

MENACES TO SOCIETY
CLASSED AS A HIGH GRADE IMBECILE, THIS GIRL, EIGHTEEN YEARS OLD, POSSESSES THE BRAIN OF A CHILD OF SEVEN.
ALTHOUGH NINETEEN YEARS OLD THIS GIRL IS ONLY SEVEN YEARS OLD MENTALLY
PHYSICALLY A WOMAN BETWEEN 25 & 30 YEARS, MENTALLY SHE IS ONLY SIX. SHE HAS A FEEBLE-MINDED SISTER
THIS MAN, THIRTY-SEVEN YEARS OLD, HAS ONLY THE MENTALITY OF A CHILD OF EIGHT AND ONE-HALF YEARS.

Scientists Are Studying How to Cut Down the Awful Cost to Mankind of Bad Heredity, Which Often Swells from a Tiny Pool to a Black Ocean of Mental Defectiveness.

Startling Examples Are Many—A Single Instance, Here Recorded, Reveals the Extension of a Crop of Wild Oats Into a Morass of Hundreds of Wretched Lives.

Popular Eugenics Americans encountered eugenics—the "science" of human breeding—through newspaper reports like this one from 1912. By offering advice on who to marry and what risky traits to look for in a potential spouse, advocates of eugenics promised to make future generations more mentally and physically fit. Grounded in racial hierarchies, eugenics resulted in forced sterilization of those deemed "unfit," particularly women of color. Chronicling America, Library of Congress.

AP® EXAM TIP

Evaluate the ways immigrant groups maintained cultural identity in the face of assimilation.

Immigrant Faiths Arriving in the United States in large numbers, Catholics and Jews wrestled with questions based on their similar experiences. To what degree should they adapt to Protestant-dominated American society? Should the education of clergy be changed? Should children attend religious or public schools? What happened if they married outside the faith? Among Catholic leaders, Bishop John Ireland of Minnesota argued that "the principles of the Church are in harmony with the interests of the Republic." But traditionalists, led by Archbishop Michael A. Corrigan of New York, disagreed. They sought to insulate Catholics from the pluralistic American environment. Indeed, by 1920, almost two million children attended Catholic elementary schools nationwide, and Catholic dioceses operated fifteen hundred high schools.

Faithful immigrant Catholics were anxious to preserve familiar traditions from Europe, and they generally supported the Church's traditional wing. But they also wanted religious life to express their ethnic identities. Italians, Poles, and other new arrivals wanted separate parishes where they could celebrate their customs, speak their languages, and establish their own parochial schools. When they became numerous enough, they also demanded their own bishops. Since agitation for ethnic parishes implied local control of church property, the Catholic hierarchy, dominated by Irish Americans, felt that the integrity of the Church was at stake. With some strain, however, the Catholic Church managed to satisfy the diverse needs of the immigrant faithful. It met the demand for representation, for example, by appointing immigrant priests as auxiliary bishops within existing dioceses.

In the same decades, many prosperous native-born Jews embraced Reform Judaism, abandoning such religious practices as keeping a kosher kitchen and conducting services in Hebrew. This was not the way of Yiddish-speaking Jews from Eastern Europe, who arrived in large numbers after the 1880s. Generally much poorer and eager to preserve their own traditions, they founded Orthodox synagogues, often in vacant stores, and practiced Judaism as they had at home.

But Eastern European Judaism had been an entire way of life, not easily replicated in an American city. "The very clothes I wore and the very food I ate had a fatal effect on my religious habits," confessed the hero of Abraham Cahan's novel *The Rise of David Levinsky* (1917). "If you . . . attempt to bend your religion to the spirit of your surroundings, it breaks. It falls to pieces." Levinsky shaved off his beard and plunged into the Manhattan clothing business. Orthodox Judaism survived the transition to America, but like other immigrant religions, it had to renounce its claims to some of the faithful. Synagogues, like Catholic parishes, faced some of the same challenges that distressed Protestants: poverty and overwork interfered with working-class people's practice of their faith, while new consumer pleasures enticed many of them to skip worship.

Protestant Innovations One of the era's dramatic religious developments — facilitated by global steamship and telegraph lines — was the rise of Protestant foreign missions. From a modest start before the Civil War, this movement peaked around 1915, when American religious organizations sponsored more than nine thousand overseas missionaries, supported at home by armies of volunteers, including more than three million women. A majority of Protestant missionaries served in Asia, with smaller numbers posted to Africa and the Middle East. Most saw American-style domesticity as a central part of evangelism, and missionary societies sent married couples into the field. Many unmarried women also served overseas as missionary teachers, doctors, and nurses, though almost never as ministers. "American woman," declared one mission leader, has "the exalted privilege of extending over the world those blessed influences, that are to renovate degraded man."

Protestant missionaries won converts, in part, by providing such modern services as medical care and women's education. Some missionaries developed deep bonds of respect with the people they served. Others showed considerable condescension toward the "poor heathen," who in turn bristled at their assumptions (see "America in the World," p. 552). One Presbyterian, who found Syrians uninterested in his gospel

Christian Missions in Japan, 1909 Through this colorful postcard, Protestant missionaries in Japan demonstrate their success in winning converts (at least a few) and their adaptation of missionary strategies to meet local needs and expectations. Here, outside their headquarters, they demonstrate "preaching by means of banners." The large characters on the vertical banner proclaim the "Association of Christian Gospel Evangelists." The horizontal banner is a Japanese translation of Matthew 11:28, "Come unto me, all ye who labor and are heavy laden, and I will give you rest." Corbis/Getty Images.

TEACHING STRATEGY

Daniel H. Bays's essay "The Foreign Missionary Movement in the Nineteenth and Early Twentieth Centuries" offers a detailed discussion of the emergence of the American overseas missions movement as an outgrowth of domestic evangelical conversion efforts. Embedded throughout the essay are numerous illustrations and photographs of missionaries and converts from around the world. The site also provides extensive links to various primary sources, including mission board archives, missionary biographies and memoirs, and digitized copies of *The American Missionary*. To access this essay, search "Bays Foreign Missionary Movement."

TEACHING STRATEGY

This chapter concentrates on changes in American religious culture within the Christian tradition and, to a lesser degree, within Judaism. But some Americans were exposed to Hinduism, Buddhism, and other Asian religions for the first time in this era as well. The World's Parliament of Religions was one place where such introductions occurred. One of the most remarkable speakers at the Parliament was Swami Vivekananda, an English-speaking Bengali educated at Calcutta University and trained in yoga and other South Asian religious traditions. He founded the Vedanta Society in the U.S. and served as a forerunner to later yogis like Swami Yogananda in the 1920s and the Maharishi Mahesh Yogi in the late 1950s. Yoga and Hindu spiritual traditions have become increasingly popular in American culture. A 2016 study by the Yoga Alliance revealed that over 36 million Americans practiced yoga in some form (nearly three-quarters of them women), spending nearly $16 billion per year on classes and products.

Source: Ramakrishna, https://www.ramakrishna .org/chcgfull.htm.

TRM Find complete suggested responses in the Teacher's Resource Materials.

Christianity in the United States and Japan

During the 1893 Chicago World's Columbian Exhibition, a Parliament of Religions brought together representatives of prominent faiths for discussion. English-speaking Protestants dominated the program, but there were several Asian representatives, including Kinzo Hirai, a lay Buddhist from Japan. In his speech, Hirai reviewed Japan's experiences with the United States since Commodore Matthew C. Perry "opened" the country in 1853.

I do not understand why the Christian lands have ignored the rights and advantages of forty million souls of Japan for forty years.... One of the excuses offered by foreign nations is that our country is not yet civilized. Is it the principle of civilized law that the rights and profits of the so-called uncivilized, or the weaker, should be sacrificed? As I understand it, the spirit and necessity of law is to protect the rights and profits of the weaker against the aggression of the stronger....

From the religious source, the claim is made that the Japanese are idolaters and heathen.... [A]dmitting for the sake of argument that we are idolaters and heathen, is it Christian morality to trample upon the rights and advantages of a non-Christian nation, coloring all their natural happiness with the dark stain of injustice?...

You send your missionaries to Japan and they advise us to be moral and believe Christianity. We like to be moral, we know that Christianity is good; and we are very thankful for this kindness. But at the same time our people are rather perplexed.... For when we think that the treaty stipulated in the time of feudalism, when we were yet in our youth, is still clung to by the powerful nations of Christendom; when we find that every year a good many western vessels of seal fishery are smuggled into our seas; when legal cases are always decided by the foreign authorities in Japan unfavorably to us; when some years ago a Japanese was not allowed to enter a university on the Pacific coast of America because of his being of a different race; when a few months ago the school board in San Francisco enacted a regulation that no Japanese should be allowed to enter the public school there; when last year the Japanese were driven out in wholesale from one of the territories of the United States; when our business men in San Francisco were compelled by some union not to employ Japanese assistants and laborers, but the Americans; when there are some in the same city who speak on the platform against those of us who are already here; when there are many who go in procession hoisting lanterns marked "Japs must go"; when the Japanese in the Hawaiian Islands were deprived of their suffrage; when we see some western people in Japan who erect before the entrance to their houses a special post upon which is the notice, "No Japanese is allowed to enter here"—just like a board upon which is written, "No dogs allowed"; when we are in such a situation, notwithstanding the kindness of the western nations from one point of view, who send their missionaries to us, that we unintelligent heathens are embarrassed and hesitate to swallow the sweet and warm liquid of the heaven of Christianity, will not be unreasonable.

SOURCE: *The World's Parliament of Religions*, ed. John Henry Barrows (Chicago: Parliament Publishing Co., 1893), 444–450.

QUESTIONS FOR ANALYSIS

1. What is Hirai's attitude toward American Christians? Describe Hirai's main argument.
2. Of what events is Hirai aware that are taking place in the United States? How does this shape his view of Christian missions in Japan? Describe the evidence Hirai uses to support his point of view.
3. How might American delegates to the Parliament, especially Protestant missionaries, have responded to Hirai? To what extent would American delegates have deemed his arguments effective?

message, angrily denounced all Muslims as "corrupt and immoral." By imposing their views of "heathen races" and attacking those who refused to convert, Christian missionaries sometimes ended up justifying Western imperialism.

American Protective Association (APA)
A powerful anti-immigrant political organization, led by Protestants, which for a brief period in the 1890s counted more than two million members. In its virulent anti-Catholicism and calls for restrictions on immigrants, the APA prefigured the revived Ku Klux Klan of the 1920s.

Cultural imperialism abroad reflected attitudes at home. Starting in Iowa in 1887, militant Protestants created a powerful political organization, the **American Protective Association (APA)**, which for a brief period in the 1890s counted more than two million members. This virulently nativist group expressed outrage at the existence of separate Catholic schools while demanding that all public school teachers be Protestants. The APA called for a ban on public officeholding by Catholics, arguing that they were beholden to an "ecclesiastic power" that was "not created and controlled by American citizens." In its anti-Catholicism and calls for restrictions on immigrants, the APA prefigured the revived Ku Klux Klan of the 1920s (see "Culture Wars" in Chapter 21).

The APA arose, in part, because Protestants found their dominance challenged. Millions of Americans, especially in the industrial working class, were now Catholics or Jews. Overall, in 1916, Protestants still constituted about 60 percent of Americans affiliated with a religious body. But they faced formidable rivals: the number of practicing Catholics in 1916 — 15.7 million — was greater than the number of Baptists, Methodists, and Presbyterians combined.

Some Protestants responded to the urban, immigrant challenge by evangelizing among the unchurched. They provided reading rooms, day nurseries, vocational classes, and other services. The goal of renewing religious faith through dedication to justice and social welfare became known as the **Social Gospel**. Its goals were epitomized by Charles Sheldon's novel *In His Steps* (1896), which told the story of a congregation that resolved to live by Christ's precepts for one year. "If church members were all doing as Jesus would do," Sheldon asked, "could it remain true that armies of men would walk the streets for jobs, and hundreds of them curse the church, and thousands of them find in the saloon their best friend?"

The Salvation Army, which arrived from Great Britain in 1879, also spread a gospel message among the urban poor, offering assistance ranging from soup kitchens to shelters for former prostitutes. When all else failed, down-and-outers knew they could count on the Salvation Army, whose bell ringers became a familiar sight on city streets. The group borrowed up-to-date marketing techniques and used the latest business slang in urging its Christian soldiers to "hustle."

The Salvation Army succeeded, in part, because it managed to bridge an emerging divide between Social Gospel reformers and Protestants who were taking a different theological path. Disturbed by what they saw as rising secularism, conservative ministers and their allies held a series of Bible Conferences at Niagara Falls between 1876 and 1897. The resulting "Niagara Creed" reaffirmed the literal truth of the Bible and the certain damnation of those not born again in Christ. By the 1910s, a network of churches and Bible institutes had emerged from these conferences. They called their movement **fundamentalism**, based on their belief in the fundamental truth of the Bible.

Fundamentalists and their allies made particularly effective use of revival meetings. Unlike Social Gospel advocates, revivalists said little about poverty or earthly justice, focusing not on the matters of the world, but on heavenly redemption. The pioneer modern evangelist was Dwight L. Moody, a former Chicago shoe salesman and YMCA official who won fame in the 1870s. Eternal life could be had for the asking, Moody promised. His listeners needed only "to come forward and take, TAKE!" Moody's successor, Billy Sunday, helped bring evangelism into the modern era. More often than his predecessors, Sunday took political stances based on his Protestant beliefs. His greatest cause was condemning the "booze traffic," but Sunday also denounced unrestricted immigration and labor radicalism. "If I had my way with these ornery wild-eyed Socialists," he once threatened, "I would stand them up before a firing squad." Sunday supported some progressive reform causes; he opposed child labor, for example, and advocated voting rights for women. In other ways, his views anticipated the nativism and antiradicalism that would dominate American politics after World War I.

Realism in the Arts

Inspired by the quest for facts, American authors rejected nineteenth-century romanticism and what they saw as its unfortunate product, sentimentality. Instead, they took up literary **realism**. In the 1880s, editor and novelist William Dean Howells called for writers "to picture the daily life in the most exact terms possible." By the

AP® EXAM TIP

Understanding reactions to immigration by nativists and social reforms is critical to success on the AP® Exam.

Social Gospel
A movement to renew religious faith through dedication to public welfare and social justice, reforming both society and the self through faith-based service. Protestant, Catholic, and Jewish denominations and lay leaders all participated.

fundamentalism
A term adopted by Protestants, between the 1890s and the 1910s, who rejected modernism and historical interpretations of scripture and asserted the literal truth of the Bible. Fundamentalists saw secularism and religious relativism as markers of sin, to be punished by God.

AP® SKILLS & PROCESSES

CAUSATION

How did America's religious life change in this era, and what prompted those changes?

realism
A movement in literature and art, from the 1880s onward, that called for writers and artists to picture daily life as precisely and truly as possible.

Rauschenbusch criticized industrial injustice and defended the rights of workers to strike and form labor unions. You can assign this essay to students as additional reading or use as the basis for a lecture on the relationship between Protestantism and industrial growth. To access this essay, search "Bateman Social Gospel."

TEACHING STRATEGY

Because the term "fundamentalism" is often used in loose, inaccurate, and pejorative terms, it is helpful to provide students with a clearer definition. Grant Wacker, a prominent scholar of fundamentalism, provides a helpful overview of the movement to help guide student understanding. His essay "The Rise of Fundamentalism" distinguishes generic fundamentalism from historic fundamentalism, offers suggestions to guide student discussion, and gives an overview of historiographic debates. Links from later periods in fundamentalist history provide images of artifacts associated with fundamentalism and an oral history of a church revival. To access the essay, search "Wacker Rise of Fundamentalism."

AP® SKILLS & PROCESSES

CAUSATION

The **CAUSATION** question asks students what factors caused changes in American religious life in this era. Students should recognize that religious change is complex, so they should look for combinations of factors, including factors that overlap with religious identity — such as race, class, and gender. Students could also identify elements of continuity within these new developments and explain which factors were most significant in bringing about changes in religious views, and why.

TRM Find complete suggested responses in the Teacher's Resource Materials.

AP® APPLY THE TIP

Using pp. 552–553, direct students to complete **Handout 17.1 — Comparison: Responses to Immigration (TRM)**. Then ask students to work in small groups and evaluate the responses to immigration in the late nineteenth century. Prompt students to think about how the same issues facing immigrants could be applied to African Americans and Native Americans, and contextualize the comparison of nativists and reformers by identifying historical processes, developments, and/or events that influenced both responses to immigration. Extend this activity by leading a class discussion about the degree to which some of the characteristics of responses in the late nineteenth century are similar to issues facing immigration today.

TRM Find **Handout 17.1 — Comparison: Responses to Immigration** in the Teacher's Resource Materials.

AP® THEME

SOC: Social Structures

In his essay "The Social Gospel and the Progressive Era," economist Bradley Bateman places the Social Gospel in the context of late nineteenth-century industrial developments. In response to the rise of Big Business, many evangelicals embraced a laissez faire ideology. In contrast, Social Gospel evangelicals like Washington Gladden and Walter

CHECK FOR UNDERSTANDING

Ask students: **In what ways did American religion become diverse and innovative in this era?** *Catholics created communities based on individual ethnicities and started schools to protect students from Protestant-influenced public schools. Reform Judaism allowed some Jews to adapt to modern circumstances, while other Jews founded Orthodox synagogues in unorthodox settings. Protestant overseas missions expanded, while nativist organizations at home sought to limit the power of Catholicism. Protestant groups like the Salvation Army and Social Gospel movement sought to apply Christian ethics to the problem of poverty.*

AP® APPLY THE TIP

Engage students in a discussion of the artistic movements in the late nineteenth to early twentieth centuries by asking them to complete **Handout 17.2 — Thematic Analysis: Realism and Modernism (TRM)**. Students should add at least two specific pieces of evidence (key term, event, person's name, etc.) related to the arts for each theme. Once students have completed the handout, re-create the diagram on the board and ask students to volunteer to add specific points with each theme. Choose several works of art that are representative of realism and modernism (works from the New York Armory Show work well for this activity), and ask students to explain the way they could use these works as evidence for their thematic analysis.

TRM Find **Handout 17.2 — Thematic Analysis: Realism and Modernism** in the Teacher's Resource Materials.

TEACHING STRATEGY

Examples of some of the art exhibited at the 1913 New York Armory Show, along with essays about this important event, are available through the University of Virginia's American Studies department. To access this resource, search "UVA New York Armory Show."

AP® SKILLS & PROCESSES

CAUSATION

Use the **CAUSATION** question to identify the effects of scientific and technological developments on the arts. Students may need to be reminded that artistic expression, like other cultural phenomena such as religion, rarely develops as a simple, direct reaction to new developments. Once students recognize this caveat, they can look for influences or inspiration prompted by dramatic economic and technological changes.

TRM Find complete suggested responses in the Teacher's Resource Materials.

AP® EXAM TIP

Evaluate the ways in which the arts reflected the social, economic, and political changes in America.

1890s, a younger generation of writers pursued this goal. Theodore Dreiser dismissed unrealistic novels that always had "a happy ending." In *Main-Travelled Roads* (1891), based on the struggles of his midwestern farm family, Hamlin Garland turned the same unsparing eye on the hardships of rural life. Stephen Crane's *Maggie: A Girl of the Streets* (1893), privately printed because no publisher would touch it, described the seduction, abandonment, and death of a slum girl.

Some authors believed realism did not go far enough to overturn sentimentalism. Jack London spent his teenage years as a factory worker, sailor, and tramp. In stories such as "The Law of Life" (1901), he echoed the ideas of Social Darwinism, dramatizing what he saw as the harsh reality of an uncaring universe. American society, he said, was "a jungle wherein wild beasts eat and are eaten." Similarly, Stephen Crane tried to capture "a world full of fists." London and Crane suggested that human beings were not so much rational shapers of their own destinies as blind victims of forces beyond their control — including their own subconscious impulses.

America's most famous writer, Samuel Langhorne Clemens, who took the pen name of Mark Twain, came to an equally bleak view. Though he achieved enormous success with such lighthearted books as *The Adventures of Tom Sawyer* (1876), Clemens courted controversy with *The Adventures of Huckleberry Finn* (1884), notable for its indictment of slavery and racism. In his novel *A Connecticut Yankee in King Arthur's Court* (1889), which ends with a bloody, technology-driven slaughter of Arthur's knights, Mark Twain became one of the bitterest critics of America's idea of progress. An outspoken critic of imperialism and foreign missions, Twain eventually denounced Christianity itself as a hypocritical delusion. Like his friend the industrialist Andrew Carnegie, Clemens "got rid of theology."

modernism
A literary and artistic movement that questioned the ideals of progress and order, rejected realism, and emphasized new cultural forms. Modernism had great cultural influence in the twentieth century and remains influential today.

By the time Clemens died in 1910, American writers and artists had laid the groundwork for **modernism**, which rejected traditional canons of artistic taste. Questioning the whole idea of progress and order, modernists focused on the subconscious and "primitive" mind. Above all, they sought to overturn convention and tradition. Poet Ezra Pound exhorted, "Make it new!" Modernism became the first great literary and artistic movement of the twentieth century.

AP® SKILLS & PROCESSES

CAUSATION
What effect did technology and scientific ideas have on literature and the arts?

In the visual arts, new technologies influenced aesthetics. By 1900, some photographers argued that their "true" representations made painting obsolete. But painters invented their own forms of realism. Nebraska-born artist Robert Henri became fascinated with life in the great cities. "The backs of tenement houses are living documents," he declared, and he set out to put them on canvas. Henri and his followers, notably John Sloan and George Bellows, called themselves the New York Realists. Critics derided them as the Ash Can school because they chose subjects that were not conventionally beautiful.

In 1913, realists participated in one of the most controversial events in American art history, the Armory Show. Housed in an enormous National Guard building in New York, the exhibit introduced America to modern art. Some painters whose work appeared at the show were experimenting with cubism, characterized by abstract, geometric forms. Along with works by Henri, Sloan, and Bellows, organizers featured paintings by European rebels such as Pablo Picasso. America's academic art world was shocked. One critic called cubism "the total destruction of the art of painting." But as the exhibition went on to Boston and Chicago, more than 250,000 people crowded to see it.

A striking feature of both realism and modernism, as they developed, was that many leading writers and artists were men. In making their work strong and modern, they also strove to assert their masculinity. Paralleling Theodore Roosevelt's call for "manly sports," they denounced nineteenth-century culture as hopelessly feminized. Stephen Crane called for "virility" in literature. Jack London described himself as a "man's man, . . . lustfully roving and conquering." Artist Robert Henri banned small brushes as "too feminine." In their own ways, these writers and artists contributed to a broad movement to masculinize American culture.

CHECK FOR UNDERSTANDING

Ask students: **How did Charles Darwin's theory of evolution and other scientific ideas impact American culture and intellectual life in the late nineteenth century? What uses did nonscientists make of such ideas?** *Charles Darwin's theory of natural selection and other scientific ideas had a significant influence on American culture in the late nineteenth century in three specific areas: sociology, eugenics, and art. Sociologists employed it to explain why some people became rich and others poor, under the so-called ideal of Social Darwinism, which held that those who were wealthy were naturally selected to be so. Advocates of eugenics, the so-called science of human breeding, used its principles to label the mentally infirm and those who did not adhere to some arbitrary standard as unworthy of social status and often political rights. Artists, meanwhile, embraced realism and modernism, artistic movements that sought to explain the world as it existed, eschewing sentimentalism and romanticism, in line with the hard realities of science.*

Arthur B. Davies, *Dancers*, 1914–1915 Artist Arthur Davies (1862–1928) was one of the primary organizers of New York's 1913 Armory Show, which introduced Americans to modernist art. An associate of John Sloan and other New York realists, Davies experimented with an array of painting styles, as well as printmaking and tapestry making. This painting dates from a three-year period, just after the Armory Show, in which Davies experimented with Cubist techniques. Detroit Institute of Arts, USA/Gift of Ralph Harman Booth/Bridgeman Images.

COMMERCE AND CULTURE

How did industrialization change the way Americans spent their leisure time, and how did this reflect evolving social identities and divisions?

As the United States industrialized and as divisions grew between rural and urban life and between the affluent and poor, the terms *middle class* and *working class* came widely into use. Americans adopted these broad identities not only in the workplace but also in their leisure time. In working-class families, wives and mothers generally took in boarders or worked for wages, as did older children, so they could contribute to the family income. In middle-class families that had access to well-paid employment for the husband and father, wives and mothers devoted themselves to domestic duties rather than to paid work, as couples sought to provide education and upward mobility for their children. At the top of the economic ladder, prosperous corporate managers and their families enjoyed rising incomes and an array of tempting ways to spend their dollars. They also generally hired household servants.

The changing technology of American homes reflected differences in class status. The rise of electricity, in particular, marked the gap between affluent urban consumers and rural and working-class families. In elite houses, domestic servants began to use — or find themselves replaced by — an array of new devices, from washing machines to vacuum cleaners. When Alexander Graham Bell invented the telephone in 1876, entrepreneurs introduced the device for business use, but it soon found eager residential customers, especially among the affluent (Figure 17.1). Telephones

AP® EXAM TIP

Analyze the differentiation of the middle class from the working class in American culture.

AP® APPLY THE TIP

Begin the discussion of the use of the terms "middle class" and "working class" in the late nineteenth century by asking students to define "middle class." Write the term on the board and in brainstorming fashion, list all the characteristics students provide to define middle class. Once students have shared all their ideas, ask them to differentiate the upper class and the working class from the descriptors listed on the board. Ask students to work in pairs to come up with a definition of the term "middle class" and "working class" that clearly distinguishes the two terms. Ask student pairs to use the text (pp. 555–558) to find evidence to support their definitions of the terms. Ask student pairs to answer the following questions:

- **Do the nineteenth century definitions of "middle class" and "working class" apply in the twenty-first century?** *Answers will vary, but should touch upon the following: distinctions are still evident in jobs, clothing, housing, etc.; less distinction because of access to consumer goods and technology, mass media, etc.*
- **What efforts were made to distinguish the middle and working class?** *Vagrancy laws were used to keep the working class from entering consumer districts for the middle class. Access to technology distinguished class.*
- **How did the definition of class relate to the rise of consumer culture in the late nineteenth century?** *The middle class could distinguish itself from the working class by owning telephones, shopping with credit in department stores, and access to amusements, including the circus, and first class rail cars.*

AP® THEME

WXT: Work, Exchange, and Technology

Use **FIGURE 17.1** to discuss how new technologies and manufacturing techniques focused the economy on, among other things, better communications systems. Though standards of living rose overall during this period, growth was not even. The expansion of residential telephones suggests variation in access to this new communication technology based on the affluence of a particular neighborhood. The questions in the caption provide useful suggestions for discussion of this subject.

TEACHING STRATEGY

The Library of Congress's "Inventing Entertainment: The Early Motion Pictures and Sound Recordings of the Edison Companies" Web site page provides essays, a collection of images, and early sound recordings and films produced by Thomas Edison and his company. To access this site, search "Library of Congress Inventing Entertainment."

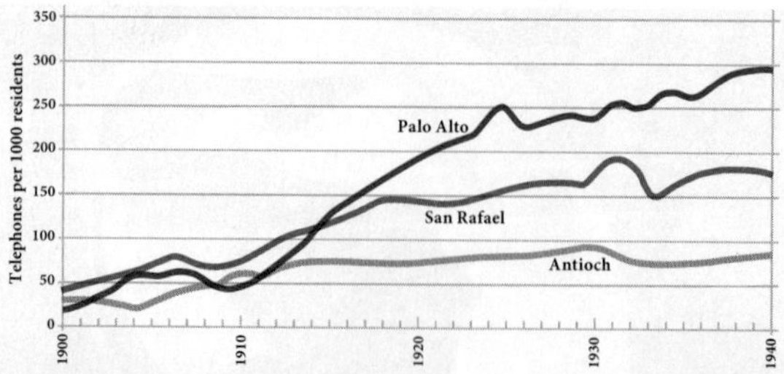

FIGURE 17.1 Estimated Number of Residential Telephones in Three California Locations, 1900–1940

This graph tracks the adoption of telephones in three California locations. Palo Alto was an affluent university town; Antioch was a working-class city; and San Rafael had a mixed economy, including some manufacturing, but served increasingly as a bedroom community for San Francisco professionals. What does the chart suggest about telephone usage? Consider, from the narrative, the changes that were occurring in family size, especially among the middle class, and note that expensive rent often led to overcrowding in working-class homes and apartments. Based on per-capita telephone adoption rates, how likely do you think it was that a person in Palo Alto had access to a private phone? A person in Antioch? Figure based on Claude S. Fischer, *A Social History of the Telephone to 1940*, copyright © 1992 by the Regents of the University of California. (Los Angeles: University of California Press, 1992). Figure 9. Reprinted by permission of the University of California Press.

changed etiquette and social relations for middle-class suburban women — while providing their working-class counterparts with new employment as operators or "hello girls."

Celebrating the new technological wonders around them, Americans hailed inventors as heroes. The most famous, Thomas Edison, operated an independent laboratory rather than working for a corporation. Edison, like many of the era's businessmen, was a shrewd entrepreneur who focused on commercial success. He and his colleagues helped introduce such lucrative products as the incandescent light bulb and the phonograph.

Even working-class Americans enjoyed cheaper products delivered by global trade and mass production, from bananas and cigarettes to colorful dime novels and magazines. Thomas Edison's moving pictures, for example, first found popularity among the urban working class. Consumer culture appeared to be democratic: anyone could eat at a restaurant or buy a rail ticket for the "ladies' car" — as long as she or he could pay. In practice, well-to-do Americans enjoyed new amenities at much higher rates. Consumer culture thus became a site of struggle over class inequality, race privilege, and proper male and female behavior.

Consumer Spaces

America's public spaces, from election polls to saloons and circus shows, had long been boisterous and male-centered. A woman who ventured there without a male chaperone risked damaging her reputation (or worse). But the rise of new businesses encouraged change. To cater to a willing public, purveyors of consumer culture invited women and families, especially those of the middle class, to linger in department stores and enjoy new amusements.

No one promoted commercial domesticity more successfully than showman P. T. Barnum, who used the country's expanding rail network to develop his famous traveling circus. Barnum condemned earlier circus managers who had opened their tents to "the rowdy element." Proclaiming children as his key audience, he created family entertainment for diverse audiences (though in the South, black audiences sat in segregated seats or attended separate shows). He promised middle-class parents that his circus would teach children courage and promote the benefits of exercise. To encourage women's attendance, Barnum emphasized the respectability and refinement of his female performers.

Department stores also lured middle-class women by offering tearooms, children's play areas, umbrellas, and clerks to wrap and carry every purchase. Store credit plans enabled well-to-do women to shop without handling money in public. Such tactics succeeded so well that New York's department store district became known as Ladies' Mile. Boston department store magnate William Filene called the department store an "Adamless Eden."

These Edens were reserved for elite and middle classes. Though bargain basements and neighborhood stores served working-class families, big department stores used vagrancy laws and police to discourage the "wrong kind" from entering. Working-class women gained access primarily as clerks, cashiers, and cash girls, who as young as age twelve began work as internal store messengers, carrying orders and change for $1.50 a week. The department store was no Eden for these women, who worked long hours on their feet, often dealing with difficult customers. Nevertheless, some clerks made enthusiastic use of employee discounts and battled employers for the right to wear their fashionable purchases while they worked in the store.

Finding prosperous Americans eager for excursions, railroad companies, like department stores, made things comfortable for middle-class women and children. Boston's South Station boasted of its modern amenities, including "everything that the traveler needs down to cradles in which the baby may be soothed." Rail cars manufactured by the famous Pullman Company of Chicago set a national standard for taste and elegance. Part of their appeal was the chance for people of modest means to emulate the rich. One experienced train conductor observed that the wives of grocers, not millionaires, were the ones most likely to "sweep . . . into a parlor car as if the very carpet ought to feel highly honored by their tread."

First-class "ladies' cars" soon became sites of struggle for racial equality. For three decades after the end of the Civil War, state laws and railroad policies on serving customers varied, and even where segregation was the rule, African Americans often succeeded in securing seats. One reformer noted, however, "There are few ordeals more nerve-wracking than the one which confronts a colored woman when she tries to secure a Pullman reservation in the South and even in some parts of the North." When they claimed first-class seats, black women often faced confrontations with conductors, resulting in numerous lawsuits in the 1870s and 1880s. Riding the Chesapeake & Ohio line in 1884, young African American journalist Ida B. Wells was told to leave. "I refused," she wrote later, "saying that the [nearest alternative] car was a smoker, and as I was in the ladies' car, I proposed to stay." Wells resisted, but the conductor and a baggage handler threw her bodily off the train. Returning home to Memphis, Wells sued and won in local courts, but Tennessee's supreme court reversed the ruling.

In 1896, the U.S. Supreme Court settled such issues decisively — but not justly. The

AP® SKILLS & PROCESSES

MAKING CONNECTIONS

How did new consumer practices arising from industrialization reshape Americans' gender, class, and race relationships?

Department Store, Detroit, Michigan, c. 1910 Department stores advertised "everything under one roof": middle-class urban women could shop for clothes, furniture, food, home goods, and other items all in one location. Successful department stores offered lounges, restaurants, postal services, and holiday concerts and events. This shopper enjoys personalized service from several clerks. A cradle stands by for any mother whose youngster needs a nap. Glasshouse Images/Alamy Stock Photo.

AP® SKILLS & PROCESSES

MAKING CONNECTIONS

The **MAKING CONNECTIONS** question asks students to identify the effects of consumerism on different social patterns. To extend this prompt, students might also consider which of these three — race, class, and gender — was most dramatically reshaped in this era and why.

TRM Find complete suggested responses in the Teacher's Resource Materials.

AP® THEME

WXT: Work, Exchange, and Technology

New technologies and manufacturing techniques focused the economy on the production of consumer goods. The venue that best showcased those consumer goods was the department store. Students can compare department stores to modern stores such as Walmart to explain whether they are more alike or more different, and why they think so.

AP® THEME

NAT: American and National Identity

In the *Plessy v. Ferguson* decision, the Supreme Court upheld racial segregation, helping to mark the end of most of the political gains African Americans made during Reconstruction. Justice John Harlan, the lone dissenter, protested the Court's decision. He denounced the Court's pretense that by providing "separate but equal" accommodations, it was protecting the civil rights of all. Today, the *Plessy* decision is considered one of the Court's most egregious miscarriages of justice. An excerpt of Harlan's dissent is available online. To access this document, search "Sage Justice Harlan's Dissent."

AP® APPLY THE TIP

Engage students in primary source analysis of the Supreme Court decision in *Plessy v. Ferguson*. Explain the background of the case by discussing the decision by Homer Plessy to violate the law requiring separate train cars for races in order to test the application of the Fourteenth Amendment to Jim Crow laws. Help students to clearly define the constitutional issue in the *Plessy* case. Provide students with excerpts from both the majority opinion by Justice Henry Brown and the dissenting opinion by Justice John Harlan. Ask students to read and analyze each opinion in the case. Ask students to use their analysis to clearly define the historical argument made by Justice Brown and Justice Harlan in the *Plessy* case. After discussing their analysis of the case and the decisions, ask students to develop a thesis statement and outline to illustrate to what degree the decision in *Plessy v. Ferguson* was a transformative moment in American history.

CHECK FOR UNDERSTANDING

Ask students: **What was the nature of consumer spaces in the late nineteenth century?** *Circuses became friendlier to women and children in an effort to attract larger audiences, department stores lured middle-class women while preventing lower-class people from entering, and homes became magnets for new technology. Many public spaces, from rail cars to schools to parks, became segregated in this era through Jim Crow laws.*

AP® APPLY THE TIP

Ask students to identify two historical continuities that occurred as a result of the *Plessy v. Ferguson* case. Give students a periodization such as 1874–1896, which will help them draw on their knowledge from Reconstruction and how the Supreme Court's decision represented both a change and continuity in national policy toward African Americans.

Plessy v. Ferguson
An 1896 Supreme Court case that ruled that racially segregated railroad cars and other public facilities, if they claimed to be "separate but equal," were permissible according to the Fourteenth Amendment.

Jim Crow
Laws that required separation of the races, especially blacks and whites, in public facilities. The post–Civil War decades witnessed many such laws, especially in southern states, and several decades of legal challenges to them. The Supreme Court upheld them in *Plessy v. Ferguson* (1896), giving national approval to a system of racial segregation in the South that lasted until the 1960s.

AP® EXAM TIP
Understanding the role of *Plessy v. Ferguson* in American History is important to know on the AP® Exam.

Plessy v. Ferguson case was brought by civil rights advocates on behalf of Homer Plessy, a New Orleans resident who was one-eighth black. Ordered to leave a first-class car and move to the "colored" car of a Louisiana train, Plessy refused and was arrested. The Court ruled that such segregation did not violate the Fourteenth Amendment as long as blacks had access to accommodations that were "separate but equal" to those of whites. "Separate but equal" was a myth: segregated facilities in the South were flagrantly inferior. Since Reconstruction, most southern states had tried to implement **Jim Crow** segregation laws, named for a stereotyped black character who appeared in minstrel shows. Though such laws clearly discriminated, the Court allowed them to stand.

Jim Crow laws applied to public schools and parks and also to emerging commercial spaces — hotels, restaurants, streetcars, trains, and eventually sports stadiums and movie theaters. Placing a national stamp of approval on segregation, the *Plessy* decision remained in place until 1954, when the Court's *Brown v. Topeka Board of Education* ruling finally struck it down. Until then, blacks' exclusion from first-class "public accommodations" was one of the most painful marks of racism. The *Plessy* decision, like the rock-bottom wages earned by twelve-year-old girls at Macy's, showed that consumer culture could be modern and innovative and at the same time hierarchical and unfair. Business and consumer culture were shaped by, and themselves shaped, racial and class injustices.

Masculinity and the Rise of Sports

Traditionally, the mark of a successful American man was economic independence: he was his own boss. In the era of industrialization, however, tens of thousands worked for other men in offices, rather than using their muscles. Would the professional American male, through his concentration on "brain work," become "weak, effeminate, [and] decaying," as one editor warned? How could well-to-do men assert their independence if work no longer required them to prove themselves physically? How could they develop toughness and strength? One answer was athletics.

Young Men's Christian Association (YMCA)
Introduced in Boston in 1851, the YMCA promoted a new model of middle-class masculinity, muscular Christianity, which combined Protestant evangelism with athletic facilities where men could make themselves "clean and strong."

"Muscular Christianity" The **Young Men's Christian Association (YMCA)** was one of the earliest and most successful promoters of athletic fitness. Introduced in Boston in 1851, the group promoted muscular Christianity, combining evangelism with gyms and athletic facilities where men could make themselves "clean and strong." Focusing first on white-collar audiences, the YMCA developed a substantial program for industrial workers after 1900. Railroad managers and other corporate titans hoped YMCAs would foster a loyal and contented workforce, discouraging labor unrest. Business leaders also relied on sports to build physical and mental discipline and help men adjust their bodies to the demands of the industrial clock. Sports honed men's competitive spirit, they believed; employer-sponsored teams instilled teamwork and company pride.

Working-class men had their own ideas about sports and leisure, and YMCAs quickly became a site of negotiation. Could workers come to the "Y" to play billiards or cards? Could they smoke? At first, YMCA leaders said no, but to attract working-class men they had to make concessions. As a result, the "Y" became a place where middle-class and working-class customs blended — or existed in uneasy tension. At the same time, YMCA leaders innovated. Searching for winter activities in the 1890s, YMCA instructors invented the new indoor games of basketball and volleyball.

AP® EXAM TIP
Evaluate changes in leisure activities that helped to define American culture.

For elite Americans, country clubs began to offer both men and women a place to enjoy tennis, golf, and swimming. By the turn of the century — perhaps because country club women were encroaching on their athletic turf — elite men took up even more aggressive physical sports, including boxing, weightlifting, and martial arts. In 1890, future president Theodore Roosevelt argued that such "virile" activities were essential to "maintain and defend this very civilization." "Most masterful nations," he claimed, "have shown a strong taste for manly sports." Roosevelt, son of a wealthy New York family, became one of the first American devotees of jujitsu. During his presidency (1901–1909), he designated a judo room in the White House and hired an expert Japanese instructor. Roosevelt also wrestled and boxed, urging other American men — especially among the elite — to increase their leadership fitness by pursuing the "strenuous life."

Baseball Before the 1860s, the only distinctively American game was Native American lacrosse, and the most popular team sport among European Americans was cricket. After the Civil War, however, team sports became a fundamental part of American manhood, none more successfully than baseball. Deriving from cricket, the game's formal rules had begun to develop in New York in the 1840s and 1850s; its popularity spread in military camps during the Civil War. Afterward, the idea that baseball "received its baptism in the bloody days of our Nation's direst danger," as one promoter put it, became part of the game's mythology.

Frank Merriwell's Chums *Tip Top Weekly*, one of many magazines and dime novels for young readers, celebrated sports and adventure. This 1902 cover story by Burt L. Standish (a pseudonymn for Gilbert Patten) featured the hero Frank Merriwell, a talented player of football, basketball, baseball, and track who eventually became a star student and athlete at Yale. Merriwell also solved crimes and mysteries while embodying clean living and honorable behavior. His exploits eventually became the basis for a comic strip, radio shows, and films. Picture Research Consultants & Archives.

TEACHING STRATEGY

The first two episodes of the Ken Burns's film *Baseball* provide information about the invention and development of baseball from the antebellum period through the 1910s. The PBS companion site to the film provides a timeline, a few lesson plans, and links to online resources that provide more information on topics like the Negro Leagues, the minor leagues, and suggestions for additional reading. To access this site, search "PBS Baseball Education."

Until the 1870s, most amateur players were clerks and white-collar workers who had leisure time to play and income to buy their own uniforms. Businessmen frowned on baseball and other sports as a waste of time, especially for working-class men. But late-nineteenth-century employers came to see baseball, like other athletic pursuits, as a benefit for workers. It provided fresh air and exercise, kept men out of saloons, and promoted discipline and teamwork. Players on company-sponsored teams, wearing uniforms emblazoned with their employers' names, began to compete on paid work time. Baseball thus set a pattern for how other American sports developed. Begun among independent craftsmen, it was taken up by elite men anxious to prove their strength and fitness. Well-to-do Americans then decided the sport could benefit the working class.

Big-time professional baseball arose with the launching of the National League in 1876. The league quickly built more than a dozen teams in large cities, from the Brooklyn Trolley Dodgers to the Cleveland Spiders. Team owners were, in their own right, profit-minded entrepreneurs who shaped the sport to please consumers. Wooden grandstands soon gave way to concrete and steel stadiums. By 1900, boys traded lithographed cards of their favorite players and the baseball cap came into fashion. In 1903, the Boston Americans defeated the Pittsburgh Pirates in the first World Series. American men could now adopt a new consumer identity — not as athletes, but as fans.

Rise of the Negro Leagues Baseball stadiums, like first-class rail cars, were sites of racial negotiation and conflict. In the 1880s and 1890s, major league managers hired a few African American players. As late as 1901, the Baltimore Orioles succeeded in signing Charlie Grant, a light-skinned black player from Cincinnati, by renaming him Charlie Tokohoma and claiming he was Cherokee. But as this subterfuge suggested, black players were increasingly barred. A Toledo team received a threatening note before one game in Richmond, Virginia: if their "negro catcher" played, he would be lynched. Toledo put a substitute on the field, and at the end of the season the club terminated the black player's contract.

Shut out of white leagues, players and fans turned to all-black professional teams, where black men could showcase athletic ability and race pride. Louisiana's top team, the New Orleans Pinchbacks, pointedly named themselves after the state's African American Reconstruction governor. By the early 1900s, such teams organized into separate **Negro leagues**. Though players suffered from erratic pay and rundown ball fields, the leagues thrived until the desegregation of baseball after World War II. In an era of stark discrimination, they celebrated black manhood and talent. "I liked the way their uniform fit, the way they wore their cap," wrote an admiring fan of the Newark Eagles. "They showed a style in almost everything they did."

Negro leagues
Professional baseball teams formed for and by black players after the 1890s, when the regular national leagues excluded African American players. Enduring until after World War II, the leagues enabled black men to showcase athletic ability and race pride, but working conditions and wages were poor.

American Football The most controversial sport of the industrializing era was football, which began at elite colleges during the 1880s. The great powerhouse was the Yale team, whose legendary coach Walter Camp went on to become a watch manufacturer. Between 1883 and 1891, under Camp's direction, Yale scored 4,660 points; its opponents scored 92. Drawing on the workplace model of scientific management, Camp emphasized drill and precision. He and other coaches argued that football offered perfect training for the competitive world of business. The game was violent: six players' deaths in the 1908 college season provoked a public outcry. Eventually, new rules protected quarterbacks and required coaches to remove injured players from the game. But such measures were adopted grudgingly, with supporters arguing that they ruined football's benefits in manly training.

Like baseball and the YMCA, football attracted sponsorship from business leaders hoping to divert workers from labor activism. The first professional teams emerged in western Pennsylvania's steel towns, soon after the defeat of the steelworkers' union. Carnegie Steel executives organized teams in Homestead and Braddock; the first league appeared during the anthracite coal strike of 1902. Other teams arose in the

Football Practice, Chilocco Indian School, 1911 Football became widely popular, spreading from Ivy League schools and state universities to schools like this one, built on Cherokee land in Oklahoma. The uniforms of this team, typical of the day, show very limited padding and protection—a factor that contributed to high rates of injury and even death on the field. As they practiced in 1911, these Chilocco students had an inspiring model to look up to: in that year Jim Thorpe, a fellow Oklahoman and a member of the Sac and Fox tribe, was winning national fame by leading the all-Indian team at Pennsylvania's Carlisle School to victory against Harvard. Thorpe, one of the finest athletes of his generation, went on to win gold medals in the pentathlon and decathlon at the 1912 Olympics in Stockholm, Sweden. National Archives, ARC Identifier 251741.

midwestern industrial heartland. The Indian-Acme Packing Company sponsored the Green Bay Packers; the future Chicago Bears, first known as the Decatur Staleys, were funded by a manufacturer of laundry starch. Like its baseball equivalent, professional football encouraged men to buy in as spectators and fans.

AP SKILLS & PROCESSES

DEVELOPMENTS AND PROCESSES

How and why did American sports evolve, and how did athletics soften or sharpen social divisions?

The Great Outdoors

As the rise of sports suggests, by the 1890s elite and middle-class Americans began to see Victorian culture as stuffy and claustrophobic. They rebelled by heading outdoors. A craze for bicycling swept the country; in 1890, at peak, U.S. manufacturers sold an astonishing ten million bikes. Women joined men in taking up athletics. By the 1890s, even elite women, long confined to corsets and heavy clothes that restricted their movement, donned lighter dresses and pursued archery and golf. Artist Charles Gibson became famous for his portraits of the Gibson Girl, an elite beauty depicted on the tennis court or swimming at the beach. The Gibson Girl personified the ideal of the "New Woman": more educated, athletic, and independent.

Those with money and leisure used railroad networks to get to the national parks of the West, which, as one senator put it, became a "breathing-place for the national lungs." People of more modest means began to take up camping. As early as 1904, California's Coronado Beach offered tent rentals for $3 a week. A decade later,

TEACHING STRATEGY

Students could compare the different goals and structure of football and baseball as varying expressions of nineteenth-century American values by exploring how they are similar and different as products of the industrial era.

CHECK FOR UNDERSTANDING

Ask students: **What ideas were associated with masculinity, and how were they connected to the rise of sports?** *Physical and mental discipline became signs of well-being and, in some cases, of Christian virtue. Baseball grew into a professional pastime that allowed elite men to prove their strength and fitness, and other sports like football followed.*

AP SKILLS & PROCESSES

DEVELOPMENTS AND PROCESSES

The **DEVELOPMENTS AND PROCESSES** question asks students to trace changes in the nature of American sport and to characterize those changes as increasing social divisions or reducing them, or both.

TRM Find complete suggested responses in the Teacher's Resource Materials.

Hikers in the Cascades, 1906 Americans in this era responded to the appeal of the outdoors. Spending time in nature offered a respite to work lives that were increasingly spent in offices and indoor spaces. Women, in particular, shed Victorian restraints and joined groups like this one, hiking past a spectacular waterfall to Paradise Valley in the Cascade range of Washington state. Enthusiasm for outdoor life led many Americans to advocate for environmental preservation. Library of Congress 09641.

AP® SKILLS & PROCESSES

MAKING CONNECTIONS

Though the National Park and Forest movement began in the late nineteenth century, students will notice how many parks and forests were designated in the early to mid-twentieth century. Ask students to connect one of the following to the creation and use of National Parks and Forests: leisure time, middle class, consumer culture. (Each of these terms are found in the Course Framework.)

campgrounds and cottages in many parts of the country catered to a working-class clientele. In an industrial society, the outdoors became associated with leisure and renewal rather than danger and hard work. One journalist, reflecting on urban life from the vantage point of a western vacation, wrote, "How stupid it all seems: the mad eagerness of money-making men, the sham pleasures of conventional society." In the wilderness, he wrote, "your blood clarifies; your brain becomes active. You get a new view of life."

As Americans searched for such renewal in remnants of unexploited land, the nation's first environmental movement arose. John Muir, who fell in love with the Yosemite Valley in 1869, became the most famous voice for wilderness. Raised in a stern Scots Presbyterian family on a Wisconsin farm, Muir knew much of the Bible by heart. He was a keen observer who developed a deeply spiritual relationship with the natural world. His contemporary Mary Austin, whose book *Land of Little Rain* (1905) celebrated the austere beauty of the California desert, called him "a devout man." In cooperation with his editor at *Century* magazine, Muir founded the **Sierra Club** in 1892. Like the earlier Appalachian Mountain Club, founded in Boston in 1876, the Sierra Club dedicated itself to preserving and enjoying America's great mountains.

Sierra Club
An organization founded in 1892 that was dedicated to the enjoyment and preservation of America's great mountains (including the Sierra Nevadas) and wilderness environments. Encouraged by such groups, national and state governments began to set aside more public lands for preservation and recreation.

Encouraged by such groups, national and state governments set aside more public lands for preservation and recreation. The United States substantially expanded its park system and, during Theodore Roosevelt's presidency, extended the reach of

MAP 17.1 National Parks and Forests, 1872–1980
Yellowstone, the first national park in the United States, dates from 1872. In 1893, the federal government began to intervene to protect national forests. Without Theodore Roosevelt, however, the national forest program might have languished; during his presidency, he added 125 million acres to the forest system, plus six national parks in addition to several that had already been created during the 1890s. America's national forest and park systems remain one of the most visible and beloved legacies of federal policy innovation in the decades between the Civil War and World War I.

national forests. Starting in 1872 with the preservation of Yellowstone in Wyoming, Congress had begun to set aside land for national parks. In 1916, President Woodrow Wilson provided comprehensive oversight of these national parks, signing an act creating the **National Park Service** (Map 17.1). A year later, the system numbered thirteen parks — including Maine's Acadia, the first east of the Mississippi River.

Environmentalists also worked to protect wildlife. By the 1890s, several state Audubon Societies, named in honor of antebellum naturalist John James Audubon, banded together to advocate broader protections for wild birds, especially herons and egrets, which were being slaughtered by the thousands for their plumes. They succeeded in winning the Lacey Act (1900), which established federal penalties for selling specified birds, animals, and plants. Soon afterward, state organizations joined together to form the National Audubon Society. Women played prominent roles in the movement, promoting boycotts of hats with plumage. In 1903, President Theodore Roosevelt created the first National Wildlife Refuge at Pelican Island, Florida.

Roosevelt also expanded preservation under the **Antiquities Act** (1906), which enabled the U.S. president, without congressional approval, to set aside "objects of historic and scientific interest" as national monuments. Two years later, Roosevelt used these powers to preserve 800,000 acres at Arizona's magnificent Grand Canyon. The act proved a mixed blessing for conservation. Monuments received weaker protection than national parks did; many fell under the authority of the U.S. Forest Service, which permitted logging and grazing. Business interests thus lobbied to have coveted lands designated as monuments rather than national parks so they could more easily exploit resources. Nonetheless, the creation of national monuments offered some protection, and many monuments (such as Alaska's Katmai) later obtained park status.

National Park Service
A federal agency founded in 1916 that provided comprehensive oversight of the growing system of national parks, established to allow Americans to access and enjoy sites of natural beauty.

Antiquities Act
A 1906 act that allowed the U.S. president to use executive powers to set aside, as federal monuments, sites of great environmental or cultural significance. Theodore Roosevelt, the first president to invoke the act's powers, used them to preserve the Grand Canyon.

TEACHING STRATEGY

The Library of Congress's "Progressive Era to New Era, 1900–1929: Conservation in the Progressive Era" Web site page gives students a deeper understanding of the efforts by Theodore Roosevelt and other reformers to conserve American wildernesses through an essay and a variety of primary sources. To access this site, search "Library of Congress Conservation in the Progressive Era."

AP® SKILLS & PROCESSES

MAKING CONNECTIONS

Use the **MAKING CONNECTIONS** question to help students identify the factors that led to the movement to create national parks. Many students who take the parks' existence for granted need to recognize the contingent nature of this development — it was not inevitable, and the U.S. might have gone in an entirely different direction. To extend this prompt, have students consider how the U.S. would be different today without the creation of a national park system.

TRM Find complete suggested responses in the Teacher's Resource Materials.

CHECK FOR UNDERSTANDING

Ask students: **How did industrialization change Americans' ideas about appropriate leisure activities for men and women of various social classes?** *Industrialization and the rise of big business undermined the workingman's sense of masculinity as he now did not use his body as much in the means of production nor was he economically independent. Encouraged by industrialists who sought to undermine their workers' potentiality for labor unrest, he sought to express himself in the great outdoors either in team sports such as baseball or American football, or in more solitary activities at the local YMCA. Upper-class men and women also sought sport as an outlet, especially at country clubs, though the sports were different and included tennis, golf, and swimming. Elite men later took up boxing, weightlifting, and martial arts as well.*

AP® APPLY THE TIP

Topics 6.10 and 6.11 in the AP® Course Framework detail some of the changes to the American family that are requisite student knowledge. Ask students to identify how the changes to the American family reflect broader historical patterns of the late nineteenth, early twentieth century. If students are struggling to make these connections, consider providing a bank of ideas such as: Urbanization, Technological Innovation, Industrialization, Education, and Social Gospel.

The expanding network of parks and monuments became popular places to hike, camp, and contemplate natural beauty.

Like other leisure venues, "wilderness" did not remain in the hands of elite men and women. As early as the late 1880s, the lakes and hiking trails of the Catskill Mountains became so thronged with working-class tourists from nearby New York City, including many Jewish immigrants, that elite visitors began to segregate themselves into gated summer communities. They thus preserved the "seclusion and privacy" they claimed as the privilege of those who could demonstrate "mental and personal worth."

At the state level, meanwhile, new game laws triggered conflicts between elite conservationists and the poor. Shifting from year-round hunting to a limited, recreational hunting season brought hardship to poor rural families who depended on game for food. Regulation brought undeniable benefits: it suppressed such popular practices as songbird hunting and the use of dynamite to kill fish. Looking back on the era before game laws, one Alabama hunter remembered that "the slaughter was terrific." But while game laws prevented further extinctions like that of the passenger pigeon, which vanished around 1900, they made it harder for rural people to support themselves through subsistence hunting and fishing.

AP® SKILLS & PROCESSES
MAKING CONNECTIONS
What changes in American society precipitated the rise of national parks and monuments?

WOMEN, MEN, AND THE SOLITUDE OF SELF

Why and how did women's public activism arise in the late nineteenth century and how did this impact American politics and society?

Speaking to Congress in 1892, women's rights advocate Elizabeth Cady Stanton described what she called the "solitude of self." Stanton rejected the claim that women did not need equal rights because they enjoyed men's protection. "The talk of sheltering woman from the fierce storms of life is the sheerest mockery," she declared. "They beat on her from every point of the compass, just as they do on man, and with more fatal results, for he has been trained to protect himself."

Stanton's argument captured one of the dilemmas of industrialization: the marketplace of labor brought both freedom and risk, and working-class women were particularly vulnerable. At the same time, middle-class women — expected to engage in selfless community service — often saw the impact of industrialization more clearly than fathers, brothers, and husbands did. In seeking to address alcoholism, poverty, and other social and economic ills, they gained a new sense of their own collective power. Women's civic engagement and reform work thus helped lay the foundations for progressivism (Chapter 19) and modern women's rights.

Changing Families

AP® EXAM TIP
Understanding the changes in family life in the late nineteenth century is critical for the AP® Exam.

The average American family, especially in the middle class, decreased in size during the industrial era. In 1800, white women who survived to menopause had borne an average of 7.0 children; by 1900, the average was 3.6. On farms and in many working-class families, youngsters counted as assets on the family balance sheet: they worked in fields or factories. But parents who had fewer sons and daughters could concentrate their resources, educating and preparing each child for success in the new economy. Among the professional classes, education became a necessity, while limiting family size became, more broadly, a key to upward mobility.

Several factors limited childbearing. Americans married at older ages, and many mothers tried to space pregnancies more widely — as their mothers and grandmothers had — by nursing children for several years, which suppressed fertility. By the late nineteenth century, as vulcanized rubber became available, couples also had access to a range of other contraceptive methods, such as condoms and diaphragms. With pressure for family limitation rising, these methods were widely used and apparently effective, though couples rarely wrote about them. Historians' evidence comes from the occasional frank diary and from the immense success of the mail-order contraceptive industry, which advertised prominently and shipped products — wrapped in discreet brown paper packages — to customers nationwide.

Reluctance to talk about contraceptives was understandable, since information about them was stigmatized and, after 1873, illegal to distribute. During Reconstruction, Anthony Comstock, crusading secretary of the New York Society for the Suppression of Vice, secured a federal law banning "obscene materials" from the U.S. mail. The **Comstock Act** (1873) prohibited circulation of almost any information about sex and birth control — even in private letters. Comstock won support for the law, in part, by appealing to parents' fears that young people were receiving sexual information through the mail, promoting the rise of "secret vice." Though critics charged Comstock with high-handed interference in private matters, many Americans supported his work, fearful of the rising tide of pornography, sexual information, and contraceptives made available by industrialization. A committee of the New York legislature declared Comstock's crusade "wholly essential to the safety and decency of the community." It appears, however, that Comstock had little success in stopping the lucrative and popular underground trade in contraceptives.

Portrait of a Middle-Class American Family This photograph of the Hedlund family was taken on July 4, 1911, on the front porch of their home in St. Paul, Minnesota. Christian, Grace, and Anna Hedlund appear on the top row, Louis and George on the bottom. Families like this one — with three children — were becoming typical among the middle class, in contrast to larger families in earlier generations. This photo was taken by twenty-one-year-old Joseph Pavlicek, a recent immigrant from Eastern Europe who was boarding with the Hedlunds. Pavlicek bought fireworks for the children to celebrate the holiday. He remembered being so proud and grateful to be in America that his heart "was nearly bursting." Minnesota Historical Society/Getty Images.

Expanding Opportunities for Education

In the industrial economy, the watchword for young people who hoped to secure good jobs was *education*. A high school diploma — now a gateway to a college degree — was valuable for boys who hoped to enter professional or managerial work. Daughters attended in even larger numbers than their brothers. Parents of the Civil War generation, who had witnessed the plight of war widows and orphans, encouraged girls to prepare themselves for teaching or office jobs and gain skills they could fall back on, "just in case." By 1900, 71 percent of Americans between the ages of five and eighteen attended school. That figure rose further in the early twentieth century, as public officials adopted laws requiring school attendance. Most high schools were coeducational, and almost every high school featured athletics. Recruited first as cheerleaders for boys' teams, girls soon established field hockey and other sports of their own.

Comstock Act
An 1873 law that prohibited circulation of "obscene literature," defined as including most information on sex, reproduction, and birth control.

AP® SKILLS & PROCESSES

CONTINUITY AND CHANGE

In what ways did the Comstock Act reflect and contradict the realities of American life in the industrial era?

CHECK FOR UNDERSTANDING

Ask students: **How did families change in this period?** *As the number of farmers declined, the need for large families declined with it. American families, particularly in the middle class, began limiting family size through extended nursing and use of contraceptives.*

AP® SKILLS & PROCESSES

CONTINUITY AND CHANGE

The **CONTINUITY AND CHANGE** question hints at the fact that laws sometimes reflect protests against changing social mores. This question may puzzle some students as it asks for ways the Comstock Act simultaneously reflected and contradicted American life. The law reflected traditional Christian acceptance of sex for the purpose of procreation, while targeting the changing (secret) practices of others — many of whom were also Christians.

TRM Find complete suggested responses in the Teacher's Resource Materials.

AP® APPLY THE TIP

Introduce students to Booker T. Washington and W. E. B. Du Bois by asking groups to research each African American leader. Students should focus on the conditions in which each leader was born and grew up, their education, and their contributions to the African American community. Once students have had the chance to familiarize themselves with each leader, provide them with excerpts from the "Atlanta Compromise" speech by Washington and the chapter "Of Booker T. Washington and Others" from *The Souls of Black Folk* by Du Bois. It is helpful to read these excerpts out loud with students so they can better understand the ideas that each leader emphasized. Stop periodically and ask students to explain the historical argument being made by each leader. Once students have read and analyzed the documents, ask them to explain the way that the author's point of view, their audience, their purpose, and the historical context of each document impacts the use of the documents as historical evidence. Contextualize the conflict between Washington and Du Bois by explaining the historical processes, developments, and events that influenced or were influenced by each of these documents.

TEACHING STRATEGY

The companion site to the PBS documentary *The Rise and Fall of Jim Crow* offers "Lesson Plan 2: Fighting Jim Crow in the Schools," which explores Booker T. Washington's vision of vocational education and reactions from contemporaries, including critics like W. E. B. Du Bois. The lesson incorporates an interactive timeline, excerpts from the film, links to relevant primary source excerpts, and suggestions for class discussion. To access this site, search "PBS Rise and Fall of Jim Crow Lesson 2."

AP® THEME

SOC: Social Structures

A challenge for many students is accounting for continuity and change simultaneously. This period in history is replete with opportunities to work on this historical reasoning skill. For instance, ask students to account for historical factors that explain how Americans both embraced and rejected social reform movements. Have students identify one example for each. Examples can be found throughout Chapter 17.

AP® EXAM TIP

Compare the leadership of Booker T. Washington and W. E. B. Du Bois.

The rate of Americans attending college had long hovered around 2 percent; driven by public universities' expansion, the rate rose in the 1880s, reaching 8 percent by 1920. Much larger numbers attended a growing network of business and technical schools. "GET A PLACE IN THE WORLD," advertised one Minneapolis business college in 1907, "where your talents can be used to the best advantage." Typically, such schools offered both day and night classes in subjects such as bookkeeping, typewriting, and shorthand.

The needs of the new economy also shaped the curriculum at more traditional collegiate institutions. State universities emphasized technical training and fed the growing professional workforce with graduates trained in fields such as engineering. Many private colleges distanced themselves from such practical pursuits; administrators argued that students who aimed to be leaders needed broad-based knowledge. But they modernized course offerings, emphasizing French and German, for example, rather than Latin and Greek. Harvard, led by dynamic president Charles W. Eliot from 1869 to 1909, pioneered the liberal arts. Students at the all-male college chose from a range of electives, as Eliot called for classes that developed each young man's "individual reality and creative power." In the South, one of the most famous educational projects was Booker T. Washington's Tuskegee Institute, founded in 1881. Washington both taught and exemplified the goal of self-help; his autobiography, *Up from Slavery* (1901), became a best-seller. Because of the deep poverty in which most southern African Americans lived, Washington concluded that "book education" for most "would be almost a waste of time." He focused instead on industrial education. Students, he argued, would "be sure of knowing how to make a living after they had left us." Tuskegee sent female graduates into teaching and nursing; men more often entered the industrial trades or farmed by the latest scientific methods.

Atlanta Compromise
An 1895 address by Booker T. Washington that urged whites and African Americans to work together for the progress of all. Delivered at the Cotton States Exposition in Atlanta, the speech was widely interpreted as approving racial segregation.

Booker T. Washington In an age of severe racial oppression, Booker T. Washington emerged as the leading public voice of African Americans. He was remarkable both for his effectiveness in speaking to white Americans and for his deep understanding of the aspirations of blacks. Born a slave, Washington had plenty of firsthand experience with racism. But having befriended several whites in his youth, he also believed that African Americans could appeal to whites of good will—and maneuver around those who were hostile—in the struggle for equality. He hoped, most of all, that economic achievement would erase white prejudice. PhotoQuest/Getty Images.

Washington gained national fame in 1895 with his **Atlanta Compromise** address, delivered at the Cotton States Exposition in Atlanta, Georgia. For the exposition's white organizers, the racial "compromise" was inviting Washington to speak at all. It was a move intended to show racial progress in the South. Washington, in turn, delivered an address that many interpreted as approving racial segregation. Stating that African Americans had, in slavery days, "proved our loyalty to you," he assured whites that "in our humble way, we shall stand by you ... ready to lay down our lives, if need be, in defense of yours." The races could remain socially detached: "In all things that are purely social we can be as separate as the fingers, yet one as the hand in all things essential to mutual progress." Washington urged, however, that whites join him in working for "the highest intelligence and development of all."

Whites greeted this address with enthusiasm, and Washington became the most prominent black leader of his generation. His soothing rhetoric and style of leadership, based on avoiding confrontation and cultivating white patronage and private influence, was well suited to the difficult years after Reconstruction. Washington believed that money was color-blind: whites would respect economic success. He represented the ideals of millions of African Americans who hoped education and hard work would erase white prejudice. That hope proved tragically overoptimistic. As the tide of disfranchisement and segregation rolled in, Washington would come under fire from a younger generation of race leaders who argued that he accommodated too much to white racism.

In addition to African American education, women's higher education expanded notably. In the Northeast and South, women most often attended single-sex institutions, including teacher-training colleges. For affluent families, private colleges offered an education equivalent to men's — for an equally high price. Vassar College started the trend when it opened in 1861; Smith, Wellesley, and others followed. Anxious doctors warned that intensive brain work would unsex young women and drain energy from their ovaries, leading them to bear weak children. But as thousands of women earned degrees and suffered no apparent harm, fears faded. Single-sex higher education for women spread from private to public institutions, especially in the South, where the Mississippi State College for Women (1885) led the way.

Coeducation was more prevalent in the Midwest and West, where many state universities opened their doors to female students after the Civil War. Women were also admitted to most African American colleges founded during Reconstruction. By 1910, 58 percent of America's colleges and universities were coeducational. While students at single-sex institutions forged strong bonds with one another, women also gained benefits from learning with men. When male students were friendly, they built comfortable working relationships; when men were hostile, women learned coping skills that served them well in later employment or reform work. One doctor who studied at the University of Iowa remembered later that he and his friends mercilessly harassed the first women who entered the medical school. But when the women showed they were good students, the men's attitudes changed to "wholesome respect."

"The Resolutes" This baseball team shows how sports mania spread — even to one of the first and most elite women's colleges, Vassar. Although college administrators doubted the propriety of their students playing baseball, a few young women persisted — while many more took up tennis, field hockey, and other athletic pursuits. By the late 1890s, basketball games became an important part of Vassar student life. Archives and Special Collections, Vassar College Library, Archives 08.17.

Whether or not they got a college education, more and more women recognized, in the words of Elizabeth Cady Stanton, their "solitude of self." In the changing economy, they could not always count on fathers and husbands. Women who needed to support themselves could choose from dozens of guidebooks such as *What Girls Can Do* (1880) and *How to Make Money Although a Woman* (1895). The Association for the Advancement of Women, founded in 1873 by women's college graduates, defended women's higher education and argued that women's paid employment was a positive good.

Today, many economists argue that education and high-quality jobs for women are keys to reducing poverty in the developing world. In the United States, that process also led to broader gains in women's political rights. As women began to earn advanced degrees, work for wages and salaries, and live independently, it became harder to argue that women were "dependents" who did not need to vote.

AP® SKILLS & PROCESSES

CONTINUITY AND CHANGE

How did educational opportunities change after the Civil War, and for whom?

AP® EXAM TIP

Analyze the changes that occurred in women's activism in the late nineteenth and early twentieth century.

Women's Civic Activism

As the United States confronted industrialization, middle-class women steadily expanded their place beyond the household, building reform movements and taking political action. Starting in the 1880s, women's clubs sprang up and began to study such problems as pollution, unsafe working conditions, and urban poverty. So many formed by 1890 that their leaders created a nationwide umbrella organization, the General Federation of Women's Clubs. Women justified such work through **maternalism**, appealing to their special role as mothers. Maternalism was an intermediate step between domesticity and modern arguments for women's equality.

maternalism
The belief that women should contribute to civic and political life through their special talents as mothers, Christians, and moral guides. Maternalists put this ideology into action by creating dozens of social reform organizations.

TEACHING STRATEGY

The growth of higher education provided an important means for middle- and upper-class American women to increase their status and opportunities. The Web site College Women offers a searchable collection of diaries, letters, scrapbooks, and photographs from the archives of a select group of the earliest women's colleges in the U.S., also known as the Seven Sisters. The site is designed to open new avenues for research in American women's history by making the dispersed writings, images, and documents of women students easily accessible through a single search. To access this site, search "College Women."

AP® SKILLS & PROCESSES

CONTINUITY AND CHANGE

The **CONTINUITY AND CHANGE** question asks students to identify postwar changes in education. Students should describe changes at both the high school and college levels and explain the significance of these changes. Students could also compare developments in college opportunities for African Americans and women, explaining particular reasons for differences between the two.

TRM Find complete suggested responses in the Teacher's Resource Materials.

AP® APPLY THE TIP

Engage students in the **AP® THINKING LIKE A HISTORIAN** document analysis activity on pp. 570–571. To extend the **AP® DBQ PRACTICE** prompt, organize students into small groups to develop a thesis and outline a response using specific evidence and documents to examine to what degree the late nineteenth century was "women's era."

CHECK FOR UNDERSTANDING

Ask students: **What were the features of education in the late nineteenth century?** *A high school diploma became a desirable commodity for both boys and girls. For boys, the diploma provided a gateway to college and professional or managerial careers. For girls, it was an opportunity for teaching or office jobs before marriage. The rate of college attendance increased from 2 to 8 percent. Vocational schools, including the Tuskegee Institute for African Americans, provided a supply of workers for technical fields. Single sex colleges for women also developed.*

"Women's place is Home," declared the journalist Rheta Childe Dorr. But she added, "Home is the community. The city full of people is the Family.... Badly do the Home and Family need their mother."

Woman's Christian Temperance Union (WCTU)
An organization advocating the prohibition of liquor that spread rapidly after 1879, when charismatic Frances Willard became its leader. Advocating suffrage and a host of reform activities, it launched tens of thousands of women into public life and was the first nationwide organization to identify and condemn domestic violence.

Women's Temperance Activism One maternalist goal was to curb alcohol abuse by prohibiting liquor sales. The **Woman's Christian Temperance Union (WCTU)**, founded after a series of women's grassroots campaigns in 1874, spread rapidly after 1879, when charismatic Frances Willard became its leader. More than any other group of the late nineteenth century, the WCTU launched women into reform. Willard knew how to frame political demands in the language of feminine self-sacrifice. "Womanliness first," she advised her followers; "afterward, what you will." WCTU members vividly described the plight of abused wives and children when men suffered in the grip of alcoholism. Willard's motto was "Home Protection," and though the WCTU placed all the blame on alcohol rather than other factors, it became the first organization to identify and combat domestic violence.

The prohibitionist movement drew activists from many backgrounds. Middle-class city dwellers worried about the link between alcoholism and crime, especially in the expanding immigrant wards. Rural citizens equated liquor with big-city sins such as prostitution and political corruption. Methodists, Baptists, Mormons, and members of other denominations condemned drinking for religious reasons. Immigrants passionately disagreed, however: Germans and Irish Catholics enjoyed their Sunday beer and saw no harm in it. Saloons were a centerpiece of working-class leisure and community life, offering free lunches, public toilets, and a place to share neighborhood news. Thus, while some labor unions advocated voluntary temperance, attitudes toward prohibition divided along ethnic, religious, and class lines.

WCTU activism led some leaders to raise radical questions about the shape of industrial society. As she investigated alcohol abuse, Willard confronted poverty, hunger, unemployment, and other industrial problems (see "Thinking Like a Historian," p. 570). Across the United States, WCTU locals founded soup kitchens and free libraries. They introduced a German educational innovation, the kindergarten. They investigated prison conditions. Though she did not persuade most prohibitionists to follow her lead, Willard declared herself a Christian Socialist and urged more attention to workers' plight. She advocated laws establishing an eight-hour workday and abolishing child labor.

Willard also called for women's voting rights, lending powerful support to the independent suffrage movement that had emerged during Reconstruction. Controversially, the WCTU threw its energies behind the Prohibition Party, which exercised considerable clout during the 1880s — challenging both major political parties, especially the Republicans. Women worked in the party as speakers, convention delegates, and even local candidates. Liquor was big business, and powerful interests mobilized to block antiliquor legislation. In many areas — particularly the cities — prohibition simply did not gain majority support. Willard retired to England, where she died in 1898, worn and discouraged by many defeats. But her legacy was powerful. Other groups took up the cause, eventually winning national prohibition after World War I.

Through its emphasis on human welfare, the WCTU encouraged women to join the national debate over poverty and inequality of wealth. Some became active in the People's Party of the 1890s, which welcomed women as organizers and stump speakers. Others led groups such as the National Congress of Mothers, founded in 1897, which promoted better child-rearing techniques in rural and working-class families. The WCTU had taught women how to lobby, raise money, and even run for office. Willard wrote that "perhaps the most significant outcome" of the movement was women's "knowledge of their own power."

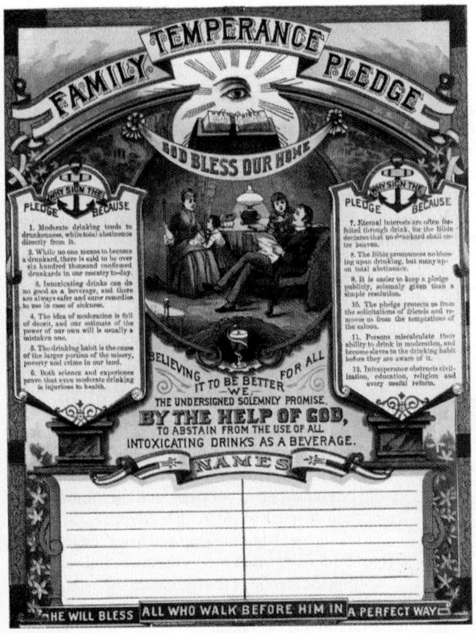

VISUAL ACTIVITY

Family Temperance Pledge This pledge form lists twelve reasons for abstaining from drinking alcoholic beverages and provides space for all family members to sign. It warns that "moderate drinking" can lead to alcoholism, "the Bible pronounces no blessing upon drinking," and "intemperance obstructs civilization, education, religion and every useful reform." Kean Collection/Getty Images.

READING THE IMAGE: Study this image carefully, including the scene in the center and the twelve reasons to "pledge because." Who do you think might have purchased this document from a temperance society or church? How might they have used or displayed it after bringing it home? Why do you think children were included in the picture and invited to sign their names?

MAKING CONNECTIONS: What larger values and goals does the pledge suggest will be fulfilled by abstaining from alcohol? Based on your reading of this chapter, what other activities and reform work might you expect family members to participate in, if they chose to sign the "temperance pledge"?

AP® THEME

SOC: Social Structures

This WCTU temperance pledge suggests the movement's evangelical roots and its continuity with the temperance efforts of the Second Great Awakening era. Ask students to compare this pledge card with one from the earlier period. Among other things, students should note the continued emphasis on voluntary efforts, which in turn assumed that people could overcome the temptation of alcohol by sheer willpower and that they would keep their word — a promise not to drink was a binding promise.

TRM Find complete suggested responses in the Teacher's Resource Materials.

Women, Race, and Patriotism As in temperance work, women played central roles in patriotic movements and African American community activism. Members of the Daughters of the American Revolution (DAR), founded in 1890, celebrated the memory of Revolutionary War heroes. Equally influential was the United Daughters of the Confederacy (UDC), founded in 1894 to extol the South's "Lost Cause." The UDC's elite southern members shaped Americans' memory of the Civil War by constructing monuments, distributing Confederate flags, and promoting school textbooks that defended the Confederacy and condemned Reconstruction. The UDC's work helped build and maintain support for segregation and disfranchisement (see Chapter 14, "Thinking Like a Historian," p. 476).

African American women did not sit idle in the face of this challenge. In 1896, they created the **National Association of Colored Women**. Through its local clubs, black women arranged for the care of orphans, founded homes for the elderly, advocated temperance, and undertook public health campaigns. Such women shared the widespread maternalist goal of carrying domesticity into the public sphere. Journalist Victoria Earle Matthews hailed the American home as "the foundation upon which nationality rests, the pride of the citizen, and the glory of the Republic." She and other African American women used the language of domesticity and respectability to justify their work.

One of the most radical voices among African American women was Ida B. Wells, who as a young Tennessee schoolteacher sued the Chesapeake & Ohio Railroad for denying her a seat in the ladies' car (see "Consumer Spaces"). In 1892, a white mob in Memphis invaded a grocery store owned by three of Wells's friends,

National Association of Colored Women
An organization created in 1896 by African American women to provide community support. NACW members arranged for the care of orphans and the elderly, undertook campaigns for public health and women's suffrage, and raised awareness of racial injustice.

AP® EXAM TIP

Evaluate the context in which Ida B. Wells became a spokeswoman for racial equality.

AP® APPLY THE TIP

Ask students to identify the ways in which Ida B. Wells contributed to the continued fight for social equality for African Americans and have them compare and contrast her goals with those of Booker T. Washington.

AP® SKILLS & PROCESSES

ANALYZING HISTORICAL EVIDENCE

The **AP® THINKING LIKE A HISTORIAN** feature addresses some of the ways that the WCTU's activism addressed issues of race in the late nineteenth century. The efforts of the WCTU and those of African American activists, most notably Wells's antilynching advocacy, came into direct contact from time to time. Northern Illinois University provides a lesson that explores the intersection between the two, as students analyze the writings of WCTU president Frances Willard and Wells to compare their views on segregation and lynching. Through this lesson, students should gain a deeper understanding of racial attitudes in the late nineteenth century, as well as the role of activist organizations in influencing politics and public opinion. To access this lesson, search "Illinois During the Gilded Age."

AP® THINKING LIKE A HISTORIAN

WCTU Women "Do Everything"

Frances Willard, one of late nineteenth-century America's most dynamic and admired reformers, rose to leadership of the Woman's Christian Temperance Union (WCTU) in the 1870s, when she was in her thirties. She built the WCTU, which had emerged from spontaneous protests in the 1870s into a powerful nationwide organization that forged alliances with African American, Catholic, and farmer-labor organizations. Urging women to view alcohol abuse in a broad context, Willard famously challenged them to "Do Everything": start libraries, soup kitchens, and kindergartens; advocate prison reform; oppose prostitution; work for women's suffrage; and elect prohibitionists to office. Though the WCTU had limited electoral success, it trained tens of thousands of women in strategies for civic engagement.

1. Consequences of Intemperance, 1874. *In songs, lectures, personal testimony, and illustrations like this one, prohibitionists described — sometimes luridly — the effects of alcoholism.*

Source: Library of Congress, 3b12591.

2. Frances E. Willard, *Hints and Helps in Our Temperance Work*, 1875. *In one of Willard's first guidebooks for WCTU members, she suggested activities for local chapters.*

Write to your state secretary for a list of the best speakers available to you.

Observe the 23rd of December, the anniversary of the [1873 Ohio] crusade, by special exercises, in which men, women, and children all participate.

Get correct statistics of intemperance in *your own town*, and have them kept before the people. These will tell more than imported figures. Interest the press in your work. Wherever practicable, edit a column in the local newspaper....

Whatever you neglect, keep up your *prayer-meeting*, and so far as possible get men and women in the bondage of strong drink to come there and sign the pledge....

Carry your peaceful war right into the ranks of the men who vote....

So far as possible, enlist *the pastors and the churches.* Seek to influence each church to become practically *a Temperance Society*....

Write in a blank-book this agreement: "We, the undersigned, believing it to be for the greatest numbers' greatest good, agree to pay our employees on Monday (or the first of the week) instead of on Saturday night, from this time henceforth." Get all the business men to sign it....

Seek to multiply places and sources of rational recreation for the young....

Homes for Inebriates — both men and women — should be established in our cities, and the Women's Unions can do much to aid in this enterprise....

Drinking fountains for "man and beast" ought to be erected by our Unions in every city, town, and village....

During the session of the legislature the Woman's State Union should plan for a convention or a series of mass-meetings at the capital....

3. Frances Willard on "Home Protection," 1879. *Early in her career Willard took on the controversial issue of women's suffrage. By the late 1880s, most state WCTUs in the Northeast, Midwest, and West took up suffrage advocacy.*

"Home Protection" is the general name given to a movement already endorsed by the W.C.T. Unions of eight states, the object of which is to secure for all women above the age of twenty-one years the ballot as one means for the protection of their homes from the devastation caused by the legalized traffic in strong drink....

We want [the] ballot because the liquor traffic is entrenched in law, and law grows out of the will of majorities.... As steam can be applied to locomotion only through an engine, and as electricity can be utilized only through a battery, so, in a Republic, we can condense the opinion of this majority of women into law only through the magical little paper which falls

As snowflakes fall upon the sod;
But executes a freeman's will
As lightnings do the will of God.

4. Frances E. W. Harper, "The Woman's Christian Temperance Union and the Colored Woman," 1888. *Writer and activist Frances E. W. Harper became one of the most prominent African American leaders in the WCTU. As Harper notes, black women*

570

worked largely in separate unions, sometimes by choice, but more often because white women insisted on maintaining all-white unions.

Victor Hugo has spoken of the nineteenth century as being woman's era, and among the most noticeable epochs of this era is the uprising of women against the twin evils of slavery and intemperance.... In the great anti-slavery conflict women had borne a part, but after the storm cloud of battle had rolled away, it was found that an enemy, old and strong and deceptive, was warring against the best interests of society; not simply an enemy to one race, but an enemy to all races....

One of the pleasantest remembrances of my connection with the Woman's Christian Temperance Union was the kind and hospitable reception I met in the Missouri State Convention, [whose] President, Mrs. Hoffman, ... declared that the color-line was eliminated. A Superintendent was chosen at that meeting for colored work in the State.... Our work is divided into about forty departments, [including] departments for parlor meetings, juvenile and evangelistic work.... The Union held meetings in Methodist and Baptist churches, and opened in the African Methodist Episcopal Church an industrial school for children.... Some of the Unions ... took the initiative for founding an orphan asylum for colored children....

In the farther South separate State Unions have been formed. Southern white women, it may be, fail to make in their minds the discrimination between social equality and Christian affiliation.... Whether or not the members of the farther South will subordinate the spirit of caste to the spirit of Christ, time will show....

5. **Frances Willard on her bicycle in Evanston, Illinois, 1893.** *Willard was in her fifties and in failing health when the United States was swept up in a bicycle craze, but she nonetheless undertook to show worried parents that bike riding was safe and fun for women and girls. As she reported in* A Wheel Within a Wheel, *biking gave girls self-confidence and an independent spirit to meet the challenges of the "wider world." Here, her two stenographers help her with her bicycle, which she nicknamed Gladys.*

Source: Courtesy of the Frances E. Willard Memorial Library and Archives.

6. **Rozette Hendrix, Minnesota's WCTU president, reports on the Union's work, 1912.** *Although Frances Willard died in 1898 and newer groups such as the Anti-Saloon League captured public attention, the WCTU continued organizing until the passage of national prohibition in 1920 (Chapter 21). This report suggests the diversity of its interests and alliances.*

Years ago the women began a war against child labor and also to procure compulsory educational laws, and sentiment has been created and much done along these lines. By the revision of our own state laws children under sixteen years of age are prohibited from employment in factories ... and children under sixteen years of age are required to be in school....

There is an aroused interest along all lines of Purity, not only in work done by our own organization but by others.... We have secured in our state such laws as are necessary for the suppression of [sex] traffic except the Injunction and Abatement measure which we failed of getting last session because of lack of time, and which we hope to get at our coming legislature....

During the past year another state has been added to those already giving full suffrage.... Women who are the home makers are the ones who are most concerned in these matters and when they have had a chance to vote, they have shown their interest....

We are out to win. We are in the midst of a battle for statewide prohibition and we shall never know defeat, victory may be delayed but it will come.... Let us ... work and pray as we never have before, for the homes, for the boys and the girls of Minnesota.

Source: (2) Frances Willard, *Hints and Helps in Our Temperance Work*, in Carolyn De Swarte Gifford and Amy R. Slagell, eds., *Let Something Good Be Said: Speeches and Writings of Frances E. Willard* (Urbana: University of Illinois Press, 2007), 12–14; (3) Frances E. Willard, *Home Protection Manual* (New York: Independent, 1879), 4–5; (4) *A.M.E. Church Review* 12 (1888): 313–316; (6) Rozette Hendrix, "President's Annual Address," *Minutes of the Thirty-Sixth Annual Meeting of the WCTU of the State of Minnesota* (Minneapolis: Thurston & Gould, 1912), in Kathryn Kish Sklar and Thomas Dublin, eds., *Women and Social Movements in the United States, 1600–2000*, accessed through Vassar College Library at library.vassar.edu, Jan. 3, 2017.

AP® ANALYZING THE EVIDENCE

1. How did Willard and other prohibitionists craft their public appeals? Use evidence from the sources to explain what values and identities WCTU leaders hoped would motivate others to join.
2. In addition to outlawing the manufacture and sale of liquor, the WCTU worked for a range of other measures. What policy recommendations appear in these documents? How might antiliquor work have led women to advocate these other policies? What is the historical situation of many WCTU reformers?
3. Which Americans were likely most receptive to the WCTU's message, and why? Who may have been indifferent or hostile, and why? Identify the audiences of WCTU's messages.

AP® DBQ PRACTICE

Using evidence from these sources and your knowledge of the period, write an essay responding to Frances Harper's comment, drawn from Victor Hugo, that the late nineteenth century was "women's era." To what extent did the WCTU fit into Hugo's views and in women's activism and women's rights more broadly?

TRM Find complete suggested responses in the Teacher's Resource Materials.

AP® SKILLS & PROCESSES

ARGUMENTATION

The **AP® DBQ PRACTICE** prompt invites students to evaluate the claim that the late nineteenth century was "women's era." In addressing this prompt, students should exercise caution to avoid exaggerating the role of groups like the WCTU. They should consider limitations to women's power — including the absence of the franchise on the national level — as well as the countervailing influences of manliness ideologies of the time.

TEACHING STRATEGY

Ida B. Wells's *Southern Horrors* is both an impassioned attack on extrajudicial violence and a well-reasoned one. Wells carefully documented all of her claims, providing clear, detailed evidence of the prevalence and racially motivated nature of lynchings. The full text is available through Project Gutenberg. *Southern Horrors* makes for very compelling reading, though teachers should exercise caution in assigning it to students, given the graphic nature of Wells's descriptions. To access this document, search "Project Gutenberg Southern Horrors."

AP® SKILLS & PROCESSES

MAKING CONNECTIONS

From the mid-nineteenth century through the early part of the twentieth century, societal expectations of women revolved around the concept of separate spheres, whereby men and women engaged in different occupations, due to gender differences. Though the Market Revolution and later Industrial Revolution questioned gender lines, women were expected to understand and be responsible for the domestic sphere. In many ways, this led to what Jane Addams referred to as political housekeeping. Put another way, women used their domestic sphere roles to affect political change. Consider having students work on creating a connection between domestic sphere responsibilities and societal change.

TRM Find complete suggested responses in the Teacher's Resource Materials.

AP® THEME

PCE: Politics and Power

The Library of Congress's primary source set *Women's Suffrage* provides a background essay exploring women's rights organizations, including NAWSA, and links to 18 high-resolution images related to the late nineteenth-century suffrage movement, guidelines for discussion, and links to additional resources for further research. To access this site, search "Library of Congress Women's Suffrage Teacher's Guide."

Ida B. Wells In 1887, Ida Wells (Wells-Barnett after she married in 1895) was thrown bodily from a train in Tennessee for refusing to vacate her seat in a section reserved for whites, launching her into a lifelong crusade for racial justice. Her mission was to expose the evil of lynching in the South. This image is the title page of a pamphlet she published in 1892. Schomburg Center, NYPL/Art Resource, NY.

angry that it competed with a nearby white-owned store. When the black store owners defended themselves, wounding several of their attackers, all three were lynched. Grieving their deaths, Wells left Memphis and urged other African Americans to join her in boycotting the city's white businesses. As a journalist, she launched a one-woman campaign against lynching. Wells's investigations demolished the myth that lynchers were reacting to the crime of rape; she showed that the real cause was more often economic competition, a labor dispute, or a consensual relationship between a white woman and a black man. Settling in Chicago, Wells became an accomplished reformer, but in an era of increasing racial injustice, few whites supported her cause.

The largest African American women's organization arose within the National Baptist Church (NBC), which by 1906 represented 2.4 million black churchgoers. Founded in 1900, the Women's Convention of the NBC funded night schools, health clinics, kindergartens, day care centers, and prison outreach programs. Adella Hunt Logan, born in Alabama, exemplified how such work could lead women to demand political rights. Educated at Atlanta University, Logan became a women's club leader, teacher, and suffrage advocate. "If white American women, with all their mutual and acquired advantage, need the ballot," she declared, "how much more do Black Americans, male and female, need the strong defense of a vote to help secure them their right to life, liberty, and the pursuit of happiness?"

Women's Rights Though it had split into two rival organizations during Reconstruction (Chapter 14), the movement for women's suffrage reunited in 1890 in the **National American Woman Suffrage Association (NAWSA)**. Soon afterward, suffragists built on earlier victories in the West, winning full ballots for women in Colorado (1893), Idaho (1896), and Utah (1896 — after being first adopted in 1870, abolished by Congress in an attempt to suppress plural marriage, and reestablished as Utah gained statehood). Afterward, movement leaders were discouraged by a decade of state-level defeats and Congress's refusal to consider a constitutional amendment. But suffrage again picked up momentum after 1911 (Map 17.2). By 1913, most women living west of the Mississippi River had the ballot. In other localities, women could vote in municipal elections, school elections, or liquor referenda.

AP® SKILLS & PROCESSES

MAKING CONNECTIONS

How did women use widespread beliefs about their "special role" to justify political activism, and for what goals?

National American Woman Suffrage Association (NAWSA)
Women's suffrage organization created in 1890 by the union of the National Woman Suffrage Association and the American Woman Suffrage Association. Up to national ratification of suffrage in 1920, the NAWSA played a central role in campaigning for women's right to vote.

feminism
The ideology that women should enter the public sphere not only to work on behalf of others, but also for their own equal rights and advancement. Feminists moved beyond advocacy of women's voting rights to seek greater autonomy in professional careers, property rights, and personal relationships.

The rising prominence of the women's suffrage movement had an ironic result: it prompted some women — and men — to organize against it, in groups such as the National Association Opposed to Woman Suffrage (1911). Antisuffragists argued that it was expensive to add so many voters to the rolls; wives' ballots would just "double their husbands' votes" or worse, cancel them out, subjecting men to "petticoat rule." Some antisuffragists also argued that voting would undermine women's special roles as disinterested reformers: no longer above the fray, they would be plunged into the "cesspool of politics." In short, women were "better citizens without the ballot." Such arguments helped delay passage of national women's suffrage until after World War I.

By the 1910s, some women moved beyond suffrage to take a public stance for what they called **feminism** — women's full political, economic, and social equality. A famous site of sexual rebellion was New York's Greenwich Village, where radical intellectuals, including many gays and lesbians, created a vibrant community. Among other political activities, women there founded the Heterodoxy Club (1912), open to any woman who pledged not to be "orthodox in her opinions." The club brought together intellectuals, journalists, and labor organizers. Almost all supported suffrage,

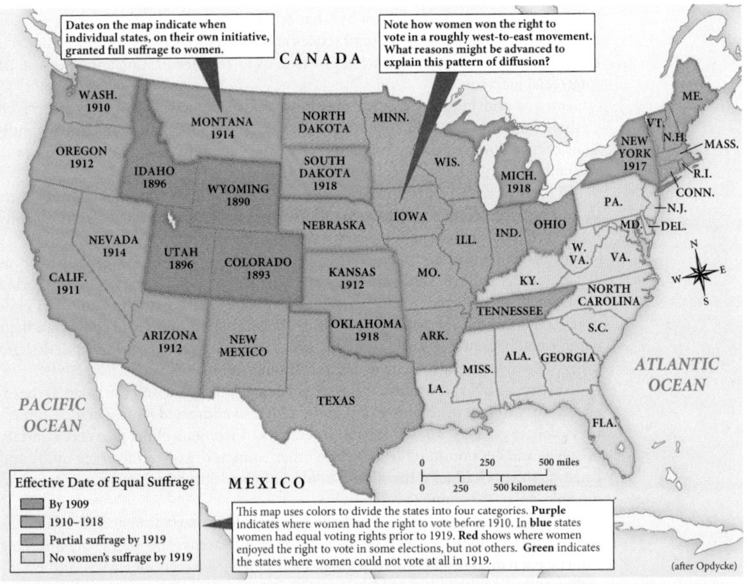

MAPPING THE PAST

MAP 17.2 Women's Suffrage, 1890–1919

By 1909, after more than sixty years of agitation, only four states had granted women full voting rights. A number of other states offered partial suffrage, limited to voting for school boards and such issues as taxes and local referenda on whether or not to permit the sale of liquor licenses (the so-called local option). Between 1910 and 1918, as the effort shifted to the struggle for a constitutional amendment, eleven states joined the list granting full suffrage.

ANALYZING THE MAP: In what regions of the country did women win full voting rights before 1910, and where did women continue to have no voting rights in 1919?

MAKING CONNECTIONS: Based on your reading of the chapter narrative — as well as prior chapters — how do you explain regional patterns in suffrage rights?

but they had a more ambitious view of what was needed for women's liberation. "I wanted to belong to the human race, not to a ladies' aid society," wrote one divorced journalist who joined Heterodoxy. Feminists argued that women should not simply fulfill expectations of feminine self-sacrifice; they should work on their own behalf. As the United States entered the modern era, then, greater advocacy for women's rights proved to be — like new consumer spaces, literary realism, and appreciation for wilderness — another unexpected transformation wrought by industrialization.

AP® EXAM TIP

Understanding the causes for the rise of feminism is important to know for the AP® Exam.

SUMMARY

In the era of industrialization, new intellectual currents, including Darwinism, challenged nineteenth-century certainties. Debates over evolution, especially its implications for the human species, proved particularly intense and long-lasting. "Survival of

TRM Find complete suggested responses in the Teacher's Resource Materials.

AP® APPLY THE TIP

Direct students to use pp. 567–573 of the text to complete **Handout 17.3 — Causation: Rise of Feminism (TRM)**. Then lead a class discussion to help students distinguish between the maternalism of the WCTU in the late nineteenth century and the ideas supported by feminism by the early twentieth century. Ask students to explain the ways that the belief in maternalism may have supported the rise of the antisuffrage movement in the U.S. in the late nineteenth century. To extend this assignment, ask students to compare the women's rights movement in the U.S. to the more radical women's rights movement in Great Britain in the late nineteenth century.

TRM Find **Handout 17.3 — Causation: Rise of Feminism** in the Teacher's Resource Materials.

CHECK FOR UNDERSTANDING

Ask students: **How did women's public activism impact American politics and society?** *Women's public activism in the late nineteenth century emphasized rectifying the ills of industrialism. While industrialization had dramatic effects on American society and culture, social structures were not in place to deal with its effects, especially on the working class. Women, either individually or collectively through such organizations as the WCTU or the NACW, sought to rectify these deficiencies and confronted poverty, hunger, unemployment, alcoholism, and other industrial problems through soup kitchens, libraries, temperance, and political advocacy for men and women, black and white (though usually in racially distinct societies). These women also took up the mantle of suffragists and advocated for the right to vote, with some success. By the passage of the nineteenth amendment in 1920, which nationalized that right, women were able to vote in many states west of the Mississippi River.*

CHECK FOR UNDERSTANDING

Use the **AP® LEARNING FOCUS** question from the beginning of the chapter to check students' understanding of the chapter as a whole: **Why and how did Americans' identities, beliefs, and culture change in the early industrial era?** *Americans' identities were in constant flux because there was no monolithic culture or beliefs. Instead, Americans continued to embrace their own sense of self, while embracing a wider national culture. For instance, Charles Darwin's theory of natural selection and other scientific ideas had a significant influence on American culture in the late nineteenth century in three specific areas: sociology, eugenics, and art. Sociologists employed it to explain why some people became rich and others poor, under the so-called ideal of Social Darwinism, which held that those who were wealthy were naturally selected to be so. Advocates of eugenics, the so-called science of human breeding, used its principles to label the mentally infirm and those who did not adhere to some arbitrary standard as unworthy of social status and often political rights. Furthermore, continued structural racism affected African Americans' access to political and social equality. Artists, meanwhile, embraced realism and modernism, artistic movements that sought to explain the world as it existed, eschewing sentimentalism and romanticism, in line with the hard realities of science. The turn of the twentieth century marked an era of dramatic technological and societal changes, which in turn, greatly affected reform movements.*

✓ LearningCurve

Remind students to go online to complete the LearningCurve quiz for this chapter.

TRM Find complete suggested responses in the Teacher's Resource Materials.

the fittest" — a term invented not by Charles Darwin, but by Herbert Spencer — was cited to justify ruthless business practices and inequalities of wealth. Eugenic "science" underlay such discriminatory practices as forced sterilization and laws against interracial marriage.

Science and modernism did not, however, displace religion. Newly arrived Catholics and Jews, as well as old-line Protestants, adapted their faiths to the conditions of modern life. Foreign missions spread the Christian gospel around the world, with mixed results for those receiving the message.

In the arts, realist and naturalist writers rejected both romanticism and the tenets of domesticity. Many Americans were shocked by the results, including the boldly modernist paintings displayed at New York's Armory Show.

Industrialization and new consumer practices created foundations for modern American culture. While middle-class families sought to preserve the Victorian domestic ideal, a variety of factors transformed family life. Families had fewer children, and a substantial majority of young people achieved more education than their parents had obtained. Across class and gender lines, Americans enjoyed athletics and the outdoors, fostering the rise of environmentalism.

Among an array of women's reform movements, the Woman's Christian Temperance Union sought prohibition of liquor, but it also addressed issues such as domestic violence, poverty, and education. Members of women's clubs pursued a variety of social and economic reforms, while other women organized for race uplift and patriotic work. Gradually, the Victorian ideal of female moral superiority gave way to modern claims for women's equal rights.

African Americans faced new challenges after Reconstruction ended. Lynchings and antiblack violence were practiced more openly across the South; the Supreme Court gave national sanction to segregation in *Plessy v. Ferguson* (1896), and by the early twentieth century, most black southerners were barred from the polls. African American leaders pursued several different strategies amid this "revolution gone backward." Booker T. Washington advised patience and accommodation, hoping that African American respectability and business success would change white minds. A younger generation of activists, including anti-lynching Ida B. Wells, began to take a more militant stance against segregation and violence.

CHAPTER 17 REVIEW

AP CONTENT REVIEW

Answer these questions to demonstrate your understanding of the chapter's main ideas.

1. How did Charles Darwin's theory of evolution impact American culture and intellectual life, and how did nonscientists make use of such ideas?
2. How did industrialization change the way Americans spent their leisure time, and how did this reflect evolving social identities and divisions?
3. Why and how did women's public activism arise in the late nineteenth century and how did this impact American politics and society?

AP TERMS TO KNOW

Identify and explain the significance of each term below.

Key Concepts and Events

Social Darwinism (p. 547)
eugenics (p. 548)
American Protective Association (APA) (p. 552)
Social Gospel (p. 553)
fundamentalism (p. 553)
realism (p. 553)
modernism (p. 554)
Plessy v. Ferguson (p. 558)
Jim Crow (p. 558)
Young Men's Christian Association (YMCA) (p. 558)
Negro leagues (p. 560)
Sierra Club (p. 562)
National Park Service (p. 563)
Antiquities Act (p. 563)

AP® SKILLS & PROCESSES

CAUSATION

AP® CONTENT REVIEW 1 asks students to consider the effects of evolution and other scientific ideas on American culture. Note: This is the same question as the section-opening prompt on p. 546.

AP® SKILLS & PROCESSES

CAUSATION

AP® CONTENT REVIEW 2 asks students to analyze the effects of industrialization on recreation activities by gender, race, and class. Note: This is the same question as the section-opening prompt on p. 555.

AP® SKILLS & PROCESSES

CAUSATION

AP® CONTENT REVIEW 3 directs students to indicate the effects of women's activism on politics and society. Note: This is the same question as the section-opening prompt on p. 564.

TRM Find definitions for these terms in the **Glossary/Glosario** in the Teacher's Resource Materials.

Comstock Act (p. 565)
Atlanta Compromise (p. 566)
maternalism (p. 567)
Woman's Christian Temperance Union (WCTU) (p. 568)
National Association of Colored Women (p. 569)
National American Woman Suffrage Association (NAWSA) (p. 572)
feminism (p. 572)

Key People

Billy Sunday (p. 553)
Mark Twain (Samuel Langhorne Clemens) (p. 554)
Thomas Edison (p. 556)
Ida B. Wells (p. 557)
John Muir (p. 562)
Booker T. Washington (p. 556)
Frances Willard (p. 568)

AP® MAKING CONNECTIONS

Recognize the larger developments and continuities within and across chapters by answering these questions.

1. This chapter explains cultural transformation as largely the result of industrialization. That's true, but it's not the whole story: the Civil War also helped bring about change. Review the material in Chapters 13 and 14, on the Civil War and its aftermath, and then write an essay in which you explain how changes in American society during the Civil War and Reconstruction laid the groundwork for cultural change in the areas of race relations, reform, science, and religious faith. Compare patterns of change in both time periods.
2. In the decades before the Civil War, middle-class Americans celebrated an ideal of domesticity, in which wives and mothers were supposed to be exempt from productive and paid labor, in order to devote themselves to motherhood and the home. Husbands' and fathers' main duty was breadwinning, though they were also expected to demonstrate Christian virtue and deference to female "influence." The ideal of domesticity reached ever-larger numbers of Americans in the post–Civil War decades, but women also used it to claim new roles in public life. How did domesticity evolve between the 1830s and the 1910s? What new groups of women justified their civic activism through ideals of motherhood and homemaking?

KEY TURNING POINTS

Refer to the timeline at the start of this chapter for help in answering the following question.

Some historians have argued that the 1890s was a crucial turning point in American culture — a decade when "modernity arrived." Based on events in this chapter, do you agree? Why or why not?

AP® PRACTICE QUESTIONS

MULTIPLE CHOICE QUESTIONS

Choose the correct answer for each question.

Questions 1–3 refer to this excerpt.

> "Private property . . . in the natural conditions of the struggle for existence produces inequalities between men. The struggle for existence is aimed against nature. It is from her . . . hand that we have to wrest the satisfactions for our needs, but our fellow-men are our competitors for the meager supply. Competition, therefore, is a law of nature. Nature is entirely neutral; she submits to him who most energetically and resolutely assails her. She grants her awards to the fittest, therefore, without regard to other considerations of any kind. . . . If we do not like it, and if we try to amend it, there is only one way in which we can do it. We can take from the better and give to the worse. . . . We shall thus lessen the inequalities. We shall favor the survival of the unfittest, and we shall accomplish this by destroying liberty."
>
> Essay by Yale Professor William Graham Sumner, 1880

AP® SKILLS & PROCESSES

CONTINUITY AND CHANGE

AP® MAKING CONNECTIONS 1 asks students to consider cultural change related to race, reform, science, and religion over a longer span of time. In this longer periodization, industrialization becomes simply one factor, rather than being the central or only factor.

AP® SKILLS & PROCESSES

CONTINUITY AND CHANGE

KEY TURNING POINTS returns to essential questions raised at the beginning of the chapter: what is "modernity" and how significant was this era at the moment of its emergence?

TRM Find complete suggested responses in the Teacher's Resource Materials.

1. The ideas in this passage most directly led to controversies in the 1880s and 1890s over
   a. increasing numbers of international migrants.
   b. business efforts to secure international markets.
   c. wages and working conditions.
   d. the moral obligations of business leaders to improve society.
2. Which of the following late eighteenth century ideas show continuity with the ideas described in the passage?
   a. Support for mercantilism by the British government
   b. Belief in the natural rights of all citizens
   c. Argument for laissez-faire economics by Adam Smith
   d. Support for Protestant Evangelism
3. Which of the following ideologies express the greatest difference from the ideas expressed in the excerpt?
   a. Populism
   b. Social Darwinism
   c. Nativism
   d. Laissez-faire capitalism

Questions 4–6 refer to this excerpt.

> "It is hardly necessary at the present day to enter a plea for athletic exercise and manly out-door sports. . . . [T]his growth can best be promoted by stimulating, within proper bounds, the spirit of rivalry on which all our games are based. . . . As a nation we have many tremendous problems to work out, and we need to bring every ounce of vital power possible to the solution. No people has ever yet done great and lasting work if its physical type was infirm and weak. . . .
>
> In college — and in most of the schools which are preparatory for college — rowing, foot-ball, base-ball, running, jumping, sparring, and the like have assumed a constantly increasing prominence. Nor is this a matter for regret . . . . [A]thletic sports, if followed properly, and not elevated into a fetish, are admirable for developing character, besides bestowing on the participants an invaluable fund of health and strength. . . ."
>
> Theodore Roosevelt, "Professionalism in Sports," 1890

4. Roosevelt's remarks in the excerpt most directly reflected which of the following developments during the late nineteenth century?
   a. New cultural opportunities in urban areas
   b. Increasing amounts of leisure time for the middle and upper classes
   c. More numerous critics championing alternative visions for U.S. society
   d. The growing income gap between rich and poor
5. Which of the following developments best represents the historical context of what is described in the excerpt?
   a. The emergence of a mass culture in entertainment and consumer spaces
   b. The increasing homogeneity of America's urban populations
   c. The expansion of higher education opportunities for women
   d. An increased support for labor organizations
6. In the late nineteenth and twentieth centuries the professionalization of athletics in the United States paralleled causes that also led most directly to a trend toward
   a. economic instability and political discontent among farmers.
   b. increasing urbanization of the United States.
   c. movements of women to seek greater equality with men.
   d. greater ethnic diversity in the industrial workforce.

SHORT ANSWER QUESTIONS

Read each question carefully and write a short response. Use evidence from the text to support your claims.

"Major league club owners were primarily men of new affluence, often Irish Catholics or German Jews. . . . These owners had important political connections that helped their sporting business succeed. . . . This created a fascinating paradox since WASPs [white, Anglo-Saxon Protestants] and other acculturated Americans regarded baseball as the institution that best epitomized the finest American beliefs, values, and traditions. Yet the baseball magnates were urban politicians, often machine politicians, who symbolized all that progressive small town Americans believed was destructive and wrong with American society."

Steven A. Reiss, *Touching Base: Professional Baseball and American Culture in the Progressive Era*, 1999

"The reserve clause would be a standard term in player contracts for nearly a century . . . the teams first considered establishing limits on salaries, but they decided that it would be easier if they simply ceased competing with each other to hire the best players. Each club was accordingly allowed to reserve . . . players for the ensuing season. . . . Once a club reserved a player, the other clubs would treat him as if he were already under contract . . . the result was an unusual system of labor relations, in which players were effectively bound for life to the teams that first signed them. . . . Even in the late nineteenth century, when workers throughout the economy had few rights enforceable against their employers, baseball stood out as a business in which the rules governing labor were conspicuously one-sided."

Stuart Banner, *The Baseball Trust: A History of Baseball's Antitrust Exemption*, 2013

1. Using the two excerpts provided, answer (a), (b), and (c).
   a. Briefly explain ONE major difference between Reiss's and Banner's historical interpretations of baseball's role in American society in the second half of the nineteenth century.
   b. Briefly explain how ONE historical event or development not directly mentioned in the excerpts could be used to support Reiss's argument.
   c. Briefly mention how ONE specific historical event or development not directly mentioned in the excerpts could be used to support Banner's argument.

2. Answer (a), (b), and (c).
   a. Briefly describe ONE specific historical change in American consumer culture during the late nineteenth century.
   b. Briefly explain ONE specific historical cause that led to the change you identified in (a).
   c. Briefly explain ONE specific historical effect that followed from the change in American consumer culture you described in (a).

3. Answer (a), (b), and (c).
   a. Briefly explain ONE important historical factor that led to reform movements during the Gilded Age.
   b. Briefly explain ONE way in which women led reform movements during the Gilded Age.
   c. Briefly explain ONE historical factor that accounts for resistance to reform efforts during the Gilded Age.

TRM Find complete suggested responses in the Teacher's Resource Materials.

18 CHAPTER

"Civilization's Inferno": The Rise and Reform of Industrial Cities

1880–1917

Chapter 18 — AP® Assessment Weight and Pacing Guide

The assessment weight on the AP® U.S. History Exam for Chapters 15–19 is 10–17 percent. Chapter 18 Sections 1 and 2 fall in Unit 6 of the AP® U.S. History Curriculum, covering Period 6: 1865–1898, and Chapter 18 Section 3 falls in Unit 7 of the AP® U.S. History Curriculum, covering Period 7: 1890–1945. These sections may be taught together or divided into separate units of study according to College Board periodization.

This pacing guide is based on a schedule with 120 sessions of 50 minutes each before the AP® U.S. History Exam. If you have a different number of sessions before the exam, you can modify the pacing to meet your needs. If you have additional time, consider incorporating quizzes, released AP® U.S. History questions, practice exams, writing practice, and other instructional activities.

	Traditional Schedule	Block Schedule
Chapter 18 Sections 1 and 2	2 days	1 day
Chapter 18 Section 3	1 day	1 day

Daily Pacing Guide

	Content Focus	Essential Question
Day 1	The New Metropolis (Period 6)	Why and how did American cities change in the late nineteenth century?
Day 2	Governing the Great City (Period 6)	Why did urban political machines arise, and what were their strengths and limitations?
Day 3	Crucibles of Progressive Reform (Period 7)	Why and how did large cities become seedbeds for political reform?

AP® Alignment

Section Heading	AP® Topic	AP® Theme
The New Metropolis	6.8, 6.9, 6.13	MIG, PCE
Governing the Great City	6.13	PCE
Crucibles of Progressive Reform	6.9, 6.13, 7.4	MIG, PCE

*Should changes be made to the Course Framework in the future, an updated alignment will be placed on our AP® updates page at go.bfwpub.com/ap-course-updates.

Chapter 18 — Overview

Chapter 18 begins by examining the dramatic technological and demographic changes that occurred with urbanization and industrialization in the late nineteenth century. These changes not only altered the city landscape but also placed greater demands on city government to provide services to city residents. In addition, the chapter looks at the dual forces of internal migration from rural to urban areas and the increase of immigration to the U.S. from Europe and Asia, resulting in the growth of ethnic communities within U.S. cities. The dramatic growth of cities associated with late nineteenth-century industrialization also gave rise to urban political machines that dominated politics in this Gilded Age. The chapter concludes by analyzing progressivism as a grassroots movement whose beginnings in response to political machines and urban issues laid the foundation for a national movement for progressive reform.

Chapter 18 — Resources

The following resources can be found in the Teacher's Resource Materials (TRM) that accompany the book. You can access the TRM via the book's digital platform, by clicking the TRM links found here in your Teacher's Edition e-book, or by contacting your representative to access the resources online. Visit **bfwpub.com/henretta10e** to learn more.

TRM Chapter 18 Lecture Presentation Slides

TRM Chapter 18 Outline with AP® Focus

TRM Chapter 18 Lecture Strategies

TRM Chapter 18 Suggested Responses

TRM Handout 18.1 — Continuity and Change: Urban Culture in the Late Nineteenth Century

TRM Handout 18.2 — Causation: Changes in Municipal Governments

TRM Handout 18.3 — Contextualization: Hull House

Chapter 18 — Essential Activity

Organize students into collaborative groups and provide each group with a set of seven primary source documents that focus on urbanization and/or political machines in the late nineteenth and early twentieth centuries. Some documents to include could be Thomas Nast's cartoons, graphs on immigrant arrivals to New York City, photographs of race riots and/or city life, and an excerpt from Lincoln Steffens, Jane Addams, William Marcy Tweed, or George Washington Plunkitt of Tammany Hall, etc. Ask students to work collaboratively to analyze each source and list ways in which the source could be used as historical evidence. Require students to extend their analysis by explaining the historical context, intended audience, purpose, and point of view of each source. Once students have analyzed the sources, ask them to write a DBQ prompt that is based on AP® Skills & Processes (causation, comparison, or continuity and change).

Chapter 18 — Bell Ringers

The following activities take no more than 5–15 minutes of your class period and offer an effective and engaging way to begin your lessons and for students to apply AP® Skills & Processes:

- Provide pairs of students with different political cartoons illustrating issues related to Tammany Hall. Ask students to explain the historical context, purpose, intended audience, and point of view of each artist. Use this analysis to lead a class discussion on the impact of Tammany Hall on immigrants and the working class in New York City.
- Ask students to analyze *New York* by George Bellows on p. 577 of the text. As a class, discuss the different elements that Bellows included in this painting. Then ask students to contextualize the image by drawing on specific elements in the painting to explain the broader historical developments, processes, or events that may have led to their inclusion in the painting.

NOTES

TEACHING STRATEGY

The chapter opener material captures the dynamic at the heart of this chapter: the increasing dominance of cities and urban life in shaping the experiences of Americans. Because the overwhelming majority of students today live in urban areas as defined by the U.S. census (2,500 inhabitants or more), they may intuitively feel that the transformation described here is unimpressive or inevitable. But it is important to emphasize the significance of a shift away from the small rural communities that had shaped American cultural patterns for three hundred years to the dynamics of urban life. The chapter introduction largely highlights the negative aspects of city life — anonymity, overcrowding, crime, and vice — that led one man to call cities "civilization's inferno." However, the text hints at some of the attractions of cities as well, including opportunities for autonomy and for escape through new forms of entertainment. Following in the tradition of antebellum reform, progressive reformers of the turn of the century perceived the city's problems and optimistically set about attacking them. For a complete suggested response to the **AP® LEARNING FOCUS** question, see p. 602.

18 CHAPTER

"Civilization's Inferno": The Rise and Reform of Industrial Cities 1880–1917

AP® LEARNING FOCUS

Why and how did the rise of big cities shape American society and politics?

Clarence Darrow, a successful lawyer from Ashtabula, Ohio, felt isolated and overwhelmed when he moved to Chicago in the 1880s. "There is no place so lonely to a young man as a great city," Darrow later wrote. "When I walked along the street I scanned every face I met to see if I could not perchance discover someone from Ohio." Instead, he saw a "sea of human units, each intent upon hurrying by." At one point, Darrow felt near despair. "If it had been possible I would have gone back to Ohio," he wrote, "but I didn't want to borrow the money, and I dreaded to confess defeat." Darrow stayed in Chicago and eventually prospered, becoming one of the nation's most famous defense attorneys.

In the era of industrialization, more and more Americans had experiences like Darrow's. In 1860, the United States was rural: less than 20 percent of Americans lived in an urban area, defined by census-takers as a place with more than 2,500 inhabitants. By 1910, more Americans lived in cities (42.1 million) than had lived in the entire nation on the eve of the Civil War (31.4 million). The country now had three of the world's ten largest cities — New York, Chicago, and Philadelphia. Though the Northeast remained by far the most urbanized region, the industrial Midwest was catching up. Seattle, San Francisco, and soon Los Angeles became hubs on the Pacific coast. Even the South boasted of thriving Atlanta and Birmingham. As journalist Frederic C. Howe declared in 1905, "Man has entered on an urban age."

The scale of industrial cities encouraged experiments that ranged from the amusement park to the art museum, the skyscraper to the subway. Yet the city's complexity also posed problems, some of them far worse than Clarence Darrow's loneliness. Brothels flourished, as did slums, pollution, disease, and corrupt political machines. Fast-talking hucksters fleeced newcomers; homeless men slept in the shadows of the mansions of the superrich. One African American observer called the city "Civilization's Inferno." The locus of urgent problems, industrial cities became important sites of political innovation and reform.

George Bellows, *New York* George Bellows, a member of the so-called Ash Can school of painters, was fascinated by urban life. In this 1911 painting, he depicts Madison Square during a winter rush hour, crowded with streetcars, horse-drawn wagons, and pedestrians. If you could enter the world of this painting, what might you hear, feel, and smell as well as see? What does Bellows suggest about the excitement and challenges of life in the big city?
Collection of Mr. and Mrs. Paul Mellon, National Gallery of Art. Courtesy National Gallery of Art, Washington.

TEACHING STRATEGY

A complete collection of George Bellows's work is available online. Search "George Bellows Complete Works" to access the site. After viewing several portrayals of New York, students might discuss in what ways and to what extent they see Bellows's paintings as "truthful" depictions of city life as described in this chapter.

AP® SKILLS & PROCESSES

CONTINUITY AND CHANGE

Use the **TIMELINE** to help students begin thinking about how the period between 1871 and 1911 could constitute a distinct historical period. Students will note that these dates are identical to the starting and ending dates of the previous chapter, and very close to those of Chapter 16. Chapter 16 largely addressed the economic developments of the industrial age, with a primary focus on big business, factory work, and immigrants who worked in factories. Chapter 17 concentrated on intellectual ideas of the era — scientific and technological change, and cultural and religious responses to them. The current chapter focuses primarily on patterns of urban life that resulted from urbanization. Students could skim through the timeline and identify three to five major developments that shaped urban life and explain their significance. They might also discuss the appropriateness of the title "Civilization's inferno," which implies that urban life destroyed civilization. To what extent is that a compelling characterization of turn-of-the-century American city life?

TIMELINE

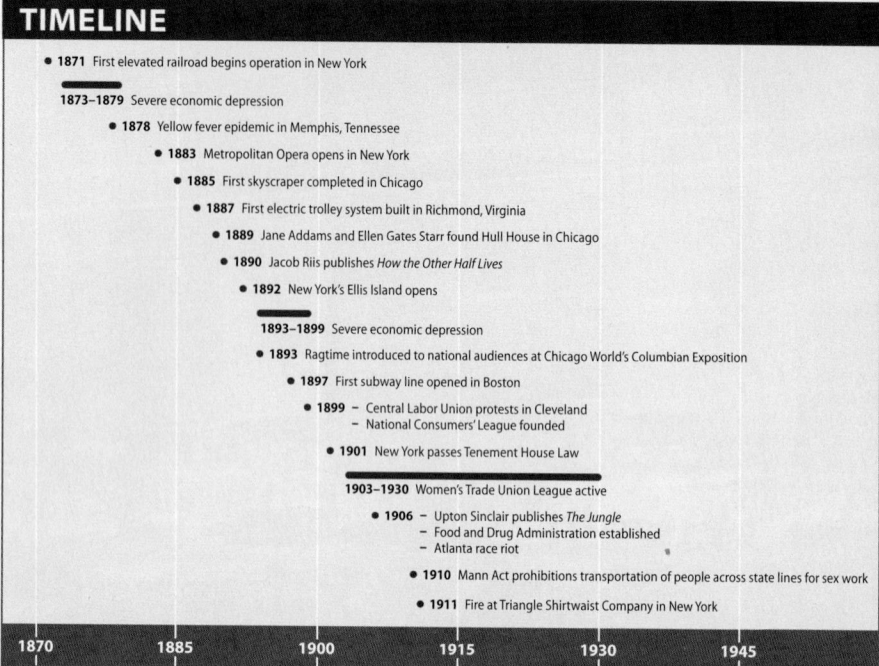

- **1871** First elevated railroad begins operation in New York
- **1873–1879** Severe economic depression
- **1878** Yellow fever epidemic in Memphis, Tennessee
- **1883** Metropolitan Opera opens in New York
- **1885** First skyscraper completed in Chicago
- **1887** First electric trolley system built in Richmond, Virginia
- **1889** Jane Addams and Ellen Gates Starr found Hull House in Chicago
- **1890** Jacob Riis publishes *How the Other Half Lives*
- **1892** New York's Ellis Island opens
- **1893–1899** Severe economic depression
- **1893** Ragtime introduced to national audiences at Chicago World's Columbian Exposition
- **1897** First subway line opened in Boston
- **1899** – Central Labor Union protests in Cleveland
  – National Consumers' League founded
- **1901** New York passes Tenement House Law
- **1903–1930** Women's Trade Union League active
- **1906** – Upton Sinclair publishes *The Jungle*
  – Food and Drug Administration established
  – Atlanta race riot
- **1910** Mann Act prohibitions transportation of people across state lines for sex work
- **1911** Fire at Triangle Shirtwaist Company in New York

1870 1885 1900 1915 1930 1945

THE NEW METROPOLIS

Why and how did American cities change in the late nineteenth century?

Mark Twain, arriving in New York in 1867, remarked, "You cannot accomplish anything in the way of business, you cannot even pay a friendly call without devoting a whole day to it. . . . [The] distances are too great." But new technologies allowed engineers and planners to reorganize urban geographies. Specialized districts began to include not only areas for finance, manufacturing, wholesaling, and warehousing but also immigrant wards and business-oriented downtowns. Department stores opened, full of tempting goods; baseball stadiums, vaudeville theaters, and other commercial venues beckoned people to spend their leisure hours — and their cash; entertainment districts like Broadway stayed open late at night, illuminated by new electric lights. It was an exciting and bewildering world.

The Landscape of the Industrial City

Before the Civil War, cities served the needs of commerce and finance, not industry. Early manufacturing sprang up mostly in the countryside, where mill owners could draw water power from streams, find plentiful fuel and raw materials, and recruit workers from farms and villages. The nation's largest cities were seaports; urban merchants bought and sold goods for distribution into the interior or to global markets.

As industrialization developed, cities became sites for manufacturing as well as finance and trade. Steam engines played a central role in this change. With them, mill operators no longer had to depend on less reliable water power. Steam power also vastly increased the scale of industry. A factory employing thousands of workers could instantly create a small city such as Aliquippa, Pennsylvania, which belonged body and soul to the Jones and Laughlin Steel Company. Older commercial cities also industrialized. Warehouse districts converted to small-scale manufacturing. Port cities that served as immigrant gateways offered abundant cheap labor, an essential element in the industrial economy.

Downtown St. Louis, c. 1890 This photograph suggests how new technologies transformed urban spaces. Architects built up; streetcars carried pedestrians from home to work and play; and telegraph and telephone wires began to crisscross streets, causing some to complain that they were dangerous eyesores. The unusual cleanliness of this street also suggests the impact of streetcars, subways, and other modern forms of transport: horses and their manure gradually disappeared from cities, replaced by fossil fuels. Library of Congress, 1s13665.

Mass Transit New technologies helped residents and visitors negotiate the industrial city. Steam-driven cable cars appeared in the 1870s. By 1887, engineer Frank Sprague designed an electric trolley system for Richmond, Virginia. A central generating plant fed electricity to trolleys through overhead power lines, which each trolley touched with a pole mounted on its roof. Trolleys soon became the primary mode of transportation in most American cities. Congestion and frequent accidents, however, led to demands that trolley lines be moved off streets. The "el" or elevated railroad, which began operation as early as 1871 in New York City, became a safer alternative. Other urban planners built down, not up. Boston opened a short underground line in 1897; by 1904, a subway running the length of Manhattan demonstrated the full potential of high-speed underground trains.

Even before the Civil War, the spread of railroads led to growth of outlying residential districts for the well-to-do. The high cost of transportation effectively segregated these wealthy districts. In the late nineteenth century, the trend accelerated. Businessmen and professionals built homes on large, beautifully landscaped lots in outlying towns such as Riverside, Illinois, and Tuxedo Park, New York. In such places, affluent wives and children enjoyed refuge from the pollution and perceived dangers of the city.

Los Angeles entrepreneur Henry Huntington, nephew of a wealthy Southern Pacific Railroad magnate, helped foster an emerging suburban ideal as he pitched the benefits of southern California sunshine. Huntington invested his family fortune in Los Angeles real estate and transportation. Along his trolley lines, he subdivided property into lots and built rows of bungalows, planting the tidy yards with lush trees and tropical fruits. Middle-class buyers flocked to purchase Huntington's houses. One exclaimed, "I have apparently found a Paradise on Earth." Anticipating twentieth-century Americans' love for affordable single-family homes near large cities, Huntington had begun to invent southern California sprawl.

Skyscrapers By the 1880s the invention of steel girders, durable plate glass, and passenger elevators began to revolutionize urban building methods. Architects invented the skyscraper, a building supported by its steel skeleton. Its walls bore little weight, serving instead as curtains to enclose the structure. Although expensive to build, skyscrapers allowed downtown landowners to profit from small plots of real estate in high-rent urban business districts. By investing in a skyscraper, a landlord could collect rent for ten or even twenty floors of space. Large corporations commissioned these striking designs as symbols of business prowess.

AP® EXAM TIP

Evaluate the impact of technological innovation in the rise of urban centers in the late nineteenth century.

AP® APPLY THE TIP

Students can use this **AP® EXAM TIP** to work on the skill of Contextualization. When students write contextualization in their Long Essay and Document-Based Questions, they need to marshal one broad historical process with a couple of supporting pieces of evidence. For this tip, have students explain the role of technological innovation in urban areas. Students then need to select two pieces of historical evidence to explain their assertion.

Chicago school
A school of architecture dedicated to the design of buildings — such as skyscrapers — whose form expressed their structure and function.

The first skyscraper was William Le Baron Jenney's ten-story Home Insurance Building (1885) in Chicago. Though unremarkable in appearance — it looked just like other downtown buildings — Jenney's steel-girder construction inspired the creativity of American architects. A **Chicago school** sprang up, dedicated to the design of buildings whose form expressed, rather than masked, their structure and function. The presiding genius of this school was architect Louis Sullivan, whose "vertical aesthetic" of set-back windows and strong columns gave skyscrapers a "proud and soaring" presence and offered plentiful natural light for workers inside. Chicago pioneered skyscraper construction, but New York, with its unrelenting demand for prime downtown space, took the lead by the late 1890s. The fifty-five-story Woolworth Building, completed in 1913, marked the beginning of Manhattan's modern skyline.

The Electric City One of the most dramatic urban amenities was electric light. Gaslight, produced from coal gas, had been used for residential light since the early nineteenth century, but gas lamps were too dim to brighten streets and public spaces. In the 1870s, as generating technology became commercially viable, electricity proved far better. Electric arc lamps, installed in Wanamaker's department store in Philadelphia in 1878, astonished viewers with their brilliant illumination. Electric streetlights soon replaced gaslights on city streets.

AP® SKILLS & PROCESSES
COMPARISON
How were America's industrial cities different from the typical city before 1860?

Before it had a significant effect on industry, electricity gave the city its modern tempo. It lifted elevators, illuminated department store windows, and turned night into day. Electric streetlights made residents feel safer; as one magazine put it in 1912, "A light is as good as a policeman." Nightlife became less risky and more appealing. One journalist described Broadway in 1894: "All the shop fronts are lighted, and the entrances to the theaters blaze out on the sidewalk." At the end of a long working day, city dwellers flocked to this free entertainment. Nothing, declared an observer, matched the "festive panorama" of Broadway "when the lights are on."

The San Francisco Earthquake California's San Andreas Fault had caused earthquakes for centuries — but when a major metropolis arose nearby, it created new potential for catastrophe. The devastating earthquake of April 18, 1906, occurred at 5:12 A.M., when many residents were sleeping. This photograph of Sacramento Street shows the resulting devastation and fires. The quake probably killed more than 2,000 people, though the exact number will never be known. A massive 296-mile rupture along the fault, felt as far away as Los Angeles, Oregon, and central Nevada, the earthquake refuted contemporary geological theories. It prompted researchers to open new lines of inquiry aimed at predicting tremors — and constructing urban buildings that could withstand them. Universal History Archive/UIG/Bridgeman Images.

AP® SKILLS & PROCESSES

COMPARISON

The **COMPARISON** question asks students to compare turn-of-the-century cities with earlier cities. Students will quickly recognize the larger size of later cities — in terms of both area and population — as well as the technologies that changed housing, transportation, and communication. While the continuities are more difficult to see, they are arguably just as important. Those who moved to cities from rural areas in the age of the Market Revolution also faced a faster-paced culture, a sense of anonymity, and the presence of vice and crime.

TRM Find complete suggested responses in the Teacher's Resource Materials.

TEACHING STRATEGY

Some students may be interested in more information about the San Francisco earthquake. "The 1906 San Francisco Earthquake and Fire Digital Collection" is a compilation of selected holdings from various sources that presents thousands of images and written texts — including many transcribed letters from survivors — related to the history of the earthquake and fire in San Francisco, as well as presenting material on other areas affected throughout the state. To access the site, search "Calisphere San Francisco Earthquake."

TEACHING STRATEGY

Modernity came in many different forms at the turn of the century. Sometimes innovation facilitated modern advancement and in other cases, modernity sprang from tragedy. Have students account for modernity from the perspective of both innovation and tragedy.

CHECK FOR UNDERSTANDI NG

Ask students: **What features characterized the shape of the industrial city?** *As seen in the photo of St. Louis on p. 579, electricity, mass transit, and skyscrapers characterized the industrial city. Mass transit sped travel, which allowed inhabitants to live farther from their place of work while simultaneously removing horse waste from city streets. New technology allowed for the construction of skyscrapers, which created denser patterns of dwelling and work. Electrification made cities brighter at night, making them generally safer and encouraging more public nightlife after work.*

Newcomers and Neighborhoods

Explosive population growth made cities a world of new arrivals, including many young women and men arriving from the countryside. Traditionally, rural daughters had provided essential labor for spinning and weaving cloth, but industrialization relocated those tasks from the household to the factory. Finding themselves without a useful household role, many farm daughters sought paid employment. In an age of declining rural prosperity, many sons also left the farm and — like immigrants arriving from other countries — set aside part of their pay to help the folks at home. Explaining why she moved to Chicago, an African American woman from Louisiana declared, "A child with any respect about herself or hisself wouldn't like to see their mother and father work so hard and earn nothing. I feel it my duty to help."

America's cities also became homes for millions of overseas immigrants. Most numerous in Boston were the Irish; in Minneapolis, Swedes; in other northern cities, Germans. Arriving in a great metropolis, immigrants confronted many difficulties. One Polish man, who had lost the address of his American cousins, felt utterly alone after disembarking at New York's main immigration facility, Ellis Island, which opened in 1892. Then he heard a kindly voice in Polish, offering to help. "From sheer joy," he recalled, "tears welled up in my eyes to hear my native tongue." Such experiences suggest why immigrants stuck together, relying on relatives and friends to get oriented and find jobs. A high degree of ethnic clustering resulted, even within a single factory. At the Jones and Laughlin steelworks in Pittsburgh, for example, the carpentry shop was German, the hammer shop Polish, and the blooming mill Serbian. "My people . . . stick together," observed a son of Ukrainian immigrants. But he added, "We who are born in this country . . . feel this country is our home."

Patterns of settlement varied by ethnic group. Many Italians, recruited by *padroni*, or labor bosses, found work in northeastern and Mid-Atlantic cities. Their urban concentration was especially marked after the 1880s, as more and more laborers arrived from southern Italy. The attraction of America was obvious to one young man, who had grown up in a poor southern Italian farm family. "I had never gotten any wages of any kind before," he reported after settling with his uncle in New Jersey. "The work here was just as hard as that on the farm; but I didn't mind it much because I would receive what seemed to me like a lot." Amadeo Peter Giannini, who started off as a produce merchant in San Francisco, soon turned to banking. After the San Francisco earthquake in 1906, his Banca d'Italia was the first financial institution to reopen in the Bay area. Expanding steadily across the West, it eventually became Bank of America.

Like Giannini's bank, institutions of many kinds sprang up to serve ethnic urban communities. Throughout America, Italian speakers avidly read the newspaper *Il Progresso Italo-Americano*; Jews read the Yiddish-language *Jewish Daily Forward*; Bohemians gathered in singing societies. By 1903, Italians in Chicago had sixty-six **mutual benefit societies**, most composed of people from a particular province or town. These societies collected dues from members and paid support in case of death or disability on the job. Mutual benefit societies also functioned as fraternal clubs. "We are strangers in a strange country," explained one member of a Chinese *tong*, or mutual benefit society, in Chicago. "We must have an organization (*tong*) to control our country fellows and develop our friendship."

Sharply defined ethnic neighborhoods such as San Francisco's Chinatown, Italian North Beach, and Jewish Hayes Valley grew up in every major city, driven by both discrimination and immigrants' desire to stick together (Map 18.1). In addition to patterns of ethnic and racial segregation, residential districts in almost all industrial cities divided along lines of economic class. Around Los Angeles's central plaza, Mexican neighborhoods diversified, incorporating Italians and Jews. Later, as the plaza became a site for business and tourism, immigrants were pushed into

AP® EXAM TIP

Understanding the ways immigrants maintained cultural identity in American cities is important to know on the AP® Exam.

mutual benefit society
An organization through which members of an ethnic immigrant group or other community, usually those from a particular province or town, pooled their funds to aid one another in case of emergency need. The societies functioned as fraternal clubs that collected dues from members in order to pay support in case of death or disability.

AP® APPLY THE TIP

Provide students with a variety of images, graphs, and maps that illustrate attempts by immigrant groups to maintain cultural identity in American cities. Be sure that each source has space for students to write at the bottom. Have students form collaborative groups and write a title and caption for each of the images based on the specific evidence presented on pp. 581–583. Then ask students to organize the images into groups as historical sources. Help students to make comparisons across chapters and topics by asking groups to use their prior knowledge to develop a thesis and outline to compare the attempts and success of immigrants and Native Americans to maintain their cultural identity in the late nineteenth century.

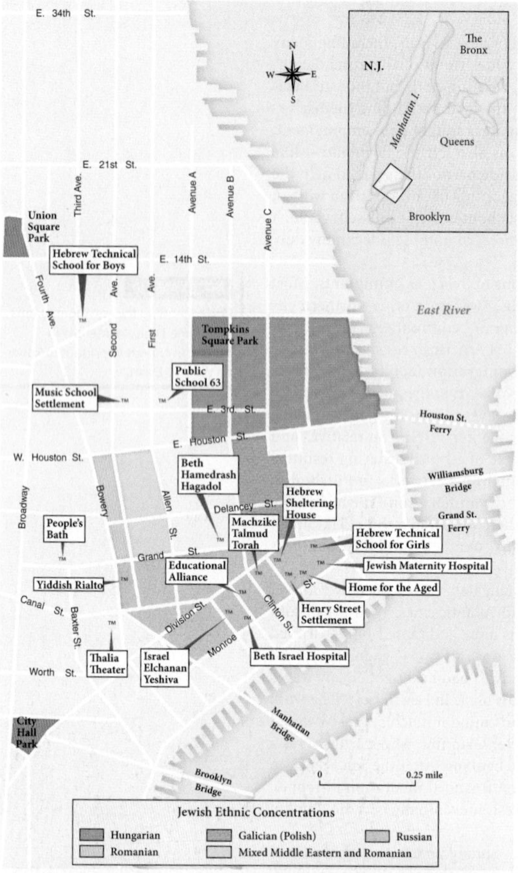

MAPPING THE PAST

MAP 18.1 The Lower East Side, New York City, 1900

As this map shows, the Jewish immigrants dominating Manhattan's Lower East Side preferred to live in neighborhoods populated by those from their home regions of Eastern Europe. Their sense of a common identity made for a remarkable flowering of educational, cultural, and social institutions on the Jewish East Side. Note that all the sites on the maps were in walking distance. Ethnic neighborhoods became a feature of almost every American city.

ANALYZING THE MAP: What institutions arose to serve this immigrant community? What does that suggest about the needs and priorities of these immigrants?

MAKING CONNECTIONS: For a newly arrived immigrant, what were the advantages and disadvantages of living in a neighborhood full of newcomers like oneself? In what ways does nativism relate to the establishment of maps such as the one above?

working-class neighborhoods like Belvedere and Boyle Heights, which sprang up to the east. Though ethnically diverse, East Los Angeles was resolutely working class; middle-class white neighborhoods grew up predominantly in West Los Angeles.

African Americans also sought urban opportunities. In 1900, almost 90 percent of American blacks still lived in the South, but increasing numbers had moved to cities such as Baton Rouge, Jacksonville, Montgomery, and Charleston, all of whose populations were more than 50 percent African American. Blacks also settled in northern cities, albeit not in the numbers that would arrive during the Great Migration of World War I. Though blacks constituted only 2 percent of New York City's population in 1910, they already numbered more than 90,000. These newcomers confronted conditions even worse than those for foreign-born immigrants. Relentlessly turned away from manufacturing jobs, most black men and women took up work in the service sector, becoming porters, laundrywomen, and domestic servants.

Blacks who moved to the city faced a threat from so-called race riots, attacks by white mobs triggered by street altercations or rumors of crime. One of the most lethal episodes occurred in Atlanta, Georgia, in 1906. The violence was fueled by a nasty political campaign that generated sensational false charges of "negro crime." Roaming bands of white men attacked black Atlantans, invading middle-class black neighborhoods and in one case lynching two barbers after seizing them in their shop. The rioters killed at least twenty-four blacks and wounded more than a hundred. The disease of hatred was not limited to the South. Race riots broke out in New York City's Tenderloin district (1900); Evansville, Indiana (1903); and Springfield, Illinois (1908). By then, one journalist observed, "In every important Northern city, a distinct race-problem already exists which must, in a few years, assume serious proportions."

Whether they arrived from the South or from Europe, Latin America, or Asia, working- class city residents needed cheap housing near their jobs. They faced grim choices. As urban land values climbed, speculators tore down houses vacated by middle-class families moving away from the industrial core. In their

AP® THEME

NAT: American and National Identity

Use **MAP 18.1** to illustrate the nature of ethnic enclaves in one of the most well-known neighborhoods of that era, New York City's Lower East Side. Ask students: **What does the map reveal about the settlement patterns of immigrant Jews?** *Several different groups of Jews formed ethnic enclaves with clearly defined boundaries provided by major city streets. The community services provided by such enclaves include schools, hospitals, religious institutions, and charitable organizations for the poor.*

TRM Find complete suggested responses in the Teacher's Resource Materials.

AP® THEME

NAT: American and National Identity

The nature of ethnic enclaves might be worth exploring with students in a bit more depth. The University of Minnesota's "Immigrants and Cities: Mapping Ethnic Enclaves in Early Twentieth Century United States" is a teaching resource that couples a visual and descriptive map of urban ethnic enclaves in Chicago with an oral interview by an immigrant growing up in New York City. Its goal is to provide different ways of "mapping" or understanding life for immigrants living in cities at the turn of the century. To access this resource, search "Immigrants and Cities: Mapping Ethnic Enclaves." Additionally, the Newberry Library provides a higher-resolution version of the descriptive map from the activity above, which can be accessed by searching "Newberry Library Polk St. to Twelfth, Chicago."

AP® THEME

MIG: Migration and Settlement

The *New York Times'* "Immigration Explorer" is an interactive mapping feature that allows users to investigate patterns of immigration. Students can change the year, select for specific countries of origin, view by number of immigrants or percentage of population, zoom in and out, and select immigrants from various regions within the U.S. To access this resource, search "NYT Immigration Explorer."

AP® THEME

MIG: Migration and Settlement

Though African Americans did not move to the north in large numbers until the early 1900s, a few preceded that larger migration and became successful. Blacks who successfully entered the middle class zealously guarded the "respectability" of their status as a protection against white racism and violence.

place, they erected five-or six-story **tenements**, buildings that housed twenty or more families in cramped, airless apartments. Tenements fostered rampant disease and horrific infant mortality. In New York's Eleventh Ward, an average of 986 persons occupied each acre. One investigator in Philadelphia described twenty-six people living in nine rooms of a tenement. "The bathroom at the rear of the house was used as a kitchen," she reported. "One privy compartment in the yard was the sole toilet accommodation for the five families living in the house." African Americans often suffered most. A study of Albany, Syracuse, and Troy, New York, noted, "The colored people are relegated to the least healthful buildings."

Tenement Life, c. 1910 Reformers who photographed the interior of tenement apartments often revealed overcrowding, squalor, and poverty — but also families determined to live with dignity amid difficult conditions. This immigrant woman poses with her seven children — all in clean, well-ironed clothes, with lace displayed on the mantelpiece and a jug of milk on the nearby table. The children's feet, however, are bare. Lewis W. Hine/George Eastman Museum/Getty Images.

Denouncing these conditions, reformers called for model tenements financed by public-spirited citizens willing to accept a limited return on their investment. When private philanthropy failed to make a dent, cities turned to housing codes. The most advanced was New York's Tenement House Law of 1901, which required interior courts, indoor toilets, and fire safeguards for new structures. The law, however, had no effect on the 44,000 tenements that already existed in Manhattan and the Bronx. Reformers were thwarted by the economic facts of urban development. Industrial workers could not afford transportation and had to live near their jobs; commercial development pushed up land values. Only high-density, cheaply built housing earned landlords a significant profit.

tenement
A high-density, cheap, five- or six-story housing unit designed for working-class urban populations. In the late nineteenth and early twentieth centuries, tenements became a symbol of urban immigrant poverty.

AP® SKILLS & PROCESSES

DEVELOPMENTS AND PROCESSES

What opportunities did urban neighborhoods provide to immigrants and African Americans, and what problems did these newcomers face?

AP® EXAM TIP

Evaluate the specific challenges facing African Americans in American cities.

City Cultures

Despite their dangers and problems, industrial cities could be exciting places to live. In the nineteenth century, white middle-class Protestants had set the cultural standard; immigrants and the poor were expected to follow their betters, seeking "uplift" and respectability. But in the cities, new mass-based entertainments emerged among the working classes, especially youth. These entertainments spread from the working class to the middle class — much to the distress of middle-class parents. At the same time, cities became stimulating centers for intellectual life.

Urban Amusements One enticing attraction was **vaudeville theater**, which arose in the 1880s and 1890s. Vaudeville customers could walk in anytime and watch a continuous sequence of musical acts, skits, magic shows, and other entertainment. First popular among the working class, vaudeville quickly broadened its appeal, creating forms that deeply influenced later radio and television. By the early 1900s, vaudeville faced competition from movie theaters, or nickelodeons, which offered short films for a nickel entry fee. With distaste, one reporter described a typical movie audience as "mothers of bawling infants" and "newsboys, bootblacks, and smudgy urchins." By the 1910s, even working girls who refrained from less respectable amusements might indulge in a movie once or twice a week.

vaudeville theater
A type of professional stage show popular in the 1880s and 1890s that included singing, dancing, and comedy routines.

AP® EXAM TIP

Evaluate the degree to which mass culture in urban areas challenged tradition in American society.

TEACHING STRATEGY

The tenement became one of the most notable features of urban life in the late nineteenth century. As the picture indicates, the dumbbell tenement, while providing access to living quarters in cities, eventually became synonymous with squalor. This example could be used as an opportunity to remind students of unintended consequences — which, in American history, have often resulted from the well-intended efforts of reformers. Columbia University hosts a site that explores the emergence of tenement housing. The site includes essays on the historical development of tenements, the design of the dumbbell tenement, and the business of tenements. The site also provides historical and contemporary photos of interiors and exteriors, including various views of the infamous dumbbell airshafts. To access this site, search "Columbia University Tenements."

AP® SKILLS & PROCESSES

DEVELOPMENTS AND PROCESSES

The **DEVELOPMENTS AND PROCESSES** question asks students to identify the costs and benefits of urban life for both immigrants and black migrants. Students are typically drawn immediately to the many very real problems of cities, so they may need to be pressed to recognize that both migrant groups continued to move to cities voluntarily — often at great cost — so they clearly perceived benefits to urban American life. Extend this prompt by asking students to explore the larger context by considering in more detail the home situations immigrants and black migrants faced.

TRM Find complete suggested responses in the Teacher's Resource Materials.

AP® APPLY THE TIP

Have students create a Venn diagram that compares the challenges facing African Americans in cities to the challenges facing African Americans in the rural South in the sharecropping system. Assign collaborative groups to investigate one of the following race riots from this period: Atlanta, GA (1906); Wilmington, NC (1898); Springfield, IL (1908); Evansville, IN (1903); Brownsville, TX (1906); etc. Students should address the following questions in their research:

- What issues or events precipitated the race riot?
- What role did local and state police forces play in the riot?
- What was the impact on African American businesses or workers?
- What was the impact on government in the city or state?
- What was the reaction of the federal government?

After students have completed their research, ask each group to present their findings. Record these findings on the board or ask students to complete a chart comparing the race riots. Then lead a class discussion on the common trends across the race riots.

CHECK FOR UNDERSTANDING

Ask students: **What newcomers came to cities in the late nineteenth century, and what kinds of neighborhoods did they form?** *European immigrants came to cities in large numbers at this time, with increasing percentages hailing from southern and eastern European countries like Italy, Poland, and Russia. Jews formed a small but noticeable element of this migration. Chinese immigrants also moved into many urban areas. African Americans moved from the South in small but measurable numbers; by 1910, there were nearly 100,000 in New York. In each case, groups lived in enclaves where they could speak their own language, practice familiar customs and eat traditional food, and form connections for aid and access to jobs.*

AP® APPLY THE TIP

Direct students to use pp. 578–587 of the text to complete **Handout 18.1 — Continuity and Change: Urban Culture in the Late Nineteenth Century (TRM)**. Once students have completed their analysis of changes associated with urbanization of the late nineteenth century, use students' findings to lead a class discussion on the degree to which these developments illustrate continuity and change.

TRM Find **Handout 18.1 — Continuity and Change: Urban Culture in the Late Nineteenth Century** in the Teacher's Resource Materials.

TEACHING STRATEGY

Long Beach was one of many coastal cities that grew as American leisure time increased and vacationers were drawn to amusement parks and to the ocean. In fact, tourism was a significant element of the local economy. When the Jack Rabbit Racer was built in 1900, the city was only three years old and had a population of 2,250; a decade later, the population had jumped to almost 18,000. More historical photos of the beach, boardwalk, pier, roller coaster, and local hotels are available from the Long Beach Public Library. To access this site, search "Long Beach Public Library digital archive."

Amusement Park, Long Beach, California The origins of the roller coaster go back to a Switchback Railway installed at New York's Coney Island in 1884, featuring gentle dips and curves. By 1900, when the Jack Rabbit Race was constructed at Long Beach, California, the goal was to create the biggest possible thrill. Angelenos journeyed by trolley to Long Beach to take a dip in the ocean as well as to ride the new roller coaster—and the whip ride in the foreground. Private Collection/Photo © GraphicaArtis/Bridgeman Images.

More spectacular were the great amusement parks that appeared around 1900, most famously at New York's Coney Island. These parks had their origins in world's fairs, whose paid entertainment areas offered giant Ferris wheels and camel rides through "a street in Cairo." Entrepreneurs found that such attractions were big business. Between 1895 and 1904 they installed several rival amusement parks near Coney Island's popular beaches. The parks offered New Yorkers a chance to come by ferry, escape the hot city, and enjoy roller coasters, lagoon plunges, and "hootchy-kootchy" dance shows. Among the amazed observers was Cuban revolutionary José Martí, working as a journalist in the United States. "What facilities for every pleasure!" Martí wrote. "What absolute absence of any outward sadness or poverty! . . . The theater, the photographers' booth, the bathhouses!" He concluded that Coney Island epitomized America's commercial society, driven not by "love or glory" but by "a desire for gain." Similar parks grew up around the United States. By the summer of 1903, Philadelphia's Willow Grove counted three million visitors annually; so did two amusement parks outside Los Angeles.

Ragtime and City Blues Music also became a booming urban entertainment. By the 1890s, Tin Pan Alley, the nickname for New York City's song-publishing district, produced such national hit tunes as "A Bicycle Built for Two" and "My Wild Irish Rose." The most famous sold more than a million copies of sheet music, as well as audio recordings for the newly invented phonograph. To find out what would sell, publishers had musicians play at New York's working-class beer gardens and dance halls. One publishing agent, who visited "sixty joints a week" to test new songs, declared that "the best songs came from the gutter."

African American musicians brought a syncopated beat that began, by the 1890s, to work its way into mainstream hits like "A Hot Time in the Old Town Tonight." Black performers became stars in their own right with the rise of ragtime. This music, apparently named for its ragged rhythm, combined a steady beat in the bass (played with the left hand on the piano) with syncopated, off-beat rhythms in the treble (played with the right). Ragtime became wildly popular among audiences of all classes and races who heard in its infectious rhythms something exciting — a decisive break with Victorian hymns and parlor songs.

For the master of the genre, composer Scott Joplin, ragtime was serious music. Joplin, the son of formerly enslaved parents, grew up along the Texas-Arkansas border and took piano lessons as a boy from a German teacher. He and other traveling performers introduced ragtime to national audiences at the Chicago World's Fair in 1893. Seeking to elevate African American music and secure a broad national audience, Joplin warned pianists, "It is never right to play 'Ragtime' fast." But his instructions were widely ignored. Young Americans embraced ragtime.

They also embraced each other, as ragtime ushered in an urban dance craze. By 1910, New York alone had more than five hundred dance halls. In Kansas City, shocked guardians of morality counted 16,500 dancers on the floor on a Saturday night; Chicago had 86,000. Some young Polish and Slovak women chose restaurant jobs rather than domestic service so they would have free time to visit dance halls "several nights a week." New dances like the Bunny Hug and Grizzly Bear were overtly sexual: they called for close body contact and plenty of hip movement. In fact, many of these dances originated in brothels. Despite widespread denunciation, dance mania quickly spread from the urban working classes to rural and middle-class youth.

By the 1910s, black music was achieving a central place in American popular culture. African American trumpet player and bandleader W. C. Handy, born in Alabama, electrified national audiences by performing music drawn from black workers in the cotton fields of the Mississippi Delta. Made famous when it reached the big city, this music became known as the **blues**. Blues music spoke of hard work and heartbreak, as in Handy's popular hit "St. Louis Blues" (1914):

blues
A form of American music that originated in the Deep South, especially from the black workers in the cotton fields of the Mississippi Delta.

> Got de St. Louis Blues jes blue as I can be,
> Dat man got a heart lak a rock cast in the sea,
> Or else he wouldn't gone so far from me.

Blues spoke to the emotional lives of young urbanites who were far from home, experiencing dislocation, loneliness, and bitter disappointment along with the thrills of city life. Like Coney Island and other leisure activities, ragtime and blues helped forge new collective experiences in a world of strangers.

Ragtime and blues had a profound influence on twentieth-century American culture. By the time Handy published "St. Louis Blues," composer Irving Berlin, a Russian Jewish immigrant, was introducing altered ragtime pieces into musical theater — which eventually transferred to radio and film. Lyrics often featured sexual innuendo, as in the title of Berlin's hit song "If You Don't Want My Peaches (You'd Better Stop Shaking My Tree)." The popularity of such music marked the arrival of modern youth culture. Its enduring features included "crossover" music that originated in the black working class and a commercial music industry that brazenly appropriated African American musical styles.

Inside a San Francisco Dance Hall, 1911 San Francisco's "Barbary Coast" had a wild reputation as a district of brothels, saloons, and other houses of ill repute. As this photo of Spider Kelly's bar suggests, however, nightclubs could provide a safe place for young couples to meet and dance. Urban singles made such bars wildly popular by the 1910s, prompting reformers and older Americans to express anxiety or condemnation of "dance madness" and its potential moral dangers. San Francisco History Center, San Francisco Public Library.

TEACHING STRATEGY

Ask students to select one of the following as the best piece of historical evidence in explaining the transformation of the city from a place solely intended for living and work to a place of entertainment: Theater, Parks, Music, and Libraries. Encourage students to make a selection they can defend with evidence.

TEACHING STRATEGY

As students engage in defining the changes in urban environments, they need to be aware of the factors that shaped those changes. For instance, rural customs and folkways directly shaped musical trends of the early twentieth century. Encourage students to connect internal migration patterns with the changes in American cities.

New Sexual Freedoms In the city, many young people found parental oversight weaker than it had been before. Amusement parks and dance halls helped foster the new custom of dating, which like other cultural innovations emerged first among the working class. Gradually, it became acceptable for a young man to escort a young woman out on the town for commercial entertainments rather than spending time at home under a chaperone's watchful eye. Dating opened a new world of pleasure, sexual adventure, and danger.

But young women, not men, proved most vulnerable in the system of dating. Having less money to spend because they earned half or less of men's wages, working-class girls relied on the "treat" to gain access to the commercialized pleasures of the big city, from amusement parks to movie theaters. Some tried to maintain strict standards of respectability, keenly aware that their prospects for marriage depended on a virtuous reputation. Others became so-called charity girls, who, as one investigator reported, "offer themselves to strangers, not for money, but for presents, attention and pleasure." For some women, sexual favors were a matter of practical necessity. "If I did not have a man," declared one waitress, "I could not get along on my wages." In the anonymous city, there was not always a clear line between working-class treats and casual prostitution.

Dating and casual sex were hallmarks of an urban world in which large numbers of residents were young and single. The 1900 census found that more than 20 percent of women in Detroit, Philadelphia, and Boston lived as boarders and lodgers, not in family units; the percentage topped 30 percent in St. Paul and Minneapolis. Single men also found social opportunities in the city. One historian has called the late nineteenth century the Age of the Bachelor, a time when being an unattached male lost its social stigma. With boardinghouses, restaurants, and abundant personal services, the city afforded bachelors all the comforts of home and, on top of that, men's clubs, saloons, and sporting events.

Many industrial cities developed robust gay subcultures. New York's gay underground, for example, included an array of drinking and meeting places, as well as clubs and drag balls. Middle-class men, both straight and gay, frequented such venues for entertainment or to find companionship. One medical student remembered being taken to a ball at which he was startled to find five hundred gay and lesbian couples waltzing to "a good band." By the 1910s, the word *queer* had come into use as slang for *homosexual*. Though harassment was frequent and moral reformers like Anthony Comstock issued regular denunciations of sexual "degeneracy," arrests were few. Gay sex shows and saloons were lucrative for those who ran them (and for police, who took bribes to look the other way, just as they did for brothels). The exuberant gay urban subculture offered a dramatic challenge to Victorian ideals.

AP® SKILLS & PROCESSES

COMPARISON

How did working-class and elite city residents differ in how they spent their money and leisure time?

High Culture For elites, the rise of great cities offered an opportunity to build museums, libraries, and other cultural institutions that could flourish only in major metropolitan centers. Millionaires patronized the arts partly to advance themselves socially but also out of a sense of civic duty and national pride. As early as the 1870s, symphony orchestras emerged in Boston and New York. Composers and conductors soon joined Europe in new experiments. The Metropolitan Opera, founded in 1883 by wealthy businessmen, drew enthusiastic crowds to hear the innovative work of Richard Wagner. In 1907, the Met shocked audiences by presenting Richard Strauss's sexually scandalous opera *Salome*.

Art museums and natural history museums also became prominent new institutions in this era. The nation's first major art museum, the Corcoran Gallery of Art, opened in Washington, D.C., in 1869, while New York's Metropolitan Museum of Art settled into its permanent home in 1880. In the same decades, public libraries grew from modest collections into major urban landmarks. The greatest library benefactor was steel magnate Andrew Carnegie, who announced in 1881 that he would build a

AP® SKILLS & PROCESSES

COMPARISON

The **COMPARISON** question asks students to identify differences in the ways two social classes spent their leisure time. Students should recognize ways that certain activities reflected greater education, social status, or access to money. Though the question focuses on differences, students should also look for similarities.

TRM Find complete suggested responses in the Teacher's Resource Materials.

library in any town or city that was prepared to maintain it. By 1907, Carnegie had spent more than $32.7 million to establish over a thousand libraries throughout the United States.

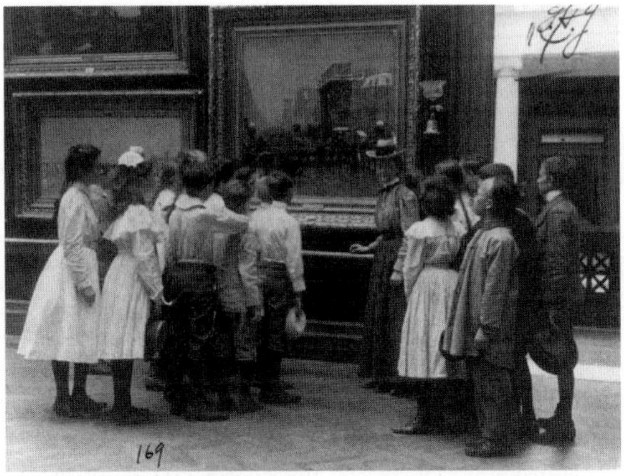

New Institutions of High Culture, 1899 This image from Washington D.C. shows public school students with their teacher, examining works of art at a local museum. The painting appears to depict the Arc de Triomphe in Paris; this class may have been visiting the Corcoran Gallery of Art, founded by a wealthy banker to foster art education and encourage the development of "American genius." Such field trips became possible in the late nineteenth century, as industrialists amassed and donated major art collections to new museums. Library of Congress, 3b15653.

Urban Journalism Patrons of Carnegie's libraries could read, in addition to books, new mass-market newspapers. Joseph Pulitzer, owner of the *St. Louis Post-Dispatch* and *New York World*, led the way in building his sales base with sensational investigations, human-interest stories, and targeted sections covering sports and high society.

By the 1890s, Pulitzer faced a challenge from William Randolph Hearst. The arrival of Sunday color comics featuring the "Yellow Kid" gave such publications the name **yellow journalism**, a derogatory term for sensationalist reporting in mass-market newspapers. Hearst's and Pulitzer's sensational coverage was often irresponsible. In the late 1890s, for example, their papers helped whip up frenzied pressure for the United States to declare war against Spain (see "The War of 1898" in Chapter 20). But Hearst and Pulitzer also exposed scandals and injustices. They believed their papers should challenge the powerful by speaking to and for ordinary Americans.

Along with Hearst's and Pulitzer's stunt reporters, other urban journalists worked to promote reform. New magazines such as *McClure's* introduced national audiences to reporters such as Ida Tarbell, who exposed the machinations of John D. Rockefeller, and David Graham Phillips, whose "Treason of the Senate," published in *Cosmopolitan* in 1906, documented the deference of U.S. senators — especially Republicans — to wealthy corporate interests. Theodore Roosevelt dismissed such writers as **muckrakers** who focused too much on the negative side of American life. The term stuck, but muckrakers' influence was profound. They inspired thousands of readers to get involved in reform movements and tackle the problems caused by industrialization.

yellow journalism
A derogatory term for newspapers that specialize in sensationalistic reporting. Yellow journalism is associated with the inflammatory reporting by the Hearst and Pulitzer newspapers leading up to the Spanish-American War in 1898.

muckrakers
A term, first applied negatively by Theodore Roosevelt but later used proudly by reformers, for investigative journalists who published exposés of political scandals and industrial abuses.

GOVERNING THE GREAT CITY

Why did urban political machines arise, and what were their strengths and limitations?

One of the most famous muckrakers was Lincoln Steffens, whose book *The Shame of the Cities* (1904), first published serially in *McClure's* magazine, denounced the corruption afflicting America's urban governments. Steffens used dramatic language to expose "swindling" politicians. He claimed, for example, that the mayor of Minneapolis had turned his city over to "outlaws." In St. Louis, "bribery was a joke," while Pittsburgh's Democratic Party operated a private company that handled most of the city's street-paving projects — at a hefty profit. Historians now believe that Steffens and other middle-class crusaders took a rather extreme view of urban politics; the reality

CHECK FOR UNDERSTANDING

Ask students: **How did American cities change in the late nineteenth century?** *American cities grew immensely, and changed accordingly, in the late nineteenth century. Industrialization was the primary catalyst; factories grew up in cities due to the availability of labor but, as they grew, they required more labor. The demand for labor brought in whites and African Americans from the countryside and immigrants from overseas, who largely lived in racially, ethnically, and socially stratified regions of the city and developed idiosyncratic social and cultural institutions in their various neighborhoods. New modes of transportation (i.e., mass transit) and building (i.e., skyscrapers) were built to accommodate larger and larger populations and businesses. New urban amusements catering to these new city dwellers, including vaudeville theater and amusement parks, emerged in and on the outskirts of these cities, as well.*

was more complex. But charges of corruption could hardly be denied. As industrial cities grew with breathtaking speed, they posed a serious problem of governance.

Urban Political Machines

AP® EXAM TIP
Understanding the role of political machines in the development of cities is important to know on the AP® Exam.

In the United States, cities relied largely on private developers to build streetcar lines and provide urgently needed water, gas, and electricity. This preference for business solutions gave birth to what one urban historian calls the "private city" — an urban environment shaped by individuals and profit-seeking businesses. Private enterprise, Americans believed, spurred great innovations — trolley cars, electric lighting, skyscrapers — and drove urban real estate development. Investment opportunities looked so tempting, in fact, that new cities sprang up almost overnight from the ruins of a catastrophic Chicago fire in 1871 and a major San Francisco earthquake in 1906. Real estate interests were often instrumental in encouraging streetcar lines to build outward from the central districts.

political machines
Complex, hierarchical party organizations, such as New York's Tammany Hall, that kept power through the strength of their political organization and their personal relationship with voters, especially working-class immigrants.

When contractors sought city business, or saloonkeepers needed licenses, they turned to **political machines** to help them: local party bureaucracies that kept an unshakable grip on both elected and appointed public offices. A machine like New York's Tammany Society — known by the name of its meeting place, Tammany Hall — consisted of layers of political functionaries. At the bottom were the party's precinct captains who knew every city neighborhood and block; above them were elected ward leaders, and at the top, powerful citywide officials, who had usually started at the bottom and worked their way up. Machines dispensed jobs and patronage, arranged for urban services, and devoted their energies to staying in office, which they did, year after year, on the strength of their political clout and popularity among urban voters. For constituents, political machines acted as a rough-and-ready social service agency, providing jobs for the jobless or a helping hand for a bereaved family. Tammany ward boss George Washington Plunkitt, for example, reported that he arranged housing for families after their apartments burned, "fix[ing] them up until they get things runnin' again." Plunkitt was an Irishman, and so were most Tammany Hall leaders. But by the 1890s, Plunkitt's Fifteenth District was filling up with Italians and Russian Jews. On a given day (as recorded in his diary), he might attend an Italian funeral in the afternoon and a Jewish wedding in the evening. Wherever he went, he brought gifts, listened to his constituents' troubles, and offered a helping hand.

The favors dispensed by urban political machines came via a system of boss control that was, as Lincoln Steffens charged, corrupt. Though rural, state, and national politics were hardly immune to such problems, cities offered flagrant opportunities for bribes and kickbacks. The level of corruption, as Plunkitt observed, was greater in cities, "accordin' to the opportunities." When politicians made contracts for city services, some of the money ended up in their pockets. In the 1860s, William Marcy Tweed, known as Boss Tweed, had made Tammany Hall a byword for corruption, until he was brought down in 1871 by flagrant overpricing of contracts for a lavish city courthouse. Thereafter, machine corruption became more surreptitious. Plunkitt declared that he had no need for outright bribes. He favored what he called "honest graft" — the profits that came to savvy insiders who knew where and when to buy land. Plunkitt made most of his money building wharves on Manhattan's waterfront.

Middle-class reformers condemned immigrants for supporting machines. But immigrant voters believed that few middle-class Americans cared about the plight of poor city folk like themselves. Machines were hardly perfect, but immigrants could rely on them for jobs, emergency aid, and the only public services they could hope to obtain. Journalist W. L. Riordan observed of a good ward boss, "Everybody knows where to find him, and nearly everybody goes to him for assistance of one sort or another. . . . He will go to the police courts to put in a good word for the 'drunks and disorderlies' or pay their fines. . . . He will attend christenings, weddings, and funerals. He will feed the hungry and help bury the dead." Ward bosses also sponsored summer picnics as well as winter balls and fancy dinners. Astute commentators saw that

AP® APPLY THE TIP

Provide students with a variety of Thomas Nast cartoons illustrating the power of the Tweed ring in New York City. Also provide students with excerpts from George Washington Plunkitt on the role of political machines in the late nineteenth century. Students should analyze the cartoons and the excerpts to define the role that political machines played in both the government of cities and in providing services to citizens in urban areas. Ask students to answer the following questions:

- **How did the rapid industrialization of the U.S. in the late nineteenth century support the rise of political machines?** *Wealthy entrepreneurs and industry leaders had access to money that was used to bribe political parties and support political machine operation; building projects provided opportunities for graft and corruption; demand for workers brought in large numbers of immigrants who became the "voters" controlled by political machines.*
- **How did political machines provide assistance to immigrants and the poor in urban areas?** *Political machines helped immigrants with the naturalization process; finding jobs and housing; assistance with sick or injured; food at special occasions like holidays, funerals, etc.*
- **What did political machines expect in exchange for their services to urban citizens?** *Votes for the machine's political candidates in elections.*
- **How did political machines benefit from the consolidation of wealth in industries in the late nineteenth century?** *The consolidation of wealth gave powerful industrialists more money to funnel into political corruption and greater power over elected officials.*

AP® THEME

NAT: American and National Identity

Thomas Nast, who is famous for his political cartoons on Reconstruction-related subjects, also became a regular critic of the Tammany Hall corruption and the leadership of William "Boss" Tweed. A blog post, available on The Museum of the City of New York (MCNY), provides a brief overview of Nast's efforts, with a photo of Nast at work and another of Tweed. There are also six Nast cartoons, though many more are available elsewhere online. To access the site, search "MCNY Thomas Nast."

bosses dominated city government because they provided for their constituents, with no condescending moral judgments (see "Thinking Like a Historian," p. 590).

Machine-style city governments achieved some notable successes on public projects as well. They arranged (at a profit) for companies to operate streetcars, bring clean water and gaslight, and remove garbage. Nowhere in the world were there more massive public projects — aqueducts, sewage systems, bridges, and spacious parks — than in the great cities of the United States. The nature of this achievement can be grasped by comparing Chicago, Illinois, with Berlin, the capital of Germany, in 1900. At that time, Chicago's waterworks pumped 500 million gallons of water a day, providing 139 gallons per resident; Berliners made do with 18 gallons each. Flush toilets, a rarity in Berlin, could be found in 60 percent of Chicago homes. Chicago lit its streets with electricity, while Berlin still relied mostly on gaslight. Chicago had twice as many parks as the German capital, and it had just completed an ambitious sanitation project that reversed the course of the Chicago River, carrying sewage into Lake Michigan, away from city residents.

These achievements were remarkable, because American municipal governments labored under severe political constraints. Judges did grant cities some authority: in 1897, for example, New York's state supreme court ruled that New York City was entirely within its rights to operate a municipally owned subway. Use of private land was also subject to whatever regulations a city might impose. But, starting with an 1868 ruling in Iowa, the American legal system largely classified the city as a "corporate entity" subject to state control. In contrast to state governments, cities had a limited police power, which they could use, for example, to stop crime but not to pass more ambitious measures for public welfare. States, not cities, held most taxation power and received most public revenues. Machines and their private allies flourished, in part, because cities were starved for legitimate cash.

Money talked; powerful economic interests warped city government. Working-class residents — even those loyal to their local machines — knew that the newest electric lights and best trolley lines served affluent neighborhoods, where citizens had the most clout. Hilda Satt, a Polish immigrant who moved into a poor Chicago neighborhood in 1893, recalled garbage-strewn streets and filthy backyard privies. "The streets were paved with wooden blocks," she later wrote, "and after a heavy rainfall the blocks would become loose and float about in the street." She remembered that on one such occasion, local pranksters posted a sign saying, "The Mayor and the Aldermen are Invited to Swim Here." As cities expanded, the problems of political machines became increasingly clear.

AP® SKILLS & PROCESSES

MAKING CONNECTIONS

How did the strengths and weaknesses of urban machines shape the experiences of Americans living in large industrial cities?

The Limits of Machine Government

The scale of urban problems became dramatically evident in the depression of the 1890s, when unemployment reached a staggering 25 percent in some cities. Homelessness and hunger were rampant; newspapers nationwide reported on cases of starvation, desperation, and suicide. To make matters worse, most cities had abolished the early nineteenth-century system of outdoor relief, which provided public support for the indigent. Fearing the system promoted laziness among the poor, middle-class reformers had insisted on private, not public, charity. Even cities that continued to provide outdoor relief in the 1890s were overwhelmed by the magnitude of the crisis. Flooded with "tramps," police stations were forced to end the long-standing practice of allowing homeless individuals to sleep inside.

Faced with this emergency, many urban voters proved none too loyal to the machines when better alternatives arose. Cleveland, Ohio, for example, experienced eighty-three labor strikes between 1893 and 1898. Workers' frustration centered on corrupt businesses with close ties to municipal officials. The city's Central Labor Union, dissatisfied with Democrats' failure to address its concerns, worked with middle-class allies to build a thriving local branch of the People's Party (see "The Populist Program" in Chapter 19). Their demands for stronger government measures,

AP® EXAM TIP

Evaluate the causes for the changes that occurred in municipal governments in the early twentieth century.

AP® SKILLS & PROCESSES

MAKING CONNECTIONS

The **MAKING CONNECTIONS** question asks students to account for strengths and weaknesses of urban political machines. In many ways, this question reflects the issue of divergent perspectives. Middle-class Americans could not see past the illegality and vote-rigging machines engaged in. Working-class people, on the other hand, generally supported machines because they were often the only agents of amelioration in cities that had outgrown existing infrastructure and governance. Even when the limits of machines' power become clear, there was often little alternative to machines' imperfect assistance.

TRM Find complete suggested responses in the Teacher's Resource Materials.

AP® APPLY THE TIP

Direct students to use pp. 589–593 of the text to complete **Handout 18.2 — Causation: Changes in Municipal Governments (TRM).** Then lead a class discussion to help students understand the changes that occurred in municipal governments that weakened the power of political machines. Ask students to explain the ways that the rise of the popular press affected challenges to the power of political machines. To extend this discussion, ask students to identify modern issues that lead to reforms in local government.

TRM Find **Handout 18.2 — Causation: Changes in Municipal Governments** in the Teacher's Resource Materials.

AP® SKILLS & PROCESSES

ANALYZING HISTORICAL EVIDENCE

The **AP® THINKING LIKE A HISTORIAN** feature asks students to think about the complexities attendant to the power and appeal of political machines, specifically ward bosses. Accounting for the appeal of the bosses might be more challenging as students tend to think only of the negative effects of machines. For the people living in urban environments, machines often offered essentials for survival. The sources provided illustrate a wide range of beliefs, including personal accounts of the appeal of machines as well as the reasons why some reformers decried machines. Students should attend to the source title for each document as that will help students understand historical change over time.

AP® THINKING LIKE A HISTORIAN

The Power and Appeal of the Ward Boss

Urban ward bosses were both corrupt and popular with their constituents. Why and how did they keep getting elected? While reformers looked for answers, successful politicians had their own explanations.

1. **Imagining Ward Bosses in Jail, 1894** In this cartoon, the humor journal *Puck* imagined citizens removing Edward Murphy Jr. from the U.S. Senate and depositing him in New York's state prison at Ossining, to sit beside convicted Coney Island ward boss John McKane. *Puck*'s prediction did not come true: despite allegations of graft, Murphy had a long, successful political career.

Source: Library of Congress, LC-DIG-ppmsca-29094.

2. **Jane Addams, Why the Ward Boss Rules, 1898** *Addams, who located her social settlement Hull House in a poverty-stricken Chicago immigrant ward, gained insight into how urban politics worked.*

The Alderman saves the very poorest of his constituents from that awful horror of burial by the county; he provides carriages for the poor, who otherwise could not have them. . . . It may be too much to say that all the relatives and friends who ride in the carriages provided by the Alderman's bounty vote for him, but they are certainly influenced by his kindness. . . . Many a man at such a time . . . has heard kindly speeches which he has remembered on election day. "Ah, well, he has a big Irish heart. He is good to the widow and the fatherless." "He knows the poor better than the big guns who are always [. . .] talking civil service and reform." Indeed, what headway can the notion of civic purity, of honesty of administration, make against this big manifestation of human friendliness, this stalking survival of village kindness? The notions of the civic reformer are negative and impotent before it. . . . Their goodness is not dramatic; it is not even concrete and human. . . .

. . . If we discover that men of low ideals and corrupt practice . . . stand by and for and with the people, then nothing remains but to obtain a like sense of identification.

3. **George Washington Plunkitt (as told to W. L. Riordan), Honest and Dishonest Graft, 1905** *Plunkitt, a Tammany Hall alderman, shared his political philosophy with journalist W. L. Riordan, who reported his words this way.*

The difference between a looter and a practical politician is the difference between the Philadelphia Republican gang and Tammany Hall. . . . The Philadelphians ain't satisfied with robbin' the bank of all its gold and paper money. They stay to pick up the nickels and pennies and the cop comes and nabs them. Tammany ain't no such fool. Why, I remember, about fifteen or twenty years ago, a Republican superintendent of the Philadelphia almshouse stole the zinc roof off the buildin' and sold it for junk. . . .

The Irish was born to rule, and they're the honestest people in the world. Show me the Irishman who would steal a roof off an almshouse! He don't exist. Of course, if an Irishman had the political pull and the roof was much worn, he might get the city authorities to put on a new one and get the contract for it himself, and buy the old roof at a bargain — but that's honest graft. It's goin' about the thing like a gentleman — and there's more money in it than in tearin' down an old roof and cartin' it to the junkman's — more money and no penal code.

4. **A Tammany Boss at Work, c. 1910–1915.** Richard E. Croker, the figure in the center wearing a silk top hat, was a Tammany Hall leader for many years. Here he appears with his wife and, to his right, Nathan Straus co-owner of what is now Macy's department store. Straus, a former commissioner of both the Parks and Health Departments, was a noted local philanthropist.

Source: Library of Congress, 17890.

5. **George Appo, Autobiography, 1916** *Appo's Irish American mother drowned at sea when he was six, and his Chinese American father ended up in jail. Growing up on the streets, Appo became addicted to opium and supported himself through petty crime. After he was attacked by a local bartender who thought Appo was informing to the police, a Tammany boss intervened in the case—on the side of Appo's enemies. Appo took his lawyer's advice and served three years at Matteawan State Hospital for the Criminally Insane.*

When my case was called for trial, there was the five men sitting together on the front bench in the courtroom ready to take the witness stand to commit perjury. These men were all friends and associates of [the bartender] and were not even in the neighbourhood at the time of the assault on me. . . . I was still suffering from the two blows I received on the head. . . . I was very weak. As the charge was read to me, I was surprised to see a lawyer named O'Reilly, a brother of [Tammany politician] Dan O'Reilly, step up beside me and say to the judge, "Your Honor, I will take this case."

. . . [My lawyer] Purdy jumped up, and in an indignant tone of voice said, "Your Honor, please, this is my client. My client is insane and devoid of reason and I demand Your Honor to form a commission and investigate his mental condition." His Honor agreed. . . . Purdy had me brought out to the counselor's room and said to me, "Who employed or assigned Counselor O'Reilly for you?"

"I do not know."

"Well, no matter. I'm glad I was there to stop him. You are in a bad fix and they are bound to put you away. . . . The best way I can see out of it is to have you sent to the hospital. . . ."

"Yes, but Counselor, this is all a frame-up job. I am the victim in the case."

"I know it, but what can we do? Everything is against you and I can't see any way out of it but the hospital."

6. **James Michael Curley, *I'd Do It Again*, 1957** *Curley rose through Boston's Democratic machine to become mayor in 1915. The "Brahmins" he refers to were elite Boston families who ruled Boston before Curley and his associates arrived.*

In my mother's day, even a job as a domestic servant was not always open to Catholics. . . . Irishmen, who often brought picks and shovels with them, were forced into jobs as day laborers, hostlers, stablers, or waiters. . . . No Irishman could get anywhere in economic or political life because the Brahmins and Yankees held the doors shut. . . .

The Irish turned to the political ladder because it was the quickest and easiest way out of the cellar. The leaders helped themselves, but in so doing they helped their people. . . .

In my day, politics was in a large measure built on personal and family contacts. The newcomers needed immediate help. The Irish leaders were rewarded with votes for favors they rendered, while the Brahmins exploited, rather than helped, the common people. In America, Democracy works from the bottom up, not from the top down.

Sources: (2) Jane Addams, "Why the Ward Boss Rules," in *Plunkitt of Tammany Hall*, ed. Terrence J. McDonald (Boston: Bedford/St. Martin's Press, 1994), 119–120, 122; (3) George Washington Plunkitt (as told to W. L. Riordan), in *Plunkitt of Tammany Hall*, ed. Terrence J. McDonald (Boston: Bedford/St. Martin's Press, 1994) 65; (5) George Appo, unpublished autobiography, in *The Urban Underworld in Late Nineteenth-Century New York*, ed. Timothy J. Gilfoyle (Boston: Bedford/St. Martin's Press, 2013), 95–96; (6) James Michael Curley, *I'd Do It Again* (Englewood Cliffs, NJ: Prentice-Hall, 1957), 10, 13–14.

ANALYZING THE EVIDENCE

1. How do Addams and Curley explain the success of urban machines? What audience do you think each of them sought to address? Identify the point of view and audience for each source.
2. Plunkitt's words were written down and published by a reform journalist, who shaped them for middle-class audiences. What do you think the journalist's goals might have been? Define the purpose of the source.
3. Based on Appo's account of his experiences, how might he have responded to the other authors' descriptions of the ward boss? Compare Appo's perspective to others' on the ward boss.
4. Most middle-class and rural Americans knew of ward bosses only as shown in the cartoon. Which of the four accounts might have confirmed that view? Which might have changed it, and how? Describe the relative credibility of each source with reasoning.

AP® DBQ PRACTICE

Using these sources, along with what you have learned in this chapter, write a short essay that explains why ward bosses flourished in the time and places they did.

TRM Find complete model answers in the Teacher's Resource Materials.

AP® SKILLS & PROCESSES

ARGUMENTATION

The **AP® DBQ PRACTICE** prompt asks students to account for the historical reasons urban machines thrived in the manner and context of the late nineteenth and early twentieth century. Students should consider information from both the primary sources and information gleaned from the textbook reading. Of particular note is the wide array of perspectives on urban machines that students should detail. Put another way, this prompt focuses on students' ability to think critically about the historical context in which urban machines flourished.

TEACHING STRATEGY

Ask students: **How does the cartoon attempt to appeal to readers? How effective do you think it would have been?** *The children, while poor, look innocent and vulnerable, playing on readers' sympathies. The depiction of skeletons is shocking and attention-grabbing. While it may have been over-the-top for some, others may have found it compelling.*

TRM Find complete suggested responses in the Teacher's Resource Materials.

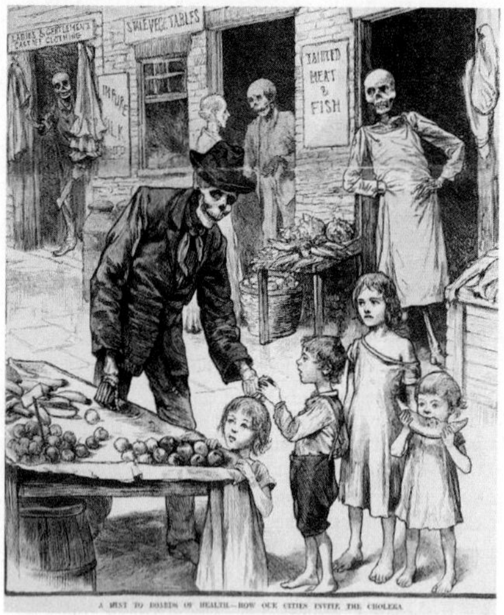

VISUAL ACTIVITY

A Hint to Boards of Health In 1884, *Frank Leslie's Illustrated Newspaper* urged municipal and state boards of health to work harder to protect urban children. When this cartoon appeared, New Yorkers were reading shocking reports of milk dealers who diluted milk with borax and other chemicals. Rutherford B. Hayes Presidential Center.

READING THE IMAGE: What threats to children in the city does the cartoon identify?

MAKING CONNECTIONS: Why do you think that progressive reformers focused on dangers to children and to women (including the young women vulnerable to "white slavery" and the victims of the Triangle Shirtwaist Fire)? Who was the most likely intended audience for this cartoon? What evidence could be used to support the artist's point of view on the rapid changes occurring in American cities?

especially to curb the power of private transit corporations and other local monopolies, culminated in citywide protests in 1899 during a strike against the hated streetcar company. That year, more than eight thousand workers participated in the city's annual Labor Day parade. As they passed the mayor's reviewing stand, the bands fell silent and the unions furled their flags in a solemn protest against the mayor's failure to support their cause.

To recapture support from working-class Clevelanders, Democrats made a dramatic change: in 1901 they nominated Tom Johnson for mayor. Johnson, a reform-minded businessman, advocated municipal ownership of utilities and a tax system in which "monopoly and privilege" bore the main burdens. (Johnson once thanked Cleveland's city appraisers for raising taxes on his own mansion.) Johnson's comfortable victory transformed the Democrats from an old-style machine into Cleveland's leading reform party. While the new mayor did not fulfill the whole agenda of the Central Labor Union and its allies, he became an advocate of publicly owned utilities and one of the nation's most famous and innovative reformers.

Like Johnson, other mayors began to transform or oust machines and launch ambitious urban services. Some modeled their municipal governments on those of Glasgow, Scotland; Düsseldorf, Germany; and other European cities on the cutting edge of innovation. In Boston, Mayor Josiah Quincy built public baths, gyms, swimming pools, and playgrounds and provided free public concerts. Like other mayors, he battled streetcar companies to bring down fares. The scope of such projects varied. In 1912, San Francisco managed to open one small municipally owned streetcar line to compete with private companies. Milwaukee, Wisconsin, on the other hand, elected socialists who experimented with a sweeping array of measures, including publicly subsidized medical care and housing.

Republican Hazen Pingree, mayor of Detroit from 1890 to 1897, worked for better streets and public transportation, and during the depression opened a network of vacant city-owned lots as community vegetable gardens. Though some people ridiculed "Pingree's Potato Patches," the gardens helped feed thousands of Detroit's working people during the harsh depression years. By 1901, a coalition of reformers who campaigned against New York's Tammany Hall began to borrow ideas from Pingree and other mayors. In the wealthier wards of New York, they promised to reduce crime and save taxpayer dollars. In working-class neighborhoods, they vowed to provide affordable housing and municipal ownership of gas and electricity. They defeated Tammany's candidates, and though they did not fulfill all of their promises, they did provide more funding for overcrowded public schools.

Reformers also experimented with new ways of organizing municipal government itself. After a devastating hurricane in 1900 killed an estimated six thousand people in Galveston, Texas, and destroyed much of the city, rebuilders adopted a commission system that became a nationwide model for efficient government. Leaders of the **National Municipal League** advised cities to elect small councils and hire professional city managers who would direct operations like a corporate executive. The league had difficulty persuading politicians to adopt its business-oriented model; it won its greatest victories in young, small cities like Phoenix, Arizona, where the professional classes held political power. Other cities chose, instead, to enhance democratic participation. As part of the Oregon System, which called for direct voting on key political questions, Portland voters participated in 129 municipal referendum votes between 1905 and 1913.

National Municipal League
A political reform organization that advised cities to elect small councils and hire professional city managers who would direct operations like a corporate executive. Some cities (especially younger and smaller ones) took up the reform.

AP® SKILLS & PROCESSES

DEVELOPMENTS AND PROCESSES
How did reformers try to address the limits of machine government? To what extent did they succeed?

CRUCIBLES OF PROGRESSIVE REFORM

Why and how did large cities become seedbeds for political reform?

The challenges posed by urban life presented rich opportunities for experimentation. As happened in Cleveland with Tom Johnson's election as mayor, working-class radicals and middle-class reformers often mounted simultaneous challenges to political machines, and these combined pressures led to dramatic change. Many reformers pointed to the plight of the urban poor, especially children. Thus it is not surprising that **progressivism**, an overlapping set of movements to combat the ills of industrialization (see "Reform Reshaped" in Chapter 19), had important roots in the city. In the slums and tenements of the metropolis, reformers invented new forms of civic participation that shaped the course of national politics.

progressivism
A loose array of reform movements that worked to clean up politics, fight poverty, increase racial and economic justice, and protect environmental resources, giving their name to the early twentieth-century Progressive Era.

A Reform Mayor in Detroit, 1891 Hazen Pingree, one of the most famous reform mayors of his era, did not forget the rural origins of many Detroit residents. During the severe depression of the 1890s Pingree opened city-owned land for community gardens. Though ridiculed as "Pingree's Potato Patches," the gardens helped thousands of poverty-stricken and unemployed Detroit residents grow fresh and nutritious food. This photograph depicts a different type of urban initiative: groundbreaking for the construction of Grand Avenue. Burton Historical Collection, Detroit Public Library.

Fighting Dirt and Vice

As early as the 1870s and 1880s, news reporters drew attention to corrupt city governments, the abuse of power by large corporations, and threats to public health. Researcher Helen Campbell reported on tenement conditions in such exposés as *Prisoners of Poverty* (1887). Using the new technique of flash photography, Danish-born journalist Jacob Riis included photographs of tenement interiors in his famous 1890 book, *How the Other Half Lives.* Riis had a profound influence on Theodore Roosevelt when the future president served as New York City's police

CHECK FOR UNDERSTANDING

Ask students: **What were urban machines? How and why did Americans debate their value?** *Urban machines were local political party bureaucracies that kept themselves in power through corruption and the rigging of votes. They dispensed jobs and patronage and provided urban services, while taking bribes and kickbacks. The* **DEVELOPMENTS AND PROCESSES** *question also discusses Americans' varied assessments of machines.*

AP® SKILLS & PROCESSES

DEVELOPMENTS AND PROCESSES

Use the **DEVELOPMENTS AND PROCESSES** question to encourage students to place reformers' anticorruption efforts in the context of late-nineteenth-century urban developments, particularly the urban problems that gave rise to political machines. The question also implicitly invites students to consider reformers' goals in light of their values, which shaped their concerns about corruption, their optimism regarding the ability to improve the situation, and their focus on rational structural changes as the way to move forward.

TRM Find complete suggested responses in the Teacher's Resource Materials.

CHECK FOR UNDERSTANDING

Ask students: **What problems did big cities pose for those who ran them, and how did political leaders try to meet those challenges?** *The massive growth of American cities in the Gilded Age presented new challenges, the scope of which had not been seen in U.S. history. Among these challenges was providing utilities and social services to a disparate number of new city dwellers. Previously, these services had been provided by the private sector, but in the late 1800s political machines (e.g., New York's Tammany Hall) took over these tasks. In exchange for votes and a blind eye to graft, many people, especially immigrants, supported political machines that helped people with public services and even jobs, food, and shelter, even as public health was undermined due to lax regulation. Nonetheless, the economic downturn in the 1890s exposed the corruption of the machines and people began to support reforms in city government, political transparency, and the employment of professional city managers.*

TEACHING STRATEGY

Frederick Law Olmsted Jr., son of the famed designer of New York's Central Park, was one of the preeminent intellectuals associated with the "City Beautiful" movement. Together with his brother, John, they formed the landscape architecture firm The Olmsted Brothers, designing dozens of civic spaces and college campuses all over the country. In a 1911 piece, Frederick articulated the key principles necessary for successful city planning: comprehensive planning, rapid transit routes, surface car routes, and carefully located playgrounds and parks boasting a variety of activities for children of all ages. The full text is available through Cornell University; to access the piece, search "Cornell Olmsted City Beautiful."

commissioner. Roosevelt asked Riis to lead him on tours around the tenements, to help him better understand the problems of poverty, disease, and crime.

Cleaning Up Urban Environments One of the most urgent problems of the big city was disease. In the late nineteenth century, scientists in Europe came to understand the role of germs and bacteria. Though researchers could not yet cure epidemic diseases, they could recommend effective measures for prevention. Following up on New York City's victory against cholera in 1866 — when government officials instituted an effective quarantine and prevented large numbers of deaths — city and state officials began to champion more public health projects. With a major clean-water initiative for its industrial cities in the late nineteenth century, Massachusetts demonstrated that it could largely eliminate typhoid fever. After a horrific yellow fever epidemic in 1878 that killed perhaps 12 percent of its population, Memphis, Tennessee, invested in state-of-the-art sewage and drainage. Though the new system did not eliminate yellow fever, it unexpectedly cut death rates from typhoid and cholera, as well as infant deaths from water-borne disease. Other cities followed suit. By 1913, a nationwide survey of 198 cities found that they were spending an average of $1.28 per resident for sanitation and other health measures.

The public health movement became one of the era's most visible and influential reforms. In cities, the impact of pollution was obvious. Children played on piles of garbage, breathed toxic air, and consumed poisoned food, milk, and water. Infant mortality rates were shocking: in the early 1900s, a baby born to a Slavic woman in an American city had a 1 in 3 chance of dying in infancy. Outraged, reformers mobilized to demand safe water and better garbage collection. Hygiene reformers taught hand-washing and other techniques to fight the spread of tuberculosis.

Americans worked in other ways to make industrial cities healthier and more beautiful to live in. Many municipalities adopted smoke-abatement laws, though they

City Garbage "How to get rid of the garbage?" was a question that bedeviled every American city. The difficulties of keeping up are all too clear in this ground-level photograph by the great urban investigator Jacob Riis, looking down Tammany Street in New York City around 1890. © Museum of the City of New York, USA/Bridgeman Images.

had limited success with enforcement until the post–World War I adoption of natural gas, which burned cleaner than coal. Recreation also received attention. Even before the Civil War, urban planners had established sanctuaries like New York's Central Park, where city people could stroll, rest, and contemplate natural landscapes. By the turn of the twentieth century, the **"City Beautiful" movement** arose to advocate more and better urban park spaces. Though most parks still featured flower gardens and tree-lined paths, they also made room for skating rinks, tennis courts, baseball fields, and swimming pools. Many included play areas with swing sets and seesaws, promoted by the National Playground Association as a way to keep urban children safe and healthy (see "Comparing Interpretations," p. 596).

"City Beautiful" movement A turn-of-the-twentieth-century movement that advocated landscape beautification, playgrounds, and more and better urban parks.

"FRIENDS" MEETING EMIGRANT GIRL AT THE DOCK

"The girl was met at New York by two 'friends' who took her in charge. These 'friends' were two of the most brutal of all the white slave traders who are in the traffic."

—U. S. Dist. Attorney Edwin W. Sims

Foreign girls are more helplessly at the mercy of white slave hunters than girls at home. Every year thousands of girls arriving in America from Italy, Sweden, Germany, etc., are never heard of again.

The Crusade Against "White Slavery" With the growth of large cities, prostitution was a major cause of concern in the Progressive Era. Though the number of sex workers per capita in the United States was probably declining by 1900, the presence of red light districts was obvious; thousands of young women (as well as a smaller number of young men) were exploited in the sex trade. This image appeared in *The Great War on White Slavery*, published by the American Purity Foundation in 1911. It illustrates how immigrant women could be ensnared in the sex trade by alleged "friends" who offered them work. Reformers' denunciations of "white slavery" show an overt racial bias: while antiprostitution campaigners reported on the exploitation of Asian and African American women, the victimization of white women received the greatest emphasis and most effectively grabbed the attention of prosperous, middle-class Americans. *The Great War on White Slavery*, by Clifford G. Roe, 1911. Courtesy Vassar College Special Collections.

Closing Red Light Districts Distressed by the commercialization of sex, progressives also launched a campaign against urban prostitution. They warned dramatically of the threat of white slavery, alleging (in spite of considerable evidence to the contrary) that large numbers of young white women were being kidnapped and forced into prostitution. In *The City's Perils* (1910), author Leona Prall Groetzinger wrote that young women arrived from the countryside "burning with high hope and filled with great resolve, but the remorseless city takes them, grinds them, crushes them, and at last deposits them in unknown graves."

Practical investigators found a more complex reality: women entered prostitution as a result of many factors, including low-wage jobs, economic desperation, abandonment, and often sexual and domestic abuse. Women who bore a child out of wedlock were often shunned by their families and forced into prostitution. Some working women and even housewives undertook casual sex work to make ends meet. For decades, female reformers had tried to "rescue" such women and retrain them for more respectable employments, such as sewing. Results were mixed. Efforts to curb demand — that is, to focus on arresting and punishing men who employed prostitutes — proved unpopular with voters.

Nonetheless, with public concern mounting over "white slavery" and the payoffs machine bosses exacted from brothel keepers, many cities appointed vice commissions in the early twentieth century. A wave of brothel closings crested between 1909 and 1912, as police shut down red light districts in cities nationwide. Meanwhile, Congress passed the Mann Act (1910) to prohibit the transportation of prostitutes across state lines.

The crusade against prostitution accomplished its main goal — closing brothels — but in the long term it worsened conditions for many sex workers. Though conditions in some brothels were horrific, sex workers who catered to wealthy clients made high wages and were relatively protected by madams, many of whom set strict rules for clients and provided medical care for their workers. In the wake of brothel closings, such women lost control of the prostitution business. Instead, almost all sex workers became "streetwalkers" or "call girls," more vulnerable to violence and often earning lower wages than they had before the antiprostitution crusade began.

AP® SKILLS & PROCESSES

CAUSATION

What prompted the rise of urban environmental and antiprostitution campaigns?

TEACHING STRATEGY

In the late nineteenth century, women were often considered the protectors of the home. Progressive-Era women reformers used this ideology to argue that women should move into the public sphere where they could exercise their moral authority over issues that affected the home. Women joined volunteer organizations in large numbers to work for reform. Efforts often began at the local level and expanded to the state and national level. Women conducted research, implemented programs, and lobbied for legislation to address social, political, and economic problems.

AP® SKILLS & PROCESSES

CAUSATION

The **CAUSATION** question asks students to identify factors that caused specific reform movements. Apart from the problems themselves, students might consider the values and beliefs of reformers as motivating factors. As with antebellum reform, scholars of progressive reform have sometimes charged reformers with being motivated by a desire for social control rather than a democratic concern for the well-being of all.

TRM Find complete suggested responses in the Teacher's Resource Materials.

CHECK FOR UNDERSTANDING

Ask students: **What forms did urban dirt and vice take? How did reforms fight both?** *Cities were often unsanitary and unhealthy; reforms lobbied for the construction of sewage and drainage systems. Reformers taught about hand-washing and other techniques to avoid the spread of contagious disease. They proposed a switch from coal to cleaner-burning natural gas. They proposed construction of urban park areas with trees, flowers, and recreational opportunities. Prostitution victimized poor and often-abused women; vice commissions attempted to crack down on brothels; and Congress passed the Mann Act to prohibit transporting prostitutes across state lines.*

AP® SKILLS & PROCESSES

ANALYZING HISTORICAL EVIDENCE

Use the **AP® COMPARING INTERPRETATIONS** feature to focus on the intersection between progressive reform and environmentalism. Though the two texts in this feature concentrate on beautifying the urban environment, it might still be helpful for students to consider the broader context of progressive support for the protection of wilderness places. Students could view the National Humanities Center's Web site page "Nature Transformed: The Environment in American History," which includes brief essays by historians, primary documents, and questions for discussion. To access the site, search "NHC Nature Transformed."

AP® COMPARING INTERPRETATIONS

How Did Urban Progressive Reformers Approach Environmentalism?

Contemporary stereotypes often associate environmentalism with wild landscapes, but environmentalism also emerged in America's cities. The urban landscapes of the late nineteenth and early twentieth centuries were the focus of reformers' efforts to manage the ill effects of industrialization and overcrowding. Though progressive environmentalists responded in different ways, they shared the view that America's cities were in danger.

The evidence was all around them. The nation's industrial factories belched plumes of coal ash. Pigs and horses wandering unpaved city streets dropped manure. The waste from overcrowded tenements spilled onto city sidewalks. With an inadequate and frequently corrupt public works infrastructure, cities were easily viewed as environmental disasters. Armed with ideals of the city, reformers embraced an environmental mission to transform America's urban spaces. What goals did different reformers prioritize? In the following excerpts, two historians, William H. Wilson and David Stradling, emphasize different approaches to Progressive Era urban environmentalism.

WILLIAM H. WILSON

SOURCE: William H. Wilson, *The City Beautiful Movement* (Baltimore: The Johns Hopkins University Press, 1989), 79–81, 86–87.

[T]hose who endorsed the City Beautiful [movement] were environmentalists. When they trumpeted the meliorative power of beauty, they were stating their belief in its capacity to shape human thought and behavior. . . . Endorsers of the City Beautiful were late-nineteenth or twentieth-century people. . . . Darwinism had compromised the old belief in man as a natural creature made in the image of God, who shared some of God's attributes and who required a beautified, naturalistic reprieve from his imprisonment in the artificial city. Man became remote from his Creator, more manipulable and malleable, a being conditioned by his environment. Therefore, the whole urban environment and the entire human experience within it were critical to the City Beautiful movement.

City Beautiful environmentalism involved social control. . . . [Its] rhetorical flights and its varied attack on urban problems occurred with a particular context — namely, Darwinian views of humanity and the city. They developed amid the proliferation of large, rapidly growing cities and of rapid advances of . . . such staple reform concerns as the juvenile problem, poverty, crime control, utilities, and housing regulation. . . .

The goal of the City Beautiful system was what Edward A. Ross, in *Social Control* (1901), termed the inculcation of "social religion," the idealized, transcendental bond among members of a community and among members of a nation or society. Ross claimed a deep emotional and instinctual basis for this civic religion, which was superior because it was an "*inward*," or internalized, control system. . . . They sought cultural hegemony by asserting control over the definition of beauty and the manipulation of civic symbols.

. . . The City Beautiful ideology was [grounded in] its enthusiastic welcome of the city. The architects, landscape architects, and planners of the era worked in cities and often lived in them or their suburbs. Some rhetorical attacks on the unnatural city persisted, but they became rarer. . . . If the city became the locus of harmony, mutual responsibility, and interdependence between classes, mediated by experts, then it would be a peaceful, productive place. . . . [A]dvocates found secular salvation for humans in their

The Movement for Social Settlements

Some urban reformers focused their energies on building a creative new institution, the **social settlement**. These community welfare centers investigated the plight of the urban poor, raised funds to address urgent needs, and helped neighborhood residents advocate on their own behalf. At the movement's peak in the early twentieth century, dozens of social settlements operated across the United States. The most famous, and one of the first, was **Hull House** on Chicago's West Side, founded in 1889 by Jane Addams and her companion Ellen Gates Starr. Their dilapidated mansion, flanked by saloons in a neighborhood of Italian and Eastern European immigrants, served as a spark plug for community improvement and political reform.

The idea for Hull House came partly from Toynbee Hall, a London settlement that Addams and Starr had visited while touring Europe. Social settlements also drew inspiration from U.S. urban missions of the 1870s and 1880s. Some of these, like the Hampton Institute, had aided former slaves during Reconstruction; others, like Grace Baptist in Philadelphia, arose in northern cities. To meet the needs of urban residents, missions

social settlement
A Progressive Era community welfare center that investigated the plight of the urban poor, advocated for change, and helped residents advocate on their own behalf.

Hull House
One of the first and most famous social settlements, founded in 1889 by Jane Addams in an impoverished, largely Italian immigrant neighborhood on Chicago's West Side.

AP® EXAM TIP
The impact of Hull House is important to know on the AP® Exam.

AP® APPLY THE TIP

Provide students with excerpts from Jane Addams on the role of Hull House and ask students to evaluate the goals and methods outlined by the excerpts. Remind students that women played vital roles in reform movements throughout the nineteenth century. Using their notes and the text, have students create a timeline of the role of women in reform movements from 1789 to 1920. Based on the content of their timelines, lead a class discussion to discuss the degree to which the establishment of the settlement house fostered change and represented continuity in the role of women in American society. Then ask students to complete **Handout 18.3 — Contextualization: Hull House (TRM)**.

TRM Find **Handout 18.3 — Contextualization: Hull House** in the Teacher's Resource Materials.

TEACHING STRATEGY

Access Jane Addams's class account of her reform work, *Twenty Years at Hull House*, online by searching "University of Pennsylvania Hull House." Additionally, the University of Illinois at Chicago offers an interactive Web site on Hull House to supplement your lecture. After an introduction page, the Web site is divided into six major sections: Historical Narrative, Timeline, Images, Geography, Teachers' Resources, and Search. Each section has a different focus and strategy to engage viewers in the subject matter. Access the site by searching "Urban Experience in Chicago: Hull-House and Its Neighborhoods."

belief in a flexible, organic city. . . . City Beautiful praised flowers, shrubs, and trees for their enhancing, softening qualities in city settings . . . [and] urged grass plots, ground covers, flowers, and plant groupings . . . [and] treated naturalistic parks and parkways as precious assets.

DAVID STRADLING

SOURCE: David Stradling, *The Nature of New York: An Environmental History of the Empire State* (Ithaca: Cornell University Press, 2010), 118–119.

Municipal health officials and city inspectors did make some advances against disease, especially through the improvement of the urban environment. They banned pigs from city streets, regulated notoriously unhealthy dairies inside city limits, and stepped up oversight of street cleaning and garbage removal. . . . In 1870 [New York City] built two bathhouses. . . . On Mondays, Wednesdays, and Fridays, women could bathe for free, and gain the use of a towel for three cents. The rest of the week, men and boys made use of the facilities. And hundreds did every day throughout the summer. By 1878 the city was operating six public baths. . . . In 1891 the New York Association for Improving the Condition of the Poor, an organization whose very name reveals the close connection between social and environmental reform, opened a new kind of public bathhouse. Located on Centre Market Place in the middle of a densely populated tenement district, the People's Bath gave residents with no bathing facilities in their own apartments — that is, most of the neighborhood — the opportunity to pay a nickel for . . . water, soap, and a towel. Unlike the city's bathhouses, the People's Bath was open year-round, and it featured clean country water piped in from outside the city. So many New Yorkers made use of the People's Bath that . . . in 1895 the state passed a law requiring cities of more than fifty thousand residents to open and operate as many public baths as local boards of health thought were required.

. . . Throughout the second half of the 1800s, improving public health remained a central goal of environmental reform. . . . [T]he Ladies Health Protective Association [was] organized in 1884 by a dozen women living in the Beekman Hill neighborhood of midtown Manhattan, who shared a concern for the vile odors emanating from a manure handler along the East River. . . . The manure heaps were eventually removed, and the women gradually expanded their concerns to the entire slaughterhouse district near their homes, including the tenements fouled by sickening smells and backed-up sewage. . . . [T]he association contacted business owners directly with their complaints, and if the nuisance persisted, they organized demonstrations at the offending location, inviting the press to witness their lay inspections. . . . The women also gained considerable publicity when they brought their complaints to the Board of Health. Successes followed, as they battled the odors emanating from fat renderers, gasworks, and other noxious industries.

Despite these victories, the Ladies Health Protective Association was circumscribed by the gender expectations of the era. Women could properly complain about issues affecting their own homes, and even the homes of other families, but they had limited access to authority. At public meetings, for example, often the association's leaders allowed men to speak for them, and women did not expect to fill the government positions . . . such as the Board of Health. Despite these limitations, women had the moral authority to keep cleanliness, odor, and public health issues in the press, and eventually they played a role in forcing broader reforms on the urban environment. . . . They inspired similar groups to form in other cities, igniting a movement that became known as "municipal housekeeping."

AP® SHORT ANSWER PRACTICE

1. What do these excerpts reveal about the historical situation of people who became urban environmentalists? What did the reformers described by Wilson and Stradling have in common? In what ways did their social standing, experience, and strategies differ?
2. What characteristics of progressivism, as discussed in this textbook, are visible in the urban environmental movements described in these excerpts? Use specific examples from the chapters to support your reasoning.
3. How does each author trace changes in reform ideas and goals over time? Compare the claims, evidence, and reasoning in each source.

TRM Find complete suggested responses in the Teacher's Resource Materials.

offered employment counseling, medical clinics, day care centers, and sometimes athletic facilities in cooperation with the Young Men's Christian Association (YMCA).

Jane Addams, a daughter of the middle class, first expected Hull House to offer art classes and other cultural programs for the poor. But Addams's views quickly changed as she got to know her new neighbors and struggled to keep Hull House open during the depression of the 1890s. Addams's views were also influenced by conversations with fellow Hull House resident Florence Kelley, who had studied in Europe and returned a committed socialist. Dr. Alice Hamilton, who opened a pediatric clinic at Hull House, wrote that Addams came to see her settlement as "a bridge between the classes. . . . She always held that this bridge was as much of a help to the well-to-do as to the poor." Settlements offered idealistic young people "a place where they could live as neighbors and give as much as they could of what they had."

Addams and her colleagues believed that working-class Americans already *knew* what they needed. What they lacked were resources to fulfill those needs, as well as a political voice. These, settlement workers tried to provide. Hull House was typical in offering a bathhouse, playground, kindergarten, and day care center. Some settlements opened libraries and gymnasiums; others operated penny savings banks and cooperative kitchens where tired mothers could purchase a meal at the end of the day. (Addams humbly closed the Hull House kitchen when she found that her bland New England cooking had little appeal for Italians; her coworker, Dr. Alice Hamilton, soon investigated the health benefits of garlic.) At the Henry Street Settlement in New York, Lillian Wald organized visiting nurses to improve health in tenement wards. Addams, meanwhile, encouraged local women to inspect the neighborhood and bring back a list of dangers to health and safety. Together, they prepared a complaint to city council. The women, Addams wrote, had shown "civic enterprise and moral conviction" in carrying out the project themselves.

Social settlements took many forms. Some attached themselves to preexisting missions and African American colleges. Others were founded by energetic college graduates. Catholics ran St. Elizabeth Center in St. Louis; Jews, the Boston Hebrew Industrial School. Whatever their origins, social settlements were, in Addams's words, "an experimental effort to aid in the solution of the social and industrial problems which are engendered by the modern condition of life in a great city."

Settlements served as a springboard for many other projects. Settlement workers often fought city hall to get better schools and lobbied state legislatures for new workplace safety laws. At Hull House, Hamilton investigated lead poisoning and other health threats at local factories. Her colleague Julia Lathrop studied the plight of teenagers caught in the criminal justice system, drafted a proposal for separate juvenile courts, and persuaded Chicago to adopt it. Pressuring the city to experiment with better rehabilitation strategies for juveniles convicted of crime, Lathrop created a model for juvenile court systems across the United States.

Another example of settlements' long-term impact was the work of Margaret Sanger, a nurse who moved to New York City in 1911 and volunteered with a Lower East Side settlement. Horrified by women's suffering from constant pregnancies — and remembering her devout Catholic mother, who had died young after bearing eleven children — Sanger

Hull House Playground, Chicago, 1906 When this postcard was made, the City of Chicago's Small Parks Commission had just taken over management of the playground from settlement workers at Hull House, who had created it. In a pattern repeated in many cities, social settlements introduced new institutions and ideas — such as safe places for urban children to play — and inspired municipal authorities to assume responsibility and control. Picture Research Consultants & Archives.

TEACHING STRATEGY

Today, students take the presence of playgrounds at public schools and parks for granted, but their ubiquity is in part a testimony to the persistent lobbying of progressive reformers. This postcard highlights Hull House's playground, a feature that "City Beautiful" landscape architects also emphasized. Ask students: **Why did reformers think playgrounds were such important components of urban reform?** *Playgrounds served several positive roles in the eyes of progressive reformers. Playgrounds encouraged physical activity so that children could be strong and healthy. They provided safe places for them to play away from trash, road traffic, and the possibility of physical harm from strangers. And they kept children occupied, preventing them from being drawn into a life of crime.*

launched a crusade for what she called birth control. Her newspaper column, "What Every Girl Should Know," soon garnered an indictment for violating obscenity laws. The publicity that resulted helped Sanger launch a national birth control movement.

Settlements were thus a crucial proving ground for many progressive experiments, as well as for the emerging profession of social work, which transformed the provision of public welfare. Social workers rejected the older model of private Christian charity, dispensed by well-meaning middle-class volunteers to those in need. Instead, social workers defined themselves as professional caseworkers who served as advocates of social justice. Like many reformers of the era, they allied themselves with the new social sciences, such as sociology and economics, and undertook statistical surveys and other systematic methods for gathering facts. Social work proved to be an excellent opportunity for educated women who sought professional careers. By 1920, women made up 62 percent of U.S. social workers.

AP® SKILLS & PROCESSES

CONTEXTUALIZATION

What were the origins of social settlements, and how did they develop over time?

Cities and National Politics

Struggles to improve factories, tenements, and neighborhoods in large cities quickly expanded into national movements for reform. In 1906, journalist Upton Sinclair exposed some of the most extreme forms of labor exploitation in his novel *The Jungle*, which described appalling conditions in Chicago meatpacking plants. What caught the nation's attention was not Sinclair's account of workers' plight, but his descriptions of rotten meat and filthy packing conditions. With constituents up in arms, Congress passed the **Pure Food and Drug Act** (1906) and created the federal Food and Drug Administration to oversee compliance with the new law.

AP® EXAM TIP

Take good notes on the role of popular media on the rise of Progressivism.

Pure Food and Drug Act
A 1906 law that created the Food and Drug Administration to regulate the food and drug industries to ensure safety.

The impact of *The Jungle* showed how urban reformers could affect national politics. Josephine Shaw Lowell, a Civil War widow from a prominent family, spent years struggling to aid poverty-stricken individuals in New York City. By 1890, she concluded that charity was not enough: she helped found the New York Consumers' League to improve wages and working conditions for female store clerks. The league encouraged shoppers to patronize only stores where wages and working conditions were known to be fair. By 1899, the organization had become the **National Consumers' League (NCL)**. At its head stood the outspoken and skillful Florence Kelley, a Hull House worker and former chief factory inspector of Illinois. Kelley believed that only government oversight could protect exploited workers. Under her crusading leadership, the NCL became one of the most powerful progressive organizations advocating worker protection laws.

National Consumers' League (NCL)
A national progressive organization that encouraged women, through their shopping decisions, to support fair wages and working conditions for industrial laborers.

Many labor organizations also began in a single city and then grew to national stature. One famous example was the **Women's Trade Union League (WTUL)**, founded in New York in 1903. Financed by wealthy women who supported its work, the league trained working-class leaders like Rose Schneiderman, who organized unions among garment workers. Although often frustrated by the patronizing attitude of elite sponsors, trade-union women joined them in the broader struggle for women's rights. When New York State held referenda on women's suffrage in 1915 and 1917, strong support came from Jewish and Italian precincts where unionized garment workers lived. Working-class voters hoped, in turn, that enfranchised women would use their ballots to help industrial workers.

Women's Trade Union League (WTUL)
A labor organization for women founded in New York in 1903 that brought elite, middle-class, and working-class women together as allies. The WTUL supported union organizing efforts among garment workers.

Residents of industrial cities, then, sought allies in state and national politics. The need for broader action was made clear in New York City by a shocking event on March 25, 1911. On that Saturday afternoon, just before quitting time, a fire broke out at the Triangle Shirtwaist Company. The **Triangle Fire** quickly spread through the three floors the company occupied at the top of a ten-story building. Panicked workers discovered that, despite fire safety laws, employers had locked the emergency doors to prevent theft. Dozens of Triangle workers, mostly young immigrant women, were trapped in the flames. Many leaped to their deaths; the rest never reached the windows. The average age of the 146 people who died was just nineteen (see "Firsthand Accounts," p. 600).

AP® EXAM TIP

The impact of the Triangle Fire on the Progressive Era is critical on the AP® Exam.

Triangle Fire
A devastating fire at the Triangle Shirtwaist Company in New York City on March 25, 1911, that killed 146 people, mostly young immigrant women. It prompted passage of state laws to increase workplace safety and regulate working hours for women and children.

AP® SKILLS & PROCESSES

CONTEXTUALIZATION

The **CONTEXTUALIZATION** question asks students to identify ways that the purposes and activities of settlement houses developed over time. Because of the label "settlement house," students tend to concentrate on the activities that took place on settlement house grounds, but the other activities that Jane Addams, Alice Hamilton, Julia Lathrop, and others engaged in may have ultimately been more important. In answering this question, students might also provide examples of the long-term effects of settlement house workers and evaluate their significance.

TRM Find complete suggested responses in the Teacher's Resource Materials.

CHECK FOR UNDERSTANDING

Ask students: **What motivated the movement for social settlements?** *Some urban reformers sought to support the plight of the poor by providing for their practical needs through an institution permanently located in the community. They aimed to provide employment counseling, medical clinics, day care centers, and other social services.*

TEACHING STRATEGY

Harvard University Library's online exhibition *Women Working, 1800–1930* explores women's impact on the economic life of the U.S. between 1800 and the Great Depression. This online research collection addresses working conditions, workplace regulations, home life, costs of living, commerce, recreation, health and hygiene, and social issues. The resources include books and pamphlets, diaries and memoirs, institutional records, magazines, manuscripts, photographs, and trade catalogs. To access this site, search "Harvard Women Working, 1800–1930."

TEACHING STRATEGY

The Triangle Shirtwaist Factory Fire was the deadliest workplace accident in New York City's history and forever changed American factories. The PBS companion site to the documentary *Triangle Fire* provides a transcript of the film, a discussion guide, a timeline of workplace accidents, a photo gallery on the era's fashions, an article explaining what shirtwaists are, and a biography of Clara Lemlich, leader of the 1909 strike by 20,000 garment workers. To access these resources, search "PBS Triangle Fire."

AP® APPLY THE TIP

Direct students to carefully analyze each source in the **AP® FIRSTHAND ACCOUNTS** feature (pp. 600–601) and provide an extended analysis by considering the author's point of view, intended audience, and purpose. After the students read the documents, organize them into collaborative groups to answer the questions on p. 601. After small groups have had a chance to discuss and answer the questions, lead a class discussion on the impact of the Triangle Fire.

AP® SKILLS & PROCESSES

ANALYZING HISTORICAL EVIDENCE

The **AP® FIRSTHAND ACCOUNTS** feature again provides students with an opportunity to investigate perspective as they read different reactions to the same event. As the introduction indicates, though all contemporaries agreed that the fire was a tragedy, their viewpoints and concerns shaped the way they attempted to make sense of that tragedy.

AP® FIRSTHAND ACCOUNTS

"These Dead Bodies Were the Answer": The Triangle Fire

Entire books have been written about the catastrophic 1911 fire at the Triangle Shirtwaist Company in New York City. The following excerpts are from documents by four contemporaries who in various ways played a part in the Triangle tragedy and its aftermath. Note the different audiences that these speakers and authors were addressing and the lessons that each one draws from this horrific event.

WILLIAM G. SHEPHERD, REPORTER

William G. Shepherd's eyewitness account appeared in newspapers across the country. Working for the United Press, Shepherd phoned the story to his editor as he watched the unfolding tragedy.

❝ I was walking through Washington Square when a puff of smoke issuing from a factory building caught my eye. I reached the building before the alarm was turned in. I saw every feature of the tragedy visible from outside the building. I learned a new sound — a more horrible sound than description can picture. It was the thud of a speeding, living body on a stone sidewalk. . . .

I looked up — saw that there were scores of girls at the windows. The flames from the floor below were beating in their faces. Somehow I knew that they, too, must come down, and something within me — something I didn't know was there — steeled me.

I even watched one girl falling. Waving her arms, trying to keep her body upright until the very instant she struck the sidewalk, she was trying to balance herself. Then came the thud — then a silent, unmoving pile of clothing and twisted, broken limbs. . . .

On the sidewalk lay heaps of broken bodies. A policeman later went about with tags, which he fastened with wire to the wrists of the dead girls, numbering each with a lead pencil, and I saw him fasten tag no. 54 to the wrist of a girl who wore an engagement ring. . . .

The floods of water from the firemen's hose that ran into the gutter were actually stained red with blood. I looked upon the heap of dead bodies and I remembered these girls were the shirtwaist makers. I remembered their great strike of last year in which these same girls had demanded more sanitary conditions and more safety precautions in the shops. These dead bodies were the answer. ❞

STEPHEN S. WISE, RABBI

A week after the fire, on April 2, 1911, a memorial meeting was held at the Metropolitan Opera House. One of the speakers, Rabbi Stephen S. Wise, a prominent figure in New York reform circles, made the following remarks.

❝ This was not an inevitable disaster which man could neither foresee nor control. We might have foreseen it, and some of us did; we might have controlled it, but we chose not to do so. . . . It is not a question of enforcement of law nor of inadequacy of law. We have the wrong kind of laws and the wrong kind of enforcement. Before insisting upon inspection and enforcement, let us lift up the industrial standards so as to make conditions worth inspecting, and, if inspected, certain to afford security to workers. . . . And when we go before the legislature of the state, and demand increased appropriations in order to ensure the possibility of a sufficient number of inspectors, we will not forever be put off with the answer: We have no money.

The lesson of the hour is that while property is good, life is better; that while possessions are valuable, life is priceless. The meaning of the hour is that the life of the lowliest worker in the nation is sacred and inviolable, and, if that sacred human right be violated, we shall stand adjudged and condemned before the tribunal of God and history. ❞

ROSE SCHNEIDERMAN, TRADE UNIONIST

Rose Schneiderman also spoke at the Metropolitan Opera House meeting. At age thirteen, she had gone to work in a garment factory like Triangle Shirtwaist's and, under the tutelage of the Women's Trade Union League, had become a labor organizer. The strike she mentions in her speech was popularly known as the Uprising of the 30,000, a nearly spontaneous walkout in 1909 that launched the union movement in the women's garment trades.

❝ I would be a traitor to these poor burned bodies if I came here to talk good fellowship. We have tried you good people of the public and we have found you wanting. The old Inquisition had its rack and its thumbscrews and its instruments of torture with iron teeth. We know what these things are

AP® EXAM TIP

Understand the causation relationship between popular media and political action in the Progressive Era.

Horrified New Yorkers responded with an outpouring of anger and grief that crossed ethnic, class, and religious boundaries. Many remembered that, only a year earlier, shirtwaist workers had walked off the job to protest abysmal safety and working conditions — and that the owners of Triangle, among other employers, had broken the strike. Facing demands for action, New York State appointed a factory commission that developed a remarkable program of labor reform: fifty-six laws dealing with such issues as fire hazards, unsafe machines, and wages and working hours

600

today; the iron teeth are our necessities, the thumbscrews are the high-powered and swift machinery close to which we must work, and the rack is here in the firetrap structures that will destroy us the minute they catch on fire.

This is not the first time girls have been burned alive in the city. . . . Every year thousands of us are maimed. The life of men and women is so cheap and property is so sacred. There are so many of us for one job it matters little if 146 of us are burned to death.

We have tried you citizens; we are trying you now, and you have a couple of dollars for the sorrowing mothers, brothers, and sisters by way of a charity gift. But every time the workers come out in the only way they know to protest against conditions which are unbearable the strong hand of the law is allowed to press down heavily upon us . . . [and] beats us back, when we rise, into the conditions that make life unbearable.

I can't talk fellowship to you who are gathered here. Too much blood has been spilled. I know from my experience it is up to the working people to save themselves. The only way they can save themselves is by a strong working-class movement. ❞

MAX D. STEUER, LAWYER

After finding physical evidence of the locked door that had blocked escape from the fire, New York's district attorney brought manslaughter charges against the Triangle proprietors, Max Blanck and Isaac Harris, who hired in their defense the best, highest-priced trial attorney in town, Max D. Steuer. In this talk, delivered some time later to a rapt audience of lawyers, Steuer described how he undermined the testimony of the key witness for the prosecution by suggesting that she had been coached to recite her answer. The trial judge instructed the jury that it could only convict Blanck and Harris if it was *certain* they had known the emergency exits were locked; as Steuer notes, the jury voted to acquit.

❝ There are many times, many times when a witness has given evidence very hurtful to your cause and you say, 'No questions,' and dismiss him or her in the hope that the jury will dismiss the evidence too. [*Laughter.*] But can you do that when the jury is weeping, and the little girl witness is weeping too? [*Laughter.*] . . . There is one [rule] that commands what not to do. Do not attack the witness. Suavely, politely, genially, toy with the story.

In the instant case, about half an hour was consumed by the examiner [Steuer]. . . . Very little progress was made; but the tears had stopped. And then [the witness] was asked, 'Now, Rose, in your own words, and in your own way will you tell the jury everything you did, everything you said, and everything you saw from the moment you first saw flames.'

The question was put in precisely the same words that the District Attorney had put it, and little Rose started her answer with exactly the same word that she had started it to the District Attorney . . . and the only change in her recital was that Rose left out one word. And then Rose was asked, 'Didn't you leave out a word that you put in when you answered it before?' . . . So Rose started to repeat to herself the answer [*laughter*], and as she came to the missing word she said, 'Oh, yes!' and supplied it; and thereupon the examiner went on to an entirely different subject. . . . [W]hen again he [asked her to repeat her story] . . . Rose started with the same word and finished with the same word, her recital being identical with her first reply to the same question.

The jurymen were not weeping. Rose had not hurt the case, and the defendants were acquitted; there was not a word of reflection at any time during that trial upon poor little Rose. ❞

Source: Excerpts from *Out of the Sweat Shop: The Struggle of Industrial Democracy* by Leon Stein, copyright © 1977 by Leon Stein, pp. 188–189, 192–193, 195–198. Used by permission of Quadrangle Books, an imprint of Random House LLC. All rights reserved. Any third party use of this material, outside of this publication, is prohibited. Interested parties must apply directly to Random House LLC for permission.

QUESTIONS FOR ANALYSIS

1. The hardest task of the historian is to conjure up the reality of the past—to say, "This is what it was really like." That's where eyewitness evidence like the reporter Shepherd's comes in. What is there in his account that you could only obtain from an eyewitness?
2. Both Rabbi Wise and Rose Schneiderman were incensed at the Triangle carnage, yet their speeches are quite different. In what ways? What conclusions do you draw about the different motivations and arguments that led to reform? Compare the historical situation of both speakers.
3. Max Steuer and Rose Schneiderman came from remarkably similar backgrounds. They were roughly the same age, grew up in poverty on the Lower East Side, and started out as child workers in the garment factories. The differences in their adult lives speak to the varieties of immigrant experience in America. What in their statements help to account for their differing life paths? How would Rose Schneiderman respond to Steuer's remarks? Use textual evidence to support your reasoning.

TRM Find complete suggested responses in the Teacher's Resource Materials.

for women and children. The chairman and vice chairman of the commission were Robert F. Wagner and Alfred E. Smith, both Tammany Hall politicians then serving in the state legislature. They established the commission, participated fully in its work, and marshaled party regulars to pass the proposals into law—all with the approval of Tammany. The labor code that resulted was the most advanced in the United States.

Tammany's response to the Triangle Fire showed that it was acknowledging its need for help. The social and economic problems of the industrial city had outgrown

Outrage after the Triangle Fire This graphic cartoon by John Sloan was titled "In Memoriam — The Real Triangle." It appeared in a prolabor newspaper, the *New York Call*. "How Long," asked the *Call's* headline, "Will the Workers Permit Themselves to be Burned As Well As Enslaved in Their Shops?" Who benefitted from the rent, interest, and profit that Sloan names as causes of the fire? The Granger Collection, New York.

the power of party machines; only stronger state and national laws could bar industrial firetraps, alleviate sweatshop conditions, and improve slums. Politicians like Wagner and Smith saw that Tammany had to change or die. The fire had unforeseen further consequences. Frances Perkins, a Columbia University student who witnessed Triangle workers leaping from the windows to their deaths, decided she would devote her efforts to the cause of labor. Already active in women's reform organizations, Perkins went to Chicago and volunteered for several years at Hull House. In 1929, she became New York State's first commissioner of labor; four years later, during the New Deal (Chapter 22), Franklin D. Roosevelt appointed her as U.S. secretary of labor — the first woman to hold a cabinet post.

The aftermath of the Triangle Fire demonstrated how challenges posed by industrial cities pushed politics in new directions, transforming urban government and initiating broader movements for reform. The nation's political and cultural standards had long been set by native-born, Protestant, middle-class Americans. By 1900, the people who thronged to the great cities helped build America into a global industrial power — and in the process, created an electorate that was far more ethnically, racially, and religiously diverse.

In the era of industrialization, some rural and native-born commentators warned that immigrants were "inferior breeds" who would "mongrelize" American culture. But urban political leaders defended cultural pluralism, expressing appreciation — even admiration — for immigrants, including Catholics and Jews, who sought a better life in the United States. At the same time, urban reformers worked to improve conditions of life for the diverse residents of American cities. Cities, then, and the innovative solutions proposed by urban leaders, held a central place in America's consciousness as the nation took on the task of progressive reform.

AP® SKILLS & PROCESSES

CAUSATION

How did urban reform movements impact state and national politics?

SUMMARY

After 1865, American cities grew at an unprecedented rate, and urban populations swelled with workers from rural areas and abroad. To move their burgeoning populations around, cities pioneered innovative forms of mass transit. Skyscrapers came to mark urban skylines, and new electric lighting systems encouraged nightlife. Neighborhoods divided along class and ethnic lines, with the working class inhabiting crowded, shoddily built tenements. Immigrants developed new ethnic cultures in their neighborhoods, while racism followed African American migrants from the country to the city. At the same time, new forms of popular urban culture bridged class and ethnic lines, some of which challenged traditional sexual norms and gender roles. Popular journalism rose to prominence and helped build rising sympathy for reform.

Industrial cities confronted a variety of new political challenges. Despite notable achievements, established machine governments could not address all urban problems locally through traditional means. Forward-looking politicians took the initiative and implemented a range of political, labor, and social reforms. Urban reformers

AP® SKILLS & PROCESSES

CAUSATION

Before answering this question, ask students to differentiate between long-term and short-term causation. There are benefits to recognizing each. However, why is there greater benefit when answering an AP® Free Response Question with short-term causation? After students have understood the concept, consider having them provide two-to-three short-term causes of urban development related to state and national politics.

TRM Find complete suggested responses in the Teacher's Resource Materials.

CHECK FOR UNDERSTANDING

Use the **AP® LEARNING FOCUS** question from the beginning of the chapter to provide a check on students' understanding of the chapter as a whole: **How and why did the rise of big cities shape American society and politics?** *After 1865, American cities grew at an unprecedented rate. To accommodate the increasing population, engineers and architects built mass transit systems, skyscrapers, and electric lighting systems. Neighborhoods within the urban environment self-segregated along class, ethnic, and racial lines. Most of the laboring class lived in tenements, while their wealthier counterparts moved to the edges of the city. At the same time, new forms of popular urban culture bridged class and ethnic lines, challenging traditional sexual norms and gender roles. Popular journalism captured the national imagination and aided those in favor of reform. The ever-growing cities encountered political challenges that could not be solved through traditional methods. Politicians, aided by urban reformers, moved to implement political, labor, and social reforms. The role of the government to help its citizens grew in this time period.*

also launched campaigns to address public health, morals, and welfare. They did so through a variety of innovative institutions, most notably social settlements, which brought affluent Americans into working-class neighborhoods to learn, cooperate, and advocate on behalf of their neighbors. Such projects began to increase Americans' acceptance of urban diversity and their confidence in government's ability to solve the problems of industrialization.

CHAPTER 18 REVIEW

AP® CONTENT REVIEW

Answer these questions to demonstrate your understanding of the chapter's main ideas.

1. Why and how did American cities change in the late nineteenth century?
2. Why did urban political machines arise, and what were their strengths and limitations?
3. Why and how did large cities become seedbeds for political reform?

AP® TERMS TO KNOW

Identify and explain the significance of each term below.

Key Concepts and Events

Chicago school (p. 580)
mutual benefit society (p. 581)
tenement (p. 583)
vaudeville theater (p. 583)
blues (p. 585)
yellow journalism (p. 587)
muckrakers (p. 587)
political machines (p. 588)
National Municipal League (p. 593)
progressivism (p. 593)
"City Beautiful" movement (p. 595)
social settlement (p. 596)
Hull House (p. 596)
Pure Food and Drug Act (p. 599)
National Consumers' League (NCL) (p. 599)
Women's Trade Union League (WTUL) (p. 599)
Triangle Fire (p. 599)

Key People

Scott Joplin (p. 585)
Tom Johnson (p. 592)
Jacob Riis (p. 593)
Jane Addams (p. 596)
Florence Kelley (p. 597)
Margaret Sanger (p. 598)
Upton Sinclair (p. 599)

AP® MAKING CONNECTIONS

Recognize the larger developments and continuities within and across chapters by answering these questions.

1. What broader economic changes that were occurring in the United States (Chapters 16 and 17) affected cities? How did urban dwellers' responses to these changes vary from those of farmers and other rural Americans?
2. Imagine that you have just arrived in a big American city in the early 1900s. Review the images and descriptions of urban life in this chapter. What do they suggest about the problems and dangers you might encounter as a newcomer? What opportunities might appeal to you? On balance, do you think you would want to stay, or turn around and head back home? Why? What factors would have shaped your decision?

KEY TURNING POINTS

Refer to the timeline at the start of the chapter for help in answering the following questions.

Based on the chapter chronology and the chapter narrative, what tipping points can you identify when Americans began to propose political solutions for urban industrial problems? What issues did they emphasize?

LearningCurve

Remind students to go online to complete the LearningCurve quiz for this chapter.

TRM Find complete suggested responses in the Teacher's Resource Materials.

AP® SKILLS & PROCESSES

CONTINUITY AND CHANGE

AP® CONTENT REVIEW 1 asks students to explain changes in the nature of cities over time. Note: This is the same question as the section-opening prompt on p. 578.

AP® SKILLS & PROCESSES

CAUSATION

AP® CONTENT REVIEW 3 probes the factors that caused reform efforts. Note: This is the same question as the section-opening prompt on p. 593.

TRM Find definitions for these terms in the **Glossary/Glosario** in the Teacher's Resource Materials.

AP® SKILLS & PROCESSES

CONTEXTUALIZATION

AP® MAKING CONNECTIONS 1 asks students to consider urbanization in the larger context of industrialization.

AP® SKILLS & PROCESSES

CONTINUITY AND CHANGE

KEY TURNING POINTS asks students to identify a turning point in the emergence of political reform efforts in the late nineteenth century.

TRM Find complete suggested responses in the Teacher's Resource Materials.

AP PRACTICE QUESTIONS

MULTIPLE CHOICE QUESTIONS *Choose the correct answer for each question.*

Questions 1–4 refer to this 1871 political cartoon by Thomas Nast depicting Boss Tweed.

Fotosearch/Archive Photos/Getty Images.

1. The political situation depicted in the image was most directly caused by
   - **a.** the First American Party System debates over the Alien Act.
   - **b.** the Second American Party System debates over the national bank.
   - **c.** large-scale international migration to cities of the United States.
   - **d.** journalists seeking government reforms during the Progressive Era.
2. The conditions depicted in the cartoon were most prevalent in which type of election race?
   - **a.** County
   - **b.** City
   - **c.** State
   - **d.** Federal
3. Which of the following would have most likely critiqued the arrangement of political power portrayed in the image?
   - **a.** Local party bureaucrats
   - **b.** Recent immigrants
   - **c.** College-educated women
   - **d.** Political machine bosses
4. Which of the following reform movements would most likely support the point of view expressed by the artist who created this cartoon?
   - **a.** Populists
   - **b.** Utopian Communities
   - **c.** Progressives
   - **d.** Women's rights advocates

Questions 5–7 refer to this excerpt.

> "There were those who made the tins for the canned meat; and their hands, too, were a maze of cuts, and each cut represented a chance for blood poisoning. Some worked at the stamping machines, and it was very seldom that one could work long there at the pace that was set, and not give out and forget himself and have a part of his hand chopped off. . . . [A]nd as for the other men, who worked in tank rooms full of steam, and in some of which there were open vats near the level of the floor, their peculiar trouble was that they fell into the vats; and when they were fished out, there was never enough of them left to be worth exhibiting, — sometimes they would be overlooked for days, till all but the bones of them had gone out to the world as Durham's Pure Beef Lard!"
>
> Upton Sinclair, *The Jungle*, 1906

5. The conditions described in the passage resulted most directly from
   - **a.** reliance on unskilled labor in meatpacking industry.
   - **b.** mechanization leading to lower meat prices.
   - **c.** an unregulated business environment emphasizing profits.
   - **d.** labor unions prioritizing pay raises over workplace safety.
6. During which earlier time period did American factory workers most commonly face comparably dangerous working conditions as those described in the excerpt?
   - **a.** 1650 to 1700
   - **b.** 1700 to 1750
   - **c.** 1750 to 1800
   - **d.** 1800 to 1850
7. The publication of muckraking accounts such as *The Jungle* most directly contributed to which of the following changes?
   - **a.** Expanded governmental oversight of businesses
   - **b.** Increased use of automation in factories
   - **c.** Consolidation of large corporations into trusts
   - **d.** Outsourcing of factories to lower wage countries

SHORT ANSWER QUESTIONS

Read each question carefully and write a short response. Use evidence from the text to support your claims.

> "[T]hose who endorsed the City Beautiful [movement] were environmentalists. When they trumpeted the meliorative power of beauty, they were stating their belief in its capacity to shape human thought and behavior. . . . [T]he whole urban environment and the entire human experience within it were critical to the City Beautiful movement. If the city became the locus of harmony, mutual responsibility, and interdependence between classes, mediated by experts, then it would be a peaceful, productive place. . . . [A]dvocates found secular salvation for humans in their belief in a flexible, organic city. . . . City Beautiful praised flowers, shrubs, and trees for their enhancing, softening qualities in city settings . . . [and] urged grass plots, ground covers, flowers, and plant groupings . . . [and] treated naturalistic parks and parkways as precious assets."
>
> William H. Wilson, *The City Beautiful Movement*, 1989
>
> "Municipal health officials and city inspectors did make some advances against disease, especially through the improvement of the urban environment. They banned pigs from city streets, regulated notoriously unhealthy dairies inside city limits, and stepped up oversight of street cleaning and garbage removal. . . . [T]he Ladies Health Protective Association . . . shared a concern for the vile odors emanating from a manure handler along the East River . . . [and] the entire slaughterhouse district near . . . the tenements fouled by sickening smells and backed-up sewage. . . . [T]he association contacted business owners directly with their complaints, and . . . organized demonstrations at the offending locations, inviting the press to witness their lay inspections. . . . The women also gained considerable publicity when they brought their complaints to the Board of Health."
>
> David Stradling, *The Nature of New York: An Environmental History of the Empire State*, 2010

1. Using the two excerpts provided, answer (a), (b), and (c).
   - **a.** Briefly explain ONE major difference between Wilson's and Stradling's historical interpretations of Progressive Era municipal reform.
   - **b.** Briefly explain how ONE specific historical event or development from the period 1880 to 1917 that is not explicitly mentioned in the excerpts could be used to support Wilson's interpretation.
   - **c.** Briefly explain how ONE specific historical event or development from the period 1880 to 1917 that is not explicitly mentioned in the excerpts could be used to support Stradling's interpretation.

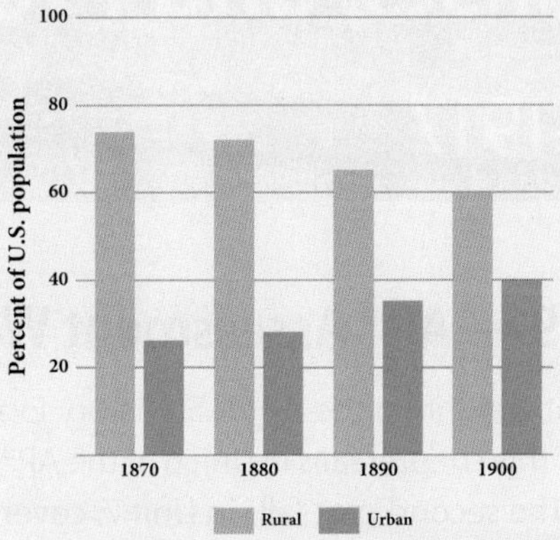

Rural and Urban Populations in the United States, 1870–1900

2. Using the graph provided, answer (a), (b), and (c).
   - **a.** Briefly explain ONE specific historical event or development that accounts for the change illustrated in the graph.
   - **b.** Briefly explain ONE specific historical political effect of the change illustrated in the graph.
   - **c.** Briefly explain ONE specific historical economic effect of the change illustrated in the graph.
3. Answer (a), (b), and (c).
   - **a.** Briefly explain ONE specific historical similarity between urban reform efforts in the period 1820 to 1860 and the period 1880 to 1920.
   - **b.** Briefly explain ONE specific historical difference between urban reform efforts in the period 1820 to 1860 and the period 1880 to 1920.
   - **c.** Briefly explain ONE specific success or failure of the urban reform movement in the period 1880 to 1920.

TRM Find complete suggested responses in the Teacher's Resource Materials.

19 CHAPTER Whose Government? Politics, Populists, and Progressives 1880–1917

Chapter 19 — AP® Assessment Weight and Pacing Guide

The assessment weight on the AP® U.S. History Exam for Chapters 15–19 is 10–17 percent. The first part of this chapter falls in Unit 6 of the AP® U.S. History Curriculum, covering Period 6: 1865–1898. The second part falls in Unit 7, covering Period 7: 1890–1945. These sections may be taught together or divided into units according to College Board periodization.

This pacing guide is based on a schedule with 120 sessions of 50 minutes each before the AP® U.S. History Exam. If you have a different number of sessions before the exam, you can modify the pacing to meet your needs. If you have additional time, consider incorporating quizzes, released AP® U.S. History questions, practice exams, writing practice, and other instructional activities.

	Traditional Schedule	Block Schedule
Chapter 19 Sections 1 and 2	2 days	1 day
Chapter 19 Sections 3 and 4	2 days	1 day

Daily Pacing Guide

	Content Focus	Essential Question
Day 1	Reform Visions, 1880–1892 (Period 6)	How did the political goals of Republicans, Democrats, and Populists differ in the years after the end of Reconstruction?
Day 2	The Political Earthquakes of the 1890s (Period 6)	Why and how did the depression of the 1890s impact federal politics and policy?
Day 3	Reform Reshaped, 1901–1912 (Period 7)	Why and to what extent did the political parties' goals change between 1900 and 1912?
Day 4	Wilson and the New Freedom, 1913–1917 (Period 7)	Why did Woodrow Wilson become a reformer after he assumed the presidency?

AP® Alignment

Section Heading	AP® Topic	AP® Theme
Reform Visions, 1880–1892	6.12, 6.13, 7.4	PCE
The Political Earthquakes of the 1890s	6.4, 6.7, 6.13	NAT, WXT, PCE
Reform Reshaped, 1901–1912	7.4	PCE, GEO
Wilson and the New Freedom, 1913–1917	7.4	PCE

*Should changes be made to the Course Framework in the future, an updated alignment will be placed on our AP® updates page at go.bfwpub.com/ap-course-updates.

Chapter 19 — Overview

Chapter 19 focuses on the efforts of radicals and reformers to address the evils of industrialization that threatened workers and farmers in the late nineteenth century. The chapter begins with analysis of the impact of calls for reform on the major political parties and the effectiveness of reform efforts. The chapter draws attention to the impact of economic crisis on political parties as well as the further entrenchment of white supremacy in the South and the continued disfranchisement of African Americans as a way to limit the popularity of populism in the agricultural South. The chapter examines the evolution of Populist ideas into the Progressive Era dominated by the middle class and elite reformers. Finally, the chapter provides a detailed analysis of the administrations of Theodore Roosevelt and Woodrow Wilson as progressive presidents.

Chapter 19 — Resources

The following resources can be found in the Teacher's Resource Materials (TRM) that accompany the book. You can access the TRM via the book's digital platform, by clicking the TRM links found here in your Teacher's Edition e-book, or by contacting your representative to access the resources online. Visit **bfwpub.com/henretta10e** to learn more.

TRM Chapter 19 Lecture Presentation Slides

TRM Chapter 19 Outline with AP® Focus

TRM Chapter 19 Lecture Strategies

TRM Chapter 19 Suggested Responses

TRM Handout 19.1 — Contextualization: Gilded Age

TRM Handout 19.2 — Contextualization: Omaha Platform

TRM Handout 19.3 — Causation: Disfranchisement of African Americans

TRM Handout 19.4 — Comparison: Progressive Era Reform

Chapter 19 — Essential Activity

Direct students to read pp. 628–629 of the text to analyze the platform positions of the Omaha Platform and the lasting legacy of the Populists on American identity and values. As students read the Omaha Platform, prompt them to break the document down into individual parts and identify historical evidence to support the position of the Populist Party. After students have assigned historical evidence to support the platform, ask them to consider the legacy of the Populist Party despite its failure to win the presidency in the election of 1896 by identifying laws, amendments, policies, etc., that show the accomplishment of Populist ideals in the nineteenth to twenty-first centuries.

Chapter 19 — Bell Ringers

The following activities take no more than 5–15 minutes of your class period and offer an effective and engaging way to begin your lessons and for students to apply AP® Skills & Processes:

- Use the **AP® COMPARING INTERPRETATIONS** feature on pp. 610–611 of the text to engage students in a discussion of the use of the names "Gilded Age" and "Progressive Era" to describe the late nineteenth to early twentieth centuries. Ask students to identify the historical argument being made by each historian. Then have students work with a partner to discuss each excerpt and identify specific historical evidence that could be used to support or challenge each historian's argument.
- Provide students with a copy of Thomas Nast's political cartoon "This is a White Man's Government." Ask students to work with a partner to identify groups represented by each character in the cartoon. (*Answers could include immigrants, Southern Redeemers, urban political machines, African Americans.*) Then ask students to contextualize the cartoon by explaining the historical processes, events, and developments that are reflected in the cartoon.
- Provide students with an excerpt from Theodore Roosevelt's *New Nationalism* and Woodrow Wilson's *New Freedom*, and prompt them to discuss the ways that each leader characterized the American economy and the role of the federal government in the economy. Ask students to consider the degree to which both leaders represented progressivism.

NOTES

TEACHING STRATEGY

While progressives "engaged in diverse, energetic movements to improve America," as discussed on pp. 623–626, progressives generally shared a few core goals, as described here that might serve as an organizing matrix for students: (1) attacking political corruption, (2) limiting the power of big business, (3) reducing poverty, and (4) promoting social justice. Students might discuss why these common problems united progressives and speculate before reading the chapter about the shapes reform might have taken. For a complete suggested response to the **AP® LEARNING FOCUS** question, see p. 634.

TEACHING STRATEGY

Despite the fact that women are not usually associated with the leadership of the Populist movement, Mary Lease was its best-known orator. History Matters provides an excerpt of her speech "In Defense of Home and Hearth," an articulation of the Populists' agrarian David and Goliath fight against Wall Street. The site also provides an excerpt of her defense of women's involvement in the movement, "A Woman's Work: Mary Lease Celebrates Women Populists." To access these resources, search "History Matters Mary Lease."

19

CHAPTER

Whose Government? Politics, Populists, and Progressives

1880–1917

AP® LEARNING FOCUS

Why and how did Progressive Era reformers seek to address the problems of industrial America, and to what extent did they succeed?

"We are living in a grand and wonderful time," declared Kansas political organizer Mary E. Lease in 1891. "Men, women and children are in commotion, discussing the mighty problems of the day." This "movement among the masses," she said, was based on the words of Jesus: "Whatsoever ye would that men should do unto you, do ye even so unto them." Between the 1880s and the 1910s, thousands of reformers like Lease confronted the problems of industrialization. Lease herself stumped not only for the People's Party, which sought more government regulation of the economy, but also for the Knights of Labor and Woman's Christian Temperance Union (WCTU), as well as for women's suffrage and public health.

Between the end of Reconstruction and the start of World War I, reformers focused on four main goals: cleaning up politics, limiting the power of big business, reducing poverty, and promoting social justice. Historians call this period of agitation and innovation the Progressive Era. In the 1880s and 1890s, labor unions and farm groups took the lead in critiquing the industrial order and demanding change. But over time, more and more middle-class and elite Americans took up the call, earning the name *progressives*. On the whole, they proposed more limited measures than farmer-labor advocates did, but since they had more political clout, they often had greater success in winning new laws.

No single group defined the Progressive Era. On the contrary, different reformers took opposite views on such questions as immigration, racial justice, women's rights, and imperialism. Leaders such as Theodore Roosevelt and Woodrow Wilson, initially hostile to the sweeping critiques of capitalism offered by radicals, gradually adopted bolder ideas. Changes in electoral politics influenced the direction of reform. Close party competition in the 1880s gave way to Republican control between 1894 and 1910, followed by a period of Democratic leadership during Wilson's presidency (1913–1919). Progressives gave the era its name, not because they acted as a unified force, but because they engaged in diverse, energetic movements to improve America.

Coxey's Army on the March, 1894 During the severe depression of the 1890s, Ohio businessman Jacob Coxey organized unemployed men for a peaceful march to the U.S. Capitol to plead for an emergency jobs program. They called themselves the Commonweal of Christ but won the nickname "Coxey's Army." Though it failed to win sympathy from Congress, the army's march on Washington — one of the nation's first — inspired similar groups to set out from many cities. Here, Coxey's group nears Washington, D.C. The man on horseback is Carl Browne, one of the group's leaders and a flamboyant publicist. As the marchers entered Washington, Coxey's seventeen-year-old daughter Mamie, dressed as the "Goddess of Peace," led the procession on a white Arabian horse. Library of Congress, 1s09215.

TEACHING STRATEGY

Ask students: **What does the photograph of Coxey's Army suggest about the nature of protest in this era?** *The photograph suggests the popular, democratic, and participatory nature of protest, as well as the often patriotic motives that inspired it.*

Extend this discussion by asking students to read and analyze the *Smithsonian* article entitled "How a Ragtag Band of Reformers Organized the First Protest March on Washington, D.C." The article highlights both the visionary and bizarre demands of Coxey's Army, suggesting that the movement's greatest legacy was the precedent of marching on the nation's capital as a means of protest. To access this article, search "Smithsonian Coxey's Army."

AP® SKILLS & PROCESSES

CONTINUITY AND CHANGE

Use the **TIMELINE** table to help students begin thinking about how the period from 1881 to 1914 could constitute a distinct historical period. At least two different features in this chapter support an investigation of the periodization of this era through a consideration of labels used to define it. **AP® COMPARING INTERPRETATIONS** (pp. 610–611) poses conflicting perspectives on the appropriateness of applying the label from an earlier era, "the Gilded Age," to the late nineteenth and early twentieth centuries.

AP® THEME

PCE: Politics and Power

The "Reform Visions, 1880–1892" section explores the ways that major political parties appealed to lingering divisions from the Civil War, while disagreeing about tariffs and currency issues.

AP® APPLY THE TIP

Introduce this chapter on the Gilded Age by providing students with an excerpt from "The Gilded Age in American History" by Vincent P. DeSantis. (To access this excerpt, search "DeSantis Gilded Age in American History.") In this excerpt, DeSantis presents an overview of the historical definitions of the term "Gilded Age" from different historians. Ask students to read the excerpt and outline the various definitions of the Gilded Age. With a partner, students should look through Chapter 19 and identify images, graphs, or excerpts that would support each definition. As a follow-up, ask students to complete **Handout 19.1 — Contextualization: Gilded Age (TRM)**.

TRM Find **Handout 19.1 — Contextualization: Gilded Age** in the Teacher's Resource Materials.

TRM Find complete suggested responses in the Teacher's Resource Materials.

TIMELINE

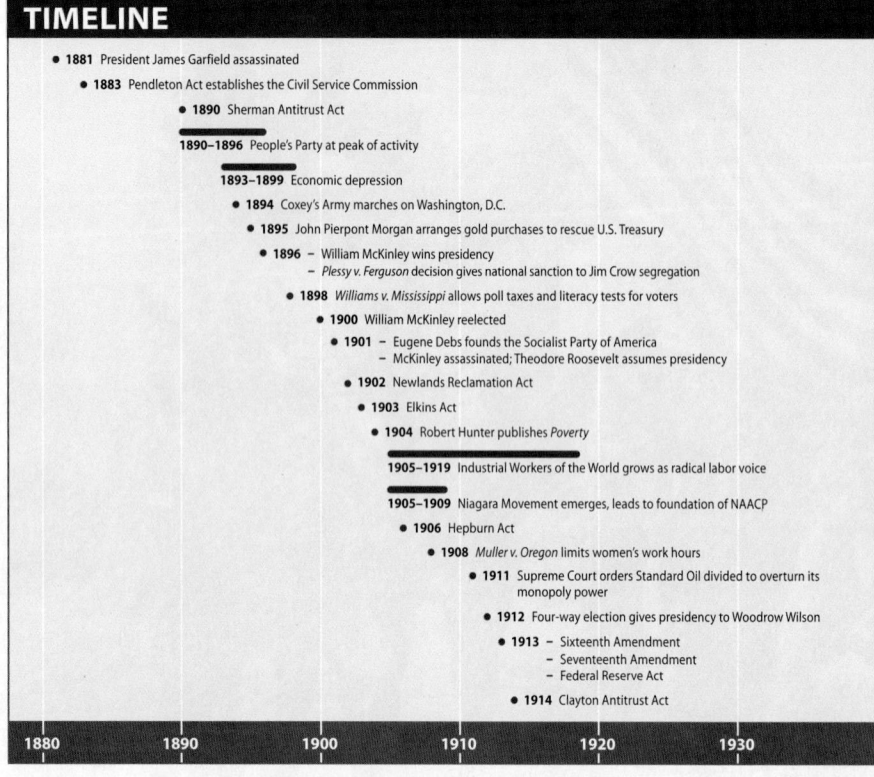

- **1881** President James Garfield assassinated
- **1883** Pendleton Act establishes the Civil Service Commission
- **1890** Sherman Antitrust Act
- **1890–1896** People's Party at peak of activity
- **1893–1899** Economic depression
- **1894** Coxey's Army marches on Washington, D.C.
- **1895** John Pierpont Morgan arranges gold purchases to rescue U.S. Treasury
- **1896** – William McKinley wins presidency
  – *Plessy v. Ferguson* decision gives national sanction to Jim Crow segregation
- **1898** *Williams v. Mississippi* allows poll taxes and literacy tests for voters
- **1900** William McKinley reelected
- **1901** – Eugene Debs founds the Socialist Party of America
  – McKinley assassinated; Theodore Roosevelt assumes presidency
- **1902** Newlands Reclamation Act
- **1903** Elkins Act
- **1904** Robert Hunter publishes *Poverty*
- **1905–1919** Industrial Workers of the World grows as radical labor voice
- **1905–1909** Niagara Movement emerges, leads to foundation of NAACP
- **1906** Hepburn Act
- **1908** *Muller v. Oregon* limits women's work hours
- **1911** Supreme Court orders Standard Oil divided to overturn its monopoly power
- **1912** Four-way election gives presidency to Woodrow Wilson
- **1913** – Sixteenth Amendment
  – Seventeenth Amendment
  – Federal Reserve Act
- **1914** Clayton Antitrust Act

1880 1890 1900 1910 1920 1930

REFORM VISIONS, 1880–1892

How did the political goals of Republicans, Democrats, and Populists differ in the years after the end of Reconstruction?

AP® EXAM TIP

Evaluate the application of the name "Gilded Age" to the late nineteenth century.

In the 1880s, radical farmers' groups and the Knights of Labor provided a powerful challenge to industrialization (Chapter 16). At the same time, groups such as the WCTU (Chapter 17) and urban settlements (Chapter 18) laid the groundwork for later progressive reform work, especially among women. Though they had different goals, these groups confronted similar dilemmas upon entering politics. Should they work through existing political parties? Create new ones? Or generate pressure from the outside? Reformers tried all these strategies.

Electoral Politics After Reconstruction

AP® SKILLS & PROCESSES

DEVELOPMENTS AND PROCESSES

What factors led to close party competition in the 1880s?

The end of Reconstruction ushered in a period of close political conflict, with neither of the major parties holding a secure national majority. Republicans and Democrats traded control of the Senate three times between 1880 and 1894, and the House majority five times. Causes of this tight competition included northerners' disillusionment with Republican policies and the resurgence of southern Democrats, who regained a strong base in Congress. Dizzying population growth also changed the size and shape of the House of Representatives. In 1875, it counted 243 seats; two decades later, that had risen to 356. Between 1889 and 1896, entry of seven new western states — Montana, North and South Dakota, Washington, Idaho, Wyoming, and Utah — contributed to political uncertainty.

Heated competition and the legacies of the Civil War evoked strong party loyalties from millions of Americans. Union veterans donned their uniforms to march in Republican parades, while ex-Confederate Democrats did the same in the South. When politicians appealed to war loyalties, critics ridiculed them for "waving the bloody shirt": whipping up old animosities that ought to be set aside. For those who had fought or lost beloved family members in the conflict, however — as well as those struggling for African American rights — war issues remained crucial. Many voters also had strong views on economic policies, especially Republicans' high protective tariffs. Proportionately more voters turned out in presidential elections from 1876 to 1892 than at any other time in American history.

Presidents of this era had limited room to maneuver in a period of narrow victories, when the opposing party often held one or both houses of Congress. Republicans Rutherford B. Hayes and Benjamin Harrison both won in the electoral college — allocated by state — but lost the popular vote. In 1884, Democrat Grover Cleveland won only 29,214 more votes than his opponent, James Blaine, while almost half a million voters rejected both major candidates (Map 19.1). With key states decided by razor-thin margins, both Republicans and Democrats engaged in vote buying and other forms of fraud. The fierce struggle for advantage also prompted innovations in political campaigning (see "Thinking Like a Historian," p. 608).

Some historians have characterized this period as a Gilded Age, when politics was corrupt and stagnant. The term *Gilded Age*, borrowed from the title of an 1873 novel cowritten by Mark Twain, suggested that America had achieved a glittery outer coating of prosperity, but underneath suffered from moral decay. Economically, the term *Gilded Age* seems apt: as we have seen in previous chapters, a handful of men made spectacular fortunes, and their triumphs belied a rising crisis of poverty, pollution, and erosion of workers' rights. But political leaders were not blind to these problems, and the political scene was hardly idle or indifferent. Rather, Americans bitterly disagreed about what to do. Nonetheless, as early as the 1880s, Congress passed important new federal measures to clean up

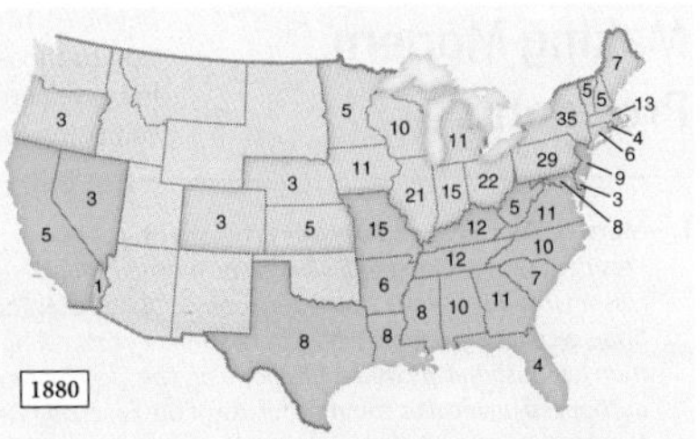

Candidate	Electoral Vote	Popular Vote	Percent of Popular Vote
James A. Garfield (Republican)	214	4,453,295	48.5
Winfield Hancock (Democrat)	155	4,414,082	48.1
James B. Weaver (Greenback-Labor)	—	308,578	3.4

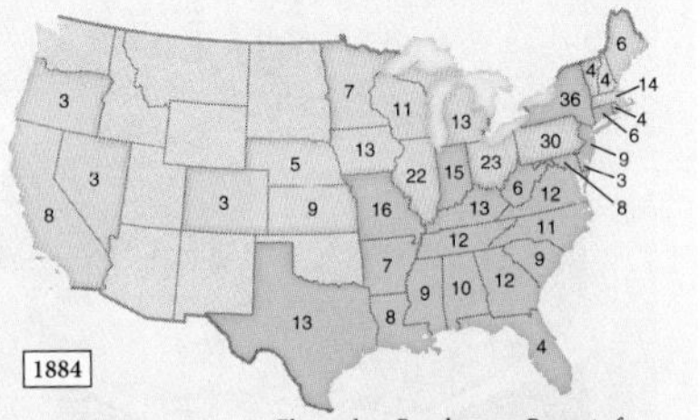

Candidate	Electoral Vote	Popular Vote	Percent of Popular Vote
Grover Cleveland (Democrat)	219	4,879,507	48.5
James G. Blaine (Republican)	182	4,850,293	48.2
Benjamin F. Butler (Greenback-Labor)	—	175,370	1.8
John P. St. John (Prohibition)	—	150,369	1.5

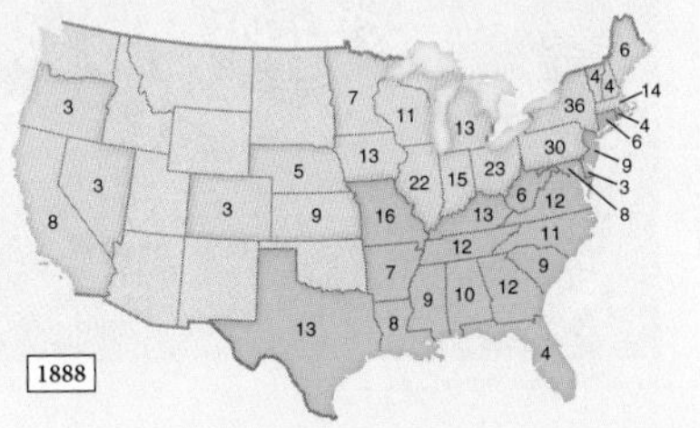

Candidate	Electoral Vote	Popular Vote	Percent of Popular Vote
Benjamin Harrison (Republican)	233	5,447,129	47.9
Grover Cleveland (Democrat)	168	5,537,857	48.6
Clinton P. Fisk (Prohibition)	—	249,506	2.2
Anson J. Streeter (Union Labor)	—	146,935	1.3

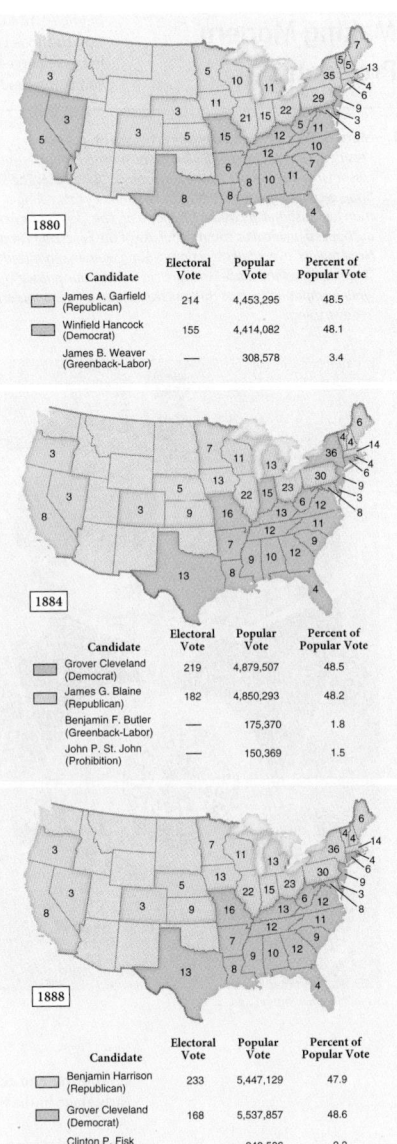

MAP 19.1 The Presidential Elections of 1880, 1884, and 1888
The anatomy of hard-fought, narrowly won presidential campaigns is evident in this trio of electoral maps. First, note the equal division of the popular vote between Republicans and Democrats. Second, note the persistent pattern of electoral votes, as states overwhelmingly went to the same party in all three elections. Here, we can identify who determined the outcomes — voters in swing states, such as New York and Indiana, whose vote shifted every four years and always in favor of the winning candidate.

TEACHING STRATEGY

Use the caption of **MAP 19.1** to highlight important voting patterns that these three maps illustrate regarding the dominant electoral trends of the era.

AP® SKILLS & PROCESSES

ANALYZING HISTORICAL EVIDENCE

The **AP® THINKING LIKE A HISTORIAN** feature invites students to consider several disparate sources in an effort to analyze the growth of presidential power in relation to changing campaign techniques. Students may need some assistance in recognizing ways that presidential candidates were responding to larger trends — or, as evident in Document 1, overtaken by them — rather than actively helping to shape them, as in Document 4. In either case, students should be attentive to the larger context and to changing dynamics in advertising, communications technology, and transportation.

AP® THINKING LIKE A HISTORIAN

Making Modern Presidents

Between 1880 and 1917, the stature and powers of the U.S. president grew in relation to those of Congress. Presidential campaign techniques also changed. The following sources shed light on candidates' increasing public visibility and new uses of campaign funds.

1. **Merrick Thread Company advertisement, c. 1886.** *President Grover Cleveland, a bachelor, married young Frances Folsom in a quiet White House ceremony in June 1886. The bride, a college graduate who was twenty-six years younger than her husband, proved wildly popular. The Clevelands never authorized political or commercial use of the First Lady's image. Nonetheless, over their objections, young women organized "Frankie Cleveland Clubs" to march in Democratic parades, while companies such as this one capitalized on her popularity in advertising.*

Source: Popperfoto/Getty Images.

2. **Account of Benjamin Harrison's front porch campaign in Indianapolis, *New York Tribune*, October 12, 1888.** *For much of the nineteenth century, presidential candidates left campaigning to their allies. A man who promoted himself risked appearing vain and greedy for office. By the 1880s, Republicans began to run "front porch campaigns": party leaders arranged for delegations to visit the candidate at home.*

This morning General Harrison's home was surrounded by visitors, who had arrived in the city in the night and on the early morning trains. . . . There were many relic-hunters among the early visitors and they swarmed about the house, taking, without protest from any one, whatever they were pleased to seize. There is no longer a fence about the house to be converted into relics, and so the visitors are taking the trees now. The shrubbery has almost disappeared. . . . The informal reception began as soon as the General got up from [breakfast] and continued until afternoon. The first delegation was composed of representatives of the Cincinnati Republican Clubs. . . . A delegation from Belleville, Ill., which . . . had patiently waited for more than four hours, were next invited to enter the house, and they were accorded the usual handshaking reception. . . .

The parade early in the afternoon was the principal feature of the day's demonstration. Two hundred or more clubs participated and they came from all parts of the State, representing various classes and interests. . . . There were mounted men and men on foot, women in wagons and women in uniform marching, brass bands. . . .

On the balcony beside General Harrison stood his wife, with several of her lady friends.

3. **Henry George on money in politics, *Wheeling Register*, September 19, 1896.** *Reformer Henry George was among many who warned of the influence of corporate contributions, solicited brilliantly in 1896 by William McKinley's campaign manager, Mark Hanna. Short of funds, Democratic candidate William Jennings Bryan undertook exhausting nationwide speaking tours.*

There is no question which of the great parties represents the house of Have and which the house of Want. . . . Democrat[s] are cramped for want of funds. . . . On the

corruption and rein in corporate power. That decade deserves to be considered an early stage in the emerging Progressive Era (see "Comparing Interpretations," p. 610).

New Initiatives One of the first reforms resulted from tragedy. On July 2, 1881, only four months after entering the White House, James Garfield was shot at a train station in Washington, D.C. ("Assassination," he had told a friend, "can no other hand there is practically "no end of money" at the disposal of the McKinley committees. . . .

As for the banks, the great railroad companies and insurance companies, who, even in ordinary times find it to their interest to help financially one, and frequently both, sides . . . , their purse strings are unloosed more freely than ever before, but only in one direction.

The danger to a republican form of government of a money interest in politics is so clear that it needs not to be dwelt upon. . . . The steady tendency of American legislation, national and state, has not merely been to create great special interests, but in the very effort to control them for the benefit of the public, to concern them directly in politics.

4. Theodore Roosevelt on the campaign trail, 1904. *Having watched Bryan's electrifying tours, Theodore Roosevelt became the first winning candidate to adopt the practice. In 1904, after a summer front porch campaign, he undertook a thirty-day speaking tour of the West. To cover as much ground as possible, Roosevelt often spoke from the last car of his train.*

Source: Library of Congress, LC-DIG-ppmsca-36689.

5. "Expenses of the Campaign," *Springfield Daily Republican*, September 22, 1900.

It is estimated that it costs $25,000,000 to elect a president of the United States. The annual allowance which the British Parliament makes to Queen Victoria is $1,925,000 . . . indicat[ing] that it is much cheaper to maintain a queen permanently than it is to elect a president. . . .

More than half of the money spent by both national and state committees goes for campaign orators. During the next three months it is estimated that the Republican national committee will have 3000 "spellbinders" traveling out of the Chicago headquarters and 2500 who will report to the New York office. . . .

The next largest item on the campaign bill is that for printing. . . . Each of the national committees will spend at least $500,000 in this way. Before the campaign is over it is estimated that both the Republican and Democratic committees will send out 100,000,000 separate documents. . . .

One more important branch of the work is the two house-to-house canvasses of the voters. . . . Hundreds of men are employed in each state, and the work of tabulating and classifying the results is by no means small. . . .

Some novel campaign methods will be adopted by both the great parties during the campaign just opening. The Republicans, it is stated, have decided to use phonographs. . . . Some eloquent party man . . . will deliver a speech before a phonographic record, from which any desired number of copies may be made . . . and sent far out into the rural districts, where it would be impossible for the more popular and important orators to go. . . .

Democrats, on the other hand, will pin their faith to stereopticons [an early slide projector].

Sources: (2) *New York Tribune*, October 12, 1888; (3) *Wheeling Register*, September 19, 1896; (5) *Springfield Daily Republican*, September 22, 1900.

ANALYZING THE EVIDENCE

1. What did a presidential candidate need in the 1880s to run an effective campaign? Two decades later, what had changed, and what had not? Describe patterns of continuity and change.
2. Based on these documents, what developments both inside and outside of politics seem to have influenced changing campaign strategies? Explain evidence from each source in your answer.

AP® DBQ PRACTICE

Historians have traced the rise of an "imperial presidency" in the late 1890s and early 1900s. How might new campaign techniques have reflected, and perhaps contributed to, this rise? Describe the historical context influencing changes in politics at the time.

more be guarded against than death by lightning, and it is best not to worry about either.") After lingering for several agonizing months, Garfield died. Most historians now believe the assassin, Charles Guiteau, suffered from mental illness. But reformers then blamed the "spoils system," arguing that Guiteau had murdered Garfield out of disappointment in the scramble for patronage, the granting of government jobs to party loyalists.

TRM Find complete suggested responses in the Teacher's Resource Materials.

AP® SKILLS & PROCESSES

ARGUMENTATION

Students might need assistance unpacking the implications of the **AP® DBQ PRACTICE** prompt. The label "imperial presidency" was coined by historian Arthur Schlesinger Jr. to describe the dramatic rise in presidential power since F.D.R. This rise in power often exceeded constitutional bounds and frequently, though not always, was associated with war-making activities overseas. In a broader sense, the term might also apply to increasing presidential initiative in establishing national policy.

AP® SKILLS & PROCESSES

ANALYZING HISTORICAL EVIDENCE

As students explore the questions posed by the **AP® COMPARING INTERPRETATIONS** feature, it might be helpful for them to discuss how much continuity or change needs to exist to consider a particular moment a turning point, rather than simply an anomaly within a single larger era. Similarly, choosing a title for an era hinges on determining what features were most characteristic of that era. These two questions — dates and labels — are intrinsically related, as changing the dates may affect the appropriateness of a particular label or vice versa. Students could also consider why these types of debates matter and what is at stake.

TEACHING STRATEGY

The National Archives provides a high-resolution facsimile edition of the Pendleton Act, along with a brief narrative that explains the act's significance, placing it in the context of previous patterns of federal government employment. To access this document, search "Our Documents Pendleton Act."

Were the "Gilded Age" and "Progressive Era" Separate Periods?

Starting in the 1920s, historians borrowed the title of *The Gilded Age*, an 1873 novel, to describe the late nineteenth-century United States. "Gilded" implies a false impression of beauty: though American politics and society glittered on the outside, according to this view, they were dull or rotten underneath. Following this standard description, historians have described the years between 1870 and 1900 as marked by political stagnation and corruption, rampant greed and corporate ruthlessness, *laissez faire* government, and ineffective "dud presidents." According to many historians, only after 1900 did a more optimistic, reform-minded "Progressive Era" begin. Some historians, including Elisabeth Israels Perry and Rebecca Edwards (one of the authors of this textbook), have identified themes that give a different perspective on the periodization of the late nineteenth-century United States.

ELISABETH ISRAELS PERRY

Source: Elisabeth Israels Perry, "Men Are from the Gilded Age, Women Are from the Progressive Era," *Journal of the Gilded Age and Progressive Era* 1, no. 1 (January 2002): 26–28, 30, 34–35, 43.

I came to this field in the mid-1970s, when . . . I began the research for a biography of Belle Moskowitz. Moskowitz was New York Governor Alfred E. Smith's political strategist in the 1920s and also my paternal grandmother. Since Moskowitz had identified herself as a Progressive, I began exploring historiography in order to place her into a wider context. . . . Moskowitz was an educated middle-class Jewish woman born in 1877 in Harlem, New York, to a family of shopkeepers. From adulthood to marriage she worked in a social settlement. After marrying she became a volunteer social reformer, most notably through membership in the Council of Jewish Women and the Society for Ethical Culture. Her earliest campaign, and one that made her known throughout New York City involved the licensing and regulating of dance halls. . . .

I found that general treatments of the progressive movement were unrecognizable from the perspective of Moskowitz's career. . . . What about all the women's voluntary associations she had been involved in? In the 1970s I could find almost nothing on them. No one had written about dance hall reform, [which] . . . in the end I came to understand . . . by connecting it to recreation, parks, and playground movements and to concerns about prostitution and other forms of commercialized urban "vice." . . . Since women did not vote in this period, political historians considered them irrelevant and wrote nothing about them.

In the past decade, Progressive-era historiography has become much more responsive to women's history than it was during the 1980s. The 1990s saw a veritable boom in historical scholarship on Progressive-era women. Historians of progressivism who do not work in women's history are now reading this work (or at least some of it). . . .

Some women activists certainly were maternalists in the sense that they envisioned a state built around the needs of mothers and tended to see women workers as mothers or as potential mothers. But other ideologies, including feminism, socialism, and a desire for "social justice" for all workers regardless of sex, also motivated women activists. . . . Historians need to broaden the meaning of the term "politics" so as to incorporate the entire spectrum of women's activism. . . . "When *was* the Progressive Era exactly?" my students ask. Roughly during the first two

Pendleton Act
An 1883 law establishing a nonpartisan Civil Service Commission to fill federal jobs by examination. The Pendleton Act dealt a major blow to the "spoils system" and sought to ensure that government positions were filled by trained, professional employees.

AP® EXAM TIP
Evaluate the impact of legislation to regulate business and industry in the late nineteenth century.

In the wake of Garfield's death, Congress passed the **Pendleton Act** (1883), establishing a nonpartisan Civil Service Commission to fill federal jobs by examination. Initially, civil service applied to only 10 percent of such jobs, but the act laid the groundwork for a major transformation of public employment. By the 1910s, Congress extended the act to cover most federal positions; cities and states across the country enacted similar laws.

Civil service laws had their downside. In the race for government jobs, they tilted the balance toward middle-class applicants who could perform well on tests. "Firemen now must know equations," complained a critic, "and be up on Euclid too." But the laws put talented professionals in office and discouraged politicians from appointing unqualified party hacks. The civil service also brought stability and consistency to government, since officials did not lose their jobs every time their party lost power. In the long run, civil service laws markedly reduced corruption and increased government efficiency.

decades of the twentieth century, I tell them. Never a precise business, periodization generally reflects the interpretive views of the historian setting its boundaries. Some historians still use 1900 as a starting date, although more recently 1890 has become popular. . . . From the perspective of women progressives, however, these boundaries need to be much more fluid. . . . The women who founded social settlements in the 1880s, along with the temperance and suffrage campaigners, comprise a group of American citizens active in conceptualizing progressive reform long before the presumed dawn of progressivism. True, they did not usually occupy positions of public authority. Nor were they holding major academic chairs in universities. But they were speaking and writing and acting on some of the major issues of the Progressive Era long before most politicians acknowledged their importance, and they laid the foundations of progressivism by building public opinion in favor of change.

REBECCA EDWARDS

Source: Rebecca Edwards, *New Spirits: Americans in the "Gilded Age," 1865–1905*, 3rd ed. (New York: Oxford University Press, 2015), 3, 5–6.

Some historians have labeled the post–Civil War era "the Gilded Age," borrowing the title of an 1873 novel by Mark Twain (the pen name of Samuel Langhorne Clemens) and his friend Charles Dudley Warner. *The Gilded Age* satirized get-rich-quick schemes and corruption in Washington, and its title suggested that America displayed a thin veneer of glitter on its outside but was rotting at its core. Twain and his contemporaries saw much cause for cynicism and despair. . . .

[Yet] the post–Civil War decades were also a time of enormous optimism. Steamships ferried wheat, cigarettes, rubber, missionaries, immigrants, and tourists all over the globe. Millions of people said farewell to friends and kin in China, Russia, Mexico, Italy, and other countries and sought their fortunes in America. Within the United States, . . . farmers' children headed to business school; the daughters and sons of slaves earned college diplomas and became teachers and insurance agents. Young American Indians pursued careers as writers and doctors. The ideal of "separate spheres" for men and women began to fade; young women graduated from high school and even college, took jobs in the corporate world, and led great reform movements. . . . Americans of the late nineteenth century embraced modernity with a passion.

Walt Whitman suggested as much in his 1871 essay "Democratic Vistas." Echoing Lincoln's call for a "new birth of freedom," Whitman proclaimed a "new spirit" in America's national experiment. . . . Whitman was in good company. Freedmen and freedwomen, immigrants, students, workers, artists, intellectuals, and grassroots reformers believed that post– Civil War America offered a chance to start anew.

This optimistic spirit has not gotten its due from historians. On the whole, they tend to depict late nineteenth-century America as dominated by corruption, political stagnation, and malaise. [But in] many ways it was a starting point for modern America. . . . Many Americans, however, worked energetically between 1865 and 1900 to purify politics, restrict the power of big business, and fight injustice. Those decades witnessed the first march on Washington, the first federal welfare programs, the first elections in which women and black men voted for president, and the first national park in the world. At the same time, problems that plagued the so-called Gilded Age continued and even intensified during the so-called Progressive Era. The global scope and power of multinational corporations, for example, created formidable new challenges, many of which remain unresolved today.

AP® DBQ PRACTICE

1. How does each of these historians challenge conventional interpretations of the Gilded Age and Progressive Era as separate periods?
2. Identify one key difference between these two assessments of the Gilded Age and Progressive Era.
3. Based on your reading of Chapters 14 to 19, how would you date and name the post- Civil War decades? Why would you choose those dates and name (or names) for the era? Support your claim with evidence from these sources and the textbook.

TEACHING STRATEGY

The tendency to see the Gilded Age as a period of corruption is addressed in each excerpt. Encourage students to highlight the phrases or examples in the excerpts that focus on positive contributions made during the Gilded Age. In particular, this will help students understand the interpretation advanced by Edwards.

TRM Find complete suggested responses in the Teacher's Resource Materials.

Leaders of the civil service movement included many classical liberals, former Republicans who became disillusioned with Reconstruction and advocated smaller, more professionalized government. Many had opposed President Ulysses S. Grant's reelection in 1872. In 1884, they again left the Republican Party because they could not stomach its scandal-tainted candidate, James Blaine. Liberal Republicans — ridiculed by their enemies as Mugwumps (fence-sitters who had their "mugs" on one side and their "wumps" on the other) — helped elect Democrat Grover Cleveland. They believed he shared their vision of smaller government.

As president, Cleveland showed that he largely did share their views. He vetoed, for example, thousands of bills providing pensions for individual Union veterans. But in 1887, responding to pressure from farmer-labor advocates in the Democratic Party who demanded action to limit corporate power, he signed the Interstate Commerce Act (see "Farmers and Workers: The Cooperative Alliance" in Chapter 16). At the same time, municipal and state-level initiatives were showing how expanded

"Political Purity," *Puck*, 1884 This Democratic cartoon suggests the disillusionment with Republicans that emerged among many voters in the 1880s. Here, the party chooses a dress, bustle, and plume to celebrate Republicans' achievements in prior decades: the Union war record, emancipation, and "high moral ideals." Her undergarments tell a different story: they are marked with scandals of the Grant era (Chapter 14), while the economic interests of tariff supporters ("protection") are depicted as her corset. The hats in the upper-right corner show Republicans' attempts to appeal to various constituencies: temperance advocates and German immigrants, workingmen and business leaders. Whitelaw Reid, staunchly Republican editor of the *New York Tribune*, appears as the party's handmaiden. Picture Research Consultants & Archives.

government could help solve industrial problems. In the 1870s and early 1880s, many states created Bureaus of Labor Statistics to investigate workplace safety and unemployment. Some appointed commissions to oversee key industries, from banking to dairy farming. By later standards, such commissions were underfunded, but even when they lacked legal power, energetic commissioners could serve as public advocates, exposing unsafe practices and generating pressure for further laws.

Republican Activism In 1888, after a decade of divided government, Republicans briefly gained control of both houses of Congress and the White House. They pursued an ambitious agenda they believed would meet the needs of a modernizing nation. In 1890, Congress extended pensions to all Union veterans and yielded to growing public outrage over trusts by passing a law to regulate interstate corporations. Though it proved difficult to enforce and was soon weakened by the Supreme Court, the **Sherman Antitrust Act** (1890) was the first federal attempt to forbid any "combination" or "conspiracy in restraint of trade." It required the federal government to investigate companies engaged in anticompetitive practices.

President Benjamin Harrison also sought to protect African American voting rights in the South. Warned during his campaign that the issue was politically risky, Harrison vowed that he would not "purchase the presidency by a compact of silence upon this question." He found allies in Congress. Massachusetts representative Henry Cabot Lodge drafted the Federal Elections Bill of 1890, or **Lodge Bill**, proposing that whenever one hundred citizens in any district appealed for intervention, a bipartisan federal board could investigate and seat the rightful winner.

Despite cries of outrage from southern Democrats, who warned that it meant "Negro supremacy," the House passed the measure. But it met resistance in the Senate. Northern classical liberals, who wanted the "best men" to govern through professional expertise, thought it provided too much democracy, while machine bosses feared the threat of federal interference in the cities. Unexpectedly, many western Republicans also opposed the bill — and with the entry of ten new states since 1863, the West had gained enormous clout. Senator William Stewart of Nevada, who had southern family ties, claimed that federal oversight of elections would bring "monarchy or revolution." He and his allies killed the bill by a single vote.

The defeat was a devastating blow to those seeking to defend black voting rights. In the verdict of one furious Republican leader who supported Lodge's proposal, the episode marked the end of the party of emancipation. "Think of it," he fumed. "Nevada, barely a respectable *county*, furnished two senators to betray the Republican Party and the rights of citizenship."

Other Republican initiatives also proved unpopular — at the polls as well as in Congress. In the Midwest, swing voters reacted against local Republican campaigns to prohibit liquor sales and end state funding for Catholic schools. Blaming high consumer prices on protective tariffs, other voters rejected Republican economic policies. In a major shift in the 1890 election, Democrats captured the House of Representatives. Two years later, by the largest margin in twenty years, voters reelected Democrat Grover Cleveland to the presidency for a nonconsecutive second term. Outnumbered, Republican congressmen abandoned any further attempt to enforce fair elections in the South.

Sherman Antitrust Act
Landmark 1890 act that forbade anti-competitive business activities, requiring the federal government to investigate trusts and any companies operating in violation of the act.

Lodge Bill
Also known as the Federal Elections Bill of 1890, a bill proposing that whenever one hundred citizens in any district appealed for intervention, a bipartisan federal board could investigate and seat the rightful winner. The defeat of the bill was a blow to those seeking to defend African American voting rights and to ensure full participation in politics.

TEACHING STRATEGY

University of Virginia's Uniting Mugwumps and the Masses: Puck's Role in Gilded Age Politics Web site provides a series of essays and political cartoons that explore the role of this particular brand of reform. The site dates from the late 1990s, so it is somewhat clunky, but the material is useful for teachers interested in exploring pre-Progressive political reform and/or the role of cartoons in critiquing political corruption and ineptitude. Among the issues articles on the site discuss is the place of gender and the ways political opponents were often depicted in feminine roles. To access this site, search "UVA Uniting Mugwumps and the Masses."

TEACHING STRATEGY

The National Archives provides a high-resolution facsimile edition of the Sherman Antitrust Act, along with a brief narrative that explains the act's significance, placing it in the context of previous patterns of federal government regulation of corporations. To access these resources, search "Our Documents Sherman Antitrust Act."

CHECK FOR UNDERSTANDING

Ask students: **What was the nature of electoral politics after Reconstruction?** *Voter participation was extremely high and the two major political parties were closely matched. They competed intensely, with victories determined by razor-thin margins, leading to regular switches in control of the House and Senate. Presidents often had little room to maneuver because one or both chambers of Congress was often controlled by the opposing party. Both Republicans and Democrats "waved the bloody shirt" by invoking the Civil War, the lives lost on both sides, and the status of African American civil rights. Despite this conflict, there was some consensus on important issues of corruption and corporate power. Congress passed the Pendleton Act to establish a nonpartisan Civil Service Commission and the Sherman Antitrust Act, designed to prevent trusts. Other Republican measures, such as the Lodge Bill, which proposed allowing the federal government to examine claims of vote tampering against blacks, were defeated. In the early 1890s, Congress and the presidency shifted to the Democrats.*

The Populist Program

As Democrats took power in Washington in 1892, they faced rising pressure from rural voters in the South and West who had organized the Farmers' Alliance. Savvy politicians responded quickly. Iowa Democrats, for example, took up some of the farmers' demands, forestalling creation of a separate farmer-labor party in that state. But other politicians listened to Alliance pleas and did nothing. It was a response they came to regret.

Republicans utterly dominated Kansas, a state chock-full of Union veterans and railroad boosters, and their leaders treated the Farmers' Alliance with contempt. In 1890, the Kansas Alliance joined with the Knights of Labor to create a People's Party. They then stunned the nation by capturing four-fifths of the lower house of the Kansas legislature and most of the state's congressional seats. The victory electrified labor and agrarian radicals nationwide. In July 1892, delegates from these groups met at Omaha, Nebraska, and formally created the national People's Party, soon known as the Populists. In recognizing an "irrepressible conflict between capital and labor," Populists split from the mainstream parties, demanding stronger government to protect ordinary Americans. Their **Omaha Platform** called for public ownership of railroad and telegraph systems, protection of land from monopoly and foreign ownership, a federal income tax on the rich, and a looser monetary policy to help borrowers. Some Populist allies went further to make their point. In New Mexico, the Gorras Blancas, a vigilante group of small-scale Mexican American farmers, protested exploitative railroads and "land grabbers" by intimidating railroad workers and cutting fences on large Anglo farms.

AP® EXAM TIP

Understanding the reforms proposed in the Omaha Platform is critical for success on the AP® Exam.

Omaha Platform
An 1892 statement by the Populists calling for public ownership of transportation and communication networks, protection of land from monopoly and foreign ownership, looser monetary policy, and a federal income tax on the rich.

Riding to a Populist Rally, Dickinson County, Kansas, 1890s Farm families in wagons carry their banners to a local meeting of the People's Party. Men, women, and children often traveled together to campaign events, which included not only stump speeches but also picnics, glee club music, and other family entertainments. Fotosearch/Getty Images.

AP® THEME

PCE: Politics and Power

The "Populist Program" section explores the ways that economic instability inspired agrarian activists to create the Populist Party, which called for a stronger governmental role in regulating the American economic system.

AP® APPLY THE TIP

Ask students to review p. 628 on the Omaha Platform. Students should pay specific attention to the platform planks in the **AP® FIRSTHAND ACCOUNTS** feature and evaluate the reasons for their inclusion in the platform. Ask students to take turns with a partner explaining why each plank is important to the members of the Populist Party, recording their findings in **Handout 19.2 — Contextualization: Omaha Platform (TRM)**. Finally, show students an image of a map illustrating the electoral successes of the Populist Party in 1892 and 1896 and discuss the reasons that the Omaha Platform failed to win over voters in industrialized areas. *(Answers could include political machines, political corruption, interference in voting by industrial bosses, etc.)*

TRM Find **Handout 19.2 — Contextualization: Omaha Platform** in the Teacher's Resource Materials.

TEACHING STRATEGY

The "William Allen White" Web site page, available through Vassar University, provides the text of William Allen White's editorial "What's the Matter with Kansas?" a scathing critique of the Populist Party by the Republican editor of the *Emporia Gazette*. Access this editorial by searching "Vassar William Allen White."

TEACHING STRATEGY

The National Humanities Center provides a series of primary sources related to issues of power in the Gilded Age entitled "Taming the Octopus." Organized around the question "How did Americans respond to the shifts in economic and political power that occurred during this period?" primary sources are grouped into a dozen different topics, each with an introductory essay and a set of related texts or images. The collection of cartoons on "the Octopus" provides a handout with detailed annotations guiding student interpretation. To access this site, search "NHC Gilded and the Gritty."

Populist leaders represented a grassroots uprising of ordinary farmers, and some won colorful nicknames. After a debate triumph based on his powerful oratory, James H. Davis of Texas became known as "Cyclone." Mary E. Lease, a fierce critic of economic policies that benefitted the wealthy, was derided as "Yellin' Mary Ellen"; her fellow Kansan Jerry Simpson was called "Sockless Jerry" after he ridiculed a wealthy opponent for wearing "fine silk hosiery," boasting that he himself wore no socks at all. The national press, based in northeastern cities, ridiculed such "hayseed politicians," but farmers insisted on being taken seriously. In the run-up to one election, a Populist writer encouraged party members to sing these lyrics to the tune of an old gospel hymn:

> I once was a tool of oppression,
> As green as a sucker could be
> And monopolies banded together
> To beat a poor hayseed like me. . . .
> But now I've roused up a little,
> And their greed and corruption I see,
> And the ticket we vote next November
> Will be made up of hayseeds like me.

Driven by farmers' votes, the People's Party had mixed success in attracting other constituencies. Its labor planks won support among Alabama steelworkers and Rocky Mountain miners, but not among many other industrial workers, who stuck with the major parties. Prohibitionist and women's suffrage leaders attended Populist conventions, hoping their issues would be taken up, but they were disappointed. The legacies of the Civil War also hampered the party. Southern Democrats, warned that Populists, were really Radical Republicans in disguise, while northeastern Republicans claimed the southern "Pops" were ex-Confederates plotting another round of treason. Despite these issues, the Populists, as they became known, captured a million votes in November. They returned to Washington with three representatives in the U.S. Senate and eleven in the House (Map 19.2) — only a sliver of congressional offices, but enough to make them one of the most successful insurgent parties in U.S. history. Amid the heated debates of the 1890s, the political system suddenly confronted an economic crisis.

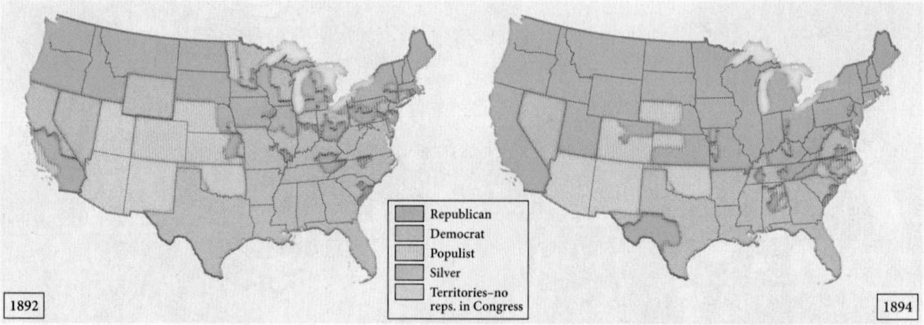

MAP 19.2 House of Representatives Elected in 1892 and 1894
Americans focus intensive effort and attention on presidential elections, but midterm congressional elections can be key turning points, as well. In response to the severe economic depression that began in 1893, American voters turned sharply away from the Democrats and toward the Republicans. That dramatic shift was first obvious not in 1896, with the election of President William McKinley, but in the midterm election that transformed Congress. These maps show the number of Democrats, Republicans, and Populists in the House of Representatives after the elections of 1892 (left) and 1894 (right). Where did Republicans make the biggest gains? How would the parties' strength in Congress have differed if Southern Populists in states such as Alabama, Arkansas, and Georgia had not been defeated through fraud?

TEACHING STRATEGY

"The Populist Party" Web site page, available through Vassar University, offers an overview of the rise of populism, its role in the 1896 election, and its legacy. The site provides a series of brief 1896 quotes from across the political spectrum assessing the meaning of the movement. To access the site, search "Vassar Populist Party."

CHECK FOR UNDERSTANDING

Ask students: **How did the political goals of Republicans, Democrats, and Populists differ in the years after the end of Reconstruction?** *In the Gilded Age, both the established parties represented established interests, albeit different ones. Republicans were beholden largely to Northern capitalists and Union veterans while Democrats were supported by Southern white elites. Both parties sought limited government intervention, especially in the economy, as laissez faire policies (excepting the Republican push for veteran's and widow's pensions) largely aided their bases. Frequently left out were small farmers and others, especially in the West. These Westerners, so-called Populists, called for public ownership of railroad and telegraph systems, protection of land from monopoly and foreign ownership, a federal income tax on the rich, and a looser monetary policy to help borrowers.*

THE POLITICAL EARTHQUAKES OF THE 1890s

Why and how did the depression of the 1890s impact federal politics and policy?

In 1893, a severe economic depression hit the United States. Though it was a global shock, and the agriculture sector had already lagged for years, Republicans blamed Grover Cleveland, who had just reentered the White House. "On every hand can be seen evidences of Democratic times," declared one Republican. "The deserted farm, the silent factory."

Apparently receptive to such appeals, voters outside the South abandoned the Democrats in 1894 and 1896. Republicans, promising prosperity, gained control of the White House and both chambers of Congress for the next sixteen years. This development created both opportunities and challenges for progressive reformers. In those same years, a different pattern emerged in the former Confederacy: Democrats deployed fraud, violence, and race-based appeals for white solidarity to defeat the Populist revolt and create a "Solid South."

Depression and Reaction

When Cleveland took the oath of office in March 1893, hard times were prompting European investors to pull money out of the United States; farm foreclosures and railroad bankruptcies signaled economic trouble. A few weeks later, a Pennsylvania railroad went bankrupt, followed by several other companies. Investors panicked; the stock market crashed. By July, major banks had drained their reserves and "suspended" withdrawals, unable to give depositors access to their money. By year's end, five hundred banks and thousands of other businesses had gone under. "Boston," one man remembered, "grew suddenly old, haggard, and thin." The unemployment rate in industrial cities soared above 20 percent.

AP® EXAM TIP

Understanding the causes of popular action against the federal government is critical for success on the AP® Exam.

For Americans who had lived through the terrible 1870s, conditions looked grimly familiar. Even fresher in the public mind were recent labor uprisings, including the 1886 Haymarket violence and the 1892 showdown at Homestead — followed, during the depression's first year, by a massive Pennsylvania coal strike and a Pullman railroad boycott that ended with bloody clashes between angry crowds and the U.S. Army. Prosperous Americans, fearful of Populism, were even more terrified that workers would embrace socialism or Marxism. Reminding Americans of upheavals such as the revolutionary Paris Commune government of 1871 and its bloody suppression, conservative commentators of the 1890s launched America's first "Red Scare" — a precursor to similar episodes of hysteria in the 1920s and 1950s.

In the summer of 1894, a further protest jolted affluent Americans. Radical businessman Jacob Coxey of Ohio proposed that the U.S. government hire the unemployed to fix America's roads. In 1894, he organized hundreds of jobless men — nicknamed Coxey's Army — to march peacefully to Washington and appeal for the program. Though public employment of the kind Coxey proposed would become central to the New Deal in the 1930s, many Americans in the 1890s viewed Coxey as a dangerous extremist. Public alarm grew when more protesters, inspired by Coxey, started out from Los Angeles, Seattle, and other cities. As they marched east, these men found support and offers of aid in Populist-leaning cities and towns. In other places, police and property owners drove marchers away at gunpoint. Coxey was stunned by what happened when he reached Capitol Hill: police jailed him for trespassing on the grass. Some of his men, arrested for vagrancy, ended up in Maryland chain gangs. The rest went home hungry.

As this response suggested, President Grover Cleveland's administration was increasingly out of step with rural and working-class demands. Any president would have been hard-pressed to cope with the depression, but Cleveland was particularly inept. He steadfastly resisted pressure to loosen the money supply by expanding federal coinage to include silver as well as gold. Advocates of this **free silver** policy

free silver
A policy of loosening the money supply by expanding federal coinage to include silver as well as gold, to encourage borrowing and stimulate industry. Democrats advocated the measure, most famously in the 1896 presidential campaign, but Republicans won and retained the gold standard.

CHECK FOR UNDERSTANDING

Ask students: **What caused the depression of 1893, and how did different groups of Americans react to it?** *Hard times led to farm foreclosures and railroad bankruptcies. Investors panicked, withdrawing funds and causing a stock market crash. Workers went on strike, which sometimes became violent, while wealthy Americans feared the coming of communism. Jacob Coxey led a march on behalf of the unemployed, asking the federal government to hire them to fix American roads.*

AP® SKILLS & PROCESSES

MAKING CONNECTIONS

The **MAKING CONNECTIONS** question asks students to explain the effects of the depression on different groups of people, as well as the consequences of their reactions. Some students may need assistance in understanding why critics of the gold standard thought that free silver would improve their situation.

TRM Find complete suggested responses in the Teacher's Resource Materials.

AP® APPLY THE TIP

Project the text of the Fourteenth and Fifteenth Amendments for students to read. Ask students to act as "constitutional historians" by explaining to a partner the historical context and purpose of each amendment. Encourage students to clarify and provide specific evidence for their arguments. After this discussion, provide students with excerpts from various Jim Crow laws, literacy test laws, and poll taxes that were passed in the southern states after Reconstruction. Students should read and analyze each excerpt and discuss the historical context and purpose of each of the excerpts. Draw students' attention to the map on p. 616 illustrating "Disfranchisement in the New South," and ask them to think about the impact that the laws and poll taxes had on the Fourteenth and Fifteenth Amendments. Lead a class discussion on the political, economic, and social impact of the disfranchisement of African Americans. Then ask students to complete **Handout 19.3 — Causation: Disfranchisement of African Americans (TRM).**

TRM Find **Handout 19.3 — Causation: Disfranchisement of African Americans** in the Teacher's Resource Materials.

("free" because, under this plan, the U.S. Mint would not charge a fee for minting silver coins) believed the policy would encourage borrowing and stimulate industry. But Cleveland clung to the gold standard. Even if ordinary people had difficulty borrowing because money was tight and interest rates high, Cleveland believed the money supply must remain tied to the nation's reserves of gold.

AP® SKILLS & PROCESSES

MAKING CONNECTIONS

How did different groups of Americans react to the economic depression of the 1890s, and what happened as a result?

As the 1894 midterm elections loomed, Democratic candidates tried to distance themselves from the president. But on election day, large numbers of voters chose Republicans, who promised to support business, put down social unrest, and bring back prosperity. Western voters turned many Populists out of office. In the next congressional session, Republicans controlled the House by a margin of 245 to 105 (see Map 19.2).

Democrats and the "Solid South"

AP® EXAM TIP

The impact of the disenfranchisement of African Americans is important to know on the AP® Exam.

In the South, the only region where Democrats gained strength in the 1890s, the People's Party lost ground for distinctive reasons. After the end of Reconstruction, African Americans in most states had continued to vote in significant numbers. As long as Democrats competed for black votes, the possibility remained that other parties could win them away. Populists proposed new measures to help farmers and wage earners — an attractive message for poverty-stricken people of both races. Some white Populists went out of their way to build cross-racial ties. "The accident of color can make no difference in the interest of farmers, croppers, and laborers," argued Georgia Populist Tom Watson. "You are kept apart that you may be separately fleeced of your earnings."

Such appeals threatened the foundations of southern politics. Democrats struck back, calling themselves the "white man's party" and denouncing Populists for advocating "Negro rule." Their arguments persuaded some voters to return to the Democratic camp. From Georgia to Texas, other poor white farmers, tenants, and wage earners ignored such appeals and continued to support the Populists in large numbers. Democrats found they could put down the Populist threat only through fraud and violence. After using such tactics, Pitchfork Ben Tillman of South Carolina openly bragged that he and his allies had "done our level best" to block "every last" vote against the Democrats, especially those cast by African Americans. "We stuffed ballot boxes," he said in 1900. "We shot them. We are not ashamed of it." "We had to do it," a Georgia Democrat later argued. "Those damned Populists would have ruined the country."

Williams v. Mississippi

An 1898 Supreme Court ruling that allowed states to impose poll taxes and literacy tests. By 1908, every southern state had adopted such measures to suppress voting by African Americans and some poor whites.

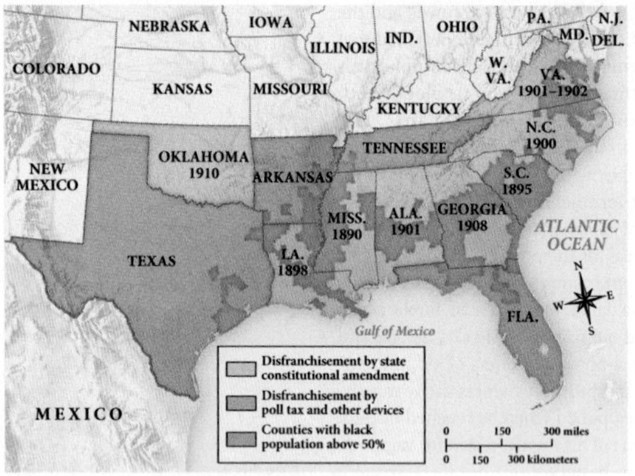

MAP 19.3 Disfranchisement in the New South
In the midst of the Populist challenge to Democratic one-party rule in the South, a movement to deprive blacks of the right to vote spread from Mississippi across the South. By 1910, every state in the region except Tennessee, Arkansas, Texas, and Florida had made constitutional changes designed to prevent blacks from voting, and these four states accomplished much the same result through poll taxes and other exclusionary methods. For the next half century, the political process in the South would be for whites only.

Having suppressed the political revolt, southern Democrats looked for new ways to enforce white supremacy. In 1890, a constitutional convention in Mississippi had adopted a key innovation: an "understanding clause" that required would-be voters to interpret parts of the state constitution, with local Democratic officials deciding who met the standard. After the Populist uprising — and after Republicans ceased their attempts to protect voting rights — such measures spread to other southern states. Louisiana's grandfather clause, which denied the ballot to any man whose grandfather had been unable to vote in slavery days, was struck down by the U.S. Supreme Court. But in ***Williams v. Mississippi*** (1898), the Court allowed poll taxes and literacy tests to stand. By 1908, every southern state had adopted such measures to suppress African American voting — and exclude some poor whites from the polls as well.

The impact of disfranchisement can hardly be overstated (Map 19.3). Across the South, voter turnout plunged, from above 70 percent to 34 percent or even lower. Not only blacks but also many poor whites ceased to vote. Since Democrats faced virtually no opposition, action shifted to the "white primaries," where Democratic candidates competed for nominations. Some former Populists joined the Democrats in openly advocating white supremacy. The racial climate hardened. Segregation laws proliferated. Lynching of African Americans increasingly occurred in broad daylight, with crowds of thousands gathered to watch.

The convict lease system, which had begun to take hold during Reconstruction, also expanded. Blacks received harsh sentences for crimes such as "vagrancy," often when they were traveling to find work or if they could not produce a current employment contract. By the 1890s, Alabama depended on convict leasing for 6 percent of its total state revenue. Prisoners were overwhelmingly black: a 1908 report showed that almost 90 percent of Georgia's leased convicts were African Americans. Calling attention to the torture and deaths of prisoners, as well as the damaging economic effect of their unpaid labor, reformers, labor unions, and Populists protested the situation strenuously. But "reforms" simply replaced convict leasing with the chain gang, in which prisoners worked directly for the state on roadbuilding and other projects, under equally cruel conditions. All these developments depended on a political Solid South in which Democrats exercised almost complete control.

The impact of the 1890s counterrevolution was dramatically illustrated in Grimes County, a cotton-growing area in east Texas where blacks comprised more than half of the population. African American voters kept the local Republican Party going after Reconstruction and regularly sent black representatives to the Texas legislature. Many local white Populists dismissed Democrats' taunts of

VISUAL ACTIVITY

Lynching in Texas Lynchings peaked between 1890 and 1910; while most common in the South, they occurred in almost every state, from Oregon to Minnesota to New York. After many lynchings — such as this one in the town of Center, Texas, in 1920 — crowds posed to have their pictures taken. Commercial photographers often, as in this case, produced photographic postcards to sell as souvenirs. The victim in this photograph, a young man named Lige Daniels, was seized from the local jail by a mob that broke down the prison door to kidnap and kill him. The inscription on the back of the postcard includes information about the killing, along with the instructions "Give this to Bud From Aunt Myrtle." Picture Research Consultants & Archives.

READING THE IMAGE: Who is in the crowd, and who is not? What might we conclude from the fact that this group of white men, some of whom may have been responsible for the lynching, felt comfortable having their photographs recorded with the body?

MAKING CONNECTIONS: What relationships can you trace between the public terror of lynching and the rising politics of white supremacy in the South? Who was the intended audience of this photo? Why?

TEACHING STRATEGY

The companion site for PBS's documentary *The Rise and Fall of Jim Crow* offers "Lesson Plan 7: Domestic Terror," which considers the problem of lynching during the Jim Crow era and the way in which a variety of documentary information was gathered and disseminated to educate people about lynching and to advocate for federal laws prohibiting its practice. While the unit is too long for teachers to use in its entirety, some elements may be useful, including various links to data on lynching. To access this lesson plan, search "PBS The Rise and Fall of Jim Crow Lesson Plans."

TRM Find complete suggested responses in the Teacher's Resource Materials.

CHECK FOR UNDERSTANDING

Ask students: **What was the "Solid South"?** *Beginning in the 1890s, Democrat-controlled legislatures passed grandfather clauses, poll taxes, and literacy tests, which quickly disfranchised African American voters as well as many poor whites. Consequently, the Democratic Party ran virtually unopposed in the "Solid South."*

AP® SKILLS & PROCESSES

DEVELOPMENTS AND PROCESSES

The **DEVELOPMENTS AND PROCESSES** question asks students to trace the emergence of the "Solid South" and the disappearance of black voters in the region. Some students may be surprised to learn that African Americans were able to participate in the political process in the post-Reconstruction period, so it may be helpful to explore how and why blacks were able to vote for a short period. Students could additionally make an inference about whether American participation in World War I affected voting conditions in the "Solid South," particularly the issue of black disfranchisement.

TRM Find complete suggested responses in the Teacher's Resource Materials.

"negro supremacy," and a Populist-Republican coalition swept the county elections in 1896 and 1898. But after their 1898 defeat, Democrats in Grimes County organized a secret brotherhood and forcibly prevented African Americans from voting in town elections, shooting two in cold blood. The Populist sheriff proved unable to bring the murderers to justice. Reconstituted in 1900 as the White Man's Party, Democrats carried Grimes County by an overwhelming margin. Gunmen then laid siege to the Populist sheriff's office, killed his brother and a friend, and drove the wounded sheriff out of the county. The White Man's Party ruled Grimes County for the next fifty years.

AP® SKILLS & PROCESSES

DEVELOPMENTS AND PROCESSES

How did politics change in the South between the 1880s and the 1910s?

Republicans Retake National Control

While their racial policies were abhorrent, that did not prevent the national Democrats from astonishing the country in 1896 by embracing parts of the Populists' radical farmer-labor program. They did so in defiance of President Cleveland, whose decisions continued to alienate him from his party's agrarian and labor base. Despite the worsening economic depression, collapsing prices, and a hemorrhage of gold to Europe, the president refused to budge from his defense of the gold standard. With gold reserves dwindling in 1895, he made a secret arrangement with a syndicate of bankers led by J. P. Morgan to arrange purchases to replenish the treasury. Morgan helped maintain America's gold supply — preserving the gold standard — and turned a tidy profit by earning interest on the bonds he provided. Cleveland's deal, once discovered, enraged fellow Democrats.

William Jennings Bryan This 1896 photograph of Bryan emphasizes the energetic, youthful appeal of the thirty-six-year-old Nebraska Democrat. A powerful orator, Bryan electrified the Democratic convention with his vow to prevent Americans from being "crucified on a cross of gold." Though Bryan secured the electoral votes of the South and a substantial majority of western states, McKinley won the election. Library of Congress, 3f06259.

In 1896, amid such outrage, Democrats rejected Cleveland and nominated a young Nebraska congressman, free silver advocate William Jennings Bryan, who passionately defended farmers and workers and attacked the gold standard. "Burn down your cities and leave our farms," Bryan declared in his famous convention speech, "and your cities will spring up again as if by magic; but destroy our farms and the grass will grow in the streets of every city in the country." He ended with a vow: "You shall not crucify mankind on a cross of gold." Cheering delegates endorsed a platform calling for free silver and a federal income tax on the wealthy that would replace tariffs as a source of revenue. Democrats, long defenders of limited government, were moving toward a more activist stance.

Populists, reeling from recent defeats, endorsed Bryan in the campaign, but their power was waning. Populist leader Tom Watson, who wanted a separate program that was more radical than Bryan's, observed that Democrats in 1896 had cast the Populists as "Jonah while they play whale": Populists had been swallowed up. The People's Party never recovered from its electoral losses in 1894 and from Democrats' two-pronged attack: ruthless opposition in the South and cooptation at the national level. By 1900, rural voters pursued reform elsewhere, particularly through the new Bryan wing of the Democratic Party.

Meanwhile, horrified Republicans denounced Bryan's platform as anarchistic. Their nominee, Ohio congressman and tariff advocate William McKinley, chose a brilliant campaign manager, coal and shipping magnate Marcus Hanna, who orchestrated an unprecedented corporate fund-raising campaign. Under his guidance, the party backed away from moral issues such as prohibition of liquor and reached out to new immigrants. Though the popular vote was closer, McKinley won big: 271 electoral votes to Bryan's 176 (Map 19.4).

Nationwide, as in the South, the realignment of the 1890s prompted new measures to exclude voters. Influenced by classical liberals' denunciations of "unfit voters," many northern states imposed literacy tests and restrictions on immigrant voting. Leaders of both major parties, determined to prevent future Populist-style threats, made it more difficult for new parties to get candidates listed on the ballot. In the wake of such laws, voter turnout declined, and the electorate narrowed in ways that favored the native-born and wealthy.

Antidemocratic restrictions on voting helped, paradoxically, to foster certain political innovations. Having excluded or reduced the number of poor, African American, and immigrant voters, elite and middle-class reformers felt more comfortable strengthening the power of the voters who remained. Both major parties increasingly turned to the direct primary, asking voters (in most states, registered party members) rather than party leaders to choose nominees. Another measure that enhanced democratic participation was the Seventeenth Amendment to the

AP® EXAM TIP

Analyze the impact of the election of 1896 on party politics and Populism.

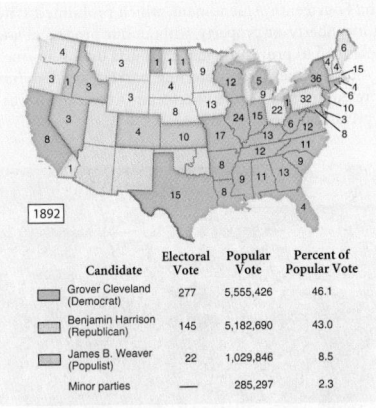

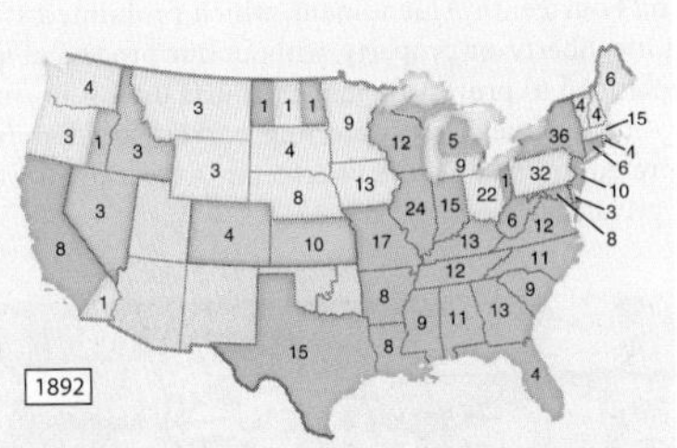

Candidate	Electoral Vote	Popular Vote	Percent of Popular Vote
Grover Cleveland (Democrat)	277	5,555,426	46.1
Benjamin Harrison (Republican)	145	5,182,690	43.0
James B. Weaver (Populist)	22	1,029,846	8.5
Minor parties	—	285,297	2.3

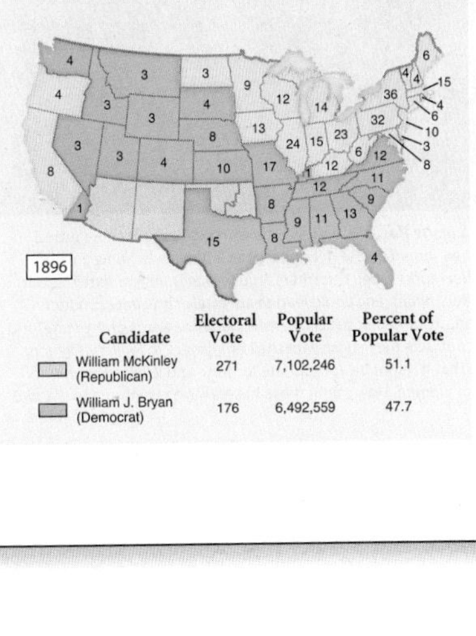

Candidate	Electoral Vote	Popular Vote	Percent of Popular Vote
William McKinley (Republican)	271	7,102,246	51.1
William J. Bryan (Democrat)	176	6,492,559	47.7

MAPPING THE PAST

MAP 19.4 The Presidential Elections of 1892 and 1896

In the 1890s, the age of political stalemate came to an end. Compare the 1892 map with Map 19.1 (p. 607) and note especially Cleveland's breakthrough in the normally Republican states of the Upper Midwest. In 1896, the pendulum swung in the opposite direction, with McKinley's consolidation of Republican control over the Northeast and Midwest far overbalancing the Democratic advances in the thinly populated western states.

ANALYZING THE MAP: Using the map, identify three changes in presidential voting patterns in 1896, as compared to 1892. Why did McKinley win in 1896, even though Bryan won so many large states?

MAKING CONNECTIONS: Compare these maps to Map 19.2, which also shows how voting patterns changed at a key moment in the mid-1890s. Based on your reading of the chapter, what issues or experiences caused Republicans to win in 1894 and 1896?

AP® APPLY THE TIP

The election of 1896 provides an opportunity for students to make connections between their understanding of the electoral process, populism, and the role of political machines (Chapter 18) in the late nineteenth century. Ask students to create a mind map with "Election of 1896" in the center. Off the central idea, have students create bubbles to represent party politics, populism, and political machines. Using text pp. 615–621, students should identify supporting details that show the impact of each bubble on the outcome of the election of 1896 and its impact on American development. Students may also review Chapter 18 as needed to complete this. Then, provide students with markers or colored pens to expand each bubble by providing supporting details from the text that illustrate the impact that the outcome of the election of 1896 had on party politics, populism, and political machines.

TRM Find complete suggested responses in the Teacher's Resource Materials.

TEACHING STRATEGY

It might be helpful to explain to students that the Supreme Court in this era was guided by "formalism" in its decisions. Judges tried to remove all appeals to emotion so decisions could be based solely on reason. Law, they thought, was a science whose principles could be discovered by the use of reason. Since all are equal before the law, none may receive special treatment. The justices also saw themselves as balancing between granting states the powers necessary to govern and protecting the liberties of the individual, free from state coercion.

The companion Web site for the PBS film *The Supreme Court* offers a clear explanation of *Lochner v. New York* that addresses the technicalities in a lucid way. To access the site, search "PBS Supreme Court Lochner."

Constitution (1913), requiring that U.S. senators be chosen not by state legislatures but by popular vote. Though many states had adopted the practice well before 1913, southern states had resisted, since Democrats feared that it might give more power to their political opponents. After disfranchisement, such objections faded and the measure passed. Thus disfranchisement enhanced the power of remaining voters in multiple, complicated ways.

At the same time, the Supreme Court proved hostile to many proposed reforms. In 1895, for example, it struck down a recently adopted federal income tax on the wealthy. The Court ruled that unless this tax was calculated on a per-state basis, rather than by the wealth of individuals, it could not be levied without a constitutional amendment. It took progressives nineteen years to achieve that goal.

Labor organizations also suffered in the new political regime, as federal courts invalidated many regulatory laws passed to protect workers. As early as 1882, in the case of *In re Jacobs*, the New York State Court of Appeals struck down a public-health law that prohibited cigar manufacturing in tenements, arguing that such regulation exceeded the state's police powers. In ***Lochner v. New York*** (1905), the U.S. Supreme Court told New York State it could not limit bakers' workdays to ten hours because that violated bakers' rights to make contracts. Judges found support for such rulings in the due process clause of the Fourteenth Amendment, which prohibited states from depriving "any person of life, liberty, or property, without due process of law." Though the clause had been intended to protect freedmen, courts used it to shield contract rights, with judges arguing that they were protecting workers' freedom *from* government regulation. Interpreted in this way, the Fourteenth Amendment was a major obstacle to regulation of private business.

Lochner v. New York
A 1905 Supreme Court ruling that New York State could not limit bakers' workday to ten hours because that violated bakers' rights to make individual contracts. This example of legal formalism did not take into account the unequal power of employers and individual workers.

New York Bakers Marching in a Labor Parade, 1909. The working hours of these proud workingmen (including Jewish bakers, as shown by the Hebrew sign at left) were left unregulated in the Supreme Court case *Lochner v. New York* (1904). Reformers argued that gruelling sixteen-hour stints beside hot ovens damaged workers' health and could lead to an unsafe consumer product (bread). A majority of justices disagreed, arguing that bakers were "in no sense wards of the state" and could, as individuals, make whatever contracts they chose with their employers. In *Muller v. Oregon*, however, the Court began to concede that it might be appropriate for state and local governments to regulate working hours — at least for women. How might these bakers have responded to the two decisions? Library of Congress, 3a24380.

Farmer and labor advocates, along with urban progressives who called for more government regulation, disagreed with such rulings. They believed judges, not state legislators, were overreaching. While courts treated employers and employees as equal parties, critics dismissed this as a legal fiction. "Modern industry has reduced 'freedom of contract' to a paper privilege," declared one labor advocate, "a mere figure of rhetoric." Supreme Court justice Oliver Wendell Holmes Jr., dissenting in the *Lochner* decision, agreed. If the choice was between working and starving, he observed, how could bakers "choose" their hours of work? Holmes's view, known as legal realism, eventually won judicial favor, but only after years of progressive and labor activism.

AP® SKILLS & PROCESSES

CONTEXTUALIZATION

What developments caused the percentage of Americans who voted to plunge after 1900, and what role did courts play in antidemocratic developments?

REFORM RESHAPED, 1901–1912

Why and to what extent did the political parties' goals change between 1900 and 1912?

William McKinley, a powerful presence in the White House, was no reformer. His victory was widely understood as a triumph for business and especially for industrial titans who had contributed heavily to his campaign. But the depression of the 1890s, by subjecting millions to severe hardship, had dramatically illustrated the problems of industrialization. At the same time, the success of McKinley's campaign managers — who spent more than $3.5 million, versus Bryan's $300,000 — raised unsettling questions about corporate power. Once the crisis of the 1890s passed, many middle-class Americans proved ready to embrace progressive ideas. The rise of such ideas was aided by historical chance, with a sudden assassination.

Theodore Roosevelt as President

On September 14, 1901, only six months after William McKinley won his second face-off against Democrat William Jennings Bryan, the president was shot as he attended the Pan-American Exposition in Buffalo, New York. He died eight days later. The murderer, Leon Czolgosz, was influenced by anarchists who had carried out recent assassinations in Europe. Though Czolgosz was American-born, many feared that McKinley's violent death was another warning of the threat posed by radical immigrants. As the nation mourned its third murdered president in less than four decades, Vice President Theodore Roosevelt was sworn into office.

AP® EXAM TIP

Evaluate Theodore Roosevelt's leadership in bringing Progressive Era reform to the federal government.

Roosevelt, from a prominent family, had chosen an unconventional path. After graduating from Harvard, he plunged into politics, winning a seat as a Republican New York assemblyman. Disillusioned by his party's resistance to reform, he left politics in the mid-1880s and moved to a North Dakota ranch. But his cattle herd was wiped out in the blizzards of 1887. He returned east, winning appointments as a U.S. Civil Service commissioner, head of the New York City Police Commission, and McKinley's assistant secretary of the navy. An energetic presence in all these jobs, Roosevelt gained broad knowledge of the problems America faced at the municipal, state, and federal levels.

After serving in the War of 1898 (see "The War of 1898" in Chapter 20), Roosevelt was elected as New York's governor. In this job, he pushed through civil service reform and a tax on corporations. Seeking to neutralize this progressive and rather unpredictable rising star, Republican bosses chose Roosevelt as McKinley's running mate in 1900, hoping the vice-presidency would be a political dead end. Instead, they found Roosevelt in the White House. The new president, who called for vigorous reform, represented a major shift for the Republicans.

CHECK FOR UNDERSTANDING

Ask students: **Why and how did the depression of the 1890s impact federal politics and policy?** *The Panic of 1893 had little effect on federal policies as the small-government moneyed interests dominated both the Democratic Cleveland (1893–1897) and the Republican McKinley (1897–1901) administrations, and reform was minimal, despite a Populist surge in the 1890s. Federal politics, however, was drastically altered. Southern Democrats increasingly appealed to racism to prevent whites from voting with the Progressives, further entrenching the race-based politics of the region. In the North, the failure of the Populists to win outright led to their absorption into the Bryan wing of the Democratic Party.*

AP® SKILLS & PROCESSES

CONTEXTUALIZATION

The **CONTEXTUALIZATION** question asks students to place two antidemocratic trends — restrictions on voters and Court decisions — in the larger context of the Progressive Era. You may need to point out to students the paradoxical nature of these antidemocratic trends in an era that reformers envisioned as a period of increased democracy.

TRM Find complete suggested responses in the Teacher's Resource Materials.

AP® THEME

PCE: Politics and Power

This portion of the text discusses the ways that progressives on the national level sought federal legislation to regulate the economy and expand democracy.

TEACHING STRATEGY

In advance of studying President Theodore Roosevelt's presidency, acknowledge the fact Roosevelt was a political centrist in many ways. That is, he took what some may consider contradictory positions because he embraced pro-business policies while also asserting the right of government to regulate industry. Too often, students will miss this nuance and alerting them early in the study may facilitate their understanding.

Antitrust Legislation Roosevelt generally supported the needs of private enterprise, but on occasion he challenged corporations in new ways. During a bitter 1902 coal strike, for example, he threatened to nationalize the big coal companies if their owners refused to negotiate with the miners' union. The owners hastily came to the table. Roosevelt also sought better enforcement of the Interstate Commerce Act and Sherman Antitrust Act. He pushed through the Elkins Act (1903), which prohibited discriminatory railway rates that favored powerful customers. That same year, he created the Bureau of Corporations, empowered to investigate business practices and bolster the Justice Department's capacity to mount antitrust suits. The department had already filed such a suit against the Northern Securities Company, arguing that this combination of northwestern railroads had created a monopoly in violation of the Sherman Antitrust Act. In a landmark decision in 1904, the Supreme Court ordered Northern Securities dissolved.

Square Deal
Theodore Roosevelt's 1904 campaign platform, calling for regulation of corporations and protection of consumers and the environment.

That year, calling for every American to get what he called a **Square Deal** — corporate regulation and consumer and environmental protection — Roosevelt handily defeated Democratic candidate Alton B. Parker. Now president in his own right, Roosevelt stepped up his attack on trusts. He regarded large-scale enterprise as the natural tendency of modern industry, but he hoped to identify and punish "malefactors of great wealth" who abused their power. After much wrangling in Congress, Roosevelt won a major victory with passage of the **Hepburn Act** (1906), which strengthened the Interstate Commerce Commission, authorizing it to set shipping rates when it found evidence of railroad collusion to fix prices.

Hepburn Act
A 1906 antitrust law that empowered the federal Interstate Commerce Commission to set railroad shipment rates wherever it believed that railroads were unfairly colluding to set prices.

At the time Roosevelt acted, trusts had partially protected themselves with the help of two friendly states, New Jersey and Delaware, whose legislatures had loosened regulations and invited trusts to incorporate under their new state laws. With its Northern Securities ruling, however, the Supreme Court began to recognize federal authority to dissolve the most egregious monopolies. Roosevelt left a powerful legacy to his successor, William Howard Taft. In its **Standard Oil decision** (1911), the Supreme Court agreed with Taft's Justice Department that John D. Rockefeller's massive oil monopoly should be broken up into several competing companies. After this ruling, Taft's attorney general undertook antitrust actions against other giant companies.

Standard Oil decision
A 1911 Supreme Court decision that directed the breakup of the Standard Oil Company into smaller companies because its overwhelming market dominance and monopoly power violated antitrust laws.

Environmental Conservation Roosevelt was an ardent outdoorsman and hunter. It was after the president went bear hunting in Mississippi in 1902, in fact, that a Russian Jewish immigrant couple in New York began to sell stuffed "Teddy's bears," which became an American childhood tradition. After John Muir gave Roosevelt a tour of Yosemite Valley, the president described the transcendent experience of camping in the open air under the giant sequoias. "The majestic trunks, beautiful in color and in symmetry," he wrote, "rose round us like the pillars of a mightier cathedral than ever was conceived."

AP® EXAM TIP
Understand the complementary as well as competing goals of conservationists and preservationists in the Progressive Era.

Roosevelt translated his love of nature into environmental action. By the end of his presidency, he had issued fifty-one executive orders creating wildlife refuges and signed a number of bills advocated by environmentalists. He also oversaw creation of three national parks, including Colorado's Mesa Verde, the first to "protect the works of man": American Indian archaeological sites. Also notable was his vigorous use of the Antiquities Act, through which he set aside such beautiful sites as Arizona's Grand Canyon and Washington's Mt. Olympus.

Some of Roosevelt's conservation policies, however, had a probusiness bent. He increased the amount of land held in federal forest reserves and turned their management over to the new, independent U.S. Forest Service, created in 1905. But his forestry chief, Gifford Pinchot, insisted on fire suppression to maximize logging potential. In addition, Roosevelt lent support to the **Newlands Reclamation Act** (1902), which had much in common with earlier Republican policies to promote economic development in the West. Under the act, the federal government sold public

Newlands Reclamation Act
A 1902 law, supported by President Theodore Roosevelt, that allowed the federal government to sell public lands to raise money for irrigation projects that expanded agriculture on arid lands.

TEACHING STRATEGY

Ohio State University's eHistory Web site offers a wide range of primary sources related to the 1902 anthracite coal strike and, more broadly, on the nature of coal mine labor. The site provides insight regarding the significance of Roosevelt's intervention in this dispute, which was unprecedented in not clearly favoring management. To access the site, search "eHistory 1902 coal strike."

AP® APPLY THE TIP

Divide the class into two teams to engage in a simulated debate on the proper role of the federal government in protecting natural resources in the late nineteenth through early twentieth centuries. (If your class is large, consider having multiple teams.) Instruct one team to represent the idea of preservation and the other team to represent the idea of conservation. Inform each team that they must do the following in preparation for the debate:

- Research the problem of destruction of natural resources in the late nineteenth century;
- Clarify the problem by explaining the causes of the problem;
- Develop a thesis statement that makes an argument for the proper role of the federal government in use of natural resources; and
- Provide evidence to support their thesis that includes specific historical documents, images, and data.

Once students have completed their research and developed their argument, bring the class together to debate preservation vs. conservation. Randomly choose students from each team to present their clarification of the issue, their thesis, and their evidence. After both teams present their ideas, allow a 5-minute "recess" to research and discuss the argument and evidence presented by the opposing team. Allow team members to question the other team in order to clarify or refute their argument, justify their use of evidence, or question their explanation of the causes of the problem. After the debate, lead a class discussion on the distinctions between preservation and conservation as well as the use of evidence to support each argument.

TEACHING STRATEGY

The *Atlantic* provides the full text of John Muir's landmark 1897 essay, "The American Forests." To access this text, search "Atlantic American Forests."

AP® THEME

GEO: Geography and Environment

The "Environmental Conservation" section discusses the ways preservationists and conservationists both supported the establishment of national parks, while advocating different government responses to the overuse of natural resources.

AP® SKILLS & PROCESSES

DEVELOPMENTS AND PROCESSES

Both preservation and conservation are specific historical terms called out in the AP® Course Framework. Have students define each with an example of those policies in practice. This essential knowledge will help students grapple with environmental debates during the Progressive Era.

lands to raise money for irrigation projects that expanded agriculture on arid lands. The law, ironically, fulfilled one of the demands of the unemployed men who had marched with Coxey's Army — a movement Roosevelt had denounced.

Roosevelt's Legacies Like the environmental laws enacted during his presidency, Theodore Roosevelt was full of contradictions. An unabashed believer in what he called "Anglo-Saxon" superiority, Roosevelt nonetheless incurred the wrath of white supremacists by inviting Booker T. Washington to dine at the White House. Roosevelt called for elite "best men" to enter politics, but he also defended the dignity of labor.

In 1908, Roosevelt chose to retire, bequeathing the Republican nomination to talented administrator William Howard Taft. Taft portrayed himself as Roosevelt's man, though he maintained a closer relationship than his predecessor with probusiness Republicans in Congress. In 1908, Taft faced off against Democrat William Jennings Bryan, who, eloquent as ever, attacked Republicans as the party of "plutocrats": men who used their wealth to buy political influence. Bryan outdid Taft in urging tougher antitrust and prolabor legislation, but Taft won comfortably.

In the wake of Taft's victory, however, rising pressure for reform began to divide Republicans. Conservatives dug in, while militant progressives within the party thought Roosevelt and his successor had not gone far enough. Reconciling these conflicting forces was a daunting task. For Taft, it spelled disaster. Through various incidents, he found himself on the opposite side of progressive Republicans, who began to call themselves "insurgents" and plot their own path.

AP® SKILLS & PROCESSES

ARGUMENTATION

To what degree — and in what ways — were Roosevelt's policies progressive?

AP® EXAM TIP

The role of local efforts and state governments in the Progressive Era is critical for success on the AP® Exam.

Diverse Progressive Goals

The revolt of Republican insurgents signaled the strength of grassroots demands for change. No one described these emerging goals more eloquently than Jane Addams, who famously declared in *Democracy and Social Ethics* (1902), "The cure for the ills of Democracy is more Democracy." It was a poignant statement, given the sharply antidemocratic direction American politics had taken since the 1890s. What, now, should more democracy look like? Various groups of progressives — women, antipoverty reformers, African American advocates — often disagreed about priorities and goals. Some, frustrated by events in the United States, traveled abroad to study inspiring experiments in other nations, hoping to bring ideas home.

Wisconsin Idea
A policy promoted by Republican governor Robert La Follette of Wisconsin for greater government intervention in the economy, with reliance on experts, particularly progressive economists, for policy recommendations.

States also served as seedbeds of change. Theodore Roosevelt dubbed Wisconsin a "laboratory of democracy" under energetic Republican governor Robert La Follette (1901–1905). La Follette promoted what he called the **Wisconsin Idea** — greater government intervention in the economy, with reliance on experts, particularly progressive economists, for policy recommendations. Like Addams, La Follette combined respect for expertise with commitment to "more Democracy." He won battles to restrict lobbying and to give Wisconsin citizens the right of recall — voting to remove unpopular politicians from office — and referendum — voting directly on a proposed law, rather than

Robert M. La Follette La Follette became a political reformer when, in 1891, a Wisconsin Republican boss attempted to bribe him to influence a judge in a railway case. As he described it in his autobiography, "Out of this awful ordeal came understanding; and out of understanding came resolution. I determined that the power of this corrupt influence . . . should be broken." This photograph captures him at the top of his form in 1897, expounding his progressive vision to a rapt audience of Wisconsin citizens at an impromptu street gathering. Library of Congress 3a03287.

CHECK FOR UNDERSTANDING

Ask students: **What was Theodore Roosevelt like as president?** *He generally struck a balance between reform and support for private enterprise, though he occasionally reined in corporations in new ways. He regulated corporations through enforcement of the Interstate Commerce Act and the Sherman Antitrust Act, and by creating the Bureau of Corporations and the Elkins Act. He won election in 1904 by promising a Square Deal to the American people and, after his victory, began attacking trusts more vigorously. He supported environmental conservation while also promoting business interests through the Newlands Reclamation Act.*

AP® SKILLS & PROCESSES

ARGUMENTATION

The **ARGUMENTATION** question essentially asks students to compare the policies of President Roosevelt to the values and goals of progressive reformers. Students should recognize that, since progressive reformers had varied and sometimes contradictory goals, Roosevelt could not align with all of them. Rather, students should consider the degree to which his major actions were consonant with at least one strain of progressivism. Students who are more advanced could evaluate the degree to which Roosevelt's probusiness policies undermine claims that he was a progressive.

TRM Find complete suggested responses in the Teacher's Resource Materials.

AP® THEME

PCE: Politics and Power

The "Diverse Progressive Goals" section explores ways that progressives were divided over many issues. Students should understand the key divisions: some supported segregation, while others ignored it. Some sought to expand participation in government, while others called for restrictions to make government more efficient.

TEACHING STRATEGY

The National Archives's Web site page "Teaching with Documents: Photographs of Lewis Hine: Documentation of Child Labor" includes a detailed background essay, more than a dozen high-quality photos with dates and titles, and suggestions for group discussion. To access the site, search "National Archives Lewis Hine."

AP® THEME

PCE: Politics and Power; SOC: Social Structures

This section of the text explains the ways that middle- and upper-class women reformers worked to effect social changes.

TEACHING STRATEGY

The Louis D. Brandeis School of Law Library provides the text of the famous *Brandeis Brief* in its entirety online. At 113 pages, it makes for daunting reading, but it might be useful for a research project for a student interested in a legal career. To access this resource, search "School of Law Brandeis Brief."

leaving it in the hands of legislators. Continuing his career in the U.S. Senate, La Follette, like Roosevelt, advocated increasingly aggressive measures to protect workers and check corporate power.

Protecting Labor The urban settlement movement called attention to poverty in America's industrial cities. In the emerging social sciences, experts argued that unemployment and crowded slums were not caused by laziness and ignorance, as elite Americans had long believed. Instead, as journalist Robert Hunter wrote in his landmark study, *Poverty* (1904), such problems resulted from "miserable and unjust social conditions."

National Child Labor Committee
A reform organization that worked (unsuccessfully) to win a federal law banning child labor. The NCLC hired photographer Lewis Hine to record brutal conditions in mines and mills where thousands of children worked.

By the early twentieth century, reformers placed particular emphasis on labor conditions for women and children. The **National Child Labor Committee**, created in 1907, hired photographer Lewis Hine to record brutal conditions in mines and mills where children worked. Impressed by the committee's investigations, Theodore Roosevelt sponsored the first White House Conference on Dependent Children in 1909, bringing national attention to child welfare issues. In 1912, momentum from the conference resulted in creation of the Children's Bureau in the U.S. Labor Department.

Muller v. Oregon
A 1908 Supreme Court case that upheld an Oregon law limiting women's workday to ten hours, based on the need to protect women's health for motherhood. *Muller* established a groundwork for states to protect workers but divided women's rights activists, some of whom saw it as discriminatory.

Those seeking to protect working-class women scored a triumph in 1908 with the Supreme Court's decision in ***Muller v. Oregon***, which upheld an Oregon law limiting women's workday to ten hours. Given the Court's ruling three years earlier in *Lochner v. New York*, it was a stunning victory. To win the case, the National Consumers' League (Chapter 18) recruited Louis Brandeis, a son of Jewish immigrants who was widely known as "the people's lawyer" for his eagerness to take on vested interests. Brandeis's legal brief in the *Muller* case devoted only two pages to the constitutional issue of state police powers. Instead, Brandeis rested his arguments on data gathered by the NCL describing the toll that long work hours took on women's health. The "Brandeis brief" cleared the way for use of social science research in court decisions. Sanctioning a more expansive role for state governments, the *Muller* decision encouraged women's organizations to lobby for further reforms. Their achievements included the first law providing public assistance for single mothers with dependent children (Illinois, 1911) and the first minimum wage law for women (Massachusetts, 1912).

Muller had drawbacks, however. Though men as well as women suffered from long work hours, the *Muller* case did not protect men. Brandeis's brief treated all women as potential mothers, focusing on the state's interest in protecting future children. Brandeis and his allies hoped this would be an "opening wedge" that would open the door to broader regulation of working hours. The Supreme Court, however, seized on motherhood as the key issue, asserting that the female worker, because of her maternal function, was "in a class by herself, and legislation for her protection may be sustained, even when like legislation is not necessary for men." This conclusion dismayed labor advocates and divided female reformers for decades afterward.

mothers' pensions
Progressive Era public payments to mothers who did not have help from a male breadwinner. Recipients had to meet standards of "respectability" defined by middle-class home visitors, reflecting a broader impulse to protect women but hold them to different standards than men.

Male workers did benefit, however, from new workmen's compensation measures. Between 1910 and 1917, all the industrial states enacted insurance laws covering on-the-job accidents, so workers' families would not starve if a breadwinner was injured or killed. Some states also experimented with so-called **mothers' pensions,** providing state assistance after a breadwinner's desertion or death. Mothers, however, were subjected to home visits to determine whether they "deserved" government aid; injured workmen were not judged on this basis, a pattern of gender discrimination that reflected the broader impulse to protect women, while also holding them to different standards than men. Mothers' pensions reached relatively small numbers of women, but they laid foundations for the national program Aid to Families with Dependent Children, an important component of the Social Security Act of 1935.

While federalism gave the states considerable freedom to innovate, state government priorities and power also limited some national reforms. In the South, for example, and in coal-mining states like Pennsylvania, companies fiercely resisted child labor laws — as did many working-class parents who relied on children's income to keep the family fed. A proposed U.S. constitutional amendment to abolish child labor never won ratification; only four states passed it. Tens of thousands of children continued to work in low-wage jobs, especially in the South. The same decentralized power that permitted innovation in Wisconsin hampered the creation of national minimum standards for pay and job safety.

Labor Militancy The skilled men in the nation's dominant union, the American Federation of Labor, had far more success in organizing but were slow to engage in electoral politics. AFL leaders like Samuel Gompers had long believed workers should improve their situation through strikes and direct negotiation with employers, not through parties and voting. But by the 1910s, as progressive reformers came forward with solutions, labor leaders in state after state began to press for political action.

The nation also confronted a daring wave of radical labor militancy. In 1905, the Western Federation of Miners (WFM), led by fiery leaders such as William "Big Bill" Haywood, helped create a new movement, the **Industrial Workers of the World (IWW)**. The Wobblies, as they were called, fervently supported the Marxist class struggle. As syndicalists, they believed that by resisting in the workplace and ultimately launching a general strike, workers could overthrow capitalism. A new society would emerge, run directly by workers. At its height, around 1916, the IWW had about 100,000 members. Though divided by internal conflicts, the group helped spark a number of local protests during the 1910s, including strikes of rail car builders in Pennsylvania, textile operatives in Massachusetts, rubber workers in Ohio, and miners in Minnesota.

Meanwhile, after midnight on October 1, 1910, an explosion ripped through the *Los Angeles Times* headquarters, killing twenty employees and wrecking the building. It turned out that John J. McNamara, a high official of the American Federation of Labor's Bridge and Structural Iron Workers Union, had planned the bombing against the fiercely antiunion *Times*. McNamara's brother and another union member had carried out the attack. The bombing created a sensation, as did the terrible Triangle Shirtwaist Company fire (see "Cities and National Politics" in Chapter 18 and the IWW's high-profile strikes. Clearly, much remained to be done to address workers' demands.

The Birth of Modern Civil Rights Reeling from disfranchisement and the sanction of racial segregation in the Supreme Court's 1896 *Plessy v. Ferguson* decision (see "Consumer Spaces" in Chapter 17), African American leaders faced even more daunting challenges facing their political goals. Given the obvious deterioration of African American rights, a new generation of black leaders proposed bolder approaches than those popularized earlier by Booker T. Washington. Harvard-educated sociologist W. E. B. Du Bois called for a **talented tenth** of educated blacks to develop new strategies. "The policy of compromise has failed," declared William Monroe Trotter, pugnacious editor of the *Boston Guardian*, in a dig at Booker T. Washington's Atlanta Compromise address. "The policy of resistance and aggression deserves a trial."

The MASSES
JUNE 1914
10 CENTS
IN THIS ISSUE
CLASS WAR IN COLORADO—Max Eastman
WHAT ABOUT MEXICO ?—John Reed

The Ludlow Massacre, 1914 This cover illustration for the popular socialist magazine *The Masses* demonstrates John Sloan's outrage at social injustice in progressive America. The drawing memorializes a tragic episode during a coal miners' strike at Ludlow, Colorado — the asphyxiation of women and children when vigilantes torched the tent city of evicted miners — and the aftermath, an armed revolt by enraged miners. Picture Research Consultants & Archives.

Industrial Workers of the World (IWW)
A radical labor group founded in 1905, dedicated to organizing unskilled workers to oppose capitalism. Nicknamed the Wobblies, they advocated direct action by workers, including sabotage and general strikes.

AP® SKILLS & PROCESSES

COMPARISON
How did various grassroots reformers define "progressivism," and how did their views differ from Theodore Roosevelt's version of "progressivism"?

AP® EXAM TIP
The role of W. E. B. Du Bois and the NAACP in challenging racial segregation and discrimination is important to know on the AP® Exam.

talented tenth
A term used by Harvard-educated sociologist W. E. B. Du Bois for the top 10 percent of educated African Americans, whom he called on to develop new strategies to advocate for civil rights.

TEACHING STRATEGY

The Colorado Coal Field War Project Web site provides several resources for teaching about the Ludlow massacre, including a background essay, high school lesson plans, and several photos of the daily life of strikers in the Ludlow tent camps. To access these resources, search "Colorado Coal Field War Project Ludlow Massacre."

AP® SKILLS & PROCESSES

COMPARISON

The **COMPARISON** question asks students to compare overlapping, and sometimes competing, definitions of progressivism. Some students may need guidance in understanding why a diverse group of people could have such divergent diagnoses of American problems and equally divergent ideas about the best cures. Students might also consider why "progress" was such a popular way of describing reform movements of the era — what did the use of this term imply about the broader views of the time?

TRM Find complete suggested responses in the Teacher's Resource Materials.

AP® APPLY THE TIP

Provide students with the following quote from the first issue of *The Crisis* written by W. E .B. Du Bois: "The object of this publication is to set forth those facts and arguments which show the danger of race prejudice, particularly as manifested today toward colored people. It takes its name from the fact that the editors believe that this is a critical time in the history of the advancement of men. . . . Finally, its editorial page will stand for the rights of men, irrespective of color or race, for the highest ideals of American democracy, and for reasonable but earnest and persistent attempts to gain these rights and realize these ideals." Students should analyze the excerpt and discuss the historical context, purpose, and intended audience. Ask students to identify the three purposes for which the National Association for the Advancement of Colored People (NAACP) was founded according to this excerpt. Lead a class discussion that addresses the ways in which the NAACP, despite being rejected or ignored by most progressives, was in essence the epitome of a progressive reform movement. Ask students to consider the historical place of the W. E. B. Du Bois and the NAACP in the origin of the civil rights movement that emerged in the post–World War II era.

Niagara Movement Leaders This superimposed image from 1905 shows some of the founders of the Niagara Movement in front of the famous waterfall near their meeting place. The men depicted came from Massachusetts, Minnesota, Kansas, Illinois, New York, Washington, D.C., and Georgia. W. E. B. DuBois, wearing a white hat and bow tie, is second from right in the middle row. The group's efforts eventually led to creation of the National Association for the Advancement of Colored People. What factors might have led Niagara leaders to include only men (and one boy, Norris B. Herndon, son of Alonzo F. Herndon of Georgia) in the photograph, though women played supportive roles in the Niagara meeting? How might we account for the dearth of participants from the South, where the majority of the nation's African American population lived? Library of Congress, LC-DIG-ppmsca-37818.

In 1905, Du Bois and Trotter called a meeting at Niagara Falls — on the Canadian side, because no hotel on the U.S. side would admit blacks. The resulting Niagara Principles called for full voting rights; an end to segregation; equal treatment in the justice system; and equal opportunity in education, jobs, health care, and military service. These principles, based on an uncompromising demand for full equality, guided the civil rights movement throughout the twentieth century.

In 1908, a bloody race riot broke out in Springfield, Illinois. Appalled by white mob violence in the hometown of Abraham Lincoln, New York settlement worker Mary White Ovington called together a group of sympathetic progressives to formulate a response. Their meeting led in 1909 to creation of the **National Association for the Advancement of Colored People (NAACP)**. Most leaders of the Niagara Movement soon joined and W. E. B. Du Bois became editor of the NAACP journal, *The Crisis*. The fledgling group found allies in African American churches and women's clubs. It also cooperated with the National Urban League (1911), a union of agencies that assisted black migrants in the North. Over the coming decades, these groups grew into a powerful force for racial justice.

The Election of 1912

Retirement did not sit comfortably with Theodore Roosevelt. Returning from a yearlong safari in Africa in 1910 to find Taft wrangling with the insurgents, Roosevelt itched to jump in. In a speech in Osawatomie, Kansas, in August 1910, he called for a **New Nationalism**. In modern America, he argued, private property had to be controlled "to whatever degree the public welfare may require it." He proposed a federal child labor law, more recognition of labor rights, and a national minimum wage for women. Pressed by friends like Jane Addams, Roosevelt also endorsed women's suffrage. Most radical was his attack on the legal system. Arguing that courts were blocking reform, Roosevelt proposed sharp curbs on their powers.

National Association for the Advancement of Colored People (NAACP)
An organization founded in 1909 by leading African American reformers and white allies as a vehicle for advocating equal rights for African Americans, especially through the courts.

New Nationalism
Theodore Roosevelt's 1910 proposal to enhance public welfare through a federal child labor law, more recognition of labor rights, a national minimum wage for women, women's suffrage, and curbs on the power of federal courts.

AP® EXAM TIP
Evaluate the election of 1912 as evidence of continuity and change in American politics as a result of the Progressive Era.

Early in 1912, Roosevelt announced himself as a Republican candidate for president. A battle within the party ensued. Roosevelt won most states that held primary elections, but Taft controlled party caucuses elsewhere. Dominated by regulars, the Republican convention chose Taft. Roosevelt then led his followers into what became known as the Progressive Party, offering his New Nationalism directly to the people. Though Jane Addams harbored private doubts (especially about Roosevelt's mania for battleships), she seconded his nomination, calling the Progressive Party "the American exponent of a world-wide movement for juster social conditions." In a nod to Roosevelt's combative stance, party followers called themselves "Bull Mooses."

Roosevelt was not the only rebel on the ballot: the major parties also faced a challenge from charismatic socialist Eugene V. Debs. In the 1890s, Debs had founded the American Railway Union (ARU), a broad-based group that included both skilled and unskilled workers. In 1894, amid the upheavals of depression and popular protest, the ARU had boycotted luxury Pullman sleeping cars, in support of a strike by workers at the Pullman Company. Railroad managers, claiming the strike obstructed

TEACHING STRATEGY

Google Books provides a fully searchable facsimile copy of each issue of *Crisis* magazine beginning with April 1911. To access this resource, search "Google Books The Crisis."

CHECK FOR UNDERSTANDING

Ask students: **What were some of the major diverse goals of progressives?** *State-level reform, such as La Follette's Wisconsin Idea, advocated greater regulation of the economy and more direct democracy through the referendum and recall. The urban settlement movement sought to improve the conditions of impoverished women and children, particularly with respect to labor. Civil rights leaders, including Du Bois, launched the Niagara Movement, calling for full equality and civil rights for African Americans. Meanwhile, the IWW sought to overthrow capitalism.*

TEACHING STRATEGY

Ohio State University's eHistory Web site features an online exhibition, *1912: Competing Visions for America*, which you can use to engage students in investigating the candidates, the issues and alternatives, and the nature of the campaign itself. To access the exhibition, search "eHistory 1912."

AP® APPLY THE TIP

Divide the class into two sections. Ask one section to discuss and develop the argument that the election of 1912 was an event that illustrated continuity in the political development of the U.S. Ask the other section to discuss and develop the argument that the election of 1912 illustrated change in American political development. Encourage students to use their textbook and additional sources to include an analysis of issues, personalities, philosophies, and party platforms, as well as the impact of the election on politics. Allow the two sides to debate their assigned arguments. After the debate, require students to write a thesis statement and outline that addresses the following Long Essay Question (LEQ) prompt: "Evaluate the extent of political change at a national level from 1900-1920." Allow students to peer review their thesis statements and use of evidence in support of the thesis in their outlines. Lead a class discussion that compares thesis statements that argue for continuity and change. To help students practice responding to LEQs, ask them to use their thesis, outline, and notes from class discussion to construct an LEQ essay.

TEACHING STRATEGY

Have students compare Roosevelt's New Nationalism platform with his progressive policies as President. Evaluating the extent of change in Roosevelt's policies will help students understand changes in the progressive movement.

The Republicans Resist Roosevelt, August 7, 1912 This cartoon appeared in the political humor journal *Puck*, six weeks after the Republican convention nominated Taft and two days after the new Progressive Party nominated Theodore Roosevelt. The baptismal choir consists of men such as Gifford Pinchot, who helped Roosevelt form the new party. The G.O.P. elephant refuses to be baptized in "Teddyism," though Preacher Roosevelt insists, "Salvation is Free." President William Howard Taft, dressed in brown with a hat, pulls on the elephant's tail. Library of Congress, LC-DIG-ppmsca-27865.

the U.S. mail, persuaded Grover Cleveland's administration to intervene against the union. The strike failed, and Debs served time in prison along with other ARU leaders. The experience radicalized him, and in 1901 he launched the Socialist Party of America. Debs translated socialism into an American idiom, emphasizing the democratic process as a means to defeat capitalism. By the early 1910s, his party had secured a minor but persistent role in politics. Both the Progressive and Socialist parties drew strength from the West, a region with vigorous urban reform movements and a legacy of farmer-labor activism. Drawing from earlier reform ideas, both the Progressive and Socialist platforms proposed sweeping changes in federal policy (see "Firsthand Accounts," p. 628).

Watching the rise of the Progressives and Socialists, Democrats were keen to build on dramatic gains they had made in the 1910 midterm election. Among their younger leaders was Virginia-born Woodrow Wilson, who as New Jersey's governor had compiled an impressive reform record, including passage of a direct primary, workers' compensation, and utility regulation. In 1912, he won the Democratic nomination. Wilson possessed, to a fault, the moral certainty that characterized many elite progressives. He had much in common with Roosevelt. "The old time of individual competition is probably gone by," he admitted, agreeing that more federal measures to restrict big business were needed. But his goals were less ambitious than Roosevelt's, and only gradually did he hammer out a reform program, calling it the New Freedom. "If America is not to have free enterprise," Wilson warned, "then she can have freedom of no sort whatever." He claimed Roosevelt's program represented collectivism, whereas the New Freedom, based on limited government, would preserve political and economic liberty.

With four candidates in the field — Taft, Roosevelt, Wilson, and Debs — the 1912 campaign generated intense excitement. Democrats continued to have an enormous blind spot: their opposition to African American rights. But Republicans, despite plentiful opportunities, had also conspicuously failed to end segregation or pass

AP® EXAM TIP

Evaluate the efforts of progressives to regulate the economy and promote social change.

AP® APPLY THE TIP

Organize students into small, collaborative groups and provide them with **Handout 19.4 — Comparison: Progressive Era Reform (TRM)**. Then provide large chart paper and ask each group to create a "checklist" or "to-do" list for the progressive movement, which should encompass the variety of progressive goals. Ask student groups to then categorize the goals under the following headings: implementing social justice, creating good government, establishing a just economy, regulating big business, and any other headings you may want to include. Once the students have grouped their goals, share the lists as a whole class noting similarities and differences. As a class, compile one organized "checklist" and ask students to evaluate the Progressive Era based on its success or failure in achieving its goals and provide a specific piece of historical evidence to support each goal that was achieved. After the students have completed the checklists, lead a class discussion regarding the effectiveness of the efforts of the progressives to achieve their goals.

TRM Find **Handout 19.4 — Comparison: Progressive Era Reform** in the Teacher's Resource Materials.

AP® SKILLS & PROCESSES

ANALYZING HISTORICAL EVIDENCE

The **AP® FIRSTHAND ACCOUNTS** feature allows students to investigate Populist views and proposals firsthand. Students should pay particular attention to the link between the problems the Preamble describes and the Platform declarations the party makes.

AP® FIRSTHAND ACCOUNTS

Three Reform Platforms

None of these three grassroots parties — the People's Party, Progressive Party, and Socialist Party — won federal power. But they proposed new ideas that inspired some Americans, shocked others, and influenced debates about how the federal government should respond to the challenges of industrialization. Their platforms outlined their aims.

OMAHA PLATFORM OF THE PEOPLE'S PARTY, 1892

Adopted by the People's Party at its first national convention a year before the terrible depression of 1893 began, the Omaha Platform demanded action to combat hardships that already existed, especially in rural areas.

SOURCE: George Brown Tindall, ed., *A Populist Reader, Selections from the Works of American Populist Leaders* (New York: Harper & Row, 1966), 90–96.

We believe that the power of government — in other words, of the people — should be expanded (as in the case of the postal service) as rapidly and as far as the good sense of an intelligent people and the teachings of experience shall justify, to the end that oppression, injustice, and poverty shall eventually cease in the land. . . .

. . . We demand free and unlimited coinage of silver and gold at the present legal ratio of l6 to 1. . . .

. . . We demand a graduated income tax. . . .

. . . We demand that postal savings banks be established by the government for the safe deposit of the earnings of the people and to facilitate exchange.

TRANSPORTATION. — . . . The government should own and operate the railroads in the interest of the people. The telegraph, like the post-office system, being a necessity for the transmission of news, should be owned and operated by the government in the interest of the people.

LAND. — . . . All land now held by railroads and other corporations in excess of their actual needs, and all lands now owned by aliens should be reclaimed by the government and held for actual settlers only.

. . . We hereby submit the following, not as a part of the Platform of the People's Party, but as resolutions expressive of the sentiment of this Convention.

. . . RESOLVED, That we demand a free ballot and a fair count in all elections and pledge ourselves to secure it to every legal voter without Federal Intervention. . . .

. . . That . . . we denounce the present ineffective laws against contract labor, and demand the further restriction of undesirable emigration.

. . . That we cordially sympathize with the efforts of organized workingmen to shorten the hours of labor, and demand a rigid enforcement of the existing eight-hour law on Government work. . . .

. . . That we commend to the favorable consideration of the people and the reform press the legislative system known as the initiative and referendum.

. . . That we favor a constitutional provision limiting the office of President and Vice-President to one term, and providing for the election of Senators of the United States by a direct vote of the people.

. . . That we oppose any subsidy or national aid to any private corporation for any purpose.

PROGRESSIVE PARTY PLATFORM, 1912

Founded by Theodore Roosevelt, who broke with the Republican Party and led an insurgent campaign for the presidency, the Progressive platform encapsulated many of the political goals of elite and middle-class reformers, including women.

SOURCE: Progressive Party Platform of 1912, American Presidency Project, UC Santa Barbara, www.presidency.ucsb.edu/documents/progressive-party-platform-1912.

. . . Political parties exist to secure responsible government and to execute the will of the people. From these great tasks both of the old parties have turned aside. Instead of instruments to promote the general welfare, they have become the tools of corrupt interests. . . .

The National Progressive party . . . declares for direct primaries for the nomination of State and National officers, for nation-wide preferential primaries for candidates for the presidency; for the direct election of United States Senators by the people; and we urge on the States . . . the initiative, referendum and recall. . . .

The Progressive party . . . pledges itself to the task of securing equal suffrage to men and women alike.

We pledge our party to legislation that will compel strict limitation of all campaign contributions and expenditures . . . .

We pledge ourselves to work unceasingly in State and Nation for:

Effective legislation looking to the prevention of industrial accidents, occupational diseases, overwork, involuntary unemployment, and other injurious effects incident to modern industry;

The fixing of minimum safety and health standards for the various occupations, and the exercise of the public authority of State and Nation . . . to maintain such standards;

The prohibition of child labor;

Minimum wage standards for working women, to provide a "living wage" in all industrial occupations;

The general prohibition of night work for women and the establishment of an eight-hour day for women and young persons;

One day's rest in seven for all wage workers;

The eight-hour day in continuous twenty-four hour industries;

The abolition of the convict contract labor system; . . .

Standards of compensation for death by industrial accident and injury and trade disease which will transfer the burden of lost earnings from the families of working people to the industry, and thus to the community;

. . . A system of social insurance adapted to American use. . . .

We favor the organization of the workers, men and women, as a means of protecting their interests. . . .

We favor the union of all the existing agencies of the Federal Government dealing with the public health into a single national health service . . . .

. . . The test of corporate efficiency shall be the ability better to serve the public. . . . We therefore demand a strong National regulation of inter-State corporations. . . . The concentration of modern business, in some degree, is both inevitable and necessary for national and international business efficiency. But the existing concentration of vast wealth under a corporate system, unguarded and uncontrolled by the Nation, has placed in the hands of a few men enormous, secret, irresponsible power. . . .

We heartily favor the policy of conservation. . . .

We believe in a graduated inheritance tax [and federal] income tax.

The Progressive party deplores the survival in our civilization of the barbaric system of warfare among nations. . . . We pledge the party to use its best endeavors to substitute judicial and other peaceful means of settling international differences.

We favor an international agreement for the limitation of naval forces. Pending such an agreement, and as the best means of preserving peace, we pledge ourselves to maintain for the present the policy of building two battleships a year. . . .

Through the establishment of industrial standards we propose to secure to the able-bodied immigrant and to his native fellow workers a larger share of American opportunity.

SOCIALIST PARTY PLATFORM, 1912

In addition to Republicans, Democrats, and Theodore Roosevelt's "Bull Moose" Progressive Party, a fourth platform outlined the vision of American socialists, led by candidate Eugene V. Debs.

SOURCE: The Socialist Party Platform of 1912, Sage American History, sageamericanhistory.net/progressive/docs/SocialistPlat1912.htm

The Socialist party declares that the capitalist system has outgrown its historical function, and has become utterly incapable of meeting the problems now confronting society. . . . Under this system the industrial equipment of the nation has passed into the absolute control of a plutocracy. . . . In spite of the multiplication of laborsaving machines and improved methods in industry which cheapen the cost of production, the share of the producers grows ever less, and the prices of all the necessities of life steadily increase. The boasted prosperity of this nation is for the owning class alone. To the rest it means only greater hardship and misery. . . .

Political parties are the expression of economic class interests. All other parties than the Socialist party represent one or another group of the ruling capitalist class. . . . The Socialist party is the political expression of the economic interests of the workers. . . . We advocate and pledge ourselves . . . to the following program:

- The collective ownership and democratic management of railroads, wire and wireless telegraphs and telephones . . . and all other social means of transportation and communication and of all large-scale industries.
- The immediate acquirement by the municipalities, the states or the federal government of all grain elevators, stock yards, storage warehouses, and other distributing agencies, in order to reduce the present extortionate cost of living.
- The extension of the public domain to include mines, quarries, oil wells, forests and water power.
- The further conservation and development of natural resources for the use and benefit of all the people. . . .
- The collective ownership and democratic management of the banking and currency system. . . .

The immediate government relief of the unemployed by the extension of all useful public works. . . .

Industrial Demands

The conservation of human resources, particularly of the lives and well-being of the workers and their families:

- By shortening the work day in keeping with the increased productiveness of machinery.
- By securing for every worker a rest period of not less than a day and a half in each week.
- By securing a more effective inspection of workshops, factories and mines.
- By forbidding the employment of children under sixteen years of age.
- By the co-operative organization of the industries in the federal penitentiaries for the benefit of the convicts and their dependents.
- By forbidding the interstate transportation of the products of child labor, of convict labor, and of all uninspected factories and mines. . . .
- By establishing minimum wage scales.
- By [creating] a system of old age pensions, a general system of insurance by the State of all its members against unemployment and invalidism and a system of compulsory insurance by employers of their workers, without cost to the latter, against industrial diseases, accidents and death.

Political Demands

- The absolute freedom of press, speech and assemblage.
- The adoption of a graduated income tax and the extension of inheritance taxes, graduated in proportion to the value of the estate. . . .
- The abolition of the monopoly ownership of patents and the substitution of collective ownership, with direct rewards to inventors by premiums or royalties.
- Unrestricted and equal suffrage for men and women.
- The adoption of the initiative, referendum and recall and of proportional representation. . . .
- The abolition of the Senate and of the veto power of the President.
- The election of the President and Vice-President by direct vote of the people. . . .

QUESTIONS FOR ANALYSIS

1. What problems does each of these platforms identify in American society?
2. To what extent does each platform propose changes in the structure of government itself, and changes in government's relationship to business? Use historical reasoning to compare each party's perspective.
3. Compare the Omaha Platform to the Progressive and Socialist platforms. Based on this comparison and the chapter narrative, how did national political debates change between 1892 and 1912? In what ways did the platforms of 1912 build on earlier proposals? Compare the party's ideologies to examine patterns of continuity and change.

TRM Find complete suggested responses in the Teacher's Resource Materials.

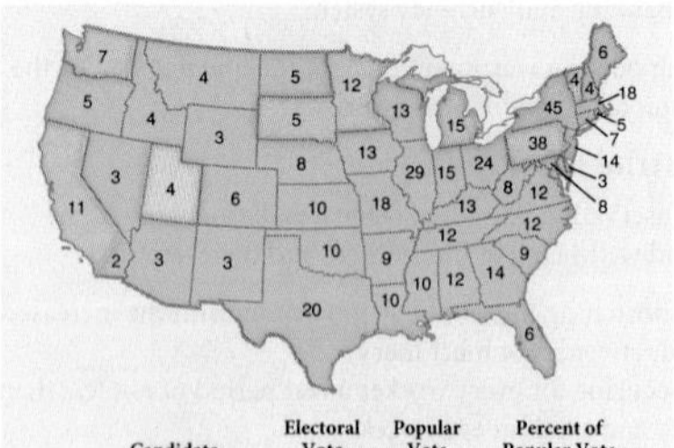

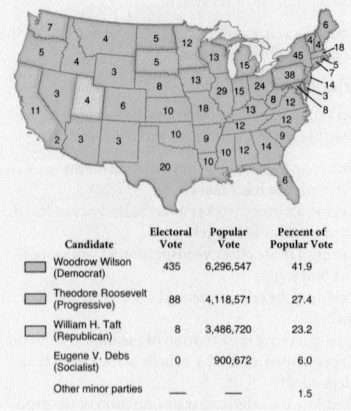

Candidate	Electoral Vote	Popular Vote	Percent of Popular Vote
Woodrow Wilson (Democrat)	435	6,296,547	41.9
Theodore Roosevelt (Progressive)	88	4,118,571	27.4
William H. Taft (Republican)	8	3,486,720	23.2
Eugene V. Debs (Socialist)	0	900,672	6.0
Other minor parties	—	—	1.5

MAP 19.5 The Presidential Election of 1912
The 1912 election reveals why the two-party system is so strongly rooted in American politics — especially in presidential elections. The Democrats, though a minority party, won an electoral landslide because the Republicans divided their vote between Roosevelt and Taft. This result indicates what is at stake when major parties splinter. The Socialist Party candidate, Eugene V. Debs, despite a record vote of 900,000, received no electoral votes.

antilynching laws. Though leaders of the NAACP had high hopes for the Progressive Party, they were crushed when the new party refused to seat southern black delegates or take a stand for racial equality. W. E. B. Du Bois considered voting for Debs, calling the Socialists the only party "which openly recognized Negro manhood." But he ultimately endorsed Wilson. Across the North, in a startling shift, thousands of African American men and women worked and voted for Wilson, hoping Democrats' reform energy would benefit Americans across racial lines. The change helped lay the foundations for Democrats' New Deal coalition of the 1930s.

Despite the intense campaign, Republicans' division between Taft and Roosevelt made the result fairly easy to predict. Wilson won, though he received only 42 percent of the popular vote and almost certainly would have lost if Roosevelt had not been in the race (Map 19.5). In comparison with Roosevelt and Debs, Wilson seemed like a rather old-fashioned choice. But Congress was restive; with labor protests cresting and progressives gaining support, Wilson faced intense pressure to act.

WILSON'S REFORMS, 1913–1917

Why did Woodrow Wilson become a reformer after he assumed the presidency?

AP® SKILLS & PROCESSES

COMPARISON

Why did the election of 1912 feature four candidates, and how did their platforms differ?

In his inaugural address, Wilson acknowledged that industrialization had precipitated a crisis. "There can be no equality of opportunity," he said, "if men and women and children be not shielded . . . from the consequences of great industrial and social processes which they cannot alter, control, or singly cope with." Wilson was a Democrat, and labor interests and farmers — some previously radicalized in the People's Party — were important components of his base. In the South, many of those voters also upheld strong support for white supremacy. Despite northern African Americans' support for Wilson, his administration did little for those constituents. But he undertook bold economic reforms.

Economic Reforms

Democrats believed workers needed stronger government to intervene on their behalf, and by 1912 they were transforming themselves into a modern, state-building party. The Wilson administration achieved a series of landmark measures — at least as significant as those enacted during earlier administrations, and perhaps more so (Table 19.1). The most enduring was the federal progressive income tax. "Progressive," in this case, referred to the fact that it was not a flat tax but rose progressively toward the top of the income scale. The tax, passed in the 1890s but rejected by the Supreme Court, was reenacted as the Sixteenth Amendment to the Constitution, ratified by the states in February 1913. The next year, Congress used the new power to enact an income tax of 1 to 7 percent on Americans with annual incomes of $4,000 or more. At a time when a white male wageworker might expect to make $800 per year, the tax affected less than 5 percent of households.

Three years later, Congress followed this with an inheritance tax. These measures created an entirely new way to fund the federal government, replacing Republicans' high tariff as the chief source of revenue. Over subsequent decades, especially between the 1930s and the 1970s, the income tax system markedly reduced America's extremes of wealth and poverty.

CHECK FOR UNDERSTANDING

Ask students: **Why and to what extent did the political parties' goals change between 1900 and 1912?** *The most important factor that transformed national politics between 1900 and 1912 was the assassination of President McKinley in September 1901, and the subsequent accession of Theodore Roosevelt to the presidency. Using the bully pulpit of the presidency, Roosevelt pushed progressive reform in the areas of trust-busting and environmental conservation. More importantly, his presidency created political cover for others, such as Robert La Follette, Lewis Hine, and the Supreme Court, to bring other progressive goals, like aiding the poor, workers' rights, and African American civil rights, to the fore.*

AP® SKILLS & PROCESSES

COMPARISON

The **COMPARISON** question asks students to compare the different candidates and their various platforms, but it implicitly addresses a larger question: why did this particular election feature so many major candidates, when American politics has traditionally been dominated by a two-party system?

TRM Find complete suggested responses in the Teacher's Resource Materials.

AP® THEME

PCE: Politics and Power

This portion of the text discusses the ways that progressives on the national level sought federal legislation to regulate the economy and expand democracy. Progressive amendments to the Constitution dealt with a federal income tax and the direct election of senators.

TEACHING STRATEGY

Have students compare the economic policies of Presidents Roosevelt, Taft, and Wilson. Students could use a three-part Venn diagram to complete this activity. The goal is for students to see the extent of change in progressive policies during each administration.

TABLE 19.1

Major Federal Progressive Measures, 1883–1921
Before 1900
Pendleton Civil Service Act (1883)
Hatch Act (1887; Chapter 16)
Interstate Commerce Act (1887; Chapter 16)
Sherman Antitrust Act (1890)
Federal income tax (1894; struck down by Supreme Court, 1895)
During Theodore Roosevelt's Presidency, 1901–1909
Newlands Reclamation Act for federal irrigation (1902)
Elkins Act (1903)
First National Wildlife Refuge (1903; Chapter 17)
Bureau of Corporations created to aid Justice Department antitrust work (1903)
U.S. Forest Service created (1905)
Antiquities Act (1906; Chapter 17)
Pure Food and Drug Act (1906; Chapter 18)
Hepburn Act (1906)
First White House Conference on Dependent Children (1909)
During William Howard Taft's Presidency, 1909–1913
Mann Act preventing interstate prostitution (1910; Chapter 18)
Children's Bureau created in the U.S. Labor Department (1912)
U.S. Commission on Industrial Relations appointed (1912)
During Woodrow Wilson's Presidency, 1913–1920
Sixteenth Amendment to the Constitution; federal income tax (1913)
Seventeenth Amendment to the Constitution; direct election of U.S. senators (1913)
Federal Reserve Act (1913)
Clayton Antitrust Act (1914)
Seamen's Act (1915)
Workmen's Compensation Act (1916)
Adamson Eight-Hour Act (1916)
National Park Service created (1916; Chapter 17)
Eighteenth Amendment to the Constitution; prohibition of liquor (1920; Chapter 21)
Nineteenth Amendment to the Constitution; women's suffrage (1920; Chapter 20)

Wilson also reorganized the financial system to address the absence of a central bank. At the time, the main function of national central banks was to back up commercial banks in case they could not meet their obligations. In the United States, the great private banks of New York (such as J. P. Morgan's) assumed this role; if they weakened, the entire system could collapse. This had nearly happened in 1907, when the Knickerbocker Trust Company failed, precipitating a panic. The **Federal Reserve Act** (1913) made the banking system more resistant to such crises. It created twelve

Federal Reserve Act
The central bank system of the United States, created in 1913. The Federal Reserve helps set the money supply level, thus influencing the rate of growth of the U.S. economy, and seeks to ensure the stability of the U.S. monetary system.

AP® SKILLS & PROCESSES

ANALYZING HISTORICAL EVIDENCE

TABLE 19.1 provides a compilation of federal laws passed during the Progressive Era. Students should note that this table does not include rulings by the Supreme Court, like the breakup of Standard Oil. Students might consider both the general trend of large-scale federal government intervention, as well as particular patterns related to antitrust activities, protections for workers, and conservation. Students could also identify three to five acts they consider the most significant and explain why they view these acts as consequential.

TEACHING STRATEGY

This political cartoon alludes to Roosevelt's well-known "big stick" policy, inviting students to discuss similarities and differences between Wilson and Roosevelt in terms of background, governing style, and progressive policies.

Wilson Chases Big Business, 1913–1914 Robert Carter, cartoonist for the *New York Sun*, drew on images of earlier president Theodore Roosevelt carrying a "big stick" in foreign policy, to show Woodrow Wilson's domestic policy toward big business. Wilson, a former schoolteacher, carries a "big ruler" instead of a big stick. Backed by Democratic working-class and agrarian interests, Wilson found himself forced as president to fight corporate monopolies and extend new protections for labor. The Granger Collection, New York.

district reserve banks funded and controlled by their member banks, with a central Federal Reserve Board to impose regulation. The Federal Reserve could issue currency — paper money based on assets held in the system — and set the interest rate that district reserve banks charged to their members. It thus indirectly set the money supply level, influencing the rate of growth in the U.S. economy. The act strengthened the banking system's stability and, to a modest degree, discouraged risky speculation on Wall Street.

Wilson and the Democratic Congress turned next to the trusts. In doing so, Wilson relied heavily on Louis D. Brandeis, the celebrated people's lawyer. Brandeis denied that monopolies were efficient. On the contrary, he believed the best source of efficiency was vigorous competition in a free market. The trick was to prevent trusts from unfairly using their power to curb such competition. The **Clayton Antitrust Act** (1914), which amended the Sherman Act, gave more power to the Justice Department to pursue antitrust cases. It specified that labor unions could not generally be prosecuted for "restraint of trade" but left the definition of illegal practices somewhat flexible. The new Federal Trade Commission received broad powers to decide what was fair, investigating companies and issuing "cease and desist" orders against anticompetitive practices.

Labor issues, meanwhile, received attention from a blue-ribbon U.S. Commission on Industrial Relations, appointed near the end of Taft's presidency and charged with investigating the conditions of labor. In its 1913 report, the commission summed up the impact of industrialization on low-skilled workers. Many earned $10 or less a week and endured regular episodes of unemployment; some faced long-term poverty and hardship. Workers held "an almost universal conviction" that they were "denied justice." The commission concluded that a major cause of industrial violence was the ruthless antiunionism of American employers. In its key recommendation, the report called for federal laws protecting workers' right to organize and engage in collective bargaining. Though Congress and Wilson were, in 1915, not ready to pass such laws, the commission helped set a new national agenda that would come to fruition in the 1930s.

Clayton Antitrust Act
A 1914 law that gave more power to the Justice Department to pursue antitrust cases to prevent corporations from exercising monopoly power; it also specified that labor unions could not generally be prosecuted for "restraint of trade."

In the meantime, guided by the commission's revelations, President Wilson warmed up to labor. In 1915 and 1916, he championed a host of bills to benefit American workers. They included the Adamson Act, which established an eight-hour day for railroad workers; the Seamen's Act, which eliminated age-old abuses of merchant sailors; and a workmen's compensation law for federal employees. Wilson, despite initial modest goals, presided over a major expansion of federal authority. The continued growth of U.S. government offices during Wilson's term reflected a reality that transcended party lines: corporations had grown in size and power, and Americans increasingly wanted federal authority to grow, too.

Wilson's reforms did not extend to the African Americans who had supported him in 1912. In fact, the president rolled back certain Republican policies, such as selected appointments of black postmasters. "I tried to help elect Wilson," W. E. B. Du Bois reflected bitterly, but "under Wilson came the worst attempt at Jim Crow legislation and discrimination in civil service that we had experienced since the Civil War." Wilson famously praised the film *Birth of a Nation* (1915), which depicted the Reconstruction-era Ku Klux Klan in heroic terms. In this way, Wilson was not "progressive" at all. His Democratic control of the White House helped set the tone for the Klan's return in the 1920s.

AP® SKILLS & PROCESSES
DEVELOPMENTS AND PROCESSES
To what degree did reforms of the Wilson era fulfill goals that various agrarian-labor advocates and progressives had sought?

AP® SKILLS & PROCESSES

DEVELOPMENTS AND PROCESSES

The **DEVELOPMENTS AND PROCESSES** question essentially asks students to evaluate the Wilson era in light of populist and progressive goals. Students may need some assistance in identifying ways that particular Wilson-era policies were in line with earlier proposals. Extend this prompt by asking students to discuss whether farm advocates or progressive workers won greater victories and why they think so.

TRM Find complete suggested responses in the Teacher's Resource Materials.

CHECK FOR UNDERSTANDING

Ask students: **What economic reforms did Democrats enact after Wilson's election?** *They passed a progressive income tax (newly authorized through the Sixteenth Amendment) and an inheritance tax, the Federal Reserve Act to institute a centralized banking system, the Clayton Antitrust Act and the Federal Trade Commission to better regulate anticompetitive practices, and various laws aimed to protect workers. African Americans were excluded from Democratic reform efforts.*

Progressive Legacies

In the industrial era, millions of Americans decided that their political system needed to adjust to new conditions. Whatever their specific goals — and whether they were rural, working-class, or middle-class — reformers faced fierce opposition from powerful business interests. When they managed to win key regulatory laws, they often found these struck down by hostile courts and were forced to try again by different means. Thus the Progressive Era in the United States should be understood partly by its limitations. Elitism and racial prejudice, embodied in new voting restrictions, limited working-class power at the polls; African Americans, their plight ignored by most white reformers, faced segregation and violence. Divided power in a federalist system blocked passage of uniform national policies on such key issues as child labor. Social welfare programs that became popular in Europe during these decades, including national health insurance and old-age pensions, scarcely made it onto the American agenda until the 1930s.

An international perspective suggests several reasons for American resistance to such programs. Business interests in the United States were exceptionally successful and powerful, flush with recent expansion. At the time, also, voters in countries with older, more native-born populations tended to support government regulation and welfare spending to a greater extent than their counterparts in countries with younger populations and large numbers of immigrants. Younger voters, understandably, seem to have been less concerned than older voters about health insurance and old-age security. Divisions in the American working class also played a role. Black, immigrant, and native-born white laborers often viewed one another as enemies or strangers rather than as members of a single class with common interests. (One of the first goals achieved by American workingmen's parties, for example, was the Chinese Exclusion Act; see "Asian Americans and Exclusion" in Chapter 16.) This helps explain why the Socialist Party drew, at peak, less than 6 percent of the U.S. vote at a time when its counterparts in Finland, Germany, and France drew 40 percent or more. Lack of pressure from a strong, self-conscious workingmen's party contributed to more limited results in the United States.

But it would be wrong to underestimate progressive achievements. Over several decades, in this period, more and more prosperous Americans began to support stronger economic regulations. Even the most cautious, elite progressives recognized that the United States had entered a new era. Multinational corporations overshadowed small businesses; in vast cities, old support systems based on village and kinship melted away. Outdated political institutions — from the spoils system to urban machines — would no longer do. Walter Lippmann, founding editor of the progressive magazine *New Republic*, observed in 1914 that Americans had "no precedents to guide us, no wisdom that wasn't made for a simpler age." Progressives created new wisdom. By 1917, they had drawn blueprints for a modern American state, one whose powers more suited the needs of an industrial era.

AP® EXAM TIP

Understanding the failure of the Progressive Era to address issues of civil rights for African Americans is important to know on the AP® Exam.

AP® SKILLS & PROCESSES

MAKING CONNECTIONS

What factors explain the limits of progressive reform in the United States?

SUMMARY

The Progressive Era emerged from the political turmoil of the 1880s and 1890s. In the 1880s, despite the limits imposed by close elections, federal and state governments managed to achieve important administrative and economic reforms. After 1888, Republican leaders undertook more sweeping efforts, including the Sherman Antitrust Act, but failed in a quest to protect black voting rights. In the South and West, the People's Party called for much stronger government intervention in the economy, but its radical program drew bitter Republican and Democratic resistance.

AP® APPLY THE TIP

Remind students that not only did progressives not achieve social justice or economic reform that benefitted African Americans, their actions actually reversed policies that supported equality (for example, Woodrow Wilson's decision to resegregate federal buildings in Washington, DC). Ask students to create a Venn diagram that compares the state of African Americans in the U.S. in 1870 (after the Civil War) and in 1920 (at the end of the Progressive Era). Remind students to use specific evidence to support their conclusions regarding similarities and differences.

CHECK FOR UNDERSTANDING

Ask students: **Why did Woodrow Wilson become a reformer after he assumed the presidency?** *Woodrow Wilson, who had demonstrated some progressive credentials as New Jersey governor, achieved significant progressive reforms when he entered the White House in 1913 largely as a result of needing to cater to his base of laborers and farmers, many of whom were radicalized by the People's Party. As such, during his first term, he enacted the income tax, created the Federal Reserve, and passed the Clayton Anti-Trust Act, among others.*

AP® SKILLS & PROCESSES

MAKING CONNECTIONS

The **MAKING CONNECTIONS** question asks students to place American reform in a larger international context, with advocates from various industrialized nations enacting different types of reform. Some students may need assistance in understanding why the factors that limited American reform efforts were unique to that nation. Students might also consider why many nations enacted similar types of reforms in this era.

TRM Find complete suggested responses in the Teacher's Resource Materials.

The depression of the 1890s brought a wave of reaction. Labor unrest threw the nation into crisis, and Cleveland's intransigence over the gold standard cost the Democrats dearly in the 1894 and 1896 elections. While Republicans took over the federal government, southern Democrats restricted voting rights in the Solid South. Federal courts struck down regulatory laws and supported southern racial discrimination.

After McKinley's assassination, Roosevelt launched a program that balanced reform and private enterprise. At both the federal and state levels, progressive reformers made extensive use of elite expertise. At the grassroots, black reformers battled racial discrimination, women reformers worked on issues ranging from public health to women's working conditions, and labor activists tried to address the problems that fueled persistent labor unrest. The election of 1912 split the Republicans, giving victory to Woodrow Wilson, who launched a Democratic program of economic and labor reform. Despite the limits of the Progressive Era, the reforms of this period laid the foundation for a modern American state.

CHECK FOR UNDERSTANDING

Use the AP® **LEARNING FOCUS** question from the beginning of the chapter to provide a check on students' understanding of the chapter as a whole: **Why and how did Progressive Era reformers seek to address the problems of industrial America, and to what extent did they succeed?** *The Progressive Era emerged from the political turmoil of the 1880s and 1890s. Following 1888, Republican leaders attempted to reform society by expanding the reach of the government. While they were able to pass the Sherman Antitrust Act, they were not able to protect black voting rights. The depression of the 1890s increased Americans' desire for government intervention. With Roosevelt's presidency, the government attempted to balance the needs of private enterprise and public interests. In the 1880s and 1890s, civil service reform, the Interstate Commerce Act, the Hatch Act, the formation of commissions at the city and state level, the Sherman Antitrust Act, agrarian reform by Populists, and political reforms like the recall and referendum altered American politics and society. With Woodrow Wilson's victory in 1912, the government continued to expand to meet the needs of its citizens. Progressive reformers decreased the power of trusts and improved industrial working conditions. However, progressives were unable to dislodge discriminatory laws and customs throughout the South.*

✓ LearningCurve

Remind students to go online to complete the LearningCurve quiz for this chapter.

TRM Find complete suggested responses in the Teacher's Resource Materials.

CHAPTER 19 REVIEW

AP CONTENT REVIEW

Answer these questions to demonstrate your understanding of the chapter's main ideas.

1. How did the political goals of Republicans, Democrats, and Populists differ in the years after the end of Reconstruction?
2. Why and how did the depression of the 1890s impact federal politics and policy?
3. Why and to what extent did the political parties' goals change between 1900 and 1912?
4. Why did Woodrow Wilson become a reformer after he assumed the presidency?

AP TERMS TO KNOW

Identify and explain the significance of each term below.

Key Concepts and Events

Pendleton Act (p. 610)
Sherman Antitrust Act (p. 612)
Lodge Bill (p. 612)
Omaha Platform (p. 613)
free silver (p. 615)
Williams v. Mississippi (p. 616)
Lochner v. New York (p. 620)
Square Deal (p. 622)
Hepburn Act (p. 622)
Standard Oil decision (p. 622)
Newlands Reclamation Act (p. 622)
Wisconsin Idea (p. 623)
National Child Labor Committee (p. 624)
Muller v. Oregon (p. 624)
mothers' pensions (p. 624)
Industrial Workers of the World (IWW) (p. 625)
talented tenth (p. 625)
National Association for the Advancement of Colored People (NAACP) (p. 626)
New Nationalism (p. 626)
Federal Reserve Act (p. 631)
Clayton Antitrust Act (p. 632)

Key People

Mary E. Lease (p. 614)
William Jennings Bryan (p. 618)
Theodore Roosevelt (p. 621)
Robert La Follette (p. 623)
Louis Brandeis (p. 624)
W. E. B. Du Bois (p. 625)
Eugene V. Debs (p. 626)

AP® SKILLS & PROCESSES

COMPARISON

AP® CONTENT REVIEW 1 asks students to compare the goals of the new Populist Party with those of the two major established parties. Note: This is the same question as the **CHECK FOR UNDERSTANDING** prompt on p. 614.

AP® SKILLS & PROCESSES

CAUSATION

AP® CONTENT REVIEW 2 encourages students to analyze the effects of the depression on government policies. Note: This is the same question as the **CHECK FOR UNDERSTANDING** prompt on p. 621.

AP® SKILLS & PROCESSES

CAUSATION

AP® CONTENT REVIEW 3 asks students to identify the factors that caused changes in the national political systems in the early twentieth century. Note: This is the same question as the **CHECK FOR UNDERSTANDING** prompt on p. 630.

AP® SKILLS & PROCESSES

CAUSATION

AP® CONTENT REVIEW 4 asks students to explain the causes of Wilson's reform posture as a president. Note: This is the same question as the **CHECK FOR UNDERSTANDING** prompt on p. 633.

TRM Find definitions for these terms in the **Glossary/Glosario** in the Teacher's Resource Materials.

AP® MAKING CONNECTIONS

Recognize the larger developments and continuities within and across chapters by answering these questions.

1. Returning to Chapter 16, review the strategies and goals of the labor and agrarian organizations that flourished in the 1870s and 1880s. The People's Party embodied many of those ideas. Imagine that you are a journalist interviewing a former People's Party leader in 1917. To what extent might he or she have said that progressives had, after 1900, fulfilled the agrarian-labor agenda? To what extent might he or she criticize progressives for failing to achieve important reforms? Compare the ideology and historical situation of populism and progressivism?
2. Compare the economic policies implemented by Republicans during the Civil War (Chapters 13 and 15) with the policies adopted in the Progressive Era. What were the main goals of legislators and presidents in each period? In what ways did those goals overlap? To what extent did progressive leaders seek to rectify problems that emerged as a result of the Civil War–era legislation?

KEY TURNING POINTS

Refer to the timeline at the start of this chapter for help in answering the following questions.

Theodore Roosevelt and Woodrow Wilson both became president under unusual circumstances: Roosevelt after the assassination of William McKinley, and Wilson in a four-way race, in which the candidate of the previously dominant Republican Party came in third. Consider the policies and achievements, as well as, the historical context of Wilson and Roosevelt. What is the legacy of each president? How does this legacy explain the importance of the presidency during the Progressive Era?

AP® PRACTICE QUESTIONS

MULTIPLE CHOICE QUESTIONS

Choose the correct answer for each question.

Questions 1–3 refer to this excerpt.

> "This is a nation of inconsistencies. . . . We fought England for our liberty and put chains on four million blacks. We wiped out slavery and by our tariff laws and national banks began a system of white wage slavery worse than the first.
>
> Wall Street owns the country. It is no longer a government of the people, by the people, and for the people, but a government of Wall Street, by Wall Street, and for Wall Street. . . .
>
> Tariff is not the paramount question. The main question is the money question. . . . Kansas now suffers from two great robbers, the Santa Fe Railroad and the loan companies. The common people are robbed to enrich their masters. . . .
>
> We want money, land and transportation. We want the abolition of national banks, and we want the power to make loans from the government. We want the accursed foreclosure system wiped out."
>
> Speech by Mary Elizabeth Lease, political activist, 1890

1. A supporter of the ideas Lease expressed in the excerpt would most likely also have supported
   - **a.** a stronger governmental role in regulating the American economic system.
   - **b.** ideas such as the Gospel of Wealth.
   - **c.** laissez-faire economic policies as pathways to growth in the long run.
   - **d.** increased sharecropping and tenant farming.
2. The ideas expressed in the excerpt had the most in common with the ideas of which of the following groups?
   - **a.** Social Darwinists in the late nineteenth century
   - **b.** Proponents of labor unions
   - **c.** Laissex-faire economists
   - **d.** Jacksonian Democrats in the 1830s
3. The ideas expressed in the excerpt resulted most directly from
   - **a.** public debates over assimilation.
   - **b.** corporate consolidation in agricultural markets.
   - **c.** battles between labor and management over wages and working conditions.
   - **d.** the promotion of the idea of a "New South."

AP® SKILLS & PROCESSES

CONTINUITY AND CHANGE

AP® MAKING CONNECTIONS 1 asks students to compare the goals of earlier agrarian reformers with those of the populist and progressive movements. In essence, students must consider the degree of continuity between these periods.

AP® SKILLS & PROCESSES

COMPARISON

AP® MAKING CONNECTIONS 2 asks students to compare federal government policies in two different eras, identifying similarities and differences and explaining the reasons for both.

TRM Find complete suggested responses in the Teacher's Resource Materials.

Questions 4–6 refer to this excerpt.

"The mechanism of modern business is so delicate that extreme care must be taken not to interfere with it in a spirit of rashness or ignorance. Many of those who have made it their vocation to denounce the great industrial combinations which are popularly . . . known as 'trusts' appeal precisely to hatred and fear. . . .

. . . . [Y]et it is also true that there are real and grave evils . . . and a resolute and practical effort must be made to correct these evils.

There is a widespread conviction in the minds of the American people that the great corporations known as trusts are in certain of their features and tendencies hurtful to the general welfare. This . . . is based upon sincere conviction that combination and concentration should be, not prohibited, but, supervised and within reasonable limits controlled; and in my judgment this conviction, is right."

Theodore Roosevelt, Message to Congress, December 3, 1901

4. The Roosevelt administration most directly acted upon the beliefs expressed in the passage through
- **a.** resolving the Anthracite Coal Strike.
- **b.** creating the Federal Trade Commission.
- **c.** supporting reduced federal rates.
- **d.** approving the corporate merger that created the United States Steel Corporation.

5. The ideas Theodore Roosevelt expressed in the excerpt share the greatest similarity to the ideas used to
- **a.** pass Federalist economic programs.
- **b.** enact New Deal legislation to mediate the effects of economic downturn.
- **c.** support legislation to help the poor.
- **d.** establish laws to ensure safe food and drugs.

6. The ideas Theodore Roosevelt expressed about regulation in the excerpt show the greatest extent of similarity to the ideas of
- **a.** the Marshall Court of 1800 to the 1820s.
- **b.** Whigs favoring the national bank in the 1830s.
- **c.** laissez-faire economists in the 1880s.
- **d.** the federal legislature in the 1890s.

TRM Find complete suggested responses in the Teacher's Resource Materials.

SHORT ANSWER QUESTIONS

Read each question carefully and write a short response. Use evidence from the text to support your claims.

"'When was the Progressive Era exactly?' my students ask. Roughly during the first two decades of the twentieth century, I tell them. . . . Some historians still use 1900 as a starting date, although more recently 1890 has become popular. . . . From the perspective of women progressives, however, these boundaries need to be much more fluid. . . . The women who founded social settlements in the 1880s, along with the temperance and suffrage campaigners, comprise a group of American citizens active in conceptualizing progressive reform long before the presumed dawn of progressivism."

Elisabeth Israels Perry, "Men Are from the Gilded Age, Women Are from the Progressive Era," 2002

"Millions of freedmen, immigrants, students, workers, artists, intellectuals, and reformers believed that post–Civil War America offered a chance to start anew. . . . Many Americans worked energetically between 1865 and 1900 to purify politics, restrict the power of big business, and fight injustice. Those decades witnessed the first march on Washington, the first federal welfare programs, the first elections in which women and black men voted for president, and the first national park in the world. At the same time, problems that plagued the so-called Gilded Age continued and even intensified during the so-called Progressive Era."

Rebecca Edwards, *New Spirits: Americans in the "Gilded Age," 1865–1905*, 2015

1. Using the two excerpts provided, answer (a), (b), and (c).
- **a.** Briefly explain ONE major difference between Perry's and Edwards's historical interpretations of the late nineteenth and early twentieth centuries.
- **b.** Briefly explain how ONE specific historical event or development not directly mentioned in the excerpts could be used to support Perry's argument.
- **c.** Briefly explain how ONE specific historical event or development not directly mentioned in the excerpts could be used to support Edwards's argument.

2. Answer (a), (b), and (c).
- **a.** Briefly explain ONE important historical difference between economic reforms sought by the Populists and the Progressives.
- **b.** Briefly explain ONE important similarity between the economic reforms sought by the Populists and the Progressives.
- **c.** Briefly explain ONE important historical factor that accounts for the similarity OR difference between the economic reforms sought by the Populists and the Progressives.

3. Answer (a), (b), and (c).
   a. Briefly explain why ONE of the following was the most significant factor contributing to political unrest between 1880 and 1917.
      - Economic instability
      - Industrial capitalism
      - Migration patterns
   b. Provide ONE specific historical example to support your argument in (a).
   c. Provide specific evidence why ONE of the other options is a less significant factor contributing to political unrest between 1880 and 1917.

TRM Find complete suggested responses in the Teacher's Resource Materials.

6 PART AP® PRACTICE ESSAY QUESTIONS

DOCUMENT-BASED QUESTION *Suggested reading period: 15 minutes. Suggested writing time: 45 minutes.*

DIRECTIONS: Question 1 is based on the accompanying documents. The documents have been edited for the purpose of this exercise.

1. Evaluate the extent to which the settlement of the American West changed American society between 1865 and 1900.

DOCUMENT 1

Source: Comanche Chief Ten Bears, Medicine Lodge Treaty Address, October 1867.

"I was born on the prairie where the wind blew free and there was nothing to break the light of the sun. I was born where there were no enclosures and where everything drew a free breath. I want to die there and not within walls. . . . When I was at Washington the Great Father told me that all the Comanche land was ours and that no one should hinder us in living upon it. So, why do you ask us to leave the rivers and the sun and the wind and live in houses? Do not ask us to give up the buffalo for the sheep. The young men have heard talk of this, and it has made them sad and angry. . . .

If the Texans had kept out of my country there might have been peace. But that which you now say we must live on is too small. The Texans have taken away the places where the grass grew the thickest and the timber was the best. Had we kept that we might have done the things you ask. But it is too late. The white man has the country which we loved, and we only wish to wander on the prairie until we die."

DOCUMENT 2

Source: Acts of the Wyoming Territorial Legislature, 1869 and 1870.

"AN ACT to confer to women all the rights of citizenship.

That every woman of the age of twenty-one years, residing in this territory, may, at every election . . . cast her vote. And her rights to the elective franchise, and to hold office, shall be the same under the election laws of the territory, as those electors.

AN ACT to protect married women in their separate property, and the enjoyment of their labor.

That all the property, both real and personal, belonging to any married woman as her sole and separate property . . . shall, notwithstanding her marriage, be and remain . . . her sole and separate property, under her sole control, and be held, owned, possessed and enjoyed by her, the same as though she were sole [single] and unmarried, and shall not be subject to the disposal, control or interference of her husband."

DOCUMENT 3

Source: A Remonstrance from the Chinese in California to the Congress of the United States, c. 1870.

"When we were first favored with the invitations of your ship-captains to emigrate to California, and heard the laudations [praises] which they published of the perfect and admirable character of your institutions, and were told of your exceeding respect and love toward the Chinese, we could hardly have calculated that we would now be the objects of your excessive hatred. . . .

If . . . you grant us, as formerly, to mine and trade here, then it is our request that you will give instructions to your courts that they shall again receive Chinese testimony; that they shall cease their incessant discussions about expelling the Chinese; that they shall quit their frequent agitations as to raising the license fees; that they shall allow the Chinese peace in the pursuit of their proper employments; and that they shall effectually repress the acts of violence common among the mountains, so that robbers shall not upon one pretext or another injure and plunder us."

DOCUMENT 4

Source: Letter from Uriah Oblinger, a Nebraska homesteader, to his wife, December 1872.

"I am confident that I can live when I have 160 [acres] of my own. . . .

[T]he longer I stay here the better I like it, there are but very few old families here. They are mostly young families just starting in life the same as we are and I find them very generous indeed. . . .

I think any one that is not able to own a farm in Indiana or any of the older states and make their living by farming are foolish for staying any longer than to just get enough to leave on. . . . It is going to be rough starting as I always told you but when started it will be ours. . . . Those that are here seem to be as happy as birds. They are all Homesteaders, yet there is not more than one in 25 that has a deed for their land yet."

DOCUMENT 5

Source: Interview of Nancy Guptil, a black migrant to Kansas, 1880.

"Came from Middle Tennessee. Heard neighbors talking of Kansas two or three years. We received two or three circulars that told about Kansas. . . . I find things here a heap better than I expected. We have forty acres. We came last May. We built our house in the fall. My husband finds enough work around here to support us. We had plenty of supplies to live on through the winter. . . . People treats us better here than they did there because they is willing to pay us what we work for. . . . I wouldn't go back for nothing. . . . All my people are mighty well satisfied here."

DOCUMENT 6

Source: Joseph Nimmo Jr., "The American Cowboy," *Harper's New Monthly Magazine*, November 1886.

"The Texas cowboys were frontiersmen, accustomed from their earliest childhood to the alarms and the struggles incident to forays of Indians of the most ferocious and warlike nature. The section of the State in which they lived was also for many years exposed to incursions of bandits from Mexico, who came with predatory intent upon the herds and the homes of the people of Texas.

The carrying of firearms and other deadly weapons was consequently a prevalent custom among them. And being scattered over vast areas, and beyond the efficient protection and restraints of civil law, they of necessity became a law unto themselves. It is not a strange thing that such an occupation and such environment should have developed a class of men whom persons accustomed to the usages of cultivated society would characterize as ruffians of the most pronounced type.

But among the better disposed of the Texas cowboys, who constitute, it is believed, much more than a majority of them, there were true and trusty men, in whom the dangers and fortunes of their lives developed generous and heroic traits of character. The same experiences, however, led the viciously inclined to give free vent to the worst passions. Upon slight provocation they would shoot down a fellow man with almost as little compunction as they fired upon the wild beasts."

DOCUMENT 7

Source: Map of major railroads and statehood in the American West.

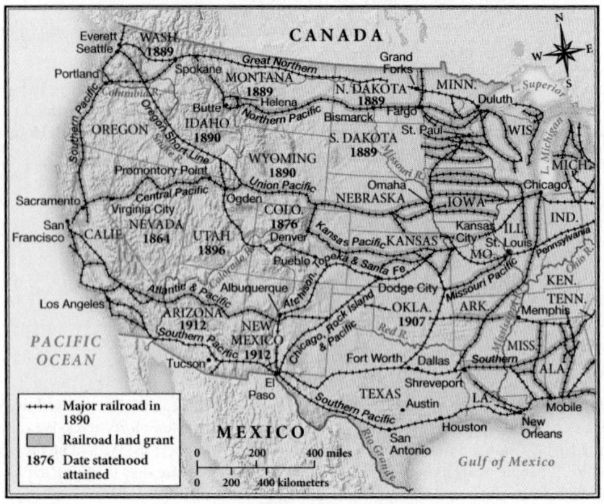

LONG ESSAY QUESTIONS *Suggested writing time: 40 minutes.*

DIRECTIONS: Please choose one of the following three questions to answer. Make a historically defensible claim and support your reasoning with specific and relevant evidence.

2. Evaluate the extent to which social reform movements between 1865 and 1900 changed American society.
3. Evaluate the extent to which urbanization changed politics in the United States between 1865 and 1900.
4. Evaluate the extent of difference between the effects of industrialization on the United States in the decades before the Civil War (1820–1860) to the effects in the decades after the Civil War (1865–1900).

7

PART

Global Ambitions and Domestic Turmoil

1890–1945

What should be the role of the United States in the world, and what is the proper relationship between government and society? If these seem like monumental questions, they are indeed. Part 7 shows how these two questions came to the fore in a tumultuous period of global warfare and domestic strife and reform. Globally, the United States expanded its empire overseas and fought on the winning side in two world wars. Domestically, the reform impulse retreated during and immediately after World War I but surged again during the crisis of the Great Depression, when Americans once more debated the responsibilities of their government.

As the chapters in this part show, on the world stage the United States acted at times in calculated self-interest and in other instances to protect democratic nations and institutions. By acquiring the Philippines, Hawaii, Guam, and Puerto Rico, the United States expanded like a traditional empire. In a nobler vein, the nation joined its European allies in the two world wars, embracing a broad international partnership against the threat of autocracy and fascism.

Those partnerships embodied President Woodrow Wilson's belief that democratic nations "cannot be separated in interest or divided in purpose."

Fifteen years later, President Franklin Delano Roosevelt called for "the warm courage of national unity" during the Great Depression. Threatened by economic catastrophe, American voters called for — and got — what Roosevelt called "action and action now," welfare programs in the form of the New Deal. We conclude Part 7 in 1945, when the United States emerged from World War II with newfound global power and the federal government with a broad mandate for sustaining a welfare state, a major turning point in modern American history. Here, in brief, are the three key dimensions of this era to explore as you read the chapters of this part. ▶

AP® CONCEPT CONNECTIONS

Why Did the United States Rise to Become a World Power?

Remember Your First Thrill of
AMERICAN LIBERTY
Library of Congress, 3g08026.

The United States grew in international power through warfare beginning in the 1890s. From victory in the War of 1898 it claimed overseas colonies in East Asia and the Caribbean to secure trade routes and protect American investments. At the start of World War I, President Wilson maintained neutrality, but trade ties and old alliances drew the United States into the conflict on the Allied side. By war's end, the United States possessed a growing empire, but it remained secondary to European powers on the world stage.

Expanding American business interests abroad shaped foreign policy in the 1920s and 1930s. Faced with isolationist sentiment at home and surging fascism in Europe and Japan, President Roosevelt avoided rushing into the brewing world war yet sent aid to Great Britain and built up American military forces. When the United States finally entered World War II in 1941, it did so in alliance with England and the Soviet Union against Germany, Japan, and Italy. Having emerged from that global war victorious, with an economy invigorated by wartime growth, the country was in a stronger international position than at any time in its history. Between the 1890s and the 1940s, the United States became a major world power in order to protect its overseas commercial interests and to safeguard democracy.

Why Did a Diversifying and Modernizing America Lead to Social Conflict?

Private Collection / © Valerie Gerrard Browne / Chicago History Museum / Bridgeman Images.

Victory in two world wars did not resolve domestic tensions in four major areas: race, immigration, labor, and religion. Those tensions arose because the nation was becoming simultaneously more diverse — through immigration, African American migration, and women's entry into politics via suffrage — and more modern — through the rise of science and the emergence of a common national culture facilitated by advertising, radio, and Hollywood, all of which challenged traditional religion and local customs. In reaction, a Red Scare, rollback of labor and immigrant rights, race riots against African Americans, and a resurgent nationwide Ku Klux Klan marked the 1920s. During the Great Depression, the U.S. government deported hundreds of thousands of people of Mexican descent, including American citizens, and during World War II it imprisoned Japanese Americans. In a mass relocation policy, the U.S. turned away most Jewish refugees fleeing Hitler and segregated African Americans in a Jim Crow military. The nation faced a fierce contest over what a modern nation would look like and who got to be considered an American.

Why Did Economic Prosperity Give Way to Calamity and How Did Policymakers Respond?

Library of Congress, LC-DIG-ppmsca-17400.

Decades of economic prosperity and the emergence of a full-blown modern consumer culture characterized this era, as radios, automobiles, and other consumer goods transformed American life. But the boom at the start of the twentieth century was followed by bust. In 1929 stock market crashes threw the country headlong into the Great Depression, which was made worse by consumer and Wall Street indebtedness and agricultural overproduction, and which left millions without jobs and few obvious solutions in sight.

Republican policymakers of the 1920s believed in hands-off government. Their policies likely helped trigger the Great Depression and deepened its subsequent impact. With little relief in sight by 1932, weary American voters elected the Democrat Franklin Roosevelt president, and his New Deal programs (1933–1938) expanded federal responsibility for the welfare of ordinary citizens. The New Deal faced considerable challenges on the political right, especially from business leaders and a hostile Supreme Court, but the popularity of its programs, such as Social Security, established a broad consensus in favor of such a welfare state.

Organized around a single theme, the Part 7 Document Set in *Sources for America's History* can be used to teach AP® Themes NAT, which deals with the ways in which two world wars, the Great Depression, the Cold War, and migration influenced evolving notions of national and racial/ethnic identities, and SOC, which deals with the ways in which class and gender roles contributed to economic, social, and cultural transformations.

AP® THEMATIC UNDERSTANDING

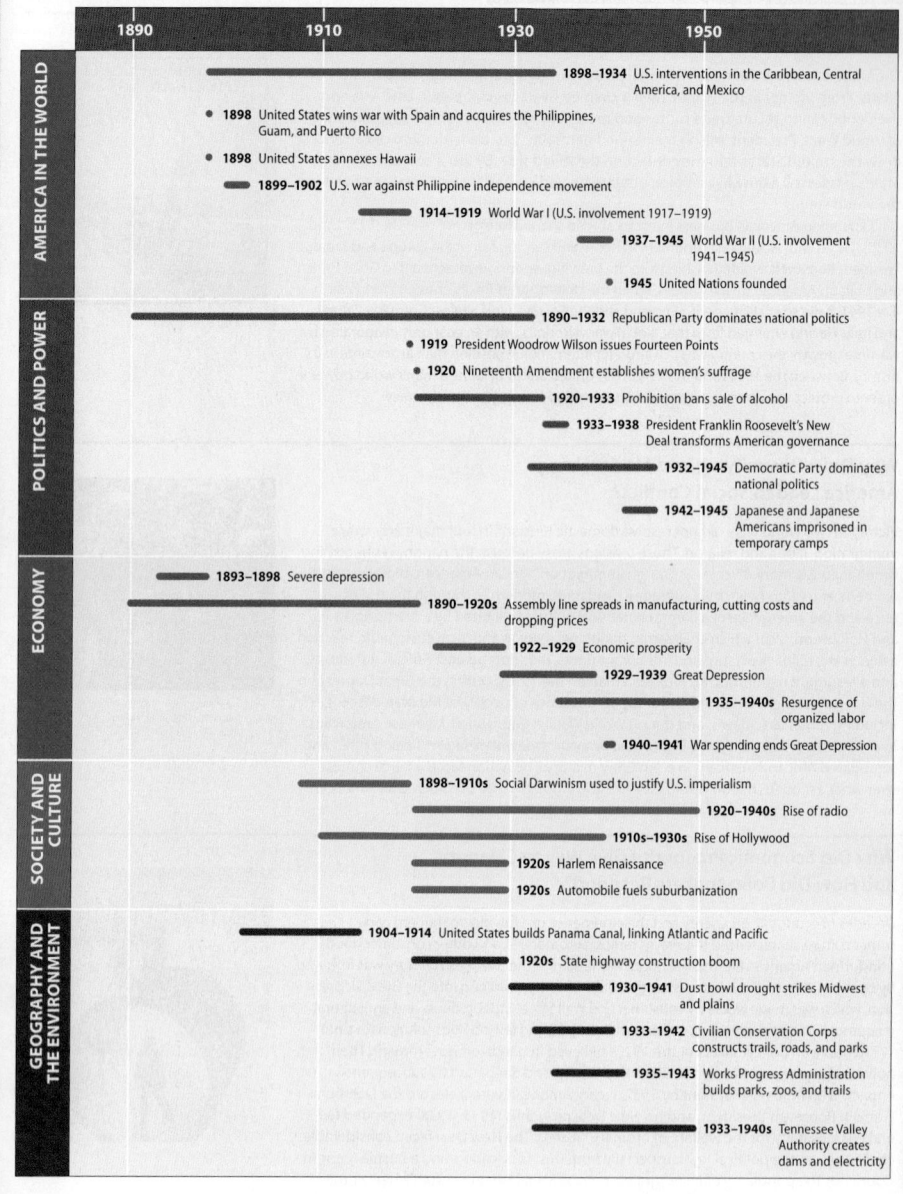

Global Ambitions and Domestic Turmoil, 1890–1945

1890 | 1910 | 1930 | 1950

AMERICA IN THE WORLD

- **1898–1934** U.S. interventions in the Caribbean, Central America, and Mexico
- **1898** United States wins war with Spain and acquires the Philippines, Guam, and Puerto Rico
- **1898** United States annexes Hawaii
- **1899–1902** U.S. war against Philippine independence movement
- **1914–1919** World War I (U.S. involvement 1917–1919)
- **1937–1945** World War II (U.S. involvement 1941–1945)
- **1945** United Nations founded

POLITICS AND POWER

- **1890–1932** Republican Party dominates national politics
- **1919** President Woodrow Wilson issues Fourteen Points
- **1920** Nineteenth Amendment establishes women's suffrage
- **1920–1933** Prohibition bans sale of alcohol
- **1933–1938** President Franklin Roosevelt's New Deal transforms American governance
- **1932–1945** Democratic Party dominates national politics
- **1942–1945** Japanese and Japanese Americans imprisoned in temporary camps

ECONOMY

- **1893–1898** Severe depression
- **1890–1920s** Assembly line spreads in manufacturing, cutting costs and dropping prices
- **1922–1929** Economic prosperity
- **1929–1939** Great Depression
- **1935–1940s** Resurgence of organized labor
- **1940–1941** War spending ends Great Depression

SOCIETY AND CULTURE

- **1898–1910s** Social Darwinism used to justify U.S. imperialism
- **1920–1940s** Rise of radio
- **1910s–1930s** Rise of Hollywood
- **1920s** Harlem Renaissance
- **1920s** Automobile fuels suburbanization

GEOGRAPHY AND THE ENVIRONMENT

- **1904–1914** United States builds Panama Canal, linking Atlantic and Pacific
- **1920s** State highway construction boom
- **1930–1941** Dust bowl drought strikes Midwest and plains
- **1933–1942** Civilian Conservation Corps constructs trails, roads, and parks
- **1935–1943** Works Progress Administration builds parks, zoos, and trails
- **1933–1940s** Tennessee Valley Authority creates dams and electricity

AP Making Connections Across Chapters

Read these questions and think about them as you read the chapters in this part. Then when you have completed reading this part, return to these questions and answer them.

1 Between 1890 and 1945, the United States emerged as a major world power. Identify and explain what you would consider the three most important turning points in that emergence. Why did you choose the turning points you did? Are there others that ought to be considered?

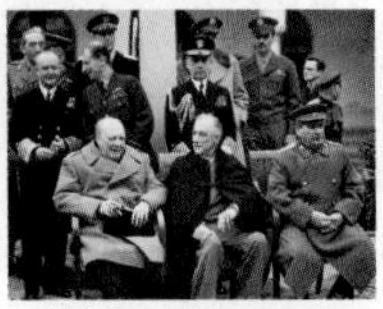

Franklin D. Roosevelt Library.

2 How was American involvement in the two world wars different? Consider the paths to war, the extent or scale of American involvement, and the aftermath for each.

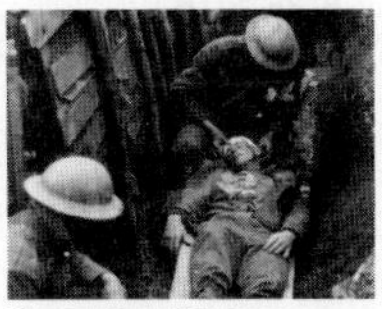

Sgt Leon H. Caverly/Getty Images.

3 What were the major transformations in American capitalism in this era? Try to identify three or four. In what ways did those transformations bring prosperity? In what ways did they contribute to economic crisis?

ullstein bild / Getty Images.

4 Consider the place of women, immigrants, and African Americans in American society in this era — as well as the place of people in territories acquired by the United States. What kinds of rights did they enjoy? Did their status change much between the 1890s and the 1940s? Why or why not?

Photo by Woodward, courtesy of the State Archives of Florida.

5 Compare and contrast the national politics of the years 1919 to 1931 and 1932 to 1945. In what ways was each period distinct? What caused the differences?

Bettmann/Getty Images.

TRM Find complete suggested responses in the Teacher's Resource Materials.

20 CHAPTER An Emerging World Power

1890–1918

Chapter 20 — AP® Assessment Weight and Pacing Guide

The assessment weight on the AP® U.S. History Exam for Chapters 20–23 is 10–17 percent. This chapter is part of Unit 7 of the AP® U.S. History Curriculum, covering Period 7: 1890–1945.

This pacing guide is based on a schedule with 120 sessions of 50 minutes each before the AP® U.S. History Exam. If you have a different number of sessions before the exam, you can modify the pacing to meet your needs. If you have additional time, consider incorporating quizzes, released AP® U.S. History questions, practice exams, writing practice, and other instructional activities.

	Traditional Schedule	Block Schedule
Chapter 20	4 days	2 days

Daily Pacing Guide

	Content Focus	Essential Question
Day 1	From Expansion to Imperialism	Through what steps did the U.S. government in the late nineteenth century begin to exert military influence in different regions of the world?
Day 2	A Power Among Powers	Why and how did U.S. actions influence Asia in this period? What impact did U.S. policies have on Latin America? In what ways were these influences similar and different?
Day 3	The United States in World War I	Why and how did participation in World War I change the economy and society of the United States?
Day 4	Catastrophe at Versailles	What arguments did U.S. political leaders make for and against ratification of the Versailles treaty?

AP® Alignment

Section Heading	AP® Topic	AP® Theme
From Expansion to Imperialism	7.2, 7.3	WOR
A Power Among Powers	7.2, 7.3	WOR
The United States in World War I	7.5, 7.6	WOR, MIG
Catastrophe at Versailles	7.5	WOR

*Should changes be made to the Course Framework in the future, an updated alignment will be placed on our AP® updates page at go.bfwpub.com/ap-course-updates.

Chapter 20 — Overview

Chapter 20 examines the processes and developments that led the U.S. to dramatically alter its role in the world. Beginning with an analysis of the reasons for supporting empire building as an extension of American expansionism, the chapter focuses on the impact of the War of 1898 on the United States's understanding of its place in the world. These dramatic changes led many Americans to seek greater involvement in the world, including the establishment of American influence in Asia and Latin America. U.S. involvement in international imperialism in the early twentieth century made it difficult for the U.S. to avoid involvement in World War I even though most Americans favored neutrality. The chapter also emphasizes the impact of America's participation in World War I on the government and society, focusing particularly on women and African Americans who saw the fight for democracy in Europe as an extension of their demands for democracy in the U.S. Finally, the chapter examines the failure of the Treaty of Versailles to address the causes of World War I or to effectively incorporate the most important concepts from Woodrow Wilson's *Fourteen Points*. The debate over ratification in the U.S. illustrated deep-rooted uncertainty regarding America's changing role in the world and a revival of neutrality to the point of isolationism.

Chapter 20 — Resources

The following resources can be found in the Teacher's Resource Materials (TRM) that accompany the book. You can access the TRM via the book's digital platform, by clicking the TRM links found here in your Teacher's Edition e-book, or by contacting your representative to access the resources online. Visit **bfwpub.com/henretta10e** to learn more.

TRM Chapter 20 Lecture Presentation Slides

TRM Chapter 20 Outline with AP® Focus

TRM Chapter 20 Lecture Strategies

TRM Chapter 20 Suggested Responses

TRM Handout 20.1 — Thematic Analysis: Foundations for Imperialism

TRM Handout 20.2 — Thematic Analysis: War of 1898

TRM Handout 20.3 — Causation: America in the Eastern Hemisphere

TRM Handout 20.4 — Comparison: Foreign Policy of the Progressives

Chapter 20 — Essential Activity

Assign each student an individual from the late nineteenth to early twentieth centuries to represent during a simulation of a symposium on imperialism. For homework, students should prepare a biography of their assigned individual and create a placard with their name, a quote, and images/symbols to reflect their ideas on imperialism.

At the start, have students divide themselves into "Imperialist" or "Anti-Imperialist" groups. In these groups, ask students to discuss their reasons for supporting or opposing imperialism. Create a list based on the AP® Themes. Then place a long table or row of desks at the front of the room. Require participation by rotating the panel of individuals while the remaining participants act as the audience. Each panel participant should present a one-minute answer to the symposium question "Is empire a noble goal?" Then students in the audience, acting as their assigned individual, should question the panel to generate discussion on imperialism.

Chapter 20 — Bell Ringers

The following activities take no more than 5–15 minutes of your class period and offer an effective and engaging way to begin your lessons and for students to apply AP® Skills & Processes:

- Provide students with a copy of the cartoon "School Begins" by Louis Dalrymple. To find an image online, search "Library of Congress School Begins." Have students work in pairs to identify the different elements of the cartoon and provide historical context for each element. Students should determine the point of view of the artist on American imperialism and explain the argument the artist is making regarding continuity and change in American history.
- Provide students with an excerpt from Theodore Roosevelt's Corollary to the Monroe Doctrine. Ask students to define the argument Roosevelt makes in support of extending U.S. influence over other nations. Then prompt students to debate the validity of Roosevelt's argument.

NOTES

TEACHING STRATEGY

Use the chapter opener material to help students understand the main themes of the chapter: imperialism, anti-imperialism, and the U.S.'s emergence as a "world power." The chapter opener ends by highlighting how contemporary debates about the role of the U.S. in the world are rooted in this period, particularly in the development of a supposedly "Wilsonian" effort to remake the world. For a complete suggested response to the **AP® LEARNING FOCUS** question, see p. 668.

TEACHING STRATEGY

To help give students a flavor of William Jennings Bryan's speaking style, consider playing an audio clip of Bryan's anti-imperialism speech, available on The History Channel. Bryan, better known for his domestic concerns, serves as a reminder of the important link between foreign policy (the focus of this chapter) and efforts to reform industrial capitalism (as the previous chapter explored), which facilitated American business interests and military expansion overseas. Access this clip by searching "History Channel Bryan anti-imperialism."

20 CHAPTER

An Emerging World Power 1890–1918

AP® LEARNING FOCUS

Why did the United States become a major power on the world stage by the 1910s, and what impact did this have at home and abroad?

Accepting the Democratic presidential nomination in 1900, William Jennings Bryan delivered a famous speech denouncing U.S. military occupations overseas. "God Himself," Bryan declared, "placed in every human heart the love of liberty. . . . He never made a race of people so low in the scale of civilization or intelligence that it would welcome a foreign master." At the time, Republican president William McKinley was leading an ambitious and popular plan of overseas expansion. The United States had asserted control over the Caribbean, claimed Hawaii, and sought to annex the Philippines. Bryan failed to convince enough voters that imperialism — the exercise of military, political, and economic power overseas — was the wrong direction. He lost the election by a landslide.

Bryan's defeat shows how popular U.S. imperialism was among voters between 1898 and the early 1910s. After that, however, American enthusiasm for empire-building began to cool. In 1917, despite efforts to stay neutral, the United States got caught up in the global catastrophe of World War I, which killed 8 million combatants, including more than 50,000 U.S. soldiers. At the war's end, with European powers' grip on their colonial empires weakening, the United States also ceased its quest for overseas territories and pursued a different path. It did so in part because the war brought dramatic changes at home, leaving Americans a postwar legacy of economic upheaval and political disillusionment.

President Woodrow Wilson, who in 1913 appointed Bryan as his secretary of state, hoped that U.S. participation in World War I would reshape the international order. America would "make the world safe for democracy," he proclaimed, while unapologetically working to advance U.S. economic interests. The U.S. Senate, however, rejected the 1919 Treaty of Versailles and with it Wilson's vision, leaving the nation's foreign policy in doubt. Should the United States try to promote democracy abroad? If so, how? Under what conditions was overseas military action justified? When, on the contrary, did it impinge on others' sovereignty, endanger U.S. soldiers, and invite disaster? Today's debates over foreign policy still center to a large degree on questions that Americans debated in the era of McKinley, Bryan, and Wilson, when the nation first asserted itself as a major world power.

The Great White Fleet The U.S. Navy's newest battle fleet, nicknamed the "Great White Fleet" and celebrated proudly by President Theodore Roosevelt, took a world tour between 1907 and 1909, demonstrating to the world that the United States now had naval power rivaling Britain and Germany. Here, the USS *Connecticut* leads the fleet of sixteen battleships on its way out of Hampton Roads, Virginia, at the start of the voyage. By 1900, global economic and military power brought the United States new prestige — and new problems. Bettmann/Getty Images.

TEACHING STRATEGY

Ask students: **In what ways does the Great White Fleet illustrate the emergence of the U.S. as a modern nation?** *The fleet reveals the development of modern American industry. Construction of these vessels required technological understanding of steamships and navigation devices, access to steel, large manufacturing facilities, and a sizable labor force. Sending the fleet on a worldwide tour suggests the nation's growing ambition. For the first time, the U.S. was seeking to be on par with the most powerful nations of the world.*

AP® SKILLS & PROCESSES

CONTINUITY AND CHANGE

Use the **TIMELINE** to help students begin thinking about how the period from 1892 to 1920 could constitute a distinct historical period in American foreign policy history. Once again, the precision — or lack of precision — in these dates is telling. For example, 1886 is a rough starting point, indicating a more general shift in national attention, while 1918 refers very specifically to the end of World War I. Prompt students to scan the events in the timeline and identify the types of foreign policy activities involving the U.S. and the locations where those activities took place. Then have students use that information to make a generalization about the U.S. as "an emerging global power" in this era. Students could also compare American foreign policy in this era with that of the 1840s, identifying both similarities and differences.

AP® APPLY THE TIP

Provide students with **Handout 20.1 — Thematic Analysis: Foundations for Imperialism (TRM).** Students should read pp. 642–643 carefully to provide at least one cause for imperialism that was related to each Theme. After students identify at least one cause for each objective, organize them into seven collaborative groups and assign each group one of the objectives on which to focus their inquiry into the rise of imperialism. Each group should use textbook pp. 643–653 and additional outside resources to identify leaders, events, and document excerpts related to their objective that illustrates the rise of imperialism in the U.S. Then ask the groups to use the research to design a document-based question (DBQ) based on one of the AP® Historical Thinking Skills and Reasoning Processes that they will share with the class. After students complete the DBQ prompt, lead a class discussion on the ways in which the documents can be used to address the prompts as well as the extended analysis and contextualization for the prompts.

TRM Find **Handout 20.1 — Thematic Analysis: Foundations for Imperialism** in the Teacher's Resource Materials.

TIMELINE

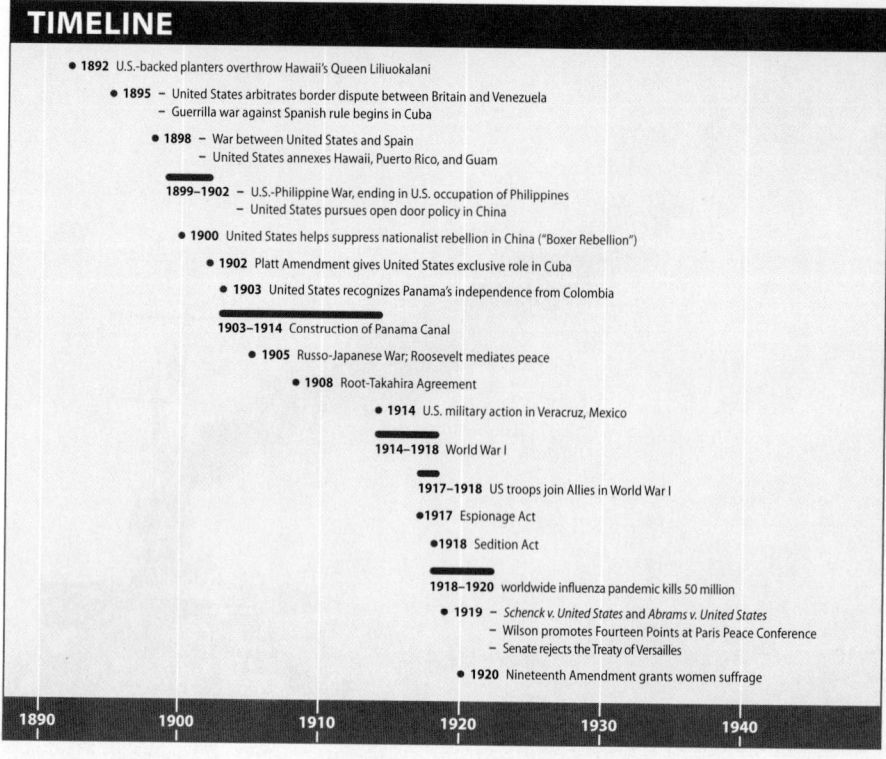

- **1892** U.S.-backed planters overthrow Hawaii's Queen Liliuokalani
- **1895** – United States arbitrates border dispute between Britain and Venezuela
  – Guerrilla war against Spanish rule begins in Cuba
- **1898** – War between United States and Spain
  – United States annexes Hawaii, Puerto Rico, and Guam
- **1899–1902** – U.S.-Philippine War, ending in U.S. occupation of Philippines
  – United States pursues open door policy in China
- **1900** United States helps suppress nationalist rebellion in China ("Boxer Rebellion")
- **1902** Platt Amendment gives United States exclusive role in Cuba
- **1903** United States recognizes Panama's independence from Colombia
- **1903–1914** Construction of Panama Canal
- **1905** Russo-Japanese War; Roosevelt mediates peace
- **1908** Root-Takahira Agreement
- **1914** U.S. military action in Veracruz, Mexico
- **1914–1918** World War I
- **1917–1918** US troops join Allies in World War I
- **1917** Espionage Act
- **1918** Sedition Act
- **1918–1920** worldwide influenza pandemic kills 50 million
- **1919** – *Schenck v. United States* and *Abrams v. United States*
  – Wilson promotes Fourteen Points at Paris Peace Conference
  – Senate rejects the Treaty of Versailles
- **1920** Nineteenth Amendment grants women suffrage

1890 | 1900 | 1910 | 1920 | 1930 | 1940

FROM EXPANSION TO IMPERIALISM

Through what steps did the U.S. government in the late nineteenth century begin to exert military influence in different regions of the world?

History books used to describe turn-of-the-twentieth-century U.S. imperialism as something new and unprecedented. Now, with the importance of Native American history more widely recognized, historians point out continuities between overseas empire building and the nation's earlier, relentless expansion across North America. Wars against Native peoples had occurred almost continuously since the country's founding; in the 1840s, the United States had annexed a third of Mexico. The United States never administered a large colonial empire, as did European powers like Spain, England, and Germany, partly because it had a plentiful supply of natural resources in the American West. But policymakers undertook a determined quest for resources and markets. Events in the 1890s opened opportunities to pursue this goal in new ways.

AP® EXAM TIP
Outline the arguments that caused the rise of imperialism in U.S. foreign policy.

Foundations of Empire

American empire builders around 1900 fulfilled a vision laid out earlier by William Seward, secretary of state under presidents Abraham Lincoln and Andrew Johnson, who saw access to global markets as key to international power (Chapter 15). Seward's ideas had won limited support at the time, but the severe economic depression of the 1890s brought Republicans into power and Seward's ideas back into vogue. Confronting high unemployment and mass protests, policymakers feared American workers would embrace socialism or Marxism. The alternative, they believed, was to create jobs and prosperity at home by selling U.S. products in overseas markets.

Intellectual and social trends also justified imperialism. As early as 1885, in his popular book *Our Country*, Congregationalist minister Josiah Strong urged Protestants to evangelize to "heathen" peoples overseas. He predicted that the American "Anglo-Saxon race," which represented "the largest liberty, the purest Christianity, the highest civilization," would "spread itself over the earth." Such arguments — and the powerful missionary efforts they helped inspire — were grounded in **American exceptionalism**, the idea that the United States had a unique destiny to foster democracy and civilization.

American exceptionalism
The idea that the United States has a unique destiny to foster democracy and civilization on the world stage.

As Strong's exhortation suggested, imperialists also drew on the popular racial theory that people of "Anglo-Saxon" descent — English and often German — were superior to all others. "Anglo-Saxon" rule over foreign people of color suited an era when, at home, the United States denied most American Indians and Asian immigrants citizenship, southern states disfranchised blacks, and the Supreme Court had justified segregation in *Plessy v. Ferguson*. Imperialists argued that "free land" on the western frontier was dwindling, and thus new outlets needed to be found for American energy and enterprise. Responding to critics of U.S. occupation of the Philippines, Theodore Roosevelt scoffed: if Filipinos should govern themselves, he declared, then America was "morally bound to return Arizona to the Apaches."

Imperialists justified their views through racialized Social Darwinism (see "Darwinism and Its Critics" in Chapter 17). Josiah Strong, for example, predicted that with the globe fully occupied, a "competition of races" would ensue and the law of "survival of the fittest" would determine the result. Fear of ruthless competition drove the United States, like European nations, to invest in the latest weaponry. Policymakers saw that European powers were amassing steel-plated battleships and carving up Africa and Asia among themselves. In his book *The Influence of Sea Power upon History* (1890), U.S. naval officer Alfred Mahan urged the United States to enter the fray, observing that naval power had been essential to past empires. As early as 1886, Congress ordered construction of two steel-hulled battleships, the USS *Texas* and USS *Maine*; in 1890, it appropriated funds for three more, a program that expanded over the next two decades as the United States built one of the world's most modern and powerful navies.

During Grover Cleveland's second term (1893–1897), his secretary of state, Richard Olney, turned to direct confrontation with European powers. He warned them to stay away from Latin America, which he saw as the United States's rightful sphere of influence. Without consulting the nation of Venezuela, Olney suddenly demanded in 1895 that Britain resolve a long-standing border dispute between Venezuela and Britain's neighboring colony, British Guiana. Invoking the Monroe Doctrine, which stated that the Western Hemisphere was off-limits to further European colonization, Olney warned that the United States would brook no challenge. Startled, Britain agreed to arbitrate. Backed by its new industrial might, the U.S. was aggressively pursuing its interests overseas.

AP® SKILLS & PROCESSES
CONTINUITY AND CHANGE
How did imperialism in the 1890s reflect both continuities and changes from earlier eras?

The War of 1898

Events in the Caribbean presented the United States with major opportunities. In 1895, Cuban patriots mounted a major guerrilla war against Spain, which had lost most of its other New World territories but continued to rule Cuba. The Spanish commander responded by rounding up Cuban civilians into concentration camps, where as many as 200,000 died of starvation, exposure, or dysentery. In the United States, "yellow journalists" such as William Randolph Hearst turned their plight into a

AP® EXAM TIP
Understanding the impact of the Spanish-American War on the U.S. is important to know on the AP® Exam.

AP® THEME
NAT: American and National Identity
It may be helpful for students to explore the arguments made by imperialists. Imperialists cited a number of arguments in favor of Americans expanding their culture and institutions to people around the globe, including economic opportunities, racial theories, competition with European empires, and the perception that by the 1890s the North American frontier was "closed." Perhaps the clearest articulation of the racial assumptions behind American empire came from Protestant clergyman and Social Gospel leader Josiah Strong in his argument for Anglo-Saxon predominance. Access his argument by searching "UVA Josiah Strong."

AP® THEME
NAT: American and National Identity
To help students better understand American interests in Latin America, consider having them read an excerpt of Richard Olney's essay "On American Jurisdiction in the Western Hemisphere." Access this essay by searching "Olney American Jurisdiction in the Western Hemisphere."

CHECK FOR UNDERSTANDING
Ask students: **What were the foundations of American empire?** *Notions of American exceptionalism emphasized the nation's unique status as a civilization based on Protestant Christianity, the Anglo-Saxon race, and democracy. Social Darwinist views reinforced the notion that a competition of races was about to ensue, and the U.S. needed to prepare for victory by building a strong navy.*

AP® SKILLS & PROCESSES
CONTINUITY AND CHANGE
Use the **CONTINUITY AND CHANGE** question for students to consider both similarities and differences in American foreign policy in the two eras. To focus discussion, students could specifically consider (1) the religious, racial, and geopolitical ideologies underlying expansion, (2) key documents and speeches that articulated this outlook, and (3) the specific nations that leaders perceived to be threats in both eras. Students could additionally offer an evaluation of whether this was a gradual evolution or a dramatic departure in American foreign policy.

TRM Find complete suggested responses in the Teacher's Resource Materials.

AP® APPLY THE TIP
Provide students with **Handout 20.2 — Thematic Analysis: War of 1898 (TRM),** and ask them to provide at least two specific pieces of historical evidence for each Theme and explain its relationship to the objective. After students have added the evidence to their handout, divide students into seven groups and assign each group one of the objectives on which to focus. Ask the groups to share their evidence related to the assigned theme and discuss the impact of the War of 1898 on the development of the U.S. in that particular thematic area. Groups should then formulate a thesis statement that addresses whether or not the War of 1898 was a transformative event in American history. Remind students that their thesis should examine the degree to which the War of 1898 resulted in change or simply represented a continuity of ideas about expansion, empire, role of the military, etc. Ask each group to write their thesis on a piece of poster paper and post in the room for the class to view. Then lead a class discussion on the impact of the War of 1898 and the use of evidence to support historical arguments.

TRM Find **Handout 20.2 — Thematic Analysis: War of 1898** in the Teacher's Resource Materials.

cause célèbre. Hearst's coverage of Spanish atrocities fed a surge of American nationalism, especially among those who feared that industrialization was causing men to lose physical strength and valor. The government should not pass up this opportunity, said Indiana senator Albert Beveridge, to "manufacture manhood." Congress called for Cuban independence.

President Cleveland had no interest in supporting the Cuban rebellion, and many of his Democratic supporters were leery of expansions of federal military power. Cleveland worried over Spain's failure to end the conflict, however, since the war disrupted trade and damaged American-owned sugar plantations on the island. Moreover, an unstable Cuba was incompatible with U.S. strategic interests, including a proposed canal whose Caribbean approaches had to be safeguarded. Flush with victory in 1897, new Republican President William McKinley took a more aggressive stance than his predecessor. In September, a U.S. diplomat informed Spain that it must ensure an "early and certain peace" or the United States would step in. At first, this hard line seemed to work: Spain's conservative regime fell, and a liberal Spanish government, taking office in October 1897, offered Cuba limited self-rule. But Spanish loyalists in Havana rioted against the proposal, while Cuban rebels held out for full independence.

In February 1898, Hearst's *New York Journal* published a private letter in which a Spanish minister to the United States belittled McKinley. The minister, Dupuy de Lôme, resigned, but exposure of the de Lôme letter intensified Americans' indignation toward Spain. The next week brought shocking news: the U.S. battle cruiser *Maine* had exploded and sunk in Havana harbor, with 260 seamen lost. "Whole Country Thrills with the War Fever," proclaimed the *New York Journal*. "Remember the *Maine*" became a national chant. Popular passions now added pressure in the march toward war.

McKinley assumed the sinking of the *Maine* had been accidental. Improbably, though, a naval board of inquiry blamed an underwater mine, fueling public outrage. (Later investigators disagreed: the more likely cause was a faulty ship design that placed explosive munitions too close to coal bunkers, which were prone to fire.) No evidence linked Spain to the purported mine, but if something in Havana harbor sank the *Maine*, then Spain was responsible for not protecting the ship.

Business leaders became impatient, believing war was preferable to an unending Cuban crisis. On March 27, McKinley cabled an ultimatum to Madrid: an immediate ceasefire in Cuba for six months and, with the United States mediating, peace negotiations with the rebels. Spain, while desperate to avoid war, balked at the United States's additional demand that mediation must result in Cuban independence. On April 11, McKinley asked Congress for authority to intervene in Cuba "in the name of civilization, [and] in behalf of endangered American interests."

Historians long referred to the ensuing fight as the Spanish-American War, but because that name ignores the pivotal role of Cuban revolutionaries, many historians now call the three-way conflict the War of 1898. Though McKinley had already demanded Cuban independence and Americans widely admired Cubans' aspirations for freedom, the McKinley administration defeated a congressional attempt to recognize the rebel government. In response, Senator Henry M. Teller of Colorado added an amendment to the war bill disclaiming any intention by the United States to occupy Cuba. The **Teller Amendment** reassured Americans that their country would respect the political independence of other nations. McKinley's expectations differed. He wrote privately, "We must keep all we get; when the war is over we must keep what we want."

Teller Amendment
An amendment to the 1898 U.S. declaration of war against Spain disclaiming any intention by the United States to occupy Cuba.

On April 24, 1898, Spain declared war on the United States. The news provoked full-blown war fever. Across the country, young men enlisted for the fight. Theodore Roosevelt, serving in the War Department, resigned to become lieutenant colonel of a cavalry regiment. The sudden mobilization was chaotic. Recruits poured into makeshift bases around Tampa, Florida, where confusion reigned. Rifles failed to arrive;

TEACHING STRATEGY

The PBS film *Crucible of Empire: The Spanish-American War* is an excellent resource for teaching about the War of 1898 given the film addresses the perspectives of Cuban and Spanish participants as well as Americans. The companion Web site offers several resources, including a timeline of the major events before, during, and after the war; photographs of the major figures involved; newspaper articles and headlines from 1890s newspapers; classroom activities; historical resources, including recent scholarship concerning the war, bibliographies, and links to other Web sites; and a quiz designed to test visitor's knowledge. McKinley's request for a declaration of war might be a good place to begin. Access these resources by searching "PBS Crucible of Empire."

AP® SKILLS & PROCESSES

CAUSATION

The causes of the Spanish-American War are important to delineate if students are to understand the effects, which are explicitly called out in the AP® Course Framework. Have students describe and weigh the relative significance of at least three causes of U.S. entry into the Spanish-American War.

food was bad and sanitation worse. No provision had been made for getting troops to Cuba, so the government hastily collected a fleet of yachts and commercial boats. Fortunately, the regular U.S. Army was a disciplined, professional force; its 28,000 seasoned troops provided a nucleus for 200,000 volunteers. The navy was in far better shape: Spain had nothing to match America's seven modern battleships and armored cruisers. The Spanish admiral predicted, sadly and accurately, that his fleet would "like Don Quixote go out to fight windmills and come back with a broken head."

An important measure of U.S. intentions was the fact that the first, decisive military engagement took place in the Pacific — not Cuba. This was the handiwork of Theodore Roosevelt, who, in his government post, had gotten intrepid Commodore George Dewey appointed commander of the Pacific fleet. In the event of war, Dewey had instructions to sail immediately for the Spanish-owned Philippines. When war was declared, Roosevelt confronted his surprised superior and pressured him into validating Dewey's instructions. On May 1, 1898, American ships cornered the Spanish fleet in Manila Bay and destroyed it. Manila, the Philippine capital, fell on August 13. "We must on no account let the [Philippines] go," declared Senator Henry Cabot Lodge. McKinley agreed. The United States now had something Republican policymakers since William Seward had wanted: a major foothold in the western Pacific.

Hawaii's Queen Hawaiian queen Liliuokalani (1838–1917) was the great-granddaughter of Keaweaheulu, founder of the Kamehameha dynasty that had ruled the islands since the late 1700s. Liliuokalani assumed the throne after her brother's death in 1891. As an outspoken critic, however, of treaties ceding power to U.S. economic interests, she was deposed three years later by a cabal of sugar planters who established a republic. When secret plans to revolt and restore the monarchy were discovered, the queen was imprisoned for a year in Iolani Palace. She lived the remainder of her life in Hawaii but never regained power. Fluent in English and influenced from childhood by Congregational missionaries, she used this background to advocate for her people; in her book *Hawaii's Story by Hawaii's Queen* (1898), she appealed for justice from fellow Christians. George Bacon Collection, Hawaii State Archives.

Dewey's victory directed attention to Hawaii, where a horde of resident American sugar planters had forcibly laid the groundwork for annexation. Nominally independent, the Hawaiian islands had long been subject to U.S. influence. An 1876 treaty between the United States and the island's monarch allowed Hawaiian-produced sugar to enter the U.S. market without tariff payments, and Hawaii pledged to sign no such agreement with any other power. When this treaty was renewed in 1887, Hawaii also granted a long-coveted lease for a U.S. naval base at Pearl Harbor. Four years later, succeeding her brother as Hawaii's monarch, Queen Liliuokalani made known her frustration with these treaties. In response, an Annexation Club led by U.S.-backed planters organized secretly and in 1892, with the help of U.S. Marines, overthrew the queen. They then negotiated a treaty of annexation, but Grover Cleveland rejected it when he entered office in 1893. Cleveland declared that it would violate America's "unbroken tradition" against acquiring territory overseas.

Dewey's victory in Manila delivered what the planters wanted: Hawaii acquired strategic value as a halfway station to the Philippines. In July 1898, Congress voted for annexation, over the protests of Hawaii's deposed queen. "Oh, honest Americans," she pleaded, "as Christians hear me for my down-trodden people! Their form of government is as dear to them as yours is precious to you. Quite as warmly as you love your country, so they love theirs." But to the great powers, Hawaii was not a country. One congressman dismissed Hawaii's monarchy as "absurd, grotesque, tottering" and declared that the "Aryan race" would "rescue" the islands.

Further U.S. annexations took on their own logic. The navy pressed for another coaling base in the central Pacific; that meant Guam, a Spanish island in the Marianas. A strategic base was needed in the Caribbean; that meant Puerto Rico. By early summer, before U.S. troops had fired a shot in Cuba, McKinley's broader war aims were crystallizing.

TEACHING STRATEGY

To help students develop a better understanding of the Hawaiian perspective on American intervention in the island nation, play a brief excerpt from the *American Experience* documentary *Hawaii's Last Queen*, detailing the overthrow of Queen Liliuokalani. To access this film, search "PBS Overthrow of Queen Liliuokalani."

TEACHING STRATEGY

In order to understand the Hawaiian perspective on U.S. intervention, have students compare and contrast the following terms germane to territorial expansion: annexation, invasion, and territorial cession. Based on their knowledge, have students choose one of these terms to describe the Hawaiian perspective on American intervention.

CHECK FOR UNDERSTANDING

Ask students: **Why did the U.S. go to war against Spain in 1898, and what led to U.S. victory?** *There were several reasons for the declaration of war. Americans were stirred by yellow journalists who highlighted the plight of Cubans imprisoned by the Spanish as a result of the island's resistance movement. Publication of the de Lôme letter mocking McKinley also fueled resentment against Spain. The explosion and subsequent sinking of the Maine fueled calls for war, as did pressure from business leaders who disliked the instability caused by the independence movement. Dewey's initiative in the Philippines, the depletion of Spanish strength by the ongoing war in Cuba, and the work of independence activists in both Cuba and the Philippines all contributed to American victory.*

TRM Find complete suggested responses in the Teacher's Resource Materials.

AP® APPLY THE TIP

When students compare the views of anti-imperialists, be sure to point out the oddity of some of the members of the group having very little in common politically, other than membership to the Anti-Imperialism League. Why would such a disparate group form together over this one issue? Have students think through categories of analysis for why this historical development occurred.

TEACHING STRATEGY

Examining the St. Louis World's Fair can provide deeper insight into white Americans' perspectives about the rest of the world at the turn of the century. Materials prepared by the Missouri Historical Society for a centennial retrospective offer a glimpse of some of the major themes raised by the Fair's exhibits. To access these resources, search "Missouri Historical Society St. Louis World Fair Education."

AP® SKILLS & PROCESSES

CAUSATION

Why did the United States go to war against Spain in 1898, and what led to U.S. victory?

AP® EXAM TIP

Compare the arguments of the anti-imperialists who expressed opposition to the Spanish-American War.

In Cuba, Spanish forces were depleted by the long guerrilla war against Cuba's homegrown revolutionaries. American forces, though poorly trained and equipped, had the advantages of a demoralized foe and knowledgeable Cuban allies. The main battle occurred on July 1 at San Juan Hill, near Santiago, where the Spanish fleet was anchored. Roosevelt's Rough Riders took the lead, but four African American regiments bore the brunt of the fighting. Observers credited much of the victory to the "superb gallantry" of these soldiers. Spanish troops retreated to a well-fortified second line, but U.S. forces were spared the test of a second assault. On July 3, the Spanish fleet in Santiago harbor tried a desperate run through the American blockade and was destroyed. Days later, Spanish forces surrendered. American combat casualties had been few; most U.S. soldiers' deaths had resulted from malaria and yellow fever.

Spoils of War

The United States and Spain quickly signed a preliminary peace agreement in which Spain agreed to liberate Cuba and cede Puerto Rico and Guam to the United States. What would happen to the Philippines, an immense archipelago that lay more than 5,000 miles from California? Initially, the United States aimed to keep only Manila, because of its fine harbor. Manila was not defensible, however, without the whole island of Luzon, on which it sat. After deliberating, McKinley found a justification for annexing all of the Philippines. He decided that "we could not leave [the Filipinos] to themselves — they were unfit for self-rule."

This declaration provoked heated debate. Under the Constitution, as Republican senator George F. Hoar argued, "no power is given to the Federal Government to acquire territory to be held and governed permanently as colonies" or "to conquer alien people and hold them in subjugation." Leading citizens and peace advocates, including Jane Addams and Mark Twain, enlisted in the anti-imperialist cause. Anti-imperialists were a diverse lot. Steel magnate Andrew Carnegie offered $20 million to purchase Philippine independence and set the islands free. Labor leader Samuel Gompers — a fierce foe of Carnegie's labor policies — nonetheless agreed with him about the Philippines, warning union members about the threat of competition from low-wage Filipino immigrants. Some anti-imperialists were also antiracists, arguing that Filipinos were perfectly capable of self-rule. Other critics of McKinley's policies warned about the dangers of annexing eight million Filipinos of an "inferior race." "No matter whether they are fit to govern themselves or not," declared a Missouri congressman, "they are not fit to govern us."

Beginning in late 1898, anti-imperialist leagues sprang up around the country, but they never sparked a mass movement. On the contrary, McKinley's "splendid little war" proved immensely popular. Confronted with that reality, Democrats waffled. Their standard-bearer, William Jennings Bryan, decided not to stake Democrats' future on opposition to a policy that he believed to be irreversible. He threw his party into turmoil by declaring last-minute support for McKinley's proposed treaty. Having met military defeat, Spanish representatives had little choice. In the Treaty of Paris, Spain ceded the Philippines to the United States for $20 million.

Philippine Exhibition at the St. Louis World's Fair, 1904 Anthropological displays were a popular feature of World's Fairs — scientific in purpose, but giving American and European tourists an opportunity to contrast their civilization, as they saw it, with various degrees of "barbarism" and "savagery." The Philippine Reservation in St. Louis was particularly controversial because it featured an array of peoples — many westernized, others traditionally tribal — from the United States's latest imperial possession. Here, Igorrote dancers rest after a performance. Some participants in such displays were lured with false promises of wealth and rapid return to their homelands; when promoters went bankrupt, some performers were stranded in the United States and never returned to their families and communities. Library of Congress, 3c11760.

AP® THEME

NAT: American and National Identity

Many students are introduced to Rudyard Kipling's poem "White Man's Burden" in the context of imperialism in World History classes. Consider reacquainting students with the poem here as it was written in response to the U.S. takeover of the Philippines. Additionally, students can explore this theme by examining editorials from American newspapers after the takeover. The National Humanities Center provides the Kipling poem and some of these editorials, along with short reading guides and sets of discussion questions. The site also provides anti-imperialist perspectives from two prominent individuals: Mark Twain and Emilio Aguinaldo. Students should use these resources to explore how the different speakers appeal to American ideals and values in making their case for or against American empire. Anti-imperialists cited principles of self-determination and invoked both racial theories and the U.S. foreign policy tradition of isolation in arguing against those who advocated extending the nation's territories overseas. To access these resources, search "NHC Empire: Manifest Destiny and Beyond."

Annexation was not as simple as U.S. policymakers had expected. On February 4, 1899, two days before the Senate ratified the treaty, fighting broke out between American and Filipino patrols on the edge of Manila. Confronted by annexation, rebel leader Emilio Aguinaldo asserted his nation's independence and turned his guns on occupying American forces. Though Aguinaldo found it difficult to organize a mass-based resistance movement, the ensuing conflict between Filipino nationalists and U.S. troops far exceeded the War of 1898 in length and ferocity. Fighting tenacious guerrillas, the U.S. Army resorted to the tactics Spain had employed in Cuba: burning crops and villages and rounding up civilians into camps. Atrocities became commonplace on both sides. In three years of warfare, 4,200 Americans and an estimated 200,000 Filipinos died; many of the latter were dislocated civilians, particularly children, who succumbed to malnutrition and disease.

McKinley's convincing victory over William Jennings Bryan in 1900 suggested popular satisfaction with America's new military efforts overseas, even in the face of dogged Filipino resistance to U.S. rule. The fighting ended in 1902, and William Howard Taft, appointed as governor-general of the Philippines, sought to make the territory a model of roadbuilding and sanitary engineering. Yet misgivings lingered as Americans confronted the brutality of the war (see "Firsthand Accounts," p. 648). Philosopher William James noted that the United States had destroyed "these islanders by the thousands, their villages and cities. . . . Could there be any more damning indictment of that whole bloated ideal termed 'modern civilization'?"

Constitutional issues also remained unresolved. The treaty, while guaranteeing freedom of religion to inhabitants of ceded Spanish territories, withheld any promise of citizenship. It specified that Congress could decide Filipinos' "civil rights and political status." In 1901, the Supreme Court upheld this provision in a set of decisions known as the ***Insular Cases***. The Constitution, declared the Court, did not automatically extend citizenship to people in acquired territories; Congress could decide. Puerto Rico, Guam, and the Philippines were thus marked as permanent colonies. For the first time, the United States had acquired new territories without providing any mechanism for them to become future states.

The next year, as a condition for withdrawing from Cuba, the United States forced the newly independent island to accept a proviso in its constitution called the **Platt Amendment** (1902). This blocked Cuba from making a treaty with any country except the United States and gave the United States the right to intervene in Cuban affairs whenever it saw fit. Cuba also granted the United States a lease on Guantánamo Bay (still in effect), where the U.S. Navy built a large base. Cubans' hard-fought independence was limited; so was that of Filipinos. Eventually, the Jones Act of 1916 committed the United States to Philippine independence but set no date. (The Philippines at last achieved independence in 1946.) The United States now had an overseas empire.

AP® EXAM TIP

Evaluate the response of the U.S. to the nationalist independence movement after the Spanish-American War.

Insular Cases
A set of Supreme Court rulings in 1901 that declared that the U.S. Constitution did not automatically extend citizenship to people in acquired territories; only Congress could decide whether to grant citizenship.

Platt Amendment
A 1902 amendment to the Cuban constitution that blocked Cuba from making a treaty with any country except the United States and gave the United States the right to intervene in Cuban affairs. The amendment was a condition for U.S. withdrawal from the newly independent island.

AP® SKILLS & PROCESSES

MAKING CONNECTIONS

What were the long-term results of the U.S. victory over Spain, in Hawaii and in former Spanish possessions?

A POWER AMONG POWERS

Why and how did U.S. actions influence Asia in this period? What impact did U.S. policies have on Latin America? In what ways were these influences similar and different?

No one appreciated America's emerging influence more than the man who, after William McKinley's assassination, became president in 1901. Theodore Roosevelt was an avid student of world affairs who called on "the civilized and orderly powers to insist on the proper policing of the world." He meant, in part, directing the affairs of "backward peoples." For Roosevelt, imperialism went hand in hand with domestic progressivism. He argued that a strong federal government, asserting itself both at home and abroad, would enhance economic stability and political order. Overseas, Roosevelt sought to arbitrate disputes and maintain a global balance of power, but he also put U.S. interests at the fore.

AP® APPLY THE TIP

As students encounter the resistance to U.S. policy in places such as the Philippines, ask students to evaluate the extent to which the United States was moving beyond its original goals for the Spanish-American War. Evaluating the nationalist movement this way will help students understand the broad nature of the U.S. response. Students may benefit from comparing the U.S. policy in the Philippines with that of Cuba.

AP® SKILLS & PROCESSES

MAKING CONNECTIONS

The **MAKING CONNECTIONS** prompt asks students to identify the effects of American victory on the various territories that it acquired. Students might indicate the different status of each territory, why that territory achieved the status it did, and what the practical implications of each status might have been. Students could additionally briefly research the current status of Hawaii, Puerto Rico, the Philippines, or Guam, explaining how that status is a result of the War of 1898.

TRM Find complete suggested responses in the Teacher's Resource Materials.

CHECK FOR UNDERSTANDING

Ask students: **Explain the steps by which the late-nineteenth-century U.S. government began to exert military influence in different regions of the world.** *The United States began to display a greater interest in using its military to spread its financial and political interests in new ways in the late nineteenth century. While the United States has always maintained its right to political hegemony in the Western Hemisphere since the Monroe Doctrine, this new wave of military action was during a time of global imperialism. The right of free trade, along with a declaration of support for nascent political movements to oust imperial powers, led the United States to support revolutionaries. Self-interest also played a role as the U.S aggressively pursued land agreements to build a canal to connect the Atlantic and Pacific Oceans. As disparate as these causes were, the factors that led to the U.S. exerting more control came together at the start of the War of 1898. Buttressing these factors was an emerging belief, promoted by jingoists, who wanted the United States to engage militarily to accomplish its foreign policy goals of free trade and political hegemony in the Caribbean and Pacific.*

AP® SKILLS & PROCESSES

ANALYZING HISTORICAL EVIDENCE

The **AP® FIRSTHAND ACCOUNTS** feature provides a relatively unique type of source — congressional testimony. Point out to students the elements that make this type of evidence, as the introduction explains, "much prized by historians," touching upon its closed-door nature and the fact that witnesses testify under oath with the threat of legal consequences for perjuring themselves. Have students identify the pieces of evidence that likely emerged only under these kinds of circumstances and explore how this type of evidence deepens our understanding of the Philippines debate.

AP® APPLY THE TIP

Provide students with **Handout 20.3 — Causation: America in the Eastern Hemisphere (TRM)** and ask them to use pp. 648–653 to complete the analysis of causation related to America's imperialism outside the Western Hemisphere. After students have completed the handout, provide them with an outline map of the world and ask them to work with a partner to label the places that the U.S. expanded its influence in the late nineteenth and early twentieth centuries (include both Western and Eastern Hemisphere so that students can make connections between imperialism in each region). Ask students to annotate the map to show the economic, political, and social reasons for U.S. interest in each place that they label. After students complete their map, ask them to consider to what degree American imperialism of the late nineteenth and early twentieth centuries was a departure from precedent in foreign policy that defined the U.S. in the previous century. Use this activity to lead a class discussion on the way in which imperialism in this period illustrated both continuity and change in American foreign policy.

TRM Find **Handout 20.3 — Causation: America in the Eastern Hemisphere** in the Teacher's Resource Materials.

AP® FIRSTHAND ACCOUNTS

Debating the Philippines

As President McKinley privately acknowledged in writing — "when the war is over we must keep what we want" — seizing the Philippines was an act of national self-interest. Of the alternatives, it was the one that seemed best calculated to serve America's strategic aims in Asia. But McKinley's geopolitical decision had unintended consequences. For one, it provoked a bloody insurrection. For another, it challenged the United States's democratic principles. As these consequences hit home, a divided Senate set up a special committee and held closed hearings. Congressional testimony is a source much prized by historians. Though some of it is prepared, once questioning begins, testimony becomes unscripted and can be especially revealing. The following documents are taken from the 1902 testimony before the Senate Committee on the Philippines.

Ideals

General Arthur MacArthur (1845–1912) was in on the action in the Philippines almost from the start. He commanded one of the first units to arrive there in 1898 and in 1900 was reassigned as the islands' military governor and general commander of the troops. His standing as a military man — holder of the Congressional Medal of Honor from the Civil War — was matched later by his more famous son, Douglas MacArthur, who fought in the Pacific during World War II. Here the elder MacArthur explains in prepared testimony his vision of America's mission to the Philippines.

SOURCE: From *Hearings Before the Committee on the Philippines of the United States Senate, April 10, 1902.* (Washington: Government Printing Office, 1902).

“ At the time I returned to Manila [May 1900] to assume the supreme command it seemed to me that . . . our occupation of the island was simply one of the necessary consequences in logical sequence of our great prosperity, and to doubt the wisdom of [occupation] was simply to doubt the stability of our own institutions and in effect to declare that a self-governing nation was incapable of successfully resisting strains arising naturally from its own productive energy. It seemed to me that our conception of right, justice, freedom, and personal liberty was the precious fruit of centuries of strife . . . [and that] we must regard ourselves simply as the custodians of imperishable ideas held in trust for the general benefit of mankind. In other words, I felt that we had attained a moral and intellectual height from which we were bound to proclaim to all as the occasion arose the true message of humanity as embodied in the principles of our own institutions. . . .

All other governments that have gone to the East have simply planted trading establishments; they have not materially affected the conditions of the people. . . . There is not a single establishment, in my judgment, in Asia to-day that would survive five years if the original power which planted it was withdrawn therefrom.

The contrasting idea with our idea is this: In planting our ideas we plant something that can not be destroyed. To my mind the archipelago is a fertile soil upon which to plant republicanism. . . . We are planting the best traditions, the best characteristics of Americanism in such a way that they can never be removed from that soil. That in itself seems to me a most inspiring thought. It encouraged me during all my efforts in those lands, even when conditions seemed most disappointing, when the people themselves, not appreciating precisely what the remote consequences of our efforts were going to be, mistrusted us; but that fact was always before me — that going deep down into that fertile soil were the indispensable ideas of Americanism. ”

Skepticism

At this point, the general was interrupted by Colorado senator Thomas Patterson, a Populist-Democrat and a vocal anti-imperialist.

“ Sen. Patterson: Do you mean that imperishable idea of which you speak is the right of self-government?

Gen. MacArthur: Precisely so; self-government regulated by law as I understand it in this Republic.

Sen. Patterson: Of course you do not mean self-government regulated by some foreign and superior power?

Gen. MacArthur: Well, that is a matter of evolution, Senator. We are putting these institutions there so they will evolve themselves just as here and everywhere else where freedom has flourished. . . .

Sen. Patterson [after the General concluded his statement]: Do I understand your claim of right and duty to

AP® EXAM TIP

Understanding imperialism's impact on U.S. foreign policy outside of the Western Hemisphere in this period is critical to success on the AP® Exam.

The Open Door in Asia

U.S. officials and business leaders had a burning interest in East Asian markets, but they were entering a crowded field (Map 20.1). In the late 1890s, following Japan's victory in the Sino-Japanese War of 1894–1895, Japan, Russia, Germany, France, and Britain divided coastal China into spheres of influence. Fearful of being shut out, U.S.

retain the Philippine Islands is based upon the proposition that they have come to us upon the basis of our morals, honorable dealing, and unassailable international integrity?

Gen. MacArthur: That proposition is not questioned by anybody in the world, excepting a few people in the United States. . . . We will be benefited, and the Filipino people will be benefited, and that is what I meant by the original proposition —

Sen. Patterson: Do you mean the Filipino people that are left alive?

Gen. MacArthur: I mean the Filipino people. . . .

Sen. Patterson: You mean those left alive after they have been subjugated?

Gen. MacArthur: I do not admit that there has been any unusual destruction of life in the Philippine Islands. The destruction is simply the incident of war, and of course it embraces only a very small percentage of the total population.

. . . I doubt if any war — either international or civil, any war on earth — has been conducted with as much humanity, with as much careful consideration, with as much self-restraint, as have been the American operations in the Philippine Archipelago. . . . ❞

Realities

Brigadier General Robert P. Hughes, a military district commander, testified as follows.

❝ *Q*: In burning towns, what would you do? Would the entire town be destroyed by fire or would only the offending portions of the town be burned?

Gen. Hughes: I do not know that we ever had a case of burning what you would call a town in this country, but probably a barrio or a sitio; probably half a dozen houses, native shacks, where the insurrectos would go in and be concealed, and if they caught a detachment passing they would kill some of them.

Q: What did I understand you to say would be the consequences of that?

Gen. Hughes: They usually burned the village.

Q: All of the houses in the village?

Gen. Hughes: Yes, every one of them.

Q: What would become of the inhabitants?

Gen. Hughes: That was their lookout.

Q: If these shacks were of no consequence what was the utility of their destruction?

Gen. Hughes: The destruction was as a punishment. They permitted these people to come in there and conceal themselves. . . .

Q: The punishment in that case would fall, not upon the men, who could go elsewhere, but mainly upon the women and little children.

Gen. Hughes: The women and children are part of the family, and where you wish to inflict a punishment you can punish the man probably worse in that way than in any other.

Q: But is that within the ordinary rules of civilized warfare? . . .

Gen. Hughes: These people are not civilized. ❞

Cruelties

Daniel J. Evans, Twelfth Infantry, describes the "water cure."

❝ *Q*: The committee would like to hear . . . whether you were the witness to any cruelties inflicted upon the natives of the Philippine Islands; and if so, under what circumstances.

Evans: The case I had reference to was where they gave the water cure to a native in the Ilicano Province at Ilocos Norte . . . about the month of August 1900. There were two native scouts with the American forces. They went out and brought in a couple of insurgents. . . . They tried to get from this insurgent . . . where the rest of the insurgents were at that time. . . . The first thing one of the Americans — I mean one of the scouts for the Americans — grabbed one of the men by the head and jerked his head back, and then they took a tomato can and poured water down his throat until he could hold no more. . . . Then they forced a gag into his mouth; they stood him up . . . against a post and fastened him so that he could not move. Then one man, an American soldier, who was over six feet tall, and who was very strong, too, struck this native in the pit of the stomach as hard as he could. . . . They kept that operation up for quite a time, and finally I thought the fellow was about to die, but I don't believe he was as bad as that, because finally he told them he would tell, and from that day on he was taken away, and I saw no more of him. ❞

QUESTIONS FOR ANALYSIS

1. The text of this chapter offers the U.S. reasons for holding on to the Philippines. In what ways does General MacArthur's testimony confirm, add to, or contradict the text account?
2. The chapter text also describes the anti-imperialist movement. What does Senator Patterson's cross-examination of General MacArthur reveal about the anti-imperialists' beliefs?
3. Identify the main ideas in the last two sources. How do the clash of ideas in these excerpts remain relevant to our own time? Use textual evidence from the sources to compare to what you might read or hear about in a news source today?

TRM Find complete suggested responses in the Teacher's Resource Materials.

Secretary of State John Hay sent those countries' governments a note in 1899, claiming the right of equal trade access — an **"open door" policy** — for all nations seeking to do business in China. The United States lacked leverage in Asia, and Hay's note elicited only noncommittal responses. But he chose to interpret this as acceptance of his position.

"open door" policy
A claim put forth by U.S. Secretary of State John Hay that all nations seeking to do business in China should have equal trade access.

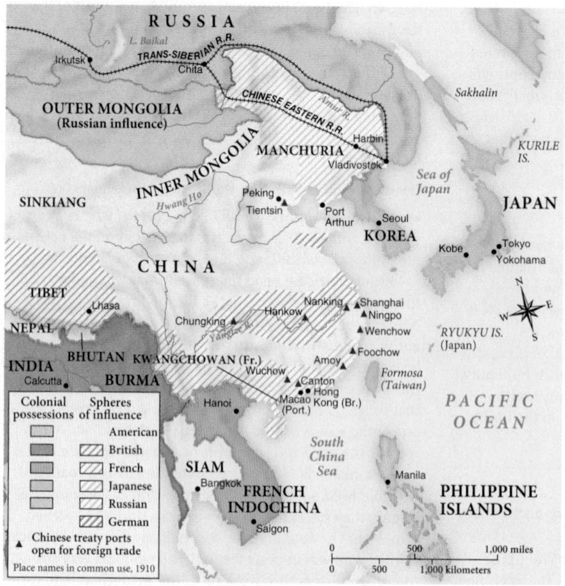

MAP 20.1 The Great Powers in East Asia, 1898–1910
European powers established dominance over China by way of "treaty ports," where the powers based their naval forces, and through "spheres of influence" that extended from the ports into the hinterland. This map reveals why the United States had a weak hand: it lacked a presence on this colonized terrain. An uprising of Chinese nationalists in 1900 gave the United States a chance to insert itself on the Chinese mainland by sending an American expeditionary force. American diplomats made the most of the opportunity to defend U.S. commercial interests in China. As noted in the key, all place names in this map are those in use in 1910: Modern *Beijing*, for example, is shown as *Peking*.

When a secret society of Chinese nationalists, known outside China as "Boxers" because of their pugnacious political stance, rebelled against foreign occupation in 1900, the United States sent 5,000 troops to join a multinational campaign to break the nationalists' siege of European offices in Beijing. Hay took this opportunity to promote a second open door principle: China must be preserved as a "territorial and administrative entity." As long as the legal fiction of an independent China survived, Americans could claim equal access to its market.

European and American plans met a challenge, however, in Japan's emergence as East Asia's dominant power. A decade after its victory over China, Japan responded to Russia's bids for control of both Korea and Manchuria, in northern China, by attacking Russia's fleet at its leased Chinese port. In a series of brilliant victories, Japanese forces smashed the Russian navy. Westerners were shocked: for the first time, a European power had been defeated by an Asian nation. Conveying both admiration and alarm, American cartoonists sketched Japan as a martial artist knocking down the Russian giant. Roosevelt mediated a settlement to the war in 1905, receiving for his efforts the first Nobel Peace Prize awarded to an American.

Though contemptuous of other Asians, Roosevelt respected the Japanese, whom he called "a wonderful and civilized people." More important, he understood Japan's rising military might and aligned himself with the mighty. The United States approved Japan's "protectorate" over Korea in 1905 and, six years later, its seizure of full control. With Japan asserting harsh authority over Manchuria, energetic Chinese diplomat Yüan Shih-k'ai tried to encourage the United States to intervene. But Roosevelt reviewed America's weak position in the Pacific and declined. He conceded that Japan had "a paramount interest in what surrounds the Yellow Sea." In 1908, the United States and Japan signed the **Root-Takahira Agreement,** confirming principles of free oceanic commerce and recognizing Japan's authority over Manchuria.

Root-Takahira Agreement
A 1908 agreement between the United States and Japan confirming principles of free oceanic commerce and recognizing Japan's authority over Manchuria.

William Howard Taft entered the White House in 1909 convinced that the United States had been shortchanged in Asia. In comparison with Roosevelt, Taft pressed for a larger role for American investors, especially in Chinese railroad construction. Eager to promote U.S. business interests abroad, he hoped that infusions of American capital would offset Japanese power. When the Chinese Revolution of 1911 toppled the Manchu dynasty, Taft supported the victorious Nationalists, who wanted to modernize their country and liberate it from Japanese domination. The United States had entangled itself in China and entered a long-term rivalry with Japan for power in the Pacific, a competition that would culminate thirty years later in World War II.

AP® THEME

WOR: America in the World

Use **MAP 20.1** to help students understand that the American victory in the War of 1898 led to the U.S. acquisition of island territories in the Caribbean and the Pacific, an increase in involvement in Asia, and the suppression of a Filipino nationalist movement. Students should note how the map indicates the extensive scale of European influence in Asia, which motivated some Americans to acquire the Philippines and to establish a foothold on the Chinese mainland.

TEACHING STRATEGY

For a contemporary perspective on the Boxer Rebellion from a Chinese Christian, students could read Fei Ch'i-hao's 1900 account on Modern Internet Sourcebook. To access this document, search "Modern History Sourcebook Boxer Rebellion."

TEACHING STRATEGY

To provide students with an American perspective on the Russo-Japanese conflict, use Indiana University's Japan-in-America Web site. This site provides a short review of the war and its outcome, framing American discourse about the war around the following issues:

- the admiration for and anxiety about Japan's military presence and expansionist ambitions;
- the need to account somehow for Japan's victories and to estimate the effect of the Russo-Japanese War on geopolitical relations, particularly concerning the role of China;
- and the pressing concern with assessing the power and the prestige of the U.S. in Asia and the Pacific at the beginning of a new century.

The site additionally offers thirty provocative cartoons for student exploration. To access this site, search "Indiana University Japan in America."

CHECK FOR UNDERSTANDING

Ask students: **How did the U.S. attempt to create an "open door" in Asia?** *Fearful of being cut out of lucrative trade with China, the U.S. established the nonbinding "open door" policy, which theoretically prevented European powers from creating exclusive spheres of influence.*

The United States and Latin America

Roosevelt famously argued that the United States should "speak softly and carry a big stick" in its relations with other countries. By "big stick," he meant naval power, and rapid access to two oceans required a canal linking the Atlantic and Pacific oceans across the Isthmus of Panama. As European powers pursued their interests in Africa, Asia, and other parts of the world, they conceded the United States's claim to control the Caribbean. Britain surrendered its Central American canal-building rights to the United States in the Hay-Pauncefote Treaty (1901). Roosevelt then persuaded Congress to authorize $10 million, plus future payments of $250,000 per year, to purchase from Colombia a six-mile strip of land across Panama, a Colombian province.

Furious when Colombia rejected this proposal, Roosevelt contemplated outright seizure of Panama but settled on a more roundabout solution. Panamanians, long separated from Colombia by remote jungle, chafed under Colombian rule. The United States lent covert assistance to an independence movement, triggering a bloodless revolution. On November 6, 1903, the United States recognized the new nation of Panama; two weeks later, it obtained a perpetually renewable lease on a canal zone. Roosevelt never regretted the venture, though in 1922 the United States paid Colombia $25 million as a kind of conscience money. (The United States returned the canal zone to Panama through a process that began in the 1970s and ended in 2000.)

Panama Canal Workers, 1910 The 51-mile-long Panama Canal includes seven sets of locks that can raise and lower fifty large ships in a twenty-four-hour period. Building the canal took eight years and required tens of thousands of workers, including immigrants from Spain and Italy and many West Indians, such as these men, who accomplished some of the worst-paid, most dangerous labor. Workers endured the horrors of rockslides, explosions, and a yellow fever epidemic that almost halted the project. But American observers hailed the canal as a triumph of modern science and engineering—especially in medical efforts to eradicate the yellow fever and malaria that had stymied earlier canal-building efforts. Theodore Roosevelt insisted on making a personal visit in November 1906. "He made the men that were building there feel like they were special people," recalled the descendant of one canal worker. "Give them pride of what they were doing for the United States." Library of Congress, 3c17214.

To build the canal, the U.S. Army Corps of Engineers hired 60,000 laborers, who came from many countries to clear vast swamps, excavate 240 million cubic yards of earth, and construct a series of immense locks. The project, a major engineering feat, took eight years and cost thousands of lives among the workers who built it. Opened in 1914, the **Panama Canal** gave the United States a commanding position in the Western Hemisphere.

Meanwhile, arguing that instability invited European intervention, Roosevelt announced in 1904 that the United States would police the whole Caribbean (Map 20.2). This so-called **Roosevelt Corollary** to the Monroe Doctrine actually turned that doctrine upside down: instead of guaranteeing that the United States would protect its neighbors from Europe and help preserve their independence, it asserted the United States's unrestricted right to regulate Caribbean affairs. The Roosevelt Corollary was not a treaty but a unilateral declaration sanctioned only by America's military and economic might. For decades after proclaiming it, the United States intervened regularly in Caribbean and Central American nations' affairs.

Entering office in 1913, Democratic president Woodrow Wilson criticized his predecessors' foreign policy. He pledged that the United States would "never again seek one additional foot of territory by conquest." This stance appealed to anti-imperialists

AP® EXAM TIP

The construction of the Panama Canal as an expression of American imperialism is important to know on the AP® Exam.

Panama Canal
A canal across the Isthmus of Panama connecting trade between the Atlantic and Pacific oceans. Built by the U.S. Army Corps of Engineers and opened in 1914, the canal gave U.S. naval vessels quick access to the Pacific and provided the United States with a commanding position in the Western Hemisphere.

Roosevelt Corollary
The 1904 assertion by President Theodore Roosevelt that the United States would act as a "policeman" in the Caribbean region and intervene in the affairs of nations that were guilty of "wrongdoing or impotence" in order to protect U.S. interests in Latin America.

TEACHING STRATEGY

The *American Experience* documentary *Panama Canal* explores the canal's construction as the beginning of America's dominance in world affairs. Show clips from the film and discuss with students how the canal marked a feat of engineering that placed the U.S. as a major player on the world stage. To access the trailer, clips, and additional resources, search "American Experience Panama Canal."

TEACHING STRATEGY

For greater understanding of Roosevelt's vision of the world, students could read details associated with his 1906 Nobel Prize award. The Nobel Prize Web site features both his lecture and acceptance speech, along with biographical information and photos of Roosevelt. To access these resources, search "Nobel Prize Roosevelt."

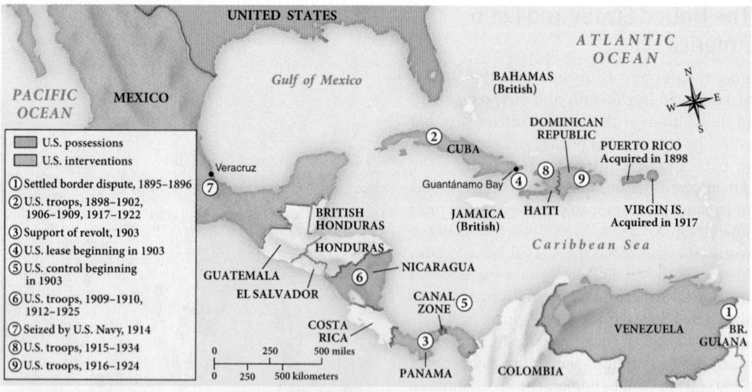

MAPPING THE PAST

MAP 20.2 Policeman of the Caribbean
After the War of 1898, the United States vigorously asserted its interest in the affairs of its neighbors to the south. As the record of interventions shows, the United States truly became the "policeman" of the Caribbean and Central America.

ANALYZING THE MAP: When did the United States first intervene in the Caribbean, during this period? When and in what nations did its last occupations end?

MAKING CONNECTIONS: Based on the narrative in this chapter, how did the United States's interventions in the Caribbean compare with U.S. assertions of American interests in other parts of the world? What were some of the broader reasons why the United States treated European nations differently than those in Latin America and Asia?

TRM Find complete suggested responses in the Teacher's Resource Materials.

in the Democratic base, including longtime supporters of William Jennings Bryan. But the new president soon showed that, when American interests called for it, his actions were not so different from those of Roosevelt and Taft.

Since the 1870s, Mexican dictator Porfirio Díaz had created a friendly climate for American companies that purchased Mexican plantations, mines, and oil fields. By the early 1900s, however, Díaz feared the extraordinary power of these foreign interests and began to nationalize — reclaim — key resources. American investors who faced the loss of Mexican holdings began to back Francisco Madero, an advocate of constitutional government who was friendly to U.S. interests. In 1911, Madero forced Díaz to resign and proclaimed himself president. Thousands of poor Mexicans took this opportunity to mobilize rural armies and demand more radical change. Madero's position was weak, and several strongmen sought to overthrow him; in 1913, he was deposed and murdered by a leading general. Immediately, several other military men vied for control.

Wilson, fearing that the unrest threatened U.S. interests, decided to intervene in the emerging Mexican Revolution. On the pretext of a minor insult to the navy, he ordered U.S. occupation of the port of Veracruz on April 21, 1914, at the cost of 19 American and 126 Mexican lives. Though the intervention helped Venustiano Carranza, the revolutionary leader whom Wilson most favored, Carranza protested it as illegitimate meddling in Mexican affairs. Carranza's forces, after nearly engaging the Americans themselves, entered Mexico City in triumph a few months later. Though Wilson had supported this outcome, his interference created lasting mistrust.

AP® EXAM TIP

Compare the foreign policies of Theodore Roosevelt, William Howard Taft, and Woodrow Wilson.

AP® APPLY THE TIP

Provide students with **Handout 20.4 — Comparison: Foreign Policy of the Progressives (TRM)** and ask them to use pp. 647–653 to complete it. Then ask students to work in collaborative groups to evaluate the degree to which the progressivism of each president in domestic policy was supported by their goals and methods in foreign policy. Students can utilize their class notes, textbook (Chapter 18), and outside sources to review each president's progressive ideas and policies in domestic policy. Students should then compare the goals and policies of each president's domestic policy to their foreign policy in the age of imperialism. Lead a class discussion that addresses the following question: Were the foreign and domestic policies of the progressive presidents consistent with progressive ideals?

TRM Access **Handout 20.4 — Comparison: Foreign Policy of the Progressives** in the Teacher's Resource Materials.

Carranza's victory did not subdue revolutionary activity in Mexico. In 1916, General Francisco "Pancho" Villa — a thug to his enemies, but a heroic Robin Hood to many poor Mexicans — crossed the U.S.-Mexico border, killing sixteen American civilians and raiding the town of Columbus, New Mexico. Wilson sent 11,000 troops to pursue Villa, a force that soon resembled an army of occupation in northern Mexico. Mexican public opinion demanded withdrawal as armed clashes broke out between U.S. and Mexican troops. At the brink of war, both governments backed off and U.S. forces departed. Policymakers in Washington, however, had shown their intention to police not only the Caribbean and Central America but also to exert military power in Mexico when they deemed it necessary.

Violence at the Border, 1916 After Mexican general Pancho Villa led a raid on Columbus, New Mexico, U.S. troops crossed the border in pursuit. Here, members of the 13th U.S. Cavalry pose for their photograph in the desert with a dead Mexican man. The cavalryman on the left holds his rifle in a position suggesting accurately, or not, that he shot the man from horseback. The Granger Collection, New York.

THE UNITED STATES IN WORLD WAR I

Why and how did participation in World War I change the economy and society of the United States?

While the United States staked claims around the globe, a war of unprecedented scale was brewing in Europe. The military buildup of Germany, a rising power, terrified its neighbors. At the same time, further east, the disintegrating Ottoman Empire was losing its grip on the Balkans. Out of these conflicts, two rival power blocs emerged: the Triple Alliance (Germany, Austria-Hungary, and Italy) and Triple Entente (Britain, France, and Russia). Within each alliance, national governments pursued their own interests but were bound to one another by public and secret treaties.

Americans had no obvious stake in these developments and in fact had a record of serving as a neutral mediator of European disputes. In 1905, when Germany suddenly challenged French control of Morocco, Theodore Roosevelt arranged an international conference to defuse the crisis. Germany got a few concessions, but France — with British backing — retained Morocco. Accomplished in the same year that Roosevelt brokered peace between Russia and Japan, the conference seemed another diplomatic triumph. One U.S. official boasted that America had kept peace by "the power of our detachment." It was not to last.

AP® EXAM TIP

Evaluate reactions in the United States to the start of World War I in Europe in 1914.

From Neutrality to War

The spark that ignited World War I came in the Balkans, where Austria-Hungary and Russia competed for control. Austria's 1908 seizure of Ottoman provinces, including Bosnia, angered the nearby Slavic nation of Serbia and its ally Russia. Serbian revolutionaries recruited Bosnian Slavs to resist Austrian rule. In June 1914, in the city of Sarajevo, university student Gavrilo Princip assassinated Archduke Franz Ferdinand, heir to the Austro-Hungarian throne.

Like dominos falling, the system of European alliances pushed all the powers into war. Austria-Hungary blamed Serbia for the assassination and declared war on July 28. Russia, tied by secret treaty to Serbia, mobilized against Austria-Hungary. This prompted

CHECK FOR UNDERSTANDING

Ask students: **Compare and contrast the factors that influenced U.S. actions in Asia and in Latin America in this period.** *At the end of the nineteenth century and the early twentieth century, U.S. policy vis-à-vis Asia and Latin America was similar in that it represented an expansion of American power and was largely guided by economic, rather than ideological or political issues. Nonetheless, there were significant differences. In Asia, where the United States had very little historical interests and, until 1898, no territorial interests, U.S. policy and actions were geared at winning a place for its business interests in China. China was dominated by European powers through their open-door policies, while at the same time Japan was recognized as a regional authority through the Root-Takahira Agreement of 1908. Latin America was different. Here, the United States had established political and military interests. Rather than seek a piece of an existing pie, Washington policymakers sought to enhance and ensure its power in the region relative to European powers through the Roosevelt Corollary, which intellectually legitimated numerous interventions (including during the Mexican Revolution), and through the construction of the Panama Canal, completed in 1914.*

TEACHING STRATEGY

American Experience's documentary *Great War* draws on unpublished diaries, memoirs, and letters to tell the complex story of World War I through the voices of nurses, journalists, aviators, and the American troops who came to be known as "doughboys." The series explores the experiences of African American and Latino soldiers, suffragists, Native American "code talkers," and others whose participation in the war to "make the world safe for democracy" has been largely forgotten. To access the film, search "American Experience Great War."

Germany to declare war on Russia and its ally France. As a preparation for attacking France, Germany launched a brutal invasion of the neutral country of Belgium, which caused Great Britain to declare war on Germany. Within a week, most of Europe was at war, with the major Allies — Great Britain, France, and Russia — confronting the Central Powers of Germany and Austria-Hungary. Two military zones emerged. On the Western Front, Germany battled the British and French; on the Eastern Front, Germany and Austria-Hungary fought Russia. Because most of the warring nations held colonial empires, the conflict soon spread to the Middle East, Africa, and Asia.

The so-called Great War wreaked terrible devastation. New technology, some of it devised in the United States, made warfare deadlier than ever before. Every soldier carried a long-range, high-velocity rifle that could hit a target at 1,000 yards — a vast technical advancement over the 300-yard range of rifles used in the U.S. Civil War. The machine gun was even more lethal. Its American-born inventor, Hiram Maxim, had moved to Britain in the 1880s to follow a friend's advice: "If you want to make your fortune, invent something which will allow those fool Europeans to kill each other more quickly." Elaborate trenches, familiar from the Civil War era, were now enhanced with barbed wire to protect soldiers in defensive positions. Once advancing Germans ran into French fortifications, they stalled. Across a swath of Belgium and northeastern France, millions of soldiers on both sides hunkered down in fortified trenches. During 1916, repeatedly trying to break through French lines at Verdun, Germans suffered 450,000 casualties. The French fared even worse, with 550,000 dead or wounded. It was all to no avail. From 1914 to 1918, the Western Front barely moved.

AP® EXAM TIP

Trace the events that led the U.S. to depart from its policy of neutrality and enter World War I in 1917.

At the war's outbreak, President Wilson called on Americans to be "neutral in fact as well as in name." If the United States remained out of the conflict, Wilson reasoned, he could influence the postwar settlement. Even if Wilson had wished to, it would have been nearly impossible in 1914 to unite Americans behind the Allies. Many Irish immigrants viewed Britain as an enemy — based on its continued occupation of Ireland — while millions of German Americans maintained ties to their homeland. Progressive-minded Republicans, such as Senator Robert La Follette of Wisconsin, vehemently opposed taking sides in a European fight, as did socialists, who condemned the war as a conflict among greedy capitalist empires. Two giants of American industry, Andrew Carnegie and Henry Ford, opposed the war. In December 1915, Ford sent a hundred men and women to Europe on a "peace ship" to urge an end to the conflict. "It would be folly," declared the *New York Sun*, "for the country to sacrifice itself to . . . the clash of ancient hatreds which is urging the Old World to destruction."

The Struggle to Remain Neutral The United States, wishing to trade with all the warring nations, might have remained neutral if Britain had not held commanding power at sea. In September 1914, the British imposed a naval blockade on the Central Powers to cut off vital supplies of food and military equipment. Though the Wilson administration protested this infringement of the rights of neutral carriers, commerce with the Allies more than made up for the economic loss. Trade with Britain and France grew fourfold over the next two years, to $3.2 billion in 1916; by 1917, U.S. banks had lent the Allies $2.5 billion. In contrast, American trade and loans to Germany stood then at a mere $56 million. This imbalance undercut U.S. neutrality. If Germany won and Britain and France defaulted on their debts, American companies would suffer catastrophic losses.

To challenge the British navy, Germany launched a devastating new weapon, the U-boat (short for *Unterseeboot*, "undersea boat," or submarine). In April 1915, Germany issued a warning that all ships flying flags of Britain or its allies were liable to destruction. A few weeks later, a U-boat torpedoed the British luxury liner *Lusitania* off the coast of Ireland, killing 1,198 people, including 128 Americans. The attack on the passenger ship (which was later revealed to have been carrying munitions) incensed Americans. The following year, in an agreement known as the Sussex pledge, Germany agreed not to target passenger liners or merchant ships unless an inspection showed the latter carried weapons. But the *Lusitania* sinking prompted Wilson to

AP® APPLY THE TIP

In the center of the board, write "U.S. declares war on Germany, 1917" and draw a large circle around the statement. Ask students to think of the area inside the circle as the immediate causes of America's decision to declare war on Germany and enter World War I. Lead a discussion in which students explain specific events that led to the U.S. declaration of war. Write these events inside the circle. Then, draw a larger box around the circle. Ask students to think of the box as representing the larger historical processes and developments that were influencing America's decision to join World War I. As students suggest ideas that belong in the larger, contextualization box, ask them to explain the relationship between the context and the specific decision to declare war on Germany. (For example, students might say that the popularization of progressivism belongs in the larger box and argue that because Americans supported the idea of using government power to solve problems inside the U.S., there was support for using the same power to address evils outside the U.S.) Continue to add ideas to the larger box to support greater understanding of contextualization. As an extension of this activity, ask students to give examples of major events that occurred before and after World War I that illustrate the same patterns of U.S. involvement or policies.

reconsider his options. After quietly trying to mediate in Europe but finding neither side interested in peace, he endorsed a $1 billion U.S. military buildup.

American public opinion still ran strongly against entering the war, a fact that shaped the election of 1916. Republicans rejected the belligerently prowar Theodore Roosevelt in favor of Supreme Court justice Charles Evans Hughes, a progressive former governor of New York. Democrats renominated Wilson, who campaigned on his domestic record and as the president who "kept us out of war." Wilson eked out a narrow victory; winning California by a mere 4,000 votes, he secured a slim majority in the electoral college.

AP® SKILLS & PROCESSES

DEVELOPMENTS AND PROCESSES

What factors led the United States to enter World War I, despite the desire of so many Americans, including the president, to stay out of the war?

America Enters the War Despite Wilson's campaign slogan, events — as well as American business interests — pushed him toward war. In February 1917, Germany resumed unrestricted submarine warfare, a decision dictated by the impasse on the Western Front. In response, Wilson broke off diplomatic relations with Germany. A few weeks later, newspapers published an intercepted dispatch from German foreign secretary Arthur Zimmermann to his minister in Mexico. The **Zimmermann telegram** urged Mexico to join the Central Powers, promising that if the United States entered the war, Germany would help Mexico recover "the lost territory of Texas, New Mexico, and Arizona." With Pancho Villa's border raids still fresh in Americans' minds, this threat jolted public opinion. Meanwhile, German U-boats began to attack U.S. ships without warning, sinking three on March 18 alone.

Zimmermann telegram
A 1917 intercepted dispatch in which German foreign secretary Arthur Zimmermann urged Mexico to join the Central Powers and promised that if the United States entered the war, Germany would help Mexico recover Texas, New Mexico, and Arizona. Published by American newspapers, the telegram outraged the American public and help precipitate the move toward U.S. entry in the war on the Allied side.

On April 2, 1917, Wilson asked Congress for a declaration of war. He argued that Germany had trampled on American rights and imperiled U.S. trade and citizens' lives. "We desire no conquest," Wilson declared, "no material compensation for the sacrifices we shall freely make." Reflecting his progressive idealism, Wilson promised that American involvement would make the world "safe for democracy." On April 6, the United States declared war on Germany. Reflecting the nation's divided views, the vote was far from unanimous. Six senators and fifty members of the House voted against entry, including Representative Jeannette Rankin of Montana, the first woman elected to Congress. "You can no more win a war than you can win an earthquake," Rankin said. "I want to stand by my country, but I cannot vote for war."

"Over There"

To Americans, Europe seemed a great distance away. Many assumed the United States would simply provide munitions and economic aid. "Good Lord," exclaimed one U.S. senator to a Wilson administration official, "you're not going to send soldiers over there, are you?" But when General John J. Pershing asked how the United States could best support the Allies, the French commander put it bluntly: "Men, men, and more men." Amid war fever, thousands of young men prepared to go "over there," in the words of George M. Cohan's popular song: "Make your Daddy glad to have had such a lad. / Tell your sweetheart not to pine, / To be proud her boy's in line."

Americans Join the War In 1917, the U.S. Army numbered fewer than 200,000 soldiers; needing more men, Congress instituted a military draft in May 1917. In contrast to the Civil War, when resistance was common in both the Union and Confederacy, conscription went smoothly, partly because local, civilian-run draft boards played a central role in the new system. Still, draft registration demonstrated government's increasing power over ordinary citizens. On a single day — June 5, 1917 — more than 9.5 million men between the ages of twenty-one and thirty registered at local voting precincts for possible military service.

AP® EXAM TIP

Evaluate the role of the American Expeditionary Force in the victory of the Allies in World War I.

President Wilson chose General Pershing to head the American Expeditionary Force (AEF), which had to be trained, outfitted, and carried across the submarine-plagued Atlantic. This required safer shipping. When the United States entered the war, German U-boats were sinking 900,000 tons of Allied ships each month. By sending merchant and troop ships in armed convoys, the U.S. Navy cut

AP® SKILLS & PROCESSES

DEVELOPMENTS AND PROCESSES

The **DEVELOPMENTS AND PROCESSES** question, which asks students to identify causes of American entry into the war, provides a good opportunity for students to distinguish between primary factors and more secondary ones. Students could additionally rank the primary factors in order of their importance in causing Wilson and Congress to change their minds about neutrality.

TRM Find complete suggested responses in the Teacher's Resource Materials.

AP® THEME

NAT: American and National Identity

After initial neutrality, the U.S. entered World War I, departing from the nation's foreign policy tradition of noninvolvement in European affairs. In asking for war, Wilson called for the defense of humanitarian and democratic principles. Students can view a facsimile copy of his original speech requesting war, a transcript of the full text, and background information at *Our Documents.* To access these resources, search "Our Documents Wilson Declaration of War."

CHECK FOR UNDERSTANDING

Ask students: **How did the U.S. move from neutrality to war?** *A series of German actions, including the sinking of the Lusitania and the Zimmermann telegram, helped the U.S. abandon neutrality.*

AP® THEME

WOR: America in the World

Students should understand how, although American forces played a relatively limited role in combat, U.S. entry helped to tip the balance in favor of the Allies.

that monthly rate to 400,000 tons by the end of 1917. With trench warfare grinding on, Allied commanders pleaded for American soldiers to fill their depleted units, but Pershing waited until the AEF reached full strength. As late as May 1918, the brunt of the fighting fell to the French and British.

The Allies' burden increased when the Eastern Front collapsed following the Bolshevik (Communist) Revolution in Russia in November 1917. To consolidate power at home, the new Bolshevik government, led by Vladimir Lenin, sought peace with the Central Powers. In a 1918 treaty that shocked the Allies, Russia surrendered its claims over vast parts of its territories in exchange for peace. Released from war against Germany, the Bolsheviks turned their attention to a civil war at home. Terrified by communism, Japan and several Allied countries, including the United States, later sent troops to fight the Bolsheviks and aid forces loyal to the deposed tsar. But after a four-year civil war, Lenin's forces established full control over Russia and reclaimed Ukraine and other former possessions.

Peace with Russia freed Germany to launch a major offensive on the Western Front. By May 1918, German troops had advanced to within 50 miles of Paris. Pershing at last committed about 60,000 U.S. soldiers to support the French defense. With American soldiers engaged in massive numbers, Allied forces brought the Germans to a halt in July; by September, they forced a retreat. Pershing then pitted more than one million American soldiers against an outnumbered and exhausted German army in the Argonne forest. By early November, this attack broke German defenses at a crucial rail hub, Sedan. The cost was high: 26,000 Americans killed and 95,000 wounded (Map 20.3). But the flood of U.S. troops and supplies determined the outcome. Recognizing inevitable defeat and facing popular uprisings at home, Germany signed an armistice on November 11, 1918. The Great War was over.

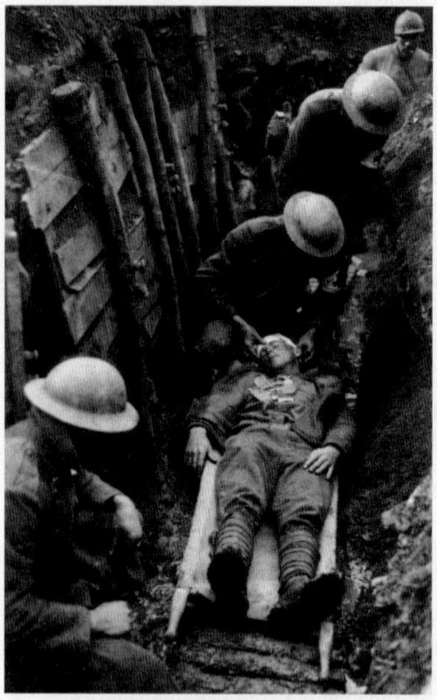

In the Trenches of the Western Front, March 1918
Red Cross medics treat a wounded American soldier and prepare to remove him to a field hospital. The photographer, Quartermaster Leon H. Caverly, a marine quartermaster, was one of the first official videographers to record U.S. troops in combat overseas; he also took many still images such as this one. By comparison with French, British, and German troops, U.S. soldiers endured trench warfare for only a short time, but the terrible conditions left a powerful impression on all who fought and survived. Sgt. Leon H. Caverly/Getty Images.

The American Fighting Force By the end of World War I, almost 4 million American men — popularly known as "doughboys" — wore U.S. uniforms, as did several thousand female nurses. The recruits reflected America's heterogeneity: one-fifth had been born outside the United States, and soldiers spoke forty-nine different languages. Though ethnic diversity worried some observers, most predicted that military service would promote Americanization.

More than 400,000 African American men enlisted, accounting for 13 percent of the armed forces. Their wartime experiences were often grim: serving in segregated units, they were given the most menial tasks. Racial discrimination hampered military efficiency and provoked violence at several camps. The worst incident occurred in August 1917, when, after suffering a string of racial attacks, black members of the 24th Infantry's Third Battalion rioted in Houston, killing 15 white civilians and police officers. The army tried 118 of the soldiers in military courts for mutiny and riot, hanged 19, and sentenced 63 to life in prison.

Unlike African Americans, American Indians served in integrated combat units. Racial stereotypes about Native Americans' prowess as warriors enhanced their military reputations, but it also prompted officers to assign them hazardous duties as scouts and snipers. About 13,000, or 25 percent, of the adult male American Indian population served during the war; roughly 5 percent died, compared to 2 percent for the military as a whole.

Most American soldiers escaped the horrors of sustained trench warfare. Still, during the brief period of U.S. participation, more than 50,000 servicemen died in action; another 63,000 died from disease, mainly the devastating influenza pandemic that began early in 1918 and, over the next two years, killed 50 million people worldwide. The nation's military deaths, though substantial, were only a tenth as many as the 500,000 American civilians who died of this terrible epidemic. In Europe, the war's casualties dwarfed those of the United States: millions of soldiers died (Germany, Russia, France, and Austria-Hungary each lost more than 1 million), and countries such as Russia, Serbia, and Bulgaria suffered heavy civilian losses as well (see "America in the World," p. 658).

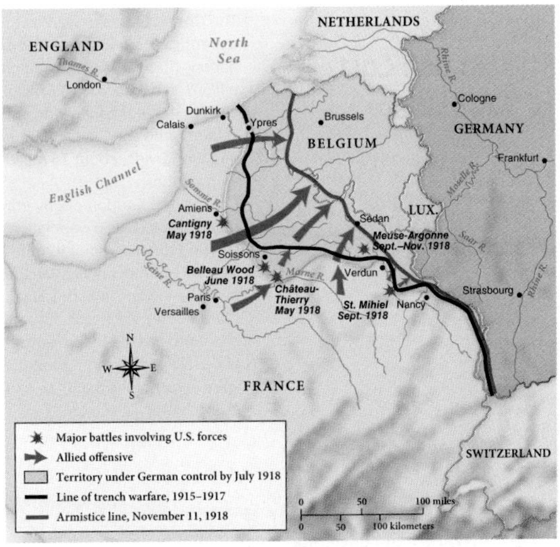

MAP 20.3 U.S. Participation on the Western Front, 1918
When American troops reached the European front in significant numbers in 1918, the Allies and Central Powers had been fighting a deadly war of attrition for almost four years. The influx of American troops and supplies helped break the stalemate. Successful offensive maneuvers by the American Expeditionary Force included those at Belleau Wood and Château-Thierry and the Meuse-Argonne campaign.

War on the Home Front

Once the United States committed to the conflict, Americans in opposition to the war became a minority. Helping the Allies triggered an economic boom that benefitted farmers and working people. Many progressives also supported the war, hoping Wilson's ideals and wartime patriotism would renew Americans' attention to reform. But the war bitterly disappointed them. Rather than enhancing democracy, it chilled the political climate as government agencies tried to enforce "100 percent loyalty."

Mobilizing the Economy American businesses made big bucks from World War I. As grain, weapons, and manufactured goods flowed to Britain and France, the United States became a creditor nation. Moreover, as the war drained British financial reserves, U.S. banks provided capital for investments around the globe.

Government powers expanded during wartime, with new federal agencies overseeing almost every part of the economy. The **War Industries Board (WIB)**, established in July 1917, directed military production. After a fumbling start that showed the limits of voluntarism, the Wilson administration reorganized the board and placed Bernard Baruch, a Wall Street financier and superb administrator, at its head. Under his direction, the WIB allocated scarce resources among industries, ordered factories to convert to war production, set prices, and standardized procedures. Though he could compel compliance, Baruch preferred to win voluntary cooperation. A man of immense charm, he usually succeeded — helped by the lucrative military contracts at his disposal. Despite higher taxes, corporate profits soared, as military production sustained a boom that continued until 1920.

Some federal agencies took dramatic measures. The **National War Labor Board (NWLB)**, formed in April 1918, established an eight-hour day for war workers with time-and-a-half pay for overtime, and it endorsed equal pay for women. In return for a no-strike pledge, the NWLB also supported workers' right to organize — a major achievement for the labor movement. The Fuel Administration, meanwhile, introduced daylight saving time to conserve coal and oil. In December 1917, the Railroad Administration seized control of the nation's hodgepodge of private railroads, seeking to facilitate rapid movement of troops and equipment — an experiment that had, at best, mixed results.

Perhaps the most successful wartime agency was the Food Administration, created in August 1917 and led by engineer Herbert Hoover. With the slogan "Food

AP® SKILLS & PROCESSES

CAUSATION

How did U.S. military entry into World War I affect the course of the war?

War Industries Board (WIB)
A federal board established in July 1917 to direct military production, including allocation of resources, conversion of factories to war production, and setting of prices.

AP® EXAM TIP

Understanding the role of war in altering the power of government and the U.S. economy is critical for success on the AP® Exam.

National War Labor Board (NWLB)
A federal agency founded in 1918 that established an eight-hour day for war workers (with time-and-a-half pay for overtime), endorsed equal pay for women, and supported workers' right to organize.

CHECK FOR UNDERSTANDING

Ask students: **What was the American experience "over there"?** *Americans largely escaped trench warfare, but over 100,000 died from war and disease as they helped to turn the tide of the war.*

AP® SKILLS & PROCESSES

CAUSATION

The **CAUSATION** question asks students to recognize the significance of American supplies and the increased morale of Allied troops, as well as military successes.

TRM Find complete suggested responses in the Teacher's Resource Materials.

AP® THEME

ARC: American and Regional Culture

Students should evaluate the rationale for war against the actions on the home front by the American government and many of its citizens. This analysis can lead to a more nuanced understanding of both the ideas behind going to war and the attendant effects on the home front. Ask students to use humanitarian and democratic processes for the rationale behind U.S. involvement in war, as is noted in the AP® Course Framework. Next, have students select two actions by the government and/or citizenry and compare those with the rationale for war.

AP® SKILLS & PROCESSES

ANALYZING HISTORICAL EVIDENCE

Use the data in the **AP® AMERICA IN THE WORLD** feature to provide students with a glimpse of the impact the war had on different countries. Students should note both the small number of American military deaths and lack of civilian deaths relative to the major belligerents, particularly as a percentage of the population. Students should keep these statistics in mind when considering the stances each of the Big Four took toward peace negotiations.

TRM Find complete suggested responses in the Teacher's Resource Materials.

AP® AMERICA IN THE WORLD

The Human Cost of World War I

The United States played a crucial role in financing World War I. In its war-related expenditures, totaling $22.6 billion, the United States ranked fourth among all nations that participated, ranking behind only Germany ($37.7 billion), Britain ($35.3 billion), and France ($24.3 billion). In human terms, however, the U.S. role was different. Note that the following figures for military casualties are rough estimates. Many soldiers who survived suffered from "shell shock" and the lifelong effects of poison gas. Worldwide, about 15 million had to learn to live with severe disabilities such as amputations.

The mobilization of governments for war led to other forms of violence and suffering. Large civilian populations, including Belgians and Polish Jews, were displaced, creating the first major international refugee crisis. Civilian casualties are uncertain: the exact number of Russians, Italians, Romanians, Serbians, and others who died will never be known. In Serbia, due to disease and starvation, far more civilians died than soldiers. The most horrific impact on civilians, made possible by wartime conditions and pressures, was the Turkish government's genocide of Armenians. At war's end, the Treaty of Versailles left minority peoples stranded in places where they had no governmental voice—one of the many ways that the aftermath of World War I created the conditions for World War II.

TABLE 20.1

World War I Casualties

Country	Total Population	Military Killed or Missing	Total Civilian Deaths
Germany	67,000,000	2,037,000	700,000
Russia	167,000,000	1,800,000	2,000,000
France	39,000,000	1,385,300	40,000
Austria-Hungary	49,900,000	1,016,200	unknown
United Kingdom	46,400,000	702,410	1,386
Italy	35,000,000	462,400	unknown
Turkey	1,300,000	236,000	2,000,000*
Romania	7,510,000	219,800	265,000–500,000
Serbia	5,000,000	127,500	600,000
Bulgaria	5,500,000	77,450	275,000
India	316,000,000	62,060	negligible
Canada	7,400,000	58,990	negligible
Australia	4,872,000	53,560	negligible
United States	92,000,000	51,822	negligible

*Mostly Armenians

QUESTIONS FOR ANALYSIS

1. What does this data suggest about the role of the United States in World War I? The experience of its soldiers? The war's impact on civilians in each nation?
2. Describe at least two patterns found in this data set. Which other countries made contributions similar to that of the United States, and why?

658

will win the war," Hoover convinced farmers to nearly double their acreage of grain. This increase allowed a threefold rise in food exports to Europe. Among citizens, the Food Administration mobilized a "spirit of self-denial" rather than mandatory rationing. Female volunteers went from door to door to persuade housekeepers to observe "Wheatless" Mondays and "Porkless" Thursdays. Hoover, a Republican, emerged from the war as one of the nation's most admired public figures.

Choctaw Code Talkers These Oklahoma soldiers of the Thirty-Sixth Division were among nineteen members of the Choctaw Nation who became, in 1918, the U.S. Army's first indigenous "code talkers." An officer, hearing several enlisted men speaking Choctaw, realized their skills could stymie Germans' skillful interception of U.S. military communications. ("We couldn't keep anything secret," one officer remembered.) Stationed at headquarters and at key points along the Meuse-Argonne line, in the closing weeks of the war, the Choctaw soldiers relayed and translated messages, resulting in a surprise attack that overwhelmed German troops. At the start of World War II, the U.S. Army remembered this triumph and specifically recruited Navajo, Comanche, Chippewa-Oneida, and Hopi tribal members. Their extensive code talking program proved vital to the European war effort. U.S. Army Photo.

Promoting National Unity Suppressing wartime dissent became a near obsession for President Wilson. In April 1917, Wilson formed the Committee on Public Information (CPI), a government propaganda agency headed by journalist George Creel. Professing lofty goals — educating citizens about democracy, assimilating immigrants, and ending the isolation of rural life — the committee set out to mold Americans into "one white-hot mass" of war patriotism. The CPI touched the lives of nearly all civilians. It distributed seventy-five million pieces of literature and enlisted thousands of volunteers — Four-Minute Men — to deliver short prowar speeches at movie theaters.

The CPI also pressured immigrant groups to become "One Hundred Percent Americans." German Americans bore the brunt of this campaign (see "Thinking Like a Historian," p. 662). With posters exhorting citizens to root out German spies, a spirit of conformity pervaded the home front. A quasi-vigilante group, the American Protective League, mobilized about 250,000 "agents," furnished them with badges issued by the Justice Department, and trained them to spy on neighbors and coworkers. In 1918, members of the league led violent raids against draft evaders and peace activists. Government propaganda helped rouse a nativist hysteria that lingered into the 1920s.

Congress also passed new laws to curb dissent. Among them was the **Sedition Act of 1918**, which prohibited any words or behavior that might "incite, provoke, or encourage resistance to the United States, or promote the cause of its enemies." Because this and an earlier Espionage Act (1917) defined treason loosely, they led to the conviction of more than a thousand people. The Justice Department prosecuted members of the Industrial Workers of the World, whose opposition to militarism threatened to disrupt war production of lumber and copper. When a Quaker pacifist teacher in New York City refused to teach a prowar curriculum, she was fired. Socialist Party leader Eugene V. Debs was sentenced to ten years in jail for the crime of arguing that wealthy capitalists had started the conflict and were forcing workers to fight.

Sedition Act of 1918
Wartime law that prohibited any words or behavior that might promote resistance to the United States or help in the cause of its enemies.

Federal courts mostly supported the acts. In *Schenck v. United States* (1919), the Supreme Court upheld the conviction of a socialist who was jailed for circulating pamphlets that urged army draftees to resist induction. The justices followed this with a similar decision in *Abrams v. United States* (1919), ruling that authorities could prosecute speech they believed to pose "a clear and present danger to the safety of the country." In an important dissent, however, Justices Oliver Wendell Holmes Jr. and Louis Brandeis objected to the *Abrams* decision. Holmes's probing questions about the definition of "clear and present danger" helped launch twentieth-century legal battles to protect free speech and civil liberties during wartime.

VISUAL ACTIVITY

Selling Liberty Bonds: Two Appeals Once the United States entered the Great War, government officials sought to enlist all Americans in the battle against the Central Powers. They carefully crafted patriotic advertising campaigns that urged Americans to buy bonds, conserve food, enlist in the military, and support the war effort in many other ways. One of these posters appeals to recent immigrants, reminding them of their debt to American Liberty. The other shows the overtly anti-German prejudices of many war appeals: it depicts the "Hun," a slur for a German soldier, with bloody hands and bayonet. Library of Congress, 3g08026 and 3g02950.

READING THE IMAGES: What situation does each poster depict? What emotions does each artist seek to evoke in the viewer?

MAKING CONNECTIONS: Compare these images with the sources in "Thinking Like a Historian: German Americans in World War I." How was the intended audience of these images similar or different? How does the purpose of the images compare?

TRM Find complete suggested responses in the Teacher's Resource Materials.

AP® EXAM TIP

Evaluate the causes and effects of the Great Migration for African Americans and American culture.

Great Migration
The migration of more than 400,000 African Americans from the rural South to the industrial cities of the North during and after World War I.

Great Migrations World War I created tremendous economic opportunities at home. Relatively well-paid work in war industries drew thousands of people to the cities. With so many men in uniform, jobs in heavy industry opened for the first time to African Americans, accelerating the pace of black migration from South to North. During World War I, more than 400,000 African Americans moved to such cities as St. Louis, Chicago, New York, and Detroit, in what became known as the **Great Migration.** The rewards were great, and taking war jobs could be a source of patriotic pride. "If it hadn't been for the negro," a Carnegie Steel manager later recalled, "we could hardly have carried on our operations."

Blacks in the North encountered discrimination in jobs, housing, and education. But in the first flush of opportunity, most celebrated their escape from the repressive racism and poverty of the South. "It is a matter of a dollar with me and I feel that God made the path and I am walking therein," one woman reported to her sister back home. "Tell your husband work is plentiful here." "I just begin to feel like a man," wrote another migrant to a friend in Mississippi. "My children are going to the same

AP® APPLY THE TIP

To help students evaluate the causes and effects of the Great Migration, divide the class into pairs or small groups and provide each group with a copy of one panel from Jacob Lawrence's *Migration Series* (search "MOMA Migration Series"). For this activity, it is best to use at least eight different images. Students should discuss what they see in the visual image and write a caption that explains the image and its historical context of the Great Migration and African American history to the viewer. Each group should share its image and caption with the whole class. Then ask students to work as a class to organize the images into correct chronological order on the board as Lawrence intended in his *Migration Series*. Allow students to move around the room to discuss the correct order for the panels. Provide feedback to reorder the panels as needed. Once the panels are in the correct chronological order, ask students to explain the causes and effects of the Great Migration.

school with the whites. . . . Will vote the next election and there isn't any 'yes sir' and 'no sir'—it's all yes and no and Sam and Bill."

Wartime labor shortages prompted Mexican Americans in the Southwest to leave farmwork for urban industrial jobs. Continued political instability in Mexico, combined with increased demand for farmworkers in the United States, also encouraged more Mexicans to move across the border. Between 1917 and 1920, at least 100,000 Mexicans entered the United States; despite discrimination, large numbers stayed. If asked why, many might have echoed the words of an African American man who left New Orleans for Chicago: they were going "north for a better chance." The same was true for Puerto Ricans such as Jésus Colón, who also confronted racism. "I came to New York to poor pay, long hours, terrible working conditions, discrimination even in the slums and in the poor paying factories," Colón recalled, "where the bosses very dexterously pitted Italians against Puerto Ricans and Puerto Ricans against American Negroes and Jews."

Women were the largest group to take advantage of wartime job opportunities. About 1 million women joined the paid labor force for the first time, while another 8 million gave up low-wage service jobs for higher-paying industrial work. Americans soon got used to the sight of female streetcar conductors, train engineers, and defense workers. Though most people expected these jobs to return to men in peacetime, the war created a new comfort level with women's employment outside the home—and with women's suffrage.

The Great Migration: Union Station, Jacksonville, Florida This photograph from 1921 shows a familiar sight across the South, especially after 1917 and 1918, when wartime jobs in Northern cities offered new opportunities for African Americans seeking to escape the Jim Crow South. Northern manufacturers, facing severe wartime labor shortages, sent labor agents to the South to recruit workers. These agents often arranged loans to pay for train fare and other travel expenses; once laborers were settled and employed in the North, they repaid the loans from their wages. In a typical pattern, some of the travelers in this photograph may have previously moved from rural parts of Florida to Jacksonville, before making the leap to the urban North. Photo by Woodward, courtesy of the State Archives of Florida.

Women's Voting Rights The National American Woman Suffrage Association (NAWSA) threw the support of its 2 million members wholeheartedly into the war effort. Its president, Carrie Chapman Catt, declared that women had to prove their patriotism to win the ballot. NAWSA members in thousands of communities promoted food conservation and distributed emergency relief through organizations such as the Red Cross.

Alice Paul and the **National Woman's Party (NWP)** took a more confrontational approach toward the promotion of women's suffrage. Paul was a Quaker who had worked in the settlement movement and earned a PhD in political science. Finding as a NAWSA lobbyist that congressmen dismissed her, Paul founded the NWP in 1916. Inspired by militant British suffragists, the group began in July 1917 to picket the White House. Standing silently with their banners, Paul and other NWP activists faced arrest for obstructing traffic and were sentenced to seven months in jail. They protested by going on a hunger strike, which prison authorities met with forced feeding. Public shock at the women's treatment drew attention to the suffrage cause.

Impressed by NAWSA's patriotism and worried by the NWP's militancy, the antisuffrage Wilson reversed his position. In January 1918, he urged support for woman suffrage as a "war measure." The constitutional amendment quickly passed the House of Representatives; it took eighteen months to get through the Senate and another year to win ratification by the states. On August 26, 1920, when Tennessee voted for ratification, the Nineteenth Amendment became law. The state thus joined Texas as one of two ex-Confederate states to ratify it. In most parts of the South, the measure meant that *white* women began to vote: in this Jim Crow era, African American women's voting rights remained restricted along with men's.

In explaining suffragists' victory, historians have debated the relative effectiveness of Catt's patriotic strategy and Paul's militant protests. Both played a role in persuading Wilson and Congress to act: the Woman's Party built public attention and pressure, while the presence of NAWSA enabled the president to justify suffrage as

National Woman's Party (NWP) A political party founded in 1916 that fought for women's suffrage, and after helping to achieve that goal in 1920, advocated for an Equal Rights Amendment to the U.S. Constitution.

AP® EXAM TIP

Evaluate the impact of World War I on immigration to the United States.

AP® EXAM TIP

The impact of war on the status of women in the United States is important to know on the AP® Exam.

AP® THEME

MIG: Migration and Settlement

Students should understand how the Great Migration represented an effort by some African Americans to escape segregation, racial violence, and limited economic opportunity in the South by moving to the North and West, where they found opportunities but also forms of discrimination. The Museum of Modern Art (MOMA)'s companion Web site to their exhibition *Jacob Lawrence: Migration Series* features biographical information on Jacob Lawrence, a series of maps and charts that visualize the Great Migration, and a high-quality image of each of the sixty different panels of the painting. To access this site, search "MOMA Jacob Lawrence Migration Series."

AP® SKILLS & PROCESSES

ANALYZING HISTORICAL EVIDENCE

The documents in the **AP® THINKING LIKE A HISTORIAN** feature highlight the wartime experiences of an ethnic minority that suffered persecution during the war. The evidence here helps students understand the complex makeup of the American populace and varied reactions to German Americans in their midst.

AP® THINKING LIKE A HISTORIAN

German Americans in World War I

Before 1917, Americans expressed diverse opinions about the war in Europe. After the United States joined the Allies, however, German Americans' loyalty became suspect. German immigrant men who were not U.S. citizens were required to register as "alien enemies," and government propaganda fueled fear of alleged German spies. In April 1918, in Collinsville, Illinois, a German-born socialist named Robert Prager — who had sought U.S. citizenship and tried to enlist in the navy — was lynched by drunken miners. The following documents shed light on German Americans' wartime experiences.

1. **Advertisement, *Fatherland*, 1915.** *This ad appeared in a political journal for German Americans. The translation of the songs offered on this recording are "Germany, Germany Above All" and "Precious Homeland."*

   Patriotic German Music on Columbia Double-Disc Records

   E2039 Deutschland, Deutschland über alles. . . .

   10 in. — 75¢ Teure Heimat. . . .

   COLUMBIA GRAMOPHONE COMPANY . . . DEALERS EVERYWHERE.

2. **C. J. Hexamer, speech, Milwaukee, 1915.** *This address by a German American community leader was widely cited during a 1918 investigation by the Senate Judiciary Committee.*

   Whoever casts his Germanism from him like an old glove, is not worthy to be spit upon. . . . We have long suffered the preachment that "you Germans must allow yourselves to be assimilated, you must merge more in the American people;" but no one will ever find us prepared to step down to a lesser culture. No, we have made it our aim to elevate the others to us. . . . Be strong, and German. Remember, you German pioneers, that we are giving to this people the best the earth affords, the benefits of Germanic *kultur*.

3. **Sign in a Chicago park, 1917.**

Source: Chicago History Museum/Getty Images.

662

4. **"Lager Uber Alles" cartoon, 1918.** *This cartoon was part of an Ohio Anti-Saloon League referendum campaign to prohibit liquor sales. Ohio voters had rejected such a measure in 1915 and 1917, but in 1918 a majority voted for prohibition. Many U.S. breweries, such as Anheuser-Busch and Pabst, were owned by German Americans. "Hun" was an epithet for Germans; "Lager (Beer) Uber Alles" refers to the German national anthem cited in source 1.*

SOURCE: Courtesy of The Ohio State University Department of History.

5. **James W. Gerard, radio address, 1917.** *Gerard was U.S. ambassador to Great Britain.*

The great majority of American citizens of German descent have, in this great crisis in our history, shown themselves splendidly loyal to our flag. Everyone has a right to sympathize with any warring nation. But now that we are in the war there are only two sides, and the time has come when every citizen must declare himself American — or traitor!

. . . The Foreign Minister of Germany once said to me ". . . we have in your country 500,000 German reservists who will rise in arms against your government if you dare to make a move against Germany." Well, I told him that that might be so, but that we had 500,001 lampposts in this country, and that that was where the reservists would be hanging the day after they tried to rise. And if there are any German-Americans here who are so ungrateful for all the benefits they have received that they are still for the Kaiser, there is only one thing to do with them. And that is to hog-tie them, give them back the wooden shoes and the rags they landed in, and ship them back. . . . There is no animal that bites and kicks and squeals . . . equal to a fat German-American, if you commenced to tie him up and told him that he was on his way back to the Kaiser.

6. **Actions by New York liederkranz reported in *New Orleans Times-Picayune*, May 16, 1918.** *Liederkranz, or singing societies, played a vital role in German immigrant communities. Before World War I the city of Wheeling, West Virginia, counted eleven such societies, with names like Harmonie, Germania, and Mozart. By 1918 most liederkranz had vanished. New York City's was one of the few that did not.*

Members of the [New York] Liederkranz, an organization founded seventy-one years ago by Germans . . . met tonight and placed on record their unqualified Americanism.

. . . They declared English the official language of the organization, and for the first time in years the sound of an enemy tongue will not be heard in the club's halls. Likewise they reiterated their offer to turn the buildings over to the government as a hospital if it were necessary.

7. **Lola Gamble Clyde, 1976 interview on life in Idaho during World War I.** *In the 1970s, historians interviewed residents of rural Latah County, Idaho, about their experiences in World War I. Frank Brocke, a farmer, recalled that neighbors on their joint telephone line would slam down the phone when his mother or sister spoke German. "We had to be so careful," he said.*

I remember when they smashed out store windows at Uniontown that said [sauer]kraut. . . . Nobody would eat kraut. Throw the Kraut out, they were Germans. . . . Even the great Williamson store, he went in and gathered up everything that was made in Germany, and had a big bonfire out in the middle of the street, you know. Although he had many good German friends all over the county that had helped make him rich. . . . And if it was a German name — we'll just change our name. . . . There were some [German American] boys that got draft deferments. . . . Some of them said that their fathers were sick and dying, and their father had so much land they had to stay home and farm it for them. . . . [Local men] tarred and feathered some of them. Some of them as old men dying still resented and remembered.

SOURCES: (1) Frederick C. Luebke, *Bonds of Loyalty: German Americans and World War I* (De Kalb: Northern Illinois University Press, 1974), 109; (2) *Hearings Before the Subcommittee on the Judiciary, United States Senate, 65th Congress, Second Session* (Washington, DC: Government Printing Office, 1918), 300; (5) Gerard speech, transcript, and recording, at Library of Congress American Memory: memory.loc.gov/ammem/nfhtml/nforSpeakers01.html; (6) *New Orleans Times-Picayune*, May 16, 1918; (7) Oral histories of Idaho residents at GMU History Matters, historymatters.gmu.edu/d/2/. Excerpt courtesy of Latah County Historical Society.

ANALYZING THE EVIDENCE

1. How did conditions change for German Americans between 1915 and 1918? Describe patterns of change during the course of WWI.
2. According to these sources, what aspects of German American culture did other Americans find threatening? What forms did anti-German hostility take? Support your claim with specific examples from the sources.
3. Compare the sources that offer a German American perspective (sources 1, 2, 6, and 7) to those that represent a threat to German Americans' way of life (3, 4, 5). How did German Americans respond to growing anti-German sentiment in this period? Corroborate sources to make an argument.

AP DBQ PRACTICE

Using these sources, along with what you have learned in this chapter, write a short essay that explains which groups were singled out as "un-American" during World War I, and what continuities you see between fears and prejudices in that period, and similar fears over "hyphenated" identities in other eras of U.S. history. Describe changes and continuity over time.

TRM Find complete suggested responses in the Teacher's Resource Materials.

Wagon Decorated for the Labor Day Parade, San Diego, California, 1910 As the woman suffrage movement grew stronger in the years before and during World War I, working-class women played increasingly prominent and visible roles in its leadership. This Labor Day parade float, created by the Women's Union Label League of San Diego, showed that activists championed equal pay for women in the workplace as well as women's voting rights. "Union Label Leagues" urged middle-class shoppers to purchase only clothing with a union label, certifying that the item had been manufactured under safe conditions and the workers who made it had received a fair wage. San Diego Historical Society.

a "reward" for loyal women's service. Neither strategy might have worked, however, without the extraordinary impact of the Great War. Across the globe, before 1914, the only places where women had full suffrage were New Zealand, Australia, Finland, and Norway. After World War I, many nations moved to enfranchise women. The new Soviet Union acted first, in 1917, with Great Britain and Canada following in 1918; by 1920, the measure had passed in Germany, Austria, Poland, Czechoslovakia, and Hungary as well as the United States. (Major exceptions were France and Italy, where women did not gain voting rights until after World War II, and Switzerland, which held out until 1971.) Thus, while World War I introduced modern horrors on the battlefield — machine guns and poison gas — its positive side effects included women's political rights and, in the United States, new economic opportunities.

AP® SKILLS & PROCESSES

COMPARISON

What were the different effects of African Americans', Mexican Americans', and women's civilian mobilization during World War I?

CATASTROPHE AT VERSAILLES

What arguments did U.S. political leaders make for and against ratification of the Versailles treaty?

The idealistic Wilson argued that no victor should be declared after World War I: only "peace among equals" could last. Having won at an incredible price, the governments of Britain and France had zero interest in such a plan. But the devastation wrought by the war created popular pressure for a just and enduring outcome. At the peace conference held in 1919 at Versailles, near Paris, Wilson scored a diplomatic victory when the Allies chose to base the talks on his **Fourteen Points**, a blueprint for peace that he had presented a year earlier in a speech to Congress.

Fourteen Points
Principles for a new world order proposed in 1919 by President Woodrow Wilson as a basis for peace negotiations at Versailles. Among them were open diplomacy, freedom of the seas, free trade, territorial integrity, arms reduction, national self-determination, and creation of the League of Nations.

AP® SKILLS & PROCESSES

COMPARISON

The **COMPARISON** question asks students to identify the different effects of the war on various groups. Because these three groups shared second-class status at the time, students should look in particular for ways the war affected this status.

TRM Find complete suggested responses in the Teacher's Resource Materials.

CHECK FOR UNDERSTANDING

Ask students: **What changes did U.S. participation in World War I bring about on the home front?** *U.S. participation in World War I had drastic effects on the home front. Like during the Civil War, the federal government seized the initiative to manage the economy in the name of wartime exigencies by directing military production through the War Industries Board and managing labor through the National War Labor Board. Also similar to what occurred during the Civil War, the federal government limited dissent, this time through the 1918 Sedition Act. Demographically, massive numbers of African Americans left their small agricultural plots in the South for war industry jobs in the North, as part of the so-called Great Migration. Women also finally achieved the right to vote in national elections per the terms of the Nineteenth Amendment (1920), which President Wilson claimed was a war measure to win suffragist support for U.S. participation in the conflict.*

Wilson's Points embodied an important strand in progressivism. They called for open diplomacy; "absolute freedom of navigation upon the seas"; arms reduction; removal of trade barriers; and national self-determination for peoples in the Austro-Hungarian, Russian, and German empires. Essential to Wilson's vision — the fourteenth of his Fourteen Points — was the creation of a "general association of nations" — eventually called the **League of Nations** — that would forge "mutual guarantees of political independence and territorial integrity by international covenant." The League would mediate disputes, supervise arms reduction, and — according to its crucial Article X — curb aggressor nations through collective military action. Wilson hoped the League would "end all wars." But his ideals had marked limits and in negotiations he confronted harsh realities.

AP® EXAM TIP

Understanding the impact of Woodrow Wilson's Fourteen Points in the post-World War I world is critical for success on the AP® Exam.

League of Nations
An international organization of nations to prevent future hostilities, proposed by President Woodrow Wilson in the aftermath of World War I. Although the League of Nations did form, the United States never became a member state.

The Fate of Wilson's Ideas

The peace conference included ten thousand representatives from around the globe, but leaders of France, Britain, and the United States dominated the proceedings. When Japan's delegation proposed a declaration for equal treatment of all races, the Allies rejected it. Similarly, the Allies ignored a global Pan-African Congress, organized by W. E. B. Du Bois and other black leaders, and snubbed Arab representatives even though they had been key military allies during the war. Wilson, like his British and French counterparts, could not imagine allowing colonized peoples of color to have an equal place at the table.

The British and French delegations further limited the talks by excluding two key players: Russia, because they distrusted its communist leaders, and Germany, because they planned to dictate terms to their defeated foe. Even Italy's prime minister — included at first among the influential "Big Four" because in 1915 Italy had switched to the Allied side — withdrew from the conference, aggrieved at the way British and French leaders marginalized him. For Wilson's "peace among equals," it was a terrible start.

Prime Minister David Lloyd George of Britain and Premier Georges Clemenceau of France imposed harsh punishments on Germany. Unbeknownst to others at the time, they had already made secret agreements to divide up Germany's African colonies and take them as spoils of war. At Versailles, they also forced the defeated nation to pay a staggering $33 billion in reparations and surrender coal supplies, merchant ships, valuable patents, and even territory along the French border. These terms caused keen resentment and economic hardship in Germany, and over the following two decades they helped lead to World War II.

Despite these conditions, Wilson managed to influence the **Treaty of Versailles** in important ways. He intervened repeatedly to soften conditions imposed on Germany. In accordance with the Fourteen Points, he worked with the other Allies to fashion nine new nations, stretching from the Baltic to the Mediterranean (Map 20.4 and Map 20.5). These were intended as a buffer to protect Western Europe from communist Russia; the plan also embodied Wilson's principle of self-determination for European states. Elsewhere in the world, the Allies dismantled their enemies' empires but did not create independent nations, keeping colonized people subordinate to European power. France, for example, refused to give up its long-standing occupation of Indochina; Clemenceau's snub of future Vietnamese leader Ho Chi Minh, who sought representation at Versailles, had grave long-term consequences for both France and the United States.

Treaty of Versailles
The 1919 treaty that ended World War I. The agreement redrew the map of the world, assigned Germany sole responsibility for the war, and saddled it with a debt of $33 billion in war damages. Its long-term impact around the globe — including the creation of British and French imperial "mandates" — was catastrophic.

The establishment of a British mandate in Palestine (now Israel) also proved crucial. During the war, British foreign secretary Sir Arthur Balfour had stated that his country would work to establish there a "national home for the Jewish people," with the condition that "nothing shall be done which may prejudice the civil and religious rights of existing non-Jewish communities in Palestine." Under the British mandate, thousands of Jews moved to Palestine and purchased land, in some cases evicting Palestinian tenants. As early as 1920, riots erupted between Jews and Palestinians — a situation that, even before World War II, escalated beyond British control.

AP® APPLY THE TIP

Provide students with a copy of Wilson's Fourteen Points. Ask them to work in pairs or small groups to analyze each point and identify in the margin which of the causes of World War I each point was designed to address. Then ask students to use **MAP 20.4** and **20.5** on p. 666 and the supporting text to highlight the ideas in Wilson's Fourteen Points that were actually included in the Treaty of Versailles. Ask them to complete a Venn diagram that compares Wilson's Fourteen Points to the Treaty of Versailles. Lead a class discussion in which students discuss the reasons for lack of consistency between the documents and the implications for the future of European politics. Ask students to additionally consider the degree to which the Treaty of Versailles addressed the causes of World War I.

CHECK FOR UNDERSTANDING

Ask students: **What was the fate of Wilson's postwar ideas?** *His ideas were only imperfectly represented in the Treaty of Versailles, primarily in the notion of self-determination, reflected in the breakup of the Central Powers' empires, and in the international framework for peace, the League of Nations. His desire to establish "war without victory" was rejected by Britain and France, which had endured the brunt of the fighting.*

MAP 20.4 and MAP 20.5 Europe and the Middle East Before and After World War I World War I and its aftermath dramatically altered the landscape of Europe and the Middle East. Before the war, the most powerful nations belonged to two alliances: the Central Powers (Germany, Austria-Hungary, and Italy) and the Entente (Great Britain, France, and Russia). The latter's victory, along with the 1917 communist revolution in Russia, dramatically reshaped power relations. Collapse of the German, Austro-Hungarian, and Russian empires allowed reconstitution of Poland and creation of a string of new states along the Baltic Sea and in Eastern Europe, based on the principle of national (ethnic) self-determination. The demise of the Ottoman Empire prompted creation of four quasi-independent territories, or "mandates": Iraq, Syria, Lebanon, and Palestine. The League of Nations stipulated that their affairs would be supervised by one of the victorious Allied powers.

The Versailles treaty thus created conditions for horrific future bloodshed, and it must be judged one of history's great catastrophes. Balfour astutely described Clemenceau, Lloyd George, and Wilson as "all-powerful, all-ignorant men, sitting there and carving up continents." Wilson, however, remained optimistic as he returned home, even though his health was beginning to fail. The president hoped the new League of Nations, authorized by the treaty, would moderate the settlement and secure peaceful resolutions of other disputes. For this to occur, U.S. participation was crucial.

AP® SKILLS & PROCESSES

ARGUMENTATION

In what ways did the Treaty of Versailles embody — or fail to embody — Wilson's Fourteen Points?

Congress Rejects the Treaty

The outlook for U.S. ratification was not promising. Though major opinion makers and religious denominations supported the treaty, openly hostile Republicans held a majority in the Senate. One group, called the "irreconcilables," consisted of western progressive Republicans such as Hiram Johnson of California and Robert La Follette of Wisconsin, who opposed U.S. involvement in European affairs. They had the popular support of many Americans, including Irish and German immigrants, who believed the League would not be truly independent but would serve as a diplomatic and political tool for the powerful British empire. Another group, led by Senator Henry Cabot Lodge of Massachusetts, worried that Article X — the provision for collective security — would prevent the United States from pursuing an independent foreign policy. Was the nation, Lodge asked, "willing to have the youth of America ordered to war" by an international body?

AP® EXAM TIP

Evaluate the causes and effects of the failure of the U.S. Senate to ratify the Treaty of Versailles.

Some Republican opponents of the treaty were isolationists who wanted to limit U.S. military engagement overseas. Others, like Lodge, strongly favored U.S. expansion and advancement of U.S. overseas interests, both economically and militarily, including interventions in Latin America. His primary concern was that the League of Nations would have the power to call up U.S. troops to protect a vulnerable nation, and might send them to war without approval from U.S. Congress.

Senators proposed an array of amendments, but Wilson refused to accept any of them, especially to placate Lodge, a hated rival. "I shall consent to nothing," the president told the French ambassador. "The Senate must take its medicine." To mobilize support, Wilson embarked on an exhausting speaking tour. His impassioned defense of the League of Nations brought audiences to tears, but the strain proved too much for the president. While visiting Colorado in September 1919, Wilson collapsed. A week later, back in Washington, he suffered a stroke that left one side of his body paralyzed.

Wilson still urged Democratic senators to reject all Republican amendments. Lodge brought the treaty to the floor with a set of reservations attached. When it came up for a vote in November 1919, it failed to win the required two-thirds majority. A second attempt, in March 1920, fell seven votes short, as a few Democratic senators joined Republicans in voting against it. The treaty was dead, and so was Wilson's leadership. The president never fully recovered from his stroke. During the last eighteen months of his administration, the government drifted as Wilson's wife, his physician, and various cabinet members secretly took charge.

The United States never ratified the Versailles treaty or joined the League of Nations. Though 63 governments joined the new League, headquartered in Geneva, the United States's absence hampered their work. League members also had to grapple with the issues the U.S. Senate had raised: Canadian delegates, for example, repeatedly sought to weaken the League's collective security provisions, because they feared the League might drag Canada into another European war. (Ironically, the League's weakness had the same result: in the 1930s, brazen acts of aggression by Germany, Italy, and Japan exposed the League's inability to protect its members and created the conditions for World War II.) When Wilson died in 1924, his dream of a just and peaceful international order lay in ruins.

The impact of World War I on future generations can hardly be overstated. Despite bids for power by Britain and France, Europe's hold on its colonial empires

AP® SKILLS & PROCESSES

ARGUMENTATION

Well-qualified arguments often recognize multiple perspectives. For this question, challenge students to account for how the Treaty of Versailles reflected a Wilsonian belief in collective security, while also acknowledging the ways in which the League failed to reflect the totality of his vision. Historical questions are not often binary; therefore, encourage students to develop a response that explains each perspective from the question. This often means students will start with broad concepts such as "collective security," as an example of embodying and "war-guilt clause," as an example of failure. Remind students Argumentation is a difficult skill and takes exercises such as this one to flesh out understandings.

TRM Find complete suggested responses in the Teacher's Resource Materials.

AP® APPLY THE TIP

Provide students with a series of political cartoons depicting the failures of the Treaty of Versailles and the failure of the U.S. Senate to ratify the treaty. There are many cartoons to use including, but not limited to, "Peace and Future Cannon Fodder", "Interrupting the Ceremony" by John McCutcheon, "Seeing Things," and "The Lamb from the Slaughter." Lead a class discussion to distinguish between the problems that Wilson believed weakened the Treaty of Versailles and those that the Senate opposed in the treaty. List these differences in a T-chart on the board. Then ask students to evaluate the causes and effects of the failure of the Treaty of Versailles.

AP® THEME

WOR: America in the World

Despite Wilson's deep involvement in postwar negotiations, the U.S. Senate refused to ratify the Treaty of Versailles or join the League of Nations. Make sure students understand how this was quickly viewed as a major weakness in the stability of the world order.

The U.S. Senate Accused, 1920 The "Treaty of Peace" lies murdered in this cartoon by *New York World* artist Rollin Kirby. "Humanity" points her finger at the U.S. Senate, which rejected Wilson's entreaties and refused to ratify the treaty. The United States's failure to join the League of Nations significantly damaged the League's prospects of success. Everett Collection Historical / Alamy Stock Photo.

never recovered. The United States appeared to turn its back on the world when it rejected the Versailles treaty. But in laying claim to Hawaii and the Philippines, asserting power in Latin America, and intervening in Asia, the United States had already entangled itself deeply in global affairs. By 1918, the nation had gained too much diplomatic clout — and was too dependent on overseas trade — for isolation to be a realistic long-term option. Future U.S. policymakers, as leaders of a rising world power, inherited many of the problems that resulted from Versailles, not only in Europe but in Palestine, Vietnam, and other locales.

On the home front, the shorter-term effects of World War I were no less dramatic. Wartime jobs and prosperity ushered in an era of exuberant consumerism, while the achievements of women's voting rights seemed to presage a new progressive era. But as peace returned, it became clear that the war had not advanced reform. Rather than embracing government activism, Americans of the 1920s proved eager to relinquish it.

SUMMARY

Between 1877 and 1918, the United States rose as a major economic and military power. Justifications for overseas expansion emphasized access to global markets, the importance of sea power, and the need to police international misconduct and trade. These justifications shaped U.S. policy toward European powers in Latin America, and victory in the War of 1898 enabled the United States to take control of former Spanish colonies in the Caribbean and Pacific. Victory, however, also led to bloody conflict in the Philippines as the United States struggled to suppress Filipino resistance to American rule.

After 1899, the United States aggressively asserted its interests in Asia and Latin America. In China, the United States used the so-called Boxer Rebellion to make good its claim to an "open door" to Chinese markets. Later, President Theodore Roosevelt strengthened relations with Japan, and his successor, William Howard Taft, supported U.S. business interests in China. In the Caribbean, the United States constructed the Panama Canal and regularly exercised the right, claimed under the Roosevelt Corollary, to intervene in the affairs of states in the region. President Woodrow Wilson publicly disparaged the imperialism of his predecessors but repeatedly used the U.S. military to "police" Mexico.

At the outbreak of World War I, the United States asserted neutrality, but its economic ties to the Allies rapidly undercut that claim. In 1917, German submarine attacks drew the United States into the war on the side of Britain and France. Involvement in the war profoundly transformed the economy, politics, and society of the nation, resulting in an economic boom, mass migrations of workers to industrial centers, and the achievement of national voting rights. At the Paris Peace Conference, Wilson attempted to implement his Fourteen Points. However, the designs of the Allies in Europe undermined the Treaty of Versailles, while Republican resistance at home prevented ratification of the treaty. Although Wilson's dream of a just international order failed, the United States had taken its place as a major world power.

CHECK FOR UNDERSTANDING

Ask students: **What arguments did U.S. political leaders make for and against ratification of the Versailles treaty?** *President Wilson and his allies, who supported the Treaty of Versailles, felt that its collective security provisions would moderate future conflicts and bring about peaceful resolutions to disputes. While most Americans supported this view, many Republican senators did not. Recognizing the cost to America's youth of the war just ended (which was, albeit, much less than the sacrifice of Germany, the United Kingdom, France, and others), some did not favor the United States entangling itself in Europe's problems. Senator Henry Cabot Lodge went even further; he did not favor American troops to be engaged anywhere on the orders of an international body like the League of Nations not responsive to the American people.*

CHECK FOR UNDERSTANDING

Use the **AP® LEARNING FOCUS** question from the beginning of the chapter to provide a check on students' understanding of the chapter as a whole: **Why did the United States become a major power on the world stage by the 1910s, and what impact did this have at home and abroad?** *Between 1877 and 1918, the United States both rose to and recoiled from responsibilities attendant to a major economic and military power. The goals of American involvement in international affairs included military strategy, expansion of economic markets, and access to natural resources. Justification for American imperialism came in the idea of American exceptionalism, the notion that Americans had a unique destiny to foster democracy and civilization across the globe. Although democracy was the justification, Americans exploited foreign nations and often remained in foreign countries despite the will of the people, as was seen in the Philippines, Cuba, and China. With the outbreak of WWI and America's eventual entry into the war, Woodrow Wilson sought to bring the world together in the League of Nations so that war might be avoided in the future. The Allies' victory in WWI introduced the United States and its goals for democratic reform onto the platform of the world stage.*

✓ LearningCurve

Remind students to go online to complete the LearningCurve quiz for this chapter.

CHAPTER 20 REVIEW

AP® CONTENT REVIEW

Answer these questions to demonstrate your understanding of the chapter's main ideas.

1. How did the U.S. government in the late nineteenth century began to exert military influence in different regions of the world?
2. Why and how did U.S. actions influence Asia in this period? What impact did U.S. policies have on Latin America? In what ways were these influences similar and different?
3. Why and how did participation in World War I change the economy and society of the United States?
4. What arguments did U.S. political leaders make for and against ratification of the Versailles treaty?

AP® TERMS TO KNOW

Identify and explain the significance of each term below.

Key Concepts and Events

American exceptionalism (p. 643)
Teller Amendment (p. 644)
Insular Cases (p. 647)
Platt Amendment (p. 647)
"open door" policy (p. 649)
Root-Takahira Agreement (p. 650)
Panama Canal (p. 651)
Roosevelt Corollary (p. 651)
Zimmermann telegram (p. 655)
War Industries Board (WIB) (p. 657)
National War Labor Board (NWLB) (p. 657)
Sedition Act of 1918 (p. 659)
Great Migration (p. 660)
National Woman's Party (NWP) (p. 661)
Fourteen Points (p. 664)
League of Nations (p. 665)
Treaty of Versailles (p. 665)

Key People

Theodore Roosevelt (p. 643)
Alfred Mahan (p. 643)
Queen Liliuokalani (p. 645)
Emilio Aguinaldo (p. 647)
Woodrow Wilson (p. 651)
Porfirio Díaz (p. 652)
Herbert Hoover (p. 657)
Alice Paul (p. 661)

AP® MAKING CONNECTIONS

Recognize the larger developments and continuities within and across chapters by answering these questions.

1. Read again the documents from "Thinking Like a Historian: Representing Indians" in Chapter 15. In what ways might ideas about Native Americans have informed attitudes toward Hawaiians, Filipinos, and other people of color overseas? How might this explain which peoples Woodrow Wilson included and excluded in his ideal of "national self-determination"? Write a short essay in which you explain how Americans' policies and attitudes toward Native peoples within North America shaped U.S. foreign policy between 1898 and 1918.
2. Review the images in this chapter that show American soldiers and civilians during World War I. What do they tell us about the opportunities and risks that the war posed for different groups of Americans? What constraints might young men and women of different ethnic backgrounds have faced, and what factors might they have considered, when deciding what wartime activities to pursue?

KEY TURNING POINTS

Refer to the timeline at the start of this chapter for help in answering the following question.

Identify at least five events from the chapter chronology that demonstrate the rising global power of the United States. Compare their consequences. How might an observer from another country have interpreted the United States's actions in each case? Include the historical situation of your observer and base your narrative on evidence from the textbook.

669

TRM Find complete suggested responses in the Teacher's Resource Materials.

AP® SKILLS & PROCESSES

CONTINUITY AND CHANGE

AP® CONTENT REVIEW 1 asks students to consider the changing role of American foreign policy — specifically military engagement — in the late nineteenth century. Note: This is the same question as the section-opening prompt on p. 642.

AP® SKILLS & PROCESSES

COMPARISON

AP® CONTENT REVIEW 2 invites students to compare American foreign policy in two different regions. Note: This is the same question as the section-opening prompt on p. 647.

AP® SKILLS & PROCESSES

CONTINUITY AND CHANGE

AP® CONTENT REVIEW 3 encourages students to think about the domestic effects of American participation in the war. Note: This is the same question as the section-opening prompt on p. 653.

AP® SKILLS & PROCESSES

COMPARISON

AP® CONTENT REVIEW 4 asks students to compare the arguments of different groups of Americans regarding a crucial foreign policy issue. Note: This is the same question as the section-opening prompt on p. 664.

TRM Find definitions for these terms in the **Glossary/Glosario** in the Teacher's Resource Materials.

AP® SKILLS & PROCESSES

CONTINUITY AND CHANGE

KEY TURNING POINTS encourages students to consider significant examples that illustrate the major theme of the era, the nation's growing global power.

TRM Find complete suggested responses in the Teacher's Resource Materials.

AP PRACTICE QUESTIONS

MULTIPLE CHOICE QUESTIONS *Choose the correct answer for each question.*

Questions 1–3 refer to this excerpt.

"It will be our wish that the processes of peace, when they are begun, shall be absolutely open and that they shall involve and permit henceforth no secret understandings of any kind. The day of conquest and aggrandizement has gone by; so is the day of secret covenants entered into in the interest of particular governments and likely at some unlooked-for moment to upset the peace of the world. . . .

We entered this war because violations of right had occurred which touched us to the quick and made the life of our own people impossible unless they were corrected and the world secure once for all against their recurrence. What we demand in this war, therefore, is nothing peculiar to ourselves. It is that the world be made fit and safe to live in. . . . All the peoples of the world are in effect partners in this interest and for our own part we see very clearly that unless justice be done to others it will not be done to us."

Woodrow Wilson, Address to Congress, January 8, 1918

1. Which of the following issues of the period was Wilson most likely concerned with in the excerpt?
   - **a.** The defense of humanitarian and democratic principles
   - **b.** The pursuit of a unilateral American foreign policy
   - **c.** The rise of fascism and totalitarianism
   - **d.** The economic opportunities presented by imperialism
2. Based on the excerpt, which of the following would Wilson most likely NOT have supported?
   - **a.** The Washington Naval Conference
   - **b.** The Selective Service Act
   - **c.** The Kellogg-Briand Pact
   - **d.** Unrestricted submarine warfare
3. In what way did Woodrow Wilson's argument in this excerpt illustrate dramatic change in the relationship of the United States and the rest of the world in comparison to earlier American foreign policy?
   - **a.** Woodrow Wilson argues for the United States to remain neutral and allow European nations to settle their own differences.
   - **b.** The argument in this excerpt illustrates Wilson's belief that the US should limit its involvement in foreign affairs.
   - **c.** The argument in this excerpt calls for the United States to limit its influence to the Western Hemisphere.
   - **d.** Woodrow Wilson argues for the US to play a significant role in the establishment of peace settlements following World War I.

Questions 4–6 refer to this excerpt.

"[The nation] is of age and it can do what it pleases; it can spurn the traditions of the past; it can repudiate the principles upon which the nation rests; it can employ force instead of reason; it can substitute might for right . . . but it cannot repeal the moral law or escape the punishment decreed for the violation of human rights. . . .

Some argue that American rule in the Philippine Islands will result in the better education of the Filipinos. Be not deceived. If we expect to maintain a colonial policy, we shall not find it to our advantage to educate the people. The educated Filipinos are now in revolt against us, and the most ignorant ones have made the least resistance to our domination. If we are to govern them without their consent and give them no voice in determining the taxes which they must pay, we dare not educate them, lest they learn to read the Declaration of Independence and Constitution of the United States and mock us for our inconsistency."

Speech by William Jennings Bryan, presidential candidate, at the Democratic National Convention, August 8, 1900

4. In highlighting how the nation could "spurn the traditions of the past," Bryan was most likely referring to
   - **a.** ideas articulated in George Washington's Farewell Address.
   - **b.** the use of government power in the confining of American Indians to reservations.
   - **c.** government policies promoting the assimilation of immigrants.
   - **d.** increased barriers to Asian migration.
5. Based on the excerpt, Bryan most likely supported which of the following?
   - **a.** Platt Amendment
   - **b.** Roosevelt Corollary to the Monroe Doctrine
   - **c.** Teller Amendment
   - **d.** Writings of Alfred Mahan
6. The excerpt best reflects which of the following?
   - **a.** Heightened public debates over America's role in the world
   - **b.** The moral obligation of the wealthy to help the less fortunate
   - **c.** The use of Social Darwinism to justify the success of nations
   - **d.** The perception that the Western frontier was "closed"

SHORT ANSWER QUESTIONS

Read each question carefully and write a short response. Use evidence from the text to support your claims.

"[T]he substance of the Draft Covenant . . . [included the] guarantee of independence and territorial integrity . . . and asserted the right of the League of Nations to concern itself about 'war or threat of war' anywhere in the world. Articles XII through XV established procedures for mediation and arbitration and called for a 'Permanent Court of International Justice.' Article XVI laid down the League's authority to impose economic boycotts and recommend the use of force. . . . [A]ll these features of Wilson's . . . were in the Draft Covenant. . . . It was a remarkable achievement, and the lion's share of the credit belonged to Wilson."

John Milton Cooper Jr., *Woodrow Wilson: A Biography*, 2009

"The U.S. and transnational labor and Left debate over the Versailles Treaty, League [of Nations] and ILO [International Labor Organization] exposed fundamental contradictions in Wilsonian internationalism. . . . [F]rom the perspective of Left activists, a League comprised of the same government elites who had caused World War I was unlikely to fundamentally alter the imperial status quo in ways that would advance the interests of the world's workers or ensure future peace and prosperity. . . . Socialist and labor activists unmasked the Wilson administration's tendencies toward . . . the belief that other nations could be immeasurably improved by reshaping them in an American mold."

Elizabeth McKillen, *Making the World Safe for Workers: Labor, the Left and Wilsonian Internationalism*, 2013

1. Using the two excerpts provided, answer (a), (b), and (c).

a. Briefly explain ONE major difference between Cooper's and McKillen's historical interpretations of the late nineteenth and early twentieth centuries.

b. Briefly explain how ONE specific historical event or development in the period 1918 to 1922 not directly mentioned in the excerpts could be used to support Cooper's argument.

c. Briefly explain how ONE specific historical event or development in the period 1918 to 1922 not directly mentioned in the excerpts could be used to support McKillen's argument.

2. Answer (a), (b), and (c).

a. Briefly explain why ONE of the following developments was the most significant factor contributing to American involvement in World War I.

- German submarine policy
- American neutrality
- Financial and commercial interests

b. Provide ONE historical example to support your argument in (a).

c. Provide specific evidence why ONE of the other options was a less influential factor contributing to American involvement in the war.

3. Answer (a), (b), and (c).

a. Briefly explain why ONE of the following developments was the most significant change in the United States that resulted from American involvement in World War I.

- Restrictions on civil liberties
- Advances for womens' rights
- Nativist campaigns

b. Provide ONE specific historical event or development to support your argument in (a).

c. Provide specific evidence why ONE of the other developments represented a less significant change in the United States that resulted from American involvement in World War I.

TRM Find complete suggested responses in the Teacher's Resource Materials.

21 CHAPTER

Unsettled Prosperity: From War to Depression

1919–1932

Chapter 21 — AP® Assessment Weight and Pacing Guide

The assessment weight on the AP® U.S. History Exam for Chapters 17–23 is 10–17 percent. This chapter falls in Unit 7 of the AP® U.S. History Curriculum, covering Period 7: 1890–1945.

This pacing guide is based on a schedule with 120 sessions of 50 minutes each before the AP® U.S. History Exam. If you have a different number of sessions before the exam, you can modify the pacing to meet your needs. If you have additional time, consider incorporating quizzes, released AP® U.S. History questions, practice exams, writing practice, and other instructional activities.

	Traditional Schedule	Block Schedule
Chapter 21	4 days	2 days

Daily Pacing Guide

	Content Focus	Essential Question
Day 1	Resurgent Conservatism	How and why did the United States take a conservative turn in the 1920s?
Day 2	Making a Modern Consumer Economy	What were the primary characteristics of the American economy in the 1920s?
Day 3	The Politics and Culture of a Diversifying Nation	What were the main causes of cultural conflict in the 1920s?
Day 4	The Coming of the Great Depression	What domestic and global economic factors caused the Great Depression?

AP® Alignment

Section Heading	AP® Topic	AP® Theme
Resurgent Conservatism	7.6, 7.8	MIG
Making a Modern Consumer Economy	7.7	WXT
The Politics and Culture of a Diversifying Nation	7.8	MIG, ARC
The Coming of the Great Depression	7.9	WXT

*Should changes be made to the Course Framework in the future, an updated alignment will be placed on our AP® updates page at go.bfwpub.com/ap-course-updates.

Chapter 21 — Overview

Chapter 21 focuses attention on the political, economic, and cultural upheavals of the 1920s and introduces the cataclysmic changes associated with the Great Depression. The chapter begins by examining the reasons for and impact of the resurgence of conservatism and rejection of Progressive ideas symbolized by the election of 1920 and the administration of Warren G. Harding. The rise of consumerism altered both the American economy and culture by establishing and supporting a national identity and popularizing a suburban lifestyle. In addition to political and economic change, the decade of the 1920s dramatically altered the culture of the U.S. forever, seen with the changing views of women and African Americans in American society. Finally, this chapter analyzes the underlying weaknesses within the American economy and political philosophy that led to the Great Depression.

Chapter 21 — Resources

The following resources can be found in the Teacher's Resource Materials (TRM) that accompany the book. You can access the TRM via the book's digital platform, by clicking the TRM links found here in your Teacher's Edition e-book, or by contacting your representative to access the resources online. Visit **bfwpub.com/henretta10e** to learn more.

TRM Chapter 21 Lecture Presentation Slides

TRM Chapter 21 Outline with AP® Focus

TRM Chapter 21 Lecture Strategies

TRM Chapter 21 Suggested Responses

TRM Handout 21.1 — Causation: Red Scare

TRM Handout 21.2 — Contextualization: Consumer Culture of the 1920s

TRM Handout 21.3 — Thematic Analysis: The Automobile

TRM Handout 21.4 — Comparison: Ku Klux Klan

Chapter 21 — Essential Activity

Assign each student to research and assume the identity of one individual important to U.S. development in the 1920s. Before class, students should research their assigned individual and prepare to introduce themselves. Arrange desks or chairs so that students can sit facing one another. Set a timer for two minutes and allow the students to introduce themselves and ask each other questions before rotating tables. Students should write the other person's name and main ideas and determine if they would be an ally or an enemy. At the end of the "speed dating" session, ask students to engage in a "reception" during which they should try to find like-minded individuals with whom they share common goals and accomplishments. Once students are in groups (or left alone), debrief the exercise by asking students to make a historical argument to explain the groupings. Discuss the different groups as representative of 1920s culture.

Chapter 21 — Bell Ringers

The following activities take no more than 5–15 minutes of your class period and offer an effective and engaging way to begin your lessons and for students to apply AP® Skills & Processes:

- Ask students to define the term "culture war" and give examples of conflicts that could fall under that definition. Then ask them to explain why culture wars are difficult to win and are almost impossible to negotiate. *Answers will vary, but should include the following: culture wars are difficult to win because it is hard to convince a group or individual that their culture is "wrong." Culture wars usually involve moral or religious issues on which people have a hard time compromising.*
- To introduce a lesson on the Harlem Renaissance or a discussion on race in the 1920s, provide students with a copy of the poem "Dinner Guest, Me" by Langston Hughes. Read the poem aloud, giving emphasis to its jazz-like rhythm. Then ask students to analyze the poem as a primary source on race relations in the 1920s. Ask students to extend their analysis by explaining the intended audience, purpose, historical context, and point of view of the author. *Answers will vary.*

NOTES

TEACHING STRATEGY

Help students identify the chapter's argument for 1919 as the start of a new era, which was dominated by three main themes: limited government, consumerism, and cultural warfare. To initiate class discussion, ask students to explore how these three themes might be related to each other. The text also suggests that the patterns established in this period have dominated American life ever since, so you might also begin this chapter by discussing ways that mass media, Hollywood, cars, and consumerism shape contemporary American life. For a complete suggested response to the **AP® LEARNING FOCUS** question, see p. 700.

21

CHAPTER

Unsettled Prosperity: From War to Depression

1919–1932

AP® LEARNING FOCUS

Why did cultural and political conflict erupt in the 1920s, and what factors led to the Great Depression?

While the United States largely avoided the destruction and disillusionment of World War I, the conflict still marked a crucial historical divide for Americans, and the country entered a distinctly new era after 1919 — one that was both prosperous and contentious. Progressivism flagged and gave way to a business-centered philosophy of limited government. A surging manufacturing economy delivered a cornucopia of consumer goods to a growing middle class. In the halls of government and in the streets, Americans clashed over what a modern society should look like — and over who defined the meaning of "American." In the economically booming and socially turbulent years between World War I and the Great Depression, the defining themes were limited government, consumerism, and cultural warfare.

The 1920s established patterns in American life that would hold for the remainder of the twentieth century. The nation had become urban. Mass media and Hollywood shaped popular culture. The automobile became an affordable mass commodity, even a necessity, and soon changed the nature of everyday life. Many Americans celebrated the dawning of what they called a "new era," defined by freer individual lifestyles, convenient consumer technologies, and "modern" ways of thinking. Others saw this emerging modernity as a threat. Groups of native-born, Protestant Americans, for instance, battled with immigrants over national belonging. White Americans frequently lashed out at black Americans — often in deadly ways — over economic opportunity. And Catholic, Protestant, Jewish, and secular Americans clashed over everything from the prohibition of alcohol to the teaching of evolution.

By the election of 1932, political and cultural divides had hardened. Decades of populist and progressive movements, dating to the 1880s, had asked "whose government?" In the 1920s, the question took on a broader cast: "whose country?" Economically, too, there were signs of distress. The abundance that fueled the "roaring twenties" proved short-lived, as the nation slid from consumer boom into the harrowing years of the Great Depression.

670

Celebrating the Fourth of July, 1926 This *Life* magazine cover celebrates two famous symbols of the 1920s: jazz music and the "flapper," in her rolled down stockings and scandalously short skirt. The flags at the top record the latest slang expressions, including "so's your old man" and "step on it" ("it" being the accelerator of an automobile, in a decade when cars were America's hottest commodity). Americans embraced new and exuberant forms of consumption and material well-being in the 1920s, but in an age of alcohol prohibition and the rise of the Ku Klux Klan, they also contended over deeply held beliefs and values. Picture Research Consultants & Archives.

TEACHING STRATEGY

Use *Life* magazine covers from the 1920s to help chronicle the stereotypical lifestyle of the Jazz Age and that of flappers in particular. Dozens of these images are available online. Students could discuss what the images convey and how they may have created, rather than simply reflected, perceptions of the era's culture.

AP® SKILLS & PROCESSES

CONTINUITY AND CHANGE

Use the **TIMELINE** to help students begin thinking about how the period from 1919 to 1932 could constitute a distinct historical period. This activity may be more challenging for students than those in other chapters. As the chapter opener suggests, 1919 reflects both the conclusion of war issues with the completion of the Treaty of Versailles and the beginning of controversies with the Red Scare, Palmer raids, and race riots. Textbooks often end the chapter on this era in 1929 or 1930, with the start of the Great Depression. However, this chapter's end date points to the election of FDR and the subsequent New Deal. In ending the chapter where it does, the authors include the stock market crash and early years of the depression within the same era, which highlights the economic expansion of the postwar period, fueled by consumer spending. This periodization provides an opportunity for students to explore different periodization choices and how they might frame an era differently. Students could discuss how the chapter might look different if the authors ended it in 1929 rather than 1932 and the message the authors seem to be giving about the economy of the 1920s.

AP® THEME

NAT: American and National Identity

Increased fear of radicalism led the government to place restrictions on speech during World War I. This anxiety continued in the early postwar years, leading to a Red Scare, as well as attacks on labor activism and immigrant culture.

TIMELINE

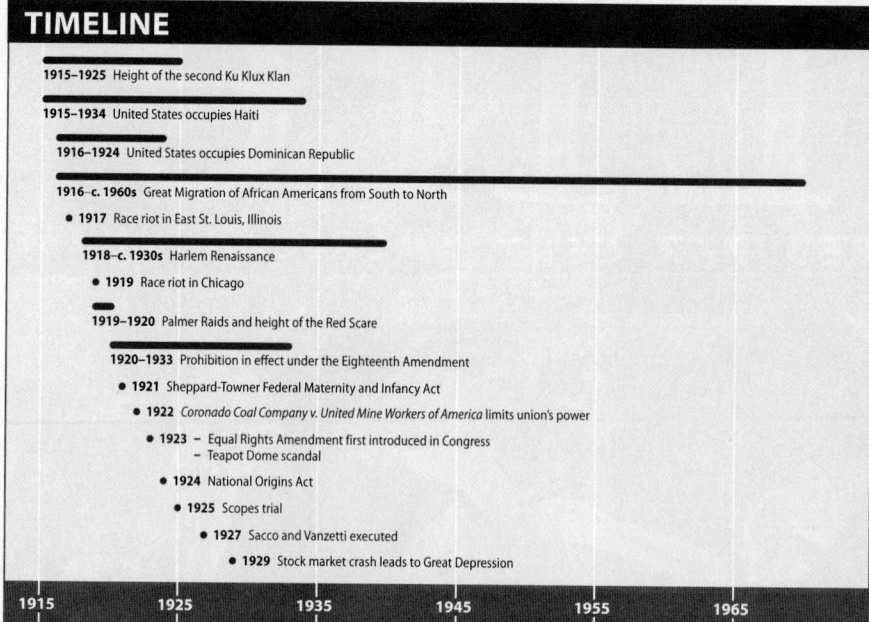

- **1915–1925** Height of the second Ku Klux Klan
- **1915–1934** United States occupies Haiti
- **1916–1924** United States occupies Dominican Republic
- **1916–c. 1960s** Great Migration of African Americans from South to North
- **1917** Race riot in East St. Louis, Illinois
- **1918–c. 1930s** Harlem Renaissance
- **1919** Race riot in Chicago
- **1919–1920** Palmer Raids and height of the Red Scare
- **1920–1933** Prohibition in effect under the Eighteenth Amendment
- **1921** Sheppard-Towner Federal Maternity and Infancy Act
- **1922** *Coronado Coal Company v. United Mine Workers of America* limits union's power
- **1923** – Equal Rights Amendment first introduced in Congress
  – Teapot Dome scandal
- **1924** National Origins Act
- **1925** Scopes trial
- **1927** Sacco and Vanzetti executed
- **1929** Stock market crash leads to Great Depression

1915 | 1925 | 1935 | 1945 | 1955 | 1965

RESURGENT CONSERVATISM

How and why did the United States take a conservative turn in the 1920s?

World War I brought an end to the long period of reform stretching from the 1880s to the 1910s. A resurgent political and social conservatism emerged in the war's aftermath. Progressivism survived, but limited government dominated national political life from 1919 until the election of Franklin D. Roosevelt as president in 1932. During the 1920s, the progressive call for economic regulation gave way to a business-first outlook. President Calvin Coolidge declared, "The man who builds a factory builds a temple. The man who works there worships there." The same theme prevailed in U.S. foreign policy: American business needs were the top priority. Socially, the conservative turn drew on postwar anxieties about a rapidly changing nation. In 1919 alone, an antiradical Red Scare, a massive strike wave, and white violence against African Americans roiled the country — a preview of an eventful but anxious era.

The Red Scare

AP® EXAM TIP

Explain the relationship between fear of radicalism and the Red Scare.

The war effort, overseen by a Democratic administration sympathetic to organized labor, had increased the size and power of labor unions. Membership in the American Federation of Labor (AFL) grew by a third during World War I, reaching more than three million by the armistice. Workers' expectations also rose as the war economy brought higher pay and better working conditions. Labor sought to preserve and expand the wartime gains after the peace. Over the course of 1919, more than four million wage laborers — one in every five — went on strike, a proportion never since equaled. A walkout of shipyard workers in Seattle sparked a general strike that shut

672

AP® APPLY THE TIP

Have students use pp. 672–674 to complete **Handout 21.1 — Causation: Red Scare (TRM)**. Then organize students into small groups to investigate the trial of Sacco and Vanzetti. Assign different groups to take on the point of view of one of the following: J. Edgar Hoover, lawyer for Sacco and Vanzetti, American Legion, NAACP, International Workers of the World, and American Federation of Labor. Ask each group to prepare a synopsis of the events associated with the trial and execution of Sacco and Vanzetti that includes at least one primary source in support of their argument. Allow each group to present their synopsis and source to the whole class to initiate a class discussion on the relationship of fear to political action in American history. In this discussion, students may reference the Salem witch trials, Alien and Sedition Acts, Lincoln's use of writs of habeas corpus, as well as current issues, including immigration restriction.

TRM Find **Handout 21.1 — Causation: Red Scare** in the Teacher's Resource Materials.

Anti-Bolshevism Cartoon, 1919 In this political cartoon published during the post–World War I Red Scare, "Bolshevism" (Russian communism) creeps under the American flag while holding a burning torch labeled "Anarchism." During the Red Scare, antiradicalism and nativism often went hand in hand, as Americans feared that European immigrants brought revolutionary ideas and tactics with them to the United States. Sarin Images/Granger, NYC.

down the entire city. Another strike disrupted the steel industry, as 350,000 workers demanded union recognition and an end to twelve-hour shifts. Union members ranging from textile workers and coal miners to city police and longshoremen joined the year's wave of worker protest. Most of the 1919 strikes sought basic economic objectives — more pay, fewer hours — rather than a socialist revolution, but the bold exercise of worker power still stoked fears of rising radicalism among labor's opponents.

That same year, the Soviet Union's new Bolshevik leaders founded the Third International, intended to foster revolutions abroad. With an eye on Europe's ongoing unrest, some Americans perceived political radicalism as an urgent threat at home. Wartime hatred of Germans quickly gave way to hostility toward Bolsheviks (labeled "Reds," after the color of communist flags). Under the banner of "one hundred percent Americanism," groups such as the newly formed American Legion decried socialists, communists, and the anticapitalist Industrial Workers of the World (IWW) as un-American. In a telling example, Ole Hanson, Seattle's mayor during the general strike, wrote a book called *Americanism Versus Bolshevism* and toured the country lecturing about the threat of revolution. Ironically, American communists remained few in number and had little political influence. Of the 63 million adults in the United States in 1920, no more than 13,000 belonged to a communist organization.

The tiny fraction of political revolutionaries who endorsed violence, however, fueled a wave of political repression. In the midst of the 1919 strike wave, radical followers of an Italian anarchist, who promised "blood and fire" and hoped to ignite a

TEACHING STRATEGY

Sometimes students struggle to ascertain the main argument in a primary source. In this particular source, have students define both Bolshevism and Anarchy before looking at the document. Once they are grounded in a basic vocabulary understanding of the words, they will be better able to apply those words to the artist's interpretation. Ask students to connect the Red Scare to the immediate aftermath of World War I on the Home Front.

TEACHING STRATEGY

To supplement your lesson on the Sacco and Vanzetti case, have students read former Supreme Court Justice Felix Frankfurter's assessment of the case in the *Atlantic*. Frankfurter argues that the trial verdict appeared to rest more on circumstantial evidence and the identity of the defendants than on their guilt. Prompt students to decide whether they find his conclusion compelling. To access this article, search "Atlantic Case of Sacco and Vanzetti."

CHECK FOR UNDERSTANDING

Ask students: **What was the Red Scare?** *The Red Scare was a panic about the growing influence of communists and other radicals in the U.S. It was fueled by the Bolshevik Revolution and subsequent formation of the Third International, designed to instigate radical revolution around the world. Bombs targeting government officials and labor strikes combined to fuel the panic. The Palmer raids, led by Attorney General A. Mitchell Palmer, and the Sacco and Vanzetti trial were key consequences.*

AP® SKILLS & PROCESSES

CAUSATION

As students contemplate the relative significance of different causes of the Red Scare, remind them these causes could stem from either foreign or domestic concerns. Additionally, ask students to weigh the relative importance of each cause — that is to say, have students determine the order of significance. Weighing categories is an expectation on the AP® U.S. History Exam and a way for students to illustrate their ability to make an interpretation.

TRM Find complete suggested responses in the Teacher's Resource Materials.

revolution, began attempting to assassinate public officials with explosives. In April, thirty-six bombs were discovered, unexploded, by alert postal workers. They were addressed to, among others, a U.S. senator, a Supreme Court justice, business magnate John D. Rockefeller, and U.S. Attorney General A. Mitchell Palmer. In June, nine similar bombs exploded in seven cities and, most gruesomely, in an effort to kill the attorney general a young man blew himself up outside Palmer's Washington, D.C. town house, obliterating its front parlor. The next day, with the vocal support of House and Senate members, Palmer vowed to find and jail every last conspirator.

Red Scare
A term for anticommunist hysteria that swept the United States, first after World War I and again after World War II, and led to government raids, deportations of radicals, and a suppression of civil liberties.

Palmer raids
A series of raids ordered by Attorney General A. Mitchell Palmer on radical organizations that peaked in January 1920, when federal agents arrested six thousand citizens and aliens and denied them access to legal counsel.

These terrifying bombings helped drive the ensuing **Red Scare** and provided the pretext for a much broader assault on political radicals of all stripes. The attorney general set up an antiradicalism unit within the Justice Department and appointed his assistant J. Edgar Hoover as head. (Hoover would go on to lead the Federal Bureau of Investigation, the FBI, from 1924 until his death in 1972.) Starting in November 1919, Palmer ordered a series of roundups that would go down in history as the **Palmer raids** but were actually planned and executed by Palmer's ambitious deputy, Hoover himself. The raids targeted the headquarters of radical organizations and indiscriminately arrested thousands, often immigrants who had committed no crimes but who held anarchist or revolutionary beliefs. Lacking the protection of U.S. citizenship, many were deported without indictment or trial. The raids peaked on a notorious night in January 1920, when federal agents invaded homes and meeting halls, arrested six thousand citizens and aliens (immigrants without U.S. citizenship) and denied the prisoners access to legal counsel.

The Red Scare's combination of antiradicalism and anti-immigrant sentiment had dire consequences in the case of Nicola Sacco and Bartolomeo Vanzetti. Though the Palmer Raids had ended in January 1920, the antiradical fervor had not ebbed. Later that year, in May, local police arrested Sacco, a shoemaker, and Vanzetti, a fish peddler, for the murder of two men during a robbery in South Braintree, Massachusetts. Sacco and Vanzetti were Italian immigrants and self-proclaimed anarchists who had evaded the draft. Convicted of the murders in 1921, they sat in jail for six years while supporters appealed their verdicts. In 1927, Judge Webster Thayer denied a motion for a new trial and sentenced them to death. Scholars still debate their guilt or innocence, but the case was clearly biased by prosecutors' emphasis on their radical ties and foreign birth. The executions of Sacco and Vanzetti became a lasting symbol of the Red Scare's hostilities and divisiveness.

AP® SKILLS & PROCESSES
CAUSATION
What ideas and developments caused the Red Scare?

Racial Backlash

Great Migration
The migration of 6 million African Americans from the South to the North and West between 1916 and 1970.

Racial repression also marked the years during and after World War I. The beginning of the **Great Migration** — a decades-long migration between 1916 and 1970 that would ultimately see 6 million black people exit the South — had drawn hundreds of thousands of African Americans from the South to northern and midwestern industrial cities for war work. These migrants found more economic clout and stronger voting rights in the North, which in turn fostered community building and a drive for racial justice (see "Firsthand Accounts," p. 676). However, the arrival of these southern migrants during the war deepened existing racial tensions, as African Americans competed with whites — including recent immigrants from Europe — for jobs and scarce housing.

AP® EXAM TIP
Evaluate the impact of social change on violent racial confrontations in the early twentieth century.

Racism had already turned such conflicts into violent confrontations during the war. One of the deadliest riots in American history occurred in 1917 in East St. Louis, Illinois, where rampaging whites burned more than three hundred black homes and murdered between 50 and 150 black men, women, and children (the exact death toll remains unknown). The East St. Louis riots were "a crime against the laws of humanity," said Marcus Garvey, the influential black leader of the Universal Negro Improvement Association.

Tensions remained high after the war, because African Americans emerged from the conflict determined to achieve citizenship rights. Millions had loyally supported

AP® APPLY THE TIP

Organize students into collaborative groups to study the causes and effects of race riots in the early twentieth century. Groups can be assigned race riots in one of the following cities: Atlanta, GA (1905); Wilmington, NC (1898); Chicago, IL (1919); Phillips County, AK (1919); Washington, DC (1919); or Harlem, NY (1919). Each group should produce a five-slide presentation that analyzes the race riots using AP® History Reasoning Processes. Require students to produce one slide to address each of the following: immediate and false causes of the race riot; impact of the race riot on the African American community; reactions from government (local, state, federal) to the riots; how the event reflects continuity; and how the event reflects change in American history.

Each group should then present to the class or post the presentations for students to view on their own to initiate a class discussion on the similarities and differences among the race riots. Ask students to draw conclusions regarding the degree to which the race riots reflect change or continuity in American history.

the war effort, and 370,000 had served in uniform. Returning veterans, empowered by their military service, often refused to accept second-class treatment at the hands of whites, whether in the North or South. The black man, one observer wrote, "realized that he was part and parcel of the great army of democracy. . . . With this realization came the consciousness of pride in himself as a man, and an American citizen."

These developments sparked white violence. In what became known as the **Red Summer** of 1919, bloody battles raged in more than two dozen cities, from major urban areas such as Washington, D.C. to small towns such as Longview, Texas. Chicago fared the worst, enduring five days of rioting in July after white youths stoned a black teenager to death on a Lake Michigan beach. The rioting led to the deaths of 23 black and 15 white Chicagoans and the destruction of more than a thousand black residences. By September, the year's death toll from racial violence across the country reached 120. Lynchings also spiked in 1919, including several murders of returning (and still uniformed) black soldiers.

Red Summer
Antiblack riots in the summer and fall of 1919 by white Americans in more than two dozen cities leading to hundreds of deaths. The worst riot occurred in Chicago, in which 38 people were killed (23 blacks, 15 whites).

Attacks on African Americans continued after 1919, as well. In June 1921, sensationalized (and false) reports of an alleged rape helped incite white mobs in the oil boomtown of Tulsa, Oklahoma. Anger focused on the eight thousand residents of Tulsa's prosperous Greenwood district, locally known as "the black Wall Street." The mobs — aided by National Guardsmen, who arrested African Americans defending their homes and businesses — burned thirty-five blocks of Greenwood and killed several dozen people. The city's leading paper acknowledged that "semi-organized bands of white men systematically applied the torch, while others shot on sight men of color." It took a decade for black residents to rebuild Greenwood. Tulsa was only one terrible incident in a steady pattern of racial violence in the early 1920s. In an equally grim episode in January 1923, mobs of furious whites in a small Florida town torched houses and hunted down African Americans, killing at least six in the Rosewood Massacre. Police and state authorities refused to intervene, and the town of Rosewood vanished from the map.

AP® SKILLS & PROCESSES

CONTEXTUALIZATION

What role did World War I play in the Red Scare and antiblack violence, and what connections might we draw among these events?

Chicago Race Riot Racial violence exploded in Chicago during the summer of 1919. The riot was sparked when a black teenager, who had violated the unofficial segregation of the city's beaches, was stoned to death by a group of white youths. The African American man pictured here was also stoned to death by a white mob as he attempted to find shelter in his home. Everett Collection.

CHECK FOR UNDERSTANDING

Ask students: **What was the racial backlash during and after World War I?** *The migration of blacks out of the South led to competition for wartime jobs, and the determination of African Americans to achieve the full rights of citizenship combined to spark several incidents of racial violence, culminating in 1919's Red Summer, where rioting took place in two dozen cities, and over two hundred blacks died from racial violence.*

AP® SKILLS & PROCESSES

CONTEXTUALIZATION

The **CONTEXTUALIZATION** question encourages students to place various forms of social violence into the same larger context, by relating these incidents to World War I and by drawing connections between them. To properly engage this question, some students may need to be reminded of the degree to which a white Protestant cultural identity still dominated the nation in this period. Students could additionally explore the other side of the question, considering factors besides the war that played into these tensions, especially long-term factors.

TRM Find complete suggested responses in the Teacher's Resource Materials.

TEACHING STRATEGY

The image depicting a scene from the Chicago race riot of 1919 suggests ways that people encountered racialized violence. To emphasize this point, you can ask students to contrast this photograph to one from a previous event in history, such as Reconstruction. Ask students to define what structural racism can look like and how images in history have captured this development. Students could also analyze documents related to the Tulsa race riot and, based on their analysis, make an inference about the event. Images, audio recordings from survivors, a Red Cross report, and testimony from several court cases are available from Tulsa Historical Society's Web site. To access these resources, search "Tulsa Historical Society Tulsa race riot." For additional information on the racial unrest of the summer of 1919, see the companion site for the PBS documentary *The Rise and Fall of Jim Crow*. To access the site, search "Rise and Fall of Jim Crow Red Summer (1919)."

AP® FIRSTHAND ACCOUNTS

AP® SKILLS & PROCESSES

ANALYZING HISTORICAL EVIDENCE

The **AP® FIRSTHAND ACCOUNTS** feature provides students with rich primary source evidence from which to study the effects of the Great Migration. A couple of concepts immediately attendant to this migration will further students' reading of the sources. Think about explaining the concept of agency and structural racism. Agency can help emphasize the role African Americans had in the choices they made to migrate north for economic work, to unite with family members, or escape the violence of the segregated southern region. Structural racism can develop students' understanding of the discriminatory actions of the government and how that affected African Americans.

African American Leaders React to the Great Migration

During the Great Migration between 1916 and 1970, 6 million African Americans moved from the South to the North and West. The first phase of the migration began during World War I and continued into the 1920s, when labor shortages in northern cities opened many jobs to African Americans for the first time. In the following excerpts, African American leaders of the era react to the migration and comment on the hopes of the migrants. (Note: The writers employ the term "Negro," a widely accepted term in the 1920s, which has long since been replaced by the terms "black" and "African American.")

MARY MCLEOD BETHUNE

"The Problems of the City Dweller," February 1925

Mary McLeod Bethune was a leading black educator and civil and women's rights advocate who founded Bethune-Cookman College, served in President Franklin Roosevelt's administration, and later became Vice President of the National Association for the Advancement of Colored People (NAACP).

SOURCE: Mary McLeod Bethune, "The Problems of the City Dweller," *Opportunity*, February 1925, 54–55.

❝ It is ever the problem of living a rational, healthy life in the midst of an environment which for the masses is for the most part, unfavorable. It is the problem of fresh air, wholesome food, sunshine and freedom within limits as pitilessly circumscribed as prison walls. It is the problem of making an increased wage, a better school, and easily accessible and cheap means of transportation, electric light, motion pictures, parades and band concerts, a policeman on the corner and propinquitous [nearby] neighbors, compensate for the sweep of the hill, the greenness of expansive meadows, and the lure of the endless road. It is the problem of getting a chance to live the abundant life, the door to which in our urban centers yields only to the touch of a golden key.

The problem has been greatly intensified in the past ten or twenty years by the rush from the rural districts. This rush has been neither sectional nor racial. Every section of the country has felt it. While there may be specific causes back of the "push" that has moved hundreds of thousands of Negroes from the Southern States to various points in the North-east and middle West, the migration can be truthfully considered as only another phase of the general movement of population from the rural toward the urban centers. In fact, for a longer period, preceding the migrations of large bodies of Negroes northward there was a steady and perceptible increase in the Negro population of Southern cities causes by a movement of this element of the population from the country to the city. . . .

The cry of the Soul to know has given another push to this modern move towards the city. Longer school terms; better equipped school buildings; more capable teachers; the broadening influence of lectures; concerts, motions pictures, libraries, parades, and festive holiday occasions, have lured many a grizzled homesteader to abandon home and ancestral acres and move cityward. The widening out and diversification of the modern high school with its facilities for teaching the technique of skilled trades and business; home economics and agriculture as well as the arts and sciences. The extending of education at the public expense in some cities to include even a college education. The offering of night courses for underprivileged boys and girls, men and women. These are advantages which even the phonograph, the motion picture machine and the radio cannot compensate for in the country. . . .

Though not so often mentioned as a cause, the desire for protection has impelled many a rural dweller to move into of nearer the city. This is especially true with Negro rural dwellers in nearly every part of the South, where the lack or indifference of constabulary or police agencies make the possession of property uncertain — often hazardous and the safeguarding of life uncertain. These people turn towards the cities for protection in the exercise of the rights guaranteed them under the constitution, and a half chance to defend themselves should these rights be infringed upon. . . .

The breaking down of racial barriers and the conceding to every man his right to own and enjoy his property wherever his means permit him to own it; the opening up of parks and playgrounds for the enjoyment and development of all citizens alike; the firm but patient tutoring of the uninitiated newcomer in the privileges and obligations of urban life, must still be the foundation of the programme of organizations like the Urban League and other great social agencies whose militant efforts in these directions have made them national in scope and purpose. ❞

ALAIN LOCKE

On Migration and the Rise of Harlem, 1925

Alain Locke was a leading African American intellectual — with a PhD in philosophy from Harvard University — who was a critical supporter of the artistic movement known as the Harlem Renaissance and the broader social and political "New Negro" movement.

SOURCE: Alain Locke, *The New Negro: An Interpretation*, 1925 original, in *The New Cavalcade: African American Writing from 1760 to the Present*, Vol. 1, eds. Arthur P. Davis, J. Saunders Redding, and Joyce Ann Joyce (Washington, DC: Howard University Press, 1991), 364–365.

In the very process of being transplanted, the Negro is becoming transformed.

The tide of Negro migration, northward and city-ward, is not to be fully explained as a blind flood started by the demands of war industry coupled with the shutting off of foreign migration, or by the pressure of poor crops coupled with increased social terrorism in certain sections of the South and Southwest. Neither labor demand, the boll-weevil nor the Ku Klux Klan is a basic factor, however contributory any or all of them may have been. The wash and rush of this human tide on the beach line of the northern city centers is to be explained primarily in terms of a new vision of opportunity, of social and economic freedom, of a spirit to seize, even in the face of an extortionate and heavy toll, a chance for the improvement of conditions. With each successive wave of it, the movement of the Negro becomes more and more a mass movement toward the larger and the more democratic chance — in the Negro's case a deliberate flight not only from countryside to city, but from medieval America to modern.

Take Harlem as an instance of this. Here in Manhattan is not merely the largest Negro community in the world, but the first concentration in history of so many diverse elements of Negro life. It has attracted the African, the West Indian, the Negro American; has brought together the Negro of the North and the Negro of the South; the man from the city and the man from the town and village; the peasant, the student, the business man, the professional man, artist, poet, musician, adventurer and worker, preacher and criminal, exploiter and social outcast. Each group has come with its own separate motives and for its own special ends, but their greatest experience has been the finding of one another. . . . Harlem, I grant you, isn't typical — but it is significant, it is prophetic. No sane observer, however sympathetic to the new trend, would contend that the great masses are articulate as yet, but they stir, they move, they are more than physically restless. . . . It is a social disservice to blunt the fact that the Negro of the northern centers has reached a stage where tutelage, even of the most interested and well-intentioned sort, must give place to new relationships, where positive self-direction must be reckoned with in ever increasing measure. The American mind must reckon with a fundamentally changed Negro.

CHARLES S. JOHNSON

Red Summer in Chicago, 1922

A professor of sociology and the first black president of Fisk University, Charles S. Johnson led a study of the causes of the 1919 Chicago Race Riot — a major event in the "Red Summer" of anti-black rioting in major cities. Though official credit for the report went to the Chicago Commission on Race Relations, for whom Johnson worked, he penned its lengthy account of the riot and its sociological causes.

SOURCE: Chicago Commission on Race Relations, *The Negro in Chicago* (Chicago: University of Chicago Press, 1922), 1–3.

A clash between whites and Negroes on the shore of Lake Michigan at Twenty-Ninth Street, which involved much stone-throwing and resulted in the drowning of a Negro boy, was the beginning of the riot. . . . Before the end came it reached out to a section of the West Side and even invaded the "Loop," the heart of Chicago's downtown business district. Of the thirty-eight killed, fifteen were whites and twenty-three Negroes; of 537 injured, 178 were whites, 342 were Negroes, and the race of seventeen was not recorded. . . .

Chicago was one of the northern cities most largely affected by the migration of Negroes from the South during the war. The Negro population increased from 44,104 in 1910 to 109,594 in 1920, an increase of 148 percent. Most of the increase came in the years 1916–1919. . . . Practically no new housing had been done in the city during the war, and it was a physical impossibility for a doubled Negro population to live in the space occupied in 1915. Negroes spread out of what had been known as the "Black Belt" into neighborhoods nearby which had been exclusively white. This movement, as described in another section of this report, developed friction, so much so that in the "invaded" neighborhoods bombs were thrown at the houses of Negroes who had moved in, and of real estate men, white and Negro, who sold or rented property to the newcomers. From July 1, 1917 to July 27, 1919, the day the riot began, twenty-four such bombs had been thrown.

QUESTIONS FOR ANALYSIS

1. What factors led to the Great Migration, according to Bethune and Locke? In what ways do they see the migration as distinctly African American, and in what ways do they see it as part of broader developments?
2. What does Locke mean that "tutelage" must give way to "new relationships" characterized by "self-direction?" Discuss relative changes in race relations.
3. After reading the excerpt from Johnson's study of the Chicago riot, assess the optimistic appraisal of the Great Migration offered by Bethune and Locke. How would you synthetize these different interpretations?

TRM Find complete suggested responses in the Teacher's Resource Materials.

American Business at Home and Abroad

American Plan
Strategy by American business in the 1920s to keep workplaces free of unions, which included refusing to negotiate with trade unions and requiring workers to sign contracts pledging not to join a union.

welfare capitalism
A system of labor relations that stressed management's responsibility for employees' well-being.

Much like African Americans, organized labor saw progress during the war years and encountered hostile, though less deadly, resistance afterward. Following the strike wave of 1919, business leaders and their political allies fought back against organized labor, which entered a decade of decline. Across the country, employers adopted what they called the **American Plan** of employment — refusing to negotiate with unions and denying workers the right to organize by forcing them to sign contracts pledging not to join a union. Facing a strike of Boston's police force, Massachusetts governor Calvin Coolidge illustrated this defiant approach by declaring, "There is no right to strike against the public safety by anybody, anywhere, anytime." A majority of the public supported the governor, and Republicans rewarded Coolidge by nominating him for the vice-presidency in 1920.

A decision by the Supreme Court contributed to organized labor's decline. In *Coronado Coal Company v. United Mine Workers of America* (1922), the Court ruled that a striking union could be penalized for illegal restraint of trade. The Coronado ruling, along with the aggressive antiunion campaigns under the American Plan, drove down membership in labor unions from 5.1 million in 1920 to 3.6 million in 1929 — just 10 percent of the nonagricultural workforce.

With unions in retreat, the 1920s marked the heyday of **welfare capitalism**, a system of labor relations that stressed a company's responsibility for its employees' well-being. Ideally, this arrangement would build a loyal workforce and head off unrest. Automaker Henry Ford, among other large industrial employers, had implemented such a system prior to World War I. Ford famously paid a generous wage of $5 a day and also offered a profit-sharing plan to employees who met the standards of its Sociological Department, which investigated workers to ensure their private lives met the company's moral standards. At a time when government unemployment compensation and Social Security did not exist, General Electric and U.S. Steel provided health insurance and old-age pensions. Other employers built athletic facilities and selectively offered paid vacations. In practice, however, the benefits of welfare capitalism proved limited. Such plans covered only about 5 percent of the industrial workforce, and they depended on employer generosity and rising profits. When faced with new financial pressures in the late 1920s, even Henry Ford cut back his $5 day, and corporate belt-tightening across the country spelled the end of this experiment.

The ascendancy of business in the 1920s shaped the nation's international outlook as well. As before the war, Latin America remained the focus of U.S. foreign policy. Under a presidential initiative launched by William Howard Taft and continued under Wilson and other presidents in the years after World War I, the State Department worked to advance U.S. business interests abroad, especially by encouraging private banks to make foreign loans in the Caribbean and South America. Policymakers hoped loans would stimulate growth in developing markets and thus increase demand for U.S. products.

Bankers, for their part, wanted government guarantees of repayment in countries they perceived as weak or unstable. Officials readily provided such assurance. In 1922, for example, when American banks offered an immense loan to Bolivia, State Department officials pressured the South American nation to accept it. A similar arrangement was reached with El Salvador's government in 1923. In other cases, the United States intervened militarily, often to force repayment of debt. The U.S. Marines occupied Nicaragua almost continuously from 1912 to 1933, the Dominican Republic from 1916 to 1924, and Haiti from 1915 to 1934. These forays were often justified through demeaning racial logic. Haitians were characterized as primitive savages or childlike people who needed U.S. guidance and supervision. One commander testified that his troops saw themselves as "trustees of a huge estate that belonged to minors. . . . The Haitians were our wards."

AP® SKILLS & PROCESSES

DEVELOPMENTS AND PROCESSES

The 1920s is often studied as a period of tremendous contrast. The bifurcated paradigm of fundamentalist and modern had a number of attendant issues. For instance, have students grapple with how this paradigm could be seen in the economic systems promoted by workers and managers. Encourage students to compare and contrast the view of those who promoted welfare capitalism with those who advocated for the American Plan.

At home, critics denounced loan guarantees and military interventions as **dollar diplomacy** — a foreign policy intended to stabilize the economies of foreign nations to benefit American commercial interests. The term was coined in 1924 by Samuel Guy Inman, a Disciples of Christ missionary who toured U.S.-occupied Haiti and the Dominican Republic. "The United States," Inman declared, "cannot go on destroying with impunity the sovereignty of other peoples, however weak." African American leaders also denounced the Haitian occupation. On behalf of the International Council of Women of the Darker Races and the Women's International League for Peace and Freedom, a delegation conducted a fact-finding tour of Haiti in 1926. Their report exposed, among other things, the sexual exploitation of Haitian women by U.S. soldiers.

Dollar diplomacy was on the defensive by the late 1920s, as its poor results spoke for themselves. Loans were repaid, securing bankers' profits, but the money more often wound up in the pockets of local elites, rather than creating markets for American exports. Military intervention had even worse results. In Haiti, for example, the marines crushed peasant protests and helped the local elite consolidate power, contributing to the rise of harsh dictatorships there. In 1933, President Roosevelt initiated the "Good Neighbor" policy with respect to Latin America — in which the U.S. pledged not to intervene in the internal affairs of countries there and to pursue reciprocal trade agreements instead — in an effort to reverse these ill effects.

While the Western Hemisphere dominated the American international outlook after World War I, many diplomats considered East Asia more important in the long run. To ease growing tensions there, the United States joined Japan, Great Britain, and France in a major naval arms limitation treaty in 1922. The so-called Four-Powers

dollar diplomacy
The use of American foreign policy to stabilize the economies of foreign nations, especially in the Caribbean and South America, in order to benefit American commercial interests, between World War I and the early 1930s.

AP® EXAM TIP

Evaluate the impact of U.S. economic imperialism in the Western Hemisphere.

Bananas
. . . a good mixer
with every fruit that grows
Oranges, apples, grapefruit, pineapples, pears, melons, grapes—all these and many others—blend perfectly with bananas. The distinctive flavor of the banana, when added to a fruit cup, a fruit salad, or any fruit combination, brings out the flavor of the other fruits and makes them taste better.
"Ripe bananas are good for little children."
"EAT plenty of fresh fruits" is now an accepted principle of diet—and the mere sight of mellow, luscious bananas is an invitation to serve many delicious and nourishing fruit combinations.
All year round from the tropics . . . Easter, Fourth of July, Thanksgiving, Christmas—every season, every day—bananas are available. Thanks to the nearness and all-year-round productiveness of the tropics, they always can be had at your grocery or fruit store.
Children crave the temptingly flavored banana instinctively. And it is well that they do, for bananas are one of the most important energy-producing foods. Doctors and dietitians consider the banana not only one of the most valuable foods, but also one of the most easily digested . . . as beneficial for grown-ups as for children.
Serve bananas with other fruits, with cereals, with milk or cream . . . or serve them plain. But always be sure they are fully ripe (generously flecked with brown spots). If they are not at the proper stage of ripeness when you buy them, let them ripen at room temperature. Never place them in the ice-box.
UNIFRUIT BANANAS
A United Fruit Company Product
Imported and Distributed by Fruit Dispatch Company
17 Battery Place, New York, N. Y.

VISUAL ACTIVITY

American Companies Abroad Both American foreign policy and overseas investment focused on Latin America in the 1920s. United Fruit was one of the many American companies that found opportunity for investment in South America and that introduced tropical produce to the United States. The company created elaborate and informative color advertisements to sell its products. Bananas were sufficiently exotic that the ads explained to consumers how to tell when bananas were ripe and how to store them ("Never place them in the ice-box.")

READING THE IMAGE: Examine the contrasting scenes, at the top and bottom of the advertisement. What does the top image suggest about the environment in which the bananas were grown and, in combination with the accompany text, what benefits does the advertisement suggest for the people in the bottom image?

MAKING CONNECTIONS: Who is the intended audience for this advertisement? Why? How did changes in family and consumerism influence this advertisement?

TRM Find complete suggested responses in the Teacher's Resource Materials.

AP® SKILLS & PROCESSES

DEVELOPMENTS AND PROCESSES

What were the economic goals of U.S. foreign policymakers in the 1920s, and what were the outcomes?

Treaty limited naval strength in the Pacific to existing levels, but stoked Japanese resentment because the status quo guaranteed Western military superiority over Japan's smaller navy. That island nation would gradually come to see the United States, not European colonial powers, as its principal adversary for dominance in Asia.

Government and Business Entangled

The postwar conservative turn was particularly evident in electoral politics. With President Woodrow Wilson ailing from a stroke, Democrats nominated Ohio governor James M. Cox for president in 1920, on a platform of U.S. participation in the League of Nations and a continuation of Wilson's progressivism. Republicans, led by their probusiness wing, tapped genial Ohio senator Warren G. Harding. In a dig at Wilson's idealism, Harding promised "not nostrums but normalcy," meaning a return to prewar life and prosperity. On election day, he won in a landslide, beginning an era of Republican political dominance that lasted until 1932.

AP® EXAM TIP

Compare the philosophy and government actions of the presidents of the 1920s to those who preceded them in the Progressive Era.

Much like dollar diplomacy, Harding's domestic policy favored business. His most energetic appointee was Secretary of Commerce Herbert Hoover, already celebrated for his work as head of the wartime Food Administration. Under Hoover's direction, the Commerce Department helped create two thousand trade associations representing companies in almost every major industry. Government officials worked closely with the associations, providing statistical research, suggesting industry-wide standards, and promoting stable prices and wages. Hoover hoped that through voluntary business cooperation with government — an associated state — he could achieve what progressives had sought via regulation.

Other changes were afoot in Washington, D.C. Lobbying Congress on behalf of business, unions, and other interests was already a long-standing tradition, but the practice became pervasive in the 1920s. Noting the change, one observer joked, "the lobbyists were so thick they were constantly falling over one another." Hundreds of groups set up offices to lobby members of Congress — from religious and civic organizations to the Anti-Saloon League — but business took the lead. The National Association of Manufacturers, the Chamber of Commerce, and public utilities (water and electric companies), among many other business organizations, assumed an ever-larger role in the legislative process.

Teapot Dome
Nickname for scandal in which Interior Secretary Albert Fall accepted $300,000 in bribes for leasing oil reserves on public land in Teapot Dome, Wyoming. It was part of a larger pattern of corruption that marred Warren G. Harding's presidency.

Ties between government and corporate interests were not always open, or honest. Corruption was widespread during the Harding years. The worst scandal concerned secret leasing of government oil reserves in **Teapot Dome**, Wyoming, and Elk Hills, California, to private companies. Secretary of the Interior Albert Fall was eventually convicted of taking over $300,000 in bribes and became the first cabinet officer in U.S. history to serve a prison sentence.

When President Harding died of a heart attack in August 1923, Vice President Calvin Coolidge ascended to the Oval Office. Over the remainder of Harding's term, Coolidge advocated limited government and tax cuts for businesses and campaigned for election in his own right in the presidential race of 1924. Democrats were deeply divided that year between rural and urban factions on issues such as prohibition and immigration restriction and deadlocked at their national convention; after 102 ballots, delegates finally nominated John W. Davis, a Wall Street lawyer. Coolidge easily defeated Davis and a third-party challenge from Senator Robert M. La Follette of Wisconsin, who tried to resuscitate the Progressive Party. The 1924 Progressive platform called for stronger government regulation at home and international efforts to reduce weapons production and prevent war. "Free men of every generation," La Follette declared in a speech, "must combat the renewed efforts of organized force and greed." In the end, Coolidge received 15.7 million votes to Davis's 8.4 million and La Follette's 4.9 million.

As the progressive spirit faded and a conservative ethos grew stronger, new patterns emerged in national political life between 1919 and 1932. Antiradicalism became

AP® SKILLS & PROCESSES

DEVELOPMENTS AND PROCESSES

The **DEVELOPMENTS AND PROCESSES** question asks students to identify the effects of American foreign policy goals. Students should consider a variety of political and economic effects in different parts of the world. They should also clearly identify the domestic effects in the U.S., which are addressed briefly in the first paragraph of this section. Students could consider whether military violence in Latin America was an unintended consequence of American policy or a necessary component of it.

TRM Find complete suggested responses in the Teacher's Resource Materials.

AP® THEME

WOR: America in the World

Presidents during the Progressive Era — Roosevelt, Taft, and Wilson — were reformers who sought to use the government as an active agent in social, political, and economic change. During the 1920s, presidents tended to be more conservative in nature, not wanting the government to be too energetic. Have students select one president from each era and conduct a comparison of the extent to which the president drove legislative reform.

CHECK FOR UNDERSTANDING

Ask students: **What was the business of America in the postwar period?** *As part of the "resurgent conservatism" this portion of the chapter addresses, American views of business at the time reflected a reversal of the Progressive Party's efforts to regulate business. Now Americans tended to support business and express suspicion of labor. Welfare capitalism reflected a compromise between labor and capital, as businesses took responsibility for employees' well-being through health insurance and pensions as a means of avoiding labor unrest.*

orthodoxy. Business and government grew closer. Lobbying grew into an established element of the legislative process. These developments would shape American politics for the remainder of the twentieth century.

AP® SKILLS & PROCESSES

MAKING CONNECTIONS

In what ways did business and government become more closely linked following World War I?

MAKING A MODERN CONSUMER ECONOMY

What were the primary characteristics of the American economy in the 1920s?

Spurred by rapid expansion during the war, and benefitting from a host of technological innovations in mass production such as the assembly line, American business thrived in the 1920s. Corporations eagerly expanded into overseas markets, and at home a truly national consumer culture — emphasizing convenience, leisure, and fun — took shape. Defined by the spread of cheaper goods, the rise of the automobile, and the growing influence of radio and movies, the decade marked a crucial turning point in the emergence of a mass consumer economy in the United States.

Postwar Abundance

Productivity proved to be the key. Manufacturing efficiencies accumulated since the turn of the century — the assembly line, mechanization, electrification — drove enormous increases in productivity. An American worker who made six toasters a day in 1920 could make ten toasters a day in 1929 working the same shift — an incredible leap in productivity. National per capita income rose an impressive 24 percent in that period. Productivity gains and rising incomes, especially among the middle class, meant an explosion of consumption. From toasters to telephones, vacuum cleaners to automobiles, a vast array of consumer products tempted Americans. Many consumers could afford to buy these goods, and their spending spurred an economic boom that lasted until the onset of the Great Depression in 1929.

AP® EXAM TIP

The rise of mass produced consumer culture in the 1920s is important to know for the AP® Exam.

Large-scale corporations continued to replace small businesses in many sectors of the economy. By 1929, after successive waves of consolidation, the two hundred largest firms had come to control almost half of the country's nonbanking corporate wealth. The greatest number of mergers occurred in rising industries such as chemicals (with DuPont in the lead) and electrical appliances (General Electric), as well as among Wall Street banks. Aided by Washington's dollar diplomats, U.S. companies exercised growing global power. Seeking cheaper livestock, giant American meatpackers opened plants in Argentina; the United Fruit Company developed plantations in Costa Rica, Honduras, and Guatemala; General Electric set up production facilities in Latin America, Asia, and Australia.

Despite the boom, some parts of the U.S. economy stumbled badly. Agriculture, which still employed one-fourth of all American workers, never fully recovered from the postwar recession. Once Europe's economy revived after the war's devastation, its farmers flooded world markets with grain and other produce, causing agricultural prices to fall. Other American industries, including coal and textiles, languished for similar reasons. Poorer Americans saw little of the decade's prosperity. The bottom 40 percent of American families earned an average annual income of only $725 (about $10,000 today). Many, especially rural tenant farmers and sharecroppers, languished in poverty and malnutrition.

Consumer Culture

But middle-class Americans readily embraced the new consumer ethos. They sat down to a breakfast of Kellogg's corn flakes before getting into Ford Model T's to drive to work or shop at Safeway. On weekends, they might head to the local theater to see the newest Charlie Chaplin film. By 1929, electric refrigerators and vacuum

AP® SKILLS & PROCESSES

MAKING CONNECTIONS

Use the **MAKING CONNECTIONS** question to help students identify specific effects of the deepening relationship between business and government in this era. To extend this prompt, have students infer the effects of a growing conservative outlook on progressive policies and leaders, apart from their decreased political power.

TRM Find complete suggested responses in the Teacher's Resource Materials.

AP® APPLY THE TIP

Ask students to work with a partner to complete **Handout 21.2 — Contextualization: Consumer Culture of the 1920s (TRM)** to evaluate the characteristics of consumer culture in the 1920s and the context in which consumer culture developed. Prompt students to use the gray circle on the handout for supporting details that help to explain the rise and importance of consumer culture, and the larger outer circle to explain the broader processes, events, and developments. Encourage students to connect the rise of consumer culture to the AP® Themes, specifically America in the World (WOR); American and National Identity (NAT); Social Structures (SOC); and Work, Exchange, and Technology (WXT). Then ask students to explain the way in which the developments of the 1920s can be related to consumer culture in current-day U.S. developments.

TRM Find **Handout 21.2 — Contextualization: Consumer Culture of the 1920s** in the Teacher's Resource Materials.

CHECK FOR UNDERSTANDING

Ask students: **What was the nature of postwar abundance?** *New manufacturing efficiency led to huge increases in productivity. Rising incomes, primarily within the middle class, fueled an explosion of consumer purchases. Large corporations replaced small businesses. But this prosperity was precarious. Some economic sectors, including agriculture and textiles languished, while over a third of the populace suffered in poverty, unable to properly feed themselves, let alone purchase the consumer goods of the era.*

AP® EXAM TIP

Analyze the influence of mass media on the rise of a national culture in the 1920s.

cleaners were common in affluent homes, and 40 percent of American households owned a radio. A burgeoning advertising industry encouraged spending, embracing what one historian calls the era of the "aggressive hard sell." The 1920s gave birth, for example, to fashion modeling and style consulting. Political consultants pioneered the "selling" of candidates — led by Albert Lasker, who shaped the public's image of presidential candidate Warren Harding in 1920 with the same techniques used to advertise oranges, soap, or franks and beans. "Sell them their dreams," one radio announcer urged advertisers in 1923. "People don't buy things to have things. . . . They buy hope — hope of what your merchandise will do for them."

To afford those hopes, both poor and affluent families stretched their incomes through forms of borrowing relatively new to most Americans, such as auto loans and installment plans. "Buy now, pay later," said the ads, and millions did. Anyone, no matter how rich, could get into debt, but **consumer credit** was particularly perilous for those living on the economic margins. In Chicago, one Lithuanian American described a neighbor's plight: "She ain't got no money. Sure she buys on credit, clothes for the children and everything." Such borrowing brought a modern lifestyle within reach for countless Americans, but the heaping debt also worsened the eventual crash.

consumer credit
Forms of borrowing, such as auto loans and installment plans, that flourished in the 1920s and worsened the crash that led to the Great Depression.

Radio, a new and fast-developing technology, hastened the spread of consumer culture in the years following World War I. Unlike magazines and newspapers, radio conveyed events as they happened, giving the medium an unprecedented immediacy and intimacy. In the first commercial radio broadcast in the United States, Pittsburgh's KDKA announced the 1920 presidential returns before the morning papers did. Households with radios shot from 260,000 in 1922 to 6.5 million in 1927 and to 12 million by the early 1930s. As thousands of stations popped up across the country, radio broadcasts came to include live theater and sporting events, news, music, variety and quiz shows, scripted comedies, and the first "soap operas." Advertising dollars fueled radio's rapid rise, laying the groundwork for the medium's "golden age" in the 1930s and 1940s.

Hollywood
The city in southern California that became synonymous with the American movie industry in the 1920s.

flapper
A young woman of the 1920s who defied conventional standards of conduct by wearing knee-length skirts and bold makeup, freely spending the money she earned on the latest fashions, dancing to jazz, and flaunting her liberated lifestyle.

Movies became a centerpiece of consumer culture. In the 1910s, the moviemaking industry had begun relocating to southern California to take advantage of low costs and sunny skies. The large studios — United Artists, Paramount, and Metro-Goldwyn-Mayer — were run mainly by Eastern European Jewish immigrants like Adolph Zukor, who arrived from Hungary in the 1880s. Zukor, a successful merchant, began his entertainment empire by investing with a partner in five-cent theaters in Manhattan. "I spent a good deal of time watching the faces of the audience," Zukor recalled. "With a little experience I could see, hear, and 'feel' the reaction to each melodrama and comedy." He used his firsthand knowledge in launching Paramount Pictures, with an eye for the emerging stars who made the studio's films successful.

Hollywood The American actress Marion Davies, playing a part in which she impersonates her male cousin to defeat a nefarious plot, in the 1926 silent film, *Beverly of Grasustark*. In the decade of the 1920s, Hollywood became the center of moviemaking in the world, and stars like Davies achieved both national and global popularity. Sound films were first introduced in the late 1920s, and they quickly became standard in the industry. John Kobal Foundation/Getty Images.

By 1920, **Hollywood** was the world's movie capital, producing nearly 90 percent of all films globally. Across the country, ornate movie palaces attracted both middle-class and working-class audiences. Idols such as Rudolph Valentino, Mary Pickford, and Douglas Fairbanks set national trends in style. Thousands of young women followed the lead of actress Clara Bow, Hollywood's famous **flapper**, who flaunted her boyish figure. Decked out in knee-length skirts, this small but influential group shocked the older generation by openly smoking and wearing bold makeup, especially around the eyes and on their lips and fingernails. Thanks to the movies and advertising, the flapper became an influential symbol of women's sexual and social emancipation. In cities, young immigrant and African American women eagerly bought makeup and the latest flapper fashions, a style that jazz stars helped popularize as much as Hollywood actresses. Mexican American teenagers joined the trend in major cities such as San Antonio and Los Angeles.

Politicians quickly saw the potential power of radio and film to shape foreign relations. In 1919, with government support, General Electric spearheaded the creation of Radio Corporation of America (RCA) to expand U.S. presence in foreign radio markets. RCA — which had a federal appointee on its board of directors — emerged as

AP® THEME

WXT: Work, Exchange, and Technology

Students should understand how the new forms of mass media described here, particularly radio and film, contributed to the spread of national culture while at the same time increased awareness of regional cultures.

TEACHING STRATEGY

Emily Spivack provides a series of five articles for *Smithsonian* on the "history of the flapper," explaining the origins, significance, and impact of the style of the 1920s. The articles include a number of images, quotes, and short film excerpts. To access the site, search "Smithsonian History of the Flapper."

a major provider of radio transmission in Latin America and East Asia. Meanwhile, by 1925, American films made up 95 percent of the movies screened in Britain, 80 percent in Latin America, and 70 percent in France. The United States was expanding what historians call **soft power** — the exercise of popular cultural influence — as radio and film exported the styles and values of American consumer culture to the world.

soft power
The exercise of popular cultural influence abroad, as American radio and movies became popular around the world in the 1920s, transmitting American consumer culture and its styles and values overseas.

The Automobile and Suburbanization

Appliances saved time, and movies thrilled audiences, but the automobile revolutionized American life inside and out. No product of the consumer boom proved more popular. The Ford Motor Company introduced the first widely affordable automobile, the Model T, in 1908, but the industry experienced its most dramatic growth in the 1920s. Car sales played a major role in the decade's economic surge: in 1929 alone, Americans spent $2.58 billion on automobiles. By the end of the decade, they owned 26 million cars — about 80 percent of the world's automobiles — or an average of one for every five people (it was one for every forty in France). The number of cars on American roads tripled in ten years (see "Thinking Like a Historian," p. 684).

The auto industry's exuberant expansion rippled through the economy. It stimulated steel, petroleum, chemical, rubber, and glass production and, directly or indirectly, created 3.7 million jobs. Highway construction became a billion-dollar-a-year enterprise, financed by federal subsidies and state gasoline taxes. Auto ownership encouraged sprawl and, in 1924, the first suburban shopping center opened: Country Club Plaza outside Kansas City, Missouri. Cars were expensive, and most Americans bought them on credit. Alfred Sloan, the president of General Motors and Henry Ford's great rival, founded the first national consumer credit agency to help Americans buy more Chevrolets. Other car companies followed GM's example. Amid a decade-long boom, few Americans worried about making big-ticket purchases on credit. When asked why her family purchased a car before installing indoor plumbing, one woman replied simply, "you can't go to town in a bathtub."

Cars changed the way Americans spent their leisure time, as proud drivers took their machines on the road. An infrastructure of gas stations, motels, and drive-in restaurants soon sprouted to serve motorists. Railroad travel faltered. The American Automobile Association, founded in 1902, estimated that by 1929 almost a third of the population took vacations by car. "I had a few days after I got my wheat cut," reported one Kansas farmer, "so I just loaded my family . . . and lit out." An elite Californian complained that automobile travel was no longer "aristocratic." "The clerks and their wives and sweethearts," observed a reporter, "driving through the Wisconsin lake country, camping at Niagara, scattering tin cans and pop bottles over the Rockies, made those places taboo for bankers."

Rising middle-class incomes, new forms of borrowing, and the automobile combined powerfully in the 1920s to produce a major suburban housing boom. Cars were central to the explosive growth. The nineteenth-century "streetcar suburbs" allowed the nation's affluent to live outside city

Automobiles Michigan Avenue in Chicago in 1930. Automobiles transformed American cities and the countryside alike. Cars also choked city streets that were once the province of horse-drawn carriages and electric trains. Cities needed new roads, traffic signs, and rules governing traffic. The booming automobile industry stimulated highway construction across the country, and auto travel created a booming business in gas stations, roadside motels, campgrounds, and sightseeing destinations. The automobile was a technology but also a consumer item that changed virtually every aspect of American life. ullstein bild/Getty Images.

AP® SKILLS & PROCESSES

MAKING CONNECTIONS

How did the radio, Hollywood movies, and the automobile exemplify the opportunities of 1920s consumer culture?

AP® EXAM TIP

Understanding the impact of the automobile on American cultural, social, and economic life is critical to success on the AP® Exam.

CHECK FOR UNDERSTANDING

Ask students: **What characterized American consumer culture in the 1920s?** *Technological and manufacturing innovations increased the number of consumer goods available to Americans, especially cars, appliances, and radios. Americans often purchased these items using credit. Film itself became a widespread consumer product, which helped to disseminate ideas and images like the flapper.*

AP® SKILLS & PROCESSES

MAKING CONNECTIONS

Technological innovation became the engine of consumer culture in the 1920s. Think about having students select one of these examples — radio, movies, or the automobile — and explain how it represented a turning point in their respective industry. In order to do this, students should examine life before and after the mass acceptance of each technological innovation.

AP® APPLY THE TIP

Divide the class into seven collaborative groups and assign each group one of the AP® Themes. Provide each group with **Handout 21.3 — Thematic Analysis: The Automobile (TRM)** and prompt students to use pp. 683–686 to identify the two most important impacts of the automobile on the U.S. according to their theme. Ask each group to share their findings.

TRM Find **Handout 21.3 — Thematic Analysis: The Automobile** and complete suggested responses in the Teacher's Resource Materials.

AP® SKILLS & PROCESSES

ANALYZING HISTORICAL EVIDENCE

Use the **AP® THINKING LIKE A HISTORIAN** feature to have students take a deep dive into the many reasons the automobile altered the American cultural and economic lifestyle of the 1920s. As the intro notes, only the personal computer is comparable to the changes wrought by the automobile. Encourage students to think of the breadth of change caused by the automobile as evidenced by the documents. While analyzing each document is crucial, encourage students to be able to explain historical trends associated with the car.

TEACHING STRATEGY

While the car is one of the best examples of modernity in American culture in the 1920s, think about having students compare and contrast other ways in which the United States embraced modernity through technological advancements. Examples such as the radio and personal appliances help students see the varied technological advancements. A question such as, Compare how technological advancement changed American cultural attitudes, can help students recognize the importance of the automobile, while accounting for a general change in cultural attitudes caused by technological advancements.

The Automobile Transforms America

No other technological innovation — only the personal computer comes close — changed American social and economic life more than the automobile powered by the internal combustion engine. The mass production of inexpensive cars, pioneered in the 1910s and 1920s, transformed countless aspects of American life. The documents that follow provide evidence of some of these transformations.

1. Charles E. Sorensen, A longtime Ford Motor Company executive's memoir, 1956. *Sorensen worked his way up from the factory floor to become a vice president in Henry Ford's company.*

Between October 1908 and May 26, 1927, we turned out 15,000,000 Model T's. I was sick of looking at them — sicker, in fact, than the public was.

The people for whom the Model T was made had outgrown the sturdy little vehicle that emancipated them from the horse, made the farm a suburb of the town, and put the automobile within the financial reach of practically everyone. Henry Ford had made a car for the common man, and now the common man was getting some uncommon ideas. He was becoming style conscious and was turning his back on Model T for the very thing that enabled him to buy it: its sameness and cheapness.

. . . Model T was notorious for its lack of glamour. It was a practical car in every sense, and it dominated its field. Attempt after attempt had failed to bring out a car which could compete with it in price and utility. But with the advent of good roads, larger cars and higher speeds were in demand. Now we had competition, not from a cheaper car, or a better-made one, but from a better-looking car — the Chevrolet.

2. American motor vehicle registration and Ford Motor Company net worth, 1920–1926. *This table provides evidence of the explosive growth of automobile ownership and the rising economic fortunes of car manufacturers like Ford.*

Year	Motor vehicle registrations in U.S.	Registrations per 1,000 people	Ford Motor Company net worth*
1920	9,231,941	86	$ 202,135,296
1921	10,463,295	96	$ 141,529,641
1922	12,238,375	111	$ 173,951,173
1923	15,090,936	134	$ 359,962,693
1924	17,591,981	154	$ 459,305,581
1925	19,937,274	172	$ 559,740,997
1926	22,001,393	187	$ 639,631,393

* Author note: These figures accurately represent the increasing valuation of Ford, because inflation was negligible, and even slightly negative, in these years.

3. Robert S. Lynd and Helen M. Lynd, *Middletown: A Study in American Culture*, 1929. Middletown *was a highly acclaimed sociological study of ordinary life in Muncie, Indiana, based on interviews with local residents in the 1920s.*

The first real automobile appeared in Middletown in 1900. . . . At the close of 1923 there were 6,221 passenger cars in the city, one for every 6.1 persons, or roughly two for every three families. . . .

According to an officer of a Middletown automobile financing company, 75 to 90 percent of the cars purchased locally are bought on time payment, and a working man earning $35.00 a week frequently plans to use one week's pay each month as payment for his car. The automobile has apparently unsettled the habit of careful saving for some families. . . . "I'll go without food before I'll see us give up the car," said one woman emphatically. . . .

Many families feel that an automobile is justified as an agency holding the family group together. . . . [But] the fact that 348 boys and 382 girls in the three upper years of the high school placed "use of the automobile" fifth and fourth respectively in a list of twelve possible sources of disagreement between them and their parents suggests that this may be an increasing decentralizing agent. . . .

If the automobile touches the rest of Middletown's living at many points, it has revolutionized its leisure . . . making leisure-time enjoyment a regularly expected part of every day and week rather than an occasional event. . . . The frequency of movie attendance of high school boys and girls is about equal, business class families tend to go more often than do working class families, and children of both groups attend more often without their parents than do all the individuals or combinations of family members put together. . . . It is probable that time formerly spent in lodges, saloons, and unions is now being spent in part at the movies, at least occasionally with other members of the family. Like the automobile and radio, the movies [break] up leisure time into an individual, family, or small group affair.

684

4. **Walter Prichard Eaton, "The Billboard Curse," November 1923.** *A writer reflects on the downsides of the automobile's takeover of American life.*

I own two automobiles. As one or the other is almost sure to go [to operate], I regard them as indispensable. To be sure, men lived rather well, and rather happily, in the house where I now dwell for the better part of a century before automobiles were invented. But they also lived without bathrooms. I have no desire to emulate them in either simplicity.

But the constantly increasing flow of motor traffic on our highways, the constantly increasing congestion in our towns and cities, the mounting toll of life from accidents, the rising taxes to meet the demand for more paved roads, and especially the desecration, in spots almost the obliteration, of our fairest landscapes by the advertising signs and ugly filling stations and cheap refreshment booths which have followed in the motor's wake, surely ought to give us some pause.

5. **Advertisement for a family car.** *Whether as symbols of individual freedom or family togetherness, advertisers presented cars as essential to the good life.*

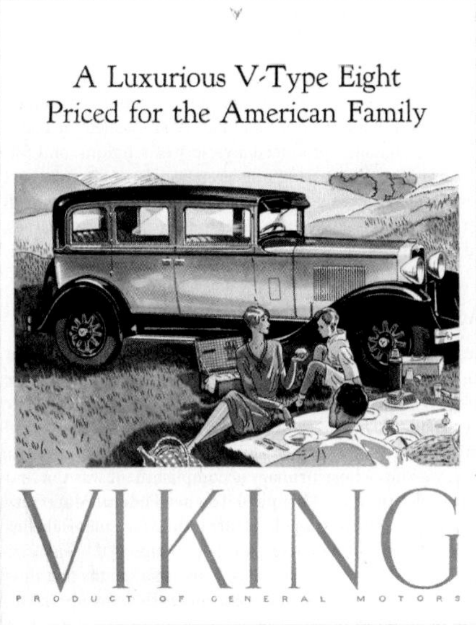
A Luxurious V-Type Eight
Priced for the American Family
VIKING
PRODUCT OF GENERAL MOTORS

Image Courtesy of The Advertising Archives.

6. **Letter to Department of Justice, 1932.** *This letter of complaint to the U.S. Department of Justice from a Chicago resident identifies a new menace: car theft.*

How can we who own automobiles feel safe in keeping one when we have here in this fair city of ours [Chicago] places to dispose of them so readily. Anyone wanting a set of wheels and tires or other accessories which are stripped from cars stolen in Indiana, Mich or other states no doubt but mostly local that is [*sic*] stolen here can get same very cheap. Our local police do not seem to prevent it. So many of our large automobile parts stores seem to have protection to handle such goods. Can something not be done about it?

Sources: (1) Charles E. Sorensen, with Samuel T. Williamson, *My Forty Years with Ford* (New York: W. W. Norton, 1956), 217–218; (2) Lawrence H. Seltzer, *A Financial History of the American Automobile Industry* (New York: Houghton Mifflin, 1928), 76, 128; (3) Excerpt from *Middletown: A Study in American Culture*, by Robert S. Lynd and Helen M. Lynd. Copyright © 1929 by Harcourt, Inc. and renewed 1957 by Robert S. and Helen M. Lynd. Reprinted by permission of Houghton Mifflin Harcourt Publishing Company. All rights reserved; (4) Walter Prichard Eaton, "The Billboard Curse," *The Forum* (November 1923): 2132; (6) John A. Heitmann and Rebecca H. Morales, *Stealing Cars: Technology and Society from the Model T to the Gran Torino* (Baltimore: Johns Hopkins University Press, 2014), 7.

ANALYZING THE EVIDENCE

1. What relationships do you see among sources 1, 2, and 3? If Sorensen (source 1) is right about the "lack of glamour" of the Model T, how does source 5 respond? Corroborate the sources to make a comparison.
2. Using sources 3, 4, and 6, identify the ways the automobile changed American life. Which of these are economic and which are cultural? Provide specific examples to support your claim.
3. Find all mentions in the sources of mobility and its advantages. What do these sources of mobility say about cultural developments in America?

AP® DBQ PRACTICE

Using these sources, along with what you have learned in this chapter, write an essay in which you examine how the increasing popularity and use of the automobile transformed American life in the 1920s. Consider the ways (cultural, economic, or social) that cars affected the lives of individuals and families.

TRM Find complete suggested responses in the Teacher's Resource Materials.

AP® SKILLS & PROCESSES

ARGUMENTATION

The **AP® DBQ PRACTICE** prompt asks students to address the larger effects of the automobile on American life. Beyond the cultural, economic, or social effects, encourage students to categorize their analysis through their own understandings from the book and class such as urban vs. rural, issues related to class, consumer culture, or modernity vs. fundamentalism. This will encourage a solid analysis to a dynamic topic.

CHECK FOR UNDERSTANDING

Ask students: **What were the primary characteristics of the American economy in the 1920s?** *Overall, the American economy boomed in the 1920s. Increasing foreign markets, business consolidations, and massive credit availability at home brought great wealth to urban and suburban dwellers, who spent it largely on new consumer goods and homes. Many of these consumer goods would have been considered luxuries in previous generations and ranged from the mundane, such as toasters and Hollywood films, to more sophisticated goods such as automobiles. This growth, which expanded the middle class significantly, did not reach rural areas, however, where agricultural prices still lagged behind.*

AP® SKILLS & PROCESSES

CAUSATION

Think about providing students with a topic that lends itself to a sound historical connection. For example, if students can examine how the automobile affected where people lived, they will understand how many people could have longer commutes to work, thus living on the geographical margins of the city increased over time. Additionally, in the 1920s Florida experienced a land boom in no small measure because of the automobile. Have students think of how the car transformed the mobility of Americans for vacation.

TRM Find complete suggested responses in the Teacher's Resource Materials.

centers, but only in communities narrowly built along the iron rail tracks of streetcar lines. After World War I, automobile suburbs grew like the crabgrass of suburban lawns — fast and everywhere. "Cities are spreading out," *National Geographic* announced in a 1923 special feature. Long Island's Nassau County, a suburban area of New York City, tripled in population, and the fifteen fastest-growing towns in Connecticut were all suburbs.

The spreading-out happened everywhere — from New York to Chicago, St. Louis to Seattle — but the growth of Los Angeles epitomized how automobiles remade American cities. New housing subdivisions opened monthly across a vast expanse of southern California, and the automobile facilitated a sprawling metropolis predicated on car travel. Los Angeles County's extensive and highly regarded electric streetcar system began to decline, as motorists clogged the roads. The region's population more than doubled in the 1920s alone, and Los Angeles went from the tenth largest American city to the fifth in just ten years. Southern California was forever linked with what historians call "automobility," and Los Angeles led the way in defining America's new "car culture."

AP® SKILLS & PROCESSES

CAUSATION

What effects did the automobile have on American culture and cities?

THE POLITICS AND CULTURE OF A DIVERSIFYING NATION

What were the main causes of cultural conflict in the 1920s?

At the dawn of the 1920s, public life in the United States had grown immeasurably more diverse. Women could now vote. More than 14 million immigrants — hailing primarily from Europe but also from Latin America and East Asia — called the country home. They spoke different languages, practiced a variety of religions, and followed unique cultural traditions (see "Comparing Interpretations," p. 688). The first phase of the Great Migration brought more than 1 million African Americans from all over the South into northern metropolises. Cities grew at the expense of rural areas. These dramatic changes led to conflict over what defined America — and Americans.

Women in a New Age

AP® EXAM TIP

Understand the causes and reactions to the rise of women as a political and cultural force in the 1920s.

Sheppard-Towner Federal Maternity and Infancy Act (1921) The first federally funded health-care legislation that provided federal funds for medical clinics, prenatal education programs, and visiting nurses.

At the start of the 1920s, many progressives hoped that women would exercise their newfound political clout on social welfare issues — and many politicians feared the power of a female voting bloc. One prominent contingent of women, veterans of the Settlement House and other Progressive-Era reform movements, did take up social welfare. They created organizations like the Women's Joint Congressional Committee, a Washington-based advocacy group whose primary accomplishment was the first federally funded health-care legislation, the **Sheppard-Towner Federal Maternity and Infancy Act** (1921). Sheppard-Towner provided federal funds for medical clinics, prenatal education programs, and visiting nurses, leading to improved health care for the poor and significantly lower infant mortality rates. It also marked the first time that Congress designated federal funds for the states to encourage them to administer a social-welfare program. But other reforms stalled, and the decade proved not to be a watershed of welfare legislation.

Another contingent of activist women focused on securing legal equality with men. In 1923, Alice Paul, founder of the National Woman's Party, persuaded congressional allies to consider an Equal Rights Amendment (ERA) to the U.S. Constitution. The proposed amendment stated simply that "men and women shall have equal rights throughout the United States." Advocates were hopeful; Wisconsin had passed a similar law two years earlier, which had helped women fight gender discrimination. But opponents pointed out that a national ERA would undermine recent labor laws that protected women from workplace abuses. Such laws recognized women's vulnerability in a heavily sex-segregated labor market. Would a theoretical statement of "equality" help poor and working women more than existing protections? This question divided women's rights advocates, and Paul's effort fizzled. The ERA would be introduced repeatedly in Congress over the next five decades, leading to eventual passage and a bitter ratification struggle in the 1970s (see "The Women's Movement and Gay Rights" in Chapter 28).

Women pushed for rights in another realm in the post–World War I years as well: reproduction. In 1921, Margaret Sanger founded the American Birth Control League, which established birth control clinics and promoted women's sexual health (it was renamed Planned Parenthood in 1942). Earlier such attempts had landed birth control advocates in jail, because contraceptive devices were illegal in most states and banned from the federal mail. But Sanger had achieved a legal victory in 1918 that permitted her to operate clinics as long as physicians prescribed contraception for medical reasons. She became an internationally recognized leader of the birth control movement in the 1920s, but women's rights activists in later decades denounced Sanger because she advocated policies based on eugenics — a theory positing the genetic superiority of white over darker races and the genetic inferiority of groups of people such as prostitutes and criminals.

The League of Women Voters The League of Women Voters was the brainchild of Carrie Chapman Catt, president of the National American Woman Suffrage Association. Formed in 1920, as the Nineteenth Amendment was about to give women the vote, the league undertook to educate Americans in responsible citizenship and to win enactment of legislation favorable to women. Library of Virginia.

National Association of Colored Women Groups such as the National Association of Colored Women (NACW) had fought for suffrage in the 1910s, just as white women had. But the constitutional right of black women to vote was meaningless in the South, where disfranchisement was law. Black women sought racial, not just gender, equality. When Addie Hunton, field secretary of the National Association for the Advancement of Colored People (NAACP), and sixty black women from the NACW urged the National Woman's Party to work against Jim Crow voting restrictions, Alice Paul refused, declaring disfranchisement to be a racial not a gender injustice. Hunton countered that "five million women in the United States cannot be denied their rights without all women of the United States feeling the effect of that denial. No women are free until all women are free."

New Woman Magazines, advertisements, and Hollywood movies crafted idealized images of an American "new woman" in the 1920s. She had thrown off Victorian modesty and claimed a place for herself alongside men in the new culture of consumption and fun. Such images, used primarily to sell products to the middle class, exaggerated reality. But women's roles — and their ambitions — were changing. The nineteenth-century notion of separate spheres for men and women had eroded considerably by 1930. More women attended college than ever before. Female athletes such as the golfer Glenna Collett, adventurers such as the celebrated pilot Amelia Earhart, and performers such as the brilliant jazz singer Josephine Baker carved out new, more liberated places for women in public life.

Social change takes time, however, and for the majority of American women in the 1920s ordinary life was far less glamorous. In some professions, such as medicine, women actually declined as a percentage of the workforce, and by the end of the decade only 3 percent of lawyers and 4 percent of physicians were women. Women's wages

CHECK FOR UNDERSTANDING

Ask students: **What does the League of Women Voters ad suggest about the importance of women's suffrage?** *The ad conveys the responsibility women bear to exercise their vote to make a positive difference. Directed by a larger-than-life female figure, perhaps a personification of Columbia or liberty, a respectable middle-class woman casts her ballot and thus makes an impact on the national government. The presence of her daughter suggests that her vote will have an important impact on families and children. The ad suggests the normative position of middle-class white women in American society.*

CHECK FOR UNDERSTANDING

Ask students: **What was life like for women in a new age?** *Women's rights activists continued to agitate for political change. They secured the Sheppard-Towner Act, which provided federal funds for maternity and childcare, and drafted the Equal Rights Amendment. African American women became politically active, forming the National Association for Colored Women. The "new woman" ideal emerged, suggesting that young middle-class women could enjoy consumer products and have fun in the same ways as men. In practical ways, however, many women's economic status languished, as their wages stagnated and they were confined to gender-specific occupations.*

AP® SKILLS & PROCESSES

ANALYZING HISTORICAL EVIDENCE

Handlin's influential interpretation of immigration in the **AP® COMPARING INTERPRETATIONS** feature persists, remaining for most Americans the default narrative of the immigrant experience. As his title indicates, Bodnar wrote his text explicitly in response to Handlin. Both titles make use of plant metaphors — uprooting and transplanting — while focusing on different elements of the process. For Handlin, immigration was a wrenching process that created a dramatic before-and-after experience, as immigrants left behind all they knew and started over in a very different America. Bodnar, by contrast, emphasizes the continuity of the immigrant experience. He suggests that modernizing processes had already come to affect Europeans in their home communities. In many cases, immigrants worked very hard to replicate the cultural patterns and social hierarchies they had established in their homelands. Thus, life in America was not as drastically different in Bodnar's estimation than Handlin made out.

AP® SKILLS & PROCESSES

ARGUMENTATION

Use the **ARGUMENTATION** question to explore unintended consequences of women receiving the right to vote. Arguably, one effect of women's achievement of the nationwide franchise through the Nineteenth Amendment was the loss of unity. The right to vote had been the primary goal of the movement for decades and the glue that held the movement together.

TRM Find complete suggested responses in the Teacher's Resource Materials.

AP® APPLY THE TIP

To help students see the common threads in the culture wars of the 1920s, prompt students to create a three-part Venn diagram labeled alcohol, education, and immigration. Students should use pp. 688–691 to identify the characteristics of each cultural conflict and add details to their Venn diagram. Then have students work with a partner to share their findings and discuss the common threads they see between each of the cultural controversies of the 1920s. Ask students to work with their partner to develop a thesis statement and outline addressing the following prompt: To what extent did the culture wars of the 1920s illustrate continuity over time in American history? Afterward, ask student groups to present their thesis statements and evidence to initiate a class discussion.

AP® COMPARING INTERPRETATIONS

How Did Immigrants Experience America at the Turn of the Century?

From the half century between the Civil War and World War I, more than 24 million people migrated to the United States. Many of these people came from Europe, but others left Asia, Latin America, and Africa in search of better opportunities or refuge in the United States. This turn-of-the-century migration included people from regions of southern and central Europe who had not previously come to the United States in such large numbers. Their presence in America's urban centers changed those places, but those immigrants were also changed. The extent to which migration from the Old to the New World affected these millions of people has, however, been a topic of debate among historians.

Oscar Handlin's classic history of the immigrant experience, *The Uprooted* (1951), defined the way historians thought about the topic for a generation. John Bodnar, writing three decades later, offered a different interpretation in *The Transplanted*. To what extent do the titles of their books hint at the argument each makes?

OSCAR HANDLIN

Source: Oscar Handlin, *The Uprooted: The Epic Story of the Great Migrations That Made the American People* (New York: Grosset & Dunlap, 1951), 144, 146, 149–150, 153, 155.

Settlement in America had snipped the continuity of the immigrants' work and ideas, of their religious life. It would also impose a new relationship to the world of space about them . . . newcomers pushed their roots into many different soils. Along the city's unyielding asphalt streets, beside the rutted roads of mill or mining towns, amidst the exciting prairie acres, they established the homes of the New World. But wherever the immigrants went, there was one common experience they shared: nowhere could they transplant the European village. Whatever the variations among environments in America, none was familiar. The pressure of that strangeness exerted a deep influence upon the character of resettlement, upon the usual forms of behavior, and upon the modes of communal action that emerged as the immigrants became Americans.

The old conditions of living could not survive in the new conditions of space. Ways long taken for granted in the village adjusted slowly and painfully to density of population in the cities, to disorder in the towns, and to distance on the farms. That adjustment was the means of creating the new communities within which these people would live. . . .

The immigrants find their first homes in quarters the old occupants no longer desire. . . . But the pressure of rising demand and the pattern of property holding gradually shaped a common form of the tenement house . . .These structures were at least six stories in height, sometimes eight. At the more moderate reckoning, twenty-four to thirty-two families could be housed on this tiny space, or more realistically, anywhere from one hundred and fifty to two hundred human beings.

. . . There were drastic social consequences to living under these dense conditions. The immigrants had left villages which counted their populations in scores (multiples of 20). . . .

The available space simply would not yield to all the demands made upon it. Where were the children to play

AP® SKILLS & PROCESSES

ARGUMENTATION

Explain why American women might have been more politically united prior to achieving the vote than afterward.

lagged far behind those of men, and women remained confined to gendered occupations: sales clerks in the new department stores, secretaries in the growing corporate world, and low-paid assembly-line workers in industry, alongside their traditional roles as domestic servants. African American and Latina women could not even get jobs as clerks and secretaries. Thus although American women in this era, especially the young, left behind the Victorian ideal of modesty and confinement to a female-only separate sphere, they had yet to fully dismantle their second-class standing.

AP® EXAM TIP

Compare the cultural controversies prevalent in the 1920s over alcohol, education, and immigration.

Culture Wars

By 1929, ninety-three U.S. cities had populations of more than 100,000. New York City exceeded 7 million inhabitants; Los Angeles's population had exploded to 1.2 million. The 1920 census marked the first time there were more urban than rural Americans, a major threshold for the nation. The lives and beliefs of urban Americans often differed dramatically from those in small towns and farming areas. One sharp critic, the writer Sinclair Lewis, wrote three satirical novels — *Main Street* (1920), *Babbitt* if the fields were gone? Where were things to be stored or clothes to be hung? . . .

Almost resignedly, the immigrants witnessed in themselves a deterioration. All relationships became less binding, all behavior more dependent on individual whim. The result was a marked personal decline and a noticeable wavering of standards. . . .

The low level of health and the high incidence of disease were certain products of overcrowding. Residents of the tenements did not need the spotted maps of later students to tell them where tuberculosis hit, a terror of illness that spread from victim to victim in the stifling rooms. . . .

The mortality rate was an indication of their helplessness against disease. The immigrants were men and women in the prime of life, yet they died more rapidly than the generality of Americans.

JOHN BODNAR

Source: John Bodnar, *The Transplanted: A History of Immigrants in Urban America* (Bloomington: Indiana University Press, 1985), 83–84.

When most working-class families had their choice, they preferred a private household consisting of parents and children. At times in the life cycle when children were able to work and contribute to finances, they were usually able to obtain their wish. The middle class was not alone in valuing the private household. But economic circumstances, primarily in the form of insufficient wages, forced parents to expand their households at specific times to embrace boarders and others in order to secure additional income.

The predisposition toward doing whatever was necessary to sustain a family-based household was nothing new. It had pervaded the immigrant homelands and received additional support ironically from the new system of industrial capitalism which restructured its labor market in a manner which facilitated the entry of groups of untrained toilers who were often related or at least acquainted with each other. Kin and friends were free to assist each other in entering America by providing access to jobs and homes and supplying important information of labor market conditions. New arrivals were adept at determining where they might enter a very large economy. The immigrant family economy survived and flourished among most newcomers in industrial America because new economic structures actually reinforced traditional ways of ordering life and, consequently, contributed to a supportive "external environment" for capitalism to proceed. In this system, individual inclinations were muted and the household, managed effectively by immigrant females, superseded all other goals and objectives. In the face of a sprawling and complex urban industrial structure, newcomers forged a relatively simple device for establishing order and purpose in their lives. This system would remain predominant among working-class families until the labor market was reshaped again after World War II. . . . Members of nearly all groups received indoctrination in the need to remain loyal to the familial and household unit. The goals of individual households could differ as a result of cultural background or positioning within the economy, and these divergences would come into play over time as separate paths of education, occupation, and mobility were taken. But in the movement to a capitalist world and in the initial decades of settlement, familial and communal networks abounded.

AP® QUESTIONS FOR ANALYSIS

1. How does Handlin's argument about immigrants as "uprooted" people differ from Bodnar's description of them as "transplanted"?
2. According to each author, what role did family and community play in the immigrant experience?
3. Which point of view — Handlin's or Bodnar's — is better supported by the chapter narrative? Give specific examples to support your argument.

TRM Find complete suggested responses in the Teacher's Resource Materials.

(1922), and *Elmer Gantry* (1927) — that mocked small-town life for its religiosity and, as Lewis saw it, hypocrisy and lack of sophistication.

In a decade of friction between traditional and modern worldviews, the urban-rural split that fascinated Lewis represented one line of conflict among several. Many of the fault lines had been in the making for decades, in some cases even centuries. Protestant versus Catholic and Jewish, religious versus secular, native born versus immigrant, and white versus black — but the cultural battles of the 1920s galvanized them into a debate over values, beliefs, and even which people could be deemed "American."

Prohibition Rural and native-born Protestants had long worked for a national prohibition on alcohol (see "Women's Civic Activism" in Chapter 17). The two principal anti-alcohol organizations, the Woman's Christian Temperance Union and the Anti-Saloon League, hailed temperance as good for health and Christian virtue. In the 1910s, some progressives joined the campaign, convinced that alcohol kept immigrant workers in poverty and that saloons bred political corruption. World War I, too, spurred the cause. Mobilizing the economy for war, Congress limited brewers' and

AP® THEME

SOC: Social Structures; NAT: American and National Identity

As the chapter opener indicated, one key feature of this era was the emergence of cultural and political controversies as Americans debated gender roles, modernism, science, religion, and issues related to race and immigration. The "Clash of Cultures in the 1910s and 1920s" Web site page, available through Ohio State University's ehistory Web site, provides materials to help students explore these controversies. To access the site, search "ehistory Clash of Cultures."

distillers' use of barley and other scarce grains, driving down consumption. Moreover, anti-German hysteria linked the many German American breweries, like Pabst and Anheuser-Busch, with the wartime enemy. A decades-long push for national prohibition culminated with Congress's passage of the **Eighteenth Amendment** in 1917. Ratified over the next two years by nearly every state and taking effect in January 1920, the amendment prohibited the "manufacture, sale, or transportation of intoxicating liquors" anywhere in the United States. It was enforced by the federal government under the 1920 **Volstead Act**.

Eighteenth Amendment
The ban on the manufacture and sale of alcohol that went into effect in January 1920. Also called "prohibition," the amendment was repealed in 1933.

Volstead Act (1920)
Officially, the National Prohibition Act, passed by Congress to enforce the provisions of the Eighteenth Amendment banning the sale of alcohol.

Prohibition's most ardent supporters were native-born, small-town Protestants, and its greatest opponents were immigrants and middle-class urbanites. Defenders of prohibition celebrated it as a victory over sin and vice. In urban areas, though, Americans flagrantly ignored the law — and mocked prohibition as old-fashioned Puritanism. Immigrants saw the ban as an attack on the working-class saloon that served as a social center. During Prohibition more affluent urban drinkers flocked to speakeasies, or illegal drinking establishments, which flourished in almost every major city; one raid on a Chicago speakeasy captured 200,000 gallons of alcohol. Profits from the speakeasies and from the illegal manufacture and transport of alcohol enriched notorious gangsters such as Chicago's Al Capone and New York's Jack Diamond.

National prohibition was a prolonged social experiment that fizzled. Alcohol consumption declined in 1921 and 1922 but then began climbing again — though it did not reach pre-1920 levels until after repeal in 1933. Among the middle class, which could afford higher prices, alcohol consumption declined hardly at all in these years. The fact that only the *sale* and not the *possession* of alcohol was illegal made prohibition exceedingly difficult to enforce. And yet the Eighteenth Amendment's most important legacy might well have been the growing influence of the Justice Department's Bureau of Investigation, the federal agency tasked with enforcing the Volstead Act ("Federal" was added in 1935, making it the now-familiar FBI). Under the shrewd direction of J. Edgar Hoover, the FBI used the Red Scare and prohibition to increase its resources, enlarge its investigative domain, and become a fixture of federal police power.

American Civil Liberties Union (ACLU)
An organization formed during the Red Scare of the 1920s to protect free speech rights.

Wine in the Gutters, Brooklyn This photograph captures America's cultural conflicts over prohibition. When the law went into effect, federal agents seized and destroyed supplies of alcohol, often dumping it in the streets. Here, working-class children in Brooklyn race to scoop it up in buckets before it drains away. In tenement neighborhoods, children eager to earn a nickel often toted buckets of beer, wine, and homemade liquor for their parents or neighbors. NY Daily News Archive via Getty Images.

Evolution in the Schools In another clash between modern and traditionalist worldviews, fundamentalist Protestants fought to keep the biblical account of creation in school curricula — and to keep the theory of evolution out. In 1925, Tennessee's legislature outlawed the teaching of "any theory that denies the story of the Divine creation of man as taught in the Bible, [and teaches] instead that man has descended from a lower order of animals." The **American Civil Liberties Union (ACLU)**, formed during the Red Scare to protect free speech rights, challenged the law's constitutionality. The trial of John T. Scopes, a high school biology teacher who admitted to teaching evolution, drew national attention to the small town of Dayton, Tennessee. Clarence Darrow, a famous criminal lawyer, defended Scopes, while William Jennings Bryan, the three-time Democratic presidential candidate, spoke for the prosecution.

TEACHING STRATEGY

To explore the development of the ACLU during the Red Scare, have students describe one way in which action taken during World War I or the Red Scare would have caused concern among citizens. What actions by the federal government or private citizens would have prompted such an organization?

Journalists dubbed the **Scopes trial** "the monkey trial." This label referred both to Darwin's argument that human beings and other primates share a common ancestor and to the circus atmosphere at the trial, which was broadcast live over a Chicago radio station. (Proving that urbanites had their own prejudices, acerbic critic and city-dweller H. L. Mencken dismissed antievolutionists, widely associated with rural areas, as "gaping primates of the upland valleys.") The jury took only eight minutes to deliver its verdict: guilty. Though the Tennessee Supreme Court later overturned Scopes's conviction on a minor technicality (the judge, not the jury, had set the fine), the law remained on the books for more than thirty years.

Scopes trial
The 1925 trial of John Scopes, a biology teacher in Dayton, Tennessee, for violating his state's ban on teaching evolution. The trial created a nationwide media frenzy and came to be seen as a showdown between urban and rural values.

AP® EXAM TIP
Evaluate the Scopes trial as an expression of the battle between modernism and fundamentalism in American society.

Nativism Some native-born Protestants saw immigration as the primary cause of a perceived moral decline. A nation of 105 million people had added more than 24 million immigrants over the previous four decades; the newcomers included many Catholics and Jews from Southern and Eastern Europe, whom one Maryland congressman referred to as "indigestible lumps" in the "national stomach." "America must be kept American," President Coolidge declared in 1924. Rising anti-immigrant views evoked the hostility toward Irish and Germans in the 1840s and 1850s. In this case, nativism fueled a momentous shift in immigration policy.

Congress had banned Chinese immigration in 1882, and Theodore Roosevelt had negotiated a so-called gentleman's agreement that limited Japanese immigration in 1907. Now nativists charged that there were too many European arrivals, some of whom, they claimed, undermined Protestantism and imported anarchism, socialism, and other radical doctrines. Responding to this pressure, Congress passed emergency immigration restrictions in 1921 and a permanent measure three years later. The **National Origins Act** (1924) used backdated census data to establish a quota system: in the future, annual immigration from each country could not exceed 2 percent of that nationality's total in the 1890 census. Since only small numbers of Italians, Greeks, Poles, Russians, and other Southern and Eastern European immigrants had arrived before 1890, the law drastically curtailed immigration from those places. In 1929, Congress imposed even more restrictive quotas, setting a cap of 150,000 immigrants per year from Europe and continuing to ban most immigrants from Asia.

National Origins Act (1924)
A federal law limiting annual immigration from each foreign country to no more than 2 percent of that nationality's percentage of the U.S. population as it had stood in 1890. The law severely limited immigration, especially from Southern and Eastern Europe.

However, the new laws did not restrict immigration from the Western Hemisphere. As a result, Latin Americans arrived in increasing numbers, finding jobs that had gone to other immigrants before exclusion. More than 1 million Mexicans entered the United States between 1900 and 1930, including many fleeing the instability caused by the Mexican Revolution. Nativists lobbied Congress to block this flow; so did labor leaders, who argued that impoverished migrants lowered wages for other American workers. But Congress heeded the pleas of employers, especially farmers in Texas and California, who wanted cheap labor.

Other anti-immigrant measures emerged at the state level. In 1913, by an overwhelming majority, California's legislature had passed a law declaring that "aliens ineligible to citizenship" could not own "real property." The aim was to prevent Asians, especially Japanese immigrants, from owning land, though some had lived in the state for decades and built up prosperous farms. In the wake of World War I, California tightened these laws, making it increasingly difficult for Asian families to establish themselves. California, Washington, and the territory of Hawaii also severely restricted any school that taught Japanese language, history, or culture. Denied both citizenship and land rights, Japanese Americans would find themselves in a vulnerable position when the United States entered World War II.

AP® EXAM TIP
Understanding the discriminatory nature of immigration restrictions in the 1920s is important to know on the AP® Exam.

The National Klan The 1920s saw a nationwide resurgence of the **Ku Klux Klan (KKK)**, a white supremacist group formed in the post–Civil War South. Soon after the premiere of *Birth of a Nation* (1915), a popular Hollywood film glorifying the Reconstruction-era Klan, a group of southerners gathered on Georgia's Stone Mountain to revive the organization. With its blunt motto of "Native, white, Protestant supremacy,"

Ku Klux Klan (KKK)
Secret society that first undertook violence against African Americans in the South after the Civil War but was reborn in 1915 to fight the perceived threats posed by African Americans, immigrants, radicals, feminists, Catholics, and Jews.

TEACHING STRATEGY

The Scopes trial is a popular classroom topic that needs to be addressed carefully and thoughtfully. The National Humanities Center's Divining America Web site provides a helpful background essay, suggestions for guiding classroom discussion, and an overview of major historiographical debates going back more than a half-century. To access the site, search "Divining America Scopes Trial."

Additionally, the *American Experience* film *Monkey Trial* offers a narrative of the trial that places it in its larger historical context while exploring its ongoing significance. To access the film, search "American Experience Monkey Trial."

AP® THEME

MIG: Migration and Settlement

Immigration from Europe peaked in the years before World War I. After the war, nativist campaigns against some ethnic groups led to the passage of quotas that restricted immigration, particularly from Southern and Eastern Europe, and also increased barriers against Asian immigration.

AP® THEME

MIG: Migration and Settlement

During and after World War I, migration to the U.S. from Mexico and elsewhere in the Western Hemisphere increased, in spite of contradictory government policies toward Mexican immigration. The photograph illustrates the willingness of some to use military force to prevent largely poor, Catholic immigrants from entering a country believed to be Protestant. As the caption indicates, this image can be connected to the development of the Johnson-Reed Bill, or National Origins Act of 1924. This tension explains the contradictory postures the U.S. adopted toward the issue. A century later, this tension remains a key element of the nation's political culture.

AP® APPLY THE TIP

Ask students to complete **Handout 21.4—Comparison: Ku Klux Klan (TRM)** using "The National Klan" section in the text (pp. 691–692) and other sources, including images and primary sources. Prompt students to include the following in their diagrams: causes for the creation or revival of the KKK in each period; groups attacked by the KKK in each period; leadership and organization in each period; events associated with the KKK in each period; political impact of the KKK in each period; and reactions to the KKK in each period.

After students have completed their diagrams, lead a class discussion on the degree to which the revival of the KKK represented change and/or continuity in the U.S. in the early twentieth century.

TRM Find **Handout 21.4—Comparison: Ku Klux Klan** in the Teacher's Resource Materials.

The U.S. Border Patrol, Laredo, Texas, 1926 Following passage of the National Origins Act in 1924, the United States established the Border Patrol, pictured here outside Laredo, Texas. Its increasing efforts to police the border slowed the casual movement of Mexican workers in and out of the United States. Photography Collection, Harry Ransom Center, The University of Texas at Austin.

AP® EXAM TIP

Compare the KKK that developed in the 1920s to the KKK that originated in the Reconstruction Era.

the Klan recruited supporters across the country. KKK members did not limit their harassment to African Americans but targeted immigrants, Catholics, and Jews as well, with physical intimidation, arson, and economic boycotts.

At the height of its influence in the early 1920s, the Klan counted more than three million members and wielded considerable political clout, particularly at the local level. A typical example was the small town of Monticello, Arkansas, where in the first half of the decade, the mayor, city marshal, half the city council, the sheriff, the county clerk, tax assessor, and treasurer, and eleven of fifteen male teachers were all Klan members. From small-town leaders to President Woodrow Wilson, who effusively praised *Birth of a Nation*, the Klan enjoyed broad support among native-born white Protestant Americans for a decade. Klan activism lent a menacing cast to political debate, as its members defined "one hundred percent Americanism" to include white racial purity, Protestantism, prohibition of alcohol, conservative sexual mores, and immigration restriction — the Klan avidly supported both the Eighteenth Amendment and the Immigration Act of 1924.

The Klan declined rapidly after 1925, owing to a wide range of factors: internal factionalism and economic mismanagement, the waning of the postwar antiradical and antiblack furor, and the achievement of immigration restriction. But its rise was part of an ugly trend that began before World War I and extended into subsequent decades. The Klan's popularity demonstrated the continued appeal of white supremacy, nativism, and Protestant Christian superiority to large numbers of Americans. Those prejudices would long outlive the Klan, and could be observed at the highest stations of American life. The most famous industrialist in the country, Henry Ford, espoused racist and anti-Semitic views. Ford used his newspaper, the *Dearborn Independent*, to rail against immigrants and warned that members of "the proud Gentile race," meaning non-Jews, must arm themselves against a Jewish conspiracy aimed at world domination. Challenged by critics, one of whom demanded that Ford choose between "democracy which is based upon equality and cooperation" and "Nazism which is based upon slavery and repression," the car-maker issued an apology in 1927. But with his paper's editorials widely circulated by the Klan and other groups, the damage was done.

The Election of 1928 Conflicts over race, religion, and ethnicity created the climate for a stormy presidential election in 1928. Democrats had traditionally drawn strength from white voters in the South and immigrants in the North, but these groups divided over prohibition, immigration restriction, and the Klan. By 1928, the party's urban wing gained firm control. Democrats nominated Governor Al Smith of New York, the first presidential candidate to reflect the aspirations of the urban working class. A grandson of Irish peasants, Smith had risen through New York City's Democratic machine to become a dynamic reformer. But he offended many small-town and rural Americans with his heavy New York accent and brown derby hat, which highlighted his ethnic working-class origins. Middle-class reformers questioned Smith's ties to Tammany Hall, the notorious Democratic political machine that controlled the city, and temperance advocates opposed him as a "wet." But the governor's greatest electoral handicap was his religion. Although Smith insisted that his Catholic beliefs would not affect his duties as president, many Protestants opposed him. "No Governor can kiss the papal ring and get within gunshot of the White House," vowed one Methodist bishop.

Smith proved no match for the Republican nominee, Secretary of Commerce Herbert Hoover. An organizational genius and a dedicated public servant, Hoover won fame during World War I for successfully managing huge food relief and refugee projects before energizing and reorganizing the Treasury Department as secretary of commerce under President Harding. Hoover ran on eight years of Republican prosperity, giving business credit for the country's rising affluence and embracing the American tradition of individualism. He won overwhelmingly, with 444 electoral votes to Smith's 87 (Map 21.1). Because many southern Protestants refused to vote for a Catholic, Hoover carried five ex-Confederate states, breaking the Democratic "Solid South" for the first time since Reconstruction. Smith, though, carried industrialized Massachusetts and Rhode Island as well as the nation's twelve largest cities, showing how urban voters were moving into the Democrats' camp.

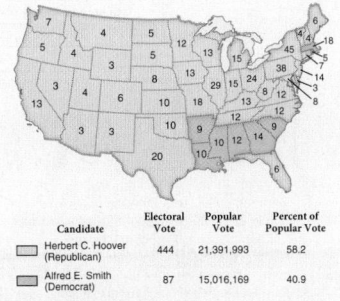

Candidate	Electoral Vote	Popular Vote	Percent of Popular Vote
Herbert C. Hoover (Republican)	444	21,391,993	58.2
Alfred E. Smith (Democrat)	87	15,016,169	40.9

MAP 21.1 The Presidential Election of 1928
Historians still debate the extent to which 1928 was a critical election — an election that produced a significant realignment in voting behavior. Although Republican Herbert Hoover swept the popular and the electoral votes, Democrat Alfred E. Smith won majorities not only in the South, his party's traditional stronghold, but also in Rhode Island, Massachusetts, and (although it is not evident on this map) all of the large cities of the North and Midwest. In subsequent elections, the Democrats won even more votes among African Americans and European ethnic groups and, until 1980, were the nation's dominant political party.

AP® SKILLS & PROCESSES

MAKING CONNECTIONS

How would you describe the view of those Americans who supported prohibition, the teaching of evolution in public schools, and immigration restriction? How would you describe their opponents' views? Can you understand the perspectives of each?

The Harlem Renaissance

Amidst these clashes over religion, morality, and Americanism, black artists and intellectuals staked a claim to unapologetic pride in their own identity. They questioned long-standing assumptions about civilization, progress, and the alleged superiority of Western cultures over so-called primitive people. A vibrant new black cultural movement took shape, centered in New York City, where the Great Migration had tripled the black population in the decade after 1910 (Map 21.2). The black neighborhood of Harlem stood as "the symbol of liberty and the Promised Land to Negroes everywhere," as one minister put it. Talented African Americans flocked there and forged a literary and artistic culture rooted in the everyday lives and experiences of black people.

AP® EXAM TIP

Evaluate the Harlem Renaissance as an expression of African American identity.

Black Writers and Artists Poet Langston Hughes voiced the upbeat spirit of the **Harlem Renaissance** when he asserted, "I am a Negro — and beautiful." Other writers and artists also championed black racial identity and pride. Claude McKay and Jean Toomer wrote poetry and novels that portrayed black people with a realism and sympathy uncommon in American letters. Painter Jacob Lawrence, who had grown up in crowded tenement districts of the urban North, used bold shapes and vivid colors to portray the daily life, aspirations, and suppressed anger of African Americans. These artists, among many others in the Renaissance, represented what

Harlem Renaissance
A flourishing of African American artists, writers, intellectuals, and social leaders in the 1920s, centered in the neighborhood of Harlem, New York City.

CHECK FOR UNDERSTANDING

Ask students: **What significant culture wars did Americans fight in the 1920s?** *Americans clashed over a number of issues that spoke to concerns about identity and values, largely launched by native-born Protestants. Prohibition reflected concerns rural, native-born Protestants had long held about the dangers of drink. Evolution threatened the authority of the Bible and the dignity of humanity. Nativism reflected anxiety about the inability of Jews and Catholics to assimilate to a presumably Protestant America. These nativist concerns were expressed most graphically in the reemergence of the KKK in the wake of the release of* Birth of a Nation.

AP® SKILLS & PROCESSES

MAKING CONNECTIONS

The **MAKING CONNECTIONS** question asks students to compare the views of opponents on both sides of several controversies in the 1920s. Students may struggle to understand the perspectives of groups they don't sympathize with, but remind them that it's helpful to develop the ability to understand different points of view even if they disagree strongly. Extend this prompt by having students explain why support for prohibition has essentially disappeared from American culture, while some opponents of evolution and some supporters of immigration restriction remain.

TRM Find complete suggested responses in the Teacher's Resource Materials.

AP® THEME

ARC: American and Regional Culture

African American migration gave rise to the Harlem Renaissance as **MAP 21.2** shows, which included new forms of art and literature expressing ethnic identity. The following online resources provide engaging, interactive ways for students to learn about African American life and culture in the era of the Harlem Renaissance:

- The Library of Congress's "The African American Odyssey: A Quest for Full Citizenship" Web site page explores how World War I galvanized the black community in its effort to make America truly democratic. To access this site, search "LOC African American Odyssey."
- The New York Public Library's "Harlem 1900–1940" Web site page provides a survey of some of the main personalities and events that shaped this Manhattan neighborhood in the early days when it became known as the "Capital of the Negro World." To access this site, search "NYPL Harlem."
- The Kennedy Center's "Drop Me Off in Harlem" Web site page invites students to discover the themes and works that emerged when creative and intellectual voices intersected during the Harlem Renaissance. To access this site, search "Kennedy Center Drop Me Off in Harlem."

TRM Find complete suggested responses in the Teacher's Resource Materials.

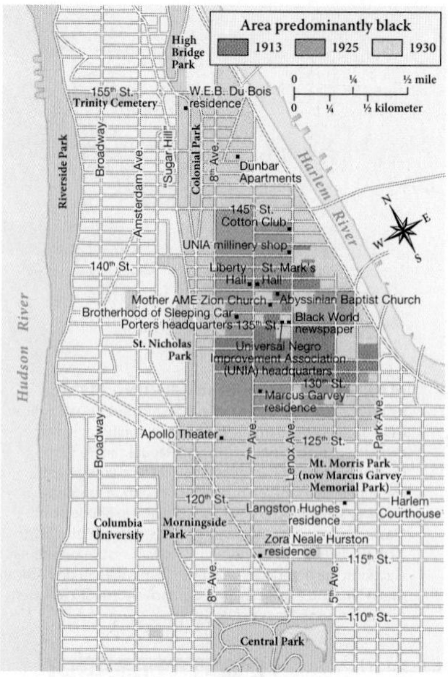

MAPPING THE PAST

MAP 21.2 Harlem, 1913–1930

African Americans had lived in New York City since its founding in 1624 as part of the Dutch settlement of New Amsterdam. A small number lived in Harlem, in the northern part of Manhattan Island until the early 1900s. Then in 1904, a subway line connecting 145th Street in Harlem to lower Manhattan and Brooklyn opened, and black tenants and homeowners began to come in larger numbers in search of better housing. During and after World War I, large numbers of southern migrants joined established black families there, bringing with them the food, music, and folkways of the South, and Harlem increasingly became a center of black life in New York City. By 1930, 165,000 African Americans, almost 75 percent of Manhattan's black population, were concentrated in Harlem.

ANALYZING THE MAP: How and when did the predominantly black areas of Harlem expand in size? What is the historical context for this development?

MAKING CONNECTIONS: How might the concentration of black residents in New York have contributed to the rise of organizations like Marcus Garvey's UNIA as well as to the literary and artistic movement known as the Harlem Renaissance? How can the identity of African Americans illustrated in this map be compared to earlier developments in African American communities and churches?

jazz
Unique American musical form with an improvisational style that emerged in New Orleans and other parts of the South before World War I. It grew in popularity during the Harlem Renaissance.

philosopher Alain Locke called, in an influential 1925 book, the "New Negro": proud and unapologetic chroniclers of the multifaceted black experience.

No one embodied the energy and optimism of the Harlem Renaissance more than Zora Neale Hurston. Born in the prosperous black community of Eatonville, Florida, Hurston had been surrounded as a child by examples of both black achievement and anti-black discrimination. After enrolling at Barnard College and studying with anthropologist Franz Boas, Hurston traveled through the South and the Caribbean for a decade, documenting folklore, songs, and religious beliefs. She incorporated this material into her short stories and novels, celebrating the humor and spiritual strength of ordinary black men and women. Like other work of the Harlem Renaissance, Hurston's stories and novels sought to articulate what it meant, as black intellectual W. E. B. Du Bois wrote, "to be both a Negro and an American."

Augusta Fells Savage, African American Sculptor Born in Florida in 1892, Augusta Fells Savage arrived in New York in 1921 to study and remained to take part in the Harlem Renaissance. Widowed at a young age and struggling to support her parents and young daughter, Savage faced both racism and poverty. Much of her work has been lost because she sculpted in clay and could not afford to cast in bronze. Savage began to speak out for racial justice after she was denied, on the basis of her race, a fellowship to study in Paris. Augusta Savage with her sculpture *Realization*, c. 1938/Andrew Herman, photographer. Federal Art Project, Photographic Division collection, c. 1920–1965, bulk 1935–1942. Archives of American Art, Smithsonian Institution.

Jazz To millions of Americans, the most famous symbol of the Harlem Renaissance was the musical form known as **jazz**. Though the origins of the word are unclear, many historians believe it was a slang term for sex — an etymology that makes sense, given the music's early association with urban vice districts. Borrowing from blues, ragtime, and other popular forms, jazz musicians developed an ensemble style in which performers, keeping a rapid ragtime beat, improvised around a basic melodic line. The majority of early jazz musicians were black, but white performers, some of whom had more formal training, injected elements of European concert music.

Jazz had first emerged in New Orleans and other parts of the South before World War I. As the sound spread nationwide in the 1920s, musicians refined what became its hallmark: the improvised solo. A key figure in this development was trumpeter Louis Armstrong. A native of New Orleans, Armstrong learned his craft playing in the saloons and brothels of the city's vice district. Like countless other African Americans, he moved north, settling in Chicago in 1922. In his recordings and live performances, Armstrong showed an inexhaustible capacity for melodic invention, and his dazzling solos inspired other musicians. By the late 1920s, soloists were the celebrities of jazz, thrilling audiences with their improvisational skill.

As jazz followed the routes of the Great Migration from the South to northern and midwestern cities, the music found eager fans. Dance halls for both black and white audiences put jazz bands on, and leading artists toured all over the country. As New Yorkers flocked to ballrooms and clubs to hear Duke Ellington and other stars, Harlem became the hub of commercially lucrative jazz performances. Many whites who thrilled at the "primitive" black music did not abandon their racial condescension: visiting a mixed-race club became known as "slumming."

Archibald Motley, *Blues*, 1929 Painter Archibald Motley (1891–1981) was born in New Orleans but arrived in Chicago as a small child, when his family—like thousands of other African Americans—moved north in search of opportunity. Motley studied at the Art Institute of Chicago and by the 1920s also showed his work in New York City. Many of his paintings depicted life in the predominantly African American neighborhood on Chicago's South Side that was widely known as the Black Belt. This piece, *Blues*, was painted when Motley was living in Paris. Private Collection/© Valerie Gerrard Browne/Chicago History Museum/Bridgeman Images.

TEACHING STRATEGY

In a ten-part documentary, filmmaker Ken Burns tells the story of jazz, the quintessential American art form. The film features thousands of rare archival music, photos, and video clips. The PBS companion Web site includes an interactive map feature that allows students to explore the places where jazz came of age and the spaces where the early sound of jazz took root and spread. A musical primer explains key jazz musical concepts, including improvisation, melody, harmony, rhythm, and instruments. To access the site, search "PBS Jazz."

TEACHING STRATEGY

The Whitney Museum of American Art provides several resources on Motley and his work to accompany the exhibition *Archibald Motley: Jazz Age Modernist*. In addition to a brief biography, the site includes more than a dozen examples of his artwork, each with a brief audio guide explaining the piece's meaning and significance. To access this site, search "Whitney Archibald Motley exhibition."

TEACHING STRATEGY

The National Humanities Center's Divining America Web site provides useful information to guide students' understanding of Marcus Garvey. The site includes an essay on Marcus Garvey and the Universal Negro Improvement Association (UNIA), suggestions for student discussion, an overview of historiographical debates, and links to a variety of online primary and secondary sources related to UNIA. To access this site, search "Divining America Marcus Garvey."

Radio also helped popularize the new sound, and the emerging record industry sold the latest tunes on 78 RPM discs. Many of those discs were so-called race records, specifically aimed at urban working-class African American listeners. In 1920, Otto K. E. Heinemann, a producer who sold immigrant records in Yiddish, Swedish, and other languages, recorded singer Mamie Smith performing "Crazy Blues." This breakthrough hit prompted big recording labels like Columbia and Paramount to copy Heinemann's approach. Even as its reception reflected the segregation of American society, jazz moved black music to the center stage of American culture. It became the signature music of the decade, so much so that novelist F. Scott Fitzgerald dubbed the 1920s the "Jazz Age."

Universal Negro Improvement Association (UNIA)
A Harlem-based group, led by charismatic, Jamaican-born Marcus Garvey, that arose in the 1920s to mobilize African American workers and champion black separatism.

Marcus Garvey and the UNIA The creative energy of the Harlem Renaissance also generated broad political aspirations. The Harlem-based **Universal Negro Improvement Association (UNIA)**, led by charismatic Jamaican-born Marcus Garvey, arose in the 1920s to mobilize African American workers and champion black nationalism. Garvey urged followers to move to Africa, arguing that people of African descent would never be treated justly in white-run countries.

The UNIA soon claimed four million members, including many recent migrants to northern cities. It published a newspaper, *Negro World*, and solicited funds for the

The Garvey Movement on the March Black Women from the Universal Negro Improvement Association (UNIA) march down Seventh Avenue in New York City in 1924. Under the leadership of Marcus Garvey, UNIA fostered collective strength and what at the time was called "race pride" within African American communities. George Rinhart/Corbis via Getty Images.

Black Star Line, a steamship company Garvey created to foster trade with the West Indies and carry black Americans to Africa. Garvey may have advocated a return to Africa, but he was outspoken about black rights in America, and this outspokenness made him a target of J. Edgar Hoover's Bureau of Investigation. Once Hoover turned his agents on the UNIA, it declined as quickly as it had risen. In 1925, Garvey was imprisoned for mail fraud because of his solicitations for the Black Star Line. President Coolidge commuted his sentence but ordered him deported to Jamaica. Without Garvey's leadership, the movement collapsed.

However, the UNIA contributed to an emerging, and ultimately more lasting, **pan-Africanism** in America. This idea held that people of African descent, in all parts of the world, shared a common destiny and should cooperate in political action. Several developments contributed to this idea: black men's military service in Europe during World War I, the Pan-African Congress that had sought representation at the Versailles peace talks, and protests against U.S. occupation of Haiti. One African American historian wrote in 1927, "The grandiose schemes of Marcus Garvey gave to the race a consciousness such as it had never possessed before."

AP® EXAM TIP

Understanding the changes that developed in political activism in the African American community is critical for success on the AP® Exam.

pan-Africanism
The idea that people of African descent, in all parts of the world, have a common heritage and destiny and should cooperate in political action.

AP® SKILLS & PROCESSES

MAKING CONNECTIONS

How did the Great Migration lead to flourishing African American culture, politics, and intellectual life, and what form did these activities take?

THE COMING OF THE GREAT DEPRESSION

What domestic and global economic factors caused the Great Depression?

By the last years of the 1920s, the mass consumer society that had emerged after World War I was in trouble. The pace of consumption slowed considerably, and the American economy as a whole was mired in debt. Consumer lending had become the tenth largest business in the country, topping $7 billion that year. Millions of farmers were trapped in the same annual cycle of debt as their forebears, and global agricultural markets were saturated, which drove down farm income. As demand for both manufactured goods and farm produce flagged, a vicious cycle ensued. Firms and farms went bankrupt and laid off workers. Unable to collect debts, banks began to fail. Warnings about the dangers of rapid growth, in which industrial production far outstripped demand, and easy credit proved painfully right. The boom that had made the 1920s "roar" stumbled and collapsed by the end of the decade, culminating in the Great Depression. The good times had been brief, the era's economic expansion lasting only seven years, from 1922 to 1929.

From Boom to Bust

The depression's precipitating event was a massive collapse of the stock market. Easy credit had fueled years of excessive stock speculation, which inflated the value of traded companies well beyond their actual worth. In a series of plunges between October 25 and November 13, 1929, the stock market lost approximately 40 percent of its value, more than the total cost to all the combatant nations of World War I. Not a mere one-day event but rather three weeks of sharply declining prices, the crash was a symptom of a weakening economy, but few onlookers understood the magnitude of the crisis. Sharp downturns had been a familiar part of the industrializing economy since the 1830s; panics tended to follow periods of rapid growth and speculation. The market recovered again in late 1929 and early 1930, and while a great deal of money had been lost, most Americans believed the aftermath of the crash would be brief.

In fact, the nation had entered the Great Depression, the most severe economic downturn to that point in the nation's history — as well as a global phenomenon, with major European and South American economies also tumbling into crisis. Over the next four years, industrial production fell 37 percent. Construction plunged

AP® EXAM TIP

Connect the causes that led to the Great Depression to the economic and political developments of the 1920s.

CHECK FOR UNDERSTANDING

Ask students: **What were the main causes of cultural conflict in the 1920s?** *The 1920s was a decade of great change. New diverse groups asserted themselves or tried to assert themselves in various arenas (economic, political, social, cultural, etc.), among them women, African Americans, and immigrants. That trend tends to create cultural conflict. But these diverse social groups also came across entrenched interests of white middle-class Protestant males, who sought to retain their social, political, economic, and cultural authority, exacerbating the situation.*

AP® SKILLS & PROCESSES

MAKING CONNECTIONS

The **MAKING CONNECTIONS** question asks students to explain how the Great Migration caused the Harlem Renaissance. Students' explanations need to move beyond the mere fact that many African Americans moved into the same section of Manhattan. To extend this prompt, ask students to explain the long-term significance of the Harlem Renaissance.

TRM Find complete suggested responses in the Teacher's Resource Materials.

TEACHING STRATEGY

Ask students: **What does FIGURE 21.1 reveal about the Great Depression?** *Figure 21.1 shows how severe the depression was, with 1 in 4 Americans unemployed at the peak in 1933. The spikes in unemployment in 1915 and 1921 suggest why some Americans did not immediately realize the depth of the coming recession. The chart also indicates that while unemployment began to drop in 1939 and 1940, it did not return to predepression levels until 1942.*

CHECK FOR UNDERSTANDING

Ask students: **How did the U.S. go from boom to bust?** *The stock market crash led to the most severe economic downturn the nation had ever experienced. Production eventually fell by more than one-third, while prices for crops fell by half. Eventually, one in four Americans was unemployed.*

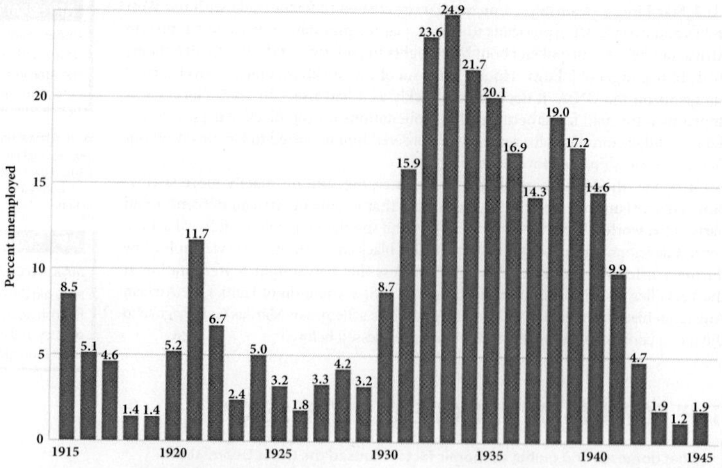

FIGURE 21.1 Unemployment, 1915–1945

During the 1920s, business prosperity and low rates of immigration resulted in historically low unemployment levels. The Great Depression threw millions of people out of work; by 1933, one in four American workers was unemployed, and the rate remained high until 1941, when the nation mobilized for World War II.

78 percent. Prices for crops and other raw materials, already low, fell by half. By 1932, unemployment had reached a staggering 24 percent (Figure 21.1).

A precipitous drop in consumer spending deepened the crisis. Facing hard times and unemployment, Americans cut back dramatically, creating a vicious cycle of falling demand and forfeited loans. Buying homes, cars, and appliances on credit had seemed like a good deal in 1925; by 1930 the deal turned sour. That year, several major banks went under, victims of overextended credit and reckless management. The following year, as industrial production slowed, a much larger wave of bank failures occurred, sending out even greater shockwaves. Since the government did not insure bank deposits, accounts in failed banks simply vanished.

The Depression's Early Years

Not all Americans were devastated by the depression; the middle class did not disappear and the rich still lived in relative luxury. But incomes plummeted even among workers who kept their jobs. Barter systems developed, as barbers traded haircuts for onions and potatoes and laborers took payment in produce or pork. "We do not dare to use even a little soap," reported one jobless Oregonian, "when it will pay for an extra egg, a few more carrots for our children." "I would be only too glad to dig ditches to keep my family from going hungry," wrote a North Carolina man.

Where did desperate people turn for aid? Their first hope lay in private charity, especially churches and synagogues. But by the winter of 1931, such institutions were overwhelmed by extraordinary need. Only eight states provided even minimal unemployment insurance. There was no public support for the elderly, statistically among the poorest citizens. Few Americans had any retirement savings, and many who did save lost it all to bank failures.

Even those who stayed afloat had to adapt to depression conditions. Couples delayed marriage and had fewer children. As a result, the marriage rate fell to a historical low, and by 1933 the birthrate dropped from 97 births per 1,000 women, its high the previous decade, to 75. Responsibility for birth control largely fell to women, becoming "one of the worst problems of women whose husbands were out of work," a Californian told a reporter. Campaigns against hiring married women were common, on the grounds that any available jobs should go to male breadwinners. Three-quarters of the nation's school districts banned married women from working as teachers — ignoring the fact that many husbands were less able to earn than ever before. Despite such restrictions, female employment increased in the depression years, as women expanded their financial contributions so families could make ends meet.

The depression hit every part of the country, though its severity varied from place to place. Bank failures clustered heavily in the Midwest and plains, while areas dependent on timber, mining, and other extractive industries suffered catastrophic declines. Although southern states endured less unemployment because of their smaller manufacturing base, farm wages plunged. In many parts of the country, unemployment rates among black men were double that of white men; joblessness among African American women was triple that of white women.

By 1932, the magnitude of the crisis was clear, and voters wanted bold action in Washington. A few years earlier, with business booming and politics placid, people had chuckled when President Coolidge disappeared on extended fishing trips. Now, in the election of 1932, Americans decisively rejected the probusiness, antiregulatory policies of the previous decade. Faced with economic cataclysm, Americans would transform their government and create a modern welfare state.

AP® SKILLS & PROCESSES

CONTEXTUALIZATION

What changed over the course of the 1920s to create the conditions for the Great Depression?

Minnesota Potato Farmers The prosperity and consumer pleasures of the 1920s hardly extended to all Americans. This Minnesota family had horses, not a tractor; many of the women's clothes were probably made by hand. Rural and working-class Americans, who often struggled in the 1920s, found conditions even harsher after 1929. On the other hand, farmers had resources to fall back on that city folks did not: they could grow their own food, and they had long experience in "making do." Minnesota Historical Society / Getty Images

AP® SKILLS & PROCESSES

CONTEXTUALIZATION

Because this focuses on contextualization, remind students to think of broader events that capture trends in history. For example, with this particular question think about providing students with a list of options such as: Maldistribution of wealth, industrialism, laissez-faire capitalism, over-production/under-consumption, and the banking system.

TRM Find complete suggested responses in the Teacher's Resource Materials.

CHECK FOR UNDERSTANDING

Ask students: **What domestic economic factors helped cause the Great Depression?** *The most significant domestic factor that caused the Great Depression was the overuse of credit, either in stocks ("buying on margin") or consumer goods, in the 1920s. When these loans began being called on in the late 1920s, the poor foundations of growth were exposed. Banks closed, jobs were lost, and farms failed.*

CHECK FOR UNDERSTANDING

Use the **AP® LEARNING FOCUS** question from the beginning of the chapter to check students' understanding of the chapter as a whole: **Why did cultural and political conflict erupt in the 1920s, and what factors led to the Great Depression?** *Conflicts between forces of modernity and traditionalism arose in the 1920s. African American progress, women's rights advocates, immigrants, those who believed in evolution, and labor unions posed a threat to white, religious Americans afraid of the deterioration of white male supremacy, the Church, and capitalism. The 1920s witnessed a battle between conservative forces anxious over change and a very modern America. Economically, the United States enjoyed a decade of prosperity and consumerism followed by a decade-long depression. Rapid and unregulated corporate expansion coupled with easy credit and fiscal instability in Europe produced the stock market crash of 1929 and the Great Depression. Economic vulnerability came to characterize the lives of Americans in the 1930s.*

LearningCurve

Remind students to go online to complete the LearningCurve quiz for this chapter.

TRM Find complete suggested responses in the Teacher's Resource Materials.

AP® SKILLS & PROCESSES

CAUSATION

AP® CONTENT REVIEW 1 asks students to explain the causes of American conservatism.

AP® SKILLS & PROCESSES

CAUSATION

AP® CONTENT REVIEW 3 invites students to identify the causes of cultural conflict in the 1920s. Note: This question is the same as the section-opening prompt on p. 686.

AP® SKILLS & PROCESSES

CAUSATION

AP® CONTENT REVIEW 4 asks students to explain the causes of the Great Depression. Note: This question is the same as the section-opening prompt on p. 697.

TRM Find definitions for these terms in the **Glossary/Glosario** in the Teacher's Resource Materials.

SUMMARY

At the end of World War I America's economy was growing and its global position was rising. But the war also unsettled the country. Racial antagonisms rose when African Americans pursued new opportunities and asserted their rights. Labor unrest grew as employers cut wages and sought to break unions. Anxieties over radicalism and immigration prompted a nationwide Red Scare.

The politics of the 1920s saw a backlash against prewar progressivism and a series of clashes over religion, morality, and national belonging. The agenda of women reformers met very limited success, despite the arrival of women's voting rights. Republican administrations embraced business at home and abroad. Prohibition and the Scopes trial demonstrated the influence religion could exert on public policy, while rising nativism fueled a resurgent Ku Klux Klan and led to sweeping new restrictions on immigration. Meanwhile, black artists and intellectuals of the Harlem Renaissance, including many inspired by pan-African ideas, explored the complexities of African American life.

But the conservative mood was not all encompassing. A booming consumer culture, exemplified by the radio, the automobile, and Hollywood films, created new forms of leisure, influencing daily life and challenging older sexual norms. Black artists and intellectuals of the Harlem Renaissance explored the complexities of African American life.

The economic boom that carried America through an unsettled decade relied on risky speculation and easy credit. The foundations of the economy showed signs of shakiness, and the 1929 stock market crash plunged the United States into the Great Depression.

CHAPTER 21 REVIEW

AP® CONTENT REVIEW

Answer these questions to demonstrate your understanding of the chapter's main ideas.

1. What accounts for the rise of conservatism during the 1920s? Explain manifestations of such conservatism.
2. What were the primary characteristics of the American economy in the 1920s?
3. What were the main causes of cultural conflict in the 1920s?
4. What domestic and global economic factors caused the Great Depression?

AP® TERMS TO KNOW

Identify and explain the significance of each term.

Key Concepts and Events

Red Scare (p. 674)
Palmer raids (p. 674)
Great Migration (p. 674)
Red Summer (p. 675)
American Plan (p. 678)
welfare capitalism (p. 678)
dollar diplomacy (p. 679)
Teapot Dome (p. 680)
consumer credit (p. 682)
Hollywood (p. 682)
flapper (p. 682)
soft power (p. 683)
Sheppard-Towner Federal Maternity and Infancy Act (p. 686)
Eighteenth Amendment (p. 690)
Volstead Act (p. 690)
American Civil Liberties Union (ACLU) (p. 690)
Scopes trial (p. 691)
National Origins Act (p. 691)
Ku Klux Klan (KKK) (p. 691)
Harlem Renaissance (p. 693)
jazz (p. 694)
Universal Negro Improvement Association (UNIA) (p. 696)
pan-Africanism (p. 697)

Key People

Nicola Sacco and Bartolomeo Vanzetti (p. 674)
Marcus Garvey (p. 674)
Henry Ford (p. 678)
Adolph Zukor (p. 682)
Zora Neale Hurston (p. 694)
Louis Armstrong (p. 695)

AP® MAKING CONNECTIONS

Recognize the larger developments and continuities within and across chapters by answering these questions.

1. The Ku Klux Klan of the Reconstruction era (Chapter 14) emerged in a specific political and social context; while the Klan of the 1920s built on its predecessor, its goals and scope were different. Using material from Chapters 14 and 21, investigate a series of Klan meetings in each era (1870s and 1920s). Where would you conduct your investigation? How might you explain the Klan's membership and activities? How would you compare the two Klans?
2. Along what lines did Americans find themselves divided in the 1920s? How were those conflicts expressed in politics? In culture and intellectual life?
3. What factors contributed to the economic boom of the 1920s and the crash that followed?

KEY TURNING POINTS

Refer to the timeline at the start of the chapter for help in answering the following questions.

American politics underwent two shifts in the period covered in this chapter: one in the aftermath of World War I, and another in 1932. What caused each turning point? What factors in American society, economics, and culture help explain each moment of political change?

AP® PRACTICE QUESTIONS

MULTIPLE CHOICE QUESTIONS

Choose the correct answer for each question.

Questions 1–4 refer to this excerpt.

> "We should stop immigration entirely until such a time as we can amend our immigration laws. . . .
>
> It is time that we act now, because within a few short years the damage will have been done. The endless tide of immigration will have filled our country with a foreign and unsympathetic element. Those who are out of sympathy with our Constitution and the spirit of our Government will be here in large numbers, and the true spirit of Americanism left us by our fathers will gradually become poisoned by this uncertain element."
>
> Representative Lucien Parrish, Congressional Debate, April 1921

1. All of the following factors contributed directly to the views expressed in the excerpt EXCEPT
   - **a.** large-scale immigration before and after World War I.
   - **b.** fears that radical ideas such as socialism or communism might spread.
   - **c.** cultural controversies arising in rapidly growing urban areas.
   - **d.** widespread support for the continuing of an imperialist foreign policy.
2. Which of the following most likely supported similar ideas as those expressed by Parrish in the excerpt?
   - **a.** Democrats in the 1840s and 1850s
   - **b.** Nativists in the 1840s and 1850s
   - **c.** Business leaders in the 1890s and 1900s
   - **d.** Preservationists in the 1890s and 1900s
3. The most direct result from the sentiments expressed in the excerpt was
   - **a.** a shortage of laborers leading to a sustained economic downturn.
   - **b.** a declaration by the Census Bureau that the frontier was "closed."
   - **c.** quotas limiting European immigration.
   - **d.** a ban on immigration from Mexico and South America.
4. Supporters of the views expressed in the excerpt would have been LEAST likely to also support political movements seeking to
   - **a.** promote traditional moral values.
   - **b.** limit the free speech of radicals.
   - **c.** arrest and deport suspected radicals.
   - **d.** repeal Prohibition.

AP® SKILLS & PROCESSES

CONTINUITY AND CHANGE

AP® MAKING CONNECTIONS 1 invites students to compare the first and second KKK, noting both significant similarities and differences.

AP® SKILLS & PROCESSES

CONTINUITY AND CHANGE

The **KEY TURNING POINTS** question asks students to consider the meaning and significance of two turning points in American history: 1919, with the end of the war, and 1932, with the onset of the Great Depression.

TRM Find complete suggested responses in the Teacher's Resource Materials.

TRM Find complete suggested responses in the Teacher's Resource Materials.

Questions 5–6 refer to this c. 1920 New York City photograph.

Library of Congress.

5. Which of the following developments most directly resulted from the context captured in the image?
   a. Increased migration of African Americans to northern cities
   b. Passage of federal anti-lynching legislation
   c. Growth of militant civil rights movements for black power
   d. Emergence of new groups promoting political violence

6. The African American community resisted segregation and discrimination in the first half of the twentieth century in all of the following ways EXCEPT by
   a. launching a series of legal challenges.
   b. developing new forms of art and literature.
   c. demanding financial reparations.
   d. appealing for greater equality in the military.

SHORT ANSWER QUESTIONS

Read each question carefully and write a short response. Use evidence from the text to support your claims.

"Settlement in America had snipped the continuity of the immigrants' work and ideas, of their religious life . . . newcomers pushed their roots into many different soils. Along the city's unyielding asphalt streets, beside the rutted roads of mill or mining towns, amidst the exciting prairie acres, they established the homes of the New World. But . . . nowhere could they transplant the European village. . . . The pressure of that strangeness exerted a deep influence upon the character of resettlement, upon the usual forms of behavior, and upon the modes of communal action that emerged as the immigrants became Americans. . . . The old conditions of living could not survive in the new conditions of space."

Oscar Handlin, *The Uprooted: The Epic Story of the Great Migrations That Made the American People*, 1951

"Kin and friends were free to assist each other in entering America by providing access to jobs and homes and supplying important information of labor market conditions. New arrivals were adept at determining where they might enter a very large economy. The immigrant family economy survived and flourished among most newcomers in industrial America because new economic structures actually reinforced traditional ways of ordering life. . . . [I]ndividual inclinations were muted and the household . . . superseded all other goals and objectives. . . . Members of nearly all groups received indoctrination in the need to remain loyal to the familial and household unit. . . . [I]n the movement to a capitalist world and in the initial decades of settlement, familial and communal networks abounded."

John Bodnar, *The Transplanted: A History of Immigrants in Urban America*, 1985

1. Using the two excerpts provided, answer (a), (b), and (c).
   a. Briefly explain ONE major difference between Handlin's and Bodnar's historical interpretations of immigration to the United States.
   b. Briefly explain how ONE specific historical event or development from the period 1900 to 1930 that is not explicitly mentioned in the excerpts could be used to support Handlin's interpretation.
   c. Briefly explain how ONE specific historical event or development from the period 1900 to 1930 that is not explicitly mentioned in the excerpts could be used to support Bodnar's interpretation.

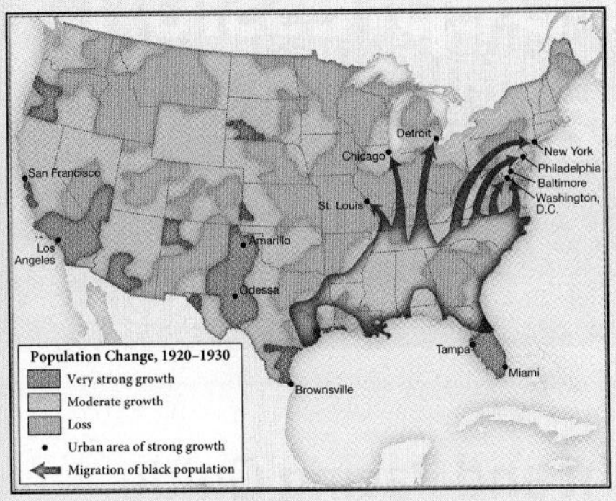

Population Change, 1920–1930

2. Using the map provided, answer (a), (b), and (c).
   - **a.** Briefly explain ONE specific historical event or development that caused a population trend illustrated in the map.
   - **b.** Briefly explain ONE specific historical event or development that caused a population trend different from what you explained in (a).
   - **c.** Briefly explain ONE significant historical result of the change you explained in (a) OR (b).

3. Answer (a), (b), and (c).
   - **a.** Briefly explain ONE specific historical similarity between the causes of the Great Depression (1929–1939) and the causes of an earlier economic recession or depression in the United States.
   - **b.** Briefly explain ONE specific historical difference in the causes of the Great Depression (1929–1939) from the causes of an earlier economic recession or depression in the United States.
   - **c.** Briefly explain how ONE specific historical event or development demonstrates a change in the United States caused by the Great Depression (1929–1939).

22

CHAPTER

Managing the Great Depression, Forging the New Deal

1929–1938

Chapter 22 — AP® Assessment Weight and Pacing Guide

The assessment weight on the AP® U.S. History Exam for Chapters 17–23 is 10–17 percent. This chapter falls in Unit 7 of the AP® U.S. History Curriculum, covering Period 7: 1890–1945.

This pacing guide is based on a schedule with 120 sessions of 50 minutes each before the AP® U.S. History Exam. If you have a different number of sessions before the exam, you can modify the pacing to meet your needs. If you have additional time, consider incorporating quizzes, released AP® U.S. History questions, practice exams, writing practice, and other instructional activities.

	Traditional Schedule	Block Schedule
Chapter 22	4 days	2 days

Daily Pacing Guide

	Content Focus	Essential Question
Day 1	Early Responses to the Depression, 1929–1932	How did Americans, from ordinary citizens to political leaders, respond to the Great Depression?
Day 2	The New Deal Arrives, 1933–1935	What were the major actions of the Hundred Days, and what were their intended purposes?
Day 3	The Second New Deal and the Redefining of Liberalism, 1935–1938	How did the Second New Deal change the purpose of American government, and what political divisions did it spark?
Day 4	The New Deal and American Society	In what ways did the New Deal promote change in American society?

AP® Alignment

Section Heading	AP® Topic	AP® Theme
Early Responses to the Depression, 1929–1932	7.9	WXT
The New Deal Arrives, 1933–1935	7.10	PCE
The Second New Deal and the Redefining of Liberalism, 1935–1938	7.10	PCE
The New Deal and American Society	7.10	PCE

*Should changes be made to the Course Framework in the future, an updated alignment will be placed on our AP® updates page at go.bfwpub.com/ap-course-updates.

Chapter 22 — Overview

Chapter 22 begins by examining the attempts of Herbert Hoover's administration to address the economic crisis brought on by the Great Depression. The despair of the Great Depression led to the landslide victory of Franklin Delano Roosevelt in the election of 1932 and the inauguration of the New Deal. This chapter analyzes the tremendous changes brought about in the First Hundred Days of FDR's administration, establishing a precedent by which all presidents are judged. Finally, the chapter examines the impact of the New Deal on American culture and the dramatic realignment of social and ethnic groups with the Democratic Party.

Chapter 22 — Resources

The following resources can be found in the Teacher's Resource Materials (TRM) that accompany the book. You can access the TRM via the book's digital platform, by clicking the TRM links found here in your Teacher's Edition e-book, or by contacting your representative to access the resources online. Visit **bfwpub.com/henretta10e** to learn more.

TRM Chapter 22 Lecture Presentation Slides

TRM Chapter 22 Outline with AP® Focus

TRM Chapter 22 Lecture Strategies

TRM Chapter 22 Suggested Responses

TRM Handout 22.1 — Causation: Herbert Hoover's Economic Policies

TRM Handout 22.2 — Causation: The Bonus Army

TRM Handout 22.3 — Comparison: Classical Liberalism vs. Keynesian Economics

Chapter 22 — Essential Activity

To help students differentiate New Deal agencies and programs, ask groups of students to research an assigned New Deal program or law to create a Public Service Announcement. The PSAs should emphasize the way that the law or agency will address a specific problem of the Great Depression. The purpose of the PSA is to convince American citizens to support these dramatic changes in the relationship between citizens and the federal government. After students create their PSA, upload the videos to YouTube or a class Web site for all students to view. Provide students with an opportunity to peer review each video and vote on the most outstanding submission. Afterward, hold an award ceremony where you give a trophy/award to the most outstanding video production.

Chapter 22 — Bell Ringers

The following activities take no more than 5–15 minutes of your class period and offer an effective and engaging way to begin your lessons and for students to apply AP® Skills & Processes:

- Provide students with an excerpt from Herbert Hoover's "Rugged Individualism" speech, and ask students to discuss the source with a partner to identify the characteristics that Hoover identifies with America's national identity. Ask students to consider the ways that the expressed philosophy could impact response to a crisis like the Great Depression. *Answers will vary.*
- Draw a political spectrum on the board and label the left side as "liberal" and the right side as "conservative." Ask students to explain where they would place the New Deal on the political spectrum (on the left) and allow students to debate how far to the left the New Deal would go by evaluating the degree to which it was a radical departure from traditional federal government policies. Then ask students to explain, in general, why individuals on the left and the right would criticize the New Deal. This activity can be used to introduce a discussion on the critics of the New Deal.
- Provide students with images of farmers dumping milk in ditches and plowing under crops. Ask students to explain why destruction of crops and commodities was a necessary part of addressing the Great Depression in 1933. *Answers will vary, but should address the following: a major reason for the Great Depression was overproduction in agriculture, which drove down farm prices and made it impossible for farmers to be consumers.*

NOTES

TEACHING STRATEGY

Use the chapter opener material to help students understand the chapter's central theme: the New Deal's redefinition of liberalism's traditional understanding of how best to protect individual rights. Since the late eighteenth century, liberals had typically assumed that individual rights were best protected through limited government. Progressives challenged this notion by advocating for government regulation of business on behalf of the individual. The Civil War and Reconstruction — through the transcontinental railroad, the Homestead Act, the Morrill Act, and the Thirteenth, Fourteenth, and Fifteenth Amendments — created a precedent for a larger federal government role in American society and economy. The New Deal dramatically expanded the definition of liberalism to include the notion of economic security, which proved controversial at the time and has remained so ever since, even as many elements of the New Deal's vision of economic security — Social Security, FDIC, SEC, FHA, NLRB, and a federal minimum wage — remain key features of the nation's economy. For a complete suggested response to the **AP® LEARNING FOCUS** question, see p. 732.

22 CHAPTER

Managing the Great Depression, Forging the New Deal

1929–1938

AP® LEARNING FOCUS

Why did the New Deal change the role of government in American life, and what were the economic and social consequences?

By virtually any measure, the American economy collapsed between 1929 and 1932. Gross domestic product fell almost by half, from $103 billion to $58 billion. Consumption dropped by 18 percent, construction by 78 percent, and private investment by 88 percent. Nearly nine thousand banks closed their doors, and one hundred thousand businesses failed. Corporate profits fell from $10 billion to $1 billion. Unemployment climbed to 25 percent. By 1933, 15 million people were out of work. "Hoover made a souphound outa me!" sang jobless harvest hands in the Southwest.

In his March 1933 inaugural address, President Franklin Delano Roosevelt acknowledged the country's precarious condition. "A host of unemployed citizens face the grim problem of existence," the new president said, "and an equally great number toil with little return. Only a foolish optimist can deny the dark realities of the moment." But Roosevelt also saw determination behind the deep distress, and he pledged to help. "This nation asks for action, and action now." He would seek from Congress "broad Executive power to wage a war against the emergency, as great as the power that would be given to me if we were in fact invaded by a foreign foe." With these words, Roosevelt launched a program of federal activism — which he called the New Deal — that would change the nature of American government.

The New Deal contributed decisively to the reinvention of liberalism, the ideology of individual rights that had long defined American politics. Classical nineteenth-century liberals believed that government should be small and relatively weak, in order not to infringe on those rights. Yet the progressives of the early twentieth century believed that state and federal checks on big business safeguarded individual freedom and opportunity. New Deal activists, known as "New Dealers," went much further: their social-welfare liberalism expanded individual rights to include economic security. Beginning in the 1930s and continuing through the 1960s, New Deal liberals sought to increase the national government's responsibility for the welfare of ordinary citizens. Their efforts did not go unchallenged. Conservative critics of the New Deal charged that its "big government" programs posed a risk to personal freedom. The divide between advocates and opponents of the New Deal would shape American politics for the next half century.

Before that long process began, the country endured several grim years. Between the onset of the depression in 1929 and when Americans went to the polls in early November 1932, the "dark realities of the moment" convinced most Americans that drastic action was required. As crisis piled upon crisis and federal initiatives under President Hoover proved ineffectual, Americans had to rethink not just the role of government but the very principles of individualism and free enterprise that had guided the nation's history.

Unemployed Workers Demonstrate in New York City Symbolizing the widespread struggles of ordinary Americans during the Great Depression, unemployed New Yorkers staged this demonstration in Times Square in late 1930. Each wears a sign stating their profession and offering to work for a dollar a week, a poverty wage.

Keystone-France/Gamma-Keystone via Getty Images.

AP® SKILLS & PROCESSES

DEVELOPMENTS AND PROCESSES

The Great Depression is sometimes referred to as the "plague of plenty," which is to say the problems of the depression could be distilled to the fact there was too much supply and not enough demand, or purchasing power. After explaining this concept to students, ask them to describe how this picture is an example of this concept. Starting the chapter with this understanding is crucial for students to understand the economic changes attendant to the depression.

AP® SKILLS & PROCESSES

CONTINUITY AND CHANGE

Use the **TIMELINE** table to help students begin thinking about how the period from 1929 to 1938 could constitute a distinct historical period. As the chronology illustrates, the New Deal's major legislation was largely packed into three years. Whether Americans love it, hate it, or fall somewhere in between, all will acknowledge that the New Deal fundamentally reshaped the American landscape. Students might note that the starting point of the chapter, 1929, overlaps with the previous chapter, taking readers back to the stock market crash, the beginning of the depression, and Hoover's response to it. The end point might be less clear to them. Textbook chapters on the New Deal often continue to 1940 or 1941 with the start of World War II. Some New Deal programs were not phased out until the 1940s (and, of course, others remain in effect today). But the "Roosevelt recession" of 1937–1938 led to major Republican congressional victories, effectively ending the New Deal as an active program; the last major piece of New Deal legislation, the Fair Labor Standards Act, was passed in 1938.

AP® APPLY THE TIP

Prompt students to use the section Crisis Management Under Hoover to complete **Handout 22.1 — Causation: Herbert Hoover's Economic Policies (TRM)**. Then provide students with images from the election of 1932 campaigns of Herbert Hoover and Franklin D. Roosevelt, and ask them to explain the relationship between the information on the handout and the campaigns of each candidate. Finally, show students a map of the results of the 1932 election to discuss the outcome of the election and the expectations for the administration of Franklin Roosevelt.

TRM Find **Handout 22.1 — Causation: Herbert Hoover's Economic Policies** in the Teacher's Resource Materials.

TIMELINE

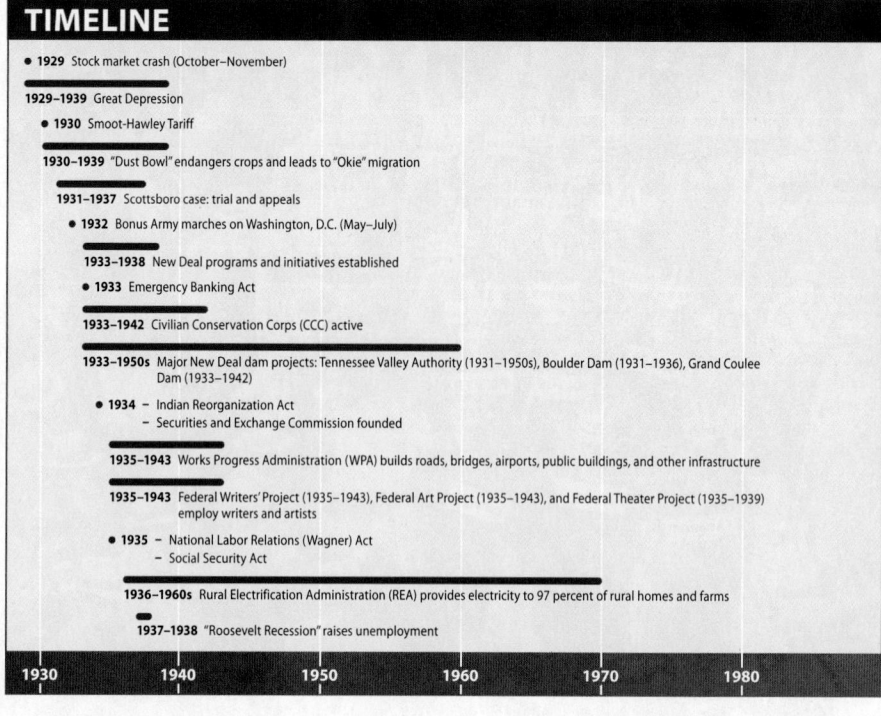

- **1929** Stock market crash (October–November)
- **1929–1939** Great Depression
- **1930** Smoot-Hawley Tariff
- **1930–1939** "Dust Bowl" endangers crops and leads to "Okie" migration
- **1931–1937** Scottsboro case: trial and appeals
- **1932** Bonus Army marches on Washington, D.C. (May–July)
- **1933–1938** New Deal programs and initiatives established
- **1933** Emergency Banking Act
- **1933–1942** Civilian Conservation Corps (CCC) active
- **1933–1950s** Major New Deal dam projects: Tennessee Valley Authority (1931–1950s), Boulder Dam (1931–1936), Grand Coulee Dam (1933–1942)
- **1934** – Indian Reorganization Act
  – Securities and Exchange Commission founded
- **1935–1943** Works Progress Administration (WPA) builds roads, bridges, airports, public buildings, and other infrastructure
- **1935–1943** Federal Writers' Project (1935–1943), Federal Art Project (1935–1943), and Federal Theater Project (1935–1939) employ writers and artists
- **1935** – National Labor Relations (Wagner) Act
  – Social Security Act
- **1936–1960s** Rural Electrification Administration (REA) provides electricity to 97 percent of rural homes and farms
- **1937–1938** "Roosevelt Recession" raises unemployment

1930 | 1940 | 1950 | 1960 | 1970 | 1980

EARLY RESPONSES TO THE DEPRESSION, 1929–1932

How did Americans, from ordinary citizens to political leaders, respond to the Great Depression?

Though the depression crippled the United States, it was a global event that crossed borders and oceans quickly. Germany preceded the United States into economic contraction in 1928, and its economy, burdened by heavy World War I reparations payments, was brought to its knees by 1929. The other major European economies, France and Britain, and the largest South American economies, Argentina and Brazil, were hard hit as well. Recovery proved difficult because the international gold standard constrained economic policymaking. The United States and most European nations had fixed the value of their currencies to the price of gold since the late nineteenth century. This system proved vulnerable during economic downturns, because the gold standard rendered nations unable to increase the supply of currency at precisely the moment when more was needed.

AP® EXAM TIP

Evaluate the impact of Hoover's economic policies as contributing factors to the Great Depression.

Crisis Management Under Hoover

Despite the global reach of the depression, like all nations the United States had to manage the crisis on its own. President Herbert Hoover and a Republican-majority Congress responded to the downturn by drawing on two influential American traditions. The first was the belief that economic circumstance flowed from individual character: success went to those who earned it. The second tradition held that the business community could recover from economic downturns without government assistance or, even worse, government regulation. Following these principles, Hoover asked Americans to tighten their belts and work hard. After the stock market crash, he cut federal taxes in an attempt to boost private spending and corporate investment. "Any lack of confidence in the economic future or the strength of business in the United States is foolish," Hoover assured the country in late 1929. Treasury secretary Andrew Mellon suggested that the downturn would encourage Americans to "work harder" and "live a more moral life."

While many factors caused the Great Depression, Hoover's adherence to the gold standard prolonged the crisis in the United States. Faced with economic catastrophe, both Britain and Germany abandoned the gold standard in 1931; when they did so, their economies recovered modestly. But the Hoover administration feared that such a move would weaken the value of the dollar. In reality, an inflexible money supply discouraged investment and prevented growth. The Roosevelt administration would ultimately remove the United States from the burdens of the gold standard in 1933. By that time, however, billions had been lost in business and bank failures, and the economy had stalled completely.

Adherence to the gold standard was not the only economic orthodoxy that would prove damaging in the downturn. Hoover and many Republicans in Congress thought high tariffs (taxes on imported goods) could stimulate American manufacturing, as they had in previous eras. In 1930, Congress passed the Smoot-Hawley Tariff Act. Despite receiving a letter from more than a thousand economists warning of catastrophe and urging him to veto the bill, Hoover signed it into law. The **Smoot-Hawley Tariff** triggered retaliatory tariffs in other countries, which further hindered global trade and worsened economic contraction throughout the industrialized world. What had served American interests in earlier eras — protecting domestic industries and agriculture — now undermined them.

Smoot-Hawley Tariff
A high tariff on imports enacted in 1930, during the Great Depression, that was designed to stimulate American manufacturing. Instead it triggered retaliatory tariffs in other countries, which hindered global trade and led to greater economic contraction.

Hoover recognized that individual initiative, business self-regulation, and high tariffs were insufficient, so he proposed government action to address the severity of the depression. He called on state and local governments to create jobs by investing in public projects, and in 1931 he secured an unprecedented increase of $700 million in federal spending for public works. Hoover's most innovative program was the Reconstruction Finance Corporation (RFC), which provided federal loans to railroads, banks, and other businesses. But like most federal initiatives under Hoover, the RFC was not nearly aggressive enough: by the end of 1932, it had loaned out only 20 percent of its $1.5 billion in funds.

Few chief executives could have survived the economic woes of 1929–1932, but Hoover's stubborn belief in the philosophy of limited government hampered recovery, and his insistence that recovery was just around the corner made him unpopular. By 1932, Americans perceived the president as insensitive to the depth of economic suffering. The nation had come a long way since the depressions of the 1870s and 1890s, when only radical figures, such as Jacob Coxey, called for direct federal aid to the unemployed (see "Depression and Reaction" in Chapter 19). Compared with previous chief executives — and in contrast to his popular image as a "do-nothing" president — Hoover had responded to the national emergency with unprecedented government action. But the country's needs were similarly unprecedented, and Hoover's programs failed to address them (Map 22.1).

AP® SKILLS & PROCESSES
CONTEXTUALIZATION
What economic principles guided President Hoover and Congress in their response to the Great Depression?

Rising Discontent

As the depression tightened its grip, new entries in the American vocabulary reflected mounting frustration. Many evicted people settled in shantytowns made of packing crates and other refuse, which they dubbed *Hoovervilles*, using *Hoover blankets* (newspapers) to keep warm. Bankrupt farmers banded together to resist the bank

AP® SKILLS & PROCESSES
MAKING CONNECTIONS
What experiences led groups of farmers, industrial workers, and veterans to protest in the early 1930s?

AP® SKILLS & PROCESSES
CONTEXTUALIZATION

Use the **CONTEXTUALIZATION** question to help students interpret the actions of Hoover and Congress in the context of the predominant economic principles of the late nineteenth and early twentieth centuries. This provides an opportunity for teachers to challenge the tendency students have to pass judgment on Hoover for inaction. Compared with what other presidents had done during earlier recessions, Hoover engaged in unprecedented economic intervention. Rather than placing Hoover and Roosevelt side-by-side as opposites, as many classroom activities do, it might be useful to think of Hoover as a steppingstone to the New Deal. To extend this prompt, ask students to point out specific actions Hoover took that could be seen as establishing a precedent for the New Deal's economic activism.

AP® SKILLS & PROCESSES
MAKING CONNECTIONS

The **MAKING CONNECTIONS** question asks students to explain the causes of protests by large numbers of everyday Americans. This phenomenon requires explanation since Americans have not historically engaged in public protest in large numbers.

TRM Find complete suggested responses in the Teacher's Resource Materials.

CHECK FOR UNDERSTANDING

Ask students: **How did Herbert Hoover respond to the onset of the Great Depression?** *Guided by a belief that individual character determined economic success and that voluntary action was the best way to respond to economic downturns, Hoover basically asked Americans to work hard and struggle on. He kept the nation on the gold standard, which discouraged investment, and approved Congress's Smoot-Hawley Tariff, which hindered global trade. His innovative Reconstruction Finance Corporation loaned funds to railroads, banks, and other businesses but was implemented too cautiously to mitigate the severity of the depression.*

AP® THEME
WXT: Work, Exchange, and Technology

As the "Rising Discontent" section illustrates, the Great Depression led to calls for a stronger financial regulatory system from a cross section of everyday Americans, not just reformers.

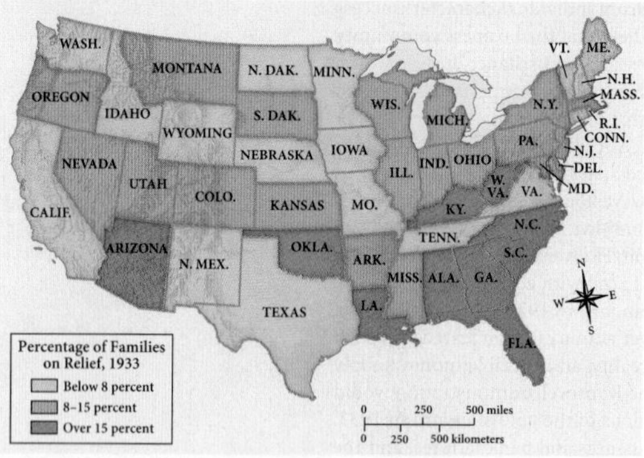

MAP 22.1 The Great Depression: Families on Relief
Although the Great Depression was a nationwide crisis, some regions were hit harder than others. Economic hardship was widespread in the agricultural South, the rural Appalachian states, and the industrial states of the Northeast and Midwest. As the depression worsened in 1931 and 1932, local and state governments, as well as charitable organizations, could not keep up with the demand for relief. After Franklin D. Roosevelt assumed the presidency in 1933, the national government began a massive program of aid through the Federal Emergency Relief Administration (FERA).

agents and sheriffs who sought to evict them from their land. Thousands of midwestern farmers took a *farmers' holiday* and joined the Farmers' Holiday Association, which protested against falling commodity prices by cutting off supplies, barricading roads, and dumping milk, vegetables, and other foodstuffs onto the roadways. Agricultural prices fell so low that the group advocated a government-supported farm program — drawing on Populist ideas from the 1890s (see "The Populist Program" in Chapter 19).

In the industrial sector, layoffs and wage cuts led to violent strikes. When coal miners in Harlan County, Kentucky, struck over a 10 percent pay cut in 1931, the mine owners called in the state's National Guard, which crushed the union. A 1932 confrontation between auto workers and security forces at the Ford Motor Company's giant River Rouge factory outside Detroit left five workers dead and dozens of strikers and police injured. In fields and on shop floors, the depression moved the producers of the nation's food and goods to organize and agitate.

Bonus Army
A group of fifteen to twenty thousand unemployed World War I veterans who set up camps near the Capitol building in 1932 to demand immediate payment of pension awards due in 1945.

AP® EXAM TIP
Recognize the Bonus Army as an expression of popular action in the Great Depression.

Veterans staged the most publicized — and tragic — protest. In the summer of 1932, the **Bonus Army**, a loose caravan of between fifteen thousand and twenty thousand unemployed World War I veterans, drove, hitchhiked, or simply walked to Washington, D.C. to demand immediate payment of pensions due in 1945. "We were heroes in 1917, but we're bums now," one veteran complained bitterly. While their leaders unsuccessfully lobbied Congress, the Bonus Army set up camps near the Capitol building. After several months of "occupation," Hoover deployed regular army troops under the command of General Douglas MacArthur, who forcefully evicted the marchers and burned their encampment to the ground. When newsreel footage showing the U.S. Army attacking veterans reached movie theaters across the nation, Hoover's popularity plunged even further. Americans had applauded when Coxey's army was scattered in 1894; their nearly opposite reaction to the demise of the Bonus Army captured the change in public attitude in 1932.

The 1932 Election

As a presidential election approached and the economic crisis intensified, most Americans believed that something new had to be tried — whatever that might be. Republicans, reluctant to dump an incumbent president, unenthusiastically renominated Hoover. The Democrats turned to New York governor Franklin Delano Roosevelt, who had overseen innovative relief and unemployment programs in his state.

Born into a wealthy family, Roosevelt was a distant cousin to former president Theodore Roosevelt. After attending Harvard College and Columbia University, Franklin Roosevelt served as assistant secretary of the navy during World War I (as Theodore Roosevelt had done before the War of 1898). In 1921, a crippling attack of polio permanently paralyzed his legs, briefly derailing his political ambitions. Supported by his wife, Eleanor, he slowly returned to public life and in 1928 he ran successfully for the governor of New York. After winning reelection in 1930, he aimed for the White House. In his 1932 campaign, Roosevelt pledged vigorous but vague action, arguing simply that "the country needs and, unless I mistake its temper, the

TEACHING STRATEGY

Use **MAP 22.1** to suggest a general pattern of deep reliance on the federal government throughout the South. Help students recognize that this map does not directly measure financial hardship, but rather the way families accessed public assistance. Students might think about factors beyond sheer need that could have influenced citizens' accessing of federal relief funds, including the robustness of state-level relief, general attitudes toward the government and direct handouts, and the level of connection between local government officials (who distributed funds) and congressional Democrats (who allocated funds).

TEACHING STRATEGY

The treatment of the Bonus Army was perhaps the most egregious public relations error of the Hoover administration. For a richer understanding of the goals of the Bonus Army, students could view a blog entry from the Library of Congress that provides brief background on the event and its significance. The site also includes a number of resources, such as a high-resolution facsimile handbill announcing the march, a series of two dozen photos of the marchers, questions for student discussion, and a webcast featuring the coauthors of a book on the Bonus Army march. To access the site, search "LOC Occupying the Bonus Army Protests."

AP® APPLY THE TIP

Ask students to complete **Handout 22.2 — Causation: The Bonus Army (TRM)** after completing a close reading of the Rising Discontent section. Then ask students to research the Bonus Army and its political action with additional resources beyond the textbook, including both text and visual primary sources. Have students utilize their handout, research, and primary sources to form small groups and produce a brief news report pretending they are reporting this event as it occurred in 1932. In their news report, students should incorporate their primary sources by using the image(s) as illustrations and their primary sources as possible interviews "on the scene" or "in the studio" segments.

TRM Find **Handout 22.2 — Causation: The Bonus Army** in the Teacher's Resource Materials.

Hooverville The depression led to the eviction of hundreds of thousands of Americans from their homes. Most found shelter with relatives, but those with little choice had to make do as they could. Encampments such as this one south of downtown Seattle, Washington, became known as Hoovervilles. The name reflected Americans' attitudes toward President Hoover, whose popularity plummeted as the depression deepened. AP Photo.

country demands bold, persistent experimentation." He won easily, receiving 22.8 million votes to Hoover's 15.7 million.

Elected in November, Roosevelt would not take office until March 1933. (The Twentieth Amendment, ratified in 1933, fixed subsequent inaugurations for January 20.) That winter, Americans waiting for Roosevelt's "action, and action now" suffered through the worst stretch of the depression. Unemployment continued to climb nationwide. In a telling measure of the woe, jobless rates in three major industrial cities in Ohio hit staggering levels: 50 percent in Cleveland, 60 percent in Akron, and 80 percent in Toledo. Across the country, private charities and public relief agencies reached only a fraction of the needy. The nation's banking system verged on collapse, and several states were approaching default, their tax revenues too low to pay for basic services. By Roosevelt's inauguration in March 1933, the nation had hit rock bottom.

THE NEW DEAL ARRIVES, 1933–1935

What were the major actions of the Hundred Days, and what were their intended purposes?

Franklin Roosevelt's ideas about how to govern did not differ radically from Hoover's. Both leaders wished to maintain the nation's economic institutions and preserve its social structure, to save capitalism by softening its worst downturns. Both believed in a balanced government budget and extolled the values of hard work, cooperation, and sacrifice. But Roosevelt's personal charm, political savvy, and willingness to experiment

TEACHING STRATEGY

Use photographs to supplement your discussion of the Great Depression. The Library of Congress features several photographs of Americans suffering during the depression, including several images of shanties and Hoovervilles. To access these images, search "LOC Photographs of the Great Depression."

TEACHING STRATEGY

The History on the Net Web site offers original recordings of a number of depression and New Deal–era songs, including "Brother, Can You Spare a Dime?" and "Big Rock Candy Mountain," giving not just a sense of the emotions of the lyrics but also popular styles of music at the time. To access these resources, search "History on the Net Depression-related music."

CHECK FOR UNDERSTANDING

Ask students: **What factors prompted rising discontent in the early years of the Great Depression?** *Low prices for farm products led farmers to dump their products in protest, as they demanded a populist-inspired government farm program to stabilize prices. Workers who were laid off or suffered severe wage cuts engaged in violent strikes. The Bonus Army included 15,000 to 20,000 unemployed World War I veterans who marched on Washington demanding early payment of pensions due to be distributed in 1945.*

AP® THEME

POL: Politics and Power; WXT: Work, Exchange, and Technology

Students should understand how Franklin Roosevelt's New Deal attempted to end the Great Depression by using government power to provide relief to the poor, stimulate recovery, and reform the American economy.

AP® APPLY THE TIP

To help students evaluate both the goals and the effectiveness of New Deal programs from the first "Hundred Days," group students into pairs and ask each pair to research and compare two New Deal programs: for example, CCC and FERA; PWA and CCC; Glass-Steagall Act and HOLC, etc. Students should develop Venn diagrams that illustrate both the goals and the impact of the programs that they are comparing. As a class, discuss the reasons that the individuals either supported or opposed the New Deal. Assign one student in each pair to assume the point of view of a person opposed to the New Deal and the other to assume the position of a person who supported the New Deal, and write a letter to President Roosevelt expressing their view using evidence from their Venn diagram and their knowledge of the era. Collect the completed letters and redistribute so students are reading a letter from a different pair. Ask students to read and analyze the letters as they would a primary source by identifying the argument and evidence used.

TEACHING STRATEGY

It is helpful for students to recognize continuity and change by considering the long-term consequences of the Glass-Steagall Act, as well as ways the law continued to be controversial until it was effectively neutralized. To help guide students' understanding, use the timeline on PBS's Frontline Web site, which charts the demise of Glass-Steagall. To access this timeline, search "*Frontline* Demise of Glass-Steagall."

made him far more effective and popular than Hoover. The programs of his New Deal helped many Americans get back to work and restored hope in the nation's future.

The First Hundred Days

fireside chats
A series of informal radio addresses Franklin Roosevelt made to the nation between 1933 and 1944 in which he explained New Deal initiatives and, later in his presidency, his wartime policies.

AP® EXAM TIP
Evaluate the impact of mass media on the relationship between citizens and government.

The wealthy patrician Roosevelt forged an unlikely rapport with ordinary Americans. Millions felt a quick kinship with the new president, calling him simply "FDR." This personal warmth proved critical to his political success. More than 450,000 letters poured into the White House in the week after his inauguration. The president's masterful use of the new medium of radio, especially his evening addresses to the American public known as **fireside chats**, in which he carefully explained his administration's policies, made him an intimate presence in home life. Thousands of citizens felt a personal relationship with FDR, saying, "He gave me a job" or "He saved my home" (see "Firsthand Accounts," p. 710).

Citing the national economic emergency, Roosevelt expanded the presidential powers that Theodore Roosevelt and Woodrow Wilson had previously increased. To draft legislation and policy, he relied heavily on financier Bernard Baruch and a "Brains Trust" of professors from Columbia, Harvard, and other leading universities. Roosevelt also assembled a talented cabinet, which included Harold L. Ickes, secretary of the interior; Frances Perkins at the Labor Department; Henry A. Wallace at Agriculture; and Henry Morgenthau Jr., secretary of the treasury. In turn, these intellectuals and administrators attracted hundreds of educated, experienced, and enthusiastic recruits to Washington. Inspired by New Deal idealism, many of them would devote their lives to public service and the principles of social-welfare liberalism.

Hundred Days
A legendary session during the first few months of Franklin Roosevelt's administration in which Congress enacted fifteen major bills that focused primarily on four problems: banking failures, agricultural overproduction, the manufacturing slump, and soaring unemployment.

Roosevelt could have accomplished little, however, without a cooperative Congress. The 1932 election swept Democratic majorities into both the House and Senate, giving the new president the lawmaking allies he needed. The first months of FDR's administration produced a whirlwind of activity on Capitol Hill. In a legendary session, known as the **Hundred Days**, the new Congress enacted fifteen major bills to fight the depression on four broad fronts: banking failures, agricultural overproduction, the manufacturing slump, and soaring unemployment. Known by some as "alphabet soup" because of their many abbreviations (CCC, WPA, AAA, etc.), the new policies and agencies born in 1933 marked a new era of American government.

AP® EXAM TIP
Compare the goals and effectiveness of New Deal programs established in banking, agriculture, manufacturing, and housing.

Banking Reform A collapsing banking system hobbled the entire economy, curtailing consumer spending and business investment. Widespread bank failures had reduced the savings of nearly nine million families, and "runs" by panicked depositors seeking to withdraw all their funds at once threatened to cause even more failures. On March 5, 1933, the day after his inauguration, FDR declared a national "bank holiday" — closing all banks — and called Congress into special session. Four days later, Congress passed the Emergency Banking Act, which permitted banks to reopen once a Treasury Department inspection showed they had sufficient cash reserves.

Glass-Steagall Act
A 1933 law that created the Federal Deposit Insurance Corporation (FDIC), which insured deposits up to $2,500 (and now up to $250,000). The act also prohibited banks from making risky investments with customers' deposits.

In the first of his Sunday night fireside chats, the president reassured a radio audience of sixty million that their money was safe. When the banking system partially reopened on March 13, calm prevailed and deposits exceeded withdrawals, restoring stability to the nation's basic financial institutions. "Capitalism was saved in eight days," quipped Roosevelt's advisor Raymond Moley. Four thousand banks had failed in the months prior to Roosevelt's inauguration; only sixty-one closed their doors in all of 1934 (Table 22.1). A second banking law, the **Glass-Steagall Act**, further restored public confidence by creating the Federal Deposit Insurance Corporation (FDIC), which insured deposits up to $2,500 (and now insures them up to $250,000). The act also prohibited banks from making risky investments with the deposits of ordinary people. And in an important economic and symbolic gesture, Roosevelt

TABLE 22.1

American Banks and Bank Failures, 1920–1940

Year	Total Number of Banks	Total Assets ($ billion)	Bank Failures
1920	30,909	53.1	168
1929	25,568	72.3	659
1931	22,242	70.1	2,294
1933	14,771	51.4	4,004
1934	15,913	55.9	61
1940	15,076	79.7	48

SOURCE: *Historical Statistics of the United States: Colonial Times to 1970* (Washington, DC: U.S. Government Printing Office, 1975), 1019, 1038–1039.

removed the U.S. Treasury from the gold standard in June 1933. This allowed the Federal Reserve to lower interest rates, which gave farms and businesses an economic lifeline in the form of low-cost loans.

Agriculture and Manufacturing With banks stabilized, Roosevelt and the New Deal Congress turned to agriculture and manufacturing. The depression led to overproduction in agriculture and underproduction in manufacturing. Reversing both problematic trends was critical. The **Agricultural Adjustment Act (AAA)** marked the first direct governmental regulation of the farm economy. To solve the problem of overproduction, which drove down prices, the AAA provided cash subsidies to farmers who cut production of seven major commodities: wheat, cotton, corn, hogs, rice, tobacco, and dairy products. By putting cash in farmers' hands to restrict supply and thereby raising prices, the AAA briefly stabilized the farm economy. But subsidies disproportionately benefitted the owners of larger farms, which often cut production by simply reducing the amount of land they rented to tenant farmers. In Mississippi, one plantation owner received $26,000 from the federal government, while thousands of black tenant farmers and sharecroppers living in the same county received only a few dollars each in relief payments.

Agricultural Adjustment Act (AAA)
New Deal legislation passed in May 1933 that aimed at cutting agricultural production to raise crop prices and thus farmers' income.

The New Deal attacked declining manufacturing production with the National Industrial Recovery Act. A new government agency, the **National Recovery Administration (NRA)**, set up separate self-governing private associations in six hundred industries. Each of these groups — ranging from large corporations producing coal, cotton textiles, and steel to small businesses making pet food and costume jewelry — regulated wages, prices, and production quotas. Participation by businesses was voluntary, but the hope was that industrial cooperation would raise wages and stabilize prices, leading to economic recovery. The AAA and the NRA sought to rescue the nation's productive industries and stabilize the economy. The measures had positive effects in some regions, but most historians agree that they did little to end the depression.

National Recovery Administration (NRA)
Federal agency established in June 1933 to promote industrial recovery during the Great Depression. It encouraged industrialists to voluntarily adopt codes that defined fair wages, set prices, and minimized competition.

Unemployment Relief and Housing Most Americans felt the reality of the depression at home, in the form of unemployment and fear of eviction. By 1933, local governments and private charities had exhausted their resources for relief and looked to Washington for assistance. Although Roosevelt wanted to avoid a budget deficit, he asked Congress to provide relief for millions of unemployed Americans. In May, Congress established the Federal Emergency Relief Administration (FERA). Directed by Harry Hopkins, a hard-driving social worker from New York, the FERA provided federal funds directly to state relief programs.

AP® SKILLS & PROCESSES

ANALYZING HISTORICAL EVIDENCE

TABLE 22.1 offers students the opportunity to analyze data that illustrates the severity of the depression. Guide students' analysis with the following questions:

- **What happened to the number of banks between the end of World War I and the beginning of World War II? Is this a mark of economic distress?** *The number of banks was cut in half. While the failure of banks caused severe economic problems, the permanent closure of some banks, largely as a result of the Emergency Banking Act, ultimately led to greater economic stability.*
- **How do bank assets illustrate the success of FDR's fireside chats and the Glass-Steagall Act? When did bank assets return to predepression levels?** *Within a year of FDR taking office, bank assets had begun to grow. They returned to predepression levels sometime in the late 1930s; by 1940, assets were higher than in 1929.*
- **How do bank failures after Glass-Steagall compare with those from before the depression began?** *The number of bank failures dramatically declined compared with the 1920s. Of course, the lower numbers from 1934 and 1940 reflect the fact that over 6,000 banks had already failed by the end of 1933, so there were significantly fewer banks left by 1934.*

AP® SKILLS & PROCESSES

ANALYZING HISTORICAL EVIDENCE

The **AP® FIRSTHAND ACCOUNTS** feature allows students to focus on evidence that is unified in type — the sources are all letters directed to the president and first lady, all written by everyday Americans — but different in perspective. As students read the letters in the feature, they might consider why so many people wrote to Eleanor Roosevelt, who had no official role or authority, what the authors hoped to accomplish with their letters, and what impact these letters may have had on the Roosevelts.

AP® FIRSTHAND ACCOUNTS

Ordinary People Respond to the New Deal

Franklin Roosevelt's fireside chats and his relief programs prompted thousands of ordinary Americans to write directly to the president and his wife, Eleanor. Taken together, their letters offer a vivid portrait of depression-era America that includes popular support for, as well as opposition to, the New Deal.

MRS. M. H. A.

Mrs. M. H. A. worked in the County Court House in Eureka, California.

Source: Robert S. McElvaine, *Down & Out in the Great Depression* (Chapel Hill: University of North Carolina Press, 1983), 54–55.

“June 14, 1934
Dear Mrs. Roosevelt:
I know you are overburdened with requests for help and if my plea cannot be recognized, I'll understand it is because you have so many others, all of them worthy. . . .

My husband and I are a young couple of very simple, almost poor families. We married eight years ago on the proverbial shoe-string but with a wealth of love. . . . We managed to build our home and furnish it comfortably. . . . Then came the depression. My work has continued and my salary alone has just been sufficient to make our monthly payments on the house and keep our bills paid. . . . But with the exception of two and one-half months work with the U.S. Coast and Geodetic Survey under the C.W.A. [Civil Works Administration], my husband has not had work since August, 1932.

My salary could continue to keep us going, but I am to have a baby. . . . I can get a leave of absence from my job for a year. But can't you, won't you do something so my husband can have a job, at least during that year? . . .

As I said before, if it were only ourselves, or if there were something we could do about it, we would never ask for help.

We have always stood on our own feet and been proud and happy. But you are a mother and you'll understand this crisis.

Very sincerely yours,
Mrs. M. H. A.”

UNSIGNED LETTER

This unsigned letter came from a factory worker in Paris, Texas.

Source: Gerald Markowitz and David Rosner, eds., *"Slaves of the Depression": Workers' Letters About Life on the Job* (Ithaca, NY: Cornell University Press, 1987), 21.

“November 23, 1936
Dear President,
[N]ow that we have had a land Slide [in the election of 1936] and done just what was best for our country . . . I do believe you Will Strain a point to help the ones who helped you mostly & that is the Working Class of People I am not smart or I would be in a different line of work & better up in ever way yet I will know you are the one & only President that ever helped a Working Class of People. . . .

I am a White Man American age, 47 married wife 2 children in high School am a Finishing room foreman I mean a Working foreman & am in a furniture Factory here in Paris Texas where thaire is 175 to 200 Working & when the NRA [National Recovery Administration] came in I was Proud to See my fellow workmen Rec 30 Per hour in Place of 8 cents to 20 cents Per hour. . . .

I can't see for my life President why a man must toil &work his life out in Such factories 10 long hours ever day except Sunday for a small sum of 15 cents to 35 cents per hour & pay the high cost of honest & deason living expences. . . .

Please see if something can be done to help this one Class of Working People the factories are a man killer not venelated or kept up just a bunch of Republickins Grafters 90/100 of them Please help us some way I Pray to God for relief. I am a Christian . . . and a truthful man & have not told you wrong & am for you to the end.

[not signed]”

R. A.

R. A. was sixty-nine years old and an architect and builder in Lincoln, Nebraska.

Source: Robert S. McElvaine, *Down & Out in the Great Depression* (Chapel Hill: University of North Carolina Press, 1983), 97.

“May 19/34
Dear Mrs Roosevelt:
In the Presidents inaugral address delivered from the capitol steps the afternoon of his inaugration he made mention of The Forgotten Man, and I with thousands of others am wondering if the folk who was borned here in America some 60 or 70 years a go are this Forgotten Man, the President had in mind, if we are this Forgotten Man then we are still Forgotten.

We who have tried to be diligent in our support of this most wonderful nation of ours boath social and other wise, we in our younger days tried to do our duty without complaining. . . .

And now a great calamity has come upon us and seemingly no cause of our own it has swept away what little savings we had accumulated and we are left in a condition that is imposible for us to correct, for two very prominent reasons if no more.

First we have grown to what is termed Old Age, this befalls every man.

Second, . . . we are confronted on every hand with the young generation, taking our places, this of corse is what we have looked forward to in training our children. But with the extra ordinary crisese which left us helpless and placed us in the position that our fathers did not have to contend with. . . .

We have been honorable citizens all along our journey, calamity and old age has forced its self upon us please do not send us to the Poor Farm but instead allow us the small pension of $40.00 per month. . . .

Mrs. Roosevelt I am asking a personal favor of you as it seems to be the only means through which I may be able to reach the President, some evening very soon, as you and Mr. Roosevelt are having dinner together privately will you ask him to read this. And we American citizens will ever remember your kindness.

Yours very truly.

R. A. ”

M. A.

M. A. was a woman who held a low-level salaried position in a corporation.

Source: Robert S. McElvaine, *Down & Out in the Great Depression* (Chapel Hill: University of North Carolina Press, 1983), 147.

“ Jan. 18, 1937

[Dear Mrs. Roosevelt:]

I . . . was simply astounded to think that anyone could be nitwit enough to wish to be included in the so called social security act if they could possibly avoid it. Call it by any name you wish it, in my opinion, (and that of many people I know) [it] is nothing but downright stealing. . . .

I am not an 'economic royalist,' just an ordinary white collar worker at $1600 per [year — about $23,600 in 2009]. Please show this to the president and ask him to remember the wishes of the forgotten man, that is, the one who dared to vote against him. We expect to be tramped on but we do wish the stepping would be a little less hard.

Security at the price of freedom is never desired by intelligent people.

M. A. ”

M. A. H.

M. A. H. was a widow who ran a small farm in Columbus, Indiana.

Source: Robert S. McElvaine, *Down & Out in the Great Depression* (Chapel Hill: University of North Carolina Press, 1983), 143.

“ December 14, 1937

Mrs. Roosevelt:

I suppose from your point of view the work relief, old age pensions, slum clearance and all the rest seems like a perfect remedy for all the ills of this country, but I would like for you to see the results, as the other half see them.

We have always had a shiftless, never-do-well class of people whose one and only aim in life is to live without work. I have been rubbing elbows with this class for nearly sixty years and have tried to help some of the most promising and have seen others try to help them, but it can't be done. We cannot help those who will not try to help themselves and if they do try a square deal is all they need, . . . let each one paddle their own canoe, or sink. . . .

I live alone on a farm and have not raised any crops for the last two years as there was no help to be had. I am feeding the stock and have been cutting the wood to keep my home fires burning. There are several reliefers around here now who have been kicked off relief but they refuse to work unless they can get relief hours and wages, but they are so worthless no one can afford to hire them. . . . They are just a fair sample of the class of people on whom so much of our hard earned tax-money is being squandered and on whom so much sympathy is being wasted. . . .

You people who have plenty of this worlds goods and whose money comes easy have no idea of the heart-breaking toil and self-denial which is the lot of the working people who are trying to make an honest living, and then to have to shoulder all these unjust burdens seems like the last straw. . . . No one should have the right to vote theirself a living at the expense of the tax payers. . . .

M. A. H. ”

QUESTIONS FOR ANALYSIS

1. How do you explain the personal, almost intimate, tone of these letters to the Roosevelts? Identify the purpose and historical situation of each source author.
2. How have specific New Deal programs helped or hurt the authors of these letters? Use evidence from the chapter to locate the New Program applicable to at least three of the sources.
3. What are the basic values of the authors? Do the values of those who support the New Deal differ from the values of those who oppose it? Use historical reasoning to compare the author's perspectives.

TRM Find complete suggested responses in the Teacher's Resource Materials.

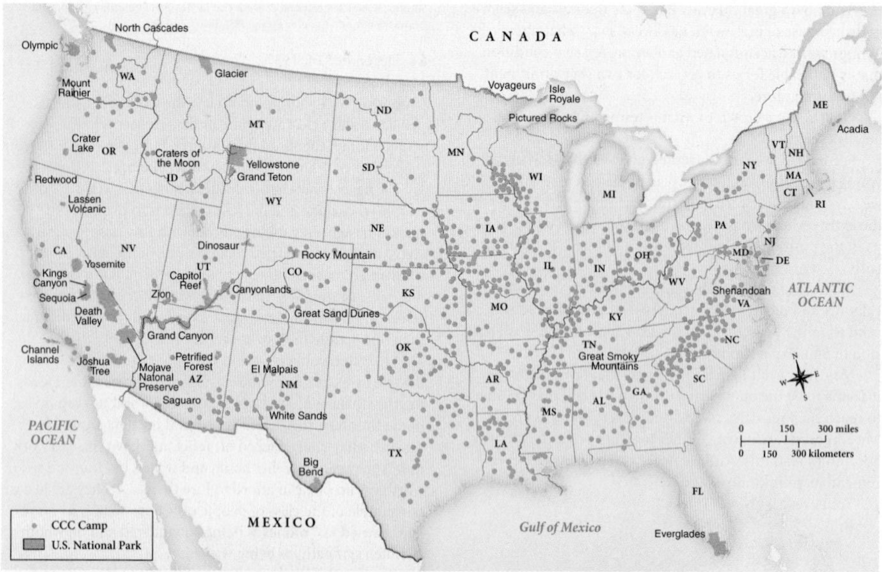

MAPPING THE PAST

MAP 22.2 Civilian Conservation Corps Camps

The Civilian Conservation Corps (CCC) gave hope to unemployed young men during the Great Depression. The first camp opened in Big Meadows, Virginia, in July 1933, and by the end of the decade CCC camps had appeared across the length of the country, located in rural, mountainous, and forested regions alike. Young men constructed bridges and roads, built hiking trails, erected public campgrounds, and performed other improvements. By the early 1940s, the CCC had planted three billion trees, among its many other contributions to the national infrastructure.

ANALYZING THE MAP: The camps are concentrated around what kinds of natural geographic features? If you follow the line of camps northward from the Gulf of Mexico, toward Illinois and Indiana as well as toward Virginia, what natural features can you identify? Are the camps in the West similarly concentrated?

MAKING CONNECTIONS: What does the concentration of the CCC camps around natural geographic features tell us about efforts of the New Deal to shape the environment?

TRM Find complete suggested responses in the Teacher's Resource Materials.

Public Works Administration (PWA) A New Deal construction program established by Congress in 1933. Designed to put people back to work, the PWA built the Boulder Dam (renamed Hoover Dam) and Grand Coulee Dam, among other large public works projects.

Civilian Conservation Corps (CCC) Federal relief program that provided jobs to millions of unemployed young men who built thousands of bridges, roads, trails, and other structures in state and national parks, bolstering the national infrastructure.

Roosevelt and Hopkins had strong reservations about the "dole," the nickname for government welfare payments. As Hopkins put it, "I don't think anybody can go year after year, month after month, accepting relief without affecting his character." To support the traditional value of individualism, the New Deal put people to work. During the Hundred Days, Congress established the **Public Works Administration (PWA)**, a large-scale construction program that would construct the Boulder and Grand Coulee Dams, and several months later Roosevelt created the Civil Works Administration (CWA) and named Hopkins its head. A stopgap measure to get the country through the winter of 1933–1934, the CWA nevertheless provided jobs for 4 million Americans, repairing bridges, laying highways, and constructing public buildings. The CWA lapsed in the spring of 1934 under Republican opposition, but a longer-term program, the **Civilian Conservation Corps (CCC)**, annually mobilized 250,000 young men to do reforestation and conservation work. Over the course of the 1930s, the "CCC boys" built thousands of bridges, roads, trails, and other structures in state and national parks, bolstering the national infrastructure (Map 22.2).

Many Americans also faced the devastating prospect of losing their homes. The economic expansion of the 1920s had created the largest housing bubble in American history to that point, a scenario in which home prices rose rapidly, fueled by widespread borrowing. In the early 1930s, real estate values collapsed, banks closed, and the jobless could not afford mortgage payments. More than half a million Americans lost their homes between 1930 and 1932. In response, Congress created the Home Owners Loan Corporation (HOLC) to refinance home mortgages. In just two years, the HOLC helped more than a million Americans keep their homes. The Federal Housing Act of 1934 would extend this program under a new agency, the **Federal Housing Administration (FHA)**. Together, the HOLC, the FHA, and the subsequent Housing Act of 1937 laid the foundation for the broad expansion of home ownership in the decades after World War II (see "A Nation of Consumers," Chapter 25).

An exhausted Congress recessed in June 1933, having passed major laws on banking reform, agricultural and industrial recovery, public works, and unemployment relief in just a few months. The new federal agencies were far from perfect and had their critics on both the radical left and the conservative right. The vigorous actions taken by Roosevelt and Congress did stabilize faltering institutions and provide a sense of hope, but their New Deal could not entirely break the depression's grip.

Grand Coulee Dam This extraordinary photo from a *Life* magazine essay shows workers hitching a ride on a 13-ton conduit as it is lowered into place on the Grand Coulee Dam in Washington state. Built to harness the awesome power of the Columbia River as it rushed to the Pacific, Grand Coulee would ultimately provide electric power to Seattle, Portland, and other West Coast cities and new irrigation waters for Washington's apple and cherry orchards, among many other crops. Library of Congress, LC-DIG-ppmsca-17400

The New Deal Under Attack

As New Dealers waited anxiously for signs of economic revival, Roosevelt turned his attention to reforming Wall Street, where reckless speculation and overleveraged buying of stocks had helped trigger the financial panic of 1929. In 1934, Congress established the **Securities and Exchange Commission (SEC)** to regulate the stock market. The commission had broad powers to determine how stocks and bonds were sold to the public, and to prevent insider trading. The Banking Act of 1935 authorized the president to appoint a new Board of Governors of the Federal Reserve System, placing control of interest rates and other money-market policies under a federal agency based in Washington rather than private bankers around the country. These initiatives represented an unprecedented centralization of financial regulation and management in the national government.

Critics on the Right Financial reforms exposed the New Deal to attack from economic conservatives — who formed a key constituency of the political right. The wealthy Roosevelt saw himself as the savior of American capitalism, declaring that "to preserve we had to reform." Many bankers and business executives felt his reforms went too far. To them, FDR became "That Man," a traitor to his class. In 1934, Republican business leaders joined with conservative Democrats in the **American Liberty League** to fight what they called the "reckless spending" and "socialist" reforms of the New Deal. The Liberty League lasted only a few years, but the **National Association of Manufacturers (NAM)** proved a durable opponent of the New Deal. In response to what many conservatives perceived as Roosevelt's antibusiness policies, the NAM produced radio programs, motion pictures, billboards, and direct mail

Federal Housing Administration (FHA)
An agency established by the Federal Housing Act of 1934 that refinanced home mortgages for mortgage holders facing possible foreclosure.

AP® SKILLS & PROCESSES

DEVELOPMENTS AND PROCESSES

What specific new roles did the American government take up as a result of the legislation passed during the first Hundred Days?

Securities and Exchange Commission (SEC)
A commission established by Congress in 1934 to regulate the stock market. The commission had broad powers to determine how stocks and bonds were sold to the public, and to prevent insider trading.

American Liberty League
A group of Republican business leaders and conservative Democrats who banded together to fight what they called the "reckless spending" and "socialist" reforms of the New Deal.

TEACHING STRATEGY

Of the many public works projects of the New Deal, Grand Coulee Dam loomed largest in America's imagination, promising to fulfill President Franklin Roosevelt's vision for a "planned promised land" where hardworking farm families would finally be free from the drought and dislocation caused by the elements. To access the site, search "American Experience Coulee."

CHECK FOR UNDERSTANDING

Ask students: **What actions did Roosevelt take in his first Hundred Days?** *FDR launched an unprecedented number of programs in this three-month period. First, he announced a bank holiday, temporarily closing all banks; he urged Congress to pass the Emergency Banking Act and the Glass-Steagall Act to reform the banking system and prevent future collapses. To improve the economy, he encouraged passage of the Agricultural Adjustment Act and the National Recovery Administration. He provided relief to the unemployed through the Federal Emergency Relief Administration, the Public Works Administration, and the Civilian Conservation Corps. Finally, he sought to reduce home foreclosures through the Federal Housing Authority.*

AP® SKILLS & PROCESSES

DEVELOPMENTS AND PROCESSES

The **DEVELOPMENTS AND PROCESSES** question asks students to identify specific effects of the first Hundred Days legislation in granting the federal government new roles. To scaffold this question, have students chart each piece of legislation; identify it as primarily addressing relief, recovery, or long-term reform; and indicate what new role the act gave the U.S. government. Students could also identify precedents from the Populist or Progressive eras for these new government roles.

TRM Find complete suggested responses in the Teacher's Resource Materials.

TEACHING STRATEGY

A close examination of the *Schechter* case provides an opportunity to understand the Supreme Court's opposition to the New Deal. The companion Web site to the PBS film *The Supreme Court* provides details about the background to the case and the legal reasoning of the Court. To access this site, search "PBS Supreme Court Schechter vs. US."

TEACHING STRATEGY

It would be helpful for students to examine the perspectives of populist critics of the New Deal in more detail. Use the following online resources to provide further information on each of the three most prominent critics:

- For Father Coughlin, have students look at a handout that provides a biography of Coughlin from historian Alan Brinkley, as well as the text of Coughlin's principles of social justice. To access these resources, search "GMU New Deal Critic."
- For Francis Townsend, the Social Security Administration provides some materials on his revolving pension fund, including a description of the plan, text from his newsletter, excerpts from congressional hearings on the plan, and related political cartoons. To access these resources, search "SSA Francis Townsend."
- For Huey Long, the Teaching History Web site offers his biography along with several primary sources, including his 1933 autobiography and his "Every Man a King Speech." To access these resources, search "Teaching History Huey Long."

National Association of Manufacturers (NAM)
An association of industrialists and business leaders opposed to government regulation. In the era of the New Deal, the group produced radio programs, motion pictures, billboards, and direct mail campaigns to promote free enterprise and unfettered capitalism.

campaigns to promote free enterprise and unfettered capitalism. After World War II, the NAM survived as a staunch critic of liberalism and it forged alliances with influential conservative politicians such as Barry Goldwater and Ronald Reagan (see "The Rise of the New Right," Chapter 29).

The Supreme Court also repudiated several cornerstones of the early New Deal. In May 1935, in *Schechter v. United States*, the Court unanimously ruled the National Industrial Recovery Act unconstitutional on two fronts: it delegated Congress's lawmaking power to the executive branch and extended federal authority to intrastate (in contrast to interstate) commerce. Roosevelt could only protest as the conservative-leaning high court struck down other New Deal legislation: the Agricultural Adjustment Act, the Railroad Retirement Act, and a debt-relief law known as the Frazier-Lemke Act.

Critics on the Left While business leaders and the Supreme Court thought that the New Deal went too far, other Americans believed it did not go far enough. Among these were activists who, in the tradition of American populism, sought to align government with ordinary citizens against corporations and the wealthy. Francis Townsend, a doctor from Long Beach, California, spoke for the nation's elderly, most of whom had no pensions or retirement savings. In 1933, Townsend proposed the Old Age Revolving Pension Plan, which would give $200 a month (nearly $4,000 today) to citizens over the age of sixty. To receive payments, the elderly would have to retire, opening their positions for younger workers. Clubs sprang up across the country in support of the **Townsend Plan**, mobilizing mass support for old-age pensions.

Townsend Plan
A plan proposed by Francis Townsend in 1933 that would give $200 a month (nearly $4,000 today) to citizens over the age of sixty; stimulated mass support for old-age pensions.

Another prominent critic of the New Deal was the "Radio Priest," Father Charles E. Coughlin, whose weekly radio broadcast reached 30 million Americans. Coughlin charged Roosevelt and the Democratic Party with insufficient action to protect the welfare of citizens. "I oppose modern capitalism," he announced, as a "detriment to civilization," and he urged Roosevelt to nationalize the banks. Politicians stayed on his good side — as one of the most recognizable and influential religious leaders in the country, a few words during his weekly radio broadcast could produce an avalanche of congressional mail. Over the course of the 1930s, his remarks grew increasingly laced with anti-Semitism (anti-Jewish sentiment), and by the end of the decade he openly embraced fascism.

Father Coughlin One of the foremost critics of the New Deal was the "Radio Priest," Father Charles E. Coughlin. In the 1930s, Coughlin's radio audience was 30 million strong, one-third of the adult population of the country, and he was among the most influential men in the country. By the early 1940s, however, Coughlin had embraced Nazi anti-Semitism and opposed U.S. entry into World War II, even after the bombing of Pearl Harbor. Forced off the air by the Catholic Archbishop, he thereafter retreated from public life. Bettmann/Getty Images.

The most direct political threat to Roosevelt came from Louisiana's Huey Long. As the Democratic governor of Louisiana from 1928 to 1932, the flamboyant Long had achieved stunning popularity. He increased taxes on corporations, lowered the utility bills of consumers, and built new highways, hospitals, and schools, which he accomplished through almost dictatorial control of state government. A U.S. senator by 1934, Long broke with the New Deal to establish his own national movement, the Share Our Wealth Society. Long believed that inequalities in the distribution of wealth prohibited millions of ordinary families from buying the goods that kept factories humming, and his organization proposed a tax of 100 percent on all income over $1 million and on all inheritances over

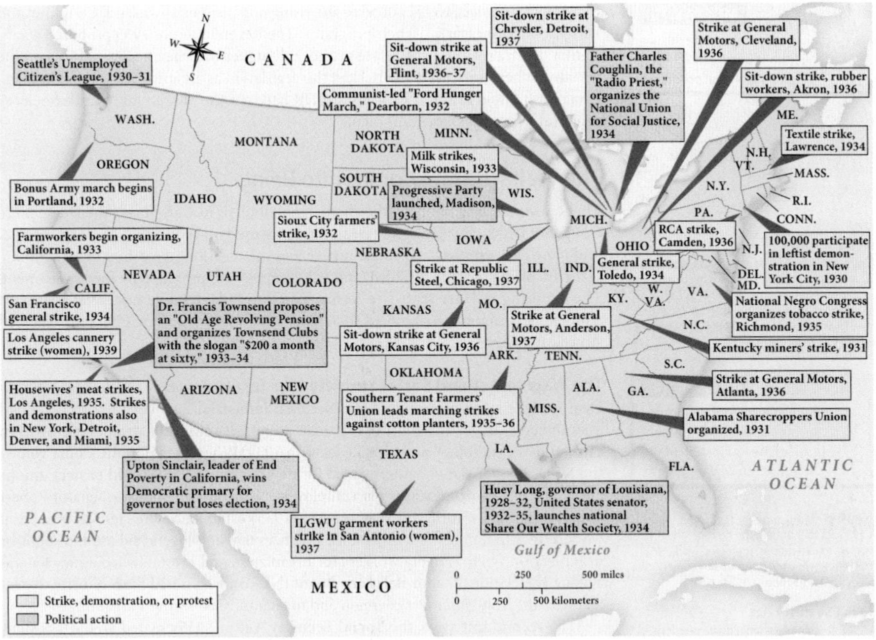

MAP 22.3 Popular Protest in the Great Depression, 1933–1939
The depression forced Americans to look closely at their society, and many of them did not like what they saw. Some citizens expressed their discontent through popular movements, and this map suggests the geography of discontent. The industrial Midwest witnessed union movements, strikes, and "Radio Priest" Charles Coughlin's demands for social reform. Simultaneously, farmers' movements — tenants in the South, smallholders in the agricultural Midwest — engaged in strikes and dumping campaigns and rallied behind the ideas of progressives in Wisconsin and Huey Long in the South. Protests took diverse forms in California, which was home to strikes by farmworkers, women, and — in San Francisco — all wageworkers. The West was also the seedbed of two important reform proposals: Upton Sinclair's End Poverty in California (EPIC) movement and Francis Townsend's Old Age Revolving Pension clubs.

$5 million. Long hoped that this populist program might carry him into the White House. Roosevelt himself feared that Long would join forces with Townsend Coughlin to form a third party, shattering the political unity of liberalism (Map 22.3).

AP® SKILLS & PROCESSES

MAKING CONNECTIONS

How did critics on the right and left represent different kinds of challenges to Roosevelt and the New Deal?

THE SECOND NEW DEAL AND THE REDEFINING OF LIBERALISM, 1935–1938

How did the Second New Deal change the purpose of American government, and what political divisions did it spark?

Reacting to the popularity of Townsend, Coughlin, and Long, and their liberal proposals, Roosevelt and his advisors moved politically to the left. Historians have labeled this shift in policy the Second New Deal. Roosevelt now openly criticized the "money classes," proudly stating, "We have earned the hatred of entrenched greed." He and the

AP® EXAM TIP

Explain the expansion of the federal government's regulatory role as a result of the Great Depression.

AP® THEME

POL: Politics and Power; WXT: Work, Exchange, and Technology

This section illustrates the competing pressures exerted on FDR. On one hand, radical, union, and Populist movements pushed Roosevelt toward more extensive efforts to change the American economic system. On the other, conservatives in Congress and the Supreme Court sought to limit the New Deal's scope. As **MAP 22.3** illustrates, popular protest was geographically widespread and took many forms, though strikes and new unions were the most common forms.

CHECK FOR UNDERSTANDING

Ask students: **What were the major components of the Hundred Days, and what was their purpose?** *Franklin Roosevelt's Hundred Days legislation in 1933 focused on four areas — banking failures, agricultural overproduction, the business slump, and soaring unemployment — in an effort to provide stabilization to the economy before his administration could embark upon reforming it. Regarding banks, Roosevelt closed the banks temporarily and passed the Glass-Steagall Act, which insured deposits through the FDIC. With regard to agricultural overproduction, the Agricultural Adjustment Act subsidized farmers not to farm. With regard to the business slump, the National Recovery Act created self-governing organizations to stabilize prices. Finally, regarding unemployment, Roosevelt created federal works programs like the Public Works Administration and the Civilian Conservation Corps.*

AP® SKILLS & PROCESSES

MAKING CONNECTIONS

Use the **MAKING CONNECTIONS** question to help students identify and compare criticisms of the New Deal from both the left and right of the political spectrum. Students may need assistance in understanding how or why particular criticisms might be viewed as liberal or conservative. Extend this prompt by asking students to indicate which type of criticism ultimately had more influence on the New Deal and why they think so.

TRM Find complete suggested responses in the Teacher's Resource Materials.

TEACHING STRATEGY

Students are required to understand the support and criticism of the New Deal. One way students can understand both perspectives is to complete a political spectrum. Explain how a political spectrum — whereby we can measure centrists, conservatives, far-right conservatives, liberals, and far-left liberals — helps explain the varied concerns people had with the New Deal. It can be useful to demonstrate what a spectrum looks like. Think about having students cite examples that match the labels provided.

AP® APPLY THE TIP

On the board or a projector, draw a line and label "Right" and "Left" to represent a political spectrum. Discuss with students the characteristics of the right and left. To help students activate prior knowledge, ask them to identify periods of history or individuals whom they would identify with each side of the spectrum. Then ask students to place "FDR and the New Deal" on the spectrum — discuss how far left it should be placed and why. Lead a class discussion on the types of criticism that the New Deal would most likely face from each side of the political spectrum. Prompt students to read pp. 713–715 and identify groups and individuals who criticized the New Deal and place them on the political spectrum. Finally, lead a class discussion on the following questions (*answers will vary*):

- **What do the critics of the New Deal have in common?**
- **What do the critics on the right have in common?**
- **Which critics would FDR be most concerned about for maintaining political support?**
- **Which critics would FDR be most concerned about for protecting reforms and laws passed in the first Hundred Days or Second New Deal?**

AP® EXAM TIP

Evaluate the impact of criticism from the right and the left on New Deal programs.

Democrats also decisively countered the rising populism of Townsend, Coughlin, and Long by adopting parts of their programs. The Revenue Act of 1935 proposed a substantial tax increase on corporate profits and higher income and estate taxes on the wealthy. When conservatives attacked this legislation as an attempt to "soak the rich," Congress tempered the tax hike, but FDR had met the Share Our Wealth Society's proposal with a tax plan of his own.

The Welfare State Comes into Being

welfare state
A term for industrial democracies that have adopted government-guaranteed social-welfare programs. The creation of Social Security and other measures of the Second New Deal established a national welfare state for the first time.

The Revenue Act symbolized the changing outlook of Roosevelt and the Democratic Congress. Unlike the First New Deal, which focused on economic recovery, the Second New Deal emphasized social justice and the creation of a safety net: economic security for the old, the disabled, and the unemployed, provided by the government. The resulting **welfare state** — a term applied to industrial democracies that have adopted government-guaranteed social-welfare programs — fundamentally changed American society.

AP® EXAM TIP

Recognize the significance of the Social Security System as the foundation of the American welfare system.

Wagner Act
A 1935 act that upheld the right of industrial workers to join unions, protected workers from employer coercion, and guaranteed collective bargaining.

Social Security Act
A 1935 act that provided old-age pensions for workers, a joint federal-state system of compensation for unemployed workers, and a program of payments to widowed mothers and the disabled.

The Wagner Act and Social Security The first beneficiary of the Second New Deal was the labor movement. The National Industrial Recovery Act (NIRA) had guaranteed workers the right to organize unions, leading to a dramatic growth in rank-and-file militancy and a strike wave in 1934. When the Supreme Court voided the NIRA in 1935, labor leaders called for new legislation that would protect unions and their collective bargaining with employers. Named for its sponsor, Senator Robert F. Wagner of New York, the **Wagner Act** (1935) established the right of industrial workers to join unions. The act banned practices that employers had used to suppress unionization, such as firing workers for organizing, and it established a new federal agency, the National Labor Relations Board (NLRB), which had the authority to protect workers from employer coercion and to guarantee collective bargaining.

The second initiative, the **Social Security Act** of 1935 created an old-age pension system. Other industrialized societies had created similar plans at the turn of the century, but American reformers had failed to secure such a program. The growing appeal of the Townsend and Long movements provided leverage for New Dealers to finally achieve the goal. Children's welfare advocates, concerned about the fate of fatherless families, also pressured the president. The resulting Social Security Act had three main provisions: old-age pensions for workers, a joint federal-state system of compensation for unemployed workers, and a program of payments to widowed mothers and the disabled. Roosevelt, however, reined in the scope of reforms. Foreseeing that compulsory pension and unemployment legislation would prove controversial, he dropped a mandate for national health insurance, fearing it would doom the entire bill.

The Social Security Act was a milestone in the creation of an American welfare state. Never before had the federal government assumed so much responsibility for the well-being of so many citizens. "Social Security," as old-age pensions were known, became one of the most popular government programs in American history. On the other hand, the assistance program for widows and children known as Aid to Dependent Children (ADC) became one of its most controversial measures. ADC covered only 700,000 youngsters in 1939; by 1994, its successor, Aid to Families with Dependent Children (AFDC), enrolled 14.1 million Americans. A minor

Workers Strike for the Forty-Hour Workweek Female employees of the Woolworth Company, a major retail employer with thousands of stores nationwide, are shown here striking for a forty-hour workweek in a branch in New York City in 1937. The 1935 Wagner Act protected unions and enabled workers like these to improve their wages and working conditions.

Underwood Archives/Getty Images.

program during the New Deal, AFDC grew enormously in the 1960s and remained an often maligned cornerstone of the welfare state until it was eliminated under President Bill Clinton in 1996.

New Deal Liberalism The legislation of the Second New Deal came to define a political ideology that historians call "New Deal liberalism." Classical liberalism saw individual liberty as the foundation of a democratic society, and the term *liberal* had traditionally denoted support for free-market policies and weak government. The Roosevelt administration and a rising generation of congressional Democrats envisioned government ensuring basic welfare and assisting the least well off. This liberal welfare state was opposed by inheritors of the nineteenth-century ideology of *laissez faire* capitalism, who gradually became known as conservatives. These competing visions of liberty and government — with liberals on one side and conservatives on the other — would serve as opposing poles of American politics for the remainder of the twentieth century.

MORE SECURITY FOR
THE AMERICAN FAMILY
THE WIDOW OF A QUALIFIED WORKER WILL RECEIVE MONTHLY BENEFITS AT AGE 65. IN CERTAIN CASES, AN AGED DEPENDENT PARENT MAY GET BENEFITS. ...
FOR INFORMATION WRITE OR CALL AT THE NEAREST FIELD OFFICE OF THE
SOCIAL SECURITY BOARD

The Birth of Social Security The Social Security Act of 1935 introduced old-age pensions (what we call simply "social security" today) as well as widows' pensions and assistance for families without a male breadwinner and disabled individuals. Such programs symbolized the New Deal's embrace of the principles of the welfare state: ensuring economic security for the country's most vulnerable citizens. Franklin D. Roosevelt Library.

From Reform to Stalemate

In Roosevelt's first term, the Democrats oversaw an extraordinary expansion of the federal state. The great burst of government action between 1933 and 1935 was unequaled in the nation's history, though President Lyndon Johnson and the Democratic-majority Congress nearly matched it in 1965 and 1966 (see "Lyndon B. Johnson and the Great Society," Chapter 27). Roosevelt's second term proved less successful, with reform stifled by a series of political reversals and a stalled economic recovery.

The 1936 Election FDR was never enthusiastic about public relief programs. But with the election of 1936 on the horizon and 10 million Americans still out of work, he won funding for the **Works Progress Administration (WPA)**. Under the energetic direction of Harry Hopkins, the WPA employed 8.5 million Americans between its establishment in 1935 and 1943. The agency's workers constructed or repaired 651,087 miles of road, 124,087 bridges, 125,110 public buildings, 8,192 parks, and 853 airports. An entire division of the agency promoted cultural programs and the arts, hiring tens of thousands of writers, poets, painters, playwrights, muralists, and others to create original works of art and to promote the varied regional cultures of ordinary Americans, from rural southern African American music to urban immigrant folkways in northern cities, and a great deal in between. The WPA was a massive program yet still only reached about one-third of the nation's unemployed.

As the 1936 election approached, the Democratic Party had a broad base of support. Many voters had personally benefitted from programs such as the WPA, or knew people who had (Table 22.2). One was Jack Reagan, a down-on-his-luck shoe salesman (and the father of future president Ronald Reagan), who took a job as a federal relief administrator in Dixon, Illinois, and became a strong supporter of the New Deal. Roosevelt could count on a powerful coalition of organized labor, midwestern

AP® SKILLS & PROCESSES

COMPARISON

How did the Second New Deal differ from the first?

Works Progress Administration (WPA)
Federal New Deal program established in 1935 that provided government-funded public works jobs to millions of unemployed Americans in areas ranging from construction to the arts.

CHECK FOR UNDERSTANDING

Ask students: **How did the welfare state come into being during the New Deal?** *Roosevelt and Congress placed the federal government firmly in support of the social welfare of American citizens through key pieces of legislation that remain in effect today. The Wagner Act established a federal right for workers to join unions, outlawed employer practices designed to discourage unions, and created the National Labor Relations Board to investigate claims of employer wrongdoing. The Social Security Act created an old-age pension system in which current workers contributed to the support of retired workers. The program also created a compensation system for the unemployed, and one for widows and the disabled.*

AP® SKILLS & PROCESSES

COMPARISON

The **COMPARISON** question asks students to identify differences between the two phases of the New Deal. Scaffold this question by asking students to categorize actions in terms of relief, recovery, reform, or some other system to make comparison easier. Though the question asks students to identify differences between the two New Deals, students could also identify similarities as well.

TRM Find complete suggested responses in the Teacher's Resource Materials.

AP® SKILLS & PROCESSES

ANALYZING HISTORICAL EVIDENCE

Use **TABLE 22.2** to organize major New Deal legislation by sector of the economy. Students could be placed in groups with each group taking responsibility for one category. After identifying the purpose of the legislation in their category and any legal challenges to the legislation, they could provide a generalization about the New Deal's impact in that economic area.

TABLE 22.2

Major New Deal Legislation

Agriculture	
1933	Agricultural Adjustment Act (AAA)
1935	Resettlement Administration (RA) Rural Electrification Administration (REA)
1937	Farm Security Administration (FSA)
1938	Agricultural Adjustment Act of 1938
Finance and Industry	
1933	Emergency Banking Act Glass-Steagall Act (created the FDIC) National Industrial Recovery Act (NIRA)
1934	Securities and Exchange Commission (SEC)
1935	Banking Act of 1935 Revenue Act (wealth tax)
Conservation and the Environment	
1933	Tennessee Valley Authority (TVA) Civilian Conservation Corps (CCC) Soil Conservation and Domestic Allotment Act
Labor and Social Welfare	
1933	Section 7(a) of NIRA
1935	National Labor Relations Act (Wagner Act) National Labor Relations Act (NLRA) Social Security Act
1937	National Housing Act
1938	Fair Labor Standards Act (FLSA)
Relief and Reconstruction	
1933	Federal Emergency Relief Administration (FERA) Civil Works Administration (CWA) Public Works Administration (PWA)
1935	Works Progress Administration (WPA) National Youth Administration (NYA)

farmers, white ethnic groups, northern African Americans, and middle-class families anxious about their savings, homes, and retirement. He also commanded the support of intellectuals and progressive Republicans. With some difficulty — mainly because of rising calls for racial justice among some New Dealers — the Democrats maintained their white southern constituency as well.

Republicans recognized that the New Deal was too popular to oppose directly. Alfred Landon, the progressive governor of Kansas and 1936 Republican presidential candidate, accepted the legitimacy of many New Deal programs but criticized their inefficiency and expense. He also pointed to the authoritarian regimes in Italy and Germany and hinted that FDR harbored similar dictatorial ambitions. These charges fell on deaf ears. Roosevelt's landslide victory in 1936 was one of the most lopsided in American history. The legislation of the Second New Deal protected Roosevelt from the populist appeals of Townsend and Long, and Long's assassination by a Louisiana political rival in September 1935 eliminated the possibility of a serious third-party challenge. Roosevelt received 60 percent of the popular vote and carried every state except Maine and Vermont. The liberal *New Republic* boasted that "it was the greatest revolution in our political history."

Even after the remarkable reforms of Roosevelt's first term, the depression still weighed heavily on American society. Unemployment remained high, at 15 percent, and average family income, measured in purchasing power, had still not returned to 1929 levels. "I see one-third of a nation ill-housed, ill-clad, ill-nourished," the president declared in his second inaugural address in January 1937. But his hopes for expansion of the liberal welfare state were quickly dashed. Within a year, staunch opposition to Roosevelt's initiatives arose in Congress, and a sharp recession undermined confidence in his economic leadership.

Court Battle and Economic Recession Roosevelt's first setback in 1937 came when he surprised the nation by seeking fundamental changes to the Supreme Court. In 1935, the Court had struck down a series of New Deal measures by the narrow margin of 5 to 4. With the Wagner Act, the Tennessee Valley Authority, and Social Security all slated to come before the Court, the future of the New Deal rested in the hands of a few elderly, conservative-minded judges. To diminish their influence, the president proposed adding a new justice to the Court for every member over the age of seventy, a scheme that would have brought six new judges to the bench at the time the legislation was proposed. Roosevelt's opponents protested that he was trying to "pack" the Court. After a long and bitter debate, Congress rejected FDR's blatant attempt to alter the judiciary to his political advantage.

Though Roosevelt lost the court fight, he won the war over the constitutionality of the New Deal. Swayed in part by the president's overwhelming electoral victory in the 1936 election, the Court upheld the Wagner and Social Security Acts. Moreover, a series of timely resignations allowed Roosevelt to reshape the Supreme Court after all. His new appointees — who included the long-serving liberal-leaning jurists Hugo

AP® SKILLS & PROCESSES
ARGUMENTATION
How had the country, as well as the Democratic Party, changed between the presidential elections of 1932 and 1936?

AP® EXAM TIP
Evaluate the causes and effects of FDR's Court Packing plan.

AP® SKILLS & PROCESSES

ARGUMENTATION

The Historical Thinking Skill of argumentation is about the ability of students to take an interpretation and extend an argument about why that interpretation is valid. This question asks about political changes as a result of the New Deal. Argument development can start with broader historical processes buttressed by specific historical evidence. For instance, give students a start by asking them to define political coalition. After you have worked through the definition, ask students to account for voting groups that were represented by the Democrats. This list includes, but is not limited to: African Americans, labor unions, urban workers, western farmers, southern farmers, and underrepresented religious groups. Have students explain the concept of President Roosevelt's political coalition with specific evidence to develop an argument.

TRM Find complete suggested responses in the Teacher's Resource Materials.

AP® APPLY THE TIP

Organize students into groups and provide each group with a variety of political cartoons from 1937 that illustrate various arguments in favor of and in opposition to FDR's plan to "pack" the Supreme Court. (Search "Political cartoons FDR Court-packing plan" for sources.) Ask groups to analyze the political cartoons by first identifying the elements represented and their potential meaning, and then by interpreting the cartoon as a historical source, explaining the point of view of the artist, purpose, and intended audience. Then have students write an explanation of each cartoon that accurately explains its message. Ask each group to select the one cartoon that they believe makes the strongest argument in favor of and in opposition to the Court-packing plan. Ask groups to share their choices with the class and discuss the use of these cartoons as political sources. Finally, lead a class discussion addressing the following questions (*answers will vary*):

- **What are the strongest arguments in opposition to the Court-packing plan?**
- **Why did some support the Court-packing plan even though it clearly endangered the system of checks and balances?**
- **Why is it important for political leaders to be willing to stand up to others in their own party?**
- **How is the Court-packing plan related to the outcome of the election of 1936? How did the Court-packing plan impact the election of 1940?**

Black, Felix Frankfurter, and William O. Douglas — viewed the Constitution as a "living document" that had to be interpreted in the light of present conditions.

The so-called Roosevelt recession of 1937–1938 dealt another blow to the New Deal. From 1933 to 1937, gross domestic product had grown by roughly 10 percent a year, bringing industrial output back to 1929 levels. Unemployment had declined from 25 percent to 14 percent. "The emergency has passed," declared Senator James F. Byrnes of South Carolina in May of 1937. Acting on this assumption, Roosevelt slashed the federal budget. Following the president's lead, Congress halved the WPA's funding, leading to the layoffs of about 1.5 million workers. The Federal Reserve, fearing rapid inflation, raised interest rates. These measures halted the recovery. The stock market dropped sharply, and unemployment jumped to 19 percent.

Roosevelt quickly reversed course, attempting to spend his way out of recession by boosting funding for the WPA and resuming public works projects. Although improvised, this spending program accorded with the theories of John Maynard Keynes, a visionary British economist. Keynes argued that government intervention could smooth out the highs and lows of the business cycle — preventing depressions and limiting inflation — through deficit spending and the adjustment of interest rates. This view was sharply criticized by Republicans and conservative Democrats in the 1930s, who opposed government management of the economy. But **Keynesian economics** gradually won wider acceptance as World War II defense spending finally ended the Great Depression. Keynesianism, as it is known, revolutionized economic thinking in the United States and other capitalist societies around the world.

In the midst of boosting WPA spending, Congress achieved a final legislative victory for the New Deal. In 1938, Congress passed the **Fair Labor Standards Act**, which outlawed child labor, standardized the forty-hour workweek, mandated overtime pay, and established a federal minimum wage. FDR considered this labor law nearly as important as the Social Security Act because of its implications for how Americans worked and what they earned. It would be the last major legislative achievement of the New Deal era.

A reformer rather than a revolutionary, Roosevelt had preserved capitalism and liberal individualism — even as he transformed them in significant ways. But the president stopped well short of more radical measures, such as the seizure of private property, that some world leaders considered (see "America in the World," p. 720). By 1938, opponents of the New Deal had reclaimed a measure of power in Congress and checked further reform. Throughout Roosevelt's second term, a conservative coalition of southern Democrats, rural Republicans, and industrial interests in both parties worked to block or impede social legislation. The era of change was over.

AP® EXAM TIP

Compare classical liberalism and Keynesian economics.

Keynesian economics
The theory, developed by British economist John Maynard Keynes in the 1930s, that deficit spending and interest rate adjustment by government could prevent depressions and limit inflation.

Fair Labor Standards Act
New Deal legislation passed in 1938 that outlawed child labor, standardized the forty-hour workweek, mandated overtime pay, and established a federal minimum wage.

THE NEW DEAL AND AMERICAN SOCIETY

In what ways did the New Deal promote change in American society?

Whatever its limits, the New Deal fundamentally altered Americans' relationship to their government. The liberal welfare state provided direct assistance to a wide range of ordinary people: the unemployed, the elderly, workers, and the poor. This required a sizable federal bureaucracy: the number of civilian federal employees increased by 80 percent between 1929 and 1940, reaching a total of 1 million. The expenditures — and deficits — of the federal government grew at an even faster rate. In 1930, the Hoover administration spent $3.1 billion and had a surplus of almost $1 billion; in 1939, New Dealers expended $9.4 billion and ran a deficit of nearly $3 billion (still small by later standards). However, the New Deal represented more than figures on a balance sheet. Across the country, it inspired new visions of America (see "Thinking Like a Historian," p. 722).

AP® APPLY THE TIP

Prompt students to use the section The Second New Deal and the Redefining of Liberalism, 1935–1938 to complete **Handout 22.3 — Comparison: Classical Liberalism vs. Keynesian Economics (TRM).** To support students' understanding of continuity and change over time, lead a class discussion in which students compare these philosophies to government actions in various periods of American history including the debate over the economic policy between Thomas Jefferson and Alexander Hamilton, the debate over the American System in the early nineteenth century, the economic policies of the Civil War era, and the industrialization of the late nineteenth century. Ask students to consider the reasons for the dominance of the Keynesian economic philosophy since the New Deal era. Discuss current economic issues and apply both philosophies to those issues to discuss varying reactions to economic problems.

TRM Find **Handout 22.3 — Comparison: Classical Liberalism vs. Keynesian Economics** in the Teacher's Resource Materials.

TEACHING STRATEGY

For a short article explaining Keynesian economic theory, see the PBS companion site to the documentary series *Commanding Heights*. To access the article, search "PBS Keynesian Theory."

CHECK FOR UNDERSTANDING

Ask students: **How did the Second New Deal change the purpose of American government, and what political divisions did it spark?** *The Second New Deal, which moved further to the left and outright attacked the "money classes," resulted in the welfare state and labor protections through the Wagner Act (1935). It highlighted differences between those who viewed the government's role in the economy as Keynesian, i.e., that the state should prime the pump of economic growth, versus those who felt that growth should come organically from private industry.*

AP® THEME

POL: Politics and Power; WXT: Work, Exchange, and Technology

Lead a class discussion on how the New Deal fostered a long-term political realignment in which many ethnic groups, African Americans, and working-class communities came to identify with the Democratic Party.

AP® SKILLS & PROCESSES

ANALYZING HISTORICAL EVIDENCE

The **AP® AMERICA IN THE WORLD** feature reminds students that the Great Depression had both global roots and global consequences. The two primary sources included in this feature illustrate contrasting responses to the crisis. When weighing discussions about whether the New Deal was "revolutionary" or not, students should keep in mind more radical options like nationalization that the U.S. did not take. While TVA is a significant exception, the New Deal overwhelmingly avoided the strategy of nationalizing industries, though there was some precedent for this, as the federal government had nationalized railroads in World War I, albeit only as a wartime measure.

TRM Find complete suggested responses in the Teacher's Resource Materials.

TEACHING STRATEGY

The Living New Deal organization is dedicated to inventorying, mapping, and publicizing the achievements of the New Deal and its public works across all fifty states. The site provides examples of individuals' general experiences of the Great Depression, their participation in programs like CCC and WPA, and the lives of those in the Greenbelt planned community outside of Washington, DC. To access this site, search "Living New Deal oral histories."

AP® AMERICA IN THE WORLD

Economic Nationalism in the United States and Mexico

President Franklin Roosevelt's New Deal sought to regulate the economy and provide a degree of economic security to American citizens while maintaining the structures of capitalism. In Mexico, President Lázaro Cárdenas (1934–1940) also hoped to achieve economic security for his country's citizens, but he took different steps than Roosevelt. His most famous action was to *nationalize* the oil industry — that is, the government took ownership of the industry away from private companies, most of which were based in Europe and the United States. In what follows, compare how each leader describes his new policies.

FRANKLIN ROOSEVELT
"Annual Message to Congress," 1936

SOURCE: Deborah Kalb, Gerhard D. Peters, and John Turner Woolley, eds., *State of the Union: Presidential Rhetoric from Woodrow Wilson to George W. Bush* (Washington, DC: CQ Press, 2007), 267.

In March, 1933, I appealed to the Congress of the United States and to the people of the United States in a new effort to restore power to those to whom it rightfully belonged. The response to that appeal resulted in the writing of a new chapter in the history of popular government. You, the members of the Legislative branch, and I, the Executive, contended for and established a new relationship between Government and people.

What were the terms of that new relationship? They were an appeal from the clamor of many private and selfish interests, yes, an appeal from the clamor of partisan interest, to the ideal of the public interest. Government became the representative and the trustee of the public interest. Our aim was to build upon essentially democratic institutions, seeking all the while the adjustment of burdens, the help of the needy, the protection of the weak, the liberation of the exploited and the genuine protection of the people's property. . . .

To be sure, in so doing, we have invited battle. We have earned the hatred of entrenched greed.

LÁZARO CÁRDENAS
"Speech to the Nation," 1938

SOURCE: Nora E. Jaffary, Edward Osowski, and Susie S. Porter, eds., *Mexican History: A Primary Source Reader* (Boulder, CO: Westview Press, 2010), 348–349.

It has been repeated *ad nauseam* that the oil industry has brought additional capital for the development and progress of the country. This assertion is an exaggeration. For many years throughout the major period of their existence, oil companies have enjoyed great privileges for development and expansion, including customs and tax exemptions and innumerable prerogatives; it is these factors of special privilege, together with the prodigious productivity of the oil deposits granted them by the Nation often against public will and law, that represent almost the total amount of this so-called capital.

Potential wealth of the Nation; miserably underpaid Native labor; tax exemptions; economic privileges; governmental tolerance — these are the factors of the boom of the Mexican oil industry.

. . . it was therefore necessary to adopt a definite and legal measure to end this permanent state of affairs in which the country sees its industrial progress held back by those who hold in their hands the power to erect obstacles as well as the motive power of all activity and who, instead of using it to high and worthy purposes, abuse their economic strength to the point of jeopardizing the very life of a Nation endeavoring to bring about the elevation of its people through its own laws, its own resources, and the free management of its own destinies.

QUESTIONS FOR ANALYSIS

1. What does Roosevelt mean by "a new relationship between Government and people"? How might the Great Depression context inform Roosevelt's perspectives?
2. What were the "economic privileges" that Cárdenas opposes? How did his goal differ from Roosevelt's? Contrast their points of view.

A More Inclusive Democracy

In 1939, writer John La Touche and musician Earl Robinson composed "Ballad for Americans," a patriotic song with lyrics calling for the solidarity of "everybody who's nobody . . . Irish, Negro, Jewish, Italian, French, and English, Spanish, Russian, Chinese, Polish, Scotch, Hungarian, Litvak, Swedish, Finnish, Canadian,

Greek, and Turk, and Czech and double Czech American." The ballad became a hit, capturing the democratic aspirations awakened by the New Deal. Millions of ordinary people — "Engineer, musician, street cleaner, carpenter, teacher . . . How about a farmer?" went the song — took inspiration from New Deal reforms and worked toward a more egalitarian national idea.

The New Deal opened fresh possibilities for realizing the more inclusive democratic society envisioned in La Touche and Robinson's song. Many New Deal initiatives touched the lives of, and sometimes empowered, groups long relegated to second-class status in American life, such as labor unions, African Americans, and Native Americans. Not every group benefitted equally, but a notable feature of the New Deal was its broad social inclusiveness.

Organized Labor Unions grew in membership and political clout under the New Deal, thanks to the Wagner Act. Organized labor had suffered in the probusiness climate of the 1920s, but by the end of the 1930s the number of unionized workers had more than doubled to an unprecedented 23 percent of the nonagricultural workforce. "The era of privilege and predatory individuals is over," the fiery labor leader John L. Lewis declared. A new union movement, led by Lewis's Congress of Industrial Organizations (CIO), promoted "industrial unionism" — organizing all the workers in an industry, from skilled machinists to unskilled janitors, into a single union. The American Federation of Labor (AFL), the other major group of unions, favored organizing workers on a craft-by-craft basis; both federations recorded massive membership increases.

Labor's new vitality translated into political power and a long-lasting alliance with the Democratic Party. The newly formed CIO encouraged support for Democratic candidates in 1936, and its political action committee became a major Democratic ally during the 1940s. The political gains of the 1930s were real but ultimately limited. Unions never enrolled a majority of American wageworkers, and antiunion employer groups such as the National Association of Manufacturers and the Chamber of Commerce remained politically influential. After a decade of progress, union labor remained a secondary, though significant, force in American industry.

Women and the New Deal Because policymakers primarily understood the depression as a crisis for male breadwinners, the New Deal did not directly challenge gender inequities. Its reforms generally enhanced women's welfare, but few addressed their specific needs and concerns. Roosevelt did bring women into the ranks of government in unprecedented numbers. Frances Perkins, the first woman to fill a cabinet post, served as secretary of labor throughout Roosevelt's presidency, and Josephine Roche served as assistant secretary of the treasury during his first term. The president also appointed the first female U.S. ambassador and the first women to the U.S. Court of Appeals. While still relatively few in number, female appointees in the New Deal era often opened up opportunities in government for other talented women.

The most prominent female figure in American politics proved to be Eleanor Roosevelt. Even before becoming First Lady, she had tirelessly worked to expand positions for women in political parties, labor unions, and education. During her years in the White House, Mrs. Roosevelt emerged as an independent public figure and the most influential First Lady in the nation's history up to that time. Descending into coal mines to view working conditions,

Roosevelts Visit Camp Tara One of Franklin Roosevelt's great political skills was the ability to connect with ordinary Americans. His wife, Eleanor, shared a similar gift, perhaps to an even greater degree. Here, he and Eleanor visit a vocational training camp for jobless women in 1934; FDR is seated on the far left while Eleanor greets two women standing beside the car. AP Photo.

TEACHING STRATEGY

The New Deal had programs that matched many different interests and occupations. Even regionally, the ideas of the New Deal reached across a vast expanse of territory and jobs. Have students select one of the following regions and explain the ways in which the New Deal sought to help constituents in that region: West, East, South, North, Midwest.

AP® SKILLS & PROCESSES

ANALYZING HISTORICAL EVIDENCE

The **AP® THINKING LIKE A HISTORIAN** feature asks students to draw connections between New Deal public works projects and a variety of different elements of the American landscape: infrastructure, art, culture, and politics. Though much of the impact of New Deal infrastructure is invisible (or unnoticed) today, it is almost impossible to exaggerate the effects. The Living New Deal Web site provides an interactive map cataloguing over 13,000 New Deal projects across the nation. While a simple glimpse of the map underscores the scale of the New Deal, students could zoom in to find out what projects were created in their state or possibly in their city. To access this map, search "Living New Deal map."

The New Deal and Public Works

More than half a dozen New Deal programs were devoted to building up the physical and cultural infrastructure of the country. The former included roads, bridges, dams, trails, and national parks. The latter included artwork, murals, plays, and other forms of literary expression. Examine the following documents and use them collectively to analyze the New Deal's relationship to infrastructure, art, culture, and politics.

1. **Harold L. Ickes, secretary of the interior, *The New Democracy*, 1934.** *The longest serving Secretary of the Interior in American history (1933–1946), Ickes was one of Roosevelt's most trusted advisors. Ickes implemented many of the major public works and conservation initiatives of the New Deal.*

   Our Government is no longer a laissez-faire Government, exercising traditional and more or less impersonal powers. There exists in Washington a sense of responsibility for the health, safety, and well-being of the people. . . . I believe that we are at the dawn of a day when the average man, woman, and child in the United States will have an opportunity for a happier and richer life. And it is just and desirable that this should be so. . . . We are not here merely to endure a purgatorial existence in anticipation of a beatific eternity after the grave closes on us. We are here with hopes and aspirations and legitimate desires that we are entitled to have satisfied to at least a reasonable degree. Nor will such a social program as we are discussing cause a strain on our economic system.

2. **Herbert Johnson cartoon, *Saturday Evening Post*, 1935.** *Critics of the New Deal charged that its public programs could only be paid for in higher taxes, which, those critics argued, burdened businesses and slowed economic growth. The New Deal debate over the relationship of taxes and growth continues today.*

3. **Federal Writers' Project interview with a WPA draftsman, Newburyport, Massachusetts, June 25, 1939.** *The Federal Writers' Project launched many different initiatives to employ struggling writers. It commissioned guidebooks for every state in the union (48 at the time), conducted thousands of oral histories with aging former slaves, and commissioned plays, novels, and poetry. Its writers also produced histories of New Deal programs, like the one of the WPA for which this interview was conducted.*

   One reason people here don't like the WPA is because they don't understand it's not all bums and drunks and aliens! Nobody ever explains to them that they'd never have had the new High School they're so [. . .] proud of if it hadn't been for the WPA. They don't stop to figure that new brick sidewalks wouldn't be there, the shade trees wouldn't be all dressed up to look at along High Street and all around town, if it weren't for WPA projects. To most in this town, and I guess it's not much different in this, than any other New England place, WPA's just a racket, set up to give a bunch of loafers and drunks steady pay to indulge in their vices! They don't stop to consider that on WPA are men and women who have traveled places and seen things, been educated and found their jobs folded up and nothing to replace them with.

SOURCE: The Granger Collection, New York.

4. Ben Shahn, WPA mural, 1938. *This is part of a three-panel mural commissioned by the Works Progress Administration (WPA) and painted at a public school in Roosevelt, New Jersey, by the well-known artist Ben Shahn.*

Source: Picture Research Consultants & Archives.

5. David E. Lilienthal, *TVA: Democracy on the March*, 1944. *This excerpt is drawn from a book written by the former chairman of the Tennessee Valley Authority (TVA), which celebrates the TVA, and the New Deal more broadly, as advancing democracy by bringing science and technology into the service of improving ordinary people's lives.*

I believe men may learn to work in harmony with the forces of nature, neither despoiling what God has given nor helpless to put them to use. I believe in the great potentialities for well-being of the machine and technology and science; and though they do hold a real threat of enslavement and frustration for the human spirit, I believe those dangers can be averted. I believe that through the practice of democracy the world of technology holds out the greatest opportunity in all history for the development of the individual, according to his own talents, aspirations, and willingness to carry the responsibilities of a free man. . . .

Such are the things that have happened in the Tennessee Valley. Here men and science and organizational skills applied to the resources of waters, land, forests, and minerals have yielded great benefits for the people. And it is just such fruits of technology and resources that people all over the world will, more and more, demand for themselves. That people believe these things can be theirs — this it is that constitutes the real revolution of our time, the dominant political fact of the generation that lies ahead.

Sources: (1) Harold L. Ickes, *The New Democracy* (New York: W. W. Norton & Company Inc., 1934), 60–61; (3) Federal Writers' Project Life Histories, Library of Congress, lcweb2.loc.gov/ammem/wpaintro/wpahome.html; (5) David E. Lilienthal, *TVA: Democracy on the March* (New York: Harper & Row Publishers, 1944), xxii, 3.

ANALYZING THE EVIDENCE

1. What sorts of reasons do the authors of sources 1 and 5 give for supporting New Deal programs? What does the "good life" look like in their view, and how is it connected to the New Deal?
2. What do sources 2 and 3 suggest about possible opposition to New Deal programs? What sorts of public burdens do New Deal opponents envision?
3. Consider source 4. What can we learn from a mural about the spirit of the New Deal? Identity specific elements of the mural and think about what they might signify about the society the muralist envisioned. What kind of faith in the federal government does the mural reveal?

AP® DBQ PRACTICE

Using evidence from the sources in this feature, alongside material from the chapter and from your knowledge of the period, write an essay in which you analyze Americans' attitudes toward New Deal public works projects. If they were positive or optimistic, what was the basis of their optimism? If they were critical, what was the basis of their criticism? From these sources, can you identify a governing spirit of New Deal reform? In your claim include a comparison of views about New Deal programs.

TRM Find complete suggested responses in the Teacher's Resource Materials.

AP® SKILLS & PROCESSES

ARGUMENTATION

Use the **AP® DBQ PRACTICE** prompt to help students analyze conflicting responses to New Deal public works projects. Students should link these responses to the larger issue this chapter raises regarding debates about the proper role of the federal government in the economy.

meeting with African Americans seeking antilynching laws, and listening to hungry Americans on breadlines, she became the conscience of the New Deal, pushing her husband to do more for the disadvantaged. "I sometimes acted as a spur," Mrs. Roosevelt later reflected, "even though the spurring was not always wanted or welcome."

Even with the contributions of Eleanor Roosevelt, Frances Perkins, and other prominent women, New Deal policymakers often ignored the needs of women. Many of the National Recovery Act's employment rules set a lower minimum wage for women than for men performing the same jobs, and only 7 percent of the workers hired by the Civil Works Administration were female. The Civilian Conservation Corps excluded women entirely. Women fared better under the Works Progress Administration; at its peak, 440,000 women were on the payroll. Most Americans agreed with such policies. A 1936 Gallup poll asked whether wives should work outside the home when their husbands had jobs, and 82 percent of those surveyed said no. Such sentiment reflected a persistent belief in women's subordinate economic status.

AP® EXAM TIP

Being able to explain the political realignment of African Americans to the Democratic Party is critical to success on the AP® Exam.

African Americans and the New Deal Across the nation, but especially in the South, African Americans faced harsh social, economic, and political discrimination. Though Roosevelt's reforms did not fundamentally change this reality, black Americans received significant benefits from New Deal relief programs and believed that the White House cared about their plight, which caused a momentous shift in their political allegiance. Since the Civil War, black voters had staunchly supported the Republican Party, the party of Lincoln, who was known as the Great Emancipator. Even in the depression year of 1932, they overwhelmingly supported Republican candidates. But in 1936, as part of the tidal wave of national support for FDR, northern African Americans gave Roosevelt 71 percent of their votes and have remained solidly Democratic ever since.

African Americans supported the New Deal partly because the Roosevelt administration appointed a number of black people to federal office, and an informal "black cabinet" of prominent black intellectuals advised New Deal agencies. Among the most important appointees was Mary McLeod Bethune, who filled the post of director of Negro Affairs in the National Youth Administration (NYA), an agency within the WPA focused on education and employment among Americans aged 16 to 25. Born in 1875 in South Carolina to former slaves, Bethune founded Bethune-Cookman College and served during the 1920s as president of the National Association of Colored Women. She joined the New Deal in 1936, confiding to a friend that she "believed in the democratic and humane program" of FDR. She saw her prominent role as an important symbolic step toward racial equality — Americans, she observed, had to become "accustomed to seeing Negroes in high places." With access to the White House and a broad mandate within the administration, Bethune pushed for New Deal programs to help African Americans.

TEACHING STRATEGY

The National Women's History Museum provides a biography of Mary McLeod Bethune and links to several sites with additional resources about her role in the New Deal. To access this site, search "NWHM Mary McLeod Bethune."

The agitation of Bethune and other members of the black cabinet proved meaningful. African Americans constituted 10 percent of the country's population but held 18 percent of WPA jobs. The Resettlement Administration, established in 1935 to help small farmers and tenants buy land, actively protected the rights of black tenant farmers. However, the New Deal's inclusion of African Americans could not undo centuries of racial subordination, nor could it temper the disproportionate power of segregationist southern whites within the Democratic Party.

Roosevelt and New Deal Democrats did not go further in support of black rights, owing to their own racial conservatism and their reliance on white southern Democrats in Congress — including powerful southern senators, many of whom held influential congressional committee posts. Most New Deal programs reflected prevailing racial attitudes. Civilian Conservation Corps camps segregated African Americans, and most NRA rules did not protect black workers from discrimination. Both the Social Security Act and the Wagner Act explicitly excluded the domestic and agricultural jobs held by most African Americans at the time. Roosevelt also refused to support legislation making lynching a federal crime, ignoring one of the most pressing black political demands. Between 1882 and 1930, more than 2,500 African Americans were lynched by white mobs; one man, woman, or child was murdered every week for fifty years. Those responsible often escaped punishment due to indifferent local and state law enforcement. Despite pleas from black leaders, and from Mrs. Roosevelt herself, FDR feared that southern white Democrats would block his other reforms in retaliation if he supported a federal antilynching law.

African Americans and the New Deal A Federal Theater Project production of *Battle Hymn* in New York City in the mid-1930s. *Battle Hymn* dramatized the life of the radical abolitionist John Brown, who led a bloody and ill-fated insurrection against slavery in 1859. New Deal programs like the Federal Theater Project fostered socially conscious artistic expression in which the improvement of society was an explicit objective. Franklin D. Roosevelt Library.

The Agricultural Adjustment Act aimed to boost the agricultural commodity process by subsidizing farmers to cut production. In the South, the AAA wound up hurting rather than helping the poorest African Americans, because many white landowners collected government payments but refused to distribute payments to tenants. Such practices forced an estimated 200,000 black families off the land. Some black farmers tried to protect themselves by joining the Southern Tenant Farmers Union (STFU), an organization notable for its racial integration. "The same chain that holds you holds my people, too," an elderly black farmer from Arkansas reminded his white neighbors. But landowners had such economic power and such support from local sheriffs that the STFU could do little.

The denial of justice for African Americans in the South attracted increasing attention nationwide. In an infamous 1931 case in Alabama, nine young black men were accused of rape by two white women hitching a ride on a freight train. The women's stories contained many inconsistencies, but within weeks a white jury in the town of Scottsboro convicted all nine defendants; eight received the death sentence. After the U.S. Supreme Court overturned the sentences because the defendants had been denied adequate legal counsel, five of the men were again convicted and sentenced to long prison terms. Across the country, the Scottsboro Boys, as they were known, inspired solidarity within African American communities. Among whites, the Communist Party took the lead in publicizing the case — and was one of the only white organizations to do so — helping to support the Scottsboro Defense Committee, which raised money for legal efforts on the defendants' behalf.

The New Deal's democratic promise inspired a generation of African American leaders, but that promise was largely unfulfilled for black Americans. From the outset, New Dealers wrestled with deeply entrenched racial politics. Many Democrats in the North and West — centers of New Deal liberalism — increasingly opposed racial discrimination. But Roosevelt and the party as a whole depended heavily on white voters in the South, who insisted on segregation and white supremacy. This meant that the nation's most liberal political forces and some of its most conservative political forces jostled side by side in the same political party. Significant progress against widespread racial injustice would not come for another generation.

Indian Policy Native Americans had long been one of the nation's most disadvantaged and powerless groups. In 1934, the average individual Indian income was only $48 per year, and the unemployment rate was three times the national average. New Dealers sought to address their plight, with mixed results. Roosevelt appointed

AP® EXAM TIP

Evaluate changes in federal policy towards Native Americans during the New Deal.

TEACHING STRATEGY

The PBS companion site to the *American Experience* film *Scottsboro: An American Tragedy* provides a variety of primary sources that allow students to explore this pivotal case in greater detail. To access this site, search "PBS American Experience Scottsboro."

AP® APPLY THE TIP

To support student understanding of continuity and change over time in relationship to Native American history, show students the TED talk by Aaron Huey. After viewing the video, ask students to work in small groups to write an explanation for the way in which federal policy changed toward Native Americans in the New Deal. After formulating this argument about change, ask each group to create a timeline that illustrates continuity and change regarding policies toward Native groups from 1789 to the present. Allow students to use their textbook as well as additional resources. Students should code their timeline by using one color to represent "change over time" and a different color to represent "continuity over time." When complete, discuss the idea of change and continuity as well as patterns that students see in the relationship between Native groups and the federal government.

TEACHING STRATEGY

Arizona State University provides a variety of lesson materials related to the Indian New Deal, focused specifically on the law's impact on the Grand Canyon region. To access this site, search "ASU New Deal at Grand Canyon education."

sociologist John Collier to head the Bureau of Indian Affairs (BIA). Collier, a progressive critic of past BIA practices, understood what Native Americans had long known: that the government's decades-long policy of forced assimilation, prohibition of traditional religions, and confiscation of lands had left most tribes poor, isolated, and without basic self-determination.

Indian Reorganization Act
A 1934 law that reversed the Dawes Act of 1887. Through the law, Indians won a greater degree of religious freedom, and tribal governments regained their status as semisovereign dependent nations.

Collier helped to write and pass the **Indian Reorganization Act** of 1934, sometimes called the "Indian New Deal." On the positive side, the law reversed the Dawes Act of 1887 (see "Breaking Up Tribal Lands" in Chapter 15), which had sought to break up tribes as social units and replace them with a system of individual land ownership. Collier's legislation instead promoted Indian self-government through formal constitutions and democratically elected tribal councils. A majority of Indian peoples — some 181 tribes — accepted the reorganization policy. Through the new law, Native people won a degree of religious freedom, and tribal governments regained their status as semisovereign dependent nations. The latter achievement would have major implications for Native rights in the second half of the twentieth century (see "The American Indian Movement" in Chapter 26).

Like so many other federal Indian policies, however, the Indian New Deal was flawed. The act imposed a model of self-government that proved incompatible with some tribal traditions and languages. The Papagos of southern Arizona, for instance, had no words for *budget* or *representative*, and they made no linguistic distinctions among *law*, *rule*, *charter*, and *constitution*. Ongoing BIA policies alienated many groups, even as the new law proposed to empower them. The nation's largest tribe, the Navajos, rejected the new policy, in large part because of controversial mandatory livestock reductions ordered by Collier's agency, to make room for the Boulder Dam project. In theory, the Indian Reorganization Act expanded Indian self-determination, and many tribes did benefit. In practice, however, the BIA and Congress

Indian New Deal Commissioner of Indian Affairs John Collier poses with chiefs of the Blackfoot Indian tribe in 1934. Collier helped reform the way the U.S. federal government treated Native Americans. As part of what many called the Indian New Deal, Collier lobbied Congress to pass the Indian Reorganization Act, which gave Indian tribes greater control over their own affairs and ended many of the most atrocious federal practices, such as forcing Indian children into white-run boarding schools and dividing up and selling reservation land. Bettmann/Getty Images.

continued to interfere in internal Indian affairs and retained financial control over reservation governments.

Immigrant Struggles in the West By the 1920s, agriculture in California had become a big business — intensive, diversified, and export-oriented. Large-scale corporate-owned farms produced specialty crops — lettuce, tomatoes, peaches, grapes, and cotton — whose staggered harvests relied on transient labor. Thousands of workers, immigrants from Mexico and Asia, as well as white migrants from the midwestern states, trooped from farm to farm and from crop to crop during the long picking season. Some migrants settled in the rapidly growing cities along the West Coast, especially the sprawling metropolis of Los Angeles. Beginning under Hoover and continuing under FDR, the federal government promoted deportation of Mexicans, in the belief that removing aliens would cut relief spending and preserve jobs for American citizens. Between 1929 and 1937, approximately half a million people of Mexican descent were deported under the guise of "repatriation." But historians estimate that more than 60 percent of those deported were in fact American citizens.

Despite these illegal deportations, many Mexican Americans benefitted from the New Deal and generally held Roosevelt and the Democratic Party in high regard. People of Mexican descent took jobs with the WPA and the CCC, and received relief in the worst years of the depression. The National Youth Administration, which employed low-income young people and sponsored a variety of school programs, proved

AP® EXAM TIP

Identify the role of the New Deal in realigning ethnic groups with the Democratic Party.

Mexican American Farm Workers Among the most hard-pressed workers during the Great Depression were those who labored in the nation's fields, orchards, and food processing plants. Here, a family of Mexican American beet workers in Minnesota gathers over coffee and conversation at the end of the workday. The New Deal era brought mixed blessings for such families. Some workers were able to join unions and improve their wages and working conditions. But others were swept up in repatriation programs, large-scale federal and state efforts to deport Mexican citizens in the United States — and even many U.S. citizens of Mexican descent — to Mexico. Library of Congress, 8b19996.

AP® APPLY THE TIP

To help students understand the changing alignments associated with political parties, provide students with a long sheet of bulletin board paper and markers to construct a timeline from 1789 to 1945. Ask students to first identify the creation of political parties in American history, e.g., Democratic-Republicans (Jeffersonians), Federalists, National Republicans, Democrats, Whigs, Republicans, Progressive Party (Bull Moose), etc. Then ask students to annotate the timeline to explain events or ideas that drew groups into political parties. Students should finalize their timeline by indicating which groups of people moved into the Democratic Party during the New Deal and provide a historical argument for the realignment. Finally, ask students to write a thesis to respond to the following prompt: What caused the realignment of political groups in the New Deal?

particularly important among Mexican Americans in southwestern cities. Even though New Deal programs did not end discriminatory practices or fundamentally reform the migrant farm labor system, the New Deal coalition attracted Mexican Americans in large numbers because of the Democrats' commitment to ordinary people. "Franklin D. Roosevelt's name was the spark that started thousands of Spanish-speaking persons to the polls," noted one Los Angeles Mexican American activist.

Americans of Asian descent — mostly from China, Japan, and the Philippines — formed a small minority of the overall population but had significant presences in West Coast areas. Immigrants from Japan and China had long faced discrimination. Increasingly strict federal statutes had curtailed immigration, and a 1913 California law prohibited them from owning land. Japanese farmers, who specialized in fruit and vegetable crops, circumvented this restriction by putting land titles in the names of their American-born children. As the depression cut farm prices and racial discrimination excluded young Japanese Americans from nonfarm jobs, as many as one in five Japanese immigrants returned to their native country.

As a group, Chinese Americans were less prosperous than their Japanese American counterparts. Only 3 percent of Chinese Americans worked in professional and technical positions, and discrimination barred them from most industrial jobs. In San Francisco, the majority of Chinese worked in small businesses: restaurants, laundries, and firms that imported textiles and ceramics. During the depression, they turned for assistance to Chinese social organizations and to the city government; in 1931, about one-sixth of San Francisco's Chinese population received public aid. But few Chinese benefitted from the New Deal. Until the repeal of Chinese exclusion in 1943, Chinese immigrants were classified as "aliens ineligible for citizenship" and therefore were ineligible for most federal programs.

Civilian Conservation Corps Members of the Civilian Conservation Corps (CCC) attend to soil conservation and reforestation following a mountainside fire in 1934. Employing about 250,000 men per year during the depth of the Great Depression, the CCC planted more than three billion trees and built trails and shelters in hundreds of parks across the country during its nine years of existence. Franklin D. Roosevelt Presidential Library.

Because Filipino immigrants came from a U.S. colonial possession, they were not affected by the ban on Asian immigration enacted in 1924. During the 1920s, their numbers swelled to about 50,000, many of whom worked on large corporate-owned farms. As the depression drove down wages, Filipino immigration slowed to a trickle, before ceasing almost entirely due to the Tydings-McDuffie Act of 1934. This law provided for gradual independence for the Philippines, classified all Filipinos in the United States as aliens, and limited immigration from the Philippines to just fifty people per year.

AP® SKILLS & PROCESSES

COMPARISON

In what ways did the New Deal assist nonwhite Americans, and in what ways did it hinder their equal standing?

Reshaping the Environment

Attention to natural resources was a consistent theme of the New Deal, and the shaping of the natural landscape among its most visible legacies. Roosevelt and Interior Secretary Harold Ickes saw themselves as conservationists in the tradition of the president's cousin, Theodore Roosevelt. Decades before the emergence of environmentalism, FDR practiced what he called the "gospel of conservation." The president primarily cared about making the land — and other natural resources — better serve human needs. National policy stressed scientific land management and maintaining ecological balance. Under Roosevelt, the federal government responded to environmental crises and reshaped the use of natural resources, especially water, in the United States.

AP® EXAM TIP

Compare the environmental policies of Franklin Roosevelt's New Deal and Theodore Roosevelt's Square Deal.

The Dust Bowl Plains farmers faced both economic and environmental catastrophe during the depression. Between 1930 and 1939, a severe drought afflicted the semiarid parts of Oklahoma, Texas, New Mexico, Colorado, Arkansas, and Kansas. Farmers in this "**dust bowl**" had stripped much of the native vegetation in favor of wheat and other crops. This upset the region's ecology and led to wind erosion of drought-parched topsoil (Map 22.4). When the winds came, huge clouds of thick dust rolled over the land, turning the day into night. This ecological disaster prompted a mass exodus. At least 350,000 "Okies" (so called whether or not they were from Oklahoma) loaded their belongings into cars and trucks and headed west to California migrant camps. John Steinbeck's novel *The Grapes of Wrath* (1939) and Dorothea Lange's haunting photography immortalized the struggle of these climate refugees.

dust bowl
An area including the semiarid states of Oklahoma, Texas, New Mexico, Colorado, Arkansas, and Kansas that experienced a severe drought and large dust storms from 1930 to 1939.

Roosevelt and Ickes believed that poor land practices made for poor people. Under their direction, government agencies tackled the dust bowl's human causes. Agents from the newly created Soil Conservation Service, for instance, taught farmers to prevent soil erosion by tilling hillsides along the contours of the land. They also encouraged (and sometimes paid) farmers to plant soil-preserving grasses instead of commercial crops. In one of the most widely publicized programs, the U.S. Forest Service planted 220 million trees in a wide "shelterbelt" that ran from Abilene, Texas, to the Canadian border, preventing soil

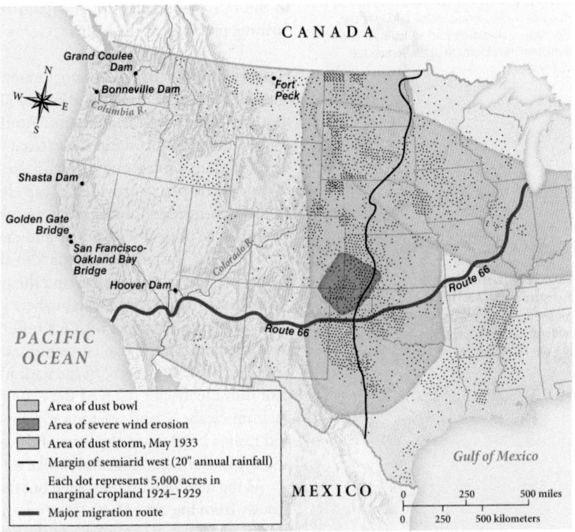

MAP 22.4 The Dust Bowl and Federal Building Projects in the West, 1930–1939
A U.S. Weather Bureau scientist called the drought of the 1930s "the worst in the climatological history of the country." Conditions were especially severe in the southern plains, where farming on marginal land threatened the environment even before the drought struck. As farm families migrated west on U.S. Route 66, the federal government began a series of massive building projects that provided flood control, irrigation, electric power, and transportation facilities to residents of the states of the far West.

AP® SKILLS & PROCESSES

COMPARISON

The **COMPARISON** question asks students to compare the effects of the New Deal on various nonwhite groups. It might be helpful to create a chart with a row for each group and columns for positive and negative consequences of the New Deal. Students could identify the group that benefitted the most and explain their answer. They could also offer a broad generalization about the New Deal's impact on nonwhites.

TRM Find complete suggested responses in the Teacher's Resource Materials.

CHECK FOR UNDERSTANDING

Ask students: **How did the New Deal attempt to create a people's democracy?** *New Deal federal programs attempted, with limited success, to make the nation more egalitarian. The Wagner Act encouraged the widespread growth of powerful new unions that helped the cause of labor, while the Indian Reorganization Act regained a measure of sovereignty lost through the Dawes Act. Women, however, reaped few benefits from New Deal programs and African Americans experienced very limited economic support, while segregation and lynching continued.*

TEACHING STRATEGY

The companion site to the PBS film *Dust Bowl* offers a number of helpful features, including an exploration of the Dust Bowl's legacy, a photo gallery, and lesson plans. To access the site, search "PBS Dust Bowl."

TEACHING STRATEGY

Use **MAP 22.4** to illustrate the connection between the natural and human factors that contributed to the Dust Bowl, while indicating its geographic scope. The map caption also hints at some of the infrastructure projects the federal government launched in the West. Through an essay and a series of ten photos, the National Archives offers a glimpse of the roads, bridges, dams, and trails created in the West. To access these resources, search "National Archives Great Depression and the New Deal."

TEACHING STRATEGY

The photo that has come to be known as *Migrant Mother* is one of a series of photos Dorothea Lange made of Florence Owens Thompson and her children in February or March of 1936 in Nipomo, California. The Library of Congress provides an overview of the series, as well as the five other images of the family Lange took at the same time. Students might compare these photos and see how Lange's framing and editing created the iconic image. To access these images, search "LOC Lange Migrant Mother."

TRM Find complete suggested responses in the Teacher's Resource Materials.

TEACHING STRATEGY

The Tennessee Valley Authority (TVA) was one of the most controversial programs of the New Deal. The government-run dam system, eventually the nation's largest energy supplier, was criticized at the time and for decades after as a socialist enterprise. Use **MAP 22.5** to indicate the extent of the project — the number of dams it created, the scale of its hydroelectric power, and the number of states it benefitted. Though the TVA lost congressional funding and became self-financing in the late 1950s, it remains a significant source of flood control, electricity, and recreation today. The TVA Web site provides the agency's perspective on its own history and ongoing legacy. To access the site, search "TVA history."

VISUAL ACTIVITY

The Human Face of the Great Depression *Migrant Mother* by Dorothea Lange is one of the most famous documentary photographs of the 1930s. On assignment for the Resettlement Administration, Lange spent only ten minutes in a pea-pickers' camp in Nipomo, California. There she captured this image (though not the name) of the woman whose despair and resignation she so powerfully recorded. In the 1970s the woman was identified as Florence Thompson, a native Cherokee from Oklahoma, who disagreed with Lange's recollections of the circumstances of the taking of the photograph. Library of Congress.

READING THE IMAGE: What do you notice about the three main figures in the photograph? What about the fourth? What state of mind is suggested by the woman's fingers resting on her cheek?

MAKING CONNECTIONS: What was Lange's purpose in capturing this image? Who was the intended audience? Why? What point of view regarding the Great Depression was Lange representing?

Tennessee Valley Authority (TVA) An agency funded by Congress in 1933 that integrated flood control, reforestation, electricity generation, and agricultural and industrial development in the Tennessee Valley area.

Rural Electrification Administration (REA) An agency established in 1935 to promote nonprofit farm cooperatives that offered loans to farmers to install power lines.

erosion and serving as a windbreak. A variety of government agencies, from the CCC to the U.S. Department of Agriculture, lent their expertise to encouraging sound farming practices in the plains.

Harnessing Nature The most extensive New Deal environmental undertaking was the **Tennessee Valley Authority (TVA)**, which Roosevelt saw as the first step in modernizing the agrarian South. Funded by Congress in 1933, the TVA integrated flood control, reforestation, electricity generation, and agricultural and industrial development under one government-owned corporation. The TVA's dams and hydroelectric plants provided cheap electric power for homes and factories and created much-needed jobs in an underdeveloped region reeling from the depression. The massive project won praise and emulation around the world (Map 22.5).

The TVA was an integral part of the Roosevelt administration's effort to keep farmers on the land by enhancing the quality of rural life. The **Rural Electrification Administration (REA)**, established in 1935, was also central to that goal. Fewer than one-tenth of the nation's 6.8 million farms had electricity at the time. The REA promoted nonprofit farm cooperatives that offered loans to farmers to install power lines. By 1940, 40 percent of the nation's farms had electricity; a decade later, 90 percent did. Electricity relieved the drudgery and isolation of farm life. Electric irons, vacuum cleaners, and washing machines particularly eased the burdens of women, and radios brightened the lives of the entire family. In concert with the automobile and the movies, electrification broke down the barriers between urban and rural life.

As the nation's least populated but fastest-growing region, the West benefitted enormously from the New Deal's attention to the environment. The region's many state and federal parks gained countless trails, bridges, cabins, and other recreational facilities, laying the groundwork for the post–World War II expansion of western tourism. On the Colorado River, Public Works Administration funds built the monumental Boulder Dam (later renamed Hoover Dam). Starting in 1936, the dam generated power for the region's growing cities such as Las Vegas, Los Angeles, and Phoenix.

The largest project in the West, however, took shape in an obscure corner of Washington state, where the PWA and the Bureau of Reclamation built the Grand Coulee Dam on the Columbia River. When it was completed in 1941, Grand Coulee was the largest electricity-producing structure in the world, and its 150-mile reservoir lake provided irrigation for the state's major crops: apples, cherries, pears, potatoes, and wheat. Inspired by the massive project and the modernizing spirit of the New Deal, folk singer Woody Guthrie wrote a song about the project. "Your power is turning our darkness to dawn," he sang, "so roll on, Columbia, roll on!"

New Deal projects made natural wonders across the country more accessible and enjoyable. CCC and WPA workers built the famous Blue Ridge Parkway, which connects the Shenandoah National Park in Virginia with the Great Smoky Mountains National Park in North Carolina. Government workers built the San Francisco Zoo, Berkeley's Tilden Park, and the canals of San Antonio. The Civilian Conservation Corps helped to complete the East Coast's Appalachian Trail and the West Coast's Pacific Crest Trail through the Sierra Nevada. The New Deal's environmental legacy included projects both monumental and modest. In parks across the country, cabins, shelters, picnic areas, lodges, and observation towers reflect the era's spirit of improvement.

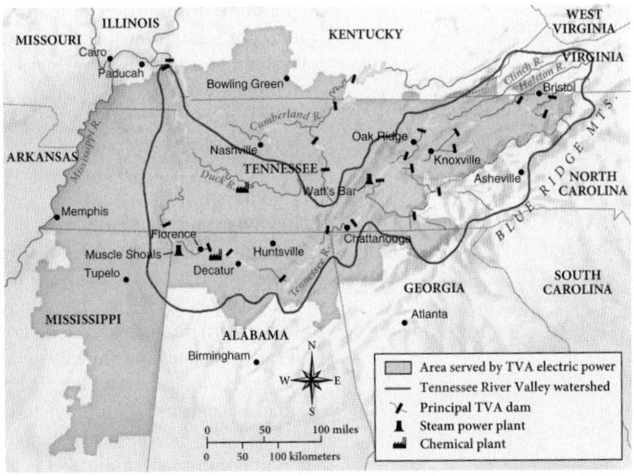

MAP 22.5 The Tennessee Valley Authority, 1933–1952
The Tennessee Valley Authority was one of the New Deal's most far-reaching environmental projects. Between 1933 and 1952, the TVA built twenty dams and improved five others, taming the flood-prone Tennessee River and its main tributaries. The cheap hydroelectric power generated by the dams brought electricity to industries as well as hundreds of thousands of area residents, and artificial lakes provided extensive recreational facilities. Widely praised at the time, the TVA came under attack in the 1970s for its practice of strip mining and the pollution caused by its power plants and chemical factories.

The New Deal and the Arts

In response to the Great Depression, many American artists and writers developed an increasing social consciousness. Never before, critic Malcolm Cowley suggested in 1939, had "literary events followed so closely on the flying coat-tails of social events." The New Deal's cultural programs enabled artists to create work meant for everyone, not just a high-brow elite. The WPA's Federal Art Project employed thousands of artists, including a number who would become leading figures in later decades, such as Jackson Pollock, Alice Neel, and Willem de Kooning. The Federal Music Project and **Federal Writers' Project (FWP)** employed fifteen thousand musicians and five thousand writers, respectively. Saul Bellow, Ralph Ellison, and John Cheever — each of whom would go on to shine in American letters — all contributed to the FWP, which also collected oral histories, including two thousand narratives by former slaves. The black folklorist and novelist Zora Neale Hurston finished three books while working for the Florida FWP, among them her best-known novel, *Their Eyes Were Watching God* (1937). Richard Wright won the 1938 *Story* magazine prize for the best tale by a WPA writer and went on to complete *Native Son* (1940), a searing novel about the consequences of white racism. The Federal Theatre Project (FTP) nurtured such talented directors, actors, and playwrights as Orson Welles, John Huston, and Arthur Miller, and mounted a wide array of productions, including the musical that featured "Ballad for Americans," the song whose ethic of inclusivity across occupational and racial differences became a hit.

AP® SKILLS & PROCESSES

MAKING CONNECTIONS

Why did the natural environment receive so much attention under New Deal programs, and with what result?

Federal Writers' Project (FWP) A New Deal program, part of the Works Progress Administration (WPA), that provided jobs for out-of-work writers, which included the collection of oral histories.

The Legacies of the New Deal

The New Deal answered the Great Depression by offering Americans security and hope. FDR and Congress created a powerful social-welfare state that took unprecedented responsibility for the well-being of all citizens. During the 1930s, millions of people began to pay taxes directly to the Social Security Administration, and more

AP® SKILLS & PROCESSES

MAKING CONNECTIONS

The **MAKING CONNECTIONS** question has both a cause element (reasons for the focus on the environment) and an effect element (the results of New Deal attention to the environment). Among the causal factors they consider, students should recognize that Progressive reformers had already expressed concern not only about conservation but also about flood control and electricity generation. Students could additionally investigate why many New Deal–era dams have become controversial.

TRM Find complete suggested responses in the Teacher's Resource Materials.

TEACHING STRATEGY

The New Deal arts projects provided work for jobless artists, but they also had a larger mission: to promote American art and culture and to give more Americans access to what Roosevelt described as "an abundant life." Despite controversy about the program, much of what these artists fashioned has survived through the efforts of museums, libraries, and archives. The National Archives exhibition *A New Deal for the Arts* explores paintings, prints, books, playbills, posters, and music transcriptions that represent an extraordinary burst of American creativity that occurred during a time of tremendous change and trial. The Web site offers a series of artworks with background information and commentary. To access these resources, search "National Archives New Deal for the Arts."

TEACHING STRATEGY

The Library of Congress's American Life Histories Web site is a collection of nearly 3,000 documents compiled and transcribed by more than 300 writers from two dozen states, working on the Folklore Project of the Federal Writers' Project. The documents vary in form from narratives to dialogues to reports to case histories, and chronicle vivid life stories of Americans who lived at the turn of the century. Students might choose one relatively short document and report on the subject and how the FWP employee contributed to the folklore of American culture by capturing that particular story. To access the site, search "LOC Federal Writers' Project."

CHECK FOR UNDERSTANDING

Ask students: **How did the New Deal reshape the environment?** *The CCC and WPA created roads and trails throughout parks, making them more accessible to the public. Massive dam-building projects throughout the nation provided electrification to millions of Americans, while changing landscapes and ecosystems.*

CHECK FOR UNDERSTANDING

Ask students: **What impact did the New Deal have on the arts?** *The government provided support to artists and writers. Through its sponsorship, artists created murals, sculptures, novels, guidebooks, and other products that, in most cases, remain available to the public today.*

than one-third of the population received direct government assistance from federal programs. New legislation regulated the stock market, reformed the banking system, and subjected business corporations to federal oversight. The New Deal's template would stand for the rest of the twentieth century. In the 1960s, Lyndon Johnson and the "Great Society" Congress dramatically expanded social-welfare programming — by creating Medicare and Medicaid, for instance — most of which remained intact even after the "Reagan Revolution" of the 1980s (Chapter 29).

Like any major political transformation, the New Deal was criticized as both doing too much and not doing enough. Conservatives, who prioritized limited government and individual freedom, felt that the New Deal state encroached on the liberty of both citizens and business. Conversely, advocates of social-welfare liberalism complained that the New Deal's safety net had too many holes: no national health-care system, welfare programs that excluded domestic workers and farm laborers, and too much leeway for state governments to limit benefits.

Even with its many critics, the New Deal unquestionably transformed the American political landscape. From 1896 to 1932, the Republican Party had commanded the votes of a majority of Americans. Franklin Roosevelt's magnetic personality and innovative programs brought millions of voters into the Democratic fold, and tilted the electoral balance. New Democratic voters included first- and second-generation immigrants from southern and central Europe — Italians, Poles, Russians, and Slavs, among others, most of them Catholic or Jewish — as well as African American migrants to northern cities. Organized labor aligned itself with a Democratic administration that recognized unions as a legitimate force in modern industrial life. The elderly and the unemployed, assisted by the Social Security Act, likewise supported FDR. This New Deal coalition of ethnic groups, city dwellers, union labor, African Americans, and middle-class progressives would support further liberal reforms in the decades to come.

AP® SKILLS & PROCESSES
ARGUMENTATION
What was the New Deal's long-term legacy?

SUMMARY

Herbert Hoover expected that the American ideals of self-reliance and self-regulation could enable the country to weather the Great Depression, but the unprecedented economic collapse required a government response of similar scope. Within days of taking office in 1933, Franklin Delano Roosevelt launched a series of reforms known as the New Deal that would radically reshape the role of government in American life. The First New Deal of 1933–1935 focused on economic recovery, providing relief to the unemployed and regulating the financial system. The Second New Deal of 1935–1938 had broader ambitions. Driven by the persistence of the depression and the growing appeal of more radical proposals, Roosevelt promoted welfare-state legislation that created a social safety net.

That safety net was not perfect, and the promise of the New Deal was not realized for all Americans — as seen in examinations of women, African Americans, union workers, immigrants, and Native Americans. However, the benefits drew many new voters into the Democratic fold, forging a coalition of the ethnic working class, African Americans, farmers, middle-class liberals, and white southerners that gave the party a firm grip on power.

The legacy of the New Deal is as complex as its programming. New Deal reforms resolved a banking crisis while preserving capitalist institutions. Through the Social Security system, farm subsidy programs, and public works projects, the New Deal birthed federal policies that touched every American. Massive infrastructure projects and conservation programs — many of them in the West, a still underdeveloped region in the 1930s — improved the national quality of life. And artistic and cultural initiatives employed thousands of writers and artists and inspired new interest in American history and regional folkways. Despite its flaws, the New Deal undeniably reimagined America, even as the depression lingered on. The coming of World War II would test the strength of a nation still recovering.

AP® THEME

POL: Politics and Power

Lead a class discussion about how although the New Deal did not end the Great Depression, it did leave a legacy of reforms and regulatory agencies.

AP® SKILLS & PROCESSES

ARGUMENTATION

Students should first either define or work through a definition with their teacher over the extent of what legacy means. Providing a periodization, or years with which students can work through, can assist students to develop a response. For instance, if you gave students the years 1932–1990, that will allow them to think through times of conservative and liberal resurgence. The challenge will be for students to connect the ideas and programs from the New Deal to other time periods. If you want to instead have students do a comparative analysis you could ask them to compare the New Deal with the Great Society and the Reagan presidency.

TRM Find complete suggested responses in the Teacher's Resource Materials.

CHECK FOR UNDERSTANDING

Use the **AP® LEARNING FOCUS** question from the beginning of the chapter to check students' understanding of the chapter as a whole: **Why did the New Deal change the role of government in American life, and what were the economic and social consequences?** *During the Great Depression, the federal government created jobs, provided transportation, water power, electricity, food, education, and homes to Americans, secured bargaining rights for laborers, documented the American experiences through photography and oral histories, and established a safety net for the needy, sick, and elderly. These new roles provided a new model for the relationship between citizen and federal government wherein the government acts as an aid and advocate for the society's most vulnerable.*

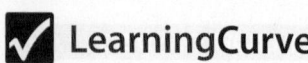

LearningCurve

Remind students to go online to complete the LearningCurve quiz for this chapter.

CHAPTER 22 REVIEW

AP® CONTENT REVIEW *Answer these questions to demonstrate your understanding of the chapter's main ideas.*

1. How did Americans, from ordinary citizens to political leaders, respond to the Great Depression?
2. What were the major actions of the Hundred Days, and what were their intended purposes?
3. How did the Second New Deal change the purpose of American government, and what political divisions did it spark?
4. In what ways did the New Deal promote change in American society?

AP® TERMS TO KNOW *Identify and explain the significance of each term.*

Key Concepts and Events

Smoot-Hawley Tariff (p. 705)
Bonus Army (p. 706)
fireside chats (p. 708)
Hundred Days (p. 708)
Glass-Steagall Act (p. 708)
Agricultural Adjustment Act (AAA) (p. 709)
National Recovery Administration (NRA) (p. 709)
Public Works Administration (PWA) (p. 712)
Civilian Conservation Corps (CCC) (p. 712)
Federal Housing Administration (FHA) (p. 713)
Securities and Exchange Commission (SEC) (p. 713)
American Liberty League (p. 713)
National Association of Manufacturers (NAM) (p. 714)
Townsend Plan (p. 714)
welfare state (p. 716)
Wagner Act (p. 716)
Social Security Act (p. 716)
Works Progress Administration (WPA) (p. 717)
Keynesian economics (p. 719)
Fair Labor Standards Act (p. 719)
Indian Reorganization Act (p. 726)
dust bowl (p. 729)
Tennessee Valley Authority (TVA) (p. 730)
Rural Electrification Administration (REA) (p. 730)
Federal Writers' Project (FWP) (p. 731)

Key People

Herbert Hoover (p. 704)
Franklin Delano Roosevelt (p. 706)
Huey Long (p. 714)
Frances Perkins (p. 708)
Eleanor Roosevelt (p. 721)
Mary McLeod Bethune (p. 724)
John Collier (p. 726)

AP® MAKING CONNECTIONS *Recognize the larger developments and continuities within and across chapters by answering these questions.*

1. People often view the New Deal as a set of government programs and policies enacted by President Roosevelt and Congress. In this version, change comes from above. Yet there is also evidence that ordinary Americans played an important role in inspiring and championing aspects of the New Deal. Find several specific examples of this, and think about the possible connections between the struggles, protests, and actions of ordinary people and the programs of the New Deal.
2. How did the lives of women, workers, and historically underrepresented racial and ethnic groups change during the Great Depression? What role did the New Deal offer those groups of Americans?

KEY TURNING POINTS *Refer to the timeline at the start of the chapter for help in answering the following question.*

Identify two critical turning points between 1934 and 1937 when the New Deal faced specific challenges.

TRM Find complete suggested responses in the Teacher's Resource Materials.

AP® SKILLS & PROCESSES

CAUSATION

AP® CONTENT REVIEW 1 asks students to describe the effects the Great Depression had on different groups of Americans.

AP® SKILLS & PROCESSES

CAUSATION

AP® CONTENT REVIEW 3 encourages students to identify the effects of the Second New Deal on the government. Note: This is the same question as the **CHECK FOR UNDERSTANDING** prompt on p. 719.

AP® SKILLS & PROCESSES

CONTINUITY AND CHANGE

AP® CONTENT REVIEW 4 asks students to describe the effects of the New Deal on American society.

TRM Find definitions for these terms in the **Glossary/Glosario** in the Teacher's Resource Materials.

AP® SKILLS & PROCESSES

CAUSATION

AP® MAKING CONNECTIONS 1 challenges students to see how citizens helped drive the reforms from the New Deal.

AP® SKILLS & PROCESSES

CAUSATION

AP® MAKING CONNECTIONS 2 asks students to identify the effects of the New Deal on different groups of people.

AP® SKILLS & PROCESSES

CONTINUITY AND CHANGE

Use the **KEY TURNING POINTS** question to help students identify smaller turning points from within the New Deal era.

TRM Find complete suggested responses in the Teacher's Resource Materials.

AP® PRACTICE QUESTIONS

MULTIPLE CHOICE QUESTIONS

Choose the correct answer for each question.

Questions 1–3 refer to this excerpt.

> "We have to limit fortunes. . . . It may be necessary, in working out of the plans, that no man's fortune would be more than $10,000,000 or $15,000,000. But be that as it may, it will still be more than any one man, or any one man and his children and their children, will be able to spend in their lifetimes; and it is not necessary or reasonable to have wealth piled up beyond that point where we cannot prevent poverty among the masses. . . . .
>
> Those are the things we propose to do. "Every Man a King." Every man to eat when there is something to eat; all to wear something when there is something to wear. That makes us all a sovereign.
>
> You cannot solve these things through these various and sundry alphabetical codes. . . . You know what the trouble is. . . . Now my friends, we have got to hit the root with the ax. Centralized power in the hands of a few, with centralized credit in the hands of a few, is the trouble."
>
> Huey Long, United States Senator, "Every Man a King" speech, 1934

1. Huey Long's ideas expressed in the excerpt participate in the 1930s trend in the United States of increasing
   - **a.** conservative attempts to limit the scope of the economic change.
   - **b.** populist-style political movements seeking change in the United States economic system.
   - **c.** calls for totalitarianism to solve economic crises.
   - **d.** state and local efforts aimed at ending the Great Depression.
2. In highlighting "these various and sundry alphabetical codes," Long referred most directly to
   - **a.** New Deal programs.
   - **b.** United States espionage against Japan.
   - **c.** efforts for industrial efficiency emphasized by Progressive reformers.
   - **d.** union movements pushing for more extensive economic change.
3. The ideas of Huey Long, as expressed in the excerpt, had most in common with the ideas of the
   - **a.** Social Darwinists of the 1880s.
   - **b.** critics of the status quo in the 1890s.
   - **c.** government reformers after 1900.
   - **d.** advocates of voting rights in the 1920s.

Questions 4–5 refer to this excerpt.

> "Sec. 2. It is hereby declared to be the policy of Congress—
>
> 1) To establish and maintain such balance between the production and consumption of agricultural commodities . . . as will reestablish prices to farmers at a level that will give agricultural commodities a purchasing power with respect to articles that farmers buy, equivalent to the purchasing power of agricultural commodities in the base period. The base period in the case of all commodities . . . shall be the prewar period. . . .
>
> 2) To approach such equality of purchasing power by gradual correction of the present inequalities therein at as rapid a rate as is deemed feasible in view of the current consumptive demand in domestic and foreign markets."
>
> The Agricultural Adjustment Act, 1933

4. The challenges faced by the agricultural sector of the economy in the 1930s were driven primarily by
   - **a.** federal deregulation of agricultural markets.
   - **b.** improvements in mechanization increasing productivity.
   - **c.** changes in regional cultures.
   - **d.** patterns of mass migration.
5. The legislation in the excerpt emerged most directly from the context of
   - **a.** Franklin Roosevelt's attempts to stimulate the economy.
   - **b.** debates over the best means to maintain traditional cultural values.
   - **c.** movement of the majority of the United States population to urban centers.
   - **d.** the expansion of popular participation in government.

SHORT ANSWER QUESTIONS

Read each question carefully and write a short response. Use evidence from the text to support your claims.

"The guarantor state . . . under the New Deal was . . . a vigorous and dynamic force in society, energizing and . . . supplanting private enterprise when the general welfare required it. . . . When social and economic problems . . . were ignored or shirked by private enterprise, then the federal government undertook to do the job. [If] private enterprise failed to provide adequate and sufficient housing for a minimum standard of welfare for the people, then the government would build houses. . . . Few areas of American life were beyond the touch of the experimenting fingers of the New Deal. . . . The New Deal Revolution has become so much a part of the American Way that no political party which aspires to high office cares now to repudiate it."

Carl N. Degler, *Out of Our Past: The Forces That Shaped Modern America*, 1959

"The critique of modern capitalism that had been so important in the early 1930s . . . was largely gone. . . . In its place was a set of liberal ideas essentially reconciled to the existing structure of the economy and committed to using the state to compensate for capitalism's inevitable flaws. . . . When liberals spoke now of government's responsibility to protect the health of the industrial world, they defined that responsibility less as a commitment to restructure the economy than as an effort to stabilize it and help it grow. They were no longer much concerned about controlling or punishing 'plutocrats' and 'economic royalists,' an impulse central to New Deal rhetoric in the mid 1930s. Instead, they spoke of their commitment to providing a healthy environment in which the corporate world could flourish and in which the economy could sustain 'full employment.'"

Alan Brinkley, *The End of Reform: New Deal Liberalism in Recession and War*, 1995

1. Using the two excerpts provided, answer (a), (b), and (c).
   - **a.** Briefly explain ONE major difference between Degler's and Brinkley's historical interpretations of the New Deal.
   - **b.** Briefly explain how ONE specific historical event or development not directly mentioned in the excerpts could be used to support Degler's argument.
   - **c.** Briefly explain how ONE specific historical event or development not directly mentioned in the excerpts could be used to support Brinkley's argument.
2. Answer (a), (b), and (c).
   - **a.** Briefly explain ONE important way in which the New Deal transformed the American economy.
   - **b.** Briefly explain ONE important way in which the New Deal transformed American politics.
   - **c.** Briefly explain ONE important way in which the New Deal represented a historical continuity in American political life.
3. Answer (a), (b), and (c).
   - **a.** Briefly explain why ONE of the following represents the most significant challenge to the ideas presented by the New Deal.
     - Populist movement
     - Conservatives in Congress
     - The Supreme Court
   - **b.** Explain ONE specific historical event or development to support your argument in (a).
   - **c.** Explain why ONE of the other options represents a less significant challenge to the ideas of the New Deal.

TRM Find complete suggested responses in the Teacher's Resource Materials.

23 CHAPTER The World at War
1937–1945

Chapter 23 — AP® Assessment Weight and Pacing Guide

The assessment weight on the AP® U.S. History Exam for Chapters 17–23 is 10–17 percent. This chapter falls in Unit 7 of the AP® U.S. History Curriculum, covering Period 7: 1890–1945.

This pacing guide is based on a schedule with 120 sessions of 50 minutes each before the AP® U.S. History Exam. If you have a different number of sessions before the exam, you can modify the pacing to meet your needs. If you have additional time, consider incorporating quizzes, released AP® U.S. History questions, practice exams, writing practice, and other instructional activities.

	Traditional Schedule	Block Schedule
Chapter 23	4 days	2 days

Daily Pacing Guide

	Content Focus	Essential Question
Day 1	The Road to War	What developments led the United States to enter World War II?
Day 2	Organizing for a Global War	How did war mobilization reshape American economic life?
Day 3	Life on the Home Front	What short-term and long-term domestic social changes were produced by the war?
Day 4	Fighting and Winning the War	How did Allied war strategy evolve between 1941 and 1945?

AP® Alignment

Section Heading	AP® Topic	AP® Theme
The Road to War	7.11	WOR
Organizing for a Global War	7.12	SOC
Life on the Home Front	7.12, 7.13	SOC, WOR
Fighting and Winning the War	7.13	WOR

*Should changes be made to the Course Framework in the future, an updated alignment will be placed on our AP® updates page at go.bfwpub.com/ap-course-updates.

Chapter 23 — Overview

Chapter 23 begins with a look at the rise of totalitarianism in Europe. As totalitarian leaders came to power in Germany and Italy, Americans were forced to consider the ways in which these systems challenged the values of American democracy. The attack on Pearl Harbor moved the nation to full mobilization. The declaration of war forever altered the U.S. economy, the role of women, and expectations of African Americans among other minorities. While the war was fought overseas, life on the home front was also dramatically altered with both demands for American society to live up to its promise of freedom and civil rights while also stripping rights away from Japanese Americans.

Chapter 23 — Resources

The following resources can be found in the Teacher's Resource Materials (TRM) that accompany the book. You can access the TRM via the book's digital platform, by clicking the TRM links found here in your Teacher's Edition e-book, or by contacting your representative to access the resources online. Visit **bfwpub.com/henretta10e** to learn more.

TRM Chapter 23 Lecture Presentation Slides

TRM Chapter 23 Outline with AP® Focus

TRM Chapter 23 Lecture Strategies

TRM Chapter 23 Suggested Response

TRM Handout 23.1 — Causation: Rise of Fascism

TRM Handout 23.2 — Comparison: Women and Minorities in World War II

TRM Handout 23.3 — Contextualization: Executive Order 8802

TRM Handout 23.4 — Causation: Migration in World War II

Chapter 23 — Essential Activity

To help students understand how the U.S. moved from neutrality to full engagement in World War II, engage them in creating a "Road Map to World War II." Divide the class into collaborative groups and provide each group with a set of images and documents. This can include the following: FDR's Quarantine Speech, Dr. Seuss appeasement cartoon, Rockwell's *Four Freedoms* posters, Churchill touring a bombed London, Adolf Hitler speaking, Nazis entering Czechoslovakia, attack on Pearl Harbor, *Guernica* by Picasso, "No 3rd Term" button from 1940 election, propaganda poster from 1936 Olympic Games, etc. Provide each group with a large sheet of bulletin board paper on which they should write 1933 in the top right corner and December 7, 1941, in the bottom right corner. Inform students that their road map should begin with two separate roads — one representing the United States and one representing Europe and Asia — to represent how the two roads eventually merge in the fight against fascism. Instruct students to use the images and documents provided to illustrate the map with signs, roadblocks, road constructions, exits, etc. Then lead a class discussion that addresses the following prompt: What were the most significant factors moving the U.S. away from neutrality leading up to the attack on Pearl Harbor?

Chapter 23 — Bell Ringers

The following activities take no more than 5–15 minutes of your class period and offer an effective and engaging way to begin your lessons and for students to apply AP® Skills & Processes:

- Provide students with a copy of the Dr. Seuss cartoon "One more lollypop . . ." Ask students to circle and analyze each element in the cartoon and explain the events or ideas each represents. Discuss the point of view expressed regarding the policy of appeasement.
- Project an image of the World War I propaganda poster "Gee, I wish I were a man, I'd join the navy" and the World War II poster of Rosie the Riveter. Ask students to compare the two posters and explain the different impact that World War I and World War II had on women. *Answers will vary.*

NOTES

23
CHAPTER

The World at War
1937–1945

TEACHING STRATEGY

The chapter introduction highlights the unprecedented global scale and destructiveness of World War II. It was inevitable that American participation in such a war would have significant consequences. The opener includes a statement on how President Roosevelt and Prime Minister Churchill defined the conflict as a "good war," which has often been applied to the American experience of World War II. Posing the question of whether this label, of World War II as a "good war" due to the fight to save democracies, is appropriate — considering both the European and Asian military theaters and the home front — could be a useful way to frame students' investigation of the chapter. In a lengthy book review essay in the *New York Times*, Adam Kirsch reflects on different answers offered to this question by historians and others, offering various dimensions of the topic students could consider in attempting to answer the question. To access this essay, search "Kirsch Is World War II Still the Good War?" For a complete suggested response to the **AP® LEARNING FOCUS** question, see p. 766.

AP® LEARNING FOCUS

Why and how did World War II transform the United States domestically and internationally?

World War II began as separate conflicts on opposite sides of the globe. Japan invaded China in 1937, and in 1939, after years of unchecked aggression, Nazi Germany unleashed its "blitzkrieg" (lightning war) against Poland, leading to British and French declarations of war in response. The two wars merged into one and drew in more and more nations. Battles were fought everywhere, from Australia to the arctic circle. Beneath the warring lay a fundamental truth: authoritarian fascism was challenging liberal democracy for dominance around the globe. The fighting ended in August 1945, after American warplanes dropped atomic bombs on the Japanese cities of Hiroshima and Nagasaki. In the years between, massive and technologically advanced forces collided in the fields of France, the forests and steppes of Russia, the river valleys of China, the volcanic islands of the Pacific, and the deserts of North Africa — slaughtering combatants and noncombatants alike in horrific numbers.

The war killed an incalculable number of people, estimated between 50 and 80 million, and wounded or displaced hundreds of millions more. At the war's end, economies and infrastructure across Europe and East Asia lay in ruins. Every industrialized nation in Europe, North America, and Asia participated in the war, as well as dozens of less-developed countries and small colonies. World War II proved the defining event of the twentieth century, leaving behind a new and volatile international order.

Long before the war's outcome was clear, and even before the United States entered hostilities in December 1941, President Roosevelt identified its ideological significance. "Armed defense of democratic existence is now being gallantly waged in four continents," FDR told the nation in his January 1941 State of the Union address. Both Roosevelt and British prime minister Winston Churchill saw the fight to protect "democratic existence" from fascism as a "good war," as it would be remembered by many. When the grim reality of the Jewish Holocaust came to light, U.S. participation in the war seemed even more just. But the war against the authoritarian regimes of Germany, Italy, and Japan was undeniably also a war to preserve British, French, and Dutch colonies in Africa, India, the Middle East, and Southeast Asia. By 1945, democracy in the industrialized world had been preserved, and a new alliance between Western Europe and the United States had taken hold. The future of colonialism, however, remained unresolved.

On the U.S. domestic front, World War II ended the Great Depression and accelerated social and political changes already underway. Racial politics and gender roles shifted in response to wartime migration and labor shortages. The pace of urbanization increased as millions of Americans uprooted themselves and moved hundreds or thousands of miles to join the military or to take a home front job. The massive war effort required an unprecedented expansion of the federal government, which became effectively permanent with the dawning of the Cold War. Though the United States fought for fewer than four years, the repercussions of World War II lasted for generations.

Black Pilots in Tuskegee, Alabama World War II was a "total war," fought on four continents by hundreds of millions of people and massive national armies. Though a late arrival to the conflict, the United States played a critical role in defeating the Axis powers. Here, African American pilots in Tuskegee, Alabama, prepare for a training flight. Afro American Newspapers/Gado/Getty Images.

TEACHING STRATEGY

The Tuskegee airmen became some of the most famed American combatants of the war, examples of the success of American minorities who fought for the chance to serve their country on the front lines, and to prove that oppressed minorities could achieve the same things as whites if given the opportunity. The Tuskegee Airmen Museum provides more detailed information about the fliers and their accomplishments, including historical photos and oral history audio. To access these resources, search "Tuskegee Museum."

AP® SKILLS & PROCESSES

CONTINUITY AND CHANGE

Use the **TIMELINE** to help students begin thinking about how the period from 1933 to 1945 could constitute a distinct historical period regarding American involvement in World War II. The chapter begins in 1937, which correlates with Japan's invasion of China. Using this date as a starting point reflects the recognition that the war actually began in Asia before the German invasion of Poland. It also reflects American interest in China, shaped by investment in the region, and the widespread work of Christian missionaries there, like the parents of famed novelist Pearl S. Buck. The year 1945 references the undisputed end of World War II, with the surrender of both Europe and Japan, the latter after suffering two atomic bomb attacks.

TIMELINE

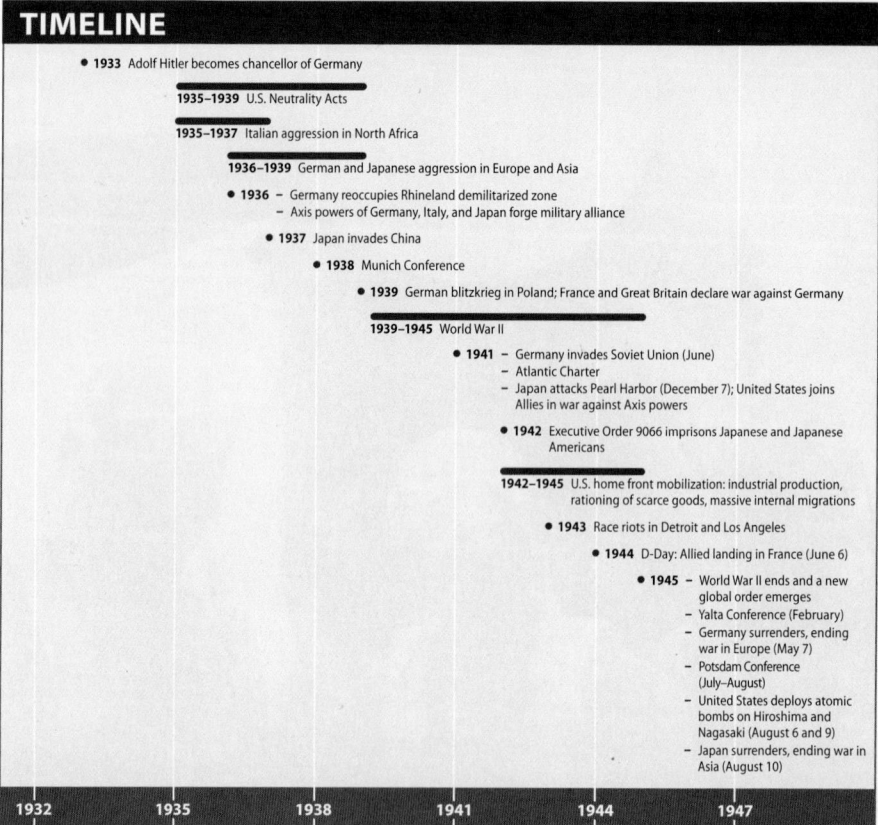

- **1933** Adolf Hitler becomes chancellor of Germany
- **1935–1939** U.S. Neutrality Acts
- **1935–1937** Italian aggression in North Africa
- **1936–1939** German and Japanese aggression in Europe and Asia
- **1936** – Germany reoccupies Rhineland demilitarized zone
  – Axis powers of Germany, Italy, and Japan forge military alliance
- **1937** Japan invades China
- **1938** Munich Conference
- **1939** German blitzkrieg in Poland; France and Great Britain declare war against Germany
- **1939–1945** World War II
- **1941** – Germany invades Soviet Union (June)
  – Atlantic Charter
  – Japan attacks Pearl Harbor (December 7); United States joins Allies in war against Axis powers
- **1942** Executive Order 9066 imprisons Japanese and Japanese Americans
- **1942–1945** U.S. home front mobilization: industrial production, rationing of scarce goods, massive internal migrations
- **1943** Race riots in Detroit and Los Angeles
- **1944** D-Day: Allied landing in France (June 6)
- **1945** – World War II ends and a new global order emerges
  – Yalta Conference (February)
  – Germany surrenders, ending war in Europe (May 7)
  – Potsdam Conference (July–August)
  – United States deploys atomic bombs on Hiroshima and Nagasaki (August 6 and 9)
  – Japan surrenders, ending war in Asia (August 10)

1932 1935 1938 1941 1944 1947

THE ROAD TO WAR

What developments led the United States to enter World War II?

The Great Depression disrupted economic life around the world and also weakened traditional political institutions. In response to the destabilization, an antidemocratic movement known as fascism emerged, promising to take stronger actions against the depression than traditional liberal political parties. By the 1930s, the template of fascism had spread from its roots in Benito Mussolini's Italy to Nazi Germany, under Adolf Hitler, and Spain, under Francisco Franco. Authoritarianism spread to East Asia as well, with Hideki Tojo's rise to power in Japan in 1940. As early as 1936, President Roosevelt warned that fascist nations had "sold their heritage of freedom" and urged Americans to work for "the survival of democracy" both at home and abroad. Although constrained by strong isolationist sentiment, FDR cautiously positioned the United States in opposition to the fascist powers.

The Rise of Fascism

World War II had its roots in the settlement of World War I. The Treaty of Versailles imposed punishing reparations on Germany, while Japan and Italy saw their desire for overseas empires thwarted by the peace settlement. These nationalist resentments and expansionist ambitions eventually fueled the rise of fascist regimes and undermined the new League of Nations, the multinational body tasked with maintaining the postwar international order.

Fascism, as typified in Germany by Hitler, combined a centralized, authoritarian state, a doctrine of Aryan racial supremacy, and fervent nationalism in a call for the spiritual reawakening of the German people. Fascist leaders worldwide disparaged democratic government, independent labor movements, and individual rights and celebrated militarism and imperialism. They opposed both the economic collectivism of the Soviet Union — where, in theory, the state managed the economy to ensure social equality — and the competitive capitalist economies of Western Europe and the United States.

AP® EXAM TIP

Evaluate the reasons why the rise of fascism concerned Americans in the 1930s.

fascism
A system of government characterized by authoritarian rule, extreme nationalism, disdain for civil society, and a conviction that militarism and imperialism make great nations. Germany under Adolf Hitler and Italy under Benito Mussolini were fascist states.

Japan and Italy The first major challenge to Versailles came from Japan. To become an industrial power, Japan required raw materials and overseas markets. Like the Western European powers and the United States before it, Japan embraced an expansionary foreign policy in pursuit of colonial possessions and regional influence. In 1931, Japanese troops occupied Manchuria, an industrialized province in northern China, followed by a full-scale invasion of China in 1937. In both instances, the League of Nations condemned Japan's actions but did nothing to stop them.

Japan's defiance of the League encouraged a fascist leader half a world away: Italy's Benito Mussolini, who had come to power in 1922. Il Duce (The Leader), as Mussolini styled himself, had long condemned the Versailles treaty, which denied Italy's colonial claims in Africa and the Middle East. Like Japan, Italy desired overseas colonies for raw materials, markets, and national prestige. In 1935, Mussolini invaded Ethiopia, one of the few remaining independent countries in Africa. Ethiopian emperor Haile Selassie appealed to the League of Nations. But the League could only impose limited sanctions and issue toothless denunciations, which did not stop Italy from completing its conquest of Ethiopia in 1936.

National Socialist (Nazi) Party
German political party led by Adolf Hitler, who became chancellor of Germany in 1933. The party's ascent was fueled by huge World War I reparation payments, economic depression, fear of communism, labor unrest, and rising unemployment.

Hitler's Germany The Nazi regime posed the gravest threat to the existing world order. Staggering war debt and reparation payments, economic depression, fear of communism, labor unrest, and rising unemployment in Germany fueled the ascent of Adolf Hitler and his **National Socialist (Nazi) Party**. When Hitler became chancellor in 1933, the Reichstag (the German legislature) granted him dictatorial powers to deal with the economic crisis. Hitler promptly outlawed other political parties, arrested many of his political rivals, and declared himself führer (leader). Under Nazi control, the Reichstag invested all legislative power in Hitler's hands.

Adolf Hitler Adolf Hitler reviews his personal guard alongside Heinrich Himmler, the head of Germany's secret police. Dispensing with the usual title of Germany's elected leader, which was "chancellor" (the equivalent of prime minister), Hitler had chosen the title of führer, symbolizing his absolute power in the national government and marking the triumph of fascism over democracy in Germany. Pictorial Press Ltd/Alamy Stock Photo.

AP® APPLY THE TIP

To help students understand the impact of events in Europe and Asia on Americans in the 1930s, prompt students to use pp. 737-740 to complete **Handout 23.1 — Causation: Rise of Fascism (TRM)**. Then provide students with excerpts from speeches by Adolf Hitler that illustrate his attempts to manipulate public opinion regarding the motivations of Germany in the pre-war years. Ask students to discuss the ways in which these primary sources help explain the justification for the policy of appeasement leading up to the invasion of Poland. Also, ask students to compare the words of Adolf Hitler from 1935 to 1939 with the actions of Germany in the Rhineland, Austria, Czechoslovakia, and the border of Poland. Engage students in a discussion of the use of propaganda by fascist dictators to control or influence popular opinion in their own nation and in their relations with other nations.

TRM Find **Handout 23.1 — Causation: Rise of Fascism** in the Teacher's Resource Materials.

TEACHING STRATEGY

Haile Selassie's speech to the League of Nations is available through Mt. Holyoke. Have students read the speech and summarize the three themes Selassie addresses in his argument. To access this speech, search "Mt. Holyoke Selassie."

CHECK FOR UNDERSTANDING

Ask students: **How did fascism rise in Europe and Japan?** *The rise of fascism in both regions was connected to the Versailles peace settlement. The humiliating terms of the treaty gave rise to fervent nationalists, eventually bringing Hitler to power in 1933. Italian and Japanese leaders desired their own empires, like the rest of the Western powers, but were thwarted by the treaty. These nations embraced militarism and eventually invaded neighbors in their quest for power.*

AP® SKILLS & PROCESSES

CAUSATION

Use the **CAUSATION** question to have students identify the causes of fascist military expansion. Students should consider both ideological and practical motives in their responses.

TRM Find complete suggested responses in the Teacher's Resource Materials.

AP® THEME

WOR: America in the World

In the 1930s, while many Americans were concerned about the rise of fascism, most opposed taking military action against the aggression of Nazi Germany and Japan. To initiate a discussion, ask students to explain how militarist ideologies changed the goals of these nations' leaders in comparison with late nineteenth-century imperialist objectives.

Hitler's goal was nothing short of European domination and world power, as he had made clear in his 1925 book *Mein Kampf* (*My Struggle*). The book outlined a plan to overturn the territorial settlements of the Versailles treaty, unite Germans living throughout central Europe in a greater fatherland, and annex large areas of Eastern Europe. The "inferior races" who lived in these regions — Jews, Gypsies, and Slavs — would be removed or subordinated to the German "master race." A virulent anti-Semite, Hitler had long blamed Jews for Germany's problems. Once in power, he began a sustained and brutal persecution of Jews, which expanded into a campaign of extermination in the early 1940s.

Axis powers
Military alliance formed in 1936 among Germany, Italy, and Japan that fought the Allied powers during World War II.

AP® SKILLS & PROCESSES

CAUSATION

What motivated Japanese, Italian, and German expansionism?

In 1935, Hitler began an open re-armament program, in violation of the Versailles treaty, without consequence. In 1936, he sent troops into the Rhineland, a demilitarized zone under the terms of Versailles. Again, there was little international opposition, with France and Britain both shrugging. Later that year, Mussolini and Hitler formed the Rome-Berlin Axis, a political and military alliance between the two fascist nations. Also in 1936, Germany agreed to a military alliance with Japan in the event of a war against the Soviet Union. With this alliance now forming a Rome-Berlin-Tokyo axis, the three nations became known as the **Axis powers**. France and Great Britain remained reluctant to oppose him, and in the absence of opposition, Hitler had seized the military advantage in Europe by 1937.

War Approaches

As Hitler pushed his initiatives in Europe, isolationist sentiment ran strong among Americans. In part, isolationism reflected disillusion with American participation in World War I. In 1934, Senator Gerald P. Nye, a progressive Republican from North Dakota, launched an investigation into the profits of munitions makers during that war. Nye's committee alleged that arms manufacturers (popularly labeled "merchants of death") had maneuvered President Wilson into World War I.

Neutrality Act of 1935
Legislation that sought to avoid entanglement in foreign wars while protecting trade. It imposed an embargo on selling arms to warring countries and declared that Americans traveling on the ships of belligerent nations did so at their own risk.

Although Nye's committee failed to prove its charge against weapon makers, its factual findings prompted Congress to pass a series of acts meant to keep the nation out of any overseas war. The **Neutrality Act of 1935** imposed an embargo on the sale of arms to warring countries and declared that Americans traveling on the ships of belligerent nations did so at their own risk. In two subsequent Neutrality Acts, Congress banned loans to belligerents in 1936 and imposed a "cash-and-carry" requirement in 1937: if a warring country wanted to purchase nonmilitary goods from the United States, it had to pay cash and carry them in its own ships, keeping the United States out of any potential naval warfare. A fourth Neutrality Act, in 1939, did permit military goods to be purchased on cash-and-carry terms.

Americans for the most part had little enthusiasm for war, and a wide variety of voices espoused isolationism. Many followed Republican Senator Robert Taft of Ohio, who distrusted both Roosevelt and European nations with equal conviction, or famed aviator Charles A. Lindbergh, who gave impassioned speeches against intervention in Europe. Some isolationists, such as the conservative National Legion of Mothers of America, combined anticommunism, Christian morality, and even anti-Semitism. Isolationists were primarily conservatives, but a contingent of progressives opposed war on pacifist or moral grounds. Whatever their philosophies, ardent isolationists forced Roosevelt to tread lightly.

Popular Front
A small, left-leaning coalition of Americans who pushed for greater U.S. intervention against fascism in Europe. It was comprised of American Communist Party members, African American civil rights activists, and trade unionists, among others.

The Popular Front A small but significant number of Americans rejected isolationism and called for the United States to confront the spread of fascism. Many of the most prominent calls for intervention came from the **Popular Front**, a broad coalition drawn from a wide range of social groups, including the American Communist Party (which had increased its membership to between fifty and seventy thousand), African American civil rights activists, trade unionists, left-wing writers and intellectuals, and even a few New Dealers. The Popular Front's ties to communism and the Soviet Union became a liability due to the brutal repression of Joseph Stalin's regime, and untenable after the Soviets made a nonaggression pact with Nazi Germany in 1939. Nevertheless American Popular Front activists were prominent among the small but vocal minority encouraging Roosevelt to take a stronger stand against European fascism.

The Failure of Appeasement Encouraged by the weak worldwide response to the invasions of China and Ethiopia and the remilitarization of the Rhineland, Hitler was further emboldened by British and French neutrality in the Spanish Civil War of 1936–1939, a clash of fascism and liberal republicanism. Growing more aggressive, in 1938 he forcefully annexed Austria and signaled his intention to seize the Sudetenland — a German-speaking border area of Czechoslovakia. Because Czechoslovakia had an alliance with France, war seemed imminent. But at the **Munich Conference** in September 1938, Britain and France capitulated, agreeing to let Germany annex the Sudetenland in return for Hitler's pledge to seek no more territory. The agreement, declared British prime minister Neville Chamberlain, guaranteed "peace for our time." Hitler drew a different conclusion, telling his generals: "Our enemies are small fry. I saw them in Munich."

Munich Conference
A conference in Munich, Germany, in September 1938 during which Britain and France agreed to allow Germany to annex the Sudetenland — a German-speaking border area of Czechoslovakia — in return for Hitler's pledge to seek no more territory.

Within six months, Hitler's forces had overrun the rest of Czechoslovakia and were threatening to march into Poland. Realizing that their policy of appeasement — capitulating to Hitler's demands — was proving disastrous, Britain and France warned Hitler that further aggression meant war. In August 1939, Hitler and Stalin shocked the world by signing a mutual nonaggression pact. This surprise agreement shielded Germany from a two-front war against Britain and France in the west and the Soviet Union in the east. On September 1, 1939, Hitler launched a blitzkrieg against Poland. Two days later, Britain and France declared war on Germany. World War II had officially begun.

Two days after the European war started, the United States declared its neutrality. But President Roosevelt made no secret of his sympathies. When war had broken

German Victory Parade in Poland German tanks roll along a major thoroughfare in Warsaw, Poland, following Hitler's successful "blitzkrieg" (lightning war) against that Eastern European nation in September 1939. Hitler's armies would in short order invade Denmark, Norway, Belgium, the Netherlands, Luxembourg, and, finally, France, conquering all of continental northern Europe by the summer of 1940. Private Collection/The Stapleton Collection/Bridgeman Images.

TEACHING STRATEGY

In retrospect, the policy of appeasement was one of the colossal failures of European policy toward Nazi Germany. However, at the time the world was divided over whether or not this was sound policy. Ask students to identify and explain at least one historical reason why someone would have supported the policy of appeasement — even though they opposed Nazi Germany — in 1938.

TEACHING STRATEGY

Even though the United States was a diplomatic, political, and economic power in the world, the nation remained somewhat removed from the decisions made in Europe in the 1930s. Have students identify and explain one historical reason for the lack of direct participation by the United States in European decisions from 1933–1938.

TEACHING STRATEGY

Fort Missoula's Web site provides a detailed, animated map of the progress of the war on the European front. While it provides more detail than you will probably want, it offers a useful overview of German territorial conquest, the rollback of Axis powers, and their defeat. The map could be helpful in a synopsis lecture or for students to view on their own. To access this site, search "Fort Missoula WWII map."

AP® APPLY THE TIP

On the board, draw a line and label the extreme points as "Isolationist" and "Interventionist" to represent a spectrum. Ask students to work in pairs to develop a definition of each term. Ask one pair to share their definition and record it under each term on the board. Then lead the class in a discussion that clarifies the definitions and provides the historical reasoning to justify the definition for the time period. Prompt students to use pp. 738–741 to add individuals, events, and other details on the spectrum to explain the points of view of those on each side. Then provide students with excerpts from Franklin Roosevelt's "Quarantine Speech" and "Four Freedoms" speech. Ask students to explain the historical argument being made by FDR in these sources. Initiate a class debate that compares the reaction of the nation to each speech and the impact of each speech on U.S. goals and ideals after the attack on Pearl Harbor.

out in 1914, Woodrow Wilson asked Americans to be neutral "in thought as well as in action." FDR, by contrast, declared in 1939 that the United States "will remain a neutral nation, but I cannot ask that every American remain neutral in thought as well." The overwhelming majority of Americans — some 84 percent, according to a poll in 1939 — supported Britain and France rather than Germany, but most wanted America to avoid another European war.

At first, any need for U.S. intervention seemed remote. After Germany quickly overran Poland, an uneasy calm settled over Europe. But on April 9, 1940, German forces invaded Denmark and Norway, rapidly defeating both Scandinavian nations. In May, the Netherlands, Belgium, and Luxembourg fell to the swift German army. The final shock came in mid-June, when the French government surrendered, and Nazi troops paraded through Paris. Britain now stood alone against Hitler.

AP® EXAM TIP

Recognize the impact of FDR's interventionist philosophy in outlining America's role in the war.

America First Committee (AFC)
A committee organized by isolationists in 1940 to oppose the entrance of the United States into World War II. The membership of the committee included senators, journalists, and publishers, and such prominent national figures as the aviator Charles Lindbergh.

Isolationists and Interventionists What *Time* magazine would later call America's "thousand-step road to war" had already begun. In 1939, after a bitter battle in Congress, Roosevelt won a change in the neutrality laws to allow the Allies to buy arms as well as nonmilitary goods on a cash-and-carry basis. Interventionists, led by journalist William Allen White and his Committee to Defend America by Aiding the Allies, became increasingly vocal in 1940 as the war in Europe escalated. In response, isolationists formed the **America First Committee (AFC)**, whose 800,000 members included journalists and publishers, as well as U.S. senators such as Gerald Nye and such prominent national figures as Lindbergh. Urging the nation to stay out of the war, the AFC held rallies across the United States, and its posters, brochures, and broadsides warning against American involvement in Europe suffused many parts of the country, especially the Midwest. The aviator Lindbergh's speeches opposing U.S. involvement accused "the British, the Jewish and the Roosevelt administration" of leading the nation into an unpopular war, also identifying "capitalists, Anglophiles, and intellectuals" as prominent among the "war agitators."

The success of America First caused Roosevelt to proceed cautiously as he moved the United States closer to involvement. The president did not want war, but he believed that most Americans "greatly underestimate the serious implications to our own future," as he confided to White. In May, Roosevelt created the National Defense Advisory Commission, which engaged in early war planning, and brought two prominent Republicans, Henry Stimson and Frank Knox, into his cabinet as secretaries of war and the navy, respectively. In the summer of 1940, the president traded fifty World War I-era destroyers to Great Britain in exchange for the right to build military bases on British possessions in the Atlantic, circumventing neutrality laws by using an executive order. In October 1940, a bipartisan vote in Congress approved a large increase in defense spending and instituted the first peacetime draft in American history. Acknowledging that Britain and the United States stood alone against fascism, FDR declared, "We must be the great arsenal of democracy."

As the war in Europe and the Pacific expanded, the United States was preparing for a presidential election. The crisis had convinced Roosevelt to seek an unprecedented third term in 1940. The Republicans nominated Wendell Willkie of Indiana, a former Democrat who supported many New Deal policies. The two parties' platforms differed only slightly. Both pledged aid to the Allies, and both candidates promised not to "send an American boy into the shambles of a European war," as Willkie put it. The challenger ran a spirited campaign, and the result was closer than that of 1932 or 1936. However, Roosevelt still swept to a third victory with 55 percent of the vote.

With the election settled, Roosevelt sought to persuade Congress to increase aid to Britain, whose survival he viewed as key to American security. In January 1941, Roosevelt delivered the State of the Union address, in what became one of his defining moments. In laying out "four essential human freedoms" — freedom of speech, freedom of religion, freedom from want, and freedom from fear — Roosevelt cast the war as a defense of democratic societies. He then linked the fate of democracy in Western Europe with the new welfare state at home. Sounding a decidedly New Deal note, Roosevelt pledged to end "special privileges for the few" and to preserve "civil liberties for all." Like President Wilson's "Fourteen Points" speech championing national self-determination at the close of World War I, Roosevelt's **"Four Freedoms"** speech outlined a liberal international order with appeal well beyond its intended European and American audiences. Since, at the time, nearly one-third of the world's peoples lived in colonies under a foreign power, FDR's words seemed to promise, as Wilson's had, liberation from external domination.

Four Freedoms
Basic human rights identified by President Franklin D. Roosevelt to justify support for Britain in World War II: freedom of speech, freedom of religion, freedom from want, and freedom from fear.

Two months later, in March 1941, with an increasingly battered Britain unable to pay cash for arms, Roosevelt persuaded Congress to pass the **Lend-Lease Act**. The legislation authorized the president to "lease, lend, or otherwise dispose of" arms and equipment, without a cash payment and with a promise of future reimbursement, to Britain or any other country whose defense was considered vital to the security of the United States. When Hitler abandoned his nonaggression pact with Stalin and launched an invasion of the Soviet Union in June 1941, the United States extended lend-lease to the Soviets. This policy marked the unofficial entrance of the United States into the European war.

Lend-Lease Act
Legislation in 1941 that enabled Britain to obtain arms from the United States without cash but with the promise of reimbursement when World War II ended. The act reflected Roosevelt's desire to assist the British in any way possible short of war.

Roosevelt underlined his support in an August 1941 meeting with British prime minister Winston Churchill (who had succeeded Chamberlain in 1940). Their joint press release, which became known as the **Atlantic Charter**, provided the ideological foundation of the Allied cause. Drawing from Wilson's Fourteen Points and Roosevelt's own Four Freedoms, the charter called for economic cooperation, national self-determination, and guarantees of political stability after the war to ensure "that all men in all the lands may live out their lives in freedom from fear and want." The charter would become the basis for a new American-led transatlantic alliance after the war's conclusion. Its promises sowed conflict in Asia and Africa, however, where European powers proved unwilling to abandon their colonial holdings.

Atlantic Charter
A press release by President Roosevelt and British prime minister Winston Churchill in August 1941 calling for economic cooperation, national self-determination, and guarantees of political stability after the war.

In the fall of 1941, outright U.S. involvement in the war drew closer. By September, Nazi U-boats and the American navy were exchanging fire in the Atlantic. With isolationists still a potent force politically, Roosevelt insisted that the United States would defend itself only against a direct attack. Behind the scenes, the president and his close advisors considered American entry into the war only a matter of time.

AP® SKILLS & PROCESSES

CONTEXTUALIZATION

How did Roosevelt use the Four Freedoms speech and the Atlantic Charter to define the war for Americans?

The Attack on Pearl Harbor

The inevitable provocation came not from Germany but from Japan. After Japan invaded China in 1937, Roosevelt had denounced "the present reign of terror and international lawlessness" and suggested that aggressors be "quarantined" by peaceful nations. Despite such rhetoric, the United States did not intervene, even after Japanese troops sacked the city of Nanjing, massacring an estimated 300,000 Chinese soldiers and civilians, and sexually assaulting thousands of women. Japanese territorial ambitions soon expanded, much like Italy in Ethiopia and Germany in Eastern Europe. In 1940, General Hideki Tojo became war minister and concluded a formal military alliance with both Italy and Germany.

Tojo, supported by Emperor Hirohito, sought to create a "Greater East Asia Co-Prosperity Sphere," under Japanese control, stretching from the Korean Peninsula south to Indonesia. The next step was the 1940 invasion of the northern part of the French colony of Indochina (present-day Vietnam, Cambodia, and Laos). When Tojo directed a full-scale invasion of Indochina in July 1941, Roosevelt froze Japanese assets in the United States and stopped all trade with Japan. This included vital oil shipments that accounted for almost 80 percent of Japanese consumption. In October 1941, General Tojo rose to prime minister and accelerated secret preparations for war against the United States. By November, American military

AP® SKILLS & PROCESSES

CONTEXTUALIZATION

The **CONTEXTUALIZATION** question offers students the opportunity to consider the role of ideas, including notions of American identity, in its articulation of war aims. Students should consider the broad context of the development of American ideals since independence, as well as in the narrower context of the war. Specifically, they should consider the circumstances of January 1941 compared with August of that year. Extend this prompt by asking students to compare the goals listed here with those indicated by Wilson in his Fourteen Points.

TRM Find complete suggested responses in the Teacher's Resource Materials.

CHECK FOR UNDERSTANDING

Ask students: **How did war approach for the U.S.?** *Through a series of neutrality acts, Congress maintained an isolationist position. As Hitler's aggression continued, however, FDR gradually persuaded Congress to modify these laws to support Britain while remaining technically neutral. Starting in 1937, neutrality laws recognized the right of belligerents to buy nonmilitary supplies, and, later, weapons, from the U.S. on a "cash and carry" basis (an option only really available to Britain). Using executive action, FDR bypassed Congress and negotiated a destroyers-for-bases deal with Britain. In 1940, Congress agreed to the first ever peacetime draft, primarily as a self-defense measure. In 1941, FDR persuaded Congress to expand cash-and-carry to lend-lease, first to Britain and then to the Soviet Union. The nation was now functionally at war. Recognizing this fact, German U-boats began attacking American ships in the Atlantic, and the U.S. Navy fired back.*

TEACHING STRATEGY

National Geographic provides a moment-by-moment animated map of the Pearl Harbor attack, with a narrative overview and links to more detailed information about each stage. To access this site, search "National Geographic Pearl Harbor."

The National WWII Museum provides a lesson that directs students to analyze two drafts and an audio recording of President Roosevelt's "Day of Infamy" speech to Congress in order to explore how primary sources are created, and how there may be as much to learn from the process of writing as from the final result. The museum also offers an essay titled "The Path to Pearl Harbor," which explains the backstory behind Japan's surprise attack. To access these resources, search "National WWII Museum Educator Resources."

CHECK FOR UNDERSTANDING

Ask students: **Explain the steps by which the United States became involved in World War II.** *The German invasion of Poland in September 1939 had dramatic effects on American foreign policy. Though many in the United States were isolationist and did not want to be involved in war and thus encouraged Congress to pass a series of Neutrality Acts, President Roosevelt prepared for that eventuality. The following are key events in the lead up to U.S. involvement in World War II: creation of the National Defense Advisory Committee (May 1940); authorization of the first peacetime draft in U.S. history (October 1940); "Four Freedoms" speech (January 1941); Lend-Lease Act (March 1941); Atlantic Charter (August 1941); attack on Pearl Harbor (December 7, 1941); and declaration of war on Japan and later Germany (December 1941).*

AP® THEME

WOR: America in the World

Ensure students understand how the mass mobilization of American society helped end the Great Depression.

AP® THEME

WOR: America in the World

The nation's strong industrial base played a pivotal role in winning the war by equipping and provisioning millions of U.S. troops and allies. Assign David Mindell's essay "The Science and Technology of World War II" or discuss in class to explore the new technologies that arose from the war such as radar, penicillin, incendiary bombs, plastics, and new "scientific" military rations, among others. To access the essay, search "David Mindell Science and Technology of WWII."

Pearl Harbor, December 7, 1941 On the morning of December 7, 1941, a surprise Japanese attack on the U.S. naval fleet in Pearl Harbor (Hawaii Territory) produced destruction and chaos. Having significantly damaged American forces in the Pacific, Japan quickly overtook virtually all of Southeast Asia. But within sixteen months, the United States had turned the tide and begun to drive the Japanese back toward their home islands. National Archives photo no. 12009098.

intelligence knew that Japan was planning an attack but did not know where it would occur.

Early on Sunday morning, December 7, 1941, Japanese warplanes attacked **Pearl Harbor** in Hawaii, the headquarters of the American Navy's Pacific Fleet. The raid killed nearly 2,400 Americans and destroyed or heavily damaged eight battleships, three cruisers, three destroyers, and almost two hundred airplanes. Although the assault was devastating, it had the unintended consequence of uniting the American people. Calling December 7th "a date which will live in infamy," President Roosevelt asked Congress for a declaration of war against Japan. The Senate voted unanimously for war, and the House concurred by a vote of 388 to 1. The lone dissenter was Jeannette Rankin of Montana, the first female member of Congress and a committed pacifist who had also voted against entry into World War I. Three days later, Germany and Italy declared war on the United States, which in turn declared war on those two Axis powers. The storm clouds of two wars, one in Asia and one in Europe, finally converged over the United States.

Pearl Harbor
A naval base in Pearl Harbor, Hawaii, that was attacked by Japanese bombers on December 7, 1941; more than 2,400 Americans were killed. The following day, President Roosevelt asked Congress for a declaration of war against Japan.

War Powers Act (1941)
The law that gave President Roosevelt unprecedented control over all aspects of the war effort during World War II.

ORGANIZING FOR A GLOBAL WAR

How did war mobilization reshape American economic life?

Fighting a global war required a massive expansion of federal power. Reorganizing industrial production, raising an army, and assembling the necessary workforce required far more authority than even the largest New Deal initiatives. The **War Powers Act**, passed in December 1941, gave President Roosevelt unprecedented control over all aspects of the war effort. This law marked the beginning of what some historians call the imperial presidency: the far-reaching use (and sometimes abuse) of executive authority during the second half of the twentieth century.

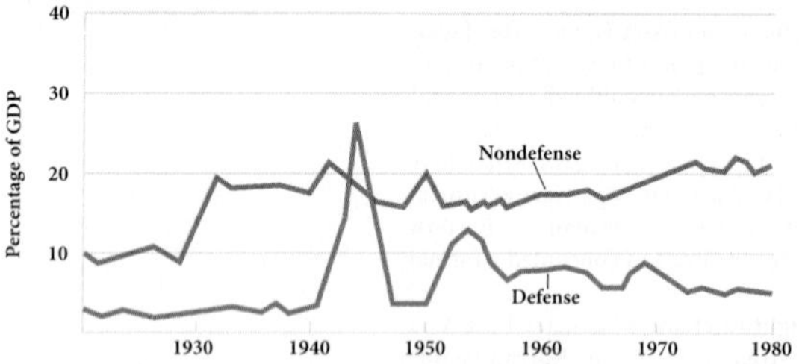

FIGURE 23.1 Government Military and Civilian Spending as a Percentage of GDP, 1920–1980
Government military spending was about 3 percent of the gross domestic product (GDP) in the 1920s and 1930s, but it ballooned to more than 25 percent during World War II, to 13 percent during the Korean War, and to nearly 10 percent during the Vietnam War. Federal government spending for civilian purposes doubled during the New Deal and has remained at about 17 to 20 percent of GDP ever since.

Financing the War

Defense mobilization, not the New Deal of the 1930s, ended the Great Depression. Between 1940 and 1945, the annual gross national product doubled, and after-tax profits of American businesses nearly doubled as well (see "America in the World," p. 743). Federal spending on war production powered this advance. By late 1943, two-thirds of the economy was directly involved in the war effort, and war-related production jumped from just 2 percent of GNP to 40 percent (Figure 23.1). Federal

AP® AMERICA IN THE WORLD

The Scales of War: Losses and Gains During World War II

World War II saw an extraordinary loss of life. Worldwide, at least 50 million people perished between 1939 and 1945 from war-related causes. The majority of those who died were civilians, though many millions of soldiers perished in battle as well. For most countries, we have reasonable estimates rather than precise figures. Figure 23.2 compares the United States with other major combatants and nations caught in this global struggle.

At the same time, the war fueled tremendous economic growth, at least in the United States, which was spared the physical devastation of Europe and East Asia. Military production for World War II lifted the United States out of the Great Depression. Gross domestic product (GDP) nearly doubled between 1938 and 1945. Economic production in other combatant nations, as shown in Figure 23.3, grew little if at all.

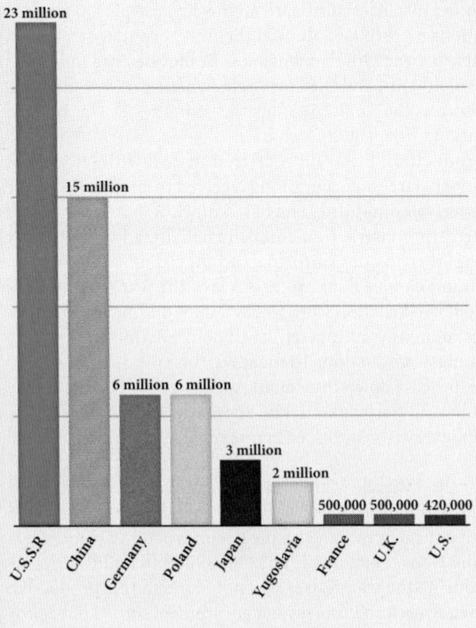

FIGURE 23.2 **World War II Military and Civilian Deaths, 1939–1945**

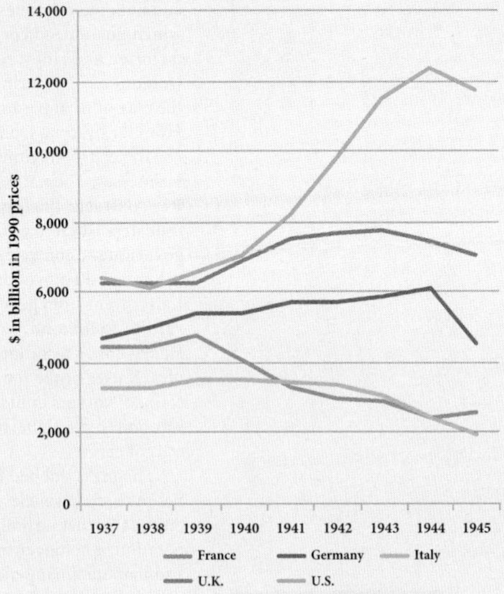

FIGURE 23.3 **Gross Domestic Product Rates Worldwide, 1938–1945**

SOURCE: GDP data from the Madison Project, Groningen Growth and Development Centre.

QUESTIONS FOR ANALYSIS

1. Why did the United States experience so many fewer deaths than other nations? Why were there so many deaths in Eastern Europe and the Soviet Union? Use specific examples from each theater of war to support your answers.
2. Describe U.S. GDP in relationship to the other industrial nations in 1938 and in 1945 included on Figure 23.3. How were some of the key domestic changes discussed in the chapter, such as rural-urban migration, racial conflict, and women's employment, linked to this economic growth?
3. Relate the patterns identified in this data to key wartime developments, such as the Holocaust, Stalin's demand for a second front, or the entry of the United States into the war?

AP® SKILLS & PROCESSES

ANALYZING HISTORICAL EVIDENCE

The **AP® AMERICA IN THE WORLD** feature gives students practice interpreting crucial data about the nature of the war: death rates and GDP productivity. The U.S. experienced the fewest casualties of any belligerent and had by far the strongest productivity. The fact that most deaths were suffered by civilians hints at ways the U.S. benefitted from not being part of the war front. Every other belligerent in this data was part of the war front in some capacity. The U.S.'s physical protection from the war front prevented large-scale civilian deaths, while preventing the destruction of American infrastructure and factories, and thus maintaining productivity. But the nation's productivity can be attributed to other factors as well: a large population, tremendous natural resources, and an innovative approach to production also played key roles. As the text on p. 744 suggests, "America's industrial might . . . proved the decisive factor in winning" the war.

TRM Find complete suggested responses in the Teacher's Resource Materials.

Revenue Act
A 1942 act that expanded the number of people paying income taxes from 3.9 million to 42.6 million. These taxes on personal incomes and business profits paid half the cost of World War II.

AP® EXAM TIP
Recognize the role of World War II in ending the Great Depression.

spending drove the surging economy, underwritten by tax increases and bond issues. The **Revenue Act** of 1942 expanded the number of people paying income taxes from 3.9 million to 42.6 million. Taxes on personal incomes and business profits paid half the cost of the war. The government borrowed the rest, both from wealthy Americans and ordinary citizens alike, who invested in popular treasury bonds (known as "war bonds").

The war effort required far-reaching cooperation between government and private business. Over the course of American involvement in the war, the number of civilians employed by the government increased almost fourfold, to 3.8 million — a far higher rate of growth than that during the New Deal. The powerful War Production Board (WPB) awarded defense contracts; allocated scarce resources such as rubber, copper, and oil; and persuaded businesses to convert to military production. For example, the WPB encouraged Ford and General Motors to build tanks rather than cars by granting generous tax advantages for re-equipping existing factories and building new ones. In other instances, the board approved "cost-plus" contracts, which guaranteed corporations a profit and allowed them to keep new steel mills, factories, and shipyards after the war. Government subsidies for defense industries would intensify during the Cold War, and the corporate beneficiaries would form the core of what became known as the "military-industrial complex" (see "Economy: From Recovery to Dominance" in Chapter 25).

To secure maximum production, the WPB preferred to deal with large-scale businesses. The nation's fifty-six largest corporations received three-fourths of the war contracts; the top ten received one-third. The best-known war contractor was industrialist Henry J. Kaiser. His construction company had already won prewar government contracts to build roads in California and played a leading role in the massive Hoover and Grand Coulee dam projects. Once the war effort began, Kaiser went from government construction work to navy shipbuilding. At his shipyard in Richmond, California, he revolutionized naval construction by applying Henry Ford's techniques of mass production. To meet wartime production schedules, Kaiser broke the work process down into small, specialized tasks that newly trained workers could handle and perform quickly. Soon, each of his work crews was building a "Liberty Ship" every two weeks, each one capable of carrying 10,000 tons of cargo.

The press dubbed Kaiser the "Miracle Man," but his success derived from close ties to federal agencies as much as industrial wizardry. The government financed the great dams that he built during the depression, and the Reconstruction Finance Corporation, a holdover from the Hoover era, lent him $300 million to build shipyards and manufacturing plants during the war. Kaiser was not alone in this productive partnership. Working together, American business and government turned out a prodigious supply of military hardware: 86,000 tanks; 296,000 airplanes; 15 million rifles and machine guns; 64,000 landing craft; and 6,500 cargo ships and naval vessels. The American way of war, wrote the Scottish historian D. W. Brogan in 1944, was "mechanized like the American farm and kitchen." America's industrial might, as much as or more than its troops, proved the decisive factor in the war.

AP® SKILLS & PROCESSES
CONTINUITY AND CHANGE
How did the war affect the relationship between corporations and the federal government?

Mobilizing the American Fighting Force

All of that war production required a huge workforce, to produce, operate, and manage. The government mobilized tens of millions of soldiers, civilians, and workers — coordinated on an unprecedented scale. During World War II, the armed forces of the United States enlisted more than sixteen million men and women, more than in any other conflict. They came from every region and economic station: black sharecroppers from Alabama; white farmers from the Midwest; the sons and daughters of European, Mexican, and Caribbean immigrants; Native men from Navajo and Choctaw reservations and other tribal communities; women from every state in the

CHECK FOR UNDERSTANDING

Ask students: **How did the U.S. finance the war?** *The government split the cost in half — financing half by taxation and the remainder through borrowing. Tax revenues grew significantly by increasing the number of Americans who paid taxes and increasing the rate of taxation on wealthy Americans. The rest was paid for through war bonds. The government favored large corporations because of the scale of production necessary for the war effort, which hastened the decline of smaller companies. Using a cost-plus formula, the government ensured that corporations made a profit irrespective of their expenditures.*

AP® SKILLS & PROCESSES

CONTINUITY AND CHANGE

The **CONTINUITY AND CHANGE** question asks students to consider changes in the relationship between corporations and the government as a result of the war. Students should think about the immediate pre-war context of the New Deal, in which the government attempted to restore business productivity, but also regulated business activity and actively supported labor organizations. Students could also place this question in the larger context of government-business relations dating back to the emergence of big business in the late nineteenth century. As the text points out, government support for defense-related corporations has remained largely intact ever since. Students might also offer an inference about why that government-business arrangement continued after the war ended.

TRM Find complete suggested responses in the Teacher's Resource Materials.

nation; even Hollywood celebrities. From urban, rural, and suburban areas, from working-class and middle-class backgrounds — they all served in the military.

In contrast to its otherwise democratic character, the American army segregated the nearly one million African Americans in uniform. The National Association for the Advancement of Colored People (NAACP) and other civil rights groups protested that a "Jim Crow army cannot fight for a free world," but the military continued to separate black soldiers and assign them menial duties. The poet Langston Hughes observed an irony: "We are elevator boys, janitors, red caps, maids — a race in uniform." But the military uniform, Hughes implied, did not suit African Americans in the eyes of whites. Native Americans and Mexican Americans, on the other hand, were never officially segregated; they rubbed elbows with the sons of European immigrants and native-born soldiers from all regions of the country.

Among the most instrumental soldiers were the Native American "**code talkers**." In the Pacific theater, native Navajo speakers served as radio men, transmitting orders in a code based on the Navajo language. At the battle of Iwo Jima — one of the war's fiercest — Navajo code talkers, working around the clock, sent and received more than eight hundred messages without error. In the European theater, Comanche, Choctaw, and Cherokee speakers transmitted crucial orders. No Axis nation ever broke these Native American codes.

Approximately 350,000 American women enlisted in the military. About 140,000 served in the Women's Army Corps (WAC), and 100,000 served in the navy's Women Accepted for Volunteer Emergency Service (WAVES). One-third of the nation's registered nurses, almost 75,000 overall, volunteered for military duty. In addition, about 1,000 Women's Airforce Service Pilots (WASPs) ferried planes and supplies in noncombat areas. However, military leadership did sharply limit the contributions of women to the war effort. Female officers could not command men, and WACs and WAVES were barred from combat duty, although nurses of both sexes served close to the front lines. Most of the jobs that women did in the military — clerical work, communications, and health care — resembled women's jobs in civilian life.

Historians still debate how to characterize the World War II American military. As an army of "citizen-soldiers," it represented a wide cross section of society. Military service provided a sense of purpose for a generation raised in economic depression. The armed forces also worked to bring the children of immigrants further into mainstream American life. But the tensions and contradictions of American society also expressed themselves in the military. The draft revealed appalling levels of health, fitness, and education among millions of Americans, spurring calls for improved literacy and nutrition. Female participation in the war effort revealed deep anxieties about the threat to "womanhood" allegedly posed by service. The racial inequalities of civilian life were re-created in the barracks. Even as it united under a common cause, the American military reflected the strengths and weaknesses of a diverse, fractious society.

Workers and the War Effort

As millions of working-age citizens joined the military, the nation faced a critical labor shortage. Women and African Americans answered the call, joining the industrial workforce in roles unavailable to them before the conflict. Unions, benefitting from the demand for labor, negotiated higher

AP® EXAM TIP

Identify the opportunities and challenges faced by women and minorities who served in World War II.

code talkers
Native American soldiers trained to use native languages to send messages in battle during World War II. The messages they sent gave the Allies great advantage in several battles.

AP® SKILLS & PROCESSES

MAKING CONNECTIONS

How did the American military reflect American society? How was it different?

Shipyards in Wartime Workers leaving the Pennsylvania shipyards in Beaumont, Texas, at the height of wartime industrial production in 1943. Across the country, cities like Beaumont became boomtowns overnight, as workers poured into suddenly roaring factories brought back to life from the Great Depression by the demands of fighting a global war. Library of Congress, 1a35442.

AP® APPLY THE TIP

To help students compare the opportunities and challenges faced by women and minorities in World War II, ask them to complete **Handout 23.2 — Comparison: Women and Minorities in World War II (TRM)**. Then organize the class into small groups and assign them to read and complete the **AP® FIRSTHAND ACCOUNTS** feature on pp. 746–747 in order to develop a DBQ prompt based on the documents. Assign each group an AP® History Reasoning Process to focus on in their prompt. Require students to find four additional primary sources to pair with those from the text to create a complete set of DBQ documents. When the prompts and documents are ready, redistribute them and have groups come up with a thesis and outline utilizing the documents and outside evidence to address the prompt.

TRM Find **Handout 23.2 — Comparison: Women and Minorities in World War II** in the Teacher's Resource Materials.

TEACHING STRATEGY

The NavajoCode Web site offers several resources for teaching about the code talkers, including a documentary film, interviews with veterans, and explanations of how cryptography works. To access this site, search "Navajo Code Talkers."

AP® SKILLS & PROCESSES

MAKING CONNECTIONS

Ask students to write at least three distinctive statements about the demographics of the United States. These statements could be about who lives where, the racial and ethnic groups in America, the migration patterns that changed during the Great Depression, or the differences between rural and urban areas. Have students identify the demographic groups the book identities from pp. 744–749. When students have the requisite background information, they should be more prepared to answer the Making Connections question.

TRM Find complete suggested responses in the Teacher's Resource Materials.

AP® SKILLS & PROCESSES

ANALYZING HISTORICAL EVIDENCE

The **AP® FIRSTHAND ACCOUNTS** feature highlights oral interviews as a particular form of historical evidence. As students read these sources, they might consider the particular usefulness of this type of evidence, as well as the ways recalling particular events years later might shape what women remember and how they think about those events long after they transpired.

AP® FIRSTHAND ACCOUNTS

Women in the Wartime Workplace

During World War II, millions of men served in the armed forces and millions of women worked in war-related industries. A generation later, some of these women workers recounted their wartime experiences to historians in oral interviews.

EVELYN GOTZION

Becoming a Union Activist

Evelyn Gotzion went to work at Rayovac, a battery company in Madison, Wisconsin, in 1935; she retired in 1978. While at Rayovac, Gotzion and her working husband raised three children.

SOURCE: *Women Remember the War, 1941–1945*, edited by Michael E. Stevens and Ellen D. Goldlust (State Historical Society of Wisconsin Press, 1993). Reprinted with permission of the Wisconsin Historical Society.

❝ I had all kinds of jobs. [During the war] we had one line, a big line, where you'd work ten hours and you'd stand in one spot or sit in one spot. It got terrible, all day long. So I suggested to my foreman, the general foreman, that we take turns of learning everybody's job and switching every half hour. Well, they [the management] didn't like it, but we were on the side, every once in a while, learning each other's job and learning how to do it, so eventually most all of us got so we could do all the jobs, [of] which there were probably fifteen or twenty on the line. We could do every job so we could go up and down the line and rotate. And then they found out that that was really a pretty good thing to do because it made the people happier. . . .

One day I was the steward, and they wouldn't listen to me. They cut our rates, so I shut off the line, and the boss came up and he said, 'What are you doing?' I said, 'Well, I have asked everybody that I know why we have gotten a cut in pay and why we're doing exactly the same amount of work as we did.' . . . So, anyhow, we wrote up a big grievance and they all signed it and then I called the president of the union and then we had a meeting. . . . At that point the president decided that I should be added to the bargaining committee so that I would go in and argue our case, because I could do it better than any of the rest of them because I knew what it was. . . . We finally got it straightened out, and we got our back pay, too. From then on I was on the bargaining committee all the years that I worked at Rayovac. ❞

DONNA JEAN HARVEY

Wartime Challenges and New Experiences

During the war Harvey raised her first child while working as a riveter and radio installer at a plant in Cheyenne, Wyoming.

SOURCE: National Park Service, *Rosie the Riveter: Women Working During World War II*, nps.gov/pwro/collection/website/donna.htm.

❝ I graduated from Cheyenne High School in 1940. I married Lewis Early Harvey in January 1941. He was drafted when the war broke out and was sent to the Aleutian Islands, and from there he transferred to the Paratroopers. In October I gave birth to my first son, Lewis Early Jr.

Labor force was critical at that time so I went to United Modification Plant and learned how to rivet, do installations of various kinds and etc. When the 'new' radar system was implemented, I asked to be put on that crew. The F.B.I. investigated me and found me to be worthy and I proceeded to install radar along with my riveting duties, while waiting for the next shipment of planes to come in. . . . I was awarded the Army-Navy E Award and was presented with a pin. I've always been very proud of that!!! I certainly got educated in more ways than I ever expected, being a very young girl. But looking back I wouldn't trade my experiences for anything.

My feeling about the war in most instances was a conglomerate of mixed emotions. I had lived a fairly sheltered life, but I listened and learned and managed to survive, but I must admit, it left a scar on my memory that can never be erased.

I was living in one of my parent's apartments during the war and since they were both retired, they baby-sat my young son. My mother decided after a while that she too would like to do something in some little way to help. So she applied for maintenance and between my father and the girl next door, I managed to have a baby-sitter available at all times. The government was asking for rubber donations so

AP® EXAM TIP

Evaluate the impact of mass mobilization in World War II on women who served in the military or entered the workforce.

wages and improved working conditions. By 1943, the war economy was at full speed, and the breadlines and double-digit unemployment of the 1930s were a memory.

Rosie the Riveter Government officials and corporate recruiters urged women to take jobs in defense industries, creating a new image of working women. "Longing won't bring him back sooner . . . GET A WAR JOB!" one poster urged, while artist Norman Rockwell's famous "Rosie the Riveter" illustration beckoned from the cover of the *Saturday Evening Post*. The government directed its publicity at housewives,

AP® APPLY THE TIP

Ask students to work with a partner to create a rough outline of the changes in the rights and status of women from the American Revolution to the 1920s. Students' outlines can take the form of a timeline or list, but remind them to be as thorough as they can with events, names, time periods, and ideas. In their outline, students should be able to identify the following events from previous chapters: Republican Motherhood, Second Great Awakening, reform movements, suffrage for women in western states, Hull House, Florence Kelley, "New Woman," and others. Ask each pair to discuss the way in which society defined women in each of the details on their outline and identify examples of continuity and change. Now, provide students with propaganda posters and photo images of women in World War II that illustrate the changing role of women in the military and in the workforce. Ask students to discuss the ways in which the images could change perceptions of women during World War II and predict the way in which the images could be viewed once the war ended.

my mother and I gave them our rubber girdles!! We liked to think that our girdles helped win the war!!!

My life took on a totally new perspective the longer I worked there. I saw many tragic accidents, none of which I care to talk about which haunt me to this day.

I couldn't do much socializing as I had a small infant at home to care for when off work and besides I was really pooped. Those midnight shifts were 'killers.' I hope I never have to do that again!! I tried to write weekly letters to my husband in between my other duties. . . .

Our community gathered together and collected scrap metals and such to help in the war effort and thanks to a good neighbor, who was growing a victory garden; we managed to get gifts of potatoes and lettuce etc. The government issued coupon books that allowed us two bananas a week, one pound of sugar and so many gallons of gas. We traded back and forth depending on our individual needs. I had a 1934 Ford and fortunately, it wasn't a gas eater and it managed to get me where I was going when I needed it. . . .

There were no unions there at that time and no baby sitting service provided. The single people formed a club and they entertained themselves after work but I was a married person with a child and so I didn't participate in any of their activities. . . .

After the war was over, most people went back to their previous jobs. I opened a beauty salon and when my husband returned home from the service he got a job with the Frontier Refinery. ❞

FANNY CHRISTINA (TINA) HILL

War Work: Social and Racial Mobility

After migrating to California from Texas and working as a domestic servant, Tina Hill, an African American, got a wartime job at North American Aircraft. After time off for a pregnancy in 1945, Hill worked there until 1980.

SOURCE: This edited version of the oral history of Fanny Christina Hill is drawn from *Rosie the Riveter Revisited*, by Sherna B. Gluck (Boston: G.K. Hall & Co., 1987). To listen to her complete oral history, go to www.csulb.edu/voaha and search for Hill, Fanny Christina.

❝ Most of the men was gone, and . . . most of the women was in my bracket, five or six years younger or older. I was twenty-four. There was a black girl that hired in with me. I went to work the next day, sixty cents an hour. . . . I could see where they made a difference in placing you in certain jobs. They had fifteen or twenty departments, but all the Negroes went to Department 17 because there was nothing but shooting and bucking rivets. You stood on one side of the panel and your partner stood on this side and he would shoot the rivets with a gun and you'd buck them with the bar. That was about the size of it. I just didn't like it . . . went over to the union and they told me what to do. I went back inside and they sent me to another department where you did bench work and I liked that much better. . . .

Some weeks I brought home twenty-six dollars . . . then it gradually went up to thirty dollars [about $420 in 2010]. . . . Whatever you make you're supposed to save some. I was also getting that fifty dollars a month from my husband and that was just saved right away. I was planning on buying a home and a car. . . . My husband came back [from the war, and] . . . looked for a job in the cleaning and pressing place, which was just plentiful. . . . That's why he didn't bother to go out to North American. But what we both weren't thinking about was that they [North American] have better benefits because they did have an insurance plan and a union to back you up. Later he did come to work there, in 1951 or 1952. . . .

When North American called me back [after I left to have a baby,] was I a happy soul! . . . It made me live better. It really did. We always say that Lincoln took the bale off of the Negroes. I think there is a statue up there in Washington, D.C., where he's lifting something off the Negro. Well, my sister always said — that's why you can't interview her because she's so radical — 'Hitler was the one that got us out of the white folks' kitchen.' ❞

QUESTIONS FOR ANALYSIS

1. How did the war change the lives of the women in these sources? Offer specific examples to support your answers.
2. Consider how the themes of identity and work, technology, and economic change connect to the lives of the women interviewed. How was their experience of the wartime industrial workplace tied to their class and gender identities? How did labor unions affect their conditions of employment?
3. These interviews occurred long after the events they describe. How might that long interval have affected the women's accounts of those years?

but many women in low-paying jobs as domestic servants or secretaries switched to higher-paying work in the defense industry. Suddenly, the nation's factories were full of women working as airplane riveters, ship welders, and drill-press operators (see "Firsthand Accounts," p. 746). Women made up 36 percent of the labor force in 1945, compared with just 24 percent at the beginning of the war.

Wartime work was a bittersweet opportunity, marked by familiar constraints. Female workers often faced sexual harassment on the job and usually received lower wages than men did. In shipyards, women at the top of the pay scale earned $7 a day, whereas top men made as much as $22. The majority of women labored

TRM Find complete suggested responses in the Teacher's Resource Materials.

AP® THEME

SOC: Social Structures

Mobilization and military service provided opportunities for women to improve their socioeconomic positions for the war's duration, though few were able to hold onto those positions when the war ended. The U.S. government actively recruited women to work for the duration of the war. The most famous images of women workers, like this one, were created by the government to present women's defense work in a positive light. The Library of Congress provides several images and other materials documenting women's wartime labor. To access this site, search "LOC Rosie the Riveter."

TEACHING STRATEGY

The quintessential Rosie the Riveter image suggests a white woman, but it is important to discuss the Latinas and African American women who also worked as well. Consider having students read excerpts from Elizabeth Escobedo's book *From Coveralls to Zoot Suits: The Lives of Mexican American Women on the World War II Home Front* (Chapel Hill: University of North Carolina Press, 2013) to supplement your discussion with this alternative perspective.

AP® APPLY THE TIP

To help students understand that World War II can be viewed as one of the major factors initiating the modern civil rights movement, provide students with a copy of excerpts from the Executive Order 8802. Ask students to read the document to identify the purpose and intended audience. Then ask them to complete **Handout 23.3 — Contextualization: Executive Order 8802 (TRM)** using the textbook and additional resources as needed. Remind students to define the characteristics and details that are directly related to the executive order in the gray circle and explain broader historical processes, developments, and events that influenced the writing of the executive order in the large outer circle. Then lead a class discussion exploring the following statement: Executive Order 8802 was a transformative event in U.S. history.

TRM Find **Handout 23.3 — Contextualization: Executive Order 8802** in the Teacher's Resource Materials.

TEACHING STRATEGY

The Our Documents Web site provides a high-resolution facsimile copy of Executive Order 8802, along with a transcription. To access this document, search "Our Documents Executive Order 8802."

Rosie the Riveter Women workers install fixtures and assemblies to a tail fuselage of a B-17 bomber at the Douglas Aircraft Company plant in Long Beach, California. To entice women to become war workers, the War Manpower Commission created the image of "Rosie the Riveter," later immortalized in posters and by a Norman Rockwell illustration on the cover of the *Saturday Evening Post*. A popular 1943 song celebrating Rosie went: "Rosie's got a boyfriend, Charlie / Charlie, he's a marine / Rosie is protecting Charlie / Working overtime on the riveting machine." Library of Congress, 1a35337.

in low-wage service jobs. Child care was often unavailable, despite the largest government-sponsored child-care program in history — the scale of demand overwhelmed the federal program. When the men returned from war, Rosie the Riveter was usually out of a job. Government propaganda switched to encouraging women back into the home — where, it was implied, their true calling lay in raising families. But many married women refused, or could not afford, to stay home. Women's participation in the paid labor force rebounded to wartime levels by the late 1940s and continued to rise for the rest of the century, bringing major changes in family life (see "Women, Work, and Family" in Chapter 25).

"Double V" campaign
An African American civil rights campaign during World War II that called for victory over Nazism abroad and over discrimination in jobs, housing, and voting at home.

Wartime Civil Rights Among African Americans, a new protest militancy emerged during the war. Pointing to parallels between anti-Semitism in Germany and racial discrimination in the United States, black leaders waged the **"Double V" campaign**: calling for victory over Nazism abroad and Jim Crow discrimination at home. The domestic struggle included renewed calls to end job and housing discrimination and sharp criticism of black voter suppression in the South. "This is a war for freedom. Whose freedom?" the renowned black leader W. E. B. Du Bois asked. If it meant "the freedom of Negroes in the Southern United States," Du Bois answered, "my gun is on my shoulder."

AP® EXAM TIP
Explain the role of World War II in generating debates over civil rights in the United States.

Even before Pearl Harbor, black activism was on the rise. In 1940, only 240 of the nation's 100,000 aircraft workers were black, and most of those were janitors. African American leaders demanded that the government require defense contractors to hire more black workers. When the Roosevelt administration took no action, A. Philip Randolph, head of the Brotherhood of Sleeping Car Porters, the largest black labor union in the country, announced plans for a march on Washington in the summer of 1941.

Executive Order 8802
An order signed by President Roosevelt in 1941 that prohibited "discrimination in the employment of workers in defense industries or government because of race, creed, color, or national origin" and established the Fair Employment Practices Commission (FEPC).

Roosevelt had no history of strong support of African American equality, but he wanted to avoid public protest and a disruption of the nation's war preparations. So the president made a deal: he issued **Executive Order 8802**, and Randolph canceled the march. The order prohibited "discrimination in the employment of workers in defense industries or government because of race, creed, color, or national origin" and established the Fair Employment Practice Committee (FEPC) as a watchdog. Mary McLeod Bethune called the wartime FEPC "a refreshing shower in a thirsty land," but its practical impact was limited. The committee had no say on segregation in the armed forces and no power to compel compliance with its orders in either the public or private sector.

Nevertheless, wartime developments laid the groundwork for the civil rights revolution of the 1950s and 1960s. The NAACP grew ninefold, with 450,000 members by 1945. In Chicago, James Farmer helped to found the Congress of Racial Equality (CORE) in 1942, a group that would rise to prominence in the 1960s with its direct action protests such as sit-ins. The FEPC inspired black organizing against employment discrimination in hundreds of cities and workplaces. That renewed militancy,

VISUAL ACTIVITY

Wartime Civil Rights Fighting fascism abroad while battling racism at home was the approach taken by black communities across the country during World War II. Securing democracy in Europe and Asia while not enjoying it in the United States did not seem just. Here picketers rally for defense jobs outside the Glenn Martin Plant in Omaha, Nebraska, in the early 1940s. Schomburg Center for Research in Black Culture, New York Public Library/Art Resource, NY.

READING THE IMAGE: What specific words are most common on the protestor's signs? What do you notice—both broadly and in detail—about how the protestors are dressed?

MAKING CONNECTIONS: What is the point of view of the artist who captured this image? Why? What is the purpose of publishing this image?

under the banner of the "Double V" campaign, combined with modest government support would advance black civil rights on multiple fronts in the postwar years.

Mexican Americans also challenged long-standing practices of discrimination and exclusion. Throughout much of the Southwest, signs reading "No Mexicans Allowed" remained common, and Mexican American workers were often limited to menial, low-paying jobs. Several organizations, including the League of United Latin American Citizens (LULAC) and the Spanish-Speaking People's Congress, pressed the government and private employers to end such discrimination. Mexican American workers themselves, often members of Congress of Industrial Organizations (CIO) unions such as the Cannery Workers and Shipyard Workers, also led efforts to enforce the FEPC's equal employment mandate.

However, exploitation persisted and sometimes worsened in the wartime economic expansion. To meet wartime labor demands, the U.S. government brought tens of thousands of Mexican contract laborers into the United States under the **Bracero Program**. Paid little and treated poorly, the braceros (who took their name from the Spanish *brazo*, "arm") exemplified the oppressive conditions of farm labor in the United States. After the war, the federal government continued to bring hundreds of thousands of Mexicans into the country to perform low-wage agricultural work—a system fraught with injustices that Mexican American civil rights leaders began battling in the 1950s.

Bracero Program
A federal program that brought hundreds of thousands of Mexican agricultural workers to the United States during and after World War II. The program continued until 1964 and was a major spur of Mexican immigration to the United States.

TRM Find complete suggested responses in the Teacher's Resource Materials.

TEACHING STRATEGY

One window into the views of African Americans during the war is Chester Himes's angry 1945 novella *If He Hollers Let Him Go*, which covers four days in the life of the protagonist, a black man employed in a naval shipyard during the war.

AP® THEME

SOC: Social Structures

Migration patterns dramatically changed as a result of World War II. Have students identify and explain two ways in which migration patterns help explain the economic changes attendant to World War II.

CHECK FOR UNDERSTANDING

Ask students: **How did workers' contributions to the war effort change American society?** *Rosie the Riveter workers from a variety of ethnic backgrounds worked in defense production. African Americans threatened to march on Washington if they were not given access to defense labor; Executive Order 8802 promised African Americans access to government-contracted work and a Fair Employment Practice Committee to investigate claims of discrimination. Organized labor increased its strength as well.*

AP® SKILLS & PROCESSES

CONTEXTUALIZATION

The **CONTEXTUALIZATION** question asks students to consider the American wartime experience — fighting an enemy who explicitly embraced racism — in the midst of a society that treated African Americans as second-class citizens, in open denial of the Fourteenth Amendment's promise. Students should identify the ways the war addressed this contradiction, as well as paving the way for postwar advancements in civil rights.

TRM Find complete suggested responses in the Teacher's Resource Materials.

CHECK FOR UNDERSTANDING

Ask students: **What aspects of the economy and American society were affected by mobilization for war?** *In response to the Japanese attack on Pearl Harbor, Congress passed the War Powers Act in December 1941 that gave President Roosevelt unprecedented powers to manage the economy. Revenues were raised through increasing the number of people who paid income taxes. Under the aegis of the War Production Board (WPB), industry was reoriented toward military production, emphasizing the conglomeration of large corporations. Socially, a broad swath of American society — men, women, whites, African Americans, and Native Americans — fought as part of the sixteen-million-strong armed forces or worked in war industries at home. The exigencies of war also had civil rights ramifications, e.g. Executive Order 8802, and labor rights ramifications, e.g. the National War Labor Board (NWLB).*

Organized Labor During the war, unions extended gains made during the New Deal and solidified their position as a powerful voice for American workers. By 1945, almost 15 million workers belonged to a union, up from 9 million in 1939. Representatives of the major unions made a no-strike pledge for the duration of the war, and Roosevelt rewarded them by creating the National War Labor Board (NWLB). Composed of representatives of labor, management, and the public, the NWLB established wages, hours, and working conditions; it also had the authority to seize manufacturing plants that did not comply.

Despite these protections, unions still faced impatience from a sometimes hostile Congress that was eager to avoid industrial shutdowns during the war. In 1943, more than half a million United Mine Workers walked out, despite the no-strike pledge. The miners sought a pay hike higher than that recommended by the NWLB. Congress responded by passing (over Roosevelt's veto) the Smith-Connally Labor Act of 1943, which allowed the president to prohibit strikes in defense industries and forbade political contributions by unions. Although organized labor would emerge from World War II more powerful than ever, its business and corporate opponents were also bolstered by the booming war economy.

AP® SKILLS & PROCESSES

CONTEXTUALIZATION

How did the slogan "A Jim Crow army cannot fight for a free world" connect the war abroad with the civil rights struggle at home?

Politics in Wartime

In his 1944 State of the Union address, FDR called for a second Bill of Rights, one that would guarantee all Americans access to education and work, adequate food and clothing, and decent housing and medical care. It would be, the president said, "a new basis of security and prosperity" guaranteed to "all regardless of station, race, or creed." Like his Four Freedoms speech of 1941, this was a call to extend the New Deal's broadening of individual rights guaranteed by government. The answer to his call, however, would have to wait for the war's conclusion. Congress authorized new government benefits only for veterans (known as GIs, short for "government issue"). The **Servicemen's Readjustment Act** of 1944, an extraordinarily influential program popularly dubbed the "GI Bill of Rights," provided education, job training, medical care, pensions, and home loans for men and women who had served in the armed forces.

Servicemen's Readjustment Act Popularly known as the GI Bill, 1944 legislation authorizing the government to provide World War II veterans with funds for education, housing, and health care, as well as loans to start businesses and buy homes.

The president's call for a second Bill of Rights sought to reinvigorate the New Deal political coalition. In the election of 1944, Roosevelt again headed the Democratic ticket for a fourth time. But party leaders, conscious of FDR's declining health and fearing that Vice President Henry Wallace's outspoken support for labor and civil rights would alienate moderates, dropped Wallace from the ticket. In his place, they chose Senator Harry S. Truman of Missouri, a plain-spoken — some thought him drab — politician with little national experience. The Republicans nominated Governor Thomas E. Dewey of New York. Dewey, who accepted the general principles of welfare-state liberalism domestically and internationalism in foreign affairs, did draw off some of Roosevelt's supporters. But a majority of voters preferred political continuity, and Roosevelt was reelected with 53.5 percent of the nationwide vote. The Democratic coalition retained its hold on government power, and the Republican political dominance of 1896–1932 slipped further into the past.

LIFE ON THE HOME FRONT

What short-term and long-term domestic social changes were produced by the war?

As in World War I, the United States escaped the physical devastations of conflict. Bombs did not fall on American cities, and civilians were not killed or displaced by the fighting. But the war profoundly changed everyday life just the same. Americans welcomed wartime prosperity but shuddered to see a Western Union boy on his bicycle, fearing that he carried a War Department telegram reporting the death of a son, husband, or father. Citizens also grumbled about annoying wartime regulations and rationing but accepted that their lives would be different "for the duration."

Mobilizing for War at Home

Spurred by both government propaganda and a desire to help the cause, people on the home front took on wartime responsibilities. They worked on civilian defense committees, recycled old newspapers and scrap metal, and served on local rationing and draft boards. About twenty million backyard "victory gardens" produced 40 percent of the nation's vegetables. Various federal agencies encouraged these efforts, especially the Office of War Information (OWI), which disseminated news and promoted patriotism. The OWI urged advertising agencies to link their clients' products to the war effort, arguing that patriotic ads would not only sell goods but also "invigorate, instruct and inspire" citizens (see "Thinking Like a Historian," p. 752).

Popular culture, especially the movies, reinforced connections between the home front and the front lines. Hollywood producers, directors, and actors offered their talents to the War Department. Director Frank Capra created a documentary series titled *Why We Fight* to explain war aims to conscripted soldiers and the wider public. Movie stars such as John Wayne and Spencer Tracy portrayed heroic American fighting men in films such as *Guadalcanal Diary* (1943) and *Thirty Seconds over Tokyo* (1944). In this pretelevision era, newsreels accompanying the feature films kept the public up-to-date on the war, as did on-the-spot radio broadcasts from CBS reporters such as Edward R. Murrow and Mary Marvin Breckenridge, the network's first female radio correspondent.

"OF COURSE I CAN!
I'm patriotic as can be—
And ration points won't worry me!"

Helping on the Home Front A U.S. government poster during World War II reminding people to conserve food so that the troops would have the supplies they required. Many government agencies, like the War Food Administration, which produced this poster, the Office of War Information, and the Office of Price Administration, used billboards, newspaper and magazine advertisements, posters, and other forms of media to get their message to ordinary Americans: unite together in patriotic sacrifice for the good of the war effort. Hi-Story/Alamy Stock Photo.

All Americans had to deal with wartime shortages of consumer goods. Beginning in 1942, federal agencies subjected almost everything Americans ate, wore, or used to rationing or regulation. The first major scarcity was rubber. The Japanese conquest of Malaysia and Dutch Indonesia cut off 97 percent of America's imports of that essential raw material. To conserve rubber for the war effort, the government rationed tires: many of the nation's thirty million car owners put their cars in storage. As more people walked, they wore out their shoes. In 1944, shoes were rationed to two pairs per person a year. By 1943, the government was rationing meat, butter, sugar, and other foods. Most citizens obeyed the complicated rationing system, but at least one-quarter of the population bought items on the black market, especially meat, gasoline, cigarettes, and nylon stockings.

Migration and the Wartime City

The war led to large-scale internal migration and changed both individual opportunities and the fate of whole regions. When men entered the armed services, their families often followed them to military bases or points of debarkation. Civilians moved to take high-paying defense jobs. About 15 million Americans changed residences during the war years, half of them moving to another state. One such migrant was Peggy Terry, who grew up in Paducah, Kentucky, worked in a shell-loading plant in

AP® EXAM TIP

Describe the causes and effects of migration from rural to urban areas in World War II.

TEACHING STRATEGY

Persuading the American public to support the war effort became a wartime "industry," as important in some ways as the manufacturing of bullets and planes. The federal government launched an aggressive propaganda campaign with clearly articulated goals and strategies to gather public support. It also recruited some of the nation's foremost intellectuals, artists, and filmmakers to wage the war on that front. An online exhibit hosted by the National Archives features images and quotes to explore the strategies of persuasion. To access this exhibit, search "National Archives Powers of Persuasion."

CHECK FOR UNDERSTANDING

Ask students: **What was life like on the home front for everyday Americans?** *The Office of War Information distributed propaganda to encourage patriotism, and popular films reinforced this message. Though Americans did not experience the hardships of civilians in other nations, they did have to adjust to the inconvenience of a shortage of consumer goods.*

AP® THEME

MIG: Migration and Settlement

The increased demand for labor during World War II led many Americans to migrate to urban areas in search of economic opportunities.

AP® APPLY THE TIP

Ask students to use pp. 751–755 to complete **Handout 23.4—Causation: Migration in World War II (TRM)**. After students complete the handout, organize the class into collaborative groups and ask each group to choose another period of migration in U.S. history that they can use as a comparison for the urban migration in World War II. Students may choose to compare migration in World War II to World War I, Oklahoma Sooners, the California gold rush, settlement of Texas, missionaries to Oregon, etc. Each group should choose a different comparative migration so that the class looks at a variety of comparisons. Then have each group create a poster to illustrate a historical argument regarding its comparison. Encourage students to determine the relative significance of the similarities and differences so that they can make a strong historical argument as to whether the two migrations were more similar or different. As a class, discuss the comparisons and historical arguments, allowing students to make suggestions to improve each group's argument. As a culminating discussion, develop a thesis statement that addresses the following prompt: To what extent did migrations in American history alter American culture and economy?

TRM Access **Handout 23.4—Causation: Migration in World War II** in the Teacher's Resource Materials.

AP® SKILLS & PROCESSES

ANALYZING HISTORICAL EVIDENCE

Use the **AP® THINKING LIKE A HISTORIAN** feature to have students consider a specific type of evidence: government propaganda. It might be helpful to remind students that in a democracy, the government must rely on persuasion, not just coercion, so wartime propaganda plays a significant role in achieving government goals. As with advice literature, propaganda tells us about what the government perceived to be a problem and what it would like to have happen, not necessarily what actually happened.

AP® THINKING LIKE A HISTORIAN

Mobilizing the Home Front

The U.S. Office of War Information (OWI) promoted everything from food rationing to carpooling during World War II, and the U.S. Treasury encouraged millions of Americans to buy war bonds. More than 20 million victory gardens were planted by ordinary Americans. By 1944 they were producing more than 40 percent of all vegetables grown in the United States. Through these and other measures, those on the home front were encouraged to see themselves as part of the war effort.

1. **U.S. government advertisement from the *Minneapolis Star Journal*, 1943.** *Notices such as this one, encouraging Americans to save steel and tin from their everyday lives for military uses, appeared in newspapers and magazines across the country.*

SOURCE: AdAccess Digital Collection, David M. Rubenstein Rare Book and Manuscript Library, Duke University.

2. **Copy from War Advertising Council/U.S. Treasury Department advertisement, 1943.** *To help finance the war, the U.S. Treasury raised nearly $200 billion by selling war bonds (a debt notice that would be repaid with interest in ten years). Government advertisements like this one enticed ordinary Americans to invest their savings in the war effort — and ultimately, 85 million did just that.*

Farmer: "Well, there's something we really want now — more than anything else . . . and I guess everybody does. It's VICTORY IN THIS WAR! We had started saving for a new milking machine and a deep-well pump that we will be needing in a few years. . . . We're still going to have that milking machine and that pump — and a lot of other new improvements after the war. When our son comes home from the fighting front, he'll help us pick them out. And we'll have the cash to pay for them. With the money we are saving now in War Bonds. And we are going to hang on to as many War Bonds as possible to take care of us after our boy takes over on the farm. For after ten years, we get four dollars back for every three we have invested."

3. **Poster from the U.S. Office of Price Administration, 1943.** *Along with salvaging metals and buying war bonds, Americans rationed the food and other consumer items they bought because of chronic shortages. This government poster explains how rationing ensures a "fair share" for everyone.*

SOURCE: United States Office of Price Administration/Northwestern University Libraries.

752

4. Girl Scouts planting a victory garden near San Francisco during the war, 1943. *To cope with food shortages, Americans planted "victory gardens" to grow their own vegetables.*

Source: Library of Congress, 8b08127

5. Oral histories about life during the war. *Two ordinary Americans, Tessie Hickam Wilson and Virginia J. Bondra, look back on their World War II experience after nearly six decades, in an oral history project conducted by the Library of Congress.*

Tessie Hickam Wilson, a young woman from Oklahoma.
It was a hard time, but we felt like we were doing our part, and all the people we knew were doing their part. We had rationing. Sugar, coffee, gasoline and meat were some of the items that were hard to come by. We had ration books every so often, and we had to use them sparingly. We bought savings bonds to help in the war effort.

We also had radios and record players, and when we could afford it, we went to the movies. And even though there were hard times, we did what we could in the war effort, and I will always be glad I was part of it.

Virginia J. Bondra, a student and clothing worker from Ohio.
The only newsreel footage we saw was in the theaters when we went to a movie. And we used to bring scrap metal or cans, and we'd get in the movies free. They needed scrap metal and they — the USA needed scrap fat. My mother used to scrap fat, you know, in a can. She'd save it, and we'd bring it to a certain place. Sugar was rationed. Each member of the family would get one pound of sugar a week. And I always had time to bake because we had sugar. . . .

Different things were rationed. We couldn't buy nylons because it was needed . . . for parachutes. So we'd — we'd — my older sisters would paint their legs with a certain makeup that came out in place of nylons. . . . It was makeup for legs.

They painted a eyebrow pencil line down the back of their leg so it would look like real nylons. And we would write V-mail. I had brother — brothers-in-law in the service. We — we'd write V-mail to them. It was called V-mail. Victory mail. . . . We couldn't put their address on because they were moved around a lot and we didn't want the enemy to know. There were a lot of secrets. They would say "zip your lip was the" — was the word of the days then. "Zip your lip" because we didn't want the enemy to get information.

Sources: (2) Digital Collections, Duke University Libraries; (5) National Park Service, *Rosie the Riveter: Real Women Workers During World War II*, and the Library of Congress Veterans History Project.

ANALYZING THE EVIDENCE

1. Examine sources 1, 2, and 3. Who created these sources, and what does this suggest about the context and purpose of these documents? Use evidence from the source to identify the intended audience.
2. Study the photograph (source 4). Who is depicted? What does this suggest about the victory garden program as well as war efforts on the home front more broadly?
3. How does the oral history in source 5 add to your understanding of home front involvement in the war effort? Does the testimony force you to question the other documents in any way, and if so, how?

AP® DBQ PRACTICE

Analyze some of the ways the U.S. government encouraged ordinary citizens to participate in the war effort, and evaluate the objectives and results of these efforts. Support your claim with evidence from the chapter and these sources.

TRM Find complete suggested responses in the Teacher's Resource Materials.

AP® SKILLS & PROCESSES

ARGUMENT DEVELOPMENT

The **AP® DBQ PRACTICE** prompt asks students to analyze both the goals and outcomes of American wartime propaganda. To answer the latter question, students will need to consider evidence from the chapter text, as the sources provided here by their very nature only address government goals. Therefore, require students to use both the primary sources and the chapter text information.

AP® SKILLS & PROCESSES

CAUSATION

Use the **CAUSATION** question to help students identify the effects of wartime migration in the U.S. Students should discuss the general increase of rural to urban migration, as well as the movement of ethnic minorities into previously white communities, which led to significant racial tensions and occasional outbreaks of violence. Students could additionally make an inference about the long-term postwar effects of these demographic patterns.

TRM Find complete suggested responses in the Teacher's Resource Materials.

nearby Viola, and then moved to a defense plant in Michigan. There, she recalled, "I met all those wonderful Polacks [Polish Americans]. They were the first people I'd ever known that were any different from me. A whole new world just opened up."

As the center of defense production for the Pacific war, California received the largest inbound migration. The state welcomed 2.5 million new residents, growing by 35 percent during the war. "The Second Gold Rush Hits the West," announced the *San Francisco Chronicle* in 1943. One-tenth of all federal dollars spent on the war flowed into California, and the state's factories turned out one-sixth of all war materials. People went where the defense jobs were: to Los Angeles, San Diego, and cities around San Francisco Bay. Some towns grew practically overnight. Within two years of the opening of the Kaiser Corporation shipyard in Richmond, California, the town's population quadrupled. Other states with major industrial centers — notably New York, Illinois, Michigan, and Ohio — also attracted migrants and federal money on a large scale.

AP® SKILLS & PROCESSES

CAUSATION

What effects did wartime migration have on the United States?

zoot-suit riots
In June 1943, a group of white sailors and soldiers in Los Angeles, seeking revenge for an earlier skirmish with Mexican American youths, attacked anyone they found wearing a zoot suit, an outfit that symbolized a rebellious style.

The growth of war industries accelerated patterns of rural-urban migration. Cities grew dramatically, as factories, shipyards, and other defense plants drew millions of citizens away from small towns and rural areas. Mobility, coupled with distance from home, loosened the authority of traditional institutions and made wartime cities vibrant and lively. Around-the-clock work shifts kept people on the streets night and day, and bars, jazz clubs, dance halls, and movie theaters thrived on the ready cash of war workers.

Zoot-Suit Youth in Los Angeles During four days of rioting in June 1943, servicemen in Los Angeles attacked young Latino men wearing distinctive zoot suits, which were widely viewed as emblems of gang membership and a delinquent youth culture. The police response was to arrest scores of zoot-suiters. Here, a group of arrested youth pose for a photographer in a jail cell. What became known as the "zoot-suit riots" were emblematic of racial tensions on the home front, even as the United States fought a war against fascism abroad. Bettmann/Getty Images.

Racial Conflict Migration and more fluid social boundaries meant that people of different races and ethnicities mixed in the booming cities. Over one million African Americans left the rural South for California, Illinois, Michigan, Ohio, and Pennsylvania — a continuation of the Great Migration earlier in the century (see "Racial Backlash" and "The Harlem Renaissance" in Chapter 21). In another echo of the World War I era, blacks and whites competed for jobs and housing, leading to racial conflicts in more than a hundred cities in 1943. Detroit saw the worst violence. In June 1943, a riot incited by southern-born whites and Polish Americans against African Americans left thirty-four people dead and hundreds injured.

Racial conflict arose in the West as well. In Los Angeles, Mexican American pachucos (male youths) often dressed in "zoot suits" — a rebellious fashion defined by broad-brimmed felt hats, thigh-length jackets with wide lapels and padded shoulders, pegged trousers, and clunky shoes. Pachucas (young women) favored long coats, huarache sandals, and pompadour hairdos. Working-class teenagers like these in Los Angeles and elsewhere took to the zoot-suit style to symbolize their rejection of middle-class values. To many adults, the zoot suit symbolized only juvenile delinquency. In June 1943, rumors swirled around Los Angeles that a pachuco gang had beaten an Anglo (white) sailor, setting off a four-day melee known as the "**zoot-suit riots**." Hundreds of Anglo servicemen roamed Mexican American neighborhoods and attacked zoot-suiters, taking special pleasure in slashing their pegged pants. In a stinging display of bias, Los Angeles police officers arrested only Mexican American youth in the wake of the unrest, and the city council passed an ordinance outlawing the wearing of the zoot suit.

Gay and Lesbian Communities Wartime migration to urban centers also enabled gay and lesbian Americans to form communities. Religious and social conventions had long treated

New Urban Communities for Laborers Folk singer Pete Seeger performs at the opening of the Washington, D.C., labor canteen in 1944, sponsored by the Congress of Industrial Organizations (CIO). Wartime migration brought people from across the country to centers of industry and military operations, opening new possibilities for urban communities.

The Granger Collection, New York.

homosexuality as taboo, and most gay men and lesbians remained closeted to avoid discrimination. During the war, however, big cities such as New York, San Francisco, Los Angeles, Chicago, and even smaller regional hubs such as Kansas City, Buffalo, and Dallas developed vibrant gay neighborhoods, sustained by a sudden influx of migrants and the relatively open wartime atmosphere. These communities would become centers of the gay rights movement of the 1960s and 1970s (see "Stonewall and Gay Liberation" in Chapter 27).

The military tried to screen out homosexuals but had limited success. The wartime armed forces were home to an extensive gay culture, which was often more apparent than that in civilian life. In the last twenty years, historians have documented thriving communities of gay and lesbian soldiers in the World War II military. Some "came out under fire," as one historian put it, but most kept their sexuality hidden from authorities who viewed homosexuality as a psychological disorder that was grounds for dishonorable discharge.

Japanese Removal

Unlike World War I, which evoked widespread harassment of German Americans, World War II produced relatively little condemnation of European Americans. Despite the presence of small but vocal groups of Nazi sympathizers and Mussolini supporters, German American and Italian American communities were largely left in peace during the war — federal officials detained fewer than fifteen thousand potentially dangerous German and Italian aliens. But this increase in tolerance did not extend to Japanese immigrants and Japanese American citizens. Immediately after the attack on Pearl Harbor, the West Coast remained relatively calm. But as residents began to fear spies, sabotage, and further attacks, a long history of racial animosity toward Asian immigrants surfaced. Local politicians and newspapers whipped up hysteria against Japanese Americans, who numbered only about 112,000, had no political power, and lived primarily in small enclaves in the Pacific coast states.

TEACHING STRATEGY

Coming Out Under Fire is an hour-long documentary based on Allan Bérubé's book of the same name. The film integrates on-camera interviews with declassified military documents and archival footage on sex education, mental health, prison compounds, and court martial hearings. The film is available to rent on Vimeo; search "Vimeo Coming Out Under Fire" to access.

CHECK FOR UNDERSTANDING

Ask students: **How did migration affect the wartime city?** *Job opportunities intensified the long-term trend toward urbanization, while the migration of minorities led to significant tensions and occasional violence.*

AP® THEME

NAT: American and National Identity

The internment of Japanese Americans represents the most egregious government-sponsored violation of civil rights during the war. The Japanese American National Museum provides extensive online resources exploring this event and its consequences. To access these resources, search "JANM Instructions to All."

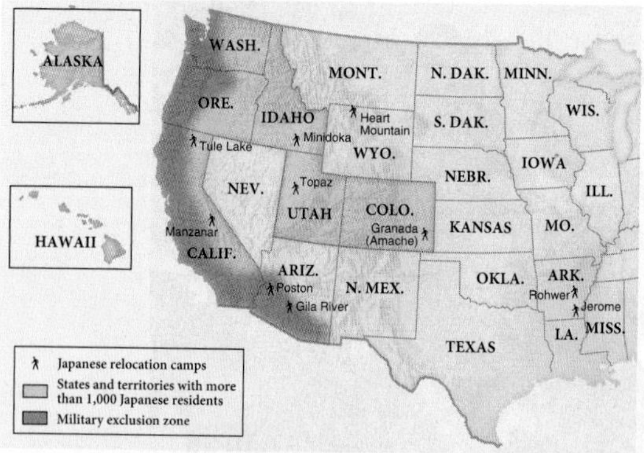

MAP 23.1 Japanese Relocation Camps
In 1942, the government ordered 112,000 Japanese Americans living on the West Coast into internment camps in the nation's interior because of their supposed threat to public safety. Some of the camps were as far away as Arkansas. The federal government rescinded the mass evacuation order in December 1944, but 44,000 people still remained in the camps when the war ended in August 1945.

Early in 1942, President Roosevelt responded to anti-Japanese sentiment by issuing **Executive Order 9066**, which authorized the War Department to force Japanese Americans from their homes and hold them in relocation camps for the duration of the war. Although there was no evidence of disloyal or seditious activity among the evacuees, few public leaders opposed the plan. "A Jap's a Jap," snapped General John DeWitt, the officer charged with defense of the West Coast. "It makes no difference whether he is an American citizen or not."

The relocation plan shocked Japanese Americans, more than two-thirds of whom were Nisei, that is, native-born children of immigrant parents (known in turn as Isei). Army officials gave families only a few days to dispose of their property. Businesses that had taken a lifetime to build were liquidated overnight. The War Relocation Authority moved the internees, prisoners in all but name, to hastily built camps in desolate areas in California, Arizona, Utah, Colorado, Wyoming, Idaho, and Arkansas (Map 23.1). Ironically, the Japanese Americans who made up one-third of the population of the territory of Hawaii, and presumably posed a greater threat because of their proximity to Japan, were not imprisoned. They provided much of the unskilled labor on the island chain, and the Hawaiian economy could not have functioned without them.

Executive Order 9066
An order signed by President Roosevelt in 1942 that authorized the War Department to force Japanese Americans from their homes and hold them in relocation camps for the rest of the war.

Cracks soon appeared in the relocation policy. A labor shortage led the government to furlough seasonal farmworkers from the camps as early as 1942. About 4,300 students were allowed to attend colleges outside the West Coast military zone. Other internees were permitted to join the armed services. The 442nd Regimental Combat Team, a unit composed almost entirely of Nisei volunteers, served with distinction in Europe.

Gordon Hirabayashi was among the Nisei who actively resisted incarceration. A student at the University of Washington, Hirabayashi was a religious pacifist who had registered with his draft board as a conscientious objector. He refused to report for evacuation and turned himself in to the FBI. "I wanted to uphold the principles of the Constitution," Hirabayashi later stated, "and the curfew and evacuation orders which singled out a group on the basis of ethnicity violated them." Tried and convicted of curfew violation in 1942, he appealed his case to the Supreme Court in *Hirabayashi v. United States* (1943). In that case and in *Korematsu v. United States* (1944), the high court allowed the removal of Japanese Americans from the West Coast on the basis of "military necessity" but avoided

Behind Barbed Wire As part of the forced relocation of 112,000 Japanese Americans, Los Angeles photographer Toyo Miyatake and his family were sent to Manzanar, a camp in the California desert east of the Sierra Nevada. Miyatake secretly began shooting photographs of the camp with a handmade camera. Eventually, he received permission from the authorities to document life in the camp—its births, weddings, deaths, and high school graduations. For Miyatake, the image gave new meaning to the phrase "prisoners of war." *The Denver Post via Getty Images.*

AP® THEME

SOC: Social Structures

The United States defined World War II as a war to defend freedom, ways of life, and democratic systems of government. Yet, on the home front, the United States struggled to connect the larger aims of the war with the treatment of ethnic and racial minorities. Have students identify and explain two ways in which the United States grappled with minority rights AND explain whether this was in support of the larger war aims or contradictory to those goals.

TEACHING STRATEGY

The Fred T. Korematsu Institute provides educational resources that explore Korematsu's story as a violation of civil rights. Teachers can request a free teaching resource kit from the Web site. To access this site, search "Korematsu Institute."

CHECK FOR UNDERSTANDING

Ask students: **Describe both the short-term and the lasting domestic social changes the war produced.** Remind students they should understand the short-term changes at this point from their reading of the textbook, but that an equally proficient understanding of the long-term changes might happen by the end of the chapter. Try splitting this in two parts. Have students create a T-Chart with short-term and long-term changes. As students encounter the requisite information, they can chart their responses.

ruling on the constitutionality of the incarceration program. These decisions underscored the fragility of civil liberties in wartime. In 1988, Congress would issue a public apology for the internment policy and pay $20,000 to each of the eighty-two thousand surviving Japanese Americans internees.

AP® SKILLS & PROCESSES

CAUSATION

Why were Japanese Americans treated differently than German and Italian Americans during the war?

FIGHTING AND WINNING THE WAR

How did Allied war strategy evolve between 1941 and 1945?

The stakes of World War II were no less than global domination. Had the Axis powers triumphed, Germany would have controlled, either directly or indirectly, all of Europe and much of Africa and the Middle East; Japan would have controlled most of East and Southeast Asia. Such an outcome would have crippled democracy in Europe and restricted American power to the Western Hemisphere. Although Pearl Harbor was the immediate cause of American entry into the war, the larger challenge to democracy and international order would have inevitably brought the United States into the conflict. The combination of the profound sacrifice of the Soviet Union and the Russian people, American industrial might, and British perseverance eventually defeated the Axis powers at great cost. The relationships among the Allies would also shape the character of the postwar world.

Wartime Aims and Tensions

Great Britain, the United States, and the Soviet Union were the key actors in the Allied coalition. China, France, and other nations played crucial but smaller roles. The leaders who became known as the Big Three — Roosevelt, Prime Minister Winston Churchill of Great Britain, and Premier Joseph Stalin of the Soviet Union — forged a grand strategy. But there were fissures in the alliance from the start. Stalin was not a party to the Atlantic Charter, which Churchill and Roosevelt had signed in August 1941, and disagreed fundamentally with some of its precepts, such as a capitalist international trading system. The Allies also disagreed about specific military plans and timing. The Big Three saw defeating Germany, rather than Japan, as the top military priority, but differed over how to stop the Nazi war machine. In 1941, the German Wehrmacht (army) had invaded the Soviet Union and raced as far as the outskirts of Moscow. The hard-pressed Red Army pushed the advance back in early 1942, but Nazi troops still besieged the major city of Leningrad and threatened to overwhelm vital areas to the south. To relieve pressure on the Soviet army, Stalin wanted the British and Americans to open a second European front by invading Nazi-controlled France.

AP® EXAM TIP

Recognize the role of Allied cooperation in the military victory of the United States in World War II.

Roosevelt informally assured Stalin that the Allies hoped to launch this counteroffensive in 1942, but Churchill opposed a hasty invasion, and American war production had yet to hit full stride. For eighteen months, Stalin's pleas went unanswered, and the Soviet Union bore the brunt of the war against Hitler. In the 1943 Battle of Kursk alone, the Soviet army suffered 860,000 casualties, several times what the Allies would suffer for the first two months of the European campaign after D-Day. In a November 1943 summit in Tehran, Roosevelt and Churchill committed to opening a second front in France within six months in return for Stalin's promise to join the fight against Japan. Both sides adhered to this agreement, but the long delay angered Stalin, who became increasingly suspicious of American and British intentions.

AP® SKILLS & PROCESSES

COMPARISON

How did the Allies disagree over military strategy?

The War in Europe

The first half of 1942 marked the low tide of the war for the Allies. Though stopped at Moscow, German armies rolled through the wheat farms of the Ukraine and into the rich oil region of the Caucasus near the Black Sea. Simultaneously, Hitler's forces

AP® SKILLS & PROCESSES

CAUSATION

The **CAUSATION** question asks students to identify causes for the different treatment of one enemy's citizens compared with another's. Students should consider both the short- and long-term causes in their answer. Extend this prompt by asking students to investigate newspaper articles from 1988 to see how Japanese internment was framed at the time of Congress's apology.

TRM Find complete suggested responses in the Teacher's Resource Materials.

AP® APPLY THE TIP

Divide the class into groups to represent the major conferences of World War II to include some or all of the following: Atlantic Conference, First Washington Conference (1941), Casablanca, Quebec Conference, Tehran Conference, Bretton Woods, Dumbarton Oaks, Yalta, or Potsdam. Student groups should research the assigned conference to identify the participants, goals, and outcomes. Then ask student groups to plan a simulation of the discussion between the participants to communicate what they learned. Remind students that they should also try to communicate the relationship between the participants. After groups present their simulation, lead a class discussion on the role of Allied cooperation on victory in the war and on the breakdown of relations and start of the Cold War in 1945.

CHECK FOR UNDERSTANDING

Ask students: **How did wartime aims differ between the Allies, and what tensions resulted?** *Stalin did not accept the capitalist aims of the Atlantic Charter. While the Big Three agreed on defeating Hitler first, they disagreed on strategy. Stalin wanted Britain and the U.S. to open a second front in France sooner than those allies were ready to launch the invasion.*

AP® SKILLS & PROCESSES

COMPARISON

In comparing the different Allied military strategies to answer the **COMPARISON** question, students should explain why motives differed and what was at stake for each. Students could also explain the consequences of these disagreements.

TRM Find complete suggested responses in the Teacher's Resource Materials.

AP® THEME

WOR: America in the World

Lead a discussion on how the U.S. and its allies achieved military victory through Allied cooperation, technological and scientific advances, and campaigns such as D-Day.

TEACHING STRATEGY

The National WWII Museum offers several downloadable PDF lesson plans on the European theater as well as several useful essays, including biographies of leaders, a glossary, a collection of statistics, and a chronology of the war in Europe. To access these resources, search "National WWII Museum."

TRM Find complete suggested responses in the Teacher's Resource Materials.

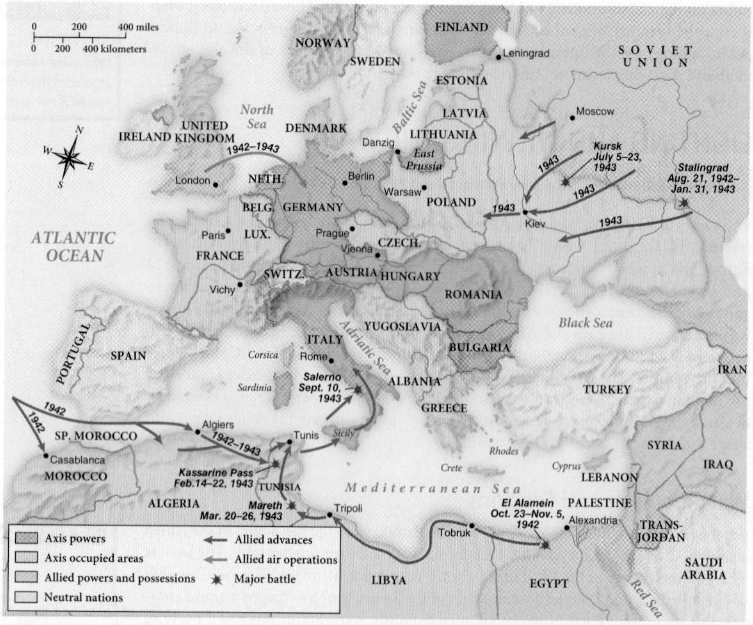

MAPPING THE PAST

MAP 23.2 World War II in Europe and North Africa, 1941–1943

Hitler's Germany reached its greatest extent in 1942, by which time Nazi forces had occupied Norway, France, North Africa, central Europe, and much of western Russia. The tide of battle turned in late 1942 when the German advance stalled at Leningrad and Stalingrad. By early 1943, the Soviet army had launched a massive counterattack at Stalingrad, and Allied forces had driven the Germans from North Africa and launched an invasion of Sicily and the Italian mainland.

ANALYZING THE MAP: Identify the combined footprint of the Axis powers and the countries they occupied. Identify both Allied and neutral nations.

MAKING CONNECTIONS: How would you characterize the relative strength of the Axis and Allied military positions from 1941 to 1943? How does the map inform your understanding of Joseph Stalin's call for a second European front?

began an offensive in North Africa aimed at seizing the critical Suez Canal. In the Atlantic, U-boats devastated American convoys carrying fuel and other vital supplies to Britain and the Soviet Union.

As 1943 approached, the tide began to turn. The Allies launched a counteroffensive in North Africa that became a temporary substitute for a European second front. In "Operation Torch," joint British-American forces invaded Algeria and Morocco in November 1942. By May 1943, combined Allied efforts led by General Dwight D. Eisenhower and General George S. Patton defeated Erwin Rommel's Afrika Korps. In the epic Battle of Stalingrad, Soviet forces halted the German advance, and the drained invaders began to lose ground. By early 1944, Stalin's troops had driven the German army out of the Soviet Union (Map 23.2).

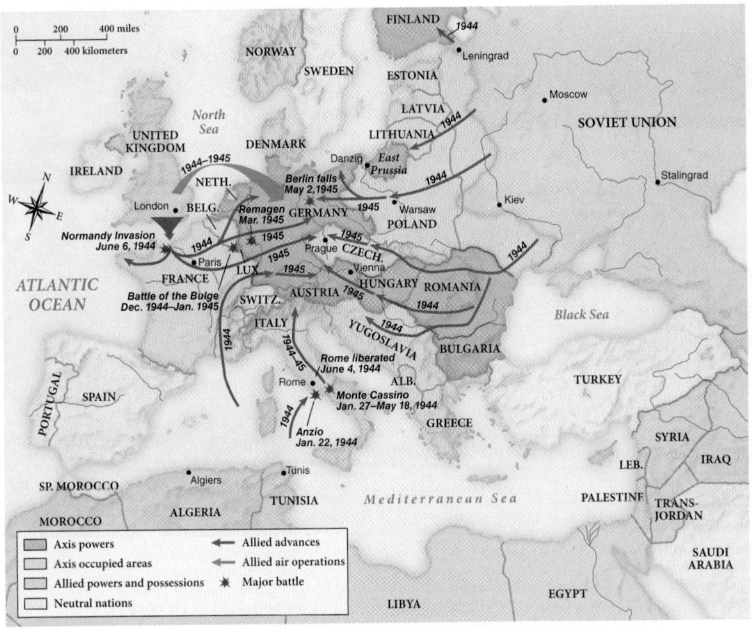

MAP 23.3 World War II in Europe, 1944–1945
By the end of 1943, the Russian army had nearly pushed the Germans out of the Soviet Union, and by June 1944, when the British and Americans finally invaded France, the Russians had liberated eastern Poland and most of southeastern Europe. By the end of 1944, British and American forces were ready to invade Germany from the west, and the Russians were poised to do the same from the east. Germany surrendered on May 7, 1945.

After victory in Africa, the Allied command followed Churchill's strategy of invading Nazi-controlled Europe via the "soft underbelly" of Italy. Allied forces landed on the island of Sicily in early July 1943, and soon after the Italian king Victor Emmanuel III ousted Mussolini's fascist regime. Italy would be officially out of the war by the time Allied forces invaded the Italian mainland in September. But German troops seized control of their former Axis partner and proved more than a match for the Allies. American and British divisions took Rome only in June 1944 and were still fighting German forces in northern Italy when the European war ended in May 1945 (Map 23.3). Churchill's southern strategy proved an immense, costly mistake, leading to hundreds of thousands of casualties but producing no strategic advantage.

AP® EXAM TIP
Explain how the impact of D-Day was a turning point event in World War II.

D-Day The long-promised invasion of France finally came on **D-Day**, June 6, 1944. That morning, the largest armada ever assembled moved across the English Channel under the command of General Eisenhower. American, British, and Canadian soldiers suffered terrible casualties storming the beaches of Normandy, but their bravery secured a foothold on Hitler's "Fortress Europe." Over the next few weeks, more than 1.5 million soldiers and countless tons of military supplies and equipment flowed into France. Much to the Allies' advantage, they never faced more than one-third of the Wehrmacht, thanks to

D-Day
June 6, 1944, the date of the Allied invasion of northern France. The largest amphibious assault in world history, the invasion opened a second front against the Germans and moved the Allies closer to victory in Europe.

AP® SKILLS & PROCESSES

DEVELOPMENTS AND PROCESSES

There are three specific references to war-related concepts in the AP® Course Framework: island hopping, D-Day, and the use of atomic weapons. Have students identify why D-Day was one of the most important events of the war in Europe. Students can accomplish this by evaluating the war in Europe from 1938–1943 and from 1944–1945.

Hitting the Beach at Normandy These U.S. soldiers were among the 156,000 Allied troops who stormed the beaches of Normandy on D-Day, June 6, 1944: on that day alone, more than 10,000 were killed or wounded. Within a month, 1 million Allied troops had come ashore. Most Americans learned of the invasion at 3:30 A.M. Eastern Time, when Edward R. Murrow, the well-known radio journalist whose reports from war-torn London had gripped the nation in 1940, read General Eisenhower's statement to the troops. "The eyes of the world are upon you," Eisenhower told the men as they prepared to invade the European mainland. Library of Congress, 3g04731

TEACHING STRATEGY

The National WWII Museum's lesson "D-Day: The Allies Invade Europe" provides a two-page overview of the attack, a ten-minute video, an oral history from a veteran, and a map exploring the Allied breakout from Normandy. To access this resource, search "National WWII Museum D-Day lesson."

Soviet pressure on the Eastern Front. In August, Allied troops liberated Paris; by September, they had driven the Germans out of most of France and Belgium. Well in advance of D-Day, Allied bombers had been pummeling military and industrial targets in the German homeland. Incendiary raids on cities such as Hamburg and Dresden destroyed vital military targets, but the resulting firestorms also killed many thousands of civilians. The human cost of the Allied bombing campaign was an estimated 305,000 civilian and military deaths, and another 780,000 injured—a grisly reminder of the war's brutality.

The Germans were not yet defeated, however. In December 1944, they mounted a final desperate offensive in Belgium, the so-called Battle of the Bulge. The push came close to a major success and saw some of the fiercest fighting of the war. But by the new year, the exhausted German forces were stopped. Soon the Allied advance would push them across the Rhine River into Germany itself. With American and British troops driving from the west, Soviet troops advanced east through Poland. On April 30, 1945, as Russian troops massed outside Berlin, Hitler committed suicide. On May 7, Germany formally surrendered.

The Holocaust As Allied troops advanced into Poland and Germany in the spring of 1945, they came face-to-face with Hitler's "final solution" for the Jewish population of Germany and the German-occupied countries: the extermination camps in which 6 million Jews had been put to death, along with another 5 to 6 million Poles, Slavs, Gypsies, homosexuals, and other "undesirables." Indelible images of the Nazi death camps at Buchenwald, Dachau, Auschwitz, and elsewhere showed bodies stacked like cordwood and survivors so emaciated that they were barely alive. Published in *Life* and other mass-circulation magazines, the photographs of the **Holocaust** horrified the American public and the world.

Holocaust
Germany's campaign during World War II to exterminate all Jews living in German-controlled lands, along with other groups the Nazis deemed "undesirable." In all, some 11 to 12 million people were killed in the Holocaust, most of them Jews.

The Horror of the Holocaust Starved and nearly dead prisoners in the Ebensee concentration camp in Austria, when it was liberated by the U.S. Army in May 1945. Ebensee was a slave labor camp whose prisoners dug vast tunnels for storing German munitions. One-third of the prisoners were near starvation at any given time, and more than 10,000 died. As horrific as life in Ebensee was, far worse were the Nazi extermination camps, such as Sobibór, Treblinka, Majdanek, Dachau, and Auschwitz-Birkenau, where more than three million people, the vast majority of them Jews, were murdered. National Archives, no. 531271

The Nazi persecution of German Jews in the 1930s was not a secret. The United States had condemned the repression but also refused to relax its strict immigration laws to take in Jewish refugees. In one notable instance, the SS *St. Louis*, a German ocean liner carrying nearly a thousand Jewish refugees, sought permission from President Roosevelt to dock at an American port in 1939. Permission was denied, and the ship was forced to return to Europe. Many of the passengers on the *St. Louis* died in Nazi extermination camps. The tight controls on immigration continued even as more and more of Europe's Jewish population fell under Hitler's control.

Various factors inhibited attempts to relax immigration barriers, but the largest was widespread anti-Semitism: in the State Department, Christian churches, and the public at large. The legacy of the immigration restriction laws of the 1920s and the isolationist attitudes of the 1930s also discouraged policymakers from embracing refugees. Taking a narrow view of the national interest, the State Department allowed only 21,000 Jewish refugees to enter the United States during the war. But the War Refugee Board, which President Roosevelt established in 1944 at the behest of Secretary of the Treasury Henry Morgenthau did help move 200,000 European Jews to safe havens in other countries.

AP® EXAM TIP

Evaluate the impact of discovery of the Holocaust on American's views of the war as a fight to protect freedom and democracy.

The War in the Pacific

Defeating Japan proved just as arduous as the campaign against the Third Reich. After crippling much of the American fleet at Pearl Harbor, the Japanese pushed out into East Asia and the wider Pacific. British colonial possessions such as Hong Kong, Singapore, Burma (Myanmar), and Malaya (Malaysia) rapidly fell to the Japanese, as did the Dutch

AP® APPLY THE TIP

To help students understand the role of anti-Semitism and the impact of the discovery of the Holocaust in World War II, have students research the U.S.'s policy toward Jewish immigrants in the pre-war and wartime era with a focus on the SS *St. Louis*. Organize the students into collaborative groups and ask each group to choose three Themes that they can use to explain the actions of the U.S. government and the impact of the discovery of the Holocaust on Americans' view of the war. Students should create an illustrated poster that highlights the ways in which the policy executed in relationship to the *St. Louis* and U.S. views of the war were in contrast with each other. Ask students to consider the ways in which the U.S.'s immigration policies and nativism impacted individuals in World War II. Lead students in a discussion of the relationship of U.S policy toward the *St. Louis* and current debates regarding immigration policy in the U.S.

AP® THEME

NAT: American and National Identity

Americans' view of the war as a fight for the survival of freedom and democracy against fascism was reinforced by revelations about Nazi concentration camps and the Holocaust. The U.S. Holocaust Memorial Museum offers several helpful resources when teaching about this subject. To access these resources, search "U.S. Holocaust Memorial Museum encyclopedia."

CHECK FOR UNDERSTANDING

Ask students: **How did the Allied fight against the Axis powers in Europe unfold?** *Soviet forces halted the German advance at the Battle of Stalingrad, which began to turn the tide of the war. British and American forces launched an attack across North Africa and into Italy, the "soft underbelly" of Europe. In mid-1944, British and American forces launched D-Day, the largest seaborne invasion in history. German forces made their final offensive at the Battle of the Bulge, but Allied forces in the West and Soviet forces in the East pressed into Germany, forcing surrender.*

AP® THEME

NAT: American and National Identity

Americans' view of the war as a fight for the survival of freedom and democracy against fascism was reinforced by revelations about Japanese wartime atrocities.

AP® THEME

WOR: America in the World

The U.S. and its allies achieved military victory through Allied cooperation, technological and scientific advances, and campaigns such as Pacific "island-hopping." Though the text doesn't discuss "island-hopping," the American advance relied on this crucial strategy of avoiding the most heavily fortified Japanese islands in favor of capturing selected islands that could bring American forces within striking distance of the Japanese homeland. The use of atomic bombs sparked debates about the morality of their use.

TEACHING STRATEGY

National Geographic provides a helpful slide show charting the progress of the Pacific War with a combination of maps, text, and images. To access the slideshow, search "National Geographic World War II in Pacific."

The National WWII Museum also provides a visual timeline, which combines photo analysis with chronological reasoning skills. In addition, it asks students to think deeply about how historians must select and prioritize historical events when writing about the past. The museum also offers a lesson that asks students to renegotiate real-life tough choices from World War II in the Pacific to help them understand history as largely the result of a multitude of individual human decisions. Another lesson invites students to analyze Japanese and American wartime propaganda to compare the combatants' ideas about each other and evaluate propaganda as a source for historical research. To access these resources, search "National WWII Museum Education."

AP® EXAM TIP

Identify the impact of "island hopping" on the military defeat of Japan.

East Indies (Indonesia). Imperial Japanese forces also seized smaller, strategically vital territories such as Wake Island, Guam, and the Solomon Islands. Their advance even threatened Australia, whose military forces were largely deployed on the other side of the globe. By May 1942, Japan forced the surrender of U.S. troops in the Philippine Islands.

At that dire moment, American naval forces scored two crucial victories. The raid on Pearl Harbor had destroyed or disabled many American battleships and cruisers, but the Pacific fleet's aircraft carriers had been away from port and were not damaged. In the Battle of the Coral Sea, off southern New Guinea in May 1942, they halted the Japanese offensive against Australia. In June, at the Battle of Midway Island, the U.S. Navy smashed the Japanese fleet and changed the course of the war. In both battles, planes launched from American aircraft carriers provided the margin of victory.

The U.S. military command in the Pacific, headed by General Douglas MacArthur and Admiral Chester W. Nimitz, then took the offensive. Following their victory at the Battle of Midway in June 1942, and extending through the summer of 1945, American forces advanced slowly toward Japan, taking one island after another in the face of determined resistance. In October 1944, MacArthur and Nimitz began the reconquest of the Philippines with a victory at the Battle of Leyte Gulf, a massive encounter in which nearly the entire Japanese navy was destroyed (Map 23.4).

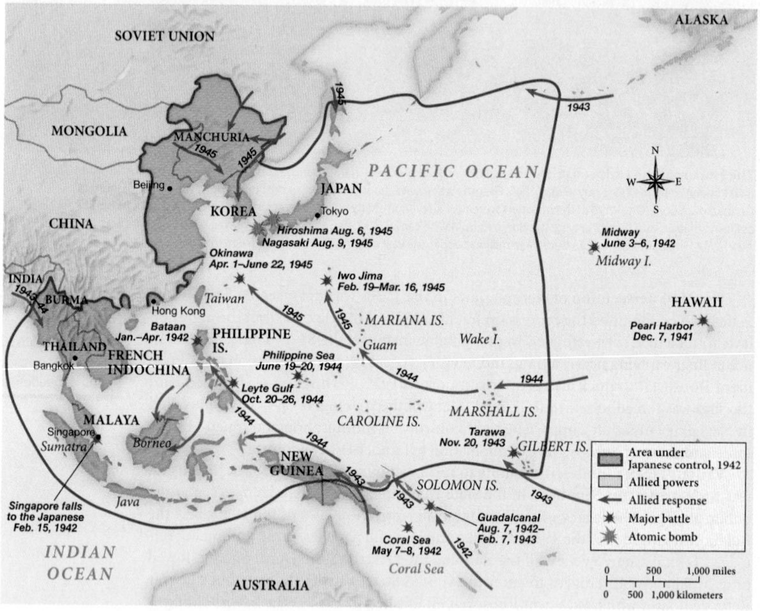

MAP 23.4 World War II in the Pacific

After the attacks on Pearl Harbor in December 1941, the Japanese rapidly extended their domination in the Pacific. The Japanese flag soon flew as far east as the Marshall and Gilbert islands and as far south as the Solomon Islands and parts of New Guinea. Japan also controlled the Philippines, much of Southeast Asia, and parts of China, including Hong Kong. By mid-1942, American naval victories at the Coral Sea and Midway stopped further Japanese expansion. Allied forces retook the islands of the central Pacific in 1943 and 1944 and ousted the Japanese from the Philippines early in 1945. Carrier-launched planes had started bombing Japan itself in 1942, but the capture of these islands gave U.S. bombers more bases from which to strike Japanese targets. As the Soviet army invaded Japanese-occupied Manchuria in August 1945, U.S. planes took off from one of the newly captured Mariana Islands to drop the atomic bombs on Hiroshima and Nagasaki. The Japanese offered to surrender on August 10.

By early 1945, victory in the Pacific was in sight. Japanese military forces had suffered devastating losses, and American bombing of the Japanese homeland had crippled the nation's industrial production, in addition to killing between 300,000 and 900,000 civilians. The human cost was horrendous, just as it was in Europe — two million Japanese soldiers were killed in the war alongside as many as three million Japanese civilians (American military deaths in the Pacific numbered fewer than 150,000). Desperate to halt the American advance and short on ammunition, Japanese pilots began to fly suicidal kamikaze missions, crashing bomb-laden planes into American ships.

The war in the Pacific was marked by vicious racial overtones. Dehumanizing logic was not limited to only one side. Japan's brutal attacks on China, its exploitation of Korean "comfort women," who were forced to have sex with Japanese soldiers, and its brutal treatment of American prisoners in the Philippines flowed from a sense of racial superiority among the Japanese. At the same time, the attack on Pearl Harbor reawakened a long tradition of anti-Asian sentiment in the United States. In the eyes of many Americans, the Japanese were "yellow monkeys," an inferior race whose humanity deserved minimal respect. Anti-Japanese attitudes in the United States would ebb in the 1950s, as the former enemy became a trusted ally. But in the 1960s, anti-Asian racial ideology would reemerge to play a major role in the U.S. war in Vietnam.

The Atomic Bomb, the Soviet Threat, and the End of the War

By early 1945, President Roosevelt was a sick man. The sixty-three-year-old had long suffered from high blood pressure and heart failure, and each successive photograph or newsreel image seemed to document his decline. He summoned his strength for a

AP® EXAM TIP

Explain the debate created regarding the use of atomic weapons despite their success in bringing a quicker end to World War II.

The Big Three at Yalta With victory in Europe at hand, Roosevelt journeyed in February 1945 to Yalta, on the Black Sea, and met for what would be the final time with Churchill and Stalin. The leaders discussed the important and controversial issues of the treatment of Germany, the status of Poland, the creation of the United Nations, and Russian entry into the war against Japan. The Yalta agreements mirrored a new balance of power and set the stage for the Cold War. Franklin D. Roosevelt Library.

CHECK FOR UNDERSTANDING

Ask students: **How did the war in the Pacific unfold?** *The Battle of Coral Sea and the Battle of Midway Island halted the Japanese advance. American forces captured strategic islands. After recapturing the Philippines, the U.S. began to attack Japan by air, killing at least 300,000 civilians. The war was fueled by brutal racism on both sides.*

TEACHING STRATEGY

Debates about the decision to drop atomic bombs on Japan are a popular classroom activity. The following Web sites offer different versions of thoughtful classroom activities on this subject:

- The National WWII Museum provides a two-page overview, along with a downloadable fifteen-page lesson with maps, a video, an audio recording of Truman's address announcing the attack, and numerous primary and secondary sources. To access these resources, search "National WWII Museum Lesson Plans."
- The Truman Library provides several dozen documents related to the Truman administration's decision to drop atomic bombs on Japan. To access these resources, search "Truman Library Decision to Drop the Atomic Bomb."

14,000-mile round trip in February to meet with Churchill and Stalin at Yalta, but his presidency was cut short. On April 12, 1945, during a short visit to his vacation home in Warm Springs, Georgia, Roosevelt suffered a cerebral hemorrhage and died.

When Harry Truman assumed the presidency, he learned for the first time about a top-secret project to develop a devastating new weapon: the atomic bomb. As early as 1939, the acclaimed physicists Leo Szilard and Albert Einstein, refugees from Nazi Germany, persuaded FDR to fund research on atomic weapons, warning that German scientists were also working on nuclear reactions. Not long after the Japanese attack on Pearl Harbor, the president brought scientists and military personnel together under a single initiative, code named the **Manhattan Project**, to carry out research and weapons development. Working at the University of Chicago in December 1942, Szilard and Enrico Fermi, a physicist who was himself a refugee from fascist Italy, produced the first controlled atomic chain reaction using highly processed uranium. The path to an atomic bomb had been established.

Manhattan Project
The research and weapons development project, authorized by President Franklin Roosevelt in 1942 that produced the first atomic bomb.

The Manhattan Project cost $2 billion, employed 120,000 people, and involved the construction of thirty-seven installations in nineteen states — with all of its activity hidden from Congress, the American people, and even Vice President Truman. Directed by Lieutenant General Leslie R. Groves Jr. and scientist J. Robert Oppenheimer, the nation's top physicists assembled the first bomb in Los Alamos, New Mexico, and successfully tested it on July 16, 1945. Overwhelmed by the frightening power of the first mushroom cloud, Oppenheimer recalled a line from the Bhagavad Gita, one of the great texts of Hindu scripture: "I am become Death, the Destroyer of Worlds."

Three weeks later, President Truman authorized the use of atomic bombs against Japanese cities: the specific targets, chosen by military commanders rather than the president, became Hiroshima on August 6 and Nagasaki on August 9. Truman's rationale for this order was straightforward. The new president and his advisors, including Secretary of War Henry Stimson and Army Chief of Staff General George Marshall, believed that Japan's military leaders would never surrender unless their country faced utter ruin. Moreover, at the Potsdam Conference in July 1945, the Allies had agreed that only the "unconditional surrender" of Japan was acceptable — the same terms to which Germany and Italy had agreed. Winning such a surrender seemed to require a direct invasion of Japan. Stimson and Marshall told Truman that such an undertaking could result in as many as one million Allied casualties.

Before giving the order, Truman considered other options. His military advisors rejected the most obvious alternative: a nonlethal demonstration of the bomb's awesome power, perhaps on a remote Pacific island. If the demonstration failed — not out of the question, as the bomb had been tested only once — it would embolden Japan further. A detailed advance warning designed to scare Japan into surrender was also rejected. Given Japan's tenacious fighting in the Pacific, the Americans believed that force alone would compel Japan's military leadership to surrender. After all, the deaths of more than 100,000 Japanese civilians in the U.S. firebombing of Tokyo and other cities in the spring of 1945 had brought Japan no closer to surrender. Although Truman's decision is still the subject of scholarly and popular debate, the atomic attacks seemingly achieved their immediate objective. Following the deaths of 100,000 people at Hiroshima on August 6 and 60,000 at Nagasaki on August 9, the Japanese government surrendered unconditionally on August 15, and signed a formal agreement ending World War II on September 2, 1945.

The atomic destruction of August 6 and 9 were not alone, however, in prompting Japanese surrender. Two days after the Hiroshima bombing, on August 8, the Soviet Union declared war on Japan, and more than one million Soviet troops launched an invasion of Japanese-occupied Manchuria, as well as Sakhalin Island and other Japanese territories north of the Sea of Japan. Japan's Supreme War Direction

Hiroshima, March 1946 Though the atomic bomb had been dropped on the port city of Hiroshima six months prior to this photo being taken, the devastation is still apparent. The U.S. Army report on the bombing described "a blinding flash in the sky, and a great rush of air and a loud rumble of noise . . . followed by the sounds of falling buildings and of growing fires, and a great cloud of dust and smoke began to cast a pall of darkness over the city." The human toll of this weapon was unprecedented: of the estimated population of 350,000, 100,000 were likely killed by the explosion, and many tens of thousands more died slowly of the effects of radiation poisoning. National Archives (342-FH-4A-49430-KE-6011).

Council, whose members set the nation's war policy, feared a Soviet invasion, and potential occupation, of their home islands as much or more than they feared an American one. Caught between these two advancing powers, the United States and the Soviet Union, from opposite sides of their contracting empire, Japan relented and surrendered.

AP® SKILLS & PROCESSES

CAUSATION

What factors influenced Truman's decision to use atomic weapons against Japan?

The Toll of the War

After the battle of Iwo Jima, one of the fiercest and bloodiest of the Pacific war, a Marine Corps rabbi chaplain delivered the eulogy for the fallen. "This shall not be in vain," he said, surveying a battlefield that witnessed the deaths of nearly 30,000 American and Japanese soldiers. Speaking of American losses, he said, "from the suffering and sorrow of those who mourn this, will come — we promise — the birth of a new freedom for the sons of man everywhere." The toll of "suffering and sorrow" from World War II was enormous. Worldwide, more than 50 million soldiers and civilians were killed, nearly 2.5 percent of the globe's population. The Holocaust took the lives of 6 million European Jews, 2.6 million from Poland alone. Nearly 100 million additional people were wounded, and 30 million people across the globe were rendered homeless. It was the most wrenching, disruptive, and terrible war in modern history.

Alongside the human toll was profound physical, economic, and political destruction. Hundreds of cities in Europe and Asia had been bombed into rubble. Some of them, such as Dresden, Warsaw, Hamburg, and Hiroshima, were simply obliterated.

CHECK FOR UNDERSTANDING

Ask students: **How did dropping atomic bombs lead to the end of the war?** *After extensive aerial bombardment of Japan, followed by the devastation of Hiroshima and Nagasaki, Japan's leaders surrendered to American forces.*

AP® SKILLS & PROCESSES

CAUSATION

This **CAUSATION** question asks student to address the crucial question of Truman's motives in dropping atomic bombs on Japan. In addition to the strategic factors that are usually discussed, students should also consider a broad range of issues, including long-term factors such as American racism, estimates of what an invasion of Japan would lead to, the bombing of cities and civilians that had already taken place (including American attacks on Japan), American investment in developing the bomb, and concerns about Soviet power.

TRM Find complete suggested responses in the Teacher's Resource Materials.

AP® THEME

WOR: America in the World

Lead a class discussion on how the war-ravaged condition of Europe and Asia as well as the U.S.'s dominant role in the Allied victory and peace settlements led the U.S. to emerge from the war as the world's most powerful nation.

CHECK FOR UNDERSTANDING

Ask students: **How did Allied strategy against the Axis powers evolve between 1941 and 1945?** *Allied strategy varied in each theater of operation and was based in large part on historical contingencies. For instance, the United States engaged in an island-hopping campaign in the Pacific due to the manner in which the Japanese fought. Attendant to this style of fighting was the decision to use incendiary weaponry from the Marianas to destroy the infrastructure on Japan, while not invading the mainland. In Europe, the United States started by engaging Nazi Germany in the so-called "soft underbelly" of southern Europe before invading France in 1944. These strategies were based on circumstance and in partnership with allies.*

CHECK FOR UNDERSTANDING

Use the **AP® LEARNING FOCUS** question from the beginning of the chapter to provide a check on students' understanding of the chapter as a whole: **Why and how did World War II transform the United States domestically and internationally?** *The outbreak of WWII saw an increase in the authority of the president in wartime, an increase in defense spending, an increase of women, African Americans, and Native Americans in the war effort, an infusion of Americans into the cities, the birth of gay culture in urban areas, and the emergence of the nation out of the Great Depression. The advent of internment camps for Japanese Americans revealed the extent of federal power and distrust following Pearl Harbor. The United States emerged from WWII as one of two superpowers on the globe, which fundamentally changed the role America played in global politics.*

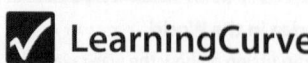

LearningCurve

Remind students to go online to complete the LearningCurve quiz for this chapter.

Much of the industrial infrastructure of Germany and Japan, two of the world's most important economies before the war, was shattered. Despite being one of the victors, Britain was no longer a global power. The independence movement in India was only the most obvious sign of Britain's weakening imperial reach. In the colonized world in Asia and Africa, many had taken the Atlantic Charter, and FDR's insistence that this was a war for *democracy*, seriously. For them, the continuation of European imperialism was unacceptable.

Even though the United States was safe from bombings and battles, the war left a great impact on the nation. More than 400,000 lives were lost, and nearly 300,000 American soldiers were wounded. In total, 16 million Americans served in the wartime military, a commitment of military service equaled in U.S. history only during the Civil War. The return of those millions of GIs to civilian life would remake American society. In 1950, World War II veterans made up one-third of all American men over the age of nineteen, and through the GI Bill they gained education and access to a middle class. Wartime spending had ended the Great Depression and given a great boost to American industry, and to the economy as a whole, that would endure for several decades. And the war indisputably left the United States a stronger, perhaps even the dominant, world power.

After incalculable costs, and the use of a new and terrible weapon, the Axis powers had finally been defeated by a fragile alliance of the capitalist West and the communist Soviet Union. The challenges of building a new international order would strain and then destroy the victorious coalition. The final chapter of European empire would see fights for independence around the globe. Even as millions celebrated a long-awaited peace, the far longer Cold War, which would pit the capitalist West against the communist East, was brewing.

SUMMARY

The rise of fascism in Germany, Italy, and Japan led to the outbreak of a second world war in 1939. Initially, the American public opposed involvement in the war. But by 1940, President Roosevelt was mobilizing support for a military buildup and preparing the nation to fight. The Japanese attack on Pearl Harbor in December 1941 brought the United States fully into the conflict. War mobilization dramatically expanded the federal government and finally ended the Great Depression. It also boosted geographical and social mobility, as women, rural whites, and southern blacks found employment in new defense plants across the country. Even as the war brought Americans closer together, inequalities like the internment of Japanese American citizens marred the idealism that defined the war effort.

In 1942, Germany and Japan seemed to be on the verge of victory. But a string of critical victories led to the Allies taking the offensive for good in 1943. With the Soviets pushing the exhausted German army back and France liberated, the Nazis looked defeated by the end of 1944. Allied victory was all but certain, and Germany surrendered in May 1945. The tide of war had turned in large part on the unprecedented industrial might of America. The federal policies that drove the war effort — the expanded income tax, a huge military establishment, and multibillion-dollar budgets, to name but a few — would become permanent fixtures in American life.

The greatest expression of America's power was the development of a nuclear weapon. After atomic bombs were dropped on the cities of Hiroshima and Nagasaki, Japan finally surrendered. The United States emerged from the war with an undamaged homeland, sole possession of atomic weapons, and a new standing in international politics and alliances. That new global role would be complicated by a lasting legacy of the war: friction with the Soviet Union, which sowed the seeds of the four-decade-long Cold War.

CHAPTER 23 REVIEW

AP® CONTENT REVIEW *Answer these questions to demonstrate your understanding of the chapter's main ideas.*

1. What developments led the United States to enter World War II?
2. How did war mobilization reshape American economic life?
3. What short-term and long-term domestic social changes were produced by the war?
4. How did Allied war strategy evolve between 1941 and 1945?

AP® TERMS TO KNOW *Identify and explain the significance of each term.*

Key Concepts and Events

fascism (p. 737)
National Socialist (Nazi) Party (p. 737)
Axis powers (p. 738)
Neutrality Act of 1935 (p. 738)
Popular Front (p. 738)
Munich Conference (p. 739)
America First Committee (AFC) (p. 740)
Four Freedoms (p. 741)
Lend-Lease Act (p. 741)
Atlantic Charter (p. 741)
Pearl Harbor (p. 742)
War Powers Act (1941) (p. 742)
Revenue Act (p. 744)
code talkers (p. 745)
"Double V" campaign (p. 748)
Executive Order 8802 (p. 748)
Bracero Program (p. 749)
Servicemen's Readjustment Act (p. 750)
zoot-suit riots (p. 754)
Executive Order 9066 (p. 756)
D-Day (p. 759)
Holocaust (p. 760)
Manhattan Project (p. 764)

Key People

Benito Mussolini (p. 736)
Adolf Hitler (p. 736)
Hideki Tojo (p. 741)
Winston Churchill (p. 741)
Harry S. Truman (p. 750)
Dwight D. Eisenhower (p. 758)

AP® MAKING CONNECTIONS *Recognize the larger developments and continuities within and across chapters by answering these questions.*

1. For the United States, the period between World War I (1914–1918) and World War II (1937–1945) was a prolonged series of conflicts and crises, both domestically and internationally. What connections can be drawn between World War I, the Great Depression, and World War II? Did this "long" conflict draw the United States and Europe closer together or drive them further apart? How did American attitudes toward involvement in European affairs change over this period?
2. How did the following developments of World War II change the relationship of the United States to other nations in the world: the Atlantic Charter, fighting a two-front war in Europe and the Pacific, the Manhattan Project and the bombing of Hiroshima and Nagasaki?
3. World War II has popularly been called the "good war." Do you agree with this assessment? Why do you think it earned that nickname?
4. Overall, what effects — positive or negative — did World War II have on social change in the United States, particularly among women and historically marginalized groups?

KEY TURNING POINTS *Refer to the timeline at the start of the chapter for help in answering the following question.*

What were the key turning points for the Allies in the European and Pacific campaigns?

TRM Find complete suggested responses in the Teacher's Resource Materials.

AP® SKILLS & PROCESSES

CAUSATION

AP® CONTENT REVIEW 1 asks students to describe the causes of American involvement in World War II. Note: This is the same question as the section-opening prompt on p. 736.

AP® SKILLS & PROCESSES

CAUSATION

AP® CONTENT REVIEW 2 asks students to identify the effects of the war on the American economy. Note: This is the same question as the section-opening prompt on p. 742.

AP® SKILLS & PROCESSES

CAUSATION

AP® CONTENT REVIEW 3 asks students to identify both short- and long-term social effects of the war on American society. Note: This is the same question as the section-opening prompt on p. 750.

AP® SKILLS & PROCESSES

CONTINUITY AND CHANGE

AP® CONTENT REVIEW 4 asks student to trace changes in American strategy over the course of the war. Note: This is the same question as the section-opening prompt on p. 757.

TRM Find definitions for these terms in the **Glossary/Glosario** in the Teacher's Resource Materials.

AP® SKILLS & PROCESSES

CONTINUITY AND CHANGE

AP® MAKING CONNECTIONS 1 asks students to consider a question of periodization: to what extent did the period between the start of World War I and the end of World War II constitute a single period?

AP® SKILLS & PROCESSES

CAUSATION

AP® MAKING CONNECTIONS 2 asks students to identify the effects of specific historical events on the U.S.'s relationship with the world.

AP® SKILLS & PROCESSES

CONTINUITY AND CHANGE

The **KEY TURNING POINTS** question asks students to find and explain turning points in Allied victory in both Europe and the Pacific.

TRM Find complete suggested responses in the Teacher's Resource Materials.

AP PRACTICE QUESTIONS

MULTIPLE CHOICE QUESTIONS *Choose the correct answer for each question.*

Questions 1–3 are based on this excerpt.

"The lend-lease policy, translated into legislative form, stunned a Congress and a nation wholly sympathetic to the cause of Great Britain. . . . It warranted my worst fears for the future of America, and it definitely stamps the President as war-minded.

The lend-lease program is the New Deal's Triple-A policy; it will plow under every fourth American boy. . . .

Approval of this legislation means war, open and complete warfare. I, therefore, ask the American people before they supinely accept it, Was the last World War worthwhile?"

Speech. Burton K. Wheeler, Senator from Montana, January 12, 1941

1. Wheeler based his appeal most directly upon the precedent of
   - **a.** Woodrow Wilson's efforts to preserve humanitarian principles through the League of Nations.
   - **b.** bi-partisan political enthusiasm for interventionism.
   - **c.** popular support for isolationism after World War I.
   - **d.** the United States' tradition of anti-imperialism.
2. Wheeler's views expressed in the excerpt best reflect the United States citizens'
   - **a.** commitment to resist totalitarianism.
   - **b.** preference for a unilateral foreign policy.
   - **c.** popular view of World War II as a fight for democracy.
   - **d.** opposition to genocide.
3. The ideas of Wheeler, as expressed in the excerpt, show the greatest difference from the ideas of
   - **a.** the Federalist Party in 1810.
   - **b.** anti-imperialists in the 1890s.
   - **c.** isolationists in the 1910s.
   - **d.** supporters of Taft's dollar diplomacy.

Questions 4–6 refer to this excerpt.

"We have built an enormous portion of our vast war plant within close range of big industries where expert management and skilled labor were at hand. Baltimore, Indianapolis, Buffalo, Hartford, St. Louis, Detroit, Los Angeles, Portland, Seattle, and numerous other cities find their manufacturing plants expanding at a rate that seemed impossible in peacetime. . . .

The meaning of these social and economic upheavals is plain. . . . The consequences will be far reaching. For in this . . . there is no chance to maintain the status quo. If strategy and geography do not thrust a community into the maelstrom of war activity, its resources will be drained into other areas where they can better serve the national interest. So the whole pattern of our economic and social life is undergoing kaleidoscopic changes, without so much as a bomb being dropped on our shores."

Merlo J. Pusey, "The Revolution at Home," *South Atlantic Quarterly*, Volume 42, pp. 207–219. Copyright 1943, Duke University Press. All rights reserved. Republished by permission of the copyright holder, Duke University Press. www.dukepress.edu

4. Which of the following most directly resulted from the changes described in the excerpt?
   - **a.** New economic opportunities for African Americans and women
   - **b.** The establishment of increased barriers to immigration
   - **c.** A reversal of the World War I Great Migration
   - **d.** The emergence of new forms of mass media
5. Pusey's observations in the excerpt most directly lead to which of the following developments?
   - **a.** The end of the Great Depression
   - **b.** Challenges to civil liberties at home
   - **c.** A decline in public confidence in government's ability to solve economic problems
   - **d.** An increase in laissez-faire policies that promoted economic growth
6. Which of the following sectors of the economy would likely cause the least amount of "upheaval" described by Pusey?
   - **a.** Defense production of weapons
   - **b.** Resource extraction
   - **c.** Entertainment and movie
   - **d.** Food production

SHORT ANSWER QUESTIONS

Read each question carefully and write a short response. Use evidence from the text to support your claims.

"Truman read the intercepts [from the Japanese]. They were very clear. They did not show a Japan ready to surrender. They show an elite ready to negotiate an armistice . . . but . . . [t]he truth is that peace would have been available only had the peace party . . . been in control. They were not. . . . [Those in control in Japan] never favored surrender, not after Saipan was lost, not after Iwo Jima was lost, not after the Philippines were lost, not after Okinawa, not even after two atoms bombs and a Soviet Declaration of War. They all supported fighting the decisive battle in the homeland during which the American invaders would take such heavy casualties that the Allies would negotiate an armistice."

Robert P. Newman, *Rhetoric & Public Affairs: Truman and the Hiroshima Cult*, 1995

"Soviet entry played an important part in the American decision to speed up the dropping of the atomic bombs. Truman was in a hurry. He was aware that the race was on between the atomic bomb and Soviet entry into the war. That was why he concocted the story of Japan's 'prompt rejection' of the Potsdam Proclamation as the justification for the atomic bomb, and that was also the reason he was ecstatic to receive the news of the Hiroshima bomb. The atomic bomb represented to Truman a solution to all the dilemmas he faced: unconditional surrender, the cost of Japan's homeland invasion, and Soviet entry into the war. He was jubilant at news of the atomic bomb on Hiroshima, not because of a perverted joy in killing the Japanese, but because of the satisfaction that everything had gone as he had planned."

Tsuyoshi Hasegawa, *Racing the Enemy: Stalin, Truman, and the Surrender of Japan*, 2009

1. Using the two excerpts provided, answer (a), (b), and (c).
   - **a.** Briefly explain ONE major difference between Newman's and Hasegawa's historical interpretations of President Truman's decision to use the atom bomb.
   - **b.** Briefly explain how ONE specific historical event or development not directly mentioned in the excerpts could be used to support Newman's argument.
   - **c.** Briefly explain how ONE specific historical event or development not directly mentioned in the excerpts could be used to support Hasegawa's argument.
2. Answer (a), (b), and (c).
   - **a.** Briefly explain why ONE of the following developments was the most significant factor contributing to military victory for the United States in the Second World War.
     - Technological and scientific advances
     - Mass mobilization of American society
     - Allied cooperation
   - **b.** Explain ONE specific historical example to support your argument in (a).
   - **c.** Explain why ONE of the other options exerted a lesser influence leading to the United States' victory.
3. Answer (a), (b), and (c).
   - **a.** Briefly explain ONE way in which involvement in World War II transformed U.S. society.
   - **b.** Briefly explain ONE way in which involvement in World War II transformed the U.S. economy.
   - **c.** Briefly explain ONE way in which involvement in World War II fostered a historical continuity in U.S. society.

TRM Find complete suggested responses in the Teacher's Resource Materials.

TRM Find complete suggested responses in the Teacher's Resource Materials.

7 PART

AP® PRACTICE ESSAY QUESTIONS

DOCUMENT-BASED QUESTION

Suggested reading period: 15 minutes. Suggested writing time: 45 minutes.

DIRECTIONS: Question 1 is based on the accompanying documents. The documents have been edited for the purpose of this exercise.

1. Evaluate the extent of change in the experiences of women in the United States from 1890 to 1940.

DOCUMENT 1

Source: *Ladies' Home Journal,* January 1890.

"Reforms in women's apparel are again being discussed, and public interest is once more awakened on this oft-mooted question. That some of the present style of dress adopted by American women are, to some extent, physically injurious and inconsistent with good taste, can scarcely be denied. But the radical reforms suggested, as, for example the substitution of the trousers for the petticoat, and similar departures from modern customs, are not destined to bring about the looked-for result . . . to advise a young woman to dress herself with any such serious departure from the prevailing fashion of her day and class is to ask her to incur a penalty that will invariably follow such an innovation.

'God has implanted in the minds of all, but especially in the female breast, the love of beauty. . . . It is a duty which every woman owes to herself, to her family, and to her society to dress tastefully, and as well as her means shall allow. It is woman's instinct to admire pretty dresses, and it is right that she should. . . .

In this matter of women's dress, then, when we sum it all up, the fact is plain that, as the love of dress in inherent in all true women, it would be as unwise as it would be useless to strive against it by any radical suggestiveness of reform."

DOCUMENT 2

Source: Labor activist Rose Schneiderman, from a speech delivered at a memorial meeting at the Metropolitan Opera House in New York City, April 2, 1911.

"I would be a traitor to those poor burned bodies if I were to come here to ask good fellowship. We have tried you good people of the public — and we have found you wanting.

The old Inquisition had its rack and its thumb screws and its instruments of torture with iron teeth. We know what these things are today: the iron teeth are our necessities, the thumbscrews are the high-powered and swift machinery close to which we must work, and the rack is here in the firetrap structures that will destroy us the minute they catch fire.

This is not the first time girls have been burned alive in this city. Every week I learn of the untimely death of one of my sister workers. Every year thousands of us are maimed. The life of men and women is so cheap and property is so sacred! There are so many of us for one job, it matters little if 140-odd are burned to death. . . .

Public officials have only words of warning for us — warning that we must be intensely orderly and must be intensely peaceable, and they have the work-house [prison] just back of all their warnings. The strong hand of the law beats us back when we rise — back into conditions that make life unbearable.

I can't talk fellowship to you who are gathered here. Too much blood has been spilled. I know from experience it is up to the working people to save themselves. And the only way is through a strong working-class movement."

767-c

DOCUMENT 3

Source: Miss N. H. Burroughs, Secretary of the Women's Auxiliary to the National Baptist Convention, "Black Women and Reform," published in *The Crisis*, August 1915.

"I was asked by a Southern white woman who is an enthusiastic worker for 'votes for (white) women,' 'What can the Negro woman do with the ballot?' I asked her, 'What can she do without it?' When the ballot is put into the hands of the American woman the world is going to get a correct estimate of the Negro woman. She is a tower of strength of which poets have never sung, orators have never spoken, and scholars have never written.

. . . The Negro woman, therefore, needs the ballot to get back, by the wise *use* of it, what the Negro man has lost by *misuse* of it. A fact worthy of note is that in every reform in which the Negro woman has taken part, during the last fifty years, she has been as aggressive, progressive, and dependable as those who inspired the reform or led it. The world has yet to learn that the Negro woman is quite superior in bearing moral responsibility. A comparison with the men of her race, in moral issues, is odious. She carries the burdens of the Church, and of the school and bears a great deal more than her economic share in the home.

The ballot, wisely used, will bring to her the respect and protection that she needs. It is her weapon of moral defence. Under present conditions, when she appears in court in defence of her virtue, she is looked upon with amused contempt. She needs the ballot to reckon with men who place no value upon her virtue, and to mould healthy public sentiment in favor of her own protection."

DOCUMENT 4

Source: Margaret Sanger, *Woman and the New Race*, 1920.

"The basic freedom of the world is woman's freedom. A free race cannot be born of slave mothers. A woman enchained cannot choose but give a measure of that bondage to her sons and daughters. No woman can call herself free who does not own and control her body. No woman can call herself free until she can choose consciously whether she will or will not be a mother. . . .

Woman must have her freedom; the fundamental freedom of choosing whether or not she shall be a mother and how many children she will have. Regardless of what man's attitude may be, that problem is hers; and before it can be his, it is hers alone.

She goes through the vale of death alone, each time a babe is born. As it is the right neither of man nor the state to coerce her into this ordeal, so it is her right to decide whether she will endure it. That right to decide imposes upon her the duty of clearing the way to knowledge by which she may make and carry out the decision.

Birth control is woman's problem. The quicker she accepts it as hers and hers alone, the quicker will society respect motherhood. The quicker, too, will the world be made a fit place for her children to live."

DOCUMENT 5

Source: Advertisement, *Good Housekeeping Magazine*, November 1924.

Her habit of measuring time in terms of dollars gives the woman in business keen insight into the true value of a Ford closed car for her personal use.
This car enables her to conserve minutes, to expedite her affairs, to widen the scope of her activities. Its low first cost, long life and inexpensive operation and upkeep convince her that it is a sound investment value.
And it is such a pleasant car to drive that it transforms the business call which might be an interruption into an enjoyable episode of her busy day.
TUDOR SEDAN, $590
FORDOR SEDAN, $685
COUPE, $525
(All prices f. o. b. Detroit)
Ford
CLOSED CARS

MPI/Archive Photos/Getty Images.

DOCUMENT 6

Source: Norman Cousins, "Will Women Lose Their Jobs?" *Current History* (New York). Reprinted with permission from *Current History* magazine 51:1, Sept. 1939. © 2017 Current History, Inc.

"There are approximately 10,000,000 people out of work in the United States today. There are also 10,000,000 or more women, married and single, who are job-holders. Simply fire the women, who shouldn't be working anyway, and hire the men. Presto! No Unemployment. No relief rolls. No depression.

This is the general idea behind the greatest assault on women's rights in two decades. . . . Of such concern is this trend that it has been called the greatest single issue to affect women since their victorious fight for suffrage. . . .

Fundamentally, the unemployment of men is not caused by women who hold jobs but by the infirmities of the economic structure itself. Nor is the depression an affliction visited exclusively upon the male; the woman must bear her part in the burden, as more than 2,000,000 unemployed women can attest. . . .

But even outside the economic sphere, arguments against the working wife reveal weakness. There is much talk about the mother's place in the home, very little about the fact that the home has changed. Housekeeping for the average family is no longer a full-time job. . . .

This change is reflected not only in employment of married women but in the growth of social and church work, and the spread of adult education, of culture and entertainment groups."

DOCUMENT 7

Source: Table, Women's Labor Force Participation Rates, 1900–1940.

Year	Percentage of All Women Working	Percentage of Married Women Working
1900	20.6%	5.6%
1920	23.7%	9.0%
1930	24.8%	11.7%
1940	25.8%	15.6%

LONG ESSAY QUESTIONS *Suggested writing time: 40 minutes.*

DIRECTIONS: Please choose one of the following two questions to answer. Make a historically defensible claim and support your reasoning with specific and relevant evidence.

2. Compare the goals of United States foreign policy in the years immediately before United States involvement in the First World War (1904–1917) to the goals of United States foreign policy in the years immediately after United States involvement in the First World War (1918–1930).

3. Compare the goals of the African American civil rights movement during the Progressive Era (1890–1920) to the goals of the African American civil rights movement during the New Deal Era (1933–1941).

4. Compare the goals of the women's rights movement during the Progressive Era (1890–1920) to the goals of the women's rights movement during the New Deal Era.

8
PART

The Modern State and the Age of Liberalism
1945–1980

Between 1945 and 1980, the United States became the world's leading economic and military power. That development defines these decades as a distinct period of American history. The dates we've chosen to bookend the period reflect two turning points. In 1945, the United States and its allies emerged victorious from World War II. In 1980, American voters turned away from the robust liberalism of the postwar years and elected a president, Ronald Reagan, backed by a conservative political movement. Each turning point, one international the other domestic, marked a new development in American history — and thus our periodization of these decades features the rise of American global power and the expansion, and later contraction, of political liberalism.

Internationally, after 1945 a prolonged period of tension and conflict known as the Cold War drew the United States into an engagement in world affairs unprecedented in the nation's history. Domestically, three decades of sustained economic growth expanded the middle class and brought into being a mass consumer society. These international and domestic developments were intertwined with the predominance of liberalism in American politics and public policy. One might think of an "age of liberalism" in this era, encompassing the social-welfare liberalism that was a legacy of the New Deal and the rights liberalism of the 1960s.

Global leadership abroad and economic prosperity at home relied on further expansions in government power — and the making of a modern state equally capable of waging global war and shaping domestic life. How that power was used proved controversial. Immediately following World War II, a national security apparatus emerged to investigate so-called subversives in the United States and, through the clandestine Central Intelligence Agency (CIA), to destabilize foreign governments. Meanwhile, American troops went to war in Korea and Vietnam. At home, African Americans, women of all racial backgrounds, the poor, and other social groups sought new laws and government initiatives to bring them greater equality in American life. Here, in brief, are three key questions about this convulsive, turbulent era to explore as you read the chapters in this part. ▶

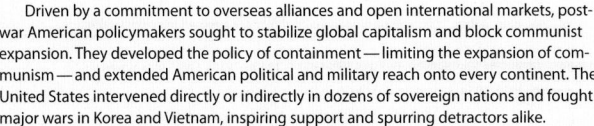

AP® CONCEPT CONNECTIONS

Why did the United States fight a Cold War and ascend to global leadership?

The National Archives.

Following their shared victory in World War II, the United States and the Soviet Union competed to reshape postwar Europe, East Asia, and the developing world. American leaders sought to restore liberal democracies in postwar conflict zones and to forge new international alliances and trading partnerships. These goals conflicted with Soviet ambition to expand its sphere of influence. Each nation feared direct military engagement with the other, so the two superpowers pursued their objectives through diplomatic and military interventions around the world that stopped short of cataclysmic nuclear war with each other. The result was a standoff that lasted four decades: the Cold War.

Driven by a commitment to overseas alliances and open international markets, postwar American policymakers sought to stabilize global capitalism and block communist expansion. They developed the policy of containment — limiting the expansion of communism — and extended American political and military reach onto every continent. The United States intervened directly or indirectly in dozens of sovereign nations and fought major wars in Korea and Vietnam, inspiring support and spurring detractors alike.

Why did liberalism define the era's politics?

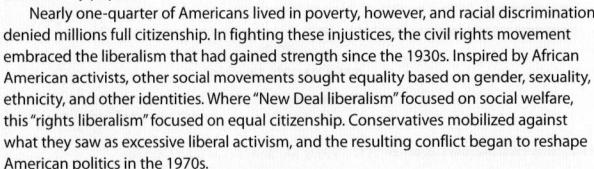

© George Ballis/Take Stock/The Image Works.

Responding to the Great Depression and World War II enlarged the federal government's involvement in the social and economic life of the country. Inspired by these examples of government as a positive force for economic growth and social stability, the Democratic Party, and many Republicans as well, undertook such postwar measures as the GI Bill, subsidies for suburban home ownership, and investment in infrastructure and education. Roosevelt's Democratic coalition of workers and the middle class, which supported these federal efforts, thrived after the war and, along with the policies themselves, made liberalism widely popular.

Nearly one-quarter of Americans lived in poverty, however, and racial discrimination denied millions full citizenship. In fighting these injustices, the civil rights movement embraced the liberalism that had gained strength since the 1930s. Inspired by African American activists, other social movements sought equality based on gender, sexuality, ethnicity, and other identities. Where "New Deal liberalism" focused on social welfare, this "rights liberalism" focused on equal citizenship. Conservatives mobilized against what they saw as excessive liberal activism, and the resulting conflict began to reshape American politics in the 1970s.

How did the rise of the postwar middle class shape culture and politics?

Justin Locke/National Geographic Creative.

The postwar American economy was driven by mass consumption and suburbanization. Rising wages, increasing access to higher education, and the availability of suburban home ownership raised living standards, and suburbanization transformed the nation's cities. But the new prosperity had mixed results. Cities declined and racial segregation hardened. Suburbanization and mass consumption raised concerns that the nation's rivers, streams, air, and open land were being damaged. And prosperity itself proved short-lived. By the 1970s, deindustrialization had eroded much of the nation's once prosperous industrial base.

A defining characteristic of the postwar decades was the growth of the American middle class, which led to numerous demographic changes. Women worked more outside the home and spurred a new feminism. Children enjoyed more purchasing power, and a "teen culture" arose on television, in popular music, and in film. The family became politicized, too, and by the late 1970s, liberals and conservatives were divided over how best to address the nation's family life.

769

Organized around a single theme, the Part 8 Document Set in *Sources for America's History* can be used to teach AP® Theme WOR (America in the World), which requires students to demonstrate how involvement in the developing world, globalization, and terrorism impacted U.S. foreign policy goals in the latter half of the twentieth century.

AP® THEMATIC UNDERSTANDING

The Modern State and the Age of Liberalism, 1945–1980

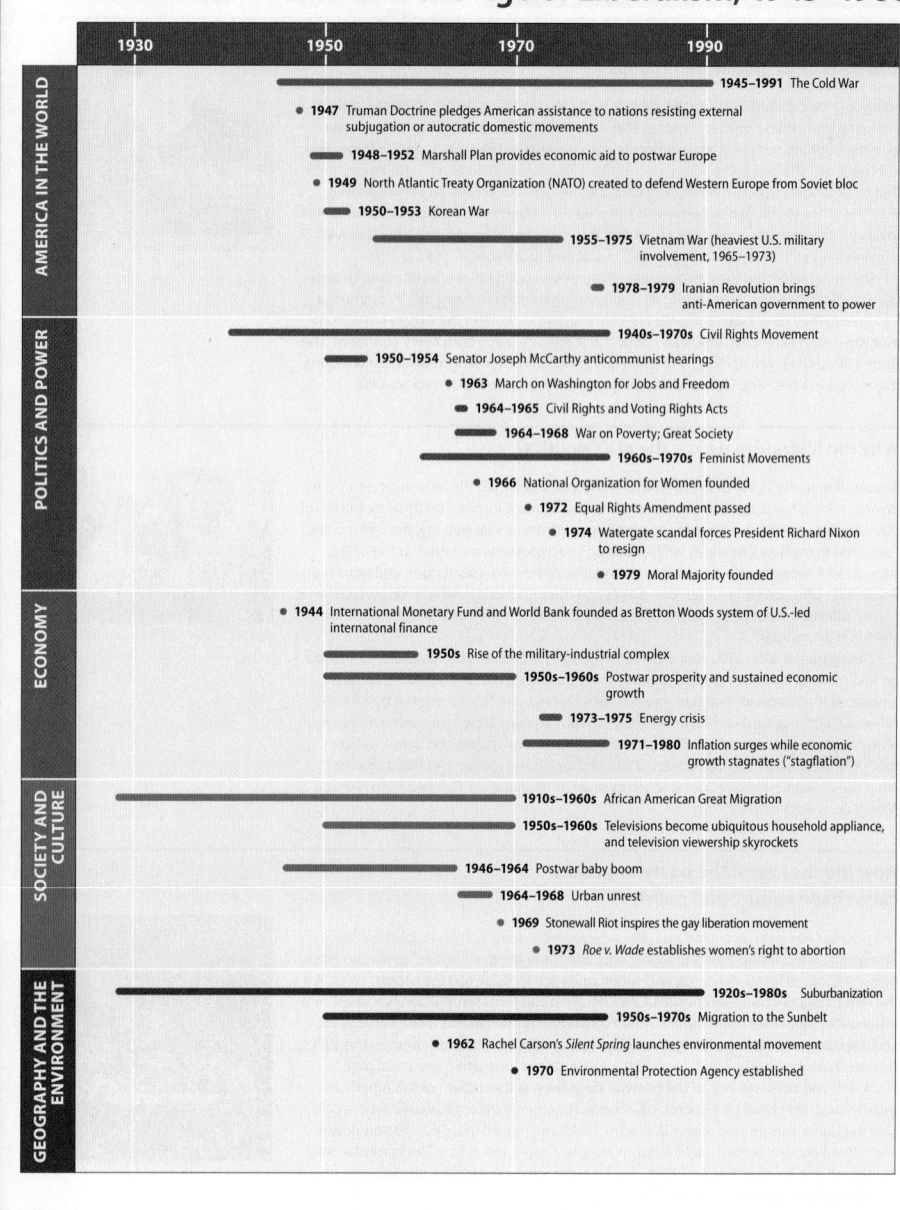

1930 | 1950 | 1970 | 1990

AMERICA IN THE WORLD

- **1945–1991** The Cold War
- **1947** Truman Doctrine pledges American assistance to nations resisting external subjugation or autocratic domestic movements
- **1948–1952** Marshall Plan provides economic aid to postwar Europe
- **1949** North Atlantic Treaty Organization (NATO) created to defend Western Europe from Soviet bloc
- **1950–1953** Korean War
- **1955–1975** Vietnam War (heaviest U.S. military involvement, 1965–1973)
- **1978–1979** Iranian Revolution brings anti-American government to power

POLITICS AND POWER

- **1940s–1970s** Civil Rights Movement
- **1950–1954** Senator Joseph McCarthy anticommunist hearings
- **1963** March on Washington for Jobs and Freedom
- **1964–1965** Civil Rights and Voting Rights Acts
- **1964–1968** War on Poverty; Great Society
- **1960s–1970s** Feminist Movements
- **1966** National Organization for Women founded
- **1972** Equal Rights Amendment passed
- **1974** Watergate scandal forces President Richard Nixon to resign
- **1979** Moral Majority founded

ECONOMY

- **1944** International Monetary Fund and World Bank founded as Bretton Woods system of U.S.-led internatonal finance
- **1950s** Rise of the military-industrial complex
- **1950s–1960s** Postwar prosperity and sustained economic growth
- **1973–1975** Energy crisis
- **1971–1980** Inflation surges while economic growth stagnates ("stagflation")

SOCIETY AND CULTURE

- **1910s–1960s** African American Great Migration
- **1950s–1960s** Televisions become ubiquitous household appliance, and television viewership skyrockets
- **1946–1964** Postwar baby boom
- **1964–1968** Urban unrest
- **1969** Stonewall Riot inspires the gay liberation movement
- **1973** *Roe v. Wade* establishes women's right to abortion

GEOGRAPHY AND THE ENVIRONMENT

- **1920s–1980s** Suburbanization
- **1950s–1970s** Migration to the Sunbelt
- **1962** Rachel Carson's *Silent Spring* launches environmental movement
- **1970** Environmental Protection Agency established

Making Connections Across Chapters

Read these questions and think about them as you read the chapters in this part. Then when you have completed reading this part, return to these questions and answer them.

1 A hallmark of the Cold War years was the interconnectedness of international and domestic developments. Each one shaped the other. Identify and explain three examples of how domestic and international events were connected to each other.

Howard Sochurek/The LIFE Picture Collection/Getty Images.

2 What effects did suburbanization have on the United States in the postwar decades? How did it influence the nation's social life, politics, and culture?

The Park Forest Historical Society.

3 What postwar developments helped the Civil Rights Movement achieve its aims, and what factors limited its reach? Did the same factors help the women's, Latino, Native American, and gay rights movements?

Rue des Archives/GRANGER.

4 How did the power of the federal government expand between 1945 and 1980? What kinds of new responsibilities did it take on? Which of its traditional roles increased and why?

Bettmann/Getty Images.

5 Can these decades be described as an "age of liberalism"? Why or why not? How does the rise, or resurgence, of conservatism in these years factor in your answer?

Charles Gorry/AP Images.

TRM Find complete suggested responses in the Teacher's Resource Materials.

24 CHAPTER

Cold War America

1945–1963

Chapter 24 — AP® Assessment Weight and Pacing Guide

The assessment weight on the AP® U.S. History Exam for Chapters 23–28 is 10–17 percent. This chapter falls in Unit 8 of the AP® U.S. History Curriculum, covering Period 8: 1945–1980.

This pacing guide is based on a schedule with 120 sessions of 50 minutes each before the AP® U.S. History Exam. If you have a different number of sessions before the exam, you can modify the pacing to meet your needs. If you have additional time, consider incorporating quizzes, released AP® U.S. History questions, practice exams, writing practice, and other instructional activities.

	Traditional Schedule	Block Schedule
Chapter 24	3 days	1–2 days

Daily Pacing Guide

	Content Focus	Essential Question
Day 1	Containment in a Divided World	What primary factors caused the Cold War?
Day 2	Cold War Liberalism	What were the defining ideas of Cold War liberalism, and why did the Democratic Party embrace them?
Day 3	Cold War in the Postcolonial World	What objectives guided U.S. foreign policy in the postcolonial world during the Cold War?

AP® Alignment

Section Heading	AP® Topic	AP® Theme
Containment in a Divided World	7.14, 8.2, 8.7	WOR
Cold War Liberalism	8.3, 8.4, 8.5	NAT, WXT, ARC
Cold War in the Postcolonial World	8.7, 8.8	WOR

*Should changes be made to the Course Framework in the future, an updated alignment will be placed on our AP® updates page at go.bfwpub.com/ap-course-updates.

Chapter 24 — Overview

Chapter 24 focuses students' attention on the changing role of the U.S. in the world that came with victory in World War II and the beginning of the Cold War. The chapter begins by analyzing the origins of the containment strategy and its first test in Asia with the fall of China to communism and the Korean War. The chapter then focuses on the impact of the beginning of the Cold War and the emergence of the Soviet Union as a nuclear power on the fear of communism in the U.S. that manifested itself in the Red Scare. Finally, the chapter places emphasis on the changing role of the U.S. in areas of the world that experience decolonization and transition to independence. The chapter concludes by looking at the U.S. response to nationalism in Vietnam that threatened the policy of containment and started the U.S. down the long path of commitment to preventing the spread of communism in that area of the world.

Chapter 24 — Resources

The following resources can be found in the Teacher's Resource Materials (TRM) that accompany the book. You can access the TRM via the book's digital platform, by clicking the TRM links found here in your Teacher's Edition e-book, or by contacting your representative to access the resources online. Visit **bfwpub.com/henretta10e** to learn more.

TRM Chapter 24 Lecture Presentation Slides

TRM Chapter 24 Outline with AP® Focus

TRM Chapter 24 Lecture Strategies

TRM Chapter 24 Suggested Responses

TRM Handout 24.1 — Contextualization: Containment

TRM Handout 24.2 — Comparison: Foreign Policy of Truman vs. Eisenhower

TRM Handout 24.3 — Comparison: National Movements in the Middle East

Chapter 24 — Essential Activity

Engage students in a document analysis activity to help them clearly formulate an understanding of the policy of containment in the Cold War era. Provide students with excerpts from the following: George Kennan's "Sources of Soviet Conduct"; Harry Truman's "Truman Doctrine"; George C. Marshall's "Marshall Plan"; Winston Churchill's "Iron Curtain" speech; Harry Truman's "Statement Announcing Soviet's A-Bomb"; and other documents that support understanding of containment. Ask students to read each document and write a clear explanation of the way in which the document clarifies the U.S. policy of containment. Ask students to extend their analysis by explaining the historical context of each document (intended audience, purpose, and point of view) and placing the documents in chronological order. Next, organize students into collaborative groups and ask each group to create a timeline illustrating the significant historical events that led to the writing of each of the above documents. Ask students to use their evidence to write a thesis statement that addresses the following prompt: What were the most significant causes for the establishment of the policy of containment in the Cold War?

Chapter 24 — Bell Ringers

The following activities take no more than 5–15 minutes of your class period and offer an effective and engaging way to begin your lessons and for students to apply AP® Skills & Processes:

- Ask students to work in pairs to read the documents provided in the **AP® COMPARING INTERPRETATIONS** feature on p. 776. Each student should read one of the sources and then explain the interpretation to his or her partner. Then students can work together to answer the **AP® SHORT ANSWER PRACTICE** questions on p. 777.
- Provide students with the text of the loyalty oath used in the 1950s (for example, Levering Act from California, 1950), but do not provide any source information. Ask students to read the text and put this question on the board: Should the U.S. government require such a loyalty oath from citizens? Lead a brief discussion in which students debate this type of policy. Use this activity as an introduction to a discussion of the Red Scare and McCarthyism.
- Display a map illustrating areas of the world in which the Peace Corps engaged in major projects in the 1960s. Search "University of Iowa Peace Corps map." Then ask students to explain how this type of volunteer service can be viewed as part of the containment policy of the U.S. in the 1960s.

NOTES

TEACHING STRATEGY

The chapter introduction provides a clear link between the domestic and foreign policy dimensions of anticommunism, as it highlights Nixon's campaign and Truman's emerging support for the French against communist forces in Vietnam. The foreign-domestic link also helps explain the tremendous economic growth of the postwar United States — especially in Sunbelt locations like Los Angeles, where Nixon delivered his speech. Though the following chapter will explore the economic boom in more detail, the current chapter provides a hint about the way government spending on weapons and aerospace production fueled the economy, a point raised in the previous chapter regarding World War II. The opener also hints at the long duration of American involvement in Vietnam, which began with Truman — well before the first regular ground troops were sent in the spring of 1965. Likewise, while McCarthyism flourished in the early 1950s, its roots were much older. The Cold War is a fascinating topic with endless possibilities for primary source investigation. The Cold War Internet History Project, housed at the Wilson Center, offers a treasure trove of thousands of primary sources related to all aspects of the Cold War, many of them formerly classified government documents. To access this site, search "Cold War Internet History Project." For a complete suggested response to the **AP® LEARNING FOCUS** question, see p. 802.

24 CHAPTER

The Cold War Dawns

1945–1963

AP® LEARNING FOCUS

Why did the international rivalry of the Cold War create a climate of fear at home and how did it affect politics and society in the United States?

In the autumn of 1950, a California congressman named Richard M. Nixon stood before reporters in Los Angeles. The little-known Nixon was running for the Senate against his fellow House member Helen Gahagan Douglas, a Hollywood actress and New Deal Democrat. Nixon told the gathered journalists that Douglas had cast "Communist-leaning" votes and that she was "pink right down to her underwear" — meaning nearly *red*, a symbol of communism. Douglas's congressional record was not much different from Nixon's, but the accusation proved potent. Nixon defeated the "pink lady" with nearly 60 percent of the vote.

A few months earlier, U.S. tanks and planes had arrived in French Indochina, a French colonial possession comprised of present-day Vietnam, Laos, and Cambodia. President Harry S. Truman authorized $15 million worth of military supplies to aid France, which was resisting an independence movement led by Ho Chi Minh, a Vietnamese communist. According to Secretary of State Dean Acheson, the military help was not meant to preserve France's empire — but to curtail the influence of communism. Both the Soviet Union and China were supporting Ho's army. "Neither national independence nor democratic evolution exists in any area dominated by Soviet imperialism," Acheson warned ominously as he announced the aid.

Though seemingly different events on the surface, Nixon's political tactics in Los Angeles and American military aid for the French empire in Vietnam were both part of the Cold War — the geopolitical and ideological struggle between the capitalist, democratic United States and the communist, authoritarian Soviet Union. Both also signaled the return of heightened anticommunism to the center of American political life. Beginning in Europe as World War II ended and extending to Asia, Latin America, the Middle East, and Africa by the mid-1950s, the Cold War reshaped international relations and dominated global politics for more than forty years (see "Comparing Interpretations," p. 776).

As the scope and stakes of the Cold War became clear, the rivalry between the United States and Soviet Union affected Americans at home in a number of ways. A hostility to "subversives" in government, education, and the media gripped the United States. The escalating arms race between the two superpowers prompted Congress to spend heavily on defense, and gave rise to the military-industrial complex, the loose alliance between the Defense Department and the network of large corporations that built planes, munitions, and electronic devices. In politics, anticommunism challenged the liberal agenda of the New Deal coalition. The international and the domestic began to run together, a process that has continued into the twenty-first century as an enduring legacy of the Cold War.

772

CD
It can happen Here
JOIN
CIVIL DEFENSE
CIVIL DEFENSE RECRUITMENT SERIES 28
Contributed in the interest
© 1951 Promotional Services, Inc.
THE DEFENSE COUNCIL OF TEANECK

The Perils of the Cold War Americans, along with the rest of the world, lived under the threat of nuclear warfare during the tense years of the Cold War between the United States and the Soviet Union. This 1951 civil defense poster, with the message "It *can* happen Here," suggests that Americans should be prepared for such a dire outcome. swin ink 2/Corbis via Getty Images.

TEACHING STRATEGY

This photo illustrates the awesome power of nuclear weapons and the fascination Americans had with them at the time. While the poster makes a plea for civilians to join in protecting against a potential Soviet attack, the image actually depicts an American bomb test.

AP® SKILLS & PROCESSES

CONTINUITY AND CHANGE

Use the **TIMELINE** to help students begin thinking about how the period from 1945 to 1963 could constitute a distinct historical period. Students should note that the chapter focuses largely on foreign policy. Domestic considerations are limited to issues that were directly affected by the Cold War, such as the Red Scare and the demise of social reform programs.

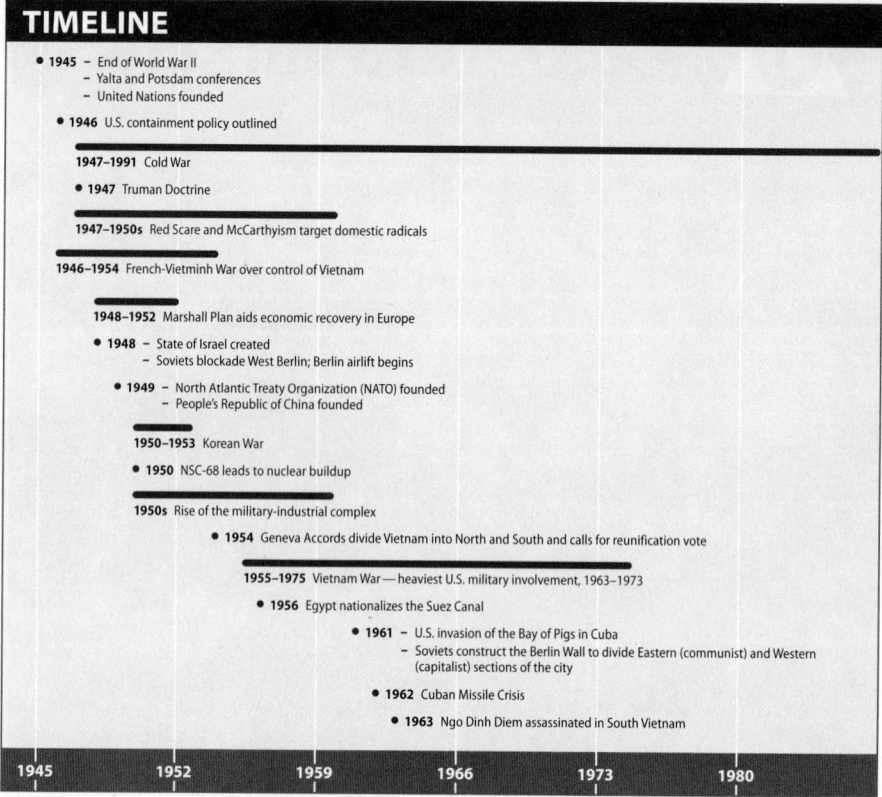

TIMELINE

- **1945** – End of World War II
  - Yalta and Potsdam conferences
  - United Nations founded
- **1946** U.S. containment policy outlined
- **1947–1991** Cold War
- **1947** Truman Doctrine
- **1947–1950s** Red Scare and McCarthyism target domestic radicals
- **1946–1954** French-Vietminh War over control of Vietnam
- **1948–1952** Marshall Plan aids economic recovery in Europe
- **1948** – State of Israel created
  - Soviets blockade West Berlin; Berlin airlift begins
- **1949** – North Atlantic Treaty Organization (NATO) founded
  - People's Republic of China founded
- **1950–1953** Korean War
- **1950** NSC-68 leads to nuclear buildup
- **1950s** Rise of the military-industrial complex
- **1954** Geneva Accords divide Vietnam into North and South and calls for reunification vote
- **1955–1975** Vietnam War—heaviest U.S. military involvement, 1963–1973
- **1956** Egypt nationalizes the Suez Canal
- **1961** – U.S. invasion of the Bay of Pigs in Cuba
  - Soviets construct the Berlin Wall to divide Eastern (communist) and Western (capitalist) sections of the city
- **1962** Cuban Missile Crisis
- **1963** Ngo Dinh Diem assassinated in South Vietnam

1945 | 1952 | 1959 | 1966 | 1973 | 1980

CONTAINMENT IN A DIVIDED WORLD

What primary factors caused the Cold War?

The Cold War followed on the heels of World War II and ended in 1991 with the dissolution of the Soviet Union. This protracted conflict placed two far-reaching questions at the center of global history: Would capitalism or communism dominate Europe and East Asia in the aftermath of war? How would the European colonies and former colonies throughout Asia, the Middle East, and Africa enter the world stage as independent nations? Each of the superpowers sought to dictate the answers, as the United States embarked on an unprecedented engagement with world affairs.

AP® EXAM TIP

Evaluate the role of the Yalta Conference in undermining wartime cooperation among the Allied powers.

Origins of the Cold War

With Germany and Japan defeated and Britain and France exhausted, only two geopolitical powers remained standing at the end of World War II. Little had united the United States and the Soviet Union, other than their commitment to defeating the Axis powers. It was likely that the Americans and Soviets would have jostled each

AP® APPLY THE TIP

Engage the class in a simulation of the Yalta Conference. Divide the class into teams to represent the following nations: U.S., Great Britain, France, Soviet Union, Germany, Poland, and Yugoslavia. Ask each team to discuss the role of their nation in World War II, the situation the nation faced in February of 1945, and the goals they would have in influencing the outcome at the Yalta Conference, using their textbook and outside resources. Each team should choose one person to represent them on the Yalta Conference panel in front of the class to stimulate the discussions that were held there. Each representative should present his or her arguments in order to get others to reach an agreement that benefits them. After the panel discusses the issues and comes to agreements, lead a class discussion debriefing the simulation and clarifying positions of nations at Yalta and shortly after it.

other as they moved to fill the postwar power vacuum, even if they shared a common set of interests. But the nations were so sharply divided — by geography, history, ideology, and strategic interest — that their rivalry hardened into a new kind of war.

Yalta President Franklin Roosevelt saw the American-Soviet alliance as essential for postwar global stability, even as World War II was still being fought. But FDR also believed that permanent peace and long-term American interests depended on the Wilsonian principles of collective security, self-determination, and free trade (see "Catastrophe at Versailles" in Chapter 20), which ran counter to Soviet aims. At the **Yalta Conference** of February 1945, these democratic ideals were trumped by the realities of power politics and military might. As Allied forces neared victory in Europe and advanced toward Japan in the Pacific, Roosevelt, Churchill, and Stalin met in Yalta, a resort on the Black Sea in southern Ukraine. Roosevelt focused on maintaining Allied unity and securing a Soviet commitment to enter the war against Japan. But the fate of Eastern Europe divided the Big Three. Stalin insisted that Russian national security required pro-Soviet governments in Eastern European nations. Roosevelt pressed for an agreement, the "Declaration on Liberated Europe," that guaranteed self-determination and democratic elections in Poland and other countries in the East. However, given that Soviet troops were already in control of much of Eastern Europe, FDR had to accept a lesser pledge from Stalin: to hold "free and unfettered elections" at a future time. The three leaders also formally committed to dividing Germany into four zones, each controlled by one Allied power (plus France), and to similarly partition the capital city, Berlin, which was located within the Soviet zone.

At the Yalta Conference, the Big Three also agreed to establish an international body to replace the discredited League of Nations. The new organization, to be known as the **United Nations**, would have both a General Assembly, in which all nations would be represented, and a Security Council composed of the five nations that prevailed over Germany and Japan — the United States, Britain, France, China, and the Soviet Union — and six other nations elected on a rotating basis (the number of rotating nations was increased to ten in 1965). The Big Three determined that the five permanent members of the Security Council would have veto power over decisions of the General Assembly. The United Nations was slated to convene for the first time in San Francisco on April 25, 1945. (The current U.N. headquarters in New York City opened in 1952.)

Potsdam Developments in the wake of the Yalta Conference hardened a split among the Allies, with the Soviets on one side and the Americans and British on the other. At the **Potsdam Conference** outside Berlin in late July and early August 1945, President Truman replaced the deceased Roosevelt. Inexperienced in world affairs, Truman found himself thrown into enormously complicated negotiations. His instinct told him to stand up to Soviet aggression. "Unless Russia is faced with an iron fist and strong language," he said, "another war is in the making." But Truman's bluster had no effect in Eastern Europe, where Soviet-imposed governments in Poland, Hungary, and Romania were backed by the Red Army. The

Yalta Conference
A meeting in Yalta of President Roosevelt, Prime Minister Churchill, and Soviet Premier Joseph Stalin in February 1945, in which the leaders discussed the treatment of Germany, the status of Poland, the creation of the United Nations, and Russian entry into the war against Japan.

United Nations
An international body founded in San Francisco in 1945, consisting of a General Assembly representing all nations, and a Security Council of the United States, Britain, France, China, the Soviet Union, and six other nations elected on a rotating basis.

Potsdam Conference
The conference, held in late July and early August 1945, in which Soviet Union leader Joseph Stalin accepted German reparations only from the Soviet zone, the eastern part of Germany, in exchange for American recognition of the Soviet-drawn Polish border. The agreement paved the way for the division of Germany into East and West.

Potsdam Conference British prime minister Winston Churchill and Soviet premier Joseph Stalin stand on opposite sides of U.S. president Harry Truman, shaking hands during the Potsdam Conference. Concluding mere days before the United States dropped an atomic bomb on Hiroshima, Japan, Potsdam determined the fate of postwar Germany and much of Eastern Europe. AFP/Getty Images

TEACHING STRATEGY

Throughout the spring of 1945, American forces continued to push German troops eastward while the Red Army pressed westward. It was only a matter of time before the two sides made contact. The first meeting was documented in morning report entries, available in high-resolution facsimile from the National Archives, along with a historic military map where contact first took place on April 25, 1945. To access these resources, search "National Archives People at War America and Russia meet."

AP® SKILLS & PROCESSES

ANALYZING HISTORICAL EVIDENCE

The **AP® COMPARING INTERPRETATIONS** feature explores the origins of the Cold War, a conflict that spanned the globe, lasted decades, and helped launch wars that led to the death of several million people in Asia and Latin America. It might be helpful for students to note that Ambrose wrote this edition of *Rise to Globalism* in early 1971, a time that was, in many ways, the height of the Cold War. Westad's text is obviously much more recent, written in a postwar context and at a time when both scholars and everyday Americans were already routinely thinking about globalism. Westad is from Norway, a founding member nation of NATO though one that was rarely at the center of U.S.-Soviet Cold War tensions. This might make him more attentive to the concerns of nations besides the two superpowers.

AP® COMPARING INTERPRETATIONS

How Did Cold War Interventions Differ Worldwide?

During World War II, the United States and the Soviet Union forged a "Grand Alliance" with Great Britain to defeat Hitler's Nazi Germany. In the wake of victory, however, this marriage of necessity quickly dissolved, leaving the Americans and Soviets to face each other in a Cold War that lasted until the dissolution of the Soviet Union (USSR) in 1991. For decades, these superpowers viewed each other's intentions with suspicion and waged proxy wars around the globe to advance the security interests they believed the other threatened. But how was the Cold War in Europe different from the Cold War in former colonized nations in Asia, Africa, and Latin America? Why did the U.S.-Soviet rivalry play out in divergent ways in these places?

Historians continue to study and debate these questions. Stephen Ambrose's account of postwar America's rise to global dominance offers a traditional explanation of the Cold War's origins in Europe. His argument differs from that of Odd Westad, who shifts the geographical focus of the Cold War rivalry from Europe itself to the rest of the globe.

STEPHEN AMBROSE

SOURCE: Stephen E. Ambrose, *Rise to Globalism: American Foreign Policy, 1938–1980* (Baltimore: Penguin Books, 1980, second revised edition), 92–94, 105.

There is no satisfactory date to mark the beginning of the Cold War, but it is certain that the issue that gave it life and shaped its early course, was East Europe. For centuries East and West have struggled with each other for control of the huge area running from the Baltic to the Balkans, an area rich in human and industrial resources and strategically vital to both sides, either to Russia as a buffer against the West, or to Germany and France as the gateway for an invasion of Russia. Neither the West nor the East has been willing to allow East Europe to be strong, independent, or neutral. Russia and the West each have wanted the area to be aligned with them.

. . . [During World War II], the West made no significant contribution to the liberation of East Europe, and when the end came the Red Army was in sole possession of the area east of a line drawn from Stettin on the Baltic to Trieste on the Adriatic. Russia controlled East Europe. This crucial result of World War II destroyed the Grand Alliance and gave birth to the Cold War.

The West, with America leading the way, was unwilling to accept Russian domination of East Europe. Although the Americans were ready to admit that Stalin had earned the right to have the major say in the politics of the region, and that Russian security demanded friendly governments there, they were not prepared to abandon East Europe altogether. They persisted in the illusion that it was possible to have East European governments that were both democratic and friendly to Russia. . . .

It was an impossible program. Given the traditions, economics, and social structures of East Europe, any freely elected government would certainly be anti-Soviet. It may be that FDR realized this fact, but if so he was unwilling to explain it to the American people. . . .

Many Americans, including leading figures in the government, believed that they could use their power to order the world in the direction of democratic capitalism on the American model. But it could not be, for a reason that most Americans did not like to think about, seldom discussed,

elections called for at Yalta eventually took place in Finland, Hungary, Bulgaria, and Czechoslovakia, with varying degrees of democratic openness. Nevertheless, Stalin got the client regimes he desired in those countries and would soon exert near-complete control over their governments. Stalin's unwillingness to honor self-determination for nations in Eastern Europe was, from the American point of view, the precipitating cause of the Cold War.

The question of Germany posed the biggest challenge at Potsdam. American officials believed that a revived German economy would ensure the prosperity of democratic regimes and capitalism throughout Western Europe — and prevent Germans from turning again to Nazism. Stalin had a more immediate objective: extracting reparations from Germany in the form of industrial machines and goods. To prevent the Soviets from dismantling German industry, and thereby impoverishing Germans for a generation, Truman and Secretary of State James Byrnes convinced Stalin to take reparations only from the Soviet zone, which was largely rural and held and frequently ignored. This was the simple fact that however great America's military and productive power was, it had limits. . . . [President] Truman [who replaced FDR in April 1945] had unprecedented power at his fingertips and a program for the world that he believed was self-evidently good. Yet he could not block Soviet expansion.

ODD WESTAD

Source: Odd Arne Westad, *The Global Cold War: Third World Interventions and the Making of Our Times* (Cambridge: Cambridge University Press, 2007), 3–5.

The concept "Third World" came into being in the early 1950s, first in French and then in English, and gained prominence after the Bandung [in Indonesia] conference of 1955, when leaders from Asia and Africa met for the first large postcolonial summit. . . . [T]he term "Third World" implied "the people" on a world scale, the global majority who had been downtrodden and enslaved through colonialism, but who were now on their way to the top of the ladder of influence. The concept also implied a distinct position in Cold War terms, the refusal to be ruled by the superpowers and their ideologies, the search for alternatives both to capitalism and Communism, a "third way" . . . for the newly liberated states.

My use of these terms may therefore be seen to point in two opposing directions: the term "Cold War" signals Western elite projects on the grandest of possible scales, while the term "Third World" indicates colonial and postcolonial processes of marginalization (and the struggle against these processes). . . .

[T]he argument that the Cold War conceptually and analytically does not belong in the south [i.e., Africa, South Asia, and Latin America] is wrong, mainly for two reasons. First, US and Soviet interventionisms to a very large extent shaped both the international and the domestic framework within which political, social, and cultural changes in Third World countries took place. Without the Cold War, Africa, Asia, and possibly also Latin America would have been very different regions today. Second, Third World elites often framed their own political agendas in conscious response to the models of development presented by the two main contenders of the Cold War, the United States and the Soviet Union. In many cases the Third World leaders' choices of ideological allegiance brought them into close collaboration with one or the other of the superpowers, and led them to subscribe to models of [economic] development that proved disastrous for their own peoples. . . .

This book argues that the United States and the Soviet Union were driven to intervene in the Third World by the ideologies inherent in their politics. Locked in conflict over the very concept of European modernity [whether "modern" people should value the individual or the collective: capitalism or socialism] — to which both states regarded themselves as successors — Washington and Moscow needed to change the world in order to prove the universal applicability of their ideologies, and the elites of the newly independent [Third World] states proved fertile ground for their competition. By helping to expand the domains of freedom or of social justice, both powers saw themselves as assisting natural trends in world history and as defending their own security at the same time. Both saw a specific mission in and for the Third World that only their own state could carry out and which without their involvement would flounder in local hands.

AP® SHORT ANSWER PRACTICE

1. Identify the major difference in these two scholars' understanding of the Cold War's geographical focus.
2. What does a focus on Eastern Europe (Ambrose) reveal about the motivations of the United States and Soviet Union in the Cold War? What does a focus on the postcolonial world or "Third World" (Westad) reveal? To what extent do these scholars agree on the factors driving the Cold War rivalry between the United States and the Soviet Union?
3. Identify in Chapter 24 the different dimensions of the Cold War discussed by Ambrose and Westad? Use evidence from the chapter to explain the policy context of each historian's perspective.

TRM Find complete suggested responses in the Teacher's Resource Materials.

little wealth or industry to plunder. In exchange, the Americans recognized a redrawn German-Polish border favored by Stalin. Compromises had been reached, but each side left Potsdam distrustful of the other (Map 24.1).

The secret negotiations at Yalta and Potsdam demonstrated that the United States and the Soviet Union had starkly different postwar objectives. A subsequent public war of words only intensified those differences. In February 1946, Stalin proclaimed in a speech that, "the unevenness of development of the capitalist countries" was likely to produce "violent disturbance" and even another war. He seemed to position blame for any future war on the capitalist West. Churchill responded in kind a month later. While visiting Truman's home state of Missouri to be honored for his wartime leadership, Churchill accused Stalin of drawing an "iron curtain" around Eastern Europe and allowing "police government" to rule its people. He went further, claiming that "the fraternal association of the English-speaking peoples," and not Russians, ought to set the terms of the postwar world.

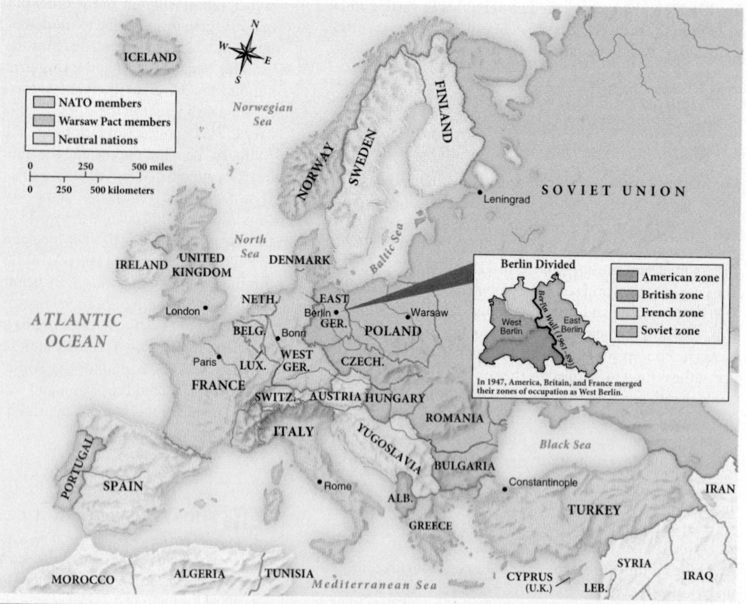

MAPPING THE PAST

MAP 24.1 Cold War in Europe, 1955

This map vividly shows the Cold War division of Europe. The NATO countries (colored green) are allies of the United States; the Warsaw Pact countries (in purple) are allied to the USSR. In 1955, West Germany had just been admitted to NATO, completing Europe's stabilization into two rival camps. But Berlin remained divided, and one can see from its location deep in East Germany why the former capital was always a flash point in Cold War controversies.

ANALYZING THE MAP: Using the map key, locate all the NATO, Warsaw Pact, and neutral countries. Note the position of Greece and Turkey relative to other NATO countries.

MAKING CONNECTIONS: How does the map illustrate the containment strategy? How does the map illustrate change in the role of the United States in the world? Why would the position of Greece and Turkey cause conflicts in the early Cold War?

AP® SKILLS & PROCESSES

COMPARISON

How did American and Soviet viewpoints differ over the postwar fate of Europe?

The nations of Europe had barely known peace before the tense standoff between the Soviet Union and the United States threatened another war. Stalin was intent on establishing client states in Eastern Europe, and the United States was equally intent on reviving Germany and establishing a system to ensure collective security in Western Europe. Among the Allies, anxiety about a Nazi victory in World War II had been quickly replaced by the threat of a potentially cataclysmic war with the Soviet Union.

The Containment Strategy

containment
The basic U.S. policy of the Cold War, which sought to contain communism within its existing geographic boundaries. Initially, containment focused on the Soviet Union and Eastern Europe, but in the 1950s it came to include China, Korea, and the postcolonial world.

In the late 1940s, American officials developed a strategy toward the Soviet Union that would become known as **containment**. Convinced that the USSR sought to methodically expand its reach, the United States would counter by limiting Soviet influence to Eastern Europe while reconstituting democratic governments in Western Europe. Three broad issues worried Truman and his advisors. First, the Soviet Union was pressing Iran for access to oil and Turkey for access to the Mediterranean. Second,

TEACHING STRATEGY

MAP 24.1 provides a clear delineation of the states that ended up in each superpower's respective sphere of influence, as well as those nations that — largely, though not completely, due to their location between the two — chose to remain neutral. Students are often confused about the division of Germany compared with the division of Berlin. It may be helpful to show them that Berlin, functionally divided in two, was deep within East Germany. Thus, West Berlin was ultimately completely surrounded by a power hostile to its independent existence.

TRM Find complete suggested responses in the Teacher's Resource Materials.

AP® SKILLS & PROCESSES

COMPARISON

Use the **COMPARISON** question to contrast the views of the two superpowers regarding the fate of postwar Europe. It might be helpful for students to create a chart that allows them to compare both economic and strategic differences between the two nations. It is worth noting that the Soviet desire for a weakened Germany had little to do with communist ideology; instead, it stemmed from a concern for security. Extend this prompt by asking students to identify points of shared interest between the U.S. and Soviet Union.

TRM Find complete suggested responses in the Teacher's Resource Materials.

CHECK FOR UNDERSTANDING

Ask students: **What factors explain the origins of the Cold War?** *The U.S. and Soviet Union were divided by geography, history, ideology, and strategic interest. At Yalta, the two nations disagreed over Eastern Europe, with FDR wanting open elections and Stalin insisting on pro-Soviet governments as a protection against future German invasion. At Potsdam, the U.S. and Soviet Union disagreed over the fate of Germany. The U.S. wanted Germany's economy restored as soon as possible to ensure a stable Europe, but the Soviet Union wanted to keep Germany weak while extracting reparations.*

a civil war roiled Greece, between monarchists backed by Great Britain and insurgents supported by the Greek and Yugoslavian Communist parties. Third, as European nations suffered through terrible privation in 1946 and 1947, Communist parties gained strength, particularly in France and Italy. All three developments, as seen from the United States, threatened to spread Soviet influence beyond Eastern Europe.

AP® EXAM TIP

Being able to explain the policy of containment is critical to success on the AP® Exam.

Toward an Uneasy Peace In this anxious context, the strategy of containment emerged gradually between 1946 and 1949. In February 1946, American diplomat George F. Kennan first proposed the idea in an 8,000-word cable — a confidential message within the U.S. State Department — sent from his post at the U.S. embassy in Moscow. Kennan argued that communism was merely a flimsy cover masking Soviet imperial aggression. A year after writing this cable (dubbed the Long Telegram), Kennan argued in an influential *Foreign Affairs* article that the West's only recourse was to meet the Soviets "with unalterable counter-force at every point where they show signs of encroaching upon the interests of a peaceful and stable world." Kennan called for "long-term, patient but firm and vigilant containment of Russian expansive tendencies."

Kennan contended that the Soviet system was unstable and would eventually collapse. Containment would work, he reasoned, as long as the United States and its allies resisted Soviet expansion worldwide. Kennan's attentive readers included Stalin himself, who quickly obtained a copy of the classified Long Telegram. Just as Kennan thought that the Soviet system was despotic and unsustainable, Stalin believed that the United States was an imperialist aggressor determined to replace Great Britain as the world's dominant capitalist power. Neither side fully understood or trusted the other, and each projected its worst fears onto its rival.

It was true that Britain was fading as an international power. Exhausted by the war, faced with budget deficits and a collapsing economy at home, and confronted with growing independence movements throughout its empire, particularly in India led by Mohandas Gandhi, the sun was finally setting on British global influence. "The reins of world leadership are fast slipping from Britain's competent but now very weak hands," read a U.S. State Department report. "These reins will be picked up either by the United States or by Russia." The United States was wedded to the notion — dating to the Wilson administration — that communism and capitalism were incompatible on the world stage. With Britain waning, American officials saw little choice but to fill its shoes as the leading capitalist nation worldwide.

In February 1947, London informed Washington that it could no longer afford to support the anticommunists in the Greek civil war. Truman worried that a communist victory in Greece would lead to Soviet domination of the eastern Mediterranean and embolden Communist parties elsewhere. In response, the president announced what became known as the **Truman Doctrine**. In a speech on March 12, he asserted an American responsibility "to support free peoples who are resisting attempted subjugation by armed minorities or by outside pressures." To that end, Truman proposed large-scale financial assistance for Greece and Turkey (then involved in a dispute with the Soviet Union over access to the Mediterranean). "If we falter in our leadership, we may endanger the peace of the world," Truman declared (see "Thinking Like a Historian," p. 780). Congress quickly approved Truman's request for $300 million in aid to Greece and $100 million for Turkey.

Truman Doctrine
President Harry S. Truman's commitment to "support free peoples who are resisting attempted subjugation by armed minorities or by outside pressures." First applied to Greece and Turkey in 1947, it became the justification for U.S. intervention into several countries during the Cold War.

Soviet expansionism was but one part of a larger unfolding drama. Europe was sliding into economic chaos. The winter of 1946–1947 brought the worst economic conditions in memory to a continent still reeling from the war. People starved, wages stagnated, and consumer markets collapsed. For both humanitarian and political reasons, Truman's advisors believed action was necessary. A global depression might ensue if the European economy, the largest foreign market for American goods, did not recover. Worse, unemployed and dispirited Western Europeans might join communist movements, threatening political stability. Secretary of State George C. Marshall came up with a remarkable proposal: a massive infusion of American capital to rebuild the European economy. In a June 1947 speech, Marshall laid out a daring

AP® EXAM TIP

Describe how the use of international aid impacted the policy of containment.

AP® APPLY THE TIP

Provide students with excerpts from "Sources of Soviet Conduct" by George Kennan. (To access this source, search "Teaching American History Sources of Soviet Conduct.") Ask students to read the excerpt closely and use the text to outline Kennan's main arguments regarding Soviet communism and the proper policy of the U.S. in response to the Soviet threat. Lead a class discussion on how Kenman's advice impacted the U.S.'s relations with nations other than the Soviet Union. As a follow-up, ask students to complete **Handout 24.1 — Contextualization: Containment (TRM)** to extend your discussion on the development of the policy of containment in the U.S.

TRM Find complete **Handout 24.1 — Contextualization: Containment** in the Teacher's Resource Materials.

AP® THEME

WOR: America in the World; WXT: Work, Exchange, and Technology

In the postwar era, tensions between the U.S. and the Soviet Union quickly dissolved the wartime alliance, and the U.S. developed a foreign policy based on collective security, international aid, and economic institutions in support of non-Communist nations.

TEACHING STRATEGY

The Our Documents Web site provides a high-resolution facsimile copy of the Truman Doctrine speech, along with a transcription and a brief introductory paragraph. To access these resources, search "Our Documents Truman Doctrine (1947)."

TEACHING STRATEGY

One of the aspects of the Truman Doctrine that students too often overlook is the importance of when political and physical geography mesh. For instance, have students locate the Dardanelles Straits and explain why this would be a contributing factor to the importance of Greece and Turkey in the context of the Truman Doctrine.

AP® SKILLS & PROCESSES

ANALYZING HISTORICAL EVIDENCE

Use the **AP® THINKING LIKE A HISTORIAN** feature to provide students with the opportunity to explore a major transformation in American foreign policy, one that has arguably shaped American policy ever since. While George Kennan primarily emphasized economic and diplomatic forms of containment, the U.S. shifted in 1950 to military intervention, beginning with the struggle in Korea and culminating nearly two decades later with 500,000 troops in South Vietnam at the peak of American involvement. Though the NSC-68 memo is not explicitly mentioned here, it should be included in students' assessment, as it provided the justification for this significant shift in U.S. policy.

AP® THINKING LIKE A HISTORIAN

The Global Cold War

Until the outbreak of the Korean War on June 25, 1950, the U.S. policy of containment was confined to economic measures, such as financial assistance to Greece and Turkey and the Marshall Plan, and focused on Europe. That changed between 1950 and 1954. In those years, containment became militarized, and its scope was expanded to include Asia and Latin America. What had begun as a limited policy to contain Soviet influence in war-torn Europe had by the mid-1950s become a global campaign against communism and social revolution.

1. **President Harry S. Truman, address before joint session of Congress, March 12, 1947.** *Known as the Truman Doctrine, this speech outlined Truman's plan to give large-scale assistance to Greece and Turkey as part of a broader anticommunist policy.*

To ensure the peaceful development of nations, free from coercion, the United States has taken a leading part in establishing the United Nations. The United Nations is designed to make possible lasting freedom and independence for all its members. We shall not realize our objectives, however, unless we are willing to help free peoples to maintain their free institutions and their national integrity against aggressive movements that seek to impose upon them totalitarian regimes. . . .

At the present moment in world history nearly every nation must choose between alternative ways of life. The choice is too often not a free one.

One way of life is based upon the will of the majority, and is distinguished by free institutions, representative government, free elections, guarantees of individual liberty, freedom of speech and religion, and freedom from political oppression.

The second way of life is based upon the will of a minority forcibly imposed upon the majority. It relies upon terror and oppression, a controlled press and radio; fixed elections, and the suppression of personal freedoms.

I believe that it must be the policy of the United States to support free peoples who are resisting attempted subjugation by armed minorities or by outside pressures.

I believe that we must assist free peoples to work out their own destinies in their own way.

I believe that our help should be primarily through economic and financial aid which is essential to economic stability and orderly political processes.

2. **President of South Korea Syngman Rhee, Criticism of U.S. policy toward Korea, 1950.** *Shortly before North Korean troops invaded South Korea on June 25, 1950, the president of South Korea, an American ally, pressed the United States for military assistance.*

A few days ago one American friend said that if the U.S. gave weapons to South Korea, she feared that South Korea would invade North Korea. This is a useless worry of some Americans, who do not know South Korea. Our present war is not a Cold War, but a real shooting war. Our troops will take all possible counter-measures. . . . In South Korea the U.S. has one foot in South Korea and one foot outside so that in case of an unfavorable situation it could pull out of the country. I daresay that if the U.S. wants to aid our country, it should not be only lip-service.

3. **Secretary of State Dean Acheson, Testimony regarding the Korean War before the Senate Armed Forces and Foreign Relations Committee, 1951.** *The American secretary of state explains North Korea's invasion of the South, which precipitated the Korean War, as a form of "aggression" that could not be met with "appeasement," employing the Munich analogy of European leaders appeasing Hitler in 1938.*

The attack on Korea was . . . a challenge to the whole system of collective security, not only in the Far East, but everywhere in the world. It was a threat to all nations newly arrived at independence. . . .

This was a test which would decide whether our collective security system would survive or would crumble. It would determine whether other nations would be intimidated by this show of force. . . .

As a people we condemn aggression of any kind. We reject appeasement of any kind. If we stood with our arms folded while Korea was swallowed up, it would have meant abandoning our principles, and it would have meant the defeat of the collective security system on which our own safety ultimately depends.

4. **Prime minister of Japan Shigeru Yoshida, speech before the Japanese Diet (parliament), July 14, 1950.** *The prime minister of Japan expresses his concern that the war in Korea might engulf his nation, which was militarily dependent on the United States.*

It is heartening . . . that America and so many members of the United Nations have gone to the rescue of an invaded country regardless of the heavy sacrifices involved. In case a war breaks out on an extensive scale how would Japan's security be preserved [since we are disarmed]? . . . This has been hotly discussed. However, the measures taken by the United Nations have done much to stabilize our people's minds.

5. Secretary of State John Foster Dulles, radio and television address to the American people about the coup in Guatemala, June 30, 1954. *Elected as Guatemala's president in 1951, Jacobo Arbenz Guzmán pursued reform policies that threatened large landholders, including the United Fruit Company, an American business. In 1954, the United States CIA engineered a coup that overthrew Arbenz Guzmán and replaced him with Carlos Castillo Armas, a colonel in the Guatemalan military.*

Tonight I should like to speak with you about Guatemala. It is the scene of dramatic events. They expose the evil purpose of the Kremlin to destroy the inter-American system, and they test the ability of the American States to maintain the peaceful integrity of the hemisphere.

For several years international communism has been probing here and there for nesting places in the Americas. It finally chose Guatemala as a spot which it could turn into an official base from which to breed subversion which would extend to other American Republics.

This intrusion of Soviet despotism was, of course, a direct challenge to our Monroe Doctrine [which declared U.S. dominion over the Western Hemisphere], the first and most fundamental of our foreign policies.

6. Guatemalan foreign minister Guillermo Toriello, speech to delegates at the Tenth Inter-American Conference of the Organization of American States in Caracas, Venezuela, March 5, 1954. *Two months before the Central Intelligence Agency (CIA) orchestrated a coup against the democratically elected president of Guatemala, that country's foreign minister sharply criticized the United States for its support of the United Fruit Company [a major American corporation in Guatemala] rather than the "legitimate desires" of the Guatemalan people.*

What is the real and effective reason for describing our government as communist? From what sources comes the accusation that we threaten continental solidarity and security? Why do they [United States] wish to intervene in Guatemala?

The answers are simple and evident. The plan of national liberation being carried out with firmness by my government has necessarily affected the privileges of the foreign enterprises that are impeding the progress and the economic development of the country. . . . With construction of publically owned ports and docks, we are putting an end to the monopoly of the United Fruit Company. . . .

They wanted to find a ready expedient to maintain the economic dependence of the American Republics and suppress the legitimate desires of their peoples, cataloguing as "communism" every manifestation of nationalism or economic independence, any desire for social progress, any intellectual curiosity, and any interest in progressive and liberal reforms.

7. Herblock cartoon from the *Washington Post*, February 11, 1962. *Many Latin American countries were beset by a wide gap between a small wealthy elite and the mass of ordinary, much poorer citizens. American officials worried that this made social revolution an attractive alternative for those at the bottom.*

Source: A 1962 Herblock Cartoon, © The Herb Block Foundation.

Sources: (1) The Avalon Project at avalon.law.yale.edu; (2) Reinhard Drifte, "Japan's Involvement in the Korean War," in *The Korean War in History*, ed. James Cotton and Ian Neary (Atlantic Highlands, NJ: Humanities Press International, 1989), 43; (3) Glenn D. Paige, *The Korean Decision* (New York: The Free Press, 1968), 175–176; (4) Drifte, 122; (5) Jonathan L. Fried et al., eds., *Guatemala in Rebellion: Unfinished History* (New York: Grove Press, 1983), 78; (6) Stephen C. Schlesinger and Stephen Kinzer, *Bitter Fruit: The Untold Story of the American Coup in Guatemala* (Garden City, NY: Doubleday, 1982), 143–144.

ANALYZING THE EVIDENCE

1. In source 1, Truman presents the choice facing the world in stark terms: totalitarianism or democracy. Why would he frame matters in this way in 1947? What was the purpose of this speech? How did Truman anticipate the militarization of the containment strategy, which did not take place until the Korean War?
2. Analyze the audience, purpose, and point of view presented in the documents dealing with the war in Korea (sources 2–4). What does Acheson mean by "collective security" and "appeasement"? Why is Yoshida thankful for the UN intervention? What can you infer about U.S. involvement in world affairs during the postwar period based on these documents?
3. In document 6, how does Toriello characterize accusations that the elected Guatemalan government is communist? What are his accusations of the United States? Compare the main ideas in documents 5 and 6. How do the documents inform the analysis of one another?
4. How does source 7 express one of the obstacles to democracy in developing nations?

AP® DBQ PRACTICE

Using these documents, and based on what you have learned in class and in this chapter, write an essay in which you analyze the role of the Korean War (1950–1953) and the 1954 Guatemalan coup in shaping American foreign policy and perceptions of the United State abroad in the early years of the Cold War.

TRM Find complete suggested responses in the Teacher's Resource Materials.

AP® SKILLS & PROCESSES

ARGUMENTATION

The **AP® DBQ PRACTICE** prompt asks students to analyze the goals of American foreign policy, specifically as it relates to the Korean War and Guatemalan coup, though to do this effectively they will need to track the nation's shifting goals, clearly identifying pre-1950 and post-1950 objectives. Students are also required to account for the global perceptions of the United States during the Cold War.

TEACHING STRATEGY

The Library of Congress provides an online exhibit on the Marshall Plan with links to more than a dozen related photographs, documents, and political cartoons. To access this exhibit, search "LOC Marshall Plan."

AP® SKILLS & PROCESSES

MAKING CONNECTIONS

The **MAKING CONNECTIONS** question asks students to explain the introduction of the Marshall Plan in the context of the post-war period and the emerging Cold War. Students might consider various reasons for the plan, including those based on altruism and those based on American self-interest. Students could also consider why the U.S. did not want the Soviet Union to participate in this program — they did, for example, accept Soviet involvement in the United Nations' Security Council — as well as factors Stalin might have weighed in deciding whether or not to join.

TRM Find complete suggested responses in the Teacher's Resource Materials.

Marshall Plan
Aid program begun in 1948 to help European economies recover from World War II.

AP® SKILLS & PROCESSES
MAKING CONNECTIONS
Why did the United States enact the Marshall Plan, and how did the program illustrate America's new role in the world?

North Atlantic Treaty Organization (NATO)
Military alliance formed in 1949 among the United States, Canada, and Western European nations to counter any possible Soviet threat.

Warsaw Pact
A military alliance established in Eastern Europe in 1955 to counter the NATO alliance; it included Albania, Bulgaria, Czechoslovakia, East Germany, Hungary, Poland, Romania, and the Soviet Union.

challenge to the nations of Europe: work out a comprehensive recovery program, and U.S. aid would finance it.

This pledge of financial assistance, known as the **Marshall Plan**, still required approval from a skeptical Congress. Republicans castigated the proposal as a huge "international WPA," their criticism harkening back to the New Deal. But on February 25, 1948, in the midst of a congressional stalemate, Stalin supported a communist-led coup in Czechoslovakia. Congress rallied and voted overwhelmingly to approve the financial plan. Over the next four years, the United States contributed $13 billion to a highly successful recovery effort. European industrial production increased by 64 percent, and Communist parties faded in Western European politics. Markets for American goods grew stronger and fostered economic interdependence between Europe and the United States. However, the Marshall Plan also intensified Cold War tensions. American officials invited the Soviets to participate but insisted on terms that virtually guaranteed Stalin's refusal. An embittered Stalin did just that, and ordered Soviet client states to follow his lead.

East and West As the most important industrial economy and the strategic linchpin of Europe, Germany remained a flash point for a potential hot war. When no agreement could be reached with the Soviet Union to unify the four zones of occupation, the Western allies consolidated their three zones in 1947. They then prepared to establish an independent federal German republic, with an economy jump-started by the Marshall Plan. Funds were also slated for West Berlin, in hopes of creating a capitalist showplace 100 miles inside the Soviet zone.

Stung by the West's plans, Stalin blockaded all traffic to West Berlin in June 1948. Instead of dropping West Berlin from Marshall Plan funding, as Stalin had expected, Truman and the British grew more resolute. "We are going to stay, period," Truman said plainly. Over the next year, American and British pilots improvised the Berlin Airlift, which flew 2.5 million tons of food and fuel into the Western zones of the city — nearly a ton for each resident. The Soviets did not retaliate against the airlift, however, and on May 12, 1949, Stalin lifted the blockade. The Berlin standoff was the closest the two sides came to actual war prior to the Cuban missile crisis of 1962 (see "Crises in Cuba and Berlin," ahead in this chapter).

The Marshall Plan A poster declaring, in German, that "The Marshall Plan Helps Europe." A waiting family sees the arrival from the United States of goods labeled "ERP," which stands for the European Recovery Program, the Marshall Plan's official name. Album/Alamy Stock Photo

The survival of a democratic West Berlin became a symbol of resistance to communism and motivated Western European nations to forge a collective security pact with the United States. In April 1949, the United States secured that pact, the **North Atlantic Treaty Organization (NATO)**, the country's first peacetime military alliance outside the Western hemisphere. Under the NATO treaty, twelve nations — Belgium, Canada, Denmark, France, Great Britain, Iceland, Italy, Luxembourg, the Netherlands, Norway, Portugal, and the United States — agreed that "an armed attack against one or more of them in Europe or North America shall be considered an attack against them all." In May 1949, those nations also agreed to the creation of the Federal Republic of Germany (West Germany), which eventually joined NATO in 1955.

In response, the Soviet Union established the German Democratic Republic (East Germany); the Council for Mutual Economic Assistance (COMECON); and, in 1955, the **Warsaw Pact**, a military alliance for Eastern Europe that included Albania, Bulgaria, Czechoslovakia, East Germany, Hungary, Poland, Romania, and the Soviet Union. These parallel steps bore out Churchill's 1946 claim that an "iron curtain" stretching "from Stettin in the Baltic to Trieste in the Adriatic" now divided Europe. Stalin's tactics were often ruthless, but they were not without reason. The Soviet Union acted out of the sort of self-interest long practiced by powerful nations — ensuring a defensive perimeter of allies, seeking access to raw materials, and pressing the advantage earned at great cost in war.

NSC-68 Atomic developments also played a critical role in the emergence of the Cold War. The United States had entertained the possibility of sharing its nuclear technology following the surrender of Japan, but did not wish to lose a key advantage over the Soviet Union. A 1946 American proposal for United Nations oversight of atomic energy would have assured near-total control of the technology by the United States. The proposal was rejected by the Soviets and only added to mounting tensions. America's brief tenure as sole nuclear power ended in late August 1949, however, when the USSR successfully tested an atomic bomb in what is now Kazakhstan.

The Berlin Airlift For 321 days, U.S. planes like this one flew missions to bring food and other supplies to Berlin after the Soviet Union had blocked all surface routes into the former German capital. The blockade was finally lifted on May 12, 1949, after the Soviets conceded that it had been a failure. AP Photo.

In the wake of this major shift in the balance of power, Truman turned to a new government advisory board for a strategic reassessment. Congress had established the U.S. National Security Council (NSC) via the National Security Act of 1947 — which brought together the State and Defense Departments, as well as intelligence analysts from the military branches and CIA — and tasked it with advising the president on vital matters of foreign affairs. In April 1950, the NSC delivered the report Truman had requested, known as **NSC-68**. Bristling with alarmist rhetoric, the document marked a decisive turning point in U.S. Cold War strategy. The report's authors described the Soviet Union not as a typical great power but as one with a "fanatic faith" that seeks to "impose its absolute authority." Going beyond even the stern language used by George Kennan, NSC-68 cast Soviet ambitions as nothing short of "the domination of the Eurasian landmass."

NSC-68
Top-secret government report of April 1950 warning that national survival in the face of Soviet communism required a massive military buildup.

To prevent that outcome, the report proposed "a bold and massive program of rebuilding the West's defensive potential to surpass that of the Soviet world." The new program would include the development of a hydrogen bomb, a thermonuclear device that would be a thousand times more destructive than the atomic bombs dropped on Japan, as well as dramatic increases in conventional forces. Critically, NSC-68 called for Americans to pay higher taxes and to accept further sacrifices out of a national unity of purpose. Many historians see the report as having "militarized" the American approach to the Cold War, which had to that point relied largely on economic measures such as the Marshall Plan. Truman was reluctant to commit to the drastic defense buildup called for in NSC-68, fearing that it would overburden the national budget. But events in Asia would soon lead him to reverse course.

AP® EXAM TIP
Summarize the debates over increasing reliance on nuclear weapons and the power of the military-industrial complex.

Containment in Asia

American officials believed that rebuilding the Japanese economy and dismantling Japan's military would ensure prosperity and contain communism in East Asia — much like their approach in the case of Germany. Following Japan's surrender, American occupation forces under General Douglas MacArthur drafted a democratic constitution and paved the way for the restoration of Japanese sovereignty in 1951. Considering the scorched-earth war that had just ended, this was a remarkable achievement, owed partly to the imperious MacArthur but mainly to the Japanese,

TEACHING STRATEGY

The PBS *American Experience* film *The Berlin Airlift* captures the drama and tension associated with this important early Cold War moment. The Truman Library provides several different lesson plans related to the Berlin Airlift. To access these resources, search "PBS Berlin Airlift" and "Truman Library Berlin Airlift lessons," respectively.

TEACHING STRATEGY

The full text of the once-secret NSC-68 memo is available online. Each section of the report is hyperlinked for quick access to specific parts of the text, including conclusions and recommendations. To access this document, search "Federation of American Scientists NSC-68."

TEACHING STRATEGY

The PBS *American Experience* film *Race for the Superbomb* explores the decision to develop and test a hydrogen bomb. The companion site provides an assortment of primary sources, timelines, biographies of key people, and a classroom guide to help students understand the development of military nuclear weapons and their significance. To access this film, search "American Experience Race for the Superbomb."

CHECK FOR UNDERSTANDING

Ask students: **What was containment strategy and how did it evolve?** *American diplomat George F. Kennan first expressed the notion of containment in a long 1946 cable sent from Moscow, arguing that the U.S. needed to forcefully contain a Soviet tendency toward expansion. President Truman enacted a containment-based foreign policy in the Truman Doctrine, providing aid to Greece and Turkey to prevent a communist overthrow. Marshall Plan support for the rebuilding of Europe was also a key element of containment, as was the formation of NATO as a defensive alliance. NSC-68 in 1950 argued that containment should be expanded to include more aggressive military confrontation.*

TEACHING STRATEGY

Ask students to weigh the relative success of different policies that were designed to support the policy of Containment. For instance, have students weight the relative success of the following actions by the United States at the start of the Cold War: Truman Doctrine, Marshall Plan, and Berlin Airlift. The goal of the exercise is not to dismiss one as not successful; rather, the objective is to have students think through the varying levels of success in Cold War policy in the immediate aftermath of World War II.

TEACHING STRATEGY

To help students understand more about Stalin, use Julia Kenny's helpful introduction to Stalin's cult of personality, which explores Stalin's tsarist roots, his emergence from Lenin's shadow, methods of enforcing his cult, and questions about whether Soviets "genuinely subscribed" to it. To access this resource, search "York Historian Stalin's cult of personality."

AP® APPLY THE TIP

In the **AP® APPLY THE TIP** on p. 779, students analyzed containment policy as expressed by George Kennan. Ask students to read pp. 784–787 and evaluate U.S. policy in the Korean War as an expression of containment policy. Organize students into groups to evaluate the ways in which the U.S.'s policy in fighting the Korean War differed from its policy in fighting World War II. Each group should write a thesis statement responding to the following prompt: To what degree was the Korean War a transformative event in American foreign policy? As a class, discuss each group's thesis statement and identify evidence that can be used to support them. Lead a discussion on the contextualization of America's policy in the Korean War.

TEACHING STRATEGY

The Truman Library provides useful resources for teaching about Executive Order 9981, including a high-resolution facsimile of the order, a transcribed version, a chronology of events surrounding the decision, and links to dozens of documents from 1938 through the end of the Korean War exploring the precursors and consequences of desegregation. To access these resources, search "Truman Library Executive Order 9981."

TEACHING STRATEGY

While millions died and many more suffered from the hostilities, the nation often collectively "forgot" about or ignored the Korean War — and its veterans — after it ended. The PBS film *Unforgettable: The Korean War* uses historical movies, photos, and personal recollections to reveal the individual stories behind the war. To access this film, search "PBS Unforgettable: The Korean War."

Communist China Chinese Communists carry placards with pictures of Joseph Stalin, premier of the Soviet Union and self-proclaimed leader of global communism. Under the leadership of General Mao Zedong, the Communist Party of China defeated its rivals in a civil war and founded the People's Republic of China in 1949. Mao's victory meant that from East Germany to the Pacific Ocean, much of the Eurasian landmass (including Eastern Europe, the Soviet Union, and China) was ruled by Communist governments. Library of Congress/Corbis/VCG via Getty Images.

who embraced peace and accepted U.S. military protection. However, events on the mainland of Asia proved much more challenging to American interests.

Civil War in China A civil war had been raging in China since the 1930s, subsiding during the Japanese occupation only to reignite in 1945. Communists led by Mao Zedong (Mao Tse-tung) battled Nationalist forces under Jiang Jieshi (Chiang Kai-shek). Fearing a Communist victory, between 1945 and 1949 the United States provided $2 billion to Jiang's army. Pressing Truman to "save" China, conservative Republican senator Robert A. Taft of Ohio predicted that "the Far East is ultimately even more important to our future peace than is Europe." By 1949, Mao's forces held the advantage, and Truman reasoned that saving Jiang would require military intervention. Unwilling to go to war in China, he cut off support and left the Nationalists to their fate. Jiang's forces retreated and ultimately fled to Taiwan, and the People's Republic of China was formally established under Mao's leadership on October 1, 1949.

AP® EXAM TIP

Recognize the Korean War as an expression of containment policy through military action.

Truman expected Mao to take an independent line from Moscow, as the Communist leader Tito had just done in Yugoslavia. But the new Chinese leader aligned himself with the Soviet Union, partly out of fear that the United States would re-arm the Nationalists and invade the mainland. As Cold War attitudes hardened, many Americans viewed Mao's success as a defeat for the United States. The pro-Chinese Nationalist "China lobby" held Truman's State Department responsible for the "loss" of China. Sensitive to these charges, the Truman administration refused to recognize "Red China" and blocked its admission to the United Nations. But the United States also pointedly declined to guarantee Taiwan's independence, and in fact accepted the outcome on the mainland.

The Korean War As a result of President Truman's 1948 Executive Order 9981, for the first time in the nation's history all troops in the Korean War served in racially integrated combat units. This photo taken during the Battle of Ch'ongch'on in 1950 shows a sergeant and his men of the 2nd Infantry Division. National Archives.

The Korean War The United States took a stronger stance in Korea. Truman and Stalin had agreed at the close of World War II to occupy the Korean peninsula jointly, temporarily dividing the former Japanese colony at the 38th parallel. As tensions rose in Europe, the 38th parallel turned into a permanent demarcation line. The Soviets supported a Communist government, led by Kim Il Sung, in North Korea; the United States backed a right-wing Nationalist, Syngman Rhee, in South Korea. The two sides had waged low-level war since 1945, and both leaders were spoiling for an opportunity to unify Korea under a single regime. However, neither Kim nor Rhee could launch an all-out offensive without the backing of his sponsor. Washington repeatedly said no, and so did Moscow. But Kim continued to press Stalin to

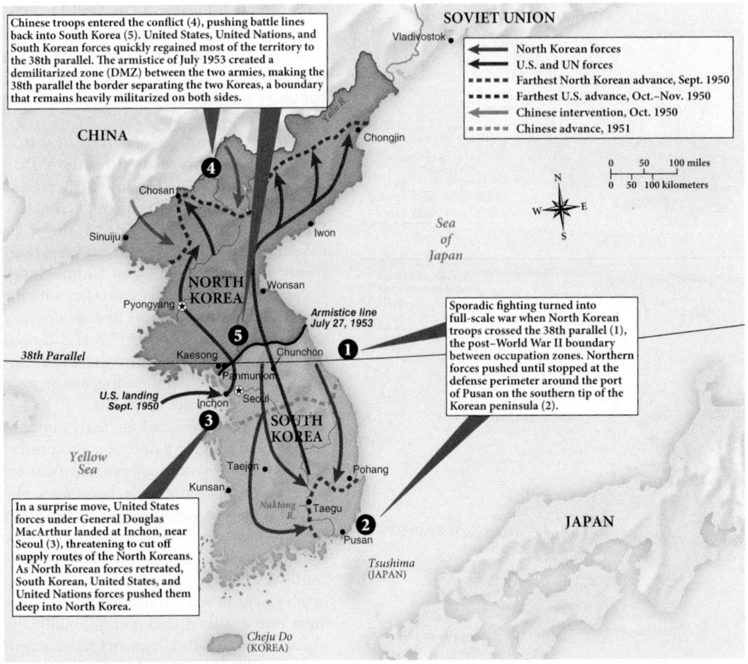

MAP 24.2 The Korean War, 1950–1953

The Korean War, which the United Nations officially deemed a "police action," lasted three years and cost the lives of more than 36,000 U.S. troops. South and North Korean deaths were estimated at more than 900,000. Although hostilities ceased in 1953, the South Korean Military (with U.S. military assistance) and the North Korean Army continue to face each other across the demilitarized zone, more than sixty years later.

permit him to reunify the nation through military action. Convinced by the North Koreans that victory would be swift, the Soviet leader finally relented in the late spring of 1950.

On June 25, 1950, the North Koreans launched a surprise attack across the 38th parallel (Map 24.2). Truman immediately asked the UN Security Council to authorize a "police action" against the invaders. The Soviet Union was boycotting the Security Council over China's exclusion from the United Nations and therefore could not veto the request. With the Security Council's approval of a "peacekeeping force," Truman ordered U.S. troops to Korea. The rapidly assembled UN army in Korea was overwhelmingly American, with General Douglas MacArthur in command. At first, the North Koreans held a distinct advantage, but MacArthur's surprise amphibious attack at Inchon gave the UN forces control of Seoul, the South Korean capital, and almost all the territory up to the 38th parallel.

The impetuous MacArthur then led his troops across the 38th parallel all the way to the Chinese border at the Yalu River. This was a major blunder, certain to draw China into the war. Sure enough, a massive Chinese counterattack forced UN forces into headlong retreat back down the Korean peninsula. Then stalemate set in. With weak public support for the war in the United States, Truman and his advisors decided to work for a negotiated peace. MacArthur disagreed, declaring, "There is

TEACHING STRATEGY

American military leaders were caught off guard by China's entrance into the five-month-old Korean War. A relatively small American force found itself surrounded and outnumbered at Chosin Reservoir, high in the mountains of North Korea. The two-week battle that followed, fought in brutally cold temperatures, is celebrated in Marine Corps annals; it helped set the course of American foreign policy in the Cold War. Incorporating interviews with more than twenty veterans of the campaign, the *American Experience* documentary *The Battle of Chosin* recounts this epic conflict through the stories of the soldiers who fought it. To access this film, search "American Experience Battle of Chosin."

AP® THEME

WOR: America in the World

Anxious about the communist ideology of expansionism and by Soviet repression, the U.S. sought to contain communism in a variety of ways, including through military engagement in Korea.

TEACHING STRATEGY

MAP 24.3 shows the growth of the military-industrial complex in Southern California, illustrating the relationship between the military, private aerospace corporations that received government contracts, and the growth of the Sunbelt. Not present in this map is the network of interstate highways, also built with government funds, which facilitated the movement of products.

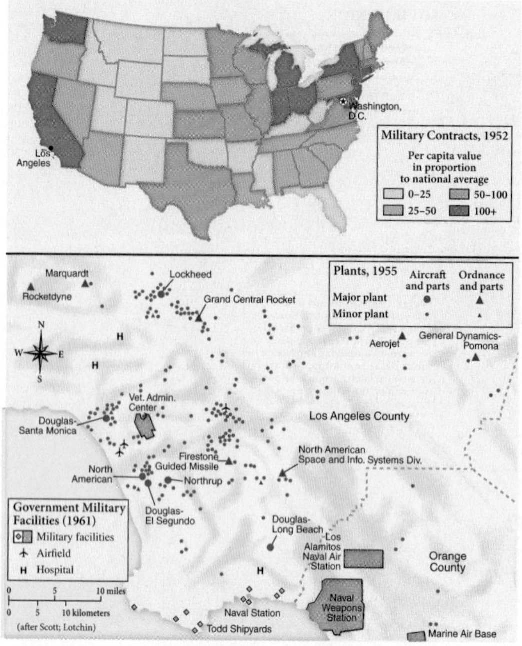

MAP 24.3 The Military-Industrial Complex
Defense spending gave a big boost to the Cold War economy, but, as the upper map suggests, the benefits were by no means equally distributed. The big winners were the Middle Atlantic states, the industrialized Upper Midwest, Washington State (with its aircraft and nuclear plants), and California. The epicenter of California's military-industrial complex was Los Angeles, which, as is evident in the lower map, was studded with military facilities and major defense contractors like Douglas Aircraft, Lockheed, and General Dynamics. There was work aplenty for engineers and rocket scientists.

no substitute for victory." On April 11, 1951, Truman relieved MacArthur of his command. Truman's decision was highly unpopular, especially among conservative Republicans, but likely saved the nation from a costly war with China.

Notwithstanding MacArthur's dismissal, the war dragged on for more than two years. An armistice in July 1953, pushed by the newly elected president, Dwight D. Eisenhower, left Korea divided at the original demarcation line. North Korea remained firmly allied with the Soviet Union; South Korea signed a mutual defense treaty with the United States. Korea was the first major proxy war between the Soviet Union and United States, in which the rivals took sides in a conflict without directly confronting one another militarily. It would not be the last.

The Korean War had far-reaching consequences. Truman's decision to commit troops without congressional approval set a precedent for future undeclared wars. His refusal to unleash atomic weapons, even when American forces were reeling under a massive Chinese attack, set ground rules for Cold War conflict. The war also expanded American involvement in Asia, transforming containment into a truly global policy. Finally, the Korean War dispelled Truman's resistance to a major military buildup (Map 24.3). Defense expenditures grew from $13 billion in 1950, roughly one-third of the federal budget, to $50 billion in 1953, nearly two-thirds of the budget (Figure 24.1). American foreign policy was now more global, more militarized, and more expensive. Even in times of peace, the United States maintained a state of permanent military mobilization.

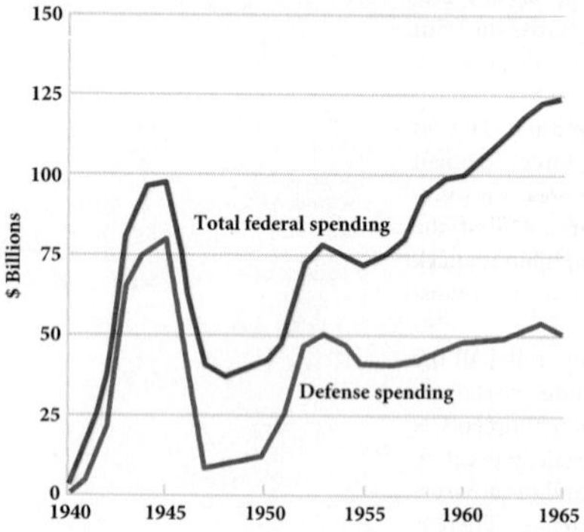

FIGURE 24.1 National Defense Spending, 1940–1965
In 1950, the U.S. defense budget was $13 billion, less than a third of total federal outlays. In 1961, U.S. defense spending reached $47 billion, fully half of the federal budget and almost 10 percent of the gross domestic product.

The Munich Analogy The memory of appeasement lay behind much of U.S. foreign policy in the first two decades of the Cold War. The generation of leaders who designed the containment strategy had witnessed the failure of the 1938 Munich conference, at which the Western democracies had appeased Hitler by offering him part of Czechoslovakia, unwittingly paving the road to World War II. Applying the lessons of Munich, American presidents believed that "appeasing" Stalin (and subsequent Soviet rulers Nikita Khrushchev and Leonid Brezhnev) would have the same result: wider war. Thus in Germany, Greece, and Korea, and later in Iran, Guatemala, and Vietnam, the United States staunchly resisted the Soviets — or what it perceived as Soviet influence. Standing up to the USSR worked in some disputes, particularly over the fate of Germany. But it also drew the Americans into armed conflicts — and convinced them to support repressive, right-wing regimes — that compromised stated American principles.

AP® SKILLS & PROCESSES

COMPARISON

How did U.S. containment strategy in Asia compare to containment in Europe?

COLD WAR LIBERALISM

What were the defining ideas of Cold War liberalism, and why did the Democratic Party embrace them?

As president, Harry Truman sought to position himself as Franklin Roosevelt's successor, using the possibilities afforded by victory in World War II to expand the New Deal at home. But the crises in Europe and Asia, combined with the swift rise of anticommunism in domestic politics, forced him along a different path. Truman went down in history as a Cold Warrior rather than a New Dealer. The Cold War consensus that he ultimately embraced — that resisting communism at home and abroad was America's foremost goal — shaped the nation's life and politics for decades to come.

Truman and the End of Reform

Truman and the Democratic Party of the late 1940s and early 1950s forged what historians call **Cold War liberalism**. They preserved the core programs of the New Deal welfare state, developed the containment policy to oppose Soviet influence throughout the world, and fought so-called subversives at home. But there would be no expansive second act for the New Deal — no national health insurance or bold initiatives to tackle poverty. Democrats adopted this combination of moderate liberal policies and anticommunism — Cold War liberalism — partly by choice and partly out of necessity. Communist victories in Eastern Europe and China, combined with several high-level espionage scandals at home, reenergized the Republican Party, which forced Truman and the Democrats to retreat to what historian Arthur Schlesinger called the "vital center." Cold War liberalism was a practical centrist program for a turbulent era. It would take hold, but only lasted until the even more turbulent 1960s tore it asunder.

Cold War liberalism
A combination of liberal policies that preserved the New Deal welfare state, anticommunism vilifying the Soviet Union abroad, and radicalism at home. Adopted by the Democratic Party after World War II.

Organized labor remained a key force in the Democratic Party and played a central role in championing Cold War liberalism. Union membership swelled to more than 14 million by 1945, making labor stronger than ever politically. Determined to redeem their wartime sacrifices and to make up for government controls that kept wages low during the war, unionized workers made aggressive demands and mounted major strikes in the automobile, steel, and coal industries after the war, as they had after World War I (for the same reasons). Probusiness Republicans responded just as aggressively. In 1946 they regained control of the House in a sweeping repudiation of Democrats and promptly passed — over Truman's veto — the **Taft-Hartley Act** (1947).

Taft-Hartley Act
Law passed by the Republican-controlled Congress in 1947 that overhauled the 1935 National Labor Relations Act, placing restrictions on organized labor that made it more difficult for unions to organize workers.

Taft-Hartley overhauled the 1935 National Labor Relations Act, introducing changes that gradually weakened the right of workers to organize and bargain collectively. Unions especially disliked Section 14b, which allowed states to pass "right-to-work" laws prohibiting the union shop (where workers are required to belong to a union — a requirement that aids union strength). Additionally, the law forced unions to purge communists, who had been among the most successful labor organizers in the 1930s, from their ranks. Trade unions would continue to support the Democratic Party, but the labor movement would penetrate neither the largely nonunion South nor the many American industries that remained unorganized. In a sense, Taft-Hartley effectively "contained" the labor movement.

AP® EXAM TIP

Identify the forces that limited the expansion of New Deal policies following World War II.

AP® SKILLS & PROCESSES

COMPARISON

Use the **COMPARISON** question to help students identify similarities and differences between containment policy in two different regions. Students should be able to identify a range of containment strategies — including alliances, economic assistance, and military support — and explain why policies in those regions differed.

TRM Find complete suggested responses in the Teacher's Resource Materials.

CHECK FOR UNDERSTANDING

Ask students: **What primary factors caused the Cold War?** *The causes of the Cold War were complex but can be boiled down to two factors: 1) the conflict between two largely incompatible ideologies, communism and capitalism, and 2) decolonization and the post–World War II geographic settlement. Through diplomacy, strategic policy, and military exploits, each side sought to secure as much territory for its side as possible while avoiding direct confrontation.*

AP® THEME

ARC: American and Regional Culture

As the decade of the 1950s approached, Americans increasingly engaged in economic changes that began during World War II. Have students explain one historical debate over the role of government in the economy during this time period and explain how that connects to a changing American culture.

Candidate	Electoral Vote	Popular Vote	Percent of Popular Vote
Harry S. Truman (Democrat)	303	24,105,182	49.6
Thomas E. Dewey (Republican)	189	21,970,065	45.1
J. Strom Thurmond (States' Rights)	39	1,169,063	2.5
Henry A. Wallace (Progressive)	—	1,157,326	2.5

MAP 24.4 The Presidential Election of 1948
Truman's electoral strategy in 1948 was to concentrate his campaign in areas where the Democrats had their greatest strength. In an election with a low turnout, Truman held on to enough support from Roosevelt's New Deal coalition of blacks, union members, and farmers to defeat Dewey by more than two million votes.

The 1948 Election Democrats would have dumped Truman in 1948 had they found a better candidate. But the party itself was in disarray. The left wing split off and formed the Progressive Party, nominating Henry A. Wallace, an avid New Dealer and former vice president whom Truman had fired as secretary of commerce in 1946 for his vocal opposition to the Cold War. A right-wing challenge came from the South. When northern liberals pushed through a strong civil rights platform at the Democratic convention, the southern delegations bolted and, calling themselves Dixiecrats, nominated for president South Carolina governor Strom Thurmond, an ardent supporter of racial segregation. The Republicans meanwhile renominated New York governor Thomas E. Dewey, a moderate who had run a strong campaign against FDR in 1944.

Truman surprised everyone. He launched a strenuous cross-country speaking tour and hammered away at the Republicans for opposing progressive legislation and running a "do-nothing" Congress. Combining these issues with attacks on the Soviet menace abroad, Truman salvaged a campaign that had appeared hopeless. An accidental president who some thought was overwhelmed by his office in 1945, Truman transformed himself into a savvy political fighter. At his rallies, enthusiastic listeners shouted, "Give 'em hell, Harry!" In the November election, Truman won 49.6 percent of the vote to Dewey's 45.1 percent (Map 24.4).

Fair Deal
The domestic policy agenda announced by President Harry S. Truman in 1949, which included civil rights, health care, public housing, and education funding. Congress rejected most of it.

This unlikely result foreshadowed coming political turmoil. Truman occupied the center of FDR's sprawling New Deal coalition. On his left were progressives, civil rights advocates, and peace activists critical of the Cold War. On his right were segregationist southerners, who opposed civil rights and were allied with Republicans on many economic and foreign policy issues. In 1948, Truman performed a delicate balancing act, largely retaining the support of Jewish and Catholic voters in the big cities, black voters in the North, union voters across the country, and a still considerable bloc of white southerners. But Thurmond's strong showing — the Dixiecrat carried four states in the Deep South — demonstrated the fragility of the Democratic coalition. As Truman wrangled opposing forces within his own party, he also faced mounting pressure from Republicans to denounce radicals at home and to take a tough stand against the Soviet Union.

Truman Triumphant In one of the most famous photographs in U.S. political history, Harry S. Truman gloats over an erroneous headline in the November 3 *Chicago Daily Tribune*. Pollsters had predicted an easy victory for Thomas E. Dewey. Their polling techniques, however, missed the dramatic surge in support for Truman during the last days of the campaign. Bettmann/Getty Images.

The Fair Deal Balancing act or no, Truman and progressive Democrats forged ahead. In his State of the Union speech on January 5, 1949, Truman proposed an ambitious extension of the New Deal, which he dubbed the **Fair Deal**: national health insurance, civil rights legislation, education funding, a housing program, expansion of Social Security, a higher minimum wage, and a new agricultural program. The Fair Deal's attention to civil rights reflected the growing influence of African Americans in the Democratic Party. In 1948, Truman had desegregated the armed forces, and his Fair Deal proposals included desegregation, fair employment, and voting rights legislation. A March

TEACHING STRATEGY

To supplement your discussion of the 1948 election, use the resources available at the Truman Library, including dozens of documents, hundreds of images, multiple political cartoons, and several audio clips related to the election. To access these resources, search "Truman Library 1948 campaign."

1949 editorial in the *Chicago Defender*, a leading African American newspaper, credited the "Negroes, labor and liberal whites who joined hands to put the Democrats in power" and promised that "the civil rights program to which the Democratic Party dedicated itself . . . is not going to be scuttled by entrenched hate-mongers."

Congress, however, remained a huge stumbling block, and the Fair Deal fared poorly. The same conservative coalition that blocked Roosevelt's initiatives in his second term stymied Truman's as well. Civil rights went nowhere, blocked by southern Democrats and probusiness Republicans. Cold War pressure shaped debates about domestic social programs, while the nation's growing paranoia over internal subversion weakened support for bold extensions of the welfare state. Truman's proposal for national health insurance, for instance, was a popular idea, with strong backing from organized labor. But the plan was denounced as "socialized medicine" by the American Medical Association and the insurance industry. In the end, the Fair Deal's only significant successes were improvements to the minimum wage and Social Security, and the National Housing Act of 1949, which authorized the construction of 810,000 low-income units.

AP® SKILLS & PROCESSES

ARGUMENTATION

Compare the years immediately following World War I (Chapter 21) and the years after World War II. In what ways were they similar, especially with respect to politics, radicalism, and organized labor?

Red Scare: The Hunt for Communists

The suspicion of subversives that helped to thwart the Fair Deal turned into a much wider Red Scare that would prove longer lasting and farther reaching than the one that followed World War I (see "The Red Scare" in Chapter 21). Many Americans believed that Communists and Communist sympathizers posed a significant threat to American life. There were legitimate reasons for concern, including leaks of information to the Soviet Union from the highest levels of government. Soviet intelligence records released after the 1991 disintegration of the USSR showed that an assistant secretary of the treasury, White House aids, scientists and technicians working on the Manhattan Project, and hundreds more across departments and agencies passed secrets to Moscow. How was this to be explained and what, many inside and outside of government asked, ought to be done about it?

Many who leaked information were idealistic New Dealers, who entered government at a moment when the Soviet-backed Popular Front made communism appear merely a more left-leaning version of liberalism and progressivism, and thus sympathetic to many liberals. But passing secrets to another country, even a wartime ally, was simply indefensible to many Americans — particularly when it came to atomic secrets. Historians generally conclude that the flow of information to the USSR had largely ceased by 1947, due to vigorous counterintelligence and the departure of many amateur spies for careers in the private sector. But the danger of espionage and Communist sympathizers remained potent — and ripe for political opportunism.

AP® EXAM TIP

Evaluate the debates over the methods and policies related to exposing communist spies in the 1950s.

Loyalty-Security Program To insulate his administration against charges of Communist infiltration, Truman issued Executive Order 9835 on March 21, 1947, which created the **Loyalty-Security Program**. The order permitted officials to investigate any employee of the federal government (some 2.5 million people) for "subversive" activities. This profound centralization of power had unforeseen consequences. Truman intended the order to apply principally to actions against the national interest (sabotage, treason, etc.), but many federal employees found themselves accused of subversion for far different reasons — for marching in a Communist-led demonstration in the 1930s, for instance, or signing a petition endorsing public housing. Even sexuality came under suspicion. Along with suspected political subversives, more than a thousand gay men and lesbians were dismissed from federal employment in the 1950s, victims of an obsessive search for anyone deemed "unfit" for government work.

Loyalty-Security Program
A program created in 1947 by President Truman that permitted officials to investigate any employee of the federal government for "subversive" activities.

Following Truman's lead, many state and local governments, universities, political organizations, churches, and businesses launched their own antisubversion campaigns, which often required that employees or members take loyalty oaths.

AP® SKILLS & PROCESSES

ARGUMENTATION

In order to answer the **ARGUMENTATION** question, students could create a chart with a row for each of the factors indicated in the question, and a column for WWI, another for WWII, and a third in the middle for shared elements. Students could also explain the reasons for major differences they note between the two eras for each factor.

TRM Find complete suggested responses in the Teacher's Resource Materials.

AP® APPLY THE TIP

Provide students with excerpts from Senator Joseph McCarthy's "Wheeling Speech" from February 9, 1950, and the "Declaration of Conscience, June 1, 1950" by Senator Margaret Chase Smith, 82nd Congress, 1st Session. Ask students to read each document and provide an analysis of the ways in which the document could be used as evidence to support or oppose McCarthyism. Then ask students to extend their analysis by explaining the intended audience, purpose, and point of view of each document. Lead a class discussion on the ways in which the documents illustrate the debate over McCarthyism. Finally, each student should choose one of the excerpts and write a response from the point of view of the senator's constituents.

TEACHING STRATEGY

There are several resources for exploring the Loyalty-Security Program and its consequences further. The American Presidency Project provides the full text of Executive Order 9835. To access this text, search "Presidency Project Executive Order 9835." Teaching American History provides the June 27, 1947, speech by California representative Chester E. Holifield expressing concern about the intrusiveness of the program. To access this speech, search "Teaching American History speech on Truman's Loyalty Program." Lastly, the Truman Library provides a lesson plan that offers a five-paragraph introduction, a guiding question, and ten documents for student exploration. To access this resource, search "Truman Library Loyalty Program."

In the labor movement, charges of Communist domination led to the expulsion of a number of unions from the Congress of Industrial Organizations (CIO) in 1949. Civil rights organizations such as the National Association for the Advancement of Colored People (NAACP) and the National Urban League also expelled Communists and "fellow travelers," as Communist sympathizers were known. From Truman's 1947 order, the Red Scare radiated outward from the federal government across the broad sweep of American public life.

House Un-American Activities Committee (HUAC)
Congressional committee especially prominent during the early years of the Cold War that investigated Americans who might be disloyal to the government or might have associated with communists or other radicals.

HUAC The Truman administration had legitimized the vague and malleable concept of "disloyalty." Other parts of the government went much further, beginning with the **House Un-American Activities Committee (HUAC)**, which Congressman Martin Dies of Texas and other conservatives had launched in 1938. In 1947, HUAC stoked the growing Red Scare with widely publicized hearings on alleged Communist infiltration in the movie industry. A group of writers and directors dubbed the Hollywood Ten went to jail for contempt of Congress after they refused to testify about their past associations. Hundreds of other actors, directors, and writers investigated by HUAC were unable to get work, victims of an unacknowledged but very real blacklist honored by industry executives.

Other HUAC investigations proved more legitimate. One was the so-called Hiss case. In 1948, Whitaker Chambers, a former Communist spy turned conservative journalist, alleged that a former State Department official named Alger Hiss — who had accompanied FDR to Yalta — was part of a secret Communist cell. Hiss denied the allegations, but California Republican congressman Richard Nixon doggedly pursued the case against him, and raised his own profile in the process. In early 1950, Hiss was found guilty not of espionage but of lying to Congress about his Communist affiliations and was sentenced to five years in federal prison. Many Americans doubted whether Hiss was a spy, although intelligence declassified in the 1990s corroborated a great deal of Chambers's testimony. No definitive proof has emerged, but many historians now recognize the strong circumstantial evidence against Hiss. Whether Hiss spied or not, the incident was a national scandal that fed the Red Scare.

McCarthyism The meteoric career of Senator Joseph McCarthy of Wisconsin marked both the height and the rapid decline of the Red Scare. In February 1950, the previously unremarkable McCarthy delivered a bombshell during a speech to the Republican Women's Club in Wheeling, West Virginia: "I have here in my hand a list of 205 . . . a list of names that were made known to the Secretary of State as being members of the Communist Party and who nevertheless are still working and shaping policy in the State Department." McCarthy would cite different numbers in different speeches, and never released any names or proof. But he had gained the attention he sought from the press and the public (see "Firsthand Accounts," p. 792).

For the next four years, McCarthy waged a virulent smear campaign from his position as chair of the Senate Permanent Subcommittee on Investigations. Critics who disagreed with him exposed themselves to charges of being "soft" on communism. McCarthy was distinctly unsuccessful in proving communist influence in the government, but he rose to national prominence by aggressively grilling witnesses he called before the committee and through his appearances on radio and television. He was poor at investigating but skilled at publicity. Truman condemned McCarthy's accusations as "slander, lies, [and] character assassination," but could do nothing to curb him. McCarthy's fellow Republicans largely refrained from publicly challenging the outspoken senator and, on the whole, were content to reap the political benefits. McCarthy's charges almost always targeted Democrats.

Despite McCarthy's failure to identify a single Communist in government, other developments gave his charges credibility with the public. The dramatic 1951 espionage trial of Julius and Ethel Rosenberg, followed around the world, was fueled by what had become known as "McCarthyism." An electrical engineer who worked with

TEACHING STRATEGY

In her book *Many Are the Crimes: McCarthyism in America* (New York: Little, Brown and Co., 1998), historian Ellen Schrecker offers one of the most influential interpretations of domestic anticommunism in the last generation. While she acknowledges the presence of a small and ineffectual Communist Party in the U.S., she suggests that it posed little threat to American security. The real significance of her argument lies in her assessment of the driving force behind anti-Communist activity: the intentional efforts of elites to stigmatize left-of-center political views — not the spontaneous panic of everyday Americans — was responsible for McCarthyism. Consider having students read the introduction (p. xiii) to evaluate her argument.

TEACHING STRATEGY

The American government has long hailed its system as one that protects democratic processes through constitutional guarantees. Ask students why, despite extreme Red Scare actions by a few, did Americans not call for broader constitutional guarantees? Did anti-communism actions challenge, appeal, or reject American constitutional values?

the U.S. Army Signal Corps, Julius Rosenberg passed atomic secrets to the Soviets in the 1940s. After a contentious trial in which Julius and Ethel were both convicted, the Rosenbergs were executed in 1953. Documents released decades later confirmed Julius Rosenberg's guilt, though not Ethel's. Their execution remains contentious — in part because some felt that anti-Semitism played a role in their sentencing. Also fueling McCarthy's investigations were a series of trials of American Communists between 1949 and 1955 for violation of the 1940 Smith Act, which prohibited Americans from advocating the violent overthrow of the government. Though civil libertarians and two Supreme Court justices vigorously objected, dozens of Communist Party members were convicted. McCarthy was not involved in either the Rosenberg trial or the Smith Act convictions, but these sensational events lent his wild charges some plausibility.

In early 1954, McCarthy finally overreached with an investigation into subversive activities in the U.S. Army. When lengthy hearings — the first of their kind broadcast on the new medium of television — brought McCarthy's tactics into the nation's living rooms, support for him plummeted. The senator's bullying and self-serving accusations, captured by live television cameras broadcasting coast to coast, offended Americans who had previously only read about McCarthy in newspapers and magazines. In December 1954, the Senate voted 67 to 22 to censure McCarthy for unbecoming conduct. He died from an alcohol-related illness three years later at the age of forty-eight. His name became the symbol of a period of political repression of which he was only the most flagrant manifestation.

AP® SKILLS & PROCESSES

CAUSATION

What factors led to the postwar Red Scare, and what were its ramifications for civil liberties in the United States?

The Army-McCarthy Hearings These 1954 hearings contributed to the downfall of Senator Joseph McCarthy by exposing his reckless accusations and bullying tactics to the huge television audience that tuned in each day. Some of the most heated exchanges took place between McCarthy (center) and Joseph Welch (seated, left), the lawyer representing the army. When the gentlemanly Welch finally asked, "Have you no sense of decency sir, at long last? Have you left no sense of decency?" he fatally punctured McCarthy's armor. The audience broke into applause because someone had finally had the courage to stand up to the senator from Wisconsin. Bettmann/Getty Images.

CHECK FOR UNDERSTANDING

Ask students: **What was the Red Scare?** *The Red Scare was a postwar panic that Communist agents had infiltrated the U.S., including the government and influential industries like Hollywood. Government agencies launched various programs and investigations to counter this threat, which, while real, was relatively limited.*

AP® SKILLS & PROCESSES

CAUSATION

The **CAUSATION** question asks students to identify both the causes of the Red Scare and its effects, especially on civil liberties. Extend this prompt by asking students to explore the question of whether investigations of possible Communist infiltration might have been pursued without violating the privacy and civil rights of government employees.

TRM Find complete suggested responses in the Teacher's Resource Materials.

AP® SKILLS & PROCESSES

ANALYZING HISTORICAL EVIDENCE

The **AP® FIRSTHAND ACCOUNTS** feature offers students the chance to explore the important question of the relationship between the Cold War and black civil rights, a topic that will be explored in more depth in the next chapter. In the postwar period, African Americans took advantage of opportunities provided by globalization — including the emergence of international organizations like the United Nations and increased international travel — to lobby for black rights. Since many conservatives already saw a link between civil rights and communism, Paul Robeson's decision to travel overseas only confirmed suspicions.

AP® FIRSTHAND ACCOUNTS

Hunting Communists: The Case of Paul Robeson

The Cold War campaigns against American communists and other radicals reached their peak between 1949 and 1954. Anticommunists searched for signs of "disloyalty" to the United States, especially among public figures such as politicians, artists, athletes, and actors. Few Americans came under greater suspicion than the black athlete, singer, civil rights advocate, and political radical Paul Robeson. Having traveled the world as a successful actor and vocalist in the 1930s, Robeson often spoke positively about the Soviet Union, where he was celebrated as a great artist. He was an outspoken advocate for black equality in the United States and a fierce critic of American political leaders for doing little to end Jim Crow and other forms of racial discrimination and racial violence after World War II.

In 1949, while speaking at a peace conference in Paris, Robeson was misquoted in the United States as having said that African Americans ("Negroes" in the standard usage of the period) would not fight in a potential war against the Soviet Union. On his return to the United States, the House Un-American Activities Committee (HUAC) held hearings at which prominent African Americans were encouraged to denounce Robeson. Among them were Thomas Young and Manning Johnson, as well as Jackie Robinson, the black baseball star who had integrated Major League Baseball in 1947. (Young was editor of a prominent black newspaper, and Johnson was a former member of the Communist Party who had turned against it.) Branded as disloyal, Robeson fought back, insisting that HUAC was disloyal for ignoring white violence and continued systematic discrimination against African Americans. This Cold War episode from 1949 shows how civil rights and anticommunism collided, with black leaders pressured by HUAC and others to choose sides.

THOMAS YOUNG

Testimony Before House Committee on Un-American Activities, July 13, 1949

SOURCE: *Hearings Regarding Communist Infiltration of Minority Groups — Part 1: Hearings Before the House Committee on Un-American Activities*, July 13, 14, and 18, 1949 (Washington, DC: Government Printing Office, 1949), 453.

" I am happy to accept the invitation extended to me to appear before this committee because I feel very strongly the need for bringing into proper perspective some of the opinions that have been expressed publicly concerning the loyalty of the American Negro. . . .

Please bear this in mind, that there is no evidence on record of the disloyalty of their country on the part of Negroes generally [sic]. It has not been charged, even, that there have been overt acts by Negroes on which suspicion of disloyalty could be predicated. On the other hand, the entire record of the American Negro's service to his country, from the Revolutionary War, in which Crispus Attucks, a Boston Negro, was among the first to shed blood for this nation's independence, down to the recent World War II, in which members of this group played important and heroic roles on every front, is a satisfactory refutation of such charges. . . .

What basis, if any, is there for believing Paul Robeson when he says that in the event of a war with Russia the Negro would not fight for his country against the Soviets? . . .

The plain truth about the matter is that in his Paris declaration Mr. Robeson has done a great disservice to his race — far greater than that done to his country. And if Mr. Robeson does not recognize the injury he has done to the cause of the Negro in this country, then that underscores his disqualification as a representative of the race. "

MANNING JOHNSON

Testimony Before House Committee on Un-American Activities, July 14, 1949

SOURCE: *Hearings Regarding Communist Infiltration of Minority Groups: Hearings Before the House Committee on Un-American Activities*, July 14, 1949 (Washington, DC: Government Printing Office, 1949), 505.

" I have met Paul Robeson a number of times in the headquarters of the national committee of the Communist Party, going to and coming from conferences with Earl Browder, Jack Stachel, and J. Peters [high-ranking officials of the Communist Party USA in the 1940s]. During the time I was a member of the Communist Party, Paul Robeson was a member of the Communist Party. . . . In the Negro commission of the national committee of the Communist Party we were told, under threat of expulsion, never to reveal that Paul Robeson was a member of the Communist Party, because Paul Robeson's assignment was highly confidential and secret. . . .

792

Paul's assignment was to work among the intellectuals, the professionals, and artists that the party was seeking to penetrate and influence along Communist lines. . . .

Of course Paul Robeson has, by background and international connections developed a complex. You recall the role he played, the role of Emperor Jones. He has delusions of grandeur. He wants to be the Black Stalin among Negroes. The Communist Party is encouraging that desire, because the Communist Party can very effectively use Robeson to further their penetration among Negroes. ”

JACK "JACKIE" ROBINSON

Testimony Before House Committee on Un-American Activities, July 18, 1949

SOURCE: *Hearings Regarding Communist Infiltration of Minority Groups: Hearings Before the House Committee on Un-American Activities*, July 18, 1949 (Washington, DC: Government Printing Office, 1949), 481.

“ We're going to make progress in other American fields besides baseball if we can get rid of some of the misunderstanding and confusion that the public still suffers from. I know I have a great desire and I think that I have some responsibility for helping to clear up that confusion. As I see it there has been a terrific lot of misunderstanding on this subject of Communism among the Negroes in this country, and it's bound to hurt my people's cause unless it is cleared up.

The white public should start toward real understanding by appreciating that every single Negro who is worth his salt is going to resent any kind of slurs and discrimination because of his race, and he is going to use every bit of intelligence such as he has to stop it. This has got absolutely nothing to do with what Communists may or may not be trying to do.

. . . I've been asked to express my views on Paul Robeson's statement in Paris to the effect that American Negroes would refuse to fight in any war against Russia because they love Russia so much. I haven't any comment to make on that statement except that if Mr. Robeson actually made it, it sounds very silly to me. But he has a right to his personal views. . . . ”

PAUL ROBESON

News Release Commenting on House Un-American Activities Committee, July 20, 1949

SOURCE: Paul Robeson, "Statement on Un-American Activities Committee," in *Paul Robeson Speaks: Writings, Speeches, Interviews, 1918–1974*, ed. Philip S. Foner (New York: Brunner/Mazel, 1978), 218.

“ Quite clearly America faces a crisis in race relations. The Un-American Activities Committee moves now to transform the Government's cold war policy against the Negro people into a hot war. Its action incites the Ku Klux Klan, that openly terrorist organization, to a reign of mob violence against my people in Florida and elsewhere. This Committee attempts to divide the Negro people from one another in order to prevent us from winning jobs, security and justice under the banner of peace.

The loyalty of the Negro people is not a subject for debate. I challenge the loyalty of the Un-American Activities Committee. This committee maintains an ominous silence in the face of the lynchings of Maceo Snipes, Robert Mallard, the two Negro veterans and their wives in Monroe, Georgia, and the violence and unpunished murders of scores of Negro veterans by white supremacists since V-J Day. . . . Every pro-war fascist-minded group in the country regards the Committee's silence as license to proceed against my people, unchecked by Government authorities and unchallenged by the courts.

Our fight for peace in America is a fight for human dignity, and an end to ghetto life. It is the fight for constitutional liberties, the civil and human rights of every American. This struggle is the decisive struggle with which my people are today concerned. . . .

It is not the Soviet Union that threatens the life, liberty and the property and the citizenship rights of Negro Americans. The threat comes from within. To destroy this threat our people need the aid of every honest American, Communist and non-Communist alike. Those who menace our lives proceed unchallenged by the Un-American Activities Committee. I shall not be drawn into any conflict dividing me from my brother victim of this terror. I am wholly committed to the struggle for peace and democratic rights of free Americans. ”

QUESTIONS FOR ANALYSIS

1. What do you think Young means by "a great disservice to his race"? What is the basis of Jackie Robinson's testimony? Why do you think Robinson insists that black resistance to discrimination has nothing to do with communism? Compare the purpose and historical situation to each source author.
2. What is Johnson's intention in identifying Robeson as a Communist? What would have been the effect of such charges in 1949?
3. How does Robeson challenge the meaning of "disloyal" in his statement? How would you compare his version of disloyalty with HUAC's?

TRM Find complete suggested responses in the Teacher's Resource Materials.

AP® THEME

WOR: America in the World

The Cold War fluctuated between periods of direct and indirect military confrontation and periods of mutual coexistence. At the Geneva Summit in 1955, Eisenhower called for "open skies," where each superpower would map its military installations and allow aerial surveillance by the other power. Eisenhower hosted Khrushchev at a Camp David summit in 1959—the first Soviet premier to visit the U.S.—and the two met in Paris the following year, though that meeting collapsed over the downing of a U.S. spy plane over the Soviet Union and the capture of its pilot. While the text does not address any of these meetings, it might be helpful for students to know that even during the height of the Cold War, with a president who had campaigned on the promise to go beyond containment and "roll back" communism, both sides still attempted to lower tension through diplomacy.

AP® SKILLS & PROCESSES

DEVELOPMENTS AND PROCESSES

This is a complex question for students who are not familiar with vernacular attendant to political parties. The chapter does provide helpful labels for students to consider. Call out the following types of Republicans explained in the book: conservative, moderate, and liberal-minded. Have students define each and identify why Republicans held divergent views on policies.

TRM Find complete suggested responses in the Teacher's Resource Materials.

Modern Republicanism and the Liberal State

As the 1952 election approached, the nation was embroiled in both the Cold War and a "hot" war in Korea. Though the opposition Republicans captured the White House, radical change was not in the offing. The new president, Dwight D. Eisenhower, was not a career politician. The former commander of Allied forces in Europe embraced what his supporters called "modern Republicanism," an updated approach that aimed at moderating, not dismantling, the New Deal. Eisenhower Republicans were as much successors of FDR as of Herbert Hoover. Foreign policy reflected a similar continuity. Like the Truman administration, the Republican leadership saw the world in Cold War polarities.

Despite Eisenhower's enormous popularity, divisions persisted among Republicans. Conservative party activists preferred Robert A. Taft of Ohio, the Republican leader in the Senate who was an outspoken opponent of the New Deal, a close friend of business, and a vocal critic of labor unions. Though an ardent anticommunist, Taft was far more of an isolationist than most Cold Warriors, and he criticized Truman's aggressive containment policy and opposed U.S. participation in NATO. Taft ran for president three times, and though he never claimed the Republican nomination, he did earn the loyalty of conservative Americans who deemed the welfare state wasteful and international initiatives dangerous.

AP® SKILLS & PROCESSES

DEVELOPMENTS AND PROCESSES

How was the Republican Party divided in the 1950s, and what were its primary constituencies?

In contrast, moderate Republicans looked to Eisenhower, a man without a political past. Believing that democracy required the military to stand aside, the career soldier had never voted. In contrast to Taft, Eisenhower was ideologically closer to more liberal-minded Republican party leaders like Nelson Rockefeller, who supported programs such as the Marshall Plan and NATO and were willing to tolerate labor unions and the welfare state. Rockefeller, the scion of one of the richest families in America, was a quintessential Cold War internationalist. He served in a variety of capacities under Eisenhower, including as an advisor on foreign affairs. Rockefeller was elected the governor of New York in 1958 and became the de facto leader of the liberal wing of the Republican Party.

Dwight Eisenhower In this photo taken during the 1952 presidential campaign, Dwight D. Eisenhower acknowledges cheers from supporters in Chicago. "Ike," as he was universally known, had been a popular five-star general in World War II (also serving as supreme allied commander in the European theater) and turned to politics in the early 1950s as a member of the Republican Party. However, Eisenhower was a centrist who did little to disrupt the liberal social policies that Democrats had pursued since the 1930s. Bettmann/Getty Images.

Between 1952 and 1960, Eisenhower maintained peace between conservative Taft Republicans and liberal Rockefeller Republicans, though more ardent conservatives considered him a closet New Dealer. "Ike," as he was widely known, proved willing to work with the mostly Democratic-controlled Congresses of those years. Eisenhower signed bills increasing federal outlays for veterans' benefits, housing, highway construction, and Social Security, and increased the minimum wage from 75 cents an hour to $1. Like Truman, Eisenhower accepted some government responsibility for the economic security of individuals as part of a broad consensus in American politics in these years.

The political landscape that birthed the containment strategy also guided Eisenhower's foreign policy. But the tone of the Cold War changed with Stalin's death in March 1953. After a prolonged power struggle, Nikita Khrushchev emerged as Stalin's successor. The new first secretary of the Communist Party soon startled the world by denouncing Stalin and detailing his crimes and blunders. He also surprised many Americans by calling for "peaceful coexistence" with the West. But the conciliatory outlook of the new Soviet leader had limits: when Hungarians rose up in 1956 to demand independence from Moscow, Khrushchev crushed the incipient revolution.

With no end to the Cold War in sight, Eisenhower focused on limiting the cost of containment. The president hoped to economize by relying on a nuclear arsenal instead of expensive conventional forces. Under this "**New Look**" defense policy, the Eisenhower administration stepped up production of the hydrogen bomb and developed long-range strike capabilities. The Soviets, however, matched the United States weapon for weapon. By 1957, both nations had intercontinental ballistic missiles. When an American nuclear submarine launched an atomic-tipped Polaris missile in 1960, Soviet engineers quickly produced an equivalent weapon. This arms race was another critical feature of the Cold War. American officials believed the best deterrent to Soviet aggression was the threat of an all-out nuclear response, dubbed "massive retaliation" by Secretary of State John Foster Dulles.

New Look
The defense policy of the Eisenhower administration that stepped up production of the hydrogen bomb and developed long-range bombing capabilities.

Although confident in the international arena, Eisenhower was a novice in domestic affairs. In the wake of the rancorous Truman years, the new president sought a less confrontational tone. He was reluctant to speak out against Joe McCarthy and did not lead on civil rights. Democrats remained strong in Congress but proved weak in the two presidential contests of the decade. In the 1952 election, Democratic nominee Adlai Stevenson was hampered by the unpopularity of the Truman administration. The deadlocked Korean War and a series of scandals that Republicans dubbed "the mess in Washington" combined to give the war-hero general an easy victory. In 1956, Ike won an even more impressive victory over Stevenson, an eloquent and sophisticated spokesman for liberalism but an ineffectual politician.

During the Eisenhower era, particularly at the national level, Democrats and Republicans seemed in broad agreement about the realities of the Cold War and how to sustain both a welfare state and a modern industrial economy. Indeed, respected commentators in the 1950s declared "the end of ideology" and wondered if the great political clashes that had wracked the 1930s were gone forever. Underneath the apparent calm, however, new forces on both right and left were stirring, with starkly opposed ideas about the direction of the nation. Their differences would bitterly divide the country in the 1960s and bring an end to the brief and fragile Cold War consensus (Chapters 26 and 27).

COLD WAR IN THE POSTCOLONIAL WORLD

What objectives guided U.S. foreign policy in the postcolonial world during the Cold War?

Even as the Cold War froze Europe, the rest of the global map changed rapidly. New nations were emerging across Asia, Africa, and the Middle East, often as the culmination of decades-long anticolonial movements. Between 1947 and 1962, the British, French, Dutch, and Belgian empires largely disintegrated in a momentous collapse of European global power. During the war years, FDR had supported the idea of national self-determination, often to the fury of his British and French allies. He saw emerging democracies as future partners in an American-led, free-market world system. But colonial revolts produced many independent- or socialist-minded regimes in the so-called Third World, as well. *Third World* was a term that came into usage after World War II to describe developing or former colonial nations in Asia, Africa, Latin America, and the Middle East that were not aligned with the Western capitalist countries led by the United States or the socialist states of Eastern Europe led by the Soviet Union. Though used throughout the Cold War, the term "Third World" has declined in usage in recent years in favor of terms like "postcolonial" or "Global South," since so many of these nations are in the southern hemisphere (see "Comparing Interpretations," p. 776).

CHECK FOR UNDERSTANDING

Ask students: **What were the components of Cold War liberalism, and why did the Democratic Party embrace them?** *Cold War liberalism was the style of liberalism embraced by the Democratic Party between the end of World War II and the 1960s. It implied preserving the New Deal programs that survived the war, containing the Soviet Union, and fighting subversives at home. In effect, it was a more moderate or centralist version of liberalism vis-à-vis New Deal liberalism, both a reaction to the rising tide of postwar conservatism and a reflection that too much intervention in the economy could be seen to be mirroring too closely the planned economies of the Soviet sphere.*

AP® APPLY THE TIP

Organize students into groups and ask them to read pp. 796–798 in order to create an illustrated timeline of the U.S. response to decolonization during the Cold War. For this timeline, students should include significant events related to the U.S. role in decolonization with a brief description of the way in which U.S. actions were related to the policy of containment. Post students' timelines throughout the classroom. Then provide each group with a different color marker and ask them to rotate around the room to view the other group's timelines. As they view the timelines, each group should use their marker to add clarifying statements or to write any questions. Then lead a class discussion on the role of the U.S. in the decolonization in the policy of containment.

TEACHING STRATEGY

The caption for **MAP 24.5** places the U.S.'s permanent membership in NATO, SEATO, and other regional alliances in the broad context of American suspicion of permanent alliances extending from President Washington to the senators who refused to join the League of Nations. In the postwar context of the Cold War, many American strategists thought that a turning point was in order.

Colonial Independence Movements

AP® EXAM TIP

Describe the goals and methods of the U.S. in seeking alliances among new nations after decolonization.

Wanting every nation to choose a side in the Cold War, the United States drew as many countries as possible into collective security agreements, with the NATO alliance as a model. Secretary of State Dulles orchestrated the 1954 creation of the Southeast Asia Treaty Organization (SEATO), which linked the United States and its major European allies with Australia, New Zealand, Pakistan, the Philippines, and Thailand. An extensive system of these defense alliances eventually tied the United States to more than forty other countries (Map 24.5). The United States also sponsored a strategically instrumental alliance between Iraq and Iran, on the southern flank of the Soviet Union.

The United States often invoked lofty rhetoric in its foreign policy, but in practice proved more interested in stability than democratic ideals. The Truman and Eisenhower administrations tended to support overtly anticommunist governments, no matter how repressive. Some of America's staunchest allies — the Philippines, South Korea, Iran, Cuba, South Vietnam, and Nicaragua — were governed by dictatorships or right-wing regimes that lacked broad-based support. Moreover, secretary of state

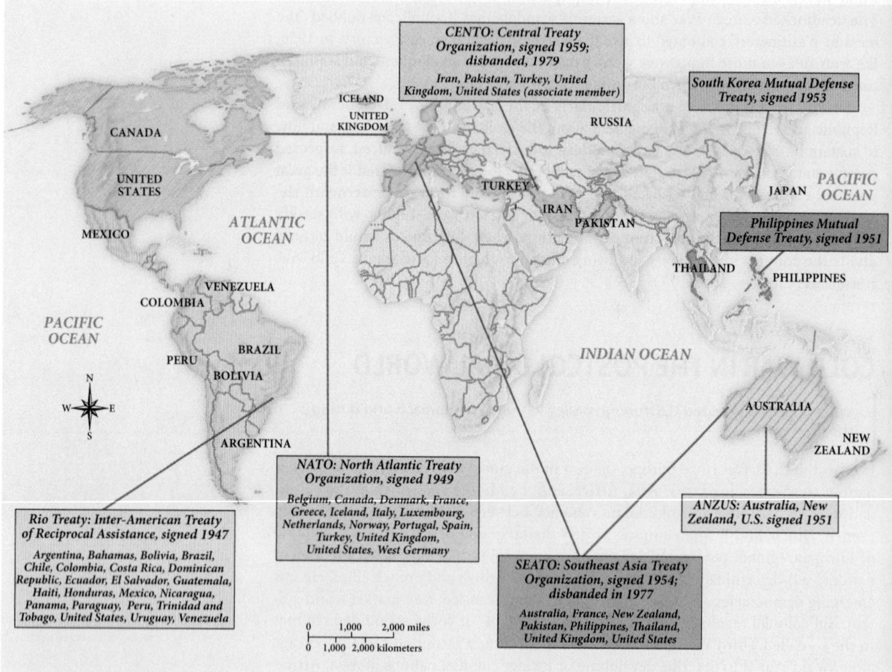

MAP 24.5 American Global Defense Treaties in the Cold War Era
The advent of the Cold War led to a major shift in American foreign policy — the signing of mutual defense treaties. Dating back to George Washington's call "to steer clear of permanent alliances with any portion of the foreign world," the United States had avoided treaty obligations that entailed the defense of other nations. As late as 1919, the U.S. Senate had rejected the principle of "collective security," the centerpiece of the League of Nations established by the Treaty of Versailles that ended World War I. But after World War II, in response to fears of Soviet global expansion, the United States entered defense alliances with much of the non-Communist world.

Dulles often resorted to secret operations against governments that, in his opinion, were too closely aligned with the Soviets.

For such clandestine work, Dulles turned to the new Central Intelligence Agency (CIA), created in 1947 and run by his brother, Allen Dulles. When Mohammad Mossadegh, the democratically elected premier of Iran, nationalized British-owned oil properties with the approval of the Iranian parliament in 1951, CIA and British agents developed a covert plan to depose him. Through Operation Ajax in 1953, those agents orchestrated Mossadegh's ouster and reinstalled Mohammad Reza Pahlavi as shah of Iran, the ancient Persian title of king. Opposition to the coup and the subsequent decades of U.S. support for the shah fueled Iranian nationalism and anti-Americanism, which would eventually spark the 1979 Iranian Revolution (see "The Carter Presidency" in Chapter 29). In 1954, the CIA also engineered a coup in Guatemala against the democratically elected president, Jacobo Arbenz Guzmán, who had seized land from the American-owned United Fruit Company. Arbenz Guzmán offered to pay United Fruit the declared value of the land, but the company rejected the overture and sought help from the U.S. government. Eisenhower specifically approved those CIA efforts and expanded the agency's mandate from gathering intelligence to intervening in the affairs of sovereign states (see "Thinking Like a Historian," p. 780).

AP® EXAM TIP

Compare the foreign policies of Harry Truman and Dwight Eisenhower.

Vietnam When covert operations failed or proved impractical, the American approach to emerging nations risked entanglement in deeper, more intractable conflicts. One example was already unfolding in a distant country unknown to most Americans: Vietnam. At the close of World War II, the Japanese occupiers of the area surrendered to China in the north of the country and to Britain in the south. The Vietminh, the nationalist movement that had led the resistance against the Japanese (and the French, prior to 1940), seized control in the north. But their leader, Ho Chi Minh, was a Communist, and this fact outweighed American and British commitment to self-determination. When France moved to restore colonial control of Vietnam, the United States and Britain sided with their European ally. President Truman rejected Ho's plea to support the Vietnamese nationhood, and France rejected Ho's offer of a negotiated independence. Shortly after the French returned in late 1946, the Vietminh resumed their war of national liberation.

Eisenhower picked up where Truman had left off. If the French failed, Eisenhower argued, all non-Communist governments in the region would fall like dominoes. This so-called **domino theory** — which represented an extension of the containment doctrine — guided U.S. policy in Southeast Asia for the next twenty years. The United States eventually provided most of the financing for the French war, but money was not enough to defeat the determined Vietminh. After a fifty-seven-day siege in early 1954, the huge French fortress at Dien Bien Phu fell, and with it France's hopes of victory. Later that year, the Geneva Accords partitioned Vietnam temporarily at the 17th parallel and called for elections within two years to form a single government for a reunited Vietnam.

domino theory
President Eisenhower's theory of containment, which warned that the fall of a non-Communist government to communism in Southeast Asia would trigger the spread of communism to neighboring countries.

The United States rejected and undermined the Geneva Accords. With the help of the CIA, a pro-American government took power in South Vietnam in June 1954. The next year, in a rigged election, the anticommunist Catholic Ngo Dinh Diem became president of an independent South Vietnam. Facing certain defeat by the popular Ho Chi Minh in the scheduled reunification vote, Diem simply called off the vote. The Eisenhower administration propped up Diem with an average of $200 million a year in aid and a contingent of 675 American military advisors. This support was just the beginning.

AP® EXAM TIP

Evaluate U.S. policy in Vietnam as a commitment to containment policy.

The Middle East Vietnam remained out of the public spotlight even as American support ramped up. The same could not be said of the Middle East, an area rich in oil, political complexity, and the legacy of European colonialism. The most volatile area was Palestine, which had a majority Arab population but was also historically the ancient land of Israel and desired by the Zionist movement as the site of a Jewish national homeland. Jewish immigration to Palestine had begun in the aftermath of

AP® APPLY THE TIP

Prompt students to use their textbooks and other sources as needed to complete **Handout 24.2 — Comparison: Foreign Policy of Truman vs. Eisenhower (TRM)**. After students have filled in the details, provide them with excerpts from the Truman Doctrine, NSC-68, Eisenhower Doctrine, and Eisenhower's Farewell Address. Students should read the excerpts and use supporting details to further clarify the comparisons in the Venn diagram. Ask students to work with a partner to write a thesis and provide evidence to address the following prompt: Were Harry S. Truman and Dwight Eisenhower more alike or more different in foreign policy?

TRM Find **Handout 24.2 — Comparison: Foreign Policy of Truman vs. Eisenhower** in the Teacher's Resource Materials.

AP® THEME

WOR: America in the World

Students should understand that, anxious about the Communist ideology of expansionism and by Soviet repression, the U.S. sought to contain communism in a variety of ways, including through military engagement in Vietnam.

TEACHING STRATEGY

Ken Burns's documentary *The Vietnam War* provides an examination of early American involvement in Vietnam. To access episodes of this documentary, search "PBS The Vietnam War."

AP® THEME

WOR: America in the World

Lead a class discussion on how economic interests, along with ideological and military concerns, shaped U.S. involvement in the Middle East.

Egyptian President Challenges the West Waving to wildly cheering crowds as he is driven through a street in Cairo on July 28, 1956, is Gamal Abdel Nasser, the president of Egypt. Nasser became beloved in the region for nationalizing the Suez Canal — seizing it from Western interests — and for advocating a pan-Arab socialism allied with neither the United States nor the Soviet Union in the Cold War. AP Photo.

World War I, and thousands of Jews arrived as anti-Semitism in Europe steadily intensified in the 1930s. After World War II, many survivors of the Nazi extermination camps resettled in Palestine, which was still controlled by Britain under a 1922 mandate from the defunct League of Nations. On November 29, 1947, the UN General Assembly voted to partition Palestine between Jewish and Arab sectors. When the British mandate ended in 1948, Palestinian leaders rejected the partition as a violation of their right to self-determination, while Zionist leaders embraced the partition and proclaimed the state of Israel. In response, the Arab nations of Lebanon, Syria, Iraq, and Egypt invaded the newly proclaimed state. The infant nation of Israel survived, and many Palestinian Arabs fled or were driven from their homes by the Israeli army during the fighting. The Arab defeat left these people permanently stranded in refugee camps or exiled in foreign countries. President Truman recognized the new state immediately, which won him crucial support from Jewish voters in the 1948 election but aroused opposition in the Arab world.

AP® EXAM TIP

Recognize the impact of U.S. policy on nationalist movements in the Middle East.

Southwest of Palestine, Egypt began to assert its presence in the region. Having gained independence from Britain several decades earlier, Egypt remained a monarchy until 1952, when Gamal Abdel Nasser led a military coup that established a constitutional republic. Caught between the Soviet Union and the United States, Nasser sought an independent route: a pan-Arab socialism designed to sever colonial relationships with the West. When negotiations with the United States over Nasser's plan to build a massive hydroelectric dam on the Nile broke down in 1956, he nationalized the Suez Canal, which was the lifeline for Western Europe's oil shipments. Britain and France, in alliance with Israel, attacked Egypt and seized the canal. Concerned that the invasion would push Egypt toward the Soviets, Eisenhower successfully pressured France and Britain to pull back. After reclaiming the Suez Canal, Nasser built the massive Aswan Dam on the Nile with Soviet support. Eisenhower had likely avoided a larger war, but the West lost a potential ally in Nasser.

Eisenhower Doctrine
President Eisenhower's 1957 declaration that the United States would actively combat communism in the Middle East.

In early 1957, concerned about Soviet presence in the region, the president delivered a "Special Message to the Congress on the Situation in the Middle East." The document outlined a policy that came to be known as the **Eisenhower Doctrine**, which stated that American forces would assist any nation in the region that required aid "against overt armed aggression from any nation controlled by International Communism." Invoking the doctrine later that year, Eisenhower helped King Hussein of Jordan put down a Nasser-backed revolt and propped up a pro-American government in Lebanon. The Eisenhower Doctrine was further evidence that the United States had extended the global reach of containment, by incorporating the Middle East into the Cold War's rigid binary logic. In search of regional allies, always with an eye on the West's vital oil supply, the United States had initiated a commitment to intervening in the region that would endure for decades.

AP® SKILLS & PROCESSES

MAKING CONNECTIONS

How did the Cold War between the United States and the Soviet Union affect disparate regions such as the Middle East and Southeast Asia?

John F. Kennedy and Renewed East-West Tensions

Eisenhower's successor in the presidency, John F. Kennedy, was a conventional Cold War politician in most regards, raised in an era defined by Munich, Yalta, and McCarthy. Kennedy would introduce new Cold War tactics without fundamentally

AP® APPLY THE TIP

Ask students to read pp. 797–798 to complete **Handout 24.3 — Comparison: Nationalist Movements in the Middle East (TRM)**. As students complete the comparison, hand out a blank map of the Middle East. After students have finished the handout, ask them to label the nations, rivers, seas, and major cities in the region. Students should research the nationalist movements in the Middle East and add annotations to the map with Post-it notes that indicate specific events related to U.S. policy regarding nationalism in the Middle East. (As an alternative, this assignment could be done digitally utilizing Thinglink.com, which allows students to tag and annotate images online.) Then lead a class discussion on the U.S. responses to nationalism in the Cold War.

TRM Find **Handout 24.3 — Comparison: Nationalist Movements in the Middle East** in the Teacher's Resource Materials.

CHECK FOR UNDERSTANDING

Ask students: **How did the Cold War intersect with colonial independence movements?** *The global and zero-sum-game nature of the Cold War led the U.S. and Soviet Union to intervene in the societies and economies of many recently formed nation-states, which tended to be weak and unstable. These nations were offered economic assistance and pressured to join regional alliances.*

AP® SKILLS & PROCESSES

MAKING CONNECTIONS

This broad question invites students to see big picture connections across time and geographic region. For instance, the Cold War introduced the concept of proxy wars in regions where the United States was historically reticent to engage in military conflict. Students can use the idea of proxy wars to examine how transformative the Cold War was to the foreign policy goals of the Soviets and Americans.

TRM Find complete suggested responses in the Teacher's Resource Materials.

altering the containment strategy pursued by American presidents since Truman. Born into a prominent Massachusetts family, Kennedy's rise was steady and fast. He performed heroically in World War II, and he had the familiar Harvard pedigree of previous leaders. But Kennedy used charisma, style, and personality — more than platforms and issues — to define a new brand of politics. Kennedy had inherited his love of political combat from his grandfathers — colorful, and often ruthless, Irish Catholic politicians in Boston. Elected to congress in 1946 and to the senate in 1952, in 1960 he set his sights on the presidency. Ambitious and image savvy, the forty-three-year-old Kennedy made use of his many advantages to become, as novelist Norman Mailer put it, "our leading man." His chief political disadvantage — that he was Catholic in a country that had never elected a Catholic president — he skillfully neutralized. Thanks to both media advisors and his youthfulness, he cultivated an air of idealism, but his international outlook relied on old-style power politics.

The Kennedy Magnetism John F. Kennedy, the 1960 Democratic candidate for president, used his youth and personality (and those of his equally personable and stylish wife) to attract voters. Here the Massachusetts senator draws an enthusiastic crowd on a campaign stop in Elgin, Illinois. AP Photo.

The Election of 1960 and the New Frontier Kennedy's Republican opponent in the 1960 presidential election was Eisenhower's vice president, Richard Nixon, a seasoned politician and Cold Warrior himself. The great innovation of the 1960 campaign was a series of four nationally televised debates. Nixon, less photogenic than Kennedy, looked pasty and unshaven under the intense studio lights. Voters who heard the first debate on the radio concluded that Nixon had won, but those who viewed it on television favored Kennedy. Despite Kennedy's success in the debates, he won the narrowest of electoral victories, receiving 49.7 percent of the popular vote to Nixon's 49.5 percent. Kennedy attracted Catholics, African Americans, and the labor vote; his vice-presidential running mate, Texas senator Lyndon Baines Johnson, helped bring in white southern Democrats. Only 120,000 votes separated the two candidates, and a shift of a few thousand votes in key states would have reversed the outcome.

Kennedy brought to Washington a host of both young, ambitious newcomers and trusted advisors and academics, who flocked to Washington to join the New Frontier — Kennedy's term for the challenges the country faced. They included Robert McNamara, a renowned systems analyst and former head of Ford Motor Company, as secretary of defense and Kennedy's younger brother Robert, who had made a name as a hard-hitting investigator of organized crime, as attorney general. Relying on an old American trope, Kennedy's New Frontier evoked masculine toughness and uncharted terrain. That terrain quickly proved treacherous, however, as the new administration faced an immediate international incident.

Crises in Cuba and Berlin In January 1961, the Soviet Union announced that it intended to support "wars of national liberation" wherever in the world they occurred. Kennedy took Soviet premier Khrushchev at his word, especially regarding Cuba, where in 1959 communist revolutionaries under Fidel Castro had overthrown the right-wing dictator Fulgencio Batista. Determined to keep Cuba out of the Soviet orbit, Kennedy followed through on Eisenhower administration plans to orchestrate a raid by Cuban exiles meant to launch an anti-Castro uprising. The invaders, trained by the CIA, proved ill-prepared for the task. Shortly after the force of 1,400 landed at

AP® EXAM TIP

The role of the United States in Latin America during the Cold War is important to know on the AP® Exam.

TEACHING STRATEGY

While Kennedy's inaugural address is often remembered for its lofty rhetoric and idealism, it devoted more time to addressing the global Cold War and the need for continued vigilance. The full text and audio file of the address is available at the Kennedy Library. To access this resource, search "Kennedy Library Inaugural Address."

TEACHING STRATEGY

The Kennedy Library's "World on the Brink" Web site page is an excellent interactive resource detailing the thirteen-day Cuban missile crisis one day at a time, with narration, maps, memos, and audio files. To access this site, search "Kennedy Library World on the Brink."

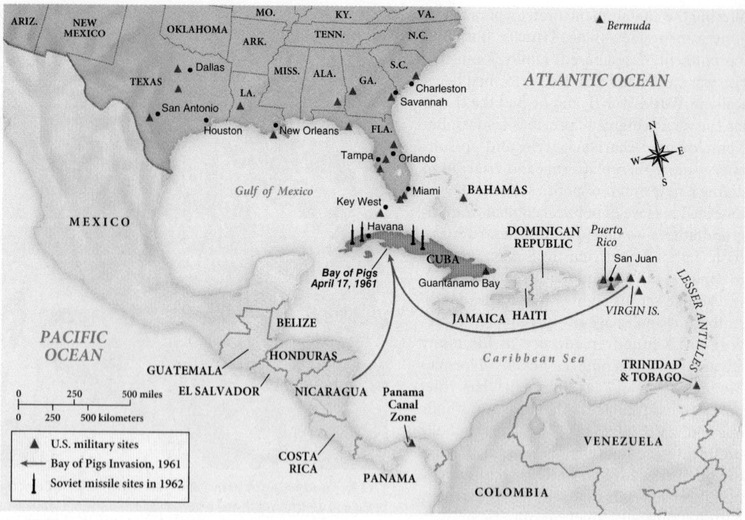

MAP 24.6 The United States and Cuba, 1961–1962
Fidel Castro's 1959 Communist takeover of Cuba brought Cold War tensions to the Caribbean. In 1961, the United States tried unsuccessfully to overthrow Castro's regime by sponsoring the Bay of Pigs invasion of Cuban exiles launched from Nicaragua and other points in the Caribbean. In 1962, the United States confronted the Soviet Union over Soviet construction of nuclear missile sites in Cuba. After President Kennedy ordered a naval blockade of the island, the Soviets backed down from the tense standoff and removed the missiles. Despite the 1991 dissolution of the Soviet Union and the official end of the Cold War, the United States continued to view Cuba, governed by Raúl Castro, Fidel's brother, since 2008, as an enemy nation until 2016, when President Barack Obama began the process of normalizing relations between the two countries.

Bay of Pigs
A failed U.S.-sponsored invasion of Cuba in 1961 by anti-Castro forces who planned to overthrow Fidel Castro's government.

Cuba's **Bay of Pigs** on April 17, 1961, Castro's troops crushed them. Kennedy prudently rejected CIA pleas for a U.S. air strike. Accepting the defeat, the new president went before the American people and took full responsibility for the fiasco (Map 24.6).

Already strained by the Bay of Pigs incident, U.S.-Soviet relations deteriorated further in June 1961 after Khrushchev stopped movement between Communist-controlled East Berlin and the city's Western sector. Kennedy responded by dispatching 40,000 additional troops to Europe. In mid-August, to stop the exodus of East Germans fleeing to the West, the Communist regime began constructing the Berlin Wall, policed by border guards under shoot-to-kill orders. Kennedy again responded, though this time rhetorically, by criticizing the wall in a June 1963 speech in West Berlin, calling it "the most obvious and vivid demonstration of the failures of the Communist system." Until the 12-foot-high concrete barrier came down in 1989, it served as the supreme symbol of the ongoing Cold War.

Perhaps the most perilous episode of that conflict arrived in Autumn 1962. In a somber televised address on October 22, Kennedy revealed that U.S. reconnaissance planes had spotted Soviet-built bases for intermediate-range ballistic missiles in Cuba — easily capable of striking the continental United States. Some of those weapons had already been installed, and more were on the way. Kennedy announced that the United States would impose a "quarantine on all offensive military equipment" bound for Cuba. As the world held its breath, ships carrying Soviet missiles turned back on October 25. After a week of tense negotiations, both sides made concessions: Kennedy pledged not to invade Cuba, and Khrushchev promised to dismantle the missile bases. Kennedy also secretly ordered U.S. missiles to be removed from Turkey,

AP® SKILLS & PROCESSES

DEVELOPMENTS AND PROCESSES

Much of the early events in the Cold War revolved around Berlin, Germany. Ask students to identify why Berlin was of such symbolic and actual importance in the Cold War for both the Americans and the Soviets.

VISUAL ACTIVITY

The Berlin Wall A West Berlin resident walks alongside a section of the Berlin Wall in August 1962, a year after its construction. The wall divided the Soviet-controlled zone, which became East Berlin, from the three zones controlled by the United States, Britain, and France, which became West Berlin. Berlin itself lay in East Germany, the independent state created in 1949 from the Soviet-occupied portion of Germany. Bettmann/Getty Images.

READING THE IMAGE: What do you notice about the materials in and around the wall? What purpose do you think the loud speakers on the East German side might have served?

MAKING CONNECTIONS: The wall divided neighborhoods and neighbors, but it also divided two nations, East and West Germany. How would the construction of the Berlin Wall be explained from the point of view of the Soviet Union? How would it be explained from the point of view of the United States? How did other events in the early Cold War impact the decision to construct the Berlin Wall?

at Khrushchev's insistence. The **Cuban missile crisis** proved the closest the Cold War came to a nuclear exchange. The terrifying stakes led to a slight thaw in U.S.-Soviet relations. As National Security Advisor McGeorge Bundy put it, both sides were chastened by "having come so close to the edge."

Cuban missile crisis
The 1962 nuclear standoff between the Soviet Union and the United States when the Soviets attempted to deploy nuclear missiles in Cuba.

Kennedy and the World Kennedy also launched a series of international initiatives that captured the idealism of the early 1960s. One was the **Peace Corps**, which embodied the call to public service put forth in his inaugural address ("Ask not what your country can do for you — ask what you can do for your country"). Thousands of men and women agreed to devote two or more years as volunteers for projects such as teaching English to Filipino schoolchildren or helping African villagers obtain clean water. The Peace Corps also proved a low-cost Cold War weapon — and an extension of American "soft power" — that showed the developing world an alternative to communism. Kennedy championed space exploration as well. In a 1962 speech, he proposed that the nation commit itself to landing a man on the moon within the decade. The Soviets had already beaten the United States into orbit with the 1957 *Sputnik* satellite and

Peace Corps
Program launched by President Kennedy in 1961 through which young American volunteers helped with education, health, and other projects in developing countries around the world.

TRM Find complete suggested responses in the Teacher's Resource Materials.

AP® SKILLS & PROCESSES

COMPARISON

President Kennedy's Peace Corps was symbolic of the mood of possibility so many Americans held in the early 1960s. It also represents a unique opportunity for students to examine how the United States waged wars in developing nations at the same time it sought to lend diplomatic and humanitarian services. Ask students to reconcile the realities of Cold War foreign policy decisions with the optimism and humanitarian goals of the Peace Corps.

the 1961 flight of cosmonaut Yuri Gagarin. Capitalizing on America's fascination with space, Kennedy persuaded Congress to increase funding for the National Aeronautics and Space Administration (NASA), which completed the research and development that pushed the United States ahead in the space race. In 1969, American astronauts would fulfill Kennedy's ambition by walking on the lunar surface.

Making a Commitment in Vietnam

When Kennedy became president, he inherited American involvement in Vietnam. Truman had sent aid to the French, and in the wake of French defeat Eisenhower had molded South Vietnam into an American client state. Like his predecessors, Kennedy understood Vietnam as another front of the Cold War. But the nuclear brinksmanship of the Cuban missile crisis led this time to a more moderate interventionism. In 1961, he increased military aid to the South Vietnamese and expanded the role of U.S. Special Forces ("Green Berets"), who would train the South Vietnamese army in unconventional, small-group warfare tactics.

But the corrupt and repressive Diem regime, propped up by Eisenhower since 1954, was losing ground in spite of American support. By 1961, Diem's opponents, with backing from North Vietnam, had formed a revolutionary movement known as the National Liberation Front (NLF). The Vietcong, as the NLF's guerrilla fighters were known, found allies among peasants harmed by Diem's "strategic hamlet" program, which had uprooted entire villages to break up support for the NLF. Furthermore, members of the country's Buddhist majority charged Diem, a Catholic, with religious persecution. Starting in May 1963, militant Buddhists staged dramatic demonstrations, which in June came to include self-immolations (burning to death) recorded by reporters covering the activities of the 16,000 U.S. military personnel then in Vietnam.

These gruesome protests, broadcast on television for a shocked global audience, illustrated the dilemma of American policy in Vietnam. To ensure a stable government in the South and check Ho Chi Minh and the North, the United States had to support Diem's authoritarian regime. But the regime's repression of its political opponents destabilized South Vietnam as a whole. The turmoil escalated with Diem's assassination on November 2, 1963. American involvement in Vietnam would massively expand, but the elemental paradox remained unchanged: in its efforts to achieve victory, the United States took actions that brought defeat ever closer.

AP® SKILLS & PROCESSES

COMPARISON

How was Kennedy's approach to the Cold War similar to and different from Eisenhower's and Truman's?

SUMMARY

The Cold War began as a conflict between the United States and the Soviet Union over the fate of post-World War II Germany and Eastern Europe. Early on, the United States adopted a strategy of containment, meant to curtail the spread of Soviet influence. After Mao Zedong and the Chinese Communist Party gained power in China, America's containment policy expanded to Asia. The first effect of that expansion was the Korean War, after which containment became America's guiding principle across the developing world—often called the Third World in that era. Cold War tensions relaxed in the late 1950s but erupted again under John F. Kennedy with the Cuban missile crisis, the building of the Berlin Wall, and major increases in American military assistance to South Vietnam. The twenty years after World War II saw a major military buildup, a massive nuclear arms race, and unprecedented entanglements across the globe.

On the domestic front, Harry S. Truman started out with high hopes for an expanded New Deal, only to be confounded by resistance from Congress and the competing demands of the Cold War. A climate of fear over internal subversion by Communists gave rise to McCarthyism and a new Red Scare. Truman's successor, Eisenhower, brought the Republicans back into power. Although personally conservative, "Ike" did not dismantle the New Deal. When Eisenhower left office and Kennedy became president, it seemed that a "liberal consensus" reigned over a nation enjoying widespread prosperity.

CHECK FOR UNDERSTANDING

Ask students: **What was John F. Kennedy's response to the Cold War?** *Kennedy was narrowly elected president in 1960 (he ran in part on a claim that his predecessor had allowed a "missile gap" to develop with the Soviet Union). In less than three years, he had several tense confrontations with the Soviet Union. He approved a disastrous CIA plan to send exiles to infiltrate Cuba, had a showdown with Soviet tanks in Berlin that led to the building of the Berlin Wall, and compelled the Soviet Union to withdraw plans to place nuclear missiles in Cuba—nearly provoking a nuclear conflict. He also increased funding and sent additional Special Forces troops to Vietnam.*

AP® SKILLS & PROCESSES

COMPARISON

It may help students to root their comparisons in policy labels such as Truman Doctrine, Eisenhower Doctrine, and Flexible Response. Have students think about the extent to which each policy embraced the overarching early Cold War policy of Containment.

TRM Find complete suggested responses in the Teacher's Resource Materials.

CHECK FOR UNDERSTANDING

Use the **AP® LEARNING FOCUS** question from the beginning of the chapter to check students' understanding of the chapter as a whole: **Why did the international rivalry of the Cold War create a climate of fear at home and how did it affect politics and society in the United States?** *The first two decades of the Cold War witnessed a competition of ideology between the Soviet Union and the United States. The Marshall Plan, the Truman Doctrine, NATO, and America's policy of containment were each informed by the theory that the USSR sought allies and adherents. Domestically, the Cold War caused fear, suspicion, and political persecution of "subversives." Conformity and loyalty to the American government became paramount issues and the federal government asserted its role in the fight against subversion in ways that caused debates over the proper balance between security and freedom.*

LearningCurve

Remind students to go online to complete the LearningCurve quiz for this chapter.

CHAPTER 24 REVIEW

AP® CONTENT REVIEW *Answer these questions to demonstrate your understanding of the chapter's main ideas.*

1. What primary factors caused the Cold War?
2. What were the defining ideas of Cold War liberalism, and why did the Democratic Party embrace them?
3. What objectives guided U.S. foreign policy in the postcolonial world during the Cold War?

AP® TERMS TO KNOW *Identify and explain the significance of each term.*

Key Concepts and Events

Yalta Conference (p. 775)
United Nations (p. 775)
Potsdam Conference (p. 775)
containment (p. 778)
Truman Doctrine (p. 779)
Marshall Plan (p. 782)
North Atlantic Treaty Organization (NATO) (p. 782)
Warsaw Pact (p. 782)
NSC-68 (p. 783)
Cold War liberalism (p. 787)
Taft-Hartley Act (p. 787)
Fair Deal (p. 788)
Loyalty-Security Program (p. 789)
House Un-American Activities Committee (HUAC) (p. 790)
New Look (p. 795)
domino theory (p. 797)
Eisenhower Doctrine (p. 798)
Bay of Pigs (p. 800)
Cuban missile crisis (p. 801)
Peace Corps (p. 801)

Key People

Joseph Stalin (p. 775)
George F. Kennan (p. 779)
Nikita Khrushchev (p. 787)
Joseph McCarthy (p. 790)
Ho Chi Minh (p. 797)
John F. Kennedy (p. 798)
Fidel Castro (p. 799)

AP® MAKING CONNECTIONS *Recognize the larger developments and continuities within and across chapters by answering these questions.*

1. How was America's Cold War foreign policy an extension of principles and policies from earlier eras, and in what ways was it a break with those traditions? Was the Cold War inevitable? Support your descriptions of continuity and change with evidence from the text.
2. Look at the map of the military-industrial complex on page 786 (Map 24.3) and the map of population changes on page 829 (Chapter 25, Map 25.2). Where were the majority of military weapons manufactured? What were the connections between weapons and geography? How did those connections affect population distribution in the United States and within individual metropolitan areas?

KEY TURNING POINTS *Refer to the timeline at the start of the chapter for help in answering the following question.*

What turning points and crises defined American containment policy between 1946 and 1954? Explain your answer with evidence from the timeline and chapter.

803

TRM Find complete suggested responses in the Teacher's Resource Materials.

AP® SKILLS & PROCESSES

CAUSATION

AP® CONTENT REVIEW 1 asks students to identify the most significant factors that caused the Cold War. Note: This question is the same as the section-opening prompt on p. 774.

TRM Find definitions for these terms in the **Glossary/Glosario** in the Teacher's Resource Materials.

AP® SKILLS & PROCESSES

CONTINUITY AND CHANGE

AP® MAKING CONNECTIONS 1 encourages students to place American foreign policy in a longer-term context.

AP® SKILLS & PROCESSES

CONTINUITY AND CHANGE

The **KEY TURNING POINTS** question asks students to identify major turning points in containment foreign policy within the early years of the Cold War.

TRM Find complete suggested responses in the Teacher's Resource Materials.

AP® PRACTICE QUESTIONS

MULTIPLE CHOICE QUESTIONS *Choose the correct answer for each question.*

Questions 1–4 refer to the excerpt provided.

"I am convinced that there would be far less hysterical anti-Sovietism in our country today if the realities of this situation were better understood by our people. There is nothing as dangerous or as terrifying as the unknown. . . .

World communism is like a malignant parasite which feeds only on diseased tissue. This is the point at which domestic and foreign policies meet. Every courageous and incisive measure to solve the internal problems of our own society . . . is a diplomatic victory over Moscow. . . .

Many foreign peoples, in Europe at least, are tired and frightened by experiences of the past, and are less interested in abstract freedom than in security. They are seeking guidance rather than responsibilities. We should be better able than Russians to give them this. And unless we do, the Russians certainly will."

George Kennan, United States diplomat in Moscow, "Long Telegram" to the Secretary of State, February 1946

1. The arguments expressed in the excerpt are best understood in the context of the
   - **a.** U.S. military involvement in the Korean and Vietnam wars.
   - **b.** fluctuation between confrontation and coexistence with the Soviet Union.
   - **c.** emergence of nationalist movements across the globe after World War II.
   - **d.** end of the wartime alliance between the United States and the Soviet Union.
2. The "hysteria" referenced by Kennan in the excerpt refers most directly to
   - **a.** widespread public protests against the draft.
   - **b.** growing scientific concern about environmental dangers of a nuclear war.
   - **c.** a domestic search for communists working in the government or mass media.
   - **d.** legislation restricting free speech and limiting criticism of U.S. foreign policy.
3. Kennan's arguments expressed in the excerpt most directly supported a foreign policy of
   - **a.** détente.
   - **b.** containment.
   - **c.** isolationism.
   - **d.** imperialism.
4. The most direct result of Kennan's ideas expressed in the excerpt was the
   - **a.** establishment of the United Nations.
   - **b.** spread of Cold War competition to Latin America.
   - **c.** North Atlantic Treaty Organization.
   - **d.** growth of a large military-industrial complex in the United States.

Questions 5–6 refer to the excerpt provided.

"In Korea the Government forces, which were armed to prevent border raids and to preserve internal security, were attacked by invading forces from North Korea. The Security Council of the United Nations called upon the invading troops to cease hostilities and to withdraw to the 38th parallel. This they have not done, but on the contrary have pressed the attack. The Security Council called upon all members of the United Nations to render every assistance to the United Nations in the execution of this resolution. In these circumstances I have ordered United States air and sea forces to give the Korean Government troops cover and support.

The attack upon Korea makes it plain beyond all doubt that communism has passed beyond the use of subversion to conquer independent nations and will now use armed invasion and war."

President Truman, Statement on the Situation in Korea, June 1950

5. The sentiments expressed in the excerpt share the greatest similarity to those who used to support U.S. entry into which of the following conflicts?
   - **a.** The Spanish-American War
   - **b.** World War I
   - **c.** Vietnam War
   - **d.** Persian Gulf War
6. The events described in the excerpt most immediately led to
   - **a.** growing power of the executive branch to conduct foreign policy.
   - **b.** the rise of independence movements in the former colonies of European countries.
   - **c.** a New Left govement challenging United States military interventionism.
   - **d.** the increasing immigration to the United States from countries in Asia.

SHORT ANSWER QUESTIONS

Read each question carefully and write a short response. Use evidence from the text to support your claims.

"Whatever date is chosen to mark the declaration of [the Cold War], it is certain that the issue that sparked it, gave it life and shaped its early course, was East Europe. For centuries East and West have struggled . . . for control of the huge area running from the Baltic to the Balkans, an area rich in human and industrial resources and one that is strategically vital to both sides. . . . Neither the West nor the East has been willing to allow East Europe to be strong, independent, or neutral. Russia and the West each have wanted the area to be aligned with them and open for their own economic exploitation. . . . [During World War II], the West made no significant contribution to the liberation of East Europe and when the end came the Red Army was in sole possession of the area. . . . This crucial result of World War II destroyed the Grand Alliance and gave birth to the Cold War."

Stephen E. Ambrose, *Rise to Globalism: American Foreign Policy Since 1938*, 1971

"[T]he argument that the Cold War conceptually and analytically does not belong in the south [i.e., Africa, South Asia, and Latin America] is wrong. . . . US and Soviet interventionisms . . . shaped both the international and the domestic framework within which political, social, and cultural changes in Third World countries took place. . . . The United States and the Soviet Union were driven to intervene in the Third World by the ideologies inherent in their politics. . . . Washington and Moscow needed to change the world in order to prove the universal applicability of their ideologies, and the elites of the newly independent [Third World] states proved fertile ground for their competition. . . . [B]oth powers saw themselves as assisting natural trends in world history and as defending their own security at the same time. Both saw a specific mission in and for the Third World that only their own state could carry out and which without their involvement would flounder in local hands."

Odd Arne Westad, *The Global Cold War: Third World Interventions and the Making of Our Times*, 2005

1. Using the two excerpts provided, answer (a), (b), and (c).
   - **a.** Briefly explain ONE major difference between Ambrose's and Westad's historical interpretations of the Cold War.
   - **b.** Briefly explain how ONE specific historical event or development from the period 1945 to 1980 that is not explicitly mentioned in the excerpts could be used to support Ambrose's interpretation.
   - **c.** Briefly explain how ONE specific historical event or development from the period 1945 to 1980 that is not explicitly mentioned in the excerpts could be used to support Westad's interpretation.

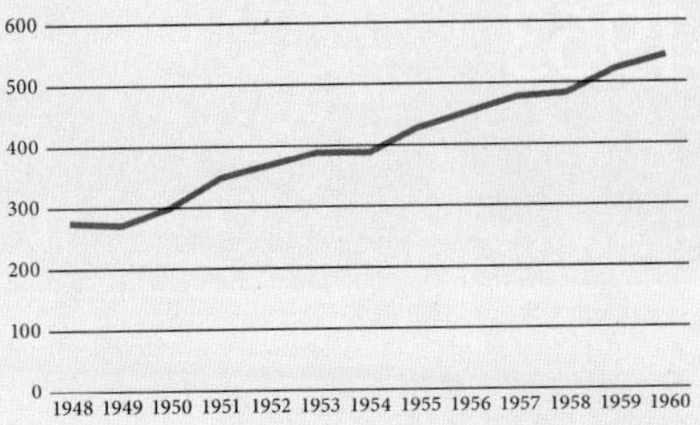

Government Military Expenditures (In Billions of Dollars)

2. Using the graph provided, answer (a), (b), and (c).
   - **a.** Briefly explain ONE specific historical event or development that caused the trend depicted in the graph.
   - **b.** Briefly explain ANOTHER specific historical event or development that caused the trend depicted in the graph.
   - **c.** Briefly explain ONE specific historical effect in United States society of the change depicted in the graph.

3. Answer (a), (b), and (c).
   - **a.** Briefly explain ONE specific historical difference between U.S. foreign policy in the period 1920–1940 from U. S. foreign policy in the period 1945–1963.
   - **b.** Briefly explain ONE specific historical similarity between U.S. foreign policy in the period 1920–1940 to U. S. foreign policy in the period 1945–1963.
   - **c.** Briefly explain ONE specific historical effect on U.S. society of the nation's foreign policy in the period 1920–1940 OR in the period 1945–1963.

TRM Find complete suggested responses in the Teacher's Resource Materials.

25 CHAPTER

Triumph of the Middle Class

1945–1963

Chapter 25 — AP® Assessment Weight and Pacing Guide

The assessment weight on the AP® U.S. History Exam for Chapters 23–28 is 10–17 percent. This chapter falls in Unit 8 of the AP® U.S. History Curriculum, covering Period 8: 1945–1980.

This pacing guide is based on a schedule with 120 sessions of 50 minutes each before the AP® U.S. History Exam. If you have a different number of sessions before the exam, you can modify the pacing to meet your needs. If you have additional time, consider incorporating quizzes, released AP® U.S. History questions, practice exams, writing practice, and other instructional activities.

	Traditional Schedule	Block Schedule
Chapter 25	3 days	1–2 days

Daily Pacing Guide

	Content Focus	Essential Question
Day 1	Postwar Prosperity and the Affluent Society	What drove the growth of the American economy after World War II?
Day 2	The Modern Nuclear Family	What was the domestic ideal, and how did Americans embrace it in the postwar decades?
Day 3	A Suburban Nation	What were the major forces that shaped postwar suburbanization?

AP® Alignment

Section Heading	AP® Topic	AP® Theme
Postwar Prosperity and the Affluent Society	8.2, 8.4, 8.5	WOR, WXT, MIG, ARC
The Modern Nuclear Family	8.4, 8.5	WXT, MIG, ARC
A Suburban Nation	8.4	WXT, MIG

*Should changes be made to the Course Framework in the future, an updated alignment will be placed on our AP® updates page at go.bfwpub.com/ap-course-updates.

Chapter 25 — Overview

Chapter 25 focuses on the cultural and economic transformation of the U.S. in the postwar era. The chapter attributes the economic prosperity of the postwar era to both the impact of federal military spending through the military-industrial complex as well as the explosion of pent-up demand for consumer goods after World War II. In this changing economic environment, the rise of the youth culture and power of teenagers as consumers are emphasized as well as the challenges these changes presented to the traditional authority of churches and parents. In addition, the changes associated with the baby boom and the role of women in the workplace and politics challenged traditional expectations regarding family life. Finally, the chapter analyzes the movement of the middle class to the suburbs and the growing divisions between urban and suburban America.

Chapter 25 — Resources

The following resources can be found in the Teacher's Resource Materials (TRM) that accompany the book. You can access the TRM via the book's digital platform, by clicking the TRM links found here in your Teacher's Edition e-book, or by contacting your representative to access the resources online. Visit **bfwpub.com/henretta10e** to learn more.

TRM Chapter 25 Lecture Presentation Slides

TRM Chapter 25 Outline with AP® Focus

TRM Chapter 25 Lecture Strategies

TRM Chapter 25 Suggested Responses

TRM Handout 25.1 — Causation: Postwar Economic Growth

TRM Handout 25.2 — Comparison: Women in the Postwar Years

TRM Handout 25.3 — Thematic Analysis: Middle Class and Suburbs

TRM Handout 25.4 — Thematic Analysis: Suburbanization

Chapter 25 — Essential Activity

Assign the **AP® THINKING LIKE A HISTORIAN** feature and questions on pp. 824–825 as homework. In class, organize students into pairs and assign each pair one of the following Historical Thinking Skills or Reasoning Processes: contextualization, causation, comparison, and continuity and change. Each pair should develop a prompt for a Document Based Question (DBQ) utilizing the six documents on pp. 824–825 as well as one additional source to support their prompt (the additional source can be found in the text or in outside sources). After students formulate their DBQ prompt, require them to create a scoring guide for their prompt to include the following: two or three acceptable thesis statements to address the prompt; a list of specific evidence outside of the documents that could be used in response to the prompt; and an extended analysis (historical context, intended audience, purpose, and point of view) for each document. As an extension of this activity, randomly assign students to write a DBQ essay in response to a prompt from a classmate.

Chapter 25 — Bell Ringers

The following activities take no more than 5–15 minutes of your class period and offer an effective and engaging way to begin your lessons and for students to apply AP® Skills & Processes:

- Provide or project images of consumer advertisements from the 1920s and the 1950s. Utilize images that illustrate the advent of the teenager as a consumer force in the 1950s. Ask students to discuss the intended audience of the ads from the 1920s versus the ads from the 1950s and discuss the impact of teenagers on consumer culture.
- Give each student a copy of the lyrics from "Little Boxes" (1962) by Malvina Reynolds. Ask students to explain the criticism of culture expressed by the lyrics of the song. Then lead a discussion on the impact of suburbanization on diversity and conformity in American society.
- Project a map of the Sunbelt that shows patterns of migration in the 1950s and 1960s. Ask students to make comparisons to other periods of migration including the Great Migration of African Americans in the 1920s–1930s and the migration of Americans to California in the gold rush. Prompt students to draw conclusions regarding the causes and effects of migration on American society.

NOTES

25 CHAPTER

Triumph of the Middle Class 1945–1963

TEACHING STRATEGY

The chapter introduction highlights the focus on postwar aspirations to middle-class status. As the text indicates, apart from a particular income threshold, middle-class identity was defined by home ownership (ideally in the suburbs) and the ability to purchase consumer goods. By that definition, the middle class *did* grow dramatically in the postwar period. However, though advertising and popular culture made this lifestyle seem ubiquitous, many Americans could not attain it. Despite dominant cultural images of conformity and tranquility, a number of problems were brewing beneath the surface. For a complete suggested response to the **AP® LEARNING FOCUS** question, see p. 832.

AP® LEARNING FOCUS

Why did consumer culture become such a fixture of American life in the postwar decades, and how did it affect politics and society?

In July of 1959, the American vice president Richard Nixon met Soviet premier Nikita Khrushchev for a rare face-to-face debate. This historic meeting did not take place at the Kremlin, or the White House, or even the United Nations, but in the kitchen of a model home at the American National Exposition in Moscow. They did not discuss ongoing tension in West Berlin, or some other Cold War flashpoint. Instead, they clashed over the merits of Pepsi-Cola, TV dinners, and electric ovens — perhaps appropriate subject matter for the setting, a showcase for the American way of life. As the two politicians walked through the exhibition, Nixon explained to Khrushchev the huge variety of goods available to American consumers. Through an interpreter, the vice president joked that the Soviet Union may have superior rockets, but the United States was ahead in other areas, such as color television.

The model home became a symbolic Cold War contest over the standard of living in the real homes of both nations. A key element of the so-called **kitchen debate** was Nixon's insistence, to a disbelieving Khrushchev, that a modern home filled with a shiny new toaster, television, and other consumer products was accessible to the average American worker. "Any steelworker could buy this house," Nixon told the Soviet leader. The kitchen debate settled little in the geopolitical rivalry between the United States and the USSR, but it speaks across the decades. By the late 1950s Americans had come to see themselves as home owners and consumers. For many, the middle-class American dream was increasingly a commercial aspiration — a lifestyle to be purchased as much as a life to be lived.

kitchen debate
A 1959 debate over the merits of their rival systems between U.S. vice president Richard Nixon and Soviet premier Nikita Khrushchev at the opening of an American exhibition in Moscow.

In the two decades following the end of World War II, a new and influential consumer class was born in the United States. *Fortune* magazine estimated that in the 1950s, the middle class — which *Fortune* defined as families with more than $5,000 in annual earnings after taxes (about $50,000 today) — was increasing at the rate of 1.1 million people per year. Riding a wave of rising incomes, American dominance in the global economy, and Cold War federal spending, this ascendant middle class enjoyed the highest standard of living in the world. That class fervently embraced a long-standing American ideal centered on home ownership, domestic fulfillment, and traditional morality. However, the success of the middle class could not mask the nation's complex contradictions. The postwar era saw challenges to conformity and mounting social strife. The persistence of racial inequality, diverging expectations for women, a rebellious youth culture, and changing sexual mores were only the most obvious sources of social tension. Suburban growth came at the expense of cities, hastening urban decay and deepening racial segregation. Nor was prosperity ever as widespread as the Moscow exhibit implied. The suburban lifestyle was beyond the reach of the working poor, the elderly, immigrants, Mexican Americans, and most African Americans — combined, nearly half of the country. The lopsided nature of postwar prosperity would become a focal point of debate and unrest in the 1960s.

TEACHING STRATEGY

The kitchen debate highlighted Nixon's view that quality of life was centrally defined by access to the newest appliances. The Teaching American History Web site provides a full transcript of the exchange between Nixon and Khrushchev that came to be known as the "kitchen debate." The two leaders used the debate as an opportunity to champion the strengths of each society's technology and system of economy. In the process, they touched on issues of gender, family, and labor. To access this transcript, search "Teaching American History Kitchen Debate."

The Middle-Class Family Ideal A family eats breakfast at a campground in Zion National Park, Utah. Americans embraced a middle-class, nuclear family ideal in the postwar decades. Justin Locke/National Geographic Creative.

TEACHING STRATEGY

Ask students: **In what ways does this image capture the middle-class ideals of the postwar family?** *The normative American family was a white, nuclear, two-parent family with two or three children. The family enjoys being together, has access to vacation time, and a personal car to drive to a national park (which cannot be accessed any other way), and — conforming to gender expectations — the mother cheerfully manages meal preparation.*

AP® SKILLS & PROCESSES

CONTINUITY AND CHANGE

Use the **TIMELINE** table to help students begin thinking about how the period from 1944 to 1965 could constitute a distinct historical period. Essentially, this chapter looks at the same period as the previous chapter, this time focused almost exclusively on domestic issues (aside from the Red Scare, which was addressed in the previous chapter). The inclusion of the kitchen debate and discussion of the military-industrial complex are intended to help remind students of the links between the Cold War — and heightened military expenditures — and the growth of the economy that made the middle-class dream available to millions. Students might compare the chronologies of the two chapters and discuss multiple links between the Cold War and postwar domestic life.

TIMELINE

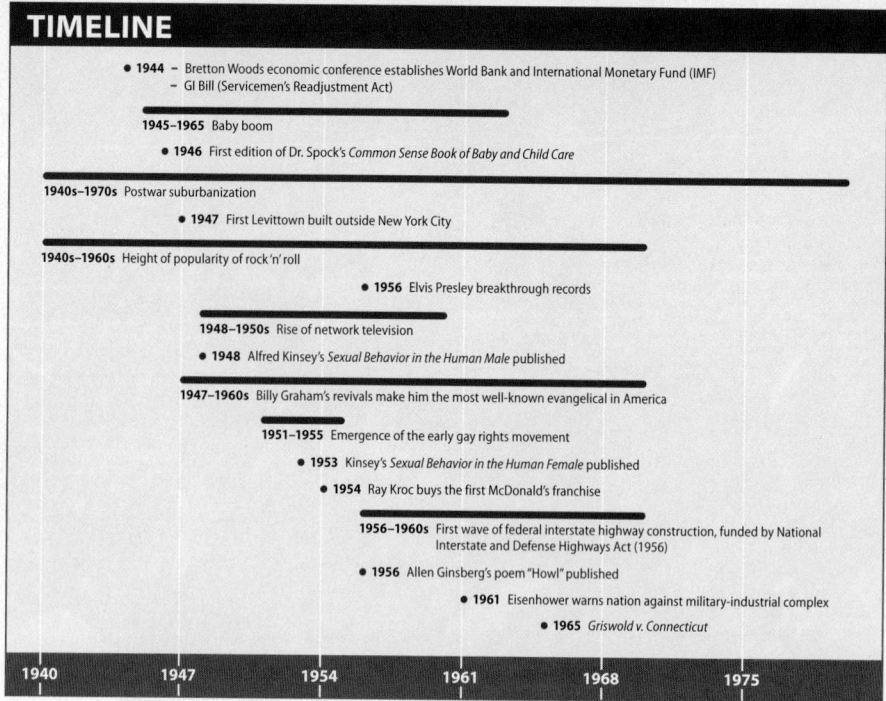

- **1944** – Bretton Woods economic conference establishes World Bank and International Monetary Fund (IMF)
  – GI Bill (Servicemen's Readjustment Act)
- **1945–1965** Baby boom
- **1946** First edition of Dr. Spock's *Common Sense Book of Baby and Child Care*
- **1940s–1970s** Postwar suburbanization
- **1947** First Levittown built outside New York City
- **1940s–1960s** Height of popularity of rock 'n' roll
- **1956** Elvis Presley breakthrough records
- **1948–1950s** Rise of network television
- **1948** Alfred Kinsey's *Sexual Behavior in the Human Male* published
- **1947–1960s** Billy Graham's revivals make him the most well-known evangelical in America
- **1951–1955** Emergence of the early gay rights movement
- **1953** Kinsey's *Sexual Behavior in the Human Female* published
- **1954** Ray Kroc buys the first McDonald's franchise
- **1956–1960s** First wave of federal interstate highway construction, funded by National Interstate and Defense Highways Act (1956)
- **1956** Allen Ginsberg's poem "Howl" published
- **1961** Eisenhower warns nation against military-industrial complex
- **1965** *Griswold v. Connecticut*

1940 | 1947 | 1954 | 1961 | 1968 | 1975

POSTWAR PROSPERITY AND THE AFFLUENT SOCIETY

What drove the growth of the American economy after World War II?

At the close of World War II, the United State occupied an unprecedented global position as the only major industrial nation not devastated by the conflict. While much of Europe and East Asia cleared away the rubble, America was poised to enter a postwar boom. The massive war effort had finally ended the Great Depression, and investments in research and development led to innovations in both technology and production. The country's internal markets were growing dramatically, and for the first time American employers generally accepted collective bargaining with labor unions. The power of union labor translated into rising wages, expanding benefits, and an increasing rate of home ownership. The federal government's outlays for military and domestic programs boosted the economy as well. Combined, these factors produced a new standard for middle-class living.

Economy: From Recovery to Dominance

Publisher Henry Luce, whose weekly *Life* magazine shaped the opinions of millions of Americans, was so confident in the nation's growing power that during World War II he had predicted the dawning of an "American century" — a global age defined by American ideals and American might, both political and economic. Luce envisioned

U.S. corporations, banks, and manufacturers dominating global markets. His vision did indeed come to pass, but it was not inevitable. America's post-1945 economic power — measured both by the productivity of its economy and by its capacity to set the rules of international trade and finance — was not simply a by-product of winning the war. Several key elements came together, internationally and at home, to support three decades of unprecedented economic growth between the late 1940s and the early 1970s.

The Kitchen Debate At the American National Exhibition in Moscow in 1959, the United States put on display the technological wonders of American home life. When Vice President Richard Nixon visited, he and Soviet premier Nikita Khrushchev got into a heated debate over the relative merits of their rival systems. Khrushchev is the man immediately to Nixon's right, pointing his finger. To Nixon's left stands Leonid Brezhnev, who would be Khrushchev's successor. Howard Sochurek/The LIFE Picture Collection/Getty Images.

The Bretton Woods System The economic foundation of American global supremacy rested partly on the institutions created at the United Nations Monetary and Financial Conference at **Bretton Woods**, New Hampshire, in July 1944. With the United States and Britain taking the lead, hundreds of delegates from the forty-four Allied countries gathered to plan a postwar financial order. The summit led to the creation of the **World Bank**, which provided loans for the reconstruction of war-torn Europe (separate from the direct aid of the Marshall Plan, which came in 1948) as well as for the economic development of previously colonized nations. The same meeting produced plans for the **International Monetary Fund (IMF)**, formally launched in 1945, which would stabilize national currencies and provide a predictable monetary environment for trade, with the U.S. dollar serving as the benchmark.

These two entities became the cornerstones of the Bretton Woods system, premised on loaning American capital, at low interest to countries that adopted free-trade capitalist economies. In 1947, the first General Agreement on Tariffs and Trade (GATT) bolstered Bretton Woods by creating an international framework for overseeing trade rules and practices. Together these agreements served the American vision of an open-market global economy and complemented the nation's ambitious diplomatic aims in the Cold War. Many critics held that Bretton Woods favored the United States at the expense of recently independent countries, because the United States could dictate lending and trading terms and stood to benefit as nations purchased more American goods. Indeed, the system was far from equitable, but it did provide much-needed economic order.

Bretton Woods
An international conference in New Hampshire in July 1944 that established the World Bank and the International Monetary Fund (IMF).

World Bank
An international bank created to provide loans for the reconstruction of war-torn Europe as well as for the development of former colonized nations.

International Monetary Fund (IMF)
A fund established to stabilize currencies and provide a predictable monetary environment for trade, with the U.S. dollar serving as the benchmark.

The Military-Industrial Complex While the Cold War raised tensions, it also drove postwar prosperity through defense spending. The business-government partnerships of the World War II era sprawled into a massive set of industries employing more than 3.5 million Americans by 1961. In that year, outgoing President Dwight D. Eisenhower used his farewell address to caution Americans about the growth of the military establishment and defense contractors, a partnership he dubbed the **military-industrial complex**, which he feared exerted undue influenced over the national government. Calling on Americans to recognize its "grave implications," Ike warned that "the potential for the disastrous rise of misplaced power exists and will persist." Some companies did so much business with the government that they in effect became private divisions of the Defense Department. Over 60 percent of the income of Boeing, General Dynamics, and Raytheon, for instance, came from military contracts, and the percentages were even higher for Lockheed and Republic Aviation. In previous peacetime years, military spending had constituted only 1 percent of

military-industrial complex
A term President Eisenhower used to refer to the military establishment and defense contractors who, he warned, exercised undue influence over the national government.

AP® THEME

WXT: Work, Exchange, and Technology
Lead a class discussion on how a growing private sector, federal spending, the baby boom, and technological developments helped spur economic growth in the postwar period.

The Military-Industrial Complex Often, technology developed for military purposes, such as the complex design of jet fighter planes, was easily transferred to the consumer market. The Boeing Aircraft Company — its Seattle plant is pictured here in the mid-1950s — became one of the leading commercial airplane manufacturers in the world in the 1960s, boosted in part by tax dollar–financed military contracts. Major American corporations — such as Boeing, McDonnell Douglas, General Electric, General Dynamics, and dozens of others — benefitted from military contracts in the years after World War II. Bettmann/Getty Images.

gross domestic product (GDP). By the time of Eisenhower's speech, it represented 10 percent.

Eisenhower's concerns about an all-consuming defense industry proved prophetic, but since economic growth relied on massive Cold War spending there was little political will to address the growing size of the military establishment. As an arms race and space race took hold, science, industry, and government became intertwined. Federal spending underwrote 90 percent of the cost of research for aviation and space, 65 percent for electricity and electronics, 42 percent for scientific instruments, and even 24 percent for automobiles. With the government footing the bill, corporations lost little time in transforming new technology into useful products. Backed by the Pentagon, for instance, IBM and Sperry Rand pressed ahead with research on integrated circuits, which later spawned the computer revolution. Cold War spending stimulated university research as well. When the Soviet Union launched the world's first satellite, ***Sputnik***, in 1957, the startled United States went into high gear to catch up. Alarmed that the United States was falling behind in science and technology, Eisenhower persuaded Congress to appropriate additional money for college scholarships and university research. The **National Defense Education Act** of 1958 funneled millions of dollars into American universities, helping institutions such as the University of California at Berkeley, Stanford University, the Massachusetts Institute of Technology, and the University of Michigan become the leading research centers in the world.

Sputnik
The world's first satellite, launched by the Soviet Union in 1957. After its launch, the United States funded research and education to catch up in the Cold War space competition.

National Defense Education Act
A 1958 act that funneled millions of dollars into American universities, helping institutions such as Stanford and the Massachusetts Institute of Technology, become leading research centers.

TEACHING STRATEGY

The Avalon Project at Yale Law School provides the full text of Eisenhower's military-industrial complex speech. To access this speech, search "Avalon Project military-industrial complex speech."

Corporate Power The massive defense industry was only one part of the nation's economy. For more than half a century, the consolidation of economic power into large corporate firms had characterized American capitalism. In the postwar decades, that tendency accelerated. By 1970, the top four U.S. automakers produced 91 percent of all motor vehicles sold in the country; the top four firms in tires produced 72 percent; those in cigarettes, 84 percent; and those in detergents, 70 percent. The head of the American Chamber of Commerce declared that "we have entered a period of accelerating bigness in all aspects of American life." Expansion into foreign markets also spurred corporate growth. During the 1950s, U.S. exports nearly doubled, giving the nation a trade surplus of close to $5 billion in 1960. By the 1970s, such firms as Coca-Cola, Gillette, IBM, and Mobil made more than half their profits abroad.

The new corporate giants required a huge army of white-collar workers. A new generation of business chieftains emerged, operating in a complex environment that demanded long-range forecasting. The culture of corporate life inspired numerous critics, who argued that the obedience demanded of white-collar workers was stifling creativity. The sociologist William Whyte studied somber "organization men" who left the home "spiritually as well as physically to take the vows of organization life." Andrew Hacker, in *The Corporation Take-Over* (1964), warned that a small handful of such organization men "can draw up an investment program calling for the expenditure of several billions of dollars" and thereby "determine the quality of life for a substantial segment of society."

Many of those "investment programs" relied on mechanization, or automation — another important factor in the postwar boom. From 1947 to 1975, worker productivity more than doubled across the whole of the economy. Many American factories replaced human muscle with machines running on cheap energy. Automation turned out products more efficiently and at lower cost but not without social costs. Over the course of the postwar decades, millions of high-wage manufacturing jobs disappeared, affecting entire cities and regions. Labor unions saw the moves as hurting both workers and markets. "How are you going to sell cars to all of these machines?" wondered Walter Reuther, president of the United Auto Workers (UAW).

AP® EXAM TIP

Evaluate the role of federal spending and the private sector in generating postwar economic growth.

The Economic Record America's annual GDP jumped from $213 billion in 1945 to more than $500 billion in 1960; by 1970, it exceeded $1 trillion (Figure 25.1). This sustained economic growth helped produce a 25 percent rise in real income for ordinary Americans between World War II and the 1960s. Even better, the new prosperity was not accompanied by inflation. After a burst of high prices in the immediate postwar period, inflation slowed to 2 to 3 percent annually, and it stayed low until the escalation of the Vietnam War in the mid-1960s. Feeling secure about the future, newly well-off Americans were eager to spend. In 1940, 43 percent of American families owned their homes; by 1960, 62 percent did. Over the same period, income inequality dropped sharply. The share of total income going to the richest tenth of the population declined by nearly one-third from the 45 percent it had been in 1940. Americans on average were both richer and more equal. The prosperity enjoyed by ordinary Americans stood in sharp contrast to the conditions of life in much of the rest of the world, where overall wealth grew slowly and was concentrated in the hands of a small elite in most countries (see "America in the World," p. 810).

Not everyone benefitted from the economic boom. Tenacious poverty persisted amidst celebrations of the new growth. In ***The Affluent Society*** (1958), which analyzed the nation's successful, "affluent" middle class, economist John Kenneth Galbraith argued that the poor were an "afterthought" in the minds of most economists and politicians. As Galbraith noted, one in thirteen families at the time

AP® EXAM TIP

Summarize the arguments on the left that criticized government for not addressing continuing problems in the U.S.

The Affluent Society

A 1958 book by John Kenneth Galbraith that analyzed the nation's successful middle class and argued that the poor were only an "afterthought" in the minds of economists and politicians.

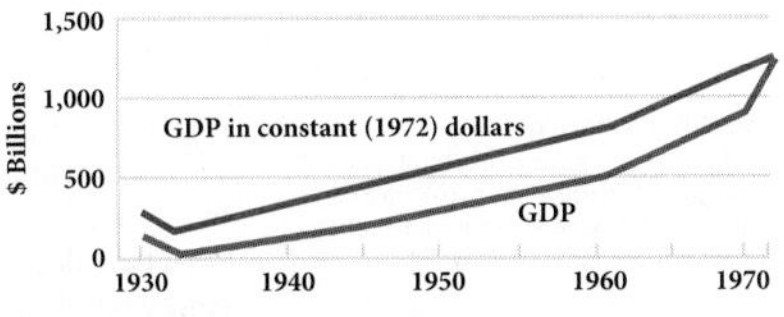

FIGURE 25.1 Gross Domestic Product, 1930–1972

After a sharp dip during the Great Depression, the GDP rose steadily in both real and constant dollars in the postwar period.

AP® APPLY THE TIP

To help students understand the factors that supported postwar economic growth, ask students to use pp. 807–809 to complete **Handout 25.1 — Causation: Postwar Economic Growth (TRM)**. After students complete the handout, ask them to assume the role of a historian being interviewed for a documentary on the postwar era to make the argument that postwar economic growth was mainly caused either by federal spending or by the private sector. After students choose a side to argue, pair them with a classmate who is taking the opposing position. Ask the pairs of students to develop a dialogue that could illustrate a debate over the main cause of economic growth in this era. You can consider utilizing phones or other platforms to record the dialogue between students.

TRM Find **Handout 25.1 — Causation: Postwar Economic Growth** in the Teacher's Resource Materials.

AP® APPLY THE TIP

To emphasize the differences in historical interpretation of a given historical context, provide pairs of students with excerpts from John Kenneth Galbraith's book *The Affluent Society* (1958) and "10 Amazing Years, 1947–1957: A Decade of Miracles (December 27, 1957)" from *U.S. News and World Report*. These sources provide a dramatically different interpretation of the impact of postwar development and the reactions to it by government. Ask one student in each pair to read Galbraith and the other to read "10 Amazing Years . . ." and summarize the historical argument of each as a thesis statement and identify the historical evidence the author provides. Then ask students to discuss the similarities and differences between the historical interpretations of each author. Lead a class discussion asking students the following (*answers will vary*):

- **On what do the authors agree about in the development of the U.S. after World War II?**
- **On what do the authors disagree?**
- **Why do these authors come to different historical interpretations of the same time period?**
- **What evidence, not explicitly mentioned in either excerpt, could be used to support or challenge the historical interpretations?**

AP® AMERICA IN THE WORLD

AP® SKILLS & PROCESSES

ANALYZING HISTORICAL EVIDENCE

The **AP® AMERICA IN THE WORLD** feature helps students examine broad, global economic trends. The first graph illustrates the effect capitalism had on the development of a global economy. The second graph illustrates economic trends from the industrial revolution of the nineteenth century to the present. The goal is for students to examine the trends concomitant to the postwar world and to consider how the war and its aftermath contributed to these processes. Use the **QUESTIONS FOR ANALYSIS** prompts to help students locate and describe broader trends and help them understand why trends can help illustrate change over time, causation, or turning points in history.

TRM Find complete suggested responses in the Teacher's Resource Materials.

TEACHING STRATEGY

Various excerpts of Harrington's *The Other America* are available online. Consider having students read excerpts to counteract the dominant impression of affluence created by many of the ads and images in this chapter. Additionally, the *New York Times* provides a review essay on the efforts of Harrington. To access this essay, search "NYT Warrior on Poverty."

Postwar Capitalism

The rise of an affluent, consumption-oriented middle class in the post–World War II United States was a distinct development within the centuries-long history of global capitalism. These two charts illustrate some of the key worldwide economic trends that explain and contextualize that distinctiveness. Each chart tracks global gross domestic product (GDP), a simple measure of how much an economy produces, in a unique way. The first highlights how relatively new the production of wealth through economic exchange is in human history. The second shows the distribution of GDP among different countries and regions since World War II.

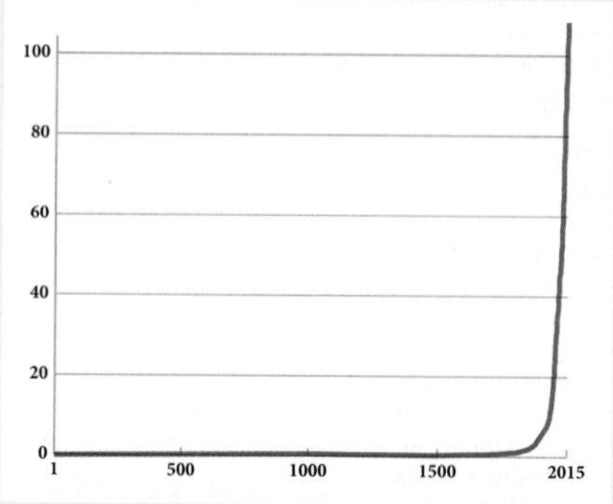

FIGURE 25.4 World GDP over the Last Two Millennia

This chart shows that the development of capitalism after 1500 dramatically increased humans' productive output and vastly expanded the per capita resources available on the planet. A conclusion one might draw from this chart is that for the majority of the last two thousand years, until just the last century, most human beings were equally poor.

Source: https://ourworldindata.org/economic-growth

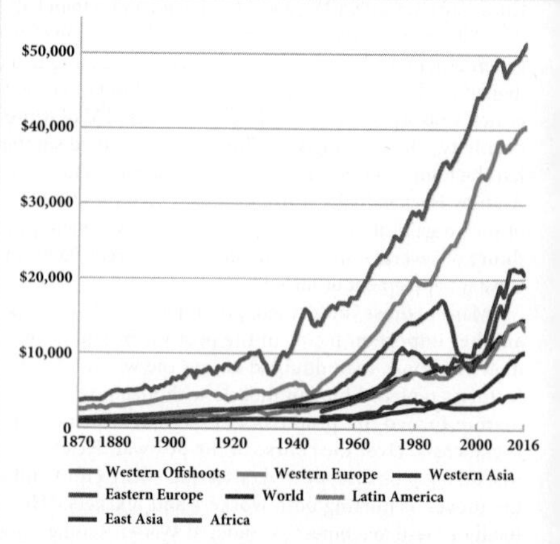

FIGURE 25.5 Global GDP Between World War II and 2016

This chart shows that per capita GDP — how much an economy produces per person — in the United States was nearly 50 percent higher than in Western Europe and more than twice as high as any other global region for most of the post–World War II decades.

Source: https://ourworldindata.org/economic-growth

Note: The label "Western offshoots" refers to the United States, Canada, and Australia.

QUESTIONS FOR ANALYSIS

1. Identify the main idea of Figure 25.4. Drawing on Chapter 25, as well as on your knowledge of the earlier periods in American history covered in Parts 1 through 6, how would you explain the change in global GDP in the twentieth century?
2. Describe at least two patterns found in Figure 25.5. Where is the U.S. in the data? What does the second chart tell us about the postwar American consumer economy? How would you give this data a social context?
3. Drawing on the material in Chapter 25, how would you explain the gaps in GDP between the United States and other parts of the world?

The Other America
A 1962 book by left-wing social critic Michael Harrington, chronicling the persistence of poverty in the United States, what he called the nation's "economic underworld."

earned less than $1,000 a year (about $9,000 in today's dollars). Four years later, in ***The Other America*** (1962), the left-wing social critic Michael Harrington chronicled the persistence of poverty in the United States, isolating millions of Americans in what he called the nation's "economic underworld." That same year, a U.S. government study, echoing a well-known sentence from Franklin Roosevelt's second inaugural address ("I see one-third of a nation ill-housed, ill-clad, ill-nourished"), declared "one-third of the nation" to be poorly paid, poorly educated, and poorly housed. As the country's top and the middle converged, the bottom remained far behind.

CHECK FOR UNDERSTANDING

Ask students: **How did the American economy move from recovery to dominance?** *The U.S. was in the forefront of developing the international postwar economic system known as Bretton Woods. It included a World Bank for loans to help war-torn European nations and recently independent former colonies, an International Monetary Fund with the U.S. dollar serving as the benchmark for international exchange, and a General Agreement on Tariffs and Trade designed to reduce tariff barriers and facilitate international commerce. At home, the aerospace industry, fueled by government funds, played a significant role in economic growth, and giant postwar corporations needed large staffs of white-collar workers.*

A Nation of Consumers

The defining development of the postwar boom was the dramatic expansion of domestic consumer markets. An avalanche of consumer goods, both in quantity and variety, awaited Americans when they went shopping. In some respects, the postwar decades echoed the 1920s: new gadgets, time-saving appliances, a car craze, and new mass media that shaped American tastes. Yet the consumerism of the 1950s bore a new significance: consumption took on an association with citizenship. Buying things, once a sign of personal indulgence, now signaled full participation in American society and, moreover, fulfilled social responsibility. To purchase a new home or car, or to buy the latest refrigerator for the kitchen or toys for the children, signaled one's social belonging — advertisers, in particular, were keen to emphasize that buying a product meant joining one's neighbors not rising above them. The appetites of a suburban family, asserted Henry Luce's *Life* magazine, helped to ensure "full employment and improved living standards for the rest of the nation."

AP® SKILLS & PROCESSES

CAUSATION

What primary factors led to the growth of the American economy after World War II?

The GI Bill This new ethic of consumption appealed to the expanding postwar middle class, the demographic sector that drove domestic market growth. Middle-class status was more accessible than ever, in part because of federal spending. The **Servicemen's Readjustment Act of 1944**, popularly known as the GI Bill, helped send 2.2 million veterans to college and another 5.6 million to trade school via government financing (the bill also provided veterans with health care and housing and loan subsidies). Before the GI Bill, commented one veteran, "I looked upon college education as likely as my owning a Rolls-Royce with a chauffeur." At one point in the mid 1950s, more than half of all U.S. college students were veterans.

Servicemen's Readjustment Act
Popularly known as the GI Bill, this 1944 legislation authorized the government to provide World War II veterans with funds for education, housing, and health care, as well as business and home loans.

Veterans Administration (VA)
A federal agency that assists former soldiers. Following World War II, the VA helped veterans purchase new homes with no down payment, sparking a building boom that created construction jobs and fueled consumer spending on home appliances and automobiles.

The government financing of education helped make the U.S. workforce the best educated in the world in the 1950s and 1960s. American colleges, universities, and trade schools grew rapidly to serve the flood of students — and would expand again when the children of the World War generation, known as baby boomers, reached college age in the 1960s. At Rutgers University, enrollment went from 7,000 before the war to 16,000 in 1947; at the University of Minnesota, from 15,000 to more than 27,000. The GI Bill trained nearly half a million engineers; 200,000 doctors, dentists, and nurses; and 150,000 scientists, among many other professions. More education meant more earning power, which turned into the consumer spending that drove the postwar economy. One observer of the GI Bill was so impressed with its achievements that he declared it responsible for "the most important educational and social transformation in American history."

The GI Bill stimulated the economy and expanded the middle class in another way: by increasing home ownership. Between the end of World War II and 1966, one of every five single-family homes built in the United States was financed through a GI Bill mortgage — 2.5 million new homes in all. In cities and suburbs across the country, the **Veterans Administration (VA)** helped former soldiers purchase new homes with no down payment, sparking a building boom that created construction jobs and fueled spending

The GI Bill The World War II veterans pictured here were purchasing books and supplies at the start of a college semester in 1945. From college and university education to vocational and industrial skill training, the federal government paid for hundreds of thousands of military veterans to receive education in the decade after World War II. As one of the largest social programs ever undertaken by the national government, the GI Bill helped forge a new middle class. College and university enrollments surged in these years, and the American workforce was among the best educated in the world. Bettmann/Getty Images.

AP® SKILLS & PROCESSES

CAUSATION

The **CAUSATION** question asks students to identify causes of economic growth after World War II. It might be helpful for them to consider this question from the standpoint of supply — the availability of new goods, advertising that made them attractive, and government support for homebuilding — and demand — increased incomes, pent-up demand from the scarcity of wartime goods, etc. Extend this prompt by having students identify elements of this economic boom that were likely to make growth unsustainable over a longer period of time.

TRM Find complete suggested responses in the Teacher's Resource Materials.

AP® SKILLS & PROCESSES

DEVELOPMENTS AND PROCESSES

One of the first steps a student needs to take is to define what the question is asking. Prior to answering this question, have students identify Americans — which Americans are they defining? Additionally, students need to define American institutions — which institutions are they defining? Look for broad categories and help students recognize answers they are less inclined to produce.

TRM Find complete suggested responses in the Teacher's Resource Materials.

AP® SKILLS & PROCESSES

DEVELOPMENTS AND PROCESSES

What were the effects of the GI Bill on Americans and on American institutions?

on home appliances and automobiles. Education and home ownership were more than personal triumphs for the families of World War II veterans (and Korean and Vietnam War veterans, eventually). They were financial *assets* that helped lift more Americans than ever before into a mass-consuming middle class.

Trade Unions Organized labor contributed to the expansion of the middle class as well. For the first time ever, trade unions and collective bargaining — the process of trade unions and employers negotiating workplace contracts — became widespread factors in the nation's economic life. Historically, organized labor had been confined to a narrow band of crafts and a few industries, primarily coal mining, railroading, and the building and metal trades. But over the Depression and war years, the power balance shifted in favor of unionized labor (Figure 25.2). By the beginning of the 1950s, the nation's major industries, including auto, steel, clothing, chemicals, and virtually all consumer product manufacturing, were operating with union contracts.

Labor's gains were the product of a hard fight. Unions staged major strikes in nearly all American industries in 1945 and 1946, much as they had done after World War I. Labor leaders such as UAW president Walter Reuther and CIO president Philip Murray declared that employers could afford a 30 percent wage increase. When employers, led by the giant General Motors, balked at that demand, the two sides seemed set for a long struggle. Instead, between 1947 and 1950 a broad "labor-management accord" gradually emerged across most industries, because each side gave a little: large manufacturers acceded to higher wages, confident their profits were secure, and unions dropped their demands for input in company decision making. This did not mean industrial peace — the country still experienced many strikes — but collective bargaining came to be accepted as the method for setting the terms of employment. The effect of labor's increased leverage was climbing wages. The average worker with three dependents gained 18 percent in spendable real income in the 1950s. That new income brought a middle-class lifestyle, which often included first-time homeownership, within reach of millions of American workers.

In addition, unions delivered greater leisure — more paid holidays and longer vacations — and a social safety net. Across postwar Europe, many of America's allies were building welfare states with some form of socialized medicine. Similar American proposals for national health care had been defeated in a bruising political battle during Truman's presidency, but by the late 1950s, union contracts commonly included pension plans and company-paid health insurance. Collective bargaining had become, in effect, the American alternative to the European welfare state and, as Reuther boasted, the passport into the middle class.

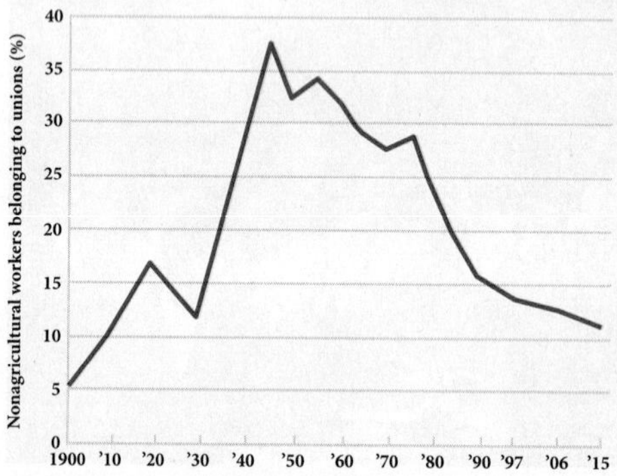

FIGURE 25.2 Labor Union Strength, 1900–2015

Labor unions reached their peak strength immediately after World War II, when they represented close to 40 percent of the nonfarm workforce. Although there was some decline after the mid-1950s, unions still represented nearly 30 percent in 1973. Thereafter, between the 1970s and the 2010s, their decline was precipitous. AFL-CIO Information Bureau, Washington, D.C.

Labor-management accord, however, was never as durable or universal as it seemed. Sheltered domestic markets were an essential condition for generous contracts, because they removed pressure on employers to lower wages to compete against less expensive goods. But in certain industries, the leading firms were already losing market share to low-cost domestic and foreign competitors — and those losses would mount considerably in later decades. Unlucky workers in unorganized industries, casual laborers, and low-wage workers in the service sector could not gain entry to the middle class. Ultimately, the greatest threat to labor's gains was the oldest: the abiding antiunionism of American employers. At heart, business regarded the heyday of collective bargaining as a negotiated truce, not a permanent peace. The postwar labor-management accord turned out to be a transitory, not permanent, fixture of American economic life.

Houses, Cars, and Children Increased levels of education, growing home ownership, and higher wages created what one historian has called a "consumers' republic." But what did its citizens buy? The postwar emphasis on nuclear families and suburbs provides the answer. In the emerging suburban nation, three elements came together to create patterns of consumption that would endure for decades: houses, cars, and children. A feature in a 1949 issue of *McCall's*, a magazine targeting middle-class women, illustrates the connections. "I now have three working centers," a housewife explains. "The baby center, a baking center and a cleaning center." Accompanying illustrations reveal the interior of a brand-new house, stocked with the latest consumer products: accessories for the baby's room; a new set of kitchen appliances; and a washer and dryer, along with cleaning products and other household goods. The article does not mention automobiles, but the photo of the house's exterior fills in the missing info: father drives home from work in a new car.

AP® EXAM TIP

Identify and explain the role of the GI Bill and the baby boom in generating economic growth in the postwar years.

Consumption for the home, which included automobiles, drove the postwar American economy as much as, or more than, the military-industrial complex. Between 1945 and 1970, more than twenty-five million new houses were built in the United States. Each required its own supply of new appliances and gadgets, from refrigerators to lawn mowers. In 1955 alone, Americans purchased four million new refrigerators, and between 1940 and 1951 the sale of power mowers rose from thirty-five thousand per year to more than one million. Moreover, as American industry discovered "planned obsolescence" — the encouragement of consumers to replace appliances and cars every few years — the home became a breeding ground for consumer wishes.

Children also spurred spending. The lives of Americans born in the "**baby boom**" between World War II and the early 1960s (peaking in 1957 with 4.3 million births) track the evolution of consumption and advertising. When the boomers were infants, companies focused on developing new baby products, from disposable diapers to instant formula. When they were toddlers and young children, new television programs, board games, fast food, TV dinners, and thousands of different kinds of toys came to market. When they were teenagers, a commodified "teen culture" — replete with clothing, music and movies, hairstyles, and other accessories — courted their considerable spending power. In 1956, a single middle-class American teenager spent on average $10 per week, close to the weekly disposable income of an entire family a generation earlier.

baby boom
The surge in the American birthrate between 1945 and 1965, which peaked in 1957 with 4.3 million births.

Television Much of the culture of the "consumers' republic" arrived through television. The dawn of TV transformed everyday life with astonishing speed. In 1947, there were seven thousand TV sets in American homes. A year later, the CBS and NBC radio networks retooled for television broadcast and began offering regular programming. By 1950 Americans owned 7.3 million sets, and ten years later 87 percent of American homes had at least one television. With this deep reach into the home, television soon became a principal mediator between the consumer and the marketplace.

Broadcast advertisers mastered the art of manufacturing consumer desire. TV stations, like radio stations before them, depended entirely on advertising for profits. Early television executives understood that selling viewers to advertisers was what kept their networks on the air. Straightforward corporate sponsorships (such as *General Electric Theater* and *U.S. Steel Hour*) and simple product jingles (such as "No matter what the time or place, let's keep up with that happy pace. 7-Up your thirst away!") gave way by the early 1960s to slick advertising campaigns that used popular music, movie stars, sports figures, and stimulating graphics to captivate viewers.

TEACHING STRATEGY

Ask students: **How does the ad reveal values and tastes of the middle class?** *The ad presents the television as a family-building device centered around the home (mentioned three times). Again, the normative family is depicted as white, middle class, and basically nuclear, and assumes that the mother is not employed. The family enjoys being together, and watching television functions as an important shared experience.*

TEACHING STRATEGY

The *Saturday Evening Post* provides an archive of advertisements from the era, including a number of ads from different car companies, which you can use to supplement students' understanding of advertising during this period. To access these advertisements, search "Saturday Evening Post advertisement archives."

TRM Find complete suggested responses in the Teacher's Resource Materials.

VISUAL ACTIVITY

Advertising in the TV Age Aggressive advertising of new products such as the color television helped fuel the surge in consumer spending during the 1950s. Marketing experts emphasized television's role in promoting family togetherness, while interior designers offered decorating tips that placed the television at the focal point of living rooms and the increasingly popular "family rooms." In this 1951 magazine advertisement, the family is watching a variety program starring singer Dinah Shore, who was the television spokeswoman for Chevrolet cars. Every American probably could hum the tune of the little song she sang in praise of the Chevy. Picture Research Consultants & Archives.

READING THE IMAGE: How are groups in the family, women, and children represented in this advertisement? What distinct groups are featured? In what direction is your eye drawn as a reader?

MAKING CONNECTIONS: What role does the advertisement suggest that television plays in family life? How would you connect this image to the chapter's discussion of domesticity and suburban patterns of consumption?

By creating powerful visual narratives of the good life, television forever changed how products were sold, in America and around the world. On the popular mid-1950s show *Queen for a Day,* women competed to see who could tell the most heart-rending story of tragedy and loss. The winner won a bonanza of household products: refrigerators, toasters, ovens, and the like. The show implied that consumer bounty cured human suffering. More mundane forms of suffering, along with their cure, were dramatized as well. In a groundbreaking advertisement for Anacin aspirin, a tiny hammer pounded inside the skull of a headache sufferer. Almost overnight, sales of Anacin increased by 50 percent.

AP® EXAM TIP

Evaluate the degree to which television represented American culture in the postwar years.

What Americans saw on television was not a mirror. The small screen mostly transmitted a narrow set of middle-class tastes and values. Both programming and commercial content centered on an overwhelmingly white, Anglo-Saxon, Protestant world of nuclear families, suburban homes, and middle-class life. A typical show was *Father Knows Best*, starring Robert Young and Jane Wyatt. Father left home each morning wearing a suit and tie and carrying a briefcase. Mother was a stereotypical full-time housewife, prone to bad driving and tears. *Leave It to Beaver*, another immensely popular series about suburban family life, embodied similar late-1950s themes. Earlier in the decade, television had featured grittier realities. *The Honeymooners*, starring Jackie Gleason as a Brooklyn bus driver, and *The Life of Riley*, a situation comedy featuring a California aircraft worker, depicted working-class lives.

AP® APPLY THE TIP

To help students understand the sometimes large gap between the images viewed on television in the 1950s and the reality of life for many Americans in the era, assign students to watch an episode of a 1950s television show for homework. This can include the following: *I Love Lucy, Leave It to Beaver, Father Knows Best,* etc. These shows are readily available on many networks and services or can be accessed with YouTube. In class the next day, organize students into groups to discuss the television shows that they watched. Ask student groups to address the following issues: race and economic class of the individuals featured; setting; issues the show dealt with; portrayal of women and children; and the conditions in which main characters lived. Then ask students to consider the degree to which they believe the show represented life and culture for most Americans. Require students to provide evidence to support their arguments regarding the degree to which television represented American culture in the postwar era.

Beulah, starring Ethel Waters and later Louise Beavers as an African American maid, and the comedic *Amos 'n' Andy*, were the only early shows to feature black actors in major roles. The first wave of television did not capture the breadth of American society, and in the second half of the 1950s broadcasting lost most of its modest ethnic, racial, and class diversity.

Youth Culture

One of the most striking developments in postwar American life was the emergence of the **teenager** as a cultural phenomenon. In 1956, only partly in jest, the CBS radio commentator Eric Sevareid questioned "whether the teenagers will take over the United States lock, stock, living room, and garage." The youth culture Sevareid lamented had emerged in the 1920s and blossomed in the 1950s thanks to lengthening years of education (high school had become nearly universal), the growing variety and influence of peer group subcultures, and the consumer tastes and spending power of young people. Market research showed a distinct teen market primed for exploitation. In 1951, *Newsweek* noted with awe that the total weekly spending money of American teenagers could buy 190 million candy bars, 130 million soft drinks, and 230 million sticks of gum. Increasingly, advertisers targeted the young, both to capture their dollars and court their influence on family purchases.

teenager
A term for a young adult. American youth culture, focused on the spending power of the "teenager," emerged as a cultural phenomenon in the 1950s.

Hollywood movies played a large role in fostering a teenage culture. Young people made up the largest audience for motion pictures, and film studios learned over the course of the 1950s to cater to them. The success of films such as *The Wild One* (1953), starring Marlon Brando; *Blackboard Jungle* (1955), with Sidney Poitier; and *Rebel Without a Cause* (1955), starring James Dean, convinced movie executives that features made for teenagers were worthy investments. Such features focused on youth rebellion so frequently that the rebel became a commodity of teen culture itself. "What are you rebelling against?" Brando is asked in *The Wild One*. "Whattaya got?" he replies. By the early 1960s, Hollywood had retooled its business model, shifting emphasis away from adults and families, the industry's primary audience since its rise in the 1920s, to teenagers. The "teenpic" soon included multiple genres: horror, rock 'n' roll, dangerous youth, and beach party, among others.

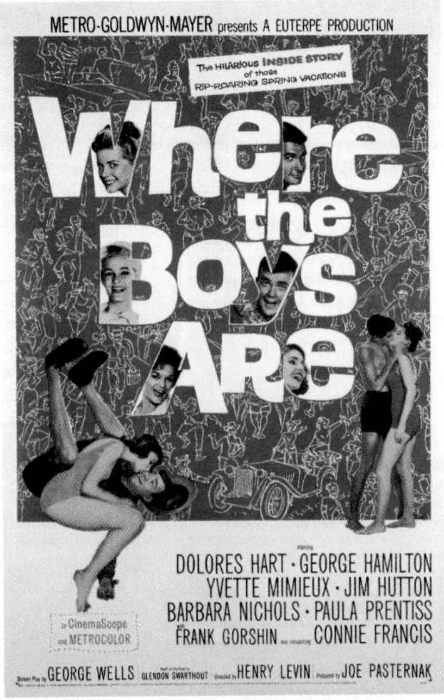

Teenagers This movie poster is from the 1960 Hollywood film *Where the Boys Are*. The plot, about the adventures of college students in Florida during spring break, was aimed squarely at teenagers. The 1950s saw the creation of the "teenager" as a distinct demographic and cultural category and, perhaps most significantly, as a consumer group—with money to spend. *Where the Boys Are* is one example of a whole new film genre, the "teenpic," invented in the 1950s by Hollywood executives eager to win over this lucrative new market. Everett Collection.

Rock 'n' Roll More than anything, music defined youth culture. Teenagers rejected the romantic pop ballads of the 1940s in favor of a louder, faster sound with roots in African American rhythm and blues, known as R&B. African American bands, as well as individual performers such as Chuck Berry, Little Richard, and Fats Domino, pioneered the R&B sound in the late 1940s and early 1950s by drawing on black gospel and blues traditions, as well as country music, a largely white musical genre. Cleveland disc jockey Alan Freed took the lead in introducing white America to black R&B and popularizing the name "rock 'n' roll." Other big-city radio DJs followed, and in the early 1950s American teenagers embraced the new sound.

Rock 'n' roll was born when this African American commercial art form met the spending power of the rising white middle class. One record company owner mused on the

CHECK FOR UNDERSTANDING

Ask students: **How did the U.S. become a nation of consumers in the postwar period?** *Fueled by a rising standard of living—aided in large part by the government through World War II spending, the GI Bill, and the military-industrial complex—Americans came to define well-being through the acquisition of consumer goods. Many products, including cars, were designed with "planned obsolescence," so replacing these goods became a regular part of American life. Many middle-class families acquired labor-saving appliances and televisions. In this period, they also often purchased two family cars.*

AP® THEME

ARC: American and Regional Culture

Mass culture became an important part of a culture driven by conformity on the one hand, with rebellion on the other. Have students select an example such as rock 'n' roll to illustrate how it both encouraged conformity, while also leading to rebellion. Asking students to explain how events can facilitate both change and continuity is an important part of historical inquiry.

TEACHING STRATEGY

The TeachRock Web site provides several different lessons that explore issues related to teenagers and rock 'n' roll. To access these lesson plans, search "Teach Rock."

TEACHING STRATEGY

Supplement students' understanding of Motown with the resources on the TeachRock Web site, which provides several images, articles, and lessons related to Motown, the Supremes, and female African American performers. To access this resource, search "TeachRock Motown."

AP® APPLY THE TIP

Project images of Norman Rockwell's *Saying Grace* (1951) and Willem de Kooning's *Woman I* (1950–1952) side-by-side on the board, and ask students to describe the visual differences in the images and try to explain the impact the differences have on the audiences of each work. Students should interpret each work by explaining the purpose and its relationship to the historical context in which it was created. After a class discussion that should emphasize rejection of conformity of the postwar society in the U.S., divide students into small, collaborative groups and assign each group one of the following topics: abstract expressionism, pop art, popular print media, popular television, popular music, and poetry. Each group should research their assigned topic and develop a thesis statement responding to the following prompt: To what degree did popular culture reject conformity in the 1950s–1960s? Students should use visual images and primary sources to support their thesis to create their presentation. Allow students to give their presentations to the class or provide the class access to all presentations digitally to view later.

TEACHING STRATEGY

Use The Beat Generation Web site to provide detailed information about the life and work of many of the artists of the Beat movement. To access this site, search "Beat Generation."

AP® SKILLS & PROCESSES

CONTEXTUALIZATION

The **CONTEXTUALIZATION** question asks students to connect broader historical concepts to the issue of consumer culture and rebellion: What aspects of consumer culture symbolized "rebellion" in the postwar decades? Students might make a larger generalization about "rebellion" as a routine pattern of a consumer culture, looking for examples in pop culture through music, television, and movies. Was rebellion more prevalent in one more than another?

TRM Find complete suggested responses in the Teacher's Resource Materials.

Rock 'n' Roll In the 1959 film *Go, Johnny Go!* the rock 'n' roll musician, Chuck Berry, and the radio disc jockey, Alan Freed, played themselves. Berry, who sang his hit song "Johnny B. Goode" in the film, was among a rising generation of black musicians that, along with a handful of white stars, created "rock 'n' roll," a fast-paced, dance-oriented, and often sexually charged musical genre derived from a variety of influences, including R&B, gospel, blues, and country. Everett Collection.

potential of the new genre: "If I could find a white man who had the Negro sound and the Negro feel, I could make a billion dollars." The first breakout performer answering that description was the Memphis performer Elvis Presley, who rocketed to instant celebrity in 1956 with his hit records "Hound Dog," originally recorded by the black artist Big Mama Thornton, and "Heartbreak Hotel." Driven by rock 'n' roll, record sales increased from $213 million to $603 million from 1953 to 1959. Both Hollywood and the music industry quickly learned that youth culture sold their products.

Cultural Dissenters Many disapproving adults perceived rock 'n' roll and other hallmarks of youth culture as dangerous provocations — encouraging rebellion, overtly sexual behavior, interracial relationships, and more. Denunciations poured forth from religious and political leaders as well as established print and television commentators, but the condemnation likely only added to the appeal. Youth rebellion was only one aspect of a broader artistic discontent with a consumer culture many found dull and mass produced. Painters, writers, musicians, and artists of all types contributed to a remarkable flowering of intensely personal expression. During and just after World War II, black musicians developed a hard-driving improvisational style known as bebop. Whether the "hot" sound of saxophonist Charlie Parker or the more subdued "cool" of the influential trumpeter Miles Davis, postwar jazz was intricate and individualistic — a striking departure from the dance-oriented commercial "swing" bands of the 1930s and 1940s.

> **AP® EXAM TIP**
> Recognize the ways that artists, intellectuals, and teenagers rejected conformity in American culture.

Bebop found eager fans not only in the African American community but also among a group of mostly white young people called the **Beats**, writers and poets gathered in cities such as New York, Los Angeles, and San Francisco. In the poem "Howl" (1956), which became an unofficial manifesto of the Beat movement, Allen Ginsberg lamented: "I saw the best minds of my generation destroyed by madness, starving hysterical naked, dragging themselves through the negro streets at dawn looking for an angry fix." (Ginsberg employed a 1950s racial stereotype, "negro streets," unselfconsciously.) So-called beatniks disdained sunny middle-class outlooks in favor of existential searching. In key works such as Jack Kerouac's novel *On the Road* (1957), the Beats glorified spontaneity, sexual adventurism, drug use, and iconoclastic spirituality. The Beats themselves were largely apolitical, but they would help to inspire the defiant counterculture of subsequent generations.

> **Beats**
> A small group of literary figures based in cities such as New York, Los Angeles, and San Francisco in the 1950s who rejected mainstream culture and instead celebrated personal freedom, which often included drug consumption and sexual adventurism.

> **AP® SKILLS & PROCESSES**
> **CONTEXTUALIZATION**
> What aspects of consumer culture symbolized "rebellion" in the postwar decades?

Religion and the Middle Class

While the Beats looked for meaning in rebellion, other Americans sought to affirm their religious faith. In an age of anxiety about nuclear annihilation and the rise of communism, which denied the existence of God, church membership jumped from 49 percent of the population in 1940 to 70 percent in 1960. Much of the growth

CHECK FOR UNDERSTANDING

Ask students: **What was the nature of youth culture in this era?** *The teenager developed as a distinct demographic in this period — including as a target for marketers. Films catered to young people, often depicting them as troubled. Rock 'n' roll, bebop, and Beat poetry offered different means of self-expression and, in some cases, rebellion against cultural mores.*

was in evangelical Protestant denominations, which emphasized human redemption from sin through the teachings, and attributed words, of Jesus Christ. Evangelical churches benefitted from a remarkable wave of new preachers. The youthful Reverend Billy Graham made brilliant use of television, radio, and advertising in spreading his message. Hundreds of thousands of Americans attended revivals — styled as "crusades" — which established Graham as the nation's leading evangelical. His 1957 revival at Madison Square Garden in New York lasted for more than three months.

Rather than clashing with the new middle-class consumer ethic, the religious reawakening accommodated materialism. Graham and his contemporaries told Americans that so long as they lived moral lives, they deserved the material blessings of modern life. The fire-and-brimstone of previous American "awakenings" gave way to a therapeutic idea of faith. No one was more influential in this regard than the minister and author Norman Vincent Peale, whose best-selling book *The Power of Positive Thinking* (1952) positioned religion as a balm for life's trials and tribulations, rather than a choice between heaven and hell. Peale taught that with faith in God and "positive thinking," anyone could overcome obstacles and become a success.

The postwar wave of evangelists were not all sunshine — they defined Americans as a righteous people at war with communist atheism. The contrast between communist "atheism" and American religiosity permeated much of the rhetoric of the Cold War. In sentencing Julius and Ethel Rosenberg to death in 1951, Judge Irving Kaufman criticized their "devoting themselves to the Russian ideology of denial of God." Catholics, Protestants, and Jews came together in an influential ecumenical movement that downplayed doctrinal differences to promote an abstract religiosity. The phrase "under God" was added to the Pledge of Allegiance in 1954, and U.S. coins carried the words "In God We Trust" after 1956. These initiatives would look distinctly moderate in comparison with the politicized evangelism that emerged in the 1960s and 1970s.

Billy Graham Charismatic and inspiring, Billy Graham brought Christian conversion to hundreds of thousands of Americans in the 1940s and 1950s, preaching to large crowds such as this one in Columbia, South Carolina. He also migrated onto the radio and television airwaves, using technology to reach even wider audiences. Graham used the Cold War to sharpen his message, telling Americans that "godless communism" was an inferior system and that democracy in America required belief in God and a constant struggle against "sin." John Dominis/The LIFE Images Collection/Getty Images.

THE MODERN NUCLEAR FAMILY

What was the domestic ideal, and how did Americans embrace it in the postwar decades?

American ideas about marriage, family, and gender roles had all shifted significantly since the turn of the twentieth century (see "Women, Men, and the Solitude of Self" in Chapter 17). By 1900, middle-class Americans had begun to understand marriage as "companionate," that is, based on romantic love and a lifetime of shared friendship. But *companionate* did not mean *equal*. Even in the mid-twentieth century, family life rested on a foundation of gender inequality: men were breadwinners and decision makers, while women cared for children and took a secondary position in public life.

The booming middle class subscribed to this paternalist, even patriarchal, vision of family life. Everyone from professional psychologists to advertisers and every organization from schools to the popular press celebrated the nuclear family. Children were prized, and women's caregiving work valorized. This ideal, especially its emphasis on female "domesticity," was bolstered by Cold War politics. Americans who deviated from prevailing gender and familial norms were viewed with suspicion, and sometimes even deemed subversive and politically dangerous.

Even as staid norms held sway, new ideas were gradually remaking marriage, gender, feminism, and sexuality. To comprehend the postwar decades, we have to keep in

AP® THEME

ARC: American and Regional Culture

The rapid and substantial growth of evangelical Christian churches and organizations was accompanied by greater political and social activism on the part of religious conservatives. Graham's Los Angeles rally took place at the time the Soviets tested their first atomic bomb. The companion site to PBS's *God in America* documentary provides additional information about Billy Graham and his ministry, including an article, interviews with several scholars of religion, and links to additional information. To access this site, search "PBS God in America."

CHECK FOR UNDERSTANDING

Ask students: **What drove the growth of the American economy after World War II?** *The American economy boomed between the end of World War II and the 1970s for a number of reasons. First, the United States did not see its infrastructure destroyed during the war, as did other nations, and thus found numerous foreign markets for its exports. Second, a large internal consumer market existed, fueled by expanding wages as a result of GI Bill-funded college graduates. Third, given the prosperity, employers widely accepted collective bargaining for the first time in U.S. history, increasing wages. Fourth, the U.S. government continually invested in new military products in light of its Cold War commitments.*

TEACHING STRATEGY

Elaine Tyler May's important study of American postwar families, *Homeward Bound: American Families in the Cold War Era* (New York: Basic Books, 2008), directly links the foreign policy concept of containment with the middle-class domestic concerns of the era. The title is a play on words, suggesting both an increased focus on the home and the constriction of being "bound" by the expectations of suburban domesticity. She suggests that applying "containment" to the domestic sphere is more than a metaphor. Consider having students read an excerpt in order to evaluate the persuasiveness of her argument.

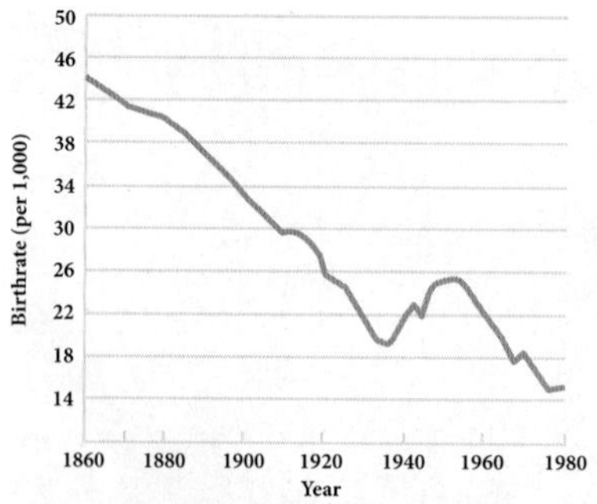

FIGURE 25.3 The American Birthrate, 1860–1980

When birthrates are viewed over more than a century, the postwar baby boom is clearly only a temporary reversal of the long-term downward trend in the American birthrate.

mind that while domesticity remained the ideal, in people's daily lives a different reality often held true.

The Baby Boom

A popular 1945 song was called "Gotta Make Up for Lost Time," and Americans followed the song's advice. The immediate postwar years saw a demographic tidal wave of weddings and births. Two things distinguished this race to "make up." First, these marriages were remarkably stable. Not until the mid-1960s did the divorce rate begin to rise sharply. Second, the newlyweds were intent on having babies. Nearly everyone expected to have several children — it was almost a civic responsibility. After a century and a half of decline, the birthrate shot up. More babies were born in the six years between 1948 and 1953 than in the previous thirty years (Figure 25.3). These developments were not a new normal, but instead temporary reversals of long-standing demographic trends. Within the twentieth century as a whole, the 1950s and early 1960s stand out as exceptions to lower birthrates, rising divorce rates, and a steadily rising marriage age.

One of the drivers of the baby boom was a drop in the average marriage age — down to twenty-two for men and twenty for women. Younger parents meant a bumper crop of children. Women who came of age in the 1930s had averaged 2.4 children; their counterparts in the 1950s averaged 3.2. Such a dramatic turnaround reflects both the younger age of marriage of the 1950s and the decade's improved economic conditions, which encouraged larger families. Originating in 1945, the baby boom peaked in 1957, and birth rates remained high until the early 1960s. The intimate decisions of couples after World War II shaped American life for decades. When boomers went to work during the 1970s, the labor market became tight. When career-oriented boomers belatedly began having children in the 1980s, the birthrate jumped. And, as noted earlier, consumer trends catered to the needs and interests of the boomer generation, from the publication of parenting books to the development of teen culture. Today, as baby boomers face retirement, the costs of their entitlements strain Social Security and Medicare.

Baby boomers and the country as a whole benefitted from a host of important advances in medicine and public health in the postwar years. "Miracle drugs" such as penicillin (introduced in 1943), streptomycin (1945), and cortisone (1948) provided ready cures for previously serious diseases. When Dr. Jonas Salk perfected a polio vaccine in 1954, he became a national hero. The free distribution of Salk's vaccine in the nation's schools, followed in 1961 by Dr. Albert Sabin's oral polio vaccine, demonstrated the potential of government-sponsored public health programs.

To keep boom babies healthy and happy, middle-class parents increasingly turned to expert advice. Published in 1946, Dr. Benjamin Spock's *Common Sense Book of Baby and Child Care* sold more copies in the postwar decades than any book other than the Bible. Spock urged mothers to abandon the rigid feeding and baby-care schedules of an earlier generation, embracing instead their own instincts and a flexible, "common sense" approach. New mothers found Spock's commonsense approach liberating. "Your little paperback is still in my cupboard, with loose pages, rather worn from use because I brought up two babies using it as my 'Bible,'" a California housewife wrote to Spock. But the advice of experts like Spock did not always reassure women. They cautioned mothers of the risks of overprotecting their children, but also urged them to be constantly available. As American mothers puzzled over such mixed messages in the 1950s, a resurgence of feminism simmered. It would boil over in the next decade.

AP® SKILLS & PROCESSES

CAUSATION

Why was there an increase in births in the decades after World War II, and what were some of the effects of this baby boom?

AP® SKILLS & PROCESSES

CAUSATION

The **CAUSATION** question essentially asks students to identify the factors that caused the baby boom and the effects of the baby boom. **FIGURE 25.3** highlights what an anomaly the baby boom constituted, and why, therefore, it needs to be explained. Students might also explore ways the long-term effects of the baby boom continue to be felt, such as the strain it puts on the Social Security and health care systems.

TRM Find complete suggested responses in the Teacher's Resource Materials.

CHECK FOR UNDERSTANDING

Ask students: **What was the baby boom?** *The baby boom was a significant upsurge in the population that lasted from roughly 1946 to 1964, peaking in 1957. A lowered marriage age, the near universality of marriage, and reduced infant mortality all contributed to this demographic anomaly.*

Women, Work, and Family

The middle-class domestic ideal of the postwar decades defined the responsibilities of women: raise children, make a home, be a devoted wife. This vision of womanhood was so prevalent that in 1957 the *Ladies' Home Journal* wondered seriously, "Is College Education Wasted on Women?" But this ideal did not agree with the reality of working-class women, who had to earn a paycheck to help their family. Contrary to the stereotype, women's paid work often helped lift many families into the middle class — the additional income made buying a home or car possible. Middle-class women faced their own barriers. Most of them, college educated or not, found professional fields closed off, for men only. For both groups, the market offered mostly "women's jobs" — in teaching, nursing, and other areas of the growing service sector — and little room for advancement (see "Firsthand Accounts," p. 820).

The idea that a woman's place was in the home was not new. The postwar obsession with femininity and motherhood bore a remarkable similarity to nineteenth-century notions of domesticity, but the updated version drew on new elements of twentieth-century science and culture for justification. Psychologists equated motherhood with "normal" female identity and suggested that career-minded mothers needed therapy. "A mother who runs out on her children to work — except in cases of absolute necessity — betrays a deep dissatisfaction with motherhood or with her marriage," wrote one leading psychiatrist. Television shows and movies depicted career-minded women as social misfits. The postwar consumer culture also emphasized women's domestic role as purchasing agents for home and family. "Can a woman ever feel right cooking on a dirty range?" asked one advertisement.

Despite the power of domestic ideals, financial necessity increasingly pushed women into the paid workforce. In 1954, married women made up half of all women workers. Six years later, the 1960 census reported that the number of mothers who worked for wages outside the home had increased four times, and over one-third of these women had children between the ages of six and seventeen. In that same year, 30 percent of married women worked, and by 1970, it was 40 percent.

Women at Work Middle-class women's lives grew increasingly complicated in the postwar decades. They may have dreamed of a suburban home with a brand-new kitchen, but laboring all day over children, dirty dishes, and a hot stove proved dissatisfying to many. Betty Friedan called the confinement of women's identities to motherhood the "feminine mystique," but did the working woman have it much better? Hardly. Most women in the 1950s and 1960s were confined to low-level secretarial work (as pictured), waitressing, and other service-sector work — or factory or domestic labor. The majority of working women also performed the "double day": a full day at work and a full day at home. Such were the expectations and double bind women faced. © Inge Morath © The Inge Morath Foundation/Magnum Photos.

Middle Class Domesticity The nuclear family, meaning a married couple plus children, stood at the heart of middle-class American culture in the postwar years. The "domestic ideal" held that men worked for wages and women labored in the home. A new generation of Americans, such as the African American family pictured here, aspired to this cultural ideal, which came within reach for many for the first time. Here a couple and their children look over blueprints of their new home in the early 1960s. ClassicStock.com/Superstock.

TEACHING STRATEGY

The *New York Times* provides an excerpt of the most famous passage of Betty Friedan's *Feminine Mystique*, from Chapter 1. To access this excerpt, search "NYT excerpt from Feminine Mystique."

AP® SKILLS & PROCESSES

ANALYZING HISTORICAL EVIDENCE

Use the **AP® FIRSTHAND ACCOUNTS** feature to provide students with an opportunity to analyze different perspectives on the nature of childhood in the postwar era, a topic that has often been presented in popular culture through a nostalgic lens. Students might recognize that class, gender, and race all deeply shaped the experience of childhood. Memoirs, often written decades after the events they recall, have a tendency toward nostalgia — especially as people recall their childhoods from their perspective as adults.

AP® APPLY THE TIP

Ask students to complete **Handout 25.2 — Comparison: Women in the Postwar Years (TRM)** using pp. 819–822 as well as their understanding of the Federal period. Then on a long sheet of bulletin board paper, ask students to construct a timeline that illustrates the changing roles of women in society and the family from 1789 to 1965. Students should identify and explain at least five major turning points as well as contextualize each point by considering the larger time period in which the event occurred. Finally, students should clarify how forces other than women's issues impacted each event on their timeline.

TRM Find **Handout 25.2 — Comparison: Women in the Postwar Years** in the Teacher's Resource Materials.

AP® FIRSTHAND ACCOUNTS

Coming of Age in the Postwar Years

At the dawn of the postwar era, Americans faced new opportunities and new anxieties. Many former soldiers attended college and purchased new homes on the GI Bill, which forever changed their lives. Women faced new pressures to realize the ideal role of housewife and mother. On the horizon, both in reality and in the American imagination, lurked communism, which Americans feared but little understood. And racial segregation continued to shape the ordinary lives of Americans. Recorded here are several different reactions to these postwar tensions, distinct experiences of coming of age in the 1940s and 1950s.

ART BUCHWALD

Studying on the GI Bill

Art Buchwald was one of the best-known humorists in American journalism. But in 1946, he was an ordinary ex-serviceman using the GI Bill to go to college.

SOURCE: From *Leaving Home: A Memoir*, by Art Buchwald (New York: G. P. Putnam's Sons, 1993). Used by permission of Joel Buchwald.

“It was time to face up to whether I was serious about attending school. My decision was to go down to the University of Southern California and find out what I should study at night to get into the place. There were at least 4,000 ex-GIs waiting to register. I stood in line with them. Hours later, I arrived at the counter and said, ‘I would like to . . .’ The clerk said, ‘Fill this out.’

Having been accepted as a full-time student under the G.I. Bill, I was entitled to seventy-five dollars a month plus tuition, books, and supplies. Meanwhile, I found a boardinghouse a few blocks from campus, run by a cheery woman who was like a mother to her thirteen boarders. . . . At the time, just after the Second World War had ended, an undeclared class war was going on at USC. The G.I.s returning home had little use for the fraternity men, since most of the frat boys were not only much younger, but considered very immature.

The G.I.s were intent on getting their educations and starting new lives.”

BETTY FRIEDAN

Living the Feminine Mystique

Like Buchwald, Betty Friedan would one day become famous as a writer — author of one of the most widely read books of the 1960s, *The Feminine Mystique*. In the late 1940s, Friedan was not yet a feminist, but she was deeply engaged in the politics of the era.

SOURCE: From *"It Changed My Life": Writings on the Women's Movement*, by Betty Friedan (Cambridge, MA: Harvard University Press, 1976). Copyright © 1963 by Betty Friedan. Reprinted by permission of Curtis Brown, Ltd.

“And then the boys our age had come back from the war. I was bumped from my job on a small labor news service by a returning veteran, and it wasn't so easy to find another job I really liked. I filled out the applications for *Time-Life* researcher, which I'd always scorned before. All the girls I knew had jobs like that, but it was official policy that no matter how good, researchers, who were women, could never become writers or editors. They could write the whole article, but the men they were working with would always get the by-line as writer. I was certainly not a feminist then — none of us were a bit interested in women's rights. But I could never bring myself to take that kind of job.

After the war, I had been very political, very involved, consciously radical. Not about women, for heaven's sake! If you were a radical in 1949, you were concerned about the Negroes, and the working class, and World War III, and the Un-American Activities Committee and McCarthy and loyalty oaths, and Communist splits and schisms, Russia, China and the UN, but you certainly didn't think about being a woman, politically.”

SUSAN ALLEN TOTH

Learning About Communism

Toth is a writer who grew up in Ames, Iowa, surrounded by cornfields. She writes here about her experience learning just how anxious people could become in the 1950s when the issue of communism was raised.

SOURCE: From Susan Allen Toth, "Boyfriend" from *Blooming: A Small-Town Girlhood*. Reprinted by permission of Molly Friedrich on behalf of the author.

“Of course, we all knew there was Communism. As early as sixth grade our teacher warned us about its dangers. I listened carefully to Mr. Casper describe what Communists wanted, which sounded terrible. World domination. Enslavement. Destruction of our way of life. I hung around school one afternoon hoping to catch Mr. Casper, whom I secretly adored, to ask him why Communism was so bad. He stayed

AP® EXAM TIP

Compare expectations of women in the postwar years to the Cult of Domesticity popularized in the nineteenth century.

Despite rising employment rates, when women sought paid work, occupational segmentation — and the inequality that came with it — still confronted them. Until 1964, the classified sections of newspapers separated employment ads into "Help Wanted Male" and "Help Wanted Female." More than 80 percent of all employed women did stereotypical women's work as sales clerks, health-care technicians, waitresses, stewardesses, domestic servants, receptionists, telephone operators, and

820

in another teacher's room so late I finally scrawled my question on our blackboard: 'Dear Mr. Casper, why is Communism so bad . . . Sue Allen' and went home. Next morning the message was still there. Like a warning from heaven it had galvanized Mr. Casper. He began class with a stern lecture, repeating everything he had said about dangerous Russians and painting a vivid picture of how we would all suffer if the Russians took over the city government in Ames. We certainly wouldn't be able to attend a school like this, he said, where free expression of opinion was allowed. At recess that day one of the boys asked me if I was a 'dirty Commie': two of my best friends shied away from me on the playground; I saw Mr. Casper talking low to another teacher and pointing at me. I cried all the way home from school and resolved never to commit myself publicly with a question like that again. ”

MELBA PATILLO BEALS

Encountering Segregation

Melba Patillo Beals was one of the "Little Rock Nine," the high school students who desegregated Central High School in Little Rock, Arkansas, in 1957. Here she recounts an experience documenting what it was like to come of age as a black southerner under Jim Crow.

SOURCE: Reprinted with permission of Atria Publishing Group, a Division of Simon & Schuster, Inc. *Warriors Don't Cry: A Searing Memoir of the Battle to Integrate Little Rock* by Melba Patillo Beals. Copyright © 1994, 1995 by Melba Beals. All rights reserved.

“ An experience I endured on a December morning would forever affect any decision I made to go 'potty' in a public place. We were Christmas shopping when I felt the twinge of emergency. I convinced Mother and Grandmother that I knew the way to restroom by myself. I was moving as fast as I could when suddenly I knew I wasn't going to make it all the way down those stairs and across the warehouse walkway to the 'Colored Ladies' toilet. So I pushed open the door marked 'White Ladies' and, taking a deep breath, I crossed the threshold. It was just as bright and pretty as I had imagined it to be. At first I could only hear voices nearby, but when I stepped through a second doorway, I saw several white ladies chatting and fussing with their makeup. Across the room, other white ladies sat on a couch reading the newspaper. Suddenly realizing I was there, two of them looked at me in astonishment. Unless I was the maid, they said, I was in the wrong place. While they shouted at me to 'get out,' my throbbing bladder consumed my attention as I frantically headed for the unoccupied stall. They kept shouting 'Good lord, do something.' I was doing something by that time, seated comfortably on the toilet, listening to the hysteria building outside my locked stall. One woman even knelt down to peep beneath the door to make certain that I didn't put my bottom on the toilet seat. She ordered me not to pee. . . . One woman waved her hand in my face, warning me that her friend had gone after the police and they would teach me a thing or two. ”

DAVID BEERS

California Suburbia

David Beers grew up in the suburbs of California, in what would eventually become known as Silicon Valley. In his memoir, he recalls the ritual of buying a house.

SOURCE: David Beers, *Blue Sky Dream: A Memoir of America's Fall from Grace* (New York: Harcourt, Brace, & Company, 1996), 39–41.

“ 'We never looked at a used house,' my father remembers of those days in the early 1960s when he and my mother went shopping for a home of their own in the Valley of Heart's Delight. 'A used house simply did not interest us.' Instead, they roved in search of balloons and bunting and the many billboards advertising *Low Interest! No Money Down!* to military veterans like my father. They would follow the signs to the model homes standing in empty fields and tour the empty floor plans and leave with notes carefully made about square footage and closet space. 'We shopped for a new house,' my father says, 'the way you shopped for a car.' . . . We were blithe conquerors, my tribe. When we chose a new homeland, invaded a place, settled it, and made it over in our image, we did so with a smiling sense of our own inevitability. At first we would establish a few outposts — a Pentagon-funded research university, say, or a bomber command center, or a missile testing range — and then, over the next decade or two, we would arrive by the thousands and tens of thousands until nothing looked or felt as it had before us. . . . We were drawn to the promise of a blank page inviting *our* design upon it. ”

QUESTIONS FOR ANALYSIS

1. What do you think Buchwald meant by "an undeclared class war"? Why would the influx of GI Bill veterans into colleges create conflict?
2. Why do you think Friedan "didn't think about being a woman, politically" in the 1940s and 1950s? Why do you think she was "bumped from" her job by a "returning veteran"?
3. What does Toth's experience as a young student suggest about American anxieties during the Cold War? Why would her question cause embarrassment and ridicule?
4. What does Beals's experience suggest about the indignities faced by young people on the front lines of challenging racial segregation? How does the source help explain why youth were so important in breaking racial barriers?
5. What do you think Beers means by "our tribe"? What was the "blank page"? What does his language tell you about postwar social order?

TRM Find complete suggested responses in the Teacher's Resource Materials.

secretaries. In 1960, only 3 percent of lawyers and 6 percent of physicians were women, while 97 percent of nurses and 85 percent of librarians were women. Along with women's jobs went women's pay, which averaged 60 percent of men's pay in 1963.

When mothers took jobs outside the home, most also bore full responsibility for child care and household management, contributing to a "double day" of paid work and family work. As one overburdened woman noted, she now had "two full-time

CHECK FOR UNDERSTANDING

Ask students: **What patterns developed regarding women's roles, the nature of work, and family life in this period?** *In the baby boom era, a strong emphasis on domesticity encouraged women to have children and remain home, carefully purchasing consumer goods for the family home. Nevertheless, many married women, including many mothers, worked in this era, though typically in highly gender-segregated patterns.*

AP® SKILLS & PROCESSES

CONTINUITY AND CHANGE

The **CONTINUITY AND CHANGE** question asks students to identify changes in women's economic roles in the postwar decades. Students should also recognize continuities from earlier periods and should be able to explain reasons for the disparity between the perception and reality of women's roles in this period.

TRM Find complete suggested responses in the Teacher's Resource Materials.

AP® SKILLS & PROCESSES

CONTINUITY AND CHANGE

In what ways did the roles of women illustrate both continuity and change in the 1950s and 1960s?

jobs instead of just one — underpaid clerical worker and unpaid housekeeper." Even so, heterosexual nuclear families with breadwinning fathers and domestic mothers were held up as symbols of a healthy nation — and paragons of American ideals in the Cold War rivalry. Americans wanted to believe in their own domestic ideal, even if it did not describe the reality of their lives.

Challenging Middle-Class Morality

AP® EXAM TIP

Explain early challenges to traditional views on moral issues.

The two decades after 1945 were in many ways culturally conservative. At the dawn of the 1960s, "going steady" in high school was understood as a prelude to marriage. College women had curfew restrictions and permission was required for male visitors. Americans married young. More than half of those who married in 1963 were under the age of twenty-one. Even after the birth control pill came on the market in 1960, few doctors prescribed it to unmarried women, and even married women did not enjoy unfettered access to contraception until the Supreme Court ruled it a "privacy" right in the 1965 *Griswold v. Connecticut* decision.

Alfred Kinsey Underneath their middle-class morality, Americans were less repressed than confused. They struggled to reconcile new freedoms with moral traditions. This was especially true with regard to sex. Two controversial studies by an unassuming Indiana University zoologist named Alfred Kinsey forced questions about sexuality into the open. Kinsey and his research team published *Sexual Behavior in the Human Male* in 1948 and followed it up in 1953 with *Sexual Behavior in the Human Female* — the latter an 842-page book that sold 270,000 copies in the first month after its publication. Taking a scientific rather than moralistic approach, Kinsey documented the full range of sexual experiences of thousands of Americans. The work of the "sex doctor," as he became known, broke numerous taboos, discussing such topics as homosexuality and marital infidelity in the detached language of science.

The Kinsey Reports Like the woman on the cover of this lighthearted 1953 book of photographs, many Americans reacted with surprise when Alfred Kinsey revealed the country's sexual habits. In his 1948 book about men and his 1953 book about women, Kinsey wrote about American sexual practices in the detached language of science. But it still made for salacious reading. Evangelical minister Billy Graham (p. 792) warned: "It is impossible to estimate the damage this book will do to the already deteriorated morals of America." Picture Research Consultants & Archives.

Both of Kinsey's studies confirmed that a quiet sexual revolution was already well underway. Kinsey estimated that 85 percent of men had had sex prior to marriage, and more than 25 percent of married women had had sex outside of marriage by the age of forty. These statistics were shocking by the moral standards of the late 1940s and early 1950s, and "hotter than the Kinsey report" became a national figure of speech. Kinsey was criticized by statisticians — because his samples were not randomly selected — and condemned by religious leaders, who charged him with encouraging promiscuity and adultery. But his research changed, or perhaps even started, the national conversation about sex.

The Homophile Movement Kinsey's work also suggested that homosexuality was more common than Americans thought. His research found that 37 percent of men and 13 percent of women had engaged in some form of homosexual activity by early adulthood. Even more shockingly, Kinsey claimed that 10 percent of American men were *exclusively* homosexual. These claims came as little surprise, but great encouragement, to a group of lesbian and gay activists who called themselves "homophiles." Organized primarily in the Mattachine Society (the first gay rights organization in the country, founded in 1951) and the Daughters of Bilitis (a lesbian organization founded in 1955), homophiles were a small but determined collection of activists who sought equal rights for lesbians and gay men at a time when the American Psychiatric Association still defined homosexuality as a mental illness. "The lesbian is a woman endowed with all the attributes of any other woman," wrote the pioneer lesbian activist Del Martin in 1956. "The salvation of the lesbian lies in her acceptance of herself without guilt or anxiety."

Building on the urban lesbian and gay communities that had coalesced during World War II, homophiles sought to change American attitudes about same-sex love. They faced daunting obstacles, since same-sex sexual relations were illegal in every state and condemned, as well as feared, by most Americans. To combat a widespread idea of gay people as marginal, homophile organizations cultivated a respectable, middle-class image. Members were encouraged to avoid bars and nightclubs, to dress in conservative shirts and ties (for men) and modest skirts and blouses (for women), and to seek out psychologists who would attest to their "normalcy." Nevertheless, the homophile movement remained invisible to most Americans, and it was not until the 1960s that homophiles began to talk about their "rights as citizens," laying the groundwork for the gay rights movement of the 1970s.

AP® SKILLS & PROCESSES

MAKING CONNECTIONS

Why did Kinsey's findings offend some Americans and embolden others?

Media and Morality Traditional morality prohibited frank public discussion of sex, but significant challenges to that prohibition emerged in popular media in the postwar years. Concerned that excessive crime, violence, and sex in comic books were encouraging juvenile delinquency, the U.S. Senate held nationally televised hearings in 1954. The Senate's final report, written largely by the Tennessee Democrat Estes Kefauver, complained of the "scantily clad women" and "penchant for violent death" common in comic books aimed at teenage audiences. Kefauver's report forced the comics industry to censor itself but did little to repress an increasing frankness about both sex and violence in other media.

A magazine entrepreneur from Chicago named Hugh Hefner became a leading, and controversial, voice in that growing frankness. Hefner founded *Playboy* magazine in 1953 to advance a countermorality against domesticity: the magazine imagined a world populated by "hip" bachelors and sexually available women. Hefner's bachelors condemned marriage and lived in sophisticated apartments filled with the latest stereo equipment and other consumer products. While domesticated fathers bought lawn mowers and patio furniture, *Playboy* encouraged men to spend money on stylish clothing, jazz albums, and on the "scantily clad women" that filled its pages. Hefner and his numerous imitators became powerful arbiters of sex in the media, but were also exceptions that proved the rule. Marriage, not swinging bachelorhood, remained the destination of the majority of men. Millions of American men read *Playboy*, but few pursued its fantasy lifestyle.

AP® SKILLS & PROCESSES

DEVELOPMENTS AND PROCESSES

What were the contradictions in postwar domesticity and middle-class morality?

A SUBURBAN NATION

What were the major forces that shaped postwar suburbanization?

By any definition, Americans prospered after World War II. Prosperity—how much an economy produces, how much people earn—is more easily measured than is quality of life. During the 1950s, however, a distinct American template for "the good life" emerged: a high value on consumption, a devotion to family and domesticity, and a preference for suburban living. The third element of that template, suburbanization, was actually a vast internal migration: millions of Americans moved from large central cities—places such as Boston, New York, Philadelphia, Baltimore, Cleveland, Chicago, and Atlanta, among a host others—to countless smaller communities on the urban periphery. That migration transformed the geography of the country and set in motion social and political changes whose effects would last for decades (see "Thinking Like a Historian," p. 824).

AP® EXAM TIP

The causes and effects of the migration of the middle class to the suburbs is important to know for the AP® Exam.

The Postwar Housing Boom

The suburbs were not a new invention. For more than a century, Americans had been moving out of densely populated cities. But what started as a trickle before World War II became a flood thereafter. In 1910, one American in fourteen lived in

CHECK FOR UNDERSTANDING

Ask students: **What was the "American Dream," and how did Americans embrace it in the postwar decades?** *The "American Dream" was marked by idyllic, at least for some, visions of what it meant to live in America. Namely, the lifestyle concomitant to suburbanization represented prosperity because of the affluence, modern technology, and established gender norms. Again, this was ideal only for some. For example, the domestic ideal, by which women were expected to remain at home, raise children, and attend to their husbands' happiness, was pervasive among the American middle-class in the middle of the twentieth century. It was so pervasive that even women who had to leave the home to work as sales clerks, waitresses, health care workers, etc.—anywhere from 30 to 50 percent of middle-class women—were still expected to maintain the household, care for the children, and keep their husbands happy. Additionally, this concept of the American Dream was racialized through government-sponsored housing programs that discriminated against minority groups.*

AP® SKILLS & PROCESSES

DEVELOPMENTS AND PROCESSES

Students need to be familiar with how to explain historical contradiction. Help students embrace this concept by pointing out a contradiction in society such as the so-called ideals of domesticity and explain why people fought against the concept. What freedoms and opportunities existed for women? How did domesticity represent a contradiction to those opportunities and freedoms?

TRM Find complete suggested responses in the Teacher's Resource Materials.

AP® THEME

MIG: Migration and Settlement

As higher education opportunities and new technologies rapidly expanded, increasing social mobility encouraged the migration of the middle class to the suburbs. Have students select at least three factors of the consumer age that connect to the rise in suburban living. Examples such as conformity, automobile, community schools, single-family homes, G.I. Bill of Rights, and shopping malls can give students an idea of some of the historical factors that led to a rise in suburban living.

AP® APPLY THE TIP

Provide groups of students with **Handout 25.3—Thematic Analysis: Middle Class and Suburbs (TRM)** and ask the groups to re-create the handout on a large, poster-sized sheet of paper. Using pp. 823–828, the groups should identify specific details to support each AP® Theme listed on the handout. Students should then draw connecting, dotted lines between details from one theme to another and provide explanations for their connection. Ask students to use their thematic analysis to construct a thesis statement to respond to the following prompt: To what degree did the popularization of suburbs in the postwar era dramatically alter American life? Allow students to share their thesis statements with each other and debate their answers.

TRM Find **Handout 25.3—Thematic Analysis: Middle Class and Suburbs** in the Teacher's Resource Materials.

AP® SKILLS & PROCESSES

ANALYZING HISTORICAL EVIDENCE

Use the **AP® THINKING LIKE A HISTORIAN** feature to encourage students to interact with critical views of suburbia. Some commentators have pushed back against negative — sometimes facile — critiques of suburbia and the supposed conformity that they generated. D. J. Waldie, who was born and raised in Lakewood, California (the West Coast equivalent to Levittown), suggests that his suburb was and is a diverse place that allowed for individuality and self-expression.

The Cold War America Suburb

Between the end of World War II and the 1980s, Americans built and populated suburban homes in an unprecedented wave of construction and migration that changed the nation forever. New home loan rules and government backing under the Federal Housing and Veterans Administrations made new suburban houses cheaper and brought home ownership within reach of more Americans than ever before. Commentators cheered these developments as a boon to ordinary citizens, but by the 1960s a generation of urban critics, led by journalist Jane Jacobs, began to find fault with the nation's suburban obsession. The following documents provide evidence of how these new suburban communities arose and how they began to transform American culture.

1. ***Life* magazine, "A *Life* Round Table on Housing," January 31, 1949.** *The nation's leading opinion magazine,* Life, *held a roundtable discussion of housing in 1949, featuring the most prominent builder of new suburbs, William J. Levitt.*

The most aggressive member of *Life's* Round Table, whether as builder or debater, was William J. Levitt, president of Levitt and Sons, Inc. of Manhasset, NY. He feels that he has started a revolution, the essence of which is size. Builders in his estimation are a poor and puny lot, too small to put pressure on materials manufacturers or the local czars of the building codes or the bankers or labor. A builder ought to be a manufacturer, he said, and to this end must be big. He himself is a nonunion operator.

The Levitt prescription for cheaper houses may be summarized as follows: 1) take infinite pains with infinite details; 2) be aggressive; 3) be big enough to throw your weight around; 4) buy at wholesale; and 5) build houses in concentrated developments where mass-production methods can be used on the site.

2. **Site plan sketch for Park Forest, Illinois, 1946.** *This sketch from a plan for a Chicago suburb shows how Americans visualized a new kind of shopping center — note the "Sears" store and expansive parking lot but also the trees and, in the far background, a church steeple.*

Source: The Park Forest Historical Society.

3. **William H. Whyte Jr., *The Organization Man*, 1956.** *Whyte, a prominent journalist, wrote about the decline of individualism and the rise of a national class of interchangeable white-collar workers.*

And is this not the whole drift of our society? We are not interchangeable in the sense of being people without differences, but in the externals of existence we are united by a culture increasingly national. And this is part of the momentum of mobility. The more people move about, the more similar American environments become, and the more similar they become, the easier it is to move about.

More and more, the young couples who move do so only physically. With each transfer the décor, the architecture, the faces, and the names may change; the people, the conversation, and the values do not — and sometimes the décor and architecture don't either. . . .

Suburban residents like to maintain that their suburbia not only looks classless but is classless. That is, they are apt to add on second thought, there are no extremes, and if the place isn't exactly without class, it is at least a one-class society — identified as the middle or upper middle, according to the inclination of the residents. "We are all," they say, "in the same boat."

4. **Jane Jacobs, *The Death and Life of Great American Cities*, 1961.** *This excerpt by New York writer and architectural critic Jane Jacobs is a classic celebration of vibrant urban neighborhoods.*

Although it is hard to believe, while looking at dull gray areas, or at housing projects or at civic centers, the fact is that big cities are natural generators of diversity and prolific incubators of new enterprises and ideas of all kinds. . . .

This is because city populations are large enough to support wide ranges of variety and choice in these things. And again we find that bigness has all the advantages in smaller settlements. Towns and suburbs, for instance, are natural homes for huge supermarkets and for little else in the way of groceries, for standard movie houses or drive-ins and for little else in the way of theater. There are simply not enough people to support further variety, although there may be people (too few of them) who would draw upon it were it there. Cities, however, are the natural homes of supermarkets and standard movie houses plus delicatessens, Viennese bakeries, foreign groceries, art movies, and so on. . . .

The diversity, of whatever kind, that is generated by cities rests on the fact that in cities so many people are so close together, and among them contain so many different tastes, skills, needs, supplies, and bees in their bonnets.

5. Crowded supermarket, early 1960s. *The vast new grocery stores that opened in suburban cities and towns in the 1950s and 1960s created a standardized look and feel, in contrast to the smaller, more specialized urban markets they replaced.*

John Dominis//Time Life Pictures/Getty Images

6. Herbert J. Gans, *The Levittowners*, 1967. *Herbert Gans wrote one of the first sociological studies of the new postwar suburbs and their residents.*

The strengths and weakness of Levittown are those of many American communities, and the Levittowners closely resemble other young middle class Americans. They are not America, for they are not a numerical majority of the population, but they represent the major constituency of the latest and more powerful economic and political institutions in American society — the favored customers and voters whom these seek to attract and satisfy. . . .

Although they are citizens of a national polity and their lives are shaped by national economic, social, and political forces, Levittowners deceive themselves into thinking that the community, or rather the home, is the single most important unit of their lives. . . .

In viewing their homes as the center of life, Levittowners are still using a societal model that fit the rural America of self-sufficient farmers and the feudal Europe of self-isolating extended families.

SOURCES: (1) *Life*, January 31, 1949, 74; (3) William H. Whyte Jr., *The Organization Man* (New York: Simon and Schuster, 1956), 276, 299; (4) Jane Jacobs, *The Death and Life of Great American Cities* (Westminster, MD: Vintage, 1992), 145–147; (6) Herbert J. Gans, *The Levittowners* (New York: Columbia University Press, 1982), 417–418.

ANALYZING THE EVIDENCE

1. Compare the main ideas of sources 3, 4, and 5. How do they reinforce or contradict one another?
2. In source 3, what does Whyte mean by "classless"? Why would suburbanites wish to think of their communities as not beset by class inequality? Were they right in this point of view? Describe the historical situation of suburbanites.
3. What is the main idea and perspective of source 1? How does Levitt's vision of the home-building industry relate to other kinds of American industries postwar?
4. In source 4, what advantages does Jacobs see in large cities over suburbs? Can you interpret sources 2 and 5 from the perspective that Jacobs outlines? How does Gans's perspective speak to these sources?

AP® DBQ PRACTICE

Write an essay in which you use the knowledge you've gained from this chapter and the documents provided above to explore postwar suburbanization. How does suburbanization affect the American economy? Ordinary Americans? What flaws did its critics see?

825

TRM Find complete suggested responses in the Teacher's Resource Materials.

AP® SKILLS & PROCESSES

ARGUMENTATION

It might be challenging for students to find a unifying theme in the **AP® DBQ PRACTICE** prompt. They could think about the prompt as a question about the effects of suburbanization on the economy, society, and culture. They also might want to consider the positive factors that drew Americans to the suburbs, not just the problems.

a suburb. By 1960, one in three did. In the years following the war, farmland on the outskirts of countless cities filled up with tract housing and shopping centers. Entire counties — such as San Mateo, south of San Francisco, or Passaic and Bergen in New Jersey, west of Manhattan — went from rural to suburban. Home construction, which had ground to a halt during the Great Depression, surged after the war. A quarter of the country's housing stock in 1960 had not even existed a decade earlier.

William J. Levitt and the FHA Two particular postwar developments remade the national housing market into a distinctly suburban shape. First, an innovative Long Island building contractor, William J. Levitt, applied mass-production techniques to construction, allowing his company to build modest, affordable houses rapidly and inexpensively. Soon his company was turning out entire neighborhoods of houses at a dizzying speed. Levitt's basic four-room house, complete with kitchen appliances, was priced at $7,990 when homes in the first **Levittown** went on sale in 1947 (about $95,000 today). Levitt did not need to advertise; word of mouth brought buyers flocking to his developments (all called Levittown) in New York, Pennsylvania, and New Jersey. Seeing Levitt's success, developers across the country snapped up cheap farmland to build their own subdivisions.

Levittown
A Long Island, New York, suburb, built by William J. Levitt in the late 1940s, that used mass-production techniques to build modest, affordable houses. Other Levittowns were built in Pennsylvania and New Jersey.

The second innovation came in home finance. Even at $7,990, Levitt's homes were beyond the means of most young families working by the traditional home-financing standard — a down payment of half the full price and ten years to pay off the balance. But the Federal Housing Administration (FHA) and the Veterans Administration (VA) — that is, the federal government — radically reshaped the home mortgage market, making home ownership more accessible than ever before. After the war, the FHA insured thirty-year mortgages with as little as 5 percent down and interest at 2 or 3 percent. The VA was even more generous, requiring only a token $1 down payment for qualified ex-GIs. Home ownership rates had hovered around 45 percent for half a century, but FHA and VA mortgages helped push the number to 60 percent by 1960.

Much about the suburbs was new, but they also reflected well-established discriminatory patterns. Levitt's houses came with restrictive covenants prohibiting occupancy "by members of other than the Caucasian Race." Levittowns were not an outlier. All across the country, formal and informal agreements barred African Americans from owning or renting homes in most suburban areas — in some places, Jews, Latinos, and Asian Americans also faced exclusion. Suburban developments from coast to coast exhibited the same age, class, and racial homogeneity. In ***Shelley v. Kraemer*** (1948), the Supreme Court outlawed restrictive covenants, but racial discrimination in housing persisted. The FHA and VA continued a practice known as redlining: refusing to insure mortgages in mixed race neighborhoods, on the grounds that such areas were "blighted" — marked on maps by a red line. It would be twenty years after *Shelley* that federal law explicitly prohibited racial discrimination, when Congress passed the Fair Housing Act in 1968.

Shelley v. Kraemer
A 1948 Supreme Court decision that outlawed racially restrictive housing occupancy covenants. However, racial discrimination persisted until the passage of the Fair Housing Act in 1968.

Interstate Highways Suburbanization on such a massive scale would have been impossible without automobiles. Planners laid out new subdivisions with the assumption that every resident drove. And drive they did — to get to work, to take the children to Little League, to shop. In 1945, Americans owned twenty-five million cars; by 1965, just two decades later, the number had tripled to seventy-five million. American oil consumption followed course, tripling as well between 1949 and 1972. But the fuel efficiency of American cars was less important than power and style. Engine sizes grew with each new model year throughout the 1950 and 1960s — when the powerful V-8 engine reached the height of its popularity — and cars were weighed down by elaborate steel tail fins and the heavy application of chrome fixtures.

Americans had more cars, and thanks to the federal government more roads on which to drive. In 1956, the **National Interstate and Defense Highways Act** authorized $26 billion over a ten-year period to fund a vast expansion of the national highway network and the integration of newly constructed highways into a single

National Interstate and Defense Highways Act
A 1956 law authorizing the construction of 42,500 miles of new highways and their integration into a single national highway system.

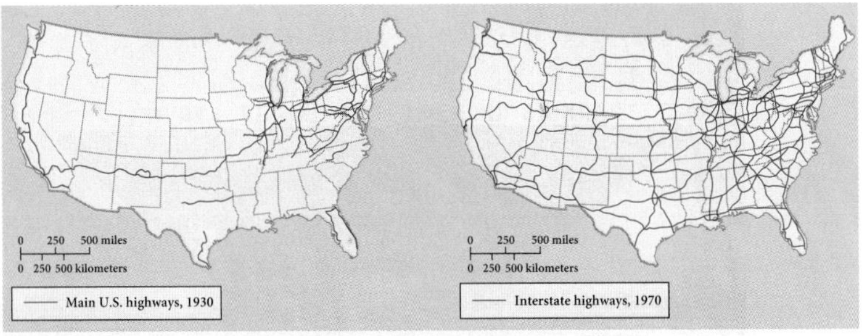

MAP 25.1 Connecting the Nation: The Interstate Highway System, 1930 and 1970
The 1956 National Interstate and Defense Highways Act paved the way for an extensive network of federal highways throughout the nation. The act not only pleased American drivers and enhanced their love affair with the automobile but also benefitted the petroleum, construction, trucking, real estate, and tourist industries. The new highway system promoted the nation's economic integration, facilitated the growth of suburbs, and contributed to the erosion of America's distinct regional identities.

system — 42,500 miles worth (Map 25.1). Cast as a Cold War necessity because broad highways made evacuating crowded cities easier in the event of a nuclear attack, the law remade driving habits and the landscape itself. An enormous public works program surpassing anything undertaken during the New Deal, and enthusiastically endorsed by a Republican administration, the interstate system became the foundation of American suburbanization. New highways rerouted traffic away from small towns and well-traveled roads such as the cross-country Route 66, and tore holes through the fabric of cities by necessitating the bulldozing of entire neighborhoods.

AP® SKILLS & PROCESSES
CONTEXTUALIZATION
How did the growing size and influence of the national government encourage suburbanization?

Fast Food and Shopping Malls Americans did not simply fill their new suburban homes with the latest appliances and gadgets; they also pioneered entirely new forms of consumption. Through World War II, downtowns remained the commercial heart of America — boasting grand department stores and five-and-dime drug stores, elegant eateries and cheap diners. But as suburbanites abandoned big-city centers in the 1950s, ambitious entrepreneurs invented two new commercial forms that would dominate the rest of the century and reconfigure American commerce: the shopping mall and the fast-food restaurant.

As Americans flocked to the suburbs, so did retailers. The first suburban shopping centers appeared outside Boston, Los Angeles, and Seattle in 1949 and 1950 and set the standard for thousands to come: an enclosed, indoor promenade featuring many small specialty shops and two or three large clothing or variety stores, all surrounded by acres of parking lots. A major developer of shopping malls in the Northeast called them "today's village green," and observed that "the fountain in the mall has replaced the downtown department clock as the gathering place for young and old alike" — centralizing otherwise dispersed lives. Malls brought "the market to the people instead of people to the market," commented the *New York Times*. In 1939, the suburban share of total metropolitan retail trade in the United States was a paltry 4 percent. By 1961, it was an astonishing 60 percent in the nation's ten largest metropolitan regions.

No one was more influential in shaping suburban consumption patterns than Ray Kroc, the Chicago-born son of Czech immigrants. A former jazz musician and traveling salesman, Kroc found his calling in 1954 when he acquired a single franchise of McDonald's Restaurant, a little-known hamburger chain in San Bernardino, California. In 1956, Kroc invested in twelve more franchises. By 1958 he owned seventy-nine. Three years later, Kroc bought the company from the McDonald brothers and proceeded to turn it into the largest chain of restaurants in the world.

AP® SKILLS & PROCESSES

CONTEXTUALIZATION

The **CONTEXTUALIZATION** question asks students to consider suburbanization in the larger context of an increased federal government role in American society. Many students struggle seeing larger structural factors as sources of change. They assume that suburbanization was a purely private decision made by individual families, but the government played a significant role in encouraging suburbanization through tax law, Federal Housing Authority loans, the GI Bill, contracts with aerospace corporations, and highway construction. Remind students to center their answers on legislation, policies, or decisions by the federal, not state, government.

TRM Find complete suggested responses in the Teacher's Resource Materials.

TEACHING STRATEGY

The National Museum of American History's online exhibit *FOOD: Transforming the American Table 1950–2000* uses text and images to explore the development of eating in the car, drive-thrus, and technological innovations that sped up food preparation. To access this exhibit, search "National Museum of American History Food exhibit."

CHECK FOR UNDERSTANDING

Ask students: **What were the causes and effects of the postwar housing boom?** *The housing boom was supported by federal programs like FHA and the VA, and the construction of interstate highways that facilitated commuting from suburban communities to urban worksites. Suburbanization facilitated the growth of the fast-food industry and shopping malls that replaced downtown department stores. While the Supreme Court declared housing covenants unenforceable, suburban communities were frequently segregated by race.*

AP® APPLY THE TIP

Ask students to work individually and use pp. 803–808 to provide at least two pieces of specific evidence of the impact of suburbanization on the U.S. to complete **Handout 25.4 — Thematic Analysis: Suburbanization (TRM)**. After students have completed their thematic analysis, organize them into seven collaborative groups and assign each group one Thematic Learning Objective from the handout. Each group should create a DBQ prompt based on their assigned objective and find seven documents that provide evidence to support their prompt. Then direct students to annotate each source with an explanation of the ways in which it could be used as evidence as well as some ways students could approach an extended analysis for each document.

TRM Find **Handout 25.4 — Thematic Analysis: Suburbanization** in the Teacher's Resource Materials.

Fast Food, 1949 The sign atop this suburban Los Angeles restaurant says it all. Suburbanization laid the foundation for a unique postwar phenomenon that would forever change American life: the rise of fast food. Cheap, convenient, and "fast," the food served in the new restaurants, modeled after the industry's pioneer, McDonald's, was not necessarily nutritious, but its chief advantage was portability. Loomis Dean/The LIFE Picture Collection/Getty Images.

McDonald's served burgers the same way Levitt built houses: quick and affordable. Kroc's vision transformed the way Americans consumed food — whether they ate in the restaurant, at home, or even in the car. "Drive-in" or "fast" food became a staple of the American diet in the subsequent decades. By the year 2000, fast food was a $100 billion industry, and Ronald McDonald, the clown in McDonald's television commercials, was as recognizable to children as Santa Claus.

Rise of the Sunbelt

AP® EXAM TIP
Recognize the reasons for the growth of the Sunbelt in the postwar years.

Sunbelt
Name applied to the Southwest and South, which grew rapidly after World War II as a center of defense industries and non-unionized labor.

Suburbanization was a national phenomenon, but its fullest expression came in an emerging region of the country — the **Sunbelt**, a broad swath of the South and Southwestern states, where defense industry jobs, low taxes, mild winters, and plenty of open space encouraged the construction of sprawling subdivisions (Map 25.2). Florida added 3.5 million people, many of them retired, between 1940 and 1970. Texas combined Sunbelt appeal with expanding petrochemical and defense industries and added 4.5 million people in the same period. Most dramatic was California's growth, spurred especially by the state's booming defense-related aircraft and electronics industries. By 1970, California contained one-tenth of the nation's population and surpassed New York as the most populous state. By the end of the century, California boasted an economy larger than that of all but a handful of countries.

A hallmark of Sunbelt suburbanization was its close relationship to the military-industrial complex. Building on World War II expansion, military bases proliferated in the South and Southwest in the postwar decades, especially in Florida, Texas, and California. In some instances, entire metropolitan regions — such as San Diego County, California, and the Houston area in Texas — expanded in tandem with nearby military outposts. Moreover, the aerospace, defense, and electronics industries were based largely in the Sunbelt. With government contracts fueling the economy and military bases providing thousands of jobs, Sunbelt politicians had added incentive to support vigorous defense spending by the federal government.

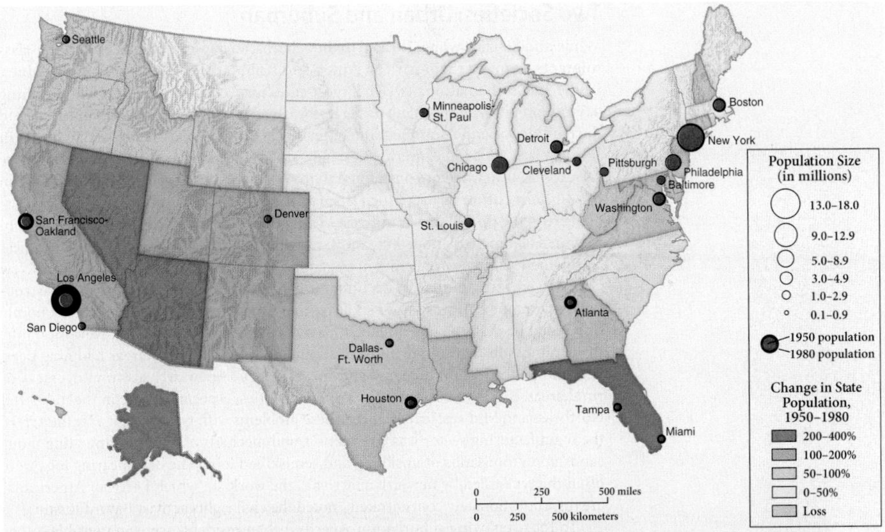

MAPPING THE PAST

MAP 25.2 Shifting Population Patterns, 1950–1980
This map shows the two major, somewhat overlapping, patterns of population movement between 1950 and 1980. Most striking is the rapid growth of the Sunbelt states. All the states experiencing increases of over 100 percent in that period are in the Southwest, plus Florida. The second pattern involves the growth of metropolitan areas, defined as a central city or urban area and its surrounding suburbs. Most central cities were not increasing in population, however, so the metropolitan growth shown in this map is evidence of expanding suburbs. And because Sunbelt growth was primarily suburban in nature, that's where we see the most rapid metropolitan growth, with Los Angeles the clear leader.

ANALYZING THE MAP: Using the map key, identify the regions with the greatest population increase in these decades. Are they more northern or more southern? Eastern or western? Where are the country's largest cities located?

MAKING CONNECTIONS: What characteristics of the high growth regions led to dramatic changes in migration patterns after World War II? How do the migration patterns illustrated above compare to earlier periods of migration in the early twentieth century and the early nineteenth century?

Orange County, California typified the Sunbelt suburb. Located southwest of Los Angeles, Orange County was until the 1940s mostly just that — abundant groves of oranges. But during World War II, local boosters attracted new bases and training facilities for the marines, navy, and army air corps (forerunner of the air force). Cold War militarization and the Korean War kept those bases humming, and Hughes Aircraft, Ford Aeronautics, and other defense-related manufacturers soon built plants in the sunny, sprawling orchards. Subdivision developers followed close behind, building so many new homes that the population of the county jumped from 130,760 in 1940 to 703,925 in 1960. In the early 1950s, the filmmaker and savvy entrepreneur Walt Disney chose Anaheim in Orange County as the site of a massive new amusement park. His Disneyland became for the postwar generation of Americans what Coney Island in New York had been to the prewar generation — a fantasy world of leisure, spectacle, entertainment, and consumption (see "City Cultures" in Chapter 18).

TEACHING STRATEGY

Use **MAP 25.2** to indicate the growth of Sunbelt states, as well as the decline of "Rustbelt" states. As with other maps presenting data, students need to read the information carefully. While the colors might suggest that Nevada, Arizona, and Florida grew the most, that is only true as a percentage of their 1950 populations; in absolute terms, California grew dramatically more.

TRM Find complete suggested responses in the Teacher's Resource Materials.

CHECK FOR UNDERSTANDING

Ask students: **What caused the rise of the Sunbelt and what were its features?** *The Sunbelt was fueled by the military-industrial complex and the federal highway system. It was characterized by suburbs, military bases and aerospace jobs, and automobile-related features like drive-thrus.*

Two Societies: Urban and Suburban

While middle-class whites flocked to the suburbs, an opposite stream of working-class migrants, many of them African Americans from the South, poured into the cities. In the 1950s, the nation's twelve largest cities lost 3.6 million whites while gaining 4.5 million nonwhites. A new phase in the decades-long Great Migration had begun during the war and continued long after 1945. As in the earlier phase that began in World War I, jobs in northern cities and a desire to escape southern Jim Crow drove the exodus. A new factor contributed to the postwar migratory surge: the automation of southern cotton farms, which displaced hundreds of thousands of rural laborers across the South and Southwest. These urban newcomers, like generations of migrants before them, hoped the move from farm to city would revive their fortunes.

By the 1950s, however, cities in the nation's industrial belt — from Chicago to New York — were struggling with declining urban economies and a decaying infrastructure. Surrounded by prosperous suburbs, the "inner city" was no longer the economic hub it had been in the late nineteenth and early twentieth centuries. New migrants, in search of jobs and opportunity, burdened it further. Urban areas had long been home to poverty, slum housing, and the struggles of new arrivals from overseas or rural areas. But in the postwar era, American cities, especially those in the industrial Northeast and Midwest, experienced these problems with new intensity. By the 1950s, the manufacturing sector was contracting, and mechanization was eliminating thousands upon thousands of unskilled and semiskilled jobs. The disappearing jobs were often the type filled by new urban arrivals, the work "in which [African Americans] are disproportionately concentrated," noted the civil rights activist Bayard Rustin.

To those enjoying suburban prosperity, urban residents were an invisible "other America," as the social critic Michael Harrington dubbed the nation's urban poor. To those living in poverty, and isolated by racial segregation, suburban prosperity was all too visible, yet inaccessible. When a wave of destructive riots swept the country in the summer of 1967, President Johnson formed the National Advisory Commission on Civil Disorders (known as the **Kerner Commission**). The group's report appeared in 1968 and warned that "our nation is moving toward two societies, one black, one white, separate and unequal."

Kerner Commission
The National Advisory Commission on Civil Disorders, which investigated the 1967 urban riots. Its 1968 report warned of the dangers of "two societies, one black, one white, separate and unequal."

The Urban Crisis The intensification of poverty, the deterioration of older housing stock, and the persistence of racial segregation produced what many called the urban crisis. Mostly unwelcome in the shiny new suburbs, African Americans instead found low-paying work and substandard housing in inner cities. Despite a growing black middle class — larger than ever before — institutional racism frustrated African Americans at every turn: housing restrictions, increasingly segregated schools, and a decaying urban infrastructure that starved for tax support as whites left for the suburbs.

Housing and job discrimination were compounded by the frenzy of urban renewal that hit black neighborhoods in the 1950s and early 1960s. Seeking to revitalize declining city centers, politicians and private developers proposed razing "blighted" neighborhoods to make way for new construction aimed at the fleeing middle class. In San Francisco, some four thousand residents of the Western Addition, a predominantly black neighborhood, lost their homes to an urban renewal program that built luxury housing, a shopping center, and an express boulevard. Under Detroit's urban renewal plans, twenty-five thousand housing units were destroyed and only fifteen thousand built. In Boston, almost one-third of the old city — including the historic Italian neighborhood in the West End — was demolished to make way for high-rise buildings and highways. Between 1949 and 1967, urban renewal demolished almost 400,000 buildings and displaced 1.4 million people nationwide.

Many of those dislocated by urban renewal were moved to federally funded housing projects, a vast expansion of New Deal housing policy. However well intended, these projects too often took the form of grim, cheaply built high-rises that isolated their inhabitants from surrounding neighborhoods. The problems of public housing

Urban Crisis In this photo of a Chicago neighborhood from 1963, a middle-class, high-rise apartment building looms over an older, low-income district. The contrast is emblematic of what many commentators in the 1960s came to call the "urban crisis," the shift of investment, commerce, good jobs, and the middle class away from central cities to either neighboring suburbs or high-rent apartment districts. Racial segregation and continued racial discrimination played a significant role in limiting the economic options available to the black working class. That reality became a major spark to the black freedom struggle in many American cities. Charles E. Knoblock/AP Images.

were especially challenging for African Americans, who often found that public housing increased racial segregation and created concentrated pockets of poverty, disconnected from jobs and thriving neighborhoods. The Robert Taylor Homes in Chicago, with twenty-eight buildings of sixteen stories each, housed twenty thousand residents, almost all of them black. The planners had imagined a huge complex of decent, affordable apartments, but instead the Taylor Homes were overcrowded, maintenance and upkeep was underfunded, and with few available jobs in close proximity residents remained poor and socially marginalized.

AP® EXAM TIP

Compare the Great Migration of the 1920s and 1930s to the movement of African Americans in the 1950s.

Urban Immigrants Despite the evident urban crisis, cities continued to attract immigrants from abroad. U.S. immigration policy had long aimed to limit "undesirable" arrivals, culminating in the overtly discriminatory National Origins Act of 1924 (see "Nativism" in Chapter 21). But World War II and the Cold War brought about a gradual change in the government's stance on immigration. The Displaced Persons Act of 1948 permitted the entry of approximately 415,000 Europeans, many of them Jewish refugees. In a gesture to an important war ally, the Chinese Exclusion Act was repealed in 1943. More far-reaching was the 1952 McCarran-Walter Act, which ended the exclusion of Japanese, Koreans, and Southeast Asians.

After the national-origins quota system went into effect in 1924, Mexico replaced Eastern and Southern Europe as the nation's labor reservoir. During World War II, the federal government introduced the Bracero Program to ease wartime labor shortages and then revived it in 1951, during the Korean War. However, the federal government

TEACHING STRATEGY

Martin Luther King Jr. is often thought of as having developed a concern for economic justice late in his career, but in his 1958 account of the Montgomery bus boycott, *Stride Toward Freedom* (New York: Harper, 1958), he talks about how he learned about the relationship between racism and economic oppression early in his life. Have students read excerpts from King's text to explore the continuity and change of the African American's experience from the Reconstruction to this period.

AP® APPLY THE TIP

To support student understanding of change and continuity over time in relationship to the migration of African Americans, ask students to construct a timeline that illustrates the various periods of migration for African Americans from the Reconstruction Era to 1960. Ask students to use pp. 830–832 as well as outside research to identify major periods of migration for African Americans. For each period of migration on the timeline, ask students to explain the causes and effects of the migration and to provide contextualization by explaining what broader historical processes, events, or developments influenced each period of migration. When the timelines are complete, ask students to respond individually to the following prompt: To what degree did the migration of African Americans in the 1950s prove similar to as well as different from earlier periods of migration?

AP® THEME

MIG: Migration and Settlement

Immigrants from around the world sought access to the political, social, and economic opportunities in the U.S., though immigration remained limited before passage of the Immigration Act in 1965. *West Side Story*, which debuted on Broadway in 1957, retells the story of Romeo and Juliet in part through Puerto Rican immigrants living on the Upper West Side of Manhattan. A popular film version of the musical was released in 1961. The *West Side Story* Web site provides images and archival materials related to both the musical and the film. To access this site, search "West Side Story."

lacked an effective mechanism to compel workers to return home. The Mexican immigrant population continued to grow, and by the time the Bracero Program ended in 1964, many of that group — an estimated 350,000 — had settled permanently in the United States. Braceros were joined by other Mexicans who immigrated to the United States to escape rural poverty or to earn money to return home and purchase land for farming.

AP® EXAM TIP

Compare the policies of the federal government toward immigrants before and after World War II.

Like generations of immigrants before them, Mexicans gravitated to major metropolitan areas. They primarily settled in Los Angeles, Long Beach, San Jose, El Paso, and other southwestern cities. But many also went north, joining well-established Mexican American communities in Chicago, Detroit, Kansas City, and Denver. Mexican Americans remained a key part of the agricultural workforce, and also became a significant presence in industrial and service work by 1960.

Another major influx of Spanish-speaking migrants came from Puerto Rico. American citizens since 1917, Puerto Ricans had an unrestricted right to move to the mainland United States. Migration increased dramatically after World War II, when mechanization of the island's sugarcane agriculture put thousands of Puerto Rican laborers out of work. Airlines began to offer low-cost direct flights between San Juan and New York City. With the fare at about $50 (two weeks' wages), Puerto Ricans became America's first migrants to arrive en masse by air. Most settled in New York, where they clustered first in East ("Spanish") Harlem and then scattered in neighborhoods across the city's five boroughs. This massive migration, which increased New York City's Puerto Rican population to 613,000 by 1960, transformed the ethnic composition of the city. More Puerto Ricans now lived in New York City than in San Juan.

Cuban refugees constituted the third largest group of Spanish-speaking immigrants. In the six years after Fidel Castro's seizure of power in 1959 an estimated 180,000 people fled Cuba for the United States. The Cuban refugee community grew so quickly that it turned Miami into a bilingual, cosmopolitan city almost overnight. Unlike other urban migrants, Miami's Cubans quickly prospered, in large part because many had arrived with middle-class skills and education.

AP® SKILLS & PROCESSES

DEVELOPMENTS AND PROCESSES

How was the United States becoming, in the language of the Kerner Commission report, "two societies" during the postwar years?

The vast majority of the nearly ten million Spanish-speaking residents of the United States in the 1960s were Mexican, Puerto Rican, or Cuban, but Latino/a communities drew immigrants from a diverse array of countries and cultures in the Americas. They gathered in urban centers, creating barrios (neighborhoods) where bilingualism flourished, the Catholic Church shaped religious life, and families sought a stake in the postwar affluence. Even as they pursued a place in mainstream economic life, these Spanish-speaking Latino/a communities remained largely segregated from white, or Anglo, areas as well as from African American districts. Though not quite 5 percent of all Americans in 1970 — in comparison, African Americans constituted 11 percent in 1970 — Latino/a populations would continue to grow over the subsequent decades, through natural increase and immigration, and in the twenty-first century would reach 18 percent of the total U.S. population.

SUMMARY

While the United States waged a costly Cold War abroad, an unparalleled prosperity reigned at home. Indeed, the Cold War was one of the engines of prosperity. The postwar economy was dominated by big corporations and defense spending. A new middle class shot up, enjoying the highest standard of living in the world. After years of depression and war-induced insecurity, Americans turned inward toward home and family. Postwar couples married young, had several children, and — if they were white and middle class — raised those children in a climate of suburban comfort. The typical 1950s family celebrated traditional gender roles, even though millions of women entered the workforce in those years. Not everyone, however, shared in the postwar prosperity. Major cities became increasingly impoverished. Black migrants, unlike earlier immigrants, encountered an urban economy that had little use for them. Pervasive racism and a lack of opportunity pushed many African Americans to the social bottom, even as sparkling new suburbs emerged outside cities. The

CHECK FOR UNDERSTANDING

Ask students: **What were the major forces that contributed to postwar suburbanization?** Students need to concentrate on including a variety of factors that contributed to suburbanization such as governmental policies, postwar economic growth, new technological developments, transportation networks, and new jobs created by the Cold War. As students respond to this question, encourage them to include two of the aforementioned subjects such as transportation networks and governmental policies.

AP® SKILLS & PROCESSES

DEVELOPMENTS AND PROCESSES

According to the Kerner Commission, the United States was becoming "two societies" as represented by black and white Americans. Think about providing students with a category of analysis such as housing, education, or economic opportunity and use that as a means to answer the prompt. Broad categories with specific historical evidence will lead to an accurate and historically defensible response.

TRM Find complete suggested responses in the Teacher's Resource Materials.

CHECK FOR UNDERSTANDING

Use the **AP® LEARNING FOCUS** question from the beginning of the chapter to check students' understanding of the chapter as a whole: **Why did consumer culture become such a fixture of American life in the postwar decades, and how did it affect politics and society?** *The rise in American prosperity, the expansion of productivity and consumer goods, the proliferation of the suburbs, the baby boom, and the new American ethic of consumption fueled the consumer culture that characterized the 1950s. The new consumer culture and the suburbanization of America created insular communities across America and particularly in the Sunbelt region that was closely related to the new military-industrial complex. Middle-class white families populated this new suburban nation whose politics were increasingly conservative. Suburbs dissected the experience of many Americans from the ongoing racial strife and impoverished conditions in many American cities.*

smoldering contradictions of the postwar period — Cold War anxiety in the midst of suburban domesticity, diverging ideas about the role of women, economic and racial inequality — would fuel the protest movements of the 1960s.

CHAPTER 25 REVIEW

AP® CONTENT REVIEW

Answer these questions to demonstrate your understanding of the chapter's main ideas.

1. What drove the growth of the American economy after World War II?
2. What was the "American Dream," and how did Americans embrace it in the postwar decades?
3. What were the major forces that shaped postwar suburbanization?

AP® TERMS TO KNOW

Identify and explain the significance of each term.

Key Concepts and Events

kitchen debate (p. 804)
Bretton Woods (p. 807)
World Bank (p. 807)
International Monetary Fund (IMF) (p. 807)
military-industrial complex (p. 807)
Sputnik (p. 808)
National Defense Education Act (p. 808)
The Affluent Society (p. 809)
The Other America (p. 810)
Servicemen's Readjustment Act (p. 811)
Veterans Administration (VA) (p. 811)
baby boom (p. 813)
teenager (p. 815)
Beats (p. 816)
Levittown (p. 826)
Shelley v. Kraemer (p. 826)
National Interstate and Defense Highways Act (p. 826)
Sunbelt (p. 828)
Kerner Commission (p. 830)

Key People

Dwight D. Eisenhower (p. 807)
Miles Davis (p. 816)
Allen Ginsberg (p. 816)
Billy Graham (p. 817)
Dr. Benjamin Spock (p. 818)

AP® MAKING CONNECTIONS

Recognize the larger developments and continuities within and across chapters by answering these questions.

1. Think back to earlier chapters that discussed gender roles, marriage, and American family life in the late nineteenth and early twentieth centuries (Chapters 17, 18, 21, and 23). How had the American family changed by the 1950s? What aspects of family life remained similar across many decades? For example, how did the working-class immigrant family of the 1890s differ from the middle-class family of the 1950s? Describe patterns of continuity and change in family life over time.
2. Examine the sections from Chapters 16, 19, 21, and 23 that explore the history of American capitalism. What key changes took place between the 1880s and the 1960s? Consider corporations, consumer society, government regulation, and the distribution of wealth.

KEY TURNING POINTS

Refer to the timeline at the start of the chapter for help in answering the following question.

What were the major turning points in the creation of postwar suburbia?

✓ LearningCurve

Remind students to go online to complete the LearningCurve quiz for this chapter.

TRM Find complete suggested responses in the Teacher's Resource Materials.

AP® SKILLS & PROCESSES

CAUSATION

AP® CONTENT REVIEW 1 asks students to identify the causes of economic growth after World War II. Note: This is the same question as the **CHECK YOUR UNDERSTANDING** prompt on p. 817.

AP® SKILLS & PROCESSES

CONTINUITY AND CHANGE

AP® CONTENT REVIEW 2 asks students to identify the "American Dream" and the extent to which it was embraced by Americans. Factors for the development of the "Dream" and contradictory policies of government (both national and local) will help students answer this question. Note: This is the same question as the **CHECK YOUR UNDERSTANDING** prompt on p. 823.

AP® SKILLS & PROCESSES

CAUSATION

AP® CONTENT REVIEW 3 asks students to identify the causes of suburbanization. Note: This is the same question as the **CHECK YOUR UNDERSTANDING** prompt on p. 832.

TRM Find definitions for these terms in the **Glossary/Glosario** in the Teacher's Resource Materials.

AP® SKILLS & PROCESSES

CONTINUITY AND CHANGE

AP® MAKING CONNECTIONS 1 asks students to track changes — and continuities — in American family life during the first half of the twentieth century.

AP® SKILLS & PROCESSES

CONTINUITY AND CHANGE

The **KEY TURNING POINTS** question asks students to identify significant events in suburbanization.

TRM Find complete suggested responses in the Teacher's Resource Materials.

AP PRACTICE QUESTIONS

MULTIPLE CHOICE QUESTIONS *Choose the correct answer for each question.*

Questions 1–3 refer to this excerpt.

"In order that you may enjoy your house, and derive the utmost pleasure from it, we have undertaken to prepare this handbook so that you may better understand our position and your responsibilities. . . .

No single feature . . . o much to the charm and beauty of the individual home and locality as well-kept lawns. Stabilization of values, yes, increase in values, will most often be found in those neighborhoods where lawns show as green carpets, and trees and shrubbery join to impart the sense of residential elegance. Where lawns and landscape material are neglected the neighborhood soon amasses a sub-standard or blighted appearance and is naturally shunned by the public. Your investment in your garden is large at the beginning, but will grow larger and larger as the years go by. For while furniture, houses, and most material things tend to depreciate with the years, your lawn, trees, and shrubs become more valuable both esthetically and monetarily."

Informational Handbook, "Homeowners Guide: Some Information for Residents of Levittown to Help Them Enjoy Their Homes," Levittown, Pennsylvania, 1957

1. The excerpt from the "Homeowner's Guide" could best be used by a historian to prove that after World War II (1945–1960) the United States experienced which of the following trends?
   - **a.** Increasing numbers of immigrants seeking access to economic opportunities
   - **b.** The rapid growth of evangelical Christian churches and organizations
   - **c.** The introduction of greater informality into U.S. culture
   - **d.** The migration of the middle class to the suburbs

2. The excerpt from the "Homeowner's Guide" was most likely intended to
   - **a.** promote an increasingly homogeneous culture in the postwar years.
   - **b.** challenge the Sunbelt as a significant political and economic force.
   - **c.** inspire critiques of conformity by artists and intellectuals.
   - **d.** advocate a link between home ownership and social mobility.

3. After World War II (1945–1960) Levittown grew most directly as a result of
   - **a.** the baby boom.
   - **b.** growing power of political machine organizations.
   - **c.** changes in sexual norms.
   - **d.** passage of new immigration laws.

Questions 4–5 refer to these song lyrics.

Little boxes on the hillside,
Little boxes made of ticky tacky,
Little boxes on the hillside,
Little boxes all the same.
There's a green one and a pink one
And a blue one and a yellow one,
And they're all made out of ticky tacky,
And they all look just the same.
And the people in the houses
All went to the university,
Where they were put in boxes
And they came out all the same,
And there's doctors and lawyers,
And business executives,
And they're all made out of ticky tacky,
And they all look just the same.
And they all play on the golf course
And drink their martinis dry,
And they all have pretty children
And the children go to school,
And the children go to summer camp,
And then to the university
Where they are put in boxes
And they come out all the same.
And the boys go into business
And marry and raise a family
In boxes made of ticky tacky
And they all look just the same.
There's a green one and a pink one
And a blue one and a yellow one,
And they're all made out of ticky tacky
And they all look just the same.

From the song, "Little Boxes." Words and music by Malvina Reynolds. Copyright © 1962 Schroder Music Co. (ASCAP) Renewed 1990. Used by permission. All rights reserved.

4. The lyrics in the excerpt are a direct response to which of the following developments during the middle of the twentieth century?
   a. The widening of the gap between the rich and the poor
   b. The expansion of higher education opportunities
   c. The decrease in child labor
   d. The increasing criticism of the expectation for conformity in American society

5. Which of the following issues of the period was the songwriter most likely concerned with?
   a. The increasingly homogenous mass culture of the postwar years
   b. The counterculture's rejection of the social and economic values of their parents' generation
   c. The persistence of poverty as a national problem despite an overall affluence
   d. The baby boom

SHORT ANSWER QUESTIONS

Read each question carefully and write a short response. Use evidence from the text to support your claims.

"Motown's commercial success put the record company in a unique position to promote a wide range of black cultural expression . . . [but its] . . . role as a producer of black culture and its ambitions in the business world did not coexist without conflict and contradiction. . . . [C]ommercial concerns about the marketability of a recording often stalled and sometimes cancelled projects that management deemed too politically controversial. . . . [T]he company wavered between willingness and caution when asked to produce recordings . . . that involved overt political or racial messages. . . . [P]opular music audiences, local activists, and national civil rights leaders . . . had their own ideas and disagreements about the meanings of Motown's music and commercial success. . . . Motown could not avoid becoming a contested symbol of racial progress. Motown's music symbolized the possibility of amicable racial integration through popular culture."

Suzanne E. Smith, *Dancing in the Street: Motown and the Cultural Politics of Detroit*, 1999

"American Bandstand encouraged the show's viewers, advertisers, and television affiliates to see it as the thread that stitched together different teenagers in different parts of the country into a coherent and recognizable national youth culture. . . . American Bandstand invited viewers to consume the sponsors' snacks and soft drinks along with the latest music and dances. . . . The central problem facing American Bandstand's producers was that their show's marketability depended on both the creative energies of black performers and the erasure of black teenagers. . . . [T]he image of youth culture American Bandstand presented to its national audiences bore little resemblance to the interracial makeup of Philadelphia's rock and roll scene. As the television program that did the most to define the image of youth in the late 1950's and early 1960's, the exclusionary racial practices of American Bandstand marginalized black teens from this imagined national youth culture."

Matthew F. Delmont, *The Nicest Kids in Town: American Bandstand, Rock 'n' Roll, and the Struggle for Civil Rights in 1950s Philadelphia*, 2012

1. Using the two excerpts provided, answer (a), (b), and (c).
   a. Briefly explain ONE major difference between Smith's and Delmot's historical interpretations of the United States music industry's influence on social change in the postwar period.
   b. Briefly explain how ONE specific historical event or development not directly mentioned in the excerpts could be used to support Smith's argument.
   c. Briefly explain how ONE specific historical event or development not directly mentioned in the excerpts could be used to support Delmot's argument.

2. Answer (a), (b), and (c).
   a. Briefly explain ONE important historical similarity between the United States consumer culture in the 1920s to that in the 1950s.
   b. Briefly explain ONE important historical difference between the United States' consumer culture in the 1920s from that in the 1950s.
   c. Briefly explain ONE important historical factor that accounts for the similarity OR difference between the United States consumer culture in the 1920s and the United States consumer culture in the 1950s.

3. Answer (a), (b), and (c).
   a. Briefly explain ONE specific historical cause of suburban growth in the U.S. after World War II.
   b. Briefly explain ANOTHER specific historical cause of suburban growth in the U.S. after World War II.
   c. Briefly explain ONE specific historical effect or consequence of suburban growth in the U.S. after World War II.

TRM Find complete suggested responses in the Teacher's Resource Materials.

26 CHAPTER

The Civil Rights Movement

1941–1973

Chapter 26 — AP® Assessment Weight and Pacing Guide

The assessment weight on the AP® U.S. History Exam for Chapters 23–28 is 10–17 percent. This chapter falls in Unit 8 of the AP® U.S. History Curriculum, covering Period 8: 1945–1980.

This pacing guide is based on a schedule with 120 sessions of 50 minutes each before the AP® U.S. History Exam. If you have a different number of sessions before the exam, you can modify the pacing to meet your needs. If you have additional time, consider incorporating quizzes, released AP® U.S. History questions, practice exams, writing practice, and other instructional activities.

	Traditional Schedule	Block Schedule
Chapter 26	3 days	1-2 days

Daily Pacing Guide

	Content Focus	Essential Question
Day 1	The Emerging Civil Rights Struggle, 1941–1957	What factors shaped the course of the civil rights movement between 1941 and 1957?
Day 2	Forging a Protest Movement, 1955–1965	How did the civil rights movement achieve its major legal and legislative victories between 1954 and 1965?
Day 3	Widening Demands for Equality, 1966–1973	Why did Americans of color seek remedies beyond formal legal equality? How successful were their efforts?

AP® Alignment

Section Heading	AP® Topic	AP® Theme
The Emerging Civil Rights Struggle, 1941–1957	7.13, 8.6	WOR, SOC
Forging a Protest Movement, 1955–1965	8.6, 8.9, 8.10	SOC, PCE
Widening Demands for Equality, 1966–1973	8.10, 8.11	SOC, PCE

*Should changes be made to the Course Framework in the future, an updated alignment will be placed on our AP® updates page at go.bfwpub.com/ap-course-updates.

Chapter 26 — Overview

Chapter 26 analyzes the popular, legislative, and judicial actions that pushed for civil rights for all Americans in the postwar era. The chapter begins by examining the forces for civil rights that were unleashed by America's crusade against Nazism in World War II. Popular action by leaders in the civil rights movement pushed the federal government to respond to state-supported limits on civil rights that had been in place since the late nineteenth century, culminating in the Supreme Court decision in *Brown v. Board of Education*. The chapter continues by emphasizing the effectiveness of nonviolent direct action in bringing about legislative victories in the Civil Rights Act of 1964 and Voting Rights Act of 1965. Finally, the chapter focuses on the divergence of the civil rights movement after 1965 with the rise of Black Power as well as movements emphasizing the civil rights of immigrant groups and Native Americans within the U.S.

Chapter 26 — Resources

The following resources can be found in the Teacher's Resource Materials (TRM) that accompany the book. You can access the TRM via the book's digital platform, by clicking the TRM links found here in your Teacher's Edition e-book, or by contacting your representative to access the resources online. Visit **bfwpub.com/henretta10e** to learn more.

TRM Chapter 26 Lecture Presentation Slides

TRM Chapter 26 Outline with AP® Focus

TRM Chapter 26 Lecture Strategies

TRM Chapter 26 Suggested Responses

TRM Handout 26.1 — Causation: Origin of the Civil Rights Movement

TRM Handout 26.2 — Comparison: Executive Action and Racial Equality

TRM Handout 26.3 — Comparison: Civil Rights Leaders

Chapter 26 — Essential Activity

For this activity, inform the class that they will simulate a team of historians who are tasked with designing a three-story museum dedicated to the American civil rights movement. Their job is to focus on three time periods: (1) 1941–1957; (2) 1955–1965; and (3) 1966–1973. To achieve their class goal of designing a museum, divide the class into three teams, assigning each team to work on one of the given time periods. Direct students to discuss with their team which events, leaders, ideas, laws, and/or cases they will focus on for their floor of the museum. Allow each of the three teams to subdivide as necessary to focus on specific parts of their museum floor plan. Assign one wall in the classroom (as available) to each team. On their wall, students should create their exhibits and display in the classroom. After the museum is in place, allow all students to circulate around the room to "experience" the museum.

Chapter 26 — Bell Ringers

The following activities take no more than 5–15 minutes of your class period and offer an effective and engaging way to begin your lessons and for students to apply AP® Skills & Processes:

- Provide students with excerpts from civil rights cases decided by the Supreme Court before *Brown v. Board of Education* (most of the cases were sponsored by the NAACP). Ask students to identify the arguments made by the NAACP in the cases leading up to the *Brown* case. Prompt students to explain why the *Brown* case is considered the turning point in comparison to the earlier cases.
- Show students the video of Martin Luther King Jr.'s "I Have a Dream" speech from the March on Washington in 1963. Ask students to discuss the reasons for the effectiveness of this statement of philosophy in the civil rights movement.
- Show students the TED talk by Aaron Huey titled "America's Native Prisoners of War." Discuss Huey's argument that a large section of the western U.S. should be returned to the Sioux. Ask students: Is returning land to Native Americans the right thing to do? Is it feasible? Allow students to discuss the demands that might be made by Native Americans under the idea of civil rights.

NOTES

TEACHING STRATEGY

The chapter introduction presents several ideas that help orient students to the civil rights movement. Help students understand that World War II played a significant role in changing national attitudes toward racism, forming a stronger national government, and creating a black middle class with buying power that could underwrite protest and withdraw its buying power in boycotts. Second, the opener addresses the notion of a "second Reconstruction," suggesting a comparison with the "unfinished Revolution" of the post–Civil War era. This notion encourages students to identify the ways the civil rights movement addressed those lingering injustices. Third, historians and other Americans debate the ambivalent legacy of the movement, which the opener captures by suggesting that the movement "swept aside systemic racial segregation" though it not did "sweep away racial inequality in its entirety." Fourth, the black civil rights movement both inspired and provided a model for many other rights movements that followed in its wake. Finally, the notion of "rights liberalism" as an identity-based extension of New Deal welfare liberalism is a helpful way to frame this topic for students, creating a link between the reform efforts of those two eras. For a complete suggested response to the **AP® LEARNING FOCUS** question, see p. 868.

26
CHAPTER

The Civil Rights Movement
1941–1973

AP® LEARNING FOCUS

Why did the civil rights movement change over time, and how did competing ideas and strategies evolve within the movement itself?

In June 1945, even as African American troops fought with distinction in the last months of World War II, Senator James O. Eastland, Democrat of Mississippi, took to the floor of the U.S. Senate and brashly asserted that "the Negro race is an inferior race." A lifetime after the Fourteenth Amendment promised "equal protection of the laws" and the Fifteenth guaranteed the right to vote regardless of "race, color, or previous condition of servitude," most white Americans held beliefs similar to Eastland's and refused to accept racial equality as a legal or social fact.

Much of the Deep South, like Eastland's Mississippi, was a "closed society": black people had no political rights and lived on the margins of white society, impoverished and exploited. While African Americans outside the South could vote and found a measure of freedom, their lives were still constrained: schools, neighborhoods, public amenities like swimming pools, and many businesses remained segregated and unequal in the North and West as well. Segregationists such as Eastland were united in their opposition to reform, and numerous and powerful enough in the U.S. Congress to block proposed civil rights legislation.

Across the nation, however, winds of change were gathering. Between World War II and the 1970s, slowly at first, and then with greater urgency in the 1960s, a civil rights movement swept aside the legal foundation of racial segregation. This wave of black activism could not sweep away racial inequality in its entirety, but the movement forged a "second Reconstruction." Civil rights became the defining social movement of the twentieth century, its model of nonviolent protest and calls for self-determination inspiring countless others to remake America. The black-led civil rights movement, joined at key moments by Latinos, Asian Americans, and Native Americans, also remade American liberalism. In the 1930s, New Deal liberalism had established a welfare state to protect citizens from economic hardship. The civil rights movement forged a new **rights liberalism**: the idea that individuals are entitled to state protection from discrimination. This version of liberalism focused on identities — such as race or gender, and eventually sexuality — and was joined to the social welfare liberalism of the New Deal. Rights liberalism proved to be both a necessary expansion of the nation's ideals and a wellspring of political backlash. Indeed, the quest for racial justice would contribute to a crisis of liberalism itself.

rights liberalism
The idea that individuals are entitled to state protection from discrimination. This version of liberalism focused on identities — such as race or gender, and eventually sexuality — and was joined to the social welfare liberalism of the New Deal.

834

The March from Selma to Montgomery, 1965 Leading a throng of 25,000 people, Martin Luther King Jr. and his wife, Coretta Scott King, marched from Selma, Alabama, to Montgomery, the state capitol, in March of 1965.
AP Photo.

TEACHING STRATEGY

Scenes of the Selma march — particularly those that include the famed Edmund Pettus Bridge — have become some of the most iconic of the movement. In his commemoration of the 50th anniversary of the march, President Barack Obama re-created part of this march, walking alongside Congressman John Lewis, who was beaten during "Bloody Sunday," the original attempt to cross the bridge in 1965. The Obama White House Web site includes Obama's speech, audio files of a half-dozen oral history testimonies about the original march, and an image of Obama, First Lady Michelle Obama, Lewis, and others walking across the bridge. To access these resources, search "Obama White House Selma 50th anniversary."

AP® SKILLS & PROCESSES

CONTINUITY AND CHANGE

Use the **TIMELINE** to help students begin thinking about how the period from 1941 to 1972 could constitute a distinct historical period. The periodization of this chapter reflects American entry into World War II as a starting point, and, along with it, A. Philip Randolph's threatened march on Washington, which prompted the Roosevelt administration to issue Executive Order 8802, guaranteeing blacks equal access to wartime jobs with companies that contracted with the federal government. The end point reflects the "Trail of Broken Treaties" protest in 1972, which suggests the diversification of the movement beyond African Americans, as well as the embrace of approaches to civil rights beyond nonviolent protest.

AP® THEME

NAT: American and National Identity; PCE: Politics and Power

Lead a class discussion on how during and after World War II, civil rights activists combatted racial discrimination with a variety of strategies, including nonviolent direct action.

AP® APPLY THE TIP

Ask students to read pp. 836-842 to complete **Handout 26.1 — Causation: Origin of the Civil Rights Movement (TRM)**. After students complete the causation exercise, ask them to determine which individual cause related to the rise of the civil rights movement was most important in the post–World War II years. Students should write their answer on a slip of paper. Then organize students into groups based on their choice. For this activity, students will research the cause they selected to make an argument in a debate format that addresses the following prompt: What was the most important reason for the rise of the modern civil rights movement? Allow groups 15 minutes to research evidence to support their argument and choose a spokesperson to present their argument. After all groups have made their argument, require each student to individually answer the prompt with a thesis statement and at least two points of evidence.

TRM Find **Handout 26.1 — Causation: Origin of the Civil Rights Movement** in the Teacher's Resource Materials.

TIMELINE

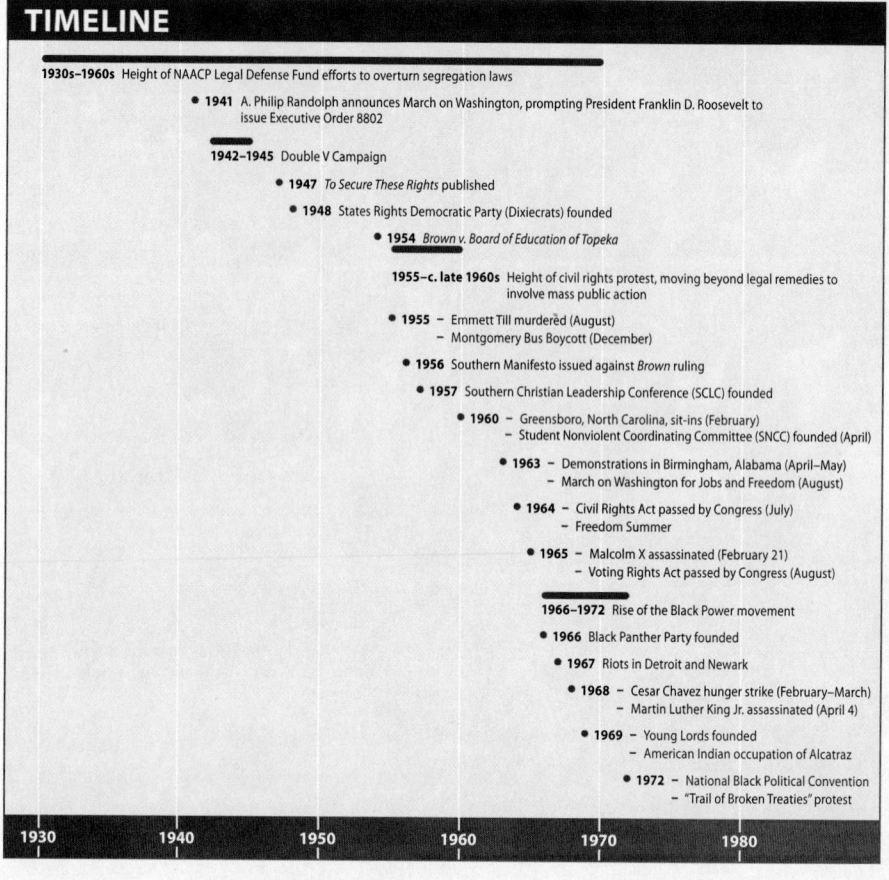

- **1930s–1960s** Height of NAACP Legal Defense Fund efforts to overturn segregation laws
- **1941** A. Philip Randolph announces March on Washington, prompting President Franklin D. Roosevelt to issue Executive Order 8802
- **1942–1945** Double V Campaign
- **1947** *To Secure These Rights* published
- **1948** States Rights Democratic Party (Dixiecrats) founded
- **1954** *Brown v. Board of Education of Topeka*
- **1955–c. late 1960s** Height of civil rights protest, moving beyond legal remedies to involve mass public action
- **1955** – Emmett Till murdered (August)
  – Montgomery Bus Boycott (December)
- **1956** Southern Manifesto issued against *Brown* ruling
- **1957** Southern Christian Leadership Conference (SCLC) founded
- **1960** – Greensboro, North Carolina, sit-ins (February)
  – Student Nonviolent Coordinating Committee (SNCC) founded (April)
- **1963** – Demonstrations in Birmingham, Alabama (April–May)
  – March on Washington for Jobs and Freedom (August)
- **1964** – Civil Rights Act passed by Congress (July)
  – Freedom Summer
- **1965** – Malcolm X assassinated (February 21)
  – Voting Rights Act passed by Congress (August)
- **1966–1972** Rise of the Black Power movement
- **1966** Black Panther Party founded
- **1967** Riots in Detroit and Newark
- **1968** – Cesar Chavez hunger strike (February–March)
  – Martin Luther King Jr. assassinated (April 4)
- **1969** – Young Lords founded
  – American Indian occupation of Alcatraz
- **1972** – National Black Political Convention
  – "Trail of Broken Treaties" protest

1930 1940 1950 1960 1970 1980

THE EMERGING CIVIL RIGHTS STRUGGLE, 1941–1957

What factors shaped the course of the civil rights movement between 1941 and 1957?

AP® EXAM TIP
Recognize the impact of World War II on the growth of the civil rights movement.

As it took shape during World War II and the early Cold War, the campaign against racial injustice proceeded along two tracks: at both grassroots and governmental levels. On the grassroots side, a loose network of organizations — churches, labor unions, and activist groups — inspired hundreds of thousands of ordinary citizens to join the movement. On the government side, civil rights lawyers and sympathetic lawmakers worked within legislative and judicial bodies, from the local to the federal, to dismantle the legal apparatus of segregation, piece by piece. Legal activists were armed with the Bill of Rights and the Reconstruction amendments to the Constitution, which guaranteed equal rights under the law to all U.S. citizens (Fourteenth Amendment) and the right to vote regardless of "race, color, or previous condition of servitude"

836

(Fifteenth Amendment). But those guarantees had been largely ignored or contradicted for African Americans since Reconstruction following the Civil War. In its most basic aims, the civil rights movement sought to restore force to those constitutional guarantees of racial equality.

Segregation in Virginia, 1962 As the law of the land in most southern states, racial segregation (known as Jim Crow) required the complete separation of blacks and whites in most public spaces. The "white only" sign on a restaurant door shown in this 1962 photograph in Hampton, Virginia, was typical. Everything from restaurants, drinking fountains, public waiting areas to libraries, public parks, schools, restrooms, and even cola vending machines was subject to strict racial segregation. © Bruce Davidson/Magnum Photos.

Life Under Jim Crow

At mid-century, a majority of the 15 million African Americans lived under a system of racial segregation and economic exploitation. African Americans made up roughly 10 percent of the overall population but comprised between 30 and 50 percent of the population of several southern states. A legal regime of social segregation and political suppression, commonly known as Jim Crow, prevailed in every aspect of life in the South, where two-thirds of all African Americans lived in 1950. Black southerners could not eat in restaurants patronized by whites or use the same waiting rooms at bus stations. Public transportation, parks, libraries, and schools were rigidly segregated by custom or by law. Even drinking fountains were labeled "White" and "Colored."

AP® EXAM TIP

Evaluate the impact World War II in bringing change and illustrating continuity for African Americans.

Underlying economic and political structures further marginalized black citizens. Virtually no African Americans could work in city or state government, and the best jobs in the private sector were reserved for whites. Black workers labored "in the back," cleaning, cooking, stocking shelves, and loading trucks for the lowest wages. Rural African Americans largely labored as sharecroppers or tenant farmers, systems that kept them stuck in poverty without access to education or other means of improvement. Political participation was low, with less than 20 percent of otherwise eligible black citizens able to cast votes as a result of barriers such as poll taxes, literacy tests, intimidation, fraud, and the "white primary" (intraparty elections in which only whites could vote). Black people made up more than a third of the population in states such as Mississippi, South Carolina, and Georgia but had no political voice. This near-total disfranchisement gave whites power that was disproportionate to their numbers — and disproportionate representation in the U.S. Congress as well.

In the North, racial segregation was less acute but just as real and routine. Segregation outside the South followed a geographic pattern: whites increasingly lived in suburbs or more affluent areas of cities, while African Americans were restricted to declining downtown neighborhoods. Often these crumbling districts were the only areas in which African Americans could find housing at all. The result was what many termed ghettos: all-black districts characterized by low wages, inadequate city services, and perversely high rents. Few jobs other than the most menial were open to African Americans. Journalists, accountants, engineers, and other highly educated graduates of all-black colleges and universities often labored as railroad porters or cooks because jobs commensurate with their skills remained for whites only. These conditions produced a self-perpetuating cycle that kept most black citizens trapped on the social and economic fringe.

African Americans did find a measure of freedom in the North and West compared to the South. They could vote, participate in politics, and more often access

AP® SKILLS & PROCESSES

DEVELOPMENTS AND PROCESSES

It is helpful if students understand the difference between personal and structural racism near the beginning of this chapter. If students understand structural racism, they will better comprehend the barriers to people of color propped up by federal, state, and local authorities. The concept of structural racism may also assist students' efforts to comprehend how and why so many Americans were allowed to be openly hostile to civil rights. The combination of both structural and personal racism are essential elements in understanding the dynamics people of color were facing as they fought for civil rights.

public accommodations. But systemic racial segregation was deeply entrenched in the country as a whole. In northern cities such as Detroit, Chicago, and Philadelphia, for instance, white homeowners used various tactics — from police harassment to thrown bricks, burning crosses, bombs, and mob violence — to keep African Americans from living near them. The Federal Housing Administration (FHA) and banks denied African Americans the easy credit that was funding the growth of suburbs, and federal urban renewal policies often demolished predominantly black neighborhoods (see "Two Societies: Urban and Suburban" in Chapter 25). Racial segregation was a national, not regional, problem.

Roots of the Civil Rights Movement

Since racial injustice had been part of American life for hundreds of years, why did the civil rights movement arise when it did? The National Association for the Advancement of Colored People (NAACP), founded in 1909, had begun challenging racial segregation in a series of court cases in the 1930s. Other organizations, such as Marcus Garvey's Universal Negro Improvement Association in the 1920s, had attracted significant popular support generations before (see "Marcus Garvey and the UNIA" in Chapter 21). These forerunners were important, but several factors came together in the middle of the twentieth century to create a much larger movement.

One such factor, or root, was the ideological justification for World War II. In the war against fascism, the Allies sought to discredit racist Nazi ideology. This commitment to fighting fascist ideology abroad drove many Americans to question and criticize their homegrown system of racism. "The Jewish people and the Negro people both know the meaning of Nordic supremacy," wrote the African American poet Langston Hughes in 1945, as he spurred the country to take up the cause of black equality. The Cold War placed added pressure on U.S. officials. To inspire other nations in the global standoff with the Soviet Union, "we must correct the remaining imperfections in our practice of democracy," President Harry S. Truman proclaimed in a "Special Message to Congress on Civil Rights" in 1948.

The emergence of a substantial black middle class, another key factor, lent more momentum to the push for equality. The historically small black middle class saw robust growth after World War II. Its ranks produced most of the civil rights leaders: ministers, teachers, trade unionists, attorneys, and other professionals. Churches, for centuries a sanctuary for black Americans, proved especially crucial. Middle-class growth was linked in crucial ways to urbanization, as cities provided jobs and education while nurturing important institutions (such as churches, labor unions, and political organizations, among others) that would aid in the struggle. In the 1960s, a sizable increase in African American college students brought new ideas and energy to the movement (Table 26.1). With access to education and media, this rising black middle class had a more powerful voice than any previous black population. Less dependent on white patronage and less vulnerable to white retaliation, middle-class African Americans were in a position to lead a movement for change.

External forces assisted the movement too. While rank-and-file white laborers did not universally back civil rights, the leaders of the United Auto Workers, the United Steelworkers, the Communications Workers of America, and other progressive trade unions became reliable allies at the national level. The new medium of television played a crucial role as well. When television networks covered early desegregation struggles — at Little Rock High School in 1957, for instance — many Americans across the country witnessed the violence of white supremacy for the first time.

TABLE 26.1

African American College Enrollment

Year	Number of African Americans Enrolled (rounded to nearest thousand)
1940	60,000
1950	110,000
1960	185,000
1970	430,000
1980	1.4 million
1990	3.6 million

CHECK FOR UNDERSTANDING

Ask students: **What was life like under Jim Crow?** *In the South, blacks were legally segregated, separated from whites in public accommodations, restaurants, and schools. They were denied access to government jobs that offered decent pay and benefits. They were also disenfranchised through mechanisms such as poll taxes and literacy tests. While segregation in the North was de facto, it was equally real, largely reflected in spatial housing patterns where blacks lived in urban ghettos and whites lived in more affluent suburbs.*

TEACHING STRATEGY

The National Association for the Advancement of Colored People (NAACP) pursued legal equality through the courts from the time of its founding in the Progressive Era. The Library of Congress provides a teacher's guide to primary source set collections the library hosts that relate to the origins and growth of the NAACP's century-long fight for freedom. To access these resources, search "LOC NAACP teacher's guide."

AP® SKILLS & PROCESSES

ANALYZING HISTORICAL EVIDENCE

Ask students: **What conclusions can you draw about African American college enrollment from TABLE 26.1? What is the significance of this data? What additional information would you need to determine more fully the significance of this data?** *The number of black college students increased dramatically, often doubling between decades. The most dramatic growth took place between 1970 and 1980, when the population more than tripled. This trend is significant because a college education is one of the most significant determinants of economic growth. It would be helpful to know how the overall black population was changing, to determine if the percentage of blacks in college was growing or shrinking. Note: The total black population rose slowly during these decades, so the percentage of blacks attending college rose more dramatically than the total number — from less than 1 percent in 1940 to nearly 30 percent in 1990.*

CHECK FOR UNDERSTANDING

Ask students: **What were the origins of the civil rights movement?** *Some black rights organizations began around the turn of the twentieth century, including the National Association for the Advancement of Colored People (NAACP) and the United Negro Improvement Association. World War II and the fight against a racist Nazi Germany prompted more Americans to condemn racism at home. The war also increased the black middle class, creating a generation of new leaders. Finally, some whites, including many in the labor movement, were sympathetic with the black plight.*

Together, these elements — the moral motives for fighting World War II, the growth of the black middle class, support from labor unions, the immediacy of television coverage — help explain why the civil rights movement emerged when it did. But no single factor was decisive on its own. None ensured an easy path. The fight for civil rights was a vast and protracted social movement, one that faced down ferocious resistance over three decades.

AP® SKILLS & PROCESSES

DEVELOPMENTS AND PROCESSES

How did the growth of the black middle class assist the civil rights movement?

World War II: The Beginnings

Even as the United States fought World War II "to make the world safe for democracy," it had long denied equality to its own black citizens. Black workers faced discrimination in wartime employment, and the more than 1 million black troops who served in World War II fought in segregated units commanded solely by whites. The war highlighted the jarring disconnect between ideas and reality, and "immeasurably magnified the Negro's awareness of the disparity between the American profession and practice of democracy," in the words of NAACP president Walter White.

AP® EXAM TIP

Evaluate the impact of executive actions in supporting racial equality.

Executive Order 8802 In early 1941, A. Philip Randolph, whose Brotherhood of Sleeping Car Porters was the most prominent black trade union, announced a march on Washington. Randolph planned to bring 100,000 protesters to the nation's capital to demand equal opportunity for black workers in war jobs — then just beginning to expand with President Franklin Roosevelt's pledge to supply the Allies with materiel. To avoid a divisive protest, FDR issued **Executive Order 8802** in June of that year, prohibiting racial discrimination in defense industries, and Randolph agreed to cancel the march. The resulting Fair Employment Practice Committee (FEPC) had few enforcement powers but set an important precedent for federal action. Randolph's efforts also showed that white leaders and institutions could be swayed by concerted African American pressure.

Executive Order 8802
An order signed by President Roosevelt in 1941 that prohibited "discrimination in the employment of workers in defense industries or government because of race, creed, color, or national origin" and established the Fair Employment Practice Committee (FEPC).

The Double V Campaign An ordinary cafeteria worker from Kansas was the spark behind another key wartime civil rights initiative. In a 1942 letter to the *Pittsburgh Courier*, James G. Thompson urged that "colored Americans adopt the double VV for a double victory" — victory over fascism abroad and victory over racism at home. Edgar Rouzeau, editor of the paper's New York office, agreed: "Black America must fight two wars and win in both." Instantly dubbed the Double V Campaign, Thompson's notion spread like wildfire through black communities across the country, with the backing of Rouzeau and the *Courier*, one of the nation's leading black newspapers. African Americans would demonstrate their loyalty and citizenship by fighting the Axis powers but simultaneously demand the defeat of racism at home.

The Double V met considerable resistance. In war industries, factories periodically shut down in Chicago, Baltimore, Philadelphia, and other cities because of "hate strikes": the refusal of white workers to labor alongside black counterparts. Detroit proved especially tense. *Life* magazine reported in 1942 that "Detroit is Dynamite. . . . It can either blow up Hitler or blow up America." A year later, the tension finally ignited. On a hot summer day, whites from the city's ethnic European neighborhoods taunted and beat African Americans in a local park. Three days of rioting ensued in which thirty-four people were killed, twenty-five of them black, and federal troops were called in to

Wartime Workers During World War II, hundreds of thousands of black migrants left the South, bound for large cities in the North and West. There they found jobs such as the welding work done by these African American women at the Landers, Frary, and Clark plant in New Britain, Connecticut. Fighting employment discrimination during the war represented one of the earliest phases in the long struggle against racial segregation in the United States. Library of Congress, 8d3978

AP® SKILLS & PROCESSES

DEVELOPMENTS AND PROCESSES

The **DEVELOPMENTS AND PROCESSES** question asks students to identify the effects of the growing strength of the black middle class on the civil rights movement. Students should identify the ways that greater skill created more leaders for the multifaceted movement, as well as autonomy from white retaliation. Extend this prompt by asking students to explain the implications of a large middle class for the strategy of boycotting; only a group with significant buying power can threaten business owners with its refusal to patronize their stores.

TRM Find complete suggested responses in the Teacher's Resource Materials.

AP® APPLY THE TIP

Ask students to complete **Handout 26.2 — Comparison: Executive Action and Racial Equality (TRM)** utilizing the textbook and online resources. Then organize students into small groups and assign each group to further research one of the following executive orders: Truman (Executive Order 99814); Eisenhower (Executive Order 10730); Kennedy (Executive Order 10925); and Johnson (Executive Order 11246). Based on their research, groups should create a contextualization diagram on a large sheet of paper that illustrates the broader historical processes, events, and developments that influenced the issuing of the executive order. (Note: Students can follow the model of the contextualization handouts in the Teacher's Research Materials.) Display the contextualization diagrams around the classroom and give students time to walk around and view the diagrams. As a class, discuss the similarities and differences between the orders and the context in which they occurred.

TRM Find **Handout 26.2 — Comparison: Executive Action and Racial Equality** in the Teacher's Resource Materials.

TEACHING STRATEGY

The Library of Congress's "African Americans at War: Fighting Two Battles" Web site page provides oral histories of African Americans' experiences both during and after the war, as they fought for rights while serving their country. To access this site, search "LOC African Americans at War."

CHECK FOR UNDERSTANDING

Ask students: **How did World War II function as the beginning of the civil rights movement?** *The need for a full labor force — as well as a strong sense of national unity — gave African Americans significant leverage to demand better conditions during the war, which resulted in Executive Order 8802 and the formation of the Fair Employment Practices Committee. Fighting a fascist foe made American racism seem especially hypocritical, prompting African Americans to fight for double victory.*

AP® SKILLS & PROCESSES

CAUSATION

The **CAUSATION** question asks students to explain the significance of World War II in helping to cause the civil rights movement. In essence, this is a turning point question, where students need to explain why the war made such a difference for blacks, since they were clearly already agitating for rights before the war began. To extend this prompt, ask students to rank the factors of the war in terms of their significance in furthering the movement.

TRM Find complete suggested responses in the Teacher's Resource Materials.

TEACHING STRATEGY

The heading "Cold War Civil Rights" is inspired by Mary Dudziak's book of the same name. Dudziak was one of the first scholars to make this link between American Cold War foreign policy and the domestic struggle for civil rights, which often hinged on federal government intervention. Her argument is helpful for students, who tend to keep these topics separate, in part because the two subjects inevitably get addressed in different textbook chapters.

TEACHING STRATEGY

Think about having students defend two historical statements about World War II and Civil Rights. Defending each of these statements will help students recognize historical change and continuity.

Statement One: World War II represented a turning point for African Americans and the struggle for civil rights.

Statement Two: World War II did not represent a turning point for African Americans and the struggle for civil rights.

restore order. The other half of the Double V — fighting abroad — also faced vigorous resistance from segregationists. Despite the fact that all-black units, such as the 761st "Black Panther" Tank Battalion and the famous Tuskegee Airmen were widely praised by military commanders, Mississippi's Senator Eastland ridiculed black troops at war's end. "The Negro soldier was an utter and dismal failure in combat," he said, a lie uttered from the floor of the U.S. Senate.

Despite such incidents, and to some degree because of them, a wave of activism spread. In New York City, employment discrimination on the city's transit lines prompted one of the first bus boycotts in the nation's history, led in 1941 by Harlem minister Adam Clayton Powell Jr. In Chicago, James Farmer and other members of the Fellowship of Reconciliation (FOR), a nonviolent peace organization, founded the **Congress of Racial Equality (CORE)** in 1942, specifically to fight for racial equality. FOR and CORE embraced the philosophy of nonviolent direct action espoused by Mahatma Gandhi of India. Another FOR member in New York and proponent of direct action, Bayard Rustin, led one of the earliest challenges to southern segregation, the 1947 Journey of Reconciliation — a two-week multiracial bus ride through the South, where buses and bus stations were strictly segregated, that met violent resistance from whites. Meanwhile, after the war, hundreds of thousands of African American veterans used the GI Bill to go to college, trade school, or graduate school, which better positioned them to push against segregation. At the war's end, Powell affirmed that "the black man . . . is ready to throw himself into the struggle to make the dream of America become flesh and blood, bread and butter."

Congress of Racial Equality (CORE) Civil rights organization founded in 1942 in Chicago by James Farmer and other members of the Fellowship of Reconciliation (FOR) that espoused nonviolent direct action.

AP® SKILLS & PROCESSES

CAUSATION

Why did World War II play such a critical role in the civil rights movement?

Cold War Civil Rights

Demands for justice persisted in the early years of the Cold War. Momentum built behind symbolic victories — such as Jackie Robinson breaking major league baseball's color line with the Brooklyn Dodgers in 1947 — but the growing black vote in northern cities proved more consequential. During World War II, more than a million African Americans migrated to northern and western cities. Leaving the Jim Crow South gave many the opportunity to vote for the first time. At the ballot box, African Americans increasingly sided with the Democratic Party of Franklin Roosevelt and the New Deal (Map 26.1). This newfound political leverage earned the attention of northern liberals, many of whom became allies of civil rights advocates. Ultimately, however, the Cold War climate produced mixed results for the movement, as the nation's growing anticommunism opened some avenues for civil rights while closing others.

Civil Rights and the New Deal Coalition African American leaders were uncertain what to expect from President Truman, a committed New Dealer who was also known to use racist language. Though Truman did not support social equality for African Americans, he did believe in equality before the law. Moreover, he understood the growing importance of the black vote in key northern states such as New York, Illinois, Pennsylvania, and Michigan. Civil rights activists Randolph and Powell — along with vocal white liberals such as Hubert Humphrey, the mayor of Minneapolis, and members of Americans for Democratic Action (ADA), a liberal organization — pressed Truman to act.

With no support for civil rights in Congress, Truman turned to executive action. In 1946, he appointed the Presidential Committee on Civil Rights, whose 1947 report, **"To Secure These Rights,"** called for robust federal action to ensure black equality. With the report's recommendations in mind, in 1948 Truman swung into action. He signed executive orders desegregating federal agencies and the armed forces, the latter after pressure from Randolph's Committee Against Jim Crow in Military Service. The president then sent a message to Congress asking that every one of the report's recommendations — including the abolition of poll taxes and the restoration of the

"To Secure These Rights" The 1947 report by the Presidential Committee on Civil Rights that called for robust federal action to ensure equality for African Americans. President Truman asked Congress to make all of the report's recommendations — including the abolition of poll taxes and the restoration of the Fair Employment Practice Committee — into law, leading to discord in the Democratic Party.

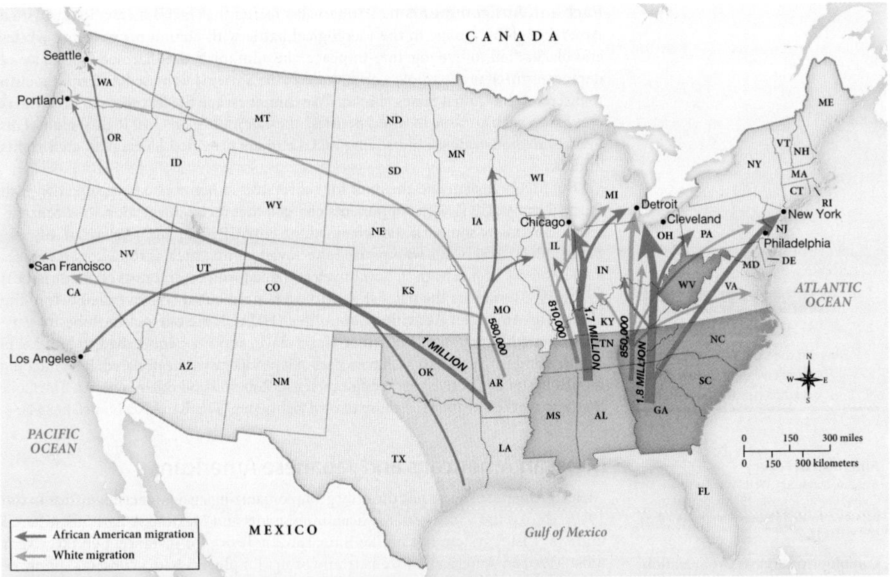

MAPPING THE PAST

MAP 26.1 Internal Migrations

The migration of African Americans from the South to other regions of the country produced one of the most remarkable demographic shifts of the mid-twentieth century. Between World War I—which marked the start of the Great Migration—and the 1970s, more than 6 million African Americans left the South. Where they settled in the North and West, they helped change the politics of entire cities and even states. Seeking black votes, which had become a key to victory in major cities, liberal Democrats and Republicans alike in New York, Illinois, California, and Pennsylvania, for instance, increasingly made civil rights part of their platform. In this way, migration advanced the political cause of black equality.

ANALYZING THE MAP: Locate the origins and the endpoints of the internal migrations represented by the map. Identify the cities and states to which people migrated. Ask yourself what forms of transportation people were most likely to use in different eras—the 1920s, for example, or the 1960s.

MAKING CONNECTIONS: Evaluate the causes for migration of African Americans that remained the same throughout the Great Migration. How did the migration of African Americans bring about change in the civil rights movement after World War II?

Fair Employment Practice Committee—become law. It was the most aggressive call for racial equality by the leader of a major political party since Reconstruction.

Truman's request was too much for southern Democrats. Under the leadership of Governor Strom Thurmond of South Carolina, white Democrats from the South formed the **States' Rights Democratic Party**, known popularly as the Dixiecrats, for the 1948 presidential election (see "The 1948 Election" in Chapter 24). This breakaway hinted at a potential long-term schism within the New Deal coalition. Would the civil rights aims of the party's liberal wing alienate southern white Democrats, as well as many suburban whites in the North? The Dixiecrat movement was a prelude to the discord that would eventually fracture the Democratic Party in the 1960s.

States' Rights Democratic Party Known popularly as the Dixiecrats, a breakaway party of white Democrats from the South that formed for the 1948 election. Its formation hinted at a potential long-term schism within the New Deal coalition.

TEACHING STRATEGY

As **MAP 26.1** indicates, not all African Americans headed to Chicago, Detroit, and New York during the Great Migration. A small but significant stream also flowed to the West Coast, most notably Los Angeles. Consider having students read an excerpt from historian Scott Kurashige's book *A Companion to Los Angeles* (Hoboken: Wiley, 2014), which captures the complex dynamics of this city, which was multiracial, not just biracial. When Japanese Americans were removed from their communities during World War II, many African Americans moved in, some of them recent arrivals of the Great Migration. After the war, the two groups had to negotiate the challenges of living side by side, which led, in some cases, to interethnic solidarity.

AP® THEME

ARC: American and Regional Culture

Think about having students compare the historical factors that led to out-migration of African Americans and whites to the West coast during and after World War II, which is a distinctive feature attendant to the years 1940–1970. What historical causes account for this movement westward?

TRM Find complete suggested responses in the Teacher's Resource Materials.

TEACHING STRATEGY

The Bracero History Archive provides a variety of resources to teach students more about race and anticommunism, including an archive of relevant documents, images, and oral histories. To access these resources, search "Bracero History Archive."

CHECK FOR UNDERSTANDING

Ask students: **How did the Cold War and civil rights advocacy intersect?** *The Cold War both encouraged and slowed civil rights. Concerned with America's image abroad, Truman was anxious to curb racism at home. At the same time, accusations that the NAACP and other civil rights organizations were infiltrated by Communists reduced support for the movement.*

AP® SKILLS & PROCESSES

CONTEXTUALIZATION

This **CONTEXTUALIZATION** note requires students to explain evidence that, at first glance, may appear contradictory. The Cold War both furthered opportunities and created obstacles for Civil Rights. Broad concepts can help students arrive at clear conclusions. For instance, the Cold War promoted democratic reforms around the world. Ask students to think of an example where the United States supported a nation seeking to enact democratic reforms. They can use this as a way to explain how that would further civil rights reforms. On the other hand, the Cold War's focus on foreign policy meant less attention to domestic events. Ask students to select an example of a foreign policy issue that took away attention from government officials.

TRM Find complete suggested responses in the Teacher's Resource Materials.

Race and Anticommunism Truman also feared that racial inequality tarnished America's global image in the ideological battle with communism. When whites and blacks "fail to live together in peace," he admonished, it harmed "the cause of democracy itself in the whole world." Indeed, the Soviet Union used American racism to discredit the United States abroad. "We cannot escape the fact that our civil rights record has been an issue in world politics," the Committee on Civil Rights wrote. This need to demonstrate an improving racial climate provided leverage to civil rights leaders.

But McCarthyism and the hunt for subversives at home also hampered the push for civil rights. Civil rights opponents charged that racial integration was "communistic," and many southern states banned the NAACP as an "anti-American" organization. Black Americans who praised the Soviet Union, such as the actor and singer Paul Robeson, or had been "fellow travelers" (allied with communists on many issues) in the 1930s, such as the pacifist Rustin, were persecuted. When called before the House Un-American Activities Committee (HUAC), the outspoken Robeson gave impassioned testimony. "My father was a slave, and my people died to build this country, and I am going to . . . have a part of it just like you," he declared. But anticommunist hysteria effectively ended the career of Robeson and other activists. The Cold War also worked *against* the cause of civil rights (see "Firsthand Accounts," p. 844).

AP® SKILLS & PROCESSES

CONTEXTUALIZATION

How did the Cold War work in the favor of civil rights? How did it work against the movement?

Mexican Americans and Japanese Americans

American GI Forum
A group founded by World War II veterans in Corpus Christi, Texas, in 1948 to protest the poor treatment of Mexican American soldiers and veterans.

Community Services Organization (CSO)
A Latino civil rights group founded in Los Angeles in 1948 that trained many Latino politicians and community activists, including Cesar Chavez and Dolores Huerta.

African Americans were not the only group organizing against racial injustice in the 1940s. Across the Southwest, Mexican immigrants and Mexican Americans suffered under a "caste" system not unlike Jim Crow. In Texas, for instance, poll taxes kept most Mexican American citizens from voting. Employers had a constant supply of cheap labor across the border, which allowed them to suppress wages. A majority of Mexican Americans were trapped near poverty, and many lived in *colonias* or barrios, segregated neighborhoods that often lacked basic infrastructure, such as reliable water and electricity.

American GI Forum Mexican American women affiliated with the American GI Forum, pictured in 1959. Founded by Mexican American veterans of World War II in Texas in 1948, the Forum was an early civil rights organization dedicated to the interests of Mexican Americans throughout the Southwest. Dr. Hector P. Garcia Papers, Collection 5, Box 427, Folder 2. Special Collections and Archives, Mary and Jeff Bell Library, Texas A&M University-Corpus Christi.

During the 1940s, labor activism, especially in Congress of Industrial Organizations (CIO) unions with large numbers of Mexican Americans, improved wages and working conditions in some industries and produced a new generation of leaders. More than 400,000 Mexican Americans also served in World War II. Many returned to the United States determined to challenge their second-class status. Additionally, a new Mexican American middle class began to take shape in major cities such as Los Angeles, San Antonio, El Paso, and Chicago, building leadership and leverage for the cause.

In Texas and California, Mexican Americans created new civil rights groups in the postwar years. In Corpus Christi, Texas, the **American GI Forum** organized in 1948 to protest the poor treatment of Mexican American soldiers and veterans. Activists in Los Angeles created the **Community Services Organization (CSO)** the same year. Both groups arose to address specific injustices (such as the segregation of military cemeteries) but quickly broadened in scope to seek political and economic justice for the larger community. Among the young activists who worked for the CSO, where they were trained in social justice organizing, were Cesar Chavez and Dolores Huerta, who would later found the United Farm Workers (UFW) and inspire the Chicano movement of the 1960s.

Mexican American activists also mounted a legal challenge to inequality. In 1947, five Mexican American fathers in California sued a local school district for placing their children in separate "Mexican" schools. The case, *Mendez v. Westminster School District*, never made it to the U.S. Supreme Court. But the Ninth Circuit Court ruled the segregation unconstitutional, laying the legal groundwork for broader challenges to racial inequality. Among those filing briefs in the case was the NAACP's Thurgood Marshall, a key architect of the legal assault on southern segregation. In another significant legal victory, the Supreme Court ruled in 1954 that Mexican Americans constituted a "distinct class" that could claim constitutional protection from discrimination.

Also on the West Coast, Japanese Americans mounted their own legal campaign against discrimination. Undeterred by rulings in the *Hirabayashi* (1943) and *Korematsu* (1944) cases upholding wartime imprisonment (see "Japanese Removal" in Chapter 23), the Japanese American Citizens League (JACL) filed lawsuits in the late 1940s to regain property lost during the war. The JACL also challenged the constitutionality of California's Alien Land Law, which prohibited Japanese immigrants from owning land, and successfully lobbied Congress to enable those same immigrants to become citizens — a right that had been denied for fifty years. The efforts of Mexican and Japanese American activists enlarged the sphere of civil rights and laid the foundation for a broader notion of racial equality in the postwar years.

AP® EXAM TIP

Explain the origins of civil rights organizations in supporting immigrant groups.

AP® SKILLS & PROCESSES

ARGUMENTATION

How were the circumstances facing Mexican and Japanese Americans similar to those facing African Americans? How were they different?

Fighting for Equality Before the Law

Southern Democrats stonewalled any congressional action on civil rights throughout the 1950s, so activists turned to northern state legislatures and to the federal courts in search of a breakthrough. Outside the South, the foremost obstacle to black progress was persistent job and housing discrimination. The states with the largest African American populations, and hence the largest share of black Democratic Party voters, became testing grounds for legislation aimed at ending such discriminatory practices.

Success depended on coalition politics. African American activists forged alliances with trade unions and liberal organizations such as the American Friends Service Committee (a Quaker group), among many others. Progress was slow and often only came after long, unglamorous struggles to win votes in state capitals such as Albany, New York; Springfield, Illinois; and Lansing, Michigan. The first fair employment laws had come in New York and New Jersey in 1945, but a decade passed before other states with significant black populations passed similar legislation. Antidiscrimination laws in housing proved even more difficult to pass, with most progress not coming until the 1960s. These legislative campaigns in northern states received little national attention, but they were instrumental in laying the groundwork for legal equality outside the South.

Thurgood Marshall The suppression of black voting rights in the South meant that the region's state legislatures were closed to the kind of organized political pressure deployed in the North. Activists looked instead to federal courts for a foothold against Jim Crow. In the late 1930s, NAACP lawyers Thurgood Marshall, Charles Hamilton Houston, and William Hastie laid a strategic foundation for challenging racial discrimination. They pursued legal actions chosen to prod courts to use the Fourteenth Amendment's "equal protection" clause, with the eventual goal of overturning the 1896 Supreme Court ruling in *Plessy v. Ferguson*, which upheld racial segregation under the "separate but equal" doctrine.

TEACHING STRATEGY

Francisco Macias provides an article "Before *Brown v. Board of Education* There Was *Mendez v. Westminster*," which explores the background and significance of the *Mendez v. Westminster* case. The article contains several dozen embedded links that offer additional historical context. To access this resource, search "LOC Mendez Westminster."

CHECK FOR UNDERSTANDING

Ask students: **What forms of racial injustice did Mexican Americans and Japanese Americans experience in the postwar period?** *Mexican Americans were often treated as a separate caste and forced into barrios separate from whites and prevented from attending white schools. They formed organizations like the CSO to lobby for rights. They pursued legal justice through the court system, winning a major victory in* Mendez v. Westminster. *Japanese Americans also formed rights organizations, like the JACL, which, though begun before World War II, began to flourish in the postwar period. And like Mexican Americans, they sought redress through the courts.*

AP® SKILLS & PROCESSES

ARGUMENTATION

Use the **ARGUMENTATION** question to help students recognize the similar elements of racial prejudice experienced by Mexican and Japanese Americans, as well as their differences. In thinking about similarities, students might consider ways in which the experiences of both groups were alike, while being different from the experiences of African Americans — for example, their concentrations in western regions, time of arrival in the U.S., and whites' perception of their foreignness. Among other factors, each group had members in its population that had been born outside the U.S. and were often denied full rights on this basis.

TRM Find complete suggested responses in the Teacher's Resource Materials.

AP® THEME

NAT: American and National Identity

Students should understand that the federal government used measures like *Brown v. Board of Education* to promote greater racial equality.

TEACHING STRATEGY

Think about having students explain ways in which the United States Supreme Court was both effecting and preventing change in racial equality in the years 1941–1954. Students should be encouraged to think across a broad spectrum of people including Mexican Americans, African Americans, and Japanese Americans.

AP® SKILLS & PROCESSES

ANALYZING HISTORICAL EVIDENCE

As the introduction to the **AP® FIRSTHAND ACCOUNTS** feature indicates, these sources trace the development of racially segregated housing patterns over the course of several decades. It might be helpful to point out to students that the housing problems blacks often faced derived from several sources — homeowners' associations, state governments, and the Federal Housing Administration — and led to the reality of a system that was structurally racist. The Kerner Commission report became a well-known document articulating the scale of the racial divide that helped to explain outbreaks of urban violence during the era, including the Watts riot of 1965 and the other incidents mentioned in the introduction to this document. The depressing conclusion that the nation constituted two different societies, "separate and unequal," intentionally echoed the language of *Brown v. Board of Education*, suggesting how far apart the promise of black equality was from its reality.

AP® FIRSTHAND ACCOUNTS

Race and Urban Space in the Civil Rights Era

Racial segregation in American cities has long been fostered by the real estate industry, white home owners, and also government policies, such as mortgage programs and interstate highway construction (which facilitated white flight to the suburbs). In the 1960s what many called the "urban crisis" became the subject of heated national debate. Poverty and lack of opportunity among people of color living in cities and their geographic exclusion from the economic growth of fast-developing suburbs stood exposed. The following excerpts explore this history, from the 1930s to the 1960s.

JOHN WING

Neighborhood Association Calls for Housing Bias, 1933

Across the United States in the mid-twentieth century, home owners banded together in neighborhood associations. These groups pursued a variety of objectives, from welcoming new residents to lobbying city government to install traffic signs and crosswalks. However, between the 1920s and the 1960s the major purpose of many of them was to prevent African Americans and other people of color from moving into white-dominated neighborhoods. In the following excerpt, from a 1933 court case originating in Evanston, Illinois, a member of just such an association discusses its actions.

Source: Becky Nicolaides and Andrew Wiese, eds., *The Suburb Reader* (New York: Routledge, 2006), 235–236.

"In 1922 the residents living in that location [Asbury Avenue] became particularly conscious of the fact that there was a likelihood of negroes moving south of Emerson Street. It was first brought to our attention in connection with the premises at 1844 Wesley Avenue, which are the premises involved in this proceeding.

. . . Because of that incident and some others, we decided that we would form some kind of an association to protect ourselves. The West Side Improvement Association was formed in 1922 and 1923, and the objective of the association is to protect the neighborhood from encroachment of all kinds, and particularly to preserve it as a place for white people to live.

. . . [W]e decided that the only method of real protection was to have the property restricted by a covenant, providing that none of the property could be occupied by negroes or sold to negroes. . . ."

FEDERAL HOUSING ADMINISTRATION

Government Endorsement of Racial Segregation, 1936

When the federal government began to regulate the market in home mortgages under the National Housing Act of 1934, it assigned lower property values to neighborhoods where people of color lived. This policy reinforced the segregation of American cities and suburbs by race and by class. Here, in one of its 1936 manuals, the Federal Housing Administration (FHA) explains that "inharmonious racial groups" should be regarded as a threat to property values.

Source: Federal Housing Administration, *Underwriting Manual: Underwriting and Valuation Procedure Under Title II of the National Housing Act with Revisions to April 1, 1936* (Washington, DC: Government Printing Office), Part II, Section 2, 229, 233.

"The Valuator [property assessor] should investigate areas surrounding the location to determine whether or not incompatible racial and social groups are present, to the end that an intelligent prediction may be made regarding the possibility or probability of the location being invaded by such groups. If a neighborhood is to retain stability it is necessary that properties shall continue to be occupied by the same social and racial classes. A change in social or racial occupancy generally leads to instability and a reduction in values. . . . Once the character of a neighborhood has been established it is usually impossible to induce a higher social class than those already in the neighborhood to purchase and occupy properties in its various locations. . . .

The Valuator should consider carefully the immunity or lack of immunity offered to the location because of its geographical position within the city. Natural or artificially established barriers will prove effective in protecting a neighborhood and the locations within it from adverse influences. Usually the protection against adverse influences afforded by these means include prevention of the infiltration of business and industrial uses, lower-class occupancy, and inharmonious racial groups."

JANE JACOBS

Urban Renewal, 1961

Jane Jacobs was one of the most influential critics of American urban policy in the twentieth century. Her book, *The Death and Life of Great American Cities* (1961), contended that American urban policy had produced lifeless cities that separated people by status. In this excerpt, she charges that the federal policy known as "urban renewal," which was implemented primarily in the 1950s and 1960s, had worsened rather than improved urban conditions.

Source: Jane Jacobs, *The Death and Life of Great American Cities* (New York: Random House, 1961), 4.

“Look what we have built with the first several billions [of federal urban renewal spending]: Low-income projects that become worse centers of delinquency, vandalism and general social hopelessness than the slums they were supposed to replace. Middle-income housing projects which are truly marvels of dullness and regimentation, sealed against any buoyancy or vitality of city life. Luxury housing projects that mitigate their inanity, or try to, with a vapid vulgarity. Cultural centers that are unable to support a good bookstore. Civic centers that are avoided by everyone but bums, who have fewer choices of loitering place than others. Commercial centers that are lackluster imitations of standardized suburban chain-store shopping. Promenades that go from no place to nowhere and have no promenaders. Expressways that eviscerate great cities. This is not the rebuilding of cities. This is the sacking of cities.”

HERBERT HILL

Race and the Urban Crisis, 1967

Herbert Hill, a prominent black NAACP official, testified before Congress in 1967, alongside dozens of witnesses to what many called the "urban crisis." Hill believed that the continued isolation of African Americans in impoverished, declining neighborhoods required an urgent response from Congress.

SOURCE: Herbert Hill, "Demographic Change and Racial Ghettos: The Crisis of American Cities," in *Urban America: Goals and Problems, Hearings Before the Subcommittee on Urban Affairs of the Joint Economic Committee, U.S. Congress* (Washington, DC: Government Printing Office, 1967), 99–153.

“Current civil rights struggles are rooted in three major demographic developments in the American Negro community: accelerated growth, increasing mobility, and rapid urbanization. Almost half of the Negro population now lives in the North, but the response of American cities to this development has been a vast increase and rigidity in the patterns of residential segregation. Thus the Negro finds that he has left the segregated South for the segregated northern slum. The growth of housing segregation has been accompanied by an extension of the ghetto pattern in major cities together with vast urban blight and the decay of central city areas. . . .

The dual migration of Negroes from the rural South to the urban North and from the rural South to the urban South is one of the major demographic changes of our time with great social and political implications for the future of American society. . . .

If migrating Negroes had freedom of choice and the economic means to acquire adequate housing on a non-segregated basis, then it is possible that our large cities would be able to absorb their entry and provide decent living conditions. But the opposite has been the case. . . .

An abundance of evidence — social, economic, political, and moral — now suggests that the time has come to give first priority to the racial problems of our great cities. But the problems of our large urban areas are inextricably intertwined with the problems of the racial ghetto. Therefore, the solution to one set of problems is, in effect, the solution of the other.”

KERNER COMMISSION

Two Societies, 1968

In the aftermath of major disturbances in Detroit, Michigan, and Newark, New Jersey, during the summer of 1967, President Johnson appointed a commission to study the causes of the uprisings. It was widely known as the Kerner Commission for its chair, Otto Kerner, the Democratic governor of Illinois. The report became known for its forthright account of race in American cities.

SOURCE: *Report of the National Advisory Commission on Civil Disorders* (New York: The New York Times Company, 1968), 1–2.

“The summer of 1967 again brought racial disorders to American cities, and with them shock, fear and bewilderment to the nation. . . .

On July 28, 1967, the President of the United States established this Commission and directed us to answer three basic questions:

What happened?

Why did it happen?

What can be done to prevent it from happening again? . . .

This is our basic conclusion: Our nation is moving toward two societies, one black, one white — separate and unequal.

Reaction to last summer's disorders has quickened the movement and deepened the division. Discrimination and segregation have long permeated much of American life; they now threaten the future of every American. . . .

What white Americans have never fully understood — but what the Negro can never forget — is that white society is deeply implicated in the ghetto. White institutions created it, white institutions maintain it, and white society condones it.

It is now time to turn with all the purpose at our command to the unfinished business of this nation. It is time to adopt strategies for action that will produce quick and visible progress. It is time to make good the promises of American democracy to all citizens — urban and rural, white and black, Spanish-surname, American Indian, and every minority group.”

QUESTIONS FOR ANALYSIS

1. How did the way neighborhoods were evaluated by government agencies in the 1930s and 1940s perpetuate racial segregation? Use evidence from source 2 to support your answer.
2. Consider how the themes of identity and geography intersect in these excerpts. How did the geographic landscapes of cities and suburbs shape racial identity? How did those geographic landscapes affect the economic resources available to different groups of people? What did the Kerner Commission mean by "two societies"? Compare the ways that segregation defined urban cultures.

TRM Find complete suggested responses in the Teacher's Resource Materials.

Marshall was the great-grandson of slaves. Of modest origins, his parents instilled in him a faith in law and the Constitution. After his 1930 graduation from Lincoln University, a prestigious African American institution near Philadelphia, Marshall applied to the University of Maryland Law School. Denied admission because the school did not accept black applicants, he enrolled instead at the all-black Howard University School of Law. There Marshall was a student of Houston's and Hastie's, both of whom were professors, and the three forged an intellectual partnership that would change the face of American legal history. Marshall, with critical strategic input from Houston and Hastie, would argue most of the NAACP's landmark cases.

Marshall, Houston, Hastie, and six other NAACP attorneys filed suit after suit, deliberately selecting their cases to bring before the courts only those most likely to produce a legal breakthrough. Slowly, with arduous effort, the strategy bore fruit. In 1936, Marshall and Houston won a state case that forced the University of Maryland Law School to admit qualified African Americans — a ruling of obvious significance to Marshall. Eight years later, in *Smith v. Allwright* (1944), Marshall convinced the U.S. Supreme Court that all-white primaries were unconstitutional. In 1950, with Marshall once again arguing the case, the high court ruled in *McLaurin v. Oklahoma* that universities could not segregate black students from others on campus. None

TEACHING STRATEGY

The Thurgood Marshall Web site is devoted to the work and legacy of this pioneering lawyer and Supreme Court justice. The site contains a biography, several photos and portraits of Marshall, and several film and news clips from throughout his career. To access this site, search "Thurgood Marshall."

Thurgood Marshall and Daisy Bates Thurgood Marshall was one of the most influential legal thinkers of the twentieth century. As director of the NAACP Legal Defense Fund during the 1940s and 1950s, he helped dismantle the legal underpinnings of racial discrimination and segregation — he argued the *Brown* case, among dozens of others, for the NAACP. In 1967, he was appointed by President Johnson to the U.S. Supreme Court. Daisy Bates was a journalist and black freedom activist whose reporting in the black press in the 1950s was widely read and influential. She headed the Arkansas NAACP and played a prominent role on the national NAACP board. Here, Marshall and Bates sit on the steps of the Supreme Court in 1958 with some of the "Little Rock Nine," the young men and women who risked their lives to desegregate public schools in Arkansas. Bettmann/Getty Images.

of these cases produced swift changes in the daily lives of most African Americans, but each struck at the legal foundation of segregation. In 1967, President Lyndon Johnson would appoint Marshall to the Supreme Court — the first African American to achieve that honor.

AP® EXAM TIP

Describe the role of the Supreme Court in supporting greater racial equality in the U.S.

Brown v. Board of Education The NAACP's legal strategy achieved its ultimate validation in a case involving Linda Brown, a young black student in Topeka, Kansas, who had been forced to attend a segregated school far from her family home rather than a nearby white elementary school. In his argument before the court in ***Brown v. Board of Education of Topeka*** (1954), Marshall contended that such segregation was unconstitutional because it denied Linda Brown the "equal protection of the laws" guaranteed by the Fourteenth Amendment (Map 26.2). In a unanimous decision on May 17, 1954, the Supreme Court agreed, overturning the "separate but equal" doctrine at last. In the decision, Chief Justice Earl Warren wrote: "We conclude that in the field of public education the doctrine of 'separate but equal' has no place. Separate educational facilities are inherently unequal." In an subsequent 1955 decision known as *Brown II*, the Court declared that desegregation should proceed "with all deliberate speed."

Brown v. Board of Education of Topeka
Supreme Court ruling of 1954 that overturned the "separate but equal" precedent established in *Plessy v. Ferguson* in 1896. The Court declared that separate educational facilities were inherently unequal and thus violated the Fourteenth Amendment.

The white South responded with a declaration of war against the *Brown* ruling. Virginia senator Harry F. Byrd issued a call for "massive resistance." Declaring May 17 "Black Monday," the Mississippi segregationist Tom P. Brady invoked the language

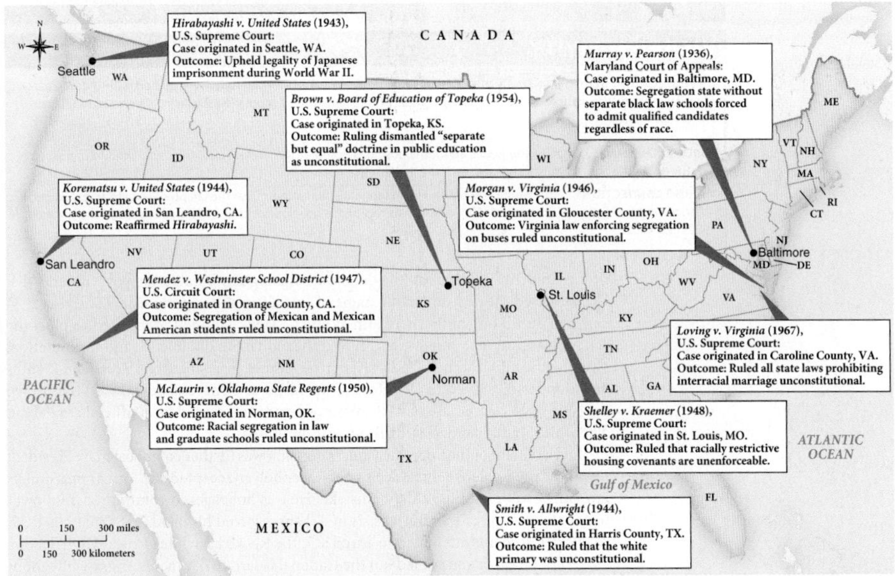

MAP 26.2 Desegregation Court Cases
Desegregation court battles were not limited to the South. Note the important California cases regarding Mexican Americans and Japanese Americans. Two seminal decisions, the 1948 housing decision in *Shelley v. Kraemer* and the 1954 school decision in *Brown v. Board of Education*, originated in Missouri and Kansas, respectively. This map helps show that racial segregation and discrimination were a national, not simply a southern, problem.

AP® APPLY THE TIP

Have students prepare a "road map" to civil rights that ends with the passage of the Voting Rights Act of 1965. To begin, provide groups of students with large poster or bulletin board paper and require students to begin in the upper left corner with "Victory in World War II." Students should use pp. 836-859 to construct a road map that illustrates the choices ("exits"), actions, leaders ("cars"), problems ("roadblocks"), setbacks ("construction zones"), and signs that help illustrate the movement of the U.S. from segregation to passage of the Voting Rights Act. Whenever possible, students should use common road map signs and images to illustrate the changes that occurred from 1945 to 1965.

TEACHING STRATEGY

While the most iconic images of the civil rights movement involve marches, speeches, and boycotts, **MAP 26.2** illustrates the significance of legal challenges to American racism. The map also shows that the civil rights movement was a national phenomenon, not just a southern one. With ten cases spanning more than two decades, the map also illustrates how piecemeal victories were chipping away at racial injustice one ruling at a time.

AP® THEME

ARC: America and Regional Culture

The civil rights movement was a national movement with distinctive problems in regions such as the Midwest, South, and West. Have students select at least two regions and give historical evidence as to what problems were unique to the region while also accounting for how each region shared common issues civil rights leaders were attempting to confront.

TEACHING STRATEGY

The PBS *News Hour* conducted an interview with seven of the Little Rock Nine in 2007 on the 50th anniversary of the beginning of their efforts to desegregate Central High School. To access this interview, search "News Hour Desegregation Pioneers."

TRM Find complete suggested responses in the Teacher's Resource Materials.

VISUAL ACTIVITY

Desegregating Schools in Nashville, Tennessee Police escorting African American mothers with children past a jeering mob of demonstrators after the desegregation of this elementary school in Nashville in September 1957.
Dan Cravens/Getty Images.

READING THE IMAGE: What do you notice about the positions occupied by different people (women, children, police, bystanders) in the photograph? Can you determine their likely emotions?

MAKING CONNECTIONS: How would you put this image together with others from the chapter to create an explanation of the movement? Evaluate the impact of images such as this on the developments of civil rights organizations in the 1950s and 1960s.

of the Cold War to discredit the decision, assailing the "totalitarian government" that had rendered the decision in the name of "socialism and communism." The year 1954 saw half a million southerners join White Citizens' Councils dedicated to blocking school integration. Some whites revived the old tactics of violence and intimidation, swelling the ranks of the Ku Klux Klan to levels not seen since the 1920s. The "Southern Manifesto," signed in 1956 by 101 members of Congress, denounced the *Brown* decision as "a clear abuse of judicial power" and encouraged local officials to defy it. The white South had declared all-out war on *Brown*.

Enforcement of the Supreme Court's decision was further complicated by President Dwight Eisenhower's reluctance to act. Eisenhower accepted the *Brown* decision as law, but considered the ruling a mistake. He was not eager to commit federal power to compel desegregation. But a crisis in Arkansas forced his hand. In September 1957, nine black students attempted to enroll at Little Rock's all-white Central High School. Governor Orval Faubus called out the National Guard to bar them. Angry white mobs gathered daily to taunt the students, chanting "Go back to the jungle." As the vicious scenes played out on television night after night, Eisenhower was forced to act. He sent federal troops to Little Rock and nationalized the state guardsmen, instructing them to protect the black students. The reluctant Eisenhower became the first president since Reconstruction to use federal troops to enforce the rights of African Americans.

AP® SKILLS & PROCESSES
MAKING CONNECTIONS
How did the NAACP develop a legal strategy to attack racial segregation?

AP® SKILLS & PROCESSES

MAKING CONNECTIONS

Use the **MAKING CONNECTIONS** question to point to an important concept for students to understand: the Supreme Court victory in *Brown v. Board of Education* was not the result of an NAACP master plan, but the consequence of shifting strategies the organization pursued over several decades. While *Brown v. Board* is popularly celebrated as a major and unambiguous victory, scholars are often more cautious.

TRM Find complete suggested responses in the Teacher's Resource Materials.

CHECK FOR UNDERSTANDING

Ask students: **What factors best explain why and how the civil rights movement developed between 1941 and 1954?** *Many factors explain the emergence of the civil rights movement in the 1940s and early 1950s. Among them are the hypocrisy of fighting racism abroad while practicing it at home during World War II, the rise of the postwar black middle class, progressive white labor leaders, and the emergence of television as a communicative medium.*

FORGING A PROTEST MOVEMENT, 1955–1965

How did the civil rights movement achieve its major legal and legislative victories between 1954 and 1965?

By declaring racial segregation integral to the South's "habits, customs, tradition, and way of life," the Southern Manifesto signaled that many whites would not accept black equality, regardless of court orders. The showdown at Central High School suggested that southern authorities were more loyal to local white custom than federal law. An unwillingness by local officials to enforce *Brown* could render the decision invalid in practice. If legal victories were nullified, citizens themselves, black and white, had to consider whether they would take to the streets to demand justice. In the years after *Brown* and the southern backlash, they did just that, in a protest movement unique in the history of the United States.

Nonviolent Direct Action

Brown had been the law of the land for barely a year when a single act of violence jolted black America. Emmett Till, a fourteen-year-old African American from the South Side of Chicago, visited relatives in Mississippi in the summer of 1955. Seen talking to a white woman in a grocery store, he was tortured and murdered by local whites during the night of August 28. Several days later, his mutilated body was found at the bottom of a river, tied with barbed wire to a heavy steel cotton gin fan. Till's mother chose to hold an open-casket funeral back in Chicago, and photos of his disfigured corpse ran in *Jet* magazine and other black publications. The gruesome images brought national attention to the heinous crime.

Two white men were arrested for Till's murder. During the trial, followed closely in black communities across the country, the lone witness to Till's kidnapping — his uncle, Mose Wright — identified both of the accused men. Feeling "the blood boil in hundreds of white people as they sat glaring in the courtroom," Wright said, "it was the first time in my life I had the courage to accuse a white man of a crime." Despite Wright's eyewitness testimony, the all-white jury found the defendants innocent. This miscarriage of justice — later, the killers even admitted their guilt in a *Look* magazine article — galvanized an entire generation of African Americans.

AP® EXAM TIP

Compare the methods and goals of civil rights leaders in the 1960s.

Montgomery Bus Boycott On December 1, 1955, less than three months after the searing Till verdict, a city bus in Montgomery, Alabama, became a crucial civil rights battleground. A black woman named Rosa Parks refused to surrender her seat on the bus to a white man. She was arrested and charged with violating a local segregation ordinance. Parks's defiance was not as spontaneous as it seemed. A longtime NAACP member familiar with protest tactics, she and other local activists, all of them women, had been contemplating such an act for some time — segregated buses were a powerful symbol of the city's racial hierarchy.

Soon after Parks's arrest, Montgomery's black community turned for leadership to the Reverend Martin Luther King Jr., the recently appointed pastor of Montgomery's Dexter Avenue Baptist Church. The son of a prominent Atlanta minister, King embraced the thinking of Mahatma Gandhi. Drawing on Gandhi's teachings, and the practical experience of Bayard Rustin, King and his fellow black ministers fashioned a response based on nonviolent direct action, which Rustin and others in the Fellowship of Reconciliation had first used in the 1940s. The **Montgomery Bus Boycott** followed a plan laid out by a local black women's organization, inspired by bus boycotts in Harlem in 1941 and Baton Rouge, Louisiana, in 1953.

For the next 381 days, Montgomery's African Americans formed car pools or walked to work. As a bus normally filled with black riders rolled by the Kings' living room window on the first day of the boycott, Coretta Scott King exclaimed to her

Montgomery Bus Boycott
Yearlong boycott of Montgomery's segregated bus system in 1955–1956 by the city's African American population. The boycott brought Martin Luther King Jr. to national prominence and ended in victory when the Supreme Court declared segregated seating on public transportation unconstitutional.

TEACHING STRATEGY

PBS's *American Experience* provides an hour-long documentary, *The Murder of Emmett Till*, exploring the brutal murder of Emmett Till, the trial, and its aftermath. The companion site provides additional articles on Moses Wright's brave court testimony, race and sex in the South in the 1950s, and the history of lynching. To access these resources, search "American Experience Emmett Till."

AP® APPLY THE TIP

Prompt students to use pp. 849–851 to complete **Handout 26.3 — Comparison: Civil Rights Leaders (TRM)**. Then lead a class discussion that examines the different methods and goals of each leader.

TRM Find **Handout 26.3 — Comparison: Civil Rights Leaders** in the Teacher's Resource Materials.

husband, "Darling, it's empty!" The transit company neared bankruptcy, and downtown stores lost business, but city authorities refused to give in. The Supreme Court ruled that segregation on public transportation is unconstitutional in November 1956, and the city finally relented. "My feets is tired, but my soul is rested," declared one woman boycotter.

The Montgomery Bus Boycott catapulted King to national prominence. In 1957, along with the Reverend Ralph Abernathy and dozens of black ministers from across the South, he founded the **Southern Christian Leadership Conference (SCLC)** in Atlanta. The black church, long the center of social and cultural life, now lent its moral authority and organizational strength to the civil rights movement. Black churchwomen proved a vital source of strength, transferring skills honed during years of church work to the movement for racial justice. The SCLC quickly joined the NAACP in the front ranks of the push for equality.

Southern Christian Leadership Conference (SCLC)
After the Montgomery Bus Boycott, Martin Luther King Jr. and other black ministers formed the SCLC in 1957 to coordinate civil rights activity in the South.

Greensboro Sit-Ins The battle for civil rights entered a new phase in Greensboro, North Carolina. On February 1, 1960, four black college students took seats at the whites-only lunch counter of a Woolworth's drugstore in Greensboro, North Carolina. Planning late at night in their dorm rooms, the students resolved to "sit in" at the counter until they were served. The New York–based Woolworth's chain announced it would "abide by local custom," which meant refusing to serve African Americans. For three weeks, hundreds of students inspired by the original foursome took turns sitting at the counters, quietly eating, doing homework, or reading. Taunted and beaten by groups of whites, pelted with food and other debris, the black students — often occupying more than sixty of the sixty-six seats — held strong. Although many were arrested, the tactic worked: the Woolworth's lunch counter was desegregated, and sit-ins quickly spread to other southern cities (see "Firsthand Accounts," p. 844).

Student Nonviolent Coordinating Committee (SNCC)
A student civil rights group founded in 1960, under the mentorship of Ella Baker, that conducted sit-ins, voter registration drives, and other actions to advance racial equality throughout the 1960s.

Ella Baker and SNCC Inspired by the sit-ins, an SCLC official named Ella Baker helped organize the **Student Nonviolent Coordinating Committee (SNCC,** pronounced "Snick") in 1960 to facilitate more student protests. By the end of the year, a wave of sit-ins had swept from North Carolina into Virginia, Maryland, and Tennessee. At protests in 126 cities, more than 50,000 people participated, and 3,600 went to jail. The sit-ins drew black college students into the movement in significant numbers for the first time. Northern students formed solidarity committees and raised money for bail, and SNCC quickly emerged as the most important student protest organization in the country.

Baker took a special interest in students because she found them receptive to her notion of participatory democracy (see "Comparing Interpretations," p. 852). The granddaughter of slaves, Baker had moved to Harlem in the 1930s, where she worked for New Deal agencies and then the NAACP. She believed in nurturing leaders from the grass roots, encouraging ordinary people to stand up for their rights rather than depend on charismatic movement stars. "My theory is, strong people don't need strong leaders," she once said. However, Baker wound up

Student Sit-Ins Demonstrators at a lunch counter sit-in in Jackson, Mississippi, are smeared with ketchup, mustard, and sugar by opponents of desegregation in 1963. Student-led sit-ins, as a nonviolent civil rights protest, spread across the South between 1960, when they first appeared in Greensboro, North Carolina, and 1963. The Granger Collection, New York.

TEACHING STRATEGY

The SNCC Digital Gateway provides a biography of Ella Baker, along with several high-quality facsimile documents related to her civil rights work, a 1974 interview with Baker, and a 2004 40th anniversary SNCC conference video that discusses her work. To access these resources, search "SNCC Digital Gateway Ella Baker."

TEACHING STRATEGY

One of the more interesting aspects of civil rights organizations is how young adults and adults each had organizations committed to the movement. Have students compare and contrast the leadership, membership, and style of SNCC and SCLC.

nurturing a generation of civil rights leaders in SNCC, including Stokely Carmichael, Anne Moody, John Lewis, and Diane Nash.

Freedom Rides Emboldened by SNCC's sit-in tactics, in 1961 the Congress of Racial Equality (CORE) organized a kind of mobile sit-in on interstate bus lines throughout the South. These so-called **Freedom Rides** aimed to call attention to ongoing segregation in interstate commerce, which had recently been ruled unconstitutional by the Supreme Court. The activists who signed on — mostly young, both black and white — knew that they were taking their lives in their hands. They found courage in song, belting out lyrics such as "I'm taking a ride on the Greyhound bus line. . . . Hallelujah, I'm traveling down freedom's main line!"

Freedom Rides
A series of multiracial sit-ins conducted on interstate bus lines throughout the South by the Congress of Racial Equality (CORE) in 1961. An early and important civil rights protest.

Courage was a necessity. Club-wielding Klansmen attacked the buses when they stopped in small towns. On May 14, 1961, outside Anniston, Alabama, a bus carrying Freedom Riders was firebombed, and fleeing passengers were brutally beaten. Freedom Riders and accompanying journalists encountered vicious attacks by Klansmen in Birmingham and Montgomery. Despite the violence, state authorities refused to intervene. "I cannot guarantee protection for this bunch of rabble rousers," declared Governor John Patterson of Alabama.

As in Little Rock and other civil rights battlegrounds, the refusal of local officials to enforce laws left matters in the hands of the federal government. The new president, John F. Kennedy, had discouraged the Freedom Riders. Elected by a thin margin, Kennedy believed that he could not afford to lose the support of powerful southern senators and had failed to deliver on his campaign promise of a civil rights bill. But footage of savage beatings, broadcast on nightly television news, proved the tactical power of nonviolent protest. The nation and the wider world became witnesses, and public pressure goaded Attorney General Robert Kennedy, with his brother's White House approval, to dispatch federal marshals to protect the riders.

From Central High School to the sit-ins to the Freedom Rides, activists had learned the tactical value of nonviolent protest that provoked violent white resistance: if white lawbreaking and violence did not prod local officials to act, federal officials could be forced to intervene, putting the national government on the side of black protesters. These victories were modest, but the groundwork had been laid for a civil rights offensive that would transform the nation. The NAACP's legal strategy had undermined the legal edifice of segregation, and the emergence of a major protest movement shook it. Now civil rights leaders focused their attention on Congress.

AP® SKILLS & PROCESSES

DEVELOPMENTS AND PROCESSES

What lessons did activists learn as the civil rights movement evolved between 1957 and 1961?

Legislating Civil Rights, 1963–1965

The first civil rights law in the nation's history, guaranteeing equality before the law, came in 1866 just after the Civil War. Its provisions were long ignored. A second law, forbidding the segregation of public spaces such as trains and hotels, was passed during Reconstruction in 1875 but struck down by the Supreme Court as unconstitutional. For nearly ninety years, southern Democrats in Congress had blocked any further civil rights legislation, save for a weak, largely symbolic act passed in 1957. But by the early 1960s, with legal precedents in their favor and nonviolent protest awakening the nation, civil rights leaders believed the time had come to pass a serious civil rights bill. The challenge was getting one through a still-reluctant Congress.

AP® EXAM TIP

Evaluate the role of the Congress in supporting greater racial equality in the U.S.

The Battle for Birmingham The road to such a bill began when Martin Luther King Jr. announced demonstrations in what he called "the most segregated city in the United States": Birmingham, Alabama. King and the SCLC sought a concrete victory in Birmingham through their strategy of nonviolent direct action. In May 1963, thousands of black marchers protested employment discrimination in Birmingham's department stores. Eugene "Bull" Connor, the city's public safety commissioner, ordered the city's police troops to meet the marchers with violent force: snarling dogs,

TEACHING STRATEGY

The excellent *American Experience* film *Freedom Riders* explores the brave efforts of the many nonviolent protesters who tested bus integration laws through the Freedom Rides. The companion site provides extensive support materials on various aspects of the movement, its leaders, the strategy of nonviolence, southern society and culture, and the Cold War climate of the era. To access these resources, search "American Experience Freedom Riders."

CHECK FOR UNDERSTANDING

Ask students: **What were the principles and strategies of nonviolent direct action?** *Nonviolence, inspired by Jesus's Sermon on the Mount and by the philosophy of Gandhi, was a refusal to respond to the violence of oppressors with violence in return. Instead, nonviolent protesters hoped to take the moral high ground, appeal to the conscience of their opponent, and try to change the opponent's mind. Strategies like boycotts and sit-ins were forms of direct action designed to gain attention and pressure business owners and civic leaders to change segregationist policies. Often, protests ended when municipal or federal leaders intervened, as in the Supreme Court's ruling on segregated city busing.*

AP® SKILLS & PROCESSES

DEVELOPMENTS AND PROCESSES

The answers to this **DEVELOPMENTS AND PROCESSES** question will vary. Think about establishing a timeline of events for students from 1957 to 1961 complete with major events and developments. From there, have students select one or two major events and have them write a one or two sentence explanation about what takeaways civil rights leaders had during this time. The key is to not explain the event; instead, students should concentrate on explaining the lesson from the event.

TRM Find complete suggested responses in the Teacher's Resource Materials.

AP® SKILLS & PROCESSES

ANALYZING HISTORICAL EVIDENCE

Like other figures in American history who have holidays in their honor — Washington and Lincoln — King has become an icon. As a result, attempting to understand the person behind the image can be challenging. King was undoubtedly a complex individual and deep thinker, and it is possible that he was both a radical and a reformer in different ways. Students should think about the different situations of the authors in the **AP® COMPARING INTERPRETATIONS** feature. Jackson is a recent historian who concentrates on the harsher, more negative assessments of King — a view that is likely less familiar to students because of the ways King's more radical views get toned down through his status as a public figure. Ransby is not offering her own assessment of King as much as she is explaining the views of Baker, a younger contemporary of King who, along with fellow members of SNCC, was restless for more aggressive strategies.

AP® COMPARING INTERPRETATIONS

Was Martin Luther King Jr. a Radical or a Reformer?

In 1983, when Congress established the national holiday that celebrates Martin Luther King Jr.'s birthday each January, members of Congress acknowledged King's pioneering work to advance the cause of black civil rights. But what was the nature of King's work? For the past few decades, scholars have debated how best to understand the civil rights movement and King's particular role in it. Some scholars have characterized King as a middle-class reformer who "dreamed" of an integrated America achieved through the actions of national civil rights leaders like himself. Others have argued that King's vision was far more radical and extended to deeper structural changes that would, for instance, combat poverty and empower local communities to shape their own destiny.

In the following excerpts, Thomas F. Jackson and Barbara Ransby present differing portraits of King. In his book, Jackson discusses King's work in the context of a campaign for human rights. Ransby, who wrote a biography of King's civil rights contemporary Ella Baker, draws a distinction between their approaches to the movement — in Ransby's view, King's reliance on his charismatic leadership style meant that he overlooked the need to empower ordinary people and communities to fight for themselves.

THOMAS F. JACKSON

SOURCE: Thomas F. Jackson, Excerpt from *Civil Rights to Human Rights: Martin Luther King, Jr., and the Struggle for Economic Justice*. Copyright © 2013 by University of Pennsylvania Press. Reprinted with permission of the University of Pennsylvania Press.

By 1965, King's radical voice rang more clearly when he confessed that his dream had turned into a "nightmare." The dream shattered when whites murdered voting rights workers in Alabama, when police battled blacks in Los Angeles, when he met jobless and "hopeless" blacks on desperate Chicago streets, and when he saw hunger and poverty in rural Mississippi and Appalachia. But King picked up the shards of his shattered dreams and reassembled them into more radical visions of emancipation for all poor people. . . . Dreams of decent jobs, affordable integrated housing, and adequate family incomes remained central to King's public ministry until his death.

. . . Since the 1956 Montgomery bus boycott, King had repeatedly urged blacks to dream of a world free of racism, militarism, and "materialism." For King, materialism encompassed the irrational inequalities of wealth under the American system, the "tragic exploitation" of a racially divided working class, and the morally corrosive and socially isolating obsession with individual success. As early as 1956, King publicly described his dream of a world in which men will no longer "take necessities from the masses to give luxuries to the classes," a "world in which men will throw down the sword" and learn to love and serve others.

Movement veterans never forgot King's radicalism. In the accurate, sardonic words of Vincent Harding, King's legacy has been compressed into "safe categories of 'civil rights leader,' 'great orator,' harmless dreamer of black and white children on the hillside." Documenting King's radicalism but overstating the degree to which the events of the 1960s radicalized him, David Garrow argued in his seminal books that King transformed himself from a "reassuring reformer" into "a radical threat" to America's class system and dominant

electric cattle prods, and highpressure fire hoses. Television cameras captured the scene for the evening news.

While serving a jail sentence for defying a court order prohibiting the march, King, scribbling in pencil on any paper he could find, composed his "Letter from Birmingham Jail." In time, the letter became one of the defining documents of nonviolent direct action, read around the world. "Why direct action?" King asked. "There is a type of constructive, nonviolent tension that is necessary for growth," he began his eloquent answer. The civil rights movement sought, King continued, "to create such a crisis and establish such a creative tension." Grounding his appeal in equal parts Christian brotherhood and democratic liberalism, King argued that Americans confronted a moral choice: they could "preserve the evil system of segregation" or take the side of "those great wells of democracy . . . the Constitution and the Declaration of Independence."

Outraged by the brutality in Birmingham and embarrassed by King's imprisonment for leading a nonviolent march, President Kennedy finally decided to act.

institutions. By November 1966, King concluded that the movement's most stubborn obstacles "were economic rather than legal, and tied much more closely to questions of class than issue of race," Garrow argues.

... Like his father, King advocated thrift, hard work, "economic individualism," and self-help, [historian Adam] Fairclough argues. Again it is true that King in 1965 stopped preaching that the Negro [a term still in use in the 1960s] should lift himself up by his "bootstraps." But King was much more radical, earlier, and more consistently, than he is credited for being. He always conceived of self-help to include collective mutual aid and black political assertion as much as individual self-improvement.... He criticized "class systems" that segmented black America, even when he did not openly call for an American class struggle.

BARBARA RANSBY

SOURCE: Barbara Ransby, From *Ella Baker and the Black Freedom Movement: A Radical Democratic Vision*. Copyright © 2003 by the University of North Carolina Press. Used by permission of the publisher. www.uncpress.org

[Ella] Baker knew that King came from a prominent family in Atlanta and could have followed in his father's footsteps rather than taking the risks that political activism entailed. She respected him for choosing a different path and trying to make a contribution to the movement.... [but] he did not seem to want to learn about the process of organizing, at least not from her.

... In the historiography of the modern Black Freedom Movement, scholars have drawn a line between charismatic leadership models and grassroots activist ones, with a parallel distinction between mobilizing (for big events) and actually organizing communities to feel empowered to assess their own needs and fight their own battles. The tensions between these two models of movement building were apparent in Montgomery during the [bus] boycott, and they persisted in SCLC as it evolved.... Her conflicted relationship with Martin Luther King Jr. turned on such questions as leadership and organization, especially the proper roles of national spokespersons and local participants in mass-based struggles.

.... The conflict between [King and Baker] reveals more fundamental conflicts between black politics and African American culture over the meanings of American democracy and the pathways toward social change. If Baker's criticisms of King were overly harsh and unforgiving, that may be because they were intensified by her disappointed hopes in King himself and by her accumulated outrage against the male leaders who had treated her in demeaning ways over many decades.

.... Baker described [King] as a pampered member of Atlanta's black elite who had the mantle of leadership handed to him rather than having had to earn it, a member of a coddled "silver spoon brigade." ... In Baker's eyes, King did not identify closely enough with the people he sought to lead. He did not situate himself among them but remained above them.... Baker felt the focus on King drained the masses of confidence in themselves.

... Baker and King had made very different choices about how to utilize their skills and privileges. They translated religious faith into their political identities in profoundly different ways. Above all, they defined the confluence of their roles as individuals and their roles as participants in a mass movement for social change quite distinctly. Baker was a militant egalitarian, and King was a sophisticated southern Baptist preacher.

AP® SHORT ANSWER PRACTICE

1. Name one key difference in the way these two historians describe King and his work in the civil rights movement.
2. What qualities does each of these historians use in defining leadership in the civil rights movement?
3. Based on your reading of the excerpts and Chapter 26's discussion of the civil rights movement, why do you think Ransby concludes that Baker was a "militant egalitarian" in contrast to King, "a sophisticated southern Baptist preacher," while Jackson's interpretation stresses King's "radicalism"? How might Baker and King's social positions have affected their relative success to achieve civil rights?

TRM Find complete suggested responses in the Teacher's Resource Materials.

On June 11, 1963, after newly elected Alabama governor George Wallace barred two black students from enrolling at the state university, Kennedy went on television to denounce racism and promise a new civil rights bill. Many black leaders felt Kennedy's action was long overdue, but they nonetheless hailed this "Second Emancipation Proclamation." That night, Medgar Evers, president of the Mississippi chapter of the NAACP, was shot and killed in the driveway of his home in Jackson by a white supremacist. Evers's tragic murder and martyrdom became a spur to further action (Map 26.3).

The March on Washington Civil rights leaders took advantage of a long-planned event for a massive demonstration in Washington set for that August to marshal support for Kennedy's bill. The idea of the demonstration in Washington had first been proposed by A. Philip Randolph in 1941. Working with Bayard Rustin, Randolph revived the idea and in early 1963 called for a march to mark the centennial of the Emancipation Proclamation. Thousands of volunteers across the country coordinated

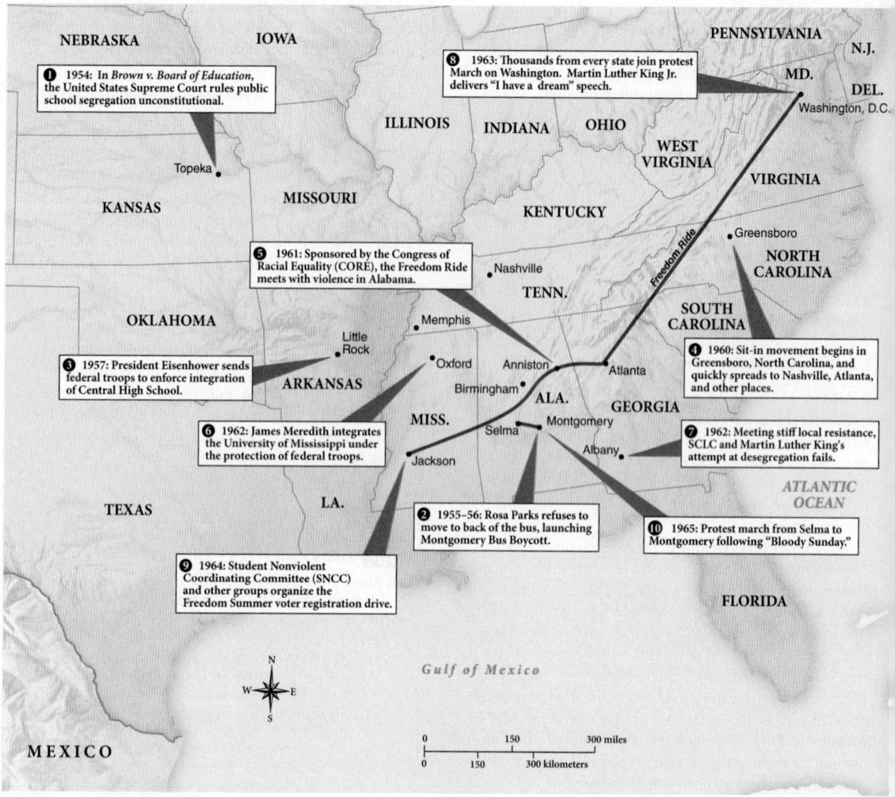

MAP 26.3 The Civil Rights Struggle, 1954–1965

In the postwar battle for black civil rights, the first major victory was the NAACP litigation of *Brown v. Board of Education*, which declared public school segregation unconstitutional. As indicated on this map, the struggle then quickly spread, raising other issues and seeding new organizations. Other organizations quickly joined the battle and shifted the focus away from the courts to mass action and organization. The year 1965 marked the high point, when violence against the Selma, Alabama, marchers spurred the passage of the Voting Rights Act.

car pools, "freedom buses," and "freedom trains" that delivered a quarter of a million people to the Lincoln Memorial on August 28, 1963. Officially named the March on Washington for Jobs and Freedom, the event became known as the **March on Washington**.

Although Randolph and Rustin had planned the event, Martin Luther King Jr. was its public face. It was King's dramatic "I Have a Dream" speech, beginning with his admonition that too many black people lived "on a lonely island of poverty" and ending with the exclamation from a traditional black spiritual — "Free at last! Free at last! Thank God almighty, we are free at last!" — that captured the nation's imagination. The sight of 250,000 blacks and whites marching solemnly together marked the high point of the civil rights movement and confirmed King's position as its leading spokesperson.

March on Washington
Officially named the March on Washington for Jobs and Freedom, on August 28, 1963, a quarter of a million people marched to the Lincoln Memorial to demand that Congress end Jim Crow racial discrimination and launch a major jobs program to bring needed employment to black communities.

To have any chance of getting the civil rights bill through Congress, King, Randolph, and Rustin believed they had to sustain a broad coalition of blacks and whites. They could not afford to lose the support of moderate whites. Young SNCC member John Lewis had planned a provocative speech for that afternoon. Lewis wrote in his original draft that a "time will come when we will not confine our marching to Washington. We will march through the South, through the Heart of Dixie, the way Sherman did." Conveying a growing restlessness among black youth, Lewis warned: "We shall fragment the South into a thousand pieces and put them back together again in the image of democracy." Rustin and others implored Lewis to tone down his rhetoric. Only minutes before he stepped up to the podium, Lewis relented. He delivered a more conciliatory speech, but his conflict with march organizers signaled an emerging rift in the movement (see "Thinking Like a Historian," p. 856).

Although the March on Washington galvanized public opinion, it changed few congressional votes. Southern senators continued to block Kennedy's legislation. Georgia senator Richard Russell, a leader of the opposition, announced he would filibuster against any bill that would "bring about social equality and intermingling and amalgamation of the races." As 1963 continued, tragic violence began to mount. In September, white supremacists bombed a Baptist church in Birmingham, killing four black girls in Sunday school. Less than two months later, President Kennedy himself was dead, the victim of assassination (see "John F. Kennedy's Promise" in Chapter 27).

On assuming the presidency, Lyndon B. Johnson made the passage of the civil rights bill a priority. A southerner and former Senate majority leader, "LBJ" was renowned for his fierce style of persuasion and tough political bargaining. By appealing to the white South's conscience, invoking the memory of the slain JFK, and playing political hardball, Johnson overcame the filibuster. He acted on both principled and personal motivations, believing that civil rights had become a generational moral imperative and that if he shepherded the bill through Congress his achievement would rank alongside those of his political idol, Franklin D. Roosevelt. In June 1964, Congress approved the most far-reaching civil rights law since Reconstruction. The keystone of the **Civil Rights Act of 1964**, Title VII, outlawed discrimination in employment on the basis of race, religion, national origin, and sex. Another section guaranteed equal access to public accommodations and schools. The law granted new enforcement powers to the U.S. attorney general and established the Equal Employment Opportunity Commission to implement the prohibition against job discrimination.

Civil Rights Act of 1964
Law that responded to demands of the civil rights movement by making discrimination illegal in employment, education, and public accommodations on the basis of race, religion, national origin, and sex.

Freedom Summer The Civil Rights Act was a law with real teeth, but it did not remove the obstacles to black voting. So protesters went back into the streets. In 1964, in what came to be known as Freedom Summer, black organizations mounted a major campaign in Mississippi, where only 5 percent of the state's eligible black residents could vote. The effort drew thousands of volunteers from across the country, including nearly one thousand white college students from the North. Led by the charismatic SNCC activist Robert "Bob" Moses, the four major civil rights organizations (SNCC, CORE, NAACP, and SCLC) spread out across the state in a major voter registration drive. This effort resulted in a brutal white backlash that left four civil rights workers murdered and thirty-seven black churches bombed or burned.

Shaken by the opposition's bloody tactics but undeterred, Moses and other Freedom Summer activists turned to electoral politics. The **Mississippi Freedom Democratic Party (MFDP)**, founded that summer, took on the state's official "whites only" Mississippi Democratic Party. MFDP leaders sought to disqualify Mississippi's segregationist delegation to the 1964 Democratic National Convention in Atlantic City, New Jersey, and take its place as the legitimate representatives of their state. MFDP co-founder Fannie Lou Hamer, a former sharecropper turned civil rights activist, eloquently challenged the Democratic power structure, including President Johnson himself. "Is this America?" Hamer asked party officials in her demand that

Mississippi Freedom Democratic Party (MFDP)
A multiracial political party founded in Mississippi during the Freedom Summer of 1964, in order protest the exclusion of black voters from the state's mainline Democratic Party.

AP® SKILLS & PROCESSES

ANALYZING HISTORICAL EVIDENCE

Teachers often introduce students to black protest in this era by contrasting King and Malcolm X, but this simplistic approach fails to capture the rich diversity of voices. As the **AP® THINKING LIKE A HISTORIAN** feature indicates, there was tremendous diversity in philosophy and strategy — and often significant tension among the leaders of various organizations. Use of terms like "movement" can sometimes give students the impression that there was a single, unified effort, rather than a range of competing voices that frequently found common cause.

AP® THINKING LIKE A HISTORIAN

Civil Rights and Black Power: Strategy and Ideology

The documents collected below reveal the range of perspectives and ideas at work within the broad civil rights, or "black freedom," struggle in the 1960s.

1. **Martin Luther King Jr., "If the Negro Wins, Labor Wins" speech, 1962.** *King, speaking to a meeting of the nation's trade union leaders, explained the economic objectives of the black freedom struggle.*

If we do not advance, the crushing burden of centuries of neglect and economic deprivation will destroy our will, our spirits and our hopes. In this way labor's historic tradition of moving forward to create vital people as consumers and citizens has become our own tradition, and for the same reasons.

This unity of purpose is not an historical coincidence. Negroes are almost entirely a working people. There are pitifully few Negro millionaires and few Negro employers. Our needs are identical with labor's needs: decent wages, fair working conditions, livable housing, old age security, health and welfare measures, conditions in which families can grow, have education for their children and respect in the community. That is why Negroes support labor's demands and fight laws which curb labor. . . .

The two most dynamic and cohesive liberal forces in the country are the labor movement and the Negro freedom movement. Together we can be architects of democracy in a South now rapidly industrializing.

2. **Police in Birmingham, Alabama, use trained German shepherds against peaceful African American protesters, 1963.** *The fight for access to jobs and equal treatment in Birmingham gripped the nation in the spring of 1963, when confrontations between protestors and police were broadcast on television.*

Source: AP Photo/Bill Hudson.

3. **Bayard Rustin, "From Protest to Politics," *Commentary*, February 1965.** *Rustin, who co-organized the 1963 March on Washington with A. Phillip Randolph, was an influential theorist of African American rights and protest tactics.*

. . . it would be hard to quarrel with the assertion that the elaborate legal structure of segregation and discrimination, particularly in relation to public accommodations, has virtually collapsed. On the other hand, without making light of the human sacrifices involved in the direct-action tactics (sit-ins, freedom rides, and the rest) that were so instrumental to this achievement, we must recognize that in desegregating public accommodations, we affected institutions which are relatively peripheral both to the American socio-economic order and to the fundamental conditions of life of the Negro people. In a highly-industrialized, 20th-century civilization, we hit Jim Crow precisely where it was most anachronistic, dispensable, and vulnerable — in hotels, lunch counters, terminals, libraries, swimming pools, and the like. . . . At issue, after all, is not civil rights, strictly speaking, but social and economic conditions.

4. **James Farmer, *Freedom, When?* 1965.** *Farmer founded the Congress of Racial Equality (CORE) in 1942 and remained an important figure in the civil rights movement in the 1960s.*

"But when will the demonstrations end?" The perpetual question. And a serious question. Actually, it is several questions, for the meaning of the question differs, depending upon who asks it.

Coming from those whose dominant consideration is peace — public peace and peace of mind — the question means: "When are you going to stop tempting violence and rioting?" Some put it more strongly: "When are you going to stop sponsoring violence?" Assumed is the necessary connection between demonstration and violence. . . .

"Isn't the patience of the white majority wearing thin? Why nourish the displeasure of 90 percent of the population with provocative demonstrations? Remember, you need allies." And the assumptions of these Cassandras of the backlash is that freedom and equality are, in the last analysis, wholly gifts in the white man's power to bestow. . . .

What the public must realize is that in a demonstration more things are happening, at more levels of human activity, than meets the eye. Demonstrations in the last few years have provided literally millions of Negroes with their first taste of self-determination and political self-expression.

5. **Stokely Carmichael and Charles Hamilton, *Black Power: The Politics of Liberation in America*, 1967.** *Carmichael brought the term "black power" into prominence in the black struggle of the 1960s and was one of the leading exponents of black nationalism. Hamilton was a professor of political science and a civil rights activist.*

Black people must redefine themselves, and only they can do that. Throughout this country, vast segments of the black communities are beginning to recognize the need to assert their own definitions, to reclaim their history, their culture; to create their own sense of community and togetherness. There is a growing resentment of the word "Negro," for example, because this term is the invention of our oppressor; it is his image of us that he describes. . . .

The concept of Black Power rests on a fundamental premise: Before a group can enter the open society, it must first close ranks. By this we mean that group solidarity is necessary before a group can operate effectively from a bargaining position of strength in a pluralistic society.

6. **Black Power salute at the 1968 Olympics in Mexico City.** *Tommie Smith and John Carlos (right) won gold and bronze medals in the 200 meters. The silver medalist, Australian Peter Norman (left), is wearing an Olympic Project for Human Rights badge to show his support. Smith and Carlos were widely condemned by white commentators.*

SOURCE: AP Photo.

SOURCES: (1) "If the Negro Wins, Labor Wins," by Martin Luther King Jr. delivered February 12, 1962. Reprinted by arrangement with the Heirs to the Estate of Martin Luther King Jr., c/o Writers House as agent for the proprietor, New York, NY. Copyright © 1962 Martin Luther King Jr. Copyright renewed 1991 Coretta Scott King; (3) *Commentary*, February 1965; (4) James Farmer, *Freedom, When?* (New York: Random House, 1965), 25–27, 42–47; (5) Stokely Carmichael and Charles V. Hamilton, *Black Power: The Politics of Liberation in America* (New York: Vintage, 1992, orig. 1967), 37, 44.

ANALYZING THE EVIDENCE

1. Compare sources 1 and 3. What does Rustin mean when he says that ending segregation in public accommodations has not affected the "fundamental conditions" of African American life? How does King's point in source 1 address such issues?
2. Examine the two photographs. What do they reveal about different kinds of protest? About different contexts among African Americans fighting for civil rights?
3. What does "self-determination" mean for Farmer and Carmichael and Hamilton? Use examples from sources 4 and 5 to explain their definitions.

AP® DBQ PRACTICE

Compose an essay in which you use the documents above, in addition to your reading of the chapter, to explore and explain different approaches to African American rights in the 1960s. In particular, think about how all of the documents come from a single movement, yet each expresses a distinct viewpoint and a distinct way of conceiving what "the struggle" is about. How do these approaches compare to the tactics of earlier struggles for civil rights?

TRM Find complete suggested responses in the Teacher's Resource Materials.

AP® SKILLS & PROCESSES

ARGUMENTATION

The **AP® DBQ PRACTICE** prompt poses several questions to students, but the main idea is the different approaches to civil rights adopted by different groups. The term "approaches" could encompass both goals and strategies, so it might be helpful for students to identify two or three major goals and then consider the strategies used by various groups to achieve those goals. Students should work to cluster several organizations together, rather than thinking of each group (SCLC, SNCC, Black Panthers) as having its own distinctive goal.

TEACHING STRATEGY

As the caption indicates, women played a significant — and often unsung — role in the movement. Besides the frequently patriarchal patterns of the movement, Fannie Lou Hamer had to overcome the challenges of her background as a poor, uneducated sharecropper from a family of twenty children. The Digital Public Library of America's "Fannie Lou Hamer and the Civil Rights Movement in Rural Mississippi" Web site page provides a primary source set exploring her key role in the movement. To access this site, search "Digital Public Library Fannie Lou Hamer."

TEACHING STRATEGY

The National Park Service's Teaching with Historic Places Web site provides a lesson plan titled "The Selma to Montgomery Voting Rights March: Shaking the Conscience of the Nation," which uses maps, texts, and images to explore this decisive campaign in the movement. To access this resource, search "NPS Teaching with Historic Places Selma."

AP® APPLY THE TIP

To help students understand the goals, provisions, and impact of the Civil Rights Act of 1964 and the Voting Rights Act of 1965, ask them to create a Venn diagram. Students should refer to pp. 855 and 858 as well as outside resources to find details related to the goals, provisions, support, and impact of each law. Ask students to extend their research by looking at challenges to these laws since 1965. Then lead a class discussion on the comparison between the laws illustrated by the Venn diagrams and responses to challenges to the laws since 1965.

Women in the Movement Though often overshadowed by men in the public spotlight, women were crucial to the black freedom movement. Here, protesting at the 1964 Democratic National Convention in Atlantic City, are (left to right) Fannie Lou Hamer, Eleanor Holmes, and Ella Baker. The men are (left to right) Emory Harris, Stokely Carmichael, and Sam Block. Hamer had been a sharecropper before she became a leader under Baker's tutelage, and Holmes was a Yale University–trained lawyer who went on to become the first female chair of the federal Equal Employment Opportunity Commission. © George Ballis/Take Stock/The Image Works.

the MFDP be recognized at the August convention. But Democratic leaders refused, and seated the white Mississippi delegation instead. Demoralized and convinced that the Democratic Party would not change, Bob Moses told television reporters: "I will have nothing to do with the political system any longer." Freedom Summer had ended with bitter disappointment.

AP® EXAM TIP

Compare the impact of the Civil Rights Act of 1964 and the Voting Rights Act of 1965.

Selma and the Voting Rights Act Martin Luther King Jr. and the SCLC did not share Moses's disillusionment. They believed that another confrontation with southern injustice could provoke further congressional action. In March 1965, James Bevel of the SCLC called for a march from Selma, Alabama, to the state capital, Montgomery, to protest the murder of a voting-rights activist. As soon as the six hundred marchers left Selma, crossing over the Edmund Pettus Bridge, state troopers attacked them with tear gas and clubs. Scenes of solemn marchers being beaten aired on national television that night, and the day became known as "Bloody Sunday." Calling the bitter spectacle "an American tragedy," President Johnson went back to Congress.

Voting Rights Act of 1965
Law passed during Lyndon Johnson's administration that outlawed measures designed to exclude African Americans, and other people of color, from voting.

The **Voting Rights Act of 1965**, which was signed by LBJ on August 6, outlawed the literacy tests and other devices that prevented African Americans and other people of color from registering to vote, and authorized the attorney general to send federal examiners to register voters in any county where registration was less than 50 percent. Together with the Twenty-Fourth Amendment (ratified in 1964), which outlawed the poll tax in federal elections, the Voting Rights Act fulfilled a promise that had been denied for a century.

The resulting shift in representation was profound. In 1960, only 20 percent of black people in the country had been registered to vote; by 1971, registration reached

62 percent (Map 26.4). Across the nation the number of black elected officials began to climb, almost quadrupling from 1,400 to 4,900 between 1970 and 1980 and doubling again by the early 1990s. Most of those elected held local offices — from sheriff to county commissioner — something unimaginable just a generation earlier. As Hartman Turnbow, a Mississippi farmer who risked his life to register in 1964, later declared, "It won't never go back where it was."

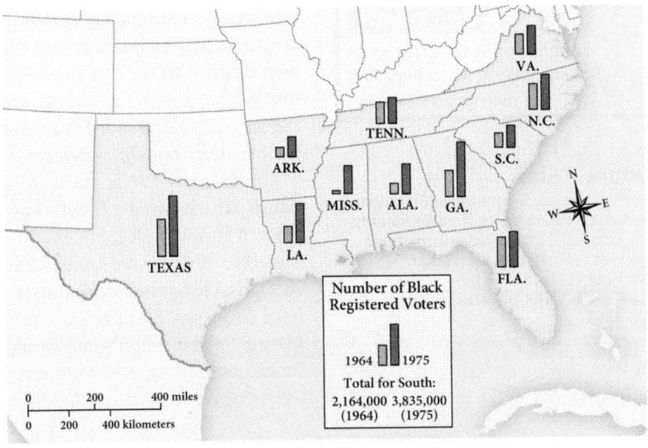

MAP 26.4 Black Voter Registration in the South, 1964 and 1975
After passage of the Voting Rights Act of 1965, black registration in the South increased dramatically. The bars on the map show the number of African Americans registered in 1964, before the act was passed, and in 1975, after it had been in effect for ten years. States in the Deep South, such as Mississippi, Alabama, and Georgia, had the biggest increases.

Neither would the liberal New Deal coalition. By the second half of the 1960s, the liberal wing of the Democratic Party had won its battle with the conservative, segregationist wing. Left-leaning Democrats had embraced the civil rights movement and made black equality a cornerstone of a new "rights" liberalism, though not without consequences. Between the 1960s and the 1980s, southern whites and many conservative northern whites responded by switching to the Republican Party. In 1964, former Dixiecrat presidential candidate Strom Thurmond, a senator from South Carolina, led the revolt by joining the Republican Party. The broad but fragile alliance that supported the New Deal consensus — working-class whites, northern African Americans, urban professionals, and white southern segregationists — had begun to fray.

AP® SKILLS & PROCESSES

DEVELOPMENTS AND PROCESSES

In what ways did white resistance hinder the civil rights movement? How does white resistance in this era compare to white resistance in the late nineteenth and early twentieth centuries?

WIDENING DEMANDS FOR EQUALITY, 1966–1973

Why did Americans of color seek remedies beyond formal legal equality? How successful were their efforts?

Beginning in the mid-1960s, civil rights advocates confronted a fresh set of complex challenges. Court victories and new laws did not mean immediate social change. Sit-ins and marches could not build institutional black power. In 1965, Bayard Rustin wrote of the need to move "from protest to politics." Some black leaders, such as the young SNCC activists Stokely Carmichael, Frances Beal, and John Lewis, grew frustrated with the slow pace of reform and the stubborn resistance of whites. Still others believed that addressing black poverty and economic disadvantage, rather than seeking legal equality by itself, was the most important objective.

A conviction that civil rights alone could not guarantee equality took hold in many communities of color in this period. African Americans were joined by Mexican Americans, Puerto Ricans, and American Indians. Each group came at the problem of inequality from different perspectives, but all asked a similar question: how much did equality before the law matter if most people of color remained in or close to poverty, if white society still regarded nonwhites as inferior, and if major social and political institutions were dominated by whites? Black leaders and representatives of other nonwhite communities increasingly weighed this question as they searched for ways to build on the achievements of the civil rights decade of 1954–1965.

AP® EXAM TIP

Explain the divergent views of the civil rights movement that emerged after 1965.

Black Nationalism

Many African Americans saw an answer to these dilemmas in **black nationalism**. The broad idea of black nationalism could mean anything from wearing African dashikis, buying from African American–owned businesses, or calling for total separatism.

black nationalism
A major strain of African American thought that emphasized black racial pride and autonomy. Present in black communities for centuries, it periodically came to the fore, as in Marcus Garvey's pan-Africanist movement in the early twentieth century and in various organizations in the 1960s and 1970s, such as the Nation of Islam and the Black Panther Party.

CHECK FOR UNDERSTANDING

Ask students: **How did the civil rights movement achieve its major legal and legislative victories between 1954 and 1965?** *After the victory in Brown, African American leaders used nonviolent action and the widespread diffusion of television to convince northern whites, and their political allies, of the justice of their cause. Through a series of high profile marches and protests — the Montgomery Bus Boycott (1955–1956), Greensboro sit-ins (1960), Freedom Rides (1961), the March on Birmingham (1963), and the March on Washington (1963) — civil rights leaders were able to convince first the John F. Kennedy administration to become interested in civil rights and to achieve, under Kennedy's successor Lyndon B. Johnson, the Civil Rights Act of 1964 and the Voting Rights Act of 1965.*

TEACHING STRATEGY

MAP 26.4 indicates the growth of black voters in terms of absolute numbers in one decade. The overall percentage growth — 177 percent — is remarkable. Likewise, the scale of change in particular states, especially in the Deep South and in Arkansas, reveals the degree of disfranchisement of blacks before the law and, thus, the significance of the Voting Rights Act in a short period of time.

AP® SKILLS & PROCESSES

DEVELOPMENTS AND PROCESSES

Students may find it more difficult to understand the second question of the **DEVELOPMENTS AND PROCESSES** prompt than the first. It may help to provide a time period, with references to historical topics, from which they can brainstorm possible answers. For instance, ask students to think of answers using the period 1877–1920. You can remind students they can choose examples from the following topics to illustrate their answer: Reconstruction, Industrial Era, Progressive Era, and World War I.

TRM Find complete suggested responses in the Teacher's Resource Materials.

AP® APPLY THE TIP

To help students understand the range of views that developed in the civil rights movement, ask them to draw a line with one end labeled "nonviolence" and the other end labeled "confrontation" to represent a spectrum. Then ask students to read the primary sources in the **AP® THINKING LIKE A HISTORIAN** feature on pp. 856–857 and place each document along the spectrum with the date it was written. Then prompt students to discuss possible historical arguments for the movement of the documents and leaders toward "confrontation" by the end of the 1960s. Consider extending the discussion to include current groups such as Black Lives Matter as well as previous eras such as the Atlanta Compromise or the leadership of W. E. B. Du Bois and the NAACP. Encourage students to draw conclusions about similarities as well as differences among groups on the spectrum.

AP® EXAM TIP

Summarize the ways that social and political unrest impacted the civil rights movement.

Nation of Islam
A religion founded in the United States that became a leading source of black nationalist thought in the 1960s. Black Muslims fused elements of traditional Islamic doctrine with black pride, a strong philosophy of self-improvement, and a rejection of white culture.

Historically, nationalism had emphasized black pride, "self-help" (African Americans creating their own community institutions), and black people's right to shape their own destiny. In the late nineteenth century, Frederick Douglass stood as a primary inspiration, and in the early twentieth century the nationalist Marcus Garvey took up the banner, calling on African Americans to take pride in their racial heritage and end their reliance on white society.

In the early 1960s, the leading exponent of black nationalism was the **Nation of Islam**, which fused a handful of elements of traditional Islamic doctrine with black pride, a strong philosophy of self-improvement, and a rejection of white culture. Black Muslims, as they were known, adhered to a strict code of personal behavior; men were recognizable by their dark suits, white shirts, and ties, women by their long dresses and head coverings. Black Muslim ministers preached an apocalyptic brand of Islam, anticipating the day when Allah would banish the white "devils" and deliver justice. While formal membership was modest, the message of the Nation of Islam found a popular following among African Americans in northern cities in the 1950s and 1960s.

Malcolm X The most charismatic Black Muslim was Malcolm X (the *X* stood for his African family name, lost under slavery). A spellbinding speaker, Malcolm X preached a militant separatism, although he advocated violence only for self-defense. "I believe in the brotherhood of man, all men," he declared, "but I don't believe in brotherhood with anybody who doesn't want brotherhood with me." Hostile to mainstream civil rights organizations, Malcolm X referred to the 1963 March on Washington caustically as the "Farce on Washington." He had little interest in changing the minds of hostile whites and saw strengthening the black community as a surer path to true equality.

In 1964, after a power struggle with founder Elijah Muhammad, Malcolm X broke with the Nation of Islam. While he remained a black nationalist, he moderated his antiwhite views and began to talk of a class struggle uniting poor whites and blacks. Following an inspiring trip to the Middle East, where he saw Muslims of all races worshipping together, Malcolm X formed the Organization of Afro-American Unity to promote black pride and to work with traditional civil rights groups. His second act proved shockingly short, however. On February 21, 1965, Malcolm X was assassinated while delivering a speech in Harlem. Three Black Muslims were later convicted of his murder.

Malcolm X Until his murder in 1965, Malcolm X was the leading proponent of black nationalism in the United States. A brilliant and dynamic orator, Malcolm had been a minister in the Nation of Islam for nearly thirteen years before he broke with the Nation in 1964. His emphasis on black pride and self-help and his unrelenting criticism of white supremacy made him one of the freedom movement's most inspirational figures, both in life and well after his death. © Topham/The Image Works.

Black Power A more secular brand of black nationalism emerged in 1966. A segment of SNCC and CORE activists, following the lead of Stokely Carmichael, called for black self-reliance under the banner of Black Power. This new initiative posed fundamental questions: If alliances with whites were necessary to achieve racial justice, as King believed, did that make African Americans dependent on the good intentions of whites? If so, could black people trust those good intentions in the long run? Those inclined toward Black Power increasingly felt that African Americans should build economic and political power in their own communities. Such power would reduce dependence on whites. Because "the institutions that function in this country are clearly racist" and "built upon racism," Carmichael told an audience in 1966, the question was how black people could "build institutions that will allow people to relate with each other as human beings."

Spurred by the Black Power slogan, African American activists sought to redress persistent economic and social disadvantages. In 1964, President Johnson had declared the War on Poverty, a slew of new federal laws designed to help the poorest Americans (see "Lyndon B. Johnson and the Great Society" in Chapter 27). Black organizers joined the effort, setting up day care centers, running job training programs, and working to improve housing and health care in urban communities. In major cities such as Philadelphia, New York, Chicago, and Pittsburgh, activists sought to open jobs in police and fire departments and in construction and transportation to black workers, who had been excluded from these occupations for decades. Others worked to end police harassment — a major problem in urban black communities — and to help black entrepreneurs secure small-business loans. CORE leader Floyd McKissick explained, "Black Power is not Black Supremacy; it is a united Black Voice reflecting racial pride."

In addition to focusing on economic disadvantage, Black Power emphasized black pride and self-determination. Some advocates rejected white society for more authentic cultural forms. Those subscribing to these beliefs often wore African clothing, chose natural hairstyles, and celebrated black history, art, and literature. The Black Arts movement thrived, and musical tastes shifted from the crossover sounds of Motown to the soul music coming out of Philadelphia, Memphis, and Chicago.

Black Panther Party One of the most radical nationalist groups was the **Black Panther Party**, founded in Oakland, California, in 1966 by college students Huey Newton and Bobby Seale. A militant organization dedicated to protecting African Americans from police violence, the Panthers took their cue from the slain Malcolm X, whose philosophy of black community empowerment and self-defense in the face of attack they embraced. They vehemently opposed the Vietnam War and declared solidarity with Third World revolutionary movements and other armed struggles (Map 26.5). In their manifesto, "What We Want, What We Believe," the Panthers

Black Panther Party
A militant organization dedicated to protecting African Americans from police violence, founded in Oakland, California, in 1966 by Huey Newton and Bobby Seale. In the late 1960s the organization spread to other cities, where members undertook a wide range of community-organizing projects, but the Panthers' radicalism and belief in armed self-defense resulted in violent clashes with police.

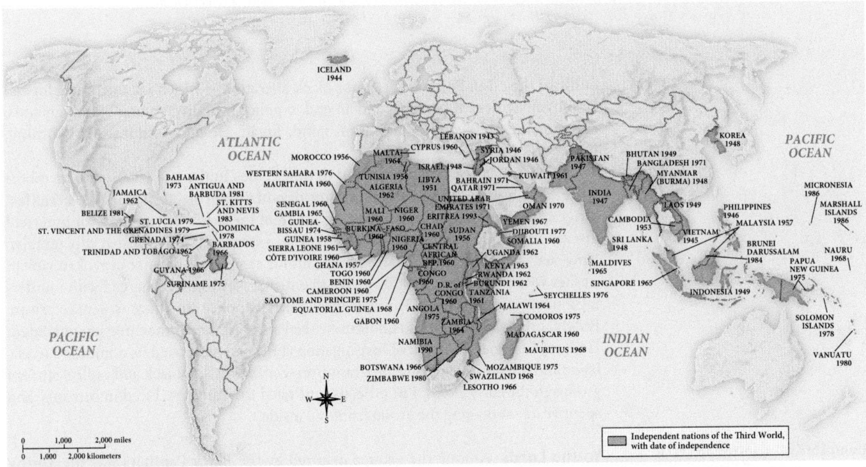

MAP 26.5 Decolonization and the Third World, 1943–1990
In the decades after World War II, African nations threw off the yoke of European colonialism. Some new nations, such as Ghana, the former British colony of Gold Coast, achieved independence rather peacefully. Others, such as Algeria and Mozambique, did so only after bloody anticolonial wars. American civil rights activists watched African decolonization with great enthusiasm, seeing the two struggles as linked. "Sure we identified with the blacks in Africa," civil rights leader John Lewis said. "Here were black people, talking of freedom and liberation and independence thousands of miles away." In 1960 alone, the year that student sit-ins swept across the American South, more than a dozen African nations gained independence.

AP® THEME

WOR: America in the World

Postwar decolonization and the emergence of nationalist movements in Asia and Africa led both sides in the Cold War to seek allies among new nations. **MAP 26.5** illustrates the dramatic growth of newly independent nations in the postwar period. Students, who have probably studied this topic in their world history courses already, should be able to recognize why this dynamic pattern was so exciting to civil rights leaders like John Lewis.

The Black Panther Party One of the most radical organizations of the 1960s, the Black Panther Party was founded in 1966 by Bobby Seale and Huey Newton (shown together in the photograph on the left) in Oakland, California. Its members carried weapons, advocated socialism, and fought police brutality in black communities, but they also ran into their own trouble with the law. Nevertheless, the party had great success in reaching ordinary people, often with programs targeted at the poor. On the right, party members distribute a free meal to the public in New Haven, Connecticut, in 1969.
LEFT: © Bruno Barbey/Magnum Photos. RIGHT: David Fenton/Getty Images.

outlined their Ten Point Program for black liberation — which included calls for full employment, decent housing, and an end to police brutality, among other demands, and concluded by stating "We want Land, Bread, Housing, Education, Clothing, Justice and Peace."

The Panther organization spread to other cities in the late 1960s, and members undertook a wide range of community-organizing projects. Their free breakfast program for children and their testing program for sickle-cell anemia, an inherited disease with a high incidence among African Americans, proved especially popular. However, the Panthers' radicalism and calls for armed self-defense provoked violent clashes with police, who saw the group as outlaws. Newton was charged with murdering a police officer, several Panthers were killed by police, and dozens went to prison. Federal officials, too, tried to undermine the Party. Still under the direction of J. Edgar Hoover, the Federal Bureau of Investigation (FBI) had redirected its domestic surveillance and counterintelligence program from communists to black and radical student groups in the early 1960s. FBI officials infiltrated the Panthers, hired informants, and spent years sabotaging the group from the inside.

Young Lords Organization (YLO)
An organization that sought self-determination for Puerto Ricans in the United States and in the Caribbean. Though immediate victories for the YLO were few, their dedicated community organizing produced a generation of leaders and awakened community consciousness.

Young Lords Among the groups inspired by the Black Panthers was the **Young Lords Organization (YLO)**, later renamed the Young Lords Party, which sought self-determination for Puerto Ricans, both on the mainland and in Puerto Rico. In practical terms, the YLO focused on improving conditions in the big-city neighborhoods where most Puerto Ricans lived. New York City allowed garbage to rot in the streets of East Harlem, home to many of the city's Puerto Ricans, and slumlords allowed the housing to become squalid. Women were especially active in the YLO, protesting sterilization campaigns that targeted Puerto Rican women and working to improve access to health care. As was true for many nationalist groups, the dedicated work of the YLO had modest immediate impact but awakened community consciousness and produced a generation of leaders, many of whom later entered electoral politics.

The New Urban Politics Black Power also inspired African Americans to work within the political system. By the mid-1960s, black residents neared 50 percent of the population in several major American cities — such as Atlanta, Cleveland, Detroit, and Washington, D.C. Black Power in these cities was not abstract; it counted in real votes. Richard Hatcher in Gary, Indiana, and Carl Stokes in Cleveland, Ohio, became the first black mayors of large cities in 1967. Hatcher and Stokes helped forge a new urban politics, registering new black voters and forging alliances with white constituencies to create a working majority. Stokes's victory seemed particularly auspicious. As one of his campaign staffers said: "If Carl Stokes could run for mayor in the eighth largest city in America, then maybe who knows. We could be senators. We could be anything we wanted."

Having met with some political success in a growing number of cities, black leaders gathered in Gary for the 1972 National Black Political Convention. In a meeting that brought together radicals, liberals, and centrists, debate centered on whether to form a third political party. Hatcher recalled that many in attendance believed that "there was going to be a black third party." In the end, however, delegates decided to "give the Democratic Party one more chance." Instead of creating a breakaway party, the convention issued the National Black Political Agenda, which called for community control of schools in black neighborhoods, national health insurance, and the elimination of the death penalty, among other objectives.

The National Black Political Agenda did not gain traction within the Democratic Party, but African Americans increasingly entered mainstream political institutions. By the end of the century, black elected officials were commonplace in major American cities. There were forty-seven African American big-city mayors by the 1990s, and blacks had led most of the nation's most prominent cities: Atlanta, Chicago, Detroit, Los Angeles, New York, Philadelphia, and Washington, D.C. These politicians and others had translated black power into a revitalized liberalism, which remains a defining feature of American urban government.

AP® SKILLS & PROCESSES

MAKING CONNECTIONS

What did Black Power and black nationalism represent to many African Americans?

Urban Unrest

Black Power was not a fundamentally violent political ideology, but violence did play a decisive role in the politics of black liberation in the mid-1960s. Few middle-class white Americans understood the depth and immediacy of the discontent simmering in poor northern black neighborhoods. The product of decades of poverty, inequality, and unanswered grievances, black discontent boiled over in a wave of riots across the nation's cities in mid-decade. The first of several "long hot summers" came in 1964. In July, a New York City police officer shot and killed a black teenager named James Powell. Rioting and looting followed the police violence — a pattern that would recur in unrest in dozens of cities over the next four years.

In August 1965, the arrest of a young black motorist in the Watts section of Los Angeles sparked six days of rioting that left thirty-four people dead. "There is a different type of Negro emerging," one riot participant told investigators. "They are not going to wait for the evolutionary process for their rights to be a man." The riots of 1967 were the most serious, engulfing twenty-two cities in July and August. Forty-three people were killed in Detroit alone, nearly all of them black,

CHECK FOR UNDERSTANDING

Ask students: **What was black nationalism?** *Black nationalism was a broad term that meant different things to different groups. In general, it indicated a critique of the civil rights movement — and often a criticism of Christianity and nonviolence — and advocacy of self-help strategies. It is associated with Malcolm X and the Nation of Islam, the radical Black Power phase of SNCC, and the militancy of the Black Panthers.*

AP® SKILLS & PROCESSES

MAKING CONNECTIONS

You can facilitate sound responses to this **MAKING CONNECTIONS** question by asking students to explain how the concepts of Black Power and black nationalism compared to groups such as SCLC, SNCC, or CORE. As a result of comparing, students may arrive at a better understanding of the transformative nature these groups represented to some African Americans.

TRM Find complete suggested responses in the Teacher's Resource Materials.

and $50 million worth of property was destroyed. President Johnson called in the National Guard and U.S. Army troops, many just returned from Vietnam, to restore order.

Johnson, who believed that the Civil Rights Act and the Voting Rights Act had immeasurably helped African Americans, was shocked by the rioting. Despondent at the news from Watts, "he refused to look at the cables from Los Angeles," recalled one aide. Virtually all black leaders condemned the rioting, though they understood its origins in poverty and deprivation. At a meeting in Watts, Martin Luther King Jr. admitted that he had "failed to take the civil rights movement to the masses of the people." His contrition appeased few. "We don't need your dreams; we need jobs!" one heckler shouted at King.

Following the gut-wrenching riots in Detroit and Newark in 1967, Johnson appointed a presidential commission, headed by (and informally named after) Illinois governor Otto Kerner, to investigate the causes of the violence. The Kerner Commission's official report landed in 1968, an unstinting and direct appraisal of how racial inequality had fed urban violence. "Our nation is moving toward two societies," the Kerner Commission Report concluded, "one black, one white — separate and unequal." The report did not excuse the brick-throwing, firebombing, and looting of the previous summers, but it did provide a sociological context for the rioting. Calling the American racial ghetto a "destructive environment," the report concluded that "White institutions created it, white institutions maintain it, and white society condones it." Shut out of white-dominated society, impoverished African Americans felt they had no stake in the social order.

Seeing the limitations of his previous work, Martin Luther King Jr. expanded his vision to the deep-seated problems of poverty and racism in America as a whole. He criticized President Johnson and Congress for prioritizing the war in Vietnam over the fight against poverty at home, and he planned a massive movement called the Poor People's Campaign to fight economic injustice. In support of that cause, he went to Memphis, Tennessee, to back a strike by predominantly black sanitation workers. There, on April 4, 1968, he was assassinated by escaped white convict James Earl Ray. The slaying of King cut short his plan for a broad assault on American poverty and touched off a further round of urban rioting, with major violence breaking out in more than a hundred cities.

As the 1960s ended, the civil rights movement could look back on a generation of success: Jim Crow segregation had collapsed, and federal law finally protected the fundamental rights of African Americans. The white monopoly on political power in the South was broken. The movement's nonviolent demonstration and methodical progress encouraged countless other groups to organize and act. It was so successful that it remade the very nature of American liberalism. Joining New Deal liberalism's attention to broad social welfare, this new liberalism affirmed the universality of the rights promised in the Constitution.

But the long and intense fight for equality brought out lasting divisions. The Democratic Party was splitting, and a new conservatism was gaining strength. Many whites resented the attention to civil rights and saw nonviolent black protestors as lawbreakers. Widespread rioting fed this belief, and many white Americans blamed Democratic Party officials for the failure to maintain law and order. The struggle for racial equality and the resistance to it unearthed fissures in American society not easily mended.

Rise of the Chicano Movement

The push for Mexican American equality gained fewer national headlines than African American campaigns but shared similar aims and tactics. In Cesar Chavez, Mexican Americans had something of a counterpart to the charismatic Martin

CHECK FOR UNDERSTANDING

Ask students: **What forms of urban disorder emerged in the 1960s?** *Police mistreatment of blacks led to several riots in the mid-1960s. While the civil rights movement had produced new laws granting legal equality, it did little to ease the economic oppression many blacks faced in urban areas. The rioting stunned Johnson, who believed that black progress had been substantial. It also motivated King to address economic issues more directly. In Memphis to support a strike by black sanitation workers, he was assassinated, which generated a new wave of rioting, this one in more than a hundred cities.*

AP® THEME

NAT: American and National Identity; PCE: Politics and Power

Latino, American Indian, and Asian American movements continued to demand social and economic equality and a redress of past injustices.

Luther King Jr. Where King took inspiration from his religious calling for moral clarity, Chavez drew from his roots in community organizing and the labor movement, as well as the Catholic Church. He and Dolores Huerta, like Chavez an emerging Mexican American activist, had worked for the Community Service Organization (CSO), a California group founded in the 1950s to promote Mexican political participation and civil rights. After leaving the CSO in 1962, Chavez concentrated on the agricultural region around Delano, California. With Huerta, he organized the **United Farm Workers (UFW)**, a union for migrant workers, some of the most vulnerable segments of the population, who faced discrimination and exploitative conditions, especially in the Southwestern states.

Huerta was a brilliant organizer, and the deeply spiritual and ascetic Chavez embodied the moral force behind what was popularly called La Causa. In support of a grape pickers' strike, the UFW called for a nationwide boycott of table grapes in 1965. The boycott won publicity and backing from the AFL-CIO. As the labor conflict continued, Chavez mounted a hunger strike to win attention for the struggle. His fast ended dramatically after twenty-eight days, with now-Senator Robert F. Kennedy at his side. A conclusive victory came in 1970, when California grape growers signed contracts recognizing the UFW. The labor campaign led by Chavez and Huerta in California's vast agriculture industry resonated beyond the picking fields, inspiring Mexican Americans, urban and rural alike, across the Southwest.

Dolores Huerta and Cesar Chavez Dolores Huerta and Cesar Chavez were two of the leading Mexican American civil rights and social justice advocates of the 1960s. Huerta, influenced by community-organizing traditions, founded two social justice and workers' rights organization before she joined with Chavez in 1962 to cofound the United Farm Workers (UFW), a union of primarily Mexican American agricultural laborers in California. Chavez, influenced equally by the Catholic Church and Mahatma Gandhi, and Huerta led the UFW's massive national grape boycott, an attempt by the UFW to force the nation's grape growers — and, by extension, the larger agriculture industry — to improve wages and working conditions and to bargain in good faith with the union. Arthur Schatz/Getty Images.

Mexican Americans shared many economic grievances with African Americans — especially limited access to jobs — but they also had unique concerns: the status of the Spanish language in schools, for instance, and immigration policy. Mexican Americans had been politically active since the 1940s, and those efforts began to pay off in the 1960s. The Mexican American Political Association (MAPA) mobilized support for the presidential campaign of John F. Kennedy and worked successfully with other organizations to elect Mexican American candidates such as Edward Roybal of California and Henry González of Texas to Congress. Two other organizations joined the fight. The **Mexican American Legal Defense and Education Fund (MALDEF)**, founded in 1967 and based on the model of the NAACP Legal Defense and Education Fund, focused on legal issues and endeavored to win protections against discrimination through court decisions. And the Southwest Voter Registration and Education Project mobilized an increasingly powerful Mexican American voting bloc.

But younger Mexican Americans grew impatient with the incremental gains of groups such as MAPA and MALDEF. A key inspiration for them was Reies Lopez Tijerina, an activist in New Mexico whose organization, known as La Alianza, called for the restoration of land owned by Mexican Americans that was confiscated by Anglos after the Mexican War. This militant spirit was picked up in Denver, Colorado, by Rodolfo (Corky) Gonzales, who in 1966 founded the Crusade for Justice to reach out to younger Mexican Americans. Just a year later, the barrios of Los Angeles and other western cities produced the militant Brown Berets, named for the hats they wore in homage to the Black Panthers.

As in the black freedom movement, young people infused the Mexican American cause with new energy and creativity. Rejecting their elders' willingness to assimilate

United Farm Workers (UFW)
A union of farmworkers founded in 1962 by Cesar Chavez and Dolores Huerta that sought to empower the mostly Mexican American migrant farmworkers who faced discrimination and exploitative conditions, especially in the Southwest.

Mexican American Legal Defense and Education Fund (MALDEF)
A Mexican American civil rights organization founded in 1967 and based on the model of the NAACP Legal Defense and Education Fund. MALDEF focused on legal issues and endeavored to win protections against discrimination through court decisions.

TEACHING STRATEGY

The California Department of Education provides model curriculum and resources on Cesar Chavez, including five lessons designed for Eleventh Grade U.S. History, a brief Chavez biography, several essays, and several dozen primary sources. To access these resources, search "CA Department of Education Chavez model curriculum."

La Raza Unida
A political party founded in Texas in 1970 by Mexican Americans as an alternative to the two major political parties; La Raza Unida (The United Race) ran candidates for state and local governments and expanded to other states.

into Anglo society, fifteen hundred Mexican American students met in Denver in 1969 to hammer out a new political and cultural agenda. Called the National Youth and Liberation Conference, the assembled activists adopted the term *Chicano* (and its feminine form, *Chicana*) to replace *Mexican American*. In Texas, Chicano/a activists organized the Mexican American Youth Organization (MAYO) in 1967 and in 1970 led the formation of a political party, **La Raza Unida** (People United), an alternative to the two major parties that would promote Chicano interests and that eventually expanded to other states. Chicano students formed El Movimiento Estudiantil Chicano/a de Aztlan, known as MEChA (pronounced "mecha"), a congress of campus-based groups that would ultimately grow to more than five hundred chapters by the 2000s. Young Chicana feminists formed a number of organizations, including Las Hijas (The Daughters), to organize women both on college campuses and in the barrios. In California and many southwestern states, students staged demonstrations to press for bilingual education, the hiring of more Chicano teachers, and the creation of Chicano studies programs.

Mexican American and Chicano activism forged significant changes in American life in subsequent decades. Government agencies and the U.S. Supreme Court recognized the right of non-English speaking Americans to access to education, and the 1974 Equal Educational Opportunities Act implemented bilingual programs in public schools. Chicano students, alongside their African American and Asian American counterparts, revolutionized college curricula, bringing ethnic studies into the mainstream and exposing students to new writers, artists, and historical figures rarely studied previously. The MALDEF developed into an important national defender of Mexican American rights, and the political organizing that followed on the heels of La Raza Unida helped elect thousands of Mexican Americans to government positions over the next decades, from local school boards to the U.S. Senate. Though activists were unable to achieve one of their foundational goals — significantly improving the wages and working conditions of the nation's farmworkers — their efforts brought legal protection and political and cultural representation to people long marginalized in national life.

The American Indian Movement

AP® EXAM TIP
Evaluate the ways that the experiences of Hispanic Americans, Native Americans, and African Americans illustrated both change and continuity in the 1960s and 1970s.

American Indians, inspired by the Black Power and Chicano movements, organized to address their unique circumstances. The country's nearly 800,000 Native people were (and are) exceedingly diverse — distinguished from one another by language, tribal history, region, and degree of integration into American life. As a group, they shared a staggering unemployment rate — ten times the national average — and huge deficits in housing, health, and access to education. Native people also had a fraught relationship with the federal government. In the 1960s, the prevailing spirit of protest swept into Native communities. Young militants challenged their elders in the National Congress of American Indians. Beginning in 1960, the National Indian Youth Council (NIYC), under the slogan "For a Greater Indian America," promoted the ideal of Native Americans as a single ethnic group — a challenging task given the importance of individual tribal culture.

American Indian Movement (AIM)
Organization established in 1968 to address the problems Indians faced in American cities, including poverty and police harassment. AIM organized Indians to end relocation and termination policies and to win greater control over their cultures and communities.

The NIYC had substantial influence within tribal communities, but two other organizations, the militant Indians of All Tribes (IAT) and the **American Indian Movement (AIM)**, attracted more attention in mainstream culture. These groups embraced the concept of Red Power, and beginning in 1968 they staged escalating protests to draw attention to indigenous issues, especially the concerns of urban Indians, many of whom had been encouraged, or forced, to leave reservations by the federal government — and faced poverty and police harassment, among other ills, in their new urban environs. In 1969, members of the IAT occupied the deserted federal penitentiary on Alcatraz Island in San Francisco Bay and proclaimed: "We will purchase said Alcatraz Island for twenty-four dollars in glass beads and red cloth, a

CHECK FOR UNDERSTANDING

Ask students: **What factors led to the rise of the Chicano movement?** *Mexican Americans experienced some of the same economic exploitation as African Americans. They faced unique challenges as Spanish speakers and, in many cases, as noncitizens. The emergence of a charismatic leader, Cesar Chavez, was one important factor. A committed Catholic, his deep spirituality gave moral force to La Causa. Together with Dolores Huerta, he formed the United Farm Workers. The group organized boycotts, and Chavez staged a hunger strike in 1968.*

AP® APPLY THE TIP

Organize students into collaborative groups to engage in a simulation called the "Civil Rights Hall of Fame." Each group should make a case for including an assigned civil rights leader, or organization, into the "hall of fame." Therefore, students must convince their classmates that their assigned individual had the greatest impact on bringing about change for minority groups from 1945 to 1975. Students may also support their individual by showing how other individuals they are competing against represent more continuity than change in American history. Be sure to remind students to think about Hispanic Americans, Native Americans, and African Americans. Individuals to assign could include (but are not limited to) Fannie Lou Hamer, Malcolm X, Medgar Evers, A. Philip Randolph, W. E. B. Du Bois, Harry S. Truman, Earl Warren, Thurgood Marshall, Ella Baker, Stokely Carmichael, Huey Newton, Dolores Huerta, Cesar Chavez, United Farm Workers, Students for Non-Violent Coordinating Committee, or American Indian Movement.

Native American Activism Members of the American Indian Movement (AIM) and local Oglala Sioux stand guard outside the Sacred Heart Catholic Church after taking control of the town and eleven hostages during a seventy-one-day standoff with the FBI and U.S. Marshalls. Founded in 1968, AIM was among several Native American groups fighting for indigenous rights in the 1960s and 1970s. In the 1973 action pictured above, AIM activists occupied the town of Wounded Knee, South Dakota, on the Pine Ridge Indian Reservation, one of the poorest such Native reservations in the country. Bettmann/Getty Images.

precedent set by the white man's purchase of a similar island [Manhattan] about 300 years ago." In 1972, AIM members joined the Trail of Broken Treaties, a march sponsored by a number of Indian groups. When AIM activists seized and ransacked the headquarters of the hated Bureau of Indian Affairs in Washington, D.C., older tribal leaders denounced them.

AIM drew national media attention with a siege at Wounded Knee, South Dakota, in February 1973. The site of the infamous 1890 U.S. military massacre of the Sioux by the U.S. military, Wounded Knee was part of the Pine Ridge Reservation, where young AIM activists had cultivated ties to sympathetic elders. For more than two months, AIM members occupied a small collection of buildings, holding off detachments of FBI agents and U.S. marshals. Several gun battles left two dead, and the siege was finally brought to a negotiated end. Although AIM's tactics were upsetting to many white onlookers and Indian elders alike, their protests attracted widespread mainstream coverage and spurred government action on tribal issues.

AP® SKILLS & PROCESSES

COMPARISON

What did the Chicano and American Indian movements have in common with the black freedom movement?

SUMMARY

The civil rights movement was comprised of a diverse set of initiatives, united by their pursuit of legal rights, a fuller participation in economic and political life, and self-determination for communities of color. African Americans waged their fight for equality both in the South, where segregation and disenfranchisement were law, and in the country as a whole, where discrimination in jobs, housing, and opportunity was pervasive. In the Southwest and West, Mexican Americans, Native Americans, and Asian Americans waged similar campaigns against unfair laws and social practices that marginalized them as second-class citizens.

CHECK FOR UNDERSTANDING

Ask students: **What social conditions prompted many Americans to seek remedies beyond formal legal equality on the basis of race? How successful were those remedies?** *Worried by the slow pace of reform and hoping to address systematic problems faced by African Americans, more radical African American reformers in the late 1960s like the Black Panthers and Malcolm X embraced black nationalism and violence. These tactics were not successful for African Americans, largely because, unlike the tactics of King and others, radical reformers were unable to win over northern whites, and after the 1970s both political parties absorbed the African American political movement to some extent. The tactics of these movements, however, influenced similar movements for Chicanos and Native Americans, who had more success in bringing their forgotten plights to the fore.*

AP® SKILLS & PROCESSES

COMPARISON

The **COMPARISON** question asks students to identify similarities between the black civil rights movement and two other movements. To scaffold this question, have students create a three-column chart that includes a central column for elements all three groups shared in common, and separate columns for elements that only Chicanos shared in common with African Americans, and for elements that only American Indians shared with African Americans. To extend this prompt, students could identify ways in which these groups differed from the black freedom movement and explain the significance of those differences.

TRM Find complete suggested responses in the Teacher's Resource Materials.

CHECK FOR UNDERSTANDING

Use the **AP® LEARNING FOCUS** question from the beginning of the chapter to check students' understanding of the chapter as a whole: **Why did the civil rights movement change over time, and how did competing ideas and strategies evolve within the movement itself?** *The civil rights movement emerged as a critique of white supremacy at the beginning of WWII, although it was not the first critique of racial inequality in the twentieth century. After the landmark Supreme Court decision,* Brown v. the Board of Education, *groups across the South began to organize and protest using various forms of civil disobedience. They wanted equal treatment under the law, the desegregation of public facilities including schools, increased job opportunities, and the right to vote. These protests were met with extreme violence. In the early 1960s, the movement became more radicalized with the movement for Black Nationalism and black power. The movement evolved in concert with the individuals who took part in the struggle for civil rights. Youth, young adults, and adults worked together; at the same time, each advocated for their own path to reform. The civil rights struggle finally gained the backing of the Democratic Party, under Kennedy and then Johnson who signed civil rights legislation into effect. The civil rights movement inspired other oppressed groups such as women, Native Americans, and Mexican Americans to organize and advocate for equal treatment under the law.*

LearningCurve

Remind students to go online to complete the LearningCurve quiz for this chapter.

TRM Find complete suggested responses in the Teacher's Resource Materials.

AP® SKILLS & PROCESSES

CONTINUITY AND CHANGE

AP® CONTENT REVIEW 1 asks students to trace the growth of and changes in the civil rights movement between the time of American entrance into World War II and the *Brown v. Board* ruling. Note: This is the same question as the section-opening prompt on p. 836.

The African American civil rights movement attacked racial inequality in three ways. First, activists sought equality under the law for all Americans, regardless of race. This required a deliberate, decades-long legal assault on the idea of "separate but equal" and the more arduous task of passing congressional legislation, such as the Civil Rights Act of 1964 and the Voting Rights Act of 1965 against a committed blockage of segregationist politicians. Second, grassroots activists, using nonviolent protest, pushed all levels of government to honor constitutionally guaranteed rights and abide by Supreme Court decisions (such as *Brown v. Board of Education*). Third, the movement worked to open economic opportunity for nonwhite populations — as illustrated by the very name of the 1963 March on Washington for Jobs and Freedom.

Although the civil rights movement succeeded in establishing equality before the law, its efforts to lift communities out of poverty proved difficult. The limitations of the civil rights model led black activists — along with Mexican Americans, Native Americans, and others — to adopt more nationalist stances in the late 1960s. Nationalism stressed the creation of political and economic power in communities of color, the celebration of racial heritage, and the rejection of white cultural standards.

CHAPTER 26 REVIEW

AP® CONTENT REVIEW

Answer these questions to demonstrate your understanding of the chapter's main ideas.

1. What factors shaped the course of the civil rights movement between 1941 and 1954?
2. How did the civil rights movement achieve its major legal and legislative victories between 1954 and 1965?
3. Why did Americans of color seek remedies beyond a legal equality? How successful were their various efforts?

AP® TERMS TO KNOW

Identify and explain the significance of each term.

Key Concepts and Events

rights liberalism (p. 834)
Executive Order 8802 (p. 839)
Congress of Racial Equality (CORE) (p. 840)
"To Secure These Rights" (p. 840)
States' Rights Democratic Party (p. 841)
American GI Forum (p. 842)
Community Services Organization (CSO) (p. 842)
Brown v. Board of Education of Topeka (p. 847)
Montgomery Bus Boycott (p. 849)
Southern Christian Leadership Conference (SCLC) (p. 850)
Student Nonviolent Coordinating Committee (SNCC) (p. 850)
Freedom Rides (p. 851)
March on Washington (p. 854)
Civil Rights Act of 1964 (p. 855)
Mississippi Freedom Democratic Party (MFDP) (p. 855)
Voting Rights Act of 1965 (p. 858)
black nationalism (p. 859)
Nation of Islam (p. 860)
Black Panther Party (p. 861)
Young Lords Organization (YLO) (p. 862)
United Farm Workers (UFW) (p. 865)
Mexican American Legal Defense and Education Fund (MALDEF) (p. 865)
La Raza Unida (p. 866)
American Indian Movement (AIM) (p. 866)

Key People

A. Philip Randolph (p. 839)
James Farmer (p. 840)
Cesar Chavez (p. 843)
Dolores Huerta (p. 843)
Thurgood Marshall (p. 843)
Rosa Parks (p. 849)
Martin Luther King Jr. (p. 849)
Stokely Carmichael (p. 851)
Malcolm X (p. 860)

AP® SKILLS & PROCESSES

CAUSATION

AP® CONTENT REVIEW 3 asks students to identify factors that caused Americans of color to adopt new strategies in their quest for justice. Note: This question is the same as the section-opening prompt on p. 859.

TRM Find definitions for these terms in the **Glossary/Glosario** in the Teacher's Resource Materials.

AP MAKING CONNECTIONS

Recognize the larger developments and continuities within and across chapters by answering these questions.

1. Why is the decade of the 1960s often referred to as the "second Reconstruction"? Think broadly about the century between the end of the Civil War in 1865 and the passage of the Voting Rights Act of 1965. What are the key turning points in African American history in that long period?

2. Examine the photograph of the desegregation of an elementary school in Nashville, Tennessee, on page 848. How does this photograph reveal the role that the media played in the civil rights struggle? Can you find similar evidence in other photographs from this chapter?

KEY TURNING POINTS

Refer to the timeline at the start of the chapter for help in answering the following question.

The history of the civil rights movement is more than a list of significant events. Pick two or three events from this timeline and explain how their timing and the broader historical context contributed to the precise role each played in the movement as a whole.

AP PRACTICE QUESTIONS

MULTIPLE CHOICE QUESTIONS

Choose the correct answer for each question.

Questions 1–3 refer to this excerpt.

> "Little Rock's Central High School is still under military occupation. The troops are still there—on the campus, in the building.
>
> The troops are still there, despite the fact that their presence is resented by the big majority of the students, the parents, and the people in general throughout the South.
>
> The troops continue to stand guard during school hours, despite the fact that there is no law or precedent—Federal or State—that permits them to do so.
>
> There is not even an order, or so much as a sanction, from the U.S. Supreme Court that makes its own 'laws' on mixing of races in the public schools. . . .
>
> Education, or attempted education, under the scrutiny of armed troops is un-American, un-Godly. . . .
>
> How much longer will Congress sit idly by and let such brazen violation of American principle and law continue on and on and on?"
>
> Editorial—"Anti-Little Rock Intervention" by Karr Shannon in *Arkansas Democrat* (March 10, 1958). Reproduced with permission.

1. In making mention of "'laws' on mixing of races," the author refers most directly to the Supreme Court's
   - **a.** *Brown v. Board of Education* case.
   - **b.** Dred Scott case.
   - **c.** *Plessy v. Ferguson* case.
   - **d.** rulings against New Deal programs.

2. Shannon's ideas show the greatest similarity to
   - **a.** antebellum advocates of states' rights.
   - **b.** proponents of Reconstruction in the 1860s and 1870s.
   - **c.** supporters of desegregation of the United States armed forces in the 1940s.
   - **d.** those calling for a Great Society in the 1960s.

3. Support for Shannon's ideas would most likely have been greatest in
   - **a.** newly politicized Protestant evangelical organizations.
   - **b.** movements for Hispanic rights.
   - **c.** groups organizing for gay and lesbian rights.
   - **d.** increasingly activist environmental organizations.

AP SKILLS & PROCESSES

CONTINUITY AND CHANGE

AP® MAKING CONNECTIONS 1 essentially encourages students to consider the experiences of African Americans in a longer-term perspective that extends backward to the era of Reconstruction. Students can consider the ways these unaddressed problems during Reconstruction contributed to black Americans' oppression, and how the civil rights movement sought to confront those problems.

AP SKILLS & PROCESSES

CONTINUITY AND CHANGE

The **KEY TURNING POINTS** question asks students to find a few events from within the three-decade period covered by this chapter and explain how they were decisive in advancing the rights and equality of many nonwhite groups.

TRM Find complete suggested responses in the Teacher's Resource Materials.

Questions 4–6 refer to this excerpt.

"This is our basic conclusion: our nation is moving toward two societies, one black, one white — separate and unequal.

"Reaction to last summer's disorders has quickened the movement and deepened the division. . . .

The alternative is . . . the realization of common opportunities for all within a single society.

This alternative will require a commitment to national action — compassionate, massive and sustained, backed by the resources of the most powerful and richest nation on earth. From every American it will require new attitudes, new understanding, and, above all, new will. . . .

What white Americans have never fully understood — but what the Negro can never forget — is that white society is deeply implicated in the ghetto. White institutions created it, white institutions maintain it, and white society condones it. . . .

We cannot escape responsibility for choosing the future of our metropolitan areas and the human relations which develop within them. . . .

Excerpt from the National Advisory Committee on Civil Disorders, 1968

4. The "division" after World War II referred to in the excerpt resulted most directly from
- **a.** suburbanization.
- **b.** economic growth.
- **c.** growing public confidence in government's ability to solve social problems.
- **d.** the baby boom.

5. The excerpt most directly demonstrates that after World War II
- **a.** liberals sought greater changes to society.
- **b.** conservatives resisted a perceived moral and cultural decline.
- **c.** Lyndon Johnson's Great Society program ended social conflict over race.
- **d.** free trade agreements improved social mobility in the United States.

6. The excerpt can best be understood as originating most directly from
- **a.** persistent economic inequality.
- **b.** nationwide efforts of the Ku Klux Klan.
- **c.** the protest tactics of the civil rights movement.
- **d.** political efforts of newly politicized Protestant evangelicalism.

TRM Find complete suggested responses in the Teacher's Resource Materials.

SHORT ANSWER QUESTIONS

Read each question carefully and write a short response. Use evidence from the text to support your claims.

"The conflict between [Martin Luther King Jr. and Ella Baker] reveals more fundamental conflicts between black politics and African American culture over the meanings of American democracy and the pathways toward social change. . . . Baker described [King] as a pampered member of Atlanta's black elite . . . a member of a coddled 'silver spoon brigade.' . . . In Baker's eyes, King did not identify closely enough with the people he sought to lead. He did not situate himself among them but remained above them. . . . Baker and King . . . translated religious faith into their political identities in profoundly different ways. Above all, they defined the confluence of their roles as individuals and their roles as participants in a mass movement for social change quite distinctly. Baker was a militant egalitarian, and King was a sophisticated southern Baptist preacher."

Barbara Ransby, *Ella Baker and the Black Freedom Movement*, 2003

"By 1965, King's radical voice rang more clearly when he confessed that his dream had turned into a 'nightmare.' The dream shattered when whites murdered voting rights workers in Alabama, when police battled blacks in Los Angeles, when he met jobless and 'hopeless' blacks on desperate Chicago streets, and when he saw hunger and poverty in rural Mississippi and Appalachia. But King picked up the shards of his shattered dreams and reassembled them into more radical visions of emancipation for all poor people. . . . Dreams of decent jobs, affordable integrated housing, and adequate family incomes remained central to King's public ministry until his death."

Thomas F. Jackson, *From Civil Rights to Human Rights: Martin Luther King, Jr., and the Struggle for Economic Justice*, 2013

1. Using the two excerpts provided, answer (a), (b), and (c).
   - **a.** Briefly explain ONE major difference between Ransby's and Jackson's historical interpretations of Martin Luther King Jr.'s leadership within the civil rights movement.
   - **b.** Briefly explain how ONE specific event, development, or circumstance not directly mentioned in the excerpts could be used to support Ransby's argument.
   - **c.** Briefly explain how ONE specific event, development, or circumstance not directly mentioned in the excerpts could be used to support Jackson's argument.
2. Answer (a), (b), and (c).
   - **a.** Briefly explain why ONE of the following developments was the most significant factor in advancing racial equality in the U.S. from 1950 to 1970.
     - *Brown v. Board of Education* decision
     - Nonviolent protest tactics
     - The Civil Rights Act of 1964
   - **b.** Explain ONE specific historical event or development to support your argument in (a).
   - **c.** Briefly explain why ONE of the other options is less convincing as a significant factor in advancing racial equality.
3. Answer (a), (b), and (c).
   - **a.** Briefly explain ONE important historical difference in the civil rights struggle of American Indians from the civil rights struggle of Asian Americans in the period 1941–1973.
   - **b.** Briefly explain ONE important historical similarity between the civil rights struggle of American Indians to the civil rights struggle of Asian Americans in the period 1941–1973.
   - **c.** Briefly explain ONE important historical factor that accounts for EITHER the similarity OR the difference that you indicated in (a) or (b).

27 CHAPTER Liberal Crisis and Conservative Rebirth 1961–1972

Chapter 27 — AP® Assessment Weight and Pacing Guide

The assessment weight on the AP® U.S. History Exam for Chapters 23–28 is 10–17 percent. This chapter falls in Unit 8 of the AP® U.S. History Curriculum, covering Period 8: 1945–1980.

This pacing guide is based on a schedule with 120 sessions of 50 minutes each before the AP® U.S. History Exam. If you have a different number of sessions before the exam, you can modify the pacing to meet your needs. If you have additional time, consider incorporating quizzes, released AP® U.S. History questions, practice exams, writing practice, and other instructional activities.

	Traditional Schedule	Block Schedule
Chapter 27	4 days	2 days

Daily Pacing Guide

	Content Focus	Essential Question
Day 1	Liberalism at High Tide	Why was there a surge in liberal politics and social policy in the early 1960s?
Day 2	The Vietnam War Begins	What factors led President Johnson to escalate the war in Vietnam, and how did Americans respond?
Day 3	Days of Rage, 1968–1972	What factors best explain the rising militancy of social change and protest movements in 1968 and afterward?
Day 4	Rise of the Silent Majority	What social issues divided Americans in the early 1970s, and how did those divisions affect the two major political parties?

AP® Alignment

Section Heading	AP® Topic	AP® Theme
Liberalism at High Tide	8.9, 8.10, 8.11	PCE, MIG, SOC
The Vietnam War Begins	8.5, 8.8, 8.12	ARC, WOR
Days of Rage, 1968–1972	8.11, 8.12, 8.14	SOC, ARC, PCE
Rise of the Silent Majority	8.8, 8.10, 8.14	WOR, PCE

*Should changes be made to the Course Framework in the future, an updated alignment will be placed on our AP® updates page at go.bfwpub.com/ap-course-updates.

Chapter 27 — Overview

Chapter 27 juxtaposes the victory of liberalism in the Great Society with the escalation of the Vietnam War between 1961 and 1972, which ultimately undermined the confidence of the American public in both foreign and domestic policy. The chapter begins with an analysis of the victory of liberalism beginning with the administration of John F. Kennedy and culminating in the Great Society in the administration of Lyndon Johnson. As the conflict in the Vietnam War escalated, Johnson's administration lost public support and the Democratic Party lost members to the Republicans, resulting in the victory of conservatism with Richard Nixon's election in 1968. Nixon took office indicating a change in policy in Vietnam with Vietnamization; however, the scope of the war expanded to include neighboring countries and the antiwar movement continued to grow.

Chapter 27 — Resources

The following resources can be found in the Teacher's Resource Materials (TRM) that accompany the book. You can access the TRM via the book's digital platform, by clicking the TRM links found here in your Teacher's Edition e-book, or by contacting your representative to access the resources online. Visit **bfwpub.com/henretta10e** to learn more.

TRM Chapter 27 Lecture Presentation Slides

TRM Chapter 27 Outline with AP® Focus

TRM Chapter 27 Lecture Strategies

TRM Chapter 27 Suggested Responses

TRM Handout 27.1 — Causation: Great Society

TRM Handout 27.2 — Contextualization: *The Feminine Mystique*

TRM Handout 27.3 — Contextualization: Tet Offensive

Chapter 27 — Essential Activity

Assign students to complete the **AP® THINKING LIKE A HISTORIAN** feature on pp. 886–887 as homework. Then lead a class discussion on the evidence provided in the documents regarding the causes for U.S. commitment to fighting the Vietnam War as well as the effects of Vietnam on domestic conflicts in the U.S. Then organize students into collaborative groups and provide them with a copy of the Port Huron Statement (1962) by Students for a Democratic Society. Have students read the document and outline the arguments expressed by the left. Then provide them with a copy of excerpts from Ronald Reagan's "A Time for Choosing" speech at the 1964 Republican National Convention as evidence of the right's criticism. Students should discuss the ways in which the right and left differ in their criticisms of the U.S. government and society.

Chapter 27 — Bell Ringers

The following activities take no more than 5–15 minutes of your class period and offer an effective and engaging way to begin your lessons and for students to apply AP® Skills & Processes:

- Provide students with two images: one of the Buddhist monk's self-immolation in Vietnam and the other, the image of the dead student on the campus of Kent State. Ask students to explain the similarities and differences between these images. Lead a discussion on the discontent with the American Vietnam War policy both in the U.S. and in Vietnam.
- Ask students to analyze the image on p. 898 and provide them with eyewitness accounts of the "hard hat riot" in New York City in 1970 at Pace University. Search "GMU Hard Hat Riot" for an account and images. Ask students to contextualize the image(s) and accounts as illustrations of the diverging beliefs of the left and the right in the U.S.

NOTES

TEACHING STRATEGY

The 1960s was a turbulent time in American history as people across the political spectrum struggled to reach consensus over what America's goals ought to be at home and abroad. More than a half-century later, the 1960s remains a cultural touchstone for those who protested, those who opposed the protesters, and the majority who watched with concern from the sidelines. For a complete suggested response to the **AP® LEARNING FOCUS** question, see p. 902.

27 CHAPTER

Liberal Crisis and Conservative Rebirth

1961–1972

AP® LEARNING FOCUS

Why did debates over liberal values in the 1960s lead to social conflict and divide the country?

The civil rights movement pushed American liberals to launch new government initiatives to advance racial equality. That progressive spirit grew in scope to inspire an expansive reform agenda that included women's rights, new social programs for the poor and the aged, job training, environmental laws, and other educational and social benefits for the middle class. All told, Congress passed more liberal legislation between 1964 and 1972 than in any period since the 1930s. The 1965–1966 legislative session, one of the most active ever, marked liberalism's high tide as the dominant ideology of American political life in the twentieth century.

But liberalism soon found itself under fire from two directions. Within liberalism itself, young activists grew frustrated with slow progress on civil rights and the Cold War logic driving America's presence in Vietnam. At the 1968 Democratic National Convention in Chicago, police teargassed and clubbed antiwar demonstrators, who chanted (as the TV cameras rolled), "The whole world is watching!" The chaos in Chicago — in the streets and inside the convention hall — became a symbol of liberalism's fracture.

The second assault came from the right, regaining momentum after two decades on the margins. Conservatives opposed the dramatic expansion of the federal government under President Lyndon B. Johnson and disdained liberalism for encouraging what they deemed a "permissive society." Embracing law and order, scorning welfare, and resisting key civil rights reforms, conservatives found new political life in the sixties. Their champion was Barry Goldwater, a Republican senator from Arizona, who warned that "a government big enough to give you everything you want is also big enough to take away everything you have."

The years from President John Kennedy's inauguration in 1961 to President Richard Nixon's landslide reelection in 1972 proved one of the most complicated, and combustible, eras in American history. From left to center to right, the entire political spectrum hummed with action and conflict. There were thousands of marches and demonstrations; massive new federal programs aimed at achieving civil rights, ending poverty, and extending the welfare state; new voices demanding to be heard; and heated rhetoric on all sides. Political assassinations and violence, both overseas and at home, heightened the volatile mood. The liberal triumphs of the mid-1960s soon gave way to a profound crisis and the resurgence of conservatism.

870

"I Want Out" Protest movements of all kinds shook the foundations of American society and national politics in the 1960s. No issue was more controversial and divisive than the war in Vietnam. Private Collection/Peter Newark American Pictures/ Bridgeman Images.

TEACHING STRATEGY

To fully appreciate the rhetoric of this poster, students should place it side by side with the original World War I recruitment poster. Guide students' analysis with the following questions:

- **How do the two posters differ?** *Uncle Sam is visibly wounded, with his head and hand covered in gauze and the shoulder of his jacket torn. His face looks weak and desperate, rather than confident. Rather than pointing to the viewer, he is reaching out to the viewer for help. The poster is no longer a call for recruitment ("I Want YOU"), but a plea to be rescued ("I Want OUT").*
- **What message does this poster communicate about the Vietnam War?** *The poster suggests that the war has made the U.S. weak and desperate, and the only appropriate response would be to exit the war as quickly as possible.*
- **How might supporters of the war have reacted to this poster?** *Supporters might have viewed the poster as disrespectful and disloyal. They might have argued that the lack of support from people like those who created the poster was the very reason the country was weak.*

AP® SKILLS & PROCESSES

CONTINUITY AND CHANGE

Use the **TIMELINE** to help students begin thinking about how the period from 1963 to 1975 could constitute a distinct historical period. Students may note that the timeline has slightly different starting and ending dates from the chapter periodization. This is actually an opportune time to discuss how historians determine chronological frameworks to understand broad developments. The timeline begins with the assassination of John F. Kennedy in 1963, which reflects Kennedy's relatively limited influence. The chapter periodization ends in 1972, reflecting the landslide reelection of Nixon and the shift from the liberalism of the 1960s to a new period of conservatism. The timeline extends a bit further, primarily to display events related to the Communist victory in Vietnam.

AP® THEME

PCE: Politics and Power

Liberalism, based on a firm belief in the efficacy of government power to achieve social goals at home, reached a high point of political influence in the mid-1960s. Nothing better illustrated the optimism of the decade and the hope that the federal government could improve society than the election of Kennedy. Much of his appeal resided in the attractiveness and sense of glamor of him and the First Lady. In honor of the centennial of Kennedy's birth in 2017, the Smithsonian hosted several exhibits with photos, artwork, and artifacts that celebrated Kennedy, his accomplishments, and his compelling image. To access this site, search "Smithsonian John F. Kennedy."

TEACHING STRATEGY

President Johnson considered President Franklin D. Roosevelt one of his political mentors. The New Deal concentrated more on economic and political reform, as opposed to social reform. Consider starting the chapter with a retrospective look at what social issues remained at the end of the New Deal, despite an increase in government programs. As students read and study the programs of the Great Society, have students explain the extent to which the Great Society addressed the shortcomings of the New Deal.

TIMELINE

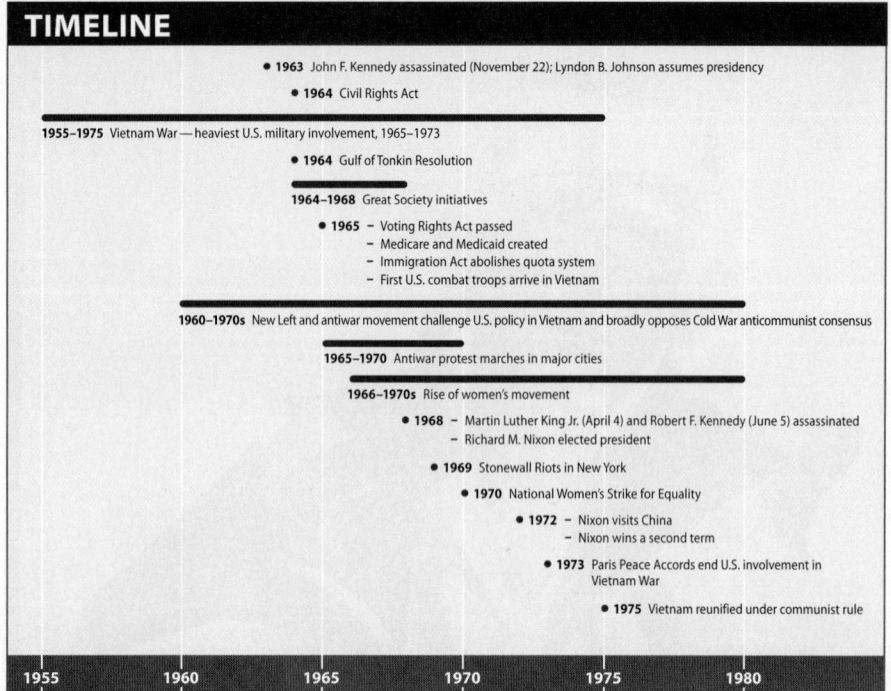

- **1963** John F. Kennedy assassinated (November 22); Lyndon B. Johnson assumes presidency
- **1964** Civil Rights Act
- **1955–1975** Vietnam War — heaviest U.S. military involvement, 1965–1973
- **1964** Gulf of Tonkin Resolution
- **1964–1968** Great Society initiatives
- **1965**
  - Voting Rights Act passed
  - Medicare and Medicaid created
  - Immigration Act abolishes quota system
  - First U.S. combat troops arrive in Vietnam
- **1960–1970s** New Left and antiwar movement challenge U.S. policy in Vietnam and broadly opposes Cold War anticommunist consensus
- **1965–1970** Antiwar protest marches in major cities
- **1966–1970s** Rise of women's movement
- **1968**
  - Martin Luther King Jr. (April 4) and Robert F. Kennedy (June 5) assassinated
  - Richard M. Nixon elected president
- **1969** Stonewall Riots in New York
- **1970** National Women's Strike for Equality
- **1972**
  - Nixon visits China
  - Nixon wins a second term
- **1973** Paris Peace Accords end U.S. involvement in Vietnam War
- **1975** Vietnam reunified under communist rule

1955 1960 1965 1970 1975 1980

LIBERALISM AT HIGH TIDE

Why was there a surge in liberal politics and social policy in the early 1960s?

Great Society
President Lyndon B. Johnson's domestic program, aimed at ending poverty, increasing individual opportunity, and enhancing national culture, which included civil rights legislation, antipoverty programs, medical insurance, aid to education, consumer protection, and aid to the arts and humanities.

In May 1964, President Lyndon B. Johnson delivered the commencement address at the University of Michigan. LBJ, as he was widely known, had only been president for six months, but he had already developed a bold vision. "We have the opportunity to move not only toward the rich society and the powerful society," he said, "but upward to the **Great Society**." As the graduates listened, Johnson described a grand objective for liberalism: "The Great Society rests on abundance and liberty for all. It demands an end to poverty and racial injustice." And this, Johnson declared, was just the beginning. He would push to renew American education, rebuild the cities, and restore the natural environment — an ambitions renewal of the New Deal's social promise. Johnson's idea was certainly ambitious, if not audacious. The path to the Great Society had started with a tragedy, however: the assassination of Johnson's predecessor in the White House.

John F. Kennedy's Promise

In 1961, three years before Johnson's Great Society speech, John F. Kennedy had voiced a different but equally lofty idea in his inaugural speech. "Let the word go forth from this time and place, to friend and foe alike," he declared, "that the torch has been passed to a new generation of Americans." He challenged his fellow citizens to "ask what you can do for your country," a call to service that inspired many Americans, particularly a generation coming of age in the Cold War. The British journalist Henry Fairlie called Kennedy's activism "the politics of expectation." These "expectations" kindled an emerging spirit of liberal reform.

Kennedy's legislative record did not live up to his promising image. This was not entirely his fault. Like many twentieth-century presidents, he faced divisions within his own party, resistance from the opposing party, and a slow-moving Congress. The Kennedy administration did not want for ideas, however. The president's domestic advisors devised bold plans for health insurance for the aged, a new antipoverty program, and a tax cut. After enormous pressure from civil rights leaders — and pushed by the demonstrations in Birmingham, Alabama, in April and May 1963 — they added a civil rights bill. None of these initiatives went anywhere in the Senate, where powerful conservatives, many of them from Kennedy's own Democratic Party, used delaying tactics. As the autumn rolled around, all of Kennedy's major bills were stalled.

In late November, the president traveled to Texas to meet with local leaders and raise campaign funds for 1964. The events of his fateful visit to Dallas would upend the political landscape. On the way to a luncheon, Kennedy and his wife Jacqueline (known as "Jackie") rode in an open car through the city's downtown. As the motorcade passed under the windows of the Texas School Book Depository, a sniper inside fired shots that struck Kennedy in the head and neck. The young president died within the hour. The accused killer, twenty-four-year-old Lee Harvey Oswald, was himself assassinated two days later while in police custody by Dallas nightclub owner Jack Ruby. Before Air Force One left Dallas to take the president's body back to Washington, a grim-faced Lyndon Johnson was sworn in as Kennedy's successor.

A sense of loss swept the nation in the wake of the assassination, heightened in part by Kennedy's youthful image and popularity. The Kennedy White House was the center of a glamorous "Camelot," where power, celebrity, and high fashion mixed. An admiring country saw in Jack and Jackie an ideal American marriage, even though JFK was in fact an obsessive womanizer. The forty-six-year-old president was celebrated for his robust health, but secretly suffered from a rare endocrine condition and chronic back pain from war injuries. Even though Camelot was a fantasy, the Kennedys' popularity was real — and proved that image mattered as much as reality in conducting the modern presidency. Kennedy took on an even more profound mystique after death.

AP® EXAM TIP

Recognizing the expression of liberal ideas in Lyndon Johnson's Great Society is critical for success on the AP® Exam.

Lyndon B. Johnson and the Great Society

In many ways, Lyndon Johnson was the opposite of Kennedy. A seasoned Texas politician and long-time Senate leader, Johnson was most at home in the back rooms of power. He was a rough-edged character who had scrambled his way up, with few scruples, to wealth and political eminence. Even after he attained considerable power, LBJ never forgot his modest origins in the hill-country of Texas or lost his sympathy for the downtrodden. Johnson lacked his predecessor's style and pedigree, but his astonishing energy and negotiating skills proved far more effective at getting legislation through Congress.

The Great Society President Lyndon Johnson toured poverty-stricken regions of the country in 1964. Here he visits with Tom Fletcher, a father of eight children in Martin County, Kentucky. Johnson envisioned a dramatic expansion of liberal social programs, both to assist the needy and to strengthen the middle class, that he called the Great Society. Bettmann/Getty Images.

TEACHING STRATEGY

The Kennedy Library provides a variety of resources that offer more information about the Kennedy assassination, including details of the Dallas trip, the funeral, and Johnson's takeover. To access these resources, search "Kennedy Library death of the President."

CHECK FOR UNDERSTANDING

Ask students: **What made John F. Kennedy's election promising to many Americans?** *Kennedy embodied expectations for the country, inspired a younger generation of Americans, and encouraged the spirit of liberalism. This perception was in part a result of careful management of Kennedy's image that conveyed the sense that he had the ideal marriage, epitomized health, and engendered a world of glamor, fashion, and celebrity.*

AP® APPLY THE TIP

Provide students with an excerpt from Lyndon Johnson's Great Society speech. Read the excerpt as a class and discuss the liberal philosophy underlying Johnson's view of American society and economy in the 1960s. Then direct students' attention to **TABLE 27.1** on p. 875 and ask students to evaluate the list of laws passed in the Great Society and organize them into a "Top 10 Liberal Ideas" list. Students should select 10 of the 18 laws from the list and organize them from least (10) to most (1) liberal. Once students have created their lists, organize the class into groups of 4–5 students. In small groups, students should compare their "Top 10" lists and discuss their differences in the evaluation of liberal ideas in the Great Society. Each group should create a single "Top 10 Liberal Ideas" list and write its top 3 on poster paper to post in the classroom. Then each group should present its top 3 and explain why they are the most liberal ideas. Lead a class discussion on the following questions (*answers will vary*):

- What are the most important characteristics of liberalism in the 1960s?
- What do the top laws on all the lists have in common?
- What other periods of American history were similar in goals and methods to the liberal era of the 1960s?
- What features of these laws might lead to challenges from conservatives in the U.S.?

AP® THEME

PCE: Politics and Power

Students should understand how liberal ideas found expression in Lyndon Johnson's Great Society, which attempted to use federal legislation and programs to end racial discrimination, eliminate poverty, and address other social issues.

On assuming the presidency, Johnson promptly pushed for civil rights legislation, pitching the reforms as a memorial to his slain predecessor. His motives were complex. As a southerner who had previously opposed civil rights for African Americans, Johnson wanted to demonstrate that he would be the president for all the people. He also wanted to make a mark on history — a noble gesture but also one fed by Johnson's considerable sense of self-importance. Politically, the move was risky. It would please the Democratic Party's liberal wing, but as most northern African Americans already voted Democratic, few additional votes would be gained. In the South, many votes might be lost if conservative white Democrats revolted. Nationally, the drive for a civil rights act threatened to undermine party unity at a critical moment for the president's broader agenda. But Johnson forged ahead, and the 1964 Civil Rights Act stands as a testament to the president's political daring and the black freedom movement's determination.

More than civil rights, Johnson's political passion was a determination to "end poverty in our time." In the midst of plenty, one-fifth of all Americans — hidden from most people's sight in Appalachia, urban ghettos, migrant labor camps, and Indian reservations — lived in poverty. Johnson saw this privation as a national disgrace but not a permanent one. He declared, "for the first time in our history, it is possible to conquer poverty." The **Economic Opportunity Act** of 1964, passed by congress at Johnson's urging, created a series of programs to help the poorest Americans in what LBJ named "the War on Poverty."

Economic Opportunity Act
A 1964 law that was the centerpiece of President Lyndon Johnson's War on Poverty. It included programs such as Head Start (free nursery school), Job Corps (job training for young people), and regional development programs to spur economic growth.

This legislation included several different initiatives. A program called Head Start provided free nursery schools to prepare disadvantaged preschoolers for kindergarten, while the Job Corps and Upward Bound provided young people with training and employment. Volunteers in Service to America (VISTA), modeled on JFK's Peace Corps, offered technical assistance to the urban and rural poor. An array of regional development programs focused on spurring economic growth in impoverished areas. Overall, the 1964 legislation did more to provide services to the poor than to create jobs, which led some critics to say it treated the symptoms of poverty rather than the underlying cause. Because of such limitations, the War on Poverty had an uneven legacy, but for the first time since the New Deal the federal government had made reducing poverty a national priority.

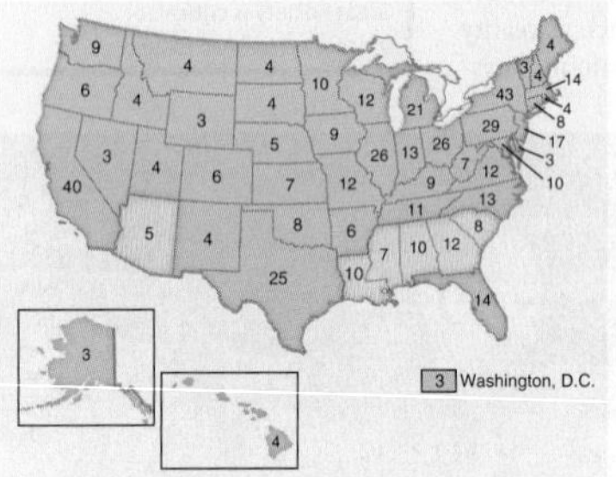

Candidate	Electoral Vote	Popular Vote	Percent of Popular Vote
Lyndon B. Johnson (Democrat)	486	43,121,085	61.1
Barry M. Goldwater (Republican)	52	27,145,161	38.5

MAP 27.1 The Presidential Election of 1964
This map reveals how one-sided was the victory of Lyndon Johnson over Barry Goldwater in 1964. Except for Arizona, his home state, Goldwater won only five states in the Deep South — not of much immediate consolation to him, but a sure indicator that the South was cutting its historic ties to the Democratic Party. Moreover, although soundly rejected in 1964, Goldwater's far-right critique of "big government" laid the foundation for a Republican resurgence in the 1980s.

The 1964 Election With the Civil Rights Act passed and his War on Poverty initiatives off the ground, Johnson turned his attention to the upcoming presidential election. Not content to deliver on the unfulfilled promise of JFK, he sought an electoral mandate of his own. Privately, Johnson saw himself as the heir not of Kennedy but Franklin Roosevelt and the expansive liberalism of the 1930s. He reminded his advisors never to forget "the meek and the humble and the lowly," because "President Roosevelt never did."

In the 1964 election, Johnson faced Republican senator Barry Goldwater of Arizona. The archconservative Goldwater ran on an anticommunist, antigovernment platform. Positioning himself as an alternative to liberalism, Goldwater campaigned against the Civil Rights Act of 1964 and promised a more vigorous Cold War foreign policy. Goldwater's strident international outlook alienated many voters — he believed, for instance, that American generals and the NATO commander should have authorization to deploy nuclear weapons. "Extremism in the defense of liberty is no vice," he had declared at the nominating convention. There remained strong national sentiment for Kennedy, and Johnson and his running mate Hubert H. Humphrey of Minnesota were happy to position themselves as fulfilling Kennedy's legacy. Johnson and Humphrey won in a landslide, garnering more than 60 percent of the popular vote (Map 27.1). Although Goldwater was soundly defeated, his candidacy marked the beginning of a

TEACHING STRATEGY

The *Washington Post* provides several retrospectives on Barry Goldwater from various perspectives that were offered at the time of his death in 1998. The site also provides the text of his famous 1964 acceptance speech for nomination as the GOP's presidential candidate. To access these resources, search "Washington Post Goldwater Remembered."

AP® SKILLS & PROCESSES

ANALYZING HISTORICAL EVIDENCE

Since the time of Andrew Jackson, the so-called "Solid South" was a stronghold for Democrats, with few exceptions. However, in 1964, the Deep South voted for the Republican candidate. Ask students to explain at least one historical factor that explains this development.

TABLE 27.1

Major Great Society Legislation		
Civil Rights		
1964	Twenty-fourth Amendment Civil Rights Act	Outlawed poll tax in federal elections Banned discrimination in employment and public accommodations on the basis of race, religion, sex, or national origin
1965	Voting Rights Act	Outlawed literacy tests for voting; provided federal supervision of registration in historically low-registration areas
Social Welfare		
1964	Economic Opportunity Act	Created Office of Economic Opportunity (OEO) to administer War on Poverty programs such as Head Start, Job Corps, and Volunteers in Service to America (VISTA)
1965	Medical Care Act	Provided medical care for the poor (Medicaid) and the elderly (Medicare)
1966	Minimum Wage Act	Raised hourly minimum wage from $1.25 to $1.60 and expanded coverage to new groups
Education		
1965	Elementary and Secondary Education Act National Endowment for the Arts and Humanities Higher Education Act	Granted federal aid for education of poor children Provided federal funding and support for artists and scholars Provided federal scholarships for postsecondary education
Housing and Urban Development		
1964	Urban Mass Transportation Act	Provided federal aid to urban mass transit
1965	Housing and Urban Development Act Omnibus Housing Act	Created Department of Housing and Urban Development (HUD) Provided federal funds for public housing and rent subsidies for low-income families
1966	Metropolitan Area Redevelopment and Demonstration Cities Acts	Designated 150 "model cities" for combined programs of public housing, social services, and job training
Environment		
1964	Wilderness Preservation Act	Designated 9.1 million acres of federal lands as "wilderness areas," barring future roads, buildings, or commercial use
1965	Air and Water Quality Acts	Set tougher air quality standards; required states to enforce water quality standards for interstate waters
Miscellaneous		
1964	Tax Reduction Act	Reduced personal and corporate income tax rates
1965	Immigration Act Appalachian Regional Development Act	Abandoned national quotas of 1924 law, allowing more non-European immigration Provided federal funding for roads, health clinics, and other public works projects in economically depressed regions

grassroots conservative revolt that would eventually transform the Republican Party. In the short run, however, Johnson's sweeping victory gave him a mandate and congressional majorities that rivaled FDR's in 1935 — just what he and liberal Democrats needed to push the Great Society forward (Table 27.1).

Great Society Initiatives One of Johnson's first successes after reelection was breaking a congressional deadlock on education and health care. Passed in April

AP® EXAM TIP

Evaluate the impact of federal legislation designed to address social and economic inequality.

AP® SKILLS & PROCESSES

ANALYZING HISTORICAL EVIDENCE

Ask students to use **TABLE 27.1** to answer the following questions:

- **Which laws had direct precedents in the New Deal?** *Antipoverty programs had direct precedents in the New Deal, most notably the first federal minimum wage law, the Fair Labor Standards Act. Medicare was an extension of Social Security. The National Endowment for the Arts and Humanities echoed arts, writing, and theater programs from the WPA. Even the model cities plan was anticipated by a handful of model communities planned during the New Deal, most notably Greenbelt, Maryland.*
- **How are some of the categories addressed in the legislation related?** *Race (as represented in civil rights legislation) and lack of economic opportunity were often related, as civil rights advocates repeatedly pointed out. Since most of the nation's poor, mostly African American, lived in cities, urban housing, in turn, was often closely related to these two issues as well.*
- **What legislation did not have New Deal precedents? What does this legislation indicate about the nature of American society compared with the 1930s?** *The New Deal avoided issues of race, so no civil rights or immigration legislation was passed. In fact, several New Deal acts had provisions that discriminated against African Americans de facto. The increased activism of civil rights groups created the impetus for addressing this issue in the 1960s. While the New Deal had flood control provisions, there were no laws targeting air and water quality. Americans became increasingly aware of issues of pollution in the postwar period. In some ways, the Great Society was even more ambitious than the New Deal, reflecting the optimism of a major reform effort undertaken in the midst of an era of prosperity, rather than a time of massive recession.*

AP® APPLY THE TIP

To help students understand the impact of Great Society legislation, ask them to use pp. 873-877 to complete **Handout 27.1 — Causation: Great Society (TRM)**. Then prompt students to research the impact of Great Society programs on the U.S. today. Ask students to create a "Then and Now" poster on the Great Society that illustrates its continuing impact on the U.S. Display the posters and use them to lead a discussion on the Great Society.

TRM Find **Handout 27.1 — Causation: Great Society** in the Teacher's Resource Materials.

1965, the Elementary and Secondary Education Act authorized $1 billion in federal funds for teacher training and other educational programs. Standing in the Texas schoolhouse where he had once taught, Johnson said: "I believe no law I have signed or will ever sign means more to the future of America." Six months later, Johnson signed the Higher Education Act, providing federal scholarships for college students. Johnson also had the votes he needed to achieve a form of national health insurance, which came later in the busy year of 1965 when he won passage of two new programs: **Medicare**, a health plan for the elderly funded by a surcharge on Social Security payroll taxes, and **Medicaid**, a health plan for the poor paid for by general tax revenues and administered by the states.

Medicare
A health plan for the elderly passed in 1965 and funded by a surcharge on Social Security payroll taxes.

Medicaid
A health plan for the poor passed in 1965 and paid for by general tax revenues and administered by the states.

The Great Society's agenda included environmental reform as well: an expanded national park system, a cleanup of the nation's air and water, protection for endangered species, stronger land-use planning, and highway beautification. Hardly pausing for breath, Johnson oversaw the creation of the Department of Housing and Urban Development (HUD); won funding for hundreds of thousands of units of public housing; secured federal support for urban mass transportation, such as the new Washington, D.C. Metro and the Bay Area Rapid Transit (BART) system in San Francisco; ushered child safety and consumer protection laws through Congress; and helped create the National Endowment for the Arts and the National Endowment for the Humanities.

There was even sufficient reform zeal to tackle the nation's discriminatory immigration policy. The Immigration Act of 1965 dismantled the quota system that favored northern Europeans, replacing it with numerical limits that did not discriminate among nations of origin. To promote family reunification, the law also stipulated that close relatives of legal residents in the United States could be admitted outside those numerical limits, an exception that helped make Asian and Latin American immigrants a more prominent part of American society after 1965.

AP® EXAM TIP
Evaluate the impact of Great Society programs on American identity and the power of the federal government.

Assessing the Great Society The Great Society's goals were too grand, and its scope too broad, to realize total success. But a number of positive changes occurred in the wake of the Great Society initiatives. The proportion of Americans living below the poverty line dropped from 20 percent to 13 percent between 1963 and 1968 (Figure 27.1). Millions of African Americans moved into the middle class, and the poverty rate among black people fell by half. Medicare and Medicaid, the most enduring of the Great Society programs, helped millions of elderly

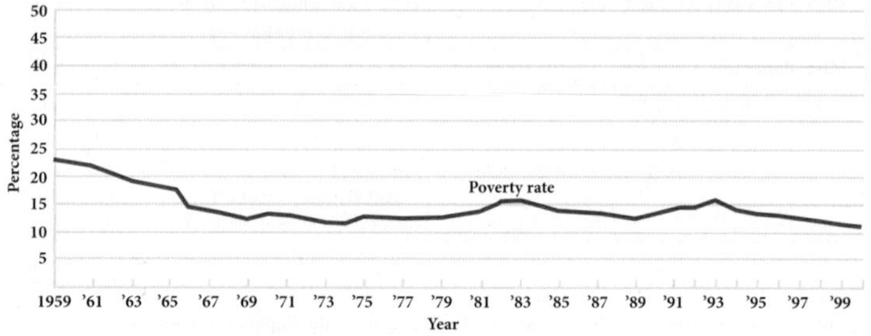

FIGURE 27.1 Americans in Poverty, 1959–2000
Between 1959 and 1973 the poverty rate among American families dropped by more than half—from 23 percent to 11 percent. There was, however, sharp disagreement about the reasons for that notable decline. Liberals credited the War on Poverty, while conservatives favored the high-performing economy, with the significant poverty dip of 1965–1966 caused by military spending, not Johnson's domestic programs.

AP® THEME

GEO: Geography and the Environment
Environmental problems and accidents led to a growing environmental movement that aimed to use legislation and public efforts to combat pollution and protect natural resources. The federal government established new environmental programs and regulations. The National Park Service's publication *Lyndon B. Johnson and the Environment* provides a helpful overview of the more than two dozen pieces of environmental legislation Johnson helped pass in his time as president. To access this site, search "NPS Johnson and the Environment."

AP® THEME

MIG: Migration and Settlement
Immigrants from around the world sought access to the political, social, and economic opportunities in the U.S., especially after the passage of the Immigration Act of 1965. This act illustrates the momentous effects that sometimes emerge from one event. It also explains the historical idea of unintended consequences. In his article titled "The Immigration Act That Inadvertently Changed America" in *The Atlantic*, Tom Gjelten argues that the Immigration Act of 1965 has dramatically—and unintentionally—reshaped the American landscape. To access this article, search "Atlantic Immigration Act."

and poor citizens access necessary health care. Early education set up children for success. American society became more diverse, as did schools, workplaces, and the public sector. Liberals believed they were on the right track. Conservatives were skeptical. They attributed these positive changes to a booming economy rather than government initiatives and spending. Indeed, critics on the right accused Johnson and other liberals of trying to solve every social problem with a government program.

In the final analysis, the Great Society dramatically improved the financial situation of the elderly, reached millions of children, and increased the racial diversity of American society and workplaces. However, entrenched poverty remained, racial segregation in the largest cities worsened, and the national distribution of wealth remained highly skewed. In relative terms, the bottom 20 percent remained as far behind as ever. In these arenas, the Great Society made little progress.

AP® SKILLS & PROCESSES

CONTEXTUALIZATION

What new roles did the federal government assume under Great Society initiatives, and how did they extend the New Deal tradition?

Rebirth of the Women's Movement

In the new era of liberal reform the women's movement reawakened. Inspired by the civil rights movement and Great Society liberalism, but critical of the lack of attention both gave to women's rights, feminists entered the political fray. A reenergized women's movement demanded not just inclusion but a rethinking of national priorities (see "Comparing Interpretations," p. 878).

AP® EXAM TIP

Evaluate the ways in which the feminism in the 1950s and 1960s illustrated continuity and change in comparison to earlier eras of American history.

Labor Feminists Even as a traditional domestic ideal dominated the postwar decades, the push for gender equity did not languish entirely. Feminist concerns were kept alive in the 1950s and early 1960s by working women, who campaigned for such policies as maternity leave and equal pay for equal work. One historian has called these women "labor feminists," because they belonged to trade unions and fought for equality and dignity in the workplace. "It became apparent to me why so many employers could legally discriminate against women — because it was written right into the law," said one such activist. Women in trade unions proved critical in the push to pass the **Equal Pay Act** in 1963, which mandated that men and women performing the same job receive the same compensation.

The increasing voice of labor feminism reflected the changing times. An unprecedented number of women — including married women (40 percent by 1970) and mothers with young children (30 percent by 1970) — were working outside the home. But they faced a labor market that undervalued their contributions. Many working women faced the "double day": they were expected to earn a paycheck and then return home to domestic labor. One woman put the problem succinctly: "The working mother has no 'wife' to care for her children."

Equal Pay Act
Law passed in 1963 that established the principle of equal pay for equal work. Trade-union women were especially critical in pushing for, and winning, congressional passage of the law.

AP® SKILLS & PROCESSES

CAUSATION

What factors accounted for the resurgence of feminism in the 1960s?

Betty Friedan and the National Organization for Women The political power of feminism was not limited to the working class. When Betty Friedan's indictment of suburban domesticity, a book entitled ***The Feminine Mystique***, appeared in 1963, it targeted college-educated, middle-class women who found themselves not working for wages but rather stifled by their domestic routines. Hundreds of thousands of women read Friedan's book and thought, "She's talking about me." *The Feminine Mystique* became a runaway best-seller, persuading many middle-class women that they needed more than the convenience foods, improved diapers, and better laundry detergents that magazines and television urged them to buy. To live rich and fulfilling lives, they needed education and work outside the home.

The domesticity that Friedan criticized was already beginning to crumble by the time *The Feminine Mystique* appeared. After the postwar baby boom, women were again having fewer children, aided by the birth control pill that first hit the market in 1960. As states liberalized divorce laws, more women were breaking away from

The Feminine Mystique
An influential book by Betty Friedan published in 1963 critiquing the ideal whereby women were encouraged to confine themselves to roles within the domestic sphere.

AP® EXAM TIP

The significance of *The Feminine Mystique* is important to know for the AP® Exam.

AP® SKILLS & PROCESSES

CONTEXTUALIZATION

The **CONTEXTUALIZATION** question asks students to place the Great Society in the larger context of federal reform extending back to the Great Depression. It might be helpful for students to compare the chart on p. 875 with the similar one on p. 718. Students should look for broadly similar thematic laws, not rigidly identical ones.

TRM Find complete suggested responses in the Teacher's Resource Materials.

CHECK FOR UNDERSTANDING

Ask students: **What was Johnson's Great Society and what did it aim to accomplish?** *It attempted to extend to all Americans the high living standard enjoyed by a greater number of Americans in the postwar period. Undertaken in the midst of an age of prosperity, it set an ambitious agenda modeled on the New Deal to reform civil rights, social welfare, education, housing, the environment, and immigration. While the Great Society led to improvements in several areas, it did not completely eradicate problems in any area.*

AP® THEME

SOC: Social Structures; NAT: American and National Identity

Discuss how feminists mobilized behind claims for legal, economic, and social equality in the 1960s and early 1970s.

AP® SKILLS & PROCESSES

CAUSATION

The **CAUSATION** question asks students to indicate the causes of the new wave of feminism in the 1960s. Students should be sure to consider the texts and introduction in the **AP® COMPARING INTERPRETATIONS** feature on pp. 878–879, which addresses this topic directly. It may be helpful for students to think about both the internal factors driving women to protest and the larger context that made protest seem urgent. Students might also compare this movement with the movement of the early twentieth century, again looking at both internal factors and the larger context.

TRM Find complete suggested responses in the Teacher's Resource Materials.

AP® APPLY THE TIP

Ask students to use pp. 877–879 to complete **Handout 27.2 — Contextualization: *The Feminine Mystique* (TRM)**. After completing the handout, discuss the broader historical developments, processes, and events the students identified. Ask students to work in pairs to analyze the sources in the **AP® COMPARING INTERPRETATIONS** feature on pp. 878–879 and answer the questions. As a class, discuss students' responses and ask students to defend each of the historical arguments by citing specific evidence related to feminism.

TRM Find **Handout 27.2 — Contextualization: *The Feminine Mystique*** in the Teacher's Resource Materials.

AP® SKILLS & PROCESSES

ANALYZING HISTORICAL EVIDENCE

Students should establish an important link between the civil rights movement and the growth of feminism, analogous in some ways to the antebellum era, when the women's rights movement emerged out of abolitionist organizing. In this way, there is a connection between the perspective of these two authors included in the **AP® COMPARING INTERPRETATIONS** feature — the notion that the civil rights movement sensitized women to their exploitation as women, though the situation for black women was compounded by racism compared with the situation of white women.

TEACHING STRATEGY

As mentioned in Chapter 25, the *New York Times* provides an excerpt of the most famous passage of the *Feminine Mystique*, from Chapter 1. To access this excerpt, search "NYT excerpt from Feminine Mystique."

TEACHING STRATEGY

As students examine the spectrum of advocates of feminism, think about providing two primary sources, which illustrate some of this breadth. The National Organization for Women (NOW) produced a "Statement of Purpose" in 1966, while the Redstockings wrote a "Manifesto" in 1969. These two documents, available in the public domain, provide a unique contrast in goals and tone for students to analyze.

AP® COMPARING INTERPRETATIONS

What Are the Origins of 1960s Feminism?

The women's rights movement has a long history, but scholars and activists talk about a "second wave" of feminist activism emerging in the 1960s. Unlike early-twentieth-century feminism, which focused on gaining the right to vote for women, this later phase attacked discrimination and gender inequalities in the workplace, in schools, and within the home and marriage. Many scholars argue that the second wave emerged in response to the 1950s "return to domesticity" following World War II, when women were expected to embrace their roles as wives and mothers. Betty Friedan's 1963 book *The Feminine Mystique* critiqued popular depictions of women's domestic roles and argued that gender discrimination limited women's potential.

Friedan's book was a catalyst for many activists who achieved such milestones as the Equal Pay Act, Title IX, and legalized abortion, but are scholars right to locate the movement's origins there? Were all feminist activists in the 1960s shaped by the constraints of domesticity? Sara Evans and Paula Giddings offer contrasting perspectives on 1960s feminism when they highlight the life experiences, work, and class characteristics of different groups of feminists.

SARA EVANS

SOURCE: Sara Evans, *Personal Politics: The Roots of Women's Liberation in the Civil Rights Movement and the New Left* (New York: Alfred A. Knopf, 1979), 19–20, 22–23.

In general, the professional women who created NOW accepted the division between the public and private spheres and chose to seek equality primarily in the public realm. . . . In contrast, however, the oppression of most women centered on their primary definition of themselves as "housewife," whether they worked solely inside the home or also outside it. Although they could vote, go to college, run for office, and enter most professions, women's primary role identification created serious obstacles both internally and in the outside world. Within themselves, women were never sure they could be womanly when not serving and nurturing. And such doubts were reinforced by a long series of experiences: the advice and urging of high school and college counselors; discrimination on the job; pressure from family and friends; a lack of social services such as child care; and social expectations on the job that continually forced women back into traditional roles.

. . . Within the context of cultural unrest and the attack on tradition made by women like Friedan, the catalyst for

unsatisfying domestic lives. Educational levels were also rising: by 1970, women made up 42 percent of the college population. All of these changes undermined traditional gender roles and enabled many women to pursue the liberation called for by Friedan and other feminists.

Presidential Commission on the Status of Women
Commission appointed by President Kennedy in 1961 that issued a 1963 report documenting job and educational discrimination.

Government action also aided feminism's resurgence. In 1961, Kennedy had appointed the **Presidential Commission on the Status of Women**, which issued a 1963 report documenting the extent of gender discrimination in jobs and education. Entitled simply *American Women*, the report struck a middle ground — calling for the elimination of most barriers to women's access to the labor market and higher education while also calling for greater support for women as mothers and caregivers. "We [as a nation] have by no means done enough," the authors of *American Women* wrote, "to strengthen family life and at the same time encourage women to make their full contribution as citizens." A bigger breakthrough came when Congress added the word "sex" to the categories protected against discrimination in Title VII of the Civil Rights Act of 1964. Women suddenly had a powerful legal tool for fighting gender discrimination.

National Organization for Women (NOW)
Women's civil rights organization formed in 1966. Initially, NOW focused on eliminating gender discrimination in public institutions and the workplace, but by the 1970s it also embraced many of the issues raised by more radical feminists.

To push for compliance with the new act, in 1966 Friedan and others, including labor feminists from around the country, founded the **National Organization for Women (NOW)**. Modeled on the NAACP, NOW intended to be a civil rights organization for women, with the aim of bringing "women into full participation in . . . American society now, exercising all the privileges and responsibilities thereof in truly equal partnership with men." Under Friedan's leadership, NOW's membership

878

a profounder criticism and a mass mobilization of American women proved to be the young female participants in the social movements of the 1960s. These daughters of the middle class had received mixed, paradoxical messages about what it meant to grow up to be women in America. On the one hand, the cultural ideal — held up by media, parents, and school — informed them that their only true happiness lay in the twin roles of wife and mother. At the same time they could observe the reality that housewifery was distinctly unsatisfactory for millions of suburban women. . . . Such contradictions left young, educated women in the 1960s dry tinder for the spark of revolt.

The stage was set. Yet the need remains to unravel the mystery of how a few young women stepped outside the assumptions on which they had been raised to articulate a radical critique of women's position in American society. For them, a particular set of experiences in the southern civil rights movement and parts of the student new left catalyzed a new feminist consciousness.

PAULA GIDDINGS

SOURCE: Paula Giddings, *When and Where I Enter: The Impact of Black Women on Race and Sex in America* (New York: William Morrow, 1984), 6–7.

In the course of my research, several themes emerged. One of them, clearly exposed through the experience of Black women, is the relationship between sexism and racism. . . . The means of oppression differed across race and sex lines, but the wellspring of that oppression was the same. Black women understood this dynamic. White women, by and large, did not. White feminists often acquiesced to racist ideology, undermining their own cause in doing so. . . .

Of course, Black women could understand the relationship between racism and sexism because they had to strive against both. In doing so, they became the linchpin between the two most important social reform movements in American history: the struggles for Black rights and women's rights. In the course of defying the imposed limitations on race and sex, they loosened the chains around both.

Throughout their history, Black women also understood the relationship between the progress of the race and their own feminism. Women's rights were an empty promise if Afro-Americans were crushed under the heel of a racist power structure. In times of racial militancy, Black women threw their considerable energies into that struggle — even at the expense of their feminist yearnings. However, when militancy faltered, Black women stepped forward to demand the rights of their race from the larger society, and their rights as women from their men. The latter demand was not seen in the context of race *versus* sex, but as one where their rights had to be secured in order to assure Black progress.

AP SHORT ANSWER PRACTICE

1. How do Evans and Giddings differ in their explanation of the origins and nature of 1960s feminism?
2. To what extent do these scholars see the domestic ideal for women as a factor in shaping second-wave feminism?
3. How does the discussion in Chapters 26 and 27 of the civil rights movement and women's activism shed light on the arguments about the origins of feminism that these two scholars make? Highlight the historical situation of the author's in your claim.

TRM Find complete suggested responses in the Teacher's Resource Materials.

grew to fifteen thousand by 1971, and the group became a powerful voice for equal rights.

One of the ironies of the 1960s was how the surge in liberal activism strained the New Deal coalition. Faced with contradictory demands from the civil rights movement, feminists, the poor, labor unions, white southerners, the suburban middle class, and urban political machines, the venerable and broad Democratic coalition began to fray. Johnson and other national leaders hoped that the center would hold as the party resolved the competing demands of its own constituents while fending off conservative attacks. In 1965, that still seemed possible. But just a few years later, the once-durable coalition would fracture beyond repair.

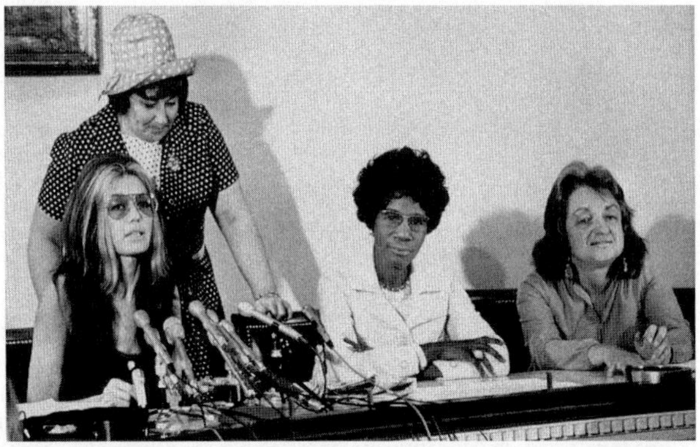

National Women's Political Caucus Leaders of the National Women's Political Caucus speak with the press in 1971. From left to right are activist and journalist Gloria Steinem, Congresswoman Bella Abzug, Congresswoman Shirley Chisholm, and author and activist Betty Friedan. Founded to advance a broad political program on behalf of American women, the Caucus called for reproductive and economic rights, women's social and legal equality, and an increase in women's participation in local, state, and national government. AP Photo/Charles Gorry.

CHECK FOR UNDERSTANDING

Ask students: **What explains the surge in liberal politics and social policy in the early 1960s?** *The civil rights movement spurred American policymakers, especially Lyndon B. Johnson, to embrace a second new deal and expand the reform agenda to a series of programs and policies for women, the poor, the environment, and the middle class.*

AP® THEME

WOR: America in the World

At ten episodes and eighteen hours, the 2017 PBS series *The Vietnam War* by Ken Burns is an epic documentary covering this long, complicated, and controversial war. The film series begins with French colonization of Indochina and ends with the American withdrawal and subsequent memorialization (and selective amnesia) about the war. It gives extensive attention not only to the American experience but also to the experience of Vietnamese soldiers and civilians on both sides of the conflict. To access this documentary, search "PBS Burns Vietnam War."

TEACHING STRATEGY

The Vietnam War Commemoration Web site, sponsored by the U.S. Department of Defense, provides several useful resources for teaching about the war, including high-resolution maps, a detailed interactive timeline, and several primary sources. To access these resources, search "Vietnam War Commemoration."

AP® APPLY THE TIP

To help students understand the expanding role of the president in military actions associated with the Vietnam War, divide the class into collaborative groups and assign each group to investigate the executive actions and decisions in Vietnam made by the following presidents: Harry Truman, Dwight Eisenhower, John F. Kennedy, Lyndon Johnson, and Richard Nixon. Students should be able to clearly explain the executive actions of the president and their relationship to their broader foreign policy. On the board, create a timeline and ask the students to help fill in the details concerning the expanded powers of the president. After adding details to the timeline for each president, provide students with an excerpt from *The Imperial Presidency* by Arthur Schlesinger Jr. Require students to write an analysis that clearly identifies Schlesinger's argument, his evidence, and the ways in which the discussion and timeline from class support the argument.

THE VIETNAM WAR BEGINS

What factors led President Johnson to escalate the war in Vietnam, and how did Americans respond?

As the accelerating rights revolution shook the Democratic coalition, the war in Vietnam rattled the entire country. In a CBS interview back in September 1963, Kennedy had remarked that it was up to the South Vietnamese whether "their war" would be won or lost. But the young president had already placed the United States on a course that could not easily be reversed. Like previous Cold War presidents, Kennedy believed that giving up in Vietnam would weaken America's "credibility" against the spread of communism. American withdrawal would likely mean victory for North Vietnam, and "would be a great mistake," he said.

AP® EXAM TIP

Explain the role of the Vietnam War in expanding the role of the president in military actions.

It is impossible to know how JFK would have managed Vietnam had he lived. What is known is that by the fall of 1963, Kennedy was frustrated with Ngo Dinh Diem, the dictatorial leader of South Vietnam whom the United States had supported since 1955 (see "Making a Commitment in Vietnam" in Chapter 24). The Catholic Diem's tenuous support among the Buddhist South Vietnamese majority had eroded during his eight years in power, and he embraced more and more repressive means to silence his critics. His failed land reform policies fueled detractors as well, turning the loyalty of many peasants to the South Vietnam National Liberation Front (NLF), or Vietcong, which was supported by North Vietnamese communists. Hoping to replace the deeply unpopular Diem with a government strong enough to repel the Vietcong and stabilize the country, Kennedy encouraged Diem's opponents to stage a coup.

It was a miscalculation. Emboldened by Kennedy's approval, a handful of South Vietnamese generals overthrew Diem on November 1, and then brutally killed him and his brother. Rather than stability, the coup brought chaos. South Vietnam fell into even deeper turmoil, with both cities and the countryside increasingly ungovernable. Kennedy himself would not live to see the long-term outcome of the coup: increasing American engagement in a long and costly, perhaps even unwinnable, war in the name of fighting communism.

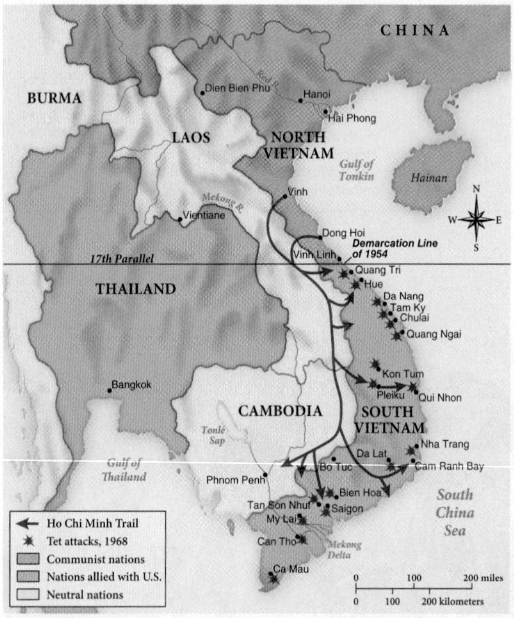

MAP 27.2 The Vietnam War, 1968
The Vietnam War was a guerrilla war, fought in skirmishes rather than set-piece battles. Despite repeated airstrikes, the United States was never able to halt the flow of North Vietnamese troops and supplies down the Ho Chi Minh Trail, which wound through Laos and Cambodia. In January 1968, Vietcong forces launched the Tet offensive, a surprise attack on cities and provincial centers across South Vietnam. Although the attackers were pushed back with heavy losses, the Tet offensive revealed the futility of American efforts to suppress the Vietcong guerrillas and marked a turning point in the war.

Escalation Under Johnson

Just as Kennedy had inherited Vietnam from Eisenhower, Lyndon Johnson inherited Vietnam from Kennedy following the latter's assassination. Johnson's inheritance proved increasingly burdensome, because it became evident that only massive American intervention could prevent the collapse of South Vietnam (Map 27.2). Johnson, like Kennedy, believed in the Cold War tenet of global containment. "I am not going to lose Vietnam," he vowed just days after taking office. "I am not going to be the President who saw Southeast Asia go the way China went."

Gulf of Tonkin Before too long, Johnson would have a chance to back up his rhetoric. During the summer of 1964, the president received reports of attacks by North Vietnamese torpedo boats on the U.S. destroyer *Maddox* in the Gulf of Tonkin. A confrontation on August 2 resulted in a single bullet hole in the *Maddox*. A second reported attack on August 4 later proved to be misread radar sightings. To Johnson, the nature of the attacks mattered little — the first had been provoked by U.S. penetration of Vietnamese waters, and the second attack later proved not to have happened. The president believed a wider war was inevitable and called on Congress to authorize "all necessary measures to repel any armed attack against the forces of the United States and to prevent further aggression." In the entire Congress, only two senators voted against his request. The **Gulf of Tonkin Resolution**, as it became known, gave Johnson unlimited authority in conducting operations in Vietnam.

Gulf of Tonkin Resolution
Resolution passed by Congress in 1964 in the wake of a naval confrontation in the Gulf of Tonkin between the United States and North Vietnam. It gave the president virtually unlimited authority in conducting the Vietnam War. The Senate terminated the resolution in 1970 following outrage over the U.S. invasion of Cambodia.

American Escalation Despite congressional approval of force, Johnson's campaign that fall included a pledge that there would be no escalation in Vietnam — no sending "American boys nine or ten thousand miles away from home to do what Asian boys ought to be doing for themselves." Privately, he doubted the pledge could be kept. Once the 1964 election was safely behind him, Johnson began an American takeover of the war in Vietnam (see "Firsthand Accounts," p. 882). The escalation, beginning in the early months of 1965, took two forms: deployment of American ground troops and intensive bombing of North Vietnam. On March 8, 1965, the first marines waded ashore near the city of Da Nang. By 1966, more than 380,000 American soldiers were stationed in Vietnam; by 1967, 485,000; and by 1968, 536,000 (Figure 27.2). General William Westmoreland, the commander of U.S. forces, and Robert McNamara, the secretary of defense, pushed Johnson to "Americanize" the ground war in an attempt to stabilize South Vietnam.

Operation Rolling Thunder
Massive bombing campaign against North Vietnam authorized by President Johnson in 1965; despite lasting three years, the bombing made North Vietnam more, not less, determined to continue fighting.

Meanwhile, Johnson authorized **Operation Rolling Thunder**, a massive bombing campaign against North Vietnam that began in March 1965 and continued for three years. Over the course of the war, the United States dropped twice as many tons of bombs on Vietnam as the Allies had dropped in Europe and the Pacific combined during the whole of World War II. To the surprise of McNamara and other American leaders, the vast aerial assault proved largely ineffectual. The North Vietnamese quickly rebuilt roads and bridges and moved munitions plants underground. Instead of demoralizing the North Vietnamese, Operation Rolling Thunder hardened their will to fight. The influx of American military power devastated Vietnam's countryside, however. After a harsh but not unusual engagement, an American commander told a reporter that "it became necessary to destroy the town in

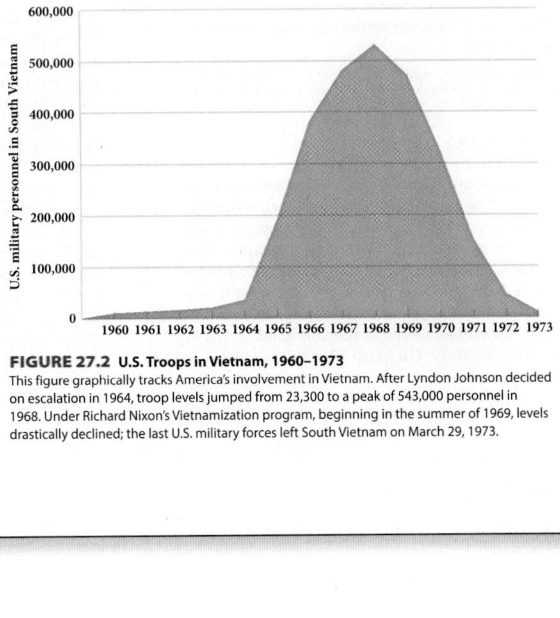

FIGURE 27.2 U.S. Troops in Vietnam, 1960–1973
This figure graphically tracks America's involvement in Vietnam. After Lyndon Johnson decided on escalation in 1964, troop levels jumped from 23,300 to a peak of 543,000 personnel in 1968. Under Richard Nixon's Vietnamization program, beginning in the summer of 1969, levels drastically declined; the last U.S. military forces left South Vietnam on March 29, 1973.

TEACHING STRATEGY

As the caption to **FIGURE 27.2** indicates, the effects of the Gulf of Tonkin Resolution are clearly visible from the sharp spike in American troops that begins in 1964. At the other end of the war, Nixon's policy of "Vietnamization" is also evident, as troop levels began to drop in 1969 as precipitously as they had increased under Johnson. The Office of the Historian provides more detail about the Gulf of Tonkin incident, the resulting resolution, and the escalation that it produced. To access these resources, search "Office of the Historian Gulf of Tonkin."

TEACHING STRATEGY

One of the historical factors the Johnson administration referenced in involving the United States in the war in Vietnam was the policy of Containment, first used during the Truman administration. Have students evaluate the extent to which U.S. involvement in Vietnam represented a historical continuity in foreign policy.

AP® SKILLS & PROCESSES

ANALYZING HISTORICAL EVIDENCE

The **AP® FIRSTHAND ACCOUNTS** feature provides insight into the deep impact the war had on American troops. The sources included here represent both men and women serving in a variety of capacities. Missing from these accounts of "the toll of war" are the experiences of Vietnamese soldiers and civilians. Estimates of Vietnamese deaths, which included North, South, civilian, and military, ranged from 1.5 million to 3.5 million.

AP® FIRSTHAND ACCOUNTS

The Toll of War

The Vietnam War drew Americans from many backgrounds and different walks of life into the military to serve in Southeast Asia. These brief selections suggest the war's profound, often horrific, impact on those Americans who experienced it firsthand.

VINCENT OKAMOTO, SOLDIER

Vincent Okamoto was a lieutenant with the 25th Infantry Division in 1968; he was interviewed some years after the war.

SOURCE: Vincent Okamoto, "Damn, I'm a Gook," in *Patriots: The Vietnam War Remembered from All Sides*, ed. Christian G. Appy (New York: Penguin, 2003), 357–362.

" I am the last of ten children, the seventh son of Japanese immigrants. I was born in Poston Relocation Camp in Arizona. In World War II, two of my older brothers served with the 442nd Regimental Combat Team. My whole life I grew up on the tradition of the 442nd. I was convinced that one of the reasons we were allowed to get out of the camps and accepted in American society to the degree that we were, was the blood shed by the 442nd. So growing up, I thought military service was an inevitable rite of passage. . . .

When I got there [Vietnam] my guys were talking about gooks, and zipperheads, and slants, and I said to myself, 'Damn, I'm a gook, I'm a zipperhead, I'm a slant.' But it didn't take too long before my mentality was just like theirs. I should have known better, yet within a relatively short time we were all thinking alike. If it became a question of maximizing protection for your men or giving some Vietnamese civilian the benefit of the doubt, after a while there was no choice. I just went with protecting my people. Even so, I was nearly killed by Americans who mistook me for a Vietnamese. "

GEORGE OLSEN, SOLDIER

George Olsen served in Vietnam from August 1969 to March 1970, when he was killed in action. He wrote this letter to a close female friend.

SOURCE: George Olsen, "Soldier," from *Dear America: Letters Home from Vietnam*, edited by Bernard Edelman for the New York Vietnam Veterans Memorial Commission, published by W.W. Norton & Company, 1985. Courtesy of Bernard Edelman.

" 31 Aug '69

Dear Red,

Last Monday I went on my first hunter-killer operation. . . . The frightening thing about it all is that it is so very easy to kill in war. There's no remorse, no theatrical "washing of the hands" to get rid of nonexistent blood, not even any regrets. When it happens, you are more afraid than you've ever been in your life — my hands shook so much I had trouble reloading. . . . You're scared, really scared, and there's no thinking about it. You kill because that little SOB is doing his best to kill you and you desperately want to live, to go home, to get drunk or walk down the street on a date again. And suddenly the grenades aren't going off any more, the weapons stop and, unbelievably fast it seems, it's all over. . . .

I have truly come to envy the honest pacifist who honestly believes that no killing is permissible and can, with a clear conscience, stay home and not take part in these conflicts. I wish I could do the same, but I can't see letting another take my place and my risks over here. . . . The only reason pacifists such as the Amish can even live in an orderly society is because someone — be they police or soldiers — is taking risks to keep the wolves away. . . . I guess that's why I'm over here, why I fought so hard to come here, and why, even though I'm scared most of the time, I'm content to be here. "

LILY ADAMS, NURSE

Lily Adams, an army nurse stationed at the 12th Evacuation Hospital near what is today Ho Chi Minh City, had an Italian American mother and a Chinese American father. She spoke with a researcher some years after the war.

SOURCE: *In the Combat Zone: An Oral History of American Women in Vietnam, 1966–1975*, ed. Kathryn Marshall (Boston: Little, Brown, 1987), 206–229.

" The majority of the people that I learned about the Vietnamese from were the infantry men. The ones that had been out in the field — yea, a lot of them had respect for the Vietnamese. I also worked with a corpsman who was a Quaker and wouldn't put up with anything — he got sent out of the field because he would call in med-evacs for [enemy] POWs, and I mean foot soldiers, nobody important. The thinking was that POWs were a waste of your time and energy, unless they were the good ones: the ones with information. . . .

I didn't realize my own strength back then — I was real proud that I could resist all the racism around me, but I didn't know my own strength as a noncomformist. It is easy to be racist, even for Asians to be racist against Asians. No, you don't have to be Ku Klux Klan to be racist.

My last two weeks in Cu Chi I was put on the surgical ward. They wanted to keep me out of trouble. Because I was hysterical — it's called short-timer's syndrome. You know, you're feeling guilty at leaving because now you're so highly skilled you can do everything blindfolded with your hands tied behind your back. New people coming in means that they are not as skilled, because the new people learn as they go. And there's a lot of ambivalence. You want to stay so you can devote yourself to the guys, but you want to leave because you want to live. ”

ARTHUR E. WOODLEY JR., SPECIAL FORCES RANGER

Special Forces Ranger Arthur E. Woodley Jr. gave this interview a decade after his return.

SOURCE: Wallace Terry, Excerpt(s) from, *Bloods: An Oral History of the Vietnam War by Black Veterans*, copyright © 1984 by Wallace Terry. Used by permission of Random House, an imprint and division of Penguin Random House LLC. All rights reserved.

“ You had to fight to survive where I grew up. Lower east Baltimore. . . . It was a mixed-up neighborhood of Puerto Ricans, Indians, Italians, and blacks. Being that I'm lightskinned, curly hair, I wasn't readily accepted in the black community. I was more accepted by Puerto Ricans and some rednecks. They didn't ask what my race classification was. I went with them to white movies, white restaurants, and so forth. But after I got older, I came to the realization that I was what I am and came to deal with my black peers. . . .

I figured I was just what my country needed. A black patriot who could do any physical job they could come up with. Six feet, one hundred and ninety pounds, and healthy. . . .

I didn't ask no questions about the war. I thought communism was spreading, and as an American citizen, it was my part to do as much as I could to defeat the Communist from coming here. Whatever America states is correct was the tradition that I was brought up in. And I thought the only way I could possibly make it out of the ghetto was to be the best soldier I possibly could. . . .

Then came the second week of February of '69. . . . We recon this area, and we came across this fella, a white guy, who was staked to the ground. His arms and legs tied down to stakes. . . . He had numerous scars on his face where he might have been beaten and mutilated. And he had been peeled from his upper part of chest to down to his waist.

Skinned. Like they slit your skin with a knife. And they take a pair of pliers or a instrument similar, and they just peel the skin off your body and expose it to the elements. . . .

And he start to cryin', beggin' to die.

He said, 'I can't go back like this. I can't live like this. I'm dying. You can't leave me here like this dying.' . . .

It took me somewhere close to 20 minutes to get my mind together. Not because I was squeamish about killing someone, because I had at that time numerous body counts. Killing someone wasn't the issue. It was killing another American citizen, another GI. . . . We buried him. We buried him. Very deep. Then I cried. . . .

When we first started going into the fields, I would not wear a finger, ear, or mutilate another person's body. Until I had the misfortune to come upon those American soldiers who were castrated. Then it got to be a game between the Communists and ourselves to see how many fingers and ears that we could capture from each other. After a kill we would cut his finger or ear off as a trophy, stuff our unit patch in his mouth, and let him die.

With 89 days left in country, I came out of the field. What I now felt was emptiness. . . . I started seeing the atrocities that we caused each other as human beings. I came to the realization that I was committing crimes against humanity and myself. That I really didn't believe in these things I was doin'. I changed. ”

GAYLE SMITH, NURSE

Gayle Smith was a nurse in a surgical unit in Vietnam in 1970–1971 and gave this interview a few years later.

SOURCE: Albert Santoli, ed., *Everything We Had* (New York: Random House, 1981), 141–148.

“ I objected to the war and I got the idea into my head of going there to bring people back. I started thinking about it in 1966 and knew that I would eventually go when I felt I was prepared enough. . . .

Boy, I remember how they came in all torn up. It was incredible. The first time a medevac came in, I got right into it. I didn't have a lot of feeling at that time. It was later on that I began to have a lot of feeling about it, after I'd seen it over and over and over again. . . . I turned that pain into anger and hatred and placed it onto the Vietnamese. . . . I did not consider the Vietnamese to be people. They were human, but they weren't people. They weren't like us, so it was okay to kill them. It was okay to hate them. . . .

I would have dreams about putting a .45 to someone's head and see it blow away over and over again. And for a long time I swore that if the Vietnamese ever came to this country I'd kill them.

It was in a Vietnam veterans group that I realized that all my hatred for the Vietnamese and my wanting to kill them was really a reflection of all the pain that I had felt for seeing all those young men die and hurt. . . . I would stand there and look at them and think to myself, 'You've just lost your leg for no reason at all.' Or 'You're going to die and it's for nothing.' For nothing. I would never, never say that to them, but they knew it. ”

QUESTIONS FOR ANALYSIS

1. Why did these five young people end up in Vietnam? How did social position affect participation? Compare their reasons for going to war.
2. Describe the experiences of those in Vietnam based on these sources and evidence from the chapter.
3. What were the authors' attitudes about the war, and how did war change the authors of each source? What do their reflections suggest about Vietnam's impact on American society?

TRM Find complete suggested responses in the Teacher's Resource Materials.

CHECK FOR UNDERSTANDING

Ask students: **How did American involvement in Vietnam escalate under Johnson?** *Using the Gulf of Tonkin incident as a pretext, Johnson requested carte blanche from Congress to increase American troop levels at his discretion. In the Gulf of Tonkin Resolution, Congress surrendered a significant element of its constitutional war-making power to the president. After a major bombing campaign of North Vietnam, Johnson began introducing ground troops. By 1968, there were over a half-million stationed in South Vietnam.*

AP® SKILLS & PROCESSES

CONTEXTUALIZATION

Think about having students start with a broad concept that predates President Johnson's time in the White House. For instance, provide students with a concept such as containment and ask them to identify the successes and setbacks of this policy prior to Johnson. Have students then examine any parallels President Johnson would have made during his time in office. The act of comparing within the larger context of the Cold War may help students arrive at a broader understanding.

TRM Find complete suggested responses in the Teacher's Resource Materials.

AP® THEME

NAT: American and National Identity

The Vietnam War inspired large, fervent antiwar protests that grew as the war escalated, and sometimes led to violence. From 1965 until 1972, the University of Michigan campus was a stronghold of political activism and discussion against the war in Vietnam. The *Anti-Vietnam War Movement* exhibit from the Michigan in the World Web site publicized research conducted by undergraduate students about the history of the antiwar movement at the University of Michigan. To access this exhibit, search "Michigan in the World Anti-Vietnam War movement."

Vietnam War An American officer shouts orders as a wounded soldier awaits evacuation near Saigon during the Vietnam War in 1969. The soldier is attended by a medic as they seek cover beside an armored troop carrier. AP Photo/Boston Globe, Oliver Noonan.

AP® SKILLS & PROCESSES

CONTEXTUALIZATION

In what larger context did President Johnson view the Vietnam conflict, and why was he determined to support South Vietnam?

AP® EXAM TIP

Recognize the causes and effects of the changing reactions of the American public to the Vietnam War over time.

order to save it" — a statement that came to symbolize the terrible logic of the war.

The Johnson administration gambled that American superiority, in both personnel and firepower, would ultimately triumph, making up for the weakness of the South Vietnam regime. This strategy was inextricably tied to political considerations. For domestic reasons, policymakers sought an elusive middle ground between all-out invasion of North Vietnam, which risked war with China, and compete disengagement. "In effect, we are fighting a war of attrition," said General Westmoreland. "The only alternative is a war of annihilation."

Public Opinion and the War

At first, Johnson's Vietnam policy enjoyed wide support. Congressional Democrats and Republicans alike had approved the escalation, and public opinion polls in 1965 and 1966 agreed. But opinion began to shift as images of the war played on television every night (see "Thinking Like a Historian," p. 886). The evening news brought the carnage of Vietnam into U.S. homes, including images of dead and wounded Americans. In the first months of fighting in 1965, television reporter Morley Safer witnessed a marine unit burning the South Vietnamese village of Cam Ne to the ground. "Today's operation is the frustration of Vietnam in miniature," Safer explained. America can "win a military victory here, but to a Vietnamese peasant whose home is [destroyed] it will take more than presidential promises to convince him that we are on his side."

What journalists saw firsthand increasingly conflicted with official statements on the progress of the fighting. War correspondents began to write about a "credibility gap." The Johnson administration, they charged, was concealing bad news about the situation in Vietnam. In February 1966, hearings by the Senate Foreign Relations Committee (chaired by J. William Fulbright, an outspoken critic of the war, and broadcast on television) raised further questions about the administration's policy. Johnson complained to his staff in 1966 that "our people can't stand firm in the face of heavy losses, and they can bring down the government." The economics of the war were politically costly as well. The war cost taxpayers $27 billion in 1967, pushing the federal deficit from $9.8 billion to $23 billion. Military spending launched an inflationary spiral that would plague the American economy throughout the 1970s.

The escalating war was felt at an intimate level as well. Between 1960 and 1966, with the draft a fixture of American life, three-quarters of a million men were inducted into the American military (another million plus would be added before the war's end), affecting families and communities in every state. During the 1964 presidential campaign, Johnson had given a speech in New Hampshire saying, "I want to be very cautious and careful and use it [military offensive] only as a last resort . . . now we lost 190 American lives, and to each one of those 190 families this is a major war." Despite his stated caution and the certainty that a wider war would multiply those 190 families many thousands of times over, Johnson believed he had no alternative than to plunge ahead. Though the deadliest years of the war still lay ahead, by the end of 1966 almost 7,000 Americans had died in Vietnam, their average age just 23.

As the military campaign in Vietnam bogged down, an antiwar movement gathered. There had been little public resistance in 1964, even after the Tonkin Resolution authorized Johnson to commit forces. But following the escalation in 1965, groups of students, clergy, civil rights advocates, antinuclear proponents, and even Dr. Benjamin Spock, whose book on child care had helped raise many young boomers, began to protest. Their launchpad was an April 1965 march of 15,000 people in Washington, D.C., that included a picket line around the White House and speeches denouncing what activist Paul Potter called "this mad war." Despite their diversity, these opponents of the war shared a deep skepticism about the aims and motivations of U.S. policy in Vietnam. They advanced a number of different charges: that intervention was antithetical to American ideals; that an independent, anticommunist South Vietnam was unattainable; and that no strategic objective justified the suffering the war was inflicting on the Vietnamese people.

The Student Movement

College students, many of them inspired by the civil rights movement, had already begun to organize and agitate for social change prior to that first antiwar march of April 1965. In Ann Arbor, Michigan, in 1960, a group called Students for a Democratic Society (SDS) formed. Two years later, they held the first national SDS convention in Port Huron, Michigan. University of Michigan student and SDS member Tom Hayden penned a manifesto — the "**Port Huron Statement**" — expressing disillusionment with complacent consumer culture, the gulf between rich and poor, and anticommunist Cold War foreign policy. "We are people of this generation," Hayden wrote, "bred in at least modest comfort, housed now in universities, looking uncomfortably to the world we inherit." Hayden and SDS sought to shake up what they saw as a complacent nation.

The New Left The SDS was the heart of a movement that called itself the **New Left**, to distinguish itself from the Old Left — communists and socialists of the 1930s and 1940s. As New Left influence spread, it hit major university towns first — places such as Ann Arbor along with Madison, Wisconsin, and Berkeley, California. One of the New Left's first major demonstrations erupted in the fall of 1964 at the University of California at Berkeley after administrators banned student political activity on university grounds. In protest, student groups formed the Free Speech Movement and organized a sit-in at the administration building. Some students had just returned from Freedom Summer in Mississippi, inspired by their experience. One such student, Mario Savio, spoke for many when he compared the conflict in Berkeley to the civil rights struggle in the South: "The same rights are at stake in both places — the right to participate as citizens in a democratic society." Implicitly comparing university administrators to southern officials defending Jim Crow, he called the events in Berkeley a "struggle against the same enemy."

Emboldened by the Berkeley movement, students across the nation were soon protesting their universities' academic policies and then, beginning in 1965, the Vietnam War. Students were on the front lines as the campaign against the war intensified. In 1967 the Spring Mobilization to End the War in Vietnam Committee organized a mass march of 250,000 protesters, Martin Luther King Jr. among them, from Central Park to the United Nations in New York, while another 100,000

The Antiwar Movement Young men burning their draft cards in Central Park in 1967. By that year, a movement opposing the Vietnam War had gained momentum and increasing media attention, and included draft resisters like those pictured here as well as peace activists, students, civil rights leaders like Martin Luther King Jr., and a growing number of religious leaders, among many others. © Burt Glinn/Magnum Photos.

AP® EXAM TIP

Explain the role of the Port Huron Statement in expressing the discontent of the left with both domestic and foreign policies.

Port Huron Statement
A 1962 manifesto by Students for a Democratic Society from its first national convention in Port Huron, Michigan, expressing disillusionment with the complacent consumer culture and the gulf between rich and poor, as well as rejecting Cold War foreign policy.

New Left
A term applied to radical students of the 1960s and 1970s, distinguishing their activism from the Old Left — the communists and socialists of the 1930s and 1940s.

CHECK FOR UNDERSTANDING

Ask students: **How and why did public opinion about the war change?** *Public support for the war remained high in 1965 and 1966. But the routine coverage of violence and devastation on American television began to change the public's mind. Journalists in Vietnam reported on the gap between the administration's statements and what they knew to be true from being in country. The high cost of the war received criticism from members of Congress.*

AP® APPLY THE TIP

Provide students with excerpts from the Port Huron Statement by the Students for a Democratic Society that illustrate the discontent of the left with both domestic and foreign policies. Students should read the excerpts and note the specific problems that the SDS points out about foreign and domestic policy. Then lead a class discussion on the ways in which evidence from the chapter supports and challenges the arguments of the Port Huron Statement. Ask students to compare the arguments in the Port Huron Statement to the arguments made by Galbraith in *The Affluent Society*.

AP® SKILLS & PROCESSES

ANALYZING HISTORICAL EVIDENCE

Use the **AP® THINKING LIKE A HISTORIAN** feature to invite students to consider reasons for American involvement in Vietnam and the significance of that involvement. With the exception of Document 2, these sources all represent American perspectives. Students might consider reading these sources in chronological order (with the recognition that Document 4, though dated 1975, reflects earlier concerns). They might also consider the statements by the presidents together, which all represent official statements defending the nation's actions. In addition to the presidential statements, Documents 2 and 5 are also position statements that attempt to explain (or criticize) the purpose of the war.

AP® THINKING LIKE A HISTORIAN

Debating the War in Vietnam

The war in Vietnam divided Americans and ultimately divided world opinion. A product of the Cold War policy of containment, the war led many to question the application of that policy to Southeast Asia. Yet every American president from Truman to Nixon believed that opposing the unification of Vietnam under communist rule was essential. Historians continue to research, and debate, what led to the war and what effects the war had on both Vietnam and the United States. The following documents help us to consider different views of the war.

1. **President Dwight Eisenhower, "Domino Theory" speech, April 7, 1954.** *Eisenhower delivered this speech, in which he anguished over how communist governments might spread throughout Southeast Asia, as the French were near defeat in their war to retain Vietnam.*

Finally, you have broader considerations that might follow what you would call the "falling domino" principle. You have a row of dominoes set up, you knock over the first one, and what will happen to the last one is the certainty that it will go over very quickly. So you could have a beginning of a disintegration that would have the most profound influences. . . .

But when we come to the possible sequence of events, the loss of Indochina, of Burma, of Thailand, of the Peninsula, and Indonesia following, now you begin to talk about areas that not only multiply the disadvantages that you would suffer through loss of materials, sources of materials, but now you're talking about millions and millions and millions of people.

2. **Manifesto of the South Vietnam National Front for Liberation (NLF), 1968.** *The National Liberation Front (as it was known) was a political and military organization, supported by the communist government in North Vietnam, dedicated to overthrowing the government of South Vietnam.*

Over the past hundred years the Vietnamese people repeatedly rose up to fight against foreign aggression for the independence and freedom of their fatherland. In 1945, the people throughout the country surged up in an armed uprising, overthrew the Japanese and French domination, and seized power. . . .

However, the American imperialists, who had in the past helped the French colonialists to massacre our people, have now replaced the French in enslaving the southern part of our country through a disguised colonial regime. They have been using their stooge — the Ngo Dinh Diem administration — in their downright repression and exploitation of our compatriots, in their maneuvers to permanently divide our country and to turn its southern part into a base in preparation for war in Southeast Asia.

3. **President Lyndon Johnson, Johns Hopkins University speech, April 7, 1965.** *Johnson delivered this address shortly after the first U.S. Marine units had been deployed to Vietnam, the first wave of the president's expansion of the war.*

Over this war — and all Asia — is another reality: the deepening shadow of Communist China. The rulers in Hanoi are urged on by Peiping [Peiking]. This is a regime which has destroyed freedom in Tibet, which has attacked India, and has been condemned by the United Nations for aggression in Korea. It is helping the forces of violence in almost every continent. The contest in Viet-Nam is part of a wider pattern of aggressive purposes.

4. **James Fallows, "What Did You Do in the Class War, Daddy?" *Washington Monthly*, October 1975.** *The journalist James Fallows highlighted the economic unfairness of the Vietnam-era draft.*

The children of the bright, good parents were spared the more immediate sort of suffering that our inferiors were undergoing. And because of that, when our parents were opposed to the war, they were opposed in a bloodless, theoretical fashion, as they might be opposed to political corruption or racism in South Africa. As long as the little gold stars [sent to parents whose son was killed in war] kept going to homes in Chelsea [a working-class part of Boston] and the backwoods of West Virginia, the mothers of Beverly Hills and Chevy Chase and Great Neck and Belmont [all affluent suburbs] were not on the telephone to their congressman screaming, "*You killed my boy*." . . . It is clear by now that if the men of Harvard had wanted to do the very most they could to help shorten the war, they should have been drafted or imprisoned en masse.

5. **Students for a Democratic Society, Call for a March on Washington to End the War, 1965.** *Students for a Democratic Society (SDS) was one of the principal New Left organizations of radical students in the 1960s.*

The current war in Vietnam is being waged on behalf of a succession of unpopular South Vietnamese dictatorships, not in behalf of freedom. No American-supported South Vietnamese regime in the past few years has gained the support of its people, for the simple reason that the people overwhelmingly want peace, self-determination, and the opportunity for development. American prosecution of the war has deprived them of all three.

The war is fundamentally a *civil* war. . . .
It is a *losing* war. . . .
It is a *self-defeating* war. . . .
It is a *dangerous* war. . . .
It is a war never declared by Congress. . . .
It is a hideously *immoral* war.

6. **Richard Nixon, address to the nation on the Vietnam War, November 3, 1969.** *Nixon delivered this speech, in which he refuses to withdraw troops but pledges to negotiate for peace, two weeks after the largest antiwar demonstration, the Moratorium to End the War in Vietnam, in Washington, D.C.*

. . . President Eisenhower sent economic aid and military equipment to assist the people of South Vietnam in their efforts to prevent a Communist takeover. Seven years ago, President Kennedy sent 16,000 military personnel to Vietnam as combat advisors. Four years ago, President Johnson sent American combat forces to South Vietnam. . . .

For these reasons, I reject the recommendation that I should end the war by immediately withdrawing all our forces. I choose instead to change American policy on both the negotiating front and the battlefront. . . .

SOURCES: (1) George Katsiaficas, ed., *Vietnam Documents: American and Vietnamese Views of the War* (Armonk, NY: M. E. Sharpe, Inc., 1992), pp. 120–121. Used by permission of the author; (2) Katsiaficas, 43–44; (3) John Clark Pratt, *Vietnam Voices: Perspectives on the War Years, 1941–1982* (New York: Penguin Books, 1984), 201; (4) *The Washington Monthly*, October 1975, 5–19; (5) Katsiaficas, 120–121; (6) Katsiaficas, 147.

7. **Evacuation of Vietnamese civilians in a burning village, c. 1965.** *The burning of villages by U.S. soldiers looking for Vietcong soldiers amongst the civilian population was one of the tragedies of the war.*

SOURCE: Dominique BERRETTY/Gamma-Rapho via Getty Images.

ANALYZING THE EVIDENCE

1. Three of the sources (1, 3, and 6) feature remarks by U.S. presidents. What common feature do they share? Are there differences among the comments? Source 2 is also an attempt by a political figure to persuade. How does the social position of the author affect the credibility of each source?
2. In source 4, which Americans does the author believe have sacrificed the most in fighting the war in Vietnam? How do socioeconomics influence participation in the war?
3. Compare sources 2 and 5. What is the main idea and intended audience of each? What common features do they share?
4. Journalists and electronic media (photography and television) played an important role in the war. How would images, such as that in source 7, shape opinion about the war both in the United States and globally?

AP® DBQ PRACTICE

Using the knowledge you have gained from this chapter, analyze the documents above to construct an essay in which you explore the politics around the Vietnam War. Describe the ways that domestic and foreign policies impacted the course of the war. Use the documents to provide evidence for your conclusions.

TRM Find complete suggested responses in the Teacher's Resource Materials.

AP® SKILLS & PROCESSES

ARGUMENTATION

To answer the **AP® DBQ PRACTICE** prompt, it might be helpful for students to consider just one or two dimensions — causes or effects, domestic or international dimensions — rather than all four simultaneously.

protesters flooded the streets of San Francisco and 100,000 more marched on the Pentagon. President Johnson counterpunched against the burgeoning antiwar movement — "The enemy's hope for victory . . . is in our division, our weariness, our uncertainty," he proclaimed — but it was clear that Johnson's war, as many called it, was no longer uniting the country.

Student resistance to the war only grew when the military's Selective Service System abolished automatic student deferments in 1967. Such controversial deferments allowed young middle-class men to avoid Vietnam so long as they remained in school — leaving military service, and thus the personal sacrifice of fighting in war, to men without the resources to be in college. To avoid the draft now, some young men enlisted in the National Guard or applied for conscientious objector status; others left the country, most often for Canada or Sweden. In public demonstrations, opponents of the war burned their draft cards, picketed induction centers, and on a few occasions broke into Selective Service offices and destroyed records. Serious antiwar activists numbered in the tens or, at most, hundreds of thousands — a small fraction of American youth — but they were vocal, visible, and determined.

Young Americans for Freedom (YAF)
The largest student political organization in the country in the 1960s, whose conservative members defended free enterprise and supported the war in Vietnam.

Sharon Statement
Manifesto drafted in 1960 by founding members of the Young Americans for Freedom (YAF), which outlined the group's principles — free enterprise, limited government, and traditional morality — and inspired young conservatives who would play important roles in the Reagan administration in the 1980s.

Young Americans for Freedom The New Left was not the only political force on college campuses. Conservative students were perhaps less noisy but just as numerous. Inspired by the group **Young Americans for Freedom (YAF)**, right-leaning students asserted their faith in "God-given free will" and charged that the federal government "accumulates power which tends to diminish order and liberty." The YAF, the largest student political organization in the country in the 1960s, defended free enterprise and supported the war in Vietnam. Its founding principles, a mixture of conservative ideals such as limited government and traditional morality, were outlined in the "**Sharon Statement**," drafted (in Sharon, Connecticut) in 1960, two years before the Port Huron Statement. Many of the students who rallied to the YAF's call would go on to play important roles in the "Reagan revolution" of the 1980s.

The Counterculture The three-day outdoor Woodstock concert in August 1969 was a defining moment in the rise of the counterculture. The event attracted 400,000 young people, like those pictured here, to Bethel, New York, for a weekend of music, drugs, and sex. The counterculture was distinct from the New Left and was less a political movement than a shifting set of cultural styles, attitudes, and practices. It rejected conformity of all kinds and placed rebellion and contrariness among its highest values. Another concept held dear by the counterculture was, simply, "love." In an era of military violence abroad and police violence at home, many in the counterculture hoped that "peace and love" would prevail instead. Bill Eppridge/The LIFE Picture Collection/Getty Images.

The Counterculture While the New Left organized against the political and economic system and the YAF defended it, many other young Americans embarked on a general revolt against authority and middle-class respectability. The "hippie" — identified by ragged blue jeans or army fatigues, flowing skirts and blouses, shirts, beads, and long unkempt hair — symbolized the new counterculture. With roots in the 1950s Beat culture of New York's Greenwich Village and San Francisco's North Beach, the counterculture was composed largely of white youth alienated by the staid manners and expectations of an older generation, which they rejected in favor of an ethic of personal freedom and authenticity. The early counterculture turned to music for inspiration, finding in song lyrics a new language questioning old ways. A countercultural folk music revival first set an idealistic tone for the era with songs such as Pete Seeger's 1961 antiwar ballad "Where Have All the Flowers Gone?" In

TEACHING STRATEGY

The Sharon Statement was adopted on September 11, 1960, by a small group of young conservatives meeting at conservative intellectual William F. Buckley's home in Sharon, Connecticut, to create the group Young Americans for Freedom (YAF). The statement emphasizes core conservative ideas of the time: limited government, religious freedom, free-market economics, and opposition to "the forces of international Communism." To access this text, search "YAF Sharon Statement."

AP® THEME

SOC: Social Structures; PCE: Politics and Power

Young people who participated in the counterculture of the 1960s rejected many of the social, economic, and political values of their parents' generation, introduced greater casualness into American culture, and advocated changes in sexual mores.

TEACHING STRATEGY

The 1968 Exhibit, curated by the Minnesota Historical Society, is an ambitious, state-of-the-art, multimedia exhibit that looks at how the experiences of the year fueled a persistent, sometimes contradictory, sense of identity for the people who lived during it. The Web site provides a wealth of resources, including oral histories, images, textual primary sources, discussion questions, and dozens of blog posts on various topics. To access this exhibit, search "Minnesota Historical Society 1968 exhibit."

AP® THEME

ARC: American and Regional Culture

In ways hitherto unseen, the youth culture of the 1960s were consumers, activists, and reformers. Have students evaluate whether this culture represented a change in American culture or a change for a small minority of youth.

the turbulent year of 1963, Bob Dylan's "Blowin' in the Wind" reflected the impatience of people whose faith in America was wearing thin. Musical artists such as Judy Collins and Joan Baez emerged alongside Dylan and pioneered a sound that would inspire a generation of female musicians.

By the mid-1960s, other forms of popular music had become the soundtrack of the counterculture. The Beatles, four working-class Brits whose awe-inspiring music, by turns lyrical and driving, spawned a commercial and cultural phenomenon known as Beatlemania. Young Americans embraced the Beatles, as well as even more rebellious bands such as the Rolling Stones, the Who, and the Doors. This new music, unfamiliar and strange sounding to older Americans, contributed to a spreading generational divide between young and old. So did the recreational use of drugs — especially marijuana and LSD, the hallucinogen popularly known as acid — which was celebrated in the psychedelic music of the late 1960s.

For a brief time, adherents of the counterculture believed that a new age was dawning. In 1967, the "world's first Human Be-In" drew 20,000 people to Golden Gate Park in San Francisco. That summer — known as the Summer of Love — San Francisco's Haight-Ashbury, New York's East Village, Chicago's Uptown neighborhood, and the Sunset Strip in Los Angeles swelled with young dropouts, drifters, and teenage runaways whom the media dubbed "flower children." Most young people had little interest in all-out revolt, or dropping out of society altogether, and media coverage often exaggerated their antipathy to social norms. But the counterculture's general antipathy to authority had a lasting influence on American youth culture — in style, clothes, music, and attitude.

AP® EXAM TIP

Recognize the role of the counterculture in challenging the status quo and expectations of a homogeneous American culture in the 1960s.

AP® SKILLS & PROCESSES

ARGUMENTATION

Contrast the political views of the SDS, the YAF, and the counterculture. How would you explain the differences?

DAYS OF RAGE, 1968–1972

What factors best explain the rising militancy of social change and protest movements in 1968 and afterward?

By 1968, urban unrest, campus protests, and a nose-thumbing counterculture had escalated into a general youth rebellion that seemed poised to tear America apart. This "watershed year for a generation," SDS founder Tom Hayden wrote, "started with legendary events, then raised hopes, only to end by immersing innocence in tragedy." The year 1968 was not simply eventful - the events themselves were explosive, with ripple effects across society. Violent clashes both in Vietnam and at home, a society and culture in turmoil, and shocking political assassinations combined to produce a palpable sense of crisis.

War Abroad, Tragedy at Home

In 1965, President Johnson had gambled on a quick victory in Vietnam. If American forces could speedily stabilize South Vietnam and get out, there would be no political cost to the escalation. But there was no quick victory. North Vietnamese and Vietcong forces fought on, the South Vietnamese government repeatedly collapsed, and American casualties mounted. By early 1968, the death rate of U.S. troops had reached several hundred a week. Johnson and his generals insisted, in a phrase widely quoted by the press, that there was "light at the end of the tunnel." Facts on the ground showed otherwise.

The Tet Offensive On January 30, 1968, the North Vietnamese and Vietcong unleashed a massive, well-coordinated assault across South Vietnam. Beginning on the Vietnamese new year holiday known as Tet, the offensive struck thirty-six provincial capitals and five of the South's six major cities, including Saigon, where the Vietcong nearly overran the U.S. embassy. In strictly military terms, the **Tet offensive** was a failure, with very heavy losses for the attackers. But psychologically, the effect in the United States was devastating. Television brought into American homes shocking

AP® EXAM TIP

Evaluate the impact of the Tet Offensive as a turning point for the war in Vietnam and the antiwar movement at home.

Tet offensive
Major campaign of attacks launched throughout South Vietnam in January 1968 by the North Vietnamese and Vietcong. A major turning point in the war, it exposed the credibility gap between official statements and the war's reality, and it shook Americans' confidence in the government.

AP® SKILLS & PROCESSES

ARGUMENTATION

The **ARGUMENTATION** question asks students to note the differences among three activist groups formed by young people in the 1960s. Apart from their differing ideologies, students should consider the identities of those drawn to each group, and the potential attraction of the ideology they adopted. Extend this prompt by asking students to identify the similarities among these three groups.

TRM Find complete suggested responses in the Teacher's Resource Materials.

CHECK FOR UNDERSTANDING

Ask students: **What led President Johnson to escalate the war in Vietnam, and how did Americans respond?** *Lyndon Johnson escalated the Vietnam War in early 1965 to win an electoral mandate for his social programs, known as the Great Society, without seeing them threatened. Once he won reelection in November 1964, U.S. ground forces went into Vietnam and U.S. planes bombed North Vietnam extensively. Public opinion, which initially favored the escalation, gradually grew against the war as the so-called credibility gap emerged, wherein public statements diverged with what Americans could see on television vis-à-vis the war's progress. The antiwar movement was led by those who the war affected most, students and others in their late teens and mid-twenties.*

AP® APPLY THE TIP

Using the textbook and other resources, students should complete **Handout 27.3 — Contextualization: Tet Offensive (TRM).** Lead a class discussion on contextualization that addresses Johnson's role as the leader of the Great Society, supporter of Civil Rights, supporter of containment policy, as well as his fear of a repeat of China's fall to communism, McCarthyism, and growing division over the war in the U.S.

TRM Find **Handout 27.3 — Contextualization: Tet Offensive** in the Teacher's Resource Materials.

TRM Find complete suggested responses in the Teacher's Resource Materials.

TEACHING STRATEGY

The *New York Times* offers an overview of the assassination of Martin Luther King Jr. and its aftermath. To access this overview, search "NYT assassination of MLK."

Additionally, the *Orange County Register* provides a brief article on the Robert F. Kennedy assassination, along with an annotated slide show of more than fifty historical images related to the killing and the subsequent funeral. To access these resources, search "Orange County Register Robert F. Kennedy assassinated."

AP SKILLS & PROCESSES

ARGUMENTATION

Why was the Tet offensive a turning point in the Vietnam War?

live images: the American embassy under siege and, in a grim testament to the casual brutality of war, the Saigon police chief placing a pistol to the head of a Vietcong suspect and executing him.

The Tet offensive made a mockery of official pronouncements that the United States was winning the war. Could an enemy truly on the verge of defeat mount such a large-scale, complex, and coordinated attack? Just before Tet, a Gallup poll found that 56 percent of Americans considered themselves "hawks" (supporters of the war), while only 28 percent identified with the "doves" (war opponents). Three months later, doves outnumbered hawks 42 to 41 percent. Without embracing the peace movement, many Americans turned against the war after simply concluding that it was unwinnable.

Johnson's war policies were effectively discredited. As the 1968 presidential primary season got under way in March, antiwar senators Eugene McCarthy of Minnesota and Robert Kennedy of New York both announced they would challenge the incumbent Johnson for the Democratic nomination. On March 31, a discouraged and fatigued LBJ stunned the nation by announcing that he would not seek reelection.

Political Assassinations On April 4, just five days after the unexpected news that a sitting president would not stand for reelection, a career criminal named James Earl Ray shot and killed Martin Luther King Jr. in Memphis. King had gone to Memphis to support striking sanitation workers, an act which alongside his 1967 speech against the war in Vietnam signaled the civil rights leader's recent shift to a broad campaign for social and economic justice — even as he remained rooted in the cause of racial justice. Cities were on edge after four successive summers of violent clashes between black communities and the police, between 1964 and 1967, and the killing of the charismatic King led to the eruption of riots in more than a hundred cities. The worst of them, in Baltimore, Chicago, and Washington, D.C., saw dozens dead and hundreds of millions of dollars of damage. The violence on the streets eerily paralleled the images of Saigon from the Tet offensive.

Robert Kennedy After the assassination of Martin Luther King Jr. and with President Johnson out of the presidential race, Robert Kennedy emerged in 1968 as the leading liberal figure in the nation. A critic of the Vietnam War, a strong supporter of civil rights, and committed to fighting poverty, Kennedy (the brother of the late President John Kennedy) ran a progressive campaign for president. In this photograph he is shown shaking hands with supporters in Detroit in May 1968. However, less than three weeks after this picture was taken, Kennedy, too, was dead, the victim of yet another assassination. Andrew Sacks/Getty Images.

Senator Robert Kennedy, the former attorney general and the youngest brother of the late president, was in Indianapolis on the day of King's slaying, campaigning for the Indiana Democratic primary election. RFK, as he was known, gave a somber speech to the city's black community on the evening of April 4, only hours after learning of the murder (Kennedy actually informed many in the unknowing crowd of the assassination, eliciting immediate gasps and tears). Americans could continue to move toward "greater polarization," Kennedy said, "black people amongst blacks, white amongst whites," or "we can replace that violence . . . with an effort to understand, compassion and love." Kennedy sympathized with African Americans' outrage at whites, but he begged them not to strike back in retribution. Impromptu and heartfelt, Kennedy's address reminded America of King's nonviolent example, even as the national mood grew darker.

With a campaign focused on racial and economic fairness and drawing on the continued popularity of his family, Kennedy had emerged as the frontrunner for the 1968 Democratic presidential nomination. But his candidacy would be cut short. On June 5, as he was celebrating his victory in the California primary over Eugene McCarthy, Kennedy was shot and killed by a young Palestinian named Sirhan Sirhan — evidence showed that Sirhan was motivated by Kennedy's support for the sale of American fighter jets to Israel. Amid the anguish over yet another assassination, one newspaper columnist declared that "the country does not work anymore." *Newsweek* asked, "Has violence become a way of life?" Kennedy's assassination was a political calamity for the Democrats — he was the only candidate able to overcome the party's fissures over Vietnam. In the space of eight weeks, American liberals had lost two great unifiers — King and RFK. With these leaders gone, the crisis of liberalism became unmanageable.

Rising Political Radicalism

Before their deaths, Martin Luther King Jr. and Robert Kennedy had spoken eloquently against the Vietnam War. To antiwar activists, however, bold speeches and marches had not produced results. "We are no longer interested in merely protesting the war," declared one. "We are out to stop it." They sought nothing short of immediate American withdrawal. Anger at Johnson and the Democratic establishment Party — fueled by the violent climate of 1968 — radicalized the movement.

Democratic Convention In August, at the **1968 Democratic National Convention** in Chicago, the political divisions generated by Vietnam finally consumed the party. Thousands of protesters descended on the city. The most visible group, led by Jerry Rubin and Abbie Hoffman, claimed to represent the Youth International Party (whose members were known as "Yippies"). In a bitter parody of the events inside the convention hall, the Yippies nominated a live pig, Pigasus, for president. These stunts were geared to draw maximum media attention. But a far larger and more serious group of activists had come to Chicago to demonstrate against the war as well — in what many came to call the Siege of Chicago.

1968 Democratic National Convention
A convention held in Chicago during which numerous antiwar demonstrators outside the convention hall were teargassed and clubbed by police. Inside the convention hall, the delegates were bitterly divided over Vietnam.

The city's four-term Democratic mayor Richard J. Daley ordered the police to break up the demonstrations. Several nights of skirmishes between protesters and police ensued, peaking on the final night of the convention. In what an official report later described as a "police riot," officers attacked protesters with teargas and clubs, turning ordinary city streets into warlike scenes of violence and chaos. As the nominating speeches proceeded, television networks broadcast scenes of the riot, cementing a public perception of the Democrats as the party of disorder. "They are going to be spending the next four years picking up the pieces," one Republican said gleefully. Inside the hall, the party dispiritedly nominated Hubert H. Humphrey, Johnson's vice president, running on a lukewarm platform that committed to continuing the fight in Vietnam while seeking a diplomatic solution.

Richard Nixon On the Republican side, former vice president Richard M. Nixon had engineered a remarkable political comeback. After losing the presidential campaign in 1960 and the California gubernatorial race in 1962, he had left public life to practice law at a high-powered New York firm. Securely outside the GOP leadership, he was insulated from blame for the liberal Johnson's rout of the conservative Goldwater, and he carefully engineered a return to electoral politics after 1964. Nixon and his advisors courted two groups of voters whose long political loyalty to the Democrats was wavering: working-class white voters in the North and white voters of all social classes in the South.

Offended by the antiwar movement and the counterculture, and disturbed by urban riots, northern blue-collar voters, especially Catholics, had drifted away from their longtime loyalty to the Democratic Party. Growing up in the Great Depression, these families were often admirers of FDR and perhaps even hung

CHECK FOR UNDERSTANDING

Ask students: **How was 1968 a significant year in terms of war abroad and tragedy at home?** *The Tet offensive marked a symbolic turning point in the Vietnam War. Though the U.S. pushed back the communist offensive, the force of the attack convinced many Americans that the war was far from over and that the government had been dishonest in claiming the opposite. Disheartened, Johnson chose not to run for reelection. Martin Luther King Jr. and Robert F. Kennedy, both critics of the war and civil rights advocates, were assassinated.*

AP® THEME

ARC: American and Regional Culture

Liberals were never a monolith on the home front during the tumultuous 1960s. Invite students to explain at least two variants of liberal reformers. Using historical developments such as Civil Rights and the Vietnam War should help students brainstorm the ways in which liberalism was represented by different beliefs and goals.

AP® SKILLS & PROCESSES

MAKING CONNECTIONS

The **MAKING CONNECTIONS** question asks students to compare supporters of FDR in the 1940s with supporters of Nixon in 1968. Students should consider the role of both economic and social factors in voters' decisions to align with each candidate. Extend this prompt by asking students to compare the profile of voters who supported Nixon in 1968 with voters in the most recent presidential election.

TRM Find complete suggested responses in the Teacher's Resource Materials.

his picture on their living-room wall. But FDR had been gone for three decades. Social scientists Ben J. Wattenberg and Richard Scammon captured the disaffection of working-class white Democrats in their study *The Real Majority* (1970). The book profiled people such as this forty-seven-year-old working-class woman from Dayton, Ohio: "[She] is afraid to walk the streets alone at night. . . . She has a mixed view about blacks and civil rights." Moreover, they wrote, "she is deeply distressed that her son is going to a community junior college where LSD was found on campus." The political backing of uneasy families like hers were increasingly up for grabs — a fact Republicans knew well.

AP® SKILLS & PROCESSES

MAKING CONNECTIONS

Why might a Democratic supporter of FDR in the 1940s have decided to vote for Republican Richard Nixon in 1968?

George Wallace It was not only Republicans who tapped working-class anxieties over student protests and urban riots. The controversial governor of Alabama, George C. Wallace, entered the 1968 presidential campaign as a third-party presidential candidate, trading on his fame as an unrepentant segregationist. He had tried to stop the federal government from desegregating the University of Alabama in 1963, and he was equally obstructive during the Selma crisis of 1965. Appealing to whites in both the North and the South, Wallace called for "law and order" and attacked welfare programs; he claimed that mothers on public assistance were, thanks to Johnson's generous Great Society, "breeding children as a cash crop."

AP® EXAM TIP

Evaluate the resurgence of conservative ideas in the late 1960s.

Wallace hoped to carry the South and deny both Nixon and Humphrey the needed electoral majority, forcing the election into the House of Representatives. He fell short of that objective, but did collect 13.5 percent of the popular vote. More significantly, Wallace's insurgent White House bid framed a set of politically effective issues — liberal elitism, welfare policies, and law and order — for the next generation of mainstream conservatives.

Nixon's Strategy Nixon offered a subtler version of Wallace's populism in a two-pronged approach. He adopted what his advisors called the "southern strategy," which aimed at attracting southern white voters fervently opposed to the civil rights gains by African Americans. Nixon won the backing of a particularly influential former Democrat, and key southerner, Senator Strom Thurmond of South Carolina, the 1948 Dixiecrat presidential nominee. Nixon quietly assured Thurmond that as a candidate he had to support civil rights, but a future Nixon administration would go easy on enforcement. Nixon also ran against the antiwar movement, urban riots, and protests, calling for a strict adherence to "law and order." He pledged to represent the "quiet voice" of the "great majority of Americans, the forgotten Americans, the nonshouters, the nondemonstrators." Here Nixon was speaking not just to the South but to the many millions of suburban voters nationwide anxious about the spread of social disorder.

Nixon's twin strategies — southern and suburban — worked. He received 43.4 percent of the vote to Humphrey's 42.7 percent, defeating him by a scant 500,000 votes out of 73 million cast (Map 27.3). The numerical closeness of the race could not disguise the devastating Democratic collapse. Humphrey received almost 12 million fewer votes than Johnson had in

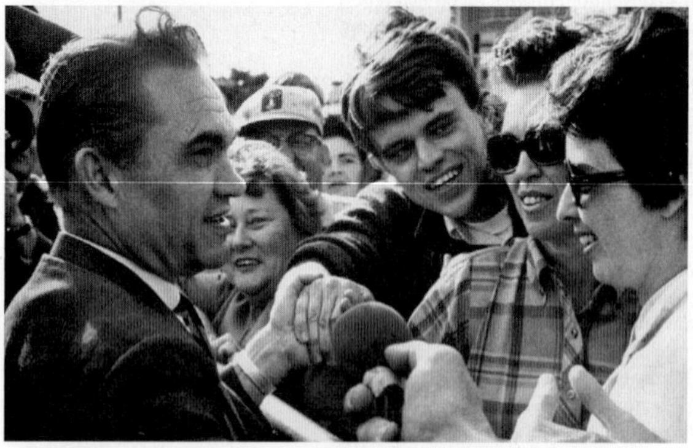

George Wallace George Wallace had become famous as the segregationist governor who stood "in the schoolhouse door" to prevent black students from enrolling at the University of Alabama in 1963 (though after being confronted by federal marshals, he stepped aside). In 1968, he campaigned for the Democratic presidential nomination on a populist "law and order" platform that appealed to many blue-collar voters concerned about antiwar protests, urban riots, and the rise of the counterculture. In this 1968 photograph, Wallace greets supporters on the campaign trail. Lee Balterman/The LIFE Picture Collection/Getty Images.

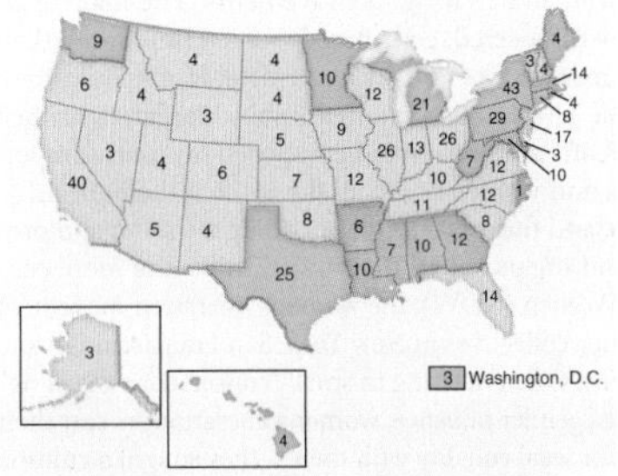

Candidate	Electoral Vote	Popular Vote	Percent of Popular Vote
Richard M. Nixon (Republican)	301	31,770,237	43.4
Hubert H. Humphrey (Democrat)	191	31,270,533	42.7
George C. Wallace (American Independent)	46	9,906,141	13.5
Minor parties	—	239,908	—

MAPPING THE PAST

MAP 27.3 The Presidential Election of 1968
With Lyndon B. Johnson's surprise withdrawal and the assassination of the party's most charismatic contender, Robert Kennedy, the Democrats faced the election of 1968 in disarray. Governor George Wallace of Alabama, who left the Democrats to run as a third-party candidate, campaigned on the backlash against the civil rights movement. As late as mid-September Wallace held the support of 21 percent of the voters. But in November he received only 13.5 percent of the vote, winning five southern states. Republican Richard M. Nixon, who like Wallace emphasized "law and order" in his campaign, defeated Hubert H. Humphrey with only 43.4 percent of the popular vote.

ANALYZING THE MAP: Identify the regional differences in support among the three candidates. Note where George Wallace had the strongest support.

MAKING CONNECTIONS: How do the regional divisions seen in this map illustrate both continuity and change in American politics? What factors contributed to the political divisions illustrated in this map?

TRM Find complete suggested responses in the Teacher's Resource Materials.

1964. The white South largely abandoned the Democratic Party, an exodus that would accelerate in the 1970s. In the North, meanwhile, both Nixon and Wallace made significant inroads among traditionally Democratic voters. The New Deal coalition that had kept Democrats unified for thirty years splintered and Nixon won the election. Nixon's 1968 victory foreshadowed—and helped propel—a decade of electoral realignment.

Black and Chicano Antiwar Activism With liberalism on the defensive and Nixon's "silent majority" movement on the rise, the antiwar movement and the wider youth rebellion were both turning fierce. So, too, were the Black Power and Chicano movements, which had broken with the liberal "rights" politics of an older generation of leaders. These new activists voiced fury at the poverty and white racism that sat beyond the reach of civil rights laws; they also saw Vietnam as an unjust war against other people of color. The Black Panther Party and the National Black Antiwar Antidraft League also sharply condemned the war. "Black Americans are considered to be the world's biggest fools," Eldridge Cleaver of the Black Panther Party wrote in his typically acerbic style, "to go to another country to fight for something they don't have for themselves." Cleaver and other radical black leaders took inspiration from Muhammad Ali, the outspoken world heavyweight boxing champion, who had refused his army induction in 1967. Sentenced to prison, Ali was eventually acquitted on appeal. But his action cost him his title, and for years he was not allowed to box professionally in the United States. In the same spirit, the **Chicano Moratorium Committee** organized demonstrations against the war. Chanting "Viva la Raza, Afuera Vietnam" ("Long live the Chicano people, Get out of Vietnam"), 20,000 Mexican Americans marched in Los Angeles in August 1970. At another Los Angeles rally in 1971, Cesar Chavez said: "For the poor it is a terrible irony that they should rise out of their misery to do battle against other poor people." He and other Mexican American activists charged that the draft was biased against those who had little.

Chicano Moratorium Committee Group founded by activist Latinos to protest the Vietnam War.

Women's Liberation and Black and Chicana Feminism

Among women, the late 1960s marked a decided break with the past and spawned new expressions of feminism: women's liberation and black and Chicana feminisms. Activists for the former were primarily younger, college-educated women, often

CHECK FOR UNDERSTANDING

Ask students: **How did the antiwar movement affect the 1968 election?** *Antiwar candidate Robert F. Kennedy's assassination left a political vacuum for the Democratic Party, since Johnson had decided not to run for reelection. At the 1968 Democratic National Convention in Chicago, delegates unenthusiastically endorsed Hubert Humphrey, Johnson's vice president, who supported continued fighting in Vietnam. Meanwhile, antiwar activists and others protesting outside spurred a "police riot" where police officers attacked protesters. The Republican Party, offended by antiwar protests, chose Richard Nixon as their candidate, who promised to bring "peace with honor" in Vietnam. Third-party candidate George Wallace, like Nixon, called for "law and order," while also appealing to whites upset with the federal government's support for the civil rights movement.*

CHECK FOR UNDERSTANDING

Ask students: **In what ways did Black and Chicano anti-war activists represent a change in the goals of social activism?** *Rejecting the "rights" politics of the civil rights movement, Black Power and Chicano activists turned to racial and ethnic nationalism.*

AP® APPLY THE TIP

Provide students with a large sheet of bulletin board paper on which they can create a timeline of the twentieth century (1900–2000). Ask students to use the textbook and class notes to place important events in women's history on the timeline. Students should indicate with a color code which events support feminism and which events were in opposition. Prompt students to create a system of periodization for the twentieth century that divides the century into distinct periods based on women's history. Students should name each period with an appropriate name (for example, remind them that the early nineteenth century had the "Cult of Domesticity"). Finally, ask the students to write a thesis statement on the timeline that responds to the prompt: To what degree does women's history in the twentieth century illustrate continuity and change?

AP® THEME

SOC: Social Structures; NAT: American and National Identity

Feminists and gay and lesbian activists mobilized behind claims for legal, economic, and social equality in the 1960s and early 1970s.

coming out of the New Left, antiwar, and civil rights movements. The male leaders of many left organizations, they discovered, considered women little more than pretty helpers who typed up their manifestoes and fetched coffee. In a manifesto of her own — entitled "Goodbye to All That" — the feminist Robin Morgan described the "counterfeit, male-dominated Left" as a movement composed of "men competing for power and status at the top, and women doing all the work at the bottom."

AP® EXAM TIP

Evaluate the degree of continuity and change in the feminist movement in the twentieth century.

Fed up with second-class status, and fluent in the tactics of organization and protest, women radicals broke away and organized on their own. Unlike the more centralized National Organization for Women (NOW), the women's liberation movement was composed of loosely tied together collectives in New York, San Francisco, Boston, and other big cities and college towns. Often meeting in small "consciousness raising" groups to discuss their experiences of gender injustice, women's liberationists cast their movement as more than a demand for legal equality with men — they sought a cultural revolution in society's treatment of women. "Women's lib," as it was dubbed by a skeptical media, went public in 1968 at the Miss America pageant. Demonstrators carried posters of female bodies labeled like butcher's diagrams — implying that society treated women as meat. Mirroring the identity politics of Black Power activists and the theatricality of the counterculture, women's liberation sought to highlight the denigration and exploitation of women. "Sisterhood is powerful!" read one women's liberationist manifesto. The nationwide Women's Strike for Equality in August 1970 brought hundreds of thousands of women into the streets for marches and demonstrations.

Women's Liberation A poster announcing a protest organized by a women's liberation group and the Black Panther Party of Connecticut in 1969, in support of six female Black Panthers who were being held in Niantic Connecticut State Women's Prison. White, black, and Chicana feminists all grew more radical in their activism and demands in the late 1960s, part of a wider radicalization of politics after 1968. Collection of the Smithsonian National Museum of African American History and Culture.

By that year, the women's movement had made new terms such as *sexism* and *male chauvinism* part of the national vocabulary. As converts flooded in, the radical and liberal offshoots of the movement began to converge. Radical women realized that key feminist goals — child care, equal pay, and reproduction rights — might be achieved by conventional political pressure. At the same time, more traditional activists, often known as "liberal feminists" to distinguish them from women's liberationists and exemplified by Betty Friedan, developed a wider view of women's oppression — and adopted some of the radical feminist positions they had earlier rejected. They came to understand that women required more than equal opportunity: a culture that primarily regarded women as sexual objects and helpmates to men had to change as well. Although still largely white and middle class, feminists of all stripes began to think of themselves as part of a broad social crusade.

"Sisterhood" did not unite all women, however. The mostly white feminist organizations such as NOW rarely addressed the concerns of women of color, and black and Chicana women primarily remained within the larger civil rights movement, linking their feminism to the crusade for racial justice. In the late 1960s, new groups such as the Combahee River Collective and the National Black Feminist Organization arose to speak for the concerns of black women. Black feminists criticized sexism but were reluctant to break completely with black men and the struggle for racial equality. "Given the mutual commitment of Black men and Black women alike to the liberation of our people," the black feminist Frances Beal wrote in 1970, "the total involvement of each individual is necessary." Mexican American feminists, or Chicana feminists as they called themselves, often came from Catholic backgrounds in which motherhood and family were held in high regard. "We want to walk hand in hand with the Chicano brothers, with our children, our *viejitos* [elders], our Familia de la Raza," one such feminist wrote. While black and Chicana feminists did embrace the larger movement for women's rights, they also sought to address specific needs in their communities.

One of the most important contributions of the new feminisms was to raise awareness about what feminist Kate Millett called "sexual politics." Liberationists, along with black and Chicana feminists, argued that women could not freely shape their destinies without control over their own bodies. They campaigned for reproductive rights, especially access to abortion, and railed against a culture that blamed women for their own sexual assault and turned a blind eye to sexual harassment in the workplace.

Progress on many of these fronts — sexual harassment in particular — was slow and would take decades, but the surging women's movement drove many changes that were more immediate and visible. Women's opportunities expanded dramatically in higher education. Starting in 1969 and continuing through the 1970s, dozens of formerly all-male bastions such as Yale, Princeton, and the U.S. military academies admitted women undergraduates for the first time, often under pressure from lawsuits filed by feminist attorneys. Women's studies programs emerged at many institutions, and the proportion of women attending graduate and professional schools rose markedly. With the adoption of **Title IX** in 1972 (of the Education Amendments bill), Congress broadened the 1964 Civil Rights Act to include educational institutions, prohibiting colleges and universities that received federal funds from discriminating on the basis of sex. Title IX guaranteed women access to the same educational opportunities as men and all but eliminated male-only institutions of higher education. By requiring comparable funding for sports programs, Title IX also made women's athletics a significant presence on college campuses.

Title IX
Law passed as part of the Education Amendments of 1972 guaranteeing women equal access and treatment in all educational institutions receiving federal funding.

AP® SKILLS & PROCESSES
COMPARISON
How did feminist movements after 1968 differ from the women's movement of the early 1960s?

Women also became an increasingly visible presence in political life. Congresswomen Bella Abzug and Shirley Chisholm joined Betty Friedan and Gloria Steinem, the founder of *Ms.* magazine, to create the National Women's Political Caucus in 1971. Abzug and Chisholm, both from New York, along with Congresswomen Patsy Mink from Hawaii and Martha Griffiths from Michigan, sponsored equal rights legislation — and helped to revive and eventually pass the Equal Rights Amendment. Congress authorized child-care tax deductions for working parents in 1972 and in 1974 passed the Equal Credit Opportunity Act, which permitted married women to get credit — including simple financial tools such as credit cards and mortgages — in their own names.

A Lesbian and Gay Rights Protest in Greenwich Village, New York City, 1970 Building on the momentum of the Black Power and women's liberation movements of the late 1960s, a gay liberation movement had emerged by the early 1970s. Its history was longer than most Americans recognized, dating to the homophile movement of the 1950s, but the struggle for gay and lesbian rights and freedoms gained new adherents after the Stonewall riots of 1969. Under the banner of "coming out," lesbian and gay Americans refused to accept second-class citizenship. Rue des Archives/GRANGER

Stonewall and Gay Liberation

The idea of liberation transformed the gay rights movement as well. Homophile activists in the 1960s had pursued rights through protest, but they adopted the respectable dress and behavior that straight society demanded (see "Challenging Middle-Class Morality" in Chapter 25). Meanwhile, the vast majority of gay men, lesbians, and transgender persons remained "in the closet." So many were closeted because homosexuality was considered immoral and was effectively illegal in the vast majority of states — sodomy statutes outlawed same-sex relations, and police used other morality laws to harass and arrest gay men, lesbians, and transgender people. In the late 1960s, however, inspired by the Black Power and women's movements, gay activists increasingly

AP® SKILLS & PROCESSES

COMPARISON

The **COMPARISON** question asks students to identify differences between the women's movement of the early 1960s and the movement at the end of the decade. Extend this prompt by asking students to explain why the movement changed, as well as the significance of the change.

TRM Find complete suggested responses in the Teacher's Resource Materials.

CHECK FOR UNDERSTANDING

Ask students: **What did the women's liberation and black and Chicana feminist movements advocate?** *Women's liberation advocates lobbied for government support for child care, equal pay, and reproduction rights, moving beyond concerns about equal opportunity in the workplace to advocate for a change in men's views of women as sex objects. While black and Chicana activists supported calls for reproductive rights, they also defended the specific concerns of their own ethnic group.*

TEACHING STRATEGY

The "Stonewall and Beyond: Lesbian and Gay Culture" Web site page, available through Columbia University, provides a number of images and texts related to the 1969 Stonewall riots and to the greater gay rights movement that it spawned. To access this site, search "Stonewall and Beyond: Lesbian and Gay Culture."

AP® SKILLS & PROCESSES

MAKING CONNECTIONS

The **MAKING CONNECTIONS** question asks students to identify the causes of the rupture between liberal politics of the early 1960s and the emergence of the antiwar movement and women's and gay liberation. To answer this question, students could explain the shared frustrations these different groups had about the nature of liberalism.

TRM Find complete suggested responses in the Teacher's Resource Materials.

CHECK FOR UNDERSTANDING

Ask students: **What factors best explain the rising militancy of social change and protest movements in 1968 and afterward?** *1968 was not a good year to be in the establishment. That year, the Tet Offensive discredited the Johnson administration, and two important reformers, Martin Luther King Jr. and Robert F. Kennedy, were assassinated. Calling on the power of the silent majority, conservative Richard Nixon was able to win the presidency. All of these events radicalized some groups of people, especially women, homosexuals, and Chicanos.*

AP® APPLY THE TIP

Divide the class into collaborative groups and assign each group to compare Richard Nixon's policies in Vietnam to another American president, including the following: Franklin Roosevelt, Harry Truman, Dwight Eisenhower, John F. Kennedy, and Lyndon Johnson. Ensure that the groups choose different presidents. Then ask each group to create a Venn diagram to discuss the similarities and differences. Display the completed Venn diagrams and discuss the similarities and differences between Nixon and his predecessors on Vietnam policy as a class. Initiate a debate to determine which president was most like and most unlike Nixon on Vietnam policy.

demanded immediate and unconditional recognition of their rights. A gay newspaper in New York bore the straightforward title *Come Out!*

This new gay liberation found expression in major cities across the country, but its defining event occurred in New York's Greenwich Village. Police had long raided gay bars, making arrests and harassing customers simply for being gay. Decades of such repression took a toll, and a routine police raid at a bar called the **Stonewall Inn** in the summer of 1969 touched off two days of clashes between gay people and the police. Local gay, lesbian, and transgender organizations proliferated after Stonewall, which became a powerful symbol of gay militancy. Activists began pushing for nondiscrimination ordinances and consensual sex laws at the city and state levels. By 1975, the National Gay Task Force and other national organizations were lobbying Congress, serving as media watchdogs, and advancing suits in the courts. Despite all this activism, progress was slow; in most arenas of life, gay men, lesbians, and transgender people did not enjoy the same legal protections and rights as other Americans.

Stonewall Inn
A gay bar in New York's Greenwich Village that was raided by police in 1969; the ensuing two-day riot contributed to the rapid rise of a gay liberation movement.

AP® SKILLS & PROCESSES
MAKING CONNECTIONS
How did the antiwar movement, women's liberation, and gay liberation break with an earlier liberal politics?

RISE OF THE SILENT MAJORITY

What social issues divided Americans in the early 1970s, and how did those divisions affect the two major political parties?

The unrest of the late 1960s had fractured the Democratic Party and left an opening for Republicans to grow in influence. Though he was an ardent anticommunist, President Nixon was a centrist by nature and temperament and not part of the archconservative Goldwater wing of the Republican Party. He accepted the basic idea that the government should play a role in the economy, and thus proved to be a transitional figure between postwar liberalism and the rightward turn of the post-Vietnam era. Nixon led rightward by capitalizing on the nation's unrest and uneasy mood through carefully timed speeches and displays of moral outrage.

In late 1969, following another massive antiwar rally in Washington, Nixon gave a televised speech in which he referred to his supporters as the **silent majority**. It was classic Nixonian rhetoric. In a single phrase, he turned a complex generational and cultural struggle into us-against-them — and placed himself on the side of ordinary Americans against rabble-rousers and troublemakers. It was an oversimplification, but *silent majority* stuck. For the remainder of his presidency, he projected himself as the defender of a reasonable middle ground under assault from the radical left.

silent majority
Term used by President Richard Nixon in a 1969 speech to describe those who supported his positions but did not publicly assert their voices, in contrast to those involved in the antiwar, civil rights, and women's movements.

Nixon in Vietnam

In Vietnam, Nixon picked up where Johnson had left off. Cold War doctrine continued to dictate presidential policy. Withdrawing, Nixon insisted, would damage America's "credibility" and make the country seem "a pitiful, helpless giant." Like everyone, the president wanted peace, but only "peace with honor." The North Vietnamese were not about to oblige him. The only reasonable outcome, from their standpoint, was a unified Vietnam under their control.

AP® EXAM TIP
Compare Richard Nixon's policies in Vietnam to previous American presidents'.

Vietnamization and Cambodia To neutralize criticism at home, Nixon decided to turn the ground fighting over to the South Vietnamese. Under this new policy of **Vietnamization**, American troop levels dropped from 543,000 in 1968 to 334,000 in 1971 and to just 24,000 by early 1973. American casualties dropped correspondingly, although the overall bloodshed continued. As Ellsworth Bunker, the U.S. ambassador to Vietnam, noted cynically, it was just a matter of changing "the color of the bodies." But even with the troop drawdown, American bombers continued, and even intensified, their aerial assault on North Vietnam.

Vietnamization
A U.S. policy, devised under President Nixon in the early 1970s, of delegating the ground fighting to the South Vietnamese in the Vietnam War. American troop levels dropped and American casualties dropped correspondingly, but the killing in Vietnam continued.

The war was far from over, and the antiwar movement, far from abating, intensified. In November 1969, half a million demonstrators gathered in Washington, D.C.,

Richard Nixon Richard Nixon completed one of the more remarkable political rehabilitations in modern times. He had lost the 1960 presidential election and the 1962 California gubernatorial election. But he came back strong in 1968 to ride — and help direct — a growing wave of reaction among conservative Americans against Great Society liberalism, the antiwar movement, civil rights, and the counterculture. In this photograph, President Nixon greets supporters in June 1969, just a few months after his inauguration. © Wally McNamee/Corbis/Corbis via Getty Images.

for the Vietnam Moratorium, one of the largest protests ever held in the capital. On April 30, 1970, Nixon announced that American forces would attack suspected enemy targets in neutral Cambodia where a secret bombing campaign had been going on for a year already. The invasion of Cambodia touched off a new wave of outrage on American campuses — and for the first time in the antiwar movement, students were killed. On May 4, 1970, at Kent State University in Ohio, panicky National Guardsmen fired into an antiwar rally, wounding nine students and killing four; of the 13 people hit, the nearest was 60 feet from the Guardsmen. Nationwide student protests led more than 450 colleges and universities to close, some for a day or two, others for weeks. Less than two weeks later, during a protest march at Jackson State College in Mississippi, Guardsmen opened fire on a dormitory, killing two black students. The Jackson State incident received slim coverage in the national media, but it was no less tragic an outcome of the escalating tensions between youth and authorities.

AP® SKILLS & PROCESSES

COMPARISON

How was President Nixon's Vietnam policy different from President Johnson's?

My Lai Massacre Though unrelated, one of the worst atrocities of the war had become public about six months before the protests at Kent State and Jackson State. On March 16, 1968, U.S. Army troops killed close to five hundred South Vietnamese civilians in the village of **My Lai**, including a large number of women and children. For the better part of a year, the massacre was effectively kept secret within the military, until journalist Seymour Hersh broke the story in November 1969 in the *St Louis Post-Dispatch*, with photos of the massacre appearing in the *Cleveland Plain Dealer*. My Lai discredited the United States in the eyes of the world. Americans, *Time* observed, "must stand in the larger dock of guilt and human conscience." Although high-ranking officers participated in the My Lai massacre and its cover-up, only one soldier, a low-ranking second lieutenant named William Calley, was convicted. Many believed that Calley was made a scapegoat for failed U.S. policies that made civilian deaths an inescapable part of the war.

My Lai
Vietnamese village where U.S. Army troops executed nearly five hundred people in 1968, including a large number of women and children.

AP® THEME

PCE: Politics and Power

In the 1960s, conservatives challenged liberal laws and court decisions, and the moral and cultural decline they perceived. They sought to limit the role of the federal government and enact more assertive foreign policies.

AP® SKILLS & PROCESSES

COMPARISON

The **COMPARISON** question asks students to identify the differences between the Vietnam policies of Johnson and Nixon. Students should explain what each hoped to accomplish and why. In their response, students could also explain the ways that Nixon's approach was a reaction to Johnson's.

TRM Find complete suggested responses in the Teacher's Resource Materials.

VISUAL ACTIVITY

Prowar Rally Under a sea of American flags, construction workers in New York City march in support of the Vietnam War. Wearing hard hats, tens of thousands of marchers jammed Broadway for four blocks opposite City Hall, and the overflow crammed the side streets. Working-class patriotism became a main source of support for Nixon's Vietnam policy. © Paul Fusco/Magnum Photos.

READING THE IMAGE: Read as many of the signs as you are able to, and identify as many different symbols as you can.

MAKING CONNECTIONS: In what ways does this image illustrate divisions in American society? How does this image relate to the development of the "southern strategy" (pg. 892) by the Republican Party?

TRM Find complete suggested responses in the Teacher's Resource Materials.

Disillusionment with the war was mounting. Notably, the disillusionment now included Americans who had served in the military. A group called Vietnam Veterans Against the War publicized other atrocities committed by U.S. troops. In a controversial protest in 1971, they returned their combat medals at demonstrations outside the U.S. Capitol, literally hurling them onto the steps of the building. "Here's my merit badge for murder," one vet said. Supporters of the war derided these veterans as disloyal, but their heartfelt antiwar protest reflected the deep personal torment that Vietnam had caused for many soldiers.

AP® EXAM TIP

Evaluate the degree to which détente fostered change and illustrated continuity in the policy of containment.

détente
The easing of conflict between the United States and the Soviet Union during the Nixon administration, which was achieved by focusing on issues of common concern, such as arms control and trade.

Détente As protests continued at home, Nixon pursued his goal of "peace with honor." Negotiations to end the war had begun in Paris in May of 1968, when Johnson was still president. With both sides avoiding agreements that looked like defeat, and each accusing the other of negotiating in bad faith, the Paris peace talks dragged on for years, as the war grew even bloodier. Nixon knew, however, that a U.S. military victory was unlikely and that the Paris talks represented the surest route to an American exit.

Nixon wanted not just "peace" but also "honor," which meant ending the war on terms favorable to the United States. He hoped to achieve those favorable terms via both diplomacy and a shift in military tactics. First, he sought **détente** (a lessening of

AP® THEME

WOR: America in the World

The Cold War fluctuated between periods of direct and indirect military confrontation and periods of coexistence, represented by the policy of détente.

tensions) with the Soviet Union and a new openness with China. Nixon reasoned that by thawing relations with these two communist adversaries, which supported North Vietnam against the U.S.-backed South, he could strike a better deal at the ongoing peace talks in Paris. In a series of meetings between 1970 and 1972, Nixon and Soviet premier Leonid Brezhnev resolved tensions over Cuba and Berlin and signed the first Strategic Arms Limitation Treaty (SALT I), the latter a symbolic step toward ending the Cold War arms race. Nixon was heavily influenced by his national security advisor, the Harvard professor Henry Kissinger, who regarded the Soviet Union not as an ideological foe to be resisted at every turn but as a traditional geopolitical rival with whom compromises were possible. Taking Kissinger's advice, Nixon sought to break the impasse that long kept the United States from any productive relationship with the Soviet Union.

Nixon took the same approach to China, and in 1972 became the first sitting U.S. president to visit that country. In a weeklong trip heavily covered by the press, the president pledged that the two nations — one capitalist, the other communist — could peacefully coexist. This was the same Nixon who had risen to prominence in the 1950s by railing against the Democrats for "losing" China and by hounding Communists and fellow travelers in the United States. Indeed, the president's impeccable anticommunist credentials gave him the political cover to travel to Beijing. Praised for his efforts to lessen Cold War tensions, Nixon also had tactical objectives in mind: he needed to end the war in Vietnam without appearing to lose it, and he hoped that better relations with the Soviet Union and China would aid in this objective.

Exit America To accompany his pursuit of détente, Nixon shifted American military tactics. In April 1972, in an attempt to strengthen his negotiating position, the president ordered large-scale bombing raids against North Vietnam. A month later, he approved laying explosive mines in North Vietnamese ports, something Johnson had never dared to do. Neither tactic worked: supplies from China and the Soviet Union still flowed in, and the communists fought on.

With the 1972 presidential election approaching, Nixon sent Kissinger back to the Paris peace talks, which had broken off in 1971. In a key concession, Kissinger accepted the presence of North Vietnamese troops in South Vietnam. North Vietnam then agreed to an interim arrangement whereby the South Vietnamese government in Saigon would stay in power while a special commission arranged a final settlement. With Kissinger's announcement that "peace is at hand," Nixon got the electoral boost he wanted and won reelection. The agreement was then sabotaged by General Nguyen Van Thieu, the South Vietnamese president. In response, Nixon, in an all-out bid to force an end to the war, unleashed the two-week "Christmas bombing" of the cities of Hanoi and Haiphong, the most intense of the entire war. Historians disagree over the bombing's impact on negotiations, but on January 27, 1973, the two sides signed the Paris Peace Accords.

New Openings with China American officials conferring with a Chinese foreign minister on their way to Beijing, China, in 1972 with President Nixon. Henry Kissinger, Nixon's national security advisor, is seated second from left. On this trip, Nixon became the first sitting president to visit mainland China, part of a larger easing of tensions between the United States and the major communist powers — the Soviet Union and China — in the early 1970s. AP Photo.

Nixon hoped that South Vietnam's Thieu regime might survive, propped up by massive American aid. But Congress was in revolt against the war and cut back aid to South Vietnam. In March 1975, North Vietnamese forces launched a final offensive, and by the end of April, Vietnam was finally reunited. That outcome was a powerful, and tragic, historical irony. The American involvement in Vietnam had begun in 1954, with Eisenhower sending money and advisors to South Vietnam just as the Diem regime refused to honor the unification vote mandated in the

CHECK FOR UNDERSTANDING

Ask students: **What was Nixon's approach to Vietnam?** *Through Vietnamization, he sought to reduce the presence of American troops. At the same time, he expanded the war against communists by bombing Cambodia and, eventually, sending in ground troops.*

Geneva Accords. Two decades later, the outcome was essentially what that unification vote would have produced. In other words, America's most disastrous military venture had not mattered. It had not changed the geopolitical outcome in Vietnam. However, although the Hanoi regime called itself communist, it refused to be a satellite of any country, least of all China, Vietnam's ancient enemy.

The price paid for the Vietnam War was steep. Those Vietnamese who had sided with the Americans lost jobs and property, spent years in "reeducation" camps, or fled the country. Millions of Vietnamese had died in the war, which included some of the heaviest aerial bombing of the twentieth century. In bordering Cambodia, the maniacal Khmer Rouge, followers of Cambodia's ruling Communist Party, took power and murdered 1.7 million people in bloody purges. More than 58,000 Americans had given their lives in Vietnam, and 300,000 had been wounded. On top of the war's $150 billion price tag, it inflicted internal wounds on the country; Americans were increasingly divided, with less confidence in their political leaders.

The Silent Majority Speaks Out

Nixon placed himself on the side of "the nonshouters, the nondemonstrators." But centrist and conservative Americans alike, those who composed the "silent majority" invoked by the president, were not in the mood to remain silent. During Nixon's first presidential term, they focused their discontent on what they believed to be the excesses of the "rights revolution" — the enormous changes in American law and society initiated by the civil rights movement and advanced by feminists and others thereafter. Periods of reform throughout American history have reliably been followed by periods of retrenchment or backlash. The backlash that followed the rights revolution of the 1960s and early 1970s rested on a specific counterargument: that liberalism had created a "permissive" society of lawbreakers and immorality while overturning natural gender roles and peaceful race relations.

Law and Order and the Supreme Court Backlash against liberalism found one of its primary targets in the U.S. Supreme Court, which had become a powerful ally of the rights revolution. The landmark civil rights case of *Brown v. Board of Education* (1954) triggered a larger judicial revolution. After *Brown*, the Court increasingly agreed to hear human rights and civil liberties cases — as opposed to its previous focus on property-related suits. Led by Chief Justice Earl Warren, a former Republican governor of California who was appointed to the bench by President Eisenhower in 1953, the Court robustly advocated civil rights and liberties from 1954 to 1969.

Warren Court
The Supreme Court under Chief Justice Earl Warren (1953–1969), which expanded the Constitution's promise of equality and civil rights. It issued landmark decisions in the areas of civil rights, criminal rights, reproductive freedom, and separation of church and state.

AP® EXAM TIP

Evaluate the role of the Supreme Court in extending liberal values through judicial decisions.

Right-wing activists fiercely opposed the **Warren Court**, which they accused of "legislating from the bench" and contributing to social breakdown. Every category of crime was up in the 1970s, with murder rates doubled since the 1950s and a 76 percent increase in burglary and theft between 1967 and 1976. Stoked by a media fixation on "crime," conservatives lamented the Supreme Court's rulings that people who are arrested have a constitutional right to counsel (1963, 1964) and, in *Miranda v. Arizona* (1966), that arrestees have to be informed by police of their right to remain silent. The Court also issued decisions that relaxed restrictions on pornography. First in *Roth v. United States* (1957) and then in *Miller v. California* (1972), the Court attempted to balance freedom of expression with rules outlining the kind of obscenity that could be legally banned. However, neither ruling slowed the proliferation of pornographic magazines, films, and live shows. Conservatives found these decisions especially distasteful, since the Court had also ruled that religious ritual of any kind in public schools — including prayers and Bible reading — violated the constitutional separation of church and state. To many religious Americans, the Court had taken the side of immorality over Christian values.

There was no known link between the increase in crime and Supreme Court decisions, given a myriad of other social factors, income inequality, enhanced statistical record-keeping, increasing drug use, and the proliferation of guns. But when many

AP® THEME

PCE: Politics and Power

Students should be aware of the series of Supreme Court decisions that expanded civil rights and individual liberties in the era of the Warren Court.

AP® APPLY THE TIP

Inform students that they will work in collaborative groups to put a Supreme Court case "In the Bag" to illustrate the ways in which judicial systems extended liberal values in the 1960s. For this activity, student groups will collect, find, create, or modify a minimum of five items to put into a small paper bag to represent different Court cases. Assign each group one case to research in order to explain the background of the case, the constitutional issue, decision of the Court, dissenting opinions (if any), and impact of the decision on extending liberal values. It is best to give students at least one night to work on this activity, as some items to collect may not be at school. When students have completed their bags, ask them to write a notecard that explains the case and the way in which each item in the bag represents a characteristic of the case. Students should then share their bag with the class. After all the cases are shared, lead a class discussion during which students should group the cases according to similarities as well as identify ways in which each case extended liberal values.

Americans looked at their cities in the 1970s, they saw pornographic theaters, X-rated bookstores, and rising crime rates. Where, they wondered, was law and order? Sensational crimes had always grabbed headlines, but now "crime" itself preoccupied politicians, the media, and the public.

An Antibusing Confrontation in Boston White and black students fighting outside Hyde Park High School in Boston, Massachusetts, in 1975. The city of Boston started a court-ordered school integration program requiring the busing of 18 percent of public school students. Wherever busing was implemented across the country, it often faced stiff resistance and protest. Many white communities resented judges dictating which children would attend which neighborhood school. Busing also had the perverse effect of speeding up "white flight" to city suburbs. AP Photo/DPG.

Busing Another major civil rights objective — desegregating schools — produced even more friction. For fifteen years, southern states, using a variety of stratagems, had fended off court directives to desegregate "with all deliberate speed." In 1968, only about one-third of all black children in the South attended schools with whites. Federal courts finally took a serious stance against noncompliance and in a series of firm decisions ordered an end to "dual school systems."

In areas where schools remained highly segregated, the courts increasingly endorsed busing students in order to achieve integration. Busing differed across the country. In some states, black children rode buses from their neighborhoods to attend previously all-white schools. In others, white children were bused to black or Latino neighborhoods, leading to fierce resistance and major protests by white parents and community members. In Charlotte, North Carolina, Vera and Darius Swann, with help from the NAACP, had forced a federal court to order the desegregation of the local school district. In an important 1971 decision, *Swann v. Charlotte-Mecklenburg*, the Supreme Court upheld the order, siding with the Swanns and affirming that federal courts had the authority to oversee and enforce school desegregation plans. Despite intense local opposition by white parents, desegregation proceeded, and many cities in the South followed suit. By the mid-1970s, 86 percent of southern black children were attending school with whites.

Postwar suburbanization produced a particularly entrenched form of school segregation in the North, and busing orders there proved less effective. Detroit exemplified the problem. To integrate Detroit schools would have required merging city and suburban school districts. A lower court ordered just such a merger in 1971, but in *Milliken v. Bradley* (1974), the Supreme Court reversed the ruling, requiring busing plans to remain within the boundaries of a single school district. Without including largely white suburbs in busing efforts, however, achieving racial balance in Detroit, and demographically similar northern cities, was impossible. Courts continued to issue busing plans for individual cities, and wherever they did, from Boston to Denver and Los Angeles, white communities erupted in protest and opposition, strengthening the silent majority's growing influence.

AP® SKILLS & PROCESSES

MAKING CONNECTIONS

How would you characterize the points of view of those who supported the Warren Court's decisions and those who opposed them?

The 1972 Election

As his reelection campaign approached, President Nixon took advantage of rising discontent over "law and order" and busing. In doing so, he became the beneficiary of a growing backlash against liberalism that was realigning American politics. The last great electoral upheaval had come between 1932 and 1936, when many Republican voters abandoned their party to support FDR, and many Americans voting for the first time likewise sided with the Democrats — forging an electoral coalition that lasted nearly four decades. The years between 1968 and 1972 proved to be a similar watershed. This time, it was Democrats who changed their votes and Republicans who captured a new electoral generation.

CHECK FOR UNDERSTANDING

Ask students: **How did the silent majority speak out in the late 1960s?** *Many conservative Americans were outraged by Supreme Court decisions that they thought reduced the public role of religion while protecting criminals and pornographers. They were also frustrated by forced busing, which they thought created unnecessary turmoil in an effort to impose social change.*

AP® SKILLS & PROCESSES

MAKING CONNECTIONS

It may help to give students categories of analysis for the Warren Court such as race-related and rights of the accused decisions. In this way, you are helping students understand the broad contours of debate over the role the Warren Court played in the political debates attendant to this period. Encourage students to select a specific Supreme Court decision to use as they explain both the support and opposition to the decisions of the Warren Court.

TRM Find complete suggested responses in the Teacher's Resource Materials.

Candidate	Electoral Vote	Popular Vote	Percent of Popular Vote
Richard Nixon (Republican)	520	47,169,911	60.7
George McGovern (Democrat)	17	29,170,383	37.5
John Hospers (Libertarian)	1	3,674	0.0

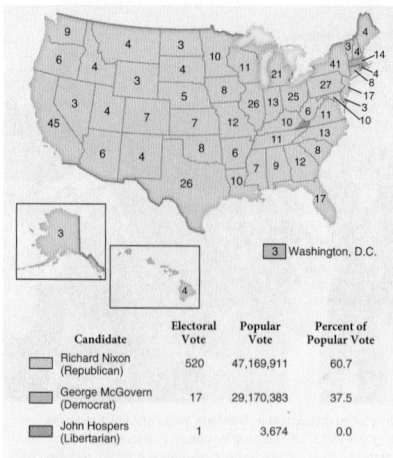

MAP 27.4 The Presidential Election of 1972
In one of the most lopsided presidential elections of the twentieth century, Republican Richard Nixon defeated Democrat George McGovern in a landslide in 1972. It was a reversal of the 1964 election, just eight years before, in which Republican Barry Goldwater had been defeated by a similar margin. Nixon hoped that his victory signaled what Kevin Phillips called "the emerging Republican majority," but the president's missteps and criminal actions in the Watergate scandal would soon bring an end to his tenure in office.

Reforms in the Democrat Party's nominating procedures had opened the door for George McGovern, a liberal South Dakota senator and favorite of the antiwar and women's movements, to capture the presidential nomination. But McGovern quickly ran afoul of the party's old guard. He failed to mollify key backers such as the AFL-CIO, which, for the first time in memory, refused to endorse the Democratic ticket. A weak campaigner, McGovern was no match for the hardboiled Nixon, whose supporters ridiculed the Democrat as the candidate of "Acid, amnesty, and abortion" — referring to McGovern's alleged support for drug legalization (which was false), amnesty for draft evaders (true), and women's reproductive rights (true). Taking advantage of incumbency, Nixon also claimed credit for a surging economy and proclaimed (prematurely) a cease-fire in Vietnam.

Appealing again to the "silent majority" of those who "care about a strong United States, about patriotism, about moral and spiritual values," Nixon won in a landslide, receiving nearly 61 percent of the popular vote and carrying every state except Massachusetts and the District of Columbia (Map 27.4). The returns revealed the fracture of traditional Democratic voting blocs. McGovern received only 38 percent of the big-city Catholic vote and, remarkably, only 60 percent of self-identified Democrats nationwide voted for him. The election results demonstrated the country's shift to the right. Yet observers legitimately asked whether 1972 proved the popularity of conservatism or only that the country had grown weary of liberalism and the changes it had wrought.

SUMMARY

Following John Kennedy's assassination in 1963, Lyndon Johnson advanced the most ambitious liberal reform program since the New Deal, securing not only civil rights legislation but also action to expand government support for education, medical care, transportation, and environmental protection. The centerpiece of Johnson's "Great Society" was the War on Poverty, a set of programs meant to help the poorest Americans share in the wide prosperity. But LBJ's visions for a Great Society were stunted by escalating involvement in Vietnam.

The war bitterly divided Americans. Galvanized by scenes of carnage and the threat of the draft, the antiwar movement spread rapidly among young people, and the spirit of rebellion spilled beyond the war. The New Left took the lead among college students, while the more apolitical counterculture preached liberation through sex, drugs, music, and personal transformation. Women's liberationists broke from the New Left and challenged society's sexism. Right-leaning students rallied in support of the war and conservative causes, but they were largely drowned out by the more demonstrative liberals and radicals.

In 1968, the nation was rocked by the assassinations of Martin Luther King Jr. and Robert F. Kennedy, as well as by a wave of urban riots, fueling a growing popular desire for law and order. Adding to the national disquiet was the Democratic National Convention that summer, which was disrupted by fierce debate over the Vietnam War inside the hall and street riots outside. Richard Nixon headed a resurgence of the Republican Party with a brand of politics that capitalized on the breakup of the New Deal coalition. The turbulent second half of the sixties had left many Americans desperate for calm and order. The years to come, full of economic crisis and further political realignment, would present the country not with a calm era free of conflict but with deepening debates about what kind of society and government role Americans wanted.

CHECK FOR UNDERSTANDING

Ask students: **What social issues divided Americans in the early 1970s, and how did those divisions affect the two major political parties?** *In the early 1970s, Americans were divided over issues such as how to extract the military forces from Vietnam and the busing of students to achieve integration. Republicans, led by Nixon, moderated their course, rejecting the far-right Goldwater segment of the party. The New Deal coalition, having fallen apart when President Johnson signed the 1964 Civil Rights Act and Southern Democrats left the party, further fractured in the 1972 election when leftists gained control of the convention and brushed aside labor leaders. This pushed the party further to the left, to its detriment in the election.*

CHECK FOR UNDERSTANDING

Use the **AP® LEARNING FOCUS** question from the beginning of the chapter to check students' understanding of the chapter as a whole: **Why did debates over liberal values in the 1960s lead to social conflict and divide the country?** *Liberalism's achievements in the 1960s included success of the civil rights movement in the form of the Civil Rights Act of 1964, the Voting Rights Act of 1965, the advances of the Great Society and War on Poverty, the gay rights movement, the women's liberation movement, the free speech movement, and the larger student movement for a more democratic society. The rise of liberalism contributed to a critique from more conservative Americans who did not agree with the growth of social programs, feminism, or the youth movement. Many believed that the American family was under attack. In addition, Americans clashed over involvement in Vietnam and the reach of the federal government abroad. Indeed, the divide in America over the Vietnam War in many ways mirrored the varied social views of the period. Fissures in American society over domestic and foreign policy defined the 1960s.*

✓ LearningCurve

Remind students to go online to complete the LearningCurve quiz for this chapter.

CHAPTER 27 REVIEW

AP® CONTENT REVIEW
Answer these questions to demonstrate your understanding of the chapter's main ideas.

1. Why was there a surge in liberal politics and social policy in the early 1960s?
2. What factors led President Johnson to escalate the war in Vietnam, and how did Americans respond?
3. What factors best explain the rising militancy of social change and protest movements in 1968 and afterward?
4. What social issues divided Americans in the early 1970s, and how did those divisions affect the two major political parties?

AP® TERMS TO KNOW
Identify and explain the significance of each term below.

Key Concepts and Events

Great Society (p. 872)
Economic Opportunity Act (p. 874)
Medicare (p. 876)
Medicaid (p. 876)
Equal Pay Act (p. 877)
The Feminine Mystique (p. 877)
Presidential Commission on the Status of Women (p. 878)
National Organization for Women (NOW) (p. 878)
Gulf of Tonkin Resolution (p. 881)
Operation Rolling Thunder (p. 881)
Port Huron Statement (p. 885)
New Left (p. 885)
Young Americans for Freedom (YAF) (p. 888)
Sharon Statement (p. 888)
Tet offensive (p. 889)
1968 Democratic National Convention (p. 891)
Chicano Moratorium Committee (p. 893)
Title IX (p. 895)
Stonewall Inn (p. 896)
silent majority (p. 896)
Vietnamization (p. 896)
My Lai (p. 897)
détente (p. 898)
Warren Court (p. 900)

Key People

Lyndon B. Johnson (p. 872)
Barry Goldwater (p. 874)
Betty Friedan (p. 877)
Ngo Dinh Diem (p. 880)
Robert Kennedy (p. 890)
Richard M. Nixon (p. 891)
George C. Wallace (p. 892)
Henry Kissinger (p. 899)

AP® MAKING CONNECTIONS
Recognize the larger developments and continuities within and across chapters by answering these questions.

1. In what ways was the Great Society an extension of the New Deal? In what ways was it different? What factors made the period between 1932 and 1972 a "liberal" era in American politics? What events and developments would you use to explain your answer?
2. Compare the photographs of the prowar rally (p. 898) and the counterculture (p. 888). Why did clothing and appearance become so important to many social movements in the 1960s — the women's movement, the Black Power movement, the antiwar movement, and others? How are these visual images historical evidence?

KEY TURNING POINTS
Refer to the timeline at the start of the chapter for helping in answering this question.

Which specific developments from the chronology made the years 1964, 1965, and 1968 turning points in politics, foreign policy, and culture, and why?

903

TRM Find complete suggested responses in the Teacher's Resource Materials.

AP® SKILLS & PROCESSES

CAUSATION

AP® CONTENT REVIEW 1 asks students to explain the causes of liberal social and political activism in the 1960s. Note: This is the same question as the section-opening prompt on p. 872.

AP® SKILLS & PROCESSES

CAUSATION

AP® CONTENT REVIEW 2 invites students to identify the causes of Johnson's escalation in Vietnam. Note: This is the same question as the section-opening prompt on p. 880.

AP® SKILLS & PROCESSES

CAUSATION

AP® CONTENT REVIEW 3 asks students to explain the causes of social and political protest in the 1960s. Note: This is the same question as the section-opening prompt on p. 889.

AP® SKILLS & PROCESSES

COMPARISON

AP® CONTENT REVIEW 4 asks students to explain the effects of social divisions on political parties. Note: This is the same question as the section-opening prompt on p. 896.

TRM Find definitions for these terms in the **Glossary/Glosario** in the Teacher's Resource Materials.

AP® SKILLS & PROCESSES

COMPARISON

AP® MAKING CONNECTIONS 1 invites students to compare two reform efforts, the New Deal and the Great Society, which was modeled on it.

AP® SKILLS & PROCESSES

CONTINUITY AND CHANGE

The **KEY TURNING POINTS** question asks students to identify turning points in American society between 1964 and 1968.

TRM Find complete suggested responses in the Teacher's Resource Materials.

AP PRACTICE QUESTIONS

MULTIPLE CHOICE QUESTIONS *Choose the correct answer for each question.*

Questions 1–4 refer to this excerpt.

> "On September 7th in Atlantic City, the Annual Miss America Pageant will again crown 'your ideal.' . . . We will protest the image of Miss America, an image that oppresses women in every area in which it purports to represent us. There will be: Picket Lines; Guerrilla Theater; Leafleting . . . a huge Freedom Trash Can (into which we will throw bras, girdles, curlers, false eyelashes, wigs, and representative issues of *Cosmopolitan, Ladies' Home Journal, Family Circle,* etc. . . . [W]e will also announce a Boycott of all those commercial products related to the Pageant. . . It should be a groovy day on the Boardwalk in the sun with our sisters. . . .
>
> Male reporters will be refused interviews. We reject patronizing reportage. Only newswomen will be recognized."
>
> "No More Miss America" press release for 1968 Pageant Protest. Excerpted with permission from *Sisterhood Is Powerful*, Robin Morgan, 1970 (Random House, NY).

1. The sentiments Morgan expressed in the excerpt are best understood as resulting from
   - a. court decisions expanding individual rights.
   - b. the rise of a youth counterculture.
   - c. the mass media.
   - d. declining public trust in the government.
2. The women's activists of the 1960s and 1970s represented by the excerpt from Morgan share the LEAST similarity with women advocates for
   - a. separate public and private spheres in the 1830s.
   - b. the Seneca Falls Declaration of Sentiments in 1848.
   - c. social reform as demonstrated by Jane Addams in the 1890s.
   - d. the Nineteenth Amendment to the Constitution in the 1910s.
3. Which of the following developments most likely resulted from women's activism as described in the excerpt?
   - a. A conservative backlash against the challenge to traditional values
   - b. Passage of the Equal Rights Amendment
   - c. Advances by women in the leadership of major corporations
   - d. The election of women to Senate and House of Representatives
4. Which rights movement most directly influenced the tactics and goals of the women's rights movement?
   - a. American Indian
   - b. Chicano/Latino
   - c. African American
   - d. Gay and Lesbian

Questions 5–7 refer to this excerpt.

> "No voting qualification or prerequisite to voting, or standard, practice, or procedure shall be imposed or applied by any State or political subdivision to deny or abridge the right of any citizen of the United States to vote on account of race or color."
>
> Voting Rights Act of 1965

5. The provisions in the Voting Rights Act share the greatest similarity in goals to the reform efforts of
   - a. abolitionists in the antebellum period from 1820 to 1860.
   - b. Republicans in the Reconstruction period from 1865 to 1877.
   - c. Progressives in the period from 1890 to 1920.
   - d. Democrats in the New Deal from 1933 to 1941.
6. The Voting Rights Act of 1965 resulted most directly from
   - a. continued efforts of southern politicians to resist school desegregation.
   - b. rulings of the Supreme Court broadening protections of civil liberties.
   - c. successful use of the protest tactic of boycotting.
   - d. President Johnson's attempt to create a Great Society.
7. The Voting Rights Act sought most directly to strengthen the
   - a. Bill of Rights.
   - b. Fourteenth Amendment.
   - c. Fifteenth Amendment.
   - d. Nineteenth Amendment.

SHORT ANSWER QUESTIONS

Read each question carefully and write a short response. Use evidence from the text to support your claims.

"Within the context of cultural unrest and the attack on tradition made by women like [Betty] Friedan, the catalyst for a profounder criticism and a mass mobilization of American women proved to be the young female participants in the social movements of the 1960s. These daughters of the middle class had received mixed, paradoxical messages about what it meant to grow up to be women in America. On the one hand, the cultural ideal . . . informed them that their only true happiness lay in the twin roles of wife and mother. At the same time they could observe the reality that housewifery was distinctly unsatisfactory for millions of suburban women. . . . Such contradictions left young, educated women in the 1960s dry tinder for the spark of revolt. . . . [Their] experiences in the southern civil rights movement and parts of the student new left catalyzed a new feminist consciousness."

Sara Evans, *Personal Politics: The Roots of Women's Liberation in the Civil Rights Movement and the New Left*, 1979

"In the course of my research, several themes emerged. One of them, clearly exposed through the experience of Black women, is the relationship between sexism and racism. . . . Of course, Black women could understand the relationship between racism and sexism because they had to strive against both. In doing so, they became the linchpin between the two most important social reform movements in American history: the struggles for Black rights and women's rights. In the course of defying the imposed limitations on race and sex, they loosened the chains around both."

Paula Giddings, *When and Where I Enter: The Impact of Black Women on Race and Sex in America*, 1984

1. Using the two excerpts provided, answer (a), (b), and (c).
   - **a.** Briefly explain ONE major difference between Evans's and Giddings's historical interpretations of the origins of 1960s feminism.
   - **b.** Briefly explain how ONE specific historical event or development from the period 1945 to 1965 that is not explicitly mentioned in the excerpts could be used to support Evans's interpretation.
   - **c.** Briefly explain how ONE specific historical event or development from the period 1945 to 1965 that is not explicitly mentioned in the excerpts could be used to support Giddings's interpretation.

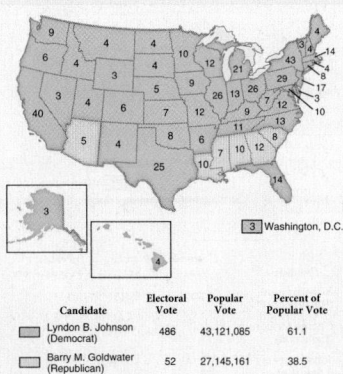

Candidate	Electoral Vote	Popular Vote	Percent of Popular Vote
Lyndon B. Johnson (Democrat)	486	43,121,085	61.1
Barry M. Goldwater (Republican)	52	27,145,161	38.5

1964 Presidential Election Map

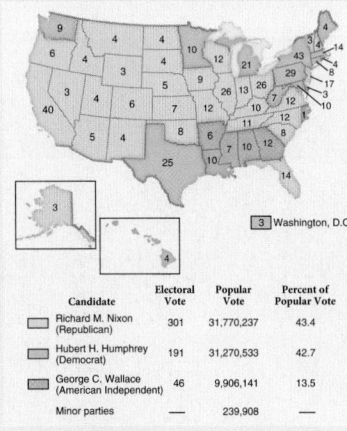

Candidate	Electoral Vote	Popular Vote	Percent of Popular Vote
Richard M. Nixon (Republican)	301	31,770,237	43.4
Hubert H. Humphrey (Democrat)	191	31,270,533	42.7
George C. Wallace (American Independent)	46	9,906,141	13.5
Minor parties	—	239,908	—

1968 Presidential Election Map

TRM Find complete suggested responses in the Teacher's Resource Materials.

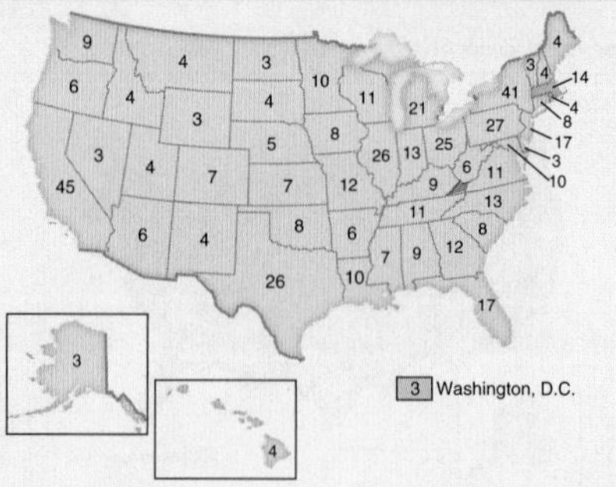

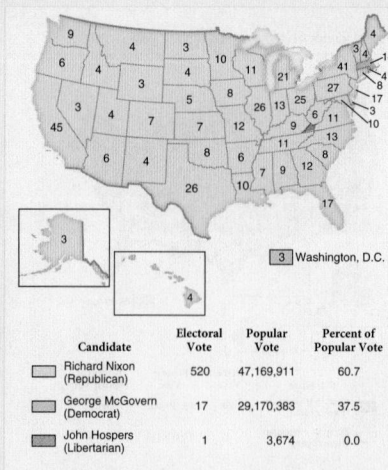

Candidate	Electoral Vote	Popular Vote	Percent of Popular Vote
Richard Nixon (Republican)	520	47,169,911	60.7
George McGovern (Democrat)	17	29,170,383	37.5
John Hospers (Libertarian)	1	3,674	0.0

1972 Presidential Election Map

2. Using the three maps provided, answer (a), (b), and (c).
   - **a.** Briefly explain ONE specific historical event or development that accounts for the change depicted in the maps.
   - **b.** Briefly explain ANOTHER specific historical event or development that accounts for the change depicted in the maps.
   - **c.** Briefly explain ONE specific historical effect of the change depicted in the maps.

3. Answer (a), (b), and (c).
   - **a.** Briefly explain ONE specific historical similarity between President Franklin Roosevelt's New Deal and President Lyndon Johnson's Great Society.
   - **b.** Briefly explain ONE specific historical difference between President Franklin Roosevelt's New Deal and President Lyndon Johnson's Great Society.
   - **c.** Briefly explain ONE specific historical effect of President Lyndon Johnson's Great Society.

28 CHAPTER The Search for Order in an Era of Limits 1973–1980

Chapter 28 — AP® Assessment Weight and Pacing Guide

The assessment weight on the AP® U.S. History Exam for Chapters 23–28 is 10–17 percent. This chapter falls in Unit 8 of the AP® U.S. History Curriculum, covering Period 8: 1945–1980.

This pacing guide is based on a schedule with 120 sessions of 50 minutes each before the AP® U.S. History Exam. If you have a different number of sessions before the exam, you can modify the pacing to meet your needs. If you have additional time, consider incorporating quizzes, released AP® U.S. History questions, practice exams, writing practice, and other instructional activities.

	Traditional Schedule	Block Schedule
Chapter 28	4 days	2 days

Daily Pacing Guide

	Content Focus	Essential Question
Day 1	Limits to Growth and Prosperity	What kind of limits, or crises, did the American economy encounter in the 1970s?
Day 2	Politics in Flux, 1973–1980	In what ways was the period between 1973 and 1980 a transitional one in American politics?
Day 3	Reform and Reaction in the 1970s	How did controversies over new individual rights shape the politics of the 1970s?
Day 4	The American Family under Stress	What were the major sources of anxiety about the American family in the decade after the 1960s?

AP® Alignment

Section Heading	AP® Topic	AP® Theme
Limits to Growth and Prosperity	8.4, 8.13, 8.14	MIG, GEO, PCE
Politics in Flux, 1973–1980	8.14	PCE
Reform and Reaction in the 1970s	8.11, 8.14	SOC, PCE
The American Family under Stress	8.11, 8.14	SOC, PCE, ARC

*Should changes be made to the Course Framework in the future, an updated alignment will be placed on our AP® updates page at go.bfwpub.com/ap-course-updates.

Chapter 28 — Overview

Chapter 28 emphasizes the dramatic shifts that occurred in the U.S. as a result of the challenges and crises of the 1970s. The chapter begins by focusing on the challenges presented by the energy crisis and economic changes that threatened American prosperity at home. Despite the loss of confidence in politics due to Vietnam, Watergate, and the energy crisis, reform groups made strides in expanding civil rights to include greater equality for women and homosexuals. Finally, the chapter focuses on the rise of New Evangelicalism as a response to those dramatic changes in American life.

Chapter 28 — Resources

The following resources can be found in the Teacher's Resource Materials (TRM) that accompany the book. You can access the TRM via the book's digital platform, by clicking the TRM links found here in your Teacher's Edition e-book, or by contacting your representative to access the resources online. Visit **bfwpub.com/henretta10e** to learn more.

TRM Chapter 28 Lecture Presentation Slides

TRM Chapter 28 Outline with AP® Focus

TRM Chapter 28 Lecture Strategies

TRM Chapter 28 Suggested Responses

TRM Handout 28.1 — Causation: Scandals and Public Confidence

TRM Handout 28.2 — Comparison: Liberals vs. Conservatives

TRM Handout 28.3 — Comparison: ERA and *Roe v. Wade*

TRM Handout 28.4 — Contextualization: Sexual Revolution

Chapter 28 — Essential Activity

As students prepare to move from the study of Period 8 (1945–1980) and into the final period in the AP® U.S. History Curriculum, Chapter 28 can serve as an opportunity to view the beginning and end of this period thematically. Divide the class into eight collaborative groups; assign four groups to create a thematic analysis of the year 1945, and the other four groups of the year 1980. Ask students to include at least one image or symbol to represent each theme for the year that they are analyzing. When groups have completed their thematic analysis, combine the two groups so that they can compare the analyses of 1945 and 1980 and discuss the ways in which the analyses illustrate continuity and change. Then lead a class discussion in which students generate a synopsis of the year 1945 and a synopsis of the year 1980 as "bookends" for understanding Period 8.

Chapter 28 — Bell Ringers

The following activities take no more than 5–15 minutes of your class period and offer an effective and engaging way to begin your lessons and for students to apply AP® Skills & Processes:

- Divide the class into seven groups and assign each group to read one document from the **AP® THINKING LIKE A HISTORIAN** feature on pp. 908–909. After students have read and analyzed their document, reorganize the class in a jigsaw activity. Prompt students to discuss the ways in which the environmental movement illustrates continuity and change. *Answers will vary, but could include the following: students might relate documents to Theodore Roosevelt's conservationism, John Muir and the Sierra Club's preservationist ideas, and the division between the left and right over environmental policy in today's politics.*
- Provide students with two political cartoons: one in support of Affirmative Action, the other opposed. Ask students to explain the message of each cartoon and evaluate the role of affirmative action in expanding civil rights.

NOTES

TEACHING STRATEGY

The chapter introduction explains the reason for the chapter periodization of 1973–1980. The reason for the periodization offered here builds on the two themes indicated in the chapter title: "order" and "limits." The social upheaval of the 1960s created a longing for a new sense of *order*. This search was complicated by the erosion of social and economic institutions that had seemed unshakeable — anticommunism, liberalism, and a strong economy — which forced a recognition of the *limits* of American values and prosperity. In many ways, of course, the "era of limits" really meant that circumstances had changed enough that middle-class Americans could not ignore them; many Americans had already experienced the limits of the nation's promise long before this time. For a complete model answer to the **AP® LEARNING FOCUS** question, see p. 932.

TEACHING STRATEGY

The National Museum of American History includes items from American television in its collection. Use the online resources to help students explore how television expresses the American identity in influential ways. To access this site, search "National Museum of American History television."

28

CHAPTER

The Search for Order in an Era of Limits

1973–1980

AP® LEARNING FOCUS

Why did the social changes of the 1960s — such as civil rights, shifting gender roles, and challenges to the family — create both new opportunities and political clashes in the 1970s?

In January 1971, Americans met a new television character. Archie Bunker was a gruff, blue-collar veteran, prone to bigoted and insensitive remarks, who often berated his wife and bemoaned his daughter's marriage to a hippie. Disdaining the liberal social movements of the 1960s, Archie expressed a conservative, hardscrabble worldview. Although to many viewers he seemed out of touch, which was the producer's intent, as the main character of the half-hour comedy *All in the Family* Archie became a folk hero to many working-class Americans in the 1970s; he said what they felt. At the opening of each episode, Archie and his wife Edith sang "Those Were the Days." The song celebrated a bygone era, when "girls were girls and men were men."

Archie Bunker proved to be more than a comic grouch with retrograde politics. The wildly popular *All in the Family* captured a national search for order. Archie's feminist daughter, liberal son-in-law, and black neighbors brought a changing world home. Not all Americans were as resistant to change as Archie. Most ordinary people were simply sorting out the consequences of a tumultuous era. The various upheavals of the late 1960s and early 1970s challenged Americans to think in new ways about race, gender roles, sexual morality, and the family. Vietnam and the Watergate scandal had produced a crisis of political authority. An "old order" had seemingly collapsed. But what would take its place was not yet clear.

Alongside cultural dislocation and political alienation, the country confronted economic setbacks. Beginning in 1973, inflation climbed at a pace unprecedented in the postwar era, and economic growth slowed. An energy crisis, aggravated by U.S. foreign policy in the Middle East, produced fuel shortages. Foreign competition in manufacturing brought less expensive, and often more reliable, goods into the U.S. market from nations such as Japan and West Germany — and drove some American plants to close. The great postwar boom was coming to an end.

The period between the energy crisis (1973) and the election of Ronald Reagan to the presidency (1980) is distinguished by a collective national search for order in the midst of rapid social change, political realignment, and economic crisis. The pillars on which postwar prosperity rested — Cold War liberalism, rising living standards, and the nuclear family — weakened and wobbled, and most Americans agreed that urgent action was needed to restore stability. For some, the search drove new forms of liberal experimentation. For others, it led instead to the conservatism of the emerging New Right, culminating in the political movement that put Reagan, a conservative Republican, in the White House.

904

Economic Troubles in a New Era Gas shortage signs like this one were common during the energy crisis of the early 1970s. Fuel rationing, and high prices when fuel was available, were evidence of the declining economic fortunes of the United States in that decade, which one American politician called "an era of limits." Owen Franken/Getty Images.

TEACHING STRATEGY

The energy crisis in the United States was caused by both domestic and foreign events. Have students connect this image to domestic issues such as stagflation and foreign events such as the formation of OPEC.

AP® SKILLS & PROCESSES

CONTINUITY AND CHANGE

Use the **TIMELINE** table to help students begin thinking about how the period from 1970 to 1979 could constitute a distinct historical period. The chronology includes Earth Day and the formation of the EPA, which ties into concerns about the environment, which became prominent in this decade. The chapter periodization differs slightly from this chronology, and the reason for this periodization is explained in the chapter opener. The year 1973 marks the start of the energy crisis (as well as the landmark Supreme Court case, *Roe v. Wade*), while 1980 references the election of Ronald Reagan, which led to a significant shift in the nation's politics and culture.

AP® THEME

GEO: Geography and the Environment

Ideological, military, and economic concerns shaped American involvement in the Middle East, and several oil crises sparked attempts to create a national energy policy. The Department of State's Office of the Historian provides more detail about the causes and effects of the 1973 OPEC oil embargo. To access this site, search "Office of the Historian 1973 oil embargo."

AP® APPLY THE TIP

To support students in understanding U.S. policy in the Middle East, write the words "Middle East Policy" in the center of the board. Off this title, write the following headings: ideology, dependence on oil, and military alliances. Prompt students to read pp. 906–907 in order to identify details to add to the diagram. Students should relate the details to current issues or issues they have heard in the news or through social media and make an argument regarding the relative significance of each of the three parts of the diagram in determining U.S. policy in the Middle East. Remind students that relative significance involves making an argument about what is most or more important between causes, effects, and comparisons. Allow students to debate the best way to address this prompt using relative significance: What is the most important factor in determining U.S. policy in the Middle East?

TIMELINE

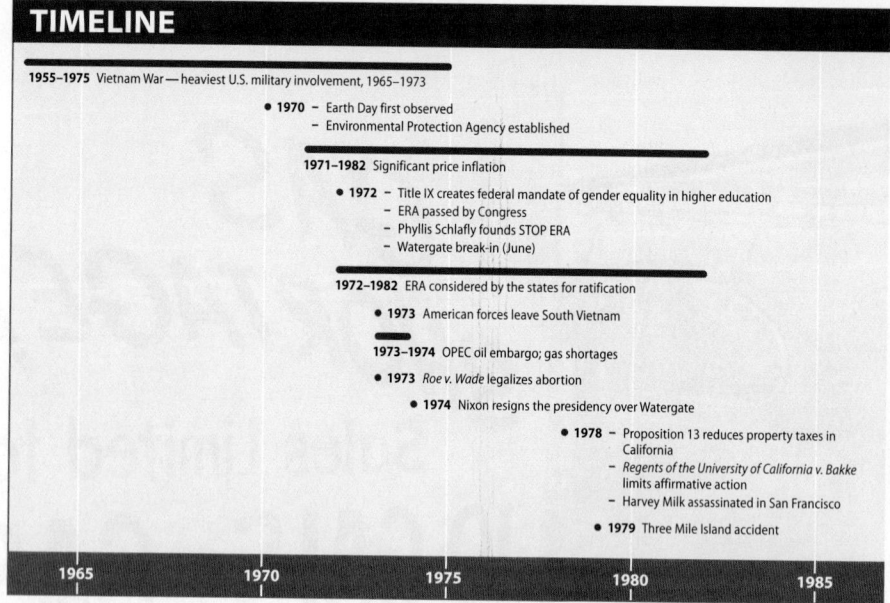

1955–1975 Vietnam War — heaviest U.S. military involvement, 1965–1973

- **1970** – Earth Day first observed
  – Environmental Protection Agency established

1971–1982 Significant price inflation

- **1972** – Title IX creates federal mandate of gender equality in higher education
  – ERA passed by Congress
  – Phyllis Schlafly founds STOP ERA
  – Watergate break-in (June)

1972–1982 ERA considered by the states for ratification

- **1973** American forces leave South Vietnam

1973–1974 OPEC oil embargo; gas shortages

- **1973** *Roe v. Wade* legalizes abortion
- **1974** Nixon resigns the presidency over Watergate
- **1978** – Proposition 13 reduces property taxes in California
  – *Regents of the University of California v. Bakke* limits affirmative action
  – Harvey Milk assassinated in San Francisco
- **1979** Three Mile Island accident

1965 1970 1975 1980 1985

LIMITS TO GROWTH AND PROSPERITY

What kind of limits, or crises, did the American economy encounter in the 1970s?

The economic downturn of the early 1970s was the deepest slump since the Great Depression. Every major economic indicator — employment, productivity, growth — turned downward, and by 1973 the economy was in a tailspin. Inflation, brought on in part by military spending on the war in Vietnam, proved especially difficult to control. An oil embargo with political roots shot prices even higher and sent tremors across a culture built around automobiles. Unemployment would stay high and productivity growth low until 1982. As twenty-five years of steady prosperity ended, Americans confronted an "era of limits," as California governor Jerry Brown first described it.

In this time of distress, Americans were forced to consider limits beyond their pocketbooks. The growth that had long defined national progress had taken a toxic toll on the natural world. A new movement called attention to the environmental impact of modern industrial capitalism. As more Americans filled up the suburbs, the urban crisis of the 1960s intensified, and several major cities verged on bankruptcy. Finally, political limits were reached as well: none of the presidents of the 1970s could reverse the nation's economic slide, though each spent years trying.

Energy Crisis

AP® EXAM TIP

Be able to describe the ways that ideology, dependence on oil, and military alliances shaped policy in the Middle East.

Modern economies run on oil. A reduction in oil supply invariably leads to higher prices, which leads to economic trouble. Americans were forced to learn this basic economic lesson in the 1970s. Once the world's leading oil producer, in the early 1970s the United States had become heavily dependent on inexpensive imported oil, mostly from the Persian Gulf (Figure 28.1). French, British, and American companies extracted the oil, but they did so under profit-sharing agreements with Persian Gulf states. In 1960, those Middle East nations and other oil-rich developing countries, such as Venezuela, formed the **Organization of Petroleum Exporting Countries (OPEC)** cartel, an alliance to set prices and regulate the market for oil.

OPEC's predominantly Arab member nations were initially reluctant to use their oil production as a political weapon, but that changed with the 1967 Six-Day War between Israel and the Arab states of Egypt, Syria, and Jordan. Following Israel's victory in that conflict, the Israeli-Arab relationship grew closer to exploding with each passing year. In October 1973, Egypt and Syria invaded Israel to regain lost territory, in what became known as the Yom Kippur War. Israel prevailed, but only after an emergency airlift of American military aid. In response to Western support for Israel, the Arab states in OPEC declared an oil embargo — exports to allies of Israel were banned and overall production reduced. Gas prices in the United States quickly jumped by 40 percent and heating oil prices by 30 percent. Demand outpaced supply, and Americans found themselves parked in long gas pump lines for much of the winter of 1973–1974.

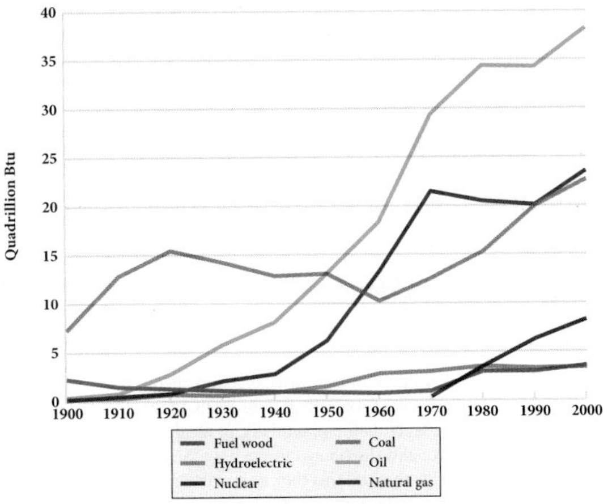

FIGURE 28.1 **U.S. Energy Consumption, 1900–2000**
Coal was the nation's primary source of energy until the 1950s, when it was surpassed by oil and natural gas. The revival of coal consumption after 1960 stemmed from new open-pit mining in the West that provided cheaper fuel for power plants. The decline in oil consumption in 1980 reflects the nation's response to the oil crisis of the 1970s, including, most notably, fuel-efficient automobiles. Nuclear energy became an important new fuel source, but after 1990 its contribution leveled off as a result of the safety concerns triggered by the Three Mile Island incident.

The United States scrambled to cope with this **energy crisis**. Just two months after the OPEC embargo began, Congress imposed a national speed limit of 55 miles per hour to conserve fuel. Americans began to buy smaller, more fuel-efficient imported cars such as Volkswagens and Toyotas — while sales of gas-guzzling American-made cars slumped. With one of every six jobs in the country generated directly or indirectly by the auto industry, a downturn for Detroit rippled across the entire economy. Compounding the distress was runaway inflation set off by the oil shortage. Prices of basic necessities, such as bread, milk, and canned goods, rose by nearly 20 percent in 1974 alone. "THINGS WILL GET WORSE," one newspaper headline warned, "BEFORE THEY GET WORSE."

Organization of Petroleum Exporting Countries (OPEC)
An alliance of oil-rich countries founded in 1960 to set prices and regulate the oil market.

energy crisis
A period of fuel shortages in the United States after the Arab states in the Organization of Petroleum Exporting Countries (OPEC) declared an oil embargo in October 1973.

Environmentalism

The oil embargo and energy crisis contributed to a growing awareness of the limits of natural resources. This idea was central to the 1970s revival of environmentalism. The environmental movement was an offshoot of sixties activism, but it had deeper historical precedents: the preservationist, conservationist, and wilderness movements of the late nineteenth century; the conservationist ethos of the New Deal; and anxiety about nuclear weapons and overpopulation in the years following World War II. The Sierra Club, Wilderness Society, and Natural Resources Council — three leading environmental organizations — were founded in 1892, 1935, and 1942, respectively. Environmental activists in the 1970s drew on these traditions in seeking to change how humans interacted with nature (see "Thinking Like a Historian," p. 908).

The movement had received a boost back in 1962 when biologist Rachel Carson published ***Silent Spring***, a stunning revelation of how human-produced pesticides

AP® EXAM TIP
Evaluate the degree of continuity and change in the environmental movement in the 1970s.

Silent Spring
Book published in 1962 by biologist Rachel Carson. Its analysis of the pesticide DDT's toxic impact on the human and natural food chains galvanized environmental activists.

TEACHING STRATEGY

FIGURE 28.1 illustrates the growth in energy consumption over the course of the twentieth century. Guide students' analysis with the following questions:

- **To what extent is the energy crisis represented in energy consumption trends in the chart?** *Both oil usage and natural gas usage leveled off during the 1970s; natural gas experienced a modest decline until the early 1980s. The shift to alternative forms of energy is indicated by the emergence of nuclear energy after 1970.*
- **What generalizations can you make about American energy consumption over the course of the twentieth century?** *Despite some variation in patterns — for example, the decline in coal usage for much of the first half of the twentieth century — Americans used more of every significant source of energy over the course of the century. Total energy usage increased roughly ten-fold.*
- **What explains the general pattern you noted?** *The population of the U.S. grew dramatically over the course of the century, and a higher standard of living — and new appliances — led to a higher per capita energy use.*

CHECK FOR UNDERSTANDING

Ask students: **What was the energy crisis and what were its consequences?** *As a means of punishing the U.S. for supporting Israel in the 1973 Yom Kippur War, the Arab states surrounding Israel, who largely dominated OPEC, embargoed the sale of oil. This dramatically reduced the overall availability of oil and led to significant increases in the price. Americans experienced long lines, reduced speed limits, and more expensive groceries (which were transported by vehicles using petroleum). Many Americans began to buy smaller foreign cars, which severely damaged the U.S. auto industry.*

AP® APPLY THE TIP

This activity requires students to review environmental policies throughout U.S. history. Students should create a list of turning points in the environmental movement, including the publication of *Silent Spring* by Rachel Carson. Students should then work with a partner to complete the **AP® THINKING LIKE A HISTORIAN** feature on pp. 908–909. As students review the documents, they should analyze the evidence that can be used to draw conclusions regarding the environmental movement and extend their analysis by identifying the historical context, intended audience, purpose, and point of view of the author of each source. After completing the activity, students should write a thesis statement and provide an outline of evidence, including documents from the activity to address the following prompt: To what degree did the publication of *Silent Spring* by Rachel Carson dramatically change environmentalism in the United States?

AP® SKILLS & PROCESSES

ANALYZING HISTORICAL EVIDENCE

The **AP® THINKING LIKE A HISTORIAN** feature encourages students to evaluate different sources that address Americans' attitudes toward the environment. Students should explain why environmentalism was initially a bipartisan concern, and how and why it quickly became part of the larger sense of division in the era. To extend this students' analysis, ask them to explore the role of environmentalism in the contemporary American political landscape.

AP® THINKING LIKE A HISTORIAN

The Environmental Movement: Reimagining the Human-Earth Relationship

The 1970s witnessed the emergence of the environmental movement in the United States. Environmentalism took a variety of forms and initially was embraced by politicians across the political spectrum, including Republican president Richard Nixon, who signed the National Environmental Policy Act in 1970. Yet environmentalism also proved to be politically divisive. The following documents provide a range of perspectives on an important social and political movement discussed in this chapter.

1. **Rachel Carson, *Silent Spring*, 1962.** *Carson, a biologist and journalist, spent four years researching pesticide use and published her findings in this influential book.*

For the first time in the history of the world, every human being is now subjected to contact with dangerous chemicals, from the moment of conception until death. In the less than two decades of their use, synthetic pesticides have been so thoroughly distributed throughout the animate and inanimate world that they occur virtually everywhere. They have been recovered from most of the major river systems and even from streams of groundwater flowing unseen through the earth.

2. **Ralph Nader, foreword to *Ecotactics: The Sierra Club Handbook for Environmental Activists*, 1970.** *In the Sierra Club's guide to environmental activism, environmental and consumer rights activist Nader discusses "environmental violence."*

Pollution is violence and environmental pollution is environmental violence. It is a violence that has different impacts, styles and time factors than the more primitive kinds of violence such as crime in the streets. Yet in the size of the population exposed and the seriousness of the harm done, environmental violence far exceeds that of street crime. . . .

To deal with a system of oppression and suppression, which characterizes the environmental violence in this country, the first priority is to deprive the polluters of their unfounded legitimacy.

3. **President Richard Nixon, State of the Union Address, January 22, 1970.** *Nixon favored action on behalf of the environment, showing early bipartisan support for that cause.*

I shall propose to this Congress a $10 billion nationwide clean waters program to put modern municipal waste treatment plants in every place in America where they are needed to make our waters clean again, and do it now. . . .

As our cities and suburbs relentlessly expand [. . .] priceless open spaces needed for recreation areas accessible to their people are swallowed up — often forever. Unless we preserve these spaces while they are available, we will have none to preserve. Therefore, I shall propose new financing methods for purchasing open space and parklands now, before they are lost to us.

The automobile is our worst polluter of the air. Adequate control requires further advances in engine design and fuel composition. We shall intensify our research, set increasingly strict standards, and strengthen enforcement procedures — and we shall do it now.

We can no longer afford to consider air and water common property, free to be abused by anyone without regard to the consequences. Instead, we should begin now to treat them as scarce resources, which we are no more free to contaminate than we are free to throw garbage into our neighbor's yard.

4. **"Earthrise" over the moon's surface, December 24, 1968.** *This photo was taken by Apollo 8 crewmember Bill Anders, as the Apollo spacecraft orbited the moon.*

NASA

908

5. **Paul Ehrlich, *The Population Bomb*, 1968.** This selection comes from a best-selling book that warned of a coming global overpopulation straining the world's resources.

Nothing could be more misleading to our children than our present affluent society. They will inherit a totally different world, a world in which the standards, politics, and economics of the 1960s are dead. As the most powerful nation in the world today, and its largest consumer, the United States cannot stand isolated. We are today involved in the events leading to famine; tomorrow we may be destroyed by its consequences.

Our position requires that we take immediate action at home and promote effective action world-wide. We must have population control at home, hopefully through a system of incentives and penalties, but by compulsion if voluntary methods fail. We must use our political power to push other countries into programs which combine agricultural development and population control. And while this is being done we must take action to reverse the deterioration of our environment before population pressure permanently ruins our planet.

6. **President Ronald Reagan, speech at the Republican National Convention, July 17, 1980.** *The president argues that environmental protection should not limit economic growth.*

Make no mistake. We will not permit the safety of our people or our environmental heritage to be jeopardized, but we are going to reaffirm that the economic prosperity of our people is a fundamental part of our environment.

Our problems are both acute and chronic, yet all we hear from those in positions of leadership are the same tired proposals for more government tinkering, more meddling, and more control — all of which led us to this state in the first place.

7. **Waste Produced by a Typical Family in a Year.** *The photographer Martyn Gaddard staged this scene to dramatize the environmental impact of a typical American family.*

Martyn Goddard/Getty Images

SOURCES: (1) Rachel Carson, *Silent Spring* (New York: Mariner Books, 2002), 15; (2) John G. Mitchell and Constance L. Hastings, eds., *Ecotactics: The Sierra Club Handbook for Environmental Activists* (New York: Trident Press, 1970), 13–15; (3 & 6) Gerhard Peters and John T. Woolley, *The American Presidency Project*, presidency.ucsb.edu; (5) Louis Warren, ed., *American Environmental History* (Malden, MA: Blackwell Publishing, 2003), 296.

ANALYZING THE EVIDENCE

1. Compare sources 1, 2, 3, 5, and 7. What are the different ways the environmental threat was understood and characterized? What kinds of solutions were proposed? Compare source claims.
2. Source 4 is one of the first photographs of the earth ever taken from space. How would this visual perspective encourage viewers to think of the earth's resources as finite?
3. How does source 6 help us understand the opposition that developed to environmentalism? Why did some Americans oppose the environmental movement?

AP® DBQ PRACTICE

Using what you have learned about the environmental movement in this chapter and the documents above, construct an essay in which you make a historical argument about the origins of the movement, the issues that it raised, and the opposition that developed. How did the movement shape politics in the 1970s?

TRM Find complete suggested responses in the Teacher's Resource Materials.

AP® SKILLS & PROCESSES

ARGUMENTATION

Because politics is often about both material interests and symbolic statements about values, to answer the **AP® DBQ PRACTICE** prompt, students might think about what economic concerns shaped the views of those who embraced and those who opposed the environmental movement, as well as the values each side believed their stance represented. Students prone to sympathize with environmentalism may struggle to understand the other side, so it may be helpful to press them to understand the antienvironmental movement.

Environmental Crisis in Cleveland On June 22, 1969, a large section of the Cuyahoga River near Cleveland on the southern shore of Lake Erie caught fire and burned for hours. Accumulated oil and other chemicals from nearby factories and refineries produced this "burning river," which received national attention and sparked renewed scrutiny of pollution and environmental degradation. Pictured here are firefighters battling an earlier fire on the same river in 1952. Between 1968 and the June 1969 blaze, there were a total of nine fires on the Cuyahoga. Together, the fires were among a series of environmental catastrophes that helped spur grassroots activism in support of new federal legislation devoted to clean air, clean water, and natural resource protection. Bettmann/Getty Images.

poisoned flora and fauna. The book shocked Americans and jump-started the resurgence of environmentalism. Further momentum built in the late 1960s. The Sierra Club successfully fought two dams in 1966 that would have flooded the Grand Canyon. And in 1969, three major events spurred the movement: an offshore drilling rig spilled millions of gallons of oil off the coast of Santa Barbara; the Cuyahoga River near Cleveland burst into flames because of the accumulation of flammable chemicals on its surface; and the Friends of the Everglades group successfully stopped plans for an airport that threatened plants and wildlife in Florida. Environmentalism became a certifiable mass movement on the first **Earth Day**, April 22, 1970, when 20 million people gathered in communities across the country to express their support for a cleaner, healthier planet.

Earth Day
An annual event honoring the environment that was first celebrated on April 22, 1970, when 20 million citizens gathered in communities across the country to express their support for a cleaner, healthier planet.

AP® SKILLS & PROCESSES

CAUSATION

What major factors led to the birth of the environmental movement in the 1970s?

Environmental Protection Agency (EPA)
Federal agency created by Congress and President Nixon in 1970 to enforce environmental laws, conduct environmental research, and reduce human health and environmental risks from pollutants.

AP® EXAM TIP

Explain how the Three Mile Island accident impacted the nation's energy policy.

Three Mile Island
A nuclear plant in Pennsylvania, where a reactor core neared meltdown in March 1979. The incident at Three Mile Island triggered a major slowdown in nuclear plant construction, though the United States is now the leading global nuclear power producer.

Environmental Protection Agency On the first day of 1970, on the heels of the Santa Barbara oil spill, Congress passed the National Environmental Policy Act, which created the **Environmental Protection Agency (EPA)**. A bipartisan bill with broad support and White House backing, the law required developers to undertake formal environmental impact studies to assess the effect of their projects on ecosystems. A spate of additional reforms followed: the Clean Air Act (1970), the Occupational Health and Safety Act (1970), the Water Pollution Control Act (1972), and the Endangered Species Act (1973).

The Democratic majority in Congress and the Republican president generally found common ground on these issues, and *Time* magazine wondered if the environment was "the gut issue that can unify a polarized nation." Despite the broad popularity of the movement, however, *Time*'s prediction was not borne out. Corporations opposed environmental regulations, as did many of their workers, who believed that tightened standards threatened jobs. "IF YOU'RE HUNGRY AND OUT OF WORK, EAT AN ENVIRONMENTALIST," read one labor union bumper sticker. By the 1980s, environmentalism starkly divided Americans, with proponents of unrestricted growth pitted against eco-activists.

Nuclear Power A brewing controversy over nuclear power foreshadowed that schism. In the 1950s, Americans had greeted the arrival of atomic energy with delight, imagining the many benefits of inexpensive electricity from splitting the atom. By 1974, U.S. utility companies were operating forty-two nuclear power plants, with a hundred more planned. Given the oil crisis, nuclear energy might have seemed a godsend. Unlike coal- or oil-driven plants, nuclear operations produced no air pollutants, but environmentalists voiced serious concerns. Reactor meltdowns loomed as potential catastrophes, and radioactive waste could poison the earth for centuries. Nuclear fears ratcheted up in March 1979, when the reactor core at the **Three Mile Island** nuclear plant near Harrisburg, Pennsylvania, came close to meltdown. More than 100,000 people fled their homes. A prompt shutdown saved the plant, but the near

AP® SKILLS & PROCESSES

CAUSATION

It may be fruitful to provide students with a periodization to answer this question. For instance, if you give students the years 1945–1970, it may help them focus on historical factors from World War II through the 1960s. Broad historical factors such as nuclear energy are effective ways of drawing sound analysis—encourage students to think about broad historical processes.

TRM Find complete suggested responses in the Teacher's Resource Materials.

catastrophe enabled environmentalists to slow the rapid expansion of nuclear energy. After the incident at Three Mile Island, no new nuclear plants were authorized for thirty years, though a handful that were already planned were built in the 1980s and 1990s. Despite this slowdown in construction, today nuclear reactors account for 20 percent of all U.S. power generation, and the United States is the leading nuclear energy producer in the world.

Economic Transformation and Decline

Beyond the energy crisis, a host of longer-term problems beset the economy. Government spending on the Vietnam War and Great Society programs drove deficits and additional inflation. In the industrial sector, the country faced increasing competition from West Germany and Japan. America's share of world trade dropped from 32 percent in 1955 to 18 percent in 1970 and continued to shrink. In a blow to national pride, nine Western European countries had surpassed the United States in per capita gross domestic product (GDP) by 1980.

AP® EXAM TIP

Recognizing how the transformation from a manufacturing to a service-based economy impacted the overall U.S. economy in the 1970s is critical for success on the AP® Exam.

Many of these economic woes highlighted a broader, multigenerational transformation in the American economy, from industrial manufacturing to provision of services. That transformation, which continues to this day, meant that the United States produced fewer automobiles, appliances, and televisions and more financial, health-care, and management consulting services — as well as millions of low-paying jobs in the restaurant, retail, and tourist industries. The shift from manufacturing to services, starting in the 1960s, exerted a broad social impact, because it changed who could become part of the middle class. Many manufacturing jobs paid middle-class wages and required only a high school education, while service jobs were sharply divided between a narrow cluster of well-paying positions, which required higher education, and a massive sea of minimum-wage positions, which didn't require more than a high school degree but which were insufficient to support a family. As the economy changed, so did individual opportunity.

In the 1970s, the U.S. economy was hit by a phenomenon called **stagflation**: a combination of high unemployment, stagnant consumer demand, and inflation. This contradicted a basic principle taught by economists: prices were not supposed

stagflation
An economic term coined in the 1970s to describe a combination of high unemployment, stagnant consumer demand, and inflation.

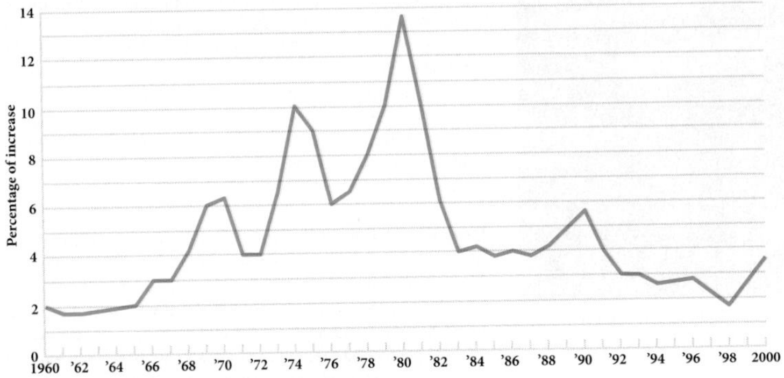

FIGURE 28.2 The Inflation Rate, 1960–2000
The impact of the oil crisis of 1973 on the inflation rate appears all too graphically in this figure. After a dip between 1974 and 1976, the inflation rate zoomed up to a staggering 14 percent in 1980. The return to normal levels after 1980 stemmed from very harsh measures by the Federal Reserve Board, which, while they succeeded, came at the cost of a painful slowdown in the economy.

CHECK FOR UNDERSTANDING

Ask students: **What were the features of the early environmental movement?** *Celebration of the first Earth Day in 1970 made environmentalism a mass movement. The same year, prompted by an oil spill off the coast of Santa Barbara, California, Congress and President Nixon passed the National Environmental Policy Act, which created the Environmental Protection Agency (EPA). Congress also passed the Clean Air and Occupational Health and Safety Acts that year, and the Water Pollution Control Act and the Endangered Species Act over the next couple of years. While these acts generally enjoyed bipartisan support, other issues were more divisive. Some favored nuclear energy as an alternative to expensive and increasingly rare petroleum, but others worried about the dangers of nuclear plants.*

AP® SKILLS & PROCESSES

ANALYZING HISTORICAL EVIDENCE

FIGURE 28.2 illustrates the dramatic growth in inflation during the 1970s. Guide students' analysis with the following questions:

- **What was the range of the average inflation rate in the 1960s? In the 1980s?** *It ranged between 2 to 6 percent. The range was roughly the same in the 1980s.*
- **What was the range between 1973 and 1981?** *Between 6 and 14 percent.*
- **What were the consequences of this inflation?** *Many Americans experienced reduced buying power, particularly with wages being stagnant. The cost of a home — central to the postwar "American dream" — became too high for many, as mortgage rates increased dramatically.*

to rise in a stagnant economy (Figure 28.2). For ordinary Americans, stagflation meant declining purchasing power, which fell by as much as 20 percent between 1973 and 1982. None of the three presidents of the decade — Richard Nixon, Gerald Ford, and Jimmy Carter — could find a solution. Nixon's New Economic Policy was perhaps the most radical attempt. He imposed temporary price and wage controls in 1971 in an effort to curb inflation, and then took an even bolder step: removing the United States from the gold standard, which effectively ended the Bretton Woods monetary system established after World War II (see "Economy: From Recovery to Dominance" in Chapter 25). These measures brought temporary relief — and contributed to Nixon's landslide reelection in 1972 — but they did not change the underlying weaknesses of the economy, and successive presidents had no more luck than Nixon.

deindustrialization
The dismantling of manufacturing in the decades after the 1960s, reversing the process of industrialization that characterized the American economy between the 1870s and 1940s.

Rust Belt
The once heavily industrialized regions of the Northeast and Midwest that went into decline after deindustrialization. By the 1980s, these regions were full of shuttered plants and distressed communities.

Deindustrialization America's economic woes struck hardest at the industrial sector. The decline of America's manufacturing backbone was sudden and shocking — nowhere more than in the steel industry. For seventy-five years steel had been the economy's crown jewel, and since World War II had enjoyed an open, hugely profitable market. But a lack of serious competition left American steelmakers without incentives to replace outdated plants and equipment. The revived West German and Japanese steel industries had new facilities with the latest technology. Less expensive but equally durable foreign steel flooded into the United States during the 1970s, and the American industry foundered rapidly. Formerly titanic steel companies began a massive dismantling. The Pittsburgh region, once a national hub of steel production, lost virtually all of its heavy industry in a single generation. By the mid-1980s, downsizing and new technologies made American steel competitive again — but its heyday was over.

Deindustrialization The old "Carrie" blast furnace in Braddock, Pennsylvania, part of the U.S. Steel Homestead Works, which was a great industrial complex in its heyday, as well as the site of the infamous 1892 battle between steelworkers and security agents hired by the steel mill's owner, Andrew Carnegie. Shuttered entirely by the 1980s, the plant was caught in the downward spiral of American industry that began in the 1970s. The result of such closures was the creation of the so-called Rust Belt in the Northeast and Midwest (Map 28.1). © Richard Kalvar/Magnum Photos

Steel was only one prominent example of **deindustrialization**, the economic transformation that left the United States largely stripped of its industrial base. A swath of the Northeast and Midwest, the country's manufacturing heartland, soon became the nation's **Rust Belt** (Map 28.1), strewn with shuttered plants and distressed communities. The automobile, tire, textile, and other consumer durable industries (appliances, electronics, furniture, and the like) all started shrinking in the 1970s. In 1959, manufacturing accounted for 25 percent of all American jobs; by 1984, the figure was 18 percent. In that same twenty-five-year period, the American population increased by one-third. As the nation continued to grow at a steady pace, industrial manufacturing jobs were losing ground. In the midst of that decline, in 1980, *Business Week* bemoaned "plant closings across the continent" and called for the "*re*industrialization of America."

Organized Labor in Decline Deindustrialization eliminated tens of thousands of well-paid union jobs and upended the lives of the newly unemployed. One study followed 4,100 steelworkers who lost their jobs in the 1977 shutdown of Youngstown Sheet & Tube Company's Campbell Works factory. Two years later, 35 percent had retired early at half pay; 10 percent had left the area; 15 percent were still jobless, with unemployment benefits long gone; and 40 percent had found local work, but mostly in low-paying, service-sector jobs. In another massive job loss, between 1978 and 1981, eight Los Angeles companies — including such giants as Ford, Uniroyal, and U.S. Steel — closed factories

TEACHING STRATEGY

As the image indicates, Pittsburgh and its surrounding suburbs epitomized the economic growth connected to industrialization from the late nineteenth century through the twentieth century. However, the economic processes of the late twentieth century would cause economic downturn in those same areas. Have students select at least one of the following cities: Pittsburgh, Detroit, or Cleveland, and provide historical evidence to explain the reason for economic decline in these areas. For an extension activity, use Deborah L. Wince-Smith's article titled "How Pittsburgh Shed Its Rust Belt Image" to help students understand how Pittsburgh moved from a Rust Belt symbol to a vibrant new city. To access this article, search "World Economic Forum Wince-Smith Pittsburgh."

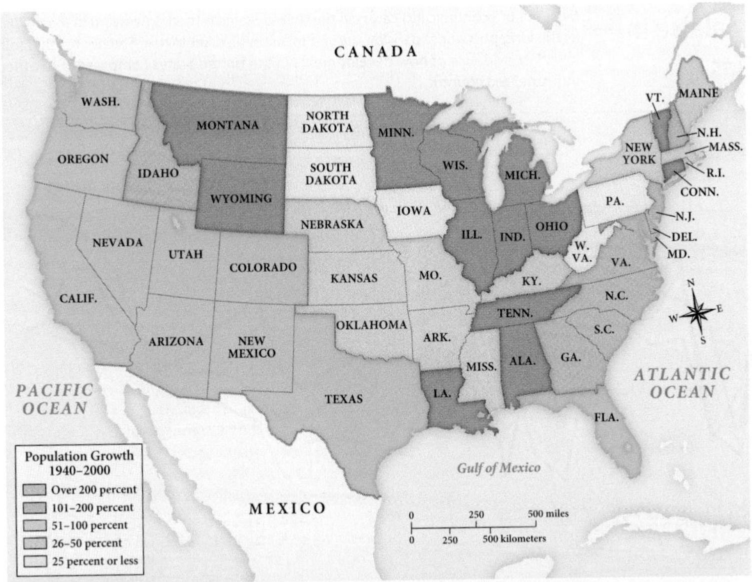

MAPPING THE PAST

MAP 28.1 From Rust Belt to Sunbelt, 1940–2000
One of the most significant developments of the post–World War II era was the growth of the Sunbelt. Sparked by federal spending for military bases, the defense industry, and the space program, states of the South and Southwest experienced an economic boom in the 1950s. This growth was further enhanced in the 1970s, as the heavily industrialized regions of the Northeast and Midwest declined and migrants from what was quickly dubbed the Rust Belt headed to the South and West in search of jobs.

ANALYZING THE MAP: Identify the regions with the highest and lowest population growth rates. Do these regions correspond to the Sunbelt and Rust Belt?

MAKING CONNECTIONS: Compare the map with Table 28.1. How did the population changes shown here affect political representation?

TRM Find complete suggested responses in the Teacher's Resource Materials.

employing a total of nearly 18,000 workers. Many of these Ohio and California workers, and hundreds of thousands of their counterparts across the nation, fell from their perch in the middle class (see "America in the World," p. 914).

Deindustrialization dealt an especially harsh blow to the labor movement, which had facilitated the postwar expansion of that middle class. In the early 1970s, as inflation hit, the number of strikes surged; 2.4 million workers participated in work stoppages in 1970 alone. But strikes produced fewer and fewer concrete results. In these hard years, the much-vaunted labor-management accord of the 1950s, which raised profits and wages by passing costs on to consumers, went bust. Instead of seeking higher wages, unions now mainly fought to save jobs. Union membership went into steep decline, and by the mid-1980s organized labor represented less than 18 percent of American workers, the lowest level since the 1920s. The impact of labor's decline on liberal politics was huge. Yet another bastion of the New Deal coalition was collapsing.

AP® SKILLS & PROCESSES

CONTEXTUALIZATION

What major developments shaped the American economy in the 1970s and contributed to its transformation?

AP® SKILLS & PROCESSES

CONTEXTUALIZATION

The **CONTEXTUALIZATION** question asks students to consider the transformation of the American economy in light of a larger context that helps explain this transformation — including global economic factors, but also including social and political factors.

TRM Find complete suggested responses in the Teacher's Resource Materials.

CHECK FOR UNDERSTANDING

Ask students: **How was the U.S. economy transformed in the 1970s?** *The most significant transformation was a shift from an economy based on industrial manufacturing — the dominant pattern for more than a half century — to one based on providing services, a pattern that remains in effect today. In competition with cheaper manufactured goods, including cars, from nations like Germany and Japan, the American steel industry went into serious decline, leading to the rise of the "Rust Belt." With deindustrialization came a reduction in the power of organized labor. "Stagflation," an unusual combination of unemployment, low consumer demand, and high inflation, plagued the U.S. during much of the 1970s, and economic efforts by Nixon, Ford, and Carter had little effect in resolving it.*

AP® AMERICA IN THE WORLD

Economic Malaise in the Seventies

Most major economic indicators in the United States turned downward in the 1970s, as the long postwar expansion ground to an unmistakable halt. The figures that follow offer evidence of how developments in the United States compared with other industrialized countries.

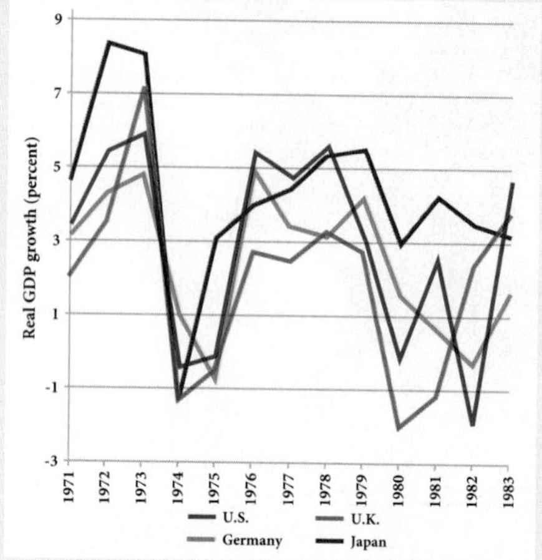

FIGURE 28.3 Falling Gross Domestic Product

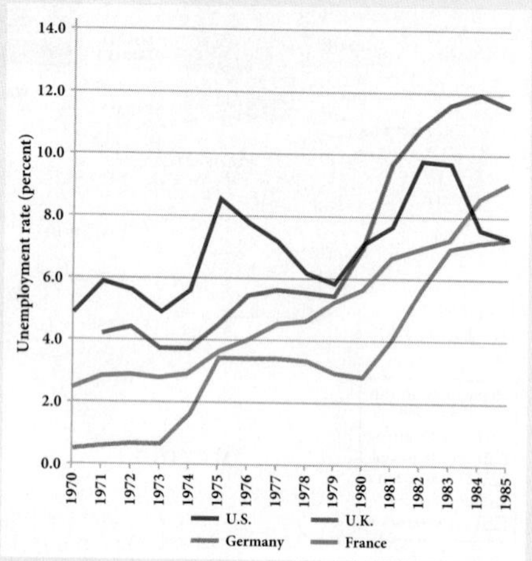

FIGURE 28.4 Rising Unemployment

AP® SKILLS & PROCESSES

ANALYZING HISTORICAL EVIDENCE

The **AP® AMERICA IN THE WORLD** feature clearly indicates the success of one element of the postwar American vision for the world: a global economy integrated through the gold standard, minimal tariffs, and the World Bank. The economic woes Americans experienced in the 1970s were largely paralleled by the experiences of other advanced industrial nations.

QUESTIONS FOR ANALYSIS

1. Identify at least one trend in Figure 28.3 and 28.4. In what ways do these figures demonstrate an integrated global economy?
2. What does the GDP graph indicate about how global economic integration affected the U.S. economy? Notice that Japan's GDP growth remained strong in the late 1970s and early 1980s. What was the historical context of the U.S. at that time? Explain the ways that these data inform "economic malaise" in the United States during the 1970s.

TRM Find complete suggested responses in the Teacher's Resource Materials.

Urban Crisis and Suburban Revolt

The economic downturn pushed already struggling American cities to the brink of fiscal collapse. Middle-class flight to the suburbs continued apace, and the "urban crisis" of the 1960s had now to contend with the "era of limits." Facing huge price inflation and mounting piles of debt — to finance social services for low-income residents and to replace disappearing tax revenue — nearly every major American city struggled to pay its bills in the 1970s. Even as suburbs prospered around them, central cities staggered toward a reckoning, their problems far outpaced the revenue available to fix them.

New York, with an annual budget in the billions, larger than that of most states, fared the worst. Unable to borrow on the tightening international bond market, the nation's largest city neared collapse in the summer of 1975; bankruptcy for America's financial capital was a real possibility. When Mayor Abraham Beame appealed to the

"Ford to City: Drop Dead" In the summer of 1975, New York City nearly went bankrupt. When Mayor Abraham Beame appealed to President Gerald Ford for federal assistance, these newspaper headlines captured the chief executive's response. Though it was ultimately saved from financial ruin, the city's brush with insolvency symbolized the larger problems facing the nation: economic stagnation, high inflation, and unemployment. Hard times had seemingly spared no one. AP Photo.

federal government for assistance, President Ford refused. "Ford to City: Drop Dead" read the headline in the *New York Daily News*. Fresh appeals ultimately produced a solution: the federal government would lend New York money, and banks would declare a three-year moratorium on municipal debt. The arrangement saved the city from defaulting, but as a condition of federal assistance Beame was forced to cut city services, freeze wages, and lay off workers. One pessimistic observer declared that "the banks have been saved, and the city has been condemned."

Cities struggled in the 1970s for many reasons, but one key was the continued loss of residents and businesses to nearby suburbs. Over the course of the decade, 13 million people (6 percent of the total U.S. population) moved to the suburbs. New suburban shopping centers opened weekly across the country, and other businesses — such as banks, insurance companies, and technology firms — increasingly sought suburban locations. More and more, people lived *and* worked in suburbs. In the San Francisco Bay area, 75 percent of all daily commutes were suburb-to-suburb, and 78 percent of New York's suburban residents worked in other suburbs. The "organization man" of the 1950s, who commuted downtown from his suburban home, had been replaced by the engineer, teacher, nurse, student, and carpenter who lived in one suburb and worked in another.

Postwar liberalism had favored generous public investment, but the troubled economy of the 1970s gave rise to the so-called tax revolt, which reversed that momentum. The premier example was California, where inflation had driven up real estate values — and property taxes. The hardest hit were suburban property owners, along with retirees and others on fixed incomes, who suddenly faced unaffordable tax bills. Into this dire situation stepped Howard Jarvis, a former anti–New Dealer and a genius at mobilizing grassroots discontent. In 1978, Jarvis proposed **Proposition 13**, an

AP® EXAM TIP

Analyze the causes and effects of the conservative backlash against New Deal and Great Society liberalism.

Proposition 13
A California measure that reduced property taxes, capped increases for present owners, and required tax measures to have a two-thirds majority in the legislature. Inspired "tax revolts" across the country and defined an enduring conservative issue: low taxes.

AP® APPLY THE TIP

To help students understand the causes and effects of the conservative backlash against liberal programs and laws, draw a political spectrum on the board and label the left as "liberal" and the right as "conservative." Write the following issues down the middle of the board: environmental protection, civil rights laws, welfare, education reform, and business regulation. Ask students to explain the goals, actions, and legislation achieved under the liberal side of the spectrum for each of these topics. Then, using pp. 906-916, identify reasons for conservative backlash against these efforts and place them on the board. Lastly, students should discuss other time periods in which these issues were important and how different views were expressed regarding them.

AP® SKILLS & PROCESSES

ARGUMENTATION

The breadth of economic crises during the 1970s was part of the reason why it was so difficult to counteract. Have students select one of the following and explain why it represents the most important economic crisis of the 1970s: stagflation, energy crisis, unemployment, high interest rates. The goal is to work on developing an interpretation, as opposed to denying the validity of a particular economic crisis.

CHECK FOR UNDERSTANDING

Ask students: **What kind of limits, or crises, did the American economy encounter in the 1970s?** *The decline of American manufacturing as well as the massive government debts incurred during the Vietnam War undercut the American economy and led to stagflation — the odd combination of a stagnant economy with inflation. As a result, the American economy witnessed deindustrialization, a decline in public investment, and an undermining of labor unions.*

AP® SKILLS & PROCESSES

COMPARISON

The **COMPARISON** question asks students to compare the effects of the economic problems of the era in cities and suburbs. Students should identify specifically how suburban residents had more flexibility to respond to these negative circumstances. They should also recognize that increasing suburbanization itself contributed to the problems faced by cities.

TRM Find complete suggested responses in the Teacher's Resource Materials.

AP® THEME

POL: Politics and Power

In the 1970s, public confidence and trust in the government's ability to solve social and economic problems declined in the wake of economic challenges, political scandals, and foreign policy crises. The Nixon Library provides dozens of excellent primary sources and brief oral history testimonies on various issues associated with the Watergate issue. The materials also include several brief oral histories reflecting on the significance of Watergate. To access these resources, search "Nixon Library Watergate."

initiative that would reduce property taxes, cap future increases for present owners, and require that all tax measures have a two-thirds majority in the legislature. Despite the opposition of virtually the entire state leadership, including politicians from both parties, Californians voted overwhelmingly for the measure.

Proposition 13 hobbled public spending in the nation's most populous state. Per capita funding of California public schools, once the envy of the nation, plunged from the top tier to the bottom, where it was ahead of only Mississippi. Moreover, Proposition 13's complicated tax rate formula benefitted well-off homeowners at the expense of poorer citizens, especially those who depended heavily on public services. Proposition 13 inspired similar "tax revolt" initiatives across the country and taught conservatives a winning political issue: low taxes.

From the New Deal to the Great Society, liberalism had overseen a remarkable decline in income inequality. In the 1970s, that trend reversed, and the wealthiest 10 percent of Americans began to pull ahead again. As corporations restructured to boost profits during the 1970s slump, they increasingly laid off high-wage workers, paid remaining employees less, and relocated overseas. Upper-class Americans benefitted, while blue-collar families who had been lifted into the middle class during the postwar boom increasingly lost out. An unmistakable trend was apparent by the end of the 1970s. The U.S. labor market was dividing in two: a vast, low-wage market at the bottom and a much narrower high-wage market at the top, with the middle squeezed smaller and smaller.

AP® SKILLS & PROCESSES

COMPARISON

How did cities and suburbs experience the "era of limits" differently, and why?

POLITICS IN FLUX, 1973–1980

In what ways was the period between 1973 and 1980 a transitional one in American politics?

Scandal is endemic to politics. Yet what became known as the Watergate affair — or simply **Watergate** — implicated President Richard Nixon in illegal behavior severe enough to bring down his presidency. Liberals benefitted from Nixon's fall in the short term, but their long-term retreat continued. Politics remained in flux because while liberals were on the defensive, conservatives had not yet put forth a clear alternative. As in the economic realm, the years from 1973 to 1980 were defined by a search for order in American politics.

Watergate
Term referring to the 1972 break-in at Democratic Party headquarters in the Watergate complex in Washington, D.C. by men working for President Nixon's reelection campaign, along with Nixon's efforts to cover it up. The Watergate scandal led to President Nixon's resignation.

Watergate and the Fall of a President

Early on the morning of June 17, 1972, something strange happened at Washington's Watergate Office Building. Five men carrying wiretapping equipment were apprehended there attempting to break into the headquarters of the Democratic National Committee (DNC). Queried by the press, a White House spokesman dismissed the episode as "a third-rate burglary attempt." In fact, the two masterminds of the break-in, former intelligence officers G. Gordon Liddy and E. Howard Hunt, worked for the Committee to Re-elect the President (CREEP), Nixon's official reelection campaign organization.

AP® EXAM TIP

Recognize the impact of political scandals on the lack of public confidence in government in the 1970s.

The Watergate burglary was no isolated incident. It was part of a broad pattern of abuse of power by a White House obsessed with its political enemies. Liddy and Hunt were on the White House payroll, part of a clandestine squad hired to stop leaks to the press but whose activities escalated far beyond that mandate — to arranging illegal wiretaps at opposition headquarters as part of a campaign of "dirty tricks" against the Democrats. There was no clear evidence tying Watergate directly to the president, and Nixon might have ridden out the scandal by firing his guilty aides, or by doing nothing at all. But it was election time, and Nixon did not trust his political future to such a strategy. Instead, he arranged hush money for the burglars and instructed

AP® APPLY THE TIP

Ask students to complete **Handout 28.1 — Causation: Scandals and Public Confidence (TRM)** using pp. 916–918. Provide pairs of students with a set of six excerpts from newspaper articles about the Watergate scandal and ask each pair to divide up the articles so that each student reads three excerpts. Remind students that in the U.S. today, knowledge of such scandals is often spread through social media such as Twitter or Facebook. Ask students to create a tweet (140 characters) or a short Facebook post for each of the articles they read. After writing their three posts, have students exchange papers with their partner and "respond" to the posts. Share some of the posts as a class and lead a class discussion on the impact of the scandal on public confidence in the government.

TRM Find **Handout 28.1 — Causation: Scandals and Public Confidence** in the Teacher's Resource Materials.

the CIA to stop an FBI investigation into the affair. His actions amounted to obstruction of justice, a criminal offense.

Nixon managed to keep the lid on the Watergate incident through his successful reelection in the fall of 1972. But early the next year, one of the burglars began to talk. In the meantime, *Washington Post* reporters Carl Bernstein and Bob Woodward uncovered CREEP's links to key White House aides. In May 1973, a Senate investigating committee began holding nationally televised hearings, at which administration officials implicated Nixon in the illegal cover-up. The president continued to deny involvement, but by June of 1974, the House Judiciary Committee began to consider articles of impeachment. With conviction in the Senate almost certain, on August 9, 1974, Nixon became the first U.S. president to resign his office. The next day, Vice President Gerald Ford was sworn in as president. Ford, the former Republican minority leader in the House of Representatives, had filled the vacancy left by Vice President Spiro Agnew, who had resigned in October 1973 for accepting kickbacks while governor of Maryland. A month after he took office, as polls showed that a majority of Americans believed Nixon to be guilty of crimes, Ford stunned the nation by granting Nixon a "full, free, and absolute" pardon.

Nixon Resignation Tourists in front of the White House reading headlines dated August 8, 1974, that proclaimed "Nixon Resigning." Richard Nixon, the 37th American president, resigned on that summer day rather than face impeachment in the House of Representatives and conviction in the Senate, which observers at the time considered a near certainty. Everett Collection Historical/Alamy Stock Photo.

As Watergate unfolded, Congress pursued an array of legislation designed to limit the power of the executive branch: the **War Powers Act** (1973), which reined in the president's ability to deploy military forces without congressional approval; amendments strengthening the **Freedom of Information Act** (1974), which gave citizens access to federal records; the **Ethics in Government Act** (1978), which required government officials to disclose their financial and employment history and limited the lobbying activities of former elected officials; and the **Foreign Intelligence Surveillance Act** (1978), which prohibited the wiretapping of foreign citizens inside the United States without a warrant.

Popular disdain for politicians, evident in declining voter turnout, deepened with Nixon's resignation in 1974. "Don't vote," read one bumper sticker in 1976. "It only encourages them." Watergate not only damaged short-term Republican prospects but also shifted the party's ideological balance to the right. Despite his effective appeal to the "silent majority," the moderate Nixon was never beloved by conservatives. His relaxation of tensions with the Soviet Union and his visit to communist China, in particular, won him no friends on the right. His disgrace gave more conservative Republicans a chance to reshape the party in their image.

War Powers Act
A law that limited the president's ability to deploy military forces without congressional approval. Congress passed the War Powers Act in 1973 as a series of laws to fight the abuses of the Nixon administration.

Freedom of Information Act
Passed in the wake of the Watergate scandal, the 1974 act that gave citizens access to federal records.

Ethics in Government Act
Passed in the wake of the Watergate scandal, the 1978 act requires government officials to disclose their financial and employment history and limits the lobbying activities of former elected officials.

Foreign Intelligence Surveillance Act
A law passed in 1978 which prohibited the wiretapping of foreign nationals on U.S. soil without a warrant.

Watergate Babies Nixon's downfall also granted Democrats a chance to recapture their eroding political fortunes. Democratic candidates in the 1974 midterm elections made the Watergate scandal and Ford's pardon of Nixon their top issues. It worked. Seventy-five new Democratic members of the House came to Washington in 1975, many of them under the age of forty-five.

Dubbed the "Watergate babies" by the press, the new Democrats solidified huge majorities in both houses of Congress and quickly pursued a reform agenda. They eliminated the House Un-American Activities Committee (HUAC), which had investigated alleged Communists in the 1940s and 1950s and antiwar activists in the 1960s.

AP® EXAM TIP
Describe the impact of the growing divide between liberals and conservatives in the 1970s.

AP® APPLY THE TIP

Direct students to complete **Handout 28.2 — Comparison: Liberals vs. Conservatives in the 1970s (TRM)** using pp. 919–926. After completing the handout, students should choose one area of the handout on which they will create an illustrated analogy. Provide students with a piece of paper containing the outline of a person (like the icon often used to indicate male and female bathrooms). Students should draw a line vertically down the outline figure, then add clothes, hair, jewelry, accessories, etc., to represent the ideas of the left and right. Make sure to NOT write out explanations of their illustrations given you will be randomly distributing them to other students. Once students have exchanged illustrations, ask them to interpret the illustration they received and create a caption for the image explaining the issue it is illustrating and the arguments of the left and right on that particular issue.

TRM Find **Handout 28.2— Comparison: Liberals v. Conservatives in the 1970s** in the Teacher's Resource Materials.

AP® SKILLS & PROCESSES

CONTINUITY AND CHANGE

This question focuses on the continuities and changes in American politics in the wake of Watergate. As students review laws passed in the wake of Watergate, they could identify the political practice a law aimed to change and explain whether it achieved its intended goal. Extend this prompt by asking students to explain why the Watergate crisis did not dramatically change politics across the board.

TRM Find complete suggested responses in the Teacher's Resource Materials.

AP® SKILLS & PROCESSES

ANALYZING HISTORICAL EVIDENCE

TABLE 28.1 indicates the growth in the power of Sunbelt states since the start of World War II. Remind students that the Constitution requires a census to be carried out every ten years, and that because the number of representatives in the House is based on population, states may receive more representatives as their population grows and, conversely, lose representatives if their state population shrinks. Because the number of representatives has been fixed at 435 since the Apportionment Act of 1911, seats withdrawn from shrinking states are reallocated to larger ones. The power of the Sunbelt should not be exaggerated. While the total number of Sunbelt seats grew by 77 percent, this put the region at almost exact parity with the Rust Belt.

CHECK FOR UNDERSTANDING

Ask students: **How did the Watergate crisis lead to the fall of President Nixon?** *Members of Nixon's reelection team broke into the headquarters of the Democratic National Committee, housed in the Watergate complex in Washington, DC. They were caught and arrested, and it quickly became clear that they had ties to the president. Nixon interfered with the investigation and refused to cooperate with requests for White House tapes to be handed over. Facing impending impeachment, he decided to resign in 1974, which made Vice President Ford the new president. Ford had only become vice president the previous year when then–Vice President Spiro Agnew resigned as a result of political corruption and tax investigation charges.*

AP® SKILLS & PROCESSES

CONTINUITY AND CHANGE

What changed and what remained the same in American politics as a result of the Watergate scandal?

In the Senate, Democrats reduced the number of votes needed to end a filibuster from 67 to 60 — a move intended to weaken the power of the minority to block legislation. In both houses, Democrats dismantled the existing committee structure, which had entrenched power in the hands of a few elite committee chairs. Overall, the Watergate babies helped to decentralize power in Washington and bring greater transparency to American government.

These changes largely succeeded in making government more transparent. But in one of the great ironies of American political history, the post-Watergate reforms made government *less* efficient and *more* susceptible to special interests — the opposite of what had been intended. Under the new committee structure, smaller subcommittees proliferated, and the size of the congressional staff doubled to more than twenty thousand. A diffuse power structure provided lobbyists more places to exert influence. As the importance of committee chairs weakened, influence shifted to party leaders, such as the Speaker of the House and the Senate majority leader. With little incentive for parties to compromise, bipartisanship became rare. Finally, with fewer votes needed to block legislation, filibustering, a seldom-used tactic largely employed by anti–civil rights southerners, increased in frequency. The Congress that we have come to know today — defined by partisan rancor, armies of lobbyists, and slow-moving response to public needs — came into being in the 1970s.

TABLE 28.1

Political Realignment: Congressional Seats

State	Apportionment 1940	Apportionment 1990
Rust Belt		
Massachusetts	14	10
Connecticut	6	6
New York	45	31
New Jersey	14	13
Pennsylvania	33	21
Ohio	23	19
Illinois	26	20
Indiana	11	10
Michigan	17	16
Wisconsin	10	9
Total	**199**	**155**
Sunbelt		
California	23	52
Arizona	2	6
Nevada	1	2
Colorado	4	6
New Mexico	2	3
Texas	21	30
Georgia	10	11
North Carolia	12	12
Virgina	9	11
Florida	6	23
Total	**90**	**156**

In the fifty years between 1940 and 1990, the Rust Belt states lost political clout, while the Sunbelt states gained it — measured here in congressional seats (which are apportioned based on population). Sunbelt states gained 66 seats, with the Rust Belt losing 44. This shifting political geography helped undermine the liberal coalition, which was strongest in industrial states with large labor unions, and paved the way for the rise of the conservative coalition, which was strongest in southern and Appalachian states, as well as California.

SOURCE: Office of the Clerk of the House, clerk.house.gov/art_history/house_history/congApp/bystate.html.

Political Realignment Despite Democratic gains in 1974, the electoral realignment that had begun with Nixon's presidential victories in 1968 and 1972 continued. As liberals failed to stop runaway inflation or speed up economic growth, conservatives gained traction with the public. The postwar liberal economic formula — sometimes known as the Keynesian consensus — consisted of micro-adjustments to the money supply coupled with federal spending. When that formula failed to revive the economy in the mid-1970s, conservatives in Congress saw an opening to articulate alternatives, especially economic deregulation and tax cuts for the well-off (see "Conservatives in Power" in Chapter 29).

The political geography of the country changed as well, with deindustrialization in the Northeast and Midwest and continued population growth in the Sunbelt. Power was shifting, incrementally but perceptibly, toward the West and South (Table 28.1). States such as New York, Illinois, and Michigan — strongholds of union labor — lost industry, jobs, and people, while libertarian- and conservative-leaning California, Arizona, Florida, and Texas gained greater political clout. The full impact of this shifting political map would not be felt until the 1980s and 1990s, but it was already a factor by the mid-1970s.

Jimmy Carter: The Outsider in Washington

When James Earl Carter Jr. told his mother that he intended to run for president, she had asked, "President of what?" Carter's mother was not the only person skeptical of his ambition, but the naval officer, peanut farmer, and former governor of Georgia emerged from the pack to win the Democratic nomination in 1976. Trading on Watergate and his down-home image, Carter pledged to restore morality to the White House. "I will never lie to you," he promised voters. The Georgian played up his credentials as a Washington outsider, although he selected Senator Walter F. Mondale of Minnesota, a seasoned liberal with decades of experience in Washington, as his running mate to ensure his ties to traditional Democratic voting blocs. In the general election, President Ford's pardon of Nixon cost him votes in key states, and Carter won with 50 percent of the popular vote to Ford's 48 percent.

Carter's outsider approach was initially effective and proved popular. He walked to the White House after the inauguration and delivered fireside chats in a cardigan sweater. His born-again Christian faith also resonated with religious Americans. But inexperience began to tell. He responded to feminists, an important Democratic constituency, by establishing a women's commission in his administration, only to dismiss that commission's concerns and engage in a public fight with prominent women's advocates. Most consequentially, his outsider strategy chilled relations with congressional leaders. Disdainful of the Democratic establishment, Carter relied heavily on inexperienced advisors from Georgia. As a detail-oriented micromanager, he exhausted himself over the fine points of policy better left to his aides.

On the domestic front, Carter's big challenge was the economy, with stagflation the most confounding fiscal problem. If the government focused on inflation — forcing prices down by raising interest rates — unemployment would rise. If the government tried to stimulate employment, inflation would worsen. None of the regular policy levers seemed to work. Carter toyed with the idea of an "industrial policy" to bail out the ailing manufacturing sector, but at heart he was an economic conservative. He moved instead in a free-market direction by lifting the New Deal–era regulation of the airline, trucking, and railroad industries. This **deregulation**, which lifted price controls and other government mandates, stimulated competition and cut prices, though it also drove firms out of business and hurt unionized workers.

Jimmy Carter President Jimmy Carter is seen here at his home in Plains, Georgia, in 1975, soon after he'd declared himself a candidate for the Democratic presidential nomination. Carter was content to portray himself as a political outsider, an ordinary American who could restore trust to Washington after the Watergate scandal. A thoughtful man and a born-again Christian, Carter nonetheless proved unable to solve the complex economic problems, especially high inflation, and international challenges of the late 1970s. AP Photo.

The president's efforts failed to reignite economic growth. In 1979, the Iranian Revolution (see "The Carter Presidency" in Chapter 29) curtailed oil supplies, and gas prices jumped again. In a major TV address in April, Carter lectured Americans about the nation's "crisis of the spirit." Citing the country's growing dependence on expensive foreign petroleum, he laid out ten broad principles for energy conservation. To emphasize the seriousness of conservation, he called it "the moral equivalent of war." The media reduced that phrase to a joke — using "MEOW" as shorthand, in order to mock the president — which aptly captured the public's opinion of the president seeming to lecture and scold, which further damaged his popularity. By then, Carter's approval rating had fallen below 30 percent. It was no wonder, given an inflation rate over 13 percent, failing industries, and long lines at the pumps. The Democrats found themselves in a political trap — Watergate had helped them regain power but also saddled them with responsibility for the economic quagmire.

deregulation
The limiting of regulation by federal agencies. In the 1970s, the lifting of price controls and other government mandates on airline, trucking, and railroad industries stimulated competition and cut prices, but also drove firms out of business and hurt unionized workers.

AP® SKILLS & PROCESSES

ARGUMENTATION

What kind of president did Jimmy Carter hope to be, and how successful was he at implementing his agenda?

REFORM AND REACTION IN THE 1970S

How did controversies over new individual rights shape the politics of the 1970s?

After a decade of churning social and political unrest — the Vietnam War, protests, riots, Watergate, recession — many Americans were exhausted with politics and cynical by the mid-1970s. But while some retreated from activism, others took reform in new directions. Civil rights efforts continued, the women's movement achieved major

TEACHING STRATEGY

It is unthinkable that any previous presidential contender would have been photographed barefooted and wearing blue jeans. This casualness was both part of his personality and an image cultivated to appeal to Americans at a particular moment. The *American Experience* film *Carter* provides a good introduction to Carter's personality, his status as an "outsider," and his longshot run for the presidency — which helps capture Americans' disillusionment with government as normal. To access the film, search "American Experience Carter."

CHECK FOR UNDERSTANDING

Ask students: **In what ways was the period between 1973 and 1980 a transitional one in American politics?** *The period between the Watergate Scandal and the election of 1980 is often referred to as a time of malaise, politically and economically. The energy crisis, controversies in the Middle East, economic crises couched under stagflation, and economic decline in manufacturing caused many Americans to question the role of the United States as world leader in the late twentieth century. This transition, as it were, concerned many Americans as they worked to regain an economic and political foothold.*

AP® SKILLS & PROCESSES

ARGUMENTATION

The **ARGUMENTATION** question invites students to compare Carter's goals with his actual agenda. In places where he was unable to accomplish his goals, students should identify the factors that led to this failure, whether they relate to his own leadership or the broader context of his presidency.

TRM Find complete suggested responses in the Teacher's Resource Materials.

gains, and gay rights blossomed. These movements pushed the "rights revolution" of the 1960s deeper into American life. In response, social conservatives pushed back, forming their own organizations to combat the emergence of what they saw as an excessively permissive society.

Civil Rights in a New Era

The 1964 Civil Rights Act required that employers hire without regard to "race, color, religion, sex, or national origin." But many liberals thought "nondiscrimination" was not enough, after centuries of slavery and decades of segregation, to allow African Americans and other people of color access to the economic mainstream. They believed that government, universities, and private employers needed to take positive steps to welcome a wider, more diverse range of Americans. That meant more people of color, more women of all backgrounds, and more people from a wide range of underrepresented groups.

This outlook gave rise to the idea of **affirmative action** — procedures designed to address the legacy of historical exclusion rather than simply guarantee fairness in the present. First advanced by the Kennedy administration in 1961, affirmative action received a boost under President Lyndon Johnson, whose Labor Department fashioned plans to encourage government contractors to recruit underrepresented racial groups. Women were added under the last of these plans, when pressure from the women's movement highlighted the problem of gender discrimination. By the early 1970s, affirmative action had been refined by court rulings into a set of legally acceptable procedures: hiring and enrollment goals, special recruitment and training programs, and set-asides (specially reserved slots) for both underrepresented racial groups and women.

Affirmative action, however, displeased many whites, who felt the deck was now stacked against them. Much of the dissent came from conservative groups that had

AP® EXAM TIP

Recognize affirmative action as part of the broader conflict over the role of federal government in issues of race.

affirmative action
Policies established in the 1960s and 1970s by governments, businesses, universities, and other institutions to address past discrimination against specific groups such as people of color and white women.

March for Affirmative Action Americans grew even more divided over the policy of affirmative action in the 1970s. For many people, such as African Americans and Latinos, affirmative action promised that groups who faced historical discrimination would have equal opportunity in jobs and education. For many whites, affirmative action looked like "reverse discrimination," and they fought its implementation. Here, supporters of affirmative action encourage the U.S. Supreme Court to overturn the California *Bakke* decision, declaring racial quotas unconstitutional. In the end, however, the Supreme Court upheld *Bakke*, and the scope of affirmative action narrowed. AP Photo/Charles Tasnadi.

AP® APPLY THE TIP

Give students the following scenario: One athlete prepares for a 50-meter dash for three years, training every day with the best equipment and coaches. Another athlete spends the same three years shackled in a small cell where he can only move a little each day. On the day of the race, both athletes are brought to the track, given the same shoes, same uniform, and placed at the starting line of the race. Do these athletes have an equal chance at success? Is equal treatment just? Lead a class discussion in which students express various reactions to this scenario. Explain to students that while the Civil Rights Act of 1964 and the enforcement of the *Brown v. Board* decision had a dramatic impact on Americans' understanding of race relations, they did not immediately change the social and economic conditions of African Americans in the U.S. One way that government attempted to address the legacy of racism in the U.S. was through the establishment of affirmative action programs to support the economic and social equality of African Americans and other minorities. Explain to students that the idea behind affirmative action was to level the playing field for those who had long been excluded from many institutions and jobs in America. Organize students into pairs to discuss the relationship of the scenario to affirmative action programs.

opposed civil rights all along. They charged affirmative action advocates with "reverse discrimination." Legal challenges abounded from white employees, job seekers, and university applicants. Some liberal groups sought a middle position. In a widely publicized 1972 letter, Jewish organizations, seared by the memory of quotas that once kept Jewish students out of elite colleges, came out against all racial quotas but nonetheless endorsed "rectifying the imbalances resulting from past discrimination."

A major shift in affirmative action policy came in 1978. Allan Bakke, a white man, sued the University of California at Davis Medical School for rejecting him in favor of less-qualified minority-group candidates. Headlines across the country sparked anti–affirmative action protest marches on college campuses and vigorous discussion on television and radio as well as in the White House. Ultimately, the Supreme Court struck down the medical school's quota system, which set aside 16 of 100 places for "disadvantaged" students. The Court ordered Bakke admitted but indicated that a more flexible affirmative action plan, in which race could be considered along with other factors, would pass constitutional muster. ***Regents of the University of California v. Bakke*** thus both upheld affirmative action but, in rejecting quotas, limited its force. More court rulings and state referenda over the following decades would further hem in affirmative action. California voters were the most aggressive, approving Proposition 209 in 1996, which prohibited public institutions — schools, universities, and government agencies — from using affirmative action to increase diversity in employment and education. Though some states followed California's lead in banning it altogether, today affirmative action is widely practiced in both public and private institutions across the country, but quotas are illegal and identities such as race and gender must be weighed alongside other factors in qualifications for admission or employment.

Regents of the University of California v. Bakke
The 1978 Supreme Court ruling that limited affirmative action by rejecting a quota system.

AP® SKILLS & PROCESSES

CONTINUITY AND CHANGE

How does affirmative action illustrate both continuity and change in the movement for civil rights?

The Women's Movement and Gay Rights

Although the civil rights movement continued and flourished into the 1970s, its major achievements had come a decade earlier. In contrast, the women's and gay rights movements had just begun to gain momentum at the dawn of the new decade. With its three influential wings — liberal, radical, and women of color (see "Women's Liberation and Black and Chicana Feminism" in Chapter 27) — the women's movement inspired both grassroots activism and legislative action across the nation. As women won notable gains, gay activists faced a fundamental set of challenges: they needed to convince Americans that same-sex relationships were natural and that gay men and lesbians deserved the equal protection of the law. Neither movement achieved all of its aims in this era, but each made meaningful progress toward equality.

Women's Activism The first half of the 1970s marked the peak of the women's liberation movement. Taking a dizzying array of forms — from lobbying legislatures to marching in the streets and establishing all-female collectives — women's liberation produced activism on the scale of the earlier black-led civil rights movement. Women's centers, as well as women-run child-care facilities, began to spring up in cities and towns. Feminist art and poetry movements flourished. Women challenged the admissions policies of all-male colleges and universities — opening such prestigious schools as Yale and Columbia and nearly bringing an end to male-only institutions entirely. The ever-increasing number of female scholars began to transform higher education: by studying women's history, pushing for the hiring of more women faculty, and by founding women's studies programs.

Women's liberationists drew a new attention to the female body — and turned it into a political battleground. Inspired by the Boston collective that published the groundbreaking book *Our Bodies, Ourselves*, the first medical/health book to focus entirely on women, the women's health movement founded dozens of medical clinics, encouraged women to become physicians, and educated millions of women about their bodies. Activists pushed against antiabortion laws in more than thirty state

AP® EXAM TIP

Evaluate the impact of legislative action and court decisions on women's rights in the 1970s.

CHECK FOR UNDERSTANDING

Ask students: **How did civil rights change in the new era of the 1970s?** *Many discussions about civil rights in the 1970s focused on the policy of affirmative action. Some whites began to complain of "reverse discrimination," winning a major victory with the Bakke decision in 1978.*

AP® SKILLS & PROCESSES

CONTINUITY AND CHANGE

Use the **CONTINUITY AND CHANGE** question to have students delineate changes in affirmative action over a fifteen-year course from Kennedy's Executive Order 10925 in 1961 to the Supreme Court's *Bakke* ruling in 1978. Students should also explain the larger social and political contexts that help explain this evolution.

TRM Find complete suggested responses in the Teacher's Resource Materials.

AP® APPLY THE TIP

Direct students to complete **Handout 28.3 — Comparison: ERA and *Roe v. Wade* (TRM)** using pp. 921–923. After students complete the handout, allow them to choose either topic — the Equal Rights Amendment or *Roe v. Wade* — to research. Tell students that they should become "30-minute experts" (or the amount of time available) on their chosen topic on the legal provisions, implications for women's rights, and especially continuing impacts of each topic for the U.S. today. Ask students to analyze the ways in which equal rights for women has been extended since 1973 despite the failure of the ERA to be ratified and the ways that the rights ensured by *Roe v. Wade* in 1973 have been challenged or limited since the decision was made. After students become "30-minute experts," ask them to form small groups to share and discuss their findings. Then lead a class discussion that addresses the following questions (*answers will vary*):

- **In what way did the debate over the Equal Rights Amendment mirror previous arguments in favor of and against women's rights?**
- **What other Supreme Court cases supported privacy rights related to the sexual revolution?**
- **How did each of these issues impact the relationship between the right and the left in American politics and society?**

TRM Find **Handout 28.3 — Comparison: ERA and *Roe v. Wade*** in the Teacher's Resource Materials.

TEACHING STRATEGY

One of the most important aspects of the rise of Conservatism was the role of evangelical Christian churches and women activists. Have students explain at least TWO reasons why women activist groups such as STOP ERA embraced conservative values in the early 1970s.

legislatures. Women's liberationists established rape crisis centers around the nation and lobbied state legislatures and Congress to reform sexual assault laws. Many of these efforts began as shoestring operations in living rooms and kitchens: *Our Bodies, Ourselves* was first published as a 35-cent mimeographed booklet, and the antirape movement began in small consciousness-raising groups that met in churches and community centers. By the end of the decade, many grassroots organizations had gone national and improved the lives of millions of American women in the process.

Equal Rights Amendment (ERA)
Constitutional amendment passed by Congress in 1972 that would require equal treatment of men and women under federal and state law. Facing fierce opposition from the New Right and the Republican Party, the ERA was defeated as time ran out for state ratification in 1982.

STOP ERA
An organization founded by Phyllis Schlafly in 1972 to fight the Equal Rights Amendment.

Equal Rights Amendment Buoyed by this flourishing of activism, the women's movement renewed the fight for an **Equal Rights Amendment (ERA)** to the Constitution. First introduced in 1923, the ERA stated, in its entirety, "Equality of rights under the law shall not be denied or abridged by the United States or any State on account of sex." Vocal congressional women from the Democratic Party, such as Patsy Mink (Hawaii), Bella Abzug (New York), and Shirley Chisholm (New York), found enthusiastic male allies — among both Democrats and Republicans — and Congress passed the amendment in 1972. Within just two years, thirty-four of the necessary thirty-eight states had ratified it, and the ERA appeared headed for adoption. While no one could predict what changes the amendment would bring — courts would have to interpret and apply its broad language — the ERA's advocates believed it would usher in an era of gender equality in employment and education, as well as between men and women in the household. But then, progress abruptly halted (Map 28.2).

Stopping the ratification of the ERA was largely the work of a remarkable woman: Phyllis Schlafly, a lawyer long active in conservative causes. Despite her own flourishing legal career, Schlafly believed in traditional roles for women. The ERA, she argued in her many public appearances, would create an unnatural "unisex

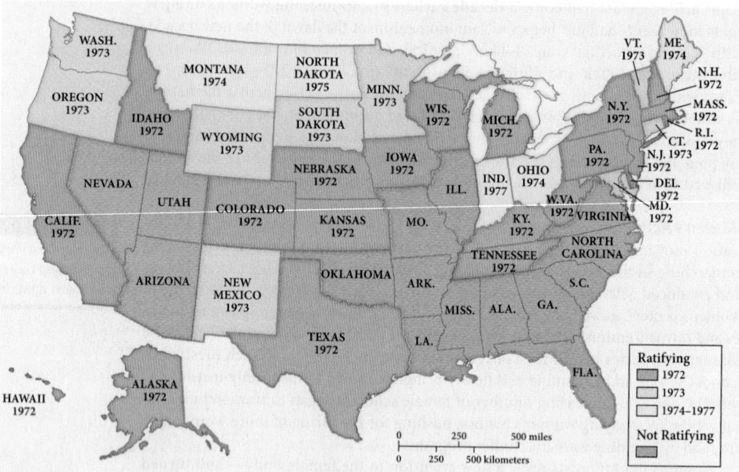

MAP 28.2 States Ratifying the Equal Rights Amendment, 1972–1977
The ratifying process for the Equal Rights Amendment (ERA) went smoothly in 1972 and 1973 but then stalled. The turning point came in 1976, when ERA advocates lobbied extensively, particularly in Florida, North Carolina, and Illinois, but failed to sway the conservative legislatures in those states. After Indiana ratified in 1977, the amendment still lacked three votes toward the three-fourths majority needed for adoption. Efforts to revive the ERA in the 1980s were unsuccessful, and it became a dead issue.

society," with women drafted into the army and forced to use unisex restrooms. Schlafly organized the **STOP ERA** group in 1972, mobilizing thousands of women to demonstrate at statehouses wielding home-baked bread and apple pies. The label on the baked goods at one anti-ERA rally captured their views: "My heart and hand went into this dough / For the sake of the family please vote no." The message resonated widely, especially among those troubled by the rapid pace of social change (see "Firsthand Accounts," p. 924). The ERA never was ratified, despite a congressional extension of the deadline to June 30, 1982.

Phyllis Schlafly Phyllis Schlafly, leader of the organization STOP ERA, leading a rally at the Illinois State Capitol in 1978, at a time when the state legislature was considering whether to ratify the Equal Rights Amendment. Schlafly described herself as a housewife and called her decades-long strenuous political career a hobby. Bettmann/Getty Images.

Roe v. Wade In the early 1960s, abortion was illegal in virtually every state. The women's movement made reproductive rights a major goal, mounting both legislative and judicial strategies to legalize abortion. By the mid-1970s, thanks to intensive lobbying by women's organizations, liberal ministers, and physicians, a handful of states (New York, Hawaii, California, and Colorado) passed laws making legal abortions easier to obtain. But progress after that was slow, and women's advocates turned to the courts.

The Supreme Court had first addressed reproductive rights in a 1965 case, *Griswold v. Connecticut*. *Griswold* struck down an 1879 state law, which prohibited the possession of contraception, as a violation of what the court called a married couples' constitutional "right of privacy." Following the logic of *Griswold*, the Court gradually expanded the right of privacy to include individuals in a series of cases in the late 1960s and early 1970s. Those cases culminated in ***Roe v. Wade*** (1973). In that landmark decision, the justices nullified a Texas law that prohibited abortion under any circumstances, even when the woman's health was at risk, and laid out a new national standard: abortions performed during the first trimester were protected by the right of privacy. In *Roe*, the Court transformed what was traditionally a matter of state policy into a national, constitutionally protected right.

Roe v. Wade
The 1973 Supreme Court ruling that the Constitution protects the right to abortion, which states cannot prohibit in the early stages of pregnancy. The decision galvanized social conservatives and made abortion a controversial policy issue for decades to come.

For the women's movement, *Roe v. Wade* represented a triumph. For evangelical and fundamentalist Christians, Catholics, and conservatives generally, it was a bitter pill. In their view, abortion was unequivocally the taking of a human life. Women's advocates responded that illegal abortions — common prior to *Roe* — were often unsafe procedures that resulted in physical harm to women and even death. *Roe* polarized opinions on a divisive subject and motivated conservatives to seek a Supreme Court reversal or, short of that, to pursue legislation that would strictly limit the conditions under which abortions could be performed. In 1976, they convinced Congress to deny Medicaid funds for abortions, the opening move in what would become a decades-long effort to weaken *Roe v. Wade* that continues today.

Harvey Milk In November 1977, Harvey Milk became the first openly gay man to be elected to public office in the United States, when he won a seat on the San Francisco Board of Supervisors. Shockingly, almost exactly a year from the day of his election, Milk was assassinated. Bettmann/Getty Images.

Harvey Milk The gay rights movement had achieved notable victories but also encountered determined conservative resistance. By the mid-1970s, more than a dozen cities had passed gay rights ordinances protecting gay men and lesbians from employment and housing discrimination. One such ordinance in Dade County, Florida, sparked a protest led by Anita Bryant, a successful pop singer and conservative Baptist activist. Her "Save Our Children" campaign in 1977,

AP® THEME

POL: Politics and Power

A series of Supreme Court decisions in the 1960s and early 1970s expanded civil rights and individual liberties. The companion site to the PBS film *The Supreme Court* provides an overview of the background to *Roe v. Wade*, details of the Court's ruling, and its significance. To access this film, search "PBS Supreme Court Roe v. Wade."

AP® THEME

SOC: Social Structures; NAT: American and National Identity

In the 1970s, feminist and gay activists continued to mobilize behind demands for legal, economic, and social equality. *The Legacy Project* provides an overview of Harvey Milk's political career and his murder, with suggestions on how to teach about him in the classroom. To access these resources, search "Legacy Project Harvey Milk lesson plans."

AP® SKILLS & PROCESSES

ANALYZING HISTORICAL EVIDENCE

The **AP® FIRSTHAND ACCOUNTS** feature explores debates about the Equal Rights Amendment, providing a clear window on the nation's deep social divisions regarding gender, the role of women, and the nature of family. Some advocates continue to lobby for passage of the ERA, nearly a century after it was first proposed.

AP® FIRSTHAND ACCOUNTS

Debating the Equal Rights Amendment

Fifty years after its introduction, the Equal Rights Amendment ("Equality of rights under the law shall not be denied or abridged by the United States or by any State on account of sex") finally met congressional approval in 1972 and was sent to the states for ratification. The amendment set off a furious debate, especially in the South and Midwest, and fell short of ratification. Following are four of the voices in that debate.

PHYLLIS SCHLAFLY

Lawyer and political activist Phyllis Schlafly was the most prominent opponent of the ERA. Her organization, STOP ERA, campaigned against the amendment in critical states and helped to halt ratification.

Source: From *The Phyllis Schlafly Report*, November 1972. Reprinted by permission. Reprinted by permission of the Eagle Forum Education & Legal Defense Fund.

❝ Women's magazines, the women's pages of newspapers, and television and radio talk shows have been filled for months with a strident advocacy of the 'rights' of women to be treated on an equal basis with men in all walks of life. But what about the rights of the woman who doesn't want to compete on an equal basis with men? Does she have the right to be treated as a woman — by her family, by society, and by the law? . . .

The laws of every one of our 50 states now guarantee the right to be a woman — protected and provided for in her career as a woman, wife, and mother. The proposed Equal Rights Amendment will wipe out all our laws which — through rights, benefits, and exemptions — guarantee this right to be a woman. . . . Is this what American women want? Is this what American men want?

The laws of every one of the 50 states now require the husband to support his wife and children — and to provide a home for them to live in. In other words, the law protects a woman's right to be a full-time wife and mother, her right not to take a job outside the home, her right to care for her own baby in her own home while being financially supported by her husband. . . .

There are two very different types of women lobbying for the Equal Rights Amendment. One group is the women's liberationists. Their motive is totally radical. They hate men, marriage, and children. They are out to destroy morality and the family. . . . There is another type of woman supporting the Equal Rights Amendment from the most sincere motives. It is easy to see why the business and professional women are supporting the Equal Rights Amendment — many of them have felt the keen edge of discrimination in their employment. ❞

JERRY FALWELL

Jerry Falwell was a fundamentalist Baptist preacher in Virginia, a television evangelist, and the founder of the political lobbying organization known as the Moral Majority.

Source: Jerry Falwell, Excerpt(s) from *Listen America!*, copyright © 1980 by Jerry Falwell. Used by permission of Doubleday, an imprint of the Knopf Doubleday Publishing Group, a division of Penguin Random House LLC. All rights reserved.

❝ I believe that at the foundation of the women's liberation movement there is a minority core of women who were once bored with life, whose real problems are spiritual problems. Many women have never accepted their God-given roles. . . . God Almighty created men and women biologically different and with differing needs and roles. He made men and women to complement each other and to love each other. . . . Women who work should be respected and accorded dignity and equal rewards for equal work. But this is not what the present feminist movement and equal rights movement are all about.

The Equal Rights Amendment is a delusion. I believe that women deserve more than equal rights. And, in families and in nations where the Bible is believed, Christian women are honored above men. Only in places where the Bible is believed and practiced do women receive more than equal rights. Men and women have differing strengths. The Equal Rights Amendment can never do for women what needs to be done for them. Women need to know Jesus Christ as their Lord and Savior and be under His Lordship. They need a man who knows Jesus Christ as his Lord and Savior, and they need to be part of a home where their husband is a godly leader and where there is a Christian family. . . .

which garnered national media attention, resulted in the repeal of the ordinance and symbolized the emergence of a conservative religious movement opposed to gay rights.

Across the country from Miami, the story of Harvey Milk, a camera-shop owner turned politician, captured both the promise and the peril of gay rights activism. A closeted businessman in New York until he was forty, in 1972 Milk arrived in San Francisco, which had become known for its vibrant gay and lesbian communities, and threw himself into public life. Fiercely independent, he ran as an openly gay candidate for city supervisor (city council) twice and the state assembly once, all three times unsuccessfully.

ERA is not merely a political issue, but a moral issue as well. A definite violation of holy Scripture, ERA defies the mandate that 'the husband is the head of the wife, even as Christ is the head of the church' (Ep. 5:23). In 1 Peter 3:7 we read that husbands are to give their wives honor as unto the weaker vessel, that they are both heirs together of the grace of life. Because a woman is weaker does not mean that she is less important. ❞

ELIZABETH DUNCAN KOONTZ

Elizabeth Duncan Koontz was a distinguished educator and the first black woman to head the National Education Association and the U.S. Women's Bureau. At the time she made this statement at state legislative hearings on the ERA in 1977, she was assistant state superintendent for public instruction in North Carolina.

SOURCE: William A. Link and Marjorie Spruill Wheeler, eds., *The South in the History of the Nation* (Boston: Bedford/St. Martin's, 1999), 295–296.

❝ A short time ago I had the misfortune to break my foot. . . . The pain . . . did not hurt me as much as when I went into the emergency room and the young woman upon asking me my name, the nature of my ailment, then asked me for my husband's social security number and his hospitalization number. I asked her what did that have to do with my emergency.

And she said, 'We have to be sure of who is going to pay your bill.' I said, 'Suppose I'm not married, then.' And she said, 'Then give me your father's name.' I did not go through that twenty years ago when I was denied the use of that emergency room because of my color.

I went through that because there is an underlying assumption that all women in our society are protected, dependent, cared for by somebody who's got a social security number and hospitalization insurance. Never once did she assume I might be a woman who might be caring for my husband, instead of him by me, because of some illness. She did not take into account the fact that one out of almost eight women heading families in poverty today [is] in the same condition as men in families and poverty. . . .

My greater concern is that so many women today . . . oppose the passage of the ERA very sincerely and . . . tell you without batting an eye, 'I don't want to see women treated that way.' And I speak up, 'What way is that?' . . . Women themselves have been a bit misguided. We have mistaken present practice for law, and women have . . . assumed too many times that their present condition cannot change. The rate of divorce, the rate of desertion, the rate of separation, and the death rate of male supporters is enough for us to say: 'Let us remove all legal barriers to women and girls making their choices — this state cannot afford it.' ❞

CAROLINE BIRD

Caroline Bird was the lead author of *What Women Want*, a report produced by women's rights advocates following the 1977 National Women's Conference, held in Houston, Texas.

SOURCE: Caroline Bird, *What Women Want* (New York: Simon & Schuster, 1979), 120–121.

❝ The Declaration of Independence, signed in 1776, stated that 'all Men are created equal' and that governments derive their powers 'from the Consent of the Governed.' Women were not included in either concept. The original American Constitution of 1787 was founded on English common law, which did not recognize women as citizens or as individuals with legal rights. A woman was expected to obey her husband or nearest male kin, and if she was married her person and her property were owned by her husband. . . .

It has been argued that the ERA is not necessary because the Fourteenth Amendment, passed after the Civil War, guarantees that no state shall deny to 'any person within its jurisdiction the equal protection of the laws.' . . .

Aside from the fact that women have been subjected to varying, inconsistent, and often unfavorable decisions under the Fourteenth Amendment, the Equal Rights Amendment is a more immediate and effective remedy to sex discrimination in Federal and State laws than case-by-case interpretation under the Fourteenth Amendment could ever be. ❞

QUESTIONS FOR ANALYSIS

1. Schlafly and Koontz have different notions of what it means to be a woman. Explain what these differences are and how they inform the authors' distinct views of the ERA.
2. Why does Schlafly believe that women will be harmed by the ERA? Use specific examples to support your claim.
3. Schlafly and Falwell argue that women need the protection and support of men. Explain the credibility of each argument with evidence. How would Koontz likely respond?
4. How do each of the four authors define women's roles and responsibilities in society? Compare the arguments of the sources and their contributions to women's rights.

TRM Find complete suggested responses in the Teacher's Resource Materials.

By mobilizing the "gay vote" into a powerful bloc, Milk finally won a supervisor seat in 1977. He was not the first openly gay elected official in the country — Kathy Kozachenko of Michigan and Elaine Noble of Massachusetts share that distinction — but he became a national symbol of emerging gay political power, after working to win passage of a rights ordinance in San Francisco. But Milk's career was cut short in 1978, when a disgruntled former fellow supervisor named Dan White assassinated him and the city's mayor, George Mascone. When White was convicted of manslaughter rather than murder, which carried a much lighter prison sentence, five thousand lesbian, gay, bisexual, transgender, and queer (LGBTQ) activists and allies

CHECK FOR UNDERSTANDING

Ask students: **How did the civil rights movement change in the 1970s?** *Women's rights activism expanded to include issues related to women's physical health, prevention of rape, and access to birth control; they won a major victory for reproductive rights when the Supreme Court ruled in* Roe v. Wade *that women had the right to an abortion in the first trimester under a new-found right to privacy. Advocates relaunched the long-dormant Equal Rights Amendment, though this movement stalled in the states. Gay activists won protection from discrimination in employment and housing.*

AP® SKILLS & PROCESSES

DEVELOPMENTS AND PROCESSES

The **DEVELOPMENTS AND PROCESSES** question asks students to identify how the civil rights movement changed by embracing new concerns (in the case of feminism) and expanding to additional groups, specifically gays and lesbians. Students should clearly explain how the expansion of the movement expressed continuity as well — that is, how the new movements were similar to earlier civil rights activism.

TRM Find complete suggested responses in the Teacher's Resource Materials.

AP® THEME

POL: Politics and Power

Conservatives challenged liberal Court decisions, seeking to limit the role of the federal government. The Burger Court played a significant role in moving the country in a more conservative direction. The Supreme Court Historical Society, founded by Burger himself, explains the nature of the Burger Court. To access this resource, search "Supreme Court Historical Society Burger Court."

CHECK FOR UNDERSTANDING

Ask students: **How did controversies over new individual rights shape the politics of the 1970s?** *The controversies over individual rights, including affirmative action, abortion rights, and non-discrimination of homosexuals, brought identity politics to the fore, worked primarily through the courts (rather than the executive or legislative branches), and exacerbated existing differences between liberals and conservatives.*

AP® SKILLS & PROCESSES

DEVELOPMENTS AND PROCESSES

How did the civil rights movement expand during the 1970s?

marched on San Francisco City Hall. Confrontations with police turned violent, and protestors attacked police vehicles and City Hall itself in what became known as the "White Night Riots." Before order was restored, dozens of police officers and more than a hundred protestors were injured.

After the Warren Court

In response to what conservatives considered a liberal judicial revolution of the Warren Court, Richard Nixon came into the presidency promising to appoint "strict constructionists" — jurists with a preference for narrower interpretations of the law. In three short years, between 1969 and 1972, he was able to appoint four new justices to the Supreme Court, including the new chief justice, Warren Burger. Surprisingly, Burger and his new conservative colleagues did not seek to overturn the work of their predecessors. In fact, in *Roe v. Wade* the Burger Court (1969–1986) dismayed conservatives by extending the "right of privacy" developed under Warren to include women's access to abortion. Other Burger Court decisions advanced women's rights in the workplace. In 1976, the Court ruled that arbitrary distinctions based on sex in the workplace and other arenas were unconstitutional, and in 1986 that sexual harassment violated the Civil Rights Act.

In all of its rulings on privacy rights the Burger Court was reluctant to move ahead of public attitudes toward homosexuality. Gay men and lesbians still had no legal recourse if state laws prohibited same-sex relations. In a controversial 1986 case, *Bowers v. Hardwick*, the Supreme Court upheld a Georgia sodomy statute that criminalized homosexuality. The majority opinion held that homosexuality was contrary to "ordered liberty" and that extending sexual privacy to gays and lesbians "would be to cast aside millennia of moral teaching." Not until 2003 (*Lawrence v. Texas*) would the Court overturn that decision, extending the right to sexual privacy to all Americans.

The Burger Court's rulings also helped to ratify the "law and order" politics embraced by many Americans in the years following the 1960s and gave it a reputation for centrist restraint. After initially striking down all existing capital punishment laws, in *Furman v. Georgia* (1972), the court subsequently restored them, in *Gregg v. Georgia* (1976). Rather than overturning the Warren Court's rulings on the rights of suspected criminals (such as the 1966 decision in *Miranda v. Arizona*), which were deeply unpopular among conservatives, the Burger Court instead limited their reach. Stretching across four presidencies (Richard Nixon, Gerald Ford, Jimmy Carter, and Ronald Reagan), the Burger Court quietly began to shift the court in a conservative direction, following the bold liberalism of the Warren Court.

THE AMERICAN FAMILY UNDER STRESS

What were the major sources of anxiety about the American family in the decade after the 1960s?

In 1973, the Public Broadcasting System (PBS) aired a twelve-part television series that followed the life of a real American family — the Louds of Santa Barbara, California. Producers wanted the show, called simply *An American Family*, to document how a middle-class white family coped with the stresses of a changing society. They did not anticipate that the family would dissolve in front of their cameras. Tensions and arguments raged, and in the final episode, Bill, the husband (who was serially unfaithful), moved out. By the time the show aired — setting the first standard for the later emergence of what would become known as "reality television" — the couple was divorced and Pat, the former wife, was a single working mom with five kids.

An American Family highlighted a traumatic moment in twentieth-century domestic life. The nuclear family was at the heart of the postwar ideal, but between 1965 and 1985, the divorce rate doubled. Children born in the 1970s had a 40 percent chance of spending part of their youth in a single-parent household. As wages stagnated and inflation pushed up prices, more and more families depended on two incomes for survival. The women's movement challenged traditional gender roles — father as provider and mother as homemaker — and middle-class baby boomers rebelled against what they saw as the puritanical sexual values of their parents' generation.

Working Families in the Age of Deindustrialization

One of the most striking developments of the 1970s and 1980s was the relative stagnation of wages. After World War II, hourly wages had grown steadily ahead of inflation, giving workers more buying power with each passing year. By 1973, that trend had stopped in its tracks. The decline of organized labor, the loss of manufacturing jobs, and runaway inflation all played a role in the sudden halt to progress. Hardest hit were blue-collar and pink-collar workers and those without college degrees.

Women Enter the Workforce Despite the presence of millions of women in the workforce, many Americans still believed in the "family wage": a breadwinner income, earned by men, sufficient to support a family. After 1973, fewer and fewer Americans brought home such an ample wage. Between 1973 and the early 1990s, every major income group except the top 10 percent saw their real earnings (accounting for inflation) either remain the same or decline. Over the same period, the typical worker saw a 10 percent drop in real wages. To keep their families from falling behind, more women went to work. Between 1950 and 1994, the proportion of women ages twenty-five to fifty-four working for pay increased from 37 to 75 percent, with much of that increase coming in the 1970s. American households were fast becoming dependent on two incomes (Figure 28.5).

The numbers tell two different stories about American life in these decades. On one hand, many women, especially those in blue-collar and pink-collar families, *had* to work for wages to sustain their family's standard of living: to buy a car, pay for college, afford medical bills, support an aging parent, or simply pay the rent. Moreover, the number of single women raising children nearly doubled between 1965 and 1990. Women's paid labor was making up for the declining earning power — or absence — of men in American households. On the other hand, women's real income overall grew during the same period. Educated baby boom women were filling higher-paying professional jobs in law and medicine, business and government, and, slowly, the sciences and engineering. Beneficiaries of feminism, these women pursued careers of which their mothers had only dreamed.

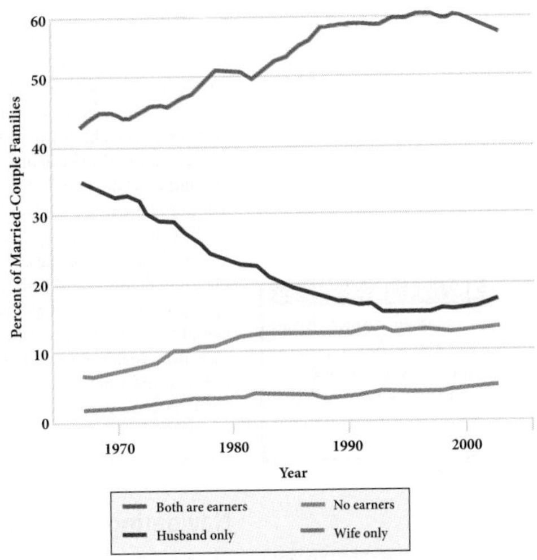

FIGURE 28.5 The Increase in Two-Worker Families

In 1968, about 43 percent of married couples sent both the husband and the wife into the workforce; thirty years later, 60 percent were two-earner families. The percentage of families in which the wife alone worked increased from 3 to 5 percent during these years, while those with no earners (welfare recipients and, increasingly, retired couples) rose from 8 to 13 percent. Because these figures do not include unmarried persons and most illegal immigrants, they do not give a complete picture of the American workplace. But there is no doubt that women now play a major role in the workforce.

Good Times The popular 1970s sitcom *Good Times* examined how the "blue-collar blues" affected a working-class black family struggling to make ends meet in tough economic times. The show's theme song spoke of "temporary layoffs . . . easy credit ripoffs . . . scratchin' and surviving." Its actors, many of them classically trained, brought a realistic portrait of working-class African American life to television. Bettmann/Getty Images.

The Working Class in the National Spotlight For a brief period in the 1970s, the trials of working men and women moved center stage in national culture. Reporters wrote of the "blue-collar blues" associated with plant closings and the hard-fought strikes of the decade. A 1972 strike at the Lordstown, Ohio, General Motors plant captivated the nation. Holding out not for higher wages but for better working conditions — the plant had the most complex assembly line in the nation — Lordstown strikers spoke out against what they saw as an inhumane industrial system. Across the nation, the number of union-led strikes surged, even as the number of Americans in the labor movement continued to decline. In Lordstown and many other sites of strikes and industrial conflict, workers won public attention but little tangible improvements.

When Americans turned on their televisions in the mid-1970s, the most popular shows reflected the prevalent theme of struggling families. *All in the Family* was joined by *The Waltons*, set during the Great Depression. *Good Times*, *Welcome Back, Kotter*, and *Sanford and Son* dealt with poverty in the inner city. *The Jeffersons* featured an upwardly mobile black couple struggling to leave working-class roots behind. *Laverne and Shirley* focused on young working women in the 1950s and *One Day at a Time* on contemporary working women making do after divorce. The most-watched television series of the decade, 1977's eight-part *Roots*, explored the history of slavery and the survival of African American culture and family roots despite the oppressive labor system. Not since the 1930s had American popular culture paid such close attention to working-class life.

The decade's popular music heavily featured artists such as Bruce Springsteen, Johnny Paycheck, and John Cougar (later Mellencamp), who turned the hardscrabble lives of people in small towns and working-class communities into rock anthems that filled arenas. Springsteen sang about characters who "sweat it out in the streets of a runaway American dream," and Paycheck famously declared, "Take this job and shove it!" to delighted audiences. Meanwhile, on the streets of Harlem and the South Bronx in New York, break dancing and rap music emerged — hybrid forms that expressed both the hardship of working-class, urban black life and the creative potential of experimentation. Early rappers emerged from the block party scene in working-class black and Latino neighborhoods, where MCs competed to put on the best dance beats and attract the biggest crowds.

AP® SKILLS & PROCESSES

MAKING CONNECTIONS

Why did the struggles of working families become more prominent in the 1970s, and what social and economic concerns did those families have?

Navigating the Sexual Revolution

The economic downturn was not the sole source of stress on American families in this era. Some people characterized changes in accepted norms about sex and love as a "sexual revolution." But the shifting sexual mores of the 1970s were less revolutionary than an evolution of developments in the first half of the twentieth century. Beginning in the 1910s, Americans increasingly viewed sex as a component of personal happiness, distinct from reproduction. Attitudes toward sex grew even more lenient in the postwar decades, a fact laid bare in the Kinsey studies of the 1940s and 1950s. By the 1960s, sex before marriage had grown more acceptable — an especially profound change for women — and frank discussions of sex in the media and popular culture had grown more common.

AP® EXAM TIP

Analyze the societal changes associated with the sexual revolution in the context of the counterculture and women's rights movements.

TEACHING STRATEGY

The Emmy Foundation's Archive of American Television provides an overview of *Good Times.* The site includes more than a dozen brief clips from writers and actors talking about the significance of the show, including the show's creator, Norman Lear. To access these resources, search "Archive of American Television Good Times."

TEACHING STRATEGY

In his article "*Born to Run* and the Decline of the American Dream," Joshua Zeitz explores Bruce Springsteen's breakout 1975 album and the way it reflected the struggles of those living in the nation's Rust Belt. Students could read the article and listen to the title song from the album to make connections. To access this resource, search "Atlantic Born to Run."

AP® SKILLS & PROCESSES

MAKING CONNECTIONS

The **MAKING CONNECTIONS** question asks students to use historical context to explain growing attention to working-class families in the 1970s. Since the struggles of this group of Americans were not new in this era, attention to this issue requires some explanation.

TRM Find complete suggested responses in the Teacher's Resource Materials.

CHECK FOR UNDERSTANDING

Ask students: **What were the experiences of working families in the age of deindustrialization?** *With real earnings either stagnant or declining for many workers due to high inflation, many families became two-income households. As divorce increased, the number of single women raising children increased substantially. These struggles made their way into popular culture through television shows and pop music, which provided an unprecedentedly frank discussion of these topics.*

AP® APPLY THE TIP

Organize the class into collaborative groups and provide students with **Handout 28.4 — Contextualization: Sexual Revolution (TRM)**. Ask students to transfer the contextualization diagram onto the large poster paper, and then read pp. 928–930 to add details to the poster. Details related directly to the sexual revolution should be placed in the inner circle, while the outer circle represents the broader historical processes, developments, and events that influenced the sexual revolution. Display the posters and discuss the cultural changes associated with the sexual revolution. Ask students to consider the ways that the sexual revolution would be explained through the following AP® Themes: American and national identity; politics and power; work, exchange, and technology; and social structures.

TRM Find **Handout 28.4 — Contextualization: Sexual Revolution** in the Teacher's Resource Materials.

Three additional developments cleared space for the sexual changes of the 1970s: the introduction of pharmaceutical birth control, the rise of a baby boomer–led counterculture, and the influence of feminism. First made available in the United States in 1960, birth control medication gave women unprecedented control over reproduction. By 1965, more than 6 million American women were using "the pill." This medical advance also changed attitudes. Middle-class baby boomers embraced a sexual ethic of greater freedom and, in many cases, a more casual approach to sex outside marriage. "I just feel I am expressing myself the way I feel at that moment in the most natural way," a female California college student, explaining her sex life, told a reporter in 1966. This stood in contrast to what a rebellious counterculture deemed the "puritanical" sexual outlook of older generations.

Many feminist critics felt that the sexual revolution was by and for men. The emphasis on casual sex seemed to perpetuate male privilege, and if anything a loosening of attitudes increased sexual harassment in the workplace. The proliferation of pornography continued to commercialize women as sex objects. But other feminists remained optimistic that the new sexual ethic could free women from those older moral constraints. They called for a revolution in sexual *values*, not simply behavior, that would end exploitation and let women enjoy the freedom to explore their sexuality on equal terms with men.

Sex and Popular Culture Whether sex was undergoing a revolution or an evolution in the 1970s, popular culture was eager to discuss every aspect. Mass-market books with titles such as *Everything You Always Wanted to Know About Sex*, *Human Sexual Response*, and *The Sensuous Man* shot up the best-seller list. William Masters and Virginia Johnson became the most famous sex researchers since Alfred Kinsey by studying couples in the act of lovemaking. In 1972, English physician Alex Comfort published *The Joy of Sex*, a guidebook for couples that became one of the most popular books of the decade. Comfort made certain to distinguish his writing from pornographic exploitation: "Sex is the one place where we today can learn to treat people as people," he wrote.

Hollywood took advantage of the new sexual ethic by making films with explicit erotic content that pushed the boundaries of middle-class tastes. Films such as *Midnight Cowboy* (1969), *Carnal Knowledge* (1971), and *Shampoo* (1975), the latter starring Hollywood's leading ladies' man, Warren Beatty, led the way. The Motion Picture Association of America (MPAA) scrambled to keep its rating system — which rated pictures G, PG, R, and X (and, after 1984, PG-13) — ahead of Hollywood's advancing sexual revolution.

On television, censorship and fears of losing advertising revenue throttled back the frankness of sexual content in the early 1970s. However, by the second half of the decade networks found ways to exploit, and criticize, the new sexual ethic. In frivolous, lighthearted shows such as the popular *Charlie's Angels*, *Three's Company*, and *The Love Boat*, heterosexual couples explored the often confusing, and usually comical, landscape of sexual morality. At the same time, between 1974 and 1981, the major networks produced more than a dozen made-for-TV movies about children in sexual danger — sensationalizing the potential risks of a looser sexual morality.

Marriage on the Rocks Couples attending a Marriage Encounter workshop near Boston in 1972. Traditional notions of marriage came under a variety of economic and psychological stresses in the 1970s. Many Americans turned to therapeutic solutions to preserve, or improve, their marriages. Marriage Encounter, founded by priests in the Catholic Church, was one organization that offered couples the opportunity to talk openly about marriage and to learn new skills for navigating the difficulties couples faced. Marriage Encounter was one among dozens of such organizations, both religious and secular, to rise to prominence in the 1970s. Spencer Grant/Getty Images.

CHECK FOR UNDERSTANDING

Ask students: **What challenges did Americans face in navigating the sexual revolution?** *Even before the 1960s, sex outside of marriage had become more socially acceptable. After 1960, this acceptance grew dramatically, as sexual activity was increasingly separated from the possibility of reproduction. Some in the women's rights movement celebrated new sexual values that would give women more freedom to explore sexuality in the same ways as men. Sex became a franker and more frequent topic in self-help books, films, and TV shows. A therapeutic industry arose to help couples sustain a healthy marriage in an age of changing sexual mores.*

AP® SKILLS & PROCESSES

CAUSATION

The **CAUSATION** question asks students to identify the effects of the "sexual revolution" of the 1960s and 1970s. Some students may need clarification on what was revolutionary about relationship patterns in this era.

TRM Find complete suggested responses in the Teacher's Resource Materials.

AP® APPLY THE TIP

After students read the "Evangelical Resurgence" section on pp. 930–931, ask the class to create a timeline on the board of the major religious movements that influenced American society and politics. Then ask students to explain if the religious movement was liberal or conservative in nature. Students may debate the characterization of various religious movements such as the "City Upon a Hill" ideal, Protestant evangelism of the Revolutionary era, First Great Awakening, Second Great Awakening, transcendentalism, Social Gospel movement, fundamentalism, etc. Then ask students to compare the resurgence of evangelism in the late 1970s and early 1980s to one of the other religious time periods. Finally, lead a class discussion that addresses the following questions (*answers will vary*):

- **Has religion been a liberal or conservative force throughout American history?**
- **In what ways have religious movements caused political change?**
- **In what ways have religious movements resulted from political change?**
- **Have religious movements contributed to greater continuity or change in American history?**

Middle-Class Marriage Many Americans worried that the sexual revolution threatened marriage itself. The notion of marriage as romantic companionship had been a middle-class norm since the nineteenth century. Throughout most of the twentieth century, Americans saw sexual satisfaction as a healthy part of the marriage bond. But what defined a healthy marriage in an age of rising divorce rates, changing sexual values, and feminist critiques of the nuclear family? Only a small minority of Americans rejected marriage outright; most continued to pursue monogamous relationships codified at some point in marriage. But many married people sought help in coping with the economic and psychological stresses of domestic life.

A therapeutic industry arose in response. Churches and secular groups alike established marriage seminars and counseling services to assist couples in sustaining a healthy union. A popular form of 1960s psychotherapy, the "encounter group," was adapted to marriage counseling: couples met in large groups to explore new methods of communicating. One of the most successful of these organizations, Marriage Encounter, was founded by the Catholic Church. It expanded into Protestant and Jewish communities in the 1970s and became one of the nation's largest counseling organizations. Such groups reflected another long-term shift in how middle-class Americans understood marriage — not simply as companionship or sexual fidelity but as a deeply felt emotional connection.

AP® SKILLS & PROCESSES
CAUSATION
What were three major consequences of the sexual revolution of the 1960s and 1970s?

Religion in the 1970s: The New Evangelicalism

For three centuries, American history has seen intermittent periods of intense religious revival — some of which historians have called Great Awakenings (Chapters 4 and 10). These phases saw a rise in church membership, the appearance of charismatic religious leaders, and religion — usually of the evangelical variety — reshaping society and politics. Between the 1960s and 1980s, one of these cycles took hold. Like its predecessors, the "New Evangelicalism" of those decades had complex causes and divergent aims, but one central feature was a concern with the family.

In the 1950s and 1960s, many mainstream Protestants had embraced the wider reform spirit of the era. Some of the most visible Protestant leaders were social activists who condemned racism and opposed the Vietnam War. Organizations such as the National Council of Churches — along with many progressive Catholics and Jews — allied with Martin Luther King Jr. and other African American ministers in the long battle for civil rights. Many mainline Protestant churches, among them the Episcopal, Methodist, and Congregationalist denominations, practiced a version of the "Social Gospel," the reform-minded Christianity of the early twentieth century.

AP® EXAM TIP
Compare the New Evangelicalism to the First and Second Great Awakenings.

Evangelical Resurgence Meanwhile, evangelicalism survived at the grass roots of American spirituality. Evangelical Protestant churches emphasized an intimate, personal salvation (being "born again"); focused on a literal interpretation of the Bible; and regarded the death and resurrection of Jesus as the central message of Christianity. These tenets, fervently cultivated in a handful of evangelical colleges, Bible schools, and seminaries in the postwar decades, set evangelicals apart from mainline Protestants as much as from Catholics and non-Christians.

No one did more to keep the evangelical fire burning than Billy Graham. A graduate of the evangelical Wheaton College in Illinois, Graham cofounded Youth for Christ in 1944 and then toured the United States and Europe preaching the gospel. Graham shot to national fame with a stunning 1949 tent revival in Los Angeles that lasted eight weeks (see "Religion and the Middle Class" in Chapter 25). His success in Los Angeles led to a popular radio program, but he continued to travel relentlessly, conducting old-fashioned revival meetings that he called "crusades." A massive sixteen-week 1957 crusade held in New York City's Madison Square Garden made Graham one of the nation's most visible religious leaders.

In the 1950s and 1960s, Graham and other evangelicals laid the groundwork for the New Evangelicalism. But a startling combination of events in the late 1960s and early 1970s dramatically magnified the evangelical revival. First, rising divorce rates, social unrest, and challenges to prevailing values led many to seek the stability of faith. Second, many Americans regarded feminism, the counterculture, sexual freedom, homosexuality, pornography, and legalized abortion not as distinct social issues, but collectively as a marker of moral decay. More and more people in response turned to evangelical ministries, especially Southern Baptist, Pentecostal, and Assemblies of God churches.

Demographics tell part of the story. As mainline churches lost about 15 percent of their membership between 1970 and 1985, evangelical church membership soared. The Southern Baptist Convention, the largest Protestant denomination, grew by 23 percent, while the Assemblies of God grew by an astounding 300 percent. *Newsweek* magazine declared 1976 "The Year of the Evangelical," and that November Jimmy Carter became the first evangelical president. In a national Gallup poll, a robust one-third of Americans answered yes when asked, "Would you describe yourself as a 'born again' or evangelical Christian?"

Much of this astonishing growth relied on the creative use of television. A new generation of preachers brought religious conversion directly into Americans' living rooms through broadcast sermons. These so-called televangelists built huge media empires through small donations from millions of avid viewers — not to mention advertising. Shows such as Jerry Falwell's *Old Time Gospel Hour*, Pat Robertson's *700 Club*, and Jim and Tammy Bakker's *PTL (Praise the Lord) Club* and preachers such as Oral Roberts and Jimmy Swaggart turned the 1970s and 1980s into the age of Christian broadcasting.

Religion and the Family A primary concern to the New Evangelism was the family. Drawing on Bible passages, evangelicals saw the nuclear family, and not the individual, as the fundamental unit of society. Their vision of the family was organized along paternalist lines: father was breadwinner and disciplinarian; mother was nurturer and supporter. "Motherhood is the highest form of femininity," the influential evangelical author Beverly LaHaye wrote. Another popular Christian author declared, "A church, a family, a nation is only as strong as its men."

Evangelicals spread their ideas about the Christian family from the pulpit and television screens, but they did not stop there. They founded publishing houses, wrote books, established foundations, and offered seminars. Helen B. Andelin, for instance, a California housewife, produced a homemade book called *Fascinating Womanhood* that eventually sold more than two million copies. She used the book as the basis for her classes, which by the early 1970s had been attended by 400,000 women and boasted 11,000 trained teachers. The message of *Fascinating Womanhood* led evangelical women in the opposite direction of feminism. Whereas the latter encouraged women to seek independence and equality, Andelin taught that "submissiveness will bring a strange but righteous power over your man." She was just one of dozens of evangelical authors and educators who encouraged women to defer to men.

Evangelical Christians believed that strict gender roles could ward off the influences of an immoral society. Many activists were especially concerned with sex education in public schools, the proliferation of pornography, legalized abortion, and the rising divorce rate. For them, the answer lay in strengthening what they called "traditional" family structures. By the early 1980s, Christians could read from among hundreds of evangelical books, take classes on how to save a marriage or how to be a Christian parent, attend countless evangelical Bible study courses, watch evangelical ministers on television, and donate to foundations that worked to promote "Christian values" in state legislatures and the U.S. Congress.

Nearly everyone, regardless of their religion or politics, agreed that American families were straining to cope with recent changes. By all accounts, the waves

AP® THEME

ARC: American and Regional Culture

The rapid growth of evangelical Christian churches and associated organizations prompted greater political and social activism among religious conservatives.

CHECK FOR UNDERSTANDING

Ask students: **What were the major sources of anxiety about the American family in the decade after the 1960s?** *Many conservatives harbored concerns about the changing structure of the family in American society. Much of these concerns found historical roots in the 1960s. Their concerns focused on groups and organizations such as feminist activists, which challenged gender roles and fought for equality. Moreover, conservatives also railed against government involvement as exemplified by the Great Society and the Warren Court, which they saw as government intrusion and a breakdown in family values.*

TRM Find complete suggested responses in the Teacher's Resource Materials.

AP® SKILLS & PROCESSES

MAKING CONNECTIONS

The **MAKING CONNECTIONS** question asks students to identify the effects of evangelicals on American society in the 1970s. While their influence on politics is evident — including in the election of Jimmy Carter in 1976 — their effects on culture should also be noted. Students should also note the factors that helped lead to the rise of evangelical influence.

TRM Find complete suggested responses in the Teacher's Resource Materials.

CHECK FOR UNDERSTANDING

Use the **AP® LEARNING FOCUS** question from the beginning of the chapter to check students' understanding of the chapter as a whole: **Why did the social changes of the 1960s — such as civil rights, shifting gender roles, and challenges to the family — create both new opportunities and political clashes in the 1970s?** *The 1970s witnessed a succession of events that originated in the 1960s including the legalization of abortion, the revival of American environmentalism, the continued migration of middle-class Americans to suburbia, the rise of a gay rights movement, the advent of the Fourth Great Awakening, a recession brought on by deindustrialization, and an oil embargo. Once again, tensions emerged over the economy and the place of power of women, blacks, and homosexuals. Referred to as culture wars, the conflicts between conservatives and liberals characterized the 1970s.*

VISUAL ACTIVITY

"Family Values" During the 1980 presidential campaign, the Reverend Jerry Falwell, pictured here with Phyllis Schlafly, supported Ronald Reagan and the Republican Party with "I Love America" rallies around the country. Falwell, head of the Moral Majority, helped to bring a new focus on "family values" to American politics in the late 1970s. This was a conservative version of the emphasis on male-breadwinner nuclear families that had long been characteristic of American values. AP Photo.

READING THE IMAGE: What symbols can you identify in the photograph? What do you notice about the people?

MAKING CONNECTIONS: How can the connection between religion and nationalism be explained as a reaction against changes in the 1960s and 1970s? What is the relationship of evangelical Christianity in the 1970s and 1980s to the resurgence of conservatism?

AP® SKILLS & PROCESSES

MAKING CONNECTIONS

How did evangelical Christianity influence American society in the 1970s?

of social liberalism and economic transformation that swept over the nation in the 1960s and 1970s had destabilized public and private life alike. But Americans did not agree about how to *re*stabilize home life. Indeed, differing attitudes on that question would further divide the country in the coming decades, as the New Right would increasingly make "family values" a political issue.

SUMMARY

The 1970s delivered a host of economic problems: inflation, energy shortages, stagnant wages, and wide deindustrialization. Postwar prosperity had finally found its limits, and for the first time since the 1930s, many Americans were forced to lower their economic expectations. Access to the middle class began to narrow rather than widen. Expectations were lowered in other ways as well. A movement for environmental protection, widely supported, led to new laws and an understanding of the limits of nature, and the energy crisis highlighted the nation's dependence on resources from abroad, especially oil.

In the midst of this gloomy economic climate, Americans also pursued political and cultural resolutions to the upheavals of the 1960s. In politics, the Watergate scandal led to a brief period of political reform. Meanwhile, the battle for civil rights entered a second stage, more concerned with concrete results than additional legislation. The movement also expanded to encompass women's rights and gay rights. Many liberals cheered these developments, but society as a whole trended toward a conservative mood that looked at liberal values with skepticism. Finally, the American family faced multiple challenges in the decade of the 1970s, and those troubles helped spur an evangelical religious revival that would shape American society for decades to come.

CHAPTER 28 REVIEW

AP® CONTENT REVIEW *Answer these questions to demonstrate your understanding of the chapter's main ideas.*

1. What kinds of limits, or crises, did the American economy encounter in the 1970s?
2. In what ways was the period between 1973 and 1980 a transitional one in American politics?
3. How did controversies over new individual rights shape the politics of the 1970s?
4. What were the major sources of anxiety about the American family in the decade after the 1960s?

AP® TERMS TO KNOW *Identify and explain the significance of each term.*

Key Concepts and Events

Organization of Petroleum Exporting Countries (OPEC) (p. 907)
energy crisis (p. 907)
Silent Spring (p. 907)
Earth Day (p. 910)
Environmental Protection Agency (EPA) (p. 910)
Three Mile Island (p. 910)
stagflation (p. 911)
deindustrialization (p. 912)
Rust Belt (p. 912)
Proposition 13 (p. 915)
Watergate (p. 916)
War Powers Act (p. 917)
Freedom of Information Act (p. 917)
Ethics in Government Act (p. 917)
Foreign Intelligence Surveillance Act (p. 917)
deregulation (p. 919)
affirmative action (p. 920)
Regents of the University of California v. Bakke (p. 921)
Equal Rights Amendment (ERA) (p. 922)
STOP ERA (p. 922)
Roe v. Wade (p. 923)

Key People

Rachel Carson (p. 907)
Gerald Ford (p. 912)
Howard Jarvis (p. 915)
Jimmy Carter (p. 918)
Phyllis Schlafly (p. 922)
Harvey Milk (p. 923)
Billy Graham (p. 930)

AP® MAKING CONNECTIONS *Recognize the larger developments and continuities within and across chapters by answering these questions.*

1. Consider the history of the American economy in the twentieth century. Compare the 1970s with other eras: the Great Depression of the 1930s, the industrial boom of the World War II years, and the growth and rising wages in the 1950s and 1960s. Using these comparisons, construct a historical narrative of the period from the 1920s through the 1970s.
2. Study the steelworks photograph on page 912 and Map 28.1. How did the economic downturn of the 1970s affect the lives of ordinary Americans and American culture broadly? What connections can you draw between the photograph and developments in the global economy and the rise of the Sunbelt?

KEY TURNING POINTS *Refer to the timeline at the start of the chapter for help in answering the following question.*

Based on this timeline, what were the three or four major political turning points of the 1970s? Defend your answer by explaining the impact of the changes.

933

✓ LearningCurve

Remind students to go online to complete the LearningCurve quiz for this chapter.

TRM Find complete suggested responses in the Teacher's Resource Materials.

AP® SKILLS & PROCESSES

CONTINUITY AND CHANGE

AP® CONTENT REVIEW 2 asks students to explain the significance of the period 1973–1980 as a turning point. Note: This is the same question as the **CHECK FOR UNDERSTANDING** prompt on p. 919.

AP® SKILLS & PROCESSES

CAUSATION

AP® CONTENT REVIEW 3 asks students to identify the effects of controversies over individual rights on national politics. Note: This is the same question as the **CHECK FOR UNDERSTANDING** prompt on p. 926.

AP® SKILLS & PROCESSES

CAUSATION

AP® CONTENT REVIEW 4 directs students to list causes of anxiety about the family in the 1970s. Note: This is the same question as the **CHECK FOR UNDERSTANDING** prompt on p. 932.

TRM Find definitions for these terms in the **Glossary/Glosario** in the Teacher's Resource Materials.

AP® SKILLS & PROCESSES

CONTINUITY AND CHANGE

AP® MAKING CONNECTIONS 1 invites students to compare economic patterns at several points during the twentieth century. The second direction, constructing a historical narrative, allows students to practice tracing continuities and changes in the economy over the course of roughly a half century.

AP® SKILLS & PROCESSES

CONTINUITY AND CHANGE

The **KEY TURNING POINTS** question asks students to identify a few factors that made the 1970s a turning point in American politics, society, and culture.

TRM Find complete suggested responses in the Teacher's Resource Materials.

AP PRACTICE QUESTIONS

MULTIPLE CHOICE QUESTIONS *Choose the correct answer for each question.*

Questions 1–3 refer to this excerpt.

"Here is the first great fault in the life of man in the ecosphere. We have broken out of the circle of life, converting its endless cycles into man-made, linear events: oil is taken from the ground, distilled into fuel, burned in an engine, converted thereby into noxious fumes, which are emitted into the air. At the end of the line is smog. Other man-made breaks in the ecosphere's cycle spew out toxic chemicals, sewage, heaps of rubbish — the testimony to our power to tear the ecological fabric that has, for millions of years, sustained the planet's life. . . .

Our assaults on the ecosystem are so powerful, so numerous, so finely interconnected, that although the damage they do is clear, it is very difficult to discover how it was done. By which weapon? In whose hand? Are we driving the ecosphere to destruction simply by our growing numbers? By our greedy accumulation of wealth? Or are the machines which we have built to gain this wealth — the magnificent technology that now feeds us out of neat packages, that clothes us in man-made fibers, that surround us with new chemical creations — at fault?"

Barry Commoner, *The Closing Circle: Nature, Man, and Technology*, 1971

1. Commoner's ideas expressed in the excerpt most likely emerged from concerns about
   - **a.** deindustrialization of the Upper Midwest and Northeast.
   - **b.** mass migration of Americans to the Sunbelt.
   - **c.** new movements to protect natural resources.
   - **d.** loss of public confidence in government's ability to solve problems.

2. The sentiments expressed in the excerpt helped prompt the federal government in the 1970s to
   - **a.** pass immigration legislation ending national quotas.
   - **b.** found the Department of the Interior.
   - **c.** establish the Environmental Protection Agency.
   - **d.** create the National Park Service.

3. Which of the following expressed the greatest opposition to Commoner's ideas?
   - **a.** American Indian organizations
   - **b.** Corporations and large manufacturers
   - **c.** Members of the baby boom generation
   - **d.** Working-class women

Questions 4–5 refer to this excerpt.

"In the place of the farmer came the industrial worker, and for the last hundred years or so the vicissitudes of the industrial worker — his claims to dignity and status, his demand for a rising share of industrial returns, his desire for a voice in the conditions which affected his work and conditions of employment — have marked the struggles of the century. . . .

Yet if one takes the industrial worker as the instrument of the future . . . then this vision is warped. For the paradoxical fact is that as one goes along the trajectory of industrialization — the increasing replacement of men with machines — one comes logically to the erosion of the industrial worker himself. . . . Instead of the industrial worker, we see the dominance of the professional and technical class in the labor force. . . A post-industrial society is based upon services. Hence, it is a game between persons. What counts is not raw muscle power, or energy, but information. The central person is the professional, for he is equipped . . . to provide the kinds of skill which are increasingly demanded in a post-industrial society."

Daniel Bell, *The Coming of Post-Industrial Society: A Venture in Social Forecasting*, 1973

4. The trends described by Bell in the excerpt resulted most directly from
   - **a.** expansions of student populations in higher education.
   - **b.** rapid and substantial growth of evangelical Christian churches.
   - **c.** increasing homogenization of mass culture.
   - **d.** policies of the Great Society.

5. A historian could best support Bell's argument from the excerpt using statistics from the 1970s about
   - **a.** industrial union members in each year as a percentage of the total workforce.
   - **b.** census data tracking migration patterns of the U.S. population.
   - **c.** changes in the real cost of living.
   - **d.** fluctuations in the international trade deficit.

SHORT ANSWER QUESTIONS

Read each question carefully and write a short response. Use evidence from the text to support your claims.

"Above all, the mid-1970's marked the end of the postwar boom. . . . Starting in the 1973–1974 years, real earnings began to stagnate and then slide. . . . By mid-decade the record-breaking strikes, rank-and-file movements, and vibrant organizing drives that had once promised a new day for workers were reduced to a trickle in the new economic climate. They were then replaced by layoffs, plant closures, and union decertification drives. White male workers' incomes . . . stagnated or fell for the next quarter century . . . driven down by oil shocks and inflation; deindustrialization, plant closings, and anti-unionism; and a global restructuring of work itself. . . . By the end of the decade working people would possess less place and meaningful identity within civic life than any time since the industrial revolution."

Jefferson Cowie, *Stayin' Alive: the 1970's and the Last Days of the Working Class*, 2010

"Forty years ago, Americans were suffering from what contemporaries called 'the energy crisis,' a crisis that in many ways defined the decade of the 1970's. During the twin oil shocks of 1973 and 1979, oil supplies dropped and prices soared, and the average citizen understood the energy crisis to mean a panic at the pump—the fear that we would not have enough oil to fill up our gas tanks, heat our homes, or run our factories. [The Arab oil] embargo stunned Americans, as if they had come under a surprise attack . . . because of the serious implications for the economy and the country's security. . . . Americans were vulnerable to scarcity and shortages as well as to higher fuel prices, which rippled through the entire economy and plagued the pocketbooks of all consumers."

Meg Jacobs, *Panic at the Pump: The Energy Crisis and the Transformation of American Politics in the 1970's*, 2016

1. Using the two excerpts provided, answer (a), (b), and (c).
   a. Briefly explain ONE major difference between Cowie's and Jacobs's historical interpretations about the 1970s.
   b. Briefly explain how ONE specific event, development, or circumstance not directly mentioned in the excerpts could be used to support Cowie's argument.
   c. Briefly explain how ONE specific event, development, or circumstance not directly mentioned in the excerpts could be used to support Jacobs's argument.
2. Answer (a), (b), and (c).
   a. Briefly explain why ONE of the following developments was the most significant factor contributing to the loss of public confidence in government in the 1970s.
   - Economic challenges
   - Political scandals
   - Foreign policy crises

   b. Briefly explain ONE historical event or development in support of your argument in (a).
   c. Briefly explain a specific historical reason why ONE of the other options contributed less to the loss of public confidence in government in the 1970s.
3. Answer (a), (b), and (c).
   a. Briefly explain ONE important historical difference in challenges faced by women's rights activists in the period after 1945 with the challenges faced by women's rights activists from 1890–1945.
   b. Briefly explain ONE important historical similarity in challenges faced by women's rights activists in the period after 1945 with the challenges faced by women's rights activists from 1890–1945.
   c. Briefly explain ONE important factor for the difference you identified in part (a).

TRM Find complete suggested responses in the Teacher's Resource Materials.

TRM Find complete suggested responses in the Teacher's Resource Materials.

8 PART AP® PRACTICE ESSAY QUESTIONS

DOCUMENT-BASED QUESTION *Suggested reading period: 15 minutes. Suggested writing time: 45 minutes.*

DIRECTIONS: Question 1 is based on the accompanying documents. The documents have been edited for the purpose of this exercise.

1. Evaluate the extent of change in United States foreign policy in the period 1945 to 1980.

DOCUMENT 1

Source: Secretary of State George Marshall, Speech at Harvard University, June 5, 1947.

"I need not tell you gentlemen that the world situation is very serious. That must be apparent to all intelligent people. I think one difficulty is that the problem is one of such enormous complexity that the very mass of facts presented to the public by press and radio make it exceedingly difficult for the man in the street to reach a clear appraisement of the situation. Furthermore, the people of this country are distant from the troubled areas of the earth and it is hard for them to comprehend the plight and consequent reaction of the long-suffering peoples, and the effect of those reactions on their governments in connection with our efforts to promote peace in the world. . . .

Aside from the demoralizing effect on the world at large and the possibilities of disturbances arising as a result of the desperation of the people concerned, the consequences to the economy of the United States should be apparent to all. It is logical that the United States should do whatever it is able to do to assist in the return of normal economic health in the world, without which there can be no political stability and no assured peace. Our policy is directed not against any country or doctrine but against hunger, poverty, desperation, and chaos. Its purpose should be the revival of working economy in the world so as to permit the emergence of political and social conditions in which free institutions can exist."

DOCUMENT 2

Source: General Douglas MacArthur, Farewell Address to Congress, April 19, 1951.

"The Communist threat is a global one. Its successful advance in one sector threatens the destruction of every other sector. You can not appease or otherwise surrender to communism in Asia without simultaneously undermining our efforts to halt its advance in Europe. . . .

But once war is forced upon us, there is no other alternative than to apply every available means to bring it to a swift end. . . . War's very object is victory, not prolonged indecision. In war there is no substitute for victory. There are some who, for varying reasons, would appease Red China. They are blind to history's clear lesson, for history teaches with unmistakable emphasis that appeasement but begets new and bloodier war. It points to no single instance where this end has justified that means, where appeasement has led to more than a sham peace. Like blackmail, it lays the basis for new and successively greater demands until, as in blackmail, violence becomes the only other alternative."

DOCUMENT 3

Source: President John F. Kennedy, Televised Address to the American Public, October 22, 1962.

"For many years, both the Soviet Union and the United States . . . have deployed strategic nuclear weapons with great care, never upsetting the precarious status quo which insured that these weapons would not be used in the absence of some vital challenge. Our own strategic missiles have never been transferred to the territory of any other nation under a cloak of secrecy and deception; and our history—unlike that of the Soviets since the end of World War II—demonstrates that we have no desire to dominate or conquer any other nation or impose our system upon its people. Nevertheless, American citizens have become adjusted to living daily on the bull's-eye of Soviet missiles located inside the U.S.S.R. or in submarines. . . .

We are prepared to discuss new proposals for the removal of tensions on both sides, including the possibilities of a genuinely independent Cuba, free to determine its own destiny. We have no wish to war with the Soviet Union—for we are a peaceful people who desire to live in peace with all other peoples.

But it is difficult to settle or even discuss these problems in an atmosphere of intimidation. That is why this latest Soviet threat—or any other threat which is made either independently or in response to our actions this week—must and will be met with determination. Any hostile move anywhere in the world against the safety and freedom of peoples to whom we are committed, including in particular the brave people of West Berlin, will be met by whatever action is needed."

DOCUMENT 4

Source: Harold Bryant, a Vietnam soldier recalling his tour of duty in August 1965.

"When I came to Vietnam, I thought we were helping another country to develop a nation. About three or four months later I found out that wasn't the case. . . .

I thought we had got into the beginning of a war. But I found out that we were just in another phase of their civil wars.

And we weren't gaining any ground. We would fight for a hill all day, spend two days or two nights there, and then abandon the hill. Then maybe two, three months later, we would have to come back and retake the same piece of territory. . . .

And they had a habit of exaggerating a body count. If we killed 7, by the time it would get back to base camp, it would have gotten to 28. Then by the time it got down to [General William] Westmoreland's office in Saigon, it done went up to 54. And by the time it left from Saigon going to Washington, it had went up to about 125. To prove we were really out there doing our jobs, doing, really, more than what we were doing."

DOCUMENT 5

Source: President Richard Nixon, State of the Union Address to Congress, January 30, 1974.

"Tonight, for the first time in 12 years, a President of the United States can report to the Congress on the state of a Union at peace with every nation of the world. . . .

In the coming year, however, increased expenditures will be needed. They will be needed to assure the continued readiness of our military forces, to preserve present force levels in the face of rising costs, and to give us the military strength we must have if our security is to be maintained and if our initiatives for peace are to succeed.

The question is not whether we can afford to maintain the necessary strength of our defense, the question is whether we can afford not to maintain it, and the answer to that question is no. We must never allow America to become the second strongest nation in the world.

I do not say this with any sense of belligerence, because I recognize the fact that is recognized around the world. America's military strength has always been maintained to keep the peace, never to break it. It has always been used to defend freedom, never to destroy it. The world's peace, as well as our own, depends on our remaining as strong as we need to be as long as we need to be.

In this year 1974, we will be negotiating with the Soviet Union to place further limits on strategic nuclear arms. Together with our allies, we will be negotiating with the nations of the Warsaw Pact on mutual and balanced reduction of forces in Europe. And we will continue our efforts to promote peaceful economic development in Latin America, in Africa, in Asia."

DOCUMENT 6

Source: U.S. Embassy Workers Being Held Hostage in Teheran, Iran, November 4, 1979.

Bettmann/Getty Images.

DOCUMENT 7

Source: U.S. Global Defense Treaties, 1945–1980.

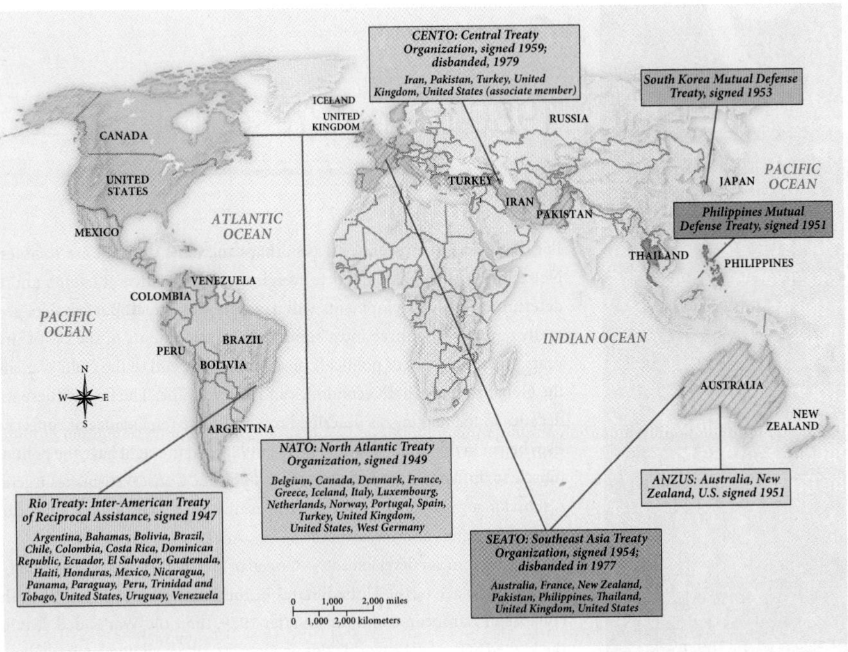

LONG ESSAY QUESTIONS *Suggested writing time: 40 minutes.*

DIRECTIONS: Please choose one of the following two questions to answer. Make a historically defensible claim and support your reasoning with specific and relevant evidence.

2. Evaluate the extent of change in United States society resulting from debates over cultural values between 1960 and 1980.

3. Evaluate the extent of change in United States society resulting from migration patterns from 1945 to 1980.

4. Evaluate the extent of change in United States society resulting from the environmental movement from 1945 to 1980.

9 PART

Globalization and the End of the American Century

1980 to the Present

For historians, the recent past is perhaps the most difficult era to assess. Not enough time has passed to weigh the significance of events and to determine which developments will have a lasting effect. But scholars generally agree on the three most significant developments of the past thirty years: the resurgence of political conservatism, the end of the Cold War, and the globalization of both economics and everyday life. The first of these was decades in the making, as described in Part 8. The renaissance of conservatism began in the 1960s, but not until the 1980s did the right have the political muscle to fundamentally reshape national politics. Conservatism's resurgence resulted in a wide-ranging and sometimes divisive debate among Americans about the nation's common values and priorities.

The other major developments—the end of the Cold War and globalization—altered the place of the United States in the international order. With the collapse of European communism after 1989, the Cold War ended, leaving the United States as the world's dominant military power. But military dominance coexisted with shrinking economic influence. In 1941, *Time* magazine publisher Henry Luce had coined the phrase "American Century" as part of a call for the country to assume the responsibility of global leadership. Luce's vision came to pass in many respects, and the fifty years after his call were ones of broad American influence around the world. But by the final years of the twentieth century, that influence was waning and Luce's "century" was over. The United States remained the world's largest economy but faced competition from a united Europe and a surging China. The decades from the 1980s to the present stand as an era of transition away from the bipolar world of the Cold War toward the multipolar world we now inhabit.

History continues to unfold to the present, and thus Part 9 is necessarily a work in progress. Nonetheless, new developments can be considered with the broad themes of this section in mind. Americans forged a new era after 1980, but the ultimate legacy of that era remains to be seen. ▶

AP CONCEPT CONNECTIONS

Why did a conservative movement transform American politics after 1980?

In the 1980s, the conservatism of Ronald Reagan and the New Right, consolidated in the Republican Party, challenged the liberalism of the 1960s and 1970s. Taking national power for the first time, conservatives reduced government regulation and eroded the welfare state of the New Deal and the Great Society. Conservative lawmakers challenged abortion rights, feminism, and gay rights, setting off a "culture war" that sharply divided Americans.

Even as the Reagan coalition ended decades of liberal government activism, much of the legacy of the New Deal was preserved. In fact, Medicare, Medicaid, and Social Security grew as a proportion of the federal budget. Conservatives were more successful in remaking U.S. foreign policy, increasing defense budgets and asserting a new doctrine of "preemptive war." Protracted and expensive involvement in Iraq and Afghanistan, along with the economic tailspin of 2008, created an opening for a moderate liberal coalition — led by Barack Obama, the first African American elected president. But the national political system subsequently moved firmly into conservative hands, culminating in the surprising and polarizing presidency of Donald Trump.

Ronald Reagan Presidential Library.

Why did the Cold War end and conflict in the Middle East ascend in its place?

Reagan had overseen a military spending hike, along with a return to the sharp Cold War rhetoric of earlier decades. Yet in the second half of the 1980s, relations between Reagan and his reform-minded Soviet counterpart Mikhail Gorbachev warmed. Communism was on the retreat in Eastern Europe, and internal reforms escalated into the sudden collapse of the Soviet Union in 1991. The United States found itself the lone military "superpower" in the world.

Absent a clear Cold War enemy, the United States intervened in civil wars, worked to disrupt terrorist activities, and provided humanitarian aid — but guided more by pragmatism than by principle. America's overseas attention centered on the Middle East, where oil reserves remained strategically paramount. Between 1991 and the present, the United States fought three wars in the region — two in Iraq and one in Afghanistan — and became further embedded in its contentious politics.

David Turnley/Corbis/VCG via Getty Images.

Why did a new era of globalized capitalism emerge between 1980 and the 2020s?

America's long postwar economic boom finally ended in the 1970s, when wages stagnated and inflation skyrocketed. In the 1980s and 1990s, however, productivity returned, military spending boosted innovation, and new industries — such as computer technology — emerged. The economy returned to a growth mode, but with an increasing emphasis on *services* rather than *goods* — as Americans increasingly bought the latter from overseas.

The globalization of trade intensified: goods and currency passed across borders easily, and multinational corporations moved production to low-wage countries — while Americans readily bought up the cheap consumer goods that resulted. Governments facilitated this process by creating new trading zones such as the European Union (EU) and the North American Free Trade Agreement (NAFTA). Inequality between the wealthiest Americans and the middle class and poor grew as labor unions weakened, manufacturing shrank, and tax policies shifted wealth upwards.

Karie Hamilton/Sygma via Getty Images.

935

Organized around a single theme, the Part 9 Document Set in *Sources for America's History* can be used to teach AP® Theme WXT (Work, Exchange, and Technology), which asks that students be able to demonstrate how changes in technology, markets, transportation, and labor have affected the economy and society since the nineteenth century.

AP® THEMATIC UNDERSTANDING

Globalization and the End of the American Century, 1980 to the Present

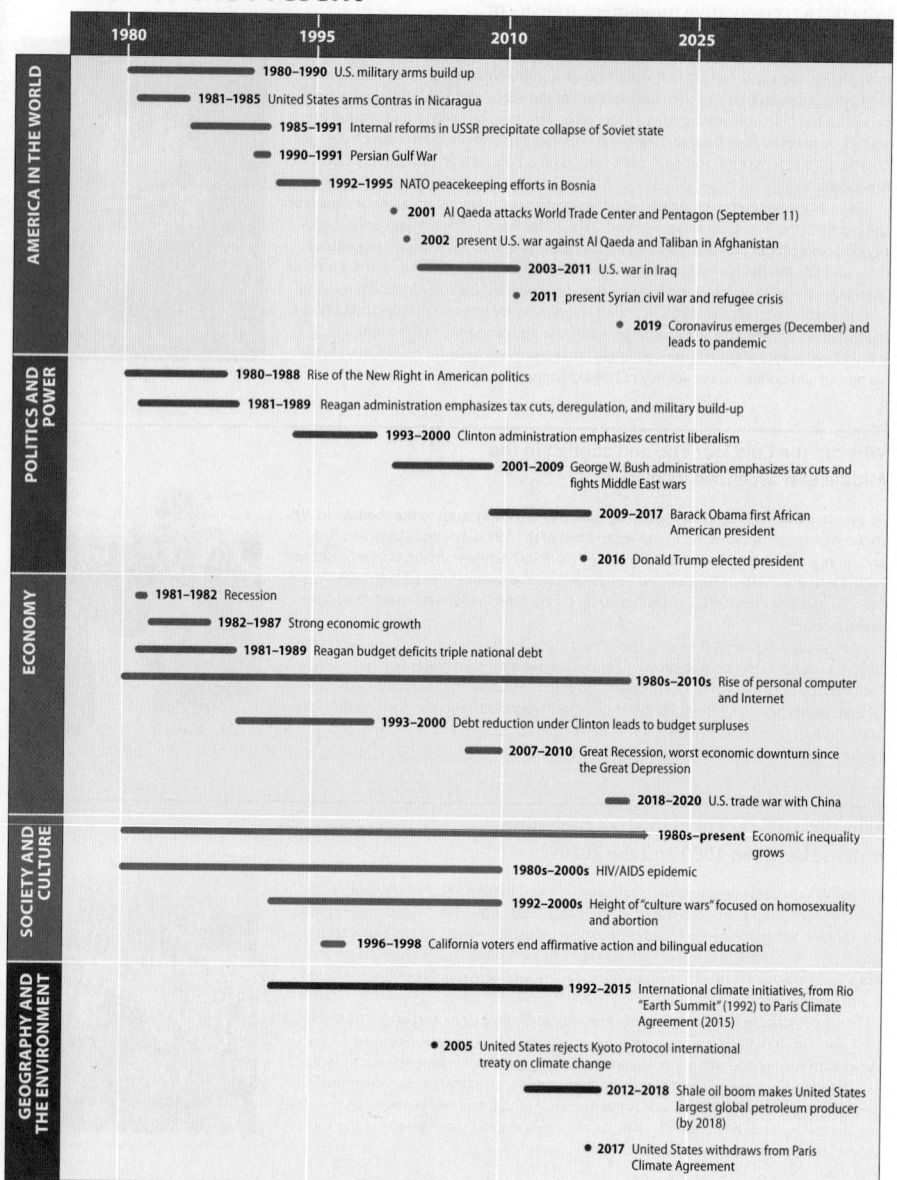

1980 | 1995 | 2010 | 2025

AMERICA IN THE WORLD

- **1980–1990** U.S. military arms build up
- **1981–1985** United States arms Contras in Nicaragua
- **1985–1991** Internal reforms in USSR precipitate collapse of Soviet state
- **1990–1991** Persian Gulf War
- **1992–1995** NATO peacekeeping efforts in Bosnia
- **2001** Al Qaeda attacks World Trade Center and Pentagon (September 11)
- **2002** present U.S. war against Al Qaeda and Taliban in Afghanistan
- **2003–2011** U.S. war in Iraq
- **2011** present Syrian civil war and refugee crisis
- **2019** Coronavirus emerges (December) and leads to pandemic

POLITICS AND POWER

- **1980–1988** Rise of the New Right in American politics
- **1981–1989** Reagan administration emphasizes tax cuts, deregulation, and military build-up
- **1993–2000** Clinton administration emphasizes centrist liberalism
- **2001–2009** George W. Bush administration emphasizes tax cuts and fights Middle East wars
- **2009–2017** Barack Obama first African American president
- **2016** Donald Trump elected president

ECONOMY

- **1981–1982** Recession
- **1982–1987** Strong economic growth
- **1981–1989** Reagan budget deficits triple national debt
- **1980s–2010s** Rise of personal computer and Internet
- **1993–2000** Debt reduction under Clinton leads to budget surpluses
- **2007–2010** Great Recession, worst economic downturn since the Great Depression
- **2018–2020** U.S. trade war with China

SOCIETY AND CULTURE

- **1980s–present** Economic inequality grows
- **1980s–2000s** HIV/AIDS epidemic
- **1992–2000s** Height of "culture wars" focused on homosexuality and abortion
- **1996–1998** California voters end affirmative action and bilingual education

GEOGRAPHY AND THE ENVIRONMENT

- **1992–2015** International climate initiatives, from Rio "Earth Summit" (1992) to Paris Climate Agreement (2015)
- **2005** United States rejects Kyoto Protocol international treaty on climate change
- **2012–2018** Shale oil boom makes United States largest global petroleum producer (by 2018)
- **2017** United States withdraws from Paris Climate Agreement

AP® Making Connections Across Chapters

Read these questions and think about them as you read the chapters in this part. Then when you have completed reading this part, return to these questions and answer them.

1 What specific issues propelled the New Right's rise to prominence in American politics between the 1980s and the 2000s?

Mark Wilson/Getty Images.

2 After 1980, in what specific ways did the nation shift away from reforms, laws, and social movements of the earlier "age of liberalism"?

AP Photo/J. Scott Applewhite.

3 What kind of U.S. foreign policy emerged in the wake of the end of the Cold War? Why did that policy take shape as it did?

Owen Franken/Corbis via Getty Images.

4 What characterized the new era of globalization that began in the late twentieth century? How did globalization affect American trade, immigration, and communications?

Blend Images/SuperStock.

5 Describe five major changes in American society in the years between the 1980s and 2010s and explain their causes.

Donaldson Collection/Getty Images.

TRM Find complete suggested responses in the Teacher's Resource Materials.

29 CHAPTER Conservative America in the Ascent 1980–1991

Chapter 29 — AP® Assessment Weight and Pacing Guide

The assessment weight on the AP® U.S. History Exam for Chapters 29–30 is 4–6 percent. This chapter falls in Unit 9 of the AP® U.S. History Curriculum, covering Period 9: 1980–present.

This pacing guide is based on a schedule with 120 sessions of 50 minutes each before the AP® U.S. History Exam. If you have a different number of sessions before the exam, you can modify the pacing to meet your needs. If you have additional time, consider incorporating quizzes, released AP® U.S. History questions, practice exams, writing practice, and other instructional activities.

	Traditional Schedule	Block Schedule
Chapter 29	3 days	1-2 days

Daily Pacing Guide

	Content Focus	Essential Question
Day 1	The Rise of the New Right	What were the major characteristics of the political movement, known as the New Right, that backed Ronald Reagan?
Day 2	The Dawning of the Conservative Age	What were the major successes and failures of the Reagan coalition?
Day 3	The End of the Cold War	What were the aims of U.S. foreign policy at the close of the Cold War?

AP® Alignment

Section Heading	AP® Topic	AP® Theme
The Rise of the New Right	8.14, 9.2	PCE, ARC
The Dawning of the Conservative Age	9.2, 9.4	PCE, WXT
The End of the Cold War	9.3	WOR

*Should changes be made to the Course Framework in the future, an updated alignment will be placed on our AP® updates page at go.bfwpub.com/ap-course-updates.

Chapter 29 — Overview

Chapter 29 emphasizes the rise of the New Right and the leadership of Ronald Reagan as the embodiment of New Right political identity and economic policy. The chapter begins by examining the philosophical underpinnings of the New Right in the leadership of Barry

Goldwater and Ronald Reagan beginning in the 1960s. The chapter examines the presidency of Jimmy Carter as a reaction against the Watergate scandal and one that faced severe limitations due to the energy crisis and the Iran hostage crisis. Following the election of Ronald Reagan in 1980, conservatism ascended in American politics with wider support than had been seen since the 1920s. Reagan represented a coalition of supporters that cemented conservative power in American politics since 1980. This coalition included the growing power of the Religious Right and powerful political action groups who influenced political, economic, and social policies. Finally, the chapter examines the policies of the Reagan and Bush years as extensions of traditional Cold War containment that ultimately helped to end the Soviet Union.

Chapter 29 — Resources

The following resources can be found in the Teacher's Resource Materials (TRM) that accompany the book. You can access the TRM via the book's digital platform, by clicking the TRM links found here in your Teacher's Edition e-book, or by contacting your representative to access the resources online. Visit **bfwpub.com/henretta10e** to learn more.

TRM Chapter 29 Lecture Presentation Slides

TRM Chapter 29 Outline with AP® Focus

TRM Chapter 29 Lecture Strategies

TRM Chapter 29 Suggested Responses

TRM Handout 29.1 — Causation: The Rise of the New Right

TRM Handout 29.2 — Causation: Shift to a Service Economy

TRM Handout 29.3 — Comparison: Ronald Reagan Foreign Policy

Chapter 29 — Essential Activity

Assign the **AP® FIRSTHAND ACCOUNTS** document exercise on pp. 944-945 as homework. In class, organize students into collaborative groups and ask them to discuss the role of religion in politics from the Colonial era to the present. Building on the documents in the text, ask students to identify five more documents from periods prior to 1980 concerning the role of religion in American public life. Engage students in a Socratic seminar that begins with this question: Do the actions of the Religious Right since the 1970s endanger the separation of church and state enshrined in the First Amendment? Require students to provide textual evidence in support of their comments and discussion. At the end of the seminar, break students back out into their collaborative groups to write a thesis statement and outline for the following prompt: To what extent does the Religious Right represent a major change in American public life since 1980?

Chapter 29 — Bell Ringers

The following activities take no more than 5–15 minutes of your class period and offer an effective and engaging way to begin your lessons and for students to apply AP® Skills & Processes:

- Provide students with quotations from excerpts from Barry Goldwater, Ronald Reagan, Phyllis Schlafly, etc. Ask students to analyze the quotes and use them to construct a definition of the "New Right" in the 1980s.
- Project an image that shows the inauguration of Ronald Reagan beside an image of the release of the hostages from Iran on January 20, 1981. Ask students to provide contextualization for these images by explaining the historical processes, developments, or events that help the viewer understand the place of the images in the rise of conservatism.
- Play a video of the 1984 Ronald Reagan campaign commercial "Morning in America." Ask students to consider the ways in which the commercial effectively communicated Reagan's conservative vision of the U.S. and to analyze the degree to which the commercial accurately illustrated life in 1984 America. Ask students to work in pairs to discuss the effectiveness of the campaign commercial and compare it to campaign ads they have seen in their lifetime.

NOTES

TEACHING STRATEGY

The chapter title captures the dominant feature of the 1980s: the ascendency of economic and cultural conservatism, focused on "economic deregulation, low taxes, Christian morality, and a reenergized Cold War foreign policy." As the end of this section indicates, conservatism had existed long before the election of Reagan, but he became a powerful symbol and shaper of the movement. Reagan's rapprochement with the Soviet Union is not the only irony of the Reagan era. The introduction to the PBS *American Experience* film on Reagan captures the many paradoxes of his presidency. To access this film, search "American Experience Reagan." For a complete suggested response to the **AP® LEARNING FOCUS** question, see p. 966.

29 CHAPTER

Conservative America in the Ascent

1980–1991

AP® LEARNING FOCUS

Why was the New Right able to ascend to national political power in the 1980s and reshape both government and society?

The 1970s began with Americans already divided by Vietnam and social strife. A decade defined by economic malaise, political scandal, and rapid change only intensified a widespread uneasiness. As a result, many ordinary Americans developed a deep distrust of the expansive liberalism of the Great Society. A revived Republican Party thrived as an alternative. With a movement known as the New Right leading the way, conservatives offered the nation a new political order based on deregulation, low taxes, Christian morality, and a reenergized Cold War foreign policy. The election of Ronald Reagan as president of the United States in 1980 marked the ascendance of this political formula, and his presidency reshaped government in the mold of this decidedly conservative republicanism.

The New Right revived confidence in "free markets" and called for a less activist government role in economic regulation and social welfare. Like the New Right generally, Reagan was profoundly skeptical of the liberal ideology that had underpinned American public policy since Franklin D. Roosevelt's New Deal. Reagan famously said, "Government is not the solution to our problem; government *is* the problem," and he duly sought to slash regulation and government programs. His conservative, domestic economic agenda was paired with aggressive anticommunism abroad — rekindling dormant tensions with the Soviet Union before Reagan, in his second term, helped orchestrate a thawing of the Cold War.

Reagan became the face of conservative ascendancy, but he did not create the New Right groundswell that brought him into office. Grassroots activists in the 1960s and 1970s built a formidable right-wing movement, and by 1980 resurgent conservatives were ready to contend for national power. Their chance came with Democratic president Jimmy Carter's mismanagement of two national crises. Raging inflation and the Iranian seizure of American hostages in Tehran undid Carter and provided an opening for the New Right, which would shape the nation's politics for the remainder of the twentieth century and the early decades of the twenty-first.

938

1984 Republican National Convention Ronald Reagan delivers his acceptance speech at the 1984 Republican National Convention. Reagan's political rise captured the spirit of conservative politics in the late 1970s and 1980s. Ronald Reagan Presidential Library.

TEACHING STRATEGY

As the text on p. 940 indicates, Ronald Reagan had been a film actor decades before he became president, a career that prepared him to carefully cultivate his appearance and persona. Though not all would agree with that critical assessment, there is no doubt that Reagan and his team carefully managed his image. To delve into this topic further, have students read the *Huffington Post's* article titled "'The Reagan Show': Acting President." To access this article, search "Huffington Post Reagan Show."

AP® SKILLS & PROCESSES

CONTINUITY AND CHANGE

Use the **TIMELINE** to help students think about how the period from 1980 to 1991 could constitute a distinct historical period. This chapter begins with Reagan's inauguration and ends with the dissolution of the Soviet Union. Students should recognize that Reagan was both a cause of significant change and a reflection of a larger wave of conservatism that he rode into the White House, as indicated in the chapter opener. Students should also recognize that this period ends in 1991, with the collapse of the Soviet Union, an event with which his legacy is closely associated.

AP® APPLY THE TIP

To focus closely on the causes for the rise of the New Right, prompt students to use pp. 940–942 to complete **Handout 29.1 — Causation: The Rise of the New Right (TRM)**. Once completed, place students in collaborative groups to compile a set of documents (primary sources, secondary sources, images, graphs) to explain the cause and effect relationships related to the rise of the New Right. On the board, write the AP® Themes, and then ask students to organize their sources according to learning objectives to show various ways of interpreting the rise of the New Right. Prompt each group to share the excerpts and other sources they compiled with the class and discuss their relationship to the learning objectives.

TRM Find complete suggested responses and **Handout 29.1 — Causation: The Rise of the New Right** in the Teacher's Resource Materials.

TIMELINE

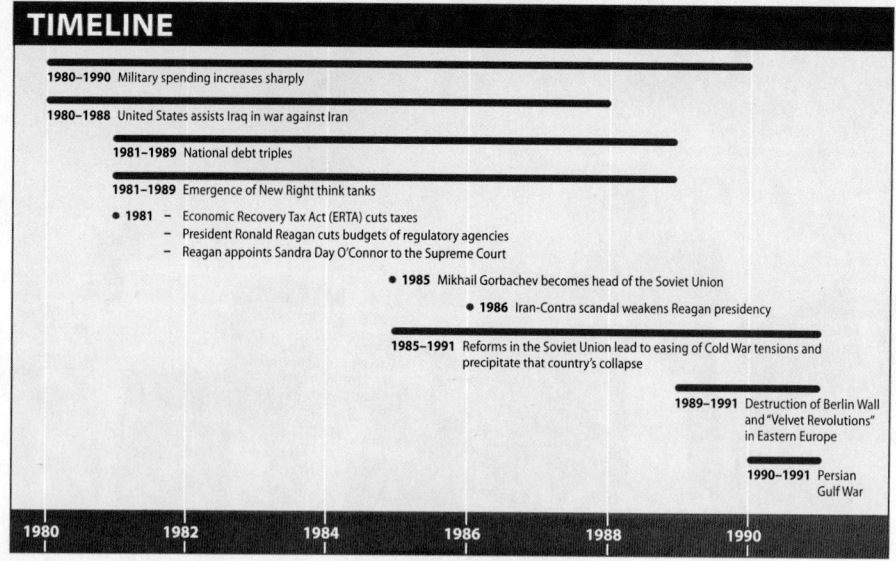

- **1980–1990** Military spending increases sharply
- **1980–1988** United States assists Iraq in war against Iran
- **1981–1989** National debt triples
- **1981–1989** Emergence of New Right think tanks
- **1981** – Economic Recovery Tax Act (ERTA) cuts taxes
  - President Ronald Reagan cuts budgets of regulatory agencies
  - Reagan appoints Sandra Day O'Connor to the Supreme Court
- **1985** Mikhail Gorbachev becomes head of the Soviet Union
- **1986** Iran-Contra scandal weakens Reagan presidency
- **1985–1991** Reforms in the Soviet Union lead to easing of Cold War tensions and precipitate that country's collapse
- **1989–1991** Destruction of Berlin Wall and "Velvet Revolutions" in Eastern Europe
- **1990–1991** Persian Gulf War

1980 1982 1984 1986 1988 1990

THE RISE OF THE NEW RIGHT

What were the major characteristics of the political movement, known as the New Right, that backed Ronald Reagan?

AP® EXAM TIP

Summarize the causes for the rising popularity of the New Right from the 1960s through the 1980s.

At midcentury, the Great Depression and World War II discredited the traditional conservative program of limited government at home and diplomatic isolationism abroad. Moderate Republicans, who came to dominate the GOP in the 1950s, sought to temper the New Deal modestly but not to dismantle it. A right-wing faction nonetheless survived within the party. Its adherents continued to oppose welfare liberalism but reversed their earlier isolationism, which gave way to anticommunist interventionism. In the postwar decades, conservatives pushed for military interventions against communism in Europe, Asia, and the developing world while calling for the broadest possible investigation of subversives at home (see "Red Scare: The Hunt for Communists" in Chapter 24).

However, conservatives still failed to sway American voters in the two decades after World War II. The Republican Party was divided, and conservatism and the GOP were not synonymous. Republican voters by and large continued to favor moderates, such as Dwight Eisenhower, Thomas Dewey, and Nelson Rockefeller. These were politicians, often called liberal Republicans, who supported much of the New Deal, endorsed the containment policy overseas, and steered a middle course on social change. The conservative faction was out of power but did not give up its hopes of a majority within the Republican electorate. In the 1960s and 1970s, those hopes rested on two dynamic figures: Barry Goldwater and Ronald Reagan. Together, the two carried the conservative banner until the national electorate grew more receptive to right-wing appeals.

Barry Goldwater and Ronald Reagan: Champions of the Right

Before World War II, Ronald Reagan was a well-known movie actor and a New Deal Democrat. However, he turned away from liberalism, partly from self-interest (he disliked paying high taxes) and partly on principle. As head of the Screen Actors Guild from 1947 to 1952, Reagan had to deal with its Communist members — the extreme left wing of the American labor movement. Dismayed by their hardline tactics and goals, he became a militant anticommunist. After nearly a decade as a spokesperson for the General Electric Corporation, Reagan joined the Republican Party in the early 1960s and began speaking for conservative causes and candidates.

One of those candidates was the forthright conservative Barry Goldwater, a Republican senator from Arizona, who surprised centrist Republicans by winning the party's 1964 presidential nomination. Goldwater's nomination previewed the coalescing conservative forces that would put Reagan in the White House sixteen years later. Indeed, Reagan the politician first came to national attention in 1964 with a televised speech at the Republican convention supporting Goldwater for the presidency. In a dramatic address titled "A Time for Choosing," Reagan warned that if Americans chose to "trade our freedom for the soup kitchen of the welfare state," the nation would "take the last step into a thousand years of darkness."

Barry Goldwater Barry Goldwater was a three-term senator from Arizona before he ran for the presidency in 1964 (this photo was taken during the campaign). Goldwater's conservative influence on the Republican Party was considerable and laid the political groundwork for the rise of Ronald Reagan a decade and a half later. Everett Collection Inc./Alamy Stock Photo.

The Conscience of a Conservative Goldwater was born in what would become the state of Arizona and inherited the Sunbelt's libertarian spirit of limited government and great personal freedom. His 1960 book, *The Conscience of a Conservative*, set forth an uncompromising conservatism. In direct and accessible prose, Goldwater attacked the New Deal state, arguing that "the natural tendency of government [is] to expand in the direction of absolutism." The problem with the Republican Party, as he saw it, was that Dwight Eisenhower had been too accommodating to liberalism. When Ike told reporters that he was "liberal when it comes to human problems," Goldwater had privately fumed.

The Conscience of a Conservative spurred a Republican grassroots movement in support of Goldwater. By distributing the book widely and mobilizing activists at state party conventions, conservatives hoped to generate enough support that Goldwater could be "drafted" to run for president in 1964, an assignment he did not relish. Meanwhile, Goldwater published another book, *Why Not Victory?*, in which he criticized the containment policy — the strategy of preventing the spread of communism embraced by both Democrats and Republicans since 1947 (see "The Containment Strategy" in Chapter 24). That policy, he would later complain in a 1964 speech, amounted to "timidly refusing to draw our own lines against aggression . . . unmarked by pride or the prospect of victory." Goldwater wanted to roll back and diminish Soviet power, not simply "contain" it. With his unapologetic views, he had enchanted a small but energetic group of conservative activists.

AP® SKILLS & PROCESSES

CONTEXTUALIZATION

Why were New Right conservatives dissatisfied with the Republican Party in the decades after World War II?

Grassroots Conservatives Because moderates dominated the Republican Party leadership, the "Draft Goldwater" movement had to work from the bottom up. They found thousands upon thousands of Americans willing to hit the streets on behalf of their political hero. Organizations such as the John Birch Society, Young Americans for Freedom, and the Liberty Lobby supplied an army of eager volunteers. They came from such conservative strongholds as Orange County, California, and the fast-growing suburbs of Phoenix, Dallas, Houston, Atlanta, and other Sunbelt metropolises. A critical boost came in the early spring of 1964, when conservatives outmaneuvered moderates at the state convention of the California Republican Party, which then enthusiastically endorsed Goldwater. The fight was bruising, and one moderate Republican warned that "sinister forces are at work to take over the whole Republican apparatus in California."

AP® THEME

MIG: Migration and Settlement; NAT: American and National Identity

After 1980, the political, economic, and cultural influence of the American South and West — the so-called Sunbelt — continued to increase as population shifted to those areas.

AP® SKILLS & PROCESSES

CONTEXTUALIZATION

When students attempt to explain the historical context of a particular situation or development, they too often sort through discrete and sometimes disparate information. Think about reminding students of the need to start with broad processes such as the Cold War, the New Deal, Great Society legislation, and Liberalism. Once students have selected a broad process, they should then move to connect specific historical evidence to establish a broader context of the reasons New Right conservatives were dissatisfied with the Republican party after the Second World War.

TRM Find complete suggested responses in the Teacher's Resource Materials.

TEACHING STRATEGY

Think about having students connect migration patterns to political developments. In this case, the rise of the Sunbelt as an economically dynamic region happened in concert with the importance of the Sunbelt as a politically important region. Have students brainstorm at least TWO historical factors that explain this connection.

TEACHING STRATEGY

Peggy Noonan, a speechwriter for Reagan, explains his switch to the conservatism of Goldwater as a matter of character — a core element of his personality, in her view, and one of the reasons for his great popularity. To access an excerpt from her essay, search "PBS Noonan Ronald Reagan."

CHECK FOR UNDERSTANDING

Ask students: **What made Barry Goldwater and Ronald Reagan champions of the political right?** *Both were willing to challenge the moderate positions that dominated the Republican Party, symbolized by Nelson Rockefeller. Both championed an uncompromising conservatism, emphasizing a strong national defense and a limited government.*

AP® THEME

WXT: Work, Exchange, and Technology

Policy debates continued in the late 1970s into the 1980s over the scope of the government social safety net and calls to reform the U.S. financial system. PBS provides the full text of Reagan's 1964 "A Time for Choosing" speech. Video versions of the speech are also widely available online. To access this speech, search "American Experience Time for Choosing."

The appearance of a book by Phyllis Schlafly, then a relatively unknown conservative activist from the Midwest, spurred on the Goldwater movement. Like *The Conscience of a Conservative*, Schlafly's *A Choice Not an Echo* accused moderate Republicans of being Democrats in all but name (that is, an "echo" of Democrats). Schlafly, who would return to the national spotlight in the early 1970s to fight the ratification of the Equal Rights Amendment (see "The Women's Movement and Gay Rights" in Chapter 28), denounced the "Rockefeller Republicans" of the Northeast and encouraged the party to embrace a defiant conservatism. Contrasting Goldwater's "grassroots Republicans" with Rockefeller's "kingmakers," Schlafly hoped to "forestall another defeat like 1940, 1944, 1948, and 1960" — all Democratic victories.

At the 1964 Republican National Convention, the conservative groundswell won the nomination for Goldwater — and shocked both moderate Republicans and reporters in the convention hall. However, Goldwater's strident tone and militarist foreign policy were too much for a nation still committed to liberalism. Aided by the legacy of John F. Kennedy, Lyndon B. Johnson defeated Goldwater in a historic landslide. Many believed that Goldwater conservatism would wither away after its brief moment. Instead the nearly four million volunteers who had campaigned for the Arizona senator built toward the future. Skilled conservative political operatives such as Richard Viguerie, a Texas-born Catholic and antiabortion activist, applied new technology to political campaigning. Viguerie took a list of 12,000 Goldwater contributors and used computerized mailing lists, which were new at the time, to solicit campaign funds, rally support for conservative causes, and get out the vote on election day. The major beneficiary of this new form of political organizing was Ronald Reagan.

Financed by wealthy southern Californians and supported by Goldwaterites, Reagan won California's governorship in 1966 and again in 1970. He succeeded with a promise of limited government and law and order — referring to campus radicals, he vowed to "clean up the mess in Berkeley" — a pledge that found broad support in the nation's most populous state. His rhetoric also made him a force in national politics, and supporters believed that he was in line to succeed Nixon as the next Republican president. Due to the Watergate scandal, however, Gerald Ford was the incumbent president, which gave him just enough of an edge to narrowly defeat Reagan for the Republican nomination in 1976. When Ford lost to Jimmy Carter in that year's election, the party's brightest star only had to wait — Reagan was a near lock for the Republican nomination in 1980.

Free-Market Economics and Religious Conservatism

Several additional developments within the New Right completed Reagan's rise. The burgeoning conservative movement increasingly resembled a three-legged stool. Each leg represented an ideological position and its political constituency: anticommunism, free-market economics, and religious traditionalism. Uniting all three into a political coalition was not simple. Traditionalists demanded strong government action to implement their faith-based agenda, but economic conservatives favored limited government and free markets. Both groups, however, were ardent anticommunists — free marketeers loathed the state-directed Soviet economy, and religious conservatives opposed the "godless" secularism of the Soviet state. The success of the New Right would come to depend on a balancing of cultural, economic, and political interests.

Beginning in the 1950s, conservative intellectuals worked to build an ideological foundation that would eventually support the New Right. Particularly prominent in this effort were William F. Buckley, the founder and editor of the conservative magazine ***National Review***, and Milton Friedman, the Nobel Prize–winning economist at the University of Chicago. Convinced that "the growth of government must be fought relentlessly," Buckley used the *National Review* to criticize liberal policy. For his part, Friedman became a national conservative icon with the publication of *Capitalism and*

National Review
A conservative magazine founded by editor William F. Buckley in 1955 that criticized liberal policy and helped lay the foundation for the New Right.

Freedom (1962), in which he argued that "economic freedom is . . . an indispensable means toward the achievement of political freedom." Friedman's free-market ideology, along with that of Friedrich von Hayek, another University of Chicago economist, found favor with wealthy conservatives, who funded think tanks during the 1980s to disseminate market-based public policy ideas. Groups such as the Heritage Foundation, the American Enterprise Institute, and the Cato Institute issued policy proposals and attacked liberal legislation they saw as strangling economic freedom. Followers of Buckley and Friedman envisioned themselves as crusaders working against what one conservative called "the despotic aspects of egalitarianism."

The **Religious Right** completed the conservative coalition. Until the 1970s, politics was an earthly concern of secondary interest to most fundamentalist and evangelical Protestants. But the perception that American society had become immoral, combined with the influence of a new generation of popular ministers, fostered a more urgent approach. Conservative Protestants and Catholics joined together in a tentative alliance to condemn divorce, abortion, premarital sex, and feminism. The route to a moral life and to "peace, pardon, purpose, and power," as one evangelical activist said, was "to plug yourself into the One, the Only One [God]."

Religious Right
Politically active religious conservatives, especially Catholics and evangelical Christians, who became particularly vocal in the 1980s against feminism, abortion, and homosexuality and who promoted "family values."

AP® EXAM TIP
Evaluate the role of the Religious Right on politics and society since 1980.

Charismatic televangelists such as Pat Robertson and Jerry Falwell emerged as the champions of a morality-based political agenda during the late 1970s. Falwell, founder of Liberty University and host of the *Old Time Gospel Hour* television program, established the Moral Majority in 1979. With 400,000 members and $1.5 million in contributions in its first year, this group would become the organizational vehicle for transforming the new evangelicalism into a religious political movement. Falwell made no secret of his views: "If you want to know where I am politically," he told reporters, "I thought Goldwater was too liberal." Falwell was not alone. Phyllis Schlafly's STOP ERA, which became Eagle Forum in 1975, continued to advocate for conservative public policy; Focus on the Family, which emphasized healthy marriages and opposed gay rights, was founded in 1977; and a succession of conservative organizations would emerge in the 1980s, including the Family Research Council, which would become one of the leading national voices for traditional marriage and family.

AP® SKILLS & PROCESSES
DEVELOPMENTS AND PROCESSES
What was the "three-legged stool" of the New Right, and how did each element develop within the context of the Cold War?

In 1964, voters had decidedly rejected the conservative message preached by Goldwater, choosing the liberal Democratic agenda instead. Then came a series of events that undermined support for liberalism: the failed war in Vietnam; urban riots; a judiciary that legalized abortion, tolerated pornography, enforced school busing, and curtailed public expression of religion; and a stagnating economy on top. By the late 1970s, the New Right had refined a conservative message with broader appeal than Goldwater's program. Religious and free-market conservatives joined with anticommunist hard-liners — alongside whites opposed to black civil rights, affirmative action, and busing — in a broad coalition that attacked welfare-state liberalism, social permissiveness, and a foreign policy deemed weak. In winning the 1980 Republican presidential nomination, Ronald Reagan expertly appealed to all of these constituencies (see "Firsthand Accounts," p. 944). It had taken almost two decades, but the New Right was on the threshold of power.

Pat Robertson Television evangelist Pat Robertson speaks before supporters at Constitution Hall, declaring God made his decision and that he is ready to run for president as soon as 3 million voters agree to pray and pay for his campaign. Robertson symbolized the rise of Christian conservatives in American politics during the 1980s. Bettmann/Getty Images.

AP® APPLY THE TIP

To help students understand the impact of the Religious Right since 1980, prompt students to read the documents in the **AP® FIRSTHAND ACCOUNTS** feature on pp. 944–945 and answer the corresponding questions. After completing the exercise, organize students into groups and prompt them to identify two documents to add to those in the text, which represent groups, ideas, or leaders who opposed the rise of the Religious Right. Additionally, ask students to identify one image (cartoon, photograph, or graph) that supports either side. In their groups, students should then write a prompt examining the role of the Religious Right in politics and society since 1980 around one of the AP® Historical Thinking Skills. Students should then exchange work with other groups; with another group's documents and prompts in hand, ask students to formulate a DBQ response.

AP® THEME

SOC: Social Structures

The dramatic growth of evangelical Christian churches and related organizations was accompanied by greater political and social activism by religious conservatives. This topic, which often becomes subject to simplistic narratives, needs careful analysis. Daniel K. Williams provides a nuanced assessment of the Religious Right's rise, suggesting that while evangelicals' allegiance to — and growing influence within — the Republican Party was new, their political activism was of long duration.

TEACHING STRATEGY

In light of the emphasis in this chapter on the role of evangelicalism in the rise of the New Right, it is worth discussing how Jimmy Carter, though not politically conservative, was also an evangelical.

CHECK FOR UNDERSTANDING

Ask students: **What role did free-market economics and religious conservatism play in the New Right?** *These two beliefs — along with anticommunism — made up the "three-legged stool" of the New Right. Of the three, religious conservatism was the newest political force, energized by concerns about divorce, abortion, premarital sex, and feminism. The support of the Moral Majority, Focus on the Family, and other Christian organizations helped propel Reagan to victory (though none of their major concerns would be addressed in any substantive way in the Reagan administration).*

AP® SKILLS & PROCESSES

DEVELOPMENTS AND PROCESSES

The **DEVELOPMENTS AND PROCESSES** question asks students to place the major elements of New Right political ideology in the context of the Cold War. Students should be clear that while each of these features may have taken on particular meaning in the Cold War, none of them was created by the Cold War. Extend this prompt by asking students to trace the role of each in their late-nineteenth and early-twentieth-century contexts.

TRM Find complete suggested responses in the Teacher's Resource Materials.

AP® SKILLS & PROCESSES

ANALYZING HISTORICAL EVIDENCE

Use the **AP® FIRSTHAND ACCOUNTS** feature to explore the controversial issue of religious involvement in political affairs. Students should pay careful attention to the specific stance each person takes regarding religion and public life, and the reasoning each provides for his position. Students might find it helpful to know that the role of religious conservatism in politics remains significant — and divisive. According to the Pew Research Center, the overwhelming majority of white evangelicals voted for Donald Trump in 2016, helping to provide his electoral victory. To access this report, search "Pew Research Center How the Faithful Voted, 2016."

AP® FIRSTHAND ACCOUNTS

Christianity and Public Life

Modern social-welfare liberalism embodies an ethic of moral pluralism and favors the separation of church and state. Conservative Christians challenge the legitimacy of pluralism and secularism and seek through political agitation and legal action to make religion an integral part of public life.

PRESIDENT RONALD REAGAN

"The Rule of Law Under God," 1983

Reagan's candidacy was strongly supported by Christian conservatives. He delivered these remarks to the National Association of American Evangelicals in 1983.

SOURCE: Reprinted with the permission of Simon & Schuster, Inc. from *Speaking My Mind* by Ronald Reagan. Copyright © 1989 Ronald W. Reagan.

" I want you to know that this administration is motivated by a political philosophy that sees the greatness of America in you, her people, and in your families, churches, neighborhoods, communities — the institutions that foster and nourish values like concern for others and respect for the rule of law under God.

Now, I don't have to tell you that this puts us in opposition to, or at least out of step with, a prevailing attitude of many who have turned to a modern-day secularism, discarding the tried and time-tested values upon which our very civilization is based. No matter how well intentioned, their value system is radically different from that of most Americans. And while they proclaim that they're freeing us from superstitions of the past, they've taken upon themselves the job of superintending us by government rule and regulation. Sometimes their voices are louder than ours, but they are not yet a majority. . . .

Freedom prospers when religion is vibrant and the rule of law under God is acknowledged. When our Founding Fathers passed the First Amendment, they sought to protect churches from government interference. They never intended to construct a wall of hostility between government and the concept of religious belief itself.

Last year, I sent the Congress a constitutional amendment to restore prayer to public schools. Already this session, there's growing bipartisan support for the amendment, and I am calling on the Congress to act speedily to pass it and to let our children pray. "

DONALD E. WILDMON

Network Television as a Moral Danger, 1985

Wildmon was a Christian minister, a grassroots religious activist, and the founder of the American Family Association.

SOURCE: From Donald E. Wildmon, *Home Invaders* (Elgin, IL: Victor Books, 1985). Copyright © 1985. Reprinted by permission of the author.

" One night during the Christmas holidays of 1976, I decided to watch television with my family. . . . Not far into the program was a scene of adultery. I reacted to the situation in the manner as I had been taught. I asked one of the children to change channels. Getting involved in the second program, we were shocked with some crude profanity. . . .

As I sat in my den that night, I became angry. I had been disturbed by the deterioration of morals I had witnessed in the media and society during the previous twenty-five years.

This was accompanied by a dramatic rise in crime, a proliferation of pornography, increasingly explicit sexual lyrics in music, increasing numbers of broken homes, a rise in drug and alcohol use among the youth, and various other negative factors. . . .

Realizing that these changes were being brought into the sanctity of my home, I decided I could and would no longer remain silent. . . .

This great struggle is one of values, particularly which ones will be the standard for our society and a base for our system of justice in the years to come. For 200 years our country has based its morals, its sense of right and wrong, on the Christian view of man. The Ten Commandments and the Sermon on the Mount have been our solid foundation. . . .

Television is the most pervasive and persuasive medium we have. At times it is larger than life. It is our only true national medium. Network television is the greatest educator we have. . . .

It is teaching that adultery is an acceptable and approved lifestyle. . . . It is teaching that hardly anyone goes to church, that very few people in our society are Christian or live by Christian principles. How? By simply censoring Christian characters, Christian values, and Christian culture from the programs. "

A. BARTLETT GIAMATTI

The Moral Majority as a Threat to Liberty, 1981

A. Bartlett Giamatti was the president of Yale University (1978–1986) and subsequently commissioner of Major League Baseball. He offered these remarks to the entering class of Yale undergraduates in 1981.

SOURCE: From Speeches and Articles by and about Presidents of Yale University (RU 65). Manuscripts and Archives, Yale University Library. Used by permission of Manuscripts and Archives, Yale University Library.

“A self-proclaimed ‘Moral Majority,’ and its satellite or client groups, cunning in the use of a native blend of old intimidation and new technology, threaten the values [of pluralism and freedom]. . . .

From the maw of this ‘morality’ come those who presume to know what justice for all is; come those who presume to know which books are fit to read, which television programs are fit to watch. . . . From the maw of this ‘morality’ rise the tax-exempt Savonarolas who believe they, and they alone, possess the ‘truth.’ There is no debate, no discussion, no dissent. They know. . . . What nonsense.

What dangerous, malicious nonsense. . . .

We should be concerned that so much of our political and religious leadership acts intimidated for the moment and will not say with clarity that this most recent denial of the legitimacy of differentness is a radical assault on the very pluralism of peoples, political beliefs, values, forms of merit and systems of religion our country was founded to welcome and foster.

Liberty protects the person from unwarranted government intrusions into a dwelling or other private places. In our tradition the State is not omnipresent in the home. And there are other spheres of our lives and existence, outside the home, where the State should not be a dominant presence.

Freedom extends beyond spatial bounds. Liberty presumes an autonomy of self that includes freedom of thought, belief, expression, and certain intimate conduct.”

ANTHONY KENNEDY

The Constitution Protects Privacy, 2003

Kennedy, a Roman Catholic, was named to the Supreme Court by Ronald Reagan in 1988. In *Lawrence v. Texas* (2003), which challenged a state antisodomy law, he wrote the opinion for five of the six justices in the majority; Sandra Day O'Connor wrote a concurring opinion.

SOURCE: *Lawrence v. Texas*, 539 U.S. 558, 562–563, 567, 571, 579 (2003).

“The question before the Court is the validity of a Texas statute making it a crime for two persons of the same sex to engage in certain intimate sexual conduct.

In Houston, Texas, officers of the Harris County Police Department were dispatched to a private residence in response to a reported weapons disturbance. They entered an apartment where one of the petitioners, John Geddes Lawrence, resided. . . . The officers observed Lawrence and another man, Tyron Garner, engaging in a sexual act. The two petitioners were arrested, held in custody over night, and charged and convicted before a Justice of the Peace.

The complaints described their crime as ‘deviate sexual intercourse, namely [. . .] sex, with a member of the same sex (man).’ . . .

We conclude the case should be resolved by determining whether the petitioners were free as adults to engage in the private conduct in the exercise of their liberty under the Due Process Clause of the Fourteenth Amendment to the Constitution.

[The Texas statute in question seeks] to control a personal relationship that, whether or not entitled to formal recognition in the law, is within the liberty of persons to choose without being punished as criminals. . . . The liberty protected by the Constitution allows homosexual persons the right to make this choice. . . .

. . . The petitioners are entitled to respect for their private lives. The State cannot demean their existence or control their destiny by making their private sexual conduct a crime. Their right to liberty under the Due Process Clause gives them the full right to engage in their conduct without intervention of the government. ‘It is a promise of the Constitution that there is a realm of personal liberty which the government may not enter.’”

QUESTIONS FOR ANALYSIS

1. Compare the Ronald Reagan and Anthony Kennedy documents. What would Reagan think of the opinion written by Justice Kennedy, his appointee? Given his condemnation of those intent on “subordinating us to government rule and regulation,” how would Reagan respond to Kennedy? Substantiate your claim with evidence.
2. According to Wildmon, what should be shown on television, and who should make those decisions? How would Giamatti answer that same question? Use historical reasoning to compare their perspectives.
3. Consider the different points of view presented here. According to these sources, when should the government police private conduct? Identify each perspective and evidence each author uses to support the argument.

TRM Find complete suggested responses in the Teacher's Resource Materials.

TEACHING STRATEGY

The University of Virginia provides an essay by Robert A. Strong that canvasses the foreign policy of the Carter administration, including the Iran hostage crisis. To access this essay, search "UVA Jimmy Carter: Foreign Affairs."

The Carter Presidency

AP® EXAM TIP

Recognize how Carter's emphasis on human rights in foreign policy represented change as well as continuity in U.S. history.

First, the Republican Party had to defeat incumbent president Jimmy Carter. Carter's outsider status and disdain for professional politicians had made him the ideal post-Watergate presidential candidate. But his ineffectiveness as an executive also made him the perfect foil for Ronald Reagan.

In foreign affairs, the idealistic Carter presented himself as the anti-Nixon, a world leader who rejected Henry Kissinger's "realism" in favor of human rights and peacemaking. "Human rights is the soul of our foreign policy," Carter asserted, "because human rights is the very soul of our sense of nationhood." He established the Bureau of Human Rights in the State Department and withdrew economic and military aid from repressive regimes in Argentina, Uruguay, and Ethiopia—although, in a concession to American strategic interests, he still funded authoritarian regimes in the Philippines, South Africa, and Iran. In Latin America, Carter removed a long-standing symbol of Yankee imperialism with a 1977 treaty handing over control of the Panama Canal to Panama—although not until December 31, 1999, as the treaty specified. Carter's most important efforts came in forging an enduring, if limited, peace in the intractable Arab-Israeli conflict. In 1978, he invited Israeli prime minister Menachem Begin and Egyptian president Anwar el-Sadat to Camp David, where they crafted a "framework for peace," under which Egypt recognized Israel and regained the Sinai Peninsula, which Israel had occupied since 1967.

Carter deplored what he called the "inordinate fear of communism," but his efforts at improving relations with the Soviet Union foundered. His criticism of the Kremlin's record on human rights offended Soviet leader Leonid Brezhnev and slowed arms reduction negotiations that had been underway since 1974. In 1979, Carter finally signed the second Strategic Arms Limitations Treaty (SALT II), limiting bombers and missiles—but Senate hawks stalled the treaty. When the Soviet Union invaded Afghanistan that December, Carter suddenly sided with the hawks and denounced the invasion as the "gravest threat to world peace since World War II." After ordering an embargo on wheat shipments to the Soviet Union and withdrawing SALT II from Senate consideration, Carter called for increased defense spending and declared an American boycott of the 1980 Summer Olympics in Moscow. In a fateful decision, the United States began to send covert assistance to anti-Soviet fighters in Afghanistan, some of whom, including Osama bin Laden, would emerge decades later as anti-American Islamic radicals.

American Hostages in Iran Images of blindfolded, handcuffed American hostages seized by Iranian militants at the U.S. embassy in Tehran in November 1979 shocked the nation and created a foreign policy crisis that eventually cost President Carter his chance for reelection. Alain Mingam/Gamma-Rapho via Getty Images.

Hostage Crisis Carter's ultimate undoing came in Iran, however. The United States had long relied on Iran as a bulwark against Soviet expansion into the Middle East and a steady source of oil. The country's shah (king) had been ousted by a democratically elected parliament in 1953, but reclaimed power in a matter of days with the support of the U.S. Central Intelligence Agency. This intervention soured Iranian views of the United States, which was regarded as an imperial nation that had violated Iranian sovereignty. Early in 1979, a revolution drove the shah into exile and brought a fundamentalist Shiite Muslim cleric, the Ayatollah Ruhollah Khomeini, to power. After the United States admitted the deposed shah into the country for cancer treatment, Iranian students seized the U.S. embassy in Tehran, taking sixty-six Americans hostage. The captors demanded that the shah be returned to Iran for trial. Carter refused. Instead, he suspended arms sales to Iran and froze Iranian assets in American banks.

TEACHING STRATEGY

As the text indicates, the 444-day ordeal paralyzed the Carter administration. The essay titled "Jimmy Carter and the Iranian Hostage Crisis" provides a lengthy narrative of the crisis and its eventual resolution. To access this essay, search "White House History Jimmy Carter and the Iranian Hostage Crisis."

For the next fourteen months, the **hostage crisis** paralyzed Carter's presidency. Night after night, humiliating pictures of blindfolded American hostages appeared on television newscasts. An attempted military rescue in April 1980 had to be aborted because of equipment failures in the desert. Several months later, however, a stunning development scrambled the situation: Iraq, led by Saddam Hussein, invaded Iran, officially because of a dispute over deep-water ports but also to prevent Iran's Shiite-led revolution from spreading across the border into Iraq, which was run by Sunni Muslims. Needing to focus his country on the war with Iraq, Khomeini opened hostage-release talks with the United States. Difficult negotiations dragged on past the American presidential election in November 1980, and the hostages were finally released the day after Carter left office — a final indignity to a well-intentioned but unsuccessful president.

hostage crisis
Crisis in 1979, in which Iranian college students seized the U.S. embassy in Tehran, took sixty-six Americans hostage, and demanded that the deposed Shah, an undemocratic ruler installed with American backing in 1954, be returned to face trial in Iran. President Carter refused, and the hostages were kept for 444 days.

AP® SKILLS & PROCESSES

ARGUMENTATION

Jimmy Carter's presidential term was sandwiched in the middle of sixteen years of Republican presidents (Nixon/Ford and Reagan). Was his presidency consistent with those others, or a break from them?

The Election of 1980 President Carter's sinking popularity made him vulnerable in the presidential primaries. After Democrats barely renominated Carter over his liberal challenger, Edward (Ted) Kennedy of Massachusetts, his approval rating was historically low: a mere 21 percent of Americans believed that he was an effective president. The reasons were clear enough: millions of citizens were feeling the pinch from stagnant wages, high inflation, crippling mortgage rates, and an unemployment rate of nearly 8 percent — in the boom years of the 1950s and 1960s, in contrast, unemployment stayed between 3 and 5 percent and only once climbed above 6 percent. In international affairs, the nation saw Carter's responses to Soviet expansion and the hostage crisis as ineffectual and weak.

With Carter on the defensive, Reagan struck an upbeat, decisive tone. "This is the greatest country in the world," Reagan reassured the nation in his warm baritone. "We have the talent, we have the drive. . . . All we need is the leadership." To emphasize his intention to be a formidable international leader, Reagan hinted that he would take strong action to free the Tehran hostages if elected. To signal his rejection of liberal policies, he also declared his opposition to affirmative action and forced busing and promised to "get the government off our backs." Most important, Reagan effectively appealed to the many Americans who felt economically insecure. In a televised debate with Carter, Reagan asked working-and middle-class Americans a powerful question: "Are you better off today than you were four years ago?"

In November, the voters gave a clear answer. They repudiated Carter, who won only 41.0 percent of the vote. Independent candidate John Anderson garnered 6.6 percent (with a few minor candidates receiving fractions of a percent), and Reagan won with 50.7 percent of the popular vote (Map 29.1). The Republicans elected thirty-three new members of the House of Representatives and twelve new senators, which gave them control of the upper chamber for the first time since 1954. The conservative landslide finally brought the New Right to national power — and signaled the arrival of a new political alignment.

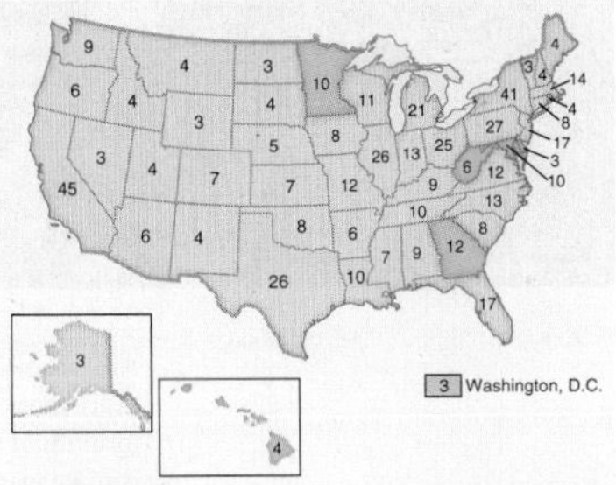

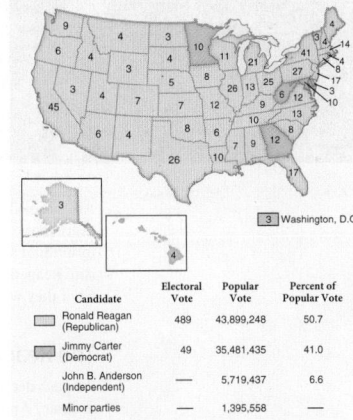

Candidate	Electoral Vote	Popular Vote	Percent of Popular Vote
Ronald Reagan (Republican)	489	43,899,248	50.7
Jimmy Carter (Democrat)	49	35,481,435	41.0
John B. Anderson (Independent)	—	5,719,437	6.6
Minor parties	—	1,395,558	—

MAP 29.1 The Presidential Election of 1980
Ronald Reagan easily defeated Democratic incumbent Jimmy Carter, taking 50.7 percent of the popular vote to Carter's 41.0 percent and winning the electoral vote in all but six states and the District of Columbia. Reagan cut deeply into the traditional Democratic coalition by wooing many southern whites, urban Catholics, and blue-collar workers. More than five million Americans expressed their discontent with Carter's ineffectiveness and Reagan's conservatism by voting for Independent candidate John Anderson, a longtime Republican member of the House of Representatives.

THE DAWNING OF THE CONSERVATIVE AGE

What were the major successes and failures of the Reagan coalition?

By the time Ronald Reagan took office in 1981, conservatism commanded wider popular support than at any time since the 1920s. As the New Deal Democratic coalition continued to fragment, the Republican Party gained voters who had been reliably Democratic since the Great Depression — which accelerated the realignment of the

AP® EXAM TIP

Be able to explain the political realignment associated with the leadership of Ronald Reagan.

AP® SKILLS & PROCESSES

ARGUMENTATION

The **ARGUMENTATION** question invites students to consider the Carter administration in the broader context of an era in which Americans were moving in a conservative direction. Encourage students to see multiple perspectives for a possible answer. One way is to extend this prompt by asking students to identify evidence that Carter followed policies largely in line with his Republican predecessors, rather than charting a dramatically different course. On the other hand, you could also ask students to marshal evidence that illustrates how Carter, at times, tried to move the country in an alternative direction to that offered by conservatives.

TRM Find complete suggested responses in the Teacher's Resource Materials.

AP® THEME

PCE: Politics and Power

Reagan's victory in the 1980 presidential election represented a major milestone, as it allowed conservatives to enact significant tax cuts and continue the deregulation of many industries. Reagan cut the budgets of many regulatory agencies like the EPA by 10 percent or more. Environmentalists feared the worst, but Reagan's record did not prove as disastrous as they feared. At the end of the Reagan administration, Philip Shabecoff offered an assessment of Reagan's environmental legacy in his article titled "Reagan and Environment: To Many, a Stalemate." To access Shabecoff's full article, search "NYT Reagan and Environment."

AP® THEME

WXT: Work, Exchange, and Technology

The 1980 election hinged in part on the fact that real wages had stagnated for the working and middle class amid growing economic inequality — a pattern that would intensify in the Reagan era.

CHECK FOR UNDERSTANDING

Ask students: **What were the major characteristics of the political movement that backed Ronald Reagan, known as the New Right?** *The New Right brought together three often divergent groups: anticommunists, free-market economists, and religious traditionalists. Formed into a difficult coalition, it won over the Republican Party in the 1970s and ultimately brought Ronald Reagan to the White House in 1981.*

TRM Find complete suggested responses in the Teacher's Resource Materials.

VISUAL ACTIVITY

President Reagan at His Ranch in Southern California Images of Reagan quickly became vital for the White House to deliver its message of conservative reform to the American people. This photo was taken by a White House photographer. Ronald Reagan Presidential Library.

READING THE IMAGE: How is Reagan dressed in this photograph, and what does he appear to be doing? What is conveyed symbolically by his clothes and his demeanor?

MAKING CONNECTIONS: How would a photograph like this have contributed at the time to Reagan's public image as a champion of conservatism? To what degree does this example of propaganda illustrate continuity and/or change in American identity?

American electorate that had begun during the 1960s. Conservatism's ascendancy did more than realign the nation politically. Its emphasis on free markets, low taxes, and individual success shaped the nation's culture and inaugurated an era of individualism. Reagan exhorted Americans, "Let the men and women of the marketplace decide what they want."

The Reagan Coalition

Reagan's decades in public life, especially his years touring the country and meeting with ordinary Americans as a national spokesman for General Electric, taught him how to articulate conservative ideas in easily understandable aphorisms. Speaking against the sprawling government that was a hallmark of the New Deal and Great Society, Reagan said, "Concentrated power has always been the enemy of liberty." In a humorous version of the same sentiment, the president joked that "The nine most terrifying words in the English language are: 'I'm from the government, and I'm here to help.'"

Under Reagan's leadership, the core of the Republican Party remained the relatively affluent, white, Protestant voters who supported balanced budgets and limited government, feared communism, and believed in strong national defense. Reagan's version of republicanism also attracted middle-class suburbanites and migrants to the Sunbelt states who endorsed the conservative agenda of combating crime and limiting social-welfare spending. Suburban growth in particular benefitted conservatives politically. The flight to the suburbs reinforced preferences for white racial homogeneity and protecting the private home, both of which inclined the residents of suburban cities toward conservative public policies.

TEACHING STRATEGY

One of the reasons the Reagan coalition was a powerful political force was how it successfully added new blocs of voters, while simultaneously taking voters previously loyal to the Democrats. Have students account for at least one relatively new bloc of voter and one group formerly loyal to the Democrats who joined the Reagan coalition.

Reagan coalition
Supporters of Ronald Reagan, including core Republican Party voters, suburbanites and Sunbelt migrants, blue-collar Catholics, and a contingent of southern whites (a key Democratic constituency).

This emerging **Reagan coalition** was joined by a large and politically vital group that had been drifting toward the Republican Party since 1964: southern whites. Reagan capitalized on the "southern strategy" developed by Richard Nixon's advisors in the late 1960s. Many southern whites had lost confidence in the Democratic Party for a wide range of reasons, but one factor stood out: the party's support for civil rights. When Reagan came to Philadelphia, Mississippi, to deliver his first official speech as the Republican presidential nominee, his ringing endorsement of "states' rights" sent a quiet but unmistakable message: he was validating twenty-five years of southern opposition to federal civil rights legislation. Some of Reagan's advisors had warned him to avoid Philadelphia, the site of the tragic murder of three civil rights workers in 1964, but Reagan believed the opportunity to launch his campaign on a states' rights note was too important. After 1980, southern whites would remain a cornerstone of his coalition.

The Religious Right proved crucial to the Republican ascendance as well. Falwell's **Moral Majority** claimed that it had registered two million new voters for the 1980 election, and the GOP platform reflected its influence. Their proposed agenda called for a constitutional ban on abortion, voluntary prayer in public schools, and a mandatory death sentence for certain crimes. Republicans also demanded an end to court-ordered busing to achieve racial integration in schools, and, for the first time in forty years, opposed the Equal Rights Amendment. Increasingly, republicanism and conservatism were inseparable.

Reagan's broad coalition attracted the allegiance of another group alienated by the direction of liberalism in the 1970s: blue-collar voters, a high number of Catholics among them, alarmed by antiwar protesters, feminism, and rising welfare expenditures. Some observers identified these voters, which many called **Reagan Democrats**, with the "silent majority" that Nixon had swung into the Republican fold in 1968 and 1972. Many lived in heavily industrialized midwestern states such as Michigan, Ohio, and Illinois and had voted Democratic for decades. Reagan's victorious coalition thus drew on a revival of right-wing conservative activism and broad dissatisfaction with liberal Democrats — a dissatisfaction that had been building since 1968 and was only briefly tempered by backlash to Watergate.

Moral Majority
A political organization established by evangelist Jerry Falwell in 1979 to mobilize conservative Christian voters on behalf of Ronald Reagan's campaign for president.

Reagan Democrats
Blue-collar Catholics from industrialized midwestern states such as Michigan, Ohio, and Illinois who were dissatisfied with the direction of liberalism in the 1970s and left the Democratic Party for the Republicans in the 1980s.

AP® SKILLS & PROCESSES
MAKING CONNECTIONS
What distinct constituencies made up the Reagan coalition, and how would you characterize their regional, geographic, class, and racial composition?

Conservatives in Power

The new president kept his political message clear and uncomplicated. "What I want to see above all," he remarked, "is that this country remains a country where someone can always get rich." Standing in the way, Reagan believed, was government. In his first year in office, Reagan and his chief advisor, James A. Baker III, quickly set new governmental priorities. They launched a three-pronged assault on federal taxes, social-welfare spending, and the regulatory bureaucracy as part of a rollback of the wider liberal state. To fight the Cold War, they advocated a vast increase in defense spending and an end to détente with the Soviet Union. In response to the resurgent economies of Germany and Japan, they set out to restore American leadership of an increasingly global market for goods and services.

Reaganomics To achieve its economic objectives, the new administration advanced a set of policies to increase the production (and thus the supply) of goods. The theory underlying **supply-side economics (Reaganomics)**, as this approach was known, emphasized investment in productive enterprises — the making of goods but also the provision of services, from financial services to fast food. According to supply-side theorists, the best way to boost that investment was to reduce the taxes paid by corporations and wealthy Americans, who could then use their windfall to expand production.

Supply-siders believed that the resulting economic expansion would increase government revenues and offset the loss of tax dollars stemming from the original tax cuts. Meanwhile, the increasing supply would generate its own demand, according to the theory, because more goods creates more wealth for the economy as a whole, which becomes new spending by individual consumers and companies alike. This approach presumed — in fact, gambled — that future tax revenues would make up for present tax cuts. The idea had a growing list of supporters in Congress, led by an ex-professional football player from Buffalo named Jack Kemp, who praised supply-side economics as "an alternative to the slow-growth, recession-oriented policies of the [Carter] administration."

Reagan took advantage of Republican control of the Senate, as well as high-profile allies such as Kemp, to win congressional approval of the 1981 **Economic Recovery Tax Act (ERTA)**, a massive tax cut that put supply-side principles into practice. The

supply-side economics (Reaganomics)
Economic theory that tax cuts encourage business investment (supply) and stimulate individual consumption (demand). In reality, supply-side economics created a massive federal budget deficit.

AP® EXAM TIP
Evaluate the goals and effects of Reaganomics.

Economic Recovery Tax Act (ERTA)
Legislation introduced by President Reagan and passed by Congress in 1981 that authorized the largest reduction in taxes in the nation's history at that time.

CHECK FOR UNDERSTANDING

Ask students: **What groups comprised the Reagan coalition?** *The New Right found strong support among wealthy whites who opposed government activism; middle-class suburban white voters, especially in Sunbelt regions; white southerners opposed to civil rights who liked Reagan's states' rights message; and some blue-collar former Democrats who tended to be socially conservative.*

AP® SKILLS & PROCESSES

MAKING CONNECTIONS

The **MAKING CONNECTIONS** question, which asks students to compare different constituencies in Reagan's coalition, would best be answered in the form of a chart, with one row for each group and a column for each factor in the question — region, class, and race.

TRM Find complete suggested responses in the Teacher's Resource Materials.

AP® APPLY THE TIP

Divide the class into two teams to set up a debate on the effectiveness of Reaganomics as an economic policy. One team should argue that Reaganomics was an effective economic policy for the U.S.; the other should argue the opposite — Reaganomics was not an effective policy. Allow each team time to find written sources, quantitative data, and excerpts from historians to support their stance, and to write a thesis statement that addresses the following prompt: To what degree did the goals and effects of Reaganomics have a positive influence on the development of the U.S.? Teams should compile their evidence into a slideshow presentation (only 8–10 slides) and present their evidence to the class. After both presentations, lead a class discussion on the ways both teams used evidence to support their thesis, and address the following questions (answers will vary):

- **Did both groups use any of the same evidence? How was the evidence used for different purposes?**
- **Does the thematic "lens" through which you look at Reaganomics impact how you evaluate its impact?**
- **Was Reaganomics a strictly economic policy? Or, was it also a rejection of social philosophy?**
- **What was the lasting legacy of Reaganomics?**

AP® THEME

PCE: Politics and Power

Lead a class discussion on how conservatives argued that liberal programs were counter-productive in fighting poverty and stimulating economic growth. Some of their efforts to reduce the size and scope of government met with inertia and liberal opposition, as many programs remained popular with voters.

AP® SKILLS & PROCESSES

ANALYZING HISTORICAL EVIDENCE

Use **FIGURE 29.1** to illustrate the way that some of Reagan's values clashed with others. On one hand, he advocated balanced budgets as a key element of government responsibility. On the other, he valued tax cuts and increased military spending (in large part to counter communism), which prompted unprecedented annual deficits and, consequently, a massive federal debt.

act reduced income tax rates for most Americans by 23 percent over three years. For the wealthiest Americans — those with millions to invest — the highest marginal tax rate dropped from 70 to 50 percent. The act also slashed estate taxes, levies dating from the Progressive Era aimed at curtailing the transmission of huge fortunes from one generation to the next. Finally, the new legislation trimmed the taxes paid by business corporations by $150 billion over a period of five years. As a result of ERTA, by 1986 the annual revenue of the federal government dropped by $200 billion (nearly half a trillion in 2020 dollars, or roughly the gross domestic product of Norway).

David Stockman, Reagan's budget director, hoped to match this reduction in tax revenue with a comparable cutback in federal expenditures on Social Security and Medicare. But Congress, and even the president himself, rejected Stockman's idea; they were not willing to antagonize middle-class and elderly voters who viewed those entitlements as sacred. As conservative columnist George Will noted ironically, "Americans are conservative. What they want to conserve is the New Deal." After defense spending, Social Security and Medicare were by far the nation's largest items on the federal budget; pruning other programs could not achieve the large spending reduction required to offset tax cuts. This contradiction between New Right Republican ideology and political reality would continue to frustrate the GOP into the twenty-first century.

There were more immediate, and embarrassing, issues related to supply-side economics. In a 1982 *Atlantic* article, Stockman admitted that the theory was based on faith, not economics. To produce optimistic projections of higher tax revenue in future years, Stockman had manipulated the figures. Worse, the White House bureaucrat told the *Atlantic* reporter candidly that supply-side theory was based on the long-discredited idea that helping the rich would eventually benefit the lower and middle classes — what was derided as "trickle-down" economics. Stockman had drawn back the curtain, much to Republicans' consternation, on the flawed reasoning of supply-side theory. But it was too late. The tax cut had passed Congress, and since Stockman could not slash major programs such as Social Security and Medicare, he had few options to balance the budget.

With budget cuts not making up for the falling tax revenue, the federal budget deficit increased dramatically. Military spending contributed a large share of the growing national debt, but President Reagan would not budge. "Defense is not a budget item," he declared. "You spend what you need." Reagan and Defense Secretary Caspar Weinberger pushed a five-year, $1.2 trillion military spending program through Congress in 1981. During Reagan's presidency, military spending accounted for one-fourth of all federal expenditures and contributed to both rising annual budget deficits (the amount overspent by the government in a single year) and a skyrocketing national debt (the cumulative total of all budget deficits). Despite pledging fiscal conservatism, Reagan oversaw a tripling of the federal debt in his two terms, rising from $930 billion in 1981 to $2.8 trillion in 1989 (Figure 29.1).

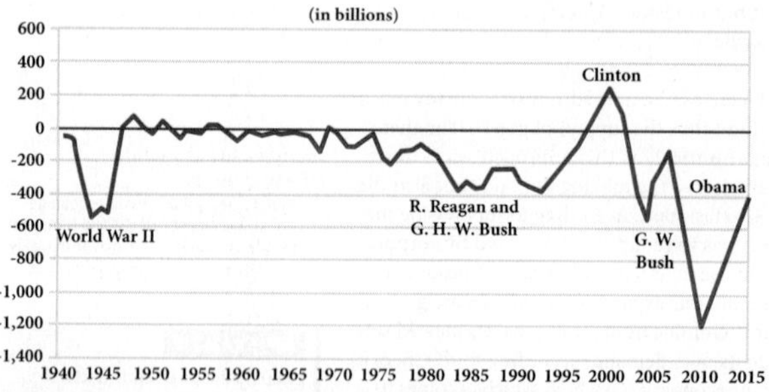

FIGURE 29.1 The Annual Federal Budget Deficit (or Surplus), 1940–2015

During World War II, the federal government incurred an enormous budget deficit. But between 1946 and 1965, it ran either an annual budget surplus or incurred a relatively small debt. The annual deficits rose significantly during the Vietnam War and the stagflation of the 1970s, but they really exploded between 1982 and 1994, in the budgets devised by the Ronald Reagan and George H. W. Bush administrations, and again between 2002 and 2005, in those prepared by George W. Bush. The Republican presidents increased military spending while cutting taxes, a budgetary policy that produced deficits.

Deregulation Advocates of Reaganomics asserted that excessive regulation by federal agencies impeded economic growth. Deregulation of prices in the trucking, airline, and railroad industries had begun under President Carter in the late 1970s, on the theory, since proven correct, that the public would reap results in lower transportation costs. But Reagan expanded the mandate to include cutting back on government protections of consumers, workers, and the environment — cuts whose benefits to the public were less clear. Some of the targeted federal bureaucracies, such as the U.S. Department of Labor, had risen to prominence during the New Deal; others, such as the Occupational Safety and Health Administration (OSHA) and the Environmental Protection Agency (EPA), had been created during the Johnson and Nixon administrations. Although these agencies provided many services to business corporations, they also increased their costs — by protecting the rights of workers, mandating safety improvements in factories, and requiring expensive equipment to comply with environmental standards. In 1981, the Reagan administration cut the budgets of these and other federal regulatory agencies by an average of 12 percent.

Reagan also weakened regulatory agencies by staffing them with leaders who were inherently opposed to the agencies' missions. James Watt, an outspoken conservative who headed the Department of the Interior, attacked environmentalism as "a left-wing cult." Acting on free-enterprise principles, Watt opened public lands for use by private businesses — oil and coal corporations, large-scale ranchers, and timber companies. Anne Gorsuch Burford, whom Reagan appointed to head the EPA, likewise disparaged environmentalists and refused to cooperate with Congress to clean up toxic waste sites around the country. The Sierra Club and other environmental groups worked to raise enough public outrage about these appointees that the administration changed its position. Both Watt and Burford left their posts before the end of Reagan's first term, and in the president's second term he significantly increased the EPA's budget and added acreage to the National Wilderness Preservation System and animals and plants to the endangered species lists — a significant turnaround from his early years in office.

"MAYBE HE SHOULD BE CITED FOR CONTEMPT OF PUBLIC INTELLIGENCE"
THIS IS A WILDERNESS PROTECTION BILL
WATT

Deregulation An editorial cartoon published in the *Washington Post* in 1982 depicting James Watt, secretary of interior during the Reagan administration, driving a steam shovel through the wilderness. According to the cartoonist, destroying nature is Watt's idea of a "Wilderness Protection Bill." Reagan appointees like Watt pursued "deregulation," the reduction or weakening of regulatory rules put in place in earlier decades to protect the environment, workplace safety, and consumers. A 1982 Herblock Cartoon, © The Herb Block Foundation.

AP® EXAM TIP

Analyze the policy of deregulation in the context of economic changes beginning in the 1970s.

Politics is sometimes called "the art of the possible," and Reagan understood the limits of what he could accomplish — and what he could not. Having attained two big goals — a major tax cut and a dramatic increase in defense spending — Reagan tempered his rollback of government regulation and the welfare state. When he left office in 1989, federal spending stood at 22.1 percent of the gross domestic product (GDP) and federal taxes at 19 percent of GDP, both virtually the same as in 1981, the first year of his presidency. In the meantime, in addition to the tripling of the federal debt, the number of government workers had increased from 2.9 to 3.1 million. The president's rhetoric about balancing budgets and downsizing government looked empty — which elicited harsh criticism from some right-wing commentators. "There was no Reagan Revolution," one conservative stated flatly. A former Reagan aide offered a more sympathetic assessment: "Ronald Reagan did far less than he had hoped . . . and a hell of a lot more than people thought he would."

AP® SKILLS & PROCESSES

CAUSATION

Why was Reagan unable to reduce federal expenditures by as much as many of his supporters wished?

TEACHING STRATEGY

One of the legacies of Ronald Reagan was his role as an advocate of lower taxes for Americans, yet he paradoxically believed Americans wanted and should have access to many of the government programs from the New Deal such as Social Security. Ask students to reconcile Reagan's legacy with that of the reality over government spending.

AP® SKILLS & PROCESSES

CAUSATION

To answer the **CAUSATION** question, students should consider the degree to which this outcome was a result of Reagan's own actions or factors beyond his control.

TRM Find complete suggested responses in the Teacher's Resource Materials.

TEACHING STRATEGY

In 1989, as the Reagan era gave way to the Bush era, the *Washington Post* ran an article titled "How Sandra Day O'Connor Became the Most Powerful Woman in 1980s America." This article is a helpful way for students to explore the significance of the first woman justice on the Supreme Court, as well as her frequent position as the swing vote on highly debated cases. To access this article, search "Washington Post Sandra Day O'Connor powerful woman."

Women on the Supreme Court In 1981, Sandra Day O'Connor, pictured here, was appointed to the Supreme Court by President Ronald Reagan, the first woman to serve on the Court. In 1993, she was joined by Ruth Bader Ginsburg, an appointee of President Bill Clinton. O'Connor emerged as a leader of the moderate bloc on the Court during the 1990s; she retired in 2006. President Barack Obama appointed two women to the court, Sonia Sotomayor in 2009 and Elena Kagan in 2010. Wally McNamee/Getty Images.

Remaking the Judiciary Even if he did not deliver everything he promised, Reagan left an indelible imprint on politics, public policy, and American culture. The federal judiciary was remade by Reagan and his attorney general, Edwin Meese, to push out the liberal judicial philosophy that had prevailed since the 1950s. During his two terms, Reagan appointed 368 federal court judges — most of them with conservative credentials — and three Supreme Court justices: Sandra Day O'Connor (1981), Antonin Scalia (1986), and Anthony Kennedy (1988). Ironically, O'Connor and Kennedy proved far less devoted to New Right conservatism than Reagan and his supporters imagined. O'Connor, the first woman to serve on the Court, became a swing vote between liberals and conservatives. Kennedy also emerged as a judicial moderate, leaving Scalia as Reagan's only genuinely conservative appointee.

But Reagan also elevated Justice William Rehnquist, a conservative Nixon appointee, to the position of chief justice. Under Rehnquist's leadership (1986–2005), the Court's conservatives took an activist stance, limiting the reach of federal laws, ending court-ordered busing, and endorsing constitutional protection of property rights. However, on controversial issues such as individual liberties, abortion rights, affirmative action, and the rights of criminal defendants, the presence of O'Connor swung the Court to a more centrist position. Under Rehnquist, the Supreme Court scaled back, but did not usually overturn, the liberal rulings of the Warren and Burger Courts. In the controversial *Webster v. Reproductive Health Services* (1989), for instance, Scalia pushed for the justices to overturn the abortion-rights decision of *Roe v. Wade* (1973). O'Connor refused, but she nonetheless approved the constitutional validity of state laws limiting the use of public funds and facilities for abortions. Centrists prevailed on only a handful of major issues, however, and the ideological tilt rightward of the federal judiciary would prove a significant institutional legacy of the Reagan presidency.

TEACHING STRATEGY

The *Frontline* film *The Age of AIDS*, which can be streamed from PBS's Web site, explores the emergence of the disease and the public response to it by various elements of the American public, including an extended look at the Reagan administration's response. The companion Web site provides extensive resources for teaching about AIDS, including primary sources, interactive maps and timeline, and interviews. To access these resources, search "PBS Frontline Age of AIDS."

HIV/AIDS
A deadly disease that killed nearly 100,000 people in the United States in the 1980s and to date has killed more than 30 million worldwide.

HIV/AIDS Reagan's complex legacy also includes the poor government response to one of the worst epidemics of the postwar decades. The human immunodeficiency virus (HIV), a slow-acting but deadly pathogen, emerged in Africa when a chimpanzee virus jumped to humans; immigrants carried it to Haiti and then to the United States during the 1970s. In 1981, American physicians identified HIV as a new virus — one that eventually led to a disease called acquired immune deficiency syndrome (AIDS). By the early 1980s, hundreds of gay men, who were prominent among the earliest carriers of the virus, were dying from AIDS and related conditions. **HIV/AIDS** spread worldwide, and by the end of the twentieth century the fast-spreading virus was carried by more than 40 million people of both sexes. To date, the virus has killed more than 30 million people around the globe.

Within the United States, AIDS took nearly one hundred thousand lives in the 1980s — more than the Korean and Vietnam Wars combined. However, because its most visible early victims were gay men, President Reagan, emboldened by New Right conservatives, hesitated in declaring a national health emergency. Some presidential advisors even asserted that this "gay disease" might be a divine retribution against homosexuals. Between 1981 and 1986, as the epidemic spread, the Reagan administration took little action, and blocked the surgeon general, C. Everett Koop, from speaking forthrightly

TEACHING STRATEGY

Students sometimes struggle to identify and explain the social issues concomitant to Reagan's era. Think about providing historical topics such as HIV/AIDS, family values of evangelical Christian churches, and the condition of inner cities. Have students explain the ways in which the Reagan administration reacted to these social issues.

HIV/AIDS and the Politics of Public Health The HIV/AIDS epidemic struck the United States in the early 1980s and has remained a major public health issue ever since. The Reagan administration's slow and ineffectual response to the crisis led gay rights activists to found ACT UP (AIDS Coalition to Unleash Power) in 1987, which engaged in militant protests designed to force the federal government to increase support for research and care. In the 1994 New York City Gay Pride parade pictured here, ACT UP supporters hold aloft posters with the ACT UP slogan "Silence = Death." Allan Tannenbaum/Getty Images.

to the nation about the disease. Late in Reagan's second term, under pressure from gay activists and health officials, the administration finally began to devote federal resources to treatment and research. Their delay came at the expense of human lives.

Morning in America

During his first run for governor of California in 1966, Reagan had a revelation while speaking with a campaign consultant. "Politics is just like the movies," Reagan told him. "You have a hell of an opening, coast for a while, and then have a hell of a close." The actor-turned-president did just that. Following a lavish inauguration, he quickly won passage of his tax cuts and launched a plan to bolster military spending for the Pentagon. But a long "coasting" period followed, during which Reagan retreated on tax cuts and navigated a major foreign policy misjudgment — known as the Iran-Contra scandal. Finally, toward the end of his two-term presidency, Reagan had his "hell of a close," leaving office as major reforms — which he had encouraged from afar — helped to tear apart the Soviet Union and end the Cold War. Through all the ups and downs, Reagan remained a master of the politics of symbolism, championing a resurgent American economy and reassuring the country that the pursuit of wealth was noble and that he had the reins of the nation firmly in hand.

AP® EXAM TIP

Compare the view of America popularized by Reagan with the view supported by Herbert Hoover.

Election of 1984 Reagan's "coasting" period began shortly after his 1981 tax reduction package passed. Reaganites cheered these supply-side cuts, but economic

CHECK FOR UNDERSTANDING

Ask students: **What were the consequences of conservatives being in power?** *Reagan instituted his policy of "supply-side economics," which assumed that tax cuts for the wealthiest Americans and lesser cuts for the middle class would generate new investments in business and industry, producing new wealth that could be taxed. At the same time, his administration hoped to slash social spending, but most Americans — and Reagan himself — resisted cuts to Social Security and Medicare. And since Reagan increased, rather than reduced, military spending, the national debt increased. Budget director David Stockman admitted that this "trickle-down" economics was a faith-based plan based on discredited economics. He pursued deregulation by reducing the staffs and budgets of federal regulatory agencies. Reagan was able to make three Supreme Court appointees, though Sandra Day O'Connor, the first woman justice, turned out to be much more of a moderate than Reagan anticipated. Finally, conservatives were slow to respond to the emerging AIDS crisis, as they often blamed gays and promiscuity for the disease.*

AP® APPLY THE TIP

Lead a class discussion by asking students to identify the ideas supported by Herbert Hoover in the Great Depression, often referred to as "Rugged Individualism," and list students' ideas on the board. Ask students to read excerpts from speeches by Ronald Reagan and think about how Reagan's views compared to Hoover's. Using pp. 949–954, which detail Reagan's policies and legislative accomplishments, students should determine if Reagan and Hoover were more similar or more different in their views of America. Then ask students to discuss the following prompt: If Reagan and Hoover had similar views, why was Reagan so popular while Hoover was generally disliked?

TEACHING STRATEGY

In his article "The Ad That Helped Reagan Sell Good Times to an Uncertain Nation," Michael Beschloss explores the famous "Morning in America" ad and explains why it resonated so well with American audiences at the time. Filled with nostalgia, the ad hearkened to a supposedly simpler time. The article imbeds the original one-minute ad for students to view. To access this article, search "NYT Beschloss Ad That Helped Reagan."

conditions forced a reversal by the president. High interest rates set by the Federal Reserve Board had eased the runaway inflation of the Carter years. But these rates — as high as 18 percent — sent the economy into a recession that put 10 million Americans out of work and shuttered 17,000 businesses in 1981–1982. Unemployment neared 10 percent, the highest rate since the Great Depression. These troubles, combined with the booming deficit, forced Reagan to negotiate a tax increase with Congress in 1982 — to the loud complaints of supply-side diehards. The president's poll numbers plummeted, and in the 1982 midterm elections Democrats increased their majority in the House of Representatives by twenty-six seats and won seven state governorships.

Fortunately for Reagan, the economy had recovered by 1983, boosting his approval rating just in time for the 1984 presidential election. During the campaign, Reagan toured the country promoting his tax policies and the nation's restored prosperity. The Democrats nominated former vice president Walter Mondale of Minnesota. With strong ties to labor unions, a variety of ethnic and racial groups, and party leaders, Mondale epitomized the remaining strength of the New Deal coalition. He selected Representative Geraldine Ferraro of New York as his running mate — the first woman to run on the presidential ticket of a major political party. Neither Ferraro's presence nor Mondale's credentials made a difference, however: Reagan won a landslide victory, losing only Minnesota and the District of Columbia. Still, Democrats retained their majority in the House and, in the 1986 midterm elections, won back the Senate. Despite the fragility of the New Deal coalition and the "Reagan revolution" pushing to topple it, the Democratic Party retained much of its congressional influence through the decade of the 1980s.

Reagan's 1984 campaign slogan, "It's Morning in America," reflected his political mythology: the sun was forever coming up on an optimistic nation of small towns, close-knit families, and kindly neighbors. "The success story of America," he once said, "is neighbor helping neighbor." The reality of the nation — which was overwhelmingly urban and suburban, with hard knock capitalism holding down as many as it elevated — mattered little. Reagan's remarkable ability to produce positive associations and feelings, alongside robust economic growth after the 1981–1982 recession, defined an era characterized by both backward-facing nostalgia and aggressive, future-oriented capitalism.

Return to Prosperity Between 1945 and the 1970s, the United States was the world's leading exporter of agricultural products, manufactured goods, and investment capital. But American manufacturers lost market share to cheaper and better-designed products from West Germany and Japan. By 1985, for the first time since 1915, the United States registered a negative balance of international payments. The country imported more goods and capital than it exported, becoming a debtor (rather than a creditor) nation. The rapid ascent of the Japanese economy to become the world's second largest was a key factor in this historic reversal. More than one-third of the American annual trade deficit of $138 billion in the 1980s belonged to Japan, whose corporations exported huge quantities of electronic goods and made nearly one-quarter of all cars bought in the United States.

Meanwhile, American businesses grappled with a slowdown in an important measure. Between 1973 and 1992, American productivity (the amount of goods or services per hour of work) grew at the meager rate of 1 percent a year — a far cry from the post- World War II rate of 3 percent. Because managers wanted to cut costs, the wages of most employees stagnated. Further, foreign competition had shrunk the number of high-paying, union-protected manufacturing jobs. By 1985, more people in the United States were slinging Big Macs at McDonald's than rolling out heavy metal in the nation's steel industry.

A brief return to competitiveness in the second half of the 1980s masked the steady long-term transformation of the economy that had begun in the 1970s. The nation's heavy industries — steel, autos, chemicals — continued to lose market share

AP® EXAM TIP

Explain why the shift from a manufacturing-based to a service-based economy continued through the 1980s and 1990s.

AP® THEME

WXT: Work, Exchange, and Technology

As discussed in the previous chapter, employment increased in service sectors and decreased in manufacturing, and union membership declined.

AP® APPLY THE TIP

Ask students to use pp. 954-958 to complete **Handout 29.2 — Causation: Shift to a Service Economy (TRM)**. Students should use quantitative data to support their understanding of the shift from manufacturing to service-based jobs in the U.S. Then organize students into collaborative groups and prompt students to pretend that they are on a task force that must make recommendations on public policy to help the U.S.'s workforce adjust to the service-based economy. Using the data collected and the textbook, groups should provide three recommendations for public policy. Have each group share its ideas with the class to lead a class discussion on the continuing impact of economic change on issues such as unemployment, education, trade, and welfare.

TRM Find complete suggested responses and **Handout 29.2 — Causation: Shift to a Service Economy** in the Teacher's Resource Materials.

to global competitors. Nevertheless, the U.S. economy grew at the impressive average rate of 2 to 3 percent per year for much of the late 1980s and 1990s (with a short recession in 1990–1991). But the direction of growth and its beneficiaries had changed. Increasingly, the expansion came in financial services, medical services, and computer technology — service industries, broadly speaking. This shift in the underlying foundation of the American economy, from manufacturing to service, from making *things* to providing *services*, would have long-term consequences for the global competitiveness of U.S. businesses and the value of the dollar.

AP® SKILLS & PROCESSES

COMPARISON

How would you compare the foundation of the American economy in the 1920s with its foundation in the 1980s?

Culture of Success Every era since the Gilded Age has had its capitalist giants, but Americans in the 1980s celebrated success in ways unseen since the 1920s. When the president christened self-made entrepreneurs "the heroes for the eighties," he probably had people like Lee Iacocca in mind. Born to Italian immigrants and trained as an engineer, Iacocca rose through the ranks to become president of the Ford Motor Corporation. In 1978, he took over the ailing Chrysler Corporation and made it profitable again — by securing a crucial $1.5 billion loan from the U.S. government, pushing the development of new cars, and selling those new Chryslers on TV. His patriotic commercials in the 1980s echoed Reagan's rhetoric: "Let's make American mean something again."

Iacocca symbolized the desire to see a resurgent American industrialism, but high-profile financial wheeler-dealers also captured the public imagination. One was Ivan Boesky, a white-collar criminal convicted of insider trading (buying or selling stock based on information from corporate insiders). "I think greed is healthy," Boesky told a business school graduating class. Boesky inspired the fictional character Gordon Gekko, who proclaimed "Greed is good!" in the hit 1987 film *Wall Street*. His outlook suited a new generation of Wall Street executives who embraced a novel business tactic: the leveraged buyout (LBO). In a typical LBO, a financier used heavily leveraged (borrowed) capital to buy a company, quickly restructured that company to make it appear spectacularly profitable, and then sold it at a higher price — repaying the borrowed purchase price and keeping the difference.

American culture still valued the ethic of hard work, but the Reagan-era public did have a certain fascination with money and celebrity — fed by magazines such as *Us* and *People* and television programs such as *Lifestyles of the Rich and Famous*. One particular money mogul captivated — and cultivated — public attention. In 1983, the flamboyant Donald Trump built the equally flamboyant Trump Tower in New York City. At the entrance of the $200 million apartment building stood two enormous bronze *T*s, a display of self-promotion that earned him a media following. Calling him "The Donald," a nickname used by Trump's first wife, TV reporters and magazines commented relentlessly on his marriages, girlfriends, and glitzy lifestyle. Trading on his celebrity as much as his business acumen, Trump would eventually forge a career on reality television and, in one of the most unexpected political developments of the early twentieth-first century, successfully run for president as a Republican in 2016.

Lifestyles of the Rich and Famous The 1980s witnessed a celebration of wealth and success unlike anything seen in the United States since the Gilded Age. Movies, television, and magazines praised the wealthy and portrayed the rich as hard-working and noble rather than selfish or greedy. Pictured here is the television host, Robin Leach, whose program *Lifestyles of the Rich and Famous*, offered ordinary Americans watching TV in their modest living rooms tours of the yachts, mansions, and palatial estates of wealthy celebrities and business executives. Donaldson Collection/Getty Images.

The Computer Revolution While Trump and other swashbuckling tycoons grabbed headlines and made splashy investments, a handful of quieter, less flashy entrepreneurs was busy reshaping the American economy. Programmers such as Bill Gates, Paul Allen, Steve Jobs, and Steve Wozniak pioneered a computer revolution in the late 1970s and 1980s (see "Thinking Like a Historian," p. 956).

AP® SKILLS & PROCESSES

COMPARISON

The **COMPARISON** question asks students to compare the growing economy of the 1980s with a similar pattern from earlier in the century. Students might identify the political context, the rate of economic growth, and the economic sectors that experienced growth. Extend this prompt by asking students to evaluate the significance of the global economy for the situation in the 1980s, a pattern that was largely the result of American postwar leadership.

TRM Find complete suggested responses in the Teacher's Resource Materials.

TEACHING STRATEGY

In his article "Meet Ivan Boesky, The Infamous Wall Streeter Who Inspired Gordon Gekko," Myles Meserve provides a biography of Boesky's rise and fall in a series of slides. Along the way, he explores the way Boesky provided the model for the protagonist of *Wall Street*. To access this article, search "Business Insider Meet Ivan Boesky."

AP® SKILLS & PROCESSES

ANALYZING HISTORICAL EVIDENCE

The **AP® THINKING LIKE A HISTORIAN** feature provides an opportunity for students to explore Americans' early relationship with computers and computer-based technology. As an extension to this discussion, it might be helpful for students to examine contemporary concerns about the growing harmful potential of artificial intelligence capabilities. *Vanity Fair* discusses Elon Musk's concern about artificial intelligence in an extended article by Maureen Dowd titled "Elon Musk's Billion-Dollar Crusade to Stop the A.I. Apocalypse." To access this article, search "Vanity Fair Maureen Dowd Elon Musk."

AP® THINKING LIKE A HISTORIAN

Personal Computing: A Technological Revolution

Considered historically, computers are a strikingly new phenomenon. The ancestors of the first computers were developed in the 1940s using vacuum tubes and transistors. Integrated circuits were introduced in the 1950s and the first microprocessor in the 1970s. Prior to the decade of the 1980s, only the federal government and large corporations and institutions used computers, which were massive in size and expensive to purchase. In the 1980s, inventors and entrepreneurs developed the first "personal" computers, which could fit on desks or tables and were soon within the price range of ordinary families. The computers we know today date from that decade. Another enormous change came in the mid-1990s, when the Internet, whose forerunner was a U.S. Defense Department computer network, became widely available to the public for the first time.

1. **Moore's law, 1965.** *In 1965, the electronics engineer Gordon Moore calculated that the number of transistors on an integrated circuit doubled roughly every two years, meaning that the power of computers was increasing at that rate.*

   The complexity for minimum component costs has increased at a rate of roughly a factor of two per year. Certainly over the short term this rate can be expected to continue, if not increase. . . . That means by 1975, the number of components per integrated circuit for minimum cost will be 65,000.

   I believe that such a large circuit can be built on a single wafer.

2. **Scene from *2001: A Space Odyssey*, 1968.** *In this scene from an acclaimed science fiction film, a space station's computer system, named HAL, defends itself against an astronaut who is determined to shut down the computer.*

   Dave Bowman: Hello, HAL. Do you read me, HAL?
   HAL: Affirmative, Dave. I read you.
   DB: Open the pod bay doors, HAL.
   HAL: I'm sorry, Dave. I'm afraid I can't do that.
   DB: What's the problem?
   HAL: I think you know what the problem is just as well as I do.
   DB: What are you talking about, HAL?
   HAL: This mission is too important for me to allow you to jeopardize it.
   DB: I don't know what you're talking about, HAL.
   HAL: I know that you and Frank were planning to disconnect me, and I'm afraid that's something I cannot allow to happen.
   DB: Where the hell did you get that idea, HAL?
   HAL: Dave, although you took very thorough precautions in the pod against my hearing you, I could see your lips move.
   DB: Alright, HAL. I'll go in through the emergency airlock.
   HAL: Without your space helmet, Dave? You're going to find that rather difficult.
   DB: HAL, I won't argue with you anymore! Open the door!
   HAL: Dave, this conversation can serve no purpose anymore. Goodbye.

3. **Neil Ardley, *World of Tomorrow: School, Work, and Play*, 1981.** *In this book written for teenagers, Neil Ardley speculated about the future of computers.*

   Imagine you are living in the future, and are doing a project on Halley's comet. It's quite some time since it last appeared in 1986, and you want to find out when it will again be seen from Earth. You also want to know the results of a space mission to the comet, and find out what the comet is made of.

   In the days when the last comet appeared, you would have had to look up Halley's comet in an encyclopedia or a book on astronomy. If you didn't possess these books, you would have gone to the library to get the information. . . .

   People still collect books as valuable antiques or for a hobby, but you get virtually all the information you need from the viewscreen of your home computer. The computer is linked to a library — not a library of books but an electronic library where information on every subject is stored in computer memory banks. . . .

   Computers will make the world of tomorrow a much safer place. They will do away with cash, so that you need no longer fear being attacked for your money. In addition, you need not worry that your home will be burgled or your car stolen. The computers in your home and car will guard them, allowing only yourself to enter or someone with your permission.

4. **Scene from *Terminator*, 1984.** *A national defense computer network called Skynet decides to exterminate humanity in the film* Terminator.

   Reese: There was a war. A few years from now. Nuclear war. The whole thing. All this — [His gesture includes the car, the city, the world.] — everything is gone. Just gone.

There were survivors. Here. There. Nobody knew who started it. (pause) It was the machines.

Sarah: I don't understand. . . .

Reese: Defense network computer. New. Powerful. Hooked into everything. Trusted to run it all. They say it got smart . . . a new order of intelligence. Then it saw all people as a threat, not just the ones on the other side. Decided our fate in a microsecond . . . extermination.

5. Interview with Steve Jobs, February 1, 1985. *Apple founder Steve Jobs, one of the pioneers of the personal computer, discusses the future of computers and computer networks.*

Question: Why should a person buy a computer?

Steve Jobs: There are different answers for different people. In business, that question is easy to answer: You can really prepare documents much faster and at a higher quality level, and you can do many things to increase office productivity. A computer frees people from much of the menial work. . . . Remember computers are tools. Tools help us do our work better. In education, computers are the first thing to come along since books that will sit there and interact with you endlessly, without judgment. . . .

Question: What will change?

Steve Jobs: The most compelling reason for most people to buy a computer for the home [in the future] will be to link it into a nationwide communications network. We're just in the beginning stages of what will be a truly remarkable breakthrough for most people — as remarkable as the telephone.

6. Percentage of Americans Using the Internet, 1990–2006. *Though ubiquitous today, Internet usage is a very recent historical development, surging primarily in the second half of the 1990s.*

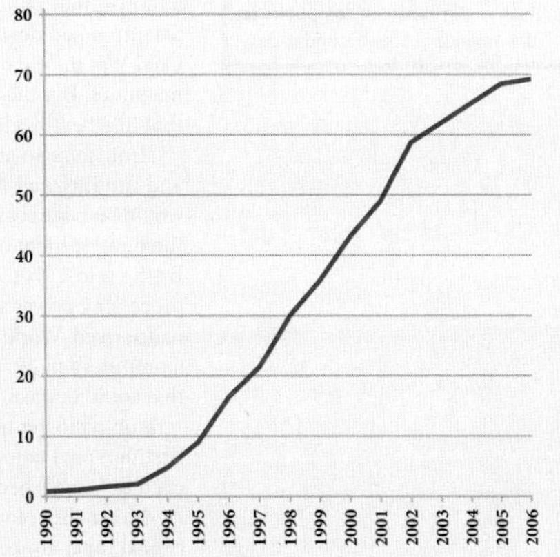

Sources: (1) G. E. Moore, "Cramming More Components onto Integrated Circuits," *Electronics*, April 19, 1965, 114; (2) *2001: A Space Odyssey*, Screenplay by Stanley Kubrick and Arthur C. Clarke (Hawk Films Ltd. and MGM Studios, 1967); (3) Neil Ardley, *World of Tomorrow: School, Work, and Play* (New York: Franklin Watts, 1981), 20–27; (4) *Terminator*, Screenplay by James Cameron and Gale Anne Hurd, Fifth Draft (Pacific Western Productions, Inc., March 11, 1984), 134; (5) *Playboy*, February 1, 1985, 52.

ANALYZING THE EVIDENCE

1. Compare sources 2 and 4. Anxiety about the extraordinary power of computers has been a regular feature of science fiction, both in writing and in film, since the late 1950s. What do the scenes from these two films tell us about the cultural reactions to computers early in their development?
2. How does source 3 offer a different vision of a future with computers? Using evidence from the chapter, account for the existence of both extreme anxiety and equally extreme optimism?
3. How does Steve Jobs's assessment of computers in source 5 compare with those in the other documents? Given Job's historical situation, how credible is this source? Explain your reasoning.

AP® DBQ PRACTICE

Using these sources, along with what you have learned in this chapter, write a short essay in which you assess the origin of the personal computer. What cultural reactions and predictions surrounded the computer's birth? What economic and social transformations did it have the potential to unleash? Compare reactions to the Industrial Revolution of the second half of the nineteenth century and the "computer revolution" of the late twentieth century. How did each development transform American society?

TRM Find complete suggested responses in the Teacher's Resource Materials.

AP® SKILLS & PROCESSES

ARGUMENTATION

In responding to the **AP® DBQ PRACTICE** prompt, encourage students to bracket what they already know about computers and how they developed after the 1980s, and try to understand as clearly as possible what Americans at that time anticipated — or failed to anticipate.

CHECK FOR UNDERSTANDING

Ask students: **What were the major political successes and failures of the Reagan coalition?** *The major successes of the Reagan coalition included deregulation to aid businesses and remaking the judiciary with conservative (non-activist) judges. Failures of the Reagan coalition include supply-side economics and the slow response to the HIV/AIDS crisis.*

AP® SKILLS & PROCESSES

DEVELOPMENTS AND PROCESSES

The 1980s ushered in a time of individualism in economic success due to a variety of factors. Have students select technological innovation, consumerism, or conformity—terms students should be familiar with from earlier in the year—to explain this historical development.

TRM Find complete suggested responses in the Teacher's Resource Materials.

AP® APPLY THE TIP

Divide students into pairs and instruct the pairs to use their notes, text, or other sources to complete **Handout 29.3 — Comparison: Ronald Reagan Foreign Policy (TRM)**. Students should discuss the key terms, goals, methods, and major events for each president listed on the handout. After students fill out the handout with details, provide pairs with a large sheet of poster paper and ask students to develop a thesis statement and outline to respond to the following prompt: To what extent were Ronald Reagan's policies responsible for the fall of communism? Then reorganize student groups so that each group contains three pairs of students. The newly formed groups should share their thesis statements and outlines in order to discuss the similarities and differences in their responses and evaluate the use of evidence in their outlines. Ask students to begin to connect their theses with AP® Themes. On a new sheet of poster paper, ask each group to write a thesis statement by either combining and modifying the different thesis statements or rewriting an entirely new thesis statement based on the group discussion. Post these new thesis statements and outlines of evidence around the room to lead a class discussion. Be sure to touch upon the similarities and differences between Reagan and the other Cold War presidents.

TRM Find **Handout 29.3 — Comparison: Ronald Reagan Foreign Policy** in the Teacher's Resource Materials.

AP® EXAM TIP

Analyze the impact of computers on the American economy and society.

They took a technology previously used only in large-scale enterprises — the military and multinational corporations — and made it accessible to individual consumers. Scientists had devised the first computers for military purposes during World War II. Cold War military research subsequently funded the construction of large mainframe machines. But these early institutional computers were bulky, cumbersome machines that filled entire climate-controlled rooms.

Ironically, in an age that celebrated free-market capitalism, government research and funding had played an enormous role in the development of a technology that would reshape society and culture. Between the 1950s and the 1970s, concluding with the development of the microprocessor in 1971, computers grew faster and smaller. By the mid-1970s, a few microchips the size of the letter *O* on this page held as much processing power as the massive early machines, and the day of the personal computer had arrived. Working in the San Francisco Bay Area, Jobs and Wozniak founded Apple Computers in 1976 and within a year were producing small, individual computers that could be easily used by a single person. As Apple found success, other companies scrambled to get into the market. International Business Machines (IBM) offered its first personal computer in 1981, but Apple's 1984 Macintosh computer (later shortened to "Mac") became personal computing's first runaway commercial success.

Meanwhile, former high school classmates, Gates, age nineteen, and Allen, age twenty-one, aimed to put "a personal computer on every desk and in every home." They recognized that software, rather than hardware, was the key. In 1975, they founded the Microsoft Corporation, whose MS-DOS and Windows operating systems soon dominated the software industry. By 2000, the company's products ran nine out of every ten personal computers in the United States and a majority of those around the world. Gates and Allen became billionaires, and Microsoft exploded into a huge company with more than 50,000 employees and annual revenues in the tens of billions of dollars. In three decades, the computer had spread from a few military research centers to thousands of corporate offices and then to millions of people's homes.

AP® SKILLS & PROCESSES

DEVELOPMENTS AND PROCESSES

In what ways did American society embrace economic success and individualism in the 1980s?

THE END OF THE COLD WAR

What were the aims of U.S. foreign policy at the close of the Cold War?

Ronald Reagan entered office determined to confront the Soviet Union diplomatically and militarily. Backed by Republican and Democratic hard-liners alike, Reagan unleashed some of the harshest Cold War rhetoric since the 1950s, labeling the Soviet Union an "evil empire" and vowing that it would end up "on the ash heap of history." However, by the end of his second term, Reagan was actively cooperating with Mikhail Gorbachev, the reform-minded Russian Communist leader. The downfall of the Soviet Union in 1991 ended the nearly fifty-year-long Cold War, but new international challenges quickly emerged.

U.S.-Soviet Relations in a New Era

AP® EXAM TIP

Compare the Cold War policies of Ronald Reagan to earlier presidents in the era.

When Reagan assumed the presidency in 1981, he broke with his immediate predecessors — especially Richard Nixon and Jimmy Carter — in Cold War strategy. Nixon had regarded himself as a "realist" in foreign affairs. Put simply, his realism meant advancing the national interest without regard to ideology. Nixon's policy of détente with the Soviet Union and China embodied this view (see "Nixon in Vietnam" in Chapter 27). President Carter endorsed détente and strove to further ease Cold War tensions. But the Soviet invasion of Afghanistan empowered hard-liners in the U.S. Congress and forced Carter to take a tougher line — which he did with the Olympic boycott and grain embargo. This was the relationship Reagan inherited in

1981: a decade of détente followed by a year of tense standoffs over Soviet advances into Central Asia, which threatened U.S. interests in the Middle East.

Reagan's Cold War Revival Most conservatives rejected both détente and the containment policy that had guided U.S. Cold War strategy since 1947. Reagan and his advisors wanted to diminish, not merely contain, Soviet influence. His administration pursued a two-pronged strategy toward that end. First, it set about re-arming America. Reagan's military budgets authorized new weapons systems and dramatically expanded military bases and the nation's nuclear arsenal. This buildup in American military strength, reasoned Secretary of Defense Caspar Weinberger, would force the Soviets into an arms race that would strain their economy and cause domestic unrest. To advance this plan, the Reagan administration entered into the Strategic Arms Reduction Talks (START) with the Soviet Union, in which the United States put forward a plan calculated to increase American advantage in sea- and air-based nuclear systems over the Soviet's ground-based system. Talks dragged on until a final settlement in 1991, but meanwhile Reagan and Weinberger had made their point to the Soviets: the Americans were ahead militarily.

Second, the president supported CIA initiatives to confront Soviet influence in the developing world, funding anticommunist movements in Angola, Mozambique, Afghanistan, and Central America. This policy often entailed supporting repressive, right-wing regimes. Nowhere was this more conspicuous than in the Central American countries of Guatemala, Nicaragua, and El Salvador. Conditions in those small countries followed a broad pattern: the United States sided with military dictatorships and oligarchies when democratically elected governments or left-wing movements sought support from the Soviet Union. In Guatemala, this approach produced a brutal military rule—thousands of opponents of the government were executed or kidnapped. In Nicaragua, Reagan actively encouraged a coup against the left-wing Sandinista government. And in El Salvador, the U.S.-backed government employed secret "death squads," which murdered larger numbers of political opponents. In each case, Soviet influence was thwarted, but at great cost to local communities and the international reputation of the United States.

Iran-Contra Determined oppositions to left-wing movements in Central America engulfed the Reagan administration in a major scandal that bridged two distinct parts of the globe. For years, Reagan had denounced Iran as an "outlaw state" and a supporter of terrorism. But in 1985, he wanted its assistance in freeing two dozen American hostages held by Hezbollah, a pro-Iranian Shiite group in Lebanon. As an enticement, the administration conducted a secret arms deal, selling weapons to Iran without public or congressional knowledge. The proceeds of this sale wound up in Nicaragua—and set off a major controversy. The CIA was already operating in the small Central American country to overthrow the democratically elected Sandinistas, a left-wing government whom the president accused of threatening U.S. business interests. Reagan ordered the intelligence agency to assist an armed opposition group called the Contras (Map 29.2). Although Reagan praised the right-wing Contras as "freedom fighters," reliable human rights groups accused them of attacking civilians and other abuses. In addition, Congress worried that the president and other executive branch agencies were

Iran-Contra The 1987 Iran-Contra congressional hearings, which lasted more than a month and were broadcast on live television, helped to uncover a secret and illegal White House scheme to provide arms to the Nicaraguan Contras. Though Lieutenant Colonial Oliver North (shown here during his testimony before Congress) concocted much of the scheme and was convicted of three felonies, he never served prison time and emerged from the hearings as a populist hero among American conservatives, who saw him as a patriot. Bettmann/Getty Images.

TEACHING STRATEGY

President Reagan's foreign policy was built on a concept called "Peace Through Strength." Have students evaluate both 'Peace' and 'Strength' with specific historical examples that explain the dual approaches of Reagan.

TEACHING STRATEGY

A May 5, 1989, article from *The Guardian* titled "Oliver North guilty of tricking Congress- archive, 1989" explains the charges against Oliver North and the guilty verdict returned by the jury. To access this article, search "Guardian Oliver North."

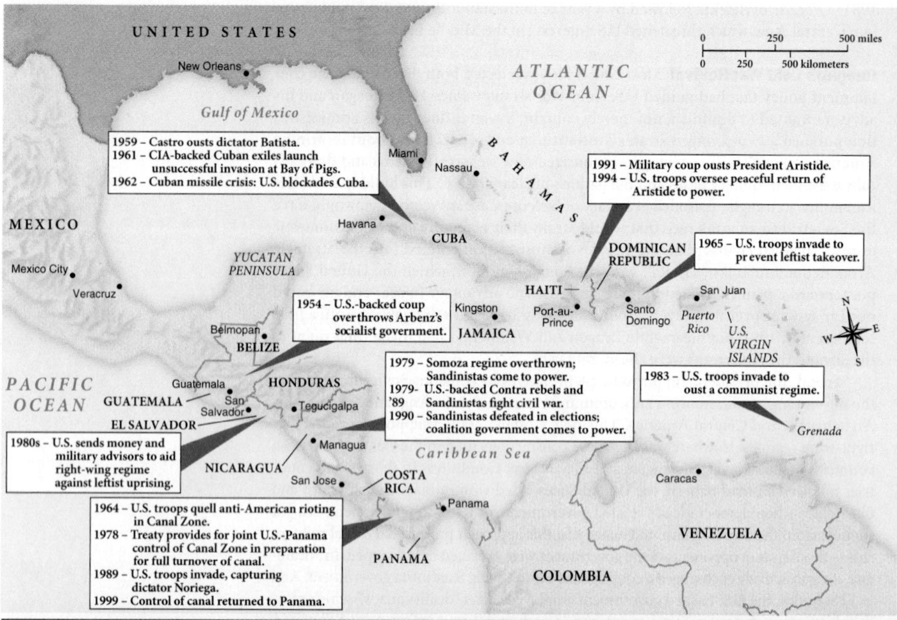

MAPPING THE PAST

MAP 29.2 U.S. Involvement in Latin America and the Caribbean, 1954–2000

Ever since the Monroe Doctrine (1823), the United States has claimed a special interest in Latin America. During the Cold War, American foreign policy throughout Latin America focused on containing instability and the appeal of communism in a region plagued by poverty and military dictatorships. Providing foreign aid was one approach to addressing social and economic needs, but the United States frequently intervened with military forces (or by supporting military coups) to remove unfriendly or socialist governments. The Reagan administration's support of the Contra rebels in Nicaragua, some of which was contrary to American law, was one of those interventions.

ANALYZING THE MAP: Study the events associated with each country, and note the dates. What kinds of events are documented and what was the American role in them?

MAKING CONNECTIONS: Was American support for the Contra rebels in Nicaragua during the 1980s similar to the involvement of the United States in other parts of the region? Using knowledge gained in this and earlier chapters in this book, explain the degree to which U.S. involvement in this region illustrates continuity as well as change over time.

assuming war-making powers that the Constitution reserved to the legislature. In 1984, Congress banned the CIA and all other government agencies from providing any military support to the Contras.

U.S. Marine Corps Lieutenant Colonial Oliver North, an aide to the National Security Council, defied that ban. With the tacit or explicit consent (whether tacit or explicit was never conclusively proved) of high-ranking administration officials, including the president, North used the profits from the Iranian arms deal to assist the Contras. When asked whether he knew of North's illegal actions, Reagan replied, "I don't remember." In an echo of the Watergate scandal, congressional hearings on what was dubbed the **Iran-Contra affair** were aired on live television for weeks in the summer of 1987, and journalists enthusiastically made comparisons to President Nixon's downfall. Called to testify, North admitted that he lied to cover up his illegal actions, but he declined to implicate Reagan in the scheme. North and several other

Iran-Contra affair
Reagan administration scandal that involved the sale of arms to Iran in exchange for its efforts to secure the release of hostages held in Lebanon and the redirection — illegal because banned by American law — of the proceeds of those sales to the Nicaraguan Contras.

TEACHING STRATEGY

MAP 29.2 places the Reagan administration's support for Nicaraguan Contra rebels in a larger historical context by illustrating American military interventions and coups over a half-century period. Also, not all interventions were designed to thwart communism; the U.S. intervened in Haiti, for example, to restore Aristide to power.

TRM Find complete suggested responses in the Teacher's Resource Materials.

AP® THEME

WOR: America in the World

Reagan asserted U.S. opposition to communism in a variety of ways — through speeches, diplomatic efforts, limited military interventions, and a buildup of both conventional and nuclear weapons. The Iran-Contra affair was one consequence of Reagan's zeal to fight communism. The Understanding the Iran-Contra Affairs Web site, available through Brown University, provides information about the rise of the Contra rebels in Nicaragua and about the Iranian Revolution, as well as the U.S. responses to both. The Web site also details the media's discovery and later press coverage of Iran-Contra, and the subsequent televised congressional hearings. To access this site, search "Brown University Understanding the Iran-Contra Affair."

officials were eventually prosecuted, and the scandal weakening Reagan at home — he proposed no bold domestic policy initiatives in his last two years. But the outcome of Watergate — a presidential resignation — was not repeated. Reagan avoided direct responsibility for North's actions and remained steadfastly engaged in international affairs, where the dramatic close to the Cold War was unfolding.

Gorbachev and Soviet Reform The Soviet system of state socialism and central planning had transformed largely agricultural Russia into an industrial society between 1917 and the 1950s. This massive change had been wrenching, and created an inefficient economy. Lacking the incentives of a market economy, most enterprises hoarded raw materials, employed too many workers, and did not develop new products. Except in military weaponry and space technology, the Russian economy fell far behind those of capitalist societies, and most people in the Soviet bloc endured a low standard of living. Moreover, the Soviet invasion of Afghanistan in 1979, like the American war in Vietnam, proved to be a major blunder — an unwinnable war that cost vast amounts of money, destroyed military morale, and undermined popular support of the government.

Mikhail Gorbachev, a relatively young Russian leader who became general secretary of the Communist Party in 1985, recognized the need for internal economic reform and an end to the quagmire in Afghanistan. The iconoclastic Gorbachev introduced policies of ***glasnost*** (openness) and ***perestroika*** (economic restructuring), which encouraged widespread criticism of the rigid institutions and authoritarian controls of the Communist regime. To lessen tensions with the United States, Gorbachev met with Reagan in 1985, and the two leaders established a warm personal rapport. By 1987, they had agreed to eliminate all intermediate-range nuclear missiles based in Europe. A year later, Gorbachev ordered Soviet troops out of Afghanistan, and Reagan replaced many of his hardline advisors with policymakers who favored a renewal of détente.

glasnost
The policy introduced by Soviet president Mikhail Gorbachev during the 1980s that involved greater openness and freedom of expression and that contributed, unintentionally, to the 1991 breakup of the Soviet Union.

perestroika
The economic restructuring policy introduced by Soviet president Mikhail Gorbachev during the 1980s that contributed, unintentionally, to the 1991 breakup of the Soviet Union.

Reagan's sudden reversal with regard to the Soviet Union worried conservatives — perhaps their cowboy-hero president had been duped by a duplicitous Gorbachev. But Reagan's gamble paid off. The easing of tensions with the United States allowed the Soviet leader to press forward with his domestic reforms. Encouraged by the loosening of control in Russia, between 1989 and 1991 the peoples of Eastern and Central Europe began to protest their own Communist governments. In Poland, the Roman Catholic Church and its pope — Polish-born John Paul II — joined with Solidarity, the trade-union movement, to overthrow the pro-Soviet regime. Twice in the 1950s, Russian troops had quashed similar popular uprisings in East Germany and Hungary. But under Gorbachev, they did not intervene, and a series of peaceful uprisings — "Velvet Revolutions" — birthed a new political order throughout the region. Communism's fall even reached into Germany, the birthplace of the Cold War. The destruction of the Berlin Wall in 1989 symbolized the end of Communist rule in Central Europe. Millions of television viewers worldwide watched jubilant Germans knock down the hated wall that had divided the city since 1961 — a vivid symbol of communist repression and the Cold War division of Europe.

Gorbachev and America The Soviet leader, Mikhail Gorbachev, and his wife Raisa, meeting with American students. Both Ronald Reagan and Mikhail Gorbachev changed the political outlook of their nations. As Reagan undermined social-welfare liberalism in the United States, Gorbachev challenged the rigidity of the Communist Party and state socialism in the Soviet Union. Although they remained ideological adversaries, by the mid-1980s the two leaders had established a personal rapport, which helped facilitate agreement on a series of arms reduction measures. Cultural exchanges between the two nations, which were uncommon during the height of the Cold War, grew more frequent as well. Yuri Lizunov and Alexander Chumichev/TASS via Getty Images.

AP® THEME

WOR: America in the World

Lead a class discussion on the factors that played a role in ending the Cold War. Students will likely identify political changes and economic problems in Eastern Europe and the Soviet Union, increased U.S. military spending, and Reagan's diplomatic initiatives.

TEACHING STRATEGY

In a November 1985 article for the *New York Times* titled "Gorbachev's Gloomy America," Philip Taubman assessed Gorbachev's view of the U.S. Assign this article for students to read to provide an interesting glimpse in perspective from the other side of the Cold War divide. To access this article, search "NYT Gorbachev's Gloomy America."

TEACHING STRATEGY

The "Making the History of 1989: The Fall of Communism in Eastern Europe" Web site page, available through George Mason University, provides extensive resources for teaching about the fall of the Berlin Wall and the collapse of communism in Eastern Europe. To access this site, search "GMU Making the History of 1989."

AP® APPLY THE TIP

Divide the class into six collaborative groups and ask each group to research the reasons for the fall of communism in their assigned nation: Poland, Czechoslovakia, Hungary, Romania, Yugoslavia, and the Soviet Union. Ask each group to identify the contextualization for the fall of communism, the role of Ronald Reagan's policies, and the sparks that led to the actual end of the rule of the Soviet Union. After students have had time to perform their research, draw a timeline on the board and assign each group a different color. Ask each group to come to the board and put significant moments that led to the fall of communism on the timeline. As needed, allow students to research additional dates and information as they see and react to their classmates' additions to the timeline. When the timeline is complete, lead a class discussion on the patterns apparent between nations and the role of Reagan's policies on the fall of communism.

The Wall Comes Down As the communist government of East Germany collapsed, West Berliners showed their contempt for the wall dividing Berlin by defacing it with graffiti. Then, in November 1989, East and West Berliners destroyed huge sections of the wall with sledgehammers, an act of psychic liberation that symbolized the end of the Cold War. Here, in a calmer moment, a man chisels away at a section of the wall. Owen Franken/Corbis via Getty Images.

Alarmed by the reforms and the increasing calls for independence from republics within the USSR, Soviet military leaders seized power in August 1991 and arrested Gorbachev. But widespread popular opposition led by Boris Yeltsin, the president of the Russian Republic, thwarted their coup and broke the dominance of the Communist Party. Inspired by the Velvet Revolutions and the weakening of the Communist Party, several Soviet republics (Estonia, Latvia, Lithuania, Ukraine, and Belarus) broke away as independent nation-states. Finally, on December 25, 1991, the USSR formally dissolved to make way for an eleven-member Commonwealth of Independent States (CIS) (Map 29.3). The remarkable and total collapse of the Soviet Union largely resulted from internal economic failure, while external pressure from the United States played an important, though secondary, role.

"Nobody — no country, no party, no person — 'won' the cold war," concluded George Kennan, the architect in 1947 of the American policy of containment, in a 1992 *New York Times* editorial. The Cold War's cost was enormous, and both sides benefitted greatly from its end. For more than forty years, the United States had fought a bitter economic and ideological battle

AP® EXAM TIP

Evaluate the role that Reagan's policies played in the fall of communism in the Soviet Union.

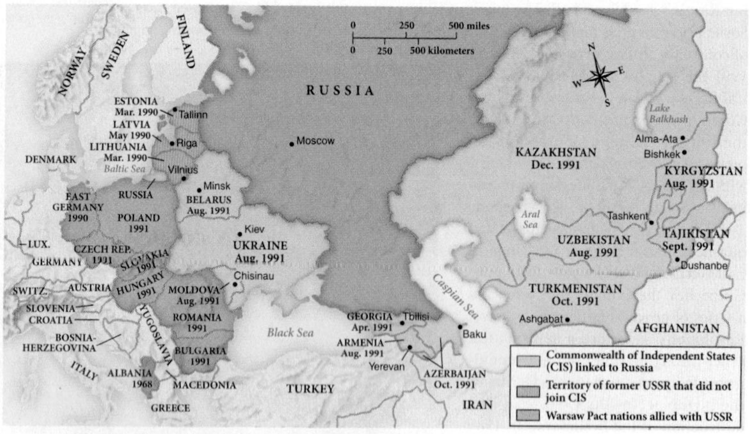

MAP 29.3 The Collapse of the Soviet Union and the Creation of Independent States, 1989–1991
The collapse of Soviet communism dramatically altered the political landscape of Central Europe and Central Asia. The Warsaw Pact, the USSR's answer to NATO, vanished. West and East Germany reunited, and the nations created by the Versailles treaty of 1919 — Estonia, Latvia, Lithuania, Poland, Czechoslovakia, Hungary, and Yugoslavia — reasserted their independence or split into smaller, ethnically defined nations. The Soviet republics bordering Russia, from Belarus in the west to Kyrgyzstan in the east, also became independent states, although remaining loosely bound with Russia in the Commonwealth of Independent States (CIS).

against its communist foe, a struggle that exerted an enormous impact on American society. Taxpayers had spent some $4 trillion on nuclear weapons and trillions more on conventional arms, placing the United States on a permanent war footing and feeding a vast military-industrial complex. The social costs were equally high, including anticommunist witch-hunts and a constant fear of nuclear annihilation. Most Americans had no qualms about proclaiming victory, however, and conservative advocates of free-market capitalism celebrated the outcome. The collapse of communism in Eastern Europe and the disintegration of the Soviet Union itself, they argued, proved that they had been right all along.

AP® SKILLS & PROCESSES

DEVELOPMENTS AND PROCESSES

How did Reagan's approach to the Soviet Union change between 1981 and 1989?

A New Political Order at Home and Abroad

Ronald Reagan's role in facilitating the end of the Cold War stood among his most important achievements. Overall, like most presidencies, his had a mixed legacy. Despite his pledge to get the federal government "off our backs," he did not reduce its size or scope. Social Security and other entitlement programs remained untouched, and increased military spending outweighed cuts in other programs. The religious right had contributed to Reagan's victorious electoral coalition, but he did not actively push their most controversial policies — such as a constitutional amendment banning abortion. He did call for tax credits for private religious schools, restrictions on abortions, and a constitutional amendment to permit prayer in public schools, but did not expend his political capital to secure these measures (see "Comparing Interpretations," p. 964).

Although Reagan failed to roll back the social welfare and regulatory state of the New Deal–Great Society eras, he did alter the dynamic of American politics. The Reagan presidency restored popular belief that the nation — and individual Americans — could enjoy ever-increasing prosperity. His antigovernment rhetoric won many adherents, as did his bold and fiscally aggressive tax cuts. Social-welfare liberalism, ascendant since 1933, remained intact but was now on the defensive. Conservatives, led by Reagan, had changed the political conversation.

Election of 1988 George H. W. Bush, Reagan's vice president and successor, was not seen by conservatives as one of their own. But he possessed an insider's familiarity with government and a long list of powerful allies, accumulated over three decades of public service. Bush's route to the White House reflected the post-Reagan alignments in American politics. In the primaries, he faced a spirited challenge from Pat Robertson, the archconservative televangelist whose influence and profile had grown during Reagan's two terms. After securing the presidential nomination, won largely because of his fierce loyalty to Reagan, Bush tapped as his vice-presidential running mate an unknown and inexperienced Indiana senator, Dan Quayle. Bush chose Quayle in part to secure the Christian "**family values**" vote — Quayle had been a quiet, but effective, advocate for the family values movement in the Senate. Robertson's challenge and Quayle's selection showed that the Religious Right had become a major force in Republican politics.

AP® EXAM TIP

Evaluate the ways American foreign policy represented change, as well as maintained continuity, after the Cold War.

family values
A political platform of conservative morality endorsed by the Religious Right in the 1980s, and subsequent decades, including support for the traditional nuclear family and opposition to homosexuality and abortion.

On the Democratic side, Jesse Jackson became the first African American to challenge for a major-party nomination, winning eleven states in primary and caucus voting. However, the more staid Michael Dukakis, the governor of Massachusetts, emerged as the Democratic nominee. The Northeast liberal Dukakis fared poorly among the constituencies Democrats had lost in the 1970s: southern whites, midwestern blue-collar Catholics, and middle-class suburbanites. Indeed, Bush made a point of attacking Dukakis as a "liberal" by calling him a "card-carrying member of the ACLU" (a prominent liberal organization), a not-so-subtle reference to J. Edgar Hoover's 1958 phrase "card-carrying communist." Bush won with 53 percent of the vote, a larger margin of victory than Reagan's in 1980. The election confirmed a pattern in presidential politics that would last through the turn of the century: every four years, Americans would refight the battles of the 1960s, with liberals on one side and conservatives on the other.

AP® SKILLS & PROCESSES

DEVELOPMENTS AND PROCESSES

Given this **DEVELOPMENTS AND PROCESSES** question is unique, point out the following to students: It focuses on one person, it pays attention to attitudes as much as actions, and it covers a relatively brief span — the eight years of Reagan's presidency. To extend this prompt, ask students to identify the reasons Reagan's views changed during this time and whether any one moment was a turning point.

TRM Find complete suggested responses in the Teacher's Resource Materials.

CHECK FOR UNDERSTANDING

Ask students: **How did U.S.-Soviet relations move into a new era during Reagan's presidency?** *Early in his presidency, Reagan ramped up American military strength, in part to cause economic turmoil within the Soviet Union. He also directed the CIA to support anticommunist movements in Angola, Mozambique, Afghanistan, and Central America. The most controversial of these programs was his support for Contra rebels, which he continued to secretly and illegally back after Congress cut off funding for their support. Mikhail Gorbachev came to power in 1985, a relatively young leader in comparison with most Soviet leaders. He sought reform of the Communist system through glasnost and perestroika. He also reached out to Reagan. The two established a warm relationship, which led to an agreement to phase out intermediate-range ballistic missiles. Gorbachev's reforms led to a coup attempt and the eventual collapse of the Soviet Union in 1991.*

AP® THEME

SOC: Social Structures; NAT: American and National Identity

As indicated in part by religious conservatives' routine use of "family values," intense political and cultural debates over issues such as diversity, gender roles, and family structures continued.

TEACHING STRATEGY

Politico Magazine's article titled "How Bush Beat Dukakis: Scenes from the 1988 Presidential Campaign" presents a series of fifteen slides with captions that trace Bush's defeat of his "card-carrying liberal" opponent. To access this article, search "Politico How Bush Beat Dukakis."

TEACHING STRATEGY

The so-called "Culture Wars" of the 1980s and 1990s were a bi-product of the political debates between liberals and conservatives. Encourage students to evaluate the emergence of culture wars at the end of this chapter.

AP® SKILLS & PROCESSES

ANALYZING HISTORICAL EVIDENCE

The **AP® COMPARING INTERPRETATIONS** feature explores the relationship between the Reagan administration and the evangelicals who helped bring him to power. There is little debate that Reagan failed to implement changes that religious conservatives wanted. The real question is whether he paid lip service to those goals without ever attempting to fight aggressively for them, in essence cynically exploiting evangelicals for their votes, or whether he was genuinely committed to the issues that mattered to religious conservatives, but was simply not skilled enough politically to accomplish their goals. Self takes the former position, while Phillips-Fein, it seems at first, takes the second. A closer read of Phillips-Fein, however, might suggest that she, like Self, thinks that Reagan wanted to "show" evangelicals that he was their candidate — without doing anything tangible for them — because his real interests were economic.

TRM Find complete suggested responses in the Teacher's Resource Materials.

AP® COMPARING INTERPRETATIONS

How Conservative Was the Reagan Presidency?

In the 1980s, Ronald Reagan's presidency seemed to define a conservative triumph. The product of a political ground game decades in the making, the conservative victory in the 1980 election fused the mobilization of Christian evangelicals, a libertarian antigovernment individualism, and a probusiness entrepreneurialism into a coalition determined to undermine the expansive legacy of sixties liberalism. Did it work?

Historians are now beginning to offer assessments of Reagan's presidency. Two scholars, Kim Phillips-Fein and Robert O. Self, one of the authors of this textbook, join this debate with perspectives on Reagan's relationship to the Christian evangelical movement. Reacting to what they saw as the permissiveness of the 1960s, the Religious Right pushed a Christian moral agenda into political debate and supported candidates pledged to "return America" to its traditional foundations. To what extent was Reagan their candidate?

KIM PHILLIPS-FEIN

Source: Kim Phillips-Fein, *Invisible Hands: The Making of the Conservative Movement from the New Deal to Reagan* (New York: W. W. Norton, 2009), 254–258.

The Reagan campaign also sought to win the support of conservative Christians. . . . The evangelical movement itself was gearing up for politics in 1980. Early in the year, Moral Majority had hosted a Key Pastors Meeting in Indianapolis, Indiana, designed to encourage ministers to start to use the pulpit to press for political engagement. All the participants received a thick packet analyzing biblical passages and showing how they could shed light on contemporary politics — always from the conservative perspective. . . . Reagan worked very hard to show conservative evangelicals that he was their candidate. In August 1980 he appeared at the National Affairs Briefing in Dallas, an event organized by the Religious Roundtable, whose leaders included virtually all of the luminaries of the Christian Right — Pat Robertson, Jerry Falwell, Tim LaHaye, and various Christian business conservatives such as the Hunt family of Texas. . . . Reagan spoke after [the Southern Baptist televangelist James Robison], the seeming answer to the prayers of the evangelicals: here was the man who would lead Christians back to the White House. . . . "We have God's promise that if we turn to him and ask His help, we shall have it," Reagan told the rapt crowd. "If we believe God has blessed America with liberty, then we have not just a *right* to vote, but a *duty* to vote." Reagan painted the Christian worldview in broad strokes that made clear its commonalities with the larger antistate agenda of his campaign, denouncing the [Federal Communications Commission] for interfering with religious broadcasting, the IRS for threatening the autonomy of religious schools, and the [National Labor Relations Board] for meddling with church employees. . . . One newspaper described the entire National Affairs Briefing as a "thinly disguised religious pep rally for Ronald Reagan."

ROBERT O. SELF

Source: Robert O. Self, *All in the Family: The Realignment of American Democracy Since the 1960s* (New York: Hill and Wang, 2012), 368–369, 376–377.

When conservative pragmatists, including Reagan himself, moved slowly or cautiously on many issues, especially abortion, religious and pro-family activists believed they had been betrayed. This produced notable tension in the [Republican Party's coalition] and led to a radicalization of disappointed far-right religious conservatives. . . . Ronald Reagan was a tax-cutter, a free-market deregulator, and a Cold War martial nationalist. He was not a moral traditionalist. He may have promised to "clean up the mess in Berkeley," in his 1966 gubernatorial campaign, but he signed California's liberal abortion laws in 1967 and opposed the antigay Briggs initiative in 1978. However, when the religious right and the pro-family movement transformed the Republican platform between 1976 and 1980 . . . the chameleonlike Reagan changed his colors. . . . The president's rhetorical support was unwavering: he gave numerous antiabortion speeches, appointed right-to-life leaders to his administration, [and] declared support for a Human Life Amendment [an amendment to the Constitution that would have outlawed abortion]. . . . But Reagan watched the polls and chose not to leap too far ahead of public opinion. His support for . . . right-to-life Senate initiatives was calibrated not to disrupt his economic agenda on Capitol Hill. And when the first chance to appoint a Supreme Court justice arrived quickly in 1981, he seized the opportunity to name the court's first woman, Sandra Day O'Connor, ignoring vocal right-to-life opposition. As an Arizona state senator in 1970, O'Connor had voted to repeal Arizona's abortion law, which had permanently disqualified her from the bench in the minds of right-to-life activists.

AP® SHORT ANSWER PRACTICE

1. How do these scholars assess Reagan's commitment to the Religious Right's political agenda? Compare the main tenets of each argument.
2. To what extent were evangelical expectations (described by Phillips-Fein) realized during Reagan's presidency (described by Self)?
3. Comparing these excerpts with Chapter 29's discussion of the 1970s and 1980s, identify two examples of the impact the Religious Right had on the era's politics.

Middle East The end of the Cold War left the United States as the sole military superpower, at the head of what Bush called a "new world order," with European and Asian allies in support. American officials and diplomats presumed that U.S. interests would prevail in this new environment, but they still faced an array of regional, religious, and ethnic conflicts that defied easy solutions. Nowhere was friction more pressing or more complex than in the Middle East — conflicts in the oil-rich lands stretching from Iran to Algeria would dominate U.S. foreign policy for the next two decades, replacing the Cold War at the center of American geopolitics.

After Carter's success negotiating the 1979 Egypt-Israel treaty at Camp David, there had been few bright spots in U.S. Middle Eastern diplomacy. In 1982, the Reagan administration sent American troops to join a multinational peacekeeping force in Lebanon, where skirmishes between Palestine Liberation Organization (PLO) fighters and Israeli-backed Lebanese forces threatened to spark a regional war. But when Lebanese militants loyal to Iran, motivated by continuing American support for Israel, killed 241 American marines, Reagan abruptly withdrew the forces. Three years later, Palestinians living in the Gaza Strip and along the West Bank of the Jordan River — territories occupied by Israel since 1967 — mounted an "intifada," a civilian uprising against Israeli authority. In response, American diplomats stepped up efforts to persuade the PLO and Arab nations to accept the legitimacy of Israel and to convince the Israelis to allow the creation of a Palestinian state. Neither initiative met with much success. Burdened in part by a history of support for undemocratic regimes in Middle Eastern countries, the United States was not viewed as an honest broker.

Persian Gulf War American interest in a reliable supply of oil from the Persian Gulf region led the United States into a short but consequential war in the Persian Gulf in the early 1990s. Ten years earlier, in September 1980, Iraq, a secular state headed by the dictator Saddam Hussein, had attacked the revolutionary Shiite Islamic nation of Iran, headed by Ayatollah Khomeini. The fighting was intense and long lasting — an eight-year war of attrition that claimed a million casualties. Reagan supported Hussein with military intelligence and other aid, in order to maintain access to Iraqi oil, undermine Iran, and preserve a balance of power in the Middle East favorable to the United States. An armistice in 1988 ended the inconclusive war, with both sides still claiming the territory that sparked the conflict.

Two years later, in August 1990, Hussein went to war again. Believing (erroneously) that he still had the support of the United States, Hussein sent in troops and quickly conquered Kuwait, Iraq's small, oil-rich neighbor, and threatened Saudi Arabia, the site of one-fifth of the world's known oil reserves and an informal ally of the United States. The Iraqi leader had miscalculated badly. To preserve the administration's preferred balance of power in the region, President George H. W. Bush sponsored a series of resolutions in the United Nations Security Council calling for Iraq to withdraw from Kuwait. When Hussein refused, Bush successfully prodded the UN to authorize the use of force, and the president organized a military coalition of thirty-four nations. Splitting mostly along party lines, the Republican-led House of Representatives authorized American participation by a vote of 250 to 183, and the Democratic-led Senate agreed by the close margin of 52 to 47.

The U.S.-led coalition forces quickly won the **Persian Gulf War** for the "liberation of Kuwait." To avoid a protracted struggle and retain French and Russian support for the UN coalition, Bush decided against occupying Iraq and removing Saddam Hussein from power. Instead, he won passage of UN Resolution 687, which imposed economic sanctions against Iraq unless it allowed exhaustive weapons inspections, destroyed all biological and chemical arms, and unconditionally abandoned any nuclear programs. The quick victory, low incidence of American casualties, and tidy ending produced a euphoric reaction at home. "By God, we've kicked the Vietnam syndrome once and for all," Bush announced, his approval spiking in the war's aftermath. But Hussein remained a formidable power in the region, and in March 2003,

Persian Gulf War
The 1991 war between Iraq and a U.S.-led international coalition that was sparked by the 1990 Iraqi invasion of Kuwait. A forty-day bombing campaign against Iraq followed by coalition troops storming into Kuwait brought a quick coalition victory.

TEACHING STRATEGY

The companion site to PBS's *Frontline* film The Gulf War provides a series of resources for teaching about the war, including maps, a chronology, oral histories, and an overview of weapons and technology that played a role in combat. To access the site, search "Frontline The Gulf War."

Additionally, in his article titled "Operation Desert Storm: 25 Years Since the First Gulf War," Alan Taylor provides an overview of the war and its consequences in a series of thirty-eight images and captions. To access this article, search "Atlantic Taylor Operation Desert Storm."

CHECK FOR UNDERSTANDING

Ask students: **What were the aims of U.S. foreign policy during the waning years of the Cold War and in its immediate aftermath?** *During the 1980s, President Reagan, more so than any president in the Cold War, confronted the Soviet Union head-on, both rhetorically, by referring to the Soviet Union as the "evil empire," and practically, by seeking to re-arm America and actively fight the Cold War. This policy had an unintended consequence of bankrupting the Soviet Union as a result of an arms race, leading to its fall in 1991. Afterward, U.S. policy was, in the words of President George H. W. Bush, aimed at creating a "new world order" with the United States, as the world's only remaining superpower, and its European and Asian allies, stabilizing the world.*

AP® SKILLS & PROCESSES

CAUSATION

The **CAUSATION** question asks students to explain the causes of American involvement in the Persian Gulf War and the Iraqi invasion of Kuwait. This question is particularly pressing because in 1990, two years after a war in which the U.S. supported Iraq, it went to war with Iraq.

TRM Find complete suggested responses in the Teacher's Resource Materials.

CHECK FOR UNDERSTANDING

Use the **AP® LEARNING FOCUS** question from the beginning of the chapter to check students' understanding of the chapter as a whole: **Why was the New Right able to ascend to national political power in the 1980s and reshape both government and society?** *The rise of the New Right in the 1980s was a long-term historical process that began decades prior, amidst the social transformations of the 1960s. In many ways, conservatives were responding to the liberalism of the Great Society. The economic and foreign policy crises of the 1970s also contributed to the rise of the New Right. Specifically, conservative forces in the late 1970s and early 1980s reacted to the expansion of government, the legalization of abortion, feminism, gay rights activism, welfare dependency, and what they believed to be the demise of the American family. They sought to cut taxes, create a more conservative Supreme Court, and deregulate the economy. Conservatives articulated ideas about American morality, the rights of the majority in America, and the benefits of capitalism and success.*

Men — and Women — at War A U.S. soldier with Norman Schwarzkopf, commander of coalition forces in the Persian Gulf War. Women comprised approximately 10 percent of American troops in that conflict. In the last decades of the twentieth century, women increasingly chose military careers and were more frequently assigned to combat zones. David Turnley/Corbis/VCG via Getty Images.

AP® SKILLS & PROCESSES

CAUSATION

Why did the United States intervene in the conflicts between Iraq and Iran and between Iraq and Kuwait?

he would become the pretext for Bush's son, President George W. Bush, to initiate another war in Iraq — one that would be much more protracted, expensive, and bloody (see "Domestic Conflict and War in the Middle East" in Chapter 30).

For half a century, the United States and the Soviet Union sought to partition the world into rival economic and ideological blocs: capitalist against communist. The end of their Cold War, and increasing U.S. involvement in the Middle East, sowed the seeds of future conflicts. The most prominent of those struggles pitted a Western-centered agenda of economic and cultural globalization against an anti-Western agenda of Muslim and Arab regionalism. But other post–Cold War shifts loomed as well. The European Union emerged as a massive united trading bloc, economic engine, and global political force; and China saw spectacular economic growth that was only beginning to coalesce in the early 1990s. The post–Cold War world promised to be a *multi*polar one, with centers of power in Europe, the United States, and East Asia — and a constant conflict brewing in the Middle East.

SUMMARY

Two central developments marked the years from 1980 to 1991: the rise of the New Right in U.S. politics and the end of the Cold War. Domestically, the New Right, which had been building in strength since the mid-1960s, rejected the liberalism of the Great Society and the perceived permissiveness of feminism and the sexual revolution. Shifting their allegiance from Barry Goldwater to Ronald Reagan, right-wing Americans built a political movement from the ground up and in 1980 came to national power with Reagan's first election as president. His predecessor, the Democrat Jimmy Carter, had championed centrist liberalism domestically and human rights abroad. But with a weak economy and mounting inflation, as well as a major conflict with Iran, Carter was no match for Reagan, the rising star of conservatism. Advocating free-market economics, lower taxes, and fewer government regulations, Reagan became a champion of the New Right. His record as president did not fully deliver on his rhetoric: Initial tax cuts were followed by tax hikes, and he frequently dismayed the Christian Right by not pursuing their interests forcefully enough, especially regarding abortion and school prayer.

Reagan also backed off an initially aggressive stance toward the USSR. His shifting approaches to the Soviets did contribute to the end of the Cold War. An already overstretched Soviet economy strained to keep up with Reagan's massive military buildup in the early 1980s. Reagan then agreed to meet with Soviet leader Mikhail Gorbachev in several summits between 1985 and 1987, lending support to Gorbachev's reform agenda. More important than Reagan's actions, however, were the contradictions of the Soviet economic structure itself. Gorbachev instituted the first significant reforms in Soviet society in half a century, which loosened Communist Party control and allowed popular movement to rise up within the USSR and both its own republics and nearby satellite states. The reforms stirred popular criticism of the Soviet Union, which finally broke apart in 1991. That same year, the United States defeated Iraq in the Gulf War — the prelude to a decades-long series of conflicts in the Middle East.

CHAPTER 29 REVIEW

AP® CONTENT REVIEW *Answer these questions to demonstrate your understanding of the chapter's main ideas.*

1. What were the major characteristics of the political movement, known as the New Right, that backed Ronald Reagan?
2. What were the major political successes and failures of the Reagan coalition?
3. What were the aims of U.S. foreign policy at the close of the Cold War?

AP® TERMS TO KNOW *Identify and explain the significance of each term.*

Key Concepts and Events

National Review (p. 942)
Religious Right (p. 943)
hostage crisis (p. 947)
Reagan coalition (p. 948)
Moral Majority (p. 949)
Reagan Democrats (p. 949)
supply-side economics (Reaganomics) (p. 949)
Economic Recovery Tax Act (ERTA) (p. 949)
HIV/AIDS (p. 952)
Iran-Contra affair (p. 960)
glasnost (p. 961)
perestroika (p. 961)
family values (p. 963)
Persian Gulf War (p. 965)

Key People

Barry Goldwater (p. 940)
Ronald Reagan (p. 940)
William F. Buckley (p. 942)
Milton Friedman (p. 942)
David Stockman (p. 950)
Sandra Day O'Connor (p. 952)
Mikhail Gorbachev (p. 958)
George H. W. Bush (p. 963)

AP® MAKING CONNECTIONS *Recognize the larger developments and continuities within and across chapters by answering these questions.*

1. Compare the two major periods of liberal legislative accomplishment — the New Deal in the 1930s (Chapter 22) and the Great Society in the 1960s (Chapter 27) — with the Reagan era in the 1980s. Did Reagan undo the legislative gains of those earlier eras? What conservative objectives were accomplished, and what limits or obstacles were encountered?
2. Examine the images in this chapter of Reagan at the Republican convention and at his ranch (pp. 939 and 948). What message do these images convey about Reagan as a person? About his policies? Together, what do they tell us about the image and reality of the Reagan presidency? Do you think that photographs are an accurate source of information for understanding the historical meaning of a particular president and his administration? Why or why not?

KEY TURNING POINTS *Refer to the timeline at the start of the chapter for help in answering this question.*

Identify some of the key moments in the decline and then end of the Cold War. What part did the United States play in these events, and how did this affect the U.S. role in world affairs more broadly?

LearningCurve

Remind students to go online to complete the LearningCurve quiz for this chapter.

TRM Find complete suggested responses in the Teacher's Resource Materials.

TRM Find definitions for these terms in the **Glossary/Glosario** in the Teacher's Resource Materials.

AP® SKILLS & PROCESSES

COMPARISON

AP® MAKING CONNECTIONS 1 asks students to compare three periods of political reform, two in which the federal government established a range of new programs and a third that attempted to undo those reforms.

AP® SKILLS & PROCESSES

CONTINUITY AND CHANGE

The **KEY TURNING POINTS** question asks students to identify significant moments in the ending of the Cold War, and then to evaluate the U.S.'s role in each of those moments.

TRM Find complete suggested responses in the Teacher's Resource Materials.

AP PRACTICE QUESTIONS

MULTIPLE CHOICE QUESTIONS *Choose the correct answer for each question.*

Questions 1–3 refer to the excerpt provided.

"We're not cutting the budget simply for the sake of sounder financial management. This is only the first step toward returning power to the States and communities, only a first step toward reordering the relationship between citizen and government. We can make government again responsive to the people not only by cutting its size and scope and thereby ensuring that its legitimate functions are performed efficiently and justly.

Because ours is a consistent philosophy of government, we can be very clear: We do not have a social agenda, separate economic agenda, and a separate foreign agenda. We have one agenda. Just as surely as we seek to put our financial house in order and rebuild our nation's defenses, so too we seek to protect the unborn, to end the manipulation of schoolchildren by utopian planners, and permit the acknowledgment of a Supreme Being in our classrooms just as we allow such acknowledgments in other public institutions."

Speech by President Ronald Reagan, March 20, 1981

1. Based upon the excerpt, Reagan would most likely support
   a. cutbacks in military programs.
   b. reductions in spending on social welfare programs.
   c. a universal health care system.
   d. a greater role of government in protecting natural resources.

2. In the decade following Reagan's election in 1980, divisions emerged between liberals and conservatives over all of the following issues EXCEPT the
   a. scope of the government social safety net.
   b. positive effects of free-trade agreements.
   c. need for deregulation of industry.
   d. foreign policies governing relations with the Soviet Union.

3. Reagan's ideas expressed in the excerpt found the greatest support among
   a. union organizations and laborers.
   b. the youth counterculture.
   c. Protestant Evangelical Christians.
   d. feminists and gay activists.

Questions 4–6 refer to the excerpt provided.

"The we-they world that emerged after 1945 is giving way to the more traditional struggles of great powers. That contest is more manageable. It permits serious negotiations. It creates new possibilities — for cooperation in combating terrorism, the spread of chemical weapons and common threats to the environment, and for shaping a less violent world.

True, Europe remains torn in two; but the place where four decades of hostility began is mending and changing in complicated patterns. True, two enormous military machines still face each other around the world; but both sides are searching for ways to reduce the burdens and risks. Values continue to clash, but less profoundly as Soviet citizens start to partake in freedom. . . .

The Bush Administration seems less attentive to these issues and more preoccupied with Mr. Gorbachev's seizing headlines worldwide. It would do better to think of him as part of the solution, not the problem. . . .

Hints dribble out about senior [Bush Administration] officials worrying that Mr. Reagan was too friendly with Mr. Gorbachev and too eager for arms-control. That's self-defeating talk. . . . It would be unfortunate if the Bush team worried too much about their right flank and tried to prove that it can out-tough Mr. Reagan. That would drain them of the imagination and boldness necessary to go beyond the cold war."

Editorial from *The New York Times*, April 2, 1989.
© 1989 *The New York Times*. All rights reserved. Used by permission and protected by the Copyright Laws of the United States. The printing, copying, redistribution, or retransmission of this Content without express written permission is prohibited.

4. The excerpt from the *New York Times* editorial placed the greatest responsibility for ending the Cold War on
   a. President Reagan's military escalations.
   b. the risks posed by the global war on terrorism.
   c. long-term success of the policy of containment.
   d. the power of the United States' unilateral foreign policy.

5. The trends described in the *New York Times* editorial contributed most directly to
   a. intensifying debates over the appropriate use of American power in the world.
   b. a greater emphasis in American foreign policy on imperialist territorial ambitions.
   c. increased calls for international isolationism in U.S. public opinion.
   d. new awareness of the dangers of permanent foreign alliances.

SHORT ANSWER QUESTIONS

Read each question carefully and write a short response. Use evidence from the text to support your claims.

"Reagan worked very hard to show conservative evangelicals that he was their candidate. In August 1980 he appeared at the National Affairs Briefing . . . an event organized by the Religious Roundtable . . . the seeming answer to the prayers of the evangelicals: here was the man who would lead Christians back to the White House. . . . Reagan painted the Christian worldview in broad strokes that made clear its commonalities with the larger antistate agenda of his campaign, denouncing the [Federal Communications Commission] for interfering with religious schools, and the [National Labor Relations Board] for meddling with church employees. . . . One newspaper described the entire National Affairs Briefing as a 'thinly disguised religious pep rally for Ronald Reagan.'"

Kim Phillips-Fein, *Invisible Hands: The Making of the Conservative Movement from the New Deal to Reagan*, 2009

"When conservative pragmatists, including Reagan himself, moved slowly or cautiously on many issues, especially abortion, religious and pro-family activists believed they had been betrayed. . . . The president's rhetorical support was unwavering: he gave . . . antiabortion speeches, appointed right-to-life leaders to his administration, [and] declared support for a Human Life Amendment [an amendment to the Constitution that would have outlawed abortion]. . . . But Reagan watched the polls and chose not to leap too far ahead of public opinion. His support for . . . right-to-life Senate initiatives was calibrated not to disrupt his economic agenda. . . . [H]e seized the opportunity to name the [Supreme] court's first woman, Sandra Day O'Connor, ignoring vocal right-to-life opposition. As an Arizona state senator in 1970, O'Connor had voted to repeal Arizona's abortion law, which had permanently disqualified her from the bench in the minds of right-to-life activists."

Robert O. Self, *All in the Family: The Realignment of American Democracy Since the 1960s*, 2012.

1. Using the two excerpts provided, answer (a), (b), and (c).
   a. Briefly explain ONE major difference between Phillips-Fein's and Self's historical interpretations of the Reagan presidency.
   b. Briefly explain how ONE specific event, development, or circumstance not directly mentioned in the excerpts could be used to support Phillips-Fein's argument.
   c. Briefly explain how ONE specific event, development, or circumstance not directly mentioned in the excerpts could be used to support Self's argument.
2. Answer (a), (b), and (c).
   a. Briefly explain why ONE of the following developments led to the most significant changes in United States society after 1980.
   - debates over family structures
   - technological changes
   - economic policies of the Reagan administration

   b. Briefly explain how ONE specific historical event or development supports your argument in (a).
   c. Briefly explain why ONE of the other options less significantly changed United States society after 1980.
3. Answer (a), (b), and (c).
   a. Briefly explain ONE important historical difference in the foreign policies of the Reagan administration from the Carter administration.
   b. Briefly explain ANOTHER important historical difference in the foreign policies of the Reagan administration from the Carter administration.
   c. Briefly explain ONE important historical similarity in the foreign policies of the Reagan administration to the Carter administration.

TRM Find complete suggested responses in the Teacher's Resource Materials.

30 CHAPTER National and Global Dilemmas

1989 to the Present

Chapter 30 — AP® Assessment Weight and Pacing Guide

The assessment weight on the AP® U.S. History Exam for Chapters 29–30 is 4–6 percent. This chapter falls in Unit 9 of the AP® U.S. History Curriculum, covering Period 9: 1980–present.

This pacing guide is based on a schedule with 120 sessions of 50 minutes each before the AP® U.S. History Exam. If you have a different number of sessions before the exam, you can modify the pacing to meet your needs. If you have additional time, consider incorporating quizzes, released AP® U.S. History questions, practice exams, writing practice, and other instructional activities.

	Traditional Schedule	Block Schedule
Chapter 30	2 days	1 day

Daily Pacing Guide

	Content Focus	Essential Question
Day 1	America in the Global Economy; Politics and Partisanship in a Contentious Era	How did globalization redefine the relationship of the United States to the rest of the world after the end of the Cold War? What were the sources of domestic division in the United States between the 1990s and the present, and how did they reshape the political landscape?
Day 2	A New Century Dawns	How did wars abroad and political turmoil at home shape the United States in the first decades of the twenty-first century?

AP® Alignment

Section Heading	AP® Topic	AP® Theme
America in the Global Economy; Politics and Partisanship in a Contentious Era	9.4, 9.5	WXT, MIG
A New Century Dawns	9.6	WOR

*Should changes be made to the Course Framework in the future, an updated alignment will be placed on our AP® updates page at go.bfwpub.com/ap-course-updates.

Chapter 30 — Overview

The final chapter focuses attention on the rise of globalization, partisanship, and conflict that continues between the left and right, and the attendant challenges faced in the administrations of George W. Bush, Barack Obama, and Donald Trump. The chapter begins by analyzing the rise of the European Union and China as global economic forces that both challenged American supremacy and provided opportunities for economic growth. The chapter then focuses on the intense partisanship that has characterized American politics since the administrations of George H. W. Bush and Bill Clinton as well as those presidents' challenges in facing a post–Cold War foreign policy. Finally, the chapter evaluates the intense partisanship and cultural fissures during the presidencies of Barack Obama and Donald Trump. The context of social reform movements and the global pandemic caused by Covid-19 are also briefly explored.

Chapter 30 — Resources

The following resources can be found in the Teacher's Resource Materials (TRM) that accompany the book. You can access the TRM via the book's digital platform, by clicking the TRM links found here in your Teacher's Edition e-book, or by contacting your representative to access the resources online. Visit **bfwpub.com/henretta10e** to learn more.

TRM Chapter 30 Lecture Presentation Slides

TRM Chapter 30 Outline with AP® Focus

TRM Chapter 30 Lecture Strategies

TRM Chapter 30 Suggested Responses

TRM Handout 30.1 — Thematic Analysis: Globalization

TRM Handout 30.2 — Causation: World Organizations

TRM Handout 30.3 — Thematic Analysis: 9/11

TRM Handout 30.4 — Comparison: Obama and Clinton

Chapter 30 — Essential Activity

Organize students into collaborative groups and ask them to create a timeline that illustrates U.S. policy on immigration from 1900 to the present. Students should identify significant laws and policies, including an explanation of the historical developments, processes, or events related to each element they add to their timeline. Then ask students to investigate the arguments for and against President Donald Trump's travel ban and wall to separate the U.S. and Mexico. Instruct students to create a Venn diagram that compares Trump's immigration policies to those of Barack Obama. Lead a class discussion on the similarities and differences between policies.

Chapter 30 — Bell Ringers

The following activities take no more than 5–15 minutes of your class period and offer an effective and engaging way to begin your lessons and for students to apply AP® Skills & Processes:

- Show students an image of the fall of the Berlin Wall and lead a class discussion on why the Berlin Wall was a symbol of the Cold War. Prompt students to examine how U.S. policies from 1980 to 1991 helped bring the Cold War to an end.
- Direct students to analyze the graph on p. 990 of the gross federal debt as a percentage of gross domestic product. Then ask students to discuss the relationship of the political party and federal debt. *Answers will vary, but should observe the following: changes in federal debt to GDP had little to do with the political party, increases in debt have occurred with both parties in power, etc. Finally, prompt students to explain what accounted for changes in debt to GDP depending on the political party in power.*

NOTES

TEACHING STRATEGY

The chapter title captures the sense of the nation being at a crossroads domestically and internationally in the last several decades since the end of the Cold War. The emotional resonance of issues related to terrorism may make it difficult for students to explore the subject dispassionately, but the chapter introduction helpfully presents the phenomenon of terrorism in the context of globalization, suggesting how globalization facilitated the terrorists' attacks. Globalization was a watchword throughout the presidency of George H. W. Bush, Reagan's vice president and successor. This theme has in many ways dominated American domestic and foreign policy concerns ever since. The Great Recession, the largest economic downturn since the Great Depression, had largely domestic causes but rippled through the global economy. For a complete suggested response to the **AP® LEARNING FOCUS** question, see p. 1000.

30 CHAPTER

National and Global Dilemmas

1989 to the Present

AP® LEARNING FOCUS

Why did the shape of American politics, economics, and society shift in response to post–Cold War globalization?

When the Cold War ended in 1991, a new era in world history began, with significant consequences for the United States. Communism was in retreat, and capitalism advanced across the world, inaugurating a period of rapid **globalization** in which we're still living. The spread of economic, political, and cultural influences and connections among countries, businesses, and individuals through trade, migration, and communication — the hallmarks of globalization — defines the decades after 1991. With this deepening worldwide interconnectedness came new domestic challenges for Americans, such as immigration policy and the effects of economic competition on industries and communities, as well as global dilemmas, such as shifting trade networks and military alliances. For the United States, globalization brought even greater urgency to the task of balancing national priorities with global realities.

Globalization was not itself new — think of the Atlantic economy of the eighteenth century linking Europe, the Americas, and Africa, for example. But Americans had turned inward in the decades of post–World War II prosperity and in the uneasy 1960s and 1970s as well — even as war in Vietnam, industrial competition from Europe and Japan, and oil politics in the Middle East exerted powerful influences. After the end of the Cold War, the country rediscovered, as it had in previous eras, just how vast and varied its connections to global cultural and economic life were. Beginning in the last decade of the twentieth century, this current era has seen the rapid spread of capitalism around the world, huge increases in global trade and commerce, and a diffusion of communications technology, including the Internet, linking the world's people to one another in ways unimaginable a generation earlier.

Globalization engulfed the United States just as the nation's politics were becoming increasingly divisive and fractious. The triumphant Reagan Revolution of the 1980s continued to inspire conservative Americans, while liberals regrouped and sought to ignite a new generation of voters. Increasingly, however, national political life seemed to offer fewer and fewer points of compromise, on issues ranging from abortion, immigration, and affirmative action to taxes and welfare spending. By the 2010s — a decade during which the nation was led by two strikingly different presidents, Barack Obama and Donald Trump — polls showed that the Democratic and Republican parties had grown starkly ideologically divided. At the same time, more Americans than ever, nearly 40 percent, labeled themselves as politically "independent," refusing to identify solely with one or the other of the major political parties.

globalization
The spread of economic, political, and cultural influences and connections among countries, businesses, and individuals through trade, migration, and communication.

Energy and the Environment At the dawn of the twenty-first century, few issues were more critical, in the United States and across the globe, than energy and the environment. This wind farm is an example of the search for nonfossil sources of new energy, a search that is among the many challenges facing the globalized world of our century. Raphael GAILLARDE/Gamma-Rapho via Getty Images.

TEACHING STRATEGY

According to the U.S. Energy Information Administration, renewable energy made up 10 percent of Americans' total energy use in 2016, with wind making up 21 percent of renewable energy use — or 2.1 percent of total energy use. To access these statistics, search "U.S. Energy Information Administration energy facts explained."

AP® SKILLS & PROCESSES

CONTINUITY AND CHANGE

Use the **TIMELINE** to help students begin thinking about how the period from 1992 to present could constitute a distinct historical period. The chronology bookends the final era, which extends to 2019, with two presidential elections. Bill Clinton's election as a "New Democrat" in 1992 reflected his party's recognition, after more than a decade out of power, of the need to move in a more centrist direction. At the other end of the timeline, the emergence of the new Democratic leadership of Barack Obama on the one hand with the rise of the Tea Party and Donald Trump on the other hand represent the intense political divisions of the early twenty-first century. During this period, the U.S. experienced several significant milestones: the worst attack on U.S. soil since Pearl Harbor, which launched wars in Afghanistan and Iraq, the latter becoming the nation's longest military struggle; the worst recession since the Great Depression; and — on a positive note — the election of the first African American president.

AP® THEME

WXT: Work, Exchange, and Technology

Economic productivity increased as improvements in digital communications enabled increased American participation in worldwide economic opportunities.

TIMELINE

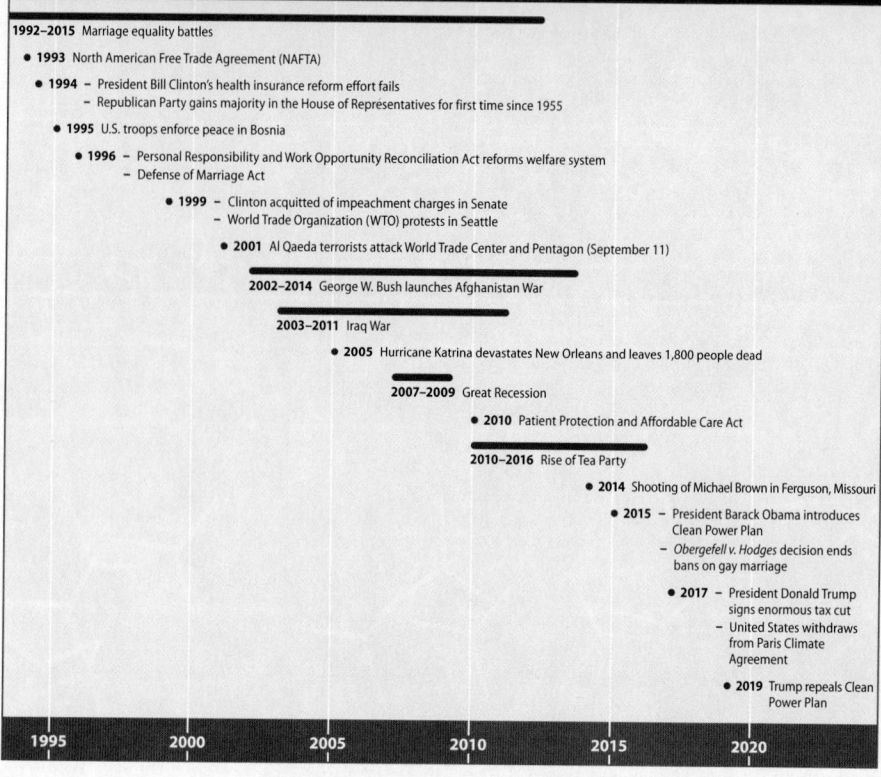

1992–2015 Marriage equality battles

- **1993** North American Free Trade Agreement (NAFTA)
- **1994** – President Bill Clinton's health insurance reform effort fails
  – Republican Party gains majority in the House of Representatives for first time since 1955
- **1995** U.S. troops enforce peace in Bosnia
- **1996** – Personal Responsibility and Work Opportunity Reconciliation Act reforms welfare system
  – Defense of Marriage Act
- **1999** – Clinton acquitted of impeachment charges in Senate
  – World Trade Organization (WTO) protests in Seattle
- **2001** Al Qaeda terrorists attack World Trade Center and Pentagon (September 11)

2002–2014 George W. Bush launches Afghanistan War

2003–2011 Iraq War

- **2005** Hurricane Katrina devastates New Orleans and leaves 1,800 people dead

2007–2009 Great Recession

- **2010** Patient Protection and Affordable Care Act

2010–2016 Rise of Tea Party

- **2014** Shooting of Michael Brown in Ferguson, Missouri
- **2015** – President Barack Obama introduces Clean Power Plan
  – *Obergefell v. Hodges* decision ends bans on gay marriage
- **2017** – President Donald Trump signs enormous tax cut
  – United States withdraws from Paris Climate Agreement
- **2019** Trump repeals Clean Power Plan

1995 | 2000 | 2005 | 2010 | 2015 | 2020

AMERICA IN THE GLOBAL ECONOMY

How did globalization redefine the relationship of the United States to the rest of the world after the end of the Cold War?

AP® EXAM TIP

Evaluate arguments for and against free trade since the 1990s.

World Trade Organization (WTO) International economic body established in 1995 through the General Agreement on Tariffs and Trade to enforce substantial tariff and import quota reductions.

As it increased connections, globalization destabilized the established order. "Profound and powerful forces are shaking and remaking our world," said a young President Bill Clinton in his first inaugural address in 1993. "The urgent question of our time is whether we can make change our friend and not our enemy." For many, globalization indeed looked like an enemy (see "Thinking Like a Historian," p. 972). In late 1999, more than 50,000 protesters took to the streets of downtown Seattle, Washington. Police, armed with pepper spray and arrayed in riot gear, worked feverishly to clear the clogged streets and usher well-dressed government ministers from around the world into a conference hall. The demonstrators jeered, chanted, and waved a sea of banners. A contingent of radicals broke away from the otherwise peaceful march and smashed the storefronts of chain stores they saw as symbols of global capitalism: Starbucks, Gap, and Old Navy.

What aroused such passion in the so-called Battle of Seattle was a meeting of the **World Trade Organization (WTO)**, a large intergovernmental economic organization that served as one of the principal advocates of unrestrained global trade. Protestors raised a question both fundamental and complicated: In whose interest was the global economy structured? Many of the Seattle activists took inspiration from the five-point "Declaration for Global Democracy," issued by the human rights organization Global Exchange during the WTO's Seattle meeting. "Global trade and investment," the document demanded, "must not be ends in themselves but rather the instruments for achieving equitable and sustainable development, including protection for workers and the environment." The WTO had been established in 1995 through the General Agreement on Tariffs and Trade (GATT), one of the international structures that emerged following World War II. In the eyes of its opponents, the WTO put profits ahead of people — and the showdown in Seattle's streets signaled the profound changes globalization had wrought.

WTO Demonstration, Seattle, 1999 In November 1999, an estimated 50,000 to 100,000 people from many states and foreign nations staged a major protest at a World Trade Organization (WTO) meeting in Seattle. The goals of the protesters were diffuse; many feared that the trend toward a system of free (capitalist-run) trade would primarily benefit multinational corporations and would hurt both developing nations and the working classes in the industrialized world. Protests have continued at subsequent meetings of the WTO and the World Bank. Karie Hamilton/Sygma via Getty Images.

The Rise of the European Union and China

The Cold War had two powerful poles, one capitalist and the other communist, and nearly all geopolitical events were understood in their relationship to the two systems. But starting in the early 1990s, a multipolar world began to emerge — with centers of power in Europe, Japan, China, and the United States, along with rising regional powers such as India and Brazil.

In 1992, the nations of Western Europe created the European Union (EU) and moved toward the creation of a single federal state, somewhat like the United States. By the first decades of the twenty-first century, the European Union included twenty-eight countries and 500 million people — collectively, the third largest population in the world, behind China and India — and accounted for a fifth of all global imports and exports (see "America in the World," p. 975). In 2002, the EU introduced a single currency, the euro, which soon rivaled the dollar and the Japanese yen as a major international currency (Map 30.1). The EU quickly became an economic juggernaut and trading rival of the United States, but faced setbacks in the Great Recession of 2007–2008. Post-recession austerity policies spearheaded by an economically dominant Germany alienated many member states, and worries about open borders fed a revival of nationalism. In a stunning referendum in 2016, the voters of the United Kingdom decided to exit the EU (known as "Brexit") on the grounds that it compromised national sovereignty and permitted unregulated immigration. Even with an uncertain future, the EU remains a major competitor to the United States in commerce and currency.

On the other side of the world, China *quadrupled* its gross domestic product (GDP) in just eight years, between 2000 and 2008. The vast nation of 1.3 billion people posted economic growth rates consistently near 10 percent — higher than the United States achieved during its own periods of furious growth in the 1950s and 1960s. Although still governed by an authoritarian Communist Party, China embraced capitalism, and its factories produced inexpensive products that Americans eagerly purchased — everything from children's toys and television sets to clothing, household appliances, and video games. To maintain this symbiotic relationship, China deliberately kept its currency weak against the American dollar during the 1990s and 2000s, ensuring that its exports remained cheap in the United States.

AP® EXAM TIP

Recognize the impact of globalization on the American economy and politics since the 1990s.

TEACHING STRATEGY

The Seattle Municipal Archives explain the consequences of the 1999 World Trade Organization (WTO) protests that took place in the city. The archives contain several photos and documents from the protests, including a flyer from protesters and various documents to and from city employees. Investigating this event might help students understand the passionate feelings evoked by an increasingly globalized economy. To access these resources, search "Seattle Municipal Archives WTO protests."

AP® APPLY THE TIP

Provide students with **Handout 30.1 — Thematic Analysis: Globalization (TRM)** at the end of class and prompt students to use Chapter 30 to complete the handout for homework. During class, divide students into pairs and ask them to complete the **AP® THINKING LIKE A HISTORIAN** document activity on p. 972. After students read the documents and answer the questions, ask them to provide an extended analysis on each document by identifying the historical context, intended audience, purpose, and point of view of each. Before students complete the **AP® DBQ PRACTICE** prompt on p. 973, ask them to find a seventh document to add to this group of documents. The document can be found in the chapter or from other sources. Students should then complete the essay assignment utilizing all seven documents as well as other evidence in response to the prompt.

TRM Find **Handout 30.1 — Thematic Analysis: Globalization** in the Teacher's Resource Materials.

AP® SKILLS & PROCESSES

ANALYZING HISTORICAL EVIDENCE

The **AP® THINKING LIKE A HISTORIAN** feature explores the uneven consequences of globalization for different economic players. Many critics have described globalization as a "race to the bottom," where the corporation that finds the cheapest source of goods or labor first "wins," with the consequence that wages are driven ever lower. In the era of globalization, countries (or regions within them) have often facilitated the race to the bottom by voluntarily deregulating and/or reducing taxes to attract investment. Students might consider whether this framework helps them make sense of the collection of documents presented here.

Globalization: Its Proponents and Its Discontents

Globalization is perhaps one of the most commonly used, yet least understood, concepts in our modern vocabulary. This chapter explores how, though there has long been an international, or global, dimension to trade, migration, and other economic activity, there is nevertheless something distinct about the post–Cold War global order. Economic integration and communications networking have created new opportunities for millions of people. Yet those same processes may not benefit all equally. The following documents offer different perspectives on the broad process called globalization.

1. **Interview with Petra Mata, Mexican immigrant to the United States, 2003.** *An immigrant from a low-wage country who was "insourced," Mata worked as a low-paid garment worker until she lost her job in the United States because it was outsourced — sent abroad to workers paid even less.*

My name is Petra Mata. I was born in Mexico. I have completed no more than the sixth grade in school. In 1969, my husband and I came to the U.S. believing we would find better opportunities for our children and ourselves. We first arrived without documents, then became legal, and finally became citizens. For years I moved from job to job until I was employed in 1976 by the most popular company in the market, Levi Strauss & Company. I earned $9.73 an hour and also had vacation and sick leave. Levi's provided me and my family with a stable situation, and in return I was a loyal employee and worked there for fourteen years.

On January 16, 1990, Levi's closed its plant in San Antonio, Texas, where I had been working, leaving 1,150 workers unemployed, a majority of whom were Mexican-American women. The company moved its factory to Costa Rica. . . .

As a result of being laid off, I personally lost my house, my method of transportation, and the tranquility of my home. My family and I had to face new problems. My husband was forced to look for a second job on top of the one he already had. He worked from seven in the morning to six at night. Our reality was very difficult. At that time, I had not the slightest idea what free trade was or meant. . . .

Our governments make agreements behind closed doors without participation from the working persons who are most affected by these decisions — decisions that to my knowledge only benefit large corporations and those in positions of power.

2. **iPhone global supply chain figure, 2011.** *This figure shows where profits in the making of iPhones accumulated and thus illustrates how globalization and free trade produced a global assembly line for the making of popular electronics.*

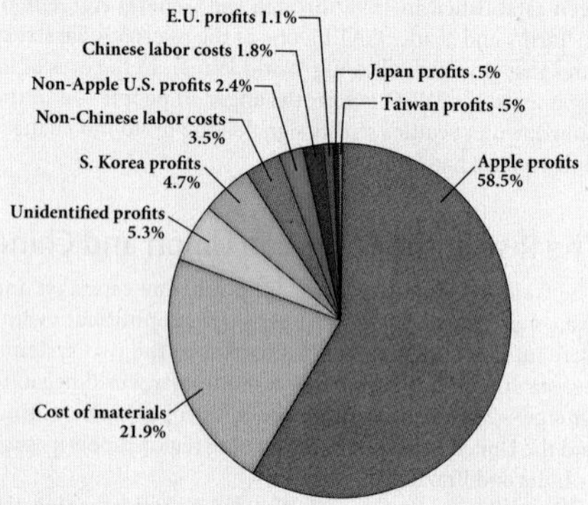

FIGURE 30.4 **Exports**

3. **Seattle Chapter, National Lawyers Guild, "Bringing in an Undemocratic Institution Brings an Undemocratic Response," 2000.** *The National Lawyers Guild, a liberal advocacy group, accuses the World Trade Organization (WTO), an international organization composed of nearly two hundred nations that regulates global trade, of lacking transparency and thwarting democracy.*

Many of the businesses that most promote the WTO and its allied institutions rely on undemocratic practices to promote their business interest. In recent years these policies have included not only monopolistic business practices but also outright interference with local governments. Frequently, to promote the interests of business, a militaristic type of government is either promoted, or even created. The effects these governments and their policies have on the citizenry of these nations are disastrous. Farms and forests are ruined and denuded. Low cost toxic waste dumps are

972

created near population centers to service skyrocketing debts. . . .

The WTO was nominally chartered as a dispute resolution organization. The problem is it is an organization with no real oversight or accountability, and a process that favors the most powerful corporations.

4. **World Trade Organization press release, 2000.** *The WTO argues that increased global trade helps poorer nations.*

- Extreme poverty is a huge problem. 1.2 billion people survive on less than a dollar a day. A further 1.6 billion, more than a quarter of the world's population, make do with one to two dollars a day.
- To alleviate poverty, developing economies need to grow faster, and the poor need to benefit from this growth. Trade can play an important part in reducing poverty, because it boosts economic growth and the poor tend to benefit from that faster growth.
- The study finds that, in general, living standards in developing countries are not catching up with those in developed countries. But some developing countries are catching up. What distinguishes them is their openness to trade. The countries that are catching up with rich ones are those that are open to trade; and the more open they are, the faster they are converging.

5. **Stuart Carlson, political cartoon from the *Milwaukee Journal-Sentinel*, 2005.** *A newspaper humorously portrays American stereotypes from the 1950s and 1990s.*

SOURCE: CARLSON ©2005 Milwaukee Journal Sentinel. Reprinted with permission of ANDREWS MCMEEL SYNDICATION. All rights reserved.

6. **Former president Bill Clinton, speech at Guildhall, London, 2006.** *Clinton, who championed free trade during his presidency (1993–2001), makes the case in favor of globalization.*

I spent a lot of time working on globalization when I was president, coming to terms with the fundamental fact of interdependence that goes far beyond economics: open border, easy travel, easy immigration, free flow of money as well as people, products, and services. I tried to figure out how to maximize the dynamism of global interdependence and still broaden its impact in terms of economics and opportunity. The one thing that I am quite sure of is that interdependence is not a choice, it's not a policy, it is the inevitable condition of our time. So, divorce is not an option. . . .

Therefore, the mission of the moment clearly is to build up the positive and reduce the negative forces of global interdependence in a way that enables us to keep score in the right way. Are people going to be better off, will our children have a better chance, will we be more united than divided?

SOURCES: (1) From *Shafted: Free Trade and America's Working Poor*, by Christine Ahn (Food First Books, 2003). Reprinted by permission of the Institute for Food and Development Policy, 398 60th Street, Oakland, CA 94618; (2) Kenneth L. Kraemer, Greg Linden, and Jason Dedrick, "Capturing Value in Global Networks: Apple's iPad and iPhone" (Paul Merage School of Business, University of California, Irvine, July 2011). Used by permission of the authors; (3) Seattle Chapter, National Lawyers Guild, "Bringing in an Undemocratic Institution Brings an Undemocratic Response," July 5, 2000, ii, 5; (4) WTO press release, June 13, 2000, quoting WTO Special Study No. 5, "Trade, Income Disparity, and Poverty," June 2000. Used by permission of the World Trade Organization; (6) collegeofpublicspeaking.co.uk/Clinton-London-2006.html.

ANALYZING THE EVIDENCE

1. Free trade means that goods can move between countries without restriction or taxation (such as tariffs or duties). Compare sources 1, 3, 5, and 6. How do the sources explain the effects of freer trade across the globe? How would you interpret the WTO's optimism about free trade alongside Petra Mata's personal experience of displacement?
2. How is increased global communication important to the trade relationships described in source 2? According to source 4, what are some other effects associated with the trade relationships shown here?
3. What tension in globalization is the cartoonist in source 5 attempting to capture? What kind of change over time has the cartoonist identified?

AP® DBQ PRACTICE

Based on this chapter's discussion of globalization, and using the preceding documents, write an essay in which you examine the economic effects of recent global integration. In particular, use your essay to define globalization and to outline potential positive and negative effects.

AP® THEME

WXT: Work, Exchange, and Technology

Employment has continued to increase in service sectors and decrease in manufacturing in the last generation. In recent decades, this process has intensified in part because of American purchases of Chinese consumer goods.

TRM Find complete suggested responses in the Teacher's Resource Materials.

AP® SKILLS & PROCESSES

ARGUMENTATION

The **AP® DBQ PRACTICE** prompt asks students to assess the positive and negative effects of globalization. Stronger essays will evaluate which quality has been predominant and why.

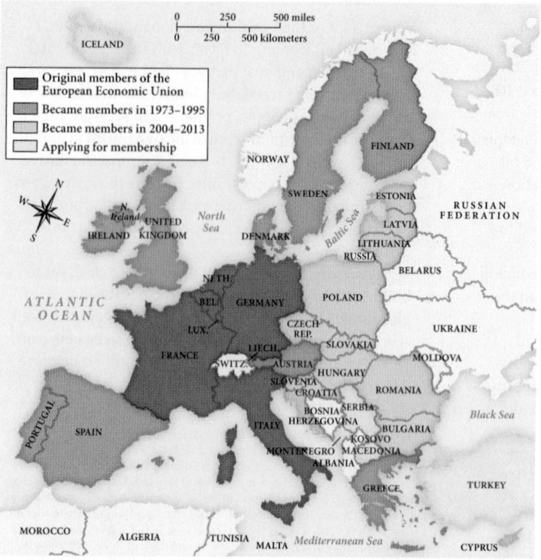

MAP 30.1 Growth of the European Community, 1951–2016
The European Community (EU) began in the 1950s as a loose organization of Western European nations. Over the course of the following decades, it created stronger common institutions, such as the European Parliament in Strasbourg, the EU Commission in Brussels, and the Court of Justice in Luxembourg. With the collapse of communism, the EU expanded to include the nations of Eastern and Central Europe. It now includes twenty-eight nations and more than 500 million people. Many states have applied for membership and are awaiting official ascension into the union, while in 2016 the United Kingdom voted to exit the EU.

Although American consumers have enjoyed the short-term benefits of inexpensive Chinese goods, China's rapid rise in manufacturing presents challenges as well. The influx of Chinese consumer goods helped to shrink further the manufacturing base in the United States, shredding jobs and fraying communities. But the more formidable economic challenge China presents may be the global trade and infrastructure network it continues to build — a combination of new roads and rail lines as well as modernized ports and shipping facilities. This multibillion-dollar initiative, known as the "Belt and Road" program, will soon link Asia, Africa, and Europe in a vast trading network with China at its center. If China captures more and more trade through this network, the United States will face a sharp uphill battle to maintain its own global economic position.

Globalization's Rules and Rulers

Americans have long depended on other countries to provide markets for export, products for import, and immigrants for domestic labor. But the *intensity* of that exchange has fluctuated over time. The end of the Cold War shattered barriers to international trade and impeded capitalist development of vast areas of the world. Perhaps most important, global financial markets became integrated to an unprecedented extent, allowing investment capital to "flow" across borders almost instantly.

AP® SKILLS & PROCESSES

CAUSATION

What were the major consequences for the United States of the economic rise of China and the European Union?

International Organizations and Corporations International governmental organizations, many of them created in the wake of World War II, set the rules for capitalism's worldwide expansion: the World Bank, the International Monetary Fund (IMF), and the General Agreement on Tariffs and Trade (GATT). During the final decade of the twentieth century, the leading capitalist industrial nations formed the **Group of Eight (G8)** to manage global economic policy. The G8 nations — the United States, Britain, Germany, France, Italy, Japan, Canada, and Russia — largely controlled the major international financial organizations (Russia was suspended from the G8 in 2014). In 1995, GATT evolved into the World Trade Organization (WTO), which formalizes and regulates trade agreements among close to 150 member states. Even more recently, in 1999, the Group of Twenty (G20) was founded, which included 19 individual countries plus the EU. With far broader membership than the G8 — including China, India, Brazil, Argentina, and Australia, among others — the G20 took a leading role in global economic policymaking.

As globalization accelerated, so did the integration of regional economies. To counter the economic clout of the European bloc, the United States, Canada, and Mexico signed the **North American Free Trade Agreement (NAFTA)** in 1993. This treaty, as ratified by the U.S. Congress, created a free-trade zone covering all

Group of Eight (G8)
An organization of the leading capitalist industrial nations — United States, Britain, Germany, France, Italy, Japan, Canada, and Russia — that manage global economic policy (Russia was suspended in 2014 for its invasion of Crimea).

North American Free Trade Agreement (NAFTA)
A 1993 treaty that eliminated all tariffs and trade barriers among the United States, Canada, and Mexico. The agreement stimulated economic growth, but critics charged that it left workers in all countries vulnerable.

CHECK FOR UNDERSTANDING

Ask students: **How did the European Union and China rise economically in the post–Cold War era?** *Twenty-eight European nations banded together to create the European Union, forming a unified trading bloc with a single currency. Through strong centralized control by the Communist Party, China has produced cheap manufactured goods, quadrupling its GDP in less than a decade.*

AP® SKILLS & PROCESSES

CAUSATION

The **CAUSATION** question asks students to indicate the effects of the emergence of China and the EU as strong trade partners. To extend this prompt, ask students to explain what the U.S. has done to mitigate the negative effects of the growth of these two economic powers.

TRM Find complete suggested responses in the Teacher's Resource Materials.

AP® THEME

PCE: Politics and Power; WXT: Work, Exchange, and Technology

Policy debates continued in this era over free-trade agreements. NAFTA, for example, was extremely controversial and a subject of significant debate during the 1992 election. On the 20th anniversary of NAFTA's ratification in November 2013, the *New York Times* hosted a forum titled "What We've Learned from NAFTA," which attempted to answer the question: Has NAFTA proved to be a success that the United States should try to replicate more widely or the type of trade agreement that should be avoided in the future? The forum provided answers from six different policy experts. To access this forum, search "NYT What We've Learned from NAFTA."

Global Trade, 1960–2020

One of the major consequences of economic globalization is an increase in trade among nations. The figures below show imports and exports for four of the world's largest economies.

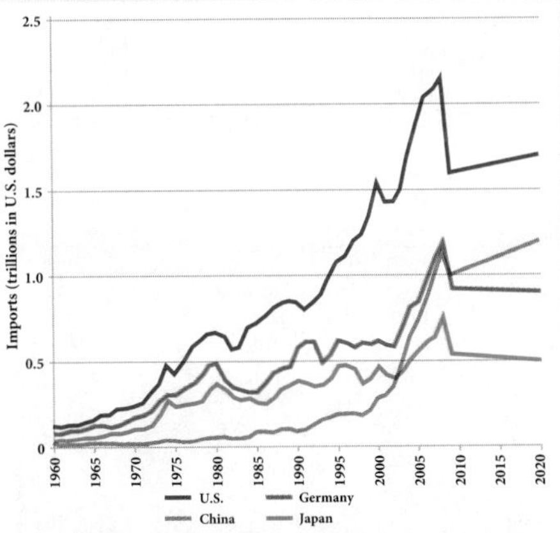

FIGURE 30.5 Imports, 1960–2009

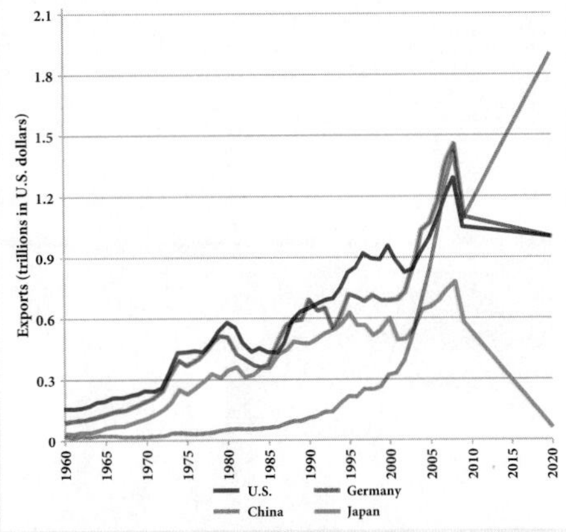

FIGURE 30.6 Exports, 1960–2009

QUESTIONS FOR ANALYSIS

1. Identify two patterns or trends pictured in Figure 30.5. According to the sources, what U.S. imports rose at roughly the same rate as those of other countries until the 1970s. What accounts for the acceleration of U.S. imports thereafter?
2. Identify two patterns or trends pictured in Figure 30.6. China's exports rose spectacularly after the 1990s. Germany increased its exports in this period dramatically as well. What evidence do you see here for increasing competition for the United States in a globalizing economy?

of North America — where goods could cross borders without tariffs or duties. Though NAFTA would eventually stimulate the economies of all three nations, critics charged that the agreement provided few protections for workers — including when manufacturing left the United States for Mexico or Canada, creating joblessness. In East Asia, the capitalist nations of Japan, South Korea, Taiwan, and Singapore consulted on economic policy; as China developed a quasi-capitalist economy and became a major exporter of manufactures, its Communist-led government joined their deliberations. The principle at work in these regional trading partnerships is that bigger is better — the larger a trading network is, and the more integrated the nations within it are, the more leverage it has in negotiating terms with competing networks.

Governmental and international organizations set the rules, but **multinational corporations (MNCs)** were the greatest facilitators of globalization. In 1970, there were 7,000 corporations with offices and factories in multiple countries; by the early 2000s, that number had exploded to 63,000. Many of the most powerful MNCs were and still are based in the United States. Walmart, the biggest American retailer, is also one of the world's largest corporations, with 7,000 stores in other nations and more than $500 billion in sales in 2018. Apple, maker of the iPhone and iPad, grew spectacularly in the 2000s and now has more than $250 billion in annual global sales. Beginning

AP® EXAM TIP

Recognize the role of world organizations in promoting global economic change.

multinational corporation (MNC) Corporate organization that owns or controls production of goods or services in a country or countries other than its home country.

AP® SKILLS & PROCESSES

ANALYZING HISTORICAL EVIDENCE

The **AP® AMERICA IN THE WORLD** feature illustrates the dynamics of the global economy, particularly the U.S.'s growing trade imbalance over the last several decades. It is important for students to notice that the two charts are indexed differently — the top of the Imports chart (on the left) ends at $2.5 trillion, while the Exports chart (on the right) stops at $2.1 trillion. Apart from noting the stunning growth in China's exports, as indicated in Question 2, students could pick a few dates and compare the value of U.S. imports v. exports and track the growing trade deficit.

TRM Find complete suggested responses in the Teacher's Resource Materials.

AP® APPLY THE TIP

Direct students to use pp. 974–977 to complete **Handout 30.2 — Causation: World Organizations (TRM)**. After completing the handout, organize students into collaborative groups to research the goals, methods, accomplishments, and controversies of one of the following: the International Monetary Fund (IMF), the General Agreement on Tariffs and Trade (GATT), the Group of 7 (G7), the Group of 8 (G8), the World Trade Organization, or the World Health Organization. After students have completed their research, engage them in a seminar-style discussion of the role of international organizations in the modern world and their impact on economic change.

TRM Find **Handout 30.2 — Causation: World Organizations** in the Teacher's Resource Materials.

VISUAL ACTIVITY

A Nike Factory in Vietnam In 2000, Nike was the largest foreign investor in Vietnam, where the company produced shoes and sportswear in ten subcontracting factories employing nearly 40,000 workers. Most of the workers were young women from small, rural villages who earned the equivalent of about $60 a month. Those wages were low, but still above the country's minimum wage. Nike in Vietnam epitomized the globalization of manufacturing and trade and the quest by American companies for a low-wage workforce. Nike also dramatically expanded its presence in China during the 2000s, where the company's products were produced in 124 subcontracted factories. AP Photo/Richard Vogel.

READING THE IMAGE: Examine the photograph for both small details and what the image as a whole shows. How are the workers organized, and can you tell what they are making? Is there anything noteworthy about gender in the photograph?

MAKING CONNECTIONS: How would you put this photograph together with information from the chapter to illustrate some of the attributes of globalization? How does this image illustrate the impact of globalization on the United States? On Vietnam?

in 1954 with Ray Kroc's original franchise in San Bernardino, California (see "Fast Food and Shopping Malls" in Chapter 25), the McDonald's restaurant chain had 1,000 outlets outside the United States by 1980; twenty years later, there were nearly 13,000, and "McWorld" had become a popular shorthand term for globalization.

These corporate giants crossed borders to access new markets — and to find cheaper sources of labor. Many American-based MNCs closed their factories at home and outsourced manufacturing jobs to plants in Mexico, Eastern Europe, and especially Asia. The athletic sportswear firm Nike was a prime example. Founded in 1964 in Oregon, Nike grew from a modest shoe retailer into a behemoth in a few short decades. By the 2010s, Nike had 700 factories in more then 40 countries worldwide employing more than 700,000 workers, most of whom received low wages, endured harsh working conditions, and had no health or pension benefits.

Financial Deregulation One principal difference between the new era of globalization and previous patterns has been the opening of national financial and currency

TRM Find complete suggested responses in the Teacher's Resource Materials.

CHECK FOR UNDERSTANDING

Ask students: **What features characterized the new era of globalization?** *The General Agreement on Tariffs and Trade (GATT), part of the Bretton Woods economic system created at the end of World War II, evolved into the World Trade Organization (WTO) in the late 1990s, comprising 150 nations that worked to formalize trade agreements. At the same time, smaller regions formed free-trade economic blocs, like NAFTA, which united the U.S., Canada, and Mexico. An increasing number of corporations became multinational corporations (MNCs), with offices and factories in multiple countries that allowed them to find the cheapest sources of labor. The neoliberal principles that governed the globalized economy generally involved deregulation of banks and investment firms. The risky investments that resulted produced dramatic profits and catastrophic failures, including a major Asian financial crisis in 1997 and a global recession in 2008.*

markets to investment from around the world. The United States and Britain led the way in the 1980s, with powerful political forces pushing for total deregulation of banks, brokerage houses, investment firms, and financial markets. In essentially letting the free market replace government oversight, the two countries led a quiet economic revolution. Financial deregulation led to spectacular profits for investors — and a more fragile, crash-prone global economy. Financial-industry profits in the United States rose from less than 10 percent of total business profits in the 1950s to more than 40 percent beginning in the 1990s. But the risks of deregulation were equally unmistakable: the bankruptcy of the American savings and loan industry in the 1980s; the near-bankruptcies of Russia in the late 1990s and of Argentina in 2001; the 1997 Asian financial crisis, centered in Thailand and Indonesia; and the Great Recession, which shook the entire global economy from 2007 to 2009. Together, the growing global power of MNCs and financial deregulation made ordinary American workers and families economically vulnerable. The American economy continued to generate wealth, but unevenly — wages stagnated and families struggled, even as corporate profits soared (Figure 30.1).

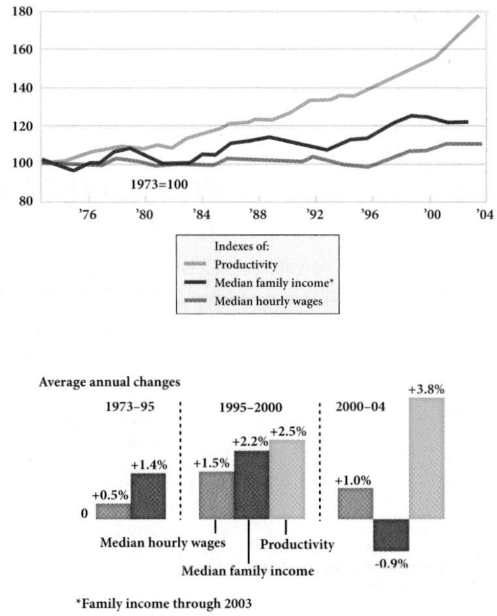

FIGURE 30.1 Productivity, Family Income, and Wages, 1970–2004 This chart tells a complex and not altogether happy story. The median hourly wages of American workers (adjusted for inflation) stagnated between 1970 and 1995. The rise in median family income reflected the increasing proportion of two-earner families, as more married women entered the workforce. The dramatic increases in productivity did not lead to higher wages for workers. Rather, businesses used those gains either to cut prices to compete in the global marketplace or to reward owners, shareholders, and, particularly, corporate executives.

Revolutions in Technology

The technological advances of the 1980s and 1990s changed the character of everyday life for millions of Americans, linking them with a global information and media environment unprecedented in world history. New communications systems — satellites, fiber-optic cables, global positioning networks — were shrinking the world's physical spaces to a degree unimaginable at the beginning of the twentieth century. Not since television was introduced to American homes in the years following World War II had technology so profoundly changed the way people lived their lives. Personal computers, cell phones and smartphones, the Internet, social media, and streaming media have since the 1990s altered work, leisure, and access to knowledge irreversibly. Like unimpeded trade, these technological advances affirmed and accelerated the globalization process.

During the 1990s, personal computers, which had emerged in the late 1970s, became the center of a massive social and consumer shift with the spread of the Internet. Like the computer itself, the Internet was the product of military-based research. During the late 1960s, the U.S. Department of Defense, in conjunction with the Massachusetts Institute of Technology, began developing a decentralized computer network, the **Advanced Research Projects Agency Network (ARPANET)**. The Internet, which grew out of the ARPANET, was soon used by government scientists, academic specialists, and military contractors to exchange data, information, and electronic mail (soon dubbed "e-mail"). By the 1980s, the Internet had spread to universities, businesses, and tech-savvy members of the general public. The debut in 1991 of the graphics-based World Wide Web — a collection of servers that allowed access to millions of documents, pictures, and other materials — enhanced the popular appeal and commercial possibilities of the Internet. Taking advantage of those possibilities,

AP® SKILLS & PROCESSES

COMPARISON

What were the potential benefits and risks of globalization to the United States and other countries?

Advanced Research Projects Agency Network (ARPANET)
A decentralized computer network developed in the late 1960s by the U.S. Department of Defense in conjunction with the Massachusetts Institute of Technology. The Internet grew out of the ARPANET.

AP® THEME

WXT: Work, Exchange, and Technology

Real wages stagnated for the working and middle classes amid growing economic inequality. As **FIGURE 30.1** indicates, median hourly wages (adjusted for inflation) stayed nearly the same over a more than thirty-year period.

AP® SKILLS & PROCESSES

COMPARISON

When comparing this concept, encourage students to think as objectively as possible. The goal is to render an interpretation, not necessarily a personal judgement of the topic in question. One way to encourage this practice is to require students to explain both a risk and reward for the United States in a globalized society. You may point out that globalization, especially economic, was a long-term development in world history

TRM Find complete suggested responses in the Teacher's Resource Materials.

AP® THEME

WXT: Work, Exchange, and Technology

Lead a class discussion on how technological innovations in computing, digital mobile technology, and the Internet transformed daily life. Students should identify the increased access to information and the emergence of new social behaviors and networks.

AP® SKILLS & PROCESSES

DEVELOPMENTS AND PROCESSES

Think about having students evaluate the societal and economic changes wrought by technological advances in the period 1980-2019. The goal is for students to recognize the broader patterns of these changes, as opposed to concentrating only on the recent past.

TEACHING STRATEGY

The Internet Society Web site provides a variety of articles explaining the historical development of the Internet, as well as more technical explanations about how it functions. To access these resources, search "Internet Society History of the Internet."

CHECK FOR UNDERSTANDING

Ask students: **How did globalization redefine the relationship of the United States to the rest of the world after the end of the Cold War?** *Starting in the 1990s, globalization radically altered the role of the United States in the world. U.S. policymakers felt pressured to engage more thoroughly in an increasing number of global organizations like the WTO and the IMF and engage with regional trading blocs like NAFTA. The rapidity of information movement increasingly connected the world and minimized regional and national differences while also leading to rapid technological developments. Globalization also brought new issues to the fore, such as increasingly specialized labor and environmental challenges.*

AP® APPLY THE TIP

Prompt students to work in collaborative groups to create a Venn diagram to illustrate the similarities and differences in the causes, effects, and historical context for the cultural conflict of the 1920s and 1950s. After the groups complete their diagrams, ask them to find one image representing each time period that best illustrates the differences and a third image to represent the most important similarity between the time periods. Ask students to place these images into a slideshow presentation; on the first slide, students should place the two images that illustrate the most important differences and on the second slide, the image that represents the similarity. Student groups should present their images and explain to the class the reasons for their choices. Once all groups have presented, lead a class discussion on the historical context in which the cultural conflicts occurred in each of the time periods.

Amazon, now the world's largest retailer, developed entirely within a digital, web-based world beginning with its founding in 1994. Five years later, the company had passed half a billion dollars in global sales and its founder, Jeff Bezos, was named *Time* magazine's "Person of the Year." By 2015, 86 percent of all Americans and more than three billion people worldwide — almost half the world's population — used the Internet to send messages, view information, and buy and sell products and services.

POLITICS AND PARTISANSHIP IN A CONTENTIOUS ERA

What were the sources of domestic division in the United States between the 1990s and the present, and how did they reshape the political landscape?

Standing at the podium at the 1992 Republican National Convention, with thousands of his supporters cheering, Patrick Buchanan did not mince words. He had already ended his campaign for the presidential nomination, but the former Nixon speechwriter and Reagan aid still hoped to shape the party's message to voters. "This election," he told the audience — including millions watching on television — "is about what we stand for as Americans." Citing Democratic support for abortion rights and the rights of lesbians and gay men, Buchanan invoked "a religious war going on in our country for the soul of America. It is a cultural war." His long list of enemies included "environmental extremists who put birds and rats and insects ahead of families, workers, and jobs."

culture war
A term derived from a 1992 speech by the Republican politician Patrick Buchanan to describe a political struggle, dating to the 1920s, between religious traditionalists and secular liberals. In the 1990s, social issues such as abortion rights and the rights of lesbians and gay men divided these groups.

Buchanan's provocative address, which became known as the "**culture war**" speech, hit two themes that came to define American politics in the 1990s and early 2000s: religious conflict and economic precarity. His "religious war" was another name for a long-standing political struggle, dating to the 1920s, between religious traditionalists and secular liberals (see "Culture Wars" in Chapter 21). The moral certainty of traditional religion is on your side, Buchanan assured his Republican followers, in the battle with Democrats "for the soul" of the country. But to address growing economic uncertainty, especially for blue-collar Americans, Buchanan had an economic message as well. "We need to let them know we know how bad they're hurting," Buchanan said of the anxious and disillusioned workers he had met on the campaign trail. Against the backdrop of globalization, American politics in the 1990s and early 2000s followed the script of Buchanan's speech, careening back and forth between contests over divisive social issues and concern over Americans' economic security.

An Increasingly Plural Society

AP® EXAM TIP
Compare the "culture war" of the 1990s to the cultural conflicts in the 1920s and 1950s.

By most demographic predictions, the United States will become a "majority-minority" nation by 2050. No single ethnic or racial group will be in the numerical majority. This was already the case in four states by 2010 — California, Texas, Hawaii, and New Mexico — where African Americans, Latinos, and Asians together constituted a majority of the state's residents. This long-range trend first became evident in the 1990s, sparking debates about identity and related public policies such as affirmative action.

AP® EXAM TIP
Recognize the impact of changes in immigration policy on American culture and the economy.

New Immigrants According to the Census Bureau, the population of the United States grew from 203 million in 1970 to 280 million in 2000 (see "Firsthand Accounts," p. 980). Of that 77-million-person increase, immigrants accounted for 28 million, with documented entrants numbering 21 million and undocumented entrants adding another 7 million (Figure 30.2). As a result, by 2010, 27 percent of California's population was foreign-born, as was 22 percent of New York's, 21 percent of New Jersey's, and 19 percent of Florida's — though 2020 census figures were not available when this textbook went to press, the number of foreign-born residents of the United States is expected to be the highest since 1910. Relatively few of the newest Americans came from

Europe, which had dominated immigration to the United States between 1880 and 1924. The overwhelming majority of immigrants — some 25 million, or 9 out of every 10 — from 1970 to 2000 came from one of two places: Latin America (16 million) and East Asia (9 million) (Map 30.2).

This extraordinary inflow was an unintended result of the **Immigration and Nationality Act** of 1965, a relatively unheralded but highly influential element of Great Society legislation (see "Great Society Initiatives" in Chapter 27). Also known as the Hart-Celler Act, the legislation eliminated the 1924 quota system, which gave preference to immigrants from Western and Northern Europe. In its place, the 1965 law created a more equal playing field among nations of origin and a slightly higher total limit on immigration. The legislation also eased the entry of immigrants who possessed skills in high demand in the United States. Finally, a provision with far reaching implications was included in the new law: immediate family members of those already legally residing in the United States were admitted outside of the total numerical limit.

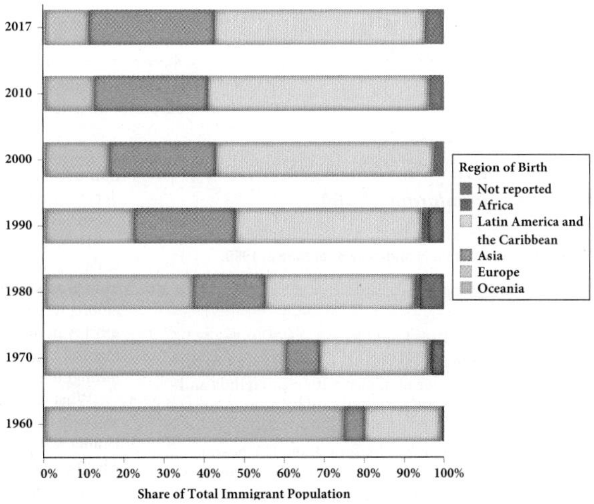

FIGURE 30.2 Regions of Birth for Immigrants in the United States, 1960–2017
This shows the foreign-born population of the United States by their region of origin between 1960 and 2017. In those decades, immigration from Europe slowed; thus the European-born population of the United States began to decline (as the children of immigrants were born in the United States). In contrast, immigration from the Caribbean and Latin America, Asia, and Africa accelerated, leading to expanding foreign-born populations from those regions. This shift in immigration patterns was made possible by the Immigration and Nationality Act of 1965. As a result, the United States continued to be a diverse nation of immigrants, with Latin America and Asia increasingly leading the way. By 2017, Asian American and Latinx people together made up 25 percent of the U.S. population.

Immigration and Nationality Act A 1965 law that eliminated the discriminatory 1924 nationality quotas, established a higher total limit on immigration, and gave immigration preferences to those with skills in high demand or immediate family members in the United States.

American residents hailing from Latin America and the Caribbean were best positioned to take advantage of the family provision. Mexican, Dominican, Salvadoran, and Guatemalan families reunited by the millions, and Latinos surpassed African Americans as a percentage of the overall population. This surge in immigration also altered the emerging global economy. The new Americans often sent substantial portions of their earnings, called remittances, back to family members in their home countries. In 2015 alone, workers in the United States sent $25 billion to Mexico, a massive remittance flow that constituted Mexico's third largest source of foreign exchange.

Asian immigration came largely from China, the Philippines, South Korea, India, and Pakistan, as well as 700,000 refugees from Southeast Asia (Vietnam, Laos, and Cambodia), who arrived during and after the Vietnam War. This inflow from Asian nations signaled more than just a population increase. As immigration from Asia increased, as Japan and China grew more influential economically, and as transoceanic trade accelerated, commentators on both sides of the ocean acknowledged an

New Immigrants In the early years of the 2000s, more immigrants lived in the United States than at any time since the first decades of the twentieth century. Most came from Asia, Latin America, and Africa. Many, like those pictured here, started small businesses that helped revive the economies of urban and suburban neighborhoods across the country. Blend Images/SuperStock.

AP® SKILLS & PROCESSES

ANALYZING HISTORICAL EVIDENCE

Use **FIGURE 30.2** to explore the dramatic growth of immigration from Latin America and Asia, as well as both a proportional and an absolute decline in immigrants from all parts of Europe as a result of the Hart-Celler Act or Immigration and Nationality Act of 1965.

AP® THEME

MIG: Migration and Settlement

International migration from Latin America and Asia increased dramatically in the last several decades. (For statistics, see the figure on p. 1001b.) The new immigrants affected U.S. culture in many ways and supplied the economy with an important labor force. Tom Gjelten, in his *Atlantic* article titled "The Immigration Act That Inadvertently Changed America," argues that the Immigration and Nationality Act of 1965 has dramatically — and unintentionally — reshaped the American landscape. To access his full article, search "Atlantic Gjelten Immigration Act."

AP® SKILLS & PROCESSES

ANALYZING HISTORICAL EVIDENCE

Since the beginning of the Trump administration, the issue of the volume and type of immigration into the U.S. has become an especially heated topic. The **AP® FIRSTHAND ACCOUNTS** feature provides a reminder that intense political and cultural debates over issues such as immigration policy have persisted for several decades.

AP® APPLY THE TIP

Provide students with an excerpt from Patrick Buchanan's "culture war" speech from 1992 and ask them to read and analyze the speech. Students should consider the ways in which the ideas expressed were like the culture conflicts of the 1920s, such as religious fundamentalism v. modernism and liberalism. Divide the class into two teams: one team representing support for immigration and a path to citizenship for illegal immigrants, and the other team representing support for immigration restriction and punishment of illegal immigrants. Allow each team to subdivide to focus on specific areas in the immigration debate, such as comprehensive immigration reform, responses to illegal immigration, reform of the green card system, Proposition 187, DREAMers, "building a wall," etc. After a research period, begin the structured debate by asking a representative from each team to step forward to address the following resolution: The U.S. has always been made stronger by open doors and unfettered immigration. Prompt students to debate the issue; require students to cite historical evidence to support their arguments. At the end of the debate, lead a class discussion to debrief on the issues surrounding the debate over multiculturalism.

AP® FIRSTHAND ACCOUNTS

Immigration After 1965: Its Defenders and Critics

As we have seen in this chapter, the immigration law passed by Congress in 1965 combined with global developments to shift the flows of people seeking entry to the United States. More and more immigrants came from Latin America, the Caribbean, Asia, and Africa. Immigration has always been politically controversial, but in the 1990s a renewed, and often polarized, debate over immigration emerged.

JOHN F. KENNEDY

A Nation of Immigrants, 1964

This selection is from a revised, and posthumously published, version of a book Kennedy originally published in 1958.

SOURCE: Nicholas Capaldi, ed., *Immigration: Debating the Issues* (Amherst, NY: Prometheus Books, 1997), 128.

❝ Immigration policy should be generous; it should be fair; it should be flexible. With such a policy we can turn to the world, and to our own past with clean hands and a clean conscience. Such a policy would be a reaffirmation of old principles. It would be an expression of our agreement with George Washington that 'The bosom of America is open to receive not only the opulent and respectable stranger, but the oppressed and persecuted of all nations and religions; whom we shall welcome to a participation of all our rights and privileges, if by decency and propriety of conduct they appear to merit the enjoyment.' ❞

ROY BECK

"A Nation of (Too Many) Immigrants?" 1996

Roy Beck is a former journalist who became an activist for immigration reduction.

SOURCE: From *The Case Against Immigration: The Moral, Economic, Social, and Environmental Reasons for Reducing U.S. Immigration Back to Traditional Levels*, by Roy H. Beck (New York: W. W. Norton & Company, 1996). Used by permission of the author.

❝ Since 1970, more than 30 million foreign citizens and their descendants have been added to the local communities and labor pools of the United States. It is the numerical equivalent of having relocated within our borders the entire present population of all Central American countries.

Demographic change on such a massive scale — primarily caused by the increased admission of *legal* immigrants — inevitably has created winners and losers among Americans. Based on opinion polls, it appears that most Americans consider themselves net losers and believe that the United States has become 'a nation of too many immigrants.'

What level of immigration is best for America, and of real help to the world? Although we often hear that the United States is a nation of immigrants, we seldom ask just what that means. It can be difficult to ask tough questions about immigration when we see nostalgic images of Ellis Island, recall our own families' coming to America, or encounter a new immigrant who is striving admirably to achieve the American dream.

But tough questions about immigration can no longer be avoided as we enter a fourth decade of unprecedentedly high immigration and struggle with its impact on our job markets, on the quality of life and social fabric of our communities, and on the state of the environment. . . .

The task before the nation in setting a fair level of immigration is not about race or some vision of a homogenous white America; it is about protecting and enhancing the United States' unique experiment in democracy for all Americans, including recent immigrants, regardless of their particular ethnicity. It is time to confront the true costs and benefits of immigration numbers, which have skyrocketed beyond our society's ability to handle them successfully. ❞

emerging "Pacific Rim" region, which included the United States, Southeast and East Asia, Canada, and Australia.

AP® EXAM TIP

Evaluate the degree to which the criticism of multiculturalism in the 1990s represented change or continuity in American history.

Multiculturalism and Its Critics Most new immigrants arrived under the terms of the 1965 law. But those who entered without legal documentation stirred political controversy. Two decades after the new law, there were between three and five million such immigrants. To remedy this situation, Congress passed the Immigration Reform and Control Act in 1986, which combined legalization for unauthorized immigrants with preventative measures to limit future immigration. The law granted citizenship to many of those who had arrived outside the law's numerical limits, but also provided incentives for employers not to hire undocumented immigrants and increased surveillance along the border with Mexico. A subsequent, more liberal law passed by Congress

VERNON M. BRIGGS JR. AND STEPHEN MOORE

"Still an Open Door?" 1994

Two academic policy analysts weigh in on the immigration debate.

SOURCE: Vernon M. Briggs Jr. and Stephen Moore, *Still an Open Door? U.S. Immigration Policy and the American Economy* (Washington, DC: The American University Press, 1994), 78.

"Immigrants are certainly not an unmixed blessing. When the newcomers first arrive, they impose short-term costs on the citizenry. Because immigration means more people, they cause more congestion of our highways, a more crowded housing market, and longer waiting lines in stores and hospitals. In states such as California, immigrants' children are heavy users of an already overburdened public school system, and so on. Some immigrants abuse the welfare system, which means that tax dollars from Americans are transferred to immigrant populations. Los Angeles County officials estimate that immigrants' use of county services costs the local government hundreds of millions of dollars each year. . . .

The benefits of immigration, however, are manifold. Perhaps the most important benefit is that immigrants come to the United States with critically needed talents, energies, and ambitions that serve as an engine for economic progress and help the United States retain economic and geopolitical leadership. Because for most of the world's immigrants, America is their first choice, the United States is in a unique position to select the most brilliant and inventive minds from the United Kingdom, Canada, China, Korea, India, Ireland, Mexico, Philippines, Russia, Taiwan, and other nations. Because most immigrants are not poor, tired, huddled masses, but rather are above the average of their compatriots in skill and education levels, the immigration process has a highly beneficial self-selection component, a skimming of the cream of the best workers and top brainpower from the rest of the world."

PRESIDENT BARACK OBAMA

June 15, 2012, Announcement at the White House Rose Garden

In 2012 the president announced a new policy allowing many immigrants to avoid deportation and apply for work authorization.

SOURCE: *New York Times*, June 15, 2012.

"This morning, Secretary Napolitano [Secretary of Department of Homeland Security] announced new actions my administration will take to mend our nation's immigration policy, to make it more fair, more efficient and more just, specifically for certain young people sometimes called DREAMers.

Now, these are young people who study in our schools, they play in our neighborhoods, they're friends with our kids, they pledge allegiance to our flag. They are Americans in their heart, in their minds, in every single way but one: on paper. They were brought to this country by their parents, sometimes even as infants, and often have no idea that they're undocumented until they apply for a job or a driver's license or a college scholarship.

Put yourself in their shoes. Imagine you've done everything right your entire life, studied hard, worked hard, maybe even graduated at the top of your class, only to suddenly face the threat of deportation to a country that you know nothing about, with a language that you may not even speak.

That's what gave rise to the Dream Act. It says that if your parents brought you here as a child, you've been here for five years and you're willing to go to college or serve in our military, you can one day earn your citizenship. And I've said time and time and time again to Congress that — send me the Dream Act, put it on my desk, and I will sign it right away. . . ."

QUESTIONS FOR ANALYSIS

1. Compare and contrast the different views on immigration presented here. According to the sources, what are the pros and cons of immigration? Identify which sources are most credible and substantiate your claim with specific examples.
2. Does the debate over immigration depend on whether immigrants are pictured as skilled and educated or unskilled and poor? How does socioeconomic status inform the arguments of these sources?
3. The Dream Act that President Obama mentions was stalled in Congress in 2012. What kinds of appeals does he make on behalf of immigrants? How do they compare with Kennedy's remarks?

TRM Find complete suggested responses in the Teacher's Resource Materials.

in 1990 increased the number of immigrants with certain in-demand job skills permitted to enter the country — in effect, expanding the category of "legal" immigrant.

These reforms did not satisfy increasingly loud immigration critics. In 1992, as he campaigned for president, Patrick Buchanan warned Americans that their country was "undergoing the greatest invasion in its history, a migration of millions of illegal aliens a year from Mexico." When Buchanan's movement sputtered at the federal level, many anti-immigrant activists began turning to the states. They garnered a quick victory in 1994, when Californians approved Proposition 187, a ballot initiative that barred undocumented immigrants from public schools, nonemergency care at public health clinics, and all other state social services. After three years in federal court, however, the controversial measure was ruled unconstitutional. State-level efforts reemerged a decade later, in 2010 and 2011, when the Arizona and Alabama

AP® SKILLS & PROCESSES

ANALYZING HISTORICAL EVIDENCE

MAP 30.2 provides a glimpse of the geographic distribution of the two largest immigrant groups since passage of the Immigration and Nationality Act of 1965. Among other patterns, students should notice significant clustering of both groups in Sun Belt areas like California. The Pew Research Center is an excellent resource on facts, statistics, and trends on many contemporary American social issues, including immigration patterns. One 2015 study, for example, included "Mexican and Asian Immigrants Compared," with tables comparing the two groups according to two dozen different demographic factors. To access this study, search "Pew Research Center Mexican and Asian Immigrants Compared 2015."

TEACHING STRATEGY

Have students evaluate at least two geographic regions where immigration caused more economic and societal changes. What factors account for this geographic trend? The maps in **MAP 30.2** should help students reach some sound conclusions.

TRM Find complete suggested responses in the Teacher's Resource Materials.

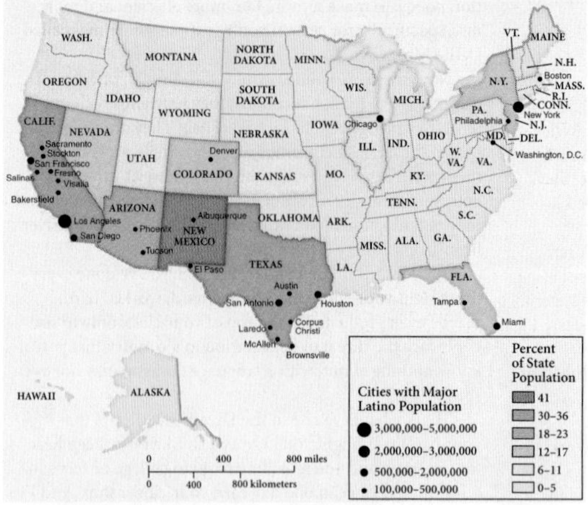

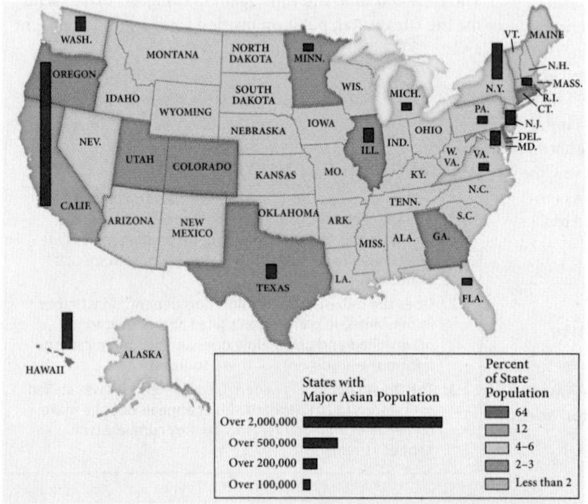

MAPPING THE PAST

MAP 30.2 Latino and Asian Populations, 2000

In 2000, people of Latin American descent made up more than 11 percent of the American population, and they now outnumber African Americans as the largest minority group. Asian Americans accounted for an additional 4 percent of the population. Demographers predict that by the year 2050 only about half of the U.S. population will be composed of non-Latino whites. Note the high percentage of Latinos and Asians in California and certain other states.

ANALYZING THE MAP: In what states and regions are immigrants from Latin America concentrated? Where are immigrants from Asia concentrated? Which specific states attract the most immigrants overall?

MAKING CONNECTIONS: How do the changes illustrated on this map relate to regional and national identity in the United States? How does the impact of immigrants on American identity illustrate both continuity and change over time?

legislatures passed modified versions of Proposition 187. The federal courts, including the Supreme Court, ruled some elements of the laws unconstitutional but allowed others, such as mandatory citizenship checks during law enforcement stops, to remain. In 2016, immigration hard-liners massed behind Republican presidential nominee Donald Trump, who pledged to "build a wall" along the border with Mexico and to deport the approximately 11 million undocumented immigrants by then residing in the United States.

Debates over post-1965 immigration resembled the argument over new arrivals in the early decades of the century. Then, many native-born white Protestants worried that predominantly Jewish and Catholic immigrants from eastern and southern Europe, along with African American migrants from the South, threatened the "purity" of the nation. In this view, the nation was white and Protestant. The conflicts looked the same, but the cultural paradigm had shifted. In the earlier era, the *melting pot* — a term borrowed from the title of a 1908 play — became the metaphor for how American society would accommodate, and assimilate, its newfound diversity. Some native-born Americans found solace in the melting-pot concept because it implied that a single "American" culture would ultimately prevail. In the 1990s, however, the idea of **multiculturalism** emerged, laying out a new definition of social diversity. Americans, this concept suggested, were not a single people that absorbed minorities. Rather, Americans as a whole comprised a diverse set of ethnic and racial groups — as well as religious and sexual — each with unique perspectives and experiences, living and working together.

Critics charged that multiculturalism sowed division and conferred preferential treatment on nonwhite groups. Many government policies, as well as a large number of private employers, continued to support affirmative action programs designed to bring African Americans and Latinos into public-roup private-sector jobs and universities in larger numbers. Conservatives argued that such governmental programs were deeply flawed because they promoted "reverse discrimination" against white men and women and awarded jobs and opportunities to less qualified applicants. As with immigration, California stood at the center of the debate. In 1995, the regents of the University of California scrapped their entire affirmative action admissions policy, and a year later

California voters approved **Proposition 209**, which outlawed affirmative action in state employment and public education. In 1995, at the height of the controversy, President Bill Clinton delivered a major speech reminding Americans that Richard Nixon, a Republican president, had endorsed affirmative action, and Clinton concluded by saying the nation should "mend it," not "end it."

As in the *Bakke* decision of the 1970s (see "Civil Rights in a New Era" in Chapter 28), the U.S. Supreme Court spoke loudest and last. In two parallel 2003 cases, the Court invalidated an affirmative action plan at the University of Michigan but allowed racial preference policies that promoted a "diverse" student body. Affirmative action had been narrowed, but its constitutional footing was preserved. States and public institutions could take race into account, as one factor among many, so long as the goal was a diversity beneficial to all.

Additional anxieties about a multicultural nation centered on language. In 1998, Silicon Valley software entrepreneur Ron Unz sponsored a California initiative calling for an end to bilingual education in public schools. Unz argued that bilingual education did not adequately prepare Spanish-speaking students to succeed in an English-speaking society. Unlike many anti-immigrant hard-liners, Unz cast his proposal, known as Proposition 227, as benefitting immigrants themselves, or at least their children. But when he unfavorably compared Latino immigrants to his own Jewish grandparents "who came to California in the 1920s and 1930s as poor European immigrants [to work] . . . not to sit back and be a burden on those who were already here," many of his opponents accused him, and his measure, of anti-Latino bias. The state's white, Anglo residents largely approved of the measure; most Mexican American, Asian American, and civil rights organizations opposed it. The passage of 227 — with a 61 percent majority in the nation's most diverse state — seemed to confirm the limits of multiculturalism.

multiculturalism
Diversity in gender, race, ethnicity, religion, and sexual preference. This political and social policy became increasingly popular in the United States during the 1980s post–civil rights era.

Proposition 209
A proposition approved by California voters in 1996 that outlawed affirmative action in state employment and public education.

AP® SKILLS & PROCESSES

CONTINUITY AND CHANGE

How did anti-immigrant sentiment increase between the 1960s and the 1990s, and what sorts of actions were taken by those opposed to immigration?

Clashes over "Family Values"

Clashes over women's rights, gay rights, and the family proved to be another cultural battleground, extending the political conflicts that had grown out of the 1960s and 1970s. New Right conservatives charged that the "abrasive experiments of two liberal decades," as a Reagan administration report put it, had eroded respect for marriage and "family values." They pointed to the divorce rate, which had doubled between 1960 and 1980 and continued to climb — nearing the point at which almost half of marriages ended in divorce. They also highlighted the nearly 60 percent rate of out-of-wedlock pregnancies among African Americans. Cultural conservatives eyed a wide range of culprits for the decline of the family: legislators who enacted liberal divorce laws and allowed welfare payments to unmarried mothers, feminists who called for equal participation for women in jobs and education, as well as judges who condoned abortion and banished religious instruction from public schools.

AP® EXAM TIP

Analyze the intense debates that continue in American society over diversity, gender, and family.

Abortion Reproductive rights provided a central stage in this cultural struggle over the family, pitting feminists against religious conservatives and turning abortion access into a defining issue between Democrats and Republicans. Feminists who described themselves as prochoice viewed the issue from the perspective of the pregnant woman; they argued that the legal right to a safe abortion was crucial to her autonomy over her body and life. Conversely, religious conservatives, who pronounced themselves prolife, viewed abortion from the perspective of the unborn fetus and claimed that its rights trumped those of the mother.

In the 1973 decision in *Roe v. Wade*, the Supreme Court had affirmed a woman's right to choose an abortion. In the generation after *Roe*, evangelical Protestants took leadership of the antiabortion movement, which grew politically powerful and developed a three-part strategy: protest, pass abortion restriction laws in the states, and methodically work through the federal courts in an attempt to overturn *Roe*. In 1987, the religious activist Randall Terry founded Operation Rescue, which mounted

CHECK FOR UNDERSTANDING

Ask students: **How did the United States become an increasingly plural society in the last several decades?** *The passage of the Hart-Celler Act, or Immigration and Nationality Act of 1965, dramatically increased the number of immigrants. The vast majority came from Latin America and Asia, which led to a significant increase in the ethnic diversity of the American population, setting in motion an historic shift toward a nation in which white Americans are likely to become a minority by 2050. Though the majority of the immigrants were Christian, the U.S. has also become more religiously diverse in the last few decades as well.*

AP® SKILLS & PROCESSES

CONTINUITY AND CHANGE

The **CONTINUITY AND CHANGE** question asks students to follow the growth of anti-immigrant sentiment over a three-decade period. Students should identify specific groups that were targeted and reasons for that targeting. They should distinguish between documented and undocumented immigrants. To extend this prompt, ask students to compare the features of the debate in the 1990s with those of the contemporary period, explaining reasons for both similarities and differences.

TRM Find complete suggested responses in the Teacher's Resource Materials.

Activists Protesting Outside the Supreme Court in 2002 In 2002 the Supreme Court considered a case in which the National Organization for Women (NOW) had challenged the legality of abortion clinic protests, such as those undertaken by Operation Rescue. The activists, and the case itself, demonstrated that the question of abortion remained far from settled, and Americans on all sides of the issue continued to hold passionate opinions. Mark Wilson/Getty Images.

protests outside abortion clinics and harassed their staffs and clients. Antiabortion activists also won a number of state laws that limited public funding for abortions, required parental notification before minors could obtain abortions, and mandated waiting periods before any woman could undergo an abortion procedure. Such laws further restricted women's reproductive choices, while still remaining constitutional under *Roe*.

Gay Rights As more gay men and women came out of the closet in the years after Stonewall (see "Stonewall and Gay Liberation" in Chapter 27), they demanded legal protections from discrimination in housing, education, and employment. Public attitude toward such protections varied by region, but by the 1990s many cities and states had banned discrimination on the basis of sexual orientation. Gay rights groups also sought legal rights for same-sex couples — such as the eligibility for workplace health-care coverage — that were akin to those enjoyed by married heterosexuals. After the turn of the century, activists pushed to expand such protections to cover transgender persons. Many of the most prominent national gay rights organizations, such as the Human Rights Campaign, focused on full marriage equality: a legal recognition of same-sex marriage that was on par with opposite-sex marriages.

The Religious Right had long condemned homosexuality on moral grounds, and public opinion was split on legal protections. In 1992, Colorado voters approved an amendment to the state constitution that prevented local governments from enacting ordinances protecting gays and lesbians — a measure that the Supreme Court subsequently overturned as unconstitutional. That same year, however, Oregon voters defeated a more radical initiative that would have prevented the state from using any

AP® THEME

SOC: Social Structures; NAT: American and National Identity

Intense political and cultural debates continued over issues such as gender roles and family structures. Debates about gay rights increasingly focused on gay marriage in the 1990s. In the early twenty-first century, views began to shift rapidly in favor of legalizing gay marriage. President Bill Clinton signed the Defense of Marriage Act in 1998. Fifteen years later, as the bill's constitutionality was challenged before the Supreme Court, Clinton wrote an op-ed piece explaining why he thought signing the bill had been a mistake. To access this article, search "Washington Post Clinton overturn DOMA."

To explore this topic further, consider using the *New York Times*'s recounting of the Court's ruling and nations' reactions to it. To access this article, search "NYT Supreme Court same sex marriage."

funds "to promote, encourage or facilitate" homosexuality. In 1996, Congress entered the fray by enacting the **Defense of Marriage Act**, which allowed states to refuse to recognize gay marriages or civil unions formed in other jurisdictions. However, following the lead of Massachusetts, which legalized same-sex marriage in 2004, in the first decades of the twenty-first century, ten states approved gay unions: California, Connecticut, Iowa, Maine, Maryland, New Hampshire, New York, Vermont, Washington, and Rhode Island. A decade later, in the 2015 decision *Obergefell v. Hodges*, the Supreme Court ruled that states could not prohibit same-sex marriage under the constitution. Remarkably, in a generation, marriage equality had prevailed.

Defense of Marriage Act
A law enacted by Congress in 1996 that allowed states to refuse to recognize gay marriages or civil unions formed in other jurisdictions. The Supreme Court ruled that DOMA was unconstitutional in 2013.

Culture Wars and the Supreme Court *Obergefell v. Hodges* highlighted a decades-long trend: as it had done since its landmark decision *Brown v. Board of Education* in 1954, the Supreme Court took up the divisive rights issues that roiled American citizens. Reproductive rights led the way, with abortion rights activists challenging the constitutionality of post-*Roe* state laws limiting access to the procedure. In ***Webster v. Reproductive Health Services*** (1989), the Supreme Court upheld the authority of state governments to limit the use of public funds and facilities for abortions. In ***Planned Parenthood of Southeastern Pennsylvania v. Casey*** (1992), the Court upheld a law requiring a twenty-four-hour waiting period prior to an abortion. Surveying these and other decisions, a reporter suggested that 1989 was "the year the Court turned right," with a conservative majority poised to overturn or restrain liberal legislation and legal precedents.

This observation was only partly correct. The Court was not yet firmly conservative. Although the *Casey* decision upheld certain restrictions on abortions, it affirmed the "essential holding" in *Roe* that women had a constitutional right to control their reproduction. In *Casey*, Justice David Souter, appointed to the Court by President George H. W. Bush in 1990, voted with Reagan appointees Sandra Day O'Connor and Anthony Kennedy. It was Kennedy who authored the majority opinions in ***Lawrence v. Texas*** (2003), where the Supreme Court limited the power of states to prohibit private homosexual activity between consenting adults, and in *Windsor v. United States* (2013), which declared the Defense of Marriage Act unconstitutional. To be certain, the court did move to the right, but it remained within the broad mainstream of American public opinion, particularly on the issues of reproduction and marriage equality.

Webster v. Reproductive Health Services
A 1989 Supreme Court ruling that upheld the authority of state governments to limit the use of public funds and facilities for abortions.

Planned Parenthood of Southeastern Pennsylvania v. Casey
A 1992 Supreme Court case that upheld a law requiring a twenty-four-hour waiting period prior to an abortion. Although the decision upheld certain restrictions on abortions, it affirmed that women had a constitutional right to control their reproduction.

Lawrence v. Texas
A 2003 landmark decision by the Supreme Court that limited the power of states to prohibit private homosexual activity between consenting adults.

AP® SKILLS & PROCESSES

CAUSATION

How did clashes over "family values" alter American politics in the 1990s?

Deepening Political Divisions

The culture wars contributed to a new, divisive partisanship in national politics. Rarely in the twentieth century had the two major parties so adamantly refused to work together. Also rare was the vitriolic rhetoric that politicians used to describe their opponents. The fractious partisanship was filtered through — or, many would argue, created by — the new twenty-four-hour cable news television networks, such as Fox News and CNN. Many commentators on these channels, finding that aggressive partisanship earned high ratings, gradually became less journalists than entertainers and sometimes provocateurs.

Partisan rancor defined the presidency of William (Bill) Jefferson Clinton. The youthful governor of Arkansas — only forty-six in 1992 — was an energetic policy wonk. In running for the 1992 Democratic nomination, he pitched himself as a "New Democrat" who would bring Reagan Democrats and middle-class voters back to the party. Opponents painted Clinton as an embodiment of the permissive social values of the 1960s: namely, that he dodged the Vietnam-era draft, smoked marijuana, and cheated on his wife. The charges were damaging, but the charismatic Clinton nonetheless secured the presidential nomination, and the Democrats mounted an aggressive campaign against the incumbent president George H. W. Bush. Clinton's domestic agenda was the centerpiece of the campaign, promising a tax cut for the

AP® EXAM TIP

Analyze the successes and failures of Bill Clinton and the New Democrats.

CHECK FOR UNDERSTANDING

Ask students: **How did Americans clash over family values in the 1990s and early 2000s?** *Americans debated the morality of abortion, with the evangelically inspired Operation Rescue mounting protests in front of abortion clinics. Americans also debated whether gay couples should have the same marriage rights as heterosexual couples. Congress passed the Defense of Marriage Act in 1996, defining marriage as between one man and one woman, and the Supreme Court overturned this ruling in 2015.*

AP® SKILLS & PROCESSES

CAUSATION

The **CAUSATION** question asks students to explain the causes of "family values" debates in the 1990s. It might be helpful for students to evaluate these debates in the larger context of the counterculture era and the conservative reaction to it that began in the 1970s. Many of the debates — and the organizations representing these views — had roots in this earlier period. In the text that immediately follows, Clinton's behavior during the 1960s, which was an issue raised during the 1992 election campaign, reflects ongoing concern with these cultural issues.

TRM Find complete suggested responses in the Teacher's Resource Materials.

TEACHING STRATEGY

PBS's *Frontline* provides a detailed chronology of Clinton's presidency, from his decision to run through the end of his second term. Imbedded throughout are several links to documents and other resources related to important events in his administration, including his impeachment. To access these resources, search "Frontline Clinton chronology."

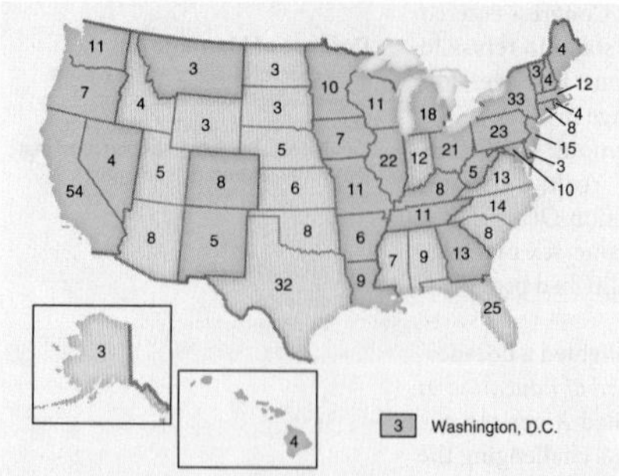

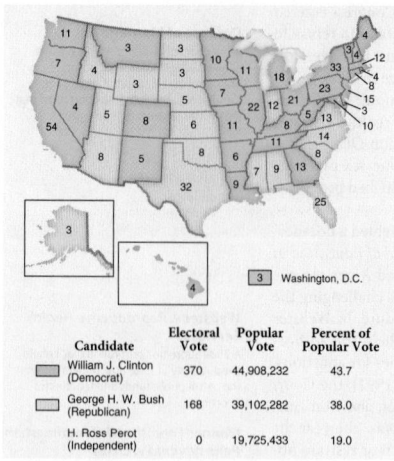

Candidate	Electoral Vote	Popular Vote	Percent of Popular Vote
William J. Clinton (Democrat)	370	44,908,232	43.7
George H. W. Bush (Republican)	168	39,102,282	38.0
H. Ross Perot (Independent)	0	19,725,433	19.0

MAP 30.3 The Presidential Election of 1992
The first national election after the end of the Cold War focused on the economy, which had fallen into a recession in 1991. The first-ever all-southern Democratic ticket of Bill Clinton (Arkansas) and Al Gore (Tennessee) won support across the country but won the election with only 43.7 percent of the popular vote. The Republican candidate, President George H. W. Bush, ran strongly in his home state of Texas and the South, an emerging Republican stronghold. Independent candidate H. Ross Perot, a wealthy technology entrepreneur, polled an impressive 19.0 percent of the popular vote by capitalizing on voter dissatisfaction with the huge federal deficits of the Reagan-Bush administrations.

middle class, universal health insurance, and a reduction of the huge Republican budget deficit — an audacious combination of traditional social-welfare liberalism and fiscal conservatism. Despite these efforts, Clinton received only 43.7 percent of the vote. It was enough to win, however, because millions of Republicans cast their ballots for independent businessman Ross Perot, who won more votes (19.0 percent) than any third-party candidate since Theodore Roosevelt in 1912 (Map 30.3). Among all post–World War II presidents, only Richard Nixon (in 1969) entered the White House with as small a share of the national vote as Clinton.

New Democrats and Public Policy Clinton tried to steer a centrist course. On his left was the Democratic Party's weakened but still vocal liberal wing. On his right were party moderates influenced by Reagan-era notions of reducing government regulation and the welfare state. Clinton's "third way," as he dubbed it, tried to satisfy these two quite different — and often antagonistic — political constituencies. Clinton had notable successes as well as spectacular failures pursuing this course.

A spectacular failure came first. Clinton's most ambitious social-welfare goal was to provide a system of health care that would cover all Americans, including the estimated 40 million who had no insurance, and reduce the burden of medical costs on the larger economy. This objective had eluded every Democratic president since Harry Truman. Clinton's health-care task force — led by First Lady Hillary Clinton — proposed a system of "managed competition" among private insurance companies, but the cost of the proposed system would fall heavily on employers, and many campaigned strongly against it. So did the powerful lobbies of the health insurance industry and the American Medical Association. By mid-1994, Democratic leaders in Congress declared that the Clintons' universal health-care proposal was dead.

Clinton's plan to reduce budget deficits, in contrast, proved an unlikely success. In 1993, he secured a five-year budget package that would reduce the federal deficit by $500 billion. Republicans unanimously opposed the proposal because it raised taxes on corporations and wealthy individuals, and liberal Democrats complained because it limited social spending. No one could complain about the results: by 1998, Clinton's fiscal policies had balanced the federal budget and begun to pay down the federal debt — at a rate of $156 billion a year between 1999 and 2001. The economy boomed, thanks in part to the low-interest rates stemming from deficit reduction.

The Republican Resurgence Clinton's victory in the 1992 presidential race did not reflect a major electoral realignment. Conservatives still had a working majority, and it had taken Perot's insurgency and a recession to open the door for the Democrats. The midterm elections of 1994 unmistakably confirmed that majority. In a well-organized campaign, dominated by grassroots appeals to the New Right, Republicans gained fifty-four seats in the House of Representatives, giving them a majority in the lower chamber for the first time since 1955. They also retook control of the Senate and captured eleven governorships. Leading the Republican charge was Representative Newt Gingrich of Georgia, who revived calls for significant tax cuts, reductions in welfare programs, anticrime initiatives, and cutbacks in federal regulations—initiatives that Gingrich promoted under the banner of a "**Contract with America**."

Contract with America
Initiatives by Representative Newt Gingrich of Georgia for significant tax cuts, reductions in welfare programs, anticrime measures, and cutbacks in federal regulations.

In response to the massive loss of Democratic congressional seats in the 1994 midterm elections, Clinton moved to the right. Claiming in 1996 that "the era of big government is over," he avoided expansive social-welfare proposals for the remainder of his presidency and instead sought Republican support for a centrist program. The signature initiative of his remaining time in office was reforming the welfare system, a measure that saved relatively little money but carried a big ideological message. Many taxpaying Americans believed that the Aid to Families with Dependent Children (AFDC) program encouraged female recipients to remain on welfare rather than seek employment. In August 1996, the federal government abolished AFDC, achieving a long-standing goal of conservatives when Clinton signed the **Personal Responsibility and Work Opportunity Reconciliation Act**, over the furious objections of liberals.

Bill Clinton President William (Bill) Clinton returned the Democratic Party to the White House after twelve years under Ronald Reagan and George H. W. Bush. Clinton was best known politically for what he called the *third way*, a phrase that described his efforts to craft policies that appealed to both liberals and moderates in his party. Here he signs the Welfare Reform Act of 1996 (officially the Personal Responsibility and Work Opportunity Reconciliation Act), which brought an end to the federal AFDC program that Democrats had created in 1935. AP Photo/J. Scott Applewhite.

Clinton's Impeachment Clinton won reelection with relative ease in 1996, but any hopes for major progress in a second term unraveled when a tawdry scandal led to his impeachment. Clinton publicly denied having had a sexual relationship with White House intern Monica Lewinsky, but Republicans concluded that Clinton was lying — and thus guilty of perjury, because he had had told the lie during a legal deposition, related to a civil lawsuit being brought against him for sexual harassment during his tenure as governor of Arkansas, while under oath. Historically, Americans have understood "high crimes and misdemeanors" — the constitutional standard for impeachment — as involving a serious abuse of public trust that endangered the republic. But in 1998, conservative Republicans favored a much lower standard, as part of a total opposition to the Clinton presidency. On December 19, the House of Representatives narrowly approved two articles of impeachment. According to a CBS News poll, 38 percent of Americans favored impeachment, whereas 58 percent opposed it. Chastened by this lack of public support, many Senate Republicans shied away from convicting Clinton, and the impeachment trial held in 1999 fell well short of the two-thirds majority needed to remove the president. But like Andrew Johnson, the only other president to be tried by the Senate up to that time, Clinton and the Democratic Party paid a high price for his acquittal. Preoccupied with defending himself, the president was unable to fashion a Democratic alternative to the Republicans' domestic agenda.

Personal Responsibility and Work Opportunity Reconciliation Act
Legislation signed by President Clinton in 1996 that replaced Aid to Families with Dependent Children with Temporary Assistance for Needy Families, which provided grants to the states to assist the poor, and limited allowable welfare payments.

AP® SKILLS & PROCESSES

MAKING CONNECTIONS

What made President Clinton a "New Democrat," and how much did his proposals differ from traditional liberal objectives?

Post–Cold War Foreign Policy

Politically weakened after the congressional losses in the 1994 midterm elections, Clinton believed he could still make a difference on the international stage, where post–Cold War developments created historic opportunities. A wide arc of independent states had emerged out of the collapsing Soviet empire, bridging Eastern Europe and central Asia. The majority of the 142 million people living in these post-Soviet states were poor, but the region boasted a sizable middle class and a wealth of natural resources, especially oil and natural gas.

AP® EXAM TIP

Evaluate the role of the U.S. as the world's leading superpower in the world since the 1990s.

CHECK FOR UNDERSTANDING

Ask students: **How did Bill Clinton and New Democrats shape the United States in the 1990s?** *New Democrats tried to increase the party's influence by bringing Reagan Democrats and middle-class voters back. To do so, they attempted to find a middle ground between two groups within the Democratic Party: liberals and moderates influenced by deregulation and reduced federal spending. In office, Clinton attempted to provide a system of health care for all Americans, but his plan was opposed by small businesses, health insurers, and the American Medical Association. He also sought to reduce budget deficits — a goal traditionally favored by conservatives —by taxing corporations and the wealthy, while reducing social spending. By the end of his presidency, he had balanced the federal budget and had begun to reduce the federal debt.*

AP® SKILLS & PROCESSES

MAKING CONNECTIONS

The **MAKING CONNECTIONS** question essentially asks students to compare "New Democrats" to the liberal Democrats of the previous generation. Students could additionally trace the specific policy initiatives in the Clinton administration that reflected New Democratic goals and discuss their consequences. They could also evaluate the degree to which recent Democratic Party goals — as reflected, for example, in the 2016 platform — continued to reflect New Democratic values.

TRM Find complete suggested responses in the Teacher's Resource Materials.

TEACHING STRATEGY

The companion site to the PBS *Frontline* film *War in Europe* provides materials on the conflict in Kosovo and the American response to it during the Clinton presidency, including a timeline, statistics, additional readings, and interviews with policymakers, analysts, and military leaders. To access this site, search "Frontline War in Europe Kosovo."

Among the challenges for the United States was the question of whether to support the admission of some of the new states into the North Atlantic Treaty Organization (NATO). Many observers worried, justifiably, that extending the NATO alliance into Eastern Europe would damage relations between the United States and Russia. Clinton, by encouraging NATO membership for the Czech Republic, Poland, and Hungary — all formerly within the Soviet bloc — nevertheless launched a process of NATO expansion that continued under his predecessors. By 2010, twelve new nations — most of them in Eastern Europe — had been admitted to the NATO alliance. Nothing symbolized the end of the Cold War more than the fact that ten of those nations were former members of the Warsaw Pact. As some observers had feared, however, NATO's expansion damaged U.S.-Russian relations, and Russian leaders made no secret of their disdain for the West's encroachment.

The Breakup of Yugoslavia Two of the new NATO states, Slovenia and Croatia, had emerged out of the communist nation of Yugoslavia, a country that had uneasily perched on the fringe of the Soviet bloc. The gradual breakup of Yugoslavia also led to the first post–Cold War conflict in Europe. Slovenia and Croatia had declared independence in 1991, and in 1992, the heavily Muslim province of Bosnia-Herzegovina followed suit. But the province's substantial Serbian population — largely Orthodox Christians — refused to live in a Muslim-run multiethnic state. Slobodan Milosevic, an uncompromising Serbian nationalist, launched a ruthless campaign of "ethnic cleansing" to create a Serbian state. Europeans and Americans failed to react swiftly to the murderous Milosevic, but Clinton finally organized a NATO-led bombing campaign and peacekeeping effort in November 1995, backed by 20,000 American troops, that ended the Serbs' vicious expansionist drive. Four years later, a new crisis emerged in Kosovo, another province of the Serbian-dominated Federal Republic of Yugoslavia. NATO intervened once more, with the United States leading the way, to preserve Kosovo's autonomy. By 2008, seven independent nations had emerged from the wreckage of Yugoslavia.

U.S./NATO Action in Yugoslavia July 29, 1999. U.S. secretary of state Madeleine Albright greeting U.S. troops during a visit to Camp Bonsteel in the U.S. sector of Kosovo, in the former Yugoslavia. Between 1989 and 1992, eight independent nations emerged from the breakup of Yugoslavia, igniting religious and ethnic tensions that lasted nearly a decade. Reuters.

America and the Middle East No post–Cold War developments proved more challenging to the United States than those in the Middle East. Muslim nations there had a long list of grievances against the West: in particular, the exploitation of the region by European imperial powers following the collapse of the Ottoman Empire in World War I and European nations' support for the founding of a Jewish state in Palestine in 1948. Subsequent events implicated the United States. In Iran, the U.S. Central Intelligence Agency had backed the overthrow of a democratically elected government in 1953, and the United States gave twenty-five years of support to the Iranian shah. America's support for Israel in the 1967 Six-Day War and the 1973 Yom Kippur War and its near-unconditional backing of Israel in the 1980s were especially galling to Muslims. Across the region, both religious and secular moderates complained about these injustices, but many also had political and economic ties to the West that constrained their criticism.

This situation left an opening for radical Islamic fundamentalists to build a movement based on opposition to Western imperialism and consumer culture. These groups interpreted the American military presence in Saudi Arabia — about 4,000 Air Force personnel — as colonial ambition reborn. Clinton had inherited from President George H. W. Bush a defeated Iraq and the troops stationed in Saudi Arabia after the war. Clinton also enforced a UN-sanctioned embargo on trade with Iraq, a policy designed to constrain Saddam Hussein's military but the primary effect of which was to deny crucial food and goods to the civilian population, causing widespread suffering. Motivated by resentment of this perceived meddling, Muslim fundamentalists soon began targeting Americans. In 1993, radicals detonated a bomb beneath the World Trade Center in New York City, killing six people and injuring more than a thousand. Radical Islamic terrorists used truck bombs to blow up U.S. embassies in Kenya and Tanzania in 1998, and packed a small boat with explosives to attack the USS *Cole* in the Yemeni port of Aden in 2000, killing 17 sailors.

The Clinton administration knew the attacks on the *Cole* and the African embassies were the work of **Al Qaeda**, a network of radical Islamic terrorists organized by the wealthy Saudi exile Osama bin Laden. In February 1998, bin Laden had issued a call for a global struggle — a "Jihad against Jews and Crusaders," claiming every Muslim had a duty to kill Americans and their allies. After the embassy bombings, Clinton ordered air strikes on Al Qaeda bases in Afghanistan, where an estimated 15,000 operatives had been trained since 1990. The strikes failed to destroy the growing network of extremists, who were already advancing plans for the attacks of September 11, 2001.

Al Qaeda
A network of radical Islamic terrorists organized by Osama bin Laden, who issued a call for holy war against Americans and their allies. Members of Al Qaeda were responsible for the 9/11 terrorist attacks.

AP® SKILLS & PROCESSES
CONTEXTUALIZATION
In what specific ways were foreign policy developments during the Clinton presidency evidence of the end of the Cold War?

A NEW CENTURY DAWNS

How did wars abroad and political turmoil at home shape the United States in the first decades of the twenty-first century?

As the twenty-first century enters its third decade, three significant developments have profoundly shaped the American present: the long war in the Middle East that began with the terrorist attack on September 11, 2001 (also known as 9/11); the 2008 election of Barack Obama as the nation's first African American president; and the 2016 election to the White House of the brazenly contrarian businessman and television personality, Donald Trump. Too little time has passed to assess precisely how these events will help to define the twenty-first century, but all three have already changed the course of history.

Domestic Conflict and War in the Middle East

The 2000 presidential election briefly offered the promise of a break with the intense partisanship of the final Clinton years. The Republican nominee, George W. Bush, the son of President George H. W. Bush, cast himself as a "uniter, not a divider" against

TEACHING STRATEGY

Osama bin Laden issued a *fatwa* in February 1998, summarizing three grievances against the U.S.: since the Iraqi invasion of Kuwait, American troops had occupied Saudi Arabia, the holy land of Islam; Americans had allied with Israel, leading to countless Muslim deaths; and the U.S. supported Israeli occupation of Jerusalem, site of the holy Al Aqsa Mosque. The full text of the *fatwa* is available at the 9/11 Memorial and Museum site. To access this document, search "9/11 Memorial Osama bin Laden fatwa."

AP® SKILLS & PROCESSES

CONTEXTUALIZATION

Use the **CONTEXTUALIZATION** question to help students place foreign policy events in the 1990s in a post–Cold War context. Students should be able to explain how significant American actions involved powers other than the Soviet Union and issues other than communism.

TRM Find complete suggested responses in the Teacher's Resource Materials.

CHECK FOR UNDERSTANDING

Ask students: **What were the sources of domestic division in the United States after 1988, and how did they reshape the political landscape?** *The major sources of domestic divisions after 1988 were multiculturalism and family values issues, including abortion and gay rights. These issues reshaped politics by moving it to the right — Republicans remained conservative but New Democrats moderated their party. The divisiveness expressed itself in the expanding mass media, which inhibited effective bipartisanship.*

his opponent, Albert ("Al") Gore, Clinton's vice president. Their race for the White House would join those of 1876 and 1960 as the closest and most contested in American history. Gore won the popular vote, amassing 50.9 million votes to Bush's 50.4 million, but fell short in the electoral college, 267 to 271.

Late on election night, the vote count in Florida had given Bush the narrowest of victories — swinging the state's 25 electoral votes into his column and edging him past Gore. As was their legal prerogative, the Democrats demanded hand recounts in several counties. A month of tumult followed, until the U.S. Supreme Court, splitting directly along conservative-liberal lines, ordered the recount stopped and let Bush's victory stand. Recounting ballots without a consistent standard to determine "voter intent," the Court reasoned, violated the rights of Floridian voters under the Fourteenth Amendment's equal protection clause. As if acknowledging the frailty of its own argument, the Court declared that *Bush v. Gore* was not to be regarded as precedent. In a dissenting opinion, Justice John Paul Stevens warned that the transparently partisan decision undermined "the Nation's confidence in the judge as an impartial guardian of the rule of law."

This controversial opening act proved a harbinger of renewed partisan politics. Although Bush had positioned himself as a moderate, countertendencies drove his administration. His vice president, the uncompromising conservative Richard (Dick) Cheney, became, with Bush's consent, virtually a copresident. Bush also brought into the administration his campaign advisor, Karl Rove, who argued that a permanent Republican majority could be built on the party's conservative base. On Capitol Hill, Rove's ambition for the GOP was reinforced by Tom DeLay, the House majority leader, who in 1995 had declared "all-out war" on the Democrats. To win that war, DeLay pushed congressional Republicans to endorse a fierce partisanship. The Senate, although more collegial, went through a similar hardening process. After 2002, with Republicans in control of both Congress and the White House, bipartisan lawmaking came to an end.

AP® EXAM TIP

Evaluate the impact of the 9/11 attacks on American foreign policy and on domestic issues of civil liberties.

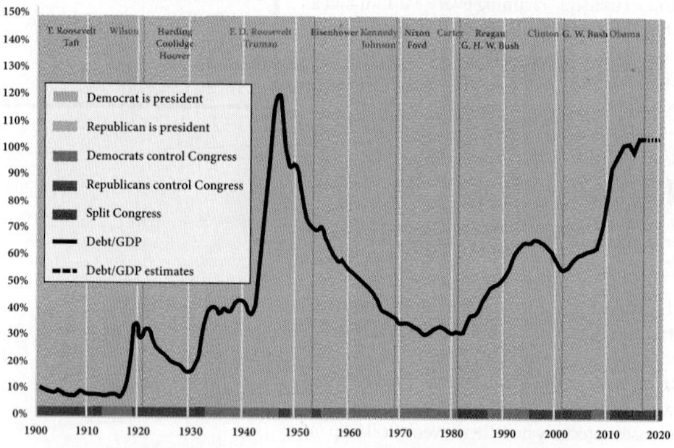

FIGURE 30.3 Gross Federal Debt as a Percentage of Gross Domestic Product

Economists argue that the best measure of a nation's debt is its size relative to the overall economy — that is, its percentage of gross domestic product (GDP). The size of the total U.S. debt declined from its World War II high until the 1980s, when it increased dramatically under President Reagan. Since then, the debt has consistently increased as a percentage of GDP, aside from a small decline under President Clinton's deficit-reduction plans in the mid-1990s.

September 11, 2001 As a candidate in 2000, George W. Bush had said little about foreign policy — and he had not needed to. With the Cold War over and few immediate threats to American power, he and many others assumed his administration would rise or fail based on his domestic program — primarily a large promised tax cut. But a sunny September morning nine months into his presidency changed everything. On that morning, September 11, 2001, a hijacked commercial airliner crashed into the south tower of the World Trade Center in lower Manhattan. Seventeen minutes later, a second airliner struck the north tower. Millions of Americans, and many more people worldwide, watched live on television and the Internet as the twin 110-story skyscrapers burned and then collapsed. Simultaneously, a third plane was flown into the Pentagon, and a

AP® APPLY THE TIP

Provide groups of students with **Handout 30.3 — Thematic Analysis: 9/11 (TRM)** and a large sheet of poster paper; ask students to transfer the diagram to a larger piece of paper. Next, distribute sets of primary sources related to 9/11 and ask the groups to use the textbook and primary sources to complete the thematic analysis. Students should identify and explain at least two pieces of evidence related to each Theme on the handout. Prompt students to consider current issues facing the U.S. and to include these in the form of questions related to the impact of 9/11 on American society and policy. Post each group's thematic analysis around the room, and then lead a class discussion on the impact of 9/11 on the development of the U.S.

TRM Find **Handout 30.3 — Thematic Analysis: 9/11** in the Teacher's Resource Materials.

AP® SKILLS & PROCESSES

ANALYZING HISTORICAL EVIDENCE

Use **FIGURE 30.3** to illustrate, for the period covered in this chapter, the notable pattern in the decline in the debt beginning in the middle of the Clinton presidency — the only decline in the debt since 1981, which ended when Bush took office and instituted new tax cuts.

fourth hijacked plane crashed in rural Pennsylvania. All told, almost 3,000 people died, with another 6,000 injured, over the course of a few hours. Before the day was over, the Federal Bureau of Investigation had determined that Al Qaeda was behind the attacks.

The 9/11 attacks were themselves products of globalization. Of the nineteen hijackers, fifteen were from Saudi Arabia, two were from the United Arab Emirates, one was from Egypt, and one was from Lebanon. Many had trained in Afghanistan, in guerrilla warfare camps operated by Osama bin Laden, Al Qaeda's leader. Four had gone to flight school in the United States. Several had lived and studied in Germany. They communicated with one another and with planners in Afghanistan through cell phones and electronic messages. A stateless Islamic guerilla organization inflicting major damage on the United States had demonstrated that global political reality had changed. The simple Cold War duality — communism versus capitalism — had long obscured regional, ethnic, and religious conflict. Absent the superpower rivalry, those conflicts moved toward the center of the world stage.

In the wake of Al Qaeda's stunning attacks, Bush found himself at the head of a wounded, and angry, nation. An outburst of patriotism swept the country in the wake of the September 11 attacks, and Bush soon proclaimed a "war on terror." Al Qaeda was the first and clearest target of that new conflict. Al Qaeda had long operated out of Afghanistan, harbored by the fundamentalist Taliban regime. In October 2001, less than a month after the hijackers struck, American planes and anti-Taliban Afghani ground troops launched a massive campaign against the regime. By early 2002, this lethal combination had ousted the Taliban, destroyed Al Qaeda's training camps, and killed or captured many of its operatives. Al Qaeda leader Osama bin Laden retreated to a mountain hideout, but U.S. forces failed to press the attack, and the terrorist planner escaped over the border into Pakistan. The hunt for the elusive bin Laden would continue for nearly ten years.

September 11, 2001 Photographers at the scene after a plane crashed into the north tower of New York City's World Trade Center on September 11 found themselves recording a defining moment in the nation's history. When a second airliner approached and then slammed into the building's south tower at 9:03 A.M., the nation knew this was no accident. The United States was under attack. Of the nearly 3,000 people killed on that day, 2,753 died at the World Trade Center.
Spencer Platt/Getty Images.

The "war on terror," as defined by the Bush administration in response to 9/11, was not confined by borders — including those of the United States. The president deemed terrorism too serious a threat for ordinary law enforcement means, and sought a wartime footing for the government's domestic surveillance. With little debate, in 2001 Congress passed the **USA PATRIOT Act**, granting the government sweeping authority to monitor citizens and apprehend suspected terrorists.

USA PATRIOT Act
A 2001 law that gave the government new powers to monitor suspected terrorists and their associates, including the ability to access personal information.

The Invasion of Iraq On the international front, on the heels of the invasion of Afghanistan, Bush used the fight against terror as the basis of a new policy of preventive war. Under international law, only an imminent threat justified a nation's right to strike first. But under what became known as the Bush doctrine, the United States claimed for itself the right to act in "anticipatory self-defense" — that is, not in response to an act of aggression but in anticipation of one. In 2002, President Bush singled out Iran, North Korea, and Iraq — "an axis of evil" — as the states most likely to trigger application of this new doctrine. Bush administration officials identified Iraq in particular as an opportunity to fulfill what they believed to be America's mission to democratize the world. Iraqis, they contended, would abandon the tyrant Saddam Hussein and embrace representative government if given the chance. According to advocates of "regime change," a wave of democratization would spread from Iraq

AP® THEME

NAT: American and National Identity; WOR: America in the World

In the wake of attacks on the World Trade Center and the Pentagon, the U.S. launched military efforts against terrorism and lengthy, controversial conflicts in Afghanistan and Iraq. The National Commission on Terrorist Attacks upon the United States (also known as the 9-11 Commission) released *The 9/11 Commission Report* on July 22, 2004. The full text of the report is available online, with downloadable individual chapters. To access the document, search "9/11 Commission Report."

TEACHING STRATEGY

In his article "Everything You Need to Know About the Patriot Act Debate," Jeremy Diamond explains the USA PATRIOT Act, a complex and controversial law. Students should note that shortly after this article was written, President Obama voted to sign the USA Freedom Act, including a provision that reauthorized Section 215. To access this article, search "CNN Diamond Patriot Act."

AP® SKILLS & PROCESSES

ANALYZING HISTORICAL EVIDENCE

Use **MAP 30.4** to illustrate the nation's involvement in the Middle East over nearly four decades, revealing multiple military interventions in this strategic, oil-rich region.

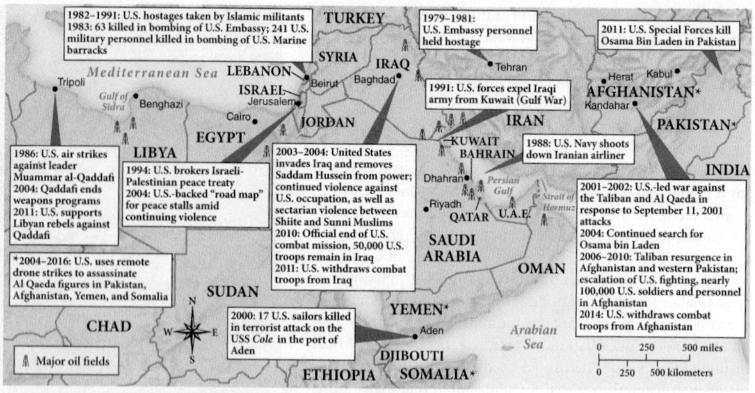

MAP 30.4 U.S. Involvement in the Middle East, 1979–2016
The United States has long played an active role in the Middle East, driven by the strategic importance of that region and, most important, by America's need to ensure a reliable supply of oil from the Persian Gulf states. This map shows the highlights of that troubled involvement, from the Tehran embassy hostage taking in 1979 to the invasion and occupation of both Iraq and Afghanistan. President Obama withdrew most combat troops from Iraq in 2011 and from Afghanistan in 2014, but U.S. involvement in the region, in the form of drone strikes, material assistance to various states and factions, and other forms of diplomatic and military assistance continues.

across the Middle East, toppling or reforming other unpopular Arab regimes and stabilizing the region — as well as securing vital oil supplies for the West. From a strategic vantage, democratization and strategic interests went hand in hand, because those planning an invasion of Iraq believed that new regimes would be allies of the United States (Map 30.4).

Neither professed democratic ideals nor oil supplies, either singly or together, met Bush's declared threshold for preventive war. So the president reluctantly acceded to the demands of anxious European allies that the United States go to the UN Security Council, which issued an ultimatum to Hussein: allow the return of the UN weapons inspectors expelled in 1998. The dictator surprisingly agreed. Still eager to invade, the Bush administration insisted that Hussein's regime constituted a "grave and gathering danger" and ignored further UN deliberations. American forces invaded in March 2003, despite widespread international criticism. Among major allies, only Great Britain joined the U.S. military action, and relations with France and Germany soured — French newspapers dubbed the invasion "Bush's War." Even neighboring Mexico and Canada condemned the invasion, and key regional ally Turkey refused transit permission, ruining the army's plan for a northern thrust into Iraq. The Arab world, rather than embrace democratic regime change, exploded in anti-American demonstrations.

Within three weeks, American troops had taken Baghdad, the Iraqi capital. Iraq's government collapsed, but despite meticulous military planning the Pentagon had made no provision for what would follow the war. The fighting shattered the infrastructure of Iraq's cities, leaving them without reliable supplies of electricity and water. In the midst of this turmoil, an insurgency began, sparked by Sunni Muslims, a minority who had nevertheless dominated the country under Hussein's Baathist regime. Iraq's Shiite majority, long oppressed by Hussein, initially welcomed the Americans, but extremist Shiite elements soon turned hostile as well. With Iraq's borders unguarded, Al Qaeda supporters flocked in from all over the Middle East, eager to do battle with the infidel Americans.

Dominant nations often underestimate the strength of religious and national identities in other people. Although it was hard for Bush administration officials to fathom, even the Iraqis who had suffered under Hussein viewed the U.S. forces as invaders. Serious misconduct by the American military contributed to the fierce insurgency. In 2004, graphic images of U.S. military guards abusing and torturing prisoners at Baghdad's **Abu Ghraib prison** shocked the world. For many Muslims, the pictures offered final proof of American treachery. At that point, the United States had spent upward of $100 billion on the invasion of Iraq. More than 1,000 American soldiers had died, and 10,000 others had been wounded, many maimed for life. But Bush and others declared that the United States would "stay the course"—for fear that a withdrawal would push Iraq further into chaos.

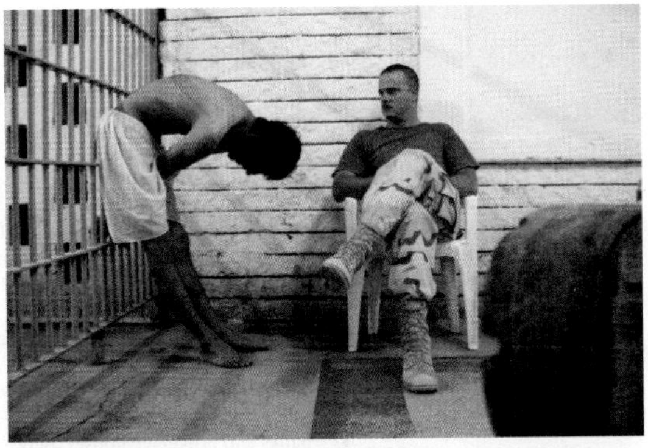

Abu Ghraib This image of one of the milder forms of torture experienced by inmates at the Abu Ghraib prison was obtained by the Associated Press in 2003. It shows a detainee bent over with his hands through the bars of a cell while being watched by a comfortably seated soldier. This photograph and others showing far worse treatment administered by sometimes jeering military personnel outraged many in the United States and abroad, particularly in the Muslim world. AP Photo.

The 2004 Election As a reelection year approached, Karl Rove, Bush's top advisor, calculated that stirring the culture wars and appealing to patriotism would mobilize conservatives to vote for Bush. Rove encouraged activists to place antigay initiatives on the ballot in key states to draw conservative voters to the polls; in all, eleven states that year would pass ballot initiatives that wrote bans on gay marriage into state constitutions. The Democratic nominee, Senator John Kerry of Massachusetts, was a decorated Vietnam veteran—in contrast to the president, who had spent the Vietnam years in the Texas Air National Guard. But when Kerry returned from service, he had joined the antiwar group Vietnam Veterans Against the War and in 1971 had delivered a blistering critique of the war to the Senate Armed Services Committee. In the logic of the culture wars, antiwar views made him vulnerable to charges of being weak and unpatriotic. Nearly 60 percent of eligible voters—the highest percentage since 1968—went to the polls. Bush won a second term, tallying 286 electoral votes to Kerry's 252. In exit polls, Bush voters cited moral "values" and national security as top concerns, saying that the incumbent made them feel "safer."

Abu Ghraib prison
A prison outside Baghdad, Iraq, where American military personnel were photographed abusing and torturing prisoners during the Iraq War.

Environmental and Economic Crises

George Bush's second term was a case study in crisis management. In 2005, Hurricane Katrina—one of the deadliest storms in the nation's history—devastated Louisiana and the Gulf Coast of Mississippi. In New Orleans, floodwaters breached the earthen barricades surrounding the city and submerged entire neighborhoods. Those who had not evacuated found themselves without food, drinking water, or shelter for days following the storm, with the worst suffering in largely low-income and African American areas. More than 1,800 people died in the aftermath of Katrina, with thousands more displaced. Initial responses to the emergency by federal and local authorities were slow to arrive, and uncoordinated and inadequate when they did. The storm revealed the vulnerability, poverty, and decay at the heart of large American cities.

AP® EXAM TIP
Evaluate the impact of tax policy under George W. Bush.

Great Recession Katrina was only the first of a series of crises. Increasing violence and a rising insurgency in Iraq made the war even more unpopular at home, despite some successes under a new military strategy. As the unpopular war dragged into a

AP® THEME

NAT: American and National Identity

The war on terror sought to improve security within the U.S. but also raised questions about the protection of civil liberties and human rights. One major controversy that surfaced involved a widespread program by the CIA to kidnap suspected terrorists, deliver them to secret "black sites" in third-party countries friendly to the U.S., and subject prisoners to what the CIA called "enhanced interrogation" and human rights critics called torture. The Senate Intelligence Committee released an unclassified version of the report of its investigation at the end of 2014. To access the full report, search "Senate Intelligence Committee CIA detention and interrogation program."

CHECK FOR UNDERSTANDING

Ask students: **What features accompanied the ascendance of George W. Bush?** *Through the Supreme Court's intervention, Bush was declared the winner of a presidential election where he lost the popular vote. He quickly instituted Reagan-style "trickle down" tax cuts. Less than a year into his presidency, the 9/11 attacks launched the "war on terror," which included the USA PATRIOT Act and wars in both Afghanistan and Iraq.*

CHECK FOR UNDERSTANDING

Ask students: **How did the nation experience violence abroad and economic collapse at home early in the new millennium?** *American military involvement in Iraq continued, despite its growing unpopularity in the U.S. Prompted largely by the subprime mortgage scheme, the housing market collapsed in 2008, launching the Great Recession, causing the closure of many businesses, a jump in unemployment to 10 percent, and defaults on home mortgages by large numbers of Americans. The Bush administration urged Congress to pass a $700 billion bailout of banks and brokerage houses that, while unpopular with the public, did help rescue the financial system.*

AP® SKILLS & PROCESSES

CONTINUITY AND CHANGE

The **CONTINUITY AND CHANGE** question asks students to compare the policies of the Reagan era with those of the George W. Bush era in terms of economic policies. It might be helpful for students to consider the larger context of the national economy at the time each administration enacted its new policies. The primary similarity is in the tax cuts both enacted, which both favored the wealthiest Americans. In their response, students might also explain why Bush did not address deregulation in the way Reagan did.

TRM Find complete suggested responses in the Teacher's Resource Materials.

sixth year, Bush's woes were compounded by economic trouble. As his final full year in the presidency unfolded, a recession turned into a full-blown economic crash — the result of highly overleveraged financial and real estate sectors collapsing under a mountain of unpayable debt. Between late 2007 and early 2009, a span of about sixteen months, the Dow Jones Industrial Average lost half its total value, and major banks, insurance companies, and financial institutions were on the verge of collapse. The entire automobile industry was near bankruptcy. Millions of Americans lost their jobs, and the unemployment rate surged to 10 percent. Housing prices dropped by as much as 40 percent in some parts of the country, and millions of Americans defaulted on their mortgages. The United States was in economic freefall. What soon became known as the Great Recession had technically begun in 2007, but its major effects were not felt until the fall of 2008.

AP® SKILLS & PROCESSES

CONTINUITY AND CHANGE

In what ways was George W. Bush a political follower of Ronald Reagan (Chapter 29)? If they embraced similar policies, how did the era of Bush's presidency, the 2000s, differ from Reagan's, the 1980s?

In September, less than two months before the end of Bush's term of office, Secretary of the Treasury Henry Paulson urged Congress to pass the Emergency Economic Stabilization Act, commonly referred to as the bailout of the financial sector. Passed in early October, the act dedicated $700 billion to rescuing many of the nation's largest banks and brokerage houses. Between Congress's actions and the independent efforts of the Treasury Department and the Federal Reserve, the U.S. government invested close to $1 trillion in saving the financial system.

From Liberal Reform to Conservative Nationalism

The 2008 presidential election took place amidst the economic meltdown. In a historically remarkable primary season, Hillary R. Clinton and Illinois senator Barack Obama — respectively, the first woman and the first African American to be major presidential contenders — vied for the Democratic nomination. After a close-fought contest, Obama emerged as the nominee by early summer.

In the general election, Obama faced Republican senator John McCain of Arizona. Obama had emerged rapidly as a unique figure in American politics. The son of a Kenyan immigrant and a white woman from Kansas, Obama was raised in Hawaii and Indonesia, and he easily connected with an increasingly diverse America. A generation younger than Bill Clinton and George W. Bush, Obama was at once a product of the 1960s, especially civil rights gains, and removed from its heated conflicts. He took the oath of office of the presidency on January 21, 2009, amid the worst economy since the Great Depression, with the United States mired in two wars in the Middle East. From the podium, the new president recognized the crises but struck an optimistic tone, encouraging the country to "begin again the work of remaking America" (Map 30.5).

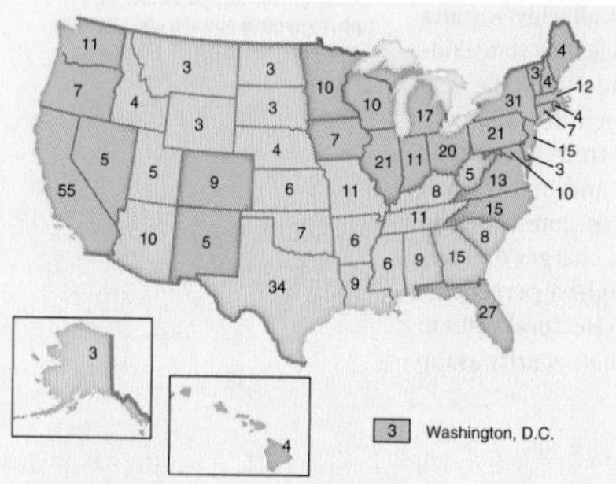

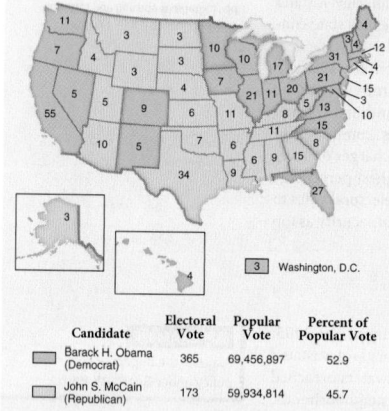

Candidate	Electoral Vote	Popular Vote	Percent of Popular Vote
Barack H. Obama (Democrat)	365	69,456,897	52.9
John S. McCain (Republican)	173	59,934,814	45.7

MAP 30.5 The Presidential Election of 2008
Illinois senator Barack Obama, a Democrat, defeated Arizona senator John McCain, the Republican nominee, to become the first African American president. Obama and his vice presidential nominee, Delaware senator Joe Biden, won 53 percent of the popular vote in an election with the highest voter turnout in four decades. The election took place against a backdrop of economic crisis — the stock market lost 25 percent of its value between September and October, as the Great Recession gained momentum. Of particular note is the fact that two-thirds of voters age eighteen to twenty-nine voted for Obama — a surge of youth voting that anchored the Democratic electorate, which was dubbed the "Obama coalition."

"Remaking America" A nation that a mere two generations prior would not allow black Americans to dine in the same restaurant with white Americans had elected a black man to the highest office. Obama himself was less interested in celebrating this historic accomplishment — part of his deliberate strategy to downplay race — than with developing a plan to deal with the nation's challenges, at home and abroad. With explicit reference to Franklin Roosevelt, Obama used the "first hundred days" of his presidency to lay out an ambitious agenda: a "stimulus package" of federal spending to invigorate the economy; plans to draw down the war in Iraq and refocus American military efforts in Afghanistan; a reform of the nation's health insurance system; and new federal regulations on Wall Street.

Remarkably, the president accomplished much of that ambitious agenda. The Democratic-controlled Congress elected alongside Obama passed the **American Recovery and Reinvestment Act**, an economic stimulus bill that provided $787 billion to state and local governments — one of the largest single packages of government spending in American history. Congress next passed the Wall Street Reform and Consumer Protection Act, a complex law that regulated the financial industry and established new consumer protections. The president's signal accomplishment, however, was the first major reform of the nation's health-care system since the introduction of Medicare in 1965: the **Patient Protection and Affordable Care Act**, signed into law by Obama on March 23, 2010. The new law, widely known as the "ACA" or "Obamacare," endeavored to extend health coverage to more people and to make it more affordable by requiring all Americans to carry coverage (as states currently do with automobile insurance) and compelling larger employers to cover all their employees. The law provided subsidies to low-income individuals for purchasing insurance and also outlawed certain discriminatory practices, such as insurance companies denying individual people coverage if they have "preexisting" conditions — meaning they have a health condition that requires treatment. Political opposition and the powerful lobbying of the private health insurance industry ensured that the new law contained enough compromises that few could predict its long-term impact — but it would ultimately reduce the number of people without health insurance by 38 percent.

Barack Obama In 2008, Barack Obama became the first African American president in U.S. history. And in 2012, he was reelected to a second term. Here, President Obama and First Lady Michelle Obama walk along Pennsylvania Avenue during his second inauguration. Chip Somodevilla/Getty Images.

American Recovery and Reinvestment Act
An economic stimulus bill passed in 2009, in response to the Great Recession, that provided $787 billion to state and local governments. It was one of the largest single packages of government spending in American history.

Patient Protection and Affordable Care Act
Sweeping 2010 health-care reform bill championed by President Obama that established nearly universal health insurance by providing subsidies and compelling larger businesses to offer coverage to employees.

Tea Party
A coalition of far-right groups, voicing an extreme antigovernment ideology, that emerged during President Obama's first term and helped the Republican Party recapture the House in 2010 and Senate in 2014.

During the fierce debate over health-care reform, a coalition of far-right groups, known collectively as the **Tea Party**, emerged to catalyze Republican opposition to the president. Thanks in part to this reenergized right, Democrats lost their majority in the House of Representatives in 2010 and in the Senate in 2014. With Tea Partiers leading the way, the Republican-controlled Congress refused to consider virtually any Democratic legislation. In the face of this legislative stalemate, Obama turned to executive authority to advance a broad, cautiously liberal agenda. In 2011, for example, the president ordered that gay men and lesbians be allowed to serve openly in the armed forces, a reversal of decades of military policy. He also made two liberal appointments to the Supreme Court: Sonia Sotomayor in 2009, the first Latina to serve on the high court, and Elena Kagan in 2010.

Climate Change In 2015, Obama directed the Environmental Protection Agency (EPA) to adopt the Clean Power Plan to combat greenhouse gases. Enforcement of this plan was subsequently blocked by a Supreme Court stay, and its guidelines subsequently weakened by Obama's successor, Donald Trump. The fight over the Clean Power Plan illustrated the political quagmire around a looming global issue. A scientific consensus has existed for decades that the production of energy through the burning of carbon-based substances (especially petroleum and coal) increases the presence of greenhouse gases in the atmosphere, warming the earth. Increasing temperatures are already producing dramatically new weather patterns and melting polar ice. Climate change threatens agricultural production, plant and animal life, and the viability of cities and regions at or near the current sea level. How to halt, or at least mitigate, climate change has become one of the most pressing public policy issues of the twenty-first century.

Arriving at the scientific consensus on climate change has proven easier than developing government policies to address it. This is especially true in the United States, where oil company lobbyists, defenders of free-market capitalism, and conservatives who deny global warming altogether have been instrumental in blocking action. The United States is not a signatory to the major international treaty — the so-called Kyoto Protocol — designed to reduce carbon emissions, and in 2017 newly elected President Trump withdrew from the one major international climate accord — known as the Paris Climate Agreement — that the United States had signed. Legislative proposals have not fared better. Cap-and-trade legislation, so named because it places a cap on individual polluters' emissions but allows those companies to trade for more emission allowances from low polluters, has stalled in Congress. Another proposal, a tax on carbon emissions, has gained little political support. Regardless of political resistance, climate change will rank among the critical issues of the twenty-first century for the United States and the rest of the planet.

AP® EXAM TIP

Compare the successes and failures of the Obama administration to the administration of Bill Clinton.

Obama and the Middle East Even as Obama pursued an ambitious domestic agenda, he faced two inherited wars in the Middle East. Determined to end the occupation of Iraq, the president began to draw down troops in 2010, with the last convoy of U.S. soldiers departing in late 2011 after a costly nine-year war. That same year, in May, U.S. Special Forces located and killed Osama bin Laden in Pakistan, where he had been hiding for many years, an action which won Obama nearly universal praise. His use of drone strikes to assassinate Al Qaeda leaders and other U.S. enemies in Afghanistan, Pakistan, and elsewhere proved more controversial — with some human rights advocates charging the president with violating international law. Despite a campaign promise to end the war in Afghanistan, the president deployed an additional 30,000 American troops there in 2009 to stem a reinvigorated Taliban. The surge temporarily stabilized the country, but long-term political and military stability proved elusive. Obama left office in 2017 with thousands of U.S. troops still in Afghanistan.

Meanwhile, a host of events in the Middle East deepened the region's volatility. In late 2010, a multinational political movement across the Middle East and North Africa roiled the politics of the Arab world. In a wave of popular demonstrations in Egypt, Tunisia, Libya, and Yemen, autocratic regimes fell, while protests in other countries led to harsh crackdowns. Obama and the U.S. State Department cautiously supported the so-called Arab Spring uprisings but were unable to significantly shape events thereafter. In Syria, for instance, an Arab Spring insurgency matured into a brutal civil war that has resulted in hundreds of thousands of deaths, nearly five million refugees, and the internal displacement of nearly six million Syrian citizens. The Islamic State, an ultraviolent, fundamentalist Sunni group that emerged in the chaos of war-torn Iraq, also plagued Syria. Starting in 2011, the extremists effectively seized control of portions of northern Iraq and northern Syria, establishing a harsh theocratic "caliphate." Between 2001, when the war against the Taliban began in Afghanistan, and 2016, when the Syrian refugee crisis and the rise of the Islamic State dominated headlines, the United States learned again that making war was far easier than controlling the events that followed.

AP® SKILLS & PROCESSES

CAUSATION

As the nation's first African American president, what kinds of unique challenges did Barack Obama face, and how did they affect his presidency?

Black Lives Matter In a reminder of the Vietnam era, violence abroad seemed to echo at home. Despite the gains of the civil rights era, African Americans continued to endure police brutality, with painful regularity. Protests against police violence have risen periodically in the United States since the late nineteenth century, and one

AP® APPLY THE TIP

Direct students to use pp. 985–987 and 994–997 to complete **Handout 30.4 — Comparison: Obama and Clinton (TRM)**. Then ask students to work in pairs to determine if the Obama and Clinton administrations were relatively more similar or more different. Students should then identify which American administration in the twentieth century they feel had the most in common with either the Obama administration or the Clinton administration. Ask students to write a thesis statement with supporting evidence in response to the following prompt: To what extent did the successes and failures of the Obama administration illustrate continuity and change in the U.S.?

TRM Find **Handout 30.4— Comparison: Obama and Clinton** in the Teacher's Resource Materials.

AP® THEME

GEO: Geography and the Environment

Conflicts in the Middle East and concerns about climate change led to debates over U.S. dependence on fossil fuels and the impact of economic consumption on the environment. Within months of taking office, President Trump decided to withdraw the U.S. from the Paris Accord, which had been negotiated by 195 nations. The *New York Times* reflects on this decision. To access this article, search "NYT Trump Paris Climate Agreement."

AP® SKILLS & PROCESSES

CAUSATION

The **CAUSATION** question asks students to consider the effects of Barack Obama's race on his presidency.

TRM Find complete suggested responses in the Teacher's Resource Materials.

such cycle began in 2014 after a police officer shot and killed an unarmed black teenager named Michael Brown in Ferguson, Missouri. Weeks of demonstrations followed, as black activists, joined by many white and Latino supporters, converged on Ferguson from around the country. Many protesters articulated calls for police reform and a renewed struggle against racism.

At the Ferguson demonstrations, an organization called Black Lives Matter (BLM) moved to the fore of an emerging movement. Formed two years earlier, in response to the 2012 killing of Trayvon Martin, an unarmed black teenager, by a civilian neighborhood watch captain in the city of Sanford, Florida, BLM put forth a comprehensive agenda of police reform, economic justice, political empowerment, and, echoing Black Power activists from the 1960s, black community control. Between 2014 and 2016, BLM and other activists staged protests in more than one hundred American cities, as police violence against African Americans came to increased public attention as a result of cell phones, surveillance, and police videos. Many activists stressed that the ongoing crisis disproved the notion that the election of a black president represented a fundamental shift in American racial history. Indeed, credible claims were made that the Tea Party's opposition to the president carried a barely disguised racial animosity. "Go back to Kenya" signs directed at Obama appeared at Tea Party rallies, and the so-called birther movement — which insisted the president was born in Indonesia — cast baseless doubts on the president's U.S. citizenship.

Nationalism and the Rise of Donald Trump From one political vantage point, President Obama and the Democratic Party looked like the beneficiaries of an electoral shift in a liberal direction. Between 1992 and 2012, Democrats won the popular vote in five of the six presidential elections, and in 2008 Obama won a greater share of the popular vote (53 percent) than any Democratic nominee since Lyndon Johnson in 1964. He won the support of 93 percent of African Americans, 71 percent of Hispanics, 73 percent of Asian Americans, 55 percent of women, and 60 percent of Americans under the age of thirty. His coalition was multiracial, heavily female, and young.

That coalition appears strong enough to win popular majorities for Democratic presidential nominees into the foreseeable future. Yet the nation's peculiar constitutional method of awarding the presidency through the electoral college allows for the possibility, as in 2000 and again in 2016, that a candidate with the lower national vote total can win. Moreover, the Constitution's awarding of two senators to each state regardless of population means that a fiercely conservative state with a small population, like North Dakota, has as much influence in the U.S. Senate as a fiercely liberal state with a massive population, like California. In that context, the Democratic coalition has struggled to sustain Senate majorities. Furthermore, changes in House districts after the 2010 Census have further disadvantaged Democrats (Table 30.1). In 2012, Democratic candidates for the House of Representatives won more votes nationally than Republican candidates did (59.6 million to 58.2 million), but Republicans still won a majority of seats. Thus, heading into the 2016 election, the long-term fate of the liberal Obama coalition remained unclear.

In the 2016 presidential election, that coalition, true to form, produced a 2.8 million-vote margin of victory for Democratic nominee Hillary Clinton. But Clinton's popular vote success could not stop the remarkable ascent of Donald Trump, the Manhattan real estate developer and one-time reality television show star, to the presidency. Despite losing the national vote by more than two percentage points (about 2.8 million votes), the Republican

TABLE 30.1

Political Realignment: Congressional Seats

As Table 28.1 (p. 918) demonstrated, between 1940 and 1990 the Rust Belt states lost population and political representation in Congress, and the Sunbelt states gained both. That trend continued between 1990 and 2010. Geographic shifts in population, especially continued population growth in California, Texas, and Florida, shaped which parts of the country had the loudest voice in Congress. In 1940, the major industrial states accounted for 45 percent of congressional seats. By 2010, they accounted for only 31 percent. Meanwhile, the Sunbelt moved in the opposite direction: in 1940, those ten states had only 20 percent of congressional seats, but by 2010 they held 40 percent. Political influence had shifted geographically over the course of seven decades.

	Apportionment	
State	**1990**	**2010**
Rust Belt		
Massachusetts	10	9
Connecticut	6	5
New York	31	27
New Jersey	13	12
Pennsylvania	21	18
Ohio	19	16
Illinois	20	18
Indiana	10	9
Michigan	16	14
Wisconsin	9	8
Total	**155**	**136**
Sunbelt		
California	52	53
Arizona	6	9
Nevada	2	4
Colorado	6	7
New Mexico	3	3
Texas	30	36
Georgia	11	14
North Carolina	12	13
Virginia	11	11
Florida	23	27
Total	**156**	**177**

SOURCE: Office of the Clerk of the House, clerk.house.gov/art_history/house_history/congApp/bystate.html.

AP® THEME

MIG: Migration and Settlement

The political, economic, and cultural influence of the American South and West has continued to increase in the last generation as population shifts to those areas. **TABLE 30.1** shows how the pattern introduced in Chapter 28 (see **TABLE 28.1** on p. 918) continued to develop. By 2010, the political clout of the Sunbelt states clearly outweighed that of the Rust Belt states.

AP® THEME

WOR: America in the World

Despite economic and foreign policy challenges, the U.S. continued as the world's leading superpower in the twenty-first century.

The Rise of Donald Trump A supporter of President Donald Trump tries to block the signs of a pair of protesters during Trump's speech at a political rally in Ohio in July 2017. Trump's 2016 election to the presidency deepened political divisions in the United States, and the president's political rallies, like this one, became symbols of those divisions. Mike Cardew/Akron Beacon Journal/Getty Images.

nominee Trump narrowly won the key states of Pennsylvania, Michigan, and Wisconsin and secured 306 electoral college votes to Clinton's 232, making him president (Map 30.6). As the first woman to lead a major-party ticket for U.S. president, Clinton boasted a resume with decades of high-level political service, including eight years as First Lady, eight years as a U.S. senator, and four years as secretary of state. In the general election campaign against Trump, Clinton proposed detailed plans of action on a wide range of issues, including climate change, criminal justice reform, workers' rights, early childhood education, tax reform, the nation's deteriorating infrastructure, and many more. For his part, Trump campaigned on building a vast wall to block immigration at the U.S.-Mexico border, temporarily banning Muslim immigration to the United States, and imposing tariffs on a variety of goods imported from other countries. Trump remained a viable presidential candidate despite revelations that many observers believed were disqualifying: that he likely avoided paying federal income taxes for decades, for instance, and his bragging in a 2005 video about sexually assaulting women.

Trump's victory surprised — even shocked — many Americans, from ordinary citizens to prominent media figures. This surprise came from the fact that Trump openly campaigned on a nationalist platform of racial animosity and economic protectionism, which most political experts predicted would doom his candidacy. He made inaccurate claims about the threat of immigration and urban crime, blaming Mexican Americans and African Americans for rising violent crime rates when in fact such rates had been declining for two decades. In the speech announcing his candidacy for the Republican nomination in 2015, Trump said of Mexican immigrants, "They're bringing drugs. They're bringing crime. They're rapists." In his first two years in office, Trump issued a ban on immigration from seven predominantly Muslim countries (an order which was adjusted following a Supreme Court ruling) and increased deportations at the U.S.-Mexico border. Trump's conservative nationalism also took the form of economic protectionism: he withdrew the United States from major trading partnerships in North America (the North American Free Trade Agreement) and East Asia (the Trans-Pacific Partnership), which had been painstakingly built over many decades, and imposed tariffs (on Mexico, Canada, China, and the EU, among other nations) instead.

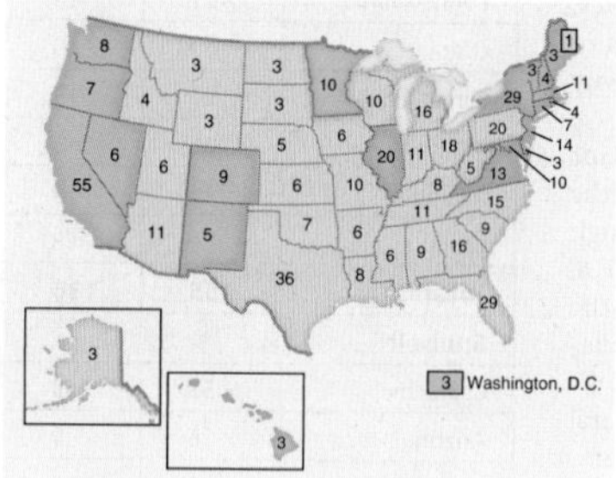

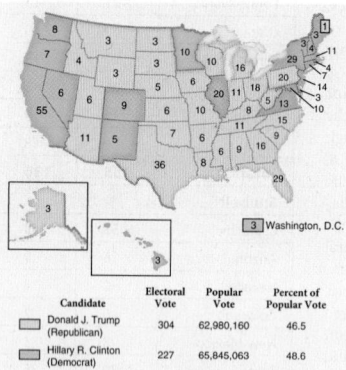

Candidate	Electoral Vote	Popular Vote	Percent of Popular Vote
Donald J. Trump (Republican)	304	62,980,160	46.5
Hillary R. Clinton (Democrat)	227	65,845,063	48.6

MAP 30.6 The Presidential Election of 2016
In an unexpected election result, the real estate mogul and television celebrity Donald Trump, the Republican nominee, defeated the former senator and U.S. secretary of state Hillary Clinton, the Democratic nominee. Clinton won the popular vote by 2.9 million, but Trump won the electoral college vote by capturing states that Obama had won in 2008 and 2016 — especially Florida, North Carolina, Pennsylvania, Ohio, and Michigan. This was the second election in sixteen years in which the winner of the popular vote (Al Gore in 2000 and Clinton in 2016) did not win the electoral college vote.

Tax Cuts President Trump has carried out most of his initiatives through the powers of the executive branch: appointing three Supreme Court justices and more than three hundred other federal judges; repealing Obama's Clean Power Plan; and imposing a series of controversial tariffs on imported goods, for example. Some of these initiatives, particularly the protectionist tariffs, have placed him at odds with political conservatism as it has evolved in the United States since the era of Ronald Reagan. But Trump's major legislative accomplishment — an enormous tax cut passed in 2017 — lies squarely within that tradition. Between 2001, when President George W. Bush and Congress launched a

A Wall at the U.S.-Mexico Border President Trump speaking with reporters in 2018 in front of prototypes of the wall he is seeking to build along the border with Mexico. During his campaign for the presidency Trump promised if elected he would construct such a wall across the entire length of the Mexican border. AP Photo/Evan Vucci.

major tax-cutting initiative, and 2018, when the Trump cuts went into effect, federal revenues have been reduced by more than $5 trillion, which has contributed to a swelling national debt. Two-thirds of that savings went directly to the richest 20 percent of Americans, which has helped to accelerate income and wealth inequality in the United States. The 2001–2018 reductions went further than even the Reagan-era cuts and have had two major consequences: placing government programs such as Social Security and Medicare on fragile financial footing and making the shoring up of those programs, or adding new social programs, more politically difficult because doing so would require raising taxes. Viewed historically, these tax reductions represent a political victory of twenty-first-century conservatism over twentieth-century liberalism's signature accomplishments (in the New Deal and Great Society eras).

AP® SKILLS & PROCESSES

MAKING CONNECTIONS

How was Hillary Clinton's loss in the 2016 presidential election part of a trend in the electoral college?

Coronavirus Pandemic With the 2020 presidential election less than a year away—and as the Democratic Party held state primaries to determine its candidate to challenge President Trump—an utterly unexpected event transformed everyday life in the United States. A new form of coronavirus (a large family of viruses that causes many illness worldwide, including the common cold) began infecting people in China in late December 2019 and within months spread around the world. This virus is easily transmitted and causes severe respiratory disease known as COVID-19, which proved fatal in vulnerable populations. Like other global disease outbreaks (pandemics) before it, COVID-19 began to overwhelm health care systems in country after country, including the United States. By the early spring of 2020, ordinary social life in the United States—from going to schools and restaurants to attending sporting events and church gatherings—had ground to a halt as cities and states took increasingly radical steps to limit the spread of the virus, treat the sick, and avoid catastrophic loss of life.

Policing Protests Resurface In the midst of the pandemic, in late May 2020, protests erupted in the United States and across the world. The long campaign against police brutality, which Black Lives Matter had reignited in 2012, surged with renewed intensity when

AP® SKILLS & PROCESSES

MAKING CONNECTIONS

The apportionment in Congress continued to favor Republicans, despite a lack of proportionality in the numbers of voters for each respective party. Though Republicans won narrow victories in 2000 and 2004, the 2016 election revealed some of the voting trends toward Republicans seen in states, especially in the Midwest.

TRM Find complete suggested responses in the Teacher's Resource Materials.

Protests against Police Brutality and Racial Bias On June 3, 2020, protesters at Black Lives Matter protest in New York City held up signs and a portrait of George Floyd, who had been asphyxiated while under arrest in Minneapolis. Protests against police brutality and bias erupted across the country in the wake of Floyd's death. ANGELA WEISS/AFP via Getty Images.

an African American man named George Floyd was killed by a police officer in Minneapolis, Minnesota. Floyd's killing was captured on video and followed soon after the killing of three other African Americans nationwide — two by police (in Louisville, Kentucky, and Tallahassee, Florida), and a third by neighborhood vigilantes in Georgia. As the video of Floyd's killing circulated around the world on social media, massive rallies and protest marches followed. The street actions spread quickly from Minneapolis and other major American cities to cities across the globe such as London and Paris, as well as major cities in Brazil, Australia, Indonesia, New Zealand, and in dozens of other countries worldwide. With the support of millions of people, marching and chanting across the country and world, protestors renewed calls for reform of policing and the criminal justice system.

As this textbook goes to press, the 2020 presidential election lies just ahead, its outcome yet unknown, and the world continues to fight the COVID-19 pandemic. Simultaneously, the protests inspired by George Floyd's death continue in major American cities as well. Together, the outcomes of the election, the battle against the coronavirus, and the renewed calls for reform of policing practices, among other events unfolding at this writing, will constitute their own historical turning point, from which new developments will unfold.

SUMMARY

Globalization — the worldwide flow of capital, goods, and people across borders — accelerated at the end of the Cold War. The number of multinational corporations, many of them based in the United States, increased dramatically. Financial markets, in particular, grew increasingly open and interconnected. Technological innovations strengthened the American economy and transformed daily life. The computer revolution and the spread of the Internet changed how Americans shopped, worked, learned, and communicated. Globalization also facilitated the immigration of millions of Asians and Latin Americans into the United States.

But even as America's connection to the wider world intensified a divisive cultural conflict emerged in domestic politics in the years after 1990. Conservatives spoke out strongly, and with increasing effectiveness, against multiculturalism and what they viewed as serious threats to "family values." Debates over access to abortion, affirmative action, and the legal rights of homosexuals intensified. The terrorist attacks of September 11, 2001, diverted attention from this increasingly bitter partisanship, but that partisanship found a new expression with the advent of the war on terror and the subsequent invasion of Iraq in 2003. Barack Obama made history in 2008 as the nation's first African American president, but faced two inherited wars and a profound economic crisis upon taking office. His, and the nation's, efforts to address these and other pressing issues found initial success before stalling in a deepening partisan stalemate, especially after his 2012 reelection. The election of celebrity businessman Donald Trump to the presidency in 2016 on a platform of right-wing nationalism affirmed that globalization and domestic cultural divisions remain at the core of American politics. Trump won the election despite losing the popular vote by a wide margin. His presidency opened with the country more divided than it had been since the turbulent 1960s.

CHECK FOR UNDERSTANDING

Ask students: **How did wars abroad and political conflicts at home reshape the United States in the first decades of the twenty-first century?** *The effects of America's overseas military commitments in the 2000s, especially in the Middle East, exacerbated an already politically polarized environment. The election of the first black president did not lead to racial healing. Instead, civil society began to divide, especially along racial lines. (e.g., the Black Lives Matter movement). This complex historical development was the result of a variety of societal changes. Moreover, a political reaction to this change resulted in a movement to support Donald Trump for president. Deep cultural fissures were illustrative of a society with competing political, economic, and cultural values.*

CHECK FOR UNDERSTANDING

Use the **AP® LEARNING FOCUS** question at the beginning of the chapter to check students' understanding of the chapter as a whole: **Why did the shape of American politics, economics, and society shift in response to post–Cold War globalization?** *Globalization — the worldwide flow of capital, goods, and people — entered a new phase after the end of the Cold War. The number of multinational corporations, many of them based in the United States, increased dramatically, and people, goods, and investment capital moved easily across political boundaries. Financial markets, in particular, grew and interconnected across the globe. The computer revolution and the spread of the Internet changed the dynamics of communication, work, and family. In addition, globalization contributed to increased immigration into the U.S. In a matter of years, Americans gained access to the global market, news, and information through technology. Globalization has also caused the nation to define its interests very broadly and to intervene economically and militarily around the world, sometimes in ways that make American foreign policy unpopular, helping to generate attacks on the U.S., like the 9/11 attacks, and to give birth to organizations like ISIS. Moreover, Americans continued to disagree on the role in which the United States played as a global economic power as illustrated by the increased tensions over trade imbalance and immigration.*

✓ LearningCurve

Remind students to go online to complete the LearningCurve quiz for this chapter.

CHAPTER 30 REVIEW

AP CONTENT REVIEW *Answer these questions to demonstrate your understanding of the chapter's main ideas.*

1. How did globalization redefine the relationship of the United States to the rest of the world after the end of the Cold War?
2. What were the sources of domestic division in the United States between the 1990s and the present, and how did they reshape the political landscape?
3. How did wars abroad and political turmoil at home shape the United States in the first decades of the twenty-first century?

AP TERMS TO KNOW *Identify and explain the significance of each term.*

Key Concepts and Events

globalization (p. 968)
World Trade Organization (WTO) (p. 970)
Group of Eight (G8) (p. 974)
North American Free Trade Agreement (NAFTA) (p. 974)
multinational corporations (MNC) (p. 975)
Advanced Research Projects Agency Network (ARPANET) (p. 977)
culture war (p. 978)
Immigration and Nationality Act (p. 979)
multiculturalism (p. 982)
Proposition 209 (p. 983)
Defense of Marriage Act (p. 985)
Webster v. Reproductive Health Services (p. 985)
Planned Parenthood of Southeastern Pennsylvania v. Casey (p. 985)
Lawrence v. Texas (p. 985)
Contract with America (p. 986)
Personal Responsibility and Work Opportunity Reconciliation Act (p. 987)
Al Qaeda (p. 989)
USA PATRIOT Act (p. 991)
Abu Ghraib prison (p. 993)
American Recovery and Reinvestment Act (p. 995)
Patient Protection and Affordable Care Act (p. 995)
Tea Party (p. 995)

Key People

William (Bill) Jefferson Clinton (p. 985)
Hillary Clinton (p. 986)
Newt Gingrich (p. 986)
Saddam Hussein (p. 989)
Osama bin Laden (p. 989)
George W. Bush (p. 989)
Barack Obama (p. 994)
Donald J. Trump (p. 997)

AP MAKING CONNECTIONS *Recognize the larger developments and continuities within and across chapters by answering these questions.*

1. How would you compare the Iraq War with previous wars in U.S. history? Compare in particular the reasons for entering the war, support for the war abroad and at home, and the outcome of the conflict.
2. How would you explain the geography of American politics after World War II? Compare Table 28.1 (p. 918) and Table 30.1 (p. 997), which show how population gains and losses over several decades shaped which states and regions had greater representation in Congress. How would you explain the significance of those changes?

KEY TURNING POINTS *Refer to the timeline at the start of the chapter for help in answering this questions.*

In what ways were the attacks of September 11, 2001, a turning point in the decades between 1989 and the present? Identify two other turning points in politics or social life in those decades. Which do you think is the most important and why?

1001

TRM Find complete suggested responses in the Teacher's Resource Materials.

AP® SKILLS & PROCESSES

CAUSATION

AP® CONTENT REVIEW 1 asks students to explain the effects of globalization on American foreign policy in the post–Cold War era. Note: This is the same question as the section-opening prompt on p. 970.

AP® SKILLS & PROCESSES

CAUSATION

AP® CONTENT REVIEW 2 invites students to explain the causes of domestic tension at the end of the Cold War, as well as their effects on national politics. Note: This is the same question as the section-opening prompt on p. 978.

AP® SKILLS & PROCESSES

CAUSATION

AP® CONTENT REVIEW 3 poses two different questions: What were the effects of war on the United States in the early twenty-first century? and What were the effects of political disagreements? Note: This is the same question as the section-opening prompt on p. 989.

TRM Find definitions for these terms in the **Glossary/Glosario** in the Teacher's Resource Materials.

AP® SKILLS & PROCESSES

COMPARISON

AP® MAKING CONNECTIONS 1 invites students to compare the Iraq War (after 9/11) with earlier wars. It might be helpful to narrow the choices for students, rather than leaving the question completely open-ended. They could compare Iraq with other wars in the half-century since World War II, which would include Afghanistan, the first Iraq War, Vietnam, and Korea.

AP® SKILLS & PROCESSES

CONTINUITY AND CHANGE

The **KEY TURNING POINTS** question asks students to situate the attacks of 9/11 as a turning point between the end of the Cold War and the present.

TRM Find complete suggested responses in the Teacher's Resource Materials.

AP® PRACTICE QUESTIONS

MULTIPLE CHOICE QUESTIONS *Choose the correct answer for each question.*

Questions 1–4 refer to this excerpt.

"[W]ithin the first 100 days of the 104th Congress, we shall bring to the House Floor the following bills . . .

1. THE FISCAL RESPONSIBILITY ACT: A balanced budget/tax limitation amendment and a legislative line-item veto to restore fiscal responsibility to an out-of-control Congress, requiring them to live under the same budget constraints as families and businesses.

2. THE TAKING BACK OUR STREETS ACT: An anti-crime package including stronger truth-in-sentencing, 'good faith' exclusionary rule exemptions, effective death penalty provisions, and cuts in social spending from this summer's 'crime' bill to fund prison construction and additional law enforcement to keep people secure in their neighborhoods and kids safe in their schools.

3. THE PERSONAL RESPONSIBILITY ACT: Discourage illegitimacy and teen pregnancy by prohibiting welfare to minor mothers and denying increased AFDC [Aid to Families with Dependent Children] for additional children while on welfare, cut spending for welfare programs, and enact a tough two-years-and-out provision with work requirements to promote individual responsibility. . . .

6. THE NATIONAL SECURITY RESTORATION ACT: No U.S. troops under U.N. command and restoration of the essential parts of our national security funding to strengthen our national defense and maintain our credibility around the world. . . .

8. THE JOB CREATION AND WAGE ENHANCEMENT ACT: Small business incentives, capital gains cut and indexation, neutral cost recovery, risk assessment/cost-benefit analysis, strengthening the Regulatory Flexibility Act and unfunded mandate reform to create jobs and raise worker wages."

Republican Party Contract with America, 1994

1. The excerpt from the Republican Party resulted most directly from
- **a.** the end of the Cold War.
- **b.** demographic shifts in the United States.
- **c.** the rise of new conservative political movements.
- **d.** the rapid nature of economic globalization.

2. The policies proposed in the excerpt from the "Contract with America" are best understood in the context of growing concerns about
- **a.** the decay of traditional United States moral values.
- **b.** the effects of growing international migration from Latin America and Asia.
- **c.** lessening the political influence of union organizations.
- **d.** international free-trade agreements.

3. The proposals in the excerpt best represent a continuation of the policies of which previous presidential administration?
- **a.** Woodrow Wilson
- **b.** Franklin Roosevelt
- **c.** Lyndon Johnson
- **d.** Ronald Reagan

4. Advocates for legislation enacting the "Contract with America" were LEAST likely to endorse which of the following policy goals?
- **a.** Promoting economic growth
- **b.** Reducing the social safety net
- **c.** Expanding civil liberties
- **d.** Deregulating businesses

Questions 5–7 refer to this graph.

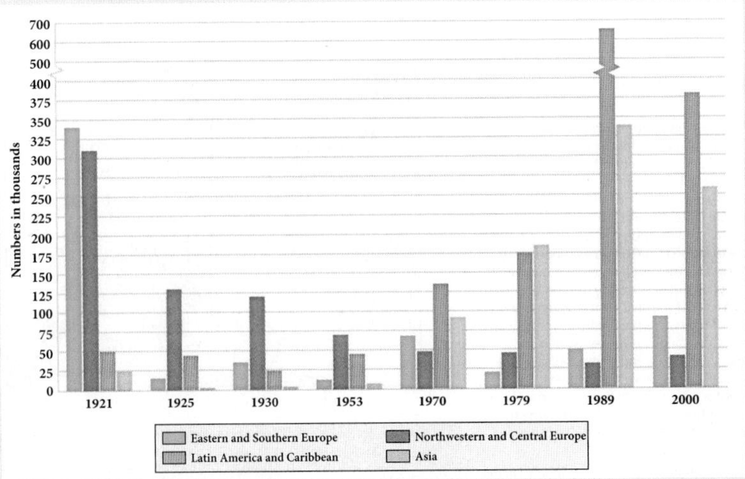

American Immigration, 1920–2000

5. The pattern depicted in the graph between 1921 and 1953 most directly resulted from

a. federal laws strictly limiting the number of immigrants.

b. nativist violence toward undocumented immigrants.

c. efforts to deport immigrants to their countries of origin.

d. increased security along the Mexican and Canadian borders.

6. The majority of immigrants who arrived in the U.S. between 1970 and 2000 settled

a. throughout the small towns of rural America.

b. in the Northeast and Midwest.

c. in the South and West.

d. along the borders with Canada and Mexico.

7. The pattern depicted in the graph between 1979 and 2000 directly contributed to all of the following EXCEPT

a. providing a vital source of labor for the American economy.

b. ongoing political debates over U.S. immigration policy.

c. fears of cultural changes diminishing traditional values.

d. declining economic productivity from a surplus of unskilled immigrant labor.

TRM Find complete suggested responses in the Teacher's Resource Materials.

SHORT ANSWER QUESTIONS

Read each question carefully and write a short response. Use evidence from the text to support your claims.

"Situating himself [Barack Obama] in a current of civil rights history that emphasized its radical currents would be political suicide.

"But there was something deeper than simple political instrumentality at work. During his journey through the polarized racial world of late twentieth-century America, Obama discovered his calling . . . to overcome the acrimonious history of racial polarization — whether it be black power or the culture wars . . . to act on the understanding that such polarization was anathema to national unity. . . . By the time that Obama was inaugurated president, he had recast himself as an agent of national unification, one who could finally bring to fruition the few lingering, unmet promises of the civil rights movement. . . . From the cacophony of the recent past, from its messiness and tumult, Obama extracts a powerful, reassuring message of progress . . . both true and mythological at the same time. Thus Barack Obama's own quest for identity and the distinctive history of the black freedom struggle, of urban politics, of civil rights and black power, became the American story. What Obama called 'my story' became 'our story.'"

Thomas J. Sugrue, *Not Even Past: Barack Obama and the Burden of Race*, 2010

"It is understandable that Obama prefers being seen as the black *president* rather than the *black* president. But his refusal to address race except when he has no choice — a kind of racial procrastination — leaves him little control of the conversation. When he is boxed into a racial corner, often as a result of black social unrest sparked by claims of police brutality, Obama has been mostly uninspiring: he has warned (black) citizens to obey the law and affirmed the status quo. Yet Obama energetically peppers his words to blacks with talk of responsibility in one public scolding after another. When Obama upbraids black folks while barely mentioning the flaws of white America, he leaves the impression that race is the concern solely of black people, and that blackness is full of pathology."

Michael Eric Dyson, *The Black Presidency: Barack Obama and the Politics of Race in America*, 2016

1. Using the two excerpts provided, answer (a), (b), and (c).
   a. Briefly explain ONE major difference between Sugrue's and Dyson's historical interpretations of the Obama presidency.
   b. Briefly explain how ONE specific historical event or development from the period 2000 to the present that is not explicitly mentioned in the excerpts could be used to support Sugrue's interpretation.
   c. Briefly explain how ONE specific historical event or development from the period 2000 to the present that is not explicitly mentioned in the excerpts could be used to support Dyson's interpretation.

Stuart Carlson © 2005 *Milwaukee Sentinel*. Reprinted with permission of UNIVERSAL UCLICK. All rights reserved.

2. Using the political cartoon provided, answer (a), (b), and (c).
   a. Briefly explain ONE historical perspective about the changes from the 1950s to the early 2000s expressed in the cartoon.
   b. Briefly explain how ONE specific event or development led to a historical change suggested by the cartoon.
   c. Briefly explain ONE specific result of a historical change suggested by the cartoon in the period 2000 to the present.
3. Answer (a), (b), and (c).
   a. Briefly explain ONE specific historical similarity between immigration to the U.S. in the period 1880 to 1920 and in the period 1980 to the present.
   b. Briefly explain ONE specific historical difference between immigration to the U.S. in the period 1880 to 1920 and in the period 1980 to the present.
   c. Briefly explain ONE specific historical effect of immigration to the U.S. in the period 1980 to the present.

AP® PRACTICE ESSAY QUESTIONS

9 PART

TRM Find complete suggested responses in the Teacher's Resource Materials.

DOCUMENT-BASED QUESTION *Suggested reading period: 15 minutes. Suggested writing time: 45 minutes.*

DIRECTIONS: Question 1 is based on the accompanying documents. The documents have been edited for the purpose of this exercise.

1. Evaluate the extent to which technological innovations have changed the American economy since 1980.

DOCUMENT 1

Source: Andrew Pollack, "Rising Trend of the Computer Age: Employees Who Work at Home," from *The New York Times*, March 12, 1981. © 1981 *The New York Times*. All rights reserved. Used by permission and protected by the Copyright Laws of the United States. The printing, copying, redistribution, or retransmission of this Content without express written permission is prohibited.

"Louise Priester used to key-punch insurance claims into a computer in the office of Blue Cross–Blue Shield of South Carolina. Now she does the same thing from a bedroom in her house in Columbia, S.C., using a terminal connected to the office's computer by telephone.

Like Mrs. Priester, a small but growing number of workers are doing office work at home on small computers or terminals with typewriter keyboards. Corporations encourage the practice, to save commuting time for their employees and to recruit some workers, such as mothers of small children, who might not be able to hold conventional jobs.

Working at home gives employees more flexibility in scheduling other activities. 'I can get up when I want to and work when I want to,' said Mrs. Priester, adding that she can now take better care of her elderly mother.

Companies and workers say the new system can transform relationships between co-workers, between employees and employers and between workers and their families.

What we're really talking about is returning production to the home, which is where it was before the Industrial Revolution."

DOCUMENT 2

Source: Ford Assembly Line, 1980.

Keystone/Hulton Archive/Getty Images.

DOCUMENT 3

Source: Martin Feldstein, American Economic Policy in the 1980s, 1995.

"The decade of the 1980s was a time of fundamental changes in American economic policy. These changes were influenced by the economic conditions that prevailed as the decade began, by the style and political philosophy of President Ronald Reagan, and by the new intellectual climate among economists and policy officials. . . . Ronald Reagan's election in 1980 . . . provided a president who was committed to achieving low inflation, to lowering tax rates, and to shrinking the role of the government in the economy."

DOCUMENT 4

Source: Thomas L. Friedman, *The World is Flat: A Brief History of the Twenty-First Century*, 2007.

"'Outsourcing is just one dimension of a much more fundamental thing happening today in the world,' Nilekani explained. 'What happened over the last [few] years is that there was a massive investment in technology. Especially in the bubble era, when hundreds of millions of dollars were invested in putting broadband connectivity around the world, undersea cables, all those things.' At the same time, he added computers became cheaper and dispersed all over the world, and there was an explosion of software-email, search engines like Google, and proprietary software that can chop up any piece of work and send one part to Boston, one part to Bangalore, and one part to Beijing, making it easy for anyone to do remote development. When all of these suddenly came together around 2000, added Nilekani, they 'created a platform where intellectual work, intellectual capital, could be delivered from anywhere. It could be disaggregated, delivered, distributed, produced, and put back together again- and this gave a whole new degree of freedom to the way we do work, especially work of an intellectual nature . . .' . . . Clearly Nandan was right: It is now possible for more people than ever to collaborate and compete in real time with more other people on more different kinds of work from more different corners of the planet and on a more equal footing than at any previous time in the history of the world- using computers, e-mail, fiber-optic networks, teleconferencing, and dynamic new software."

DOCUMENT 5

Source: Bureau of Labor Statistics, U.S. Department of Labor, November 2001.

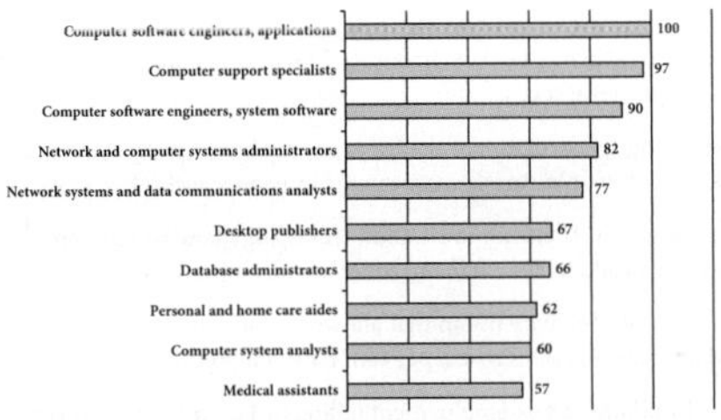

Fastest Growing Occupations (by percentage), 2000 to 2010

DOCUMENT 6

Source: Leroy McClelland Sr., a steelworker, Interview with Bill Barry, 2006.

"Mr. McClelland: [W]ith technology being advanced and computers and what have you, we've had operations that would never ever operate unless you had a person there. Now, that's not necessary. In fact, it can have a crew —it used to be six people on a mill reduced to three. Why? Computer, and then it advances further on down the road for technology. When that happened, too, you've got to understand that the idea of the union was to protect jobs, create jobs, not eliminate jobs. Well, I had the unfortunate experience of being the zone committeeman at the time when a lot of this technology was starting to really grow.

Mr. Barry: When was this?

Mr. McClelland: Well, it really started in 1975, from '75 on, '80, '90s, biggest part being in the '80s really, the advanced technology. But when these other things started to take place, guys and gals sort of looked at this change coming down, felt hey, that's a God send, not realizing that when that takes place you ain't going to be there to see it because your job is going to be gone. . . . I mean reality is technology is the future and competitiveness is strong. If you can't deal with competitiveness, if you don't have tons per hour and manpower per hour was the way it was, and that's what had to happen. . . .

Mr. Barry: These were people who were eligible to retire and the technology in effect drove them out?

Mr. McClelland: Yes, absolutely it did. And change is tough for anybody."

DOCUMENT 7

Source: Robin Harding, "Technology Shakes Up U.S. Economy," *Financial Times*, March 26, 2014. Used under license from the *Financial Times*. All rights reserved.

"New technologies are transforming the structure of the US economy but creating only modest numbers of jobs, according to the biggest official survey of businesses, conducted only once every five years. . . .

It highlights concerns that recent innovations in information technology tend to raise productivity by replacing existing workers, rather than creating new products that demand more labour to produce. . . .

In manufacturing, the story is of a productivity boom that allowed a solid increase in sales, coupled with falling employment and payrolls. Manufacturing sales rose 8 per cent between 2007 and 2012 to reach $5.8 trillion.

However, the industry shed 2.1 million jobs — employment falling to 11.3 million — and its payroll dropped $20 billion to $593 billion.

The relatively greater drop in jobs than payrolls highlights how remaining jobs in the sector are becoming more skilled. Annual payroll per employee in the manufacturing sector rose from $45,818 in 2007 to $52,686 in 2012.

That is among the highest of any big industry, but highlights how manufacturing increasingly employs skilled engineers to tend complex equipment, rather than being a source of well-paid jobs for less-skilled workers."

LONG ESSAY QUESTIONS *Suggested writing time: 40 minutes.*

DIRECTIONS: Please choose one of the following two questions to answer. Make a historically defensible claim and support your reasoning with specific and relevant evidence.

1. Evaluate the extent to which demographic shifts changed politics in the United States from 1980 to 2000.
2. Evaluate the extent to which demographic shifts changed culture in the United States from 1980 to 2000.
3. Evaluate the extent to which the end of the Cold War changed U.S. foreign policy from 1980 to 2010.

AP® UNITED STATES HISTORY PRACTICE EXAM

EXAM OVERVIEW

Section	Question Type	Number of Questions	Timing	% of Total Exam Score
Section I	Part A: Multiple-Choice Questions	55 questions	55 minutes	40%
	Part B: Short-Answer Questions	3 questions	40 minutes	20%
Section II	Part A: Document-Based Question	1 question	60 minutes	25%
	Part B: Long Essay Question	1 question	40 minutes	15%

SECTION I
PART A: MULTIPLE-CHOICE QUESTIONS
55 minutes

DIRECTIONS: Choose the correct answer for each question.

Questions 1–3 refer to the excerpt provided.

> "The extremely heterogeneous population confronted Pennsylvania with a unique set of problems that could have impeded the creation of a stable society. Nevertheless, despite the inevitable tensions, exacerbated by waves of new immigration, wars, and religious conflict, colonial Pennsylvanians managed to develop new ideals of pluralism and tolerance on which they built their province. . . . William Penn . . . set forth a new, ideological basis for pluralism and tolerance that transformed the tentative pattern of relative harmony and toleration into one of official policy.
>
> . . . [H]e drafted a series of constitutions that guaranteed religious freedom and promoted his colony not only in the British Isles but on the Continent as well."
>
> Sally Schwartz, *"A Mixed Multitude": The Struggle for Toleration in Colonial Pennsylvania*, 1987

1. Which of the following later developments can best be used to support Schwartz's argument regarding the colonial culture in Pennsylvania?

a. A strong abolitionist movement developed in Pennsylvania in the eighteenth and nineteenth centuries.
b. Relations with American Indians deteriorated over time as colonists demanded more land.
c. Pennsylvania's nineteenth-century leaders rejected the development of a strong national government.
d. The overt resistance of African Americans revolting against slavery.

2. Which of the following best explains the context in which Pennsylvania's culture in the colonial era developed?

a. Leaders' insistence on tolerance in accordance with religious policy in England
b. The colony's strong emphasis on economic goods as Pennsylvania was founded as a corporate colony
c. The Anglicization of diverse migrants to Pennsylvania
d. The Quaker founders' established policies favoring tolerance and individual freedom of conscience

3. In the seventeenth century, Pennsylvania merchants engaged in the transatlantic trade most extensively by

a. exporting tobacco from Pennsylvania to England.
b. importing enslaved Africans to Pennsylvania.
c. exporting staple crop rice from Pennsylvania to the Caribbean.
d. importing goods manufactured in England.

Questions 4–6 refer to the image provided.

The Great Migration: Union Station, Jacksonville, Florida

Photo by Woodward, courtesy of the State Archives of Florida.

4. This image illustrates which of the following trends in African Americans' experience in the period 1917–1945?

a. The expansion of civil rights and suffrage that accompanied new opportunities for African Americans in the North

b. The restrictions placed on African American voting rights in the North and the South

c. The expansion of job opportunities in the North because of wartime labor shortages

d. The tendency of African Americans to abandon Northern industrial jobs in favor of agricultural opportunities in the South

5. This image can best be understood as a contributing factor to the development of which of the following?

a. Progressive Era

b. Harlem Renaissance

c. Great Depression

d. New Deal Legislation

6. Which of the following was likely the most important contributing factor in the decisions made by the individuals pictured in this image?

a. Support for an expansion of civil rights for African Americans in the North

b. Continued racial segregation in the South

c. Large urban enclaves on the West Coast

d. Economic opportunities within the South

Questions 7–9 refer to the excerpt provided.

> "A government of our own is our natural right: And when a man seriously reflects on the precariousness of human affairs, he will become convinced, that it is infinitely wiser and safer, to form a constitution of our own in a cool deliberate manner, while we have it in our power, than to trust such an interesting event to time and chance. If we omit it now, some, Massanello may hereafter arise, who laying hold of popular disquietudes, may collect together the desperate and discontented, and by assuming to themselves the powers of government, may sweep away the liberties of the continent like a deluge. Should the government of America return again into the hands of Britain, the tottering situation of things, will be a temptation for some desperate adventurer to try his fortune; and in such a case, what relief can Britain give? Ere she could hear the news, the fatal business might be done; and ourselves suffering like the wretched Britons under the oppression of the Conqueror. Ye that oppose independence now, ye know not what ye do; ye are opening a door to eternal tyranny, by keeping vacant the seat of government. There are thousands, and tens of thousands, who would think it glorious to expel from the continent, that barbarous and hellish power, which hath stirred up the Indians and Negroes to destroy us, the cruelty hath a double guilt, it is dealing brutally by us, and treacherously by them.
>
> To talk of friendship with those in whom our reason forbids us to have faith, and our affections wounded through a thousand pores instruct us to detest, is madness and folly. Every day wears out the little remains of kindred between us and them, and can there be any reason to hope, that as the relationship expires, the affection will increase, or that we shall agree better, when we have ten times more and greater concerns to quarrel over than ever?"
>
> Thomas Paine, *Common Sense*, 1776

7. The excerpt could be best used as evidence to support an argument that
- **a.** Enlightenment ideals spread through transatlantic print culture influenced colonial political ideology.
- **b.** American Indian political systems such as the Iroquois League shaped colonial ideas about government.
- **c.** British North American colonies developed an original political philosophy.
- **d.** Parliament failed in efforts to control American political developments.

8. The excerpt from "Common Sense" expresses ideas most similar to those in the House of Burgesses, the Virginia representative assembly founded in 1619, that emphasized
- **a.** the importance of religion in government.
- **b.** the rights of citizens to self-govern.
- **c.** a rigid social hierarchy.
- **d.** royal authority.

9. The ideas expressed by Thomas Paine in this excerpt share the most continuity with the later ideas of
- **a.** The Declaration of Independence.
- **b.** the U.S. Constitution.
- **c.** the Declaration Sentiments.
- **d.** the Emancipation Proclamation.

Questions 10–13 refer to the image provided.

"The Boston Massacre," Engraving, Silversmith Paul Revere, 1790

Library of Congress.

10. Historians could use this as historical evidence for which of the following reasons?
- **a.** Explain the ideological varieties of colonial resistance
- **b.** Illustrate the strength of loyalist support for Great Britain
- **c.** Illustrate the concept of salutary neglect
- **d.** Explain how moderate groups were a part of revolutionary rhetoric

11. This image best represents the ideology of
- **a.** colonial governors.
- **b.** Patriots.
- **c.** British soldiers.
- **d.** the Great Awakening.

12. Which of the following most directly led to the events represented in this image?
- **a.** British enforcement of mercantilist policies in the colonies
- **b.** Dissenting ideas of Protestant evangelicalism
- **c.** George Washington's appointment as general of the Continental army
- **d.** British royal decrees that formally recognized American Indian lands west of the Appalachians

13. The image could best be used as evidence to support an argument that colonial leaders
- **a.** incorporated popular movements into calls for changes in British policy.
- **b.** used the free press to secure European allies to support colonial independence.
- **c.** placed political freedom and liberty above economic interests.
- **d.** rejected compromise in conflicts over British colonial rule as early as 1770.

Questions 14–16 refer to the excerpt provided.

> "The President assumes, what no one doubts, that the late rebel States have lost their constitutional relations to the Union, and are incapable of representation in Congress, except by permission of the Government. It matters but little, with this admission, whether you call them States out of the Union, and now conquered territories, or assert that because the Constitution forbids them to do what they did do, that they are therefore only dead as to all national and political action, and will remain so until the Government shall breathe into them the breath of life anew and permit them to occupy their former position. In other words, that they are not out of the Union, but are only dead carcasses lying within the Union. In either case, it is very plain that it requires the action of Congress to enable them to form a State government and send representatives to Congress. Nobody, I believe, pretends that with their old constitutions and frames of government they can be permitted to claim their old rights under the Constitution. . . . Dead men cannot raise themselves. Dead States cannot restore their existence '*as it was.*' Whose especial duty is it to do it? In whom does the Constitution place the power? Not in the judicial branch of Government, for it only adjudicates and does not prescribe laws. Not in the Executive, for he only executes and cannot make laws. Not in the Commander-in-Chief of the armies, for he can only hold them under military rule until the sovereign legislative power of the conqueror shall give them law."
>
> Thaddeus Stevens, Speech to Congress, December 18, 1865

14. Which of the following best explains the context in which Thaddeus Stevens delivered this speech?
- **a.** The assassination of President Lincoln reopening debates over presidential Reconstruction
- **b.** Political resistance to radical Republican use of military districts in Reconstruction
- **c.** Debate over passage of the Thirteenth Amendment in Congress
- **d.** The challenge presented by the passage in southern states of Black Codes after the Civil War

15. Thaddeus Stevens's arguments regarding which branch of the federal government holds power over the status of lands and admission of states shows the greatest similarity to the Constitutional argument presented during which of the following historical events?
- **a.** Louisiana Purchase
- **b.** Missouri Compromise
- **c.** Kansas-Nebraska
- **d.** Dred Scott decision

16. Arguments such as those presented by Thaddeus Stevens in the excerpt revealed which of the following controversies during Reconstruction?
- **a.** Balance of power between Congress and the president
- **b.** Economic mobilization during the war
- **c.** New efforts by those supportive of women's rights
- **d.** The role of the Supreme Court in establishing rights for African Americans

Questions 17–19 are based on the image provided.

King Andrew the First, 1833

Library of Congress.

17. The cartoon most reflects the political views of the

a. Federalist Party.
b. Democratic Party.
c. Whig Party.
d. Republican Party.

18. At the time of its publication in 1833, the cartoon criticized political developments in the federal government that increased the

a. role of Congress in promoting national economic growth.
b. power of the president.
c. power of the Supreme Court in enforcing judicial decisions.
d. role of the people in electing federal politicians.

19. All of the following developments during the 1820s and 1830s reveal similar political party divisions as those reflected in the image EXCEPT

a. federal investment in roads, canals, and railroads.
b. the gag rule passed in Congress to avoid confrontations over slavery.
c. resistance to Indian Removal by federal politicians.
d. refusal to recharter the national bank.

Questions 20–23 refer to the excerpt provided.

"Most of the men was gone, and . . . most of the women was in my bracket, five or six years younger or older. I was twenty-four. There was a black girl that hired in with me. I went to work the next day, sixty cents an hour. . . . I could see where they made a difference in placing you in certain jobs. They had fifteen or twenty departments, but all the Negroes went to Department 17 because there was nothing but shooting and bucking rivets. . . . Some weeks I brought home twenty-six dollars . . . then it gradually went up to thirty dollars. . . . Whatever you make you're supposed to save some. I was also getting that fifty dollars a month from my husband and that was just saved right away. I was planning on buying a home and a car. . . . My husband came back [from the war, and] . . . looked for a job in the cleaning and pressing place. . . . But what we both weren't thinking about was that they [North American] have better benefits because they did have an insurance plan and a union to back you up. Later he did come to work there, in 1951 or 1952. . . . [After I left to have a baby] North American called me back [and] was I a happy soul! . . . It made me live better. It really did. We always say that Lincoln took the bale off of the Negroes. I think there is a statue up there in Washington, D.C., where he's lifting something off the Negro. Well, my sister always said — that's why you can't interview her because she's so radical — 'Hitler was the one that got us out of the white folks' kitchen.' "

Fanny Christina (Tina) Hill, "War Work: Social and Racial Mobility," from *Rosie the Riveter Revisited*, by Sherna B. Gluck, 1987.

20. Fanny Hill's experiences working in World War II differed most from those of women working in World War I in that
- **a.** during World War I industries hired almost exclusively white workers.
- **b.** when World War I ended most female workers left the industrial workforce.
- **c.** the World War II factory jobs were concentrated in the Sunbelt.
- **d.** women working during World War II refused to join labor unions.

21. The story told by Fanny Hill in the excerpt could be used to support all of the following arguments EXCEPT
- **a.** employers allowed women significant roles in producing war supplies in World War II.
- **b.** women experienced more respect for their work in World War II than in World War I.
- **c.** World War II led to improvements in working conditions.
- **d.** labor unions advocated on behalf of women workers during World War I.

22. Fanny Hill's comments about her sister can best be understood as resulting most directly from the
- **a.** international concerns leading to the founding of the United Nations.
- **b.** political and cultural expressions of domestic anticommunism.
- **c.** increasingly confrontational African American civil rights movement.
- **d.** foreign policies aiming at containment.

23. The excerpt from Fanny Hill related developments that most directly participated in the trend after World War II toward
- **a.** suburbanization.
- **b.** the baby boom.
- **c.** conservatism.
- **d.** a more educated populace.

Questions 24–26 refer to the excerpt provided.

> "The question whether or no there shall be slavery in the new territories . . . is a question between the grand body of white workingmen, the millions of mechanics, farmers, and operatives of our country, with their interests on the one side — and the interests of the few thousand rich, 'polished,' and aristocratic owners of slaves at the South, on the other side.
>
> Experience has proved . . . that a stalwart mass of respectable workingmen, cannot exist, much less flourish, in a thorough slave State. Let any one think for a moment what a different appearance New York, Pennsylvania, or Ohio, would present — how much less sturdy independence and family happiness there would be — were slaves the workmen there, instead of each man as a general thing being his own workman. . . .
>
> Slavery is a good thing enough . . . to the rich — the one out of thousands; but it is destructive to the dignity and independence of all who work, and to labor itself. . . . All practice and theory . . . are strongly arrayed in favor of limiting slavery to where it already exists."
>
> Walt Whitman, Editorial, September 1, 1847

24. Which of the following developments led most directly to this editorial by Walt Whitman?
- **a.** The U.S.-Mexico War
- **b.** Conflicts with Britain over Oregon
- **c.** The discovery of gold in California
- **d.** The abolitionist activism of Harriet Tubman and Frederick Douglass

25. The ideas expressed by Whitman in the third paragraph share the most continuity to the later political platform of the
- **a.** antebellum Republican Party.
- **b.** Reconstruction-era Democratic Party.
- **c.** Populist Party.
- **d.** Bull Moose Party.

26. The ideas of Walt Whitman in the excerpt show the most similarity to
    a. the Cult of Domesticity.
    b. free soil ideology.
    c. the Supreme Court decisions of the Marshall Court.
    d. abolitionist ideology.

Questions 27–30 refer to the map provided.

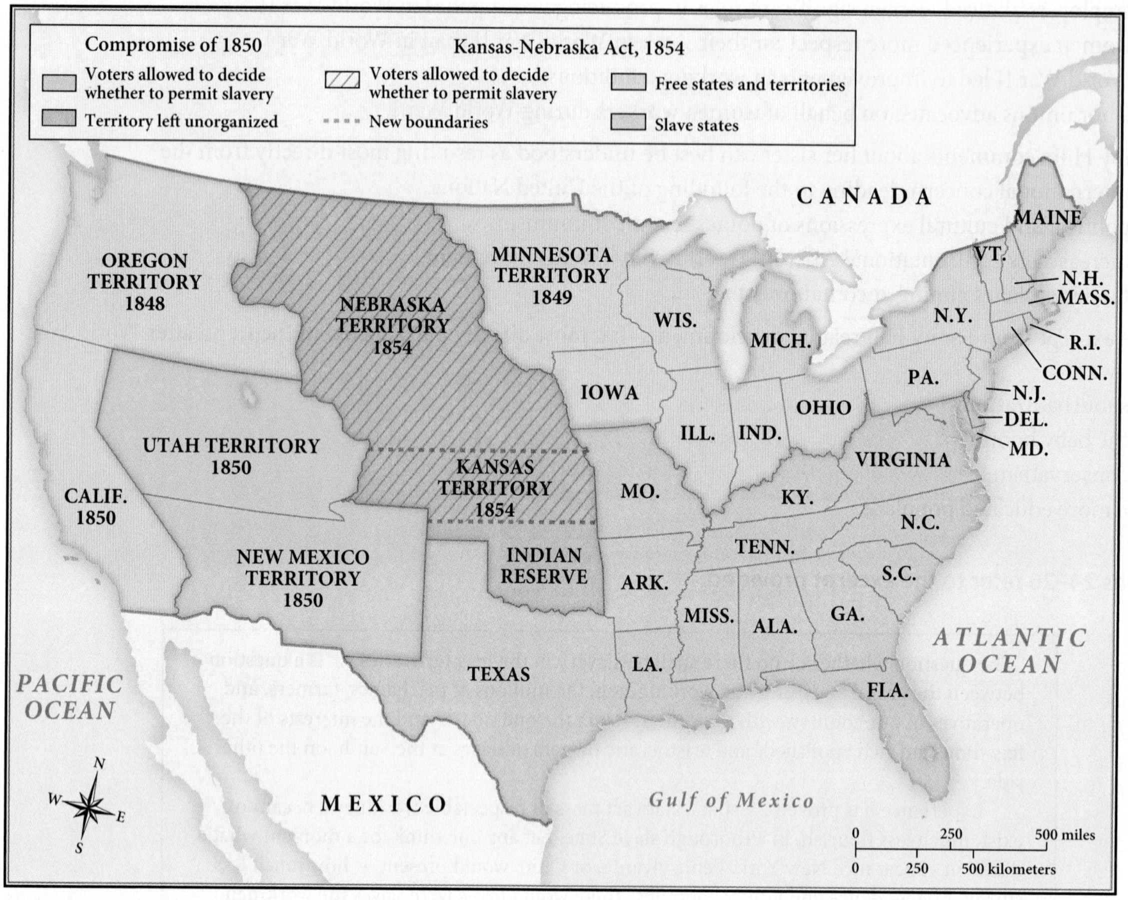

The Compromise of 1850 and the Kansas–Nebraska Act of 1854

27. In reference to territorial agreements shown in this map, which of the following was the most important concession made to southern Congressmen in exchange for the agreement regarding California?
    a. The passage of a new Fugitive Slave Law
    b. The establishment of popular sovereignty in the Kansas Territory
    c. The repeal of the Missouri Compromise
    d. The federal government investment in a transcontinental railroad

28. The map illustrates a trend after the U.S.-Mexico War in the direction of
    a. compromise avoiding violent conflict over slavery.
    b. expansion of women's rights to vote granted by western states.
    c. more extensive efforts to assimilate and incorporate American Indians.
    d. allowing local autonomy in decisions over slavery.

29. The Kansas-Nebraska Act changed federal policy most significantly by
    a. eliminating the 36°30' division in territory gained in the Louisiana Purchase.
    b. introducing measures reducing American Indian tribal lands.
    c. promoting the establishment of Homestead Act settlements by farmers.
    d. opening western lands to migrations of African American farmers such as the Exodusters.

30. Agreements made in the Kansas-Nebraska Act and the Compromise of 1850 show the greatest continuity with the
    a. Three-Fifths Compromise.
    b. Missouri Compromise.
    c. Treaty of Guadalupe Hidalgo.
    d. Compromise of 1877.

Questions 31–33 refer to the excerpt provided.

> "It was upon these gentle lambs, imbued by the Creator with all the qualities we have mentioned, that from the very first day they clapped eyes on them the Spanish fell like ravening wolves upon the fold, or like tigers and savage lions who have not eaten meat for days. The pattern established at the outset has remained unchanged to this day, and the Spaniards still do nothing save tear the natives to shreds, murder them and inflict upon them untold misery, suffering and distress, tormenting, harrying and persecuting them mercilessly. . . . When the Spanish first journeyed there, the indigenous population of the island of Hispaniola stood at some three million; today only two hundred survive. The island of Cuba, which extends for a distance almost as great as that separating Valladolid from Rome, is now to all intents and purposes uninhabited; and two other large, beautiful and fertile islands, Puerto Rico and Jamaica, have been similarly devastated. Not a living soul remains today on any of the islands of the Bahamas. . . . On the mainland, we know for sure that our fellow-countrymen have, through their cruelty and wickedness, depopulated and laid waste an area which once boasted more than ten kingdoms, each of them larger in area than the whole of the Iberian Peninsula. . . . At a conservative estimate, the despotic and diabolical behaviour of the Christians has, over the last forty years, led to the unjust and totally unwarranted deaths of more than twelve million souls, women and children among them, and there are grounds for believing my own estimate of more than fifteen million to be nearer the mark."
>
> Bartolomé de las Casas, *A Short Account of the Destruction of the Indies*, 1542

31. The immediate result of the influence of this document was the
    a. exile of de las Casas from the Spanish colonies.
    b. passage of the New Laws ending Native American slavery under Charles V.
    c. establishment of the Atlantic slave trade with Africa.
    d. abolition of slavery in all Spanish colonies.
32. The most direct effect of the ideas expressed by de las Casas in the excerpt was
    a. the Columbian Exchange.
    b. European competition for lands in the Americas.
    c. debates over Spanish imperial policies.
    d. King Philip's War.
33. The excerpt from de las Casas could best be used as evidence to support an argument that the Spanish
    a. utilized advanced technology in colonizing.
    b. allied with American Indians to create a mestizo society.
    c. creoles held preferred status in the Spanish caste system.
    d. prioritized use of native labor in the *encomienda* system above other interests.

Questions 34–36 refer to the image provided.

Cartoon Demonstrating Anti-Chinese Racism, By Shober and Carqueville, 1886

Library of Congress

34. Which of the following most directly led to the situation that preceded the 1870s conflict portrayed in the image?

a. Job opportunities created by rapid expansion of railroads
b. Victory of the United States in the U.S.-Mexico War
c. Limitations on Mexican immigration established by nativist quotas
d. Increasing acceptance of Irish immigrants into the Democratic Party

35. This cartoon could best be used as evidence to support the conclusion about the late nineteenth century that

a. Republicans expressed a partisan support for Chinese immigration in opposition to the Democratic Party.
b. labor unions consistently opposed Chinese immigration.
c. nativist ideology grew in strength.
d. most Progressive-era reformers advocated for protections of Chinese American interests.

36. Which of the following best summarizes the trend in federal government immigration policy from the late nineteenth century through 1930?

a. Immigration restrictions focused on the Chinese while allowing Europeans open immigration.
b. Immigration restrictions against the Chinese were viewed as failed policies and reversed by the early twentieth century.
c. Immigration restrictions lost the bipartisan support of Congress as business leaders advocated for more cheap labor.
d. Immigration restrictions began with the Chinese and expanded to limit other groups, including Europeans.

Questions 37–39 refer to the excerpt provided.

> "Municipal health officials and city inspectors did make some advances against disease, especially through the improvement of the urban environment. They banned pigs from city streets, regulated notoriously unhealthy dairies inside city limits, and stepped up oversight of street cleaning and garbage removal. . . . [T]he Ladies Health Protective Association . . . shared a concern for the vile odors emanating from a manure handler along the East River . . . [and] the entire slaughter-house district near . . . the tenements fouled by sickening smells and backed-up sewage. . . . [T]he association contacted business owners directly with their complaints, and . . . organized demonstrations at the offending locations, inviting the press to witness their lay inspections. . . . The women also gained considerable publicity when they brought their complaints to the Board of Health."
>
> David Stradling, *The Nature of New York: An Environmental History of the Empire State*, 2010

37. Based on the goals and methods described in this excerpt, which historical period is most likely being described?

a. Market Revolution
b. Progressive Era
c. New Deal
d. World War I

38. The developments described by Stradling most reflect the context of

a. an increasing role of the federal government in protection of the environment through propaganda campaigns.
b. an expanding role of state governments ensuring public health through legislation.
c. both lessening and modification of gender roles defined by domesticity.
d. stable support for *laissez-faire* economic policies.

39. The actions of women described in this excerpt are most similar to the role of women reformers active during

a. the First Great Awakening.
b. the American Revolution.
c. the Second Great Awakening.
d. Reconstruction.

Questions 40–42 refer to the image provided.

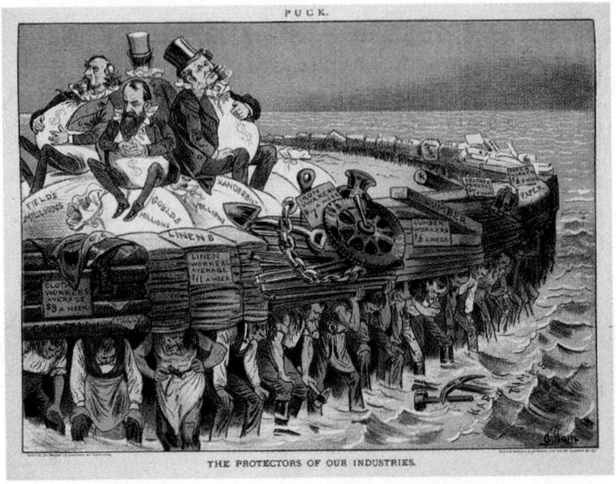

"The Protectors of Our Industries," 1883

Library of Congress

40. The image is best understood as a response to conditions justified most directly by the ideology of
  a. the Social Gospel.
  b. the Gospel of Wealth.
  c. *laissez faire.*
  d. late nineteenth-century domesticity.

41. People sharing the ideas supported in the image also most likely supported
  a. the application of Social Darwinist philosophy to explain poverty.
  b. the passage of labor reforms, including a minimum wage and workplace safety laws.
  c. the creation of federal regulations to protect the natural environment.
  d. continuing federal government policies denying legal sanction to labor unions.

42. Images and political cartoons like this one were most effectively used to sway public opinion to support
  a. local ordinances to protect workers in the workplace.
  b. federal legislation to limit working hours.
  c. state laws to limit the power of railroads.
  d. expansion of suffrage rights to women.

Questions 43–45 refer to the excerpt provided.

> "In March, 1933, I appealed to the Congress of the United States and to the people of the United States in a new effort to restore power to those to whom it rightfully belonged. The response to that appeal resulted in the writing of a new chapter in the history of popular government. You, the members of the Legislative branch, and I, the Executive, contended for and established a new relationship between Government and people. What were the terms of that new relationship? They were an appeal from the clamor of many private and selfish interests, yes, an appeal from the clamor of partisan interest, to the ideal of the public interest. Government became the representative and the trustee of the public interest. Our aim was to build upon essentially democratic institutions, seeking all the while the adjustment of burdens, the help of the needy, the protection of the weak, the liberation of the exploited and the genuine protection of the people's property. . . . To be sure, in so doing, we have invited battle. We have earned the hatred of entrenched greed."
>
> Franklin Roosevelt, "Annual Message to Congress," 1936

43. In the excerpt, Roosevelt most directly contradicts the ideology of
  a. liberalism.
  b. *laissez faire.*
  c. the Social Gospel.
  d. prohibition.

44. The ideas expressed by Roosevelt in the excerpt contributed most directly to a trend leading to
  a. a new and unique conception of federal government power.
  b. limitations on the powers of the federal government in favor of states' rights.
  c. a renewal of federal activism building on Progressive-era policies.
  d. a return to ideas about government common among elected office holders during the Gilded Age of the late nineteenth century.

45. Which of the following leaders would most likely have supported Franklin Roosevelt's argument regarding use of federal power in this excerpt?
  a. Thomas Jefferson
  b. Andrew Jackson
  c. Lyndon Johnson
  d. Ronald Reagan

Questions 46–47 refer to the excerpt provided.

> "Within the context of cultural unrest and the attack on tradition made by women like [Betty] Friedan, the catalyst for a profounder criticism and a mass mobilization of American women proved to be the young female participants in the social movements of the 1960s. These daughters of the middle class had received mixed, paradoxical messages about what it meant to grow up to be women in America. On the one hand, the cultural ideal . . . informed them that their only true happiness lay in the twin roles of wife and mother. At the same time they could observe the reality that housewifery was distinctly unsatisfactory for millions of suburban women. . . . Such contradictions left young, educated women in the 1960s dry tinder for the spark of revolt. . . . [Their] experiences in the southern civil rights movement and parts of the student new left catalyzed a new feminist consciousness."
>
> Sara Evans, *Personal Politics: The Roots of Women's Liberation in the Civil Rights Movement and the New Left*, 1979

46. Which of the following best represents the "social movements of the 1960s" in which women's experiences led to greater activism?
- **a.** The movement for a Great Society
- **b.** African American civil rights movement
- **c.** The environmental movement
- **d.** The antinuclear movement

47. Women's activism experienced the greatest success in the 1960s and 1970s from
- **a.** policies requiring equal pay.
- **b.** passage of a constitutional amendment for equal rights.
- **c.** elimination of the cultural double standard in sexual norms.
- **d.** overcoming social expectations of domesticity.

Questions 48–50 refer to the excerpt provided.

> "I want you to know that this administration is motivated by a political philosophy that sees the greatness of America in you, her people, and in your families, churches, neighborhoods, communities — the institutions that foster and nourish values like concern for others and respect for the rule of law under God.
>
> Now, I don't have to tell you that this puts us in opposition to, or at least out of step with, a prevailing attitude of many who have turned to a modern-day secularism, discarding the tried and time-tested values upon which our very civilization is based. No matter how well intentioned, their value system is radically different from that of most Americans. And while they proclaim that they're freeing us from superstitions of the past, they've taken upon themselves the job of superintending us by government rule and regulation. Sometimes their voices are louder than ours, but they are not yet a majority. . . .
>
> Freedom prospers when religion is vibrant and the rule of law under God is acknowledged. When our Founding Fathers passed the First Amendment, they sought to protect churches from government interference. They never intended to construct a wall of hostility between government and the concept of religious belief itself. Last year, I sent the Congress a constitutional amendment to restore prayer to public schools. . . ."
>
> Ronald Reagan, "The Rule of Law Under God," National Association of American Evangelicals, 1983

48. The ideas expressed by Reagan in the excerpt most directly appeal to a late twentieth-century trend toward
- **a.** increasing environmental regulation.
- **b.** politically active Christian evangelical churches and organizations.
- **c.** free-trade agreements.
- **d.** increased rights for women.

49. Reagan's ideas expressed in the excerpt led most directly to policies
- **a.** increasing military spending.
- **b.** deregulating major industries.
- **c.** ending legalized abortion.
- **d.** decreasing taxes.

50. In the 1980s Reagan and the national Republican Party captured more votes from all of the following demographics EXCEPT
- **a.** suburbanites.
- **b.** former Democrats in the South.
- **c.** college graduates in urban areas.
- **d.** wealthy white Protestants.

Questions 51–53 refer to the excerpt provided.

> "His [Alexander Hamilton's] plans . . . were not only a catalyst for sectional confrontation. They seemed an excellent confirmation of persistent Antifederalist suspicions of an engulfing federal power. . . . Coming in conjunction with the high style of the new government, the antipopulistic pronouncements of some of its supporters, and measures such as an excise tax and a professional army, the Hamiltonian program might as well have been designed to awaken specific expectations about the course and nature of governmental decay that were never very far beneath the surface of revolutionary minds."
>
> Lance Banning, *The Jeffersonian Persuasion: Evolution of a Party Ideology*, 1978

51. Which of the following evidence best supports Banning's argument in the excerpt?
- **a.** Fear of popular rebellion expressed in the Annapolis Convention
- **b.** Failure of state government control as seen in Shays's Rebellion
- **c.** Anger at federal tax policy expressed in the Whiskey Rebellion
- **d.** Dissatisfaction with trade policy established with Pinckney's Treaty

52. The most immediate cause for the formulation of Hamilton's financial plans in the Early Federal Period was the
- **a.** threat of war with France and Great Britain created by the Napoleonic Wars.
- **b.** crisis over issues of debt generated by the American Revolution.
- **c.** establishment of the first cabinet during Washington's administration.
- **d.** ratification debates that led to a loss of trust in the federal government.

53. Which of the following is the best example of the type of "sectional confrontation" referred to by Banning in the excerpt?
- **a.** The state of Virginia's resistance to the assumption of state debts
- **b.** The state of Massachusetts's opposition to establishment of a federal navy
- **c.** State competitions over land claims in the trans-Appalachian West
- **d.** Refusal of city leaders in New York and Philadelphia to support creation of a national bank

Questions 54–55 refer to the figure provided.

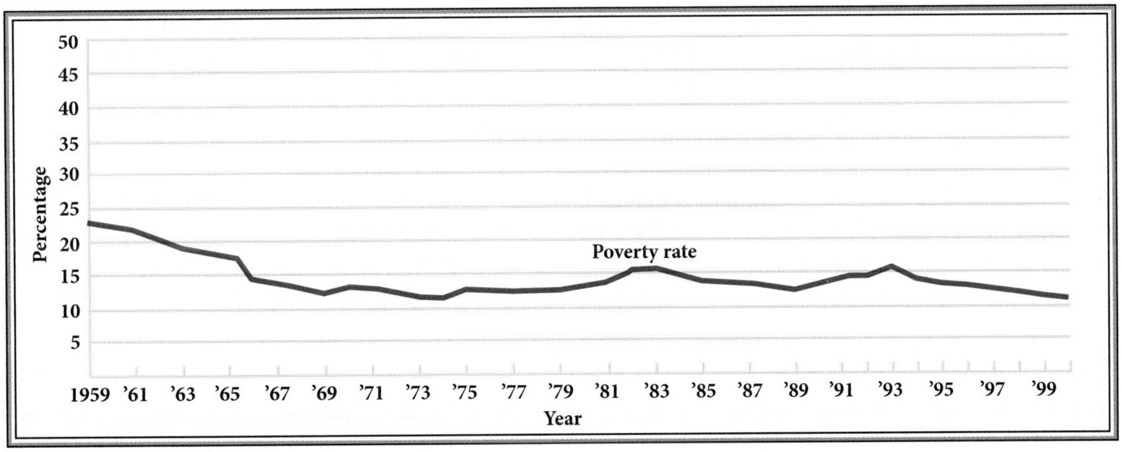

Americans in Poverty, 1959–2000

54. The information from this graph would likely be utilized by a liberal to argue that

a. Great Society programs dramatically reduced poverty in the U.S.

b. U.S. involvement in the Vietnam War undermined the accomplishments of the Johnson administration.

c. federal aid to those in poverty did not drastically alter living conditions in urban areas.

d. the early accomplishments of the Great Society were reversed by use of block grants to states.

55. Which of the following presidential policies was inspired by the level of poverty in the U.S. in the period 1959–1961?

a. New Frontier

b. Dynamic Conservatism

c. War on Poverty

d. Reaganomics

SECTION I
PART B: SHORT-ANSWER QUESTIONS
40 minutes

DIRECTIONS: Answer all parts of every question using complete sentences.

"[T]he guarantor state . . . under the New Deal was . . . a vigorous and dynamic force in the society, energizing and . . . supplanting private enterprise when the general welfare required it. . . . When social and economic problems . . . were ignored or shirked by private enterprise, then the federal government undertook to do the job. [If] private enterprise failed to provide adequate and sufficient housing for a minimum standard of welfare for the people, then the government would build houses. . . . Few areas of American life were beyond the touch of the experimenting fingers of the New Deal. . . . The New Deal Revolution has become so much a part of the American Way that no political party which aspires to high office dares now to repudiate it."

Carl N. Degler, *Out of Our Past: The Forces That Shaped Modern America*, 1959

> "The critique of modern capitalism that had been so important in the early 1930s . . . was largely gone. . . . In its place was a set of liberal ideas essentially reconciled to the existing structure of the economy and committed to using the state to compensate for capitalism's inevitable flaws. . . . When liberals spoke now of government's responsibility to protect the health of the industrial world, they defined that responsibility less as a commitment to restructure the economy than as an effort to stabilize it and help it to grow. They were no longer much concerned about controlling or punishing 'plutocrats' and 'economic royalists,' an impulse central to New Deal rhetoric in the mid-1930s. Instead, they spoke of their commitment to providing a healthy environment in which the corporate world could flourish and in which the economy could sustain 'full employment.' "
>
> Alan Brinkley, *The End of Reform: New Deal Liberalism in Recession and War*, 1995

1. Using the two excerpts provided, answer (a), (b), and (c).

a. Briefly describe ONE major difference between Degler's and Brinkley's historical interpretations of the New Deal.

b. Briefly explain how ONE specific piece of historical evidence from the period 1933 to 1945 that is not explicitly mentioned in the excerpts could be used to support Degler's interpretation.

c. Briefly explain how ONE specific piece of historical evidence from the period 1933 to 1945 that is not explicitly mentioned in the excerpts could be used to support Brinkley's interpretation.

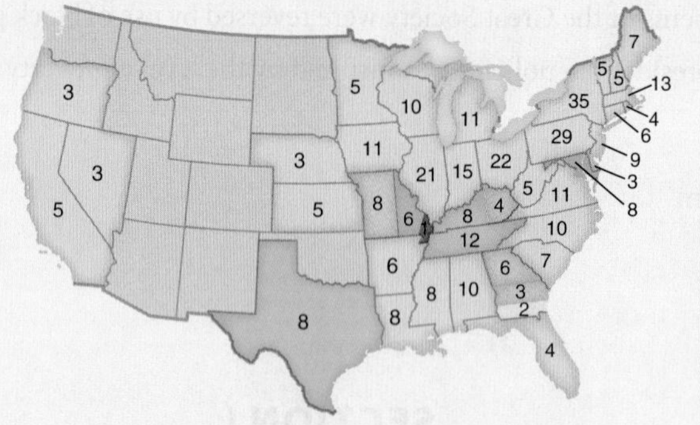

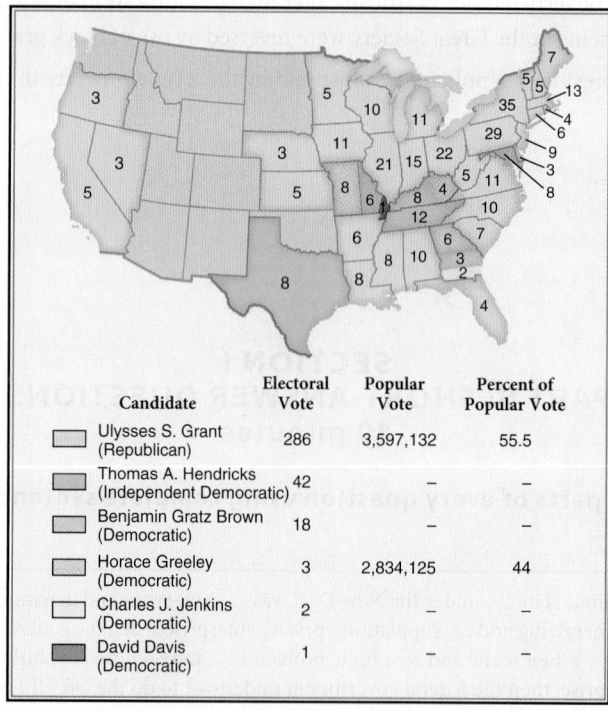

Candidate	Electoral Vote	Popular Vote	Percent of Popular Vote
Ulysses S. Grant (Republican)	286	3,597,132	55.5
Thomas A. Hendricks (Independent Democratic)	42	–	–
Benjamin Gratz Brown (Democratic)	18	–	–
Horace Greeley (Democratic)	3	2,834,125	44
Charles J. Jenkins (Democratic)	2	–	–
David Davis (Democratic)	1	–	–

The Presidential Election of 1872

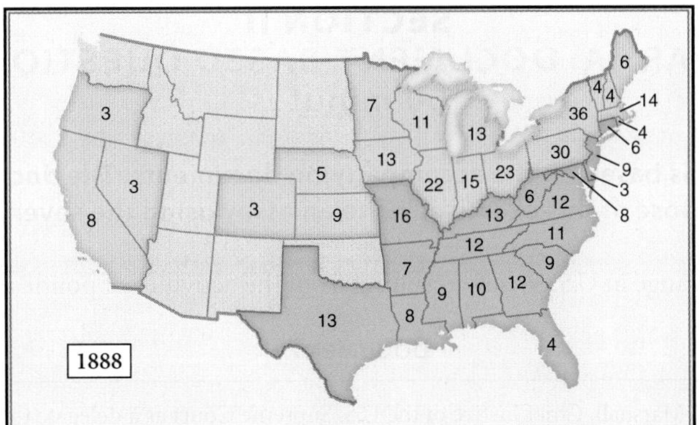

Candidate	Electoral Vote	Popular Vote	Percent of Popular Vote
Benjamin Harrison (Republican)	233	5,447,129	47.9
Grover Cleveland (Democrat)	168	5,537,857	48.6
Clinton P. Fisk (Prohibition)	—	249,506	2.2
Anson J. Streeter (Union Labor)	—	146,935	1.3

The Presidential Election of 1888

2. Using the two maps provided, answer (a), (b), and (c).

a. Describe ONE specific late nineteenth-century event or development in the South that can be used to explain the change in election patterns from 1872 to 1888.

b. Explain ONE specific historical change in the society of the South in the period between 1872 and 1900 that resulted from the political changes shown in the maps.

c. Describe how one or both of the maps can be used to explain the impact of the role of the federal government on the American South from 1865 to 1900.

DIRECTIONS: Choose EITHER Question 3 OR Question 4.

3. a. Briefly explain ONE specific historical difference between Westward expansion from 1800–1840 and Westward expansion from 1848–1890.

b. Briefly explain ONE specific historical similarity between Westward expansion from 1800–1840 and Westward expansion from 1848–1890.

c. Briefly explain ONE specific historical event or development that accounts for the difference in Westward expansion you identified in part a from 1800–1890.

4. a. Briefly describe ONE specific historical difference between the experiences of women in the 1920s and that of women in the 1950s.

b. Briefly describe ONE specific historical similarity between the experiences of women in the 1920s and that of women in the 1950s.

c. Briefly explain ONE specific historical effect of the experiences of women in either the 1920s OR the 1950s.

SECTION II
PART A: DOCUMENT-BASED QUESTION
60 minutes

DIRECTIONS: Question 1 is based on the accompanying documents. The documents have been edited for the purpose of this exercise. Write an essay using the seven documents provided.

1. Evaluate the extent of change in U.S. society resulting from the activities of political parties from 1824 to 1840.

DOCUMENT 1

Source: John Marshall, Chief Justice of the U.S. Supreme Court as a delegate to the Virginia Convention to revise the state constitution, "Memorial of the Non-Freeholders of Virginia," 1829.

"Surely it were much to be desired that every citizen should be qualified for the proper exercise of all his rights and the due performance of all his duties. But the same qualifications that entitle him to assume the management of his private affairs and to claim all other privileges of citizenship equally entitle him, in the judgment of your memorialists, to be entrusted with this, the dearest of all privileges, the most important of all his concerns. . . .

Virtue, intelligence are not products of the soil. Attachment to property, often a sordid sentiment, is not to be confounded with the sacred flame of patriotism. The love of country, like that of parents and offspring, is engrafted in our nature. It exists in all climates, among all classes, under every possible form of government. Riches more often impair it than poverty."

DOCUMENT 2

Source: Henry Clay, "Speech Against President Jackson on the Removal of the Deposits," 1833.

"The eyes and hopes of the American people are turned to Congress. They feel that they have been deceived and insulted; their confidence abused; their interests betrayed; and their liberties in danger. They see a rapid and alarming concentration of all power in one man's hands. They see that, by the exercise of the positive authority of the executive, and his negative power asserted over Congress, the will of one man alone prevails and governs the republic. The question is no longer what laws will Congress pass, but what will the executive not veto?"

DOCUMENT 3

Source: Andrew Jackson, Veto Message to Congress on the National Bank, July 10, 1832.

"Equality of talents, of education, or of wealth, cannot be produced by human institutions. . . . [E]very man is equally entitled to protection by law. But when laws undertake to add to these natural and just advantages, artificial distinctions, to grant titles, gratuities, and exclusive privileges, and to make the rich richer and the potent more powerful, the humble members of society, the farmers, mechanics, and laborers who have neither the time nor the means of securing the like favors to themselves, have a right to complain against their government. . . .

Nor is our government to be maintained, or our Union preserved, by invasions of the rights and powers of the several states. In thus attempting to make our government strong, we make it weak. Its true strength consists in leaving individuals and states as much as possible, to themselves; in making itself felt, not in its power, but in its beneficence; not in its control, but in its protection; not in its binding the states more closely to the centre, but leaving each to move, unobstructed, in its proper orbit."

DOCUMENT 4

Source: Margaret Byrd Smith, Washington socialite, letter to son, March 1829.

"But at the White House reception following the inauguration, what a scene did we witness!! The majesty of the people had disappeared, and instead a rabble, a mob . . . scrambling, fighting, romping. . . . The president after having literally been nearly pressed to death . . . escaped to his lodgings at Gadsby's. Cut glass and bone china to the amount of several thousand dollars had been broken in the struggle to get refreshments. . . . Ladies fainted, men were seen with bloody noses. . . . Ladies and gentlemen only had been expected at this reception, not the people en masse. But it was the people's day, and the people's president. . . . The . . . rabble in the president's house brought to my mind descriptions I had read of the mobs in the Tuileries and at Versailles."

DOCUMENT 5

Source: Harriet Martineau, a British author, reporting on her 1834 visit to the United States in *Society in America* (New York, 1837).

"I had been less than three weeks in the country and was in a state of something like awe at the prevalence of not only external competence but also intellectual ability. The striking effect upon a stranger of witnessing, for the first time, the absence of poverty, of gross ignorance, of all servility, of all insolence of manner cannot be exaggerated in description. I had seen every man in the towns an independent citizen; every man in the country a landowner. I had seen that the villages had their newspapers, the factory girls their libraries. I had witnessed controversies between candidates for office on some difficult subjects, of which the people were to be the judges.

With all these things in my mind, and with evidence of prosperity about me in the comfortable homesteads which every turn in the road and every reach of the lake brought into view, I was thrown into painful amazement by being told that the grand question of the time was 'whether the people should be encouraged to govern themselves, or whether the wise should save them from themselves.' "

DOCUMENT 6

Source: John C. Calhoun, South Carolina Exposition and Protest, 1828.

"[The Federal] Government is one of specific powers, and it can rightfully exercise only the powers expressly granted, and those that may be 'necessary and proper' to carry them into effect; all others being reserved expressly to the States, or to the people. It results necessarily, that those who claim to exercise a power under the Constitution, are bound to shew [sic], that it is expressly granted, or that it is necessary and proper, as a means to some of the granted powers. The advocates of the Tariff have offered no such proof. It is true, that the third [sic; eighth] section of the first article of the Constitution of the United States authorizes Congress to lay and collect an impost duty, but it is granted as a tax power, for the sole purpose of revenue; a power in its nature essentially different from that of imposing protective or prohibitory duties. . . . The Constitution grants to Congress the power of imposing a duty on imports for revenue; which power is abused by being converted into an instrument for rearing up the industry of one section of the country on the ruins of another. The violation then consists in using a power, granted for one object, to advance another, and that by the sacrifice of the original object. . . ."

DOCUMENT 7

Source: King Andrew the First, New York, 1833. Library of Congress.

SECTION II
PART B: LONG ESSAY QUESTIONS
40 minutes

DIRECTIONS: Choose one of the following three questions to answer.

2. Evaluate the extent to which the ideology of "republican motherhood" fostered changes in the roles of women in the United States from 1789 to 1820.
3. Evaluate the extent to which the Declaration of Sentiments fostered changes in the roles of women in the United States between 1820 and 1877.
4. Evaluate the extent to which the Progressive Era suffrage movement fostered changes in the roles of women in the United States between 1890 and 1940.

Documents

The Declaration of Independence

In Congress, July 4, 1776, The Unanimous Declaration of the Thirteen United States of America

When in the Course of human events, it becomes necessary for one people to dissolve the political bands which have connected them with another, and to assume among the Powers of the earth, the separate and equal station to which the Laws of Nature and of Nature's God entitle them, a decent respect to the opinions of mankind requires that they should declare the causes which impel them to the separation.

We hold these truths to be self-evident, that all men are created equal, that they are endowed by their Creator with certain unalienable rights, that among these are Life, Liberty, and the pursuit of Happiness. That to secure these rights, Governments are instituted among Men, deriving their just powers from the consent of the governed. That whenever any Form of Government becomes destructive of these ends, it is the Right of the People to alter or to abolish it, and to institute new Government, laying its foundation on such principles and organizing its powers in such form, as to them shall seem most likely to effect their Safety and Happiness. Prudence, indeed, will dictate that Governments long established should not be changed for light and transient causes; and accordingly all experience hath shown, that mankind are more disposed to suffer, while evils are sufferable, than to right themselves by abolishing the forms to which they are accustomed. But when a long train of abuses and usurpations, pursuing invariably the same Object evinces a design to reduce them under absolute Despotism, it is their right, it is their duty, to throw off such Government, and to provide new Guards for their future security. — Such has been the patient sufferance of these Colonies; and such is now the necessity which constrains them to alter their former Systems of Government. The history of the present King of Great Britain is a history of repeated injuries and usurpations, all having in direct object the establishment of an absolute Tyranny over these States. To prove this, let Facts be submitted to a candid world.

He has refused his Assent to Laws, the most wholesome and necessary for the public good.

He has forbidden his Governors to pass Laws of immediate and pressing importance, unless suspended in their operation till his Assent should be obtained; and, when so suspended, he has utterly neglected to attend to them.

He has refused to pass other Laws for the accommodation of large districts of people, unless those people would relinquish the right of Representation in the Legislature, a right inestimable to them and formidable to tyrants only.

He has called together legislative bodies at places unusual, uncomfortable, and distant from the depository of their public Records, for the sole purpose of fatiguing them into compliance with his measures.

He has dissolved Representative Houses repeatedly, for opposing with manly firmness his invasions on the rights of the people.

He has refused for a long time, after such dissolutions, to cause others to be elected; whereby the Legislative powers, incapable of Annihilation, have returned to the People at large for their exercise; the State remaining in the mean time exposed to all the dangers of invasion from without and convulsions within.

He has endeavoured to prevent the population of these States; for that purpose obstructing the Laws of Naturalization of Foreigners; refusing to pass others to encourage their migrations hither, and raising the conditions of new Appropriations of Lands.

He has obstructed the Administration of Justice, by refusing his Assent to Laws for establishing Judiciary powers.

He has made Judges dependent on his Will alone, for the tenure of their offices, and the amount and payment of their salaries.

He has erected a multitude of New Offices, and sent hither swarms of Officers to harass our People, and eat out their substance.

He has kept among us, in times of peace, Standing Armies without the Consent of our legislature.

He has affected to render the Military independent of and superior to the Civil Power.

He has combined with others to subject us to a jurisdiction foreign to our constitution, and unacknowledged by our laws; giving his Assent to their Acts of pretended Legislation:

For quartering large bodies of armed troops among us:

For protecting them, by a mock Trial, from Punishment for any Murders which they should commit on the Inhabitants of these States:

For cutting off our Trade with all parts of the world:

For imposing taxes on us without our Consent:

For depriving us, in many cases, of the benefits of Trial by jury:

For transporting us beyond Seas to be tried for pretended offences:

For abolishing the free System of English Laws in a neighbouring Province, establishing therein an Arbitrary government, and enlarging its Boundaries so as to render it at once an example and fit instrument for introducing the same absolute rule into these Colonies:

For taking away our Charters, abolishing our most valuable Laws, and altering fundamentally the Forms of our Governments:

For suspending our own Legislatures, and declaring themselves invested with Power to legislate for us in all cases whatsoever.

He has abdicated Government here, by declaring us out of his Protection and waging War against us.

He has plundered our seas, ravaged our Coasts, burnt our towns, and destroyed the lives of our people.

He is at this time transporting large armies of foreign mercenaries to compleat the works of death, desolation, and tyranny, already begun with circumstances of Cruelty & perfidy scarcely paralleled in the most barbarous ages, and totally unworthy the Head of a civilized nation.

He has constrained our fellow Citizens taken Captive on the high Seas to bear Arms against their Country, to become the executioners of their friends and Brethren, or to fall themselves by their Hands.

He has excited domestic insurrections amongst us, and has endeavoured to bring on the inhabitants of our frontiers, the merciless Indian Savages, whose known rule of warfare, is an undistinguished destruction of all ages, sexes, and conditions.

In every stage of these Oppressions We have Petitioned for Redress in the most humble terms: Our repeated Petitions have been answered only by repeated injury. A Prince, whose character is thus marked by every act which may define a Tyrant, is unfit to be the ruler of a free people.

Nor have We been wanting in attention to our British brethren. We have warned them from time to time of attempts by their legislature to extend an unwarrantable jurisdiction over us. We have reminded them of the circumstances of our emigration and settlement here. We have appealed to their native justice and magnanimity, and we have conjured them by the ties of our common kindred to disavow these usurpations, which would inevitably interrupt our connections and correspondence. They too have been deaf to the voice of justice and of consanguinity. We must, therefore, acquiesce in the necessity, which denounces our Separation, and hold them, as we hold the rest of mankind, Enemies in War, in Peace Friends.

We, therefore, the Representatives of the United States of America, in General Congress, Assembled, appealing to the Supreme Judge of the world for the rectitude of our intentions, do, in the Name, and by Authority of the good People of these Colonies, solemnly publish and declare, That these United Colonies are, and of Right ought to be FREE AND INDEPENDENT STATES; that they are Absolved from all Allegiance to the British Crown, and that all political connection between them and the State of Great Britain, is and ought to be totally dissolved; and that as Free and Independent States, they have full Power to levy War, conclude Peace, contract Alliances, establish Commerce, and to do all other Acts and Things which Independent States may of right do. And for the support of this Declaration, with a firm reliance on the Protection of Divine Providence, we mutually pledge to each other our Lives, our Fortunes, and our sacred Honor.

John Hancock

Button Gwinnett
Lyman Hall
Geo. Walton
Wm. Hooper
Joseph Hewes
John Penn
Edward Rutledge
Thos. Heyward, Junr.
Thomas Lynch, Junr.
Arthur Middleton
Samuel Chase
Wm. Paca
Thos. Stone
Charles Carroll of Carrollton

George Wythe
Richard Henry Lee
Th. Jefferson
Benja. Harrison
Thos. Nelson, Jr.
Francis Lightfoot Lee
Carter Braxton
Robt. Morris
Benjamin Rush
Benja. Franklin
John Morton
Geo. Clymer
Jas. Smith
Geo. Taylor

James Wilson
Geo. Ross
Caesar Rodney
Geo. Read
Thos. M'Kean
Wm. Floyd
Phil. Livingston
Frans. Lewis
Lewis Morris
Richd. Stockton
John Witherspoon
Fras. Hopkinson
John Hart
Abra. Clark

Josiah Bartlett
Wm. Whipple
Matthew Thornton
Saml. Adams
John Adams
Robt. Treat Paine
Elbridge Gerry
Step. Hopkins
William Ellery
Roger Sherman
Sam'el Huntington
Wm. Williams
Oliver Wolcott

The Constitution of the United States of America

Agreed to by Philadelphia Convention, September 17, 1787
Implemented March 4, 1789

We the People of the United States, in Order to form a more perfect Union, establish Justice, insure domestic Tranquility, provide for the common defence, promote the general Welfare, and secure the Blessings of Liberty to ourselves and our Posterity, do ordain and establish this Constitution for the United States of America.

Article I

Section 1. All legislative Powers herein granted shall be vested in a Congress of the United States, which shall consist of a Senate and a House of Representatives.

Section 2. The House of Representatives shall be composed of Members chosen every second Year by the People of the several States, and the Electors in each State shall have the Qualifications requisite for Electors of the most numerous Branch of the State Legislature.

No Person shall be a Representative who shall not have attained to the Age of twenty-five Years, and been seven Years a Citizen of the United States, and who shall not, when elected, be an Inhabitant of that State in which he shall be chosen.

Representatives and direct Taxes shall be apportioned among the several States which may be included within this Union, according to their respective Numbers, *which shall be determined by adding to the whole Number of free Persons, including those bound to Service for a Term of Years, and excluding Indians not taxed, three fifths of all other Persons.** The actual Enumeration shall be made within three Years after the first Meeting of the Congress of the United States, and within every subsequent Term of ten Years, in such Manner as they shall by Law direct. The Number of Representatives shall not exceed one for every thirty Thousand, but each State shall have at Least one Representative; and *until such enumeration shall be made, the State of New Hampshire shall be entitled to chuse three, Massachusetts eight, Rhode Island and Providence Plantations one, Connecticut five, New York six, New Jersey four, Pennsylvania eight, Delaware one, Maryland six, Virginia ten, North Carolina five, South Carolina five, and Georgia three.*

When vacancies happen in the Representation from any State, the Executive Authority thereof shall issue Writs of Election to fill such Vacancies.

The House of Representatives shall chuse their Speaker and other Officers; and shall have the sole Power of Impeachment.

Section 3. The Senate of the United States shall be composed of two Senators from each State, *chosen by the Legislature thereof,*† for six Years; and each Senator shall have one Vote.

Immediately after they shall be assembled in Consequence of the first Election, they shall be divided as equally as may be into three Classes. The Seats of the Senators of the first Class shall be vacated at the Expiration of the second Year, of the second Class at the Expiration of the fourth Year, and of the third Class at the Expiration of the sixth Year, so that one-third may be chosen every second Year; and if Vacancies happen by Resignation, or otherwise, during the Recess of the Legislature of any State, the Executive thereof may make temporary Appointments until the next Meeting of the Legislature, which shall then fill such Vacancies.‡

No person shall be a Senator who shall not have attained to the Age of thirty Years, and been nine Years a Citizen of the United States, and who shall not, when elected, be an Inhabitant of that State for which he shall be chosen.

The Vice President of the United States shall be President of the Senate, but shall have no Vote, unless they be equally divided.

The Senate shall chuse their other Officers, and also a President pro tempore, in the absence of the Vice President, or when he shall exercise the Office of President of the United States.

The Senate shall have the sole Power to try all Impeachments. When sitting for that Purpose, they shall be on Oath or Affirmation. When the President of the United States is tried, the Chief Justice shall preside: And no Person shall be convicted without the Concurrence of two-thirds of the Members present.

Judgment in Cases of Impeachment shall not extend further than to removal from Office, and disqualification to hold and enjoy any Office of honor, Trust or Profit under the United States: but the Party convicted shall nevertheless be liable and subject to Indictment, Trial, Judgment and Punishment, according to Law.

Section 4. The Times, Places and Manner of holding Elections for Senators and Representatives, shall be prescribed in each State by the Legislature thereof; but the Congress may at any time by Law make or alter such Regulations, except as to the Places of Chusing Senators.

Note: The Constitution became effective March 4, 1789. Provisions in italics are no longer relevant or have been changed by constitutional amendment.

*Changed by Section 2 of the Fourteenth Amendment.

†Changed by Section 1 of the Seventeenth Amendment.

‡Changed by Clause 2 of the Seventeenth Amendment.

The Congress shall assemble at least once in every Year, and such Meeting *shall be on the first Monday in December, unless they shall by Law appoint a different Day.**

Section 5. Each House shall be the Judge of the Elections, Returns and Qualifications of its own Members, and a Majority of each shall constitute a Quorum to do Business; but a smaller number may adjourn from day to day, and may be authorized to compel the Attendance of absent Members, in such Manner, and under such Penalties, as each House may provide.

Each House may determine the Rules of its Proceedings, punish its Members for disorderly Behavior, and, with the Concurrence of two-thirds, expel a Member.

Each House shall keep a Journal of its Proceedings, and from time to time publish the same, excepting such Parts as may in their Judgment require Secrecy; and the Yeas and Nays of the Members of either House on any question shall, at the Desire of one-fifth of those Present, be entered on the Journal.

Neither House, during the Session of Congress, shall, without the Consent of the other, adjourn for more than three days, nor to any other Place than that in which the two Houses shall be sitting.

Section 6. The Senators and Representatives shall receive a Compensation for their Services, to be ascertained by Law, and paid out of the Treasury of the United States. They shall in all Cases, except Treason, Felony and Breach of the Peace, be privileged from Arrest during their Attendance at the Session of their respective Houses, and in going to and returning from the same; and for any Speech or Debate in either House, they shall not be questioned in any other Place.

No Senator or Representative shall, during the Time for which he was elected, be appointed to any civil Office under the Authority of the United States, which shall have been created, or the Emoluments whereof shall have been increased, during such time; and no Person holding any Office under the United States, shall be a Member of either House during his Continuance in Office.

Section 7. All Bills for raising Revenue shall originate in the House of Representatives; but the Senate may propose or concur with Amendments as on other Bills.

Every Bill which shall have passed the House of Representatives and the Senate, shall, before it becomes a Law, be presented to the President of the United States; If he approve he shall sign it, but if not he shall return it, with his Objections to that House in which it shall have originated, who shall enter the Objections at large on their Journal, and proceed to reconsider it. If after such Reconsideration two-thirds of that House shall agree to pass the Bill, it shall be sent, together with the Objections, to the other House, by which it shall likewise be reconsidered, and if approved by two-thirds of that House, it shall become a Law. But in all such Cases the Votes of both Houses shall be determined by Yeas and Nays, and the Names of the Persons voting for and against the Bill shall be entered on the Journal of each House respectively. If any Bill shall not be returned by the President within ten Days (Sundays excepted) after it shall have been presented to him, the Same shall be a Law, in like Manner as if he had signed it, unless the Congress by their Adjournment prevent its Return, in which Case it shall not be a Law.

Every Order, Resolution, or Vote to which the Concurrence of the Senate and the House of Representatives may be necessary (except on a question of Adjournment) shall be presented to the President of the United States; and before the Same shall take Effect, shall be approved by him, or being disapproved by him, shall be repassed by two-thirds of the Senate and House of Representatives, according to the Rules and Limitations prescribed in the Case of a Bill.

Section 8. The Congress shall have Power To lay and collect Taxes, Duties, Imposts and Excises, to pay the Debts and provide for the common Defence and general Welfare of the United States; but all Duties, Imposts and Excises shall be uniform throughout the United States;

To borrow Money on the credit of the United States;

To regulate Commerce with foreign Nations, and among the several States, and with the Indian Tribes;

To establish an uniform Rule of Naturalization, and uniform Laws on the subject of Bankruptcies throughout the United States;

To coin Money, regulate the Value thereof, and of foreign Coin, and fix the Standard of Weights and Measures;

To provide for the Punishment of counterfeiting the Securities and current Coin of the United States;

To establish Post Offices and post Roads;

To promote the Progress of Science and useful Arts, by securing for limited Times to Authors and Inventors the exclusive Right to their respective Writings and Discoveries;

To constitute Tribunals inferior to the supreme Court;

To define and punish Piracies and Felonies committed on the high Seas, and Offenses against the Law of Nations;

To declare War, grant Letters of Marque and Reprisal, and make Rules concerning Captures on Land and Water;

To raise and support Armies, but no Appropriation of Money to that Use shall be for a longer Term than two Years;

To provide and maintain a Navy;

To make Rules for the Government and Regulation of the land and naval Forces;

To provide for calling forth the Militia to execute the Laws of the Union, suppress Insurrections and repel Invasions;

To provide for organizing, arming, and disciplining the Militia, and for governing such Part of them as may be employed in the Service of the United States, reserving to the States respectively, the Appointment of the Officers, and the Authority of training the Militia according to the discipline prescribed by Congress;

To exercise exclusive Legislation in all Cases whatsoever, over such District (not exceeding ten Miles square) as may,

*Changed by Section 2 of the Twentieth Amendment.

by Cession of particular States, and the acceptance of Congress, become the Seat of Government of the United States, and to exercise like Authority over all Places purchased by the Consent of the Legislature of the State in which the Same shall be, for the Erection of Forts, Magazines, Arsenals, dock-Yards, and other needful Buildings; — And

To make all Laws which shall be necessary and proper for carrying into Execution the foregoing Powers, and all other Powers vested by this Constitution in the Government of the United States, or in any Department or Officer thereof.

Section 9. The Migration or Importation of such Persons as any of the States now existing shall think proper to admit, shall not be prohibited by the Congress prior to the Year one thousand eight hundred and eight but a tax or duty may be imposed on such Importation, not exceeding ten dollars for each Person.

The privilege of the Writ of Habeas Corpus shall not be suspended, unless when in Cases of Rebellion or Invasion the public Safety may require it.

No Bill of Attainder or ex post facto Law shall be passed.

*No capitation, or other direct, Tax shall be laid, unless in Proportion to the Census or Enumeration herein before directed to be taken.**

No Tax or Duty shall be laid on Articles exported from any State.

No Preference shall be given by any Regulation of Commerce or Revenue to the Ports of one State over those of another: nor shall Vessels bound to, or from, one State, be obliged to enter, clear, or pay Duties in another.

No Money shall be drawn from the Treasury, but in Consequence of Appropriations made by law; and a regular Statement and Account of the Receipts and Expenditures of all public Money shall be published from time to time.

No Title of Nobility shall be granted by the United States: And no Person holding any Office of Profit or Trust under them, shall, without the Consent of the Congress, accept of any present, Emolument, Office, or Title, of any kind whatever, from any King, Prince, or foreign State.

Section 10. No State shall enter into any Treaty, Alliance, or Confederation; grant Letters of Marque and Reprisal; coin Money; emit Bills of Credit; make any Thing but gold and silver Coin a Tender in Payment of Debts; pass any Bill of Attainder, ex post facto Law, or Law impairing the Obligation of Contracts, or grant any Title of Nobility.

No State shall, without the Consent of the Congress, lay any Imposts or Duties on Imports or Exports, except what may be absolutely necessary for executing its inspection Laws: and the net Produce of all Duties and Imposts, laid by any State on Imports or Exports, shall be for the Use of the Treasury of the United States; and all such Laws shall be subject to the Revision and Control of the Congress.

No State shall, without the Consent of the Congress, lay any duty of Tonnage, keep Troops, or Ships of War in time of Peace, enter into any Agreement or Compact with another State, or with a foreign Power, or engage in War, unless actually invaded, or in such imminent Danger as will not admit of delay.

Article II

Section 1. The executive Power shall be vested in a President of the United States of America. He shall hold his Office during the Term of four Years, and, together with the Vice President, chosen for the same Term, be elected, as follows:

Each State shall appoint, in such Manner as the Legislature thereof may direct, a Number of Electors, equal to the whole Number of Senators and Representatives to which the State may be entitled in the Congress; but no Senator or Representative, or Person holding an Office of Trust or Profit under the United States, shall be appointed an Elector.

The Electors shall meet in their respective States, and vote by Ballot for two Persons, of whom one at least shall not be an Inhabitant of the same State with themselves. And they shall make a List of all the Persons voted for, and of the Number of Votes for each; which List they shall sign and certify, and transmit sealed to the Seat of the Government of the United States, directed to the President of the Senate. The President of the Senate shall, in the Presence of the Senate and House of Representatives, open all the Certificates, and the Votes shall then be counted. The Person having the greatest Number of Votes shall be the President, if such Number be a Majority of the whole Number of Electors appointed; and if there be more than one who have such Majority, and have an equal Number of Votes, then the House of Representatives shall immediately chuse by Ballot one of them for President; and if no Person have a Majority, then from the five highest on the List the said House shall in like Manner chuse the President. But in chusing the President, the Votes shall be taken by States, the Representation from each State having one Vote; a quorum for this Purpose shall consist of a Member or Members from two thirds of the States, and a Majority of all the States shall be necessary to a Choice. In every Case, after the Choice of the President, the Person having the greatest Number of Votes of the Electors shall be the Vice President. But if there should remain two or more who have equal Votes, the Senate shall chuse from them by Ballot the Vice President.†

The Congress may determine the Time of chusing the Electors, and the Day on which they shall give their Votes; which Day shall be the same throughout the United States.

No Person except a natural born Citizen, or a Citizen of the United States, at the time of the Adoption of this Constitution, shall be eligible to the Office of President; neither shall any Person be eligible to that Office who shall not have attained to the Age of thirty five Years, and been fourteen Years a Resident within the United States.

In Case of the Removal of the President from Office, or of his Death, Resignation, or Inability to discharge the Powers

*Changed by the Sixteenth Amendment.

†Superseded by the Twelfth Amendment.

and Duties of the said Office, the same shall devolve on the Vice President, *and the Congress may by Law provide for the Case of Removal, Death, Resignation, or Inability, both of the President and Vice President, declaring what Officer shall then act as President, and such Officer shall act accordingly, until the Disability be removed, or a President shall be elected.**

The President shall, at stated Times, receive for his Services a Compensation, which shall neither be increased nor diminished during the Period for which he shall have been elected, and he shall not receive within that Period any other Emolument from the United States, or any of them.

Before he enter on the Execution of his Office, he shall take the following Oath or Affirmation: — "I do solemnly swear (or affirm) that I will faithfully execute the Office of President of the United States, and will to the best of my Ability, preserve, protect and defend the Constitution of the United States."

Section 2. The President shall be Commander in Chief of the Army and Navy of the United States, and of the Militia of the several States, when called into the actual Service of the United States; he may require the Opinion, in writing, of the principal Officer in each of the executive Departments, upon any Subject relating to the Duties of their respective Offices, and he shall have Power to Grant Reprieves and Pardons for Offences against the United States, except in Cases of Impeachment.

He shall have Power, by and with the Advice and Consent of the Senate, to make Treaties, provided two thirds of the Senators present concur; and he shall nominate, and by and with the Advice and Consent of the Senate, shall appoint Ambassadors, other public Ministers and Consuls, Judges of the supreme Court, and all other Officers of the United States, whose Appointments are not herein otherwise provided for, and which shall be established by Law: but the Congress may by Law vest the Appointment of such inferior Officers, as they think proper, in the President alone, in the Courts of Law, or in the Heads of Departments.

The President shall have Power to fill up all Vacancies that may happen during the Recess of the Senate, by granting Commissions which shall expire at the End of their next Session.

Section 3. He shall from time to time give to the Congress Information of the State of the Union, and recommend to their Consideration such Measures as he shall judge necessary and expedient; he may, on extraordinary Occasions, convene both Houses, or either of them, and in Case of Disagreement between them, with Respect to the Time of Adjournment, he may adjourn them to such Time as he shall think proper; he shall receive Ambassadors and other public Ministers; he shall take Care that the Laws be faithfully executed, and shall Commission all the Officers of the United States.

Section 4. The President, Vice President and all civil Officers of the United States, shall be removed from Office on Impeachment for, and Conviction of, Treason, Bribery, or other high Crimes and Misdemeanors.

*Modified by the Twenty-Fifth Amendment.

Article III

Section 1. The judicial Power of the United States, shall be vested in one supreme Court, and in such inferior Courts as the Congress may from time to time ordain and establish. The Judges, both of the supreme and inferior Courts, shall hold their Offices during good Behaviour, and shall, at stated Times, receive for their Services a Compensation, which shall not be diminished during their Continuance in Office.

Section 2. The judicial Power shall extend to all Cases, in Law and Equity, arising under this Constitution, the Laws of the United States, and Treaties made, or which shall be made, under their Authority; — to all Cases affecting Ambassadors, other public Ministers and Consuls; — to all Cases of admiralty and maritime Jurisdiction; — to Controversies to which the United States shall be a Party; — to Controversies between two or more States; — *between a State and Citizens of another State;*† — between Citizens of different States; — between Citizens of the same State claiming Lands under Grants of different States, and between a State, or the Citizens thereof, and foreign States, Citizens or Subjects.

In all Cases affecting Ambassadors, other public Ministers and Consuls, and those in which a State shall be Party, the supreme Court shall have original Jurisdiction. In all the other Cases before mentioned, the supreme Court shall have appellate Jurisdiction, both as to Law and Fact, with such Exceptions, and under such Regulations as the Congress shall make.

The trial of all Crimes, except in Cases of Impeachment, shall be by Jury; and such Trial shall be held in the State where said Crimes shall have been committed; but when not committed within any State, the Trial shall be at such Place or Places as the Congress may by Law have directed.

Section 3. Treason against the United States, shall consist only in levying War against them, or in adhering to their Enemies, giving them Aid and Comfort. No Person shall be convicted of Treason unless on the Testimony of two Witnesses to the same overt Act, or on Confession in open Court.

The Congress shall have Power to declare the Punishment of Treason, but no Attainder of Treason shall work Corruption of Blood, or Forfeiture except during the Life of the Person attainted.

Article IV

Section 1. Full Faith and Credit shall be given in each State to the public Acts, Records, and judicial Proceedings of every other State. And the Congress may by general Laws prescribe the Manner in which such Acts, Records, and Proceedings shall be proved, and the Effect thereof.

Section 2. The Citizens of each State shall be entitled to all Privileges and Immunities of Citizens in the several States.

A Person charged in any State with Treason, Felony, or other Crime, who shall flee from Justice, and be found in another State, shall on demand of the executive Authority of

†Restricted by the Eleventh Amendment.

the State from which he fled, be delivered up, to be removed to the State having Jurisdiction of the Crime.

*No Person held to Service or Labour in one State, under the Laws thereof, escaping into another, shall, in Consequence of any Law or Regulation therein, be discharged from such Service or Labour, but shall be delivered up on Claim of the Party to whom such Service or Labour may be due.**

Section 3. New States may be admitted by the Congress into this Union; but no new State shall be formed or erected within the Jurisdiction of any other State; nor any State be formed by the Junction of two or more States, or parts of States, without the Consent of the Legislatures of the States concerned as well as of the Congress.

The Congress shall have Power to dispose of and make all needful Rules and Regulations respecting the Territory or other Property belonging to the United States; and nothing in this Constitution shall be so construed as to Prejudice any Claims of the United States, or of any particular State.

Section 4. The United States shall guarantee to every State in this Union a Republican Form of Government, and shall protect each of them against Invasion; and on Application of the Legislature, or of the Executive (when the Legislature cannot be convened) against domestic Violence.

Article V

The Congress, whenever two-thirds of both Houses shall deem it necessary, shall propose Amendments to this Constitution, or, on the Application of the Legislatures of two-thirds of the several States, shall call a Convention for proposing Amendments, which, in either Case, shall be valid to all Intents and Purposes, as Part of this Constitution, when ratified by the Legislatures of three-fourths of the several States, or by Conventions in three-fourths thereof, as the one or the other Mode of Ratification may be proposed by the Congress; *Provided that no Amendment which may be made prior to the Year One thousand eight hundred and eight shall in any Manner affect the first and fourth Clauses in the Ninth Section of the first Article; and* that no State, without its Consent, shall be deprived of its equal Suffrage in the Senate.

Article VI

All Debts contracted and Engagements entered into, before the Adoption of this Constitution, shall be as valid against the United States under this Constitution, as under the Confederation.

This Constitution, and the Laws of the United States which shall be made in Pursuance thereof; and all Treaties made, or which shall be made, under the Authority of the United States, shall be the supreme Law of the Land; and the Judges in every State shall be bound thereby, any Thing in the Constitution or Laws of any State to the Contrary notwithstanding.

The Senators and Representatives before mentioned, and the Members of the several State Legislatures, and all executive and judicial Officers, both of the United States and of the several States, shall be bound by Oath or Affirmation, to support this Constitution; but no religious Test shall ever be required as a Qualification to any Office or public Trust under the United States.

Article VII

The Ratification of the Conventions of nine States shall be sufficient for the Establishment of this Constitution between the States so ratifying the Same.

Done in Convention by the Unanimous Consent of the States present the Seventeenth Day of September in the Year of our Lord one thousand seven hundred and Eighty seven and of the Independence of the United States of America the Twelfth. In Witness whereof We have hereunto subscribed our Names.

Go. Washington
President and deputy from Virginia

New Hampshire
John Langdon
Nicholas Gilman

Connecticut
Wm. Saml. Johnson
Roger Sherman

New Jersey
Wil. Livingston
David Brearley
Wm. Paterson
Jona. Dayton

Pennsylvania
B. Franklin
Thomas Mifflin
Robt. Morris
Geo. Clymer
Thos. FitzSimons

Massachusetts
Nathaniel Gorham
Rufus King
Jared Ingersoll
James Wilson
Gouv. Morris

Delaware
Geo. Read
Gunning Bedford jun

New York
Alexander Hamilton
John Dickinson
Richard Bassett
Jaco. Broom

Maryland
James McHenry
Dan. of St. Thos. Jenifer
Danl. Carroll

Virginia
John Blair
James Madison, Jr.

North Carolina
Wm. Blount
Richd. Dobbs Spaight
Hu Williamson

South Carolina
J. Rutledge
Charles Cotesworth Pinckney
Charles Pinckney
Pierce Butler

Georgia
William Few
Abr. Baldwin

*Superseded by the Thirteenth Amendment.

Amendments to the Constitution (Including the Six Unratified Amendments)

Amendment I [1791]*

Congress shall make no law respecting an establishment of religion, or prohibiting the free exercise thereof; or abridging the freedom of speech, or of the press; or the right of the people peaceably to assemble, and to petition the Government for a redress of grievances.

Amendment II [1791]

A well regulated Militia, being necessary to the security of a free State, the right of the people to keep and bear Arms shall not be infringed.

Amendment III [1791]

No Soldier shall, in time of peace, be quartered in any house, without the consent of the Owner, nor in time of war, but in a manner to be prescribed by law.

Amendment IV [1791]

The right of the people to be secure in their persons, houses, papers, and effects, against unreasonable searches and seizures, shall not be violated, and no Warrants shall issue, but upon probable cause, supported by Oath or affirmation, and particularly describing the place to be searched, and the persons or things to be seized.

Amendment V [1791]

No person shall be held to answer for a capital or otherwise infamous crime, unless on a presentment or indictment of a Grand Jury, except in cases arising in the land or naval forces, or in the Militia, when in actual service in time of War or public danger; nor shall any person be subject for the same offence to be twice put in jeopardy of life or limb; nor shall be compelled in any criminal case to be a witness against himself, nor be deprived of life, liberty, or property, without due process of law; nor shall private property be taken for public use, without just compensation.

Amendment VI [1791]

In all criminal prosecutions, the accused shall enjoy the right to a speedy and public trial, by an impartial jury of the State and district wherein the crime shall have been committed, which district shall have been previously ascertained by law, and to be informed of the nature and cause of the accusation; to be confronted with the witnesses against him; to have compulsory process for obtaining witnesses in his favor, and to have the Assistance of Counsel for his defence.

*The dates in brackets indicate when the amendment was ratified.

Amendment VII [1791]

In suits at common law, where the value in controversy shall exceed twenty dollars, the right of trial by jury shall be preserved, and no fact tried by a jury, shall be otherwise reexamined in any Court of the United States, than according to the Rules of the common law.

Amendment VIII [1791]

Excessive bail shall not be required, nor excessive fines imposed, nor cruel and unusual punishments inflicted.

Amendment IX [1791]

The enumeration in the Constitution, of certain rights, shall not be construed to deny or disparage others retained by the people.

Amendment X [1791]

The powers not delegated to the United States by the Constitution, nor prohibited by it to the States, are reserved to the States respectively, or to the people.

Unratified Amendment

Reapportionment Amendment
(proposed by Congress September 25, 1789, along with the Bill of Rights)

After the first enumeration required by the first article of the Constitution, there shall be one Representative for every thirty thousand, until the number shall amount to one hundred, after which the proportion shall be so regulated by Congress, that there shall be not less than one hundred Representatives, nor less than one Representative for every forty thousand persons, until the number of Representatives shall amount to two hundred; after which the proportion shall be so regulated by Congress, that there shall not be less than two hundred Representatives, nor more than one Representative for every fifty thousand persons.

Amendment XI [1795]

The Judicial power of the United States shall not be construed to extend to any suit in law or equity, commenced or prosecuted against one of the United States by Citizens of another State, or by Citizens or subjects of any foreign state.

Amendment XII [1804]

The Electors shall meet in their respective States and vote by ballot for President and Vice-President, one of whom, at least, shall not be an inhabitant of the same State with themselves; they shall name in their ballots the person voted for as President, and in distinct ballots the person voted for as

Vice-President, and they shall make distinct lists of all persons voted for as President, and of all persons voted for as Vice-President, and of the number of votes for each, which lists they shall sign and certify, and transmit sealed to the seat of government of the United States, directed to the President of the Senate; — the President of the Senate shall, in the presence of the Senate and House of Representatives, open all the certificates and the votes shall then be counted; — The person having the greatest number of votes for President, shall be the President, if such number be a majority of the whole number of Electors appointed; and if no person have such majority, then from the persons having the highest numbers not exceeding three on the list of those voted for as President, the House of Representatives shall choose immediately, by ballot, the President. But in choosing the President, the votes shall be taken by States, the representation from each State having one vote; a quorum for this purpose shall consist of a member or members from two-thirds of the States, and a majority of all the States shall be necessary to a choice. And if the House of Representatives shall not choose a President whenever the right of choice shall devolve upon them, before *the fourth day of March* next following, then the Vice-President shall act as President, as in the case of the death or other constitutional disability of the President.* — The person having the greatest number of votes as Vice-President, shall be the Vice-President, if such number be a majority of the whole number of Electors appointed; and if no person have a majority, then from the two highest numbers on the list, the Senate shall choose the Vice-President; a quorum for the purpose shall consist of two-thirds of the whole number of Senators, and a majority of the whole number shall be necessary to a choice. But no person constitutionally ineligible to the office of President shall be eligible to that of Vice-President of the United States.

Unratified Amendment

Titles of Nobility Amendment
(proposed by Congress May 1, 1810)

If any citizen of the United States shall accept, claim, receive or retain any title of nobility or honor or shall, without the consent of Congress, accept and retain any present, pension, office or emolument of any kind whatever, from any emperor, king, prince or foreign power, such person shall cease to be a citizen of the United States, and shall be incapable of holding any office of trust or profit under them, or either of them.

Unratified Amendment

Corwin Amendment
(proposed by Congress March 2, 1861)

No amendment shall be made to the Constitution which will authorize or give to Congress the power to abolish or interfere, within any State, with the domestic institutions thereof, including that of persons held to labor or service by the laws of said State.

*Superseded by Section 3 of the Twentieth Amendment.

Amendment XIII [1865]

Section 1. Neither slavery nor involuntary servitude, except as a punishment for crime whereof the party shall have been duly convicted, shall exist within the United States, or any place subject to their jurisdiction.

Section 2. Congress shall have power to enforce this article by appropriate legislation.

Amendment XIV [1868]

Section 1. All persons born or naturalized in the United States, and subject to the jurisdiction thereof, are citizens of the United States and of the State wherein they reside. No State shall make or enforce any law which shall abridge the privileges or immunities of citizens of the United States; nor shall any State deprive any person of life, liberty, or property, without due process of law; nor deny to any person within its jurisdiction the equal protection of the laws.

Section 2. Representatives shall be apportioned among the several States according to their respective numbers, counting the whole number of persons in each State, excluding Indians not taxed. But when the right to vote at any election for the choice of electors for President and Vice-President of the United States, Representatives in Congress, the Executive and Judicial officers of a State, or the members of the Legislature thereof, is denied to any of the *male* inhabitants of such State, being *twenty-one* years of age and citizens of the United States, or in any way abridged, except for participation in rebellion, or other crime, the basis of representation therein shall be reduced in the proportion which the number of such *male* citizens shall bear to the whole number of *male* citizens *twenty-one* years of age in such State.

Section 3. No person shall be a Senator or Representative in Congress, or Elector of President and Vice-President, or hold any office, civil or military, under the United States, or under any State, who, having previously taken an oath, as a member of Congress, or as an officer of the United States, or as a member of any State legislature, or as an executive or judicial officer of any State, to support the Constitution of the United States, shall have engaged in insurrection or rebellion against the same, or given aid or comfort to the enemies thereof. Congress may, by a vote of two-thirds of each house, remove such disability.

Section 4. The validity of the public debt of the United States, authorized by law, including debts incurred for payment of pensions and bounties for services in suppressing insurrection or rebellion, shall not be questioned. But neither the United States nor any State shall assume or pay any debt or obligation incurred in aid of insurrection or rebellion against the United States, or any claim for the loss or emancipation of any slave; but all such debts, obligations, and claims shall be held illegal and void.

Section 5. The Congress shall have power to enforce, by appropriate legislation, the provisions of this article.

Amendment XV [1870]

Section 1. The right of citizens of the United States to vote shall not be denied or abridged by the United States or by any State on account of race, color, or previous condition of servitude —

Section 2. The Congress shall have power to enforce this article by appropriate legislation.

Amendment XVI [1913]

The Congress shall have power to lay and collect taxes on incomes, from whatever source derived, without apportionment among the several States, and without regard to any census or enumeration.

Amendment XVII [1913]

Section 1. The Senate of the United States shall be composed of two Senators from each State, elected by the people thereof, for six years; and each Senator shall have one vote. The electors in each State shall have the qualifications requisite for electors of [voters for] the most numerous branch of the State legislatures.

Section 2. When vacancies happen in the representation of any State in the Senate, the executive authority of such State shall issue writs of election to fill such vacancies: Provided, that the Legislature of any State may empower the executive thereof to make temporary appointments until the people fill the vacancies by election as the Legislature may direct.

Section 3. *This amendment shall not be so construed as to affect the election or term of any Senator chosen before it becomes valid as part of the Constitution.*

Amendment XVIII [1919; repealed 1933 by Amendment XXI]

Section 1. *After one year from the ratification of this article the manufacture, sale, or transportation of intoxicating liquors within, the importation thereof into, or the exportation thereof from the United States and all territory subject to the jurisdiction thereof, for beverage purposes, is hereby prohibited.*

Section 2. *The Congress and the several States shall have concurrent power to enforce this article by appropriate legislation.*

Section 3. *This article shall be inoperative unless it shall have been ratified as an amendment to the Constitution by the legislatures of the several States, as provided by the Constitution, within seven years from the date of the submission thereof to the States by the Congress.*

Amendment XIX [1920]

Section 1. The right of citizens of the United States to vote shall not be denied or abridged by the United States or by any State on account of sex.

Section 2. Congress shall have the power to enforce this article by appropriate legislation.

Unratified Amendment

Child Labor Amendment
(proposed by Congress June 2, 1924)

Section 1. *The Congress shall have power to limit, regulate, and prohibit the labor of persons under eighteen years of age.*

Section 2. *The power of the several States is unimpaired by this article except that the operation of State laws shall be suspended to the extent necessary to give effect to legislation enacted by Congress.*

Amendment XX [1933]

Section 1. The terms of the President and Vice-President shall end at noon on the 20th day of January, and the terms of Senators and Representatives at noon on the 3rd day of January, of the years in which such terms would have ended if this article had not been ratified; and the terms of their successors shall then begin.

Section 2. The Congress shall assemble at least once in every year, and such meeting shall begin at noon on the 3rd day of January, unless they shall by law appoint a different day.

Section 3. If, at the time fixed for the beginning of the term of the President, the President-elect shall have died, the Vice-President-elect shall become President. If a President shall not have been chosen before the time fixed for the beginning of his term, or if the President-elect shall have failed to qualify, then the Vice-President-elect shall act as President until a President shall have qualified; and the Congress may by law provide for the case wherein neither a President-elect nor a Vice-President-elect shall have qualified, declaring who shall then act as President, or the manner in which one who is to act shall be selected, and such person shall act accordingly until a President or Vice-President shall have qualified.

Section 4. The Congress may by law provide for the case of the death of any of the persons from whom the House of Representatives may choose a President whenever the right of choice shall have devolved upon them, and for the case of the death of any of the persons from whom the Senate may choose a Vice-President whenever the right of choice shall have devolved upon them.

Section 5. Sections 1 and 2 shall take effect on the 15th day of October following the ratification of this article.

Section 6. This article shall be inoperative unless it shall have been ratified as an amendment to the Constitution by the Legislatures of three-fourths of the several States within seven years from the date of its submission.

Amendment XXI [1933]

Section 1. The eighteenth article of amendment to the Constitution of the United States is hereby repealed.

Section 2. The transportation or importation into any State, Territory, or Possession of the United States for delivery or use therein of intoxicating liquors, in violation of the laws thereof, is hereby prohibited.

Section 3. This article shall be inoperative unless it shall have been ratified as an amendment to the Constitution by conventions in the several States, as provided in the Constitution, within seven years from the date of the submission thereof to the States by the Congress.

Amendment XXII [1951]

Section 1. No person shall be elected to the office of the President more than twice, and no person who has held the office of President, or acted as President, for more than two years of a term to which some other person was elected President shall be elected to the office of President more than once. But this article shall not apply to any person holding the office of President when this Article was proposed by the Congress, and shall not prevent any person who may be holding the office of President, or acting as President, during the term within which this Article becomes operative from holding the office of President or acting as President during the remainder of such term.

Section 2. This article shall be inoperative unless it shall have been ratified as an amendment to the Constitution by the legislatures of three-fourths of the several States within seven years from the date of its submission to the States by the Congress.

Amendment XXIII [1961]

Section 1. The District constituting the seat of Government of the United States shall appoint in such manner as the Congress may direct: A number of electors of President and Vice-President equal to the whole number of Senators and Representatives in Congress to which the District would be entitled if it were a State, but in no event more than the least populous State; they shall be in addition to those appointed by the States, but they shall be considered for the purposes of the election of President and Vice-President, to be electors appointed by a State; and they shall meet in the District and perform such duties as provided by the twelfth article of amendment.

Section 2. The Congress shall have the power to enforce this article by appropriate legislation.

Amendment XXIV [1964]

Section 1. The right of citizens of the United States to vote in any primary or other election for President or Vice-President, for electors for President or Vice-President, or for Senator or Representative in Congress, shall not be denied or abridged by the United States or any State by reason of failure to pay any poll tax or other tax.

Section 2. The Congress shall have the power to enforce this article by appropriate legislation.

Amendment XXV [1967]

Section 1. In case of the removal of the President from office or of his death or resignation, the Vice-President shall become President.

Section 2. Whenever there is a vacancy in the office of the Vice-President, the President shall nominate a Vice-President who shall take office upon confirmation by a majority vote of both Houses of Congress.

Section 3. Whenever the President transmits to the President pro tempore of the Senate and the Speaker of the House of Representatives his written declaration that he is unable to discharge the powers and duties of his office, and until he transmits to them a written declaration to the contrary, such powers and duties shall be discharged by the Vice-President as Acting President.

Section 4. Whenever the Vice-President and a majority of either the principal officers of the executive departments or of such other body as Congress may by law provide, transmit to the President pro tempore of the Senate and the Speaker of the House of Representatives their written declaration that the President is unable to discharge the powers and duties of his office, the Vice-President shall immediately assume the powers and duties of the office as Acting President.

Thereafter, when the President transmits to the President pro tempore of the Senate and the Speaker of the House of Representatives his written declaration that no inability exists, he shall resume the powers and duties of his office unless the Vice-President and a majority of either the principal officers of the executive department[s] or of such other body as Congress may by law provide, transmit within four days to the President pro tempore of the Senate and the Speaker of the House of Representatives their written declaration that the President is unable to discharge the powers and duties of his office. Thereupon Congress shall decide the issue, assembling within forty-eight hours for that purpose if not in session. If the Congress, within twenty-one days after receipt of the latter written declaration, or, if Congress is not in session, within twenty-one days after Congress is required to assemble, determines by two-thirds vote of both Houses that the President is unable to discharge the powers and duties of his office, the Vice-President shall continue to discharge the same as Acting President; otherwise, the President shall resume the powers and duties of his office.

Amendment XXVI [1971]

Section 1. The right of citizens of the United States, who are eighteen years of age or older, to vote shall not be denied or abridged by the United States or by any State on account of age.

Section 2. The Congress shall have power to enforce this article by appropriate legislation.

Unratified Amendment

Equal Rights Amendment (proposed by Congress March 22, 1972; seven-year deadline for ratification extended to June 30, 1982)

Section 1. *Equality of rights under the law shall not be denied or abridged by the United States or by any State on account of sex.*

Section 2. *The Congress shall have the power to enforce, by appropriate legislation, the provisions of this article.*

Section 3. *This amendment shall take effect two years after the date of ratification.*

Unratified Amendment

District of Columbia Statehood Amendment (proposed by Congress August 22, 1978)

Section 1. *For purposes of representation in the Congress, election of the President and Vice President, and article V of this Constitution, the District constituting the seat of government of the United States shall be treated as though it were a State.*

Section 2. *The exercise of the rights and powers conferred under this article shall be by the people of the District constituting the seat of government, and as shall be provided by Congress.*

Section 3. *The twenty-third article of amendment to the Constitution of the United States is hereby repealed.*

Section 4. *This article shall be inoperative, unless it shall have been ratified as an amendment to the Constitution by the legislatures of three-fourths of the several states within seven years from the date of its submission.*

Amendment XXVII [1992]

No law varying the compensation for the services of the Senators and Representatives, shall take effect, until an election of Representatives shall have intervened.

Appendix

The American Nation

Admission of States into the Union

State	Date of Admission	State	Date of Admission	State	Date of Admission
1. Delaware	December 7, 1787	18. Louisiana	April 30, 1812	35. West Virginia	June 20, 1863
2. Pennsylvania	December 12, 1787	19. Indiana	December 11, 1816	36. Nevada	October 31, 1864
3. New Jersey	December 18, 1787	20. Mississippi	December 10, 1817	37. Nebraska	March 1, 1867
4. Georgia	January 2, 1788	21. Illinois	December 3, 1818	38. Colorado	August 1, 1876
5. Connecticut	January 9, 1788	22. Alabama	December 14, 1819	39. North Dakota	November 2, 1889
6. Massachusetts	February 6, 1788	23. Maine	March 15, 1820	40. South Dakota	November 2, 1889
7. Maryland	April 28, 1788	24. Missouri	August 10, 1821	41. Montana	November 8, 1889
8. South Carolina	May 23, 1788	25. Arkansas	June 15, 1836	42. Washington	November 11, 1889
9. New Hampshire	June 21, 1788	26. Michigan	January 26, 1837	43. Idaho	July 3, 1890
10. Virginia	June 25, 1788	27. Florida	March 3, 1845	44. Wyoming	July 10, 1890
11. New York	July 26, 1788	28. Texas	December 29, 1845	45. Utah	January 4, 1896
12. North Carolina	November 21, 1789	29. Iowa	December 28, 1846	46. Oklahoma	November 16, 1907
13. Rhode Island	May 29, 1790	30. Wisconsin	May 29, 1848	47. New Mexico	January 6, 1912
14. Vermont	March 4, 1791	31. California	September 9, 1850	48. Arizona	February 14, 1912
15. Kentucky	June 1, 1792	32. Minnesota	May 11, 1858	49. Alaska	January 3, 1959
16. Tennessee	June 1, 1796	33. Oregon	February 14, 1859	50. Hawaii	August 21, 1959
17. Ohio	March 1, 1803	34. Kansas	January 29, 1861		

Presidential Elections

Year	Candidates	Parties	Percentage of Popular Vote*	Electoral Vote
1789	**George Washington**	No party designations		69
	John Adams†			34
	Other candidates			35
1792	**George Washington**	No party designations		132
	John Adams			77
	George Clinton			50
	Other candidates			5

SOURCES: U.S. Bureau of the Census, *Historical Statistics of the United States, Colonial Times to 1970* (1975); *Statistical Abstract of the United States, 2001*; *Statistical Abstract of the United States, 2006*.

*Prior to 1824, most presidential electors were chosen by state legislators rather than by popular vote. For elections after 1824, candidates receiving less than 1.0 percent of the popular vote have been omitted from this chart. Hence the popular vote does not total 100 percent for all elections.

†Before the Twelfth Amendment was passed in 1804, the electoral college voted for two presidential candidates; the runner-up became vice president.

Year	Candidates	Parties	Percentage of Popular Vote	Electoral Vote
1796	**John Adams**	Federalist		71
	Thomas Jefferson	Democratic-Republican		68
	Thomas Pinckney	Federalist		59
	Aaron Burr	Democratic-Republican		30
	Other candidates			48
1800	**Thomas Jefferson**	Democratic-Republican		73
	Aaron Burr	Democratic-Republican		73
	John Adams	Federalist		65
	Charles C. Pinckney	Federalist		64
	John Jay	Federalist		1
1804	**Thomas Jefferson**	Democratic-Republican		162
	Charles C. Pinckney	Federalist		14
1808	**James Madison**	Democratic-Republican		122
	Charles C. Pinckney	Federalist		47
	George Clinton	Democratic-Republican		6
1812	**James Madison**	Democratic-Republican		128
	DeWitt Clinton	Federalist		89
1816	**James Monroe**	Democratic-Republican		183
	Rufus King	Federalist		34
1820	**James Monroe**	Democratic-Republican		231
	John Quincy Adams	Independent Republican		1
1824	**John Quincy Adams**	Democratic-Republican	30.5	84
	Andrew Jackson	Democratic-Republican	43.1	99
	Henry Clay	Democratic-Republican	13.2	37
	William H. Crawford	Democratic-Republican	13.1	41
1828	**Andrew Jackson**	Democratic	56.0	178
	John Quincy Adams	National Republican	44.0	83
1832	**Andrew Jackson**	Democratic	54.5	219
	Henry Clay	National Republican	37.5	49
	William Wirt	Anti-Masonic	8.0	7
	John Floyd	Democratic	‡	11
1836	**Martin Van Buren**	Democratic	50.9	170
	William H. Harrison	Whig	49.1	73
	Hugh L. White	Whig		26
	Daniel Webster	Whig		14
	W. P. Mangum	Whig		11
1840	**William H. Harrison**	Whig	53.1	234
	Martin Van Buren	Democratic	46.9	60
1844	**James K. Polk**	Democratic	49.6	170
	Henry Clay	Whig	48.1	105
	James G. Birney	Liberty	2.3	
1848	**Zachary Taylor**	Whig	47.4	163
	Lewis Cass	Democratic	42.5	127
	Martin Van Buren	Free Soil	10.1	

‡Independent Democrat John Floyd received the 11 electoral votes of South Carolina; that state's presidential electors were still chosen by its legislature, not by popular vote.

Year	Candidates	Parties	Percentage of Popular Vote	Electoral Vote
1852	**Franklin Pierce**	Democratic	50.9	254
	Winfield Scott	Whig	44.1	42
	John P. Hale	Free Soil	5.0	
1856	**James Buchanan**	Democratic	45.3	174
	John C. Frémont	Republican	33.1	114
	Millard Fillmore	American	21.6	8
1860	**Abraham Lincoln**	Republican	39.8	180
	Stephen A. Douglas	Democratic	29.5	12
	John C. Breckinridge	Democratic	18.1	72
	John Bell	Constitutional Union	12.6	39
1864	**Abraham Lincoln**	Republican	55.0	212
	George B. McClellan	Democratic	45.0	21
1868	**Ulysses S. Grant**	Republican	52.7	214
	Horatio Seymour	Democratic	47.3	80
1872	**Ulysses S. Grant**	Republican	55.6	286
	Horace Greeley	Democratic	43.9	
1876	**Rutherford B. Hayes**	Republican	48.0	185
	Samuel J. Tilden	Democratic	51.0	184
1880	**James A. Garfield**	Republican	48.5	214
	Winfield S. Hancock	Democratic	48.1	155
	James B. Weaver	Greenback-Labor	3.4	
1884	**Grover Cleveland**	Democratic	48.5	219
	James G. Blaine	Republican	48.2	182
	Benjamin F. Butler	Greenback-Labor	1.8	
	John P. St. John	Prohibition	1.5	
1888	**Benjamin Harrison**	Republican	47.9	233
	Grover Cleveland	Democratic	48.6	168
	Clinton P. Fisk	Prohibition	2.2	
	Anson J. Streeter	Union Labor	1.3	
1892	**Grover Cleveland**	Democratic	46.1	277
	Benjamin Harrison	Republican	43.0	145
	James B. Weaver	People's	8.5	22
	John Bidwell	Prohibition	2.2	
1896	**William McKinley**	Republican	51.1	271
	William J. Bryan	Democratic	47.7	176
1900	**William McKinley**	Republican	51.7	292
	William J. Bryan	Democratic; Populist	45.5	155
	John C. Wooley	Prohibition	1.5	
1904	**Theodore Roosevelt**	Republican	57.4	336
	Alton B. Parker	Democratic	37.6	140
	Eugene V. Debs	Socialist	3.0	
	Silas C. Swallow	Prohibition	1.9	
1908	**William H. Taft**	Republican	51.6	321
	William J. Bryan	Democratic	43.1	162
	Eugene V. Debs	Socialist	2.8	
	Eugene W. Chafin	Prohibition	1.7	

Year	Candidates	Parties	Percentage of Popular Vote	Electoral Vote
1912	**Woodrow Wilson**	Democratic	41.9	435
	Theodore Roosevelt	Progressive	27.4	88
	William H. Taft	Republican	23.2	8
	Eugene V. Debs	Socialist	6.0	
	Eugene W. Chafin	Prohibition	1.4	
1916	**Woodrow Wilson**	Democratic	49.4	277
	Charles E. Hughes	Republican	46.2	254
	A. L. Benson	Socialist	3.2	
	J. Frank Hanly	Prohibition	1.2	
1920	**Warren G. Harding**	Republican	60.4	404
	James M. Cox	Democratic	34.2	127
	Eugene V. Debs	Socialist	3.4	
	P. P. Christensen	Farmer-Labor	1.0	
1924	**Calvin Coolidge**	Republican	54.0	382
	John W. Davis	Democratic	28.8	136
	Robert M. La Follette	Progressive	16.6	13
1928	**Herbert C. Hoover**	Republican	58.2	444
	Alfred E. Smith	Democratic	40.9	87
1932	**Franklin D. Roosevelt**	Democratic	57.4	472
	Herbert C. Hoover	Republican	39.7	59
	Norman Thomas	Socialist	2.2	
1936	**Franklin D. Roosevelt**	Democratic	60.8	523
	Alfred M. Landon	Republican	36.5	8
	William Lemke	Union	1.9	
1940	**Franklin D. Roosevelt**	Democratic	54.8	449
	Wendell L. Willkie	Republican	44.8	82
1944	**Franklin D. Roosevelt**	Democratic	53.5	432
	Thomas E. Dewey	Republican	46.0	99
1948	**Harry S. Truman**	Democratic	49.6	303
	Thomas E. Dewey	Republican	45.1	189
	J. Strom Thurmond	States' Rights	2.4	
	Henry Wallace	Progressive	2.4	
1952	**Dwight D. Eisenhower**	Republican	55.1	442
	Adlai E. Stevenson	Democratic	44.4	89
1956	**Dwight D. Eisenhower**	Republican	57.6	457
	Adlai E. Stevenson	Democratic	42.1	73
1960	**John F. Kennedy**	Democratic	49.7	303
	Richard M. Nixon	Republican	49.5	219
1964	**Lyndon B. Johnson**	Democratic	61.1	486
	Barry M. Goldwater	Republican	38.5	52
1968	**Richard M. Nixon**	Republican	43.4	301
	Hubert H. Humphrey	Democratic	42.7	191
	George C. Wallace	American Independent	13.5	46
1972	**Richard M. Nixon**	Republican	60.7	520
	George S. McGovern	Democratic	37.5	17
	John G. Schmitz	American	1.4	

Year	Candidates	Parties	Percentage of Popular Vote	Electoral Vote
1976	**Jimmy Carter**	Democratic	50.1	297
	Gerald R. Ford	Republican	48.0	240
1980	**Ronald W. Reagan**	Republican	50.7	489
	Jimmy Carter	Democratic	41.0	49
	John B. Anderson	Independent	6.6	0
	Ed Clark	Libertarian	1.1	
1984	**Ronald W. Reagan**	Republican	58.4	525
	Walter F. Mondale	Democratic	41.6	13
1988	**George H. W. Bush**	Republican	53.4	426
	Michael Dukakis	Democratic	45.6	111*
1992	**Bill Clinton**	Democratic	43.7	370
	George H. W. Bush	Republican	38.0	168
	H. Ross Perot	Independent	19.0	0
1996	**Bill Clinton**	Democratic	49	379
	Robert J. Dole	Republican	41	159
	H. Ross Perot	Reform	8	0
2000	**George W. Bush**	Republican	47.8	271
	Albert Gore	Democratic	48.4	267
	Ralph Nader	Green	2.7	0
2004	**George W. Bush**	Republican	50.7	286
	John Kerry	Democratic	48.3	252
2008	**Barack Obama**	Democratic	52.9	365
	John McCain	Republican	45.7	173
2012	**Barack Obama**	Democratic	51	332
	Mitt Romney	Republican	47.2	206
2016	**Donald Trump**	Republican	46.4	306
	Hillary Clinton	Democratic	48.5	232

*One Dukakis elector cast a vote for Lloyd Bentsen.

Population Growth*

Year	Population	Percentage Increase	Year	Population	Percentage Increase
1610	350	—	1820	9,638,453	33.1
1620	2,300	557.1	1830	12,866,020	33.5
1630	4,600	100.0	1840	17,069,453	32.7
1640	26,600	478.3	1850	23,191,876	35.9
1650	50,400	90.8	1860	31,443,321	35.6
1660	75,100	49.0	1870	39,818,449	26.6
1670	111,900	49.0	1880	50,155,783	26.0
1680	151,500	35.4	1890	62,947,714	25.5
1690	210,400	38.9	1900	75,994,575	20.7
1700	250,900	19.2	1910	91,972,266	21.0
1710	331,700	32.2	1920	105,710,620	14.9
1720	466,200	40.5	1930	122,775,046	16.1
1730	629,400	35.0	1940	131,669,275	7.2
1740	905,600	43.9	1950	150,697,361	14.5
1750	1,170,800	29.3	1960	179,323,175	19.0
1760	1,593,600	36.1	1970	203,235,298	13.3
1770	2,148,100	34.8	1980	226,545,805	11.5
1780	2,780,400	29.4	1990	248,709,873	9.8
1790	3,929,214	41.3	2000	281,421,906	13.2
1800	5,308,483	35.1	2010	308,745,538	9.7
1810	7,239,881	36.4			

SOURCES: U.S. Bureau of the Census, *Historical Statistics of the United States, Colonial Times to 1970* (1975); *Statistical Abstract of the United States, 2010*.

*Note: Until 1890, census takers never made any effort to count the Native American people who lived outside their reserved political areas and compiled only casual and incomplete enumerations of those living within their jurisdictions. In 1890, the federal government attempted a full count of the Indian population: the Census found 125,719 Indians in 1890, compared with only 12,543 in 1870 and 33,985 in 1880.

Immigration by Decade

Year	Number	Immigrants During This Decade as a Percentage of Total Population	Year	Number	Immigrants During This Decade as a Percentage of Total Population
1821–1830	151,824	1.6	1921–1930	4,107,209	3.9
1831–1840	599,125	4.6	1931–1940	528,431	0.4
1841–1850	1,713,251	10.0	1941–1950	1,035,039	0.7
1851–1860	2,598,214	11.2	1951–1960	2,515,479	1.6
1861–1870	2,314,824	7.4	1961–1970	3,321,677	1.8
1871–1880	2,812,191	7.1	1971–1980	4,493,000	2.2
1881–1890	5,246,613	10.5	1981–1990	7,338,000	3.0
1891–1900	3,687,546	5.8	1991–2000	9,095,083	3.7
1901–1910	8,795,386	11.6	2001–2010	10,501,053	3.7
1911–1920	5,735,811	6.2	2011–2015	5,151,773	NA
Total	**33,654,785**		**Total**	**48,086,744**	
			1821–2000		
			GRAND TOTAL	**81,741,529**	

SOURCES: U.S. Bureau of the Census, *Historical Statistics of the United States, Colonial Times to 1970* (1975), part 1, 105–106; *Statistical Abstract of the United States, 2001*. U.S. Department of Homeland Security, *Yearbook of Immigration Statistics, 2015*.

Regional Origins

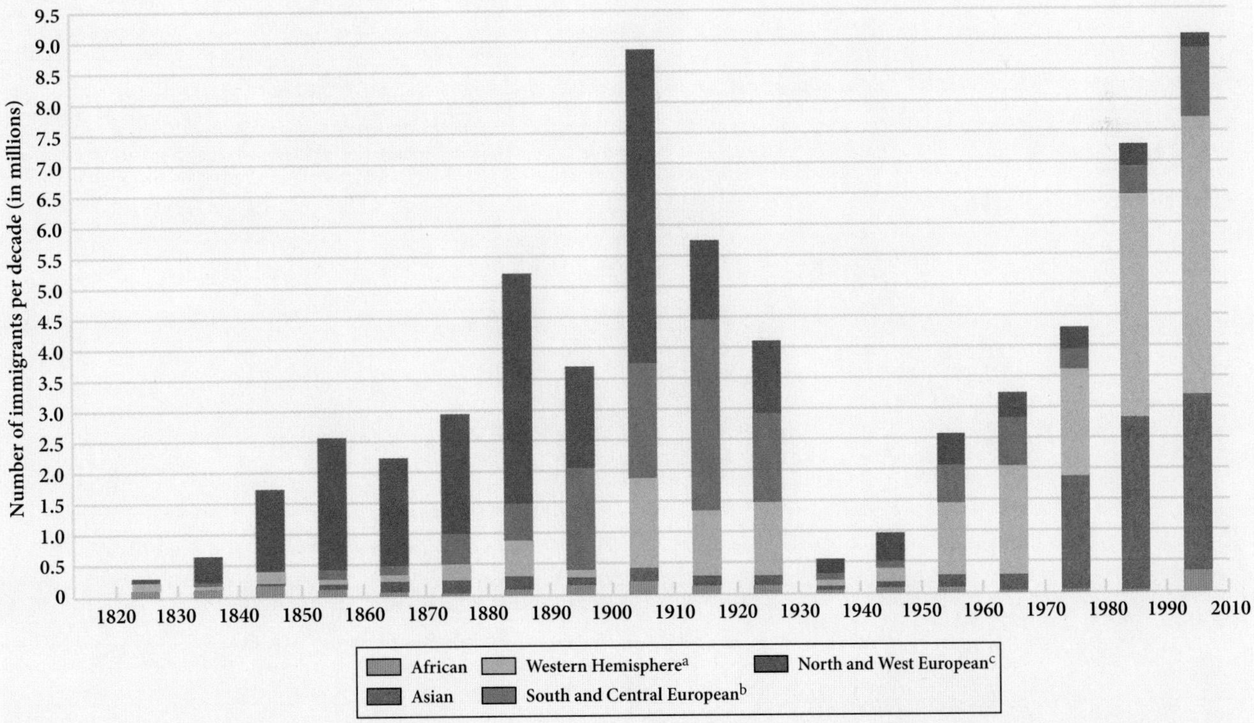

[a] Canada and all countries in South America and Central America.
[b] Italy, Spain, Portugal, Greece, Germany (Austria included, 1938–1945), Poland, Czechoslovakia (since 1920), Yugoslavia (since1920), Hungary (since 1861), Austria (since 1861, except 1938–1945), former USSR (excludes Asian USSR between 1931 and 1963), Latvia, Estonia, Lithuania, Finland, Romania, Bulgaria, Turkey (in Europe), and other European countries not classified elsewhere.
[c] Great Britain, Ireland, Norway, Sweden, Denmark, Iceland, Netherlands, Belgium, Luxembourg, Switzerland, and France.

SOURCES: Stephan Thernstrom, ed., *Harvard Encyclopedia of American Ethnic Groups* (1980), 480; U.S. Bureau of the Census, *Statistical Abstract of the United States, 1991*; U.S. Immigration and Naturalization Service, *Statistical Yearbook, 2010*.

Glossary/Glosario

abolitionism: The social reform movement to end slavery immediately and without compensation that began in the United States in the 1830s. (p. 335)

Abu Ghraib prison: A prison outside Baghdag, Iraq, where American military personnel were photographed abusing and torturing prisoners during the Iraq war. (p. 993)

Adams-Onís Treaty: An 1819 treaty in which John Quincy Adams persuaded Spain to cede the Florida territory to the United States. In return, the American government accepted Spain's claim to Texas and agreed to a compromise on the western boundary for the state of Louisiana. (p. 240)

Advanced Research Projects Agency Network (ARPANET): A decentralized computer network developed in the late 1960s by the U.S. Department of Defense in conjunction with the Massachusetts Institute of Technology. The Internet grew out of the ARPANET. (p. 977)

affirmative action: Policies established in the 1960s and 1970s by governments, businesses, universities, and other institutions to address past discrimination against specific groups such as people of color and white women. (p. 920)

African Methodist Episcopal Church: Church founded in 1816 by African Americans who were discriminated against by white Protestants. The church spread across the Northeast and Midwest and even founded a few congregations in the slave states of Missouri, Kentucky, Louisiana, and South Carolina. (p. 334)

Agricultural Adjustment Act: New Deal legislation passed in May 1933 that aimed at cutting agricultural production to raise crop prices and thus farmers' income. (p. 709)

Al Qaeda: A network of radical Islamic terrorists organized by Osama bin Laden, who issued a call for holy war against Americans and their allies. Members of Al Qaeda were responsible for the 9/11 terrorist attacks. (p. 989)

Alamo: The 1836 defeat by the Mexican army of the Texan garrison defending the Alamo in San Antonio. Newspapers urged Americans to "Remember the Alamo," and American adventurers, lured by offers of land grants, flocked to Texas to join the rebel forces. (p. 353)

Algonquian cultures/languages: A Native American language family whose speakers were widespread in the eastern woodlands, Great Lakes, and subarctic regions of eastern North America. The Algonquian language family should not be confused

abolicionismo: Movimiento de reforma social que comenzó en los Estados Unidos en la década de 1830, cuyo objetivo fue ponerle fin a la esclavitud de forma inmediata y sin compensación. (pág. 335)

Prisión de Abu Ghraib: Prisión en las afueras de Bagdad, Irak, donde los guardias estadounidenses fueron fotografiados abusando y torturando a presuntos insurgentes. (pág. 993)

Tratado de Adams-Onís: Tratado que tuvo lugar en 1819 en el que John Quincy Adams persuadió a Espana a que cediera el territorio de la Florida a los Estados Unidos. A cambio, el gobierno estadounidense aceptó el reclamo de España sobre Texas y aceptó negociar el límite occidental del estado de Luisiana. (pág. 240)

Advanced Research Projects Agency Network (Red de la Agencia de Proyectos de Investigación Avanzada, ARPANET): Red de computadoras descentralizadas desarrollada a finales de la década de 1960 por el Departamento de Defensa de Estados Unidos en colaboración con el Massachusetts Institute of Technology. La Internet surgió a partir de ARPANET. (pág. 977)

acción afirmativa (o discriminación positiva): Políticas establecidas en las décadas de 1960 y 1970 por gobiernos, negocios, universidades y otras instituciones para superar los efectos de discriminaciones del pasado contra grupos específicos como minorías raciales y étnicas, y mujeres. (pág. 920)

Iglesia Episcopal Metodista Africana: Iglesia fundada en 1816 por afroamericanos discriminados por protestantes blancos. La iglesia se extendió por el noreste y el medio oeste del país e incluso fundó un número de congregaciones en los estados esclavistas de Misuri, Kentucky, Luisiana y Carolina del Sur. (pág. 334)

Ley de Ajuste Agrícola: Legislación del "Nuevo Trato" aprobada en mayo de 1933 que buscaba recortar la producción agrícola para aumentar el precio de los cultivos y por lo tanto, el ingreso de los agricultores. (pág. 709)

Al Qaeda: Red de terroristas islámicos radicales organizada por Osama Bin Laden, quien convocó a una guerra santa contra los estadounidenses y sus aliados. Miembros de Al Qaeda fueron responsables de los ataques terroristas del 11 de septiembre. (pág. 989)

Álamo: Derrota, a manos del ejército mexicano en 1836, de la guarnición texana que defendía el Álamo en San Antonio. Los periódicos instaron a los estadounidenses a que "Recuerden el Álamo", y los aventureros estadounidenses, atraídos por las ofertas de concesiones de tierras, acudieron a Texas para unirse a las fuerzas rebeldes. (pág. 353)

algonquinas, culturas y lenguas: Familia de lenguas nativas americanas cuyos hablantes se extendieron por los bosques orientales, los Grandes Lagos y las regiones subárticas del este de América del Norte. La familia de las lenguas algonquinas no debe confundirse

with the Algonquins, who were a single nation inhabiting the St. Lawrence Valley at the time of first contact. (p. 12)

America First Committee: A committee organized by isolationists in 1940 to oppose the entrance of the United States into World War II. The membership of the committee included senators, journalists, and publishers and such prominent national figures as the aviator Charles Lindbergh. (p. 740)

American Anti-Slavery Society: The first interracial social justice movement in the United States, which advocated the immediate, unconditional end of slavery on the basis of human rights, without compensation to slave masters. (p. 336)

American Civil Liberties Union: An organization formed during the Red Scare of the 1920s to protect free speech rights. (p. 690)

American Colonization Society: Founded by Henry Clay and other prominent citizens in 1817, the society argued that slaves had to be freed and then resettled, in Africa or elsewhere. (p. 289)

American exceptionalism: The idea that the United States has a unique destiny to foster democracy and civilization on the world stage. (p. 643)

American Federation of Labor: Organization of skilled workers created by Samuel Gompers in 1886 that called for direct negotiation with employers in order to achieve better pay and benefits. The AFL became the largest and most enduring workers' organization of the industrial era. (p. 541)

American GI Forum: A group founded by World War II veterans in Corpus Christi, Texas, in 1948 to protest the poor treatment of Mexican American soldiers and veterans. (p. 842)

American Indian Movement (AIM): Organization established in 1968 to address the problems Indians faced in American cities, including poverty and police harassment. AIM organized Indians to end relocation and termination policies and to win greater control over their cultures and communities. (p. 866)

American, or Know-Nothing, Party: An anti-immigrant, anti-Catholic political party formed in 1851 that arose in response to mass immigration in the 1840s, especially from Ireland and Germany. In 1854, the party gained control of the state governments of Massachusetts and Pennsylvania. (p. 399)

American Liberty League: A group of Republican business leaders and conservative Democrats who banded together to fight what they called the "reckless spending" and "socialist" reforms of the New Deal. (p. 713)

American Plan: Strategy by American business in the 1920s to keep workplaces free of unions, which included refusing to negotiate with trade unions and requiring workers to sign contracts pledging not to join a union. (p. 678)

American Protective Association: A powerful anti-immigrant political organization, led by Protestants, which for a brief period

con los algonquinos, la nación-pueblo que habitaba el valle de San Lorenzo cuando ocurrió el primer contacto. (pág. 12)

Comité América Primero: Comité organizado por aislacionistas en 1940 en oposición a la entrada de Estados Unidos a la Segunda Guerra Mundial. Entre los miembros del comité había senadores, periodistas, editores y figuras respetadas como el piloto Charles Lindbergh. (pág. 740)

Sociedad Antiesclavista Americana: Fue el primer movimiento interracial de justicia social en los Estados Unidos que abogó por el final inmediato e incondicional de la esclavitud sobre la base de los derechos humanos, sin compensación para los dueños de esclavos. (pág. 336)

Unión Americana de Libertades Civiles: Organización formada durante el Temor rojo para proteger los derechos de libertad de expresión. (pág. 690)

Sociedad Americana de Colonización: Fundada en 1817 por Henry Clay y otros ciudadanos prominentes, esta sociedad argumentaba que los esclavos debían ser liberados y reubicados en África o en otro lugar. (pág. 289)

Excepcionalismo americano: La idea de que Estados Unidos tiene como destino único fomentar la democracia y civilización en el escenario internacional. (pág. 643)

Federación Americana del Trabajo (AFL): Organización creada por Samuel Gompers en 1886 que coordinó las actividades de los gremios y pidió negociaciones directas con los patrones para obtener beneficios para la mano de obra calificada. La AFL se convirtió en la organización obrera más grande y duradera de la era industrial. (pág. 541)

Foro Americano G.I.: Grupo fundado en 1948 por veteranos de la Segunda Guerra Mundial en Corpus Christi, Texas, para protestar el maltrato a soldados y veteranos mexicano-americanos. (pág. 842)

Movimiento Indígena Estadounidense (AIM): Organización establecida en 1968 para responder a los problemas que enfrentaban los indígenas en las ciudades estadounidenses, entre ellos, la pobreza y el acoso de la policía. El AIM organizó a los indígenas para terminar con las políticas de terminación y desplazamiento y lograr mayor control sobre sus comunidades y culturas. (pág. 866)

Partido Americano o Know-Nothing (lit. "Saber nada"): Partido político antiinmigrante y anticatólico formado en 1851 que surgió en respuesta a la inmigración masiva de la década de 1840, especialmente desde Irlanda y Alemania. En 1854, el partido obtuvo el control de los gobiernos estatales de Massachusetts y Pensilvania. (pág. 399)

Liga Americana para la Libertad: Grupo de líderes empresariales republicanos y demócratas conservadores que se unieron para combatir lo que llamaron el "gasto desmedido" y las reformas "socialistas" del Nuevo Trato. (pág. 713)

Plan Americano: Estrategia diseñada por negocios estadounidenses en la década de 1920 para excluir a los sindicatos de los lugares de trabajo con medidas como negarse a negociar con sindicatos y requerir que los trabajadores firmen contratos donde se comprometían a no unirse a un sindicato. (pág. 678)

Asociación Protectora Americana: Poderosa organización política de militancia protestante, que durante un periodo breve en la

in the 1890s counted more than two million members. In its virulent anti-Catholicism and calls for restrictions on immigrants, the APA prefigured the revived Ku Klux Klan of the 1920s. (p. 552)

American Recovery and Reinvestment Act: An economic stimulus bill passed in 2009, in response to the Great Recession, that provided $787 billion to state and local governments. It was one of the largest single packages of government spending in American history. (p. 995)

American Renaissance: A literary explosion during the 1840s inspired in part by Emerson's ideas on the liberation of the individual. (p. 319)

American System: The mercantilist system of national economic development advocated by Henry Clay and adopted by John Quincy Adams, with a national bank to manage the nation's financial system; protective tariffs to provide revenue and encourage industry; and a nationally funded network of roads, canals, and railroads. (p. 291)

American Woman Suffrage Association: A women's suffrage organization led by Lucy Stone, Henry Blackwell, and others who remained loyal to the Republican Party, despite its failure to include women's voting rights in the Reconstruction amendments. Stressing the urgency of voting rights for African American men, AWSA leaders held out hope that once Reconstruction had been settled, it would be women's turn. (p. 458)

Antifederalists: Opponents of ratification of the Constitution. Antifederalists feared that a powerful and distant central government would be out of touch with the needs of citizens. They also complained that it failed to guarantee individual liberties in a bill of rights. (p. 205)

Antiquities Act: A 1906 act that allowed the U.S. president to use executive powers to set aside, as federal monuments, sites of great environmental or cultural significance. Theodore Roosevelt, the first president to invoke the act's powers, used them to preserve the Grand Canyon. (p. 563)

Articles of Confederation: The written document defining the structure of the government from 1781 to 1788, under which the Union was a confederation of equal states, with no executive and limited powers, existing mainly to foster a common defense. (p. 194)

artisan republicanism: An ideology of production that celebrated small-scale producers and emphasized liberty and equality. It flourished after the American Revolution and gradually declined as a result of industrialization. (p. 270)

Atlanta Compromise: An 1895 address by Booker T. Washington that urged whites and African Americans to work together for the progress of all. Delivered at the Cotton States Exposition in Atlanta, the speech was widely interpreted as approving racial segregation. (p. 566)

Atlantic Charter: A press release by President Roosevelt and British prime minister Winston Churchill in August 1941 calling

década de 1890, tuvo más de dos millones de miembros. En su anticatolicismo virulento y su llamado a imponer restricciones sobre inmigrantes, la APA prefiguró a la reactivada Ku Klux Klan de la década de 1920. (pág. 552)

Ley de Reinversión y Recuperación de Estados Unidos: Ley de estímulo económico promulgada en 2009 como respuesta a la Gran Recesión que brindó $787 mil millones de dólares a gobiernos estatales y locales para escuelas, hospitales y proyectos de transporte. Ha sido uno de los paquetes de egreso gubernamental más grandes en la historia del país. (pág. 995)

Renacimiento Americano: Explosión literaria que ocurrió durante la década de 1840 inspirada en parte por las ideas de Emerson sobre la liberación del individuo. (pág. 319)

sistema americano: Sistema mercantilista de desarrollo económico nacional, defendido por Henry Clay y adoptado por John Quincy Adams, que contaba con un banco nacional para administrar el sistema financiero de la nación, tarifas protectoras para proporcionar ingresos y estimular a la industria, y una red de carreteras, canales y ferrocarriles financiados a nivel nacional. (pág. 291)

Asociación Americana pro Sufragio de la Mujer (AWSA): Organización de mujeres sufragistas dirigida por Lucy Stone, Henry Blackwell y otros que permanecieron fieles al Partido Republicano pese a que no incluyó a los derechos de voto de la mujer en las Enmiendas de Reconstrucción. Haciendo hincapié en la urgencia de otorgar derechos de voto a los hombres afroamericanos, los líderes de la AWSA esperaban que una vez que asentara la Reconstrucción el turno de las mujeres llegaría. (pág. 458)

antifederalistas: Oponentes de la ratificación de la Constitución. Los antifederalistas temían que un gobierno central poderoso y distante estaría alejado de la realidad de las necesidades de los ciudadanos. También reclamaban que el gobierno no había garantizado las libertades individuales con una declaración de derechos. (pág. 205)

Ley de Antigüedades: Ley promulgada en 1906 que permitía al presidente de los Estados Unidos el uso de poderes ejecutivos para apartar y designar sitios de gran importancia cultural o natural, como monumentos federales. Theodore Roosevelt, primer presidente en invocar los poderes de la ley, los usó para preservar el Gran Cañón. (pág. 563)

Artículos de la Confederación: Documento escrito que definió la estructura del gobierno de 1781 a 1788, según el cual la Unión era una confederación de estados igualitarios, sin poderes ejecutivos y cuyos otros poderes estaban limitados, que existió principalmente para fomentar una defensa común. (pág. 194)

republicanismo artesanal: Ideología que conmemoraba a los pequeños productores y resaltaba la igualdad y la libertad. Tuvo su auge después de la Revolución de los Estados Unidos y declinó gradualmente como resultado de la industrialización. (pág. 270)

Compromiso de Atlanta: Discurso de Booker T. Washington en 1895 que llamaba a los blancos y a los afroamericanos a trabajar juntos para el progreso de todos. Pronunciado durante la Exposición de Estados Algodoneros en Atlanta, el discurso fue interpretado por muchos como una aprobación de la segregación racial. (pág. 566)

Carta del Atlántico: Boletín de prensa emitido por el presidente Roosevelt y el primer ministro británico, Winston Churchill, en

for economic cooperation, national self-determination, and guarantees of political stability after the war. (p. 741)

Axis powers: Military alliance formed in 1936 among Germany, Italy, and Japan that fought the Allied powers during World War II. (p. 738)

baby boom: The surge in the American birthrate between 1945 and 1965, which peaked in 1957 with 4.3 million births. (p. 813)

Bacon's Rebellion: The rebellion in 1675–1676 in Virginia that began when vigilante colonists started a war with neighboring Indians. When Governor William Berkeley refused to support them, the rebels — led by Nathaniel Bacon — formed an army that marched on the capital. The rebellion was finally crushed but prompted reforms in Virginia's government. (p. 72)

Bank of the United States: A bank chartered in 1790 and jointly owned by private stockholders and the national government. Alexander Hamilton argued that the bank would provide stability to the American economy, which was chronically short of capital, by making loans to merchants, handling government funds, and issuing bills of credit. (p. 215)

Battle of Little Big Horn: The 1876 battle begun when American cavalry under George Armstrong Custer attacked an encampment of Sioux, Arapaho, and Cheyenne Indians who were resisting removal to a reservation. Custer's force was annihilated, but with whites calling for U.S. soldiers to retaliate, the Native American military victory was short-lived. (p. 505)

Battle of Long Island (1776): First major engagement of the new Continental army against 32,000 British troops; Washington's army was defeated and forced to retreat to Manhattan Island. (p. 179)

Battle of Saratoga (1777): A multistage battle in New York ending with the surrender of British general John Burgoyne. The victory ensured the diplomatic success of American representatives in Paris, who won a military alliance with France. (p. 181)

Battle of Tippecanoe: An attack on Shawnee Indians and their allies at Prophetstown on the Tippecanoe River in 1811 by American forces headed by William Henry Harrison, Indiana's territorial governor. The governor's troops traded heavy casualties with the confederacy's warriors and then destroyed the holy village. (p. 233)

Battle of Yorktown (1781): A battle in which French and American troops and a French fleet trapped the British army under the command of General Charles Cornwallis at Yorktown, Virginia. The Franco-American victory broke the resolve of the British government and led to peace negotiations. (p. 188)

Bay of Pigs: A failed U.S.-sponsored invasion of Cuba in 1961 by anti-Castro forces who planned to overthrow Fidel Castro's government. (p. 800)

agosto de 1941 llamando a la cooperación económica, a la auto determinación nacional y a las garantías de estabilidad política cuando concluyera la guerra. (pág. 741)

potencias del Eje: Alianza militar formada en 1963 entre Alemania, Italia y Japón que luchó contra los Aliados durante la Segunda Guerra Mundial. (pág. 738)

baby boom: El aumento en la tasa de nacimientos en los Estados Unidos entre 1945 y 1965, que tuvo su cúspide en 1957 con 4.3 millones de nacimientos. (pág. 813)

La Rebelión de Bacon: Rebelión que tuvo lugar en Virginia entre 1675 y 1676 cuando colonos justicieros iniciaron una guerra contra los nativos americanos de la zona. Cuando el gobernador William Berkeley se negó a apoyarlos, los rebeldes — bajo el mando de Nathaniel Bacon — formaron un ejército que se dirigió a la capital. La rebelión fue finalmente sofocada, pero impulsó reformas en el gobierno de Virginia. (pág. 72)

Banco de los Estados Unidos: Banco constituido en 1790 que fue propiedad conjunta de accionistas privados y del gobierno nacional. Alexander Hamilton argumentó que el banco proporcionaría estabilidad a la economía estadounidense, que carecía constantemente de capital, haciendo préstamos a comerciantes, manejando fondos del gobierno y emitiendo cuentas de crédito. (pág. 215)

Batalla de Little Big Horn: La batalla ocurrida en 1876 inició cuando una caballería estadounidense comandada por George Armstrong Custer atacó un campamento de indígenas Sioux, Arapaho y Cheyenne que se resistían a ser desplazados a una reserva. Las fuerzas de Custer fueron aniquiladas, pero el llamado de los blancos a los soldados estadounidenses a tomar represalias significó que la victoria del ejercito indígena duró poco. (pág. 505)

Batalla de Long Island (1776): Primer gran encuentro bélico del nuevo ejército continental, que luchó contra 32,000 tropas británicas. El ejército de Washington fue derrotado y obligado a retroceder a la isla de Manhattan. (pág. 179)

Batalla de Saratoga (1777): Batalla que se desplegó en varias etapas en Nueva York y que concluyó con la rendición del general británico John Burgoyne. La victoria aseguró el éxito diplomático de los representantes estadounidenses en París, que lograron una alianza militar con Francia. (pág. 181)

Batalla de Tippecanoe: Ataque a los indios shawnee en Prophetstown sobre el río Tippecanoe en 1811 por fuerzas estadounidenses encabezadas por William Henry Harrison, gobernador territorial de Indiana. Las tropas del gobernador entablaron una batalla con los soldados de la confederación, que causó grandes bajas de ambos lados, y luego destruyeron la aldea sagrada. (pág. 233)

Batalla de Yorktown (1781): Batalla en la cual las tropas francesas y americanas, con el apoyo de una flota francesa, atraparon al ejército británico bajo el mando del general Charles Cornwallis en Yorktown, Virginia. La victoria francoamericana causó que el gobierno británico finalmente desistiera y se negoció la paz. (pág. 188)

Bahía de Cochinos: Invasión fallida de Cuba llevada a cabo por anticastristas apoyados por los Estados Unidos en 1961, con la intención de derrocar al gobierno de Fidel Castro. (pág. 800)

Bear Flag Republic: A short-lived republic created in California by American emigrants to sponsor a rebellion against Mexican authority in 1846. (p. 372)

Beats: A small group of literary figures based in cities such as New York, Los Angeles, and San Francisco in the 1950s who rejected mainstream culture and instead celebrated personal freedom, which often included drug consumption and sexual adventurism. (p. 816)

Benevolent Empire: A web of reform organizations, heavily Whig in their political orientation, built by evangelical Protestant men and women influenced by the Second Great Awakening. (p. 318)

Bill of Rights: The first ten amendments to the Constitution, officially ratified by 1791. The amendments safeguarded fundamental personal rights, including freedom of speech and religion, and mandated legal procedures, such as trial by jury. (p. 213)

Black Codes: Laws passed by southern states after the Civil War that denied ex-slaves the civil rights enjoyed by whites, punished vague crimes such as "vagrancy" or failing to have a labor contract, and tried to force African Americans back to plantation labor systems that closely mirrored those in slavery times. (p. 453)

black nationalism: A major strain of African American thought that emphasized black racial pride and autonomy. Present in black communities for centuries, it periodically came to the fore, as in Marcus Garvey's pan-Africanist movement in the early twentieth century and in various organizations in the 1960s and 1970s, such as the Nation of Islam and the Black Panther Party. (p. 859)

Black Panther Party: A militant organization dedicated to protecting African Americans from police violence, founded in Oakland, California, in 1966 by Huey Newton and Bobby Seale. In the late 1960s the organization spread to other cities, where members undertook a wide range of community-organizing projects, but the Panthers' radicalism and belief in armed self-defense resulted in violent clashes with police. (p. 861)

blues: A form of American music that originated in the Deep South, especially from the black workers in the cotton fields of the Mississippi Delta. (p. 585)

Bonus Army: A group of fifteen to twenty thousand unemployed World War I veterans who set up camps near the Capitol building in 1932 to demand immediate payment of pension awards due in 1945. (p. 706)

Bracero Program: A federal program that brought hundreds of thousands of Mexican agricultural workers to the United States during and after World War II. The program continued until 1964 and was a major spur of Mexican immigration to the United States. (p. 749)

República de la Bandera del Oso: República efímera creada en California por emigrantes estadounidenses con el fin de patrocinar una rebelión contra la autoridad mexicana en 1846. (pág. 372)

Generación de los Beats: Pequeño grupo de figuras literarias basado en las ciudades de Nueva York y San Francisco en la década de 1950. Rechazaban a la cultura establecida y celebraban, más bien, la libertad personal, que con frecuencia incluía consumo de drogas y sexo casual. (pág. 816)

imperio benévolo: Red de organizaciones reformistas, con fuertes tendencias Whig en su orientación política, construida por hombres y mujeres protestantes evangélicos influenciados por el Segundo Gran Despertar. (pág. 318)

Declaración de Derechos: Las primeras diez enmiendas a la Constitución, ratificadas oficialmente en 1791. Las enmiendas salvaguardan los derechos personales fundamentales, incluidos la libertad de expresión y de religión, y los procedimientos legales obligatorios, como derecho a jucio ante un jurado. (pág. 213)

Códigos Negros: Leyes aprobadas por los estados sureños después de la Guerra Civil que negaban los derechos civiles de los blancos a los esclavos liberados, castigaban delitos ambiguos como el "vagabundeo" o no tener un contrato laboral y trataron de obligar a los afroamericanos a volver a los sistemas de trabajo de las plantaciones, que eran muy similares a aquellos en tiempos de la esclavitud. (pág. 453)

nacionalismo negro: Corriente principal del pensamiento afroamericano que enfatiza el orgullo racial negro y la autonomía. Existe desde hace siglos entre las comunidades negras y periódicamente ha retomado protagonismo, como ocurrió con el movimiento pan-africanista de Marcus Garvey a principios del siglo XX y con varias organizaciones de las décadas de 1960 y 1970, como la Nación del Islam y el Partido de las Panteras Negras. (pág. 859)

Partido de las Panteras Negras: Organización militante fundada en Oakland, California, en 1966 por Huey Newton y Bobby Seale para proteger a los afroamericanos de la violencia policial. A finales de la década de 1960, la organización se expandió a otras ciudades, donde los miembros asumieron una gran variedad de proyectos de organización comunitaria, pero el radicalismo de las Panteras y su creencia en la auto-defensa armada resultó en choques con la policía. (pág. 861)

blues: Tipo de música americana originada en el Sur Profundo, especialmente entre los trabajadores negros de las plantaciones de algodón en la boca del río Misisipi. (pág. 585)

Bonus Army: Grupo de 15 mil a 20 mil veteranos de la Primera Guerra Mundial que establecieron campamentos cerca del edificio del Capitolio para exigir el pago inmediato de las pensiones que estaban programadas para pagarse en 1945. (pág. 706)

Programa Bracero: Con el nombre oficial, Programa de Trabajadores Agrícolas Mexicanos el Programa Bracero (acordado con México) llevó a cientos de miles de trabajadores agrícolas a Estados Unidos durante y después de la Segunda Guerra Mundial. El programa continuó hasta 1964 y fue uno de los principales incentivos de immigración mexicana a los Estados Unidos. (pág. 749)

Bretton Woods: An international conference in New Hampshire in July 1944 that established the World Bank and the International Monetary Fund (IMF). (p. 807)

Brown v. Board of Education of Topeka: Supreme Court ruling of 1954 that overturned the "separate but equal" precedent established in *Plessy v. Ferguson* in 1896. The Court declared that separate educational facilities were inherently unequal and thus violated the Fourteenth Amendment. (p. 847)

Burlingame Treaty: An 1868 treaty that guaranteed the rights of U. S. missionaries in China and set official terms for the emigration of Chinese laborers to work in the United States. (p. 483)

Californios: The elite Mexican ranchers in the province of California. (p. 365)

casta system: A hierarchical system of racial classification developed by colonial elites in Latin America to make sense of the complex patterns of racial mixing that developed there. (p. 43)

caucus: A meeting held by a political party to choose candidates, make policies, and enforce party discipline. (p. 286)

chain migration: A pattern by which immigrants find housing and work and learn to navigate a new environment, and then assist other immigrants from their family or home area to settle in the same location. (p. 395)

chattel slavery: A system of bondage in which a slave has the legal status of property and so can be bought and sold. (p. 40)

Chicago school: A school of architecture dedicated to the design of buildings — such as skyscrapers — whose form expressed their structure and function. (p. 580)

Chicano Moratorium Committee: Group founded by activist Latinos to protest the Vietnam War. (p. 893)

Chinese Exclusion Act: The 1882 race-based law that barred Chinese laborers from entering the United States. Later applied to other Asian immigrants as well, it was not repealed until 1943. (p. 533)

Christianity: A religion that holds the belief that Jesus Christ was himself divine. For centuries, the Roman Catholic Church was the great unifying institution in Western Europe, and it was from Europe that Christianity spread to the Americas. (p. 22)

Church of Jesus Christ of Latter-day Saints, or Mormons: Founded by Joseph Smith in 1830. After Smith's death at the hands of an angry mob, in 1846 Brigham Young led many followers of Mormonism to lands in present-day Utah. (p. 324)

"City Beautiful" movement: A turn-of-the-twentieth-century movement that advocated landscape beautification, playgrounds, and more and better urban parks. (p. 595)

Civilian Conservation Corps: Federal relief program that provided jobs to millions of unemployed young men who built thousands of bridges, roads, trails, and other structures in state and national parks, bolstering the national infrastructure. (p. 712)

Bretton Woods: Conferencia internacional sostenida en New Hampshire en julio de 1944 que estableció al Banco Mundial y al Fondo Monetario Internacional (FMI). (pág. 807)

Caso Brown contra el Consejo de Educación de Topeka: Sentencia de la Corte Suprema en 1954 que anuló el precedente "separados pero iguales" establecido en Plessy v. Ferguson en 1896. La Corte declaró que las instalaciones educativas separadas eran intrínsecamente desiguales y atentaban contra la Decimocuarta Enmienda de la Constitución. (pág. 847)

Tratado de Burlingame: Tratado de 1868 que garantizaba los derechos de misioneros estadounidenses en China y establecía condiciones oficiales a la emigración de peones chinos que se iban a trabajar en Estados Unidos. (pág. 483)

californios: Nombre que se le dio a los rancheros mexicanos de élite en la provincia de California. (pág. 365)

sistema de castas: Sistema jerárquico de clasificación racial desarrollado por las elites coloniales en América Latina para dar sentido a los complejos patrones de mezcla racial que se desarrollaron allí. (pág. 43)

asamblea de partidos: Reunión celebrada por un partido político para elegir candidatos, formular políticas y hacer cumplir la disciplina del partido. (pág. 286)

migración en cadena: Patrón según el cual los inmigrantes encuentran vivienda y trabajo y aprenden a desenvolverse en un nuevo entorno, y luego ayudan a otros inmigrantes de su familia o región a establecerse en el mismo sitio. (pág. 395)

propiedad de esclavos: Sistema de esclavismo en que el estado legal de los esclavos es igual que el de una propiedad que puede comprarse y venderse. (pág. 40)

Escuela de Chicago: Escuela de arquitectura dedicada al diseño de edificios (como los rascacielos) cuya forma expresaba su estructura y función en lugar de ocultarla. (pág. 580)

Comité Nacional de Moratoria Chicana: Grupo fundado por activistas latinos para protestar contra la Guerra de Vietnam. (pág. 893)

Ley de Exclusión de Chinos: Ley promulgada en 1882 que impidió que trabajadores chinos entraran a los Estados Unidos. Posteriormente fue aplicada a otros inmigrantes asiáticos y no fue derogada hasta 1943. (pág. 533)

cristianismo: Religión que sostiene la creencia de que Jesucristo es Dios. Durante siglos, la Iglesia Católica Romana fue la gran institución unificadora en Europa Occidental; y fue desde Europa que el cristianismo se extendió a las Américas. (pág. 22)

Iglesia de Jesucristo de los Santos de los Últimos Días, o mormones: Fundada por Joseph Smith en 1830. Después de la muerte de Smith a manos de una turba enfurecida en 1846, Brigham Young condujo a muchos seguidores del mormonismo a tierras ubicadas en la actual Utah. (pág. 324)

movimiento "Ciudad Bella": Movimiento del cambio de siglo que promovió el embellecimiento de paisajes, parques infantiles y buscó mejores parques urbanos. (pág. 595)

Cuerpo Civil de Conservación: Programa federal de auxilio que ofreció empleo a millones de hombres desempleados en la construcción de miles de puentes, caminos, senderos y otras estructuras dentro de parques nacionales y estatales que reforzaron la infraestructura nacional. (pág. 712)

Civil Rights Act of 1866: Legislation passed by Congress that nullified the Black Codes and affirmed that African Americans should have equal benefit of the law. (p. 454)

Civil Rights Act of 1875: A law that required "full and equal" access to jury service and to transportation and public accommodations, irrespective of race. (p. 468)

Civil Rights Act of 1964: Law that responded to demands of the civil rights movement by making discrimination illegal in employment, education, and public accommodations on the basis of race, religion, national origin, and sex. (p. 855)

Civil Rights Cases: A series of 1883 Supreme Court decisions that struck down the Civil Rights Act of 1875, rolling back key Reconstruction laws and paving the way for later decisions that sanctioned segregation. (p. 475)

classical liberalism, or laissez-faire: The political ideology of individual liberty, private property, a competitive market economy, free trade, and limited government. The ideal is a *laissez faire* or "let alone" policy in which government does the least possible. (pp. 304; 470)

Clayton Antitrust Act: A 1914 law that gave more power to the Justice Department to pursue antitrust cases to prevent corporations from exercising monopoly power; it also specified that labor unions could not generally be prosecuted for "restraint of trade." (p. 632)

coastal trade: The domestic slave trade with routes along the Atlantic coast that sent thousands of slaves to sugar plantations in Louisiana and cotton plantations in the Mississippi Valley. (p. 264)

code talkers: Native American soldiers trained to use native languages to send messages in battle during World War II. The messages they sent gave the Allies great advantage in several battles. (p. 745)

Coercive Acts: Four British acts of 1774 meant to punish Massachusetts for the destruction of three shiploads of tea. Known in America as the Intolerable Acts, they led to open rebellion in the northern colonies. (p. 164)

Cold War liberalism: A combination of liberal policies that preserved the New Deal welfare state, anticommunism vilifying the Soviet Union abroad, and radicalism at home. Adopted by the Democratic Party after World War II. (p. 787)

Columbian Exchange: The massive global exchange of living things, including people, animals, plants, and diseases, between the Eastern and Western Hemispheres that began after the voyages of Columbus. (p. 43)

committees of correspondence: A communications network established among colonial assemblies between 1772 and 1773 to provide for rapid dissemination of news about important political developments. (p. 163)

Commonwealth System: The republican system of political economy implemented by state governments in the early nineteenth century that funneled aid to private businesses whose projects would improve the general welfare. (p. 254)

Ley de Derechos Civiles de 1866: Legislación promulgada por el Congreso que anuló los Códigos Negros y afirmó que los afroamericanos debían tener el mismo beneficio de la ley. (pág. 454)

Ley de Derechos Civiles de 1875: Ley que requería acceso "pleno e igualitario" al servicio de jurado, al transporte y al alojamiento público, sin importar la raza de la persona. (pág. 468)

Ley de Derechos Civiles de 1964: Ley que respondió a las exigencias del movimiento de derechos civiles al ilegalizar la discriminación en el empleo, la educación y la vivienda pública por raza, religión, nacionalidad y género. (pág. 855)

Casos de derechos civiles: Serie de decisiones de la Corte Suprema en 1883 que abolieron la Ley de Derechos Civiles de 1875 y revocaron importantes leyes de Reconstrucción, que más adelante marcaron la pauta de las decisiones que sancionaron la segregación. (pág. 475)

liberalismo clásico o laissez-faire: Ideología política de libertad individual, propiedad privada, economía competitiva de mercado, libre comercio y gobierno limitado. Lo ideal es una política de laissez faire o "dejar ser", en la cual el gobierno hace lo mínimo posible. (pág. 304, 470)

Ley Clayton Antimonopolio: Ley de 1914 que fortaleció las definiciones federales de "monopolio" y aumentó los poderes del Departamento de Justicia para perseguir casos antimonopolio; también especificó que, en general, no se podía perseguir a los sindicatos por "restricciones al comercio". (pág. 632)

comercio costero: Trata doméstica de esclavos con rutas a lo largo de la costa atlántica que enviaba miles de esclavos a plantaciones de azúcar en Luisiana y plantaciones de algodón en el valle del Misisipi. (pág. 264)

locutores de claves: Soldados nativos americanos en la Segunda Guerra Mundial entrenados para usar idiomas nativos para enviar mensajes durante el combate. Sus mensajes dieron grandes ventajas a los Aliados en muchas batallas. (pág. 745)

Leyes Coactivas: Cuatro leyes británicas de 1774 cuyo objetivo fue castigar a Massachusetts por la destrucción de tres cargamentos de té. Conocidas en los Estados Unidos como las Leyes Intolerables, condujeron a la rebelión abierta en las colonias del norte. (pág. 164)

Liberalismo de la Guerra Fría: Combinación de políticas liberales moderadas que preservaron programas del estado benefactor del Nuevo Trato y del anticomunismo directo, que vilificó a la Unión Soviética en el extranjero y al radicalismo en casa. Fueron adoptadas por el Partido Demócrata después de la Segunda Guerra Mundial. (pág. 787)

intercambio colombino: Intercambio mundial masivo de seres vivos — como personas, animales, plantas y enfermedades — entre los hemisferios oriental y occidental que comenzó después de los viajes de Colón. (pág. 43)

comités de correspondencia: Red de comunicaciones establecida entre las ciudades en las colonias y entre las asambleas coloniales entre 1772 y 1773 para proporcionar la rápida difusión de noticias sobre acontecimientos políticos importantes. (pág. 163)

sistema de mancomunidad: Sistema republicano de economía política creado por los gobiernos estatales para 1820, mediante el cual los estados canalizaban subsidios hacia empresas privadas cuyos proyectos mejorarían el bienestar general. (pág. 254)

Community Services Organization (CSO): A Latino civil rights group founded in Los Angeles in 1948 that trained many Latino politicians and community activists, including Cesar Chavez and Dolores Huerta. (p. 842)

competency: The ability of a family to keep a household solvent and independent and to pass that ability on to the next generation. (p. 113)

Compromise of 1850: Laws passed in 1850 that were meant to resolve the dispute over the status of slavery in the territories. Key elements included the admission of California as a free state and a new Fugitive Slave Act. (p. 391)

Comstock Act: An 1873 law that prohibited circulation of "obscene literature," defined as including most information on sex, reproduction, and birth control. (p. 565)

Comstock Lode: A vein of silver ore discovered in Nevada in 1859, leading to one of the West's most important mining booms. The lode was so rich that a Confederate expedition tried unsuccessfully to capture it during the Civil War; its output significantly altered the ratio of silver in circulation, leading to changes in monetary policy. (p. 489)

Congress of Racial Equality (CORE): Civil rights organization founded in 1942 in Chicago by James Farmer and other members of the Fellowship of Reconciliation (FOR) that espoused nonviolent direct action. (p. 840)

constitutional monarchy: A monarchy limited in its rule by a constitution — in England's case, the Declaration of Rights (1689), which formally limited the power of its king. (p. 85)

consumer credit: Forms of borrowing, such as auto loans and installment plans, that flourished in the 1920s and worsened the crash that led to the Great Depression. (p. 682)

consumer revolution: An increase in consumption in English manufactures in Britain and the colonies that was fueled by the Industrial Revolution. The consumer revolution raised living standards but landed many colonists in debt. (p. 136)

containment: The basic U.S. policy of the Cold War, which sought to contain communism within its existing geographic boundaries. Initially, containment focused on the Soviet Union and Eastern Europe, but in the 1950s it came to include China, Korea, and the postcolonial world. (p. 778)

Continental Association: An association established in 1774 by the First Continental Congress to enforce a boycott of British goods. (p. 168)

Continental Congress: September 1774 gathering of delegates in Philadelphia to discuss the crisis caused by the Coercive Acts. The Congress issued a declaration of rights and agreed to a boycott of trade with Britain. (p. 164)

contrabands: Slaves who fled plantations and sought protection behind Union lines during the Civil War. (p. 423)

Organización de Servicios Comunitarios (CSO): Grupo latino de derechos civiles fundado en Los Ángeles en 1948 que entrenó a muchos políticos y activistas comunitarios latinos, entre ellos, César Chávez y Dolores Huerta. (pág. 842)

competencia: Capacidad de una familia de mantener un hogar en estado de solvencia e independencia y transmitir esa capacidad a la próxima generación. (pág. 113)

Compromiso de 1850: Leyes aprobadas en 1850 que resolverían la disputa sobre el estado de la esclavitud en los territorios. Algunos elementos claves fueron: la admisión de California como estado libre y una nueva Ley de Esclavos Fugitivos. (pág. 391)

Ley Comstock: Ley de 1873 que prohibió la circulación de "literatura obscena", definida como aquella que incluía información sobre sexo, reproducción y anticoncepción. (pág. 565)

Comstock Lode: Veta de mineral de plata, descubierta en Nevada en 1859, que condujo a uno de los auges mineros más importantes del Oeste. La veta tenía tal riqueza que una expedición confederada intentó tomarla sin éxito durante la Guerra Civil; su producción alteró significativamente la proporción de la plata en circulación, lo que generó cambios en la política monetaria. (pág. 489)

Congreso para la Igualdad Racial (CORE): Organización de derechos civiles fundada en Chicago en 1942 por James Farmer y otros miembros de la Fellowship of Reconciliation (FOR) que defendió la acción directa no violenta. (pág. 840)

monarquía constitucional: Monarquía limitada en su gobierno por una constitución, que en el caso de Inglaterra fue la Declaración de Derechos (1689), que limitaba formalmente el poder del rey. (pág. 85)

crédito al consumo: Nuevas formas de préstamo, como el préstamo automotriz y planes de financiación, que florecieron en la década de 1920, y empeoraron la caída que llevó a la Gran Depresión. (pág. 682)

revolución del consumidor: Aumento en el consumo de manufacturas inglesas en Gran Bretaña y las colonias británicas impulsado por la Revolución Industrial. Aunque la revolución del consumidor elevó los niveles de vida, causó que muchos consumidores, y a las colonias en conjunto, cayeran en deuda. (pág. 136)

contención: Política básica de Estados Unidos durante la Guerra Fría que buscó contener al comunismo dentro de sus fronteras geográficas existentes. En un principio, la contención se enfocó en la Unión Soviética y Europa del Este, pero en la década de 1950 llegó a incluir a China, Corea del Norte y otras partes del mundo en vías del desarrollo. (pág. 778)

Asociación Continental: Asociación establecida en 1774 por el Primer Congreso Continental con el fin hacer cumplir un boicot a los productos británicos. (pág. 168)

Congreso Continental: Reunión de delegados coloniales en Filadelfia que tuvo lugar en septiembre de 1774 para discutir la crisis precipitada por las Leyes Coactivas. El Congreso generó una declaración de derechos y un acuerdo para imponer un boicot limitado al comercio con Gran Bretaña. (pág. 164)

"contrabando": Esclavos que huyeron de las plantaciones y buscaron protección detrás de las líneas de la Unión durante la Guerra Civil. (pág. 423)

Contract with America: Initiatives by Representative Newt Gingrich of Georgia for significant tax cuts, reductions in welfare programs, anticrime measures, and cutbacks in federal regulations. (p. 986)

Contrato con América; Iniciativas del congresista, Newt Gingrich, de Georgia, a favor de significativas reducciones de impuestos, reducciones en programas de asistencia social, medidas anti-crimen y recortes en regulaciones federales. (pág. 986)

convict leasing: Notorious system, begun during Reconstruction, whereby southern state officials allowed private companies to hire out prisoners to labor under brutal conditions in mines and other industries. (p. 466)

arrendamiento de convictos: Sistema notorio que tuvo sus orígenes durante la Reconstrucción, mediante el cual los funcionarios estatales del sur permitieron a las empresas privadas contratar a prisioneros para que hicieran trabajos en condiciones brutales en minas y otras industrias. (pág. 466)

corrupt bargain: When Speaker of the House Henry Clay used his influence to select John Quincy Adams as president in 1824, and then Adams appointed Clay secretary of state, Andrew Jackson's supporters called it a corrupt bargain. (p. 292)

negociación corrupta: Los partidarios de Andrew Jackson emplearon este término cuando el presidente de la Cámara de Representantes, Henry Clay, usó su influencia para elegir a John Quincy Adams como presidente en 1824, que posteriormente designó a Clay como secretario de estado. (pág. 292)

cotton complex: The economic system that developed in the first half of the nineteenth century binding together southern cotton production with northern clothmaking, shipping, and capital. (p. 258)

complejo algodonero: Sistema económico que se desarrolló en la primera mitad del siglo XIX y que unía la producción de algodón del sur con la fabricación de telas, el transporte marítimo y el capital del norte. (pág. 258)

Counter-Reformation: A reaction in the Catholic Church triggered by the Reformation that sought change from within and created new monastic and missionary orders, including the Jesuits, who saw themselves as soldiers of Christ. (p. 24)

Contrarreforma: Reacción en la Iglesia Católica, desencadenada por la Reforma, que buscaba el cambio desde dentro y creó nuevas órdenes monásticas y misioneras, incluida la orden de los jesuitas (fundada en 1540), que se veían a sí mismos como soldados de Cristo. (pág. 24)

Covenant Chain: The alliance of the Iroquois, first with the colony of New York, then with the British Empire and its other colonies. The Covenant Chain became a model for relations between the British Empire and other Native American peoples. (p. 87)

Cadena del Pacto: Alianza de los iroqueses, primero con la colonia de Nueva York y luego con el Imperio Británico y sus demás colonias. La Cadena del Pacto se convirtió en un modelo para las relaciones entre el Imperio Británico y otros pueblos nativos americanos. (pág. 87)

covenant of grace: The Christian idea that God's elect are granted salvation as a pure gift of grace. This doctrine holds that nothing people do can erase their sins or earn them a place in heaven. (p. 63)

pacto de gracia: Idea cristiana de que los elegidos de Dios reciben la salvación como un regalo puro de la gracia. Esta doctrina sostiene que las personas no pueden hacer nada para borrar sus pecados o ganarse un lugar en el cielo. (pág. 63)

covenant of works: The Christian idea that God's elect must do good works in their earthly lives to earn their salvation. (p. 63)

pacto de obras: Idea cristiana de que los elegidos de Dios deben hacer buenas obras en sus vidas terrenales para ganar su salvación. (pág. 63)

coverture: A principle in English law that placed wives under the protection and authority of their husbands, so that they did not have independent legal standing. (p. 116)

coverture: Principio en la ley inglesa que coloca a las esposas bajo la protección y la autoridad de sus maridos, de modo que carecen de una posición legal independiente. (pág. 116)

Crédit Mobilier: A sham corporation set up by shareholders in the Union Pacific Railroad to secure government grants at an enormous profit. Organizers of the scheme protected it from investigation by providing gifts of its stock to powerful members of Congress. (p. 471)

Crédit Mobilier: Corporación fraudulenta creada por los accionistas de Union Pacific Railroad para obtener subvenciones del gobierno con enormes ganancias. Los organizadores del plan lo protegieron de la investigación al proporcionar obsequios de sus acciones a poderosos miembros del Congreso. (pág. 471)

crop-lien laws: Nineteenth-century laws that enforced lenders' rights to a portion of harvested crops as repayment for debts. Once they owed money to a country store, sharecroppers were trapped in debt and became targets for unfair pricing. (p. 462)

leyes de gravámenes sobre cultivos: Leyes del siglo XIX que otorgaban derechos a los prestamistas a una parte de los cultivos cosechados como pago de deudas. Cuando les debían dinero a tiendas de la zona, los aparceros quedaban atrapados en deudas y solían ser blanco de tarifas desleales. (pág. 462)

Crusades: A series of wars undertaken by Christian armies between A.D. 1096 and 1291 to reverse the Muslim advance in Europe and win back the holy lands where Christ had lived. (p. 22)

Cruzadas: Serie de guerras emprendidas por los ejércitos cristianos entre los años 1096 y 1291d.C. para revertir el avance de los musulmanes en Europa y recuperar las tierras santas donde vivió Cristo. (pág. 22)

Cuban missile crisis: The 1962 nuclear standoff between the Soviet Union and the United States when the Soviets attempted to deploy nuclear missiles in Cuba. (p. 801)

Crisis de los misiles en Cuba: Conflicto nuclear entre la Unión Soviética y Estados Unidos causado por el intento de los soviéticos de enviar misiles nucleares a Cuba en 1962. (pág. 801)

culture war: A term derived from a 1992 speech by the Republican politician Patrick Buchanan to describe a political struggle, dating to the 1920s, between religious traditionalists and secular liberals. In the 1990s, social issues such as abortion rights and the rights of lesbians and gay men divided these groups. (p. 978)

currency tax: A hidden tax on farmers and artisans who accepted Continental bills in payment for supplies and on the thousands of soldiers who took them as pay. Rampant inflation caused Continental currency to lose much of its value during the war, implicitly taxing those who accepted it as payment. (p. 189)

David Walker's *Appeal*: The radical 1829 pamphlet by free African American David Walker in which he protested slavery and racial oppression, called for solidarity among people of African descent, and warned that slaves would revolt if the cause of freedom was not served. (p. 334)

Dawes Severalty Act: The 1887 law that gave Native Americans severalty (individual ownership of land) by dividing reservations into homesteads. The law was a disaster for Native peoples, resulting over several decades in the loss of 66 percent of lands held by Indians at the time of the law's passage. (p. 504)

D-Day: June 6, 1944, the date of the Allied invasion of northern France. The largest amphibious assault in world history, the invasion opened a second front against the Germans and moved the Allies closer to victory in Europe. (p. 759)

Declaration of Independence: A document containing philosophical principles and a list of grievances that declared separation from Britain. Adopted by the Second Continental Congress on July 4, 1776, it ended a period of intense debate with moderates still hoping to reconcile with Britain. (p. 173)

Declaratory Act of 1766: Law asserting Parliament's unassailable right to legislate for its British colonies "in all cases whatsoever." (p. 156)

Defense of Marriage Act: A law enacted by Congress in 1998 that allowed states to refuse to recognize gay marriages or civil unions formed in other jurisdictions. The Supreme Court ruled that DOMA was unconstitutional in 2013. (p. 985)

deindustrialization: The dismantling of manufacturing in the decades after the 1960s, reversing the process of industrialization that characterized the American economy between the 1870s and the 1940s. (p. 912)

deism: The Enlightenment-influenced belief that God created the universe and then left it to run according to natural laws. Deists relied on reason rather than scripture to interpret God's will. (p. 124)

demographic transition: The sharp decline in birthrate in the United States beginning in the 1790s that was caused by changes in cultural behavior, including the use of birth control. The migration of thousands of young men to the trans-Appalachian west was also a factor in this decline. (p. 287)

guerra cultural: Término usado por Patrick Buchanan en 1992 para describir la larga lucha política, que comenzó en la década de 1920, entre tradicionalistas religiosos y liberales seculares. En la década de 1990, los grupos estaban divididos por temas como derechos de aborto, y los derechos de gays y lesbianas. (pág. 978)

impuesto a las divisas: impuesto oculto sobre los granjeros y artesanos que aceptaron billetes continentales como pago por suministros y sobre los miles de soldados que los aceptaron como pago. Debido a la inflación desenfrenada, la moneda continental perdió gran parte de su valor durante la guerra; de ahí el impuesto implícito sobre quienes lo aceptaron como pago. (pág. 189)

***Apelación* de David Walker:** Folleto radical escrito en 1829 por el afroamericano libre David Walker en el que protestaba contra la esclavitud y la opresión racial, proclamaba la solidaridad entre afrodescendientes y advertía que los esclavos se rebelarían si no se atendía la causa de la libertad. (pág. 334)

Ley de Dawes Severalty: Ley de 1887 que otorgó separabilidad (propiedad individual de tierras) a los nativos americanos al dividir las reservas en fincas. La ley fue un desastre para los pueblos nativos, y resultó tras varias décadas en la pérdida del 66 por ciento de las tierras que ocupaban los indios en el momento de la aprobación de la ley. (pág. 504)

Día D: 6 de junio de 1944, fecha de la invasión de los Aliados en el norte de Francia. El Día D fue el ataque anfibio más grande en la historia del mundo. La invasión abrió un segundo frente contra los alemanes y acercó a los Aliados a la victoria en Europa. (pág. 759)

Declaración de la independencia: Documento que contiene principios filosóficos y una lista de agravios con los cuales se declaró la separación de Gran Bretaña. Adoptada por el Segundo Congreso Continental el 4 de julio de 1776, puso fin a un intenso debate con los moderados que todavía esperaban reconciliarse con Gran Bretaña. (pág. 173)

Ley Declaratoria de 1766: Ley emitida por el Parlamento para hacer valer el derecho inexpugnable del Parlamento de legislar para sus colonias británicas "en todos los casos". (pág. 156)

Ley de Defensa del Matrimonio (DOMA): Ley promulgada por el Congreso en 1998 que permitió a los estados el derecho a negarse a reconocer los matrimonios o uniones civiles gays formadas en otras jurisdicciones. En 2013, la Corte Suprema sentenció a DOMA como anticonstitucional. (pág. 985)

desindustrialización: Desmantelamiento de la manufactura en las décadas posteriores a 1960, que representó un revés en el proceso de industrialización que dominó a la economía americana desde la década de 1870 hasta después de 1940. (pág. 912)

deísmo: Creencia influida por la Iluminación en la cual el Dios cristiano creó el universo y luego lo dejó funcionar de acuerdo con las leyes naturales. Los deístas interpretaban la voluntad de Dios desde la razón en lugar de las escrituras. (pág. 124)

transición demográfica: Fuerte declive de la tasa de natalidad en los Estados Unidos a partir de la década de 1790 que fue causada por cambios en el comportamiento cultural, incluido el uso de métodos anticonceptivos. La migración de miles de hombres jóvenes al oeste de los Apalaches también fue un factor en este declive. (pág. 287)

deregulation: The limiting of regulation by federal agencies. In the 1970s, the lifting of price controls and other government mandates on airline, trucking, and railroad industries stimulated competition and cut prices, but also drove firms out of business and hurt unionized workers. (p. 919)

deskilling: A system in which unskilled workers complete discrete, small-scale tasks to build a standardized item, rather than crafting an entire product. This process accelerated in the late nineteenth century as mechanized manufacturing expanded. With deskilling, employers found they could pay workers less and replace them more easily. (p. 523)

détente: The easing of conflict between the United States and the Soviet Union during the Nixon administration, which was achieved by focusing on issues of common concern, such as arms control and trade. (p. 898)

dollar diplomacy: The use of American foreign policy to stabilize the economies of foreign nations, especially in the Caribbean and South America, in order to benefit American commercial interests, between World War I and the early 1930s. (p. 679)

domesticity: A middle-class ideal of "separate spheres" that celebrated women's special mission as homemakers, wives, and mothers who exercised a Christian influence on their families and communities; it excluded women from professional careers, politics, and civic life. (p. 339)

Dominion of New England: A royal province created by King James II in 1686 that would have absorbed Connecticut, Rhode Island, Massachusetts Bay, Plymouth, New York, and New Jersey into a single colony and eliminated their chartered rights. James's plan was canceled by the Glorious Revolution, which removed him from the throne. (p. 84)

domino theory: President Eisenhower's theory of containment, which warned that the fall of a non-Communist government to communism in Southeast Asia would trigger the spread of communism to neighboring countries. (p. 797)

"Double V" campaign: An African American civil rights campaign during World War II that called for victory over Nazism abroad and over discrimination in jobs, housing, and voting at home. (p. 748)

draft (conscription): The system for selecting individuals for conscription, or compulsory military service, first implemented during the Civil War. (p. 428)

draft riots: Violent protests against military conscription that occurred in the North, most dramatically in New York City; led by working-class men who could not buy exemption from the draft. (p. 429)

***Dred Scott* decision:** The 1857 Supreme Court decision that ruled the Missouri Compromise unconstitutional. The Court ruled against slave Dred Scott, who claimed that travels with his master into free states and territories made him and his family free. The decision also denied the federal government the right to exclude slavery from the territories and declared that African Americans were not citizens. (p. 402)

Dunmore's War: A 1774 war led by Virginia's royal governor, the Earl of Dunmore, against the Ohio Shawnees, who claimed

desregulación: La limitación de la regulación de agencias federales. La desregulación de los precios en las industrias camioneras, de aerolíneas y ferroviarias en la década de 1970 esimuló la competencia pero también causó el cierre de muchos negocios y afectó a trabajadores sindicalizados. (pág. 919)

reducción de la especialización: La eliminación del trabajo calificado bajo un nuevo sistema de manufactura mecanizada, donde los trabajadores se dedican a tareas discretas de menor escala en lugar de fabricar un producto entero. Con este proceso, los empleadores encontraron que podían reducir los salarios de los trabajadores y reemplazarlos con mayor facilidad. (pág. 523)

détente: La relajación del conflicto entre Estados Unidos y la Unión Soviética durante la administración de Nixon, que fue lograda mediante un enfoque sobre temas que preocupaban a ambos países, como el control de armas y el comercio. (pág. 898)

diplomacia del dólar: El uso de la política exterior de los Estados Unidos entre la Primera Guerra Mundial y el principio de la década de 1930 para estabilizar las economías de otros países, especialmente en el Caribe y Sudamérica, con el fin de beneficiar intereses comerciales americanos. (pág. 679)

domesticidad: Ideal de clase media de "esferas separadas" que celebraba la misión especial de las mujeres como amas de casa, esposas y madres que ejercían una influencia cristiana en sus familias y comunidades; excluía a las mujeres de las carreras profesionales, la política y la vida cívica. (pág. 339)

Dominio de Nueva Inglaterra: Provincia real creada por Jacobo II de Inglaterra en 1686 que habría absorbido Connecticut, Rhode Island, la bahía de Massachusetts, Plymouth, Nueva York y Nueva Jersey en una colonia grande y única, y habría eliminado sus asambleas y otros derechos constituidos. El plan de Jacobo II fue cancelado por la Revolución Gloriosa en 1688, que lo derrocó. (pág. 84)

teoría dominó: Teoría de contención del presidente Eisenhower, que advertía que la caída de un gobierno no comunista del sureste de Asia ante el comunismo provocaría el esparcimiento del comunismo a sus países aledaños. (pág. 797)

Campaña de Doble V: Campaña afroamericana de derechos civiles durante la Segunda Guerra Mundial que proclamaba la victoria sobre el nazismo en el extranjero y sobre la discriminación en el trabajo, la vivienda y la votación en el país. (pág. 748)

draft (reclutamiento): Sistema que selecciona individuos para el servicio militar obligatorio o conscripto, implementado por primera vez durante la Guerra Civil. (pág. 428)

draft riots: (disturbios): Protestas violentas contra el reclutamiento militar que ocurrieron en el norte, con mayor notoriedad en la ciudad de Nueva York; dirigidas por hombres de la clase trabajadora que no podían comprar la exención al reclutamiento. (pág. 429)

decisión del caso *Dred Scott*: Decisión de la Corte Suprema de 1857 que dictaminó la inconstitucionalidad del Compromiso de Misuri. La Corte falló en contra del esclavo Dred Scott, que afirmó que viajar con su amo hacia estados y territorios libres lo liberaba a él y a su familia. La decisión también denegó al gobierno federal el derecho a excluir la esclavitud de los territorios y declaró que los afroamericanos no eran ciudadanos. (pág. 402)

Guerra de Dunmore: Guerra dirigida por el Conde de Dunmore, gobernador real de Virginia, que tuvo lugar en 1774 contra los

Kentucky as a hunting ground. The Shawnees were defeated and Virginians claimed Kentucky as their own. (p. 170)

dust bowl: An area including the semiarid states of Oklahoma, Texas, New Mexico, Colorado, Arkansas, and Kansas that experienced a severe drought and large dust storms from 1930 to 1939. (p. 729)

Earth Day: An annual event honoring the environment that was first celebrated on April 22, 1970, when 20 million citizens gathered in communities across the country to express their support for a cleaner, healthier planet. (p. 910)

eastern woodlands: A culture area of Native Americans that extended from the Atlantic Ocean westward to the Great Plains, and from the Great Lakes to the Gulf of Mexico. The eastern woodlands could be subdivided into the southeastern and northeastern woodlands. Eastern woodlands peoples were generally semisedentary, with agriculture based on maize, beans, and squash. Most, but not all, were chiefdoms. (p. 12)

Economic Opportunity Act: A 1964 law that was the centerpiece of President Lyndon Johnson's War on Poverty. It included programs such as Head Start (free nursery school), Job Corps (job training for young people), and regional development programs to spur economic growth. (p. 874)

Economic Recovery Tax Act (ERTA): Legislation introduced by President Reagan and passed by Congress in 1981 that authorized the largest reduction in taxes in the nation's history at that time. (p. 949)

Eighteenth Amendment: The ban on the manufacture and sale of alcohol that went into effect in January 1920. Also called "prohibition," the amendment was repealed in 1933. (p. 690)

Eisenhower Doctrine: President Eisenhower's 1957 declaration that the United States would actively combat communism in the Middle East. (p. 798)

Emancipation Proclamation: President Abraham Lincoln's proclamation issued on January 1, 1863, that legally abolished slavery in all states that remained out of the Union. While the Emancipation Proclamation did not immediately free a single slave, it signaled an end to the institution of slavery. (p. 425)

Embargo Act of 1807: An act of Congress that prohibited U.S. ships from traveling to foreign ports in an attempt to deter Britain and France from halting U.S. ships at sea. The embargo caused grave hardships for Americans engaged in overseas commerce. (p. 232)

encomienda: A grant of Indian labor in Spanish America given in the sixteenth century by the Spanish kings to prominent men. *Encomenderos* extracted tribute from these Indians in exchange for granting them protection and Christian instruction. (p. 43)

energy crisis: A period of fuel shortages in the United States after the Arab states in the Organization of Petroleum Exporting

shawnees de Ohio, que reclamaban su derecho histórico sobre Kentucky como campo de caza. Los shawnees fueron derrotados y Dunmore y sus fuerzas de las milicias reclamaron Kentucky como propio. (pág. 170)

***dust bowl* (cuenco de polvo):** Zona semiárida de los estados de Oklahoma, Texas, Nuevo México, Colorado, Arkansas y Kansas que vivió una sequía severa y sufrió grandes tormentas de polvo entre 1930 y 1941. (pág. 729)

bosques orientales: Área cultural de nativos americanos que se extendía desde el océano Atlántico hacia el oeste hasta las Grandes Llanuras, y desde los Grandes Lagos hasta el golfo de México. Los bosques orientales podrían subdividirse en los bosques del sureste y el noreste. Los pueblos de los bosques orientales generalmente eran semisedentarios, con una agricultura basada en maíz, frijoles y calabaza. La mayoría, aunque no todos, eran jefaturas. (pág. 12)

Día de la Tierra: Evento anual en honor del medio ambiente, celebrado por primera vez el 22 de abril de 1970, cuando 20 millones de ciudadanos se reunieron en comunidades de todo el país para expresar su apoyo hacia un planeta más limpio y sano. (pág. 910)

Ley de Oportunidades Económicas: Ley de 1964 que fue la pieza central de la Guerra Contra la Pobreza del presidente Lyndon Johnson. Incluyó una serie de programas, entre ellos el programa Head Start (preescolar gratuito), Job Corps (capacitación laboral para jóvenes) y programas de desarrollo regional para estimular el crecimiento económico. (pág. 874)

Ley del Impuesto para la Recuperación Económica (ERTA): Legislación introducida por el presidente Reagan y aprobada por el Congreso en 1981 que autorizó la mayor reducción de impuestos en la historia del país. (pág. 949)

Decimoctava Enmienda: La prohibición de la manufactura y venta de alcohol que entró en vigencia en enero de 1920. La enmienda, también conocida como la "prohibición", fue revocada en 1933. (pág. 690)

Doctrina Eisenhower: Declaración de 1957 del presidente Eisenhower, que estableció que Estados Unidos combatiría el comunismo en el Medio Oriente. (pág. 798)

Proclamación de Emancipación: Proclamación del presidente Abraham Lincoln emitida el 1 de enero de 1863 que abolió legalmente la esclavitud en todos los estados que permanecieron fuera de la Unión. Si bien en un principio la Proclamación de Emancipación no liberó a un solo esclavo, señaló el fin de la esclavitud como institución. (pág. 425)

Ley de Embargo de 1807: Ley del Congreso que, en un intento de disuadir a Gran Bretaña y Francia de detener los barcos estadounidenses en altamar, prohibió a los barcos estadounidenses viajar a puertos extranjeros. El embargo causó graves dificultades para los estadounidenses que participaban en el comercio exterior. (pág. 232)

encomienda: Concesión de mano de obra indígena en Hispanoamérica otorgada en el siglo XVI por los reyes españoles a hombres prominentes. Los encomenderos extrajeron tributos de estos indios a cambio de otorgarles protección e instrucción cristiana. (pág. 43)

crisis energética: Periodo de escasez en Estados Unidos como consecuencia del embargo petrolero declarado en octubre de 1973

Countries (OPEC) declared an oil embargo in October 1973. (p. 907)

Enforcement Laws: Acts passed in Congress in 1870 and signed by President U. S. Grant that were designed to protect freedmen's rights under the Fourteenth and Fifteenth Amendments. Authorizing federal prosecutions, military intervention, and martial law to suppress terrorist activity, the Enforcement Laws largely succeeded in shutting down Klan activities. (p. 474)

English common law: The centuries-old body of legal rules and procedures that protected the lives and property of the British monarch's subjects. (p. 153)

Enlightenment: An eighteenth-century philosophical movement that emphasized the use of reason to reevaluate previously accepted doctrines and traditions and the power of reason to understand and shape the world. (p. 122)

Environmental Protection Agency (EPA): Federal agency created by Congress and President Nixon in 1970 to enforce environmental laws, conduct environmental research, and reduce human health and environmental risks from pollutants. (p. 910)

Equal Pay Act: Law passed in 1963 that established the principle of equal pay for equal work. Trade-union women were especially critical in pushing for, and winning, congressional passage of the law. (p. 877)

Equal Rights Amendment (ERA): Constitutional amendment passed by Congress in 1972 that would require equal treatment of men and women under federal and state law. Facing fierce opposition from the New Right and the Republican Party, the ERA was defeated as time ran out for state ratification in 1982. (p. 922)

Erie Canal: A 364-mile waterway connecting the Hudson River and Lake Erie. The Erie Canal brought prosperity to the entire Great Lakes region, and its benefits prompted civic and business leaders in Philadelphia and Baltimore to propose canals to link their cities to the Midwest. (p. 256)

Ethics in Government Act: Passed in the wake of the Watergate scandal, the 1978 act requires government officials to disclose their financial and employment history and limits the lobbying activities of former elected officials. (p. 917)

eugenics: An emerging "science" of human breeding in the late nineteenth century that argued that mentally deficient people should be prevented from reproducing. (p. 548)

Executive Order 8802: An order signed by President Roosevelt in 1941 that prohibited "discrimination in the employment of workers in defense industries or government because of race, creed, color, or national origin" and established the Fair Employment Practices Commission (FEPC). (p. 748)

Executive Order 9066: An order signed by President Roosevelt in 1942 that authorized the War Department to force Japanese Americans from their homes and hold them in relocation camps for the rest of the war. (p. 756)

por los países árabes de la Organización de Países Exportadores de Petróleo (OPEC). (pág. 907)

Leyes de aplicación: Leyes aprobadas por el Congreso en 1870 y ratificadas por el presidente U. S. Grant, que fueron diseñadas para proteger los derechos de los liberados bajo la Decimocuarta y Decimoquinta Enmienda. Las Leyes de aplicación lograron en gran medida poner fin a las actividades del Klan al autorizar los enjuiciamientos federales, la intervención militar y la ley marcial con el propósito de reprimir la actividad terrorista. (pág. 474)

Derecho consuetudinario inglés: Estructura jurídica centenaria de reglas y procedimientos legales que protegía la vida y la propiedad de los súbditos del monarca británico. (pág. 153)

Ilustración: Movimiento filosófico del siglo XVIII que enfatizó el uso de la razón para reevaluar doctrinas y tradiciones previamente aceptadas y el poder de la razón para comprender y dar forma al mundo. (pág. 122)

Agencia de Protección Ambiental (EPA): Agencia Federal creada por el Congreso y el presidente Nixon en 1970 para vigilar el cumplimiento de leyes ambientales, conducir estudios del medio ambiente y reducir los riesgos de los contaminantes para la salud humana y el medio ambiente. (pág. 910)

Ley de Igualdad de Salario: Ley aprobada en 1963 que estableció el principio de igualdad de pago por trabajos iguales. Las mujeres sindicalizadas tuvieron un papel particularmente importante en impulsar y conseguir la aprobación de la ley en el Congreso. (pág. 877)

Enmienda de Igualdad de Derechos (ERA): Enmienda constitucional aprobada por el Congreso en 1972, que exige por ley estatal y federal trato igual para los hombres y las mujeres. Ante la feroz oposición de la Nueva Derecha y el Partido Republicano, ERA fue derrotada sobre el tiempo límite para su ratificación en 1982. (pág. 922)

Canal de Erie: Canal de 364 millas que conecta el río Hudson y el lago Erie. El Canal de Erie trajo prosperidad a toda la región de los Grandes Lagos, y sus beneficios impulsaron a los líderes cívicos y empresariales de Filadelfia y Baltimore a proponer canales para unir sus ciudades con el medio oeste del país. (pág. 256)

Ley de Ética Gubernamental: Aprobada tras el escándalo de Watergate, esta ley de 1978 obligaría a los candidatos políticos a revelar sus contribuciones financieras y limitó las actividades de cabildeo de funcionarios que previamente habían ocupado cargos de elección pública. (pág. 917)

eugenesia: "Ciencia" de la reproducción humana que surgió a finales del siglo XIX y que argumentaba que se debía impedir la reproducción de personas con deficiencias mentales. (pág. 548)

Orden Ejecutiva 8802: Orden firmada por el presidente Roosevelt en 1941 para prohibir la "discriminación en el empleo de trabajadores en las industrias de defensa o gobierno por raza, creencia religiosa, color u origen nacional" y establecer la Fair Employment Practices Comission (Comisión para las Prácticas Laborales Justas, FEPC). (pág. 748)

Orden Ejecutiva 9066: Orden firmada por el presidente Roosevelt en 1942 que autorizó al Departamento de Guerra a obligar a los japoneses americanos de la Costa Oeste a abandonar sus hogares para ser enviados a campos de internamiento durante el resto de la guerra. (pág. 756)

Fair Deal: The domestic policy agenda announced by President Harry S. Truman in 1949, which included civil rights, health care, public housing, and education funding. Congress rejected most of it. (p. 788)

Fair Labor Standards Act: New Deal legislation passed in 1938 that outlawed child labor, standardized the forty-hour workweek, mandated overtime pay, and established a federal minimum wage. (p. 719)

family values: A political platform of conservative morality endorsed by the Religious Right in the 1980s, and subsequent decades, including support for the traditional nuclear family and opposition to homosexuality and abortion. (p. 963)

Farmers' Alliance: A rural movement founded in Texas during the depression of the 1870s that spread across the plains and the South. Advocating cooperative stores to circumvent middlemen, the Alliance also called for greater government aid to farmers and stricter regulation of railroads. (p. 539)

fascism: A system of government characterized by authoritarian rule, extreme nationalism, disdain for civil society, and a conviction that militarism and imperialism make great nations. Germany under Adolf Hitler and Italy under Benito Mussolini were fascist states. (p. 737)

Federal Housing Administration: An agency established by the Federal Housing Act of 1934 that refinanced home mortgages for mortgage holders facing possible foreclosure. (p. 713)

Federal Reserve Act: The central bank system of the United States, created in 1913. The Federal Reserve helps set the money supply level, thus influencing the rate of growth of the U.S. economy, and seeks to ensure the stability of the U.S. monetary system. (p. 631)

Federal Writers' Project: A New Deal program, part of the Works Progress Administration (WPA) that provided jobs for out-of-work writers, which included the collection of oral histories. (p. 731)

Federalist No. 10: An essay by James Madison in *The Federalist* (1787–1788) that challenged the view that republican governments only worked in small polities; it argued that a geographically expansive national government would better protect republican liberty. (p. 206)

Federalists: Supporters of the Constitution of 1787, which created a strong central government; their opponents, the Antifederalists, feared that a strong central government would corrupt the nation's newly won liberty. (p. 204)

Female Moral Reform Society: An organization led by middle-class Christian women who viewed prostitutes as victims of male lust and sought to expose their male customers while "rescuing" sex workers and encouraging them to pursue respectable trades. (p. 341)

feminism: The ideology that women should enter the public sphere not only to work on behalf of others, but also for their own equal rights and advancement. Feminists moved beyond

Trato Justo: Agenda de política doméstica anunciada por el presidente Harry S. Truman en 1949. La iniciativa de Truman incluyó derechos civiles, salud pública y reformas educativas, pero sólo fue parcialmente exitosa en el Congreso. (pág. 788)

Ley de Normas Laborales Justas: Fue una de las leyes principales del Nuevo Trato y prohibió el trabajo de menores, estableció el estándar de semana laboral de 40 horas (con pago obligatorio de horas extra) y estableció un salario mínimo nacional. (pág. 719)

valores de familia: Valores promovidos por la Derecha Religiosa que incluyen el apoyo a la familia nuclear tradicional y la oposición al matrimonio entre personas del mismo sexo y al aborto. (pág. 963)

Alianza de Granjeros: Movimiento rural fundado en Texas durante la depresión de la década de 1870 que se esparció por los estados de la planicie y el Sur. La Alianza de Granjeros abogaba por tiendas cooperativas e intercambios que eliminarían la necesidad de intermediarios y pedía más apoyos gubernamentales para las granjas y mayor regulación de los ferrocarriles. (pág. 539)

fascismo: Sistema autoritario de gobierno caracterizado por el régimen dictatorial, el nacionalismo extremo, el desprecio por la sociedad civil y la convicción de que el imperialismo y la guerra son los medios para conseguir la grandeza nacional. Estados Unidos luchó contra el fascismo cuando enfrentó a la Alemania Nazi de Adolf Hitler y a la Italia de Benito Mussolini durante la Segunda Guerra Mundial. (pág. 737)

Administración Federal de la Vivienda: Agencia creada por la Ley de Vivienda Federal de 1934 que refinanció hipotecas de deudores hipotecarios que enfrentaban una posible ejecución hipotecaria. (pág. 713)

Ley de la Reserva Federal: Sistema bancario central de los Estados Unidos creado en 1913. La reserva federal ayuda a establecer el nivel de dinero en circulación y, por lo tanto, influye sobre la tasa de crecimiento de la economía de Estados Unidos y busca asegurar la estabilidad del sistema monetario de Estados Unidos. (pág. 631)

Federal Writers' Project: Programa del Nuevo Trato que, como parte de la Administración de Obras Públicas (WAP), dio trabajo a escritores desempleados, que incluyó la recolección de historias orales. (pág. 731)

Federalista No. 10: Ensayo de James Madison en The Federalist (1787–1788) que puso en tela de juico la opinión de que los gobiernos republicanos sólo trabajaban en pequeñas entidades políticas; argumentó que un gobierno nacional geográficamente expansivo protegería mejor la libertad republicana. (pág. 206)

Federalistas: Partidarios de la Constitución de 1787, que creó un gobierno central fuerte; sus oponentes, los antifederalistas, temían que un gobierno central fuerte corrompiera la recién obtenida libertad de la nación. (pág. 204)

Sociedad Reformista Femenina: Organización dirigida por cristianas de clase media, quienes veían a las prostitutas como víctimas de la lujuria machista y buscaban poner en evidencia a sus victimarios mientras "rescataban" a las trabajadoras sexuales y las alentaban a buscar profesiones respetables. (pág. 341)

feminismo: Ideología bajo la cual las mujeres deben entrar a la esfera pública no sólo para trabajar a nombre de otros, sino también por la igualdad de sus derechos y su desarrollo personal.

advocacy of women's voting rights to seek greater autonomy in professional careers, property rights, and personal relationships. (p. 572)

Fetterman massacre: A massacre in December 1866 in which 1,500 Sioux warriors lured Captain William Fetterman and 80 soldiers from a Wyoming fort and attacked them. With the Fetterman massacre the Sioux succeeded in closing the Bozeman Trail, the main route into Montana. (p. 499)

Fifteenth Amendment: Constitutional amendment ratified in 1870 that forbade states to deny citizens the right to vote on grounds of race, color, or "previous condition of servitude." (p. 457)

"Fifty-four forty or fight!": Democratic candidate Governor James K. Polk's slogan in the election of 1844 calling for American sovereignty over the entire Oregon Country, which stretched from California to Russian-occupied Alaska and at the time was shared with Great Britain. (p. 368)

filibustering: Private paramilitary campaigns, mounted particularly by southern proslavery advocates in the 1850s, to seize additional territory in the Caribbean or Latin America in order to establish control by U.S.-born leaders, with an expectation of eventual annexation by the United States. (p. 394)

fireside chats: A series of informal radio addresses Franklin Roosevelt made to the nation between 1933 and 1944 in which he explained New Deal initiatives and, later in his presidency, his wartime policies. (p. 708)

flapper: A young woman of the 1920s who defied conventional standards of conduct by wearing knee-length skirts and bold makeup, freely spending the money she earned on the latest fashions, dancing to jazz, and flaunting her liberated lifestyle. (p. 682)

Foreign Intelligence Surveillance Act: A law passed in 1978 which prohibited the wiretapping of foreign nationals on U.S. soil without a warrant. (p. 917)

Foreign Miner's Tax: A discriminatory tax, adopted in 1850 in California Territory, that forced Chinese and Latin American immigrant miners to pay high taxes for the right to prospect for gold. The tax effectively drove these miners from the goldfields. (p. 387)

Four Freedoms: Basic human rights identified by President Franklin D. Roosevelt to justify support for Britain in World War II: freedom of speech, freedom of religion, freedom from want, and freedom from fear. (p. 741)

Fourteen Points: Principles for a new world order proposed in 1919 by President Woodrow Wilson as a basis for peace negotiations at Versailles. Among them were open diplomacy, freedom of the seas, free trade, territorial integrity, arms reduction, national self-determination, and creation of the League of Nations. (p. 664)

Las feministas fueron más allá de buscar el derecho femenino al voto para buscar mayor autonomía en sus carreras profesionales, derechos de propiedad y relaciones personales. (pág. 572)

Masacre de Fetterman: Masacre que tuvo lugar en diciembre de 1866 en la cual 1500 guerreros siux hicieron salir al Capitán William Fetterman y 80 soldados de un fuerte de Wyoming y los atacaron. Con la masacre de Fetterman, los siux lograron cerrar el sendero Bozeman, que era la ruta principal hacia Montana. (pág. 499)

Decimoquinta Enmienda: Enmienda constitucional ratificada en 1869 que prohibió a los estados negar a los ciudadanos el derecho de voto por raza, color o "condición previa de servidumbre". (pág. 457)

"Fifty-four forty or fight!" ("¡Cincuenticuatro cuarenta o lucha!"): Lema del gobernador James K. Polk, candidato demócrata en las elecciones de 1844, que pedía la soberanía americana sobre todo el Territorio de Oregón, es decir, desde California hasta la Alaska ocupada por Rusia, que en ese momento se compartía con Gran Bretaña. (pág. 368)

filibusterismo: Campañas paramilitares privadas, impulsadas especialmente por los defensores de la esclavitud sureña en la década de 1850, para apoderarse de territorios adicionales en el Caribe o América Latina con el propósito de controlar a los líderes nacidos en EE. UU., con la expectativa de una futura anexión por parte de los Estados Unidos. (pág. 394)

cantos de fuego (fireside chats): Serie de discursos informales pronunciados vía radio por Franklin Roosevelt explicando al país las iniciativas del Nuevo Trato y posteriormente, sus políticas para los tiempos de guerra. (pág. 708)

chica a la moda (flapper): Mujeres jóvenes de la década de 1920 que desafiaron los estándares convencionales de conducta usando faldas cortas y maquillaje, gastando libremente el dinero ganado de su trabajo en la última moda, bailando jazz y haciendo alarde de su estilo de vida liberado. (pág. 682)

Ley de Vigilancia de la Inteligencia Extranjera: Ley sancionada en 1978 que prohibía espiar telefónicamente a los ciudadanos extranjeros en suelo estadounidense sin una orden judicial. (pág. 917)

Impuesto al Minero Extranjero: Impuesto discriminatorio adoptado en 1850 en el Territorio de California, que obligó a los mineros inmigrantes chinos y latinoamericanos a pagar impuestos elevados por el derecho a buscar oro. El impuesto efectivamente expulsó a estos mineros de los yacimientos de oro. (pág. 387)

Cuatro Libertades: De acuerdo con el presidente Franklin D. Roosevelt, los derechos humanos fundamentales son: libertad de expresión, libertad de culto, libertad de vivir sin penuria y libertad de vivir sin miedo. El presidente usó estas ideas de libertad para justificar el apoyo a Inglaterra durante la Segunda Guerra Mundial, que a su vez involucró a Estados Unidos en la guerra. (pág. 741)

Catorce Puntos: Principios para un nuevo orden mundial propuestos en 1919 por el presidente Woodrow Wilson como la base de las negociaciones para la paz en Versalles. Entre los Catorce Puntos estaba la diplomacia abierta, la libertad de los mares, el comercio libre, la integridad territorial, la reducción de armas, la auto-determinación de los pueblos y la creación de la Liga de las Naciones. (pág. 664)

Fourteenth Amendment: Constitutional amendment ratified in 1868 that made all native-born or naturalized persons U.S. citizens and prohibited states from abridging the rights of national citizens, thus giving primacy to national rather than state citizenship. (p. 455)

Decimocuarta Enmienda: Enmienda constitucional ratificada en 1868 que convertía a todas las personas naturalizadas o nacidas en Estados Unidos en ciudadanos americanos y prohibía a los estados restringir los derechos de los ciudadanos nacionales, otorgando así primacía a la ciudadanía nacional en lugar de la estatal. (pág. 455)

franchise: The right to vote. Between 1820 and 1860, most states revised their constitutions to extend the vote to all adult white males. Black adult men gained the right to vote with the passage of the Fourteenth Amendment. The Nineteenth Amendment granted adult women the right to vote. (p. 284)

sufragio: Derecho a votar. Entre 1820 y 1860, la mayoría de los estados revisaron sus constituciones para extender el voto a todos los hombres blancos adultos. Los hombres adultos negros obtuvieron el derecho al voto con la ratificación de la Decimocuarta Enmienda (1868). La Decimonovena Enmienda (1920) otorgó a las mujeres adultas el derecho al voto. (pág. 284)

Free African Societies: Organizations in northern free black communities that sought to help community members and work against racial discrimination, inequality, and political slavery. (p. 334)

Sociedades Africanas Libres: Organizaciones en las comunidades negras libres del norte que buscaban ayudar a los miembros de la comunidad y militaban contra la discriminación racial, la desigualdad y la esclavitud política. (pág. 334)

Freedmen's Bureau: Government organization created in March 1865 to aid displaced blacks and other war refugees. Active until the early 1870s, it was the first federal agency in history that provided direct payments to assist those in poverty and to foster social welfare. (p. 454)

Oficina de Libertos: Organización gubernamental creada en marzo de 1865 para proporcionar asistencia a los negros desplazados y otros refugiados de guerra. Activa hasta principios de la década de 1870, fue la primera agencia federal en la historia que proporcionó pagos directos para ayudar a las personas indigentes y fomentar el bienestar social. (pág. 454)

Freedom of Information Act: Passed in the wake of the Watergate scandal, the 1974 act that gave citizens access to federal records. (p. 917)

Ley de Libertad de Información: Fue aprobada tras el escándalo de Watergate en 1974 y dio acceso público a los registros federales. (pág. 917)

Freedom Rides: A series of multiracial sit-ins conducted on interstate bus lines throughout the South by the Congress of Racial Equality (CORE) in 1961. An early and important civil rights protest. (p. 851)

viajes de la libertad: Serie de protestas multirraciales que realizó en 1961 la organización Congreso de Igualdad Racial (CORE) en líneas de autobuses interestatales en todo el sur del país. Protesta precoz e importante por los derechos civiles. (pág. 851)

freeholds: Land owned in its entirety, without feudal dues or landlord obligations. Freeholders had the legal right to improve, transfer, or sell their landed property. (p. 53)

propiedades absolutas: Tierra poseída en su totalidad, sin obligaciones feudales ni obligaciones a terratenientes. Los propietarios absolutos tenían el derecho legal de mejorar, transferir o vender sus propiedades. (pág. 53)

free silver: A policy of loosening the money supply by expanding federal coinage to include silver as well as gold, to encourage borrowing and stimulate industry. Democrats advocated the measure, most famously in the 1896 presidential campaign, but Republicans won and retained the gold standard. (p. 615)

Política "free silver": Política para relajar la oferta de dinero mediante la inclusión de la plata, junto con el oro, en el sistema monetario federal para estimular los préstamos y la industria. Los demócratas promovieron la medida, particularmente en la campaña presidencial de 1896, pero los republicanos ganaron y mantuvieron el patrón oro. (pág. 615)

free soil movement: A political movement that opposed the expansion of slavery. In 1848, the free soilers organized the Free Soil Party, which depicted slavery as a threat to republicanism and to the Jeffersonian ideal of a freeholder society, arguments that won broad support among aspiring white farmers. (p. 385)

movimiento de suelo libre: Movimiento político que se opuso a la expansión de la esclavitud. En 1848, los partidarios de este movimiento organizaron el Partido de Suelo Libre, que describía la esclavitud como una amenaza para el republicanismo y para el ideal jeffersoniano de una sociedad libre, argumentos que lograron amplio apoyo entre los blancos que aspiraban a convertirse en agricultores. (pág. 385)

French Revolution: A revolution in France (1789–1799) that was initially welcomed by most Americans because it began by abolishing feudalism and establishing a constitutional monarchy, but eventually came to seem too radical to many. (p. 216)

Revolución francesa: Revolución que tuvo lugar en Francia en 1789. Fue bien recibida inicialmente por la mayoría de los americanos porque abolió el feudalismo y estableció una monarquía constitucional, pero finalmente terminó siendo considerada por muchos como demasiado radical. (pág. 216)

Fugitive Slave Act of 1850: A federal law that set up special federal courts to facilitate capture of anyone accused of being a runaway slave. These courts could consider a slaveowner's sworn affidavit as proof, but defendants could not testify or receive a jury trial.

Ley de Esclavos Fugitivos de 1850: Ley federal que estableció tribunales federales especiales para facilitar la captura de toda persona acusada de ser un esclavo fugitivo. Los tribunales podían considerar la declaración jurada del amo de esclavos como

The controversial law led to armed conflict between U.S. marshals and abolitionists. (p. 392)

prueba, pero los acusados no podían testificar ni tener un juicio justo. La controvertida ley provocó un conflicto armado entre los agentes federales estadounidenses y los abolicionistas. (pág. 392)

fundamentalism: A term adopted by Protestants, between the 1890s and the 1910s, who rejected modernism and historical interpretations of scripture and asserted the literal truth of the Bible. Fundamentalists saw secularism and religious relativism as markers of sin, to be punished by God. (p. 553)

fundamentalismo: Término adoptado entre 1890 y 1910 por protestantes que rechazaban el modernismo y las interpretaciones históricas de las escrituras y hacían valer la verdad literal de la Biblia. Históricamente, los fundamentalistas han percibido al secularismo y al relativismo religioso como indicadores del pecado que será castigado por Dios. (pág. 553)

gag rule: A procedure in the House of Representatives from 1836 to 1844 by which antislavery petitions were automatically tabled when they were received so that they could not become the subject of debate. (p. 332)

ley mordaza: Procedimiento en la Cámara de Representantes entre 1836 y 1844 mediante el cual las peticiones antiesclavistas quedaban automáticamente pospuestas cuando se recibían para que no pudieran ser objeto de debate. (pág. 332)

gang-labor system: A system of work discipline used on southern cotton plantations in the mid-nineteenth century in which white overseers or black drivers supervised gangs of enslaved laborers to achieve greater productivity. (p. 276)

sistema de trabajo grupal: Sistema de disciplina laboral utilizado en las plantaciones de algodón del Sur a mediados del siglo XIX, en el que los capataces blancos o los conductores negros supervisaban a los grupos de trabajadores esclavos para lograr una mayor productividad. (pág. 276)

gentility: A refined style of living and elaborate manners that came to be highly prized among well-to-do English families after 1600 and strongly influenced leading colonists after 1700. (p. 102)

refinamiento: Estilo de vida elegante y de modales distinguidos que llegó a ser muy apreciado entre familias acomodadas inglesas después de 1600 y que influyeron fuertemente en los primeros colonos después de 1700. (pág. 102)

German Coast uprising: The largest slave revolt in nineteenth-century North America, it began on January 8, 1811, on Louisiana sugar plantations and involved more than two hundred enslaved workers. About ninety-five slaves were killed in the fighting or executed as a result of their involvement. (p. 358)

Levantamiento de la Costa Alemana: La mayor revuelta de esclavos en América del Norte del siglo XIX, que tuvo lugar el 8 de enero de 1811 en las plantaciones de azúcar de Luisiana e involucró a más de doscientos esclavos. Alrededor de noventa y cinco esclavos murieron en la lucha o fueron ejecutados por haber participado. (pág. 358)

Gettysburg Address: Abraham Lincoln's November 1863 speech dedicating a national cemetery at the Gettysburg battlefield. Lincoln declared the nation's founding ideal to be that "all men are created equal," and he urged listeners to dedicate themselves out of the carnage of war to a "new birth of freedom" for the United States. (p. 437)

Discurso de Gettysburg: Discurso de Abraham Lincoln en noviembre de 1863 con motivo de la dedicación de un cementerio nacional en el campo de batalla de Gettysburg. Lincoln declaró que el ideal fundacional de la nación era que "todos los hombres son creados iguales" e instó a los oyentes a abandonar la hecatombe de la guerra y dedicarse a un "nuevo nacimiento de la libertad" para los Estados Unidos. (pág. 437)

Ghost Dance movement: Religion of the late 1880s and early 1890s that combined elements of Christianity and traditional Native American religion. It fostered Plains Indians' hope that they could, through sacred dances, resurrect the great bison herds and call up a storm to drive whites back across the Atlantic. (p. 506)

Movimiento de la Danza de los espíritus: Religión de finales de la década de 1880 y principios de la de 1890 que combinaba elementos del cristianismo y de las religiones nativas americanas tradicionales. Despertó la esperanza de los indios de las Llanuras de que podían, mediante danzas sagradas, resucitar las grandes manadas de bisontes y convocar a una tormenta para conducir a los blancos de vuelta al otro lado del Atlántico. (pág. 506)

glasnost: The policy introduced by Soviet president Mikhail Gorbachev during the 1980s that involved greater openness and freedom of expression and that contributed, unintentionally, to the 1991 breakup of the Soviet Union. (p. 961)

glasnost: Política introducida por el presidente soviético Mihkail Gorbachev durante la década de 1980, que creo mayor apertura y libertad de expresión y que, sin querer, contribuyó al fin de la Unión Soviética en 1991. (pág. 961)

Glass-Steagall Act: A 1933 law that created the Federal Deposit Insurance Corporation (FDIC), which insured deposits up to $2,500 (and now up to $250,000). The act also prohibited banks from making risky investments with customers' deposits. (p. 708)

Ley Glass-Steagall: Ley de 1933 que creó la Corporación Federal de Seguro de Depósitos (FDIC), que aseguraba depósitos de hasta $2,500 (actualmente hasta $250,000). Esta ley además prohibió que los bancos hicieran inversiones arriesgadas no garantizadas con depósitos de sus clientes. (pág. 708)

globalization: The spread of economic, political, and cultural influences and connections among countries, businesses, and individuals through trade, migration, and communication. (p. 968)

globalización: El aumento de influencias y conexiones políticas, culturales y económicas entre países, negocios e individuos de todo el mundo a través del comercio, la inmigración, la comunicación y otros medios. (pág. 968)

Glorious Revolution: A quick and nearly bloodless coup in 1688 in which members of Parliament invited William of Orange to overthrow James II. Whig politicians forced the new King William and Queen Mary to accept the Declaration of Rights, creating a constitutional monarchy that enhanced the powers of the House of Commons at the expense of the crown. (p. 85)

gold standard: The practice of backing a country's currency with its reserves of gold. In 1873 the United States, following Great Britain and other European nations, began converting to the gold standard. (p. 488)

Gospel of Wealth: Andrew Carnegie's argument that corporate leaders' success showed their "fitness" to lead society and that poverty demonstrated, on the contrary, lack of "fitness" to compete in the new economy. Carnegie advocated, however, that wealthy men should use their fortunes for the public good. (p. 519)

gradual emancipation: The practice of ending slavery in the distant future while recognizing white property rights to the slaves they owned. Gradual emancipation statutes only applied to enslaved laborers born after the passage of the statute, and only after they had first labored for their owners for a term of years. (p. 261)

Granger laws: Economic regulatory laws that aimed to limit the power of railroads and other corporations, and that midwestern states passed in the late 1870s in response to pressure from farmers and the Greenback-Labor Party. (p. 537)

Great American Desert: A term coined by Major Stephen H. Long in 1820 to describe the grasslands of the southern plains from the ninety-fifth meridian west to the Rocky Mountains, which he believed was "almost wholly unfit for cultivation." (p. 352)

Great Basin: An arid basin-and-range region bounded by the Rocky Mountains on the east and the Sierra Mountains on the west. All of its water drains or evaporates within the basin. A resource-scarce environment, the Great Basin was thinly populated by Native American hunter-gatherers who ranged long distances to support themselves. (p. 16)

Great Lakes: Five enormous, interconnected freshwater lakes — Ontario, Erie, Huron, Michigan, and Superior — that dominate eastern North America. In the era before long-distance overland travel, they comprised the center of the continent's transportation system. (p. 15)

Great Migration: The migration of more than 400,000 African Americans from the rural South to the industrial cities of the North during and after World War I. (pp. 660; 674)

Great Plains: A broad plateau region that stretches from central Texas in the south to the Canadian plains in the north, bordered on the east by the eastern woodlands and on the west by the Rocky Mountains. Averaging around 20 inches of rainfall a year, the Great Plains are primarily grasslands that support grazing but not crop agriculture. (p. 15)

Great Railroad Strike of 1877: A nationwide strike of thousands of railroad workers and labor allies, who protested the growing

Revolución Gloriosa: Golpe de estado rápido y casi incruento que ocurrió en 1688 en el que Jacobo II de Inglaterra fue derrocado por Guillermo de Orange. Los políticos *whig* forzaron al nuevo rey Guillermo y a la reina María a aceptar la Declaración de Derechos, creando una monarquía constitucional que aumentó los poderes de la Cámara de los Comunes a expensas de la corona. (pág. 85)

patrón oro: Práctica de respaldar la moneda de un país con sus reservas de oro. En 1873, Estados Unidos, siguiendo el ejemplo de Gran Bretaña y otras naciones europeas, comenzó su conversión al patrón oro. (pág. 488)

Evangelio de la riqueza: Argumento de Andrew Carnegie que dice que el éxito de los lideres corporativos demostraba su "condición" para dirigir a la sociedad y que la pobreza demostraba, en cambio, no tener la "condición" para competir en la nueva economía. Sin embargo, Carnegie sostenía que los hombres ricos debían usar sus fortunas para el bien público. (pág. 519)

emancipación gradual: Práctica de acabar con la esclavitud en un futuro lejano sin dejar de reconocer los derechos de propiedad de los blancos sobre los esclavos que poseen. En general, los esclavos vivos no fueron liberados por estatutos de emancipación gradual; estos se aplicaron sólo a los esclavos nacidos después de la aprobación del estatuto, y sólo después de que hubieran trabajado en un principio para sus dueños por un período de ciertos años. (pág. 261)

Leyes Granger: Leyes de regulación económica aprobadas en algunos estados del medio oeste a finales de la década de 1870, que fueron la consecuencia de presiones de los granjeros y el Partido Greenback-Labor. (pág. 537)

Gran Desierto Americano: Término acuñado por el mayor Stephen H. Long en 1820 para describir las praderas de las llanuras sureñas desde el meridiano noventa y cinco hasta las Rocallosas, que él creía que eran "casi totalmente inservibles para el cultivo". (pág. 352)

Gran Cuenca: Región árida de cuenca y cordillera delimitada por las Rocallosas en el este y las montañas de la Sierra en el oeste. Toda su agua se drena o se evapora dentro de la cuenca. Por ser un entorno de pocos recursos, la Gran Cuenca estaba escasamente poblada por cazadores-recolectores nativos americanos que recorrían largas distancias para sustentarse. (pág. 16)

Grandes Lagos: Cinco enormes lagos de agua dulce que están interconectados: Ontario, Erie, Hurón, Míchigan y Superior, que dominan el este de América del Norte. Antes de que se popularizaran los viajes terrestres a larga distancia, estos constituían el centro del sistema de transporte del continente. (pág. 15)

Gran Migración: La migración de más de 400 mil afroamericanos del Sur rural a las ciudades industriales del Norte durante y después de la Primera Guerra Mundial. (pág. 660; 674)

Grandes Llanuras: Amplia región de meseta que se extiende desde el centro de Texas en el sur hasta las llanuras canadienses en el norte; limita al este con los bosques orientales y al oeste con las Rocallosas. Con un promedio de 20 pulgadas de lluvia al año, las Grandes Llanuras son principalmente pastizales que sustentan el pastoreo, pero no la agricultura de cultivos. (pág. 15)

Gran Huelga Ferroviaria de 1877: Huelga nacional de miles de trabajadores del ferrocarril y aliados laborales en protesta del

power of railroad corporations and the steep wage cuts imposed by railroad managers amid a severe economic depression that had begun in 1873. (p. 534)

Great Society: President Lyndon B. Johnson's domestic program, aimed at ending poverty, increasing individual opportunity, and enhancing national culture, which included civil rights legislation, antipoverty programs, medical insurance, aid to education, consumer protection, and aid to the arts and humanities. (p. 872)

Greenback-Labor Party: A political movement of the 1870s and 1880s that called on the government to protect worker rights, regulate corporations, continue Reconstruction policies in the South, and increase the money supply in order to assist borrowers. (p. 536)

greenbacks: Paper money issued by the U.S. Treasury during the Civil War to finance the war effort. (p. 426)

Group of Eight (G8): An organization of the leading capitalist industrial nations — United States, Britain, Germany, France, Italy, Japan, Canada, and Russia — that manage global economic policy (Russia was suspended in 2014 for its invasion of Crimea). (p. 974)

Gulf of Tonkin Resolution: Resolution passed by Congress in 1964 in the wake of a naval confrontation in the Gulf of Tonkin between the United States and North Vietnam. It gave the president virtually unlimited authority in conducting the Vietnam War. The Senate terminated the resolution in 1970 following outrage over the U.S. invasion of Cambodia. (p. 881)

Gullah dialect: A Creole language that combined English and African words in an African grammatical structure. It remained widespread in the South Carolina and Georgia low country throughout the nineteenth century and is still spoken in a modified form today. (p. 355)

habeas corpus: A legal writ forcing government authorities to justify their arrest and detention of an individual. During the Civil War, Lincoln suspended habeas corpus to stop protests against the draft and other anti-Union activities. (p. 418)

Haitian Revolution: An uprising against French colonial rule in Saint-Domingue (1791–1804) involving *gens de coleur* and liberated slaves from the island and armies from three European countries. In 1803, Saint-Domingue became the independent black republic of Haiti, in which former slaves were citizens. (p. 220)

hard war: The philosophy and tactics used by Union general William Tecumseh Sherman, by which he treated civilians as combatants. (p. 441)

Harlem Renaissance: A flourishing of African American artists, writers, intellectuals, and social leaders in the 1920s, centered in the neighborhood of Harlem, New York City. (p. 693)

Haymarket Square: The May 4, 1886, conflict in Chicago in which both workers and policemen were killed or wounded during a

creciente poder de las corporaciones ferroviarias y los fuertes recortes salariales impuestos en plena depresión económica, que comenzó en 1873. (pág. 534)

Gran Sociedad: Programa doméstico del presidente Lyndon B. Johnson, que incluyó legislación sobre derechos civiles, programas anti-pobreza, subsidio gubernamental de la salud, apoyo federal para la educación, protección al consumidor y apoyos para las artes y humanidades. (pág. 872)

Partido Greenback-Labor: Movimiento nacional que llamó al gobierno a incrementar la oferta monetaria para asistir a los prestatarios y fomentar el crecimiento económico; los "Greenbackers" también buscaban mayor regulación de las corporaciones y leyes que impusieran jornadas laborales de ocho horas. (pág. 536)

greenbacks: Papel moneda emitido por el Departamento del Tesoro de los Estados Unidos durante la Guerra Civil para financiar el esfuerzo bélico. (pág. 426)

Grupo de los Ocho (G8): Organización internacional de los países capitalistas industriales líderes: Estados Unidos, Bretaña, Alemania, Francia, Italia, Japón, Canadá y Rusia. El G8 controla en gran medida a las grandes organizaciones financieras internacionales en el mundo: el Fondo Monetario Internacional (FMI) y a la Organización Mundial del Comercio (OMC). Rusia fue suspendida en 2014 por invadir Crimea. (pág. 974)

Resolución del Golfo de Tonkin: Resolución aprobada por el Congreso en 1964 tras la confrontación naval en el Golfo de Tonkin entre Estados Unidos y Vietnam del Norte. Le confirió autoridad prácticamente ilimitada al presidente para conducir la Guerra de Vietnam. El Senado terminó la resolución en 1970 después de la indignación por la invasión de Estados Unidos en Camboya. (pág. 881)

dialecto gullah: Idioma criollo que combina palabras del inglés y de una variedad de lenguas africanas en una estructura gramatical africana. Aunque permaneció diseminado en las tierras bajas de Carolina del Sur y Georgia a lo largo del siglo XIX y aún hoy se habla en forma modificada. (pág. 355)

habeas corpus: Orden judicial que obliga a las autoridades gubernamentales a justificar el arresto y la detención de un individuo. Durante la Guerra Civil, Lincoln suspendió el habeas corpus para detener las protestas contra el reclutamiento y otras actividades anti-Unión. (pág. 418)

Revolución haitiana: Levantamiento contra el dominio colonial en Saint-Domingue (1791–1804), que involucró *gens de coloeur* y esclavos liberados y ejércitos de tres países europeos. En 1803, Saint-Domingue se convirtió en la república negra independiente de Haití, en la cual las personas que fueron esclavos se convirtieron en ciudadanos. (pág. 220)

guerra total: Filosofía y tácticas utilizadas por el general de la Unión William Tecumseh Sherman, por las cuales trataba a los civiles como combatientes. (pág. 441)

Renacimiento de Harlem: Florecimiento, en la década de 1920, de artistas, escritores, intelectuales y líderes afroamericanos centrados en los vecindarios de Harlem, en la ciudad de Nueva York. (pág. 693)

Haymarket Square: Conflicto ocurrido el 4 de mayo de 1886 donde trabajadores y policías fueron heridos o perdieron la

labor demonstration called by local anarchists. The incident created a backlash against all labor organizations, including the Knights of Labor. (p. 538)

headright system: A system of land distribution, pioneered in Virginia and used in several other colonies, that granted land — usually 50 acres — to anyone who paid the passage of a new arrival. By this means, large planters amassed huge landholdings as they imported large numbers of servants and slaves. (p. 53)

Hepburn Act: A 1906 antitrust law that empowered the federal Interstate Commerce Commission to set railroad shipment rates wherever it believed that railroads were unfairly colluding to set prices. (p. 622)

HIV/AIDS: A deadly disease that killed nearly 100,000 people in the United States in the 1980s and to date has killed more than 30 million worldwide. (p. 952)

Hollywood: The city in southern California that became synonymous with the American movie industry in the 1920s. (p. 682)

Holocaust: Germany's campaign during World War II to exterminate all Jews living in German-controlled lands, along with other groups the Nazis deemed "undesirable." In all, some 11 to 12 million people were killed in the Holocaust, most of them Jews. (p. 960)

Homestead Act: The 1862 act that gave 160 acres of free western land to any applicant who occupied and improved the property. This policy led to the rapid development of the American West after the Civil War; facing arid conditions in the West, however, many homesteaders found themselves unable to live on their land. (p. 488)

horizontal integration: A business concept invented in the late nineteenth century to force rivals to merge their companies into a single conglomerate. John D. Rockefeller of Standard Oil pioneered this model. (p. 518)

hostage crisis: Crisis in 1979, in which Iranian college students seized the U.S. embassy in Tehran, taking sixty-six Americans hostage, and demanded that the deposed Shah, an undemocratic ruler installed with American backing in 1954, be returned to face trial in Iran. President Carter refused, and the hostages were kept for 444 days. (p. 947)

household mode of production: The system of exchanging goods and labor that helped eighteenth-century New England freeholders survive on ever-shrinking farms as available land became more scarce. (p. 116)

House of Burgesses: Organ of government in colonial Virginia made up of an assembly of representatives elected by the colony's inhabitants. (p. 49)

House Un-American Activities Committee (HUAC): Congressional committee especially prominent during the early years of the Cold War that investigated Americans who might be disloyal

vida durante una protesta convocada por anarquistas locales. El incidente tuvo consecuencias para todas las organizaciones laborales, incluyendo a los Knights of Labor. (pág. 538)

sistema de reparto de tierras *headright*: Sistema de distribución de tierras, iniciado en Virginia y utilizado en varias otras colonias, que otorgaba tierras, generalmente de 50 acres, a cualquier persona que pagara el pasaje a otra persona para que se mudara allí. De esta manera, los grandes plantadores acumularon muchas propiedades ya que importaron grandes cantidades de sirvientes y esclavos. (pág. 53)

Ley Hepburn: Ley anti-monopolio de 1906 que confirió poderes a la Comisión Interestatal del Comercio para imponer tarifas de envíos por ferrocarril cuando los ferrocarriles coludían injustamente para establecer precios. (pág. 622)

VIH/SIDA: Enfermedad mortal que mató a cerca de 100 mil personas en Estados unidos durante la década de 1980. (pág. 952)

Hollywood: Ciudad del sur de California que se convirtió en sinónimo de la industria cinematográfica de Estados Unidos en la década de 1920. (pág. 682)

Holocausto: Campaña de Alemania durante la Segunda Guerra Mundial para exterminar a todos los judíos que vivían en territorios bajo control alemán, y a otros grupos que los nazis veían como "indeseables". En total, cerca de 11 millones de personas murieron en el Holocausto, la mayoría de ellas judías. (pág. 960)

Ley de Asentamientos Rurales: Ley de 1862 que otorgó 160 acres de tierra libre occidental a cualquier solicitante que ocupara y mejorara la propiedad. Esta política condujo al rápido desarrollo del Oeste Americano después de la Guerra Civil; sin embargo, por las condiciones áridas del Oeste, muchos colonos se encontraron incapaces de vivir en su tierra. (pág. 488)

integración horizontal: Concepto de negocios inventado a finales del siglo XIX para presionar a los competidores y forzar a los rivales a fusionar sus compañías para formar un conglomerado. John D. Rockefeller de Standard Oil fue el pionero de este modelo de negocios. (pág. 518)

crisis de los rehenes: Crisis que comenzó en 1979 cuando estudiantes ingresaron a la embajada de Estados Unidos en Teherán y tomaron como rehenes a 66 americanos. Exigían que el shah derrocado, líder antidemocrático instalado en 1954 con respaldo de Estados Unidos, fuera llevado a Irán para ser juzgado. El presidente Carter se negó y los 66 americanos fueron mantenidos como rehenes por 444 días. (pág. 947)

modo de producción doméstica: Sistema de intercambio de bienes y mano de obra que ayudó a los terratenientes libres de Nueva Inglaterra del siglo XVIII a sobrevivir en granjas cada vez más pequeñas a medida que las tierras disponibles se tornaban más escasas. (pág. 116)

Casa de Burguesses: Órgano de gobierno en la Virginia colonial compuesto por una asamblea de representantes elegidos por los habitantes de la colonia. (pág. 49)

Comité de Actividades Antiestadounidenses (HUAC): Comité del congreso particularmente importante durante los primeros años de la Guerra Fría que se dedicó a investigar a estadounidenses

to the government or might have associated with communists or other radicals. (p. 790)

Hull House: One of the first and most famous social settlements, founded in 1889 by Jane Addams in an impoverished, largely Italian immigrant neighborhood on Chicago's West Side. (p. 596)

Hundred Days: A legendary session during the first few months of Franklin Roosevelt's administration in which Congress enacted fifteen major bills that focused primarily on four problems: banking failures, agricultural overproduction, the manufacturing slump, and soaring unemployment. (p. 708)

hunters and gatherers: Societies whose members gather food by hunting, fishing, and collecting wild plants rather than relying on agriculture or animal husbandry. Because hunter-gatherers are mobile, moving seasonally through their territory to exploit resources, they have neither fixed townsites nor weighty material goods. (p. 8)

Immigration and Nationality Act: A 1965 law that eliminated the discriminatory 1924 nationality quotas, established a higher total limit on immigration, and gave immigration preferences to those with skills in high demand or immediate family members in the United States. (p. 979)

indentured servitude: System in which workers contracted for service for a specified period. In exchange for agreeing to work for four or five years (or more) without wages in the colonies, indentured workers received passage across the Atlantic, room and board, and status as a free person at the end of the contract period. (p. 55)

Indian Removal Act of 1830: Act that directed the mandatory relocation of eastern tribes to territory west of the Mississippi. Jackson insisted that his goal was to save the Indians and their culture. Indians resisted the controversial act, but in the end most were forced to comply. (p. 301)

Indian Reorganization Act: A 1934 law that reversed the Dawes Act of 1887. Through the law, Indians won a greater degree of religious freedom, and tribal governments regained their status as semisovereign dependent nations. (p. 726)

individualism: Word coined by Alexis de Tocqueville in 1835 to describe Americans as people no longer bound by social attachments to classes, castes, associations, and families. (p. 314)

Industrial Revolution: A burst of major inventions and economic expansion based on water and steam power, reorganized work routines, and the use of machine technology that transformed certain industries, such as cotton textiles and iron, between 1790 and 1860. (p. 258)

Industrial Workers of the World: A radical labor group founded in 1905, dedicated to organizing unskilled workers to oppose capitalism. Nicknamed the Wobblies, they advocated direct action by workers, including sabotage and general strikes. (p. 625)

posiblemente desleales al gobierno o que podían estar asociados con comunistas u otros radicales. (pág. 790)

Casa Hull: Uno de los primeros y más reconocidos asentamientos sociales, fundado en 1889 por Jane Addams y su acompañante Ellen Gates Starr en un vecindario empobrecido y poblado principalmente de inmigrantes italianos en el oeste de Chicago. (pág. 596)

Cien Días: Sesión legendaria durante los primeros meses de la administración de Franklin Roosevelt, en la cual el congreso promulgó quince leyes enfocadas principalmente sobre cuatro problemas: fallos bancarios, sobreproducción en la agricultura, depresión de los negocios y el aumento desmedido del desempleo. (pág. 708)

cazadores y recolectores: Sociedades cuyos miembros recolectan alimentos mediante la caza, la pesca y la colecta de plantas silvestres en lugar de depender de la agricultura o la cría de animales. Debido a que los cazadores-recolectores eran móviles, es decir, se desplazaban según las estaciones a través de su territorio para explotar los recursos, no tenían ciudades ni bienes materiales fijos. (pág. 8)

Ley de Inmigración y Nacionalidad: Ley de 1965 que eliminó las cuotas discriminatorias de 1924 de nacionalidades, incrementó ligeramente los límites totales de inmigrantes, incluyó disposiciones para facilitar la entrada de inmigrantes con habilidades en alta demanda y de familiares inmediatos de residentes legales en los Estados Unidos. (pág. 979)

trabajador no abonado: Sistema en el cual los trabajadores son contratados para un servicio por un período específico. A cambio de trabajar durante cuatro o cinco años (o más) sin salario en las colonias, los trabajadores no abonados recibían un pasaje para cruzar el Atlántico, alojamiento y comida, y el estado de persona libre al final del período del contrato. (pág. 55)

Ley de Traslado Forzoso de los Indios de 1830: Ley que dirigió la reubicación obligatoria de tribus orientales al territorio al oeste del Misisipi. Jackson insistió en que su objetivo era salvar a los indios y su cultura. Los indios resistieron la ley controvertida, pero al final la mayoría se vio obligada a acatarla. (pág. 301)

Ley de Reorganización Indígena: Ley de 1934 que revirtió la Ley Dawes de 1887. Por medio de esta ley, los indígenas obtuvieron mayores libertades religiosas y los gobiernos tribales recuperaron su estatus de naciones dependientes semi-soberanas. (pág. 726)

individualismo: Palabra acuñada por Alexis de Tocqueville en 1835 para describir a los estadounidenses como personas que ya no están atadas por los vínculos sociales con las clases, las castas, las asociaciones y las familias. (pág. 314)

Revolución Industrial: Explosión de grandes inventos y expansión económica basada en el poder del agua y el vapor y el uso de la tecnología de máquinas que transformó ciertas industrias, como los textiles de algodón y el hierro, entre 1790 y 1860. (pág. 258)

Trabajadores Industriales del Mundo: Sindicato general y grupo radical político fundado en 1905, dedicado a la organización de trabajadores no calificados para oponerse al capitalismo. Apodado los Wobblies, promovía la acción directa de los trabajadores, incluyendo el sabotaje y las huelgas generales. (pág. 625)

inland system: The slave trade system in the interior of the country that fed slaves to the Cotton South. (p. 266)

Insular Cases: A set of Supreme Court rulings in 1901 that declared that the U.S. Constitution did not automatically extend citizenship to people in acquired territories; only Congress could decide whether to grant citizenship. (p. 647)

internal improvements: Government-funded public works such as roads and canals. (p. 291)

International Monetary Fund (IMF): A fund established to stabilize currencies and provide a predictable monetary environment for trade, with the U.S. dollar serving as the benchmark. (p. 807)

Interstate Commerce Commission (ICC): Formed in 1887 to oversee the railroad industry and prevent unfair rates, the ICC was an important early effort by Congress to regulate corporate practices. (p. 539)

Iran-Contra affair: Reagan administration scandal that involved the sale of arms to Iran in exchange for its efforts to secure the release of hostages held in Lebanon and the redirection — illegal because banned by American law — of the proceeds of those sales to the Nicaraguan Contras. (p. 960)

Iroquoian cultures/languages: A Native American language family whose speakers were concentrated in the eastern woodlands. The Iroquoian language family should not be confused with the nations of the Iroquois Confederacy, which inhabited the territory of modern-day upstate New York at the time of first contact. (p. 13)

Iroquois Confederacy: A league of five Native American nations — the Mohawks, Oneidas, Onondagas, Cayugas, and Senecas — probably formed around A.D. 1450. A sixth nation, the Tuscaroras, joined the confederacy around 1720. Condolence ceremonies introduced by a Mohawk named Hiawatha formed the basis for the league. Positioned between New France and New Netherland (later New York), the Iroquois played a central role in the era of European colonization. (p. 15)

Islam: A religion that considers Muhammad to be God's last prophet. Following the death of Muhammad in A.D. 632, the newly converted Arab peoples of North Africa used force and fervor to spread the Muslim faith into sub-Saharan Africa, India, Indonesia, Spain, and the Balkan regions of Europe. (p. 22)

Jay's Treaty: A 1795 treaty between the United States and Britain, negotiated by John Jay. The treaty accepted Britain's right to stop neutral ships and required the U.S. government to provide restitution for the pre–Revolutionary War debts of British merchants. In return, it allowed Americans to submit claims for illegal seizures and required the British to remove their troops and Indian agents from the Northwest Territory. (p. 217)

jazz: Unique American musical form with an improvisational style that emerged in New Orleans and other parts of the South before World War I. It grew in popularity during the Harlem Renaissance. (p. 694)

Jim Crow: Laws that required separation of the races, especially blacks and whites, in public facilities. The post–Civil War

sistema interior: sistema de trata de esclavos en el interior del país que surtía esclavos al sur algodonero. (pág. 266)

Casos Insulares: Conjunto de sentencias de la Corte Suprema en 1901 que declararon que la Constitución de los Estados Unidos no otorgaba ciudadanía automática a las personas de territorios adquiridos; sólo el Congreso tenía el poder de decisión para otorgar ciudadanía. (pág. 647)

mejoras internas: obras públicas como carreteras y canales. (pág. 291)

Fondo Monetario Internacional (FMI): Fondo establecido para estabilizar las monedas y ofrecer un entorno predecible para el intercambio monetario, donde el dolar estadounidense es el referente. (pág. 807)

Ley de Comercio Interestatal: Ley de 1887 que creo la Comisión Interestatal del Comercio (ICC), agencia federal reguladora diseñada para vigilar la industria ferroviaria y prevenir colusiones y tarifas injustas. (pág. 539)

Escándalo Irán-Contra: Escándalo de la administración de Reagan que involucró la venta de armas a Irán a cambio de sus esfuerzos para asegurar la liberación de rehenes en Líbano y la desviación — ilegal porque estaba prohibida por la ley estadounidense — de las ganancias de esas ventas a los Contras nicaragüenses. (pág. 960)

culturas y lenguas iroquesas: Familia de lenguas nativas americanas cuyos hablantes se concentraron en los bosques orientales. La familia de lenguas iroquesas no debe confundirse con las naciones de la Confederación Iroquesa, que habitaban el territorio del estado actual de Nueva York cuando ocurrió el primer contacto. (pág. 13)

Confederación Iroquesa: Liga de cinco naciones nativas de América — mohawks, oneidas, onondagas, cayugas y senecas — que probablemente se formó alrededor del año 1450 d.C. Una sexta nación, los tuscaroras, se unió a la confederación alrededor de 1720. Las ceremonias de condolencias introducidas por un mohawk llamado Hiawatha formaron la base de la liga. Ubicados entre Nueva Francia y Nuevos Países Bajos (más tarde Nueva York), los iroqueses desempeñaron un papel central en la era de la colonización europea. (pág. 15)

islam: Religión que considera a Mahoma como el último profeta de Dios. Tras la muerte de Mahoma en 632 d.C. los pueblos árabes recién convertidos del norte de África utilizaron la fuerza y el fervor para difundir la fe musulmana en el África subsahariana, la India, Indonesia, España y las regiones de los Balcanes en Europa. (pág. 22)

Tratado Jay: Tratado que se firmó en 1795 entre los Estados Unidos y Gran Bretaña, negociado por John Jay. El tratado aceptó el derecho de Gran Bretaña de detener barcos neutrales. A cambio, permitió a los estadounidenses presentar reclamaciones por incautaciones ilegales y exigió a los británicos que retiraran sus tropas y agentes indios del Territorio del Noroeste. (pág. 217)

jazz: Música americana que surgió en Nueva Orleans y otras partes del Sur antes de la Primera Guerra Mundial. Su popularidad aumentó durante el Renacimiento de Harlem. (pág. 694)

Jim Crow: Leyes que requirieron la separación de las razas, particularmente blancos y negros, en lugares públicos. En las décadas decades witnessed many such laws, especially in southern states, and several decades of legal challenges to them. The Supreme Court upheld them in *Plessy v. Ferguson* (1896), giving national approval to a system of racial segregation in the South that lasted until the 1960s. (p. 558)

posteriores a la Guerra Civil se promulgaron muchas leyes con este fin, particularmente en los estados del sur, y a lo largo de estas décadas se buscó revertirlas por la vía legal. La Suprema Corte las mantuvo luego de *Plessy v. Ferguson* (1896) y con ello se aprobó un sistema de segregación racial en el Sur que duró hasta la década de 1960. (pág. 558)

joint-stock corporation: A financial organization devised by English merchants around 1550 that facilitated the colonization of North America. In these companies, a number of investors pooled their capital and received shares of stock in the enterprise in proportion to their share of the total investment. (p. 48)

sociedad por acciones: Organización financiera ideada por comerciantes ingleses alrededor de 1550 que facilitó la colonización de América del Norte. En estas compañías, varios inversores agrupaban su capital y recibían acciones en la empresa en proporción a su participación en la inversión total. (pág. 48)

Judiciary Act of 1789: Act that established a federal district court in each state and three circuit courts to hear appeals from the districts, with the Supreme Court serving as the highest appellate court in the federal system. (p. 213)

Ley Judicial de 1789: Ley que estableció un tribunal federal de distrito en cada estado y tres tribunales de circuito para escuchar las apelaciones de los distritos; el Tribunal Supremo tendría la última palabra. (pág. 213)

Kansas-Nebraska Act: A controversial 1854 law that divided Indian Territory into Kansas and Nebraska, repealed the Missouri Compromise, and left the new territories to decide the issue of slavery on the basis of popular sovereignty. Far from clarifying the status of slavery in the territories, the act led to violent conflict in "Bleeding Kansas." (p. 400)

Ley de Kansas-Nebraska: Ley controvertida de 1854 que dividió el Territorio indio en Kansas y Nebraska, derogó el Compromiso de Misuri y bajo el argumento de la soberanía popular, dejó la decisión sobre la esclavitud en manos de los nuevos territorios. Lejos de aclarar el estado de la esclavitud en los territorios, la ley condujo al conflicto violento de "*Bleeding Kansas*" (Kansas sangrienta). (pág. 400)

Kerner Commission: The National Advisory Commission on Civil Disorders, which investigated the 1967 urban riots. Its 1968 report warned of the dangers of "two societies, one black, one white, separate and unequal." (p. 830)

Comisión Kerner: Nombre informal para el Comité Nacional Consultivo sobre los Desórdenes Civiles formado por el presidente para investigar las causas de los disturbios urbanos de 1967. Su reporte, elaborado en 1968, advirtió que "nuestro país se está convirtiendo en dos sociedades, una negra, una blanca, separada y desigual." (pág. 830)

Keynesian economics: The theory, developed by British economist John Maynard Keynes in the 1930s, that deficit spending and interest rate adjustment by government could prevent depressions and limit inflation. (p. 719)

Economía keynesiana: Teoría desarrollada por el economista británico, John Maynard Keynes, en la década de 1930, en la cual la intervención intencionada del gobierno en la economía (a través de reducciones o aumentos de impuestos, tasas de interés y gasto público) puede afectar el nivel general de actividad económica y, por lo tanto, prevenir severas depresiones e inflación desmedida. (pág. 719)

King Cotton: The Confederates' belief during the Civil War that their cotton was so important to the British and French economies that those governments would recognize the South as an independent nation and supply it with loans and arms. (p. 417)

Algodón es rey, el: Creencia de los confederados durante la Guerra Civil de que su algodón era tan importante para las economías británica y francesa que aquellos gobiernos reconocerían al Sur como una nación independiente y le proporcionarían préstamos y armas. (pág. 417)

kitchen debate: A 1959 debate over the merits of their rival systems between U.S. vice president Richard Nixon and Soviet premier Nikita Khrushchev at the opening of an American exhibition in Moscow. (p. 804)

debate de cocina: Debate en 1959 entre Richard Nixon, presidente de los Estados Unidos, y Nikita Khruschev, premier soviético, sobre los méritos de sus sistemas rivales, sostenido en la inauguración de una exhibición estadounidense en Moscú. (pág. 804)

Knights of Labor: The first mass labor organization of nationwide scope, which sought to bridge differences of occupation, race, and gender to unite all workers. The Knights peaked in strength in the mid-1880s. (p. 537)

Knights of Labor (Caballeros del Trabajo): Primera organización laboral masiva creada entre la clase trabajadora de Estados Unidos. Fundada en 1869, alcanzó su punto máximo a mediados de la década de 1880. Los Knights of Labor intentaron eliminar fronteras de etnicidad, género, ideología, raza y ocupación para crear una "hermandad universal" de todos los trabajadores. (pág. 537)

Ku Klux Klan: Secret society that first undertook violence against African Americans in the South after the Civil War but was reborn in 1915 to fight the perceived threats posed by African Americans, immigrants, radicals, feminists, Catholics, and Jews. (pp. 471; 691)

Ku Klux Klan: Sociedad secreta que en sus principios cometió actos de violencia contra los afroamericanos en el sur después de la Guerra Civil, pero renació en 1915 para luchar contra las amenazas percibidas en afroamericanos, inmigrantes, radicales, feministas, católicos y judíos. (págs. 471; 691)

labor theory of value: The belief that human labor produces economic value. Adherents argued that the price of a product should be determined not by the market but by the amount of work required to make it, and that most of the price should be paid to the person who produced it. (p. 272)

teoría del valor-trabajo: Creencia de que el trabajo humano produce valor económico. Los adherentes argumentaron que el precio de un producto debería determinarse no por el mercado (oferta y demanda) sino por la cantidad de trabajo requerido para hacerlo, y que la mayor parte del precio debería pagarse a la persona que lo produjo. (pág. 272)

land-grant colleges: Authorized by the Morrill Act of 1862, land-grant colleges were public universities founded to broaden educational opportunities and foster technical and scientific expertise. These universities were funded by the Morrill Act, which authorized the sale of federal lands to raise money for higher education. (p. 489)

Universidades con Dotación de Terrenos Federales: Autorizadas por la Ley Morrill de 1862, estas universidades públicas fueron fundadas para ampliar las oportunidades educativas y fomentar la experiencia técnica y científica. Estas universidades fueron financiadas por la Ley Morrill, que autorizó la venta de tierras federales para recaudar dinero para la educación superior. (pág. 489)

La Raza Unida: A political party founded in Texas in 1970 by Mexican Americans as an alternative to the two major political parties; La Raza Unida (The United Race) ran candidates for state and local governments and expanded to other states. (p. 866)

La Raza Unida: Organización fundada por mexicanos-americanos en Texas en 1970 como alternativa a los dos principales partidos políticos; La Raza Unida postuló a candidatos para gobernador estatal y otros cargos gubernamentales locales. (pág. 866)

Lawrence v. Texas: A 2003 landmark decision by the Supreme Court that limited the power of states to prohibit private homosexual activity between consenting adults. (p. 985)

Lawrence v. Texas: Decisión histórica de la Corte Suprema que limitó los poderes de los estados para prohibir actividades homosexuales privadas consentidas entre adultos. (pág. 985)

League of Nations: An international organization of nations to prevent future hostilities, proposed by President Woodrow Wilson in the aftermath of World War I. Although the League of Nations did form, the United States never became a member state. (p. 665)

Liga de las Naciones: Organización internacional, propuesta por el presidente Woodrow Wilson, que reunió a los gobiernos del mundo para prevenir hostilidades futuras tras las secuelas de la Primera Guerra Mundial. Si bien se logró la formación de la Liga de las Naciones, Estados Unidos nunca fue un estado miembro. (pág. 665)

Lend-Lease Act: Legislation in 1941 that enabled Britain to obtain arms from the United States without cash but with the promise of reimbursement when World War II ended. The act reflected Roosevelt's desire to assist the British in any way possible short of war. (p. 741)

Ley de Préstamo y Arriendo: Legislación de 1941 que permitió que Bretaña obtuviera armas de Estados Unidos sin un pago en efectivo con la promesa de reembolsar a Estados Unidos al concluir la guerra. La ley reflejó el deseo de asistir a Bretaña como fuera posible sin tener que ir a la guerra. (pág. 741)

Levittown: A Long Island, New York, suburb, built by William J. Levitt in the late 1940s, that used mass-production techniques to build modest, affordable houses. Other Levittowns were built in Pennsylvania and New Jersey. (p. 826)

Levittown: Suburbio de Long Island, Nueva York, construido por William J. Levitt a fines de la década de 1940 donde se usaron técnicas de producción en masa para construir casas modestas y asequibles. Luego se construirían otros Levittowns en Pennsylvania y en Nueva Jersey. (pág. 826)

Liberty Party: An antislavery political party that ran its first presidential candidate in 1844, controversially challenging both the Democrats and Whigs. (p. 339)

Partido Libertad: Partido político antiesclavista que presentó su primer candidato presidencial en 1844, desafiando de manera controvertida tanto a los demócratas como a los whigs. (pág. 339)

Lieber Code: Union guidelines for the laws of war, issued in April 1863. The code ruled that soldiers and prisoners must be treated equally without respect to color or race; justified a range of military actions if they were based on "necessity" that would "hasten surrender"; and outlawed use of torture. The code provided a foundation for later international agreements on the laws of war. (p. 432)

Código Lieber: Directrices sindicales para las leyes de la guerra, emitidas en abril de 1863. El código dictaminó que los soldados y los presos debían ser tratados por igual sin importar color o raza; justificó una serie de acciones militares siempre y cuando fueran por una "necesidad" que "aceleraría la rendición"; y proscribió el uso de la tortura. El código proporcionó una base para posteriores acuerdos internacionales sobre las leyes de la guerra. (pág. 432)

Lochner v. New York: A 1905 Supreme Court ruling that New York State could not limit bakers' workday to ten hours because that violated bakers' rights to make individual contracts. This example of legal formalism did not take into account the unequal power of employers and individual workers. (p. 620)

Lochner v. New York: Sentencia de la Corte Suprema en 1905 que dictaminó que el estado de Nueva York no podría limitar la jornada laboral de los panaderos a diez horas porque violaba el derecho de los panaderos de hacer contratos. Este ejemplo de formalismo legal no tomaba en cuenta los poderes desiguales entre empleadores y trabajadores individuales. (pág. 620)

Lodge Bill: Also known as the Federal Elections Bill of 1890, a bill proposing that whenever one hundred citizens in any district appealed for intervention, a bipartisan federal board could investigate and seat the rightful winner. The defeat of the bill

Propuesta de Ley Lodge: También conocida como la Propuesta de Ley de Elecciones Federales de 1890, proponía que si 100 ciudadanos de cualquier distrito apelaban a favor de una intervención, un comité federal integrado por ambos partidos podría investigar y otorgar la victoria al ganador legítimo. La derrota de was a blow to those seeking to defend African American voting rights and to ensure full participation in politics. (p. 612)

la propuesta fue un golpe duro para quienes buscaban defender los derechos del voto afroamericano y asegurar la participación plena en la política. (pág. 612)

Lone Wolf v. Hitchcock: A 1903 Supreme Court ruling that Congress could make whatever Indian policies it chose, ignoring all existing treaties. (p. 504)

Lone Wolf v. Hitchcock: Sentencia de la Corte Suprema de 1903 que dictaminó que el Congreso podía adoptar cualquier política india, ignorando todos los tratados existentes. (pág. 504)

Louisiana Purchase: The 1803 purchase of French territory west of the Mississippi River that stretched from the Gulf of Mexico to Canada and nearly doubled the size of the United States. The purchase required President Thomas Jefferson to exercise powers not explicitly granted to him by the Constitution. (p. 229)

Compra de Luisiana: Compra en 1803 del territorio francés al oeste del río Misisipi, que se extendía desde el golfo de México hasta Canadá. La Compra de Luisiana casi duplicó el tamaño de los Estados Unidos y abrió el camino para la futura expansión estadounidense hacia el oeste. La compra requirió que el presidente Thomas Jefferson ejerciera poderes que la Constitución no otorgaba explícitamente. (pág. 229)

Loyalty-Security Program: A program created in 1947 by President Truman that permitted officials to investigate any employee of the federal government for "subversive" activities. (p. 789)

Programa de Lealtad: Programa creado en 1947 por el presidente Truman que permitió a oficiales gubernamentales investigar a cualquier empleado del gobierno por "actividades subversivas". (pág. 789)

machine tools: Machines that made standardized metal parts for other machines, like textile looms and sewing machines. The development of machine tools by American inventors in the early nineteenth century accelerated industrialization. (p. 269)

máquinas herramienta: Máquinas de corte, perforación y taladro utilizadas para producir piezas metálicas estandarizadas, que luego se ensamblaban en productos tales como telares textiles y máquinas de coser. El rápido desarrollo de las máquinas herramienta por parte de los inventores estadounidenses a principios del siglo XIX fue un factor en la rápida expansión de la industrialización. (pág. 269)

Maine Law: The nation's first state law for the prohibition of liquor manufacture and sales, passed in 1851. (p. 318)

Ley de Maine: Primera ley estatal de la nación que prohibió la fabricación y la venta de licor, aprobada en 1851. (pág. 318)

management revolution: An internal management structure adopted by large corporations that departmentalized operations and distinguished top executives from those responsible for day-to-day operations. (p. 517)

revolución de la administración: Estructura interna de administración adoptada por muchas corporaciones grandes y complejas que distinguió a los altos ejecutivos de las personas responsables de las operaciones diarias y creo departamentos para separar las operaciones de acuerdo con su función. (pág. 517)

Manhattan Project: The research and weapons development project, authorized by President Franklin Roosevelt in 1942 that produced the first atomic bomb. (p. 764)

Proyecto Manhattan: Proyecto secreto autorizado por Franklin Roosevelt en 1942 para desarrollar la primera bomba atómica. (pág. 764)

Manifest Destiny: A term coined by John L. O'Sullivan in 1845 to express the idea that Euro-Americans were fated by God to settle the North American continent from the Atlantic to the Pacific Ocean. (p. 359)

Destino manifiesto: Término acuñado por John L. O'Sullivan en 1845 para expresar la idea de que los euroamericanos estaban predestinados por Dios para establecer el continente norteamericano, desde el Atlántico hasta el océano Pacífico. (pág. 359)

manumission: The legal act of relinquishing property rights in slaves. Worried that a large free black population would threaten the institution of slavery, the Virginia assembly repealed Virginia's 1782 manumission law in 1792. (p. 262)

manumisión: Acto legal de renunciar a los derechos de propiedad de los esclavos. Bajo la preocupación de que una gran población negra libre amenazara la institución de la esclavitud, la asamblea de Virginia derogó la ley de manumisión de 1782 de Virginia en 1792. (pág. 262)

Marbury v. Madison: A Supreme Court case that established the principle of judicial review in finding that parts of the Judiciary Act of 1789 were in conflict with the Constitution. For the first time, the Supreme Court assumed legal authority to overrule acts of other branches of the government. (p. 228)

***Marbury v. Madison* (1803):** Caso de la Corte Suprema que estableció el principio de revisión judicial al constatar que algunas partes de la Ley Judicial de 1789 estaban en conflicto con la Constitución. Por primera vez, la Corte Suprema asumió la autoridad legal para anular leyes de otras ramas del gobierno. (pág. 228)

March on Washington: Officially named the March on Washington for Jobs and Freedom, on August 28, 1963, a quarter of a million people marched to the Lincoln Memorial to demand that Congress end Jim Crow racial discrimination and launch a major jobs program to bring needed employment to black communities. (p. 854)

Marcha sobre Washington: De nombre oficial Marcha sobre Washington por el Trabajo y la Libertad con fecha del 28 de agosto de 1963, convocó a 250 mil personas que marcharon al Monumento a Lincoln para exigir que el Congreso eliminara la discriminación racial de Jim Crow y lanzara un programa masivo de empleos para llevar a las comunidades negras de vuelta al trabajo. (pág. 854)

Market Revolution: The dramatic increase between 1820 and 1850 in the exchange of goods and services in market transactions. The Market Revolution reflected the increased output of farms and factories, the entrepreneurial activities of traders and merchants, and the creation of a transportation network of roads, canals, and railroads. (p. 256)

married women's property laws: Laws enacted between 1839 and 1860 in New York and other states that permitted married women to own, inherit, and bequeath property. (p. 343)

Marshall Plan: Aid program begun in 1948 to help European economies recover from World War II. (p. 782)

maternalism: The belief that women should contribute to civic and political life through their special talents as mothers, Christians, and moral guides. Maternalists put this ideology into action by creating dozens of social reform organizations. (p. 567)

McCulloch v. Maryland (1819): A Supreme Court case that denied the right of states to tax the Second Bank of the United States, thereby asserting the dominance of national over state statutes. (p. 239)

mechanics: A term used in the nineteenth century to refer to skilled craftsmen and inventors who built and improved machinery and machine tools for industry. (p. 259)

Medicaid: A health plan for the poor passed in 1965 and paid for by general tax revenues and administered by the states. (p. 876)

Medicare: A health plan for the elderly passed in 1965 and funded by a surcharge on Social Security payroll taxes. (p. 876)

mercantilism: A system of political economy based on government regulation. Beginning in 1650, Britain enacted Navigation Acts that controlled colonial commerce and manufacturing for the enrichment of Britain. (p. 46)

Metacom's War: Also known as King Philip's War, it pitted a coalition of Native Americans led by the Wampanoag leader Metacom against the New England colonies in 1675–1676. A thousand colonists were killed and twelve colonial towns destroyed, but the colonies prevailed. Metacom and his allies lost some 4,500 people. (p. 69)

Mexican American Legal Defense and Education Fund (MALDEF): A Mexican American civil rights organization founded in 1967 and based on the model of the NAACP Legal Defense and Education Fund. MALDEF focused on legal issues and endeavored to win protections against discrimination through court decisions. (p. 865)

Mexican cession: Lands taken by the United States in the U.S.-Mexico War (1846–1848). (p. 389)

middle class: An economic group of prosperous farmers, artisans, and traders that emerged in the early nineteenth century. Its rise reflected a dramatic increase in prosperity. This surge in income, along with an abundance of inexpensive mass-produced goods, fostered a distinct middle-class urban culture. (p. 277)

revolución mercantil: Aumento drástico en el intercambio de bienes y servicios en las transacciones de mercado que tuvo lugar entre 1820 y 1850. La revolución mercantil reflejó el aumento de la producción de granjas y fábricas, las actividades empresariales de los comerciantes y mercantes, y la creación de una red de transporte de carreteras, canales y ferrocarriles. (pág. 256)

leyes de propiedad de mujeres casadas: Leyes promulgadas entre 1839 y 1860 en Nueva York y otros estados, que permitieron a las mujeres casadas poseer, heredar y ceder propiedades. (pág. 343)

Plan Marshall: Programa de asistencia comenzado en 1948 para asistir a la recuperación de las economías europeas después de la Segunda Guerra Mundial. (pág. 782)

maternalismo: La creencia de que las mujeres deben contribuir a la vida política y cívica a través de sus talentos especiales como madres, cristianas y líderes morales. Las maternalistas pusieron en marcha esta ideología mediante la creación de docenas de organizaciones de reforma social. (pág. 567)

***McCulloch v. Maryland* (1819):** Caso de la Corte Suprema que afirmó el dominio de los estatutos nacionales sobre los estatales. (pág. 239)

mecánicos: Término utilizado en el siglo XIX para referirse a los artesanos e inventores expertos que construyeron y mejoraron la maquinaria y las máquinas herramienta para la industria. (pág. 259)

Medicaid: Plan de salud para los pobres aprobado en 1965, financiado con ingresos fiscales generales y administrado por los estados. (pág. 876)

Medicare: Plan de salud para la tercera edad aprobado en 1965 financiado por un recargo en los impuestos sobre nóminas de Seguridad Social. (pág. 876)

mercantilismo: Sistema de economía política basado en la regulación gubernamental. A partir de 1650, Gran Bretaña promulgó leyes de navegación que controlaban el comercio y la fabricación colonial para el enriquecimiento de Gran Bretaña. (pág. 46)

Guerra de Metacomet: También conocida como la Guerra del rey Felipe, enfrentó a una coalición de nativos americanos encabezada por el líder wampanoag Metacomet contra las colonias de Nueva Inglaterra en 1675–1676. Mil colonos fueron asesinados y doce ciudades coloniales destruidas, pero las colonias prevalecieron. Metacomet y sus aliados perdieron unas 4,500 personas. (pág. 69)

Fondo Mexicano-Americano de Defensa Legal y Educación (MALDEF): Organización mexicano-americana de derechos civiles fundada en 1967 basada en el modelo del Fondo de Defensa Legal y Educación de la NAACP. MALDEF se enfocó en asuntos legales y buscó lograr protecciones contra la discriminación por medio de decisiones judiciales. (pág. 865)

Cesión mexicana: Tierras tomadas por los Estados Unidos en la Guerra de Estados Unidos-México (1846–1848). (pág. 389)

clase media: Grupo económico de agricultores, artesanos y comerciantes prósperos que surgió a principios del siglo XIX. Su crecimiento reflejó un aumento drástico en la prosperidad. Este aumento en los ingresos, junto con una abundancia de bienes de bajo costo producidos, fomentó una cultura urbana de clase media singular. (pág. 277)

Middle Passage: The brutal sea voyage that carried about 12.5 million Africans toward enslavement in the Americas, of whom about 1.8 million died en route. (p. 94)

military-industrial complex: A term President Eisenhower used to refer to the military establishment and defense contractors who, he warned, exercised undue influence over the national government. (p. 807)

Minor v. Happersett: A Supreme Court decision in 1875 that ruled that suffrage rights were not inherent in citizenship and had not been granted by the Fourteenth Amendment, as some women's rights advocates argued. Women were citizens, the Court ruled, but state legislatures could deny women the vote if they wished. (p. 459)

minstrel shows: Popular theatrical entertainment begun around 1830 in which white actors in blackface presented comic routines that combined racist caricature and social criticism. (p. 327)

Minutemen: Colonial militiamen ready to mobilize on short notice during the imperial crisis of the 1770s. These volunteers formed the core of the citizens' army that met British troops at Lexington and Concord in April 1775. (p. 171)

miscegenation: A derogatory word for interracial sexual relationships coined by Democrats in the 1864 election, as they claimed that emancipation would allow African American men to gain sexual access to white women and produce mixed-race children. (p. 443)

Mississippian culture: A Native American culture complex that flourished in the Mississippi River basin and the Southeast from around A.D. 850 to around 1700. Characterized by maize agriculture, moundbuilding, and distinctive pottery styles, Mississippian communities were complex chiefdoms usually located along the floodplains of rivers. The largest of these communities was Cahokia, in modern-day Illinois. (p. 12)

Mississippi Freedom Democratic Party: A multiracial political party founded in Mississippi during the Freedom Summer of 1964, in order to protest the exclusion of black voters from the state's mainline Democratic Party. (p. 855)

Missouri Compromise: A series of political agreements devised by Speaker of the House Henry Clay. Maine entered the Union as a free state and Missouri followed as a slave state, preserving a balance in the Senate between North and South. Farther west, it set the northern boundary of slavery at the southern boundary of Missouri. (p. 290)

mixed government: A political theory that called for three branches of government, each representing one function: executive, legislative, and judicial. This system of dispersed authority was devised to maintain a balance of power in government. (p. 192)

modernism: A literary and artistic movement that questioned the ideals of progress and order, rejected realism, and emphasized new cultural forms. Modernism had great cultural influence in the twentieth century and remains influential today. (p. 554)

travesía del Atlántico: Brutal viaje por mar desde África hasta las Américas que llevó a 12.5 millones de africanos a la esclavitud. Cerca de 1.8 millones murieron en el camino. (pág. 94)

complejo industrial-militar: Término empleado por el presidente Eisenhower para referirse al establecimiento militar y a los contratistas de defensa que, advirtió, ejercían demasiada influencia sobre el gobierno nacional. (pág. 807)

Minor v. Happersett: Decisión de la Corte Suprema en 1875 que dictaminó que los derechos de sufragio no eran inherentes a la ciudadanía y no habían sido otorgados por la Decimocuarta Enmienda, como argumentaban algunos defensores de los derechos de las mujeres. Las mujeres eran ciudadanas, dictaminó la Corte, pero las legislaturas estatales podían negarles el voto si así lo deseaban. (pág. 459)

minstrel: Entretenimiento teatral popular que tuvo sus comienzos alrededor de 1830, en el que los actores blancos, con la cara pintada de negro, presentaban rutinas cómicas que combinaban la caricatura racista y la crítica social. (pág. 327)

minutemen: Milicianos coloniales que estaban listos para movilizarse sin antelación durante la crisis imperial de la década de 1770. Estos voluntarios formaron el núcleo del ejército de ciudadanos que se reunió con las tropas británicas en Lexington y Concord en abril de 1775. (pág. 171)

mestizaje: Palabra despectiva acuñada por los demócratas en las elecciones de 1864 para referirse a las relaciones interraciales. Los demócratas afirmaban que la emancipación les permitiría a los hombres afroamericanos obtener acceso sexual a mujeres blancas y producir niños de raza mixta. (pág. 443)

cultura misisipiana: Complejo de cultura nativa americana que floreció en la cuenca del río Misisipi y en el Sureste entre los años 850 d.C. y aproximadamente 1700. Caracterizadas por la agricultura de maíz, la construcción de montículos y los estilos distintivos de cerámica, las comunidades misisipianas eran jefaturas complejas que generalmente se ubicaban a lo largo de los terrenos inundables de los ríos. La mayor de estas comunidades fue Cahokia, en la actual Illinois. (pág. 12)

Partido Demócrata de la Libertad de Misisipi: Partido multi-racial fundado en Misisipi durante el Verano de la Libertad de 1964 para protestar contra la exclusión de votantes negros del Partido Demócrata del estado. (pág. 855)

Compromiso de Misuri: Serie de acuerdos políticos ideados por el presidente de la Cámara, Henry Clay. Maine ingresó a la Unión como un estado libre en 1820 y Misuri le siguió como un estado esclavista en 1821, preservando un equilibrio en el Senado entre el Norte y el Sur. Hacia el oeste, estableció la frontera norte de la esclavitud en la frontera sur de Misuri. (pág. 290)

gobierno mixto: Teoría política que propone tres poderes gubernamentales, cada uno con una función particular: ejecutivo, legislativo y judicial. Este sistema de autoridad distribuida fue diseñado para mantener el equilibrio de poderes en el gobierno. (pág. 192)

modernismo: Movimiento que cuestionó los ideales del orden y progreso, rechazó al realismo y enfatizó nuevas formas culturales. El modernismo fue el primer gran movimiento literario y artístico del siglo XX y a la fecha permanece su influencia. (pág. 554)

Monroe Doctrine: The 1823 declaration by President James Monroe that the Western Hemisphere was closed to any further colonization or interference by European powers. In exchange, Monroe pledged that the United States would not become involved in European struggles. (p. 240)

Doctrina Monroe: Declaración de 1823 del presidente James Monroe de que el hemisferio occidental estaba cerrado a cualquier colonización o interferencia de las potencias europeas. A cambio, Monroe se comprometió a no involucrar a los Estados Unidos en las luchas europeas. (pág. 240)

Montgomery Bus Boycott: Yearlong boycott of Montgomery's segregated bus system in 1955–1956 by the city's African American population. The boycott brought Martin Luther King Jr. to national prominence and ended in victory when the Supreme Court declared segregated seating on public transportation unconstitutional. (p. 849)

Boicot de autobuses de Montgomery: Boicot de la población afroamericana al sistema segregado de autobuses de la ciudad durante un año entre 1955–1956. El boicot le dio prominencia nacional a Martin Luther King Jr. y tuvo un final victorioso cuando la Corte Suprema declaró que la segregación de asientos en el transporte público era inconstitucional. (pág. 849)

Moral Majority: A political organization established by evangelist Jerry Falwell in 1979 to mobilize conservative Christian voters on behalf of Ronald Reagan's campaign for president. (p. 949)

Mayoría Moral: Organización política establecida por el evangelista Jerry Falwell en 1979 para movilizar a los votantes cristianos conservadores en favor de la campaña presidencial de Ronald Reagan. (pág. 949)

mothers' pensions: Progressive Era public payments to mothers who did not have help from a male breadwinner. Recipients had to meet standards of "respectability" defined by middle-class home visitors, reflecting a broader impulse to protect women but hold them to different standards than men. (p. 624)

pensiones maternales: Apoyo gubernamental durante la Era Progresiva para madres cuyos maridos fallecieron, habían sido incapacitados o abandonaron a la familia. Las beneficiarias debían cumplir con estándares de "respetabilidad" definidos por visitantes de clase media que acudían a los hogares, lo cual reflejaba una preferencia por proteger a las mujeres y, a su vez, someterlas a diferentes criterios que a los hombres. (pág. 624)

muckrakers: A term, first applied negatively by Theodore Roosevelt but later used proudly by reformers, for investigative journalists who published exposés of political scandals and industrial abuses. (p. 587)

muckrakers: Término crítico empleado por Theodore Roosevelt para periodistas investigadores que desenmascararon escándalos políticos y abusos industriales. (pág. 587)

Muller v. Oregon: A 1908 Supreme Court case that upheld an Oregon law limiting women's workday to ten hours, based on the need to protect women's health for motherhood. *Muller* established a groundwork for states to protect workers but divided women's rights activists, some of whom saw it as discriminatory. (p. 624)

Muller v. Oregon: Caso de la Corte Suprema en 1908 para mantener una ley que limitaba la jornada laboral de las mujeres a diez horas, con base en la necesidad de proteger la salud de las mujeres para la maternidad. *Muller* sentó las bases para que los estados pudieran proteger a los trabajadores. Sin embargo, dividió a los activistas de derechos de las mujeres, al considerar que algunas de sus disposiciones eran discriminatorias. (pág. 624)

multiculturalism: Diversity in gender, race, ethnicity, religion, and sexual preference. This political and social policy became increasingly popular in the United States during the 1980s post–civil rights era. (p. 982)

multiculturalismo: Promoción de la diversidad de género, raza, etnicidad, religión y preferencia sexual. Esta política en materia social y gubernamental fue cada vez más popular en Estados Unidos en la década de 1980, durante la etapa posterior a la era de los derechos civiles. (pág. 982)

multinational corporation: Corporate organization that owns or controls production of goods or services in a country or countries other than its home country. (p. 975)

corporaciones multinacionales: Corporaciones que tienen oficionas y fábricas en países que no son su país de origen. (pág. 975)

Munich Conference: A conference in Munich, Germany, held in September 1938 during which Britain and France agreed to allow Germany to annex the Sudetenland — a German-speaking border area of Czechoslovakia — in return for Hitler's pledge to seek no more territory. (p. 739)

Conferencia de Munich: Conferencia celebrada en septiembre de 1938 en Munich durante la cual Bretaña y Francia aceptaron que Alemania anexara la región de los Sudetes — región fronteriza de Checoslovaquia de habla alemana — a cambio del compromiso de Hitler de no buscar más territorio. (pág. 739)

Munn v. Illinois: An 1877 Supreme Court case that affirmed that states could regulate key businesses, such as railroads and grain elevators, if those businesses were "clothed in the public interest." (p. 487)

Munn v. Illinois: Caso de la Corte Suprema de 1877 que afirmaba que los estados podían regular negocios clave, como ferrocarriles y elevadores de granos, si esos negocios estaban "eran de interés público". (pág. 487)

mutual benefit society: An organization through which members of an ethnic immigrant group or other community, usually those from a particular province or town, pooled their funds to aid one another in case of emergency need. The societies functioned as fraternal clubs that collected dues from members in order to pay support in case of death or disability. (p. 581)

sociedad de asistencia mutua: Organización a través de la cual los miembros de minorías étnicas o de otra comunidad, generalmente una provincia o un pueblo, recaudaban fondos para ayudarse entre sí en caso de emergencia. Las sociedades funcionaban como clubes que cobraban cuotas a los miembros para pagar gastos en casos de muerte o incapacidad. (pág. 581)

My Lai: Vietnamese village where U.S. Army troops executed nearly five hundred people in 1968, including a large number of women and children. (p. 897)

National American Woman Suffrage Association: Women's suffrage organization created in 1890 by the union of the National Woman Suffrage Association and the American Woman Suffrage Association. Up to national ratification of suffrage in 1920, the NAWSA played a central role in campaigning for women's right to vote. (p. 572)

National Association for the Advancement of Colored People (NAACP): An organization founded in 1909 by leading African American reformers and white allies as a vehicle for advocating equal rights for African Americans, especially through the courts. (p. 626)

National Association of Colored Women: An organization created in 1896 by African American women to provide community support. NACW members arranged for the care of orphans and the elderly, undertook campaigns for public health and women's suffrage, and raised awareness of racial injustice. (p. 569)

National Association of Manufacturers: An association of industrialists and business leaders opposed to government regulation. In the era of the New Deal, the group produced radio programs, motion pictures, billboards, and direct mail campaigns to promote free enterprise and unfettered capitalism. (p. 714)

National Child Labor Committee: A reform organization that worked (unsuccessfully) to win a federal law banning child labor. The NCLC hired photographer Lewis Hine to record brutal conditions in mines and mills where thousands of children worked. (p. 624)

National Consumers' League: A national progressive organization that encouraged women, through their shopping decisions, to support fair wages and working conditions for industrial laborers. (p. 599)

National Defense Education Act: A 1958 act that funneled millions of dollars into American universities, helping institutions such as Stanford and the Massachusetts Institute of Technology, become leading research centers. (p. 808)

National Interstate and Defense Highways Act: A 1956 law authorizing the construction of 42,500 miles of new highways and their integration into a single national highway system. (p. 826)

National Municipal League: A political reform organization that advised cities to elect small councils and hire professional city managers who would direct operations like a corporate executive. Some cities (especially younger and smaller ones) took up the reform. (p. 593)

National Organization for Women (NOW): Women's civil rights organization formed in 1966. Initially, NOW focused on eliminating gender discrimination in public institutions and the workplace, but by the 1970s it also embraced many of the issues raised by more radical feminists. (p. 878)

My Lai: Pueblo vietnamita donde tropas del ejército estadounidense ejecutaron a cerca de 500 personas en 1968, incluyendo a mujeres y niños. (pág. 897)

Asociación Nacional Americana pro Sufragio de la Mujer (NAWSA): Organización de mujeres sufragistas creada en 1890 tras la unión de la Asociación Nacional pro Sufragio de la Mujer y la Asociación Americana pro Sufragio de la Mujer. Hasta el momento de la ratificación del sufragio en 1920, la NAWSA desempeñó un papel central en las campañas para el derecho de voto de las mujeres. (pág. 572)

Asociación Nacional para el Progreso de las Personas de Color (NAACP): Organización fundada en 1909 por líderes reformistas afroamericanos y aliados blancos para defender la igualdad de derechos de los afroamericanos, especialmente en los tribunales. (pág. 626)

Asociación Nacional de Mujeres de Color (NACW): Organización creada en 1896 por mujeres afroamericanas para ofrecer apoyo al a comunidad. A través de sus clubes locales, la NACW ayudó a cuidar huérfanos, fundó hogares para la tercera edad, emprendió campañas de salud pública, lanzó campañas para el sufragio de la mujer y creo conciencia de la injusticia racial. (pág. 569)

Asociación Nacional de Manufacturas: Asociación de industrialistas y líderes empresariales que se oponen a la regulación gubernamental. En la era del Nuevo Trato, el grupo promovió la empresa libre y el capitalismo a través de campañas de radio, películas, carteleras y correo directo. (pág. 714)

Comité Nacional del Trabajo Infantil (NCLC): Organización de reforma que trabajó (sin éxito) para lograr una ley federal que prohibiera el trabajo infantil. La NCLC contrató al fotógrafo Lewis Hine para documentar las condiciones brutales en minas y plantas donde trabajaban miles de niños. (pág. 624)

Liga Nacional de Consumidores: Organización nacional progresista, que promovió que las mujeres, a través de sus decisiones de compra, apoyaran el salario justo y las condiciones laborales de los trabajadores industriales. (pág. 599)

Ley Nacional de Educación de Defensa: Ley de 1958 aprobada en respuesta al lanzamiento soviético del satélite *Sputnik*, que encauzó millones de dólares hacia las universidades estadounidenses y ayudó a instituciones como la Universidad de Berkeley en California y el Massachusetts Institute of Technology, entre otras, a convertirse en centros de investigación líderes a nivel mundial. (pág. 808)

Ley Nacional de Autopistas Interestatales y de Defensa: Ley de 1956 que autorizó la construcción de un sistema nacional de carreteras. (pág. 826)

Liga Nacional Municipal: Organización de reforma política que aconsejó a pequeños condados que contrataran a gestores municipales para dirigir sus operaciones como un ejecutivo corporativo. Algunas ciudades, particularmente las más nuevas y pequeñas, asumieron la reforma. (pág. 593)

Organización Nacional de Mujeres (NOW): Organización de derechos civiles de mujeres, formada en 1966. En un principio, la NOW se enfocó en la eliminación de la discriminación de género en las instituciones públicas y en el trabajo, y para la década de 1970 asumió muchas de las causas de feministas más radicales. (pág. 878)

National Origins Act (1924): A federal law limiting annual immigration from each foreign country to no more than 2 percent of that nationality's percentage of the U.S. population as it had stood in 1890. The law severely limited immigration, especially from Southern and Eastern Europe. (p. 691)

National Park Service: A federal agency founded in 1916 that provided comprehensive oversight of the growing system of national parks, established to allow Americans to access and enjoy sites of natural beauty. (p. 563)

National Recovery Administration: Federal agency established in June 1933 to promote industrial recovery during the Great Depression. It encouraged industrialists to voluntarily adopt codes that defined fair wages, set prices, and minimized competition. (p. 709)

National Review: A conservative magazine founded by editor William F. Buckley in 1955 that criticized liberal policy and helped lay the foundation for the New Right. (p. 942)

National Socialist (Nazi) Party: German political party led by Adolf Hitler, who became chancellor of Germany in 1933. The party's ascent was fueled by huge World War I reparation payments, economic depression, fear of communism, labor unrest, and rising unemployment. (p. 737)

National War Labor Board: A federal agency founded in 1918 that established an eight-hour day for war workers (with time-and-a-half pay for overtime), endorsed equal pay for women, and supported workers' right to organize. (p. 657)

National Woman's Party: A political party founded in 1916 that fought for women's suffrage, and after helping to achieve that goal in 1920, advocated for an Equal Rights Amendment to the U.S. Constitution. (p. 661)

National Woman Suffrage Association: A suffrage group headed by Elizabeth Cady Stanton and Susan B. Anthony that stressed the need for women to lead organizations on their own behalf. The NWSA focused exclusively on women's rights — sometimes denigrating men of color in the process — and took up the battle for a federal women's suffrage amendment. (p. 572)

Nation of Islam: A religion founded in the United States that became a leading source of black nationalist thought in the 1960s. Black Muslims fused elements of traditional Islamic doctrine with black pride, a strong philosophy of self-improvement, and a rejection of white culture. (p. 860)

nativism: Opposition to immigration and to full citizenship for recent immigrants or to immigrants of a particular ethnic or national background, as expressed, for example, by anti-Irish discrimination in the 1850s and Asian exclusion laws between the 1880s and 1940s. (p. 398)

Naturalization, Alien, and Sedition Acts: Three laws passed in 1798 that limited individual rights and threatened the fledgling party system. The Naturalization Act lengthened the residency requirement for citizenship, the Alien Act authorized the deportation of foreigners, and the Sedition Act prohibited the publication of insults or malicious attacks on the president or members of Congress. (p. 222)

Ley de Orígenes Nacionales: Ley de 1924 que limitó la inmigración anual de cada país a no más del 2 por ciento del porcentaje de esa nacionalidad en la población de Estados Unidos con respecto a 1890. La ley limitó la inmigración notablemente, especialmente del sur y del este de Europa. (pág. 691)

Servicio de Parques Nacionales: Agencia federal fundada en 1916 que ofreció supervisión integral del creciente sistema de parques nacionales. (pág. 563)

Administración para la Recuperación Nacional: Agencia federal establecida en junio de 1933 para promover la recuperación industrial durante la Gran Depresión. Alentó a industrialistas a adaptar voluntariamente códigos que definieran condiciones laborales justas, precios fijos y minimizaron la competencia. (pág. 709)

National Review: Revista conservadora fundada en 1955 por el editor William F. Buckley, quien la usó para criticar la política liberal. (pág. 942)

Partido Nacional Socialista (Nazi): Partido político alemán dirigido por Adolf Hitler, que fue canciller alemán en 1933. El ascenso del partido fue causado en parte por los enormes pagos de reparación de la Primera Guerra Mundial, por la depresión económica, el miedo al comunismo, el malestar laboral y el aumento del desempleo. (pág. 737)

Comité Nacional de Trabajos de Guerra: Agencia federal fundada en 1918 que estableció la jornada laboral de ocho horas para los trabajadores de guerra (con pagos de tiempo y medio por horas extra), aprobó el pago igualitario para mujeres y apoyó el derecho de organización de los trabajadores. (pág. 657)

Partido Nacional de Mujeres: Partido político fundado en 1916 que luchó por el sufragio de la mujer y, al ayudar a obtenerlo en 1920, abogó por la Enmienda de Igualdad de Derechos de la Constitución de los Estados Unidos. (pág. 661)

Asociación Nacional pro Sufragio de la Mujer (NWSA): Grupo de sufragio encabezado por Elizabeth Cady Stanton y Susan B. Anthony que enfatizó la necesidad de que las mujeres lideren organizaciones en representación propia. La NWSA se centró exclusivamente en los derechos de las mujeres — a veces denigrando a los hombres de color en el proceso — y emprendió la batalla por una enmienda federal al sufragio de las mujeres. (pág. 572)

Nación de Islam: Religión fundada en Estados Unidos que se convirtió en una fuente de pensamiento nacionalista negro en la década de 1960. Los Musulmanes Negros juntaron elementos de la doctrina islámica tradicional con el orgullo negro, una fuerte filosofía de autosuperación y un rechazo de la cultura blanca. (pág. 860)

nativismo: Oposición a la inmigración y a la ciudadanía plena para inmigrantes recientes o inmigrantes de ciertos orígenes étnicos o nacionales. Un ejemplo fue la discriminación antiirlandesa que tuvo lugar en la década de 1850 y las leyes de exclusión asiáticas entre los años 1880 y 1940. (pág. 398)

Leyes de Naturalización, Extranjería y Sedición: Tres leyes aprobadas en 1798 que limitaron derechos individuales y amenazaron al incipiente sistema de partidos. La Ley de Naturalización aumentó el tiempo de residencia requerido para obtener la ciudadanía, la Ley de Extranjería autorizó la deportación de extranjeros y la Ley de Sedición prohibió la publicación de insultos o ataques malignos contra el presidente o miembros del Congreso. (pág. 222)

natural rights: The rights to life, liberty, and property. John Locke argued that political authority was not given by God to monarchs but instead derived from social compacts that people made to preserve their natural rights. (p. 124)

derechos naturales: El derecho a la vida, la libertad y la propiedad. Según el filósofo John Locke en su obra *Dos tratados sobre el gobierno civil* (1690), no era Dios quien concedía autoridad política a los monarcas. En cambio, la autoridad derivaba de contratos sociales que las personas hacían para preservar sus derechos naturales. (pág. 124)

Navigation Acts: English laws passed, beginning in the 1650s and 1660s, requiring that certain English colonial goods be shipped through English ports on English ships manned primarily by English sailors in order to benefit English merchants, shippers, and seamen. (p. 83)

Actas de Navegación: Leyes aprobadas, apartir de la década de 1650 y 1660, que requerían que ciertos bienes coloniales ingleses fueran importados a través de puertos ingleses, a bordo de embarcaciones inglesas tripuladas por navegantes ingleses con el fin de beneficiar a los mercantes, exportadores y marineros ingleses. (pág. 83)

Negro leagues: Professional baseball teams formed for and by black players after the 1890s, when the regular national leagues excluded African American players. Enduring until after World War II, the leagues enabled black men to showcase athletic ability and race pride, but working conditions and wages were poor. (p. 560)

Ligas Negras: Equipos profesionales de béisbol formados por y para jugadores negros, tras la exclusión de todos los jugadores afroamericanos de las principales ligas nacionales en la década de 1890. Las ligas duraron hasta la abolición de la segregación racial en el béisbol, al concluir la Segunda Guerra Mundial, y permitieron a los hombres negros mostrar sus capacidades atléticas y orgullo racial, pero bajo condiciones y salarios mucho menos deseables que aquellos de los jugadores en las ligas blancas. (pág. 560)

neo-Europes: Term for colonies in which colonists sought to replicate, or at least approximate, economies and social structures they knew at home. (p. 40)

neoeuropeos: Término para las colonias en las cuales los colonos buscaron recrear, o al menos aproximar, las estructuras económicas o sociales que conocían en sus países de origen. (pág. 40)

neomercantilism: A system of government-assisted economic development embraced by state legislatures in the first half of the nineteenth century, especially in the Northeast. This system of activist government encouraged entrepreneurs to enhance the public welfare through private economic initiatives. (p. 250)

neomercantilismo: Sistema de desarrollo económico asistido por el gobierno que fue adoptado por las legislaturas de los estados republicanos por todo el país, particularmente en el noreste. Este sistema de gobierno activista invitaba a emprendedores privados a buscar oportunidades individuales y al bienestar público a través del intercambio de mercados. (pág. 250)

Neutrality Act of 1935: Legislation that sought to avoid entanglement in foreign wars while protecting trade. It imposed an embargo on selling arms to warring countries and declared that Americans traveling on the ships of belligerent nations did so at their own risk. (p. 738)

Ley de Neutralidad de 1935: Legislación que buscó evitar la participación en guerras extranjeras y al mismo tiempo proteger al comercio. Impuso un embargo a la venta de armas a países en guerra y declaró que los estadounidenses que viajaran en las embarcaciones de países beligerantes lo hacían bajo su propio riesgo. (pág. 738)

New Jersey Plan: Alternative to the Virginia Plan drafted by delegates from small states, retaining the Confederation's single-house congress with one vote per state. It shared with the Virginia Plan enhanced congressional powers to raise revenue, control commerce, and make binding requisitions on the states. (p. 202)

Plan de Nueva Jersey: Alternativa para el Plan de Virginia redactado por delegados de estados para mantener el Congreso de una cámara única en la confederación, con un voto por estado. De manera similar al Plan de Virginia, ampliaba los poderes del Congreso para aumentar las rentas, controlar el comercio y hacer requisitos vinculantes a los estados. (pág. 202)

Newlands Reclamation Act: A 1902 law, supported by President Theodore Roosevelt, that allowed the federal government to sell public lands to raise money for irrigation projects that expanded agriculture on arid lands. (p. 622)

Ley de Recuperación de Newlands: Ley de 1902 apoyada por el presidente Theodore Roosevelt, que permitió al gobierno federal vender tierras públicas para recaudar fondos para los proyectos de irrigación que expandieron la agricultura en tierras áridas. (pág. 622)

New Left: A term applied to radical students of the 1960s and 1970s, distinguishing their activism from the Old Left — the communists and socialists of the 1930s and 1940s. (p. 855)

Nueva Izquierda: Término usado para estudiantes radicales de las décadas de 1960 y 1970 que distinguía su activismo del de la Vieja Izquierda, representada por comunistas y socialistas de las décadas de 1930 y 1940. (pág. 885)

New Lights: Evangelical preachers who decried a Christian faith that was merely intellectual; they emphasized instead the importance of a spiritual rebirth. (p. 128)

luces nuevas: Predicadores evangélicos que menospreciaban a la fe cristiana meramente intelectual y resaltaban la importancia de un renacimiento espiritual. (pág. 128)

New Look: The defense policy of the Eisenhower administration that stepped up production of the hydrogen bomb and developed long-range bombing capabilities. (p. 795)

Política "New Look" (Nueva Apariencia): Política de defensa de la administración de Eisenhower que aumentó la producción de bombas de hidrógeno y desarrolló la capacidad de bombardeo de larga distancia. (pág. 795)

New Nationalism: Theodore Roosevelt's 1910 proposal to enhance public welfare through a federal child labor law, more recognition

Nuevo Nacionalismo: En un discurso pronunciado en 1910, Theodore Roosevelt, llamó a un "Nuevo Nacionalismo" que of labor rights, a national minimum wage for women, women's suffrage, and curbs on the power of federal courts. (p. 626)

promovía la intervención del gobierno para mejorar el bienestar público, incluyendo una ley de trabajo infantil, mayor reconocimiento de los derechos laborales, un salario mínimo nacional para las mujeres, sufragio para las mujeres, y reducciones al poder de las cortes federales para impedir reformas. (pág. 626)

New South: A term describing economic diversification and growth of industry in the post–Civil War South. Because of the region's poverty, much work was extractive (such as coal and timber production), and some (like textiles) was low-wage and involved child labor. (p. 526)

Nuevo Sur: Apodo para los antiguos estados Confederados, usado por sus adeptos para describir la diversificación económica y el aumento de empleos industriales en la región durante la era posterior a la Guerra Civil. Debido a la pobreza de la región, muchas de esas industrias eran de extracción (de carbón y madera) y algunas (como la industria de textiles) pagaban salarios bajos y practicaban en gran medida el trabajo infantil. (pág. 526)

1968 Democratic National Convention: A convention held in Chicago during which numerous antiwar demonstrators outside the convention hall were teargassed and clubbed by police. Inside the convention hall, the delegates were bitterly divided over Vietnam. (p. 881)

Convención Nacional Demócrata de 1968: Convención celebrada en Chicago en la que la policía lanzó gas y golpeó a una gran cantidad de manifestantes pacifistas fuera del salón de convenciones. Dentro del salón de convenciones, los delegados tenían posiciones muy divididas con respecto a la Guerra de Vietnam. (pág. 881)

nonimportation movement: The effort to protest parliamentary legislation by boycotting British goods. This occurred in 1766, in response to the Stamp Act; in 1768, after the Townshend duties; and in 1774, after the Coercive Acts. (p. 155)

movimiento de no importación: Los colonos intentaron firmar acuerdos de no importación tres veces: en 1766, en respuesta a la Ley del Timbre; en 1768, en respuesta a los Actos Townshend; y en 1774, en respuesta a las Leyes Coactivas. (pág. 155)

North American Free Trade Agreement (NAFTA): A 1993 treaty that eliminated all tariffs and trade barriers among the United States, Canada, and Mexico. The agreement stimulated economic growth, but critics charged that it left workers in all countries vulnerable. (p. 974)

Tratado de Libre Comercio de América del Norte (TLCAN): Tratado firmado en 1993 que eliminó todos los aranceles y barreras comerciales entre Estados Unidos, Canadá y México. El tratado estimuló el crecimiento económico, pero los críticos argumentaban que dejaría a los trabajadores de los tres países en una posición vulnerable. (pág. 974)

North Atlantic Treaty Organization (NATO): Military alliance formed in 1949 among the United States, Canada, and Western European nations to counter any possible Soviet threat. (p. 782)

Organización del Tratado del Atlántico Norte (OTAN): Alianza militar formada en 1949 entre Estados Unidos, Canadá y los países del occidente de Europa para contrarrestar cualquier amenaza soviética. (pág. 782)

Northwest Ordinance of 1787: A land act that provided for orderly settlement and established a process by which settled territories would become the states of Ohio, Indiana, Illinois, Michigan, and Wisconsin. It also banned slavery in the Northwest Territory. (p. 197)

Ordenanza Noroeste de 1787: Ley de tierras que estableció un asentamiento ordenado y un proceso por medio del cual los territorios poblados se convertirían en los estados de Ohio, Indiana, Illinois, Michigan y Wisconsin. También prohibió la esclavitud en el Territorio Noroeste. (pág. 197)

notables: Northern landlords, slave-owning planters, and seaport merchants who dominated the political system of the early nineteenth century. (p. 284)

notables: Terratenientes norteños, colonos dueños de esclavos y comerciantes de puertos marítimos que dominaron el sistema político del siglo XIX. (pág. 284)

NSC-68: Top-secret government report of April 1950 warning that national survival in the face of Soviet communism required a massive military buildup. (p. 783)

NSC-68 (Reporte 68 del Consejo de Seguridad Nacional): Reporte ultra-secreto del gobierno, redactado en 1950, que advirtió que sobrevivir al comunismo soviético implicaría un aumento drástico en el armamento militar. (pág. 783)

nullification: The constitutional argument advanced by John C. Calhoun that a state legislature or convention could void a law passed by Congress. (p. 296)

anulación: Argumento constitucional impulsado por John C. Calhoun en el cual una legislatura o convención estatal puede vetar una ley aprobada por el Congreso. (pág. 296)

Old Lights: Conservative ministers opposed to the passion displayed by evangelical New Light preachers; they preferred to emphasize the importance of cultivating a virtuous Christian life. (p. 128)

luces viejas: Ministros conservadores que se opusieron a la pasión mostrada por predicadores evangélicos; preferían resaltar la importancia de cultuivar una vida cristiana virtuosa. (pág. 128)

Omaha Platform: An 1892 statement by the Populists calling for public ownership of transportation and communication networks, protection of land from monopoly and foreign ownership, looser monetary policy, and a federal income tax on the rich. (p. 613)

Plataforma de Omaha: Declaración de los populistas en 1892 que exigió que las redes de transporte y comunicación fueran propiedad pública, que se protegiera a la tierra de monopolios y propiedad extranjera, que se relajaran las políticas monetarias y que se cobraran impuestos federales a los ricos. (pág. 613)

one-tenth tax: A tax adopted by the Confederacy in 1863 that required all farmers to turn over a tenth of their crops and livestock to the government for military use. The tax demonstrated the southern government's strong use of centralized power; it caused great hardship for poor families. (p. 427)

impuesto del décimo: Impuesto adoptado por la Confederación en 1863 que requería que todos los agricultores entregaran al gobierno una décima parte de sus cultivos y ganado para uso militar. El impuesto demostró el fuerte uso del gobierno sureño del poder centralizado; causó grandes dificultades para las familias pobres. (pág. 427)

"open door" policy: A claim put forth by U.S. Secretary of State John Hay that all nations seeking to do business in China should have equal trade access. (p. 649)

política de puertas abiertas: Afirmación de John Hay, Secretario de Estado de Estados Unidos, quien dijo que todos los países que deseen hacer negocios en China deben tener el mismo nivel de acceso comercial. (pág. 649)

Operation Rolling Thunder: Massive bombing campaign against North Vietnam authorized by President Johnson in 1965; despite lasting three years, the bombing made North Vietnam more, not less, determined to continue fighting. (p. 881)

Operación Rolling Thunder: Campaña masiva de bombardeos contra Vietnam del Norte autorizada por el presidente Johnson en 1965; contra toda expectativa, alimentó y fortaleció al deseo de los vietnamitas del norte de mantenerse en la pelea. (pág. 881)

Oregon Trail: An emigrant route that originally led from Independence, Missouri, to the Willamette Valley in Oregon, a distance of some 2,000 miles. Alternate routes included the California Trail, the Mormon Trail, and the Bozeman Trail. Together they conveyed several hundred thousand migrants to the Far West in the 1840s, 1850s, and 1860s. (p. 363)

senda de Oregon: Ruta emigrante que originalmente iniciaba en Independence, Misuri, y llegaba hasta el valle de Willamette en Oregón, tras un recorrido de unas dos mil millas. Entre las rutas alternas estaba la senda de California, la senda de los Mormones y la senda Bozeman. Las tres rutas llevaron a cientos de miles de migrantes al Lejano Oeste durante las décadas de 1840, 1850 y 1860. (pág. 363)

Organization of Petroleum Exporting Countries (OPEC): An alliance of oil-rich countries founded in 1960 to set prices and regulate the oil market. (p. 907)

Organización de Países Exportadores de Petróleo (OPEC, en inglés): Cartel formado en 1960 por países de riqueza petrolera que permitió a sus miembros ejercer mayor control sobre el precio del petróleo. (pág. 907)

Ostend Manifesto: An 1854 manifesto that urged President Franklin Pierce to seize the slave-owning province of Cuba from Spain. Northern Democrats denounced this aggressive initiative, and the plan was scuttled. (p. 394)

manifiesto de Ostende: Manifiesto de 1854 que exhortó al presidente Franklin Pierce a apoderarse de la provincia esclavista de Cuba que pertenecía a España. Los Demócratas del Norte denunciaron esta agresiva iniciativa y el plan fue desechado. (pág. 394)

Palmer Raids: A series of raids ordered by Attorney General A. Mitchell Palmer on radical organizations that peaked in January 1920, when federal agents arrested six thousand citizens and aliens and denied them access to legal council. (p. 674)

Redadas de Palmer: Serie de redadas dirigidas por el fiscal general, A. Mitchell Palmer, sobre las organizaciones radicales que tuvieron su auge en enero de 1920, cuando agentes federales arrestaron a seis mil ciudadanos y extranjeros y les negaron acceso a un abogado. (pág. 674)

pan-Africanism: The idea that people of African descent, in all parts of the world, have a common heritage and destiny and should cooperate in political action. (p. 697)

pan-africanismo: La idea de que las personas de descendencia africana en todo el mundo tienen una herencia y destino común y deben cooperar en la acción política. (pág. 697)

Panama Canal: A canal across the Isthmus of Panama connecting trade between the Atlantic and Pacific oceans. Built by the U.S. Army Corps of Engineers and opened in 1914, the canal gave U.S. naval vessels quick access to the Pacific and provided the United States with a commanding position in the Western Hemisphere. (p. 651)

Canal de Panamá: Canal que atraviesa el Istmo de Panamá y conecta el comercio entre el océano Pacífico y el Atlántico. Construido por los Cuerpos de Ingenieros del Ejército de los Estados Unidos e inaugurado en 1914, el canal le dio acceso rápido a las embarcaciones navales estadounidenses al Pacífico y ofreció a los Estados Unidos una posición dominante en el Hemisferio Occidental. (pág. 651)

Panic of 1819: First major economic crisis of the United States. Farmers and planters faced an abrupt 30 percent drop in world agricultural prices, and as farmers' income declined, they could not pay debts owed to stores and banks, many of which went bankrupt. (p. 252)

crisis de 1819: Primera gran crisis económica de Estados Unidos. Granjeros y hacendados enfrentaron una caída repentina del 30 por ciento en los precios mundiales de la agricultura, y al disminuir los ingresos de los granjeros, les fue imposible pagar las deudas contraídas en tiendas y bancos que, a su vez, terminaron en bancarrota. (pág. 252)

Panic of 1837: Triggered by a sharp reduction in English capital and credit flowing into the United States, the cash shortage caused a panic while the collapse of credit led to a depression — the second major economic crisis of the United States — that lasted from 1837 to 1843. (p. 307)

crisis de 1837: Provocada por una fuerte reducción de la entrada de capital y crédito inglés a Estados Unidos, la escasez de efectivo causó pánico y el colapso del crédito llevó a una depresión — la segunda crisis económica mayor en Estados Unidos — que duró de 1837 a 1843. (pág. 307)

paternalism: The ideology held by slave owners who considered themselves committed to the welfare of their slaves. (p. 267)

Patient Protection and Affordable Care Act: Sweeping 2010 health-care reform bill championed by President Obama that established nearly universal health insurance by providing subsidies and compelling larger businesses to offer coverage to employees. (p. 995)

patronage: The power of elected officials to grant government jobs and favors to their supporters; also the jobs and favors themselves. (p. 107)

Peace Corps: Program launched by President Kennedy in 1961 through which young American volunteers helped with education, health, and other projects in developing countries around the world. (p. 801)

Pearl Harbor: A naval base in Pearl Harbor, Hawaii, that was attacked by Japanese bombers on December 7, 1941; more than 2,400 Americans were killed. The following day, President Roosevelt asked Congress for a declaration of war against Japan. (p. 742)

peasants: The traditional term for farmworkers in Europe. Some peasants owned land, whereas others leased or rented small plots from landlords. (p. 19)

Pendleton Act: An 1883 law establishing a nonpartisan Civil Service Commission to fill federal jobs by examination. The Pendleton Act dealt a major blow to the "spoils system" and sought to ensure that government positions were filled by trained, professional employees. (p. 610)

Pennsylvania constitution of 1776: It granted all taxpaying men the right to vote and hold office and created a unicameral (one-house) legislature with complete power; there was no governor to exercise a veto. It also mandated a system of elementary education and protected citizens from imprisonment for debt. (p. 191)

penny papers: Sensational and popular urban newspapers that built large circulations by reporting crime and scandals. (p. 329)

perestroika: The economic restructuring policy introduced by Soviet president Mikhail Gorbachev during the 1980s that contributed, unintentionally, to the 1991 breakup of the Soviet Union. (p. 961)

Persian Gulf War: The 1991 war between Iraq and a U.S.-led international coalition that was sparked by the 1990 Iraqi invasion of Kuwait. A forty-day bombing campaign against Iraq followed by coalition troops storming into Kuwait brought a quick coalition victory. (p. 965)

personal liberty laws: Laws enacted in many northern states that guaranteed to all residents, including alleged fugitives, the right to a jury trial. (p. 393)

Personal Responsibility and Work Opportunity Reconciliation Act: Legislation signed by President Clinton in 1996 that replaced Aid to Families with Dependent Children with

paternalismo: Ideología de los dueños de esclavos que consideraban que estaban comprometidos con el bienestar de sus esclavos. (pág. 267)

Ley de Protección al Paciente y Cuidado de Salud Asequible: Arrolladora reforma del cuidado de salud en 2010 impulsada por el presidente Obama que estableció un seguro de saludo casi universal al ofrecer subsidios y obligando a las empresas más grandes a ofrecer cobertura a sus empleados. (pág. 955)

mecenazgo: El poder de oficiales electos para conceder cargos gubernamentales y favores a sus seguidores; también los trabajos y favores mismos. (pág. 107)

Cuerpos de Paz: Programa lanzado por el presidente Kennedy en 1961 a través del cual jóvenes voluntarios estadounidenses asistieron en la educación, salud y otros proyectos en países en desarrollo alrededor del mundo. (pág. 801)

Pearl Harbor: Base naval en Pearl Harbor, Hawái, que el 7 de diciembre de 1941 fue atacada por bombarderos japoneses; más de 2,400 estadounidenses murieron en el ataque. Al día siguiente, el presidente Roosevelt pidió al Congreso que declarara la guerra contra Japón. (pág. 742)

campesinos: Término tradicional para los trabajadores agrícolas en Europa. Algunos campesinos poseían tierras mientras que otros rentaban pequeños terrenos de sus terratenientes. (pág. 19)

Ley Pendleton: Ley de 1883 que estableció una Comisión de Servicio Civil independiente para ocupar cargos federales con base en méritos. La Ley Pendleton significó un fuerte golpe para el "sistema de concesión de favores" y buscó asegurar que los cargos de gobierno fueran ocupados por empleados profesionales y educados. (pág. 610)

Constitución de Pennsylvania de 1776: Constitución que otorgó a todos los hombres contribuyentes el derecho a votar y ocupar cargos públicos y creó una legislatura de una cámara con poderes completos; no incluyó la figura de un gobernador que pudiera ejercer un veto. Otras disposiciones ordenaron un sistema de educación primaria y protegía a los ciudadanos de ser encarcelados por deudas. (pág. 191)

penny press: Periódicos urbanos sensacionalistas y populares que lograron gran circulación al informar sobre crímenes y escándalos. (pág. 329)

perestroika: Política de reestructuración económica introducida por el presidente soviético Mikhail Gorbachev durante la década de 1980 que contribuyó, sin quererlo, a la desintegración de la Unión Soviética en 1991. (pág. 961)

Guerra del Golfo Pérsico: Guerra de 1991 entre Irak y una coalición internacional comandada por Estados Unidos y que fue causada por la invasión de Irak a Kuwait. Tras una campaña de bombardeos de 40 días contra Irak, las tropas de la coalición entraron a Kuwait y lograron rápidamente la victoria para la coalición. (pág. 965)

leyes de libertad personal: Leyes promulgadas en muchos estados del norte que garantizaban a todos los residentes, incluidos los presuntos fugitivos, el derecho a un juicio ante un jurado. (pág. 393)

Ley de Responsabilidad Personal y Reconciliación de Oportunidades: Legislación firmada por el presidente Clinton en 1996 que reemplazó el programa de Asistencia a Familias con Niños

Temporary Assistance for Needy Families, which provided grants to the states to assist the poor, and limited allowable welfare payments. (p. 987)

Dependientes con el programa Asistencia Temporal para Familias Necesitadas, que ofreció subsidios a los estados para asistir a los pobres y limitó los pagos de asistencia. (pág. 987)

Philipsburg Proclamation: A 1779 proclamation that declared that any slave who deserted a rebel master would receive protection, freedom, and land from Great Britain. (p. 184)

Proclamación de Philipsburg: Proclamación de 1779 que declaraba que cualquier esclavo que escapara de un maestro rebelde recibiría protección, libertad y tierras de Gran Bretaña. (pág. 184)

Pietism: A Christian revival movement characterized by Bible study, the conversion experience, and the individual's personal relationship with God that became widely influential in Britain and its colonies in the eighteenth century. (p. 122)

pietismo: Movimiento de renacimiento cristiano caracterizado por el estudio de la Biblia, la experiencia de la conversión y la relación personal del individuo con Dios. Comenzó como esfuerzo para reformar la Iglesia Luterana Alemana a mediados del siglo XVII y tuvo gran influencia en Bretaña y sus colonias en el siglo XVIII. (pág. 122)

Pilgrims: One of the first Protestant groups to come to America, seeking a separation from the Church of England. They founded Plymouth, the first permanent community in New England, in 1620. (p. 62)

peregrinos: Uno de los primeros grupos protestantes que llegaron a América buscando separarse de la Iglesia de Inglaterra. Fundaron Plymouth, la primera comunidad permanente en Nueva Inglaterra en 1620. (pág. 62)

Planned Parenthood of Southeastern Pennsylvania v. Casey: A 1992 Supreme Court case that upheld a law requiring a twenty-four-hour waiting period prior to an abortion. Although the decision upheld certain restrictions on abortions, it affirmed that women had a constitutional right to control their reproduction. (p. 985)

Planned Parenthood of Southeastern Pennsylvania v. Casey (Planificación de la Familia del Sureste de Pennsylvania contra Casey): Caso de la Corte Suprema de 1992 que mantuvo una ley que requiere un periodo de 24 horas de espera antes de un aborto. Si bien la decisión mantuvo ciertas restricciones sobre el aborto, sostuvo la "determinación esencial" de *Roe v. Wade* (1973), que estableció que las mujeres tienen el derecho constitucional de controlar su reproducción. (pág. 985)

plantation system: A system of production characterized by unfree labor producing cash crops for distant markets. The plantation complex developed in sugar-producing areas of the Mediterranean world and was transferred to the Americas, where it took hold in tropical and subtropical areas, including Brazil, the West Indies, and southeastern North America. In addition to sugar, the plantation complex was adapted to produce tobacco, rice, indigo, and cotton. (p. 37)

sistema de plantación: Sistema de producción caracterizado por usar esclavos, que produce cultivos comerciales para mercados lejanos. El sistema de plantación comenzó en las zonas azucareras del mundo mediterráneo y fue transferido a las Américas donde se instaló en zonas tropicales y subtropicales, inclyendo a Brasil, las Indias Occidentales y el sureste de Norteamérica. Aparte del azúcar, las plantaciones fueron adaptadas para producir arroz, tabaco, índigo y algodón. (pág. 37)

Platt Amendment: A 1902 amendment to the Cuban constitution that blocked Cuba from making a treaty with any country except the United States and gave the United States the right to intervene in Cuban affairs. The amendment was a condition for U.S. withdrawal from the newly independent island. (p. 647)

Enmienda Platt: Enmienda de 1902 a la constitución cubana que impidió a Cuba firmar tratados con ningún otro país que no fuera Estados Unidos y dio a Estados Unidos el derecho a intervenir en asuntos cubanos. La enmienda fue una condición para el retiro de Estados Unidos de la isla recién independizada. (pág. 647)

Plessy v. Ferguson: An 1896 Supreme Court case that ruled that racially segregated railroad cars and other public facilities, if they claimed to be "separate but equal," were permissible according to the Fourteenth Amendment. (p. 558)

Plessy v. Ferguson: Caso de la Corte Suprema en 1896 que dictaminó que la segregación racial en vagones de tren y otras instalaciones era permisible bajo la Decimocuarta Enmienda si se aseguraba que eran "separadas pero iguales". (pág. 558)

plural marriage: The practice of men taking multiple wives, which Mormon prophet Joseph Smith argued was biblically sanctioned and divinely ordained as a family system. (p. 325)

matrimonio plural: Práctica en la cual los hombres tienen varias esposas, que según el profeta mormón, Joseph Smith, estaba autorizada por la biblia y divinamente ordenado como sistema familiar. (pág. 325)

political machine(s): A highly organized group of insiders that directs a political party. These complex, hierarchical party organizations, such as New York's Tammany Hall, kept power through the strength of their political organization and their personal relationship with voters, especially working-class immigrants. Political machines were replaced by disciplined political parties usually run by professional politicians. (pp. 286; 588)

máquina política: Grupo altamente organizado de personas con información interna que dirigen a un partido. Estas complejas organizaciones jerárquicas, como Tammany Hall de Nueva York, conservaban el poder a través de su organización política y su relación personal con los votantes, particularmente inmigrantes de clase trabajadora. Las máquinas políticas fueron reemplazadas por partidos políticos dirigidos normalmente por políticos profesionales. (pág. 286; 588)

Popular Front: A small, left-leaning coalition of Americans who pushed for greater U.S. intervention against fascism in Europe.

Frente Popular: Pequeño grupo de estadounidenses izquierdistas que hizo escuchar su deseo de aumentar la injerencia de los

It was comprised of American Communist Party members, African American civil rights activists, and trade unionists, among others (p. 738)

popular sovereignty: The principle that ultimate power lies in the hands of the electorate. Also a plan, first promoted by Democratic candidate Senator Lewis Cass as "squatter sovereignty," then revised as "popular sovereignty" by fellow Democratic presidential aspirant Stephen Douglas, under which Congress would allow settlers in each territory to determine its status as free or slave. (p. 390)

Port Huron Statement: A 1962 manifesto by Students for a Democratic Society from its first national convention in Port Huron, Michigan, expressing disillusionment with the complacent consumer culture and the gulf between rich and poor, as well as rejecting Cold War foreign policy. (p. 885)

"positive good": In 1837, South Carolina Senator John C. Calhoun argued on the floor of the Senate that slavery was not a necessary evil but a positive good "indispensable to the peace and happiness" of blacks and whites alike. (p. 266)

Potsdam Conference: The conference, held in late July and early August 1945, in which Soviet Union leader Joseph Stalin accepted German reparations only from the Soviet zone, the eastern part of Germany, in exchange for American recognition of the Soviet-drawn Polish border. The agreement paved the way for the division of Germany into East and West. (p. 775)

predatory pricing: A tactic developed by large corporations in the late nineteenth century, in which a corporation drops prices below cost, in a limited area, to drive small competitors out of business and take control of a local market. (p. 518)

Presidential Commission on the Status of Women: Commission appointed by President Kennedy in 1961 that issued a 1963 report documenting job and educational discrimination. (p. 878)

Proclamation of Neutrality: A proclamation issued by President George Washington in 1793, allowing U.S. citizens to trade with all belligerents in the war between France and Great Britain. (p. 217)

producerism: An argument, made by late nineteenth century farmers' and workers' movements, that real economic wealth is created by workers engaged in physical labor, and that merchants, bankers, and other middlemen unfairly gain their wealth from such "producers." (p. 536)

progressivism: A loose array of reform movements that worked to clean up politics, fight poverty, increase racial and economic justice, and protect environmental resources, giving their name to the early twentieth-century Progressive Era. (p. 593)

Proposition 13: A California measure that reduced property taxes, capped increases for present owners, and required tax measures

Estados Unidos contra el fascismo en Europa. Lo integraban miembros del Partido Comunista Americano, activistas de derechos civiles afroamericanos y sindicalistas, entre otros. (pág. 738)

soberanía popular: Principio que establece que el poder descansa finalmente en las manos del electorado. También fue un plan, promovido en un principio por el Senador Lewis Cass, candidato demócrata, como "soberanía de los ocupantes", que luego fue revisada como "soberanía popular" por el aspirante demócrata a la presidencia, Stephen Douglas. Bajo este plan el Congreso permitiría a los pobladores determinar si su territorio sería libre o esclavista. (págs. 390)

Declaración de Port Huron: Manifiesto de 1962 de los Students for a Democratic Society (Estudiantes para una Sociedad Democrática) en su primera convención nacional en Port Huron, Michigan, que expresaba la desilusión de los estudiantes con la cultura de consumo del país y la enorme brecha entre ricos y pobres, además de rechazar la política exterior de la Guerra Fría, incluyendo la Guerra de Vietnam. (pág. 885)

"bien positivo": En 1837, el senador de Carolina del Sur John C. Calhoun argumentó ante el Senado que la esclavitud no era un mal necesario, sino un bien positivo, "indispensable para la paz y la felicidad" de los negros y los blancos por igual. (pág. 266)

Conferencia de Potsdam: Conferencia llevada a cabo en 1945 en la cual oficiales americanos convencieron a Iósif Stalin, líder de la Unión Soviética, para que aceptara únicamente compensaciones por la zona de ocupación soviética, o la región más oriental de Alemania. El acuerdo pavimentó el camino para la división de Alemania en Oriental y Occidental. (pág. 775)

fijación de precios predatorios: Táctica desarrollada por grandes corporaciones a fines del siglo XIX mediante la que una empresa baja los precios por debajo del costo en un área determinada para expulsar a los pequeños competidores del negocio y tomar el control del mercado local. (pág. 518)

Comisión Presidencial para el Estatus de las Mujeres: Comisión designada por el presidente Kennedy en 1961 que expidió un reporte en 1963 documentando la discriminación laboral y educativa. (pág. 878)

Proclamación de neutralidad: Proclamación emitida por el presidente George Washington en 1793 que permitió a los ciudadanos de Estados Unidos comerciar con todos los beligerantes durante la guerra entre Francia y Gran Bretaña. (pág. 217)

productorismo: Argumento según el cual la verdadera riqueza económica es creada por trabajadores que se ganan la vida mediante el trabajo físico, como lo hacen los granjeros y artesanos mientras que los comerciantes, abogados, banqueros y demás intermediarios logran su riqueza injustamente a costa de los verdaderos "productores". (pág. 536)

progresismo: Término general para describir la causa que buscaban los reformistas políticos que trabajaron para mejorar el sistema político, combatir la pobreza, conservar recursos ambientales y aumentar la participación del gobierno en la economía. Los reformistas le dieron su nombre a la "Era Progresista" de inicios del siglo XX. (pág. 593)

Proposición 13: Medida aprobada por una mayoría aplastante de californianos para reducir impuestos sobre la propiedad, limitar to have a two-thirds majority in the legislature. Inspired "tax revolts" across the country and defined an enduring conservative issue: low taxes. (p. 915)

los aumentos futuros para propietarios actuales y requerir que toda medida fiscal sea aprobada por mayoría de dos terceras partes en la legislatura. La Proposición 13 inspiró "revueltas contra los impuestos" en todo el país y ayudó a los conservadores a definir un tema duradero: los bajos impuestos. (pág. 915)

Proposition 209: A proposition approved by California voters in 1996 that outlawed affirmative action in state employment and public education. (p. 983)

Proposición 209: Proposición aprobada por votantes californianos en 1996 que proscribió la acción afirmativa en el empleo estatal y la educación pública. (pág. 983)

proprietorship: A colony created through a grant of land from the English monarch to an individual or group who then set up a form of government largely independent from royal control. (p. 82)

propiedad: Colonia creada a través de tierras concedidas por un monarca inglés a una persona o grupo, que entonces crea un gobierno independiente, a grandes rasgos, del control real. (pág. 82)

protective tariff: A tax or duty on foreign producers of goods imported into the United States; tariffs gave U.S. manufacturers a competitive advantage in America's gigantic domestic market. (p. 482)

tarifa protectora: Impuesto a productores extranjeros de bienes que entran o son importados a los Estados Unidos; los aranceles le dieron una ventaja competitiva a los fabricantes estadounidenses dentro del enorme mercado doméstico del país. (pág. 482)

Protestant Reformation: The reform movement that began in 1517 with Martin Luther's critiques of the Roman Catholic Church and that precipitated an enduring schism that divided Protestants from Catholics. (p. 24)

Reforma Protestante: Movimiento de reforma que comenzó en 1517 con las críticas de Martín Lutero a la Iglesia Católica Romana y que precipitó un cisma duradero que dividió a los protestantes de los católicos. (pág. 24)

Public Works Administration: A New Deal construction program established by Congress in 1933. Designed to put people back to work, the PWA built the Boulder Dam (renamed Hoover Dam) and Grand Coulee Dam, among other large public works projects. (p. 712)

Administración de Obras Públicas (PWA): Programa de construcción de la época del Nuevo Trato establecido por el Congreso en 1933. Diseñada para devolver a las personas al empleo, la PWA sirvió para construir la Presa de Boulder (cuyo nombre cambió después a Presa de Hoover) y la Presa Grand Coulee y otras grandes obras. (pág. 712)

Pueblo Revolt: Also known as Popé's Rebellion, the revolt in 1680 was an uprising of 46 Native American pueblos against Spanish rule. Spaniards were driven out of New Mexico. When they returned in the 1690s, they granted more autonomy to the pueblos they claimed to rule. (p. 70)

Rebelión de los Indios: También conocida como la Rebelión de Popé, la revuelta de 1680 fue un levantamiento de 46 pueblos nativos americanos contra el dominio español. Los españoles fueron expulsados de Nuevo México. Cuando regresaron en la década de 1690, concedieron mayor autonomía a los pueblos a quienes afirmaban gobernar. (pág. 70)

Pure Food and Drug Act: A 1906 law that created the Food and Drug Administration to regulate the food and drug industries to ensure safety. (p. 599)

Ley de Pureza de Alimentos y Medicamentos: Ley de 1906 que reguló las condiciones en las industrias de alimentos y medicamentos para asegurar un abastecimiento seguro de alimentos y medicinas. (pág. 599)

Puritans: Dissenters from the Church of England who wanted a genuine Reformation rather than the partial Reformation sought by Henry VIII. The Puritans' religious principles emphasized the importance of an individual's relationship with God developed through Bible study, prayer, and introspection. (p. 62)

puritanos: Disidentes de la Iglesia de Inglaterra que deseaban una reforma genuina en lugar de la reforma parcial buscada por Enrique VIII. Los principios religiosos de los puritanos resaltaban la importancia de la relación del individuo con Dios, que se desarrolla a través del estudio de la Biblia, la oración y la introspección. (pág. 62)

Quakers: Epithet for members of the Society of Friends. Their belief that God spoke directly to each individual through an "inner light" and that neither the Bible nor ministers were essential to discovering God's Word put them in conflict with both the Church of England and orthodox Puritans. (p. 83)

cuáqueros: Epíteto para miembros de la Sociedad de Amigos. Por creer que Dios le hablaba directamente a cada individuo a través de una "luz interna" y que ni los ministros ni la Biblia eran esenciales para descubrir la Palabra de Dios, entraron en conflicto con la Iglesia de Inglaterra y los puritanos ortodoxos. (pág. 83)

Quartering Act of 1765: A British law passed by Parliament at the request of General Thomas Gage, the British military commander in America, that required colonial governments to provide barracks and food for British troops. (p. 151)

Ley del Alojamiento de 1765: Ley británica aprobada por el Parlamento por solicitud del general Thomas Gage, comandante militar británico en América, que requería que los gobiernos proveyeran cuarteles y alimento para las tropas británicas. (pág. 151)

Radical Republicans: The members of the Republican Party who were bitterly opposed to slavery and to southern slave owners since the mid-1850s. With the Confiscation Act in 1861, Radical Republicans began to use wartime legislation to destroy slavery. (p. 455)

republicanos radicales: Miembros del Partido Republicano que se opusieron amargamente a la esclavitud y a los dueños de esclavos desde mediados de la década de 1850. Con la Ley de Confiscación en 1861, los republicanos radicales empezaron a usar la legislación de tiempos de guerra para destruir la esclavitud. (pág. 424; 455)

Reagan coalition: Supporters of Ronald Reagan, including core Republican Party voters, suburbanites and Sunbelt migrants, blue-collar Catholics, and a contingent of southern whites (a key Democratic constituency). (p. 948)

Reagan Democrats: Blue-collar Catholics from industrialized midwestern states such as Michigan, Ohio, and Illinois who were dissatisfied with the direction of liberalism in the 1970s and left the Democratic Party for the Republicans in the 1980s. (p. 949)

realism: A movement in literature and art, from the 1880s onward, that called for writers and artists to picture daily life as precisely and truly as possible. (p. 553)

Reconstruction Act of 1867: An act that divided the conquered South into five military districts, each under the command of a U.S. general. To reenter the Union, former Confederate states had to grant the vote to freedmen and deny it to leading ex-Confederates. (p. 455)

redemptioner: A type of indentured servant in the Middle colonies in the eighteenth century who did not sign a contract before leaving Europe but instead negotiated employment after arriving in America. (p. 110)

Red Scare: A term for anticommunist hysteria that swept the United States, first after World War I and then again after World War II, and led to government raids, deportations of radicals, and a suppression of civil liberties. (p. 674)

Red Summer: Antiblack riots in the summer and fall of 1919 by white Americans in more than two dozen cities leading to hundreds of deaths. The worst riot occurred in Chicago, in which 38 people were killed (23 blacks, 15 whites). (p. 675)

Regents of the University of California v. Bakke: The 1978 Supreme Court ruling that limited affirmative action by rejecting a quota system. (p. 921)

Regulators: Landowning protestors who organized in North and South Carolina in the 1760s and 1770s to demand that the eastern-controlled government provide western districts with more courts, fairer taxation, and greater representation in the assembly. (p. 138)

Religious Right: Politically active religious conservatives, especially Catholics and evangelical Christians, who became particularly vocal in the 1980s against feminism, abortion, and homosexuality and who promoted "family values." (p. 943)

Report on Manufactures: A proposal by treasury secretary Alexander Hamilton in 1791 calling for the federal government to urge the expansion of American manufacturing while imposing tariffs on foreign imports. (p. 215)

Report on the Public Credit: Alexander Hamilton's 1790 report recommending that the federal government should assume all

Coalición Reagan: Coalición en favor de Ronald Reagan que incluyó al núcleo tradicional de votantes del Partido Republicano, personas de clase media de los suburbios y migrantes habitantes de los estados del Sur y Suroeste, obreros católicos y un gran contingente de blancos sureños, grupo clave, en términos electorales. (pág. 948)

Demócratas por Reagan: Obreros católicos de los estados industrializados del Medio Oeste como Michigan, Ohio e Illinois, que se encontraban insatisfechos con la dirección del liberalismo en la década de 1970 y que dejaron al Partido Demócrata por los republicanos. (pág. 949)

realismo: Movimiento que llamaba a artistas y escritores a relatar la vida diaria de la manera más precisa y fidedigna posible. (pág. 553)

Ley de Reconstrucción de 1867: Ley que dividió al Sur conquistado en cinco distritos militares, cada uno bajo el mando de un general de los Estados Unidos. Para reingresar a la Unión, los antiguos estados Confederados debían otorgar el derecho de voto a los libertos y negárselo a los dirigentes ex confederados. (pág. 455)

redemptioner: Tipo común de sirviente aprendiz en las colonias medias del siglo XVIII. A diferencia de otros sirvientes como ellos, los redemptioners no firmaban un contrato antes de dejar Europa. En cambio, encontraban patrones al llegar a América. (pág. 110)

Temor Rojo: Término para describir la histeria anticomunista que cimbró a los Estados Unidos al concluir la Primera Guerra Mundial, y que condujo a una serie de redadas gubernamentales a supuestas personas subversivas y a la supresión de libertades civiles. (pág. 674)

Verano Rojo: El verano y otoño de 1919, en los cuales los disturbios anti-negros perpetrados por americanos blancos en más de dos docenas de ciudades ocasionaron cientos de muertes. Obtuvo su nombre por los choques sangrientos. El peor sucedió en Chicago, donde murieron 38 personas (23 negros, 15 blancos), 537 personas fueron heridas y más de mil familias negras se quedaron sin hogar. (pág. 675)

Regents of the University of California v. Bakke: Fallo de la Corte Suprema de 1978 que limitó la discriminación positiva al rechazar un sistema de cuotas. (pág. 921)

reguladores: Manifestantes terratenientes que, en las décadas de 1760 y 1770 en Carolina del Norte y del Sur, se organizaron para exigir que el gobierno controlado por el este proveyera más tribunales, impuestos más justos y mayor representación en la asamblea a los distritos del oeste. (pág. 138)

Derecha Religiosa: Conservadores religiosos políticamente activos, especialmente católicos y cristianos evangélicos, que en la década de 1980 fueron particularmente activos en su postura contra el feminismo, el aborto, los homosexuales y que promovían los "valores de la familia". (pág. 943)

Informe sobre manufacturas: Propuesta del secretario de la tesorería, Alexander Hamilton, en 1791 pidiendo al gobierno federal la expansión de la manufactura estadounidense y al mismo tiempo la imposición de aranceles sobre exportaciones extranjeras. (pág. 215)

Informe sobre el crédito público: Reporte de Alexander Hamilton en 1790 que recomendó que el gobierno federal debe asumir state debts and fund the national debt — that is, offer interest on it rather than repaying it — at full value. Hamilton's goal was to make the new country creditworthy, not debt-free. (p. 213)

todas las deudas estatales y financiar la deuda nacional–es decir, que ofrezcan interés sobre la deuda en lugar de pagarla–en su valor total. El objetivo de Hamilton fue lograr que el país fuera solvente, no que estuviera libre de deudas. (pág. 213)

republic: A state without a monarch or prince that is governed by representatives of the people. (p. 20)

república: Estado sin monarca o príncipe gobernado por representantes del pueblo. (pág. 20)

republican aristocracy: The Old South gentry who envisioned themselves as an American aristocracy and feared federal government interference with their slave property. (p. 349)

aristocracia republicana: La pequeña nobleza del Viejo Sur que construyó mansiones impresionantes, adoptó las maneras y valores de la nobleza inglesa y temía que el gobierno interfiriera con su propiedad de esclavos. (pág. 349)

republican motherhood: The idea that the primary political role of American women was to instill a sense of patriotic duty and republican virtue in their sons and husbands and mold them into exemplary citizens. (p. 287)

maternidad republicana: La idea de que el papel principal de las mujeres americanas era instaurar un sentido de deber patriótico y de virtud republicana en sus hijos para forjar ciudadanos republicanos ejemplares. (pág. 287)

Revenue Act: A 1942 act that expanded the number of people paying income taxes from 3.9 million to 42.6 million. These taxes on personal incomes and business profits paid half the cost of World War II. (p. 744)

Ley de Ingresos: Ley de 1942 que aumentó el número de personas que pagaban impuestos sobre la renta de de 3.9 millones a 42.6 millones. Estos impuestos sobre ingresos personales y de ganancias de negocios pagaron la mitad del costo de la Segunda Guerra Mundial. (pág. 744)

revival: A renewal of religious enthusiasm in a Christian congregation. In the eighteenth century, revivals were often inspired by evangelical preachers who urged their listeners to experience a rebirth. (p. 125)

renacimiento: Renovación del entusiasmo religioso en una congreagación cristiana. En el siglo XVIII, los renacimientos fueron inspirados normalmente por predicadores evangélicos que exhortaban a sus seguidores a vivir un renacer. (pág. 125)

rights liberalism: The idea that individuals are entitled to state protection from discrimination. This version of liberalism focused on identities — such as race or gender, and eventually sexuality — and was joined to the social welfare liberalism of the New Deal. (p. 834)

liberalismo de derechos: La convicción de que los individuos requieren protección gubernamental contra la discriminación. Esta versión del liberalismo fue promovida por los movimientos de derechos civiles de las mujeres y se enfocaba en la identidad — de raza o de género — más que en el bienestar social general del liberalismo del Nuevo Trato. (pág. 834)

Rocky Mountains: A high mountain range that spans some 3,000 miles, the Rocky Mountains are bordered by the Great Plains on the east and the Great Basin on the west. Native peoples fished; gathered roots and berries; and hunted elk, deer, and bighorn sheep there. Silver mining boomed in the Rockies in the nineteenth century. (p. 16)

Rocallosas: Cadena montañosa elevada que se extiende sobre aproximadamente 3000 millas. Las Rocallosas están bordeadas por las Grandes Llanuras al este y la Gran Cuenca al oeste. Ahí, los pueblos nativos pescaban, recolectaban raíces comestibles y moras, y cazaban alces, venado y borregos cimarrones. La minería de plata tuvo un auge en las Rocalloseas a mediados del siglo XIX. (pág. 16)

Roe v. Wade: The 1973 Supreme Court ruling that the Constitution protects the right to abortion, which states cannot prohibit in the early stages of pregnancy. The decision galvanized social conservatives and made abortion a controversial policy issue for decades to come. (p. 923)

Roe v. Wade: Decisión de la Corte Suprema en 1973 que protege el derecho a abortar, que los estados no pueden prohibir en las etapas iniciales del embarazo. La decisión impulsó a los conservadores sociales y convirtió al aborto en un tema político controvertido en las décadas siguientes. (pág. 923)

romanticism: A European philosophy that rejected the ordered rationality of the eighteenth-century Enlightenment, embracing human passion, spiritual quest, and self-knowledge. Romanticism strongly influenced American transcendentalism. (p. 319)

romanticismo: Filosofía europea que rechazaba la racionalidad ordenada de la Ilustración del siglo XVIII para adoptar la pasión humana, la búsqueda espiritual y el auto-conocimiento. El romanticismo influyó en gran medida sobre el trascendentalismo americano. (pág. 319)

Roosevelt Corollary: The 1904 assertion by President Theodore Roosevelt that the United States would act as a "policeman" in the Caribbean region and intervene in the affairs of nations that were guilty of "wrongdoing or impotence" in order to protect U.S. interests in Latin America. (p. 651)

Corolario Roosevelt: Declaración del presidente Theodore Roosevelt en 1904, afirmando que Estados Unidos actuaría como "policía" en la región del Caribe e intervendría en los asuntos de naciones que fueran culpables de "obrar mal o de impotencia" y así proteger los intereses de los Estados Unidos en América Latina. (pág. 651)

Root-Takahira Agreement: A 1908 agreement between the United States and Japan confirming principles of free oceanic commerce and recognizing Japan's authority over Manchuria. (p. 650)

Acuerdo Root-Takahira: Acuerdo firmado en 1908 entre los Estados Unidos y Japón confirmando los principios de comercio marítimo libre y en reconocimiento de la autoridad japonesa sobre Manchuria. (pág. 650)

royal colony: In the English system, a royal colony was chartered by the crown. The colony's governor was appointed by the crown and served according to the instructions of the Board of Trade. (p. 49)

Rural Electrification Administration: An agency established in 1935 to promote nonprofit farm cooperatives that offered loans to farmers to install power lines. (p. 730)

Rust Belt: The once heavily industrialized regions of the Northeast and Midwest that went into decline after deindustrialization. By the 1980s, these regions were full of shuttered plants and distressed communities. (p. 912)

salutary neglect: A term used to describe British colonial policy during the reigns of George I and George II. By relaxing their supervision of internal colonial affairs, royal bureaucrats inadvertently assisted the rise of self-government in North America. (p. 106)

Sand Creek massacre: The November 29, 1864, massacre of more than a hundred peaceful Cheyennes, largely women and children, by John M. Chivington's Colorado militia. (p. 499)

scientific management: A system of organizing work, developed by Frederick W. Taylor in the late nineteenth century, designed to coax maximum output from the individual worker, increase efficiency, and reduce production costs. (p. 523)

Scopes trial: The 1925 trial of John Scopes, a biology teacher in Dayton, Tennessee, for violating his state's ban on teaching evolution. The trial created a nationwide media frenzy and came to be seen as a showdown between urban and rural values. (p. 691)

Second Bank of the United States: National bank with multiple branches chartered in 1816 for twenty years. Intended to help regulate the economy, the bank became a major issue in Andrew Jackson's reelection campaign in 1832. (p. 296)

Second Continental Congress: Legislative body that governed the United States from May 1775 through the war's duration. It established an army, created its own money, and declared independence. (p. 171)

Second Great Awakening: A series of evangelical Protestant revivals extending from the 1790s to the 1830s that prompted thousands of conversions and widespread optimism about Americans' capacity for progress and reform. (p. 316)

Second Hundred Years' War: An era of warfare between England and France beginning in 1689 and lasting until 1815. In that time, England fought in seven major wars; the longest era of peace lasted only twenty-six years. (p. 86)

secret ballot: Form of voting that allows the voter to enter a choice privately rather than making a public declaration for a candidate. (p. 353)

colonia real: En el sistema inglés, la corona decretaba las colonias reales. La corona designaba al gobernador de la colonia y éste servía de acuerdo a las instrucciones de la Junta de Comercio. (pág. 49)

Administración de la Electrificación Rural: Agencia establecida en 1935 para promover cooperativas rurales sin fines de lucro que ofrecieron préstamos a granjeros para que instalaran cables de suministro eléctrico. (pág. 730)

Rust Belt (región): Las regiones que anteriormente estuvieron altamente industrializadas en el Noreste y Medio Oeste y que empezaron a declinar con la desindustrialización. Para las décadas de 1970 y 1980, en estas regiones abundaban las plantas abandonadas y las comunidades afligidas. (pág. 912)

negligencia saludable: Término usado para describir al proyecto colonial británico durante el reinado de George I (r. 1714–1727) y George II (r. 1727–1760). Al relajar la supervisión de los asuntos internos coloniales, los burócratas reales inadvertidamente asistieron al surgimiento del auto-gobierno en América del Norte. (pág. 106)

Masacre de Sand Creek: En la masacre ocurrida el 29 de noviembre de 1964, murieron más de cien indígenas cheyenne pacíficos, en su mayoría mujeres y niños, a manos de la milicia de John M. Chivington en Colorado. (pág. 499)

administración científica: Sistema de organización del trabajo desarrollado por Frederick W. Taylor a finales del siglo XIX. Fue diseñado para obtener la producción máxima de cada trabajador individual, aumentar la eficiencia y reducir los costos de producción. (pág. 523)

Juicio de Scopes: El juicio en 1925 del maestro de biología, John Scopes, en Dayton, Tennessee, por violar la prohibición estatal de la enseñanza de la evolución. El juicio causó un frenesí mediático a nivel nacional y llegó a ser percibido como un enfrentamiento entre valores urbanos y rurales. (pág. 691)

Segundo Banco de los Estados Unidos: Banco nacional con múltiples sucursales constituido en 1816 por 20 años. Creado con la intención de ayudar a regular la economía, el banco se convirtió en uno de los puntos principales de la campaña de reelección de Andrew Jackson en 1832. (pág. 296)

Segundo Congreso Continental: Órgano legislativo que gobernó a los Estados Unidos desde mayo de 1775 hasta que terminó la guerra. Estableció un ejército, creó su propio dinero y declaró la independencia. (pág. 171)

Segundo Gran Despertar: Serie de renacimientos evangélicos protestantes que duraron desde la década de 1790 hasta la década de 1830 y que fue causa de miles de conversiones y de un optimismo generalizado sobre la capacidad de los estadounidenses para el progreso y la reforma. (pág. 316)

Segunda Guerra de los Cien Años: Era de conflictos bélicos que comenzó con la guerra de la Liga de Augsburgo en 1689 y que duró hasta la derrota de Napoleón en Waterloo en 1815. Durante ese tiempo, Inglaterra estuvo en siete grandes guerras; el periodo de paz más largo duró a penas 26 años. (pág. 86)

voto secreto: forma de votación que permite que el votante elija en privado en vez de hacer una declaración pública sobre un candidato (pág. 353)

Securities and Exchange Commission: A commission established by Congress in 1934 to regulate the stock market. The commission had broad powers to determine how stocks and bonds were sold to the public, and to prevent insider trading. (p. 713)

Comisión de Bolsa y Valores: Comisión establecida por el Congreso en 1934 para regular la bolsa de valores. La comisión contaba con amplios poderes para determinar cómo se venderían las acciones y los bonos al público, para establecer las reglas de operaciones marginales (de crédito) y para prevenir la venta de acciones por aquellos con información interna sobre planes corporativos. (pág. 713)

Sedition Act of 1918: Wartime law that prohibited any words or behavior that might promote resistance to the United States or help in the cause of its enemies. (p. 659)

Ley de Sedición de 1918: Ley de tiempos de guerra que prohibió cualquier expresión o comportamiento que pudiera promover la resistencia contra los Estados Unidos o servir a la causa de sus enemigos. (pág. 659)

self-made man: A nineteenth-century ideal that celebrated men who rose to wealth or social prominence from humble origins through self-discipline, hard work, and temperate habits. (p. 279)

hombre que prosperó: Ideal del siglo XIX que celebraba a los hombres que habían alcanzado la riqueza o la prominencia social desde orígenes humildes gracias a la disciplina, el esfuerzo y los hábitos moderados. (pág. 279)

semisedentary societies: Societies whose members combine slash-and-burn agriculture with hunting and fishing. Semisedentary societies often occupy large village sites near their fields in the summer, then disperse during the winter months into smaller hunting, fishing, and gathering camps, regathering again in spring to plant their crops. (p. 8)

sociedades semisedentarias: Sociedades cuyos miembros combinan la agricultura despiadada con la pesca y la cacería. Las sociedades semisedentarias suelen ocupar grandes villas cerca de sus cultivos en el verano para dispersarse durante el invierno en campamentos de cacería, pesca y recolección, y juntarse de nuevo en primavera para sembrar sus cultivos. (pág. 8)

Seneca Falls Convention: The first women's rights convention in the United States. Held in Seneca Falls, New York, in 1848, it resulted in a manifesto extending to women the egalitarian republican ideology of the Declaration of Independence. (p. 343)

Convención de Seneca Falls: Primera convención de derechos de la mujer en Estados Unidos. Celebrada en 1848 en Seneca Falls, Nueva York, dio como resultado un manifiesto que extendió la ideologia igualitaria republicana de la Declaración de Independencia para incluir a las mujeres. (pág. 343)

Servicemen's Readjustment Act: Popularly known as the GI Bill, 1944 legislation authorizing the government to provide World War II veterans with funds for education, housing, and health care, as well as loans to start businesses and buy homes. (p. 750)

Ley de Reajuste del Personal de las Fuerzas Armadas: Conocida popularmente como el GI Bill, esta legislación de 1944 autorizó al gobierno para ofrecer fondos para educación, vivienda y salud a los veteranos de la Segunda Guerra Mundial, así como préstamos para comprar casas y emprender negocios. (pág. 750)

Sharon Statement: Manifesto drafted in 1960 by founding members of the Young Americans for Freedom (YAF), which outlined the group's principles — free enterprise, limited government, and traditional morality — and inspired young conservatives who would play important roles in the Reagan administration in the 1980s. (p. 888)

Declaración de Sharon: Redactada por integrantes de Young Americans for Freedom (Jóvenes Americanos por la Libertad, YAF), este manifiesto delineó los principios de este grupo (empresa libre, gobierno limitado y moral tradicional) e inspiró a jóvenes conservadores que tuvieron un papel importante en la administración de Reagan en la década de 1980. (pág. 888)

Shays's Rebellion: A 1786–1787 uprising led by dissident farmers in western Massachusetts, many of them Revolutionary War veterans, protesting the taxation policies of the eastern elites who controlled the state's government. (p. 197)

Rebelión de Shays: Levantamiento ocurrido en 1786–1787 encabezado por agricultores disidentes en el oeste de Massachussets, muchos de los cuales eran veteranos de la Guerra de Revolución que protestaban las políticas de impuestos de las élites del este que controlaban al gobierno del estado. (pág. 197)

Shelley v. Kraemer: A 1948 Supreme Court decision that outlawed racially restrictive housing occupancy covenants. However, racial discrimination persisted until the passage of the Fair Housing Act in 1968. (p. 826)

Shelley v. Kraemer: Decisión de la Corte Suprema en 1948 que proscribió los pactos restrictivos sobre la ocupación de desarrollos de vivienda por afroamericanos, asiáticos americanos y otras minorías. Debido a que la decisión de la Corte no prohibió en sí la discriminación racial en la vivienda, las prácticas injustas contra las minorías continuaron hasta que se aprobó la Ley de Vivienda Justa en 1968. (pág. 826)

Sheppard-Towner Federal Maternity and Infancy Act (1921): The first federally funded health-care legislation that provided federal funds for medical clinics, prenatal education programs, and visiting nurses. (p. 686)

Ley Federal Sheppard Towner de Protección de la Maternidad y la Infancia: Primera legislación de cuidados de salud de financiamiento federal que ofreció fondos federales a clínicas médicas, programas de educación prenatales y enfermeras que realizaban visitas a hogares. (pág. 686)

Sherman Antitrust Act: Landmark 1890 act that forbade anticompetitive business activities, requiring the federal government to

Ley Sherman Antimonopolio: Ley histórica de 1890 que prohibió las actividades de negocios anti-competitivas y requirió que el investigate trusts and any companies operating in violation of the act. (p. 612)

Sierra Club: An organization founded in 1892 that was dedicated to the enjoyment and preservation of America's great mountains (including the Sierra Nevadas) and wilderness environments. Encouraged by such groups, national and state governments began to set aside more public lands for preservation and recreation. (p. 562)

silent majority: Term used by President Richard Nixon in a 1969 speech to describe those who supported his positions but did not publicly assert their voices, in contrast to those involved in the antiwar, civil rights, and women's movements. (p. 896)

Silent Spring: Book published in 1962 by biologist Rachel Carson. Its analysis of the pesticide DDT's toxic impact on the human and natural food chains galvanized environmental activists. (p. 907)

Slaughter-House Cases: A group of decisions begun in 1873 in which the Court began to undercut the power of the Fourteenth Amendment to protect African American rights. (p. 474)

"slave power" conspiracy: The political argument, made by abolitionists, free soilers, and Republicans in the pre–Civil War years, that southern slaveholders were using their unfair representative advantage under the three-fifths compromise of the Constitution, as well as their clout within the Democratic Party, to demand extreme federal proslavery policies (such as annexation of Cuba) that the majority of American voters would not support. (p. 384)

slave society: A society in which the institution of slavery affects all aspects of life. (p. 349)

Smoot-Hawley Tariff: A high tariff on imports enacted in 1930, during the Great Depression, that was designed to stimulate American manufacturing. Instead it triggered retaliatory tariffs in other countries, which hindered global trade and led to greater economic contraction. (p. 705)

Social Darwinism: An idea, actually formulated not by Charles Darwin but by British philosopher and sociologist Herbert Spencer, that human society advanced through ruthless competition and the "survival of the fittest." (p. 547)

Social Gospel: A movement to renew religious faith through dedication to public welfare and social justice, reforming both society and the self through faith-based service. Protestant, Catholic, and Jewish denominations and lay leaders all participated. (p. 553)

Social Security Act: A 1935 act that provided old-age pensions for workers, a joint federal-state system of compensation for unemployed workers, and a program of payments to widowed mothers and the disabled. (p. 716)

social settlement: A Progressive Era community welfare center that investigated the plight of the urban poor, advocated for change, and helped residents advocate on their own behalf. (p. 596)

gobierno federal investigara los trusts y cualquier compañía que actuara contra esta ley. (pág. 612)

Sierra Club: Organización fundada en 1892 dedicada a la preservación y goce de las grandes montañas (incluyendo la Sierra Nevada) y los entornos naturales. Gracias a la inspiración de estos grupos, los gobiernos nacionales y estatales empezaron a apartar más tierras públicas para la preservación y la recreación. (pág. 562)

mayoría silenciosa: Término retomado por Nixon en un discurso de 1969 para describir a aquellos que apoyaron sus posturas pero no lo pronunciaron públicamente, en contraste con aquellos involucrados en los movimientos antiguerra, de derechos civiles y de mujeres. (pág. 896)

Primavera silenciosa: Libro publicado por la bióloga Rachel Carson en 1962. Su análisis de los impactos tóxicos del pesticida DDT sobre los humanos y las cadenas alimenticias impulsó a los activistas ambientales. (pág. 907)

Casos del matadero: Conjunto de decisiones tomadas a partir de 1873, en las cuales la Corte empezó a debilitar el poder de la Decimocuarta Enmienda para proteger los derechos de los afroamericanos. (pág. 474)

conspiración de la "potencia negra": Argumento político de abolicionistas, partidarios del suelo libre y republicanos en los años previos a la Guerra Civil, que decía que los dueños de esclavos usaban injustamente sus ventajas representativas, bajo el Compromiso de los Tres Quintos de la Constitución, así como su influencia con el Partido Demócrata, para exigir políticas antiesclavistas federales extremas (como la anexión de Cuba) que la mayoría de los votantes americanos no apoyarían. (pág. 384)

sociedad esclavista: Sociedad en la cual la institución de la esclavitud afecta todos los aspectos de la vida. (pág. 349)

Tarifa Smoot-Hawley: Tarifa promulgada en 1930 durante la Gran Depresión. Al colocar impuestos sobre los bienes importados, el Congreso esperaba estimular la manufactura estadounidense, pero la tarifa causó represalias en otros países, que impidieron el comercio global aún más y llevaron a una contracción económica más fuerte. (pág. 705)

Darwinismo Social: Idea formulada, no por Charles Darwin, sino por el filósofo y sociólogo inglés Herbert Spencer, en la cual la sociedad humana avanza gracias a la competencia despiadada y la "supervivencia de los más aptos". (pág. 547)

Evangelio Social: Movimiento para renovar la fe religiosa mediante la dedicación al bienestar público y la justicia social, y para reformar tanto a la sociedad como al individuo a través del servicio cristiano. Participaron líderes protestantes, católicos, judíos y laicos. (pág. 553)

Ley de Seguridad Social: Ley de 1935 que incluyó tres disposiciones principales: pensiones para trabajadores de la tercera edad; un sistema federal-estatal conjunto para compensar a trabajadores desempleados; y un programa de pagos para madres viudas y para los ciegos, sordos y discapacitados. (pág. 716)

asentamiento social: Centros de bienestar comunitario que investigaban la situación de los pobres, recaudaban fondos para responder a necesidades urgentes y ayudaban a los residentes del vecindario a abogar por sí mismos. (pág. 596)

soft power: The exercise of popular cultural influence abroad, as American radio and movies became popular around the world in the 1920s, transmitting American consumer culture and its styles and values overseas. (p. 683)

poder suave: El ejercicio de la influencia de la cultura popular en el extranjero con la creciente popularidad de películas y radio estadounidenses en el mundo durante la década de 1920, que transmitieron ideales culturales de Estados Unidos a otros países. (pág. 683)

Sons of Liberty: Colonists — primarily middling merchants and artisans — who banded together to protest the Stamp Act and other imperial reforms of the 1760s. The group originated in Boston in 1765 but soon spread to all the colonies. (p. 152)

Hijos de la Libertad: Colonos — principalmente comerciantes y artesanos medianos — que se juntaron para protestar la Ley del Timbre y otras reformas imperiales de la década de 1760. El grupo se originó en Boston en 1765 y rápidamente se esparció a todas las colonias. (pág. 152)

South Atlantic System: A new agricultural and commercial order that produced sugar, tobacco, rice, and other tropical and subtropical products for an international market. Its plantation societies were ruled by European planter-merchants and worked by hundreds of thousands of enslaved Africans. (p. 90)

Sistema del Atlántico Sur: Nueva orden agricultora y comercial que produjo azúcar, tabaco, arroz y otros productos tropicales y subtropicales para el mercado internacional. Sus sociedades de plantación fueron dominadas por comerciantes-hacendados y fueron trabajadas por cientos de miles de africanos esclavizados. (pág. 90)

Southern Christian Leadership Conference (SCLC): After the Montgomery Bus Boycott, Martin Luther King Jr. and other black ministers formed the SCLC in 1957 to coordinate civil rights activity in the South. (p. 850)

Conferencia Sur de Liderazgo Cristiano (SCLC): Después del boicot de autobuses en Montgomery, en 1957 Martin Luther King Jr. y otros líderes de derechos civiles fundaron la SLCS para coordinar actividades de derechos civiles en el Sur. (pág. 850)

Special Field Order No. 15: An order by General William T. Sherman, later reversed by policymakers, that granted confiscated land to formerly enslaved families in Georgia and South Carolina so they could farm independently. (p. 445)

Orden militar especial n.º 15: Orden emitida por el general William T. Sherman, posteriormente revocada por legisladores, que concedía tierras confiscadas a familias anteriormente esclavizadas en Georgia y Carolina del Sur para que pudieran cosecharlas independientemente. (pág. 445)

Specie Circular: An executive order in 1836 that required the Treasury Department to accept only gold and silver in payment for lands in the national domain. (p. 310)

Specie Circular: Orden ejecutiva de 1836 que requería que el Departamento de Tesorería aceptara únicamente oro y plata como pago por tierras en el dominio nacional. (pág. 310)

spoils system: The widespread award of public jobs to political supporters after an electoral victory. In 1829, Andrew Jackson instituted the system on the national level, arguing that the rotation of officeholders was preferable to a permanent group of bureaucrats. (p. 295)

clientelismo: La entrega generalizada de empleos públicos a seguidores políticos después una victoria electoral. En 1829, Andrew Jackson instituyó este sistema a nivel nacional, argumentando que la rotación de cargos era mejor que un grupo de burócratas permanentes. (pág. 295)

***Sputnik*:** The world's first satellite, launched by the Soviet Union in 1957. After its launch, the United States funded research and education to catch up in the Cold War space competition. (p. 808)

***Sputnik*:** Primer satélite en el mundo, lanzado por la Unión Soviética en 1957. Después del lanzamiento, Estados Unidos financió la investigación y la educación para ponerse al tanto en la competencia por el espacio de la Guerra Fría. (pág. 808)

Square Deal: Theodore Roosevelt's 1904 campaign platform, calling for regulation of corporations and protection of consumers and the environment. (p. 622)

***Square Deal* (Trato justo y honesto):** Plataforma de campaña de Theodore Roosevelt en 1904 que proclamaba el control de las grandes empresas, así como la protección de los consumidores y del medio ambiente. (pág. 622)

squatter: Someone who settles on land he or she does not own or rent. Many eighteenth-century migrants settled on land before it was surveyed and entered for sale, requesting the first right to purchase the land when sales began. (p. 117)

ocupante: Persona que se asienta en tierras que no posee ni renta. Muchos pobladores del siglo XVIII se asentaron en la tierra antes de que fuera inspeccionada y colocada en venta, exigiendo el derecho primordial de adquirir las tierras cuando comenzaran las ventas. (pág. 117)

stagflation: An economic term coined in the 1970s to describe a combination of high unemployment, stagnant consumer demand, and inflation. (p. 911)

estagflación: Término económico acuñado en la década de 1970 para describir la condición en la cual la inflación y el desempleo crecen al mismo tiempo. (pág. 911)

Stamp Act Congress: A congress of delegates from nine assemblies that met in New York City in October 1765 to protest the loss of American "rights and liberties." The congress challenged Parliament by declaring that only the colonists' elected representatives could tax them. (p. 152)

Congreso de la Ley del Timbre: Congreso de delegados de nueve asambleas que se reunieron en la Ciudad de Nueva York en octubre de 1765 para protestar la pérdida de "derechos y libertades" americanas y el derecho a ser juzgado ante un jurado. El congreso cuestionó la constitucionalidad de las Leyes del Timbre y del Azúclar, al declarar que sólo los representantes elegidos por colonos podían cobrarles impuestos. (pág. 152)

Stamp Act of 1765: British law imposing a tax on all paper used in the colonies. Widespread resistance to the Stamp Act prevented it from taking effect and led to its repeal in 1766. (p. 150)

Standard Oil decision: A 1911 Supreme Court decision that directed the breakup of the Standard Oil Company into smaller companies because its overwhelming market dominance and monopoly power violated antitrust laws. (p. 622)

States' Rights Democratic Party: Known popularly as the Dixiecrats, a breakaway party of white Democrats from the South that formed for the 1948 election. Its formation hinted at a potential long-term schism within the New Deal coalition. (p. 841)

Stonewall Inn: A gay bar in New York's Greenwich Village that was raided by police in 1969; the ensuing two-day riot contributed to the rapid rise of a gay liberation movement. (p. 896)

Stono Rebellion: Slave uprising in 1739 along the Stono River in South Carolina in which a group of slaves armed themselves, plundered six plantations, and killed more than 20 colonists. Colonists quickly suppressed the rebellion. (p. 101)

STOP ERA: An organization founded by Phyllis Schlafly in 1972 to fight the Equal Rights Amendment. (p. 922)

Student Nonviolent Coordinating Committee (SNCC): A student civil rights group founded in 1960, under the mentorship of Ella Baker, that conducted sit-ins, voter registration drives, and other actions to advance racial equality throughout the 1960s. (p. 850)

Sugar Act of 1764: British law that lowered the duty on French molasses and raised penalties for smuggling. New England merchants opposed both the tax and the provision that they would be tried in a vice-admiralty court. (p. 149)

Sunbelt: Name applied to the Southwest and South, which grew rapidly after World War II as a center of defense industries and non-unionized labor. (p. 828)

supply-side economics (Reaganomics): Economic theory that tax cuts encourage business investment (supply) and stimulate individual consumption (demand). In reality, supply-side economics created a massive federal budget deficit. (p. 949)

Taft-Hartley Act: Law passed by the Republican-controlled Congress in 1947 that overhauled the 1935 National Labor Relations Act, placing restrictions on organized labor that made it more difficult for unions to organize workers. (p. 787)

Ley del Timbre de 1765: Ley británica que colocó impuestos sobre todo el papel usado en las colonias. La resistencia generalizada a la Ley del Timbre impidió que entrara en vigencia y llevó a su revocación en 1766. (pág. 150)

Decisión Standard Oil: Decisión de la Corte Suprema en 1911 de desintegrar a la Standard Oil Company en compañías más pequeñas porque su apabullante influencia en el mercado y su poder monopólico violaba leyes antimonopolio. (pág. 622)

Partido Demócrata por los Derechos de los Estados: Conocido popularmente como los Dixiecrats, este partido fue una escisión de demócratas del Sur que se formó para la elección de 1948. Su formación reveló las luchas internas entre los objetivos de derechos civiles del ala liberal del partido y los demócratas blancos del Sur. (pág. 841)

Stonewall Inn: Bar gay en Greenwich Village en Nueva York donde la policía condujo una redada en 1969; los disturbios consecuentes, con duración de dos días, contribuyeron al rápido crecimiento del movimiento de liberación gay. (pág. 896)

Rebelión de Stono: Levantamiento de esclavos en 1739 en Stono River, Carolina del Sur, donde un grupo de esclavos armados saquearon seis plantaciones y mataron a más de veinte colonos. Los colonos rápidamente contuvieron esta rebelión. (pág. 101)

STOP ERA (siglas de la campaña Stop Taking Our Privileges Equal Rights Amendment): Organización fundada por Phyllis Schlafly en 1972 para luchar contra la Enmienda de Igualdad de Derechos. (pág. 922)

Comité Coordinador Estudiantil No Violento (SNCC): Grupo de derechos civiles fundado en 1960 guiado por la activista Ella Baker que llevó a cabo manifestaciones, campañas de registro de votantes y otras medidas para impulsar la igualdad racial en la década de 1960. (pág. 850)

Ley del Azúcar de 1764: Ley británica que redujo el arancel en la melaza francesa, de tal manera que los exportadores tuvieron más motivos para obedecer la ley. Al mismo tiempo, aumentaron los castigos por el contrabando. Esta ley enfureció a los comerciantes de Nueva Inglaterra, que se oponían al impuesto y al hecho de que los comerciantes perseguidos serían juzgados por jueces de designación británica en un tribunal de vicealmirante. (pág. 149)

Sunbelt (o Franja del Sol, región de los Estados Unidos): Nombre aplicado a la región del Sur y al Suroeste, que creció rápidamente después de la Segunda Guerra Mundial como centro para las industrias de defensa y la mano de obra no sindicalizada. (pág. 828)

economía de la oferta (reaganomía): Teoría económica en la cual los recortes de impuestos para negocios e individuos invitan a la inversión y a la producción (oferta) y estimulan el consumo (demanda) gracias a que los individuos logran conservar una parte mayor de sus ingresos. En realidad, la economía de la oferta creó un enorme déficit en el presupuesto federal. (pág. 949)

Ley Taft-Harley: Ley aprobada por el Congreso de mayoría republicana en 1947 que revisó la Ley Nacional de Relaciones Laborales de 1935, misma que colocó restricciones sobre el trabajo organizado e hizo más difícil que los sindicatos organizaran a los trabajadores. (pág. 787)

talented tenth: A term used by Harvard-educated sociologist W. E. B. Du Bois for the top 10 percent of educated African Americans, whom he called on to develop new strategies to advocate for civil rights. (p. 625)

El décimo talentoso: Término usado por el sociólogo formado en Harvard, W. E. B. Du Bois, para el 10 por ciento de afroamericanos educados, a quienes llamó a desarrollar nuevas estrategias para abogar por sus derechos civiles. (pág. 625)

Tariff of Abominations: A tariff enacted in 1828 that raised duties significantly on raw materials, textiles, and iron goods. It enraged the South, which had no industries that needed protection and resented the higher cost of imported goods. (p. 293)

arancel de las abominaciones: Arancel aprobado en 1828 que aumentó significativamente los impuestos sobre materia prima, textiles y bienes de hierro. El senador van Buren de Nueva York esperaba ganarse el apoyo de los agricultores de Nueva York, Ohio y Kentucky con el arancel, pero enfureció al Sur que no tenía industrias y necesitaba protección arancelaria, por lo cual resintieron el costo de bienes importados con gravámenes. (pág. 293)

task system: A system of labor common in the rice-growing regions of South Carolina in which a slave was assigned a daily task to complete and was allowed to do as he wished upon its completion. (p. 357)

sistema de tareas: Sistema de trabajo común en las regiones arroceras de Carolina del Sur, donde a los esclavos se les asignaba una tarea diaria y al completarla podían usar su tiempo como quisieran. (pág. 357)

Tea Act of May 1773: British act that lowered the existing tax on tea and granted exemptions to the East India Company to make their tea cheaper in the colonies and entice boycotting Americans to buy it. (p. 163)

Ley del Té de mayo de 1773: Ley británica que redujo el impuesto existente sobre el té y otorgó exenciones a la East India Company para reducir el precio de su té en las colonias y convencer a los americanos, que lo estaban boicoteando, de comprarlo. (pág. 163)

Tea Party: A coalition of far-right groups, voicing an extreme anti-government ideology, that emerged during President Obama's first term and helped the Republican Party recapture the House in 2010 and Senate in 2014. (p. 995)

Partido del Té: Conjunto de grupos de oposición de extrema derecha que surgieron durante el primer término del presidente Obama que dieron voz al sentimiento antigobierno y contribuyeron a que el Partido Republicano recuperara la cámara baja en 2010 y el senado en 2014. (pág. 995)

Teapot Dome: Nickname for scandal in which Interior Secretary Albert Fall accepted $300,000 in bribes for leasing oil reserves on public land in Teapot Dome, Wyoming. It was part of a larger pattern of corruption that marred Warren G. Harding's presidency. (p. 680)

Teapot Dome: Apodo para el escándalo en el cual el Secretario de Interior, Albert Fall, aceptó sobornos de $300,000 a cambio de arrendar reservas petroleras en terrenos públicos en Teapot Dome, Wyoming. Fue parte de un patrón de corrupción más grande, que manchó la presidencia de Warren G. Harding. (pág. 680)

teenager: A term for a young adult. American youth culture, focused on the spending power of the "teenager," emerged as a cultural phenomenon in the 1950s. (p. 815)

adolescente (teenager): Término para un adulto joven. La cultura juvenil americana, enfocada sobre el poder adquisitivo de los "teenagers," surgió como fenómeno cultural en las décadas de la posguerra. (pág. 815)

Teller Amendment: An amendment to the 1898 U.S. declaration of war against Spain disclaiming any intention by the United States to occupy Cuba. (p. 644)

Enmienda Teller: Enmienda a la declaración de Guerra de los Estados Unidos contra España en 1898 que negó cualquier intención de Estados Unidos de ocupar Cuba. (pág. 644)

tenancy: The rental of property. To attract tenants in New York's Hudson River Valley, Dutch and English manorial lords granted long tenancy leases, with the right to sell improvements — houses and barns, for example — to the next tenant. (p. 117)

tenencia: Renta de una propiedad. Para atraer inquilinos a la cuenca del río Hudson, terratenientes señoriales ingleses y holandeses concedieron arrendamientos de largo plazo con derecho a vender las mejoras–casas y establos, por ejemplo–al siguiente inquilino. (pág. 117)

tenement: A high-density, cheap, five- or six-story housing unit designed for working-class urban populations. In the late nineteenth and early twentieth centuries, tenements became a symbol of urban immigrant poverty. (p. 583)

vecindad: Unidad de vivienda de alta densidad, bajo costo y de cinco o seis pisos diseñada para las poblaciones urbanas de clase trabajadora. A finales del siglo XIX y principios del siglo XX, las vecindades se convirtieron en símbolo de la pobreza inmigrante urbana. (pág. 583)

Tennessee Valley Authority: An agency funded by Congress in 1933 that integrated flood control, reforestation, electricity generation, and agricultural and industrial development in the Tennessee Valley area. (p. 730)

Autoridad del Valle de Tennessee: Agencia fundada por el Congreso en 1933 que integraba el control de inundaciones, la reforestación, la generación de electricidad y el desarrollo cultural en la región del Valle de Tennessee. (pág. 730)

Ten Percent Plan: A plan proposed by President Abraham Lincoln during the Civil War, but never implemented, that would have

Plan del diez por ciento: Plan propuesto por el presidente Abraham Lincoln durante la Guerra Civil, que nunca fue implementado y granted amnesty to most ex-Confederates and allowed each rebellious state to return to the Union as soon as 10 percent of its voters had taken a loyalty oath and the state had approved the Thirteenth Amendment. (p. 452)

que hubiera otorgado amnistía a la mayoría de los ex Confederados para permitir que cada estado rebelde regresara a la Unión una vez que el 10 por ciento de sus votantes hayan profesado su lealtad y una vez que cada estado aprobara la Decimotercera Enmienda. (pág. 452)

Tet offensive: Major campaign of attacks launched throughout South Vietnam in January 1968 by the North Vietnamese and Vietcong. A major turning point in the war, it exposed the credibility gap between official statements and the war's reality, and it shook Americans' confidence in the government. (p. 889)

Ofensiva del Tet: Campaña mayor de ataques lanzados sobre el Sur de Vietnam por los vietnamitas del norte y el Vietcong en enero de 1968. Fue un importante punto de transición en la guerra, reveló la brecha de credibilidad entre los comunicados oficiales y la realidad de la guerra y afectó la confianza de los estadounidenses en el gobierno. (pág. 889)

The Affluent Society: A 1958 book by John Kenneth Galbraith that analyzed the nation's successful middle class and argued that the poor were only an "afterthought" in the minds of economists and politicians. (p. 809)

La sociedad opulenta: Libro escrito en 1958 por John Kenneth Galbraith, que analizó a la exitosa clase media del país y argumentó que los pobres sólo eran una consideración secundaria en las mentes de economistas y políticos. (pág. 809)

The Feminine Mystique: An influential book by Betty Friedan published in 1963 critiquing the ideal whereby women were encouraged to confine themselves to roles within the domestic sphere. (p. 877)

La mística de la feminidad: Título de un influyente libro escrito en 1963 por Betty Friedan, que criticaba el ideal en el cual las mujeres debían limitarse a labores domésticas. (pág. 877)

The Other America: A 1962 book by left-wing social critic Michael Harrington, chronicling the persistence of poverty in the United States, what he called the nation's "economic underworld." (p. 810)

La otra América: Libro publicado en 1962 por Michael Harrington, crítico social de izquierdas que documentó "el submundo económico de la vida americana". (pág. 810)

Three Mile Island: A nuclear plant in Pennsylvania, where a reactor core neared meltdown in March 1979. The incident at Three Mile Island triggered a major slowdown in nuclear plant construction, though the United States is now the leading global nuclear power producer. (p. 910)

Three Mile Island: Planta nuclear en Pennsylvania, donde, en marzo de 1979, el núcleo de un reactor estuvo cerca de sufrir una fusión. Si bien después del incidente en Three Mile Island la construcción de plantas nucleares disminuyó, ahora Estados Unidos es líder en la producción de energía nuclear. (pág. 910)

Title IX: Law passed as part of the Education Amendments of 1972 guaranteeing women equal access and treatment in all educational institutions receiving federal funding. (p. 895)

Título IX: Ley aprobada por el Congreso en 1972 como parte de la enmienda educativa que garantizó a las mujeres trato y acceso igualitario a instituciones educativas en universidades y colegios que recibieran fondos federales. (pág. 895)

toleration: The allowance of different religious practices. Lord Baltimore persuaded the Maryland assembly to enact the Toleration Act (1649), which granted all Christians the right to follow their beliefs and hold church services. The crown imposed toleration on Massachusetts Bay in its new royal charter of 1691. (p. 63)

tolerancia social: Permiso para distintas prácticas religiosas. Lord Baltimore convenció a la asamblea de Maryland para que promulgara la Ley de Tolerancia (1649), que concedió a todos los cristianos el derecho de seguir sus creencias y celebrar ceremonias religiosas. La corona impuso la tolerancia en Massachusetts Bay en su nueva carta real de 1691. (pág. 63)

"To Secure These Rights": The 1947 report by the Presidential Committee on Civil Rights that called for robust federal action to ensure equality for African Americans. President Truman asked Congress to make all of the report's recommendations — including the abolition of poll taxes and the restoration of the Fair Employment Practice Committee — into law, leading to discord in the Democratic Party. (p. 840)

"Para asegurar estos derechos": Reporte de 1947 elaborado por el Comité Presidencial de Derechos Civiles que llamaba a tomar medidas federales para asegurar la igualdad para los afroamericanos. El presidente Truman pidió al congreso que convirtiera todas las recomendaciones del reporte — incluidas la abolición de impuestos de capitación y la restauración del Comité de Prácticas de Empleo Justo — en ley, lo que llevó a desacuerdos en el Partido Demócrata. (pág. 840)

town meeting: A system of local government in New England in which all male heads of households met regularly to elect selectmen; levy local taxes; and regulate markets, roads, and schools. (p. 67)

gobierno asambleario: Sistema de gobierno local de Nueva Inglaterra donde todos los hombres, jefes de hogar, se reunían regularmente para elegir concejales, recaudar impuestos locales y regular mercados, vías y escuelas. (pág. 67)

Townsend Plan: A plan proposed by Francis Townsend in 1933 that would give $200 a month (nearly $4,000 today) to citizens over the age of sixty; stimulated mass support for old-age pensions. (p. 714)

Plan Townsend: Plan propuesto por Francis Townsend en 1933 que entregaría $200 mensuales (cerca de $3,600 en la actualidad) a ciudadanos mayores de sesenta años. Los Clubes Townsend aparecieron en todo el país para apoyar al plan y movilizar el apoyo para las pensiones de la tercera edad. (pág. 714)

Townshend Act of 1767: British law that established new duties on tea, glass, lead, paper, and painters' colors imported into the colonies. The Townshend duties led to boycotts and heightened tensions between Britain and the American colonies. (p. 154)

Trail of Tears: Forced westward journey of Cherokees from their lands in Georgia to present-day Oklahoma in 1838. Nearly a quarter of the Cherokees died in route. (p. 303)

transcendentalism: A nineteenth-century American intellectual movement that posited the importance of an ideal world of mystical knowledge and harmony beyond the immediate grasp of the senses. Influenced by romanticism, transcendentalists Ralph Waldo Emerson and Henry David Thoreau called for the critical examination of society and emphasized individuality, self-reliance, and nonconformity. (p. 319)

transcontinental railroad: The railway line completed on May 10, 1869, that connected the Central Pacific and Union Pacific lines, enabling goods to move by railway from the eastern United States all the way to California. (p. 480)

Treaty of Ghent: The treaty signed on Christmas Eve 1814 that ended the War of 1812. It retained the prewar borders of the United States. (p. 238)

Treaty of Greenville: A 1795 treaty between the United States and various Indian tribes in Ohio. American negotiators acknowledged Indian ownership of the land, and, in return for various payments, the Western Confederacy ceded most of Ohio to the United States. (p. 224)

Treaty of Kanagawa: An 1854 treaty in which, after a show of military force by U.S. Commodore Matthew Perry, leaders of Japan agreed to permit American ships to refuel at two Japanese ports. (p. 393)

Treaty of Paris of 1783: The treaty that ended the Revolutionary War. By its terms, Great Britain formally recognized American independence and relinquished its claims to lands south of the Great Lakes and east of the Mississippi River. (p. 190)

Treaty of Versailles: The 1919 treaty that ended World War I. The agreement redrew the map of the world, assigned Germany sole responsibility for the war, and saddled it with a debt of $33 billion in war damages. Its long-term impact around the globe — including the creation of British and French imperial "mandates" — was catastrophic. (p. 665)

Triangle Fire: A devastating fire at the Triangle Shirtwaist Company in New York City on March 25, 1911, that killed 146 people, mostly young immigrant women. It prompted passage of state laws to increase workplace safety and regulate working hours for women and children. (p. 599)

tribalization: The adaptation of stateless peoples to the demands imposed on them by neighboring states. (p. 86)

Truman Doctrine: President Harry S. Truman's commitment to "support free peoples who are resisting attempted subjugation by armed minorities or by outside pressures." First applied to

Ley Townshend de 1767: Ley británica que colocó nuevos impuestos sobre té, vidrio, plomo y los colores para pintores importados a las colonias. Los impuestos de Townshend condujero a boicots y tensiones entre Bretaña y las colonias americanas. (pág. 154)

Sendero de lágrimas: Viaje de los cheroquis que fueron forzosamente removidos de sus tierras en Georgia en 1838 para reubicarse en lo que ahora es Oklahoma. Cerca de una cuarta parte de los cheroquis murieron en el camino. (pág. 303)

trascendentalismo: Movimiento intelectual estadounidense del siglo XIX que plantea la importancia de un mundo ideal de conocimientos místicos y armonía más allá del alcance de los sentidos. Con la influencia del romanticismo, los trascendentalistas Ralph Waldo Emerson y Henry David Thoreau llamaron al análisis crítico de la sociedad y destacaron la individualidad, la dependencia de uno mismo y el inconformismo. (pág. 319)

ferrocarril transcontinental: Ferrocarril completado el 10 de mayo de 1869, que conectó las líneas de Central Pacific y Union Pacific y permitió el tránsito de bienes por ferrocarril desde el este de Estados Unidos hasta California. (pág. 480)

Tratado de Gante: Tratado firmado en Nochebuena de 1814 que dio fin a la Guerra de 1812. Como resultado, las fronteras de los Estados Unidos previas a la guerra se mantuvieron. (pág. 238)

Tratado de Greenville: Tratado que se firmó en 1795 entre los Estados Unidos varias tribus indígenas en Ohio. Los negociadores americanos reconocieron la propiedad indígena de la tierra, y, a cambio de varios pagos, la Confederación del Oeste cedió la mayoría de Ohio a los Estados Unidos. (pág. 224)

Tratado de Kanagawa: Tratado de 1854 en el cual, después de un despliegue de fuerza militar por parte del comodoro de Estados Unidos, Matthew Perry, los líderes de Japón dieron permiso a las embarcaciones estadounidenses de cargar combustible en dos puertos japoneses. (pág. 393)

Tratado de París de 1783: Tratado que dio fin a la guerra de Independencia de los Estados Unidos. En el tratado, Gran Bretaña reconoció formalmente la independencia americana y renunció a sus derechos sobre las tierras del sur de los Grandes Lagos y al este del Río Misisipi. (pág. 190)

Tratado de Versalles: Tratado de 1919 que dio fin a la Primera Guerra Mundial. El acuerdo cambió el mapa del mundo, responsabilizó únicamente a Alemania por la guerra y la dejó con una deuda de $33 mil millones por daños de la guerra. Su impacto en el largo plazo alrededor de la tierra — incluyendo los "mandatos" imperiales de Bretaña y Francia — fue catastrófico. (pág. 665)

Incendio en la fábrica Triangle Shirtwaist: Devastador incendio que el 25 de marzo de 1911 se extendió rápidamente por la Triangle Shirtwaist Company en la ciudad de Nueva York y costó la vida de 146 personas. Tras la tragedia se aprobaron 56 leyes estatales para regular temas como peligros de incendio, equipamiento peligroso y salarios y horarios de mujeres y niños. (pág. 599)

tribalización La adaptación de personas apátridas a las demandas impuestas sobre ellos por estados vecinos. (pág. 86)

Doctrina Truman: Compromiso del presidente Harry S. Truman de "apoyar a las personas libres que se resisten a la subyugación de minorías armadas o presiones externas". Aplicada por primera

Greece and Turkey in 1947, it became the justification for U.S. intervention into several countries during the Cold War. (p. 779)

trust: A small group of associates who hold stock from multiple firms and manage them as a single entity. Trusts quickly evolved into other centralized business forms, but critics continued to refer to giant firms with monopoly power as "trusts." (p. 518)

twenty-Negro rule: A law adopted by the Confederate Congress that exempted one man from military conscription for every twenty slaves owned by a family. The law showed how dependence on coerced slave labor could be a military disadvantage, and it exacerbated class resentments among nonslaveholding whites who were required to serve in the army. (p. 428)

Underground Railroad: An informal network of whites and free blacks in the South that assisted fugitive slaves to reach freedom in the North. (p. 336)

unions: Organizations of workers that began during the Industrial Revolution to bargain with employers over wages, hours, benefits, and control of the workplace. (p. 271)

United Farm Workers (UFW): A union of farmworkers founded in 1962 by Cesar Chavez and Dolores Huerta that sought to empower the mostly Mexican American migrant farmworkers who faced discrimination and exploitative conditions, especially in the Southwest. (p. 865)

United Nations: An international body founded in San Francisco in 1945, consisting of a General Assembly representing all nations, and a Security Council of the United States, Britain, France, China, the Soviet Union, and six other nations elected on a rotating basis. (p. 775)

Universal Negro Improvement Association: A Harlem-based group, led by charismatic, Jamaican-born Marcus Garvey, that arose in the 1920s to mobilize African American workers and champion black separatism. (p. 696)

USA PATRIOT Act: A 2001 law that gave the government new powers to monitor suspected terrorists and their associates, including the ability to access personal information. (p. 981)

U.S. Fish and Wildlife Service: A federal bureau established in 1871 that made recommendations to stem the decline in wild fish. Its creation was an important step toward wildlife conservation and management. (p. 497)

U.S. Sanitary Commission: An organization that supported the Union war effort through professional and volunteer medical aid. (p. 432)

utopias: Communities founded by reformers and transcendentalists to help realize their spiritual and moral potential and to escape from the competition of modern industrial society. (p. 322)

vez a Grecia y Turquía en 1947, se convirtió en una justificación para la intervención de Estados Unidos en varios países durante la Guerra Fría. (pág. 779)

trust: Pequeño grupo de asociados que poseen acciones en un grupo de empresas combinadas que administran como una sola entidad. Los trusts evolucionaron rápidamente para convertirse en otras formas de negocio centralizado, pero los críticos progresistas no dejaron de referirse a compañías gigantes como "trusts". (pág. 518)

Regla de los veinte esclavos: Ley adoptada por el Congreso Confederado que eximía a un hombre de la conscripción militar por cada veinte esclavos pertenecientes a una familia. La ley mostraba cómo la dependencia del trabajo esclavo forzado podía ser una desventaja militar, y exacerbaba los resentimientos de clase entre los blancos no esclavistas que debían servir en el ejército. (pág. 428)

ferrocarril subterráneo: Red informal de blancos y negros libres en el Sur que asistieron a los esclavos fugitivos a alcanzar la libertad en el Norte. (pág. 336)

sindicatos: Organizaciones de trabajadores que comenzaron con la Revolución Industrial para negociar con patrones sobre salarios, horarios, beneficios y control del sitio de trabajo. (pág. 271)

Unión de Trabajadores Campesinos (UFW): Unión de campesinos fundada en 1962 por César Chávez y Dolores Huerta con el fin de empoderar a la mayoría de trabajadores migrantes mexicano-americanos que enfrentaban discriminación y condiciones de explotación, particularmente en el Suroeste. (pág. 865)

Naciones Unidas: Cuerpo internacional acordado a partir de la Conferencia de Yalta y fundado en una conferencia en San Francisco en 1945, que consistiría en una Asamblea General donde todos los países están representados, y en un Consejo de Seguridad de los cinco principales poderes aliados — Estados Unidos, Bretaña, Francia, China y la Unión Soviética — además de seis naciones más que serían elegidas por rotación. (pág. 775)

Asociación Universal de Desarrollo Negro: Grupo basado en Harlem, dirigido por el carismático Marcus Garvey, nacido en Jamaica, que surgió en la década de 1920 para mobilizar a los trabajadores afroamericanos y abogar por el separatismo negro. (pág. 696)

Ley USA PATRIOT: Ley de 2001 que dio nuevos poderes al gobierno para vigilar a sospechosos de terrorismo y sus asociados, incluso permitiendo acceso a su información personal. (pág. 981)

Comisión de Pesca de los Estados Unidos: Agencia federal establecida en 1871 que hizo recomendaciones para detener el declive de peces salvajes. Su creación representó un paso importante hacia la conservación y administración de la vida salvaje. (pág. 497)

Comisión Sanitaria de los Estados Unidos: Organización que apoyó el esfuerzo bélico de la Unión por medio de auxilios médicos voluntarios. (pág. 432)

utopías: Comunidades fundadas por reformistas y trascendentalistas para ayudar a realizar su potencial moral y espiritual, y escapar de la competencia de la sociedad industrial moderna. (pág. 322)

Valley Forge: A military camp in which George Washington's army of 12,000 soldiers and hundreds of camp followers suffered horribly in the winter of 1777–1778. (p. 183)

Valley Forge: Campo militar en el cual el ejército de George Washington, compuesto por 12 mil soldados y cientos de seguidores del campamento, sufrieron horriblemente en el invierno de 1777–1778. (pág. 183)

vaudeville theater: A type of professional stage show popular in the 1880s and 1890s that included singing, dancing, and comedy routines. (p. 583)

teatro vaudeville: Tipo de espectáculo escénico profesional popularizado en las décadas de 1880 y 1890 que incluyó cantos, bailes y rutinas de comedia; creó una forma de entretenimiento familiar que tuvo profunda influencia sobre otros formatos más tardíos, como los programas de radio y las comedias en televisión. (pág. 583)

vertical integration: A business model, pioneered by late nineteenth-century entrepreneurs such as Gustavus Swift and Andrew Carnegie, in which a corporation controlled all aspects of production from raw materials to packaged products. (p. 517)

integración vertical: Modelo de negocios en el cual una corporación controlaba todos los aspectos de la producción, desde la materia prima hasta los productos empaquetados. Los "robber barons" (capitalistas inescrupulosos) o innovadores industriales como Gustavus Swift y Andrew Carnegie, fueron pioneros de este tipo de negocios tras la Guerra Civil. (pág. 517)

Veterans Administration: A federal agency that assists former soldiers. Following World War II, the VA helped veterans purchase new homes with no down payment, sparking a building boom that created construction jobs and fueled consumer spending on home appliances and automobiles. (p. 811)

Departamento de Asuntos Veteranos (VA): Agencia federal que asiste a ex soldados. Después de la Segunda Guerra Mundial, la VA ayudó a los veteranos a adquirir nuevos hogares sin requerir un depósito, resultando en un boom en la construcción que creó empleos en la industria constructora y alimentó el gasto de consumidores en aparatos eléctricos y automóviles. (pág. 811)

Vietnamization: A U.S. policy, devised under President Nixon in the early 1970s, of delegating the ground fighting to the South Vietnamese in the Vietnam War. American troop levels dropped and American casualties dropped correspondingly, but the killing in Vietnam continued. (p. 896)

Vietnamización Nueva política de los Estados Unidos, diseñada por el presidente Nixon a principios de la década de 1970, de delegar el combate terrestre a los vietnamitas del sur durante la Guerra de Vietnam. Se redujo la cantidad de tropas estadounidenses las muertes estadounidenses disminuyeron, pero la matanza en Vietnam continuó. (pág. 896)

Virginia and Kentucky Resolutions: Resolutions by the Virginia and Kentucky state legislatures in 1798 condemning the Alien and Sedition Acts. The resolutions tested the idea that state legislatures could judge the legitimacy of federal laws. (p. 222)

Resoluciones de Virginia y Kentucky: Resoluciones emitidas en 1798 condenando las leyes de Extranjería y Sedición que fueron presentadas al gobierno federal por las legislaturas estatales de Virginia y Kentucky. Las resoluciones pusieron a prueba la idea de que las legislaturas estatales podían juzgar la constitucionalidad de las leyes federales y anularlas. (pág. 222)

Virginia Plan: A plan drafted by James Madison that was presented at the Philadelphia Constitutional Convention. It designed a powerful three-branch government, with representation in both houses of the congress tied to population; this plan would have eclipsed the voice of small states in the national government. (p. 199)

Plan de Virginia: Plan escrito por James Madison, presentado en la Convención Constitucional de Filadelfia. Diseñó un poderoso gobierno de tres ramas, con la representación de ambas cámaras del congreso vinculadas a la población; este plan hubiera eclipsado la voz de los estados pequeños en el gobierno nacional. (pág. 199)

Volstead Act (1920): Officially, the National Prohibition Act, passed by Congress to enforce the provisions of the Eighteenth Amendment banning the sale of alcohol. (p. 690)

Ley Volstead: Oficialmente, Ley Nacional de Prohibición, aprobada por el Congreso en 1920 para aplicar las disposiciones de la Decimoctava Enmienda que prohibió la venta de alcohol. (pág. 690)

Voting Rights Act of 1965: Law passed during Lyndon Johnson's administration that outlawed measures designed to exclude African Americans, and other people of color, from voting. (p. 858)

Ley de Derecho al Voto de 1965: Ley aprobada durante la administración de Lyndon Johnson que confirió poderes al gobierno federal para intervenir y asegurar el acceso de las minorías a las urnas. (pág. 858)

Wade-Davis Bill: A bill proposed by Congress in July 1864 that required an oath of allegiance by a majority of each state's adult white men, new governments formed only by those who had never taken up arms against the Union, and permanent disenfranchisement of Confederate leaders. The plan was passed but pocket vetoed by President Abraham Lincoln. (p. 452)

Proyecto de Ley Wade-Davis: Ley propuesta por el Congreso en Julio de 1864 que requirió que la mayoría de los hombres blancos adultos de cada estado hicieran un juramento de lealtad, que los nuevos gobiernos fueran formados por personas que no se habían levantado en armas contra la Unión y la inhabilitación política permanente de los líderes confederados. El plan fue aprobado pero el presidente Lincoln lo vetó "de bolsillo". (pág. 452)

Wagner Act: A 1935 act that upheld the right of industrial workers to join unions, protected workers from employer coercion, and guaranteed collective bargaining. (p. 716)

Ley Wagner: Ley de 1935 que mantuvo el derecho de los trabajadores industriales de formar sindicatos y establecer la Junta Nacional de Relaciones Laborales (NLRB), agencia federal autorizada para proteger a los trabajadores de la coacción de sus empleadores y garantizar negociaciones colectivas. (pág. 716)

Waltham-Lowell System: A labor system employing young farm women in New England factories that originated in 1822 and declined after 1860, when immigrant labor became predominant. The women lived in company boardinghouses with strict rules and curfews and were often required to attend church. (p. 260)

sistema Waltham-Lowell: Sistema de trabajo que reclutó a mujeres jóvenes de familias agricultoras para trabajar en fábricas entre 1822 que declinó después de 1860 con el auge de la mano de obra inmigrante. Las mujeres vivían en dormitorios de la compañía con reglas estrictas y toques de queda, y con frecuencia se les requería asistir a la iglesia. (pág. 260)

War Industries Board: A federal board established in July 1917 to direct military production, including allocation of resources, conversion of factories to war production, and setting of prices. (p. 657)

Consejo de Industrias de Guerra: Consejo federal establecido en 1917 para dirigir la producción militar, incluyendo la asignación de recursos, la conversión de fábricas a la producción para la guerra y la definición de precios. (pág. 657)

War Powers Act (1941): The law that gave President Roosevelt unprecedented control over all aspects of the war effort during World War II. (p. 742)

Ley de Poderes de Guerra (1941): Ley que confirió al presidente Roosevelt un nivel de control sin precedentes sobre todos los aspectos del esfuerzo bélico durante la Segunda Guerra Mundial. (pág. 742)

Warren Court: The Supreme Court under Chief Justice Earl Warren (1953–1969), which expanded the Constitution's promise of equality and civil rights. It issued landmark decisions in the areas of civil rights, criminal rights, reproductive freedom, and separation of church and state. (p. 900)

La Corte de Warren: La Corte Suprema bajo la presidente del tribunal, Earl Warren, (1953–1969), que expandió la promesa de igualdad y derechos civiles de la Constitución. Emitió decisiones históricas en el terreno de derechos civiles, derechos de los criminales, libertades reproductivas y separación de iglesia y estado. (pág. 900)

Warsaw Pact: A military alliance established in Eastern Europe in 1955 to counter the NATO alliance; it included Albania, Bulgaria, Czechoslovakia, East Germany, Hungary, Poland, Romania, and the Soviet Union. (p. 782)

Pacto de Varsovia: Alianza militar establecida en Europa del Este en 1955 en respuesta a la alianza de la OTAN; incluyó a Albania, Bulgaria, Checoslovaquia, Alemania Oriental, Hungría, Polonia, Rumania y la Unión Soviética. (pág. 782)

Watergate: Term referring to the 1972 break-in at Democratic Party headquarters in the Watergate complex in Washington, D.C. by men working for President Nixon's reelection campaign, along with Nixon's efforts to cover it up. The Watergate scandal led to President Nixon's resignation. (p. 916)

Watergate: Término que describe la intrusión en la sede del Partido Demócrata ubicada en el complejo de Watergate de Washington D.C. en 1972, perpetrada por hombres que trabajan para la campaña de reelección de Nixon y el esfuerzo de Nixon para encubrir este acto. El escándalo de Watergate condujo a la renuncia del presidente Nixon. (pág. 916)

Webster v. Reproductive Health Services: A 1989 Supreme Court ruling that upheld the authority of state governments to limit the use of public funds and facilities for abortions. (p. 985)

Webster v. Reproductive Health Services (Caso Webster contra los Servicios de Salud Reproductiva): Decisión de la Corte Suprema en 1989 que mantuvo la autoridad de los estados para limitar el uso de fondos públicos en instalaciones para abortos. (pág. 985)

welfare capitalism: A system of labor relations that stressed management's responsibility for employees' well-being. (p. 678)

capitalismo de bienestar: Sistema de relaciones laborales que resaltaban que el bienestar de los empleados es responsabilidad de la administración. (pág. 678)

welfare state: A term for industrial democracies that have adopted government-guaranteed social-welfare programs. The creation of Social Security and other measures of the Second New Deal established a national welfare state for the first time. (p. 716)

estado de bienestar: Término aplicado a las democracias industriales que adoptan varios programas de bienestar social garantizados por el gobierno. La creación de la Seguridad Social junto con otras medidas del Segundo Nuevo Trato, cambió fundamentalmente a la sociedad estadounidense y estableció por primera vez un estado nacional de bienestar. (pág. 716)

Whig Party: The Whig Party arose in 1834 when a group of congressmen contested Andrew Jackson's policies and conduct. The party identified itself with the pre-Revolutionary American and British parties — also called Whigs — that had opposed the arbitrary actions of British monarchs. (p. 305)

whigs: El segundo partido nacional, el Partido de los Whigs, surgió en 1834 cuando un grupo de congresistas impugnaron la conducta y las políticas de Andrew Jackson. El partidio se identificaba con la América pre-revolucionaria y con los partidos británicos — también llamados *whigs* — que se habían opuesto a las acciones de los monarcas británicos. (pág. 305)

Whiskey Rebellion: A 1794 uprising by farmers in western Pennsylvania in response to enforcement of an unpopular excise tax on whiskey. (p. 216)

***Williams v. Mississippi*:** An 1898 Supreme Court ruling that allowed states to impose poll taxes and literacy tests. By 1908, every southern state had adopted such measures to suppress voting by African Americans and some poor whites. (p. 616)

Wilmot Proviso: The 1846 proposal by Representative David Wilmot of Pennsylvania to ban slavery in territory acquired from the U.S.-Mexico War. (p. 383)

Wisconsin Idea: A policy promoted by Republican governor Robert La Follette of Wisconsin for greater government intervention in the economy, with reliance on experts, particularly progressive economists, for policy recommendations. (p. 623)

Woman's Christian Temperance Union: An organization advocating the prohibition of liquor that spread rapidly after 1879, when charismatic Frances Willard became its leader. Advocating suffrage and a host of reform activities, it launched tens of thousands of women into public life and was the first nationwide organization to identify and condemn domestic violence. (p. 568)

Woman's Loyal National League: An organization of Unionist women that worked to support the war effort, hoping the Union would recognize women's patriotism with voting rights after the war. (p. 433)

Women's Trade Union League: A labor organization for women founded in New York in 1903 that brought elite, middle-class, and working-class women together as allies. The WTUL supported union organizing efforts among garment workers. (p. 599)

Works Progress Administration: Federal New Deal program established in 1935 that provided government-funded public works jobs to millions of unemployed Americans in areas ranging from construction to the arts. (p. 717)

World Bank: An international bank created to provide loans for the reconstruction of war-torn Europe as well as for the development of former colonized nations. (p. 807)

World Trade Organization (WTO): International economic body established in 1995 through the General Agreement on Tariffs and Trade to enforce substantial tariff and import quota reductions. (p. 970)

Wounded Knee: The 1890 massacre of Sioux Indians by American cavalry at Wounded Knee Creek, South Dakota. Sent to suppress the Ghost Dance, soldiers caught up with fleeing Lakotas and killed as many as 300. (p. 507)

XYZ Affair: A 1797 incident in which American negotiators in France were rebuffed for refusing to pay a substantial bribe. The

Rebelión del Whisky: Levantamiento en 1794 de agricultores en el oeste de Pennsylvania como respuesta a un impopular impuesto especial sobre el whiskey. (pág. 216)

***Williams v. Mississippi*:** Dictamen de la Corte Suprema que permitió a los estados imponer impuestos de capitación y pruebas de alfabetización. Para 1908, todos los estados del Sur habían adoptado estas medidas para suprimir el voto de afroamericanos y blancos pobres. (pág. 616)

Enmienda Wilmot: Propuesta presentada por el Representante David Wilmot en 1846 para prohibir la esclavitud en los territorios adquiridos durante la Intervención estadounidense en México. (pág. 383)

Idea de Wisconsin: Política promovida por el gobernador republicano, Robert La Follette, de Wisconsin, para una mayor intervención del gobierno en la economía que se apoyaría en expertos, particularmente economistas progresistas, para recomendaciones de políticas. (pág. 623)

Unión Cristiana de Mujeres por la Templanza: Organización que abogó por la prohibición del licor, que a partir de 1879 se expandió rápidamente cuando Frances Willard se convirtió en su líder. Abogaba por el sufragio y varias actividades reformistas, lanzó a decenas de miles de mujeres hacia la vida pública y fue la primera organización nacional que condenó la violencia doméstica. (pág. 568)

Woman's Loyal National League: Organización de mujeres de la Unión que trabajaron para apoyar el esfuerzo bélico con la esperanza de que la Unión correspondería el patriotismo de las mujeres con derechos de voto después de la guerra. (pág. 433)

Liga del Sindicato de Mujeres (WTUL): Organización laboral para mujeres fundada en Nueva York en 1903 que unió a mujeres de las élites, de la clase media y de la clase trabajadora como aliadas. La WTUL apoyó los esfuerzos para organizar un sindicato de trabajadores de manufactura de prendas. (pág. 599)

Administración del Progreso de Obras: Programa federal del Nuevo Trato establecido en 1935 para ofrecer empleos públicos financiados por el gobierno a los millones de estadounidenses desempleados durante la Gran Depresión en industrias desde la construcción hasta las artes. (pág. 717)

Banco Mundial: Banco internacional creado para brindar préstamos de reconstrucción a Europa tras la devastación de la guerra y para el desarrollo de los países en vías de desarrollo que fueron colonias. (pág. 807)

Organización Mundial del Comercio (OMC o WTO en inglés): Entidad económica internacional establecida en 1995 por medio del Acuerdo General sobre Aranceles Aduaneros y Comercio, para imponer reducciones substanciales en cuotas de importación y aranceles. (pág. 970)

Masacre de Wounded Knee: Suceso que tuvo lugar en 1890 en Wounded Knee Creek, Dakota del Sur, en el que los indios siux fueron masacrados por la caballería estadounidense. Enviados para reprimir la Danza de los espíritus, los soldados alcanzaron a los lakotas cuando huían y mataron a unos trescientos de ellos. (pág. 507)

caso XYZ: Incidente en 1797 en el cual negociadores estadounidenses en Francia fueron rechazados por negarse a pagar un incident led the United States into an undeclared war that curtailed American trade with the French West Indies. (p. 222)

soborno considerable. El incidente llevó a los Estados Unidos a una guerra no declarada que redujo el comercio estadounidense con las Antillas Francesas. (pág. 222)

Yalta Conference: A meeting in Yalta of President Roosevelt, Prime Minister Churchill, and Soviet Premier Joseph Stalin in February 1945, in which the leaders discussed the treatment of Germany, the status of Poland, the creation of the United Nations, and Russian entry into the war against Japan. (p. 775)

Conferencia de Yalta Reunión en Yalta del presidente Roosevelt, el primer ministro Churchill y Iósif Stalin en febrero de 1945 donde se discutió el trato hacia Alemania, el estatus de Polonia, la creación de las Naciones Unidas y el ingreso ruso a la guerra contra Japón. (pág. 775)

yellow journalism: A derogatory term for newspapers that specialize in sensationalistic reporting. Yellow journalism is associated with the inflammatory reporting by the Hearst and Pulitzer newspapers leading up to the Spanish-American War in 1898. (p. 587)

periodismo amarillista: Nombre peyorativo que se da a los periódicos que se especializan en reportajes sensacionalistas. El periodismo amarillista se asocia con los reportajes incendiarios de los periódicos Hearst y Pulitzer que llevaron a la guerra hispano-estadounidense de 1898. (pág. 587)

Yellowstone National Park: Established in 1872 by Congress, Yellowstone was the first national park in the United States. (p. 496)

Parque Nacional de Yellowstone: Establecido en 1872 por el Congreso, Yellowstone fue el primer parque nacional de los Estados Unidos. (pág. 496)

Young Americans for Freedom (YAF): The largest student political organization in the country in the 1960s, whose conservative members defended free enterprise and supported the war in Vietnam. (p. 888)

Jóvenes Americanos por la Libertad (YAF): Organización política estudiantil más grande del país cuyos miembros conservadores defendieron a la empresa libre y apoyaron a la guerra en Vietnam. (pág. 888)

Young Lords Organization (YLO): An organization that sought self-determination for Puerto Ricans in the United States and in the Caribbean. Though immediate victories for the YLO were few, their dedicated community organizing produced a generation of leaders and awakened community consciousness. (p. 862)

Organización Young Lords (YLO): Organización que buscó la autodeterminación para los puertorriqueños en Estados Unidos y el Caribe. Si bien los YLO obtuvieron pocas victorias inmediatas, su dedicación a la organización de la comunidad produjo una generación de líderes y despertó la conciencia comunitaria. (pág. 862)

Young Men's Christian Association: Introduced in Boston in 1851, the YMCA promoted a new model of middle-class masculinity, muscular Christianity, which combined Protestant evangelism with athletic facilities where men could make themselves "clean and strong." (p. 558)

Asociación Cristiana de Jóvenes (YMCA): Introducida en Boston en 1851, la YMCA promovió una nueva forma de masculinidad de clase media: la cristiandad muscular, combinando el evangelismo con las instalaciones deportivas donde los hombres pudieran convertirse en "limpios y fuertes". (pág. 558)

Zimmermann telegram: A 1917 intercepted dispatch in which German foreign secretary Arthur Zimmermann urged Mexico to join the Central Powers and promised that if the United States entered the war, Germany would help Mexico recover Texas, New Mexico, and Arizona. Published by American newspapers, the telegram outraged the American public and help precipitate the move toward U.S. entry in the war on the Allied side. (p. 655)

telegrama Zimmermann: Envío interceptado en 1917 donde el secretario de exterior alemán llamaba a México a unirse a los Poderes Centrales y prometía que si Estados Unidos entraba a la guerra, Alemania ayudaría a México a recuperar Texas, Nuevo México y Arizona. Publicado por periódicos estadounidenses, el telegrama indignó al público americano y ayudó a precipitar la decisión de Estados Unidos de involucrarse en la guerra del lado de los Aliados. (pág. 655)

zoot-suit riots: In June 1943, a group of white sailors and soldiers in Los Angeles, seeking revenge for an earlier skirmish with Mexican American youths, attacked anyone they found wearing a zoot suit, an outfit that symbolized a rebellious style. (p. 754)

zoot suits (vestimenta): Trajes de tamaño excesivo que estuvieron de moda en la década de 1940, particularmente entre hombres afroamericanos y mexicano-americanos jóvenes. En junio de 1943, un grupo de marinos y soldados blancos, buscando vengarse de un conflicto anterior con jóvenes mexicano-americanos, atacaron a cualquiera que portara un zoot suit en lo que se conoce como los disturbios zoot-suit. (pág. 754)

Index

A note about the index: Names of individuals appear in boldface; biographical dates are included for U.S. presidents. Letters in parentheses following page numbers refer to:
(f) figures, including charts and graphs;
(i) illustrations, including photographs and artifacts; *(m)* maps; and *(t)* tables.